THE HISTORY OF THE DECLINE AND FALL OF THE ROMAN EMPIRE

'David Womersley's edition supersedes all others ... [it] gives us the best text we have ever had, a vigorously intelligent introduction and an indispensable collection of ancillary documents: work of the highest calibre, reader-friendly ... and handsome in physical format ... this work will reach the audience it deserves' – Claude Rawson in *The Times Literary Supplement*

'This new edition will be invaluable for those interested not merely in reading Gibbon, but in mapping his place in European intellectual history' – Jose Harris in *The Times Higher Education Supplement*

'A cultivated book for cultivated people ... David Womersley has produced a splendid critical edition' – Daniel Johnson in *The Times*

'David Womersley's edition is an enormous achievement ... These volumes give us *The Decline and Fall of the Roman Empire* on a scale worthy of the original' – J. G. A. Pocock in the *London Review of Books*

'The full greatness of Gibbon's achievement is superbly set out in David Womersley's introduction ... It is a fitting monument to the greatest of all English historians' – Niall Ferguson in the *Sunday Telegraph*

ABOUT THE AUTHOR AND EDITOR

EDWARD GIBBON was born in 1737, in Putney, and was the only child of his parents to survive infancy. Although his education was frequently interrupted by ill health, his knowledge was far-reaching. His brief career as an undergraduate at Magdalen College, Oxford, ended when he joined the Catholic Church. His father sent him to Lausanne, in Switzerland, where, while studying Greek and French for the next five years, he rejoined the Protestant Church. In 1761 he published his *Essai sur l'étude de la littérature*; the English version appeared in 1764. Meanwhile, Gibbon served as a captain in the Hampshire Militia until 1763, when he returned to the Continent. It was while he was in Rome in 1764 that he first conceived the work that was eventually to become *The History of the Decline and Fall of the Roman Empire*. After the death of his father, Gibbon settled in London and in 1774 was elected to Parliament, where he sat for the next eight years, although he never once spoke in the Commons. He also took his place among the literary circles of London. The first volume of his famous *History* was published in 1776; it was highly praised for its learning and style but incurred some censure for its treatment of the early Christians. The second and third volumes appeared in 1781 and the final three, which were written in Lausanne, in 1788. He died while on a visit to his friend Lord Sheffield, who posthumously edited Gibbon's autobiographical papers and published them in 1796.

DAVID WOMERSLEY is a Fellow and Tutor in English Literature at Jesus College, Oxford. His book *The Transformation of the Decline and Fall of the Roman Empire* was published by Cambridge University Press in 1988.

EDWARD GIBBON

THE HISTORY OF THE DECLINE AND FALL OF THE ROMAN EMPIRE

Volume the Fifth

(1788)

AND

Volume the Sixth

(1788)

Edited by David Womersley

PENGUIN BOOKS

PENGUIN BOOKS

Published by the Penguin Group
Penguin Books Ltd, 80 Strand, London WC2R 0RL, England
Penguin Putnam Inc., 375 Hudson Street, New York, New York 10014, USA
Penguin Books Australia Ltd, 250 Camberwell Road, Camberwell, Victoria 3124, Australia
Penguin Books Canada Ltd, 10 Alcorn Avenue, Toronto, Ontario, Canada M4V 3B2
Penguin Books India (P) Ltd, 11 Community Centre, Panchsheel Park, New Delhi – 110 017, India
Penguin Books (NZ) Ltd, Cnr Rosedale and Airborne Roads, Albany, Auckland, New Zealand
Penguin Books (South Africa) (Pty) Ltd, 24 Sturdee Avenue, Rosebank 2196, South Africa

Penguin Books Ltd, Registered Offices: 80 Strand, London WC2R 0RL, England

www.penguin.com

Volumes 5 and 6 first published 1788
This edition first published by Allen Lane The Penguin Press 1994
Published in Penguin Classics 1995

020

Printed and bound in Great Britain by Clays Ltd, Elcograf S.p.A.

CONTENTS

Table of Contents of the Fifth Volume 1
Table of Contents of the Sixth Volume 10

THE DECLINE AND FALL
OF THE ROMAN EMPIRE
Volume the Fifth 21
Volume the Sixth 555

Appendix 1 Deviations from Copy Text 1087
Appendix 2 Gibbon's Marginalia 1093
Appendix 3 A Vindication (1779) 1106

Bibliographical Index 1185

General Index (1788) 1278

TABLE OF CONTENTS OF THE FIFTH VOLUME.

CHAP. XLVIII.

Plan of the Fifth and Sixth Volumes. – Succession and Characters of the Greek Emperors of Constantinople, from the Time of Heraclius to the Latin Conquest.

A.D.
Defects of the Byzantine History 23
Its Connection with the Revolutions of the World 25
Plan of the Fifth and Sixth Volumes ib.
Second Marriage and Death of Heraclius 27
641 Constantine III. 28
Heracleonas ib.
Punishment of Martina and Heracleonas 29
Constans II. ib.
668 Constantine IV. Pogonatus 30
685 Justinian II. 32
695–705. His Exile 33
705–711. His Restoration and Death 34
711 Philippicus 35
713 Anastasius II. 36
716 Theodosius III. ib.
718 Leo III. the Isaurian ib.
741 Constantine V. Copronymus 37
775 Leo IV. 38
780 Constantine VI. and Irene 40
792 Irene 41
802 Nicephorus I. 42
811 Stauracius ib.
Michael I. Rhangabe ib.
813 Leo V. the Armenian 43
A.D.
820 Michael II. the Stammerer 44
829 Theophilus 45
842 Michael III. 47
867 Basil I. the Macedonian 49
886 Leo VI. the Philosopher 53
911 Alexander, Constantine VII. Porphyrogenitus 54
919 Romanus I. Lecapenus 55
Christopher, Stephen, Constantine VIII. ib.
945 Constantine VII. 56
959 Romanus II. junior 57
963 Nicephorus II. Phocas ib.
969 John Zimisces, Basil II. Constantine IX. 58
976 Basil II. and Constantine IX. 66
1025 Constantine IX. 61
1028 Romanus III. Argyrus ib.
1034 Michael IV. the Paphlagonian 62
1041 Michael V. Calaphates ib.
1042 Zoe and Theodora 63
1042 Constantine X. Monomachus ib.
1054 Theodora ib.
1056 Michael VI. Stratioticus ib.
1057 Isaac I. Comnenus 64
1059 Constantine XI. Ducas 65
1067 Eudocia 66
Romanus III. Diogenes ib.
1071 Michael VII. Parapinaces, Andronicus I. ib.
Constantine XII. ib.
1078 Nicephorus III. Botaniates 67
1081 Alexius I. Comnenus 69
1118 John, or Calo-Johannes 70
1143 Manuel 72

A.D.
1180 Alexius II. 74
Character and first Adventures of Andronicus ib.
1183 Andronicus I. Comnenus 81
1185 Isaac II. Angelus 83

CHAP. XLIX.

Introduction, Worship, and Persecution of Images. – Revolt of Italy and Rome. – Temporal Dominion of the Popes. – Conquest of Italy by the Franks. – Establishment of Images. – Character and Coronation of Charlemagne. – Restoration and Decay of the Roman Empire in the West. – Independence of Italy. – Constitution of the Germanic Body.

A.D.
Introduction of Images into the Christian Church 86
Their Worship 87
The Image of Edessa 89
Its Copies 90
Opposition to Image-worship 91
726–840. Leo the Iconoclast, and his Successors 93
754 Their Synod of Constantinople 94
Their Creed ib.
726–775. Their Persecution of the Images and Monks 95
State of Italy 97
727 Epistles of Gregory II. to the Emperor 99
728 Revolt of Italy 101
Republic of Rome 104
730–752. Rome attacked by the Lombards 105
754 Her Deliverance by Pepin 107
774 Conquest of Lombardy by Charlemagne 109
751, 753, 768. Pepin and Charlemagne, Kings of France ib.
Patricians of Rome 111

A.D.
Donations of Pepin and Charlemagne to the Popes 113
Forgery of the Donation of Constantine 115
780 Restoration of Images in the East by the Empress Irene 117
787 VIIth General Council, II[d] of Nice 118
842 Final Establishment of Images by the Empress Theodora 119
794 Reluctance of the Franks and of Charlemagne 120
774–800. Final Separation of the Popes from the Eastern Empire ib.
800 Coronation of Charlemagne as Emperor of Rome and of the West 122
768–814. Reign and Character of Charlemagne 124
Extent of his Empire 127
France ib.
Spain 128
Italy 129
Germany ib.
Hungary 130
His Neighbours and Enemies ib.
His Successors 132
814–887. In Italy ib.
911 In Germany ib.
987 In France ib.
814–840. Lewis the Pious ib.
840–856. Lothaire I. ib.
856–875. Lewis II. 133
888 Division of the Empire ib.
962 Otho, King of Germany, restores and appropriates the Western Empire ib.
Transactions of the Western and Eastern Empires 134
800–1060. Authority of the Emperors in the Elections of the Popes 136
Disorders 137
1073 Reformation and Claims of the Church 139
Authority of the Emperors in Rome ib.
932 Revolt of Alberic 140
967 Of Pope John XII. 141

A.D.
998 Of the Consul Crescentius 141
774–1250. The Kingdom of Italy 142
1152–1190. Frederic I. 143
1198–1250. Frederic II. 144
814–1250. Independence of the Princes of Germany 145
1250 The Germanic Constitution 146
1347–1378. Weakness and Poverty of the German Emperor Charles IV. 147
1356 His Ostentation 148
Contrast of the Power and Modesty of Augustus 149

CHAP. L.

Description of Arabia and its Inhabitants. – Birth, Character, and Doctrine of Mahomet. – He preaches at Mecca. – Flies to Medina. – Propagates his Religion by the Sword. – Voluntary or reluctant Submission of the Arabs. – His Death and Successors. – The Claims and Fortunes of Ali and his Descendants.

A.D.
Description of Arabia 151
The Soil and Climate 152
Division of the Sandy, the Stony, and the Happy, Arabia 153
Manners of the Bedoweens, or Pastoral Arabs 154
The Horse 155
The Camel ib.
Cities of Arabia 156
Mecca 157
Her Trade ib.
National Independence of the Arabs 158
Their domestic Freedom and Character 160
Civil Wars and private Revenge 162
Annual Truce 163
Their social Qualifications and Virtues 164
Love of Poetry 164
Examples of Generosity 165
Ancient Idolatry 166
The Caaba, or Temple of Mecca 167
Sacrifices and Rites 168
Introduction of the Sabians 170
The Magians 171
The Jews ib.
The Christians ib.
569–609. Birth and Education of Mahomet 172
Deliverance of Mecca 173
Qualifications of the Prophet 174
One God 176
Mahomet, the Apostle of God, and the last of the Prophets 178
Moses 179
Jesus ib.
The Koran 181
Miracles 182
Precepts of Mahomet – Prayer, Fasting, Alms 184
Resurrection 187
Hell and Paradise ib.
609 Mahomet preaches at Mecca 190
613–622. Is opposed by the Koreish 192
622 And driven from Mecca 193
622 Received as Prince of Medina 194
622–632. His regal Dignity 195
He declares War against the Infidels 196
His defensive Wars against the Koreish of Mecca 199
623 Battle of Beder ib.
Of Ohud 200
625 The Nations, or the Ditch 201
623–627. Mahomet subdues the Jews of Arabia ib.
629 Submission of Mecca 203
629–632. Conquest of Arabia 205
629, 630. First War of the Mahometans against the Roman Empire 207
632 Death of Mahomet 210
His Character 212
Private Life of Mahomet 214
His Wives 215
And Children 217
Character of Ali 218

A.D.
632 Reign of Abubeker 218
634 —— of Omar 219
644 —— of Othman 220
Discord of the Turks and Persians ib.
655 Death of Othman 222
655–660. Reign of Ali ib.
655, or 661–680. Reign of Moawiyah 224
680 Death of Hosein 225
Posterity of Mahomet and Ali 228
Success of Mahomet 229
Permanency of his Religion 230
His Merit towards his Country 231

CHAP. LI.

The Conquest of Persia, Syria, Egypt, Africa, and Spain, by the Arabs or Saracens. – Empire of the Caliphs, or Successors of Mahomet. – State of the Christians, &c. under their Government.

A.D.
632 Union of the Arabs 233
Character of their Caliphs 235
Their conquests 237
Invasion of PERSIA 239
636 Battle of Cadesia ib.
Foundation of Bassora 241
637 Sack of Madayn 242
Foundation of Cufa 243
637–651. Conquest of Persia 244
651 Death of the last King 246
710 The Conquest of Transoxiana 247
632 Invasion of SYRIA 248
Siege of Bosra 250
633 —— of Damascus 252
Battle of Aiznadin 253
The Arabs return to Damascus 255
634 The City is taken by Storm and Capitulation 257
Pursuit of the Damascenes 259
Fair of Abyla 261
635 Sieges of Heliopolis and Emesa 262
636 Battle of Yermuk 264

A.D.
637 Conquest of Jerusalem 267
638 —— of Aleppo and Antioch 269
Flight of Heraclius 271
End of the Syrian War 272
633–639. The Conquerors of Syria 273
639–655. Progress of the Syrian Conquerors 274
EGYPT. Character and Life of Amrou 276
638 Invasion of Egypt 277
The Cities of Memphis, Babylon, and Cairo 278
Voluntary Submission of the Copts or Jacobites 280
Siege and Conquest of Alexandria 282
The Alexandrian Library 284
Administration of Egypt 286
Riches and Populousness 287
647 AFRICA. First Invasion by Abdallah 290
The Præfect Gregory and his Daughter 291
Victory of the Arabs 292
665–689. Progress of the Saracens in Africa 294
670–675. Foundation of Cairoan 296
692–698. Conquest of Carthage 298
698–709. Final Conquest of Africa 299
Adoption of the Moors 301
709 SPAIN. First Temptations and Designs of the Arabs ib.
State of the Gothic Monarchy 302
710 The first Descent of the Arabs 304
711 Their second Descent and Victory 304–5
Ruin of the Gothic Monarchy 306
712, 713. Conquest of Spain by Musa 308
714 Disgrace of Musa 311
Prosperity of Spain under the Arabs 313
Religious Toleration 315
Propagation of Mahometism ib.
Fall of the Magians of Persia 316
749 Decline and Fall of Christianity in Africa 318
1149 And Spain 319

A.D.
Toleration of the Christians 320
Their Hardships 321
718 The Empire of the Caliphs ib.

CHAP. LII.

The Two Sieges of Constantinople by the Arabs. – Their Invasion of France, and Defeat by Charles Martel. – Civil War of the Ommiades and Abbassides. – Learning of the Arabs. – Luxury of the Caliphs. – Naval Enterprises on Crete, Sicily, and Rome. – Decay and Division of the Empire of the Caliphs. – Defeats and Victories of the Greek Emperors.

A.D.
The Limits of the Arabian Conquests 323
668–675. First Siege of Constantinople by the Arabs ib.
677 Peace and Tribute 325
716–718. Second Siege of Constantinople 327
Failure and Retreat of the Saracens 330
Invention and Use of the Greek Fire ib.
721 Invasion of France by the Arabs 333
731 Expedition and Victories of Abderame 335
732 Defeat of the Saracens by Charles Martel 336
They retreat before the Franks 338
746–750. Elevation of the Abbassides 339
750 Fall of the Ommiades 341
755 Revolt of Spain 342
Triple Division of the Caliphate 343
750–960. Magnificence of the Caliphs ib.
Its Consequences on private and public Happiness 345

A.D.
754, &c. 813, &c. Introduction of Learning among the Arabians 347
Their real Progress in the Sciences 349
Want of Erudition, Taste, and Freedom 352
781–805. Wars of Harun al Rashid against the Romans 353
823 The Arabs subdue the Isle of Crete 356
827–878. And of Sicily 357
846 Invasion of Rome by the Saracens 359
849 Victory and Reign of Leo IV. 360
852 Foundation of the Leonine City 362
838 The Amorian War between Theophilus and Motassem ib.
841–870. Disorders of the Turkish Guards 365
890–951. Rise and Progress of the Carmathians 367
900 Their Military Exploits ib.
929 They pillage Mecca 368
800–936. Revolt of the Provinces 369
The independent Dynasties 370
800–941. The Aglabites ib.
829–907. The Edrisites ib.
813–872. The Taherites ib.
872–902. The Soffarides ib.
874–999. The Samanides 371
868–905. The Toulonides ib.
934–968. The Ikshidites ib.
892–1001. The Hamadanites ib.
933–1055. The Bowides 372
936 Fallen State of the Caliphs of Bagdad ib.
960 Enterprises of the Greeks 374
Reduction of Crete ib.
963–975. The Eastern Conquests of Nicephorus Phocas, and John Zimisces 375
Conquest of Cilicia ib.
Invasion of Syria 376
Recovery of Antioch ib.
Passage of the Euphrates 377
Danger of Bagdad ib.

CHAP. LIII.

State of the Eastern Empire in the Tenth Century. – Extent and Division. – Wealth and Revenue. – Palace of Constantinople. – Titles and Offices. – Pride and Power of the Emperors. – Tactics of the Greeks, Arabs, and Franks. – Loss of the Latin Tongue. – Studies and Solitude of the Greeks.

A.D.
Memorials of the Greek Empire 379
Works of Constantine Porphyrogenitus ib.
Their Imperfections 380
Embassy of Liutprand 382
The Themes, or Provinces of the Empire, and its Limits in every Age 383
General Wealth and Populousness 384
State of Peloponesus: Sclavonians 385
Freemen of Laconia 386
Cities and Revenue of Peloponesus 387
Manufactures – especially of Silk ib.
Transported from Greece to Sicily 389
Revenue of the Greek Empire 390
Pomp and Luxury of the Emperors 391
The Palace of Constantinople ib.
Furniture and Attendants 393
Honours and Titles of the Imperial Family 394
Offices of the Palace, the State, and the Army 395
Adoration of the Emperor 397
Reception of Ambassadors ib.
Processions and Acclamations 398
Marriage of the Cæsars with foreign Nations 399
Imaginary Law of Constantine 400
A.D.
733 The first Exception 401
941 The second ib.
943 The third ib.
972 Otho of Germany 402
988 Wolodomir of Russia ib.
Despotic Power 403
Coronation Oath ib.
Military Force of the Greeks, the Saracens, and the Franks 404
Navy of the Greeks ib.
Tactics and Character of the Greeks 407
Character and Tactics of the Saracens 409
The Franks or Latins 411
Their Character and Tactics 412
Oblivion of the Latin Language 414
The Greek Emperors and their Subjects retain and assert the Name of Romans 416
Period of Ignorance ib.
Revival of Greek Learning 417
Decay of Taste and Genius 419
Want of national Emulation 421

CHAP. LIV.

Origin and Doctrine of the Paulicians. – Their Persecution by the Greek Emperors. Revolt in Armenia, &c. – Transplantation into Thrace. – Propagation in the West. – The Seeds, Character, and Consequences of the Reformation.

A.D.
Supine Superstition of the Greek Church 423
660 Origin of the Paulicians, or Disciples of St. Paul 424
Their Bible 425
The Simplicity of their Belief and Worship 426
They hold the two Principles of the Magians and Manichæans 427
The Establishment of the Paulicians in Armenia, Pontus, &c. ib.

A.D.
Persecution of the Greek Emperors 428
845–880. Revolt of the Paulicians 430
They fortify Tephrice ib.
And pillage Asia Minor 431
Their Decline 432
Their Transplantation from Armenia to Thrace 432
Their Introduction into Italy and France 434
1200 Persecution of the Albigeois 435
Character and Consequences of the Reformation 436

CHAP. LV.

The Bulgarians. – Origin, Migrations, and Settlement of the Hungarians. – Their Inroads in the East and West. – The Monarchy of Russia. – Geography and Trade. – Wars of the Russians against the Greek Empire. – Conversion of the Barbarians.

A.D.
680 Emigration of the Bulgarians 441
900 Croats or Sclavonians of Dalmatia 442
640–1017. First Kingdom of the Bulgarians 443
884 Emigration of the Turks or Hungarians 445
Their Fennic Origin 447
900 Tactics and Manners of the Hungarians and Bulgarians 448
889 Establishment and Inroads of the Hungarians 450
934 Victory of Henry the Fowler 452
955 —— of Otho the Great 453
839 Origin of the Russian Monarchy 455
The Varangians of Constantinople 456
950 Geography and Trade of Russia 457
Naval Expeditions of the Russians against Constantinople 460
865 The first 461
904 The second ib.
941 The third 462
1043 The fourth ib.
Negociations and Prophecy ib.
955–973. Reign of Swatoslaus 463
970–973. His Defeat by John Zimisces 464
864 Conversion of Russia 466
955 Baptism of Olga 467
988 —— of Wolodomir ib.
800–1100. Christianity of the North 468

CHAP. LVI.

The Saracens, Franks, and Greeks, in Italy. – First Adventures and Settlement of the Normans. – Character and Conquests of Robert Guiscard, Duke of Apulia. – Deliverance of Sicily by his Brother Roger. – Victories of Robert over the Emperors of the East and West. – Roger, King of Sicily, invades Africa and Greece. – The Emperor Manuel Comnenus. – Wars of the Greeks and Normans. – Extinction of the Normans.

A.D.
840–1017. Conflict of the Saracens, Latins, and Greeks, in Italy 471
871 Conquest of Bari 472
890 New Province of the Greeks in Italy 473
983 Defeat of Otho III. 474
Anecdotes ib.
1016 Origin of the Normans in taly 477
1029 Foundation of Aversa 479
1038 The Normans serve in Sicily ib.
1040–1043. Their Conquest of Apulia 480
Character of the Normans 481
1046 Oppression of Apulia 482

A.D.

1049–1054. League of the Pope and the two Empires 483

1053 Expedition of Pope Leo IX. against the Normans 484

His Defeat and Captivity ib.

Origin of the Papal Investitures to the Normans 485

1020–1085. Birth and Character of Robert Guiscard 485

1054–1080. His Ambition and Success 488

1060 Duke of Apulia 489

His Italian Conquests ib.

School of Salerno 490

Trade of Amalphi 491

1060–1090. Conquest of Sicily by Count Roger 492

1081 Robert invades the Eastern Empire 494

Siege of Durazzo 496

The Army and March of the Emperor Alexius 498

Battle of Durazzo 500

1082 Durazzo taken 501

Return of Robert, and Actions of Bohemond 502

1081 The Emperor Henry III. invited by the Greeks 503

1081–1084. Besieges Rome 504

Flies before Robert 505

1084 Second Expedition of Robert into Greece 506

1085 His Death 507

1101–1154. Reign and Ambition of Roger, great Count of Sicily 508

1127 Duke of Apulia 509

1130–1139. First King of Sicily 510

1122–1152. His Conquests in Africa ib.

1146 His Invasion of Greece 512

His Admiral delivers Louis VII. of France 513

Insults Constantinople ib.

1148, 1149. The Emperor Manuel repulses the Normans ib.

1155 He reduces Apulia and Calabria 514

A.D.

1155–1174. His Design of acquiring Italy and the Western Empire 514

Failure of his Designs 516

1156 Peace with the Normans 517

1185 Last War of the Greeks and Normans ib.

1154–1166. William I. the Bad, King of Sicily 518

1166–1189. William II. the Good ib.

Lamentation of the Historian Falcandus 519

1194 Conquest of the Kingdom of Sicily by the Emperor Henry VI. 520

1204 Final Extinction of the Normans 522

CHAP. LVII.

The Turks of the House of Seljuk. – Their Revolt against Mahmud Conqueror of Hindostan. – Togrul subdues Persia, and protects the Caliphs. – Defeat and Captivity of the Emperor Romanus Diogenes by Alp Arslan. – Power and Magnificence of Malek Shah. – Conquest of Asia Minor and Syria. – State and Oppression of Jerusalem. – Pilgrimages to the Holy Sepulchre.

A.D.

THE TURKS 523

997–1028. Mahmud, the Gaznevide ib.

His twelve Expeditions into Hindostan 524

His Character 526

980–1028. Manners and Emigration of the Turks, or Turkmans 527

1038 They defeat the Gaznevides, and subdue Persia 529

1038–1152. Dynasty of the Seljukians 530

1038–1063. Reign and Character of Togrul Beg ib.

1055 He delivers the Caliph of Bagdad 532

A.D.
His Investiture 532
1063 And Death 533
1050 The Turks invade the Roman Empire ib.
1063–1072. Reign of Alp Arslan 534
1065–1068. Conquest of Armenia and Georgia ib.
1068–1071. The Emperor Romanus Diogenes 535
1071 Defeat of the Romans 536
Captivity and Deliverance of the Emperor 538
1072 Death of Alp Arslan 540
1072–1092. Reign and Prosperity of Malek Shah 541

A.D.
1092 His Death 543
Division of the Seljukian Empire 544
1074–1084. Conquest of Asia Minor by the Turks 545
The Seljukian Kingdom of Roum 546
638–1099. State and Pilgrimage of Jerusalem 548
969–1076. Under the Fatimite Caliphs 550
1009 Sacrilege of Hakem 551
1024 Encrease of Pilgrimages 552
1076–1096. Conquest of Jerusalem by the Turks 553

TABLE OF CONTENTS OF THE SIXTH VOLUME.

CHAP. LVIII.

Origin and Numbers of the First Crusade. – Characters of the Latin Princes. – Their March to Constantinople. – Policy of the Greek Emperor Alexius. – Conquest of Nice, Antioch, and Jerusalem, by the Franks. – Deliverance of the Holy Sepulchre. – Godfrey of Bouillon, First King of Jerusalem. – Institutions of the French or Latin Kingdom.

A.D.
1095–1099. The first Crusade 557
Peter the Hermit ib.
1095 Urban II. in the Council of Placentia 558
Council of Clermont 560
Justice of the Crusades 563
Spiritual Motives and Indulgences 565
Temporal and carnal Motives 567
Influence of Example 569
1096 Departure of the first Crusaders 570
Their Destruction in Hungary and Asia 571
The Chiefs of the first Crusade 574
I. Godfrey of Bouillon ib.
II. Hugh of Vermandois, Robert of Normandy, Robert of Flanders, Stephen of Chartres, &c. 575
III. Raymond of Tholouse 576
IV. Bohemond and Tancred 577
Chivalry ib.
A.D.
1096, 1097. March of the Princes to Constantinople 580
Policy of the Emperor Alexius Comnenus 582
He obtains the Homage of the Crusaders 584
Insolence of the Franks 586
1097 Their Review and Numbers 587
Siege of Nice 589
Battle of Dorylæum 591
March through the Lesser Asia 592
1097–1151. Baldwin founds the Principality of Edessa 593
1097, 1098. Siege of Antioch ib.
1098 Victory of the Crusaders 596
Their Famine and Distress at Antioch ib.
Legend of the Holy Lance 598
Celestial Warriors 600
The State of the Turks and Caliphs of Egypt ib.
1098, 1099. Delay of the Franks 602
1099 Their March to Jerusalem ib.
Siege and Conquest of Jerusalem 603
1099, 1100. Election and Reign of Godfrey of Bouillon 606
1099 Battle of Ascalon ib.
1099–1187. The Kingdom of Jerusalem 607
1099–1369. Assise of Jerusalem 610
Court of Peers 611
Law of judicial Combats 612
Court of Burgesses 613
Syrians ib.
Villains and Slaves 614

CHAP. LIX.

Preservation of the Greek Empire. – Numbers, Passage, and Event, of the Second and Third Crusades. – St. Bernard. – Reign of Saladin in Egypt and Syria. – His Conquest of Jerusalem. – Naval Crusades. – Richard the First of England. – Pope Innocent the Third; and the Fourth and Fifth Crusades. – The Emperor Frederic the Second. – Louis the Ninth of France; and the Two last Crusades. – Expulsion of the Latins or Franks by the Mamalukes.

A.D.
1097–1118. Success of Alexius 615
Expeditions by Land 617
1101 The first Crusade ib.
1147 The second, of Conrad III. and Louis VII. ib.
1189 The third, of Frederic I. ib.
Their Numbers 618
Passage through the Greek Empire 619
Turkish Warfare 621
Obstinacy of the Enthusiasm of the Crusades 624
1091–1153. Character and Mission of St. Bernard ib.
Progress of the Mahometans 626
The Atabeks of Syria 627
1127–1145. Zenghi ib.
1145–1174. Noureddin ib.
1163–1169. Conquest of Egypt by the Turks 628
1171 End of the Fatimite Caliphs 631
1171–1193. Reign and Character of Saladin ib.
1187 His Conquest of the Kingdom 634
And City of Jerusalem 636
1188 The third Crusade, by Sea 638
1189–1191. Siege of Acre 639
1191, 1192. Richard of England, in Palestine 640
1192 His Treaty and Departure 643
A.D.
1193 Death of Saladin 644
1198–1216. Innocent III. ib.
1203 The fourth Crusade 645
1218 The fifth ib.
1228 The emperor Frederic II. in Palestine 646
1243 Invasion of the Carizmians 648
1248–1254. St. Louis, and the sixth Crusade 649
1249 He takes Damietta 650
1250 His Captivity in Egypt ib.
1270 His Death before Tunis, in the seventh Crusade 651
1250–1517. The Mamalukes of Egypt 652
1268 Loss of Antioch 653
1291 The Loss of Acre and the Holy Land 654

CHAP. LX.

Schism of the Greeks and Latins. – State of Constantinople. – Revolt of the Bulgarians. – Isaac Angelus dethroned by his Brother Alexius. – Origin of the Fourth Crusade. – Alliance of the French and Venetians with the Son of Isaac. – Their naval Expedition to Constantinople. – The Two Sieges and final Conquest of the City by the Latins.

A.D.
Schism of the Greeks 655
Their Aversion to the Latins ib.
Procession of the Holy Ghost 656
Variety of ecclesiastical Discipline ib.
857–886. Ambitious Quarrels of Photius, Patriarch of Constantinople, with the Popes 657
1054 The Popes excommunicate the Patriarch of Constantinople and the Greeks 659
1100–1200. Enmity of the Greeks and Latins ib.

A.D.
The Latins at Constantinople 660
1183 Their Massacre 661
1185–1195. Reign and Character of Isaac Angelus 662
1186 Revolt of the Bulgarians 663
1195–1203. Usurpation and Character of Alexius Angelus 664
1198 The fourth Crusade 665
Embraced by the Barons of France 666
697–1200. State of the Venetians 668
1201 Alliance of the French and Venetians 670
1202 Assembly and Departure of the Crusade from Venice 672
Siege of Zara 673
Alliance of the Crusaders with the Greek Prince, the young Alexius 674
1203 Voyage from Zara to Constantinople 676
Fruitless Negociation of the Emperor 678
Passage of the Bosphorus 679
First Siege and Conquest of Constantinople by the Latins 681
Restoration of the Emperor Isaac Angelus, and his son Alexius 683
Quarrels of the Greeks and Latins 685
1204 The War renewed 687
Alexius and his Father deposed by Mourzoufle 688
Second Siege ib.
Pillage of Constantinople 691
Division of the Spoil 692
Misery of the Greeks 693
Sacrilege and Mockery 694
Destruction of the Statues 695

CHAP. LXI.

Partition of the Empire by the French and Venetians. – Five Latin Emperors of the Houses of Flanders and Courtenay. – Their Wars against the Bulgarians and Greeks. – Weakness and Poverty of the Latin Empire. – Recovery of Constantinople by the Greeks. – General Consequences of the Crusades.

A.D.
1204 Election of the Emperor Baldwin I. 699
Division of the Greek Empire 701
1204 Revolt of the Greeks 704
1204–1222. Theodore Lascaris, Emperor of Nice 705
The Dukes and Emperors of Trebizond 706
The Despots of Epirus ib.
1205 The Bulgarian War 707
Defeat and Captivity of Baldwin 709
Retreat of the Latins ib.
Death of the Emperor 710
1206–1216. Reign and Character of Henry 711
1217 Peter of Courtenay, Emperor of Constantinople 713
1217–1219. His Captivity and Death 714
1221–1228. Robert, Emperor of Constantinople 715
1228–1237. Baldwin II. and John of Brienne, Emperors of Constantinople 716
1237–1261. Baldwin II. 718
The Holy Crown of Thorns 720
1237–1261. Progress of the Greeks 721
1259 Michael Palæologus, the Greek Emperor 722
1261 Constantinople recovered by the Greeks 723
General Consequences of the Crusades 725

Digression on the Family of Courtenay.

1020 Origin of the Family of Courtenay 729

A.D.
1101–1152. I. The Counts of Edessa 729
II. The Courtenays of France 730
1150 Their Alliance with the Royal Family 731
III. The Courtenays of ngland 734
The Earls of Devonshire ib.

CHAP. LXII.

The Greek Emperors of Nice and Constantinople. – Elevation and Reign of Michael Palæologus. – His false Union with the Pope and the Latin Church. – Hostile Designs of Charles of Anjou. – Revolt of Sicily. – War of the Catalans in Asia and Greece. – Revolutions and present State of Athens.

A.D.
Restoration of the Greek Empire 737
1204–1222. Theodore Lascaris ib.
1222–1255. John Ducas Vataces ib.
1255–1259. Theodore Lascaris II. 739
1259 Minority of John Lascaris 740
Family and Character of Michael Palæologus 741
His Elevation to the Throne 743
1260 Michael Palæologus Emperor 745
1261 Recovery of Constantinople ib.
Return of the Greek Emperor 746
Palæologus blinds and banishes the young Emperor 747
1262–1268. Is excommunicated by the Patriarch Arsenius 748
1266–1312. Schism of the Arsenites 749
1259–1282. Reign of Michael Palæologus 750
1273–1332. Reign of Andronicus the Elder ib.
1274–1277. His Union with the Latin Church 751
1277–1282. His Persecution of the Greeks 753
1283 The Union dissolved 754
A.D.
1266 Charles of Anjou subdues Naples and Sicily 754
1270 Threatens the Greek Empire 755
1280 Palæologus instigates the Revolt of Sicily 756
1282 The Sicilian Vespers 757
Defeat of Charles 758
1303–1307. The Service and War of the Catalans in the Greek Empire 759
1204–1456. Revolutions of Athens 762
Present State of Athens 764

CHAP. LXIII.

Civil Wars, and Ruin of the Greek Empire. – Reigns of Andronicus, the Elder and Younger, and John Palæologus. – Regency, Revolt, Reign, and Abdication of John Cantacuzene. – Establishment of a Genoese Colony at Pera or Galata. – Their Wars with the Empire and City of Constantinople.

A.D.
1282–1320. Superstition of Andronicus and the Times 766
1320 First Disputes between the Elder and Younger Andronicus 768
1321–1328. Three Civil Wars between the two Emperors 770
1325 Coronation of the Younger Andronicus ib.
1328 The Elder Andronicus abdicates the Government 771
1332 His Death 772
1328–1341. Reign of Andronicus the Younger ib.
His two Wives 773
1341–1391. Reign of John Palæologus 774
Fortune of John Cantacuzenus ib.
He is left Regent of the Empire 775
1341 His Regency is attacked ib.
By Apocaucus, the Empress Anne of Savoy, and the Patriarch ib.

A.D.
Cantacuzene assumes the Purple 777
1341–1347. The Civil War 778
Victory of Cantacuzene ib.
1347 He re-enters Constantinople 780
1347–1355. Reign of John Cantacuzene ib.
1353 John Palæologus takes up Arms against him 782
1355 Abdication of Cantacuzene 783
1341–1351. Dispute concerning the Light of Mount Thabor ib.
1261–1347. Establishment of the Genoese at Pera or Galata 785
Their Trade and Insolence 786
1348 Their War with the Emperor Cantacuzene 787
1349 Destruction of his Fleet 788
1352 Victory of the Genoese over the Venetians and Greeks 789
Their Treaty with the Empire 790

CHAP. LXIV.

Conquests of Zingis Khan and the Moguls from China to Poland. – Escape of Constantinople and the Greeks. – Origin of the Ottoman Turks in Bithynia. – Reigns and Victories of Othman, Orchan, Amurath the First, and Bajazet the First. – Foundation and Progress of the Turkish Monarchy in Asia and Europe. – Danger of Constantinople and the Greek Empire.

A.D.
1206–1227. Zingis Khan, first Emperor of the Moguls and Tartars 791
His Laws 793
1210–1214. His Invasion of China 795
1218–1224. Of Carizme, Transoxiana, and Persia 796
1227 His Death 798
1227–1295. Conquests of the Moguls under the Successors of Zingis ib.

A.D.
1234 Of the Northern Empire of China 798
1279 Of the Southern 799
1258 Of Persia, and the Empire of the Caliphs 800
1242–1272. Of Anatolia 801
1235–1245. Of Kipzak, Russia, Poland, Hungary, &c. 802
1242 Of Siberia 804
1227–1259. The Successors of Zingis ib.
1259–1368. Adopt the Manners of China 805
1259–1300. Division of the Mogul Empire 806
1240–1304. Escape of Constantinople and the Greek Empire from the Moguls 807
1304 Decline of the Mogul Khans of Persia 808
1240 Origin of the Ottomans 809
1299–1326. Reign of Othman ib.
1326–1360. Reign of Orchan 811
1326–1339. His Conquest of Bithynia ib.
1300 Division of Anatolia among the Turkish Emirs 812
1312 Loss of the Asiatic Provinces ib.
1310–1523. The Knights of Rhodes ib.
1341–1347. First Passage of the Turks into Europe 813
1346 Marriage of Orchan with a Greek Princess 814
1353 Establishment of the Ottomans in Europe 815
Death of Orchan and his Son Soliman 816
1360–1389. The Reign and European Conquests of Amurath I. ib.
The Janizaries 817
1389–1403. The Reign of Bajazet I. Ilderim 818
His Conquests, from the Euphrates to the Danube ib.
1396 Battle of Nicopolis 820
1396–1398. Crusade and Captivity of the French Princes ib.
1355–1391. The Emperor John Palæologus 823
Discord of the Greeks ib.

A.D.
1391–1425. The Emperor Manuel 824
1395–1402. Distress of Constantinople ib.

CHAP. LXV.

Elevation of Timour or Tamerlane to the Throne of Samarcand. – His Conquests in Persia, Georgia, Tartary, Russia, India, Syria, and Anatolia. – His Turkish War. – Defeat and Captivity of Bajazet. – Death of Timour. – Civil War of the Sons of Bajazet. – Restoration of the Turkish Monarchy by Mahomet the First. – Siege of Constantinople by Amurath the Second.

A.D.
Histories of TIMOUR, or *Tamerlane* 826
1361–1370. His first Adventures 828
1370 He ascends the Throne of Zagatai 829
1370–1400. His Conquests 830
1380–1393. I. Of Persia ib.
1370–1383. II. Of Turkestan 831
1390–1396. Of Kipzak, Russia, &c. 832
1398, 1399. III. Of Hindostan 833
1400 His War against Sultan Bajazet 835
Timour invades Syria 837
Sacks Aleppo 838
1401 Damascus 839
And Bagdad ib.
1402 Invades Anatolia 840
Battle of Angora 841
Defeat and Captivity of Bajazet 842
The Story of his Iron Cage disproved by the Persian Historian of Timour 843
Attested, 1. by the French 844
——, 2. by the Italians ib.
——, 3. by the Arabs 845
——, 4. by the Greeks 846
——, 5. by the Turks ib.
Probable Conclusion ib.
1403 Death of Bajazet 847
Term of the Conquests of Timour ib.
1404, 1405. His Triumph at Samarcand 849
1405 His Death on the Road to China 850
Character and Merits of Timour ib.
1403–1421. Civil Wars of the Sons of Bajazet 853
1. Mustapha ib.
2. Isa 854
1403–1410. 3. Soliman ib.
1410 4. Mousa ib.
1413–1421. 5. Mahomet I. 855
1421–1451. Reign of Amurath II. ib.
1421 Re-union of the Ottoman Empire ib.
1402–1425. State of the Greek Empire 856
1422 Siege of Constantinople by Amurath II. 858
1425–1448. The Emperor John Palæologus II. 859
Hereditary Succession and Merit of the Ottomans ib.
Education and Discipline of the Turks 860
Invention and Use of Gunpowder 862

CHAP. LXVI.

Applications of the Eastern Emperors to the Popes. – Visits to the West, of John the First, Manuel, and John the Second, Palæologus. – Union of the Greek and Latin Churches, promoted by the Council of Basil, and concluded at Ferrara and Florence. – State of Literature at Constantinople. – Its Revival in Italy by the Greek Fugitives. – Curiosity and Emulation of the Latins.

A.D.
1339 Embassy of the Younger Andronicus to Pope Benedict XII. 864

A.D.
The Arguments for a Crusade and Union 865
1348 Negociation of Cantacuzene with Clement VI. 866
1355 Treaty of John Palæologus I. with Innocent VI. 868
1369 Visit of John Palæologus to Urban V. at Rome 869
1370 His Return to Constantinople 871
Visit of the Emperor Manuel ib.
1400 To the Court of France 872
Of England ib.
1402 His Return to Greece 873
Greek Knowledge and Descriptions 874
Of Germany ib.
Of France 875
Of England ib.
1402–1417. Indifference of Manuel towards the Latins 876
1417–1425. His Negociations 877
His private Motives ib.
His Death 878
1425–1437. Zeal of John Palæologus II. 879
Corruption of the Latin Church ib.
1377–1429. Schism 880
1409 Council of Pisa ib.
1414–1418. Of Constance ib.
1431–1443. Of Basil 881
Their Opposition to Eugenius IV. ib.
1434–1437. Negociations with the Greeks ib.
1437 John Palæologus embarks in the Pope's Gallies 882
1438 His triumphal Entry at Venice 885
—— into Ferrara 886
1438, 1439. Council of the Greeks and Latins at Ferrara and Florence 887
Negociations with the Greeks 890
1438 Eugenius deposed at Basil 892
Re-union of the Greeks at Florence ib.
1440 Their Return to Constantinople 893
1449 Final Peace of the Church ib.

A.D.
1300–1453. State of the Greek Language at Constantinople 894
Comparison of the Greeks and Latins 895
Revival of the Greek Learning in Italy 896
1339 Lessons of Barlaam 897
1339–1374. Studies of Petrarch 898
1360 Of Boccace 899
1360–1363. Leo Pilatus, first Greek Professor at Florence, and in the West ib.
1390–1415. Foundation of the Greek Language in Italy by Manuel Chrysoloras 900
1400–1500. The Greeks in Italy 902
Cardinal Bessarion, &c. 903
Their Faults and Merits ib.
The Platonic Philosophy 905
Emulation and Progress of the Latins 906
1447–1455. Nicholas V. ib.
1428–1492. Cosmo and Lorenzo of Medicis 907
Use and Abuse of ancient Learning 908

CHAP. LXVII.

Schism of the Greeks and Latins. – Reign and Character of Amurath the Second. – Crusade of Ladislaus King of Hungary. – His Defeat and Death. – John Huniades. – Scanderbeg. – Constantine Palæologus last Emperor of the East.

A.D.
Comparison of Rome and Constantinople 910
1440–1448. The Greek Schism after the Council of Florence 912
Zeal of the Orientals and Russians 914
1421–1451. Reign and Character of Amurath II. 915
1442–1444. His double Abdication 916

A.D.
1443 Eugenius forms a League against the Turks 917
Ladislaus, King of Poland and Hungary, marches against them 919
The Turkish Peace 920
1444 Violation of the Peace ib.
Battle of Warna 922
Death of Ladislaus 923
The Cardinal Julian ib.
John Corvinus Huniades 924
1456 His Defence of Belgrade, and Death 925
1404–1413. Birth and Education of Scanderbeg, Prince of Albania 926
1443 His Revolt from the Turks 927
His Valour 928
1467 And Death 929
1448–1453. Constantine, the last of the Roman or Greek Emperors 930
1450–1452. Embassies of Phranza 931
State of the Byzantine Court 933

CHAP. LXVIII.

Reign and Character of Mahomet the Second. – Siege, Assault, and final Conquest of Constantinople by the Turks. – Death of Constantine Palæologus. – Servitude of the Greeks. – Extinction of the Roman Empire in the East. – Consternation of Europe. – Conquests and Death of Mahomet the Second.

A.D.
Character of Mahomet II. 934
1451–1481. His Reign 936
1451 Hostile Intentions of Mahomet 937
1452 He builds a Fortress on the Bosphorus 939
The Turkish War 940
1452, 1453. Preparations for the Siege of Constantinople 941
The great Cannon of Mahomet 943

A.D.
1453 Mahomet II. forms the Siege of Constantinople 944
Forces of the Turks 945
—— of the Greeks 946
1452 False Union of the two Churches 947
Obstinacy and Fanaticism of the Greeks 948
1453 Siege of Constantinople by Mahomet II. 950
Attack and Defence 951
Succour and Victory of four Ships 952
Mahomet transports his Navy over Land 955
Distress of the City 957
Preparations of the Turks for the general Assault ib.
Last Farewel of the Emperor and the Greeks 959
The general Assault 960
Death of the Emperor Constantine Palælogus 962
Loss of the City and Empire 963
The Turks enter and pillage Constantinople ib.
Captivity of the Greeks 964
Amount of the Spoil 966
Mahomet II. visits the City, St. Sophia, the Palace, &c. 967
His Behaviour to the Greeks 968
He repeoples and adorns Constantinople 969
Extinction of the Imperial Families of Comnenus and Palæologus 971
1460 Loss of the Morea 972
1461 —— of Trebizond 973
1453 Grief and Terror of Europe 974
1481 Death of Mahomet II. 976

CHAP. LXIX.

State of Rome from the Twelfth Century. – Temporal Dominion of the Popes. – Seditions of the City. – Political Heresy of Arnold of Brescia. – Restoration of the

Republic. – The Senators. – Pride of the Romans. – Their Wars. – They are deprived of the Election and Presence of the Popes, who retire to Avignon. – The Jubilee. – Noble Families of Rome. – Feud of the Colonna and Ursini.

A.D.
1100–1500. State and Revolutions of Rome 978
800–1100. The French and German Emperors of Rome 979
Authority of the Popes in Rome 980
From Affection ib.
—— Right 981
—— Virtue ib.
—— Benefits ib.
Inconstancy of Superstition 982
Seditions of Rome against the Popes 983
1086–1305. Successors of Gregory VII. 984
1099–1118. Paschal II. ib.
1118, 1119. Gelasius II. 985
1144, 1145. Lucius II. ib.
1181–1185. Lucius III. ib.
1119–1124. Calistus II. 986
1130–1143. Innocent II. ib.
Character of the Romans by St. Bernard ib.
1140 Political Heresy of Arnold of Brescia 987
1144–1154. He exhorts the Romans to restore the Republic 989
1155 His Execution 990
1144 Restoration of the Senate 991
The Capitol 992
The Coin 993
The Præfect of the City 994
Number and Choice of the Senate 995
The Office of Senator ib.
1252–1258. Brancaleone 996
1265–1278. Charles of Anjou 997
1281 Pope Martin IV. 998
1328 The Emperor Lewis of Bavaria ib.

A.D.
Addresses of Rome to the Emperors ib.
1144 Conrad III. ib.
1155 Frederic I. 999
Wars of the Romans against the neighbouring Cities 1002
1167 Battle of Tusculum 1003
1234 —— of Viterbo 1004
The Election of the Popes ib.
1179 Right of the Cardinals established by Alexander III. 1005
1274 Institution of the Conclave by Gregory X. ib.
Absence of the Popes from Rome 1007
1294–1303. Boniface VIII. 1008
1309 Translation of the Holy See to Avignon 1009
1300 Institution of the Jubilee, or Holy Year 1010
1350 The second Jubilee 1012
The Nobles or Barons of Rome ib.
Family of Leo the Jew 1013
The Colonna 1014
And Ursini 1017
Their hereditary Feuds ib.

CHAP. LXX.

Character and Coronation of Petrarch. – Restoration of the Freedom and Government of Rome by the Tribune Rienzi. – His Virtues and Vices, his Expulsion and Death. – Return of the Popes from Avignon. – Great Schism of the West. – Reunion of the Latin Church. – Last Struggles of Roman Liberty. – Statutes of Rome. – Final Settlement of the Ecclesiastical State.

A.D.
1304–1374. Petrarch 1019
1341 His poetic Coronation at Rome 1021
Birth, Character, and patriotic Designs of Rienzi 1023

A.D.
1347 He assumes the Government of Rome 1025
With the Title and Office of Tribune 1026
Laws of the good Estate ib.
Freedom and Prosperity of the Roman Republic 1028
The Tribune is respected in Italy, &c. 1029
And celebrated by Petrarch 1030
His Vices and Follies 1031
1347 The Pomp of his Knighthood 1032
And Coronation 1033
Fear and Hatred of the Nobles of Rome 1034
They oppose Rienzi in Arms 1035
Defeat and Death of the Colonna 1036
Fall and Flight of the Tribune Rienzi 1037
1347–1354. Revolutions of Rome 1038
Adventures of Rienzi 1039
1351 A Prisoner at Avignon ib.
1354 Rienzi, Senator of Rome 1040
His Death 1041
1355 Petrarch invites and upbraids the Emperor Charles IV. ib.
He solicits the Popes of Avignon to fix their Residence at Rome 1042
1367–1370. Return of Urban V. 1043
1377 Final Return of Gregory XI. 1044
1378 His Death 1045
Election of Urban VI. ib.
Election of Clement VII. 1046
1378–1418. Great Schism of the West 1047
Calamities of Rome ib.
1392–1407. Negociations for Peace and Union 1048
1409 Council of Pisa 1049
1414–1418. Council of Constance 1050
Election of Martin V. 1051
1417 Martin V. ib.
1431 Eugenius IV. ib.
1447 Nicholas V. ib.
1434 Last Revolt of Rome ib.
1452 Last Coronation of a German Emperor, Frederic III. 1052

A.D.
The Statutes and Government of Rome 1052
1453 Conspiracy of Porcaro 1054
Last Disorders of the Nobles of Rome 1056
1500 The Popes acquire the absolute Dominion of Rome ib.
The Ecclesiastical Government 1058
1585–1590. Sixtus V. 1059

CHAP. LXXI.

Prospect of the Ruins of Rome in the Fifteenth Century. – Four Causes of Decay and Destruction. – Example of the Coliseum. – Renovation of the City. – Conclusion of the whole Work.

A.D.
1430 View and Discourse of Poggius from the Capitoline Hill 1062
His Description of the Ruins 1063
Gradual Decay of Rome 1064
Four Causes of Destruction 1065
I. The Injuries of Nature ib.
Hurricanes and Earthquakes 1066
Fires ib.
Inundations 1067
II. The hostile Attacks of the Barbarians and Christians 1068
III. The Use and Abuse of the Materials 1070
IV. The domestic Quarrels of the Romans 1073
The Coliseum or Amphitheatre of Titus 1076
Games of Rome 1077
1332 A Bull-feast in the Coliseum 1078
Injuries 1079
And Consecration of the Coliseum 1080
Ignorance and Barbarism of the Romans ib.
1420 Restoration and Ornaments of the City 1082
Final Conclusion 1084

THE

HISTORY

OF THE

DECLINE AND FALL

OF THE

ROMAN EMPIRE.

By EDWARD GIBBON, Esq;

VOLUME THE FIFTH.

LONDON:
PRINTED FOR A. STRAHAN; AND T. CADELL, IN THE STRAND.
MDCCLXXXVIII.

CHAPTER XLVIII

Plan of the Fifth and Sixth Volumes. – Succession and Characters of the Greek Emperors of Constantinople, from the Time of Heraclius to the Latin Conquest.

Defects of the Byzantine history.

I have now deduced from Trajan to Constantine, from Constantine to Heraclius, the regular series of the Roman emperors; and faithfully exposed the prosperous and adverse fortunes of their reigns. Five centuries of the decline and fall of the empire have already elapsed; but a period of more than eight hundred years still separates me from the term of my labours, the taking of Constantinople by the Turks. Should I persevere in the same course, should I observe the same measure, a prolix and slender thread would be spun through many a volume, nor would the patient reader find an adequate reward of instruction or amusement. At every step, as we sink deeper in the decline and fall of the Eastern empire, the annals of each succeeding reign would impose a more ungrateful and melancholy task. These annals must continue to repeat a tedious and uniform tale of weakness and misery; the natural connection of causes and events would be broken by frequent and hasty transitions, and a minute accumulation of circumstances must destroy the light and effect of those general pictures which compose the use and ornament of a remote history. From the time of Heraclius, the Byzantine theatre is contracted and darkened: the line of empire, which had been defined by the laws of Justinian and the arms of Belisarius, recedes on all sides from our view: the Roman name, the proper subject of our enquiries, is reduced to a narrow corner of Europe, to the lonely suburbs of Constantinople; and the fate of the Greek empire has been compared to that of the Rhine, which loses itself in the sands, before its waters can mingle with the ocean. The scale of dominion is diminished to our view by the distance of time and place: nor is the loss of external splendour compensated by the nobler gifts of virtue and genius. In the last moments of her decay, Constantinople was doubtless more opulent and populous than Athens at her most flourishing æra, when a scanty sum of six thousand talents, or twelve hundred thousand pounds sterling, was possessed by twenty-one thousand male citizens of an adult age. But each of these citizens was a freeman, who dared to assert the liberty of his thoughts, words, and actions; whose person and property were guarded by equal law; and who exercised his independent vote in the government of the republic. Their numbers seem to be multiplied by the strong and various discriminations of character: under the shield of freedom, on the wings of emulation and vanity, each Athenian aspired to the level of the national dignity: from this commanding eminence, some chosen spirits soared beyond the reach of a vulgar eye; and the chances of superior merit in a great and populous kingdom, as they are proved by experience, would excuse the computation of imaginary millions. The territories of Athens, Sparta, and their allies, do not exceed a moderate province of France or England: but after the trophies of Salamis and Platæa, they expand in our fancy to the gigantic size of Asia, which had been trampled under the feet of the victorious Greeks. But the subjects of the Byzantine empire, who assume and dishonour the names both of Greeks and Romans, present a dead uniformity of abject vices, which are neither softened by the weakness of humanity, nor animated by the vigour of memorable crimes. The freemen of antiquity might repeat with generous enthusiasm the sentence of Homer, "that on the first day of his servitude, the captive is deprived of one half of his manly virtue." But the poet had only seen the effects of civil or domestic slavery, nor could he foretell that the second moiety of manhood must be annihilated by the spiritual despotism, which shackles, not only the actions, but even the thoughts of the prostrate votary. By this double yoke, the Greeks were oppressed under the successors of Heraclius; the tyrant, a law of eternal justice, was degraded by the vices of his subjects; and on the throne, in the camp, in the schools, we search, perhaps with fruitless diligence, the names and characters that may deserve to be rescued from oblivion. Nor are the defects of the subject compensated by the skill and variety of the painters. Of a space of eight hundred years, the four first centuries are overspread with a cloud interrupted by some faint and broken rays of historic light: in the lives of the emperors, from Maurice to Alexius, Basil the Macedonian has alone been the theme of a separate work; and the absence, or loss, or imperfection of contemporary evidence, must be poorly supplied by the doubtful authority of more recent compilers. The four last centuries are exempt from the reproach of penury: and with the Comnenian family, the historic muse of Constantinople again revives, but her apparel is gaudy, her motions are without elegance or grace. A succession of priests, or courtiers, treads in each other's footsteps in the same path of servitude and superstition: their views are narrow, their judgment is feeble or corrupt; and we close the volume of copious barrenness, still ignorant of the causes of events, the characters of the actors, and the manners of the times, which they celebrate or deplore. The observation which has been applied to a man, may be extended to a whole people, that the energy of the sword is communicated to the pen; and it will be found by experience, that the tone of history will rise or fall with the spirit of the age.

Its connection with the revolutions of the world.

From these considerations, I should have abandoned without regret the Greek slaves and their servile historians, had I not reflected that the fate of the Byzantine monarchy is *passively* connected with the most splendid and important revolutions which have changed the state of the world. The space of the lost provinces was immediately replenished with new colonies and rising kingdoms: the active virtues of peace and war deserted from the vanquished to the victorious nations; and it is in their origin and conquests, in their religion and government, that we must explore the causes and effects of the decline and fall of the Eastern empire. Nor will this scope of narrative, the riches and variety of these materials, be incompatible with the unity of design and composition. As, in his daily prayers, the Musulman of Fez or Delhi still turns his face towards the temple of Mecca, the historian's eye shall be always fixed on the city of Constantinople. The excursive line may embrace the wilds of Arabia and Tartary, but the circle will be ultimately reduced to the decreasing limit of the Roman monarchy.

Plan of the fifth and sixth volumes.

On this principle I shall now establish the plan of the two last volumes of the present work. The first chapter will contain, in a regular series, the emperors who reigned at Constantinople during a period of six hundred years, from the days of Heraclius to the Latin conquest: a rapid abstract, which may be supported by a *general* appeal to the order and text of the original historians. In this introduction, I shall confine myself to the revolutions of the throne, the succession of families, the personal characters of the Greek princes, the mode of their life and death, the maxims and influence of their domestic government, and the tendency of their reign to accelerate or suspend the downfal of the Eastern empire. Such a chronological review will serve to illustrate the various argument of the subsequent chapters; and each circumstance of the eventful story of the Barbarians will adapt itself in a proper place to the Byzantine annals. The internal state of the empire, and the dangerous heresy of the Paulicians, which shook the East and enlightened the West, will be the subject of two separate chapters; but these enquiries must be postponed till our farther progress shall have opened the view of the world in the ninth and tenth centuries of the Christian æra. After this foundation of Byzantine history, the following nations will pass before our eyes, and each will occupy the space to which it may be entitled by greatness or merit, or the degree of connection with the Roman world and the present age. I. The FRANKS; a general appellation which includes all the Barbarians of France, Italy, and Germany, who were united by the sword and sceptre of Charlemagne. The persecution of images and their votaries, separated Rome and Italy from the Byzantine throne, and prepared the restoration of the Roman empire in the West. II. The ARABS or SARACENS. Three ample chapters will be devoted to this curious and interesting object. In the first, after a picture of the country and its inhabitants, I shall investigate the character of Mahomet; the character, religion, and success of the prophet. In the second I shall lead the Arabs to the conquest of Syria, Egypt, and Africa, the provinces of the Roman empire; nor can I check their victorious career till they have overthrown the monarchies of Persia and Spain. In the third I shall enquire how Constantinople and Europe were saved by the luxury and arts, the division and decay, of the empire of the caliphs. A single chapter will include, III. The BULGARIANS, IV. HUNGARIANS, and, V. RUSSIANS, who assaulted by sea or by land the provinces and the capital; but the last of these, so important in their present greatness, will excite some curiosity in their origin and infancy. VI. The NORMANS; or rather the private adventurers of that warlike people, who founded a powerful kingdom in Apulia and Sicily, shook the throne of Constantinople, displayed the trophies of chivalry, and almost realized the wonders of romance. VII. The LATINS; the subjects of the pope, the nations of the West, who enlisted under the banner of the cross for the recovery or relief of the holy sepulchre. The Greek emperors were terrified and preserved by the myriads of pilgrims who marched to Jerusalem with Godfrey of Bouillon and the peers of Christendom. The second and third crusades trod in the footsteps of the first: Asia and Europe were mingled in a sacred war of two hundred years; and the Christian powers were bravely resisted, and finally expelled, by Saladin and the Mamalukes of Egypt. In these memorable crusades, a fleet and army of French and Venetians were diverted from Syria to the Thracian Bosphorus: they assaulted the capital, they subverted the Greek monarchy: and a dynasty of Latin princes was seated near threescore years on the throne of Constantine. VIII. The GREEKS themselves, during this period of captivity and exile, must be considered as a foreign nation; the enemies, and again the sovereigns, of Constantinople. Misfortune had rekindled a spark of national virtue; and the Imperial series may be continued with some dignity from their restoration to the Turkish conquest. IX. The MOGULS and TARTARS. By the arms of Zingis and his descendants, the globe was shaken from China to Poland and Greece: the sultans were overthrown: the caliphs fell, and the Cæsars trembled on their throne. The victories of Timour suspended above fifty years the final ruin of the Byzantine empire. X. I have already noticed the first appearance of the TURKS, and the names of the fathers, of *Seljuk* and *Othman*, discriminate the two successive dynasties of the nation, which emerged in the eleventh century from the Scythian wilderness. The former established a potent and splendid kingdom from the banks of the Oxus to Antioch and Nice; and the first crusade was provoked by the violation of Jerusalem and the danger of Constantinople. From an humble origin, the *Ottomans* arose, the scourge and terror of Christendom. Constantinople was besieged and taken by Mahomet II. and his triumph annihilates the remnant, the image, the title, of the Roman empire in the East. The schism of the Greeks will be connected with their last calamities, and the restoration of learning in the Western world. I shall return from the captivity of the new, to the ruins of ancient ROME: and the venerable name, the interesting theme, will shed a ray of glory on the conclusion of my labours.

* * *

Second marriage and death of Heraclius.

The emperor Heraclius had punished a tyrant and ascended his throne; and the memory of his reign is perpetuated by the transient conquest, and irreparable loss, of the Eastern provinces. After the death of Eudocia, his first wife, he disobeyed the patriarch, and violated the laws, by his second marriage with his niece Martina; and the superstition of the Greeks beheld the judgment of heaven in the diseases of the father and the deformity of his offspring. But the opinion of an illegitimate birth is sufficient to distract the choice, and loosen the obedience, of the people: the ambition of Martina was quickened by maternal love, and perhaps by the envy of a step-mother; and the aged husband was too feeble to withstand the arts of conjugal allurements. Constantine, his eldest son, enjoyed in a mature age the title of Augustus; but the weakness of his constitution required a colleague and a guardian, and he yielded with secret reluctance to the partition of the empire. The senate was summoned to the palace to ratify or attest the association of Heracleonas, the son of Martina: the imposition of the diadem was consecrated by the prayer and blessing of

A.D. 638, July 4.

the patriarch; the senators and patricians adored the majesty of the great emperor and the partners of his reign; and as soon as the doors were thrown open, they were hailed by the tumultuary but important voice of the soldiers. After an interval of five months, the pompous ceremonies which formed the essence of the Byzantine state were celebrated in the cathedral and the hippodrome: the concord of the royal brothers was affectedly displayed by the younger leaning on the arm of the elder; and the name of Martina was mingled in the reluctant or venal acclamations of the people. Heraclius survived this association about two years: his last testament declared his two sons the equal heirs of the Eastern empire, and commanded them to honour his widow Martina as their mother and their sovereign.

A.D. 639, January.

A.D. 641, February 11.

Constantine III. A.D. 641, February.

When Martina first appeared on the throne with the name and attributes of royalty, she was checked by a firm, though respectful, opposition; and the dying embers of freedom were kindled by the breath of superstitious prejudice. "We reverence," exclaimed the voice of a citizen, "we reverence the mother of our princes; but to those princes alone our obedience is due; and Constantine, the elder emperor, is of an age to sustain, in his own hands, the weight of the sceptre. Your sex is excluded by nature from the toils of government. How could you combat, how could you answer, the Barbarians, who, with hostile or friendly intentions, may approach the royal city? May heaven avert from the Roman republic this national disgrace, which would provoke the patience of the slaves of Persia." Martina descended from the throne with indignation, and sought a refuge in the female apartment of the palace. The reign of Constantine the third lasted only one hundred and three days: he expired in the thirtieth year of his age, and, although his life had been a long malady, a belief was entertained that poison had been the means, and his cruel step-mother the author, of his untimely fate. Martina reaped indeed the harvest of his death, and assumed the government in the name of the surviving emperor; but the incestuous widow of Heraclius was universally abhorred; the jealousy of the people was awakened, and the two orphans whom Constantine had left, became the objects of the public care. It was in vain that the son of Martina, who was no more than fifteen years of age, was taught to declare himself the guardian of his nephews, one of whom he had presented at the baptismal font: it was in vain that he swore on the wood of the true cross, to defend them against all their enemies. On his death-bed, the late emperor had dispatched a trusty servant to arm the troops and provinces of the East in the defence of his helpless

Heracleonas, A.D. 641, May 25.

children: the eloquence and liberality of Valentin had been successful, and from his camp of Chalcedon, he boldly demanded the punishment of the assassins, and the restoration of the lawful heir. The licence of the soldiers who devoured the grapes and drank the wine of their Asiatic vineyards, provoked the citizens of Constantinople against the domestic authors of their calamities, and the dome of St. Sophia re-echoed, not with prayers and hymns, but with the clamours and imprecations of an enraged multitude. At their imperious command, Heracleonas appeared in the pulpit with the eldest of the royal orphans; Constans alone was saluted as emperor of the Romans, and a crown of gold, which had been taken from the tomb of Heraclius, was placed on his head, with the solemn benediction of the patriarch. But in the tumult of joy and indignation, the church was pillaged, the sanctuary was polluted by a promiscuous crowd of Jews and Barbarians; and the Monothelite Pyrrhus, a creature of the empress, after dropping a protestation on the altar, escaped by a prudent flight from the zeal of the Catholics. A more serious and bloody task was reserved for the senate, who derived a temporary strength from the consent of the soldiers and people. The spirit of Roman freedom revived the ancient and awful examples of the judgment of tyrants, and the Imperial culprits were deposed and condemned as the authors of the death of Constantine. But the severity of the conscript fathers was stained by the indiscriminate punishment of the innocent and the guilty: Martina and Heracleonas were sentenced to the amputation, the former of her tongue, the latter of his nose; and after this cruel execution, they consumed the remainder of their days in exile and oblivion. The Greeks who were capable of reflection might find some consolation for their servitude, by observing the abuse of power when it was lodged for a moment in the hands of an aristocracy.

Punishment of Martina and Heracleonas, A.D. 641, September.

We shall imagine ourselves transported five hundred years backwards to the age of the Antonines, if we listen to the oration which Constans II. pronounced in the twelfth year of his age before the Byzantine senate. After returning his thanks for the just punishment of the assassins who had intercepted the fairest hopes of his father's reign, "By the divine providence," said the young emperor, "and by your righteous decree, Martina and her incestuous progeny have been cast headlong from the throne. Your majesty and wisdom have prevented the Roman state from degenerating into lawless tyranny. I therefore exhort and beseech you to stand forth as the counsellors and judges of the common safety." The senators were gratified by the respectful address

Constans II. A.D. 641, September.

and liberal donative of their sovereign; but these servile Greeks were unworthy and regardless of freedom; and in his mind, the lesson of an hour was quickly erazed by the prejudices of the age and the habits of despotism. He retained only a jealous fear lest the senate or people should one day invade the right of primogeniture, and seat his brother Theodosius on an equal throne. By the imposition of holy orders, the grandson of Heraclius was disqualified for the purple; but this ceremony, which seemed to profane the sacraments of the church, was insufficient to appease the suspicions of the tyrant, and the death of the deacon Theodosius could alone expiate the crime of his royal birth. His murder was avenged by the imprecations of the people, and the assassin, in the fulness of power, was driven from his capital into voluntary and perpetual exile. Constans embarked for Greece; and, as if he meant to retort the abhorrence which he deserved, he is said, from the Imperial galley, to have spit against the walls of his native city. After passing the winter at Athens, he sailed to Tarentum in Italy, visited Rome, and concluded a long pilgrimage of disgrace and sacrilegious rapine, by fixing his residence at Syracuse. But if Constans could fly from his people, he could not fly from himself. The remorse of his conscience created a phantom who pursued him by land and sea, by day and by night; and the visionary Theodosius, presenting to his lips a cup of blood, said, or seemed to say, "Drink, brother, drink;" a sure emblem of the aggravation of his guilt, since he had received from the hands of the deacon the mystic cup of the blood of Christ. Odious to himself and to mankind, Constans perished by domestic, perhaps by episcopal, treason, in the capital of Sicily. A servant who waited in the bath, after pouring warm water on his head, struck him violently with the vase. He fell, stunned by the blow and suffocated by the water; and his attendants, who wondered at the tedious delay, beheld with indifference the corpse of their lifeless emperor. The troops of Sicily invested with the purple an obscure youth, whose inimitable beauty eluded, and it might easily elude, the declining art of the painters and sculptors of the age.

Constantine IV. Pogonatus, A.D. 668, September.

Constans had left in the Byzantine palace three sons, the eldest of whom had been clothed in his infancy with the purple. When the father summoned them to attend his person in Sicily, these precious hostages were detained by the Greeks, and a firm refusal informed him that they were the children of the state. The news of his murder was conveyed with almost supernatural speed from Syracuse to Constantinople; and Constantine, the eldest of his sons, inherited his throne without being the heir of the public hatred. His subjects contributed, with zeal and alacrity, to chastise the guilt and presumption of a province which had usurped the rights of the senate and people; the young emperor sailed from the Hellespont with a powerful fleet; and the legions of Rome and Carthage were assembled under his standard in the harbour of Syracuse. The defeat of the Sicilian tyrant was easy, his punishment just, and his beauteous head was exposed in the hippodrome: but I cannot applaud the clemency of a prince, who, among a crowd of victims, condemned the son of a patrician, for deploring with some bitterness the execution of a virtuous father. The youth was castrated: he survived the operation, and the memory of this indecent cruelty is preserved by the elevation of Germanus to the rank of a patriarch and saint. After pouring this bloody libation on his father's tomb, Constantine returned to his capital, and the growth of his young beard during the Sicilian voyage, was announced by the familiar surname of Pogonatus, to the Grecian world. But his reign, like that of his predecessor, was stained with fraternal discord. On his two brothers, Heraclius and Tiberius, he had bestowed the title of Augustus: an empty title, for they continued to languish without trust or power in the solitude of the palace. At their secret instigation, the troops of the Anatolian *theme* or province approached the city on the Asiatic side, demanded for the royal brothers, the partition or exercise of sovereignty, and supported their seditious claim by a theological argument. They were Christians (they cried), and orthodox Catholics; the sincere votaries of the holy and undivided Trinity. Since there are three equal persons in heaven, it is reasonable there should be three equal persons upon earth. The emperor invited these learned divines to a friendly conference, in which they might propose their arguments to the senate: they obeyed the summons, but the prospect of their bodies hanging on the gibbet in the suburb of Galata, reconciled their companions to the unity of the reign of Constantine. He pardoned his brothers, and their names were still pronounced in the public acclamations: but on the repetition or suspicion of a similar offence, the obnoxious princes were deprived of their titles and noses, in the presence of the Catholic bishops who were assembled at Constantinople in the sixth general synod. In the close of his life, Pogonatus was anxious only to establish the right of primogeniture: the hair of his two sons, Justinian and Heraclius, was offered on the shrine of St. Peter, as a symbol of their spiritual adoption by the pope; but the elder was alone exalted to the rank of Augustus and the assurance of the empire.

After the decease of his father, the inheritance of the Roman world

Justinian II. A.D. 685, September. devolved to Justinian II.; and the name of a triumphant lawgiver was dishonoured by the vices of a boy, who imitated his namesake only in the expensive luxury of building. His passions were strong; his understanding was feeble; and he was intoxicated with a foolish pride, that his birth had given him the command of millions, of whom the smallest community would not have chosen him for their local magistrate. His favourite ministers were two beings the least susceptible of human sympathy, an eunuch and a monk: to the one he abandoned the palace, to the other the finances; the former corrected the emperor's mother with a scourge, the latter suspended the insolvent tributaries, with their heads downwards, over a slow and smoaky fire. Since the days of Commodus and Caracalla, the cruelty of the Roman princes had most commonly been the effect of their fear; but Justinian, who possessed some vigour of character, enjoyed the sufferings, and braved the revenge, of his subjects about ten years, till the measure was full, of his crimes and of their patience. In a dark dungeon, Leontius, a general of reputation, had groaned above three years, with some of the noblest and most deserving of the patricians: he was suddenly drawn forth to assume the government of Greece; and this promotion of an injured man was a mark of the contempt rather than of the confidence of his prince. As he was followed to the port by the kind offices of his friends, Leontius observed with a sigh that he was a victim adorned for sacrifice, and that inevitable death would pursue his footsteps. They ventured to reply, that glory and empire might be the recompense of a generous resolution; that every order of men abhorred the reign of a monster; and that the hands of two hundred thousand patriots expected only the voice of a leader. The night was chosen for their deliverance; and in the first effort of the conspirators, the præfect was slain, and the prisons were forced open: the emissaries of Leontius proclaimed in every street, "Christians, to St. Sophia;" and the seasonable text of the patriarch, "this is the day of the Lord!" was the prelude of an inflammatory sermon. From the church the people adjourned to the hippodrome: Justinian, in whose cause not a sword had been drawn, was dragged before these tumultuary judges, and their clamours demanded the instant death of the tyrant. But Leontius, who was already clothed with the purple, cast an eye of pity on the prostrate son of his own benefactor and of so many emperors. The life of Justinian was spared; the amputation of his nose, perhaps of his tongue, was imperfectly performed: the happy flexibility of the Greek language could impose the name of Rhinotmetus; and the mutilated tyrant was banished to Chersonæ in

Crim-Tartary, a lonely settlement, where corn, wine, and oil, were imported as foreign luxuries.

His exile, A.D. 695–705.

On the edge of the Scythian wilderness, Justinian still cherished the pride of his birth and the hope of his restoration. After three years exile, he received the pleasing intelligence that his injury was avenged by a second revolution, and that Leontius in his turn had been dethroned and mutilated by the rebel Apsimar, who assumed the more respectable name of Tiberius. But the claim of lineal succession was still formidable to a plebeian usurper; and his jealousy was stimulated by the complaints and charges of the Chersonites, who beheld the vices of the tyrant in the spirit of the exile. With a band of followers, attached to his person by common hope or common despair, Justinian fled from the inhospitable shore to the hord of the Chozars, who pitched their tents between the Tanais and Borysthenes. The khan entertained with pity and respect the royal suppliant: Phanagoria, once an opulent city, on the Asiatic side of the lake Mœotis, was assigned for his residence; and every Roman prejudice was stifled in his marriage with the sister of the Barbarian, who seems, however, from the name of Theodora, to have received the sacrament of baptism. But the faithless Chozar was soon tempted by the gold of Constantinople; and had not the design been revealed by the conjugal love of Theodora, her husband must have been assassinated, or betrayed into the power of his enemies. After strangling, with his own hands, the two emissaries of the khan, Justinian sent back his wife to her brother, and embarked on the Euxine in search of new and more faithful allies. His vessel was assaulted by a violent tempest; and one of his pious companions advised him to deserve the mercy of God by a vow of general forgiveness, if he should be restored to the throne. "Of forgiveness?" replied the intrepid tyrant: "may I perish this instant – may the Almighty whelm me in the waves – if I consent to spare a single head of my enemies!" He survived this impious menace, sailed into the mouth of the Danube, trusted his person in the royal village of the Bulgarians, and purchased the aid of Terbelis, a Pagan conqueror, by the promise of his daughter and a fair partition of the treasures of the empire. The Bulgarian kingdom extended to the confines of Thrace; and the two princes besieged Constantinople at the head of fifteen thousand horse. Apsimar was dismayed by the sudden and hostile apparition of his rival, whose head had been promised by the Chozar, and of whose evasion he was yet ignorant. After an absence of ten years, the crimes of Justinian were faintly remembered, and the birth and misfortunes of their hereditary sovereign excited the pity of the multitude, ever discontented with the ruling powers; and by the active diligence of his adherents he was introduced into the city and palace of Constantine.

His restoration and death, A.D. 705–711.

In rewarding his allies and recalling his wife, Justinian displayed some sense of honour and gratitude; and Terbelis retired, after sweeping away an heap of gold coin, which he measured with his Scythian whip. But never was vow more religiously performed than the sacred oath of revenge which he had sworn amidst the storms of the Euxine. The two usurpers, for I must reserve the name of tyrant for the conqueror, were dragged into the hippodrome, the one from his prison, the other from his palace. Before their execution, Leontius and Apsimar were cast prostrate in chains beneath the throne of the emperor; and Justinian, planting a foot on each of their necks, contemplated above an hour the chariot-race, while the inconstant people shouted, in the words of the Psalmist, "Thou shalt trample on the asp and basilisk, and on the lion and dragon shalt thou set thy foot!" The universal defection which he had once experienced might provoke him to repeat the wish of Caligula, that the Roman people had but one head. Yet I shall presume to observe, that such a wish is unworthy of an ingenious tyrant, since his revenge and cruelty would have been extinguished by a single blow, instead of the slow variety of tortures which Justinian inflicted on the victims of his anger. His pleasures were inexhaustible: neither private virtue nor public service could expiate the guilt of active, or even passive, obedience to an established government; and during the six years of his new reign, he considered the axe, the cord, and the rack, as the only instruments of royalty. But his most implacable hatred was pointed against the Chersonites, who had insulted his exile and violated the laws of hospitality. Their remote situation afforded some means of defence, or at least of escape; and a grievous tax was imposed on Constantinople, to supply the preparations of a fleet and army. "All are guilty, and all must perish," was the mandate of Justinian; and the bloody execution was entrusted to his favourite Stephen, who was recommended by the epithet of the savage. Yet even the savage Stephen imperfectly accomplished the intentions of his sovereign. The slowness of his attack allowed the greater part of the inhabitants to withdraw into the country; and the minister of vengeance contented himself with reducing the youth of both sexes to a state of servitude, with roasting alive seven of the principal citizens, with drowning twenty in the sea, and with reserving forty-two in chains to receive their doom from the mouth of the emperor. In their return, the fleet was driven on the rocky shores of Anatolia; and Justinian applauded the obedience of the Euxine, which had involved so many thousands of his subjects and enemies in a common shipwreck: but the tyrant was still insatiate of blood; and a second expedition was commanded to extirpate the remains of the proscribed colony. In the short interval, the Chersonites had returned to their city, and were prepared to die in arms; the khan of the Chozars had renounced the cause of his odious brother; the exiles of every province were assembled in Tauris; and Bardanes, under the name of Philippicus, was invested with the purple. The Imperial troops, unwilling and unable to perpetrate the revenge of Justinian, escaped his displeasure by abjuring his allegiance: the fleet, under their new sovereign, steered back a more auspicious course to the harbours of Sinope and Constantinople; and every tongue was prompt to pronounce, every hand to execute, the death of the tyrant. Destitute of friends, he was deserted by his Barbarian guards; and the stroke of the assassin was praised as an act of patriotism and Roman virtue. His son Tiberius had taken refuge in a church; his aged grandmother guarded the door; and the innocent youth, suspending round his neck the most formidable relics, embraced with one hand the altar, with the other the wood of the true cross. But the popular fury that dares to trample on superstition, is deaf to the cries of humanity; and the race of Heraclius was extinguished after a reign of one hundred years.

Philippicus, A.D. 711, December.

Between the fall of the Heraclian and the rise of the Isaurian dynasty, a short interval of six years is divided into three reigns. Bardanes, or Philippicus, was hailed at Constantinople as an hero who had delivered his country from a tyrant; and he might taste some moments of happiness in the first transports of sincere and universal joy. Justinian had left behind him an ample treasure, the fruit of cruelty and rapine: but this useful fund was soon and idly dissipated by his successor. On the festival of his birth-day, Philippicus entertained the multitude with the games of the hippodrome; from thence he paraded through the streets with a thousand banners and a thousand trumpets; refreshed himself in the baths of Zeuxippus, and, returning to the palace, entertained his nobles with a sumptuous banquet. At the meridian hour he withdrew to his chamber, intoxicated with flattery and wine, and forgetful that his example had made every subject ambitious, and that every ambitious subject was his secret enemy. Some bold conspirators introduced themselves in the disorder of the feast; and the slumbering monarch was surprised, bound, blinded, and deposed, before he was sensible of his danger. Yet the traitors were deprived of their reward; and the free voice of the senate and people promoted Artemius from the office of

Anastasius II. A.D. 713, June 4.

secretary to that of emperor: he assumed the title of Anastasius the second, and displayed in a short and troubled reign the virtues both of peace and war. But, after the extinction of the Imperial line, the rule of obedience was violated, and every change diffused the seeds of new revolutions. In a mutiny of the fleet, an obscure and reluctant officer of the revenue was forcibly invested with the purple: after some months of a naval war, Anastasius resigned the sceptre; and the conqueror, Theodosius the third, submitted in his turn to the superior ascendant of Leo, the general and emperor of the Oriental troops. His two predecessors were permitted to embrace the ecclesiastical profession: the restless impatience of Anastasius tempted him to risk and to lose his life in a treasonable enterprise; but the last days of Theodosius were honourable and secure. The single sublime word "HEALTH," which he inscribed on his tomb, expresses the confidence of philosophy or religion; and the fame of his miracles was long preserved among the people of Ephesus. This convenient shelter of the church might sometimes impose a lesson of clemency; but it may be questioned whether it is for the public interest to diminish the perils of unsuccessful ambition.

Theodosius III. A.D. 716, January.

Leo III. the Isaurian, A.D. 718, March 25.

I have dwelt on the fall of a tyrant; I shall briefly represent the founder of a new dynasty, who is known to posterity by the invectives of his enemies, and whose public and private life is involved in the ecclesiastical story of the Iconoclasts. Yet in spite of the clamours of superstition, a favourable prejudice for the character of Leo the Isaurian, may be reasonably drawn from the obscurity of his birth, and the duration of his reign. – I. In an age of manly spirit, the prospect of an Imperial reward would have kindled every energy of the mind, and produced a crowd of competitors as deserving as they were desirous to reign. Even in the corruption and debility of the modern Greeks, the elevation of a plebeian from the last to the first rank of society, supposes some qualifications above the level of the multitude. He would probably be ignorant and disdainful of speculative science; and in the pursuit of fortune, he might absolve himself from the obligations of benevolence and justice: but to his character we may ascribe the useful virtues of prudence and fortitude, the knowledge of mankind, and the important art of gaining their confidence and directing their passions. It is agreed that Leo was a native of Isauria, and that Conon was his primitive name. The writers, whose awkward satire is praise, describe him as an itinerant pedlar who drove an ass with some paltry merchandise to the country fairs; and foolishly relate that he met on the road some Jewish fortune-tellers, who promised him the Roman empire, on condition that he should abolish the worship of idols. A more probable account relates the migration of his father from Asia Minor to Thrace, where he exercised the lucrative trade of a grazier; and he must have acquired considerable wealth, since the first introduction of his son was procured by a supply of five hundred sheep to the Imperial camp. His first service was in the guards of Justinian, where he soon attracted the notice, and by degrees the jealousy, of the tyrant. His valour and dexterity were conspicuous in the Colchian war: from Anastasius he received the command of the Anatolian legions, and by the suffrage of the soldiers he was raised to the empire with the general applause of the Roman world. – II. In this dangerous elevation, Leo the third supported himself against the envy of his equals, the discontent of a powerful faction, and the assaults of his foreign and domestic enemies. The Catholics, who accuse his religious innovations, are obliged to confess that they were undertaken with temper and conducted with firmness. Their silence respects the wisdom of his administration and the purity of his manners. After a reign of twenty-four years, he peaceably expired in the palace of Constantinople; and the purple which he had acquired, was transmitted by the right of inheritance to the third generation.

Constantine V. Copronymus, A.D. 741, June 18.

In a long reign of thirty-four years, the son and successor of Leo, Constantine the fifth, surnamed Copronymus, attacked with less temperate zeal the images or idols of the church. Their votaries have exhausted the bitterness of religious gall, in their portrait of this spotted panther, this anti-christ, this flying dragon of the serpent's seed, who surpassed the vices of Elagabalus and Nero. His reign was a long butchery of whatever was most noble, or holy, or innocent, in his empire. In person, the emperor assisted at the execution of his victims, surveyed their agonies, listened to their groans, and indulged, without satiating, his appetite for blood: a plate of noses was accepted as a grateful offering, and his domestics were often scourged or mutilated by the royal hand. His surname was derived from his pollution of his baptismal font. The infant might be excused; but the manly pleasures of Copronymus degraded him below the level of a brute; his lust confounded the eternal distinctions of sex and species; and he seemed to extract some unnatural delight from the objects most offensive to human sense. In his religion, the Iconoclast was an Heretic, a Jew, a Mahometan, a Pagan, and an Atheist; and his belief of an invisible power could be discovered only in his magic rites, human victims, and nocturnal sacrifices to Venus and the dæmons of antiquity. His life was stained with the most opposite vices, and the ulcers which covered his body, anticipated before his death the sentiment of hell-tortures. Of these accusations, which I have so patiently copied, a part is refuted by its own absurdity; and in the private anecdotes of the life of princes, the lie is more easy as the detection is more difficult. Without adopting the pernicious maxim, that where much is alleged, something must be true, I can however discern, that Constantine the fifth was dissolute and cruel. Calumny is more prone to exaggerate than to invent; and her licentious tongue is checked in some measure by the experience of the age and country to which she appeals. Of the bishops and monks, the generals and magistrates, who are said to have suffered under his reign, the numbers are recorded, the names were conspicuous, the execution was public, the mutilation visible and permanent. The Catholics hated the person and government of Copronymus; but even their hatred is a proof of their oppression. They dissemble the provocations which might excuse or justify his rigour, but even these provocations must gradually inflame his resentment, and harden his temper in the use or the abuse of despotism. Yet the character of the fifth Constantine was not devoid of merit, nor did his government always deserve the curses or the contempt of the Greeks. From the confession of his enemies, I am informed of the restoration of an ancient aqueduct, of the redemption of two thousand five hundred captives, of the uncommon plenty of the times, and of the new colonies with which he repeopled Constantinople and the Thracian cities. They reluctantly praise his activity and courage; he was on horseback in the field at the head of his legions; and, although the fortune of his arms was various, he triumphed by sea and land, on the Euphrates and the Danube, in civil and Barbarian war. Heretical praise must be cast into the scale, to counterbalance the weight of orthodox invective. The Iconoclasts revered the virtues of the prince: forty years after his death, they still prayed before the tomb of the saint. A miraculous vision was propagated by fanaticism or fraud: and the Christian hero appeared on a milk-white steed, brandishing his lance against the pagans of Bulgaria: "An absurd fable," says the Catholic historian, "since Copronymus is chained with the dæmons in the abyss of hell."

Leo IV. A.D. 775, Sept. 14. Leo the fourth, the son of the fifth and the father of the sixth Constantine, was of a feeble constitution both of mind and body, and the principal care of his reign was the settlement of the succession. The association of the young Constantine was urged by the officious zeal of his subjects; and the emperor, conscious of his decay, complied, after a prudent hesitation, with their unanimous wishes. The royal infant, at the age of five years, was crowned with his mother Irene; and the national consent was ratified by every circumstance of pomp and solemnity, that could dazzle the eyes, or bind the conscience, of the Greeks. An oath of fidelity was administered in the palace, the church, and the hippodrome, to the several orders of the state, who adjured the holy names of the son, and mother, of God. "Be witness, O Christ! that we will watch over the safety of Constantine the son of Leo, expose our lives in his service, and bear true allegiance to his person and posterity." They pledged their faith on the wood of the true cross, and the act of their engagement was deposited on the altar of St. Sophia. The first to swear, and the first to violate their oath, were the five sons of Copronymus by a second marriage; and the story of these princes is singular and tragic. The right of primogeniture excluded them from the throne; the injustice of their elder brother defrauded them of a legacy of about two millions sterling; some vain titles were not deemed a sufficient compensation for wealth and power; and they repeatedly conspired against their nephew, before and after the death of his father. Their first attempt was pardoned; for the second offence they were condemned to the ecclesiastical state: and for the third treason, Nicephorus, the eldest and most guilty, was deprived of his eyes, and his four brothers, Christopher, Nicetas, Anthemeus, and Eudoxas, were punished, as a milder sentence, by the amputation of their tongues. After five years confinement, they escaped to the church of St. Sophia, and displayed a pathetic spectacle to the people. "Countrymen and Christians," cried Nicephorus for himself and his mute brethren, "behold the sons of your emperor, if you can still recognise our features in this miserable state. A life, an imperfect life, is all that the malice of our enemies has spared. It is now threatened, and we now throw ourselves on your compassion." The rising murmur might have produced a revolution, had it not been checked by the presence of a minister, who soothed the unhappy princes with flattery and hope, and gently drew them from the sanctuary to the palace. They were speedily embarked for Greece, and Athens was allotted for the place of their exile. In this calm retreat, and in their helpless condition, Nicephorus and his brothers were tormented by the thirst of power, and tempted by a Sclavonian chief, who offered to break their prison, and to lead them in arms, and in the purple, to the gates of Constantinople. But the Athenian people, ever zealous in the cause of Irene, prevented her justice or cruelty; and the five sons of Copronymus were plunged in eternal darkness and oblivion.

Constantine VI. and Irene, A.D. 780, September 8.

For himself, that emperor had chosen a Barbarian wife, the daughter of the khan of the Chozars: but in the marriage of his heir, he preferred an Athenian virgin, an orphan, seventeen years old, whose sole fortune must have consisted in her personal accomplishments. The nuptials of Leo and Irene were celebrated with royal pomp; she soon acquired the love and confidence of a feeble husband, and in his testament he declared the empress, guardian of the Roman world, and of their son Constantine the sixth, who was no more than ten years of age. During his childhood, Irene most ably and assiduously discharged, in her public administration, the duties of a faithful mother; and her zeal in the restoration of images has deserved the name and honours of a saint, which she still occupies in the Greek calendar. But the emperor attained the maturity of youth; the maternal yoke became more grievous; and he listened to the favourites of his own age, who shared his pleasures, and were ambitious of sharing his power. Their reasons convinced him of his right, their praises of his ability, to reign; and he consented to reward the services of Irene by a perpetual banishment to the isle of Sicily. But her vigilance and penetration easily disconcerted their rash projects; a similar, or more severe, punishment was retaliated on themselves and their advisers; and Irene inflicted on the ungrateful prince the chastisement of a boy. After this contest, the mother and the son were at the head of two domestic factions; and, instead of mild influence and voluntary obedience, she held in chains a captive and an enemy. The empress was overthrown by the abuse of victory; the oath of fidelity which she exacted to herself alone, was pronounced with reluctant murmurs; and the bold refusal of the Armenian guards encouraged a free and general declaration, that Constantine the sixth was the lawful emperor of the Romans. In this character he ascended his hereditary throne, and dismissed Irene to a life of solitude and repose. But her haughty spirit condescended to the arts of dissimulation: she flattered the bishops and eunuchs, revived the filial tenderness of the prince, regained his confidence, and betrayed his credulity. The character of Constantine was not destitute of sense or spirit; but his education had been studiously neglected; and his ambitious mother exposed to the public censure the vices which she had nourished and the actions which she had secretly advised: his divorce and second marriage offended the prejudices of the clergy, and by his imprudent rigour he forfeited the attachment of the Armenian guards. A powerful conspiracy was formed for the restoration of Irene; and the secret, though widely diffused, was faithfully kept above eight months, till the emperor, suspicious of his danger, escaped from Constantinople, with the design of appealing to the provinces and armies. By this hasty flight, the empress was left on the brink of the precipice; yet before she implored the mercy of her son, Irene addressed a private epistle to the friends whom she had placed about his person, with a menace, that unless *they* accomplished, *she* would reveal, their treason. Their fear rendered them intrepid; they seized the emperor on the Asiatic shore, and he was transported to the porphyry apartment of the palace, where he had first seen the light. In the mind of Irene, ambition had stifled every sentiment of humanity and nature; and it was decreed in her bloody council, that Constantine should be rendered incapable of the throne: her emissaries assaulted the sleeping prince, and stabbed their daggers with such violence and precipitation into his eyes, as if they meant to execute a mortal sentence. An ambiguous passage of Theophanes persuaded the annalist of the church that death was the immediate consequence of this barbarous execution. The Catholics have been deceived or subdued by the authority of Baronius; and protestant zeal has re-echoed the words of a cardinal, desirous, as it should seem, to favour the patroness of images. Yet the blind son of Irene survived many years, oppressed by the court and forgotten by the world: the Isaurian dynasty was silently extinguished; and the memory of Constantine was recalled only by the nuptials of his daughter Euphrosyne with the emperor Michael the second.

Irene, A.D. 792, August 19.

The most bigotted orthodoxy has justly execrated the unnatural mother, who may not easily be paralleled in the history of crimes. To her bloody deed, superstition has attributed a subsequent darkness of seventeen days; during which many vessels in mid-day were driven from their course, as if the sun, a globe of fire so vast and so remote, could sympathise with the atoms of a revolving planet. On earth, the crime of Irene was left five years unpunished; her reign was crowned with external splendour; and if she could silence the voice of conscience, she neither heard nor regarded the reproaches of mankind. The Roman world bowed to the government of a female; and as she moved through the streets of Constantinople, the reins of four milk-white steeds were held by as many patricians, who marched on foot before the golden chariot of their queen. But these patricians were for the most part eunuchs; and their black ingratitude justified, on this occasion, the popular hatred and contempt. Raised, enriched, entrusted with the first dignities of the empire, they basely conspired against their benefactress: the great treasurer Nicephorus was secretly invested with the purple; her successor was introduced into the palace, and crowned at St. Sophia by the venal patriarch. In their first interview, she recapitulated with dignity the revolutions of her life, gently accused the perfidy of Nicephorus, insinuated that he owed his life to her unsuspicious clemency, and, for the throne and treasures which she resigned, solicited a decent and honourable retreat. His avarice refused this modest compensation; and, in her exile of the isle of Lesbos, the empress earned a scanty subsistence by the labours of her distaff.

Nicephorus I. A.D. 802, October 31.

Many tyrants have reigned undoubtedly more criminal than Nicephorus, but none perhaps have more deeply incurred the universal abhorrence of their people. His character was stained with the three odious vices of hypocrisy, ingratitude, and avarice: his want of virtue was not redeemed by any superior talents, nor his want of talents by any pleasing qualifications. Unskilful and unfortunate in war, Nicephorus was vanquished by the Saracens, and slain by the Bulgarians; and the advantage of his death overbalanced, in the public opinion, the destruction of a Roman army. His son and heir Stauracius escaped from the field with a mortal wound: yet six months of an expiring life were sufficient to refute his indecent, though popular declaration, that he would in all things avoid the example of his father. On the near prospect of his decease, Michael, the great master of the palace, and the husband of his sister Procopia, was named by every person of the palace and city, except by his envious brother. Tenacious of a sceptre now falling from his hand, he conspired against the life of his successor, and cherished the idea of changing to a democracy the Roman empire. But these rash projects served only to inflame the zeal of the people and to remove the scruples of the candidate: Michael the first accepted the purple, and before he sunk into the grave, the son of Nicephorus implored the clemency of his new sovereign. Had Michael in an age of peace ascended an hereditary throne, he might have reigned and died the father of his people: but his mild virtues were adapted to the shade of private life, nor was he capable of controlling the ambition of his equals, or of resisting the arms of the victorious Bulgarians. While his want of ability and success exposed him to the contempt of the soldiers, the masculine spirit of his wife Procopia awakened their indignation. Even the Greeks of the ninth century were provoked by the insolence of a female, who, in the front of the standards, presumed to direct their discipline and animate their valour; and their licentious clamours advised the new Semiramis to reverence the majesty of a Roman camp. After an unsuccessful campaign, the emperor left in their winter-quarters of Thrace, a disaffected army under the command of his enemies;

Stauracius, A.D. 811, July 25.

Michael I. Rhangabe, A.D. 811, October 2.

and their artful eloquence persuaded the soldiers to break the dominion of the eunuchs, to degrade the husband of Procopia, and to assert the right of a military election. They marched towards the capital: yet the clergy, the senate, and the people of Constantinople, adhered to the cause of Michael; and the troops and treasures of Asia might have protracted the mischiefs of civil war. But his humanity (by the ambitious, it will be termed his weakness) protested, that not a drop of Christian blood should be shed in his quarrel, and his messengers presented the conquerors with the keys of the city and the palace. They were disarmed by his innocence and submission; his life and his eyes were spared; and the Imperial monk enjoyed the comforts of solitude and religion above thirty-two years after he had been stripped of the purple and separated from his wife.

Leo V. the Armenian, A.D. 813, July 11.

A rebel, in the time of Nicephorus, the famous and unfortunate Bardanes, had once the curiosity to consult an Asiatic prophet, who, after prognosticating his fall, announced the fortunes of his three principal officers, Leo the Armenian, Michael the Phrygian, and Thomas the Cappadocian, the successive reigns of the two former, the fruitless and fatal enterprise of the third. This prediction was verified, or rather was produced, by the event. Ten years afterwards, when the Thracian camp rejected the husband of Procopia, the crown was presented to the same Leo, the first in military rank and the secret author of the mutiny. As he affected to hesitate, "With this sword," said his companion Michael, "I will open the gates of Constantinople to your Imperial sway; or instantly plunge it into your bosom, if you obstinately resist the just desires of your fellow-soldiers." The compliance of the Armenian was rewarded with the empire, and he reigned seven years and an half under the name of Leo the fifth. Educated in a camp, and ignorant both of laws and letters, he introduced into his civil government the rigour and even cruelty of military discipline; but if his severity was sometimes dangerous to the innocent, it was always formidable to the guilty. His religious inconstancy was taxed by the epithet of Chameleon, but the Catholics have acknowledged by the voice of a saint and confessors, that the life of the Iconoclast was useful to the republic. The zeal of his companion Michael was repaid with riches, honours, and military command; and his subordinate talents were beneficially employed in the public service. Yet the Phrygian was dissatisfied at receiving as a favour a scanty portion of the Imperial prize which he had bestowed on his equal; and his discontent, which sometimes evaporated in hasty discourse, at length assumed a more threatening and hostile aspect against a prince whom he represented as a cruel tyrant. That tyrant, however, repeatedly detected, warned, and dismissed the old companion of his arms, till fear and resentment prevailed over gratitude; and Michael, after a scrutiny into his actions and designs, was convicted of treason, and sentenced to be burnt alive in the furnace of the private baths. The devout humanity of the empress Theophano was fatal to her husband and family. A solemn day, the twenty-fifth of December, had been fixed for the execution: she urged, that the anniversary of the Saviour's birth would be profaned by this inhuman spectacle, and Leo consented with reluctance to a decent respite. But on the vigil of the feast, his sleepless anxiety prompted him to visit at the dead of night the chamber in which his enemy was confined: he beheld him released from his chain, and stretched on his gaoler's bed in a profound slumber: Leo was alarmed at these signs of security and intelligence; but, though he retired with silent steps, his entrance and departure were noticed by a slave who lay concealed in a corner of the prison. Under the pretence of requesting the spiritual aid of a confessor, Michael informed the conspirators, that their lives depended on his discretion, and that a few hours were left to assure their own safety, by the deliverance of their friend and country. On the great festivals, a chosen band of priests and chanters was admitted into the palace by a private gate to sing matins in the chapel; and Leo, who regulated with the same strictness the discipline of the choir and of the camp, was seldom absent from these early devotions. In the ecclesiastical habit, but with swords under their robes, the conspirators mingled with the procession, lurked in the angles of the chapel, and expected, as the signal of murder, the intonation of the first psalm by the emperor himself. The imperfect light, and the uniformity of dress, might have favoured his escape, while their assault was pointed against an harmless priest; but they soon discovered their mistake, and encompassed on all sides the royal victim. Without a weapon and without a friend, he grasped a weighty cross, and stood at bay against the hunters of his life; but as he asked for mercy, "This is the hour, not of mercy, but of vengeance," was the inexorable reply. The stroke of a well-aimed sword separated from his body the right arm and the cross, and Leo the Armenian was slain at the foot of the altar.

Michael II. the Stammerer, A.D. 820, Dec. 25.

A memorable reverse of fortune was displayed in Michael the second, who, from a defect in his speech, was surnamed the Stammerer. He was snatched from the fiery furnace to the sovereignty of an empire; and as in the tumult a smith could not readily be found, the fetters remained on his legs several hours after he was seated on the throne of the Cæsars. The royal blood which had been the price of his elevation, was unprofitably spent: in the purple he retained the ignoble vices of his origin; and Michael lost his provinces with as supine indifference as if they had been the inheritance of his fathers. His title was disputed by Thomas, the last of the military triumvirate, who transported into Europe fourscore thousand Barbarians from the banks of the Tigris and the shores of the Caspian. He formed the siege of Constantinople; but the capital was defended with spiritual and carnal weapons; a Bulgarian king assaulted the camp of the Orientals, and Thomas had the misfortune, or the weakness, to fall alive into the power of the conqueror. The hands and feet of the rebel were amputated; he was placed on an ass, and, amidst the insults of the people, was led through the streets, which he sprinkled with his blood. The depravation of manners, as savage as they were corrupt, is marked by the presence of the emperor himself. Deaf to the lamentations of a fellow-soldier, he incessantly pressed the discovery of more accomplices, till his curiosity was checked by the question of an honest or guilty minister: "Would you give credit to an enemy, against the most faithful of your friends?" After the death of his first wife, the emperor, at the request of the senate, drew from her monastery Euphrosyne, the daughter of Constantine the sixth. Her august birth might justify a stipulation in the marriage-contract, that her children should equally share the empire with their elder brother. But the nuptials of Michael and Euphrosyne were barren; and she was content with the title of mother of Theophilus, his son and successor.

Theophilus, A.D. 829, October 3.

The character of Theophilus is a rare example in which religious zeal has allowed, and perhaps magnified, the virtues of an heretic and a persecutor. His valour was often felt by the enemies, and his justice by the subjects, of the monarchy; but the valour of Theophilus was rash and fruitless, and his justice arbitrary and cruel. He displayed the banner of the cross against the Saracens; but his five expeditions were concluded by a signal overthrow; Amorium, the native city of his ancestors, was levelled with the ground, and from his military toils, he derived only the surname of the Unfortunate. The wisdom of a sovereign is comprised in the institution of laws and the choice of magistrates, and while he seems without action, his civil government revolves round his centre with the silence and order of the planetary system. But the justice of Theophilus was fashioned on the model of the Oriental despots, who, in personal and irregular acts of authority, consult the reason or passion of the moment, without measuring the sentence by the law or the penalty by the offence. A poor woman threw herself at the emperor's feet to complain of a powerful neighbour, the brother of the empress, who had raised his palace wall to such an inconvenient height, that her humble dwelling was excluded from light and air! On the proof of the fact, instead of granting, like an ordinary judge, sufficient or ample damages to the plaintiff, the sovereign adjudged to her use and benefit the palace and the ground. Nor was Theophilus content with this extravagant satisfaction: his zeal converted a civil trespass into a criminal act; and the unfortunate patrician was stripped and scourged in the public place of Constantinople. For some venial offences, some defect of equity or vigilance, the principal ministers, a præfect, a quæstor, a captain of the guards, were banished or mutilated, or scalded with boiling pitch, or burnt alive in the hippodrome; and as these dreadful examples might be the effects of error or caprice, they must have alienated from his service the best and wisest of the citizens. But the pride of the monarch was flattered in the exercise of power, or, as he thought, of virtue; and the people, safe in their obscurity, applauded the danger and debasement of their superiors. This extraordinary rigour was justified, in some measure, by its salutary consequences; since, after a scrutiny of seventeen days, not a complaint or abuse could be found in the court or city: and it might be alleged that the Greeks could be ruled only with a rod of iron, and that the public interest is the motive and law of the supreme judge. Yet in the crime, or the suspicion, of treason, that judge is of all others the most credulous and partial. Theophilus might inflict a tardy vengeance on the assassins of Leo and the saviours of his father; but he enjoyed the fruits of their crime; and his jealous tyranny sacrificed a brother and a prince to the future safety of his life. A Persian of the race of the Sassanides died in poverty and exile at Constantinople, leaving an only son, the issue of a plebeian marriage. At the age of twelve years, the royal birth of Theophobus was revealed, and his merit was not unworthy of his birth. He was educated in the Byzantine palace, a Christian and a soldier; advanced with rapid steps in the career of fortune and glory; received the hand of the emperor's sister; and was promoted to the command of thirty thousand Persians, who, like his father, had fled from the Mahometan conquerors. These troops, doubly infected with mercenary and fanatic vices, were desirous of revolting against their benefactor, and erecting the standard of their native king: but the loyal Theophobus rejected their offers, disconcerted their schemes, and escaped from their hands to the camp or palace of his royal brother. A generous confidence might have secured a faithful and able guardian for his wife and his infant son, to whom Theophilus, in the flower of his age, was compelled to leave the inheritance of the empire. But his jealousy was exasperated by envy and disease: he feared the dangerous virtues which might either support or oppress their infancy and weakness; and the dying emperor demanded the head of the Persian prince. With savage delight, he recognised the familiar features of his brother: "Thou art no longer Theophobus," he said; and, sinking on his couch, he added, with a faultering voice, "Soon, too soon, I shall be no more Theophilus!"

The Russians, who have borrowed from the Greeks the greatest part of their civil and ecclesiastical policy, preserved, till the last century, a singular institution in the marriage of the Czar. They collected, not the virgins of every rank and of every province, a vain and romantic idea, but the daughters of the principal nobles, who awaited in the palace the choice of their sovereign. It is affirmed, that a similar method was adopted in the nuptials of Theophilus. With a golden apple in his hand, he slowly walked between two lines of contending beauties: his eye was detained by the charms of Icasia, and, in the awkwardness of a first declaration, the prince could only observe, that, in this world, women had been the cause of much evil: "And surely, sir," she pertly replied, "they have likewise been the occasion of much good." This affectation of unseasonable wit displeased the Imperial lover: he turned aside in disgust; Icasia concealed her mortification in a convent; and the modest silence of Theodora was rewarded with the golden apple. She deserved the love, but did not escape the severity, of her lord. From the palace garden he beheld a vessel deeply laden, and steering into the port: on the discovery that the precious cargo of Syrian luxury was the property of his wife, he condemned the ship to the flames, with a sharp reproach, that her avarice had degraded the character of an empress into that of a merchant. Yet his last choice entrusted her with the guardianship of the empire and her son Michael, who was left an orphan in the fifth year of his age. The restoration of images, and the final extirpation of the Iconoclasts, has endeared her name to the devotion of the Greeks; but in the fervour of religious zeal, Theodora entertained a grateful regard for the memory and salvation of her husband. After thirteen years of a prudent and frugal administration, she perceived the decline of her influence; but the second Irene imitated only the virtues of her predecessor. Instead of conspiring against the life or government of her son, she retired, without a struggle, though not without a murmur, to the solitude of private life, deploring the ingratitude, the vices, and the inevitable ruin, of the worthless youth.

Michael III. A.D. 842, January 20.

Among the successors of Nero and Elagabalus, we have not hitherto found the imitation of their vices, the character of a Roman prince who considered pleasure as the object of life, and virtue as the enemy of pleasure. Whatever might have been the maternal care of Theodora in the education of Michael the third, her unfortunate son was a king before he was a man. If the ambitious mother laboured to check the progress of reason, she could not cool the ebullition of passion; and her selfish policy was justly repaid by the contempt and ingratitude of the headstrong youth. At the age of eighteen, he rejected her authority, without feeling his own incapacity to govern the empire and himself. With Theodora, all gravity and wisdom retired from the court; their place was supplied by the alternate dominion of vice and folly; and it was impossible, without forfeiting the public esteem, to acquire or preserve the favour of the emperor. The millions of gold and silver which had been accumulated for the service of the state, were lavished on the vilest of men, who flattered his passions and shared his pleasures; and in a reign of thirteen years, the richest of sovereigns was compelled to strip the palace and the churches of their precious furniture. Like Nero, he delighted in the amusements of the theatre, and sighed to be surpassed in the accomplishments in which he should have blushed to excel. Yet the studies of Nero in music and poetry, betrayed some symptoms of a liberal taste; the more ignoble arts of the son of Theophilus were confined to the chariot-race of the hippodrome. The four factions which had agitated the peace, still amused the idleness, of the capital: for himself, the emperor assumed the blue livery; the three rival colours were distributed to his favourites, and in the vile though eager contention he forgot the dignity of his person and the safety of his dominions. He silenced the messenger of an invasion, who presumed to divert his attention in the most critical moment of the race; and by his command, the importunate beacons were extinguished, that too frequently spread the alarm from Tarsus to Constantinople. The most skilful charioteers obtained the first place in his confidence and esteem; their merit was profusely rewarded; the emperor feasted in their houses, and presented their children at the baptismal font; and while he applauded his own popularity, he affected to blame the cold and stately reserve of his predecessors. The unnatural lusts which had degraded even the manhood of Nero, were banished from the world; yet the strength of Michael was consumed by the indulgence of love and intemperance. In his midnight revels, when his passions were inflamed by wine, he was provoked to issue the most sanguinary commands; and if any feelings of humanity were left, he was reduced, with the return of sense, to approve the salutary disobedience of his servants. But the most extraordinary feature in the character of Michael, is the profane mockery of the religion of his country. The superstition of the Greeks might indeed excite the smile of a philosopher: but his smile would have been rational and temperate, and he must have condemned the ignorant folly of a youth who insulted the objects of public veneration. A buffoon of the court was invested in the robes of the patriarch: his twelve metropolitans, among whom the emperor was ranked, assumed their ecclesiastical garments: they used or abused the sacred vessels of the altar; and in their bacchanalian feasts, the holy communion was administered in a nauseous compound of vinegar and mustard. Nor were these impious spectacles concealed from the eyes of the city. On the day of a solemn festival, the emperor, with his bishops or buffoons, rode on asses through the streets, encountered the true patriarch at the head of his clergy; and by their licentious shouts and obscene gestures, disordered the gravity of the Christian procession. The devotion of Michael appeared only in some offence to reason or piety: he received his theatrical crowns from the statue of the Virgin; and an imperial tomb was violated for the sake of burning the bones of Constantine the Iconoclast. By this extravagant conduct, the son of Theophilus became as contemptible as he was odious: every citizen was impatient for the deliverance of his country; and even the favourites of the moment were apprehensive that a caprice might snatch away what a caprice had bestowed. In the thirtieth year of his age, and in the hour of intoxication and sleep, Michael the third was murdered in his chamber by the founder of a new dynasty, whom the emperor had raised to an equality of rank and power.

Basil I. the Macedonian, A.D. 867, Sept. 24.

The genealogy of Basil the Macedonian (if it be not the spurious offspring of pride and flattery) exhibits a genuine picture of the revolution of the most illustrious families. The Arsacides, the rivals of Rome, possessed the sceptre of the East near four hundred years: a younger branch of these Parthian kings continued to reign in Armenia; and their royal descendants survived the partition and servitude of that ancient monarchy. Two of these, Artabanus and Chlienes, escaped or retired to the court of Leo the first: his bounty seated them in a safe and hospitable exile, in the province of Macedonia: Adrianople was their final settlement. During several generations they maintained the dignity of their birth; and their Roman patriotism rejected the tempting offers of the Persian and Arabian powers, who recalled them to their native country. But their splendour was insensibly clouded by time and poverty; and the father of Basil was reduced to a small farm, which he cultivated with his own hands: yet he scorned to disgrace the blood of the Arsacides by a plebeian alliance: his wife, a widow of

Adrianople, was pleased to count among her ancestors, the great Constantine; and their royal infant was connected by some dark affinity of lineage or country with the Macedonian Alexander. No sooner was he born, than the cradle of Basil, his family, and his city, were swept away by an inundation of the Bulgarians: he was educated a slave in a foreign land; and in this severe discipline, he acquired the hardiness of body and flexibility of mind which promoted his future elevation. In the age of youth or manhood he shared the deliverance of the Roman captives, who generously broke their fetters, marched through Bulgaria to the shores of the Euxine, defeated two armies of Barbarians, embarked in the ships which had been stationed for their reception, and returned to Constantinople, from whence they were distributed to their respective homes. But the freedom of Basil was naked and destitute: his farm was ruined by the calamities of war: after his father's death, his manual labour, or service, could no longer support a family of orphans; and he resolved to seek a more conspicuous theatre, in which every virtue and every vice may lead to the paths of greatness. The first night of his arrival at Constantinople, without friends or money, the weary pilgrim slept on the steps of the church of St. Diomede: he was fed by the casual hospitality of a monk; and was introduced to the service of a cousin and namesake of the emperor Theophilus; who, though himself of a diminutive person, was always followed by a train of tall and handsome domestics. Basil attended his patron to the government of Peloponnesus; eclipsed, by his personal merit, the birth and dignity of Theophilus, and formed an useful connection with a wealthy and charitable matron of Patras. Her spiritual or carnal love embraced the young adventurer, whom she adopted as her son. Danielis presented him with thirty slaves; and the produce of her bounty was expended in the support of his brothers, and the purchase of some large estates in Macedonia. His gratitude or ambition still attached him to the service of Theophilus; and a lucky accident recommended him to the notice of the court. A famous wrestler, in the train of the Bulgarian ambassadors, had defied, at the royal banquet, the boldest and most robust of the Greeks. The strength of Basil was praised; he accepted the challenge; and the Barbarian champion was overthrown at the first onset. A beautiful but vicious horse was condemned to be hamstrung: it was subdued by the dexterity and courage of the servant of Theophilus; and his conqueror was promoted to an honourable rank in the Imperial stables. But it was impossible to obtain the confidence of Michael, without complying with his vices; and his new favourite, the great chamberlain of the palace, was raised and supported by a disgraceful marriage with a royal concubine, and the dishonour of his sister, who succeeded to her place. The public administration had been abandoned to the Cæsar Bardas, the brother and enemy of Theodora; but the arts of female influence persuaded Michael to hate and to fear his uncle: he was drawn from Constantinople, under the pretence of a Cretan expedition, and stabbed in the tent of audience, by the sword of the chamberlain, and in the presence of the emperor. About a month after this execution, Basil was invested with the title of Augustus and the government of the empire. He supported this unequal association till his influence was fortified by popular esteem. His life was endangered by the caprice of the emperor; and his dignity was profaned by a second colleague, who had rowed in the gallies. Yet the murder of his benefactor must be condemned as an act of ingratitude and treason; and the churches which he dedicated to the name of St. Michael, were a poor and puerile expiation of his guilt.

The different ages of Basil the first, may be compared with those of Augustus. The situation of the Greek did not allow him in his earliest youth to lead an army against his country, or to proscribe the noblest of her sons; but his aspiring genius stooped to the arts of a slave; he dissembled his ambition and even his virtues, and grasped, with the bloody hand of an assassin, the empire which he ruled with the wisdom and tenderness of a parent. A private citizen may feel his interest repugnant to his duty; but it must be from a deficiency of sense or courage, that an absolute monarch can separate his happiness from his glory, or his glory from the public welfare. The life or panegyric of Basil has indeed been composed and published under the long reign of his descendants; but even their stability on the throne may be justly ascribed to the superior merit of their ancestor. In his character, his grandson Constantine has attempted to delineate a perfect image of royalty: but that feeble prince, unless he had copied a real model, could not easily have soared so high above the level of his own conduct or conceptions. But the most solid praise of Basil is drawn from the comparison of a ruined and a flourishing monarchy, that which he wrested from the dissolute Michael, and that which he bequeathed to the Macedonian dynasty. The evils which had been sanctified by time and example, were corrected by his master-hand; and he revived, if not the national spirit, at least the order and majesty of the Roman empire. His application was indefatigable, his temper cool, his understanding vigorous and decisive; and in his practice he observed that rare and salutary moderation, which pursues each virtue, at an equal distance between the opposite vices. His military service had been confined to the palace; nor was the emperor endowed with the spirit or the talents of a warrior. Yet under his reign the Roman arms were again formidable to the Barbarians. As soon as he had formed a new army by discipline and exercise, he appeared in person on the banks of the Euphrates, curbed the pride of the Saracens, and suppressed the dangerous though just revolt of the Manichæans. His indignation against a rebel who had long eluded his pursuit, provoked him to wish and to pray, that, by the grace of God, he might drive three arrows into the head of Chrysochir. That odious head, which had been obtained by treason rather than by valour, was suspended from a tree, and thrice exposed to the dexterity of the Imperial archer: a base revenge against the dead, more worthy of the times, than of the character of Basil. But his principal merit was in the civil administration of the finances and of the laws. To replenish an exhausted treasury, it was proposed to resume the lavish and ill-placed gifts of his predecessor: his prudence abated one moiety of the restitution; and a sum of twelve hundred thousand pounds was instantly procured to answer the most pressing demands, and to allow some space for the mature operations of œconomy. Among the various schemes for the improvement of the revenue, a new mode was suggested of capitation, or tribute, which would have too much depended on the arbitrary discretion of the assessors. A sufficient list of honest and able agents was instantly produced by the minister; but on the more careful scrutiny of Basil himself, only two could be found, who might be safely entrusted with such dangerous powers; and they justified his esteem by declining his confidence. But the serious and successful diligence of the emperor established by degrees an equitable balance of property and payment, of receipt and expenditure: a peculiar fund was appropriated to each service; and a public method secured the interest of the prince and the property of the people. After reforming the luxury, he assigned two patrimonial estates to supply the decent plenty, of the Imperial table: the contributions of the subject were reserved for his defence; and the residue was employed in the embellishment of the capital and provinces. A taste for building, however costly, may deserve some praise and much excuse: from thence industry is fed, art is encouraged, and some object is attained of public emolument or pleasure: the use of a road, an aqueduct, or an hospital, is obvious and solid; and the hundred churches that arose by the command of Basil, were consecrated to the devotion of the age. In the character of a judge, he was assiduous and impartial; desirous to save, but not afraid to strike: the oppressors of the people were severely chastised; but his personal foes, whom it might be unsafe to pardon, were condemned, after the loss of their eyes, to a life of solitude and repentance. The change of language and manners demanded a revision of the obsolete jurisprudence of Justinian: the voluminous body of his Institutes, Pandects, Code, and Novels, was digested under forty titles, in the Greek idiom; and the *Basilics*, which were improved and completed by his son and grandson, must be referred to the original genius of the founder of their race. This glorious reign was terminated by an accident in the chace. A furious stag entangled his horns in the belt of Basil, and raised him from his horse: he was rescued by an attendant, who cut the belt and slew the animal; but the fall, or the fever, exhausted the strength of the aged monarch, and he expired in the palace, amidst the tears of his family and people. If he struck off the head of the faithful servant, for presuming to draw his sword against his sovereign; the pride of despotism, which had lain dormant in his life, revived in the last moments of despair, when he no longer wanted or valued the opinion of mankind.

Leo VI. the Philosopher, A.D. 886, March 1.

Of the four sons of the emperor, Constantine died before his father, whose grief and credulity were amused by a flattering impostor and a vain apparition. Stephen, the youngest, was content with the honours of a patriarch and a saint; both Leo and Alexander were alike invested with the purple, but the powers of government were solely exercised by the elder brother. The name of Leo the sixth has been dignified with the title of *philosopher*; and the union of the prince and the sage, of the active and speculative virtues, would indeed constitute the perfection of human nature. But the claims of Leo are far short of this ideal excellence. Did he reduce his passions and appetites under the dominion of reason? His life was spent in the pomp of the palace, in the society of his wives and concubines; and even the clemency which he shewed, and the peace which he strove to preserve, must be imputed to the softness and indolence of his character. Did he subdue his prejudices, and those of his subjects? His mind was tinged with the most puerile superstition; the influence of the clergy, and the errors of the people, were consecrated by his laws; and the oracles of Leo, which reveal, in prophetic style, the fates of the empire, are founded on the arts of astrology and divination. If we still enquire the reason of his sage appellation, it can only be replied, that the son of Basil was less ignorant than the greater part of his contemporaries in church and state; that his education had been directed by the learned Photius; and that several books of profane and ecclesiastical science were composed by the pen, or in the name, of the Imperial *philosopher*. But the reputation of his philosophy and religion was overthrown by a domestic vice, the repetition of his nuptials. The primitive ideas of the merit and holiness of celibacy, were preached by the monks and entertained by the Greeks. Marriage was allowed as a necessary means for the propagation of mankind; after the death of either party, the survivor might satisfy by a *second* union, the weakness or the strength of the flesh: but a *third* marriage was censured as a state of legal fornication; and a *fourth* was a sin or scandal as yet unknown to the Christians of the East. In the beginning of his reign, Leo himself had abolished the state of concubines, and condemned, without annulling, third marriages: but his patriotism and love soon compelled him to violate his own laws, and to incur the penance, which in a similar case he had imposed on his subjects. In his three first alliances, his nuptial bed was unfruitful; the emperor required a female companion, and the empire a legitimate heir. The beautiful Zoe was introduced into the palace as a concubine; and after a trial of her fecundity, and the birth of Constantine, her lover declared his intention of legitimating the mother and the child, by the celebration of his fourth nuptials. But the patriarch Nicholas refused his blessing: the Imperial baptism of the young prince was obtained by a promise of separation; and the contumacious husband of Zoe was excluded from the communion of the faithful. Neither the fear of exile, nor the desertion of his brethren, nor the authority of the Latin church, nor the danger of failure or doubt in the succession to the empire,* could bend the spirit of the inflexible monk. After the death of Leo, he was recalled from exile to the civil and ecclesiastical administration; and the edict of union which was promulgated in the name of Constantine, condemned the future scandal of fourth marriages, and left a tacit imputation on his own birth.

Alexander, Constantine VII. Porphyrogenitus, A.D. 911, May 11.

In the Greek language, *purple* and *porphyry* are the same word: and as the colours of nature are invariable, we may learn, that a dark deep red was the Tyrian dye which stained the purple of the ancients. An apartment of the Byzantine palace was lined with porphyry: it was reserved for the use of the pregnant empresses; and the royal birth of their children was expressed by the appellation of *porphyrogenite*, or born in the purple. Several of the Roman princes had been blessed with an heir; but this peculiar surname was first applied to Constantine the seventh. His life and titular reign were of equal duration; but of fifty-four years, six had elapsed before his father's death; and the son of Leo was ever the voluntary or reluctant subject of those who oppressed his weakness or abused his confidence. His uncle Alexander, who had long been invested with the title of Augustus, was the first colleague and governor of the young prince: but in a rapid career of vice and folly, the brother of Leo already emulated the reputation of Michael; and when he was extinguished by a timely death, he entertained a project of castrating his nephew, and leaving the empire to a worthless favourite. The succeeding years of the minority of Constantine were occupied by his mother Zoe, and a succession or council of seven regents, who pursued their interest, gratified their passions, abandoned the republic, supplanted each other, and finally vanished in the presence of a soldier. From an obscure origin, Romanus Lecapenus had raised himself to the command of the naval armies; and in the anarchy of the times, had deserved, or at least had obtained, the national esteem. With a victorious and affectionate fleet, he sailed from the mouth of the Danube into the harbour of Constantinople, and was hailed as the deliverer of the people, and the guardian of the prince. His supreme office was at first defined by the new appellation of father of the emperor; but Romanus soon disdained the subordinate powers of a minister, and assumed, with the titles of Cæsar and Augustus, the full independence of royalty, which he held near five and twenty years. His three sons, Christopher, Stephen, and Constantine, were successively adorned with the same honours, and the lawful emperor was degraded from the first to the fifth rank in this college of princes. Yet, in the preservation of his life and crown, he might still applaud his own fortune and the clemency of the usurper. The examples of ancient and modern history would have excused the ambition of Romanus: the powers and the laws of the empire were in his hand; the spurious birth of Constantine would have justified his exclusion; and the grave or the monastery was open to receive the son of the concubine. But Lecapenus does not appear to have possessed either the virtues or the vices of a tyrant. The spirit and activity of his private life dissolved away in the sunshine of the throne; and in his licentious pleasures, he forgot the safety both of the republic and of his family. Of a mild and religious character, he respected the sanctity of oaths, the innocence of the youth, the memory of his parents and the attachment of the people. The studious temper and retirement of Constantine, disarmed the jealousy of power: his books and music, his pen and his pencil, were a constant source of amusement; and if he could improve a scanty allowance by the sale of his pictures, if their price was not enhanced by the name of the artist, he was endowed with a personal talent, which few princes could employ in the hour of adversity.

Romanus I. Lecapenus, A.D. 919, Dec. 24. Christopher, Stephen, Constantine VIII.

Constantine VII. A.D. 945, January 27. The fall of Romanus was occasioned by his own vices and those of his children. After the decease of Christopher, his eldest son, the two surviving brothers quarrelled with each other, and conspired against their father. At the hour of noon, when all strangers were regularly excluded from the palace, they entered his apartment with an armed force, and conveyed him, in the habit of a monk, to a small island in the Propontis, which was peopled by a religious community. The rumour of this domestic revolution excited a tumult in the city; but Porphyrogenitus alone, the true and lawful emperor, was the object of the public care; and the sons of Lecapenus were taught, by tardy experience, that they had atchieved a guilty and perilous enterprise for the benefit of their rival. Their sister Helena, the wife of Constantine, revealed, or supposed, their treacherous design of assassinating her husband at the royal banquet. His loyal adherents were alarmed; and the two usurpers were prevented, seized, degraded from the purple, and embarked for the same island and monastery where their father had been so lately confined. Old Romanus met them on the beach with a sarcastic smile, and, after a just reproach of their folly and ingratitude, presented his Imperial colleagues with an equal share of his water and vegetable diet. In the fortieth year of his reign, Constantine the seventh obtained the possession of the Eastern world, which he ruled, or seemed to rule, near fifteen years. But he was devoid of that energy of character which could emerge into a life of action and glory; and the studies which had amused and dignified his leisure, were incompatible with the serious duties of a sovereign. The emperor neglected the practice, to instruct his son Romanus in the theory, of government: while he indulged the habits of intemperance and sloth, he dropt the reins of the administration into the hands of Helena his wife; and, in the shifting scene of her favour and caprice, each minister was regretted in the promotion of a more worthless successor. Yet the birth and misfortunes of Constantine had endeared him to the Greeks; they excused his failings; they respected his learning, his innocence, and charity, his love of justice; and the ceremony of his funeral was mourned with the unfeigned tears of his subjects. The body, according to ancient custom, lay in state in the vestibule of the palace; and the civil and military officers, the patricians, the senate, and the clergy, approached in due order to adore and kiss the inanimate corpse of their sovereign. Before the procession moved towards the Imperial sepulchre, an herald proclaimed this awful admonition: "Arise, O king of the world, and obey the summons of the King of kings!"

The death of Constantine was imputed to poison; and his son Romanus, who derived that name from his maternal grandfather, ascended the throne of Constantinople. A prince who, at the age of twenty, could be suspected of anticipating his inheritance, must have been already lost in the public esteem; yet Romanus was rather weak than wicked; and the largest share of the guilt was transferred to his wife, Theophano, a woman of base origin, masculine spirit, and flagitious manners. The sense of personal glory and public happiness, the true pleasures of royalty, were unknown to the son of Constantine; and, while the two brothers, Nicephorus and Leo, triumphed over the Saracens, the hours which the emperor owed to his people were consumed in strenuous idleness. In the morning he visited the circus; at noon he feasted the senators; the greater part of the afternoon he spent in the *sphæristerium*, or tennis-court, the only theatre of his victories; from thence he passed over to the Asiatic side of the Bosphorus, hunted and killed four wild boars of the largest size, and returned to the palace, proudly content with the labours of the day. In strength and beauty he was conspicuous above his equals: tall and streight as a young cypress, his complexion was fair and florid, his eyes sparkling, his shoulders broad, his nose long and aquiline. Yet even these perfections were insufficient to fix the love of Theophano; and, after a reign of four years, she mingled for her husband the same deadly draught which she had composed for his father.

Romanus II. junior, A.D. 959, Nov. 15.

By his marriage with this impious woman, Romanus the younger left two sons, Basil the second and Constantine the ninth, and two daughters, Theophano and Anne. The eldest sister was given to Otho the second, emperor of the West; the younger became the wife of Wolodomir, great duke and apostle of Russia, and, by the marriage of her grand-daughter with Henry the first, king of France, the blood of the Macedonians, and perhaps of the Arsacides, still flows in the veins of the Bourbon line. After the death of her husband, the empress aspired to reign in the name of her sons, the elder of whom was five, and the younger only two, years of age; but she soon felt the instability of a throne, which was supported by a female who could not be esteemed, and two infants who could not be feared. Theophano looked around for a protector, and threw herself into the arms of the bravest soldier; her heart was capacious; but the deformity of the new favourite rendered it more than probable that interest was the motive and excuse of her love. Nicephorus Phocas united, in the popular opinion, the double merit of an hero and a saint. In the former character,

Nicephorus II. Phocas, A.D. 963, August 6.

his qualifications were genuine and splendid: the descendant of a race, illustrious by their military exploits, he had displayed, in every station and in every province, the courage of a soldier and the conduct of a chief; and Nicephorus was crowned with recent laurels, from the important conquest of the isle of Crete. His religion was of a more ambiguous cast; and his haircloth, his fasts, his pious idiom, and his wish to retire from the business of the world, were a convenient mask for his dark and dangerous ambition. Yet he imposed on an holy patriarch, by whose influence, and by a decree of the senate, he was entrusted, during the minority of the young princes, with the absolute and independent command of the Oriental armies. As soon as he had secured the leaders and the troops, he boldly marched to Constantinople, trampled on his enemies, avowed his correspondence with the empress, and, without degrading her sons, assumed with the title of Augustus, the pre-eminence of rank and the plenitude of power. But his marriage with Theophano was refused by the same patriarch who had placed the crown on his head: by his second nuptials he incurred a year of canonical penance; a bar of spiritual affinity was opposed to their celebration; and some evasion and perjury were required to silence the scruples of the clergy and people. The popularity of the emperor was lost in the purple: in a reign of six years he provoked the hatred of strangers and subjects; and the hypocrisy and avarice of the first Nicephorus were revived in his successor. Hypocrisy I shall never justify or palliate; but I will dare to observe, that the odious vice of avarice is of all others most hastily arraigned, and most unmercifully condemned. In a private citizen, our judgment seldom expects an accurate scrutiny into his fortune and expence; and in a steward of the public treasure, frugality is always a virtue, and the encrease of taxes too often an indispensable duty. In the use of his patrimony, the generous temper of Nicephorus had been proved; and the revenue was strictly applied to the service of the state: each spring the emperor marched in person against the Saracens; and every Roman might compute the employment of his taxes in triumphs, conquests, and the security of the Eastern barrier.

John Zimisces, Basil II. Constantine IX. A.D. 969, Dec. 25.

Among the warriors who promoted his elevation, and served under his standard, a noble and valiant Armenian had deserved and obtained the most eminent rewards. The stature of John Zimisces was below the ordinary standard; but this diminutive body was endowed with strength, beauty, and the soul of an hero. By the jealousy of the emperor's brother, he was degraded from the office of general of the East, to that of director of the posts, and his murmurs were chastised with disgrace and exile. But Zimisces was ranked among the numerous lovers of the empress: on her intercession, he was permitted to reside at Chalcedon, in the neighbourhood of the capital: her bounty was repaid in his clandestine and amorous visits to the palace; and Theophano consented, with alacrity, to the death of an ugly and penurious husband. Some bold and trusty conspirators were concealed in her most private chambers: in the darkness of a winter night, Zimisces, with his principal companions, embarked in a small boat, traversed the Bosphorus, landed at the palace stairs, and silently ascended a ladder of ropes, which was cast down by the female attendants. Neither his own suspicions, nor the warnings of his friends, nor the tardy aid of his brother Leo, nor the fortress which he had erected in the palace, could protect Nicephorus from a domestic foe, at whose voice every door was opened to the assassins. As he slept on a bear-skin, on the ground, he was roused by their noisy intrusion, and thirty daggers glittered before his eyes. It is doubtful whether Zimisces imbrued his hands in the blood of his sovereign; but he enjoyed the inhuman spectacle of revenge. The murder was protracted by insult and cruelty; and as soon as the head of Nicephorus was shewn from the window, the tumult was hushed, and the Armenian was emperor of the East. On the day of his coronation, he was stopped on the threshold of St. Sophia, by the intrepid patriarch; who charged his conscience with the deed of treason and blood; and required, as a sign of repentance, that he should separate himself from his more criminal associate. This sally of apostolic zeal was not offensive to the prince, since he could neither love nor trust a woman who had repeatedly violated the most sacred obligations; and Theophano, instead of sharing his Imperial fortune, was dismissed with ignominy from his bed and palace. In their last interview, she displayed a frantic and impotent rage; accused the ingratitude of her lover; assaulted, with words and blows, her son Basil, as he stood silent and submissive in the presence of a superior colleague; and avowed her own prostitution, in proclaiming the illegitimacy of his birth. The public indignation was appeased by her exile, and the punishment of the meaner accomplices: the death of an unpopular prince was forgiven; and the guilt of Zimisces was forgotten in the splendour of his virtues. Perhaps his profusion was less useful to the state than the avarice of Nicephorus; but his gentle and generous behaviour delighted all who approached his person; and it was only in the paths of victory that he trod in the footsteps of his predecessor. The greatest part of his reign was employed in the camp and the field: his personal valour and activity were signalized on the Danube and the

Tigris, the ancient boundaries of the Roman world; and by his double triumph over the Russians and the Saracens, he deserved the titles of saviour of the empire, and conqueror of the East. In his last return from Syria, he observed that the most fruitful lands of his new provinces were possessed by the eunuchs. "And is it for them," he exclaimed, with honest indignation, "that we have fought and conquered? Is it for them that we shed our blood, and exhaust the treasures of our people?" The complaint was re-echoed to the palace, and the death of Zimisces is strongly marked with the suspicion of poison.

Basil II. and Constantine IX. A.D. 976, January 10.

Under this usurpation, or regency, of twelve years, the two lawful emperors, Basil and Constantine, had silently grown to the age of manhood. Their tender years had been incapable of dominion: the respectful modesty of their attendance and salutation, was due to the age and merit of their guardians: the childless ambition of those guardians had no temptation to violate their right of succession: their patrimony was ably and faithfully administered; and the premature death of Zimisces was a loss, rather than a benefit, to the sons of Romanus. Their want of experience detained them twelve years longer the obscure and voluntary pupils of a minister, who extended his reign by persuading them to indulge the pleasures of youth, and to disdain the labours of government. In this silken web, the weakness of Constantine was for ever entangled; but his elder brother felt the impulse of genius and the desire of action; he frowned, and the minister was no more. Basil was the acknowledged sovereign of Constantinople and the provinces of Europe; but Asia was oppressed by two veteran generals, Phocas and Sclerus, who, alternately friends and enemies, subjects and rebels, maintained their independence, and laboured to emulate the example of successful usurpation. Against these domestic enemies, the son of Romanus first drew his sword, and they trembled in the presence of a lawful and high-spirited prince. The first in the front of battle was thrown from his horse, by the stroke of poison, or an arrow: the second, who had been twice loaded with chains, and twice invested with the purple, was desirous of ending in peace the small remainder of his days. As the aged suppliant approached the throne, with dim eyes and faultering steps, leaning on his two attendants, the emperor exclaimed, in the insolence of youth and power, "And is this the man who has so long been the object of our terror?" After he had confirmed his own authority, and the peace of the empire, the trophies of Nicephorus and Zimisces would not suffer their royal pupil to sleep in the palace. His long and frequent expeditions against the Saracens were rather glorious, than useful to the empire; but the final destruction of the kingdom of Bulgaria appears, since the time of Belisarius, the most important triumph of the Roman arms. Yet instead of applauding their victorious prince, his subjects detested the rapacious and rigid avarice of Basil; and in the imperfect narrative of his exploits, we can only discern the courage, patience, and ferociousness, of a soldier. A vicious education, which could not subdue his spirit, had clouded his mind; he was ignorant of every science; and the remembrance of his learned and feeble grandsire might encourage his real or affected contempt of laws and lawyers, of artists and arts. Of such a character, in such an age, superstition took a firm and lasting possession; after the first licence of his youth, Basil the second devoted his life, in the palace and the camp, to the penance of an hermit, wore the monastic habit under his robes and armour, observed a vow of continence, and imposed on his appetites a perpetual abstinence from wine and flesh. In the sixty-eighth year of his age, his martial spirit urged him to embark in person for a holy war against the Saracens of Sicily; he was prevented by death, and Basil, surnamed the Slayer of the Bulgarians, was dismissed from the world, with the blessings of the clergy and the curses of the people. After his decease, his brother Constantine enjoyed, about three years, the power, or rather the pleasures, of royalty; and his only care was the settlement of the succession. He had enjoyed, sixty-six years, the title of Augustus; and the reign of the two brothers is the longest, and most obscure, of the Byzantine history.

Constantine IX. A.D. 1025, December.

A lineal succession of five emperors, in a period of an hundred and sixty years, had attached the loyalty of the Greeks to the Macedonian dynasty, which had been thrice respected by the usurpers of their power. After the death of Constantine the ninth, the last male of the royal race, a new and broken scene presents itself, and the accumulated years of twelve emperors do not equal the space of his single reign. His elder brother had preferred his private chastity to the public interest, and Constantine himself had only three daughters; Eudocia, who took the veil, and Zoe and Theodora, who were preserved till a mature age in a state of ignorance and virginity. When their marriage was discussed in the council of their dying father, the cold or pious Theodora refused to give an heir to the empire, but her sister Zoe presented herself a willing victim at the altar. Romanus Argyrus, a patrician of a graceful person and fair reputation, was chosen for her husband, and, on his declining that honour, was informed, that blindness or death was the second alternative. The motive of his reluctance

Romanus III. Argyrus, A.D. 1028, Nov. 12.

was conjugal affection, but his faithful wife sacrificed her own happiness to his safety and greatness; and her entrance into a monastery removed the only bar to the Imperial nuptials. After the decease of Constantine, the sceptre devolved to Romanus the third; but his labours at home and abroad were equally feeble and fruitless; and the mature age, the forty-eight years of Zoe, were less favourable to the hopes of pregnancy than to the indulgence of pleasure. Her favourite chamberlain was an handsome Paphlagonian of the name of Michael, whose first trade had been that of a money-changer; and Romanus, either from gratitude or equity, connived at their criminal intercourse, or accepted a slight assurance of their innocence. But Zoe soon justified the Roman maxim, that every adultress is capable of poisoning her husband; and the death of Romanus was instantly followed by the scandalous marriage and elevation of Michael the fourth. The expectations of Zoe were however disappointed: instead of a vigorous and grateful lover, she had placed in her bed, a miserable wretch, whose health and reason were impaired by epileptic fits, and whose conscience was tormented by despair and remorse. The most skilful physicians of the mind and body were summoned to his aid; and his hopes were amused by frequent pilgrimages to the baths, and to the tombs of the most popular saints; the monks applauded his penance, and, except restitution (but to whom should he have restored?) Michael sought every method of expiating his guilt. While he groaned and prayed in sackcloth and ashes, his brother, the eunuch John, smiled at his remorse, and enjoyed the harvest of a crime of which himself was the secret and most guilty author. His administration was only the art of satiating his avarice, and Zoe became a captive in the palace of her fathers and in the hands of her slaves. When he perceived the irretrievable decline of his brother's health, he introduced his nephew, another Michael, who derived his surname of Calaphates from his father's occupation in the careening of vessels: at the command of the eunuch, Zoe adopted for her son, the son of a mechanic; and this fictitious heir was invested with the title and purple of the Cæsars, in the presence of the senate and clergy. So feeble was the character of Zoe, that she was oppressed by the liberty and power which she recovered by the death of the Paphlagonian; and at the end of four days, she placed the crown on the head of Michael the fifth, who had protested, with tears and oaths, that he should ever reign the first and most obedient of her subjects. The only act of his short reign, was his base ingratitude to his benefactors, the eunuch and the empress. The disgrace of the former was pleasing to

Michael IV. the Paphlagonian, A.D. 1034, April 11.

Michael V. Calaphates, A.D. 1041, Dec. 14.

the public; but the murmurs, and at length the clamours, of Constantinople deplored the exile of Zoe, the daughter of so many emperors; her vices were forgotten, and Michael was taught, that there is a period in which the patience of the tamest slaves rises into fury and revenge. The citizens of every degree assembled in a formidable tumult which lasted three days; they besieged the palace, forced the gates, recalled their *mothers*, Zoe from her prison, Theodora from her monastery, and condemned the son of Calaphates to the loss of his eyes or of his life. For the first time, the Greeks beheld with surprise the two royal sisters seated on the same throne, presiding in the senate, and giving audience to the ambassadors of the nations. But this singular union subsisted no more than two months; the two sovereigns, their tempers, interests, and adherents, were secretly hostile to each other; and as Theodora was still averse to marriage, the indefatigable Zoe, at the age of sixty, consented, for the public good, to sustain the embraces of a third husband, and the censures of the Greek church. His name and number were Constantine the tenth, and the epithet of *Monomachus*, the single combatant, must have been expressive of his valour and victory in some public or private quarrel. But his health was broken by the tortures of the gout, and his dissolute reign was spent in the alternative of sickness and pleasure. A fair and noble widow had accompanied Constantine in his exile to the isle of Lesbos, and Sclerena gloried in the appellation of his mistress. After his marriage and elevation, she was invested with the title and pomp of *Augusta*, and occupied a contiguous apartment in the palace. The lawful consort (such was the delicacy or corruption of Zoe) consented to this strange and scandalous partition; and the emperor appeared in public between his wife and his concubine. He survived them both; but the last measures of Constantine to change the order of succession were prevented by the more vigilant friends of Theodora; and after his decease, she resumed, with the general consent, the possession of her inheritance. In her name, and by the influence of four eunuchs, the Eastern world was peaceably governed about nineteen months; and as they wished to prolong their dominion, they persuaded the aged princess to nominate for her successor Michael the sixth. The surname of *Stratioticus* declares his military profession; but the crazy and decrepit veteran could only see with the eyes, and execute with the hands, of his ministers. Whilst he ascended the throne, Theodora sunk into the grave; the last of the Macedonian or Basilian dynasty. I have hastily reviewed, and gladly

Zoe and Theodora, A.D. 1042, April 21.

Constantine X. Monomachus, A.D. 1042, June 11.

Theodora, A.D. 1054, Nov. 30.

Michael VI. Stratioticus, A.D. 1056, August 22.

dismiss, this shameful and destructive period of twenty-eight years, in which the Greeks, degraded below the common level of servitude, were transferred like a herd of cattle by the choice or caprice of two impotent females.

Isaac I. Comnenus, A.D. 1057, August 31.

From this night of slavery, a ray of freedom, or at least of spirit, begins to emerge: the Greeks either preserved or revived the use of surnames, which perpetuate the fame of hereditary virtue; and we now discern the rise, succession, and alliances of the last dynasties of Constantinople and Trebizond. The *Comneni*, who upheld for a while the fate of the sinking empire, assumed the honour of a Roman origin: but the family had been long since transported from Italy to Asia. Their patrimonial estate was situate in the district of Castamona in the neighbourhood of the Euxine; and one of their chiefs, who had already entered the paths of ambition, revisited with affection, perhaps with regret, the modest though honourable dwelling of his fathers. The first of their line was the illustrious Manuel, who, in the reign of the second Basil, contributed by war and treaty to appease the troubles of the East: he left in a tender age, two sons, Isaac and John, whom, with the consciousness of desert, he bequeathed to the gratitude and favour of his sovereign. The noble youths were carefully trained in the learning of the monastery, the arts of the palace, and the exercises of the camp: and from the domestic service of the guards, they were rapidly promoted to the command of provinces and armies. Their fraternal union doubled the force and reputation of the Comneni, and their ancient nobility was illustrated by the marriage of the two brothers, with a captive princess of Bulgaria, and the daughter of a patrician, who had obtained the name of *Charon* from the number of enemies whom he had sent to the infernal shades. The soldiers had served with reluctant loyalty a series of effeminate masters; the elevation of Michael the sixth was a personal insult to the more deserving generals; and their discontent was inflamed by the parsimony of the emperor and the insolence of the eunuchs. They secretly assembled in the sanctuary of St. Sophia, and the votes of the military synod would have been unanimous in favour of the old and valiant Catacalon, if the patriotism or modesty of the veteran had not suggested the importance of birth as well as merit in the choice of a sovereign. Isaac Comnenus was approved by general consent, and the associates separated without delay to meet in the plains of Phrygia at the head of their respective squadrons and detachments. The cause of Michael was defended in a single battle by the mercenaries of the Imperial guard, who were aliens to the public interest, and animated only by a principle of honour and gratitude. After their defeat, the fears of the emperor solicited a treaty, which was almost accepted by the moderation of the Comnenian. But the former was betrayed by his ambassadors, and the latter was prevented by his friends. The solitary Michael submitted to the voice of the people; the patriarch annulled their oath of allegiance; and as he shaved the head of the royal monk, congratulated his beneficial exchange of temporal royalty for the kingdom of heaven: an exchange, however, which the priest, on his own account, would probably have declined. By the hands of the same patriarch, Isaac Comnenus was solemnly crowned: the sword which he inscribed on his coins, might be an offensive symbol, if it implied his title by conquest; but this sword would have been drawn against the foreign and domestic enemies of the state. The decline of his health and vigour suspended the operation of active virtue; and the prospect of approaching death determined him to interpose some moments between life and eternity. But instead of leaving the empire as the marriage portion of his daughter, his reason and inclination concurred in the preference of his brother John, a soldier, a patriot, and the father of five sons, the future pillars of an hereditary succession. His first modest reluctance might be the natural dictates of discretion and tenderness, but his obstinate and successful perseverance, however it may dazzle with the shew of virtue, must be censured as a criminal desertion of his duty, and a rare offence against his family and country. The purple which he had refused was accepted by Constantine Ducas, a friend of the Comnenian house, and whose noble birth was adorned with the experience and reputation of civil policy. In the monastic habit, Isaac recovered his health, and survived two years his voluntary abdication. At the command of his abbot, he observed the rule of St. Basil, and executed the most servile offices of the convent: but his latent vanity was gratified by the frequent and respectful visits of the reigning monarch, who revered in his person the character of a benefactor and a saint.

Constantine XI. Ducas, A.D. 1059, Dec. 25.

If Constantine the eleventh were indeed the subject most worthy of empire, we must pity the debasement of the age and nation in which he was chosen. In the labour of puerile declamations he sought, without obtaining, the crown of eloquence, more precious, in his opinion, than that of Rome; and, in the subordinate functions of a judge, he forgot the duties of a sovereign and a warrior. Far from imitating the patriotic indifference of the authors of his greatness, Ducas was anxious only to secure, at the expence of the republic, the power and prosperity of his children. His three sons, Michael the seventh, Andronicus the first, and Constantine the twelfth, were

Eudocia, A.D. 1067, May.

invested, in a tender age, with the equal title of Augustus; and the succession was speedily opened by their father's death. His widow, Eudocia, was entrusted with the administration; but experience had taught the jealousy of the dying monarch to protect his sons from the danger of her second nuptials; and her solemn engagement, attested by the principal senators, was deposited in the hands of the patriarch. Before the end of seven months, the wants of Eudocia, or those of the state, called aloud for the male virtues of a soldier; and her heart had already chosen Romanus Diogenes, whom she raised from the scaffold to the throne. The discovery of a treasonable attempt had exposed him to the severity of the laws: his beauty and valour absolved him in the eyes of the empress; and Romanus, from a mild exile, was recalled on the second day to the command of the Oriental armies. Her royal choice was yet unknown to the public; and the promise which would have betrayed her falsehood and levity, was stolen by a dextrous emissary from the ambition of the patriarch. Xiphilin at first alleged the sanctity of oaths and the sacred nature of a trust; but a whisper, that his brother was the future emperor, relaxed his scruples, and forced him to confess

Romanus III. Diogenes, A.D. 1067, August.

that the public safety was the supreme law. He resigned the important paper; and when his hopes were confounded by the nomination of Romanus, he could no longer regain his security, retract his declarations, nor oppose the second nuptials of the empress. Yet a murmur was heard in the palace; and the Barbarian guards had raised their battle-axes in the cause of the house of Ducas, till the young princes were soothed by the tears of their mother and the solemn assurances of the fidelity of their guardian, who filled the Imperial station with dignity and honour. Hereafter I shall relate his valiant, but unsuccessful, efforts to resist the progress of the Turks. His defeat and captivity inflicted a deadly wound on the Byzantine monarchy of the East; and after he was released from the chains of the sultan, he vainly sought his wife and his subjects. His wife had been thrust into a monastery, and the subjects of Romanus had embraced the rigid maxim of the civil law, that a prisoner in the hands of the enemy is deprived, as by the stroke of death, of all the public and private rights of a citizen. In the general

Michael VII. Parapinaces, Andronicus I. Constantine XII. A.D. 1071, August.

consternation, the Cæsar John asserted the indefeasible right of his three nephews: Constantinople listened to his voice; and the Turkish captive was proclaimed in the capital, and received on the frontier, as an enemy of the republic. Romanus was not more fortunate in domestic than in foreign war: the loss of two battles compelled him to yield, on the assurance of fair and honourable treatment; but his enemies were devoid of faith or humanity; and, after the cruel extinction of his sight, his wounds were left to bleed and corrupt, till in a few days he was relieved from a state of misery. Under the triple reign of the house of Ducas, the two younger brothers were reduced to the vain honours of the purple; but the eldest, the pusillanimous Michael, was incapable of sustaining the Roman sceptre; and his surname of *Parapinaces* denotes the reproach which he shared with an avaricious favourite, who enhanced the price, and diminished the measure, of wheat. In the school of Psellus, and after the example of his mother, the son of Eudocia made some proficiency in philosophy and rhetoric; but his character was degraded, rather than ennobled, by the virtues of a monk and the learning of a sophist. Strong in the contempt of their sovereign and their own esteem, two generals, at the head of the European and Asiatic legions, assumed the purple at Adrianople and Nice. Their revolt was in the same month; they bore the same name of Nicephorus; but the two candidates were distinguished by the surnames of Bryennius and Botaniates; the former in the maturity of wisdom and courage, the latter conspicuous only by the memory of his past exploits. While Botaniates advanced with cautious and dilatory steps, his active competitor stood in arms before the gates of Constantinople. The name of Bryennius was illustrious; his cause was popular; but his licentious troops could not be restrained from burning and pillaging a suburb; and the people, who would have hailed the rebel, rejected and repulsed the incendiary of his country. This change of the public opinion was favourable to Botaniates, who at length, with an army of Turks, approached the shores of Chalcedon. A formal invitation, in the name of the patriarch, the synod, and the senate, was circulated through the streets of Constantinople; and the general assembly, in the dome of St. Sophia, debated, with order and calmness, on the choice of their sovereign. The guards of Michael would have dispersed this unarmed multitude; but the feeble emperor, applauding his own moderation and clemency, resigned the ensigns of royalty, and was rewarded with the monastic habit, and the title of archbishop of Ephesus. He left a son, a Constantine, born and educated in the purple; and a daughter of the house of Ducas illustrated the blood, and confirmed the succession, of the Comnenian dynasty.

Nicephorus III. Botaniates, A.D. 1078, March 25.

John Comnenus, the brother of the emperor Isaac, survived in peace and dignity his generous refusal of the sceptre. By his wife Anne, a woman of masculine spirit and policy, he left eight children: the three daughters multiplied the Comnenian alliances with the noblest of the Greeks: of the five sons, Manuel was stopped by a premature death; Isaac and Alexius restored the Imperial greatness of their house, which was enjoyed without toil or danger, by the two younger brethren, Adrian and Nicephorus. Alexius, the third and most illustrious of the brothers, was endowed by nature with the choicest gifts both of mind and body: they were cultivated by a liberal education, and exercised in the school of obedience and adversity. The youth was dismissed from the perils of the Turkish war, by the paternal care of the emperor Romanus; but the mother of the Comneni, with her aspiring race, was accused of treason, and banished, by the sons of Ducas, to an island in the Propontis. The two brothers soon emerged into favour and action, fought by each other's side against the rebels and Barbarians, and adhered to the emperor Michael, till he was deserted by the world and by himself. In his first interview with Botaniates, "Prince," said Alexius, with a noble frankness, "my duty rendered me your enemy; the decrees of God and of the people have made me your subject. Judge of my future loyalty, by my past opposition." The successor of Michael entertained him with esteem and confidence: his valour was employed against three rebels, who disturbed the peace of the empire, or at least of the emperors. Ursel, Bryennius, and Basilacius, were formidable by their numerous forces and military fame: they were successively vanquished in the field, and led in chains to the foot of the throne; and whatever treatment they might receive from a timid and cruel court, they applauded the clemency, as well as the courage, of their conqueror. But the loyalty of the Comneni was soon tainted by fear and suspicion; nor is it easy to settle between a subject and a despot, the debt of gratitude, which the former is tempted to claim by a revolt, and the latter to discharge by an executioner. The refusal of Alexius to march against a fourth rebel, the husband of his sister, destroyed the merit or memory of his past services: the favourites of Botaniates provoked the ambition which they apprehended and accused; and the retreat of the two brothers might be justified by the defence of their life or liberty. The women of the family were deposited in a sanctuary, respected by tyrants: the men, mounted on horseback, sallied from the city, and erected the standard of civil war. The soldiers, who had been gradually assembled in the capital and the neighbourhood, were devoted to the cause of a victorious and injured leader: the ties of common interest and domestic alliance secured the attachment of the house of Ducas; and the generous dispute of the Comneni was terminated by the decisive resolution of Isaac, who was the first to invest his younger brother with the name and ensigns of royalty. They returned to Constantinople, to threaten rather than besiege that impregnable fortress; but the fidelity of the guards was corrupted; a gate was surprised; and the fleet was occupied by the active courage of George Palæologus, who fought against his father, without foreseeing that he laboured for his posterity. Alexius ascended the throne; and his aged competitor disappeared in a monastery. An army of various nations was gratified with the pillage of the city; but the public disorders were expiated by the tears and fasts of the Comneni, who submitted to every penance compatible with the possession of the empire.

Alexius I. Comnenus, A.D. 1081, April 1.

The life of the emperor Alexius has been delineated by a favourite daughter, who was inspired by a tender regard for his person and a laudable zeal to perpetuate his virtues. Conscious of the just suspicion of her readers, the princess Anne Comnena repeatedly protests, that, besides her personal knowledge, she had searched the discourse and writings of the most respectable veterans: that after an interval of thirty years, forgotten by, and forgetful of, the world, her mournful solitude was inaccessible to hope and fear; and that truth, the naked perfect truth, was more dear and sacred than the memory of her parent. Yet instead of the simplicity of style and narrative which wins our belief, an elaborate affectation of rhetoric and science, betrays in every page the vanity of a female author. The genuine character of Alexius is lost in a vague constellation of virtues; and the perpetual strain of panegyric and apology, awakens our jealousy, to question the veracity of the historian and the merit of the hero. We cannot however refuse her judicious and important remark, that the disorders of the times were the misfortune and the glory of Alexius; and that every calamity which can afflict a declining empire was accumulated on his reign by the justice of Heaven and the vices of his predecessors. In the East, the victorious Turks had spread, from Persia to the Hellespont, the reign of the Koran and the Crescent: the West was invaded by the adventurous valour of the Normans; and, in the moments of peace, the Danube poured forth new swarms, who had gained, in the science of war, what they had lost in the ferociousness of manners. The sea was not less hostile than the land; and while the frontiers were assaulted by an open enemy, the palace was distracted with secret treason and conspiracy. On a sudden, the banner of the Cross was displayed by the Latins: Europe was precipitated on Asia; and Constantinople had almost been swept away by this impetuous deluge. In the tempest Alexius steered the Imperial vessel with dexterity and courage. At the head of his armies, he was bold in action, skilful in stratagem, patient of fatigue, ready to improve his advantages, and rising from his defeats with inexhaustible vigour. The discipline of the camp was revived, and a new generation of men and soldiers was created by the example and the precepts of their leader. In his intercourse with the Latins, Alexius was patient and artful: his discerning eye pervaded the new system of an unknown world; and I shall hereafter describe the superior policy with which he balanced the interests and passions of the champions of the first crusade. In a long reign of thirty-seven years, he subdued and pardoned the envy of his equals: the laws of public and private order were restored: the arts of wealth and science were cultivated: the limits of the empire were enlarged in Europe and Asia; and the Comnenian sceptre was transmitted to his children of the third and fourth generation. Yet the difficulties of the times betrayed some defects in his character; and have exposed his memory to some just or ungenerous reproach. The reader may possibly smile at the lavish praise which his daughter so often bestows on a flying hero: the weakness or prudence of his situation might be mistaken for a want of personal courage; and his political arts are branded by the Latins with the names of deceit and dissimulation. The increase of the male and female branches of his family adorned the throne and secured the succession; but their princely luxury and pride offended the patricians, exhausted the revenue, and insulted the misery of the people. Anna is a faithful witness that his happiness was destroyed, and his health was broken, by the cares of a public life: the patience of Constantinople was fatigued by the length and severity of his reign; and before Alexius expired, he had lost the love and reverence of his subjects. The clergy could not forgive his application of the sacred riches to the defence of the state; but they applauded his theological learning and ardent zeal for the orthodox faith, which he defended with his tongue, his pen, and his sword. His character was degraded by the superstition of the Greeks; and the same inconsistent principle of human nature enjoined the emperor to found an hospital for the poor and infirm, and to direct the execution of an heretic, who was burnt alive in the square of St. Sophia. Even the sincerity of his moral and religious virtues was suspected by the persons who had passed their lives in his familiar confidence. In his last hours, when he was pressed by his wife Irene to alter the succession, he raised his head, and breathed a pious ejaculation on the vanity of this world. The indignant reply of the empress may be inscribed as an epitaph on his tomb, "You die, as you have lived – AN HYPOCRITE!"

John, or Calo-Johannes, A.D. 1118, August 15.

It was the wish of Irene to supplant the eldest of her surviving sons, in favour of her daughter the princess Anne, whose philosophy would not have refused the weight of a diadem. But the order of male succession was asserted by the friends of their country; the lawful heir drew the royal signet from the finger of his insensible or conscious father, and the empire obeyed the master of the palace. Anna Comnena was stimulated by ambition and revenge to conspire against the life of her brother, and when the design was prevented by the fears or scruples of her husband, she passionately exclaimed, that nature had mistaken the two sexes, and had endowed Bryennius with the soul of a woman. The two sons of Alexius, John and Isaac, maintained the fraternal concord, the hereditary virtue of their race; and the younger brother was content with the title of *Sebastocrator*, which approached the dignity, without sharing the power, of the emperor. In the same person, the claims of primogeniture and merit were fortunately united; his swarthy complexion, harsh features, and diminutive stature, had suggested the ironical surname of Calo-Johannes, or John the Handsome, which his grateful subjects more seriously applied to the beauties of his mind. After the discovery of her treason, the life and fortune of Anne were justly forfeited to the laws. Her life was spared by the clemency of the emperor, but he visited the pomp and treasures of her palace, and bestowed the rich confiscation on the most deserving of his friends. That respectable friend, Axuch, a slave of Turkish extraction, presumed to decline the gift, and to intercede for the criminal: his generous master applauded and imitated the virtue of his favourite, and the reproach or complaint of an injured brother was the only chastisement of the guilty princess. After this example of clemency, the remainder of his reign was never disturbed by conspiracy or rebellion: feared by his nobles, beloved by his people, John was never reduced to the painful necessity of punishing, or even of pardoning, his personal enemies. During his government of twenty-five years, the penalty of death was abolished in the Roman empire, a law of mercy most delightful to the humane theorist, but of which the practice, in a large and vicious community, is seldom consistent with the public safety. Severe to himself, indulgent to others, chaste, frugal, abstemious, the philosophic Marcus would not have disdained the artless virtues of his successor, derived from his heart, and not borrowed from the schools. He despised and moderated the stately magnificence of the Byzantine court, so oppressive to the people, so contemptible to the eye of reason. Under such a prince, innocence had nothing to fear, and merit had every thing to hope; and without assuming the tyrannic office of a censor, he introduced a gradual though visible reformation in the public and private manners of Constantinople. The only defect of this accomplished character, was the frailty of noble minds, the love of arms and military glory. Yet the frequent expeditions of John the Handsome may be justified, at least in their principle, by the necessity of repelling the Turks from the Hellespont and the Bosphorus. The sultan of Iconium was confined to his capital, the Barbarians were driven to the mountains, and the maritime provinces of Asia enjoyed the transient blessings of their deliverance. From Constantinople to Antioch and Aleppo, he repeatedly marched at the head of a victorious army, and in the sieges and battles of this holy war, his Latin allies were astonished by the superior spirit and prowess of a Greek. As he began to indulge the ambitious hope of restoring the ancient limits of the empire, as he revolved in his mind, the Euphrates and Tigris, the dominion of Syria, and the conquest of Jerusalem, the thread of his life and of the public felicity was broken by a singular accident. He hunted the wild boar in the valley of Anazarbus, and had fixed his javelin in the body of the furious animal: but in the struggle, a poisoned arrow dropt from his quiver, and a slight wound in his hand, which produced a mortification, was fatal to the best and greatest of the Comnenian princes.

Manuel, A.D. 1143, April 8.

A premature death had swept away the two eldest sons of John the Handsome; of the two survivors, Isaac and Manuel, his judgment or affection preferred the younger; and the choice of their dying prince was ratified by the soldiers who had applauded the valour of his favourite in the Turkish war. The faithful Axuch hastened to the capital, secured the person of Isaac in honourable confinement, and purchased with a gift of two hundred pounds of silver, the leading ecclesiastics of St. Sophia, who possessed a decisive voice in the consecration of an emperor. With his veteran and affectionate troops, Manuel soon visited Constantinople; his brother acquiesced in the title of Sebastocrator; his subjects admired the lofty stature and martial graces of their new sovereign, and listened with credulity to the flattering promise, that he blended the wisdom of age with the activity and vigour of youth. By the experience of his government, they were taught, that he emulated the spirit, and shared the talents, of his father, whose social virtues were buried in the grave. A reign of thirty-seven years is filled by a perpetual though various warfare against the Turks, the Christians, and the hordes of the wilderness beyond the Danube. The arms of Manuel were exercised on mount Taurus, in the plains of Hungary, on the coast of Italy and Egypt, and on the seas of Sicily and Greece: the influence of his negociations extended from Jerusalem to Rome and Russia; and the Byzantine monarchy, for a while, became an object of respect or terror to the powers of Asia and Europe. Educated in the silk and purple of the East, Manuel possessed the iron temper of a soldier, which cannot easily be paralleled, except in the lives of Richard the first of England, and of Charles the twelfth of Sweden. Such was his strength and exercise in arms, that Raymond, surnamed the Hercules of Antioch, was incapable of wielding the lance and buckler of the Greek emperor. In a famous tournament, he entered the lists on a fiery courser, and overturned in his first career two of the stoutest of the Italian knights. The first in the charge, the last in the retreat, his friends and his enemies alike trembled, the former for *his* safety, and the latter for their own. After posting an ambuscade in a wood, he rode forwards in search of some perilous adventure, accompanied only by his brother and the faithful Axuch, who refused to desert their sovereign. Eighteen horsemen, after a short combat, fled before them: but the numbers of the enemy encreased; the march of the reinforcement was tardy and fearful, and Manuel, without receiving a wound, cut his way through a squadron of five hundred Turks. In a battle against the Hungarians, impatient of the slowness of his troops, he snatched a standard from the head of the column, and was the first, almost alone, who passed a bridge that separated him from the enemy. In the same country, after transporting his army beyond the Save, he sent back the boats, with an order, under pain of death, to their commander, that he should leave him to conquer or die on that hostile land. In the siege of Corfu, towing after him a captive galley, the emperor stood aloft on the poop, opposing against the vollies of darts and stones, a large buckler and a flowing sail, nor could he have escaped inevitable death, had not the Sicilian admiral enjoined his archers to respect the person of an hero. In one day, he is said to have slain above forty of the Barbarians with his own hand; he returned to the camp, dragging along four Turkish prisoners, whom he had tied to the rings of his saddle: he was ever the foremost to provoke or to accept a single combat; and the *gigantic* champions, who encountered his arm, were transpierced by the lance, or cut asunder by the sword, of the invincible Manuel. The story of his exploits, which appear as a model or a copy of the romances of chivalry, may induce a reasonable suspicion of the veracity of the Greeks: I will not, to vindicate their credit, endanger my own; yet I may observe, that in the long series of their annals, Manuel is the only prince who has been the subject of similar exaggeration. With the valour of a soldier, he did not unite the skill or prudence of a general: his victories were not productive of any permanent or useful conquest; and his Turkish laurels were blasted in his last unfortunate campaign, in which he lost his army in the mountains of Pisidia, and owed his deliverance to the generosity of the sultan. But the most singular feature in the character of Manuel, is the contrast and vicissitude of labour and sloth, of hardiness and effeminacy. In war he seemed ignorant of peace, in peace he appeared incapable of war. In the field he slept in the sun or in the snow, tired in the longest marches the strength of his men and horses, and shared with a smile the abstinence or diet of the camp. No sooner did he return to Constantinople, than he resigned himself to the arts and pleasures of a life of luxury: the expence of his dress, his table, and his palace, surpassed the measure of his predecessors, and whole summer days were idly wasted in the delicious isles of the Propontis, in the incestuous love of his niece Theodora. The double cost of a warlike and dissolute prince, exhausted the revenue, and multiplied the taxes; and Manuel, in the distress of his last Turkish campaign, endured a bitter reproach from the mouth of a desperate soldier. As he quenched his thirst, he complained that the water of a fountain was mingled with Christian blood. "It is not the first time," exclaimed a voice from the crowd, "that you have drank, O emperor, the blood of your Christian subjects." Manuel Comnenus was twice married, to the virtuous Bertha or Irene of Germany, and to the beauteous Maria, a French or Latin princess of Antioch. The only daughter of his first wife was destined for Bela an Hungarian prince, who was educated at Constantinople under the name of Alexius: and the consummation of their nuptials might have transferred the Roman sceptre to a race of free and warlike Barbarians. But as soon as Maria of Antioch had given a son and heir to the empire, the presumptive rights of Bela were abolished, and he was deprived of his promised bride; but the Hungarian prince resumed his name and the kingdom of his fathers, and displayed such virtues as might excite the regret and envy of the Greeks. The son of Maria was named Alexius; and at the age of ten years, he ascended the Byzantine throne, after his father's decease had closed the glories of the Comnenian line.

Alexius II. A.D. 1180, Sept. 24. Character and first adventures of Andronicus.

The fraternal concord of the two sons of the great Alexius, had been sometimes clouded by an opposition of interest and passion. By ambition, Isaac the Sebastocrator was excited to flight and rebellion, from whence he was reclaimed by the firmness and clemency of John the Handsome. The errors of Isaac, the father of the emperors of Trebizond, were short and venial; but John, the elder of his sons, renounced for ever his religion. Provoked by a real or imaginary insult of his uncle, he escaped from the Roman to the Turkish camp: his apostacy was rewarded with the Sultan's daughter, the title of Chelebi, or noble, and the inheritance of a princely estate; and, in the fifteenth century, Mahomet the second boasted of his Imperial descent from the Comnenian family. Andronicus, younger brother of John, son of Isaac, and grandson of Alexius Comnenus, is one of the most conspicuous characters of the age; and his genuine adventures might form the subject of a very singular romance. To justify the choice of three ladies of royal birth, it is incumbent on me to observe, that their fortunate lover was cast in the best proportions of strength and beauty; and that the want of the softer graces was supplied by a manly countenance, a lofty stature, athletic muscles, and the air and deportment of a soldier. The preservation, in his old age, of health and vigour, was the reward of temperance and exercise. A piece of bread and a draught of water was often his sole and evening repast; and if he tasted of a wild boar, or a stag, which he had roasted with his own hands, it was the well-earned fruit of a laborious chace. Dextrous in arms, he was ignorant of fear: his persuasive eloquence could bend to every situation and character of life: his style, though not his practice, was fashioned by the example of St. Paul; and, in every deed of mischief, he had a heart to resolve, a head to contrive, and a hand to execute. In his youth, after the death of the emperor John, he followed the retreat of the Roman army; but, in the march through Asia Minor, design or accident tempted him to wander in the mountains; the hunter was encompassed by the Turkish huntsmen, and he remained some time a reluctant or willing captive in the power of the sultan. His virtues and vices recommended him to the favour of his cousin: he shared the perils and the pleasures of Manuel; and while the emperor lived in public incest with his niece Theodora, the affections of her sister Eudocia were seduced and enjoyed by Andronicus. Above the decencies of her sex and rank, she gloried in the name of his concubine; and both the palace and the camp could witness that she slept, or watched, in the arms of her lover. She accompanied him to his military command of Cilicia, the first scene of his valour and imprudence. He pressed, with active ardour, the siege of Mopsuestia: the day was employed in the boldest attacks; but the night was wasted in song and dance; and a band of Greek comedians formed the choicest part of his retinue. Andronicus was surprised by the sally of a vigilant foe; but, while his troops fled in disorder, his invincible lance transpierced the thickest ranks of the Armenians. On his return to the Imperial camp in Macedonia, he was received by Manuel with public smiles and a private reproof; but the dutchies of Naissus, Braniseba, and Castoria, were the reward or consolation of the unsuccessful general. Eudocia still attended his motions: at midnight, their tent was suddenly attacked by her angry brothers, impatient to expiate her infamy in his blood: his daring spirit refused her advice, and the disguise of a female habit; and boldly starting from his couch, he drew his sword, and cut his way through the numerous assassins. It was here that he first betrayed his ingratitude and treachery: he engaged in a treasonable correspondence with the king of Hungary and the German emperor: approached the royal tent at a suspicious hour, with a drawn sword, and, under the mask of a Latin soldier, avowed an intention of revenge against a mortal foe; and imprudently praised the fleetness of his horse, as an instrument of flight and safety. The monarch dissembled his suspicions; but, after the close of the campaign, Andronicus was arrested and strictly confined in a tower of the palace of Constantinople.

In this prison he was left above twelve years; a most painful restraint, from which the thirst of action and pleasure perpetually urged him to escape. Alone and pensive, he perceived some broken bricks in a corner of the chamber, and gradually widened the passage, till he had explored a dark and forgotten recess. Into this hole he conveyed himself, and the remains of his provisions, replacing the bricks in their former position, and erasing with care the footsteps of his retreat. At the hour of the customary visit, his guards were amazed by the silence and solitude of the prison, and reported, with shame and fear, his incomprehensible flight. The gates of the palace and city were instantly shut: the strictest orders were dispatched into the provinces, for the recovery of the fugitive; and his wife, on the suspicion of a pious act, was basely imprisoned in the same tower. At the dead of night, she beheld a spectre: she recognized her husband: they shared their provisions; and a son was the fruit of these stolen interviews, which alleviated the tediousness of their confinement. In the custody of a woman, the vigilance of the keepers was insensibly relaxed; and the captive had accomplished his real escape, when he was discovered, brought back to Constantinople, and loaded with a double chain. At length he found the moment, and the means, of his deliverance. A boy, his domestic servant, intoxicated the guards, and obtained in wax the impression of the keys. By the diligence of his friends, a similar key, with a bundle of ropes, was introduced into the prison, in the bottom of a hogshead. Andronicus employed, with industry and courage, the instruments of his safety, unlocked the doors, descended from the tower, concealed himself all day among the bushes, and scaled in the night the garden-wall of the palace. A boat was stationed for his reception: he visited his own house, embraced his children, cast away his chain, mounted a fleet horse, and directed his rapid course towards the banks of the Danube. At Anchialus in Thrace, an intrepid friend supplied him with horses and money: he passed the river, traversed with speed the desert of Moldavia and the Carpathian hills, and had almost reached the town of Halicz, in the Polish Russia, when he was intercepted by a party of Walachians, who resolved to convey their important captive to Constantinople. His presence of mind again extricated him from this danger. Under the pretence of sickness, he dismounted in the night, and was allowed to step aside from the troop: he planted in the ground his long staff; clothed it with his cap and upper garment; and, stealing into the wood, left a phantom to amuse, for some time, the eyes of the Walachians. From Halicz he was honourably conducted to Kiow, the residence of the great duke: the subtle Greek soon obtained the esteem and confidence of Ieroslaus: his character could assume the manners of every climate; and the Barbarians applauded his strength and courage in the chace of the elks and bears of the forest. In this northern region he deserved the forgiveness of Manuel, who solicited the Russian prince to join his arms in the invasion of Hungary. The influence of Andronicus atchieved this important service: his private treaty was signed with a promise of fidelity on one side, and of oblivion on the other; and he marched at the head of the Russian cavalry, from the Borysthenes to the Danube. In his resentment Manuel had ever sympathised with the martial and dissolute character of his cousin; and his free pardon was sealed in the assault of Zemlin, in which he was second, and second only, to the valour of the emperor.

No sooner was the exile restored to freedom and his country, than his ambition revived, at first to his own, and at length to the public, misfortune. A daughter of Manuel was a feeble bar to the succession of the more deserving males of the Comnenian blood: her future marriage with the prince of Hungary was repugnant to the hopes or prejudices of the princes and nobles. But when an oath of allegiance was required to the presumptive heir, Andronicus alone asserted the honour of the Roman name, declined the unlawful engagement, and boldly protested against the adoption of a stranger. His patriotism was offensive to the emperor, but he spoke the sentiments of the people, and was removed from the royal presence, by an honourable banishment, a second command of the Cilician frontier, with the absolute disposal of the revenues of Cyprus. In this station, the Armenians again exercised his courage and exposed his negligence; and the same rebel, who baffled all his operations, was unhorsed, and almost slain by the vigour of his lance. But Andronicus soon discovered a more easy and pleasing conquest, the beautiful Philippa, sister of the empress Maria, and daughter of Raymond of Poitou, the Latin prince of Antioch. For her sake, he deserted his station, and wasted the summer in balls and tournaments: to his love she sacrificed her innocence, her reputation, and the offer of an advantageous marriage. But the resentment of Manuel for this domestic affront, interrupted his pleasures: Andronicus left the indiscreet princess to weep and to repent; and, with a band of desperate adventurers, undertook the pilgrimage of Jerusalem. His birth, his martial renown, and professions of zeal, announced him as the champion of the cross: he soon captivated both the clergy and the king; and the Greek prince was invested with the lordship of Berytus, on the coast of Phœnicia. In his neighbourhood resided a young and handsome queen, of his own nation and family, great-grand-daughter of the emperor Alexis, and widow of Baldwin the third, king of Jerusalem. She visited and loved her kinsman. Theodora was the third victim of his amorous seduction; and her shame was more public and scandalous than that of her predecessors. The emperor still thirsted for revenge; and his subjects and allies of the Syrian frontier, were repeatedly pressed to seize the person, and put out the eyes, of the fugitive. In Palestine he was no longer safe; but the tender Theodora revealed his danger and accompanied his flight. The queen of Jerusalem was exposed to the East, his obsequious concubine; and two illegitimate children were the living monuments of her weakness. Damascus was his first refuge; and, in the characters of the great Noureddin and his servant Saladin, the superstitious Greek might learn to revere the virtues of the Musulmans. As the friend of Noureddin he visited, most probably, Bagdad, and the courts of Persia; and, after a long circuit round the Caspian sea and the mountains of Georgia, he finally settled among the Turks of Asia Minor, the hereditary enemies of his country. The sultan of Colonia afforded an hospitable retreat to Andronicus, his mistress, and his band of outlaws: the debt of gratitude was paid by frequent inroads in the Roman province of Trebizond; and he seldom returned without an ample harvest of spoil and of Christian captives. In the story of his adventures, he was fond of comparing himself to David, who escaped, by a long exile, the snares of the wicked. But the royal prophet (he presumed to add) was content to lurk on the borders of Judæa, to slay an Amalekite, and to threaten, in his miserable state, the life of the avaricious Nabal. The excursions of the Comnenian prince had a wider range; and he had spread over the Eastern world the glory of his name and religion. By a sentence of the Greek church, the licentious rover had been separated from the faithful; but even this excommunication may prove, that he never abjured the profession of Christianity.

His vigilance had eluded or repelled the open and secret persecution of the emperor; but he was at length ensnared by the captivity of his female companion. The governor of Trebizond succeeded in his attempt to surprise the person of Theodora: the queen of Jerusalem and her two children were sent to Constantinople, and their loss embittered the tedious solitude of banishment. The fugitive implored and obtained a final pardon, with leave to throw himself at the feet of his sovereign, who was satisfied with the submission of this haughty spirit. Prostrate on the ground, he deplored with tears and groans the guilt of his past rebellion; nor would he presume to arise unless some faithful subject would drag him to the foot of the throne, by an iron chain with which he had secretly encircled his neck. This extraordinary penance excited the wonder and pity of the assembly; his sins were forgiven by the church and state; but the just suspicion of Manuel fixed his residence at a distance from the court, at Oenoe, a town of Pontus, surrounded with rich vineyards, and situate on the coast of the Euxine. The death of Manuel, and the disorders of the minority, soon opened the fairest field to his ambition. The emperor was a boy of twelve or fourteen years of age, without vigour, or wisdom, or experience: his mother, the empress Mary, abandoned her person and government to a favourite of the Comnenian name; and his sister, another Mary, whose husband, an Italian, was decorated with the title of Cæsar, excited a conspiracy, and at length an insurrection, against her odious stepmother. The provinces were forgotten, the capital was in flames, and a century of peace and order was overthrown in the vice and weakness of a few months. A civil war was kindled in Constantinople; the two factions fought a bloody battle in the square of the palace, and the rebels sustained a regular siege in the cathedral of St. Sophia. The patriarch laboured with honest zeal to heal the wounds of the republic, the most respectable patriots called aloud for a guardian and avenger, and every tongue repeated the praise of the talents and even the virtues of Andronicus. In his retirement, he affected to revolve the solemn duties of his oath: "If the safety or honour of the Imperial family be threatened, I will reveal and oppose the mischief to the utmost of my power." His correspondence with the patriarch and patricians, was seasoned with apt quotations from the psalms of David and the epistles of St. Paul; and he patiently waited till he was called to her deliverance by the voice of his country. In his march from Oenoe to Constantinople, his slender train insensibly swelled to a crowd and an army; his professions of religion and loyalty were mistaken for the language of his heart; and the simplicity of a foreign dress, which shewed to advantage his majestic stature, displayed a lively image of his poverty and exile. All opposition sunk before him;

he reached the streights of the Thracian Bosphorus; the Byzantine navy sailed from the harbour to receive and transport the saviour of the empire: the torrent was loud and irresistible, and the insects who had basked in the sunshine of royal favour disappeared at the blast of the storm. It was the first care of Andronicus to occupy the palace, to salute the emperor, to confine his mother, to punish her minister, and to restore the public order and tranquillity. He then visited the sepulchre of Manuel: the spectators were ordered to stand aloof, but as he bowed in the attitude of prayer, they heard, or thought they heard, a murmur of triumph and revenge. "I no longer fear thee, my old enemy, who hast driven me a vagabond to every climate of the earth. Thou art safely deposited under a sevenfold dome, from whence thou canst never arise till the signal of the last trumpet. It is now my turn, and speedily will I trample on thy ashes and thy posterity." From his subsequent tyranny we may impute such feelings to the man, and the moment: but it is not extremely probable that he gave an articulate sound to his secret thoughts. In the first months of his administration, his designs were veiled by a fair semblance of hypocrisy, which could delude only the eyes of the multitude: the coronation of Alexius was performed with due solemnity, and his perfidious guardian, holding in his hands the body and blood of Christ, most fervently declared, that he lived, and was ready to die, for the service of his beloved pupil. But his numerous adherents were instructed to maintain, that the sinking empire must perish in the hands of a child, that the Romans could only be saved by a veteran prince, bold in arms, skilful in policy, and taught to reign by the long experience of fortune and mankind; and that it was the duty of every citizen to force the reluctant modesty of Andronicus to undertake the burthen of the public care. The young emperor was himself constrained to join his voice to the general acclamation, and to solicit the association of a colleague, who instantly degraded him from the supreme rank, secluded his person, and verified the rash declaration of the patriarch, that Alexius might be considered as dead, so soon as he was committed to the custody of his guardian. But his death was preceded by the imprisonment and execution of his mother. After blackening her reputation, and inflaming against her the passions of the multitude, the tyrant accused and tried the empress for a treasonable correspondence with the king of Hungary. His own son, a youth of honour and humanity, avowed his abhorrence of this flagitious act, and three of the judges had the merit of preferring their conscience to their safety: but the obsequious tribunal, without requiring any proof, or hearing any defence, condemned the widow of Manuel;

and her unfortunate son subscribed the sentence of her death. Maria was strangled, her corpse was buried in the sea, and her memory was wounded by the insult most offensive to female vanity, a false and ugly representation of her beauteous form. The fate of her son was not long deferred: he was strangled with a bowstring, and the tyrant, insensible to pity or remorse, after surveying the body of the innocent youth, struck it rudely with his foot: "Thy father," he cried, "was a *knave*, thy mother a *whore*, and thyself a *fool*!"

Andronicus I. Comnenus, A.D. 1183, October.

The Roman sceptre, the reward of his crimes, was held by Andronicus about three years and a half as the guardian or sovereign of the empire. His government exhibited a singular contrast of vice and virtue. When he listened to his passions, he was the scourge; when he consulted his reason, the father, of his people. In the exercise of private justice, he was equitable and rigorous: a shameful and pernicious venality was abolished, and the offices were filled with the most deserving candidates by a prince who had sense to chuse, and severity to punish. He prohibited the inhuman practice of pillaging the goods and persons of shipwrecked mariners; the provinces, so long the objects of oppression or neglect, revived in prosperity and plenty; and millions applauded the distant blessings of his reign, while he was cursed by the witnesses of his daily cruelties. The ancient proverb, That blood-thirsty is the man who returns from banishment to power, had been applied with too much truth to Marius and Tiberius; and was now verified for the third time in the life of Andronicus. His memory was stored with a black list of the enemies and rivals, who had traduced his merit, opposed his greatness, or insulted his misfortunes; and the only comfort of his exile was the sacred hope and promise of revenge. The necessary extinction of the young emperor and his mother, imposed the fatal obligation of extirpating the friends, who hated, and might punish, the assassin; and the repetition of murder rendered him less willing, and less able, to forgive. An horrid narrative of the victims whom he sacrificed by poison or the sword, by the sea or the flames, would be less expressive of his cruelty than the appellation of the Halcyon-days, which was applied to a rare and bloodless week of repose: the tyrant strove to transfer, on the laws and the judges, some portion of his guilt; but the mask was fallen, and his subjects could no longer mistake the true author of their calamities. The noblest of the Greeks, more especially those who, by descent or alliance, might dispute the Comnenian inheritance, escaped from the monster's den: Nice or Prusa, Sicily or Cyprus, were their places of refuge; and as their flight was already criminal, they aggravated their offence by an open revolt, and the Imperial title. Yet Andronicus resisted the daggers and swords of his most formidable enemies: Nice and Prusa were reduced and chastised: the Sicilians were content with the sack of Thessalonica; and the distance of Cyprus was not more propitious to the rebel than to the tyrant. His throne was subverted by a rival without merit, and a people without arms. Isaac Angelus, a descendant in the female line from the great Alexius, was marked as a victim, by the prudence or superstition of the emperor. In a moment of despair, Angelus defended his life and liberty, slew the executioner, and fled to the church of St. Sophia. The sanctuary was insensibly filled with a curious and mournful crowd, who, in his fate, prognosticated their own. But their lamentations were soon turned to curses, and their curses to threats: they dared to ask, "Why do we fear? why do we obey? We are many, and he is one; our patience is the only bond of our slavery." With the dawn of day the city burst into a general sedition, the prisons were thrown open, the coldest and most servile were roused to the defence of their country, and Isaac, the second of the name, was raised from the sanctuary to the throne. Unconscious of his danger, the tyrant was absent; withdrawn from the toils of state, in the delicious islands of the Propontis. He had contracted an indecent marriage with Alice, or Agnes, daughter of Lewis the seventh, of France, and relict of the unfortunate Alexius; and his society, more suitable to his temper than to his age, was composed of a young wife and a favourite concubine. On the first alarm he rushed to Constantinople, impatient for the blood of the guilty; but he was astonished by the silence of the palace, the tumult of the city, and the general desertion of mankind. Andronicus proclaimed a free pardon to his subjects; they neither desired, nor would grant, forgiveness: he offered to resign the crown to his son Manuel; but the virtues of the son could not expiate his father's crimes. The sea was still open for his retreat; but the news of the revolution had flown along the coast: when fear had ceased, obedience was no more: the Imperial galley was pursued and taken by an armed brigantine; and the tyrant was dragged to the presence of Isaac Angelus, loaded with fetters, and a long chain round his neck. His eloquence, and the tears of his female companions, pleaded in vain for his life; but, instead of the decencies of a legal execution, the new monarch abandoned the criminal to the numerous sufferers, whom he had deprived of a father, an husband, or a friend. His teeth and hair, an eye and a hand, were torn from him, as a poor compensation for their loss; and a short respite was allowed, that he might feel the bitterness of death. Astride on a camel, without any danger of a rescue, he was carried through the city, and the basest of the populace rejoiced to trample on the fallen majesty of their prince. After a thousand blows and outrages, Andronicus was hung by the feet, between two pillars that supported the statues of a wolf and a sow; and every hand that could reach the public enemy, inflicted on his body some mark of ingenious or brutal cruelty, till two friendly or furious Italians, plunging their swords into his body, released him from all human punishment. In this long and painful agony, "Lord have mercy upon me! and why will you bruise a broken reed?" were the only words that escaped from his mouth. Our hatred for the tyrant is lost in pity for the man; nor can we blame his pusillanimous resignation, since a Greek Christian was no longer master of his life.

Isaac II. Angelus, A.D. 1185, Sept. 12.

I have been tempted to expatiate on the extraordinary character and adventures of Andronicus; but I shall here terminate the series of the Greek emperors since the time of Heraclius. The branches that sprang from the Comnenian trunk had insensibly withered; and the male line was continued only in the posterity of Andronicus himself, who, in the public confusion, usurped the sovereignty of Trebizond, so obscure in history, and so famous in romance. A private citizen of Philadelphia, Constantine Angelus, had emerged to wealth and honours, by his marriage with a daughter of the emperor Alexius. His son Andronicus is conspicuous only by his cowardice. His grandson Isaac punished and succeeded the tyrant; but he was dethroned by his own vices, and the ambition of his brother; and their discord introduced the Latins to the conquest of Constantinople, the first great period in the fall of the Eastern empire.

A.D. 1204, April 12.

If we compute the number and duration of the reigns, it will be found, that a period of six hundred years is filled by sixty emperors, including in the Augustan list some female sovereigns; and deducting some usurpers who were never acknowledged in the capital, and some princes who did not live to possess their inheritance. The average proportion will allow ten years for each emperor, far below the chronological rule of Sir Isaac Newton, who, from the experience of more recent and regular monarchies, has defined about eighteen or twenty years as the term of an ordinary reign. The Byzantine empire was most tranquil and prosperous when it could acquiesce in hereditary succession: five dynasties, the Heraclian, Isaurian, Amorian, Basilian, and Comnenian families enjoyed and transmitted the royal patrimony during their respective series, of five, four, three, six, and four generations; several princes number the years of their reign with those of their infancy; and Constantine the seventh and his two grandsons occupy the space of an entire century. But in the intervals of the Byzantine dynasties, the succession is rapid and broken, and the name of a successful candidate is speedily erazed by a more fortunate competitor. Many were the paths that led to the summit of royalty: the fabric of rebellion was overthrown by the stroke of conspiracy, or undermined by the silent arts of intrigue: the favourites of the soldiers or people, of the senate or clergy, of the women and eunuchs, were alternately clothed with the purple: the means of their elevation were base, and their end was often contemptible or tragic. A being of the nature of man, endowed with the same faculties, but with a longer measure of existence, would cast down a smile of pity and contempt on the crimes and follies of human ambition, so eager, in a narrow span, to grasp at a precarious and short-lived enjoyment. It is thus that the experience of history exalts and enlarges the horizon of our intellectual view. In a composition of some days, in a perusal of some hours, six hundred years have rolled away, and the duration of a life or reign is contracted to a fleeting moment: the grave is ever beside the throne; the success of a criminal is almost instantly followed by the loss of his prize; and our immortal reason survives and disdains the sixty phantoms of kings who have passed before our eyes, and faintly dwell on our remembrance. The observation, that, in every age and climate, ambition has prevailed with the same commanding energy, may abate the surprise of a philosopher; but while he condemns the vanity, he may search the motive, of this universal desire to obtain and hold the sceptre of dominion. To the greater part of the Byzantine series, we cannot reasonably ascribe the love of fame and of mankind. The virtue alone of John Comnenus was beneficent and pure: the most illustrious of the princes, who precede or follow that respectable name, have trod with some dexterity and vigour the crooked and bloody paths of a selfish policy: in scrutinizing the imperfect characters of Leo the Isaurian, Basil the first, and Alexius Comnenus, of Theophilus, the second Basil, and Manuel Comnenus, our esteem and censure are almost equally balanced; and the remainder of the Imperial crowd could only desire and expect to be forgotten by posterity. Was personal happiness the aim and object of their ambition? I shall not descant on the vulgar topics of the misery of kings; but I may surely observe, that their condition, of all others, is the most pregnant with fear, and the least susceptible of hope. For these opposite passions, a larger scope was allowed in the revolutions of antiquity, than in the smooth and solid temper of the modern world, which cannot easily repeat either the triumph of Alexander or the fall of Darius. But the peculiar infelicity of the Byzantine princes exposed them to domestic perils, without affording any lively promise of foreign conquest. From the pinnacle of greatness, Andronicus was precipitated by a death more cruel and shameful than that of the vilest malefactor; but the most glorious of his predecessors had much more to dread from their subjects than to hope from their enemies. The army was licentious without spirit, the nation turbulent without freedom: the Barbarians of the East and West pressed on the monarchy, and the loss of the provinces was terminated by the final servitude of the capital.

The entire series of Roman emperors, from the first of the Cæsars to the last of the Constantines, extends above fifteen hundred years: and the term of dominion, unbroken by foreign conquest, surpasses the measure of the ancient monarchies; the Assyrians or Medes, the successors of Cyrus, or those of Alexander.

CHAPTER XLIX

Introduction, Worship, and Persecution of Images. – Revolt of Italy and Rome. – Temporal Dominion of the Popes. – Conquest of Italy by the Franks. – Establishment of Images. – Character and Coronation of Charlemagne. – Restoration and Decay of the Roman Empire in the West. – Independence of Italy. – Constitution of the Germanic Body.

Introduction of images into the Christian church.

In the connection of the church and state, I have considered the former as subservient only, and relative, to the latter; a salutary maxim, if in fact, as well as in narrative, it had ever been held sacred. The oriental philosophy of the Gnostics, the dark abyss of predestination and grace, and the strange transformation of the Eucharist from the sign to the substance of Christ's body,[1] I have purposely abandoned to the curiosity of speculative divines. But I have reviewed, with diligence and pleasure, the objects of ecclesiastical history, by which the decline and fall of the Roman empire were materially affected, the propagation of Christianity, the constitution of the Catholic church, the ruin of Paganism, and the sects that arose from the mysterious controversies concerning the Trinity and incarnation. At the head of this class, we may justly rank the worship of images, so fiercely disputed in the eighth and ninth centuries; since a question of popular superstition produced the revolt of Italy, the temporal power of the popes, and the restoration of the Roman empire in the West.

The primitive Christians were possessed with an unconquerable repugnance to the use and abuse of images; and this aversion may be ascribed to their descent from the Jews, and their enmity to the Greeks. The Mosaic law had severely proscribed all representations of the Deity; and that precept was firmly established in the principles and practice of the chosen people. The wit of the Christian apologists was pointed against the foolish idolaters, who bowed before the workmanship of their own

1. The learned Selden has given the history of transubstantiation in a comprehensive and pithy sentence. "This opinion is only rhetoric turned into logic." (His Works, vol. iii. p. 2073. in his Table-talk.)

hands; the images of brass and marble, which, had *they* been endowed with sense and motion, should have started rather from the pedestal to adore the creative powers of the artist.[2] Perhaps some recent and imperfect converts of the Gnostic tribe, might crown the statues of Christ and St. Paul with the profane honours which they paid to those of Aristotle and Pythagoras;[3] but the public religion of the Catholics was uniformly simple and spiritual; and the first notice of the use of pictures is in the censure of the council of Illiberis, three hundred years after the Christian æra. Under the successors of Constantine, in the peace and luxury of the triumphant church, the more prudent bishops condescended to indulge a visible superstition, for the benefit of the multitude; and, after the ruin of Paganism, they were no longer restrained by the apprehension of an odious parallel. The first introduction of a symbolic worship was in the veneration of the cross, and of relics. The saints and martyrs, whose intercession was implored, were seated on the right-hand of God; but the gracious and often supernatural favours, which, in the popular belief, were showered round their tomb, conveyed an unquestionable sanction of the devout pilgrims, who visited, and touched, and kissed, these lifeless remains, the memorials of their merits and sufferings.[4] But a memorial, more interesting than the skull or the sandals of a departed worthy, is the faithful copy of his person and features, delineated by the arts of painting or sculpture. In every age, such copies, so congenial to human feelings, have been cherished by the zeal of private friendship, or public esteem: the images of the Roman emperors were adored with civil, and almost religious honours; a reverence less ostentatious, but more sincere, was applied to the statues of sages and patriots; and these profane virtues, these splendid sins, disappeared in the presence of the holy men, who had died for their celestial and everlasting country. At first, the experiment was made with caution and scruple; and the venerable pictures were discreetly allowed to instruct the ignorant, to awaken the cold, and to gratify the prejudices of the heathen proselytes. By a slow though

Their worship.

2. Nec intelligunt homines ineptissimi, quôd si sentire simulacra et moveri possent, adoratura hominem fuissent a quo sunt expolita (Divin. Institut. l. ii. c. 2.). Lactantius is the last, as well as the most eloquent, of the Latin apologists. Their raillery of idols attacks not only the object, but the form and matter.

3. See Irenæus, Epiphanius, and Augustin (Basnage, Hist. des Eglises Reformées, tom. ii. p. 1313.). This Gnostic practice has a singular affinity with the private worship of Alexander Severus (Lampridius, c. 29. Lardner, Heathen Testimonies, vol. iii. p. 34.).

4. See this History, vol. i. p. 736. 836.; vol. ii. p. 90–97.

inevitable progression, the honours of the original were transferred to the copy: the devout Christian prayed before the image of a saint; and the Pagan rites of genuflexion, luminaries, and incense, again stole into the Catholic church. The scruples of reason, or piety, were silenced by the strong evidence of visions and miracles; and the pictures which speak, and move, and bleed, must be endowed with a divine energy, and may be considered as the proper objects of religious adoration. The most audacious pencil might tremble in the rash attempt of defining, by forms and colours, the infinite Spirit, the eternal Father, who pervades and sustains the universe.[5] But the superstitious mind was more easily reconciled to paint and to worship the angels, and, above all, the Son of God, under the human shape, which, on earth, they have condescended to assume. The second person of the Trinity had been clothed with a real and mortal body; but that body had ascended into heaven; and, had not some similitude been presented to the eyes of his disciples, the spiritual worship of Christ might have been obliterated by the visible relics and representations of the saints. A similar indulgence was requisite, and propitious, for the Virgin Mary: the place of her burial was unknown; and the assumption of her soul and body into heaven was adopted by the credulity of the Greeks and Latins. The use, and even the worship, of images, was firmly established before the end of the sixth century: they were fondly cherished by the warm imagination of the Greeks and Asiatics: the Pantheon and Vatican were adorned with the emblems of a new superstition; but this semblance of idolatry was more coldly entertained by the rude Barbarians and the Arian clergy of the West. The bolder forms of sculpture, in brass or marble, which peopled the temples of antiquity, were offensive to the fancy or conscience of the Christian Greeks; and a smooth surface of colours has ever been esteemed a more decent and harmless mode of imitation.[6]

5. *Ου γαρ το Θειον απλουν υπαρχον και αληπτον μορφαις τισι και σχημασιν απεικαζομεν. ουτε κηρῳ και ξυλοις την ὑπερουσιον και προαναρχον ουσιαν τιμαν ἡμεις διεγνωκαμεν* (Concilium Nicenum, ii. in Collect. Labb. tom. viii. p. 1025. edit. Venet.). Il seroit peutêtre à-propos de ne point souffrir d'images de la Trinité ou de la Divinité; les defenseurs les plus zelés des images ayant condamne celles ci, et le concile de Trente ne parlant que des images de Jesus Christ et des Saints (Dupin, Bibliot. Eccles. tom. vi. p. 154.).

6. This general history of images is drawn from the xxii[d] book of the Hist. des Eglises Reformées of Basnage, tom. ii. p. 1310–1337. He was a protestant, but of a manly spirit; and on this head the protestants are so notoriously in the right, that they can venture to be impartial. See the perplexity of poor friar Pagi, Critica, tom. i. p. 42.

The image of Edessa.

The merit and effect of a copy depends on its resemblance with the original; but the primitive Christians were ignorant of the genuine features of the Son of God, his mother, and his apostles: the statue of Christ at Paneas in Palestine[7] was more probably that of some temporal saviour; the Gnostics and their profane monuments were reprobated; and the fancy of the Christian artists could only be guided by the clandestine imitation of some heathen model. In this distress, a bold and dextrous invention assured at once the likeness of the image and the innocence of the worship. A new superstructure of fable was raised on the popular basis of a Syrian legend, on the correspondence of Christ and Abgarus, so famous in the days of Eusebius, so reluctantly deserted by our modern advocates. The bishop of Cæsarea[8] records the epistle,[9] but he most strangely forgets the picture, of Christ;[10] the perfect impression of his face on a linen, with which he gratified the faith of the royal stranger, who had invoked his healing power, and offered the strong city of Edessa to protect him against the malice of the Jews. The ignorance of the

7. After removing some rubbish of miracle and inconsistency, it may be allowed, that as late as the year 300, Paneas in Palestine was decorated with a bronze statue, representing a grave personage wrapt in a cloak, with a grateful or suppliant female kneeling before him, and that an inscription – τῳ Σωτηρι, τῳ ευεργετῃ – was perhaps inscribed on the pedestal. By the Christians, this groupe was foolishly explained of their founder and the *poor* woman whom he had cured of the bloody flux (Euseb. vii. 18. Philostorg. vii. 3, &c.). M. de Beausobre more reasonably conjectures the philosopher Apollonius, or the emperor Vespasian: in the latter supposition, the female is a city, a province, or perhaps the queen Berenice (Bibliothéque Germanique, tom. xiii. p. 1–92.).

8. Euseb. Hist. Eccles. l. i. c. 13. The learned Assemannus has brought up the collateral aid of three Syrians, St. Ephrem, Josua Stylites, and James bishop of Sarug; but I do not find any notice of the Syriac original or the archives of Edessa (Bibliot. Orient., tom. i. p. 318. 420. 554.); their vague belief is probably derived from the Greeks.

9. The evidence for these epistles is stated and rejected by the candid Lardner (Heathen Testimonies, vol. i. p. 297–309.). Among the herd of bigots who are forcibly driven from this convenient, but untenable, post, I am ashamed, with the Grabes, Caves, Tillemonts, &c. to discover Mr. Addison, an English gentleman (his Works, vol. i. p. 528. Baskerville's edition); but his superficial tract on the Christian religion owes its credit to his name, his style, and the interested applause of our clergy.

10. From the silence of James of Sarug (Asseman. Bibliot. Orient. p. 289. 318.), and the testimony of Evagrius (Hist. Eccles. l. iv. c. 27.), I conclude that this fable was invented between the years 521 and 594, most probably after the siege of Edessa in 540 (Asseman. tom. i. p. 416. Procopius, de Bell. Persic. l. ii.). It is the sword and buckler of Gregory II. (in Epist. i. ad Leon. Isaur. Concil. tom. viii. p. 656, 657.) of John Damascenus (Opera, tom. i. p. 281. edit. Lequien), and of the second Nicene Council (Actio v. p. 1030.). The most perfect edition may be found in Cedrenus (Compend. p. 175–178.).

primitive church is explained by the long imprisonment of the image in a niche of the wall, from whence, after an oblivion of five hundred years, it was released by some prudent bishop, and seasonably presented to the devotion of the times. Its first and most glorious exploit was the deliverance of the city from the arms of Chosroes Nushirvan; and it was soon revered as a pledge of the divine promise, that Edessa should never be taken by a foreign enemy. It is true indeed, that the text of Procopius ascribes the double deliverance of Edessa to the wealth and valour of her citizens, who purchased the absence and repelled the assaults of the Persian monarch. He was ignorant, the profane historian, of the testimony which he is compelled to deliver in the ecclesiastical page of Evagrius, that the Palladium was exposed on the rampart, and that the water which had been sprinkled on the holy face, instead of quenching, added new fewel to the flames of the besieged. After this important service, the image of Edessa was preserved with respect and gratitude; and if the Armenians rejected the legend, the more credulous Greeks adored the similitude, which was not the work of any mortal pencil, but the immediate creation of the divine original. The style and sentiments of a Byzantine hymn will declare how far their worship was removed from the grossest idolatry. "How can we with mortal eyes contemplate this image, whose celestial splendour the host of heaven presumes not to behold? HE who dwells in heaven condescends this day to visit us by his venerable image: HE who is seated on the cherubim, visits us this day by a picture, which the Father has delineated with his immaculate hand, which he has formed in an ineffable manner, and which we sanctify by adoring it with fear and love." Before the end of the sixth century, these images, *made without hands* (in Greek, it is a single word[11]), were propagated in the camps and cities of the Eastern empire:[12] they were the objects of worship, and the instruments of miracles: and in the hour of danger or tumult, their

Its copies. venerable presence could revive the hope, rekindle the courage,

11. *Αχειροποιητος*. See Ducange, in Gloss. Græc. et Lat. The subject is treated with equal learning and bigotry by the Jesuit Gretser (Syntagma de Imaginibus non Manû factis, ad calcem Codini de Officiis, p. 289–330.), the ass, or rather the fox, of Ingoldstadt (see the Scaligerana); with equal reason and wit by the protestant Beausobre, in the ironical controversy which he has spread through many volumes of the Bibliothéque Germanique (tom. xviii. p. 1–50. xx. p. 27–68. xxv. p. 1–36. xxvii. p. 85–118. xxviii. p. 1–33. xxxi. p. 111–148. xxxii. p. 75–107. xxxiv. p. 67–96.).

12. Theophylact Simocatta (l. ii. c. 3. p. 34. l. iii. c. 1. p. 63.) celebrates the *θεανδρικον εικασμα*, which he styles *αχειροποιητον*; yet it was no more than a copy, since he adds, *αρχετυπον το εκεινον οι Ρωμαιοι* (of Edessa) *θρησκευουσι τι αρρητον*. See Pagi, tom. ii. A.D. 586, N° 11.

or repress the fury, of the Roman legions. Of these pictures, the far greater part, the transcripts of a human pencil, could only pretend to a secondary likeness and improper title: but there were some of higher descent, who derived their resemblance from an immediate contact with the original, endowed, for that purpose, with a miraculous and prolific virtue. The most ambitious aspired from a filial to a fraternal relation with the image of Edessa; and such is the *veronica* of Rome, or Spain, or Jerusalem, which Christ in his agony and bloody sweat applied to his face, and delivered to an holy matron. The fruitful precedent was speedily transferred to the Virgin Mary, and the saints and martyrs. In the church of Diospolis in Palestine, the features of the Mother of God[13] were deeply inscribed in a marble column: the East and West have been decorated by the pencil of St. Luke; and the evangelist, who was perhaps a physician, has been forced to exercise the occupation of a painter, so profane and odious in the eyes of the primitive Christians. The Olympian Jove, created by the muse of Homer and the chissel of Phidias, might inspire a philosophic mind with momentary devotion: but these Catholic images were faintly and flatly delineated by monkish artists in the last degeneracy of taste and genius.[14]

Opposition to image-worship.

The worship of images had stolen into the church by insensible degrees, and each petty step was pleasing to the superstitious mind, as productive of comfort and innocent of sin. But in the beginning of the eighth century, in the full magnitude of the abuse, the more timorous Greeks were awakened by an apprehension, that under the mask of Christianity, they had restored the religion of their fathers: they heard, with grief and impatience, the name of idolaters; the incessant charge of the Jews and Mahometans,[15] who derived from the Law and the Koran an immortal hatred to graven images and all relative worship. The servitude of the Jews might curb their zeal and depreciate their authority; but the triumphant Musulmans, who reigned

13. See, in the genuine or supposed works of John Damascenus, two passages on the Virgin and St. Luke, which have not been noticed by Gretser, nor consequently by Beausobre (Opera Joh. Damascen. tom. i. p. 618. 631.).

14. "Your scandalous figures stand quite out from the canvass: they are as bad as a group of statues!" It was thus that the ignorance and bigotry of a Greek priest applauded the pictures of Titian, which he had ordered, and refused to accept.

15. By Cedrenus, Zonaras, Glycas, and Manasses, the origin of the Iconoclasts is imputed to the caliph Yezid and two Jews, who promised the empire to Leo; and the reproaches of these hostile sectaries are turned into an absurd conspiracy for restoring the purity of the Christian worship (see Spanheim, Hist. Imag. c. 2.).

at Damascus, and threatened Constantinople, cast into the scale of reproach the accumulated weight of truth and victory. The cities of Syria, Palestine, and Egypt, had been fortified with the images of Christ, his mother, and his saints; and each city presumed on the hope or promise of miraculous defence. In a rapid conquest of ten years, the Arabs subdued those cities and these images; and, in their opinion, the Lord of Hosts pronounced a decisive judgment between the adoration and contempt of these mute and inanimate idols. For a while Edessa had braved the Persian assaults; but the chosen city, the spouse of Christ, was involved in the common ruin; and his divine resemblance became the slave and trophy of the infidels. After a servitude of three hundred years, the Palladium was yielded to the devotion of Constantinople, for a ransom of twelve thousand pounds of silver, the redemption of two hundred Musulmans, and a perpetual truce for the territory of Edessa.[16] In this season of distress and dismay, the eloquence of the monks was exercised in the defence of images; and they attempted to prove, that the sin and schism of the greatest part of the Orientals had forfeited the favour, and annihilated the virtue, of these precious symbols. But they were now opposed by the murmurs of many simple or rational Christians, who appealed to the evidence of texts, of facts, and of the primitive times, and secretly desired the reformation of the church. As the worship of images had never been established by any general or positive law, its progress in the Eastern empire had been retarded, or accelerated, by the differences of men and manners, the local degrees of refinement, and the personal characters of the bishops. The splendid devotion was fondly cherished by the levity of the capital, and the inventive genius of the Byzantine clergy; while the rude and remote districts of Asia were strangers to this innovation of sacred luxury. Many large congregations of Gnostics and Arians maintained, after their conversion, the simple worship which had preceded their separation; and the Armenians, the most warlike subjects of Rome, were not reconciled, in the twelfth century, to the sight of images.[17] These various denominations of men

16. See Elmacin (Hist. Saracen. p. 267.), Abulpharagius (Dynast. p. 201.), and Abulfeda (Annal. Moslem. p. 264.), and the Criticisms of Pagi (tom. iii. A.D. 944). The prudent Franciscan refuses to determine whether the image of Edessa now reposes at Rome or Genoa; but its repose is inglorious, and this ancient object of worship is no longer famous or fashionable.

17. *Αρμενιοις και Αλαμανοις επισης ἡ ἁγιων εικονων προσκυνησις απηγορευται* (Nicetas, l. ii. p. 258.). The Armenian churches are still content with the Cross (Missions du Levant, tom. iii. p. 148.): but surely the superstitious Greek is unjust to the superstition of the Germans of the xii[th] century.

afforded a fund of prejudice and aversion, of small account in the villages of Anatolia or Thrace, but which, in the fortune of a soldier, a prelate, or an eunuch, might be often connected with the powers of the church and state.

Leo the Iconoclast, and his successors, A.D. 726–840.

Of such adventurers, the most fortunate was the emperor Leo the third,[18] who, from the mountains of Isauria, ascended the throne of the East. He was ignorant of sacred and profane letters; but his education, his reason, perhaps his intercourse with the Jews and Arabs, had inspired the martial peasant with an hatred of images; and it was held to be the duty of a prince, to impose on his subjects the dictates of his own conscience. But in the outset of an unsettled reign, during ten years of toil and danger, Leo submitted to the meanness of hypocrisy, bowed before the idols which he despised, and satisfied the Roman pontiff with the annual professions of his orthodoxy and zeal. In the reformation of religion, his first steps were moderate and cautious: he assembled a great council of senators and bishops, and enacted, with their consent, that all the images should be removed from the sanctuary and altar to a proper height in the churches, where they might be visible to the eyes, and inaccessible to the superstition, of the people. But it was impossible on either side to check the rapid though adverse impulse of veneration and abhorrence: in their lofty position, the sacred images still edified their votaries and reproached the tyrant. He was himself provoked by resistance and invective; and his own party accused him of an imperfect discharge of his duty, and urged for his imitation, the example of the Jewish king, who had broken without scruple the brazen serpent of the temple. By a second edict, he proscribed the existence as well as the use of religious pictures; the churches of Constantinople and the provinces were cleansed from idolatry; the images of Christ, the Virgin, and the Saints, were demolished, or a smooth surface of plaster was spread over the walls of the edifice. The sect of the Iconoclasts was supported by the zeal and despotism of six emperors, and the East and West were involved in a noisy conflict of one hundred and

18. Our original, but not impartial, monuments of the Iconoclasts must be drawn from the Acts of the Councils, tom. viii and ix. Collect. Labbé, edit. Venet. and the historical writings of Theophanes, Nicephorus, Manasses, Cedrenus, Zonaras, &c. Of the modern Catholics, Baronius, Pagi, Natalis Alexander (Hist. Eccles. Seculum viii and ix.), and Maimbourg (Hist. des Iconoclastes), have treated the subject with learning, passion, and credulity. The protestant labours of Frederic Spanheim (Historia Imaginum Restituta) and James Basnage (Hist. des Eglises Reformées, tom. ii. l. xxiii. p. 1339–1385.) are cast into the Iconoclast scale. With this mutual aid, and opposite tendency, it is easy for *us* to poise the balance with philosophic indifference.

twenty years. It was the design of Leo the Isaurian to pronounce the condemnation of images, as an article of faith, and by the authority of a general council: but the convocation of such an assembly was reserved for his son Constantine;[19] and though it is stigmatised by triumphant bigotry as a meeting of fools and atheists, their own partial and mutilated acts betray many symptoms of reason and piety. The debates and decrees of many provincial synods introduced the summons of the general council which met in the suburbs of Constantinople, and was composed of the respectable number of three hundred and thirty-eight bishops of Europe and Anatolia; for the patriarchs of Antioch and Alexandria were the slaves of the caliph, and the Roman pontiff had withdrawn the churches of Italy and the West from the communion of the Greeks. This Byzantine synod assumed the rank and powers of the seventh general council: yet even this title was a recognition of the six preceding assemblies which had laboriously built the structure of the Catholic faith. After a serious deliberation of six months, the three hundred and thirty-eight bishops pronounced and subscribed an unanimous decree, that all visible symbols of Christ, except in the Eucharist, were either blasphemous or heretical; that image-worship was a corruption of Christianity and a renewal of Paganism; that all such monuments of idolatry should be broken or erazed; and that those who should refuse to deliver the objects of their private superstition, were guilty of disobedience to the authority of the church and of the emperor. In their loud and loyal acclamations, they celebrated the merits of their temporal redeemer; and to his zeal and justice they entrusted the execution of their spiritual censures. At Constantinople, as in the former councils, the will of the prince was the rule of episcopal faith; but on this occasion, I am inclined to suspect that a large majority of the prelates sacrificed their secret conscience to the temptations of hope and fear. In the long night of superstition, the Christians had wandered far away from the simplicity of the gospel: nor was it easy for them to discern the clue, and tread back the mazes, of the labyrinth. The worship of images was inseparably blended, at least to a pious fancy, with the Cross,

Their synod of Constantinople, A.D. 754.

Their creed.

19. Some flowers of rhetoric are *Συνοδον παρανομον και αθεον*, and the bishops *τοις ματαιοφροσιν*. By Damascenus it is styled *ακυρος και αδεκτος* (Opera, tom. i. p. 623.). Spanheim's Apology for the Synod of Constantinople (p. 171, &c.) is worked up with truth and ingenuity, from such materials as he could find in the Nicene Acts (p. 1046, &c.). The witty John of Damascus converts *επισκοπους* into *επισκοτους* makes them *κοιλιοδουλους*, slaves of their belly, &c. Opera, tom. i. p. 306.

the Virgin, the Saints and their relics: the holy ground was involved in a cloud of miracles and visions; and the nerves of the mind, curiosity and scepticism, were benumbed by the habits of obedience and belief. Constantine himself is accused of indulging a royal licence to doubt, or deny, or deride the mysteries of the Catholics,[20] but they were deeply inscribed in the public and private creed of his bishops; and the boldest Iconoclast might assault with a secret horror, the monuments of popular devotion, which were consecrated to the honour of his celestial patrons. In the reformation of the sixteenth century, freedom and knowledge had expanded all the faculties of man; the thirst of innovation superseded the reverence of antiquity, and the vigour of Europe could disdain those phantoms which terrified the sickly and servile weakness of the Greeks.

Their persecution of the images and monks, A.D. 726–775.

The scandal of an abstract heresy can be only proclaimed to the people by the blast of the ecclesiastical trumpet; but the most ignorant can perceive, the most torpid must feel, the profanation and downfal of their visible deities. The first hostilities of Leo were directed against a lofty Christ on the vestibule, and above the gate, of the palace. A ladder had been planted for the assault, but it was furiously shaken by a crowd of zealots and women: they beheld, with pious transport, the ministers of sacrilege tumbling from on high, and dashed against the pavement; and the honours of the ancient martyrs were prostituted to these criminals, who justly suffered for murder and rebellion.[21] The execution of the Imperial edicts was resisted by frequent tumults in Constantinople and the provinces: the person of Leo was endangered, his officers were massacred, and the popular enthusiasm was quelled by the strongest efforts of the civil and military power. Of the Archipelago, or Holy Sea, the numerous islands were filled with images and monks: their votaries abjured, without scruple, the enemy of Christ, his mother, and the saints: they armed a fleet of boats and gallies, displayed their consecrated banners, and boldly steered for the harbour of Constantinople, to place on the throne a new favourite of God and the people. They depended on the succour of a

20. He is accused of proscribing the title of saint; styling the Virgin, mother of *Christ*; comparing her after her delivery to an empty purse; of Arianism, Nestorianism, &c. In his defence, Spanheim (c. iv. p. 207.) is somewhat embarrassed between the interest of a protestant and the duty of an orthodox divine.

21. The holy confessor Theophanes approves the principle of their rebellion, *θειῳ κινουμενοι ζηλῳ* (p. 339.). Gregory II. (in Epist. i. ad Imp. Leon. Concil. tom. viii. p. 661. 664.) applauds the zeal of the Byzantine women who killed the Imperial officers.

miracle; but their miracles were inefficient against the *Greek fire*; and, after the defeat and conflagration of their fleet, the naked islands were abandoned to the clemency or justice of the conqueror. The son of Leo, in the first year of his reign, had undertaken an expedition against the Saracens: during his absence, the capital, the palace, and the purple, were occupied by his kinsman Artavasdes, the ambitious champion of the orthodox faith. The worship of images was triumphantly restored: the patriarch renounced his dissimulation, or dissembled his sentiments; and the righteous claim of the usurper was acknowledged, both in the new, and in ancient, Rome. Constantine flew for refuge to his paternal mountains; but he descended at the head of the bold and affectionate Isaurians; and his final victory confounded the arms and predictions of the fanatics. His long reign was distracted with clamour, sedition, conspiracy, and mutual hatred, and sanguinary revenge: the persecution of images was the motive, or pretence, of his adversaries; and, if they missed a temporal diadem, they were rewarded by the Greeks with the crown of martyrdom. In every act of open and clandestine treason, the emperor felt the unforgiving enmity of the monks, the faithful slaves of the superstition to which they owed their riches and influence. They prayed, they preached, they absolved, they inflamed, they conspired: the solitude of Palestine poured forth a torrent of invective; and the pen of St. John Damascenus,[22] the last of the Greek fathers, devoted the tyrant's head, both in this world and the next.[23] I am not at leisure to examine how far the monks provoked, nor how much they have exaggerated, their real and pretended sufferings, nor how many lost their lives or limbs, their eyes or their beards, by the cruelty of the emperor. From the chastisement of individuals, he proceeded to the abolition of the order;

22. John, or Mansur, was a noble Christian of Damascus, who held a considerable office in the service of the caliph. His zeal in the cause of images exposed him to the resentment and treachery of the Greek emperor; and on the suspicion of a treasonable correspondence, he was deprived of his right hand, which was miraculously restored by the Virgin. After this deliverance, he resigned his office, distributed his wealth, and buried himself in the monastery of St. Sabas, between Jerusalem and the Dead Sea. The legend is famous; but his learned editor, father Lequien, has unluckily proved that St. John Damascenus was already a monk before the Iconoclast dispute (Opera, tom. i. Vit. St. Joan. Damascen. p. 10–13. et Notas ad loc.).

23. After sending Leo to the devil, he introduces his heir – *το μιαρον αυτου γεννημα, και της κακιας αυτου κληρονομος εν διπλῳ γενομενος* (Opera Damascen. tom. i. p. 625.). If the authenticity of this piece be suspicious, we are sure that in other works, no longer extant, Damascenus bestowed on Constantine the titles of *νεον Μωαμεθ, Χριστομαχον, μισαγιον* (tom. i. p. 306.).

and, as it was wealthy and useless, his resentment might be stimulated by avarice and justified by patriotism. The formidable name and mission of the *Dragon*,[24] his visitor-general, excited the terror and abhorrence of the *black* nation: the religious communities were dissolved; the buildings were converted into magazines, or barracks; the lands, moveables, and cattle, were confiscated; and our modern precedents will support the charge, that much wanton or malicious havock was exercised against the relics, and even the books, of the monasteries. With the habit and profession of monks, the public and private worship of images was rigorously proscribed; and it should seem, that a solemn abjuration of idolatry was exacted from the subjects, or at least from the clergy, of the Eastern empire.[25]

State of Italy.

The patient East abjured, with reluctance, her sacred images; they were fondly cherished, and vigorously defended, by the independent zeal of the Italians. In ecclesiastical rank and jurisdiction, the patriarch of Constantinople and the pope of Rome were nearly equal. But the Greek prelate was a domestic slave under the eye of his master, at whose nod he alternately passed from the convent to the throne, and from the throne to the convent. A distant and dangerous station, amidst the Barbarians of the West, excited the spirit and freedom of the Latin bishops. Their popular election endeared them to the Romans: the public and private indigence was relieved by their ample revenue; and the weakness or neglect of the emperors compelled them to consult, both in peace and war, the temporal safety of the city. In the school of adversity the priest insensibly imbibed the virtues and the ambition of a prince; the same character was assumed, the same policy was adopted, by the Italian, the Greek, or the Syrian, who ascended the chair of St. Peter; and, after the loss of her legions and provinces, the genius and fortune of the popes again restored the supremacy of Rome. It is agreed, that in the eighth century their dominion was founded on rebellion, and that the rebellion was produced, and justified, by the heresy of the Iconoclasts; but the conduct of the second and third Gregory, in this memorable contest, is variously interpreted by the wishes of their friends and enemies. The

24. In the narrative of this persecution from Theophanes and Cedrenus, Spanheim (p. 235–238.) is happy to compare the *Draco* of Leo with the dragoons (*Dracones*) of Louis XIV.; and highly solaces himself with this controversial pun.

25. Προγραμμα γαρ εξεπεμψε κατα πασαν εξαρχιαν την ὑπο της χειρος αυτου, παντας ὑπογραψαι και ομνυναι του αθετησαι την προσκυνησιν των σεπτων εικονων (Damascen. Op. tom. i. p. 625.). This oath and subscription I do not remember to have seen in any modern compilation.

Byzantine writers unanimously declare, that, after a fruitless admonition, they pronounced the separation of the East and West, and deprived the sacrilegious tyrant of the revenue and sovereignty of Italy. Their excommunication is still more clearly expressed by the Greeks, who beheld the accomplishment of the papal triumphs; and as they are more strongly attached to their religion than to their country, they praise, instead of blaming, the zeal and orthodoxy of these apostolical men.[26] The modern champions of Rome are eager to accept the praise and the precedent: this great and glorious example of the deposition of royal heretics is celebrated by the cardinals Baronius and Bellarmine;[27] and if they are asked, why the same thunders were not hurled against the Neros and Julians of antiquity? they reply, that the weakness of the primitive church was the sole cause of her patient loyalty.[28] On this occasion, the effects of love and hatred are the same; and the zealous protestants, who seek to kindle the indignation, and to alarm the fears, of princes and magistrates, expatiate on the insolence and treason of the two Gregories against their lawful sovereign.[29] They are defended only by the moderate Catholics, for the most part, of the Gallican church,[30] who respect the saint, without approving the sin. These common advocates of the crown and the mitre circumscribe the truth of facts by the rule of equity,

26. *Και την Ρωμην σου παση Ιταλιᾳ της βασιλειας ἀυτου απεστησε*, says Theophanes (Chronograph. p. 343.). For this Gregory is styled by Cedrenus *ανηρ αποστολικος* (p. 450.). Zonaras specifies the thunder, *αναθηματι συνοδικῳ* (tom. ii. l. xv. p. 104, 105.). It may be observed, that the Greeks are apt to confound the times and actions of two Gregories.

27. See Baronius, Annal. Eccles. A.D. 730, N° 4, 5.: dignum exemplum! Bellarmin, de Romano Pontifice, l. v. c. 8.: mulctavit eum parte imperii. Sigonius, de Regno Italiæ, l. iii, Opera, tom. ii. p. 169. Yet such is the change of Italy, that Sigonius is corrected by the editor of Milan, Philippus Argelatus, a Bolognese, and subject of the pope.

28. Quod si Christiani olim non deposuerunt Neronem aut Julianum, id fuit quia deerant vires temporales Christianis (honest Bellarmine, de Rom. Pont. l. v. c. 7.). Cardinal Perron adds a distinction more honourable to the first Christians, but not more satisfactory to modern princes – the *treason* of heretics and apostates, who break their oath, belie their coin, and renounce their allegiance to Christ and his vicar (Perroniana, p. 89.).

29. Take, as a specimen, the cautious Basnage (Hist. de l'Eglise, p. 1350, 1351.) and the vehement Spanheim (Hist. Imaginum), who, with an hundred more, tread in the footsteps of the centuriators of Magdeburgh.

30. See Launoy (Opera, tom. v. pars ii. epist. vii. 7. p. 456–474.), Natalis Alexander (Hist. Nov. Testamenti, secul. viii. dissert. i. p. 92–96.), Pagi (Critica, tom. iii. p. 215, 216.), and Giannone (Istoria Civile di Napoli, tom. i. p. 317–320.), a disciple of the Gallican school. In the field of controversy I always pity the moderate party, who stand on the open middle ground exposed to the fire of both sides.

scripture, and tradition; and appeal to the evidence of the Latins,[31] and the lives[32] and epistles of the popes themselves.

Epistles of Gregory II. to the emperor, A.D. 727.

Two original epistles, from Gregory the second to the emperor Leo, are still extant;[33] and if they cannot be praised as the most perfect models of eloquence and logic, they exhibit the portrait, or at least the mask, of the founder of the papal monarchy. "During ten pure and fortunate years," says Gregory to the emperor, "we have tasted the annual comfort of your royal letters, subscribed in purple ink, with your own hand, the sacred pledges of your attachment to the orthodox creed of our fathers. How deplorable is the change! how tremendous the scandal! You now accuse the Catholics of idolatry; and, by the accusation, you betray your own impiety and ignorance. To this ignorance we are compelled to adapt the grossness of our style and arguments: the first elements of holy letters are sufficient for your confusion; and were you to enter a grammar-school, and avow yourself the enemy of our worship, the simple and pious children would be provoked to cast their horn-books at your head." After this decent salutation, the pope attempts the usual distinction between the idols of antiquity and the Christian images. The former were the fanciful representations of phantoms or dæmons, at a time when the true God had not manifested his person in any visible likeness. The latter are the genuine forms of Christ, his mother, and his saints, who had approved, by a crowd of miracles, the innocence and merit of this relative worship.

31. They appeal to Paul Warnefrid, or Diaconus (de Gestis Langobard. l. vi. c. 49. p. 506, 507. in Script. Ital. Muratori, tom. i. pars i.), and the nominal Anastasius (de Vit. Pont. in Muratori, tom. iii. pars i. Gregorius II. p. 154. Gregorius III. p. 158. Zacharias, p. 161. Stephanus III. p. 165. Paulus, p. 172. Stephanus IV. p. 174. Hadrianus, p. 179. Leo III. p. 195.). Yet I may remark, that the true Anastasius (Hist. Eccles. p. 134. edit. Reg.) and the Historia Miscella (l. xxi. p. 151. in tom. i. Script. Ital.), both of the ix[th] century, translate and approve the Greek text of Theophanes.

32. With some minute difference, the most learned critics, Lucas Holstenius, Schelestrate, Ciampini, Bianchini, Muratori (Prolegomena ad tom. iii. pars i.), are agreed that the Liber Pontificalis was composed and continued by the apostolical librarians and notaries of the viii[th] and ix[th] centuries; and that the last and smallest part is the work of Anastasius, whose name it bears. The style is barbarous, the narrative partial, the details are trifling – yet it must be read as a curious and authentic record of the times. The epistles of the popes are dispersed in the volumes of Councils.

33. The two epistles of Gregory II. have been preserved in the Acts of the Nicene Council (tom. viii. p. 651–674.). They are without a date, which is variously fixed, by Baronius in the year 726, by Muratori (Annali d'Italia, tom. vi. p. 120.) in 729, and by Pagi in 730. Such is the force of prejudice, that some *papists* have praised the good sense and moderation of these letters.

He must indeed have trusted to the ignorance of Leo, since he could assert the perpetual use of images, from the apostolic age, and their venerable presence in the six synods of the Catholic church. A more specious argument is drawn from present possession and recent practice: the harmony of the Christian world supersedes the demand of a general council; and Gregory frankly confesses, that such assemblies can only be useful under the reign of an orthodox prince. To the impudent and inhuman Leo, more guilty than an heretic, he recommends peace, silence, and implicit obedience to his spiritual guides of Constantinople and Rome. The limits of civil and ecclesiastical powers are defined by the pontiff. To the former he appropriates the body; to the latter, the soul: the sword of justice is in the hands of the magistrate: the more formidable weapon of excommunication is entrusted to the clergy; and in the exercise of their divine commission, a zealous son will not spare his offending father: the successor of St. Peter may lawfully chastise the kings of the earth. "You assault us, O tyrant! with a carnal and military hand: unarmed and naked, we can only implore the Christ, the prince of the heavenly host, that he will send unto you a devil, for the destruction of your body and the salvation of your soul. You declare, with foolish arrogance, I will dispatch my orders to Rome: I will break in pieces the image of St. Peter; and Gregory, like his predecessor Martin, shall be transported in chains, and in exile, to the foot of the Imperial throne. Would to God, that I might be permitted to tread in the footsteps of the holy Martin; but may the fate of Constans serve as a warning to the persecutors of the church. After his just condemnation by the bishops of Sicily, the tyrant was cut off, in the fulness of his sins, by a domestic servant: the saint is still adored by the nations of Scythia, among whom he ended his banishment and his life. But it is our duty to live for the edification and support of the faithful people; nor are we reduced to risk our safety on the event of a combat. Incapable as you are of defending your Roman subjects, the maritime situation of the city may perhaps expose it to your depredation; but we can remove to the distance of four-and-twenty *stadia*,[34] to the first fortress of the Lombards, and then – you

34. *Εικοσι τεσσαρα σταδια ὑποχωρησει ὁ Αρχιερευς Ρωμης εις την χωραν της Καμπανιας, και ὑπαγε διωξον τους ανεμους* (Epist. i. p. 664.). This proximity of the Lombards is hard of digestion. Camillo Pellegrini (dissert. iv. de Ducatû Beneventi, in the Script. Ital. tom. v. p. 172, 173.) forcibly reckons the xxivth stadia, not from Rome, but from the limits of the Roman dutchy, to the first fortress, perhaps Sora, of the Lombards. I rather believe that Gregory, with the pedantry of the age, employs *stadia* for miles, without much enquiry into the genuine measure.

may pursue the winds. Are you ignorant that the popes are the bond of union, the mediators of peace, between the East and West? The eyes of the nations are fixed on our humility; and they revere, as a God upon earth, the apostle St. Peter, whose image you threaten to destroy.[35] The remote and interior kingdoms of the West present their homage to Christ and his vicegerent; and we now prepare to visit one of their most powerful monarchs, who desires to receive from our hands the sacrament of baptism.[36] The Barbarians have submitted to the yoke of the gospel, while you alone are deaf to the voice of the Shepherd. These pious Barbarians are kindled into rage: they thirst to avenge the persecution of the East. Abandon your rash and fatal enterprise; reflect, tremble, and repent. If you persist, we are innocent of the blood that will be spilt in the contest; may it fall on your own head."

Revolt of Italy, A.D. 728, &c.

The first assault of Leo against the images of Constantinople had been witnessed by a crowd of strangers from Italy and the West, who related with grief and indignation the sacrilege of the emperor. But on the reception of his proscriptive edict, they trembled for their domestic deities; the images of Christ and the Virgin, of the angels, martyrs, and saints, were abolished in all the churches of Italy; and a strong alternative was proposed to the Roman pontiff, the royal favour as the price of his compliance, degradation and exile as the penalty of his disobedience. Neither zeal nor policy allowed him to hesitate; and the haughty strain in which Gregory addressed the emperor displays his confidence in the truth of his doctrine or the powers of resistance. Without depending on prayers or miracles, he boldly armed against the public enemy, and his pastoral letters admonished the Italians of their danger and their duty.[37] At this signal, Ravenna, Venice, and the cities of

35. *‘Ον ἁι πασαι Βασιλειαι της δυσεως ως Θεον επιγειον εχουσι.*

36. *Απο της εσωτερου δυσεως του λεγομενου Σεπτετου* (p. 665.). The pope appears to have imposed on the ignorance of the Greeks: he lived and died in the Lateran; and in his time all the kingdoms of the West had embraced Christianity. May not this unknown *Septetus* have some reference to the chief of the Saxon *Heptarchy*, to Ina king of Wessex, who, in the pontificate of Gregory the second, visited Rome, for the purpose, not of baptism, but of pilgrimage (Pagi, A.D. 689, N° 2. A.D. 726, N° 15.).

37. I shall transcribe the important and decisive passage of the Liber Pontificalis. Respiciens ergo pius vir profanam principis jussionem, jam contra Imperatorem quasi contra *hostem* se armavit, renuens hæresim ejus, scribens ubique se cavere Christianos eo quod orta fuisset, impietas talis. *Igitur* permoti omnes Pentapolenses, atque Venetiarum exercitus contra Imperatoris jussionem restiterunt: dicentes se nunquam in ejusdem pontificis condescendere necem, sed pro ejus magis defensione viriliter decertare (p. 156.).

the Exarchate and Pentapolis, adhered to the cause of religion; their military force by sea and land consisted, for the most part, of the natives; and the spirit of patriotism and zeal was transfused into the mercenary strangers. The Italians swore to live and die in the defence of the pope and the holy images; the Roman people was devoted to their father, and even the Lombards were ambitious to share the merit and advantage of this holy war. The most treasonable act, but the most obvious revenge, was the destruction of the statues of Leo himself: the most effectual and pleasing measure of rebellion, was the withholding the tribute of Italy, and depriving him of a power which he had recently abused by the imposition of a new capitation.[38] A form of administration was preserved by the election of magistrates and governors; and so high was the public indignation, that the Italians were prepared to create an orthodox emperor, and to conduct him with a fleet and army to the palace of Constantinople. In that palace, the Roman bishops, the second and third Gregory, were condemned as the authors of the revolt, and every attempt was made either by fraud or force to seize their persons, and to strike at their lives. The city was repeatedly visited or assaulted by captains of the guards, and dukes and exarchs of high dignity or secret trust; they landed with foreign troops, they obtained some domestic aid, and the superstition of Naples may blush that her fathers were attached to the cause of heresy. But these clandestine or open attacks were repelled by the courage and vigilance of the Romans; the Greeks were overthrown and massacred, their leaders suffered an ignominious death, and the popes, however inclined to mercy, refused to intercede for these guilty victims. At Ravenna,[39] the several quarters of the city had long exercised a bloody and hereditary feud; in religious controversy they found a new aliment of faction: but the votaries of images were superior in numbers or spirit, and the exarch, who attempted to stem the torrent, lost his life in a popular sedition. To punish this flagitious deed, and restore his dominion

38. A *census*, or capitation, says Anastasius (p. 156.); a most cruel tax, unknown to the Saracens themselves, exclaims the zealous Maimbourg (Hist. des Iconoclastes, l. i.), and Theophanes (p. 344.), who talks of Pharaoh's numbering the male children of Israel. This mode of taxation was familiar to the Saracens; and, most unluckily for the historian, it was imposed a few years afterwards in France by his patron Lewis XIV.

39. See the Liber Pontificalis of Agnellus (in the Scriptores Rerum Italicarum of Muratori, tom. ii. pars. i.), whose deeper shade of Barbarism marks the difference between Rome and Ravenna. Yet we are indebted to him for some curious and domestic facts – the quarters and factions of Ravenna (p. 154.), the revenge of Justinian II. (p. 160, 161.), the defeat of the Greeks (p. 170, 171.), &c.

in Italy, the emperor sent a fleet and army into the Adriatic gulf. After suffering from the winds and waves much loss and delay, the Greeks made their descent in the neighbourhood of Ravenna: they threatened to depopulate the guilty capital, and to imitate, perhaps to surpass, the example of Justinian the second, who had chastised a former rebellion by the choice and execution of fifty of the principal inhabitants. The women and clergy, in sackcloth and ashes, lay prostrate in prayer; the men were in arms for the defence of their country; the common danger had united the factions, and the event of a battle was preferred to the slow miseries of a siege. In a hard-fought day, as the two armies alternately yielded and advanced, a phantom was seen, a voice was heard, and Ravenna was victorious by the assurance of victory. The strangers retreated to their ships, but the populous sea-coast poured forth a multitude of boats; the waters of the Po were so deeply infected with blood, that during six years, the public prejudice abstained from the fish of the river; and the institution of an annual feast perpetuated the worship of images, and the abhorrence of the Greek tyrant. Amidst the triumph of the Catholic arms, the Roman pontiff convened a synod of ninety-three bishops against the heresy of the Iconoclasts. With their consent, he pronounced a general excommunication against all who by word or deed should attack the tradition of the fathers and the images of the saints: in this sentence the emperor was tacitly involved,[40] but the vote of a last and hopeless remonstrance may seem to imply that the anathema was yet suspended over his guilty head. No sooner had they confirmed their own safety, the worship of images, and the freedom of Rome and Italy, than the popes appear to have relaxed of their severity, and to have spared the relics of the Byzantine dominion. Their moderate counsels delayed and prevented the election of a new emperor, and they exhorted the Italians not to separate from the body of the Roman monarchy. The exarch was permitted to reside within the walls of Ravenna, a captive rather than a master; and till the Imperial coronation of Charlemagne, the government of Rome and Italy was exercised in the name of the successors of Constantine.[41]

40. Yet Leo was undoubtedly comprised in the si quis . . . imaginum sacrarum . . . destructor . . . extiterit sit extorris a corpore D.N. Jesu Christi vel totius ecclesiæ unitate. The canonists may decide whether the guilt or the name constitutes the excommunication; and the decision is of the last importance to their safety, since, according to the oracle (Gratian Caus. xxiii. q. 5. c. 47. apud Spanheim, Hist. Imag. p. 112.), homicidas non esse qui excommunicatos trucidant.

41. Compescuit tale consilium Pontifex, sperans conversionem principis (Anastas.

Republic of Rome. The liberty of Rome, which had been oppressed by the arms and arts of Augustus, was rescued, after seven hundred and fifty years of servitude, from the persecution of Leo the Isaurian. By the Cæsars, the triumphs of the consuls had been annihilated: in the decline and fall of the empire, the god Terminus, the sacred boundary, had insensibly receded from the ocean, the Rhine, the Danube, and the Euphrates; and Rome was reduced to her ancient territory from Viterbo to Terracina, and from Narni to the mouth of the Tyber.[42] When the kings were banished, the republic reposed on the firm basis which had been founded by their wisdom and virtue. Their perpetual jurisdiction was divided between two annual magistrates: the senate continued to exercise the powers of administration and counsel; and the legislative authority was distributed in the assemblies of the people, by a well-proportioned scale of property and service. Ignorant of the arts of luxury, the primitive Romans had improved the science of government and war: the will of the community was absolute: the rights of individuals were sacred: one hundred and thirty thousand citizens were armed for defence or conquest; and a band of robbers and outlaws was moulded into a nation, deserving of freedom and ambitious of glory.[43] When the sovereignty of the Greek emperors was extinguished, the ruins of Rome presented the sad image of depopulation and decay: her slavery was an habit, her liberty an accident; the effect of superstition, and the object of her own amazement and terror. The last vestige of the substance, or even the forms, of the constitution, was obliterated from the practice and memory of the Romans; and they were devoid of knowledge, or virtue, again to build the fabric of a commonwealth. Their scanty remnant, the offspring of slaves and strangers, was despicable in the eyes of the victorious Barbarians. As often as the Franks or Lombards expressed their most bitter contempt of a foe, they called him a Roman; "and in this name,"

p. 156.). Sed ne desisterent ab amore et fide R. J. admonebat (p. 157.). The popes style Leo and Constantine Copronymus, Imperatores et Domini, with the strange epithet of *Piissimi*. A famous Mosaic of the Lateran (A.D. 798) represents Christ, who delivers the keys to St. Peter and the banner to Constantine V. (Muratori, Annali d'Italia, tom. vi. p. 337.)

42. I have traced the Roman dutchy according to the maps, and the maps according to the excellent dissertation, of father Beretti (de Chorographia Italiæ Medii Ævi, sect. xx. p. 216–232.). Yet I must nicely observe, that Viterbo is of Lombard foundation (p. 211.), and that Terracina was usurped by the Greeks.

43. On the extent, population, &c. of the Roman kingdom, the reader may peruse, with pleasure, the *Discours Preliminaire* to the Republique Romaine of M. de Beaufort (tom. i.), who will not be accused of too much credulity for the early ages of Rome.

says the bishop Liutprand, "we include whatever is base, whatever is cowardly, whatever is perfidious, the extremes of avarice and luxury, and every vice that can prostitute the dignity of human nature."[44] By the necessity of their situation, the inhabitants of Rome were cast into the rough model of a republican government: they were compelled to elect some judges in peace and some leaders in war: the nobles assembled to deliberate, and their resolves could not be executed without the union and consent of the multitude. The style of the Roman senate and people was revived,[45] but the spirit was fled; and their new independence was disgraced by the tumultuous conflict of licentiousness and oppression. The want of laws could only be supplied by the influence of religion, and their foreign and domestic counsels were moderated by the authority of the bishop. His alms, his sermons, his correspondence with the kings and prelates of the West, his recent services, their gratitude, and oath, accustomed the Romans to consider him as the first magistrate or prince of the city. The Christian humility of the popes was not offended by the name of *Dominus*, or Lord; and their face and inscription are still apparent on the most ancient coins.[46] Their temporal dominion is now confirmed by the reverence of a thousand years; and their noblest title is the free choice of a people, whom they had redeemed from slavery.

Rome attacked by the Lombards, A.D. 730–752.

In the quarrels of ancient Greece, the holy people of Elis enjoyed a perpetual peace, under the protection of Jupiter, and in the exercise of the Olympic games.[47] Happy would it have been for the Romans, if a similar privilege had guarded the patrimony of St. Peter from the calamities of war; if the Christians,

44. Quos (*Romanos*) nos, Longobardi scilicet, Saxones, Franci, Lotharingi, Bajoarii, Suevi, Burgundiones, tanto dedignamur ut inimicos nostros commoti, nil aliud contumeliarum nisi Romane, dicamus: hoc solo, id est Romanorum nomine, quicquid ignobilitatis, quicquid timiditatis, quicquid avaritiæ, quicquid luxuriæ, quicquid mendacii, immo quicquid vitiorum est comprehendentes (Liutprand, in Legat. Script. Ital. tom. ii. pars i. p. 481.). For the sins of Cato or Tully, Minos might have imposed, as a fit penance, the daily perusal of this barbarous passage.

45. Pipino regi Francorum, omnis senatus, atque universa populi generalitas a Deo servatæ Romanæ urbis. Codex Carolin. epist. 36. in Script. Ital. tom. iii. pars ii. p. 160. The names of senatus and senator were never totally extinct (Dissert. Chorograph. p. 216, 217.); but in the middle ages they signified little more than nobiles optimates, &c. (Ducange, Gloss. Latin.).

46. See Muratori, Antiquit. Italiæ Medii Ævi, tom. ii. dissertat. xxvii. p. 548. On one of these coins we read Hadrianus Papa (*A.D.* 772); on the reverse, Vict. DDNN. with the word *CONOB*, which the Pére Joubert (Science des Medailles, tom. ii. p. 42.) explains by *CON*stantinopoli Officina *B (secunda)*.

47. See West's Dissertation on the Olympic Games (Pindar, vol. ii. p. 32–36.

who visited the holy threshold, would have sheathed their swords in the presence of the apostle and his successor. But this mystic circle could have been traced only by the wand of a legislator and a sage: this pacific system was incompatible with the zeal and ambition of the popes: their Romans were not addicted, like the inhabitants of Elis, to the innocent and placid labours of agriculture; and the Barbarians of Italy, though softened by the climate, were far below the Grecian states in the institutions of public and private life. A memorable example of repentance and piety was exhibited by Liutprand king of the Lombards. In arms, at the gate of the Vatican, the conqueror listened to the voice of Gregory the second,[48] withdrew his troops, resigned his conquests, respectfully visited the church of St. Peter, and, after performing his devotions, offered his sword and dagger, his cuirass and mantle, his silver cross, and his crown of gold, on the tomb of the apostle. But this religious fervour was the illusion, perhaps the artifice, of the moment; the sense of interest is strong and lasting; the love of arms and rapine was congenial to the Lombards; and both the prince and people were irresistibly tempted by the disorders of Italy, the nakedness of Rome, and the unwarlike profession of her new chief. On the first edicts of the emperor, they declared themselves the champions of the holy images: Liutprand invaded the province of Romagna, which had already assumed that distinctive appellation; the Catholics of the Exarchate yielded without reluctance to his civil and military power; and a foreign enemy was introduced for the first time into the impregnable fortress of Ravenna. That city and fortress were speedily recovered by the active diligence and maritime forces of the Venetians; and those faithful subjects obeyed the exhortation of Gregory himself, in separating the personal guilt of Leo from the general cause of the Roman empire.[49] The Greeks were less mindful of the service, than the Lombards of the injury: the two nations, hostile in their faith, were reconciled in a dangerous and unnatural alliance; the king and

edition in 12mo), and the judicious reflections of Polybius (tom. i. l. iv. p. 466. edit. Gronov.).

48. The speech of Gregory to the Lombard is finely composed by Sigonius (de Regno Italiæ, l. iii. Opera, tom. ii. p. 173.), who imitates the licence and the spirit of Sallust or Livy.

49. The Venetian historians, John Sagorninus (Chron. Venet. p. 13.) and the doge Andrew Dandolo (Scriptores Rer. Ital. tom. xii. p. 135.), have preserved this epistle of Gregory. The loss and recovery of Ravenna are mentioned by Paulus Diaconus (de Gest. Langobard. l. vi. c. 49. 54. in Script. Ital. tom. i. pars i. p. 506. 508.); but our chronologists, Pagi, Muratori, &c. cannot ascertain the date or circumstances.

the exarch marched to the conquest of Spoleto and Rome: the storm evaporated without effect, but the policy of Liutprand alarmed Italy with a vexatious alternative of hostility and truce. His successor Astolphus declared himself the equal enemy of the emperor and the pope: Ravenna was subdued by force or treachery,[50] and this final conquest extinguished the series of the exarchs, who had reigned with a subordinate power since the time of Justinian and the ruin of the Gothic kingdom. Rome was summoned to acknowledge the victorious Lombard as her lawful sovereign; the annual tribute of a piece of gold was fixed as the ransom of each citizen, and the sword of destruction was unsheathed to exact the penalty of her disobedience. The Romans hesitated; they entreated; they complained; and the threatening Barbarians were checked by arms and negociations, till the popes had engaged the friendship of an ally and avenger beyond the Alps.[51]

Her deliverance by Pepin, A.D. 754.

In his distress, the first Gregory had implored the aid of the hero of the age, of Charles Martel, who governed the French monarchy with the humble title of mayor or duke; and who, by his signal victory over the Saracens, had saved his country, and perhaps Europe, from the Mahometan yoke. The ambassadors of the pope were received by Charles with decent reverence; but the greatness of his occupations, and the shortness of his life, prevented his interference in the affairs of Italy, except by a friendly and ineffectual mediation. His son Pepin, the heir of his power and virtues, assumed the office of champion of the Roman church; and the zeal of the French prince appears to have been prompted by the love of glory and religion. But the danger was on the banks of the Tyber, the succour on those of the Seine; and our sympathy is cold to the relation of distant misery. Amidst the tears of the city, Stephen the third embraced the generous resolution of visiting in person the courts of Lombardy and France, to deprecate the injustice of his enemy, or to excite the pity and indignation of his friend. After soothing the public despair by litanies and orations, he undertook this laborious journey with the ambassadors of the French monarch and

50. The option will depend on the various readings of the MSS. of Anastasius – *deceperat*, or *decerpserat* (Script. Ital. tom. iii. pars i. p. 167.).

51. The Codex Carolinus is a collection of the Epistles of the Popes to Charles Martel (whom they style *Subregulus*), Pepin, and Charlemagne, as far as the year 791, when it was formed by the last of these princes. His original and authentic MS. (Bibliothecæ Cubicularis) is now in the Imperial library of Vienna, and has been published by Lambecius and Muratori (Script. Rerum Ital. tom. iii. pars ii. p. 75, &c.).

the Greek emperor. The king of the Lombards was inexorable; but his threats could not silence the complaints, nor retard the speed, of the Roman pontiff, who traversed the Pennine Alps, reposed in the abbey of St. Maurice, and hastened to grasp the right-hand of his protector; a hand which was never lifted in vain, either in war or friendship. Stephen was entertained as the visible successor of the apostle; at the next assembly, the field of March or of May, his injuries were exposed to a devout and warlike nation, and he repassed the Alps, not as a suppliant, but as a conqueror, at the head of a French army, which was led by the king in person. The Lombards, after a weak resistance, obtained an ignominious peace, and swore to restore the possessions, and to respect the sanctity, of the Roman church. But no sooner was Astolphus delivered from the presence of the French arms, than he forgot his promise and resented his disgrace. Rome was again encompassed by his arms; and Stephen, apprehensive of fatiguing the zeal of his Transalpine allies, enforced his complaint and request, by an eloquent letter in the name and person of St. Peter himself.[52] The apostle assures his adoptive sons, the king, the clergy, and the nobles of France, that dead in the flesh, he is still alive in the spirit; that they now hear, and must obey, the voice of the founder and guardian of the Roman church: that the Virgin, the angels, the saints, and the martyrs, and all the host of heaven, unanimously urge the request, and will confess the obligation; that riches, victory, and paradise, will crown their pious enterprise, and that eternal damnation will be the penalty of their neglect, if they suffer his tomb, his temple, and his people, to fall into the hands of the perfidious Lombards. The second expedition of Pepin was not less rapid and fortunate than the first: St. Peter was satisfied, Rome was again saved, and Astolphus was taught the lessons of justice and sincerity by the scourge of a foreign master. After this double chastisement, the Lombards languished about twenty years in a state of languor and decay. But their minds were not yet humbled to their condition; and instead of affecting the pacific virtues of the feeble, they peevishly harassed the Romans with a repetition of claims, evasions, and inroads, which they undertook without reflection and terminated without glory. On either side, their expiring monarchy was pressed by

52. See this most extraordinary letter in the Codex Carolinus, epist. iii. p. 92. The enemies of the popes have charged them with fraud and blasphemy; yet they surely meant to persuade rather than deceive. This introduction of the dead, or of immortals, was familiar to the ancient orators, though it is executed on this occasion in the rude fashion of the age.

the zeal and prudence of pope Adrian the first, the genius, the fortune, and greatness of Charlemagne the son of Pepin; these heroes of the church and state were united in public and domestic friendship, and while they trampled on the prostrate, they varnished their proceedings with the fairest colours of equity and moderation.[53] The passes of the Alps, and the walls of Pavia, were the only defence of the Lombards; the former were surprised, the latter were invested, by the son of Pepin; and after a blockade of two years, Desiderius, the last of their native princes, surrendered his sceptre and his capital. Under the dominion of a foreign king, but in the possession of their national laws, the Lombards became the brethren, rather than the subjects, of the Franks; who derived their blood, and manners, and language, from the same Germanic origin.[54]

Conquest of Lombardy by Charlemagne, A.D. 774.

The mutual obligations of the popes and the Carlovingian family, form the important link of ancient and modern, of civil and ecclesiastical, history. In the conquest of Italy, the champions of the Roman church obtained a favourable occasion, a specious title, the wishes of the people, the prayers and intrigues of the clergy. But the most essential gifts of the popes to the Carlovingian race were the dignities of king of France,[55] and of patrician of Rome. I. Under the sacerdotal monarchy of St. Peter, the nations began to resume the practice of seeking, on the banks of the Tyber, their kings, their laws, and the oracles of their fate. The Franks were perplexed between the name and substance of their government. All the powers of royalty were exercised by Pepin, mayor of the palace; and nothing, except the regal title, was wanting to his ambition. His

Pepin and Charlemagne, kings of France, A.D. 751. 753. 768.

53. Except in the divorce of the daughter of Desiderius, whom Charlemagne repudiated sine aliquo crimine. Pope Stephen IV. had most furiously opposed the alliance of a noble Frank – cum perfidâ, horridâ, nec dicendâ, fœtentissima natione Longobardorum – to whom he imputes the first stain of leprosy (Cod. Carolin. epist. 45. p. 178, 179.). Another reason against the marriage was the existence of a first wife (Muratori, Annali d'Italia, tom. vi. p. 232, 233. 236, 237.). But Charlemagne indulged himself in the freedom of polygamy or concubinage.

54. See the Annali d'Italia of Muratori, tom. vi. and the three first dissertations of his Antiquitates Italiæ Medii Ævi, tom. i.

55. Besides the common historians, three French critics, Launoy (Opera, tom. v. pars ii. l. vii. epist. 9. p. 477–487.), Pagi (Critica, A.D. 751, N° 1–6. A.D. 752, N° 1–10.), and Natalis Alexander (Hist. Novi Testamenti, dissertat. ii. p. 96–107.), have treated this subject of the deposition of Childeric with learning and attention, but with a strong bias to save the independence of the crown. Yet they are hard pressed by the texts which they produce of Eginhard, Theophanes, and the old annals, Laureshamenses, Fuldenses, Loisielani.

enemies were crushed by his valour; his friends were multiplied by his liberality; his father had been the saviour of Christendom; and the claims of personal merit were repeated and ennobled in a descent of four generations. The name and image of royalty was still preserved in the last descendant of Clovis, the feeble Childeric; but his obsolete right could only be used as an instrument of sedition: the nation was desirous of restoring the simplicity of the constitution; and Pepin, a subject and a prince, was ambitious to ascertain his own rank and the fortune of his family. The mayor and the nobles were bound, by an oath of fidelity, to the royal phantom: the blood of Clovis was pure and sacred in their eyes; and their common ambassadors addressed the Roman pontiff, to dispel their scruples, or to absolve their promise. The interest of pope Zachary, the successor of the two Gregories, prompted him to decide, and to decide in their favour: he pronounced that the nation might lawfully unite, in the same person, the title and authority of king; and that the unfortunate Childeric, a victim of the public safety, should be degraded, shaved, and confined in a monastery for the remainder of his days. An answer, so agreeable to their wishes, was accepted by the Franks, as the opinion of a casuist, the sentence of a judge, or the oracle of a prophet: the Merovingian race disappeared from the earth; and Pepin was exalted on a buckler by the suffrage of a free people, accustomed to obey his laws and to march under his standard. His coronation was twice performed, with the sanction of the popes, by their most faithful servant St. Boniface, the apostle of Germany, and by the grateful hands of Stephen the third, who, in the monastery of St. Denys, placed the diadem on the head of his benefactor. The royal unction of the kings of Israel was dextrously applied:[56] the successor of St. Peter assumed the character of a divine ambassador: a German chieftain was transformed into the Lord's anointed; and this Jewish rite has been diffused and maintained by the superstition and vanity of modern Europe. The Franks were absolved from their ancient oath; but a dire anathema was thundered against them and their posterity, if they should dare to renew the same freedom of choice, or to elect a king, except in the holy and meritorious race of the

56. Not absolutely for the first time. On a less conspicuous theatre, it had been used, in the vi[th] and vii[th] centuries, by the provincial bishops of Britain and Spain. The royal unction of Constantinople was borrowed from the Latins in the last age of the empire. Constantine Manasses mentions that of Charlemagne as a foreign, Jewish, incomprehensible ceremony. See Selden's Titles of Honour, in his Works, vol. iii. part i. p. 234–249.

Carlovingian princes. Without apprehending the future danger, these princes gloried in their present security: the secretary of Charlemagne affirms, that the French sceptre was transferred by the authority of the popes;[57] and, in their boldest enterprises, they insist, with confidence, on this signal and successful act of temporal jurisdiction.

Patricians of Rome.

II. In the change of manners and language, the patricians of Rome[58] were far removed from the senate of Romulus, or the palace of Constantine, from the free nobles of the republic, or the fictitious parents of the emperor. After the recovery of Italy and Africa by the arms of Justinian, the importance and danger of those remote provinces required the presence of a supreme magistrate; he was indifferently styled the exarch or the patrician; and these governors of Ravenna, who fill their place in the chronology of princes, extended their jurisdiction over the Roman city. Since the revolt of Italy and the loss of the Exarchate, the distress of the Romans had exacted some sacrifice of their independence. Yet, even in this act, they exercised the right of disposing of themselves; and the decrees of the senate and people successively invested Charles Martel and his posterity, with the honours of patrician of Rome. The leaders of a powerful nation would have disdained a servile title and subordinate office; but the reign of the Greek emperors was suspended; and, in the vacancy of the empire, they derived a more glorious commission from the pope and the republic. The Roman ambassadors presented these patricians with the keys of the shrine of St. Peter, as a pledge and symbol of sovereignty; with a holy banner, which it was their right and duty to unfurl in the defence of the church and city.[59]

57. See Eginhard, in Vitâ Caroli Magni, c. i. p. 9, &c. c. iii. p. 24. Childeric was deposed – *jussû*, the Carlovingians were established – *auctoritate*, Pontificis Romani. Launoy, &c. pretend that these strong words are susceptible of a very soft interpretation. Be it so; yet Eginhard understood the world, the court, and the Latin language.

58. For the title and powers of patrician of Rome, see Ducange (Gloss. Latin. tom. v. p. 149–151.), Pagi (Critica, A.D. 740, N° 6–11.), Muratori (Annali d'Italia, tom. vi. p. 308–329.), and St. Marc (Abregé Chronologique de l'Italie, tom. i. p. 379–382.). Of these, the Franciscan Pagi is the most disposed to make the patrician a lieutenant of the church, rather than of the empire.

59. The papal advocates can soften the symbolic meaning of the banner and the keys; but the style of ad *regnum* dimisimus, or direximus (Codex Carolin. epist. i. tom. iii. pars ii. p. 76.), seems to allow of no palliation or escape. In the MS. of the Vienna library, they read, instead of *regnum*, *rogum*, prayer or request (see Ducange); and the royalty of Charles Martel is subverted by this important correction (Catalani, in his Critical Prefaces Annali d'Italia, tom. xvii. p. 95–99.).

In the time of Charles Martel and of Pepin, the interposition of the Lombard kingdom covered the freedom, while it threatened the safety, of Rome; and the *patriciate* represented only the title, the service, the alliance, of these distant protectors. The power and policy of Charlemagne annihilated an enemy, and imposed a master. In his first visit to the capital, he was received with all the honours which had formerly been paid to the exarch, the representative of the emperor; and these honours obtained some new decorations from the joy and gratitude of pope Adrian the first.[60] No sooner was he informed of the sudden approach of the monarch, than he dispatched the magistrates and nobles of Rome to meet him, with the banner, about thirty miles from the city. At the distance of one mile, the Flaminian way was lined with the *schools*, or national communities, of Greeks, Lombards, Saxons, &c.: the Roman youth was under arms; and the children of a more tender age, with palms and olive branches in their hands, chaunted the praises of their great deliverer. At the aspect of the holy crosses, and ensigns of the saints, he dismounted from his horse, led the procession of his nobles to the Vatican, and, as he ascended the stairs, devoutly kissed each step of the threshold of the apostles. In the portico, Adrian expected him at the head of his clergy: they embraced, as friends and equals; but in their march to the altar, the king or patrician assumed the right-hand of the pope. Nor was the Frank content with these vain and empty demonstrations of respect. In the twenty-six years that elapsed, between the conquest of Lombardy and his Imperial coronation, Rome, which had been delivered by the sword, was subject, as his own, to the sceptre, of Charlemagne. The people swore allegiance to his person and family: in his name money was coined, and justice was administered; and the election of the popes was examined and confirmed by his authority. Except an original and self-inherent claim of sovereignty, there was not any prerogative remaining, which the title of emperor could add to the patrician of Rome.[61]

60. In the authentic narrative of this reception, the Liber Pontificalis observes – obviam illi ejus sanctitas dirigens venerabiles cruces, id est signa; sicut mos est ad exarchum, aut patricium suscipiendum, eum cum ingenti honore suscipi fecit (tom. iii. pars i. p. 185.).

61. Paulus Diaconus, who wrote before the *empire* of Charlemagne, describes Rome as his subject city – vestræ civitates (ad Pompeium Festum), suis addidit sceptris (de Metensis Ecclesiæ Episcopis). Some Carlovingian medals, struck at Rome, have engaged Le Blanc to write an elaborate, though partial, dissertation on their authority at Rome, both as patricians and emperors (Amsterdam, 1692, in 4to).

Donations of Pepin and Charlemagne to the popes.

The gratitude of the Carlovingians was adequate to these obligations, and their names are consecrated, as the saviours and benefactors of the Roman church. Her ancient patrimony of farms and houses was transformed by their bounty into the temporal dominion of cities and provinces; and the donation of the exarchate was the first fruits of the conquests of Pepin.[62] Astolphus with a sigh relinquished his prey; the keys and the hostages of the principal cities were delivered to the French ambassador; and, in his master's name, he presented them before the tomb of St. Peter. The ample measure of the Exarchate[63] might comprise all the provinces of Italy which had obeyed the emperor and his vicegerent; but its strict and proper limits were included in the territories of Ravenna, Bologna, and Ferrara: its inseparable dependency was the Pentapolis, which stretched along the Adriatic from Rimini to Ancona, and advanced into the midland country as far as the ridges of the Apennine. In this transaction, the ambition and avarice of the popes has been severely condemned. Perhaps the humility of a Christian priest should have rejected an earthly kingdom, which it was not easy for him to govern without renouncing the virtues of his profession. Perhaps a faithful subject, or even a generous enemy, would have been less impatient to divide the spoils of the Barbarian; and if the emperor had entrusted Stephen to solicit in his name the restitution of the Exarchate, I will not absolve the pope from the reproach of treachery and falsehood. But in the rigid interpretation of the laws, every one may accept, without injury, whatever his benefactor can bestow without injustice. The Greek emperor had abdicated or forfeited his right to the Exarchate; and the sword of Astolphus was broken by the stronger sword of the Carlovingian. It was not in the cause of the Iconoclast that Pepin had exposed his person and army in a double expedition beyond the Alps: he possessed, and might lawfully alienate, his conquests; and to the importunities of the Greeks, he piously replied, that no human consideration should tempt him to resume the gift which he had

62. Mosheim (Institution Hist. Eccles. p. 263.) weighs this donation with fair and deliberate prudence. The original act has never been produced; but the Liber Pontificalis represents (p. 171.), and the Codex Carolinus supposes, this ample gift. Both are contemporary records; and the latter is the more authentic, since it has been preserved, not in the papal, but the Imperial, library.

63. Between the exorbitant claims, and narrow concessions, of interest and prejudice, from which even Muratori (Antiquitat. tom. i. p. 63–68.) is not exempt, I have been guided, in the limits of the Exarchate and Pentapolis, by the Dissertatio Chorographica Italiæ Medii Ævi, tom. x. p. 160–180.

conferred on the Roman pontiff for the remission of his sins and the salvation of his soul. The splendid donation was granted in supreme and absolute dominion, and the world beheld for the first time a Christian bishop invested with the prerogatives of a temporal prince; the choice of magistrates, the exercise of justice, the imposition of taxes, and the wealth of the palace of Ravenna. In the dissolution of the Lombard kingdom, the inhabitants of the dutchy of Spoleto[64] sought a refuge from the storm, shaved their heads after the Roman fashion, declared themselves the servants and subjects of St. Peter, and completed, by this voluntary surrender, the present circle of the ecclesiastical state. That mysterious circle was enlarged to an indefinite extent, by the verbal or written donation of Charlemagne,[65] who, in the first transports of his victory, despoiled himself and the Greek emperor of the cities and islands which had formerly been annexed to the Exarchate. But, in the cooler moments of absence and reflection, he viewed, with an eye of jealousy and envy, the recent greatness of his ecclesiastical ally. The execution of his own and his father's promises was respectfully eluded: the king of the Franks and Lombards asserted the inalienable rights of the empire; and, in his life and death, Ravenna,[66] as well as Rome, was numbered in the list of his metropolitan cities. The sovereignty of the Exarchate melted away in the hands of the popes: they found in the archbishops of Ravenna a dangerous and domestic rival:[67] the nobles and people disdained the yoke of a priest; and, in the disorders of the times, they could only retain the memory of an ancient claim, which, in a more prosperous age, they have revived and realized.

64. Spoletini deprecati sunt, ut eos in servitio B. Petri reciperet et more Romanorum tonsurari faceret (Anastasius, p. 185.). Yet it may be a question whether they gave their own persons or their country.

65. The policy and donations of Charlemagne are carefully examined by St. Marc (Abregé, tom. i. p. 390–408.), who has well studied the Codex Carolinus. I believe, with him, that they were only verbal. The most ancient act of donation that pretends to be extant, is that of the emperor Lewis the Pious (Sigonius, de Regno Italiæ, l. iv. Opera, tom. ii. p. 267–270.). Its authenticity, or at least its integrity, are much questioned (Pagi, A.D. 817, N° 7, &c. Muratori, Annali, tom. vi. p. 432, &c. Dissertat. Chorographica, p. 33, 34.); but I see no reasonable objection to these princes so freely disposing of what was not their own.

66. Charlemagne solicited and obtained from the proprietor, Hadrian I. the mosaics of the palace of Ravenna, for the decoration of Aix-la-Chapelle (Cod. Carolin. epist. 67. p. 223.).

67. The popes often complain of the usurpations of Leo of Ravenna (Codex Carolin. epist. 51, 52, 53. p. 200–205.). Si corpus St. Andreæ fratris germani St. Petri hîc humasset, nequaquam nos Romani pontifices sic subjugassent (Agnellus, Liber Pontificalis, in Scriptores Rerum Ital. tom. ii. pars i. p. 107.).

Forgery of the donation of Constantine.

Fraud is the resource of weakness and cunning; and the strong, though ignorant, Barbarian was often entangled in the net of sacerdotal policy. The Vatican and Lateran were an arsenal and manufacture, which, according to the occasion, have produced or concealed a various collection of false or genuine, of corrupt or suspicious, acts, as they tended to promote the interest of the Roman church. Before the end of the eighth century, some apostolical scribe, perhaps the notorious Isidore, composed the decretals, and the donation of Constantine, the two magic pillars of the spiritual and temporal monarchy of the popes. This memorable donation was introduced to the world by an epistle of Adrian the first, who exhorts Charlemagne to imitate the liberality, and revive the name, of the great Constantine.[68] According to the legend, the first of the Christian emperors was healed of the leprosy, and purified in the waters of baptism, by St. Silvester, the Roman bishop; and never was physician more gloriously recompensed. His royal proselyte withdrew from the seat and patrimony of St. Peter: declared his resolution of founding a new capital in the East; and resigned to the popes the free and perpetual sovereignty of Rome, Italy, and the provinces of the West.[69] This fiction was productive of the most beneficial effects. The Greek princes were convicted of the guilt of usurpation; and the revolt of Gregory was the claim of his lawful inheritance. The popes were delivered from their debt of gratitude; and the nominal gifts of the Carlovingians were no more than the just and irrevocable restitution of a scanty portion of the ecclesiastical state. The sovereignty of Rome no longer depended on the choice of a fickle people; and the successors of St. Peter and Constantine were invested with the purple and prerogatives of the Cæsars. So deep was the ignorance and credulity of the times, that the most absurd of fables was received, with equal reverence, in Greece and in France, and is still enrolled among the decrees of the canon law.[70]

68. Piissimo Constantino magno, per ejus largitatem S. R. Ecclesia elevata et exaltata est, et potestatem in his Hesperiæ partibus largiri dignatus est . . . . Quia ecce novus Constantinus his temporibus, &c. (Codex Carolin. epist. 49. in tom. iii. part ii. p. 195.). Pagi (Critica, A.D. 324, N° 16.) ascribes them to an impostor of the viii[th] century, who borrowed the name of St. Isidore: his humble title of *Peccator* was ignorantly, but aptly, turned into *Mercator*; his merchandise was indeed profitable, and a few sheets of paper were sold for much wealth and power.

69. Fabricius (Bibliot. Græc. tom. vi. p. 4–7.) has enumerated the several editions of this Act, in Greek and Latin. The copy which Laurentius Valla recites and refutes, appears to be taken either from the spurious Acts of St. Silvester or from Gratian's Decree, to which, according to him and others, it has been surreptitiously tacked.

70. In the year 1059, it was believed (was it believed?) by pope Leo IX. cardinal Peter

The emperors, and the Romans, were incapable of discerning a forgery, that subverted their rights and freedom; and the only opposition proceeded from a Sabine monastery, which, in the beginning of the twelfth century, disputed the truth and validity of the donation of Constantine.[71] In the revival of letters and liberty this fictitious deed was transpierced by the pen of Laurentius Valla, the pen of an eloquent critic and a Roman patriot.[72] His contemporaries of the fifteenth century were astonished at his sacrilegious boldness; yet such is the silent and irresistible progress of reason, that before the end of the next age, the fable was rejected by the contempt of historians[73] and poets,[74] and the tacit or modest censure of the advocates of the Roman church.[75] The popes themselves have indulged a smile at the credulity of the vulgar;[76] but a false and obsolete title still

---

Damianus, &c. Muratori places (Annali d'Italia, tom. ix. p. 23, 24.) the fictitious donations of Lewis the Pious, the Othos, &c. de Donatione Constantini. See a Dissertation of Natalis Alexander, seculum iv. diss. 25. p. 335–350.

71. See a large account of the controversy (A.D. 1105), which arose from a private law-suit, in the Chronicon Farfense (Script. Rerum Italicarum, tom. ii. pars ii. p. 637, &c.), a copious extract from the archives of that Benedictine abbey. They were formerly accessible to curious foreigners (Le Blanc and Mabillon), and would have enriched the first volume of the Historia Monastica Italiæ of Quirini. But they are now imprisoned (Muratori, Scriptores R.I. tom. ii. pars ii. p. 269.) by the timid policy of the court of Rome; and the future cardinal yielded to the voice of authority and the whispers of ambition (Quirini, Comment. pars ii. p. 123–136.).

72. I have read in the collection of Schardius (de Potestate Imperiali Ecclesiasticâ, p. 734–780.), this animated discourse, which was composed by the author, A.D. 1440, six years after the flight of pope Eugenius IV. It is a most vehement party pamphlet: Valla justifies and animates the revolt of the Romans, and would even approve the use of a dagger against their sacerdotal tyrant. Such a critic might expect the persecution of the clergy; yet he made his peace, and is buried in the Lateran (Bayle, Dictionaire Critique, VALLA; Vossius, de Historicis Latinis, p. 580.).

73. See Guicciardini, a servant of the popes, in that long and valuable digression, which has resumed its place in the last edition, correctly published from the author's MS. and printed in four volumes in quarto, under the name of Friburgo, 1775 (Istoria d'Italia, tom. i. p. 385–395.).

74. The Paladin Astolpho found it in the moon, among the things that were lost upon earth (Orlando Furioso, xxxiv. 80.).

> Di vari fiore ad un grand monte passa,
> Ch'ebbe già buono odore, or puzza forte
> Questo era il dono (se però dir lece)
> Che Costantino al buon Silvestro fece.

Yet this incomparable poem has been approved by a bull of Leo X.

75. See Baronius, A.D. 324, N° 117–123. A.D. 1191, N° 51, &c. The cardinal wishes to suppose that Rome was offered by Constantine, and *refused* by Silvester. The act of donation he considers, strangely enough, as a forgery of the Greeks.

76. Baronius n'en dit gueres contre: encore en a-t'il trop dit, et l'on vouloit sans moi, *(Cardinal du Perron)*, qui l'empechai, censurer cette partie de son histoire. J'en

sanctifies their reign; and, by the same fortune which has attended the decretals and the Sibylline oracles, the edifice has subsisted after the foundations have been undermined.

Restoration of images in the East by the empress Irene, A.D. 780, &c.

While the popes established in Italy their freedom and dominion, the images, the first cause of their revolt, were restored in the Eastern empire.[77] Under the reign of Constantine the fifth, the union of civil and ecclesiastical power had overthrown the tree, without extirpating the root, of superstition. The idols, for such they were now held, were secretly cherished by the order and the sex most prone to devotion; and the fond alliance of the monks and females, obtained a final victory over the reason and authority of man. Leo the fourth maintained with less rigour the religion of his father and grandfather; but his wife, the fair and ambitious Irene, had imbibed the zeal of the Athenians, the heirs of the idolatry, rather than the philosophy, of their ancestors. During the life of her husband, these sentiments were inflamed by danger and dissimulation, and she could only labour to protect and promote some favourite monks whom she drew from their caverns, and seated on the metropolitan thrones of the East. But as soon as she reigned in her own name and that of her son, Irene more seriously undertook the ruin of the Iconoclasts; and the first step of her future persecution, was a general edict for liberty of conscience. In the restoration of the monks, a thousand images were exposed to the public veneration; a thousand legends were invented of their sufferings and miracles. By the opportunities of death or removal, the episcopal seats were judiciously filled; the most eager competitors for earthly or celestial favour, anticipated and flattered the judgment of their sovereign; and the promotion of her secretary Tarasius, gave Irene the patriarch of Constantinople, and the command of the Oriental church. But the decrees of a general council could only be repealed by a similar

---

devisai un jour avec le Pape, et il ne me repondit autre chose que "che volete? i Canonici la tengono," il le disoit *en riant* (Perroniana, p. 77.).

77. The remaining history of images, from Irene to Theodora, is collected, for the Catholics, by Baronius and Pagi (A.D. 780–840), Natalis Alexander (Hist. N.T. seculum viii. Panoplia adversus Hæreticos, p. 118–178.), and Dupin (Bibliot. Eccles. tom. vi. p. 136–154.); for the protestants, by Spanheim (Hist. Imag. p. 305–639.), Basnage (Hist. de l'Eglise, tom. i. p. 556–572. tom. ii. p. 1362–1385.), and Mosheim (Institut. Hist. Eccles. secul. viii et ix.). The protestants, except Mosheim, are soured with controversy; but the Catholics, except Dupin, are inflamed by the fury and superstition of the monks; and even Le Beau (Hist. du Bas Empire), a gentleman and a scholar, is infected by the odious contagion.

assembly;[78] the Iconoclasts whom she convened, were bold in possession, and averse to debate; and the feeble voice of the bishops was re-echoed by the more formidable clamour of the soldiers and people of Constantinople. The delay and intrigues of a year, the separation of the disaffected troops, and the choice of Nice for a second orthodox synod, removed these obstacles; and the episcopal conscience was again, after the Greek fashion, in the hands of the prince. No more than eighteen days were allowed for the consummation of this important work: the Iconoclasts appeared, not as judges, but as criminals or penitents; the scene was decorated by the legates of pope Adrian and the Eastern patriarchs,[79] the decrees were framed by the president Tarasius, and ratified by the acclamations and subscriptions of three hundred and fifty bishops. They unanimously pronounced, that the worship of images is agreeable to scripture and reason, to the fathers and councils of the church: but they hesitate whether that worship be relative or direct; whether the Godhead, and the figure, of Christ be entitled to the same mode of adoration. Of this second Nicene council, the acts are still extant; a curious monument of superstition and ignorance, of falsehood and folly. I shall only notice the judgment of the bishops, on the comparative merit of image-worship and morality. A monk had concluded a truce with the dæmon of fornication, on condition of interrupting his daily prayers to a picture that hung in his cell. His scruples prompted him to consult the abbot. "Rather than abstain from adoring Christ and his Mother in their holy images, it would be better for you," replied the casuist, "to enter every brothel, and visit every prostitute, in the city."[80]

VIIth general council, II[d] of Nice, A.D. 787, Sept. 24–Oct. 23.

78. See the Acts, in Greek and Latin, of the second Council of Nice, with a number of relative pieces, in the viii[th] volume of the Councils, p. 645–1600. A faithful version, with some critical notes, would provoke, in different readers, a sigh or a smile.

79. The pope's legates were casual messengers, two priests without any special commission, and who were disavowed on their return. Some vagabond monks were persuaded by the Catholics to represent the Oriental patriarchs. This curious anecdote is revealed by Theodore Studites (epist. i. 38. in Sirmond. Opp. tom. v. p. 1319.), one of the warmest Iconoclasts of the age.

80. *Συμφερει δε σοι μη καταλιπειν εν τη πολει ταυτη πορνειον εις ὁ μη εισελθης, η ἱνα αρνηση το προσκυνειν τον κυριον ἡμων και θεον Ιησουν Χριστον μετα της ιδιας αυτου μητρος εν εικονι.* These visits could not be innocent, since the *Δαιμων πορνειας* (the dæmon of fornication) *επολεμει δε αοτον . . . εν μιᾳ ουν ὡς επεκειτο αυτῳ σφοδρα*, &c. Actio iv. p. 901. Actio v. p. 1031.

Final establishment of images by the empress Theodora, A.D. 842.

For the honour of orthodoxy, at least the orthodoxy of the Roman church, it is somewhat unfortunate, that the two princes who convened the two councils of Nice, are both stained with the blood of their sons. The second of these assemblies was approved and rigorously executed by the despotism of Irene, and she refused her adversaries the toleration which at first she had granted to her friends. During the five succeeding reigns, a period of thirty-eight years, the contest was maintained, with unabated rage and various success, between the worshippers and the breakers of the images; but I am not inclined to pursue with minute diligence the repetition of the same events. Nicephorus allowed a general liberty of speech and practice; and the only virtue of his reign is accused by the monks as the cause of his temporal and eternal perdition. Superstition and weakness formed the character of Michael the first, but the saints and images were incapable of supporting their votary on the throne. In the purple, Leo the fifth asserted the name and religion of an Armenian; and the idols, with their seditious adherents, were condemned to a second exile. Their applause would have sanctified the murder of an impious tyrant, but his assassin and successor, the second Michael, was tainted from his birth with the Phrygian heresies: he attempted to mediate between the contending parties; and the intractable spirit of the Catholics insensibly cast him into the opposite scale. His moderation was guarded by timidity; but his son Theophilus, alike ignorant of fear and pity, was the last and most cruel of the Iconoclasts. The enthusiasm of the times ran strongly against them; and the emperors, who stemmed the torrent, were exasperated and punished by the public hatred. After the death of Theophilus, the final victory of the images was atchieved by a second female, his widow Theodora, whom he left the guardian of the empire. Her measures were bold and decisive. The fiction of a tardy repentance absolved the fame and the soul of her deceased husband: the sentence of the Iconoclast patriarch was commuted from the loss of his eyes to a whipping of two hundred lashes: the bishops trembled, the monks shouted, and the festival of orthodoxy preserves the annual memory of the triumph of the images. A single question yet remained, whether they are endowed with any proper and inherent sanctity: it was agitated by the Greeks of the eleventh century;[81] and as this opinion has the strongest recommendation of absurdity, I am surprised that it was not more

81. See an account of this controversy in the Alexius of Anna Comnena (l. v. p. 129.) and Mosheim (Institut. Hist. Eccles. p. 371, 372.).

explicitly decided in the affirmative. In the West, pope Adrian the first accepted and announced the decrees of the Nicene assembly, which is now revered by the Catholics as the seventh in rank of the general councils. Rome and Italy were docile to the voice of their father; but the greatest part of the Latin Christians were far behind in the race of superstition. The churches of France, Germany, England, and Spain, steered a middle course between the adoration and the destruction of images, which they admitted into their temples, not as objects of worship, but as lively and useful memorials of faith and history. An angry book of controversy was composed and published in the name of Charlemagne;[82] under his authority a synod of three hundred bishops was assembled at Frankfort:[83] they blamed the fury of the Iconoclasts, but they pronounced a more severe censure against the superstition of the Greeks, and the decrees of their pretended council, which was long despised by the Barbarians of the West.[84] Among them the worship of images advanced with a silent and insensible progress; but a large atonement is made for their hesitation and delay, by the gross idolatry of the ages which precede the reformation, and of the countries, both in Europe and America, which are still immersed in the gloom of superstition.

Reluctance of the Franks and of Charlemagne, A.D. 794, &c.

It was after the Nicene synod, and under the reign of the pious Irene, that the popes consummated the separation of Rome and Italy, by the translation of the empire to the less orthodox Charlemagne. They were compelled to chuse between the rival nations: religion was not the sole motive of their choice; and while they dissembled the failings of their friends,

Final separation of the popes from the Eastern empire, A.D. 774–800.

82. The Libri Carolini (Spanheim, p. 443–529.), composed in the palace or winter-quarters of Charlemagne, at Worms, A.D. 790; and sent by Engebert to pope Hadrian I. who answered them by a grandis et verbosa epistola (Concil. tom. viii. p. 1553.). The Carolines propose 120 objections against the Nicene synod, and such words as these are the flowers of their rhetoric – dementiam priscæ Gentilitatis obsoletum errorem . . . argumenta insanissima et absurdissima . . . derisione dignas nænias, &c. &c.

83. The assemblies of Charlemagne were political, as well as ecclesiastical; and the three hundred members (Nat. Alexander, sec. viii. p. 53.) who sat and voted at Franckfort must include not only the bishops, but the abbots, and even the principal laymen.

84. Qui supra sanctissima patres nostri (episcopi et sacerdotes) *omnimodis* servitium et adorationem imaginum renuentes contempserunt, atque consentientes condemnaverunt (Concil. tom. ix. p. 101. Canon ii. Franckfurd). A polemic must be hard-hearted indeed, who does not pity the efforts of Baronius, Pagi, Alexander, Maimbourg, &c. to elude this unlucky sentence.

they beheld, with reluctance and suspicion, the Catholic virtues of their foes. The difference of language and manners had perpetuated the enmity of the two capitals; and they were alienated from each other by the hostile opposition of seventy years. In that schism the Romans had tasted of freedom, and the popes of sovereignty: their submission would have exposed them to the revenge of a jealous tyrant; and the revolution of Italy had betrayed the impotence, as well as the tyranny, of the Byzantine court. The Greek emperors had restored the images, but they had not restored the Calabrian estates[85] and the Illyrian diocese,[86] which the Iconoclasts had torn away from the successors of St. Peter; and pope Adrian threatens them with a sentence of excommunication unless they speedily abjure this practical heresy.[87] The Greeks were now orthodox, but their religion might be tainted by the breath of the reigning monarch: the Franks were now contumacious; but a discerning eye might discern their approaching conversion from the use, to the adoration, of images. The name of Charlemagne was stained by the polemic acrimony of his scribes; but the conqueror himself conformed, with the temper of a statesman, to the various practice of France and Italy. In his four pilgrimages or visits to the Vatican, he embraced the popes in the communion of friendship and piety; knelt before the tomb, and consequently before the image, of the apostle; and joined, without scruple, in all the prayers and processions of the Roman liturgy. Would prudence or gratitude allow the pontiffs to renounce their benefactor? Had they a right to alienate his gift of the Exarchate? Had they power to abolish his

85. Theophanes (p. 343.) specifies those of Sicily and Calabria, which yielded an annual rent of three talents and a half of gold (perhaps 7000 l. sterling). Liutprand more pompously enumerates the patrimonies of the Roman church in Greece, Judæa, Persia, Mesopotamia, Babylonia, Egypt, and Libya, which were detained by the injustice of the Greek emperor (Legat. ad Nicephorum, in Script. Rerum Italicarum, tom. ii. pars i. p. 481.).

86. The great diocese of the Eastern Illyricum, with Apulia, Calabria, and Sicily (Thomassin, Discipline de l'Eglise, tom. i. p. 145.): by the confession of the Greeks, the patriarch of Constantinople had detached from Rome the metropolitans of Thessalonica, Athens, Corinth, Nicopolis, and Patræ (Luc. Holsten. Geograph. Sacra, p. 22.); and his spiritual conquests extended to Naples and Amalphi (Giannone, Istoria Civile di Napoli, tom. i. p. 517–524. Pagi, A.D. 730, N° 11.).

87. In hoc ostenditur, quia ex uno capitulo ab errore reversis, in aliis duobus, in *eodem* (was it the same?) permaneant errore . . . de diocesi S.R.E. seu de patrimoniis iterum increpantes commonemus, ut si ea restituere noluerit hereticum eum pro hujusmodi errore persevantiâ decernemus (Epist. Hadrian. Papæ ad Carolum Magnum, in Concil. tom. viii. p. 1598.); to which he adds a reason, most directly opposite to his conduct, that he preferred the salvation of souls and rule of faith to the goods of this transitory world.

government of Rome? The title of patrician was below the merit and greatness of Charlemagne; and it was only by reviving the Western empire that they could pay their obligations or secure their establishment. By this decisive measure they would finally eradicate the claims of the Greeks: from the debasement of a provincial town, the majesty of Rome would be restored: the Latin Christians would be united, under a supreme head, in their ancient metropolis; and the conquerors of the West would receive their crown from the successors of St. Peter. The Roman church would acquire a zealous and respectable advocate; and, under the shadow of the Carlovingian power, the bishop might exercise, with honour and safety, the government of the city.[88]

Coronation of Charlemagne as emperor of Rome and of the West, A.D. 800, Dec. 25.

Before the ruin of paganism in Rome, the competition for a wealthy bishopric had often been productive of tumult and bloodshed. The people was less numerous, but the times were more savage, the prize more important, and the chair of St. Peter was fiercely disputed by the leading ecclesiastics who aspired to the rank of sovereign. The reign of Adrian the first[89] surpasses the measure of past or succeeding ages;[90] the walls of Rome, the sacred patrimony, the ruin of the Lombards, and the friendship of Charlemagne, were the trophies of his fame: he secretly edified the throne of his successors, and displayed in a narrow space the virtues of a great prince. His memory was revered; but in the next election, a priest of the Lateran, Leo the third, was preferred to the nephew and the favourite of Adrian, whom he had promoted to the first dignities of the church. Their acquiescence or repentance disguised, above four years, the blackest

88. Fontanini considers the emperors as no more than the advocates of the church (advocatus et defensor S.R.E. See Ducange, Gloss. Lat. tom. i. p. 97.). His antagonist Muratori reduces the popes to be no more than the exarchs of the emperor. In the more equitable view of Mosheim (Institut. Hist. Eccles. p. 264, 265.), they held Rome under the empire as the most honourable species of fief or benefice – premuntur nocte caliginosâ!

89. His merits and hopes are summed up in an epitaph of thirty-eight verses, of which Charlemagne declares himself the author (Concil. tom. viii. p. 520.).

Post patrem lacrymans Carolus hæc carmina scripsi.
Tu mihi dulcis amor, te modo plango pater . . .
Nomina jungo simul titulis, clarissime, nostra
Adrianus, Carolus, rex ego, tuque pater.

The poetry might be supplied by Alcuin; but the tears, the most glorious tribute, can only belong to Charlemagne.

90. Every new pope is admonished – "Sancte Pater, non videbis annos Petri," twenty-five years. On the whole series the average is about eight years – a short hope for an ambitious cardinal.

intention of revenge, till the day of a procession, when a furious band of conspirators dispersed the unarmed multitude, and assaulted with blows and wounds the sacred person of the pope. But their enterprise on his life or liberty was disappointed, perhaps by their own confusion and remorse. Leo was left for dead on the ground; on his revival from the swoon, the effect of his loss of blood, he recovered his speech and sight; and this natural event was improved to the miraculous restoration of his eyes and tongue, of which he had been deprived, twice deprived, by the knife of the assassins.[91] From his prison, he escaped to the Vatican; the duke of Spoleto hastened to his rescue, Charlemagne sympathised in his injury, and in his camp of Paderborn in Westphalia, accepted or solicited a visit from the Roman pontiff. Leo repassed the Alps with a commission of counts and bishops, the guards of his safety and the judges of his innocence; and it was not without reluctance, that the conqueror of the Saxons delayed till the ensuing year the personal discharge of this pious office. In his fourth and last pilgrimage, he was received at Rome with the due honours of king and patrician: Leo was permitted to purge himself by oath of the crimes imputed to his charge: his enemies were silenced, and the sacrilegious attempt against his life was punished by the mild and insufficient penalty of exile. On the festival of Christmas, the last year of the eighth century, Charlemagne appeared in the church of St. Peter; and, to gratify the vanity of Rome, he had exchanged the simple dress of his country for the habit of a patrician.[92] After the celebration of the holy mysteries, Leo suddenly placed a precious crown on his head,[93] and the dome resounded with the acclamations of the

91. The assurance of Anastasius (tom. iii. pars i. p. 197, 198.) is supported by the credulity of some French annalists; but Eginhard, and other writers of the same age, are more natural and sincere. "Unus ei occulus paullulum est læsus," says John the deacon of Naples (Vit. Episcop. Napol. in Scriptores Muratori, tom. i. pars ii. p. 312.). Theodulphus, a contemporary bishop of Orleans, observes with prudence (l. iii. carm. 3.),

> Reddita sunt? mirum est: mirum est auferre nequîsse.
> Est tamen in dubio, hinc mirer aut inde magis.

92. Twice, at the request of Hadrian and Leo, he appeared at Rome – longâ tunicâ et chlamyde amictus, et calceamentis quoque Romano more formatis. Eginhard (c. xxiii. p. 109–113.) describes, like Suetonius, the simplicity of his dress, so popular in the nation, that when Charles the Bald returned to France in a foreign habit, the patriotic dogs barked at the apostate (Gaillard, Vie de Charlemagne, tom. iv. p. 109.).

93. See Anastasius (p. 199.) and Eginhard (c. xxviii. p. 124–128.). The unction is mentioned by Theophanes (p. 399.), the oath by Sigonius (from the Ordo Romanus), and the pope's adoration, more

people, "Long life and victory to Charles, the most pious Augustus, crowned by God the great and pacific emperor of the Romans!" The head and body of Charlemagne were consecrated by the royal unction: after the example of the Cæsars, he was saluted or adored by the pontiff; his coronation oath represents a promise to maintain the faith and privileges of the church; and the first fruits were paid in his rich offerings to the shrine of the apostle. In his familiar conversation, the emperor protested his ignorance of the intentions of Leo, which he would have disappointed by his absence on that memorable day. But the preparations of the ceremony must have disclosed the secret; and the journey of Charlemagne reveals his knowledge and expectation: he had acknowledged that the Imperial title was the object of his ambition, and a Roman synod had pronounced, that it was the only adequate reward of his merit and services.[94]

Reign and character of Charlemagne, A.D. 768–814.

The appellation of *great* has been often bestowed and sometimes deserved, but CHARLEMAGNE is the only prince in whose favour the title has been indissolubly blended with the name. That name, with the addition of *saint*, is inserted in the Roman calendar; and the saint, by a rare felicity, is crowned with the praises of the historians and philosophers of an enlightened age.[95] His *real* merit is doubtless enhanced by the barbarism of the nation and the times from which he emerged: but the *apparent* magnitude of an object is likewise enlarged by an unequal comparison; and the ruins of Palmyra derive a casual splendour from the nakedness of the surrounding desert. Without injustice to his fame, I may discern some blemishes in the sanctity and greatness of the restorer of the Western empire. Of his moral

antiquorum principum, by the Annales Bertiniani (Script. Murator. tom. ii. pars ii. p. 505.).

94. This great event of the translation or restoration of the empire, is related and discussed by Natalis Alexander, secul. ix. (dissert. i. p. 390–397.), Pagi (tom. iii. p. 418.), Muratori (Annali d'Italia, tom. vi. p. 339–352.), Sigonius (de Regno Italiæ, l. iv. Opp. tom. ii. p. 247–251.), Spanheim (de fictâ Translatione Imperii), Giannone (tom. i. p. 395–405.), St. Marc (Abregé Chronologique, tom. i. p. 438–450.), Gaillard (Hist. de Charlemagne, tom. ii. p. 386–446.). Almost all these moderns have some religious or national bias.

95. By Mably (Observations sur l'Histoire de France), Voltaire (Histoire Generale), Robertson (History of Charles V.), and Montesquieu (Esprit des Loix, l. xxxi. c. 18.). In the year 1782, M. Gaillard published his Histoire de Charlemagne (in 4 vols. in 12mo), which I have freely and profitably used. The author is a man of sense and humanity; and his work is laboured with industry and elegance. But I have likewise examined the original monuments of the reigns of Pepin and Charlemagne, in the vth volume of the Historians of France.

virtues, chastity is not the most conspicuous:[96] but the public happiness could not be materially injured by his nine wives or concubines, the various indulgence of meaner or more transient amours, the multitude of his bastards whom he bestowed on the church, and the long celibacy and licentious manners of his daughters,[97] whom the father was suspected of loving with too fond a passion. I shall be scarcely permitted to accuse the ambition of a conqueror; but in a day of equal retribution, the sons of his brother Carloman, the Merovingian princes of Aquitain, and the four thousand five hundred Saxons who were beheaded on the same spot, would have something to allege against the justice and humanity of Charlemagne. His treatment of the vanquished Saxons[98] was an abuse of the right of conquest; his laws were not less sanguinary than his arms, and in the discussion of his motives, whatever is subtracted from bigotry must be imputed to temper. The sedentary reader is amazed by his incessant activity of mind and body; and his subjects and enemies were not less astonished at his sudden presence, at the moment when they believed him at the most distant extremity of the empire; neither peace nor war, nor summer nor winter, were a season of repose; and our fancy cannot easily reconcile the annals of his reign with the geography of his expeditions. But this activity was a national rather than a personal virtue; the vagrant life of a Frank was spent in the chace, in pilgrimage, in military adventures; and the journies of Charlemagne were distinguished only by a more numerous train and a more important purpose. His military renown must be tried by the scrutiny of his troops, his enemies, and his actions. Alexander conquered with the arms of Philip, but the *two* heroes who preceded Charlemagne, bequeathed him their name, their examples, and the companions of their victories. At the head of his

96. The vision of Weltin, composed by a monk, eleven years after the death of Charlemagne, shews him in purgatory, with a vulture, who is perpetually gnawing the guilty member, while the rest of his body, the emblem of his virtues, is sound and perfect (see Gaillard, tom. ii. p. 317–360.).

97. The marriage of Eginhard with Imma, daughter of Charlemagne, is, in my opinion, sufficiently refuted by the *probrum* and *suspicio* that sullied these fair damsels, without excepting his own wife (c. xix. p. 98–100. cum Notis Schmincke). The husband must have been too strong for the historian.

98. Besides the massacres and transmigrations, the pain of death was pronounced against the following crimes: 1. The refusal of baptism. 2. The false pretence of baptism. 3. A relapse to idolatry. 4. The murder of a priest or bishop. 5. Human sacrifices. 6. Eating meat in Lent. But every crime might be expiated by baptism or penance (Gaillard, tom. ii. p. 241–247.): and the Christian Saxons became the friends and equals of the Franks (Struv. Corpus Hist. Germanicæ, p. 133.).

veteran and superior armies, he oppressed the savage or degenerate nations, who were incapable of confederating for their common safety: nor did he ever encounter an equal antagonist in numbers, in discipline, or in arms. The science of war has been lost and revived with the arts of peace; but his campaigns are not illustrated by any siege or battle, of singular difficulty and success; and he might behold, with envy, the Saracen trophies of his grandfather. After his Spanish expedition, his rear-guard was defeated in the Pyrenæan mountains; and the soldiers, whose situation was irretrievable and whose valour was useless, might accuse, with their last breath, the want of skill or caution of their general.[99] I touch with reverence the laws of Charlemagne, so highly applauded by a respectable judge. They compose not a system, but a series, of occasional and minute edicts, for the correction of abuses, the reformation of manners, the œconomy of his farms, the care of his poultry, and even the sale of his eggs. He wished to improve the laws and the character of the Franks; and his attempts, however feeble and imperfect, are deserving of praise: the inveterate evils of the times were suspended or mollified by his government;[100] but in his institutions I can seldom discover the general views and the immortal spirit of a legislator, who survives himself for the benefit of posterity. The union and stability of his empire depended on the life of a single man: he imitated the dangerous practice of dividing his kingdoms among his sons; and, after his numerous diets, the whole constitution was left to fluctuate between the disorders of anarchy and despotism. His esteem for the piety and knowledge of the clergy tempted him to entrust that aspiring order with temporal dominion and civil jurisdiction; and his son Lewis, when he was stripped and degraded by the bishops, might accuse, in some measure, the imprudence of his father. His laws enforced the imposition of tythes, because the dæmons had proclaimed in the air that the default of payment had been the cause of the last scarcity.[101] The literary merits of Charlemagne are attested by the

99. In this action the famous Rutland, Rolando, Orlando, was slain – cum compluribus aliis. See the truth in Eginhard (c. 9. p. 51–56.), and the fable in an ingenious Supplement of M. Gaillard (tom. iii. p. 474.). The Spaniards are too proud of a victory, which history ascribes to the Gascons, and romance to the Saracens.

100. Yet Schmidt, from the best authorities, represents the interior disorders and oppression of his reign (Hist. des Allemands, tom. ii. p. 45–49.).

101. Omnis homo ex suâ proprietate legitimam decimam ad ecclesiam conferat. Experimento enim didicimus, in anno, quo illa valida fames irrepsit, ebullire vacuas annonas a dæmonibus devoratas, et voces exprobationis auditas. Such is the decree and assertion of the great Council of Franckfort (canon xxv. tom. ix. p. 105.).

foundation of schools, the introduction of arts, the works which were published in his name, and his familiar connection with the subjects and strangers whom he invited to his court to educate both the prince and people. His own studies were tardy, laborious, and imperfect; if he spoke Latin, and understood Greek, he derived the rudiments of knowledge from conversation, rather than from books; and, in his mature age, the emperor strove to acquire the practice of writing, which every peasant now learns in his infancy.[102] The grammar and logic, the music and astronomy, of the times, were only cultivated as the handmaids of superstition; but the curiosity of the human mind must ultimately tend to its improvement, and the encouragement of learning reflects the purest and most pleasing lustre on the character of Charlemagne.[103] The dignity of his person,[104] the length of his reign, the prosperity of his arms, the vigour of his government, and the reverence of distant nations, distinguish him from the royal crowd; and Europe dates a new æra from his restoration of the Western empire.

Extent of his empire in France,

That empire was not unworthy of its title;[105] and some of the fairest kingdoms of Europe were the patrimony or conquest of a prince, who reigned at the same time in France, Spain, Italy, Germany, and Hungary.[106] I. The Roman province of Gaul had

Both Selden (Hist. of Tythes; Works, vol. iii. part ii. p. 1146.) and Montesquieu (Esprit des Loix, l. xxxi. c. 12.) represent Charlemagne as the first *legal* author of tythes. Such obligations have country gentlemen to his memory!

102. Eginhard (c. 25. p. 119.) clearly affirms, tentabat et scribere . . . sed parum prospere successit labor præposterus et sero inchoatus. The moderns have perverted and corrected this obvious meaning, and the title of M. Gaillard's Dissertation (tom. iii. p. 247–260.) betrays his partiality.

103. See Gaillard, tom. iii. p. 138–176. and Schmidt, tom. ii. p. 121–129.

104. M. Gaillard (tom. iii. p. 372.) fixes the true stature of Charlemagne (see a Dissertation of Marquard Freher ad calcem Eginhart. p. 220, &c.) at five feet nine inches of French, about six feet one inch and a fourth English, measure. The romance writers have increased it to eight feet, and the giant was endowed with matchless strength and appetite: at a single stroke of his good sword *Joyeuse*, he cut asunder an horseman and his horse; at a single repast he devoured a goose, two fowls, a quarter of mutton, &c.

105. See the concise, but correct and original, work of d'Anville (Etats formés en Europe après la Chute de l'Empire Romain en Occident, Paris, 1771, in 4to), whose map includes the empire of Charlemagne; the different parts are illustrated, by Valesius (Notitia Galliarum) for France, Beretti (Dissertatio Chorographica) for Italy, De Marca (Marca Hispanica) for Spain. For the middle geography of Germany, I confess myself poor and destitute.

106. After a brief relation of his wars and conquests (Vit. Carol. c. 5–14.), Eginhard recapitulates, in a few words (c. 15.), the countries subject to his empire. Struvius (Corpus Hist. German. p. 118–149.) has inserted in his Notes the texts of the old Chronicles.

been transformed into the name and monarchy of FRANCE; but, in the decay of the Merovingian line, its limits were contracted by the independence of the *Britons* and the revolt of *Aquitain*. Charlemagne pursued, and confined, the Britons on the shores of the ocean; and that ferocious tribe, whose origin and language are so different from the French, was chastised by the imposition of tribute, hostages, and peace. After a long and evasive contest, the rebellion of the dukes of Aquitain was punished by the forfeiture of their province, their liberty, and their lives. Harsh and rigorous would have been such treatment of ambitious governors, who had too faithfully copied the mayors of the palace. But a recent discovery[107] has proved that these unhappy princes were the last and lawful heirs of the blood and sceptre of Clovis, a younger branch, from the brother of Dagobert, of the Merovingian house. Their ancient kingdom was reduced to the dutchy of Gascogne, to the counties of Fesenzac and Armagnac, at the foot of the Pyrenees: their race was propagated till the beginning of the sixteenth century; and, after surviving their Carlovingian tyrants, they were reserved to feel the injustice, or the favours, of a third dynasty. By the re-union of Aquitain, France was enlarged to its present boundaries, with the additions of the Netherlands

Spain, and Spain, as far as the Rhine. II. The Saracens had been expelled from France by the grandfather and father of Charlemagne; but they still possessed the greatest part of SPAIN, from the rock of Gibraltar to the Pyrenees. Amidst their civil divisions, an Arabian emir of Saragossa implored his protection in the diet of Paderborn. Charlemagne undertook the expedition, restored the emir, and, without distinction of faith, impartially crushed the resistance of the Christians, and rewarded the obedience and service of the Mahometans. In his absence he instituted the *Spanish march*,[108] which extended from the Pyrenees to the river Ebro: Barcelona was the residence of the French governor: he possessed the

107. Of a charter granted to the monastery of Alaon (A.D. 845) by Charles the Bald, which deduces this royal pedigree. I doubt whether some subsequent links of the ix[th] and x[th] centuries are equally firm; yet the whole is approved and defended by M. Gaillard (tom. ii. p. 60–81. 203–206.), who affirms, that the family of Montesquiou (not of the president de Montesquieu) is descended, in the female line, from Clotaire and Clovis – an innocent pretension!

108. The governors or counts of the Spanish march revolted from Charles the Simple about the year 900; and a poor pittance, the Rousillon, has been recovered in 1642 by the kings of France (Longuerue, Description de la France, tom. i. p. 220–222.). Yet the Rousillon contains 188,900 subjects, and annually pays 2,600,000 livres (Necker, Administration des Finances, tom. i. p. 278, 279.); more people, perhaps, and doubtless more money, than the march of Charlemagne.

counties of *Rousillon* and *Catalonia*; and the infant kingdoms of *Navarre* and *Arragon* were subject to his jurisdiction. III. As king of the Lombards, and patrician of Rome, he reigned over the greatest part of ITALY,[109] *Italy,* a tract of a thousand miles from the Alps to the borders of Calabria. The dutchy of *Beneventum*, a Lombard fief, had spread, at the expence of the Greeks, over the modern kingdom of Naples. But Arrechis, the reigning duke, refused to be included in the slavery of his country; assumed the independent title of prince; and opposed his sword to the Carlovingian monarchy. His defence was firm, his submission was not inglorious, and the emperor was content with an easy tribute, the demolition of his fortresses, and the acknowledgment, on his coins, of a supreme lord. The artful flattery of his son Grimoald added the appellation of father, but he asserted his dignity with prudence, and Beneventum insensibly escaped from the French yoke.[110] IV. Charlemagne was the first who united GERMANY under the same sceptre. The name of *Oriental France* *Germany,* is preserved in the circle of *Franconia*; and the people of *Hesse* and *Thuringia* were recently incorporated with the victors, by the conformity of religion and government. The *Alemanni*, so formidable to the Romans, were the faithful vassals and confederates of the Franks; and their country was inscribed within the modern limits of *Alsace*, *Swabia*, and *Switzerland*. The *Bavarians*, with a similar indulgence of their laws and manners, were less patient of a master: the repeated treasons of Tasillo justified the abolition of their hereditary dukes; and their power was shared among the counts, who judged and guarded that important frontier. But the north of Germany, from the Rhine and beyond the Elbe, was still hostile and Pagan; nor was it till after a war of thirty-three years that the Saxons bowed under the yoke of Christ and of Charlemagne. The idols and their votaries were extirpated: the foundation of eight bishoprics, of Munster, Osnaburgh, Paderborn, and Minden, of Bremen, Verden, Hildesheim, and Halberstadt, define, on either side of the Weser, the bounds of ancient Saxony; these episcopal seats were the first schools and cities of that savage land; and the religion and humanity of the children atoned, in some degree, for the massacre of the parents. Beyond the Elbe, the *Slavi*, or Sclavonians, of similar manners and various denominations, overspread the modern dominions of Prussia, Poland, and Bohemia, and some transient marks of obedience have tempted the French historian to extend the empire to the Baltic and the Vistula. The conquest or conversion of

109. Schmidt, Hist. des Allemands, tom. ii. p. 200, &c.

110. See Giannone, tom. i. p. 374, 375. and the Annals of Muratori.

those countries is of a more recent age; but the first union of *Bohemia* with the Germanic body may be justly ascribed to the arms of Charlemagne. V.

Hungary. He retaliated on the Avars, or Huns of Pannonia, the same calamities which they had inflicted on the nations. Their rings, the wooden fortifications which encircled their districts and villages, were broken down by the triple effort of a French army, that was poured into their country by land and water, through the Carpathian mountains and along the plain of the Danube. After a bloody conflict of eight years, the loss of some French generals was avenged by the slaughter of the most noble Huns: the relics of the nation submitted: the royal residence of the chagan was left desolate and unknown; and the treasures, the rapine of two hundred and fifty years, enriched the victorious troops, or decorated the churches of Italy and Gaul.[111] After the reduction of Pannonia, the empire of Charlemagne was bounded only by the conflux of the Danube with the Teyss and the Save: the provinces of Istria, Liburnia, and Dalmatia, were an easy, though unprofitable, accession; and it was an effect of his moderation, that he left the maritime cities under the real or nominal sovereignty of the Greeks. But these distant possessions added more to the reputation than to the power of the Latin emperor; nor did he risk any ecclesiastical foundations to reclaim the Barbarians from their vagrant life and idolatrous worship. Some canals of communication between the rivers, the Saône and the Meuse, the Rhine and the Danube, were faintly attempted.[112] Their execution would have vivified the empire; and more cost and labour were often wasted in the structure of a cathedral.

His neighbours and enemies. If we retrace the outlines of this geographical picture, it will be seen that the empire of the Franks extended, between east and west, from the Ebro to the Elbe or Vistula; between the north and south, from the dutchy of Beneventum to the river Eyder, the perpetual boundary of Germany and Denmark. The personal and political importance of Charlemagne was magnified by the distress and

111. Quot prælia in eo gesta! quantum sanguinis effusum sit! Testatur vacua omni habitatione Pannonia, et locus in quo regia Cagani fuit ita desertus, ut ne vestigium quidem humanæ habitationis appareat. Tota in hoc bello Hunnorum nobilitas periit, tota gloria decidit, omnis pecunia et congesti ex longo tempore thesauri direpti sunt.

112. The junction of the Rhine and Danube was undertaken only for the service of the Pannonian war (Gaillard, Vie de Charlemagne, tom. ii. p. 312–315.). The canal, which would have been only two leagues in length, and of which some traces are still extant in Swabia, was interrupted by excessive rains, military avocations, and superstitious fears (Schæpflin, Hist. de l'Academie des Inscriptions, tom. xviii. p. 256. Molimina fluviorum, &c. jungendorum, p. 59–62.).

division of the rest of Europe. The islands of Great Britain and Ireland were disputed by a crowd of princes of Saxon or Scottish origin; and, after the loss of Spain, the Christian and Gothic kingdom of Alphonso the chaste, was confined to the narrow range of the Asturian mountains. These petty sovereigns revered the power or virtue of the Carlovingian monarch, implored the honour and support of his alliance, and styled him their common parent, the sole and supreme emperor of the West.[113] He maintained a more equal intercourse with the caliph Harun al Rashid,[114] whose dominion stretched from Africa to India, and accepted from his ambassadors a tent, a water-clock, an elephant, and the keys of the holy sepulchre. It is not easy to conceive the private friendship of a Frank and an Arab, who were strangers to each other's person, and language, and religion: but their public correspondence was founded on vanity, and their remote situation left no room for a competition of interest. Two-thirds of the Western empire of Rome were subject to Charlemagne, and the deficiency was amply supplied by his command of the inaccessible or invincible nations of Germany. But in the choice of his enemies, we may be reasonably surprised that he so often preferred the poverty of the north to the riches of the south. The three-and-thirty campaigns laboriously consumed in the woods and morasses of Germany, would have sufficed to assert the amplitude of his title by the expulsion of the Greeks from Italy and the Saracens from Spain. The weakness of the Greeks would have ensured an easy victory: and the holy crusade against the Saracens would have been prompted by glory and revenge, and loudly justified by religion and policy. Perhaps, in his expeditions beyond the Rhine and the Elbe, he aspired to save his monarchy from the fate of the Roman empire, to disarm the enemies of civilized society, and to eradicate the seed of future emigrations. But it has been wisely observed, that in a light of precaution, all conquest must be ineffectual, unless it could be universal; since the encreasing circle must be involved in a larger sphere of hostility.[115] The subjugation of Germany withdrew the veil which had so long concealed the continent or islands of

113. See Eginhard, c. 16. and Gaillard, tom. ii. p. 361–385. who mentions, with a loose reference, the intercourse of Charlemagne and Egbert, the emperor's gift of his own sword, and the modest answer of his Saxon disciple. The anecdote, if genuine, would have adorned our English histories.

114. The correspondence is mentioned only in the French annals, and the Orientals are ignorant of the caliph's friendship for the *Christian dog* – a polite appellation, which Harun bestows on the emperor of the Greeks.

115. Gaillard, tom. ii. p. 361–365. 471–476. 492. I have borrowed his judicious

Scandinavia from the knowledge of Europe, and awakened the torpid courage of their barbarous natives. The fiercest of the Saxon idolaters escaped from the Christian tyrant to their brethren of the north; the Ocean and Mediterranean were covered with their pyratical fleets; and Charlemagne beheld with a sigh the destructive progress of the Normans, who, in less than seventy years, precipitated the fall of his race and monarchy.

His successors. A.D. 814–887 in Italy; 911 in Germany; 987 in France.

Had the pope and the Romans revived the primitive constitution, the titles of emperor and Augustus were conferred on Charlemagne for the term of his life; and his successors, on each vacancy, must have ascended the throne by a formal or tacit election. But the association of his son Lewis the Pious asserts the independent right of monarchy and conquest, and the emperor seems on this occasion to have foreseen and prevented the latent claims *A.D. 813.* of the clergy. The royal youth was commanded to take the crown from the altar, and with his own hands to place it on his head, as a gift which he held from God, his father, and the nation.[116] The same ceremony was repeated, though with less energy, in the subsequent associations of Lothaire and Lewis the second; the Carlovingian sceptre was transmitted from father to son in a lineal descent of four generations; and the ambition of the popes was reduced to the empty honour of crowning and anointing these hereditary princes who were already invested with

Lewis the Pious, A.D. 814–840.

their power and dominions. The pious Lewis survived his brothers, and embraced the whole empire of Charlemagne; but the nations and the nobles, his bishops and his children, quickly discerned that this mighty mass was no longer inspired by the same soul; and the foundations were undermined to the centre, while the external surface was yet fair and entire. After a war, or battle, which consumed one hundred thousand Franks, the empire was divided by treaty between his three sons, who had violated every filial and fraternal duty. The

Lothaire I. A.D. 840–856.

kingdoms of Germany and France were for ever separated; the provinces of Gaul, between the Rhone and the Alps, the Meuse and the Rhine, were assigned, with Italy, to the Imperial dignity

---

remarks on Charlemagne's plan of conquest, and the judicious distinction of his enemies of the first and the second *enceinte* (tom. ii. p. 184. 509, &c.).

116. Thegan, the biographer of Lewis, relates this coronation; and Baronius has honestly transcribed it (A.D. 813, N° 13, &c. See Gaillard, tom. ii. p. 506, 507, 508.), howsoever adverse to the claims of the popes. For the series of the Carlovingians, see the historians of France, Italy, and Germany; Pfeffel, Schmidt, Velly, Muratori, and even Voltaire, whose pictures are sometimes just, and always pleasing.

of Lothaire. In the partition of his share, Lorraine and Arles, two recent and transitory kingdoms, were bestowed on the younger children; and Lewis the second, his eldest son, was content with the realm of Italy, the proper and sufficient patrimony of a Roman emperor. On his death without any male issue, the vacant throne was disputed by his uncles and cousins, and the popes most dextrously seized the occasion of judging the claims and merits of the candidates, and of bestowing on the most obsequious or most liberal, the Imperial office of advocate of the Roman church. The dregs of the Carlovingian race no longer exhibited any symptoms of virtue or power, and the ridiculous epithets of the *bald*, the *stammerer*, the *fat*, and the *simple*, distinguished the tame and uniform features of a crowd of kings alike deserving of oblivion. By the failure of the collateral branches, the whole inheritance devolved to Charles the Fat, the last emperor of his family: his insanity authorised the desertion of Germany, Italy, and France: he was deposed in a diet, and solicited his daily bread from the rebels, by whose contempt his life and liberty had been spared. According to the measure of their force, the governors, the bishops, and the lords, usurped the fragments of the falling empire; and some preference was shewn to the female or illegitimate blood of Charlemagne. Of the greater part, the title and possession were alike doubtful, and the merit was adequate to the contracted scale of their dominions. Those who could appear with an army at the gates of Rome were crowned emperors in the Vatican; but their modesty was more frequently satisfied with the appellation of kings of Italy: and the whole term of seventy-four years may be deemed a vacancy, from the abdication of Charles the Fat to the establishment of Otho the first.

Lewis II. A.D. 856–875.

Division of the empire, A.D. 888.

Otho[117] was of the noble race of the dukes of Saxony; and if he truly descended from Witikind, the adversary and proselyte of Charlemagne, the posterity of a vanquished people was exalted to reign over their conquerors. His father Henry the Fowler was elected, by the suffrage of the nation, to save and institute the kingdom of Germany. Its

Otho king of Germany restores and appropriates the Western empire, A.D. 962.

117. He was the son of Otho, the son of Ludolph, in whose favour the dutchy of Saxony had been instituted, A.D. 858. Ruotgerus, the biographer of a St. Bruno (Bibliot. Bunavianæ Catalog. tom. iii. vol. ii. p. 679.), gives a splendid character of his family. Atavorum atavi usque ad hominum memoriam omnes nobilissimi; nullus in eorum stirpe ignotus nullus degener facile reperitur (apud Struvium, Corp. Hist. German. p. 216.). Yet Gundling (in Henrico Aucupe) is not satisfied of his descent from Witikind.

limits[118] were enlarged on every side by his son, the first and greatest of the Othos. A portion of Gaul to the west of the Rhine, along the banks of the Meuse and the Moselle, was assigned to the Germans, by whose blood and language it has been tinged since the time of Cæsar and Tacitus. Between the Rhine, the Rhone, and the Alps, the successors of Otho acquired a vain supremacy over the broken kingdoms of Burgundy and Arles. In the north, Christianity was propagated by the sword of Otho, the conqueror and apostle of the Slavic nations of the Elbe and Oder: the marches of Brandenburg and Sleswick were fortified with German colonies; and the king of Denmark, the dukes of Poland and Bohemia, confessed themselves his tributary vassals. At the head of a victorious army, he passed the Alps, subdued the kingdom of Italy, delivered the pope, and for ever fixed the Imperial crown in the name and nation of Germany. From that memorable æra, two maxims of public jurisprudence were introduced by force and ratified by time. I. *That* the prince, who was elected in the German diet, acquired from that instant the subject kingdoms of Italy and Rome. II. But that he might not legally assume the titles of emperor and Augustus, till he had received the crown from the hands of the Roman pontiff.[119]

Transactions of the Western and Eastern empires.

The Imperial dignity of Charlemagne was announced to the East by the alteration of his style; and instead of saluting his fathers, the Greek emperors, he presumed to adopt the more equal and familiar appellation of brother.[120] Perhaps in his connection with Irene he aspired to the name of husband: his embassy to Constantinople spoke the language of peace and friendship, and might conceal a treaty of marriage with that ambitious princess, who had renounced the most sacred duties of a mother. The nature, the duration, the probable consequences of such an union between two distant and dissonant empires, it is impossible to conjecture; but the unanimous

118. See the treatise of Conringius (de Finibus Imperii Germanici, Francofurt. 1680, in 4[to]): he rejects the extravagant and improper scale of the Roman and Carlovingian empires, and discusses with moderation the rights of Germany, her vassals, and her neighbours.

119. The power of custom forces me to number Conrad I. and Henry I. the Fowler, in the list of emperors, a title which was never assumed by those kings of Germany. The Italians, Muratori for instance, are more scrupulous and correct, and only reckon the princes who have been crowned at Rome.

120. Invidiam tamen suscepti nominis (C.P. imperatoribus super hoc indignantibus magnâ tulit patientiâ, vicitque eorum contumaciam . . . mittendo ad eos crebras legationes, et in epistolis fratres eos appellando. Eginhard, c. 28. p. 128.). Perhaps it was on their account that, like Augustus, he affected some reluctance to receive the empire.

silence of the Latins may teach us to suspect, that the report was invented by the enemies of Irene, to charge her with the guilt of betraying the church and state to the strangers of the West.[121] The French ambassadors were the spectators, and had nearly been the victims, of the conspiracy of Nicephorus, and the national hatred. Constantinople was exasperated by the treason and sacrilege of ancient Rome: a proverb, "That the Franks were good friends and bad neighbours," was in every one's mouth; but it was dangerous to provoke a neighbour who might be tempted to reiterate, in the church of St. Sophia, the ceremony of his Imperial coronation. After a tedious journey of circuit and delay, the ambassadors of Nicephorus found him in his camp, on the banks of the river Sala; and Charlemagne affected to confound their vanity by displaying, in a Franconian village, the pomp, or at least the pride, of the Byzantine palace.[122] The Greeks were successively led through four halls of audience: in the first they were ready to fall prostrate before a splendid personage in a chair of state, till he informed them that he was only a servant, the constable, or master of the horse of the emperor. The same mistake, and the same answer, were repeated in the apartments of the count palatine, the steward, and the chamberlain; and their impatience was gradually heightened, till the doors of the presence-chamber were thrown open, and they beheld the genuine monarch, on his throne, enriched with the foreign luxury which he despised, and encircled with the love and reverence of his victorious chiefs. A treaty of peace and alliance was concluded between the two empires, and the limits of the East and West were defined by the right of present possession. But the Greeks[123] soon forgot this humiliating equality, or remembered it only to hate the Barbarians by whom it was extorted. During the short union of virtue and power, they respectfully saluted the *august* Charlemagne with the acclamations of *basileus*, and emperor of the Romans. As soon as these

121. Theophanes speaks of the coronation and unction of Charles, *Καρουλλος* (Chronograph. p. 399.), and of his treaty of marriage with Irene (p. 402.), which is unknown to the Latins. Gaillard relates his transactions with the Greek empire (tom. ii. p. 446–468.).

122. Gaillard very properly observes, that this pageant was a farce suitable to children only; but that it was indeed represented in the presence, and for the benefit, of children of a larger growth.

123. Compare, in the original texts collected by Pagi (tom. iii. A.D. 812, N° 7. A.D. 824, N° 10, &c.), the contrast of Charlemagne and his son: to the former the ambassadors of Michael (who were indeed disavowed) more suo, id est linguâ Græcâ laudes dixerunt, imperatorem eum et *Βασιλεα* appellantes; to the latter, *Vocato* imperatori *Francorum*, &c.

qualities were separated in the person of his pious son, the Byzantine letters were inscribed, "To the king, or, as he styles himself, the emperor of the Franks and Lombards." When both power and virtue were extinct, they despoiled Lewis the second of his hereditary title, and, with the barbarous appellation of rex or *rega*, degraded him among the crowd of Latin princes. His reply[124] is expressive of his weakness: he proves, with some learning, that, both in sacred and profane history, the name of king is synonymous with the Greek word *basileus*: if, at Constantinople, it were assumed in a more exclusive and imperial sense, he claims from his ancestors, and from the pope, a just participation of the honours of the Roman purple. The same controversy was revived in the reign of the Othos; and their ambassador describes, in lively colours, the insolence of the Byzantine court.[125] The Greeks affected to despise the poverty and ignorance of the Franks and Saxons; and in their last decline, refused to prostitute to the kings of Germany the title of Roman emperors.

Authority of the emperors in the elections of the popes, A.D. 800–1060.

These emperors, in the election of the popes, continued to exercise the powers which had been assumed by the Gothic and Grecian princes; and the importance of this prerogative encreased with the temporal estate and spiritual jurisdiction of the Roman church. In the Christian aristocracy, the principal members of the clergy still formed a senate to assist the administration, and to supply the vacancy, of the bishop. Rome was divided into twenty-eight parishes, and each parish was governed by a cardinal-priest, or presbyter, a title which, however common and modest in its origin, has aspired to emulate the purple of kings. Their number was enlarged by the association of the seven deacons of the most considerable hospitals, the seven palatine judges of the Lateran, and some dignitaries of the church. This ecclesiastical senate was directed by the seven cardinal-bishops of the Roman province, who were less occupied in the suburb dioceses of Ostia, Porto, Velitræ, Tusculum, Præneste, Tibur, and the Sabines, than by their weekly service in the Lateran, and their superior

124. See the epistle, in Paralipomena, of the anonymous writer of Salerno (Script. Ital. tom. ii. pars ii. p. 243–254. c. 93–107.), whom Baronius (A.D. 871, N° 51–71.) mistook for Erchempert, when he transcribed it in his Annals.

125. Ipse enim vos, non *imperatorem*, id est *Βασιλεα* suâ lingua, sed ob indignationem *Ρηγα*, id est *regem* nostrâ vocabat (Liutprand, in Legat. in Script. Ital. tom. ii. pars i. p. 479.). The pope had exhorted Nicephorus, emperor of the *Greeks*, to make peace with Otho, the august emperor of the *Romans* – quæ inscriptio secundum Græcos peccatria et temeraria . . . imperatorem inquiunt, *universalem*, *Romanorum*, *Augustum*, *magnum*, *solum*, Nicephorum (p. 486.).

share in the honours and authority of the apostolic see. On the death of the pope, these bishops recommended a successor to the suffrage of the college of cardinals,[126] and their choice was ratified or rejected by the applause or clamour of the Roman people. But the election was imperfect; nor could the pontiff be legally consecrated till the emperor, the advocate of the church, had graciously signified his approbation and consent. The royal commissioner examined, on the spot, the form and freedom of the proceedings; nor was it, till after a previous scrutiny into the qualifications of the candidates, that he accepted an oath of fidelity, and confirmed the donations which had successively enriched the patrimony of St. Peter. In the frequent schisms, the rival claims were submitted to the sentence of the emperor; and in a synod of bishops he presumed to judge, to condemn, and to punish, the crimes of a guilty pontiff. Otho the first imposed a treaty on the senate and people, who engaged to prefer the candidate most acceptable to his majesty:[127] his successors anticipated or prevented their choice: they bestowed the Roman benefice, like the bishoprics of Cologne or Bamberg, on their chancellors or preceptors; and whatever might be the merit of a Frank or Saxon, his name sufficiently attests the interposition of foreign power. These acts of prerogative were most speciously excused by the vices of a popular election. The competitor who had been excluded by the cardinals, appealed to the passions or avarice of the multitude: the Vatican and the Lateran were stained with blood; and the most powerful senators, the marquisses of Tuscany and the counts of Tusculum, held the apostolic see in a long and disgraceful servitude. The Roman pontiffs, of the *Disorders.* ninth and tenth centuries, were insulted, imprisoned, and murdered, by their tyrants; and such was their indigence after the loss and usurpation of the ecclesiastical patrimonies, that they could neither support the state

126. The origin and progress of the title of cardinal may be found in Thomassin (Discipline de l'Eglise, tom. i. p. 1261–1298.), Muratori (Antiquitat. Italiæ Medii Ævi, tom. vi. dissert. lxi. p. 159–182.), and Mosheim (Institut. Hist. Eccles. p. 345–347.), who accurately remarks the forms and changes of the election. The cardinal-bishops, so highly exalted by Peter Damianus, are sunk to a level with the rest of the sacred college.

127. Firmiter jurantes, nunquam se papam electuros aut ordinaturos, præter consensum et electionem Othonis et filii sui (Liutprand, l. vi. c. 6. p. 472.). This important concession may either supply or confirm the decree of the clergy and people of Rome, so fiercely rejected by Baronius, Pagi, and Muratori (A.D. 964), and so well defended and explained by St. Marc (Abregé, tom. ii. p. 808–816. tom. iv. p. 1167–1185.). Consult that historical critic, and the Annals of Muratori, for the election and confirmation of each pope.

of a prince nor exercise the charity of a priest.[128] The influence of two sister prostitutes, Marozia, and Theodora, was founded on their wealth and beauty, their political and amorous intrigues: the most strenuous of their lovers were rewarded with the Roman mitre, and their reign[129] may have suggested to the darker ages[130] the fable[131] of a female pope.[132] The bastard son, the grandson and the great-grandson of Marozia, a rare genealogy, were seated in the chair of St. Peter, and it was at the age of nineteen years that the second of these became the head of the Latin church. His youth and manhood were of a suitable complexion; and the nations of pilgrims could bear testimony to the charges that were urged against him in a Roman synod, and in the presence of Otho the great. As John XII. had renounced the dress and decencies of his profession, the *soldier* may not perhaps be dishonoured by the wine which he drank,

128. The oppression and vices of the Roman church in the xth century are strongly painted in the history and legation of Liutprand (see p. 440. 450. 471–476. 479, &c.); and it is whimsical enough to observe Muratori tempering the invectives of Baronius against the popes. But these popes had been chosen, not by the cardinals, but by lay-patrons.

129. The time of pope Joan *(papissa Joanna)* is placed somewhat earlier than Theodora or Marozia; and the two years of her imaginary reign are forcibly inserted between Leo IV. and Benedict III. But the contemporary Anastasius indissolubly links the death of Leo and the elevation of Benedict (illico, mox, p. 247.); and the accurate chronology of Pagi, Muratori, and Leibnitz, fixes both events to the year 857.

130. The advocates for pope Joan produce one hundred and fifty witnesses, or rather echoes, of the xiv[th], xv[th], and xvi[th] centuries. They bear testimony against themselves and the legend, by multiplying the proof that so curious a story *must* have been repeated by writers of every description to whom it was known. On those of the ix[th] and x[th] centuries, the recent event would have flashed with a double force. Would Photius have spared such a reproach? Could Liutprand have missed such scandal? It is scarcely worth while to discuss the various readings of Martinus Polonus, Sigebert of Gemblours, or even Marianus Scotus; but a most palpable forgery is the passage of pope Joan, which has been foisted into some MSS. and editions of the Roman Anastasius.

131. As *false*, it deserves that name; but I would not pronounce it incredible. Suppose a famous French chevalier of our own times to have been born in Italy, and educated in the church, instead of the army: *her* merit or fortune *might* have raised her to St. Peter's chair; her amours would have been natural; her delivery in the streets unlucky, but not improbable.

132. Till the reformation, the tale was repeated and believed without offence; and Joan's female statue long occupied her place among the popes in the cathedral of Sienna (Pagi, Critica, tom. iii. p. 624–626.). She has been annihilated by two learned protestants, Blondel and Bayle (Dictionaire Critique, PAPESSE, POLONUS, BLONDEL); but their brethren were scandalised by this equitable and generous criticism. Spanheim and Lenfant attempt to save this poor engine of controversy; and even Mosheim condescends to cherish some doubt and suspicion (p. 289.).

the blood that he spilt, the flames that he kindled, or the licentious pursuits of gaming and hunting. His open simony might be the consequence of distress: and his blasphemous invocation of Jupiter and Venus, if it be true, could not possibly be serious. But we read with some surprise, that the worthy grandson of Marozia lived in public adultery with the matrons of Rome; that the Lateran palace was turned into a school for prostitution, and that his rapes of virgins and widows had deterred the female pilgrims from visiting the tomb of St. Peter, lest, in the devout act, they should be violated by his successor.[133] The protestants have dwelt with malicious pleasure on these characters of anti-christ; but to a philosophic eye, the vices of the clergy are far less dangerous than their virtues. After a long series of scandal, the apostolic see was reformed and exalted by the austerity and zeal of Gregory VII. That ambitious monk devoted his life to the execution of two projects. I. To fix in the college of cardinals the freedom and independence of election, and for ever to abolish the right or usurpation of the emperors and the Roman people. II. To bestow and resume the Western empire as a fief or benefice[134] of the church, and to extend his temporal dominion over the kings and kingdoms of the earth. After a contest of fifty years, the first of these designs was accomplished by the firm support of the ecclesiastical order, whose liberty was connected with that of their chief. But the second attempt, though it was crowned with some partial and apparent success, has been vigorously resisted by the secular power, and finally extinguished by the improvement of human reason.

Reformation and claims of the church, A.D. 1073, &c.

In the revival of the empire of Rome, neither the bishop nor the people could bestow on Charlemagne or Otho, the provinces which were lost, as they had been won, by the chance of arms. But the Romans were free to chuse a master for themselves; and the powers which had been delegated to the patrician, were irrevocably

Authority of the emperors in Rome.

133. Lateranense palatium . . . prostibulum meretricum . . . Testis omnium gentium, præterquam Romanorum, absentia mulierum, quæ sanctorum apostolorum limina orandi gratiâ timent visere, cum nonnullas ante dies paucos, hunc audierint conjugatas viduas, virgines vi oppressisse (Liutprand, Hist. l. vi. c. 6. p. 471. See the whole affair of John XII. p. 471–476.).

134. A new example of the mischief of equivocation is the *beneficium* (Ducange, tom. i. p. 617, &c.) which the pope conferred on the emperor Frederic I. since the Latin word may signify either a legal fief, or a simple favour, an obligation (we want the word *bienfait*). See Schmidt, Hist. des Allemands, tom. iii. p. 393–408. Pfeffel, Abregé Chronologique, tom. i. p. 229. 296. 317. 324. 420. 430. 500. 505. 509, &c.).

granted to the French and Saxon emperors of the West. The broken records of the times[135] preserve some remembrance of their palace, their mint, their tribunal, their edicts, and the sword of justice, which, as late as the thirteenth century, was derived from Cæsar to the præfect of the city.[136] Between the arts of the popes and the violence of the people, this supremacy was crushed and annihilated. Content with the titles of emperor and Augustus, the successors of Charlemagne neglected to assert this local jurisdiction. In the hour of prosperity, their ambition was diverted by more alluring objects; and in the decay and division of the empire, they were oppressed by the defence of their hereditary provinces. Amidst the ruins of Italy, the famous Marozia invited one of the usurpers to assume the character of her third husband; and Hugh, king of Burgundy, was introduced by her faction into the mole of Hadrian or castle of St. Angelo, which commands the principal bridge and entrance of Rome. Her son by the first marriage, Alberic, was compelled to attend at the nuptial banquet; but his reluctant and ungraceful service was chastised with a blow by his new father. The blow was productive of a revolution. "Romans," exclaimed the youth, "once you were the masters of the world, and these Burgundians the most abject of your slaves. They now reign, these voracious and brutal savages, and my injury is the commencement of your servitude."[137] The alarum-bell rung to arms in every quarter of the city: the Burgundians retreated with haste and shame; Marozia was imprisoned by her victorious son; and his brother, pope John XI. was reduced to the exercise of his spiritual functions. With the title of prince, Alberic possessed above twenty years the government of Rome, and he is said to have gratified the popular prejudice, by restoring the office, or at least the title, of consuls and tribunes. His son and heir Octavian assumed, with the pontificate, the name of John XII.; like his predecessor, he was provoked by the Lombard princes to seek a deliverer for the church and republic; and the services

Revolt of Alberic, A.D. 932.

135. For the history of the emperors in Rome and Italy, see Sigonius, de Regno Italiæ; Opp. tom. ii. with the Notes of Saxius, and the Annals of Muratori, who might refer more distinctly to the authors of his great collection.

136. See the Dissertation of Le Blanc at the end of his Treatise des Monnoyes de France, in which he produces some Roman coins of the French emperors.

137. Romanorum aliquando servi, scilicet Burgundiones, Romanis imperent? . . . Romanæ urbis dignitas ad tantam est stultitiam ducta, ut meretricum etiam imperio pareat? (Liutprand, l. iii. c. 12. p. 450.) Sigonius (l. vi. p. 400.) positively affirms the renovation of the consulship; but in the old writers Albericus is more frequently styled princeps Romanorum.

of Otho were rewarded with the Imperial dignity. But the Saxon was imperious, the Romans were impatient, the festival of the coronation was disturbed by the secret conflict of prerogative and freedom, and Otho commanded his sword-bearer not to stir from his person, lest he should be assaulted and murdered at the foot of the altar.[138] Before he repassed the Alps, the emperor chastised the revolt of the people and the ingratitude of John XII. The pope was degraded in a synod; the præfect was mounted on an ass, whipped through the city and cast into a dungeon; thirteen of the most guilty were hanged, others were mutilated or banished; and this severe process was justified by the ancient laws of Theodosius and Justinian. The voice of fame has accused the second Otho of a perfidious and bloody act, the massacre of the senators, whom he had invited to his table under the fair semblance of hospitality and friendship.[139] In the minority of his son Otho the third, Rome made a bold attempt to shake off the Saxon yoke, and the consul Crescentius was the Brutus of the republic. From the condition of a subject and an exile, he twice rose to the command of the city, oppressed, expelled, and created the popes, and formed a conspiracy for restoring the authority of the Greek emperors. In the fortress of St. Angelo, he maintained an obstinate siege, till the unfortunate consul was betrayed by a promise of safety: his body was suspended on a gibbet, and his head was exposed on the battlements of the castle. By a reverse of fortune, Otho, after separating his troops, was besieged three days, without food, in his palace; and a disgraceful escape saved him from the justice or fury of the Romans. The senator Ptolemy was the leader of the people, and the widow of Crescentius enjoyed the pleasure or the fame of revenging her husband, by a poison which she administered to her Imperial lover. It was the design of Otho the third to abandon the ruder countries of the north, to erect his throne in Italy, and to revive the institutions of the Roman monarchy. But his successors only once in their lives appeared on the banks of the Tyber, to receive their crown in the Vatican.[140] Their absence was contemptible, their

Of pope John XII. A.D. 967.

Of the consul Crescentius. A.D. 998.

138. Ditmar, p. 354. apud Schmidt, tom. iii. p. 439.

139. This bloody feast is described in Leonine verse, in the Pantheon of Godfrey of Viterbo (Script. Ital. tom. vii. p. 436, 437.), who flourished towards the end of the xii[th] century (Fabricius, Bibliot. Latin. med. et infimi Ævi, tom. iii. p. 69. edit. Mansi); but his evidence, which imposed on Sigonius, is reasonably suspected by Muratori (Annali, tom. viii. p. 177.).

140. The coronation of the emperor, and some original ceremonies of the xth century, are preserved in the Panegyric on Berengarius (Script. Ital. tom. ii. pars i. p. 405–414.), illustrated by the Notes of

presence odious and formidable. They descended from the Alps, at the head of their Barbarians, who were strangers and enemies to the country; and their transient visit was a scene of tumult and bloodshed.[141] A faint remembrance of their ancestors still tormented the Romans; and they beheld with pious indignation the succession of Saxons, Franks, Swabians, and Bohemians, who usurped the purple and prerogatives of the Cæsars.

The kingdom of Italy, A.D. 774–1250.

There is nothing perhaps more adverse to nature and reason than to hold in obedience remote countries and foreign nations, in opposition to their inclination and interest. A torrent of Barbarians may pass over the earth, but an extensive empire must be supported by a refined system of policy and oppression: in the centre, an absolute power, prompt in action, and rich in resources: a swift and easy communication with the extreme parts: fortifications to check the first effort of rebellion: a regular administration to protect and punish; and a well-disciplined army to inspire fear, without provoking discontent and despair. Far different was the situation of the German Cæsars, who were ambitious to enslave the kingdom of Italy. Their patrimonial estates were stretched along the Rhine, or scattered in the provinces; but this ample domain was alienated by the imprudence or distress of successive princes; and their revenue, from minute and vexatious prerogative, was scarcely sufficient for the maintenance of their household. Their troops were formed by the legal or voluntary service of their feudal vassals, who passed the Alps with reluctance, assumed the licence of rapine and disorder, and capriciously deserted before the end of the campaign. Whole armies were swept away by the pestilential influence of the climate; the survivors brought back the bones of their princes and nobles,[142] and the effects of their own intemperance were often imputed to the treachery and malice of the Italians, who rejoiced at least in the calamities of the Barbarians. This irregular tyranny might contend on equal terms with the petty tyrants of Italy; nor can the

---

Hadrian Valesius, and Leibnitz. Sigonius has related the whole process of the Roman expedition, in good Latin, but with some errors of time and fact (l. vii. p. 441–446.).

141. In a quarrel at the coronation of Conrad II. Muratori takes leave to observe – doveano ben essere allora, indisciplinati, Barbari, e *bestiali* i Tedeschi. Annal. tom. viii. p. 368.

142. After boiling away the flesh. The caldrons for that purpose were a necessary piece of travelling furniture; and a German who was using it for his brother, promised it to a friend, after it should have been employed for himself (Schmidt, tom. iii. p. 423, 424.). The same author observes, that the whole Saxon line was extinguished in Italy (tom. ii. p. 440.).

people, or the reader, be much interested in the event of the quarrel. But in the eleventh and twelfth centuries, the Lombards rekindled the flame of industry and freedom; and the generous example was at length imitated by the republics of Tuscany. In the Italian cities a municipal government had never been totally abolished; and their first privileges were granted by the favour and policy of the emperors, who were desirous of erecting a plebeian barrier against the independence of the nobles. But their rapid progress, the daily extension of their power and pretensions, were founded on the numbers and spirit of these rising communities.[143] Each city filled the measure of her diocese or district: the jurisdiction of the abbots and bishops, of the marquisses and counts, was banished from the land; and the proudest nobles were persuaded or compelled to desert their solitary castles, and to embrace the more honourable character of freemen and magistrates. The legislative authority was inherent in the general assembly; but the executive powers were entrusted to three consuls, annually chosen from the three orders of *captains*, *valvassors*,[144] and commons, into which the republic was divided. Under the protection of equal law, the labours of agriculture and commerce were gradually revived; but the martial spirit of the Lombards was nourished by the presence of danger; and as often as the bell was rung, or the standard[145] erected, the gates of the city poured forth a numerous and intrepid band, whose zeal in their own cause was soon guided by the use and discipline of arms. At the foot of these popular ramparts, the pride of the Cæsars was overthrown; and the invincible genius of liberty prevailed over the two Frederics, the greatest princes of the middle age: the first, superior perhaps in military prowess; the second, who undoubtedly excelled in the softer accomplishments of peace and learning.

Frederic the first, A.D. 1152–1190.

Ambitious of restoring the splendour of the purple, Frederic the first invaded the republics of Lombardy, with the arts of a statesman, the valour of a soldier, and the cruelty of

143. Otho bishop of Frisingen has left an important passage on the Italian cities (l. ii. c. 13. in Script. Ital. tom. vi. p. 707–710.); and the rise, progress, and government, of these republics are perfectly illustrated by Muratori (Antiquitat. Ital. Medii Ævi, tom. iv. dissert. xlv–lii. p. 1–675. Annal. tom. viii, ix, x.).

144. For these titles, see Selden (Titles of Honour, vol. iii. part i. p. 488.), Ducange (Gloss. Latin. tom. ii. p. 140. tom. vi p. 776.), and St. Marc (Abregé Chronologique, tom. ii. p. 719.).

145. The Lombards invented and used the *carocium*, a standard planted on a car or waggon, drawn by a team of oxen (Ducange, tom. ii. p. 194, 195. Muratori, Antiquitat. tom. ii. diss. xxvi. p. 489–493.).

a tyrant. The recent discovery of the Pandects had renewed a science most favourable to despotism; and his venal advocates proclaimed the emperor the absolute master of the lives and properties of his subjects. His royal prerogatives, in a less odious sense, were acknowledged in the diet of Roncaglia; and the revenue of Italy was fixed at thirty thousand pounds of silver,[146] which were multiplied to an indefinite demand, by the rapine of the fiscal officers. The obstinate cities were reduced by the terror or the force of his arms: his captives were delivered to the executioner, or shot from his military engines; and, after the siege and surrender of Milan, the buildings of that stately capital were razed to the ground, three hundred hostages were sent into Germany, and the inhabitants were dispersed in four villages, under the yoke of the inflexible conqueror.[147] But Milan soon rose from her ashes; and the league of Lombardy was cemented by distress: their cause was espoused by Venice, pope Alexander the third, and the Greek emperor: the fabric of oppression was overturned in a day; and in the treaty of Constance, Frederic subscribed, with some reservations, the freedom of four-and-twenty cities. His grandson contended with their vigour and maturity; but Frederic the second[148] was endowed with some personal and peculiar advantages. His birth and education recommended him to the Italians; and in the implacable discord of the two factions, the Ghibelins were attached to the emperor, while the Guelfs displayed the banner of liberty and the church. The court of Rome had slumbered, when his father Henry the sixth was permitted to unite with the empire the kingdoms of Naples and Sicily; and from these hereditary realms, the son derived an ample and ready supply of troops and treasure. Yet Frederic the second was finally oppressed by the arms of the Lombards and the thunders of the Vatican; his kingdom was given to a stranger, and the last of his family was beheaded at Naples on a public scaffold. During sixty years, no emperor appeared in Italy, and the name was remembered only by the ignominious sale of the last relics of sovereignty.

Frederic the second, A.D. 1198–1250.

146. Gunther Ligurinus, l. viii. 584, et seq. apud Schmidt, tom. iii. p. 399.

147. Solus imperator faciem suam firmavit ut petram (Burcard. de Excidio Mediolani, Script. Ital. tom. vi. p. 917.). This volume of Muratori contains the originals of the history of Frederic the first, which must be compared with due regard to the circumstances and prejudices of each German or Lombard writer.

148. For the history of Frederic II. and the house of Swabia at Naples, see Giannone, Istoria Civile, tom. ii. l. xiv–xix.

Independence of the princes of Germany, A.D. 814–1250, &c.

The Barbarian conquerors of the West were pleased to decorate their chief with the title of emperor; but it was not their design to invest him with the despotism of Constantine and Justinian. The persons of the Germans were free, their conquests were their own, and their national character was animated by a spirit which scorned the servile jurisprudence of the new or the ancient Rome. It would have been a vain and dangerous attempt to impose a monarch, on the armed freemen who were impatient of a magistrate; on the bold, who refused to obey; on the powerful, who aspired to command. The empire of Charlemagne and Otho was distributed among the dukes of the nations or provinces, the counts of the smaller districts, and the margraves of the marches or frontiers, who all united the civil and military authority as it had been delegated to the lieutenants of the first Cæsars. The Roman governors, who, for the most part, were soldiers of fortune, seduced their mercenary legions, assumed the Imperial purple, and either failed or succeeded in their revolt, without wounding the power and unity of government. If the dukes, margraves, and counts of Germany, were less audacious in their claims, the consequences of their success were more lasting and pernicious to the state. Instead of aiming at the supreme rank, they silently laboured to establish and appropriate their provincial independence. Their ambition was seconded by the weight of their estates and vassals, their mutual example and support, the common interest of the subordinate nobility, the change of princes and families, the minorities of Otho the third and Henry the fourth, the ambition of the popes, and the vain pursuit of the fugitive crowns of Italy and Rome. All the attributes of regal and territorial jurisdiction were gradually usurped by the commanders of the provinces; the right of peace and war, of life and death, of coinage and taxation, of foreign alliance and domestic œconomy. Whatever had been seized by violence, was ratified by favour or distress, was granted as the price of a doubtful vote or a voluntary service; whatever had been granted to one, could not, without injury, be denied to his successor or equal; and every act of local or temporary possession was insensibly moulded into the constitution of the Germanic kingdom. In every province, the visible presence of the duke or count was interposed between the throne and the nobles; the subjects of the law became the vassals of a private chief; and the standard, which *he* received from his sovereign, was often raised against him in the field. The temporal power of the clergy was cherished and exalted by the superstition or policy of the Carlovingian and Saxon dynasties, who blindly depended on their moderation and fidelity; and the bishoprics of

Germany were made equal in extent and privilege, superior in wealth and population, to the most ample states of the military order. As long as the emperors retained the prerogative of bestowing on every vacancy these ecclesiastic and secular benefices, their cause was maintained by the gratitude or ambition of their friends and favourites. But in the quarrel of the investitures, they were deprived of their influence over the episcopal chapters; the freedom of election was restored, and the sovereign was reduced, by a solemn mockery, to his *first prayers*, the recommendation, once in his reign, to a single prebend in each church. The secular governors, instead of being recalled at the will of a superior, could be degraded only by the sentence of their peers. In the first age of the monarchy, the appointment of the son to the dutchy or county of his father, was solicited as a favour; it was gradually obtained as a custom, and extorted as a right: the lineal succession was often extended to the collateral or female branches; the states of the empire (their popular, and at length their legal, appellation) were divided and alienated by testament and sale; and all idea of a public trust was lost in that of a private and perpetual inheritance. The emperor could not even be enriched by the casualties of forfeiture and extinction: within the term of a year, he was obliged to dispose of the vacant fief, and in the choice of the candidate, it was his duty to consult either the general or the provincial diet.

The Germanic constitution, A.D. 1250.

After the death of Frederic the second, Germany was left a monster with an hundred heads. A crowd of princes and prelates disputed the ruins of the empire: the lords of innumerable castles were less prone to obey, than to imitate, their superiors; and according to the measure of their strength, their incessant hostilities received the names of conquest or robbery. Such anarchy was the inevitable consequence of the laws and manners of Europe; and the kingdoms of France and Italy were shivered into fragments by the violence of the same tempest. But the Italian cities and the French vassals were divided and destroyed, while the union of the Germans has produced, under the name of an empire, a great system of a fœderative republic. In the frequent and at last the perpetual institution of diets, a national spirit was kept alive, and the powers of a common legislature are still exercised by the three branches or colleges of the electors, the princes, and the free and Imperial cities of Germany. I. Seven of the most powerful feudataries were permitted to assume, with a distinguished name and rank, the exclusive privilege of chusing the Roman emperor; and these electors were the king of Bohemia, the duke of Saxony, the margrave of Brandenburgh, the count palatine of the Rhine, and the three archbishops of Mentz, of Treves, and of Cologne. II. The college of princes and prelates purged themselves of a promiscuous multitude: they reduced to four representative votes, the long series of independent counts, and excluded the nobles or equestrian order, sixty thousand of whom, as in the Polish diets, had appeared on horseback in the field of election. III. The pride of birth and dominion, of the sword and the mitre, wisely adopted the commons as the third branch of the legislature, and, in the progress of society, they were introduced about the same æra into the national assemblies of France, England, and Germany. The Hanseatic league commanded the trade and navigation of the north: the confederates of the Rhine secured the peace and intercourse of the inland country: the influence of the cities has been adequate to their wealth and policy, and their negative still invalidates the acts of the two superior colleges of electors and princes.[149]

Weakness and poverty of the German emperor Charles IV. A.D. 1347–1378.

It is in the fourteenth century, that we may view in the strongest light the state and contrast of the Roman empire of Germany, which no longer held, except on the borders of the Rhine and Danube, a single province of Trajan or Constantine. Their unworthy successors were the counts of Hapsburgh, of Nassau, of Luxemburgh, and of Schwartzenburgh: the emperor Henry the seventh procured for his son the crown of Bohemia, and his grandson Charles the fourth was born among a people, strange and barbarous in the estimation of the Germans themselves.[150] After the excommunication of Lewis of Bavaria, he received the gift or promise of

149. In the immense labyrinth of the *jus publicum* of Germany, I must either quote one writer or a thousand; and I had rather trust to one faithful guide, than transcribe, on credit, a multitude of names and passages. That guide is M. Pfeffel, the author of the best legal and constitutional history that I know of any country (Nouvel Abregé Chronologique de l'Histoire et du Droit Public d'Allemagne; Paris, 1776, 2 vols. in 4to). His learning and judgment have discerned the most interesting facts; his simple brevity comprises them in a narrow space; his chronological order distributes them under the proper dates; and an elaborate index collects them under their respective heads. To this work, in a less perfect state, Dr. Robertson was gratefully indebted for that masterly sketch which traces even the modern changes of the Germanic body. The Corpus Historiæ Germanicæ of Struvius has been likewise consulted, the more usefully, as that huge compilation is fortified in every page with the original texts.

150. Yet, *personally*, Charles IV. must not be considered as a Barbarian. After his education at Paris, he recovered the use of the Bohemian, his native, idiom; and the emperor conversed and wrote with equal facility in French, Latin, Italian, and German (Struvius, p. 615, 616.). Petrarch always represents him as a polite and learned prince.

the vacant empire from the Roman pontiffs, who, in the exile and captivity of Avignon, affected the dominion of the earth. The death of his competitors united the electoral college, and Charles was unanimously saluted king of the Romans, and future emperor: a title which in the same age was prostituted to the Cæsars of Germany and Greece. The German emperor was no more than the elective and impotent magistrate of an aristocracy of princes, who had not left him a village that he might call his own. His best prerogative was the right of presiding and proposing in the national senate, which was convened at his summons; and his native kingdom of Bohemia, less opulent than the adjacent city of Nurembergh, was the firmest seat of his power and the richest source of *A.D. 1355.* his revenue. The army with which he passed the Alps, consisted of three hundred horse. In the cathedral of St. Ambrose, Charles was crowned with the *iron* crown, which tradition ascribed to the Lombard monarchy; but he was admitted only with a peaceful train; the gates of the city were shut upon him; and the king of Italy was held a captive by the arms of the Visconti, whom he confirmed in the sovereignty of Milan. In the Vatican he was again crowned with the *golden* crown of the empire; but, in obedience to a secret treaty, the Roman emperor immediately withdrew, without reposing a single night within the walls of Rome. The eloquent Petrarch,[151] whose fancy revived the visionary glories of the Capitol, deplores and upbraids the ignominious flight of the Bohemian; and even his contemporaries could observe, that the sole exercise of his authority was in the lucrative sale of privileges and titles. The gold of Italy secured the election of his son; but such was the shameful poverty of the Roman emperor, that his person was arrested by a butcher in the streets of Worms, and was detained in the public inn, as a pledge or hostage for the payment of his expences.

His ostentation. A.D. 1356. From this humiliating scene, let us turn to the apparent majesty of the same Charles in the diets of the empire. The golden bull, which fixes the Germanic constitution, is promulgated in the style of a sovereign and legislator. An hundred princes bowed before his throne, and exalted their own dignity by the voluntary honours which they yielded to their chief or minister. At the royal banquet, the hereditary great officers, the seven electors, who in rank and title were equal to

151. Besides the German and Italian historians, the expedition of Charles IV. is painted in lively and original colours in the curious Memoires sur la Vie de Petrarque, tom. iii. p. 376–430. by the abbé de Sade, whose prolixity has never been blamed by any reader of taste and curiosity.

kings, performed their solemn and domestic service of the palace. The seals of the triple kingdom were borne in state by the archbishops of Mentz, Cologne, and Treves, the perpetual arch-chancellors of Germany, Italy, and Arles. The great marshal, on horseback, exercised his function with a silver measure of oats, which he emptied on the ground, and immediately dismounted to regulate the order of the guests. The great steward, the count palatine of the Rhine, placed the dishes on the table. The great chamberlain, the margrave of Brandenburgh, presented, after the repast, the golden ewer and bason, to wash. The king of Bohemia, as great cup-bearer, was represented by the emperor's brother, the duke of Luxemburgh and Brabant; and the procession was closed by the great huntsmen, who introduced a boar and a stag, with a loud chorus of horns and hounds.[152] Nor was the supremacy of the emperor confined to Germany alone: the hereditary monarchs of Europe confessed the pre-eminence of his rank and dignity: he was the first of the Christian princes, the temporal head of the great republic of the West:[153] to his person the title of majesty was long appropriated; and he disputed with the pope the sublime prerogative of creating kings and assembling councils. The oracle of the civil law, the learned Bartolus, was a pensioner of Charles the fourth; and his school resounded with the doctrine, that the Roman emperor was the rightful sovereign of the earth, from the rising to the setting sun. The contrary opinion was condemned, not as an error, but as an heresy, since even the gospel had pronounced, "And there went forth a decree from Cæsar Augustus, that *all the world* should be taxed."[154]

Contrast of the power and modesty of Augustus.

If we annihilate the interval of time and space between Augustus and Charles, strong and striking will be the contrast between the two Cæsars; the Bohemian, who concealed his weakness under the mask of ostentation, and the Roman, who disguised his strength under the semblance of modesty. At the head of his victorious legions, in his reign over the sea and land, from the Nile and Euphrates to the Atlantic ocean, Augustus professed himself the servant of the state and the equal of his fellow-citizens. The conqueror of Rome and her provinces assumed the popular and legal form of a censor, a consul, and a tribune. His will was the law of mankind, but in the declaration of his laws he borrowed the voice of the senate and

152. See the whole ceremony, in Struvius, p. 629.

153. The republic of Europe, with the pope and emperor at its head, was never represented with more dignity than in the council of Constance. See Lenfant's History of that assembly.

154. Gravina, Origines Juris Civilis, p. 108.

people; and, from their decrees, their master accepted and renewed his temporary commission to administer the republic. In his dress, his domestics,[155] his titles, in all the offices of social life, Augustus maintained the character of a private Roman; and his most artful flatterers respected the secret of his absolute and perpetual monarchy.

155. Six thousand urns have been discovered of the slaves and freedmen of Augustus and Livia. So minute was the division of office, that one slave was appointed to weigh the wool which was spun by the empress's maids, another for the care of her lap-dog, &c. (Camere Sepolchrale, &c. by Bianchini. Extract of his work, in the Bibliotheque Italique, tom. iv. p. 175. His Eloge, by Fontenelle, tom. vi. p. 356.). But these servants were of the same rank, and possibly not more numerous than those of Pollio or Lentulus. They only prove the general riches of the city.

CHAPTER L

Description of Arabia and its Inhabitants. – Birth, Character, and Doctrine of Mahomet. – He preaches at Mecca. – Flies to Medina. – Propagates his Religion by the Sword. – Voluntary or reluctant Submission of the Arabs. – His Death and Successors. – The Claims and Fortunes of Ali and his Descendants.

After pursuing above six hundred years the fleeting Cæsars of Constantinople and Germany, I now descend, in the reign of Heraclius, on the eastern borders of the Greek monarchy. While the state was exhausted by the Persian war, and the church was distracted by the Nestorian and Monophysite sects, Mahomet, with the sword in one hand and the Koran in the other, erected his throne on the ruins of Christianity and of Rome. The genius of the Arabian prophet, the manners of his nation, and the spirit of his religion, involve the causes of the decline and fall of the Eastern empire; and our eyes are curiously intent on one of the most memorable revolutions, which have impressed a new and lasting character on the nations of the globe.[1]

Description of Arabia.

In the vacant space between Persia, Syria, Egypt, and Æthiopia, the Arabian peninsula[2] may be conceived as a triangle

1. As in this and the following chapter I shall display much Arabic learning, I must profess my total ignorance of the Oriental tongues, and my gratitude to the learned interpreters, who have transfused their science into the Latin, French, and English languages. Their collections, versions, and histories, I shall occasionally notice.

2. The geographers of Arabia may be divided into three classes: 1. The *Greeks* and *Latins*, whose progressive knowledge may be traced in Agatharcides (de Mari Rubro, in Hudson, Geograph. Minor. tom. i.), Diodorus Siculus (tom. i. l. ii. p. 159–167. l. iii. p. 211–216. edit. Wesseling), Strabo (l. xvi. p. 1112–1114. from Eratosthenes, p. 1122–1132. from Artemidorus), Dionysius (Periegesis, 927–969.), Pliny (Hist. Natur. v. 12. vi. 32.), and Ptolemy (Descript. et Tabulæ Urbium, in Hudson, tom. iii.). 2. The *Arabic writers*, who have treated the subject with the zeal of patriotism or devotion: the extracts of Pocock (Specimen Hist. Arabum, p. 125–128.) from the Geography of the Sherif al Edrissi, render us still more dissatisfied with the version or abridgment (p. 24–27. 44–56. 108, &c. 119, &c.) which the Maronites have published under the absurd title of Geographia Nubiensis (Paris, 1619); but the Latin and French translators, Greaves (in Hudson, tom. iii.) and Galland (Voyage de la Palestine par La Roque, p. 265–346.), have opened to us the Arabia of Abulfeda,

of spacious but irregular dimensions. From the northern point of Beles[3] on the Euphrates, a line of fifteen hundred miles is terminated by the streights of Babelmandel and the land of frankincense. About half this length may be allowed for the middle breadth, from east to west, from Bassora to Suez, from the Persian Gulf to the Red Sea.[4] The sides of the triangle are gradually enlarged, and the southern basis presents a front of a thousand miles to the Indian ocean. The entire surface of the peninsula exceeds in a fourfold proportion that of Germany or France; but the far greater part has been justly stigmatised with the epithets of the *stony* and the *sandy*. Even the wilds of Tartary are decked, by the hand of nature, with lofty trees and luxuriant herbage; and the lonesome traveller derives a sort of comfort and society from the presence of vegetable life. But in the dreary waste of Arabia, a boundless level of sand is intersected by sharp and naked mountains; and the face of the desert, without shade or shelter, is scorched by the direct and intense rays of a tropical sun. Instead of refreshing breezes, the winds, particularly from the south-west, diffuse a noxious and even deadly vapour; the hillocks of sand which they alternately raise and scatter, are compared to the billows of the ocean, and whole caravans, whole armies, have been lost and buried in the whirlwind. The common benefits of water are an object of desire and contest; and such is the scarcity of wood, that some art is requisite to preserve and propagate the element of fire. Arabia is destitute of navigable rivers, which fertilize the soil, and convey its produce to the adjacent regions: the torrents that fall from the hills are imbibed by the thirsty earth: the rare and hardy plants, the tamarind or the acacia, that strike their roots into the clefts of the rocks, are nourished by the dews of the night: a scanty supply of rain is collected in cisterns and aqueducts:

The soil and climate.

---

the most copious and correct account of the peninsula, which may be enriched, however, from the Bibliotheque Orientale of d'Herbelot, p. 120. et alibi passim. 3. The *European travellers*; among whom Shaw (p. 438–455.) and Niebuhr (Description, 1773. Voyages, tom. i. 1776) deserve an honourable distinction: Busching (Geographie par Berenger, tom. viii. p. 416–510.) has compiled with judgment; and d'Anville's Maps (Orbis Veteribus Notus, and 1re Partie de l'Asie) should lie before the reader, with his Geographie Ancienne, tom. ii. p. 208–231.

3. Abulfed. Descript. Arabiæ, p. 1. D'Anville, l'Euphrate et le Tigre, p. 19, 20. It was in this place, the paradise or garden of a satrap, that Xenophon and the Greeks first passed the Euphrates (Anabasis, l. i. c. 10. p. 29. edit. Wells).

4. Reland has proved, with much superfluous learning, 1. That our Red Sea (the Arabian Gulf) is no more than a part of the *Mare Rubrum*, the Ερυθρα θαλασση of the ancients, which was extended to the indefinite space of the Indian ocean. 2. That the synonymous words ερυθρος, αιθιοψς, allude to the colour of the blacks or negroes (Dissert. Miscell. tom. i. p. 59–117.).

the wells and springs are the secret treasure of the desert; and the pilgrim of Mecca,[5] after many a dry and sultry march, is disgusted by the taste of the waters, which have rolled over a bed of sulphur or salt. Such is the general and genuine picture of the climate of Arabia. The experience of evil enhances the value of any local or partial enjoyments. A shady grove, a green pasture, a stream of fresh water, are sufficient to attract a colony of sedentary Arabs to the fortunate spots which can afford food and refreshment to themselves and their cattle, and which encourage their industry in the cultivation of the palm-tree and the vine. The high lands that border on the Indian ocean are distinguished by their superior plenty of wood and water: the air is more temperate, the fruits are more delicious, the animals and the human race more numerous; the fertility of the soil invites and rewards the toil of the husbandman; and the peculiar gifts of frankincense[6] and coffee have attracted in different ages the merchants of the world. If it be compared with the rest of the peninsula, this sequestered region may truly deserve the appellation of the *happy*; and the splendid colouring of fancy and fiction has been suggested by contrast and countenanced by distance. It was for this earthly paradise that nature had reserved her choicest favours and her most curious workmanship: the incompatible blessings of luxury and innocence were ascribed to the natives: the soil was impregnated with gold[7] and gems, and both the land and sea were taught to exhale the odours of aromatic sweets. This division of the *sandy*, and *stony*, and the *happy*, so familiar to the Greeks and Latins, is unknown to the Arabians themselves; and it is singular enough, that a country, whose language and inhabitants have ever been the same, should scarcely retain a vestige of its ancient geography. The maritime districts of *Bahrein* and *Oman* are opposite to the realm of Persia. The kingdom of *Yemen* displays the limits, or at least the situation, of Arabia Fœlix: the name of *Neged* is extended over the inland space; and the birth

Division of the sandy, the stony, and the happy, Arabia.

5. In the thirty days, or stations, between Cairo and Mecca, there are fifteen destitute of good water. See the route of the Hadjees, in Shaw's Travels, p. 477.

6. The aromatics, especially the *thus* or frankincense, of Arabia, occupy the xii[th] book of Pliny. Our great poet (Paradise Lost, l. iv.) introduces, in a simile, the spicy odours that are blown by the north-east wind from the Sabæan coast:

—— Many a league,
Pleas'd with the grateful scent, old
Ocean smiles.
(Plin. Hist. Natur. xii. 42.)

7. Agatharcides affirms, that lumps of pure gold were found, from the size of an olive to that of a nut; that iron was twice, and silver ten times, the value of gold (de Mari Rubro, p. 60.). These real or imaginary treasures are vanished; and no gold mines are at present known in Arabia (Niebuhr, Description, p. 124.).

of Mahomet has illustrated the province of *Hejaz* along the coast of the Red Sea.[8]

Manners of the Bedoweens, or pastoral Arabs.

The measure of population is regulated by the means of subsistence; and the inhabitants of this vast peninsula might be out-numbered by the subjects of a fertile and industrious province. Along the shores of the Persian gulf, of the ocean, and even of the Red Sea, the *Icthyophagi*,[9] or fish-eaters, continued to wander in quest of their precarious food. In this primitive and abject state, which ill deserves the name of society, the human brute, without arts or laws, almost without sense or language, is poorly distinguished from the rest of the animal creation. Generations and ages might roll away in silent oblivion, and the helpless savage was restrained from multiplying his race, by the wants and pursuits which confined his existence to the narrow margin of the sea-coast. But in an early period of antiquity the great body of the Arabs had emerged from this scene of misery; and as the naked wilderness could not maintain a people of hunters, they rose at once to the more secure and plentiful condition of the pastoral life. The same life is uniformly pursued by the roving tribes of the desert, and in the portrait of the modern *Bedoweens*, we may trace the features of their ancestors,[10] who, in the age of Moses or Mahomet, dwelt under similar tents, and conducted their horses, and camels, and sheep, to the same springs and the same pastures. Our toil is lessened, and our wealth is encreased, by our dominion over the useful animals; and the Arabian shepherd had acquired the absolute possession of a faithful friend and a laborious slave.[11] Arabia, in the opinion of the naturalist, is the genuine

8. Consult, peruse, and study, the Specimen Historia Arabum of Pocock! (Oxon. 1650, in 4[to]). The thirty pages of text and version are extracted from the Dynasties of Gregory Abulpharagius, which Pocock afterwards translated (Oxon. 1663, in 4to): the three hundred and fifty-eight notes form a classic and original work on the Arabian antiquities.

9. Arrian remarks the Icthyophagi of the coast of Hejaz (Periplus Maris Erythræi, p. 12.) and beyond Aden (p. 15.). It seems probable that the shores of the Red Sea (in the largest sense) were occupied by these savages in the time, perhaps, of Cyrus; but I can hardly believe that any cannibals were left among the savages in the reign of Justinian (Procop. de Bell. Persic. l. i. c. 19.).

10. See the Specimen Historiæ Arabum of Pocock, p. 2. 5. 86, &c. The journey of M. d'Arvieux, in 1664, to the camp of the emir of Mount Carmel (Voyage de la Palestine, Amsterdam, 1718), exhibits a pleasing and original picture of the life of the Bedoweens, which may be illustrated from Niebuhr (Description de l'Arabie, p. 327–344.) and Volney (tom. i. p. 343–385.), the last and most judicious of our Syrian travellers.

11. Read (it is no unpleasing task) the incomparable articles of the *Horse* and the *Camel*, in the Natural History of M. de Buffon.

and original country of the *horse*; the climate most propitious, *The horse.* not indeed to the size, but to the spirit and swiftness, of that generous animal. The merit of the Barb, the Spanish, and the English breed, is derived from a mixture of Arabian blood:[12] the Bedoweens preserve, with superstitious care, the honours and the memory of the purest race: the males are sold at a high price, but the females are seldom alienated: and the birth of a noble foal was esteemed, among the tribes, as a subject of joy and mutual congratulation. These horses are educated in the tents, among the children of the Arabs, with a tender familiarity, which trains them in the habits of gentleness and attachment. They are accustomed only to walk and to gallop: their sensations are not blunted by the incessant abuse of the spur and the whip: their powers are reserved for the moments of flight and pursuit; but no sooner do they feel the touch of the hand or the stirrup, than they dart away with the swiftness of the wind; and if their friend be dismounted in the rapid career, they instantly stop till he has recovered his seat. In the sands of Afric and Arabia, the *camel* is a sacred and precious gift. That strong and patient beast *The camel.* of burthen can perform, without eating or drinking, a journey of several days; and a reservoir of fresh water is preserved in a large bag, a fifth stomach of the animal, whose body is imprinted with the marks of servitude: the larger breed is capable of transporting a weight of a thousand pounds; and the dromedary, of a lighter and more active frame, outstrips the fleetest courser in the race. Alive or dead, almost every part of the camel is serviceable to man: her milk is plentiful and nutritious: the young and tender flesh has the taste of veal:[13] a valuable salt is extracted from the urine: the dung supplies the deficiency of fuel; and the long hair, which falls each year and is renewed, is coarsely manufactured into the garments, the furniture, and the tents, of the Bedoweens. In the rainy seasons they consume the rare and insufficient herbage of the desert: during the heats of summer and the scarcity of winter, they remove their

12. For the Arabian horses, see d'Arvieux (p. 159–173.) and Niebuhr (p. 142–144.). At the end of the xiii[th] century, the horses of Neged were esteemed sure-footed, those of Yemen strong and serviceable, those of Hejaz most noble. The horses of Europe, the tenth and last class, were generally despised, as having too much body and too little spirit (d'Herbelot, Bibliot. Orient. p. 339.): their strength was requisite to bear the weight of the knight and his armour.

13. Qui carnibus camelorum vesci solent odii tenaces sunt, was the opinion of an Arabian physician (Pocock, Specimen, p. 88.). Mahomet himself, who was fond of milk, prefers the cow, and does not even mention the camel; but the diet of Mecca and Medina was already more luxurious (Gagnier, Vie de Mahomet, tom. iii. p. 404.).

encampments to the sea-coast, the hills of Yemen, or the neighbourhood of the Euphrates, and have often extorted the dangerous licence of visiting the banks of the Nile, and the villages of Syria and Palestine. The life of a wandering Arab is a life of danger and distress; and though sometimes, by rapine or exchange, he may appropriate the fruits of industry, a private citizen in Europe is in the possession of more solid and pleasing luxury than the proudest emir, who marches in the field at the head of ten thousand horse.

Cities of Arabia: Yet an essential difference may be found between the hords of Scythia and the Arabian tribes, since many of the latter were collected into towns, and employed in the labours of trade and agriculture. A part of their time and industry was still devoted to the management of their cattle: they mingled, in peace and war, with their brethren of the desert; and the Bedoweens derived from their useful intercourse, some supply of their wants, and some rudiments of art and knowledge. Among the forty-two cities of Arabia,[14] enumerated by Abulfeda, the most ancient and populous were situate in the *happy* Yemen: the towers of Saana,[15] and the marvellous reservoir of Merab,[16] were constructed by the kings of the Homerites; but their profane lustre was eclipsed by the prophetic glories of MEDINA[17] and MECCA,[18] near the Red Sea, and at the distance

14. Yet Marcian of Heraclea (in Periplo, p. 16. in tom. i. Hudson, Minor Geograph.) reckons one hundred and sixty-four towns in Arabia Fœlix. The size of the towns might be small – the faith of the writer might be large.

15. It is compared by Abulfeda (in Hudson, tom. iii. p. 54) to Damascus, and is still the residence of the Imam of Yemen (Voyages de Niebuhr, tom. i. p. 331–342.). Saana is twenty-four parasangs from Dafar (Abulfeda, p. 51.), and sixty-eight from Aden (p. 53.).

16. Pocock, Specimen, p. 57. Geograph. Nubiensis, p. 52. Meriaba, or Merab, six miles in circumference, was destroyed by the legions of Augustus (Plin. Hist. Nat. vi. 32.), and had not revived in the xiv^th^ century (Abulfed. Descript. Arab. p. 58.).

17. The name of *city*, *Medina*, was appropriated, κατ'ἐξοχην, to Yatreb (the Iatrippa of the Greeks), the seat of the prophet. The distances from Medina are reckoned by Abulfeda in stations, or days journey of a caravan (p. 15.): to Bahrein, xv; to Bassora, xviii; to Cufah, xx; to Damascus or Palestine, xx; to Cairo, xxv; to Mecca, x; from Mecca to Saana (p. 52.) or Aden, xxx; to Cairo, xxxi days, or 412 hours (Shaw's Travels, p. 477.); which, according to the estimate of d'Anville (Mesures Itineraires, p. 99.), allows about twenty-five English miles for a day's journey. From the land of frankincense (Hadramaut, in Yemen, between Aden and Cape Fartasch) to Gaza, in Syria, Pliny (Hist. Nat. xii. 32.) computes lxv mansions of camels. These measures may assist fancy and elucidate facts.

18. Our notions of Mecca must be drawn from the Arabians (d'Herbelot, Bibliotheque Orientale, p. 368–371. Pocock, Specimen, p. 125–128. Abulfeda, p. 11–40.). As no unbeliever is permitted to enter

from each other of two hundred and seventy miles. The last of these holy places was known to the Greeks under the name of Macoraba; and the termination of the word is expressive of its greatness, which has not indeed, in the most flourishing period, exceeded the size and populousness of Marseilles. Some latent motive, perhaps of superstition, must have impelled the founders, in the choice of a most unpromising situation. They erected their habitations of mud or stone, in a plain about two miles long and one mile broad, at the foot of three barren mountains: the soil is a rock; the water even of the holy well of Zemzem is bitter or brackish; the pastures are remote from the city; and grapes are transported above seventy miles from the gardens of Tayef. The fame and spirit of the Koreishites, who reigned in Mecca, were conspicuous among the Arabian tribes; but their ungrateful soil refused the labours of agriculture, and their position was favourable to the enterprises of trade. By the sea-port of Gedda, at the distance only of forty miles, they maintained an easy correspondence with Abyssinia; and that Christian kingdom afforded the first refuge to the disciples of Mahomet. The treasures of Africa were conveyed over the peninsula to Gerrha or Katif, in the province of Bahrein, a city built, as it is said, of rock-salt, by the Chaldean exiles:[19] and from thence, with the native pearls of the Persian Gulf, they were floated on rafts to the mouth of the Euphrates. Mecca is placed almost at an equal distance, a month's journey, between Yemen on the right, and Syria on the left hand. The former was the winter, the latter the summer, station of her caravans; and their seasonable arrival relieved the ships of India from the tedious and troublesome navigation of the Red Sea. In the markets of Saana and Merab, in the harbours of Oman and Aden, the camels of the Koreishites were laden with a precious cargo of aromatics; a supply of corn and manufactures was purchased in the fairs of Bostra and Damascus; the lucrative exchange diffused plenty and riches in the streets of Mecca; and the noblest of her sons united the love of arms with the profession of merchandise.[20]

Mecca;

her trade.

---

the city, our travellers are silent; and the short hints of Thevenot (Voyages du Levant, part i. p. 490.) are taken from the suspicious mouth of an African renegado. Some Persians counted 6000 houses (Chardin, tom. iv. p. 167.).

19. Strabo, l. xvi. p. 1110. See one of these salt houses near Bassora, in d'Herbelot, Bibliot. Orient. p. 6.

20. Mirum dictû ex innumeris populis pars æqua in *commerciis* aut in latrociniis degit (Plin. Hist. Nat. vi. 32.). See Sale's Koran. Surat cvi. p. 503. Pocock, Specimen, p. 2. D'Herbelot, Bibliot. Orient. p. 361. Prideaux's Life of Mahomet, p. 5. Gagnier, Vie de Mahomet, tom. i. p. 72. 120. 126, &c.

National independence of the Arabs. The perpetual independence of the Arabs has been the theme of praise among strangers and natives; and the arts of controversy transform this singular event into a prophecy and a miracle, in favour of the posterity of Ismael.[21] Some exceptions, that can neither be dissembled nor eluded, render this mode of reasoning as indiscreet as it is superfluous: the kingdom of Yemen has been successively subdued by the Abyssinians, the Persians, the sultans of Egypt,[22] and the Turks:[23] the holy cities of Mecca and Medina have repeatedly bowed under a Scythian tyrant; and the Roman province of Arabia[24] embraced the peculiar wilderness in which Ismael and his sons must have pitched their tents in the face of their brethren. Yet these exceptions are temporary or local; the body of the nation has escaped the yoke of the most powerful monarchies: the arms of Sesostris and Cyrus, of Pompey and Trajan, could never atchieve the conquest of Arabia; the present sovereign of the Turks[25] may exercise a shadow of jurisdiction, but his pride is reduced to solicit the friendship of a people, whom it is dangerous to provoke and fruitless to attack. The obvious causes of their freedom are inscribed on the character and country of the Arabs. Many ages before

21. A nameless doctor (Universal Hist. vol. xx. octavo edition) has formally *demonstrated* the truth of Christianity by the independence of the Arabs. A critic, besides the exceptions of fact, might dispute the meaning of the text (Genes. xvi. 12.), the extent of the application, and the foundation of the pedigree.

22. It was subdued, A.D. 1173, by a brother of the great Saladin, who founded a dynasty of Curds or Ayoubites (Guignes, Hist. des Huns, tom. i. p. 425. D'Herbelot, p. 477.).

23. By the lieutenant of Soliman I. (A.D. 1538) and Selim II. (1568). See Cantemir's Hist. of the Othman empire, p. 201. 221. The Pasha, who resided at Saana, commanded twenty-one Beys, but no revenue was ever remitted to the Porte (Marsigli, Stato Militare dell' Imperio Ottomanno, p. 124.), and the Turks were expelled about the year 1630 (Niebuhr. p. 167, 168.).

24. Of the Roman province, under the name of Arabia and the third Palestine, the principal cities were Bostra and Petra, which dated their æra from the year 105, when they were subdued by Palma a lieutenant of Trajan (Dion Cassius, l. lxviii.). Petra was the capital of the Nabathæans; whose name is derived from the eldest of the sons of Ismael (Genes. xxv. 12, &c. with the Commentaries of Jerom, Le Clerc, and Calmet). Justinian relinquished a palm country of ten days journey to the south of Ælah (Procop. de Bell. Persic. l. i. c. 19.), and the Romans maintained a centurion and a custom-house (Arrian in Periplo Maris Erythræi, p. 11. in Hudson, tom. i.), at a place (λευκη κωμη, Pagus Albus Hawara) in the territory of Medina (d'Anville Memoire sur l'Egypte, p. 243.). These real possessions, and some naval inroads of Trajan (Peripl. p. 14, 15.), are magnified by history and medals into the Roman conquest of Arabia.

25. Niebuhr (Description de l'Arabie, p. 302, 303. 329–331.) affords the most recent and authentic intelligence of the Turkish empire in Arabia.

Mahomet,[26] their intrepid valour had been severely felt by their neighbours in offensive and defensive war. The patient and active virtues of a soldier are insensibly nursed in the habits and discipline of a pastoral life. The care of the sheep and camels is abandoned to the women of the tribe; but the martial youth under the banner of the emir, is ever on horseback, and in the field, to practise the exercise of the bow, the javelin, and the scymetar. The long memory of their independence is the firmest pledge of its perpetuity, and succeeding generations are animated to prove their descent and to maintain their inheritance. Their domestic feuds are suspended on the approach of a common enemy; and in their last hostilities against the Turks, the caravan of Mecca was attacked and pillaged by fourscore thousand of the confederates. When they advance to battle, the hope of victory is in the front; in the rear, the assurance of a retreat. Their horses and camels, who in eight or ten days can perform a march of four or five hundred miles, disappear before the conqueror; the secret waters of the desert elude his search; and his victorious troops are consumed with thirst, hunger, and fatigue, in the pursuit of an invisible foe, who scorns his efforts, and safely reposes in the heart of the burning solitude. The arms and deserts of the Bedoweens are not only the safeguards of their own freedom, but the barriers also of the happy Arabia, whose inhabitants, remote from war, are enervated by the luxury of the soil and climate. The legions of Augustus melted away in disease and lassitude;[27] and it is only by a naval power that the reduction of Yemen has been successfully attempted. When Mahomet erected his holy standard,[28] that kingdom was a province of the Persian empire; yet seven princes of the Homerites still reigned in the mountains; and the vicegerent of Chosroes was tempted to forget his distant country and his unfortunate master. The historians of the age of Justinian represent the state of the independent Arabs, who were divided by interest or affection in the long quarrel of the East: the tribe of *Gassan* was allowed to encamp on the Syrian territory: the princes of *Hira* were permitted to form a city

26. Diodorus Siculus (tom. ii. l. xix. p. 390–393. edit. Wesseling) has clearly exposed the freedom of the Nabathæan Arabs, who resisted the arms of Antigonus and his son.

27. Strabo, l. xvi. p. 1127–1129. Plin. Hist. Natur. vi. 32. Ælius Gallus landed near Medina, and marched near a thousand miles into the part of Yemen between Mareb and the Ocean. The non ante devictis Sabeæ regibus (Od. i. 29.), and the intacti Arabum thesauri (Od. iii. 24.) of Horace, attest the virgin purity of Arabia.

28. See the imperfect history of Yemen in Pocock, Specimen. p. 55–66. of Hira, p. 66–74. of Gassan, p. 75–78. as far as it could be known or preserved in the time of ignorance.

about forty miles to the southward of the ruins of Babylon. Their service in the field was speedy and vigorous; but their friendship was venal, their faith inconstant, their enmity capricious: it was an easier task to excite than to disarm these roving Barbarians; and, in the familiar intercourse of war, they learned to see, and to despise, the splendid weakness both of Rome and of Persia. From Mecca to the Euphrates, the Arabian tribes[29] were confounded by the Greeks and Latins, under the general appellation of SARACENS,[30] a name which every Christian mouth has been taught to pronounce with terror and abhorrence.

Their domestic freedom and character.

The slaves of domestic tyranny may vainly exult in their national independence; but the Arab is personally free; and he enjoys, in some degree, the benefits of society, without forfeiting the prerogatives of nature. In every tribe, superstition, or gratitude, or fortune, has exalted a particular family above the heads of their equals. The dignities of sheich and emir invariably descend in this chosen race; but the order of succession is loose and precarious; and the most worthy or aged of the noble kinsmen are preferred to the simple, though important, office of composing disputes by their advice, and guiding valour by their example. Even a female of sense and spirit has been permitted to command the countrymen of Zenobia.[31] The momentary junction of several tribes produces an army: their more lasting union constitutes a nation; and the supreme chief, the emir of emirs, whose banner is displayed at their head, may deserve, in the eyes of strangers, the honours of the kingly name. If the Arabian princes abuse their power, they are

29. The *Σαρακηνικα φυλα, μυριαδες ταυτα, και πο πλειστον αυτων ερημονομοι, και αδεσποτοι*, are described by Menander (Excerpt. Legation. p. 149.), Procopius (de Bell. Persic. l. i. c. 17. 19. l. ii. c. 10.); and, in the most lively colours, by Ammianus Marcellinus (l. xiv. c. 4.), who had spoken of them as early as the reign of Marcus.

30. The name which, used by Ptolemy and Pliny in a more confined, by Ammianus and Procopius in a larger, sense, has been derived, ridiculously, from *Sarah*, the wife of Abraham, obscurely from the village of *Saraka* (*μετα Ναβαταιους*. Stephan. de Urbibus), more plausibly from the Arabic words, which signify a *thievish* character, or *Oriental* situation, (Hottinger, Hist. Oriental. l. i. c. i. p. 7, 8. Pocock, Specimen, p. 33–35. Asseman. Bibliot. Orient. tom. iv. p. 567.). Yet the last and most popular of these etymologies, is refuted by Ptolemy (Arabia, p. 2. 18. in Hudson, tom. iv.), who expressly remarks the western and southern position of the Saracens, then an obscure tribe on the borders of Egypt. The appellation cannot therefore allude to any *national* character; and, since it was imposed by strangers, it must be found, not in the Arabic, but in a foreign language.

31. Saraceni . . . mulieres aiunt in eos regnare (Expositio totius Mundi, p. 3. in Hudson, tom. iii.). The reign of Mavia is famous in ecclesiastical story. Pocock, Specimen, p. 69. 83.

quickly punished by the desertion of their subjects, who had been accustomed to a mild and parental jurisdiction. Their spirit is free, their steps are unconfined, the desert is open, and the tribes and families are held together by a mutual and voluntary compact. The softer natives of Yemen supported the pomp and majesty of a monarch; but if he could not leave his palace without endangering his life,[32] the active powers of government must have been devolved on his nobles and magistrates. The cities of Mecca and Medina present, in the heart of Asia, the form, or rather the substance, of a commonwealth. The grandfather of Mahomet, and his lineal ancestors, appear in foreign and domestic transactions as the princes of their country; but they reigned, like Pericles at Athens, or the Medici at Florence, by the opinion of their wisdom and integrity; their influence was divided with their patrimony; and the sceptre was transferred from the uncles of the prophet to a younger branch of the tribe of Koreish. On solemn occasions they convened the assembly of the people; and, since mankind must be either compelled or persuaded to obey, the use and reputation of oratory among the ancient Arabs is the clearest evidence of public freedom.[33] But their simple freedom was of a very different cast from the nice and artificial machinery of the Greek and Roman republics, in which each member possessed an undivided share of the civil and political rights of the community. In the more simple state of the Arabs, the nation is free, because each of her sons disdains a base submission to the will of a master. His breast is fortified with the austere virtues of courage, patience, and sobriety: the love of independence prompts him to exercise the habits of self-command; and the fear of dishonour guards him from the meaner apprehension of pain, of danger, and of death. The gravity and firmness of the mind is conspicuous in his outward demeanor: his speech is slow, weighty, and concise, he is seldom provoked to laughter, his only gesture is that of stroking his beard, the venerable symbol of manhood; and the sense of his own importance teaches him to accost his equals without levity, and his superiors without awe.[34] The liberty of the Saracens survived their

32. *Μη εξειναι εκ των βασιλειων*, is the report of Agatharades (de Mari Rubro, p. 63, 64. in Hudson, tom. i.), Diodorus Siculus (tom. i. l. iii. c. 47. p. 215.), and Strabo (l. xvi. p. 1124.). But I much suspect that this is one of the popular tales, or extraordinary accidents, which the credulity of travellers so often transforms into a fact, a custom, and a law.

33. Non gloriabantur antiquitus Arabes, nisi gladio, hospite, et *eloquentiâ* (Sephadius, apud Pocock, Specimen, p. 161, 162.). This gift of speech they shared only with the Persians; and the sententious Arabs would probably have disdained the simple and sublime logic of Demosthenes.

34. I must remind the reader that d'Arvieux, d'Herbelot, and Niebuhr, represent,

conquests: the first caliphs indulged the bold and familiar language of their subjects: they ascended the pulpit to persuade and edify the congregation; nor was it before the seat of empire was removed to the Tigris, that the Abbassides adopted the proud and pompous ceremonial of the Persian and Byzantine courts.

Civil wars and private revenge.

In the study of nations and men, we may observe the causes that render them hostile or friendly to each other, that tend to narrow or enlarge, to mollify or exasperate, the social character. The separation of the Arabs from the rest of mankind, has accustomed them to confound the ideas of stranger and enemy; and the poverty of the land has introduced a maxim of jurisprudence, which they believe and practise to the present hour. They pretend, that in the division of the earth the rich and fertile climates were assigned to the other branches of the human family; and that the posterity of the outlaw Ismael might recover, by fraud or force, the portion of inheritance of which he had been unjustly deprived. According to the remark of Pliny, the Arabian tribes are equally addicted to theft and merchandise: the caravans that traverse the desert are ransomed or pillaged; and their neighbours, since the remote times of Job and Sesostris,[35] have been the victims of their rapacious spirit. If a Bedoween discovers from afar a solitary traveller, he rides furiously against him, crying, with a loud voice, "Undress thyself, thy aunt (*my wife*) is without a garment." A ready submission entitles him to mercy; resistance will provoke the aggressor, and his own blood must expiate the blood which he presumes to shed in legitimate defence. A single robber, or a few associates, are branded with their genuine name; but the exploits of a numerous band assume the character of lawful and honourable war. The temper of a people, thus armed against mankind, was doubly inflamed by the domestic licence of rapine, murder, and revenge. In the constitution of Europe, the right of peace and war is now confined to a small, and the actual exercise to a much smaller, list of respectable potentates; but each Arab, with impunity and renown, might point his javelin against the life of his countryman. The union of the nation consisted only in a vague resemblance of language and manners;

---

in the most lively colours, the manners and government of the Arabs, which are illustrated by many incidental passages in the life of Mahomet.

35. Observe the first chapter of Job, and the long wall of 1500 stadia, which Sesostris built from Pelusium to Heliopolis (Diodor. Sicul. tom. i. l. i. p. 67.). Under the name of *Hycsos*, the shepherd-kings, they had formerly subdued Egypt (Marsham, Canon. Chron. p. 98–163, &c.).

and in each community, the jurisdiction of the magistrate was mute and impotent. Of the time of ignorance which preceded Mahomet, seventeen hundred battles[36] are recorded by tradition: hostility was embittered with the rancour of civil faction; and the recital, in prose or verse, of an obsolete feud was sufficient to rekindle the same passions among the descendents of the hostile tribes. In private life, every man, at least every family, was the judge and avenger of its own cause. The nice sensibility of honour, which weighs the insult rather than the injury, sheds its deadly venom on the quarrels of the Arabs: the honour of their women, and of their *beards*, is most easily wounded; an indecent action, a contemptuous word, can be expiated only by the blood of the offender; and such is their patient inveteracy, that they expect whole months and years the opportunity of revenge. A fine or compensation for murder is familiar to the Barbarians of every age: but in Arabia the kinsmen of the dead are at liberty to accept the atonement, or to exercise with their own hands the law of retaliation. The refined malice of the Arabs refuses even the head of the murderer, substitutes an innocent to the guilty person, and transfers the penalty to the best and most considerable of the race by whom they have been injured. If he falls by their hands, they are exposed in their turn to the danger of reprisals, the interest and principal of the bloody debt are accumulated; the individuals of either family lead a life of malice and suspicion, and fifty years may sometimes elapse before the account of vengeance be finally settled.[37] This sanguinary spirit, ignorant of pity or forgiveness, has been moderated, however, by the maxims of honour, which require in every private encounter some decent equality of age and strength, of numbers and weapons. An annual festival of two, perhaps of four, months, was observed by the Arabs before the time of Mahomet, during which their swords were religiously sheathed both in foreign and domestic hostility; and this partial truce is more strongly expressive of the habits of anarchy and warfare.[38]

Annual truce.

36. Or, according to another account, 1200 (d'Herbelot, Bibliotheque Orientale, p. 75.): the two historians who wrote of the *Ayam al Arab*, the battles of the Arabs, lived in the ixth and xth century. The famous war of Dahes and Gabrah was occasioned by two horses, lasted forty years, and ended in a proverb (Pocock, Specimen, p. 48.).

37. The modern theory and practice of the Arabs in the revenge of murder, are described by Niebuhr (Description, p. 26–31.). The harsher features of antiquity may be traced in the Koran, c. 2. p. 20. c. 17. p. 230. with Sale's Observations.

38. Procopius (de Bell. Persic. l. i. c. 16.) places the *two* holy months about the summer solstice. The Arabians consecrate *four* months of the year – the first, seventh, eleventh, and twelfth; and pretend, that in a long series of ages the truce was infringed only four or six times (Sale's Preliminary Discourse, p. 147–150. and Notes on the

Their social qualifications and virtues. But the spirit of rapine and revenge was attempered by the milder influence of trade and literature. The solitary peninsula is encompassed by the most civilized nations of the ancient world: the merchant is the friend of mankind; and the annual caravans imported the first seeds of knowledge and politeness into the cities, and even the camps of the desert. Whatever may be the pedigree of the Arabs, their language is derived from the same original stock with the Hebrew, the Syriac, and the Chaldæan tongues; the independence of the tribes was marked by their peculiar dialects;[39] but each, after their own, allowed a just preference to the pure and perspicuous idiom of Mecca. In Arabia as well as in Greece, the perfection of language outstripped the refinement of manners; and her speech could diversify the fourscore names of honey, the two hundred of a serpent, the five hundred of a lion, the thousand of a sword, at a time when this copious dictionary was entrusted to the memory of an illiterate people. The monuments of the Homerites were inscribed with an obsolete and mysterious character; but the Cufic letters, the ground-work of the present alphabet, were invented on the banks of the Euphrates; and the recent invention was taught at Mecca by a stranger who settled in that city after the birth of Mahomet. The arts of grammar, of metre, and of rhetoric, were unknown to the freeborn eloquence of the Arabians; but their penetration was sharp, their fancy luxuriant, their wit strong and sententious,[40] and their more elaborate compositions were addressed with energy and effect to the minds of their hearers. The genius *Love of poetry.* and merit of a rising poet was celebrated by the applause of his own and the kindred tribes. A solemn banquet was prepared, and a chorus of women, striking their tymbals, and displaying the pomp of their nuptials, sung in the presence of their sons and husbands the felicity of their native tribe; that a champion had now appeared to vindicate

---

ix[th] chapter of the Koran, p. 154, &c. Casiri, Bibliot. Hispano-Arabica, tom. ii. p. 20, 21.).

39. Arrian, in the second century, remarks (in Periplo Maris Erythræi, p. 12.) the partial or total difference of the dialects of the Arabs. Their language and letters are copiously treated by Pocock (Specimen, p. 150–154.), Casiri (Bibliot. Hispano-Arabica, tom. i. p. 1. 83. 292. tom. ii. p. 25, &c.), and Niebuhr (Description de l'Arabie, p. 72–86.). I pass slightly; I am not fond of repeating words like a parrot.

40. A familiar tale in Voltaire's Zadig (le Chien et le Cheval) is related, to prove the natural sagacity of the Arabs (d'Herbelot, Bibliot. Orient. p. 120, 121. Gagnier, Vie de Mahomet, tom. i. p. 37–46.); but d'Arvieux, or rather La Roque (Voyage de Palestine, p. 92.), denies the boasted superiority of the Bedoweens. The one hundred and sixty-nine sentences of Ali (translated by Ockley, London, 1718) afford a just and favourable specimen of Arabian wit.

their rights; that a herald had raised his voice to immortalise their renown. The distant or hostile tribes resorted to an annual fair which was abolished by the fanaticism of the first Moslems; a national assembly that must have contributed to refine and harmonise the Barbarians. Thirty days were employed in the exchange, not only of corn and wine, but of eloquence and poetry. The prize was disputed by the generous emulation of the bards; the victorious performance was deposited in the archives of princes and emirs; and we may read in our own language, the seven original poems which were inscribed in letters of gold, and suspended in the temple of Mecca.[41] The Arabian poets were the historians and moralists of the age; and if they sympathised with the prejudices, they inspired and crowned the virtues, of their countrymen. The indissoluble union of generosity and valour was the darling theme of their song; and when they pointed their keenest satire against a despicable race, they affirmed, in the bitterness of reproach, that the men knew not how to give, nor the women to deny.[42] The same hospitality, which was practised by Abraham and celebrated by Homer, is still renewed in the camps of the Arabs. The ferocious Bedoweens, the terror of the desert, embrace, without enquiry or hesitation, the stranger who dares to confide in their honour and to enter their tent. His treatment is kind and respectful: he shares the wealth or the poverty of his host; and, after a needful repose, he is dismissed on his way, with thanks, with blessings, and perhaps with gifts. The heart and hand are more largely expanded by the wants of a brother or a friend; but the heroic acts that could deserve the public applause, must have surpassed the narrow measure of discretion and experience. A dispute had arisen, who, among the citizens of Mecca, was entitled to the prize of generosity; and a successive application was made to the three who were deemed most worthy of the trial. Abdallah, the son of Abbas, had undertaken a distant journey, and his foot was in the stirrup when he heard the voice of a suppliant, "O son of the uncle of the apostle of God, I am a traveller and in distress." He instantly dismounted to present the pilgrim with his camel, her rich caparison, and a purse of four thousand pieces of gold, excepting only

Examples of generosity.

41. Pocock (Specimen, p. 158–161.) and Casiri (Bibliot. Hispano-Arabica, tom. i. p. 48. 84, &c. 119. tom. ii. p. 17, &c.) speak of the Arabian poets before Mahomet: the seven poems of the Caaba have been published in English by Sir William Jones; but his honourable mission to India has deprived us of his own notes, far more interesting than the obscure and obsolete text.

42. Sale's Preliminary Discourse, p. 29, 30.

the sword, either for its intrinsic value, or as the gift of an honoured kinsman. The servant of Kais informed the second suppliant that his master was asleep; but he immediately added, "Here is a purse of seven thousand pieces of gold (it is all we have in the house), and here is an order, that will entitle you to a camel and a slave;" the master, as soon as he awoke, praised and enfranchised his faithful steward, with a gentle reproof, that by respecting his slumbers he had stinted his bounty. The third of these heroes, the blind Arabah, at the hour of prayer, was supporting his steps on the shoulders of two slaves. "Alas!" he replied, "my coffers are empty! but these you may sell; if you refuse, I renounce them." At these words, pushing away the youths, he groped along the wall with his staff. The character of Hatem is the perfect model of Arabian virtue;[43] he was brave and liberal, an eloquent poet and a successful robber: forty camels were roasted at his hospitable feasts; and at the prayer of a suppliant enemy, he restored both the captives and the spoil. The freedom of his countrymen disdained the laws of justice: they proudly indulged the spontaneous impulse of pity and benevolence.

Ancient idolatry. The religion of the Arabs,[44] as well as of the Indians, consisted in the worship of the sun, the moon, and the fixed stars, a primitive and specious mode of superstition. The bright luminaries of the sky display the visible image of a Deity: their number and distance convey to a philosophic, or even a vulgar, eye, the idea of boundless space: the character of eternity is marked on these solid globes, that seem incapable of corruption or decay: the regularity of their motions may be ascribed to a principle of reason or instinct; and their real or imaginary influence encourages the vain belief that the earth and its inhabitants are the object of their peculiar care. The science of astronomy was cultivated at Babylon; but the school of the Arabs was a clear firmament and a naked plain. In their nocturnal marches, they steered by the guidance of the stars: their names, and order, and daily station, were familiar to the curiosity and devotion of the Bedoween; and he was taught by experience

43. D'Herbelot, Bibliot. Orient. p. 458. Gagnier, Vie de Mahomet, tom. iii. p. 118. Caab and Hesnus (Pocock, Specimen, p. 43. 46. 48.) were likewise conspicuous for their liberality; and the latter is elegantly praised by an Arabian poet: "Videbis eum cum accesseris exultantem, ac si dares illi quod ab illo petis."

44. Whatever can now be known of the idolatry of the ancient Arabians, may be found in Pocock (Specimen, p. 89–136. 163, 164.). His profound erudition is more clearly and concisely interpreted by Sale (Preliminary Discourse, p. 14–24.); and Assemanni (Bibliot. Orient. tom. iv. p. 580–590.) has added some valuable remarks.

to divide in twenty-eight parts, the zodiac of the moon, and to bless the constellations who refreshed, with salutary rains, the thirst of the desert. The reign of the heavenly orbs could not be extended beyond the visible sphere; and some metaphysical powers were necessary to sustain the transmigration of souls and the resurrection of bodies: a camel was left to perish on the grave, that he might serve his master in another life; and the invocation of departed spirits implies that they were still endowed with consciousness and power. I am ignorant, and I am careless, of the blind mythology of the Barbarians; of the local deities, of the stars, the air, and the earth, of their sex or titles, their attributes or subordination. Each tribe, each family, each independent warrior, created and changed the rites and the object of his fantastic worship; but the nation, in every age, has bowed to the religion, as well as to the language, of Mecca. The genuine antiquity of the CAABA ascends beyond the Christian æra: in describing the coast of the Red Sea, the Greek historian Diodorus[45] has remarked, between the Thamudites and the Sabæans, a famous temple, whose superior sanctity was revered by *all* the Arabians: the linen or silken veil, which is annually renewed by the Turkish emperor, was first offered by a pious king of the Homerites, who reigned seven hundred years before the time of Mahomet.[46] A tent or a cavern might suffice for the worship of the savages, but an edifice of stone and clay has been erected in its place; and the art and power of the monarchs of the East have been confined to the simplicity of the original model.[47] A spacious portico incloses the quadrangle of the Caaba; a square chapel, twenty-four cubits long, twenty-three broad, and twenty-

The Caaba, or temple of Mecca.

45. *Ιερον αγιωτατον ιδρυται τιμωμενον ὑπο παντων Αραβων περιττοτερον* (Diodor. Sicul. tom. i. l. iii. p. 211.). The character and position are so correctly apposite, that I am surprised how this curious passage should have been read without notice or application. Yet this famous temple had been overlooked by Agatharcides (de Mari Rubro, p. 58. in Hudson, tom. i.), whom Diodorus copies in the rest of the description. Was the Sicilian more knowing than the Egyptian? Or was the Caaba built between the years of Rome 650 and 746, the dates of their respective histories? (Dodwell, in Dissert. ad tom. i. Hudson, p. 72. Fabricius, Bibliot. Græc. tom. ii. p. 770.)

46. Pocock, Specimen, p. 60, 61. From the death of Mahomet we ascend to 68, from his birth to 129, years, before the Christian æra. The veil or curtain, which is now of silk and gold, was no more than a piece of Egyptian linen (Abulfeda, in Vit. Mohammed. c. 6. p. 14.).

47. The original plan of the Caaba (which is servilely copied in Sale, the Universal History, &c.) was a Turkish draught, which Reland (de Religione Mohammedicâ, p. 113–123.) has corrected and explained from the best authorities. For the description and legend of the Caaba, consult Pocock (Specimen, p. 115–122.), the

seven high: a door and a window admit the light; the double roof is supported by three pillars of wood; a spout (now of gold) discharges the rain-water, and the well Zemzem is protected by a dome from accidental pollution. The tribe of Koreish, by fraud or force, had acquired the custody of the Caaba: the sacerdotal office devolved through four lineal descents to the grandfather of Mahomet; and the family of the Hashemites, from whence he sprung, was the most respectable and sacred in the eyes of their country.[48] The precincts of Mecca enjoyed the rights of sanctuary; and, in the last month of each year, the city and the temple were crowded with a long train of pilgrims, who presented their vows and offerings in the house of God. The same rites, which are now accomplished by the faithful Musulman, were invented and practised by the superstition of the idolaters. At an awful distance they cast away their garments: seven times, with hasty steps, they encircled the Caaba, and kissed the black stone: seven times they visited and adored the adjacent mountains: seven times they threw stones into the valley of Mina; and the pilgrimage was atchieved, as at the present hour, by a sacrifice of sheep and camels, and the burial of their hair and nails in the consecrated ground. Each tribe either found or introduced in the Caaba their domestic worship: the temple was adorned, or defiled, with three hundred and sixty idols of men, eagles, lions, and antelopes; and most conspicuous was the statue of Hebal, of red agate, holding in his hand seven arrows, without heads or feathers, the instruments and symbols of profane divination. But this statue was a monument of Syrian arts: the devotion of the ruder ages was content with a pillar or a tablet; and the rocks of the desert were hewn into gods or altars, in imitation of the black stone[49] of Mecca, which is deeply tainted with the reproach of an idolatrous origin.

Sacrifices and rites.

From Japan to Peru, the use of sacrifice has universally prevailed; and the votary has expressed his gratitude, or fear, by destroying

---

Bibliotheque Orientale of d'Herbelot (*Caaba, Hagier, Zemzem*, &c.), and Sale (Preliminary Discourse, p. 114–122.).

48. Cosa, the fifth ancestor of Mahomet, must have usurped the Caaba A.D. 440; but the story is differently told by Jannabi (Gagnier, Vie de Mahomet, tom. i. p. 65–69.) and by Abulfeda (in Vit. Moham. c. 6. p. 13.).

49. In the second century, Maximus of Tyre attributes to the Arabs the worship of a stone – *Αραβιοι σεβουσι μεν, οντινα δε ουκ οιδα, το δε αγαλμα ειδον; λιθος ην τετραγωνος* (dissert. viii. tom. i. p. 142. edit. Reiske); and the reproach is furiously re-echoed by the Christians (Clemens Alex. in Protreptico, p. 40. Arnobius contra Gentes, l. vi. p. 246.). Yet these stones were no other than the *βαιτυλα* of Syria and Greece, so renowned in sacred and profane antiquity (Euseb. Præp. Evangel. l. i. p. 37. Marsham, Canon. Chron. p. 54–56.).

or consuming, in honour of the gods, the dearest and most precious of their gifts. The life of a man[50] is the most precious oblation to deprecate a public calamity: the altars of Phœnicia and Egypt, of Rome and Carthage, have been polluted with human gore: the cruel practice was long preserved among the Arabs; in the third century, a boy was annually sacrificed by the tribe of the Dumatians;[51] and a royal captive was piously slaughtered by the prince of the Saracens, the ally and soldier of the emperor Justinian.[52] A parent who drags his son to the altar, exhibits the most painful and sublime effort of fanaticism: the deed, or the intention, was sanctified by the example of saints and heroes; and the father of Mahomet himself was devoted by a rash vow, and hardly ransomed for the equivalent of an hundred camels. In the time of ignorance, the Arabs, like the Jews and Egyptians, abstained from the taste of swine's flesh;[53] they circumcised[54] their children at the age of puberty: the same customs, without the censure or the precept of the Koran, have been silently transmitted to their posterity and proselytes. It has been sagaciously conjectured, that the artful legislator indulged the stubborn prejudices of his countrymen. It is more simple to believe that he adhered to the habits and opinions of his youth, without foreseeing that a practice congenial

50. The two horrid subjects of *Ανδροθυσια* and *Παιδοθυσια*, are accurately discussed by the learned Sir John Marsham (Canon. Chron. p. 76–78. 301–304.). Sanchoniatho derives the Phœnician sacrifices from the example of Chronus; but we are ignorant whether Chronus lived before or after Abraham, or indeed whether he lived at all.

51. *Κατ' ετος εκαστον παιδα εθυον*, is the reproach of Porphyry; but he likewise imputes to the Roman the same barbarous custom, which, A.U.C. 657, had been finally abolished. Dumætha, Daumat al Gendal, is noticed by Ptolemy (Tabul. p. 37. Arabia, p. 9–29.) and Abulfeda (p. 57.); and may be found in d'Anville's maps, in the mid-desert between Chaibar and Tadmor.

52. Procopius (de Bell. Persico, l. i. c. 28.), Evagrius (l. vi. c. 21.), and Pocock (Specimen, p. 72. 86.), attest the human sacrifices of the Arabs in the vi^th^ century. The danger and escape of Abdallah, is a tradition rather than a fact (Gagnier, Vie de Mahomet, tom. i. p. 82–84.).

53. Suillis carnibus abstinent, says Solinus (Polyhistor. c. 33.), who copies Pliny (l. viii. c. 68.) in the strange supposition, that hogs cannot live in Arabia. The Egyptians were actuated by a natural and superstitious horror for that unclean beast (Marsham, Canon. p. 205.). The old Arabians likewise practised, *post coitum*, the rite of ablution (Herodot. l. i. c. 80.), which is sanctified by the Mahometan law (Reland, p. 75, &c. Chardin, or rather the *Mollah* of Shaw Abbas, tom. iv. p. 71, &c.).

54. The Mahometan doctors are not fond of the subject; yet they hold circumcision necessary to salvation, and even pretend that Mahomet was miraculously born without a foreskin (Pocock, Specimen, p. 319, 320. Sale's Preliminary Discourse, p. 106, 107.).

to the climate of Mecca, might become useless or inconvenient on the banks of the Danube or the Volga.

Introduction of the Sabians. Arabia was free: the adjacent kingdoms were shaken by the storms of conquest and tyranny, and the persecuted sects fled to the happy land where they might profess what they thought, and practice what they professed. The religions of the Sabians and Magians, of the Jews and Christians, were disseminated from the Persian Gulf to the Red Sea. In a remote period of antiquity, Sabianism was diffused over Asia by the science of the Chaldæans[55] and the arms of the Assyrians. From the observations of two thousand years, the priests and astronomers of Babylon[56] deduced the eternal laws of nature and providence. They adored the seven gods or angels who directed the course of the seven planets, and shed their irresistible influence on the earth. The attributes of the seven planets, with the twelve signs of the zodiac, and the twenty-four constellations of the northern and southern hemisphere, were represented by images and talismans; the seven days of the week were dedicated to their respective deities; the Sabians prayed thrice each day; and the temple of the moon at Haran was the term of their pilgrimage.[57] But the flexible genius of their faith was always ready either to teach or to learn: in the tradition of the creation, the deluge, and the patriarchs, they held a singular agreement with their Jewish captives; they appealed to the secret books of Adam, Seth, and Enoch; and a slight infusion of the gospel has transformed the last remnant of the Polytheists into the Christians of St. John, in the territory of Bassora.[58] The altars of Babylon

55. Diodorus Siculus (tom. i. l. ii. p. 142–145.) has cast on their religion the curious but superficial glance of a Greek. Their astronomy would be far more valuable: they had looked through the telescope of reason, since they could doubt whether the sun were in the number of the planets or of the fixed stars.

56. Simplicius (who quotes Porphyry), de Cœlo, l. ii. com. xlvi. p. 123. lin. 18. apud Marsham, Canon. Chron. p. 474. who doubts the fact, because it is adverse to his systems. The earliest date of the Chaldean observations is the year 2234 before Christ. After the conquest of Babylon by Alexander, they were communicated, at the request of Aristotle, to the astronomer Hipparchus. What a moment in the annals of science!

57. Pocock (Specimen, p. 138–146.), Hottinger (Hist. Oriental. p. 162–203.), Hyde (de Religione Vet. Persarum, p. 124. 128, &c.), d'Herbelot (*Sabi*, p. 725, 726.), and Sale (Preliminary Discourse, p. 14, 15.), rather excite than gratify our curiosity; and the last of these writers confounds Sabianism with the primitive religion of the Arabs.

58. D'Anville (l'Euphrate et le Tigre, p. 130–147.) will fix the position of these ambiguous Christians; Assemannus (Bibliot. Oriental. tom. iv. p. 607–614.) may explain their tenets. But it is a slippery task to ascertain the creed of an ignorant people, afraid and ashamed to disclose their secret traditions.

were overturned by the Magians; but the injuries of the Sabians *The Magians.* were revenged by the sword of Alexander; Persia groaned above five hundred years under a foreign yoke; and the purest disciples of Zoroaster escaped from the contagion of idolatry, and breathed with their adversaries the freedom of the desert.[59] Seven hundred years before the death of Mahomet, the Jews were settled in Arabia: and a far greater *The Jews.* multitude was expelled from the holy land in the wars of Titus and Hadrian. The industrious exiles aspired to liberty and power: they erected synagogues in the cities and castles in the wilderness, and their Gentile converts were confounded with the children of Israel, whom they resembled in the outward mark of circumcision. The Christian *The Christians.* missionaries were still more active and successful: the Catholics asserted their universal reign; the sects whom they oppressed successively retired beyond the limits of the Roman empire; the Marcionites and Manichæans dispersed their *phantastic* opinions and apocryphal gospels; the churches of Yemen, and the princes of Hira and Gassan, were instructed in a purer creed by the Jacobite and Nestorian bishops.[60] The liberty of choice was presented to the tribes: each Arab was free to elect or to compose his private religion: and the rude superstition of his house was mingled with the sublime theology of saints and philosophers. A fundamental article of faith was inculcated by the consent of the learned strangers; the existence of one supreme God, who is exalted above the powers of heaven and earth, but who has often revealed himself to mankind by the ministry of his angels and prophets, and whose grace or justice has interrupted, by seasonable miracles, the order of nature. The most rational of the Arabs acknowledged his power, though they neglected his worship;[61] and it was habit rather than conviction that still attached them to the relics of idolatry. The Jews and Christians were the people of the *book*; the bible was already translated into the Arabic language,[62] and the

59. The Magi were fixed in the province of Bahrein (Gagnier, Vie de Mahomet, tom. iii. p. 114.), and mingled with the old Arabians (Pocock, Specimen, p. 146–150.).

60. The state of the Jews and Christians in Arabia, is described by Pocock from Sharestani, &c. (Specimen, p. 60. 134, &c.), Hottinger (Hist. Orient. p. 212–238), d'Herbelot (Bibliot. Orient. p. 474–476.), Basnage (Hist. des Juifs, tom. vii. p. 185. tom. viii. p. 280.), and Sale (Preliminary Discourse, p. 22, &c. 33, &c.).

61. In their offerings it was a maxim to defraud God for the profit of the idol, not a more potent, but a more irritable patron (Pocock, Specimen, p. 108, 109.).

62. Our versions now extant, whether Jewish or Christian, appear more recent than the Koran; but the existence of a prior translation may be fairly inferred, 1. From the perpetual practice of the synagogue, of expounding the Hebrew lesson by a paraphrase in the vulgar tongue of the country. 2. From the analogy of the

volume of the old testament was accepted by the concord of these implacable enemies. In the story of the Hebrew patriarchs, the Arabs were pleased to discover the fathers of their nation. They applauded the birth and promises of Ismael; revered the faith and virtue of Abraham; traced his pedigree and their own to the creation of the first man, and imbibed with equal credulity, the prodigies of the holy text, and the dreams and traditions of the Jewish rabbis.

Birth and education of Mahomet, A.D. 569–609.

The base and plebeian origin of Mahomet is an unskilful calumny of the Christians,[63] who exalt instead of degrading the merit of their adversary. His descent from Ismael was a national privilege or fable; but if the first steps of the pedigree[64] are dark and doubtful, he could produce many generations of pure and genuine nobility: he sprung from the tribe of Koreish and the family of Hashem, the most illustrious of the Arabs, the princes of Mecca, and the hereditary guardians of the Caaba. The grandfather of Mahomet was Abdol Motalleb, the son of Hashem, a wealthy and generous citizen, who relieved the distress of famine with the supplies of commerce. Mecca, which had been fed by the liberality of the father, was saved by the courage of the son. The kingdom of Yemen was subject to the Christian princes of Abyssinia; their vassal Abrahah was provoked by an insult to avenge the honour of the cross; and the holy city was invested by a train of elephants and an army of Africans. A treaty was proposed; and in the first audience, the grandfather of Mahomet demanded the restitution of his cattle. "And why," said Abrahah, "do you not rather implore my clemency in favour of your temple, which I have threatened to destroy?" "Because," replied the intrepid chief, "the cattle is my own; the Caaba belongs to the gods, and *they* will defend their house from

Armenian, Persian, Æthiopic versions, expressly quoted by the fathers of the fifth century, who assert that the Scriptures were translated into *all* the Barbaric languages (Walton, Prolegomena ad Biblia Polyglot. p. 34. 93–97.). Simon, Hist. Critique du V. et du N. Testament, tom. i. p. 180, 181, 282–286. 293. 305, 306. tom. iv. p. 206.).

63. In eo conveniunt omnes, ut plebeio vilique genere ortum, &c. (Hottinger, Hist. Orient. p. 136.). Yet Theophanes, the most ancient of the Greeks, and the father of many a lie, confesses that Mahomet was of the race of Ismael, εκ μιας γενικωτατης φυλης (Chronograph. p. 277.).

64. Abulfeda (in Vit. Mohammed. c. 1, 2.) and Gagnier (Vie de Mahomet, p. 25–97.) describe the popular and approved genealogy of the prophet. At Mecca, I would not dispute its authenticity; at Lausanne, I will venture to observe, 1. *That* from Ismael to Mahomet, a period of 2500 years, they reckon thirty, instead of seventy-five, generations. 2. *That* the modern Bedoweens are ignorant of their history and careless of their pedigree (Voyage de d'Arvieux, p. 100. 103.).

injury and sacrilege." The want of provisions, or the valour of the Koreish, compelled the Abyssinians to a disgraceful retreat; their discomfiture has been adorned with a miraculous flight of birds, who showered down stones on the heads of the infidels; and the deliverance was long commemorated by the æra of the elephant.[65] The glory of Abdol Motalleb was crowned with domestic happiness, his life was prolonged to the age of one hundred and ten years, and he became the father of six daughters and thirteen sons. His best beloved Abdallah was the most beautiful and modest of the Arabian youth; and in the first night, when he consummated his marriage with Amina, of the noble race of the Zahrites, two hundred virgins are said to have expired of jealousy and despair. Mahomet, or more properly Mohammed, the only son of Abdallah and Amina, was born at Mecca, four years after the death of Justinian, and two months after the defeat of the Abyssinians,[66] whose victory would have introduced into the Caaba the religion of the Christians. In his early infancy, he was deprived of his father, his mother, and his grandfather; his uncles were strong and numerous; and in the division of the inheritance, the orphan's share was reduced to five camels and an Æthiopian maid-servant. At home and abroad, in peace and war, Abu Taleb, the most respectable of his uncles, was the guide and guardian of his youth; in his twenty-fifth year, he entered into the service of Cadijah, a rich and noble widow of Mecca, who soon rewarded his fidelity with the gift of her hand and fortune. The marriage-contract, in the simple style of antiquity, recites the mutual love of Mahomet and Cadijah;

Deliverance of Mecca.

65. The seed of this history, or fable, is contained in the cv[th] chapter of the Koran; and Gagnier (in Præfat. ad Vit. Moham. p. 18, &c.) has translated the historical narrative of Abulfeda, which may be illustrated from d'Herbelot. (Bibliot. Orientale, p. 12.), and Pocock (Specimen, p. 64.). Prideaux (Life of Mahomet, p. 48.) calls it a lie of the coinage of Mahomet; but Sale (Koran, p. 501–503.), who is half a Musulman, attacks the inconsistent faith of the Doctor for believing the miracles of the Delphic Apollo. Maracci (Alcoran, tom. i. part ii. p. 14. tom. ii. p. 823.) ascribes the miracle to the devil, and extorts from the Mahometans the confession, that God would not have defended against the Christians the idols of the Caaba.

66. The safest æras of Abulfeda (in Vit. c. i. p. 2.), of Alexander, or the Greeks, 882, of Bocht Naser, or Nabonasser, 1316, equally lead us to the year 569. The old Arabian calendar is too dark and uncertain to support the Benedictines (Art de verifier les Dates, p. 15.), who from the day of the month and week deduce a new mode of calculation, and remove the birth of Mahomet to the year of Christ 570, the 10th of November. Yet this date would agree with the year 882 of the Greeks, which is assigned by Elmacin (Hist. Saracen. p. 5.) and Abulpharagius (Dynast. p. 101. and Errata Pocock's version). While we refine our chronology, it is possible that the illiterate prophet was ignorant of his own age.

describes him as the most accomplished of the tribe of Koreish; and stipulates a dowry of twelve ounces of gold and twenty camels, which was supplied by the liberality of his uncle.[67] By this alliance, the son of Abdallah was restored to the station of his ancestors; and the judicious matron was content with his domestic virtues, till, in the fortieth year of his age,[68] he assumed the title of a prophet, and proclaimed the religion of the Koran.

Qualifications of the prophet.

According to the tradition of his companions, Mahomet[69] was distinguished by the beauty of his person, an outward gift which is seldom despised, except by those to whom it has been refused. Before he spoke, the orator engaged on his side the affections of a public or private audience. They applauded his commanding presence, his majestic aspect, his piercing eye, his gracious smile, his flowing beard, his countenance that painted every sensation of the soul, and his gestures that enforced each expression of the tongue. In the familiar offices of life he scrupulously adhered to the grave and ceremonious politeness of his country: his respectful attention to the rich and powerful was dignified by his condescension and affability to the poorest citizens of Mecca: the frankness of his manner concealed the artifice of his views; and the habits of courtesy were imputed to personal friendship or universal benevolence. His memory was capacious and retentive, his wit easy and social, his imagination sublime, his judgment clear, rapid, and decisive. He possessed the courage both of thought and action; and, although his designs might gradually expand with his success, the first idea which he entertained of his divine mission bears the stamp of an original and superior genius.

67. I copy the honourable testimony of Abu Taleb to his family and nephew. Laus Dei, qui nos a stirpe Abrahami et femine Ismaelis constituit, et nobis regionem sacram dedit, et nos judices hominibus statuit. Porro Mohammed filius Abdollahi nepotis mei *(nepos meus)* quo cum ex æquo librabitur e Koraishidis quispiam cui non præponderaturus est, bonitate et excellantiâ, et intellectû et gloria et acumine etsi opum inops fuerit (et certe opes umbra transiens sunt et depositum quod reddi debet), desiderio Chadijæ filiæ Chowailedi tenetur, et illa vicissim ipsius, quicquid autem dotis vice petieritis, ego in me suscipiam (Pocock, Specimen, e septimâ parte libri Ebn Hamduni).

68. The private life of Mahomet, from his birth to his mission, is preserved by Abulfeda (in Vit. c. 3–7.), and the Arabian writers of genuine or apocryphal note, who are alleged by Hottinger (Hist. Orient. p. 204–211.), Maracci (tom. i. p. 10–14.), and Gagnier (Vie de Mahomet, tom. i. p. 97–134.).

69. Abulfeda, in Vit. c. lxv, lxvi. Gagnier, Vie de Mahomet, tom. iii. p. 272–289.; the best traditions of the person and conversation of the prophet are derived from Ayesha, Ali and Abu Horaira (Gagnier, tom. ii. p. 267. Ockley's Hist. of the Saracens, vol. ii. p. 149.), surnamed the father of a cat, who died in the year 59 of the Hegira.

The son of Abdallah was educated in the bosom of the noblest race, in the use of the purest dialect of Arabia; and the fluency of his speech was corrected and enhanced by the practice of discreet and seasonable silence. With these powers of eloquence, Mahomet was an illiterate Barbarian: his youth had never been instructed in the arts of reading and writing;[70] the common ignorance exempted him from shame or reproach, but he was reduced to a narrow circle of existence, and deprived of those faithful mirrors, which reflect to our mind the minds of sages and heroes. Yet the book of nature and of man was open to his view; and some fancy has been indulged in the political and philosophical observations which are ascribed to the Arabian *traveller*.[71] He compares the nations and the religions of the earth; discovers the weakness of the Persian and Roman monarchies; beholds, with pity and indignation, the degeneracy of the times; and resolves to unite, under one God and one king, the invincible spirit and primitive virtues of the Arabs. Our more accurate enquiry will suggest, that instead of visiting the courts, the camps, the temples of the East, the two journies of Mahomet into Syria were confined to the fairs of Bostra and Damascus: that he was only thirteen years of age when he accompanied the caravan of his uncle, and that his duty compelled him to return as soon as he had disposed of the merchandise of Cadijah. In these hasty and superficial excursions, the eye of genius might discern some objects invisible to his grosser companions; some seeds of

70. Those who believe that Mahomet could read or write, are incapable of reading what is written, with another pen, in the Surats, or chapters of the Koran vii. xxix. xcvi. These texts, and the traditions of the Sonna, are admitted, without doubt, by Abulfeda (in Vit. c. vii.), Gagnier (Not. ad Abulfed. p. 15.), Pocock (Specimen, p. 151.), Reland (de Religione Mohammedicâ, p. 236.), and Sale (Preliminary Discourse, p. 42.). Mr. White, almost alone, denies the ignorance, to accuse the imposture, of the prophet. His arguments are far from satisfactory. Two short trading journies to the fairs of Syria, were surely not sufficient to infuse a science so rare among the citizens of Mecca: it was not in the cool deliberate act of a treaty, that Mahomet would have dropt the mask; nor can any conclusion be drawn from the words of disease and delirium. The *lettered* youth, before he aspired to the prophetic character, must have often exercised, in private life, the arts of reading and writing; and his first converts, of his own family, would have been the first to detect and upbraid his scandalous hypocrisy (White's Sermons, p. 203. 204. Notes, p. xxxvi–xxxviii.).

71. The Count de Boulainvilliers (Vie de Mahomed, p. 202–228.) leads his Arabian pupil, like the Telemachus of Fenelon, or the Cyrus of Ramsay. His journey to the court of Persia is probably a fiction; nor can I trace the origin of his exclamation, "Les Grecs sont pourtant des hommes." The two Syrian journies are expressed by almost all the Arabian writers, both Mahometans and Christians (Gagnier ad Abulfed. p. 10.).

knowledge might be cast upon a fruitful soil; but his ignorance of the Syriac language must have checked his curiosity; and I cannot perceive, in the life or writings of Mahomet, that his prospect was far extended beyond the limits of the Arabian world. From every region of that solitary world, the pilgrims of Mecca were annually assembled, by the calls of devotion and commerce: in the free concourse of multitudes, a simple citizen, in his native tongue, might study the political state and character of the tribes, the theory and practice of the Jews and Christians. Some useful strangers might be tempted, or forced, to implore the rights of hospitality; and the enemies of Mahomet have named the Jew, the Persian, and the Syrian monk, whom they accuse of lending their secret aid to the composition of the Koran.[72] Conversation enriches the understanding, but solitude is the school of genius; and the uniformity of a work denotes the hand of a single artist. From his earliest youth, Mahomet was addicted to religious contemplation: each year, during the month of Ramadan, he withdrew from the world, and from the arms of Cadijah: in the cave of Hera, three miles from Mecca,[73] he consulted the spirit of fraud or enthusiasm, whose abode is not in the heavens, but in the mind of the prophet. The faith which, under the name of *Islam*, he preached to his family and nation, is compounded of an eternal truth, and a necessary fiction, THAT THERE IS ONLY ONE GOD, AND THAT MAHOMET IS THE APOSTLE OF GOD.

One God. It is the boast of the Jewish apologists, that while the learned nations of antiquity were deluded by the fables of polytheism, their simple ancestors of Palestine preserved the knowledge and worship of the true God. The moral attributes of Jehovah may not easily be reconciled with the standard of *human* virtue: his metaphysical qualities are darkly expressed; but each page of the Pentateuch and the Prophets is an evidence of his power: the unity of his name is inscribed on the first table of the law; and his sanctuary was never defiled by any visible image of the invisible essence. After the ruin of the temple, the faith of the Hebrew exiles was purified, fixed, and enlightened, by the spiritual devotion of the

72. I am not at leisure to pursue the fables or conjectures which name the strangers accused or suspected by the infidels of Mecca (Koran, c. 16. p. 223. c. 35. p. 297. with Sale's Remarks. Prideaux's Life of Mahomet, p. 22–27. Gagnier, Not. ad Abulfed. p. 11. 74. Maracci, tom. ii. p. 400.). Even Prideaux has observed, that the transaction must have been secret, and that the scene lay in the heart of Arabia.

73. Abulfeda in Vit. c. 7. p. 15. Gagnier, tom. i. p. 133. 135. The situation of mount Hera is remarked by Abulfeda (Geograph. Arab. p. 4.). Yet Mahomet had never read of the cave of Egeria, ubi nocturnæ Numa constituebat amicæ, of the Idæan mount, where Minos conversed with Jove, &c.

synagogue; and the authority of Mahomet will not justify his perpetual reproach, that the Jews of Mecca or Medina adored Ezra as the son of God.[74] But the children of Israel had ceased to be a people; and the religions of the world were guilty, at least in the eyes of the prophet, of giving sons, or daughters, or companions, to the supreme God. In the rude idolatry of the Arabs, the crime is manifest and audacious: the Sabians are poorly excused by the pre-eminence of the first planet, or intelligence, in their cœlestial hierarchy; and in the Magian system the conflict of the two principles betrays the imperfection of the conqueror. The Christians of the seventh century had insensibly relapsed into a semblance of paganism: their public and private vows were addressed to the relics and images that disgraced the temples of the East: the throne of the Almighty was darkened by a cloud of martyrs, and saints, and angels, the objects of popular veneration; and the Collyridian heretics, who flourished in the fruitful soil of Arabia, invested the Virgin Mary with the name and honours of a goddess.[75] The mysteries of the Trinity and Incarnation *appear* to contradict the principle of the divine unity. In their obvious sense, they introduce three equal deities, and transform the man Jesus into the substance of the son of God:[76] an orthodox commentary will satisfy only a believing mind: intemperate curiosity and zeal had torn the veil of the sanctuary; and each of the Oriental sects was eager to confess that all, except themselves, deserved the reproach of idolatry and polytheism. The creed of Mahomet is free from suspicion or ambiguity; and the Koran is a glorious testimony to the unity of God. The prophet of Mecca rejected the worship of idols and men, of stars and planets, on the rational principle that whatever rises must set, that

74. Koran, c. 9. p. 153. Al Beidawi, and the other commentators quoted by Sale, adhere to the charge; but I do not understand that it is coloured by the most obscure or absurd tradition of the Talmudists.

75. Hottinger, Hist. Orient. p. 225–228. The Collyridian heresy was carried from Thrace to Arabia by some women, and the name was borrowed from the κολλυρις, or cake, which they offered to the goddess. This example, that of Beryllus bishop of Bostra (Euseb. Hist. Eccles. l. vi. c. 33.), and several others, may excuse the reproach, Arabia hærefeωn ferax.

76. The three gods in the Koran, (c. 4. p. 81. c. 5. p. 92.) are obviously directed against our Catholic mystery: but the Arabic commentators understand them of the Father, the Son, and the Virgin Mary, an heretical Trinity, maintained, as it is said, by some Barbarians at the council of Nice (Eutych. Annal. tom. i. p. 440.). But the existence of the *Marianites* is denied by the candid Beausobre (Hist. de Manicheisme, tom. i. p. 532.): and he derives the mistake from the word *Rouah*, the Holy Ghost, which in some Oriental tongues is of the feminine gender, and is figuratively styled the mother of Christ in the gospel of the Nazarenes.

whatever is born must die, that whatever is corruptible must decay and perish.[77] In the Author of the universe, his rational enthusiasm confessed and adored an infinite and eternal being, without form or place, without issue or similitude, present to our most secret thoughts, existing by the necessity of his own nature, and deriving from himself all moral and intellectual perfection. These sublime truths, thus announced in the language of the prophet,[78] are firmly held by his disciples, and defined with metaphysical precision by the interpreters of the Koran. A philosophic theist might subscribe the popular creed of the Mahometans;[79] a creed too sublime perhaps for our present faculties. What object remains for the fancy, or even the understanding, when we have abstracted from the unknown substance all ideas of time and space, of motion and matter, of sensation and reflection? The first principle of reason and revelation was confirmed by the voice of Mahomet: his proselytes, from India to Morocco, are distinguished by the name of *Unitarians*; and the danger of idolatry has been prevented by the interdiction of images. The doctrine of eternal decrees and absolute predestination is strictly embraced by the Mahometans; and they struggle with the common difficulties, *how* to reconcile the prescience of God with the freedom and responsibility of man; *how* to explain the permission of evil under the reign of infinite power and infinite goodness.

Mahomet, the apostle of God, and the last of the prophets.

The God of nature has written his existence on all his works, and his law in the heart of man. To restore the knowledge of the one and the practice of the other, has been the real or pretended aim of the prophets of every age: the liberality of Mahomet allowed to his predecessors the same credit which he claimed for himself; and the chain of inspiration was prolonged from the fall of Adam to the promulgation of the Koran.[80] During that period,

77. This train of thought is philosophically exemplified in the character of Abraham, who opposed in Chaldæa the first introduction of idolatry (Koran, c. 6. p. 106. d'Herbelot, Bibliot. Orient. p. 13.).

78. See the Koran, particularly the second (p. 30.), the fifty-seventh (p. 437.), the fifty-eighth (p. 441.) chapter, which proclaim the omnipotence of the Creator.

79. The most orthodox creeds are translated by Pocock (Specimen, p. 274. 284–292.), Ockley (Hist. of the Saracens, vol. ii. p. lxxxii–xcv.), Reland (de Religion. Moham. l. i. p. 7–13.), and Chardin (Voyages en Perse, tom. iv. p. 4–28.). The great truth, that God is without similitude, is foolishly criticised by Maracci (Alcoran, tom. i. part iii. p. 87–94.), because he made man after his own image.

80. Reland, de Relig. Moham. l. i. p. 17–47. Sale's Preliminary Discourse, p. 73–76. Voyage de Chardin, tom. iv. p. 28–37. and 37–47. for the Persian addition, "Ali is the vicar of God!" Yet the precise number of prophets is not an article of faith.

some rays of prophetic light had been imparted to one hundred and twenty-four thousand of the elect, discriminated by their respective measure of virtue and grace; three hundred and thirteen apostles were sent with a special commission to recal their country from idolatry and vice; one hundred and four volumes have been dictated by the holy spirit; and six legislators of transcendent brightness have announced to mankind the six successive revelations of various rites, but of one immutable religion. The authority and station of Adam, Noah, Abraham, Moses, Christ, and Mahomet, rise in just gradation above each other; but whosoever hates or rejects any one of the prophets, is numbered with the infidels. The writings of the patriarchs were extant only in the apocryphal copies of the Greeks and Syrians:[81] the conduct of Adam had not entitled him to the gratitude or respect of his children; the seven precepts of Noah were observed by an inferior and imperfect class of the proselytes of the synagogue;[82] and the memory of Abraham was obscurely revered by the Sabians in his native land of Chaldæa: of the myriads of prophets, Moses and Christ alone lived and reigned; and the remnant of the inspired writings was comprised in the books of the Old and the New Testament. The miraculous story of Moses is consecrated and embellished in the Koran;[83] and the captive Jews enjoy the secret revenge of imposing their own belief on the nations whose recent creeds they deride. For the author of Christianity, the Mahometans are taught by the prophet to entertain an high and mysterious reverence.[84] "Verily, Christ Jesus, the son of Mary, is the apostle of God, and his word, which he conveyed unto Mary, and a Spirit proceeding from him: honourable in this world, and in the world to come; and one of those who approach near to the presence of God."[85] The wonders of the genuine and apocryphal gospels[86] are profusely heaped on his head; and

Moses.

Jesus.

81. For the apocryphal books of Adam, see Fabricius, Codex Pseudepigraphus V. T. p. 27–29.; of Seth, p. 154–157.; of Enoch, p. 160–219. But the book of Enoch is consecrated, in some measure, by the quotation of the apostle St. Jude; and a long legendary fragment is alleged by Syncellus and Scaliger.

82. The seven precepts of Noah are explained by Marsham (Canon. Chronicus, p. 154–180.), who adopts, on this occasion, the learning and credulity of Selden.

83. The articles of *Adam, Noah, Abraham, Moses*, &c. in the Bibliotheque of d'Herbelot, are gaily bedecked with the fanciful legends of the Mahometans, who have built on the ground-work of Scripture and the Talmud.

84. Koran, c. 7. p. 128, &c. c. 10. p. 173, &c. D'Herbelot, p. 647, &c.

85. Koran, c. 3. p. 40. c. 4. p. 80. D'Herbelot, p. 399, &c.

86. See the gospel of St. Thomas, or of the Infancy, in the Codex Apocryphus N. T. of Fabricius, who collects the various testimonies concerning it (p. 128–158.). It

the Latin church has not disdained to borrow from the Koran the immaculate conception[87] of his virgin mother. Yet Jesus was a mere mortal; and, at the day of judgment, his testimony will serve to condemn both the Jews, who reject him as a prophet, and the Christians, who adore him as the Son of God. The malice of his enemies aspersed his reputation, and conspired against his life; but their intention only was guilty, a phantom or a criminal was substituted on the cross, and the innocent saint was translated to the seventh heaven.[88] During six hundred years the gospel was the way of truth and salvation; but the Christians insensibly forgot both the laws and the example of their founder; and Mahomet was instructed by the Gnostics to accuse the church, as well as the synagogue, of corrupting the integrity of the sacred text.[89] The piety of Moses and of Christ rejoiced in the assurance of a future prophet, more illustrious than themselves: the evangelic promise of the *Paraclete*, or Holy Ghost, was prefigured in the name, and accomplished in the person, of Mahomet,[90] the greatest and the last of the apostles of God.

---

was published in Greek by Cotelier, and in Arabic by Sike, who thinks our present copy more recent than Mahomet. Yet his quotations agree with the original about the speech of Christ in his cradle, his living birds of clay, &c. (*Sike*, c. 1. p. 168, 169. c. 36. p. 198, 199. c. 46. p. 206. *Cotelier*, c. 2. p. 160, 161.).

87. It is darkly hinted in the Koran (c. 3. p. 39.), and more clearly explained by the tradition of the Sonnites (Sale's Note, and Maracci, tom. ii. p. 112.). In the xii[th] century, the immaculate conception was condemned by St. Bernard as a presumptuous novelty (Fra Paolo, Istoria del Concilio di Trento, l. ii.).

88. See the Koran, c. 3. v. 53. and c. 4. v. 156. of Maracci's edition. Deus est præstantissimus dolose agentium (an odd praise) . . . nec crucifixerunt eum, sed objecta est eis similitudo: an expression that may suit with the system of the Docetes; but the commentators believe (Maracci, tom. ii. p. 113–115. 173. Sale, p. 42. 43. 79.), that another man, a friend or an enemy, was crucified in the likeness of Jesus; a fable which they had read in the gospel of St. Barnabas, and which had been started as early as the time of Irenæus, by some Ebionite heretics (Beausobre, Hist. du Manicheisme, tom. ii. p. 25. Mosheim de Reb. Christ. p. 353.).

89. This charge is obscurely urged in the Koran (c. 3. p. 45.): but neither Mahomet, nor his followers, are sufficiently versed in languages and criticism to give any weight or colour to their suspicions. Yet the Arians and Nestorians could relate some stories, and the illiterate prophet might listen to the bold assertions of the Manichæans. See Beausobre, tom. i. p. 291–305.

90. Among the prophecies of the Old and New Testament, which are perverted by the fraud or ignorance of the Musulmans, they apply to the prophet the promise of the *Paraclete*, or Comforter, which had been already usurped by the Montanists and Manichæans (Beausobre, Hist. Critique du Manicheisme, tom. i. p. 263, &c.); and the easy change of letters, περικλυτος for παρακλητος, affords the etymology of the name of Mohammed (Maracci, tom. i. part i. p. 15–28.).

The communication of ideas requires a similitude of thought *The Koran.* and language: the discourse of a philosopher would vibrate without effect on the ear of a peasant; yet how minute is the distance of *their* understandings, if it be compared with the contact of an infinite and a finite mind, with the word of God expressed by the tongue or the pen of a mortal? The inspiration of the Hebrew prophets, of the apostles and evangelists of Christ, might not be incompatible with the exercise of their reason and memory; and the diversity of their genius is strongly marked in the style and composition of the books of the Old and New Testament. But Mahomet was content with a character, more humble, yet more sublime, of a simple editor: the substance of the Koran,[91] according to himself or his disciples, is uncreated and eternal; subsisting in the essence of the Deity, and inscribed with a pen of light on the table of his everlasting decrees. A paper copy in a volume of silk and gems, was brought down to the lowest heaven by the angel Gabriel, who, under the Jewish œconomy, had indeed been dispatched on the most important errands; and this trusty messenger successively revealed the chapters and verses to the Arabian prophet. Instead of a perpetual and perfect measure of the divine will, the fragments of the Koran were produced at the discretion of Mahomet; each revelation is suited to the emergencies of his policy or passion; and all contradiction is removed by the saving maxim, that any text of scripture is abrogated or modified by any subsequent passage. The word of God, and of the apostle, was diligently recorded by his disciples on palm-leaves and the shoulder-bones of mutton; and the pages, without order or connection, were cast into a domestic chest in the custody of one of his wives. Two years after the death of Mahomet, the sacred volume was collected and published by his friend and successor Abubeker: the work was revised by the caliph Othman, in the thirtieth year of the Hegira; and the various editions of the Koran assert the same miraculous privilege of an uniform and incorruptible text. In the spirit of enthusiasm or vanity, the prophet rests the truth of his mission on the merit of his book, audaciously challenges both men and angels to imitate the beauties of a single page, and presumes to assert that God alone could dictate this incomparable performance.[92] This argument is most powerfully addressed to a devout Arabian, whose mind is attuned to faith and rapture, whose ear is delighted by the

91. For the Koran, see d'Herbelot, p. 85–88. Maracci, tom. i. in Vit. Mohammed. p. 32–45. Sale, Preliminary Discourse, p. 56–70.

92. Koran, c. 17. v. 89. In Sale, p. 235, 236. In Maracci, p. 410.

music of sounds, and whose ignorance is incapable of comparing the productions of human genius.[93] The harmony and copiousness of style will not reach, in a version, the European infidel: he will peruse with impatience the endless incoherent rhapsody of fable, and precept, and declamation, which seldom excites a sentiment or an idea, which sometimes crawls in the dust, and is sometimes lost in the clouds. The divine attributes exalt the fancy of the Arabian missionary; but his loftiest strains must yield to the sublime simplicity of the book of Job, composed in a remote age, in the same country and in the same language.[94] If the composition of the Koran exceed the faculties of a man, to what superior intelligence should we ascribe the Iliad of Homer or the Philippics of Demosthenes? In all religions, the life of the founder supplies the silence of his written revelation: the sayings of Mahomet were so many lessons of truth; his actions so many examples of virtue; and the public and private memorials were preserved by his wives and companions. At the end of two hundred years, the *Sonna* or oral law was fixed and consecrated by the labours of Al Bochari, who discriminated seven thousand two hundred and seventy-five genuine traditions, from a mass of three hundred thousand reports, of a more doubtful or spurious character. Each day the pious author prayed in the temple of Mecca, and performed his ablutions with the water of Zemzem: the pages were successively deposited on the pulpit, and the sepulchre of the apostle; and the work has been approved by the four orthodox sects of the Sonnites.[95]

Miracles. The mission of the ancient prophets, of Moses and of Jesus, had been confirmed by many splendid prodigies; and Mahomet was repeatedly urged, by the inhabitants of Mecca and Medina, to produce a similar evidence of his divine legation; to call down from heaven the angel or the volume of his revelation, to create a garden in the desert, or to kindle a conflagration in the unbelieving city. As often as he is pressed

93. Yet a sect of Arabians was persuaded, that it might be equalled or surpassed by an human pen (Pocock, Specimen, p. 221, &c.); and Maracci (the polemic is too hard for the translator) derides the rhyming affectation of the most applauded passage (tom. i. part ii. p. 69–75.).

94. Colloquia (whether real or fabulous) in media Arabia atque ab Arabibus habita (Lowth, de Poesi Hebræorum Prælect. xxxii, xxxiii, xxxiv. with his German editor Michaelis, Epimetron iv.). Yet Michaelis (p. 671–673.) has detected many Egyptian images, the elephantiasis, papyrus, Nile, crocodile, &c. The language is ambiguously styled, *Arabico-Hebræa*. The resemblance of the sister dialects was much more visible in their childhood than in their mature age (Michaelis, p. 682. Schultens, in Præfat. Job).

95. Al Bochari died A.H. 224. See d'Herbelot, p. 208. 416. 827. Gagnier, Not. ad Abulfed. c. 19. p. 33.

by the demands of the Koreish, he involves himself in the obscure boast of vision and prophecy, appeals to the internal proofs of his doctrine, and shields himself behind the providence of God, who refuses those signs and wonders that would depreciate the merit of faith and aggravate the guilt of infidelity. But the modest or angry tone of his apologies betrays his weakness and vexation; and these passages of scandal establish, beyond suspicion, the integrity of the Koran.[96] The votaries of Mahomet are more assured than himself of his miraculous gifts, and their confidence and credulity encrease as they are farther removed from the time and place of his spiritual exploits. They believe or affirm that trees went forth to meet him; that he was saluted by stones; that water gushed from his fingers; that he fed the hungry, cured the sick, and raised the dead; that a beam groaned to him; that a camel complained to him; that a shoulder of mutton informed him of its being poisoned; and that both animate and inanimate nature were equally subject to the apostle of God.[97] His dream of a nocturnal journey is seriously described as a real and corporeal transaction. A mysterious animal, the Borak, conveyed him from the temple of Mecca to that of Jerusalem: with his companion Gabriel, he successively ascended the seven heavens, and received and repaid the salutations of the patriarchs, the prophets, and the angels, in their respective mansions. Beyond the seventh heaven, Mahomet alone was permitted to proceed; he passed the veil of unity, approached within two bow-shots of the throne, and felt a cold that pierced him to the heart, when his shoulder was touched by the hand of God. After this familiar though important conversation, he again descended to Jerusalem, remounted the Borak, returned to Mecca, and performed in the tenth part of a night the journey of many thousand years.[98] According to another legend, the apostle confounded in a national assembly the malicious challenge of

96. See more remarkably, Koran, c. 2. 6. 12. 13. 17. Prideaux (Life of Mahomet, p. 18, 19.) has confounded the impostor. Maracci, with a more learned apparatus, has shewn that the passages which deny his miracles are clear and positive (Alcoran, tom. i. part ii. p. 7–12.), and those which seem to assert them, are ambiguous and insufficient (p. 12–22.).

97. See the Specimen Hist. Arabum, the text of Abulpharagius, p. 17. the notes of Pocock, p. 187–190. D'Herbelot Bibliotheque Orientale, p. 76, 77. Voyages de Chardin, tom. iv. p. 200–203. Maracci (Alcoran, tom. i. p. 22–64.) has most laboriously collected and confuted the miracles and prophecies of Mahomet, which, according to some writers, amount to three thousand.

98. The nocturnal journey is circumstantially related by Abulfeda (in Vit. Mohammed. c. 19. p. 33.), who wishes to think it a vision; by Prideaux (p. 31–40.), who aggravates the absurdities; and by Gagnier (tom. i. p. 252–343.), who declares, from the zealous Al Jannabi, that to deny this journey, is to disbelieve the Koran. Yet the Koran, without naming

the Koreish. His resistless word split asunder the orb of the moon: the obedient planet stooped from her station in the sky, accomplished the seven revolutions round the Caaba, saluted Mahomet in the Arabian tongue, and suddenly contracting her dimensions, entered at the collar, and issued forth through the sleeve, of his shirt.[99] The vulgar are amused with these marvellous tales; but the gravest of the Musulman doctors imitate the modesty of their master, and indulge a latitude of faith or interpretation.[100] They might speciously allege, that in preaching the religion, it was needless to violate the harmony, of nature; that a creed unclouded with mystery may be excused from miracles; and that the sword of Mahomet was not less potent than the rod of Moses.

Precepts of Mahomet – prayer, fasting, alms.

The polytheist is oppressed and distracted by the variety of superstition: a thousand rites of Egyptian origin were interwoven with the essence of the Mosaic law; and the spirit of the gospel had evaporated in the pageantry of the church. The prophet of Mecca was tempted by prejudice, or policy, or patriotism, to sanctify the rites of the Arabians, and the custom of visiting the holy stone of the Caaba. But the precepts of Mahomet himself inculcate a more simple and rational piety: prayer, fasting, and alms, are the religious duties of a Musulman; and he is encouraged to hope, that prayer will carry him half way to God, fasting will bring him to the door of his palace, and alms will gain him admittance.[101] I. According to the tradition of the nocturnal journey, the apostle, in his personal conference with the

---

either heaven, or Jerusalem, or Mecca, has only dropt a mysterious hint: Laus illi qui transtulit servum suum ab oratorio Haram ad oratorium remotissimum (Koran, c. 17. v. 1. in Maracci, tom. ii. p. 407.; for Sale's version is more licentious). A slender basis for the aërial structure of tradition.

99. In the prophetic style, which uses the present or past for the future, Mahomet had said: Appropinquavit hora et scissa est luna (Koran, c. 54. v. 1. in Maracci, tom. ii. p. 688.). This figure of rhetoric has been converted into a fact, which is said to be attested by the most respectable eyewitnesses (Maracci, tom. ii. p. 690.). The festival is still celebrated by the Persians (Chardin, tom. iv. p. 201.); and the legend is tediously spun out by Gagnier (Vie de Mahomet, tom. i. p. 183–234.) on the faith, as it should seem, of the credulous Al Jannabi. Yet a Mahometan doctor has arraigned the credit of the principal witness (apud Pocock, Specimen, p. 187.); the best interpreters are content with the simple sense of the Koran (Al Beidawi, apud Hottinger, Hist. Orient. l. ii. p. 302); and the silence of Abulfeda is worthy of a prince and a philosopher.

100. Abulpharagius, in Specimen Hist. Arab. p. 17.; and his scepticism is justified in the notes of Pocock, p. 190–194. from the purest authorities.

101. The most authentic account of these precepts, pilgrimage, prayer, fasting, alms, and ablutions, is extracted from the Persian and Arabian theologians by Maracci (Prodrom. part iv. p. 9–24.). Reland (in his excellent treatise de Religione Moham-

Deity, was commanded to impose on his disciples the daily obligation of fifty prayers. By the advice of Moses, he applied for an alleviation of this intolerable burthen; the number was gradually reduced to five; without any dispensation of business or pleasure, or time or place: the devotion of the faithful is repeated at day-break, at noon, in the afternoon, in the evening, and at the first watch of the night; and, in the present decay of religious fervour, our travellers are edified by the profound humility and attention of the Turks and Persians. Cleanliness is the key of prayer: the frequent lustration of the hands, the face, and the body, which was practised of old by the Arabs, is solemnly enjoined by the Koran; and a permission is formally granted to supply with sand the scarcity of water. The words and attitudes of supplication, as it is performed either sitting, or standing, or prostrate on the ground, are prescribed by custom or authority, but the prayer is poured forth in short and fervent ejaculations; the measure of zeal is not exhausted by a tedious liturgy; and each Musulman, for his own person, is invested with the character of a priest. Among the theists, who reject the use of images, it has been found necessary to restrain the wanderings of the fancy, by directing the eye and the thought towards a *kebla*, or visible point of the horizon. The prophet was at first inclined to gratify the Jews by the choice of Jerusalem; but he soon returned to a more natural partiality; and five times every day the eyes of the nations at Astracan, at Fez, at Delhi, are devoutly turned to the holy temple of Mecca. Yet every spot for the service of God is equally pure: the Mahometans indifferently pray in their chamber or in the street. As a distinction from the Jews and Christians, the Friday in each week is set apart for the useful institution of public worship: the people is assembled in the mosch and the imam: some respectable elder ascends the pulpit, to begin the prayer and pronounce the sermon. But the Mahometan religion is destitute of priesthood or sacrifice; and the independent spirit of fanaticism looks down with contempt on the ministers and the slaves of superstition. II. The voluntary[102] penance of the ascetics, the torment and glory of their lives, was odious to a prophet who censured in his companions a rash vow of abstaining from flesh, and

---

medicâ, Utrecht, 1717, p. 67–123.); and Chardin (Voyages en Perse, tom. iv. p. 47–195.). Maracci is a partial accuser; but the jeweller, Chardin, had the eyes of a philosopher; and Reland, a judicious student, had travelled over the East in his closet at Utrecht. The xiv[th] letter of Tournefort (Voyage du Levant, tom. ii. p. 325–360. in octavo) describes what he had seen of the religion of the Turks.

102. Mahomet (Sale's Koran, c. 9. p. 153.) reproaches the Christians with taking their priests and monks for their lords, besides God. Yet Maracci (Prodromus, part iii.

women, and sleep; and firmly declared, that he would suffer no monks in his religion.[103] Yet he instituted, in each year, a fast of thirty days; and strenuously recommended the observance, as a discipline which purifies the soul and subdues the body, as a salutary exercise of obedience to the will of God and his apostle. During the month of Ramadan, from the rising to the setting of the sun, the Musulman abstains from eating, and drinking, and women, and baths, and perfumes; from all nourishment that can restore his strength, from all pleasure that can gratify his senses. In the revolution of the lunar year, the Ramadan coincides by turns with the winter cold and the summer heat; and the patient martyr, without assuaging his thirst with a drop of water, must expect the close of a tedious and sultry day. The interdiction of wine, peculiar to some orders of priests or hermits, is converted by Mahomet alone into a positive and general law;[104] and a considerable portion of the globe has abjured, at his command, the use of that salutary, though dangerous, liquor. These painful restraints are, doubtless, infringed by the libertine and eluded by the hypocrite; but the legislator, by whom they are enacted, cannot surely be accused of alluring his proselytes by the indulgence of their sensual appetites. III. The charity of the Mahometans descends to the animal creation; and the Koran repeatedly inculcates, not as a merit, but as a strict and indispensable duty, the relief of the indigent and unfortunate. Mahomet, perhaps, is the only lawgiver who has defined the precise measure of charity: the standard may vary with the degree and nature of property, as it consists either in money, in corn or cattle, in fruits or merchandise; but the Musulman does not accomplish the law, unless he bestows a *tenth* of his revenue; and if his conscience accuses him of fraud or extortion, the tenth, under the idea of restitution, is enlarged to a *fifth*.[105] Benevolence is the foundation of justice, since we are forbid to

---

p. 69, 70.) excuses the worship, especially of the pope, and quotes, from the Koran itself, the case of Eblis, or Satan, who was cast from heaven for refusing to adore Adam.

103. Koran, c. 5. p. 94. and Sale's note, which refers to the authority of Jallaloddin and Al Beidawi. D'Herbelot declares, that Mahomet condemned *la vie religieuse*; and that the first swarms of fakirs, dervises, &c. did not appear till after the year 300 of the Hegira (Bibliot. Orient. p. 292. 718.).

104. See the double prohibition (Koran, c. 2. p. 25. c. 5. p. 94.); the one in the style of a legislator, the other in that of a fanatic. The public and private motives of Mahomet are investigated by Prideaux (Life of Mahomet, p. 62–64.); and Sale (Preliminary Discourse, p. 124.).

105. The jealousy of Maracci (Prodromus, part iv. p. 33.) prompts him to enumerate the more liberal alms of the Catholics of Rome. Fifteen great hospitals are open to many thousand patients and pilgrims, fifteen hundred maidens are annually portioned, fifty-six charity schools are

injure those whom we are bound to assist. A prophet may reveal the secrets of heaven and of futurity; but in his moral precepts he can only repeat the lessons of our own hearts.

Resurrection.

The two articles of belief, and the four practical duties of Islam, are guarded by rewards and punishments; and the faith of the Musulman is devoutly fixed on the event of the judgment and the last day. The prophet has not presumed to determine the moment of that awful catastrophe, though he darkly announces the signs, both in heaven and earth, which will precede the universal dissolution, when life shall be destroyed, and the order of creation shall be confounded in the primitive chaos. At the blast of the trumpet, new worlds will start into being; angels, genii, and men, will arise from the dead, and the human soul will again be united to the body. The doctrine of the resurrection was first entertained by the Egyptians;[106] and their mummies were embalmed, their pyramids were constructed, to preserve the ancient mansion of the soul, during a period of three thousand years. But the attempt is partial and unavailing; and it is with a more philosophic spirit that Mahomet relies on the omnipotence of the Creator, whose word can reanimate the breathless clay, and collect the innumerable atoms, that no longer retain their form or substance.[107] The intermediate state of the soul it is hard to decide; and those who most firmly believe her immaterial nature are at a loss to understand how she can think or act without the agency of the organs of sense.

Hell and paradise.

The re-union of the soul and body will be followed by the final judgment of mankind; and, in his copy of the Magian picture, the prophet has too faithfully represented the forms of proceeding, and even the slow and successive operations of an earthly tribunal. By his intolerant adversaries he is upbraided for extending, even to themselves, the hope of salvation, for asserting the blackest heresy, that every man who believes in God, and accomplishes good works, may expect in the last day a favourable sentence. Such rational indifference is ill adapted to the

---

founded for both sexes, one hundred and twenty confraternities relieve the wants of their brethren, &c. The benevolence of London is still more extensive; but I am afraid that much more is to be ascribed to the humanity, than to the religion, of the people.

106. See Herodotus (l. ii. c. 123.) and our learned countryman Sir John Marsham (Canon. Chronicus, p. 46.). The *Αδης* of the same writer (p. 254–274.) is an elaborate sketch of the infernal regions, as they were painted by the fancy of the Egyptians and Greeks, of the poets and philosophers of antiquity.

107. The Koran (c. 2. p. 259, &c.; of Sale, p. 32.; of Maracci, p. 97.) relates an ingenious miracle, which satisfied the curiosity, and confirmed the faith, of Abraham.

character of a fanatic; nor is it probable that a messenger from heaven should depreciate the value and necessity of his own revelation. In the idiom of the Koran,[108] the belief of God is inseparable from that of Mahomet: the good works are those which he has enjoined; and the two qualifications imply the profession of Islam, to which all nations and all sects are equally invited. Their spiritual blindness, though excused by ignorance and crowned with virtue, will be scourged with everlasting torments; and the tears which Mahomet shed over the tomb of his mother, for whom he was forbidden to pray, display a striking contrast of humanity and enthusiasm.[109] The doom of the infidels is common: the measure of their guilt and punishment is determined by the degree of evidence which they have rejected, by the magnitude of the errors which they have entertained: the eternal mansions of the Christians, the Jews, the Sabians, the Magians, and the idolaters, are sunk below each other in the abyss; and the lowest hell is reserved for the faithless hypocrites who have assumed the mask of religion. After the greater part of mankind has been condemned for their opinions, the true believers only will be judged by their actions. The good and evil of each Musulman will be accurately weighed in a real or allegorical balance, and a singular mode of compensation will be allowed for the payment of injuries: the aggressor will refund an equivalent of his own good actions, for the benefit of the person whom he has wronged; and if he should be destitute of any moral property, the weight of his sins will be loaded with an adequate share of the demerits of the sufferer. According as the shares of guilt or virtue shall preponderate, the sentence will be pronounced, and all, without distinction, will pass over the sharp and perilous bridge of the abyss; but the innocent, treading in the footsteps of Mahomet, will gloriously enter the gates of paradise, while the guilty will fall into the first and mildest of the seven hells. The term of expiation will vary from nine hundred to seven thousand years; but the prophet has judiciously promised, that *all* his disciples, whatever may be their sins, shall be saved, by their own faith and his intercession, from eternal damnation. It is not

108. The candid Reland has demonstrated, that Mahomet damns all unbelievers (de Religion. Moham. p. 128–142.), that devils will not be finally saved (p. 196–199.); that paradise will not *solely* consist of corporeal delights (p. 199–205.); and that women's souls are immortal (p. 205–209.).

109. Al Beidawi, apud Sale, Koran, c. 9. p. 164. The refusal to pray for an unbelieving kindred, is justified, according to Mahomet, by the duty of a prophet, and the example of Abraham, who reprobated his own father as an enemy of God. Yet Abraham (he adds, c. 9. v. 116. Maracci, tom. ii. p. 317.) fuit sane pius, mitis.

surprising that superstition should act most powerfully on the fears of her votaries, since the human fancy can paint with more energy the misery than the bliss of a future life. With the two simple elements of darkness and fire, we create a sensation of pain, which may be aggravated to an infinite degree by the idea of endless duration. But the same idea operates with an opposite effect on the continuity of pleasure; and too much of our present enjoyments is obtained from the relief or the comparison of evil. It is natural enough that an Arabian prophet should dwell with rapture on the groves, the fountains, and the rivers, of paradise; but instead of inspiring the blessed inhabitants with a liberal taste for harmony and science, conversation and friendship, he idly celebrates the pearls and diamonds, the robes of silk, palaces of marble, dishes of gold, rich wines, artificial dainties, numerous attendants, and the whole train of sensual and costly luxury, which becomes insipid to the owner, even in the short period of this mortal life. Seventy-two *Houris*, or black-eyed girls, of resplendent beauty, blooming youth, virgin purity, and exquisite sensibility, will be created for the use of the meanest believer; a moment of pleasure will be prolonged to a thousand years, and his faculties will be encreased an hundred fold, to render him worthy of his felicity. Notwithstanding a vulgar prejudice, the gates of heaven will be open to both sexes; but Mahomet has not specified the male companions of the female elect, lest he should either alarm the jealousy of their former husbands, or disturb their felicity, by the suspicion of an everlasting marriage. This image of a carnal paradise has provoked the indignation, perhaps the envy, of the monks: they declaim against the impure religion of Mahomet; and his modest apologists are driven to the poor excuse of figures and allegories. But the sounder and more consistent party adhere, without shame, to the literal interpretation of the Koran: useless would be the resurrection of the body, unless it were restored to the possession and exercise of its worthiest faculties; and the union of sensual and intellectual enjoyment is requisite to complete the happiness of the double animal, the perfect man. Yet the joys of the Mahometan paradise will not be confined to the indulgence of luxury and appetite; and the prophet has expressly declared, that all meaner happiness will be forgotten and despised by the saints and martyrs, who shall be admitted to the beatitude of the divine vision.[110]

110. For the day of judgment, hell, paradise, &c. consult the Koran (c. 2. v. 25. c. 56. 78, &c.); with Maracci's virulent, but learned, refutation (in his notes, and in the Prodromus, part iv. p. 78. 120. 122, &c.); d'Herbelot, Bibliotheque Orientale,

Mahomet preaches at Mecca, A.D. 609.

The first and most arduous conquests of Mahomet[111] were those of his wife, his servant, his pupil, and his friend;[112] since he presented himself as a prophet to those who were most conversant with his infirmities as a man. Yet Cadijah believed the words, and cherished the glory, of her husband; the obsequious and affectionate Zeid was tempted by the prospect of freedom; the illustrious Ali, the son of Abu Taleb, embraced the sentiments of his cousin with the spirit of a youthful hero; and the wealth, the moderation, the veracity of Abubeker, confirmed the religion of the prophet whom he was destined to succeed. By his persuasion, ten of the most respectable citizens of Mecca were introduced to the private lessons of Islam; they yielded to the voice of reason and enthusiasm; they repeated the fundamental creed; "there is but one God, and Mahomet is the apostle of God;" and their faith, even in this life, was rewarded with riches and honours, with the command

---

p. 368. 375. Reland, p. 47–61.); and Sale (p. 76–103.). The original ideas of the Magi are darkly and doubtfully explored by their apologist Dr. Hyde (Hist. Religionis Persarum, c. 33. p. 402–412. Oxon. 1760). In the article of Mahomet, Bayle has shewn how indifferently wit and philosophy supply the absence of genuine information.

111. Before I enter on the history of the prophet, it is incumbent on me to produce my evidence. The Latin, French, and English versions of the Koran, are preceded by historical discourses, and the three translators, Maracci (tom. i. p. 10–32.), Savary (tom. i. p. 1–248.), and Sale (Preliminary Discourse, p. 33–56.), had accurately studied the language and character of their author. Two professed lives of Mahomet have been composed by Dr. Prideaux (Life of Mahomet, seventh edition, London, 1718, in octavo) and the count de Boulainvilliers (Vie de Mahomed, Londres, 1730, in octavo); but the adverse wish of finding an impostor or an hero, has too often corrupted the learning of the doctor and the ingenuity of the count. The article in d'Herbelot (Bibliot. Orient. p. 598–603.), is chiefly drawn from Novairi and Mircond; but the best and most authentic of our guides is M. Gagnier, a Frenchman by birth, and professor at Oxford of the Oriental tongues. In two elaborate works (Ismael Abulfeda de Vita et Rebus gestis Mohammedis, &c. Latine vertit, Præfatione et Notis illustravit Johannes Gagnier, Oxon. 1723, in folio. La Vie de Mahomet traduite et compilée de l'Alcoran, des Traditions authentiques de la Sonna et des meilleurs Auteurs Arabes; Amsterdam, 1748, 3 vols. in 12mo) he has interpreted, illustrated, and supplied the Arabic text of Abulfeda and Al Jannabi; the first, an enlightened prince, who reigned at Hamah, in Syria, A.D. 1310–1332 (see Gagnier Præfat. ad Abulfed.); the second, a credulous doctor, who visited Mecca A.D. 1556 (d'Herbelot, p. 397. Gagnier, tom. iii. p. 209, 210.). These are my general vouchers, and the inquisitive reader may follow the order of time, and the division of chapters. Yet I must observe, that both Abulfeda and Al Jannabi are modern historians, and that they cannot appeal to any writers of the first century of the Hegira.

112. After the Greeks, Prideaux (p. 8.) discloses the secret doubts of the wife of Mahomet. As if he had been a privy counsellor of the prophet, Boulainvilliers (p. 272, &c.) unfolds the sublime and patriotic views of Cadijah and the first disciples.

of armies and the government of kingdoms. Three years were silently employed in the conversion of fourteen proselytes, the first fruits of his mission; but in the fourth year he assumed the prophetic office, and resolving to impart to his family the light of divine truth, he prepared a banquet, a lamb, as it is said, and a bowl of milk, for the entertainment of forty guests of the race of Hashem. "Friends and kinsmen," said Mahomet to the assembly, "I offer you, and I alone can offer, the most precious of gifts, the treasures of this world and of the world to come. God has commanded me to call you to his service. Who among you will support my burthen? Who among you will be my companion and my vizir?"[113] No answer was returned, till the silence of astonishment, and doubt, and contempt, was at length broken by the impatient courage of Ali, a youth in the fourteenth year of his age. "O prophet, I am the man: whosoever rises against thee, I will dash out his teeth, tear out his eyes, break his legs, rip up his belly. O prophet, I will be thy vizir over them." Mahomet accepted his offer with transport, and Abu Taleb was ironically exhorted to respect the superior dignity of his son. In a more serious tone, the father of Ali advised his nephew to relinquish his impracticable design. "Spare your remonstrances," replied the intrepid fanatic to his uncle and benefactor; "if they should place the sun on my right-hand and the moon on my left, they should not divert me from my course." He persevered ten years in the exercise of his mission; and the religion which has overspread the East and the West, advanced with a slow and painful progress within the walls of Mecca. Yet Mahomet enjoyed the satisfaction of beholding the encrease of his infant congregation of Unitarians, who revered him as a prophet, and to whom he seasonably dispensed the spiritual nourishment of the Koran. The number of proselytes may be esteemed by the absence of eighty-three men and eighteen women, who retired to Æthiopia in the seventh year of his mission: and his party was fortified by the timely conversion of his uncle Hamza, and of the fierce and inflexible Omar, who signalised in the cause of Islam the same zeal which he had exerted for its destruction. Nor was the charity of Mahomet confined to the tribe of Koreish or the precincts of Mecca: on solemn festivals, in the days of pilgrimage, he frequented the Caaba, accosted the strangers of every tribe, and urged, both in private converse and public discourse, the belief and worship of a sole Deity.

113. *Vezirus, portitor, bajulus, onus ferens*; and this plebeian name was transferred by an apt metaphor to the pillars of the state (Gagnier, Not. ad Abulfed. p. 19.). I endeavour to preserve the Arabian idiom, as far as I can feel it myself, in a Latin or French translation.

Conscious of his reason and of his weakness, he asserted the liberty of conscience, and disclaimed the use of religious violence:[114] but he called the Arabs to repentance, and conjured them to remember the ancient idolaters of Ad and Thamud, whom the divine justice had swept away from the face of the earth.[115]

Is opposed by the Koreish, A.D. 613–622.

The people of Mecca was hardened in their unbelief by superstition and envy. The elders of the city, the uncles of the prophet, affected to despise the presumption of an orphan, the reformer of his country: the pious orations of Mahomet in the Caaba were answered by the clamours of Abu Taleb. "Citizens and pilgrims, listen not to the tempter, hearken not to his impious novelties. Stand fast in the worship of Al Lâta and Al Uzzah." Yet the son of Abdallah was ever dear to the aged chief; and he protected the fame and person of his nephew against the assaults of the Koreishites, who had long been jealous of the pre-eminence of the family of Hashem. Their malice was coloured with the pretence of religion: in the age of Job, the crime of impiety was punished by the Arabian magistrate;[116] and Mahomet was guilty of deserting and denying the national deities. But so loose was the policy of Mecca, that the leaders of the Koreish, instead of accusing a criminal, were compelled to employ the measures of persuasion or violence. They repeatedly addressed Abu Taleb in the style of reproach and menace. "Thy nephew reviles our religion; he accuses our wise forefathers of ignorance and folly; silence him quickly, lest he kindle tumult and discord in the city. If he persevere, we shall draw our swords against him and his adherents, and thou wilt be responsible for the blood of thy fellow-citizens." The weight and moderation of Abu Taleb eluded the violence of religious faction; the most helpless or timid of the disciples retired to

114. The passages of the Koran in behalf of toleration, are strong and numerous: c. 2. v. 257. c. 16. 129. c. 17. 54. c. 45. 15. c. 50. 39. c. 88. 21, &c. with the notes of Maracci and Sale. This character alone may generally decide the doubts of the learned, whether a chapter was revealed at Mecca or Medina.

115. See the Koran (passim, and especially c. 7. p. 123, 124, &c.), and the tradition of the Arabs (Pocock, Specimen, p. 35–37.). The caverns of the tribe of Thamud, fit for men of the ordinary stature, were shewn in the midway between Medina and Damascus (Abulfed. Arabiæ Descript. p. 43, 44.), and may be probably ascribed to the Troglodytes of the primitive world (Michaelis, ad Lowth de Poesi Hebræor. p. 131–134. Recherches sur les Egyptiens, tom. ii. p. 48, &c.).

116. In the time of Job, the crime of impiety was punished by the Arabian magistrate (c. 31. v. 26, 27, 28.). I blush for a respectable prelate (de Poesi Hebræorum, p. 650, 651. edit. Michaelis; and letter of a late professor in the university of Oxford, p. 15–53.), who justifies and applauds this patriarchal inquisition.

Æthiopia, and the prophet withdrew himself to various places of strength in the town and country. As he was still supported by his family, the rest of the tribe of Koreish engaged themselves to renounce all intercourse with the children of Hashem, neither to buy nor sell, neither to marry nor to give in marriage, but to pursue them with implacable enmity, till they should deliver the person of Mahomet to the justice of the gods. The decree was suspended in the Caaba before the eyes of the nation; the messengers of the Koreish pursued the Musulman exiles in the heart of Africa: they besieged the prophet and his most faithful followers, intercepted their water, and inflamed their mutual animosity by the retaliation of injuries and insults. A doubtful truce restored the appearances of concord; till the death of Abu Taleb abandoned Mahomet to the power of his enemies, at the moment when he was deprived of his domestic comforts by the loss of his faithful and generous Cadijah. Abu Sophian, the chief of the branch of Ommiyah, succeeded to the principality of the republic of Mecca. A zealous votary of the idols, a mortal foe of the line of Hashem, he convened an assembly of the Koreishites and their allies, to decide the fate of the apostle. His imprisonment might provoke the despair of his enthusiasm; and the exile of an eloquent and popular fanatic would diffuse the mischief through the provinces of Arabia. His death was resolved; and they agreed that a sword from each tribe should be buried in his heart, to divide the guilt of his blood and baffle the vengeance of the Hashemites. An angel or a spy revealed their conspiracy; and flight was the only resource of Mahomet.[117] At the dead of night, accompanied by his friend Abubeker, he silently escaped from his house: the assassins watched at the door; but they were deceived by the figure of Ali, who reposed on the bed, and was covered with the green vestment of the apostle. The Koreish respected the piety of the heroic youth; but some verses of Ali, which are still extant, exhibit an interesting picture of his anxiety, his tenderness, and his religious confidence. Three days Mahomet and his companion were concealed in the cave of Thor, at the distance of a league from Mecca; and in the close of each evening, they received from the son and daughter of Abubeker, a secret supply of intelligence and food. The diligence of the Koreish explored every haunt in the neighbourhood of the city, they arrived at the entrance of the cavern; but the providential deceit of a spider's web and a pigeon's nest, is

and driven from Mecca, A.D. 622.

117. D'Herbelot, Bibliot. Orient. p. 445. He quotes a particular history of the flight of Mahomet.

supposed to convince them that the place was solitary and inviolate. "We are only two," said the trembling Abubeker. "There is a third," replied the prophet; "it is God himself." No sooner was the pursuit abated, than the two fugitives issued from the rock, and mounted their camels: on the road to Medina, they were overtaken by the emissaries of the Koreish; they redeemed themselves with prayers and promises from their hands. In this eventful moment, the lance of an Arab might have changed the history of the world. The flight of the prophet from Mecca to Medina has fixed the memorable æra of the *Hegira*,[118] which, at the end of twelve centuries, still discriminates the lunar years of the Mahometan nations.[119]

Received as prince of Medina, A.D. 622.

The religion of the Koran might have perished in its cradle, had not Medina embraced with faith and reverence the holy outcasts of Mecca. Medina, or the *city*, known under the name of Yathreb, before it was sanctified by the throne of the prophet, was divided between the tribes of the Charegites and the Awsites, whose hereditary feud was rekindled by the slightest provocations: two colonies of Jews, who boasted a sacerdotal race, were their humble allies, and without converting the Arabs, they introduced the taste of science and religion, which distinguished Medina as the city of the book. Some of her noblest citizens, in a pilgrimage to the Caaba, were converted by the preaching of Mahomet; on their return they diffused the belief of God and his prophet, and the new alliance was ratified by their deputies in two secret and nocturnal interviews on a hill in the suburbs of Mecca. In the first, ten Charegites and two Awsites united in faith and love, protested in the name of their wives, their children, and their absent brethren, that they would for ever profess the creed, and observe the precepts, of the Koran. The second was a political association, the first vital spark of the empire of the Saracens.[120] Seventy-three men and two women of Medina held a solemn conference with Mahomet, his kinsmen,

118. The *Hegira* was instituted by Omar, the second caliph, in imitation of the æra of the martyrs of the Christians (d'Herbelot, p. 444.); and properly commenced sixty-eight days before the flight of Mahomet, with the first of Moharren, or first day of that Arabian year, which coincides with Friday July 16th, A.D. 622 (Abulfeda, Vit. Moham. c. 22, 23. p. 45–50.; and Greaves's edition of Ullug Beig's Epochæ Arabum, &c. c. 1. p. 8. 10, &c.).

119. Mahomet's life, from his mission to the Hegira, may be found in Abulfeda (p. 14–45.) and Gagnier (tom. i. p. 134–251. 342–383.). The legend from p. 187–234. is vouched by Al Jannabi, and disdained by Abulfeda.

120. The triple inauguration of Mahomet is described by Abulfeda (p. 30. 33. 40. 86.) and Gagnier (tom. i. p. 342, &c. 349, &c. tom. ii. p. 223, &c.).

and his disciples; and pledged themselves to each other by a mutual oath of fidelity. They promised in the name of the city, that if he should be banished, they would receive him as a confederate, obey him as a leader, and defend him to the last extremity, like their wives and children. "But if you are recalled by your country," they asked with a flattering anxiety, "will you not abandon your new allies?" "All things," replied Mahomet with a smile, "are now common between us; your blood is as my blood, your ruin as my ruin. We are bound to each other by the ties of honour and interest. I am your friend, and the enemy of your foes." "But if we are killed in your service, what," exclaimed the deputies of Medina, "will be our reward?" "PARADISE," replied the prophet. "Stretch forth thy hand." He stretched it forth, and they reiterated the oath of allegiance and fidelity. Their treaty was ratified by the people, who unanimously embraced the profession of Islam; they rejoiced in the exile of the apostle, but they trembled for his safety, and impatiently expected his arrival. After a perilous and rapid journey along the sea-coast, he halted at Koba, two miles from the city, and made his public entry into Medina, sixteen days after his flight from Mecca. Five hundred of the citizens advanced to meet him; he was hailed with acclamations of loyalty and devotion; Mahomet was mounted on a she-camel, an umbrella shaded his head, and a turban was unfurled before him to supply the deficiency of a standard. His bravest disciples, who had been scattered by the storm, assembled round his person: and the equal, though various, merit of the Moslems was distinguished by the names of *Mohagerians* and *Ansars*, the fugitives of Mecca, and the auxiliaries of Medina. To eradicate the seeds of jealousy, Mahomet judiciously coupled his principal followers with the rights and obligations of brethren, and when Ali found himself without a peer, the prophet tenderly declared, that *he* would be the companion and brother of the noble youth. The expedient was crowned with success; the holy fraternity was respected in peace and war, and the two parties vied with each other in a generous emulation of courage and fidelity. Once only the concord was slightly ruffled by an accidental quarrel; a patriot of Medina arraigned the insolence of the strangers, but the hint of their expulsion was heard with abhorrence, and his own son most eagerly offered to lay at the apostle's feet the head of his father.

His regal dignity, A.D. 622–632.

From his establishment at Medina, Mahomet assumed the exercise of the regal and sacerdotal office; and it was impious to appeal from a judge whose decrees were inspired by the divine wisdom. A small portion of ground, the patrimony of two orphans, was acquired by gift or purchase;[121] on that chosen spot, he built an house and a mosch more venerable in their rude simplicity than the palaces and temples of the Assyrian caliphs. His seal of gold, or silver, was inscribed with the apostolic title; when he prayed and preached in the weekly assembly, he leaned against the trunk of a palm-tree; and it was long before he indulged himself in the use of a chair or pulpit of rough timber.[122] After a reign of six years, fifteen hundred Moslems, in arms and in the field, renewed their oath of allegiance; and their chief repeated the assurance of protection till the death of the last member, or the final dissolution of the party. It was in the same camp that the deputy of Mecca was astonished by the attention of the faithful to the words and looks of the prophet, by the eagerness with which they collected his spittle, an hair that dropt on the ground, the refuse water of his lustrations, as if they participated in some degree of the prophetic virtue. "I have seen," said he, "the Chosroes of Persia and the Cæsar of Rome, but never did I behold a king among his subjects like Mahomet among his companions." The devout fervour of enthusiasm acts with more energy and truth than the cold and formal servility of courts.

He declares war against the infidels.

In the state of nature every man has a right to defend, by force of arms, his person and his possessions; to repel, or even to prevent, the violence of his enemies, and to extend his hostilities to a reasonable measure of satisfaction and retaliation. In the free society of the Arabs, the duties of subject and citizen imposed a feeble restraint; and Mahomet, in the exercise of a peaceful and benevolent mission, had been despoiled and banished by the injustice of his countrymen. The choice of an independent people had exalted the fugitive of Mecca to the rank of a sovereign; and he was invested with the just prerogative of forming alliances, and of waging offensive or defensive war. The imperfection of human rights was supplied and armed by the plenitude

121. Prideaux (Life of Mahomet, p. 44.) reviles the wickedness of the impostor, who despoiled two poor orphans, the sons of a carpenter; a reproach which he drew from the Disputatio contra Saracenos, composed in Arabic before the year 1130; but the honest Gagnier (ad Abulfed. p. 53.) has shewn that they were deceived by the word *Al Nagjar*, which signifies, in this place, not an obscure trade, but a noble tribe of Arabs. The desolate state of the ground is described by Abulfeda; and his worthy interpreter has proved, from Al Bochari, the offer of a price; from Al Jannabi, the fair purchase; and from Ahmed Ben Joseph, the payment of the money by the generous Abubeker. On these grounds the prophet must be honourably acquitted.

122. Al Jannabi (apud Gagnier, tom. ii. p. 246. 324.) describes the seal and pulpit, as two venerable relics of the apostle of God; and the portrait of his court is taken from Abulfeda (c. 44. p. 85.).

of divine power: the prophet of Medina assumed, in his new revelations, a fiercer and more sanguinary tone, which proves that his former moderation was the effect of weakness:[123] the means of persuasion had been tried, the season of forbearance was elapsed, and he was now commanded to propagate his religion by the sword, to destroy the monuments of idolatry, and, without regarding the sanctity of days or months, to pursue the unbelieving nations of the earth. The same bloody precepts, so repeatedly inculcated in the Koran, are ascribed by the author to the Pentateuch and the Gospel. But the mild tenor of the evangelic style may explain an ambiguous text, that Jesus did not bring peace on the earth, but a sword: his patient and humble virtues should not be confounded with the intolerant zeal of princes and bishops, who have disgraced the name of his disciples. In the prosecution of religious war, Mahomet might appeal with more propriety to the example of Moses, of the judges and the kings of Israel. The military laws of the Hebrews are still more rigid than those of the Arabian legislator.[124] The Lord of hosts marched in person before the Jews: if a city resisted their summons, the males, without distinction, were put to the sword: the seven nations of Canaan were devoted to destruction; and neither repentance nor conversion could shield them from the inevitable doom, that no creature within their precincts should be left alive. The fair option of friendship, or submission, or battle, was proposed to the enemies of Mahomet. If they professed the creed of Islam, they were admitted to all the temporal and spiritual benefits of his primitive disciples, and marched under the same banner to extend the religion which they had embraced. The clemency of the prophet was decided by his interest, yet he seldom trampled on a prostrate enemy; and he seems to promise, that, on the payment of a tribute, the least guilty of his unbelieving subjects might be indulged in their worship, or at least in their imperfect faith. In the first months of his reign, he practised the lessons of holy warfare, and displayed his white banner before the gates of Medina: the martial apostle fought in person at nine battles or sieges;[125] and fifty enterprises of war were atchieved in

123. The viii[th] and ix[th] chapters of the Koran are the loudest and most vehement; and Maracci (Prodromus, part iv. p. 59–64.) has inveighed with more justice than discretion against the double-dealing of the impostor.

124. The xth and xx[th] chapters of Deuteronomy, with the practical comments of Joshua, David, &c. are read with more awe than satisfaction by the pious Christians of the present age. But the bishops, as well as the rabbis of former times, have beat the drum-ecclesiastic with pleasure and success (Sale's Preliminary Discourse, p. 142, 143.).

125. Abulfeda, in Vit. Moham. p. 156. The private arsenal of the apostle consisted of

ten years by himself or his lieutenants. The Arab continued to unite the professions of a merchant and a robber; and his petty excursions for the defence or the attack of a caravan insensibly prepared his troops for the conquest of Arabia. The distribution of the spoil was regulated by a divine law:[126] the whole was faithfully collected in one common mass: a fifth of the gold and silver, the prisoners and cattle, the moveables and immoveables, was reserved by the prophet for pious and charitable uses; the remainder was shared in adequate portions by the soldiers who had obtained the victory or guarded the camp: the rewards of the slain devolved to their widows and orphans; and the encrease of cavalry was encouraged by the allotment of a double share to the horse and to the man. From all sides the roving Arabs were allured to the standard of religion and plunder: the apostle sanctified the licence of embracing the female captives as their wives or concubines; and the enjoyment of wealth and beauty was a feeble type of the joys of paradise prepared for the valiant martyrs of the faith. "The sword," says Mahomet, "is the key of heaven and of hell: a drop of blood shed in the cause of God, a night spent in arms, is of more avail than two months of fasting or prayer: whosoever falls in battle, his sins are forgiven: at the day of judgment his wounds shall be resplendent as vermillion and odoriferous as musk; and the loss of his limbs shall be supplied by the wings of angels and cherubim." The intrepid souls of the Arabs were fired with enthusiasm: the picture of the invisible world was strongly painted on their imagination; and the death which they had always despised became an object of hope and desire. The Koran inculcates, in the most absolute sense, the tenets of fate and predestination, which would extinguish both industry and virtue, if the actions of man were governed by his speculative belief. Yet their influence in every age has exalted the courage of the Saracens and Turks. The first companions of Mahomet advanced to battle with a fearless confidence: there is no danger where there is no chance: they were ordained to perish in their beds; or they were safe and invulnerable amidst the darts of the enemy.[127]

---

nine swords, three lances, seven pikes or half-pikes, a quiver and three bows, seven cuirasses, three shields, and two helmets (Gagnier, tom. iii. p. 328–334.), with a large white standard, a black banner (p. 335.), twenty horses (p. 322.), &c. Two of his martial sayings are recorded by tradition (Gagnier, tom. ii. p. 88. 337.).

126. The whole subject de jure belli Mohammedanorum, is exhausted in a separate dissertation by the learned Reland (Dissertationes Miscellaneæ, tom. iii. Dissert. x. p. 3–53.).

127. The doctrine of absolute predestination, on which few religions can reproach each other, is sternly exposed in

His defensive wars against the Koreish of Mecca.

Perhaps the Koreish would have been content with the flight of Mahomet, had they not been provoked and alarmed by the vengeance of an enemy, who could intercept their Syrian trade as it passed and repassed through the territory of Medina. Abu Sophian himself, with only thirty or forty followers, conducted a wealthy caravan of a thousand camels: the fortune or dexterity of his march escaped the vigilance of Mahomet; but the chief of the Koreish was informed that the holy robbers were placed in ambush to await his return. He dispatched a messenger to his brethren of Mecca, and they were roused, by the fear of losing their merchandise and their provisions, unless they hastened to his relief with the military force of the city. The sacred band of Mahomet was formed of three hundred and thirteen Moslems, of whom seventy-seven were fugitives, and the rest auxiliaries: they mounted by turns a train of seventy camels (the camels of Yathreb were formidable in war); but such was the poverty of his first disciples, that only two could appear on horseback in the field.[128] In the fertile and famous vale of Beder,[129] three stations from Medina, he was informed by his scouts of the caravan that approached on one side; of the Koreish, one hundred horse, eight hundred and fifty foot, who advanced on the other. After a short debate, he sacrificed the prospect of wealth to the pursuit of glory and revenge; and a slight intrenchment was formed, to cover his troops, and a stream of fresh water that glided through the valley. "O God," he exclaimed as the numbers of the Koreish descended from the hills, "O God, if these are destroyed, by whom wilt thou be worshipped on the earth? – Courage, my children, close your ranks; discharge your arrows, and the day is your own." At these words he placed himself, with Abubeker, on a throne or pulpit,[130]

Battle of Beder, A.D. 623.

---

the Koran (c. 3. p. 52, 53. c. 4. p. 70, &c. with the notes of Sale, and c. 17. p. 413. with those of Maracci). Reland (de Relig. Mohamm. p. 61–64.) and Sale (Prelim. Discourse, p. 103.) represent the opinions of the doctors, and our modern travellers the confidence, the fading confidence, of the Turks.

128. Al Jannabi (apud Gagnier, tom. ii. p. 9.) allows him seventy or eighty horse; and on two other occasions prior to the battle of Ohud, he enlists a body of thirty (p. 10.), and of 500 (p. 66.) troopers. Yet the Musulmans, in the field of Ohud, had no more than two horses, according to the better sense of Abulfeda (in Vit. Mohamm. p. xxxi. p. 65.). In the *stony* province, the camels were numerous; but the horse appears to have been less common than in the *Happy* or the *Desert* Arabia.

129. Bedder Houneene, twenty miles from Medina, and forty from Mecca, is on the high road of the caravan of Egypt; and the pilgrims annually commemorate the prophet's victory by illuminations, rockets, &c. Shaw's Travels, p. 477.

130. The place to which Mahomet retired during the action is styled by Gagnier (in

and instantly demanded the succour of Gabriel and three thousand angels. His eye was fixed on the field of battle: the Musulmans fainted and were pressed: in that decisive moment the prophet started from his throne, mounted his horse, and cast a handful of sand into the air; "Let their faces be covered with confusion." Both armies heard the thunder of his voice: their fancy beheld the angelic warriors:[131] the Koreish trembled and fled: seventy of the bravest were slain; and seventy captives adorned the first victory of the faithful. The dead bodies of the Koreish were despoiled and insulted: two of the most obnoxious prisoners were punished with death; and the ransom of the others, four thousand drams of silver, compensated in some degree the escape of the caravan. But it was in vain that the camels of Abu Sophian explored a new road through the desert and along the Euphrates: they were overtaken by the diligence of the Musulmans; and wealthy must have been the prize, if twenty thousand drams could be set apart for the fifth of the apostle. The resentment of the public and private loss stimulated Abu Sophian to collect a body of three thousand men, seven hundred of whom were armed with cuirasses, and two hundred were mounted on horseback: three thousand camels attended his march; and his wife Henda, with fifteen matrons of Mecca, incessantly sounded their timbrels to animate the troops, and to magnify
of Ohud, A.D. 623. the greatness of Hobal, the most popular deity of the Caaba. The standard of God and Mahomet was upheld by nine hundred and fifty believers: the disproportion of numbers was not more alarming than in the field of Beder; and their presumption of victory prevailed against the divine and human sense of the apostle. The second battle was fought on mount Ohud, six miles to the north of Medina:[132] the Koreish

---

Abulfeda, c. 27. p. 58. Vie de Mahomet, tom. ii. p. 30. 33.), *Umbraculum, une loge de bois avec une porte.* The same Arabic word is rendered by Reiske (Annales Moslemici Abulfedæ, p. 23.) by *Solium, Suggestus editior*; and the difference is of the utmost moment for the honour both of the interpreter and of the hero. I am sorry to observe the pride and acrimony with which Reiske chastises his fellow-labourer. Sæpe sic vertit, ut integræ paginæ nequeant nisi unâ liturâ corrigi: Arabice non satis callebat et carebat judicio critico. J. J. Reiske, Prodidagmata ad Hagji Chalisæ Tabulas, p. 228. ad calcem Abulfedæ Syriæ Tabulæ; Lipsiæ, 1766, in 4to.

131. The loose expressions of the Koran (c. 3. p. 124, 125. c. 8. p. 9.) allow the commentators to fluctuate between the numbers of 1000, 3000, or 9000 angels; and the smallest of these might suffice for the slaughter of seventy of the Koreish (Marracci, Alcoran, tom. ii. p. 131.). Yet the same scholiasts confess, that this angelic band was not visible to any mortal eye (Marracci, p. 297.). They refine on the words (c. 8. 16.), "not thou, but God, &c." (d'Herbelot, Bibliot. Orientale, p. 600, 601.).

132. Geograph. Nubiensis, p. 47.

advanced in the form of a crescent; and the right wing of cavalry was led by Caled, the fiercest and most successful of the Arabian warriors. The troops of Mahomet were skilfully posted on the declivity of the hill; and their rear was guarded by a detachment of fifty archers. The weight of their charge impelled and broke the centre of the idolaters; but in the pursuit they lost the advantage of their ground: the archers deserted their station: the Musulmans were tempted by the spoil, disobeyed their general, and disordered their ranks. The intrepid Caled, wheeling his cavalry on their flank and rear, exclaimed, with a loud voice, that Mahomet was slain. He was indeed wounded in the face with a javelin: two of his teeth were shattered with a stone; yet, in the midst of tumult and dismay, he reproached the infidels with the murder of a prophet; and blessed the friendly hand that staunched his blood, and conveyed him to a place of safety. Seventy martyrs died for the sins of the people: they fell, said the apostle, in pairs, each brother embracing his lifeless companion:[133] their bodies were mangled by the inhuman females of Mecca; and the wife of Abu Sophian tasted the entrails of Hamza, the uncle of Mahomet. They might applaud their superstition and satiate their fury; but the Musulmans soon rallied in the field, and the Koreish wanted strength or courage to undertake the siege of Medina. It was attacked the ensuing year by an army of ten thousand enemies; and this third expedition is variously named from the *nations*, which marched under the banner of Abu Sophian, from the *ditch* which was drawn before the city, and a camp of three thousand Musulmans. The prudence of Mahomet, declined a general engagement: the valour of Ali was signalized in single combat; and the war was protracted twenty days, till the final separation of the confederates. A tempest of wind, rain, and hail, overturned their tents: their private quarrels were fomented by an insidious adversary; and the Koreish, deserted by their allies, no longer hoped to subvert the throne, or to check the conquests, of their invincible exile.[134]

The nations, or the ditch, A.D. 625.

The choice of Jerusalem for the first kebla of prayer, discovers the early propensity of Mahomet in favour of the Jews; and happy would it have been for their temporal interest, had they recognised, in the Arabian prophet, the hope of Israel

Mahomet subdues the Jews of Arabia, A.D. 623–627.

133. In the iii[d] chapter of the Koran (p. 50–53. with Sale's notes), the prophet alleges some poor excuses for the defeat of Ohud.

134. For the detail of the three Koreish wars, of Beder, of Ohud, and of the ditch, peruse Abulfeda (p. 56–61. 64–69. 73–77.), Gagnier (tom. ii. p. 23–45. 70–96. 120–139.), with the proper articles of d'Herbelot, and the abridgments of Elmacin (Hist. Saracen. p. 6, 7.) and Abulpharagius (Dynast. p. 102.).

and the promised Messiah. Their obstinacy converted his friendship into implacable hatred, with which he pursued that unfortunate people to the last moment of his life: and in the double character of an apostle and a conqueror, his persecution was extended to both worlds.[135] The Kainoka dwelt at Medina under the protection of the city; he seized the occasion of an accidental tumult, and summoned them to embrace his religion, or contend with him in battle. "Alas," replied the trembling Jews, "we are ignorant of the use of arms, but we persevere in the faith and worship of our fathers; why wilt thou reduce us to the necessity of a just defence?" The unequal conflict was terminated in fifteen days; and it was with extreme reluctance that Mahomet yielded to the importunity of his allies, and consented to spare the lives of the captives. But their riches were confiscated, their arms became more effectual in the hands of the Musulmans; and a wretched colony of seven hundred exiles was driven with their wives and children to implore a refuge on the confines of Syria. The Nadhirites were more guilty, since they conspired in a friendly interview to assassinate the prophet. He besieged their castle three miles from Medina, but their resolute defence obtained an honourable capitulation; and the garrison, sounding their trumpets and beating their drums, was permitted to depart with the honours of war. The Jews had excited and joined the war of the Koreish: no sooner had the *nations* retired from the *ditch*, than Mahomet, without laying aside his armour, marched on the same day to extirpate the hostile race of the children of Koraidha. After a resistance of twenty-five days, they surrendered at discretion. They trusted to the intercession of their old allies of Medina: they could not be ignorant that fanaticism obliterates the feelings of humanity. A venerable elder, to whose judgment they appealed, pronounced the sentence of their death: seven hundred Jews were dragged in chains to the market-place of the city: they descended alive into the grave prepared for their execution and burial; and the apostle beheld with an inflexible eye the slaughter of his helpless enemies. Their sheep and camels were inherited by the Musulmans: three hundred cuirasses, five hundred pikes, a thousand lances, composed the most useful portion of the spoil. Six days journey to the north-east of Medina, the ancient and wealthy town of Chaibar was the seat of the Jewish power in Arabia; the territory, a fertile spot in the desert, was covered with plantations and cattle, and

135. The wars of Mahomet against the Jewish tribes, of Kainoka, the Nadhirites, Koraidha, and Chaibar, are related by Abulfeda (p. 61. 71. 77. 87, &c.) and Gagnier (tom. ii. p. 61–65. 107–112. 139–148. 268–294.).

protected by eight castles, some of which were esteemed of impregnable strength. The forces of Mahomet consisted of two hundred horse and fourteen hundred foot: in the succession of eight regular and painful sieges they were exposed to danger, and fatigue, and hunger; and the most undaunted chiefs despaired of the event. The apostle revived their faith and courage by the example of Ali, on whom he bestowed the surname of the Lion of God: perhaps we may believe that an Hebrew champion of gigantic stature was cloven to the chest by his irresistible scymetar; but we cannot praise the modesty of romance, which represents him as tearing from its hinges the gate of a fortress, and wielding the ponderous buckler in his left-hand.[136] After the reduction of the castles, the town of Chaibar submitted to the yoke. The chief of the tribe was tortured, in the presence of Mahomet, to force a confession of his hidden treasure: the industry of the shepherds and husbandmen was rewarded with a precarious toleration: they were permitted, so long as it should please the conqueror, to improve their patrimony, in equal shares, for *his* emolument and their own. Under the reign of Omar, the Jews of Chaibar were transplanted to Syria; and the caliph alleged the injunction of his dying master, that one and the true religion should be professed in his native land of Arabia.[137]

Submission of Mecca, A.D. 629.

Five times each day the eyes of Mahomet were turned towards Mecca,[138] and he was urged by the most sacred and powerful motives to revisit, as a conqueror, the city and the temple from whence he had been driven as an exile. The Caaba was present to his waking and sleeping fancy: an idle dream was translated into vision and prophecy; he unfurled the holy banner; and a rash promise of success too hastily dropped from the lips of the apostle. His march from Medina to Mecca, displayed the peaceful and solemn pomp of a pilgrimage: seventy camels chosen and bedecked for sacrifice, preceded the van; the sacred territory was respected, and the captives were dismissed without ransom

136. Abu Rafe, the servant of Mahomet, is said to affirm, that he himself, and seven other men, afterwards tried, without success, to move the same gate from the ground (Abulfeda, p. 90.). Abu Rafe was an eye-witness, but who will witness for Abu Rafe?

137. The banishment of the Jews is attested by Elmacin (Hist. Saracen. p. 9.) and the great Al Zabari (Gagnier, tom. ii. p. 285.). Yet Niebuhr (Description de l'Arabie, p. 324.) believes, that the Jewish religion, and Kareite sect, are still professed by the tribe of Chaibar; and that in the plunder of the caravans, the disciples of Moses are the confederates of those of Mahomet.

138. The successive steps of the reduction of Mecca are related by Abulfeda (p. 84–87. 97–100. 102–111.) and Gagnier (tom. ii. p. 209–245. 309–322. tom. iii. p. 1–58.), Elmacin (Hist. Saracen. p. 8, 9, 10.), Abulpharagius (Dynast. p. 103.).

to proclaim his clemency and devotion. But no sooner did Mahomet descend into the plain, within a day's journey of the city, than he exclaimed, "they have clothed themselves with the skins of tygers;" the numbers and resolution of the Koreish opposed his progress; and the roving Arabs of the desert might desert or betray a leader whom they had followed for the hopes of spoil. The intrepid fanatic sunk into a cool and cautious politician: he waved in the treaty his title of apostle of God, concluded with the Koreish and their allies a truce of ten years, engaged to restore the fugitives of Mecca who should embrace his religion, and stipulated only, for the ensuing year, the humble privilege of entering the city as a friend, and of remaining three days to accomplish the rites of the pilgrimage. A cloud of shame and sorrow hung on the retreat of the Musulmans, and their disappointment might justly accuse the failure of a prophet who had so often appealed to the evidence of success. The faith and hope of the pilgrims were rekindled by the prospect of Mecca: their swords were sheathed; seven times in the footsteps of the apostle they encompassed the Caaba: the Koreish had retired to the hills, and Mahomet, after the customary sacrifice, evacuated the city on the fourth day. The people was edified by his devotion; the hostile chiefs were awed or divided, or seduced; and both Caled and Amrou, the future conquerors of Syria and Egypt, most seasonably deserted the sinking cause of idolatry. The power of Mahomet was encreased by the submission of the Arabian tribes; ten thousand soldiers were assembled for the conquest of Mecca, and the idolaters, the weaker party, were easily convicted of violating the truce. Enthusiasm and discipline impelled the march and preserved the secret, till the blaze of ten thousand fires proclaimed to the astonished Koreish, the design, the approach, and the irresistible force of the enemy. The haughty Abu Sophian presented the keys of the city, admired the variety of arms and ensigns that passed before him in review; observed that the son of Abdallah had acquired a mighty kingdom, and confessed, under the scymetar of Omar, that he was the apostle of the true God. The return of Marius and Sylla was stained with the blood of the Romans: the revenge of Mahomet was stimulated by religious zeal, and his injured followers were eager to execute or to prevent the order of a massacre. Instead of indulging their passions and his own,[139] the victorious exile forgave the guilt, and united the factions, of Mecca. His troops, in three

139. After the conquest of Mecca, the Mahomet of Voltaire imagines and perpetrates the most horrid crimes. The poet confesses, that he is not supported by the truth of history, and can only allege, que celui qui fait la guerre à sa patrie au nom

divisions, marched into the city: eight and twenty of the inhabitants were slain by the sword of Caled; eleven men and six women were proscribed by the sentence of Mahomet; but he blamed the cruelty of his lieutenant; and several of the most obnoxious victims were indebted for their lives to his clemency or contempt. The chiefs of the Koreish were prostrate at his feet. "What mercy can you expect from the man whom you have wronged?" "We confide in the generosity of our kinsman." "And you shall not confide in vain: begone! you are safe, you are free." The people of Mecca deserved their pardon by the profession of Islam; and after an exile of seven years, the fugitive missionary was inthroned as the prince and prophet of his native country.[140] But the three hundred and sixty idols of the Caaba were ignominiously broken: the house of God was purified and adorned; as an example to future times, the apostle again fulfilled the duties of a pilgrim; and a perpetual law was enacted that no unbeliever should dare to set his foot on the territory of the holy city.[141]

Conquest of Arabia, A.D. 629–632.

The conquest of Mecca determined the faith and obedience of the Arabian tribes;[142] who, according to the vicissitudes of fortune, had obeyed or disregarded the eloquence or the arms of the prophet. Indifference for rites and opinions still marks the character of the Bedoweens; and they might accept, as loosely as they hold, the doctrine of the Koran. Yet an obstinate remnant still adhered to the religion and liberty of their ancestors, and the war of Honain derived a proper appellation from the *idols*, whom Mahomet had vowed to destroy, and whom the confederates of Tayef had sworn to defend.[143] Four

de Dieu, est capable de tout (Oeuvres de Voltaire, tom. xv. p. 282.). The maxim is neither charitable nor philosophic; and some reverence is surely due to the fame of heroes and the religion of nations. I am informed that a Turkish ambassador at Paris was much scandalized at the representation of this tragedy.

140. The Mahometan doctors still dispute, whether Mecca was reduced by force or consent (Abulfeda, p. 107, et Gagnier ad locum); and this verbal controversy is of as much moment, as our own about William the *Conqueror*.

141. In excluding the Christians from the peninsula of Arabia, the province of Hejaz, or the navigation of the Red Sea, Chardin (Voyages en Perse, tom. iv. p. 166.) and Reland (Dissert. Miscell. tom. iii. p. 51.) are more rigid than the Musulmans themselves. The Christians are received without scruple into the ports of Mocha, and even of Gedda, and it is only the city and precincts of Mecca that are inaccessible to the profane (Niebuhr, Description de l'Arabie, p. 308, 309. Voyage en Arabie, tom. i. p. 205. 248, &c.).

142. Abulfeda, p. 112–115. Gagnier, tom. iii. p. 67–88. D'Herbelot, MOHAMMED.

143. The siege of Tayef, division of the spoil, &c. are related by Abulfeda (p. 117–123.); and Gagnier, (tom. iii. p. 88–111.). It is Al Jannabi who mentions the engines and engineers of the tribe of Daws. The

thousand pagans advanced with secrecy and speed to surprise the conqueror; they pitied and despised the supine negligence of the Koreish, but they depended on the wishes, and perhaps the aid, of a people who had so lately renounced their gods, and bowed beneath the yoke of their enemy. The banners of Medina and Mecca were displayed by the prophet; a crowd of Bedoweens encreased the strength or numbers of the army, and twelve thousand Musulmans entertained a rash and sinful presumption of their invincible strength. They descended without precaution into the valley of Honain: the heights had been occupied by the archers and slingers of the confederates; their numbers were oppressed, their discipline was confounded, their courage was appalled, and the Koreish smiled at their impending destruction. The prophet, on his white mule, was encompassed by the enemies; he attempted to rush against their spears in search of a glorious death: ten of his faithful companions interposed their weapons and their breasts; three of these fell dead at his feet: "O my brethren," he repeatedly cried with sorrow and indignation, "I am the son of Abdallah, I am the apostle of truth! O man stand fast in the faith! O God send down thy succour!" His uncle Abbas, who, like the heroes of Homer, excelled in the loudness of his voice, made the valley resound with the recital of the gifts and promises of God: the flying Moslems returned from all sides to the holy standard; and Mahomet observed with pleasure, that the furnace was again rekindled: his conduct and example restored the battle, and he animated his victorious troops to inflict a merciless revenge on the authors of their shame. From the field of Honain, he marched without delay to the siege of Tayef, sixty miles to the south-east of Mecca, a fortress of strength, whose fertile lands produce the fruits of Syria in the midst of the Arabian desert. A friendly tribe, instructed (I know not how) in the art of sieges, supplied him with a train of battering rams and military engines, with a body of five hundred artificers. But it was in vain that he offered freedom to the slaves of Tayef; that he violated his own laws by the extirpation of the fruit-trees; that the ground was opened by the miners; that the breach was assaulted by the troops. After a siege of twenty days, the prophet sounded a retreat, but he retreated with a song of devout triumph, and affected to pray for the repentance and safety of the unbelieving city. The spoil of this fortunate expedition amounted to six thousand captives, twenty-four

---

fertile spot of Tayef was supposed to be a piece of the land of Syria detached and dropped in the general deluge.

thousand camels, forty thousand sheep, and four thousand ounces of silver: a tribe who had fought at Honain, redeemed their prisoners by the sacrifice of their idols; but Mahomet compensated the loss, by resigning to the soldiers his fifth of the plunder, and wished for their sake, that he possessed as many head of cattle as there were trees in the province of Tehama. Instead of chastising the disaffection of the Koreish, he endeavoured to cut out their tongues (his own expression), and to secure their attachment by a superior measure of liberality: Abu Sophian alone was presented with three hundred camels and twenty ounces of silver; and Mecca was sincerely converted to the profitable religion of the Koran. The *fugitives* and *auxiliaries* complained, that they who had borne the burthen were neglected in the season of victory. "Alas," replied their artful leader, "suffer me to conciliate these recent enemies, these doubtful proselytes, by the gift of some perishable goods. To your guard I entrust my life and fortunes. You are the companions of my exile, of my kingdom, of my paradise." He was followed by the deputies of Tayef, who dreaded the repetition of a siege. "Grant us, O apostle of God! a truce of three years, with the toleration of our ancient worship." "Not a month, not an hour." "Excuse us at least from the obligation of prayer." "Without prayer religion is of no avail." They submitted in silence; their temples were demolished, and the same sentence of destruction was executed on all the idols of Arabia. His lieutenants, on the shores of the Red Sea, the Ocean, and the Gulf of Persia, were saluted by the acclamations of a faithful people; and the ambassadors who knelt before the throne of Medina, were as numerous (says the Arabian proverb) as the dates that fall from the maturity of a palm-tree. The nation submitted to the God and the sceptre of Mahomet: the opprobrious name of tribute was abolished: the spontaneous or reluctant oblations of alms and tithes were applied to the service of religion: and one hundred and fourteen thousand Moslems accompanied the last pilgrimage of the apostle.[144]

First war of the Mahometans against the Roman empire, A.D. 629, 630.

When Heraclius returned in triumph from the Persian war, he entertained, at Emesa, one of the ambassadors of Mahomet, who invited the princes and nations of the earth to the profession of Islam. On this foundation the zeal of the Arabians has supposed the secret conversion of the Christian emperor:

144. The last conquests and pilgrimage of Mahomet are contained in Abulfeda (p. 121–133.), Gagnier (tom. iii. p. 119–219.), Elmacin (p. 10, 11.), Abulpharagius (p. 103.). The ix[th] of the Hegira was styled the Year of Embassies (Gagnier, Not. ad Abulfed. p. 121.).

the vanity of the Greeks has feigned a personal visit of the prince of Medina, who accepted from the royal bounty a rich domain, and a secure retreat, in the province of Syria.[145] But the friendship of Heraclius and Mahomet was of short continuance: the new religion had inflamed rather than assuaged the rapacious spirit of the Saracens; and the murder of an envoy afforded a decent pretence for invading, with three thousand soldiers, the territory of Palestine, that extends to the eastward of the Jordan. The holy banner was entrusted to Zeid; and such was the discipline or enthusiasm of the rising sect, that the noblest chiefs served, without reluctance, under the slave of the prophet. On the event of his decease, Jaafar and Abdallah were successively substituted to the command; and if the three should perish in the war, the troops were authorised to elect their general. The three leaders were slain in the battle of Muta,[146] the first military action which tried the valour of the Moslems against a foreign enemy. Zeid fell, like a soldier, in the foremost ranks: the death of Jaafar was heroic and memorable; he lost his right-hand; he shifted the standard to his left; the left was severed from his body; he embraced the standard with his bleeding stumps, till he was transfixed to the ground with fifty honourable wounds. "Advance," cried Abdallah, who stepped into the vacant place, "advance with confidence; either victory or paradise is our own." The lance of a Roman decided the alternative; but the falling standard was rescued by Caled, the proselyte of Mecca: nine swords were broken in his hand; and his valour withstood and repulsed the superior numbers of the Christians. In the nocturnal council of the camp he was chosen to command: his skilful evolutions of the ensuing day secured either the victory or the retreat of the Saracens; and Caled is renowned among his brethren and his enemies by the glorious appellation of the *Sword of God*. In the pulpit, Mahomet described, with prophetic rapture, the crowns of the blessed martyrs; but in private he betrayed the feelings of human nature: he was surprised as he wept over the daughter of Zeid: "What do I see?" said the astonished votary. "You see," replied the apostle, "a friend, who is deploring the loss of his most faithful friend." After the conquest of Mecca the sovereign of Arabia affected to prevent the hostile preparations of Heraclius; and

145. Compare the bigotted Al Jannabi (apud Gagnier, tom. ii. p. 232–255.) with the no less bigotted Greeks, Theophanes (p. 276–278.), Zonaras (tom. ii. l. xiv. p. 86.), and Cedrenus (p. 421.).

146. For the battle of Muta, and its consequences, see Abulfeda (p. 100–102.) and Gagnier (tom. ii. p. 327–343.). *Καλεδος* (says Theophanes) *ὀν λεγουσι μαχαιραν του Θεου*.

solemnly proclaimed war against the Romans, without attempting to disguise the hardships and dangers of the enterprise.[147] The Moslems were discouraged: they alleged the want of money, or horses, or provisions: the season of harvest, and the intolerable heat of the summer: "Hell is much hotter," said the indignant prophet. He disdained to compel their service; but on his return he admonished the most guilty, by an excommunication of fifty days. Their desertion enhanced the merit of Abubeker, Othman, and the faithful companions who devoted their lives and fortunes; and Mahomet displayed his banner at the head of ten thousand horse and twenty thousand foot. Painful indeed was the distress of the march: lassitude and thirst were aggravated by the scorching and pestilential winds of the desert: ten men rode by turns on the same camel; and they were reduced to the shameful necessity of drinking the water from the belly of that useful animal. In the mid-way, ten days journey from Medina and Damascus, they reposed near the grove and fountain of Tabuc. Beyond that place, Mahomet declined the prosecution of the war; he declared himself satisfied with the peaceful intentions, he was more probably daunted by the martial array, of the emperor of the East. But the active and intrepid Caled spread around the terror of his name; and the prophet received the submission of the tribes and cities, from the Euphrates to Ailah, at the head of the Red Sea. To his Christian subjects, Mahomet readily granted the security of their persons, the freedom of their trade, the property of their goods, and the toleration of their worship.[148] The weakness of their Arabian brethren had restrained them from opposing his ambition; the disciples of Jesus were endeared to the

147. The expedition of Tabuc is recorded by our ordinary historians, Abulfeda (Vit. Moham. p. 123–127.) and Gagnier (Vie de Mahomet, tom. iii. p. 147–163.); but we have the advantage of appealing to the original evidence of the Koran (c. 9. p. 154. 165.), with Sale's learned and rational notes.

148. The *Diploma securitatis Ailensibus*, is attested by Ahmed Ben Joseph, and the author *Libri Splendorum* (Gagnier, Not. ad Abulfedam, p. 125.); but Abulfeda himself, as well as Elmacin (Hist. Saracen. p. 11.), though he owns Mahomet's regard for the Christians (p. 13.), only mention peace and tribute. In the year 1630, Sionita published at Paris the text and version of Mahomet's patent in favour of the Christians; which was admitted and reprobated by the opposite taste of Salmasius and Grotius (Bayle, MAHOMET. Rem. AA.). Hottinger doubts of its authenticity (Hist. Orient. p. 237.); Renaudot urges the consent of the Mahometans (Hist. Patriarch. Alex. p. 169.); but Mosheim (Hist. Eccles. p. 244.) shews the futility of their opinion, and inclines to believe it spurious. Yet Abulpharagius quotes the impostor's treaty with the Nestorian patriarch (Asseman. Bibliot. Orient. tom. ii. p. 418.); but Abulpharagius was primate of the Jacobites.

enemy of the Jews; and it was the interest of a conqueror to propose a fair capitulation to the most powerful religion of the earth.

Death of Mahomet, A.D. 632, June 7.

Till the age of sixty-three years, the strength of Mahomet was equal to the temporal and spiritual fatigues of his mission. His epileptic fits, an absurd calumny of the Greeks, would be an object of pity rather than abhorrence;[149] but he seriously believed that he was poisoned at Chaibar by the revenge of a Jewish female.[150] During four years, the health of the prophet declined; his infirmities encreased; but his mortal disease was a fever of fourteen days, which deprived him by intervals of the use of reason. As soon as he was conscious of his danger, he edified his brethren by the humility of his virtue or penitence. "If there be any man," said the apostle from the pulpit, "whom I have unjustly scourged, I submit my own back to the lash of retaliation. Have I aspersed the reputation of a Musulman? let him proclaim *my* faults in the face of the congregation. Has any one been despoiled of his goods? the little that I possess shall compensate the principal and the interest of the debt." "Yes," replied a voice from the crowd, "I am entitled to three drams of silver." Mahomet heard the complaint, satisfied the demand, and thanked his creditor for accusing him in this world rather than at the day of judgment. He beheld with temperate firmness the approach of death; enfranchised his slaves (seventeen men, as they are named, and eleven women); minutely directed the order of his funeral, and moderated the lamentations of his weeping friends, on whom he bestowed the benediction of peace. Till the third day before his death, he regularly performed the function of public prayer: the choice of Abubeker to supply his place, appeared to mark that ancient and faithful friend as his successor in the sacerdotal and regal office; but he prudently declined the risk and envy of a more explicit nomination. At a moment when his faculties were visibly impaired, he called for pen and ink, to write, or,

149. The epilepsy, or falling-sickness, of Mahomet, is asserted by Theophanes, Zonaras, and the rest of the Greeks; and is greedily swallowed by the gross bigotry of Hottinger (Hist. Orient. p. 10, 11.), Prideaux (Life of Mahomet, p. 12.), and Maracci (tom. ii.), Alcoran (p. 762, 763.). The titles *(the wrapped-up, the covered)* of two chapters of the Koran (73, 74.), can hardly be strained to such an interpretation; the silence, the ignorance of the Mahometan commentators, is more conclusive than the most peremptory denial; and the charitable side is espoused by Ockley (Hist. of the Saracens, tom. i. p. 301.), Gagnier (ad Abulfeda, p. 9. Vie de Mahomet. tom. i. p. 118.), and Sale (Koran. p. 469–474.).

150. This poison (more ignominious since it was offered as a test of his prophetic knowledge) is frankly confessed by his zealous votaries, Abulfeda (p. 92.), and Al Jannabi (apud Gagnier, tom. ii. p. 286–288.).

more properly, to dictate, a divine book, the sum and accomplishment of all his revelations: a dispute arose in the chamber, whether he should be allowed to supersede the authority of the Koran; and the prophet was forced to reprove the indecent vehemence of his disciples. If the slightest credit may be afforded to the traditions of his wives and companions, he maintained, in the bosom of his family, and to the last moments of his life, the dignity of an apostle and the faith of an enthusiast; described the visits of Gabriel, who bade an everlasting farewel to the earth, and expressed his lively confidence, not only of the mercy, but of the favour, of the Supreme Being. In a familiar discourse he had mentioned his special prerogative, that the angel of death was not allowed to take his soul till he had respectfully asked the permission of the prophet. The request was granted; and Mahomet immediately fell into the agony of his dissolution: his head was reclined on the lap of Ayesha, the best beloved of all his wives; he fainted with the violence of pain; recovering his spirits, he raised his eyes towards the roof of the house, and, with a steady look, though a faultering voice, uttered the last broken, though articulate, words: "O God! . . . pardon my sins. . . . Yes, . . . I come, . . . among my fellow-citizens on high:" and thus peaceably expired on a carpet spread upon the floor. An expedition for the conquest of Syria was stopped by this mournful event: the army halted at the gates of Medina; the chiefs were assembled round their dying master. The city, more especially the house, of the prophet was a scene of clamorous sorrow or silent despair: fanaticism alone could suggest a ray of hope and consolation. "How can he be dead, our witness, our intercessor, our mediator, with God? By God he is not dead; like Moses and Jesus he is wrapt in a holy trance, and speedily will he return to his faithful people." The evidence of sense was disregarded; and Omar, unsheathing his scymetar, threatened to strike off the heads of the infidels, who should dare to affirm that the prophet was no more. The tumult was appeased by the weight and moderation of Abubeker. "Is it Mahomet," said he to Omar and the multitude, "or the God of Mahomet, whom you worship. The God of Mahomet liveth for ever, but the apostle was a mortal like ourselves, and according to his own prediction, he has experienced the common fate of mortality." He was piously interred by the hands of his nearest kinsman, on the same spot on which he expired;[151] Medina has

151. The Greeks and Latins have invented and propagated the vulgar and ridiculous story, that Mahomet's iron tomb is suspended in the air at *Mecca* (*σημα μετεωριζομενον*. Laonicus Chalcocondyles de Rebus Turcicis, l. iii. p. 66.), by the action

been sanctified by the death and burial of Mahomet; and the innumerable pilgrims of Mecca often turn aside from the way, to bow, in voluntary devotion,[152] before the simple tomb of the prophet.[153]

His character. At the conclusion of the life of Mahomet, it may perhaps be expected, that I should balance his faults and virtues, that I should decide whether the title of enthusiast or impostor more properly belongs to that extraordinary man. Had I been intimately conversant with the son of Abdallah, the task would still be difficult, and the success uncertain: at the distance of twelve centuries, I darkly contemplate his shade through a cloud of religious incense; and could I truly delineate the portrait of an hour, the fleeting resemblance would not equally apply to the solitary of mount Hera, to the preacher of Mecca, and to the conqueror of Arabia. The author of a mighty revolution appears to have been endowed with a pious and contemplative disposition: so soon as marriage had raised him above the pressure of want, he avoided the paths of ambition and avarice; and till the age of forty, he lived with innocence, and would have died without a name. The unity of God is an idea most congenial to nature and reason; and a slight conversation with the Jews and Christians would teach him to despise and detest the idolatry of Mecca. It was the duty of a man and a citizen to impart the doctrine of salvation, to rescue his country from the dominion of sin and error. The energy of a mind incessantly bent on the same object, would convert a general obligation into a particular call; the warm suggestions of the understanding or the fancy, would be felt as the inspirations of heaven; the labour of thought would expire in rapture and vision; and the inward sensation, the invisible monitor, would be described with the form and attributes of an angel of

---

of equal and potent loadstones (Dictionaire de Bayle, MAHOMET, Rem. EE. FF.). Without any philosophical enquiries, it may suffice, that, 1. The prophet was not buried at Mecca; and, 2. That his tomb at Medina, which has been visited by millions, is placed on the ground (Reland de Relig. Moham. l. ii. c. 19. p. 209–211.), Gagnier (Vie de Mahomet, tom. iii. p. 263–268.).

152. Al Jannabi enumerates (Vie de Mahomet. tom. iii. p. 372–391.) the multifarious duties of a pilgrim who visits the tombs of the prophet and his companions; and the learned casuist decides, that this act of devotion is nearest in obligation and merit to a divine precept. The doctors are divided which, of Mecca or Medina, be the most excellent (p. 391–394.).

153. The last sickness, death, and burial of Mahomet, are described by Abulfeda and Gagnier (Vit. Moham. p. 133–142. Vie de Mahomet, tom. iii. p. 220–271.). The most private and interesting circumstances were originally received from Ayesha, Ali, the sons of Abbas, &c.; and as they dwelt at Medina, and survived the prophet many years, they might repeat the pious tale to a second or third generation of pilgrims.

God.[154] From enthusiasm to imposture, the step is perilous and slippery: the dæmon of Socrates[155] affords a memorable instance, how a wise man may deceive himself, how a good man may deceive others, how the conscience may slumber in a mixed and middle state between self-illusion and voluntary fraud. Charity may believe that the original motives of Mahomet were those of pure and genuine benevolence; but a human missionary is incapable of cherishing the obstinate unbelievers who reject his claims, despise his arguments, and persecute his life; he might forgive his personal adversaries, he may lawfully hate the enemies of God; the stern passions of pride and revenge were kindled in the bosom of Mahomet, and he sighed, like the prophet of Niniveh, for the destruction of the rebels whom he had condemned. The injustice of Mecca, and the choice of Medina, transformed the citizen into a prince, the humble preacher into the leader of armies; but his sword was consecrated by the example of the saints; and the same God who afflicts a sinful world with pestilence and earthquakes, might inspire for their conversion or chastisement the valour of his servants. In the exercise of political government, he was compelled to abate of the stern rigour of fanaticism, to comply in some measure with the prejudices and passions of his followers, and to employ even the vices of mankind as the instruments of their salvation. The use of fraud and perfidy, of cruelty and injustice, were often subservient to the propagation of the faith; and Mahomet commanded or approved the assassination of the Jews and idolaters who had escaped from the field of battle. By the repetition of such acts, the character of Mahomet must have been gradually stained; and the influence of such

154. The Christians, rashly enough, have assigned to Mahomet a tame pigeon, that seemed to descend from heaven and whisper in his ear. As this pretended miracle is urged by Grotius (de Veritate Religionis Christianæ), his Arabic translator, the learned Pocock, enquired of him the names of his authors; and Grotius confessed, that it is unknown to the Mahometans themselves. Lest it should provoke their indignation and laughter, the pious *lie* is suppressed in the Arabic version; but it has maintained an edifying place in the numerous editions of the Latin text (Pocock, Specimen Hist. Arabum, p. 186, 187. Reland, de Religion. Moham. l. ii. c. 39. p. 259–262.).

155. *Εμοι δε τουτο εστιν εκ παιδος αρξαμενον, φωνη τις γιγνομενη ἡ ὁταν γενηται αει αποτρεπει με τουτου ὁ αν μελλω πραττειν, προτρεπει δε ουποτε* (Plato, in Apolog. Socrat. c. 19. p. 121, 122. edit. Fischer). The familiar examples, which Socrates urges in his Dialogue with Theages (Platon. Opera, tom. i. p. 128, 129. edit. Hen. Stephan), are beyond the reach of human foresight; and the divine inspiration (the *Δαιμονιον*) of the philosopher, is clearly taught in the Memorabilia of Xenophon. The ideas of the most rational Platonists are expressed by Cicero (de Divinat. i. 54.) and in the xiv[th] and xv[th] Dissertations of Maximus of Tyre (p. 153–172. edit. Davis).

pernicious habits would be poorly compensated by the practice of the personal and social virtues which are necessary to maintain the reputation of a prophet among his sectaries and friends. Of his last years, ambition was the ruling passion; and a politician will suspect, that he secretly smiled (the victorious impostor!) at the enthusiasm of his youth and the credulity of his proselytes.[156] A philosopher will observe, that *their* credulity and *his* success, would tend more strongly to fortify the assurance of his divine mission, that his interest and religion were inseparably connected, and that his conscience would be soothed by the persuasion, that he alone was absolved by the Deity from the obligation of positive and moral laws. If he retained any vestige of his native innocence, the sins of Mahomet may be allowed as an evidence of his sincerity. In the support of truth, the arts of fraud and fiction may be deemed less criminal; and he would have started at the foulness of the means, had he not been satisfied of the importance and justice of the end. Even in a conqueror or a priest, I can surprise a word or action of unaffected humanity; and the decree of Mahomet, that, in the sale of captives, the mothers should never be separated from their children, may suspend or moderate the censure of the historian.[157]

Private life of Mahomet.

The good sense of Mahomet[158] despised the pomp of royalty: the apostle of God submitted to the menial offices of the family: he kindled the fire, swept the floor, milked the ewes, and mended with his own hands his shoes and his woollen garment. Disdaining the penance and merit of an hermit, he observed without effort or vanity, the abstemious diet of an Arab and a soldier. On solemn occasions he feasted his companions with rustic and hospitable plenty; but in his domestic life, many weeks would elapse without a fire being kindled on the hearth of the prophet. The interdiction of wine was confirmed by his example; his

156. In some passage of his voluminous writings, Voltaire compares the prophet, in his old age, to a fakir: "qui detache la chaine de son cou pour en donner sur les oreilles à ses confreres."

157. Gagnier relates, with the same impartial pen, this humane law of the prophet, and the murders of Caab, and Sophian, which he prompted and approved (Vie de Mahomet, tom. ii. p. 69. 97. 208.).

158. For the domestic life of Mahomet, consult Gagnier, and the corresponding chapters of Abulfeda; for his diet (tom. iii. p. 285–288.); his children (p. 189. 289.); his wives (p. 290–303.); his marriage with Zeineb (tom. ii. p. 152–160.); his amour with Mary (p. 303–309.); the false accusation of Ayesha (p. 186–199.). The most original evidence of the three last transactions, is contained in the xxiv[th], xxxiii[d], and lxvi[th] chapters of the Koran, with Sale's Commentary. Prideaux (Life of Mahomet, p. 80–90.) and Maracci (Prodrom. Alcoran, part iv. p. 49–59.) have maliciously exaggerated the frailties of Mahomet.

hunger was appeased with a sparing allowance of barley-bread; he delighted in the taste of milk and honey: but his ordinary food consisted of dates and water. Perfumes and women were the two sensual enjoyments which his nature required and his religion did not forbid: and Mahomet affirmed, that the fervour of his devotion was encreased by these innocent pleasures. The heat of the climate inflames the blood of the Arabs; and their libidinous complexion has been noticed by the writers of antiquity.[159] Their incontinence was regulated by the civil and religious laws of the Koran: their incestuous alliances were blamed, the boundless licence of polygamy was reduced to four legitimate wives or concubines; their rights, both of bed and of dowry, were equitably determined; the freedom of divorce was discouraged, adultery was condemned as a capital offence, and fornication, in either sex, was punished with an hundred stripes.[160] Such were the calm and rational precepts of the legislator: but in his private conduct, Mahomet indulged the appetites of a man, and abused the claims of a prophet. A special revelation dispensed him from the laws which he had imposed on his nation; the female sex, without reserve, was abandoned to his desires; and this singular prerogative excited the envy, rather than the scandal, the veneration, rather than the envy, of the devout Musulmans. If we remember the seven hundred wives *His wives,* and three hundred concubines of the wise Solomon, we shall applaud the modesty of the Arabian who espoused no more than seventeen or fifteen wives; eleven are enumerated who occupied at Medina their separate apartments round the house of the apostle, and enjoyed in their turns the favour of his conjugal society. What is singular enough, they were all widows, excepting only Ayesha, the daughter of Abubeker. *She* was doubtless a virgin, since Mahomet consummated his nuptials (such is the premature ripeness of the climate) when she was only nine years of age. The youth, the beauty, the spirit of Ayesha, gave her a superior ascendant: she was beloved and trusted by the prophet; and, after his death, the daughter of Abubeker was long revered as the mother of the faithful. Her behaviour had been ambiguous and indiscreet: in a nocturnal march, she was accidentally left behind; and in the morning Ayesha returned to the camp with a man. The temper of Mahomet was inclined to jealousy; but a divine revelation assured him of her innocence: he

159. Incredibile est quo ardore apud eos in Venerem uterque solvitur sexus (Ammian. Marcellin. l. xiv. c. 4.).

160. Sale (Preliminary Discourse, p. 133–137.) has recapitulated the laws of marriage, divorce, &c.; and the curious reader of Selden's Uxor Hebraica will recognize many Jewish ordinances.

chastised her accusers, and published a law of domestic peace, that no woman should be condemned unless four male witnesses had seen her in the act of adultery.[161] In his adventures with Zeineb, the wife of Zeid, and with Mary, an Egyptian captive, the amorous prophet forgot the interest of his reputation. At the house of Zeid, his freedman and adopted son, he beheld, in a loose undress, the beauty of Zeineb, and burst forth into an ejaculation of devotion and desire. The servile, or grateful, freedman understood the hint, and yielded without hesitation to the love of his benefactor. But as the filial relation had excited some doubt and scandal, the angel Gabriel descended from heaven to ratify the deed, to annul the adoption, and gently to reprove the apostle for distrusting the indulgence of his God. One of his wives, Hafna, the daughter of Omar, surprised him on her own bed, in the embraces of his Egyptian captive: she promised secrecy and forgiveness: he swore that he would renounce the possession of Mary. Both parties forgot their engagements; and Gabriel again descended with a chapter of the Koran, to absolve him from his oath, and to exhort him freely to enjoy his captives and concubines, without listening to the clamours of his wives. In a solitary retreat of thirty days, he laboured, alone with Mary, to fulfil the commands of the angel. When his love and revenge were satiated, he summoned to his presence his eleven wives, reproached their disobedience and indiscretion, and threatened them with a sentence of divorce, both in this world and in the next: a dreadful sentence, since those who had ascended the bed of the prophet were for ever excluded from the hope of a second marriage. Perhaps the incontinence of Mahomet may be palliated by the tradition of his natural or preternatural gifts:[162] he united the manly virtue of thirty of the children of Adam; and the apostle might rival the thirteenth labour[163] of the Grecian Hercules.[164] A more serious and decent excuse

161. In a memorable case, the caliph Omar decided that all presumptive evidence was of no avail; and that all the four witnesses must have actually seen stylum in pyxide (Abulfedæ Annales Moslemici, p. 71. vers. Reiske).

162. Sibi robur ad generationem, quantum triginta viri habent, inesse jactaret: ita ut unicâ hora posset undecim fœminis *satisfacere*, ut ex Arabum libris refert S[tus] Petrus Paschasius, c. 2. (Maracci, Prodromus Alcoran, p. iv. p. 55. See likewise Observations de Belon, l. iii. c. 10. fol. 179. recto). Al Jannabi (Gagnier, tom. iii. p. 287.) records his own testimony, that he surpassed all men in conjugal vigour; and Abulfeda mentions the exclamation of Ali, who washed his body after his death, "O propheta, certe penis tuus cœlum versus erectus est" (in Vit. Mohammed. p. 140.).

163. I borrow the style of a father of the church, εναθλευων Ἡρακλης τρισκαιδεκατον αθλον (Greg. Nazianzen, Orat. iii. p. 108.).

164. The common and most glorious legend includes, in a single night, the fifty

may be drawn from his fidelity to Cadijah. During the twenty-four years of their marriage, her youthful husband abstained from the right of polygamy, and the pride or tenderness of the venerable matron was never insulted by the society of a rival. After her death, he placed her in the rank of the four perfect women, with the sister of Moses, the mother of Jesus, and Fatima, the best beloved of his daughters. "Was she not old?" said Ayesha, with the insolence of a blooming beauty; "has not God given you a better in her place?" "No, by God," said Mahomet, with an effusion of honest gratitude, "there never can be a better! She believed in me, when men despised me: she relieved my wants, when I was poor and persecuted by the world."[165]

and children.

In the largest indulgence of polygamy, the founder of a religion and empire might aspire to multiply the chances of a numerous posterity and a lineal succession. The hopes of Mahomet were fatally disappointed. The virgin Ayesha, and his ten widows of mature age and approved fertility, were barren in his potent embraces. The four sons of Cadijah died in their infancy. Mary, his Egyptian concubine, was endeared to him by the birth of Ibrahim. At the end of fifteen months the prophet wept over his grave; but he sustained with firmness the raillery of his enemies, and checked the adulation or credulity of the Moslems, by the assurance that an eclipse of the sun was *not* occasioned by the death of the infant. Cadijah had likewise given him four daughters, who were married to the most faithful of his disciples: the three eldest died before their father; but Fatima, who possessed his confidence and love, became the wife of her cousin Ali, and the mother of an illustrious progeny. The merit and misfortunes of Ali and his descendants will lead me to anticipate, in this place, the series of the Saracen caliphs, a title which describes the commanders of the faithful as the vicars and successors of the apostle of God.[166]

---

victories of Hercules over the virgin daughters of Thestius (Diodor. Sicul. tom. i. l. iv. p. 274. Pausanias, l. ix. p. 763. Statius Sylv. l. i. eleg. iii. v. 42.). But Athenæus allows seven nights (Deipnosophist. l. xiii. p. 556.), and Apollodorus fifty, for this arduous atchievement of Hercules, who was then no more than eighteen years of age (Bibliot. l. ii. c. 4. p. 111. cum notis Heyne, part i. p. 332.).

165. Abulfeda in Vit. Moham. p. 12, 13, 16, 17. cum notis Gagnier.

166. This outline of the Arabian history is drawn from the Bibliotheque Orientale of d'Herbelot (under the names of *Aboubecre, Omar, Othman, Ali,* &c.); from the Annals of Abulfeda, Abulpharagius, and Elmacin (under the proper years of the *Hegira*), and especially from Ockley's History of the Saracens (vol. i. p. 1–10. 115–122. 229. 249. 363–372. 378–391. and almost the whole of the second volume). Yet we should weigh with caution the traditions of the hostile sects; a stream which becomes still more

Character of Ali. The birth, the alliance, the character of Ali, which exalted him above the rest of his countrymen, might justify his claim to the vacant throne of Arabia. The son of Abu Taleb was, in his own right, the chief of the family of Hashem, and the hereditary prince or guardian of the city and temple of Mecca. The light of prophecy was extinct; but the husband of Fatima might expect the inheritance and blessing of her father: the Arabs had sometimes been patient of a female reign; and the two grandsons of the prophet had often been fondled in his lap, and shewn in his pulpit, as the hope of his age, and the chief of the youth of paradise. The first of the true believers might aspire to march before them in this world and in the next; and if some were of a graver and more rigid cast, the zeal and virtue of Ali were never outstripped by any recent proselyte. He united the qualifications of a poet, a soldier, and a saint: his wisdom still breathes in a collection of moral and religious sayings;[167] and every antagonist, in the combats of the tongue or of the sword, was subdued by his eloquence and valour. From the first hour of his mission, to the last rites of his funeral, the apostle was never forsaken by a generous friend, whom he delighted to name his brother, his vicegerent, and the faithful Aaron of a second Moses. The son of Abu Taleb was afterwards reproached for neglecting to secure his interest by a solemn declaration of his right, which would have silenced all competition, and sealed his succession by the decrees of heaven. But the unsuspecting hero confided in himself: the jealousy of empire, and perhaps the fear of opposition, might suspend the resolutions of Mahomet; and the bed of sickness was besieged by the artful Ayesha, the daughter of Abubeker, and the enemy of Ali.

Reign of Abubeker; A.D. 632, June 7. The silence and death of the prophet restored the liberty of the people; and his companions convened an assembly to deliberate on the choice of his successor. The hereditary claim and lofty spirit of Ali, were offensive to an aristocracy of elders, desirous of bestowing and resuming the sceptre by a free and frequent election: the Koreish could never be reconciled to the proud pre-eminence of the line of Hashem; the ancient discord of the tribes was rekindled; the *fugitives* of Mecca and the *auxiliaries* of Medina asserted

---

muddy as it flows farther from the source. Sir John Chardin has too faithfully copied the fables and errors of the modern Persians (Voyages, tom. ii. p. 235–250, &c.).

167. Ockley (at the end of his second volume) has given an English version of 169 sentences, which he ascribes, with some hesitation, to Ali, the son of Abu Taleb. His preface is coloured by the enthusiasm of a translator: yet these sentences delineate a characteristic, though dark, picture of human life.

their respective merits, and the rash proposal of chusing two independent caliphs would have crushed in their infancy the religion and empire of the Saracens. The tumult was appeased by the disinterested resolution of Omar, who, suddenly renouncing his own pretensions, stretched forth his hand, and declared himself the first subject of the mild and venerable Abubeker. The urgency of the moment, and the acquiescence of the people, might excuse this illegal and precipitate measure; but Omar himself confessed from the pulpit, that if any Musulman should hereafter presume to anticipate the suffrage of his brethren, both the elector and the elected would be worthy of death.[168] After the simple inauguration of Abubeker, he was obeyed in Medina, Mecca, and the provinces of Arabia; the Hashemites alone declined the oath of fidelity; and their chief, in his own house, maintained, above six months, a sullen and independent reserve; without listening to the threats of Omar, who attempted to consume with fire the habitation of the daughter of the apostle. The death of Fatima, and the decline of his party, subdued the indignant spirit of Ali: he condescended to salute the commander of the faithful, accepted his excuse of the necessity of preventing their common enemies, and wisely rejected his courteous offer of abdicating the government of the Arabians. After a reign of two years, the aged caliph was summoned by the angel of death. In his testament, with the tacit approbation of the companions, he bequeathed the sceptre to the firm and intrepid virtue of Omar. "I have no occasion," said the modest candidate, "for the place." "But the place has occasion for you," replied Abubeker; who expired with a fervent prayer, that the God of Mahomet would ratify his choice, and direct the Musulmans in the way of concord and obedience. The prayer was not ineffectual, since Ali himself, in a life of privacy and prayer, professed to revere the superior worth and dignity of his rival; who comforted him for the loss of empire, by the most flattering marks of confidence and esteem. In the twelfth year of his reign, Omar received a mortal wound from the hand of an assassin: he rejected with equal impartiality the names of his son and of Ali, refused to load his conscience with the sins of his successor, and devolved on six of the most respectable companions, the arduous task of electing a commander of the faithful. On this occasion, Ali was again

of Omar; A.D. 634, July 24.

168. Ockley (Hist. of the Saracens, vol. i. p. 5, 6.) from an Arabian MS. represents Ayesha as adverse to the substitution of her father in the place of the apostle. This fact, so improbable in itself, is unnoticed by Abulfeda, Al Jannabi, and Al Bochari, the last of whom quotes the tradition of Ayesha herself (Vit. Mohammed, p. 136. Vie de Mahomet, tom. iii. p. 236.).

blamed by his friends[169] for submitting his right to the judgment of men, for recognizing their jurisdiction by accepting a place among the six electors. He might have obtained their suffrage, had he deigned to promise a strict and servile conformity, not only to the Koran and tradition, but likewise to the determinations of two *seniors*.[170] With these limitations, Othman, the secretary of Mahomet, accepted the government; nor was it till after the third caliph, twenty-four years after the death of the prophet, that Ali was invested, by the popular choice, with the regal and sacerdotal office. The manners of the Arabians retained their primitive simplicity, and the son of Abu Taleb despised the pomp and vanity of this world. At the hour of prayer, he repaired to the mosch of Medina, clothed in a thin cotton gown, a coarse turban on his head, his slippers in one hand, and his bow in the other, instead of a walking staff. The companions of the prophet and the chiefs of the tribes saluted their new sovereign, and gave him their right hands as a sign of fealty and allegiance.

of Othman, A.D. 644, November 6.

Discord of the Turks and Persians.

The mischiefs that flow from the contests of ambition are usually confined to the times and countries in which they have been agitated. But the religious discord of the friends and enemies of Ali has been renewed in every age of the Hegira, and is still maintained in the immortal hatred of the Persians and Turks.[171] The former, who are branded with the appellation of *Shiites* or sectaries, have enriched the Mahometan creed with a new article of faith; and if Mahomet be the apostle, his companion Ali is the vicar, of God. In their private converse, in their public worship, they bitterly execrate the three usurpers who intercepted his indefeasible right to the dignity of Imam and Caliph; and the name of Omar expresses in their tongue the perfect

169. Particularly by his friend and cousin Abdallah, the son of Abbas, who died A.D. 687, with the title of grand doctor of the Moslems. In Abulfeda he recapitulated the important occasions in which Ali had neglected his salutary advice (p. 76. vers. Reiske); and concludes (p. 85.), O princeps fidelium, absque controversia tu quidem vere fortis es, at inops boni consilii, et rerum gerendarum parum callens.

170. I suspect that the two seniors (Abulpharagius, p. 115. Ockley, tom. i. p. 371.) may signify not two actual counsellors, but his two predecessors, Abubeker and Omar.

171. The schism of the Persians is explained by all our travellers of the last century, especially in the ii[d] and iv[th] volume of their master, Chardin. Niebuhr, though of inferior merit, has the advantage of writing so late as the year 1764 (Voyages en Arabie, &c. tom. ii. p. 208–233.), since the ineffectual attempt of Nadir Shah to change the religion of the nation (see his Persian History translated into French by Sir William Jones, tom. ii. p. 5. 6. 47, 48. 144–155.).

accomplishment of wickedness and impiety.[172] The *Sonnites*, who are supported by the general consent and orthodox tradition of the Musulmans, entertain a more impartial, or at least a more decent opinion. They respect the memory of Abubeker, Omar, Othman, and Ali, the holy and legitimate successors of the prophet. But they assign the last and most humble place to the husband of Fatima, in the persuasion that the order of succession was determined by the degrees of sanctity.[173] An historian who balances the four caliphs with a hand unshaken by superstition, will calmly pronounce, that their manners were alike pure and exemplary; that their zeal was fervent, and probably sincere; and that, in the midst of riches and power, their lives were devoted to the practice of moral and religious duties. But the public virtues of Abubeker and Omar, the prudence of the first, the severity of the second, maintained the peace and prosperity of their reigns. The feeble temper and declining age of Othman were incapable of sustaining the weight of conquest and empire. He chose, and he was deceived; he trusted, and he was betrayed: the most deserving of the faithful became useless or hostile to his government, and his lavish bounty was productive only of ingratitude and discontent. The spirit of discord went forth in the provinces, their deputies assembled at Medina, and the Charegites, the desperate fanatics who disclaimed the yoke of subordination and reason, were confounded among the free-born Arabs, who demanded the redress of their wrongs and the punishment of their oppressors. From Cufa, from Bassora, from Egypt, from the tribes of the desert, they rose in arms, encamped about a league from Medina, and dispatched an haughty mandate to their sovereign, requiring him to execute justice, or to descend from the throne. His repentance began to disarm and disperse the insurgents; but their fury was rekindled by the arts of his enemies; and the forgery of a perfidious secretary was contrived to blast his reputation and precipitate his fall. The caliph had lost the only guard of his predecessors, the esteem and confidence of the Moslems; during a siege of six weeks his water and provisions were intercepted,

172. Omar is the name of the devil; his murderer is a saint. When the Persians shoot with the bow, they frequently cry, "May this arrow go to the heart of Omar!" (Voyages de Chardin, tom. ii. p. 239, 240. 259, &c.).

173. This gradation of merit is distinctly marked in a creed illustrated by Reland (de Relig. Mohamm. l. i. p. 37.); and a Sonnite argument inserted by Ockley (Hist. of the Saracens, tom. ii. p. 230.). The practice of cursing the memory of Ali was abolished, after forty years, by the Ommiades themselves (d'Herbelot, p. 690.); and there are few among the Turks who presume to revile him as an infidel (Voyages de Chardin, tom. iv. p. 46.).

and the feeble gates of the palace were protected only by the scruples of the more timorous rebels. Forsaken by those who had abused his simplicity, the helpless and venerable caliph expected the approach of death: the brother of Ayesha marched at the head of the assassins; and Othman, with the Koran in his lap, was pierced with a multitude of wounds. A tumultuous anarchy of five days was appeased by the inauguration of Ali; his refusal would have provoked a general massacre. In this painful situation he supported the becoming pride of the chief of the Hashemites; declared that he had rather serve than reign; rebuked the presumption of the strangers; and required the formal, if not the voluntary, assent of the chiefs of the nation. He has never been accused of prompting the assassin of Omar; though Persia indiscreetly celebrates the festival of that holy martyr. The quarrel between Othman and his subjects was assuaged by the early mediation of Ali; and Hassan, the eldest of his sons, was insulted and wounded in the defence of the caliph. Yet it is doubtful whether the father of Hassan was strenuous and sincere in his opposition to the rebels; and it is certain that he enjoyed the benefit of their crime. The temptation was indeed of such magnitude as might stagger and corrupt the most obdurate virtue. The ambitious candidate no longer aspired to the barren sceptre of Arabia: the Saracens had been victorious in the East and West; and the wealthy kingdoms of Persia, Syria, and Egypt, were the patrimony of the commander of the faithful.

Death of Othman, A.D. 655, June 18.

Reign of Ali, A.D. 655–660.

A life of prayer and contemplation had not chilled the martial activity of Ali; but in a mature age, after a long experience of mankind, he still betrayed in his conduct the rashness and indiscretion of youth. In the first days of his reign, he neglected to secure, either by gifts or fetters, the doubtful allegiance of Telha and Zobeir, two of the most powerful of the Arabian chiefs. They escaped from Medina to Mecca, and from thence to Bassora; erected the standard of revolt; and usurped the government of Irak, or Assyria, which they had vainly solicited as the reward of their services. The mask of patriotism is allowed to cover the most glaring inconsistencies; and the enemies, perhaps the assassins, of Othman now demanded vengeance for his blood. They were accompanied in their flight by Ayesha, the widow of the prophet, who cherished, to the last hour of her life, an implacable hatred against the husband and the posterity of Fatima. The most reasonable Moslems were scandalised, that the mother of the faithful should expose in a camp her person and character; but the superstitious crowd was confident that her presence would sanctify the justice, and assure the success, of their cause.

At the head of twenty thousand of his loyal Arabs, and nine thousand valiant auxiliaries of Cufa, the caliph encountered and defeated the superior numbers of the rebels under the walls of Bassora. Their leaders, Telha and Zobeir, were slain in the first battle that stained with civil blood the arms of the Moslems. After passing through the ranks to animate the troops, Ayesha had chosen her post amidst the dangers of the field. In the heat of the action, seventy men, who held the bridle of her camel, were successively killed or wounded; and the cage or litter in which she sat, was stuck with javelins and darts like the quills of a porcupine. The venerable captive sustained with firmness the reproaches of the conqueror, and was speedily dismissed to her proper station, at the tomb of Mahomet, with the respect and tenderness that was still due to the widow of the apostle. After this victory, which was styled the Day of the Camel, Ali marched against a more formidable adversary; against Moawiyah, the son of Abu Sophian, who had assumed the title of caliph, and whose claim was supported by the forces of Syria and the interest of the house of Ommiyah. From the passage of Thapsacus, the plain of Siffin[174] extends along the western bank of the Euphrates. On this spacious and level theatre, the two competitors waged a desultory war of one hundred and ten days. In the course of ninety actions or skirmishes, the loss of Ali was estimated at twenty-five, that of Moawiyah at forty-five, thousand soldiers; and the list of the slain was dignified with the names of five and twenty veterans who had fought at Beder under the standard of Mahomet. In this sanguinary contest, the lawful caliph displayed a superior character of valour and humanity. His troops were strictly enjoined to await the first onset of the enemy, to spare their flying brethren, and to respect the bodies of the dead, and the chastity of the female captives. He generously proposed to save the blood of the Moslems by a single combat; but his trembling rival declined the challenge as a sentence of inevitable death. The ranks of the Syrians were broken by the charge of a hero who was mounted on a pyebald horse, and wielded with irresistible force his ponderous and two-edged sword. As often as he smote a rebel, he shouted the Allah Acbar, "God is victorious;" and in the tumult of a nocturnal battle, he was heard to repeat four hundred times that tremendous exclamation. The prince of Damascus already meditated his flight, but the certain victory was snatched from the grasp of Ali by the disobedience and enthusiasm of his troops. Their conscience

174. The plain of Siffin is determined by d'Anville (l'Euphrate et le Tigre, p. 29.) to be the Campus Barbaricus of Procopius.

was awed by the solemn appeal to the books of the Koran which Moawiyah exposed on the foremost lances; and Ali was compelled to yield to a disgraceful truce and an insidious compromise. He retreated with sorrow and indignation to Cufa; his party was discouraged; the distant provinces of Persia, of Yemen, and of Egypt, were subdued or seduced by his crafty rival; and the stroke of fanaticism which was aimed against the three chiefs of the nation, was fatal only to the cousin of Mahomet. In the temple of Mecca, three Charegites or enthusiasts discoursed of the disorders of the church and state: they soon agreed, that the deaths of Ali, of Moawiyah, and of his friend Amrou, the viceroy of Egypt, would restore the peace and unity of religion. Each of the assassins chose his victim, poisoned his dagger, devoted his life, and secretly repaired to the scene of action. Their resolution was equally desperate: but the first mistook the person of Amrou, and stabbed the deputy who occupied his seat; the prince of Damascus was dangerously hurt by the second; the lawful caliph, in the mosch of Cufa, received a mortal wound from the hand of the third. He expired in the sixty-third year of his age, and mercifully recommended to his children, that they would dispatch the murderer by a single stroke. The sepulchre of Ali[175] was concealed from the tyrants of the house of Ommiyah;[176] but in the fourth age of the Hegira, a tomb, a temple, a city, arose near the ruins of Cufa.[177] Many thousands of the Shiites repose in holy ground at the feet of the vicar of God; and the desert is vivified by the numerous and annual visits of the Persians, who esteem their devotion not less meritorious than the pilgrimage of Mecca.

Reign of Moawiyah, A.D. 655, or 661–680.

The persecutors of Mahomet usurped the inheritance of his children; and the champions of idolatry became the supreme heads of his religion and empire. The opposition of Abu Sophian had been fierce and obstinate; his conversion was tardy

175. Abulfeda, a moderate Sonnite, relates the different opinions concerning the burial of Ali, but adopts the sepulchre of Cufa, hodie famâ numeroque religiose frequentantium celebratum. This number is reckoned by Niebuhr to amount annually to 2000 of the dead, and 5000 of the living (tom. ii. p. 208, 209.).

176. All the tyrants of Persia, from Adhad el Dowlat (A.D. 977, d'Herbelot, p. 58, 59. 95.) to Nadir Shah (A.D. 1743, Hist. de Nadir Shah, tom. ii. p. 155.), have enriched the tomb of Ali with the spoils of the people. The dome is copper, with a bright and massy gilding, which glitters to the sun at the distance of many a mile.

177. The city of Meshed Ali, five or six miles from the ruins of Cufa, and one hundred and twenty to the south of Bagdad, is of the size and form of the modern Jerusalem. Meshed Hosein, larger and more populous, is at the distance of thirty miles.

and reluctant; his new faith was fortified by necessity and interest; he served, he fought, perhaps he believed; and the sins of the time of ignorance were expiated by the recent merits of the family of Ommiyah. Moawiyah, the son of Abu Sophian, and of the cruel Henda, was dignified in his early youth with the office or title of secretary of the prophet: the judgment of Omar entrusted him with the government of Syria; and he administered that important province above forty years either in a subordinate or supreme rank. Without renouncing the fame of valour and liberality, he affected the reputation of humanity and moderation: a grateful people was attached to their benefactor; and the victorious Moslems were enriched with the spoils of Cyprus and Rhodes. The sacred duty of pursuing the assassins of Othman was the engine and pretence of his ambition. The bloody shirt of the martyr was exposed in the mosch of Damascus: the emir deplored the fate of his injured kinsman; and sixty thousand Syrians were engaged in his service by an oath of fidelity and revenge. Amrou, the conqueror of Egypt, himself an army, was the first who saluted the new monarch, and divulged the dangerous secret, that the Arabian caliphs might be created elsewhere than in the city of the prophet.[178] The policy of Moawiyah eluded the valour of his rival; and, after the death of Ali, he negociated the abdication of his son Hassan, whose mind was either above or below the government of the world, and who retired without a sigh from the palace of Cufa to an humble cell near the tomb of his grandfather. The aspiring wishes of the caliph were finally crowned by the important change of an elective to an hereditary kingdom. Some murmurs of freedom or fanaticism attested the reluctance of the Arabs, and four citizens of Medina refused the oath of fidelity; but the designs of Moawiyah were conducted with vigour and address; and his son Yezid, a feeble and dissolute youth, was proclaimed as the commander of the faithful and the successor of the apostle of God.

Death of Hosein, A.D. 680, October 10.

A familiar story is related of the benevolence of one of the sons of Ali. In serving at table, a slave had inadvertently dropt a dish of scalding broth on his master: the heedless wretch fell prostrate, to deprecate his punishment, and repeated a verse of the Koran: "Paradise is for those who command their anger:" – "I am not angry:" – "and for those who pardon offences:" – "I pardon your offence:" – "and for those who return good for evil:" – "I give you your

178. I borrow, on this occasion, the strong sense and expression of Tacitus (Hist. i. 4.): Evulgato imperii arcano posse imperatorem alibi quam Romæ fieri.

liberty, and four hundred pieces of silver." With an equal measure of piety, Hosein, the younger brother of Hassan, inherited a remnant of his father's spirit, and served with honour against the Christians in the siege of Constantinople. The primogeniture of the line of Hashem, and the holy character of grandson of the apostle, had centered in his person, and he was at liberty to prosecute his claim against Yezid the tyrant of Damascus, whose vices he despised, and whose title he had never deigned to acknowledge. A list was secretly transmitted from Cufa to Medina, of one hundred and forty thousand Moslems, who professed their attachment to his cause, and who were eager to draw their swords so soon as he should appear on the banks of the Euphrates. Against the advice of his wisest friends, he resolved to trust his person and family in the hands of a perfidious people. He traversed the desert of Arabia with a timorous retinue of women and children; but as he approached the confines of Irak, he was alarmed by the solitary or hostile face of the country, and suspected either the defection or ruin of his party. His fears were just; Obeidollah, the governor of Cufa, had extinguished the first sparks of an insurrection; and Hosein, in the plain of Kerbela, was encompassed by a body of five thousand horse, who intercepted his communication with the city and the river. He might still have escaped to a fortress in the desert, that had defied the power of Cæsar and Chosroes, and confided in the fidelity of the tribe of Tai, which would have armed ten thousand warriors in his defence. In a conference with the chief of the enemy, he proposed the option of three honourable conditions; that he should be allowed to return to Medina, or be stationed in a frontier garrison against the Turks, or safely conducted to the presence of Yezid. But the commands of the caliph, or his lieutenant, were stern and absolute; and Hosein was informed that he must either submit as a captive and a criminal to the commander of the faithful, or expect the consequences of his rebellion. "Do you think," replied he, "to terrify me with death?" And, during the short respite of a night, he prepared with calm and solemn resignation to encounter his fate. He checked the lamentations of his sister Fatima, who deplored the impending ruin of his house. "Our trust," said Hosein, "is in God alone. All things, both in heaven and earth, must perish and return to their Creator. My brother, my father, my mother, were better than me; and every Musulman has an example in the prophet." He pressed his friends to consult their safety by a timely flight: they unanimously refused to desert or survive their beloved master; and their courage was fortified by a fervent prayer and the assurance of paradise. On the morning of the fatal day, he mounted on horseback, with his sword in one hand and the Koran in the other: his generous band of martyrs consisted only of thirty-two horse and forty foot; but their flanks and rear were secured by the tent-ropes, and by a deep trench which they had filled with lighted faggots, according to the practice of the Arabs. The enemy advanced with reluctance; and one of their chiefs deserted, with thirty followers, to claim the partnership of inevitable death. In every close onset, or single combat, the despair of the Fatimites was invincible; but the surrounding multitudes galled them from a distance with a cloud of arrows, and the horses and men were successively slain: a truce was allowed on both sides for the hour of prayer; and the battle at length expired by the death of the last of the companions of Hosein. Alone, weary, and wounded, he seated himself at the door of his tent. As he tasted a drop of water, he was pierced in the mouth with a dart; and his son and nephew, two beautiful youths, were killed in his arms. He lifted his hands to heaven, they were full of blood, and he uttered a funeral prayer for the living and the dead. In a transport of despair his sister issued from the tent, and adjured the general of the Cufians, that he would not suffer Hosein to be murdered before his eyes: a tear trickled down his venerable beard; and the boldest of his soldiers fell back on every side as the dying hero threw himself among them. The remorseless Shamer, a name detested by the faithful, reproached their cowardice; and the grandson of Mahomet was slain with three and thirty strokes of lances and swords. After they had trampled on his body, they carried his head to the castle of Cufa, and the inhuman Obeidollah struck him on the mouth with a cane: "Alas!" exclaimed an aged Musulman, "on these lips have I seen the lips of the apostle of God!" In a distant age and climate the tragic scene of the death of Hosein will awaken the sympathy of the coldest reader.[179] On the annual festival of his martyrdom, in the devout pilgrimage to his sepulchre, his Persian votaries abandon their souls to the religious frenzy of sorrow and indignation.[180]

179. I have abridged the interesting narrative of Ockley (tom. ii. p. 170–231.). It is long and minute; but the pathetic, almost always, consists in the detail of little circumstances.

180. Niebuhr the Dane (Voyages en Arabie, &c. tom. ii. p. 208, &c.) is perhaps the only European traveller who has dared to visit Meshed Ali and Meshed Hosein. The two sepulchres are in the hands of the Turks, who tolerate and tax the devotion of the Persian heretics. The festival of the death of Hosein is amply described by Sir John Chardin, a traveller whom I have often praised.

Posterity of Mahomet and Ali. When the sisters and children of Ali were brought in chains to the throne of Damascus, the caliph was advised to extirpate the enmity of a popular and hostile race, whom he had injured beyond the hope of reconciliation. But Yezid preferred the counsels of mercy; and the mourning family was honourably dismissed to mingle their tears with their kindred at Medina. The glory of martyrdom superseded the right of primogeniture; and the twelve IMAMS,[181] or pontiffs, of the Persian creed are Ali, Hassan, Hosein, and the lineal descendants of Hosein to the ninth generation. Without arms, or treasures, or subjects, they successively enjoyed the veneration of the people, and provoked the jealousy of the reigning caliphs: their tombs at Mecca or Medina, on the banks of the Euphrates, or in the province of Chorasan, are still visited by the devotion of their sect. Their names were often the pretence of sedition and civil war; but these royal saints despised the pomp of the world, submitted to the will of God and the injustice of man, and devoted their innocent lives to the study and practice of religion. The twelfth and last of the Imams, conspicuous by the title of *Mahadi*, or the Guide, surpassed the solitude and sanctity of his predecessors. He concealed himself in a cavern near Bagdad: the time and place of his death are unknown; and his votaries pretend, that he still lives, and will appear before the day of judgment to overthrow the tyranny of Dejal, or the Antichrist.[182] In the lapse of two or three centuries the posterity of Abbas, the uncle of Mahomet, had multiplied to the number of thirty-three thousand:[183] the race of Ali might be equally prolific; the meanest individual was above the first and greatest of princes; and the most eminent were supposed to excel the perfection of angels. But their adverse fortune, and the wide extent of the Musulman empire, allowed an ample scope for every bold and artful impostor, who claimed affinity with the holy seed: the sceptre of the Almohades in Spain and Afric, of the Fatimites in Egypt and Syria,[184] of the Sultans of Yemen, and of the

181. The general article of *Imam*, in d'Herbelot's Bibliotheque, will indicate the succession; and the lives of the *twelve* are given under their respective names.

182. The name of *Antichrist* may seem ridiculous, but the Mahometans have liberally borrowed the fables of every religion (Sale's Preliminary Discourse, p. 80. 82.). In the royal stable of Ispahan, two horses were always kept saddled, one for the Mahadi himself, the other for his lieutenant, Jesus the son of Mary.

183. In the year of the Hegira 200 (A.D. 815). See d'Herbelot, p. 546.

184. D'Herbelot, p. 342. The enemies of the Fatimites disgraced them by a Jewish origin. Yet they accurately deduced their genealogy from Jaafar, the sixth Imam; and the impartial Abulfeda allows (Annal. Moslem. p. 230.) that they were owned by many, qui absque controversiâ genuini sunt Alidarum, homine propaginum suæ gentis

Sophis of Persia,[185] has been consecrated by this vague and ambiguous title. Under their reigns it might be dangerous to dispute the legitimacy of their birth; and one of the Fatimite caliphs silenced an indiscreet question, by drawing his scymetar: "This," said Moez, "is my pedigree; and these," casting an handful of gold to his soldiers, "and these are my kindred and my children." In the various conditions of princes, or doctors, or nobles, or merchants, or beggars, a swarm of the genuine or fictitious descendants of Mahomet and Ali is honoured with the appellation of sheiks, or sherifs, or emirs. In the Ottoman empire, they are distinguished by a green turban, receive a stipend from the treasury, are judged only by their chief, and, however debased by fortune or character, still assert the proud pre-eminence of their birth. A family of three hundred persons, the pure and orthodox branch of the caliph Hassan, is preserved without taint or suspicion in the holy cities of Mecca and Medina, and still retains, after the revolutions of twelve centuries, the custody of the temple and the sovereignty of their native land. The fame and merit of Mahomet would ennoble a plebeian race, and the ancient blood of the Koreish transcends the recent majesty of the kings of the earth.[186]

Success of Mahomet.

The talents of Mahomet are entitled to our applause, but his success has perhaps too strongly attracted our admiration. Are we surprised that a multitude of proselytes should embrace the doctrine and the passions of an eloquent fanatic? In the heresies of the church, the same seduction has been tried and repeated from the time of the apostles to that of the reformers. Does it seem incredible that a private citizen should grasp the sword and the sceptre, subdue his native country, and erect a monarchy by his victorious arms? In the moving picture of the dynasties of the East, an hundred fortunate usurpers have arisen from a

---

exacte callentes. He quotes some lines from the celebrated *Scherif or Rahdi*, Egone humilitatem induam in terris hostium? (I suspect him to be an Edrissite of Sicily) cum in Ægypto sit Chalifa de gente Alii, quocum ego communem habeo patrem et vindicem.

185. The kings of Persia of the last dynasty are descended from Sheik Sefi, a saint of the xiv[th] century, and through him from Moussa Cassem, the son of Hosein, the son of Ali (Olearius, p. 957. Chardin, tom. iii. p. 288.). But I cannot trace the intermediate degrees in any genuine or fabulous pedigree. If they were truly Fatimites, they might draw their origin from the princes of Mazanderan, who reigned in the ix[th] century (d'Herbelot, p. 96.).

186. The present state of the family of Mahomet and Ali is most accurately described by Demetrius Cantemir (Hist. of the Othman Empire, p. 94.); and Niebuhr (Description de l'Arabie, p. 9–16. 317, &c.). It is much to be lamented, that the Danish traveller was unable to purchase the chronicles of Arabia.

baser origin, surmounted more formidable obstacles, and filled a larger scope of empire and conquest. Mahomet was alike instructed to preach and to fight, and the union of these opposite qualities, while it enhanced his merit, contributed to his success: the operation of force and persuasion, of enthusiasm and fear, continually acted on each other, till every barrier yielded to their irresistible power. His voice invited the Arabs to freedom and victory, to arms and rapine, to the indulgence of their darling passions in this world and the other; the restraints which he imposed were requisite to establish the credit of the prophet, and to exercise the obedience of the people; and the only objection to his success, was his rational creed of the unity and perfections of God. It is

Permanency of his religion.

not the propagation but the permanency of his religion that deserves our wonder: the same pure and perfect impression which he engraved at Mecca and Medina, is preserved, after the revolutions of twelve centuries, by the Indian, the African, and the Turkish proselytes of the Koran. If the Christian apostles, St. Peter or St. Paul, could return to the Vatican, they might possibly enquire the name of the Deity who is worshipped with such mysterious rites in that magnificent temple: at Oxford or Geneva, they would experience less surprise; but it might still be incumbent on them to peruse the catechism of the church, and to study the orthodox commentators on their own writings and the words of their master. But the Turkish dome of St. Sophia, with an encrease of splendor and size, represents the humble tabernacle erected at Medina by the hands of Mahomet. The Mahometans have uniformly withstood the temptation of reducing the object of their faith and devotion to a level with the senses and imagination of man. "I believe in one God, and Mahomet the apostle of God," is the simple and invariable profession of Islam. The intellectual image of the Deity has never been degraded by any visible idol; the honours of the prophet have never transgressed the measure of human virtue; and his living precepts have restrained the gratitude of his disciples within the bounds of reason and religion. The votaries of Ali have indeed consecrated the memory of their hero, his wife, and his children, and some of the Persian doctors pretend that the divine essence was incarnate in the person of the Imams; but their superstition is universally condemned by the Sonnites; and their impiety has afforded a seasonable warning against the worship of saints and martyrs. The metaphysical questions on the attributes of God, and the liberty of man, have been agitated in the schools of the Mahometans, as well as in those of the Christians; but among the former they have never engaged the passions of the people or disturbed the tranquillity of the state. The cause of this important difference may be found in the separation or union of the regal and sacerdotal characters. It was the interest of the caliphs, the successors of the prophet and commanders of the faithful, to repress and discourage all religious innovations: the order, the discipline, the temporal and spiritual ambition of the clergy, are unknown to the Moslems; and the sages of the law are the guides of their conscience and the oracles of their faith. From the Atlantic to the Ganges, the Koran is acknowledged as the fundamental code, not only of theology but of civil and criminal jurisprudence; and the laws which regulate the actions and the property of mankind, are guarded by the infallible and immutable sanction of the will of God. This religious servitude is attended with some practical disadvantage; the illiterate legislator had been often misled by his own prejudices and those of his country; and the institutions of the Arabian desert may be ill-adapted to the wealth and numbers of Ispahan and Constantinople. On these occasions, the Cadhi respectfully places on his head the holy volume, and substitutes a dextrous interpretation more apposite to the principles of equity, and the manners and policy of the times.

His merit towards his country.

His beneficial or pernicious influence on the public happiness is the last consideration in the character of Mahomet. The most bitter or most bigotted of his Christian or Jewish foes, will surely allow that he assumed a false commission to inculcate a salutary doctrine, less perfect only than their own. He piously supposed, as the basis of his religion, the truth and sanctity of *their* prior revelations, the virtues and miracles of their founders. The idols of Arabia were broken before the throne of God; the blood of human victims was expiated by prayer, and fasting, and alms, the laudable or innocent arts of devotion; and his rewards and punishments of a future life were painted by the images most congenial to an ignorant and carnal generation. Mahomet was perhaps incapable of dictating a moral and political system for the use of his countrymen: but he breathed among the faithful a spirit of charity and friendship, recommended the practice of the social virtues, and checked, by his laws and precepts, the thirst of revenge and the oppression of widows and orphans. The hostile tribes were united in faith and obedience, and the valour which had been idly spent in domestic quarrels, was vigorously directed against a foreign enemy. Had the impulse been less powerful, Arabia, free at home, and formidable abroad, might have flourished under a succession of her native monarchs. Her sovereignty was lost by the extent and rapidity of conquest. The colonies of the nation were scattered over the East and West, and their blood was mingled with the blood of their converts and captives. After the reign of three caliphs, the throne was transported from Medina to the valley of Damascus and the banks of the Tigris; the holy cities were violated by impious war; Arabia was ruled by the rod of a subject, perhaps of a stranger; and the Bedoweens of the desert, awakening from their dream of dominion, resumed their old and solitary independence.[187]

187. The writers of the Modern Universal History (vol. i. and ii.) have compiled, in 850 folio pages, the life of Mahomet and the annals of the caliphs. They enjoyed the advantage of reading, and sometimes correcting, the Arabic texts; yet, notwithstanding their high-sounding boasts, I cannot find, after the conclusion of my work, that they have afforded me much (if any) additional information. The dull mass is not quickened by a spark of philosophy or taste: and the compilers indulge the criticism of acrimonious bigotry against Boulainvilliers, Sale, Gagnier, and all who have treated Mahomet with favour, or even justice.

CHAPTER LI

The Conquest of Persia, Syria, Egypt, Africa, and Spain, by the Arabs or Saracens. – Empire of the Caliphs, or Successors of Mahomet. – State of the Christians, &c. under their Government.

Union of the Arabs, A.D. 632.

The revolution of Arabia had not changed the character of the Arabs: the death of Mahomet was the signal of independence; and the hasty structure of his power and religion tottered to its foundations. A small and faithful band of his primitive disciples had listened to his eloquence, and shared his distress; had fled with the apostle from the persecution of Mecca, or had received the fugitive in the walls of Medina. The encreasing myriads, who acknowledged Mahomet as their king and prophet, had been compelled by his arms, or allured by his prosperity. The polytheists were confounded by the simple idea of a solitary and invisible God: the pride of the Christians and Jews disdained the yoke of a mortal and contemporary legislator. Their habits of faith and obedience were not sufficiently confirmed; and many of the new converts regretted the venerable antiquity of the law of Moses, or the rites and mysteries of the Catholic church, or the idols, the sacrifices, the joyous festivals, of their Pagan ancestors. The jarring interests and hereditary feuds of the Arabian tribes had not yet coalesced in a system of union and subordination; and the Barbarians were impatient of the mildest and most salutary laws that curbed their passions, or violated their customs. They submitted with reluctance to the religious precepts of the Koran, the abstinence from wine, the fast of the Ramadan, and the daily repetition of five prayers; and the alms and tithes, which were collected for the treasury of Medina, could be distinguished only by a name from the payment of a perpetual and ignominious tribute. The example of Mahomet had excited a spirit of fanaticism or imposture, and several of his rivals presumed to imitate the conduct and defy the authority of the living prophet. At the head of the *fugitives* and *auxiliaries*, the first caliph was reduced to the cities of Mecca, Medina, and Tayef; and perhaps the Koreish would have restored the idols of the Caaba, if their levity had not been checked by a seasonable reproof. "Ye men of Mecca, will ye be the last to embrace and the first to abandon the religion of Islam?" After exhorting the Moslems to confide in the aid of God and his apostle, Abubeker resolved, by a vigorous attack, to prevent the junction of the rebels. The women and children were safely lodged in the cavities of the mountains: the warriors, marching under eleven banners, diffused the terror of their arms; and the appearance of a military force revived and confirmed the loyalty of the faithful. The inconstant tribes accepted, with humble repentance, the duties of prayer, and fasting, and alms; and, after some examples of success and severity, the most daring apostates fell prostrate before the sword of the Lord and of Caled. In the fertile province of Yemanah,[1] between the Red Sea and the Gulph of Persia, in a city not inferior to Medina itself, a powerful chief, his name was Moseilama, had assumed the character of a prophet, and the tribe of Hanifa listened to his voice. A female prophetess was attracted by his reputation: the decencies of words and actions were spurned by these favourites of heaven;[2] and they employed several days in mystic and amorous converse. An obscure sentence of his Koran, or book, is yet extant;[3] and, in the pride of his mission, Moseilama condescended to offer a partition of the earth. The proposal was answered by Mahomet with contempt; but the rapid progress of the impostor awakened the fears of his successor: forty thousand Moslems were assembled under the standard of Caled; and the existence of their faith was resigned to the event of a decisive battle. In

1. See the description of the city and country of Al Yamanah, in Abulfeda, Descript. Arabiæ, p. 60, 61. In the xiii[th] century, there were some ruins, and a few palms; but in the present century, the same ground is occupied by the visions and arms of a modern prophet, whose tenets are imperfectly known (Niebuhr, Description de l'Arabie, p. 296–302.).

2. Their first salutation may be transcribed, but cannot be translated. It was thus that Moseilama said or sung:

> Surge tandem itaque strenue permolenda; nam stratus tibi thorus est.
> Aut in propatulo tentorio si velis, aut in abditiore cubiculo si malis;
> Aut supinam te humi exporrectam fustigabo, si velis, aut si malis manibus pedibusque nixam.
> Aut si velis ejus (*Priapi*) gemino triente, aut si malis totus veniam.
> Imo, totus venito, O Apostole Dei clamabat fœmina. Id ipsum dicebat
> Moseilama mihi quoque suggessit Deus.

The prophetess Segjah, after the fall of her lover, returned to idolatry; but, under the reign of Moawiyah, she became a Musulman, and died at Bassora (Abulfeda, Annal. vers. Reiske, p. 63.).

3. See this text, which demonstrates a God from the work of generation, in Abulpharagius (Specimen, Hist. Arabum, p. 13. and Dynast. p. 103.) and Abulfeda (Annal. p. 63.).

the first action, they were repulsed with the loss of twelve hundred men; but the skill and perseverance of their general prevailed: their defeat was avenged by the slaughter of ten thousand infidels; and Moseilama himself was pierced by an Ethiopian slave with the same javelin which had mortally wounded the uncle of Mahomet. The various rebels of Arabia, without a chief or a cause, were speedily suppressed by the power and discipline of the rising monarchy; and the whole nation again professed, and more stedfastly held, the religion of the Koran. The ambition of the caliphs provided an immediate exercise for the restless spirit of the Saracens: their valour was united in the prosecution of an holy war; and their enthusiasm was equally confirmed by opposition and victory.

Character of their caliphs.

From the rapid conquests of the Saracens a presumption will naturally arise, that the first caliphs commanded in person the armies of the faithful, and sought the crown of martyrdom in the foremost ranks of the battle. The courage of Abubeker,[4] Omar,[5] and Othman,[6] had indeed been tried in the persecution and wars of the prophet; and the personal assurance of paradise must have taught them to despise the pleasures and dangers of the present world. But they ascended the throne in a venerable or mature age, and esteemed the domestic cares of religion and justice the most important duties of a sovereign. Except the presence of Omar at the siege of Jerusalem, their longest expeditions were the frequent pilgrimage from Medina to Mecca; and they calmly received the tidings of victory as they prayed or preached before the sepulchre of the prophet. The austere and frugal measure of their lives was the effect of virtue or habit, and the pride of their simplicity insulted the vain magnificence of the kings of the earth. When Abubeker assumed the office of caliph, he enjoined his daughter Ayesha to take a strict account of his private patrimony, that it might be evident whether he were enriched or impoverished by the service of the state. He thought himself entitled to a stipend of three pieces of gold, with the sufficient maintenance of a single camel and a black slave; but on the Friday of each week, he distributed the residue of his own and the public money, first to the most worthy, and then to the most indigent, of the Moslems. The

4. His reign in Eutychius, tom. ii. p. 251. Elmacin, p. 18. Abulpharagius, p. 108. Abulfeda, p. 60. D'Herbelot, p. 58.

5. His reign in Eutychius, p. 264. Elmacin, p. 24. Abulpharagius, p. 110. Abulfeda, p. 66. D'Herbelot, p. 686.

6. His reign in Eutychius, p. 323. Elmacin, p. 36. Abulpharagius, p. 115. Abulfeda, p. 75. D'Herbelot, p. 695.

remains of his wealth, a coarse garment, and five pieces of gold, were delivered to his successor, who lamented with a modest sigh his own inability to equal such an admirable model. Yet the abstinence and humility of Omar were not inferior to the virtues of Abubeker; his food consisted of barley-bread or dates; his drink was water; he preached in a gown that was torn or tattered in twelve places; and a Persian satrap who paid his homage to the conqueror, found him asleep among the beggars on the steps of the mosch of Medina. Oeconomy is the source of liberality, and the encrease of the revenue enabled Omar to establish a just and perpetual reward for the past and present services of the faithful. Careless of his own emolument, he assigned to Abbas, the uncle of the prophet, the first and most ample allowance of twenty-five thousand drams or pieces of silver. Five thousand were allotted to each of the aged warriors, the relics of the field of Beder, and the last and meanest of the companions of Mahomet was distinguished by the annual reward of three thousand pieces. One thousand was the stipend of the veterans who had fought in the first battles against the Greeks and Persians, and the decreasing pay, as low as fifty pieces of silver, was adapted to the respective merit and seniority of the soldiers of Omar. Under his reign, and that of his predecessor, the conquerors of the East, were the trusty servants of God and the people: the mass of the public treasure was consecrated to the expences of peace and war; a prudent mixture of justice and bounty, maintained the discipline of the Saracens, and they united, by a rare felicity, the dispatch and execution of despotism, with the equal and frugal maxims of a republican government. The heroic courage of Ali,[7] the consummate prudence of Moawiyah,[8] excited the emulation of their subjects; and the talents which had been exercised in the school of civil discord, were more usefully applied to propagate the faith and dominion of the prophet. In the sloth and vanity of the palace of Damascus, the succeeding princes of the house of Ommiyah were alike destitute of the qualifications of statesmen and of saints.[9] Yet the spoils of unknown nations were continually laid at the foot of their throne, and the uniform ascent of the Arabian greatness must be ascribed to the spirit of the nation

7. His reign in Eutychius, p. 343. Elmacin, p. 51. Abulpharagius, p. 117. Abulfeda, p. 83. D'Herbelot, p. 89.

8. His reign in Eutychius, p. 344. Elmacin, p. 54. Abulpharagius, p. 123. Abulfeda, p. 101. D'Herbelot, p. 586.

9. Their reigns in Eutychius, tom. ii. p. 360–395. Elmacin, p. 59–108. Abulpharagius, Dynast. ix. p. 124–139. Abulfeda, p. 111–141. D'Herbelot, Bibliotheque Orientale, p. 691. and the particular articles of the Ommiades.

rather than the abilities of their chiefs. A large deduction must be allowed for the weakness of their enemies. The birth of Mahomet was fortunately placed in the most degenerate and disorderly period of the Persians, the Romans, and the Barbarians of Europe: the empires of Trajan, or even of Constantine or Charlemagne, would have repelled the assault of the naked Saracens, and the torrent of fanaticism might have been obscurely lost in the sands of Arabia.

Their conquests.

In the victorious days of the Roman republic, it had been the aim of the senate to confine their counsels and legions to a single war, and completely to suppress a first enemy before they provoked the hostilities of a second. These timid maxims of policy were disdained by the magnanimity or enthusiasm of the Arabian caliphs. With the same vigour and success they invaded the successors of Augustus and those of Artaxerxes; and the rival monarchies at the same instant became the prey of an enemy whom they had been so long accustomed to despise. In the ten years of the administration of Omar, the Saracens reduced to his obedience thirty-six thousand cities or castles, destroyed four thousand churches or temples of the unbelievers, and edified fourteen hundred moschs for the exercise of the religion of Mahomet. One hundred years after his flight from Mecca, the arms and the reign of his successors extended from India to the Atlantic Ocean, over the various and distant provinces, which may be comprised under the names of, I. Persia; II. Syria; III. Egypt; IV. Africa; and, V. Spain. Under this general division, I shall proceed to unfold these memorable transactions; dispatching with brevity the remote and less interesting conquests of the East, and reserving a fuller narrative for those domestic countries, which had been included within the pale of the Roman empire. Yet I must excuse my own defects by a just complaint of the blindness and insufficiency of my guides. The Greeks, so loquacious in controversy, have not been anxious to celebrate the triumphs of their enemies.[10] After a century of ignorance, the first annals of the Musulmans were collected in a great measure from the

10. For the vii[th] and viii[th] century, we have scarcely any original evidence of the Byzantine historians, except the Chronicles of Theophanes (Theophanis Confessoris Chronographia, Gr. et Lat. cum notis Jacobi Goar. Paris, 1655, in folio); and the Abridgement of Nicephorus (Nicephori Patriarchæ, C. P. Breviarium Historicum, Gr. et Lat. Paris, 1648, in folio), who both lived in the beginning of the ix[th] century (see Hanckius de Scriptor. Byzant. p. 200–246.). Their contemporary Photius does not seem to be more opulent. After praising the style of Nicephorus, he adds, *Και ὁλως πολλους εστι τον προ αυτου αποκρυπτομενος τηδε της ἱστοριας τῃ συγγραφῃ*, and only complains of his extreme brevity (Phot. Bibliot. cod. lxvi.

voice of tradition.[11] Among the numerous productions of Arabic and Persian literature,[12] our interpreters have selected the imperfect sketches of a more recent age.[13] The art and genius of history have ever been unknown to the Asiatics;[14] they are ignorant of the laws of criticism; and our monkish chronicles of the same period may be compared to their most popular works, which are never vivified by the spirit of philosophy and freedom. The *Oriental library* of a Frenchman[15] would instruct the

---

p. 100.). Some additions may be gleaned from the more recent histories of Cedrenus and Zonaras of the xii[th] century.

11. Tabari, or Al Tabari, a native of Taborestan, a famous Imam of Bagdad, and the Livy of the Arabians, finished his general history in the year of the Hegira 302 (A.D. 914). At the request of his friends, he reduced a work of 30,000 sheets to a more reasonable size. But his Arabic original is known only by the Persian and Turkish versions. The Saracenic history of Ebn Amid, or Elmacin, is said to be an abridgment of the great Tabari (Ockley's Hist. of the Saracens, vol. ii. preface p. xxxix. and, list of authors, d'Herbelot, p. 866. 870. 1014.).

12. Besides the lists of authors framed by Prideaux (Life of Mahomet, p. 179–189.), Ockley (at the end of his second volume), and Petit de la Croix (Hist. de Gengiscan. p. 525–550.), we find in the Bibliotheque Orientale *Tarikh*, a catalogue of two or three hundred histories or chronicles of the East, of which not more than three or four are older than Tabari. A lively sketch of Oriental literature is given by Reiske (in his Prodidagmata ad Hagji Chalifæ librum memorialem ad calcem Abulfedæ Tabulæ Syriæ, Lipsiæ, 1766); but his project and the French version of Petit de la Croix (Hist. de Timur Bec. tom. i. preface, p. xlv.) have fallen to the ground.

13. The particular historians and geographers will be occasionally introduced. The four following titles represent the annals, which have guided me in this general narrative. 1. *Annales Eutychii, Patriarchæ Alexandrini, ab Edwardo Pocockio, Oxon*, 1656, 2 *vols.* in 4to. A pompous edition of an indifferent author, translated by Pocock to gratify the presbyterian prejudices of his friend Selden. 2. *Historia Saracenica Georgii Elmacini, operâ et studio Thomæ Erpenii, in* 4to *Lugd. Batavorum*, 1625. He is said to have hastily translated a corrupt MS. and his version is often deficient in style and sense. 3. *Historia compendiosa Dynastiarum a Gregorio Abulpharagio, interprete Edwardo Pocockio, in* 4to *Oxon*, 1663. More useful for the literary than the civil history of the East. 4. *Abulfedæ Annales Moslemici ad Ann. Hegiræ*, ccccvi. *a Jo. Jac. Reiske, in* 4to *Lipsiæ*, 1754. The best of our Chronicles, both for the original and version, yet how far below the name of Abulfeda. We know that he wrote at Hamah, in the xiv[th] century. The three former were Christians of the xth, xii[th], and xiii[th] centuries; the two first, natives of Egypt, a Melchite patriarch, and a Jacobite scribe.

14. M. de Guignes (Hist. des Huns, tom. i. pref. p. xix, xx.) has characterised, with truth and knowledge, the two sorts of Arabian historians, the dry annalist, and the tumid and flowery orator.

15. Bibliotheque Orientale, par M. d'Herbelot, in folio, Paris, 1697. For the character of the respectable author, consult his friend Thevenot (Voyages du Levant, part i. ch. 1.). His work is an agreeable miscellany, which must gratify every taste; but I never can digest the alphabetical order, and I find him more satisfactory in the Persian than the Arabic history. The recent supplement from the papers of M. M. Visdelou and

most learned mufti of the East; and perhaps the Arabs might not find in a single historian, so clear and comprehensive a narrative of their own exploits, as that which will be deduced in the ensuing sheets.

Invasion of Persia, A.D. 632.

I. In the first year of the first caliph, his lieutenant Caled, the sword of God, and the scourge of the infidels, advanced to the banks of the Euphrates, and reduced the cities of Anbar and Hira. Westward of the ruins of Babylon, a tribe of sedentary Arabs had fixed themselves on the verge of the desert; and Hira was the seat of a race of kings who had embraced the Christian religion, and reigned above six hundred years under the shadow of the throne of Persia.[16] The last of the Mondars was defeated and slain by Caled; his son was sent a captive to Medina; his nobles bowed before the successor of the prophet; the people was tempted by the example and success of their countrymen; and the caliph accepted as the first fruits of foreign conquest, an annual tribute of seventy thousand pieces of gold. The conquerors, and even their historians, were astonished by the dawn of their future greatness: "In the same year," says Elmacin, "Caled fought many signal battles; an immense multitude of the infidels was slaughtered; and spoils, infinite and innumerable, were acquired by the victorious Moslems."[17] But the invincible Caled was soon transferred to the Syrian war: the invasion of the Persian frontier was conducted by less active or less prudent commanders: the Saracens were repulsed with loss in the passage of the Euphrates; and, though they chastised the insolent pursuit of the Magians, their remaining forces still hovered in the desert of Babylon.

Battle of Cadesia, A.D. 636.

The indignation and fears of the Persians suspended for a moment their intestine divisions. By the unanimous sentence of the priests and nobles, their queen Arzema was deposed; the sixth of the transient usurpers, who had arisen and vanished in three or four years, since the death of Chosroes and the retreat of Heraclius. Her tiara

---

Galland (in folio, La Haye, 1779) is of a different cast, a medley of tales, proverbs, and Chinese antiquities.

16. Pocock will explain the chronology (Specimen, Hist. Arabum, p. 66–74.), and d'Anville the Geography (l'Euphrate et le Tigre, p. 125.), of the Dynasty of the Almondars. The English scholar understood more Arabic than the Mufti of Aleppo (Ockley, vol. ii. p. 34.): the French geographer is equally at home in every age and every climate of the world.

17. Fecit et Chaled plurima in hoc anno prœlia, in quibus vicerunt Muslimi, et *infidelium* immensâ multitudine occisâ spolia infinita et innumera sunt nacti (Hist. Saracenica, p. 20.). The Christian annalist slides into the national and compendious term of *infidels*, and I often adopt (I hope without scandal) this characteristic mode of expression.

was placed on the head of Yezdegerd, the grandson of Chosroes; and the same æra, which coincides with an astronomical period,[18] has recorded the fall of the Sassanian dynasty and the religion of Zoroaster.[19] The youth and inexperience of the prince, he was only fifteen years of age, declined a perilous encounter: the royal standard was delivered into the hands of his general Rustam; and a remnant of thirty thousand regular troops was swelled in truth, or in opinion, to one hundred and twenty thousand subjects, or allies, of the great king. The Moslems, whose numbers were reinforced from twelve to thirty thousand, had pitched their camp in the plains of Cadesia:[20] and their line, though it consisted of fewer *men*, could produce more *soldiers* than the unwieldy host of the infidels. I shall here observe what I must often repeat, that the charge of the Arabs was not like that of the Greeks and Romans, the effort of a firm and compact infantry: their military force was chiefly formed of cavalry and archers; and the engagement, which was often interrupted and often renewed by single combats and flying skirmishes, might be protracted without any decisive event to the continuance of several days. The periods of the battle of Cadesia were distinguished by their peculiar appellations. The first, from the well-timed appearance of six thousand of the Syrian brethren, was denominated the day of *succour*. The day of *concussion* might express the disorder of one, or perhaps of both, of the contending armies. The third, a nocturnal tumult, received the whimsical name of the night of *barking*, from the discordant clamours, which were compared to the inarticulate sounds of the fiercest animals. The morning of the succeeding day determined the fate of Persia; and a seasonable

18. A cycle of 120 years, the end of which an intercalary month of 30 days supplied the use of our Bissextile, and restored the integrity of the solar year. In a great revolution of 1440 years, this intercalation was successively removed from the first to the twelfth month; but Hyde and Freret are involved in a profound controversy, whether the twelve, or only eight of these changes were accomplished before the æra of Yezdegerd, which is unanimously fixed to the 16th of June A.D. 632. How laboriously does the curious spirit of Europe explore the darkest and most distant antiquities (Hyde, de Religione Persarum, c. 14–18. p. 181–211. Freret in the Mem. de l'Academie des Inscriptions, tom. xvi. p. 233–267.)!

19. Nine days after the death of Mahomet (7th June A.D. 632), we find the æra of Yezdegerd (16th June A.D. 632), and his accession cannot be postponed beyond the end of the first year. His predecessors could not therefore resist the arms of the caliph Omar, and these unquestionable dates overthrow the thoughtless chronology of Abulpharagius. See Ockley's Hist. of the Saracens, vol. i. p. 130.

20. Cadesia, says the Nubian geographer (p. 121.), is in margine solitudinis, 61 leagues from Bagdad, and two stations from Cufa. Otter (Voyage, tom. i. p. 163.) reckons 15 leagues, and observes, that the place is supplied with dates and water.

whirlwind drove a cloud of dust against the faces of the unbelievers. The clangor of arms was re-echoed to the tent of Rustam, who, far unlike the ancient hero of his name, was gently reclining in a cool and tranquil shade, amidst the baggage of his camp, and the train of mules that were laden with gold and silver. On the sound of danger he started from his couch; but his flight was overtaken by a valiant Arab, who caught him by the foot, struck off his head, hoisted it on a lance, and instantly returning to the field of battle, carried slaughter and dismay among the thickest ranks of the Persians. The Saracens confess a loss of seven thousand five hundred men; and the battle of Cadesia is justly described by the epithets of obstinate and atrocious.[21] The standard of the monarchy was overthrown and captured in the field – a leathern apron of a blacksmith, who, in ancient times, had arisen the deliverer of Persia; but this badge of heroic poverty was disguised, and almost concealed by a profusion of precious gems.[22] After this victory, the wealthy province of Irak or Assyria submitted to the caliph, and his conquests were firmly established by the speedy foundation of Bassora,[23] a place which ever commands the trade and navigation of the Persians. At the distance of fourscore miles from the Gulf, the Euphrates and Tigris unite in a broad and direct current, which is aptly styled the river of the Arabs. In the mid-way between the junction and the mouth of these famous streams, the new settlement was planted on the western bank: the first colony was composed of eight hundred Moslems; but the influence of the situation soon reared a flourishing and populous capital. The air, though excessively hot, is pure and healthy: the meadows are filled with palm-trees and cattle; and one of the adjacent vallies has been celebrated among the four paradises or gardens of Asia. Under the first caliphs, the jurisdiction of this Arabian colony extended over the southern provinces of Persia: the city has been sanctified by the tombs of the companions and martyrs; and the vessels of Europe still frequent the port of Bassora, as a convenient station and passage of the Indian trade.

Foundation of Bassora.

21. Atrox, contumax, plus semel renovatum, are the well-chosen expressions of the translator of Abulfeda (Reiske, p. 69.).

22. D'Herbelot, Bibliotheque Orientale, p. 297. 348.

23. The reader may satisfy himself on the subject of Bassora, by consulting the following writers: Geograph. Nubiens. p. 121. D'Herbelot, Bibliotheque Orientale, p. 192. D'Anville, L'Euphrate et le Tigre, p. 130. 133. 145. Raynal, Hist. Philosophique des deux Indes, tom. ii. p. 92–100. Voyages di Pietro della Valle, tom. iv. p. 370–391. De Tavernier, tom. i. p. 240–247. De Thevenot, tom. ii. p. 545–584. D'Otter, tom. ii. p. 45–78. De Niebuhr, tom. ii. p. 172–199.

Sack of Madayn, A.D. 637, March.

After the defeat of Cadesia, a country intersected by rivers and canals might have opposed an insuperable barrier to the victorious cavalry; and the walls of Ctesiphon or Madayn, which had resisted the battering-rams of the Romans, would not have yielded to the darts of the Saracens. But the flying Persians were overcome by the belief, that the last day of their religion and empire was at hand: the strongest posts were abandoned by treachery or cowardice; and the king, with a part of his family and treasures, escaped to Holwan at the foot of the Median hills. In the third month after the battle, Said, the lieutenant of Omar, passed the Tigris without opposition; the capital was taken by assault; and the disorderly resistance of the people gave a keener edge to the sabres of the Moslems, who shouted with religious transport, "This is the white palace of Chosroes, this is the promise of the apostle of God!" The naked robbers of the desert were suddenly enriched beyond the measure of their hope or knowledge. Each chamber revealed a new treasure secreted with art, or ostentatiously displayed; the gold and silver, the various wardrobes and precious furniture, surpassed (says Abulfeda) the estimate of fancy or numbers; and another historian defines the untold and almost infinite mass, by the fabulous computation of three thousands of thousands of thousands of pieces of gold.[24] Some minute though curious facts represent the contrast of riches and ignorance. From the remote islands of the Indian Ocean, a large provision of camphire[25] had been imported, which is employed with a mixture of wax to illuminate the palaces of the East. Strangers to the name and properties of that odoriferous gum, the Saracens, mistaking it for salt, mingled the camphire in their bread, and were astonished at the bitterness of the taste. One of the apartments of the palace was decorated with a carpet of silk, sixty cubits in length, and as many in breadth: a paradise or garden was depictured on the ground; the flowers, fruits, and shrubs were imitated by the figures of the gold embroidery, and the colours of the precious

24. Mente vix potest numerove comprehendi quanta spolia . . . nostris cesserint. Abulfeda, p. 69. Yet I still suspect, that the extravagant numbers of Elmacin may be the error, not of the text, but of the version. The best translators from the Greek, for instance, I find to be very poor arithmeticians.

25. The Camphire tree grows in China and Japan; but many hundred weight of those meaner sorts are exchanged for a single pound of the more precious gum of Borneo and Sumatra (Raynal, Hist. Philosoph. tom. i. p. 362–365. Dictionnaire d'Hist. Naturelle par Bomare. Millar's Gardener's Dictionary). These may be the islands of the first climate from whence the Arabians imported their camphire (Geograph. Nub. p. 34, 35. d'Herbelot, p. 232.).

stones; and the ample square was encircled by a variegated and verdant border. The Arabian general persuaded his soldiers to relinquish their claim, in the reasonable hope, that the eyes of the caliph would be delighted with the splendid workmanship of nature and industry. Regardless of the merit of art and the pomp of royalty, the rigid Omar divided the prize among his brethren of Medina: the picture was destroyed; but such was the intrinsic value of the materials, that the share of Ali alone was sold for twenty thousand drams. A mule that carried away the tiara and cuirass, the belt and bracelets of Chosroes, was overtaken by the pursuers; the gorgeous trophy was presented to the commander of the faithful, and the gravest of the companions condescended to smile when they beheld the white beard, hairy arms, and uncouth figure of the veteran, who was invested with the spoils of the great king.[26] The sack of Ctesiphon was followed by its desertion and gradual decay. The Saracens disliked the air and situation of the place, and Omar was advised by his general to remove the seat of government to the western side of the Euphrates. In every age the foundation and ruin of the Assyrian cities has been easy and rapid; the country is destitute of stone and timber, and the most solid structures[27] are composed of bricks baked in the sun, and joined by a cement of the native bitumen. The name of *Cufa*[28] describes an habitation of reeds and earth; but the importance of the new capital was supported by the numbers, wealth, and spirit of a colony of veterans; and their licentiousness was indulged by the wisest caliphs who were apprehensive of provoking the revolt of an hundred thousand swords: "Ye men of Cufa," said Ali, who solicited their aid, "you have been always conspicuous by your valour. You conquered the Persian king, and scattered his forces, till you had taken possession of his inheritance." This mighty conquest was atchieved by the battles of Jalula and Nehavend. After the loss of the former, Yezdegerd fled from Holwan, and concealed his shame and despair in the mountains of Farsistan, from whence Cyrus had descended with his equal and valiant companions. The courage of the nation survived that of the monarch; among the hills to the south of Ecbatana or Hamadan, one hundred and

Foundation of Cufa.

26. See Gagnier, Vie de Mahomet, tom. i. p. 376, 377. I may credit the fact, without believing the prophecy.

27. The most considerable ruins of Assyria are the tower of Belus, at Babylon, and the hall of Chosroes, at Ctesiphon: they have been visited by that vain and curious traveller Pietro della Valle (tom. i. p. 713–718. 731–735.).

28. Consult the article of *Coufah* in the Bibliotheque of d'Herbelot (p. 277, 278.), and the second volume of Ockley's history, particularly p. 40. and 153.

fifty thousand Persians made a third and final stand for their religion and country; and the decisive battle of Nehavend was styled by the Arabs the victory of victories. If it be true that the flying general of the Persians was stopt and overtaken in a crowd of mules and camels laden with honey, the incident, however slight or singular, will denote the luxurious impediments of an Oriental army.[29]

Conquest of Persia, A.D. 637–651.

The geography of Persia is darkly delineated by the Greeks and Latins; but the most illustrious of her cities appear to be more ancient than the invasion of the Arabs. By the reduction of Hamadan and Ispahan, of Caswin, Tauris, and Rei, they gradually approached the shores of the Caspian Sea; and the orators of Mecca might applaud the success and spirit of the faithful, who had already lost sight of the northern bear, and had almost transcended the bounds of the habitable world.[30] Again turning towards the West and the Roman empire, they repassed the Tigris over the bridge of Mosul, and, in the captive provinces of Armenia and Mesopotamia, embraced their victorious brethren of the Syrian army. From the palace of Madayn their Eastern progress was not less rapid or extensive. They advanced along the Tigris and the Gulf; penetrated through the passes of the mountains into the valley of Estachar or Persepolis; and profaned the last sanctuary of the Magian empire. The grandson of Chosroes was nearly surprised among the falling columns and mutilated figures; a sad emblem of the past and present fortune of Persia:[31] he fled with accelerated haste over the desert of Kirman, implored the aid of the warlike Segestans, and sought an humble refuge on the verge of the Turkish and Chinese power. But a victorious army is insensible of fatigue: the Arabs divided their forces in the pursuit of a timorous enemy; and the caliph Othman promised the government of Chorasan to the first general who should

29. See the article of *Nehavend*, in d'Herbelot, p. 667, 668.; and Voyages en Turquie et en Perse, par Otter, tom. i. p. 191.

30. It is in such a style of ignorance and wonder that the Athenian orator describes the Arctic conquests of Alexander, who never advanced beyond the shores of the Caspian. *Αλεξανδρος εξω της αρκτου και της οικουμενης, ολιγου δειν, πασης μεθηστηκει.* Eschines contra Ctesiphontem, tom. iii. p. 554, edit. Græc. Orator. Reiske. This memorable cause was pleaded at Athens, Olymp. cxii. 3. (before Christ 330); in the autumn (Tayler, præfat. p. 370, &c.), about a year after the battle of Arbela; and Alexander, in the pursuit of Darius, was marching towards Hyrcania and Bactriana.

31. We are indebted for this curious particular to the Dynasties of Abulpharagius, p. 116; but it is needless to prove the identity of Estachar and Persepolis (d'Herbelot, p. 327.); and still more needless to copy the drawings and descriptions of Sir John Chardin, or Corneille le Bruyn.

enter that large and populous country, the kingdom of the ancient Bactrians. The condition was accepted; the prize was deserved; the standard of Mahomet was planted on the walls of Herat, Merou, and Balch; and the successful leader neither halted nor reposed till his foaming cavalry had tasted the waters of the Oxus. In the public anarchy, the independent governors of the cities and castles obtained their separate capitulations: the terms were granted or imposed by the esteem, the prudence, or the compassion, of the victors; and a simple profession of faith established the distinction between a brother and a slave. After a noble defence, Harmozan, the prince or satrap of Ahwaz and Susa, was compelled to surrender his person and his state to the discretion of the caliph; and their interview exhibits a portrait of the Arabian manners. In the presence, and by the command, of Omar, the gay Barbarian was despoiled of his silken robes embroidered with gold, and of his tiara bedecked with rubies and emeralds: "Are you now sensible," said the conqueror to his naked captive; "are you now sensible of the judgment of God, and of the different rewards of infidelity and obedience?" "Alas!" replied Harmozan, "I feel them too deeply. In the days of our common ignorance, we fought with the weapons of the flesh, and my nation was superior. God was then neuter: since he has espoused your quarrel, you have subverted our kingdom and religion." Oppressed by this painful dialogue, the Persian complained of intolerable thirst, but discovered some apprehension lest he should be killed whilst he was drinking a cup of water. "Be of good courage," said the caliph, "your life is safe till you have drank this water:" the crafty satrap accepted the assurance, and instantly dashed the vase against the ground. Omar would have avenged the deceit; but his companions represented the sanctity of an oath; and the speedy conversion of Harmozan entitled him not only to a free pardon, but even to a stipend of two thousand pieces of gold. The administration of Persia was regulated by an actual survey of the people, the cattle, and the fruits of the earth;[32] and this monument which attests the vigilance of the caliphs, might have instructed the philosophers of every age.[33]

32. After the conquest of Persia, Theophanes adds, *αυτῳ δε τῳ χρονῳ εκελευσεν Ουμαρος αναγραφηναι πασαν την ὑπ' αυτον οικουμενην. εγενετο δε ἡ αναγραφη και ανθρωπων και κτηνων και φυτων* (Chronograph. p. 283.).

33. Amidst our meagre relations, I must regret, that d'Herbelot has not found and used a Persian translation of Tabari, enriched, as he says, with many extracts from the native historians of the Ghebers or Magi (Bibliotheque Orientale, p. 1014.).

Death of the last king, A.D. 651.

The flight of Yezdegerd had carried him beyond the Oxus, and as far as the Jaxartes, two rivers[34] of ancient and modern renown, which descend from the mountains of India towards the Caspian Sea. He was hospitably entertained by Tarkhan, prince of Fargana,[35] a fertile province on the Jaxartes; the king of Samarcand, with the Turkish tribes of Sogdiana and Scythia, were moved by the lamentations and promises of the fallen monarch; and he solicited by a suppliant embassy, the more solid and powerful friendship of the emperor of China.[36] The virtuous Taitsong,[37] the first of the dynasty of the Tang, may be justly compared with the Antonines of Rome: his people enjoyed the blessings of prosperity and peace; and his dominion was acknowledged by forty-four hords of the Barbarians of Tartary. His last garrisons of Cashgar and Khoten maintained a frequent intercourse with their neighbours of the Jaxartes and Oxus; a recent colony of Persians had introduced into China the astronomy of the Magi; and Taitsong might be alarmed by the rapid progress and dangerous vicinity of the Arabs. The influence, and perhaps the supplies, of China revived the hopes of Yezdegerd and the zeal of the worshippers of fire; and he returned with an army of Turks to conquer the inheritance of his fathers. The fortunate Moslems, without unsheathing their swords, were the spectators of his ruin and death. The grandson of Chosroes was betrayed by his servant, insulted by the seditious inhabitants of Merou, and oppressed, defeated, and pursued, by his Barbarian allies. He reached the banks of a river, and offered his rings and bracelets for an instant passage in a miller's boat. Ignorant or insensible of royal distress, the rustic replied, that four drams of silver were the daily profit of his mill, and that he would not suspend his work unless the loss were repaid. In this moment of hesitation and delay, the last of the Sassanian kings was overtaken and slaughtered by the

34. The most authentic accounts of the two rivers, the Sihon (Jaxartes), and the Gihon (Oxus), may be found in Sherif al Edrisi (Geograph. Nubiens. p. 138.). Abulfeda (Descript. Chorasan. in Hudson, tom. iii. p. 23.). Abulghazi Khan, who reigned on their banks (Hist. Genealogique des Tatars, p. 32. 57. 766.), and the Turkish Geographer, a MS. in the king of France's library (Examen Critique des Historiens d'Alexandre, p. 194–360.).

35. The territory of Fergana is described by Abulfeda, p. 76, 77.

36. Eo redegit angustiarum eundem regem exsulem, ut Turcici regis, et Sogdiani, et Sinensis, auxilia missis literis imploraret (Abulfed. Annal. p. 74.). The connection of the Persian and Chinese history is illustrated by Freret (Mem. de l'Academie, tom. xvi. p. 245–255.), and de Guignes (Hist. des Huns, tom. i. p. 54–59.), and for the geography of the borders, tom. ii. p. 1–43.).

37. Hist. Sinica, p. 41–46. in the iii[d] part of the Relations Curieuses of Thevenot.

Turkish cavalry, in the nineteenth year of his unhappy reign.[38] His son Firuz, an humble client of the Chinese emperor, accepted the station of captain of his guards; and the Magian worship was long preserved by a colony of loyal exiles in the province of Bucharia. His grandson inherited the regal name; but after a faint and fruitless enterprise, he returned to China, and ended his days in the palace of Sigan. The male line of the Sassanides was extinct; but the female captives, the daughters of Persia, were given to the conquerors in servitude or marriage; and the race of the caliphs and imams was ennobled by the blood of their royal mothers.[39]

The conquest of Transoxiana, A.D. 710.

After the fall of the Persian kingdom, the river Oxus divided the territories of the Saracens and of the Turks. This narrow boundary was soon overleaped by the spirit of the Arabs: the governors of Chorasan extended their successive inroads; and one of their triumphs was adorned with the buskin of a Turkish queen, which she dropt in her precipitate flight beyond the hills of Bochara.[40] But the final conquest of Transoxiana,[41] as well as of Spain, was reserved for the glorious reign of the inactive Walid; and the name of Catibah, the camel-driver, declares the origin and merit of his successful lieutenant. While one of his colleagues displayed the first Mahometan banner on the banks of the Indus, the spacious regions between the Oxus, the Jaxartes, and the Caspian Sea, were reduced by the arms of Catibah to the obedience of the prophet and of the caliph.[42] A tribute of two millions

38. I have endeavoured to harmonize the various narratives of Elmacin (Hist. Saracen. p. 37.), Abulpharagius (Dynast. p. 116.), Abulfeda (Annal. p. 74. 79.), and d'Herbelot (p. 485.). The end of Yezdegerd was not only unfortunate but obscure.

39. The two daughters of Yezdegerd married Hassan, the son of Ali, and Mohammed, the son of Abubeker; and the first of these was the father of a numerous progeny. The daughter of Phirouz became the wife of the caliph Walid, and their son Yezid derived his genuine or fabulous descent from the Chosroes of Persia, the Cæsars of Rome, and the Chagans of the Turks or Avars (d'Herbelot, Bibliot. Orientale, p. 96. 487.).

40. It was valued at 2000 pieces of gold, and was the prize of Obeidollah, the son of Ziyad, a name afterwards infamous by the murder of Hosein (Ockley's History of the Saracens, vol. ii. p. 142, 143.). His brother Salem was accompanied by his wife, the first Arabian woman (A.D. 680.) who passed the Oxus: she borrowed, or rather stole, the crown and jewels of the princess of the Sogdians (p. 231, 232.).

41. A part of Abulfeda's geography is translated by Greaves, inserted in Hudson's collection of the minor geographers (tom. iii.), and entitled, Descriptio Chorasmiæ et *Mawaralnahræ*, id est, regionum extra fluvium, Oxum, p. 80. The name of *Transoxiana*, softer in sound, equivalent in sense, is aptly used by Petit de la Croix (Hist. de Gengiscan, &c.), and some modern Orientalists, but they are mistaken in ascribing it to the writers of antiquity.

42. The conquests of Catibah are faintly marked by Elmacin (Hist. Saracen. p. 84.),

of pieces of gold was imposed on the infidels; their idols were burnt or broken; the Musulman chief pronounced a sermon in the new mosch of Carizme; after several battles, the Turkish hords were driven back to the desert; and the emperors of China solicited the friendship of the victorious Arabs. To their industry, the prosperity of the province, the Sogdiana of the ancients, may in a great measure be ascribed; but the advantages of the soil and climate had been understood and cultivated since the reign of the Macedonian kings. Before the invasion of the Saracens, Carizme, Bochara, and Samarcand, were rich and populous under the yoke of the shepherds of the north. These cities were surrounded with a double wall; and the exterior fortification, of a larger circumference, inclosed the fields and gardens of the adjacent district. The mutual wants of India and Europe were supplied by the diligence of the Sogdian merchants; and the inestimable art of transforming linen into paper, has been diffused from the manufacture of Samarcand over the western world.[43]

Invasion of SYRIA, *A.D. 632.*

II. No sooner had Abubeker restored the unity of faith and government, than he dispatched a circular letter to the Arabian tribes. "In the name of the most merciful God, to the rest of the true believers. Health and happiness, and the mercy and blessing of God be upon you. I praise the most high God, and I pray for his prophet Mahomet. This is to acquaint you, that I intend to send the true believers into Syria[44] to take it out of the hands of the infidels. And I would have you know, that the fighting for religion is an act of obedience to God." His messengers returned with the tidings of pious and martial ardour

---

d'Herbelot (Bibliot. Orient. *Catbah, Samarcand Valid.*), and de Guignes (Hist. des Huns, tom. i. p. 58, 59).

43. A curious description of Samarcand is inserted in the Bibliotheca Arabico-Hispana, tom. i. p. 208, &c. The librarian Casiri (tom. ii. 9.) relates, from credible testimony, that paper was first imported from China to Samarcand, A.H. 30. and *invented*, or rather introduced, at Mecca, A. H. 88. The Escurial library contains paper MSS. as old as the iv[th] or v[th] century of the Hegira.

44. A separate history of the conquest of Syria has been composed by Al Wakidi, cadi of Bagdad, who was born A.D. 748, and died A.D. 822: he likewise wrote the conquest of Egypt, of Diarbekir, &c. Above the meagre and recent chronicles of the Arabians, Al Wakidi has the double merit of antiquity and copiousness. His tales and traditions afford an artless picture of the men and the times. Yet his narrative is too often defective, trifling, and improbable. Till something better shall be found, his learned and spirited interpreter (Ockley, in his history of the Saracens, vol. i. p. 21–342.) will not deserve the petulant animadversion of Reiske (Prodidagmata ad Hagji Chalifæ Tabulas, p. 236.). I am sorry to think that the labours of Ockley were consummated in a jail (see his two prefaces to the 1st vol. A.D. 1708, to the 2[d], 1718, with the list of authors at the end.

which they had kindled in every province; and the camp of Medina was successively filled with the intrepid bands of the Saracens, who panted for action, complained of the heat of the season and the scarcity of provisions; and accused with impatient murmurs the delays of the caliph. As soon as their numbers were complete, Abubeker ascended the hill, reviewed the men, the horses, and the arms, and poured forth a fervent prayer for the success of their undertaking. In person, and on foot, he accompanied the first day's march; and when the blushing leaders attempted to dismount, the caliph removed their scruples by a declaration, that those who rode, and those who walked, in the service of religion, were equally meritorious. His instruction[45] to the chiefs of the Syrian army, were inspired by the warlike fanaticism which advances to seize, and affects to despise, the objects of earthly ambition. "Remember," said the successor of the prophet, "that you are always in the presence of God, on the verge of death, in the assurance of judgment, and the hope of paradise. Avoid injustice and oppression; consult with your brethren, and study to preserve the love and confidence of your troops. When you fight the battles of the Lord, acquit yourselves like men, without turning your backs; but let not your victory be stained with the blood of women or children. Destroy no palm-trees, nor burn any fields of corn. Cut down no fruit-trees, nor do any mischief to cattle, only such as you kill to eat. When you make any covenant or article, stand to it, and be as good as your word. As you go on, you will find some religious persons who live retired in monasteries, and propose to themselves to serve God that way: let them alone, and neither kill them nor destroy their monasteries:[46] And you will find another sort of people that belong to the synagogue of Satan, who have shaven crowns;[47] be sure you cleave their skulls, and give them no quarter till they either turn Mahometans or pay tribute." All profane or frivolous conversation; all dangerous

45. The instructions, &c. of the Syrian war, are described by Al Wakidi and Ockley, tom. i. p. 22–27, &c. In the sequel it is necessary to contract, and needless to quote their circumstantial narrative. My obligations to others shall be noticed.

46. Notwithstanding this precept, M. Pauw (Recherches sur les Egyptiens, tom. ii. p. 192. edit. Lausanne) represents the Bedoweens as the implacable enemies of the Christian monks. For my own part I am more inclined to suspect the avarice of the Arabian robbers, and the prejudices of the German philosopher.

47. Even in the seventh century, the monks were generally laymen; they wore their hair long and dishevelled, and shaved their heads when they were ordained priests. The circular tonsure was sacred and mysterious: it was the crown of thorns; but it was likewise a royal diadem, and every priest was a king, &c. (Thomassin, Discipline de l'Eglise, tom. i. p. 721–758. especially p. 737, 738.).

recollection of ancient quarrels was severely prohibited among the Arabs; in the tumult of a camp, the exercises of religion were assiduously practised; and the intervals of action were employed in prayer, meditation, and the study of the Koran. The abuse, or even the use, of wine was chastised by fourscore strokes on the soals of the feet, and in the fervour of their primitive zeal many secret sinners revealed their fault, and solicited their punishment. After some hesitation the command of the Syrian army was delegated to Abu Obeidah, one of the fugitives of Mecca and companions of Mahomet; whose zeal and devotion were assuaged, without being abated, by the singular mildness and benevolence of his temper. But in all the emergencies of war, the soldiers demanded the superior genius of Caled; and whoever might be the choice of the prince, the *sword of God* was both in fact and fame the foremost leader of the Saracens. He obeyed without reluctance; he was consulted without jealousy; and such was the spirit of the man, or rather of the times, that Caled professed his readiness to serve under the banner of the faith, though it were in the hands of a child or an enemy. Glory, and riches, and dominion, were indeed promised to the victorious Musulman; but he was carefully instructed, that if the goods of this life were his only incitement, *they* likewise would be his only reward.

Siege of Bosra. One of the fifteen provinces of Syria, the cultivated lands to the eastward of the Jordan, had been decorated by Roman vanity with the name of *Arabia*;[48] and the first arms of the Saracens were justified by the semblance of a national right. The country was enriched by the various benefits of trade; by the vigilance of the emperors it was covered with a line of forts; and the populous cities of Gerasa, Philadelphia, and Bosra,[49] were secure, at least from a surprise, by the solid structure of their walls. The last of these cities was the eighteenth station from Medina: the road was familiar to the caravans of Hejaz and Irak, who annually visited this plenteous market of the province and the desert: the perpetual jealousy of the Arabs had trained the inhabitants to arms; and

48. Huic Arabia est conserta, ex alio latere Nabathæis contigua; opima varietate commerciorum, castrisque oppleta validis et castellis, quæ ad repellendos gentium vicinarum excursus, solicitudo perviget veterum per opportunos saltos erexit et cautos. Ammian. Marcellin xiv. 8. Reland. Palestin. tom. i. p. 85, 86.

49. With Gerasa and Philadelphia, Ammianus praises the fortifications of Bosra firmitate cautissimas. They deserved the same praise in the time of Abulfeda (Tabul. Syriæ, p. 99.), who describes this city, the metropolis of Hawran (Auranitis), four days journey from Damascus. The Hebrew etymology I learn from Reland, Palestin. tom. ii. p. 666.

twelve thousand horse could sally from the gates of Bosra, an appellation which signifies, in the Syriac language, a strong tower of defence. Encouraged by their first success against the open towns and flying parties of the borders, a detachment of four thousand Moslems presumed to summon and attack the fortress of Bosra. They were oppressed by the numbers of the Syrians; they were saved by the presence of Caled, with fifteen hundred horse: he blamed the enterprise, restored the battle, and rescued his friend, the venerable Serjabil, who had vainly invoked the unity of God and the promises of the apostle. After a short repose, the Moslems performed their ablutions with sand instead of water;[50] and the morning prayer was recited by Caled before they mounted on horseback. Confident in their strength, the people of Bosra threw open their gates, drew their forces into the plain, and swore to die in the defence of their religion. But a religion of peace was incapable of withstanding the fanatic cry of "Fight, fight! Paradise, paradise!" that re-echoed in the ranks of the Saracens; and the uproar of the town, the ringing of bells,[51] and the exclamations of the priests and monks encreased the dismay and disorder of the Christians. With the loss of two hundred and thirty men, the Arabs remained masters of the field; and the ramparts of Bosra, in expectation of human or divine aid, were crowded with holy crosses and consecrated banners. The governor Romanus had recommended an early submission: despised by the people, and degraded from his office, he still retained the desire and opportunity of revenge. In a nocturnal interview, he informed the enemy of a subterraneous passage from his house under the wall of the city; the son of the caliph, with an hundred volunteers, were committed to the faith of this new ally, and their successful intrepidity gave an easy entrance to their companions. After Caled had imposed the terms of servitude and tribute, the apostate or convert avowed in the assembly of the people his meritorious treason. "I renounce your society,"

50. The apostle of a desert and an army was obliged to allow this ready succedaneum for water (Koran, c. iii. p. 66. c. v. p. 83.); but the Arabian and Persian casuists have embarrassed his free permission with many niceties and distinctions (Reland de Relig. Mohammed, l. i. p. 82, 83. Chardin, Voyages en Perse, tom. iv.).

51. *The bells rung!* Ockley, vol. i. p. 38. Yet I much doubt whether this expression can be justified by the text of Al Wakidi, or the practice of the times. Ad Græcos, says the learned Ducange (Glossar. med. et in fin. Græcitat. tom. i. p. 774.) campanarum usus serius transit et etiamnum rarissimus est. The oldest example which he can find in the Byzantine writers is of the year 1040; but the Venetians pretend, that they introduced bells at Constantinople in the ix[th] century.

said Romanus, "both in this world, and the world to come. And I deny him that was crucified, and whosoever worships him. And I chuse God for my Lord, Islam for my faith, Mecca for my temple, the Moslems for my brethren, and Mahomet for my prophet; who was sent to lead us into the right way, and to exalt the true religion in spite of those who join partners with God."

Siege of Damascus, A.D. 633.

The conquest of Bosra, four days journey from Damascus,[52] encouraged the Arabs to besiege the ancient capital of Syria.[53] At some distance from the walls, they encamped among the groves and fountains of that delicious territory,[54] and the usual option of the Mahometan faith, of tribute or of war, was proposed to the resolute citizens, who had been lately strengthened by a reinforcement of five thousand Greeks. In the decline as in the infancy of the military art, an hostile defiance was frequently offered and accepted by the generals themselves:[55] many a lance was shivered in the plain of Damascus, and the personal prowess of Caled was signalized in the first sally of the besieged. After an obstinate combat, he had overthrown and made prisoner one of the Christian leaders, a stout and worthy antagonist. He instantly mounted a fresh horse, the gift of the governor of Palmyra, and pushed forwards to the front of the battle. "Repose yourself, for a moment," said his friend Derar, "and permit me to supply your place: you are fatigued with fighting with this dog." "O Derar!" replied the

52. Damascus is amply described by the Sherif al Edrisi (Geograph. Nub. p. 116, 117.); and his translator, Sionita (Appendix, c. 4.); Abulfeda (Tabula Syriæ, p. 100.); Schultens (Index Geograph. ad Vit. Saladin); d'Herbelot (Bibliot. Orient. p. 291.); Thevenot, Voyage du Levant (part i. p. 688–698.); Maundrell (Journey from Aleppo to Jerusalem, p. 122–130.); and Pocock (Description of the East, vol. ii. p. 117–127.).

53. Nobilissima civitas, says Justin. According to the Oriental traditions, it was older than Abraham or Semiramis. Joseph. Antiq. Jud. l. i. c. 6, 7. p. 24. 29. edit. Havercamp. Justin. xxxvi. 2.

54. *Εδει γαρ οιμαι την Διος πολιν αληθως, και της ʽΕωας ἁπασης οφθαλμον, την ιεραν και μεγιστην Δαμασκον λεγω, τοις τε αλλοις συμπασιν, ὁιον ἱερων καλλει, και νεων μεγεθει. και ὡρων ευκαιρια και πηγων αγλαια και ποταμων πληθει, και γης ευφορια νικωσαν*, &c. Julian, epist. xxiv. p. 392. These splendid epithets are occasioned by the figs of Damascus, of which the author sends an hundred to his friend Serapion, and this rhetorical theme is inserted by Petavius, Spanheim, &c. (p. 390–396.) among the genuine epistles of Julian. How could they overlook that the writer is an inhabitant of Damascus (he thrice affirms, that this peculiar fig grows only *παρι ἡμιν*), a city which Julian never entered or approached?

55. Voltaire, who casts a keen and lively glance over the surface of history, has been struck with the resemblance of the first Moslems and the heroes of the Iliad; the siege of Troy and that of Damascus (Hist. Generale, tom. i. p. 348.).

indefatigable Saracen, "we shall rest in the world to come. He that labours to-day, shall rest to-morrow." With the same unabated ardour, Caled answered, encountered and vanquished a second champion; and the heads of his two captives who refused to abandon their religion were indignantly hurled into the midst of the city. The event of some general and partial actions reduced the Damascenes to a closer defence: but a messenger whom they dropt from the walls, returned with the promise of speedy and powerful succour, and their tumultuous joy conveyed the intelligence to the camp of the Arabs. After some debate it was resolved by the generals to raise or rather to suspend the siege of Damascus, till they had given battle to the forces of the emperor. In the retreat, Caled would have chosen the more perilous station of the rear-guard; he modestly yielded to the wishes of Abu Obeidah. But in the hour of danger he flew to the rescue of his companion, who was rudely pressed by a sally of six thousand horse and ten thousand foot, and few among the Christians could relate at Damascus the circumstances of their defeat. The importance of the contest required the junction of the Saracens who were dispersed on the frontiers of Syria and Palestine; and I shall transcribe one of the circular mandates which was addressed to Amrou the future conqueror of Egypt. "In the name of the most merciful God: from Caled to Amrou, health and happiness. Know that thy brethren the Moslems design to march to Aiznadin, where there is an army of seventy thousand Greeks, who purpose to come against us, *that they may extinguish the light of God with their mouths; but God preserveth his light in spite of the infidels.*[56] As soon therefore as this letter of mine shall be delivered to thy hands, come with those that are with thee to Aiznadin, where thou shall find us if it please the most high God." The summons were cheerfully obeyed, and the forty-five thousand Moslems who met on the same day, on the same spot, ascribed to the blessing of providence the effects of their activity and zeal.

Battle of Aiznadin, A.D. 633, July 13.

About four years after the triumphs of the Persian war, the repose of Heraclius and the empire was again disturbed by a new enemy, the power of whose religion was more strongly felt than it was clearly understood by the Christians of the East. In his palace of Constantinople or Antioch, he was awakened by the invasion of Syria, the loss of Bosra, and the danger of Damascus. An army of

56. These words are a text of the Koran, c. ix. 32. lxi. 8. Like our fanatics of the last century, the Moslems, on every familiar or important occasion, spoke the language of *their* scriptures; a style more natural in their mouths, than the Hebrew idiom transplanted into the climate and dialect of Britain.

seventy thousand veterans, or new levies, was assembled at Hems or Emesa, under the command of his general Werdan;[57] and these troops, consisting chiefly of cavalry, might be indifferently styled either Syrians, or Greeks, or Romans: *Syrians* from the place of their birth or warfare; *Greeks* from the religion and language of their sovereign; and *Romans*, from the proud appellation which was still profaned by the successors of Constantine. On the plain of Aiznadin, as Werdan rode on a white mule decorated with gold chains, and surrounded with ensigns and standards, he was surprised by the near approach of a fierce and naked warrior, who had undertaken to view the state of the enemy. The adventurous valour of Derar was inspired, and has perhaps been adorned, by the enthusiasm of his age and country. The hatred of the Christians, the love of spoil, and the contempt of danger, were the ruling passions of the audacious Saracen; and the prospect of instant death could never shake his religious confidence, or ruffle the calmness of his resolution, or even suspend the frank and martial pleasantry of his humour. In the most hopeless enterprises, he was bold, and prudent, and fortunate: after innumerable hazards, after being thrice a prisoner in the hands of the infidels, he still survived to relate the atchievements, and to enjoy the rewards, of the Syrian conquest. On this occasion, his single lance maintained a flying fight against thirty Romans, who were detached by Werdan; and after killing or unhorsing seventeen of their number, Derar returned in safety to his applauding brethren. When his rashness was mildly censured by the general, he excused himself with the simplicity of a soldier. "Nay," said Derar, "I did not begin first: but they came out to take me, and I was afraid that God should see me turn my back; and indeed I fought in good earnest, and without doubt God assisted me against them; and had I not been apprehensive of disobeying your orders, I should not have come away as I did; and I perceive already that they will fall into our hands." In the presence of both armies, a venerable Greek advanced from the ranks with a liberal offer of peace; and the departure of the Saracens would have been purchased by a gift to each soldier, of a turban, a robe, and a piece of gold; ten robes, and an hundred pieces to their leader; one hundred robes, and a thousand pieces to the caliph. A smile of indignation

57. The name of Werdan is unknown to Theophanes, and, though it might belong to an Armenian chief, has very little of a Greek aspect or sound. If the Byzantine historians have mangled the Oriental names, the Arabs, in this instance, likewise have taken ample revenge on their enemies. In transposing the Greek character from right to left, might they not produce, from the familiar appellation of *Andrew*, something like the anagram *Werdan*?

expressed the refusal of Caled. "Ye Christian dogs, you know your option; the Koran, the tribute, or the sword. We are a people whose delight is in war, rather than in peace; and we despise your pitiful alms, since we shall be speedily masters of your wealth, your families, and your persons." Notwithstanding this apparent disdain, he was deeply conscious of the public danger: those who had been in Persia, and had seen the armies of Chosroes, confessed that they never beheld a more formidable array. From the superiority of the enemy, the artful Saracen derived a fresh incentive of courage: "You see before you, said he, the united force of the Romans, you cannot hope to escape, but you may conquer Syria in a single day. The event depends on your discipline and patience. Reserve yourselves till the evening. It was in the evening that the prophet was accustomed to vanquish." During two successive engagements, his temperate firmness sustained the darts of the enemy, and the murmurs of his troops. At length, when the spirits and quivers of the adverse line were almost exhausted, Caled gave the signal of onset and victory. The remains of the Imperial army fled to Antioch, or Cæsarea, or Damascus; and the death of four hundred and seventy Moslems was compensated by the opinion that they had sent to hell above fifty thousand of the infidels. The spoil was inestimable; many banners and crosses of gold and silver, precious stones, silver and gold chains, and innumerable suits of the richest armour and apparel. The general distribution was postponed till Damascus should be taken; but the seasonable supply of arms became the instrument of new victories. The glorious intelligence was transmitted to the throne of the caliph, and the Arabian tribes, the coldest or most hostile to the prophet's mission, were eager and importunate to share the harvest of Syria.

The Arabs return to Damascus.

The sad tidings were carried to Damascus by the speed of grief and terror; and the inhabitants beheld from their walls the return of the heroes of Aiznadin. Amrou led the van at the head of nine thousand horse: the bands of the Saracens succeeded each other in formidable review; and the rear was closed by Caled in person, with the standard of the black eagle. To the activity of Derar he entrusted the commission of patrolling round the city with two thousand horse, of scouring the plain, and of intercepting all succour or intelligence. The rest of the Arabian chiefs were fixed in their respective stations before the seven gates of Damascus; and the siege was renewed with fresh vigour and confidence. The art, the labour, the military engines, of the Greeks and Romans are seldom to be found in the simple, though successful, operations of the Saracens: it was sufficient for them to invest a city with arms, rather than with trenches; to repel the sallies of the besieged; to attempt a stratagem or an assault; or to expect the progress of famine and discontent. Damascus would have acquiesced in the trial of Aiznadin, as a final and peremptory sentence between the emperor and the caliph: her courage was rekindled by the example and authority of Thomas, a noble Greek, illustrious in a private condition by the alliance of Heraclius.[58] The tumult and illumination of the night proclaimed the design of the morning sally; and the Christian hero, who affected to despise the enthusiasm of the Arabs, employed the resource of a similar superstition. At the principal gate, in the sight of both armies, a lofty crucifix was erected; the bishop with his clergy, accompanied the march, and laid the volume of the New Testament before the image of Jesus; and the contending parties were scandalised or edified by a prayer, that the Son of God would defend his servants and vindicate his truth. The battle raged with incessant fury; and the dexterity of Thomas,[59] an incomparable archer, was fatal to the boldest Saracens, till their death was revenged by a female heroine. The wife of Aban, who had followed him to the holy war, embraced her expiring husband. "Happy," said she, "happy art thou, my dear; thou art gone to thy Lord who first joined us together, and then parted us asunder. I will revenge thy death, and endeavour to the utmost of my power to come to the place where thou art, because I love thee. Henceforth shall no man ever touch me more, for I have dedicated myself to the service of God." Without a groan, without a tear, she washed the corpse of her husband, and buried him with the usual rites. Then grasping the manly weapons, which in her native land she was accustomed to wield, the intrepid widow of Aban sought the place where his murderer fought in the thickest of the battle. Her first arrow pierced the hand of his standard-bearer; her second wounded Thomas in the eye; and the fainting Christians no longer beheld their ensign or their leader. Yet the generous champion of Damascus refused to withdraw to his palace: his wound was dressed on the rampart; the fight was continued till the evening; and the Syrians rested on their arms. In the silence of

58. Vanity prompted the Arabs to believe, that Thomas was the son-in-law of the emperor. We know the children of Heraclius by his two wives; and his *august* daughter would not have married in exile at Damascus (see Ducange, Fam. Byzantin. p. 118, 119.). Had he been less religious, I might only suspect the legitimacy of the damsel.

59. Al Wakidi (Ockley, p. 101.) says, "with poisoned arrows;" but this savage invention is so repugnant to the practice of the Greeks and Romans, that I must suspect, on this occasion, the malevolent credulity of the Saracens.

the night, the signal was given by a stroke on the great bell; the gates were thrown open, and each gate discharged an impetuous column on the sleeping camp of the Saracens. Caled was the first in arms; at the head of four hundred horse he flew to the post of danger, and the tears trickled down his iron cheeks, as he uttered a fervent ejaculation; "O God, who never sleepest, look upon thy servants, and do not deliver them into the hands of their enemies." The valour and victory of Thomas were arrested by the presence of the *sword of God*; with the knowledge of the peril, the Moslems recovered their ranks, and charged the assailants in the flank and rear. After the loss of thousands, the Christian general retreated with a sigh of despair, and the pursuit of the Saracens was checked by the military engines of the rampart.

The city is taken by storm and capitulation, A.D. 634.

After a siege of seventy days,[60] the patience, and perhaps the provisions, of the Damascenes were exhausted; and the bravest of their chiefs submitted to the hard dictates of necessity. In the occurrences of peace and war, they had been taught to dread the fierceness of Caled, and to revere the mild virtues of Abu Obeidah. At the hour of midnight, one hundred chosen deputies of the clergy and people were introduced to the tent of that venerable commander. He received and dismissed them with courtesy. They returned with a written agreement, on the faith of a companion of Mahomet, that all hostilities should cease; that the voluntary emigrants might depart in safety, with as much as they could carry away of their effects; and that the tributary subjects of the caliph should enjoy their lands and houses, with the use and possession of seven churches. On these terms, the most respectable hostages, and the gate nearest to his camp, were delivered into his hands: his soldiers imitated the moderation of their chief; and he enjoyed the submissive gratitude of a people whom he had rescued from destruction. But the success of the treaty had relaxed their vigilance, and in the same moment the opposite quarter of the city was betrayed and taken by assault. A party of an hundred Arabs had

60. Abulfeda allows only seventy days for the siege of Damascus (Annal. Moslem. p. 67. vers. Reiske); but Elmacin, who mentions this opinion, prolongs the term to six months, and notices the use of *balistæ* by the Saracens (Hist. Saracen. p. 25. 32.). Even this longer period is insufficient to fill the interval between the battle of Aiznadin (July, A.D. 633) and the accession of Omar (24 July, A.D. 634), to whose reign the conquest of Damascus is unanimously ascribed (Al Wakidi, apud Ockley, vol. i. p. 115. Abulpharagius, Dynast. p. 112. vers. Pocock). Perhaps, as in the Trojan war, the operations were interrupted by excursions and detachments, till the last seventy days of the siege.

opened the eastern gate to a more inexorable foe. "No quarter," cried the rapacious and sanguinary Caled, "no quarter to the enemies of the Lord:" his trumpets sounded, and a torrent of Christian blood was poured down the streets of Damascus. When he reached the church of St. Mary, he was astonished and provoked by the peaceful aspect of his companions: their swords were in the scabbard, and they were surrounded by a multitude of priests and monks. Abu Obeidah saluted the general: "God," said he, "has delivered the city into my hands by way of surrender, and has saved the believers the trouble of fighting." "And am *I* not," replied the indignant Caled, "am *I* not the lieutenant of the commander of the faithful? Have I not taken the city by storm? The unbelievers shall perish by the sword. Fall on." The hungry and cruel Arabs would have obeyed the welcome command: and Damascus was lost, if the benevolence of Abu Obeidah had not been supported by a decent and dignified firmness. Throwing himself between the trembling citizens and the most eager of the Barbarians, he adjured them by the holy name of God, to respect his promise, to suspend their fury, and to wait the determination of their chiefs. The chiefs retired into the church of St. Mary; and after a vehement debate, Caled submitted in some measure to the reason and authority of his colleague; who urged the sanctity of a covenant, the advantage as well as the honour which the Moslems would derive from the punctual performance of their word, and the obstinate resistance which they must encounter from the distrust and despair of the rest of the Syrian cities. It was agreed that the sword should be sheathed, that the part of Damascus which had surrendered to Abu Obeidah, should be immediately entitled to the benefit of his capitulation, and that the final decision should be referred to the justice and wisdom of the caliph.[61] A large majority of the people accepted the terms of toleration and tribute; and Damascus is still peopled by twenty thousand Christians. But the valiant Thomas, and the free-born patriots who had fought under his banner, embraced the alternative of poverty and exile. In the adjacent meadow, a numerous encampment was formed of priests and laymen, of soldiers and citizens, of women and children: they collected, with haste and terror, their most precious moveables; and abandoned, with loud lamentations or silent anguish, their native homes, and the pleasant banks

61. It appears from Abulfeda (p. 125.) and Elmacin (p. 32.), that this distinction of the two parts of Damascus was long remembered, though not always respected, by the Mahometan sovereigns. See likewise Eutychius (Annal. tom. ii. p. 379, 380. 383.).

of the Pharphar. The inflexible soul of Caled was not touched by the spectacle of their distress: he disputed with the Damascenes the property of a magazine of corn; endeavoured to exclude the garrison from the benefit of the treaty; consented, with reluctance, that each of the fugitives should arm himself with a sword, or a lance, or a bow; and sternly declared, that, after a respite of three days, they might be pursued and treated as the enemies of the Moslems.

Pursuit of the Damascenes.

The passion of a Syrian youth completed the ruin of the exiles of Damascus. A nobleman of the city, of the name of Jonas,[62] was betrothed to a wealthy maiden; but her parents delayed the consummation of his nuptials, and their daughter was persuaded to escape with the man whom she had chosen. They corrupted the nightly watchmen of the gate Keisan: the lover, who led the way, was encompassed by a squadron of Arabs; but his exclamation in the Greek tongue, "the bird is taken," admonished his mistress to hasten her return. In the presence of Caled, and of death, the unfortunate Jonas professed his belief in one God, and his apostle Mahomet; and continued, till the season of his martyrdom, to discharge the duties of a brave and sincere Musulman. When the city was taken, he flew to the monastery, where Eudocia had taken refuge; but the lover was forgotten; the apostate was scorned; she preferred her religion to her country; and the justice of Caled, though deaf to mercy, refused to detain by force a male or female inhabitant of Damascus. Four days was the general confined to the city by the obligation of the treaty, and the urgent cares of his new conquest. His appetite for blood and rapine would have been extinguished by the hopeless computation of time and distance; but he listened to the importunities of Jonas, who assured him that the weary fugitives might yet be overtaken. At the head of four thousand horse, in the disguise of Christian Arabs, Caled undertook the pursuit. They halted only for the moments of prayer; and their guide had a perfect knowledge of the country. For a long way the footsteps of the Damascenes were plain and conspicuous:

62. On the fate of these lovers, whom he names Phocyas and Eudocia, Mr. Hughes has built the Siege of Damascus, one of our most popular tragedies, and which possesses the rare merit of blending nature and history, the manners of the times and the feelings of the heart. The foolish delicacy of the players compelled him to soften the guilt of the hero and the despair of the heroine. Instead of a base renegado, Phocyas serves the Arabs as an honourable ally; instead of prompting their pursuit, he flies to the succour of his countrymen, and after killing Caled and Derar, is himself mortally wounded, and expires in the presence of Eudocia, who professes her resolution to take the veil at Constantinople. A frigid catastrophe!

they vanished on a sudden; but the Saracens were comforted by the assurance that the caravan had turned aside into the mountains, and must speedily fall into their hands. In traversing the ridges of the Libanus, they endured intolerable hardships, and the sinking spirits of the veteran fanatics were supported and cheered by the unconquerable ardour of a lover. From a peasant of the country, they were informed that the emperor had sent orders to the colony of exiles, to pursue without delay the road of the sea-coast, and of Constantinople; apprehensive, perhaps, that the soldiers and people of Antioch might be discouraged by the sight and the story of their sufferings. The Saracens were conducted through the territories of Gabala[63] and Laodicea, at a cautious distance from the walls of the cities; the rain was incessant, the night was dark, a single mountain separated them from the Roman army; and Caled, ever anxious for the safety of his brethren, whispered an ominous dream in the ear of his companion. With the dawn of day, the prospect again cleared, and they saw before them, in a pleasant valley, the tents of Damascus. After a short interval of repose and prayer, Caled divided his cavalry into four squadrons, committing the first to his faithful Derar, and reserving the last for himself. They successively rushed on the promiscuous multitude, insufficiently provided with arms, and already vanquished by sorrow and fatigue. Except a captive who was pardoned and dismissed, the Arabs enjoyed the satisfaction of believing that not a Christian of either sex escaped the edge of their scymetars. The gold and silver of Damascus was scattered over the camp, and a royal wardrobe of three hundred load of silk might clothe an army of naked Barbarians. In the tumult of the battle, Jonas sought and found the object of his pursuit; but her resentment was inflamed by the last act of his perfidy; and as Eudocia struggled in his hateful embraces, she struck a dagger to her heart. Another female, the widow of Thomas, and the real or supposed daughter of Heraclius, was spared and released without a ransom; but the generosity of Caled was the effect of his contempt; and the haughty Saracen insulted, by a message of defiance, the throne of the Cæsars. Caled had penetrated above an hundred and fifty miles into the heart of the Roman province: he

63. The towns of Gabala and Laodicea, which the Arabs passed, still exist in a state of decay (Maundrell, p. 11, 12. Pocock, vol. ii. p. 13.). Had not the Christians been overtaken, they must have crossed the Orontes on some bridge in the sixteen miles between Antioch and the sea, and might have rejoined the high road of Constantinople at Alexandria. The itineraries will represent the directions and distances (p. 146. 148. 581, 582. edit. Wesseling).

returned to Damascus with the same secrecy and speed. On the accession of Omar, the *sword of God* was removed from the command; but the caliph, who blamed the rashness, was compelled to applaud the vigour and conduct, of the enterprise.

Fair of Abyla.

Another expedition of the conquerors of Damascus will equally display their avidity and their contempt for the riches of the present world. They were informed that the produce and manufactures of the country were annually collected in the fair of Abyla,[64] about thirty miles from the city; that the cell of a devout hermit was visited at the same time by a multitude of pilgrims; and that the festival of trade and superstition would be ennobled by the nuptials of the daughter of the governor of Tripoli. Abdallah, the son of Jaafar, a glorious and holy martyr, undertook, with a banner of five hundred horse, the pious and profitable commission of despoiling the infidels. As he approached the fair of Abyla, he was astonished by the report of the mighty concourse of Jews and Christians, Greeks and Armenians, of natives of Syria, and of strangers of Egypt, to the number of ten thousand, besides a guard of five thousand horse that attended the person of the bride. The Saracens paused: "For my own part," said Abdallah, "I *dare not* go back: our foes are many, our danger is great, but our reward is splendid and secure, either in this life or in the life to come. Let every man, according to his inclination, advance or retire." Not a Musulman deserted his standard. "Lead the way," said Abdallah to his Christian guide, "and you shall see what the companions of the prophet can perform." They charged in five squadrons; but after the first advantage of the surprise they were encompassed and almost overwhelmed by the multitude of their enemies; and their valiant band is fancifully compared to a white spot in the skin of a black camel.[65] About the hour of sunset, when their weapons dropped from their hands, when they panted on the verge of eternity, they discovered an approaching cloud of dust, they heard the welcome sound of the *tecbir*,[66] and they soon perceived the standard of Caled, who flew

64. *Dair Abil Kodos*. After retrenching the last word, the epithet, *holy*, I discover the Abila of Lysanias between Damascus and Heliopolis: the name (*Abil* signifies a vineyard) concurs with the situation to justify my conjecture (Reland, Palestin. tom. i. p. 317. tom. ii. p. 525. 527.).

65. I am bolder than Mr. Ockley (vol. i. p. 164.), who dares not insert this figurative expression in the text, though he observes in a marginal note, that the Arabians often borrow their similies from that useful and familiar animal. The rein-deer may be equally famous in the songs of the Laplanders.

66.

We heard the *tecbir*; so the Arabs call

to their relief with the utmost speed of his cavalry. The Christians were broken by his attack, and slaughtered in their flight as far as the river of Tripoli. They left behind them the various riches of the fair; the merchandises that were exposed for sale, the money that was brought for purchase, the gay decorations of the nuptials, and the governor's daughter, with forty of her female attendants. The fruits, provisions, and furniture, the money, plate, and jewels, were diligently laden on the backs of horses, asses, and mules; and the holy robbers returned in triumph to Damascus. The hermit, after a short and angry controversy with Caled, declined the crown of martyrdom, and was left alive in the solitary scene of blood and devastation.

Sieges of Heliopolis and Emesa, A.D. 635.

Syria,[67] one of the countries that have been improved by the most early cultivation, is not unworthy of the preference.[68] The heat of the climate is tempered by the vicinity of the sea and mountains, by the plenty of wood and water; and the produce of a fertile soil affords the subsistence, and encourages the propagation, of men and animals. From the age of David to that of Heraclius, the country was overspread with ancient and flourishing cities: the inhabitants were numerous and wealthy; and, after the slow ravage of despotism and superstition, after the recent calamities of the Persian war, Syria could still attract and reward the rapacious tribes of the desert. A plain, of ten

---

Their shout of onset, when with loud appeal
They challenge heaven, as if demanding conquest.

This word, so formidable in their holy wars, is a verb active (says Ockley in his index) of the second conjugation, from *Kabbara*, which signifies saying *Alla Acbar*, God is most mighty!

67. In the geography of Abulfeda, the description of Syria, his native country, is the most interesting and authentic portion. It was published in Arabic and Latin, Lipsiæ, 1766, in quarto, with the learned notes of Kochler and Reiske, and some extracts of geography and natural history from Ibn Ol Wardii. Among the modern travels, Pocock's Description of the East (of Syria and Mesopotamia, vol. ii. p. 88–209.) is a work of superior learning and dignity; but the author too often confounds what he had seen and what he had read.

68. The praises of Dionysius are just and lively. *Και την μεν* (Syria) *πολλοι τε και ολβιοι ανδρες εχουσιν* (in Periegesi, v. 902. in tom. iv. Geograph. Minor. Hudson). In another place, he styles the country *πολυπτολιν αιαν* (v. 898.). He proceeds to say,

Πασα δε τοι λιπαρη τε και ευβοτος επλετο χωρη
Μηλα τε φερβεμεναι και δενδρεσι καρπον αεξειν.

v. 921, 922.

This poetical geographer lived in the age of Augustus, and his description of the world is illustrated by the Greek commentary of Eustathius, who paid the same compliment to Homer and Dionysius (Fabric. Bibliot. Græc. l. iv. c. 2. tom. iii. p. 21, &c.).

days journey, from Damascus to Aleppo and Antioch, is watered, on the western side, by the winding course of the Orontes. The hills of Libanus and Anti-Libanus are planted from north to south, between the Orontes and the Mediterranean; and the epithet of *hollow* (Cœlesyria) was applied to a long and fruitful valley, which is confined in the same direction by the two ridges of snowy mountains.[69] Among the cities, which are enumerated by Greek and Oriental names in the geography and conquest of Syria, we may distinguish Emesa or Hems, Heliopolis or Baalbec, the former as the metropolis of the plain, the latter as the capital of the valley. Under the last of the Cæsars, they were strong and populous: the turrets glittered from afar: an ample space was covered with public and private buildings; and the citizens were illustrious by their spirit, or at least by their pride; by their riches, or at least by their luxury. In the days of paganism, both Emesa and Heliopolis were addicted to the worship of Baal, or the sun; but the decline of their superstition and splendour has been marked by a singular variety of fortune. Not a vestige remains of the temple of Emesa, which was equalled in poetic style to the summits of mount Libanus,[70] while the ruins of Baalbec, invisible to the writers of antiquity, excite the curiosity and wonder of the European traveller.[71] The measure of the temple is two hundred feet in length, and one hundred in breadth: the front is adorned with a double portico of eight columns; fourteen may be counted on either side; and each column, forty-five feet in height, is composed of three massy blocks of stone or marble. The proportions and ornaments of the Corinthian order express

69. The topography of the Libanus and Anti-Libanus is excellently described by the learning and sense of Reland (Palestin. tom. i. p. 311–326.).

70.

——Emesæ fastigia celsa renident
Nam diffusa solo latus explicat; ac subit auras
Turribus in cœlum nitentibus: incola claris
Cor studiis acuit . . .
Denique flammicomo devoti pectora soli
Vitam agitant. Libanus frondosa cacumina turget,
Et tamen bis certant celsi fastigia templi.

These verses of the Latin version of Rufus Avienus are wanting in the Greek original of Dionysius; and since they are likewise unnoticed by Eustatius, I must, with Fabricius (Bibliot. Latin. tom. iii. p. 153. edit. Ernesti), and against Salmasius (ad Vopiscum, p. 366, 367. in Hist. August.), ascribe them to the fancy rather than the MSS. of Avienus.

71. I am much better satisfied with Maundrell's slight octavo (Journey, p. 134–139.), than with the pompous folio of Doctor Pocock (Description of the East, vol. ii. p. 106–113.); but every preceding account is eclipsed by the magnificent description and drawings of M. M. Dawkins and Wood, who have transported into England the ruins of Palmyra and Baalbeck.

the architecture of the Greeks; but as Baalbec has never been the seat of a monarch, we are at a loss to conceive how the expence of these magnificent structures could be supplied by private or municipal liberality.[72] From the conquest of Damascus the Saracens proceeded to Heliopolis and Emesa; but I shall decline the repetition of the sallies and combats which have been already shewn on a larger scale. In the prosecution of the war, their policy was not less effectual than their sword. By short and separate truces they dissolved the union of the enemy; accustomed the Syrians to compare their friendship with their enmity; familiarised the idea of their language, religion, and manners; and exhausted, by clandestine purchase, the magazines and arsenals of the cities which they returned to besiege. They aggravated the ransom of the more wealthy, or the more obstinate; and Chalcis alone was taxed at five thousand ounces of gold, five thousand ounces of silver, two thousand robes of silk, and as many figs and olives as would load five thousand asses. But the terms of truce or capitulation were faithfully observed; and the lieutenant of the caliph, who had promised not to enter the walls of the captive Baalbec, remained tranquil and immoveable in his tent till the jarring factions solicited the interposition of a foreign master. The conquest of the plain and valley of Syria was atchieved in less than two years. Yet the commander of the faithful reproved the slowness of their progress, and the Saracens, bewailing their fault with tears of rage and repentance, called aloud on their chiefs to lead them forth to fight the battles of the Lord. In a recent action, under the walls of Emesa, an Arabian youth, the cousin of Caled, was heard aloud to exclaim, "Methinks I see the black-eyed girls looking upon me; one of whom, should she appear in this world, all mankind would die for love of her. And I see in the hand of one of them, an handkerchief of green silk, and a cap of precious stones, and she beckons me, and calls out, come hither quickly, for I love thee." With these words, charging the Christians, he made havock wherever he went, till, observed at length by the governor of Hems, he was struck through with a javelin.

Battle of Yermuk, It was incumbent on the Saracens to exert the full powers of their valour and enthusiasm against the forces of the emperor,

72. The Orientals explain the prodigy by a never-failing expedient. The edifices of Baalbec were constructed by the fairies or the genii (Hist. de Timour Bec, tom. iii. l. v. c. 23. p. 311, 312. Voyage d'Otter, tom. i. p. 83.). With less absurdity, but with equal ignorance, Abulfeda and Ibn Chaukel ascribe them to the Sabæans or Aadites. Non sunt in omni Syria ædificia magnificentiora his (Tabula Syriæ, p. 103.).

who was taught by repeated losses, that the rovers of the desert had undertaken, and would speedily atchieve, a regular and permanent conquest. From the provinces of Europe and Asia, fourscore thousand soldiers were transported by sea and land to Antioch and Cæsarea: the light troops of the army consisted of sixty thousand Christian Arabs of the tribe of Gassan. Under the banner of Jabalah, the last of their princes, they marched in the van; and it was a maxim of the Greeks, that, for the purpose of cutting diamond, a diamond was the most effectual. Heraclius withheld his person from the dangers of the field; but his presumption, or perhaps his despondency, suggested a peremptory order, that the fate of the province and the war should be decided by a single battle. The Syrians were attached to the standard of Rome and of the cross; but the noble, the citizen, the peasant, were exasperated by the injustice and cruelty of a licentious host, who oppressed them as subjects, and despised them as strangers and aliens.[73] A report of these mighty preparations was conveyed to the Saracens in their camp of Emesa; and the chiefs, though resolved to fight, assembled a council: the faith of Abu Obeidah would have expected on the same spot the glory of martyrdom; the wisdom of Caled advised an honourable retreat to the skirts of Palestine and Arabia, where they might await the succours of their friends and the attack of the unbelievers. A speedy messenger soon returned from the throne of Medina, with the blessings of Omar and Ali, the prayers of the widows of the prophet, and a reinforcement of eight thousand Moslems. In their way they overturned a detachment of Greeks, and when they joined at Yermuk the camp of their brethren, they found the pleasing intelligence, that Caled had already defeated and scattered the Christian Arabs of the tribe of Gassan. In the neighbourhood of Bosra, the springs of mount Hermon descend in a torrent to the plain of Decapolis, or ten cities; and the Hieromax, a name which has been corrupted to Yermuk, is lost after a short course in the lake of Tiberias.[74] The banks of this obscure stream were illustrated by a long and bloody encounter. On this momentous

A.D. 636, November.

73. I have read somewhere in Tacitus, or Grotius, Subjectos habent tanquam suos, viles tanquam alienos. Some Greek officers ravished the wife, and murdered the child, of their Syrian landlord; and Manuel smiled at his undutiful complaint.

74. See Reland, Palestin. tom. i. p. 272. 283. tom. ii. p. 773. 775. This learned professor was equal to the task of describing the Holy Land, since he was alike conversant with Greek and Latin, with Hebrew and Arabian literature. The Yermuk, or Hieromax, is noticed by Cellarius (Geograph. Antiq. tom. ii. p. 392.) and d'Anville (Geographie Ancienne, tom. ii. p. 185.). The Arabs, and even Abulfeda himself, do not seem to recognize the scene of their victory.

occasion, the public voice, and the modesty of Abu Obeidah, restored the command to the most deserving of the Moslems. Caled assumed his station in the front, his colleague was posted in the rear, that the disorder of the fugitives might be checked by his venerable aspect and the sight of the yellow banner which Mahomet had displayed before the walls of Chaibar. The last line was occupied by the sister of Derar, with the Arabian women who had enlisted in this holy war, who were accustomed to wield the bow and the lance, and who in a moment of captivity had defended, against the uncircumcised ravishers, their chastity and religion.[75] The exhortation of the generals was brief and forcible: "Paradise is before you, the devil and hell-fire in your rear." Yet such was the weight of the Roman cavalry, that the right wing of the Arabs was broken and separated from the main body. Thrice did they retreat in disorder, and thrice were they driven back to the charge by the reproaches and blows of the women. In the intervals of action, Abu Obeidah visited the tents of his brethren, prolonged their repose, by repeating at once the prayers of two different hours; bound up their wounds with his own hands, and administered the comfortable reflection, that the infidels partook of their sufferings without partaking of their reward. Four thousand and thirty of the Moslems were buried in the field of battle; and the skill of the Armenian archers enabled seven hundred to boast that they had lost an eye in that meritorious service. The veterans of the Syrian war acknowledged that it was the hardest and most doubtful of the days which they had seen. But it was likewise the most decisive: many thousands of the Greeks and Syrians fell by the swords of the Arabs; many were slaughtered, after the defeat in the woods and mountains; many, by mistaking the ford, were drowned in the waters of the Yermuk; and however the loss may be magnified,[76] the Christian writers confess and bewail the bloody punishment of their sins.[77] Manuel, the Roman general, was either killed at Damascus, or took refuge in the monastery of mount

75. These women were of the tribe of the Hamyarites, who derived their origin from the ancient Amalekites. Their females were accustomed to ride on horseback, and to fight like the Amazons of old (Ockley, vol. i. p. 67.).

76. We killed of them, says Abu Obeidah to the caliph, one hundred and fifty thousand, and made prisoners forty thousand (Ockley, vol. i. p. 241.). As I cannot doubt his veracity, nor believe his computation, I must suspect that the Arabic historians indulged themselves in the practice of composing speeches and letters for their heroes.

77. After deploring the sins of the Christians, Theophanes adds (Chronograph. p. 276.), *ανεστη ὁ ερημικος Αμαληκ τυπτων ἡμας τον λαον του Χριστου, και γινεται πρωτη φορα πτωσις του Ρωμαικου*

Sinai. An exile in the Byzantine court, Jabalah lamented the manners of Arabia, and his unlucky preference of the Christian cause.[78] He had once inclined to the profession of Islam; but in the pilgrimage of Mecca, Jabalah was provoked to strike one of his brethren, and fled with amazement from the stern and equal justice of the caliph. The victorious Saracens enjoyed at Damascus a month of pleasure and repose: the spoil was divided by the discretion of Abu Obeidah: an equal share was allotted to a soldier and to his horse, and a double portion was reserved for the noble coursers of the Arabian breed.

Conquest of Jerusalem, A.D. 637.

After the battle of Yermuk, the Roman army no longer appeared in the field; and the Saracens might securely chuse among the fortified towns of Syria, the first object of their attack. They consulted the caliph whether they should march to Cæsarea or Jerusalem; and the advice of Ali determined the immediate siege of the latter. To a profane eye, Jerusalem was the first or second capital of Palestine; but after Mecca and Medina, it was revered and visited by the devout Moslems, as the temple of the Holy Land which had been sanctified by the revelation of Moses, of Jesus, and of Mahomet himself. The son of Abu Sophian was sent with five thousand Arabs to try the first experiment of surprise or treaty: but on the eleventh day, the town was invested by the whole force of Abu Obeidah. He addressed the customary summons to the chief commanders and people of *Ælia*.[79] "Health and happiness to every one that follows the right way! We require of you to testify that there is but one God, and that Mahomet is his apostle. If you refuse this, consent to pay tribute, and be under us

---

στρατου ἥ κατα το Γαβιθαν λεγω (does he mean Aiznadin?) *και Ιερμουκαν, και την αθεσμον ἁιματοχυσιαν*. His account is brief and obscure, but he accuses the numbers of the enemy, the adverse wind, and the cloud of dust: *μη δυνηθειτες* (the Romans) *αντηπροσωπησαι εχθροις δια τον κονιορτον ἥττωνται, και ἕαυτους βαλλοντες εις τας στενοδους του Ιερμοχθου ποταμου εκει απωλοντο αρδην* (Chronograph. p. 280.).

78. See Abulfeda (Annal. Moslem. p. 70, 71.), who transcribes the poetical complaint of Jabalah himself, and some panegyrical strains of an Arabian poet, to whom the chief of Gassan sent from Constantinople a gift of five hundred pieces of gold by the hands of the ambassador of Omar.

79. In the name of the city, the profane prevailed over the sacred; *Jerusalem* was known to the devout Christians (Euseb. de Martyr. Palest. c. xi.); but the legal and popular appellation of *Ælia* (the colony of Ælius Hadrianus) has passed from the Romans to the Arabs (Reland, Palestin. tom. i. p. 207. tom. ii. p. 835. d'Herbelot, Bibliotheque Orientale, *Cods*, p. 269. *Ilia*, p. 420.). The epithet of *Al Cods*, the Holy, is used as the proper name of Jerusalem.

forthwith. Otherwise I shall bring men against you who love death better than you do the drinking of wine or eating hogs flesh. Nor will I ever stir from you, if it please God, till I have destroyed those that fight for you, and made slaves of your children." But the city was defended on every side by deep vallies and steep ascents; since the invasion of Syria, the walls and towers had been anxiously restored; the bravest of the fugitives of Yermuk had stopped in the nearest place of refuge; and in the defence of the sepulchre of Christ, the natives and strangers might feel some sparks of the enthusiasm which so fiercely glowed in the bosoms of the Saracens. The siege of Jerusalem lasted four months; not a day was lost without some action of sally or assault; the military engines incessantly played from the ramparts; and the inclemency of the winter was still more painful and destructive to the Arabs. The Christians yielded at length to the perseverance of the besiegers. The patriarch Sophronius appeared on the walls, and by the voice of an interpreter demanded a conference. After a vain attempt to dissuade the lieutenant of the caliph from his impious enterprise, he proposed, in the name of the people, a fair capitulation, with this extraordinary clause, that the articles of security should be ratified by the authority and presence of Omar himself. The question was debated in the council of Medina; the sanctity of the place, and the advice of Ali, persuaded the caliph to gratify the wishes of his soldiers and enemies, and the simplicity of his journey is more illustrious than the royal pageants of vanity and oppression. The conqueror of Persia and Syria was mounted on a red camel, which carried, besides his person, a bag of corn, a bag of dates, a wooden dish, and a leathern bottle of water. Wherever he halted, the company, without distinction, was invited to partake of his homely fare, and the repast was consecrated by the prayer and exhortation of the commander of the faithful.[80] But in this expedition or pilgrimage, his power was exercised in the administration of justice; he reformed the licentious polygamy of the Arabs, relieved the tributaries from extortion and cruelty, and chastised the luxury of the Saracens, by despoiling them of their rich silks, and dragging them on their faces in the dirt. When he came within sight of Jerusalem, the caliph cried with a loud voice, "God is victorious. O Lord give us an easy conquest;" and, pitching his tent of coarse hair, calmly seated himself on the ground. After signing the capitulation, he entered the city without fear or precaution; and courteously discoursed with the patriarch con-

80. The singular journey and equipage of Omar are described (besides Ockley, vol i. p. 250.) by Murtadi (Merveilles de l'Egypte, p. 200–202.).

cerning its religious antiquities.[81] Sophronius bowed before his new master, and secretly muttered, in the words of Daniel, "The abomination of desolation is in the holy place."[82] At the hour of prayer, they stood together in the church of the Resurrection; but the caliph refused to perform his devotions, and contented himself with praying on the steps of the church of Constantine. To the patriarch he disclosed his prudent and honourable motive. "Had I yielded," said Omar, "to your request, the Moslems of a future age would have infringed the treaty under colour of imitating my example." By his command, the ground of the temple of Solomon was prepared for the foundation of a mosch;[83] and, during a residence of ten days, he regulated the present and future state of his Syrian conquests. Medina might be jealous, lest the caliph should be detained by the sanctity of Jerusalem or the beauty of Damascus; her apprehensions were dispelled by his prompt and voluntary return to the tomb of the apostle.[84]

Of Aleppo and Antioch, A.D. 638.

To atchieve what yet remained of the Syrian war, the caliph had formed two separate armies; a chosen detachment, under Amrou and Yezid, was left in the camp of Palestine; while the larger division, under the standard of Abu Obeidah and Caled, marched away to the north against Antioch and Aleppo. The latter of these, the Beræa of the Greeks, was not yet illustrious as the capital of a province or a kingdom; and the inhabitants, by anticipating their submission and pleading their poverty, obtained a moderate composition for their lives

81. The Arabs boast of an old prophecy preserved at Jerusalem, and describing the name, the religion, and the person of Omar, the future conqueror. By such arts the Jews are said to have soothed the pride of their foreign masters, Cyrus and Alexander (Joseph. Ant. Jud. l. xi. c. 1. 8. p. 547. 579–582.).

82. *Το βδελυγμα της ερυμοσεως το ῥηθεν δια Δανιηλ του προφητου εστως εν τοπῳ αγιῳ.* Theophan. Chronograph. p. 281. This prediction, which had already served for Antiochus and the Romans, was again refitted for the present occasion, by the œconomy of Sophronius, one of the deepest theologians of the Monothelite controversy.

83. According to the accurate survey of d'Anville (Dissertation sur l'ancienne Jerusalem, p. 42–54.), the mosch of Omar, enlarged and embellished by succeeding caliphs, covered the ground of the ancient temple (*παλαιον του μεγαλου ναου δαπεδον*, says Phocas), a length of 215, a breadth of 172, *toises*. The Nubian geographer declares, that this magnificent structure was second only in size and beauty to the great mosch of Cordova (p. 113.), whose present state Mr. Swinburne has so elegantly represented (Travels into Spain, p. 296–302.).

84. Of the many Arabic tarikhs or chronicles of Jerusalem (d'Herbelot, p. 867.), Ockley found one among the Pocock MSS. of Oxford (vol.i.p. 257.), which he has used to supply the defective narrative of Al Wakidi.

and religion. But the castle of Aleppo,[85] distinct from the city, stood erect on a lofty artificial mound: the sides were sharpened to a precipice, and faced with freestone; and the breadth of the ditch might be filled with water from the neighbouring springs. After the loss of three thousand men, the garrison was still equal to the defence; and Youkinna, their valiant and hereditary chief, had murdered his brother, an holy monk, for daring to pronounce the name of peace. In a siege of four or five months, the hardest of the Syrian war, great numbers of the Saracens were killed and wounded: their removal to the distance of a mile could not reduce the vigilance of Youkinna; nor could the Christians be terrified by the execution of three hundred captives, whom they beheaded before the castle wall. The silence, and at length the complaints, of Abu Obeidah informed the caliph that their hope and patience were consumed at the foot of this impregnable fortress. "I am variously affected," replied Omar, "by the difference of your success; but I charge you by no means to raise the siege of the castle. Your retreat would diminish the reputation of our arms, and encourage the infidels to fall upon you on all sides. Remain before Aleppo till God shall determine the event, and forage with your horse round the adjacent country." The exhortation of the commander of the faithful was fortified by a supply of volunteers from all the tribes of Arabia, who arrived in the camp on horses or camels. Among these was Dames, of a servile birth, but of gigantic size and intrepid resolution. The forty-seventh day of his service he proposed, with only thirty men, to make an attempt on the castle. The experience and testimony of Caled recommended his offer; and Abu Obeidah admonished his brethren not to despise the baser origin of Dames, since he himself, could he relinquish the public care, would cheerfully serve under the banner of the slave. His design was covered by the appearance of a retreat; and the camp of the Saracens was pitched about a league from Aleppo. The thirty adventurers lay in ambush at the foot of the hill; and Dames at length succeeded in his enquiries, though he was provoked by the ignorance of his Greek captives. "God curse these dogs," said the illiterate Arab, "what a strange barbarous language they speak!" At the darkest hour of the night, he scaled the most accessible

85. The Persian historian of Timur (tom. iii. l. v. c. 21. p. 300.) describes the castle of Aleppo as founded on a rock one hundred cubits in height, a proof, says the French translator, that he had never visited the place. It is now in the midst of the city, of no strength, with a single gate, the circuit is about 5 or 600 paces, and the ditch half full of stagnant water (Voyages de Tavernier, tom. i. p. 149. Pocock, vol. ii. part i. p. 150.). The fortresses of the East are contemptible to an European eye.

height which he had diligently surveyed, a place where the stones were less entire, or the slope less perpendicular, or the guard less vigilant. Seven of the stoutest Saracens mounted on each others shoulders, and the weight of the column was sustained on the broad and sinewy back of the gigantic slave. The foremost in this painful ascent could grasp and climb the lowest part of the battlements: they silently stabbed and cast down the sentinels; and the thirty brethren, repeating a pious ejaculation, "O apostle of God, help and deliver us!" were successively drawn up by the long folds of their turbans. With bold and cautious footsteps, Dames explored the palace of the governor, who celebrated, in riotous merriment, the festival of his deliverance. From thence, returning to his companions, he assaulted on the inside the entrance of the castle. They overpowered the guard, unbolted the gate, let down the drawbridge, and defended the narrow pass, till the arrival of Caled, with the dawn of day, relieved their danger and assured their conquest. Youkinna, a formidable foe, became an active and useful proselyte; and the general of the Saracens expressed his regard for the most humble merit, by detaining the army at Aleppo till Dames was cured of his honourable wounds. The capital of Syria was still covered by the castle of Aazaz and the iron bridge of the Orontes. After the loss of those important posts, and the defeat of the last of the Roman armies, the luxury of Antioch[86] trembled and obeyed. Her safety was ransomed with three hundred thousand pieces of gold; but the throne of the successors of Alexander, the seat of the Roman government in the East, which had been decorated by Cæsar with the titles of free, and holy, and inviolate, was degraded under the yoke of the caliphs to the secondary rank of a provincial town.[87]

Flight of Heraclius, A.D. 638.

In the life of Heraclius, the glories of the Persian war are clouded on either hand by the disgrace and weakness of his more early and his later days. When the successors of Mahomet

86. The date of the conquest of Antioch by the Arabs is of some importance. By comparing the years of the world in the chronography of Theophanes with the years of the Hegira in the history of Elmacin, we shall determine, that it was taken between January 23^{d} and September 1st of the year of Christ 638 (Pagi Critica, in Baron. Annal. tom. ii. p. 812, 813.). Al Wakidi (Ockley, vol. i. p. 314.) assigns that event to Tuesday, August 21st, an inconsistent date; since Easter fell that year on April 5th, the 21st of August must have been a Friday (see the Tables of the Art de Verifier les Dates).

87. His bounteous edict, which tempted the grateful city to assume the victory of Pharsalia for a perpetual æra, is given *εν Αντιοχεια τη μητροπολει, ιερᾳ και ασυλῳ και αυτονομῳ και αρχουσῃ και προκαθημενῃ της ανατολης*. John Malela, in Chron. p. 91. edit. Venet. We may distinguish his authentic information of domestic facts from his gross ignorance of general history.

unsheathed the sword of war and religion, he was astonished at the boundless prospect of toil and danger; his nature was indolent, nor could the infirm and frigid age of the emperor be kindled to a second effort. The sense of shame, and the importunities of the Syrians, prevented his hasty departure from the scene of action; but the hero was no more; and the loss of Damascus and Jerusalem, the bloody fields of Aiznadin and Yermuk, may be imputed in some degree to the absence or misconduct of the sovereign. Instead of defending the sepulchre of Christ, he involved the church and state in a metaphysical controversy for the unity of his will; and while Heraclius crowned the offspring of his second nuptials, he was tamely stripped of the most valuable part of their inheritance. In the cathedral of Antioch, in the presence of the bishops, at the foot of the crucifix, he bewailed the sins of the prince and people; but his confession instructed the world, that it was vain, and perhaps impious, to resist the judgment of God. The Saracens were invincible in fact, since they were invincible in opinion; and the desertion of Youkinna, his false repentance and repeated perfidy, might justify the suspicion of the emperor, that he was encompassed by traitors and apostates, who conspired to betray his person and their country to the enemies of Christ. In the hour of adversity, his superstition was agitated by the omens and dreams of a falling crown; and after bidding an eternal farewel to Syria, he secretly embarked with a few attendants, and absolved the faith of his subjects.[88] Constantine, his eldest son, had been stationed with forty thousand men at Cæsarea, the civil metropolis of the three provinces of Palestine. But his private interest recalled him to the Byzantine court; and, after the flight of his father, he felt himself an unequal champion to the united force of the caliph. His vanguard was boldly attacked by three hundred Arabs and a thousand black slaves, who, in the depth of winter, had climbed the snowy mountains of Libanus, and who were speedily followed by the victorious squadrons of Caled himself. From the north and south the troops of Antioch and Jerusalem advanced along the sea shore, till their banners were joined under the walls of the Phœnician cities: Tripoli and Tyre were betrayed; and a fleet of fifty transports, which entered without distrust the captive harbours, brought a seasonable supply of arms and provisions to the camp of the

End of the Syrian war.

88. See Ockley (vol. i. p. 308. 312.), who laughs at the credulity of his author. When Heraclius bade farewel to Syria, Vale Syria et ultimum vale, he prophesied that the Romans should never re-enter the province till the birth of an inauspicious child, the future scourge of the empire. Abulfeda, p. 68. I am perfectly ignorant of the mystic sense, or nonsense, of this prediction.

Saracens. Their labours were terminated by the unexpected surrender of Cæsarea: the Roman prince had embarked in the night;[89] and the defenceless citizens solicited their pardon with an offering of two hundred thousand pieces of gold. The remainder of the province Ramlah, Ptolemais or Acre, Sichem or Neapolis, Gaza, Ascalon, Berytus, Sidon, Gabala, Laodicea, Apamea, Hierapolis, no longer presumed to dispute the will of the conqueror; and Syria bowed under the sceptre of the caliphs seven hundred years after Pompey had despoiled the last of the Macedonian kings.[90]

The conquerors of Syria, A.D. 633–639.

The sieges and battles of six campaigns had consumed many thousands of the Moslems. They died with the reputation and the cheerfulness of martyrs; and the simplicity of their faith may be expressed in the words of an Arabian youth, when he embraced, for the last time, his sister and mother: "It is not," said he, "the delicacies of Syria, or the fading delights of this world, that have prompted me to devote my life in the cause of religion. But I seek the favour of God and his apostle; and I have heard, from one of the companions of the prophet, that the spirits of the martyrs will be lodged in the crops of green birds, who shall taste the fruits, and drink of the rivers, of paradise. Farewel, we shall meet again among the groves and fountains which God has provided for his elect." The faithful captives might exercise a passive and more arduous resolution; and a cousin of Mahomet is celebrated for refusing, after an abstinence of three days, the wine and pork, the only nourishment that was allowed by the malice of the infidels. The frailty of some weaker brethren exasperated the implacable spirit of fanaticism; and the father of Amer deplored, in pathetic strains, the apostacy and damnation of a son, who had renounced the promises of God, and the intercession of the prophet, to occupy, with the priests and deacons, the lowest mansions of hell. The more fortunate Arabs, who survived the war and persevered in the faith, were restrained

89. In the loose and obscure chronology of the times, I am guided by an authentic record (in the book of ceremonies of Constantine Porphyrogenitus), which certifies that, June 4, A.D. 638, the emperor crowned his younger son Heraclius in the presence of his eldest Constantine, and in the palace of Constantinople; that January 1, A.D. 639, the royal procession visited the great church, and on the 4th of the same month, the hippodrome.

90. Sixty-five years before Christ, *Syria Pontusque monumenta sunt Cn. Pompeii virtutis* (Vell. Patercul. ii. 38.), rather of his fortune and power: he adjudged Syria to be a Roman province, and the last of the Seleucides were incapable of drawing a sword in the defence of their patrimony (see the original texts collected by Usher, Annal. p. 420.).

by their abstemious leader from the abuse of prosperity. After a refreshment of three days, Abu Obeidah withdrew his troops from the pernicious contagion of the luxury of Antioch, and assured the caliph that their religion and virtue could only be preserved by the hard discipline of poverty and labour. But the virtue of Omar, however rigorous to himself, was kind and liberal to his brethren. After a just tribute of praise and thanksgiving, he dropt a tear of compassion; and sitting down on the ground, wrote an answer, in which he mildly censured the severity of his lieutenant: "God," said the successor of the prophet, "has not forbidden the use of the good things of this world to faithful men, and such as have performed good works. Therefore you ought to have given them leave to rest themselves, and partake freely of those good things which the country affordeth. If any of the Saracens has no family in Arabia, they may marry in Syria; and whosoever of them wants any female slaves, he may purchase as many as he hath occasion for." The conquerors prepared to use, or to abuse, this gracious permission; but the year of their triumph was marked by a mortality of men and cattle; and twenty-five thousand Saracens were snatched away from the possession of Syria. The death of Abu Obeidah might be lamented by the Christians; but his brethren recollected that he was one of the ten elect whom the prophet had named as the heirs of paradise.[91] Caled survived his brethren about three years; and the tomb of the sword of God is shewn in the neighbourhood of Emesa. His valour, which founded in Arabia and Syria the empire of the caliphs, was fortified by the opinion of a special providence; and as long as he wore a cap, which had been blessed by Mahomet, he deemed himself invulnerable amidst the darts of the infidels.

Progress of the Syrian conquerors, A.D. 639–655.

The place of the first conquerors was supplied by a new generation of their children and countrymen; Syria became the seat and support of the house of Ommiyah; and the revenue, the soldiers, the ships of that powerful kingdom, were consecrated to enlarge on every side the empire of the caliphs. But the Saracens despise a superfluity of fame; and their historians scarcely condescend to mention the subordinate conquests which are lost in the splendour and rapidity of their victorious career. To the *north* of Syria, they passed mount Taurus, and reduced to their obedience the province

91. Abulfeda, Annal. Moslem. p. 73. Mahomet could artfully vary the praises of his disciples. Of Omar he was accustomed to say, that if a prophet could arise after himself, it would be Omar; and that in a general calamity, Omar would be excepted by the divine justice (Ockley, vol. i. p. 221.).

of Cilicia, with its capital Tarsus, the ancient monument of the Assyrian kings. Beyond a second ridge of the same mountains, they spread the flame of war, rather than the light of religion, as far as the shores of the Euxine and the neighbourhood of Constantinople. To the *east* they advanced to the banks and sources of the Euphrates and Tigris:[92] the long-disputed barrier of Rome and Persia was for ever confounded; the walls of Edessa and Amida, of Dara and Nisibis, which had resisted the arms and engines of Sapor or Nushirvan, were levelled in the dust; and the holy city of Abgarus might vainly produce the epistle or the image of Christ to an unbelieving conqueror. To the *west*, the Syrian kingdom is bounded by the sea: and the ruin of Aradus, a small island or peninsula on the coast, was postponed during ten years. But the hills of Libanus abounded in timber, the trade of Phœnicia was populous in mariners; and a fleet of seventeen hundred barks was equipped and manned by the natives of the desert. The Imperial navy of the Romans fled before them from the Pamphylian rocks to the Hellespont; but the spirit of the emperor, a grandson of Heraclius, had been subdued before the combat by a dream and a pun.[93] The Saracens rode masters of the sea; and the islands of Cyprus, Rhodes, and the Cyclades, were successively exposed to their rapacious visits. Three hundred years before the Christian æra, the memorable though fruitless siege of Rhodes[94] by Demetrius, had furnished that maritime republic with the materials and the subject of a trophy. A gigantic statue of Apollo or the sun, seventy cubits in height, was erected at the entrance of the harbour, a monument of the freedom and the arts of Greece. After standing fifty-six years, the colossus

92. Al Wakidi had likewise written an history of the conquest of Diarbekir, or Mesopotamia (Ockley, at the end of the ii[d] vol.), which our interpreters do not appear to have seen. The Chronicle of Dionysius of Telmar, the Jacobite patriarch, records the taking of Edessa, A.D. 637, and of Dara A.D. 641 (Asseman, Bibliot. Orient. tom. ii. p. 103.); and the attentive may glean some doubtful information from the Chronography of Theophanes (p. 285–287.). Most of the towns of Mesopotamia yielded by surrender (Abulpharag. p. 112.).

93. He dreamt that he was at Thessalonica, an harmless and unmeaning vision; but his soothsayer, or his cowardice, understood the sure omen of a defeat concealed in that inauspicious word *θες αλλῳ νικην*, Give to another the victory (Theophan. p. 286, Zonaras, tom. ii. l. xiv. p. 88.).

94. Every passage and every fact that relates to the isle, the city, and the colossus of Rhodes, are compiled in the laborious treatise of Meursius, who has bestowed the same diligence on the two larger islands of Crete and Cyprus. See in the iii[d] vol. of his works, the *Rhodus* of Meursius (l. i. c. 15. p. 715–719.). The Byzantine writers, Theophanes and Constantine, have ignorantly prolonged the term to 1360 years, and ridiculously divide the weight among 30,000 camels.

of Rhodes was overthrown by an earthquake: but the massy trunk, and huge fragments, lay scattered eight centuries on the ground, and are often described as one of the wonders of the ancient world. They were collected by the diligence of the Saracens, and sold to a Jewish merchant of Edessa, who is said to have laden nine hundred camels with the weight of the brass metal: an enormous weight, though we should include the hundred colossal figures,[95] and the three thousand statues, which adorned the prosperity of the city of the sun.

Egypt. Character and life of Amrou.

II. The conquest of Egypt may be explained by the character of the victorious Saracen, one of the first of his nation, in an age when the meanest of the brethren was exalted above his nature by the spirit of enthusiasm. The birth of Amrou was at once base and illustrious: his mother, a notorious prostitute, was unable to decide among five of the Koreish; but the proof of resemblance adjudged the child to Aasi the oldest of her lovers.[96] The youth of Amrou was impelled by the passions and prejudices of his kindred: his poetic genius was exercised in satirical verses against the person and doctrine of Mahomet; his dexterity was employed by the reigning faction to pursue the religious exiles who had taken refuge in the court of the Æthiopian king.[97] Yet he returned from this embassy, a secret proselyte; his reason or his interest determined him to renounce the worship of idols; he escaped from Mecca with his friend Caled, and the prophet of Medina enjoyed at the same moment the satisfaction of embracing the two firmest champions of his cause. The impatience of Amrou to lead the armies of the faithful, was checked by the reproof of Omar, who advised him not to seek power and dominion, since he who is a subject to-day, may be a prince tomorrow. Yet his merit was not overlooked by the two first successors of Mahomet; they were indebted to his arms for the conquest of Palestine; and in all the battles and sieges of Syria, he united with the temper of a chief, the valour of an adventurous soldier. In a visit to Medina, the caliph expressed a wish to survey the sword which had cut down so many Christian warriors: the son of Aasi unsheathed a short and ordinary

95. Centum colossi alium nobilitaturi locum, says Pliny, with his usual spirit. Hist. Natur. xxxiv. 18.

96. We learn this anecdote from a spirited old woman, who reviled to their faces the caliph and his friend. She was encouraged by the silence of Amrou and the liberality of Moawiyah (Abulfeda, Annal. Moslem. p. 111.).

97. Gagnier, Vie de Mahomet, tom. ii. p. 46, &c. who quotes the Abyssinian history, or romance, of Abdel Balcides. Yet the fact of the embassy and ambassador may be allowed.

scymetar; and as he perceived the surprise of Omar, "Alas," said the modest Saracen, "the sword itself, without the arm of its master, is neither sharper nor more weighty than the sword of Pharezdak the poet."[98] After the conquest of Egypt, he was recalled by the jealousy of the caliph Othman; but in the subsequent troubles, the ambition of a soldier, a statesman, and an orator, emerged from a private station. His powerful support, both in council and in the field, established the throne of the Ommiades; the administration and revenue of Egypt were restored by the gratitude of Moawiyah to a faithful friend who had raised himself above the rank of a subject; and Amrou ended his days in the palace and city which he had founded on the banks of the Nile. His dying speech to his children is celebrated by the Arabians as a model of eloquence and wisdom: he deplored the errors of his youth; but if the penitent was still infected by the vanity of a poet, he might exaggerate the venom and mischief of his impious compositions.[99]

Invasion of Egypt, A.D. 638, June.

From his camp, in Palestine, Amrou had surprised or anticipated the caliph's leave for the invasion of Egypt.[100] The magnanimous Omar trusted in his God and his sword, which had shaken the thrones of Chosroes and Cæsar: but when he compared the slender force of the Moslems with the greatness of the enterprise, he condemned his own rashness, and listened to his timid companions. The pride and the greatness of Pharaoh were familiar to the readers of the Koran; and a tenfold repetition of prodigies had been scarcely sufficient to effect, not the victory, but the flight, of six hundred thousand of the children of Israel: the cities of Egypt were many and populous; their architecture was strong and solid; the Nile, with its numerous branches, was alone an insuperable barrier; and the granary of the Imperial city would be obstinately defended by the Roman powers.

98. This saying is preserved by Pocock (Not. ad Carmen Tograi, p. 184.), and justly applauded by Mr. Harris (Philosophical Arrangements, p. 350.).

99. For the life and character of Amrou, see Ockley (Hist. of the Saracens, vol. i. p. 28. 63. 94. 328. 342. 344. and to the end of the volume; vol. ii. p. 51. 55. 57. 74. 110–112. 162.) and Otter (Mem. de l'Academie des Inscriptions, tom. xxi. p. 131, 132.). The readers of Tacitus may aptly compare Vespasian and Mucianus, with Moawiyah and Amrou. Yet the resemblance is still more in the situation, than in the characters, of the men.

100. Al Wakidi had likewise composed a separate history of the conquest of Egypt, which Mr. Ockley could never procure; and his own enquiries (vol. i. p. 344–362.) have added very little to the original text of Eutychius (Annal. tom. ii. p. 296–323. vers. Pocock), the Melchite patriarch of Alexandria, who lived three hundred years after the revolution.

In this perplexity, the commander of the faithful resigned himself to the decision of chance, or, in his opinion, of providence. At the head of only four thousand Arabs, the intrepid Amrou had marched away from his station of Gaza when he was overtaken by the messenger of Omar. "If you are still in Syria," said the ambiguous mandate, "retreat without delay; but if, at the receipt of this epistle, you have already reached the frontiers of Egypt, advance with confidence, and depend on the succour of God and of your brethren." The experience, perhaps the secret intelligence, of Amrou had taught him to suspect the mutability of courts; and he continued his march till his tents were unquestionably pitched on Egyptian ground. He there assembled his officers, broke the seal, perused the epistle, gravely enquired the name and situation of the place, and declared his ready obedience to the commands of the caliph. After a siege of thirty days, he took possession of Farmah or Pelusium; and that key of Egypt, as it has been justly named, unlocked the entrance of the country, as far as the ruins of Heliopolis and the neighbourhood of the modern Cairo.

The cities of Memphis, Babylon, and Cairo.

On the western side of the Nile, at a small distance to the east of the pyramids, at a small distance to the south of the Delta, Memphis, one hundred and fifty furlongs in circumference, displayed the magnificence of ancient kings. Under the reign of the Ptolemies and Cæsars, the seat of government was removed to the sea-coast; the ancient capital was eclipsed by the arts and opulence of Alexandria; the palaces, and at length the temples, were reduced to a desolate and ruinous condition: yet, in the age of Augustus, and even in that of Constantine, Memphis was still numbered among the greatest and most populous of the provincial cities.[101] The banks of the Nile, in this place of the breadth of three thousand feet, were united by two bridges of sixty and of thirty boats, connected in the middle stream by the small island of Rouda, which was covered with gardens and habitations.[102] The

101. Strabo, an accurate and attentive spectator, observes of Heliopolis νυνι μεν ουν εστι πανερημος ἡ πολις (Geograph. l. xvii. p. 1158.); but of Memphis, he declares, πολις δ'εστι μεγαλη τε και ευανδρος δευτερα μετ' Αλεξανδρειαν (p. 1161.); he notices, however, the mixture of inhabitants, and the ruin of the palaces. In the proper Egypt, Ammianus enumerates Memphis among the four cities, maximis urbibus quibus provincia nitet (xxii. 16.); and the name of Memphis appears with distinction in the Roman Itinerary and episcopal lists.

102. These rare and curious facts, the breadth (2946 feet) and the bridge of the Nile, are only to be found in the Danish traveller and the Nubian geographer (p. 98.).

eastern extremity of the bridge was terminated by the town of Babylon and the camp of a Roman legion, which protected the passage of the river and the second capital of Egypt. This important fortress, which might fairly be described as a part of Memphis or *Misrah*, was invested by the arms of the lieutenant of Omar: a reinforcement of four thousand Saracens soon arrived in his camp; and the military engines, which battered the walls, may be imputed to the art and labour of his Syrian allies. Yet the siege was protracted to seven months; and the rash invaders were encompassed and threatened by the inundation of the Nile.[103] Their last assault was bold and successful: they passed the ditch, which had been fortified with iron spikes, applied their scaling-ladders, entered the fortress with the shout of "God is victorious!" and drove the remnant of the Greeks to their boats and the isle of Rouda. The spot was afterwards recommended to the conqueror by the easy communication with the gulf and the peninsula of Arabia: the remains of Memphis was deserted: the tents of the Arabs were converted into permanent habitations; and the first mosch was blessed by the presence of fourscore companions of Mahomet.[104] A new city arose in their camp on the eastward bank of the Nile; and the contiguous quarters of Babylon and Fostat are confounded in their present decay by the appellation of old Misrah or Cairo, of which they form an extensive suburb. But the name of Cairo, the town of victory, more strictly belongs to the modern capital, which was founded in the tenth century by the Fatimite caliphs.[105] It has gradually receded from the river, but the continuity of buildings may be traced by an attentive eye from the monuments of Sesostris to those of Saladin.[106]

103. From the month of April, the Nile begins imperceptibly to rise: the swell becomes strong and visible in the moon after the summer solstice (Plin. Hist. Nat. v. 10.), and is usually proclaimed at Cairo on St. Peter's day (June 29.). A register of thirty successive years marks the greatest height of the waters between July 25 and August 18 (Maillet, Description de l'Egypte, lettre xi. p. 67, &c. Pocock's Description of the East, vol. i. p. 200. Shaw's Travels, p. 383.).

104. Murtadi, Merveilles de l'Egypte, p. 243–259. He expatiates on the subject with the zeal and minuteness of a citizen and a bigot, and his local traditions have a strong air of truth and accuracy.

105. D'Herbelot, Bibliotheque Orientale, p. 233.

106. The position of New and of Old Cairo is well known, and has been often described. Two writers, who were intimately acquainted with ancient and modern Egypt, have fixed, after a learned enquiry, the city of Memphis at *Gizeh*, directly opposite the Old Cairo (Sicard, Nouveaux Memoires des Missions du Levant, tom. vi. p. 5. 6. Shaw's Observations and Travels, p. 296–304.). Yet we may not disregard the authority or the arguments of Pocock (vol. i. p. 25–41.), Niebuhr (Voyage, tom. i. 77–106.), and,

Voluntary submission of the Copts or Jacobites, A.D. 638.

Yet the Arabs, after a glorious and profitable enterprise, must have retreated to the desert, had they not found a powerful alliance in the heart of the country. The rapid conquest of Alexander was assisted by the superstition and revolt of the natives: they abhorred their Persian oppressors, the disciples of the Magi, who had burnt the temples of Egypt, and feasted with sacrilegious appetite on the flesh of the god Apis.[107] After a period of ten centuries the same revolution was renewed by a similar cause; and in the support of an incomprehensible creed, the zeal of the Coptic Christians was equally ardent. I have already explained the origin and progress of the Monophysite controversy, and the persecution of the emperors, which converted a sect into a nation, and alienated Egypt from their religion and government. The Saracens were received as the deliverers of the Jacobite church; and a secret and effectual treaty was opened during the siege of Memphis between a victorious army and a people of slaves. A rich and noble Egyptian, of the name of Mokawkas, had dissembled his faith to obtain the administration of his province: in the disorders of the Persian war he aspired to independence: the embassy of Mahomet ranked him among princes; but he declined, with rich gifts and ambiguous compliments, the proposal of a new religion.[108] The abuse of his trust exposed him to the resentment of Heraclius; his submission was delayed by arrogance and fear; and his conscience was prompted by interest to throw himself on the favour of the nation and the support of the Saracens. In his first conference with Amrou, he heard without indignation the usual option of the Koran, the tribute or the sword. "The Greeks," replied Mokawkas, "are determined to abide the determination of the sword; but with the Greeks I desire no communion, either in this world or in the next, and I abjure for ever the Byzantine tyrant, his synod of

---

above all, of d'Anville (Description de l'Egypte, p. 111, 112. 130–149.), who have removed Memphis towards the village of Mohannah, some miles farther to the south. In their heat, the disputants have forgot that the ample space of a metropolis covers and annihilates the far greater part of the controversy.

107. See Herodotus, l. iii. c. 27, 28, 29. Ælian. Hist. Var. l. iv. c. 8. Suidas in Ωχος tom. ii. p. 774. Diodor. Sicul. tom. ii. l. xvii. p. 197. edit. Wesseling. *Των Περσων ησεβηκοτων εις τα ιερα*, says the last of these historians.

108. Mokawkas sent the prophet two Coptic damsels, with two maids, and one eunuch, an alabaster vase, an ingot of pure gold, oil, honey, and the finest white linen of Egypt, with an horse, a mule, and an ass, distinguished by their respective qualifications. The embassy of Mahomet was dispatched from Medina in the seventh year of the Hegira (A.D. 628). See Gagnier (Vie de Mahomet, tom. ii. p. 255, 256. 303.), from Al Jannabi.

Chalcedon, and his Melchite slaves. For myself and my brethren, we are resolved to live and die in the profession of the gospel and unity of Christ. It is impossible for us to embrace the revelations of your prophet; but we are desirous of peace, and cheerfully submit to pay tribute and obedience to his temporal successors." The tribute was ascertained at two pieces of gold for the head of every Christian; but old men, monks, women, and children, of both sexes, under sixteen years of age, were exempted from this personal assessment: the Copts above and below Memphis swore allegiance to the caliph, and promised an hospitable entertainment of three days to every Musulman who should travel through their country. By this charter of security, the ecclesiastical and civil tyranny of the Melchites was destroyed:[109] the anathemas of St. Cyril were thundered from every pulpit; and the sacred edifices, with the patrimony of the church, were restored to the national communion of the Jacobites, who enjoyed without moderation the moment of triumph and revenge. At the pressing summons of Amrou, their patriarch Benjamin emerged from his desert; and, after the first interview, the courteous Arab affected to declare, that he had never conversed with a Christian priest of more innocent manners and a more venerable aspect.[110] In the march from Memphis to Alexandria the lieutenant of Omar entrusted his safety to the zeal and gratitude of the Egyptians: the roads and bridges were diligently repaired; and in every step of his progress, he could depend on a constant supply of provisions and intelligence. The Greeks of Egypt, whose numbers could scarcely equal a tenth of the natives, were overwhelmed by the universal defection; they had ever been hated, they were no longer feared: the magistrate fled from his tribunal, the bishop from his altar; and the distant garrisons were surprised or starved by the surrounding multitudes. Had not the Nile afforded a safe and ready conveyance to the sea, not an individual could have escaped, who by birth, or language, or office, or religion, was connected with their odious name.

109. The præfecture of Egypt, and the conduct of the war, had been trusted by Heraclius to the patriarch Cyrus (Theophan. p. 280, 281.). "In Spain," said James II. "do you not consult your priests?" "We do," replied the Catholic ambassador, "and our affairs succeed accordingly." I know not how to relate the plans of Cyrus, of paying tribute without impairing the revenue, and of converting Omar by his marriage with the emperor's daughter (Nicephor. Breviar. p. 17, 18.).

110. See the life of Benjamin, in Renaudot (Hist. Patriarch. Alexandrin. p. 156–172.), who has enriched the conquest of Egypt with some facts from the Arabic text of Severus the Jacobite historian.

Siege and conquest of Alexandria.

By the retreat of the Greeks from the provinces of Upper Egypt, a considerable force was collected in the island of Delta: the natural and artificial channels of the Nile afforded a succession of strong and defensible posts; and the road to Alexandria was laboriously cleared by the victory of the Saracens in two and twenty days of general or partial combat. In their annals of conquest, the siege of Alexandria[111] is perhaps the most arduous and important enterprise. The first trading city in the world was abundantly replenished with the means of subsistence and defence. Her numerous inhabitants fought for the dearest of human rights, religion and property; and the enmity of the natives seemed to exclude them from the common benefit of peace and toleration. The sea was continually open; and if Heraclius had been awake to the public distress, fresh armies of Romans and Barbarians might have been poured into the harbour to save the second capital of the empire. A circumference of ten miles would have scattered the forces of the Greeks, and favoured the stratagems of an active enemy; but the two sides of an oblong square were covered by the sea and the lake Maræotis, and each of the narrow ends exposed a front of no more than ten furlongs. The efforts of the Arabs were not inadequate to the difficulty of the attempt and the value of the prize. From the throne of Medina, the eyes of Omar were fixed on the camp and city: his voice excited to arms the Arabian tribes and the veterans of Syria; and the merit of an holy war was recommended by the peculiar fame and fertility of Egypt. Anxious for the ruin or expulsion of their tyrants, the faithful natives devoted their labours to the service of Amrou; some sparks of martial spirit were perhaps rekindled by the example of their allies; and the sanguine hopes of Mokawkas had fixed his sepulchre in the church of St. John of Alexandria. Eutychius the patriarch observes, that the Saracens fought with the courage of lions; they repulsed the frequent and almost daily sallies of the besieged, and soon assaulted in their turn the walls and towers of the city. In every attack, the sword, the banner of Amrou, glittered in the van of the Moslems. On a memorable day, he was betrayed by his imprudent valour: his followers who had entered the citadel were

111. The local description of Alexandria is perfectly ascertained by the master hand of the first of geographers (d'Anville, Memoire sur l'Egypte, p. 52–63.); but we may borrow the eyes of the modern travellers, more especially of Thevenot (Voyage au Levant, part i. p. 381–395.), Pocock (vol. i. p. 2–13.), and Niebuhr (Voyage en Arabie, tom. i. p. 34–43.). Of the two modern rivals, Savary and Volney, the one may amuse, the other will instruct.

driven back; and the general, with a friend and a slave, remained a prisoner in the hands of the Christians. When Amrou was conducted before the præfect, he remembered his dignity and forgot his situation; a lofty demeanour, and resolute language, revealed the lieutenant of the caliph, and the battle-axe of a soldier was already raised to strike off the head of the audacious captive. His life was saved by the readiness of his slave, who instantly gave his master a blow on the face, and commanded him, with an angry tone, to be silent in the presence of his superiors. The credulous Greek was deceived; he listened to the offer of a treaty, and his prisoners were dismissed in the hope of a more respectable embassy, till the joyful acclamations of the camp announced the return of their general, and insulted the folly of the infidels. At length, after a siege of fourteen months,[112] and the loss of three and twenty thousand men, the Saracens prevailed: the Greeks embarked their dispirited and diminished numbers, and the standard of Mahomet was planted on the walls of the capital of Egypt. "I have taken," said Amrou to the caliph, "the great city of the West. It is impossible for me to enumerate the variety of its riches and beauty; and I shall content myself with observing, that it contains four thousand palaces, four thousand baths, four hundred theatres or places of amusement, twelve thousand shops for the sale of vegetable food, and forty thousand tributary Jews. The town has been subdued by force of arms, without treaty or capitulation, and the Moslems are impatient to seize the fruits of their victory."[113] The commander of the faithful rejected with firmness the idea of pillage, and directed his lieutenant to reserve the wealth and revenue of Alexandria for the public service and the propagation of the faith: the inhabitants were numbered; a tribute was imposed; the zeal and resentment of the Jacobites were curbed, and the Melchites who submitted to the Arabian yoke, were indulged in the obscure but tranquil exercise of their worship. The intelligence of this disgraceful and calamitous event afflicted the declining health of the emperor; and Heraclius died of a dropsy about seven weeks

112. Both Eutychius (Annal. tom. ii. p. 319.) and Elmacin (Hist. Saracen. p. 28.) concur in fixing the taking of Alexandria to Friday of the new moon of Moharram of the twentieth year of the Hegira (December 22, A.D. 640). In reckoning backwards fourteen months spent before Alexandria, seven months before Babylon, &c. Amrou might have invaded Egypt about the end of the year 638: but we are assured, that he entered the country the 12th of Bayni, 6th of June (Murtadi, Merveilles de l'Egypte, p. 164. Severus, apud Renaudot, p. 162.). The Saracen, and afterwards Lewis IX. of France, halted at Pelusium, or Damietta, during the season of the inundation of the Nile.

113. Eutych. Annal. tom. ii. p. 316. 319.

after the loss of Alexandria.[114] Under the minority of his grandson, the clamours of a people, deprived of their daily sustenance, compelled the Byzantine court to undertake the recovery of the capital of Egypt. In the space of four years, the harbour and fortifications of Alexandria were twice occupied by a fleet and army of Romans. They were twice expelled by the valour of Amrou, who was recalled by the domestic peril from the distant wars of Tripoli and Nubia. But the facility of the attempt, the repetition of the insult, and the obstinacy of the resistance, provoked him to swear, that if a third time he drove the infidels into the sea, he would render Alexandria as accessible on all sides as the house of a prostitute. Faithful to his promise, he dismantled several parts of the walls and towers, but the people was spared in the chastisement of the city, and the mosch of *Mercy* was erected on the spot where the victorious general had stopped the fury of his troops.

The Alexandrian library. I should deceive the expectation of the reader, if I passed in silence the fate of the Alexandrian library, as it is described by the learned Abulpharagius. The spirit of Amrou was more curious and liberal than that of his brethren, and in his leisure hours, the Arabian chief was pleased with the conversation of John, the last disciple of Ammonius, and who derived the surname of *Philoponus*, from his laborious studies of grammar and philosophy.[115] Emboldened by this familiar intercourse, Philoponus presumed to solicit a gift, inestimable in *his* opinion, contemptible in that of the Barbarians; the royal library, which alone, among the spoils of Alexandria, had not been appropriated by the visit and the seal of the conqueror. Amrou was inclined to gratify the wish of the grammarian, but his rigid integrity refused to alienate the minutest object without the consent of the caliph; and the well-known answer of Omar was inspired by the ignorance of a fanatic. "If these writings of the Greeks agree with the book of God, they are useless

114. Notwithstanding some inconsistencies of Theophanes and Cedrenus, the accuracy of Pagi (Critica, tom. ii. p. 824.) has extracted from Nicephorus and the Chronicon Orientale the true date of the death of Heraclius, February 11th, A.D. 641, fifty days after the loss of Alexandria. A fourth of that time was sufficient to convey the intelligence.

115. Many treatises of this lover of labour (φιλοπονος) are still extant; but for readers of the present age, the printed and unpublished are nearly in the same predicament. Moses and Aristotle are the chief objects of his verbose commentaries, one of which is dated as early as May 10th, A.D. 617 (Fabric. Bibliot. Græc. tom. ix. p. 458–468.). A modern (John Le Clerc), who sometimes assumed the same name, was equal to old Philoponus in diligence, and far superior in good sense and real knowledge.

and need not be preserved: if they disagree, they are pernicious and ought to be destroyed." The sentence was executed with blind obedience: the volumes of paper or parchment were distributed to the four thousand baths of the city; and such was their incredible multitude, that six months were barely sufficient for the consumption of this precious fuel. Since the Dynasties of Abulpharagius[116] have been given to the world in a Latin version, the tale has been repeatedly transcribed; and every scholar, with pious indignation, has deplored the irreparable shipwreck of the learning, the arts, and the genius, of antiquity. For my own part, I am strongly tempted to deny both the fact and the consequences. The fact is indeed marvellous; "Read and wonder!" says the historian himself: and the solitary report of a stranger who wrote at the end of six hundred years on the confines of Media, is overbalanced by the silence of two annalists of a more early date, both Christians, both natives of Egypt, and the most ancient of whom, the patriarch Eutychius, has amply described the conquest of Alexandria.[117] The rigid sentence of Omar is repugnant to the sound and orthodox precept of the Mahometan casuists: they expressly declare, that the religious books of the Jews and Christians, which are acquired by the right of war, should never be committed to the flames; and that the works of profane science, historians or poets, physicians or philosophers, may be lawfully applied to the use of the faithful.[118] A more destructive zeal may perhaps be attributed to the first successors of Mahomet; yet in this instance, the conflagration would have speedily expired in the deficiency of materials. I shall not recapitulate the disasters of the Alexandrian library, the involuntary flame that was kindled by Cæsar in his own defence,[119] or the mischievous bigotry of the Christians

116. Abulpharag. Dynast. p. 114. vers. Pocock. Audi quid factum sit et mirare. It would be endless to enumerate the moderns who have wondered and believed, but I may distinguish with honour the rational scepticism of Renaudot (Hist. Alex. Patriarch. p. 170.): historia . . . habet aliquid απιστον ut Arabibus familiare est.

117. This curious anecdote will be vainly sought in the annals of Eutychius, and the Saracenic history of Elmacin. The silence of Abulfeda, Murtadi, and a crowd of Moslems, is less conclusive from their ignorance of Christian literature.

118. See Reland, de Jure Militari Mohammedanorum, in his iii[d] volume of Dissertations, p. 37. The reason for not burning the religious books of the Jews or Christians, is derived from the respect that is due to the *name* of God.

119. Consult the collections of Frensheim (Supplement. Livian. c. 12. 43.) and Usher (Annal. p. 469.). Livy himself had styled the Alexandrian library, elegantiæ regum curæque egregium opus; a liberal encomium, for which he is pertly criticised by the narrow stoicism of Seneca (De Tranquillitate Animi, c. 9.), whose wisdom, on this occasion, deviates into nonsense.

who studied to destroy the monuments of idolatry.[120] But if we gradually descend from the age of the Antonines to that of Theodosius, we shall learn from a chain of contemporary witnesses, that the royal palace and the temple of Serapis, no longer contained the four, or the seven, hundred thousand volumes, which had been assembled by the curiosity and magnificence of the Ptolemies.[121] Perhaps the church and seat of the patriarchs might be enriched with a repository of books; but if the ponderous mass of Arian and Monophysite controversy were indeed consumed in the public baths,[122] a philosopher may allow, with a smile, that it was ultimately devoted to the benefit of mankind. I sincerely regret the more valuable libraries which have been involved in the ruin of the Roman empire; but when I seriously compute the lapse of ages, the waste of ignorance, and the calamities of war, our treasures, rather than our losses, are the object of my surprise. Many curious and interesting facts are buried in oblivion; the three great historians of Rome have been transmitted to our hands in a mutilated state, and we are deprived of many pleasing compositions of the lyric, iambic, and dramatic poetry of the Greeks. Yet we should gratefully remember, that the mischances of time and accident have spared the classic works to which the suffrage of antiquity[123] had adjudged the first place of genius and glory: the teachers of ancient knowledge, who are still extant, had perused and compared the writings of their predecessors;[124] nor can it fairly be presumed that any important truth, any useful discovery in art or nature, has been snatched away from the curiosity of modern ages.

Administration of Egypt.

In the administration of Egypt,[125] Amrou balanced the demands of justice and policy; the interest of the people of

120. See this History, vol. ii. p. 83. quarto edition.

121. Aulus Gellius (Noctes Atticæ, vi. 17.), Ammianus Marcellinus (xxii. 16.), and Orosius (l. vi. c. 15.). They all speak in the *past* tense, and the words of Ammianus are remarkably strong: fuerunt Bibliothecæ innumerabiles; et loquitur monumentorum veterum concinens fides, &c.

122. Renaudot answers for versions of the Bible, Hexapla, *Catenæ Patrum*, Commentaries, &c. (p. 170.). Our Alexandrian MS. if it came from Egypt, and not from Constantinople, or mount Athos (Wetstein, Prolegom. ad N. T. p. 8, &c.), might *possibly* be among them.

123. I have often perused with pleasure a chapter of Quintilian (Institut. Orator. x. 1.), in which that judicious critic enumerates and appreciates the series of Greek and Latin classics.

124. Such as Galen, Pliny, Aristotle, &c. On this subject Wotton (Reflections on ancient and modern Learning, p. 85–95.) argues, with solid sense, against the lively exotic fancies of Sir William Temple. The contempt of the Greeks for *Barbaric* science, would scarcely admit the Indian or Æthiopic books into the library of Alexandria; nor is it proved that philosophy has sustained any real loss from their exclusion.

125. This curious and authentic intel-

the law, who were defended by God; and of the people of the alliance, who were protected by man. In the recent tumult of conquest and deliverance, the tongue of the Copts and the sword of the Arabs were most adverse to the tranquillity of the province. To the former, Amrou declared, that faction and falsehood would be doubly chastised; by the punishment of the accusers, whom he should detest as his personal enemies, and by the promotion of their innocent brethren, whom their envy had laboured to injure and supplant. He excited the latter by the motives of religion and honour to sustain the dignity of their character, to endear themselves by a modest and temperate conduct to God and the caliph, to spare and protect a people who had trusted to their faith, and to content themselves with the legitimate and splendid rewards of their victory. In the management of the revenue he disapproved the simple but oppressive mode of a capitation, and preferred with reason a proportion of taxes, deducted on every branch from the clear profits of agriculture and commerce. A third part of the tribute was appropriated to the annual repairs of the dykes and canals, so essential to the public welfare. Under his administration the fertility of Egypt supplied the dearth of Arabia; and a string of camels, laden with corn and provisions, covered almost without an interval the long road from Memphis to Medina.[126] But the genius of Amrou soon renewed the maritime communication which had been attempted or atchieved by the Pharaohs, the Ptolemies, or the Cæsars; and a canal, at least eighty miles in length, was opened from the Nile to the Red Sea. This inland navigation, which would have joined the Mediterranean and the Indian ocean, was soon discontinued as useless and dangerous: the throne was removed from Medina to Damascus; and the Grecian fleets might have explored a passage to the holy cities of Arabia.[127]

Riches and populousness.

Of his new conquest, the caliph Omar had an imperfect knowledge from the voice of fame and the legends of the Koran. He requested that his lieutenant would place before his eyes the

ligence of Murtadi (p. 284–289.) has not been discovered either by Mr. Ockley, or by the self-sufficient compilers of the Modern Universal History.

126. Eutychius, Annal. tom. ii. p. 320. Elmacin, Hist. Saracen. p. 35.

127. On these *obscure* canals, the reader may try to satisfy himself from d'Anville (Mem. sur l'Egypte, p. 108–110. 124. 132.), and a learned thesis maintained and printed at Strasburg in the year 1770 (Jungendorum marium fluviorumque molimina, p. 39–47. 68–70.). Even the supine Turks have agitated the old project of joining the two seas (Memoires du Baron de Tott, tom. iv.).

realm of Pharaoh and the Amalekites; and the answer of Amrou exhibits a lively and not unfaithful picture of that singular country.[128] "O commander of the faithful, Egypt is a compound of black earth and green plants, between a pulverised mountain and a red sand. The distance from Syene to the sea is a month's journey for an horseman. Along the valley descends a river, on which the blessing of the Most High reposes both in the evening and morning, and which rises and falls with the revolutions of the sun and moon. When the annual dispensation of providence unlocks the springs and fountains that nourish the earth, the Nile rolls his swelling and sounding waters through the realm of Egypt: the fields are overspread by the salutary flood; and the villages communicate with each other in their painted barks. The retreat of the inundation deposits a fertilizing mud for the reception of the various seeds: the crowds of husbandmen who blacken the land may be compared to a swarm of industrious ants; and their native indolence is quickened by the lash of the task-master, and the promise of the flowers and fruits of a plentiful encrease. Their hope is seldom deceived; but the riches which they extract from the wheat, the barley, and the rice, the legumes, the fruit-trees, and the cattle, are unequally shared between those who labour and those who possess. According to the vicissitudes of the seasons, the face of the country is adorned with a *silver* wave, a verdant *emerald*, and the deep yellow of a *golden* harvest."[129] Yet this beneficial order is sometimes interrupted; and the long delay and sudden swell of the river in the first year of the conquest might afford some colour to an edifying fable. It is

128. A small volume, des Merveilles, &c. de l'Egypte, composed in the xiii[th] century by Murtadi of Cairo, and translated from an Arabic MS. of cardinal Mazarin, was published by Pierre Vatier, Paris, 1666. The antiquities of Egypt are wild and legendary: but the writer deserves credit and esteem for his account of the conquest and geography of his native country (See the correspondence of Amrou and Omar, p. 279–289.).

129. In a twenty years residence at Cairo, the consul Maillet had contemplated that varying scene, the Nile (lettre ii. particularly p. 70. 75.); the fertility of the land (lettre ix.). From a college at Cambridge, the poetic eye of Gray had *seen* the same objects with a keener glance:

What wonder in the sultry climes that spread,
Where Nile, redundant o'er his summer bed,
From his broad bosom life and verdure flings,
And broods o'er Egypt with his wat'ry wings;
If with advent'rous oar, and ready sail,
The dusky people drive before the gale:
Or on frail floats to neighbouring cities ride,
That rise and glitter o'er the ambient tide.

(Mason's Works and Memoirs of Gray, p. 199, 200.)

said, that the annual sacrifice of a virgin[130] had been interdicted by the piety of Omar; and that the Nile lay sullen and inactive in his shallow bed, till the mandate of the caliph was cast into the obedient stream, which rose in a single night to the height of sixteen cubits. The admiration of the Arabs for their new conquest encouraged the licence of their romantic spirit. We may read, in the gravest authors, that Egypt was crowded with twenty thousand cities or villages:[131] *that*, exclusive of the Greeks and Arabs, the Copts alone were found, on the assessment, six millions of tributary subjects,[132] or twenty millions of either sex and of every age: *that* three hundred millions of gold or silver were annually paid to the treasury of the caliph.[133] Our reason must be startled by these extravagant assertions; and they will become more palpable, if we assume the compass and measure the extent of habitable ground: a valley from the tropic to Memphis, seldom broader than twelve miles, and the triangle of the Delta, a flat surface of two thousand one hundred square leagues, compose a twelfth part of the magnitude of France.[134] A more accurate research will justify a more reasonable estimate. The three hundred millions, created by the error of a scribe, are reduced to the decent revenue of four millions three hundred thousand pieces of gold, of which nine hundred thousand were consumed by the pay of the soldiers.[135] Two

130. Murtadi, p. 164–167. The reader will not easily credit an human sacrifice under the Christian emperors, or a miracle of the successors of Mahomet.

131. Maillet, Description de l'Egypte, p. 22. He mentions this number as the *common* opinion; and adds, that the generality of these villages contain two or three thousand persons, and that many of them are more populous than our large cities.

132. Eutych. Annal. tom. ii. p. 308. 311. The twenty millions are computed from the following *data*: one-twelfth of mankind above sixty, one-third below sixteen, the proportion of men to women as seventeen to sixteen (Recherches sur la Population de la France, p. 71, 72.). The president Goguet (Origine des Arts, &c. tom. iii. p. 26, &c.) bestows twenty-seven millions on ancient Egypt, because the seventeen hundred companions of Sesostris were born on the same day.

133. Elmacin, Hist. Saracen. p. 218.; and this gross lump is swallowed without scruple by d'Herbelot (Bibliot. Orient. p. 1031.), Arbuthnot (Tables of ancient Coins, p. 262.), and de Guignes (Hist. des Huns, tom. iii. p. 135.). They might allege the not less extravagant liberality of Appian in favour of the Ptolemies (in præfat.) of seventy-four myriads, 740,000 talents, an annual income of 185, or near 300, millions of pounds sterling, according as we reckon by the Egyptian or the Alexandrian talent (Bernard de Ponderibus Antiq. p. 186.).

134. See the measurement of d'Anville (Mem. sur l'Egypte, p. 23, &c.). After some peevish cavils, M. Pauw (Recherches sur les Egyptiens, tom. i. p. 118–121.) can only enlarge his reckoning to 2250 square leagues.

135. Renaudot, Hist. Patriarch. Alexand. p. 334. who calls the common reading or version of Elmacin, *error librarii*. His own

authentic lists, of the present and of the twelfth century, are circumscribed within the respectable number of two thousand seven hundred villages and towns.[136] After a long residence at Cairo, a French consul has ventured to assign about four millions of Mahometans, Christians, and Jews, for the ample, though not incredible, scope, of the population of Egypt.[137]

Africa. First invasion by Abdallah, A.D. 647.

IV. The conquest of Africa, from the Nile to the Atlantic ocean,[138] was first attempted by the arms of the caliph Othman. The pious design was approved by the companions of Mahomet and the chiefs of the tribes; and twenty thousand Arabs marched from Medina, with the gifts and the blessing of the commander of the faithful. They were joined in the camp of Memphis by twenty thousand of their countrymen; and the conduct of the war was entrusted to Abdallah,[139] the son of Said and the foster-brother of the caliph, who had lately supplanted the conqueror and lieutenant of Egypt. Yet the favour of the prince, and the merit of his favourite, could not obliterate the guilt of his apostacy. The early conversion of Abdallah, and his skilful

---

emendation, of 4,300,000 pieces, in the ix[th] century, maintains a probable medium between the 3,000,000 which the Arabs acquired by the conquest of Egypt (idem, p. 168.), and the 2,400,000 which the sultan of Constantinople levied in the last century (Pietro della Valle, tom. i. p. 352.; Thevenot, part i. p. 824.). Pauw (Recherches, tom. ii. p. 365–373.) gradually raises the revenue of the Pharaohs, the Ptolemies, and the Cæsars, from six to fifteen millions of German crowns.

136. The list of Schultens (Index Geograph. ad calcem Vit. Saladin. p. 5.) contains 2396 places; that of d'Anville (Mem. sur l'Egypte, p. 29.), from the divan of Cairo, enumerates 2696.

137. See Maillet (Description de l'Egypte, p. 28.), who seems to argue with candour and judgment. I am much better satisfied with the observations than with the reading of the French consul. He was ignorant of Greek and Latin literature, and his fancy is too much delighted with the fictions of the Arabs. Their best knowledge is collected by Abulfeda (Descript. Ægypt. Arab. et Lat. à Joh. David Michaelis, Gottingæ, in 4to, 1776): and in two recent voyages into Egypt, we are amused by Savary, and instructed by Volney. I wish the latter could travel over the globe.

138. My conquest of Africa is drawn from two French interpreters of Arabic literature, Cardonne (Hist. de l'Afrique et de l'Espagne sous la Domination des Arabes, tom. i. p. 8–55.) and Otter (Hist. de l'Academie des Inscriptions, tom. xxi. p. 111–125. and 136.). They derive their principal information from Novairi, who composed, A.D. 1331, an Encyclopædia in more than twenty volumes. The five general parts successively treat of, 1. Physics, 2. Man, 3. Animals, 4. Plants, and, 5. History; and the African affairs are discussed in the vi[th] chapter of the vth section of this last part (Reiske, Prodidagmata ad Hagji Chalifæ Tabulas, p. 232–234.). Among the older historians who are quoted by Novairi we may distinguish the original narrative of a soldier who led the van of the Moslems.

139. See the history of Abdallah, in Abulfeda (Vit. Mohammed. p. 109.) and Gagnier (Vie de Mahomet, tom. iii. p. 45–48.).

pen, had recommended him to the important office of transcribing the sheets of the Koran: he betrayed his trust, corrupted the text, derided the errors which he had made, and fled to Mecca to escape the justice, and expose the ignorance, of the apostle. After the conquest of Mecca, he fell prostrate at the feet of Mahomet: his tears, and the entreaties of Othman, extorted a reluctant pardon; but the prophet declared that he had so long hesitated, to allow time for some zealous disciple to avenge his injury in the blood of the apostate. With apparent fidelity and effective merit, he served the religion which it was no longer his interest to desert: his birth and talents gave him an honourable rank among the Koreish; and, in a nation of cavalry, Abdallah was renowned as the boldest and most dextrous horseman of Arabia. At the head of forty thousand Moslems, he advanced from Egypt into the unknown countries of the West. The sands of Barca might be impervious to a Roman legion; but the Arabs were attended by their faithful camels; and the natives of the desert beheld without terror the familiar aspect of the soil and climate. After a painful march, they pitched their tents before the walls of Tripoli,[140] a maritime city, in which the *name*, the wealth, and the inhabitants, of the province had gradually centered, and which now maintains the third rank among the states of Barbary. A reinforcement of Greeks was surprised and cut in pieces on the sea-shore; but the fortifications of Tripoli resisted the first assaults; and the Saracens were tempted by the approach of the præfect Gregory[141] to relinquish the labours of the siege for the perils and the hopes of a decisive action. If his standard was followed by one hundred and twenty thousand men, the regular bands of the empire must have been lost in the naked and disorderly crowd of Africans and Moors, who formed the strength, or rather the numbers, of his host. He rejected with indignation the option of the Koran or the tribute; and during several days, the two armies were fiercely

The præfect Gregory and his daughter.

140. The province and city of Tripoli are described by Leo Africanus (in Navigatione et Viaggi di Ramusio, tom. i. Venetia, 1550, fol. 76. *verso*) and Marmol (Description de l'Afrique, tom. ii. p. 562.). The first of these writers was a Moor, a scholar, and a traveller, who composed or translated his African geography in a state of captivity at Rome, where he had assumed the name and religion of pope Leo X. In a similar captivity among the Moors, the Spaniard Marmol, a soldier of Charles V. compiled his Description of Africa, translated by d'Ablancourt into French (Paris, 1667, 3 vols. in 4to). Marmol had read and seen, but he is destitute of the curious and extensive observation which abounds in the original work of Leo the African.

141. Theophanes, who mentions the defeat, rather than the death, of Gregory. He brands the præfect with the name of *Τυραννος*; he had probably assumed the purple (Chronograph. p. 285.).

engaged from the dawn of light to the hour of noon, when their fatigue and the excessive heat compelled them to seek shelter and refreshment in their respective camps. The daughter of Gregory, a maid of incomparable beauty and spirit, is said to have fought by his side: from her earliest youth she was trained to mount on horseback, to draw the bow, and to wield the scymetar; and the richness of her arms and apparel were conspicuous in the foremost ranks of the battle. Her hand, with an hundred thousand pieces of gold, was offered for the head of the Arabian general, and the youths of Africa were excited by the prospect of the glorious prize. At the pressing solicitation of his brethren, Abdallah withdrew his person from the field; but the Saracens were discouraged by the retreat of their leader, and the repetition of these equal or unsuccessful conflicts.

Victory of the Arabs. A noble Arabian, who afterwards became the adversary of Ali and the father of a caliph, had signalized his valour in Egypt, and Zobeir[142] was the first who planted a scaling-ladder against the walls of Babylon. In the African war he was detached from the standard of Abdallah. On the news of the battle, Zobeir, with twelve companions, cut his way through the camp of the Greeks, and pressed forwards, without tasting either food or repose, to partake of the dangers of his brethen. He cast his eyes round the field: "Where," said he, "is our general?" "In his tent." "Is the tent a station for the general of the Moslems?" Abdallah represented with a blush the importance of his own life, and the temptation that was held forth by the Roman præfect. "Retort," said Zobeir, "on the infidels their ungenerous attempt. Proclaim through the ranks, that the head of Gregory shall be repaid with his captive daughter, and the equal sum of one hundred thousand pieces of gold." To the courage and discretion of Zobeir the lieutenant of the caliph entrusted the execution of his own stratagem, which inclined the long-disputed balance in favour of the Saracens. Supplying by activity and artifice the deficiency of numbers, a part of their forces lay concealed in their tents, while the remainder prolonged an irregular skirmish with the enemy, till the sun was high in the heavens. On both sides they retired with fainting steps: their horses were unbridled, their armour was laid aside, and the hostile nations prepared, or seemed to prepare, for the

142. See in Ockley (Hist. of the Saracens, vol. ii. p. 45.), the death of Zobeir, which was honoured with the tears of Ali, against whom he had rebelled. *His* valour at the siege of Babylon, if indeed it be the same person, is mentioned by Eutychius (Annal. tom. ii. p. 308.).

refreshment of the evening, and the encounter of the ensuing day. On a sudden, the charge was sounded; the Arabian camp poured forth a swarm of fresh and intrepid warriors; and the long line of the Greeks and Africans was surprised, assaulted, overturned, by new squadrons of the faithful, who, to the eye of fanaticism, might appear as a band of angels descending from the sky. The præfect himself was slain by the hand of Zobeir: his daughter, who sought revenge and death, was surrounded and made prisoner; and the fugitives involved in their disaster the town of Sufetula, to which they escaped from the sabres and lances of the Arabs. Sufetula was built one hundred and fifty miles to the south of Carthage: a gentle declivity is watered by a running stream, and shaded by a grove of juniper-trees; and, in the ruins of a triumphal arch, a portico, and three temples of the Corinthian order, curiosity may yet admire the magnificence of the Romans.[143] After the fall of this opulent city, the provincials and Barbarians implored on all sides the mercy of the conqueror. His vanity or his zeal might be flattered by offers of tribute or professions of faith: but his losses, his fatigues, and the progress of an epidemical disease, prevented a solid establishment; and the Saracens, after a campaign of fifteen months, retreated to the confines of Egypt, with the captives and the wealth of their African expedition. The caliph's fifth was granted to a favourite, on the nominal payment of five hundred thousand pieces of gold;[144] but the state was doubly injured by this fallacious transaction, if each foot-soldier had shared one thousand, and each horseman three thousand, pieces, in the real division of the plunder. The author of the death of Gregory was expected to have claimed the most precious reward of the victory: from his silence it might be presumed that he had fallen in the battle, till the tears and exclamations of the præfect's daughter at the sight of Zobeir revealed the valour and modesty of that gallant soldier. The unfortunate virgin was offered, and almost rejected as a slave, by her father's murderer, who coolly declared that his sword was consecrated to the service of religion; and that he laboured for a recompense far above the charms of mortal beauty, or the riches of this transitory life. A reward congenial to his temper, was the honourable commission of announcing to the caliph Othman the success of his arms. The companions, the chiefs, and the people, were assembled in the

143. Shaw's Travels, p. 118, 119.

144. Mimica emptio, says Abulfeda, erat hæc, et mira donatio; quandoquidem Othman, ejus nomine nummos ex ærario prius ablatos ærario præstabat (Annal. Moslem. p. 78.). Elmacin (in his cloudy version, p. 39.) seems to report the same job. When the Arabs besieged the palace of Othman, it stood high in their catalogue of grievances.

mosch of Medina, to hear the interesting narrative of Zobeir; and, as the orator forgot nothing except the merit of his own counsels and actions, the name of Abdallah was joined by the Arabians with the heroic names of Caled and Amrou.[145]

Progress of the Saracens in Africa, A.D. 665–689.

The western conquests of the Saracens were suspended near twenty years, till their dissensions were composed by the establishment of the house of Ommiyah: and the caliph Moawiyah was invited by the cries of the Africans themselves. The successors of Heraclius had been informed of the tribute which they had been compelled to stipulate with the Arabs; but instead of being moved to pity and relieve their distress, they imposed, as an equivalent or a fine, a second tribute of a similar amount. The ears of the Byzantine ministers were shut against the complaints of their poverty and ruin: their despair was reduced to prefer the dominion of a single master; and the extortions of the patriarch of Carthage, who was invested with civil and military power, provoked the sectaries, and even the Catholics, of the Roman province to abjure the religion as well as the authority of their tyrants. The first lieutenant of Moawiyah acquired a just renown, subdued an important city, defeated an army of thirty thousand Greeks, swept away fourscore thousand captives, and enriched with their spoils the bold adventurers of Syria and Egypt.[146] But the title of conqueror of Africa is more justly due to his successor Akbah. He marched from Damascus at the head of ten thousand of the bravest Arabs; and the genuine force of the Moslems was enlarged by the doubtful aid and conversion of many thousand Barbarians. It would be difficult, nor is it necessary, to trace the accurate line of the progress of Akbah. The interior regions have been peopled by the Orientals with fictitious armies and imaginary citadels. In the warlike province of Zab or Numidia, fourscore thousand of the natives might assemble in arms; but the number of three hundred and sixty towns is incompatible with the ignorance or decay of husbandry;[147]

145. *Επεστρατευσαν Σαρακηνοι την Αφρικην, και συμβαλοντες τῳ τυραννῳ Γρηγοριῳ τουτον τρεπουσι και τους συν αυτω κτεινουσι και στοιχησαντες φορους μετα των Αφρων υπεστρεψαν*. Theophan. Chronograph. p. 285. edit. Paris. His chronology is loose and inaccurate.

146. Theophanes (in Chronograph. p. 293.) inserts the vague rumours that might reach Constantinople, of the western conquests of the Arabs; and I learn from Paul Warnefrid, deacon of Aquileia (de Gestis Langobard. l. v. c. 13.), that at this time they sent a fleet from Alexandria into the Sicilian and African seas.

147. See Novairi (apud Otter, p. 118.), Leo Africanus (fol. 81. *verso*), who reckons only cinque citta è infinite casale, Marmol (Description de l'Afrique, tom. iii. p. 33.), and Shaw (Travels, p. 57. 65–68.).

and a circumference of three leagues will not be justified by the ruins of Erbe or Lambesa, the ancient metropolis of that inland country. As we approach the sea-coast, the well-known cities of Bugia[148] and Tangier[149] define the more certain limits of the Saracen victories. A remnant of trade still adheres to the commodious harbour of Bugia, which, in a more prosperous age, is said to have contained about twenty thousand houses; and the plenty of iron which is dug from the adjacent mountains might have supplied a braver people with the instruments of defence. The remote position and venerable antiquity of Tingi, or Tangier, have been decorated by the Greek and Arabian fables; but the figurative expressions of the latter, that the walls were constructed of brass, and that the roofs were covered with gold and silver, may be interpreted as the emblems of strength and opulence. The province of Mauritania Tingitana,[150] which assumed the name of the capital, had been imperfectly discovered and settled by the Romans; the five colonies were confined to a narrow pale, and the more southern parts were seldom explored except by the agents of luxury, who searched the forests for ivory and the citron wood,[151] and the shores of the ocean for the purple shell-fish. The fearless Akbah plunged into the heart of the country, traversed the wilderness in which his successors erected the splendid capitals of Fez and Morocco,[152] and at length penetrated to the verge of the Atlantic and

148. Leo African. fol. 58. verso 59. recto. Marmol, tom. ii. p. 415. Shaw, p. 43.

149. Leo African. fol. 52. Marmol, tom. ii. p. 228.

150. Regio ignobilis, et vix quicquam illustre sortita, parvis oppidis habitatur, parva flumina emittit, solo quam viris melior et segnitie gentis obscura. Pomponius Mela, i. 5. iii. 10. Mela deserves the more credit, since his own Phœnician ancestors had migrated from Tingitana to Spain (see, in ii. 6. a passage of that geographer so cruelly tortured by Salmasius, Isaac Vossius, and the most virulent of critics, James Gronovius). He lived at the time of the final reduction of that country by the emperor Claudius: yet almost thirty years afterwards, Pliny (Hist. Nat. v. 1.) complains of his authors, too lazy to enquire, too proud to confess their ignorance of that wild and remote province.

151. The foolish fashion of this citron wood prevailed at Rome among the men, as much as the taste for pearls among the women. A round board or table, four or five feet in diameter, sold for the price of an estate (latefundii taxatione), eight, ten, or twelve thousand pounds sterling (Plin. Hist. Natur. xiii. 29.). I conceive that I must not confound the tree *citrus*, with that of the fruit *citrum*. But I am not botanist enough to define the former (it is like the wild cypress) by the vulgar or Linnæan name; nor will I decide whether the *citrum* be the orange or the lemon. Salmasius appears to exhaust the subject, but he too often involves himself in the web of his disorderly erudition (Plinian. Exercitat. tom. ii. p. 666, &c.).

152. Leo African. fol. 16. verso. Marmol, tom. ii. p. 28. This province, the first scene of the exploits and greatness of the *cherifs*, is often mentioned in the curious history of that dynasty at the end of the iii[d] volume of

the great desert. The river Sus descends from the western sides of mount Atlas, fertilises, like the Nile, the adjacent soil, and falls into the sea at a moderate distance from the Canary, or Fortunate, islands. Its banks were inhabited by the last of the Moors, a race of savages, without laws, or discipline, or religion: they were astonished by the strange and irresistible terrors of the Oriental arms; and as they possessed neither gold nor silver, the richest spoil was the beauty of the female captives, some of whom were afterwards sold for a thousand pieces of gold. The career, though not the zeal, of Akbah was checked by the prospect of a boundless ocean. He spurred his horse into the waves, and raising his eyes to heaven, exclaimed with the tone of a fanatic: "Great God! if my course were not stopped by this sea, I would still go on, to the unknown kingdoms of the West, preaching the unity of thy holy name, and putting to the sword the rebellious nations who worship any other gods than thee."[153] Yet this Mahometan Alexander, who sighed for new worlds, was unable to preserve his recent conquests. By the universal defection of the Greeks and Africans, he was recalled from the shores of the Atlantic, and the surrounding multitudes left him only the resource of an honourable death. The last scene was dignified by an example of national virtue. An ambitious chief, who had disputed the command and failed in the attempt, was led about as a prisoner in the camp of the Arabian general. The insurgents had trusted to his discontent and revenge; he disdained their offers and revealed their designs. In the hour of danger, the grateful Akbah unlocked his fetters, and advised him to retire; he chose to die under the banner of his rival. Embracing as friends and martyrs, they unsheathed their scymetars, broke their scabbards, and maintained an obstinate combat, till they fell by each other's side on the last of their slaughtered countrymen. The third general or governor of Africa, Zuheir, avenged and encountered the fate of his predecessor. He vanquished the natives in many battles; he was overthrown by a powerful army, which Constantinople had sent to the relief of Carthage.

Foundation of Cairoan, A.D. 670–675.

It had been the frequent practice of the Moorish tribes to join the invaders, to share the plunder, to profess the faith, and to revolt to their savage state of independence and idolatry, on

---

Marmol, Description de l'Afrique. The iii[d] vol. of the Recherches Historiques sur les Maures (lately published at Paris) illustrates the history and geography of the kingdoms of Fez and Morocco.

153. Otter (p. 119.) has given the strong tone of fanaticism to this exclamation, which Cardonne (p. 37.) has softened to a pious wish of *preaching* the Koran. Yet they had both the same text of Novairi before their eyes.

the first retreat or misfortune of the Moslems. The prudence of Akbah had proposed to found an Arabian colony in the heart of Africa; a citadel that might curb the levity of the Barbarians, a place of refuge to secure, against the accidents of war, the wealth and the families of the Saracens. With this view, and under the modest title of the station of a caravan, he planted this colony in the fiftieth year of the Hegira. In its present decay, Cairoan[154] still holds the second rank in the kingdom of Tunis, from which it is distant about fifty miles to the south:[155] its inland situation, twelve miles westward of the sea, has protected the city from the Greek and Sicilian fleets. When the wild beasts and serpents were extirpated, when the forest, or rather wilderness, was cleared, the vestiges of a Roman town were discovered in a sandy plain: the vegetable food of Cairoan is brought from afar; and the scarcity of springs constrains the inhabitants to collect in cisterns and reservoirs a precarious supply of rain-water. These obstacles were subdued by the industry of Akbah; he traced a circumference of three thousand and six hundred paces, which he encompassed with a brick wall; in the space of five years, the governor's palace was surrounded with a sufficient number of private habitations; a spacious mosch was supported by five hundred columns of granite, porphyry, and Numidian marble; and Cairoan became the seat of learning as well as of empire. But these were the glories of a later age; the new colony was shaken by the successive defeats of Akbah and Zuheir, and the western expeditions were again interrupted by the civil discord of the Arabian monarchy. The son of the valiant Zobeir maintained a war of twelve years, a siege of seven months against the house of Ommiyah. Abdallah was said to unite the fierceness of the lion with the subtlety of the fox; but if he inherited the courage, he was devoid of the generosity, of his father.[156]

154. The foundation of Cairoan is mentioned by Ockley (Hist. of the Saracens, vol. ii. p. 129, 130.); and the situation, mosch, &c. of the city, are described by Leo Africanus (fol. 75.), Marmol (tom. ii. p. 532.), and Shaw (p. 115.).

155. A portentous, though frequent mistake, has been the confounding, from a slight similitude of name, the *Cyrene* of the Greeks, and the *Cairoan* of the Arabs, two cities which are separated by an interval of a thousand miles along the sea-coast. The great Thuanus has not escaped this fault, the less excusable as it is connected with a formal and elaborate description of Africa (Historiar. l. vii. c. 2. in tom. i. p. 240. edit. Buckley).

156. Besides the Arabic chronicles of Abulfeda, Elmacin, and Abulpharagius, under the lxxiii[d] year of the Hegira, we may consult d'Herbelot (Bibliot. Orient. p. 7.) and Ockley (Hist. of the Saracens, vol. ii. p. 339–349.). The latter has given the last and pathetic dialogue between Abdallah and his mother; but he has forgot a physical effect of *her* grief for his death, the return, at the age of ninety, and fatal consequences, of her *menses*.

Conquest of Carthage, A.D. 692–698.

The return of domestic peace allowed the caliph Abdalmalek to resume the conquest of Africa; the standard was delivered to Hassan governor of Egypt, and the revenue of that kingdom, with an army of forty thousand men, was consecrated to the important service. In the vicissitudes of war, the interior provinces had been alternately won and lost by the Saracens. But the sea-coast still remained in the hands of the Greeks; the predecessors of Hassan had respected the name and fortifications of Carthage; and the number of its defenders was recruited by the fugitives of Cabes and Tripoli. The arms of Hassan were bolder and more fortunate: he reduced and pillaged the metropolis of Africa; and the mention of scaling-ladders may justify the suspicion that he anticipated, by a sudden assault, the more tedious operations of a regular siege. But the joy of the conquerors was soon disturbed by the appearance of the Christian succours. The præfect and patrician John, a general of experience and renown, embarked at Constantinople the forces of the Eastern empire;[157] they were joined by the ships and soldiers of Sicily, and a powerful reinforcement of Goths[158] was obtained from the fears and religion of the Spanish monarch. The weight of the confederate navy broke the chain that guarded the entrance of the harbour; the Arabs retired to Cairoan, or Tripoli; the Christians landed; the citizens hailed the ensign of the cross, and the winter was idly wasted in the dream of victory or deliverance. But Africa was irrecoverably lost: the zeal and resentment of the commander of the faithful[159] prepared in the ensuing spring a more numerous armament by

157. *Λεοντιος . . . απαντα τα Ρωμαικα εξωπλισε πλοιμα, στρατηγον τε επ' αυτοις Ιωαννην τον Πατρικιον εμπειρον των πολεμιων προχειρισαμενος προς Καρχηδονα κατα των Σαρακηνων εξεπεμψεν.* Nicephori Constantinopolitani Breviar. p. 28. The patriarch of Constantinople, with Theophanes (Chronograph. p. 309.), have slightly mentioned this last attempt for the relief of Africa. Pagi (Critica, tom. iii. p. 129. 141.) has nicely ascertained the chronology by a strict comparison of the Arabic and Byzantine historians, who often disagree both in time and fact. See likewise a note of Otter (p. 121.).

158. Dove s'erano ridotti i nobili Romani e i *Gotti*; and afterwards, i Romani fuggirono e i *Gotti*, lasciarono Carthagine (Leo African. fol. 72. recto). I know not from what Arabic writer the African derived his Goths, but the fact, though new, is so interesting and so probable, that I will accept it on the slightest authority.

159. This commander is styled by Nicephorus *Βασιλευς Σαρακηνων*, a vague though not improper definition of the caliph. Theophanes introduces the strange appellation of *Προτοσυμβολος*, which his interpreter Goar explains by *Vizir Azem*. They may approach the truth, in assigning the active part to the minister, rather than the prince; but they forget that the Ommiades had only a *kateb*, or secretary, and that the office of vizir was not revived or instituted till the 132[d] year of the Hegira (d'Herbelot, p. 912.).

sea and land; and the patrician in his turn was compelled to evacuate the post and fortifications of Carthage. A second battle was fought in the neighbourhood of Utica: the Greeks and Goths were again defeated; and their timely embarkation saved them from the sword of Hassan, who had invested the slight and insufficient rampart of their camp. Whatever yet remained of Carthage, was delivered to the flames, and the colony of Dido[160] and Cæsar lay desolate above two hundred years, till a part, perhaps a twentieth, of the old circumference was repeopled by the first of the Fatimite caliphs. In the beginning of the sixteenth century, the second capital of the West was represented by a mosch, a college without students, twenty-five or thirty shops, and the huts of five hundred peasants, who, in their abject poverty, displayed the arrogance of the Punic senators. Even that paltry village was swept away by the Spaniards whom Charles the Fifth had stationed in the fortress of the Goletta. The ruins of Carthage have perished; and the place might be unknown if some broken arches of an aqueduct did not guide the footsteps of the inquisitive traveller.[161]

Final conquest of Africa, A.D. 698–709.

The Greeks were expelled, but the Arabians were not yet masters of the country. In the interior provinces the Moors or *Berbers*,[162] so feeble under the first Cæsars, so formidable to the Byzantine princes, maintained a disorderly resistance to the religion and power of the successors of Mahomet. Under the standard of their

160. According to Solinus (l. 27. p. 36. edit. Salmas.), the Carthage of Dido stood either 677 or 737 years; a various reading, which proceeds from the difference of MSS. or editions (Salmas. Plinian. Exercit. tom. i. p. 228.). The former of these accounts, which gives 823 years before Christ, is more consistent with the well-weighed testimony of Velleius Paterculus: but the latter is preferred by our chronologists (Marsham, Canon. Chron. p. 398.), as more agreeable to the Hebrew and Tyrian annals.

161. Leo African. fol. 71, verso; 72, recto. Marmol, tom. ii. p. 445–447. Shaw, p. 80.

162. The history of the word *Barbar* may be classed under four periods. 1. In the time of Homer, when the Greeks and Asiatics might probably use a common idiom, the imitative sound of Bar-bar was applied to the ruder tribes, whose pronunciation was most harsh, whose grammar was most defective. *Καρες Βαρβαροφωνοι* (Iliad ii. 867. with the Oxford scholiast, Clarke's Annotation, and Henry Stephens's Greek Thesaurus, tom. i. p. 720.). 2. From the time, at least, of Herodotus, it was extended to *all* the nations who were strangers to the language and manners of the Greeks. 3. In the age of Plautus, the Romans submitted to the insult (Pompeius Festus, l. ii. p. 48. edit. Dacier), and freely gave themselves the name of Barbarians. They insensibly claimed an exemption for Italy, and her subject provinces; and at length removed the disgraceful appellation to the savage or hostile nations beyond the pale of the empire. 4. In every sense, it was due to the Moors; the familiar word was borrowed from the Latin provincials by the Arabian conquerors, and has justly settled as a local denomination (Barbary) along the northern coast of Africa.

queen Cahina the independent tribes acquired some degree of union and discipline; and as the Moors respected in their females the character of a prophetess, they attacked the invaders with an enthusiasm similar to their own. The veteran bands of Hassan were inadequate to the defence of Africa: the conquests of an age were lost in a single day; and the Arabian chief, overwhelmed by the torrent, retired to the confines of Egypt, and expected, five years, the promised succours of the caliph. After the retreat of the Saracens, the victorious prophetess assembled the Moorish chiefs, and recommended a measure of strange and savage policy. "Our cities," said she, "and the gold and silver which they contain, perpetually attract the arms of the Arabs. These vile metals are not the objects of *our* ambition; we content ourselves with the simple productions of the earth. Let us destroy these cities; let us bury in their ruins those pernicious treasures; and when the avarice of our foes shall be destitute of temptation, perhaps they will cease to disturb the tranquillity of a warlike people." The proposal was accepted with unanimous applause. From Tangier to Tripoli the buildings, or at least the fortifications, were demolished, the fruit-trees were cut down, the means of subsistence were extirpated, a fertile and populous garden was changed into a desert, and the historians of a more recent period could discern the frequent traces of the prosperity and devastation of their ancestors. Such is the tale of the modern Arabians. Yet I strongly suspect that their ignorance of antiquity, the love of the marvellous, and the fashion of extolling the philosophy of Barbarians, has induced them to describe, as one voluntary act, the calamities of three hundred years since the first fury of the Donatists and Vandals. In the progress of the revolt Cahina had most probably contributed her share of destruction; and the alarm of universal ruin might terrify and alienate the cities that had reluctantly yielded to her unworthy yoke. They no longer hoped, perhaps they no longer wished, the return of their Byzantine sovereigns: their present servitude was not alleviated by the benefits of order and justice; and the most zealous Catholic must prefer the imperfect truths of the Koran to the blind and rude idolatry of the Moors. The general of the Saracens was again received as the saviour of the province: the friends of civil society conspired against the savages of the land; and the royal prophetess was slain in the first battle which overturned the baseless fabric of her superstition and empire. The same spirit revived under the successor of Hassan: it was finally quelled by the activity of Musa and his two sons; but the number of the rebels may be presumed from that of three hundred thousand captives; sixty thousand of whom, the caliph's fifth, were sold for the profit of the public treasury. Thirty thousand of the Barbarian youth were enlisted in the troops; and the pious labours of Musa, to inculcate the knowledge and practice of the Koran, accustomed the Africans to obey the apostle of God and the commander of the faithful. In their climate and government, their diet and habitation, the wandering Moors resembled the Bedoweens of the desert. With the religion, they were proud to adopt the language, name, and origin, of Arabs: the blood of the strangers and natives was insensibly mingled; and from the Euphrates to the Atlantic the same nation might seem to be diffused over the sandy plains of Asia and Africa. Yet I will not deny that fifty thousand tents of pure Arabians might be transported over the Nile, and scattered through the Libyan desert; and I am not ignorant that five of the Moorish tribes still retain their *barbarous* idiom, with the appellation and character of *white* Africans.[163]

Adoption of the Moors.

Spain.
First temptations and designs of the Arabs, A.D. 709.

V. In the progress of conquest from the north and south, the Goths and the Saracens encountered each other on the confines of Europe and Africa. In the opinion of the latter, the difference of religion is a reasonable ground of enmity and warfare.[164] As early as the time of Othman[165] their piratical squadrons had ravaged the coast of Andalusia;[166] nor had they forgotten the relief of Carthage by the Gothic succours. In that age, as well as in the present, the kings of Spain were possessed of the fortress of Ceuta; one of the columns of Hercules, which is divided by a narrow streight from the opposite pillar or point of Europe. A small portion of Mauritania was still wanting to the African conquest; but Musa, in the pride of

163. The first book of Leo Africanus, and the observations of Dr. Shaw (p. 220. 223. 227. 247, &c.), will throw some light on the roving tribes of Barbary, of Arabian or Moorish descent. But Shaw had seen these savages with distant terror; and Leo, a captive in the Vatican, appears to have lost more of his Arabic, than he could acquire of Greek or Roman, learning. Many of his gross mistakes might be detected in the first period of the Mahometan history.

164. In a conference with a prince of the Greeks, Amrou observed that their religion was different; upon which score it was lawful for brothers to quarrel. Ockley's History of the Saracens, vol. i. p. 328.

165. Abulfeda, Annal. Moslem. p. 78. vers. Reiske.

166. The name of Andalusia is applied by the Arabs not only to the modern province, but to the whole peninsula of Spain (Geograph. Nub. p. 151. d'Herbelot, Bibliot. Orient. p. 114, 115.). The etymology has been most improbably deduced from Vandalusia, country of the Vandals (d'Anville Etats de l'Europe, p. 146, 147, &c.). But the Handalusia of Casiri, which signifies in Arabic the region of the evening, of the West, in a word, the Hesperia of the Greeks, is perfectly apposite (Bibliot. Arabico-Hispana, tom. ii. p. 327, &c.).

victory, was repulsed from the walls of Ceuta, by the vigilance and courage of count Julian, the general of the Goths. From his disappointment and perplexity, Musa was relieved by an unexpected message of the Christian chief, who offered his place, his person, and his sword, to the successors of Mahomet, and solicited the disgraceful honour of introducing their arms into the heart of Spain.[167] If we enquire into the cause of his treachery, the Spaniards will repeat the popular story of his daughter Cava;[168] of a virgin who was seduced, or ravished, by her sovereign; of a father who sacrificed his religion and country to the thirst of revenge. The passions of princes have often been licentious and destructive; but this well-known tale, romantic in itself, is indifferently supported by external evidence; and the history of Spain will suggest some motives of interest and policy more congenial to the breast of a veteran statesman.[169]

State of the Gothic monarchy.

After the decease or deposition of Witiza, his two sons were supplanted by the ambition of Roderic, a noble Goth, whose father, the duke or governor of a province, had fallen a victim to the preceding tyranny. The monarchy was still elective; but the sons of Witiza, educated on the steps of the throne, were impatient of a private station. Their resentment was the more dangerous, as it was varnished with the dissimulation of courts: their followers were excited by the remembrance of favours and the promise of a revolution; and their uncle Oppas, archbishop of Toledo and Seville, was the first person in the

167. The fall and resurrection of the Gothic monarchy are related by Mariana (tom. i. p. 238–260. l. vi. c. 19–26. l. vii. c. 1, 2.). That historian has infused into his noble work (Historiæ de Rebus Hispaniæ, libri xxx. Hagæ Comitum 1733, in four volumes in folio, with the Continuation of Miniana), the style and spirit of a Roman classic; and after the xii[th] century, his knowledge and judgment may be safely trusted. But the Jesuit is not exempt from the prejudices of his order; he adopts and adorns, like his rival Buchanan, the most absurd of the national legends; he is too careless of criticism and chronology, and supplies, from a lively fancy, the chasms of historical evidence. These chasms are large and frequent; Roderic archbishop of Toledo, the father of the Spanish history, lived five hundred years after the conquest of the Arabs; and the more early accounts are comprised in some meagre lines of the blind chronicles of Isidore of Badajoz (Pacensis), and of Alphonso III. king of Leon, which I have seen only in the Annals of Pagi.

168. Le viol (says Voltaire) est aussi difficile à faire qu'à prouver. Des Evêques se seroient ils ligués pour une fille? (Hist. Generale, c. xxvi.) His argument is not logically conclusive.

169. In the story of Cava, Mariana (l. vi. c. 21. p. 241, 242.) seems to vie with the Lucretia of Livy. Like the ancients, he seldom quotes; and the oldest testimony of Baronius (Annal. Eccles. A.D. 713, N° 19.), that of Lucas Tudensis, a Galician deacon of the xiii[th] century, only says, Cava quam pro concubinâ utebatur.

church, and the second in the state. It is probable that Julian was involved in the disgrace of the unsuccessful faction, that he had little to hope and much to fear from the new reign; and that the imprudent king could not forget or forgive the injuries which Roderic and his family had sustained. The merit and influence of the count rendered him an useful or formidable subject: his estates were ample, his followers bold and numerous, and it was too fatally shewn that, by his Andalusian and Mauritanian commands, he held in his hand the keys of the Spanish monarchy. Too feeble, however, to meet his sovereign in arms, he sought the aid of a foreign power; and his rash invitation of the Moors and Arabs produced the calamities of eight hundred years. In his epistles, or in a personal interview, he revealed the wealth and nakedness of his country; the weakness of an unpopular prince; the degeneracy of an effeminate people. The Goths were no longer the victorious Barbarians, who had humbled the pride of Rome, despoiled the queen of nations, and penetrated from the Danube to the Atlantic ocean. Secluded from the world by the Pyrenæan mountains, the successors of Alaric had slumbered in a long peace: the walls of the cities were mouldered into dust: the youth had abandoned the exercise of arms; and the presumption of their ancient renown would expose them in a field of battle to the first assault of the invaders. The ambitious Saracen was fired by the ease and importance of the attempt; but the execution was delayed till he had consulted the commander of the faithful; and his messenger returned with the permission of Walid to annex the unknown kingdoms of the West to the religion and throne of the caliphs. In his residence of Tangier, Musa, with secrecy and caution, continued his correspondence and hastened his preparations. But the remorse of the conspirators was soothed by the fallacious assurance that he should content himself with the glory and spoil, without aspiring to establish the Moslems beyond the sea that separates Africa from Europe.[170]

170. The Orientals, Elmacin, Abulpharagius, Abulfeda, pass over the conquest of Spain in silence, or with a single word. The text of Novairi, and the other Arabian writers, is represented, though with some foreign alloy, by M. de Cardonne (Hist. de l'Afrique et de l'Espagne sous la Domination des Arabes, Paris 1765, 3 vol. in 12mo. tom. i. p. 55–114.), and more concisely by M. de Guignes (Hist. des Huns, tom. i. p. 347–350.). The librarian of the Escurial has not satisfied my hopes: yet he appears to have searched with diligence his broken materials; and the history of the conquest is illustrated by some valuable fragments of the *genuine* Razis (who wrote at Corduba, A. H. 300), of Ben Hazil, &c. See Bibliot. Arabico-Hispana, tom. ii. p. 32. 105, 106. 182. 252. 319–332. On this occasion, the industry of Pagi has been aided by the Arabic

The first descent of the Arabs, A.D. 710, July. Before Musa would trust an army of the faithful to the traitors and infidels of a foreign land, he made a less dangerous trial of their strength and veracity. One hundred Arabs, and four hundred Africans, passed over, in four vessels, from Tangier or Ceuta; the place of their descent on the opposite shore of the streight, is marked by the name of Tarif their chief; and the date of this memorable event[171] is fixed to the month of Ramadan, of the ninety-first year of the Hegira, to the month of July, seven hundred and forty-eight years from the Spanish æra of Cæsar,[172] seven hundred and ten after the birth of Christ. From their first station, they marched eighteen miles through an hilly country to the castle and town of Julian;[173] on which (it is still called Algezire) they bestowed the name of the Green island, from a verdant cape that advances into the sea. Their hospitable entertainment, the Christians who joined their standard, their inroad into a fertile and unguarded province, the richness of their spoil, and the safety of their return, announced to their brethren the most favourable omens of victory. In the ensuing spring, five thousand veterans and volunteers were embarked under the command of Tarik, a dauntless and skilful soldier, who surpassed the expectation of his chief; and the necessary transports were provided by the industry of their too faithful ally. The Saracens landed[174] at the pillar or point of Europe; the corrupt *Their second descent,*

---

learning of his friend the Abbé de Longuerue, and to their joint labours I am deeply indebted.

171. A mistake of Roderic of Toledo, in comparing the lunar years of the Hegira with the Julian years of the Æra, has determined Baronius, Mariana, and the crowd of Spanish historians, to place the first invasion in the year 713, and the battle of Xeres in November 714. This anachronism of three years, has been detected by the more correct industry of modern chronologists, above all, of Pagi (Critica, tom. iii. p. 169. 171–174.), who have restored the genuine date of the revolution. At the present time, an Arabian scholar like Cardonne, who adopts the ancient error (tom. i. p. 75.), is inexcusably ignorant or careless.

172. The Æra of Cæsar, which in Spain was in legal and popular use till the xivth century, begins thirty-eight years before the birth of Christ. I would refer the origin to the general peace by sea and land, which confirmed the power and *partition* of the Triumvirs (Dion Cassius, l. xlviii. p. 547. 553. Appian de Bell. Civil. l. v. p. 1034. edit. fol.). Spain was a province of Cæsar Octavian; and Tarragona, which raised the first temple to Augustus (Tacit. Annal. i. 78.), might borrow from the Orientals this mode of flattery.

173. The road, the country, the old castle of count Julian, and the superstitious belief of the Spaniards of hidden treasures, &c. are described by Pere Labat (Voyages en Espagne et en Italie, tom. i. p. 207–217.) with his usual pleasantry.

174. The Nubian geographer (p. 154.) explains the topography of the war; but it is highly incredible that the lieutenant of Musa should execute the desperate and useless measure of burning his ships.

and familiar appellation of Gibraltar (*Gebel al Tarik*) describes the mountain of Tarik; and the intrenchments of his camp were the first outline of those fortifications, which, in the hands of our countrymen, have resisted the art and power of the house of Bourbon. The adjacent governors informed the court of Toledo of the descent and progress of the Arabs; and the defeat of his lieutenant Edeco, who had been commanded to seize and bind the presumptuous strangers, admonished Roderic of the magnitude of the danger. At the royal summons, the dukes and counts, the bishops and nobles of the Gothic monarchy, assembled at the head of their followers; and the title of king of the Romans, which is employed by an Arabic historian, may be excused by the close affinity of language, religion, and manners, between the nations of Spain. His army consisted of ninety or an hundred thousand men; a formidable power, if their fidelity and discipline had been adequate to their numbers. The troops of Tarik had been augmented to twelve thousand Saracens; but the Christian malecontents were attracted by the influence of Julian, and a crowd of Africans most greedily tasted the temporal blessings of the Koran. In the neighbourhood of Cadiz, the town of Xeres[175] has been illustrated by the encounter which determined the fate of the kingdom; the stream of the Guadalete, which falls into the bay, divided the two camps, and marked the advancing and retreating skirmishes of three successive and bloody days. On the fourth day, the two armies joined a more serious and decisive issue; but Alaric would have blushed at the sight of his unworthy successor, sustaining on his head a diadem of pearls, incumbered with a flowing robe of gold and silken embroidery, and reclining on a litter or car of ivory drawn by two white mules. Notwithstanding the valour of the Saracens, they fainted under the weight of multitudes, and the plain of Xeres was overspread with sixteen thousand of their dead bodies. "My brethren," said Tarik to his surviving companions, "the enemy is before you, the sea is behind; whither would ye fly? Follow your general: I am resolved either to lose my life, or to trample on the prostrate king of the Romans." Besides the resource of despair, he confided in the secret correspondence and nocturnal interviews of count Julian, with the sons and the brother of Witiza. The two princes and the archbishop of Toledo, occupied the

A.D. 711, April;

and victory, July 19–26.

175. Xeres (the Roman colony of Asta Regia) is only two leagues from Cadiz. In the xvi[th] century it was a granary of corn; and the wine of Xeres is familiar to the nations of Europe (Lud. Nonii Hispania, c. 13. p. 54–56. a work of correct and concise knowledge; d'Anville, Etats de l'Europe, &c. p. 154.).

most important post: their well-timed defection broke the ranks of the Christians; each warrior was prompted by fear or suspicion to consult his personal safety; and the remains of the Gothic army were scattered or destroyed in the flight and pursuit of the three following days. Amidst the general disorder, Roderic started from his car, and mounted Orelia, the fleetest of his horses; but he escaped from a soldier's death to perish more ignobly in the waters of the Bœtis or Guadalquivir. His diadem, his robes, and his courser, were found on the bank; but as the body of the Gothic prince was lost in the waves, the pride and ignorance of the caliph must have been gratified with some meaner head, which was exposed in triumph before the palace of Damascus. "And such," continues a valiant historian of the Arabs, "is the fate of those kings who withdraw themselves from a field of battle."[176]

Ruin of the Gothic monarchy, A.D. 711.

Count Julian had plunged so deep into guilt and infamy, that his only hope was in the ruin of his country. After the battle of Xeres he recommended the most effectual measures to the victorious Saracen. "The king of the Goths is slain; their princes have fled before you, the army is routed, the nation is astonished. Secure with sufficient detachments the cities of Bœtica; but in person, and without delay, march to the royal city of Toledo, and allow not the distracted Christians either time or tranquillity for the election of a new monarch." Tarik listened to his advice. A Roman captive and proselyte, who had been enfranchised by the caliph himself, assaulted Cordova with seven hundred horse: he swam the river, surprised the town, and drove the Christians into the great church, where they defended themselves above three months. Another detachment reduced the sea-coast of Bœtica, which in the last period of the Moorish power has comprised in a narrow space the populous kingdom of Grenada. The march of Tarik from the Bœtis to the Tagus,[177] was directed through the Sierra Morena, that separates Andalusia and Castille, till he appeared in arms under the

176. Id sane infortunii regibus pedem ex acie referentibus sæpe contingit. Ben Hazil of Grenada, in Bibliot. Arabico-Hispana, tom. ii. p. 327. Some credulous Spaniards believe that king Roderic, or Rodrigo, escaped to an hermit's cell; and others, that he was cast alive into a tub full of serpents, from whence he exclaimed, with a lamentable voice, "they devour the part with which I have so grievously sinned" (Don Quixote, part ii. l. iii. c. 1.).

177. The direct road from Corduba to Toledo was measured by Mr. Swinburne's mules in 72½ hours; but a larger computation must be adopted for the slow and devious marches of an army. The Arabs traversed the province of La Mancha, which the pen of Cervantes has transformed into classic ground to the readers of every nation.

walls of Toledo.[178] The most zealous of the Catholics had escaped with the relics of their saints; and if the gates were shut, it was only till the victor had subscribed a fair and reasonable capitulation. The voluntary exiles were allowed to depart with their effects; seven churches were appropriated to the Christian worship; the archbishop and his clergy were at liberty to exercise their functions, the monks to practise or neglect their penance; and the Goths and Romans were left in all civil and criminal cases to the subordinate jurisdiction of their own laws and magistrates. But if the justice of Tarik protected the Christians, his gratitude and policy rewarded the Jews, to whose secret or open aid he was indebted for his most important acquisitions. Persecuted by the kings and synods of Spain, who had often pressed the alternative of banishment or baptism, that outcast nation embraced the moment of revenge: the comparison of their past and present state was the pledge of their fidelity; and the alliance between the disciples of Moses and of Mahomet, was maintained till the final æra of their common expulsion. From the royal seat of Toledo, the Arabian leader spread his conquests to the north, over the modern realms of Castille and Leon; but it is needless to enumerate the cities that yielded on his approach, or again to describe the table of emerald,[179] transported from the East by the Romans, acquired by the Goths among the spoils of Rome, and presented by the Arabs to the throne of Damascus. Beyond the Asturian mountains, the maritime town of Gijon was the term[180] of the lieutenant of Musa, who had performed, with the speed of a traveller, his victorious march, of seven hundred miles, from the rock of Gibraltar to the bay of Biscay. The failure of land compelled him to retreat; and he was recalled to Toledo, to excuse his presumption of subduing a kingdom in the absence of his general. Spain,

178. The antiquities of Toledo, *Urbs Parva* in the Punic wars, *Urbs Regia* in the vi^th^ century, are briefly described by Nonius (Hispania, c. 59. p. 181–186.). He borrows from Roderic the *fatale palatium* of Moorish portraits; but modestly insinuates, it was no more than a Roman amphitheatre.

179. In the Historia Arabum (c. 9. p. 17. ad calcem Elmacin), Roderic of Toledo describes the emerald table, and inserts the name of Medinat Almeyda in Arabic words and letters. He appears to be conversant with the Mahometan writers; but I cannot agree with M. de Guignes (Hist. des Huns, tom. i. p. 350.), that he had read and transcribed Novairi; because he was dead an hundred years before Novairi composed his history. This mistake is founded on a still grosser error. M. de Guignes confounds the historian Roderic Ximenes archbishop of Toledo in the xiii[th] century, with cardinal Ximenes who governed Spain in the beginning of the xvi[th], and was the subject, not the author, of historical compositions.

180. Tarik might have inscribed on the last rock, the boast of Regnard and his companions in their Lapland journey, "Hic tandem stetimus, nobis ubi defuit orbis."

which, in a more savage and disorderly state, had resisted, two hundred years, the arms of the Romans, was overrun in a few months by those of the Saracens; and such was the eagerness of submission and treaty, that the governor of Cordova is recorded as the only chief who fell, without conditions, a prisoner into their hands. The cause of the Goths had been irrevocably judged in the field of Xeres; and, in the national dismay, each part of the monarchy declined a contest with the antagonist who had vanquished the united strength of the whole.[181] That strength had been wasted by two successive seasons of famine and pestilence; and the governors, who were impatient to surrender, might exaggerate the difficulty of collecting the provisions of a siege. To disarm the Christians, superstition likewise contributed her terrors: and the subtle Arab encouraged the report of dreams, omens, and prophecies, and of the portraits of the destined conquerors of Spain, that were discovered on breaking open an apartment of the royal palace. Yet a spark of the vital flame was still alive: some invincible fugitives preferred a life of poverty and freedom in the Asturian vallies; the hardy mountaineers repulsed the slaves of the caliph; and the sword of Pelagius has been transformed into the sceptre of the Catholic kings.[182]

Conquest of Spain by Musa, A.D. 712, 713.

On the intelligence of this rapid success, the applause of Musa degenerated into envy; and he began, not to complain, but to fear, that Tarik would leave him nothing to subdue. At the head of ten thousand Arabs and eight thousand Africans, he passed over in person from Mauritania to Spain: the first of his companions were the noblest of the Koreish; his eldest son was left in the command of Africa; the three younger brethren were of an age and spirit to second the boldest enterprises of their father. At his landing in Algezire, he was respectfully entertained by count Julian, who stifled his inward remorse, and testified, both in words and actions, that the victory of the Arabs had not impaired his attachment to their cause. Some enemies yet remained for the sword of Musa. The tardy repentance of the Goths had compared their own numbers and those of the invaders; the cities from which the march of Tarik had declined, considered themselves as impregnable; and the bravest patriots defended the for-

181. Such was the argument of the traitor Oppas, and every chief to whom it was addressed did not answer with the spirit of Pelagius: Omnis Hispania dudum sub unò regimine Gothorum, omnis exercitus Hispaniæ in uno congregatus Ismaelitarum non valuit sustinere impetum. Chron. Alphonsi Regis, apud Pagi, tom. iii. p. 177.

182. The revival of the Gothic kingdom in the Asturias is distinctly though concisely noticed by d'Anville (Etats de l'Europe, p. 159.).

tifications of Seville and Merida. They were successively besieged and reduced by the labour of Musa, who transported his camp from the Bœtis to the Anas, from the Guadalquivir to the Guadiana. When he beheld the works of Roman magnificence, the bridge, the aqueducts, the triumphal arches, and the theatre, of the ancient metropolis of Lusitania, "I should imagine," said he to his four companions, "that the human race must have united their art and power in the foundation of this city: happy is the man who shall become its master!" He aspired to that happiness, but the *Emeritans* sustained on this occasion the honour of their descent from the veteran legionaries of Augustus.[183] Disdaining the confinement of their walls, they gave battle to the Arabs on the plain; but an ambuscade rising from the shelter of a quarry, or a ruin, chastised their indiscretion and intercepted their return. The wooden turrets of assault were rolled forwards to the foot of the rampart; but the defence of Merida was obstinate and long; and the *castle of the martyrs* was a perpetual testimony of the losses of the Moslems. The constancy of the besieged was at length subdued by famine and despair; and the prudent victor disguised his impatience under the names of clemency and esteem. The alternative of exile or tribute was allowed; the churches were divided between the two religions; and the wealth of those who had fallen in the siege, or retired to Gallicia, was confiscated as the reward of the faithful. In the midway between Merida and Toledo, the lieutenant of Musa saluted the vicegerent of the caliph, and conducted him to the palace of the Gothic kings. Their first interview was cold and formal: a rigid account was exacted of the treasures of Spain: the character of Tarik was exposed to suspicion and obloquy; and the hero was imprisoned, reviled, and ignominiously scourged by the hand, or the command, of Musa. Yet so strict was the discipline, so pure the zeal, or so tame the spirit, of the primitive Moslems, that, after this public indignity, Tarik could serve and be trusted in the reduction of the Tarragonese province. A mosch was erected at Saragossa, by the liberality of the Koreish: the port of Barcelona was opened to the vessels of Syria; and the Goths were pursued beyond the Pyrenean mountains into their Gallic province of Septimania or Languedoc.[184] In the church of St. Mary at Carcassone, Musa found, but

183. The honourable relics of the Cantabrian war (Dion Cassius, l. liii. p. 720.) were planted in this metropolis of Lusitania, perhaps of Spain (submittit cui tota suos Hispania fasces). Nonius (Hispania, c. 31. p. 106–110.) enumerates the ancient structures, but concludes with a sigh: Urbs hæc olim nobilissima ad magnam incolarum infrequentiam delapsa est et præter priscæ claritatis ruinas nihil ostendit.

184. Both the interpreters of Novairi, de Guignes (Hist. des Huns, tom. i. p. 349.) and

it is improbable that he left, seven equestrian statues of massy silver; and from his *term* or column of Narbonne, he returned on his footsteps to the Gallician and Lusitanian shores of the ocean. During the absence of the father, his son Abdelaziz chastised the insurgents of Seville, and reduced, from Malaga to Valentia, the sea-coast of the Mediterranean: his original treaty with the discreet and valiant Theodemir[185] will represent the manners and policy of the times. "*The conditions of peace agreed and sworn between Abdelaziz, the son of Musa, the son of Nassir, and Theodemir, prince of the Goths.* In the name of the most merciful God, Abdelaziz makes peace on these conditions: *that* Theodemir shall not be disturbed in his principality; nor any injury be offered to the life or property, the wives and children, the religion and temples, of the Christians: *that* Theodemir shall freely deliver his seven cities, Orihuela, Valentola, Alicant, Mola, Vacasora, Bigerra (now Bejar), Ora (or Opta), and Lorca: *that* he shall not assist or entertain the enemies of the caliph, but shall faithfully communicate his knowledge of their hostile designs: *that* himself, and each of the Gothic nobles, shall annually pay one piece of gold, four measures of wheat, as many of barley, with a certain proportion of honey, oil, and vinegar; and that each of their vassals shall be taxed at one moiety of the said imposition. Given the fourth of Regeb, in the year of the Hegira ninety-four, and subscribed with the names of four Musulman witnesses."[186] Theodemir and his subjects were treated with uncommon lenity; but the rate of tribute appears to have fluctuated from a tenth to a fifth, according to the submission or obstinacy of the Christians.[187] In this revolution, many partial calamities were inflicted by

---

Cardonne (Hist. de l'Afrique et de l'Espagne, tom. i. p. 93, 94. 104, 105.), lead Musa into the Narbonnese Gaul. But I find no mention of this enterprise either in Roderic of Toledo, or the MSS. of the Escurial, and the invasion of the Saracens is postponed by a French chronicle till the ix[th] year after the conquest of Spain, A.D. 721 (Pagi Critica, tom. iii. p. 177. 195. Historians of France, tom. iii.). I much question whether Musa ever passed the Pyrenees.

185. Four hundred years after Theodemir, his territories of Murcia and Carthagena retain in the Nubian geographer Edrisi (p. 154–161.) the name of Tadmir (d'Anville, Etats de l'Europe, p. 156. Pagi, tom. iii. p. 174.). In the present decay of Spanish agriculture, Mr. Swinburne (Travels into Spain, p. 119.) surveyed with pleasure the delicious valley from Murcia to Orihuela, four leagues and a half of the finest corn, pulse, lucern, oranges, &c.

186. See the treaty in Arabic and Latin, in the Bibliotheca Arabico-Hispana, tom. ii. p. 105, 106. It is signed the 4th of the month of Regeb, A.H. 94. the 5th of April, A.D. 713, a date which seems to prolong the resistance of Theodemir and the government of Musa.

187. From the history of Sandoval, p. 87. Fleury (Hist. Eccles. tom. ix. p. 261.) has given the substance of another treaty concluded A. Æ. C. 782. A.D. 734, between an Arabian chief, and the Goths and Romans,

the carnal or religious passions of the enthusiasts: some churches were profaned by the new worship: some relics or images were confounded with idols: the rebels were put to the sword; and one town (an obscure place between Cordova and Seville) was razed to its foundations. Yet if we compare the invasion of Spain by the Goths, or its recovery by the kings of Castille and Arragon, we must applaud the moderation and discipline of the Arabian conquerors.

Disgrace of Musa, A.D. 714.

The exploits of Musa were performed in the evening of life, though he affected to disguise his age by colouring with a red powder the whiteness of his beard. But in the love of action and glory, his breast was still fired with the ardour of youth; and the possession of Spain was considered only as the first step to the monarchy of Europe. With a powerful armament by sea and land, he was preparing to repass the Pyrenees, to extinguish in Gaul and Italy the declining kingdoms of the Franks and Lombards, and to preach the unity of God on the altar of the Vatican. From thence, subduing the Barbarians of Germany, he proposed to follow the course of the Danube from its source to the Euxine sea, to overthrow the Greek or Roman empire of Constantinople, and returning from Europe to Asia, to unite his new acquisitions with Antioch and the provinces of Syria.[188] But his vast enterprise, perhaps of easy execution, must have seemed extravagant to vulgar minds; and the visionary conqueror was soon reminded of his dependence and servitude. The friends of Tarik had effectually stated his services and wrongs: at the court of Damascus, the proceedings of Musa were blamed, his intentions were suspected, and his delay in complying with the first invitation was chastised by an harsher and more peremptory summons. An intrepid messenger of the caliph entered his camp at Lugo in Gallicia, and in the presence of the Saracens and Christians arrested the bridle of his horse. His own loyalty, or that of his troops, inculcated the duty of obedience: and his disgrace was alleviated by the recal of his rival, and the permission of investing with his two governments his two sons, Abdallah and

---

of the territory of Coimbra in Portugal. The tax of the churches is fixed at twenty-five pounds of gold; of the monasteries, fifty; of the cathedrals, one hundred: the Christians are judged by their count, but in capital cases he must consult the alcaide. The church doors must be shut, and they must respect the name of Mahomet. I have not the original before me; it would confirm or destroy a dark suspicion, that the piece has been forged to introduce the immunity of a neighbouring convent.

188. This design, which is attested by *several* Arabian historians (Cardonne, tom. i. p. 95, 96.), may be compared with that of Mithridates, to march from the Crimæa to Rome; or with that of Cæsar, to conquer the East, and return home by the North: and all three are perhaps surpassed by the *real* and successful enterprise of Hannibal.

Abdelaziz. His long triumph from Ceuta to Damascus displayed the spoils of Afric and the treasures of Spain: four hundred Gothic nobles, with gold coronets and girdles, were distinguished in his train; and the number of male and female captives, selected for their birth or beauty, was computed at eighteen, or even at thirty, thousand persons. As soon as he reached Tiberias in Palestine, he was apprised of the sickness and danger of the caliph, by a private message from Soliman, his brother and presumptive heir; who wished to reserve for his own reign, the spectacle of victory. Had Walid recovered, the delay of Musa would have been criminal: he pursued his march, and found an enemy on the throne. In his trial before a partial judge, against a popular antagonist, he was convicted of vanity and falsehood; and a fine of two hundred thousand pieces of gold either exhausted his poverty or proved his rapaciousness. The unworthy treatment of Tarik was revenged by a similar indignity; and the veteran commander, after a public whipping, stood a whole day in the sun before the palace gate, till he obtained a decent exile, under the pious name of a pilgrimage to Mecca. The resentment of the caliph might have been satiated with the ruin of Musa; but his fears demanded the extirpation of a potent and injured family. A sentence of death was intimated with secrecy and speed to the trusty servants of the throne both in Africa and Spain; and the forms, if not the substance, of justice were superseded in this bloody execution. In the mosch or palace of Cordova, Abdelaziz was slain by the swords of the conspirators; they accused their governor of claiming the honours of royalty; and his scandalous marriage with Egilona, the widow of Roderic, offended the prejudices both of the Christians and Moslems. By a refinement of cruelty, the head of the son was presented to the father with an insulting question, whether he acknowledged the features of the rebel? "I know his features," he exclaimed with indignation: "I assert his innocence; and I imprecate the same, a juster, fate, against the authors of his death." The age and despair of Musa raised him above the power of kings; and he expired at Mecca of the anguish of a broken heart. His rival was more favourably treated: his services were forgiven; and Tarik was permitted to mingle with the crowd of slaves.[189] I am ignorant whether count Julian

189. I much regret our loss, or my ignorance, of two Arabic works of the viii[th] century, a Life of Musa, and a Poem on the Exploits of Tarik. Of these authentic pieces, the former was composed by a grandson of Musa, who had escaped from the massacre of his kindred; the latter, by the Vizir of the first Abdalrahman caliph of Spain, who might have conversed with some of the veterans of the conqueror (Bibliot. Arabico-Hispana, tom. ii. p. 36. 139.).

was rewarded with the death which he deserved indeed, though not from the hands of the Saracens; but the tale of their ingratitude to the sons of Witiza is disproved by the most unquestionable evidence. The two royal youths were reinstated in the private patrimony of their father; but on the decease of Eba the elder, his daughter was unjustly despoiled of her portion by the violence of her uncle Sigebut. The Gothic maid pleaded her cause before the caliph Hashem, and obtained the restitution of her inheritance; but she was given in marriage to a noble Arabian, and their two sons, Isaac and Ibrahim, were received in Spain with the consideration that was due to their origin and riches.

Prosperity of Spain under the Arabs.

A province is assimilated to the victorious state by the introduction of strangers and the imitative spirit of the natives; and Spain, which had been successively tinctured with Punic, and Roman, and Gothic blood, imbibed, in a few generations, the name and manners of the Arabs. The first conquerors, and the twenty successive lieutenants of the caliphs, were attended by a numerous train of civil and military followers, who preferred a distant fortune to a narrow home: the private and public interest was promoted by the establishment of faithful colonies; and the cities of Spain were proud to commemorate the tribe or country of their Eastern progenitors. The victorious though motley bands of Tarik and Musa asserted, by the name of *Spaniards*, their original claim of conquest; yet they allowed their brethren of Egypt to share their establishments of Murcia and Lisbon. The royal legion of Damascus was planted at Cordova; that of Emesa at Seville; that of Kinnisrin or Chalcis at Jaen; that of Palestine at Algezire and Medina Sidonia. The natives of Yemen and Persia were scattered round Toledo and the inland country; and the fertile seats of Grenada were bestowed on ten thousand horsemen of Syria and Irak, the children of the purest and most noble of the Arabian tribes.[190] A spirit of emulation, sometimes beneficial, more frequently dangerous, was nourished by these hereditary factions. Ten years after the conquest, a map of the province was presented to the caliph: the seas, the rivers, and the harbours, the inhabitants and

190. Bibliot. Arab. Hispana, tom. ii. p. 32. 252. The former of these quotations is taken from a *Biographia Hispanica*, by an Arabian of Valentia (see the copious Extracts of Casiri, tom. ii. p. 30–121.); and the latter from a general Chronology of the Caliphs, and of the African and Spanish Dynasties, with a particular History of the Kingdom of Grenada, of which Casiri has given almost an entire version (Bibliot. Arabico-Hispana, tom. ii. p. 177–319.). The author, Ebn Khateb, a native of Grenada, and a contemporary of Novairi and Abulfeda (born A.D. 1313, died A.D. 1374), was an historian, geographer, physician, poet, &c. (tom. ii. p. 71–72.).

cities, the climate, the soil, and the mineral productions of the earth.[191] In the space of two centuries, the gifts of nature were improved by the agriculture,[192] the manufactures, and the commerce of an industrious people; and the effects of their diligence have been magnified by the idleness of their fancy. The first of the Ommiades who reigned in Spain solicited the support of the Christians; and, in his edict of peace and protection, he contents himself with a modest imposition of ten thousand ounces of gold, ten thousand pounds of silver, ten thousand horses, as many mules, one thousand cuirasses, with an equal number of helmets and lances.[193] The most powerful of his successors derived from the same kingdom the annual tribute of twelve millions and forty-five thousand dinars or pieces of gold, about six millions of sterling money;[194] a sum which, in the tenth century, most probably surpassed the united revenues of the Christian monarchs. His royal seat of Cordova contained six hundred moschs, nine hundred baths, and two hundred thousand houses: he gave laws to eighty cities of the first, to three hundred of the second and third order; and the fertile banks of the Guadalquivir were adorned with twelve thousand villages and hamlets. The Arabs might exaggerate the truth, but they created and they describe the most prosperous æra of the riches, the cultivation, and the populousness of Spain.[195]

191. Cardonne, Hist. de l'Afrique et de l'Espagne, tom. i. p. 116, 117.

192. A copious treatise of husbandry, by an Arabian of Seville, in the xii[th] century, is in the Escurial library, and Casiri had some thoughts of translating it. He gives a list of the authors quoted, Arabs, as well as Greeks, Latins, &c.; but it is much if the Andalusian saw these strangers through the medium of his countryman Columella (Casiri, Bibliot. Arabico-Hispana, tom. i. p. 323–338.).

193. Bibliot. Arabico-Hispana, tom. ii. p. 104. Casiri translates the original testimony of the historian Rasis, as it is alleged in the Arabic Biographia Hispanica, pars ix. But I am most exceedingly surprised at the address, Principibus cæterisque Christianis Hispanis suis *Castellæ*. The name of Castellæ was unknown in the viii[th] century; the kingdom was not erected till the year 1022, an hundred years after the time of Rasis (Bibliot. tom. ii. p. 330.), and the appellation was always expressive, not of a tributary province, but of a line of *castles* independent of the Moorish yoke (d'Anville, Etats de l'Europe, p. 166–170.). Had Casiri been a critic, he would have cleared a difficulty, perhaps of his own making.

194. Cardonne, tom. i. p. 337, 338. He computes the revenue at 130,000,000 of French livres. The entire picture of peace and prosperity relieves the bloody uniformity of the Moorish annals.

195. I am happy enough to possess a splendid and interesting work, which has only been distributed in presents by the court of Madrid: *Bibliotheca Arabico-Hispana Escurialensis, operâ et studio Michaelis Casiri, Syro Maronitæ. Matriti, in folio, tomus prior,* 1760. *tomus posterior,* 1770. The execution of this work does honour to the Spanish press; the MSS. to the number of MDCCCLI, are judiciously classed by the editor, and his copious extracts throw *some* light on the Mahometan literature and history of Spain.

Religious toleration.

The wars of the Moslems were sanctified by the prophet; but, among the various precepts and examples of his life, the caliphs selected the lessons of toleration that might tend to disarm the resistance of the unbelievers. Arabia was the temple and patrimony of the God of Mahomet; but he beheld with less jealousy and affection the nations of the earth. The polytheists and idolaters who were ignorant of his name, might be lawfully extirpated by his votaries;[196] but a wise policy supplied the obligation of justice; and after some acts of intolerant zeal, the Mahometan conquerors of Hindostan have spared the pagods of that devout and populous country. The disciples of Abraham, of Moses, and of Jesus, were solemnly invited to accept the more *perfect* revelation of Mahomet; but if they preferred the payment of a moderate tribute, they were entitled to the freedom of conscience and religious worship.[197] In a field of battle, the forfeit lives of the prisoners were redeemed by the profession of *Islam*; the females were bound to embrace the religion of their masters, and a race of sincere proselytes was gradually multiplied by the education of the infant captives. But the millions of African and Asiatic converts, who swelled the native band of the faithful Arabs, must have been allured, rather than constrained, to declare their belief in one God and the apostle of God. By the repetition of a sentence and the loss of a foreskin, the subject or the slave, the captive or the criminal, arose in a moment the free and equal companion of the victorious Moslems. Every sin was expiated, every engagement was dissolved: the vow of celibacy was superseded by the indulgence of nature; the active spirits who slept in the cloister were awakened by the trumpet of the Saracens; and in the convulsion of the world, every member of a new society ascended to the natural level of his capacity and courage. The minds of the multitude were tempted by the invisible

Propagation of Mahometism.

These relics are now secure, but the task has been supinely delayed, till in the year 1671 a fire consumed the greatest part of the Escurial library, rich in the spoils of Grenada and Morocco.

196. The *Harbii*, as they are styled, qui tolerari nequeunt, are, 1. Those who, *besides* God, worship the sun, moon, or idols. 2. Atheists. Utrique, quamdiu princeps aliquis inter Mohammedanos superest oppugnari debent donec religionem amplectantur, nec requies iis concedenda est, nec pretium acceptandum pro obtinendâ conscientiæ libertate (Reland, Dissertat. x. de Jure Militari Mohammedan. tom. iii. p. 14.): A rigid theory!

197. The distinction between a proscribed and a tolerated sect, between the *Harbii* and the People of the Book, the believers in some divine revelation is correctly defined in the conversation of the caliph Al Mamun with the idolaters or Sabæans of Charræ. Hottinger, Hist. Orient. p. 107, 108.

as well as temporal blessings of the Arabian prophet; and charity will hope that many of his proselytes entertained a serious conviction of the truth and sanctity of his revelation. In the eyes of an inquisitive polytheist, it must appear worthy of the human and the divine nature. More pure than the system of Zoroaster, more liberal than the law of Moses, the religion of Mahomet might seem less inconsistent with reason, than the creed of mystery and superstition, which, in the seventh century, disgraced the simplicity of the gospel.

Fall of the Magians of Persia.

In the extensive provinces of Persia and Africa, the national religion has been eradicated by the Mahometan faith. The ambiguous theology of the Magi stood alone among the sects of the East: but the profane writings of Zoroaster[198] might, under the reverend name of Abraham, be dextrously connected with the chain of divine revelation. Their evil principle, the dæmon Ahriman, might be represented as the rival or as the creature of the God of light. The temples of Persia were devoid of images; but the worship of the sun and of fire might be stigmatized as a gross and criminal idolatry.[199] The milder sentiment was consecrated by the practice of[200] Mahomet and the prudence of the caliphs; the Magians or Ghebers were ranked with the Jews and Christians among the people of the written law;[201] and as late as the third century of the Hegira, the city of Herat will afford a lively contrast

198. The Zend or Pazend, the bible of the Ghebers, is reckoned by themselves, or at least by the Mahometans, among the ten books which Abraham received from heaven; and their religion is honourably styled the religion of Abraham (d'Herbelot, Bibliot. Orient. p. 701.; Hyde, de Religione veterum Persarum, c. iii. p. 27, 28, &c.). I much fear that we do not possess any pure and *free* description of the system of Zoroaster. Dr. Prideaux (Connection, vol. i. p. 300. octavo) adopts the opinion, that he had been the slave and scholar of some Jewish prophet in the captivity of Babylon. Perhaps the Persians, who have been the masters of the Jews, would assert the honour, a poor honour, of being *their* masters.

199. The Arabian Nights, a faithful and amusing picture of the Oriental world, represent in the most odious colours the Magians, or worshippers of fire, to whom they attribute the annual sacrifice of a Musulman. The religion of Zoroaster has not the least affinity with that of the Hindoos, yet they are often confounded by the Mahometans; and the sword of Timour was sharpened by this mistake (Hist. de Timour Bec, par Cherefeddin Ali Yezdi, l. v.).

200. Vie de Mahomet, par Gagnier, tom. iii. p. 114, 115.

201. Hæ tres sectæ, Judæi, Christiani, et qui inter Persas Magorum institutis addicti sunt, κατ' ἐξοχην, *populi libri* dicuntur (Reland, Dissertat. tom. iii. p. 15.). The caliph Al Mamun confirms this honourable distinction in favour of the three sects, with the vague and equivocal religion of the Sabæans, under which the ancient polytheists of Charræ were allowed to shelter their idolatrous worship (Hottinger, Hist. Orient. p. 167, 168.).

of private zeal and public toleration.[202] Under the payment of an annual tribute, the Mahometan law secured to the Ghebers of Herat, their civil and religious liberties: but the recent and humble mosch was overshadowed by the antique splendour of the adjoining temple of fire. A fanatic Imam deplored, in his sermons, the scandalous neighbourhood, and accused the weakness or indifference of the faithful. Excited by his voice, the people assembled in tumult; the two houses of prayer were consumed by the flames, but the vacant ground was immediately occupied by the foundations of a new mosch. The injured Magi appealed to the sovereign of Chorasan; he promised justice and relief; when, behold! four thousand citizens of Herat, of a grave character and mature age, unanimously swore that the idolatrous fane had *never* existed; the inquisition was silenced, and their conscience was satisfied (says the historian Mirchond)[203] with this holy and meritorious perjury.[204] But the greatest part of the temples of Persia were ruined by the insensible and general desertion of their votaries. It was *insensible*, since it is not accompanied with any memorial of time or place, of persecution or resistance. It was *general*, since the whole realm, from Shiraz to Samarcand, imbibed the faith of the Koran; and the preservation of the native tongue reveals the descent of the Mahometans of Persia.[205] In the mountains and deserts, an

202. This singular story is related by d'Herbelot (Bibliot. Orient. p. 448, 449.) on the faith of Khondemir, and by Mirchond himself (Hist. priorum Regum Persarum, &c. p. 9, 10. not. p. 88, 89.).

203. Mirchond (Mohammed Emir Khoondah Shah), a native of Herat, composed in the Persian language a general history of the East, from the creation to the year of the Hegira 875 (A.D. 1471). In the year 904 (A.D. 1498) the historian obtained the command of a princely library, and his applauded work, in seven or twelve parts, was abbreviated in three volumes by his son Khondemir, A. H. 927. A.D. 1520. The two writers most accurately distinguished by Petit de la Croix (Hist. de Genghizcan, p. 537, 538. 544, 545.), are loosely confounded by d'Herbelot (p. 358. 410. 994, 995.): but his numerous extracts, under the improper name of Khondemir, belong to the father rather than the son. The historian of Genghizcan refers to a MS. of Mirchond, which he received from the hands of his friend d'Herbelot himself. A curious fragment (the Taherian and Soffarian Dynasties) has been lately published in Persic and Latin (Viennæ, 1782, in 4to, cum notis Bernard de Jenisch); and the editor allows us to hope for a continuation of Mirchond.

204. Quo testimonio boni se quidpiam præstitisse opinabantur. Yet Mirchond must have condemned their zeal, since he approved the legal toleration of the Magi, cui (the fire temple) peracto singulis annis censû, uti sacra Mohammedis lege cautum, ab omnibus molestiis ac oneribus libero esse licuit.

205. The last Magian of name and power appears to be Mardavige the Dilemite, who, in the beginning of the xth century, reigned in the northern provinces of Persia, near the Caspian Sea (d'Herbelot, Bibliot. Orient. p. 355.). But his soldiers and successors, the *Bowides*, either professed or embraced the Mahometan faith; and under their dynasty (A.D. 933–1020) I should place the fall of the religion of Zoroaster.

obstinate race of unbelievers adhered to the superstition of their fathers; and a faint tradition of the Magian theology is kept alive in the province of Kirman, along the banks of the Indus, among the exiles of Surat, and in the colony which, in the last century, was planted by Shaw Abbas at the gates of Ispahan. The chief pontiff has retired to mount Elbourz, eighteen leagues from the city of Yezd: the perpetual fire (if it continue to burn) is inaccessible to the profane; but his residence is the school, the oracle, and the pilgrimage, of the Ghebers, whose hard and uniform features attest the unmingled purity of their blood. Under the jurisdiction of their elders, eighty thousand families maintain an innocent and industrious life; their subsistence is derived from some curious manufactures and mechanic trades; and they cultivate the earth with the fervour of a religious duty. Their ignorance withstood the despotism of Shaw Abbas, who demanded with threats and tortures the prophetic books of Zoroaster; and this obscure remnant of the Magians is spared by the moderation or contempt of their present sovereigns.[206]

Decline and fall of Christianity in Africa,

The northern coast of Africa is the only land in which the light of the Gospel, after a long and perfect establishment, has been totally extinguished. The arts, which had been taught by Carthage and Rome, were involved in a cloud of ignorance; the doctrine of Cyprian and Augustin was no longer studied. Five hundred episcopal churches were overturned by the hostile fury of the Donatists, the Vandals, and the Moors. The zeal and numbers of the clergy declined; and the people, without discipline, or knowledge, or hope, submissively
A.D. 749. sunk under the yoke of the Arabian prophet. Within fifty years after the expulsion of the Greeks, a lieutenant of Africa informed the caliph that the tribute of the infidels was abolished by their conversion;[207] and, though he sought to disguise his fraud and rebellion, his specious
A.D. 837. pretence was drawn from the rapid and extensive progress of the Mahometan faith. In the next age, an extraordinary mission of five bishops was detached from Alexandria to Cairoan. They were ordained by the Jacobite patriarch to cherish and revive the dying embers of

206. The present state of the Ghebers in Persia, is taken from Sir John Chardin, not indeed the most learned, but the most judicious and inquisitive, of our modern travellers (Voyages en Perse, tom. ii. p. 109. 179–187. in 4to). His brethren, Pietro della Valle, Olearius, Thevenot, Tavernier, &c. whom I have fruitlessly searched, had neither eyes nor attention for this interesting people.

207. The letter of Abdoulrahman, governor or tyrant of Africa, to the caliph Aboul Abbas, the first of the Abassides, is dated A. H. 132 (Cardonne, Hist. de l'Afrique et de l'Espagne, tom. i. p. 168.).

Christianity:[208] but the interposition of a foreign prelate, a stranger to the Latins, an enemy to the Catholics, supposes the decay and dissolution of the African hierarchy. It was no longer the time when the successor of St. Cyprian, at the head of a numerous synod, could maintain an equal contest with the ambition of the Roman pontiff. In the *A.D. 1053–1076.* eleventh century, the unfortunate priest who was seated on the ruins of Carthage, implored the alms and the protection of the Vatican; and he bitterly complains that his naked body had been scourged by the Saracens, and that his authority was disputed by the four suffragans, the tottering pillars of his throne. Two epistles of Gregory the seventh[209] are destined to soothe the distress of the Catholics and the pride of a Moorish prince. The pope assures the sultan that they both worship the same God, and may hope to meet in the bosom of Abraham; but the complaint, that three bishops could no longer be found to consecrate a brother, announces the speedy and inevitable ruin of the episcopal order. The Christians of Africa and Spain had long since submitted to the practice of *and Spain,* circumcision and the legal abstinence from wine and pork; and *A.D. 1149,* the name of *Mozarabes*[210] (adoptive Arabs) was applied to their *&c.* civil or religious conformity.[211] About the middle of the twelfth century the worship of Christ and the succession of pastors were abolished along the coast of Barbary, and in the kingdoms of Cordova and Seville, of Valencia and Grenada.[212] The throne of the Almohades, or Unitarians, was founded on the blindest fanaticism, and their extraordinary rigour

208. Bibliotheque Orientale, p. 66. Renaudot, Hist. Patriarch. Alex. p. 287, 288.

209. Among the Epistles of the Popes, see Leo IX. epist. 3. Gregor. VII. l. i. epist. 22, 23. l. iii. epist. 19, 20, 21.; and the criticisms of Pagi (tom. iv. A.D. 1053, N° 14. A.D. 1073, N° 13.), who investigates the name and family of the Moorish prince, with whom the proudest of the Roman pontiffs so politely corresponds.

210. Mozarabes, or Mostarabes, *adscititii*, as it is interpreted in Latin (Pocock, Specimen Hist. Arabum, p. 39, 40. Bibliot. Arabico-Hispana, tom. ii. p. 18.). The Mozarabic liturgy, the ancient ritual of the church of Toledo, has been attacked by the popes, and exposed to the doubtful trials of the sword and of fire (Marian. Hist. Hispan. tom. i. l. ix. c. 18. p. 378.). It was, or rather it is, in the Latin tongue; yet in the xi[th] century it was found necessary (A. Æ. C. 1687, A.D. 1039) to transcribe an Arabic version of the canons of the councils of Spain (Bibliot. Arab. Hisp. tom. i. p. 547.), for the use of the bishops and clergy in the Moorish kingdoms.

211. About the middle of the xth century, the clergy of Cordova was reproached with this criminal compliance, by the intrepid envoy of the emperor Otho I. (Vit. Johan. Gorz, in Secul. Benedict. V. N° 115. apud Fleury, Hist. Eccles. tom. xii. p. 91.).

212. Pagi, Critica, tom. iv. A.D. 1149, N° 8, 9. He justly observes, that when Seville, &c. were retaken by Ferdinand of Castille, no Christians, except captives, were found in the place; and that the Mozarabic

might be provoked or justified by the recent victories and intolerant zeal of the princes of Sicily and Castille, of Arragon and Portugal. The faith of the Mozarabes was occasionally revived by the papal missionaries; and, *A.D. 1535.* on the landing of Charles the fifth, some families of Latin Christians were encouraged to rear their heads at Tunis and Algiers. But the seed of the gospel was quickly eradicated, and the long province from Tripoli to the Atlantic has lost all memory of the language and religion of Rome.[213]

Toleration of the Christians. After the revolution of eleven centuries, the Jews and Christians of the Turkish empire enjoy the liberty of conscience which was granted by the Arabian caliphs. During the first age of the conquest, they suspected the loyalty of the Catholics, whose name of Melchites betrayed their secret attachment to the Greek emperor, while the Nestorians and Jacobites, his inveterate enemies, approved themselves the sincere and voluntary friends of the Mahometan government.[214] Yet this partial jealousy was healed by time and submission: the churches of Egypt were shared with the Catholics;[215] and all the Oriental sects were included in the common benefits of toleration. The rank, the immunities, the domestic jurisdiction, of the patriarchs, the bishops, and the clergy, were protected by the civil magistrate: the learning of individuals recommended them to the employments of secretaries and physicians: they were enriched by the lucrative collection of the revenue; and their merit was sometimes raised to the command of cities and provinces. A caliph of the house of Abbas was heard to declare that the Christians were most

---

churches of Africa and Spain, described by James à Vitriaco, A.D. 1218 (Hist. Hierosol. c. 80. p. 1095. in Gest. Dei per Francos), are copied from some older book. I shall add, that the date of the Hegira 677 (A.D. 1278) must apply to the copy, not the composition, of a treatise of jurisprudence, which states the civil rights of the Christians of Cordova (Bibliot. Arab. Hisp. tom. i. p. 471.); and that the Jews were the only dissenters whom Abul Waled, king of Grenada (A.D. 1313), could either discountenance or tolerate (tom. ii. p. 288.).

213. Renaudot, Hist. Patriarch. Alex. p. 288. Leo Africanus would have flattered his Roman masters, could he have discovered any latent relics of the Christianity of Africa.

214. Absit (said the Catholic to the Vizir of Bagdad) ut pari loco habeas Nestorianos, quorum præter Arabas nullus alius rex est, et Græcos quorum reges amovendo Arabibus bello non desistunt, &c. See in the Collections of Assemannus (Bibliot. Orient. tom. iv. p. 94–101.), the state of the Nestorians under the caliphs. That of the Jacobites is more concisely exposed in the Preliminary Dissertation of the second volume of Assemannus.

215. Eutych. Annal. tom. ii. p. 384. 387, 388. Renaudot, Hist. Patriarch. Alex. p. 205, 206. 257. 332. A taint of the Monothelite heresy might render the first of these Greek patriarchs less loyal to the emperors and less obnoxious to the Arabs.

worthy of trust in the administration of Persia. "The Moslems," said he, "will abuse their present fortune; the Magians regret their fallen greatness; and the Jews are impatient for their approaching deliverance."[216] But the slaves of despotism are exposed to the alternatives of favour and disgrace. The captive churches of the East have been afflicted in every age by the avarice or bigotry of their rulers; and the ordinary and legal restraints must be offensive to the pride or the zeal of the Christians.[217] About two hundred years after Mahomet, they were separated from their fellow-subjects by a turban or girdle of a less honourable colour; instead of horses or mules, they were condemned to ride on asses, in the attitude of women. Their public and private buildings were measured by a diminutive standard; in the streets or the baths it is their duty to give way or bow down before the meanest of the people; and their testimony is rejected, if it may tend to the prejudice of a true believer. The pomp of processions, the sound of bells or of psalmody, is interdicted in their worship: a decent reverence for the national faith is imposed on their sermons and conversations; and the sacrilegious attempt to enter a mosch, or to seduce a Musulman, will not be suffered to escape with impunity. In a time however of tranquillity and justice the Christians have never been compelled to renounce the Gospel or to embrace the Koran; but the punishment of death is inflicted for the apostates who have professed and deserted the law of Mahomet. The martyrs of Cordova provoked the sentence of the cadhi, by the public confession of their inconstancy, or their passionate invectives against the person and religion of the prophet.[218]

Their hardships.

At the end of the first century of the Hegira, the caliphs were the most potent and absolute monarchs of the globe. Their prerogative was not circumscribed, either in right or in

The empire of the caliphs, A.D. 718.

216. Motadhed, who reigned from A.D. 892 to 902. The Magians still held their name and rank among the religions of the empire (Assemanni, Bibliot. Orient. tom. iv. p. 97.).

217. Reland explains the general restraints of the Mahometan policy and jurisprudence (Dissertat. tom. iii. p. 16–20.). The oppressive edicts of the caliph Motawakkel (A.D. 847–861), which are still in force, are noticed by Eutychius (Annal. tom. ii. p. 448.) and d'Herbelot (Bibliot. Orient. p. 640.). A persecution of the caliph Omar II. is related, and most probably magnified, by the Greek Theophanes (Chron. p. 334.).

218. The martyrs of Cordova (A.D. 850, &c.) are commemorated and justified by St. Eulogius, who at length fell a victim himself. A synod, convened by the caliph, ambiguously censured their rashness. The moderate Fleury cannot reconcile their conduct with the discipline of antiquity, toutefois l'autorité de l'eglise, &c. (Fleury, Hist. Eccles. tom. x. p. 415–522. particularly p. 451. 508, 509.) Their authentic acts throw a strong though transient light on the Spanish church in the ix[th] century.

fact, by the power of the nobles, the freedom of the commons, the privileges of the church, the votes of a senate, or the memory of a free constitution. The authority of the companions of Mahomet expired with their lives; and the chiefs or emirs of the Arabian tribes left behind, in the desert, the spirit of equality and independence. The regal and sacerdotal characters were united in the successors of Mahomet; and if the Koran was the rule of their actions, they were the supreme judges and interpreters of that divine book. They reigned by the right of conquest over the nations of the East, to whom the name of liberty was unknown, and who were accustomed to applaud in their tyrants the acts of violence and severity that were exercised at their own expence. Under the last of the Ommiades, the Arabian empire extended two hundred days journey from east to west, from the confines of Tartary and India to the shores of the Atlantic ocean. And if we retrench the sleeve of the robe, as it is styled by their writers, the long and narrow province of Africa, the solid and compact dominion from Fargana to Aden, from Tarsus to Surat, will spread on every side to the measure of four or five months of the march of a caravan.[219] We should vainly seek the indissoluble union and easy obedience that pervaded the government of Augustus and the Antonines; but the progress of the Mahometan religion diffused over this ample space a general resemblance of manners and opinions. The language and laws of the Koran were studied with equal devotion at Samarcand and Seville: the Moor and the Indian embraced as countrymen and brothers in the pilgrimage of Mecca; and the Arabian language was adopted as the popular idiom in all the provinces to the westward of the Tigris.[220]

219. See the article *Eslamiah* (as we say Christendom), in the Bibliotheque Orientale (p. 325.). This chart of the Mahometan world is suited by the author, Ebn Alwardi, to the year of the Hegira 385 (A.D. 995). Since that time, the losses in Spain have been overbalanced by the conquests in India, Tartary, and the European Turkey.

220. The Arabic of the Koran is taught as a dead language in the college of Mecca. By the Danish traveller, this ancient idiom is compared to the Latin; the vulgar tongue of Hejaz and Yemen to the Italian; and the Arabian dialects of Syria, Egypt, Africa, &c. to the Provençal, Spanish, and Portuguese (Niebuhr, Description de l'Arabie, p. 74, &c.).

CHAPTER LII

The Two Sieges of Constantinople by the Arabs. – Their Invasion of France, and Defeat by Charles Martel. – Civil War of the Ommiades and Abbassides. – Learning of the Arabs. – Luxury of the Caliphs. – Naval Enterprises on Crete, Sicily, and Rome. – Decay and Division of the Empire of the Caliphs. – Defeats and Victories of the Greek Emperors.

The limits of the Arabian conquests.

When the Arabs first issued from the desert, they must have been surprised at the ease and rapidity of their own success. But when they advanced in the career of victory to the banks of the Indus and the summit of the Pyrenees; when they had repeatedly tried the edge of their scymetars and the energy of their faith, they might be equally astonished that any nation could resist their invincible arms, that any boundary should confine the dominion of the successor of the prophet. The confidence of soldiers and fanatics may indeed be excused, since the calm historian of the present hour, who strives to follow the rapid course of the Saracens, must study to explain by what means the church and state were saved from this impending, and, as it should seem, from this inevitable danger. The deserts of Scythia and Sarmatia might be guarded by their extent, their climate, their poverty, and the courage of the northern shepherds; China was remote and inaccessible; but the greatest part of the temperate zone was subject to the Mahometan conquerors, the Greeks were exhausted by the calamities of war and the loss of their fairest provinces, and the Barbarians of Europe might justly tremble at the precipitate fall of the Gothic monarchy. In this enquiry I shall unfold the events that rescued our ancestors of Britain, and our neighbours of Gaul from the civil and religious yoke of the Koran; that protected the majesty of Rome, and delayed the servitude of Constantinople; that invigorated the defence of the Christians, and scattered among their enemies the seeds of division and decay.

First siege of Constantinople

Forty-six years after the flight of Mahomet from Mecca, his disciples appeared in arms under the walls of Constantinople.[1]

1. Theophanes places the *seven* years of the siege of Constantinople in the year of *our* Christian æra 673 (of the Alexandrian 665, Sept. 1.), and the peace of the Saracens, *four*

by the Arabs, A.D. 668–675.

They were animated by a genuine or fictitious saying of the prophet, that, to the first army which besieged the city of the Cæsars, their sins were forgiven: the long series of Roman triumphs would be meritoriously transferred to the conquerors of New Rome; and the wealth of nations was deposited in this well-chosen seat of royalty and commerce. No sooner had the caliph Moawiyah suppressed his rivals and established his throne, than he aspired to expiate the guilt of civil blood, by the success and glory of this holy expedition;[2] his preparations by sea and land were adequate to the importance of the object; his standard was entrusted to Sophian, a veteran warrior, but the troops were encouraged by the example and presence of Yezid the son and presumptive heir of the commander of the faithful. The Greeks had little to hope, nor had their enemies any reasons of fear, from the courage and vigilance of the reigning emperor, who disgraced the name of Constantine, and imitated only the inglorious years of his grandfather Heraclius. Without delay or opposition, the naval forces of the Saracens passed through the unguarded channel of the Hellespont, which even now, under the feeble and disorderly government of the Turks, is maintained as the natural bulwark of the capital.[3] The Arabian fleet cast anchor, and the troops were disembarked near the palace of Hebdomon, seven miles from the city. During many days, from the dawn of light to the evening, the line of assault was extended from the golden gate to the eastern promontory, and the foremost warriors were impelled by the weight and effort of the succeeding columns. But the besiegers had formed an insufficient estimate of the strength and resources of Constantinople. The solid and lofty walls were guarded by numbers and discipline: the spirit of the Romans was rekindled by the last danger of

---

years afterwards; a glaring inconsistency! which Petavius, Goar, and Pagi (Critica, tom. iv. p. 63, 64.), have struggled to remove. Of the Arabians, the Hegira 52 (A.D. 672, January 8.) is assigned by Elmacin, the year 48 (A.D. 668, Feb. 20.) by Abulfeda, whose testimony I esteem the most convenient and creditable.

2. For this first siege of Constantinople, see Nicephorus (Breviar. p. 21, 22.); Theophanes (Chronograph. p. 294.); Cedrenus (Compend. p. 437.); Zonaras (Hist. tom. ii. l. xiv. p. 89.); Elmacin (Hist. Saracen, p. 56, 57.); Abulfeda (Annal. Moslem. p. 107, 108. vers. Reiske); d'Herbelot (Bibliot. Orient. Constantin.); Ockley's Hist. of the Saracens, vol. ii. p. 127, 128.

3. The state and defence of the Dardannelles is exposed in the memoirs of the Baron de Tott (tom. iii. p. 39–97.), who was sent to fortify them against the Russians. From a principal actor, I should have expected more accurate details; but he seems to write for the amusement, rather than the instruction, of his reader. Perhaps, on the approach of the enemy, the minister of Constantine was occupied, like that of Mustapha, in finding two Canary birds, who should sing precisely the same note.

their religion and empire: the fugitives from the conquered provinces more successfully renewed the defence of Damascus and Alexandria; and the Saracens were dismayed by the strange and prodigious effects of artificial fire. This firm and effectual resistance diverted their arms to the more easy attempts of plundering the European and Asiatic coasts of the Propontis; and, after keeping the sea from the month of April to that of September, on the approach of winter they retreated fourscore miles from the capital, to the isle of Cyzicus, in which they had established their magazine of spoil and provisions. So patient was their perseverance, or so languid were their operations, that they repeated in the six following summers the same attack and retreat, with a gradual abatement of hope and vigour, till the mischances of shipwreck and disease, of the sword and of fire, compelled them to relinquish the fruitless enterprise. They might bewail the loss or commemorate the martyrdom of thirty thousand Moslems, who fell in the siege of Constantinople; and the solemn funeral of Abu Ayub, or Job, excited the curiosity of the Christians themselves. That venerable Arab, one of the last of the companions of Mahomet, was numbered among the *ansars*, or auxiliaries, of Medina, who sheltered the head of the flying prophet. In his youth he fought, at Beder and Ohud, under the holy standard: in his mature age he was the friend and follower of Ali; and the last remnant of his strength and life was consumed in a distant and dangerous war against the enemies of the Koran. His memory was revered; but the place of his burial was neglected and unknown, during a period of seven hundred and eighty years, till the conquest of Constantinople by Mahomet the second. A seasonable vision (for such are the manufacture of every religion) revealed the holy spot at the foot of the walls and the bottom of the harbour; and the mosch of Ayub has been deservedly chosen for the simple and martial inauguration of the Turkish sultans.[4]

Peace and tribute, A.D. 677.

The event of the siege revived, both in the East and West, the reputation of the Roman arms, and cast a momentary shade over the glories of the Saracens. The Greek ambassador was favourably received at Damascus, in a general council of the emirs or Koreish: a peace, or truce, of thirty years was ratified between the two empires; and the stipulation of an annual tribute, fifty horses of a noble breed, fifty

4. Demetrius Cantemir's Hist. of the Othman empire, p. 105, 106. Rycaut's State of the Ottoman Empire, p. 10, 11. Voyages de Thevenot, part i. p. 189. The Christians, who suppose that the martyr Abu Ayub is vulgarly confounded with the patriarch Job, betray their own ignorance rather than that of the Turks.

slaves, and three thousand pieces of gold, degraded the majesty of the commander of the faithful.[5] The aged caliph was desirous of possessing his dominions, and ending his days in tranquillity and repose: while the Moors and Indians trembled at his name, his palace and city of Damascus was insulted by the Mardaites, or Maronites, of mount Libanus, the firmest barrier of the empire, till they were disarmed and transplanted by the suspicious policy of the Greeks.[6] After the revolt of Arabia and Persia, the house of Ommiyah[7] was reduced to the kingdoms of Syria and Egypt: their distress and fear enforced their compliance with the pressing demands of the Christians; and the tribute was encreased to a slave, an horse, and a thousand pieces of gold, for each of the three hundred and sixty-five days of the solar year. But as soon as the empire was again united by the arms and policy of Abdalmalek, he disclaimed a badge of servitude not less injurious to his conscience than to his pride: he discontinued the payment of the tribute; and the resentment of the Greeks was disabled from action by the mad tyranny of the second Justinian, the just rebellion of his subjects, and the frequent change of his antagonists and successors. Till the reign of Abdalmalek, the Saracens had been content with the free possession of the Persian and Roman treasures, in the coin of Chosroes and Cæsar. By the command of that Caliph, a national mint was established, both for silver and gold, and the inscription of the Dinar, though it might be censured by some timorous casuists, proclaimed the unity of the God of Mahomet.[8] Under the reign

5. Theophanes, though a Greek, deserves credit for these tributes (Chronograph. p. 295, 296. 300, 301.), which are confirmed, with some variation, by the Arabic history of Abulpharagius (Dynast. p. 128. vers. Pocock).

6. The censure of Theophanes is just and pointed, *την Ρωμαικην δυναστειαν ακρωτηριασασ . . . πανδεινα κακα πεπονθεν ἡ Ρωμανια ὑπο των Αραβων μεχρι του νυν* (Chronograph. p. 302, 303.). The series of these events may be traced in the Annals of Theophanes, and in the Abridgement of the Patriarch Nicephorus, p. 22. 24.

7. These domestic revolutions are related in a clear and natural style, in the second volume of Ockley's History of the Saracens, p. 253–370. Besides our printed authors, he draws his materials from the Arabic MSS. of Oxford, which he would have more deeply searched, had he been confined to the Bodleian library instead of the city jail; a fate how unworthy of the man and of his country!

8. Elmacin, who dates the first coinage A. H. 76, A.D. 695, five or six years later than the Greek historians, has compared the weight of the best or common gold dinar, to the drachm or dirhem of Egypt (p. 77.), which may be equal to two pennies (48 grains) of our Troy weight (Hooper's Enquiry into Ancient Measures, p. 24–36.), and equivalent to eight shillings of our sterling money. From the same Elmacin and the Arabian physicians, some dinars as high as two dirhems, as low as half a dirhem, may be deduced. The piece of silver was the dirhem, both in value and weight; but

of the caliph Waled, the Greek language and characters were excluded from the accounts of the public revenue.[9] If this change was productive of the invention or familiar use of our present numerals, the Arabic or Indian cyphers, as they are commonly styled, a regulation of office has promoted the most important discoveries of arithmetic, algebra, and the mathematical sciences.[10]

Second siege of Constantinople, A.D. 716–718.

Whilst the caliph Waled sat idle on the throne of Damascus, while his lieutenants atchieved the conquest of Transoxiana and Spain, a third army of Saracens overspread the provinces of Asia Minor, and approached the borders of the Byzantine capital. But the attempt and disgrace of the second siege was reserved for his brother Soliman, whose ambition appears to have been quickened by a more active and martial spirit. In the revolutions of the Greek empire, after the tyrant Justinian had been punished and avenged, an humble secretary, Anastasius or Artemius, was promoted by chance or merit to the vacant purple. He was alarmed by the sound of war; and his ambassador returned from Damascus with the tremendous news, that the Saracens were preparing an armament by sea and land, such as would transcend the experience of the past, or the belief of the present, age. The precautions of Anastasius were not unworthy of his station, or of the impending danger. He issued a peremptory mandate, that all persons who were not provided with the means of subsistence for a three years siege, should evacuate the city: the public granaries and arsenals were abundantly replenished; the walls were restored and strengthened; and the engines for casting stones, or darts, or fire, were stationed along the ramparts, or in the brigantines of war, of which an additional number was hastily constructed. To prevent, is safer, as well as more honourable, than to repel, an attack; and a design was meditated, above the usual spirit of the

---

an old, though fair coin, struck at Waset, A. H. 88, and preserved in the Bodleian library, wants four grains of the Cairo standard (see the Modern Universal History, tom. i. p. 548. of the French translation).

9. *Και εκωλυσε γραφεσθαι ἑλληνιστι τους δημοσιους των λογοθεσιων κωδικας, αλλ' Αραβιοις αυτα παρασεμαινεσθαι χωρις των ψηφων, επειδη αδυνατον τῃ εκεινων γλωσσῃ μοναδα, η δυαδα, η τριαδα, η οκτω ημισυ η τρια γραφεσθαι.* Theophan. Chronograph. p. 314. This defect, if it really existed, must have stimulated the ingenuity of the Arabs to invent or borrow.

10. According to a new, though probable notion, maintained by M. de Villoison (Anecdota Græca, tom. ii. p. 152–157.), our cyphers are not of Indian or Arabic invention. They were used by the Greek and Latin arithmeticians long before the age of Boethius. After the extinction of science in the West, they were adopted by the Arabic versions from the original MSS. and *restored* to the Latins about the xi[th] century.

Greeks, of burning the naval stores of the enemy, the cypress timber that had been hewn in mount Libanus, and was piled along the sea-shore of Phœnicia, for the service of the Egyptian fleet. This generous enterprise was defeated by the cowardice or treachery of the troops, who, in the new language of the empire, were styled of the *Obsequian Theme.*[11] They murdered their chief, deserted their standard in the isle of Rhodes, dispersed themselves over the adjacent continent, and deserved pardon or reward by investing with the purple a simple officer of the revenue. The name of Theodosius might recommend him to the senate and people; but, after some months, he sunk into a cloyster, and resigned, to the firmer hand of Leo the Isaurian, the urgent defence of the capital and empire. The most formidable of the Saracens, Moslemah the brother of the caliph, was advancing at the head of one hundred and twenty thousand Arabs and Persians, the greater part mounted on horses or camels; and the successful sieges of Tyana, Amorium, and Pergamus, were of sufficient duration to exercise their skill and to elevate their hopes. At the well-known passage of Abydus, on the Hellespont, the Mahometan arms were transported, for the first time, from Asia to Europe. From thence, wheeling round the Thracian cities of the Propontis, Moslemah invested Constantinople on the land side, surrounded his camp with a ditch and rampart, prepared and planted his engines of assault, and declared, by words and actions, a patient resolution of expecting the return of seed-time and harvest, should the obstinacy of the besieged prove equal to his own. The Greeks would gladly have ransomed their religion and empire, by a fine or assessment of a piece of gold on the head of each inhabitant of the city; but the liberal offer was rejected with disdain, and the presumption of Moslemah was exalted by the speedy approach and invincible force of the navies of Egypt and Syria. They are said to have amounted to eighteen hundred ships: the number betrays their inconsiderable size; and of the twenty stout and capacious vessels, whose magnitude impeded their progress, each was manned with no more than one hundred heavy armed soldiers. This huge Armada proceeded on a smooth sea and with a gentle gale, towards the mouth of the

11. In the division of the *Themes*, or provinces described by Constantine Porphyrogenitus (de Thematibus, l. i. p. 9, 10.), the *Obsequium*, a Latin appellation of the army and palace, was the fourth in the public order. Nice was the metropolis, and its jurisdiction extended from the Hellespont over the adjacent parts of Bithynia and Phrygia (see the two maps prefixed by Delisle to the Imperium Orientale of Banduri).

Bosphorus; the surface of the streight was overshadowed, in the language of the Greeks, with a moving forest, and the same fatal night had been fixed by the Saracen chief for a general assault by sea and land. To allure the confidence of the enemy, the emperor had thrown aside the chain that usually guarded the entrance of the harbour; but while they hesitated whether they should seize the opportunity, or apprehend the snare, the ministers of destruction were at hand. The fireships of the Greeks were launched against them, the Arabs, their arms, and vessels, were involved in the same flames, the disorderly fugitives were dashed against each other or overwhelmed in the waves; and I no longer find a vestige of the fleet, that had threatened to extirpate the Roman name. A still more fatal and irreparable loss was that of the caliph Soliman, who died of an indigestion[12] in his camp near Kinnisrin or Chalcis in Syria, as he was preparing to lead against Constantinople the remaining forces of the East. The brother of Moslemah was succeeded by a kinsman and an enemy; and the throne of an active and able prince was degraded by the useless and pernicious virtues of a bigot. While he started and satisfied the scruples of a blind conscience, the siege was continued through the winter by the neglect rather than by the resolution of the caliph Omar.[13] The winter proved uncommonly rigorous: above an hundred days the ground was covered with deep snow, and the natives of the sultry climes of Egypt and Arabia lay torpid and almost lifeless in their frozen camp. They revived on the return of spring; a second effort had been made in their favour; and their distress was relieved by the arrival of two numerous fleets, laden with corn, and arms, and soldiers, the first from Alexandria, of four hundred transports and gallies; the second of three hundred and sixty vessels from the ports of Africa. But the Greek fires were again kindled, and if the destruction was less complete, it was owing to the

12. The caliph had emptied two baskets of eggs and of figs, which he swallowed alternately, and the repast was concluded with marrow and sugar. In one of his pilgrimages to Mecca, Soliman ate, at a single meal, seventy pomgranates, a kid, six fowls, and a huge quantity of the grapes of Tayef. If the bill of fare be correct, we must admire the appetite rather than the luxury of the sovereign of Asia (Abulfeda, Annal. Moslem. p. 126.).

13. See the article of Omar Ben Abdalaziz, in the Bibliotheque Orientale (p. 689, 690.), præferens, says Elmacin (p. 91.), religionem suam rebus suis mundanis. He was so desirous of being with God, that he would not have anointed his ear (his own saying) to obtain a perfect cure of his last malady. The caliph had only one shirt, and in an age of luxury, his annual expence was no more than two drachms (Abulpharagius, p. 131.). Haud diu gavisus eo principe fuit orbis Moslemus (Abulfeda, p. 127.).

experience which had taught the Moslems to remain at a safe distance, or to the perfidy of the Egyptian mariners, who deserted with their ships to the emperor of the Christians. The trade and navigation of the capital were restored; and the produce of the fisheries supplied the wants, and even the luxury, of the inhabitants. But the calamities of famine and disease were soon felt by the troops of Moslemah, and as the former was miserably assuaged, so the latter was dreadfully propagated, by the pernicious nutriment which hunger compelled them to extract from the most unclean or unnatural food. The spirit of conquest, and even of enthusiasm, was extinct: the Saracens could no longer straggle beyond their lines, either single or in small parties, without exposing themselves to the merciless retaliation of the Thracian peasants. An army of Bulgarians was attracted from the Danube by the gifts and promises of Leo; and these savage auxiliaries made some atonement for the evils which they had inflicted on the empire, by the defeat and slaughter of twenty-two thousand Asiatics. A report was dextrously scattered, that the Franks, the unknown nations of the Latin world, were arming by sea and land in the defence of the Christian cause, and their formidable aid was expected with far different sensations in the camp and city. At length, after a siege of thirteen months,[14] the hopeless Moslemah received from the caliph the welcome permission of retreat. The march of the Arabian cavalry over the Hellespont and through the provinces of Asia, was executed without delay or molestation; but an army of their brethren had been cut in pieces on the side of Bithynia, and the remains of the fleet were so repeatedly damaged by tempest and fire, that only five gallies entered the port of Alexandria to relate the tale of their various and almost incredible disasters.[15]

Failure and retreat of the Saracens.

Invention and use of the Greek fire.

In the two sieges, the deliverance of Constantinople may be chiefly ascribed to the novelty, the terrors, and the real efficacy of the *Greek fire.*[16] The important secret of compounding and

14. Both Nicephorus and Theophanes agree that the siege of Constantinople was raised the 15th of August (A.D. 718); but as the former, our best witness, affirms that it continued thirteen months, the latter must be mistaken in supposing that it began on the same day of the preceding year. I do not find that Pagi has remarked this inconsistency.

15. In the second siege of Constantinople, I have followed Nicephorus (Brev. p. 33–36.), Theophanes (Chronograph. p. 324–334.), Cedrenus (Compend. p. 449–452.), Zonaras (tom. ii. p. 98–102.), Elmacin (Hist. Saracen. p. 88.), Abulfeda (Annal. Moslem. p. 126.), and Abulpharagius (Dynast. p. 130.), the most satisfactory of the Arabs.

16. Our sure and indefatigable guide in the middle ages and Byzantine history,

directing this artificial flame was imparted by Callinicus, a native of Heliopolis in Syria, who deserted from the service of the caliph to that of the emperor.[17] The skill of a chymist and engineer was equivalent to the succour of fleets and armies; and this discovery or improvement of the military art was fortunately reserved for the distressful period, when the degenerate Romans of the East were incapable of contending with the warlike enthusiasm and youthful vigour of the Saracens. The historian who presumes to analize this extraordinary composition should suspect his own ignorance and that of his Byzantine guides, so prone to the marvellous, so careless, and, in this instance, so jealous of the truth. From their obscure, and perhaps fallacious hints, it should seem that the principal ingredient of the Greek fire was the *naptha*,[18] or liquid bitumen, a light, tenacious, and inflammable oil,[19] which springs from the earth, and catches fire as soon as it comes in contact with the air. The naptha was mingled, I know not by what methods or in what proportions, with sulphur and with the pitch that is extracted from evergreen firs.[20] From

---

Charles du Fresne du Cange, has treated in several places of the Greek fire, and his collections leave few gleanings behind. See particularly Glossar. Med. et Infim. Græcitat. p. 1275. sub voce *Πυρ θαλασσιον, υγρον*. Glossar. Med. et Infim. Latinitat. *Ignis Græcus*. Observations sur Villehardouin, p. 305, 306. Observations sur Joinville, p. 71, 72.

17. Theophanes styles him *αρχιτεκτων* (p. 295.). Cedrenus (p. 437.) brings this artist from (the ruins of) Heliopolis in Egypt; and chemistry was indeed the peculiar science of the Egyptians.

18. The naptha, the oleum incendiarium of the history of Jerusalem (Gest. Dei per Francos, p. 1167.), the Oriental fountain of James de Vitry (l. iii. c. 84.), is introduced on slight evidence and strong probability. Cinnamus (l. vi. p. 165.) calls the Greek fire *πυρ Μηδικον*; and the naptha is known to abound between the Tigris and the Caspian Sea. According to Pliny (Hist. Natur. ii. 109.), it was subservient to the revenge of Medea, and in either etymology the *ελαιον Μηδιας*, or *Μηδειας* (Procop. de Bell. Gothic. l. iv. c. 11.), may fairly signify this liquid bitumen.

19. On the different sorts of oils and bitumens, see Dr. Watson's (the present bishop of Llandaff's) Chemical Essays, vol. iii. essay i. a classic book, the best adapted to infuse the taste and knowledge of chemistry. The less perfect ideas of the ancients may be found in Strabo (Geograph. l. xvi. p. 1078.) and Pliny (Hist. Natur. ii. 108, 109.). Huic *(Napthæ)* magna cognatio est ignium, transiliuntque protinus in eam undecunque visam. Of our travellers I am best pleased with Otter (tom. i. p. 153. 158.).

20. Anna Comnena has partly drawn aside the curtain. *Απο της πευκης, και αλλων τινων τοιουτων δενδρων αειθαλων συναγεται δακρυον ακαυστον. Τουτο μετα θειου τριβομενον εμβαλλεται εις αυλισκους καλαμων και εμφυσαται παρα του παιζοντος λαβρῳ και συνεχει πνευματι* (Alexiad, l. xiii. p. 383.). Elsewhere (l. xi. p. 336.) she mentions the property of burning, *κατα το πρανες και εφ' ἑκατερα*. Leo, in the xix[th] chapter of his Tactics (Opera Meursii, tom. vi. p. 843. edit. Lami, Florent. 1745), speaks of the new invention of *πυρ μετα βροντης και καπνου*. These are genuine and *Imperial* testimonies.

this mixture, which produced a thick smoke and a loud explosion, proceeded a fierce and obstinate flame, which not only rose in perpendicular ascent, but likewise burnt with equal vehemence in descent or lateral progress; instead of being extinguished, it was nourished and quickened, by the element of water; and sand, urine, or vinegar, were the only remedies that could damp the fury of this powerful agent, which was justly denominated by the Greeks, the *liquid*, or the *maritime*, fire. For the annoyance of the enemy, it was employed with equal effect, by sea and land, in battles or in sieges. It was either poured from the rampart in large boilers, or launched in red-hot balls of stone and iron, or darted in arrows and javelins, twisted round with flax and tow, which had deeply imbibed the inflammable oil: sometimes it was deposited in fire-ships, the victims and instruments of a more ample revenge, and was most commonly blown through long tubes of copper, which were planted on the prow of a galley, and fancifully shaped into the mouths of savage monsters, that seemed to vomit a stream of liquid and consuming fire. This important art was preserved at Constantinople, as the palladium of the state: the gallies and *artillery* might occasionally be lent to the allies of Rome; but the composition of the Greek fire was concealed with the most jealous scruple, and the terror of the enemies was encreased and prolonged by their ignorance and surprise. In the treatise of the administration of the empire, the royal author[21] suggests the answers and excuses that might best elude the indiscreet curiosity and importunate demands of the Barbarians. They should be told that the mystery of the Greek fire had been revealed by an angel to the first and greatest of the Constantines, with a sacred injunction, that this gift of heaven, this peculiar blessing of the Romans, should never be communicated to any foreign nation: that the prince and subject were alike bound to religious silence under the temporal and spiritual penalties of treason and sacrilege; and that the impious attempt would provoke the sudden and supernatural vengeance of the God of the Christians. By these precautions, the secret was confined, above four hundred years, to the Romans of the East; and, at the end of the eleventh century, the Pisans, to whom every sea and every art were familiar, suffered the effects, without understanding the composition, of the Greek fire. It was at length either discovered or stolen by the Mahometans; and, in the holy wars of Syria and Egypt, they retorted an invention, contrived against themselves, on the heads of the Christians. A knight, who despised the swords and lances of the

21. Constantin. Porphyrogenit. de Administrat. Imperii, c. xiii. p. 64, 65.

Saracens, relates, with heartfelt sincerity, his own fears, and those of his companions, at the sight and sound of the mischievous engine that discharged a torrent of the Greek fire, the *feu Gregeois*, as it is styled by the more early of the French writers. It came flying through the air, says Joinville,[22] like a winged long-tailed dragon, about the thickness of an hogshead, with the report of thunder and the velocity of lightning; and the darkness of the night was dispelled by this deadly illumination. The use of the Greek, or, as it might now be called, of the Saracen, fire, was continued to the middle of the fourteenth century,[23] when the scientific or casual compound of nitre, sulphur, and charcoal, effected a new revolution in the art of war and the history of mankind.[24]

Invasion of France by the Arabs, A.D. 721, &c.

Constantinople and the Greek fire might exclude the Arabs from the eastern entrance of Europe; but in the West, on the side of the Pyrenees, the provinces of Gaul were threatened and invaded by the conquerors of Spain.[25] The decline of the French monarchy invited the attack of these insatiate fanatics. The

22. Histoire de St. Louis, p. 39. Paris, 1668, p. 44. Paris, de l'Imprimerie Royale, 1761. The former of these editions is precious for the observations of Ducange; the latter, for the pure and original text of Joinville. We must have recourse to that text to discover, that the feu Gregeois was shot with a pile or javeline, from an engine that acted like a sling.

23. The vanity, or envy, of shaking the established property of Fame, has tempted some moderns to carry gunpowder above the xiv[th] (see Sir William Temple, Dutens, &c.), and the Greek fire above the vii[th] century (see the Saluste du President des Brosses, tom. ii. p. 381.). But their evidence, which precedes the vulgar æra of the invention, is seldom clear or satisfactory, and subsequent writers may be suspected of fraud or credulity. In the earliest sieges, some combustibles of oil and sulphur have been used, and the Greek fire has *some* affinities with gunpowder both in nature and effects: for the antiquity of the first, a passage of Procopius (de Bell. Goth. l. iv. c. 11.); for that of the second, some facts in the Arabic history of Spain (A.D. 1249. 1312. 1332. Bibliot. Arab. Hisp. tom. ii. p. 6, 7, 8.), are the most difficult to elude.

24. That extraordinary man, Friar Bacon, reveals two of the ingredients, saltpetre and sulphur, and conceals the third in a sentence of mysterious gibberish, as if he dreaded the consequences of his own discovery (Biographia Britannica, vol. i. p. 430. new edition).

25. For the invasion of France, and the defeat of the Arabs by Charles Martel, see the Historia Arabum (c. 11, 12, 13, 14.) of Roderic Ximenes, archbishop of Toledo, who had before him the Christian chronicle of Isidore Pacensis, and the Mahometan history of Novairi. The Moslems are silent or concise in the account of their losses, but M. Cardonne (tom. i. p. 129, 130, 131.) has given a *pure* and simple account of all that he could collect from Ibn Halikan, Hidjazi, and an anonymous writer. The texts of the chronicles of France, and lives of saints, are inserted in the collection of Bouquet (tom. iii.) and the Annals of Pagi, who (tom. iii. under the proper years) has restored the chronology, which is anticipated six years in the

descendants of Clovis had lost the inheritance of his martial and ferocious spirit; and their misfortune or demerit has affixed the epithet of *lazy* to the last kings of the Merovingian race.[26] They ascended the throne without power, and sunk into the grave without a name. A country palace, in the neighbourhood of Compiegne,[27] was allotted for their residence or prison; but each year, in the month of March or May, they were conducted in a waggon drawn by oxen to the assembly of the Franks, to give audience to foreign ambassadors, and to ratify the acts of the mayor of the palace. That domestic officer was become the minister of the nation and the master of the prince. A public employment was converted into the patrimony of a private family: the elder Pepin left a king of mature years under the guardianship of his own widow and her child; and these feeble regents were forcibly dispossessed by the most active of his bastards. A government, half savage and half corrupt, was almost dissolved; and the tributary dukes, the provincial counts, and the territorial lords, were tempted to despise the weakness of the monarch, and to imitate the ambition of the mayor. Among these independent chiefs, one of the boldest and most successful was Eudes, duke of Aquitain, who, in the southern provinces of Gaul, usurped the authority and even the title of king. The Goths, the Gascons, and the Franks, assembled under the standard of this Christian hero: he repelled the first invasion of the Saracens; and Zama, lieutenant of the caliph, lost his army and his life under the walls of Tholouse. The ambition of his successors was stimulated by revenge; they repassed the Pyrenees with the means and the resolution of conquest. The advantageous situation which had recommended Narbonne[28] as the first Roman colony, was again chosen by the Moslems: they claimed the province of Septemania or Languedoc

---

Annals of Baronius. The Dictionary of Bayle (*Abderame* and *Munuza*) has more merit for lively reflection than original research.

26. Eginhart, de Vita Caroli Magni, c. ii. p. 13–18. edit. Schmink, Utrecht, 1711. Some modern critics accuse the minister of Charlemagne of exaggerating the weakness of the Merovingians: but the general outline is just, and the French reader will for ever repeat the beautiful lines of Boileau's Lutrin.

27. *Mamaccæ* on the Oyse, between Compiegne and Noyon, which Eginhart calls perparvi reditûs villam (see the notes, and the map of ancient France for Dom. Bouquet's Collection). Compendium, or Compiegne was a palace of more dignity (Hadrian Valesii Notitia Galliarum, p. 152), and that laughing philosopher, the Abbé Galliani (Dialogues sur le Commerce des Bleds), may truly affirm, that it was the residence of the rois très Chretiens et très chevelûs.

28. Even before that colony, A. U. C. 630 (Velleius Patercul. i. 15.), in the time of Polybius (Hist. l. iii. p. 265. edit. Gronov.), Narbonne was a Celtic town of the first

as a just dependence of the Spanish monarchy: the vineyards of Gascony and the city of Bourdeaux were possessed by the sovereign of Damascus and Samarcand; and the south of France, from the mouth of the Garonne to that of the Rhône, assumed the manners and religion of Arabia.

Expedition and victories of Abderame, A.D. 731.

But these narrow limits were scorned by the spirit of Abdalrahman, or Abderame, who had been restored by the caliph Hashem to the wishes of the soldiers and people of Spain. That veteran and daring commander adjudged to the obedience of the prophet whatever yet remained of France or of Europe; and prepared to execute the sentence, at the head of a formidable host, in the full confidence of surmounting all opposition either of nature or of man. His first care was to suppress a domestic rebel, who commanded the most important passes of the Pyrenees: Munuza, a Moorish chief, had accepted the alliance of the duke of Aquitain; and Eudes, from a motive of private or public interest, devoted his beauteous daughter to the embraces of the African misbeliever. But the strongest fortresses of Cerdagne were invested by a superior force; the rebel was overtaken and slain in the mountains; and his widow was sent a captive to Damascus, to gratify the desires, or more probably the vanity, of the commander of the faithful. From the Pyrenees, Abderame proceeded without delay to the passage of the Rhône and the siege of Arles. An army of Christians attempted the relief of the city: the tombs of their leaders were yet visible in the thirteenth century; and many thousands of their dead bodies were carried down the rapid stream into the Mediterranean sea. The arms of Abderame were not less successful on the side of the ocean. He passed without opposition the Garonne and Dordogne, which unite their waters in the gulf of Bourdeaux; but he found, beyond those rivers, the camp of the intrepid Eudes, who had formed a second army, and sustained a second defeat, so fatal to the Christians, that, according to their sad confession, God alone could reckon the number of the slain. The victorious Saracen overran the provinces of Aquitain, whose Gallic names are disguised, rather than lost, in the modern appellations of Perigord, Saintonge, and Poitou: his standards were planted on the walls, or at least before the gates, of Tours and of Sens; and his detachments overspread the kingdom of Burgundy as far as the well-known cities of Lyons and Besançon. The

---

eminence, and one of the most northern places of the known world (d'Anville, Notice de l'Ancienne Gaule, p. 473.).

memory of these devastations, for Abderame did not spare the country or the people, was long preserved by tradition; and the invasion of France by the Moors or Mahometans, affords the ground-work of those fables, which have been so wildly disfigured in the romances of chivalry, and so elegantly adorned by the Italian muse. In the decline of society and art, the deserted cities could supply a slender booty to the Saracens; their richest spoil was found in the churches and monasteries, which they stripped of their ornaments and delivered to the flames: and the tutelar saints, both Hilary of Poitiers and Martin of Tours, forgot their miraculous powers in the defence of their own sepulchres.[29] A victorious line of march had been prolonged above a thousand miles from the rock of Gibraltar to the banks of the Loire; the repetition of an equal space would have carried the Saracens to the confines of Poland and the Highlands of Scotland: the Rhine is not more impassable than the Nile or Euphrates, and the Arabian fleet might have sailed without a naval combat into the mouth of the Thames. Perhaps the interpretation of the Koran would now be taught in the schools of Oxford, and her pulpits might demonstrate to a circumcised people the sanctity and truth of the revelation of Mahomet.[30]

Defeat of the Saracens by Charles Martel, A.D. 732.

From such calamities was Christendom delivered by the genius and fortune of one man. Charles, the illegitimate son of the elder Pepin, was content with the titles of mayor or duke of the Franks, but he deserved to become the father of a line of kings. In a laborious administration of twenty-four years, he restored and supported the dignity of the throne, and the rebels of Germany and Gaul were successively crushed by the activity of a warrior, who, in the same campaign, could display his banner on the Elbe, the Rhône, and the shores of the ocean. In the public danger, he was summoned by the voice of his country; and his rival, the duke of Aquitain, was reduced to appear among the fugitives and suppliants. "Alas!" ex-

29. With regard to the sanctuary of St. Martin of Tours, Roderic Ximenes accuses the Saracens of the *deed*. Turonis civitatem, ecclesiam et palatia vastatione et incendio simili diruit et consumpsit. The continuator of Fredegarius imputes to them no more than the *intention*. Ad domum beatissimi Martini evertendam destinant. At Carolus, &c. The French annalist was more jealous of the honour of the saint.

30. Yet I sincerely doubt whether the Oxford mosch would have produced a volume of controversy so elegant and ingenious as the sermons lately preached by Mr. White, the Arabic professor, at Mr. Bampton's lecture. His observations on the character and religion of Mahomet, are always adapted to his argument, and generally founded in truth and reason. He sustains the part of a lively and eloquent advocate; and sometimes rises to the merit of an historian and philosopher.

claimed the Franks, "what a misfortune! what an indignity! We have long heard of the name and conquests of the Arabs: we were apprehensive of their attack from the East; they have now conquered Spain, and invade our country on the side of the West. Yet their numbers, and (since they have no buckler) their arms, are inferior to our own." "If you follow my advice," replied the prudent mayor of the palace, "you will not interrupt their march, nor precipitate your attack. They are like a torrent, which it is dangerous to stem in its career. The thirst of riches, and the consciousness of success, redouble their valour, and valour is of more avail than arms or numbers. Be patient till they have loaded themselves with the incumbrance of wealth. The possession of wealth will divide their counsels and assure your victory." This subtle policy is perhaps a refinement of the Arabian writers; and the situation of Charles will suggest a more narrow and selfish motive of procrastination; the secret desire of humbling the pride, and wasting the provinces, of the rebel duke of Aquitain. It is yet more probable, that the delays of Charles were inevitable and reluctant. A standing army was unknown under the first and second race: more than half the kingdom was now in the hands of the Saracens: according to their respective situation, the Franks of Neustria and Austrasia were too conscious or too careless of the impending danger; and the voluntary aids of the Gepidæ and Germans were separated by a long interval from the standard of the Christian general. No sooner had he collected his forces, than he sought and found the enemy in the centre of France, between Tours and Poitiers. His well-conducted march was covered by a range of hills, and Abderame appears to have been surprised by his unexpected presence. The nations of Asia, Africa, and Europe, advanced with equal ardour to an encounter which would change the history of the world. In the six first days of desultory combat, the horsemen and archers of the East maintained their advantage: but in the closer onset of the seventh day, the Orientals were oppressed by the strength and stature of the Germans, who, with stout hearts and *iron* hands,[31] asserted the civil and religious freedom of their posterity. The epithet of *Martel*, the *Hammer*, which has been added to the name of Charles, is expressive of his weighty and irresistible strokes: the valour of Eudes was excited by resentment and emulation; and their companions, in the eye of history, are the true Peers and Paladins of French chivalry.

31. Gens Austriæ membrorum preeminentiâ valida, et gens Germana corde et corpore præstantissima, quasi in ictû oculi manû ferreâ et pectore arduo Arabes extinxerunt (Roderic. Toletan. c. xiv.).

After a bloody field, in which Abderame was slain, the Saracens, in the close of the evening, retired to their camp. In the disorder and despair of the night, the various tribes of Yemen and Damascus, of Africa and Spain, were provoked to turn their arms against each other: the remains of their host were suddenly dissolved, and each *emir* consulted his safety by an hasty and separate retreat. At the dawn of day, the stillness of an hostile camp was suspected by the victorious Christians: on the report of their spies, they ventured to explore the riches of the vacant tents; but, if we except some celebrated relics, a small portion of the spoil was restored to the innocent and lawful owners. The joyful tidings were soon diffused over the Catholic world, and the monks of Italy could affirm and believe that three hundred and fifty, or three hundred and seventy-five thousand of the Mahometans had been crushed by the hammer of Charles;[32] while no more than fifteen hundred Christians were slain in the field of Tours. But this incredible tale is sufficiently disproved by the caution of the French general, who apprehended the snares and accidents of a pursuit, and dismissed his German allies to their native forests. The inactivity of a conqueror betrays the loss of strength and blood, and the most cruel execution is inflicted, not in the ranks of battle, but on the backs of a flying enemy. Yet the victory of the Franks was complete and final; Aquitain was recovered by the arms of Eudes; the Arabs never resumed the conquest of Gaul, and they were soon driven beyond the Pyrenees by Charles Martel and his valiant race.[33] It might have been expected that the saviour of Christendom would have been canonized, or at least applauded, by the gratitude of the clergy, who are indebted to his sword for their present existence. But in the public distress, the mayor of the palace had been compelled to apply the riches, or at least the revenues, of the bishops and abbots, to the relief of the state and the reward of the soldiers. His merits were forgotten, his sacrilege alone was remembered, and, in an epistle to a

They retreat before the Franks.

32. These numbers are stated by Paul Warnefrid, the deacon of Aquileia (de Gestis Langobard. l. vi. p. 921. edit. Grot.), and Anastasius, the librarian of the Roman church (in Vit. Gregorii II.), who tells a miraculous story of three consecrated spunges, which rendered invulnerable the French soldiers among whom they had been shared. It should seem, that in his letters to the pope, Eudes usurped the honour of the victory, for which he is chastised by the French annalists, who, with equal falsehood, accuse him of inviting the Saracens.

33. Narbonne, and the rest of Septimania, was recovered by Pepin, the son of Charles Martel, A.D. 755 (Pagi, Critica, tom. iii. p. 300.). Thirty-seven years afterwards it was pillaged by a sudden inroad of the Arabs, who employed the captives in the construction of the mosch of Cordova (de Guignes, Hist. des Huns, tom. i. p. 354.).

Carlovingian prince, a Gallic synod presumes to declare that his ancestor was damned; that on the opening of his tomb, the spectators were affrighted by a smell of fire and the aspect of an horrid dragon; and that a saint of the times was indulged with a pleasant vision of the soul and body of Charles Martel, burning, to all eternity, in the abyss of hell.[34]

Elevation of the Abbassides, A.D. 746–750.

The loss of an army, or a province, in the Western world, was less painful to the court of Damascus than the rise and progress of a domestic competitor. Except among the Syrians, the caliphs of the house of Ommiyah had never been the objects of the public favour. The life of Mahomet recorded their perseverance in idolatry and rebellion: their conversion had been reluctant, their elevation irregular and factious, and their throne was cemented with the most holy and noble blood of Arabia. The best of their race, the pious Omar, was dissatisfied with his own title: their personal virtues were insufficient to justify a departure from the order of succession; and the eyes and wishes of the faithful were turned towards the line of Hashem and the kindred of the apostle of God. Of these the Fatimites were either rash or pusillanimous; but the descendants of Abbas cherished, with courage and discretion, the hopes of their rising fortunes. From an obscure residence in Syria, they secretly dispatched their agents and missionaries, who preached in the Eastern provinces their hereditary indefeasible right; and Mohammed, the son of Ali, the son of Abdallah, the son of Abbas, the uncle of the prophet, gave audience to the deputies of Chorasan, and accepted their free gift of four hundred thousand pieces of gold. After the death of Mohammed, the oath of allegiance was administered in the name of his son Ibrahim to a numerous band of votaries, who expected only a signal and a leader; and the governor of Chorasan continued to deplore his fruitless admonitions and the deadly slumber of the caliphs of Damascus, till he himself with all his adherents was driven from the city and palace of Meru, by the rebellious arms of Abu Moslem.[35] That maker of kings, the author, as he is named, of the *call* of the Abbassides, was at

34. This pastoral letter, addressed to Lewis the Germanic, the grandson of Charlemagne, and most probably composed by the pen of the artful Hincmar, is dated in the year 858, and signed by the bishops of the provinces of Rheims and Rouen (Baronius, Annal. Eccles. A.D. 741. Fleury, Hist. Eccles. tom. x. p. 514–516.). Yet Baronius himself, and the French critics, reject with contempt this episcopal fiction.

35. The steed and the saddle which had carried any of his wives, were instantly killed or burnt, lest they should be afterwards mounted by a male. Twelve hundred mules, or camels, were required for his kitchen furniture; and the daily

length rewarded for his presumption of merit with the usual gratitude of courts. A mean, perhaps a foreign, extraction could not repress the aspiring energy of Abu Moslem. Jealous of his wives, liberal of his wealth, prodigal of his own blood and of that of others, he could boast with pleasure, and possibly with truth, that he had destroyed six hundred thousand of his enemies; and such was the intrepid gravity of his mind and countenance, that he was never seen to smile except on a day of battle. In the visible separation of parties the *green* was consecrated to the Fatimites; the Ommiades were distinguished by the *white*, and the *black*, as the most adverse, was naturally adopted by the Abbassides. Their turbans and garments were stained with that gloomy colour: two black standards, on pike-staves nine cubits long, were borne aloft in the van of Abu Moslem; and their allegorical names of the *night* and the *shadow* obscurely represented the indissoluble union and perpetual succession of the line of Hashem. From the Indus to the Euphrates the East was convulsed by the quarrel of the white and the black factions: the Abbassides were most frequently victorious; but their public success was clouded by the personal misfortune of their chief. The court of Damascus, awakening from a long slumber, resolved to prevent the pilgrimage of Mecca, which Ibrahim had undertaken with a splendid retinue, to recommend himself at once to the favour of the prophet and of the people. A detachment of cavalry intercepted his march and arrested his person; and the unhappy Ibrahim, snatched away from the promise of untasted royalty, expired in iron fetters in the dungeons of Haran. His two younger brothers, Saffah and Almansor, eluded the search of the tyrant, and lay concealed at Cufa, till the zeal of the people and the approach of his eastern friends allowed them to expose their persons to the impatient public. On Friday, in the dress of a caliph, in the colours of the sect, Saffah proceeded with religious and military pomp to the mosch: ascending the pulpit, he prayed and preached as the lawful successor of Mahomet; and, after his departure, his kinsmen bound a willing people by an oath of fidelity. But it was on the banks of the Zab, and not in the mosch of Cufa, that this important controversy was determined. Every advantage appeared to be on the side of the white faction: the authority of established government; an army of an hundred and twenty thousand soldiers, against a sixth part of that number; and the presence and merit of the caliph Mervan, the fourteenth and last of

---

consumption amounted to three thousand cakes, an hundred sheep, besides oxen, poultry, &c. (Abulpharagius, Hist. Dynast. p. 140.)

the house of Ommiyah. Before his accession to the throne, he had deserved, by his Georgian warfare, the honourable epithet of the ass of Mesopotamia;[36] and he might have been ranked among the greatest princes, had not, says Abulfeda, the eternal order decreed that moment for the ruin of his family; a decree against which all human prudence and fortitude must struggle in vain. The orders of Mervan were mistaken or disobeyed: the return of his horse, from which he had dismounted on a necessary occasion, impressed the belief of his death; and the enthusiasm of the black squadrons was ably conducted by Abdallah, the uncle of his competitor. After an irretrievable defeat, the caliph escaped to Mosul; but the colours of the Abbassides were displayed from the rampart; he suddenly repassed the Tigris, cast a melancholy look on his palace of Haran, crossed the Euphrates, abandoned the fortifications of Damascus, and, without halting in Palestine, pitched his last and fatal camp at Busir on the banks of the Nile.[37] His speed was urged by the incessant diligence of Abdallah, who in every step of the pursuit acquired strength and reputation: the remains of the white faction were finally vanquished in Egypt; and the lance, which terminated the life and anxiety of Mervan, was not less welcome perhaps to the unfortunate than to the victorious chief. The merciless inquisition of the conqueror eradicated the most distant branches of the hostile race: their bones were scattered, their memory was accursed, and the martyrdom of Hossein was abundantly revenged on the posterity of his tyrants. Fourscore of the Ommiades, who had yielded to the faith or clemency of their foes, were invited to a banquet at Damascus. The laws of hospitality were violated by a promiscuous massacre: the board was spread over their fallen bodies; and the festivity of the guests was enlivened by the music of their dying groans. By the event of the civil war the dynasty of the Abbassides was firmly established; but the Christians only

Fall of the Ommiades, A.D. 750, February 10.

36. *Al Hemar.* He had been governor of Mesopotamia, and the Arabic proverb praises the courage of that warlike breed of asses who never fly from an enemy. The surname of Mervan may justify the comparison of Homer (Iliad *Λ*, 557, &c.), and both will silence the moderns, who consider the ass as a stupid and ignoble emblem (d'Herbelot, Bibliot. Orient. p. 558.).

37. Four several places, all in Egypt, bore the name of Busir, or Busiris, so famous in Greek fable. The first where Mervan was slain, was to the west of the Nile, in the province of Fium, or Arsinoe; the second in the Delta, in the Sebennytic nome; the third, near the pyramids; the fourth, which was destroyed by Diocletian (see above, vol. i. p. 370.), in the Thebais. I shall here transcribe a note of the learned and orthodox Michaelis: Videntur in pluribus Ægypti superioris urbibus Busiri Coptoque arma sumpsisse Christiani, libertatemque de religione sentiendi defendisse, sed succubuisse quo in bello Coptus

could triumph in the mutual hatred and common loss of the disciples of Mahomet.[38]

Revolt of Spain, A.D. 755.

Yet the thousands who were swept away by the sword of war might have been speedily retrieved in the succeeding generation, if the consequences of the revolution had not tended to dissolve the power and unity of the empire of the Saracens. In the proscription of the Ommiades, a royal youth of the name of Abdalrahman alone escaped the rage of his enemies, who hunted the wandering exile from the banks of the Euphrates to the vallies of mount Atlas. His presence in the neighbourhood of Spain revived the zeal of the white faction. The name and cause of the Abbassides had been first vindicated by the Persians: the West had been pure from civil arms; and the servants of the abdicated family still held, by a precarious tenure, the inheritance of their lands and the offices of government. Strongly prompted by gratitude, indignation, and fear, they invited the grandson of the caliph Hashem to ascend the throne of his ancestors; and in his desperate condition, the extremes of rashness and prudence were almost the same. The acclamations of the people saluted his landing on the coast of Andalusia; and, after a successful struggle, Abdalrahman established the throne of Cordova, and was the father of the Ommiades of Spain, who reigned above two hundred and fifty years from the Atlantic to the Pyrenees.[39] He slew in battle a lieutenant of the Abbassides, who had invaded his dominions with a fleet and army: the head of Ala, in salt and camphire, was suspended by a daring messenger before the palace of Mecca; and the caliph Almansor rejoiced in his safety, that he was removed by seas and lands from such a formidable adversary. Their mutual designs or

---

et Busiris diruta, et circa Esnam magna strages edita. Bellum narrant sed causam belli ignorant scriptores Byzantini, alioqui Coptum et Busirim non rebellasse dicturi, sed causam Christianorum suscepturi (Not. 211. p. 100.). For the geography of the four Busirs, see Abulfeda (Descript. Ægypt. p. 9. vers. Michaelis. Gottingæ, 1776, in 4to), Michaelis (Not. 122–127. p. 58–63.), and d'Anville (Memoire sur l'Egypte, p. 85. 147. 205.).

38. See Abulfeda (Annal. Moslem. p. 136–145.), Eutychius (Annal. tom. ii. p. 392. vers. Pocock), Elmacin (Hist. Saracen. p. 109–121.), Abulpharagius (Hist. Dynast. p. 134–140.), Roderic of Toledo (Hist. Arabum, c. 18. p. 33.), Theophanes (Chronograph. p. 356, 357. who speaks of the Abbassides under the names of *Χωρασανιται* and *Μαυροφοροι*), and the Bibliotheque of d'Herbelot, in the articles of *Ommiades, Abassides, Mærvan, Ibrahim, Saffah, Abou Moslem.*

39. For the revolution of Spain, consult Roderic of Toledo (c. xviii. p. 34, &c.), the Bibliotheca Arabico-Hispana (tom. ii. p. 30. 198.), and Cardonne (Hist. de l'Afrique et de l'Espagne, tom. i. p. 180–197. 205. 272. 323, &c.).

declarations of offensive war evaporated without effect; but instead of opening a door to the conquest of Europe, Spain was dissevered from the trunk of the monarchy, engaged in perpetual hostility with the East, and inclined to peace and friendship with the Christian sovereigns of Constantinople and France. The example of the Ommiades was imitated by the real or fictitious progeny of Ali, the Edrissites of Mauritania, and the more powerful Fatimites of Africa and Egypt. In the tenth century, the chair of Mahomet was disputed by three caliphs or commanders of the faithful, who reigned at Bagdad, Cairoan, and Cordova, excommunicated each other, and agreed only in a principle of discord, that a sectary is more odious and criminal than an unbeliever.[40]

Triple division of the caliphate.

Mecca was the patrimony of the line of Hashem, yet the Abbassides were never tempted to reside either in the birth-place or the city of the prophet. Damascus was disgraced by the choice, and polluted with the blood, of the Ommiades; and after some hesitation, Almansor, the brother and successor of Saffah, laid the foundations of Bagdad,[41] the Imperial seat of his posterity during a reign of five hundred years.[42] The chosen spot is on the eastern bank of the Tigris about fifteen miles above the ruins of Modain: the double wall was of a circular form; and such was the rapid encrease of a capital, now dwindled to a provincial town, that the funeral of a popular saint might be attended by eight hundred thousand men and sixty thousand women of Bagdad and the adjacent villages. In this *city of peace*,[43] amidst the riches

Magnificence of the caliphs, A.D. 750–960.

40. I shall not stop to refute the strange errors and fancies of Sir William Temple (his works, vol. iii. p. 371–374. octavo edition) and Voltaire (Histoire Generale, c. xxviii. tom. ii. p. 124, 125. edition de Lausanne), concerning the division of the Saracen empire. The mistakes of Voltaire proceeded from the want of knowledge or reflection; but Sir William was deceived by a Spanish impostor, who has framed an apocryphal history of the conquest of Spain by the Arabs.

41. The geographer d'Anville (l'Euphrate et le Tigre, p. 121–123.), and the Orientalist d'Herbelot (Bibliotheque, p. 167, 168.), may suffice for the knowledge of Bagdad. Our travellers, Pietro della Valle (tom. i. p. 688–698.), Tavernier (tom. i. p. 230–238.), Thevenot (part ii. p. 209–212.), Otter (tom. i. p. 162–168.), and Niebuhr (Voyage en Arabie, tom. ii. p. 239–271.), have seen only its decay; and the Nubian geographer (p. 204.) and the travelling Jew, Benjamin of Tudela (Itinerarium, p. 112–123. à Const. l'Empereur, apud Elzevir, 1633), are the only writers of my acquaintance, who have known Bagdad under the reign of the Abbassides.

42. The foundations of Bagdad were laid A.H. 145, A.D. 762. Mostasem, the last of the Abbassides, was taken and put to death by the Tartars, A.H. 656, A.D. 1258, the 20th of February.

43. Medinat al Salem, Dar al Salam. Urbs pacis, or as it is more neatly compounded by the Byzantine writers, Ειρηνοπολις (Irenopolis). There is some dispute

of the East, the Abbassides soon disdained the abstinence and frugality of the first caliphs, and aspired to emulate the magnificence of the Persian kings. After his wars and buildings, Almansor left behind him in gold and silver about thirty millions sterling;[44] and this treasure was exhausted in a few years by the vices or virtues of his children. His son Mahadi, in a single pilgrimage to Mecca, expended six millions of dinars of gold. A pious and charitable motive may sanctify the foundation of cisterns and caravanseras, which he distributed along a measured road of seven hundred miles; but his train of camels, laden with snow, could serve only to astonish the natives of Arabia, and to refresh the fruits and liquors of the royal banquet.[45] The courtiers would surely praise the liberality of his grandson Almamon, who gave away four fifths of the income of a province, a sum of two millions four hundred thousand gold dinars, before he drew his foot from the stirrup. At the nuptials of the same prince, a thousand pearls of the largest size were showered on the head of the bride,[46] and a lottery of lands and houses displayed the capricious bounty of fortune. The glories of the court were brightened rather than impaired in the decline of the empire; and a Greek ambassador might admire or pity the magnificence of the feeble Moctader. "The caliph's whole army," says the historian Abulfeda, "both horse and foot, was under arms, which together made a body of one hundred and sixty thousand men. His state-officers, the favourite slaves, stood near him in splendid apparel, their belts glittering with gold and gems. Near them were seven thousand eunuchs, four thousand of them white, the remainder black. The porters or door-keepers were in number seven hundred. Barges and boats, with the most superb decorations, were seen swimming

---

concerning the etymology of Bagdad, but the first syllable is allowed to signify a garden in the Persian tongue; the garden of Dad, a Christian hermit, whose cell had been the only habitation on the spot.

44. Reliquit in ærario sexcenties millies mille stateres, et quater et vicies millies mille aureos aureos. Elmacin, Hist. Saracen. p. 126. I have reckoned the gold pieces at eight shillings, and the proportion to the silver as twelve to one. But I will never answer for the numbers of Erpenius; and the Latins are scarcely above the savages in the language of arithmetic.

45. D'Herbelot, p. 530. Abulfeda, p. 154. Nivem Meccam apportavit, rem ibi aut nunquam aut rarissime visam.

46. Abulfeda, p. 184. 189. describes the splendour and liberality of Almamon. Milton has alluded to this Oriental custom:

– Or where the gorgeous East, with richest hand,
Showers on her kings Barbaric pearls and gold.

I have used the modern word *lottery*, to express the *Missilia* of the Roman emperors, which entitled to some prize the person who caught them, as they were thrown among the crowd.

upon the Tigris. Nor was the palace itself less splendid, in which were hung up thirty-eight thousand pieces of tapestry, twelve thousand five hundred of which were of silk embroidered with gold. The carpets on the floor were twenty-two thousand. An hundred lions were brought out with a keeper to each lion.[47] Among the other spectacles of rare and stupendous luxury, was a tree of gold and silver spreading into eighteen large branches, on which, and on the lesser boughs, sat a variety of birds made of the same precious metals, as well as the leaves of the tree. While the machinery affected spontaneous motions, the several birds warbled their natural harmony. Through this scene of magnificence, the Greek ambassador was led by the visir to the foot of the caliph's throne."[48] In the West, the Ommiades of Spain supported, with equal pomp, the title of commander of the faithful. Three miles from Cordova, in honour of his favourite sultana, the third and greatest of the Abdalrahmans constructed the city, palace, and gardens of Zehra. Twenty-five years, and above three millions sterling, were employed by the founder: his liberal taste invited the artists of Constantinople, the most skilful sculptors and architects of the age; and the buildings were sustained or adorned by twelve hundred columns of Spanish and African, of Greek and Italian marble. The hall of audience was encrusted with gold and pearls, and a great bason in the centre, was surrounded with the curious and costly figures of birds and quadrupeds. In a lofty pavilion of the gardens, one of these basons and fountains, so delightful in a sultry climate, was replenished not with water, but with the purest quicksilver. The seraglio of Abdalrahman, his wives, concubines, and black eunuchs, amounted to six thousand three hundred persons; and he was attended to the field by a guard of twelve thousand horse, whose belts and scymetars were studded with gold.[49]

Its consequences on private and public happiness.

In a private condition, our desires are perpetually repressed by poverty and subordination; but the lives and labours of millions are devoted to the service of a despotic prince, whose

47. When Bell of Antermony (Travels, vol. i. p. 99) accompanied the Russian ambassador to the audience of the unfortunate Shah Hussein of Persia, *two* lions were introduced, to denote the power of the king over the fiercest animals.

48. Abulfeda, p. 237. d'Herbelot, p. 590. This embassy was received at Bagdad A.H. 305, A.D. 917. In the passage of Abulfeda, I have used, with some variations, the English translation of the learned and amiable Mr. Harris of Salisbury (Philological Enquiries, p. 363, 364.).

49. Cardonne, Histoire de l'Afrique et de l'Espagne, tom. i. p. 330–336. A just idea of the taste and architecture of the Arabians of Spain, may be conceived from the description and plates of the Alhambra of Grenada (Swinburne's Travels, p. 171–188.).

laws are blindly obeyed, and whose wishes are instantly gratified. Our imagination is dazzled by the splendid picture; and whatever may be the cool dictates of reason, there are few among us who would obstinately refuse a trial of the comforts and the cares of royalty. It may therefore be of some use to borrow the experience of the same Abdalrahman, whose magnificence has perhaps excited our admiration and envy, and to transcribe an authentic memorial which was found in the closet of the deceased caliph. "I have now reigned above fifty years in victory or peace; beloved by my subjects, dreaded by my enemies, and respected by my allies. Riches and honours, power and pleasure, have waited on my call, nor does any earthly blessing appear to have been wanting to my felicity. In this situation, I have diligently numbered the days of pure and genuine happiness which have fallen to my lot: they amount to FOURTEEN: – O man! place not thy confidence in this present world."[50] The luxury of the caliphs, so useless to their private happiness, relaxed the nerves, and terminated the progress, of the Arabian empire. Temporal and spiritual conquest had been the sole occupation of the first successors of Mahomet; and after supplying themselves with the necessaries of life, the whole revenue was scrupulously devoted to that salutary work. The Abbassides were impoverished by the multitude of their wants and their contempt of œconomy. Instead of pursuing the great object of ambition, their leisure, their affections, the powers of their mind, were diverted by pomp and pleasure: the rewards of valour were embezzled by women and eunuchs, and the royal camp was encumbered by the luxury of the palace. A similar temper was diffused among the subjects of the caliph. Their stern enthusiasm was softened by time and prosperity: they sought riches in the occupations of industry, fame in the pursuits of literature, and happiness in the tranquillity of domestic life. War was no longer the passion of the Saracens; and the encrease of pay, the repetition of donatives, were insufficient to allure the posterity of those voluntary champions who had crowded to the standard of Abubeker and Omar for the hopes of spoil and of paradise.

50. Cardonne, tom. i. p. 329, 330. This confession, the complaints of Solomon of the vanity of this world (read Prior's verbose but eloquent poem), and the happy ten days of the emperor Seghed (Rambler, N° 204, 205.), will be triumphantly quoted by the detractors of human life. Their expectations are commonly immoderate, their estimates are seldom impartial. If I may speak of myself (the only person of whom I can speak with certainty), *my* happy hours have far exceeded, and far exceed, the scanty numbers of the caliph of Spain; and I shall not scruple to add, that many of them are due to the pleasing labour of the present composition.

Introduction of learning among the Arabians, A.D. 754, &c. 813, &c.

Under the reign of the Ommiades, the studies of the Moslems were confined to the interpretation of the Koran, and the eloquence and poetry of their native tongue. A people continually exposed to the dangers of the field, must esteem the healing powers of medicine or rather of surgery: but the starving physicians of Arabia murmured a complaint, that exercise and temperance deprived them of the greatest part of their practice.[51] After their civil and domestic wars, the subjects of the Abbassides, awakening from this mental lethargy, found leisure and felt curiosity for the acquisition of profane science. This spirit was first encouraged by the caliph Almansor, who, besides his knowledge of the Mahometan law, had applied himself with success to the study of astronomy. But when the sceptre devolved to Almamon, the seventh of the Abbassides, he completed the designs of his grandfather, and invited the muses from their ancient seats. His ambassadors at Constantinople, his agents in Armenia, Syria, and Egypt, collected the volumes of Grecian science: at his command they were translated by the most skilful interpreters into the Arabic language: his subjects were exhorted assiduously to peruse these instructive writings; and the successor of Mahomet assisted with pleasure and modesty at the assemblies and disputations of the learned. "He was not ignorant," says Abulpharagius, "that *they* are the elect of God, his best and most useful servants, whose lives are devoted to the improvement of their rational faculties. The mean ambition of the Chinese or the Turks may glory in the industry of their hands or the indulgence of their brutal appetites. Yet these dextrous artists must view, with hopeless emulation, the hexagons and pyramids of the cells of a bee-hive:[52] these fortitudinous heroes are awed by the superior fierceness of the lions and tigers; and in their amorous enjoyments, they are much inferior to the

51. The Gulistan (p. 239.) relates the conversation of Mahomet and a physician (Epistol. Renaudot. in Fabricius, Bibliot. Græc. tom. i. p. 814.). The prophet himself was skilled in the art of medicine; and Gagnier (Vie de Mahomet, tom. iii. p. 394–405.) has given an extract of the aphorisms which are extant under his name.

52. See their curious architecture in Reaumur (Hist. des Insectes, tom. v. Memoire viii.). These hexagons are closed by a pyramid; the angles of the three sides of a similar pyramid, such as would accomplish the given end with the smallest quantity possible of materials, were determined by a mathematician, at 109 degrees 26 minutes for the larger, 70 degrees 34 minutes for the smaller. The actual measure is 109 degrees 28 minutes, 70 degrees 32 minutes. Yet this perfect harmony raises the work at the expence of the artist: the bees are not masters of transcendant geometry.

vigour of the grossest and most sordid quadrupeds. The teachers of wisdom are the true luminaries and legislators of a world, which, without their aid, would again sink in ignorance and barbarism."[53] The zeal and curiosity of Almamon were imitated by succeeding princes of the line of Abbas: their rivals, the Fatimites of Africa and the Ommiades of Spain, were the patrons of the learned, as well as the commanders of the faithful: the same royal prerogative was claimed by their independent emirs of the provinces; and their emulation diffused the taste and the rewards of science from Samarcand and Bochara to Fez and Cordova. The visir of a sultan consecrated a sum of two hundred thousand pieces of gold to the foundation of a college at Bagdad, which he endowed with an annual revenue of fifteen thousand dinars. The fruits of instruction were communicated, perhaps at different times, to six thousand disciples of every degree, from the son of the noble to that of the mechanic: a sufficient allowance was provided for the indigent scholars; and the merit or industry of the professors was repaid with adequate stipends. In every city the productions of Arabic literature were copied and collected by the curiosity of the studious and the vanity of the rich. A private doctor refused the invitation of the sultan of Bochara, because the carriage of his books would have required four hundred camels. The royal library of the Fatimites consisted of one hundred thousand manuscripts, elegantly transcribed and splendidly bound, which were lent, without jealousy or avarice, to the students of Cairo. Yet this collection must appear moderate, if we can believe that the Ommiades of Spain had formed a library of six hundred thousand volumes, forty-four of which were employed in the mere catalogue. Their capital, Cordova, with the adjacent towns of Malaga, Almeria, and Murcia, had given birth to more than three hundred writers, and above seventy public libraries were opened in the cities of the Andalusian kingdom. The age of Arabian learning continued about five hundred years, till the great eruption of the Moguls, and was coæval with the darkest and most slothful period of European annals; but since the sun of science has arisen in the West, it should seem that the Oriental studies have languished and declined.[54]

53. Saed Ebn Ahmed, cadhi of Toledo, who died A.H. 462, A.D. 1069, has furnished Abulpharagius (Dynast. p. 160.) with this curious passage, as well as with the text of Pocock's Specimen Historiæ Arabum. A number of literary anecdotes of philosophers, physicians, &c. who have flourished under each caliph, form the principal merit of the Dynasties of Abulpharagius.

54. These literary anecdotes are borrowed from the Bibliotheca Arabico-Hispana (tom. ii. p. 38. 71. 201, 202.), Leo Africanus (de Arab. Medicis et Philosophis, in Fabric.

Their real progress in the sciences.

In the libraries of the Arabians, as in those of Europe, the far greater part of the innumerable volumes were possessed only of local value or imaginary merit.[55] The shelves were crowded with orators and poets, whose style was adapted to the taste and manners of their countrymen; with general and partial histories, which each revolving generation supplied with a new harvest of persons and events; with codes and commentaries of jurisprudence, which derived their authority from the law of the prophet; with the interpreters of the Koran, and orthodox tradition; and with the whole theological tribe, polemics, mystics, scholastics, and moralists, the first or the last of writers, according to the different estimate of sceptics or believers. The works of speculation or science may be reduced to the four classes of philosophy, mathematics, astronomy, and physic. The sages of Greece were translated and illustrated in the Arabic language, and some treatises, now lost in the original, have been recovered in the versions of the East,[56] which possessed and studied the writings of Aristotle and Plato, of Euclid and Apollonius, of Ptolemy, Hippocrates, and Galen.[57] Among the ideal systems, which have varied with the fashion of the times, the Arabians adopted the philosophy of the Stagirite, alike intelligible or alike obscure for the readers of every age. Plato wrote for the Athenians, and his allegorical genius is too closely blended with the language and religion of Greece. After the fall of that

Bibliot. Græc. tom. xiii. p. 259–298. particularly p. 274.), and Renaudot (Hist. Patriarch. Alex. p. 274, 275. 536, 537.), besides the chronological remarks of Abulpharagius.

55. The Arabic catalogue of the Escurial will give a just idea of the proportion of the classes. In the library of Cairo, the MSS. of astronomy and medicine amounted to 6500, with two fair globes, the one of brass, the other of silver (Bibliot. Arab. Hisp. tom. i. p. 417.).

56. As for instance, the fifth, sixth, and seventh books (the eighth is still wanting) of the Conic Sections of Apollonius Pergæus, which were printed from the Florence MS. 1661 (Fabric. Bibliot. Græc. tom. ii. p. 559.). Yet the fifth book had been previously restored by the mathematical divination of Viviani (see his eloge in Fontenelle, tom. v. p. 59, &c.).

57. The merit of these Arabic versions is freely discussed by Renaudot (Fabric. Bibliot. Græc. tom. i. p. 812–816.), and piously defended by Casiri (Bibliot. Arab. Hispana, tom. i. p. 238–240.). Most of the versions of Plato, Aristotle, Hippocrates, Galen, &c. are ascribed to Honain, a physician of the Nestorian sect, who flourished at Bagdad in the court of the caliphs, and died A.D. 876. He was at the head of a school or manufacture of translations, and the works of his sons and disciples were published under his name. See Abulpharagius (Dynast. p. 88. 115. 171–174. and apud Asseman, Bibliot. Orient. tom. ii. p. 438.), d'Herbelot (Bibliot. Orientale, p. 456.), Asseman (Bibliot. Orient. tom. iii. p. 164.), and Casiri (Bibliot. Arab. Hispana, tom. i. p. 238, &c. 251. 286–290. 302. 304, &c.).

religion, the Peripatetics, emerging from their obscurity, prevailed in the controversies of the Oriental sects, and their founder was long afterwards restored by the Mahometans of Spain to the Latin schools.[58] The physics, both of the Academy and the Lycæum, as they are built, not on observation, but on argument, have retarded the progress of real knowledge. The metaphysics of infinite, or finite, spirit, have too often been enlisted in the service of superstition. But the human faculties are fortified by the art and practice of dialectics; the ten predicaments of Aristotle collect and methodise our ideas,[59] and his syllogism is the keenest weapon of dispute. It was dextrously wielded in the schools of the Saracens, but as it is more effectual for the detection of error than for the investigation of truth, it is not surprising that new generations of masters and disciples should still revolve in the same circle of logical argument. The mathematics are distinguished by a peculiar privilege, that, in the course of ages, they may always advance, and can never recede. But the ancient geometry, if I am not misinformed, was resumed in the same state by the Italians of the fifteenth century; and whatever may be the origin of the name, the science of algebra is ascribed to the Grecian Diophantus by the modest testimony of the Arabs themselves.[60] They cultivated with more success the sublime science of astronomy, which elevates the mind of man to disdain his diminutive planet and momentary existence. The costly instruments of observation were supplied by the caliph Almamon, and the land of the Chaldæans still afforded the same spacious level, the same unclouded horizon. In the plains of Sinaar, and a second time in those of Cufa, his mathematicians accurately measured a degree of the great circle of the earth, and determined at twenty-four thousand miles the entire circumference of our globe.[61] From the reign of the Abbassides

58. See Mosheim, Institut. Hist. Eccles. p. 181. 214. 236. 257. 315. 338. 396. 438, &c.

59. The most elegant commentary on the Categories or Predicaments of Aristotle, may be found in the Philosophical Arrangements of Mr. James Harris (London, 1775, in octavo), who laboured to revive the studies of Grecian literature and philosophy.

60. Abulpharagius, Dynast. p. 81. 222. Bibliot. Arab. Hisp. tom. i. p. 370, 371. In quem (says the primate of the Jacobites) si immiserit se lector, oceanum hoc in genere *(algebræ)* inveniet. The time of Diophantus of Alexandria is unknown, but his six books are still extant, and have been illustrated by the Greek Planudes and the Frenchman Meziriac (Fabric. Bibliot. Græc. tom. iv. p. 12–15.).

61. Abulfeda (Annal. Moslem. p. 210, 211. vers. Reiske) describes this operation according to Ibn Challecan, and the best historians. This degree most accurately contains 200,000 royal or Hashemite cubits, which Arabia had derived from the sacred and legal practice both of Palestine and Egypt. This ancient cubit is repeated 400

to that of the grandchildren of Tamerlane, the stars, without the aid of glasses, were diligently observed; and the astronomical tables of Bagdad, Spain, and Samarcand,[62] correct some minute errors, without daring to renounce the hypothesis of Ptolemy, without advancing a step towards the discovery of the solar system. In the eastern courts, the truths of science could be recommended only by ignorance and folly, and the astronomer would have been disregarded, had he not debased his wisdom or honesty by the vain predictions of astrology.[63] But in the science of medicine, the Arabians have been deservedly applauded. The names of Mesua and Geber, of Razis and Avicenna, are ranked with the Grecian masters; in the city of Bagdad, eight hundred and sixty physicians were licensed to exercise their lucrative profession:[64] in Spain, the life of the Catholic princes was entrusted to the skill of the Saracens,[65] and the school of Salerno, their legitimate offspring, revived in Italy and Europe the precepts of the healing art.[66] The success of each professor must have been influenced by personal and accidental causes; but we may form a less fanciful estimate of their general knowledge of anatomy,[67] botany,[68] and chemistry,[69] the threefold basis of their theory and practice. A

---

times in each basis of the great pyramid, and seems to indicate the primitive and universal measures of the East. See the Metrologie of the laborious M. Paucton, p. 101–195.

62. See the Astronomical Tables of Ulugh Begh, with the preface of Dr. Hyde, in the 1st volume of his Syntagma Dissertationum, Oxon. 1767.

63. The truth of astrology was allowed by Albumazar, and the best of the Arabian astronomers, who drew their most certain predictions, not from Venus and Mercury, but from Jupiter and the sun (Abulpharag. Dynast. p. 161–163.). For the state and science of the Persian astronomers, see Chardin (Voyages en Perse, tom. iii. p. 162–203.).

64. Bibliot. Arabico-Hispana, tom. i. p. 438. The original relates a pleasant tale, of an ignorant but harmless practitioner.

65. In the year 956, Sancho the fat, king of Leon, was cured by the physicians of Cordova (Mariana, l. viii. c. 7. tom. i. p. 318.).

66. The school of Salerno, and the introduction of the Arabian sciences into Italy, are discussed with learning and judgment by Muratori (Antiquitat. Italiæ Medii Ævi, tom. iii. p. 932–940.) and Giannone (Istoria Civile di Napoli, tom. ii. p. 119–127.).

67. See a good view of the progress of anatomy in Wotton (Reflections on ancient and modern Learning, p. 208–256.). His reputation has been unworthily depreciated by the wits in the controversy of Boyle and Bentley.

68. Bibliot. Arab. Hispanica, tom. i. p. 275. Al Beithar of Malaga, their greatest botanist, had travelled into Africa, Persia, and India.

69. Dr. Watson (Elements of Chemistry, vol. i. p. 17, &c.) allows the *original* merit of the Arabians. Yet he quotes the modest confession of the famous Geber of the ixth century (d'Herbelot, p. 387.), that he had drawn most of his science, perhaps of the transmutation of metals, from the ancient sages. Whatever might be the origin or extent of their knowledge, the arts of

superstitious reverence for the dead confined both the Greeks and the Arabians to the dissection of apes and quadrupeds; the more solid and visible parts were known in the time of Galen, and the finer scrutiny of the human frame was reserved for the microscope and the injections of modern artists. Botany is an active science, and the discoveries of the torrid zone might enrich the herbal of Dioscorides with two thousand plants. Some traditionary knowledge might be secreted in the temples and monasteries of Egypt; much useful experience had been acquired in the practice of arts and manufactures; but the *science* of chemistry owes its origin and improvement to the industry of the Saracens. They first invented and named the alembic for the purposes of distillation, analysed the substances of the three kingdoms of nature, tried the distinction and affinities of alcalis and acids, and converted the poisonous minerals into soft and salutary medicines. But the most eager search of Arabian chemistry was the transmutation of metals, and the elixir of immortal health: the reason and the fortunes of thousands were evaporated in the crucibles of alchymy, and the consummation of the great work was promoted by the worthy aid of mystery, fable, and superstition.

Want of erudition, taste, and freedom. But the Moslems deprived themselves of the principal benefits of a familiar intercourse with Greece and Rome, the knowledge of antiquity, the purity of taste, and the freedom of thought. Confident in the riches of their native tongue, the Arabians disdained the study of any foreign idiom. The Greek interpreters were chosen among their Christian subjects; they formed their translations, sometimes on the original text, more frequently perhaps on a Syriac version: and in the crowd of astronomers and physicians, there is no example of a poet, an orator, or even an historian, being taught to speak the language of the Saracens.[70] The mythology of Homer would have provoked the abhorrence of those stern fanatics: they possessed in lazy ignorance the colonies of the Macedonians, and the provinces of Carthage and Rome: the heroes of Plutarch and Livy were buried in oblivion; and the history of the world before Mahomet was reduced to a short legend of the

chemistry and alchymy appear to have been known in Egypt at least three hundred years before Mahomet (Wotton's Reflections, p. 121–133. Pauw, Recherches sur les Egyptiens et les Chinois, tom. i. p. 376–429.).

70. Abulpharagius (Dynast. p. 26. 148.) mentions a *Syriac* version of Homer's two poems, by Theophilus, a Christian Maronite of mount Libanus, who professed astronomy at Roha or Edessa towards the end of the viiith century. His work would be a literary curiosity. I have read somewhere, but I do not believe, that Plutarch's Lives were translated into Turkish for the use of Mahomet the second.

patriarchs, the prophets, and the Persian kings. Our education in the Greek and Latin schools may have fixed in our minds a standard of exclusive taste; and I am not forward to condemn the literature and judgment of nations, of whose language I am ignorant. Yet I *know* that the classics have much to teach, and I *believe* that the Orientals have much to learn: the temperate dignity of style, the graceful proportions of art, the forms of visible and intellectual beauty, the just delineation of character and passion, the rhetoric of narrative and argument, the regular fabric of epic and dramatic poetry.[71] The influence of truth and reason is of a less ambiguous complexion. The philosophers of Athens and Rome enjoyed the blessings, and asserted the rights, of civil and religious freedom. Their moral and political writings might have gradually unlocked the fetters of Eastern despotism, diffused a liberal spirit of enquiry and toleration, and encouraged the Arabian sages to suspect that their caliph was a tyrant and their prophet an impostor.[72] The instinct of superstition was alarmed by the introduction even of the abstract sciences; and the more rigid doctors of the law condemned the rash and pernicious curiosity of Almamon.[73] To the thirst of martyrdom, the vision of paradise, and the belief of predestination, we must ascribe the invincible enthusiasm of the prince and people. And the sword of the Saracens became less formidable, when their youth was drawn away from the camp to the college, when the armies of the faithful presumed to read and to reflect. Yet the foolish vanity of the Greeks was jealous of their studies, and reluctantly imparted the sacred fire to the Barbarians of the East.[74]

Wars of Harun al Rashid

In the bloody conflict of the Ommiades and Abbassides, the Greeks had stolen the opportunity of avenging their

71. I have perused, with much pleasure, Sir William Jones's Latin Commentary on Asiatic poetry (London, 1774, in octavo), which was composed in the youth of that wonderful linguist. At present, in the maturity of his taste and judgment, he would perhaps abate of the fervent, and even partial, praise which he has bestowed on the Orientals.

72. Among the Arabian philosophers, Averroes has been accused of despising the religions of the Jews, the Christians, and the Mahometans (see his article in Bayle's Dictionary). Each of these sects would agree, that in two instances out of three, his contempt was reasonable.

73. D'Herbelot, Bibliotheque Orientale, p. 546.

74. *Θεοφιλος ατοπον κρινας ει την των οντων γνωσιν, δι ἣν το Ρωμαιων γενος θαυμαζεται εκδοτον ποιησει τοις εθνεσι*, &c. Cedrenus, p. 548. who relates how manfully the emperor refused a mathematician to the instances and offers of the caliph Almamon. This absurd scruple is expressed almost in the same words, by the continuator of Theophanes (Scriptores post Theophanem, p. 118.).

against the Romans, A.D. 781–805. wrongs and enlarging their limits. But a severe retribution was exacted by Mohadi, the third caliph of the new dynasty, who seized in his turn the favourable opportunity, while a woman and a child, Irene and Constantine, were seated on the Byzantine throne. An army of ninety-five thousand Persians and Arabs was sent from the Tigris to the Thracian Bosphorus, under the command of Harun,[75] or Aaron, the second son of the commander of the faithful. His encampment on the opposite heights of Chrysopolis or Scutari, informed Irene, in her palace of Constantinople, of the loss of her troops and provinces. With the consent or connivance of their sovereign her ministers subscribed an ignominious peace; and the exchange of some royal gifts could not disguise the annual tribute of seventy thousand dinars of gold, which was imposed on the Roman empire. The Saracens had too rashly advanced into the midst of a distant and hostile land: their retreat was solicited by the promise of faithful guides and plentiful markets; and not a Greek had courage to whisper, that their weary forces might be surrounded and destroyed in their necessary passage between a slippery mountain and the river Sangarius. Five years after this expedition, Harun ascended the throne of his father and his elder brother; the most powerful and vigorous monarch of his race, illustrious in the West, as the ally of Charlemagne, and familiar to the most childish readers, as the perpetual hero of the Arabian tales. His title to the name of *Al Rashid* (the *Just*) is sullied by the extirpation of the generous, perhaps the innocent, Barmecides; yet he could listen to the complaint of a poor widow who had been pillaged by his troops, and who dared, in a passage of the Koran, to threaten the inattentive despot with the judgment of God and posterity. His court was adorned with luxury and science; but, in a reign of three-and-twenty years, Harun repeatedly visited his provinces from Chorasan to Egypt; nine times he performed the pilgrimage of Mecca; eight times he invaded the territories of the Romans; and as often as they declined the payment of the tribute, they were taught to feel that a month of depredation was more costly than a year of submission. But when the unnatural mother of Constantine was deposed and banished, her successor Nicephorus resolved to obliterate this badge of servitude and disgrace. The epistle of the emperor to the caliph was pointed with an allusion to the game of chess, which had already spread from Persia to Greece. "The

75. See the reign and character of Harun al Rashid, in the Bibliotheque Orientale, p. 431–433, under his proper title; and in the relative articles to which M. d'Herbelot refers. That learned collector has shewn much taste in stripping the Oriental chronicles of their instructive and amusing anecdotes.

queen (he spoke of Irene) considered you as a rook and herself as a pawn. That pusillanimous female submitted to pay a tribute, the double of which she ought to have exacted from the Barbarians. Restore therefore the fruits of your injustice, or abide the determination of the sword." At these words the ambassadors cast a bundle of swords before the foot of the throne. The caliph smiled at the menace, and drawing his scymetar, *samsamah*, a weapon of historic or fabulous renown, he cut asunder the feeble arms of the Greeks, without turning the edge, or endangering the temper, of his blade. He then dictated an epistle of tremendous brevity: "In the name of the most merciful God, Harun al Rashid, commander of the faithful, to Nicephorus, the Roman dog. I have read thy letter, O thou son of an unbelieving mother. Thou shalt not hear, thou shalt behold my reply." It was written in characters of blood and fire on the plains of Phrygia; and the warlike celerity of the Arabs could only be checked by the arts of deceit and the shew of repentance. The triumphant caliph retired, after the fatigues of the campaign, to his favourite palace of Racca on the Euphrates;[76] but the distance of five hundred miles, and the inclemency of the season, encouraged his adversary to violate the peace. Nicephorus was astonished by the bold and rapid march of the commander of the faithful, who repassed, in the depth of winter, the snows of mount Taurus: his stratagems of policy and war were exhausted; and the perfidious Greek escaped with three wounds from a field of battle overspread with forty thousand of his subjects. Yet the emperor was ashamed of submission, and the caliph was resolved on victory. One hundred and thirty-five thousand regular soldiers received pay, and were inscribed in the military roll; and above three hundred thousand persons of every denomination marched under the black standard of the Abbassides. They swept the surface of Asia Minor far beyond Tyana and Ancyra, and invested the Pontic Heraclea,[77] once a flourishing state, now a paltry town; at that time capable of sustaining in her antique walls a month's siege against the forces of the East. The ruin was complete, the spoil was

76. For the situation of Racca, the old Nicephorium, consult d'Anville (l'Euphrate et le Tigre, p. 24–27.). The Arabian Nights represent Harun al Rashid as almost stationary in Bagdad. He respected the royal seat of the Abbassides, but the vices of the inhabitants had driven him from the city (Abulfed. Annal. p. 167.).

77. M. de Tournefort, in his coasting voyage from Constantinople to Trebizond, passed a night at Heraclea or Eregri. His eye surveyed the present state, his reading collected the antiquities, of the city (Voyage du Levant, tom. iii. lettre xvi. p. 23–35.). We have a separate history of Heraclea in the fragments of Memnon, which are preserved by Photius.

ample; but if Harun had been conversant with Grecian story, he would have regretted the statue of Hercules, whose attributes, the club, the bow, the quiver, and the lion's hide, were sculptured in massy gold. The progress of desolation by sea and land, from the Euxine to the isle of Cyprus, compelled the emperor Nicephorus to retract his haughty defiance. In the new treaty, the ruins of Heraclea were left for ever as a lesson and a trophy; and the coin of the tribute was marked with the image and superscription of Harun and his three sons.[78] Yet this plurality of lords might contribute to remove the dishonour of the Roman name. After the death of their father, the heirs of the caliph were involved in civil discord, and the conqueror, the liberal Almamon, was sufficiently engaged in the restoration of domestic peace and the introduction of foreign science.

The Arabs subdue the isle of Crete, A.D. 823.

Under the reign of Almamon at Bagdad, of Michael the Stammerer at Constantinople, the islands of Crete[79] and Sicily were subdued by the Arabs. The former of these conquests is disdained by their own writers, who were ignorant of the fame of Jupiter and Minos, but it has not been overlooked by the Byzantine historians, who now begin to cast a clearer light on the affairs of their own times.[80] A band of Andalusian volunteers, discontented with the climate or government of Spain, explored the adventures of the sea; but as they sailed in no more than ten or twenty gallies, their warfare must be branded with the name of piracy. As the subjects and sectaries of the

78. The wars of Harun al Rashid against the Roman empire, are related by Theophanes (p. 384, 385. 391. 396. 407, 408.), Zonaras (tom. ii. l. xv. p. 115. 124.), Cedrenus (p. 477, 478.), Eutychius (Annal. tom. ii. p. 407.), Elmacin (Hist. Saracen. p. 136. 151. 152.), Abulpharagius (Dynast. p. 147. 151.), and Abulfeda (p. 156. 166–168.).

79. The authors from whom I have learned the most of the ancient and modern state of Crete, are Belon (Observations, &c. c. 3–20. Paris, 1555), Tournefort (Voyage du Levant, tom. i. lettre ii. et iii.), and Meursius (CRETA, in his works, tom. iii. p. 343–544.). Although Crete is styled by Homer *Πιειρα*, by Dionysius *λιπαρη τε και ευβοτος*, I cannot conceive that mountainous island to surpass, or even to equal, in fertility the greater part of Spain.

80. The most authentic and circumstantial intelligence is obtained from the four books of the Continuation of Theophanes, compiled by the pen or the command of Constantine Porphyrogenitus, with the Life of his father Basil the Macedonian (Scriptores post Theophanem, p. 1–162. à Francisc. Combefis, Paris, 1685). The loss of Crete and Sicily is related, l. ii. p. 46–52. To these we may add the secondary evidence of Joseph Genesius (l. ii. p. 21. Venet. 1733), George Cedrenus (Compend. p. 506–508.), and John Scylitzes Curopalata (apud Baron. Annal. Eccles. A.D. 827. N° 24, &c.). But the modern Greeks are such notorious plagiaries, that I should only quote a plurality of names.

white party, they might lawfully invade the dominions of the *black* caliphs. A rebellious faction introduced them into Alexandria;[81] they cut in pieces both friends and foes, pillaged the churches and the moschs, sold above six thousand Christian captives, and maintained their station in the capital of Egypt, till they were oppressed by the forces and the presence of Almamon himself. From the mouth of the Nile to the Hellespont, the islands and sea-coasts both of the Greeks and Moslems were exposed to their depredations; they saw, they envied, they tasted, the fertility of Crete, and soon returned with forty gallies to a more serious attack. The Andalusians wandered over the land fearless and unmolested; but when they descended with their plunder to the sea-shore, their vessels were in flames, and their chief, Abu Caab, confessed himself the author of the mischief. Their clamours accused his madness or treachery. "Of what do you complain?" replied the crafty emir. "I have brought you to a land flowing with milk and honey. Here is your true country; repose from your toils, and forget the barren place of your nativity." "And our wives and children?" "Your beauteous captives will supply the place of your wives, and in their embraces you will soon become the fathers of a new progeny." The first habitation was their camp, with a ditch and rampart, in the bay of Suda; but an apostate monk led them to a more desirable position in the eastern parts; and the name of Candax, their fortress and colony, has been extended to the whole island, under the corrupt and modern appellation of *Candia*. The hundred cities of the age of Minos were diminished to thirty; and of these, only one, most probably Cydonia, had courage to retain the substance of freedom and the profession of Christianity. The Saracens of Crete soon repaired the loss of their navy; and the timbers of mount Ida were launched into the main. During an hostile period, of one hundred and thirty-eight years, the princes of Constantinople attacked these licentious corsairs with fruitless curses and ineffectual arms.

and of Sicily, A.D. 827–878.

The loss of Sicily[82] was occasioned by an act of superstitious rigour. An amorous youth who had stolen a nun from her cloyster, was sentenced by the emperor to the amputation of his tongue.

81. Renaudot (Hist. Patriarch. Alex. p. 251–256. 268–270.) has described the ravages of the Andalusian Arabs in Egypt, but has forgot to connect them with the conquest of Crete.

82. *Δηλοι* (says the continuator of Theophanes, l. ii. p. 51.) *δε ταυτα σαφεστατα και πλατικωτερον ἡ τοτε γραφεισα Θεογνωστῳ και εις χειρας ελθουσα ἡμων*. This history of the loss of Sicily is no longer extant. Muratori (Annali d'Italia, tom. vii. p. 7. 19. 21, &c.) has added some circumstances from the Italian chronicles.

Euphemius appealed to the reason and policy of the Saracens of Africa; and soon returned with the Imperial purple, a fleet of one hundred ships, and an army of seven hundred horse and ten thousand foot. They landed at Mazara near the ruins of the ancient Selinus; but after some partial victories, Syracuse[83] was delivered by the Greeks, the apostate was slain before her walls, and his African friends were reduced to the necessity of feeding on the flesh of their own horses. In their turn they were relieved by a powerful reinforcement of their brethren of Andalusia; the largest and western part of the island was gradually reduced, and the commodious harbour of Palermo was chosen for the seat of the naval and military power of the Saracens. Syracuse preserved about fifty years the faith which she had sworn to Christ and to Cæsar. In the last and fatal siege, her citizens displayed some remnant of the spirit which had formerly resisted the powers of Athens and Carthage. They stood above twenty days against the battering-rams and *catapultæ*, the mines and tortoises of the besiegers, and the place might have been relieved, if the mariners of the Imperial fleet had not been detained at Constantinople in building a church to the Virgin Mary. The deacon Theodosius, with the bishop and clergy, was dragged in chains from the altar to Palermo, cast into a subterraneous dungeon, and exposed to the hourly peril of death or apostacy. His pathetic, and not inelegant complaint, may be read as the epitaph of his country.[84] From the Roman conquest to this final calamity, Syracuse, now dwindled to the primitive isle of Ortygea, had insensibly declined. Yet the relics were still precious; the plate of the cathedral weighed five thousand pounds of silver; the entire spoil was computed at one million of pieces of gold (about four hundred thousand pounds sterling), and the captives must out-number the seventeen thousand Christians, who were transported from the sack of Tauromenium into African servitude. In Sicily, the religion and language of the Greeks were eradicated; and such was the docility of the rising generation, that fifteen thousand boys were circumcised and clothed on the same day with the son of the Fatimite caliph. The Arabian squadrons issued from the harbours of Palermo, Biserta, and Tunis; an hundred and fifty towns

83. The splendid and interesting tragedy of *Tancrede* would adapt itself much better to this epoch, than to the date (A.D. 1005) which Voltaire himself has chosen. But I must gently reproach the poet, for infusing into the Greek subjects the spirit of modern knights and ancient republicans.

84. The narrative or lamentation of Theodosius, is transcribed and illustrated by Pagi (Critica, tom. iii. p. 719, &c.). Constantine Porphyrogenitus (in Vit. Basil. c. 69, 70. p. 190–192.) mentions the loss of Syracuse and the triumph of the demons.

of Calabria and Campania were attacked and pillaged; nor could the suburbs of Rome be defended by the name of the Cæsars and apostles. Had the Mahometans been united, Italy must have fallen an easy and glorious accession to the empire of the prophet. But the caliphs of Bagdad had lost their authority in the West; the Aglabites and Fatimites usurped the provinces of Africa; their emirs of Sicily aspired to independence; and the design of conquest and dominion was degraded to a repetition of predatory inroads.[85]

Invasion of Rome by the Saracens, A.D. 846.

In the sufferings of prostrate Italy, the name of Rome awakens a solemn and mournful recollection. A fleet of Saracens from the African coast presumed to enter the mouth of the Tyber, and to approach a city which even yet, in her fallen state, was revered as the metropolis of the Christian world. The gates and ramparts were guarded by a trembling people; but the tombs and temples of St. Peter and St. Paul were left exposed in the suburbs of the Vatican and of the Ostian way. Their invisible sanctity had protected them against the Goths, the Vandals, and the Lombards; but the Arabs disdained both the gospel and the legend; and their rapacious spirit was approved and animated by the precepts of the Koran. The Christian *idols* were stripped of their costly offerings; a silver altar was torn away from the shrine of St. Peter; and if the bodies or the buildings were left entire, their deliverance must be imputed to the haste, rather than the scruples, of the Saracens. In their course along the Appian way, they pillaged Fundi and besieged Gayeta; but they had turned aside from the walls of Rome, and, by their divisions, the Capitol was saved from the yoke of the prophet of Mecca. The same danger still impended on the heads of the Roman people; and their domestic force was unequal to the assault of an African emir. They claimed the protection of their Latin sovereign; but the Carlovingian standard was overthrown by a detachment of the Barbarians: they meditated the restoration of the Greek emperors; but the attempt was treasonable, and the succour remote and precarious.[86] Their distress

85. The extracts from the Arabic histories of Sicily are given in Abulfeda (Annal. Moslem. p. 271–273.), and in the first volume of Muratori's Scriptores Rerum Italicarum. M. de Guignes (Hist. des Huns, tom. i. p. 363, 364.) has added some important facts.

86. One of the most eminent Romans (Gratianus, magister militum et Romani palatii superista) was accused of declaring, Quia Franci nihil nobis boni faciunt, neque adjutorium præbent, sed magis quæ nostra sunt violenter tollunt. Quare non advocamus Græcos, et cum eis fœdus pacis componentes, Francorum regem et gentem de nostro regno et dominatione expellimus? Anastasius in Leone IV. p. 199.

appeared to receive some aggravation from the death of their spiritual and temporal chief; but the pressing emergency superseded the forms and intrigues of an election; and the unanimous choice of pope Leo the fourth[87] was the safety of the church and city. This pontiff was born a Roman; the courage of the first ages of the republic glowed in his breast; and, amidst the ruins of his country, he stood erect, like one of the firm and lofty columns that rear their heads above the fragments of the Roman forum. The first days of his reign were consecrated to the purification and removal of relics, to prayers and processions, and to all the solemn offices of religion, which served at least to heal the imagination, and restore the hopes, of the multitude. The public defence had been long neglected, not from the presumption of peace, but from the distress and poverty of the times. As far as the scantiness of his means, and the shortness of his leisure would allow, the ancient walls were repaired by the command of Leo; fifteen towers, in the most accessible stations, were built or renewed; two of these commanded on either side the Tyber; and an iron chain was drawn across the stream to impede the ascent of an hostile navy. The Romans were assured of a short respite by the welcome news, that the siege of Gayeta had been raised, and that a part of the enemy, with their sacrilegious plunder, had perished in the waves.

Victory and reign of Leo IV. A.D. 849.

But the storm, which had been delayed, soon burst upon them with redoubled violence. The Aglabite,[88] who reigned in Africa, had inherited from his father a treasure and an army: a fleet of Arabs and Moors, after a short refreshment in the harbours of Sardinia, cast anchor before the mouth of the Tyber, sixteen miles from the city; and their discipline and numbers appeared to threaten, not a transient inroad, but a serious design of conquest and dominion. But the vigilance of Leo had formed an alliance with the vassals of the Greek empire, the free and maritime states of Gayeta, Naples, and Amalfi; and in the hour of danger, their gallies appeared in the port of Ostia under the command of Cæsarius the son of the Neapolitan duke, a noble and valiant youth, who had already vanquished the fleets of the Saracens. With his principal companions, Cæsarius was invited to the Lateran

87. Voltaire (Hist. Generale, tom. ii. c. 38. p. 124.) appears to be remarkably struck with the character of pope Leo IV. I have borrowed his general expression, but the sight of the forum has furnished me with a more distinct and lively image.

88. De Guignes, Hist. Generale des Huns, tom. i. p. 363, 364. Cardonne, Hist. de l'Afrique et de l'Espagne, sous la Domination des Arabes, tom. ii. p. 24, 25. I observe, and cannot reconcile, the difference of these writers in the succession of the Aglabites.

palace, and the dextrous pontiff affected to enquire their errand, and to accept with joy and surprise their providential succour. The city bands, in arms, attended their father to Ostia, where he reviewed and blessed his generous deliverers. They kissed his feet, received the communion with martial devotion, and listened to the prayer of Leo, that the same God who had supported St. Peter and St. Paul on the waves of the sea, would strengthen the hands of his champions against the adversaries of his holy name. After a similar prayer, and with equal resolution, the Moslems advanced to the attack of the Christian gallies, which preserved their advantageous station along the coast. The victory inclined to the side of the allies, when it was less gloriously decided in their favour by a sudden tempest, which confounded the skill and courage of the stoutest mariners. The Christians were sheltered in a friendly harbour, while the Africans were scattered and dashed in pieces among the rocks and islands of an hostile shore. Those who escaped from shipwreck and hunger, neither found nor deserved mercy at the hands of their implacable pursuers. The sword and the gibbet reduced the dangerous multitude of captives; and the remainder was more usefully employed, to restore the sacred edifices which they had attempted to subvert. The pontiff, at the head of the citizens and allies, paid his grateful devotion at the shrines of the apostles; and, among the spoils of this naval victory, thirteen Arabian bows of pure and massy silver were suspended round the altar of the fisherman of Galilee. The reign of Leo the fourth was employed in the defence and ornament of the Roman state. The churches were renewed and embellished: near four thousand pounds of silver were consecrated to repair the losses of St. Peter; and his sanctuary was decorated with a plate of gold of the weight of two hundred and sixteen pounds; embossed with the portraits of the pope and emperor, and encircled with a string of pearls. Yet this vain magnificence reflects less glory on the character of Leo, than the paternal care with which he rebuilt the walls of Horta and Ameria; and transported the wandering inhabitants of Centumcellæ to his new foundation of Leopolis, twelve miles from the sea-shore.[89] By his liberality, a colony of Corsicans, with their wives and children, was planted in the station of Porto at the mouth of the Tyber: the falling city was restored for their use, the fields and vineyards were divided among the new settlers: their first efforts were assisted by a gift of horses and cattle; and the hardy exiles, who breathed revenge against the Saracens,

89. Beretti (Chorographia Italiæ Medii Ævi, p. 106. 108.) has illustrated Centumcellæ, Leopolis, Civitas Leonina, and the other places of the Roman dutchy.

swore to live and die under the standard of St. Peter. The nations of the west and north who visited the threshold of the apostles had gradually formed the large and populous suburb of the Vatican, and their various habitations were distinguished in the language of the times, as the *schools* of the Greeks and Goths, of the Lombards and Saxons. But this venerable spot was still open to sacrilegious insult: the design of inclosing it with walls and towers exhausted all that authority could command, or charity would supply: and the pious labour of four years was animated in every season, and at every hour, by the presence of the indefatigable pontiff. The love of fame, a generous but worldly passion, may be detected in the name of the *Leonine city*, which he bestowed on the Vatican, yet the pride of the dedication was tempered with Christian pennance and humility. The boundary was trod by the bishop and his clergy, barefoot, in sackcloth, and ashes; the songs of triumph were modulated to psalms and litanies; the walls were besprinkled with holy water; and the ceremony was concluded with a prayer, that under the guardian care of the apostles and the angelic host, both the old and the new Rome might ever be preserved pure, prosperous, and impregnable.[90]

Foundation of the Leonine city, A.D. 852.

The Amorian war between Theophilus and Motassem, A.D. 838.

The emperor Theophilus, son of Michael the Stammerer, was one of the most active and high-spirited princes who reigned at Constantinople during the middle age. In offensive or defensive war, he marched in person five times against the Saracens, formidable in his attack, esteemed by the enemy in his losses and defeats. In the last of these expeditions he penetrated into Syria, and besieged the obscure town of Sozopetra; the casual birth-place of the caliph Motassem, whose father Harun was attended in peace or war by the most favoured of his wives and concubines. The revolt of a Persian impostor employed at that moment the arms of the Saracen, and he could only intercede in favour of a place for which he felt and acknowledged some degree of filial affection. These solicitations determined the emperor to wound his pride in so sensible a part. Sozopetra was levelled with the ground, the Syrian prisoners were marked or

90. The Arabs and the Greeks are alike silent concerning the invasion of Rome by the Africans. The Latin chronicles do not afford much instruction (see the Annals of Baronius and Pagi). Our authentic and contemporary guide for the popes of the ix[th] century, is Anastasius, librarian of the Roman church. His Life of Leo IV. contains twenty-four pages (p. 175–199. edit. Paris); and if a great part consists of superstitious trifles, we must blame or commend his hero, who was much oftener in a church than in a camp.

mutilated with ignominious cruelty, and a thousand female captives were forced away from the adjacent territory. Among these a matron of the house of Abbas invoked, in an agony of despair, the name of Motassem; and the insults of the Greeks engaged the honour of her kinsman to avenge his indignity, and to answer her appeal. Under the reign of the two elder brothers, the inheritance of the youngest had been confined to Anatolia, Armenia, Georgia, and Circassia; this frontier station had exercised his military talents; and among his accidental claims to the name of *Octonary*,[91] the most meritorious are the *eight* battles which he gained or fought against the enemies of the Koran. In this personal quarrel, the troops of Irak, Syria, and Egypt, were recruited from the tribes of Arabia and the Turkish hords: his cavalry might be numerous, though we should deduct some myriads from the hundred and thirty thousand horses of the royal stables; and the expence of the armament was computed at four millions sterling, or one hundred thousand pounds of gold. From Tarsus, the place of assembly, the Saracens advanced in three divisions along the high road of Constantinople: Motassem himself commanded the centre, and the vanguard was given to his son Abbas, who, in the trial of the first adventures, might succeed with the more glory, or fail with the least reproach. In the revenge of his injury, the caliph prepared to retaliate a similar affront. The father of Theophilus was a native of Amorium[92] in Phrygia: the original seat of the Imperial house had been adorned with privileges and monuments; and, whatever might be the indifference of the people, Constantinople itself was scarcely of more value in the eyes of the sovereign and his court. The name of AMORIUM was inscribed on the shields of the Saracens; and their three armies were again united under the walls of the devoted city. It had been proposed by the wisest counsellors, to evacuate Amorium, to remove the inhabitants, and to abandon the empty structures to the vain resentment of the Barbarians. The emperor embraced the more generous resolution of defending, in a siege and battle, the country of his ancestors. When the armies drew near, the front of the Mahometan line appeared to a

91. The same number was applied to the following circumstances in the life of Motassem: he was the *eighth* of the Abbassides; he reigned *eight* years, *eight* months, and *eight* days; left *eight* sons, *eight* daughters, *eight* thousand slaves, *eight* millions of gold.

92. Amorium is seldom mentioned by the old geographers, and totally forgotten in the Roman Itineraries. After the vi[th] century, it became an episcopal see, and at length the metropolis of the new Galatia (Carol. S[cto] Paulo, Geograph. Sacra, p. 234.). The city rose again from its ruins, if we should read *Ammuria*, not *Anguria*, in the text of the Nubian geographer (p. 236.).

Roman eye more closely planted with spears and javelins; but the event of the action was not glorious on either side to the national troops. The Arabs were broken, but it was by the swords of thirty thousand Persians, who had obtained service and settlement in the Byzantine empire. The Greeks were repulsed and vanquished, but it was by the arrows of the Turkish cavalry; and had not their bow-strings been damped and relaxed by the evening rain, very few of the Christians could have escaped with the emperor from the field of battle. They breathed at Dorylæum, at the distance of three days; and Theophilus, reviewing his trembling squadrons, forgave the common flight both of the prince and people. After this discovery of his weakness, he vainly hoped to deprecate the fate of Amorium: the inexorable caliph rejected with contempt his prayers and promises; and detained the Roman ambassadors to be the witnesses of his great revenge. They had nearly been the witnesses of his shame. The vigorous assaults of fifty-five days were encountered by a faithful governor, a veteran garrison, and a desperate people; and the Saracens must have raised the siege, if a domestic traitor had not pointed to the weakest part of the wall, a place which was decorated with the statues of a lion and a bull. The vow of Motassem was accomplished with unrelenting rigour: tired, rather than satiated, with destruction, he returned to his new palace of Samara, in the neighbourhood of Bagdad, while the *unfortunate*[93] Theophilus implored the tardy and doubtful aid of his Western rival the emperor of the Franks. Yet in the siege of Amorium above seventy thousand Moslems had perished: their loss had been revenged by the slaughter of thirty thousand Christians, and the sufferings of an equal number of captives, who were treated as the most atrocious criminals. Mutual necessity could sometimes extort the exchange or ransom of prisoners;[94] but in the national and religious conflict of the two empires, peace was without confidence, and war without mercy. Quarter was seldom given in the field; those who escaped the edge of the sword were condemned to hopeless servitude, or exquisite torture; and a Catholic emperor relates, with visible satisfaction, the execution of the Saracens of Crete, who were flayed alive, or plunged into chaldrons

93. In the East he was styled *Δυστυχης* (Continuator Theophan. l. iii. p. 84.); but such was the ignorance of the West, that his ambassadors, in public discourse, might boldly narrate, de victoriis, quas adversus exteras bellando gentes cœlitus fuerat assecutus. (Annalist Bertinian, apud Pagi, tom. iii. p. 720.).

94. Abulpharagius (Dynast. p. 167, 168.) relates one of these singular transactions on the bridge of the river Lamus in Cilicia, the limit of the two empires, and one day's journey westward of Tarsus (d'Anville, Geographie Ancienne, tom. ii. p. 91.). Four

of boiling oil.[95] To a point of honour Motassem had sacrificed a flourishing city, two hundred thousand lives, and the property of millions. The same caliph descended from his horse, and dirtied his robe to relieve the distress of a decrepit old man, who, with his laden ass, had tumbled into a ditch. On which of these actions did he reflect with the most pleasure, when he was summoned by the angel of death?[96]

Disorders of the Turkish guards, A.D. 841–870, &c.

With Motassem, the eighth of the Abbassides, the glory of his family and nation expired. When the Arabian conquerors had spread themselves over the East, and were mingled with the servile crowds of Persia, Syria, and Egypt, they insensibly lost the freeborn and martial virtues of the desert. The courage of the south is the artificial fruit of discipline and prejudice; the active power of enthusiasm had decayed, and the mercenary forces of the caliphs were recruited in those climates of the north, of which valour is the hardy and spontaneous production. Of the Turks[97] who dwelt beyond the Oxus and Jaxartes, the robust youths, either taken in war, or purchased in trade, were educated in the exercises of the field, and the profession of the Mahometan faith. The Turkish guards stood in arms round the throne of their benefactor, and their chiefs usurped the dominion of the palace and the provinces. Motassem, the first author of this dangerous example, introduced into the capital above fifty thousand Turks: their licentious conduct provoked the public indignation, and the quarrels of the soldiers and people induced the caliph to retire from Bagdad, and establish his own residence and the camp of his Barbarian favourites at

---

thousand four hundred and sixty Moslems, eight hundred women and children, one hundred confederates, were exchanged for an equal number of Greeks. They passed each other in the middle of the bridge, and when they reached their respective friends, they shouted *Allah Acbar*, and *Kyrie Eleison*. Many of the prisoners of Amorium were probably among them, but in the same year (A.H. 231.), the most illustrious of them, the forty-two martyrs, were beheaded by the caliph's order.

95. Constantin. Porphyrogenitus, in Vit. Basil. c. 61. p. 186. These Saracens were indeed treated with peculiar severity as pirates and renegadoes.

96. For Theophilus, Motassem, and the Amorian war, see the Continuator of Theophanes (l. iii. p. 77–84.), Genesius (l. iii. p. 24–34.), Cedrenus (p. 528–532.), Elmacin (Hist. Saracen. p. 180.), Abulpharagius (Dynast. p. 165, 166.), Abulfeda (Annal. Moslem, p. 191.), d'Herbelot (Bibliot. Orientale, p. 639–640.).

97. M. de Guignes, who sometimes leaps, and sometimes stumbles, in the gulph between Chinese and Mahometan story, thinks he can see, that these Turks are the *Hoei-ke*, alias the *Kao-tche*, or *high waggons*; that they were divided into fifteen hords, from China and Siberia to the dominions of the caliphs and Samanides, &c. (Hist. des Huns, tom. iii. p. 1–33. 124–131.).

Samara on the Tigris, about twelve leagues above the city of Peace.[98] His son Motawakkel was a jealous and cruel tyrant: odious to his subjects, he cast himself on the fidelity of the strangers, and these strangers, ambitious and apprehensive, were tempted by the rich promise of a revolution. At the instigation, or at least in the cause of his son, they burst into his apartment at the hour of supper, and the caliph was cut into seven pieces by the same swords which he had recently distributed among the guards of his life and throne. To this throne, yet streaming with a father's blood, Montasser was triumphantly led; but in a reign of six months, he found only the pangs of a guilty conscience. If he wept at the sight of an old tapestry which represented the crime and punishment of the son of Chosroes; if his days were abridged by grief and remorse, we may allow some pity to a parricide, who exclaimed in the bitterness of death, that he had lost both this world, and the world to come. After this act of treason, the ensigns of royalty, the garment and walking-staff of Mahomet, were given and torn away by the foreign mercenaries, who in four years created, deposed, and murdered three commanders of the faithful. As often as the Turks were inflamed by fear, or rage, or avarice, these caliphs were dragged by the feet, exposed naked to the scorching sun, beaten with iron clubs, and compelled to purchase, by the abdication of their dignity, a short reprieve of inevitable fate.[99] At length, however, the fury of the tempest was spent or diverted: the Abbassides returned to the less turbulent residence of Bagdad; the insolence of the Turks was curbed with a firmer and more skilful hand, and their numbers were divided and destroyed in foreign warfare. But the nations of the East had been taught to trample on the successors of the prophet; and the blessings of domestic peace were obtained by the relaxation of strength and discipline. So uniform are the mischiefs of military despotism, that I seem to repeat the story of the prætorians of Rome.[100]

98. He changed the old name of Sumere, or Samara, into the fanciful title of *Ser-mēn-raï*, that which gives pleasure at first sight (d'Herbelot, Bibliotheque Orientale, p. 808. d'Anville, l'Euphrate et le Tigre, p. 97, 98.).

99. Take a specimen, the death of the caliph Motaz, correptum pedibus pertrahunt, et sudibus probe permulcant, et spoliatum laceris vestibus in sole collocant, præ cujus, acerrimo æstû pedes alternis attollebat et demittebat. Adstantium aliquis misero colaphos continuo ingerebat, quos ille objectis manibus avertere studebat . . . Quo facto traditus tortori fuit totoque triduo cibo potuque prohibitus . . . Suffocatus, &c. (Abulfeda, p. 206.). Of the caliph Mohtadi, he says, cervices ipsi perpetuis ictibus contundebant, testiculosque pedibus conculcabant (p. 208.).

100. See under the reigns of Motassem, Motawakkel, Montasser, Mostain, Motaz,

Rise and progress of the Carmathians, A.D. 890–951.

While the flame of enthusiasm was damped by the business, the pleasure, and the knowledge, of the age, it burnt with concentrated heat in the breasts of the chosen few, the congenial spirits, who were ambitious of reigning either in this world or in the next. How carefully soever the book of prophecy had been sealed by the apostle of Mecca, the wishes, and (if we may profane the word) even the reason, of fanaticism, might believe that, after the successive missions of Adam, Noah, Abraham, Moses, Jesus, and Mahomet, the same God, in the fulness of time, would reveal a still more perfect and permanent law. In the two hundred and seventy-seventh year of the Hegira, and in the neighbourhood of Cufa, an Arabian preacher, of the name of Carmath, assumed the lofty and incomprehensible style of the Guide, the Director, the Demonstration, the Word, the Holy Ghost, the Camel, the Herald of the Messiah, who had conversed with him in a human shape, and the representative of Mohammed the son of Ali, of St. John the Baptist, and of the angel Gabriel. In his mystic volume, the precepts of the Koran were refined to a more spiritual sense; he relaxed the duties of ablution, fasting, and pilgrimage; allowed the indiscriminate use of wine and forbidden food; and nourished the fervour of his disciples by the daily repetition of fifty prayers. The idleness and ferment of the rustic crowd awakened the attention of the magistrates of Cufa; a timid persecution assisted the progress of the new sect; and the name of the prophet became more revered after his person had been withdrawn from the world. His twelve apostles dispersed themselves among the Bedoweens, "a race of men," says Abulfeda, "equally devoid of reason and of religion;" and the success of their preaching seemed to threaten Arabia with a new revolution. The Carmathians were ripe for rebellion, since they disclaimed the title of the house of Abbas, and abhorred the worldly pomp of the caliphs of Bagdad. They were susceptible of discipline, since they vowed a blind and absolute submission to their Imam, who was called to the prophetic office by the voice of God and the people. Instead of the legal tithes, he claimed the fifth of their substance and spoil; the most flagitious sins were no more than the type of disobedience; and the brethren were united and concealed by an oath of secresy. After a bloody conflict, they prevailed in the province of Bahrein, along the Persian Gulf: far and wide, the tribes of the desert were subject to the

Their military exploits, A.D. 900, &c.

Mohtadi, and Motamed, in the Bibliotheque of d'Herbelot, and the now familiar Annals of Elmacin, Abulpharagius, and Abulfeda.

sceptre, or rather to the sword, of Abu Said and his son Abu Taher; and these rebellious imams could muster in the field an hundred and seven thousand fanatics. The mercenaries of the caliph were dismayed at the approach of an enemy who neither asked nor accepted quarter; and the difference between them, in fortitude and patience, is expressive of the change which three centuries of prosperity had effected in the character of the Arabians. Such troops were discomfited in every action; the cities of Racca and Baalbec, of Cufa and Bassora, were taken and pillaged; Bagdad was filled with consternation; and the caliph trembled behind the veils of his palace. In a daring inroad beyond the Tigris, Abu Taher advanced to the gates of the capital with no more than five hundred horse. By the special order of Moctader, the bridges had been broken down, and the person or head of the rebel was expected every hour by the commander of the faithful. His lieutenant, from a motive of fear or pity, apprised Abu Taher of his danger, and recommended a speedy escape. "Your master," said the intrepid Carmathian to the messenger, "is at the head of thirty thousand soldiers: three such men as these are wanting in his host:" at the same instant, turning to three of his companions, he commanded the first to plunge a dagger into his breast, the second to leap into the Tigris, and the third to cast himself headlong down a precipice. They obeyed without a murmur. "Relate," continued the imam, "what you have seen: before the evening your general shall be chained among my dogs." Before the evening, the camp was surprised and the menace was executed. The rapine of the Carmathians was sanctified by their aversion to the worship of Mecca: they robbed a caravan of pilgrims, and twenty thousand devout Moslems were abandoned on the burning sands to a death of hunger and thirst. Another year they suffered the pilgrims to proceed without interruption; but, in the festival of devotion, Abu Taher stormed the holy city, and trampled on the most venerable relics of the Mahometan faith. Thirty thousand citizens and strangers were put to the sword; the sacred precincts were polluted by the burial of three thousand dead bodies; the well of Zemzem overflowed with blood; the golden spout was forced from its place; the veil of the Caaba was divided among these impious sectaries; and the black stone, the first monument of the nation, was borne away in triumph to their capital. After this deed of sacrilege and cruelty, they continued to infest the confines of Irak, Syria, and Egypt; but the vital principle of enthusiasm had withered at the root. Their scruples or their avarice again opened the pilgrimage of Mecca, and restored the black stone of the Caaba; and it is needless to enquire

They pillage Mecca, A.D. 929.

into what factions they were broken, or by whose swords they were finally extirpated. The sect of the Carmathians may be considered as the second visible cause of the decline and fall of the empire of the caliphs.[101]

Revolt of the provinces, A.D. 800–936.

The third and most obvious cause was the weight and magnitude of the empire itself. The caliph Almamon might proudly assert, that it was easier for him to rule the East and the West, than to manage a chess-board of two feet square;[102] yet I suspect, that in both those games, he was guilty of many fatal mistakes; and I perceive, that in the distant provinces, the authority of the first and most powerful of the Abbassides was already impaired. The analogy of despotism invests the representative with the full majesty of the prince; the division and balance of powers might relax the habits of obedience, might encourage the passive subject to enquire into the origin and administration of civil government. He who is born in the purple is seldom worthy to reign; but the elevation of a private man, of a peasant perhaps, or a slave, affords a strong presumption of his courage and capacity. The viceroy of a remote kingdom aspires to secure the property and inheritance of his precarious trust; the nations must rejoice in the presence of their sovereign; and the command of armies and treasures are at once the object and the instrument of his ambition. A change was scarcely visible as long as the lieutenants of the caliph were content with their vicarious title; while they solicited for themselves or their sons a renewal of the Imperial grant, and still maintained on the coin, and in the public prayers, the name and prerogative of the commander of the faithful. But in the long and hereditary exercise of power, they assumed the pride and attributes of royalty; the alternative of peace or war, of reward or punishment, depended solely on their will; and the revenues of their government were reserved for local services or private magnificence. Instead of a regular supply of men and money, the successors of the prophet were flattered with the ostentatious gift of an elephant, or a cast of hawks, a suit of silk hangings, or some pounds of musk and amber.[103]

101. For the sect of the Carmathians, consult Elmacin (Hist. Saracen. p. 219. 224. 229. 231. 238. 241. 243.), Abulpharagius (Dynast. p. 179–182.), Abulfeda (Annal. Moslem. p. 218, 219, &c. 245. 265. 274.), and d'Herbelot (Bibliotheque Orientale, p. 256–258. 635.). I find some inconsistencies of theology and chronology, which it would not be easy nor of much importance to reconcile.

102. Hyde, Syntagma Dissertat. tom. ii. p. 57. in Hist. Shahiludii.

103. The dynasties of the Arabian empire may be studied in the Annals of Elmacin, Abulpharagius, and Abulfeda, under the *proper* years, in the dictionary of

The independent dynasties. After the revolt of Spain, from the temporal and spiritual supremacy of the Abbassides, the first symptoms of disobedience broke forth in the province of Africa. Ibrahim, the son of Aglab, the lieutenant of the vigilant and rigid Harun, bequeathed to the dynasty of the *Aglabites* the inheritance of his name and power. *The Aglabites, A.D. 800–941.* The indolence or policy of the caliphs dissembled the injury and loss, and pursued only with poison the founder of the *Edrisites*,[104] who erected the kingdom and city of Fez on the shores of the western ocean.[105] *The Edrisites, A.D. 829–907.* In the East, the first dynasty was that of the *Taherites*;[106] the posterity of the valiant Taher, *The Taherites, A.D. 813–872.* who, in the civil wars of the sons of Harun, had served with too much zeal and success the cause of Almamon the younger brother. He was sent into honourable exile, to command on the banks of the Oxus; and the independence of his successors, who reigned in Chorasan till the fourth generation, was palliated by their modest and respectful demeanour, the happiness of their subjects, and the security of their frontier. They were supplanted by one of those adventurers so frequent in the annals of the East, who left his trade of a brazier (from whence the name of *Soffarides*) for the profession of a robber. *The Soffarides, A.D. 872–902.* In a nocturnal visit to the treasure of the prince of Sistan, Jacob, the son of Leith, stumbled over a lump of salt, which he unwarily tasted with his tongue. Salt, among the Orientals, is the symbol of hospitality, and the pious robber immediately retired without spoil or damage. The discovery of this honourable behaviour recommended Jacob to pardon and trust; he led an army at first for his benefactor, at last for himself, subdued

---

d'Herbelot, under the *proper* names. The tables of M. de Guignes (Hist. des Huns, tom. i.) exhibit a general chronology of the East, interspersed with some historical anecdotes; but his attachment to national blood has sometimes confounded the order of time and place.

104. The Aglabites and Edrisites are the professed subject of M. de Cardonne (Hist. de l'Afrique et de l'Espagne sous la Domination des Arabes, tom. ii. p. 1–63.).

105. To escape the reproach of error, I must criticise the inaccuracies of M. de Guignes (tom. i. p. 359.) concerning the Edrisites. 1. The dynasty and city of Fez could not be founded in the year of the Hegira 173, since the founder was a *posthumous* child of a descendant of Ali, who fled from Mecca in the year 168. 2. This founder, Edris the son of Edris, instead of living to the improbable age of 120 years, A.H. 313, died A.H. 214, in the prime of manhood. 3. The dynasty ended A.H. 307, twenty-three years sooner than it is fixed by the historian of the Huns. See the accurate Annals of Abulfeda, p. 158, 159. 185. 238.

106. The dynasties of the Taherites and Soffarides, with the rise of that of the Samanides, are described in the original history and Latin version of Mirchond: yet the most interesting facts had already been drained by the diligence of M. d'Herbelot.

Persia, and threatened the residence of the Abbassides. On his march towards Bagdad, the conqueror was arrested by a fever. He gave audience in bed to the ambassador of the caliph; and beside him on a table were exposed a naked scymetar, a crust of brown bread, and a bunch of onions. "If I die," said he, "your master is delivered from his fears. If I live, *this* must determine between us. If I am vanquished, I can return without reluctance to the homely fare of my youth." From the height where he stood, the descent would not have been so soft or harmless: a timely death secured his own repose and that of the caliph, who paid with the most lavish concessions the retreat of his brother Amrou to the palaces of Shiraz and Ispahan. The Abbassides were too feeble to contend, too proud to forgive; they invited the powerful dynasty of the *Samanides*, who passed the Oxus with ten thousand horse, so poor, that their stirrups were of wood; so brave, that they vanquished the Soffarian army, eight times more numerous than their own. The captive Amrou was sent in chains, a grateful offering to the court of Bagdad; and as the victor was content with the inheritance of Transoxiana and Chorasan, the realms of Persia returned for a while to the allegiance of the caliphs. The provinces of Syria and Egypt were twice dismembered by their Turkish slaves, of the race of *Toulun* and *Ikshid*.[107] These Barbarians, in religion and manners the countrymen of Mahomet, emerged from the bloody factions of the palace to a provincial command and an independent throne: their names became famous and formidable in their time; but the founders of these two potent dynasties confessed, either in words or actions, the vanity of ambition. The first on his death-bed implored the mercy of God to a sinner, ignorant of the limits of his own power: the second, in the midst of four hundred thousand soldiers and eight thousand slaves, concealed from every human eye the chamber where he attempted to sleep. Their sons were educated in the vices of kings; and both Egypt and Syria were recovered and possessed by the Abbassides during an interval of thirty years. In the decline of their empire, Mesopotamia, with the important cities of Mosul and Aleppo, was occupied by the Arabian princes of the tribe of *Hamadan*. The poets of their court could repeat without a blush, that nature had formed their countenances for beauty, their

The Samanides, A.D. 874–999.

The Toulonides, A.D. 868–905.

The Ikshidites, A.D. 934–968.

The Hamadanites, A.D. 892–1001.

107. M. de Guignes (Hist. des Huns, tom. iii. p. 124–154.) has exhausted the Toulonides and Ikshidites of Egypt, and thrown some light on the Carmathians and Hamadanites.

tongues for eloquence, and their hands for liberality and valour: but the genuine tale of the elevation and reign of the *Hamadanites*, exhibits a scene of treachery, murder, and parricide. At the same fatal period, the Persian kingdom was again usurped by the dynasty of the *Bowides*, by the sword of three brothers, who, under various names, were styled the support and columns of the state, and who, from the Caspian sea to the ocean, would suffer no tyrants but themselves. Under their reign, the language and genius of Persia revived, and the Arabs, three hundred and four years after the death of Mahomet, were deprived of the sceptre of the East.

The Bowides, A.D. 933–1055.

Fallen state of the caliphs of Bagdad, A.D. 936, &c.

Rahdi, the twentieth of the Abbassides, and the thirty-ninth of the successors of Mahomet, was the last who deserved the title of commander of the faithful:[108] the last (says Abulfeda) who spoke to the people, or conversed with the learned: the last who, in the expence of his household, represented the wealth and magnificence of the ancient caliphs. After him, the lords of the Eastern world were reduced to the most abject misery, and exposed to the blows and insults of a servile condition. The revolt of the provinces circumscribed their dominions within the walls of Bagdad; but that capital still contained an innumerable multitude, vain of their past fortune, discontented with their present state, and oppressed by the demands of a treasury which had formerly been replenished by the spoil and tribute of nations. Their idleness was exercised by faction and controversy. Under the mask of piety, the rigid followers of Hanbal[109] invaded the pleasures of domestic life, burst into the houses of plebeians and princes, spilt the wine, broke the instruments, beat the musicians, and dishonoured, with

108. Hic est ultimus chalifah qui multum atque sæpius pro concione perorarit . . . Fuit etiam ultimus qui otium cum eruditis et facetis hominibus fallere hilariterque agere soleret. Ultimus tandem chalifarum cui sumtus, stipendia, reditus, et thesauri, culinæ, cæteraque omnis aulica pompa priorum chalifarum ad instar comparata fuerint. Videbimus enim paullo post quam indignis et servilibus ludibriis exagitati, quam ad humilem fortunam ultimumque contemptum abjecti fuerint hi quondam potentissimi totius terratum Orientalium orbis domini. Abulfed. Annal. Moslem. p. 261. I have given this passage as the manner and tone of Abulfeda, but the cast of Latin eloquence belongs more properly to Reiske. The Arabian historian (p. 255. 257. 261–269. 283, &c.) has supplied me with the most interesting facts of this paragraph.

109. Their master, on a similar occasion, shewed himself of a more indulgent and tolerating spirit. Ahmed Ebn Hanbal, the head of one of the four orthodox sects, was born at Bagdad A.H. 164, and died there A.H. 241. He fought and suffered in the dispute concerning the creation of the Koran.

infamous suspicions, the associates of every handsome youth. In each profession, which allowed room for two persons, the one was a votary, the other an antagonist, of Ali; and the Abbassides were awakened by the clamorous grief of the sectaries, who denied their title and cursed their progenitors. A turbulent people could only be repressed by a military force; but who could satisfy the avarice or assert the discipline of the mercenaries themselves? The African and the Turkish guards drew their swords against each other, and the chief commanders, the emirs at Omra,[110] imprisoned or deposed their sovereigns, and violated the sanctuary of the mosch and haram. If the caliphs escaped to the camp or court of any neighbouring prince, their deliverance was a change of servitude, till they were prompted by despair to invite the Bowides, the sultans of Persia, who silenced the factions of Bagdad by their irresistible arms. The civil and military powers were assumed by Moezaldowlat, the second of the three brothers, and a stipend of sixty thousand pounds sterling was assigned by his generosity for the private expence of the commander of the faithful. But on the fortieth day, at the audience of the ambassadors of Chorasan, and in the presence of a trembling multitude, the caliph was dragged from his throne to a dungeon, by the command of the stranger, and the rude hands of his Dilemites. His palace was pillaged, his eyes were put out, and the mean ambition of the Abbassides aspired to the vacant station of danger and disgrace. In the school of adversity, the luxurious caliphs resumed the grave and abstemious virtues of the primitive times. Despoiled of their armour and silken robes, they fasted, they prayed, they studied the Koran and the tradition of the Sonnites; they performed, with zeal and knowledge, the functions of their ecclesiastical character. The respect of nations still waited on the successors of the apostle, the oracles of the law and conscience of the faithful; and the weakness or division of their tyrants sometimes restored the Abbassides to the sovereignty of Bagdad. But their misfortunes had been embittered by the triumph of the Fatimites, the real or spurious progeny of Ali. Arising from the extremity of Africa, these successful rivals extinguished, in Egypt and Syria, both the spiritual and temporal authority of the Abbassides; and the monarch of the Nile insulted the humble pontiff on the banks of the Tigris.

110. The office of vizir was superseded by the emir al Omra, Imperator Imperatorum, a title first instituted by Rahdi, and which merged at length in the Bowides and Seljukides: vectigalibus, et tributis et curiis per omnes regiones præfecit, jussitque in omnibus suggestis nominis ejus in concionibus mentionem fieri (Abulpharagius, Dynast. p. 199.). It is likewise mentioned by Elmacin (p. 254, 255.).

Enterprises of the Greeks, A.D. 960.

In the declining age of the caliphs, in the century which elapsed after the war of Theophilus and Motassem, the hostile transactions of the two nations were confined to some inroads by sea and land, the fruits of their close vicinity and indelible hatred. But when the Eastern world was convulsed and broken, the Greeks were roused from their lethargy by the hopes of conquest and revenge. The Byzantine empire, since the accession of the Basilian race, had reposed in peace and dignity; and they might encounter with their entire strength the front of some petty emir, whose rear was assaulted and threatened by his national foes of the Mahometan faith. The lofty titles of the morning star, and the death of the Saracens,[111] were applied in the public acclamations to Nicephorus Phocas, a prince as renowned in the camp as he was unpopular in the city. In the subordinate station of great domestic, or general of the East, he reduced the island of Crete, and extirpated the nest of pirates who had so long defied, with impunity, the majesty of the empire.[112] His military genius was displayed in the conduct and success of the enterprise, which had so often failed with loss and dishonour. The Saracens were confounded by the landing of his troops on safe and level bridges, which he cast from the vessels to the shore. Seven months were consumed in the siege of Candia; the despair of the native Cretans was stimulated by the frequent aid of their brethren of Africa and Spain; and, after the massy wall and double ditch had been stormed by the Greeks, an hopeless conflict was still maintained in the streets and houses of the city. The whole island was subdued in the capital, and a submissive people accepted, without resistance, the baptism of the conqueror.[113] Constantinople applauded

Reduction of Crete.

111. Liutprand, whose choleric temper was embittered by his uneasy situation, suggests the names of reproach and contempt more applicable to Nicephorus than the vain titles of the Greeks, Ecce venit stella matutina, surgit Eous, reverberat obtutû solis radios, pallida Saracenorum mors, Nicephorus μεδων.

112. Notwithstanding the insinuation of Zonaras, και ει μη, &c. (tom. ii. l. xvi. p. 197.), it is an undoubted fact, that Crete was completely and finally subdued by Nicephorus Phocas (Pagi, Critica, tom. iii. p. 873–875. Meursius, Creta, l. iii. c. 7. tom. iii. p. 464, 465.).

113. A Greek life of St. Nicon the Armenian was found in the Sforza library, and translated into Latin by the Jesuit Sirmond for the use of cardinal Baronius. This contemporary legend casts a ray of light on Crete and Peloponnesus in the xth century. He found the newly recovered island, fœdis detestandæ Agarenorum superstitionis vestigiis adhuc plenam ac refertam . . . but the victorious missionary, perhaps with some carnal aid, ad baptismum omnes veræque fidei disciplinam pepulit. Ecclesiis per totam insulam ædificatis, &c. (Annal. Eccles. A.D. 961.)

the long-forgotten pomp of a triumph; but the Imperial diadem was the sole reward that could repay the services, or satisfy the ambition, of Nicephorus.

The Eastern conquests of Nicephorus Phocas, and John Zimisces, A.D. 963–975.

After the death of the younger Romanus, the fourth in lineal descent of the Basilian race, his widow Theophania successively married Nicephorus Phocas and his assassin John Zimisces, the two heroes of the age. They reigned as the guardians and colleagues of her infant sons; and the twelve years of their military command form the most splendid period of the Byzantine annals. The subjects and confederates, whom they led to war, appeared, at least in the eyes of an enemy, two hundred thousand strong; and of these about thirty thousand were armed with cuirasses:[114] a train of four thousand mules attended their march; and their evening camp was regularly fortified with an enclosure of iron spikes. A series of bloody and undecisive combats is nothing more than an anticipation of what would have been effected in a few years by the course of nature; but I shall briefly prosecute the conquests of the two emperors from the hills of Cappadocia to the desert of Bagdad. The sieges of Mopsuestia and Tarsus in Cilicia first exercised the skill and perseverance of their troops, on whom, at this moment, I shall not hesitate to bestow the name of Romans. In the double city of Mopsuestia, which is divided by the river Sarus, two hundred thousand Moslems were predestined to death or slavery,[115] a surprising degree of population, which must at least include the inhabitants of the dependent districts. They were surrounded and taken by assault; but Tarsus was reduced by the slow progress of famine; and no sooner had the Saracens yielded on honourable terms than they were mortified by the distant and unprofitable view of the naval succours of Egypt. They were dismissed with a safe-conduct to the confines of Syria; a part of the old Christians had quietly lived under their dominion; and the vacant habitations were replenished by a new colony. But the mosch was converted into a stable;

Conquest of Cilicia.

114. Elmacin, Hist. Saracen. p. 278, 279. Liutprand was disposed to depreciate the Greek power, yet he owns that Nicephorus led against Assyria an army of eighty thousand men.

115. Ducenta fere millia hominum numerabat urbs (Abulfeda, Annal. Moslem. p. 231.) of Mopsuestia, or Masifa, Mampsysta, Mansista, Mamista, as it is corruptly, or perhaps more correctly, styled in the middle ages (Wesseling, Itinerar. p. 580.). Yet I cannot credit this extreme populousness a few years after the testimony of the emperor Leo, ου γαρ πολυπληθια στρατου τοις Κιλιξι βαρβαροις εστιν (Tactica, c. xviii. in Meursii Oper. tom. vi. p. 817.).

the pulpit was delivered to the flames; many rich crosses of gold and gems, the spoil of Asiatic churches, were made a grateful offering to the piety or avarice of the emperor; and he transported the gates of Mopsuestia and Tarsus, which were fixed in the wall of Constantinople, an eternal monument of his victory. After they had forced and secured the narrow passes of mount Amanus, the two Roman princes repeatedly carried their arms into the heart of Syria. Yet, instead of assaulting the walls of Antioch, the humanity or superstition of Nicephorus appeared to respect the ancient metropolis of the East: he contented himself with drawing round the city a line of circumvallation; left a stationary army; and instructed his lieutenant to expect, without impatience, the return of spring. But in the depth of winter, in a dark and rainy night, an adventurous subaltern, with three hundred soldiers, approached the rampart, applied his scaling-ladders, occupied two adjacent towers, stood firm against the pressure of multitudes, and bravely maintained his post till he was relieved by the tardy, though effectual, support of his reluctant chief. The first tumult of slaughter and rapine subsided; the reign of Cæsar and of Christ was restored; and the efforts of an hundred thousand Saracens, of the armies of Syria and the fleets of Afric, were consumed without effect before the walls of Antioch. The royal city of Aleppo was subject to Seifeddowlat, of the dynasty of Hamadan, who clouded his past glory by the precipitate retreat which abandoned his kingdom and capital to the Roman invaders. In his stately palace that stood without the walls of Aleppo, they joyfully seized a well-furnished magazine of arms, a stable of fourteen hundred mules, and three hundred bags of silver and gold. But the walls of the city withstood the strokes of their battering-rams; and the besiegers pitched their tents on the neighbouring mountain of Jaushan. Their retreat exasperated the quarrel of the townsmen and mercenaries; the guard of the gates and ramparts was deserted; and, while they furiously charged each other in the market-place, they were surprised and destroyed by the sword of a common enemy. The male sex was exterminated by the sword; ten thousand youths were led into captivity; the weight of the precious spoil exceeded the strength and number of the beasts of burthen; the superfluous remainder was burnt; and, after a licentious possession of ten days, the Romans marched away from the naked and bleeding city. In their Syrian inroads they commanded the husbandmen to cultivate their lands, that they themselves, in the ensuing season, might reap the benefit: more than an hundred cities were reduced to obedience; and eighteen pulpits of the principal moschs were committed to the flames to expiate

Invasion of Syria.

Recovery of Antioch.

the sacrilege of the disciples of Mahomet. The classic names of Hierapolis, Apamea, and Emesa, revive for a moment in the list of conquest: the emperor Zimisces encamped in the paradise of Damascus, and accepted the ransom of a submissive people; and the torrent was only stopped by the impregnable fortress of Tripoli, on the sea-coast of Phœnicia. Since the days of Heraclius, the Euphrates, below the passage of mount Taurus, had been impervious, and almost invisible, to the Greeks. The river yielded a free passage to the victorious Zimisces; and the historian may imitate the speed with which he overran the once famous cities of Samosata, Edessa, Martyropolis, Amida,[116] and Nisibis, the ancient limit of the empire in the neighbourhood of the Tigris. His ardour was quickened by the desire of grasping the virgin treasures of Ecbatana,[117] a well-known name, under which the Byzantine writer has concealed the capital of the Abbassides. The consternation of the fugitives had already diffused the terror of his name; but the fancied riches of Bagdad had already been dissipated by the avarice and prodigality of domestic tyrants. The prayers of the people, and the stern demands of the lieutenant of the Bowides, required the caliph to provide for the defence of the city. The helpless Mothi replied, that his arms, his revenues, and his provinces, had been torn from his hands, and that he was ready to abdicate a dignity which he was unable to support. The emir was inexorable; the furniture of the palace was sold; and the paltry price of forty thousand pieces of gold was instantly consumed in private luxury. But the apprehensions of Bagdad were relieved by the retreat of the Greeks: thirst and hunger guarded the desert of Mesopotamia; and the emperor, satiated with glory, and laden with Oriental spoils, returned to Constantinople, and displayed, in his triumph, the silk, the aromatics, and three hundred myriads of gold and silver. Yet the powers of the East

Passage of the Euphrates.

Danger of Bagdad.

116. The text of Leo the deacon, in the corrupt names of Emeta and Myctarsim, reveals the cities of Amida and Martyropolis (Miafarekin. See Abulfeda Geograph. p. 245. vers. Reiske). Of the former, Leo observes, urbs munita et illustris; of the latter, clara atque conspicua opibusque et pecore, reliquis ejus provinciis urbibus atque oppidis longe præstans.

117. Ut et Ecbatana pergeret Agarenorumque regiam everteret . . . aiunt enim urbium quæ usquam sunt ac toto orbe existunt felicissimam esse auroque ditissimam (Leo Diacon. apud Pagium, tom. iv. p. 34.). This splendid description suits only with Bagdad, and cannot possibly apply either to Hamadan, the true Ecbatana (d'Anville, Geog. Ancienne, tom. ii. p. 237.), or Tauris, which has been commonly mistaken for that city. The name of Ecbatana, in the same indefinite sense, is transferred by a more classic authority (Cicero pro Lege Maniliâ, c. 4.) to the royal seat of Mithridates king of Pontus.

had been bent, not broken, by this transient hurricane. After the departure of the Greeks, the fugitive princes returned to their capitals; the subjects disclaimed their involuntary oaths of allegiance; the Moslems again purified their temples, and overturned the idols of the saints and martyrs; the Nestorians and Jacobites preferred a Saracen to an orthodox master; and the numbers and spirit of the Melchites were inadequate to the support of the church and state. Of these extensive conquests, Antioch, with the cities of Cilicia and the isle of Cyprus, was alone restored, a permanent and useful accession to the Roman empire.[118]

118. See the Annals of Elmacin, Abulpharagius, and Abulfeda, from A.H. 351, to A.H. 361; and the reigns of Nicephorus Phocas and John Zimisces, in the Chronicles of Zonaras (tom. ii. l. xvi. p. 199– l. xvii. 215.) and Cedrenus (Compend. p. 649–684.). Their manifold defects are partly supplied by the MS. history of Leo the deacon, which Pagi obtained from the Benedictines, and has inserted almost entire, in a Latin version (Critica, tom. iii. p. 873. tom. iv. p. 37.).

CHAPTER LIII

State of the Eastern Empire in the Tenth Century. – Extent and Division. – Wealth and Revenue. – Palace of Constantinople. – Titles and Offices. – Pride and Power of the Emperors. – Tactics of the Greeks, Arabs, and Franks. – Loss of the Latin Tongue. – Studies and Solitude of the Greeks.

Memorials of the Greek empire.

A ray of historic light seems to beam from the darkness of the tenth century. We open with curiosity and respect the royal volumes of Constantine Porphyrogenitus,[1] which he composed at a mature age for the instruction of his son, and which promise to unfold the state of the Eastern empire, both in peace and war, both at home and abroad. In the first of these works he minutely describes the pompous ceremonies of the church and palace of Constantinople, according to his own practice and that of his predecessors.[2] In the second, he attempts an accurate survey of the provinces, the *themes*, as they were then denominated, both of Europe and Asia.[3] The system of Roman tactics, the discipline and order of the troops, and the military operations by land and sea, are explained in the third of these didactic collections, which may be ascribed to Constantine

Works of Constantine Porphyrogenitus.

1. The epithet of *Πορφυρογεννητος*, Porphyrogenitus, born in the purple, is elegantly defined by Claudian:

> Ardua privatos nescit fortuna Penates;
> Et regnum cum luce dedit. Cognata potestas
> Excepit Tyrio venerabile pignus in ostro.

And Ducange, in his Greek and Latin Glossaries, produces many passages expressive of the same idea.

2. A splendid MS. of Constantine, de Cæremoniis Aulæ et Ecclesiæ Byzantinæ, wandered from Constantinople to Buda, Frankfort and Leipsic, where it was published in a splendid edition by Leich and Reiske (A.D. 1751, in folio), with such lavish praise as editors never fail to bestow on the worthy or worthless object of their toil.

3. See, in the first volume of Banduri's Imperium Orientale, Constantinius de Thematibus, p. 1–24. de Administrando Imperio, p. 45–127. edit. Venet. The text of the old edition of Meursius is corrected from a MS. of the royal library of Paris, which Isaac Casaubon had formerly seen (Epist. ad Polybium, p. 10.), and the sense is illustrated by two maps of William Delisle, the prince of geographers, till the appearance of the greater d'Anville.

or his father Leo.[4] In the fourth, of the administration of the empire, he reveals the secrets of the Byzantine policy, in friendly or hostile intercourse with the nations of the earth. The literary labours of the age, the practical systems of law, agriculture, and history, might redound to the benefit of the subject and the honour of the Macedonian princes. The sixty books of the *Basilics*,[5] the code and pandects of civil jurisprudence, were gradually framed in the three first reigns of that prosperous dynasty. The art of agriculture had amused the leisure, and exercised the pens, of the best and wisest of the ancients; and their chosen precepts are comprised in the twenty books of the *Geoponics*[6] of Constantine. At his command, the historical examples of vice and virtue were methodised in fifty-three books,[7] and every citizen might apply, to his contemporaries or himself, the lesson or the warning of past times. From the august character of a legislator, the sovereign of the East descends to the more humble office of a teacher and a scribe: and if his successors and subjects were regardless of his paternal cares, *we* may inherit and enjoy the everlasting legacy.

Their imperfections.

A closer survey will indeed reduce the value of the gift, and the gratitude of posterity: in the possession of these Imperial treasures, we may still deplore our poverty and ignorance; and the fading glories of their authors will be obliterated by indifference or contempt.

4. The Tactics of Leo and Constantine are published with the aid of some new MSS. in the great edition of the works of Meursius, by the learned John Lami (tom. vi. p. 531–920. 1211–1417. Florent. 1745), yet the text is still corrupt and mutilated, the version is still obscure and faulty. The Imperial library of Vienna would afford some valuable materials to a new editor (Fabric. Bibliot. Græc. tom. vi. p. 369, 370.).

5. On the subject of the *Basilics*, Fabricius (Bibliot. Græc. tom. xii. p. 425–514.), and Heineccius (Hist. Juris Romani, p. 396–399.), and Giannone (Istoria civile di Napoli, tom. i. p. 450–458.), as historical civilians may be usefully consulted. XLI books of this Greek code have been published, with a Latin version, by Charles Annibal Fabrottus (Paris, 1647), in seven tomes in folio; IV other books have been since discovered, and are inserted in Gerard Meerman's Novus Thesaurus Juris Civ. et Canon. tom. v. Of the whole work, the sixty books, John Leunclavius has printed (Basil, 1575) an *eclogue*, or synopsis. The CXIII novels, or new laws, of Leo, may be found in the Corpus Juris Civilis.

6. I have used the last and best edition of the Geoponics (by Nicolas Niclas, Lipsiæ, 1781, 2 vols. in octavo). I read in the preface, that the same emperor restored the long-forgotten systems of rhetoric and philosophy: and his two books of *Hippiatrica*, or Horse-physic, were published at Paris, 1530, in folio (Fabric. Bibliot. Græc. tom. vi. p. 493–500.).

7. Of these LIII books, or titles, only two have been preserved and printed, de Legationibus (by Fulvius Ursinus, Antwerp, 1582, and Daniel Hæschelius, August. Vindel. 1603), and de Virtutibus et Vitiis (by Henry Valesius, or de Valois, Paris, 1634).

The Basilics will sink to a broken copy, a partial and mutilated version in the Greek language, of the laws of Justinian; but the sense of the old civilians is often superseded by the influence of bigotry: and the absolute prohibition of divorce, concubinage, and interest for money, enslaves the freedom of trade and the happiness of private life. In the historical book, a subject of Constantine might admire the inimitable virtues of Greece and Rome: he might learn to what a pitch of energy and elevation the human character had formerly aspired. But a contrary effect must have been produced by a new edition of the lives of the saints, which the great logothete or chancellor of the empire was directed to prepare: and the dark fund of superstition was enriched by the fabulous and florid legends of Simon the *Metaphrast*.[8] The merits and miracles of the whole calendar are of less account in the eyes of a sage than the toil of a single husbandman, who multiplies the gifts of the Creator and supplies the food of his brethren. Yet the royal authors of the *Geoponics* were more seriously employed in expounding the precepts of the destroying art, which has been taught since the days of Xenophon,[9] as the art of heroes and kings. But the *Tactics* of Leo and Constantine are mingled with the baser alloy of the age in which they lived. It was destitute of original genius; they implicitly transcribe the rules and maxims which had been confirmed by victories. It was unskilled in the propriety of style and method; they blindly confound the most distant and discordant institutions, the phalanx of Sparta and that of Macedon, the legions of Cato and Trajan, of Augustus and Theodosius. Even the use, or at least the importance, of these military rudiments may be fairly questioned: their general theory is dictated by reason; but the merit, as well as difficulty, consists in the application. The discipline of a soldier is formed by exercise rather than by study: the talents of a commander are appropriated to those calm though rapid minds, which nature produces to decide the fate of armies and nations: the former is the habit of a life, the latter the glance of a

8. The life and writings of Simeon Metaphrastes are described by Hankius (de Scriptoribus Byzant. p. 418–460.). This biographer of the saints indulged himself in a loose paraphrase of the sense or nonsense of more ancient acts. His Greek rhetoric is again paraphrased in the Latin version of Surius, and scarcely a thread can be now visible of the original texture.

9. According to the first book of the Cyropædia, professors of tactics, a small part of the science of war, were already instituted in Persia, by which Greece must be understood. A good edition of all the Scriptores Tactici would be a task not unworthy of a scholar. His industry might discover some new MSS. and his learning might illustrate the military history of the ancients. But this scholar should be likewise a soldier; and, alas! Quintus Icilius is no more.

moment; and the battles won by lessons of tactics may be numbered with the epic poems created from the rules of criticism. The book of ceremonies is a recital, tedious yet imperfect, of the despicable pageantry which had infected the church and state since the gradual decay of the purity of the one and the power of the other. A review of the themes or provinces might promise such authentic and useful information, as the curiosity of government only can obtain, instead of traditionary fables on the origin of the cities, and malicious epigrams on the vices of their inhabitants.[10] Such information the historian would have been pleased to record; nor should his silence be condemned if the most interesting objects, the population of the capital and provinces, the amount of the taxes and revenues, the numbers of subjects and strangers who served under the Imperial standard, have been unnoticed by Leo the philosopher, and his son Constantine. His treatise of the public administration is stained with the same blemishes; yet it is discriminated by peculiar merit: the antiquities of the nations may be doubtful or fabulous; but the geography and manners of the Barbaric world are delineated with curious accuracy. Of these nations, the Franks alone were qualified to observe in their turn, and to describe, the metropolis of the East. The ambassador of the great Otho, a bishop of Cremona, has painted the state of Constantinople about the middle of the tenth century: his style is glowing, his narrative lively, his observation keen; and even the prejudices and passions of Liutprand are stamped with an original character of freedom and genius.[11] From this scanty fund of foreign and domestic materials I shall investigate the form and substance of the Byzantine empire; the provinces and wealth, the civil government and military force, the character and literature, of the Greeks in a period of six hundred years, from the reign of Heraclius to the successful invasion of the Franks or Latins.

Embassy of Liutprand.

10. After observing that the demerit of the Cappadocians rose in proportion to their rank and riches, he inserts a more pointed epigram, which is ascribed to Demodocus:

> *Καππαδοκην ποτ' εχιδνα κακη δακεν,*
> *αλλα και αυτη*
> *Κατθανε, γευσαμενη ἁιματος ιοβολου.*

The sting is precisely the same with the French epigram against Freron: Un serpent mordit Jean Freron – Eh bien? Le serpent en mourut. But as the Paris wits are seldom read in the Anthology, I should be curious to learn through what channel it was conveyed for their imitation (Constantin. Porphyrogen. de Themat. c. ii. Brunk. Analect. Græc. tom. ii. p. 56. Brodæi Anthologia, l. ii. p. 244.).

11. The Legatio Liutprandi Episcopi Cremonensis ad Nicephorum Phocam, is inserted in Muratori, Scriptores Rerum Italicarum, tom. ii. pars i.

The themes, or provinces of the empire, and its limits in every age.

After the final division between the sons of Theodosius, the swarms of Barbarians from Scythia and Germany overspread the provinces and extinguished the empire of ancient Rome. The weakness of Constantinople was concealed by extent of dominion: her limits were inviolate, or at least entire; and the kingdom of Justinian was enlarged by the splendid acquisition of Africa and Italy. But the possession of these new conquests was transient and precarious; and almost a moiety of the Eastern empire was torn away by the arms of the Saracens. Syria and Egypt were oppressed by the Arabian caliphs; and, after the reduction of Africa, their lieutenants invaded and subdued the Roman province which had been changed into the Gothic monarchy of Spain. The islands of the Mediterranean were not inaccessible to their naval powers; and it was from their extreme stations, the harbours of Crete and the fortresses of Cilicia, that the faithful or rebel emirs insulted the majesty of the throne and capital. The remaining provinces under the obedience of the emperors, were cast into a new mould; and the jurisdiction of the presidents, the consulars, and the counts, was superseded by the institution of the *themes*,[12] or military governments, which prevailed under the successors of Heraclius, and are described by the pen of the royal author. Of the twenty-nine themes, twelve in Europe and seventeen in Asia, the origin is obscure, the etymology doubtful or capricious: the limits were arbitrary and fluctuating; but some particular names that sound the most strangely to our ear were derived from the character and attributes of the troops that were maintained at the expence, and for the guard, of the respective divisions. The vanity of the Greek princes most eagerly grasped the shadow of conquest and the memory of lost dominion. A new Mesopotamia was created on the western side of the Euphrates: the appellation and prætor of Sicily were transferred to a narrow slip of Calabria; and a fragment of the dutchy of Beneventum was promoted to the style and title of the theme of Lombardy. In the decline of the Arabian empire, the successors of Constantine might indulge their pride in more solid advantages. The victories of Nicephorus, John Zimisces, and Basil the second, revived the fame and enlarged the boundaries of the Roman name: the province of Cilicia, the metropolis of Antioch, the islands of Crete and Cyprus,

12. See Constantine de Thematibus, in Banduri, tom. i. p. 1–30. who owns, that the word is *ουκ παλαια*. *Θεμα* is used by Maurice (Stratagem. l. ii. c. 2.) for a legion, from whence the name was easily transferred to its post or province (Ducange, Gloss. Græc. tom. i. p. 487, 488.). Some etymologies are attempted for the Opsician, Optimatian, Thracesian, themes.

were restored to the allegiance of Christ and Cæsar: one third of Italy was annexed to the throne of Constantinople: the kingdom of Bulgaria was destroyed; and the last sovereigns of the Macedonian dynasty extended their sway from the sources of the Tigris to the neighbourhood of Rome. In the eleventh century, the prospect was again clouded by new enemies and new misfortunes: the relics of Italy were swept away by the Norman adventurers; and almost all the Asiatic branches were dissevered from the Roman trunk by the Turkish conquerors. After these losses, the emperors of the Comnenian family continued to reign from the Danube to Peloponesus, and from Belgrade to Nice, Trebizond, and the winding stream of the Meander. The spacious provinces of Thrace, Macedonia, and Greece, were obedient to their sceptre; the possession of Cyprus, Rhodes, and Crete, was accompanied by the fifty islands of the Ægean or Holy Sea;[13] and the remnant of their empire transcends the measure of the largest of the European kingdoms.

General wealth and populousness.

The same princes might assert, with dignity and truth, that of all the monarchs of Christendom they possessed the greatest city,[14] the most ample revenue, the most flourishing and populous state. With the decline and fall of the empire, the cities of the West had decayed and fallen; nor could the ruins of Rome, or the mud walls, wooden hovels, and narrow precincts, of Paris and London, prepare the Latin stranger to contemplate the situation and extent of Constantinople, her stately palaces and churches, and the arts and luxury of an innumerable people. Her treasures might attract, but her virgin strength had repelled, and still promised to repel, the audacious invasion of the Persian and Bulgarian, the Arab and the Russian. The provinces were less fortunate and impregnable; and few districts, few cities, could be discovered which had not been violated by some fierce Barbarian, impatient to despoil, because he was hopeless to possess. From the age of Justinian the Eastern

13. *Αγιος πελαγος*, as it is styled by the modern Greeks, from which the corrupt names of Archipelago, l'Archipel, and the Arches, have been transformed by geographers and seamen (d'Anville, Geographie Ancienne, tom. i. p. 281. Analyse de la Carte de la Grece, p. 60.). The numbers of monks or caloyers in all the islands and the adjacent mountain of Athos (Observations de Belon, fol. 32. verso), monte santo, might justify the epithet of holy, *αγιος*, a slight alteration from the original *αιγαιος*, imposed by the Dorians, who, in their dialect, gave the figurative name of *αιγες*, or goats, to the bounding waves (Vossius, apud Cellarium, Geograph. Antiq. tom. i. p. 829.).

14. According to the Jewish traveller who had visited Europe and Asia, Constantinople was equalled only by Bagdad, the great city of the Ismaelites (Voyage de Benjamin de Tudele, par Baratier, tom. i. c. 5. p. 46.).

empire was sinking below its former level: the powers of destruction were more active than those of improvement; and the calamities of war were embittered by the more permanent evils of civil and ecclesiastical tyranny. The captive who had escaped from the Barbarians was often stripped and imprisoned by the ministers of his sovereign: the Greek superstition relaxed the mind by prayer, and emaciated the body by fasting; and the multitude of convents and festivals diverted many hands and many days from the temporal service of mankind. Yet the subjects of the Byzantine empire were still the most dextrous and diligent of nations; their country was blessed by nature with every advantage of soil, climate, and situation; and, in the support and restoration of the arts, their patient and peaceful temper was more useful than the warlike spirit and feudal anarchy of Europe. The provinces that still adhered to the empire were repeopled and enriched by the misfortunes of those which were irrecoverably lost. From the yoke of the caliphs, the Catholics of Syria, Egypt, and Africa, retired to the allegiance of their prince, to the society of their brethren: the moveable wealth, which eludes the search of oppression, accompanied and alleviated their exile; and Constantinople received into her bosom the fugitive trade of Alexandria and Tyre. The chiefs of Armenia and Scythia, who fled from hostile or religious persecution, were hospitably entertained: their followers were encouraged to build new cities and to cultivate waste lands; and many spots, both in Europe and Asia, preserved the name, the manners, or at least the memory, of these national colonies. Even the tribes of Barbarians, who had seated themselves in arms on the territory of the empire, were gradually reclaimed to the laws of the church and state; and as long as they were separated from the Greeks, their posterity supplied a race of faithful and obedient soldiers. Did we possess sufficient materials to survey the twenty-nine themes of the Byzantine monarchy, our curiosity might be satisfied with a chosen example: it is fortunate enough that the clearest light should be thrown on the most interesting province, and the name of PELOPONESUS will awaken the attention of the classic reader.

State of Peloponesus: Sclavonians.

As early as the eighth century, in the troubled reign of the Iconoclasts, Greece, and even Peloponesus,[15] were overrun by some Sclavonian bands who outstripped the royal standard of

15. *Εσθλαβωθη δε πασα ἡ χωρα και γεγονε βαρβαρος*, says Constantine (Thematibus, l. ii. c. 6. p. 25.), in a style as barbarous as the idea, which he confirms, as usual, by a foolish epigram. The epitomizer of Strabo likewise observes, *και νυν δε πασαν Ηπειρον, και Ελλαδασχεδον και Μακεδονιαν, και Πελοπονησον Σκυθαι Σκλαβοι νεμονται* (l.vii. p. 98. edit. Hudson): a passage which leads Dodwell a

Bulgaria. The strangers of old, Cadmus, and Danaus, and Pelops, had planted in that fruitful soil, the seeds of policy and learning; but the savages of the north eradicated what yet remained of their sickly and withered roots. In this irruption, the country and the inhabitants were transformed; the Grecian blood was contaminated; and the proudest nobles of Peloponesus were branded with the names of foreigners and *slaves*. By the diligence of succeeding princes, the land was in some measure purified from the Barbarians; and the humble remnant was bound by an oath of obedience, tribute, and military service, which they often renewed and often violated. The siege of Patras was formed by a singular concurrence of the Sclavonians of Peloponesus and the Saracens of Africa. In their last distress, a pious fiction of the approach of the prætor of Corinth, revived the courage of the citizens. Their sally was bold and successful; the strangers embarked, the rebels submitted, and the glory of the day was ascribed to a phantom or a stranger, who fought in the foremost ranks under the character of St. Andrew the apostle. The shrine which contained his relics was decorated with the trophies of victory, and the captive race was for ever devoted to the service and vassalage of the Metropolitan church of Patras. By the revolt of two Sclavonian tribes in the neighbourhood of Helos and Lacedæmon, the peace of the peninsula was often disturbed. They sometimes insulted the weakness, and sometimes resisted the oppression, of the Byzantine government, till at length the approach of their hostile brethren extorted a golden bull to define the rights and obligations of the Ezzerites and Milengi, whose annual tribute was defined at twelve hundred pieces of gold. From these strangers the Imperial geographer has accurately distinguished a domestic and perhaps original race, who, in some degree, might derive their blood from the much injured Helots. The liberality of the Romans, and especially of Augustus, had enfranchised the maritime cities from the dominion of Sparta; and the continuance of the same benefit ennobled them with the title of *Eleuthero-* or free-Laconians.[16] In the time of Constantine Porphyrogenitus, they had acquired the name of *Mainotes*, under which they dishonour the claim of liberty by the inhuman pillage of all that is shipwrecked on their rocky shores. Their territory, barren of corn, but fruitful of olives, extended to

Freemen of Laconia.

weary dance (Geograph. Minor. tom. ii. dissert. vi. p. 170–191.), to enumerate the inroads of the Sclavi, and to fix the date (A.D. 980) of this petty geographer.

16. Strabon. Geograph. l. viii. p. 562. Pausanias, Græc. Descriptio, l. iii. c. 21. p. 264, 265. Plin. Hist. Natur. l. iv. c. 8.

the Cape of Malea: they accepted a chief or prince from the Byzantine prætor, and a light tribute of four hundred pieces of gold was the badge of their immunity rather than of their dependence. The freemen of Laconia assumed the character of Romans, and long adhered to the religion of the Greeks. By the zeal of the emperor Basil, they were baptized in the faith of Christ: but the altars of Venus and Neptune had been crowned by these rustic votaries five hundred years after they were proscribed in the Roman world. In the theme of Peloponnesus,[17] forty cities were still numbered, and the declining state of Sparta, Argos, and Corinth, may be suspended in the tenth century, at an equal distance, perhaps, between their antique splendour and their present desolation. The duty of military service either in person or by substitute, was imposed on the lands or benefices of the province: a sum of five pieces of gold was assessed on each of the substantial tenants; and the same capitation was shared among several heads of inferior value. On the proclamation of an Italian war, the Peloponesians excused themselves by a voluntary oblation of one hundred pounds of gold (four thousand pounds sterling), and a thousand horses with their arms and trappings. The churches and monasteries furnished their contingent; a sacrilegious profit was extorted from the sale of ecclesiastical honours, and the indigent bishop of Leucadia[18] was made responsible for a pension of one hundred pieces of gold.[19]

Cities and revenue of Peloponesus.

But the wealth of the province, and the trust of the revenue, were founded on the fair and plentiful produce of trade and manufactures: and some symptoms of liberal policy may be traced in a law which exempts from all personal taxes the mariners of Peloponesus, and the workmen in parchment and purple. This denomination may be fairly applied or extended to the manufactures of linen, woollen, and more especially of silk: the two former of which had flourished in Greece since the days of Homer; and the last was introduced perhaps as early as the reign of Justinian. These arts, which were exercised at Corinth, Thebes, and Argos, afforded food and occupation to a numerous people: the men, women, and children, were distributed according to their age

Manufactures, especially of silk,

17. Constantin. de Administrando Imperio. l. ii. c. 50, 51, 52.

18. The rock of Leucate, was the southern promontory of his island and diocese. Had he been the exclusive guardian of the Lover's Leap, so well known to the readers of Ovid (Epist. Sappho) and the Spectator, he might have been the richest prelate of the Greek church.

19. Leucatensis mihi juravit episcopus, quotannis ecclesiam suam debere Nicephoro aureos centum persolvere, similiter et ceteras plus minusve secundum vires suas (Liutprand in Legat. p. 489.).

and strength; and if many of these were domestic slaves, their masters, who directed the work and enjoyed the profit, were of a free and honourable condition. The gifts which a rich and generous matron of Peloponesus presented to the emperor Basil, her adopted son, were doubtless fabricated in the Grecian looms. Danielis bestowed a carpet of fine wool, of a pattern which imitated the spots of a peacock's tail, of a magnitude to overspread the floor of a new church, erected in the triple name of Christ, of Michael the archangel, and of the prophet Elijah. She gave six hundred pieces of silk and linen, of various use and denomination: the silk was painted with the Tyrian dye, and adorned by the labours of the needle; and the linen was so exquisitely fine, that an entire piece might be rolled in the hollow of a cane.[20] In his description of the Greek manufactures, an historian of Sicily discriminates their price, according to the weight and quality of the silk, the closeness of the texture, the beauty of the colours, and the taste and materials of the embroidery. A single, or even a double or treble thread was thought sufficient for ordinary sale; but the union of six threads composed a piece of stronger and more costly workmanship. Among the colours, he celebrates, with affectation of eloquence, the fiery blaze of the scarlet, and the softer lustre of the green. The embroidery was raised either in silk or gold: the more simple ornament of stripes or circles was surpassed by the nicer imitation of flowers: the vestments that were fabricated for the palace or the altar often glittered with precious stones; and the figures were delineated in strings of Oriental pearls.[21] Till the twelfth century, Greece alone, of all the countries of Christendom, was possessed of the insect who is taught by nature, and of the workmen who are instructed by art, to prepare this elegant luxury. But the secret had been stolen by the dexterity and diligence of the Arabs: the caliphs of the East and West scorned to borrow from the unbelievers their furniture and apparel; and two cities of Spain, Almeria and Lisbon, were famous for the manufacture, the use, and

20. See Constantine (in Vit. Basil, c. 74, 75, 76. p. 195. 197. in Script. post Theophanem) who allows himself to use many technical or barbarous words: barbarous, says he, *τῃ των πολλων αμαθιᾳ καλον γαρ επι τουτοις κοινολεκτειν*. Ducange labours on some; but he was not a weaver.

21. The manufactures of Palermo, as they are described by Hugo Falcandus (Hist. Sicula in proem. in Muratori Script. Rerum Italicarum, tom. v. p. 256.) is a copy of those of Greece. Without transcribing his declamatory sentences, which I have softened in the text, I shall observe, that in this passage, the strange word *exarentasmata* is very properly changed for *exanthemata* by Carisius, the first editor. Falcandus lived about the year 1190.

transported from Greece to Sicily.

perhaps the exportation, of silk. It was first introduced into Sicily by the Normans; and this emigration of trade distinguishes the victory of Roger from the uniform and fruitless hostilities of every age. After the sack of Corinth, Athens, and Thebes, his lieutenant embarked with a captive train of weavers and artificers of both sexes, a trophy glorious to their master, and disgraceful to the Greek emperor.[22] The king of Sicily was not insensible of the value of the present; and, in the restitution of the prisoners, he excepted only the male and female manufacturers of Thebes and Corinth, who labour, says the Byzantine historian, under a barbarous lord, like the old Eretrians in the service of Darius.[23] A stately edifice, in the palace of Palermo, was erected for the use of this industrious colony;[24] and the art was propagated by their children and disciples to satisfy the encreasing demand of the western world. The decay of the looms of Sicily may be ascribed to the troubles of the island, and the competition of the Italian cities. In the year thirteen hundred and fourteen, Lucca alone, among her sister republics, enjoyed the lucrative monopoly.[25] A domestic revolution dispersed the manufacturers to Florence, Bologna, Venice, Milan, and even the countries beyond the Alps; and thirteen years after this event, the statutes of Modena enjoin the planting of mulberry trees, and regulate the duties on raw silk.[26] The northern climates are less propitious to the education of the silk-worm; but the industry of France and England[27] is supplied and enriched by the productions of Italy and China.

22. Inde ad interiora Græciæ progressi Corinthum, Thebas, Athenas, antiquâ nobilitate celebres expugnant; et maxima ibidem prædâ direptâ, opifices etiam qui Sericos pannos texere solent, ob ignominiam Imperatoris illius, suique principis gloriam, captivos deducunt. Quos Rogerius, in Palermo Siciliæ metropoli collocans, artem texendi suos edocere præcepit; et exhinc prædicta ars illa, prius à Græcis tantum inter Christianos habita, Romanis patere cœpit ingeniis (Otho Frisingen. de Gestis. Frederici I. l. i. c. 33. in Muratori Script. Ital. tom. vi. p. 668.). This exception allows the bishop to celebrate Lisbon and Almeria in sericorum pannorum opificio prænobilissimæ (in Chron. apud Muratori, Annali d'Italia, tom. ix. p. 415.).

23. Nicetas in Manuel, l. ii. c. 8. p. 65. He describes these Greeks as skilled *ευητριους οθονας ὑφαινειν*, as *ιστῳ προσανοεχοντας των ἑξαμιτων και χρυσοπαστων στολων*.

24. Hugo Falcandus styles them nobiles officinas. The Arabs had not introduced silk, though they had planted canes and made sugar in the plain of Palermo.

25. See the Life of Castruccio Casticani, not by Machiavel, but by his more authentic biographer Nicholas Tegrimi. Muratori, who has inserted it in the xi^th^ volume of his Scriptores, quotes this curious passage in his Italian Antiquities (tom. i. dissert. xxv. p. 378.).

26. From the MS. statutes, as they are quoted by Muratori in his Italian Antiquities (tom. ii. dissert. xxx. p. 46–48.).

27. The broad silk manufacture was

Revenue of the Greek empire.

I must repeat the complaint that the vague and scanty memorials of the times will not afford any just estimate of the taxes, the revenue, and the resources, of the Greek empire. From every province of Europe and Asia, the rivulets of gold and silver discharged into the Imperial reservoir a copious and perennial stream. The separation of the branches from the trunk encreased the relative magnitude of Constantinople; and the maxims of despotism contracted the state to the capital, the capital to the palace, and the palace to the royal person. A Jewish traveller, who visited the East in the twelfth century, is lost in his admiration of the Byzantine riches. "It is here," says Benjamin of Tudela, "in the queen of cities, that the tributes of the Greek empire are annually deposited, and the lofty towers are filled with precious magazines of silk, purple, and gold. It is said, that Constantinople pays each day to her sovereign twenty thousand pieces of gold; which are levied on the shops, taverns, and markets, on the merchants of Persia and Egypt, of Russia and Hungary, of Italy and Spain, who frequent the capital by sea and land."[28] In all pecuniary matters, the authority of a Jew is doubtless respectable; but as the three hundred and sixty-five days would produce a yearly income exceeding seven millions sterling, I am tempted to retrench at least the numerous festivals of the Greek calendar. The mass of treasure that was saved by Theodora and Basil the second, will suggest a splendid, though indefinite, idea of their supplies and resources. The mother of Michael, before she retired to a cloister, attempted to check or expose the prodigality of her ungrateful son, by a free and faithful account of the wealth which he inherited; one hundred and nine thousand pounds of gold, and three hundred thousand of silver, the fruits of her own œconomy and that of her deceased husband.[29] The avarice of Basil is not less renowned than his valour and fortune: his victorious armies were paid and rewarded without breaking into the mass of two hundred thousand pounds of gold (about eight millions sterling), which he had buried in the subterraneous vaults of the palace.[30] Such accumu-

---

established in England in the year 1620 (Anderson's Chronological Deduction, vol. ii. p. 4.): but it is to the revocation of the edict of Nantes, that we owe the Spitalfields colony.

28. Voyage de Benjamin de Tudele, tom. i. c. 5. p. 44–52. The Hebrew text has been translated into French by that marvellous child Baratier, who has added a volume of crude learning. The errors and fictions of the Jewish rabbi, are not a sufficient ground to deny the reality of his travels.

29. See the continuator of Theophanes (l. iv. p. 107.), Cedrenus (p. 544.), and Zonaras (tom. ii. l. xvi. p. 157.).

30. Zonaras (tom. ii. l. xvii. p. 225.), instead of pounds, uses the more classic

lation of treasure is rejected by the theory and practice of modern policy; and we are more apt to compute the national riches by the use and abuse of the public credit. Yet the maxims of antiquity are still embraced by a monarch formidable to his enemies; by a republic respectable to her allies; and both have attained their respective ends, of military power, and domestic tranquillity.

Pomp and luxury of the emperors.

Whatever might be consumed for the present wants, or reserved for the future use, of the state, the first and most sacred demand was for the pomp and pleasure of the emperor; and his discretion only could define the measure of his private expence. The princes of Constantinople were far removed from the simplicity of nature; yet, with the revolving seasons, they were led by taste or fashion to withdraw to a purer air, from the smoke and tumult of the capital. They enjoyed, or affected to enjoy, the rustic festival of the vintage: their leisure was amused by the exercise of the chace and the calmer occupation of fishing, and, in the summer heats, they were shaded from the sun, and refreshed by the cooling breezes from the sea. The coasts and islands of Asia and Europe were covered with their magnificent villas: but, instead of the modest art which secretly strives to hide itself and to decorate the scenery of nature, the marble structure of their gardens served only to expose the riches of the lord, and the labours of the architect. The successive casualties of inheritance and forfeiture, had rendered the sovereign proprietor of many stately houses in the city and suburbs, of which twelve were appropriated to the ministers of state; but the great palace,[31] the centre of the Imperial residence, was fixed during eleven centuries to the same position, between the hippodrome, the cathedral of St. Sophia, and the gardens, which descended by many a terrace to the shores of the Propontis. The primitive edifice of the first Constantine was a copy or rival of ancient Rome; the gradual improvements of his successors aspired to emulate the wonders of the old world,[32]

The palace of Constantinople.

---

appellation of talents, which, in a literal sense and strict computation, would multiply sixty fold the treasure of Basil.

31. For a copious and minute description of the Imperial palace, see the Constantinop. Christiana (l. ii. c. 4. p. 113–123.) of Ducange, the Tillemont of the middle ages. Never has laborious Germany produced two antiquarians more laborious and accurate, than these two natives of lively France.

32. The Byzantine palace surpasses the Capitol, the palace of Pergamus, the Rufinian wood (φαιδρον αγαλμα), the temple of Adrian at Cyzicus, the pyramids, the Pharus, &c. according to an epigram (Antholog. Græc. l. iv. p. 488, 489. Brodæi, apud Wechel) ascribed to Julian, ex-præfect of Egypt. Seventy-one of his epigrams, some lively, are collected by Brunck (Analect. Græc. tom. ii. p. 493–510.); but this is wanting.

and in the tenth century, the Byzantine palace excited the admiration, at least of the Latins, by an unquestionable pre-eminence of strength, size, and magnificence.[33] But the toil and treasure of so many ages had produced a vast and irregular pile: each separate building was marked with the character of the times and of the founder; and the want of space might excuse the reigning monarch who demolished, perhaps with secret satisfaction, the works of his predecessors. The œconomy of the emperor Theophilus allowed a more free and ample scope for his domestic luxury and splendour. A favourite ambassador who had astonished the Abbassides themselves by his pride and liberality, presented on his return the model of a palace, which the caliph of Bagdad had recently constructed on the banks of the Tigris. The model was instantly copied and surpassed: the new buildings of Theophilus[34] were accompanied with gardens, and with five churches, one of which was conspicuous for size and beauty: it was crowned with three domes, the roof of gilt brass reposed on columns of Italian marble, and the walls were incrusted with marbles of various colours. In the face of the church, a semi-circular portico, of the figure and name of the Greek *sigma* was supported by fifteen columns of Phrygian marble, and the subterraneous vaults were of a similar construction. The square before the sigma was decorated with a fountain, and the margin of the bason was lined and encompassed with plates of silver. In the beginning of each season, the bason, instead of water, was replenished with the most exquisite fruits, which were abandoned to the populace for the entertainment of the prince. He enjoyed this tumultuous spectacle from a throne resplendent with gold and gems, which was raised by a marble stair-case to the height of a lofty terrace. Below the throne were seated the officers of his guards, the magistrates, the chiefs of the factions of the circus; the inferior steps were occupied by the people, and the place below was covered with troops of dancers, singers, and pantomimes. The square was surrounded by the hall of justice, the arsenal, and the various offices of business and pleasure; and the *purple* chamber was named from the annual distribution of robes of scarlet and purple by the hand of the empress herself. The long series of the apartments was adapted to the seasons, and decorated with marble and porphyry, with painting, sculpture, and mosaics, with a profusion of gold, silver, and

33. Constantinopolitanum Palatium non pulchritudine solum, verum etiam fortitudine, omnibus quas unquam videram munitionibus præstat (Liutprand, Hist. l. v. c. 9. p. 465.).

34. See the anonymous continuator of Theophanes (p. 59. 61. 86.), whom I have followed in the neat and concise abstract of Le Beau (Hist. du Bas-Empire, tom. xiv. p. 436. 438.).

precious stones. His fanciful magnificence employed the skill and patience of such artists as the times could afford: but the taste of Athens would have despised their frivolous and costly labours; a golden tree, with its leaves and branches, which sheltered a multitude of birds, warbling their artificial notes, and two lions of massy gold, and of the natural size, who looked and roared like their brethren of the forest. The successors of Theophilus, of the Basilian and Comnenian dynasties, were not less ambitious of leaving some memorial of their residence; and the portion of the palace most splendid and august, was dignified with the title of the golden *triclinium*.[35] With becoming modesty, the rich and noble Greeks aspired to imitate their sovereign, and when they passed through the streets on horseback, in their robes of silk and embroidery, they were mistaken by the children for kings.[36] A matron of Peloponesus,[37] who had cherished the infant fortunes of Basil the Macedonian, was excited by tenderness or vanity to visit the greatness of her adopted son. In a journey of five hundred miles from Patras to Constantinople, her age or indolence declined the fatigue of an horse or carriage: the soft litter or bed of Danielis was transported on the shoulders of ten robust slaves; and as they were relieved at easy distances, a band of three hundred was selected for the performance of this service. She was entertained in the Byzantine palace with filial reverence, and the honours of a queen; and whatever might be the origin of her wealth, her gifts were not unworthy of the regal dignity. I have already described the fine and curious manufactures of Peloponesus, of linen, silk, and woollen; but the most acceptable of her presents consisted in three hundred beautiful youths, of whom one hundred were eunuchs;[38] "for she was not ignorant," says the historian, "that the air of the palace is more

Furniture and attendants.

35. In aureo triclinio quæ præstantior est pars potentissimus (*the usurper Romanus*) degens cæteras partes (*filiis*) distribuerat (Liutprand. Hist. l. v. c. 9. p. 469.). For this lax signification of Triclinium (ædificium tria vel plura κλινη scilicet στεγε complectens), see Ducange (Gloss. Græc. et Observations sur Joinville, p. 240.) and Reiske (ad Constantinum de Ceremoniis, p. 7.).

36. In equis vecti (says Benjamin of Tudela) regum filiis videntur persimiles. I prefer the Latin version of Constantine l'Empereur (p. 46.), to the French of Baratier (tom. i. p. 49.).

37. See the account of her journey, munificence, and testament, in the Life of Basil, by his grandson Constantine (c. 74, 75, 76. p. 195–197.).

38. *Carsamatium* (καρξιμαδες, Ducange, Gloss.) Græci vocant, amputatis virilibus et virgâ, puerum eunuchum quos Verdunenses mercatores ob immensum lucrum facere solent et in Hispaniam ducere (Liutprand, l. vi. c. 3. p. 470.) – The last abomination of the abominable slave-trade! Yet I am surprised to find in the xth century, such active speculations of commerce in Lorraine.

congenial to such insects, than a shepherd's dairy to the flies of the summer." During her lifetime, she bestowed the greater part of her estates in Peloponesus, and her testament instituted Leo the son of Basil her universal heir. After the payment of the legacies, fourscore villas or farms were added to the Imperial domain; and three thousand slaves of Danielis were enfranchised by their new lord, and transplanted as a colony to the Italian coast. From this example of a private matron, we may estimate the wealth and magnificence of the emperors. Yet our enjoyments are confined by a narrow circle; and, whatsoever may be its value, the luxury of life is possessed with more innocence and safety by the master of his own, than by the steward of the public, fortune.

Honours and titles of the Imperial family.

In an absolute government, which levels the distinctions of noble and plebeian birth, the sovereign is the sole fountain of honour; and the rank, both in the palace and the empire, depends on the titles and offices which are bestowed and resumed by his arbitrary will. Above a thousand years, from Vespasian to Alexius Comnenus,[39] the *Cæsar* was the second person, or at least the second degree, after the supreme title of *Augustus* was more freely communicated to the sons and brothers of the reigning monarch. To elude without violating his promise to a powerful associate, the husband of his sister; and, without giving himself an equal, to reward the piety of his brother Isaac, the crafty Alexius interposed a new and supereminent dignity. The happy flexibility of the Greek tongue allowed him to compound the names of Augustus and emperor (Sebastos and Autocrator), and the union produced the sonorous title of *Sebastocrator.* He was exalted above the Cæsar on the first step of the throne: the public acclamations repeated his name; and he was only distinguished from the sovereign by some peculiar ornaments of the head and feet. The emperor alone could assume the purple or red buskins, and the close diadem or tiara, which imitated the fashion of the Persian kings.[40] It was an high pyramidal cap of cloth or silk, almost concealed by a profusion of pearls and jewels: the crown was formed by an horizontal circle and two arches of gold: at the summit, the point of their intersection was placed a globe or cross, and two strings

39. See the Alexiad (l. iii. p. 78, 79.) of Anna Comnena, who, except in filial piety, may be compared to Mademoiselle de Montpensier. In her awful reverence for titles and forms, she styles her father *Επιστημοναρχης*, the inventor of this royal art, the *τεχνη τεχνων*, and *επιστημη επι στημων*.

40. *Στεμμα, στεφανος, διαδημα*, see Reiske, ad Ceremoniale, p. 14, 15. Ducange has given a learned dissertation on the crowns of Constantinople, Rome, France, &c. (sur Joinville xxv. p. 289–303.): but of his thirty-four models, none exactly tally with Anne's description.

or lappets of pearl depended on either cheek. Instead of red, the buskins of the Sebastocrator and Cæsar were green; and on their *open* coronets or crowns, the precious gems were more sparingly distributed. Beside and below the Cæsar, the fancy of Alexius created the *Panhypersebastos* and the *Protosebastos*, whose sound and signification will satisfy a Grecian ear. They imply a superiority and a priority above the simple name of Augustus; and this sacred and primitive title of the Roman prince was degraded to the kinsmen and servants of the Byzantine court. The daughter of Alexius applauds, with fond complacency, this artful gradation of hopes and honours; but the science of words is accessible to the meanest capacity; and this vain dictionary was easily enriched by the pride of his successors. To their favourite sons or brothers, they imparted the more lofty appellation of Lord or *Despot*, which was illustrated with new ornaments and prerogatives, and placed immediately after the person of the emperor himself. The five titles of, 1. *Despot*; 2. *Sebastocrator*; 3. *Cæsar*; 4. *Panhypersebastos*; and, 5. *Protosebastos*; were usually confined to the princes of his blood: they were the emanations of his majesty; but as they exercised no regular functions, their existence was useless, and their authority precarious.

Offices of the palace, the state, and the army.

But in every monarchy the substantial powers of government must be divided and exercised by the ministers of the palace and treasury, the fleet and army. The titles alone can differ; and in the revolution of ages, the counts and præfects, the prætor and quæstor, insensibly descended, while their servants rose above their heads to the first honours of the state. 1. In a monarchy, which refers every object to the person of the prince, the care and ceremonies of the palace form the most respectable department. The *Curopalata*,[41] so illustrious in the age of Justinian, was supplanted by the *Protovestiare*, whose primitive functions were limited to the custody of the wardrobe. From thence his jurisdiction was extended over the numerous menials of pomp and luxury; and he presided with his silver wand at the public and private audience. 2. In the ancient system of Constantine, the name of *Logothete*, or accountant, was applied to the receivers of the finances: the

41.

Par exstans curis, solo diademate dispar
Ordine pro rerum vocitatus *Cura-Palati*;

says the African Corippus (de Laudibus Justini, l. i. 136.); and in the same century (the vi[th]), Cassiodorius represents him, who, virgâ aureâ decoratus, inter numerosa obsequia primus ante pedes incederet (Variar. vii. 5.). But this great officer, unknown, *ανεπιγνωστος*, exercising no function, *νυν δε ουδεμιαν*, was cast down by the modern Greeks to the xv[th] rank (Codin. c. 5. p. 65.).

principal officers were distinguished as the Logothetes of the domain, of the posts, the army, the private and public treasure; and the *great Logothete*, the supreme guardian of the laws and revenues, is compared with the chancellor of the Latin monarchies.[42] His discerning eye pervaded the civil administration; and he was assisted, in due subordination, by the eparch or præfect of the city, the first secretary, and the keepers of the privy seal, the archives, and the red or purple ink which was reserved for the sacred signature of the emperor alone.[43] The introductor and interpreter of foreign ambassadors were the great *Chiauss*[44] and the *Dragoman*,[45] two names of Turkish origin, and which are still familiar to the sublime Porte. 3. From the humble style and service of guards, the *Domestics* insensibly rose to the station of generals; the military themes of the East and West, the legions of Europe and Asia, were often divided, till the *great Domestic* was finally invested with the universal and absolute command of the land forces. The *Protostrator*, in his original functions, was the assistant of the emperor when he mounted on horseback: he gradually became the lieutenant of the great Domestic in the field; and his jurisdiction extended over the stables, the cavalry, and the royal train of hunting and hawking. The *Stratopedarch* was the great judge of the camp; the *Protospathaire* commanded the guards; the *Constable*,[46] the *great Æteriarch*, and the *Acolyth*, were the separate chiefs of the Franks, the Barbarians, and the Varangi, or English, the mercenary strangers, who, in the decay of the national spirit, formed the nerve of the Byzantine armies. 4. The naval powers were under the command of the *great Duke*; in his absence they obeyed the *great Drungaire* of the fleet; and, in *his*

42. Nicetas (in Manuel, l. vii. c. 1.) defines him *ως ἡ Λατινων φωνη Καγκελαριον, ως δ' Ελληνες ειποιεν Λογοθετην*. Yet the epithet of *μεγας* was added by the elder Andronicus (Ducange, tom. i. p. 822, 823.).

43. From Leo I. (A.D. 470) the Imperial ink, which is still visible on some original acts, was a mixture of vermillion and cinnabar, or purple. The emperor's guardians, who shared in this prerogative, always marked in green ink the indiction, and the month. See the Dictionaire Diplomatique (tom. i. p. 511–513.), a valuable abridgment.

44. The sultan sent a *Σιαους* to Alexius (Anna Comnena, l. vi. p. 170. Ducange ad loc.); and Pachymer often speaks of the *μεγας τζαους* (l. vii. c. 1. l. xii. c. 30. l. xiii. c. 22.). The Chiaoush basha is now at the head of 700 officers (Rycaut's Ottoman Empire, p. 349. octavo edition).

45. *Tagerman* is the Arabic name of an interpreter (d'Herbelot, p. 854, 855.), *πρωτος των ερμενευων ὁυς κοινως ονομαζουσι δραγομανους*, says Codinus (c. 5. N° 70. p. 67.). See Villehardouin (N° 96.), Busbequius (Epist. iv. p. 338.), and Ducange (Observations sur Villehardouin, and Gloss. Græc. et Latin.).

46. *Κονοσταυλος*, or *κοντοσταυλος*, a corruption from the Latin Comes stabuli, or the French Connêtable. In a military sense, it was used by the Greeks in the xi[th] century, at least as early as in France.

place, the *Emir*, or *admiral*, a name of Saracen extraction,[47] but which has been naturalized in all the modern languages of Europe. Of these officers, and of many more whom it would be useless to enumerate, the civil and military hierarchy was framed. Their honours and emoluments, their dress and titles, their mutual salutations and respective pre-eminence, were balanced with more exquisite labour, than would have fixed the constitution of a free people; and the code was almost perfect when this baseless fabric, the monument of pride and servitude, was for ever buried in the ruins of the empire.[48]

Adoration of the emperor.

The most lofty titles, and the most humble postures, which devotion has applied to the Supreme Being, have been prostituted by flattery and fear to creatures of the same nature with ourselves. The mode of *adoration*,[49] of falling prostrate on the ground, and kissing the feet of the emperor, was borrowed by Diocletian from Persian servitude; but it was continued and aggravated till the last age of the Greek monarchy. Excepting only on Sundays, when it was waved, from a motive of religious pride, this humiliating reverence was exacted from all who entered the royal presence, from the princes invested with the diadem and purple, and from the ambassadors who represented their independent sovereigns, the caliphs of Asia, Egypt, or Spain, the kings of France and Italy, and the Latin emperors of ancient Rome. In his transactions of business, Liutprand, bishop of Cremona,[50] asserted the free spirit of a Frank and the dignity of his master Otho. Yet his sincerity cannot disguise the abasement of his first audience. When he approached the throne, the birds of the golden tree began to warble their notes, which were accompanied by the roarings of the two lions of gold. With his two companions, Liutprand was compelled to bow and to fall prostrate; and thrice he touched the ground with his forehead. He

Reception of ambassadors.

47. It was directly borrowed from the Normans. In the xii[th] century, Giannone reckons the admiral of Sicily among the great officers.

48. This sketch of honours and offices is drawn from George Codinus Curopalata, who survived the taking of Constantinople by the Turks: his elaborate though trifling work (de Officiis Ecclesiæ et Aulæ C. P.) has been illustrated by the notes of Goar, and the three books of Gretser, a learned Jesuit.

49. The respectful salutation of carrying the hand to the mouth, *ad os*, is the root of the Latin word, *adoro adorare*. See our learned Selden (vol. iii. p. 143–145. 942.), in his Titles of Honour. It seems, from the 1st book of Herodotus, to be of Persian origin.

50. The two embassies of Liutprand to Constantinople, all that he saw or suffered in the Greek capital, are pleasantly described by himself (Hist. l. vi. c. 1–4. p. 469–471. Legatio ad Nicephorum Phocam, p. 479–489.).

arose, but in the short interval, the throne had been hoisted by an engine from the floor to the cieling, the Imperial figure appeared in new and more gorgeous apparel, and the interview was concluded in haughty and majestic silence. In this honest and curious narrative, the bishop of Cremona represents the ceremonies of the Byzantine court, which are still practised in the sublime Porte, and which were preserved in the last age by the dukes of Muscovy or Russia. After a long journey by the sea and land, from Venice to Constantinople, the ambassador halted at the golden gate, till he was conducted by the formal officers to the hospitable palace prepared for his reception; but this palace was a prison, and his jealous keepers prohibited all social intercourse either with strangers or natives. At his first audience, he offered the gifts of his master, slaves, and golden vases, and costly armour. The ostentatious payment of the officers and troops displayed before his eyes the riches of the empire: he was entertained at a royal banquet,[51] in which the ambassadors of the nations were marshalled by the esteem or contempt of the Greeks: from his own table, the emperor, as the most signal favour, sent the plates which he had tasted; and his favourites were dismissed with a robe of honour.[52] In the morning and evening of each day, his civil and military servants attended their duty in the palace; their labour was repaid by the sight, perhaps by the smile, of their lord; his commands were signified by a nod or a sign: but all earthly greatness *stood* silent and submissive in his presence. In his regular or extraordinary processions through the capital, he unveiled his person to the public view: the rites of policy were connected with those of religion, and his visits to the principal churches were regulated by the festivals of the Greek calendar. On the eve of these processions, the gracious or devout intention of the monarch was proclaimed by the heralds. The streets were cleared and purified; the pavement was strewed with flowers; the most precious furniture, the gold and silver plate, and silken hangings, were displayed from the windows and balconies, and a severe discipline restrained and silenced the tumult of the populace. The march was opened by the military officers at the head of their troops; they were followed in long

Procesions and acclamations.

51. Among the amusements of the feast, a boy balanced, on his forehead, a pike, or pole, twenty-four feet long, with a cross bar of two cubits a little below the top. Two boys, naked, though cinctured (*campestrati*) together, and singly, climbed, stood, played, descended, &c. ita me stupidum redidit: utrum mirabilius nescio (p. 470.). At another repast an homily of Chrysostom on the Acts of the Apostles was read elata voce non Latine (p. 483.).

52. *Gala* is not improbably derived from Cala, or Caloat, in Arabic, a robe of honour (Reiske, Not. in Ceremon. p. 84.).

order by the magistrates and ministers of the civil government: the person of the emperor was guarded by his eunuchs and domestics, and at the church-door, he was solemnly received by the patriarch and his clergy. The task of applause was not abandoned to the rude and spontaneous voices of the crowd. The most convenient stations were occupied by the bands of the blue and green factions of the circus; and their furious conflicts, which had shaken the capital, were insensibly sunk to an emulation of servitude. From either side they echoed in responsive melody the praises of the emperor; their poets and musicians directed the choir, and long life[53] and victory were the burthen of every song. The same acclamations were performed at the audience, the banquet, and the church; and as an evidence of boundless sway, they were repeated in the Latin,[54] Gothic, Persian, French, and even English language,[55] by the mercenaries who sustained the real or fictitious character of those nations. By the pen of Constantine Porphyrogenitus, this science of form and flattery has been reduced into a pompous and trifling volume,[56] which the vanity of succeeding times might enrich with an ample supplement. Yet the calmer reflection of a prince would surely suggest, that the same acclamations were applied to every character and every reign: and if he had risen from a private rank, he might remember, that his own voice had been the loudest and most eager in applause, at the very moment, when he envied the fortune, or conspired against the life, of his predecessor.[57]

Marriage of the Cæsars with foreign nations.

The princes of the North, of the nations, says Constantine, without faith or fame, were ambitious of mingling their blood with the blood of the Cæsars, by their marriage with a royal

53. *Πολυχρονιζειν* is explained by *ευφημιζειν* (Codin. c. 7. Ducange, Gloss. Græc. tom. i. p. 1199.).

54. *Κωνσερβετ Δεους ἡμπεριυμ βεστρουμ – βικτορ σις σεμπερ – βηβητε Δομινι Ημπερατορες ην μουλτος αννος* (Ceremon. c. 75. p. 215.). The want of the Latin V, obliged the Greeks to employ their *β*; nor do they regard quantity. Till he recollected the true language, these strange sentences might puzzle a professor.

55. *Βαραγγοι κατα την πατριαν γλωσσαν και ουτοι, ηγουν Ινκλινιστι πολυχρονιζουσι* (Codin. p. 90.). I wish he had preserved the words, however corrupt, of their English acclamation.

56. For all these ceremonies, see the professed work of Constantine Porphyrogenitus, with the notes, or rather dissertations, of his German editors, Leich and Reiske. For the rank of the *standing* courtiers, p. 80. not. 23. 62.; for the adoration, except on Sundays, p. 95. 240. not. 131.; the processions, p. 2, &c. not. p. 3, &c. the acclamations, passim. not. 25, &c.; the factions and Hippodrome, p. 177–214. not. 9. 93, &c.; the Gothic games, p. 221. not. 111.; vintage, p. 217. not. 109.: much more information is scattered over the work.

57. Et privato Othoni et nuper eadem dicenti nota adulatio (Tacit. Hist. i. 85.).

virgin, or by the nuptials of their daughters with a Roman prince.[58] The aged monarch, in his instructions to his son, reveals the secret maxims of policy and pride; and suggests the most decent reasons for refusing these insolent and unreasonable demands. Every animal, says the discreet emperor, is prompted by nature to seek a mate among the animals of his own species; and the human species is divided into various tribes, by the distinction of language, religion, and manners. A just regard to the purity of descent preserves the harmony of public and private life; but the mixture of foreign blood is the fruitful source of disorder and discord. Such had ever been the opinion and practice of the sage Romans: their jurisprudence proscribed the marriage of a citizen and a stranger: in the days of freedom and virtue, a senator would have scorned to match his daughter with a king: the glory of Mark Anthony was sullied by an Egyptian wife;[59] and the emperor Titus was compelled, by popular censure, to dismiss with reluctance the reluctant Berenice.[60] This perpetual interdict was ratified by the fabulous sanction of the great Constantine. The ambassadors of the nations, more especially of the unbelieving nations, were solemnly admonished, that such strange alliances had been condemned by the founder of the church and city.

Imaginary law of Constantine.

The irrevocable law was inscribed on the altar of St. Sophia; and the impious prince who should stain the majesty of the purple was excluded from the civil and ecclesiastical communion of the Romans. If the ambassadors were instructed by any false brethren in the Byzantine history, they might produce three memorable examples of the violation of this imaginary law: the marriage of Leo, or rather of his father Constantine the fourth, with the daughter of the king of the Chozars, the nuptials of the grand-daughter of Romanus with a Bulgarian prince, and the union of Bertha of France or Italy with young Romanus, the son of Constantine Porphyrogenitus himself. To these objections, three answers were prepared, which solved the difficulty and established

58. The xiii[th] chapter, de Administratione Imperii, may be explained and rectified by the Familiæ Byzantinæ of Ducange.

59. Sequiturque nefas Ægyptia conjunx (Virgil, Æneid viii. 688.). Yet this Egyptian wife was the daughter of a long line of kings. Quid te mutavit (says Antony in a private letter to Augustus) an quod reginam ineo? Uxor mea est (Sueton. in August. c. 69.). Yet I much question (for I cannot stay to enquire), whether the triumvir ever dared to celebrate his marriage either with Roman or Egyptian rites.

60. Berenicem invitus invitam dimisit (Suetonius in Tito, c. 7.). Have I observed elsewhere, that this Jewish beauty was at this time above fifty years of age? The judicious Racine has most discreetly suppressed both her age and her country.

The first exception, A.D. 733. the law. I. The deed and the guilt of Constantine Copronymus were acknowledged. The Isaurian heretic, who sullied the baptismal font, and declared war against the holy images, had indeed embraced a Barbarian wife. By this impious alliance, he accomplished the measure of his crimes, and was devoted to the just censure of the church and of posterity. *The second, A.D. 941.* II. Romanus could not be alleged as a legitimate emperor; he was a plebeian usurper, ignorant of the laws, and regardless of the honour, of the monarchy. His son Christopher, the father of the bride, was the third in rank in the college of princes, at once the subject and the accomplice of a rebellious parent. The Bulgarians were sincere and devout Christians; and the safety of the empire, with the redemption of many thousand captives, depended on this preposterous alliance. Yet no consideration could dispense from the law of Constantine; the clergy, the senate, and the people, disapproved the conduct of Romanus; and he was reproached, both in his life and death, as the author of the public disgrace. *The third, A.D. 943.* III. For the marriage of his own son with the daughter of Hugo king of Italy, a more honourable defence is contrived by the wise Porphyrogenitus. Constantine, the great and holy, esteemed the fidelity and valour of the Franks;[61] and his prophetic spirit beheld the vision of their future greatness. They alone were excepted from the general prohibition: Hugo king of France was the lineal descendant of Charlemagne;[62] and his daughter Bertha inherited the prerogatives of her family and nation. The voice of truth and malice insensibly betrayed the fraud or error of the Imperial court. The patrimonial estate of Hugo was reduced from the monarchy of France to the simple county of Arles; though it was not denied, that, in the confusion of the times, he had usurped the sovereignty of Provence, and invaded the kingdom of Italy. His father was a private noble; and if Bertha derived her female descent from the Carlovingian line, every step was polluted with illegitimacy or vice. The grandmother of Hugo was the famous Valdrada, the concubine, rather than the wife, of the second Lothair; whose adultery, divorce, and second nuptials, had provoked against him the thunders of the Vatican. His mother, as she was styled the great

61. Constantine was made to praise the *ευγενεια* and *περιφανεια* of the Franks, with whom he claimed a private and public alliance. The French writers (Isaac Casaubon in Dedicat. Polybii) are highly delighted with these compliments.

62. Constantine Porphyrogenitus (de Administrat. Imp. c. 26.) exhibits a pedigree and life of the illustrious king Hugo *περιβλεπτου ρηγος Ουγονως*. A more correct idea may be formed from the Criticism of Pagi, the Annals of Muratori, and the Abridgement of St. Marc, A.D. 925–946.

Bertha, was successively the wife of the count of Arles and of the marquis of Tuscany: France and Italy were scandalised by her gallantries; and, till the age of threescore, her lovers, of every degree, were the zealous servants of her ambition. The example of maternal incontinence was copied by the king of Italy; and the three favourite concubines of Hugo were decorated with the classic names of Venus, Juno, and Semele.[63] The daughter of Venus was granted to the solicitations of the Byzantine court: her name of Bertha was changed to that of Eudoxia; and she was wedded, or rather betrothed, to young Romanus, the future heir of the empire of the East. The consummation of this foreign alliance was suspended by the tender age of the two parties; and, at the end of five years, the union was dissolved by the death of the virgin spouse. The second wife of the emperor Romanus was a maiden of plebeian, but of Roman, birth; and their two daughters, Theophano and Anne, were given in marriage to the princes of the earth. The eldest was bestowed, as the pledge of peace,

Otho of Germany, A.D. 972.

on the eldest son of the great Otho, who had solicited this alliance with arms and embassies. It might legally be questioned how far a Saxon was entitled to the privilege of the French nation: but every scruple was silenced by the fame and piety of a hero who had restored the empire of the West. After the death of her father-in-law and husband, Theophano governed Rome, Italy, and Germany, during the minority of her son, the third Otho; and the Latins have praised the virtues of an empress, who sacrificed to a superior duty the remembrance of her country.[64] In the nuptials of her sister Anne, every prejudice was lost, and every consideration of dignity was superseded, by the stronger

Wolodomir of Russia, A.D. 988.

argument of necessity and fear. A Pagan of the north, Wolodomir, great prince of Russia, aspired to a daughter of the Roman purple; and his claim was enforced by the threats of war, the promise of conversion, and the offer of a powerful succour against a domestic rebel. A victim of her religion and country, the Grecian princess was torn from the palace of her fathers, and condemned to a savage reign and an hopeless exile on the banks of the Borysthenes, or in the

63. After the mention of the three goddesses, Liutprand very naturally adds, et quoniam non rex solus iis abutebatur, earum nati ex incertis patribus originem ducunt (Hist. l. iv. c. 6.): for the marriage of the younger Bertha, see Hist. l. v. c. 5.; for the incontinence of the elder, dulcis exercitio Hymenæi, l. ii. c. 15.; for the virtues and vices of Hugo, l. iii. c. 5. Yet it must not be forgot, that the bishop of Cremona was a lover of scandal.

64. Licet illa Imperatrix Græca sibi et aliis fuisset satis utilis et optima, &c. is the preamble of an inimical writer, apud Pagi, tom. iv. A.D. 989, N° 3. Her marriage and principal actions may be found in Muratori, Pagi, and St. Marc, under the proper years.

neighbourhood of the Polar circle.[65] Yet the marriage of Anne was fortunate and fruitful: the daughter of her grandson Jeroslaus was recommended by her Imperial descent; and the king of France, Henry I. sought a wife on the last borders of Europe and Christendom.[66]

Despotic power.

In the Byzantine palace, the emperor was the first slave of the ceremonies which he imposed, of the rigid forms which regulated each word and gesture, besieged him in the palace, and violated the leisure of his rural solitude. But the lives and fortunes of millions hung on his arbitrary will: and the firmest minds, superior to the allurements of pomp and luxury, may be seduced by the more active pleasure of commanding their equals. The legislative and executive power were centered in the person of the monarch, and the last remains of the authority of the senate, were finally eradicated by Leo the philosopher.[67] A lethargy of servitude had benumbed the minds of the Greeks; in the wildest tumults of rebellion they never aspired to the idea of a free constitution; and the private character of the prince was the only source and measure of their public happiness. Superstition rivetted their chains; in the church of St. Sophia, he was solemnly crowned by the patriarch; at the foot of the altar, they pledged their passive and unconditional obedience to his government and family. On his side he engaged to abstain as much as possible from the capital punishments of death and mutilation; his orthodox creed was subscribed with his own hand, and he promised to obey the decrees of the seven synods, and the canons of the holy church.[68] But the assurance of mercy was loose and

Coronation oath.

65. Cedrenus, tom. ii. p. 699. Zonaras, tom. ii. p. 221. Elmacin, Hist. Saracenica, l. iii. c. 6. Nestor apud Levesque, tom. ii. p. 112. Pagi, Critica, A.D. 987, N° 6. a singular concourse! Wolodomir and Anne are ranked among the saints of the Russian church. Yet we know his vices, and are ignorant of her virtues.

66. Henricus primus duxit uxorem Scythicam, Russam, filiam regis Jeroslai. An embassy of bishops was sent into Russia, and the father gratanter filiam cum multis donis misit. This event happened in the year 1051. See the passages of the original chronicles in Bouquet's Historians of France (tom. xi. p. 29. 159. 161. 319. 384. 481.). Voltaire might wonder at this alliance; but he should not have owned his ignorance of the country, religion, &c. of Jeroslaus – a name so conspicuous in the Russian annals.

67. A constitution of Leo the Philosopher (lxxviii.) ne senatusconsulta amplius fiant, speaks the language of naked despotism, εξ ὁυ το μοναρχον κρατος την τουτων ανηπται διοικησιν, και ακαιρον και ματαιον το αχρηστον μετα των χρειαν παρεχομενων συναπτεσθαι.

68. Codinus (de Officiis, c. xvii. p. 120, 121.) gives an idea of this oath so strong to the church πιστος και γνησιος δουλος και υιος της ἁγαις εκκλησιας, so weak to the people και απεχεσθαι φονων και ακρωτηριασμων και ὁμοιων τουτοις κατα το δυνατον.

indefinite: he swore, not to his people, but to an invisible judge, and except in the inexpiable guilt of heresy, the ministers of heaven were always prepared to preach the indefeasible right, and to absolve the venial transgressions, of their sovereign. The Greek ecclesiastics were themselves the subjects of the civil magistrate: at the nod of a tyrant, the bishops were created, or transferred, or deposed, or punished, with an ignominious death: whatever might be their wealth or influence, they could never succeed like the Latin clergy in the establishment of an independent republic; and the patriarch of Constantinople condemned, what he secretly envied, the temporal greatness of his Roman brother. Yet the exercise of boundless despotism is happily checked by the laws of nature and necessity. In proportion to his wisdom and virtue, the master of an empire is confined to the path of his sacred and laborious duty. In proportion to his vice and folly, he drops the sceptre too weighty for his hands; and the motions of the royal image are ruled by the imperceptible thread of some minister or favourite, who undertakes for his private interest to exercise the task of the public oppression. In some fatal moment, the most absolute monarch may dread the reason or the caprice of a nation of slaves; and experience has proved, that whatever is gained in the extent, is lost in the safety and solidity, of regal power.

Military force of the Greeks, the Saracens, and the Franks.

Whatever titles a despot may assume, whatever claims he may assert, it is on the sword that he must ultimately depend to guard him against his foreign and domestic enemies. From the age of Charlemagne to that of the Crusades, the world (for I overlook the remote monarchy of China) was occupied and disputed by the three great empires or nations of the Greeks, the Saracens, and the Franks. Their military strength may be ascertained by a comparison of their courage, their arts and riches, and their obedience to a supreme head, who might call into action all the energies of the state. The Greeks, far inferior to their rivals in the first, were superior to the Franks, and at least equal to the Saracens, in the second and third of these warlike qualifications.

Navy of the Greeks.

The wealth of the Greeks enabled them to purchase the service of the poorer nations, and to maintain a naval power for the protection of their coasts and the annoyance of their enemies.[69] A commerce of mutual benefit exchanged the gold of Constantinople for

69. If we listen to the threats of Nicephorus, to the ambassador of Otho, Nec est in mari domino tuo classium numerus. Navigantium fortitudo mihi soli inest, qui

the blood of the Sclavonians and Turks, the Bulgarians and Russians: their valour contributed to the victories of Nicephorus and Zimisces; and if an hostile people pressed too closely on the frontier, they were recalled to the defence of their country, and the desire of peace, by the well-managed attack of a more distant tribe.[70] The command of the Mediterranean, from the mouth of the Tanais to the columns of Hercules, was always claimed, and often possessed, by the successors of Constantine. Their capital was filled with naval stores and dextrous artificers: the situation of Greece and Asia, the long coasts, deep gulfs, and numerous islands, accustomed their subjects to the exercise of navigation; and the trade of Venice and Amalfi supplied a nursery of seamen to the Imperial fleet.[71] Since the time of the Peloponesian and Punic wars, the sphere of action had not been enlarged; and the science of naval architecture appears to have declined. The art of constructing those stupendous machines which displayed three, or six, or ten, ranges of oars, rising above, or falling behind, each other, was unknown to the ship-builders of Constantinople, as well as to the mechanicians of modern days.[72] The *Dromones*,[73] or light gallies of the Byzantine empire, were content with two tire of oars; each tire was composed of five and twenty benches; and two rowers were seated on each bench, who plyed their oars on either side of the vessel. To these we must add the captain or centurion, who, in time of action, stood erect with his armour-bearer on the poop, two steersmen at the helm, and two officers at the prow, the one to manage

---

eum classibus aggrediar, bello maritimas ejus civitates demoliar; et quæ fluminibus sunt vicina redigam in favillam. (Liutprand in Legat. ad Nicephorum Phocam, in Muratori Scriptores rerum Italicarum, tom. ii. pars i. p. 481.). He observes in another place, qui cæteris præstant Venetici sunt et Amalphitani.

70. Nec ipsa capiet eum (the emperor Otho) in quâ ortus est pauper et pellicea Saxonia: pecuniâ quâ pollemus omnes nationes super eum invitabimus; et quasi Keramicum confringemus (Liutprand in Legat. p. 487.). The two books, de administrando Imperio, perpetually inculcate the same policy.

71. The xix[th] chapter of the Tactics of Leo (Meurs. Opera, tom. vi. p. 825–848.), which is given more correct from a manuscript of Gudius, by the laborious Fabricius (Bibliot. Græc. tom. vi. p. 372–379.), relates to the *Naumachia* or naval war.

72. Even of fifteen and sixteen rows of oars, in the navy of Demetrius Poliorcetes. These were for real use: the forty rows of Ptolemy Philadelphus were applied to a floating palace, whose tonnage, according to Dr. Arbuthnot (Tables of ancient Coins, &c. p. 231–236.), is compared as $4\frac{1}{2}$ to one, with an English 100 gun ship.

73. The Dromones of Leo, &c. are so clearly described with two tire of oars, that I must censure the version of Meursius and Fabricius, who pervert the sense by a blind attachment to the classic appellation of *Triremes*. The Byzantine historians are sometimes guilty of the same inaccuracy.

the anchor, the other to point and play against the enemy the tube of liquid fire. The whole crew, as in the infancy of the art, performed the double service of mariners and soldiers; they were provided with defensive and offensive arms, with bows and arrows, which they used from the upper deck, with long pikes, which they pushed through the port holes of the lower tire. Sometimes indeed the ships of war were of a larger and more solid construction; and the labours of combat and navigation were more regularly divided between seventy soldiers and two hundred and thirty mariners. But for the most part they were of the light and manageable size; and as the cape of Malea in Peloponesus was still clothed with its ancient terrors, an Imperial fleet was transported five miles over land across the Isthmus of Corinth.[74] The principles of maritime tactics had not undergone any change since the time of Thucydides: a squadron of gallies still advanced in a crescent, charged to the front, and strove to impel their sharp beaks against the feeble sides of their antagonists. A machine for casting stones and darts was built of strong timbers in the midst of the deck; and the operation of boarding was effected by a crane that hoisted baskets of armed men. The language of signals, so clear and copious in the naval grammar of the moderns, was imperfectly expressed by the various positions and colours of a commanding flag. In the darkness of the night the same orders to chace, to attack, to halt, to retreat, to break, to form, were conveyed by the lights of the leading galley. By land, the fire signals were repeated from one mountain to another; a chain of eight stations commanded a space of five hundred miles; and Constantinople in a few hours was apprized of the hostile motions of the Saracens of Tarsus.[75] Some estimate may be formed of the power of the Greek emperors, by the curious and minute detail of the armament which was prepared for the reduction of Crete. A fleet of one hundred and twelve gallies, and seventy-five vessels of the Pamphylian style, was equipped in the capital, the islands of the Ægæan sea, and the

74. Constantin. Porphyrogen. in Vit. Basil. c. lxi. p. 185. He calmly praises the stratagem as a *βουλην συνετην και σοφην*; but the sailing round Peloponesus is described by his terrified fancy as a circumnavigation of a thousand miles.

75. The continuator of Theophanes (l. iv. p. 122, 123.) names the successive stations, the castle of Lulum near Tarsus, mount Argæus, Isamus, Ægilus, the hill of Mamas, Cyrisus, Mocilus, the hill of Auxentius, the sun-dial of the Pharus of the great palace. He affirms, that the news were transmitted *εν ακαρει* in an indivisible moment of time. Miserable amplification, which, by saying too much, says nothing. How much more forcible and instructive would have been the definition of three, or six, or twelve hours.

sea-ports of Asia, Macedonia, and Greece. It carried thirty-four thousand mariners, seven thousand three hundred and forty soldiers, seven hundred Russians, and five thousand and eighty-seven Mardaites, whose fathers had been transplanted from the mountains of Libanus. Their pay, most probably of a month, was computed at thirty-four centenaries of gold, about one hundred and thirty-six thousand pounds sterling. Our fancy is bewildered by the endless recapitulation of arms and engines, of clothes and linen, of bread for the men and forage for the horses, and of stores and utensils of every description, inadequate to the conquest of a petty island, but amply sufficient for the establishment of a flourishing colony.[76]

Tactics and character of the Greeks.

The invention of the Greek fire did not, like that of gun-powder, produce a total revolution in the art of war. To these liquid combustibles, the city and empire of Constantine owed their deliverance; and they were employed in sieges and sea-fights with terrible effect. But they were either less improved, or less susceptible of improvement: the engines of antiquity, the catapultæ, balistæ, and battering-rams, were still of most frequent and powerful use in the attack and defence of fortifications; nor was the decision of battles reduced to the quick and heavy *fire* of a line of infantry, whom it were fruitless to protect with armour against a similar fire of their enemies. Steel and iron were still the common instruments of destruction and safety; and the helmets, cuirasses, and shields, of the tenth century did not, either in form or substance, essentially differ from those which had covered the companions of Alexander or Achilles.[77] But instead of accustoming the modern Greeks, like the legionaries of old, to the constant and easy use of this salutary weight; their armour was laid aside in light chariots, which followed the march, till, on the approach of an enemy, they resumed with haste and reluctance the unusual incumbrance. Their offensive weapons consisted of swords, battle-axes, and spears; but the Macedonian pike was shortened a fourth of its length, and reduced to the more convenient measure of twelve cubits or feet. The sharpness of the Scythian

76. See the Ceremoniale of Constantine Porphyrogenitus, l. ii. c. 44. p. 176–192. A critical reader will discern some inconsistencies in different parts of this account; but they are not more obscure or more stubborn than the establishment and effectives, the present and fit for duty, the rank and file and the private, of a modern return, which retain in proper hands the knowledge of these profitable mysteries.

77. See the fifth, sixth, and seventh chapters, *περι οπλων*, *περι οπλισεως*, and *περι γυμνασιας* in the Tactics of Leo, with the corresponding passages in those of Constantine.

and Arabian arrows had been severely felt; and the emperors lament the decay of archery as a cause of the public misfortunes, and recommend, as an advice, and a command, that the military youth, till the age of forty, should assiduously practise the exercise of the bow.[78] The *bands*, or regiments, were usually three hundred strong; and, as a medium between the extremes of four and sixteen, the foot soldiers of Leo and Constantine were formed eight, deep; but the cavalry charged in four ranks from the reasonable consideration, that the weight of the front could not be encreased by any pressure of the hindmost horses. If the ranks of the infantry or cavalry were sometimes doubled, this cautious array betrayed a secret distrust of the courage of the troops, whose numbers might swell the appearance of the line, but of whom only a chosen band would dare to encounter the spears and swords of the Barbarians. The order of battle must have varied according to the ground, the object, and the adversary; but their ordinary disposition, in two lines and a reserve, presented a succession of hopes and resources most agreeable to the temper as well as the judgment of the Greeks.[79] In case of a repulse, the first line fell back into the intervals of the second; and the reserve, breaking into two divisions, wheeled round the flanks to improve the victory or cover the retreat. Whatever authority could enact was accomplished, at least in theory, by the camps and marches, the exercises and evolutions, the edicts and books, of the Byzantine monarch.[80] Whatever art could produce from the forge, the loom, or the laboratory, was abundantly supplied by the riches of the prince, and the industry of his numerous workmen. But neither authority nor art could frame the most important machine, the soldier himself; and if the *ceremonies* of Constantine always suppose the safe and triumphal return of the emperor,[81] his *tactics* seldom soar above the means of escaping a defeat, and procrastinating the

78. They observe της γαρ τοξειας παντελως αμεληθεισης . . . εν τοις Ρωμαιοις τα πολλα νυν ειωθε σφαλματα γινεσθαι (Leo, Tactic. p. 581. Constantin. p. 1216.). Yet such were not the maxims of the Greeks and Romans, who despised the loose and distant practice of archery.

79. Compare the passages of the Tactics, p. 669, and 721, and the xii[th] with the xviii[th] chapter.

80. In the preface to his Tactics, Leo very freely deplores the loss of discipline and the calamities of the times, and repeats, without scruple (proem. p. 537.), the reproaches of αμελεια, αταξια, αγυμνασια, δειλια, &c. nor does it appear that the same censures were less deserved in the next generation by the disciples of Constantine.

81. See in the Ceremonial (l. ii. c. 19. p. 353.) the form of the emperor's trampling on the necks of the captive Saracens, while the singers chanted, "thou hast made my enemies my footstool!" and the people shouted forty times the kyrie eleison.

war.[82] Notwithstanding some transient success, the Greeks were sunk in their own esteem and that of their neighbours. A cold hand and a loquacious tongue was the vulgar description of the nation: the author of the tactics was besieged in his capital; and the last of the Barbarians, who trembled at the name of the Saracens, or Franks, could proudly exhibit the medals of gold and silver which they had extorted from the feeble sovereign of Constantinople. What spirit their government and character denied, might have been inspired in some degree by the influence of religion; but the religion of the Greeks could only teach them to suffer and to yield. The emperor Nicephorus, who restored for a moment the discipline and glory of the Roman name, was desirous of bestowing the honours of martyrdom on the Christians who lost their lives in an holy war against the infidels. But this political law was defeated by the opposition of the patriarch, the bishops, and the principal senators; and they strenuously urged the canons of St. Basil, that all who were polluted by the bloody trade of a soldier, should be separated, during three years, from the communion of the faithful.[83]

Character and tactics of the Saracens.

These scruples of the Greeks have been compared with the tears of the primitive Moslems when they were held back from battle; and this contrast of base superstition, and high-spirited enthusiasm, unfolds to a philosophic eye the history of the rival nations. The subjects of the last caliphs[84] had undoubtedly degenerated from the zeal and faith of the companions of the prophet. Yet their martial creed still represented the deity as the author of war:[85] the vital though latent spark of fanaticism still glowed in the heart of their religion, and among the Saracens who dwelt on the Christian borders, it was frequently rekindled to a lively and active flame. Their regular force was formed of the valiant slaves who had been educated to guard the person and

82. Leo observes (Tactic. p. 668.), that a fair open battle against any nation whatsoever, is *επισφαλες* and *επικινδυνον*; the words are strong, and the remark is true; yet if such had been the opinion of the old Romans, Leo had never reigned on the shores of the Thracian Bosphorus.

83. Zonaras (tom. ii. l. xvi. p. 202, 203.) and Cedrenus (Compend. p. 668.), who relate the design of Nicephorus, must unfortunately apply the epithet of *γενναιως* to the opposition of the patriarch.

84. The xvii[th] chapter of the tactics of the different nations, is the most historical and useful of the whole Collection of Leo. The manners and arms of the Saracens (Tactic. p. 809–817. and a fragment from the Medicean MS. in the preface of the vi[th] volume of Meursius), the Roman emperor was too frequently called upon to study.

85. *Παντος δε και κακου εργου τον Θεον αιτιον ὑπο τιθενται, και πολεμοις χαιρειν λεγοισι τον Θεον τον διασκορπιζοντα εθνη τα τους πολεμους θελοντα.* Leon. Tactic. p. 809.

accompany the standard of their lord; but the Musulman people of Syria and Cilicia, of Africa and Spain, was awakened by the trumpet which proclaimed an holy war against the infidels. The rich were ambitious of death or victory in the cause of God; the poor were allured by the hopes of plunder, and the old, the infirm, and the women, assumed their share of meritorious service by sending their substitutes, with arms and horses, into the field. These offensive and defensive arms were similar in strength and temper to those of the Romans, whom they far excelled in the management of the horse and the bow; the massy silver of their belts, their bridles, and their swords, displayed the magnificence of a prosperous nation, and except some black archers of the south, the Arabs disdained the naked bravery of their ancestors. Instead of waggons, they were attended by a long train of camels, mules, and asses; the multitude of these animals, whom they bedecked with flags and streamers, appeared to swell the pomp and magnitude of their host; and the horses of the enemy were often disordered by the uncouth figure and odious smell of the camels of the East. Invincible by their patience of thirst and heat, their spirits were frozen by a winter's cold, and the consciousness of their propensity to sleep exacted the most rigorous precautions against the surprises of the night. Their order of battle was a long square of two deep and solid lines; the first of archers, the second of cavalry. In their engagements by sea and land, they sustained with patient firmness the fury of the attack, and seldom advanced to the charge till they could discern and oppress the lassitude of their foes. But if they were repulsed and broken, they knew not how to rally or renew the combat; and their dismay was heightened by the superstitious prejudice, that God had declared himself on the side of their enemies. The decline and fall of the caliphs countenanced this fearful opinion; nor were there wanting, among the Mahometans and Christians, some obscure prophecies[86] which prognosticated their alternate defeats. The unity of the Arabian empire was dissolved, but the independent fragments were equal to populous and powerful kingdoms; and in their naval and military armaments, an emir of Aleppo or Tunis might command no despicable fund of skill and industry and treasure. In their transactions of peace and war with the Saracens, the princes of Constantinople too often felt that these Bar-

86. Liutprand (p. 484, 485.) relates and interprets the oracles of the Greeks and Saracens, in which, after the fashion of prophecy, the past is clear and historical, the future is dark, ænigmatical, and erroneous. From this boundary of light and shade, an impartial critic may commonly determine the date of the composition.

barians had nothing barbarous in their discipline; and that if they were destitute of original genius, they had been endowed with a quick spirit of curiosity and imitation. The model was indeed more perfect than the copy: their ships, and engines, and fortifications, were of a less skilful construction; and they confess, without shame, that the same God who has given a tongue to the Arabians, had more nicely fashioned the hands of the Chinese, and the heads of the Greeks.[87]

The Franks or Latins.

A name of some German tribes between the Rhine and the Weser had spread its victorious influence over the greatest part of Gaul, Germany, and Italy; and the common appellation of FRANKS[88] was applied by the Greeks and Arabians to the Christians of the Latin church, the nations of the West, who stretched beyond *their* knowledge to the shores of the Atlantic Ocean. The vast body had been inspired and united by the soul of Charlemagne; but the division and degeneracy of his race soon annihilated the Imperial power, which would have rivalled the Cæsars of Byzantium, and revenged the indignities of the Christian name. The enemies no longer feared, nor could the subjects any longer trust, the application of a public revenue, the labours of trade and manufactures in the military service, the mutual aid of provinces and armies, and the naval squadrons which were regularly stationed from the mouth of the Elbe to that of the Tyber. In the beginning of the tenth century, the family of Charlemagne had almost disappeared; his monarchy was broken into many hostile and independent states; the regal title was assumed by the most ambitious chiefs; their revolt was imitated in a long subordination of anarchy and discord, and the nobles of every province disobeyed their sovereign, oppressed their vassals, and exercised perpetual hostilities against their equals and neighbours. Their private wars, which overturned the fabric of government, fomented the martial spirit of the nation. In the system of modern Europe, the power of the sword is possessed, at least in fact, by five or six mighty potentates; their operations are conducted on a distant frontier, by an order of men who devote their lives to the study and practice of the military art: the rest of the country

87. The sense of this distinction is expressed by Abulpharagius (Dynast. p. 2. 62. 101.), but I cannot recollect the passage in which it is conveyed by this lively apothegm.

88. Ex Francis, quo nomine tam Latinos quam Teutones comprehendit, ludum habuit (Liutprand. in Legat. ad Imp. Nicephorum, p. 483, 484.). This extension of the name may be confirmed from Constantine (de administrando Imperio, l. ii. c. 27, 28.) and Eutychius (Annal. tom. i. p. 55, 56.), who both lived before the crusades. The testimonies of Abulpharagius (Dynast. p. 69.) and Abulfeda (Præfat. ad Geograph.) are more recent.

and community enjoys in the midst of war the tranquillity of peace, and is only made sensible of the change by the aggravation or decrease of the public taxes. In the disorders of the tenth and eleventh centuries, every peasant was a soldier, and every village a fortification; each wood or valley was a scene of murder and rapine; and the lords of each castle were compelled to assume the character of princes and warriors. To their own courage and policy, they boldly trusted for the safety of their family, the protection of their lands, and the revenge of their injuries; and, like the conquerors of a larger size, they were too apt to transgress the privilege of defensive war. The powers of the mind and body were hardened by the presence of danger and necessity of resolution: the same spirit refused to desert a friend and to forgive an enemy; and, instead of sleeping under the guardian care of the magistrate, they proudly disdained the authority of the laws. In the days of feudal anarchy, the instruments of agriculture and art were converted into the weapons of bloodshed: the peaceful occupations of civil and ecclesiastical society were abolished or corrupted; and the bishop who exchanged his mitre for an helmet, was more forcibly urged by the manners of the times than by the obligation of his tenure.[89]

Their character and tactics.

The love of freedom and of arms was felt, with conscious pride, by the Franks themselves, and is observed by the Greeks with some degree of amazement and terror. "The Franks," says the emperor Constantine, "are bold and valiant to the verge of temerity; and their dauntless spirit is supported by the contempt of danger and death. In the field and in close onset, they press to the front, and rush headlong against the enemy, without deigning to compute either his numbers or their own. Their ranks are formed by the firm connections of consanguinity and friendship; and their martial deeds are prompted by the desire of saving or revenging their dearest companions. In their eyes, a retreat is a shameful flight; and flight is indelible infamy."[90] A nation

89. On this subject of ecclesiastical and beneficiary discipline, father Thomassin (tom. iii. l. i. c. 40. 45, 46, 47.) may be usefully consulted. A general law of Charlemagne exempted the bishops from personal service, but the opposite practice, which prevailed from the ix[th] to the xv[th] century, is countenanced by the example or silence of saints and doctors. . . . You justify your cowardice by the holy canons, says Ratherius of Verona; the canons likewise forbid you to whore, and yet ——

90. In the xviii[th] chapter of his Tactics, the emperor Leo has fairly stated the military vices and virtues of the Franks (whom Meursius ridiculously translates by *Galli*), and the Lombards, or Langobards. See likewise the xxvi[th] Dissertation of Muratori de Antiquitatibus Italiæ medii Ævi.

endowed with such high and intrepid spirit, must have been secure of victory, if these advantages had not been counterbalanced by many weighty defects. The decay of their naval power, left the Greeks and Saracens in possession of the sea, for every purpose of annoyance and supply. In the age which preceded the institution of knighthood, the Franks were rude and unskilful in the service of cavalry;[91] and, in all perilous emergencies, their warriors were so conscious of their ignorance, that they chose to dismount from their horses and fight on foot. Unpractised in the use of pikes, or of missile weapons, they were encumbered by the length of their swords, the weight of their armour, the magnitude of their shields, and, if I may repeat the satire of the meagre Greeks, by their unwieldy intemperance. Their independent spirit disdained the yoke of subordination, and abandoned the standard of their chief, if he attempted to keep the field beyond the term of their stipulation or service. On all sides they were open to the snares of an enemy, less brave, but more artful, than themselves. They might be bribed, for the Barbarians were venal; or surprised in the night, for they neglected the precautions of a close encampment or vigilant centinels. The fatigues of a summer's campaign exhausted their strength and patience, and they sunk in despair if their voracious appetite was disappointed of a plentiful supply of wine and of food. This general character of the Franks was marked with some national and local shades, which I should ascribe to accident, rather than to climate, but which were visible both to natives and to foreigners. An ambassador of the great Otho declared, in the palace of Constantinople, that the Saxons could dispute with swords better than with pens; and that they preferred inevitable death to the dishonour of turning their backs to an enemy.[92] It was the glory of the nobles of France, that, in their humble dwellings, war and rapine were the only pleasure, the sole occupation, of their lives. They affected to deride the palaces, the banquets, the polished manners, of the Italians, who, in the estimate of the Greeks themselves, had degenerated from the liberty and valour of the ancient Lombards.[93]

91. Domini tui milites (says the proud Nicephorus) equitandi ignari pedestris pugnæ sunt inscii: scutorum magnitudo, loricarum gravitudo, ensium longitudo, galearumque pondus neutrâ parte pugnare eos sinit; ac subridens, impedit, inquit, et eos gastrimargia hoc est ventris ingluvies, &c. Liutprand. in Legat. p. 480, 481.

92. In Saxonia certe scio . . . decentius ensibus pugnare quam calamis et prius mortem obire quam hostibus terga dare (Liutprand, p. 482.).

93. *Φραγγοι τοινυν και Λογιβαρδοι λογον ελευθεριας περι πολλου ποιουνται, αλλ' δι μεν Λογιβαρδοι το πλεον της τοιαυτης αρετης νυν απωλεσαν.* Leonis Tactica,

Oblivion of the Latin language. By the well-known edict of Caracalla, his subjects, from Britain to Egypt, were entitled to the name and privileges of Romans, and their national sovereign might fix his occasional or permanent residence in any province of their common country. In the division of the East and West, an ideal unity was scrupulously preserved, and in their titles, laws, and statutes, the successors of Arcadius and Honorius announced themselves as the inseparable colleagues of the same office, as the joint sovereigns of the Roman world and city, which were bounded by the same limits. After the fall of the Western monarchy, the majesty of the purple resided solely in the princes of Constantinople; and of these, Justinian was the first, who after a divorce of sixty years regained the dominion of ancient Rome, and asserted, by the right of conquest, the august title of emperor of the Romans.[94] A motive of vanity or discontent solicited one of his successors, Constans the second, to abandon the Thracian Bosphorus, and to restore the pristine honours of the Tyber: an extravagant project (exclaims the malicious Byzantine), as if he had despoiled a beautiful and blooming virgin, to enrich, or rather to expose, the deformity of a wrinkled and decrepit matron.[95] But the sword of the Lombards opposed his settlement in Italy: he entered Rome,

---

c. 18. p. 805. The emperor Leo died A.D. 911: an historical poem, which ends in 916, and appears to have been composed in 940, by a native of Venetia, discriminates in these verses the manners of Italy and France:

—— Quid inertia bello
Pectora (Ubertus ait) duris prætenditis armis
O Itali? Potius vobis sacra pocula cordi;
Sæpius et stomachum nitidis laxare saginis
Elatasque domos rutilo fulcire metallo.
Non eadem Gallos similis vel cura remordet;
Vicinas quibus est studium devincere terras
Depressumque larem spoliis hinc inde coactis
Sustentare. ——

(Anonym. Carmen Panegyricum de Laudibus Berengarii Augusti, l. ii. in Muratori Script. Rerum Italic. tom. ii. pars i. p. 393.).

94. Justinian, says the historian Agathias (l. v. p. 157.), *πρωτος Ρωμαιων αυτοκρατωρ ονοματι και πραγματι*. Yet the specific title of emperor of the Romans was not used at Constantinople, till it had been claimed by the French and German emperors of old Rome.

95. Constantine Manasses reprobates this design in his barbarous verse:

Την πολιν την βασιλειαν αποκοσμησαι θελων,
Και την αρχην χαρισασθαι τριπεμπελῳ Ρωμῃ,
Ως ειτις αβροστολιστον αποκοσμησει νυμφην,
Και γραυν τινα τρικορωνον ὡς κορην ωρᾶισει.

and it is confirmed by Theophanes, Zonaras, Cedrenus, and the Historia Miscella. voluit in urbem Romam Imperium transferre (l. xix. p. 157. in tom. i. pars i. of the Scriptores Rer. Ital. of Muratori).

not as a conqueror, but as a fugitive, and after a visit of twelve days, he pillaged, and for ever deserted, the ancient capital of the world.[96] The final revolt and separation of Italy was accomplished about two centuries after the conquests of Justinian, and from his reign we may date the gradual oblivion of the Latin tongue. That legislator had composed his Institutes, his Code, and his Pandects, in a language which he celebrates as the proper and public style of the Roman government, the consecrated idiom of the palace and senate of Constantinople, of the camps and tribunals of the East.[97] But this foreign dialect was unknown to the people and soldiers of the Asiatic provinces, it was imperfectly understood by the greater part of the interpreters of the laws and the ministers of the state. After a short conflict, nature and habit prevailed over the obsolete institutions of human power: for the general benefit of his subjects, Justinian promulgated his novels in the two languages; the several parts of his voluminous jurisprudence were successively translated:[98] the original was forgotten, the version was studied, and the Greek, whose intrinsic merit deserved indeed the preference, obtained a legal as well as popular establishment in the Byzantine monarchy. The birth and residence of succeeding princes estranged them from the Roman idiom: Tiberius by the Arabs,[99] and Maurice by the Italians,[100] are distinguished as the first of the Greek Cæsars, as the founders of a new dynasty and empire: the silent revolution was accomplished before the death of Heraclius; and

96. Paul. Diacon. l. v. c. 11. p. 480. Anastasius in Vitis Pontificum, in Muratori's Collection, tom. iii. pars i. p. 141.

97. Consult the preface of Ducange (ad Gloss. Græc. medii Ævi), and the novels of Justinian (vii. lxvi.). The Greek language was *κοινος*, the Latin was *πατριος* to himself, *πυριωτατος* to the *πολιτειας σχημα*, the system of government.

98. *Ου μεν αλλα και Λατινικη λεξις και φρασις εις επι τους νομους τους συνειναι ταυτην μη δυναμενους απετειχιζε* (Matth. Blastares, Hist. Juris, apud Fabric. Bibliot. Græc. tom. xii. p. 369.). The Code and Pandects (the latter by Thalelæus) were translated in the time of Justinian (p. 358. 366.). Theophilus, one of the original triumvirs, has left an elegant, though diffuse, paraphrase of the Institutes. On the other hand, Julian, antecessor of Constantinople (A.D. 570), cxx. Novellas Græcas eleganti Latinitate donavit (Heineccius, Hist. J. R. p. 396.) for the use of Italy and Africa.

99. Abulpharagius assigns the vii[th] Dynasty to the Franks or Romans, the viii[th] to the Greeks, the ix[th] to the Arabs. A tempore Augusti Cæsaris donec imperaret Tiberius Cæsar spatio circiter annorum 600 fuerunt Imperatores C. P. Patricii, et præcipua pars exercitûs Romani: extra quod, consiliarii, scribæ et populus, omnes Græci fuerunt: deinde regnum etiam Græcanicum factum est (p. 96. vers. Pocock). The Christian and ecclesiastical studies of Abulpharagius gave him some advantage over the more ignorant *Moslems*.

100. Primus ex Græcorum genere in Imperio confirmatus est; or, according to another MS. of Paulus Diaconus (l. iii. c. 15. p. 443.), in Græcorum Imperio.

the ruins of the Latin speech were darkly preserved in the terms of jurisprudence and the acclamations of the palace. After the restoration of the Western empire by Charlemagne and the Othos, the names of Franks and Latins acquired an equal signification and extent; and these haughty Barbarians asserted, with some justice, their superior claim to the language and dominion of Rome. They insulted the aliens of the East who had renounced the dress and idiom of Romans; and their reasonable practice will justify the frequent appellation of Greeks.[101] But this contemptuous appellation was indignantly rejected by the prince and people to whom it is applied. Whatsoever changes had been introduced by the lapse of ages, they alleged a lineal and unbroken succession from Augustus and Constantine; and, in the lowest period of degeneracy and decay, the name of ROMANS adhered to the last fragments of the empire of Constantinople.[102]

The Greek emperors and their subjects retain and assert the name of Romans.

Period of ignorance.

While the government of the East was transacted in Latin, the Greek was the language of literature and philosophy; nor could the masters of this rich and perfect idiom be tempted to envy the borrowed learning and imitative taste of their Roman disciples. After the fall of Paganism, the loss of Syria and Egypt, and the extinction of the schools of Alexandria and Athens, the studies of the Greeks insensibly retired to some regular monasteries, and above all to the royal college of Constantinople, which was burnt in the reign of Leo the Isaurian.[103] In the pompous style of the age, the president of that foundation was named the Sun of Science: his twelve associates, the professors in the different

101. Quia linguam, mores, vestesque mutâstis, putavit Sanctissimus Papa (an audacious irony), ita vos (vobis) displicere Romanorum nomen. His nuncios, rogabant Nicephorum Imperatorem Græcorum, ut cum Othone Imperatore Romanorum amicitiam faceret (Liutprand in Legatione, p. 486.).

102. By Laonicus Chalcocondyles, who survived the last siege of Constantinople, the account is thus stated (l. i. p. 3.). Constantine transplanted his Latins of Italy to a Greek city of Thrace: they adopted the language and manners of the natives, who were confounded with them under the name of Romans. The kings of Constantinople, says the historian, επι το σφας αυτους σεμνυνεσθαι Ρωμαιων βασιλεις τε και αυτοκρατορας αποκαλειν, Ελληνων δε βασιλεις ουκετι ουδαμη αξιουν.

103. See Ducange (C. P. Christiana, l. ii. p. 150, 151.), who collects the testimonies, not of Theophanes, but at least of Zonaras (tom. ii. l. xv. p. 104.), Cedrenus (p. 454.), Michael Glycas (p. 281.), Constantine Manasses (p. 87.). After refuting the absurd charge against the emperor, Spanheim (Hist. Imaginum, p. 99–111.), like a true advocate, proceeds to doubt or deny the reality of the fire, and almost of the library.

arts and faculties, were the twelve signs of the zodiac; a library of thirty-six thousand five hundred volumes was open to their enquiries; and they could shew an ancient manuscript of Homer, on a roll of parchment one hundred and twenty feet in length, the intestines, as it was fabled, of a prodigious serpent.[104] But the seventh and eighth centuries were a period of discord and darkness; the library was burnt, the college was abolished, the Iconoclasts are represented as the foes of antiquity; and a savage ignorance and contempt of letters has disgraced the princes of the Heraclean and Isaurian dynasties.[105]

Revival of Greek learning.

In the ninth century, we trace the first dawnings of the restoration of science.[106] After the fanaticism of the Arabs had subsided, the caliphs aspired to conquer the arts, rather than the provinces, of the empire: their liberal curiosity rekindled the emulation of the Greeks, brushed away the dust from their ancient libraries, and taught them to know and reward the philosophers, whose labours had been hitherto repaid by the pleasure of study and the pursuit of truth. The Cæsar Bardas, the uncle of Michael the third, was the generous protector of letters, a title which alone has preserved his memory and excused his ambition. A particle of the treasures of his nephew was sometimes diverted from the indulgence of vice and folly; a school was opened in the palace of Magnaura; and the presence of Bardas excited the emulation of the masters and students. At their head was the philosopher Leo, archbishop of Thessalonica: his profound skill in astronomy and the mathematics was admired by the strangers of the East; and this occult science was magnified by vulgar credulity, which modestly supposes that all knowledge superior to its own must be the effect of inspiration or magic. At the pressing entreaty of the Cæsar, his friend, the celebrated Photius,[107] renounced the freedom of a secular and studious life, ascended the patriarchal throne, and was alternately excommunicated and absolved by the synods of the East and West. By the confession even of priestly

104. According to Malchus (apud Zonar. l. xiv. p. 53.), this Homer was burnt in the time of Basiliscus. The MS. might be renewed – But on a serpent's skin? Most strange and incredible!

105. The *αλογια* of Zonaras, the *αγρια και αμαθια* of Cedrenus, are strong words, perhaps not ill-suited to these reigns.

106. See Zonaras (l. xvi. p. 160, 161.) and Cedrenus (p. 549, 550.). Like fryar Bacon, the philosopher Leo has been transformed by ignorance into a conjurer: yet not so undeservedly, if he be the author of the oracles more commonly ascribed to the emperor of the same name. The physics of Leo in MS. are in the library of Vienna (Fabricius, Bibliot. Græc. tom. vi. p. 366. tom. xii. p. 781.). Quiescant!

107. The ecclesiastical and literary character of Photius, is copiously discussed by Hanckius (de Scriptoribus Byzant. p. 269–396.) and Fabricius.

hatred, no art or science, except poetry, was foreign to this universal scholar, who was deep in thought, indefatigable in reading, and eloquent in diction. Whilst he exercised the office of protospathaire, or captain of the guards, Photius was sent ambassador to the caliph of Bagdad.[108] The tedious hours of exile, perhaps of confinement, were beguiled by the hasty composition of his *Library*, a living monument of erudition and criticism. Two hundred and fourscore writers, historians, orators, philosophers, theologians, are reviewed without any regular method: he abridges their narrative or doctrine, appreciates their style and character, and judges even the fathers of the church with a discreet freedom, which often breaks through the superstition of the times. The emperor Basil, who lamented the defects of his own education, entrusted to the care of Photius his son and successor Leo the philosopher; and the reign of that prince and of his son Constantine Porphyrogenitus forms one of the most prosperous æras of the Byzantine literature. By their munificence the treasures of antiquity were deposited in the Imperial library; by their pens, or those of their associates, they were imparted in such extracts and abridgments as might amuse the curiosity, without oppressing the indolence, of the public. Besides the *Basilics*, or code of laws, the arts of husbandry and war, of feeding or destroying the human species, were propagated with equal diligence; and the history of Greece and Rome was digested into fifty-three heads or titles, of which two only (of embassies, and of virtues and vices) have escaped the injuries of time. In every station, the reader might contemplate the image of the past world, apply the lesson or warning of each page, and learn to admire, perhaps to imitate, the examples of a brighter period. I shall not expatiate on the works of the Byzantine Greeks, who, by the assiduous study of the ancients, have deserved in some measure the remembrance and gratitude of the moderns. The scholars of the present age may still enjoy the benefit of the philosophical common-place book of Stobæus, the grammatical and historic lexicon of Suidas, the Chiliads of Tzetzes, which comprise six hundred narratives in twelve thousand verses, and the commentaries on Homer of Eustathius archbishop of Thessalonica, who, from his horn

108. *Εις Ασσυριους* can only mean Bagdad, the seat of the caliph; and the relation of his embassy might have been curious and instructive. But how did he procure his books? A library so numerous could neither be found at Bagdad, nor transported with his baggage, nor preserved in his memory. Yet the last, however incredible, seems to be affirmed by Photius himself, *οσας αυτων ἡ μνημη διεσοζε*. Camusat (Hist. Critique des Journaux, p. 87–94.) gives a good account of the Myriobiblon.

of plenty, has poured the names and authorities of four hundred writers. From these originals, and from the numerous tribe of scholiasts and critics,[109] some estimate may be formed of the literary wealth of the twelfth century: Constantinople was enlightened by the genius of Homer and Demosthenes, of Aristotle and Plato; and in the enjoyment or neglect of our present riches, we must envy the generation that could still peruse the history of Theopompus, the orations of Hyperides, the comedies of Menander,[110] and the odes of Alcæus and Sappho. The frequent labour of illustration attests not only the existence but the popularity of the Grecian classics: the general knowledge of the age may be deduced from the example of two learned females, the empress Eudocia, and the princess Anna Comnena, who cultivated, in the purple, the arts of rhetoric and philosophy.[111] The vulgar dialect of the city was gross and barbarous: a more correct and elaborate style distinguished the discourse, or at least the compositions, of the church and palace, which sometimes affected to copy the purity of the Attic models.

Decay of taste and genius.

In our modern education, the painful though necessary attainment of two languages, which are no longer living, may consume the time and damp the ardour of the youthful student. The poets and orators were long imprisoned in the barbarous dialects of our Western ancestors, devoid of harmony or grace; and their genius, without precept or example, was abandoned to the rude and native powers of

109. Of these modern Greeks, see the respective articles in the Bibliotheca Græca of Fabricius; a laborious work, yet susceptible of a better method and many improvements: of Eustathius (tom. i. p. 289–292. 306–329.), of the Pselli (a diatribe of Leo Allatius, ad calcem tom. v.), of Constantine Porphyrogenitus (tom. vi. p. 486–509.), of John Stobæus (tom. viii. 665–728.), of Suidas (tom. ix. p. 620–827.), John Tzetzes (tom. xii. p. 245–273.). Mr. Harris, in his Philological Arrangements, opus senile, has given a sketch of this Byzantine learning (p. 287–300.).

110. From obscure and hearsay evidence, Gerard Vossius (de Poetis Græcis, c. 6.) and le Clerc (Bibliotheque Choisie, tom. xix. p. 285.) mention a commentary of Michael Psellus on twenty-four plays of Menander, still extant in MS. at Constantinople. Yet such classic studies seem incompatible with the gravity or dulness of a schoolman, who pored over the categories (de Psellis, p. 42.): and Michael has probably been confounded with Homerus *Sellius*, who wrote arguments to the comedies of Menander. In the xth century, Suidas quotes fifty plays, but he often transcribes the old scholiast of Aristophanes.

111. Anna Comnena may boast of her Greek style (*το Ελληνιζειν ες ακρον εσπουδακυια*), and Zonaras, her contemporary, but not her flatterer, may add with truth, *γλωτταν ειχεν ακριβως Αττικιζουσαν*. The princess was conversant with the artful dialogues of Plato; and had studied the *τετρακυς*, or *quadrivium* of astrology, geometry, arithmetic, and music (see her preface to the Alexiad, with Ducange's notes).

their judgment and fancy. But the Greeks of Constantinople, after purging away the impurities of their vulgar speech, acquired the free use of their ancient language, the most happy composition of human art, and a familiar knowledge of the sublime masters who had pleased or instructed the first of nations. But these advantages only tend to aggravate the reproach and shame of a degenerate people. They held in their lifeless hands the riches of their fathers, without inheriting the spirit which had created and improved that sacred patrimony: they read, they praised, they compiled, but their languid souls seemed alike incapable of thought and action. In the revolution of ten centuries, not a single discovery was made to exalt the dignity or promote the happiness of mankind. Not a single idea has been added to the speculative systems of antiquity, and a succession of patient disciples became in their turn the dogmatic teachers of the next servile generation. Not a single composition of history, philosophy, or literature, has been saved from oblivion by the intrinsic beauties of style or sentiment, of original fancy, or even of successful imitation. In prose, the least offensive of the Byzantine writers are absolved from censure by their naked and unpresuming simplicity: but the orators, most eloquent[112] in their own conceit, are the farthest removed from the models whom they affect to emulate. In every page our taste and reason are wounded by the choice of gigantic and obsolete words, a stiff and intricate phraseology, the discord of images, the childish play of false or unseasonable ornament, and the painful attempt to elevate themselves, to astonish the reader, and to involve a trivial meaning in the smoke of obscurity and exaggeration. Their prose is soaring to the vicious affectation of poetry: their poetry is sinking below the flatness and insipidity of prose. The tragic, epic, and lyric muses, were silent and inglorious: the bards of Constantinople seldom rose above a riddle or epigram, a panegyric or tale; they forgot even the rules of prosody; and with the melody of Homer yet sounding in their ears, they confound all measure of feet and syllables in the impotent strains which have received the name of *political* or city verses.[113] The minds of the Greeks were bound in the fetters of a base and imperious superstition, which extends

112. To censure the Byzantine taste, Ducange (Prefat. Gloss. Græc. p. 17.) strings the authorities of Aulus Gellius, Jerom Petronius, George Hamartolus, Longinus; who give at once the precept and the example.

113. The *versus politici*, those common prostitutes, as, from their easiness, they are styled by Leo Allatius, usually consist of fifteen syllables. They are used by Constantine Manasses, John Tzetzes, &c. (Ducange, Gloss. Latin. tom. iii. p. i. p. 345, 346. edit. Basil, 1762.)

her dominion round the circle of profane science. Their understandings were bewildered in metaphysical controversy: in the belief of visions and miracles, they had lost all principles of moral evidence, and their taste was vitiated by the homilies of the monks, an absurd medley of declamation and scripture. Even these contemptible studies were no longer dignified by the abuse of superior talents: the leaders of the Greek church were humbly content to admire and copy the oracles of antiquity, nor did the schools or pulpit produce any rivals of the fame of Athanasius and Chrysostom.[114]

Want of national emulation.

In all the pursuits of active and speculative life, the emulation of states and individuals is the most powerful spring of the efforts and improvements of mankind. The cities of ancient Greece were cast in the happy mixture of union and independence, which is repeated on a larger scale, but in a looser form, by the nations of modern Europe: the union of language, religion, and manners, which renders them the spectators and judges of each others merit:[115] the independence of government and interest, which asserts their separate freedom, and excites them to strive for pre-eminence in the career of glory. The situation of the Romans was less favourable; yet in the early ages of the republic, which fixed the national character, a similar emulation was kindled among the states of Latium and Italy; and, in the arts and sciences, they aspired to equal or surpass their Grecian masters. The empire of the Cæsars undoubtedly checked the activity and progress of the human mind; its magnitude might indeed allow some scope for domestic competition; but when it was gradually reduced, at first to the East and at last to Greece and Constantinople, the Byzantine subjects were degraded to an abject and languid temper, the natural effect of their solitary and insulated state. From the North they were oppressed by nameless tribes of Barbarians, to whom they scarcely imparted the appellation of men. The language and religion of the more polished Arabs were an insurmountable bar to all social intercourse. The conquerors of Europe were their brethren in the Christian faith; but the speech of the Franks or Latins was unknown, their manners were rude, and they were rarely connected, in peace or war, with the successors of Heraclius. Alone in the universe, the self-satisfied pride of the Greeks was not disturbed by the comparison of foreign merit; and it is no wonder if they fainted in the race, since they had neither competitors to urge their speed, nor

114. As St. Bernard of the Latin, so St. John Damascenus in the viii[th] century, is revered as the last father of the Greek, church.

115. Hume's Essays, vol. i. p. 125.

judges to crown their victory. The nations of Europe and Asia were mingled by the expeditions to the Holy Land; and it is under the Comnenian dynasty that a faint emulation of knowledge and military virtue was rekindled in the Byzantine empire.

CHAPTER LIV

Origin and Doctrine of the Paulicians. – Their Persecution by the Greek Emperors. – Revolt in Armenia, &c. – Transplantation into Thrace. – Propagation in the West. – The Seeds, Character, and Consequences of the Reformation.

Supine superstition of the Greek church.

In the profession of Christianity, the variety of national characters may be clearly distinguished. The natives of Syria and Egypt abandoned their lives to lazy and contemplative devotion: Rome again aspired to the dominion of the world; and the wit of the lively and loquacious Greeks was consumed in the disputes of metaphysical theology. The incomprehensible mysteries of the Trinity and Incarnation, instead of commanding their silent submission, were agitated in vehement and subtle controversies, which enlarged their faith at the expence perhaps of their charity and reason. From the council of Nice to the end of the seventh century, the peace and unity of the church was invaded by these spiritual wars; and so deeply did they affect the decline and fall of the empire, that the historian has too often been compelled to attend the synods, to explore the creeds, and to enumerate the sects, of this busy period of ecclesiastical annals. From the beginning of the eighth century to the last ages of the Byzantine empire the sound of controversy was seldom heard: curiosity was exhausted, zeal was fatigued; and, in the decrees of six councils, the articles of the Catholic faith had been irrevocably defined. The spirit of dispute, however vain and pernicious, requires some energy and exercise of the mental faculties; and the prostrate Greeks were content to fast, to pray, and to believe, in blind obedience to the patriarch and his clergy. During a long dream of superstition, the Virgin and the Saints, their visions and miracles, their relics and images, were preached by the monks and worshipped by the people; and the appellation of people might be extended without injustice to the first ranks of civil society. At an unseasonable moment, the Isaurian emperors attempted somewhat rudely to awaken their subjects: under their influence, reason might obtain some proselytes, a far greater number was swayed by interest or fear; but the Eastern world embraced or deplored their visible deities, and the restoration of images was celebrated as the feast of orthodoxy. In this passive and unanimous state the ecclesiastical rulers were relieved from the toil, or deprived of the pleasure, of persecution. The Pagans had disappeared; the Jews were silent and obscure; the disputes with the Latins were rare and remote hostilities against a national enemy; and the sects of Egypt and Syria enjoyed a free toleration, under the shadow of the Arabian caliphs. About the middle of the seventh century, a branch of Manichæans was selected as the victims of spiritual tyranny: their patience was at length exasperated to despair and rebellion; and their exile has scattered over the West the seeds of reformation. These important events will justify some enquiry into the doctrine and story of the PAULICIANS;[1] and, as they cannot plead for themselves, our candid criticism will magnify the *good*, and abate or suspect the *evil*, that is reported by their adversaries.

Origin of the Paulicians, or disciples of St. Paul, A.D. 660, &c.

The Gnostics, who had distracted the infancy, were oppressed by the greatness and authority, of the church. Instead of emulating or surpassing the wealth, learning, and numbers, of the Catholics, their obscure remnant was driven from the capitals of the East and West, and confined to the villages and mountains along the borders of the Euphrates. Some vestige of the Marcionites may be detected in the fifth century;[2] but the numerous sects were finally lost in the odious name of the Manichæans; and these heretics, who presumed to reconcile the doctrines of Zoroaster and Christ, were pursued by the two religions with equal and unrelenting hatred. Under the grandson of Heraclius, in the neighbourhood of Samosata, more famous for the birth of Lucian than for the title of a Syrian kingdom, a reformer arose, esteemed by the *Paulicians* as the chosen messenger of truth. In his humble dwelling of Mananalis, Constantine entertained a deacon, who returned from Syrian captivity, and received the inestimable gift of the New Testament, which was already concealed from the vulgar by the prudence of the Greek, and perhaps of the Gnostic,

1. The errors and virtues of the Paulicians are weighed, with his usual judgment and candour, by the learned Mosheim (Hist. Ecclesiast. seculum ix. p. 311, &c.). He draws his original intelligence from Photius (contra Manichæos, l. i.) and Peter Siculus (Hist. Manichæorum). The first of these accounts has not fallen into my hands; the second, which Mosheim prefers, I have read in a Latin version inserted in the Maxima Bibliotheca Patrum (tom. xvi. p. 754–764.), from the edition of the Jesuit Raderus (Ingolstadii, 1604, in 4to).

2. In the time of Theodoret, the diocese of Cyrrhus, in Syria, contained eight hundred villages. Of these, two were inhabited by Arians and Eunomians, and eight by *Marcionites*, whom the laborious bishop reconciled to the Catholic church (Dupin, Bibliot. Ecclesiastique, tom. iv. p. 81, 82.).

clergy.[3] These books became the measure of his studies and the rule of his faith; and the Catholics, who dispute his interpretation, acknowledge that his text was genuine and sincere. But he attached himself with peculiar devotion to the writings and character of St. Paul: the name of the Paulicians is derived by their enemies from some unknown and domestic teacher; but I am confident that they gloried in their affinity to the apostle of the Gentiles. His disciples, Titus, Timothy, Sylvanus, Tychichus, were represented by Constantine and his fellow-labourers: the names of the apostolic churches were applied to the congregations which they assembled in Armenia and Cappadocia; and this innocent allegory revived the example and memory of the first ages. In *Their bible.* the gospel, and the epistles of St. Paul, his faithful follower investigated the creed of primitive Christianity; and, whatever might be the success, a protestant reader will applaud the spirit, of the enquiry. But if the scriptures of the Paulicians were pure, they were not perfect. Their founders rejected the two epistles of St. Peter,[4] the apostle of the circumcision, whose dispute with their favourite for the observance of the law could not easily be forgiven.[5] They agreed with their Gnostic brethren in the universal contempt for the Old Testament, the books of Moses and the prophets, which have been consecrated by the decrees of the Catholic church. With equal boldness, and doubtless with more reason, Constantine, the new Sylvanus, disclaimed the visions, which, in so many bulky and splendid volumes, had been published by the Oriental sects;[6] the fabulous productions of the Hebrew patriarchs and the sages of the East; the spurious gospels, epistles, and acts, which in the first age had

3. Nobis profanis ista *(sacra Evangelia)* legere non licet sed sacerdotibus duntaxat, was the first scruple of a Catholic when he was advised to read the Bible (Petr. Sicul. p. 761.).

4. In rejecting the *second* epistle of St. Peter, the Paulicians are justified by some of the most respectable of the ancients and moderns (see Wetstein ad loc. Simon, Hist. Critique du Nouveau Testament, c. 17.). They likewise overlooked the Apocalypse (Petr. Sicul. p. 756.); but as such neglect is not imputed as a crime, the Greeks of the ix[th] century must have been careless of the credit and honour of the Revelations.

5. This contention, which has not escaped the malice of Porphyry, supposes some error and passion in one or both of the apostles. By Chrysostom, Jerom, and Erasmus, it is represented as a sham quarrel, a pious fraud, for the benefit of the Gentiles and the correction of the Jews (Middleton's Works, vol. ii. p. 1–20.).

6. Those who are curious of this heterodox library, may consult the researches of Beausobre (Hist. Critique du Manicheisme, tom. i. p. 305–437.). Even in Africa, St. Austin could describe the Manichæan books, tam multi, tam grandes, tam pretiosi codices (contra Faust. xiii. 14.); but he adds, without pity, Incendite omnes illas membranas: and his advice has been rigorously followed.

overwhelmed the orthodox code; the theology of Manes, and the authors of the kindred heresies; and the thirty generations, or æons, which had been created by the fruitful fancy of Valentine. The Paulicians sincerely condemned the memory and opinions of the Manichæan sect, and complained of the injustice which impressed that invidious name on the simple votaries of St. Paul and of Christ.

The simplicity of their belief and worship.

Of the ecclesiastical chain, many links had been broken by the Paulician reformers; and their liberty was enlarged, as they reduced the number of masters, at whose voice profane reason must bow to mystery and miracle. The early separation of the Gnostics had preceded the establishment of the Catholic worship; and against the gradual innovations of discipline and doctrine, they were as strongly guarded by habit and aversion, as by the silence of St. Paul and the evangelists. The objects which had been transformed by the magic of superstition, appeared to the eyes of the Paulicians in their genuine and naked colours. An image made without hands, was the common workmanship of a mortal artist, to whose skill alone the wood and canvas must be indebted for their merit or value. The miraculous relics were an heap of bones and ashes, destitute of life or virtue, or of any relation, perhaps, with the person to whom they were ascribed. The true and vivifying cross was a piece of sound or rotten timber; the body and blood of Christ, a loaf of bread and a cup of wine, the gifts of nature and the symbols of grace. The mother of God was degraded from her celestial honours and immaculate virginity; and the saints and angels were no longer solicited to exercise the laborious office, of mediation in heaven, and ministry upon earth. In the practice, or at least in the theory of the sacraments, the Paulicians were inclined to abolish all visible objects of worship, and the words of the gospel were, in their judgment, the baptism and communion of the faithful. They indulged a convenient latitude for the interpretation of scripture; and as often as they were pressed by the literal sense, they could escape to the intricate mazes of figure and allegory. Their utmost diligence must have been employed to dissolve the connection between the old and the new testament; since they adored the latter as the oracles of God, and abhorred the former, as the fabulous and absurd invention of men or dæmons. We cannot be surprised, that they should have found in the gospel, the orthodox mystery of the trinity: but instead of confessing the human nature and substantial sufferings of Christ, they amused their fancy with a celestial body that passed through the virgin like water through a pipe; with a phantastic crucifixion, that eluded the vain and impotent malice of the Jews. A creed thus simple

They hold the two principles of the Magians and Manichæans.

and spiritual was not adapted to the genius of the times;[7] and the rational Christian who might have been contented with the light yoke and easy burthen of Jesus and his apostles, was justly offended, that the Paulicians should dare to violate the unity of God, the first article of natural and revealed religion. Their belief and their trust was in the Father, of Christ, of the human soul, and of the invisible world. But they likewise held the eternity of matter; a stubborn and rebellious substance, the origin of a second principle, of an active being, who has created this visible world, and exercises his temporal reign till the final consummation of death and sin.[8] The appearances of moral and physical evil had established the two principles in the ancient philosophy and religion of the East; from whence this doctrine was transfused to the various swarms of the Gnostics. A thousand shades may be devised in the nature and character of *Ahriman*, from a rival god to a subordinate dæmon, from passion and frailty to pure and perfect malevolence: but, in spite of our efforts, the goodness, and the power, of Ormusd are placed at the opposite extremities of the line; and every step that approaches the one must recede in equal proportion from the other.[9]

The establishment of the Paulicians in Armenia, Pontus, &c.

The apostolic labours of Constantine-Sylvanus, soon multiplied the number of his disciples, the secret recompence of spiritual ambition. The remnant of the Gnostic sects, and especially the Manichæans of Armenia, were united under his standard; many Catholics were converted or seduced by his arguments; and he preached with success in the regions of Pontus[10] and Cappadocia, which had long since imbibed the religion of Zoroaster. The Paulician teachers were distinguished only by their scriptural names, by the modest title of fellow-pilgrims, by the austerity of their lives, their zeal or knowledge, and the credit of some extraordinary gifts of the holy spirit. But they were incapable of desiring, or at least of obtaining, the wealth

7. The six capital errors of the Paulicians are defined by Peter Siculus (p. 756.) with much prejudice and passion.

8. Primum illorum axioma est, duo rerum esse principia; Deum malum et Deum bonum aliumque hujus mundi conditorem et principem, et alium futuri ævi (Petr. Sicul. p. 756.).

9. Two learned critics, Beausobre (Hist. Critique du Manicheisme, l. i. iv, v, vi.) and Mosheim (Institut. Hist. Eccles. and de Rebus Christianis ante Constantinum, sec. i, ii, iii.), have laboured to explore and discriminate the various systems of the Gnostics on the subject of the two principles.

10. The countries between the Euphrates and the Halys, were possessed above 350 years by the Medes (Herodot. l. i. c. 103.) and Persians; and the kings of Pontus were of the royal race of the Achæmenides (Salust. Fragment. l. iii. with the French supplement and notes of the president de Brosses).

and honours of the Catholic prelacy: such anti-christian pride they bitterly censured; and even the rank of elders or presbyters was condemned as an institution of the Jewish synagogue. The new sect was loosely spread over the provinces of Asia Minor to the westward of the Euphrates; six of their principal congregations represented the churches to which St. Paul had addressed his epistles; and their founder chose his residence in the neighbourhood of Colonia,[11] in the same district of Pontus which had been celebrated by the altars of Bellona[12] and the miracles of Gregory.[13] After a mission of twenty-seven years, Sylvanus, who had retired from the tolerating government of the Arabs, fell a sacrifice to Roman persecution. The laws of the pious emperors, which seldom touched the lives of less odious heretics, proscribed without mercy or disguise the tenets, the books, and the persons of the Montanists and Manichæans: the books were delivered to the flames; and all who should presume to secrete such writings, or to profess such opinions, were devoted to an ignominious death.[14] A Greek minister, armed with legal and military powers, appeared at Colonia to strike the shepherd, and to reclaim, if possible, the lost sheep. By a refinement of cruelty, Simeon placed the unfortunate Sylvanus before a line of his disciples, who were commanded, as the price of their pardon and the proof of their repentance, to massacre their spiritual father. They turned aside from the impious office; the stones dropt from their filial hands, and of the whole number, only one executioner could be found,

Persecution of the Greek emperors.

11. Most probably founded by Pompey after the conquest of Pontus. This Colonia, on the Lycus above Neo-Cæsarea, is named by the Turks Coulei-hisar, or Chonac, a populous town in a strong country (d'Anville, Geographie Ancienne, tom. ii. p. 34. Tournefort, Voyage du Levant, tom. iii. lettre xxi. p. 293.).

12. The temple of Bellona at Comana in Pontus, was a powerful and wealthy foundation, and the high priest was respected as the second person in the kingdom. As the sacerdotal office had been occupied by his mother's family, Strabo (l. xii. p. 809. 835. 836, 837.) dwells with peculiar complacency on the temple, the worship, and festival, which was twice celebrated every year. But the Bellona of Pontus had the features and character of the goddess, not of war, but of love.

13. Gregory, bishop of Neo-Cæsarea (A.D. 240–265), surnamed Thaumaturgus, or the Wonder-worker. An hundred years afterwards, the history or romance of his life was composed by Gregory of Nyssa, his namesake and countryman, the brother of the great St. Basil.

14. Hoc cæterum ad sua egregia facinora, divini atque orthodoxi Imperatores addiderunt, ut Manichæos Montanosque capitali puniri sententiâ juberent, eorumque libros, quocunque in loco inventi essent, flammis tradi; quòd siquis uspiam eosdem occultasse deprehenderetur, hunc eundem mortis pœnæ addici, ejusque bona in fiscum inferri (Petr. Sicul. p. 759.). What more could bigotry and persecution desire?

a new David, as he is styled by the Catholics, who boldly overthrew the giant of heresy. This apostate, Justus was his name, again deceived and betrayed his unsuspecting brethren, and a new conformity to the acts of St. Paul may be found in the conversion of Simeon: like the apostle, he embraced the doctrine which he had been sent to persecute, renounced his honours and fortunes, and acquired among the Paulicians the fame of a missionary and a martyr. They were not ambitious of martyrdom,[15] but in a calamitous period of one hundred and fifty years, their patience sustained whatever zeal could inflict: and power was insufficient to eradicate the obstinate vegetation of fanaticism and reason. From the blood and ashes of the first victims, a succession of teachers and congregations repeatedly arose: amidst their foreign hostilities, they found leisure for domestic quarrels: they preached, they disputed, they suffered; and the virtues, the apparent virtues, of Sergius, in a pilgrimage of thirty-three years, are reluctantly confessed by the orthodox historians.[16] The native cruelty of Justinian the second was stimulated by a pious cause, and he vainly hoped to extinguish in a single conflagration the name and memory of the Paulicians. By their primitive simplicity, their abhorrence of popular superstition, the Iconoclast princes might have been reconciled to some erroneous doctrines; but they themselves were exposed to the calumnies of the monks, and they chose to be the tyrants, lest they should be accused as the accomplices, of the Manichæans. Such a reproach has sullied the clemency of Nicephorus, who relaxed in their favour the severity of the penal statutes, nor will his character sustain the honour of a more liberal motive. The feeble Michael the first, the rigid Leo the Armenian, were foremost in the race of persecution; but the prize must doubtless be adjudged to the sanguinary devotion of Theodora, who restored the images to the Oriental church. Her inquisitors explored the cities and mountains of the lesser Asia, and the flatterers of the empress have affirmed that, in a short reign, one hundred thousand Paulicians were extirpated by the sword, the gibbet, or the flames. Her guilt or merit has perhaps been stretched beyond the measure of truth: but if the

15. It should seem, that the Paulicians allowed themselves some latitude of equivocation and mental reservation: till the Catholics discovered the pressing questions, which reduced them to the alternative of apostacy or martyrdom (Petr. Sicul. p. 760.).

16. The persecution is told by Petrus Siculus (p. 579–763.) with satisfaction and pleasantry. Justus *justa* persolvit. Simeon was not *τιτος* but *κητος* (the pronunciation of the two vowels must have been nearly the same), a great whale that drowned the mariners who mistook him for an island. See likewise Cedrenus (p. 432–435.).

account be allowed, it must be presumed that many simple Iconoclasts were punished under a more odious name; and that some who were driven from the church, unwillingly took refuge in the bosom of heresy.

Revolt of the Paulicians, A.D. 845–880. The most furious and desperate of rebels are the sectaries of a religion long persecuted, and at length provoked. In an holy cause they are no longer susceptible of fear or remorse: the justice of their arms hardens them against the feelings of humanity; and they revenge their fathers wrongs on the children of their tyrants. Such have been the Hussites of Bohemia and the Calvinists of France, and such, in the ninth century, were the Paulicians of Armenia and the adjacent provinces.[17] They were first awakened to the massacre of a governor and bishop, who exercised the Imperial mandate of converting or destroying the heretics; and the deepest recesses of mount Argæus protected their independence and revenge. A more dangerous and consuming flame was kindled by the persecution of Theodora, and the revolt of Carbeas, a valiant Paulician, who commanded the guards of the general of the East. His father had been impaled by the Catholic inquisitors; and religion, or at least nature, might justify his desertion and revenge. Five thousand of his brethren were united by the same motives; they renounced the allegiance of anti-christian Rome; a Saracen emir introduced Carbeas to the caliph; and the commander of the faithful extended his sceptre to the implacable enemy of the Greeks. In the mountains *They fortify Tephrice,* between Siwas and Trebizond he founded or fortified the city of Tephrice,[18] which is still occupied by a fierce and licentious people, and the neighbouring hills were covered with the Paulician fugitives, who now reconciled the use of the Bible and the sword. During more than thirty years, Asia was afflicted by the calamities of foreign and domestic war: in their hostile inroads the disciples of St. Paul were joined with those of Mahomet; and the peaceful Christians, the aged parent and tender virgin, who were delivered into barbarous servitude, might justly accuse the intolerant spirit of their sovereign. So urgent was the mischief, so intolerable the shame, that even the dissolute Michael, the son of Theodora, was compelled to march in person against the Paulicians: he

17. Petrus Siculus (p. 763, 764.), the continuator of Theophanes (l. iv. c. 4. p. 103, 104.), Cedrenus (p. 541, 542. 545.), and Zonaras (tom. ii. l. xvi. p. 156.), describe the revolt and exploits of Carbeas and his Paulicians.

18. Otter (Voyage en Turquie et en Perse, tom. ii.) is probably the only Frank who has visited the independent Barbarians of Tephrice, now Divrigni, from whom he fortunately escaped in the train of a Turkish officer.

was defeated under the walls of Samosata; and the Roman emperor fled before the heretics whom his mother had condemned to the flames. The Saracens fought under the same banners, but the victory was ascribed to Carbeas; and the captive generals, with more than an hundred tribunes, were either released by his avarice, or tortured by his fanaticism. The valour and ambition of Chrysocheir,[19] his successor, embraced a wider circle of rapine and revenge. In alliance with his faithful Moslems, he boldly penetrated into the heart of Asia; the troops of the frontier and the palace were repeatedly overthrown; the edicts of persecution were answered by the pillage of Nice and Nicomedia, of Ancyra and *and pillage* Ephesus; nor could the apostle St. John protect from violation *Asia Minor.* his city and sepulchre. The cathedral of Ephesus was turned into a stable for mules and horses; and the Paulicians vied with the Saracens in their contempt and abhorrence of images and relics. It is not unpleasing to observe the triumph of rebellion over the same despotism which has disdained the prayers of an injured people. The emperor Basil, the Macedonian, was reduced to sue for peace, to offer a ransom for the captives, and to request, in the language of moderation and charity, that Chrysocheir would spare his fellow-christians, and content himself with a royal donative of gold and silver and silk garments. "If the emperor," replied the insolent fanatic, "be desirous of peace, let him abdicate the East, and reign without molestation in the West. If he refuse, the servants of the Lord will precipitate him from the throne." The reluctant Basil suspended the treaty, accepted the defiance, and led his army into the land of heresy, which he wasted with fire and sword. The open country of the Paulicians was exposed to the same calamities which they had inflicted; but when he had explored the strength of Tephrice, the multitude of the Barbarians, and the ample magazines of arms and provisions, he desisted with a sigh from the hopeless siege. On his return to Constantinople he laboured, by the foundation of convents and churches, to secure the aid of his celestial patrons, of Michael the archangel and the prophet Elijah; and it was his daily prayer that he might live to transpierce, with three arrows, the head of his impious adversary. Beyond his expectations, the wish was accomplished: after a successful inroad, Chrysocheir was surprised and slain in his retreat; and the rebel's head was triumphantly

19. In the history of Chrysocheir, Genesius (Chron. p. 67–70. edit. Venet.) has exposed the nakedness of the empire. Constantine Porphyrogenitus (in Vit. Basil. c. 37–43. p. 166–171.) has displayed the glory of his grandfather. Cedrenus (p. 570–573.) is without their passions or their knowledge.

presented at the foot of the throne. On the reception of this welcome trophy, Basil instantly called for his bow, discharged three arrows with unerring aim, and accepted the applause of the court, who hailed the victory of the royal archer. With Chrysocheir, the glory of the Paulicians faded and withered;[20] on the second expedition of the emperor, the impregnable Tephrice was deserted by the heretics, who sued for mercy or escaped to the borders. The city was ruined, but the spirit of independence survived in the mountains: the Paulicians defended, above a century, their religion and liberty, infested the Roman limits, and maintained their perpetual alliance with the enemies of the empire and the gospel.

Their decline.

Their transplantation from Armenia to Thrace.

About the middle of the eighth century, Constantine, surnamed Copronymus by the worshippers of images, had made an expedition into Armenia, and found, in the cities of Melitene and Theodosiopolis, a great number of Paulicians, his kindred heretics. As a favour or punishment, he transplanted them from the banks of the Euphrates to Constantinople and Thrace; and by this emigration their doctrine was introduced and diffused in Europe.[21] If the sectaries of the metropolis were soon mingled with the promiscuous mass, those of the country struck a deep root in a foreign soil. The Paulicians of Thrace resisted the storms of persecution, maintained a secret correspondence with their Armenian brethren, and gave aid and comfort to their preachers, who solicited, not without success, the infant faith of the Bulgarians.[22] In the tenth century, they were restored and multiplied by a more powerful colony, which John Zimisces[23] transported from the Chalybian hills to the vallies of mount Hæmus. The Oriental clergy, who would have preferred the destruction, impatiently sighed for the absence, of the Manichæans: the warlike emperor had felt and esteemed their valour; their attachment to the Saracens was pregnant

20. *Συναπεμαρανθη πασα ἡ ανθουσα της Τεφρικης ευανδια.* How elegant is the Greek tongue, even in the mouth of Cedrenus!

21. Copronymus transported his *συγγενεις*, heretics; and thus *επλατυνθη ἡ αιρεσις Παυλικιανον*, says Cedrenus (p. 463.), who has copied the annals of Theophanes.

22. Petrus Siculus, who resided nine months at Tephrice (A.D. 870) for the ransom of captives (p. 764.), was informed of their intended mission, and addressed his preservative, the Historia Manichæorum, to the new archbishop of the Bulgarians (p. 754.).

23. The colony of Paulicians and Jacobites, transplanted by John Zimisces (A.D. 970.) from Armenia to Thrace, is mentioned by Zonaras (tom. ii. l. xvii. p. 209.) and Anna Comnena (Alexiad, l. xiv. p. 450, &c.).

with mischief; but, on the side of the Danube, against the Barbarians of Scythia, their service might be useful, and their loss would be desirable. Their exile in a distant land was softened by a free toleration: the Paulicians held the city of Philippopolis and the keys of Thrace; the Catholics were their subjects; the Jacobite emigrants their associates: they occupied a line of villages and castles in Macedonia and Epirus; and many native Bulgarians were associated to the communion of arms and heresy. As long as they were awed by power and treated with moderation, their voluntary bands were distinguished in the armies of the empire; and the courage of these *dogs*, ever greedy of war, ever thirsty of human blood, is noticed with astonishment, and almost with reproach, by the pusillanimous Greeks. The same spirit rendered them arrogant and contumacious: they were easily provoked by caprice or injury; and their privileges were often violated by the faithless bigotry of the government and clergy. In the midst of the Norman war, two thousand five hundred Manichæans deserted the standard of Alexius Comnenus,[24] and retired to their native homes. He dissembled till the moment of revenge; invited the chiefs to a friendly conference; and punished the innocent and guilty by imprisonment, confiscation, and baptism. In an interval of peace, the emperor undertook the pious office of reconciling them to the church and state: his winter-quarters were fixed at Philippopolis; and the thirteenth apostle, as he is styled by his pious daughter, consumed whole days and nights in theological controversy. His arguments were fortified, their obstinacy was melted, by the honours and rewards which he bestowed on the most eminent proselytes; and a new city, surrounded with gardens, enriched with immunities, and dignified with his own name, was founded by Alexius, for the residence of his vulgar converts. The important station of Philippopolis was wrested from their hands; the contumacious leaders were secured in a dungeon, or banished from their country; and their lives were spared by the prudence, rather than the mercy, of an emperor, at whose command a poor and solitary heretic was burnt alive before the church of St. Sophia.[25] But the proud hope of eradicating the prejudices of a nation was speedily overturned by the invincible zeal of the Paulicians, who ceased to dissemble or refused to obey. After the departure and

24. The Alexiad of Anna Comnena (l. v. p. 131. l. vi. p. 154, 155. l. xiv. p. 450–457. with the annotations of Ducange) records the transactions of her apostolic father with the Manichæans, whose abominable heresy she was desirous of refuting.

25. Basil, a monk, and the author of the Bogomiles, a sect of Gnostics, who soon vanished (Anna Comnena, Alexiad, l. xv. p. 486–494. Mosheim, Hist. Ecclesiastica, p. 420.).

death of Alexius, they soon resumed their civil and religious laws. In the beginning of the thirteenth century, their pope or primate (a manifest corruption) resided on the confines of Bulgaria, Croatia, and Dalmatia, and governed, by his vicars, the filial congregations of Italy and France.[26] From that æra, a minute scrutiny might prolong and perpetuate the chain of tradition. At the end of the last age, the sect or colony still inhabited the vallies of mount Hæmus, where their ignorance and poverty were more frequently tormented by the Greek clergy than by the Turkish government. The modern Paulicians have lost all memory of their origin; and their religion is disgraced by the worship of the cross, and the practice of bloody sacrifice, which some captives have imported from the wilds of Tartary.[27]

Their introduction into Italy and France.

In the West, the first teachers of the Manichæan theology had been repulsed by the people or suppressed by the prince. The favour and success of the Paulicians in the eleventh and twelfth centuries must be imputed to the strong, though secret, discontent which armed the most pious Christians against the church of Rome. Her avarice was oppressive, her despotism odious: less degenerate perhaps than the Greeks in the worship of saints and images, her innovations were more rapid and scandalous: she had rigorously defined and imposed the doctrine of transubstantiation: the lives of the Latin clergy were more corrupt, and the Eastern bishops might pass for the successors of the apostles, if they were compared with the lordly prelates, who wielded by turns the crosier, the sceptre, and the sword. Three different roads might introduce the Paulicians into the heart of Europe. After the conversion of Hungary, the pilgrims who visited Jerusalem might safely follow the course of the Danube: in their journey and return they passed through Philippopolis; and the sectaries, disguising their name and heresy, might accompany the French or German caravans to their respective countries. The trade and dominion of Venice pervaded the coast of the Adriatic, and the hospitable republic opened her bosom to foreigners of every climate and religion. Under the Byzantine standard, the Paulicians were often transported to the Greek provinces of Italy and Sicily; in peace and war they freely conversed with strangers and natives, and their opinions were silently propagated in Rome, Milan, and the kingdoms

26. Matt. Paris, Hist. Major. p. 267. This passage of our English historian is alleged by Ducange in an excellent note on Villehardouin (N° 208.), who found the Paulicians at Philippopolis the friends of the Bulgarians.

27. See Marsigli, Stato Militare dell' Impero Ottomano, p. 24.

beyond the Alps.[28] It was soon discovered, that many thousand Catholics of every rank, and of either sex, had embraced the Manichæan heresy; and the flames which consumed twelve canons of Orleans, was the first act and signal of persecution. The Bulgarians,[29] a name so innocent in its origin, so odious in its application, spread their branches over the face of Europe. United in common hatred of idolatry and Rome, they were connected by a form of episcopal and presbyterian government; their various sects were discriminated by some fainter or darker shades of theology; but they generally agreed in the two principles, the contempt of the old testament, and the denial of the body of Christ, either on the cross or in the Eucharist. A confession of simple worship and blameless manners is extorted from their enemies; and so high was their standard of perfection, that the encreasing congregations were divided into two classes of disciples, of those who practised, and of those who aspired. It was in the country of the Albigeois,[30] in the southern provinces of France, that the Paulicians were most deeply implanted; and the same vicissitudes of martyrdom and revenge which had been displayed in the neighbourhood of the Euphrates, were repeated in the thirteenth century on the banks of the Rhône. The laws of the Eastern emperors were revived by Frederic the second. The insurgents of Tephrice were represented by the barons and cities of Languedoc: Pope Innocent III. surpassed the sanguinary fame of Theodora. It was in cruelty alone that her soldiers could equal the heroes of

Persecution of the Albigeois, A.D. 1200, &c.

28. The introduction of the Paulicians into Italy and France, is amply discussed by Muratori (Antiquitat. Italiæ medii Ævi, tom. v. dissert. lx. p. 81–152.), and Mosheim (p. 379–382. 419–422.). Yet both have overlooked a curious passage of William the Appulian, who clearly describes them in a battle between the Greeks and Normans, A.D. 1040 (in Muratori, Script. Rerum Ital. tom. v. p. 256.).

Cum Græcis aderant, quidem quos pessimus error,
Fecerat amentes, et ab ipso nòmen habebant.

But he is so ignorant of their doctrine as to make them a kind of Sabellians or Patripassians.

29. *Bulgari, Boulgres, Bougres*, a national appellation, has been applied by the French as a term of reproach to usurers and unnatural sinners. The *Paterini*, or *Patelini*, has been made to signify a smooth and flattering hypocrite, such as *l'Avocat Patelin* of that original and pleasant farce (Ducange, Gloss. Latinitat. medii et infimi Ævi). The Manichæans were likewise named *Cathari*, or the pure, by corruption, *Gazari*, &c.

30. Of the laws, crusade, and persecution against the Albigeois, a just, though general idea, is expressed by Mosheim (p. 477–481.). The detail may be found in the ecclesiastical historians, ancient and modern, Catholics and Protestants; and among these Fleury is the most impartial and moderate.

the Crusades, and the cruelty of her priests was far excelled by the founders of the inquisition;[31] an office more adapted to confirm, than to refute, the belief of an evil principle. The visible assemblies of the Paulicians, or Albigeois, were extirpated by fire and sword; and the bleeding remnant escaped by flight, concealment, or catholic conformity. But the invincible spirit which they had kindled still lived and breathed in the Western world. In the state, in the church, and even in the cloister, a latent succession was preserved of the disciples of St. Paul; who protested against the tyranny of Rome, embraced the bible as the rule of faith, and purified their creed from all the visions of the Gnostic theology. The struggles of Wickliff in England, of Huss in Bohemia, were premature and ineffectual; but the names of Zuinglius, Luther, and Calvin, are pronounced with gratitude as the deliverers of nations.

Character and consequences of the reformation.

A philosopher, who calculates the degree of their merit and the value of their reformation, will prudently ask from what articles of faith, *above* or *against* our reason, they have enfranchised the Christians; for such enfranchisement is doubtless a benefit so far as it may be compatible with truth and piety. After a fair discussion we shall rather be surprised by the timidity, than scandalised by the freedom, of our first reformers.[32] With the Jews, they adopted the belief and defence of all the Hebrew scriptures, with all their prodigies, from the garden of Eden to the visions of the prophet Daniel; and they were bound, like the Catholics, to justify against the Jews the abolition of a divine law. In the great mysteries of the Trinity and Incarnation the reformers were severely orthodox: they freely adopted the theology of the four, or the six first councils; and with the Athanasian creed, they pronounced the eternal damnation of all who did not believe the Catholic faith. Transubstantiation, the invisible change of the bread and wine into the body and blood of Christ, is a tenet that may defy the power of argument and pleasantry; but instead of consulting the evidence of their senses, of their sight, their feeling, and their taste, the first protestants

31. The Acts (Liber Sententiarum) of the Inquisition of Tholouse (A.D. 1307–1323) have been published by Limborch (Amstelodami, 1692), with a previous History of the Inquisition in General. They deserved a more learned and critical editor. As we must not calumniate even Satan, or the Holy Office, I will observe, that of a list of criminals which fills nineteen folio pages, only fifteen men and four women were delivered to the secular arm.

32. The opinions and proceedings of the reformers are exposed in the second part of the general history of Mosheim: but the balance, which he has held with so clear an eye, and so steady an hand, begins to incline in favour of his Lutheran brethren.

were entangled in their own scruples, and awed by the words of Jesus in the institution of the sacrament. Luther maintained a *corporeal*, and Calvin a *real*, presence of Christ in the eucharist; and the opinion of Zuinglius, that it is no more than a spiritual communion, a simple memorial, has slowly prevailed in the reformed churches.[33] But the loss of one mystery was amply compensated by the stupendous doctrines of original sin, redemption, faith, grace, and predestination, which have been strained from the epistles of St. Paul. These subtle questions had most assuredly been prepared by the fathers and schoolmen; but the final improvement and popular use may be attributed to the first reformers, who enforced them as the absolute and essential terms of salvation. Hitherto the weight of supernatural belief inclines against the Protestants; and many a sober Christian would rather admit that a wafer is God, than that God is a cruel and capricious tyrant.

Yet the services of Luther and his rivals are solid and important; and the philosopher must own his obligations to these fearless enthusiasts.[34] I. By their hands the lofty fabric of superstition, from the abuse of indulgences to the intercession of the Virgin, has been levelled with the ground. Myriads of both sexes of the monastic profession were restored to the liberty and labours of social life. An hierarchy of saints and angels, of imperfect and subordinate deities, were stripped of their temporal power, and reduced to the enjoyment of celestial happiness: their images and relics were banished from the church; and the credulity of the people was no longer nourished with the daily repetition of miracles and visions. The imitation of Paganism was supplied by a pure and spiritual worship of prayer and thanksgiving, the most worthy of man, the least unworthy of the Deity. It only remains to observe, whether such sublime simplicity be consistent with popular devotion; whether the vulgar, in the absence of all visible objects, will not be inflamed by enthusiasm, or insensibly subside in languor and indifference. II. The chain of authority was broken, which restrains the bigot from thinking as he pleases, and the slave from speaking as he thinks: the popes, fathers, and councils, were no longer the supreme and infallible judges of the world; and each

33. Under Edward VI. our reformation was more bold and perfect: but in the fundamental articles of the church of England, a strong and explicit declaration against the real presence was obliterated in the original copy, to please the people, or the Lutherans, or Queen Elizabeth (Burnet's History of the Reformation, vol. ii. p. 82. 128. 302.).

34. "Had it not been for such men as Luther and myself," said the fanatic Whiston to Halley the philosopher, "you would now be kneeling before an image of St. Winifred."

Christian was taught to acknowledge no law but the scriptures, no interpreter but his own conscience. This freedom however was the consequence, rather than the design, of the reformation. The patriot reformers were ambitious of succeeding the tyrants whom they had dethroned. They imposed with equal rigour their creeds and confessions; they asserted the right of the magistrate to punish heretics with death. The pious or personal animosity of Calvin proscribed in Servetus[35] the guilt of his own rebellion;[36] and the flames of Smithfield, in which he was afterwards consumed, had been kindled for the Anabaptists by the zeal of Cranmer.[37] The nature of the tyger was the same, but he was gradually deprived of his teeth and fangs. A spiritual and temporal kingdom was possessed by the Roman pontiff: the Protestant doctors were subjects of an humble rank, without revenue or jurisdiction. *His* decrees were consecrated by the antiquity of the Catholic church: *their* arguments and disputes were submitted to the people; and their appeal to private judgment was accepted beyond their wishes, by curiosity and enthusiasm. Since the days of Luther and Calvin, a secret reformation has been silently working in the bosom of the reformed churches; many weeds of prejudice were eradicated; and the disciples of Erasmus[38] diffused a spirit of freedom and moderation. The liberty of conscience has been claimed as a common benefit, an inalienable right:[39] the free governments

35. The article of *Servet* in the Dictionaire Critique of Chauffepié, is the best account which I have seen of this shameful transaction. See likewise the Abbé d'Artigny, Nouveaux Memoires d'Histoire, &c. tom. ii. p. 55–154.

36. I am more deeply scandalised at the single execution of Servetus, than at the hecatombs which have blazed in the Auto da Fès of Spain and Portugal. 1. The zeal of Calvin seems to have been envenomed by personal malice, and perhaps envy. He accused his adversary before their common enemies, the judges of Vienna, and betrayed, for his destruction, the sacred trust of a private correspondence. 2. The deed of cruelty was not varnished by the pretence of danger to the church or state. In his passage through Geneva, Servetus was an harmless stranger, who neither preached, nor printed, nor made proselytes. 3. A Catholic inquisitor yields the same obedience which he requires, but Calvin violated the golden rule of doing as he would be done by; a rule which I read in a moral treatise of Isocrates (in Nicocle, tom. i. p. 93. edit. Battie), four hundred years before the publication of the gospel. *'Α πασχοντες ὑφ' ἑτερων οργιζεσθε, ταυτα τοις αλλοις μη ποιειτε.*

37. See Burnet, vol. ii. p. 84–86. The sense and humanity of the young king were oppressed by the authority of the primate.

38. Erasmus may be considered as the father of rational theology. After a slumber of an hundred years, it was revived by the Arminians of Holland, Grotius, Limborch, and Le Clerc: in England by Chillingworth, the latitudinarians of Cambridge (Burnet, Hist. of own Times, vol. i. p. 261–268. octavo edition), Tillotson, Clarke, Hoadley, &c.

39. I am sorry to observe, that the three writers of the last age, by whom the rights

of Holland[40] and England[41] introduced the practice of toleration; and the narrow allowance of the laws has been enlarged by the prudence and humanity of the times. In the exercise, the mind has understood the limits, of its powers, and the words and shadows that might amuse the child can no longer satisfy his manly reason. The volumes of controversy are overspread with cobwebs: the doctrine of a Protestant church is far removed from the knowledge or belief of its private members; and the forms of orthodoxy, the articles of faith, are subscribed with a sigh or a smile by the modern clergy. Yet the friends of Christianity are alarmed at the boundless impulse of enquiry and scepticism. The predictions of the Catholics are accomplished: the web of mystery is unravelled by the Arminians, Arians, and Socinians, whose numbers must not be computed from their separate congregations. And the pillars of revelation are shaken by those men who preserve the name without the substance of religion, who indulge the licence without the temper of philosophy.[42]

---

of toleration have been so nobly defended, Bayle, Leibnitz, and Locke, are all laymen and philosophers.

40. See the excellent chapter of Sir William Temple on the religion of the United Provinces. I am not satisfied with Grotius (de Rebus Belgicis, Annal. l. i. p. 13, 14. edit. in 12[mo]), who approves the Imperial laws of persecution, and only condemns the bloody tribunal of the inquisition.

41. Sir William Blackstone (Commentaries, vol. iv. p. 53, 54.) explains the law of England as it was fixed at the Revolution. The exceptions of Papists, and of those who deny the Trinity, would still leave a tolerable scope for persecution, if the national spirit were not more effectual than an hundred statutes.

42. I shall recommend to public animadversion two passages in Dr. Priestley, which betray the ultimate tendency of his opinions. At the first of these (Hist. of the Corruptions of Christianity, vol. i. p. 275, 276.), the priest; at the second (vol. ii. p. 484.), the magistrate, may tremble!

CHAPTER LV

The Bulgarians. – Origin, Migrations, and Settlement of the Hungarians. – Their Inroads in the East and West. – The Monarchy of Russia. – Geography and Trade. – Wars of the Russians against the Greek Empire. – Conversion of the Barbarians.

Under the reign of Constantine the grandson of Heraclius, the ancient barrier of the Danube, so often violated and so often restored, was irretrievably swept away by a new deluge of Barbarians. Their progress was favoured by the caliphs, their unknown and accidental auxiliaries: the Roman legions were occupied in Asia; and after the loss of Syria, Egypt, and Africa, the Cæsars were twice reduced to the danger and disgrace of defending their capital against the Saracens. If in the account of this interesting people, I have deviated from the strict and original line of my undertaking, the merit of the subject will hide my transgression or solicit my excuse. In the East, in the West, in war, in religion, in science, in their prosperity, and in their decay, the Arabians press themselves on our curiosity: the first overthrow of the church and empire of the Greeks may be imputed to their arms; and the disciples of Mahomet still hold the civil and religious sceptre of the Oriental world. But the same labour would be unworthily bestowed on the swarms of savages, who, between the seventh and the twelfth century, descended from the plains of Scythia, in transient inroad or perpetual emigration.[1] Their names are uncouth, their origins doubtful, their actions obscure, their superstition was blind, their valour brutal, and the uniformity of their public and private lives was neither softened by innocence nor refined by policy. The majesty of the Byzantine throne repelled and survived their disorderly attacks; the greater part of these Barbarians has disappeared without leaving any

1. *All* the passages of the Byzantine history which relate to the Barbarians, are compiled, methodised, and transcribed in a Latin version, by the laborious John Gotthelf Stritter, in his Memoriæ Populorum, ad Danubium, Pontum Euxinum, Paludem Mæotidem, Caucasum, Mare Caspium, et inde magis ad Septemtriones incolentium, Petropoli, 1771–1779, in four tomes, or six volumes, in 4to. But the fashion has not enhanced the price of these raw materials.

memorial of their existence, and the despicable remnant continues, and may long continue, to groan under the dominion of a foreign tyrant. From the antiquities of, I. *Bulgarians*, II. *Hungarians*, and, III. *Russians*, I shall content myself with selecting such facts as yet deserve to be remembered. The conquests of the, IV. NORMANS, and the monarchy of the, V. TURKS, will naturally terminate in the memorable Crusades to the Holy Land, and the double fall of the city and empire of Constantine.

Emigration of the Bulgarians, A.D. 680, &c.

In his march to Italy, Theodoric[2] the Ostrogoth had trampled on the arms of the Bulgarians. After this defeat the name and the nation are lost during a century and an half; and it may be suspected that the same or a similar appellation was revived by strange colonies from the Borysthenes, the Tanais, or the Volga. A king of the ancient Bulgaria[3] bequeathed to his five sons a last lesson of moderation and concord. It was received as youth has ever received the counsels of age and experience: the five princes buried their father; divided his subjects and cattle; forgot his advice; separated from each other; and wandered in quest of fortune, till we find the most adventurous in the heart of Italy, under the protection of the exarch of Ravenna.[4] But the stream of emigration was directed or impelled towards the capital. The modern Bulgaria, along the southern banks of the Danube, was stamped with the name and image which it has retained to the present hour: the new conquerors successively acquired, by war or treaty, the Roman provinces of Dardania, Thessaly, and the two Epirus';[5] the ecclesiastical supremacy was translated from the native city of Justinian; and, in their prosperous age, the obscure town of Lychnidus, or Achrida, was honoured with the throne of a king and a patriarch.[6] The unquestionable

2. Hist. vol. ii. p. 537.

3. Theophanes, p. 296–299. Anastasius, p. 113. Nicephorus, C.P. p. 22, 23. Theophanes places the old Bulgaria on the banks of the Atell or Volga; but he deprives himself of all geographical credit, by discharging that river into the Euxine Sea.

4. Paul. Diacon. de Gestis Langobard. l. v. c. 29. p. 881, 882. The apparent difference between the Lombard historian and the above mentioned Greeks, is easily reconciled by Camillo Pellegrino (de Ducatû Beneventano, dissert. vii. in the Scriptores Rerum Ital. tom. v. p. 186, 187.) and Beretti (Chorograph. Italiæ medii Ævi, p. 273, &c.). This Bulgarian colony was planted in a vacant district of Samnium, and learned the Latin, without forgetting their native, language.

5. These provinces of the Greek idiom and empire, are assigned to the Bulgarian kingdom in the dispute of ecclesiastical jurisdiction between the patriarchs of Rome and Constantinople (Baronius, Annal. Eccles. A.D. 869, N° 75.).

6. The situation and royalty of Lychnidus, or Achrida, are clearly expressed in Cedrenus (p. 713.). The removal of an archbishop or patriarch from Justinianea prima, to Lychnidus, and at length to Ternovo, has produced some perplexity in the ideas or language of the Greeks (Nicephorus

evidence of language attests the descent of the Bulgarians from the original stock of the Sclavonian, or more properly Slavonian, race;[7] and the kindred bands of Servians, Bosnians, Rascians, Croatians, Walachians,[8] &c. followed either the standard or the example of the leading tribe. From the Euxine to the Adriatic, in the state of captives, or subjects, or allies, or enemies, of the Greek empire, they overspread the land; and the national appellation of the SLAVES[9] has been degraded by chance or malice from the signification of glory to that of servitude.[10] Among these

Croats or Sclavonians of Dalmatia, A.D. 900, &c.

colonies, the Chrobatians,[11] or Croats, who now attend the motions of an Austrian army, are the descendants of a mighty people, the conquerors and sovereigns of Dalmatia. The maritime cities, and of these the infant republic of Ragusa, implored the aid and instructions of the Byzantine court: they were advised by the magnanimous Basil to reserve a small acknowledgment of their fidelity to the Roman empire, and to appease, by an annual tribute, the wrath of these irresistible Barbarians. The kingdom of Croatia was shared by eleven *Zoupans*, or feudatory lords; and their united forces were numbered at sixty thousand horse and one hundred thousand foot. A long sea-coast, indented with capacious harbours, covered with a string

---

Gregoras, l. ii. c. 2. p. 14, 15. Thomassin, Discipline de l'Eglise, tom. i. l. i. c. 19. 23.); and a Frenchman (d'Anville) is more accurately skilled in the geography of their own country (Hist. de l'Academie des Inscriptions, tom. xxxi.).

7. Chalcocondyles, a competent judge, affirms the identity of the language of the Dalmatians, Bosnians, Servians, *Bulgarians*, Poles (de Rebus Turcicis, l. x. p. 283.), and elsewhere of the Bohemians (l. ii. p. 38.). The same author has marked the separate idiom of the Hungarians.

8. See the work of John Christopher de Jordan, de Originibus Sclavicis, Vindobonæ, 1745, in four parts, or two volumes in folio. His collections and researches are useful to elucidate the antiquities of Bohemia and the adjacent countries: but his plan is narrow, his style barbarous, his criticism shallow, and the Aulic counsellor is not free from the prejudices of a Bohemian.

9. Jordan subscribes to the well-known and probable derivation from *Slava*, *laus*, *gloria*, a word of familiar use in the different dialects and parts of speech, and which forms the termination of the most illustrious names (de Originibus Sclavicis, pars i. p. 40. pars iv. p. 101, 102.).

10. This conversion of a national into an appellative name, appears to have arisen in the viii[th] century, in the Oriental France, where the princes and bishops were rich in Sclavonian captives, not of the Bohemian (exclaims Jordan), but of Sorabian race. From thence the word was extended to general use, to the modern languages, and even to the style of the last Byzantines (see the Greek and Latin Glossaries of Ducange). The confusion of the *Σερβλοι*, or Servians, with the Latin *Servi*, was still more fortunate and familiar (Constant. Porphyr. de administrando Imperio, c. 32. p. 99.).

11. The emperor Constantine Porphyrogenitus, most accurate for his own times, most fabulous for preceding ages, describes the Sclavonians of Dalmatia (c. 29–36.).

of islands, and almost in sight of the Italian shores, disposed both the natives and strangers to the practice of navigation. The boats or brigantines of the Croats were constructed after the fashion of the old Liburnians: one hundred and eighty vessels may excite the idea of a respectable navy; but our seamen will smile at the allowance of ten, or twenty, or forty, men for each of these ships of war. They were gradually converted to the more honourable service of commerce; yet the Sclavonian pirates were still frequent and dangerous; and it was not before the close of the tenth century that the freedom and sovereignty of the Gulf were effectually vindicated by the Venetian republic.[12] The ancestors of these Dalmatian kings were equally removed from the use and abuse of navigation: they dwelt in the White Croatia, in the inland regions of Silesia and Little Poland, thirty days journey, according to the Greek computation, from the sea of darkness.

First kingdom of the Bulgarians, A.D. 640–1017.

The glory of the Bulgarians[13] was confined to a narrow scope both of time and place. In the ninth and tenth centuries, they reigned to the south of the Danube; but the more powerful nations that had followed their emigration, repelled all return to the north and all progress to the west. Yet, in the obscure catalogue of their exploits, they might boast an honour which had hitherto been appropriated to the Goths; that of slaying in battle one of the successors of Augustus and Constantine. The emperor Nicephorus had lost his fame in the Arabian, he lost his life in the Sclavonian, war. In his first operations he advanced with boldness and success into the centre of Bulgaria, and burnt the *royal court*, which was probably no more than an edifice and village of timber. But, while he searched the spoil and refused all offers of treaty, his enemies collected their spirits and their forces: the passes of retreat were insuperably barred; and the trembling Nicephorus was heard to exclaim: "Alas, alas! unless we could assume the wings of birds, we cannot hope to escape." Two days he waited his fate in the inactivity of despair; but, on the morning of the third, the Bulgarians surprised the camp, and the Roman prince, with the great officers of the empire, were slaughtered in their tents. The body of Valens had been saved *A.D. 811.*

12. See the anonymous Chronicle of the xi[th] century, ascribed to John Sagorninus (p. 94–102.), and that composed in the xiv[th] by the Doge Andrew Dandolo (Script. Rerum Ital. tom. xii. p. 227–230.); the two oldest monuments of the history of Venice.

13. The first kingdom of the Bulgarians may be found under the proper dates in the Annals of Cedrenus and Zonaras. The Byzantine materials are collected by Stritter (Memoriæ Populorum, tom. ii. pars ii. p. 441–647.); and the series of their kings is disposed and settled by Ducange (Fam. Byzant. p. 305–318.).

from insult; but the head of Nicephorus was exposed on a spear, and his skull, enchased with gold, was often replenished in the feasts of victory. The Greeks bewailed the dishonour of the throne; but they acknowledged the just punishment of avarice and cruelty. This savage cup was deeply tinctured with the manners of the Scythian wilderness; but they were softened before the end of the same century by a peaceful intercourse with the Greeks, the possession of a cultivated region, and the introduction of the Christian worship. The nobles of Bulgaria were educated in the schools and palace of Constantinople; and Simeon,[14] a youth of the royal line, was instructed in the rhetoric of Demosthenes and the logic of Aristotle. He relinquished the profession of a monk for that of a king and warrior; and in his reign, of more than forty years, Bulgaria assumed a rank among the civilized powers of the earth. The Greeks, whom he repeatedly attacked, derived a faint consolation from indulging themselves in the reproaches of perfidy and sacrilege. They purchased the aid of the Pagan Turks; but Simeon, in a second battle, redeemed the loss of the first, at a time when it was esteemed a victory to elude the arms of that formidable nation. The Servians were overthrown, made captive, and dispersed; and those who visited the country before their restoration could discover no more than fifty vagrants, without women or children, who extorted a precarious subsistence from the chace. On classic ground, on the banks of the Achelous, the Greeks were defeated; their horn was broken by the strength of the Barbaric Hercules.[15] He formed the siege of Constantinople; and, in a personal conference with the emperor, Simeon imposed the conditions of peace. They met with the most jealous precautions: the royal galley was drawn close to an artificial and well-fortified platform; and the majesty of the purple was emulated by the pomp of the Bulgarian. "Are you a Christian?" said the humble Romanus; "It is your duty to abstain from the blood of your fellow-Christians. Has the thirst of riches seduced you from the blessings of peace? Sheath your sword, open your hand, and I will satiate the utmost measure of your desires." The reconciliation was sealed by a domestic alliance; the freedom of trade was granted or

A.D. 888–927, or 932.

14. Simeonem semi-Græcum esse aiebant, eo quod a pueritia Byzantii Demosthenis rhetoricam et Aristotelis syllogismos didicerat. Liutprand, l. iii. c. 8. He says in another place, Simeon, fortis bellator, Bulgariæ præerat; Christianus sed vicinis Græcis valde inimicus (l. i. c. 2.).

15.

—— Rigidum fera dexterâ cornu
Dum tenet infregit, truncâque a fronte revellit.

Ovid (Metamorph. ix. 1–100.) has boldly painted the combat of the river-god and the hero; the native and the stranger.

restored; the first honours of the court were secured to the friends of Bulgaria, above the ambassadors of enemies or strangers;[16] and her princes were dignified with the high and invidious title of *Basileus*, or emperor. But this friendship was soon disturbed: after the death of Simeon the nations were again in arms; his feeble successors were divided and extinguished; and, in the beginning of the eleventh century, the second Basil, who was born in the purple, deserved the appellation of conqueror of the Bulgarians. His avarice was in some measure gratified by a treasure of four hundred thousand pounds sterling (ten thousand pound weight of gold), which he found in the palace of Lychnidus. His cruelty inflicted a cool and exquisite vengeance on fifteen thousand captives who had been guilty of the defence of their country. They were deprived of sight, but to one of each hundred a single eye was left, that he might conduct his blind century to the presence of their king. Their king is said to have expired of grief and horror; the nation was awed by this terrible example; the Bulgarians were swept away from their settlements, and circumscribed within a narrow province; the surviving chiefs bequeathed to their children the advice of patience and the duty of revenge.

A.D. 950, &c.

II. When the black swarm of Hungarians first hung over Europe, about nine hundred years after the Christian æra, they were mistaken by fear and superstition for the Gog and Magog of the scriptures, the signs and forerunners of the end of the world.[17] Since the introduction of letters, they have explored their own antiquities with a strong and laudable impulse of patriotic curiosity.[18] Their rational criticism can no longer be amused with a vain pedigree of

Emigration of the Turks or Hungarians, A.D. 884.

16. The ambassador of Otho was provoked by the Greek excuses, cum Christophori filiam Petrus Bulgarorum *Vasileus* conjugem duceret, *Symphona*, idest consonantia, scripto juramento firmata sunt ut omnium gentium *Apostolis* idest nunciis penes nos Bulgarorum Apostoli præponantur, honorentur, diligentur (Liutprand in Legatione, p. 482.). See the Ceremoniale of Constantine Porphyrogenitus, tom. i. p. 82. tom. ii. p. 429, 430. 434, 435. 443, 444. 446, 447. with the annotations of Reiske.

17. A bishop of Wurtzburgh submitted this opinion to a reverend abbot; but *he* more gravely decided, that Gog and Magog were the spiritual persecutors of the church; since Gog signifies the roof, the pride of the Heresiarchs, and Magog what comes from the roof, the propagation of their sects. Yet these men once commanded the respect of mankind (Fleury, Hist. Eccles. tom. xi. p. 594, &c.).

18. The two national authors, from whom I have derived the most assistance, are George Pray (Dissertationes ad Annales veterum Hungarorum, &c. Vindobonæ, 1775, in folio), and Stephen Katona (Hist. Critica Ducum et Regum Hungariæ stirpis Arpadianæ, Pæstini, 1778–1781, 5 vols. in octavo). The first embraces a large and often conjectural space: the latter, by his learning, judgment, and perspicuity, deserves the name of a critical historian.

Attila and the Huns; but they complain that their primitive records have perished in the Tartar war; that the truth or fiction of their rustic songs is long since forgotten; and that the fragments of a rude chronicle[19] must be painfully reconciled with the contemporary though foreign intelligence of the Imperial geographer.[20] *Magiar* is the national and oriental denomination of the Hungarians; but, among the tribes of Scythia, they are distinguished by the Greeks under the proper and peculiar name of *Turks*, as the descendants of that mighty people who had conquered and reigned from China to the Volga. The Pannonian colony preserved a correspondence of trade and amity with the eastern Turks on the confines of Persia; and after a separation of three hundred and fifty years, the missionaries of the king of Hungary discovered and visited their ancient country near the banks of the Volga. They were hospitably entertained by a people of Pagans and Savages who still bore the name of Hungarians; conversed in their native tongue, recollected a tradition of their long-lost brethren, and listened with amazement to the marvellous tale of their new kingdom and religion. The zeal of conversion was animated by the interest of consanguinity; and one of the greatest of their princes had formed the generous, though fruitless design, of replenishing the solitude of Pannonia by this domestic colony from the heart of Tartary.[21] From this primitive country, they were driven to the west by the tide of war and emigration, by the weight of the more distant tribes, who at the same time were fugitives and conquerors. Reason or fortune directed their course towards the frontiers of the Roman empire; they halted in the usual stations along the banks of the great rivers; and in the territories of Moscow, Kiow, and Moldavia, some vestiges have been discovered of their temporary residence. In this long and various peregrination, they could not always escape the dominion of the stronger;

19. The author of this Chronicle is styled the notary of king Bela. Katona has assigned him to the xii[th] century, and defends his character against the hyper-criticism of Pray. This rude annalist must have transcribed some historical records, since he could affirm with dignity, rejectis falsis fabulis rusticorum, et garrulo cantû joculatorum. In the xv[th] century, these fables were collected by Thurotzius, and embellished by the Italian Bonfinius. See the Preliminary Discourse in the Hist. Critica Ducum, p. 7–33.

20. See Constantine de Administrando Imperio, c. 3, 4. 13. 38–42. Katona has nicely fixed the composition of this work to the years 949, 950, 951. (p. 4–7.). The critical historian (p. 34–107.) endeavours to prove the existence, and to relate the actions, of a first duke *Almus*, the father of Arpad, who is tacitly rejected by Constantine.

21. Pray (Dissert. p. 37–39, &c.) produces and illustrates the original passages of the Hungarian missionaries, Bonfinius and Æneas Sylvius.

and the purity of their blood was improved or sullied by the mixture of a foreign race: from a motive of compulsion or choice, several tribes of the Chazars were associated to the standard of their ancient vassals; introduced the use of a second language; and obtained by their superior renown the most honourable place in the front of battle. The military force of the Turks and their allies marched in seven equal and artificial divisions; each division was formed of thirty thousand eight hundred and fifty-seven warriors, and the proportion of women, children, and servants, supposes and requires at least a million of emigrants. Their public counsels were directed by seven *vayvods* or hereditary chiefs, but the experience of discord and weakness recommended the more simple and vigorous administration of a single person. The sceptre which had been declined by the modest Lebedias, was granted to the birth or merit of Almus and his son Arpad, and the authority of the supreme khan of the Chazars confirmed the engagement of the prince and people; of the people to obey his commands, of the prince to consult their happiness and glory.

Their Fennic origin.

With this narrative we might be reasonably content, if the penetration of modern learning had not opened a new and larger prospect of the antiquities of nations. The Hungarian language stands alone, and as it were insulated, among the Sclavonian dialects; but it bears a close and clear affinity to the idioms of the Fennic race,[22] of an obsolete and savage race, which formerly occupied the northern regions of Asia and Europe. The genuine appellation of *Ugri* or *Igours* is found on the western confines of China;[23] their migration to the banks of the Irtish is attested by Tartar evidence;[24] a similar name and language are detected in the southern parts of Siberia;[25] and the remains of the Fennic

22. Fischer, in the Quæstiones Petropolitanæ, de Origine Ungrorum, and Pray, Dissertat. i, ii, iii. &c. have drawn up several comparative tables of the Hungarian with the Fennic dialects. The affinity is indeed striking, but the lists are short, the words are purposely chosen; and I read in the learned Bayer (Comment. Academ. Petropol. tom. x. p. 374.), that although the Hungarian has adopted many Fennic words (innumeras voces), it essentially differs toto genio et naturâ.

23. In the region of Turfan, which is clearly and minutely described by the Chinese geographers (Gaubil, Hist. du Grand Gengiscan, p. 13. de Guignes, Hist. des Huns, tom. ii. p. 31, &c.).

24. Hist. Genealogique des Tartars, par Abulghazi Bahadur Khan, partie ii. p. 90–98.

25. In their journey to Pekin, both Isbrand Ives (Harris's Collection of Voyages and Travels, vol. ii. p. 920, 921.) and Bell (Travels, vol. i. p. 174.) found the Vogulitz in the neighbourhood of Tobolsky. By the tortures of the etymological art, *Ugur* and *Vogul* are reduced to the same name; the circumjacent mountains really bear the appellation of *Ugrian*; and of all the Fennic dialects, the Vogulian is the nearest to the Hungarian (Fischer, Dissert. i. p. 20–30. Pray, Dissert. ii. p. 31–34.).

tribes are widely, though thinly, scattered from the sources of the Oby to the shores of Lapland.[26] The consanguinity of the Hungarians and Laplanders would display the powerful energy of climate on the children of a common parent; the lively contrast between the bold adventurers, who are intoxicated with the wines of the Danube, and the wretched fugitives who are immersed beneath the snows of the polar circle. Arms and freedom have ever been the ruling, though too often the unsuccessful, passion of the Hungarians, who are endowed by nature with a vigorous constitution of soul and body.[27] Extreme cold has diminished the stature and congealed the faculties of the Laplanders; and the Arctic tribes, alone among the sons of men, are ignorant of war, and unconscious of human blood: an happy ignorance, if reason and virtue were the guardians of their peace![28]

Tactics and manners of the Hungarians and Bulgarians, A.D. 900, &c.

It is the observation of the Imperial author of the Tactics,[29] that all the Scythian hords resembled each other in their pastoral and military life, that they all practised the same means of subsistence, and employed the same instruments of destruction. But he adds, that the two nations of Bulgarians and Hungarians were superior to their brethren, and similar to each other, in the improvements, however rude, of their discipline and government; their visible likeness determines Leo to confound his friends and enemies in one common description; and the picture may be heightened by some strokes from their contemporaries of the tenth century. Except the merit and fame of military prowess, all that is valued by mankind appeared vile and contemptible to these Barbarians, whose native fierceness was stimulated by the consciousness of numbers and freedom. The

26. The eight tribes of the Fennic race, are described in the curious work of M. Levesque (Hist. des Peuples soumis à la Domination de la Russie, tom. i. p. 361–561.).

27. This picture of the Hungarians and Bulgarians is chiefly drawn from the Tactics of Leo, p. 796–801. and the Latin Annals which are alleged by Baronius, Pagi, and Muratori, A.D. 889, &c.

28. Buffon, Hist. Naturelle, tom. v. p. 6. in 12mo. Gustavus Adolphus attempted, without success, to form a regiment of Laplanders. Grotius says of these Arctic tribes, arma arcus et pharetra sed adversus feras (Annal. l. iv. p. 236.), and attempts, after the manner of Tacitus, to varnish with philosophy their brutal ignorance.

29. Leo has observed, that the government of the Turks was monarchical, and that their punishments were rigorous (Tactic. p. 896. απεωεις και βαρειας). Rhegino (in Chron. A.D. 889) mentions theft as a capital crime, and his jurisprudence is confirmed by the original code of St. Stephen (A.D. 1016). If a slave were guilty, he was chastised, for the first time, with the loss of his nose, or a fine of five heifers; for the second, with the loss of his ears, or a similar fine; for the third, with death; which the freeman did not incur till the fourth offence, as his first penalty was the loss of liberty (Katona, Hist. Regum Hungar. tom. i. p. 231, 232.).

tents of the Hungarians were of leather, their garments of fur; they shaved their hair and scarified their faces: in speech they were slow, in action prompt, in treaty perfidious; and they shared the common reproach of Barbarians, too ignorant to conceive the importance of truth, too proud to deny or palliate the breach of their most solemn engagements. Their simplicity has been praised; yet they abstained only from the luxury they had never known; whatever they saw, they coveted; their desires were insatiate, and their sole industry was the hand of violence and rapine. By the definition of a pastoral nation, I have recalled a long description of the œconomy, the warfare, and the government that prevail in that stage of society; I may add, that to fishing as well as to the chace, the Hungarians were indebted for a part of their subsistence, and since they *seldom* cultivated the ground, they must, at least in their new settlements, have sometimes practised a slight and unskilful husbandry. In their emigrations, perhaps in their expeditions, the host was accompanied by thousands of sheep and oxen, who encreased the cloud of formidable dust, and afforded a constant and wholesome supply of milk and animal food. A plentiful command of forage was the first care of the general, and if the flocks and herds were secure of their pastures, the hardy warrior was alike insensible of danger and fatigue. The confusion of men and cattle that overspread the country exposed their camp to a nocturnal surprise, had not a still wider circuit been occupied by their light cavalry, perpetually in motion to discover and delay the approach of the enemy. After some experience of the Roman tactics, they adopted the use of the sword and spear, the helmet of the soldier, and the iron breast-plate of his steed: but their native and deadly weapon was the Tartar bow: from the earliest infancy, their children and servants were exercised in the double science of archery and horsemanship; their arm was strong; their aim was sure; and in the most rapid career, they were taught to throw themselves backwards, and to shoot a volley of arrows into the air. In open combat, in secret ambush, in flight, or pursuit, they were equally formidable: an appearance of order was maintained in the foremost ranks, but their charge was driven forwards by the impatient pressure of succeeding crowds. They pursued, headlong and rash, with loosened reins and horrific outcries; but if they fled, with real or dissembled fear, the ardour of a pursuing foe was checked and chastised by the same habits of irregular speed and sudden evolution. In the abuse of victory, they astonished Europe, yet smarting from the wounds of the Saracen and the Dane: mercy they rarely asked, and more rarely bestowed; both sexes were accused as equally inaccessible to pity, and their appetite for raw flesh might countenance the popular tale, that they drank the blood and feasted on the hearts of the slain. Yet the Hungarians were not devoid of those principles of justice and humanity, which nature has implanted in every bosom. The licence of public and private injuries was restrained by laws and punishments; and in the security of an open camp, theft is the most tempting and most dangerous offence. Among the Barbarians, there were many, whose spontaneous virtue supplied their laws and corrected their manners, who performed the duties, and sympathised with the affections, of social life.

Establishment and inroads of the Hungarians, A.D. 889.

After a long pilgrimage of flight or victory, the Turkish hords approached the common limits of the French and Byzantine empires. Their first conquests and final settlements extended on either side of the Danube above Vienna, below Belgrade, and beyond the measure of the Roman province of Pannonia, or the modern kingdom of Hungary.[30] That ample and fertile land was loosely occupied by the Moravians, a Sclavonian name and tribe, which were driven by the invaders into the compass of a narrow province. Charlemagne had stretched a vague and nominal empire as far as the edge of Transylvania; but, after the failure of his legitimate line, the dukes of Moravia forgot their obedience and tribute to the monarchs of Oriental France. The bastard Arnulph was provoked to invite the arms of the Turks; they rushed through the real or figurative wall, which his indiscretion had thrown open; and the king of Germany has been justly reproached as a traitor to the civil and ecclesiastical society of the Christians. During

A.D. 900, &c.

the life of Arnulph, the Hungarians were checked by gratitude or fear; but in the infancy of his son Lewis they discovered and invaded Bavaria; and such was their Scythian speed, that in a single day a circuit of fifty miles was stript and consumed. In the battle of Augsburgh the Christians maintained their advantage till the seventh hour of the day: they were deceived and vanquished by the flying stratagems of the Turkish cavalry. The conflagration spread over the provinces of Bavaria, Swabia, and Franconia; and the Hungarians[31] promoted the reign of anarchy, by forcing the stoutest barons to discipline their vassals and fortify their castles. The origin of walled towns is ascribed to this calamitous period; nor could any distance be secure against an enemy, who, almost at the same instant, laid in ashes the Helvetian monastery of St. Gall, and the

30. See Katona, Hist. Ducum Hungar. p. 321–352.

31. Hungarorum gens, cujus omnes fere nationes expertæ sævitiam, &c. is the preface of Liutprand (l. i. c. 2.), who frequently expatiates on the calamities of his own times. See l. i. c. 5. l. ii. c. 1, 2. 4, 5, 6, 7. l. iii. c. 1, &c. l. v. c. 8. 15. in Legat. p. 485. His colours are glaring, but his chronology must be rectified by Pagi and Muratori.

city of Bremen, on the shores of the northern ocean. Above thirty years the Germanic empire or kingdom was subject to the ignominy of tribute; and resistance was disarmed by the menace, the serious and effectual menace, of dragging the women and children into captivity, and of slaughtering the males above the age of ten years. I have neither power nor inclination to follow the Hungarians beyond the Rhine; but I must observe with surprise, that the southern provinces of France were blasted by the tempest, and that Spain, behind her Pyrenees, was astonished at the approach of these formidable strangers.[32] The vicinity of Italy *A.D. 900.* had tempted their early inroads; but, from their camp on the Brenta, they beheld with some terror the apparent strength and populousness of the new-discovered country. They requested leave to retire; their request was proudly rejected by the Italian king; and the lives of twenty thousand Christians paid the forfeit of his obstinacy and rashness. Among the cities of the West, the royal Pavia was conspicuous in fame and splendour; and the pre-eminence of Rome itself was only derived from the relics of the apostles. The Hungarians appeared; Pavia was in flames; forty- *A.D. 924.* three churches were consumed; and, after the massacre of the people, they spared about two hundred wretches, who had gathered some bushels of gold and silver (a vague exaggeration) from the smoking ruins of their country. In these annual excursions from the Alps to the neighbourhood of Rome and Capua, the churches, that yet escaped, resounded with a fearful litany: "O save and deliver us from the arrows of the Hungarians!" But the saints were deaf or inexorable; and the torrent rolled forwards, till it was stopped by the extreme land of Calabria.[33] A composition was offered and accepted for the head of each Italian subject; and ten bushels of silver were poured forth in the Turkish camp. But falsehood is the natural antagonist of violence; and the robbers were defrauded both in

32. The three bloody reigns of Arpad, Zoltan, and Toxus, are critically illustrated by Katona (Hist. Ducum, &c. p. 107–499.). His diligence has searched both natives and foreigners, yet to the deeds of mischief or glory, I have been able to add the destruction of Bremen (Adam Bremensis, i. 43.).

33. Muratori has considered with patriotic care the danger and resources of Modena. The citizens besought St. Geminianus, their patron, to avert, by his intercession, the *rabies*, *flagellum*, &c.

Nunc te rogamus licet servi pessimi
Ab Ungerorum nos defendas jaculis.

The bishop erected walls for the public defence, not contra dominos serenos (Antiquitat. Ital. med. Ævi, tom. i. dissertat. i. p. 21, 22.), and the song of the nightly watch is not without elegance or use (tom. iii. diss. xl. p. 709.). The Italian annalist has accurately traced the series of their inroads (Annali d'Italia, tom. vii. p. 365. 367. 393. 401. 437. 440. tom. viii. p. 19. 41. 52, &c.).

the numbers of the assessment and the standard of the metal. On the side of the East the Hungarians were opposed in doubtful conflict by the equal arms of the Bulgarians, whose faith forbade an alliance with the Pagans, and whose situation formed the barrier of the Byzantine empire.

A.D. 924. The barrier was overturned; the emperor of Constantinople beheld the waving banners of the Turks; and one of their boldest warriors presumed to strike a battle-axe into the golden gate. The arts and treasures of the Greeks diverted the assault; but the Hungarians might boast in their retreat, that they had imposed a tribute on the spirit of Bulgaria and the majesty of the Cæsars.[34] The remote and rapid operations of the same campaign, appear to magnify the power and numbers of the Turks; but their courage is most deserving of praise, since a light troop of three or four hundred horse would often attempt and execute the most daring inroads to the gates of Thessalonica and Constantinople. At this disastrous æra of the ninth and tenth centuries, Europe was afflicted by a triple scourge from the North, the East, and the South: the Norman, the Hungarian, and the Saracen, sometimes trod the same ground of desolation; and these savage foes might have been compared by Homer to the two lions growling over the carcase of a mangled stag.[35]

Victory of Henry the Fowler, A.D. 934.

The deliverance of Germany and Christendom was atchieved by the Saxon princes, Henry the Fowler and Otho the Great, who, in two memorable battles, for ever broke the power of the Hungarians.[36] The valiant Henry was roused from a bed of sickness by the invasion of his country: but his mind was vigorous and his prudence successful. "My companions," said he on the morning of the combat, "maintain your ranks, receive on your bucklers the first

34. Both the Hungarian and Russian annals suppose, that they besieged, or attacked, or insulted Constantinople (Pray, dissertat. x. p. 239. Katona, Hist. Ducum, p. 354–360.); and the fact is *almost* confessed by the Byzantine historians (Leo Grammaticus, p. 506. Cedrenus, tom. ii. p. 629.): yet, however glorious to the nation, it is denied or doubted by the critical historian, and even by the notary of Bela. Their scepticism is meritorious; they could not safely transcribe or believe the rusticorum fabulas; but Katona might have given due attention to the evidence of Liutprand, Bulgarorum gentem atque *Græcorum* tributariam fecerant (Hist. l. ii. c. 4. p. 435.).

35.

—— λεονθ' ὡς δηρινθητην
Οτι ουρεος κορυφησι περι κταμενης ελαφοιο
Αμφω πειναοντε μεγα φρονεοντε μαχεσθον.

36. They are amply and critically discussed by Katona (Hist. Ducum, p. 360–368. 427–470.). Liutprand (l. ii. c. 8, 9.) is the best evidence for the former, and Witichind (Annal. Saxon. l. iii.) of the latter: but the critical historian will not even overlook the horn of a warrior, which is said to be preserved at Jaz-berin.

arrows of the Pagans, and prevent their second discharge by the equal and rapid career of your lances." They obeyed and conquered: and the historical picture of the castle of Merseburgh, expressed the features, or at least the character, of Henry, who, in an age of ignorance, entrusted to the finer arts the perpetuity of his name.[37] At the end of twenty years, the children of the Turks who had fallen by his sword invaded the empire of his son; and their force is defined, in the lowest estimate, at one hundred thousand horse. They were invited by domestic faction; the gates of Germany were treacherously unlocked, and they spread far beyond the Rhine and the Meuse, into the heart of Flanders. But the vigour and prudence of Otho dispelled the conspiracy; the princes were made sensible, that unless they were true to each other, their religion and country were irrecoverably lost; and the national powers were reviewed in the plains of Augsburgh. They marched and fought in eight legions, according to the division of provinces and tribes; the first, second, and third, were composed of Bavarians; the fourth of Franconians; the fifth of Saxons, under the immediate command of the monarch; the sixth and seventh consisted of Swabians; and the eighth legion, of a thousand Bohemians, closed the rear of the host. The resources of discipline and valour were fortified by the arts of superstition, which, on this occasion, may deserve the epithets of generous and salutary. The soldiers were purified with a fast; the camp was blessed with the relics of saints and martyrs; and the Christian hero girded on his side the sword of Constantine, grasped the invincible spear of Charlemagne, and waved the banner of St. Maurice, the præfect of the Thebæan legion. But his firmest confidence was placed in the holy lance,[38] whose point was fashioned of the nails of the cross, and which his father had extorted from the king of Burgundy, by the threats of war and the gift of a province. The Hungarians were expected in the front; they secretly passed

of Otho the Great, A.D. 955.

37. Hunc vero triumphum tam laude quam memoria dignum, ad Meresburgum rex in superiori cœnaculo domûs per *ζωγραφιαν*, id est, picturam notari, precepit, adeo ut rem veram potius quam verisimilem videas: an high encomium (Liutprand, l. ii. c. 9.). Another palace in Germany had been painted with holy subjects, by the order of Charlemagne; and Muratori may justly affirm, nulla sæcula fuere in quibus pictores desiderati fuerint (Antiquitat. Ital. medii Ævi, tom. ii. dissert. xxiv. p. 360, 361.). Our domestic claims to antiquity of ignorance and original imperfection (Mr. Walpole's lively words), are of a much more recent date (Anecdotes of Painting, vol. i. p. 2, &c.).

38. See Baronius, Annal. Eccles. A.D. 929, N° 2–5. The lance of Christ is taken from the best evidence, Liutprand (l. iv. c. 12.), Sigebert, and the acts of St. Gerard: but the other military relics depend on the faith of the Gesta Anglorum post Bedam, l. ii. c. 8.

the Lech, a river of Bavaria that falls into the Danube; turned the rear of the Christian army; plundered the baggage, and disordered the legions of Bohemia and Swabia. The battle was restored by the Franconians, whose duke, the valiant Conrad, was pierced with an arrow as he rested from his fatigues: the Saxons fought under the eyes of their king; and his victory surpassed, in merit and importance, the triumphs of the last two hundred years. The loss of the Hungarians was still greater in the flight than in the action; they were encompassed by the rivers of Bavaria; and their past cruelties excluded them from the hope of mercy. Three captive princes were hanged at Ratisbon, the multitude of prisoners was slain or mutilated, and the fugitives, who presumed to appear in the face of their country, were condemned to everlasting poverty and disgrace.[39] Yet the spirit of the nation was humbled, and the most accessible passes of Hungary were fortified with a ditch and rampart. Adversity suggested *A.D. 972.* the counsels of moderation and peace: the robbers of the West acquiesced in a sedentary life; and the next generation was taught by a discerning prince, that far more might be gained by multiplying and exchanging the produce of a fruitful soil. The native race, the Turkish or Fennic blood, was mingled with new colonies of Scythian or Sclavonian origin;[40] many thousands of robust and industrious captives had been imported from all the countries of Europe;[41] and after the marriage of Geisa with a Bavarian princess, he bestowed honours and estates on the nobles of Germany.[42] The son of Geisa was invested with the regal title,

39. Katona, Hist. Ducum Hungariæ, p. 500, &c.

40. Among these colonies we may distinguish, 1. The Chazars, or Cabari, who joined the Hungarians on their march (Constant. de admin. Imp. c. 39, 40. p. 108, 109.). 2. The Jazyges, Moravians, and Siculi, whom they found in the land; the last were *perhaps* a remnant of the Huns of Attila, and were entrusted with the guard of the borders. 3. The Russians, who, like the Swiss in France, imparted a general name to the royal porters. 4. The Bulgarians, whose chiefs (A.D. 956) were invited, cum magnâ multitudine *Hismahelitarum*. Had any of these Sclavonians embraced the Mahometan religion? 5. The Bisseni and Cumans, a mixed multitude of Patzinacites, Uzi, Chazars, &c. who had spread to the lower Danube. The last colony of 40,000 Cumans, A.D. 1239, was received and converted by the kings of Hungary, who derived from that tribe a new regal appellation (Pray, Dissert. vi. vii. p. 109–173. Katona, Hist. Ducum, p. 95–99. 259–264. 476. 479–483, &c.).

41. Christiani autem, quorum pars major populi est, qui ex omni parte mundi illuc tracti sunt captivi, &c. Such was the language of Piligrinus, the first missionary who entered Hungary, A.D. 973. Pars major is strong. Hist. Ducum, p. 517.

42. The fideles Teutonici of Geisa are authenticated in old charters; and Katona, with his usual industry, has made a fair estimate of these colonies, which had been so loosely magnified by the Italian Ranzanus (Hist. Critic. Ducum, p. 667–681.).

and the house of Arpad reigned three hundred years in the kingdom of Hungary. But the freeborn Barbarians were not dazzled by the lustre of the diadem, and the people asserted their indefeasible right of chusing, deposing, and punishing the hereditary servant of the state.

Origin of the Russian monarchy.

III. The name of RUSSIANS[43] was first divulged, in the ninth century, by an embassy from Theophilus, emperor of the East, to the emperor of the West, Lewis, the son of Charlemagne. The Greeks were accompanied by the envoys of the great duke, or chagan, or *czar*, of the Russians. In their journey to Constantinople, they had traversed many hostile nations; and they hoped to escape the dangers of their return by requesting the French monarch to transport them by sea to their native country. A closer examination detected their origin: they were the brethren of the Swedes and Normans, whose name was already odious and formidable in France; and it might justly be apprehended that these Russian strangers were not the messengers of peace, but the emissaries of war. They were detained, while the Greeks were dismissed; and Lewis expected a more satisfactory account, that he might obey the laws of hospitality or prudence, according to the interest of both empires.[44] This Scandinavian origin of the people, or at least the princes, of Russia, may be confirmed and illustrated by the national annals[45] and the general history of the North. The Normans, who had so long been concealed by a veil of impenetrable darkness, suddenly burst forth in the spirit of naval and military enterprise. The vast, and, as it is said, the populous, regions of Denmark, Sweden, and Norway, were crowded with independent chieftains and desperate adventurers, who sighed in the laziness of peace, and smiled in the agonies

A.D. 839.

43. Among the Greeks, this national appellation has a singular form, Ρως, as an undeclinable word, of which many fanciful etymologies have been suggested. I have perused, with pleasure and profit, a dissertation de Origine Russorum (Comment. Academ. Petropolitanæ, tom. viii. p. 388–436.), by Theophilus Sigefrid Bayer, a learned German, who spent his life and labours in the service of Russia. A geographical tract of d'Anville, de l'Empire de Russie son Origine, et ses Accroissemens (Paris, 1772, in 12mo), has likewise been of use.

44. See the entire passage (dignum, says Bayer, ut aureis in tabulis figatur) in the Annales Bertiniani Francorum (in Script. Ital. Muratori, tom. ii. pars i. p. 525.), A.D. 839, twenty-two years before the Æra of Ruric. In the xth century, Liutprand (Hist. l. v. c. 6.) speaks of the Russians and Normans as the same Aquilonares homines of a red complexion.

45. My knowledge of these annals is drawn from M. Levesque, Histoire de Russie. Nestor, the first and best of these ancient annalists, was a monk of Kiow, who died in the beginning of the xii^th^ century; but his Chronicle was obscure, till it was published at Petersburgh, 1767, in 4to. Levesque, Hist. de Russie, tom. i. p. xvi. Coxe's Travels, vol. ii. p. 184.

of death. Piracy was the exercise, the trade, the glory, and the virtue, of the Scandinavian youth. Impatient of a bleak climate and narrow limits, they started from the banquet, grasped their arms, sounded their horn, ascended their vessels, and explored every coast that promised either spoil or settlement. The Baltic was the first scene of their naval atchievements; they visited the eastern shores, the silent residence of Fennic and Sclavonian tribes, and the primitive Russians of the lake Ladoga paid a tribute, the skins of white squirrels, to these strangers, whom they saluted with the title of *Varangians*[46] or Corsairs. Their superiority in arms, discipline, and renown, commanded the fear and reverence of the natives. In their wars against the more inland savages, the Varangians condescended to serve as friends and auxiliaries, and gradually, by choice or conquest, obtained the dominion of a people whom they were qualified to protect. Their tyranny was expelled, their valour was again recalled, *A.D. 862.* till at length, Ruric, a Scandinavian chief, became the father of a dynasty which reigned above seven hundred years. His brothers extended his influence: the example of service and usurpation was imitated by his companions in the southern provinces of Russia; and their establishments, by the usual methods of war and assassination, were cemented into the fabric of a powerful monarchy.

The Varangians of Constantinople.

As long as the descendants of Ruric were considered as aliens and conquerors, they ruled by the sword of the Varangians, distributed estates and subjects to their faithful captains, and supplied their numbers with fresh streams of adventurers from the Baltic coast.[47] But when the Scandinavian chiefs had struck a deep and permanent root into the soil, they mingled with the Russians in blood, religion, and language, and the first Waladimir had the merit of delivering his country from these foreign mercenaries. They had seated him on the throne; his riches were insufficient to satisfy their demands; but they listened to his pleasing advice, that they should seek, not a more grateful, but a more wealthy, master; that they should embark for Greece, where, instead of the skins of squirrels, silk and gold would be the recompence of their service. At the same time the Russian prince admonished his Byzantine ally to disperse and employ, to recompense

46. Theophil. Sig. Bayer de Varagis (for the name is differently spelt), in Comment. Academ. Petropolitanæ, tom. iv. p. 275–311.

47. Yet, as late as the year 1018, Kiow and Russia were still guarded, ex fugitivorum servorum robore, confluentium et maxime Danorum. Bayer, who quotes (p. 292.) the Chronicle of Dithmar of Merseburgh, observes, that it was unusual for the Germans to enlist in a foreign service.

and restrain, these impetuous children of the North. Contemporary writers have recorded the introduction, name, and character, of the *Varangians*: each day they rose in confidence and esteem; the whole body was assembled at Constantinople to perform the duty of guards; and their strength was recruited by a numerous band of their countrymen from the island of Thule. On this occasion, the vague appellation of Thule is applied to England; and the new Varangians were a colony of English and Danes who fled from the yoke of the Norman conqueror. The habits of pilgrimage and piracy had approximated the countries of the earth; these exiles were entertained in the Byzantine court; and they preserved, till the last age of the empire, the inheritance of spotless loyalty, and the use of the Danish or English tongue. With their broad and double-edged battle-axes on their shoulders, they attended the Greek emperor to the temple, the senate, and the hippodrome; he slept and feasted under their trusty guard; and the keys of the palace, the treasury, and the capital, were held by the firm and faithful hands of the Varangians.[48]

Geography and trade of Russia, A.D. 950.

In the tenth century, the geography of Scythia was extended far beyond the limits of ancient knowledge; and the monarchy of the Russians obtains a vast and conspicuous place in the map of Constantine.[49] The sons of Ruric were masters of the spacious province of Wolodomir, or Moscow; and, if they were confined on that side by the hords of the East, their western frontier in those early days was enlarged to the Baltic sea and the country of the Prussians. Their northern reign ascended above the sixtieth degree of latitude, over the Hyperborean regions, which fancy had peopled with monsters, or clouded with eternal darkness. To the south they followed the course of the Borysthenes, and approached with that river the neighbourhood of the Euxine sea. The tribes that dwelt, or wandered,

48. Ducange has collected from the original authors the state and history of the Varangi at Constantinople (Glossar. Med. et Infimæ Græcitatis, sub voce *Βαραγγοι*. Med. et. Infimæ Latinitatis, sub voce *Vagri*. Not. ad Alexiad, Annæ Comnenæ, p. 256, 257, 258. Notes sur Villehardouin, p. 296–299.). See likewise the Annotations of Reiske to the Ceremoniale Aulæ Byzant. of Constantine, tom. ii. p. 149, 150. Saxo Grammaticus affirms, that they spoke Danish; but Codinus maintains them till the fifteenth century in the use of their native English: *Πολυχρονιζουσι οι Βαραγγοι κατα των πατριον γλωσσαν αυτων ητοι Ιγκληνιστι*.

49. The original record of the geography and trade of Russia is produced by the emperor Constantine Porphyrogenitus (de Administrat. Imperii, c. 2. p. 55, 56. c. 9. p. 59–61. c. 13. p. 63–67. c. 37. p. 106. c. 42. p. 112, 113.), and illustrated by the diligence of Bayer (de Geographiâ Russiæ vicinarumque Regionum circiter A.C. 948, in Comment. Academ. Petropol. tom. ix. p. 367–422. tom. x. p. 371–421.), with the aid of the chronicles and traditions of Russia, Scandinavia, &c.

in this ample circuit were obedient to the same conqueror, and insensibly blended into the same nation. The language of Russia is a dialect of the Sclavonian; but, in the tenth century, these two modes of speech were different from each other; and, as the Sclavonian prevailed in the South, it may be presumed that the original Russians of the North, the primitive subjects of the Varangian chief, were a portion of the Fennic race. With the emigration, union, or dissolution, of the wandering tribes, the loose and indefinite picture of the Scythian desert has continually shifted. But the most ancient map of Russia affords some places which still retain their name and position; and the two capitals, Novogorod[50] and Kiow,[51] are coeval with the first age of the monarchy. Novogorod had not yet deserved the epithet of great, nor the alliance of the Hanseatic league, which diffused the streams of opulence and the principles of freedom. Kiow could not yet boast of three hundred churches, an innumerable people, and a degree of greatness and splendour, which was compared with Constantinople by those who had never seen the residence of the Cæsars. In their origin, the two cities were no more than camps or fairs, the most convenient stations in which the Barbarians might assemble for the occasional business of war or trade. Yet even these assemblies announce some progress in the arts of society; a new breed of cattle was imported from the southern provinces; and the spirit of commercial enterprise pervaded the sea and land from the Baltic to the Euxine, from the mouth of the Oder to the port of Constantinople. In the days of idolatry and barbarism, the Sclavonic city of Julin was frequented and enriched by the Normans, who had prudently secured a free mart of purchase and exchange.[52] From this harbour, at the entrance of the Oder, the corsair, or merchant, sailed in forty-three days to the eastern shores

50. The haughty proverb, "Who can resist God and the great Novogorod?" is applied by M. Levesque (Hist. de Russie, tom. i. p. 60.) even to the times that preceded the reign of Ruric. In the course of his history he frequently celebrates this republic, which was suppressed A.D. 1475 (tom. ii. p. 252–266.). That accurate traveller, Adam Olearius, describes (in 1635) the remains of Novogorod, and the route by sea and land of the Holstein ambassadors (tom. i. p. 123–129.).

51. In hac magna civitate, quæ est caput regni, plus trecentæ ecclesiæ habentur et nundinæ octo, populi etiam ignota manus (Eggehardus ad A.D. 1018, apud Bayer, tom. ix. p. 412.). He likewise quotes (tom. x. p. 397.) the words of the Saxon annalist, Cujus *(Russiæ)* metropolis est Chive, æmula sceptri Constantinopolitani quæ est clarissimam decus Græciæ. The fame of Kiow, especially in the xi[th] century, had reached the German and the Arabian geographers.

52. In Odoræ ostio quâ Scythicas alluit paludes, nobilissima civitas Julinum, celeberrimam, Barbaris et Græcis qui sunt in circuitû præstans stationem; est sane maxima omnium quas Europa claudit civitatum (Adam Bremensis, Hist.

of the Baltic, the most distant nations were intermingled, and the holy groves of Curland *are said* to have been decorated with *Grecian* and Spanish gold.[53] Between the sea and Novogorod an easy intercourse was discovered; in the summer, through a gulf, a lake, and a navigable river; in the winter season, over the hard and level surface of boundless snows. From the neighbourhood of that city, the Russians descended the streams that fall into the Borysthenes; their canoes, of a single tree, were laden with slaves of every age, furs of every species, the spoil of their bee-hives, and the hides of their cattle; and the whole produce of the North was collected and discharged in the magazines of Kiow. The month of June was the ordinary season of the departure of the fleet: the timber of the canoes was framed into the oars and benches of more solid and capacious boats; and they proceeded without obstacle down the Borysthenes, as far as the seven or thirteen ridges of rocks, which traverse the bed, and precipitate the waters, of the river. At the more shallow falls it was sufficient to lighten the vessels; but the deeper cataracts were impassable; and the mariners, who dragged their vessels and their slaves six miles over land, were exposed in this toilsome journey to the robbers of the desert.[54] At the first island below the falls, the Russians celebrated the festival of their escape; at a second, near the mouth of the river, they repaired their shattered vessels for the longer and more perilous voyage of the Black Sea. If they steered along the coast, the Danube was accessible; with a fair wind they could reach in thirty-six or forty hours the opposite shores of Anatolia; and Constantinople admitted the annual visit of the strangers of the North. They returned at the stated season with a rich cargo of

---

Eccles. p. 19.). A strange exaggeration even in the xi[th] century. The trade of the Baltic, and the Hanseatic league, are carefully treated in Anderson's Historical Deduction of Commerce; at least, in *our* languages, I am not acquainted with any book so satisfactory.

53. According to Adam of Bremen (de Sitû Daniæ, p. 58.), the old Curland extended eight days journey along the coast; and by Peter Teutoburgicus (p. 68. A.D. 1326), Memel is defined as the common frontier of Russia, Curland, and Prussia. Aurum ibi plurimum (says Adam) divinis, auguribus atque necromanticis omnes domus sunt plenæ . . . a toto orbe ibi responsa petuntur maxime ab Hispanis (forsan *Zupanis*, id est regulis Lettoviæ) et Græcis. The name of Greeks was applied to the Russians even before their conversion; an imperfect conversion, if they still consulted the wizards of Curland (Bayer, tom. x. p. 378. 402, &c. Grotius, Prolegomen. ad Hist. Goth. p. 99.).

54. Constantine only reckons seven cataracts, of which he gives the Russian and Sclavonic names; but thirteen are enumerated by the Sieur de Beauplan, a French engineer, who had surveyed the course and navigation of the Dnieper or Borysthenes (Description d'Ukranie, Rouen, 1660, a thin quarto); but the map is unluckily wanting in my copy.

corn, wine, and oil, the manufactures of Greece, and the spices of India. Some of their countrymen resided in the capital and provinces; and the national treaties protected the persons, effects, and privileges, of the Russian merchant.[55]

Naval expeditions of the Russians against Constantinople.

But the same communication which had been opened for the benefit, was soon abused for the injury, of mankind. In a period of one hundred and ninety years, the Russians made four attempts to plunder the treasures of Constantinople: the event was various, but the motive, the means, and the object, were the same in these naval expeditions.[56] The Russian traders had seen the magnificence and tasted the luxury of the city of the Cæsars. A marvellous tale, and a scanty supply, excited the desires of their savage countrymen: they envied the gifts of nature which their climate denied; they coveted the works of art which they were too lazy to imitate and too indigent to purchase: the Varangian princes unfurled the banners of piratical adventure, and their bravest soldiers were drawn from the nations that dwelt in the northern isles of the ocean.[57] The image of their naval armaments was revived in the last century, in the fleets of the Cosacks, which issued from the Borysthenes, to navigate the same seas, for a similar purpose.[58] The Greek appellation of *monoxyla*, or single canoes, might be justly applied to the bottom of their vessels. It was scooped out of the long stem of a beech or willow, but the slight and narrow foundation was raised and continued on either side with planks, till it attained the length of sixty, and the height of about twelve, feet. These boats were built without a deck, but with two rudders and a mast; to move with sails and oars; and to contain from forty to seventy men, with their arms, and provisions of fresh water and salt fish. The first trial of the Russians was made with two hundred boats; but when the national force was exerted,

55. Nestor, apud Levesque, Hist. de Russie, tom. i. p. 78–80. From the Dnieper or Borysthenes, the Russians went to Black Bulgaria, Chazaria, and *Syria*. To Syria, how, where, when? May we not, instead of *Συρια*, read *Συανια* (de Administrat. Imp. c. 42. p. 113.)? The alteration is slight; the position of Suania, between Chazaria and Lazica, is perfectly suitable; and the name was still used in the xi[th] century (Cedren. tom. ii. p. 770.).

56. The wars of the Russians and Greeks in the ix[th], x[th], and xi[th] centuries, are related in the Byzantine Annals, especially those of Zonaras and Cedrenus; and all their testimonies are collected in the *Russica* of Stritter, tom. ii. pars ii. p. 939–1044.

57. *Προσεταιρισαμενος δε και συμμαχικον ουκ ολιγον απο των κατοικουντων εν τοις προσαρκτιοις του Οκεανου νησοις εθνων*. Cedrenus, in Compend. p. 758.

58. See Beauplan (Description de l'Ukranie, p. 54–61.): his descriptions are lively, his plans accurate, and, except the circumstance of fire-arms, we may read old Russians, for modern Cosacks.

they might arm against Constantinople a thousand or twelve hundred vessels. Their fleet was not much inferior to the royal navy of Agamemnon, but it was magnified in the eyes of fear to ten or fifteen times the real proportion of its strength and numbers. Had the Greek emperors been endowed with foresight to discern, and vigour to prevent, perhaps they might have sealed with a maritime force the mouth of the Borysthenes. Their indolence abandoned the coast of Anatolia to the calamities of a piratical war, which, after an interval of six hundred years, again infested the Euxine; but as long as the capital was respected, the sufferings of a distant province escaped the notice both of the prince and the historian. The storm which had swept along from the Phasis and Trebizond, at length burst on the Bosphorus of Thrace; a streight of fifteen miles, in which the rude vessels of the Russian might have been stopped and destroyed by a more skilful adversary. In their first enterprise[59] under the princes of Kiow, they passed without opposition, and occupied the port of Constantinople in the absence of the emperor Michael, the son of Theophilus. Through a crowd of perils, he landed at the palace-stairs, and immediately repaired to a church of the Virgin Mary.[60] By the advice of the patriarch, her garment, a precious relic, was drawn from the sanctuary and dipped in the sea; and a seasonable tempest, which determined the retreat of the Russians, was devoutly ascribed to the mother of God.[61] The silence of the Greeks may inspire some doubt of the truth, or at least of the importance, of the second attempt by Oleg the guardian of the sons of Ruric.[62] A strong barrier of arms and fortifications defended the Bosphorus: they were eluded by the usual expedient of drawing the boats over the isthmus; and this simple operation is described in the national chronicles, as if the Russian fleet had sailed over dry land with a brisk and favourable gale.

The first, A.D. 865.

The second, A.D. 904.

59. It is to be lamented, that Bayer has only given a Dissertation de Russorum *primâ* Expeditione Constantinopolitanâ (Comment. Academ. Petropol. tom. vi. p. 365–391.). After disentangling some chronological intricacies, he fixes it in the years 864 or 865, a date which might have smoothed some doubts and difficulties in the beginning of M. Levesque's history.

60. When Photius wrote his encyclic epistle on the conversion of the Russians, the miracle was not yet sufficiently ripe; he reproaches the nation as εις ωμοτητα και μιαιφονιαν παντας δευτερους ταττομενον.

61. Leo Grammaticus, p. 463, 464. Constantini Continuator, in Script. post Theophanem, p. 121, 122. Symeon Logothet. p. 445, 446. Georg. Monach. p. 535, 536. Cedrenus, tom. ii. p. 551. Zonaras, tom. ii. p. 162.

62. See Nestor and Nicon, in Levesque's Hist. de Russie, tom. i. p. 74–80. Katona (Hist. Ducum, p. 75–79.) uses his advantage to disprove this Russian victory, which would cloud the siege of Kiow by the Hungarians.

The third, A.D. 941. The leader of the third armament, Igor, the son of Ruric, had chosen a moment of weakness and decay, when the naval powers of the empire were employed against the Saracens. But if courage be not wanting, the instruments of defence are seldom deficient. Fifteen broken and decayed gallies were boldly launched against the enemy; but instead of the single tube of Greek fire usually planted on the prow, the sides and stern of each vessel were abundantly supplied with that liquid combustible. The engineers were dextrous; the weather was propitious; many thousand Russians, who chose rather to be drowned than burnt, leaped into the sea; and those who escaped to the Thracian shore were inhumanly slaughtered by the peasants and soldiers. Yet one third of the canoes escaped into shallow water; and the next spring Igor was again prepared to retrieve his disgrace and claim his revenge.[63] *The fourth, A.D. 1043.* After a long peace, Jaroslaus, the great-grandson of Igor, resumed the same project of a naval invasion. A fleet, under the command of his son, was repulsed at the entrance of the Bosphorus by the same artificial flames. But in the rashness of pursuit the vanguard of the Greeks was encompassed by an irresistible multitude of boats and men; their provision of fire was probably exhausted; and twenty-four gallies were either taken, sunk, or destroyed.[64]

Negociations and prophecy. Yet the threats or calamities of a Russian war were more frequently diverted by treaty than by arms. In these naval hostilities, every disadvantage was on the side of the Greeks: their savage enemy afforded no mercy; his poverty promised no spoil; his impenetrable retreat deprived the conqueror of the hopes of revenge; and the pride or weakness of empire indulged an opinion, that no honour could be gained or lost in the intercourse with Barbarians. At first their demands were high and inadmissible, three pounds of gold for each soldier or mariner of the fleet: the Russian youth adhered to the design of conquest and glory; but the counsels of moderation were recommended by the hoary sages. "Be content," they said, "with the liberal offers of Cæsar; is it not far better to obtain without a combat, the possession of gold, silver, silks, and all the objects of our desires? Are we sure of victory? Can we

63. Leo Grammaticus, p. 506, 507. Incert. Contin. p. 263, 264. Symeon Logothet. p. 490, 491. George Monach. p. 588, 589. Cedren. tom. ii. p. 629. Zonaras, tom. ii. p. 190, 191. and Liutprand, l. v. c. 6. who writes from the narratives of his father-in-law, then ambassador at Constantinople, and corrects the vain exaggeration of the Greeks.

64. I can only appeal to Cedrenus (tom. ii. p. 758, 759.) and Zonaras (tom. ii. p. 253, 254.); but they grow more weighty and credible as they draw near to their own times.

conclude a treaty with the sea? We do not tread on the land; we float on the abyss of water, and a common death hangs over our heads."[65] The memory of these Arctic fleets that seemed to descend from the Polar circle, left a deep impression of terror on the Imperial city. By the vulgar of every rank, it was asserted and believed, that an equestrian statue in the square of Taurus, was secretly inscribed with a prophecy, how the Russians, in the last days, should become masters of Constantinople.[66] In our own time, a Russian armament, instead of sailing from the Borysthenes, has circumnavigated the continent of Europe; and the Turkish capital has been threatened by a squadron of strong and lofty ships of war, each of which, with its naval science and thundering artillery, could have sunk or scattered an hundred canoes such as those of their ancestors. Perhaps the present generation may yet behold the accomplishment of the prediction, of a rare prediction, of which the style is unambiguous and the date unquestionable.

Reign of Swatoslaus, A.D. 955–973.

By land the Russians were less formidable than by sea; and as they fought for the most part on foot, their irregular legions must often have been broken and overthrown by the cavalry of the Scythian hords. Yet their growing towns, however slight and imperfect, presented a shelter to the subject and a barrier to the enemy: the monarchy of Kiow, till a fatal partition, assumed the dominion of the North; and the nations from the Volga to the Danube were subdued or repelled by the arms of Swatoslaus,[67] the son of Igor, the son of Oleg, the son of Ruric. The vigour of his mind and body was fortified by the hardships of a military and savage life. Wrapt in a bear-skin, Swatoslaus usually slept on the ground, his head reclining on a saddle; his diet was coarse and frugal, and, like the heroes of Homer,[68] his meat (it was often horse-flesh) was broiled or roasted on the coals. The exercise

65. Nestor, apud Levesque, Hist. de Russie, tom. i. p. 87.

66. This brazen statue, which had been brought from Antioch, and was melted down by the Latins, was supposed to represent either Joshua or Bellerophon, an odd dilemma. See Nicetas Choniates (p. 413, 414.), Codinus (de Originibus C. P. p. 24.), and the anonymous writer de Antiquitat. C. P. (Banduri, Imp. Orient. tom. i. p. 17, 18.), who lived about the year 1100. They witness the belief of the prophecy; the rest is immaterial.

67. The life of Swatoslaus, or Sviatoslaf, or Sphendosthlabus, is extracted from the Russian Chronicles by M. Levesque (Hist. de Russie, tom. i. p. 94–107.).

68. This resemblance may be clearly seen in the ninth book of the Iliad (205–221.), in the minute detail of the cookery of Achilles. By such a picture, a modern epic poet would disgrace his work and disgust his reader; but the Greek verses are harmonious, a dead language can seldom appear low or familiar; and at the distance of two thousand seven hundred years, we are amused with the primitive manners of antiquity.

of war gave stability and discipline to his army; and it may be presumed, that no soldier was permitted to transcend the luxury of his chief. By an embassy from Nicephorus, the Greek emperor, he was moved to undertake the conquest of Bulgaria, and a gift of fifteen hundred pounds of gold was laid at his feet to defray the expence, or reward the toils, of the expedition. An army of sixty thousand men was assembled and embarked; they sailed from the Borysthenes to the Danube; their landing was effected on the Mæsian shore; and, after a sharp encounter, the swords of the Russians prevailed against the arrows of the Bulgarian horse. The vanquished king sunk into the grave; his children were made captive; and his dominions, as far as mount Hæmus, were subdued or ravaged by the northern invaders. But instead of relinquishing his prey, and performing his engagements, the Varangian prince was more disposed to advance than to retire; and, had his ambition been crowned with success, the seat of empire in that early period might have been transferred to a more temperate and fruitful climate. Swatoslaus enjoyed and acknowledged the advantages of his new position, in which he could unite, by exchange or rapine, the various productions of the earth. By an easy navigation he might draw from Russia the native commodities of furs, wax, and hydromel: Hungary supplied him with a breed of horses and the spoils of the West; and Greece abounded with gold, silver, and the foreign luxuries, which his poverty had affected to disdain. The bands of Patzinacites, Chozars, and Turks, repaired to the standard of victory; and the ambassador of Nicephorus betrayed his trust, assumed the purple, and promised to share with his new allies the treasures of the Eastern world. From the banks of the Danube the Russian prince pursued his march as far as Adrianople; a formal summons to evacuate the Roman province was dismissed with contempt; and Swatoslaus fiercely replied, that Constantinople might soon expect the presence of an enemy and a master.

His defeat by John Zimisces, A.D. 970–973.

Nicephorus could no longer expel the mischief which he had introduced; but his throne and wife were inherited by John Zimisces,[69] who, in a diminutive body, possessed the spirit and abilities of an hero. The first victory of his lieutenants deprived the Russians of their foreign allies, twenty thousand of whom were either

69. This singular epithet is derived from the Armenian language, and Τζιμισκης is interpreted in Greek by μουζακιζης, or μοιρα κιζης. As I profess myself equally ignorant of *these* words, I may be indulged in the question in the play, "Pray which of you is the interpreter?" From the context, they seem to signify *Adolescentulus* (Leo Diacon, l. iv. MS. apud Ducange, Glossar. Græc. p. 1570.).

destroyed by the sword, or provoked to revolt, or tempted to desert. Thrace was delivered, but seventy thousand Barbarians were still in arms; and the legions that had been recalled from the new conquests of Syria, prepared, with the return of the spring, to march under the banners of a warlike prince, who declared himself the friend and avenger of the injured Bulgaria. The passes of mount Hæmus had been left unguarded; they were instantly occupied; the Roman vanguard was formed of the *immortals* (a proud imitation of the Persian style); the emperor led the main body of ten thousand five hundred foot; and the rest of his forces followed in slow and cautious array with the baggage and military engines. The first exploit of Zimisces was the reduction of Marcianapolis, or Peristhlaba,[70] in two days: the trumpets sounded; the walls were scaled; eight thousand five hundred Russians were put to the sword; and the sons of the Bulgarian king were rescued from an ignominious prison, and invested with a nominal diadem. After these repeated losses, Swatoslaus retired to the strong post of Dristra, on the banks of the Danube, and was pursued by an enemy who alternately employed the arms of celerity and delay. The Byzantine gallies ascended the river; the legions completed a line of circumvallation; and the Russian prince was encompassed, assaulted, and famished, in the fortifications of the camp and city. Many deeds of valour were performed; several desperate sallies were attempted; nor was it till after a siege of sixty-five days that Swatoslaus yielded to his adverse fortune. The liberal terms which he obtained announce the prudence of the victor, who respected the valour, and apprehended the despair, of an unconquered mind. The great duke of Russia bound himself by solemn imprecations to relinquish all hostile designs; a safe passage was opened for his return; the liberty of trade and navigation was restored; a measure of corn was distributed to each of his soldiers; and the allowance of twenty-two thousand measures attests the loss and the remnant of the Barbarians. After a painful voyage, they again reached the mouth of the Borysthenes; but their provisions were exhausted, the season was unfavourable; they passed the winter on the ice; and, before they could prosecute their march, Swatoslaus was surprised and oppressed by the neighbouring tribes, with whom the Greeks entertained a perpetual and

70. In the Sclavonic tongue, the name of Peristhlaba implied the great or illustrious city, μεγαλη και ουσα και λεγομενη, says Anna Comnena (Alexiad, l. vii. p. 194.). From its position between Mount Hæmus and the Lower Danube, it appears to fill the ground, or at least the station, of Marcianopolis. The situation of Durostolus, or Dristra, is well known and conspicuous (Comment. Academ. Petropol. tom. ix. p. 415, 416. d'Anville, Geographie Ancienne, tom. i. p. 307. 311.).

useful correspondence.[71] Far different was the return of Zimisces, who was received in his capital like Camillus or Marius, the saviours of ancient Rome. But the merit of the victory was attributed by the pious emperor to the mother of God; and the image of the Virgin Mary, with the divine infant in her arms, was placed on a triumphal car, adorned with the spoils of war and the ensigns of Bulgarian royalty. Zimisces made his public entry on horseback; the diadem on his head, a crown of laurel in his hand; and Constantinople was astonished to applaud the martial virtues of her sovereign.[72]

Conversion of Russia, A.D. 864.

Photius of Constantinople, a patriarch whose ambition was equal to his curiosity, congratulates himself and the Greek church on the conversion of the Russians.[73] Those fierce and bloody Barbarians had been persuaded by the voice of reason and religion, to acknowledge Jesus for their God, the Christian missionaries for their teachers, and the Romans for their friends and brethren. His triumph was transient and premature. In the various fortune of their piratical adventures, some Russian chiefs might allow themselves to be sprinkled with the waters of baptism; and a Greek bishop with the name of metropolitan, might administer the sacraments in the church of Kiow, to a congregation of slaves and natives. But the seed of the Gospel was sown on a barren soil: many were the apostates, the converts were few; and the baptism of Olga may be fixed as the æra of Russian Christianity.[74] A female, perhaps of the basest origin, who could revenge the death, and assume the sceptre, of her husband Igor, must have been endowed with those active virtues which command the fear and obedience of Barbarians. In a moment of foreign and domestic peace, she sailed from Kiow to Constantinople; and the emperor Constantine Porphyrogenitus has described with minute diligence the ceremonial of her reception in

71. The political management of the Greeks, more especially with the Patzinacites, is explained in the seven first chapters, de Administratione Imperii.

72. In the narrative of this war, Leo the Deacon (apud Pagi, Critica, tom. iv. A.D. 968–973) is more authentic and circumstantial than Cedrenus (tom. ii. p. 660–683.) and Zonaras (tom. ii. p. 205–214.). These declaimers have multiplied to 308,000 and 330,000 men, those Russian forces, of which the contemporary had given a moderate and consistent account.

73. Phot. Epistol. ii. N° 35. p. 58. edit. Montacut. It was unworthy of the learning of the editor to mistake the Russian nation, το 'Ρως, for a war-cry of the Bulgarians; nor did it become the enlightened patriarch to accuse the Sclavonian idolaters της Ελληνικης και αθεου δοξης. They were neither Greeks nor Atheists.

74. M. Levesque has extracted, from old chronicles and modern researches, the most satisfactory account of the religion of the *Slavi*, and the conversion of Russia (Hist. de Russie, tom. i. p. 35–54. 59. 92, 93. 113–121. 124–129. 148, 149, &c.).

his capital and palace. The steps, the titles, the salutations, the banquet, the presents, were exquisitely adjusted, to gratify the vanity of the stranger, with due reverence to the superior majesty of the purple.[75] In the sacrament of baptism, she received the venerable name of the empress Helena; and her conversion might be preceded or followed by her uncle, two interpreters, sixteen damsels, of an higher, and eighteen of a lower rank, twenty-two domestics or ministers, and forty-four Russian merchants, who composed the retinue of the great princess Olga. After her return to Kiow and Novogorod, she firmly persisted in her new religion; but her labours in the propagation of the Gospel were not crowned with success; and both her family and nation adhered with obstinacy or indifference to the gods of their fathers. Her son Swatoslaus was apprehensive of the scorn and ridicule of his companions; and her grandson Wolodomir devoted his youthful zeal to multiply and decorate the monuments of ancient worship. The savage deities of the North were still propitiated with human sacrifices: in the choice of the victim, a citizen was preferred to a stranger, a Christian to an idolater; and the father, who defended his son from the sacerdotal knife, was involved in the same doom by the rage of a fanatic tumult. Yet the lessons and example of the pious Olga had made a deep, though secret, impression on the minds of the prince and people: the Greek missionaries continued to preach, to dispute, and to baptise; and the ambassadors or merchants of Russia compared the idolatry of the woods with the elegant superstition of Constantinople. They had gazed with admiration on the dome of St. Sophia; the lively pictures of saints and martyrs, the riches of the altar, the number and vestments of the priests, the pomp and order of the ceremonies; they were edified by the alternate succession of devout silence and harmonious song; nor was it difficult to persuade them, that a choir of angels descended each day from heaven to join in the devotion of the Christians.[76] But the conversion of Wolodomir was determined or hastened by his desire of a Roman bride. At the same time, and in the city of Cherson, the rites of baptism and marriage were celebrated by the Christian pontiff: the city he restored to the emperor Basil, the brother of his spouse; but the brazen

Baptism of Olga, A.D. 955.

of Wolodomir, A.D. 988.

75. See the Ceremoniale Aulæ Byzant. tom. ii. c. 15. p. 343–345.: the style of Olga, or Elga, is *Αρχοντισσα ‛Ρωσιας*. For the chief of Barbarians the Greeks whimsically borrowed the title of an Athenian magistrate, with a female termination, which would have astonished the ear of Demosthenes.

76. See an anonymous fragment published by Banduri (Imperium Orientale, tom. ii. p. 112, 113.), de Conversione Russorum.

gates were transported, as it is said, to Novogorod, and erected before the first church as a trophy of his victory and faith.[77] At his despotic command, Peroun, the god of thunder, whom he had so long adored, was dragged through the streets of Kiow; and twelve sturdy Barbarians battered with clubs, the mishapen image, which was indignantly cast into the waters of the Borysthenes. The edict of Wolodomir had proclaimed, that all who should refuse the rites of baptism would be treated as the enemies of God and their prince; and the rivers were instantly filled with many thousands of obedient Russians, who acquiesced in the truth and excellence of a doctrine which had been embraced by the great duke and his boyars. In the next generation, the relics of paganism were finally extirpated; but as the two brothers of Wolodomir had died without baptism, their bones were taken from the grave, and sanctified by an irregular and posthumous sacrament.

Christianity of the North, A.D. 800–1100.

In the ninth, tenth, and eleventh centuries of the Christian æra, the reign of the gospel and of the church, was extended over Bulgaria, Hungary, Bohemia, Saxony, Denmark, Norway, Sweden, Poland, and Russia.[78] The triumphs of apostolic zeal were repeated in the iron age of Christianity; and the northern and eastern regions of Europe submitted to a religion, more different in theory than in practice, from the worship of their native idols. A laudable ambition excited the monks, both of Germany and Greece, to visit the tents and huts of the Barbarians: poverty, hardships, and dangers, were the lot of the first missionaries; their courage was active and patient; their motive pure and meritorious; their present reward consisted in the testimony of their conscience and the respect of a grateful people; but the fruitful harvest of their toils was inherited and enjoyed by the proud and wealthy prelates of succeeding times. The first conversions were free and spontaneous: an holy life and an eloquent tongue were the only arms of the missionaries; but the domestic fables of the Pagans were silenced

77. Cherson, or Corsun, is mentioned by Herberstein (apud Pagi, tom. iv. p. 56.) as the place of Wolodomir's baptism and marriage; and both the tradition and the gates are still preserved at Novogorod. Yet an observing traveller transports the brazen gates from Magdeburgh in Germany (Coxe's Travels into Russia, &c. vol. i. p. 452.); and quotes an inscription, which seems to justify his opinion. The modern reader must not confound this old Cherson of the Tauric or Crimæan peninsula with a new city of the same name, which has arisen near the mouth of the Borysthenes, and was lately honoured by the memorable interview of the empress of Russia with the emperor of the West.

78. Consult the Latin text, or English version, of Mosheim's excellent History of the Church, under the first head or section of each of these centuries.

by the miracles and visions of the strangers; and the favourable temper of the chiefs was accelerated by the dictates of vanity and interest. The leaders of nations, who were saluted with the titles of kings and saints,[79] held it lawful and pious to impose the Catholic faith on their subjects and neighbours: the coast of the Baltic, from Holstein to the gulf of Finland, was invaded under the standard of the cross; and the reign of idolatry was closed by the conversion of Lithuania in the fourteenth century. Yet truth and candour must acknowledge, that the conversion of the North imparted many temporal benefits both to the old and the new Christians. The rage of war, inherent to the human species, could not be healed by the evangelic precepts of charity and peace; and the ambition of Catholic princes has renewed in every age the calamities of hostile contention. But the admission of the Barbarians into the pale of civil and ecclesiastical society delivered Europe from the depredations, by sea and land, of the Normans, the Hungarians, and the Russians, who learned to spare their brethren and cultivate their possessions.[80] The establishment of law and order was promoted by the influence of the clergy; and the rudiments of art and science were introduced into the savage countries of the globe. The liberal piety of the Russian princes engaged in their service the most skilful of the Greeks, to decorate the cities and instruct the inhabitants: the dome and the paintings of St. Sophia were rudely copied in the churches of Kiow and Novogorod: the writings of the fathers were translated into the Sclavonic idiom; and three hundred noble youths were invited or compelled to attend the lessons of the college of Jaroslaus. It should appear that Russia might have derived an early and rapid improvement from her peculiar connection with the church and state of Constantinople, which in that age so justly despised the ignorance of the Latins. But the Byzantine nation was servile, solitary, and verging to an hasty decline: after the fall of Kiow, the navigation of

79. In the year 1000, the ambassadors of St. Stephen received from pope Silvester the title of king of Hungary, with a diadem of Greek workmanship. It had been designed for the duke of Poland; but the Poles, by their own confession, were yet too barbarous to deserve an *angelical* and *apostolical* crown (Katona, Hist. Critic. Regum Stirpis Arpadianæ, tom. i. p. 1–20.).

80. Listen to the exultations of Adam of Bremen (A.D. 1080), of which the substance is agreeable to truth: Ecce illa ferocissima Danorum, &c. natio . . . jamdudum novit in Dei laudibus Alleluia resonare . . . Ecce populus ille piraticus . . . suis nunc finibus contentus est. Ecce patria horribilis semper inaccessa propter cultum idolorum . . . prædicatores veritatis ubique certatim admittit, &c. &c. (de Situ Daniæ, &c. p. 40, 41. edit. Elzevir: a curious and original prospect of the north of Europe, and the introduction of Christianity).

the Borysthenes was forgotten; the great princes of Wolodomir and Moscow were separated from the sea and Christendom; and the divided monarchy was oppressed by the ignominy and blindness of Tartar servitude.[81] The Sclavonic and Scandinavian kingdoms, which had been converted by the Latin missionaries, were exposed, it is true, to the spiritual jurisdiction and temporal claims of the popes;[82] but they were united, in language and religious worship, with each other, and with Rome; they imbibed the free and generous spirit of the European republic, and gradually shared the light of knowledge which arose on the western world.

81. The great princes removed in 1156 from Kiow, which was ruined by the Tartars in 1240. Moscow became the seat of empire in the xiv[th] century. See the i[st] and ii[d] volumes of Levesque's History, and Mr. Coxe's Travels into the North, tom. i. p. 241, &c.

82. The ambassadors of St. Stephen had used the reverential expressions of *regnum oblatum, debitam obedientiam*, &c. which were most rigorously interpreted by Gregory VII.; and the Hungarian Catholics are distressed between the sanctity of the pope and the independence of the crown (Katona, Hist. Critica, tom. i. p. 20–25. tom. ii. p. 304. 346. 360, &c.).

CHAPTER LVI

The Saracens, Franks, and Greeks, in Italy. – First Adventures and Settlement of the Normans. – Character and Conquests of Robert Guiscard, Duke of Apulia. – Deliverance of Sicily by his Brother Roger. – Victories of Robert over the Emperors of the East and West. – Roger, King of Sicily, invades Africa and Greece. – The Emperor Manuel Comnenus. – Wars of the Greeks and Normans. – Extinction of the Normans.

Conflict of the Saracens, Latins, and Greeks, in Italy, A.D. 840–1017.

The three great nations of the world, the Greeks, the Saracens, and the Franks, encountered each other on the theatre of Italy.[1] The southern provinces, which now compose the kingdom of Naples, were subject, for the most part, to the Lombard dukes and princes of Beneventum;[2] so powerful in war, that they checked for a moment the genius of Charlemagne; so liberal in peace, that they maintained in their capital an academy of thirty-two philosophers and grammarians. The division of this flourishing state produced the rival principalities of Benevento, Salerno, and Capua; and the thoughtless ambition or revenge of the competitors invited the Saracens to the ruin of their common inheritance. During a calamitous period of two hundred years, Italy was exposed to a repetition of wounds, which the invaders were not capable of healing by the union and tranquillity of a perfect conquest. Their frequent and almost annual squadrons

1. For the general history of Italy in the ix[th] and x[th] centuries, I may properly refer to the vth, vi[th], and vii[th] books of Sigonius de Regno Italiæ (in the second volume of his works, Milan, 1732); the Annals of Baronius, with the Criticism of Pagi; the vii[th] and viii[th] books of the Istoria Civile del Regno di Napoli of Giannone; the vii[th] and viii[th] volumes (the octavo edition) of the Annali d'Italia of Muratori, and the ii[d] volume of the Abregé Chronologique of M. de Saint Marc, a work which, under a superficial title, contains much genuine learning and industry. But my long-accustomed reader will give me credit for saying, that I myself have ascended to the fountain-head, as often as such ascent could be either profitable or possible; and that I have diligently turned over the originals in the first volumes of Muratori's great collection of the *Scriptores Rerum Italicarum.*

2. Camillo Pellegrino, a learned Capuan of the last century, has illustrated the history of the dutchy of Beneventum, in his two books, Historia Principum Longobardorum, in the Scriptores of Muratori, tom. ii. pars i. p. 221–345. and tom. v. p. 159–245.

issued from the port of Palermo, and were entertained with too much indulgence by the Christians of Naples: the more formidable fleets were prepared on the African coast; and even the Arabs of Andalusia were sometimes tempted to assist or oppose the Moslems of an adverse sect. In the revolution of human events, a new ambuscade was concealed in the Caudine forks, the fields of Cannæ were bedewed a second time with the blood of the Africans, and the sovereign of Rome again attacked or defended the walls of Capua and Tarentum. A colony of Saracens had been planted at Bari, which commands the entrance of the Adriatic Gulf; and their impartial depredations provoked the resentment, and conciliated the union, of the two emperors. An offensive alliance was concluded between Basil the Macedonian, the first of his race, and Lewis, the great-grandson of Charlemagne;[3] and each party supplied the deficiencies of his associate. It would have been imprudent in the Byzantine monarch to transport his stationary troops of Asia to an Italian campaign; and the Latin arms would have been insufficient, if *his* superior navy had not occupied the mouth of the Gulf. The fortress of Bari was invested by the infantry of the Franks, and by the cavalry and gallies of the Greeks; and, after a defence of four years, the Arabian emir submitted to the clemency of Lewis, who commanded in person the operations of the siege. This important conquest had been atchieved by the concord of the East and West; but their recent amity was soon embittered by the mutual complaints of jealousy and pride. The Greeks assumed as their own the merit of the conquest and the pomp of the triumph; extolled the greatness of their powers, and affected to deride the intemperance and sloth of the handful of Barbarians who appeared under the banners of the Carlovingian prince. His reply is expressed with the eloquence of indignation and truth: "We confess the magnitude of your preparations," says the great-grandson of Charlemagne. "Your armies were indeed as numerous as a cloud of summer locusts, who darken the day, flap their wings, and, after a short flight, tumble weary and breathless to the ground. Like them, ye sunk after a feeble effort; ye were vanquished by your own cowardice; and withdrew from the scene of action to injure and despoil our Christian subjects of the Sclavonian coast. We were few in number, and why were we few? because, after a tedious expectation of your arrival, I had dismissed my host, and retained only a chosen band of warriors to continue the blockade of the city. If they indulged their

Conquest of Bari, A.D. 871.

3. See Constantin. Porphyrogen. de Thematibus, l. ii. c. xi. in Vit. Basil. c. 55. p. 181.

hospitable feasts in the face of danger and death, did these feasts abate the vigour of their enterprise? Is it by your fasting that the walls of Bari have been overturned? Did not these valiant Franks, diminished as they were by languor and fatigue, intercept and vanquish the three most powerful emirs of the Saracens? and did not their defeat precipitate the fall of the city? Bari is now fallen; Tarentum trembles; Calabria will be delivered; and, if we command the sea, the island of Sicily may be rescued from the hands of the infidels. My brother (a name most offensive to the vanity of the Greek), accelerate your naval succours, respect your allies, and distrust your flatterers."[4]

New province of the Greeks in Italy, A.D. 890.

These lofty hopes were soon extinguished by the death of Lewis, and the decay of the Carlovingian house; and whoever might deserve the honour, the Greek emperors, Basil, and his son Leo, secured the advantage, of the reduction of Bari. The Italians of Apulia and Calabria were persuaded or compelled to acknowledge their supremacy, and an ideal line from mount Garganus to the bay of Salerno, leaves the far greater part of the kingdom of Naples under the dominion of the Eastern empire. Beyond that line, the dukes or republics of Amalfi[5] and Naples, who had never forfeited their voluntary allegiance, rejoiced in the neighbourhood of their lawful sovereign; and Amalfi was enriched by supplying Europe with the produce and manufactures of Asia. But the Lombard princes of Benevento, Salerno, and Capua,[6] were reluctantly torn from the communion of the Latin world, and too often violated their oaths of servitude and tribute. The city of Bari rose to dignity and wealth, as the metropolis of the new theme or province of Lombardy; the title of patrician, and afterwards the singular name of *Catapan*,[7] was assigned to the supreme governor; and the

4. The original epistle of the emperor Lewis II. to the emperor Basil, a curious record of the age, was first published by Baronius (Annal. Eccles. A.D. 871, N° 51–71.), from the Vatican MS. of Erchempert, or rather of the anonymous historian of Salerno.

5. See an excellent dissertation de Republica Amalphitanâ, in the Appendix (p. 1–42.) of Henry Brencmann's Historia Pandectarum (Trajecti ad Rhenum, 1722, in 4to).

6. Your master, says Nicephorus, has given aid and protection principibus Capuano et Beneventano, servis meis, quos oppugnare dispono . . . Nova (potius *nota*) res est quòd eorum patres et avi nostro Imperio tributa dederunt (Liutprand, in Legat. p. 484.). Salerno is not mentioned, yet the prince changed his party about the same time, and Camillo Pellegrino (Script. Rer. Ital. tom. ii. pars i. p. 285.) has nicely discerned this change in the style of the anonymous Chronicle. On the rational ground of history and language, Liutprand (p. 480.) had asserted the Latin claim to Apulia and Calabria.

7. See the Greek and Latin Glossaries of

policy both of the church and state was modelled in exact subordination to the throne of Constantinople. As long as the sceptre was disputed by the princes of Italy, their efforts were feeble and adverse; and the Greeks resisted or eluded the forces of Germany, which descended from the Alps under the Imperial standard of the Othos. The first and greatest of those Saxon princes was compelled to relinquish the siege of Bari: the second, after the loss of his stoutest bishops and barons, escaped with honour from the bloody field of Crotona. On that day the scale of war was turned against the Franks by the valour of the Saracens.[8] These corsairs had indeed been driven by the Byzantine fleets from the fortresses and coasts of Italy; but a sense of interest was more prevalent than superstition or resentment, and the caliph of Egypt had transported forty thousand Moslems to the aid of his Christian ally. The successors of Basil amused themselves with the belief, that the conquest of Lombardy had been atchieved, and was still preserved, by the justice of their laws, the virtues of their ministers, and the gratitude of a people whom they had rescued from anarchy and oppression. A series of rebellions might dart a ray of truth into the palace of Constantinople; and the illusions of flattery were dispelled by the easy and rapid success of the Norman adventurers.

Defeat of Otho III. A.D. 983.

Anecdotes.

The revolution of human affairs had produced in Apulia and Calabria, a melancholy contrast between the age of Pythagoras and the tenth century of the Christian æra. At the former period, the coast of Great Greece (as it was then styled) was planted with free and opulent cities: these cities were peopled with soldiers, artists, and philosophers; and the military strength of Tarentum, Sybaris, or Crotona, was not inferior to that of a powerful kingdom. At the second æra, these once flourishing provinces were clouded with ignorance, impoverished by tyranny, and depopulated by Barbarian war; nor can we severely accuse

---

Ducange (*Κατεπανω, catapanus*), and his notes on the Alexias (p. 275.). Against the contemporary notion, which derives it from *Κατα παν, juxta omne,* he treats it as a corruption of the Latin *capitaneus*. Yet M. de St. Marc has accurately observed (Abregé Chronologique, tom. ii. p. 924.), that in this age the capitanei were not *captains*, but only nobles of the first rank, the great valvassors of Italy.

8. *Ου μονον δια πολεμων ἀκριβως ετεταγμενων το τοιουτον υπηγαγε το εθνος* (the Lombards), *αλλα και αγχινοιᾳ χρησαμενος και δικαιοσυνῃ και χρηστοτητι επιεικως τε τοις προσερχομενοις προσφερομενος και την ελευθεριαν αυτοις πασης τε δουλειας, και των αλλων φορολογικων χαριζομενος* (Leon. Tactic. c. xv. p. 741.). The little Chronicle of Beneventum (tom. ii. pars i. p. 280.) gives a far different character of the Greeks during the five years (A.D. 891–896) that Leo was master of the city.

the exaggeration of a contemporary, that a fair and ample district was reduced to the same desolation which had covered the earth after the general deluge.[9] Among the hostilities of the Arabs, the Franks, and the Greeks, in the southern Italy, I shall select two or three anecdotes expressive of their national manners. 1. It was the amusement of *A.D. 873.* the Saracens to profane, as well as to pillage, the monasteries and churches. At the siege of Salerno, a Musulman chief spread his couch on the communion-table, and on that altar sacrificed each night the virginity of a Christian nun. As he wrestled with a reluctant maid, a beam in the roof was accidentally or dextrously thrown down on his head; and the death of the lustful emir was imputed to the wrath of Christ, which was at length awakened to the defence of his faithful spouse.[10] 2. The *A.D. 874.* Saracens besieged the cities of Beneventum and Capua: after a vain appeal to the successors of Charlemagne, the Lombards implored the clemency and aid of the Greek emperor.[11] A fearless citizen dropt from the walls, passed the intrenchments, accomplished his commission, and fell into the hands of the Barbarians, as he was returning with the welcome news. They commanded him to assist their enterprise, and deceive his countrymen with the assurance that wealth and honours should be the reward of his falsehood, and that his sincerity would be punished with immediate death. He affected to yield, but as soon as he was conducted within hearing of the Christians on the rampart, "Friends and brethren," he cried with a loud voice, "be bold and patient, maintain the city; your sovereign is informed of your distress, and your deliverers are at hand. I know my doom, and commit my wife and children to your gratitude." The rage of the Arabs confirmed his evidence; and the self-devoted patriot was transpierced with an hundred spears. He deserves to live in

9. Calabriam adeunt, eamque inter se divisam reperientes funditus depopulati sunt (or depopularunt), ita ut deserta sit velut in diluvio. Such is the text of Herempert, or Erchempert, according to the two editions of Caraccioli (Rer. Italic. Script. tom. v. p. 23.) and of Camillo Pellegrino (tom. ii. pars i. p. 246.). Both were extremely scarce, when they were reprinted by Muratori.

10. Baronius (Annal. Eccles. A.D. 874, N° 2.) has drawn this story from a MS. of Erchempert, who died at Capua only fifteen years after the event. But the cardinal was deceived by a false title, and we can only quote the anonymous Chronicle of Salerno (Paralipomena, c. 110.), composed towards the end of the xth century, and published in the second volume of Muratori's Collection. See the Dissertations of Camillo Pellegrino (tom. ii. pars i. p. 231–281, &c.).

11. Constantine Porphyrogenitus (in Vit. Basil. c. 58. p. 183.) is the original author of this story. He places it under the reigns of Basil and Lewis II.; yet the reduction of Beneventum by the Greeks is dated A.D. 891, after the decease of both of those princes.

the memory of the virtuous, but the repetition of the same story in ancient and modern times, may sprinkle some doubts on the reality of

A.D. 930. this generous deed.[12] 3. The recital of the third incident may provoke a smile amidst the horrors of war. Theobald, marquis of Camerino and Spoleto,[13] supported the rebels of Beneventum; and his wanton cruelty was not incompatible in that age with the character of an hero. His captives of the Greek nation or party, were castrated without mercy, and the outrage was aggravated by a cruel jest, that he wished to present the emperor with a supply of eunuchs, the most precious ornaments of the Byzantine court. The garrison of a castle had been defeated in a sally, and the prisoners were sentenced to the customary operation. But the sacrifice was disturbed by the intrusion of a frantic female, who, with bleeding cheeks, dishevelled hair, and importunate clamours, compelled the marquis to listen to her complaint. "Is it thus," she cried, "ye magnanimous heroes, that ye wage war against women, against women who have never injured ye, and whose only arms are the distaff and the loom?" Theobald denied the charge, and protested, that, since the Amazons, he had never heard of a female war. "And how," she furiously exclaimed, "can you attack us more directly, how can you wound us in a more vital part, than by robbing our husbands of what we most dearly cherish, the source of our joys and the hope of our posterity? The plunder of our flocks and herds I have endured without a murmur, but this fatal injury, this irreparable loss, subdues my patience, and calls aloud on the justice of heaven and earth." A general laugh applauded her eloquence; the savage Franks, inaccessible to pity, were moved by her ridiculous, yet rational, despair; and with the deliverance of the captives, she obtained the restitution of her effects. As she returned in triumph to the castle, she was overtaken by a messenger, to enquire, in the name of Theobald, what punishment should be inflicted on her husband, were he again

12. In the year 663, the same tragedy is described by Paul the Deacon (de Gestis Langobard. l. v. c. 7, 8. p. 870, 871. edit. Grot.), under the walls of the same city of Beneventum. But the actors are different, and the guilt is imputed to the Greeks themselves, which in the Byzantine edition is applied to the Saracens. In the late war in Germany, M. d'Assas, a French officer of the regiment of Auvergne, *is said* to have devoted himself in a similar manner. His behaviour is the more heroic, as mere silence was required by the enemy who had made him prisoner (Voltaire, Siecle de Louis XV. c. 33. tom. ix. p. 172.).

13. Theobald, who is styled *Heros* by Liutprand, was properly duke of Spoleto and marquis of Camerino, from the year 926 to 935. The title and office of marquis (commander of the march or frontier) was introduced into Italy by the French emperors (Abregé Chronologique, tom. ii. p. 645–732, &c.).

taken in arms? "Should such," she answered without hesitation, "be his guilt and misfortune, he has eyes, and a nose, and hands, and feet. These are his own, and these he may deserve to forfeit by his personal offences. But let my lord be pleased to spare what his little handmaid presumes to claim as her peculiar and lawful property."[14]

Origin of the Normans in Italy, A.D. 1016.

The establishment of the Normans in the kingdoms of Naples and Sicily,[15] is an event most romantic in its origin, and in its consequences most important both to Italy and the Eastern empire. The broken provinces of the Greeks, Lombards, and Saracens, were exposed to every invader, and every sea and land were invaded by the adventurous spirit of the Scandinavian pirates. After a long indulgence of rapine and slaughter, a fair and ample territory was accepted, occupied, and named, by the Normans of France; they renounced their gods for the God of the Christians;[16] and the dukes of Normandy acknowledged themselves the vassals of the successors of Charlemagne and Capet. The savage fierceness which they had brought from the snowy mountains of Norway, was refined, without being corrupted, in a warmer climate; the companions of Rollo insensibly mingled with the natives; they imbibed the manners, language,[17] and gallantry, of the French nation; and, in a martial age, the Normans might claim the palm of valour and glorious atchievements. Of the fashionable

14. Liutprand, Hist. l. iv. c. 4. in the Rerum Italic. Script. tom. i. pars i. p. 453, 454. Should the licentiousness of the tale be questioned, I may exclaim, with poor Sterne, that it is hard if I may not transcribe with caution, what a bishop could write without scruple. What if I had translated, ut viris certetis testiculos amputare, in quibus nostri corporis refocillatio, &c.?

15. The original monuments of the Normans in Italy are collected in the vth volume of Muratori, and among these we may distinguish the poem of William Appulus (p. 245–278.) and the history of Galfridus *(Jeffrey)* Malaterra (p. 537–607.). Both were natives of France, but they wrote on the spot, in the age of the first conquerors (before A.D. 1100), and with the spirit of freemen. It is needless to recapitulate the compilers and critics of Italian history, Sigonius, Baronius, Pagi, Giannone, Muratori, St. Marc, &c. whom I have always consulted, and never copied.

16. Some of the first converts were baptised ten or twelve times, for the sake of the white garment usually given at this ceremony. At the funeral of Rollo, the gifts to monasteries for the repose of his soul, were accompanied by a sacrifice of one hundred captives. But in a generation or two, the national change was pure and general.

17. The Danish language was still spoken by the Normans of Bayeux on the sea-coast, at a time (A.D. 940) when it was already forgotten at Rouen, in the court and capital. Quem (Richard I.) confestim pater Baiocas mittens Botoni militiæ suæ principi nutriendum tradidit, ut ibi *lingua* eruditus *Danica* suis exterisque hominibus sciret aperte dare responsa (Wilhelm. Gemeticensis de Ducibus Normannis, l. iii. c. 8. p. 623. edit. Cambden). Of the vernacular and favourite idiom of William

superstitions, they embraced with ardour the pilgrimages of Rome, Italy, and the Holy Land. In this active devotion, their minds and bodies were invigorated by exercise: danger was the incentive, novelty the recompence: and the prospect of the world was decorated by wonder, credulity, and ambitious hope. They confederated for their mutual defence; and the robbers of the Alps who had been allured by the garb of a pilgrim, were often chastised by the arm of a warrior. In one of these pious visits to the cavern of mount Garganus in Apulia, which had been sanctified by the apparition of the archangel Michael,[18] they were accosted by a stranger in the Greek habit, but who soon revealed himself as a rebel, a fugitive, and a mortal foe of the Greek empire. His name was Melo; a noble citizen of Bari, who, after an unsuccessful revolt, was compelled to seek new allies and avengers of his country. The bold appearance of the Normans revived his hopes and solicited his confidence: they listened to the complaints, and still more to the promises, of the patriot. The assurance of wealth demonstrated the justice of his cause; and they viewed as the inheritance of the brave, the fruitful land which was oppressed by effeminate tyrants. On their return to Normandy, they kindled a spark of enterprise; and a small but intrepid band was freely associated for the deliverance of Apulia. They passed the Alps by separate roads, and in the disguise of pilgrims; but in the neighbourhood of Rome they were saluted by the chief of Bari, who supplied the more indigent with arms and horses, and instantly led them to the field of action. In the first conflict, their valour prevailed; but in the second engagement they were overwhelmed by the numbers and military engines of the Greeks, and indignantly retreated with their faces to the enemy. The unfortunate Melo ended his life, a suppliant at the court of Germany: his Norman followers, excluded from their native and their promised land, wandered among the hills and vallies of Italy, and earned their daily subsistence by the sword. To that formidable sword, the princes of Capua, Beneventum, Salerno, and Naples, alternately appealed in their domestic quarrels; the superior spirit and discipline of the Normans gave victory to the side which they espoused; and their cautious policy observed the balance of power, lest the preponderance of any rival state should render

---

the conqueror (A.D. 1035), Selden (Opera, tom. ii. p. 1640–1656.) has given a specimen, obsolete and obscure even to antiquarians and lawyers.

18. See Leandro Alberti (Descrizione d'Italia, p. 250.) and Baronius (A.D. 493, N° 43). If the archangel inherited the temple and oracle, perhaps the cavern, of old Calchas the soothsayer (Strab. Geograph. l. vi. p. 435, 436.), the Catholics (on this occasion) have surpassed the Greeks in the elegance of their superstition.

their aid less important and their service less profitable. Their first asylum was a strong camp in the depth of the marshes of Campania; but they were soon endowed by the liberality of the duke of Naples with a more plentiful and permanent seat. Eight miles from his residence, as a bulwark against Capua, the town of Aversa was built and fortified for their use; and they enjoyed as their own, the corn and fruits, the meadows and groves, of that fertile district. The report of their success attracted every year new swarms of pilgrims and soldiers: the poor were urged by necessity; the rich were excited by hope; and the brave and active spirits of Normandy were impatient of ease and ambitious of renown. The independent standard of Aversa afforded shelter and encouragement to the outlaws of the province, to every fugitive who had escaped from the injustice or justice of his superiors; and these foreign associates were quickly assimilated in manners and language to the Gallic colony. The first leader of the Normans was count Rainulf; and in the origin of society, pre-eminence of rank is the reward and the proof of superior merit.[19]

Foundation of Aversa, A.D. 1029.

Since the conquest of Sicily by the Arabs, the Grecian emperors had been anxious to regain that valuable possession; but their efforts, however strenuous, had been opposed by the distance and the sea. Their costly armaments, after a gleam of success, added new pages of calamity and disgrace to the Byzantine annals: twenty thousand of their best troops were lost in a single expedition; and the victorious Moslems derided the policy of a nation, which entrusted eunuchs not only with the custody of their women but with the command of their men.[20] After a reign of two hundred years, the Saracens were ruined by their divisions.[21] The emir disclaimed the authority of the king of Tunis; the people rose against the emir; the cities were usurped by the chiefs; each meaner rebel was independent in his village or castle; and

The Normans serve in Sicily, A.D. 1038.

19. See the 1st book of William Appulus. His words are applicable to every swarm of Barbarians and freebooters:

> Si vicinorum quis *pernitiosus* ad illos
> Confugiebat, eum gratanter suscipiebant
> Moribus et lingua quoscumque venire videbant
> Informant propria; gens efficiatur ut una.

And elsewhere, of the native adventurers of Normandy:

> Pars parat exiguæ vel opes aderant quia nullæ.
> Pars quia de magnis majora subire volebant.

20. Liutprand in Legatione, p. 485. Pagi has illustrated this event from the MS. history of the deacon Leo (tom. iv. A.D. 965, N° 17–19.).

21. See the Arabian Chronicle of Sicily, apud Muratori Script. Rerum Ital. tom. i. p. 253.

the weaker of two rival brothers implored the friendship of the Christians. In every service of danger the Normans were prompt and useful; and five hundred *knights*, or warriors on horseback, were enrolled by Arduin, the agent and interpreter of the Greeks, under the standard of Maniaces governor of Lombardy. Before their landing, the brothers were reconciled; the union of Sicily and Africa was restored; and the island was guarded to the water's edge. The Normans led the van, and the Arabs of Messina felt the valour of an untried foe. In a second action the emir of Syracuse was unhorsed and transpierced by the *iron arm* of William of Hauteville. In a third engagement his intrepid companions discomfited the host of sixty thousand Saracens, and left the Greeks no more than the labour of the pursuit: a splendid victory; but of which the pen of the historian may divide the merit with the lance of the Normans. It is, however, true that they essentially promoted the success of Maniaces, who reduced thirteen cities and the greater part of Sicily under the obedience of the emperor. But his military fame was sullied by ingratitude and tyranny. In the division of the spoil, the deserts of his brave auxiliaries were forgotten; and neither their avarice nor their pride could brook this injurious treatment. They complained, by the mouth of their interpreter: their complaint was disregarded; their interpreter was scourged; the sufferings were *his*; the insult and resentment belonged to *those* whose sentiments he had delivered. Yet they dissembled till they had obtained, or stolen, a safe passage to the Italian continent: their brethren of Aversa sympathised in their indignation, and the province of Apulia was invaded as the forfeit of the debt.[22] Above twenty years after the first emigration, the Normans took the field with no more than seven hundred horse and five hundred foot; and after the recall of the Byzantine legions[23] from the Sicilian war, their numbers are magnified to the amount of threescore thousand men. Their herald proposed the option of battle or retreat; "of battle," was the unanimous cry of the Normans; and one of their stoutest warriors, with a stroke of his fist, felled to the ground the horse of the Greek messenger. He was dismissed with a fresh horse; the insult was concealed from the Imperial

Their conquest of Apulia, A.D. 1040–1043.

22. Jeffrey Malaterra, who relates the Sicilian war, and the conquest of Apulia (l. i. c. 7, 8, 9, 19.). The same events are described by Cedrenus (tom. ii. p. 741–743. 755, 756.) and Zonaras (tom. ii. p. 237, 238.); and the Greeks are so hardened to disgrace, that their narratives are impartial enough.

23. Cedrenus specifies the *ταγμα* of the Obsequium (Phrygia), and the *μερος* of the Thracesians (Lydia; consult Constantine de Thematibus, i. 3, 4. with Delisle's map); and afterwards names the Pisidians and Lycaonians, with the fœderati.

troops; but in two successive battles they were more fatally instructed of the prowess of their adversaries. In the plains of Cannæ, the Asiatics fled before the adventurers of France; the duke of Lombardy was made prisoner; the Apulians acquiesced in a new dominion; and the four places of Bari, Otranto, Brundusium, and Tarentum, were alone saved in the shipwreck of the Grecian fortunes. From this æra we may date the establishment of the Norman power, which soon eclipsed the infant colony of Aversa. Twelve counts[24] were chosen by the popular suffrage; and age, birth, and merit, were the motives of their choice. The tributes of their peculiar districts were appropriated to their use; and each count erected a fortress in the midst of his lands, and at the head of his vassals. In the centre of the province, the common habitation of Melphi was reserved as the metropolis and citadel of the republic; an house and separate quarter was allotted to each of the twelve counts; and the national concerns were regulated by this military senate. The first of his peers, their president and general, was entitled count of Apulia; and this dignity was conferred on William of the iron arm, who, in the language of the age, is styled a lion in battle, a lamb in society, and an angel in council.[25] The manners of his countrymen are fairly delineated by a contemporary and national historian.[26] "The Normans," says Malaterra, "are a cunning and revengeful people; eloquence and dissimulation

Character of the Normans.

24.

Omnes conveniunt et bis sex nobiliores
Quos genus et gravitas morum decorabat et ætas,
Elegere duces. Provectis ad comitatum
His alii parent. Comitatus nomen honoris
Quo donantur erat. Hi totas undique terras
Divisere sibi, ni sors inimica repugnet
Singula proponunt loca quæ contingere sorte
Cuique duci debent, et quæque tributa locorum.

And after speaking of Melphi, William Appulus adds,

Pro numero comitum bis sex statuere plateas
Atque domus comitum totidem fabricantur in urbe.

Leo Ostiensis (l. ii. c. 67.) enumerates the divisions of the Apulian cities, which it is needless to repeat.

25. Gulielm. Appulus. l. ii. c. 12. according to the reference of Giannone (Istoria Civile di Napoli, tom. ii. p. 31.), which I cannot verify in the original. The Apulian praises indeed his *validas vires, probitas animi*, and *vivida virtus*; and declares, that had he lived, no poet could have equalled his merits (l. i. p. 258. l. ii. p. 259.). He was bewailed by the Normans, quippe qui tanti consilii virum (says Malaterra, l. i. c. 12. p. 552.) tam armis strenuum, tam sibi munificum, affabilem, morigeratum ulterius se habere diffidebant.

26. The gens astutissima, injuriarum ultrix . . . adulari sciens . . . eloquentiis inserviens, of Malaterra (l. i. c. 3. p. 550.), are expressive of the popular and proverbial character of the Normans.

appear to be their hereditary qualities: they can stoop to flatter; but unless they are curbed by the restraint of law, they indulge the licentiousness of nature and passion. Their princes affect the praise of popular munificence; the people observe the medium, or rather blend the extremes, of avarice and prodigality; and, in their eager thirst of wealth and dominion, they despise whatever they possess, and hope whatever they desire. Arms and horses, the luxury of dress, the exercises of hunting and hawking,[27] are the delight of the Normans; but, on pressing occasions, they can endure with incredible patience the inclemency of every climate, and the toil and abstinence of a military life."[28]

Oppression of Apulia, A.D. 1046, &c.

The Normans of Apulia were seated on the verge of the two empires; and, according to the policy of the hour, they accepted the investiture of their lands from the sovereigns of Germany or Constantinople. But the firmest title of these adventurers was the right of conquest: they neither loved nor trusted; they were neither trusted nor beloved: the contempt of the princes was mixed with fear, and the fear of the natives was mingled with hatred and resentment. Every object of desire, an horse, a woman, a garden, tempted and gratified the rapaciousness of the strangers;[29] and the avarice of their chiefs was only coloured by the more specious names of ambition and glory. The twelve counts were sometimes joined in a league of injustice: in their domestic quarrels they disputed the spoils of the people: the virtues of William were buried in his grave; and Drogo, his brother and successor, was better qualified to lead the valour, than to restrain the violence, of his peers. Under the reign of Constantine Monomachus, the policy, rather than benevolence, of the Byzantine court attempted to relieve Italy from this adherent mischief, more grievous than a flight of Barbarians;[30] and Argyrus, the son of Melo, was invested for this purpose

27. The hunting and hawking more properly belong to the *descendants* of the Norwegian sailors; though they might import from Norway and Iceland the finest casts of falcons.

28. We may compare this portrait with that of William of Malmsbury (de Gestis Anglorum, l. iii. p. 101, 102.), who appreciates, like a philosophic historian, the vices and virtues of the Saxons and Normans. England was assuredly a gainer by the conquest.

29. The biographer of St. Leo IX. pours his holy venom on the Normans. Videns indisciplinatam et alienam gentem Normannorum, crudeli et inauditâ rabie et plusquam Paganâ impietate adversus ecclesias Dei insurgere, passim Christianos trucidare, &c. (Wibert, c. 6.). The honest Apulian (l. ii. p. 259.) says calmly of their accuser, Veris commiscens fallacia.

30. The policy of the Greeks, revolt of Maniaces, &c. must be collected from Cedrenus (tom. ii. p. 757, 758.), William Appulus (l. i. p. 257, 258. l. ii. p. 259.), and the two Chronicles of Bari, by Lupus

with the most lofty titles[31] and the most ample commission. The memory of his father might recommend him to the Normans; and he had already engaged their voluntary service to quell the revolt of Maniaces, and to avenge their own and the public injury. It was the design of Constantine to transplant this warlike colony from the Italian provinces to the Persian war; and the son of Melo distributed among the chiefs the gold and manufactures of Greece, as the first fruits of the Imperial bounty. But his arts were baffled by the sense and spirit of the conquerors of Apulia: his gifts, or at least his proposals, were rejected; and they unanimously refused to relinquish their possessions and their hopes for the distant prospect of Asiatic fortune. After the means of persuasion had failed, Argyrus resolved to compel or to destroy: the Latin powers were solicited against the common enemy; and an offensive alliance was formed of the pope, and the two emperors of the East and West. The throne of St. Peter was occupied by Leo the ninth, a simple saint,[32] of a temper most apt to deceive himself and the world, and whose venerable character would consecrate with the name of piety, the measures least compatible with the practice of religion. His humanity was affected by the complaints, perhaps the calumnies, of an injured people: the impious Normans had interrupted the payment of tithes; and the temporal sword might be lawfully unsheathed against the sacrilegious robbers, who were deaf to the censures of the church. As a German of noble birth and royal kindred, Leo had free access to the court and confidence of the emperor Henry the third; and in search of arms and allies, his ardent zeal transported him from Apulia to Saxony, from the Elbe to the Tiber. During these hostile preparations, Argyrus indulged himself in the use of secret and guilty weapons: a crowd of Normans became the victims of public or private revenge; and the valiant Drogo was murdered in a church. But his spirit survived in his brother Humphrey, the third count of Apulia. The assassins were chastised; and

League of the pope and the two empires, A.D. 1049–1054.

A.D. 1051.

Protospata (Muratori, Script. Ital. tom. v. p. 42, 43, 44.), and an anonymous writer (Antiquitat. Italiæ medii Ævi, tom. i. p. 31–35.). This last is a fragment of some value.

31. Argyrus received, says the anonymous Chronicle of Bari, imperial letters, Fœderatûs et Patriciatûs, et Catapani et Vestatûs. In his Annals, Muratori (tom. viii. p. 426.) very properly reads, or interprets, *Sevestatus*, the title of Sebastos or Augustus. But in his Antiquities, he was taught by Ducange to make it a palatine office, master of the wardrobe.

32. A Life of St. Leo IX. deeply tinged with the passions and prejudices of the age, has been composed by Wibert, printed at Paris, 1615, in octavo, and since inserted in the Collections of the Bollandists, of Mabillon, and of Muratori. The public and private history of that pope is diligently treated by M. de St. Marc (Abregé, tom. ii. p. 140–210. and p. 25–95. 2[d] column).

the son of Melo, overthrown and wounded, was driven from the field to hide his shame behind the walls of Bari, and to await the tardy succour of his allies.

Expedition of pope Leo IX. against the Normans, A.D. 1053.

But the power of Constantine was distracted by a Turkish war; the mind of Henry was feeble and irresolute; and the pope, instead of repassing the Alps with a German army, was accompanied only by a guard of seven hundred Swabians and some volunteers of Lorraine. In his long progress from Mantua to Beneventum, a vile and promiscuous multitude of Italians was enlisted under the holy standard:[33] the priest and the robber slept in the same tent; the pikes and crosses were intermingled in the front; and the martial saint repeated the lessons of his youth in the order of march, of encampment, and of combat. The Normans of Apulia could muster in the field no more than three thousand horse, with an handful of infantry: the defection of the natives intercepted their provisions and retreat; and their spirit, incapable of fear, was chilled for a moment by superstitious awe. On the hostile approach of Leo, they knelt without disgrace or reluctance before their spiritual father. But the pope was inexorable; his lofty Germans affected to deride the diminutive stature of their adversaries; and the Normans were informed that death or exile was their only alternative. Flight they disdained, and, as many of them had been three days without tasting food, they embraced the assurance of a more easy and honourable death. They climbed the hill of Civitella, descended into the plain, and charged in three divisions the army of the pope. On the left, and in the centre, Richard count of Aversa, and Robert the famous

His defeat and captivity, June 18.

Guiscard, attacked, broke, routed, and pursued the Italian multitudes, who fought without discipline and fled without shame. A harder trial was reserved for the valour of count Humphrey, who led the cavalry of the right wing. The Germans[34] have been described as unskilful in the management of the horse and lance: but on foot they formed a strong and impenetrable phalanx; and neither

33. See the expedition of Leo IX. against the Normans. See William Appulus (l. ii. p. 259–261.) and Jeffrey Malaterra (l. i. c. 13, 14, 15. p. 253.). They are impartial, as the national, is counterbalanced by the clerical, prejudice.

34.

Teutonici quia cæsaries et forma decoros
Fecerat egregie proceri corporis illos
Corpora derident Normannica quæ breviora
Esse videbantur.

The verses of the Apulian are commonly in this strain, though he heats himself a little in the battle. Two of his similies from hawking and sorcery are descriptive of manners.

man, nor steed, nor armour, could resist the weight of their long and two-handed swords. After a severe conflict, they were encompassed by the squadrons returning from the pursuit; and died in their ranks with the esteem of their foes, and the satisfaction of revenge. The gates of Civitella were shut against the flying pope, and he was overtaken by the pious conquerors, who kissed his feet to implore his blessing and the absolution of their sinful victory. The soldiers beheld in their enemy and captive, the vicar of Christ; and, though we may suppose the policy of the chiefs, it is probable that they were infected by the popular superstition. In the calm of retirement, the well-meaning pope deplored the effusion of Christian blood, which must be imputed to his account: he felt, that he had been the author of sin and scandal; and as his undertaking had failed, the indecency of his military character was universally condemned.[35] With these dispositions, he listened to the offers of a beneficial treaty; deserted an alliance which he had preached as the cause of God; and ratified the past and future conquests of the Normans. By whatever hands they had been usurped, the provinces of Apulia and Calabria were a part of the donation of Constantine and the patrimony of St. Peter: the grant and the acceptance confirmed the mutual claims of the pontiff and the adventurers. They promised to support each other with spiritual and temporal arms; a tribute or quit-rent of twelve-pence was afterwards stipulated for every ploughland; and since this memorable transaction, the kingdom of Naples has remained above seven hundred years a fief of the Holy See.[36]

Origin of the papal investitures to the Normans.

The pedigree of Robert Guiscard[37] is variously deduced from the peasants and the dukes of Normandy: from the peasants,

Birth and character

35. Several respectable censures or complaints are produced by M. de St. Marc (tom. ii. p. 200–204.). As Peter Damianus, the oracle of the times, had denied the popes the right of making war, the hermit (lugens eremi incola) is arraigned by the cardinal, and Baronius (Annal. Eccles. A.D. 1053, N° 10–17.) most strenuously asserts the two swords of St. Peter.

36. The origin and nature of the papal investitures are ably discussed by Giannone (Istoria Civile di Napoli, tom. ii. p. 37–49. 57–66.) as a lawyer and antiquarian. Yet he vainly strives to reconcile the duties of patriot and catholic, adopts an empty distinction of "Ecclesia Romana non dedit sed accepit," and shrinks from an honest but dangerous confession of the truth.

37. The birth, character, and first actions of Robert Guiscard, may be found in Jeffrey Malaterra (l. i. c. 3, 4. 11. 16, 17, 18. 38, 39, 40.), William Appulus (l. ii. p. 260–262.), William Gemeticensis or of Jumieges (l. xi. c. 30. p. 663, 664. edit. Cambden), and Anna Comnena (Alexiad, l. i. p. 23–27. l. vi. p. 165, 166.), with the annotations of Ducange (Not. in Alexiad. p. 230–232. 320.), who has swept all the French and Latin chronicles for supplemental intelligence.

of Robert Guiscard, A.D. 1020–1085.

by the pride and ignorance of a Grecian princess;[38] from the dukes, by the ignorance and flattery of the Italian subjects.[39] His genuine descent may be ascribed to the second or middle order of private nobility.[40] He sprang from a race of *valvassors* or *bannerets*, of the diocese of Coutances, in the lower Normandy: the castle of Hauteville was their honourable seat; his father Tancred was conspicuous in the court and army of the duke; and his military service was furnished by ten soldiers or knights. Two marriages, of a rank not unworthy of his own, made him the father of twelve sons, who were educated at home by the impartial tenderness of his second wife. But a narrow patrimony was insufficient for this numerous and daring progeny; they saw around the neighbourhood the mischiefs of poverty and discord, and resolved to seek in foreign wars a more glorious inheritance. Two only remained to perpetuate the race, and cherish their father's age: their ten brothers, as they successively attained the vigour of manhood, departed from the castle, passed the Alps, and joined the Apulian camp of the Normans. The elder were prompted by native spirit; their success encouraged their younger brethren; and the three first in seniority, William, Drogo, and Humphrey, deserved to be the chiefs of their nation and the founders of the new republic. Robert was the eldest of the seven sons of the second marriage; and even the reluctant praise of his foes has endowed him with the heroic qualities of a soldier and a statesman. His lofty stature surpassed the tallest of his army: his limbs were cast in the true proportion of strength and gracefulness; and to the decline of life, he maintained the patient vigour of health and the commanding dignity of his form. His complexion was ruddy, his shoulders were broad, his hair and beard were

38. *Ο δε Ρομπερτος* (a Greek corruption) *ουτος ην Νορμαννος το γενος, την τυχην ασημος* . . . again, *εξ αφανους πανυ τυχης περιφανης*, and elsewhere (l. iv. p. 84.), *απο εσχατης πενιας και τυχης αφανους*. Anna Comnena was born in the purple; yet her father was no more than a private though illustrious subject, who raised himself to the empire.

39. Giannone (tom. ii. p. 2.) forgets all his original authors, and rests this princely descent on the credit of Inveges, an Augustine monk of Palermo in the last century. They continue the succession of dukes from Rollo to William II. the Bastard or Conqueror, whom they hold (comunemente si tiene) to be the father of Tancred of Hauteville: a most strange and stupendous blunder! The sons of Tancred fought in Appulia, before William II. was three years old (A.D. 1037).

40. The judgment of Ducange is just and moderate: Certe humilis fuit ac tenuis Roberti familia, si ducalem et regium spectemus apicem, ad quem postea pervenit; quæ honesta tamen et præter nobilium vulgarium statum et conditionem illustris habita est, "quæ nec humi reperet nec altum quid tumeret" (Wilhelm. Malmsbur. de Gestis Anglorum, l. iii. p. 107. Not. ad Alexiad. p. 230.).

long and of a flaxen colour, his eyes sparkled with fire, and his voice, like that of Achilles, could impress obedience and terror amidst the tumult of battle. In the ruder ages of chivalry, such qualifications are not below the notice of the poet or historian: they may observe that Robert, at once, and with equal dexterity, could wield in the right-hand his sword, his lance in the left; that in the battle of Civitella, he was thrice unhorsed; and that in the close of that memorable day he was adjudged to have borne away the prize of valour from the warriors of the two armies.[41] His boundless ambition was founded on the consciousness of superior worth: in the pursuit of greatness, he was never arrested by the scruples of justice, and seldom moved by the feelings of humanity: though not insensible of fame, the choice of open or clandestine means was determined only by his present advantage. The surname of *Guiscard*[42] was applied to this master of political wisdom, which is too often confounded with the practice of dissimulation and deceit; and Robert is praised by the Apulian poet for excelling the cunning of Ulysses and the eloquence of Cicero. Yet these arts were disguised by an appearance of military frankness: in his highest fortune, he was accessible and courteous to his fellow-soldiers; and while he indulged the prejudices of his new subjects, he affected in his dress and manners to maintain the ancient fashion of his country. He grasped with a rapacious, that he might distribute with a liberal, hand: his primitive indigence had taught the habits of frugality; the gain of a merchant was not below his attention; and his prisoners were tortured with slow and unfeeling cruelty to force a discovery of their secret treasure. According to the Greeks, he departed from Normandy with only five followers on horseback and thirty on foot; yet even this allowance appears too bountiful; the sixth son of Tancred of Hauteville passed the Alps as a pilgrim; and his first military band was

41. I shall quote with pleasure some of the best lines of the Apulian (l. ii. p. 270.):

Pugnat utrâque manû, nec lancea cassa, nec ensis
Cassus erat, quocunque manû deducere vellet.
Ter dejectus equo, ter viribus ipse resumptis
Major in arma redit: stimulos furor ipse ministrat.
Ut Leo cum frendens, &c.
. . . .
Nullus in hoc bello sicuti post bella probatum est
Victor vel victus, tam magnos edidit ictus.

42. The Norman writers and editors most conversant with their own idiom, interpret *Guiscard* or *Wiscard*, by *Callidus*, a cunning man. The root *(wise)* is familiar to our ear; and in the old word *Wiseacre*, I can discern something of a similar sense and termination. *Την ψυχην πανουργοτατος*, is no bad translation of the surname and character of Robert.

levied among the adventurers of Italy. His brothers and countrymen had divided the fertile lands of Apulia; but they guarded their shares with the jealousy of avarice: the aspiring youth was driven forwards to the mountains of Calabria, and in his first exploits against the Greeks and the natives, it is not easy to discriminate the hero from the robber. To surprise a castle or a convent, to ensnare a wealthy citizen, to plunder the adjacent villages for necessary food, were the obscure labours which formed and exercised the powers of his mind and body. The volunteers of Normandy adhered to his standard; and, under his command, the peasants of Calabria assumed the name and character of Normans.

His ambition and success, A.D. 1054–1080.

As the genius of Robert expanded with his fortune, he awakened the jealousy of his elder brother, by whom, in a transient quarrel, his life was threatened and his liberty restrained. After the death of Humphrey, the tender age of his sons excluded them from the command; they were reduced to a private estate by the ambition of their guardian and uncle; and Guiscard was exalted on a buckler, and saluted count of Apulia and general of the republic. With an encrease of authority and of force, he resumed the conquest of Calabria, and soon aspired to a rank that should raise him for ever above the heads of his equals. By some acts of rapine or sacrilege, he had incurred a papal excommunication: but Nicholas the second was easily persuaded, that the divisions of friends could terminate only in their mutual prejudice; that the Normans were the faithful champions of the Holy See; and it was safer to trust the alliance of a prince than the caprice of an aristocracy. A synod of one hundred bishops was convened at Melphi; and the count interrupted an important enterprise to guard the person and execute the decrees of the Roman pontiff. His gratitude and policy conferred on Robert and his posterity, the ducal title,[43] with the investiture of Apulia, Calabria, and all the lands, both in Italy and Sicily, which his sword could rescue from the schismatic Greeks and the unbelieving Saracens.[44] This apostolic sanction might justify his arms; but the obedience of a free and victorious people could not be transferred

43. The acquisition of the ducal title by Robert Guiscard is a nice and obscure business. With the good advice of Giannone, Muratori, and St. Marc, I have endeavoured to form a consistent and probable narrative.

44. Baronius (Annal. Eccles. A.D. 1059, N° 69.) has published the original act. He professes to have copied it from the *Liber Censuum*, a Vatican MS. Yet a Liber Censuum of the xiith century has been printed by Muratori (Antiquit. medii Ævi, tom. v. p. 851–908.): and the names of Vatican and Cardinal awaken the suspicions of a protestant, and even of a philosopher.

without their consent; and Guiscard dissembled his elevation till the ensuing campaign had been illustrated by the conquest of Consenza and Reggio. In the hour of triumph, he assembled his troops, and solicited the Normans to confirm by their suffrage the judgment of the vicar of Christ: the soldiers hailed with joyful acclamations their valiant duke; and the counts, his former equals, pronounced the oath of fidelity, with hollow smiles and secret indignation. After this inauguration, Robert styled himself, "by the grace of God and St. Peter, duke of Apulia, Calabria, and hereafter of Sicily;" and it was the labour of twenty years to deserve and realize these lofty appellations. Such tardy progress, in a narrow space, may seem unworthy of the abilities of the chief and the spirit of the nation: but the Normans were few in number; their rescources were scanty; their service was voluntary and precarious. The bravest designs of the duke were sometimes opposed by the free voice of his parliament of barons: the twelve counts of popular election, conspired against his authority; and against their perfidious uncle, the sons of Humphrey demanded justice and revenge. By his policy and vigour, Guiscard discovered their plots, suppressed their rebellions, and punished the guilty with death or exile: but in these domestic feuds, his years, and the national strength, were unprofitably consumed. After the defeat of his foreign enemies, the Greeks, Lombards, and Saracens, their broken forces retreated to the strong and populous cities of the sea-coast. They excelled in the arts of fortification and defence; the Normans were accustomed to serve on horseback in the field, and their rude attempts could only succeed by the efforts of persevering courage. The resistance of Salerno was maintained above eight months: the siege or blockade of Bari lasted near four years. In these actions the Norman duke was the foremost in every danger; in every fatigue the last and most patient. As he pressed the citadel of Salerno, an huge stone from the rampart shattered one of his military engines; and by a splinter he was wounded in the breast. Before the gates of Bari, he lodged in a miserable hut or barrack, composed of dry branches, and thatched with straw; a perilous station, on all sides open to the inclemency of the winter and the spears of the enemy.[45]

Duke of Apulia, A.D. 1060.

The Italian conquests of Robert correspond with the limits of the present kingdom of Naples; and the countries united by his arms have not been dissevered by the revolutions of seven hundred

His Italian conquests.

45. Read the life of Guiscard in the second and third books of the Apulian, the first and second books of Malaterra.

years.[46] The monarchy has been composed of the Greek provinces of Calabria and Apulia, of the Lombard principality of Salerno, the republic of Amalphi, and the inland dependencies of the large and ancient duchy of Beneventum. Three districts only were exempted from the common law of subjection; the first for ever, and the two last till the middle of the succeeding century. The city and immediate territory of Benevento had been transferred, by gift or exchange, from the German emperor to the Roman pontiff; and although this holy land was sometimes invaded, the name of St. Peter was finally more potent than the sword of the Normans. Their first colony of Aversa subdued and held the state of Capua; and her princes were reduced to beg their bread before the palace of their fathers. The dukes of Naples, the present metropolis, maintained the popular freedom, under the shadow of the Byzantine empire. Among the new acquisitions of Guiscard, the science of Salerno,[47] and the trade of Amalphi,[48] may detain for a moment the curiosity of the reader. I. Of the learned faculties, jurisprudence implies the previous establishment of laws and property; and theology may perhaps be superseded by the full light of religion and reason. But the savage and the sage must alike implore the assistance of physic; and, if *our* diseases are inflamed by luxury, the mischiefs of blows and wounds would be more frequent in the ruder ages of society. The treasures of Grecian medicine had been communicated to the Arabian colonies of Africa, Spain, and Sicily; and in the intercourse of peace and war, a spark of knowledge had been kindled and cherished at Salerno, an illustrious city, in which the men were honest and the women beautiful.[49] A school, the first that arose in the darkness of Europe, was consecrated to the healing

School of Salerno.

46. The conquests of Robert Guiscard and Roger I. the exemption of Benevento and the XII provinces of the kingdom, are fairly exposed by Giannone in the second volume of his Istoria Civile, l. ix, x, xi. and l. xvii. p. 460–470. This modern division was not established before the time of Frederic II.

47. Giannone (tom. ii. p. 119–127.), Muratori (Antiquitat. medii Ævi, tom. iii. dissert. xliv. p. 935, 936.), and Tiraboschi (Istoria della Letteratura Italiana), have given an historical account of these physicians; their medical knowledge and practice must be left to our physicians.

48. At the end of the Historia Pandectarum of Henry Brencman (Trajecti ad Rhenum, 1722, in 4to), the indefatigable author has inserted two dissertations, de Republicâ Amalphitanâ, and de Amalphi a Pisanis direpta, which are built on the testimonies of one hundred and forty writers. Yet he has forgotten two most important passages of the embassy of Liutprand (A.D. 969), which compare the trade and navigation of Amalphi with that of Venice.

49.

Urbs Latii non est hac delitiosior, urbe,
Frugibus arboribus vino redundat; et unde

art: the conscience of monks and bishops was reconciled to that salutary and lucrative profession; and a crowd of patients, of the most eminent rank and most distant climates, invited or visited the physicians of Salerno. They were protected by the Norman conquerors; and Guiscard, though bred in arms, could discern the merit and value of a philosopher. After a pilgrimage of thirty-nine years, Constantine, an African Christian, returned from Bagdad, a master of the language and learning of the Arabians; and Salerno was enriched by the practice, the lessons, and the writings, of the pupil of Avicenna. The school of medicine has long slept in the name of an university; but her precepts are abridged in a string of aphorisms, bound together in the Leonine verses, or Latin rhymes, of the twelfth century.[50] II. Seven miles to the west of Salerno, and thirty to the south of Naples, the obscure town of Amalphi displayed the power and rewards of industry. The land, however fertile, was of narrow extent; but the sea was accessible and open: the inhabitants first assumed the office of supplying the western world with the manufactures and productions of the East; and this useful traffic was the source of their opulence and freedom. The government was popular, under the administration of a duke and the supremacy of the Greek emperor. Fifty thousand citizens were numbered in the walls of Amalphi; nor was any city more abundantly provided with gold, silver, and the objects of precious luxury. The mariners who swarmed in her port excelled in the theory and practice of navigation and astronomy; and the discovery of the compass, which has opened the globe, is due to their ingenuity or good fortune. Their trade was extended to the coasts, or at least to the commodities, of Africa, Arabia, and India; and their settlements in Constantinople, Antioch, Jerusalem, and Alexandria, acquired the privileges of independent colonies.[51] After three hundred years of prosperity, Amalphi was oppressed by the arms of the Normans, and sacked by the

Trade of Amalphi.

Non tibi poma, nuces, non pulchra palatia desunt,
Non species muliebris abest probitasque virorum.
(Gulielmus Appulus, l. iii. p. 267.)

50. Muratori carries their antiquity above the year (1066) of the death of Edward the Confessor, the *rex Anglorum* to whom they are addressed. Nor is this date affected by the opinion, or rather mistake, of Pasquier (Recherches de la France, l. vii. c. 2.) and Ducange (Glossar. Latin.). The practice of rhyming, as early as the vii[th] century, was borrowed from the languages of the North and East (Muratori, Antiquitat. tom. iii. dissert. xl. p. 686–708.).

51. The description of Amalphi, by William the Apulian (l. iii. p. 267.), contains much truth and some poetry; and the third line may be applied to the sailor's compass:

Nulla magis locuples argento, vestibus, auro
Partibus innumeris: hâc plurimus urbe moratur

jealousy of Pisa; but the poverty of one thousand fishermen is yet dignified by the remains of an arsenal, a cathedral, and the palaces of royal merchants.

Conquest of Sicily by count Roger, A.D. 1060–1090.

Roger, the twelfth and last of the sons of Tancred, had been long detained in Normandy by his own and his father's age. He accepted the welcome summons; hastened to the Apulian camp; and deserved at first the esteem, and afterwards the envy, of his elder brother. Their valour and ambition were equal; but the youth, the beauty, the elegant manners, of Roger, engaged the disinterested love of the soldiers and people. So scanty was his allowance, for himself and forty followers, that he descended from conquest to robbery, and from robbery to domestic theft; and so loose were the notions of property, that, by his own historian, at his special command, he is accused of stealing horses from a stable at Melphi.[52] His spirit emerged from poverty and disgrace: from these base practices he rose to the merit and glory of a holy war; and the invasion of Sicily was seconded by the zeal and policy of his brother Guiscard. After the retreat of the Greeks, the *idolaters*, a most audacious reproach of the Catholics, had retrieved their losses and possessions; but the deliverance of the island, so vainly undertaken by the forces of the Eastern empire, was atchieved by a small and private band of adventurers.[53] In the first attempt, Roger braved, in an open boat, the real and fabulous dangers of Scylla and Charybdis; landed with only sixty soldiers on a hostile shore; drove the Saracens to the gates of Messina; and safely returned with the spoils of

---

Nauta *maris cœlique vias aperire peritus.*
Huc et Alexandri diversa feruntur ab urbe
Regis, et Antiochi. Gens hæc freta plurima transit.
His Arabes, Indi, Siculi nascuntur et Afri.
Hæc gens est totum prope nobilitata per orbem,
Et mercando ferens, et amans mercata referre.

52. Latrocinio armigerorum suorum in multis sustentabatur, quod quidem ad ejus ignominiam non dicimus; sed ipso ita præcipiente adhuc viliora et reprehensibiliora dicturi sumus ut pluribus patescat, quàm laboriose et cum quantâ angustiâ a profundâ paupertate ad summum culmen divitiarum vel honoris attigerit. Such is the preface of Malaterra (l. i. c. 25.) to the horse-stealing. From the moment (l. i. c. 19.) that he has mentioned his patron Roger, the elder brother sinks into the second character. Something similar in Velleius Paterculus may be observed of Augustus and Tiberius.

53. Duo sibi proficua deputans animæ scilicet et corporis si terram Idolis deditam ad cultum divinum revocaret (Galfrid Malaterra, l. ii. c. 1.). The conquest of Sicily is related in the three last books, and he himself has given an accurate summary of the chapters (p. 544–546.).

the adjacent country. In the fortress of Trani, his active and patient courage were equally conspicuous. In his old age he related with pleasure, that, by the distress of the siege, himself, and the countess his wife, had been reduced to a single cloak or mantle, which they wore alternately: that in a sally his horse had been slain, and he was dragged away by the Saracens; but that he owed his rescue to his good sword, and had retreated with his saddle on his back, lest the meanest trophy might be left in the hands of the miscreants. In the siege of Trani, three hundred Normans withstood and repulsed the forces of the island. In the field of Ceramio, fifty thousand horse and foot were overthrown by one hundred and thirty-six Christian soldiers, without reckoning St. George, who fought on horseback in the foremost ranks. The captive banners, with four camels, were reserved for the successor of St. Peter; and had these Barbaric spoils been exposed not in the Vatican, but in the Capitol, they might have revived the memory of the Punic triumphs. These insufficient numbers of the Normans most probably denote their knights, the soldiers of honourable and equestrian rank, each of whom was attended by five or six followers in the field;[54] yet, with the aid of this interpretation, and after every fair allowance on the side of valour, arms, and reputation, the discomfiture of so many myriads will reduce the prudent reader to the alternative of a miracle or a fable. The Arabs of Sicily derived a frequent and powerful succour from their countrymen of Africa: in the siege of Palermo, the Norman cavalry was assisted by the gallies of Pisa; and, in the hour of action, the envy of the two brothers was sublimed to a generous and invincible emulation. After a war of thirty years,[55] Roger, with the title of great count, obtained the sovereignty of the largest and most fruitful island of the Mediterranean; and his administration displays a liberal and enlightened mind above the limits of his age and education. The Moslems were maintained in the free enjoyment of their religion and property:[56] a philosopher and physician of Mazara, of the race of Mahomet, harangued the conqueror, and was invited to court; his

54. See the word *milites*, in the Latin Glossary of Ducange.

55. Of odd particulars, I learn from Malaterra, that the Arabs had introduced into Sicily the use of camels (l. i. c. 33.) and of carrier-pigeons (c. 42.); and that the bite of the tarantula provokes a windy disposition, quæ per anum inhoneste crepitando emergit: a symptom most ridiculously felt by the whole Norman army in their camp near Palermo (c. 36.). I shall add an etymology not unworthy of the xi[th] century: *Messana* is derived from *Messis*, the place from whence the harvests of the isle were sent in tribute to Rome (l. ii. c. 1.).

56. See the capitulation of Palermo in Malaterra, l. ii. c. 45. and Giannone, who remarks the general toleration of the Saracens (tom. ii. p. 72.).

geography of the seven climates was translated into Latin; and Roger, after a diligent perusal, preferred the work of the Arabian to the writings of the Grecian Ptolemy.[57] A remnant of Christian natives had promoted the success of the Normans: they were rewarded by the triumph of the Cross. The island was restored to the jurisdiction of the Roman pontiff; new bishops were planted in the principal cities; and the clergy was satisfied by a liberal endowment of churches and monasteries. Yet the Catholic hero asserted the rights of the civil magistrate. Instead of resigning the investiture of benefices, he dextrously applied to his own profit the papal claims: the supremacy of the crown was secured and enlarged, by the singular bull which declares the princes of Sicily hereditary and perpetual legates of the Holy See.[58]

Robert invades the Eastern empire, A.D. 1081.

To Robert Guiscard, the conquest of Sicily was more glorious than beneficial: the possession of Apulia and Calabria was inadequate to his ambition; and he resolved to embrace or create the first occasion of invading, perhaps of subduing, the Roman empire of the East.[59] From his first wife, the partner of his humble fortunes, he had been divorced under the pretence of consanguinity; and her son Bohemond was destined to imitate, rather than to succeed, his illustrious father. The second wife of Guiscard was the daughter of the princes of Salerno; the Lombards acquiesced in the lineal succession of their son Roger; their five daughters were given in honourable nuptials,[60] and one of them was betrothed in a tender age, to

57. John Leo Afer, de Medicis et Philosophis Arabibus, c. 14. apud Fabric. Bibliot. Græc. tom. xiii. p. 278, 279. This philosopher is named Esseriph Essachalli, and he died in Africa, A.H. 516. A.D. 1122. Yet this story bears a strange resemblance to the Sherif al Edrissi, who presented his book (Geographia Nubiensis, see preface, p. 88. 90. 170.) to Roger king of Sicily, A.H. 548. A.D. 1153 (d'Herbelot, Bibliotheque Orientale, p. 786. Prideaux's Life of Mahomet, p. 188. Petit de la Croix, Hist. de Gengiscan, p. 535, 536. Casiri, Bibliot. Arab. Hispan. tom. ii. p. 9–13.); and I am afraid of some mistake.

58. Malaterra remarks the foundation of the bishoprics (l. iv. c. 7.), and produces the original of the bull (l. iv. c. 29.). Giannone gives a rational idea of this privilege, and the tribunal of the monarchy of Sicily (tom. ii. p. 95–102.); and St. Marc (Abregé, tom. iii. p. 217–301. 1st column) labours the case with the diligence of a Sicilian lawyer.

59. In the first expedition of Robert against the Greeks, I follow Anna Comnena (the ist, iiid, ivth, and vth books of the Alexiad), William Appulus (l. ivth and vth, p. 270–275.), and Jeffrey Malaterra (l. iii. c. 13, 14. 24–29. 39.). Their information is contemporary and authentic, but none of them were eye-witnesses of the war.

60. One of them was married to Hugh, the son of Azzo, or Axo, a marquis of Lombardy, rich, powerful, and *noble* (Gulielm. Appul. l. iii. p. 267.), in the xith century, and whose ancestors in the xth and ixth are explored by the critical industry of Leibnitz and Muratori. From the two elder sons of the marquis Azzo, are derived the

Constantine, a beautiful youth, the son and heir of the emperor Michael.[61] But the throne of Constantinople was shaken by a revolution: the Imperial family of Ducas was confined to the palace or the cloister; and Robert deplored, and resented, the disgrace of his daughter and the expulsion of his ally. A Greek, who styled himself the father of Constantine, soon appeared at Salerno, and related the adventures of his fall and flight. That unfortunate friend was acknowledged by the duke, and adorned with the pomp and titles of Imperial dignity: in his triumphal progress through Apulia and Calabria, Michael[62] was saluted with the tears and acclamations of the people; and pope Gregory the seventh exhorted the bishops to preach, and the Catholics to fight, in the pious works of his restoration. His conversations with Robert were frequent and familiar; and their mutual promises were justified by the valour of the Normans and the treasures of the East. Yet this Michael, by the confession of the Greeks and Latins, was a pageant and impostor; a monk who had fled from his convent, or a domestic who had served in the palace. The fraud had been contrived by the subtle Guiscard; and he trusted, that after this pretender had given a decent colour to his arms, he would sink, at the nod of the conqueror, into his primitive obscurity. But victory was the only argument that could determine the belief of the Greeks; and the ardour of the Latins was much inferior to their credulity: the Norman veterans wished to enjoy the harvest of their toils, and the unwarlike Italians trembled at the known and unknown dangers of a transmarine expedition. In his new levies, Robert exerted the influence of gifts and promises, the terrors of civil and ecclesiastical authority; and some acts of violence might justify the reproach, that age and infancy were pressed without distinction into the service of their unrelenting prince. After two years incessant preparations, the land and naval forces were assembled at Otranto, at the heel, or extreme promontory, of Italy; and Robert was

---

illustrious lines of Brunswick and Este. See Muratori, Antichita Estense.

61. Anna Comnena, somewhat too wantonly, praises and bewails that handsome boy, who, after the rupture of his barbaric nuptials (l. i. p. 23.), was betrothed as her husband; he was *αγαλμα φυσεως . . . Θεου χειρων φιλοτιμημα . . . χρυσου γενους απορροη*, &c. (p. 27.). Elsewhere, she describes the red and white of his skin, his hawk's eyes, &c. l. iii. p. 71.

62. Anna Comnena, l. i. p. 28, 29. Guilelm. Appul. l. iv. p. 271. Galfrid Malaterra, l. iii. c. 13. p. 579, 580. Malaterra is more cautious in his style: but the Apulian is bold and positive.

—— Mentitus se Michaelem
Venerat a Danais quidam seductor ad illum.

As Gregory VII. had believed, Baronius, almost alone, recognizes the emperor Michael (A.D. 1080, N° 44.).

accompanied by his wife, who fought by his side, his son Bohemond, and the representative of the emperor Michael. Thirteen hundred knights[63] of Norman race or discipline, formed the sinews of the army, which might be swelled to thirty thousand[64] followers of every denomination. The men, the horses, the arms, the engines, the wooden towers, covered with raw hides, were embarked on board one hundred and fifty vessels: the transports had been built in the ports of Italy, and the gallies were supplied by the alliance of the republic of Ragusa.

Siege of Durazzo, A.D. 1081, June 17.

At the mouth of the Adriatic gulf, the shores of Italy and Epirus incline towards each other. The space between Brundusium and Durazzo, the Roman passage, is no more than one hundred miles;[65] at the last station of Otranto, it is contracted to fifty;[66] and this narrow distance had suggested to Pyrrhus and Pompey the sublime or extravagant idea of a bridge. Before the general embarkation, the Norman duke dispatched Bohemond with fifteen gallies to seize or threaten the isle of Corfu, to survey the opposite coast, and to secure an harbour in the neighbourhood of Vallona for the landing of the troops. They passed and landed without perceiving an enemy; and this successful experiment displayed the neglect and decay of the naval power of the Greeks. The islands of Epirus and the maritime towns were subdued by the arms or the name of Robert, who led his fleet and army from Corfu (I use the modern appellation) to the siege of Durazzo. That city, the western key of the empire, was guarded by ancient renown, and recent fortifications, by George Palæologus, a patrician, victorious in the Oriental wars, and a numerous garrison of Albanians and Macedonians, who, in every age, have maintained the character of soldiers. In the prosecution

63. Ipse armatæ militiæ non plusquam MCCC milites secum habuisse, ab eis qui eidem negotio interfuerunt attestatur (Malaterra, l. iii. c. 24. p. 583.). These are the same whom the Apulian (l. iv. p. 273.) styles the equestris gens ducis, equites de gente ducis.

64. *Εις τριακοντα χιλιαδας*, says Anna Comnena (Alexias, l. i. p. 37.); and her account tallies with the number and lading of the ships. Ivit in Dyrrachium cum XV millibus hominum, says the Chronicon Breve Normannicum (Muratori, Scriptores, tom. v. p. 278.). I have endeavoured to reconcile these reckonings.

65. The Itinerary of Jerusalem (p. 609. edit. Wesseling) gives a true and reasonable space of a thousand stadia, or one hundred miles, which is strangely doubled by Strabo (l. vi. p. 433.) and Pliny (Hist. Natur. iii. 16.).

66. Pliny (Hist. Nat. iii. 6. 16.) allows *quinquaginta* millia for this brevissimus cursus, and agrees with the real distance from Otranto to La Vallona, or Aulon (d'Anville, Analyse de sa Carte des Cotes de la Gréce, &c. p. 3–6.). Hermolaus Barbarus, who substitutes *centum* (Harduin, Not. lxvi. in Plin. l. iii.), might have been corrected by every Venetian pilot who had sailed out of the gulph.

of his enterprise, the courage of Guiscard was assailed by every form of danger and mischance. In the most propitious season of the year, as his fleet passed along the coast, a storm of wind and snow unexpectedly arose: the Adriatic was swelled by the raging blast of the south, and a new shipwreck confirmed the old infamy of the Acroceraunian rocks.[67] The sails, the masts, and the oars, were shattered or torn away; the sea and shore were covered with the fragments of vessels, with arms and dead bodies; and the greatest part of the provisions were either drowned or damaged. The ducal galley was laboriously rescued from the waves, and Robert halted seven days on the adjacent cape, to collect the relics of his loss and revive the drooping spirits of his soldiers. The Normans were no longer the bold and experienced mariners who had explored the ocean from Greenland to mount Atlas, and who smiled at the petty dangers of the Mediterranean. They had wept during the tempest; they were alarmed by the hostile approach of the Venetians, who had been solicited by the prayers and promises of the Byzantine court. The first day's action was not disadvantageous to Bohemond, a beardless youth,[68] who led the naval powers of his father. All night the gallies of the republic lay on their anchors in the form of a crescent; and the victory of the second day was decided by the dexterity of their evolutions, the station of their archers, the weight of their javelins, and the borrowed aid of the Greek fire. The Apulian and Ragusian vessels fled to the shore, several were cut from their cables and dragged away by the conqueror; and a sally from the town carried slaughter and dismay to the tents of the Norman duke. A seasonable relief was poured into Durazzo, and as soon as the besiegers had lost the command of the sea, the islands and maritime towns withdrew from the camp the supply of tribute and provision. That camp was soon afflicted with a pestilential disease; five hundred knights perished by an inglorious death; and the list of burials (if all could obtain a decent burial) amounted to ten thousand persons. Under these calamities, the mind of Guiscard alone was firm and invincible: and while he collected new forces from Apulia and Sicily, he battered, or scaled, or sapped, the walls of Durazzo. But his industry and valour were

67. Infames scopulos Acroceraunia, Horat. carm. i. 3. The precipitem Africum decertantem Aquilonibus et rabiem Noti, and the monstra natantia of the Adriatic, are somewhat enlarged; but Horace trembling for the life of Virgil, is an interesting moment in the history of poetry and friendship.

68. *Των δε εις τον πωγωνα αυτου εφυβρισαντων* (Alexias, l. iv. p. 106.). Yet the Normans shaved, and the Venetians wore, their beards; they must have derided the *no*-beard of Bohemond; an harsh interpretation! (Ducange, Not. ad Alexiad. p. 283.)

encountered by equal valour and more perfect industry. A moveable turret, of a size and capacity to contain five hundred soldiers, had been rolled forwards to the foot of the rampart: but the descent of the door or drawbridge was checked by an enormous beam, and the wooden structure was instantly consumed by artificial flames.

The army and march of the emperor Alexius, April–September.

While the Roman empire was attacked by the Turks in the East and the Normans in the West, the aged successor of Michael surrendered the sceptre to the hands of Alexius, an illustrious captain, and the founder of the Comnenian dynasty. The princess Anne, his daughter and historian, observes, in her affected style, that even Hercules was unequal to a double combat; and, on this principle, she approves an hasty peace with the Turks, which allowed her father to undertake in person the relief of Durazzo. On his accession, Alexius found the camp without soldiers and the treasury without money; yet such were the vigour and activity of his measures, that in six months he assembled an army of seventy thousand men,[69] and performed a march of five hundred miles. His troops were levied in Europe and Asia, from Peloponesus to the Black Sea; his majesty was displayed in the silver arms and rich trappings of the companies of horse-guards; and the emperor was attended by a train of nobles and princes, some of whom, in rapid succession, had been clothed with the purple, and were indulged by the lenity of the times in a life of affluence and dignity. Their youthful ardour might animate the multitude; but their love of pleasure and contempt of subordination were pregnant with disorder and mischief; and their importunate clamours for speedy and decisive action disconcerted the prudence of Alexius, who might have surrounded and starved the besieging army. The enumeration of provinces recalls a sad comparison of the past and present limits of the Roman world: the raw levies were drawn together in haste and terror; and the garrisons of Anatolia, or Asia Minor, had been purchased by the evacuation of the cities which were immediately occupied by the Turks. The strength of the Greek army consisted in the Varangians, the Scandinavian

69. Muratori (Annali d'Italia, tom. ix. p. 136, 137.) observes, that some authors (Petrus Diacon. Chron. Casinen. l. iii. c. 49.) compose the Greek army of 170,000 men, but that the *hundred* may be struck off, and that Malaterra reckons only 70,000: a slight inattention. The passage to which he alludes, is in the Chronicle of Lupus Protospata (Script. Ital. tom. v. p. 45.). Malaterra (l. iv. c. 27.) speaks in high, but indefinite, terms of the emperor, cum copiis innumerabilibus: like the Apulian poet (l. iv. p. 272.):

> More locustarum montes et plana teguntur.

guards, whose numbers were recently augmented by a colony of exiles and volunteers from the British island of Thule. Under the yoke of the Norman conqueror, the Danes and English were oppressed and united: a band of adventurous youths resolved to desert a land of slavery; the sea was open to their escape; and, in their long pilgrimage, they visited every coast that afforded any hope of liberty and revenge. They were entertained in the service of the Greek emperor; and their first station was in a new city on the Asiatic shore: but Alexius soon recalled them to the defence of his person and palace; and bequeathed to his successors the inheritance of their faith and valour.[70] The name of a Norman invader revived the memory of their wrongs: they marched with alacrity against the national foe, and panted to regain in Epirus, the glory which they had lost in the battle of Hastings. The Varangians were supported by some companies of Franks or Latins; and the rebels, who had fled to Constantinople from the tyranny of Guiscard, were eager to signalise their zeal and gratify their revenge. In this emergency the emperor had not disdained the impure aid of the Paulicians or Manichæans of Thrace and Bulgaria; and these heretics united with the patience of martyrdom, the spirit and discipline of active valour.[71] The treaty with the sultan had procured a supply of some thousand Turks; and the arrows of the Scythian horse were opposed to the lances of the Norman cavalry. On the report and distant prospect of these formidable numbers, Robert assembled a council of his principal officers. "You behold," said he, "your danger: it is urgent and inevitable. The hills are covered with arms and standards; and the emperor of the Greeks is accustomed to wars and triumphs. Obedience and union are our only safety; and I am ready to yield the command to a more worthy leader." The vote and acclamation, even of his secret enemies, assured him, in that perilous moment, of their esteem and confidence; and the duke thus continued: "Let us trust in the rewards of victory, and deprive cowardice of the means of escape. Let us burn our vessels and our baggage, and give battle on this spot, as if it were the place of our nativity and our burial." The resolution was unanimously approved; and, without confining himself to his lines, Guiscard awaited in battle-array the nearer approach of the enemy. His rear was covered

70. See William of Malmsbury de Gestis Anglorum, l. ii. p. 92. Alexius fidem Anglorum suscipiens præcipuis familiaritatibus suis eos applicabat, amorem eorum filio transcribens. Ordericus Vitalis (Hist. Eccles. l. iv. p. 508. l. vii. p. 641.) relates their emigration from England, and their service in Greece.

71. See the Apulian (l. i. p. 256.). The character and story of these Manichæans has been the subject of the liv[th] chapter.

by a small river; his right wing extended to the sea, his left to the hills: nor was he conscious, perhaps, that on the same ground Cæsar and Pompey had formerly disputed the empire of the world.[72]

Battle of Durazzo, A.D. 1081, October 18.

Against the advice of his wisest captains, Alexius resolved to risk the event of a general action, and exhorted the garrison of Durazzo to assist their own deliverance by a well-timed sally from the town. He marched in two columns to surprise the Normans before daybreak on two different sides: his light cavalry was scattered over the plain; the archers formed the second line; and the Varangians claimed the honours of the van-guard. In the first onset, the battle-axes of the strangers made a deep and bloody impression on the army of Guiscard, which was now reduced to fifteen thousand men. The Lombards and Calabrians ignominiously turned their backs: they fled towards the river and the sea; but the bridge had been broken down to check the sally of the garrison, and the coast was lined with the Venetian gallies, who played their engines among the disorderly throng. On the verge of ruin, they were saved by the spirit and conduct of their chiefs. Gaita, the wife of Robert, is painted by the Greeks as a warlike Amazon, a second Pallas; less skilful in arts, but not less terrible in arms, than the Athenian goddess:[73] though wounded by an arrow, she stood her ground, and strove, by her exhortation and example, to rally the flying troops.[74] Her female voice was seconded by the more powerful voice and arm of the Norman duke, as calm in action as he was magnanimous in council: "Whither," he cried aloud, "whither do ye fly? Your enemy is implacable; and death is less grievous than servitude." The moment was decisive: as the Varangians advanced before the line, they discovered the nakedness

72. See the simple and masterly narrative of Cæsar himself (Comment. de Bell. Civil. iii. 41–75.). It is pity that Quintus Icilius (M. Guischard) did not live to analyse these operations, as he has done the campaigns of Africa and Spain.

73. *Παλλας αλλη καν μη Αθηνη*, which is very properly translated by the president Cousin (Hist. de Constantinople, tom. iv. p. 131, in 12mo), qui combattoit comme une Pallas, quoiquelle ne fût pas aussi savante que celle d'Athénes. The Grecian goddess was composed of two discordant characters, of Neith, the workwoman of Sais in Egypt, and of a virgin Amazon of the Tritonian lake in Libya (Banier, Mythologie, tom. iv. p. 1–31. in 12mo).

74. Anna Comnena (l. iv. p. 116.) admires, with some degree of terror, her masculine virtues. They were more familiar to the Latins; and though the Apulian (l. iv. p. 273.) mentions her presence and her wound, he represents her as far less intrepid.

> Uxor in hoc bello Roberti forte sagittâ
> Quâdam læsa fuit: quo vulnere *territa* nullam
> Dum sperabat opem se pœne *subegerat* hosti.

The last is an unlucky word for a female prisoner.

of their flanks; the main battle of the duke, of eight hundred knights, stood firm and entire; they couched their lances, and the Greeks deplore the furious and irresistible shock of the French cavalry.[75] Alexius was not deficient in the duties of a soldier or a general; but he no sooner beheld the slaughter of the Varangians, and the flight of the Turks, than he despised his subjects and despaired of his fortune. The princess Anne, who drops a tear on this melancholy event, is reduced to praise the strength and swiftness of her father's horse, and his vigorous struggle, when he was almost overthrown by the stroke of a lance, which had shivered the Imperial helmet. His desperate valour broke through a squadron of Franks who opposed his flight; and, after wandering two days and as many nights in the mountains, he found some repose, of body, though not of mind, in the walls of Lychnidus. The victorious Robert reproached the tardy and feeble pursuit which had suffered the escape of so illustrious a prize; but he consoled his disappointment by the trophies and standards of the field, the wealth and luxury of the Byzantine camp, and the glory of defeating an army five times more numerous than his own. A multitude of Italians had been the victims of their own fears; but only thirty of his knights were slain in this memorable day. In the Roman host, the loss of Greeks, Turks, and English, amounted to five or six thousand:[76] the plain of Durazzo was stained with noble and royal blood; and the end of the impostor Michael was more honourable than his life.

Durazzo taken, A.D. 1082, February 8.

It is more than probable that Guiscard was not afflicted by the loss of a costly pageant, which had merited only the contempt and derision of the Greeks. After their defeat, they still persevered in the defence of Durazzo; and a Venetian commander supplied the place of George Palæologus, who had been imprudently called away from his station. The tents of the besiegers were converted into barracks, to sustain the inclemency of the winter; and in answer to the defiance of the garrison, Robert insinuated, that his patience was at least equal to their obstinacy.[77] Perhaps he already trusted to his secret correspondence

75. *Απο της του Ρομπερτου προηγησαμενης μαχης, γινοσκων την πρωτην κατα των εναντιων ἱππασιαν των Κελτων ανυποιστον* (Anna, l. v. p. 133.); and elsewhere *και γαρ Κελτος ανηρ πας εποχουμενος μεν ανυποιστος την ορμην, και την θεαν εστιν* (p. 140.). The pedantry of the princess in the choice of classic appellations, encouraged Ducange to apply to his countrymen the characters of the ancient Gauls.

76. Lupus Protospata (tom. iii. p. 45.) says 6000; William the Apulian more than 5000 (l. iv. p. 273.). Their modesty is singular and laudable: they might with so little trouble have slain two or three myriads of schismatics and infidels!

77. The Romans had changed the inauspicious name of *Epi-damnus* to Dyrrachium (Plin. iii. 26.); and the vulgar corruption of Duracium (see Malaterra) bore some

with a Venetian noble, who sold the city for a rich and honourable marriage. At the dead of night several rope-ladders were dropped from the walls; the light Calabrians ascended in silence; and the Greeks were awakened by the name and trumpets of the conqueror. Yet they defended the streets three days against an enemy already master of the rampart; and near seven months elapsed between the first investment and the final surrender of the place. From Durazzo, the Norman duke advanced into the heart of Epirus or Albania; traversed the first mountains of Thessaly; surprised three hundred English in the city of Castoria; approached Thessalonica; and made Constantinople tremble. A more pressing duty suspended the prosecution of his ambitious designs. By shipwreck, pestilence, and the sword, his army was reduced to a third of the original numbers; and instead of being recruited from Italy, he was informed, by plaintive epistles, of the mischiefs and dangers which had been produced by his absence: the revolt of the cities and barons of Apulia; the distress of the pope; and the approach or invasion of Henry king of Germany.

Return of Robert, and actions of Bohemond.

Highly presuming that his person was sufficient for the public safety, he repassed the sea in a single brigantine, and left the remains of the army under the command of his son and the Norman counts, exhorting Bohemond to respect the freedom of his peers, and the counts to obey the authority of their leader. The son of Guiscard trod in the footsteps of his father; and the two destroyers are compared by the Greeks to the caterpillar and the locust, the last of whom devours whatever has escaped the teeth of the former.[78] After winning two battles against the emperor, he descended into the plain of Thessaly, and besieged Larissa, the fabulous realm of Achilles,[79] which contained the treasure and magazines of the Byzantine camp. Yet a just praise must not be refused to the fortitude and prudence of Alexius, who bravely struggled with the calamities of the times. In the poverty of the state, he presumed to borrow the superfluous ornaments of the churches;

---

affinity to *hardness*. One of Robert's names was Durand, a *durando*: poor wit! (Alberic. Monach. in Chron. apud Muratori Annali d'Italia, tom. ix. p. 137.)

78. *Βρουχους και ακριδας ειπεν αν τις αυτους πατερα και ὑιον* (Anna, l. i. p. 35.). By these similies, so different from those of Homer, she wishes to inspire contempt as well as horror for the little, noxious animal, a conqueror. Most unfortunately, the common sense, or common nonsense, of mankind resists her laudable design.

79.

> Prodiit hâc auctor Trojanæ cladis Achilles.

The supposition of the Apulian (l. v. p. 275.) may be excused by the more classic poetry of Virgil (Æneid II. 197.) Larissæus Achilles, but it is not justified by the geography of Homer.

the desertion of the Manichæans was supplied by some tribes of Moldavia; a reinforcement of seven thousand Turks replaced and revenged the loss of their brethren; and the Greek soldiers were exercised to ride, to draw the bow, and to the daily practice of ambuscades and evolutions. Alexius had been taught by experience, that the formidable cavalry of the Franks on foot was unfit for action, and almost incapable of motion;[80] his archers were directed to aim their arrows at the horse rather than the man; and a variety of spikes and snares was scattered over the ground on which he might expect an attack. In the neighbourhood of Larissa the events of war were protracted and balanced. The courage of Bohemond was always conspicuous, and often successful; but his camp was pillaged by a stratagem of the Greeks; the city was impregnable; and the venal or discontented counts deserted his standard, betrayed their trusts, and enlisted in the service of the emperor. Alexius returned to Constantinople with the advantage, rather than the honour, of victory. After evacuating the conquests which he could no longer defend, the son of Guiscard embarked for Italy, and was embraced by a father who esteemed his merit and sympathised in his misfortune.

The emperor Henry III. invited by the Greeks, A.D. 1081.

Of the Latin princes, the allies of Alexius and enemies of Robert, the most prompt and powerful was Henry the third or fourth, king of Germany and Italy, and future emperor of the West. The epistle of the Greek monarch[81] to his brother is filled with the warmest professions of friendship, and the most lively desire of strengthening their alliance by every public and private tie. He congratulates Henry on his success in a just and pious war, and complains that the prosperity of his own empire is disturbed by the audacious enterprises of the Norman Robert. The list of his presents expresses the manners of the age, a radiated crown of gold, a cross set with pearls to hang on the breast, a case of relics, with the names and titles of the saints, a vase of chrystal, a vase of sardonyx, some balm, most probably of Mecca, and one hundred pieces of purple. To these he added a more solid present,

80. The *των πεδιλων προαλματα,* which incumbered the knights on foot, have been ignorantly translated spurs (Anna Comnena, Alexias, l. v. p. 140.). Ducange has explained the true sense by a ridiculous and inconvenient fashion, which lasted from the xi[th] to the xv[th] century. These peaks, in the form of a scorpion, were sometimes two foot, and fastened to the knee with a silver chain.

81. The epistle itself (Alexias, l. iii. p. 93, 94, 95.) well deserves to be read. There is one expression, *αστροπελεκυν δεδεμενον μετα χρυσαφιου,* which Ducange does not understand. I have endeavoured to grope out a tolerable meaning: *χρυσαφιον,* is a golden crown; *αστροπελεκυς,* is explained by Simon Portius (in Lexico Græco-Barbar.), by *κεραυνος, πρηστηρ,* a flash of lightning.

of one hundred and forty-four thousand Byzantines of gold, with a farther assurance of two hundred and sixteen thousand, so soon as Henry should have entered in arms the Apulian territories, and confirmed by an oath the league against the common enemy. The German,[82] who was already in Lombardy at the head of an army and a faction, accepted these liberal offers, and marched towards the south: his speed was checked by the sound of the battle of Durazzo; but the influence of his arms or name, in the hasty return of Robert, was a full equivalent for the Grecian bribe. Henry was the sincere adversary of the Normans, the allies and vassals of Gregory the seventh, his implacable foe. The long quarrel of the throne and mitre had been recently kindled by the zeal and ambition of that haughty priest:[83] the king and the pope had degraded each other; and each had seated a rival on the temporal or spiritual throne of his antagonist. After the defeat and death of his Swabian rebel, Henry descended into Italy to assume the Imperial crown, and to drive from the Vatican the tyrant of the church.[84] But the Roman people adhered to the cause of Gregory: their resolution was fortified by supplies of men and money

Besieges Rome, A.D. 1081–1084.

from Apulia; and the city was thrice ineffectually besieged by the king of Germany. In the fourth year he corrupted, as it is said, with Byzantine gold, the nobles of Rome, whose estates and castles had been ruined by the war. The gates, the bridges, and fifty

A.D. 1084, March 21, —— 24, —— 31.

hostages, were delivered into his hands: the antipope, Clement the third, was consecrated in the Lateran: the grateful pontiff crowned his protector in the Vatican; and the emperor Henry fixed his residence in the Capitol, as the lawful successor of Augustus and Charlemagne. The ruins of the Septizonium were still defended by the nephew of Gregory: the pope himself was invested in the castle of St. Angelo; and his last hope was in the courage and fidelity

82. For these general events I must refer to the general historians Sigonius, Baronius, Muratori, Mosheim, St. Marc, &c.

83. The lives of Gregory VII. are either legends or invectives (St. Marc, Abregé, tom. iii. p. 235, &c.): and his miraculous or magical performances are alike incredible to a modern reader. He will, as usual, find some instruction in Le Clerc (Vie de Hildebrand, Bibliot. ancienne et moderne, tom. viii.), and much amusement in Bayle (Dictionaire Critique, *Gregoire* VII.). That pope was undoubtedly a great man, a second Athanasius, in a more fortunate age of the church. May I presume to add, that the portrait of Athanasius is one of the passages of my history (vol. i. p. 796, &c.) with which I am the least dissatisfied?

84. Anna, with the rancour of a Greek schismatic, calls him *καταπτυστος ουτος Παπας* (l. i. p. 32.), a pope, or priest, worthy to be spit upon; and accuses him of scourging, shaving, perhaps of castrating, the ambassadors of Henry (p. 31, 33.). But this outrage is improbable and doubtful (see the sensible preface of Cousin).

of his Norman vassal. Their friendship had been interrupted by some reciprocal injuries and complaints; but, on this pressing occasion, Guiscard was urged by the obligation of his oath, by his interest, more potent than oaths, by the love of fame, and his enmity to the two emperors. Unfurling the holy banner, he resolved to fly to the relief of the prince of the apostles: the most numerous of his armies, six thousand horse and thirty thousand foot, was instantly assembled; and his march from Salerno to Rome was animated by the public applause and the promise of the divine favour. Henry, invincible in sixty-six battles, trembled at his approach; recollected some indispensible affairs that required his presence in Lombardy; exhorted the Romans to persevere in their allegiance; and hastily retreated three days before the entrance of the Normans. *Flies before Robert, May.* In less than three years, the son of Tancred of Hauteville enjoyed the glory of delivering the pope, and of compelling the two emperors, of the East and West, to fly before his victorious arms.[85] But the triumph of Robert was clouded by the calamities of Rome. By the aid of the friends of Gregory, the walls had been perforated or scaled; but the Imperial faction was still powerful and active; on the third day, the people rose in a furious tumult; and an hasty word of the conqueror, in his defence or revenge, was the signal of fire and pillage.[86] The Saracens of Sicily, the subjects of Roger, and auxiliaries of his brother, embraced this fair occasion of rifling and profaning the holy city of the Christians: many thousands of the citizens, in the sight, and by the allies, of their spiritual father, were exposed to violation, captivity, or death; and a spacious quarter of the city, from the Lateran to the Coliseum, was consumed by the flames, and devoted to perpetual solitude.[87] From a city, where he was now hated, and might be no longer feared, Gregory retired to

85.

Sic uno tempore victi
Sunt terræ Domini duo: rex Alemannicus iste,
Imperii rector Romani maximus ille.
Alter ad arma ruens armis superatur; et alter
Nominis auditi solâ formidine cessit.

It is singular enough, that the Apulian, a Latin, should distinguish the Greek as the ruler of the Roman empire (l. iv. p. 274.).

86. The narrative of Malaterra (l. iii. c. 37. p. 587, 588.) is authentic, circumstantial, and fair. Dux ignem exclamans urbe incensa, &c. The Apulian softens the mischief (inde *quibusdam* ædibus exustis), which is again exaggerated in some partial Chronicles (Muratori Annali, tom. ix. p. 147.).

87. After mentioning this devastation, the Jesuit Donatus (de Roma veteri et nova, l. iv. c. 8. p. 489.) prettily adds, Duraret hodieque in Cœlio monte interque ipsum et capitolium miserabilis facies prostratæ urbis, nisi in hortorum vinetorumque amænitatem Roma resurrexisset ut perpetuâ viriditate contegeret vulnera et ruinas suas.

end his days in the palace of Salerno. The artful pontiff might flatter the vanity of Guiscard, with the hope of a Roman or Imperial crown; but this dangerous measure, which would have inflamed the ambition of the Norman, must for ever have alienated the most faithful princes of Germany.

Second expedition of Robert into Greece, A.D. 1084, October.

The deliverer and scourge of Rome might have indulged himself in a season of repose; but in the same year of the flight of the German emperor, the indefatigable Robert resumed the design of his Eastern conquests. The zeal or gratitude of Gregory had promised to his valour the kingdoms of Greece and Asia;[88] his troops were assembled in arms, flushed with success, and eager for action. Their numbers, in the language of Homer, are compared by Anna to a swarm of bees;[89] yet the utmost and moderate limits of the powers of Guiscard have been already defined; they were contained in this second occasion in one hundred and twenty vessels; and as the season was far advanced, the harbour of Brundusium[90] was preferred to the open road of Otranto. Alexius, apprehensive of a second attack, had assiduously laboured to restore the naval forces of the empire; and obtained from the republic of Venice an important succour of thirty-six transports, fourteen gallies, and nine galeots or ships of extraordinary strength and magnitude. Their services were liberally paid by the licence or monopoly of trade, a profitable gift of many shops and houses in the port of Constantinople, and a tribute to St. Mark, the more acceptable, as it was the produce of a tax on their rivals of Amalphi. By the union of the Greeks and Venetians, the Adriatic was covered with an hostile fleet, but their own neglect, or the vigilance of Robert, the change of a wind, or the shelter of a mist, opened a free passage; and the Norman troops were safely disembarked on the coast of Epirus. With twenty strong and well-appointed gallies, their intrepid duke immediately sought the enemy,

88. The royalty of Robert, either promised or bestowed by the pope (Anna, l. i. p. 32.), is sufficiently confirmed by the Apulian (l. iv. p. 270.).

> Romani regni sibi promisisse coronam
> Papa ferebatur.

Nor can I understand why Gretser, and the other papal advocates, should be displeased with this new instance of apostolic jurisdiction.

89. See Homer Iliad *B.* (I hate this pedantic mode of quotation by the letters of the Greek alphabet) 87, &c. His bees are the image of a disorderly crowd: their discipline and public works seem to be the ideas of a later age (Virgil. Æneid, l. i.).

90. Guilielm. Appulus, l. v. p. 276. The admirable port of Brundusium was double; the outward harbour was a gulph covered by an island, and narrowing by degrees, till it communicated by a small gullet with the inner harbour, which embraced the city on both sides. Cæsar and Nature have laboured for its ruin; and against such agents, what are the feeble efforts of the Neapolitan government? (Swinburne's Travels in the two Sicilies, vol. i. p. 384–390.).

and though more accustomed to fight on horseback, he trusted his own life, and the lives of his brother and two sons, to the event of a naval combat. The dominion of the sea was disputed in three engagements, in sight of the isle of Corfu: in the two former, the skill and numbers of the allies were superior; but in the third, the Normans obtained a final and complete victory.[91] The light brigantines of the Greeks were scattered in ignominious flight: the nine castles of the Venetians maintained a more obstinate conflict; seven were sunk, two were taken; two thousand five hundred captives implored in vain the mercy of the victor; and the daughter of Alexius deplores the loss of thirteen thousand of his subjects or allies. The want of experience had been supplied by the genius of Guiscard; and each evening, when he had sounded a retreat, he calmly explored the causes of his repulse, and invented new methods how to remedy his own defects, and to baffle the advantages of the enemy. The winter season suspended his progress: with the return of spring he again aspired to the conquest of Constantinople; but, instead of traversing the hills of Epirus, he turned his arms against Greece and the islands, where the spoils would repay the labour, and where the land and sea forces might pursue their joint operations with vigour and effect. But, in the isle of Cephalonia, his projects were fatally blasted by an epidemical disease; Robert himself, in the seventieth year of his age, expired in his tent; and a suspicion of poison was imputed, by public rumour, to his wife, or to the Greek emperor.[92] *His death, A.D. 1085, July 17.* This premature death might allow a boundless scope for the imagination of his future exploits; and the event sufficiently declares, that the Norman greatness was founded on his life.[93] Without the appearance of an enemy, a victorious army dispersed or retreated in disorder and consternation; and

91. William of Apulia (l. v. p. 276.) describes the victory of the Normans, and forgets the two previous defeats, which are diligently recorded by Anna Comnena (l. vi. p. 159, 160, 161.). In her turn, she invents or magnifies a fourth action, to give the Venetians revenge and rewards. Their own feelings were far different, since they deposed their doge, propter excidium stoli (Dandulus in Chron. in Muratori, Script. Rerum Italicarum, tom. xii. p. 249.).

92. The most authentic writers, William of Apulia (l. v. 277.), Jeffrey Malaterra (l. iii. c. 41. p. 589.), and Romuald of Salerno (Chron. in Muratori, Script. Rerum Ital. tom. vii.), are ignorant of this crime so apparent to our countrymen William of Malmsbury (l. iii. p. 107.) and Roger de Hoveden (p. 710. in Script. post Bedam): and the latter can tell, how the just Alexius married, crowned, and burnt alive, his female accomplice. The English historian is indeed so blind, that he ranks Robert Guiscard, or Wiscard, among the knights of Henry I. who ascended the throne fifteen years after the duke of Apulia's death.

93. The joyful Anna Comnena scatters some flowers over the grave of an enemy (Alexiad, l. v. p. 162–166.): and his best praise is the esteem and envy of William the Conqueror, the sovereign of his family.

Alexius, who had trembled for his empire, rejoiced in his deliverance. The galley which transported the remains of Guiscard was shipwrecked on the Italian shore; but the duke's body was recovered from the sea, and deposited in the sepulchre of Venusia,[94] a place more illustrious for the birth of Horace,[95] than for the burial of the Norman heroes. Roger, his second son and successor, immediately sunk to the humble station of a duke of Apulia: the esteem or partiality of his father left the valiant Bohemond to the inheritance of his sword. The national tranquillity was disturbed by his claims, till the first crusade against the infidels of the East opened a more splendid field of glory and conquest.[96]

Reign and ambition of Roger, great count of Sicily, A.D. 1101–1154, February 26.

Of human life, the most glorious or humble prospects are alike and soon bounded by the sepulchre. The male line of Robert Guiscard was extinguished, both in Apulia and at Antioch, in the second generation; but his younger brother became the father of a line of kings; and the son of the great count was endowed with the name, the conquests, and the spirit, of the first Roger.[97] The heir of that Norman adventurer was born in Sicily; and, at the age of only four years, he succeeded to the sovereignty of the island, a lot which reason might envy, could she indulge for a moment the visionary, though virtuous, wish of dominion. Had Roger been content with his fruitful patrimony, an happy and grateful people might have blessed their benefactor; and, if a wise administration could have restored the prosperous times of the Greek colonies,[98] the opulence

---

Græcia (says Malaterra) hostibus recedentibus libera læta quievit: Apulia tota sive Calabria turbatur.

94.

> Urbs Venusina nitet tantis decorata sepulchris,

is one of the last lines of the Apulian's poem (l. v. p. 278.). William of Malmsbury (l. iii. p. 107.) inserts an epitaph on Guiscard, which is not worth transcribing.

95. Yet Horace had few obligations to Venusia: he was carried to Rome in his childhood (Sermon. i. 6.); and his repeated allusions to the doubtful limit of Apulia and Lucania (Carm. iii. 4. Serm. ii. 1.) are unworthy of his age and genius.

96. See Giannone (tom. ii. p. 88–93.), and the historians of the first crusade.

97. The reign of Roger, and the Norman kings of Sicily, fills four books of the Istoria Civile of Giannone (tom. ii. l. xi–xiv. p. 136–340.), and is spread over the ix[th] and x[th] volumes of the Italian Annals of Muratori. In the Bibliotheque Italique (tom. i. p. 175–222.) I find an useful abstract of Capecelatro, a modern Neapolitan, who has composed, in two volumes, the history of his country from Roger I. to Frederic II. inclusive.

98. According to the testimony of Philistus and Diodorus, the tyrant Dionysius of Syracuse could maintain a standing force of 10,000 horse, 100,000 foot, and 400 gallies. Compare Hume (Essays, vol. i. p. 268. 435.) and his adversary Wallace (Numbers of Mankind, p. 306, 307.). The ruins of Agrigentum are the theme of every traveller, d'Orville, Reidesel, Swinburne, &c.

and power of Sicily alone might have equalled the widest scope that could be acquired and desolated by the sword of war. But the ambition of the great count was ignorant of these noble pursuits; it was gratified by the vulgar means of violence and artifice. He sought to obtain the undivided possession of Palermo, of which one moiety had been ceded to the elder branch; struggled to enlarge his Calabrian limits beyond the measure of former treaties; and impatiently watched the declining health of his cousin William of Apulia, the grandson of Robert. On the first intelligence of his premature death, Roger sailed from Palermo with seven gallies, cast anchor in the bay of Salerno, received, after ten days negociation, an oath of fidelity from the Norman capital, commanded the submission of the barons, and extorted a legal investiture from the reluctant popes, who could not long endure either the friendship or enmity of a powerful vassal. The sacred spot of Benevento was respectfully spared, as the patrimony of St. Peter; but the reduction of Capua and Naples completed the design of his uncle Guiscard; and the sole inheritance of the Norman conquests was possessed by the victorious Roger. A conscious superiority of power and merit prompted him to disdain the titles of duke and of count; and the isle of Sicily, with a third perhaps of the continent of Italy, might form the basis of a kingdom[99] which would only yield to the monarchies of France and England. The chiefs of the nation who attended his coronation at Palermo, might doubtless pronounce under what name he should reign over them; but the example of a Greek tyrant or a Saracen emir were insufficient to justify his regal character; and the nine kings of the Latin world[100] might disclaim their new associate, unless he were consecrated by the authority of the supreme pontiff. The pride of Anacletus was pleased to confer a title, which the pride of the Norman had stooped to solicit;[101]

Duke of Apulia, A.D. 1127.

99. A contemporary historian of the Acts of Roger from the year 1127 to 1135, founds his title on merit and power, the consent of the barons, and the ancient royalty of Sicily and Palermo, without introducing pope Anacletus (Alexand. Cœnobii Telesini Abbatis de Rebus gestis Regis Rogerii, lib. iv. in Muratori, Script. Rerum Ital. tom. v. p. 607–645.).

100. The kings of France, England, Scotland, Castille, Arragon, Navarre, Sweden, Denmark, and Hungary. The three first were more ancient than Charlemagne: the three next were created by their sword, the three last by their baptism; and of these the king of Hungary alone was honoured or debased by a papal crown.

101. Fazellus, and a crowd of Sicilians, had imagined a more early and independent coronation (A.D. 1130, May 1.), which Giannone unwillingly rejects (tom. ii. p. 137–144.). This fiction is disproved by the silence of contemporaries; nor can it be restored by a spurious charter of Messina (Muratori, Annali d'Italia, tom. ix. p. 340. Pagi, Critica, tom. iv. p. 467, 468.).

First king of Sicily, A.D. 1130, Dec. 25– A.D. 1139, July 25.

but his own legitimacy was attacked by the adverse election of Innocent the second; and while Anacletus sat in the Vatican, the successful fugitive was acknowledged by the nations of Europe. The infant monarchy of Roger was shaken, and almost overthrown, by the unlucky choice of an ecclesiastical patron; and the sword of Lothaire the second of Germany, the excommunications of Innocent, the fleets of Pisa, and the zeal of St. Bernard, were united for the ruin of the Sicilian robber. After a gallant resistance, the Norman prince was driven from the continent of Italy; a new duke of Apulia was invested by the pope and the emperor, each of whom held one end of the *gonfanon*, or flag-staff, as a token that they asserted their right, and suspended their quarrel. But such jealous friendship was of short and precarious duration: the German armies soon vanished in disease and desertion:[102] the Apulian duke, with all his adherents, was exterminated by a conqueror, who seldom forgave either the dead or the living; like his predecessor Leo the ninth, the feeble though haughty pontiff became the captive and friend of the Normans; and their reconciliation was celebrated by the eloquence of Bernard, who now revered the title and virtues of the king of Sicily.

His conquests in Africa, A.D. 1122–1152.

As a penance for his impious war against the successor of St. Peter, that monarch might have promised to display the banner of the cross, and he accomplished with ardour a vow so propitious to his interest and revenge. The recent injuries of Sicily might provoke a just retaliation on the heads of the Saracens: the Normans, whose blood had been mingled with so many subject streams, were encouraged to remember and emulate the naval trophies of their fathers, and in the maturity of their strength they contended with the decline of an African power. When the Fatimite caliph departed for the conquest of Egypt, he rewarded the real merit and apparent fidelity of his servant Joseph, with a gift of his royal mantle, and forty Arabian horses, his palace with its sumptuous furniture, and the government of the kingdoms of Tunis and Algiers. The Zeirides,[103] the descendants of Joseph, forgot their allegiance and gratitude to a distant benefactor, grasped and abused the fruits of prosperity; and after running the little course of an Oriental dynasty, were now fainting in their own weakness.

102. Roger corrupted the second person of Lothaire's army, who sounded, or rather cried, a retreat: for the Germans (says Cinnamus, l. iii. c. 1. p. 51.) are ignorant of the use of trumpets. Most ignorant himself!

103. See de Guignes, Hist. Generale des Huns, tom. i. p. 369–373. and Cardonne, Hist. de l'Afrique, &c. sous la Domination des Arabes, tom. ii. p. 70–144. Their common original appears to be Novairi.

On the side of the land, they were oppressed by the Almohades, the fanatic princes of Morocco, while the sea-coast was open to the enterprises of the Greeks and Franks, who, before the close of the eleventh century, had extorted a ransom of two hundred thousand pieces of gold. By the first arms of Roger, the island or rock of Malta, which has been since ennobled by a military and religious colony, was inseparably annexed to the crown of Sicily. Tripoli,[104] a strong and maritime city, was the next object of his attack; and the slaughter of the males, the captivity of the females, might be justified by the frequent practice of the Moslems themselves. The capital of the Zeirides was named Africa from the country, and Mahadia[105] from the Arabian founder: it is strongly built on a neck of land, but the imperfection of the harbour is not compensated by the fertility of the adjacent plain. Mahadia was besieged by George the Sicilian admiral, with a fleet of one hundred and fifty gallies, amply provided with men and the instruments of mischief: the sovereign had fled, the Moorish governor refused to capitulate, declined the last and irresistible assault, and secretly escaping with the Moslem inhabitants, abandoned the place and its treasures to the rapacious Franks. In successive expeditions, the king of Sicily or his lieutenants reduced the cities of Tunis, Safax, Capsia, Bona, and a long tract of the sea-coast;[106] the fortresses were garrisoned, the country was tributary, and a boast, that it held Africa in subjection, might be ascribed with some flattery on the sword of Roger.[107] After his death, that sword was broken; and these transmarine possessions were neglected, evacuated, or lost, under the troubled reign of his successor.[108] The triumphs of Scipio and Belisarius have proved, that the African continent is neither inaccessible nor invincible: yet the great princes and powers of Christendom have repeatedly

104. Tripoli (says the Nubian geographer, or more properly the Sherif al Edrisi) urbs fortis, saxeo muro vallata, sita prope litus maris. Hanc expugnavit Rogerius, qui mulieribus captivis ductis, viros peremit.

105. See the geography of Leo Africanus (in Ramusio, tom. i. fol. 74. verso, fol. 75. recto), and Shaw's Travels (p. 110.), the vii[th] book of Thuanus, and the xi[th] of the Abbé de Vertot. The possession and defence of the place was offered by Charles V. and wisely declined by the knights of Malta.

106. Pagi has accurately marked the African conquests of Roger; and his criticism was supplied by his friend the Abbé de Longuerue, with some Arabic memorials (A.D. 1147, N° 26, 27. A.D. 1148, N° 16. A.D. 1153, N° 16.).

107.

Appulus et Calaber, Siculus mihi
servit et Afer.

A proud inscription, which denotes, that the Norman conquerors were still discriminated from their Christian and Moslem subjects.

108. Hugo Falcandus (Hist. Sicula, in Muratori Script. tom. vii. p. 270, 271.) ascribes these losses to the neglect or treachery of the admiral Majo.

failed in their armaments against the Moors, who may still glory in the easy conquest and long servitude of Spain.

His invasion of Greece, A.D. 1146. Since the decease of Robert Guiscard, the Normans had relinquished, above sixty years, their hostile designs against the empire of the East. The policy of Roger solicited a public and private union with the Greek princes, whose alliance would dignify his regal character: he demanded in marriage a daughter of the Comnenian family, and the first steps of the treaty seemed to promise a favourable event. But the contemptuous treatment of his ambassadors exasperated the vanity of the new monarch; and the insolence of the Byzantine court was expiated, according to the laws of nations, by the sufferings of a guiltless people.[109] With a fleet of seventy gallies, George the admiral of Sicily appeared before Corfu: and both the island and city were delivered into his hands by the disaffected inhabitants, who had yet to learn that a siege is still more calamitous than a tribute. In this invasion, of some moment in the annals of commerce, the Normans spread themselves by sea, and over the provinces of Greece; and the venerable age of Athens, Thebes, and Corinth, was violated by rapine and cruelty. Of the wrongs of Athens no memorial remains. The ancient walls, which encompassed without guarding the opulence of Thebes, were scaled by the Latin Christians; but their sole use of the Gospel was to sanctify an oath, that the lawful owners had not secreted any relic of their inheritance or industry. On the approach of the Normans the lower town of Corinth was evacuated: the Greeks retired to the citadel, which was seated on a lofty eminence, abundantly watered by the classic fountain of Pirene; an impregnable fortress, if the want of courage could be balanced by any advantages of art or nature. As soon as the besiegers had surmounted the labour (their sole labour) of climbing the hill; their general, from the commanding eminence, admired his own victory, and testified his gratitude to heaven, by tearing from the altar the precious image of Theodore the tutelary saint. The silk weavers of both sexes, whom George transported to Sicily, composed the most valuable part of the spoil, and in comparing the skilful industry of the mechanic with the sloth and cowardice of the soldier, he was heard to exclaim, that the distaff and loom were the only weapons which the Greeks were capable of using.

109. The silence of the Sicilian historians, who end too soon or begin too late, must be supplied by Otho of Frisingen, a German (de Gestis Frederici I. l. i. c. 33. in Muratori Script. tom. vi. p. 668.), the Venetian Andrew Dandulus (Id. tom. xii. p. 282, 283.), and the Greek writers Cinnamus (l. iii. c. 2–5.) and Nicetas (in Manuel. l. ii. c. 1–6.).

His admiral delivers Louis VII. of France:

The progress of this naval armament was marked by two conspicuous events, the rescue of the king of France, and the insult of the Byzantine capital. In his return by sea from an unfortunate crusade, Louis the seventh was intercepted by the Greeks, who basely violated the laws of honour and religion. The fortunate encounter of the Norman fleet delivered the royal captive; and after a free and honourable entertainment in the court of Sicily, Louis continued his journey to Rome and Paris.[110] In the absence of the emperor, Constantinople and the Hellespont were left without defence and without the suspicion of danger. The clergy and people, for the soldiers had followed the standard of Manuel, were astonished and dismayed at the hostile appearance of a line of gallies, which boldly cast anchor in the front of the Imperial city. The forces of the Sicilian admiral were inadequate to the siege or assault of an immense and populous metropolis: but George enjoyed the glory of humbling the Greek arrogance, and of marking the path of conquest to the navies of the West. He landed some soldiers to rifle the fruits of the royal gardens, and pointed with silver, or more probably with fire, the arrows which he discharged against the palace of the Cæsars.[111] This playful outrage of the pirates of Sicily, who had surprised an unguarded moment, Manuel affected to despise, while his martial spirit, and the forces of the empire, were awakened to revenge. The Archipelago and Ionian sea were covered with his squadrons and those of Venice, but I know not by what favourable allowance of transports, victuallers, and pinnaces, our reason, or even our fancy, can be reconciled to the stupendous account of fifteen hundred vessels, which is proposed by a Byzantine historian. These operations were directed with prudence and energy: in his homeward voyage, George lost nineteen of his gallies, which were separated and taken: after an obstinate defence, Corfu implored the clemency of her lawful sovereign; nor could a ship, a soldier of the Norman prince, be found,

insults Constantinople.

The emperor Manuel repulses the Normans, A.D. 1148, 1149.

110. To this imperfect capture and speedy rescue, I apply the *παρ' ὀλιγον ηλθε του αλωναι*, of Cinnamus, l. ii. c. 19. p. 49. Muratori, on tolerable evidence (Annali d'Italia, tom. ix. p. 420, 421.), laughs at the delicacy of the French, who maintain, marisque nullo impediente periculo ad regnum proprium reversum esse; yet I observe that their advocate, Ducange, is less positive as the commentator on Cinnamus, than as the editor of Joinville.

111. In palatium regium sagittas igneas injecit, says Dandulus; but Nicetas, l. ii. c. 8. p. 66. transforms them into *Βελη αργεντεους εχοντα ατρακτους*, and adds, that Manuel styled this insult *παιγνιον*, and *γελωτα . . . ληστευοντα*. These arrows, by the compiler, Vincent de Beauvais, are again transmuted into gold.

unless as a captive, within the limits of the Eastern empire. The prosperity and the health of Roger were already in a declining state: while he listened in his palace of Palermo to the messengers of victory or defeat, the invincible Manuel, the foremost in every assault, was celebrated by the Greeks and Latins as the Alexander or Hercules of the age.

He reduces Apulia and Calabria, A.D. 1155.

A prince of such a temper could not be satisfied with having repelled the insolence of a Barbarian. It was the right and duty, it might be the interest and glory, of Manuel to restore the ancient majesty of the empire, to recover the provinces of Italy and Sicily, and to chastise this pretended king, the grandson of a Norman vassal.[112] The natives of Calabria were still attached to the Greek language and worship, which had been inexorably proscribed by the Latin clergy: after the loss of her dukes, Apulia was chained as a servile appendage to the crown of Sicily: the founder of the monarchy had ruled by the sword; and his death had abated the fear, without healing the discontent, of his subjects: the feudal government was always pregnant with the seeds of rebellion; and a nephew of Roger himself invited the enemies of his family and nation. The majesty of the purple, and a series of Hungarian and Turkish wars, prevented Manuel from embarking his person in the Italian expedition. To the brave and noble Palæologus, his lieutenant, the Greek monarch entrusted a fleet and army: the siege of Bari was his first exploit; and, in every operation, gold as well as steel was the instrument of victory. Salerno, and some places along the western coast, maintained their fidelity to the Norman king; but he lost in two campaigns the greater part of his continental possessions; and the modest emperor, disdaining all flattery and falsehood, was content with the reduction of three hundred cities or villages of Apulia and Calabria, whose names and titles were inscribed on all the walls of the palace. The prejudices of the Latins were gratified by a genuine or fictitious donation, under the seal of the German Cæsars;[113] but the successor of Constantine soon

His design of acquiring Italy and the

renounced this ignominious pretence, claimed the indefeasible dominion of Italy, and professed his design of chacing the Barbarians beyond the Alps. By the artful speeches, liberal gifts,

112. For the invasion of Italy, which is almost overlooked by Nicetas, see the more polite history of Cinnamus (l. iv. c. 1–15. p. 78–101.), who introduces a diffuse narrative by a lofty profession, *περι πης Σικελιας τε, και της Ιταλων εσκεπτετο γης, ὡς και ταυτας Ρωμαιοις ανασωσαιτο.*

113. The Latin, Otho (de Gestis Frederici I. l. ii. c. 30. p. 734.), attests the forgery: the Greek, Cinnamus (l. i. c. 4. p. 78.), claims a promise of restitution from Conrad and Frederic. An act of fraud is always credible when it is told of the Greeks.

Western empire, A.D. 1155–1174, &c.

and unbounded promises, of their Eastern ally, the free cities were encouraged to persevere in their generous struggle against the despotism of Frederic Barbarossa: the walls of Milan were rebuilt by the contributions of Manuel; and he poured, says the historian, a river of gold into the bosom of Ancona, whose attachment to the Greeks was fortified by the jealous enmity of the Venetians.[114] The situation and trade of Ancona rendered it an important garrison in the heart of Italy: it was twice besieged by the arms of Frederic; the Imperial forces were twice repulsed by the spirit of freedom; that spirit was animated by the ambassador of Constantinople; and the most intrepid patriots, the most faithful servants were rewarded by the wealth and honours of the Byzantine court.[115] The pride of Manuel disdained and rejected a Barbarian colleague; his ambition was excited by the hope of stripping the purple from the German usurpers, and of establishing, in the West, as in the East, his lawful title of sole emperor of the Romans. With this view, he solicited the alliance of the people and the bishop of Rome. Several of the nobles embraced the cause of the Greek monarch; the splendid nuptials of his niece with Odo Frangipani, secured the support of that powerful family,[116] and his royal standard or image was entertained with due reverence in the ancient metropolis.[117] During the quarrel between Frederic and Alexander the third, the pope twice received in the Vatican the ambassadors of Constantinople. They flattered his piety by the long-promised union of the two churches, tempted the avarice of his venal court, and exhorted the Roman pontiff to seize the just provocation, the favourable moment, to humble the savage insolence of the Alemanni, and to acknowledge the true representative of Constantine and Augustus.[118]

114. Quod Anconitani Græcum imperium nimis diligerent . . . Veneti speciali odio Anconam oderunt. The cause of love, perhaps of envy, were the beneficia, flumen aureum of the emperor; and the Latin narrative is confirmed by Cinnamus (l. iv. c. 14. p. 98.).

115. Muratori mentions the two sieges of Ancona; the first in 1167, against Frederic I. in person (Annali, tom. x. p. 39, &c.); the second, in 1173, against his lieutenant Christian, archbishop of Mentz, a man unworthy of his name and office (p. 76, &c.). It is of the second siege, that we possess an original narrative, which he has published in his great collection (tom. vi. p. 921–946.).

116. We derive this anecdote from an anonymous chronicle of Fossa Nova, published by Muratori (Script. Ital. tom. vii. p. 874.).

117. The *Βασιλειον σημειον* of Cinnamus (l. iv. c. 14. p. 99.), is susceptible of this double sense. A standard is more Latin, an image more Greek.

118. Nihilominus quoque petebat, ut quia occasio justa et tempus opportunum et acceptabile se obtulerant, Romani corona imperii a sancto apostolo sibi redderetur; quoniam non ad Frederici Alamanni, sed

Failure of his designs. But these Italian conquests, this universal reign, soon escaped from the hand of the Greek emperor. His first demands were eluded by the prudence of Alexander the third, who paused on this deep and momentous revolution;[119] nor could the pope be seduced by a personal dispute to renounce the perpetual inheritance of the Latin name. After his re-union with Frederic, he spoke a more peremptory language, confirmed the acts of his predecessors, excommunicated the adherents of Manuel, and pronounced the final separation of the churches, or at least the empires, of Constantinople and Rome.[120] The free cities of Lombardy no longer remembered their foreign benefactor, and without preserving the friendship of Ancona, he soon incurred the enmity of Venice.[121] By his own avarice or the complaints of his subjects, the Greek emperor was provoked to arrest the persons, and confiscate the effects, of the Venetian merchants. This violation of the public faith exasperated a free and commercial people: one hundred gallies were launched and armed in as many days; they swept the coasts of Dalmatia and Greece; but after some mutual wounds, the war was terminated by an agreement, inglorious to the empire, insufficient for the republic; and a complete vengeance of these and of fresh injuries, was reserved for the succeeding generation. The lieutenant of Manuel had informed his sovereign that he was strong enough to quell any domestic revolt of Apulia and Calabria; but that his forces were inadequate to resist the impending attack of the king of Sicily. His prophecy was soon verified: the death of Palæologus devolved the command on several chiefs, alike eminent in rank, alike defective in military talents; the Greeks were oppressed by land and sea; and a captive remnant that escaped the swords of the Normans and Saracens, abjured all future hostility against the person or dominions of their conqueror.[122] Yet the king of Sicily esteemed the courage and

---

ad suum jus asseruit pertinere (Vit. Alexandri III. a Cardinal. Arragoniæ, in Script. Rerum Ital. tom. iii. par. i. p. 458.). His second embassy was accompanied cum immensa multitudine pecuniarum.

119. Nimis alta et perplexa sunt (Vit. Alexandri III. p. 460, 461.), says the cautious pope.

120. Μηδεν μεσον ειναι λεγων Ρωμῃ τῃ νεοτερᾳ προς την πρεσβυτεραν παλαι αποῤῥαγεισων (Cinnamus, l. iv. c. 14. p. 99.).

121. In his vi[th] book, Cinnamus describes the Venetian war, which Nicetas has not thought worthy of his attention. The Italian accounts, which do not satisfy our curiosity, are reported by the annalist Muratori, under the years 1171, &c.

122. This victory is mentioned by Romuald of Salerno (in Muratori, Script. Ital. tom. vii. p. 198.). It is whimsical enough, that in the praise of the king of Sicily, Cinnamus (l. iv. c. 13. p. 97, 98.) is much warmer and copious than Falcandus (p. 268. 270.). But the Greek is fond of description, and the Latin historian is not fond of William the Bad.

constancy of Manuel, who had landed a second army on the Italian shore: he respectfully addressed the new Justinian; solicited a peace or truce of thirty years, accepted as a gift, the regal title; and acknowledged himself the military vassal of the Roman empire.[123] The Byzantine Cæsars acquiesced in this shadow of dominion, without expecting, perhaps without desiring, the service of a Norman army; and the truce of thirty years was not disturbed by any hostilities between Sicily and Constantinople. About the end of that period, the throne of Manuel was usurped by an inhuman tyrant, who had deserved the abhorrence of his country and mankind: the sword of William the second, the grandson of Roger, was drawn by a fugitive of the Comnenian race; and the subjects of Andronicus might salute the strangers as friends, since they detested their sovereign as the worst of enemies. The Latin historians[124] expatiate on the rapid progress of the four counts who invaded Romania with a fleet and army, and reduced many castles and cities to the obedience of the king of Sicily. The Greeks[125] accuse and magnify the wanton and sacrilegious cruelties that were perpetrated in the sack of Thessalonica the second city of the empire. The former deplore the fate of those invincible but unsuspecting warriors who were destroyed by the arts of a vanquished foe. The latter applaud, in songs of triumph, the repeated victories of their countrymen on the sea of Marmora or Propontis, on the banks of the Strymon, and under the walls of Durazzo. A revolution which punished the crimes of Andronicus, had united against the Franks the zeal and courage of the successful insurgents: ten thousand were slain in battle, and Isaac Angelus, the new emperor, might indulge his vanity or vengeance in the treatment of four thousand captives. Such was the event of the last contest between the Greeks and Normans: before the

Peace with the Normans, A.D. 1156.

Last war of the Greeks and Normans, A.D. 1185.

123. For the Epistle of William I. see Cinnamus (l. iv. c. 15. p. 101, 102.), and Nicetas (l. ii. c. 8.). It is difficult to affirm, whether these Greeks deceived themselves, or the public, in these flattering portraits of the grandeur of the empire.

124. I can only quote of original evidence, the poor chronicles of Sicard of Cremona (p. 603.), and of Fossa Nova (p. 875.), as they are published in the vii[th] tome of Muratori's historians. The king of Sicily sent his troops contra nequitiam Andronici . . . ad acquirendum imperium C.P. They were capti aut confusi . . . decepti captique, by Isaac.

125. By the failure of Cinnamus, we are now reduced to Nicetas (in Andronico, l. i. c. 7, 8, 9. l. ii. c. 1. in Isaac Angelo, l. i. c. 1–4.), who now becomes a respectable contemporary. As he survived the emperor and the empire, he is above flattery: but the fall of Constantinople exasperated his prejudices against the Latins. For the honour of learning I shall observe that Homer's great commentator, Eustathius archbishop of Thessalonica, refused to desert his flock.

expiration of twenty years, the rival nations were lost or degraded in foreign servitude; and the successors of Constantine did not long survive to insult the fall of the Sicilian monarchy.

William I. the Bad, king of Sicily, A.D. 1154, Feb. 26– A.D. 1166, May 7.

The sceptre of Roger successively devolved to his son and grandson: they might be confounded under the name of William; they are strongly discriminated by the epithets of the *bad* and the *good*: but these epithets, which appear to describe the perfection of vice and virtue, cannot strictly be applied to either of the Norman princes. When he was roused to arms by danger and shame, the first William did not degenerate from the valour of his race; but his temper was slothful; his manners were dissolute; his passions headstrong and mischievous; and the monarch is responsible, not only for his personal vices, but for those of Majo, the great admiral, who abused the confidence, and conspired against the life, of his benefactor. From the Arabian conquest, Sicily had imbibed a deep tincture of Oriental manners; the despotism, the pomp, and even the haram, of a sultan; and a Christian people was oppressed and insulted by the ascendant of the eunuchs, who openly professed, or secretly cherished, the religion of Mahomet. An eloquent historian of the times[126] has delineated the misfortunes of his country:[127] the ambition and fall of the ungrateful Majo; the revolt and punishment of his assassins; the imprisonment and deliverance of the king himself; the private feuds that arose from the public confusion; and the various forms of calamity and discord which afflicted Palermo, the island, and the continent, during the reign of William the first, and the minority of his son. The youth, innocence, and beauty of William the second,[128] endeared

William II. the Good,

126. The Historia Sicula of Hugo Falcandus, which properly extends from 1154 to 1169, is inserted in the vii[th] volume of Muratori's Collection (tom. vii. p. 259–344.), and preceded by an eloquent preface or epistle (p. 251–258.), de Calamitatibus Siciliæ. Falcandus has been styled the Tacitus of Sicily; and, after a just, but immense, abatement, from the i[st] to the xii[th] century, from a senator to a monk, I would not strip him of his title: his narrative is rapid and perspicuous, his style bold and elegant, his observation keen; he had studied mankind, and feels like a man. I can only regret the narrow and barren field on which his labours have been cast.

127. The laborious Benedictines (l'Art de verifier les Dates, p. 896.) are of opinion, that the true name of Falcandus, is Fulcandus, or Foucault. According to them, Hugues Foucault, a Frenchman by birth, and at length abbot of St. Denys, had followed into Sicily his patron Stephen de la Perche, uncle to the mother of William II. archbishop of Palermo, and great chancellor of the kingdom. Yet Falcandus has all the feelings of a Sicilian: and the title of *Alumnus* (which he bestows on himself), appears to indicate, that he was born, or at least educated, in the island.

128. Falcand. p. 303. Richard de St. Germano begins his history from the death

him to the nation: the factions were reconciled; the laws were revived; and from the manhood to the premature death of that amiable prince, Sicily enjoyed a short season of peace, justice, and happiness, whose value was enhanced by the remembrance of the past and the dread of futurity. The legitimate male posterity of Tancred of Hauteville, was extinct in the person of the second William; but his aunt, the daughter of Roger, had married the most powerful prince of the age; and Henry the sixth, the son of Frederic Barbarossa, descended from the Alps, to claim the Imperial crown and the inheritance of his wife. Against the unanimous wish of a free people, this inheritance could only be acquired by arms; and I am pleased to transcribe the style and sense of the historian Falcandus, who writes at the moment and on the spot, with the feelings of a patriot and the prophetic eye of a statesman. "Constantia, the daughter of Sicily, nursed from her cradle in the pleasures and plenty, and educated in the arts and manners, of this fortunate isle, departed long since to enrich the Barbarians with our treasures, and now returns, with her savage allies, to contaminate the beauties of her venerable parent. Already I behold the swarms of angry Barbarians: our opulent cities, the places flourishing in a long peace, are shaken with fear, desolated by slaughter, consumed by rapine, and polluted by intemperance and lust. I see the massacre or captivity of our citizens, the rapes of our virgins and matrons.[129] In this extremity (he interrogates a friend) how must the Sicilians act? By the unanimous election of a king of valour and experience, Sicily and Calabria might yet be preserved;[130] for in the levity of the Apulians, ever eager for new revolutions, I can repose neither confidence nor hope.[131]

A.D. 1166, May 7– A.D. 1189, Nov. 16.

Lamentation of the historian Falcandus.

---

and praises of William II. After some unmeaning epithets, he thus continues: legis et justitiæ cultus tempore suo vigebat in regno: suâ erat quilibet sorte contentus; (were they mortals?) ubique pax, ubique securitas, nec latronum metuebat viator insidias, nec maris nauta offendicula piratarum (Scrip. Rerum Ital. tom. vii. p. 969.).

129. Constantia, primis a cunabulis in deliciarum tuarum affluentiâ diutius educata, tuisque institutis, doctrinis et moribus informata, tandem opibus tuis Barbaros delatura discessit: et nunc cum ingentibus copiis revertitur, ut pulcherrima nutricis ornamenta barbaricâ fœditate contaminet . . . Intueri mihi jam videor turbulentas barbarorum acies . . . civitates opulentas et loca diuturnâ pace florentia, metû concutere, cæde vastare, rapinis atterere, et fœdare luxuriâ: hinc cives aut gladiis intercepti, aut servitute depressi, virgines constupratæ, matronæ, &c.

130. Certe si regem non dubiæ virtutis elegerint, nec a Saracenis Christiani dissentiant, poterit rex creatus rebus licet quasi desperatis et perditis subvenire, et incursus hostium, si prudenter egerit, propulsare.

131. In Apulis, qui, semper novitate gaudentes, novarum rerum studiis aguntur, nihil arbitror spei aut fiduciæ reponendum.

Should Calabria be lost, the lofty towers, the numerous youth, and the naval strength, of Messina,[132] might guard the passage against a foreign invader. If the savage Germans coalesce with the pirates of Messina; if they destroy with fire the fruitful region, so often wasted by the fires of mount Ætna,[133] what resource will be left for the interior parts of the island, these noble cities which should never be violated by the hostile footsteps of a Barbarian?[134] Catana has again been overwhelmed by an earthquake: the ancient virtue of Syracuse expires in poverty and solitude;[135] but Palermo is still crowned with a diadem, and her triple walls inclose the active multitudes of Christians and Saracens. If the two nations, under one king, can unite for their common safety, they may rush on the Barbarians with invincible arms. But if the Saracens, fatigued by a repetition of injuries, should now retire and rebel; if they should occupy the castles of the mountains and sea-coast, the unfortunate Christians, exposed to a double attack, and placed as it were between the hammer and the anvil, must resign themselves to hopeless and inevitable servitude."[136] We must not forget, that a priest here prefers his country to his religion; and that the Moslems, whose alliance he seeks, were still numerous and powerful in the state of Sicily.

Conquest of the kingdom of Sicily by the emperor Henry VI. A.D. 1194.

The hopes, or at least the wishes, of Falcandus, were at first gratified by the free and unanimous election of Tancred, the grandson of the first king, whose birth was illegitimate, but whose civil and military virtues shone without a blemish. During four years, the term of his life and reign, he stood in

132. Si civium tuorum virtutem et audaciam attendas, . . . murorum etiam ambitum densis turribus circumseptum.

133. Cum crudelitate piraticâ Theutonum confligat atrocitas, et inter ambustos lapides, et Ethnæ flagrantis incendia, &c.

134. Eam partem, quam nobilissimarum civitatum fulgor illustrat, quæ et toti regno singulari meruit privilegio præminere, nefarium esset . . . vel barbarorum ingressû pollui. I wish to transcribe his florid, but curious, description of the palace, city, and luxuriant plain of Palermo.

135. Vires non suppetunt, et conatus tuos tam inopia civium, quam paucitas bellatorum elidunt.

136. At vero, quia difficile est Christianos in tanto rerum turbine, sublato regis timore Saracenos non opprimere, si Saraceni injuriis fatigati ab eis cœperint dissidere, et castella forte maritima vel montanas munitiones occupaverint; ut hinc cum Theutonicis summâ virtute pugnandum illinc Saracenis crebris insultibus occurrendum, quid putas acturi sunt Siculi inter has depressi angustias, et velut inter malleum et incudem multo cum discrimine constituti? hoc utique agent quod poterunt, ut se Barbaris miserabili conditione dedentes, in eorum se conferant potestatem. O utinam plebis et procerum, Christianorum et Saracenorum vota conveniant; ut regem sibi concorditer eligentes, barbaros totis viribus, toto conanime, totisque desideriis proturbare contendant. The Normans and Sicilians appear to be confounded.

arms on the farthest verge of the Apulian frontier, against the powers of Germany; and the restitution of a royal captive, of Constantia herself, without injury or ransom, may appear to surpass the most liberal measure of policy or reason. After his decease, the kingdom of his widow and infant son fell without a struggle; and Henry pursued his victorious march from Capua to Palermo. The political balance of Italy was destroyed by his success; and if the pope and the free cities had consulted their obvious and real interest, they would have combined the powers of earth and heaven to prevent the dangerous union of the German empire with the kingdom of Sicily. But the subtle policy, for which the Vatican has so often been praised or arraigned, was on this occasion blind and inactive; and if it were true that Celestine the third had kicked away the Imperial crown from the head of the prostrate Henry,[137] such an act of impotent pride could serve only to cancel an obligation and provoke an enemy. The Genoese, who enjoyed a beneficial trade and establishment in Sicily, listened to the promise of his boundless gratitude and speedy departure:[138] their fleet commanded the streights of Messina, and opened the harbour of Palermo; and the first act of his government was to abolish the privileges, and to seize the property, of these imprudent allies. The last hope of Falcandus was defeated by the discord of the Christians and Mahometans: they fought in the capital; several thousands of the latter were slain; but their surviving brethren fortified the mountains, and disturbed above thirty years the peace of the island. By the policy of Frederic the second, sixty thousand Saracens were transplanted to Nocera in Apulia. In their wars against the Roman church, the emperor and his son Mainfroy were strengthened and disgraced by the service of the enemies of Christ; and this national colony maintained their religion and manners in the heart of Italy, till they were extirpated, at the end of the thirteenth century, by the zeal and revenge of the house of Anjou.[139] All the calamities which the prophetic orator had deplored, were surpassed

137. The testimony of an Englishman, of Roger de Hoveden (p. 689.), will lightly weigh against the silence of German and Italian history (Muratori, Annali d'Italia, tom. x. p. 156.). The priests and pilgrims, who returned from Rome, exalted, by every tale, the omnipotence of the holy father.

138. Ego enim in eo cum Teutonicis manere non debeo (Caffari, Annal. Genuenses, in Muratori, Script. Rerum Italicarum, tom. vi. p. 367, 368.).

139. For the Saracens of Sicily and Nocera, see the Annals of Muratori (tom. x. p. 149. and A.D. 1223, 1247), Giannone (tom. ii. p. 385.), and of the originals, in Muratori's Collection, Richard de St. Germano (tom. vii. p. 996.), Matteo Spinelli de Giovenazzo (tom. vii. p. 1064.), Nicholas de Jamsilla (tom. x. p. 494.), and Matteo Villani (tom. xiv. l. vii. p. 103.). The last of these insinuates, that in reducing the Saracens of

by the cruelty and avarice of the German conqueror. He violated the royal sepulchres, and explored the secret treasures of the palace, Palermo, and the whole kingdom: the pearls and jewels, however precious, might be easily removed; but one hundred and sixty horses were laden with the gold and silver of Sicily.[140] The young king, his mother and sisters, and the nobles of both sexes, were separately confined in the fortresses of the Alps; and, on the slightest rumour of rebellion, the captives were deprived of life, of their eyes, or of the hope of posterity. Constantia herself was touched with sympathy for the miseries of her country; and the heiress of the Norman line might struggle to check her despotic husband, and to save the patrimony of her new-born son, of an emperor so famous in the next age under the name of Frederic the second. Ten years after this revolution, the French monarchs annexed to their crown the duchy of Normandy: the sceptre of her ancient dukes had been transmitted, by a grand-daughter of William the Conqueror, to the house of Plantagenet; and the adventurous Normans, who had raised so many trophies in France, England, and Ireland, in Apulia, Sicily, and the East, were lost, either in victory or servitude, among the vanquished nations.

Final extinction of the Normans, A.D. 1204.

Nocera, Charles II. of Anjou employed rather artifice than violence.

140. Muratori quotes a passage from Arnold of Lubec (l. iv. c. 20.): Reperit thesauros absconditos, et omnem lapidum pretiosorum et gemmarum gloriam, ita ut oneratis 160 somariis, gloriose ad terram suam redierit. Roger de Hoveden, who mentions the violation of the royal tombs and corpses, computes the spoil of Salerno at 200,000 ounces of gold (p. 746.). On these occasions, I am almost tempted to exclaim with the listening maid in La Fontaine, "Je voudrois bien avoir ce qui manque."

CHAPTER LVII

The Turks of the House of Seljuk. – Their Revolt against Mahmud Conqueror of Hindostan. – Togrul subdues Persia, and protects the Caliphs. – Defeat and Captivity of the Emperor Romanus Diogenes by Alp Arslan. – Power and Magnificence of Malek Shah. – Conquest of Asia Minor and Syria. – State and Oppression of Jerusalem. – Pilgrimages to the holy Sepulchre.

From the isle of Sicily, the reader must transport himself beyond the Caspian Sea, to the original seat of the Turks or Turkmans, against whom the first crusade was principally directed. Their Scythian empire of the sixth century was long since dissolved; but the name was still famous among the Greeks and Orientals; and the fragments of the nation, each a powerful and independent people, were scattered over the desert from China to the Oxus and the Danube: the colony of Hungarians was admitted into the republic of Europe, and the thrones of Asia were occupied by slaves and soldiers of Turkish extraction. While Apulia and Sicily were subdued by the Norman lance, a swarm of these northern shepherds overspread the kingdoms of Persia: their princes of the race of Seljuk, erected a splendid and solid empire from Samarcand to the confines of Greece and Egypt; and the Turks have maintained their dominion in Asia Minor, till the victorious crescent has been planted on the dome of St. Sophia. *THE TURKS.*

One of the greatest of the Turkish princes, was Mamood or Mahmud,[1] the Gaznevide, who reigned in the eastern provinces of Persia, one thousand years after the birth of Christ. His father Sebectagi was the slave of the slave of the slave of the commander of the faithful. But in this descent of servitude, the first degree *Mahmud, the Gaznevide, A.D. 997–1028.*

1. I am indebted for his character and history to d'Herbelot (Bibliotheque Orientale, *Mahmud*, p. 533–537.), M. de Guignes (Histoire des Huns, tom. iii. p. 155–173.), and our countryman Colonel Alexander Dow (vol. i. p. 23–83.). In the two first volumes of his History of Hindostan, he styles himself the translator of the Persian Ferishta; but in his florid text, it is not easy to distinguish the version and the original.

was merely titular, since it was filled by the sovereign of Transoxiana and Chorasan, who still paid a nominal allegiance to the caliph of Bagdad. The second rank was that of a minister of state, a lieutenant of the Samanides,[2] who broke, by his revolt, the bonds of political slavery. But the third step was a state of real and domestic servitude in the family of that rebel; from which Sebectagi, by his courage and dexterity, ascended to the supreme command of the city and province of Gazna,[3] as the son-in-law and successor of his grateful master. The falling dynasty of the Samanides was at first protected, and at last overthrown, by their servants; and, in the public disorders, the fortune of Mahmud continually encreased. For him, the title of *sultan*[4] was first invented; and his kingdom was enlarged from Transoxiana to the neighbourhood of Ispahan, from the shores of the Caspian to the mouth of the Indus. But the principal source of his fame and riches was the holy war which he waged against the Gentoos of Hindostan. In this foreign narrative I may not consume a page; and a volume would scarcely suffice to recapitulate the battles and sieges of his twelve expeditions. Never was the Musulman hero dismayed by the inclemency of the seasons, the height of the mountains, the breadth of the rivers, the barrenness of the desert, the multitudes of the enemy, or the formidable array of their elephants of war.[5] The sultan of Gazna surpassed the limits of the con-

His twelve expeditions into Hindostan.

2. The dynasty of the Samanides, continued 125 years, A.D. 874–999, under ten princes. See their succession and ruin, in the Tables of M. de Guignes (Hist. des Huns, tom. i. p. 404–406.). They were followed by the Gaznevides, A.D. 999–1183 (see tom. i. p. 239, 240.). His division of nations often disturbs the series of time and place.

3. Gaznah hortos non habet: est emporium et domicilium mercaturæ Indicæ. Abulfedæ Geograph. Reiske, tab. xxiii. p. 349. d'Herbelot, p. 364. It has not been visited by any modern traveller.

4. By the ambassador of the caliph of Bagdad, who employed an Arabian or Chaldaic word that signifies *lord* and *master* (d'Herbelot, p. 825.). It is interpreted *Αυτοκρατωρ, Βασιλευς Βασιλεων*, by the Byzantine writers of the xi[th] century; and the name (*Σουλτανος*, Soldanus) is familiarly employed in the Greek and Latin languages, after it had passed from the Gaznevides to the Seljukides, and other emirs of Asia and Egypt. Ducange (Dissertation xvi. sur Joinville, p. 238–240. Gloss. Græc. et Latin.) labours to find the title of sultan in the ancient kingdom of Persia; but his proofs are mere shadows: a proper name in the Themes of Constantine (ii. 11.), an anticipation of Zonaras, &c. and a medal of Kai Khosrou, not (as he believes) the Sassanide of the vi[th], but the Seljukide of Iconium of the xiii[th], century (de Guignes, Hist. des Huns, tom. i. p. 246.).

5. Ferishta (apud Dow, Hist. of Hindostan, vol. i. p. 49.) mentions the report of a *gun* in the Indian army. But as I am slow in believing this premature (A.D. 1008) use of artillery, I must desire to scrutinize first the text, and then the authority of Ferishta, who lived in the Mogul court in the last century.

quests of Alexander: after a march of three months, over the hills of Cashmir and Thibet, he reached the famous city of Kinnoge,[6] on the Upper Ganges; and, in a naval combat on one of the branches of the Indus, he fought and vanquished four thousand boats of the natives. Delhi, Lahor, and Multan, were compelled to open their gates: the fertile kingdom of Guzarat attracted his ambition and tempted his stay; and his avarice indulged the fruitless project of discovering the golden and aromatic isles of the Southern Ocean. On the payment of a tribute, the *rajahs* preserved their dominions; the people, their lives and fortunes; but to the religion of Hindostan, the zealous Musulman was cruel and inexorable: many hundred temples, or pagodas, were levelled with the ground; many thousand idols were demolished; and the servants of the prophet were stimulated and rewarded by the precious materials of which they were composed. The pagoda of Sumnat was situate on the promontory of Guzarat, in the neighbourhood of Diu, one of the last remaining possessions of the Portuguese.[7] It was endowed with the revenue of two thousand villages; two thousand Brahmins were consecrated to the service of the Deity, whom they washed each morning and evening in water from the distant Ganges: the subordinate ministers consisted of three hundred musicians, three hundred barbers, and five hundred dancing girls, conspicuous for their birth or beauty. Three sides of the temple were protected by the ocean, the narrow isthmus was fortified by a natural or artificial precipice; and the city and adjacent country were peopled by a nation of fanatics. They confessed the sins and the punishment of Kinnoge and Dehli; but if the impious stranger should presume to approach *their* holy precincts, he would surely be overwhelmed by a blast of the Divine vengeance. By this challenge, the faith of Mahmud was animated to a personal trial of the strength of this Indian deity. Fifty thousand of his worshippers were pierced by the spear of the Moslems: the walls were scaled; the sanctuary was profaned; and the conqueror aimed a blow of his iron mace at the head of the idol. The trembling Brahmins are said to have offered ten millions sterling for his ransom; and it was urged by the wisest counsellors, that the destruction

6. Kinnouge, or Canouge (the old Palimbothra) is marked in latitude 27° 3', longitude 80° 13'. See d'Anville (Antiquité de l'Inde, p. 60–62.), corrected by the local knowledge of Major Rennel (in his excellent Memoir on his map of Hindostan, p. 37–43.): 300 jewellers, 30,000 shops for the arreca nut, 60,000 bands of musicians, &c. (Abulfed. Geograph. tab. xv. p. 274. Dow, vol. i. p. 16.), will allow an ample deduction.

7. The idolaters of Europe, says Ferishta (Dow, vol. i. p. 66.). Consult Abulfeda (p. 272.), and Rennel's map of Hindostan.

of a stone image would not change the hearts of the Gentoos; and that such a sum might be dedicated to the relief of the true believers. "Your reasons," replied the Sultan, "are specious and strong; but never in the eyes of posterity shall Mahmud appear as a merchant of idols." He repeated his blows, and a treasure of pearls and rubies, concealed in the belly of the statue, explained in some degree the devout prodigality of the Brahmins. The fragments of the idol were distributed to Gazna, Mecca, and Medina. Bagdad listened to the edifying tale; and Mahmud was saluted by the caliph with the title of guardian of the fortune and faith of Mahomet.

His character. From the paths of blood, and such is the history of nations, I cannot refuse to turn aside to gather some flowers of science or virtue. The name of Mahmud the Gaznevide is still venerable in the East: his subjects enjoyed the blessings of prosperity and peace; his vices were concealed by the veil of religion; and two familiar examples will testify his justice and magnanimity. I. As he sat in the Divan, an unhappy subject bowed before the throne to accuse the insolence of a Turkish soldier who had driven him from his house and bed. "Suspend your clamours," said Mahmud; "inform me of his next visit, and ourself in person will judge and punish the offender." The sultan followed his guide, invested the house with his guards, and extinguishing the torches, pronounced the death of the criminal, who had been seized in the act of rapine and adultery. After the execution of his sentence, the lights were rekindled, Mahmud fell prostrate in prayer, and rising from the ground, demanded some homely fare, which he devoured with the voraciousness of hunger. The poor man, whose injury he had avenged, was unable to suppress his astonishment and curiosity; and the courteous monarch condescended to explain the motives of this singular behaviour. "I had reason to suspect that none except one of my sons could dare to perpetrate such an outrage; and I extinguished the lights, that my justice might be blind and inexorable. My prayer was a thanksgiving on the discovery of the offender; and so painful was my anxiety, that I had passed three days without food since the first moment of your complaint." II. The sultan of Gazna had declared war against the dynasty of the Bowides, the sovereigns of the western Persia: he was disarmed by an epistle of the sultana mother, and delayed his invasion till the manhood of her son.[8] "During the life of my husband," said the artful regent, "I was ever

8. D'Herbelot, Bibliotheque Orientale, p. 527. Yet these letters, apothegms, &c. are rarely the language of the heart, or the motives of public action.

apprehensive of your ambition: he was a prince and a soldier worthy of your arms. He is now no more; his sceptre has passed to a woman and a child, and you *dare not* attack their infancy and weakness. How inglorious would be your conquest, how shameful your defeat! and yet the event of war is in the hand of the Almighty." Avarice was the only defect that tarnished the illustrious character of Mahmud; and never has that passion been more richly satiated. The Orientals exceed the measure of credibility in the account of millions of gold and silver, such as the avidity of man has never accumulated; in the magnitude of pearls, diamonds, and rubies, such as have never been produced by the workmanship of nature.[9] Yet the soil of Hindostan is impregnated with precious minerals; her trade, in every age, has attracted the gold and silver of the world; and her virgin spoils were rifled by the first of the Mahometan conquerors. His behaviour, in the last days of his life, evinces the vanity of these possessions, so laboriously won, so dangerously held, and so inevitably lost. He surveyed the vast and various chambers of the treasury of Gazna; burst into tears; and again closed the doors, without bestowing any portion of the wealth which he could no longer hope to preserve. The following day he reviewed the state of his military force; one hundred thousand foot, fifty-five thousand horse, and thirteen hundred elephants of battle.[10] He again wept the instability of human greatness; and his grief was embittered by the hostile progress of the Turkmans, whom he had introduced into the heart of his Persian kingdom.

Manners and emigration of the Turks, or Turkmans, A.D. 980–1028.

In the modern depopulation of Asia, the regular operation of government and agriculture is confined to the neighbourhood of cities; and the distant country is abandoned to the pastoral tribes of Arabs, Curds, and *Turkmans*.[11] Of the last-mentioned people, two considerable branches extend on

9. For instance, a ruby of four hundred and fifty miskals (Dow, vol. i. p. 53.), or six pounds three ounces: the largest in the treasury of Delhi weighed seventeen miskals (Voyages de Tavernier, partie ii. p. 280.). It is true, that in the East all coloured stones are called rubies (p. 355.), and that Tavernier saw three larger and more precious among the jewels de notre grand roi, le plus puissant et plus magnifique de tous les Rois de la terre (p. 376.).

10. Dow, vol. i. p. 65. The sovereign of Kinoge is said to have possessed 2500 elephants (Abulfed. Geograph. tab. xv. p. 274.). From these Indian stories, the reader may correct a note in my first volume (p. 226.); or from that note he may correct these stories.

11. See a just and natural picture of these pastoral manners, in the history of William archbishop of Tyre (l. i. c. vii. in the Gesta Dei per Francos, p. 633, 634.), and a valuable note by the editor of the Histoire Genealogique des Tatars, p. 535–538.

either side of the Caspian Sea: the western colony can muster forty thousand soldiers; the eastern, less obvious to the traveller, but more strong and populous, has encreased to the number of one hundred thousand families. In the midst of civilized nations, they preserve the manners of the Scythian desert, remove their encampments with the change of seasons, and feed their cattle among the ruins of palaces and temples. Their flocks and herds are their only riches; their tents, either black or white, according to the colour of the banner, are covered with felt, and of a circular form; their winter apparel is a sheep-skin; a robe of cloth or cotton their summer garment: the features of the men are harsh and ferocious; the countenance of their women is soft and pleasing. Their wandering life maintains the spirit and exercise of arms; they fight on horseback; and their courage is displayed in frequent contests with each other and with their neighbours. For the licence of pasture they pay a slight tribute to the sovereign of the land; but the domestic jurisdiction is in the hands of the chiefs and elders. The first emigration of the eastern Turkmans, the most ancient of their race, may be ascribed to the tenth century of the Christian æra.[12] In the decline of the caliphs, and the weakness of their lieutenants, the barrier of the Jaxartes was often violated: in each invasion, after the victory or retreat of their countrymen, some wandering tribe, embracing the Mahometan faith, obtained a free encampment in the spacious plains and pleasant climate of Transoxiana and Carizme. The Turkish slaves who aspired to the throne encouraged these emigrations, which recruited their armies, awed their subjects and rivals, and protected the frontier against the wilder natives of Turkestan; and this policy was abused by Mahmud the Gaznevide beyond the example of former times. He was admonished of his error by a chief of the race of Seljuk, who dwelt in the territory of Bochara. The sultan had enquired what supply of men he could furnish for military service. "If you send," replied Ismael, "one of these arrows into our camp, fifty thousand of your servants will mount on horseback." "And if that number," continued Mahmud, "should not be sufficient?" "Send this second arrow to the hord of Balik, and you will find fifty thousand more." "But," said the Gaznevide, dissembling his anxiety, "if I should stand in need of the whole force of your kindred tribes?" "Dispatch my

12. The first emigrations of the Turkmans, and doubtful origin of the Seljukians, may be traced in the laborious History of the Huns, by M. de Guignes (tom. i. Tables Chronologiques, l. v. tom. iii. l. vii. ix. x.), and the Bibliotheque Orientale of d'Herbelot, (p. 799–802. 897–901.), Elmacin (Hist. Saracen. p. 331–333.), and Abulpharagius (Dynast. p. 221, 222.).

bow," was the last reply of Ismael, "and as it is circulated around, the summons will be obeyed by two hundred thousand horse." The apprehension of such formidable friendship induced Mahmud to transport the most obnoxious tribes into the heart of Chorasan, where they would be separated from their brethren by the river Oxus, and inclosed on all sides by the walls of obedient cities. But the face of the country was an object of temptation rather than terror; and the vigour of government was relaxed by the absence and death of the sultan of Gazna. The shepherds were converted into robbers; the bands of robbers were collected into an army of conquerors: as far as Ispahan and the Tigris, Persia was afflicted by their predatory inroads; and the Turkmans were not ashamed or afraid to measure their courage and numbers with the proudest sovereigns of Asia. Massoud, the son and successor of Mahmud, had too long neglected the advice of his wisest Omrahs. "Your enemies," they repeatedly urged, "were in their origin a swarm of ants; they are now little snakes; and, unless they be instantly crushed, they will acquire the venom and magnitude of serpents." After some alternatives of truce and hostility, after the repulse or partial success of his lieutenants, the sultan marched in person against the Turkmans, who attacked him on all sides with barbarous shouts and irregular onset. "Massoud," says the Persian historian,[13] "plunged singly to oppose the torrent of gleaming arms, exhibiting such acts of gigantic force and valour as never king had before displayed. A few of his friends, roused by his words and actions, and that innate honour which inspires the brave, seconded their lord so well, that wheresoever he turned his fatal sword, the enemies were mowed down, or retreated before him. But now, when victory seemed to blow on his standard, misfortune was active behind it; for when he looked round, he beheld almost his whole army, excepting that body he commanded in person, devouring the paths of flight." The Gaznevide was abandoned by the cowardice or treachery of some generals of Turkish race; and this memorable day of Zendecan[14] founded in Persia the dynasty of the shepherd kings.[15]

They defeat the Gaznevides, and subdue Persia, A.D. 1038.

13. Dow, Hist. of Hindostan, vol. i. p. 89. 95–98. I have copied this passage as a specimen of the Persian manner; but I suspect, that by some odd fatality, the style of Ferishta has been improved by that of Ossian.

14. The Zendekan of d'Herbelot (p. 1028.), the Dindaka of Dow (vol. i. p. 97.), is probably the Dandanekan of Abulfeda (Geograph. p. 345. Reiske), a small town of Chorasan, two days journey from Marû, and renowned through the East for the production and manufacture of cotton.

15. The Byzantine historians (Cedrenus, tom. ii. p. 766, 767. Zonaras, tom. ii.

Dynasty of the Seljukians, A.D. 1038–1152.

The victorious Turkmans immediately proceeded to the election of a king; and, if the probable tale of a Latin historian[16] deserves any credit, they determined by lot the choice of their new master. A number of arrows were successively inscribed with the name of a tribe, a family, and a candidate; they were drawn from the bundle by the hand of a child; and the important prize was obtained by Togrul Beg, the son of Michael, the son of Seljuk, whose surname was immortalised in the greatness of his posterity. The sultan Mahmud, who valued himself on his skill in national genealogy, professed his ignorance of the family of Seljuk; yet the father of that race appears to have been a chief of power and renown.[17] For a daring intrusion into the haram of his prince, Seljuk was banished from Turkestan: with a numerous tribe of his friends and vassals, he passed the Jaxartes, encamped in the neighbourhood of Samarcand, embraced the religion of Mahomet, and acquired the crown of martyrdom in a war against the infidels. His age, of an hundred and seven years, surpassed the life of his son, and Seljuk adopted the care of his two grandsons, Togrul and Jaafar; the eldest of whom, at the age of forty-five, was invested with the title of sultan, in the royal city of Nishabur. The blind determination of chance was justified by the virtues of the successful candidate. It would be superfluous to praise the valour of a Turk; and the ambition of Togrul[18] was equal to his valour. By his arms, the Gaznevides were expelled from the eastern kingdoms of Persia, and gradually driven to the banks of the Indus,

Reign and character of Togrul Beg, A.D. 1038–1063.

---

p. 255. Nicephorus Bryennius, p. 21.) have confounded, in this revolution, the truth of time and place, of names and persons, of causes and events. The ignorance and errors of these Greeks (which I shall not stop to unravel) may inspire some distrust of the story of Cyaxares and Cyrus, as it is told by their most eloquent predecessors.

16. Willerm. Tyr. l. i. c. 7. p. 633. The divination by arrows is ancient and famous in the East.

17. D'Herbelot, p. 801. Yet after the fortune of his posterity, Seljuk became the thirty-fourth in lineal descent from the great Afrasiab, emperor of Touran (p. 800.). The Tartar pedigree of the house of Zingis gave a different cast to flattery and fable; and the historian Mirkhond derives the Seljukides from Alankavah, the virgin mother (p. 801. col. 2.). If they be the same as the *Zalzuts* of Abulghazi Bahadur Khan (Hist. Genealogique, p. 148.), we quote in their favour the most weighty evidence of a Tartar prince himself, the descendant of Zingis, Alankavah, or Alancu, and Oguz Khan.

18. By a slight corruption, Togrul Beg is the Tangroli-pix of the Greeks. His reign and character are faithfully exhibited by d'Herbelot (Bibliot. Orient. p. 1027, 1028.) and de Guignes (Hist. des Huns, tom. iii. p. 189–201.).

in search of a softer and more wealthy conquest. In the West he annihilated the dynasty of the Bowides; and the sceptre of Irak passed from the Persian to the Turkish nation. The princes who had felt, or who feared, the Seljukian arrows, bowed their heads in the dust; by the conquest of Aderbijan, or Media, he approached the Roman confines; and the shepherd presumed to dispatch an ambassador or herald to demand the tribute and obedience of the emperor of Constantinople.[19] In his own dominions, Togrul was the father of his soldiers and people; by a firm and equal administration Persia was relieved from the evils of anarchy; and the same hands which had been imbrued in blood became the guardians of justice and the public peace. The more rustic, perhaps the wisest, portion of the Turkmans[20] continued to dwell in the tents of their ancestors; and, from the Oxus to the Euphrates, these military colonies were protected and propagated by their native princes. But the Turks of the court and city were refined by business and softened by pleasure: they imitated the dress, language, and manners, of Persia; and the royal palaces of Nishabur and Rei displayed the order and magnificence of a great monarchy. The most deserving of the Arabians and Persians were promoted to the honours of the state; and the whole body of the Turkish nation embraced with fervour and sincerity the religion of Mahomet. The northern swarms of Barbarians, who overspread both Europe and Asia, have been irreconcilably separated by the consequences of a similar conduct. Among the Moslems, as among the Christians, their vague and local traditions have yielded to the reason and authority of the prevailing system, to the fame of antiquity, and the consent of nations. But the triumph of the Koran is more pure and meritorious, as it was not assisted by any visible splendour of worship which might allure the Pagans by some resemblance of idolatry. The first of the Seljukian sultans was conspicuous by his zeal and faith: each day he repeated the five prayers which are enjoined to the true believers: of each week, the two first days were consecrated by an extraordinary fast; and in

19. Cedrenus, tom. ii. p. 774, 775. Zonaras, tom. ii. p. 257. With their usual knowledge of Oriental affairs, they describe the ambassador as a *sherif*, who, like the syncellus of the patriarch, was the vicar and successor of the caliph.

20. From William of Tyre, I have borrowed this distinction of Turks and Turkmans, which at least is popular and convenient. The names are the same, and the addition of *man*, is of the same import in the Persic and Teutonic idioms. Few critics will adopt the etymology of James de Vitry (Hist. Hierosol. l. i. c. 11. p. 1061.), of Turcomani, quasi *Turci* et *Comani*, a mixed people.

every city a mosch was completed, before Togrul presumed to lay the foundations of a palace.[21]

He delivers the caliph of Bagdad, A.D. 1055.

With the belief of the Koran, the son of Seljuk imbibed a lively reverence for the successor of the prophet. But that sublime character was still disputed by the caliphs of Bagdad and Egypt, and each of the rivals was solicitous to prove his title in the judgment of the strong though illiterate Barbarians. Mahmud the Gaznevide had declared himself in favour of the line of Abbas; and had treated with indignity the robe of honour which was presented by the Fatimite ambassador. Yet the ungrateful Hashemite had changed with the change of fortune; he applauded the victory of Zendecan, and named the Seljukian sultan his temporal vicegerent over the Moslem world. As Togrul executed and enlarged this important trust, he was called to the deliverance of the caliph Cayem, and obeyed the holy summons, which gave a new kingdom to his arms.[22] In the palace of Bagdad, the commander of the faithful still slumbered, a venerable phantom. His servant or master, the prince of the Bowides, could no longer protect him from the insolence of meaner tyrants; and the Euphrates and Tigris were oppressed by the revolt of the Turkish and Arabian emirs. The presence of a conqueror was implored as a blessing; and the transient mischiefs of fire and sword were excused as the sharp but salutary remedies which alone could restore the health of the republic. At the head of an irresistible force, the sultan of Persia marched from Hamadan: the proud were crushed, the prostrate were spared; the prince of the Bowides disappeared; the heads of the most obstinate rebels were laid at the feet of Togrul; and he inflicted a lesson of obedience on the people of Mosul and Bagdad. After the chastisement of the guilty, and the restoration of peace, the royal shepherd accepted the reward of his labours; and a solemn comedy represented the triumph of religious prejudice over Barbarian power.[23] The Turkish sultan embarked on the Tigris, landed at the gate of Racca, and made his public entry on horseback. At the palace-gate he respectfully dismounted, and walked on foot, preceded by his emirs without arms. The caliph was seated behind his black veil: the

His investiture,

21. Hist. Generale des Huns, tom. iii. p. 165, 166, 167. M. de Guignes quotes Abulmahasen, an historian of Egypt.

22. Consult the Bibliotheque Orientale, in the articles of the *Abbassides*, *Caher*, and *Caiem*, and the Annals of Elmacin and Abulpharagius.

23. For this curious ceremony I am indebted to M. de Guignes (tom. iii. p. 197, 198.), and that learned author is obliged to Bondari, who composed in Arabic the history of the Seljukides (tom. v. p. 365.). I am ignorant of his age, country, and character.

black garment of the Abbassides was cast over his shoulders, and he held in his hand the staff of the apostle of God. The conqueror of the East kissed the ground, stood some time in a modest posture, and was led towards the throne by the vizir and an interpreter. After Togrul had seated himself on another throne, his commission was publicly read, which declared him the temporal lieutenant of the vicar of the prophet. He was successively invested with seven robes of honour, and presented with seven slaves, the natives of the seven climates of the Arabian empire. His mystic veil was perfumed with musk; two crowns were placed on his head, two scymetars were girded to his side, as the symbols of a double reign over the East and West. After this inauguration, the sultan was prevented from prostrating himself a second time; but he twice kissed the hand of the commander of the faithful, and his titles were proclaimed by the voice of heralds and the applause of the Moslems. In a second visit to Bagdad, the Seljukian prince again rescued the caliph from his enemies; and devoutly, on foot, led the bridle of his mule from the prison to the palace. Their alliance was cemented by the marriage of Togrul's sister with the successor of the prophet. Without reluctance he had introduced a Turkish virgin into his haram; but Cayem proudly refused his daughter to the sultan, disdained to mingle the blood of the Hashemites with the blood of a Scythian shepherd; and protracted the negociation many months, till the gradual diminution of his revenue admonished him that he was still in the hands of a master. The royal nuptials were followed by the death of Togrul himself;[24] as he left no children, his nephew Alp Arslan succeeded to the title and prerogatives of sultan; and his name, after that of the caliph, was pronounced in the public prayers of the Moslems. Yet in this revolution, the Abbassides acquired a larger measure of liberty and power. On the throne of Asia, the Turkish monarchs were less jealous of the domestic administration of Bagdad; and the commanders of the faithful were relieved from the ignominious vexations to which they had been exposed by the presence and poverty of the Persian dynasty.

and death, A.D. 1063.

The Turks invade the Roman empire, A.D. 1050.

Since the fall of the caliphs, the discord and degeneracy of the Saracens respected the Asiatic provinces of Rome; which, by the victories of Nicephorus, Zimisces, and Basil, had been extended as far as Antioch and the eastern boundaries of Armenia. Twenty-five years after the death of Basil, his successors were

24. Eodem anno (A.H. 455) obiit princeps Togrulbecus . . . rex fuit clemens, prudens, et peritus regnandi, cujus terror corda mortalium invaserat, ita ut obedirent ei reges atque ad ipsum scriberent. Elmacin, Hist. Saracen. p. 342. vers. Erpenii.

suddenly assaulted by an unknown race of Barbarians, who united the Scythian valour with the fanaticism of new proselytes, and the art and riches of a powerful monarchy.[25] The myriads of Turkish horse overspread a frontier of six hundred miles from Tauris to Arzeroum, and the blood of one hundred and thirty thousand Christians was a grateful sacrifice to the Arabian prophet. Yet the arms of Togrul did not make any deep or lasting impression on the Greek empire. The torrent rolled away from the open country; the sultan retired without glory or success from the siege of an Armenian city; the obscure hostilities were continued or suspended with a vicissitude of events; and the bravery of the Macedonian legions renewed the fame of the conqueror of Asia.[26] The name of Alp Arslan, the valiant lion, is expressive of the popular idea of the perfection of man; and the successor of Togrul displayed the fierceness and generosity of the royal animal. He passed the Euphrates at the head of the Turkish cavalry, and entered Cæsarea, the metropolis of Cappadocia, to which he had been attracted by the fame and wealth of the temple of St. Basil. The solid structure resisted the destroyer: but he carried away the doors of the shrine incrusted with gold and pearls, and profaned the relics of the tutelar saint, whose mortal frailties were now covered by the venerable rust of antiquity. The final conquest of Armenia and Georgia was atchieved by Alp Arslan. In Armenia, the title of a kingdom, and the spirit of a nation, were annihilated: the artificial fortifications were yielded by the mercenaries of Constantinople; by strangers without faith, veterans without pay or arms, and recruits without experience or discipline. The loss of this important frontier was the news of a day; and the Catholics were neither surprised nor displeased, that a people so deeply infected with the Nestorian and Eutychian errors, had been delivered by Christ and his mother into the hands of the infidels.[27] The

Reign of Alp Arslan, A.D. 1063–1072.

Conquest of Armenia and Georgia, A.D. 1065–1068.

25. For these wars of the Turks and Romans, see in general the Byzantine histories of Zonaras and Cedrenus, Scylitzes the continuator of Cedrenus, and Nicephorus Bryennius Cæsar. The two first of these were monks, the two latter statesmen; yet such were the Greeks, that the difference of style and character is scarcely discernible. For the Orientals, I draw as usual on the wealth of d'Herbelot (see titles of the first Seljukides) and the accuracy of de Guignes (Hist. des Huns, tom. iii. l. x.).

26. *Ἐφερετο γαρ εν Τουρκοις λογος, ως ειη πεπρωμενον καταστραφηναι το Τουρκων γενος απο της τοιαυτης δυναμεως, ὁποιαν ὁ Μακεδων Αλεξανδρος εχων καταστρεψατο Περσας*. Cedrenus, tom. ii. p. 791. The credulity of the vulgar is always probable; and the Turks had learned from the Arabs the history or legend of Escander Dulcarnein (d'Herbelot, p. 317, &c.).

27. *Ὁι και Ιβηριαν και Μεσοποταμιαν, και Αρμενιαν οικουσιν· και ὁι την Ιου-*

woods and vallies of mount Caucasus were more strenuously defended by the native Georgians[28] or Iberians: but the Turkish sultan and his son Malek were indefatigable in this holy war; their captives were compelled to promise a spiritual as well as temporal obedience; and, instead of their collars and bracelets, an iron horse-shoe, a badge of ignominy, was imposed on the infidels who still adhered to the worship of their fathers. The change, however, was not sincere or universal; and, through ages of servitude, the Georgians have maintained the succession of their princes and bishops. But a race of men, whom nature has cast in her most perfect mould, is degraded by poverty, ignorance, and vice; their profession, and still more their practice, of Christianity is an empty name; and if they have emerged from heresy, it is only because they are too illiterate to remember a metaphysical creed.[29]

The emperor Romanus Diogenes, A.D. 1068–1071.

The false or genuine magnanimity of Mahmud the Gaznevide, was not imitated by Alp Arslan; and he attacked without scruple the Greek empress Eudocia and her children. His alarming progress compelled her to give herself and her sceptre to the hand of a soldier; and Romanus Diogenes was invested with the Imperial purple. His patriotism, and perhaps his pride, urged him from Constantinople within two months after his accession; and the next campaign he most scandalously took the field during the holy festival of Easter. In the palace, Diogenes was no more than the husband of Eudocia: in the camp, he was the emperor of the Romans, and he sustained that character with feeble resources and invincible courage. By his spirit and success, the soldiers were taught to act, the subjects to hope, and the

---

διακηυ του Νεστοριου και των Ακεφαλων θρησκευουσιν αιρεσιν (Scylitzes, ad calcem Cedreni, tom. ii. p. 834. whose ambiguous construction shall not tempt me to suspect that he confounded the Nestorian and Monophysite heresies). He familiarly talks of the μηνις, χολος, οργη, Θεου, qualities, as I should apprehend, very foreign to the perfect Being; but his bigotry is forced to confess, that they were soon afterwards discharged on the orthodox Romans.

28. Had the name of Georgians been known to the Greeks (Stritter, Memoriæ Byzant. tom. iv. *Iberica*), I should derive it from their agriculture, as the Σκυθαι γεωργοι of Herodotus (l. iv. c. 18. p. 289. edit. Wesseling). But it appears only since the crusades, among the Latins (Jac. a Vitriaco, Hist. Hierosol. c. 79. p. 1095.) and Orientals (d'Herbelot, p. 407.), and was devoutly borrowed from St. George of Cappadocia.

29. Mosheim, Institut. Hist. Eccles. p. 632. See in Chardin's Travels (tom. i. p. 171–174.), the manners and religion of this handsome but worthless nation. See the pedigree of their princes from Adam to the present century, in the Tables of M. de Guignes (tom. i. p. 433–438.).

enemies to fear. The Turks had penetrated into the heart of Phrygia; but the sultan himself had resigned to his emirs the prosecution of the war; and their numerous detachments were scattered over Asia in the security of conquest. Laden with spoil and careless of discipline, they were separately surprised and defeated by the Greeks: the activity of the emperor seemed to multiply his presence; and while they heard of his expedition to Antioch, the enemy felt his sword on the hills of Trebizond. In three laborious campaigns, the Turks were driven beyond the Euphrates: in the fourth and last, Romanus undertook the deliverance of Armenia. The desolation of the land obliged him to transport a supply of two months provisions; and he marched forwards to the siege of Malazkerd,[30] an important fortress in the midway between the modern cities of Arzeroum and Van. His army amounted, at the least, to one hundred thousand men. The troops of Constantinople were reinforced by the disorderly multitudes of Phrygia and Cappadocia; but the real strength was composed of the subjects and allies of Europe, the legions of Macedonia, and the squadrons of Bulgaria; the Uzi, a Moldavian hord, who were themselves of the Turkish race;[31] and, above all, the mercenary and adventurous bands of French and Normans. Their lances were commanded by the valiant Ursel of Baliol, the kinsman or father of the Scottish kings,[32] and were allowed to excel in the exercise of arms, or, according to the Greek style, in the practice of the Pyrrhic dance.

Defeat of the Romans, A.D. 1071, August.

On the report of this bold invasion, which threatened his hereditary dominions, Alp Arslan flew to the scene of action at

30. This city is mentioned by Constantine Porphyrogenitus (de Administrat. Imperii, l. ii. c. 44. p. 119.), and the Byzantines of the xi^th^ century, under the name of Mantzikierte, and by some is confounded with Theodosiopolis; but Delisle, in his notes and maps has very properly fixed the situation. Abulfeda (Geograph. tab. xviii. p. 310.) describes Malasgerd as a small town, built with black stone, supplied with water, without trees, &c.

31. The Uzi of the Greeks (Stritter, Memor. Byzant. tom. iii. p. 923–948.) are the Gozz of the Orientals (Hist. des Huns, tom. ii. p. 522. tom. iii. p. 133, &c.). They appear on the Danube and the Volga, in Armenia, Syria, and Chorasan, and the name seems to have been extended to the whole Turkman race.

32. Urselius (the Russelius of Zonaras) is distinguished by Jeffrey Malaterra (l. i. c. 33.) among the Norman conquerors of Sicily, and with the surname of *Baliol*: and our own historians will tell how the Baliols came from Normandy to Durham, built Bernard's-castle on the Tees, married an heiress of Scotland, &c. Ducange (Not. ad Nicephor. Bryennium, l. ii. N° 4.) has laboured the subject in honour of the president de Bailleul, whose father had exchanged the sword for the gown.

the head of forty thousand horse.[33] His rapid and skilful evolutions distressed and dismayed the superior numbers of the Greeks; and in the defeat of Basilacius, one of their principal generals, he displayed the first example of his valour and clemency. The imprudence of the emperor had separated his forces after the reduction of Malazkerd. It was in vain that he attempted to recal the mercenary Franks: they refused to obey his summons; he disdained to await their return: the desertion of the Uzi filled his mind with anxiety and suspicion; and against the most salutary advice he rushed forwards to speedy and decisive action. Had he listened to the fair proposals of the sultan, Romanus might have secured a retreat, perhaps a peace; but in these overtures he supposed the fear or weakness of the enemy, and his answer was conceived in the tone of insult and defiance. "If the Barbarian wishes for peace, let him evacuate the ground which he occupies for the encampment of the Romans, and surrender his city and palace of Rei as a pledge of his sincerity." Alp Arslan smiled at the vanity of the demand, but he wept the death of so many faithful Moslems; and, after a devout prayer, proclaimed a free permission to all who were desirous of retiring from the field. With his own hands he tied up his horse's tail, exchanged his bow and arrows for a mace and scymetar, clothed himself in a white garment, perfumed his body with musk, and declared that if he were vanquished, that spot should be the place of his burial.[34] The sultan himself had affected to cast away his missile weapons; but his hopes of victory were placed in the arrows of the Turkish cavalry, whose squadrons were loosely distributed in the form of a crescent. Instead of the successive lines and reserves of the Grecian tactics, Romanus led his army in a single and solid phalanx, and pressed with vigour and impatience the artful and yielding resistance of the Barbarians. In this desultory and fruitless combat he wasted the greater part of a summer's day, till prudence and fatigue compelled him to return to his camp. But a retreat is always perilous in the face of an active foe; and no sooner had the standard been turned to the rear than the phalanx was broken by the base cowardice, or the baser jealousy, of Andronicus, a rival prince, who

33. Elmacin (p. 343, 344.) assigns this probable number, which is reduced by Abulpharagius to 15,000 (p. 227.), and by d'Herbelot (p. 102.) to 12,000 horse. But the same Elmacin gives 300,000 men to the emperor, of whom Abulpharagius says, cum centum hominum millibus, multisque equis et magnâ pompâ instructus. The Greeks abstain from any definition of numbers.

34. The Byzantine writers do not speak so distinctly of the presence of the sultan; he committed his forces to an eunuch, had retired to a distance, &c. Is it ignorance, or jealousy, or truth?

disgraced his birth and the purple of the Cæsars.[35] The Turkish squadrons poured a cloud of arrows on this moment of confusion and lassitude; and the horns of their formidable crescent were closed in the rear of the Greeks. In the destruction of the army and pillage of the camp, it would be needless to mention the number of the slain or captives. The Byzantine writers deplore the loss of an inestimable pearl: they forget to mention, that in this fatal day the Asiatic provinces of Rome were irretrievably sacrificed.

Captivity and deliverance of the emperor.

As long as a hope survived, Romanus attempted to rally and save the relics of his army. When the centre, the Imperial station, was left naked on all sides, and encompassed by the victorious Turks, he still, with desperate courage, maintained the fight till the close of day, at the head of the brave and faithful subjects who adhered to his standard. They fell around him: his horse was slain, the emperor was wounded; yet he stood alone and intrepid, till he was oppressed and bound by the strength of multitudes. The glory of this illustrious prize was disputed by a slave and a soldier; a slave who had seen him on the throne of Constantinople, and a soldier whose extreme deformity had been excused on the promise of some signal service. Despoiled of his arms, his jewels, and his purple, Romanus spent a dreary and perilous night on the field of battle, amidst a disorderly crowd of the meaner Barbarians. In the morning the royal captive was presented to Alp Arslan, who doubted of his fortune, till the identity of the person was ascertained by the report of his ambassadors, and by the more pathetic evidence of Basilacius, who embraced with tears the feet of his unhappy sovereign. The successor of Constantine, in a plebeian habit, was led into the Turkish divan, and commanded to kiss the ground before the lord of Asia. He reluctantly obeyed; and Alp Arslan, starting from his throne, is said to have planted his foot on the neck of the Roman emperor.[36] But the fact is doubtful; and if, in this moment of insolence, the sultan complied with a national custom, the rest of his conduct has extorted the praise of his bigotted foes, and may afford a lesson to the most civilized ages. He instantly raised the royal captive from the ground; and

35. He was the son of the Cæsar John Ducas, brother of the emperor Constantine (Ducange, Fam. Byzant. p. 165.). Nicephorus Bryennius applauds his virtues and extenuates his faults (l. i. p. 30. 38. l. ii. p. 53.). Yet he owns his enmity to Romanus, *ου πανυ δε φιγιως εχων προς βασιλεα*. Scylitzes speaks more explicitly of his treason.

36. This circumstance, which we read and doubt in Scylitzes and Constantine Manasses, is more prudently omitted by Nicephorus and Zonaras.

thrice clasping his hand with tender sympathy, assured him, that his life and dignity should be inviolate in the hands of a prince who had learned to respect the majesty of his equals and the vicissitudes of fortune. From the divan, Romanus was conducted to an adjacent tent, where he was served with pomp and reverence by the officers of the sultan, who, twice each day, seated him in the place of honour at his own table. In a free and familiar conversation of eight days, not a word, not a look, of insult, escaped from the conqueror; but he severely censured the unworthy subjects who had deserted their valiant prince in the hour of danger, and gently admonished his antagonist of some errors which he had committed in the management of the war. In the preliminaries of negociation, Alp Arslan asked him what treatment he expected to receive, and the calm indifference of the emperor displays the freedom of his mind. "If you are cruel," said he, "you will take my life; if you listen to pride, you will drag me at your chariot wheels; if you consult your interest, you will accept a ransom, and restore me to my country." "And what," continued the sultan, "would have been your own behaviour, had fortune smiled on your arms?" The reply of the Greek betrays a sentiment, which prudence, and even gratitude, should have taught him to suppress. "Had I vanquished," he fiercely said, "I would have inflicted on thy body many a stripe." The Turkish conqueror smiled at the insolence of his captive; observed that the Christian law inculcated the love of enemies and forgiveness of injuries; and nobly declared, that he would not imitate an example which he condemned. After mature deliberation, Alp Arslan dictated the terms of liberty and peace, a ransom of a million, an annual tribute of three hundred and sixty thousand pieces of gold,[37] the marriage of the royal children, and the deliverance of all the Moslems who were in the power of the Greeks. Romanus, with a sigh, subscribed this treaty, so disgraceful to the majesty of the empire; he was immediately invested with a Turkish robe of honour; his nobles and patricians were restored to their sovereign; and the sultan, after a courteous embrace, dismissed him with rich presents and a military guard. No sooner did he reach the confines of the empire, than he was informed that the palace and provinces had disclaimed their allegiance to a captive: a sum of two hundred thousand pieces was painfully collected; and the fallen monarch

37. The ransom and tribute are attested by reason and the Orientals. The other Greeks are modestly silent; but Nicephorus Bryennius dares to affirm, that the terms were *ουκ αναξιας Ῥωμαιων αρχης*, and that the emperor would have preferred death to a shameful treaty.

transmitted this part of his ransom, with a sad confession of his impotence and disgrace. The generosity, or perhaps the ambition, of the sultan, prepared to espouse the cause of his ally; but his designs were prevented by the defeat, imprisonment, and death, of Romanus Diogenes.[38]

Death of Alp Arslan, A.D. 1072.

In the treaty of peace, it does not appear that Alp Arslan extorted any province or city from the captive emperor; and his revenge was satisfied with the trophies of his victory, and the spoils of Anatolia, from Antioch to the Black Sea. The fairest part of Asia was subject to his laws: twelve hundred princes, or the sons of princes, stood before his throne; and two hundred thousand soldiers marched under his banners. The sultan disdained to pursue the fugitive Greeks; but he meditated the more glorious conquest of Turkestan, the original seat of the house of Seljuk. He moved from Bagdad to the banks of the Oxus; a bridge was thrown over the river; and twenty days were consumed in the passage of his troops. But the progress of the great king was retarded by the governor of Berzem; and Joseph the Carizmian presumed to defend his fortress against the powers of the East. When he was produced a captive in the royal tent, the sultan, instead of praising his valour, severely reproached his obstinate folly; and the insolent replies of the rebel provoked a sentence, that he should be fastened to four stakes and left to expire in that painful situation. At this command the desperate Carizmian, drawing a dagger, rushed headlong towards the throne: the guards raised their battle-axes; their zeal was checked by Alp Arslan, the most skilful archer of the age; he drew his bow, but his foot slipped, the arrow glanced aside, and he received in his breast the dagger of Joseph, who was instantly cut in pieces. The wound was mortal; and the Turkish prince bequeathed a dying admonition to the pride of kings. "In my youth," said Alp Arslan, "I was advised by a sage, to humble myself before God; to distrust my own strength; and never to despise the most contemptible foe. I have neglected these lessons; and my neglect has been deservedly punished. Yesterday, as from an eminence I beheld the

38. The defeat and captivity of Romanus Diogenes may be found in John Scylitzes ad calcem Cedreni, tom. ii. p. 835–843. Zonaras, tom. ii. p. 281–284. Nicephorus Bryennius, l. i. p. 25–32. Glycas, p. 325–327. Constantine Manasses, p. 134. Elmacin, Hist. Saracen. p. 343, 344. Abulpharag. Dynast. p. 227. d'Herbelot, p. 102, 103. de Guignes, tom. iii. p. 207–211. Besides my old acquaintance Elmacin and Abulpharagius, the historian of the Huns has consulted Abulfeda, and his epitomizer Benschounah, a Chronicle of the Caliphs, by Soyouthi, Abulmahasen of Egypt, and Novairi of Africa.

numbers, the discipline, and the spirit, of my armies, the earth seemed to tremble under my feet; and I said in my heart, surely thou art the king of the world, the greatest and most invincible of warriors. These armies are no longer mine; and in the confidence of my personal strength, I now fall by the hand of an assassin."[39] Alp Arslan possessed the virtues of a Turk and a Musulman; his voice and stature commanded the reverence of mankind; his face was shaded with long whiskers; and his ample turban was fashioned in the shape of a crown. The remains of the sultan were deposited in the tomb of the Seljukian dynasty; and the passenger might read and meditate this useful inscription:[40] "O YE WHO HAVE SEEN THE GLORY OF ALP ARSLAN EXALTED TO THE HEAVENS, REPAIR TO MARU, AND YOU WILL BEHOLD IT BURIED IN THE DUST!" The annihilation of the inscription, and the tomb itself, more forcibly proclaims the instability of human greatness.

Reign and prosperity of Malek Shah, A.D. 1072–1092.

During the life of Alp Arslan, his eldest son had been acknowledged as the future sultan of the Turks. On his father's death, the inheritance was disputed by an uncle, a cousin, and a brother: they drew their scymetars, and assembled their followers; and the triple victory of Malek Shah[41] established his own reputation and the right of primogeniture. In every age, and more especially in Asia, the thirst of power has inspired the same passions and occasioned the same disorders; but, from the long series of civil war, it would not be easy to extract a sentiment more pure and magnanimous than is contained in a saying of the Turkish prince. On the eve of the battle, he performed his devotions at Thous, before the tomb of the Imam Riza. As the sultan rose from the ground, he asked his vizir Nizam, who had knelt beside him, what had been the object of his secret petition, "that your arms may be crowned with victory," was the prudent, and most probably the sincere answer of the minister. "For my part," replied

39. This interesting death is told by d'Herbelot (p. 103, 104.), and M. de Guignes (tom. iii. p. 212, 213.), from their Oriental writers; but neither of them have transfused the spirit of Elmacin (Hist. Saracen. p. 344, 345.).

40. A critic of high renown (the late Dr. Johnson), who has severely scrutinised the epitaphs of Pope, might cavil in this sublime inscription at the words "repair to Maru," since the reader must already be at Maru before he could peruse the inscription.

41. The Bibliotheque Orientale has given the text of the reign of Malek (p. 542, 543, 544. 654, 655.); and the Histoire Generale des Huns, tom. iii. p. 214–224. has added the usual measure of repetition, emendation, and supplement. Without those two learned Frenchmen, I should be blind indeed in the Eastern world.

the generous Malek, "I implored the Lord of hosts, that he would take from me my life and crown, if my brother be more worthy than myself to reign over the Moslems." The favourable judgment of heaven was ratified by the caliph; and for the first time, the sacred title of commander of the faithful was communicated to a Barbarian. But this Barbarian, by his personal merit, and the extent of his empire, was the greatest prince of his age. After the settlement of Persia and Syria, he marched at the head of innumerable armies, to atchieve the conquest of Turkestan, which had been undertaken by his father. In his passage of the Oxus, the boatmen, who had been employed in transporting some troops, complained, that their payment was assigned on the revenues of Antioch. The sultan frowned at this preposterous choice; but he smiled at the artful flattery of his vizir. "It was not to postpone their reward, that I selected those remote places, but to leave a memorial to posterity, that under your reign, Antioch and the Oxus were subject to the same sovereign." But this description of his limits was unjust and parsimonious: beyond the Oxus, he reduced to his obedience the cities of Bochara, Carizme, and Samarcand, and crushed each rebellious slave, or independent savage, who dared to resist. Malek passed the Sihon or Jaxartes, the last boundary of Persian civilization: the hords of Turkestan yielded to his supremacy; his name was inserted on the coins, and in the prayers of Cashgar, a Tartar kingdom on the extreme borders of China. From the Chinese frontier, he stretched his immediate jurisdiction or feudatory sway to the west and south, as far as the mountains of Georgia, the neighbourhood of Constantinople, the holy city of Jerusalem, and the spicy groves of Arabia Fœlix. Instead of resigning himself to the luxury of his Haram, the shepherd king, both in peace and war, was in action and in the field. By the perpetual motion of the royal camp, each province was successively blessed with his presence; and he is said to have perambulated twelve times the wide extent of his dominions, which surpassed the *Asiatic* reign of Cyrus and the caliphs. Of these expeditions, the most pious and splendid was the pilgrimage of Mecca: the freedom and safety of the caravans were protected by his arms; the citizens and pilgrims were enriched by the profusion of his alms; and the desert was cheared by the places of relief and refreshment, which he instituted for the use of his brethren. Hunting was the pleasure, and even the passion, of the sultan, and his train consisted of forty-seven thousand horses; but after the massacre of a Turkish chace, for each piece of game, he bestowed a piece of gold on the poor, a slight atonement, at the expence of the people, for the cost and mischief of the amusement of kings. In the peaceful prosperity of his reign, the cities of Asia were adorned with palaces and hospitals, with moschs and colleges; few departed from his Divan without reward, and none without justice. The language and literature of Persia revived under the house of Seljuk;[42] and if Malek emulated the liberality of a Turk less potent than himself,[43] his palace might resound with the songs of an hundred poets. The sultan bestowed a more serious and learned care on the reformation of the calendar which was effected by a general assembly of the astronomers of the East. By a law of the prophet, the Moslems are confined to the irregular course of the lunar months; in Persia, since the age of Zoroaster, the revolution of the sun has been known and celebrated as an annual festival;[44] but, after the fall of the Magian empire, the intercalation had been neglected; the fractions of minutes and hours were multiplied into days; and the date of the Spring was removed from the sign of Aries to that of Pisces. The reign of Malek was illustrated by the *Gelalæan* æra; and all errors, either past or future, were corrected by a computation of time, which surpasses the Julian, and approaches the accuracy of the Gregorian, style.[45]

His death, A.D. 1092.

In a period when Europe was plunged in the deepest Barbarism, the light and splendour of Asia may be ascribed to the docility rather than the knowledge of the Turkish conquerors. An ample share of their wisdom and virtue is due to a Persian vizir, who ruled the empire under the reigns of Alp Arslan and his son. Nizam, one of the most illustrious ministers of the East, was honoured by the caliph as an oracle of religion and science; he was trusted by the sultan as the faithful vicegerent of his power and justice. After an administration of thirty years, the fame of the vizir, his wealth, and even his services, were transformed into crimes. He was overthrown by the insidious arts of a

42. See an excellent discourse at the end of Sir William Jones's History of Nadir Shah, and the articles of the poets, Amak, Anvari, Raschidi, &c. in the Bibliotheque Orientale.

43. His name was Kheder Khan. Four bags were placed round his sopha, and as he listened to the song, he cast handfuls of gold and silver to the poets (d'Herbelot, p. 107). All this may be true; but I do not understand how he could reign in Transoxiana in the time of Malek Shah, and much less how Kheder could surpass him in power and pomp. I suspect that the beginning, not the end, of the xi[th] century, is the true æra of his reign.

44. See Chardin, Voyages en Perse, tom. ii. p. 235.

45. The Gelalæan æra (Gelaleddin, Glory of the Faith, was one of the names or titles of Malek Shah) is fixed to the 15th of March, A.H. 471, A.D. 1079. Dr. Hyde has produced the original testimonies of the Persians and Arabians (de Religione veterum Persarum, c. 16. p. 200–211.).

woman and a rival; and his fall was hastened by a rash declaration, that his cap and ink-horn, the badges of his office, were connected by the divine decree with the throne and diadem of the sultan. At the age of ninety-three years, the venerable statesman was dismissed by his master, accused by his enemies, and murdered by a fanatic: the last words of Nizam attested his innocence, and the remainder of Malek's life was short and inglorious. From Ispahan, the scene of this disgraceful transaction, the sultan moved to Bagdad with the design of transplanting the caliph, and of fixing his own residence in the capital of the Moslem world. The feeble successor of Mahomet obtained a respite of ten days; and before the expiration of the term, the Barbarian was summoned by the angel of death. His ambassadors at Constantinople had asked in marriage a Roman princess; but the proposal was decently eluded; and the daughter of Alexius, who might herself have been the victim, expresses her abhorrence of this unnatural conjunction.[46] The daughter of the sultan was bestowed on the caliph Moctadi, with the imperious condition, that, renouncing the society of his wives and concubines, he should for ever confine himself to this honourable alliance.

Division of the Seljukian empire.

The greatness and unity of the Turkish empire expired in the person of Malek Shah. His vacant throne was disputed by his brother and his four sons; and, after a series of civil wars, the treaty which reconciled the surviving candidates confirmed a lasting separation in the *Persian* dynasty, the eldest and principal branch of the house of Seljuk. The three younger dynasties were those of *Kerman*, of *Syria*, and of *Roum*: the first of these commanded an extensive, though obscure,[47] dominion on the shores of the Indian ocean:[48] the second expelled the Arabian princes of Aleppo and Damascus; and the third, our peculiar care, invaded the Roman provinces of Asia Minor. The generous policy of Malek contributed to their elevation; he allowed the princes of his blood, even those whom he had vanquished in the field, to seek new

46. She speaks of this Persian royalty as *απασης κακοδαιμονεστερον πενιας*. Anna Comnena was only nine years old at the end of the reign of Malek Shah (A.D. 1092), and when she speaks of his assassination, she confounds the sultan with the vizir (Alexias, l. vi. p. 177, 178.).

47. So obscure, that the industry of M. de Guignes could only copy (tom. i. p. 244. tom. iii. part i. p. 269, &c.) the history, or rather list, of the Seljukides of Kerman, in Bibliotheque Orientale. They were extinguished before the end of the xii[th] century.

48. Tavernier, perhaps the only traveller who has visited Kerman, describes the capital as a great ruinous village, twenty-five days journey from Ispahan, and twenty-seven from Ormus, in the midst of a fertile country (Voyages en Turquie et en Perse, p. 107. 110.).

kingdoms worthy of their ambition; nor was he displeased that they should draw away the more ardent spirits, who might have disturbed the tranquillity of his reign. As the supreme head of his family and nation, the great sultan of Persia commanded the obedience and tribute of his royal brethren: the thrones of Kerman and Nice, of Aleppo and Damascus; the Atabeks, and emirs of Syria and Mesopotamia, erected their standards under the shadow of his sceptre;[49] and the hords of Turkmans overspread the plains of the western Asia. After the death of Malek, the bands of union and subordination were relaxed and finally dissolved: the indulgence of the house of Seljuk invested their slaves with the inheritance of kingdoms; and, in the Oriental style, a crowd of princes arose from the dust of their feet.[50]

Conquest of Asia Minor by the Turks, A.D. 1074–1084.

A prince of the royal line, Cutulmish, the son of Izrail, the son of Seljuk, had fallen in a battle against Alp Arslan; and the humane victor had dropt a tear over his grave. His five sons, strong in arms, ambitious of power, and eager for revenge, unsheathed their scymetars against the son of Alp Arslan. The two armies expected the signal, when the caliph, forgetful of the majesty which secluded him from vulgar eyes, interposed his venerable mediation. "Instead of shedding the blood of your brethren, your brethren both in descent and faith, unite your forces in an holy war against the Greeks, the enemies of God and his apostle." They listened to his voice; the sultan embraced his rebellious kinsmen; and the eldest, the valiant Soliman, accepted the royal standard, which gave him the free conquest and hereditary command of the provinces of the Roman empire, from Arzeroum to Constantinople, and the unknown regions of the West.[51] Accompanied by his four brothers, he passed the Euphrates: the Turkish camp was soon seated in the neighbourhood of Kutaieh in Phrygia; and his flying cavalry laid waste the country as far as the Hellespont and the Black Sea. Since the decline of the empire, the peninsula of Asia Minor

49. It appears from Anna Comnena, that the Turks of Asia Minor obeyed the signet and chiauss of the great sultan (Alexias, l. vi. p. 170.); and that the two sons of Soliman were detained in his court (p. 180.).

50. This expression is quoted by Petit de la Croix (Vie de Gengiscan, p. 161.), from some poet, most probably a Persian.

51. On the conquest of Asia Minor, M. de Guignes has derived no assistance from the Turkish or Arabian writers, who produce a naked list of the Seljukides of Roum. The Greeks are unwilling to expose their shame, and we must extort some hints from Scylitzes (p. 860. 863.), Nicephorus Bryennius (p. 88. 91, 92, &c. 103, 104.), and Anna Comnena (Alexias, p. 91, 92, &c. 168, &c.).

had been exposed to the transient, though destructive, inroads of the Persians and Saracens; but the fruits of a lasting conquest were reserved for the Turkish sultan; and his arms were introduced by the Greeks, who aspired to reign on the ruins of their country. Since the captivity of Romanus, six years the feeble son of Eudocia had trembled under the weight of the Imperial crown, till the provinces of the East and West were lost in the same month by a double rebellion: of either chief Nicephorus was the common name; but the surnames of Bryennius and Botoniates distinguish the European and Asiatic candidates. Their reasons, or rather their promises, were weighed in the divan; and, after some hesitation, Soliman declared himself in favour of Botoniates, opened a free passage to his troops in their march from Antioch to Nice, and joined the banner of the crescent to that of the cross. After his ally had ascended the throne of Constantinople, the sultan was hospitably entertained in the suburb of Chrysopolis or Scutari; and a body of two thousand Turks was transported into Europe, to whose dexterity and courage the new emperor was indebted for the defeat and captivity of his rival Bryennius. But the conquest of Europe was dearly purchased by the sacrifice of Asia: Constantinople was deprived of the obedience and revenue of the provinces beyond the Bosphorus and Hellespont; and the regular progress of the Turks, who fortified the passes of the rivers and mountains, left not a hope of their retreat or expulsion. Another candidate implored the aid of the sultan: Melissenus, in his purple robes and red buskins, attended the motions of the Turkish camp; and the desponding cities were tempted by the summons of a Roman prince, who immediately surrendered them into the hands of the Barbarians. These acquisitions were confirmed by a treaty of peace with the emperor Alexius: his fear of Robert compelled him to seek the friendship of Soliman; and it was not till after the sultan's death that he extended as far as Nicomedia, about sixty miles from Constantinople, the eastern boundary of the Roman world. Trebizond alone, defended on either side by the sea and mountains, preserved at the extremity of the Euxine the ancient character of a Greek colony, and the future destiny of a Christian empire.

The Seljukian kingdom of Roum.

Since the first conquests of the caliphs, the establishment of the Turks in Anatolia or Asia Minor was the most deplorable loss which the church and empire had sustained. By the propagation of the Moslem faith, Soliman deserved the name of *Gazi*, a holy champion; and his new kingdom, of the Romans, or of *Roum*, was added to the tables of Oriental geography. It is described as extending from the Euphrates to Constantinople, from the Black Sea to the confines of Syria;

pregnant with mines of silver and iron, of allum and copper, fruitful in corn and wine, and productive of cattle and excellent horses.[52] The wealth of Lydia, the arts of the Greeks, the splendour of the Augustan age, existed only in books and ruins, which were equally obscure in the eyes of the Scythian conquerors. Yet, in the present decay, Anatolia still contains *some* wealthy and populous cities; and, under the Byzantine empire, they were far more flourishing in numbers, size, and opulence. By the choice of the sultan, Nice, the metropolis of Bithynia, was preferred for his palace and fortress: the seat of the Seljukian dynasty of Roum was planted one hundred miles from Constantinople; and the divinity of Christ was denied and derided in the same temple in which it had been pronounced by the first general synod of the Catholics. The unity of God, and the mission of Mahomet, were preached in the moschs; the Arabian learning was taught in the schools; the Cadhis judged according to the law of the Koran; the Turkish manners and language prevailed in the cities; and Turkman camps were scattered over the plains and mountains of Anatolia. On the hard conditions of tribute and servitude, the Greek Christians might enjoy the exercise of their religion; but their most holy churches were profaned; their priests and bishops were insulted;[53] they were compelled to suffer the triumph of the *Pagans*, and the apostacy of their brethren; many thousand children were marked by the knife of circumcision; and many thousand captives were devoted to the service or the pleasures of their masters.[54] After the loss of Asia, Antioch still maintained her primitive allegiance to Christ and Cæsar; but the solitary province was separated from all Roman aid, and surrounded on all sides by the Mahometan powers. The despair of Philaretus the governor prepared the sacrifice of his religion and loyalty, had not his

52. Such is the description of Roum by Haiton the Armenian, whose Tartar history may be found in the collections of Ramusio and Bergeron. (See Abulfeda, Geograph. climat. xvii. p. 301–305.)

53. Dicit eos quendam abusione Sodomitica intervertisse episcopum (Guibert, Abbat. Hist. Hierosol. l. i. p. 468.). It is odd enough, that we should find a parallel passage of the same people in the present age. "Il n'est point d'horreur que ces Turcs n'ayent commis, et semblables aux soldats effrenés, qui dans le sac d'une ville non contens de disposer de tout à leur gre pretendent encore aux succès les moins desirables. Quelque Sipahis ont porté leurs attentats sur la personne du vieux rabbi de la synagogue, et celle de l'Archêveque Grec." (Memoires du Baron de Tott, tom. ii. p. 193.)

54. The emperor, or abbot, describe the scenes of a Turkish camp as if they had been present. Matres correptæ in conspectû filiarum multipliciter repetitis diversorum coitibus vexabantur (is that the true reading?); cum filiæ assistentes carmina præcinere saltando cogerentur. Mox eadem passio ad filias, &c.

guilt been prevented by his son, who hastened to the Nicene palace, and offered to deliver this valuable prize into the hands of Soliman. The ambitious sultan mounted on horseback, and in twelve nights (for he reposed in the day) performed a march of six hundred miles. Antioch was oppressed by the speed and secrecy of his enterprise; and the dependent cities, as far as Laodicea and the confines of Aleppo,[55] obeyed the example of the metropolis. From Laodicea to the Thracian Bosphorus, or arm of St. George, the conquests and reign of Soliman extended thirty days journey in length, and in breadth about ten or fifteen, between the rocks of Lycia and the Black Sea.[56] The Turkish ignorance of navigation protected, for a while, the inglorious safety of the emperor; but no sooner had a fleet of two hundred ships been constructed by the hands of the captive Greeks, than Alexius trembled behind the walls of his capital. His plaintive epistles were dispersed over Europe, to excite the compassion of the Latins, and to paint the danger, the weakness, and the riches, of the city of Constantine.[57]

State and pilgrimage of Jerusalem, A.D. 638–1099.

But the most interesting conquest of the Seljukian Turks, was that of Jerusalem,[58] which soon became the theatre of nations. In their capitulation with Omar, the inhabitants had stipulated the assurance of their religion and property; but the articles were interpreted by a master against whom it was dangerous to dispute; and in the four hundred years of the reign of the caliphs, the political climate of Jerusalem was exposed to the vicissitudes of storms and sunshine.[59] By the encrease of proselytes and population, the Mahometans might excuse their usurpation of three-fourths of the city: but a peculiar

55. See Antioch, and the death of Soliman, in Anna Comnena (Alexias, l. vi. p. 168, 169.), with the notes of Ducange.

56. William of Tyre (l. i. c. 9, 10. p. 635.) gives the most authentic and deplorable account of these Turkish conquests.

57. In his epistle to the count of Flanders, Alexius seems to fall too low beneath his character and dignity: yet it is approved by Ducange (Not. ad Alexiad, p. 335, &c.), and paraphrased by the abbot Guibert, a contemporary historian. The Greek text no longer exists; and each translator and scribe might say with Guibert (p. 475.), verbis vestita meis, a privilege of most indefinite latitude.

58. Our best fund for the history of Jerusalem from Heraclius to the crusades, is contained in two large and original passages of William Archbishop of Tyre (l. i. c. 1–10. l. xviii. c. 5, 6.), the principal author of the Gesta Dei per Francos. M. de Guignes has composed a very learned Memoire sur le Commerce des François dans le Levant avant les Croisades, &c. (Mem. de l'Academie des Inscriptions, tom. xxxvii. p. 467–500.)

59. Secundum Dominorum dispositionem plerumque lucida plerumque nubila recepit intervalla, et ægrotantium more temporum præsentium gravabatur aut respirabat qualitate (l. i. c. 3. p. 630.). The latinity of William of Tyre is by no means contemptible: but in his account of

quarter was reserved for the patriarch with his clergy and people; a tribute of two pieces of gold was the price of protection; and the sepulchre of Christ, with the church of the Resurrection, was still left in the hands of his votaries. Of these votaries, the most numerous and respectable portion were strangers to Jerusalem: the pilgrimages to the Holy Land had been stimulated, rather than suppressed, by the conquest of the Arabs; and the enthusiasm which had always prompted these perilous journies, was nourished by the congenial passions of grief and indignation. A crowd of pilgrims from the East and West continued to visit the holy sepulchre, and the adjacent sanctuaries, more especially at the festival of Easter: and the Greeks and Latins, the Nestorians and Jacobites, the Copts and Abyssinians, the Armenians and Georgians, maintained the chapels, the clergy, and the poor of their respective communions. The harmony of prayer in so many various tongues, the worship of so many nations in the common temple of their religion, might have afforded a spectacle of edification and peace; but the zeal of the Christian sects was embittered by hatred and revenge; and in the kingdom of a suffering Messiah, who had pardoned his enemies, they aspired to command and persecute their spiritual brethren. The pre-eminence was asserted by the spirit and numbers of the Franks; and the greatness of Charlemagne[60] protected both the Latin pilgrims, and the Catholics of the East. The poverty of Carthage, Alexandria, and Jerusalem, were relieved by the alms of that pious emperor; and many monasteries of Palestine were founded or restored by his liberal devotion. Harun Alrashid, the greatest of the Abassides, esteemed in his Christian brother a similar supremacy of genius and power: their friendship was cemented by a frequent intercourse of gifts and embassies; and the caliph, without resigning the substantial dominion, presented the emperor with the keys, of the holy sepulchre, and perhaps of the city of Jerusalem. In the decline of the Carlovingian monarchy, the republic of Amalphi promoted the interest of trade and religion in the East. Her vessels transported the Latin pilgrims to the coasts of Egypt and Palestine, and deserved, by their useful imports, the favour and alliance of the Fatimite caliphs:[61] an annual fair was instituted

---

490 years, from the loss to the recovery of Jerusalem, he exceeds the true account by thirty years.

60. For the transactions of Charlemagne with the Holy Land, see Eginhard (de Vita Caroli Magni, c. 16. p. 79–82.), Constantine Porphyrogenitus (de Administratione Imperii, l. ii. c. 26. p. 80.), and Pagi (Critica, tom. iii. A.D. 800, N° 13, 14, 15.).

61. The caliph granted his privileges, Amalphitanis viris amicis et utilium

on mount Calvary; and the Italian merchants founded the convent and hospital of St. John of Jerusalem, the cradle of the monastic and military order, which has since reigned in the isles of Rhodes and of Malta. Had the Christian pilgrims been content to revere the tomb of a prophet, the disciples of Mahomet, instead of blaming, would have imitated, their piety: but these rigid *Unitarians* were scandalised by a worship which represents the birth, death, and resurrection, of a God; the Catholic images were branded with the name of idols; and the Moslems smiled with indignation[62] at the miraculous flame, which was kindled on the eve of Easter in the holy sepulchre.[63] This pious fraud, first devised in the ninth century,[64] was devoutly cherished by the Latin crusaders, and is annually repeated by the clergy of the Greek, Armenian, and Coptic sects,[65] who impose on the credulous spectators[66] for their own benefit, and that of their tyrants. In every age, a principle of toleration has been fortified by a sense of interest; and the revenue of the prince and his emir was encreased each year, by the expence and tribute of so many thousand strangers.

Under the Fatimite caliphs, A.D. 969–1076.

The revolution which transferred the sceptre from the Abassides to the Fatimites was a benefit, rather than an injury, to the Holy Land. A sovereign resident in Egypt, was more sensible of the importance of Christian trade; and the emirs of Palestine were less remote from the justice and power of the throne. But the third

---

introductoribus (Gesta Dei, p. 934.). The trade of Venice to Egypt and Palestine cannot produce so old a title, unless we adopt the laughable translation of a Frenchman who mistook the two factions of the circus (Veneti et Prasini) for the Venetians and Parisians.

62. An Arabic chronicle of Jerusalem (apud Asseman. Bibliot. Orient. tom. i. p. 628. tom. iv. p. 368.) attests the unbelief of the caliph and the historian; yet Cantacuzene presumes to appeal to the Mahometans themselves for the truth of this perpetual miracle.

63. In his Dissertations on Ecclesiastical History, the learned Mosheim has separately discussed this pretended miracle (tom. ii. p. 214–306.), de lumine sancti sepulchri.

64. William of Malmsbury (l. iv. c. 2. p. 209.) quotes the Itinerary of the monk Bernard, an eye-witness, who visited Jerusalem A.D. 870. The miracle is confirmed by another pilgrim some years older; and Mosheim ascribes the invention to the Franks, soon after the decease of Charlemagne.

65. Our travellers, Sandys (p. 134), Thevenot (p. 621–627), Maundrell (p. 94, 95.), &c. describe this extravagant farce. The Catholics are puzzled to decide, *when* the miracle ended, and the trick began.

66. The Orientals themselves confess the fraud, and plead necessity and edification (Memoires du Chevalier d'Arvieux, tom. ii. p. 140. Joseph. Abudacni, Hist. Copt. c. 20.): but I will not attempt, with Mosheim, to explain the mode. Our travellers have failed with the blood of St. Januarius at Naples.

of these Fatimite caliphs was the famous Hakem,[67] a frantic youth, who was delivered by his impiety and despotism from the fear either of God or man; and whose reign was a wild mixture of vice and folly. Regardless of the most ancient customs of Egypt, he imposed on the women an absolute confinement: the restraint excited the clamours of both sexes; their clamours provoked his fury; a part of Old Cairo was delivered to the flames; and the guards and citizens were engaged many days in a bloody conflict. At first the caliph declared himself a zealous Musulman, the founder or benefactor of moschs and colleges: twelve hundred and ninety copies of the Koran were transcribed at his expence in letters of gold; and his edict extirpated the vineyards of the upper Egypt. But his vanity was soon flattered by the hope of introducing a new religion; he aspired above the fame of a prophet, and styled himself the visible image of the most high God, who, after nine apparitions on earth, was at length manifest in his royal person. At the name of Hakem, the lord of the living and the dead, every knee was bent in religious adoration: his mysteries were performed on a mountain near Cairo: sixteen thousand converts had signed his profession of faith; and at the present hour, a free and warlike people, the Druses of mount Libanus, are persuaded of the life and divinity of a madman and tyrant.[68] In his divine character, Hakem hated the Jews and Christians, as the servants of his rivals: while some remains of prejudice or prudence still pleaded in favour of the law of Mahomet. Both in Egypt and Palestine, his cruel and wanton persecution made some martyrs and many apostates: the common rights, and special privileges of the sectaries were equally disregarded; and a general interdict was laid on the devotion of strangers and natives. The temple of the Christian world, the church of the resurrection, was demolished to its foundations; the luminous prodigy of Easter was interrupted, and much profane labour was exhausted to destroy the cave in the rock which properly constitutes the holy sepulchre. At the

Sacrilege of Hakem, A.D. 1009.

67. See d'Herbelot (Bibliot. Orientale, p. 411.), Renaudot (Hist. Patriarch Alex. p. 390. 397. 400, 401.), Elmacin (Hist. Saracen. p. 321–323.), and Marei (p. 384–386.), an historian of Egypt, translated by Reiske from Arabic into German, and verbally interpreted to me by a friend.

68. The religion of the Druses is concealed by their ignorance and hypocrisy. Their secret doctrines are confined to the elect who profess a contemplative life; and the vulgar Druses, the most indifferent of men, occasionally conform to the worship of the Mahometans and Christians of their neighbourhood. The little that is, or deserves to be, known, may be seen in the industrious Niebuhr (Voyages, tom. ii. p. 354–357.), and the second volume of the recent and instructive Travels of M. de Volney.

report of this sacrilege, the nations of Europe were astonished and afflicted: but instead of arming in the defence of the Holy Land, they contented themselves with burning, or banishing, the Jews, as the secret advisers of the impious Barbarian.[69] Yet the calamities of Jerusalem were in some measure alleviated by the inconstancy or repentance of Hakem himself; and the royal mandate was sealed for the restitution of the churches, when the tyrant was assassinated by the emissaries of his sister. The succeeding caliphs resumed the maxims of religion and policy; a free toleration was again granted; with the pious aid of the emperor of Constantinople, the holy sepulchre arose from its ruins; and, after a short abstinence, the pilgrims returned with an encrease of appetite to the spiritual feast.[70] In the sea-voyage of Palestine, the dangers were frequent, and the opportunities rare: but the conversion of Hungary opened a safe communication between Germany and Greece. The charity of St. Stephen, the apostle of his kingdom, relieved and conducted his itinerant brethren;[71] and from Belgrade to Antioch, they traversed fifteen hundred miles of a Christian empire. Among the Franks, the zeal of pilgrimage prevailed beyond the example of former times: and the roads were covered with multitudes of either sex, and of every rank, who professed their contempt of life, so soon as they should have kissed the tomb of their Redeemer. Princes and prelates abandoned the care of their dominions; and the numbers of these pious caravans were a prelude to the armies which marched in the ensuing age under the banner of the cross. About thirty years before the first crusade, the archbishop of Mentz, with the bishops of Utrecht, Bamberg, and Ratisbon, undertook this laborious journey from the Rhine to the Jordan; and the multitude of their followers amounted to seven thousand persons. At Constantinople, they were hospitably entertained by the emperor, but the ostentation of their wealth provoked the assault of the wild Arabs; they drew their swords with scrupulous reluctance, and sustained a siege in the village of Capernaum, till they were rescued by

Encrease of pilgrimages, A.D. 1024, &c.

69. See Glaber, l. iii. c. 7. and the Annals of Baronius and Pagi, A.D. 1009.

70. Per idem tempus ex universo orbe tam innumerabilis multitudo cœpit confluere ad sepulchrum salvatoris Hierosolymis, quantum nullus hominum prius sperare poterat. Ordo inferioris plebis . . . mediocres . . . reges et comites . . . præsules . . . mulieres multæ nobiles cum pauperioribus . . . Pluribus enim erat mentis desiderium mori priusquam ad propria reverterentur (Glaber. l. iv. c. 6. Bouquet, Historians of France, tom. x. p. 50.).

71. Glaber. l. iii. c. 1. Katona (Hist. Critic. Regum Hungariæ, tom. i. p. 304–311.), examines whether St. Stephen founded a monastery at Jerusalem.

the venal protection of the Fatimite emir. After visiting the holy places, they embarked for Italy, but only a remnant of two thousand arrived in safety in their native land. Ingulphus, a secretary of William the conqueror, was a companion of this pilgrimage: he observes that they sallied from Normandy, thirty stout and well-appointed horsemen; but that they repassed the Alps, twenty miserable palmers, with the staff in their hand, and the wallet at their back.[72]

Conquest of Jerusalem by the Turks, A.D. 1076–1096.

After the defeat of the Romans, the tranquillity of the Fatimite caliphs was invaded by the Turks.[73] One of the lieutenants of Malek Shah, Atsiz the Carizmian, marched into Syria at the head of a powerful army, and reduced Damascus by famine and the sword. Hems, and the other cities of the province, acknowledged the caliph of Bagdad and the sultan of Persia; and the victorious emir advanced without resistance to the banks of the Nile: the Fatimite was preparing to fly into the heart of Africa; but the negroes of his guard and the inhabitants of Cairo made a desperate sally, and repulsed the Turk from the confines of Egypt. In his retreat, he indulged the licence of slaughter and rapine: the judge and notaries of Jerusalem were invited to his camp; and their execution was followed by the massacre of three thousand citizens. The cruelty or the defeat of Atsiz was soon punished by the sultan Toucush, the brother of Malek Shah, who, with a higher title and more formidable powers, asserted the dominion of Syria and Palestine. The house of Seljuk reigned about twenty years in Jerusalem;[74] but the hereditary command of the holy city and territory was entrusted or abandoned to the emir Ortok, the chief of a tribe of Turkmans, whose children, after their expulsion from Palestine, formed two dynasties on the borders of Armenia and Assyria.[75]

72. Baronius (A.D. 1064, N° 43–56.) has transcribed the greater part of the original narratives of Ingulphus, Marianus, and Lambertus.

73. See Elmacin (Hist. Saracen. p. 349, 350.), and Abulpharagius (Dynast. p. 237. vers. Pocock.), M. de Guignes (Hist. des Huns, tom. iii. part i. p. 215, 216.) adds the testimonies, or rather the names, of Abulfeda and Novairi.

74. From the expedition of Isar Atsiz (A.D. 469, A.D. 1076), to the expulsion of the Ortokides (A.D. 1096). Yet William of Tyre (l. i. c. 6. p. 633.) asserts, that Jerusalem was thirty-eight years in the hands of the Turks; and an Arabic chronicle, quoted by Pagi (tom. iv. p. 202.), supposes, that the city was reduced by a Carizmian general to the obedience of the caliph of Bagdad, A.H. 463, A.D. 1070. These early dates are not very compatible with the general history of Asia; and I am sure, that as late as A.D. 1064, the regnum Babylonicum (of Cairo) still prevailed in Palestine (Baronius, A.D. 1064, N° 56.).

75. De Guignes, Hist. des Huns, tom. i. p. 249–252.

The Oriental Christians and the Latin pilgrims deplored a revolution, which, instead of the regular government and old alliance of the caliphs, imposed on their necks the iron yoke of the strangers of the North.[76] In his court and camp the great sultan had adopted in some degree the arts and manners of Persia; but the body of the Turkish nation, and more especially the pastoral tribes, still breathed the fierceness of the desert. From Nice to Jerusalem, the western countries of Asia were a scene of foreign and domestic hostility; and the shepherds of Palestine, who held a precarious sway on a doubtful frontier, had neither leisure nor capacity to await the slow profits of commercial and religious freedom. The pilgrims who, through innumerable perils, had reached the gates of Jerusalem were the victims of private rapine or public oppression, and often sunk under the pressure of famine and disease, before they were permitted to salute the holy sepulchre. A spirit of native barbarism, or recent zeal, prompted the Turkmans to insult the clergy of every sect: the patriarch was dragged by the hair along the pavement, and cast into a dungeon, to extort a ransom from the sympathy of his flock; and the divine worship in the church of the resurrection was often disturbed by the savage rudeness of its masters. The pathetic tale excited the millions of the West to march under the standard of the cross to the relief of the holy land: and yet how trifling is the sum of these accumulated evils, if compared with the single act of the sacrilege of Hakem, which had been so patiently endured by the Latin Christians! A slighter provocation inflamed the more irascible temper of their descendants: a new spirit had arisen of religious chivalry and papal dominion: a nerve was touched of exquisite feeling; and the sensation vibrated to the heart of Europe.

76. Willerm. Tyr. l. i. c. 8. p. 634. who strives hard to magnify the Christian grievances. The Turks exacted an *aureus* from each pilgrim! The *caphar* of the Franks is now fourteen dollars: and Europe does not complain of this voluntary tax.

END OF THE FIFTH VOLUME.

THE

HISTORY

OF THE

DECLINE AND FALL

OF THE

ROMAN EMPIRE.

By EDWARD GIBBON, Esq;

VOLUME THE SIXTH.

LONDON:

PRINTED FOR A. STRAHAN; AND T. CADELL, IN THE STRAND.

MDCCLXXXVIII.

CHAPTER LVIII

Origin and Numbers of the First Crusade. – Characters of the Latin Princes. – Their March to Constantinople. – Policy of the Greek Emperor Alexius. – Conquest of Nice, Antioch, and Jerusalem, by the Franks. – Deliverance of the Holy Sepulchre. – Godfrey of Bouillon, First King of Jerusalem. – Institutions of the French or Latin Kingdom.

The first crusade, A.D. 1095–1099. Peter the Hermit.

About twenty years after the conquest of Jerusalem by the Turks, the holy sepulchre was visited by an hermit of the name of Peter, a native of Amiens, in the province of Picardy[1] in France. His resentment and sympathy were excited by his own injuries and the oppression of the Christian name; he mingled his tears with those of the patriarch, and earnestly enquired, if no hopes of relief could be entertained from the Greek emperors of the East. The patriarch exposed the vices and weakness of the successors of Constantine. "I will rouse," exclaimed the hermit, "the martial nations of Europe in your cause;" and Europe was obedient to the call of the hermit. The astonished patriarch dismissed him with epistles of credit and complaint, and no sooner did he land at Bari, than Peter hastened to kiss the feet of the Roman pontiff. His stature was small, his appearance contemptible; but his eye was keen and lively; and he possessed that vehemence of speech, which seldom fails to impart the persuasion of the soul.[2] He was born of a gentleman's family (for we must now adopt a modern idiom), and his military service was under the neighbouring counts of Boulogne, the heroes of the first crusade. But he soon relinquished the sword and the world; and if it be true, that his wife, however noble, was aged and ugly,

1. Whimsical enough is the origin of the name of *Picards*, and from thence of *Picardie*, which does not date earlier than A.D. 1200. It was an academical joke, an epithet first applied to the quarrelsome humour of those students, in the university of Paris, who came from the frontier of France and Flanders (Valesii Notitia Galliarum, p. 447. Longuerue, Description de la France, p. 54.).

2. William of Tyre (l. i. c. 11. p. 637, 638.) thus describes the hermit: pusillus, persona contemptibilis, vivacis ingenii, et occulum habens perspicacem gratumque, et sponte fluens ei non deerat eloquium. See Albert Aquensis, p. 185. Guibert, p. 482. Anna Comnena in Alexiad, l. x. p. 284, &c. with Ducange's notes, p. 349.

he might withdraw, with the less reluctance, from her bed to a convent, and at length to an hermitage. In this austere solitude, his body was emaciated, his fancy was inflamed; whatever he wished, he believed; whatever he believed, he *saw* in dreams and revelations. From Jerusalem, the pilgrim returned an accomplished fanatic; but as he excelled in the popular madness of the times, pope Urban the second received him as a prophet, applauded his glorious design, promised to support it in a general council, and encouraged him to proclaim the deliverance of the Holy Land. Invigorated by the approbation of the pontiff, his zealous missionary traversed, with speed and success, the provinces of Italy and France. His diet was abstemious, his prayers long and fervent, and the alms which he received with one hand, he distributed with the other: his head was bare, his feet naked, his meagre body was wrapt in a coarse garment; he bore and displayed a weighty crucifix; and the ass on which he rode, was sanctified in the public eye by the service of the man of God. He preached to innumerable crowds in the churches, the streets, and the highways: the hermit entered with equal confidence the palace and the cottage; and the people, for all was people, was impetuously moved by his call to repentance and arms. When he painted the sufferings of the natives and pilgrims of Palestine, every heart was melted to compassion; every breast glowed with indignation, when he challenged the warriors of the age to defend their brethren and rescue their Saviour: his ignorance of art and language was compensated by sighs, and tears, and ejaculations; and Peter supplied the deficiency of reason by loud and frequent appeals to Christ and his Mother, to the saints and angels of paradise, with whom he had personally conversed. The most perfect orator of Athens might have envied the success of his eloquence: the rustic enthusiast inspired the passions which he felt, and Christendom expected with impatience the counsels and decrees of the supreme pontiff.

Urban II. in the council of Placentia, A.D. 1095, March.

The magnanimous spirit of Gregory the seventh had already embraced the design of arming Europe against Asia; the ardour of his zeal and ambition still breathes in his epistles: from either side of the Alps, fifty thousand Catholics had enlisted under the banner of St. Peter;[3] and his successor reveals *his* intention of marching at their head against the impious sectaries of Mahomet. But the glory or reproach of executing, though not in person, this holy

3. Ultra quinquaginta millia, si me possunt in expeditione pro duce et pontifice habere, armatâ manû volunt in inimicos Dei insurgere et ad sepulchrum Domini ipso ducente pervenire (Gregor. vii. epist. ii. 31. in tom. xii. p. 322. concil.).

enterprise, was reserved for Urban the second,[4] the most faithful of his disciples. He undertook the conquest of the East, whilst the larger portion of Rome was possessed and fortified by his rival Guibert of Ravenna, who contended with Urban for the name and honours of the pontificate. He attempted to unite the powers of the West, at a time when the princes were separated from the church, and the people from their princes, by the excommunication which himself and his predecessors had thundered against the emperor and the king of France. Philip the first, of France, supported with patience the censures which he had provoked by his scandalous life and adulterous marriage. Henry the fourth, of Germany, asserted the right of investitures, the prerogative of confirming his bishops by the delivery of the ring and crosier. But the emperor's party was crushed in Italy by the arms of the Normans and the countess Mathilda; and the long quarrel had been recently envenomed by the revolt of his son Conrad and the shame of his wife,[5] who, in the synods of Constance and Placentia, confessed the manifold prostitutions to which she had been exposed by an husband regardless of her honour and his own.[6] So popular was the cause of Urban, so weighty was his influence, that the council which he summoned at Placentia[7] was composed of two hundred bishops of Italy, France, Burgundy, Swabia, and Bavaria. Four thousand of the clergy, and thirty thousand of the laity, attended this important meeting; and, as the most spacious cathedral would have been inadequate to the multitude, the session of seven days was held in a plain adjacent to the city. The ambassadors of the Greek emperor, Alexius Comnenus, were introduced to plead the distress of their sovereign and the danger of

4. See the original lives of Urban II. by Pandulphus Pisanus and Bernardus Guido, in Muratori, Rer. Ital. Script. tom. iii. pars i. p. 352, 353.

5. She is known by the different names of Praxes, Eupræcia, Eufrasia, and Adelais; and was the daughter of a Russian prince, and the widow of a margrave of Brandenburgh. Struv. Corpus Hist. Germanicæ, p. 340.

6. Henricus odio eam cœpit habere: ideo incarceravit eam, et concessit ut plerique vim ei inferrent; immo filium hortans ut eam subagitaret (Dodechin, Continuat. Marian. Scot. apud Baron. A.D. 1093, N° 4.). In the synod of Constance, she is described by Bertholdus, rerum inspector: quæ se tantas et tam inauditas fornicationum spurcitias, et a tantis passam fuisse conquesta est, &c. and again at Placentia: satis misericorditer suscepit, eo quòd ipsam tantas spurcitias non tam commisisse quam invitam pertulisse pro certo cognoverit papa cum sanctâ synodo. Apud Baron. A.D. 1093, N° 4. 1094, N° 3. A rare subject for the infallible decision of a pope and council. These abominations are repugnant to every principle of human nature, which is not altered by a dispute about rings and crosiers. Yet it should seem, that the wretched woman was tempted by the priests to relate or subscribe some infamous stories of herself and her husband.

7. See the narrative and acts of the synod of Placentia, Concil. tom. xii. p. 821, &c.

Constantinople, which was divided only by a narrow sea from the victorious Turks, the common enemies of the Christian name. In their suppliant address they flattered the pride of the Latin princes; and, appealing at once to their policy and religion, exhorted them to repel the Barbarians on the confines of Asia, rather than to expect them in the heart of Europe. At the sad tale of the misery and perils of their Eastern brethren the assembly burst into tears: the most eager champions declared their readiness to march; and the Greek ambassadors were dismissed with the assurance of a speedy and powerful succour. The relief of Constantinople was included in the larger and most distant project of the deliverance of Jerusalem; but the prudent Urban adjourned the final decision to a second synod, which he proposed to celebrate in some city of France in the autumn of the same year. The short delay would propagate the flame of enthusiasm; and his firmest hope was in a nation of soldiers,[8] still proud of the pre-eminence of their name, and ambitious to emulate their hero Charlemagne,[9] who, in the popular romance of Turpin,[10] had atchieved the conquest of the Holy Land. A latent motive of affection or vanity might influence the choice of Urban: he was himself a native of France, a monk of Clugny, and the first of his countrymen who ascended the throne of St. Peter. The pope had illustrated his family and province; nor is there perhaps a more exquisite gratification than to revisit, in a conspicuous dignity, the humble and laborious scenes of our youth.

Council of Clermont, A.D. 1095, November.

It may occasion some surprise that the Roman pontiff should erect, in the heart of France, the tribunal from whence he hurled his anathemas against the king. But our surprise will vanish so soon as we form a just estimate of a king of France of the eleventh

8. Guibert himself, a Frenchman, praises the piety and valour of the French nation, the author and example of the crusades: Gens nobilis, prudens, bellicosa, dapsilis et nitida ... Quos enim Britones, *Anglos*, Ligures, si bonis eos moribus videamus, non illico *Francos homines* appellemus? (p. 478.) He owns, however, that the vivacity of the French degenerates into petulance among foreigners (p. 483.), and vain loquaciousness (p. 502.).

9. Per viam quam jamdudum Carolus Magnus mirificus rex Francorum aptari fecit usque C. P. (Gesta Francorum, p. 1. Robert. Monach. Hist. Hieros. l. i. p. 33, &c.).

10. John Tilpinus, or Turpinus, was archbishop of Rheims, A.D. 773. After the year 1000 this romance was composed in his name, by a monk of the borders of France and Spain: and such was the idea of ecclesiastical merit, that he describes himself as a fighting and drinking priest! Yet the book of lies was pronounced authentic by pope Calixtus II. (A.D. 1122), and is respectfully quoted by the abbot Suger, in the great Chronicles of St. Denys (Fabric. Bibliot. Latin. medii Ævi, edit. Mansi, tom. iv. p. 161.).

century.[11] Philip the first was the great-grandson of Hugh Capet the founder of the present race, who, in the decline of Charlemagne's posterity, added the regal title to his patrimonial estates of Paris and Orleans. In this narrow compass, he was possessed of wealth and jurisdiction; but in the rest of France, Hugh and his first descendants were no more than the feudal lords of about sixty dukes and counts, of independent and hereditary power,[12] who disdained the control of laws and legal assemblies, and whose disregard of their sovereign was revenged by the disobedience of their inferior vassals. At Clermont, in the territories of the count of Auvergne,[13] the pope might brave with impunity the resentment of Philip; and the council which he convened in that city was not less numerous or respectable than the synod of Placentia.[14] Besides his court and council of Roman cardinals, he was supported by thirteen archbishops and two hundred and twenty-five bishops; the number of mitred prelates was computed at four hundred; and the fathers of the church were blessed by the saints, and enlightened by the doctors of the age. From the adjacent kingdoms, a martial train of lords and knights of power and renown, attended the council,[15] in high expectation of its resolves; and such was the ardour of zeal and curiosity, that the city was filled, and many thousands, in the month of November, erected their tents or huts in the open field. A session of eight days produced some useful or edifying canons for the reformation of manners; a severe censure was pronounced against the licence of private war; the truce of God[16] was confirmed, a suspension of hostilities during four days of the week; women and priests were placed under the safeguard of the church; and a

11. See Etat de la France, by the Count de Boulainvilliers, tom. i. p. 180–182. and the second volume of the Observations sur l'Histoire de France, by the Abbé de Mably.

12. In the provinces to the south of the Loire, the first *Capetians* were scarcely allowed a feudal supremacy. On all sides, Normandy, Bretagne, Aquitain, Burgundy, Lorraine, and Flanders, contracted the name and limits of the *proper* France. See Hadrian Vales. Notitia Galliarum.

13. These counts, a younger branch of the dukes of Aquitain, were at length despoiled of the greatest part of their country by Philip Augustus. The bishops of Clermont gradually became princes of the city. Melanges, tirés d'une grande Bibliotheque, tom. xxxvi. p. 288, &c.

14. See the acts of the council of Clermont, Concil. tom. xii. p. 829, &c.

15. Confluxerunt ad concilium e multis regionibus, viri potentes et honorati, innumeri quamvis cingulo laicalis militiæ superbi (Baldric, an eye witness, p. 86–88. Robert. Mon. p. 31, 32. Will. Tyr. i. 14, 15. p. 639–641. Guibert, p. 478–480. Fulcher. Carnot. p. 382.).

16. The Truce of God (Treva, or Treuga Dei) was first invented in Aquitain, A.D. 1032; blamed by some bishops as an occasion of perjury, and rejected by the Normans as contrary to their privileges (Ducange, Gloss. Latin. tom. vi. p. 682–685.).

protection of three years was extended to husbandmen and merchants, the defenceless victims of military rapine. But a law, however venerable be the sanction, cannot suddenly transform the temper of the times; and the benevolent efforts of Urban deserve the less praise, since he laboured to appease some domestic quarrels that he might spread the flames of war from the Atlantic to the Euphrates. From the synod of Placentia, the rumour of his great design had gone forth among the nations: the clergy on their return had preached in every diocese the merit and glory of the deliverance of the Holy Land; and when the pope ascended a lofty scaffold in the market-place of Clermont, his eloquence was addressed to a well prepared and impatient audience. His topics were obvious, his exhortation was vehement, his success inevitable. The orator was interrupted by the shout of thousands, who with one voice, and in their rustic idiom, exclaimed aloud, "God wills it, God wills it."[17] "It is indeed the will of God," replied the pope; "and let this memorable word, the inspiration surely of the Holy Spirit, be for ever adopted as your cry of battle, to animate the devotion and courage of the champions of Christ. His cross is the symbol of your salvation; wear it, a red, a bloody cross, as an external mark on your breasts or shoulders, as a pledge of your sacred and irrevocable engagement." The proposal was joyfully accepted; great numbers both of the clergy and laity impressed on their garments the sign of the cross,[18] and solicited the pope to march at their head. This dangerous honour was declined by the more prudent successor of Gregory, who alleged the schism of the church, and the duties of his pastoral office, recommending to the faithful, who were disqualified by sex or profession, by age or infirmity, to aid, with their prayers and alms, the personal service of their robust brethren. The name and powers of his legate he devolved on Adhemar bishop of Puy, the first who had received the cross at his hands. The foremost of the temporal chiefs was

17. *Deus vult, Deus vult!* was the pure acclamation of the clergy who understood Latin (Robert. Mon. l. i. p. 32.). By the illiterate laity, who spoke the *Provincial* or *Limousin* idiom, it was corrupted to *Deus lo volt*, or *Diex el volt.* See Chron. Casinense, l. iv. c. 11. p. 497. in Muratori, Script. Rerum Ital. tom. iv. and Ducange (Dissertat. xi. p. 207. sur Joinville, and Gloss. Latin. tom. ii. p. 690.), who, in his preface, produces a very difficult specimen of the dialect of Rovergue, A.D. 1100, very near, both in time and place, to the council of Clermont (p. 15, 16.).

18. Most commonly on their shoulders, in gold, or silk, or cloth, sewed on their garments. In the first crusade, all were red: in the third, the French alone preserved that colour, while green crosses were adopted by the Flemings, and white by the English (Ducange, tom ii. p. 651.). Yet in England, the red ever appears the favourite, and, as it were, the national, colour of our military ensigns and uniforms.

Raymond count of Thoulouse, whose ambassadors in the council excused the absence, and pledged the honour, of their master. After the confession and absolution of their sins, the champions of the cross were dismissed with a superfluous admonition to invite their countrymen and friends; and their departure for the Holy Land was fixed to the festival of the Assumption, the fifteenth of August, of the ensuing year.[19]

Justice of the crusades?

So familiar, and as it were so natural to man, is the practice of violence, that our indulgence allows the slightest provocation, the most disputable right, as a sufficient ground of national hostility. But the name and nature of an *holy war* demands a more rigorous scrutiny; nor can we hastily believe, that the servants of the Prince of peace would unsheathe the sword of destruction, unless the motive were pure, the quarrel legitimate, and the necessity inevitable. The policy of an action may be determined from the tardy lessons of experience; but, before we act, our conscience should be satisfied of the justice and propriety of our enterprise. In the age of the crusades, the Christians, both of the East and West, were persuaded of their lawfulness and merit; their arguments are clouded by the perpetual abuse of scripture and rhetoric; but they seem to insist on the right of natural and religious defence, their peculiar title to the Holy Land, and the impiety of their Pagan and Mahometan foes.[20] I. The right of a just defence may fairly include our civil and spiritual allies: it depends on the existence of danger; and that danger must be estimated by the two-fold consideration of the malice, and the

19. Bongarsius, who has published the original writers of the crusades, adopts, with much complacency, the fanatic title of Guibertus, Gesta Dei per Francos; though some critics propose to read Gesta *Diaboli* per Francos (Hanoviæ, 1611, two vols. in folio). I shall briefly enumerate, as they stand in this collection, the authors whom I have used for the first crusade. I. Gesta Francorum. II. Robertus Monachus. III. Baldricus. IV. Raimundus de Agiles. V. Albertus Aquensis. VI. Fulcherius Carnotensis. VII. Guibertus. VIII. Willielmus Tyriensis. Muratori has given us, IX. Radulphus Cadomensis de Gestis Tancredi (Script. Rer. Ital. tom. v. p. 285–333.), and, X. Bernardus Thesaurarius de Acquisitione Terræ Sanctæ (tom. vii. p. 664–848.). The last of these was unknown to a late French historian, who has given a large and critical list of the writers of the crusades (Esprit des Croisades, tom. i. p. 13–141.), and most of whose judgments my own experience will allow me to ratify. It was late before I could obtain a sight of the French historians collected by Duchesne. I. Petri Tudebodi Sacerdotis Sivracensis Historia de Hierosolymitano Itinere (tom. iv. p. 773–815.), has been transfused into the first anonymous writer of Bongarsius. II. The Metrical History of the first Crusade, in vii books (p. 890–912.), is of small value or account.

20. If the reader will turn to the first scene of the first part of Henry the Fourth, he will see in the text of Shakspeare the natural feelings of enthusiasm; and in the notes of Dr. Johnson, the workings of a bigotted though vigorous mind, greedy of every pretence to hate and persecute those who dissent from his creed.

power, of our enemies. A pernicious tenet has been imputed to the Mahometans, the duty of *extirpating* all other religions by the sword. This charge of ignorance and bigotry is refuted by the Koran, by the history of the Musulman conquerors, and by their public and legal toleration of the Christian worship. But it cannot be denied, that the Oriental churches are depressed under their iron yoke; that, in peace and war, they assert a divine and indefeasible claim of universal empire; and that, in their orthodox creed, the unbelieving nations are continually threatened with the loss of religion or liberty. In the eleventh century, the victorious arms of the Turks presented a real and urgent apprehension of these losses. They had subdued in less than thirty years the kingdoms of Asia, as far as Jerusalem and the Hellespont; and the Greek empire tottered on the verge of destruction. Besides an honest sympathy for their brethren, the Latins had a right and interest in the support of Constantinople, the most important barrier of the West; and the privilege of defence must reach to prevent, as well as to repel, an impending assault. But this salutary purpose might have been accomplished by a moderate succour; and our calmer reason must disclaim the innumerable hosts and remote operations, which overwhelmed Asia and depopulated Europe. II. Palestine could add nothing to the strength or safety of the Latins; and fanaticism alone could pretend to justify the conquest of that distant and narrow province. The Christians affirmed that their inalienable title to the promised land had been sealed by the blood of their divine Saviour: it was their right and duty to rescue their inheritance from the unjust possessors, who profaned his sepulchre, and oppressed the pilgrimage of his disciples. Vainly would it be alleged that the pre-eminence of Jerusalem, and the sanctity of Palestine, have been abolished with the Mosaic law; that the God of the Christians is not a local deity, and that the recovery of Bethlem or Calvary, his cradle or his tomb, will not atone for the violation of the moral precepts of the gospel. Such arguments glance aside from the leaden shield of superstition; and the religious mind will not easily relinquish its hold on the sacred ground of mystery and miracle. III. But the holy wars which have been waged in every climate of the globe, from Egypt to Livonia, and from Peru to Hindostan, require the support of some more general and flexible tenet. It has been often supposed, and sometimes affirmed, that a difference of religion is a worthy cause of hostility; that obstinate unbelievers may be slain or subdued by the champions of the cross; and that grace is the sole fountain of dominion as well as of mercy. Above four hundred years before the first crusade, the eastern and western provinces of the Roman empire had been acquired about the same time, and in the same manner, by the Barbarians of Germany and Arabia. Time and treaties had legitimated the conquests of the *Christian* Franks; but in the eyes of their subjects and neighbours, the Mahometan princes were still tyrants and usurpers, who, by the arms of war or rebellion, might be lawfully driven from their unlawful possession.[21]

Spiritual motives and indulgences.

As the manners of the Christians were relaxed, their discipline of penance[22] was enforced; and with the multiplication of sins, the remedies were multiplied. In the primitive church, a voluntary and open concession prepared the work of atonement. In the middle ages, the bishops and priests interrogated the criminal; compelled him to account for his thoughts, words, and actions; and prescribed the terms of his reconciliation with God. But as this discretionary power might alternately be abused by indulgence and tyranny, a rule of discipline was framed, to inform and regulate the spiritual judges. This mode of legislation was invented by the Greeks; their *penitentials*[23] were translated, or imitated, in the Latin church; and, in the time of Charlemagne, the clergy of every diocese were provided with a code, which they prudently concealed from the knowledge of the vulgar. In this dangerous estimate of crimes and punishments, each case was supposed, each difference was remarked, by the experience or penetration of the monks; some sins are enumerated which innocence could not have suspected, and others which reason cannot believe; and the more ordinary offences of fornication and adultery, of perjury and sacrilege, of rapine and murder, were expiated by a penance, which, according to the various circumstances, was prolonged from forty days to seven years. During this term of mortification, the patient was healed, the criminal was absolved, by a salutary regimen of fasts and prayers: the disorder of his dress was expressive of grief and remorse; and he humbly abstained from all the business and pleasure of social life. But the rigid execution of these laws would have depopulated the palace, the camp, and the city: the Barbarians of the West believed and

21. The vi[th] Discourse of Fleury on Ecclesiastical History (p. 223–261.) contains an accurate and rational view of the causes and effects of the crusades.

22. The penance, indulgences, &c. of the middle ages are amply discussed by Muratori (Antiquitat. Italiæ medii Ævi, tom. v. dissert. lxviii. p. 709–768.), and by M. Chais (Lettres sur les Jubiles et les Indulgences, tom. ii. lettres 21 & 22. p. 478–556.), with this difference, that the abuses of superstition are mildly, perhaps faintly, exposed by the learned Italian, and peevishly magnified by the Dutch minister.

23. Schmidt (Histoire des Allemands, tom. ii. p. 211–220. 452–462.) gives an abstract of the Penitential of Rhegino in the ninth, and of Burchard in the tenth, century. In one year, five-and-thirty murders were perpetrated at Worms.

trembled; but nature often rebelled against principle; and the magistrate laboured without effect to enforce the jurisdiction of the priest. A literal accomplishment of penance was indeed impracticable; the guilt of adultery was multiplied by daily repetition; that of homicide might involve the massacre of a whole people; each act was separately numbered; and, in those times of anarchy and vice, a modest sinner might easily incur a debt of three hundred years. His insolvency was relieved by a commutation, or *indulgence*: a year of penance was appreciated at twenty-six *solidi*[24] of silver, about four pounds sterling, for the rich; at three solidi, or nine shillings, for the indigent: and these alms were soon appropriated to the use of the church, which derived, from the redemption of sins, an inexhaustible source of opulence and dominion. A debt of three hundred years, or twelve hundred pounds, was enough to impoverish a plentiful fortune; the scarcity of gold and silver was supplied by the alienation of land; and the princely donations of Pepin and Charlemagne are expressly given for the *remedy* of their soul. It is a maxim of the civil law, that whosoever cannot pay with his purse, must pay with his body; and the practice of flagellation was adopted by the monks, a cheap, though painful, equivalent. By a fantastic arithmetic, a year of penance was taxed at three thousand lashes;[25] and such was the skill and patience of a famous hermit, St. Dominic of the Iron Cuirass,[26] that in six days he could discharge an entire century, by a whipping of three hundred thousand stripes. His example was followed by many penitents of both sexes; and, as a vicarious sacrifice was accepted, a sturdy disciplinarian might expiate on his own back the sins of his benefactors.[27] These compensations of the purse and the person introduced, in the eleventh century, a more honourable mode of satisfaction. The merit of military service against the Saracens of Africa and Spain, had been allowed by the predecessors

24. Till the xii[th] century, we may support the clear account of xii *denarii*, or pence, to the *solidus*, or shilling; and xx *solidi* to the pound weight of silver, about the pound sterling. Our money is diminished to a third, and the French to a fiftieth, of this primitive standard.

25. Each century of lashes was sanctified with the recital of a psalm; and the whole Psalter, with the accompaniment of 15,000 stripes, was equivalent to five years.

26. The Life and Atchievements of St. Dominic Loricatus, was composed by his friend and admirer, Peter Damianus. See Fleury, Hist. Eccles. tom. xiii. p. 96–104. Baronius, A.D. 1056, N° 7. who observes from Damianus, how fashionable, even among ladies of quality (sublimis generis), this expiation (purgatorii genus) was grown.

27. At a quarter, or even half a rial a lash, Sancho Panza was a cheaper, and possibly not a more dishonest, workman. I remember in Pére Labat (Voyages en Italie, tom. vii. p. 16–29.) a very lively picture of the *dexterity* of one of these artists.

of Urban the second. In the council of Clermont, that pope proclaimed a *plenary indulgence* to those who should enlist under the banner of the cross; the absolution of *all* their sins, and a full receipt for *all* that might be due of canonical penance.[28] The cold philosophy of modern times is incapable of feeling the impression that was made on a sinful and fanatic world. At the voice of their pastor, the robber, the incendiary, the homicide, arose by thousands to redeem their souls, by repeating on the infidels the same deeds which they had exercised against their Christian brethren; and the terms of atonement were eagerly embraced by offenders of every rank and denomination. None were pure; none were exempt from the guilt and penalty of sin; and those who were the least amenable to the justice of God and the church, were the best entitled to the temporal and eternal recompence of their pious courage. If they fell, the spirit of the Latin clergy did not hesitate to adorn their tomb with the crown of martyrdom;[29] and should they survive, they could expect without impatience the delay and encrease of their heavenly reward. They offered their blood to the Son of God, who had laid down his life for their salvation: they took up the cross, and entered with confidence into the way of the Lord. His providence would watch over their safety; perhaps his visible and miraculous power would smooth the difficulties of their holy enterprise. The cloud and pillar of Jehovah had marched before the Israelites into the promised land. Might not the Christians more reasonably hope that the rivers would open for their passage; that the walls of the strongest cities would fall at the sound of their trumpets; and that the sun would be arrested in his mid-career, to allow them time for the destruction of the infidels?

Temporal and carnal motives.

Of the chiefs and soldiers who marched to the holy sepulchre, I will dare to affirm, that *all* were prompted by the spirit of enthusiasm; the belief of merit, the hope of reward, and the assurance of divine aid. But I am equally persuaded, that in *many* it was not the sole, that in *some* it was not the leading, principle of action. The use and abuse of religion are feeble to stem, they are strong and irresistible to impel, the stream of national manners. Against the private wars of the

28. Quicunque pro solâ devotione, non pro honoris vel pecuniæ adeptione, ad liberandam ecclesiam Dei Jerusalem profectus fuerit, iter illud pro omni pœnitentia reputetur. Canon. Concil. Claromont. ii. p. 829. Guibert styles it novum salutis genus (p. 471.), and is almost philosophical on the subject.

29. Such at least was the belief of the crusaders, and such is the uniform style of the historians (Esprit des Croisades, tom. iii. p. 477.); but the prayers for the repose of their souls, is inconsistent in orthodox theology with the merits of martyrdom.

Barbarians, their bloody tournaments, licentious loves, and judicial duels, the popes and synods might ineffectually thunder. It is a more easy task to provoke the metaphysical disputes of the Greeks, to drive into the cloister the victims of anarchy or despotism, to sanctify the patience of slaves and cowards, or to assume the merit of the humanity and benevolence of modern Christians. War and exercise were the reigning passions of the Franks or Latins; they were enjoined, as a penance, to gratify those passions, to visit distant lands, and to draw their swords against the nations of the East. Their victory, or even their attempt, would immortalise the names of the intrepid heroes of the cross; and the purest piety could not be insensible to the most splendid prospect of military glory. In the petty quarrels of Europe, they shed the blood of their friends and countrymen, for the acquisition perhaps of a castle or a village. They could march with alacrity against the distant and hostile nations who were devoted to their arms: their fancy already grasped the golden sceptres of Asia; and the conquest of Apulia and Sicily by the Normans might exalt to royalty the hopes of the most private adventurer. Christendom, in her rudest state, must have yielded to the climate and cultivation of the Mahometan countries; and their natural and artificial wealth had been magnified by the tales of pilgrims, and the gifts of an imperfect commerce. The vulgar, both the great and small, were taught to believe every wonder, of lands flowing with milk and honey, of mines and treasures, of gold and diamonds, of palaces of marble and jasper, and of odoriferous groves of cinnamon and frankincense. In this earthly paradise, each warrior depended on his sword to carve a plenteous and honourable establishment, which he measured only by the extent of his wishes.[30] Their vassals and soldiers trusted their fortunes to God and their master: the spoils of a Turkish emir might enrich the meanest follower of the camp; and the flavour of the wines, the beauty of the Grecian women,[31] were temptations more adapted to the nature, than to the profession, of the champions of the cross. The love of freedom was a powerful incitement to the multitudes who were oppressed by feudal or

30. The same hopes were displayed in the letters of the adventurers ad animandos qui in Francia residerant. Hugh de Reiteste could boast, that his share amounted to one abbey and ten castles, of the yearly value of 1500 marks, and that he should acquire an hundred castles by the conquest of Aleppo (Guibert, p. 554, 555.).

31. In his genuine or fictitious letter to the count of Flanders, Alexius mingles with the danger of the church, and the relics of saints, the auri et argenti amor, and pulcherrimarum fœminarum voluptas (p. 476.); as if, says the indignant Guibert, the Greek women were handsomer than those of France.

ecclesiastical tyranny. Under this holy sign the peasants and burghers, who were attached to the servitude of the glebe, might escape from an haughty lord, and transplant themselves and their families to a land of liberty. The monk might release himself from the discipline of his convent: the debtor might suspend the accumulation of usury, and the pursuit of his creditors; and outlaws and malefactors of every cast might continue to brave the laws and elude the punishment of their crimes.[32]

Influence of example.

These motives were potent and numerous: when we have singly computed their weight on the mind of each individual, we must add the infinite series, the multiplying powers of example and fashion. The first proselytes became the warmest and most effectual missionaries of the cross: among their friends and countrymen they preached the duty, the merit, and the recompence, of their holy vow; and the most reluctant hearers were insensibly drawn within the whirlpool of persuasion and authority. The martial youths were fired by the reproach or suspicion of cowardice; the opportunity of visiting with an army the sepulchre of Christ, was embraced by the old and infirm, by women and children, who consulted rather their zeal than their strength; and those who in the evening had derided the folly of their companions, were the most eager, the ensuing day, to tread in their footsteps. The ignorance, which magnified the hopes, diminished the perils, of the enterprise. Since the Turkish conquest, the paths of pilgrimage were obliterated; the chiefs themselves had an imperfect notion of the length of the way and the state of their enemies; and such was the stupidity of the people, that, at the sight of the first city or castle beyond the limits of their knowledge, they were ready to ask whether that was not the Jerusalem, the term and object of their labours. Yet the more prudent of the crusaders, who were not sure that they should be fed from heaven with a shower of quails, or manna, provided themselves with those precious metals, which, in every country, are the representatives of every commodity. To defray, according to their rank, the expences of the road, princes alienated their provinces, nobles their lands and castles, peasants their cattle and the instruments of husbandry. The value of property was depreciated by the eager competition of multitudes; while the price of arms and horses was raised to an exorbitant height by the wants and impatience of the buyers.[33] Those who remained at home, with sense and money, were enriched by the

32. See the privileges of the *Crucesignati*, freedom from debt, usury, injury, secular justice, &c. The pope was their perpetual guardian (Ducange, tom. ii. p. 651, 652.).

33. Guibert (p. 481.) paints in lively colours this general emotion. He was one of the few contemporaries who had genius enough to feel the astonishing scenes that

epidemical disease: the sovereigns acquired at a cheap rate the domains of their vassals; and the ecclesiastical purchasers completed the payment by the assurance of their prayers. The cross, which was commonly sewed on the garment, in cloth or silk, was inscribed by some zealots on their skin: an hot iron, or indelible liquor, was applied to perpetuate the mark; and a crafty monk, who shewed the miraculous impression on his breast, was repaid with the popular veneration and the richest benefices of Palestine.[34]

Departure of the first crusaders, A.D. 1096, March, May, &c.

The fifteenth of August had been fixed in the council of Clermont for the departure of the pilgrims: but the day was anticipated by the thoughtless and needy crowd of plebeians; and I shall briefly dispatch the calamities which they inflicted and suffered, before I enter on the more serious and successful enterprise of the chiefs. Early in the spring, from the confines of France and Lorraine, above sixty thousand of the populace of both sexes flocked round the first missionary of the crusade, and pressed him with clamorous importunity to lead them to the holy sepulchre. The hermit, assuming the character, without the talents or authority, of a general, impelled or obeyed the forward impulse of his votaries along the banks of the Rhine and Danube. Their wants and numbers soon compelled them to separate, and his lieutenant, Walter the Pennyless, a valiant though needy soldier, conducted a vanguard of pilgrims, whose condition may be determined from the proportion of eight horsemen to fifteen thousand foot. The example and footsteps of Peter were closely pursued by another fanatic, the monk Godescal, whose sermons had swept away fifteen or twenty thousand peasants from the villages of Germany. Their rear was again pressed by an herd of two hundred thousand, the most stupid and savage refuse of the people, who mingled with their devotion a brutal licence of rapine, prostitution, and drunkenness. Some counts and gentlemen, at the head of three thousand horse, attended the motions of the multitude to partake in the spoil; but their genuine leaders (may we credit such folly?) were a goose and a goat, who were carried in the front, and to whom these worthy Christians ascribed an infusion of the divine spirit.[35] Of these, and of other bands of enthusiasts, the first and most easy warfare

---

were passing before their eyes. Erat itaque videre miraculum caro omnes emere, atque vili vendere, &c.

34. Some instances of these *stigmata* are given in the Esprit des Croisades (tom. iii. p. 169, &c.), from authors whom I have not seen.

35. Fuit et aliud scelus detestabile in hac congregatione pedestris populi stulti et vesanæ levitatis, *anserem* quendam divino spiritû asserebant afflatum, et *capellam* non minus eodem repletam, et has sibi duces

was against the Jews, the murderers of the Son of God. In the trading cities of the Moselle and the Rhine, their colonies were numerous and rich; and they enjoyed, under the protection of the emperor and the bishops, the free exercise of their religion.[36] At Verdun, Treves, Mentz, Spires, Worms, many thousands of that unhappy people were pillaged and massacred:[37] nor had they felt a more bloody stroke since the persecution of Hadrian. A remnant was saved by the firmness of their bishops, who accepted a feigned and transient conversion; but the more obstinate Jews opposed their fanaticism to the fanaticism of the Christians, barricadoed their houses, and precipitating themselves, their families, and their wealth, into the rivers or the flames, disappointed the malice, or at least the avarice, of their implacable foes.

Their destruction in Hungary and Asia, A.D. 1096.

Between the frontiers of Austria and the seat of the Byzantine monarchy, the crusaders were compelled to traverse an interval of six hundred miles; the wild and desolate countries of Hungary[38] and Bulgaria. The soil is fruitful, and intersected with rivers; but it was then covered with morasses and forests, which spread to a boundless extent, whenever man has ceased to exercise his dominion over the earth. Both nations had imbibed the rudiments of Christianity; the Hungarians were ruled by their native princes; the Bulgarians by a lieutenant of the Greek emperor; but, on the slightest provocation, their ferocious nature was rekindled, and ample provocation was afforded by the disorders of the first pilgrims. Agriculture must have been unskilful and languid among a people, whose cities were built of reeds and timber, which were deserted in the summer season for the tents of hunters and shepherds. A scanty supply of provisions was rudely demanded, forcibly seized, and greedily consumed; and on the first

---

secundæ viæ fecerant, &c. (Albert. Aquensis, l. i. c. 31. p. 196.) Had these peasants founded an empire, they might have introduced, as in Egypt, the worship of animals, which their philosophic descendants would have glossed over with some specious and subtle allegory.

36. Benjamin of Tudela describes the state of his Jewish brethren from Cologne along the Rhine: they were rich, generous, learned, hospitable, and lived in the eager hope of the Messiah (Voyage, tom. i. p. 243–245. par Baratier). In seventy years (he wrote about A.D. 1170) they had recovered from these massacres.

37. These massacres and depredations on the Jews, which were renewed at each crusade, are *coolly* related. It is true, that St. Bernard (epist. 363. tom. i. p. 329.) admonishes the Oriental Franks, non sunt persequendi Judæi, non sunt trucidandi. The contrary doctrine had been preached by a *rival* monk.

38. See the contemporary description of Hungary in Otho of Frisingen, l. ii. c. 31. in Muratori, Script. Rerum Italicarum, tom. vi. p. 665, 666.

quarrel, the crusaders gave a loose to indignation and revenge. But their ignorance of the country, of war, and of discipline, exposed them to every snare. The Greek præfect of Bulgaria commanded a regular force; at the trumpet of the Hungarian king, the eighth or the tenth of his martial subjects bent their bows and mounted on horseback; their policy was insidious, and their retaliation on these pious robbers was unrelenting and bloody.[39] About a third of the naked fugitives, and the hermit Peter was of the number, escaped to the Thracian mountains; and the emperor, who respected the pilgrimage and succour of the Latins, conducted them by secure and easy journies to Constantinople, and advised them to await the arrival of their brethren. For a while they remembered their faults and losses; but no sooner were they revived by the hospitable entertainment, than their venom was again inflamed; they stung their benefactor, and neither gardens, nor palaces, nor churches, were safe from their depredations. For his own safety, Alexius allured them to pass over to the Asiatic side of the Bosphorus; but their blind impetuosity soon urged them to desert the station which he had assigned, and to rush headlong against the Turks, who occupied the road of Jerusalem. The hermit, conscious of his shame, had withdrawn from the camp to Constantinople; and his lieutenant, Walter the Pennyless, who was worthy of a better command, attempted without success to introduce some order and prudence among the herd of savages. They separated in quest of prey, and themselves fell an easy prey to the arts of the sultan. By a rumour that their foremost companions were rioting in the spoils of his capital, Soliman tempted the main body to descend into the plain of Nice; they were overwhelmed by the Turkish arrows; and a pyramid of bones[40] informed their companions of the place of their defeat. Of the first crusaders, three hundred thousand had already perished, before a single city was rescued from the infidels, before their graver and more noble brethren had completed the preparations of their enterprise.[41]

39. The old Hungarians, without excepting Turotzius, are ill informed of the first crusade, which they involve in a single passage. Katona, like ourselves, can only quote the writers of France; but he compares with local science the ancient and modern geography. *Ante portam Cyperon*, is Sopron or Poson; *Mallevilla*, Zemlin; *Fluvius Maroe*, Savus; *Lintax*, Leith; *Mesebroch*, or *Merseburg*, Ouar, or Moson; *Tollenburg*, Pragg (de Regibus Hungariæ, tom. iii. p. 19–53.).

40. Anna Comnena (Alexias, l. x. p. 287.) describes this *οστων κολωνος* as a mountain *ὑψηλον και βαθος και πλατος αξιολογωτατον*. In the siege of Nice, such were used by the Franks themselves as the materials of a wall.

41. To save time and space, I shall represent, in a short table [see p. 573], the particular references to the great events of the first crusade.

	The Crowd.	The Chiefs.	The Road to Constantinople.	Alexius.	Nice and Asia Minor.	Edessa.	Antioch.	The Battle.	The Holy Lance.	Conquest of Jerusalem.
I. Gesta Francorum	p. 1, 2.	p. 2.	p. 2, 3.	p. 4, 5.	p. 5–7.	–	p. 9–15.	p. 15–22.	p. 18–20.	p. 26–29.
II. Robertus Monachus	p. 33, 34.	p. 35, 36.	p. 36, 37.	p. 37, 38.	p. 39–45.	–	p. 45–55.	p. 56–66.	p. 61, 62.	p. 74–81.
III. Baldricus	p. 89.	–	p. 91–93.	p. 91–94.	p. 94–101.	–	p. 101, 111.	p. 111–122.	p. 116–119.	p. 130–138.
IV. Raimundus des Agiles	–	–	p. 139, 140.	p. 140, 141.	p. 142.	–	p. 142–149.	p. 149–155.	p. 150. 152. 156.	p. 173–183.
V. Albertus Aquensis	l. i. c. 7–31.	–	l. ii. c. 1–8.	l. ii. c. 9–19	l. ii. c. 20–43. l. iii. c. 1–4.	l. iii. c. 5–32. l. iv. 9. 12. l. v. 15–22.	l. iii. c. 33–66. iv. 1–26.	l. iv. c. 7–56.	l. iv. c. 43.	l. v. c. 45, 46. l. vi. c. 1–50.
VI. Fulcherius Carnotensis	p. 384.	–	p. 385, 386.	p. 386.	p. 387–389.	p. 389, 390.	p. 390–392.	p. 392–395.	p. 392.	p. 396–400.
VII. Guibertus	p. 482. 485.	–	p. 485. 489.	p. 485–490.	p. 491–493. 498.	p. 496, 497.	p. 498. 506. 512.	p. 512–523.	p. 520. 530. 533.	p. 523–537.
VIII. Willermus Tyriensis	l. i. c. 18–30.	l. i. c. 17.	l. ii. c. 1–4. 13. 17. 22.	l. ii. c. 5–23.	l. iii. c. 1–12. l. iv. c. 13–25.	l. iv. c. 1–6.	l. iv. 9–24. l. v. 1–23.	l. vi. c.1–23.	l. vi. c. 14.	l. vii. c. 1–25. l. viii. c. 1–24.
IX. Radulphus Cadomensis	–	c. 1–3. 15.	c. 4–7. 17.	c. 8–13. 18, 19.	c. 14–16. 21–47.	–	c. 48–71.	c. 72–91.	c. 100–109.	c.111–138.
X. Bernardus Thesaurarius	c. 7–11.	–	c. 11–20.	c. 11–20.	c. 21–25.	c. 26.	c. 27–38.	c. 39–52.	c. 45.	c. 54–77.

The chiefs of the first crusade.

None of the great sovereigns of Europe embarked their persons in the first crusade. The emperor Henry the fourth was not disposed to obey the summons of the pope: Philip the first of France was occupied by his pleasures; William Rufus of England by a recent conquest; the kings of Spain were engaged in a domestic war against the Moors; and the northern monarchs of Scotland, Denmark,[42] Sweden, and Poland, were yet strangers to the passions and interests of the South. The religious ardour was more strongly felt by the princes of the second order, who held an important place in the feudal system. Their situation will naturally cast under four distinct heads the review of their names and characters; but I may escape some needless repetition, by observing at once, that courage and the exercise of arms are the common attribute of these Christian adventurers. I. The first rank both in war and council is justly due to Godfrey of Bouillon; and happy would it have been for the crusaders, if they had trusted themselves to the sole conduct of that accomplished hero, a worthy representative of Charlemagne, from whom he was descended in the female line. His father was of the noble race of the counts of Boulogne: Brabant, the lower province of Lorraine,[43] was the inheritance of his mother; and by the emperor's bounty, he was himself invested with that ducal title, which has been improperly transferred to his lordship of Bouillon in the Ardennes.[44] In the service of Henry the fourth, he bore the great standard of the empire, and pierced with his lance the breast of Rodolph, the rebel king: Godfrey was the first who ascended the walls of Rome; and his sickness, his vow, perhaps his remorse for bearing arms against the pope, confirmed an early resolution of visiting the holy sepulchre, not as a pilgrim, but a deliverer. His valour was matured by prudence and moderation; his piety, though blind, was sincere; and, in the tumult of a camp, he practised the real and fictitious virtues of a convent. Superior to the private factions of the chiefs, he reserved his enmity for the enemies of Christ; and though he gained a kingdom by

I. Godfrey of Bouillon.

42. The author of the Esprit des Croisades has doubted, and might have disbelieved, the crusade and tragic death of prince Sueno, with 1500 or 15,000 Danes, who was cut off by sultan Soliman in Cappadocia, but who still lives in the poem of Tasso (tom. iv. p. 111–115.).

43. The fragments of the kingdoms of Lotharingia, or Lorraine, were broken into the two duchies, of the Moselle, and of the Meuse; the first has preserved its name, which in the latter has been changed into that of Brabant (Vales. Notit. Gall. p. 283–288.).

44. See, in the Description of France, by the Abbe de Longuerue, the articles of *Boulogne*, part i. p. 54. *Brabant*, part ii. p. 47, 48. *Bouillon*, p. 134. On his departure, Godfrey sold or pawned Bouillon to the church for 1300 marks.

the attempt, his pure and disinterested zeal was acknowledged by his rivals. Godfrey of Bouillon[45] was accompanied by his two brothers, by Eustace the elder, who had succeeded to the county of Boulogne, and by the younger, Baldwin, a character of more ambiguous virtue. The duke of Lorraine was alike celebrated on either side of the Rhine: from his birth and education he was equally conversant with the French and Teutonic languages: the barons of France, Germany, and Lorraine, assembled their vassals; and the confederate force that marched under his banner was composed of fourscore thousand foot and about ten thousand horse. II. In the parliament that was held at Paris, in the king's presence, about two months after the council of Clermont, Hugh count of Vermandois was the most conspicuous of the princes who assumed the cross. But the appellation of *the great* was applied, not so much to his merit or possessions (though neither were contemptible), as to the royal birth of the brother of the king of France.[46] Robert duke of Normandy was the eldest son of William the Conqueror; but on his father's death he was deprived of the kingdom of England, by his own indolence and the activity of his brother Rufus. The worth of Robert was degraded by an excessive levity and easiness of temper: his cheerfulness seduced him to the indulgence of pleasure; his profuse liberality impoverished the prince and people; his indiscriminate clemency multiplied the number of offenders; and the amiable qualities of a private man became the essential defects of a sovereign. For the trifling sum of ten thousand marks he mortgaged Normandy during his absence to the English usurper;[47] but his engagement and behaviour in the holy war, announced in Robert a reformation of manners, and restored him in some degree to the public esteem. Another Robert was count of Flanders, a royal province, which, in this century, gave three queens to the thrones of France, England, and Denmark: he was surnamed the sword and lance of the Christians; but in the exploits of a soldier, he sometimes forgot the duties of a general.

II. Hugh of Vermandois, Robert of Normandy, Robert of Flanders, Stephen of Chartres, &c.

45. See the family character of Godfrey, in William of Tyre, l. ix. c. 5–8.; his previous design on Guibert (p. 485.), his sickness and vow, in Bernard. Thesaur. (c. 78.).

46. Anna Comnena supposes, that Hugh was proud of his nobility, riches, and power (l. x. p. 288.): the two last articles appear more equivocal; but an ευγενεια, which seven hundred years ago was famous in the palace of Constantinople, attests the ancient dignity of the Capetian family of France.

47. Will. Gemeticensis, l. vii. c. 7. p. 672, 673. in Camden. Normanicis. He pawned the duchy for one hundredth part of the present yearly revenue. Ten thousand marks may be equal to five hundred thousand livres, and Normandy annually yields fifty-seven millions to the king (Necker, Administration des Finances, tom. i. p. 287.).

Stephen, count of Chartres, of Blois, and of Troyes, was one of the richest princes of the age; and the number of his castles has been compared to the three hundred and sixty-five days of the year. His mind was improved by literature; and in the council of the chiefs, the eloquent Stephen[48] was chosen to discharge the office of their president. These four were the principal leaders of the French, the Normans, and the pilgrims of the British isles: but the list of the barons who were possessed of three or four towns, would exceed, says a contemporary, the catalogue of the Trojan war.[49] III. In the south of France, the command was assumed by Adhemar, bishop of Puy, the pope's legate, and by Raymond, count of St. Giles and Tholouse, who added the prouder titles of duke of Narbonne and marquis of Provence. The former was a respectable prelate, alike qualified for this world and the next. The latter was a veteran warrior, who had fought against the Saracens of Spain, and who consecrated his declining age, not only to the deliverance, but to the perpetual service, of the holy sepulchre. His experience and riches gave him a strong ascendant in the Christian camp, whose distress he was often able, and sometimes willing, to relieve. But it was easier for him to extort the praise of the Infidels, than to preserve the love of his subjects and associates. His eminent qualities were clouded by a temper, haughty, envious, and obstinate; and, though he resigned an ample patrimony, for the cause of God, his piety, in the public opinion, was not exempt from avarice and ambition.[50] A mercantile, rather than a martial spirit, prevailed among his *provincials,*[51] a common name, which included the natives of Auvergne and Languedoc[52], the vassals of the kingdom of Burgundy or Arles. From the adjacent frontier of Spain, he drew a band of hardy

III. Raymond of Tholouse.

48. His original letter to his wife, is inserted in the Spicilegium of Dom. Luc. d'Acheri, tom. iv. and quoted in the Esprit des Croisades, tom. i. p. 63.

49. Unius enim, duûm, trium seu quatuor oppidorum dominos quis numeret? quorum tanta fuit copia, ut non vix totidem Trojana obsidio coegisse putetur (Ever the lively and interesting Guibert, p. 486.).

50. It is singular enough, that Raymond of St. Giles, a second character in the genuine history of the crusades, should shine as the first of heroes in the writings of the Greeks (Anna Comnen. Alexiad, l. x, xi.) and the Arabians (Longueruana, p. 129.).

51. Omnes de Burgundiâ, et Alverniâ, et Vasconiâ, et Gothi (of *Languedoc*), provinciales appellabantur, cæteri vero Francigenæ et hoc in exercitu; inter hostes autem Franci dicebantur. Raymond des Agiles, p. 144.

52. The town of his birth, or first appanage, was consecrated to St. Ægidius, whose name as early as the first crusade, was corrupted by the French into St. Gilles, or St Giles. It is situate in the Lower Languedoc, between Nismes and the Rhône, and still boasts a collegiate church of the foundation of Raymond (Melanges tirés d'une grande Bibliotheque, tom. xxxvii. p. 51.).

adventurers; as he marched through Lombardy, a crowd of Italians flocked to his standard, and his united force consisted of one hundred thousand horse and foot. If Raymond was the first to enlist and the last to depart, the delay may be excused by the greatness of his preparation and the promise of an everlasting farewell. IV. The name of Bohemond, the son of Robert Guiscard, was already famous by his double victory over the Greek emperor: but his father's will had reduced him to the principality of Tarentum, and the remembrance of his Eastern trophies, till he was awakened by the rumour and passage of the French pilgrims. It is in the person of this Norman chief that we may seek for the coolest policy and ambition with a small allay of religious fanaticism. His conduct may justify a belief that he had secretly directed the design of the pope, which he affected to second with astonishment and zeal: at the siege of Amalphi, his example and discourse inflamed the passions of a confederate army; he instantly tore his garment to supply crosses for the numerous candidates, and prepared to visit Constantinople and Asia at the head of ten thousand horse and twenty thousand foot. Several princes of the Norman race accompanied this veteran general; and his cousin Tancred[53] was the partner, rather than the servant, of the war. In the accomplished character of Tancred, we discover all the virtues of a perfect knight,[54] the true spirit of chivalry, which inspired the generous sentiments and social offices of man, far better than the base philosophy, or the baser religion, of the times.

IV. Bohemond and Tancred.

Between the age of Charlemagne and that of the crusades, a revolution had taken place among the Spaniards, the Normans, and the French, which was gradually extended to the rest of Europe. The service of the infantry was degraded to the plebeians; the cavalry formed the

Chivalry.

53. The mother of Tancred was Emma, sister of the great Robert Guiscard; his father, the marquis Odo the Good. It is singular enough, that the family and country of so illustrious a person should be unknown; but Muratori reasonably conjectures that he was an Italian, and perhaps of the race of the marquisses of Montferrat in Piedmont (Script. tom. v. p. 281, 282.).

54. To gratify the childish vanity of the house of Este, Tasso has inserted in his poem, and in the first crusade, a fabulous hero, the brave and amorous Rinaldo (x. 75. xvii. 66–94.). He might borrow his name from a Rinaldo, with the Aquila bianca Estense, who vanquished, as the standard-bearer of the Roman church, the emperor Frederic I. (Storia Imperiale di Ricobaldo, in Muratori Script. Ital. tom. ix. p. 360. Ariosto, Orlando Furioso, iii. 30.). But, 1. The distance of sixty years between the youth of the two Rinaldos, destroys their identity. 2. The Storia Imperiale is a forgery of the conte Boyardo, at the end of the xv[th] century (Muratori, p. 281–289.). 3. This Rinaldo, and his exploits, are not less chimerical than the hero of Tasso (Muratori, Antichità Estense, tom. i. p. 350.).

strength of the armies, and the honourable name of *miles*, or soldier, was confined to the gentlemen[55] who served on horseback, and were invested with the character of knighthood. The dukes and counts, who had usurped the rights of sovereignty, divided the provinces among their faithful barons: the barons distributed among their vassals the fiefs or benefices of their jurisdiction; and these military tenants, the peers of each other and of their lord, composed the noble or equestrian order, which disdained to conceive the peasant or burgher as of the same species with themselves. The dignity of their birth was preserved by pure and equal alliances; their sons alone, who could produce four quarters or lines of ancestry, without spot or reproach, might legally pretend to the honour of knighthood; but a valiant plebeian was sometimes enriched and ennobled by the sword, and became the father of a new race. A single knight could impart, according to his judgment, the character which he received; and the warlike sovereigns of Europe derived more glory from this personal distinction, than from the lustre of their diadem. This ceremony, of which some traces may be found in Tacitus and the woods of Germany,[56] was in its origin simple and profane; the candidate, after some previous trial, was invested with his sword and spurs; and his cheek or shoulder were touched with a slight blow, as an emblem of the last affront, which it was lawful for him to endure. But superstition mingled in every public and private action of life; in the holy wars, it sanctified the profession of arms; and the order of chivalry was assimilated in its rights and privileges to the sacred orders of priesthood. The bath and white garment of the novice, were an indecent copy of the regeneration of baptism: his sword, which he offered on the altar, was blessed by the ministers of religion; his solemn reception was preceded by fasts and vigils; and he was created a knight in the name of God, of St. George, and of St. Michael the archangel. He swore to accomplish the duties of his profession; and education, example, and the public opinion, were the inviolable guardians of his oath. As the champion of God and the ladies (I blush to unite such discordant names), he devoted himself to speak the truth; to maintain the right; to protect the distressed; to practise *courtesy*, a virtue less familiar to the ancients; to pursue the

55. Of the words *gentilis, gentilhomme, gentleman*, two etymologies are produced: 1. From the Barbarians of the fifth century, the soldiers, and at length the conquerors of the Roman empire, who were vain of their foreign nobility; and, 2. From the sense of the civilians, who consider *gentilis* as synonymous with *ingenuus*. Selden inclines to the first, but the latter is more pure, as well as probable.

56. Framea scutoque juvenem ornant. Tacitus, Germania, c. 13.

infidels; to despise the allurements of ease and safety; and to vindicate in every perilous adventure the honour of his character. The abuse of the same spirit provoked the illiterate knight to disdain the arts of industry and peace; to esteem himself the sole judge and avenger of his own injuries; and proudly to neglect the laws of civil society and military discipline. Yet the benefits of this institution, to refine the temper of Barbarians, and to infuse some principles, of faith, justice, and humanity, were strongly felt, and have been often observed. The asperity of national prejudice was softened; and the community of religion and arms spread a similar colour and generous emulation over the face of Christendom. Abroad, in enterprise and pilgrimage, at home in martial exercise, the warriors of every country were perpetually associated; and impartial taste must prefer a Gothic tournament to the Olympic games of classic antiquity.[57] Instead of the naked spectacles which corrupted the manners of the Greeks, and banished from the stadium the virgins and matrons; the pompous decoration of the lists was crowned with the presence of chaste and high-born beauty, from whose hands the conqueror received the prize of his dexterity and courage. The skill and strength that were exerted in wrestling and boxing, bear a distant and doubtful relation to the merit of a soldier; but the tournaments, as they were invented in France, and eagerly adopted both in the East and West, presented a lively image of the business of the field. The single combats, the general skirmish, the defence of a pass, or castle, were rehearsed as in actual service; and the contest, both in real and mimic war, was decided by the superior management of the horse and lance. The lance was the proper and peculiar weapon of the knight: his horse was of a large and heavy breed; but this charger, till he was roused by the approaching danger, was usually led by an attendant, and he quietly rode a pad or palfrey of a more easy pace. His helmet, and sword, his greaves, and buckler, it would be superfluous to describe; but I may remark, that at the period of the crusades, the armour was less ponderous than in later times; and that, instead of a massy cuirass, his breast was defended by an hauberk or coat of mail. When their long lances were fixed in the rest, the warriors furiously spurred their horses against the foe; and the light cavalry of the Turks and Arabs could seldom stand against the direct and impetuous

57. The athletic exercises, particularly the cœstus and pancratium, were condemned by Lycurgus, Philopœmen, and Galen, a lawgiver, a general, and a physician. Against their authority and reasons, the reader may weigh the apology of Lucian, in the character of Solon. See West on the Olympic Games, in his Pindar, vol. ii. p. 86–96. 245–248.

weight of their charge. Each knight was attended to the field by his faithful squire, a youth of equal birth and similar hopes; he was followed by his archers and men at arms, and four, or five, or six soldiers, were computed as the furniture of a complete *lance*. In the expeditions to the neighbouring kingdoms or the Holy Land, the duties of the feudal tenure no longer subsisted; the voluntary service of the knights and their followers was either prompted by zeal or attachment, or purchased with rewards and promises; and the numbers of each squadron were measured by the power, the wealth, and the fame of each independent chieftain. They were distinguished by his banner, his armorial coat, and his cry of war; and the most ancient families of Europe must seek in these atchievements the origin and proof of their nobility. In this rapid portrait of chivalry, I have been urged to anticipate on the story of the crusades, at once an effect, and a cause, of this memorable institution.[58]

March of the princes to Constantinople, A.D. 1096, August 15– A.D. 1097, May.

Such were the troops, and such the leaders, who assumed the cross for the deliverance of the holy sepulchre. As soon as they were relieved by the absence of the plebeian multitude, they encouraged each other, by interviews and messages, to accomplish their vow and hasten their departure. Their wives and sisters were desirous of partaking the danger and merit of the pilgrimage; their portable treasures was conveyed in bars of silver and gold; and the princes and barons were attended by their equipage of hounds and hawks to amuse their leisure and to supply their table. The difficulty of procuring subsistence for so many myriads of men and horses, engaged them to separate their forces; their choice or situation determined the road; and it was agreed to meet in the neighbourhood of Constantinople, and from thence to begin their operations against the Turks. From the banks of the Meuse and the Moselle, Godfrey of Bouillon followed the direct way of Germany, Hungary, and Bulgaria: and, as long as he exercised the sole command, every step afforded some proof of his prudence and virtue. On the confines of Hungary he was stopped three weeks by a Christian people, to whom the name, or at least the abuse, of the cross was justly odious. The Hungarians still smarted with the wounds which they had received from the first pilgrims: in their turn they had abused the right of defence and retaliation; and they had reason to

58. On the curious subjects of knighthood, knights-service, nobility, arms, cry of war, banners, and tournaments, an ample fund of information may be sought in Selden (Opera, tom. iii. part i. Titles of Honour, part ii. c. 1. 3. 5. 8.), Ducange (Gloss. Latin. tom. iv. p. 398–412, &c.), Dissertations sur Joinville (i. vi–xii. p. 127–142. p. 165–222.), and M. de St. Palaye (Memoires sur la Chevalerie).

apprehend a severe revenge from an hero of the same nation, and who was engaged in the same cause. But, after weighing the motives and the events, the virtuous duke was content to pity the crimes and misfortunes of his worthless brethren; and his twelve deputies, the messengers of peace, requested in his name a free passage and an equal market. To remove their suspicions, Godfrey trusted himself, and afterwards his brother, to the faith of Carloman king of Hungary, who treated them with a simple but hospitable entertainment: the treaty was sanctified by their common gospel; and a proclamation, under pain of death, restrained the animosity and licence of the Latin soldiers. From Austria to Belgrade, they traversed the plains of Hungary, without enduring or offering any injury; and the proximity of Carloman, who hovered on their flanks with his numerous cavalry, was a precaution not less useful for their safety than for his own. They reached the banks of the Save; and no sooner had they passed the river, than the king of Hungary restored the hostages, and saluted their departure with the fairest wishes for the success of their enterprise. With the same conduct and discipline, Godfrey pervaded the woods of Bulgaria and the frontiers of Thrace; and might congratulate himself, that he had almost reached the first term of his pilgrimage, without drawing his sword against a Christian adversary. After an easy and pleasant journey through Lombardy, from Turin to Aquileia, Raymond and his provincials marched forty days through the savage country of Dalmatia[59] and Sclavonia. The weather was a perpetual fog; the land was mountainous and desolate; the natives were either fugitive or hostile: loose in their religion and government, they refused to furnish provisions or guides; murdered the stragglers; and exercised by night and day the vigilance of the count, who derived more security from the punishment of some captive robbers than from his interview and treaty with the prince of Scodra.[60] His march between Durazzo and Constantinople was harassed, without being stopped, by the peasants and soldiers of the Greek emperor; and the same faint and ambiguous hostility was prepared for the remaining chiefs, who passed the Adriatic from the

59. The Familiæ Dalmaticæ of Ducange are meagre and imperfect; the national historians are recent and fabulous, the Greeks remote and careless. In the year 1104, Coloman reduced the maritime country as far as Trau and Salona (Katona, Hist. Crit. tom. iii. p. 195–207.).

60. Scodras appears in Livy as the capital and fortress of Gentius king of the Illyrians, arx munitissima, afterwards a Roman colony (Cellarius, tom. i. p. 393, 394.). It is now called Iscodar, or Scutari (d'Anville, Geographie Ancienne, tom. i. p. 164.). The sanjiak (now a pasha) of Scutari, or Schendeire, was the viii[th] under the Beglerbeg of Romania, and furnished 600 soldiers on a revenue of 78,787 rix-dollars (Marsigli, Stato Militare del Impero Ottomano, p. 128.).

coast of Italy. Bohemond had arms and vessels, and foresight and discipline; and his name was not forgotten in the provinces of Epirus and Thessaly. Whatever obstacles he encountered were surmounted by his military conduct and the valour of Tancred; and if the Norman prince affected to spare the Greeks, he gorged his soldiers with the full plunder of an heretical castle.[61] The nobles of France pressed forwards with the vain and thoughtless ardour of which their nation has been sometimes accused. From the Alps to Apulia the march of Hugh the Great, of the two Roberts, and of Stephen of Chartres, through a wealthy country, and amidst the applauding Catholics, was a devout or triumphant progress: they kissed the feet of the Roman pontiff; and the golden standard of St. Peter was delivered to the brother of the French monarch.[62] But in this visit of piety and pleasure, they neglected to secure the season, and the means, of their embarkation: the winter was insensibly lost; their troops were scattered and corrupted in the towns of Italy. They separately accomplished their passage, regardless of safety or dignity: and within nine months from the feast of the Assumption, the day appointed by Urban, all the Latin princes had reached Constantinople. But the count of Vermandois was produced as a captive; his foremost vessels were scattered by a tempest; and his person, against the law of nations, was detained by the lieutenants of Alexius. Yet the arrival of Hugh had been announced by four-and-twenty knights in golden armour, who commanded the emperor to revere the general of the Latin Christians, the brother of the King of kings.[63]

Policy of the emperor Alexius Comnenus,

In some Oriental tale I have read the fable of a shepherd, who was ruined by the accomplishment of his own wishes: he had prayed for water; the Ganges was turned into his grounds, and his flock and cottage were swept away by the inundation.

61. In Pelagonia castrum hæreticûm ... spoliatum cum suis habitatoribus igne combussere. *Nec id eis injuria contigit*: quia illorum detestabilis sermo et cancer serpebat, jamque circumjacentes regiones suo pravo dogmate fœdaverat (Robert. Mon. p. 36, 37.). After coolly relating the fact, the archbishop Baldric adds, as a praise, Omnes siquidem illi viatores, Judeos, hæreticos, Saracenos æqualiter habent exosos; quos omnes appellant inimicos Dei (p. 92.).

62. *Αναλαβομενος απο Ρωμης την χρυσην του Ἁγιου Πετρου σημαιαν* (Alexiad, l. x. p. 288.).

63. *Ὁ Βασιλευς των βασιλεων, και αρχηγος του Φραγγικου στρατευματος απαντος*. This Oriental pomp is extravagant in a count of Vermandois; but the patriot Ducange repeats with much complacency (Not. ad Alexiad. p. 352, 353. Dissert. xxvii. sur Joinville, p. 315.), the passages of Matthew Paris (A.D. 1254.) and Froissard (vol. iv. p. 201.), which style the king of France, rex regum, and chef de tous les rois Chretiens.

A.D. 1096, December– A.D. 1097, May.

Such was the fortune, or at least the apprehension, of the Greek emperor Alexius Comnenus, whose name has already appeared in this history, and whose conduct is so differently represented by his daughter Anne,[64] and by the Latin writers.[65] In the council of Placentia, his ambassadors had solicited a moderate succour, perhaps of ten thousand soldiers: but he was astonished by the approach of so many potent chiefs and fanatic nations. The emperor fluctuated between hope and fear, between timidity and courage; but in the crooked policy which he mistook for wisdom, I cannot believe, I cannot discern, that he maliciously conspired against the life or honour of the French heroes. The promiscuous multitudes of Peter the hermit, were savage beasts, alike destitute of humanity and reason: nor was it possible for Alexius to prevent or deplore their destruction. The troops of Godfrey and his peers were less contemptible, but not less suspicious, to the Greek emperor. Their motives *might* be pure and pious; but he was equally alarmed by his knowledge of the ambitious Bohemond, and his ignorance of the Transalpine chiefs: the courage of the French was blind and headstrong; they might be tempted by the luxury and wealth of Greece, and elated by the view and opinion of their invincible strength; and Jerusalem might be forgotten in the prospect of Constantinople. After a long march and painful abstinence, the troops of Godfrey encamped in the plains of Thrace; they heard with indignation, that their brother, the count of Vermandois, was imprisoned by the Greeks; and their reluctant duke was compelled to indulge them in some freedom of retaliation and rapine. They were appeased by the submission of Alexius; he promised to supply their camp; and as they refused in the midst of winter, to pass the Bosphorus, their quarters were assigned among the gardens and palaces on the shores of that narrow sea. But an incurable jealousy still rankled in the minds of the two nations, who despised each other as slaves and Barbarians. Ignorance is the ground of suspicion, and suspicion was inflamed into daily provocations: prejudice is blind, hunger is deaf; and

64. Anna Comnena was born the 1st of December, A.D. 1083, indiction vii. (Alexiad, l. vi. p. 166, 167.). At thirteen, the time of the first crusade, she was nubile, and perhaps married to the younger Nicephorus Bryennius, whom she fondly styles *τον εμον Καισαρα* (l. x. p. 295, 296.). Some moderns have *imagined*, that her enmity to Bohemond was the fruit of disappointed love. In the transactions of Constantinople and Nice, her partial accounts (Alex. l. x, xi. p. 283–317.) may be opposed to the partiality of the Latins, but in their subsequent exploits she is brief and ignorant.

65. In their views of the character and conduct of Alexius, Maimbourg has favoured the *Catholic* Franks, and Voltaire has been partial to the *schismatic* Greeks. The prejudice of a philosopher is less excusable than that of a Jesuit.

Alexius is accused of a design to starve or assault the Latins in a dangerous post, on all sides encompassed with the waters.[66] Godfrey sounded his trumpets, burst the net, overspread the plain, and insulted the suburbs: but the gates of Constantinople were strongly fortified; the ramparts were lined with archers; and after a doubtful conflict, both parties listened to the voice of peace and religion. The gifts and promises of the emperor insensibly soothed the fierce spirit of the western strangers; as a Christian warrior, he rekindled their zeal for the prosecution of their holy enterprise, which he engaged to second with his troops and treasures. On the return of spring, Godfrey was persuaded to occupy a pleasant and plentiful camp in Asia; and no sooner had he passed the Bosphorus, than the Greek vessels were suddenly recalled to the opposite shore. The same policy was repeated with the succeeding chiefs, who were swayed by the example, and weakened by the departure, of their foremost companions. By his skill and diligence, Alexius prevented the union of any two of the confederate armies at the same moment under the walls of Constantinople; and before the feast of the Pentecost not a Latin pilgrim was left on the coast of Europe.

He obtains the homage of the crusaders.

The same arms which threatened Europe, might deliver Asia, and repel the Turks from the neighbouring shores of the Bosphorus and Hellespont. The fair provinces from Nice to Antioch were the recent patrimony of the Roman emperor; and his ancient and perpetual claim still embraced the kingdoms of Syria and Egypt. In his enthusiasm, Alexius indulged, or affected, the ambitious hope of leading his new allies to subvert the thrones of the East: but the calmer dictates of reason and temper dissuaded him from exposing his royal person to the faith of unknown and lawless Barbarians. His prudence, or his pride, was content with extorting from the French princes an oath of homage and fidelity, and a solemn promise, that they would either restore, or hold, their Asiatic conquests, as the humble and loyal vassals of the Roman empire. Their independent spirit was fired at the mention of this foreign and voluntary servitude: they successively yielded to the dextrous application of gifts and flattery; and the first proselytes became the most eloquent and effectual missionaries to multiply the companions of their shame. The pride of Hugh of Vermandois was

66. Between the Black Sea, the Bosphorus, and the river Barbyses, which is deep in summer, and runs fifteen miles through a flat meadow. Its communication with Europe and Constantinople is by the stone bridge of the *Blachernæ*, which in successive ages was restored by Justinian and Basil (Gyllius de Bosphoro Thracio, l. ii. c. 3. Ducange, C. P. Christiana, l. iv. c. 2. p. 179.).

soothed by the honours of his captivity; and in the brother of the French king, the example of submission was prevalent and weighty. In the mind of Godfrey of Bouillon every human consideration was subordinate to the glory of God and the success of the crusade. He had firmly resisted the temptations of Bohemond and Raymond, who urged the attack and conquest of Constantinople. Alexius esteemed his virtues, deservedly named him the champion of the empire, and dignified his homage with the filial name and the rites of adoption.[67] The hateful Bohemond was received as a true and ancient ally; and if the emperor reminded him of former hostilities, it was only to praise the valour that he had displayed, and the glory that he had acquired, in the fields of Durazzo and Larissa. The son of Guiscard was lodged and entertained, and served with Imperial pomp: one day, as he passed through the gallery of the palace, a door was carelessly left open to expose a pile of gold and silver, of silk and gems, of curious and costly furniture, that was heaped in seeming disorder, from the floor to the roof of the chamber. "What conquests," exclaimed the ambitious miser, "might not be atchieved by the possession of such a treasure?" "It is your own," replied a Greek attendant who watched the motions of his soul; and Bohemond, after some hesitation, condescended to accept this magnificent present. The Norman was flattered by the assurance of an independent principality, and Alexius eluded, rather than denied, his daring demand of the office of great domestic, or general, of the East. The two Roberts, the son of the conqueror of England, and the kinsman of three queens,[68] bowed in their turn before the Byzantine throne. A private letter of Stephen of Chartres attests his admiration of the emperor, the most excellent and liberal of men, who taught him to believe that he was a favourite, and promised to educate and establish his youngest son. In his southern province, the count of St. Giles and Tholouse faintly recognized the supremacy of the king of France, a prince of a foreign nation and language. At the head of an hundred thousand men, he declared, that he was the soldier and servant of Christ alone, and that the Greek might be satisfied with an equal treaty of alliance and friendship. His obstinate resistance enhanced the value and the price of his submission; and he shone, says the princess Anne, among the Barbarians, as the sun amidst the stars of heaven. His disgust of the

67. There were two sorts of adoption, the one by arms, the other by introducing the son between the shirt and skin of his father. Ducange (sur Joinville, diss. xxii. p. 270.) supposes Godfrey's adoption to have been of the latter sort.

68. After his return, Robert of Flanders became the *man* of the king of England, for a pension of four hundred marks. See the first act in Rymer's Fœdera.

noise and insolence of the French, his suspicions of the designs of Bohemond, the emperor imparted to his faithful Raymond; and that aged statesman might clearly discern, that however false in friendship, he was sincere in his enmity.[69] The spirit of chivalry was last subdued in the person of Tancred; and none could deem themselves dishonoured by the imitation of that gallant knight. He disdained the gold and flattery of the Greek monarch; assaulted in his presence an insolent patrician; escaped to Asia in the habit of a private soldier; and yielded with a sigh to the authority of Bohemond and the interest of the Christian cause. The best and most ostensible reason was the impossibility of passing the sea and accomplishing their vow, without the licence and the vessels of Alexius; but they cherished a secret hope, that as soon as they trod the continent of Asia, their swords would obliterate their shame, and dissolve the engagement, which on his side might not be very faithfully performed. The ceremony of their homage was grateful to a people who had long since considered pride as the substitute of power. High on his throne, the emperor sat mute and immovable: his majesty was adored by the Latin princes; and they submitted to kiss either his feet or his knees, an indignity which their own writers are ashamed to confess and unable to deny.[70]

Insolence of the Franks. Private or public interest suppressed the murmurs of the dukes and counts; but a French baron (he is supposed to be Robert of Paris[71]) presumed to ascend the throne, and to place himself by the side of Alexius. The sage reproof of Baldwin provoked him to exclaim, in his barbarous idiom, "Who is this rustic, that keeps his seat, while so many valiant captains are standing round him?" The emperor maintained his silence, dissembled his indignation, and questioned his interpreter concerning the meaning of the words, which he partly suspected from the universal language of gesture and countenance. Before the departure of

69. Sensit vetus regnandi, falsos in amore, odia non fingere, Tacit. vi. 44.

70. The proud historians of the crusades slide and stumble over this humiliating step. Yet, since the heroes knelt to salute the emperor as he sat motionless on his throne, it is clear that they must have kissed either his feet or knees. It is only singular, that Anna should not have amply supplied the silence or ambiguity of the Latins. The abasement of their princes, would have added a fine chapter to the Ceremoniale Aulæ Byzantinæ.

71. He called himself *Φραγγος καθαρος των ευγενων* (Alexias, l. x. p. 301.). What a title of *noblesse* of the xi[th] century, if any one could now prove his inheritance! Anna relates, with visible pleasure, that the swelling Barbarian, *Λατινος τετυφωμενος*, was killed, or wounded, after fighting in the front in the battle of Dorylæum (l. xi. p. 317.). This circumstance may justify the suspicion of Ducange (Not. p. 362.), that he was no other than Robert of Paris, of the district most peculiarly styled the Duchy or Island of France (*L'Isle de France*).

the pilgrims, he endeavoured to learn the name and condition of the audacious baron. "I am a Frenchman," replied Robert, "of the purest and most ancient nobility of my country. All that I know is, that there is a church in my neighbourhood,[72] the resort of those who are desirous of approving their valour in single combat. Till an enemy appears, they address their prayers to God and his saints. That church I have frequently visited, but never have I found an antagonist who dared to accept my defiance." Alexius dismissed the challenger with some prudent advice for his conduct in the Turkish warfare; and history repeats with pleasure this lively example of the manners of his age and country.

Their review and numbers, A.D. 1097, May.

The conquest of Asia was undertaken and atchieved by Alexander, with thirty-five thousand Macedonians and Greeks;[73] and his best hope was in the strength and discipline of his phalanx of infantry. The principal force of the crusaders consisted in their cavalry; and when that force was mustered in the plains of Bithynia, the knights and their martial attendants on horseback amounted to one hundred thousand fighting men, completely armed with the helmet and coat of mail. The value of these soldiers deserved a strict and authentic account; and the flower of European chivalry might furnish, in a first effort, this formidable body of heavy horse. A part of the infantry might be enrolled for the service of scouts, pioneers, and archers; but the promiscuous crowd were lost in their own disorder; and we depend not on the eyes or knowledge, but on the belief and fancy, of a chaplain of count Baldwin,[74] in the estimate of six hundred thousand pilgrims able to bear arms, besides the priests and monks, the women and children, of the Latin camp. The reader starts; and before he is recovered from his surprise, I shall add, on the same testimony, that if all who took the cross had accomplished their vow, above SIX MILLIONS would have migrated from Europe to Asia. Under this oppression of faith, I derive some relief from a more sagacious and thinking writer,[75]

72. With the same penetration, Ducange discovers his church to be that of St. Drausus, or Drosin, of Soissons, quem duello dimicaturi solent invocare: pugiles qui ad memoriam ejus *(his tomb)* pernoctant invictos reddit, ut et de Burgundiâ et Italia tali necessitate confugiatur ad eum. Joan. Sariberiensis, epist. 139.

73. There is some diversity on the numbers of his army: but no authority can be compared with that of Ptolemy, who states it at five thousand horse and thirty thousand foot (see Usher's Annales, p. 152.).

74. Fulcher. Carnotensis, p. 387. He enumerates nineteen nations of different names and languages (p. 389.); but I do not clearly apprehend his difference between the *Franci* and *Galli, Itali* and *Apuli*. Elsewhere (p. 385.) he contemptuously brands the deserters.

who, after the same review of the cavalry, accuses the credulity of the priest of Chartres, and even doubts whether the *Cisalpine* regions (in the geography of a Frenchman) were sufficient to produce and pour forth such incredible multitudes. The coolest scepticism will remember, that of these religious volunteers great numbers never beheld Constantinople and Nice. Of enthusiasm the influence is irregular and transient: many were detained at home by reason or cowardice, by poverty or weakness; and many were repulsed by the obstacles of the way, the more insuperable as they were unforeseen to these ignorant fanatics. The savage countries of Hungary and Bulgaria were whitened with their bones: their vanguard was cut in pieces by the Turkish sultan; and the loss of the first adventure by the sword, or climate, or fatigue, has already been stated at three hundred thousand men. Yet the myriads that survived, that marched, that pressed forwards on the holy pilgrimage, were a subject of astonishment to themselves and to the Greeks. The copious energy of her language sinks under the efforts of the princess Anne:[76] the images of locusts, of leaves and flowers, of the sands of the sea, or the stars of heaven, imperfectly represent what she had seen and heard; and the daughter of Alexius exclaims, that Europe was loosened from its foundations, and hurled against Asia. The ancient hosts of Darius and Xerxes labour under the same doubt of a vague and indefinite magnitude; but I am inclined to believe, that a larger number has never been contained within the lines of a single camp than at the siege of Nice, the first operation of the Latin princes. Their motives, their characters, and their arms, have been already displayed. Of their troops, the most numerous portion were natives of France: the Low Countries, the banks of the Rhine and Apulia, sent a powerful reinforcement: some bands of adventurers were drawn from Spain, Lombardy, and England;[77] and from the distant bogs and mountains

75. Guibert, p. 556. Yet even his gentle opposition implies an immense multitude. By Urban II. in the fervour of his zeal, it is only rated at 300,000 pilgrims (epist. xvi. Concil. tom. xii. p. 731.).

76. Alexias, l. x. p. 283. 305. Her fastidious delicacy complains of their strange and inarticulate names, and indeed there is scarcely one that she has not contrived to disfigure with the proud ignorance, so dear and familiar to a polished people. I shall select only one example, *Sangeles*, for the count of St. Giles.

77. William of Malmsbury (who wrote about the year 1130) has inserted in his history (l. iv. p. 130–154.) a narrative of the first crusade: but I wish that, instead of listening to the tenue murmur which had passed the British ocean (p. 143.), he had confined himself to the numbers, families, and adventures of his countrymen. I find in Dugdale, that an English Norman, Stephen earl of Albemarle and Holdernesse, led the rearguard with duke Robert, at the battle of Antioch (Baronage, part i. p. 61.).

of Ireland or Scotland[78] issued some naked and savage fanatics, ferocious at home but unwarlike abroad. Had not superstition condemned the sacrilegious prudence of depriving the poorest or weakest Christian of the merit of the pilgrimage, the useless crowd, with mouths, but without hands, might have been stationed in the Greek empire, till their companions had opened and secured the way of the Lord. A small remnant of the pilgrims, who passed the Bosphorus, was permitted to visit the holy sepulchre. Their northern constitution was scorched by the rays, and infected by the vapours, of a Syrian sun. They consumed, with heedless prodigality, their stores of water and provision: their numbers exhausted the inland country; the sea was remote, the Greeks were unfriendly, and the Christians of every sect fled before the voracious and cruel rapine of their brethren. In the dire necessity of famine, they sometimes roasted and devoured the flesh of their infant or adult captives. Among the Turks and Saracens, the idolaters of Europe were rendered more odious by the name and reputation of cannibals: the spies who introduced themselves into the kitchen of Bohemond, were shewn several human bodies turning on the spit; and the artful Norman encouraged a report, which encreased at the same time the abhorrence and the terror of the infidels.[79]

Siege of Nice, A.D. 1097, May 14– June 20.

I have expatiated with pleasure on the first steps of the crusaders, as they paint the manners and character of Europe: but I shall abridge the tedious and uniform narrative of their blind atchievements, which were performed by strength and are described by ignorance. From their first station in the neighbourhood of Nicomedia, they advanced in successive divisions; passed the contracted limit of the Greek empire; opened a road through the hills, and commenced by the siege of his capital, their pious warfare against the Turkish sultan. His kingdom of Roum extended from the Hellespont to the confines of Syria, and barred the pilgrimage of Jerusalem: his name was Kilidge-Arslan, or Soliman,[80] of the race of Seljuk, and son of the

78. Videres Scotorum apud se ferocium alias imbellium cuneos (Guibert, p. 471.): the *crus intectum*, and *hispida chlamys*, may suit the Highlanders; but the finibus uliginosis, may rather apply to the Irish bogs. William of Malmsbury expressly mentions the Welsh and Scots, &c. (l. iv. p. 133.) who quitted, the former venationem saltuum, the latter familiaritatem pulicum.

79. This cannibal hunger, sometimes real, more frequently an artifice or a lye, may be found in Anna Comnena (Alexias, l. x. p. 288.), Guibert (p. 546.), Radulph. Cadom. (c. 97.). The stratagem is related by the author of the Gesta Francorum, the monk Robert Baldric, and Raymond des Agiles, in the siege and famine of Antioch.

80. His Musulman appellation of Soliman is used by the Latins, and his character is highly embellished by Tasso. His Turkish

first conqueror; and in the defence of a land which the Turks considered as their own, he deserved the praise of his enemies, by whom alone he is known to posterity. Yielding to the first impulse of the torrent, he deposited his family and treasure in Nice; retired to the mountains with fifty thousand horse; and twice descended to assault the camps or quarters of the Christian besiegers, which formed an imperfect circle of above six miles. The lofty and solid walls of Nice were covered by a deep ditch, and flanked by three hundred and seventy towers; and on the verge of Christendom, the Moslems were trained in arms and inflamed by religion. Before this city, the French princes occupied their stations, and prosecuted their attacks without correspondence or subordination: emulation prompted their valour; but their valour was sullied by cruelty, and their emulation degenerated into envy and civil discord. In the siege of Nice, the arts and engines of antiquity were employed by the Latins; the mine and the battering-ram, the tortoise, and the belfrey or moveable turret, artificial fire, and the *catapult* and *balist*, the sling, and the cross-bow for the casting of stones and darts.[81] In the space of seven weeks, much labour and blood were expended, and some progress, especially by count Raymond, was made on the side of the besiegers. But the Turks could protract their resistance and secure their escape, as long as they were masters of the lake[82] Ascanius, which stretches several miles to the westward of the city. The means of conquest were supplied by the prudence and industry of Alexius; a great number of boats was transported on sledges from the sea to the lake; they were filled with the most dextrous of his archers; the flight of the sultana was intercepted; Nice was invested by land and water; and a Greek emissary persuaded the inhabitants to accept his master's protection, and to save themselves, by a timely surrender, from the rage of the savages of Europe. In the moment of victory, or at least of hope, the crusaders, thirsting for blood and plunder, were awed by the Imperial banner that streamed from the citadel; and Alexius

---

name of Kilidge-Arslan (A.H. 485–500. A.D. 1092–1106. See de Guignes's Tables, tom. i. p. 245.) is employed by the Orientals, and with some corruption by the Greeks: but little more than his name can be found in the Mahometan writers, who are dry and sulky on the subject of the first crusade (de Guignes, tom. iii. p. ii. p. 10–30.).

81. On the fortifications, engines, and sieges of the middle ages, see Muratori (Antiquitat. Italiæ, tom. ii. dissert. xxvi. p. 452–524.). The *belfredus*, from whence our belfrey, was the moveable tower of the ancients (Ducange, tom. i. p. 608.).

82. I cannot forbear remarking the resemblance between the siege and lake of Nice, with the operations of Hernan Cortez before Mexico. See Dr. Robertson, Hist. of America, l. v.

guarded with jealous vigilance this important conquest. The murmurs of the chiefs were stifled by honour or interest; and after an halt of nine days, they directed their march towards Phrygia under the guidance of a Greek general, whom they suspected of a secret connivance with the sultan. The consort and the principal servants of Soliman had been honourably restored without ransom; and the emperor's generosity to the *miscreants*[83] was interpreted as treason to the Christian cause.

Battle of Dorylæum, A.D. 1097, July 4.

Soliman was rather provoked than dismayed by the loss of his capital: he admonished his subjects and allies of this strange invasion of the western Barbarians; the Turkish emirs obeyed the call of loyalty or religion; the Turkman hords encamped round his standard; and his whole force is loosely stated by the Christians at two hundred, or even three hundred and sixty, thousand horse. Yet he patiently waited till they had left behind them the sea and the Greek frontier; and hovering on the flanks, observed their careless and confident progress in two columns beyond the view of each other. Some miles before they could reach Dorylæum in Phrygia, the left, and least numerous, division was surprised, and attacked, and almost oppressed, by the Turkish cavalry.[84] The heat of the weather, the clouds of arrows, and the barbarous onset, overwhelmed the crusaders; they lost their order and confidence, and the fainting fight was sustained by the personal valour, rather than by the military conduct, of Bohemond, Tancred, and Robert of Normandy. They were revived by the welcome banners of duke Godfrey, who flew to their succours with the count of Vermandois, and sixty thousand horse; and was followed by Raymond of Tholouse, the bishop of Puy, and the remainder of the sacred army. Without a moment's pause, they formed in new order, and advanced to a second battle. They were received with equal resolution; and, in their common disdain for the unwarlike people of Greece and Asia, it was confessed on both sides, that the Turks and the Franks were the only nations entitled to the appellation of soldiers.[85] Their encounter was varied and balanced by the

83. *Mecreant*, a word invented by the French crusaders, and confined in that language to its primitive sense. It should seem, that the zeal of our ancestors boiled higher, and that they branded every unbeliever as a rascal. A similar prejudice still lurks in the minds of many who think themselves Christians.

84. Baronius has produced a very doubtful letter to his brother Roger (A.D. 1098, N° 15.) The enemies consisted of Medes, Persians, Chaldæans: be it so. The first attack was cum nostro incommodo; true and tender. But why Godfrey of Bouillon and Hugh *brothers*? Tancred is styled *filius*; of whom? certainly not of Roger, nor of Bohemond.

85. Veruntamen dicunt se esse de Francorum generatione; et quia nullus homo naturaliter debet esse miles nisi Franci et

contrast of arms and discipline; of the direct charge, and wheeling evolutions; of the couched lance, and the brandished javelin; of a weighty broad-sword, and a crooked sabre; of cumbrous armour, and thin flowing robes; and of the long Tartar bow, and the *arbalist* or cross-bow, a deadly weapon, yet unknown to the Orientals.[86] As long as the horses were fresh and the quivers full, Soliman maintained the advantage of the day; and four thousand Christians were pierced by the Turkish arrows. In the evening, swiftness yielded to strength; on either side, the numbers were equal, or at least as great as any ground could hold, or any generals could manage; but in turning the hills, the last division of Raymond and his *provincials* was led, perhaps without design, on the rear of an exhausted enemy; and the long contest was determined. Besides a nameless and unaccounted multitude, three thousand *Pagan* knights were slain in the battle and pursuit; the camp of Soliman was pillaged; and in the variety of precious spoil, the curiosity of the Latins was amused with foreign arms and apparel, and the new aspect of dromedaries and camels. The importance of the victory was proved by the hasty retreat of the sultan: reserving ten thousand guards of the relics of his army, Soliman evacuated the kingdom of Roum, and hastened to implore the aid, and kindle the resentment, of his Eastern brethren. In a march of five hundred miles, the crusaders traversed the Lesser Asia, through a wasted land and deserted towns, without finding either a friend or an enemy. The geographer[87] may trace the position of Dorylæum, Antioch of Pisidia, Iconium, Archelais, and Germanicia, and may compare those classic appellations with the modern names of Eskishehr the old city, Akshehr the white city, Cogni, Erekli, and Marash. As the pilgrims passed over a desert, where a draught of water is exchanged for silver, they were tormented by intolerable thirst; and on the banks of the first rivulet, their haste and intemperance were still more pernicious to the disorderly throng. They climbed with toil and danger the steep and slippery sides of mount Taurus: many of the

March through the Lesser Asia, July–September.

Turci (Gesta Francorum, p. 7.). The same community of blood and valour is attested by archbishop Baldric (p. 99.).

86. *Balista, Balestra, Arbalestre.* See Muratori, Antiq. tom. ii. p. 517–524. Ducange, Gloss. Latin. tom. i. p. 531, 532. In the time of Anna Comnena, this weapon, which she describes under the name of *tzangra*, was unknown in the East (l. x. p. 291.). By an humane inconsistency, the pope strove to prohibit it in Christian wars.

87. The curious reader may compare the classic learning of Cellarius, and the geographical science of d'Anville. William of Tyre is the only historian of the crusades who has any knowledge of antiquity; and M. Otter trod almost in the footsteps of the Franks from Constantinople to Antioch (Voyage en Turquie et en Perse, tom. i. p. 35–88.).

soldiers cast away their arms to secure their footsteps; and had not terror preceded their van, the long and trembling file might have been driven down the precipice by an handful of resolute enemies. Two of their most respectable chiefs, the duke of Lorraine and the count of Tholouse, were carried in litters: Raymond was raised, as it is said by miracle, from an hopeless malady; and Godfrey had been torn by a bear, as he pursued that rough and perilous chace in the mountains of Pisidia.

Baldwin founds the principality of Edessa, A.D. 1097–1151.

To improve the general consternation, the cousin of Bohemond and the brother of Godfrey were detached from the main army with their respective squadrons of five, and of seven, hundred knights. They over-ran in a rapid career the hills and sea-coast of Cilicia, from Cogni to the Syrian gates: the Norman standard was first planted on the walls of Tarsus and Malmistra; but the proud injustice of Baldwin at length provoked the patient and generous Italian; and they turned their consecrated swords against each other in a private and profane quarrel. Honour was the motive, and fame the reward, of Tancred; but fortune smiled on the more selfish enterprise of his rival.[88] He was called to the assistance of a Greek or Armenian tyrant, who had been suffered under the Turkish yoke to reign over the Christians of Edessa. Baldwin accepted the character of his son and champion; but no sooner was he introduced into the city, than he inflamed the people to the massacre of his father, occupied the throne and treasure, extended his conquests over the hills of Armenia and the plain of Mesopotamia, and founded the first principality of the Franks or Latins, which subsisted fifty-four years beyond the Euphrates.[89]

Siege of Antioch, A.D. 1097, October 21– A.D. 1098, June 3.

Before the Franks could enter Syria, the summer, and even the autumn, were completely wasted: the siege of Antioch, or the separation and repose of the army during the winter season, was strongly debated in their council: the love of arms and the holy sepulchre urged them to advance; and reason perhaps was on the side of resolution, since every hour of delay abates the fame and force of the invader, and multiplies the resources of defensive war. The capital of Syria was protected by the river Orontes; and the *iron bridge*, of nine arches, derives its name from the massy gates

88. This detached conquest of Edessa is best represented by Fulcherius Carnotensis, or of Chartres (in the collections of Bongarsius, Duchesne, and Martenne), the valiant chaplain of count Baldwin (Esprit des Croisades, tom. i. p. 13, 14.). In the disputes of that prince with Tancred, his partiality is encountered by the partiality of Radulphus Cadomensis, the soldier and historian of the gallant marquis.

89. See de Guignes, Hist. des Huns, tom. i. p. 456.

of the two towers which are constructed at either end. They were opened by the sword of the duke of Normandy: his victory gave entrance to three hundred thousand crusaders, an account which may allow some scope for losses and desertion, but which clearly detects much exaggeration in the review of Nice. In the description of Antioch,[90] it is not easy to define a middle term between her ancient magnificence, under the successors of Alexander and Augustus, and the modern aspect of Turkish desolation. The Tetrapolis, or four cities, if they retained their name and position, must have left a large vacuity in a circumference of twelve miles; and that measure, as well as the number of four hundred towers, are not perfectly consistent with the five gates, so often mentioned in the history of the siege. Yet Antioch must have still flourished as a great and populous capital. At the head of the Turkish emirs, Baghisian, a veteran chief, commanded in the place: his garrison was composed of six or seven thousand horse, and fifteen or twenty thousand foot: one hundred thousand Moslems are said to have fallen by the sword; and their numbers were probably inferior to the Greeks, Armenians, and Syrians, who had been no more than fourteen years the slaves of the house of Seljuk. From the remains of a solid and stately wall, it appears to have arisen to the height of threescore feet in the vallies; and wherever less art and labour had been applied, the ground was supposed to be defended by the river, the morass, and the mountains. Notwithstanding these fortifications, the city had been repeatedly taken by the Persians, the Arabs, the Greeks, and the Turks; so large a circuit must have yielded many pervious points of attack; and in a siege that was formed about the middle of October, the vigour of the execution could alone justify the boldness of the attempt. Whatever strength and valour could perform in the field was abundantly discharged by the champions of the cross: in the frequent occasions of sallies, of forage, of the attack and defence of convoys, they were often victorious; and we can only complain, that their exploits are sometimes enlarged beyond the scale of probability and truth. The sword of Godfrey[91] divided a Turk from the shoulder to the

90. For Antioch, see Pococke (Description of the East, vol. ii. p. i. p. 188–193.), Otter (Voyage en Turquie, &c. tom. i. p. 81, &c.), the Turkish geographer (in Otter's notes), the Index Geographicus of Schultens (ad calcem Bohadin. Vit. Saladin.), and Abulfeda (Tabula Syriæ, p. 115, 116. vers. Reiske).

91. Ensem elevat, eumque a sinistrâ parte scapularum, tanta virtute intorsit ut quòd pectus medium disjunxit spinam et vitalia interrupit, et sic lubricus ensis super crus dextrum integer exivit; sicque caput integrum cum dextrâ parte corporis immersit gurgite, partemque quæ equo præsidebat remisit civitati (Robert. Mon. p. 50.). Cujus ense trajectus, Turcus duo factus est Turci; ut inferior alter in urbem equitaret,

haunch; and one half of the infidel fell to the ground, while the other was transported by his horse to the city gate. As Robert of Normandy rode against his antagonist, "I devote thy head," he piously exclaimed, "to the dæmons of hell;" and that head was instantly cloven to the breast by the resistless stroke of his descending faulchion. But the reality or the report of such gigantic prowess[92] must have taught the Moslems to keep within their walls; and against those walls of earth or stone, the sword and the lance were unavailing weapons. In the slow and successive labours of a siege, the crusaders were supine and ignorant, without skill to contrive, or money to purchase, or industry to use, the artificial engines and implements of assault. In the conquest of Nice, they had been powerfully assisted by the wealth and knowledge of the Greek emperor: his absence was poorly supplied by some Genoese and Pisan vessels, that were attracted by religion or trade to the coast of Syria: the stores were scanty, the return precarious, and the communication difficult and dangerous. Indolence or weakness had prevented the Franks from investing the entire circuit; and the perpetual freedom of two gates relieved the wants and recruited the garrison of the city. At the end of seven months, after the ruin of their cavalry, and an enormous loss by famine, desertion, and fatigue, the progress of the crusaders was imperceptible, and their success remote, if the Latin Ulysses, the artful and ambitious Bohemond, had not employed the arms of cunning and deceit. The Christians of Antioch were numerous and discontented: Phirouz, a Syrian renegado, had acquired the favour of the emir and the command of three towers; and the merit of his repentance disguised to the Latins, and perhaps to himself, the foul design of perfidy and treason. A secret correspondence, for their mutual interest, was soon established between Phirouz and the prince of Tarento; and Bohemond declared in the council of the chiefs, that he could deliver the city into their hands. But he claimed the sovereignty of Antioch as the reward of his service; and the proposal which had been rejected by the envy, was at length extorted from the distress, of his equals. The nocturnal surprise was executed by the French and Norman princes, who ascended in person the scaling-ladders that were thrown from the walls: their new proselyte,

---

alter arcitenens in flumine nataret (Radulph. Cadom. c. 53. p. 304.). Yet he justifies the deed by the *stupendis* viribus of Godfrey; and William of Tyre covers it by ostupuit populus facti novitate ... mirabilis (l. v. c. 6. p. 701.). Yet it must not have appeared incredible to the knights of that age.

92. See the exploits of Robert, Raymond, and the modest Tancred, who imposed silence on his squire (Radulph. Cadom. c. 53.).

after the murder of his too scrupulous brother, embraced and introduced the servants of Christ; the army rushed through the gates; and the Moslems soon found, that although mercy was hopeless, resistance was impotent. But the citadel still refused to surrender; and the victors themselves were speedily encompassed and besieged by the innumerable forces of Kerboga, prince of Mosul, who, with twenty-eight Turkish emirs, advanced to the deliverance of Antioch. Five-and-twenty days the Christians spent on the verge of destruction; and the proud lieutenant of the caliph and the sultan left them only the choice of servitude or death.[93] In this extremity they collected the relics of their strength, sallied from the town, and in a single memorable day annihilated or dispersed the host of Turks and Arabians, which they might safely report to have consisted of six hundred thousand men.[94] Their supernatural allies I shall proceed to consider: the human causes of the victory of Antioch were the fearless despair of the Franks; and the surprise, the discord, perhaps the errors, of their unskilful and presumptuous adversaries. The battle is described with as much disorder as it was fought; but we may observe the tent of Kerboga, a moveable and spacious palace, enriched with the luxury of Asia, and capable of holding above two thousand persons; we may distinguish his three thousand guards, who were cased, the horses as well as the men, in complete steel.

Victory of the crusaders, A.D. 1098, June 28.

Their famine and distress at Antioch.

In the eventful period of the siege and defence of Antioch, the crusaders were alternately exalted by victory or sunk in despair; either swelled with plenty or emaciated with hunger. A speculative reasoner might suppose, that their faith had a strong and serious influence on their practice; and that the soldiers of the cross, the deliverers of the holy sepulchre, prepared themselves by a sober and virtuous life for the daily contemplation of martyrdom. Experience blows away this charitable illusion: and seldom does the history of profane war display such scenes of intemperance and prostitution as were exhibited

93. After mentioning the distress and humble petition of the Franks, Abulpharagius adds the haughty reply of Codbuka, or Kerboga; non evasuri estis nisi per gladium (Dynast. p. 242.).

94. In describing the host of Kerboga, most of the Latin historians, the author of the Gesta (p. 17.), Robert Monachus (p. 56.), Baldric (p. 111.), Fulcherius Carnotensis (p. 392.), Guibert (p. 512.), William of Tyre (l. vi. c. 3. p. 714.), Bernard Thesaurarius (c. 39. p. 695.), are content with the vague expressions of infinita multitudo, immensum agmen, innumeræ copiæ or gentes, which correspond with the *μετα αναριθμητων χιλιαδων* of Anna Comnena (Alexias, l. xi. p. 318–320.). The numbers of the Turks are fixed by Albert Aquensis at 200,000 (l. iv. c. 10. p. 242.), and by Radulphus Cadomensis at 400,000 horse (c. 72. p. 309.).

under the walls of Antioch. The grove of Daphne no longer flourished; but the Syrian air was still impregnated with the same vices; the Christians were seduced by every temptation[95] that nature either prompts or reprobates; the authority of the chiefs was despised; and sermons and edicts were alike fruitless against those scandalous disorders, not less pernicious to military discipline, than repugnant to evangelic purity. In the first days of the siege and the possession of Antioch, the Franks consumed with wanton and thoughtless prodigality the frugal subsistence of weeks and months: the desolate country no longer yielded a supply; and from that country they were at length excluded by the arms of the besieging Turks. Disease, the faithful companion of want, was envenomed by the rains of the winter, the summer heats, unwholesome food, and the close imprisonment of multitudes. The pictures of famine and pestilence are always the same, and always disgustful; and our imagination may suggest the nature of their sufferings and their resources. The remains of treasure or spoil were eagerly lavished in the purchase of the vilest nourishment; and dreadful must have been the calamities of the poor, since, after paying three marks of silver for a goat and fifteen for a lean camel,[96] the count of Flanders was reduced to beg a dinner, and duke Godfrey to borrow an horse. Sixty thousand horses had been reviewed in the camp: before the end of the siege they were diminished to two thousand, and scarcely two hundred fit for service could be mustered on the day of the battle. Weakness of body, and terror of mind, extinguished the ardent enthusiasm of the pilgrims; and every motive of honour and religion was subdued by the desire of life.[97] Among the chiefs, three heroes may be found without fear or reproach: Godfrey of Bouillon was supported by his magnanimous piety; Bohemond by ambition and interest; and Tancred declared, in the true spirit of chivalry, that as long as he was at the head of forty knights, he would never relinquish the enterprise of Palestine. But the count of Tholouse and Provence was suspected of a voluntary indisposition; the duke of Normandy was recalled from the sea-shore by

95. See the tragic and scandalous fate of an archdeacon of royal birth, who was slain by the Turks as he reposed in an orchard, playing at dice with a Syrian concubine.

96. The value of an ox rose from five solidi (fifteen shillings) at Christmas to two marks (four pounds), and afterwards much higher: a kid or lamb, from one shilling to eighteen of our present money: in the second famine, a loaf of bread, or the head of an animal, sold for a piece of gold. More examples might be produced; but it is the ordinary, not the extraordinary, prices, that deserve the notice of the philosopher.

97. Alii multi, quorum nomina non tenemus, quia deleta de libro vitæ præsenti operi non sunt inserenda (Will. Tyr. l. vi. c. 5. p. 715.). Guibert (p. 518. 523.) attempts to excuse Hugh the Great, and even Stephen of Chartres.

the censures of the church; Hugh the Great, though he led the vanguard of the battle, embraced an ambiguous opportunity of returning to France; and Stephen count of Chartres basely deserted the standard which he bore, and the council in which he presided. The soldiers were discouraged by the flight of William viscount of Melun, surnamed the *Carpenter*, from the weighty strokes of his axe; and the saints were scandalised by the fall of Peter the Hermit, who, after arming Europe against Asia, attempted to escape from the penance of a necessary fast. Of the multitude of recreant warriors, the names (says an historian) are blotted from the book of life; and the opprobrious epithet of the rope-dancers was applied to the deserters who dropt in the night from the walls of Antioch. The emperor Alexius,[98] who seemed to advance to the succour of the Latins, was dismayed by the assurance of their hopeless condition. They expected their fate in silent despair; oaths and punishments were tried without effect; and to rouse the soldiers to the defence of the walls, it was found necessary to set fire to their quarters.

Legend of the Holy Lance. For their salvation and victory, they were indebted to the same fanaticism which had led them to the brink of ruin. In such a cause, and in such an army, visions, prophecies, and miracles, were frequent and familiar. In the distress of Antioch, they were repeated with unusual energy and success: St. Ambrose had assured a pious ecclesiastic, that two years of trial must precede the season of deliverance and grace; the deserters were stopped by the presence and reproaches of Christ himself; the dead had promised to arise and combat with their brethren; the Virgin had obtained the pardon of their sins; and their confidence was revived by a visible sign, the seasonable and splendid discovery of the HOLY LANCE. The policy of their chiefs has on this occasion been admired, and might surely be excused; but a pious fraud is seldom produced by the cool conspiracy of many persons; and a voluntary impostor might depend on the support of the wise and the credulity of the people. Of the diocese of Marseilles, there was a priest of low cunning and loose manners, and his name was Peter Bartholemy. He presented himself at the door of the council-chamber, to disclose an apparition of St. Andrew, which had been thrice reiterated in his sleep, with a dreadful menace, if he presumed to suppress the commands of heaven. "At Antioch," said the apostle, "in the church of my brother St. Peter, near the high altar, is concealed the steel head of the lance that pierced the

98. See the progress of the crusade, the retreat of Alexius, the victory of Antioch, and the conquest of Jerusalem, in the Alexiad, l. xi. p. 317–327. Anna was so prone to exaggeration, that she magnifies the exploits of the Latins.

side of our Redeemer. In three days, that instrument of eternal, and now of temporal, salvation, will be manifested to his disciples. Search and ye shall find: bear it aloft in battle; and that mystic weapon shall penetrate the souls of the miscreants." The pope's legate, the bishop of Puy, affected to listen with coldness and distrust; but the revelation was eagerly accepted by count Raymond, whom his faithful subject, in the name of the apostle, had chosen for the guardian of the holy lance. The experiment was resolved; and on the third day, after a due preparation of prayer and fasting, the priest of Marseilles introduced twelve trusty spectators, among whom were the count and his chaplain; and the church-doors were barred against the impetuous multitude. The ground was opened in the appointed place; but the workmen, who relieved each other, dug to the depth of twelve feet without discovering the object of their search. In the evening, when count Raymond had withdrawn to his post, and the weary assistants began to murmur, Bartholemy, in his shirt, and without his shoes, boldly descended into the pit; the darkness of the hour and of the place enabled him to secrete and deposit the head of a Saracen lance; and the first sound, the first gleam, of the steel, was saluted with a devout rapture. The holy lance was drawn from its recess, wrapt in a veil of silk and gold, and exposed to the veneration of the crusaders; their anxious suspense burst forth in a general shout of joy and hope, and the desponding troops were again inflamed with the enthusiasm of valour. Whatever had been the arts, and whatever might be the sentiments of the chiefs, they skilfully improved this fortunate revolution by every aid that discipline and devotion could afford. The soldiers were dismissed to their quarters with an injunction to fortify their minds and bodies for the approaching conflict, freely to bestow their last pittance on themselves and their horses, and to expect with the dawn of day the signal of victory. On the festival of St. Peter and St. Paul, the gates of Antioch were thrown open; a martial psalm, "Let the Lord arise, and let his enemies be scattered!" was chaunted by a procession of priests and monks; the battle array was marshalled in twelve divisions, in honour of the twelve apostles; and the holy lance, in the absence of Raymond, was entrusted to the hands of his chaplain. The influence of this relic or trophy was felt by the servants, and perhaps by the enemies, of Christ;[99] and its potent energy was heightened by an accident, a stratagem, or a rumour, of a miraculous

99. The Mahometan Aboulmahasen (apud de Guignes, tom. ii. p. ii. p. 95.) is more correct in his account of the holy lance than the Christians, Anna Comnena and Abulpharagius: the Greek princess confounds it with a nail of the cross (l. xi. p. 326.); the Jacobite primate, with St. Peter's staff (p. 242.).

Celestial warriors. complexion. Three knights, in white garments and resplendent arms, either issued, or seemed to issue, from the hills: the voice of Adhemar, the pope's legate, proclaimed them as the martyrs St. George, St. Theodore, and St. Maurice; the tumult of battle allowed no time for doubt or scrutiny; and the welcome apparition dazzled the eyes or the imagination of a fanatic army. In the season of danger and triumph, the revelation of Bartholemy of Marseilles was unanimously asserted; but as soon as the temporary service was accomplished, the personal dignity and liberal alms which the count of Tholouse derived from the custody of the holy lance, provoked the envy, and awakened the reason, of his rivals. A Norman clerk presumed to sift, with a philosophic spirit, the truth of the legend, the circumstances of the discovery, and the character of the prophet; and the pious Bohemond ascribed their deliverance to the merits and intercession of Christ alone. For a while, the Provincials defended their national palladium with clamours and arms; and new visions condemned to death and hell the profane sceptics, who presumed to scrutinise the truth and merit of the discovery. The prevalence of incredulity compelled the author to submit his life and veracity to the judgment of God. A pile of dry faggots, four feet high, and fourteen long, was erected in the midst of the camp; the flames burnt fiercely to the elevation of thirty cubits; and a narrow path of twelve inches was left for the perilous trial. The unfortunate priest of Marseilles traversed the fire with dexterity and speed; but his thighs and belly were scorched by the intense heat; he expired the next day; and the logic of believing minds will pay some regard to his dying protestations of innocence and truth. Some efforts were made by the Provincials to substitute a cross, a ring, or a tabernacle, in the place of the holy lance, which soon vanished in contempt and oblivion.[100] Yet the revelation of Antioch is gravely asserted by succeeding historians; and such is the progress of credulity, that miracles, most doubtful on the spot and at the moment, will be received with implicit faith at a convenient distance of time and space.

The state of the Turks and caliphs of Egypt. The prudence or fortune of the Franks had delayed their invasion till the decline of the Turkish empire.[101] Under the manly government of the three first sultans, the kingdoms

100. The two antagonists who express the most intimate knowledge and the strongest conviction of the *miracle*, and of the *fraud*, are Raymond des Agiles, and Radulphus Cadomensis, the one attached to the count of Thoulouse, the other to the Norman prince. Fulcherius Carnotensis presumes to say, audite fraudem et non fraudem! and afterwards, invenit lanceam, fallaciter occultatam forsitan. The rest of the herd are loud and strenuous.

101. See M. de Guignes (tom. ii. p. ii. p.

of Asia were united in peace and justice; and the innumerable armies which they led in person were equal in courage, and superior in discipline, to the Barbarians of the West. But at the time of the crusade, the inheritance of Malek Shaw was disputed by his four sons; their private ambition was insensible of the public danger; and, in the vicissitudes of their fortune, the royal vassals were ignorant, or regardless, of the true object of their allegiance. The twenty-eight emirs, who marched with the standard of Kerboga, were his rivals or enemies; their hasty levies were drawn from the towns and tents of Mesopotamia and Syria; and the Turkish veterans were employed or consumed in the civil wars beyond the Tigris. The caliph of Egypt embraced this opportunity of weakness and discord, to recover his ancient possessions; and his sultan Aphdal besieged Jerusalem and Tyre, expelled the children of Ortok, and restored in Palestine the civil and ecclesiastical authority of the Fatimites.[102] They heard with astonishment of the vast armies of Christians that had passed from Europe to Asia, and rejoiced in the sieges and battles which broke the power of the Turks, the adversaries of their sect and monarchy. But the same Christians were the enemies of the prophet; and from the overthrow of Nice and Antioch, the motive of their enterprise, which was gradually understood, would urge them forwards to the banks of the Jordan, or perhaps of the Nile. An intercourse of epistles and embassies, which rose and fell with the events of war, was maintained between the throne of Cairo and the camp of the Latins; and their adverse pride was the result of ignorance and enthusiasm. The ministers of Egypt declared in an haughty, or insinuated in a milder, tone, that their sovereign, the true and lawful commander of the faithful, had rescued Jerusalem from the Turkish yoke; and that the pilgrims, if they would divide their numbers, and lay aside their arms, should find a safe and hospitable reception at the sepulchre of Jesus. In the belief of their lost condition, the caliph Mostali despised their arms and imprisoned their deputies: the conquest and victory of Antioch prompted him to solicit those formidable champions with gifts of horses and silk robes, of vases, and purses of gold and silver; and in his estimate of their merit or power, the first place was assigned to Bohemond, and the second to Godfrey. In either fortune, the

223, &c.); and the articles of *Barkiarok*, *Mohammed*, *Sangiar*, in d'Herbelot.

102. The emir, or sultan Aphdal, recovered Jerusalem and Tyre, A.H. 489 (Renaudot, Hist. Patriarch. Alexandrin. p. 478. de Guignes, tom. i. p. 249. from Abulfeda and Ben Schounah). Jerusalem ante adventum vestrum recuperavimus, Turcos ejecimus, say the Fatimite ambassadors.

answer of the crusaders was firm and uniform: they disdained to enquire into the private claims or possessions of the followers of Mahomet: whatsoever was his name or nation, the usurper of Jerusalem was their enemy; and instead of prescribing the mode and terms of their pilgrimage, it was only by a timely surrender of the city and province, their sacred right, that he could deserve their alliance, or deprecate their impending and irresistible attack.[103]

Delay of the Franks, A.D. 1098, July–A.D. 1099, May.

Yet this attack, when they were within the view and reach of their glorious prize, was suspended above ten months after the defeat of Kerboga. The zeal and courage of the crusaders were chilled in the moment of victory: and instead of marching to improve the consternation, they hastily dispersed to enjoy the luxury, of Syria. The causes of this strange delay may be found in the want of strength and subordination. In the painful and various service of Antioch, the cavalry was annihilated; many thousands of every rank had been lost by famine, sickness, and desertion: the same abuse of plenty had been productive of a third famine; and the alternative of intemperance and distress, had generated a pestilence, which swept away above fifty thousand of the pilgrims. Few were able to command, and none were willing to obey: the domestic feuds, which had been stifled by common fear, were again renewed in acts, or at least in sentiments, of hostility; the fortune of Baldwin and Bohemond excited the envy of their companions; the bravest knights were enlisted for the defence of their new principalities; and count Raymond exhausted his troops and treasures in an idle expedition into the heart of Syria. The winter was consumed in discord and disorder; a sense of honour and religion was rekindled in the spring; and the private soldiers, less susceptible of ambition and jealousy, awakened with angry clamours the indolence of their chiefs. In the month of May, the relics of this mighty host proceeded from Antioch to Laodicea; about forty thousand Latins, of whom no more than fifteen hundred horse, and twenty thousand foot, were capable of immediate service. Their easy march was continued between mount Libanus and the sea-shore; their wants were liberally supplied by the coasting traders of Genoa and Pisa; and they drew large contributions from the emirs of Tripoli, Tyre, Sidon, Acre, and Cæsarea, who granted a free passage, and promised to follow

Their march to Jerusalem, A.D. 1099, May 13–June 6.

103. See the transactions between the caliph of Egypt and the crusaders, in William of Tyre (l. iv. c. 24. l. vi. c. 19.) and Albert Aquensis (l. iii. c. 59.), who are more sensible of their importance, than the contemporary writers.

the example of Jerusalem. From Cæsarea they advanced into the midland country; their clerks recognised the sacred geography of Lydda, Ramla, Emaus, and Bethlem, and as soon as they descried the holy city, the crusaders forgot their toils and claimed their reward.[104]

Siege and conquest of Jerusalem, A.D. 1099, June 7–July 15.

Jerusalem has derived some reputation from the number and importance of her memorable sieges. It was not till after a long and obstinate contest that Babylon and Rome could prevail against the obstinacy of the people, the craggy ground that might supersede the necessity of fortifications, and the walls and towers that would have fortified the most accessible plain.[105] These obstacles were diminished in the age of the crusades. The bulwarks had been completely destroyed and imperfectly restored: the Jews, their nation and worship, were for ever banished; but nature is less changeable than man, and the site of Jerusalem, though somewhat softened and somewhat removed, was still strong against the assaults of an enemy. By the experience of a recent siege and a three years possession, the Saracens of Egypt had been taught to discern, and in some degree to remedy, the defects of a place, which religion as well as honour forbade them to resign. Aladin or Iftikhar, the caliph's lieutenant, was entrusted with the defence: his policy strove to restrain the native Christians by the dread of their own ruin and that of the holy sepulchre; to animate the Moslems by the assurance of temporal and eternal rewards. His garrison is said to have consisted of forty thousand Turks and Arabians; and if he could muster twenty thousand of the inhabitants, it must be confessed that the besieged were more numerous than the besieging army.[106] Had the diminished strength and numbers of the Latins allowed them to grasp the whole circumference of four thousand yards (about two English miles and an half[107]), to what useful purpose should they have descended into

104. The greatest part of the march of the Franks is traced, and most accurately traced, in Maundrell's Journey from Aleppo to Jerusalem (p. 11–67.), un des meilleurs morceaux, sans contredit, qu'on ait dans ce genre (d'Anville, Memoire sur Jerusalem, p. 27.).

105. See the masterly description of Tacitus (Hist. v. 11, 12, 13.), who supposes, that the Jewish lawgivers had provided for a perpetual state of hostility against the rest of mankind.

106. The lively scepticism of Voltaire is balanced with sense and erudition by the French author of the Esprit des Croisades (tom. iv. p. 386–388.), who observes, that according to the Arabians, the inhabitants of Jerusalem must have exceeded 200,000; that in the siege of Titus, Josephus collects 1,300,000 Jews; that they are stated by Tacitus himself at 600,000, and that the largest defalcation, that his *accepimus* can justify, will still leave them more numerous than the Roman army.

107. Maundrell, who diligently perambulated the walls, found a circuit of 4630

the valley of Ben Himmon and torrent of Cedron,[108] or approached the precipices of the South and East, from whence they had nothing either to hope or fear? Their siege was more reasonably directed against the northern and western sides of the city. Godfrey of Bouillon erected his standard on the first swell of mount Calvary: to the left, as far as St. Stephen's gate, the line of attack was continued by Tancred and the two Roberts; and count Raymond established his quarters from the citadel to the foot of mount Sion, which was no longer included within the precincts of the city. On the fifth day, the crusaders made a general assault in the fanatic hope of battering down the walls without engines, and of scaling them without ladders. By the dint of brutal force, they burst the first barrier, but they were driven back with shame and slaughter to the camp: the influence of vision and prophecy was deadened by the too frequent abuse of those pious stratagems; and time and labour were found to be the only means of victory. The time of the siege was indeed fulfilled in forty days, but they were forty days of calamity and anguish. A repetition of the old complaint of famine may be imputed in some degree to the voracious or disorderly appetite of the Franks; but the stony soil of Jerusalem is almost destitute of water; the scanty springs and hasty torrents were dry in the summer season; nor was the thirst of the besiegers relieved, as in the city, by the artificial supply of cisterns and aqueducts. The circumjacent country is equally destitute of trees for the uses of shade or building; but some large beams were discovered in a cave by the crusaders: a wood near Sichem, the enchanted grove of Tasso,[109] was cut down: the necessary timber was transported to the camp by the vigour and dexterity of Tancred; and the engines were framed by some Genoese artists, who had fortunately landed in the harbour of Jaffa. Two moveable turrets were constructed at the expence, and in the stations, of the duke

---

paces, or 4167 English yards (p. 109, 110.): from an authentic plan, d'Anville concludes a measure nearly similar of 1960 French *toises* (p. 23–29.), in his scarce and valuable tract. For the topography of Jerusalem, see Reland (Palestina, tom. ii. p. 832–860.).

108. Jerusalem was possessed only of the torrent of Kedron, dry in summer, and of the little spring or brook of Siloe (Reland, tom. i. p. 294. 300.). Both strangers and natives complained of the want of water, which in time of war was studiously aggravated. Within the city, Tacitus mentions a perennial fountain, an aqueduct, and cisterns for rain water. The aqueduct was conveyed from the rivulet Tekoe or Etham, which is likewise mentioned by Bohadin (in Vit. Saladin. p. 238.).

109. Gierusalemme Liberata, canto xiii. It is pleasant enough to observe how Tasso has copied and embellished the minutest details of the siege.

of Lorraine and the count of Tholouse, and rolled forwards with devout labour, not to the most accessible, but to the most neglected, parts of the fortification. Raymond's tower was reduced to ashes by the fire of the besieged, but his colleague was more vigilant and successful; the enemies were driven by his archers from the rampart; the draw-bridge was let down; and on a Friday at three in the afternoon, the day and hour of the Passion, Godfrey of Bouillon stood victorious on the walls of Jerusalem. His example was followed on every side by the emulation of valour; and about four hundred and sixty years after the conquest of Omar, the holy city was rescued from the Mahometan yoke. In the pillage of public and private wealth, the adventurers had agreed to respect the exclusive property of the first occupant; and the spoils of the great mosch, seventy lamps and massy vases of gold and silver, rewarded the diligence, and displayed the generosity, of Tancred. A bloody sacrifice was offered by his mistaken votaries to the God of the Christians: resistance might provoke, but neither age nor sex could mollify, their implacable rage: they indulged themselves three days in a promiscuous massacre;[110] and the infection of the dead bodies produced an epidemical disease. After seventy thousand Moslems had been put to the sword, and the harmless Jews had been burnt in their synagogue, they could still reserve a multitude of captives, whom interest or lassitude persuaded them to spare. Of these savage heroes of the cross, Tancred alone betrayed some sentiments of compassion; yet we may praise the more selfish lenity of Raymond, who granted a capitulation and safe conduct to the garrison of the citadel.[111] The holy sepulchre was now free; and the bloody victors prepared to accomplish their vow. Bareheaded and barefoot, with contrite hearts, and in an humble posture, they ascended the hill of Calvary, amidst the loud anthems of the clergy; kissed the stone which had covered the Saviour of the world; and bedewed with tears of joy and penitence the monument of their redemption. This union of the fiercest and most tender passions has been variously considered by two philosophers; by the one,[112] as easy and natural; by the other,[113] as absurd and incredible.

110. Besides the Latins, who are not ashamed of the massacre, see Elmacin (Hist. Saracen. p. 363.), Abulpharagius (Dynast. p. 243.), and M. de Guignes (tom. ii. p. ii. p. 99.), from Aboulmahasen.

111. The old tower Psephina, in the middle ages Neblosa, was named Castellum Pisanum, from the patriarch Daimbert. It is still the citadel, the residence of the Turkish aga, and commands a prospect of the Dead Sea, Judea, and Arabia (d'Anville, p. 19–23.). It was likewise called the Tower of David, πυργος παμμεγεθεστατος.

112. Hume, in his History of England, vol. i. p. 311, 312. octavo edition.

113. Voltaire, in his Essai sur l'Histoire Generale, tom. ii. c. 54. p. 345, 346.

Perhaps it is too rigorously applied to the same persons and the same hour: the example of the virtuous Godfrey awakened the piety of his companions; while they cleansed their bodies, they purified their minds; nor shall I believe that the most ardent in slaughter and rapine were the foremost in the procession to the holy sepulchre.

Election and reign of Godfrey of Bouillon, A.D. 1099, July 23–A.D. 1100, July 18.

Eight days after this memorable event, which pope Urban did not live to hear, the Latin chiefs proceeded to the election of a king, to guard and govern their conquests in Palestine. Hugh the Great, and Stephen of Chartres, had retired with some loss of reputation, which they strove to regain by a second crusade and an honourable death. Baldwin was established at Edessa, and Bohemond at Antioch, and two Roberts, the duke of Normandy[114] and the count of Flanders, preferred their fair inheritance in the West to a doubtful competition or a barren sceptre. The jealousy and ambition of Raymond were condemned by his own followers, and the free, the just, the unanimous voice of the army, proclaimed Godfrey of Bouillon the first and most worthy of the champions of Christendom. His magnanimity accepted a trust as full of danger as of glory; but in a city where his Saviour had been crowned with thorns, the devout pilgrim rejected the name and ensigns of royalty; and the founder of the kingdom of Jerusalem contented himself with the modest title of Defender and Baron of the Holy Sepulchre. His government of a single year,[115] too short for the public happiness, was interrupted in the first fortnight by a summons to the field, by the approach of the vizir or sultan of Egypt, who had been too slow to prevent, but who was impatient to avenge, the loss of Jerusalem. His total overthrow in the

Battle of Ascalon, A.D. 1099, August 12.

battle of Ascalon sealed the establishment of the Latins in Syria, and signalized the valour of the French princes, who in this action bade a long farewel to the holy wars. Some glory might be derived from the prodigious inequality of numbers, though I shall not count the myriads of horse and foot on the side of the Fatimites; but, except three thousand Ethiopians or blacks, who were armed with flails or scourges of iron, the Barbarians of the South fled on the first

114. The English ascribe to Robert of Normandy, and the Provincials to Raymond of Tholouse, the glory of refusing the crown; but the honest voice of tradition has preserved the memory of the ambition and revenge (Villehardouin, N° 136.) of the count of St. Giles. He died at the siege of Tripoli, which was possessed by his descendants.

115. See the election, the battle of Ascalon, &c. in William of Tyre, l. ix. c. 1–12. and in the conclusion of the Latin historians of the first crusade.

onset, and afforded a pleasing comparison between the active valour of the Turks and the sloth and effeminacy of the natives of Egypt. After suspending before the holy sepulchre the sword and standard of the sultan, the new king (he deserves the title) embraced his departing companions, and could retain only with the gallant Tancred three hundred knights, and two thousand foot soldiers, for the defence of Palestine. His sovereignty was soon attacked by a new enemy, the only one against whom Godfrey was a coward. Adhemar, bishop of Puy, who excelled both in council and action, had been swept away in the last plague of Antioch: the remaining ecclesiastics preserved only the pride and avarice of their character; and their seditious clamours had required that the choice of a bishop should precede that of a king. The revenue and jurisdiction of the lawful patriarch were usurped by the Latin clergy: the exclusion of the Greeks and Syrians was justified by the reproach of heresy or schism;[116] and, under the iron yoke of their deliverers, the Oriental Christians regretted the tolerating government of the Arabian caliphs. Daimbert, archbishop of Pisa, had long been trained in the secret policy of Rome: he brought a fleet of his countrymen to the succour of the Holy Land, and was installed, without a competitor, the spiritual and temporal head of the church. The new patriarch[117] immediately grasped the sceptre which had been acquired by the toil and blood of the victorious pilgrims; and both Godfrey and Bohemond submitted to receive at his hands the investiture of their feudal possessions. Nor was this sufficient; Daimbert claimed the immediate property of Jerusalem and Jaffa: instead of a firm and generous refusal, the hero negociated with the priest; a quarter of either city was ceded to the church; and the modest bishop was satisfied with an eventual reversion of the rest, on the death of Godfrey without children, or on the future acquisition of a new seat at Cairo or Damascus.

The kingdom of Jerusalem, A.D. 1099–1187.

Without this indulgence, the conqueror would have almost been stripped of his infant kingdom, which consisted only of Jerusalem and Jaffa, with about twenty villages and towns of the adjacent country.[118] Within this narrow verge, the Mahometans

116. Renaudot, Hist. Patriarch. Alex. p. 479.

117. See the claims of the patriarch Daimbert, in William of Tyre (l. ix. c. 15–18. x. 4. 7. 9.), who asserts with marvellous candour the independence of the conquerors and kings of Jerusalem.

118. Willerm. Tyr. l. x. 19. The Historia Hierosolimita of Jacobus à Vitriaco (l. i. c. 21–50.), and the Secreta Fidelium Crucis of Marinus Sanutus (l. iii. p. i.), describe the state and conquests of the Latin kingdom of Jerusalem.

were still lodged in some impregnable castles; and the husbandman, the trader, and the pilgrim, were exposed to daily and domestic hostility. By the arms of Godfrey himself, and of the two Baldwins, his brother and cousin, who succeeded to the throne, the Latins breathed with more ease and safety; and at length they equalled, in the extent of their dominions, though not in the millions of their subjects, the ancient princes of Judah and Israel.[119] After the reduction of the maritime cities of Laodicea, Tripoli, Tyre, and Ascalon,[120] which were powerfully assisted by the fleets of Venice, Genoa, and Pisa, and even of Flanders and Norway,[121] the range of sea-coast from Scanderoon to the borders of Egypt was possessed by the Christian pilgrims. If the prince of Antioch disclaimed his supremacy, the counts of Edessa and Tripoli owned themselves the vassals of the king of Jerusalem: the Latins reigned beyond the Euphrates; and the four cities of Hems, Hamah, Damascus, and Aleppo, were the only relics of the Mahometan conquests in Syria.[122] The laws and language, the manners and titles, of the French nation and Latin church, were introduced into these transmarine colonies. According to the feudal jurisprudence, the principal states and subordinate baronies descended in the line of male and female succession;[123] but the children of the first conquerors,[124] a motley and degenerate race, were dissolved by the luxury

119. An actual muster, not including the tribes of Levi and Benjamin, gave David an army of 1,300,000, or 1,574,000 fighting men; which, with the addition of women, children, and slaves, may imply a population of thirteen millions, in a country sixty leagues in length, and thirty broad. The honest and rational Le Clerc (Comment. on 2[d] Samuel xxiv. and 1st Chronicles xxi.) æstuat angusto in limite, and mutters his suspicion of a false transcript; a dangerous suspicion!

120. These sieges are related, each in its proper place, in the great history of William of Tyre, from the ix[th] to the xviii[th] book, and more briefly told by Bernardus Thesaurarius (de Acquisitione Terræ Sanctæ, c. 89–98. p. 732–740.). Some domestic facts are celebrated in the Chronicles of Pisa, Genoa, and Venice, in the vi[th], ix[th], and xii[th] tomes of Muratori.

121. Quidam populus de insulis occidentis egressus, et maxime de eâ parte quæ Norvegia dicitur. William of Tyre (l. xi. c. 14. p. 804.) marks their course per Britannicum mare et Calpen to the siege of Sidon.

122. Benelathir, apud de Guignes, Hist. des Huns, tom. ii. part ii. p. 150, 151. A.D. 1127. He must speak of the inland country.

123. Sanut very sensibly descants on the mischiefs of female succession, in a land hostibus circumdata, ubi cuncta virilia et virtuosa esse deberent. Yet, at the summons, and with the approbation, of her feudal lord, a noble damsel was obliged to chuse a husband and champion (Assises de Jerusalem, c. 242, &c.). See in M. de Guignes (tom. i. p. 441–471.) the accurate and useful tables of these dynasties, which are chiefly drawn from the *Lignages d'Outremer*.

124. They were called by derision *Poullains, Pullani*, and their name is never pronounced without contempt (Ducange, Gloss. Latin. tom. v. p. 535. and Observations sur Joinville, p. 84, 85. Jacob à Vitriaco, Hist. Hierosol. l. i. c. 67. 72. and Sanut, l. iii. p. viii. c. 2. p. 182.). Illustrium

of the climate; the arrival of new crusaders from Europe, was a doubtful hope and a casual event. The service of the feudal tenures[125] was performed by six hundred and sixty-six knights, who might expect the aid of two hundred more under the banner of the count of Tripoli; and each knight was attended to the field by four squires or archers on horseback.[126] Five thousand and seventy-five *serjeants*, most probably foot-soldiers, were supplied by the churches and cities; and the whole legal militia of the kingdom could not exceed eleven thousand men, a slender defence against the surrounding myriads of Saracens and Turks.[127] But the firmest bulwark of Jerusalem was founded on the knights of the hospital of St. John,[128] and of the temple of Solomon;[129] on the strange association of a monastic and military life, which fanaticism might suggest, but which policy must approve. The flower of the nobility of Europe aspired to wear the cross, and to profess the vows, of these respectable orders; their spirit and discipline were immortal; and the speedy donation of twenty-eight thousand farms, or manors,[130] enabled them to support a regular force of cavalry and infantry for the defence of Palestine. The austerity of the convent soon evaporated in the exercise of arms: the world was scandalised by the pride, avarice, and corruption of these Christian soldiers; their claims of immunity and jurisdiction disturbed the harmony of the church and state; and the public peace was endangered by their

---

virorum qui ad Terræ Sanctæ ... liberationem in ipsâ manserunt degeneres filii ... in deliciis enutriti, molles et effæminati, &c.

125. This authentic detail is extracted from the Assises de Jerusalem (c. 324. 326–331.). Sanut (l. iii. p. viii. c. 1. p. 174.) reckons only 518 knights, and 5775 followers.

126. The sum total, and the division, ascertain the service of the three great baronies at 100 knights each; and the text of the Assises, which extends the number to 500, can only be justified by this supposition.

127. Yet on great emergencies (says Sanut) the barons brought a voluntary aid, decentem comitivam militum juxta statum suum.

128. William of Tyre (l. xviii. c. 3, 4, 5.) relates the ignoble origin, and early insolence, of the Hospitalers, who soon deserted their humble patron, St. John the Eleemosynary, for the more august character of St. John the Baptist (see the ineffectual struggles of Pagi, Critica, A.D. 1099, N° 14–18.). They assumed the profession of arms about the year 1120; the Hospital was *mater*, the Temple, *filia*; the Teutonic order was founded A.D. 1190, at the siege of Acre (Mosheim, Institut. p. 389, 390.).

129. See St. Bernard de Laude Novæ Militiæ Templi, composed A.D. 1132–1136, in Opp. tom. i. p. ii. p. 547–563. edit. Mabillon, Venet. 1750. Such an encomium, which is thrown away on the dead Templars, would be highly valued by the historians of Malta.

130. Matthew Paris, Hist. Major, p. 544. He assigns to the Hospitalers 19,000, to the Templars 9,000 *maneria*, a word of much higher import (as Ducange has rightly observed) in the English than in the French idiom. *Manor* is a lordship, *manoir* a dwelling.

jealous emulation. But in their most dissolute period, the knights of the hospital and temple maintained their fearless and fanatic character: they neglected to live, but they were prepared to die, in the service of Christ; and the spirit of chivalry, the parent and offspring of the crusades, has been transplanted by this institution from the holy sepulchre to the isle of Malta.[131]

Assise of Jerusalem, A.D. 1099–1369.

The spirit of freedom, which pervades the feudal institutions, was felt in its strongest energy by the volunteers of the cross, who elected for their chief the most deserving of his peers. Amidst the slaves of Asia, unconscious of the lesson or example, a model of political liberty was introduced: and the laws of the French kingdom are derived from the purest source of equality and justice. Of such laws, the first and indispensable condition is the assent of those, whose obedience they require, and for whose benefit they are designed. No sooner had Godfrey of Bouillon accepted the office of supreme magistrate, than he solicited the public and private advice of the Latin pilgrims, who were the best skilled in the statutes and customs of Europe. From these materials, with the counsel and approbation of the patriarch and barons, of the clergy and laity, Godfrey composed the ASSISE OF JERUSALEM,[132] a precious monument of feudal jurisprudence. The new code, attested by the seals of the king, the patriarch, and the viscount of Jerusalem, was deposited in the holy sepulchre, enriched with the improvements of succeeding times, and respectfully consulted as often as any doubtful question arose in the tribunals of Palestine. With the kingdom and city, all was lost:[133] the fragments of the written law were preserved by jealous tradition[134] and variable practice till the middle of

131. In the three first books of the Histoire des Chevaliers de Malthe, par l'Abbé de Vertot, the reader may amuse himself with a fair, and sometimes flattering, picture of the order, while it was employed for the defence of Palestine. The subsequent books pursue their emigrations to Rhodes and Malta.

132. The Assises de Jerusalem, in old law French, were printed with Beaumanoir's Coutumes de Beauvoisis (Bourges and Paris, 1690, in folio), and illustrated by Gaspard Thaumas de la Thaumassiere, with a comment and glossary. An Italian version had been published in 1535, at Venice, for the use of the kingdom of Cyprus.

133. A la terre perdue, tout fut perdû, is the vigorous expression of the Assise (c. 281.). Yet Jerusalem capitulated with Saladin; the queen and the principal Christians departed in peace; and a code so precious and so portable could not provoke the avarice of the conquerors. I have sometimes suspected the existence of this original copy of the Holy Sepulchre, which might be invented to sanctify and authenticate the traditionary customs of the French in Palestine.

134. A noble lawyer, Raoul de Tabarie, denied the prayer of king Amauri (A.D. 1195–1205), that he would commit his knowledge to writing, and frankly

the thirteenth century: the code was restored by the pen of John d'Ibelin, count of Jaffa, one of the principal feudatories;[135] and the final revision was accomplished in the year thirteen hundred and sixty-nine, for the use of the Latin kingdom of Cyprus.[136]

Court of peers.

The justice and freedom of the constitution were maintained by two tribunals of unequal dignity, which were instituted by Godfrey of Bouillon after the conquest of Jerusalem. The king, in person, presided in the upper-court, the court of the barons. Of these the four most conspicuous were the prince of Galilee, the lord of Sidon and Cæsarea, and the counts of Jaffa and Tripoli, who, perhaps with the constable and marshal,[137] were in a special manner the compeers and judges of each other. But all the nobles, who held their lands immediately of the crown, were entitled and bound to attend the king's court; and each baron exercised a similar jurisdiction in the subordinate assemblies of his own feudatories. The connection of lord and vassal was honourable and voluntary: reverence was due to the benefactor, protection to the dependent; but they mutually pledged their faith to each other; and the obligation on either side might be suspended by neglect or dissolved by injury. The cognizance of marriages and testaments was blended with religion, and usurped by the clergy; but the civil and criminal causes of the nobles, the inheritance and tenure of their fiefs, formed the proper occupation of the supreme court. Each member was the judge and guardian both of public and private rights. It was his duty to assert with his tongue and sword the lawful claims of the lord; but if an unjust superior presumed to violate the freedom or property of a vassal, the confederate peers stood forth to maintain his quarrel by word and deed. They boldly affirmed his innocence and his wrongs; demanded the restitution of his liberty or his lands; suspended, after a fruitless demand,

---

declared, que de ce qu'il savoit, ne feroit-il ja nul borjois son pareill, ne nul sage homme lettré (c. 281.).

135. The compiler of this work, Jean d'Ibelin, was count of Jaffa and Ascalon, lord of Baruth (Berytus) and Rames, and died A.D. 1266 (Sanut, l. iii. p. ii. c. 5. 8.). The family of Ibelin, which descended from a younger brother of a count of Chartres in France, long flourished in Palestine and Cyprus (see the Lignages de deça Mer, or d'Outremer, c. 6. at the end of the Assises de Jerusalem, an original book, which records the pedigrees of the French adventurers).

136. By sixteen commissioners chosen in the states of the island: the work was finished the 3[d] of November 1369, sealed with four seals, and deposited in the cathedral of Nicosia (see the preface to the Assises).

137. The cautious John d'Ibelin argues, rather than affirms, that Tripoli is the fourth barony, and expresses some doubt concerning the right or pretension of the constable and marshal (c.323.).

their own service; rescued their brother from prison; and employed every weapon in his defence, without offering direct violence to the person of their lord, which was ever sacred in their eyes.[138] In their pleadings, replies, and rejoinders, the advocates of the court were subtle and copious; but the use of argument and evidence was often superseded by judicial combat; and the Assise of Jerusalem admits in many cases this barbarous institution, which has been slowly abolished by the laws and manners of Europe.

Law of judicial combats.

The trial by battle was established in all criminal cases, which affected the life, or limb, or honour, of any person; and in all civil transactions, of or above the value of one mark of silver. It appears, that in criminal cases the combat was the privilege of the accuser, who, except in a charge of treason, avenged his personal injury, or the death of those persons whom he had a right to represent; but wherever, from the nature of the charge, testimony could be obtained, it was necessary for him to produce witnesses of the fact. In civil cases, the combat was not allowed as the means of establishing the claim of the demandant; but he was obliged to produce witnesses who had, or assumed to have, knowledge of the fact. The combat was then the privilege of the defendant; because he charged the witness with an attempt by perjury to take away his right. He came therefore to be in the same situation as the appellant in criminal cases. It was not then as a mode of proof that the combat was received, nor as making negative evidence (according to the supposition of Montesquieu[139]); but in every case the right to offer battle was founded on the right to pursue by arms the redress of any injury; and the judicial combat was fought on the same principle, and with the same spirit, as a private duel. Champions were only allowed to women, and to men maimed or past the age of sixty. The consequence of a defeat was death to the person accused, or to the champion or witness, as well as to the accuser himself; but in civil cases, the demandant was punished with infamy and the loss of his suit, while his witness and champion suffered an ignominious death. In many cases it was in the option of the judge to award or to refuse the combat: but two are specified, in which

138. Entre seignor et homme ne n'a que la foi; ... mais tant que l'homme doit à son seignor reverence en toutes choses (c.206.). Tous les hommes dudit royaume sont par ladite Assise tenus les uns as autres ... et en celle maniere que le seignor mette main ou facè mettre au cors ou au fié d'aucun d'yaus sans esgard et sans connoissance de court, que tous les autres doivent venir devant le seignor, &c. (212.). The form of their remonstrances is conceived with the noble simplicity of freedom.

139. See l'Esprit des Loix, l. xxviii. In the forty years since its publication, no work has been more read and criticised; and the spirit of enquiry which it has excited, is not the least of our obligations to the author.

it was the inevitable result of the challenge; if a faithful vassal gave the lie to his compeer, who unjustly claimed any portion of their lord's demesnes; or if an unsuccessful suitor presumed to impeach the judgment and veracity of the court. He might impeach them, but the terms were severe and perilous: in the same day he successively fought *all* the members of the tribunal, even those who had been absent: a single defeat was followed by death and infamy; and where none could hope for victory, it is highly probable that none would adventure the trial. In the Assise of Jerusalem, the legal subtlety of the count of Jaffa is more laudably employed to elude, than to facilitate, the judicial combat, which he derives from a principle of honour rather than of superstition.[140]

Court of burgesses.

Among the causes which enfranchised the plebeians from the yoke of feudal tyranny, the institution of cities and corporations is one of the most powerful; and if those of Palestine are coeval with the first crusade, they may be ranked with the most ancient of the Latin world. Many of the pilgrims had escaped from their lords under the banner of the cross; and it was the policy of the French princes to tempt their stay by the assurance of the rights and privileges of freemen. It is expressly declared in the Assize of Jerusalem, that after instituting, for his knights and barons, the court of peers, in which he presided himself, Godfrey of Bouillon established a second tribunal, in which his person was represented by his viscount. The jurisdiction of this inferior court extended over the burgesses of the kingdom; and it was composed of a select number of the most discreet and worthy citizens, who were sworn to judge, according to the laws, of the actions and fortunes of their equals.[141] In the conquest and settlement of new cities, the example of Jerusalem was imitated by the kings and their great vassals; and above thirty similar corporations were founded before the loss of the Holy Land. Another class of subjects, the Syrians,[142] or Oriental *Syrians.*

140. For the intelligence of this obscure and obsolete jurisprudence (c. 80–111.), I am deeply indebted to the friendship of a learned lord, who, with an accurate and discerning eye, has surveyed the philosophic history of law. By his studies, posterity might be enriched: the merit of the orator and the judge can be *felt* only by his contemporaries.

141. Louis le Gros, who is considered as the father of this institution in France, did not begin his reign till nine years (A.D. 1108) after Godfrey of Bouillon (Assises, c. 2. 324.). For its origin and effects, see the judicious remarks of Dr. Robertson (History of Charles V. vol. i. p. 30–36. 251–265. quarto edition).

142. Every reader conversant with the historians of the crusades, will understand by the peuple des Suriens, the Oriental Christians, Melchites, Jacobites, or Nestorians, who had all adopted the use of the Arabic language (vol. iv. p. 593.).

Christians, were oppressed by the zeal of the clergy, and protected by the toleration of the state. Godfrey listened to their reasonable prayer, that they might be judged by their own national laws. A third court was instituted for their use, of limited and domestic jurisdiction: the sworn members were Syrians, in blood, language, and religion; but the office of the president (in Arabic, of the *rais*) was sometimes exercised by the viscount of the city. At an immeasurable distance below the *nobles*, the *burgesses*, and the *strangers*, the Assise of Jerusalem condescends to mention

Villains and slaves. the *villains* and *slaves*, the peasants of the land and the captives of war, who were almost equally considered as the objects of property. The relief or protection of these unhappy men was not esteemed worthy of the care of the legislator; but he diligently provides for the recovery, though not indeed for the punishment, of the fugitives. Like hounds, or hawks, who had strayed from the lawful owner, they might be lost and claimed: the slave and falcon were of the same value; but three slaves, or twelve oxen, were accumulated to equal the price of the war-horse; and a sum of three hundred pieces of gold was fixed, in the age of chivalry, as the equivalent of the more noble animal.[143]

143. See the Assises de Jerusalem (310, 311, 312.). These laws were enacted as late as the year 1350, in the kingdom of Cyprus. In the same century, in the reign of Edward I. I understand, from a late publication (of his Book of Account), that the price of a war-horse was not less exorbitant in England.

CHAPTER LIX

Preservation of the Greek Empire. – Numbers, Passage, and Event, of the Second and Third Crusades. – St. Bernard. – Reign of Saladin in Egypt and Syria. – His Conquest of Jerusalem. – Naval Crusades. – Richard the First of England. – Pope Innocent the Third; and the Fourth and Fifth Crusades. – The Emperor Frederic the Second. – Louis the Ninth of France; and the two last Crusades. – Expulsion of the Latins or Franks by the Mamalukes.

Success of Alexius, A.D. 1097–1118.

In a style less grave than that of history, I should perhaps compare the emperor Alexius[1] to the jackall, who is said to follow the steps, and to devour the leavings, of the lion. Whatever had been his fears and toils in the passage of the first crusade, they were amply recompensed by the subsequent benefits which he derived from the exploits of the Franks. His dexterity and vigilance secured their first conquest of Nice; and from this threatening station the Turks were compelled to evacuate the neighbourhood of Constantinople. While the crusaders, with blind valour, advanced into the midland countries of Asia, the crafty Greek improved the favourable occasion when the emirs of the sea-coast were recalled to the standard of the sultan. The Turks were driven from the isles of Rhodes and Chios: the cities of Ephesus and Smyrna, of Sardes, Philadelphia, and Laodicea, were restored to the empire, which Alexius enlarged from the Hellespont to the banks of the Mæander, and the rocky shores of Pamphylia. The churches resumed their splendour; the towns were rebuilt and fortified; and the desert country was peopled with colonies of Christians, who were gently removed from the more distant and dangerous frontier. In these paternal cares, we may forgive Alexius, if he forgot the deliverance of the holy sepulchre; but, by the Latins, he was stigmatized with the foul reproach of treason and desertion. They had sworn fidelity and obedience to his throne; but *he* had promised to assist their enterprise in person, or, at

1. Anna Comnena relates her father's conquests in Asia Minor, Alexiad, l. xi. p. 321–325. l. xiv. p. 419.; his Cilician war against Tancred and Bohemond, p. 328–342; the war of Epirus, with tedious prolixity, l. xii, xiii. p. 345–406; the death of Bohemond, l. xiv. p. 419.

least, with his troops and treasures: his base retreat dissolved their obligations; and the sword, which had been the instrument of their victory, was the pledge and title of their just independence. It does not appear that the emperor attempted to revive his obsolete claims over the kingdom of Jerusalem;[2] but the borders of Cilicia and Syria were more recent in his possession, and more accessible to his arms. The great army of the crusaders was annihilated or dispersed; the principality of Antioch was left without a head, by the surprise and captivity of Bohemond: his ransom had oppressed him with a heavy debt; and his Norman followers were insufficient to repel the hostilities of the Greeks and Turks. In this distress, Bohemond embraced a magnanimous resolution, of leaving the defence of Antioch to his kinsman, the faithful Tancred; of arming the West against the Byzantine empire, and of executing the design which he inherited from the lessons and example of his father Guiscard. His embarkation was clandestine: and if we may credit a tale of the princess Anne, he passed the hostile sea, closely secreted in a coffin.[3] But his reception in France was dignified by the public applause, and his marriage with the king's daughter: his return was glorious, since the bravest spirits of the age enlisted under his veteran command; and he repassed the Adriatic at the head of five thousand horse and forty thousand foot, assembled from the most remote climates of Europe.[4] The strength of Durazzo, and prudence of Alexius, the progress of famine, and approach of Winter, eluded his ambitious hopes; and the venal confederates were seduced from his standard. A treaty of peace[5] suspended the fears of the Greeks; and they were finally delivered by the death of an adversary, whom neither oaths could bind, nor dangers could appal, nor prosperity could satiate. His children succeeded to the principality of Antioch; but the boundaries were strictly defined, the homage was clearly stipulated, and the cities of Tarsus and Malmistra were restored to the Byzantine emperors. Of the coast of Anatolia, they possessed the entire circuit from

2. The kings of Jerusalem submitted however to a nominal dependence, and in the dates of their inscriptions (one is still legible in the church of Bethlem), they respectfully placed before their own, the name of the reigning emperor (Ducange, Dissertations sur Joinville, xxvii. p. 319.).

3. Anna Comnena adds, that to complete the imitation, he was shut up with a dead cock; and condescends to wonder how the Barbarian could endure the confinement and putrefaction. This absurd tale is unknown to the Latins.

4. *Απο Θυλης*, in the Byzantine Geography, must mean England; yet we are more credibly informed, that our Henry I. would not suffer him to levy any troops in his kingdom (Ducange, Not. ad Alexiad, p. 41.).

5. The copy of the treaty (Alexiad, l. xiii. p. 406–416.) is an original and curious piece, which would require, and might afford, a good map of the principality of Antioch.

Trebizond to the Syrian gates. The Seljukian dynasty of Roum[6] was separated on all sides from the sea and their Musulman brethren; the power of the sultans was shaken by the victories, and even the defeats of the Franks; and after the loss of Nice, they removed their throne to Cogni or Iconium, an obscure and inland town above three hundred miles from Constantinople.[7] Instead of trembling for their capital, the Comnenian princes waged an offensive war against the Turks, and the first crusade prevented the fall of the declining empire.

Expeditions by land: the first crusade, A.D. 1101. the second, of Conrad III. and Louis VII. A.D. 1147. the third, of Frederic I. A.D. 1189.

In the twelfth century, three great emigrations marched by land from the West to the relief of Palestine. The soldiers and pilgrims of Lombardy, France, and Germany, were excited by the example and success of the first crusade.[8] Forty-eight years after the deliverance of the holy sepulchre, the emperor, and the French king, Conrad the third, and Louis the seventh, undertook the second crusade to support the falling fortunes of the Latins.[9] A grand division of the third crusade was led by the emperor Frederic Barbarossa,[10] who sympathised with his brothers of France and England in the common loss of Jerusalem. These three expeditions may be compared in their resemblance of the greatness of numbers, their passage through the Greek empire, and the nature and event of their Turkish warfare, and a brief parallel may save the repetition of a tedious narrative. However splendid it may seem,

6. See in the learned work of M. de Guignes (tom. ii. part ii.), the history of the Seljukians of Iconium, Aleppo, and Damascus, as far as it may be collected from the Greeks, Latins, and Arabians. The last are ignorant or regardless of the affairs of *Roum*.

7. Iconium is mentioned as a station by Xenophon, and by Strabo, with the ambiguous title of Κωμοπολις (Cellarius, tom. ii. p. 121.). Yet St. Paul found in that place a multitude (πληθος) of Jews and Gentiles. Under the corrupt name of *Kunijah*, it is described as a great city, with a river and gardens, three leagues from the mountains, and decorated (I know not why) with Plato's tomb (Abulfeda, tabul. xvii. p. 303. vers. Reiske; and the Index Geographicus of Schultens from Ibn Said).

8. For this supplement to the first crusade, see Anna Comnena (Alexias, l. xi. p. 331, &c. and the viii[th] book of Albert Aquensis).

9. For the second crusade of Conrad III. and Lewis VII. see William of Tyre (l. xvi. c. 18–29.), Otho of Frisingen (l. i. c. 34–45. 59, 60.), Matthew Paris (Hist. Major. p. 68.), Struvius (Corpus, Hist. Germanicæ, p. 372, 373.), Scriptores Rerum Francicarum à Duchesne, tom. iv. Nicetas, in Vit. Manuel, l. i. c. 4, 5, 6. p. 41–48. Cinnamus, l. ii. p. 41–49.

10. For the third crusade, of Frederic Barbarossa, see Nicetas in Isaac. Angel. l. ii. c. 3–8. p. 257–266. Struv. (Corpus, Hist. Germ. p. 414.), and two historians, who probably were spectators, Tagino (in Scriptor. Freher. tom. i. p. 406–416. edit. Struv.), and the Anonymus de Expeditione Asiaticâ, Fred. I. (in Canisii, Antiq. Lection. tom. iii. p. ii. p. 498–526. edit. Basnage).

a regular story of the crusades would exhibit the perpetual return of the same causes and effects; and the frequent attempts for the defence or recovery of the Holy Land, would appear so many faint and unsuccessful copies of the original.

Their numbers. I. Of the swarms that so closely trod in the footsteps of the first pilgrims, the chiefs were equal in rank, though unequal in fame and merit, to Godfrey of Bouillon and his fellow adventurers. At their head were displayed the banners of the dukes of Burgundy, Bavaria, and Aquitain: the first a descendant of Hugh Capet, the second a father of the Brunswick line: the archbishop of Milan, a temporal prince, transported, for the benefit of the Turks, the treasures and ornaments of his church and palace; and the veteran crusaders, Hugh the Great, and Stephen of Chartres, returned to consummate their unfinished vow. The huge and disorderly bodies of their followers moved forwards in two columns; and if the first consisted of two hundred and sixty thousand persons, the second might possibly amount to sixty thousand horse, and one hundred thousand foot.[11] The armies of the second crusade might have claimed the conquest of Asia: the nobles of France and Germany were animated by the presence of their sovereigns; and both the rank and personal characters of Conrad and Louis, gave a dignity to their cause, and a discipline to their force, which might be vainly expected from the feudatory chiefs. The cavalry of the emperor, and that of the king, was each composed of seventy thousand knights and their immediate attendants in the field;[12] and if the light-armed troops, the peasant infantry, the women and children, the priests and monks, be rigorously excluded, the full account will scarcely be satisfied with four hundred thousand souls. The West, from Rome to Britain, was called into action; the kings of Poland and Bohemia obeyed the summons of Conrad; and it is affirmed by the Greeks and Latins, that in the passage of a streight or river, the Byzantine agents, after a tale of nine hundred thousand, desisted from the endless and formidable computation.[13] In the third crusade, as the French and English preferred the navigation of the Mediterranean, the

11. Anne, who states these later swarms at 40,000 horse, and 100,000 foot, calls them Normans, and places at their head two brothers of Flanders. The Greeks were strangely ignorant of the names, families and possessions of the Latin princes.

12. William of Tyre, and Matthew Paris, reckon 70,000 loricati in each of the armies.

13. The imperfect enumeration is mentioned by Cinnamus (*εννενηκοντα μυριαδες*), and confirmed by Odo de Diogilo apud Ducange ad Cinnamum, with the more precise sum of 900,556. Why must therefore the version and comment suppose the modest and insufficient reckoning of 90,000? Does not

host of Frederic Barbarossa was less numerous. Fifteen thousand knights, and as many squires, were the flower of the German chivalry: sixty thousand horse, and one hundred thousand foot, were mustered by the emperor in the plains of Hungary; and after such repetitions we shall no longer be startled at the six hundred thousand pilgrims, which credulity has ascribed to this last emigration.[14] Such extravagant reckonings prove only the astonishment of contemporaries; but their astonishment most strongly bears testimony to the existence of an enormous though indefinite multitude. The Greeks might applaud their superior knowledge of the arts and stratagems of war, but they confessed the strength and courage of the French cavalry and the infantry of the Germans;[15] and the strangers are described as an iron race, of gigantic stature, who darted fire from their eyes, and spilt blood like water on the ground. Under the banners of Conrad, a troop of females rode in the attitude and armour of men; and the chief of these Amazons, from her gilt spurs and buskins, obtained the epithet of the Golden-footed Dame.

Passage through the Greek empire.

II. The numbers and character of the strangers was an object of terror to the effeminate Greeks, and the sentiment of fear is nearly allied to that of hatred. This aversion was suspended or softened by the apprehension of the Turkish power; and the invectives of the Latins will not biass our more candid belief, that the emperor Alexius dissembled their insolence, eluded their hostilities, counselled their rashness, and opened to their ardour the road of pilgrimage and conquest. But when the Turks had been driven from Nice and the sea-coast, when the Byzantine princes no longer dreaded the distant Sultans of Cogni, they felt with purer indignation the free and frequent passage of the western Barbarians, who violated the majesty, and endangered the safety, of the empire. The second and third crusades were undertaken under the reign of Manuel Comnenus and Isaac

---

Godfrey of Viterbo (Pantheon, p. xix. in Muratori, tom. vii. p. 462.) exclaim?

—— Numerum si poscere quæras.
Millia millena milites agmen erat.

14. This extravagant account is given by Albert of Stade (apud Struvium, p. 414.); my calculation is borrowed from Godfrey of Viterbo, Arnold of Lubeck, apud eundem, and Bernard Thesaur. (c. 169. p. 804.). The original writers are silent. The Mahometans gave him 200,000, or 260,000 men (Bohadin, in Vit. Saladin. p. 110.).

15. I must observe, that in the second and third crusades, the subjects of Conrad and Frederic are styled by the Greeks and Orientals *Alamanni*. The Lechi and Tzechi of Cinnamus, are the Poles and Bohemians; and it is for the French, that he reserves the ancient appellation of Germans. He likewise names the *Βριττοι*, or *Βριταννοι*.

Angelus. Of the former, the passions were always impetuous, and often malevolent; and the natural union of a cowardly and a mischievous temper was exemplified in the latter, who, without merit or mercy, could punish a tyrant, and occupy his throne. It was secretly, and perhaps tacitly, resolved by the prince and people to destroy, or at least to discourage, the pilgrims, by every species of injury and oppression; and their want of prudence and discipline continually afforded the pretence or the opportunity. The Western monarchs had stipulated a safe passage and fair market in the country of their Christian brethren; the treaty had been ratified by oaths and hostages; and the poorest soldier of Frederic's army was furnished with three marks of silver to defray his expences on the road. But every engagement was violated by treachery and injustice; and the complaints of the Latins are attested by the honest confession of a Greek historian, who has dared to prefer truth to his country.[16] Instead of an hospitable reception, the gates of the cities, both in Europe and Asia, were closely barred against the crusaders; and the scanty pittance of food was let down in baskets from the walls. Experience or foresight might excuse this timid jealousy; but the common duties of humanity prohibited the mixture of chalk, or other poisonous ingredients, in the bread; and should Manuel be acquitted of any foul connivance, he is guilty of coining base money for the purpose of trading with the pilgrims. In every step of their march they were stopped or misled: the governors had private orders to fortify the passes and break down the bridges against them: the stragglers were pillaged and murdered; the soldiers and horses were pierced in the woods by arrows from an invisible hand; the sick were burnt in their beds; and the dead bodies were hung on gibbets along the highways. These injuries exasperated the champions of the cross, who were not endowed with evangelical patience; and the Byzantine princes, who had provoked the unequal conflict, promoted the embarkation and march of these formidable guests. On the verge of the Turkish frontier Barbarossa spared the guilty Philadelphia,[17] rewarded the hospitable Laodicea, and deplored the hard necessity that had stained his sword with any drops of Christian blood. In their intercourse with the

16. Nicetas was a child at the second crusade, but in the third he commanded against the Franks the important post of Philippopolis. Cinnamus is infected with national prejudice and pride.

17. The conduct of the Philadelphians is blamed by Nicetas, while the anonymous German accuses the rudeness of his countrymen (culpâ nostrâ). History would be pleasant, if we were embarrassed only by *such* contradictions. It is likewise from Nicetas, that we learn the pious and humane sorrow of Frederic.

monarchs of Germany and France, the pride of the Greeks was exposed to an anxious trial. They might boast that on the first interview the seat of Louis was a low stool, beside the throne of Manuel;[18] but no sooner had the French king transported his army beyond the Bosphorus, than he refused the offer of a second conference, unless his brother would meet him on equal terms, either on the sea or land. With Conrad and Frederic, the ceremonial was still nicer and more difficult: like the successors of Constantine, they styled themselves emperors of the Romans;[19] and firmly maintained the purity of their title and dignity. The first of these representatives of Charlemagne would only converse with Manuel on horseback in the open field; the second, by passing the Hellespont rather than the Bosphorus, declined the view of Constantinople and its sovereign. An emperor, who had been crowned at Rome, was reduced in the Greek epistles to the humble appellation of *Rex*, or prince of the Alemanni; and the vain and feeble Angelus affected to be ignorant of the name of one of the greatest men and monarchs of the age. While they viewed with hatred and suspicion the Latin pilgrims, the Greek emperors maintained a strict, though secret, alliance with the Turks and Saracens. Isaac Angelus complained, that by his friendship for the great Saladin he had incurred the enmity of the Franks; and a mosch was founded at Constantinople for the public exercise of the religion of Mahomet.[20]

III. The swarms that followed the first crusade, were destroyed in Anatolia by famine, pestilence, and the Turkish arrows: and the princes only escaped with some squadrons of horse to accomplish their lamentable pilgrimage. A just opinion may be formed of their knowledge and humanity; of their knowledge from the design of subduing Persia and Chorasan in their way to Jerusalem; of their humanity from the massacre of the Christian people, a friendly city, who came out to meet them with palms and crosses in their hands. The arms of Conrad and Louis were less cruel and imprudent; but the event of the second

Turkish warfare.

18. *Χθαμαλη εδρα*, which Cinnamus translates into Latin by the word *Σελλιον*. Ducange works very hard to save his king and country from such ignominy (sur Joinville, dissertat. xxvii. p. 317–320.). Louis afterwards insisted on a meeting in mari ex æquo, not ex equo, according to the laughable readings of some MSS.

19. Ego Romanorum imperator sum, ille Romaniorum (Anonym. Canis. p. 512.). The public and historical style of the Greeks was *Ρηξ* ... *princeps*. Yet Cinnamus owns, that *Ιμπερατορ* is synonymous to *Βασιλευς*.

20. In the Epistles of Innocent III. (xiii. p. 184.), and the History of Bohadin (p. 129, 130.), see the views of a pope and a cadhi on this *singular* toleration.

crusade was still more ruinous to Christendom; and the Greek Manuel is accused by his own subjects of giving seasonable intelligence to the sultan, and treacherous guides to the Latin princes. Instead of crushing the common foe, by a double attack at the same time but on different sides, the Germans were urged by emulation, and the French were retarded by jealousy. Louis had scarcely passed the Bosphorus when he was met by the returning emperor, who had lost the greatest part of his army in glorious, but unsuccessful, action on the banks of the Mæander. The contrast of the pomp of his rival hastened the retreat of Conrad: the desertion of his independent vassals reduced him to his hereditary troops; and he borrowed some Greek vessels to execute by sea the pilgrimage of Palestine. Without studying the lessons of experience, or the nature of the war, the king of France advanced through the same country to a similar fate. The vanguard, which bore the royal banner and the oriflamme of St. Denys,[21] had doubled their march with rash and inconsiderate speed; and the rear which the king commanded in person no longer found their companions in the evening camp. In darkness and disorder they were encompassed, assaulted, and overwhelmed, by the innumerable host of Turks, who in the art of war were superior to the Christians of the twelfth century. Louis, who climbed a tree in the general discomfiture, was saved by his own valour and the ignorance of his adversaries; and with the dawn of day he escaped alive, but almost alone to the camp of the vanguard. But instead of pursuing his expedition by land, he was rejoiced to shelter the relics of his army in the friendly sea-port of Satalia. From thence he embarked for Antioch; but so penurious was the supply of Greek vessels, that they could only afford room for his knights and nobles; and the plebeian crowd of infantry was left to perish at the foot of the Pamphylian hills. The emperor and the king embraced and wept at Jerusalem; their martial trains, the remnant of mighty armies, were joined to the Christian powers of Syria, and a fruitless siege of Damascus was the final effort of the second crusade. Conrad and Louis embarked for Europe with the personal fame of piety and courage; but the Orientals had braved these potent monarchs of the Franks, with whose names and military forces they had been

21. As counts of Vexin, the kings of France were the vassals and advocates of the monastery of St. Denys. The saint's peculiar banner, which they received from the abbot, was of a square form, and a red or *flaming* colour. The *oriflamme* appeared at the head of the French armies from the xiith to the xvth century (Ducange sur Joinville, dissert. xviii. p. 244–253.).

so often threatened.[22] Perhaps they had still more to fear from the veteran genius of Frederic the first, who in his youth had served in Asia under his uncle Conrad. Forty campaigns in Germany and Italy had taught Barbarossa to command; and his soldiers, even the princes of the empire, were accustomed under his reign to obey. As soon as he lost sight of Philadelphia and Laodicea, the last cities of the Greek frontier, he plunged into the salt and barren desert, a land (says the historian) of horror and tribulation.[23] During twenty days, every step of his fainting and sickly march was besieged by the innumerable hords of Turkmans,[24] whose numbers and fury seemed after each defeat to multiply and inflame. The emperor continued to struggle and to suffer; and such was the measure of his calamities, that when he reached the gates of Iconium, no more than one thousand knights were able to serve on horseback. By a sudden and resolute assault, he defeated the guards, and stormed the capital of the sultan,[25] who humbly sued for pardon and peace. The road was now open, and Frederic advanced in a career of triumph, till he was unfortunately drowned in a petty torrent of Cilicia.[26] The remainder of his Germans was consumed by sickness and desertion; and the emperor's son expired with the greatest part of his Swabian vassals at the siege of Acre. Among the Latin heroes, Godfrey of Bouillon and Frederic Barbarossa could alone atchieve the passage of the Lesser Asia; yet even their success was a warning; and in the last and most experienced age of the crusades, every nation preferred the sea to the toils and perils of an inland expedition.[27]

22. The original French histories of the second crusade, are the Gesta Ludovici VII. published in the iv[th] volume of Duchesne's Collection. The same volume contains many original letters of the king, of Suger his minister, &c. the best documents of authentic history.

23. Terram horroris et salsuginis, terram siccam, sterilem inamænam. Anonym. Canis. p. 517. The emphatic language of a sufferer.

24. Gens innumera, sylvestris, indomita, prædones sine ductore. The sultan of Cogni might sincerely rejoice in their defeat. Anonym. Canis. p. 517, 518.

25. See in the anonymous writer in the collection of Canisius, Tagino, and Bohadin (Vit. Saladin. p. 119, 120.), the ambiguous conduct of Kilidge Arslan, sultan of Cogni, who hated and feared both Saladin and Frederic.

26. The desire of comparing two great men, has tempted many writers to drown Frederic in the river Cydnus, in which Alexander so imprudently bathed (Q. Curt. l. iii. c. 4, 5.). But from the march of the emperor, I rather judge, that his Saleph is the Calycadnus, a stream of less fame, but of a longer course.

27. Marinus Sanutus, A.D. 1321, lays it down as a precept, Quod stolus Ecclesiæ per terram nullatenus est ducenda. He resolves, by the Divine aid, the objection, or rather exception, of the first crusade (Secreta Fidelium Crucis, l. ii. pars ii. c. i. p. 37.).

Obstinacy of the enthusiasm of the crusades.

The enthusiasm of the first crusade is a natural and simple event, while hope was fresh, danger untried, and enterprise congenial to the spirit of the times. But the obstinate perseverance of Europe may indeed excite our pity and admiration; that no instruction should have been drawn from constant and adverse experience; that the same confidence should have repeatedly grown from the same failures; that six succeeding generations should have rushed headlong down the precipice that was open before them; and that men of every condition should have staked their public and private fortunes, on the desperate adventure of possessing or recovering a tomb-stone two thousand miles from their country. In a period of two centuries after the council of Clermont, each spring and summer produced a new emigration of pilgrim warriors for the defence of the Holy Land; but the seven great armaments or crusades were excited by some impending or recent calamity: the nations were moved by the authority of their pontiffs, and the example of their kings: their zeal was kindled, and their reason was silenced, by the voice of their holy orators; and among these,

Character and mission of St. Bernard, A.D. 1091–1153.

Bernard,[28] the monk, or the saint, may claim the most honourable place. About eight years before the first conquest of Jerusalem, he was born of a noble family in Burgundy; at the age of three-and-twenty, he buried himself in the monastery of Citeaux, then in the primitive fervour of the institution; at the end of two years he led forth her third colony, or daughter, to the valley of Clairvaux[29] in Champagne; and was content, till the hour of his death, with the humble station of Abbot of his own community. A philosophic age has abolished, with too liberal and indiscriminate disdain, the honours of these spiritual heroes. The meanest among them are distinguished by some energies of the mind; they were at least superior to their votaries and disciples; and, in the race of superstition, they

28. The most authentic information of St. Bernard must be drawn from his own writings, published in a correct edition by Pére Mabillon, and reprinted at Venice 1750, in six volumes in folio. Whatever friendship could recollect, or superstition could add, is contained in the two lives, by his disciples, in the vi[th] volume: whatever learning and criticism could ascertain, may be found in the prefaces of the Benedictine editor.

29. Clairvaux, surnamed the Valley of Absynth, is situate among the woods near Bar sur Aube in Champagne. St. Bernard would blush at the pomp of the church and monastery; he would ask for the library, and I know not whether he would be much edified by a tun of 800 muids ($914\frac{1}{7}$ hogsheads), which almost rivals that of Heidelberg (Melangés Tirés d'une Grande Bibliotheque, tom. xlvi. p. 15–20.).

attained the prize for which such numbers contended. In speech, in writing, in action, Bernard stood high above his rivals and contemporaries; his compositions are not devoid of wit and eloquence; and he seems to have preserved as much reason and humanity as may be reconciled with the character of a saint. In a secular life, he would have shared the seventh part of a private inheritance; by a vow of poverty and penance, by closing his eyes against the visible world,[30] by the refusal of all ecclesiastical dignities, the abbot of Clairvaux became the oracle of Europe, and the founder of one hundred and sixty convents. Princes and pontiffs trembled at the freedom of his apostolical censures: France, England, and Milan, consulted and obeyed his judgment in a schism of the church: the debt was repaid by the gratitude of Innocent the second; and his successor Eugenius the third was the friend and disciple of the holy Bernard. It was in the proclamation of the second crusade that he shone as the missionary and prophet of God, who called the nations to the defence of his holy sepulchre.[31] At the parliament of Vezelay he spoke before the king; and Louis the seventh, with his nobles, received their crosses from his hand. The abbot of Clairvaux then marched to the less easy conquest of the emperor Conrad: a phlegmatic people, ignorant of his language, was transported by the pathetic vehemence of his tone and gestures; and his progress, from Constance to Cologne, was the triumph of eloquence and zeal. Bernard applauds his own success in the depopulation of Europe; affirms that cities and castles were emptied of their inhabitants; and computes, that only one man was left behind for the consolation of seven widows.[32] The blind fanatics were desirous of electing him for their general; but the example of the hermit Peter was before his eyes; and while he assured the Crusaders of the divine favour, he prudently declined a military command, in which failure and victory would have been almost equally disgraceful to

30. The disciples of the saint (Vit. 1ma, l. iii. c. 2. p. 1232. Vit. ii.^da^, c. 16. N° 45. p. 1383.) record a marvellous example of his pious apathy. Juxta lacum etiam Lausannensem totius diei itinere pergens, penitus non attendit aut se videre non vidit. Cum enim vespere facto de eodem lacû socii colloquerentur, interrogabat eos ubi lacus ille esset; et mirati sunt universi. To admire or despise St. Bernard as he ought, the reader, like myself, should have before the windows of his library the beauties of that incomparable landskip.

31. Otho Frising. l. i. c. 4. Bernard, Epist. 363. ad Francos Orientales, Opp. tom. i. p. 328. Vit. 1ma, l. iii. c. 4. tom. vi. p. 1235.

32. Mandastis et obedivi ... multiplicati sunt super numerum; vacuantur urbes et castella; et *pene* jam non inveniunt quem apprehendant septem mulieres unum virum; adeo ubique viduæ vivis remanent viris. Bernard. Epist. p. 247. We must be careful not to construe *pene* as a substantive.

his character.[33] Yet, after the calamitous event, the abbot of Clairvaux was loudly accused as a false prophet, the author of the public and private mourning; his enemies exulted, his friends blushed, and his apology was slow and unsatisfactory. He justifies his obedience to the commands of the pope; expatiates on the mysterious ways of providence; imputes the misfortunes of the pilgrims to their own sins; and modestly insinuates, that his mission had been approved by signs and wonders.[34] Had the fact been certain, the argument would be decisive; and his faithful disciples, who enumerate twenty or thirty miracles in a day, appeal to the public assemblies of France and Germany, in which they were performed.[35] At the present hour, such prodigies will not obtain credit beyond the precincts of Clairvaux; but in the preternatural cures of the blind, the lame, and the sick, who were presented to the man of God, it is impossible for us to ascertain the separate shares of accident, of fancy, of imposture, and of fiction.

Progress of the Mahometans. Omnipotence itself cannot escape the murmurs of its discordant votaries; since the same dispensation which was applauded as a deliverance in Europe, was deplored, and perhaps arraigned, as a calamity in Asia. After the loss of Jerusalem, the Syrian fugitives diffused their consternation and sorrow: Bagdad mourned in the dust; the cadhi Zeineddin of Damascus tore his beard in the caliph's presence; and the whole divan shed tears at his melancholy tale.[36] But the commanders of the faithful could only weep; they were themselves captives in the hands of the Turks: some temporal power was restored to the last age of the Abbassides; but their humble ambition was confined to Bagdad and the adjacent province. Their tyrants, the Seljukian sultans, had followed the common law of the Asiatic dynasties, the unceasing round of valour, greatness, discord, degeneracy, and decay: their spirit and power were unequal to the defence of religion; and, in his distant realm of Persia, the Christians were strangers to the name and the arms

33. Quis ego sum ut disponam acies, ut egrediar ante facies armatorum, aut quid tam remotum a professione meâ, si vires, si peritia, &c. epist. 256. tom. i. p. 259. He speaks with contempt of the hermit Peter, vir quidam, epist. 363.

34. Sic dicunt forsitan iste, unde scimus quòd a Domino sermo egressus sit? Quæ signa tu facis ut credamus tibi? Non est quod ad ista ipse respondeam; percendum verecundiæ meæ, responde tu pro me, et pro te ipso, secundum quæ vidisti et audisti, et secundum quod te inspiraverit Deus. Consolat. l. ii. c. 1. Opp. tom. ii. p. 421–423.

35. See the testimonies in Vita 1ma l. iv. c. 5, 6. Opp. tom. vi. p. 1258–1261. l. vi. c. 1–17. p. 1286–1314.

36. Abulmahasen apud de Guignes, Hist. des Huns, tom. ii. P. ii. p. 99.

of Sangiar, the last hero of his race.[37] While the sultans were involved in the silken web of the haram, the pious task was undertaken by their slaves, the Atabeks;[38] a Turkish name, which, like the Byzantine patricians, may be translated by Father of the Prince. Ascansar, a valiant Turk, had been the favourite of Malek Shaw, from whom he received the privilege of standing on the right-hand of the throne; but, in the civil wars that ensued on the monarch's death, he lost his head and the government of Aleppo. His domestic emirs persevered in their attachment to his son Zenghi, who proved his first arms against the Franks in the defeat of Antioch: thirty campaigns in the service of the caliph and sultan established his military fame; and he was invested with the command of Mosul, as the only champion that could avenge the cause of the prophet. The public hope was not disappointed: after a siege of twenty-five days, he stormed the city of Edessa, and recovered from the Franks their conquests beyond the Euphrates:[39] the martial tribes of Curdistan were subdued by the independent sovereign of Mosul and Aleppo: his soldiers were taught to behold the camp as their only country; they trusted to his liberality for their rewards; and their absent families were protected by the vigilance of Zenghi. At the head of these veterans, his son Noureddin gradually united the Mahometan powers; added the kingdom of Damascus to that of Aleppo, and waged a long and successful war against the Christians of Syria; he spread his ample reign from the Tigris to the Nile, and the Abbassides rewarded their faithful servant with all the titles and prerogatives of royalty. The Latins themselves were compelled to own the wisdom and courage, and even the justice and piety, of this implacable adversary.[40] In his life and government, the holy warrior revived the zeal

The Atabeks of Syria.

Zenghi, A.D. 1127–1145.

Noureddin, A.D. 1145–1174.

37. See his *article* in the Bibliotheque Orientale of d'Herbelot, and de Guignes, tom. ii. P. i. p.230–261. Such was his valour, that he was styled the second Alexander; and such the extravagant love of his subjects, that they prayed for the sultan a year after his decease. Yet Sangiar might have been made prisoner by the Franks, as well as by the Uzes. He reigned near fifty years (A.D. 1103–1152.), and was a munificent patron of Persian poetry.

38. See the Chronology of the Atabeks of Irak and Syria, in de Guignes, tom. i. p. 254; and the reigns of Zenghi and Noureddin in the same writer (tom. ii. P. ii. p. 147–221.), who uses the Arabic text of Benelathir, Ben Schounah, and Abulfeda; the Bibliotheque Orientale, under the articles *Atabeks* and *Noureddin*, and the Dynasties of Abulpharagius, p. 250–267. vers. Pocock.

39. William of Tyre (l. xvi. c. 4, 5. 7.) describes the loss of Edessa, and the death of Zenghi. The corruption of his name into *Sanguin*, afforded the Latins a comfortable allusion to his *sanguinary* character and end, fit sanguine sanguinolentus.

40. Noradinus (says William of Tyre, l. xx. 33.) maximus nominis et fidei Christianæ persecutor; princeps tamen justus, vafer,

and simplicity of the first caliphs. Gold and silk were banished from his palace; the use of wine from his dominions; the public revenue was scrupulously applied to the public service; and the frugal household of Noureddin was maintained from his legitimate share of the spoil which he vested in the purchase of a private estate. His favourite Sultana sighed for some female object of expence. "Alas," replied the king, "I fear God, and am no more than the treasurer of the Moslems. Their property I cannot alienate; but I still possess three shops in the city of Hems: these you may take; and these alone can I bestow." His chamber of justice was the terror of the great and the refuge of the poor. Some years after the sultan's death, an oppressed subject called aloud in the streets of Damascus, "O Noureddin, Noureddin, where art thou now? Arise, arise, to pity and protect us!" A tumult was apprehended, and a living tyrant blushed or trembled at the name of a departed monarch.

Conquest of Egypt by the Turks, A.D. 1163–1169.

By the arms of the Turks and Franks, the Fatimites had been deprived of Syria. In Egypt, the decay of their character and influence was still more essential. Yet they were still revered as the descendants and successors of the prophet; they maintained their invisible state in the palace of Cairo; and their person was seldom violated by the profane eyes of subjects or strangers. The Latin ambassadors[41] have described their own introduction through a series of gloomy passages, and glittering porticoes: the scene was enlivened by the warbling of birds and the murmur of fountains: it was enriched by a display of rich furniture, and rare animals; of the Imperial treasures, something was shewn, and much was supposed; and the long order of unfolding doors was guarded by black soldiers and domestic eunuchs. The sanctuary of the presence chamber was veiled with a curtain; and the vizir, who conducted the ambassadors, laid aside his scymetar, and prostrated himself three times on the ground; the veil was then removed; and they beheld the commander of the faithful, who signified his pleasure to the first slave of the throne. But this slave was his master: the vizirs or

---

providus, et secundum gentis suæ traditiones religiosus. To this catholic witness, we may add the primate of the Jacobites (Abulpharag. p. 267.), quo non alter erat inter reges vitæ ratione magis laudabili, aut quæ pluribus justitiæ experimentis abundaret. The true praise of kings is after their death, and from the mouth of their enemies.

41. From the ambassador, William of Tyre (l. xix. c. 17, 18.) describes the palace of Cairo. In the caliphs treasure were found a pearl as large as a pigeon's egg, a ruby weighing seventeen Egyptian drams, an emerald a palm and an half in length, and many vases of chrystal and porcelain of China (Renaudot, p. 536.).

sultans had usurped the supreme administration of Egypt; the claims of the rival candidates were decided by arms; and the name of the most worthy, of the strongest, was inserted in the royal patent of command. The factions of Dargham and Shawer alternately expelled each other from the capital and country; and the weaker side implored the dangerous protection of the sultan of Damascus or the king of Jerusalem, the perpetual enemies of the sect and monarchy of the Fatimites. By his arms and religion, the Turk was most formidable; but the Frank, in an easy direct march, could advance from Gaza to the Nile; while the intermediate situation of his realm compelled the troops of Noureddin to wheel round the skirts of Arabia, a long and painful circuit, which exposed them to thirst, fatigue, and the burning winds of the desert. The secret zeal and ambition of the Turkish prince aspired to reign in Egypt under the name of the Abbassides; but the restoration of the suppliant Shawer was the ostensible motive of the first expedition; and the success was entrusted to the emir Shiracouh, a valiant and veteran commander. Dargham was oppressed and slain; but the ingratitude, the jealousy, the just apprehensions, of his more fortunate rival, soon provoked him to invite the king of Jerusalem to deliver Egypt from his insolent benefactors. To this union, the forces of Shiracouh were unequal; he relinquished the premature conquest; and the evacuation of Belbeis or Pelusium was the condition of his safe retreat. As the Turks defiled before the enemy, and their general closed the rear, with a vigilant eye, and a battle-axe in his hand, a Frank presumed to ask him if he were not afraid of an attack? "It is doubtless in your power to begin the attack," replied the intrepid emir; "but rest assured, that not one of my soldiers will go to paradise till he has sent an infidel to hell." His report of the riches of the land, the effeminacy of the natives, and the disorders of the government, revived the hopes of Noureddin; the caliph of Bagdad applauded the pious design; and Shiracouh descended into Egypt a second time with twelve thousand Turks and eleven thousand Arabs. Yet his forces were still inferior to the confederate armies of the Franks and Saracens; and I can discern an unusual degree of military art, in his passage of the Nile, his retreat into Thebais, his masterly evolutions in the battle of Babain, the surprise of Alexandria, and his marches and counter-marches in the flats and valley of Egypt, from the tropic to the sea. His conduct was seconded by the courage of his troops, and on the eve of action a Mamaluke[42]

42. *Mamluc*, plur. *Mamalic*, is defined by Pocock (Prolegom. ad Abulpharag. p. 7.), and d'Herbelot (p. 545.), servum emptitium, seu qui pretio numerato in domini

exclaimed, "If we cannot wrest Egypt from the Christian dogs, why do we not renounce the honours and rewards of the sultan, and retire to labour with the peasants, or to spin with the females of the haram?" Yet, after all his efforts in the field,[43] after the obstinate defence of Alexandria[44] by his nephew Saladin, an honourable capitulation and retreat concluded the second enterprise of Shiracouh; and Noureddin reserved his abilities for a third and more propitious occasion. It was soon offered by the ambition and avarice of Amalric or Amaury, king of Jerusalem, who had imbibed the pernicious maxim, that no faith should be kept with the enemies of God. A religious warrior, the great master of the hospital, encouraged him to proceed; the emperor of Constantinople, either gave, or promised, a fleet to act with the armies of Syria; and the perfidious Christian, unsatisfied with spoil and subsidy, aspired to the conquest of Egypt. In this emergency, the Moslems turned their eyes towards the sultan of Damascus; the vizir, whom danger encompassed on all sides, yielded to their unanimous wishes, and Noureddin seemed to be tempted by the fair offer of one third of the revenue of the kingdom. The Franks were already at the gates of Cairo; but the suburbs, the old city, were burnt on their approach; they were deceived by an insidious negociation; and their vessels were unable to surmount the barriers of the Nile. They prudently declined a contest with the Turks, in the midst of an hostile country; and Amaury retired into Palestine, with the shame and reproach that always adhere to unsuccessful injustice. After this deliverance, Shiracouh was invested with a robe of honour, which he soon stained with the blood of the unfortunate Shawer. For a while, the Turkish emirs condescended to hold the office of vizir; but this foreign conquest precipitated the fall of the Fatimites themselves; and the bloodless change was accomplished by a message and a word. The caliphs had been degraded by their own weakness and the tyranny of the vizirs: their subjects blushed, when the descendant and successor of the prophet presented his naked hand to the rude gripe of a Latin ambassador; they

possessionem cedit. They frequently occur in the wars of Saladin (Bohadin, p. 236, &c.); and it was only the *Bahartie* Mamalukes that were first introduced into Egypt by his descendants.

43. Jacobus à Vitriaco (p. 1116.) gives the king of Jerusalem no more than 374 knights. Both the Franks and the Moslems report the superior numbers of the enemy; a difference which may be solved by counting or omitting the unwarlike Egyptians.

44. It was the Alexandria of the Arabs, a middle term in extent and riches between the period of the Greeks and Romans, and that of the Turks (Savary, Lettres sur l'Egypte, tom. i. p. 25, 26.).

wept when he sent the hair of his women, a sad emblem of their grief and terror, to excite the pity of the sultan of Damascus. By the command of Noureddin, and the sentence of the doctors, the holy names of Abubeker, Omar, and Othman, were solemnly restored: the caliph Mosthadi, of Bagdad, was acknowledged in the public prayers as the true commander of the faithful; and the green livery of the sons of Ali was exchanged for the black colour of the Abbassides. The last of his race, the caliph Adhed, who survived only ten days, expired in happy ignorance of his fate: his treasures secured the loyalty of the soldiers and silenced the murmurs of the sectaries; and in all subsequent revolutions, Egypt has never departed from the orthodox tradition of the Moslems.[45]

End of the Fatimite caliphs, A.D. 1171.

The hilly country beyond the Tigris is occupied by the pastoral tribes of the Curds:[46] a people hardy, strong, savage, impatient of the yoke, addicted to rapine, and tenacious of the government of their national chiefs. The resemblance of name, situation, and manners, seem to identify them with the Carduchians of the Greeks;[47] and they still defend against the Ottoman Porte the antique freedom which they asserted against the successors of Cyrus. Poverty and ambition prompted them to embrace the profession of mercenary soldiers: the service of his father and uncle prepared the reign of the great Saladin;[48] and the son of Job or Ayub, a simple Curd, magnanimously smiled at his pedigree, which flattery deduced from the

Reign and character of Saladin, A.D. 1171–1193.

45. For this great revolution of Egypt, see William of Tyre (l. xix. 5, 6, 7. 12–31. xx. 5–12.), Bohadin (in Vit. Saladin. p. 30–39.), Abulfeda (in Excerpt. Schultens, p. 1–12.), d'Herbelot (Bibliot. Orient. *Adhed, Fathemah*, but very incorrect), Renaudot (Hist. Patriarch. Alex. p. 522–525. 532–537.), Vertot (Hist. des Chevaliers de Malthe, tom. i. p. 141–163. in 4to), and M. de Guignes (tom. ii. p. ii. p. 185–215.).

46. For the Curds, see de Guignes, tom. i. p. 416, 417. the Index Geographicus of Schultens, and Tavernier, Voyages, p. i. p. 308, 309. The Ayoubites descended from the tribe of the Rawadiæi, one of the noblest; but as *they* were infected with the heresy of the Metempsychosis, the orthodox sultans insinuated, that their descent was only on the mother's side, and that their ancestor was a stranger who settled among the Curds.

47. See the iv[th] book of the Anabasis of Xenophon. The ten thousand suffered more from the arrows of the free Carduchians, than from the splendid weakness of the great king.

48. We are indebted to the professor Schultens (Lugd. Bat. 1755, in folio) for the richest and most authentic materials, a life of Saladin by his friend and minister the Cadhi Bohadin, and copious extracts from the history of his kinsman the prince Abulfeda of Hamah. To these we may add, the article of *Salaheddin* in the Bibliotheque Orientale, and all that may be gleaned from the Dynasties of Abulpharagius.

Arabian caliphs.[49] So unconscious was Noureddin of the impending ruin of his house, that he constrained the reluctant youth to follow his uncle Shiracouh into Egypt: his military character was established by the defence of Alexandria; and if we may believe the Latins, he solicited and obtained from the Christian general the *profane* honours of knighthood.[50] On the death of Shiracouh, the office of grand vizir was bestowed on Saladin, as the youngest and least powerful of the emirs; but with the advice of his father, whom he invited to Cairo, his genius obtained the ascendant over his equals, and attached the army to his person and interest. While Noureddin lived, these ambitious Curds were the most humble of his slaves; and the indiscreet murmurs of the divan were silenced by the prudent Ayub, who loudly protested that at the command of the sultan he himself would lead his son in chains to the foot of the throne. "Such language," he added in private, "was prudent and proper in an assembly of your rivals; but we are now above fear and obedience; and the threats of Noureddin shall not extort the tribute of a sugar-cane." His seasonable death relieved them from the odious and doubtful conflict: his son, a minor of eleven years of age, was left for a while to the emirs of Damascus; and the new lord of Egypt was decorated by the caliph with every title[51] that could sanctify his usurpation in the eyes of the people. Nor was Saladin long content with the possession of Egypt; he despoiled the Christians of Jerusalem, and the Atabeks of Damascus, Aleppo, and Diarbekir: Mecca and Medina acknowledged him for their temporal protector: his brother subdued the distant regions of Yemen, or the happy Arabia; and at the hour of his death, his empire was spread from the African Tripoli to the Tigris, and from the Indian ocean to the mountains of Armenia. In the judgment of his character, the reproaches of treason and ingratitude strike forcibly on *our* minds, impressed, as they are, with the principle and experience of law and loyalty. But his ambition may in some measure be excused by the revolutions of Asia,[52] which had

49. Since Abulfeda was himself an Ayoubite, he may share the praise, for imitating, at least tacitly, the modesty of the founder.

50. Hist. Hierosol. in the Gesta Dei per Francos, p. 1152. A similar example may be found in Joinville (p. 42. edition du Louvre); but the pious St. Louis refused to dignify infidels with the order of Christian knighthood (Ducange, Observations, p. 70.).

51. In these Arabic titles, *religionis* must always be understood; *Noureddin*, lumen r.; *Ezzodin*, decus; *Amadoddin*, columen: our hero's proper name was Joseph, and he was styled *Salahoddin*, salus; *Al Malichus, Al Nasirus*, rex defensor; *Abu Modaffir*, pater victoriæ. Schultens, Præfat.

52. Abulfeda, who descended from a brother of Saladin, observes from many examples, that the founders of dynasties

erased every notion of legitimate succession; by the recent example of the Atabeks themselves; by his reverence to the son of his benefactor, his humane and generous behaviour to the collateral branches; by *their* incapacity and *his* merit; by the approbation of the caliph, the sole source of all legitimate power; and, above all, by the wishes and interest of the people, whose happiness is the first object of government. In *his* virtues, and in those of his patron, they admired the singular union of the hero and the saint; for both Noureddin and Saladin are ranked among the Mahometan saints; and the constant meditation of the holy war appears to have shed a serious and sober colour over their lives and actions. The youth of the latter[53] was addicted to wine and women; but his aspiring spirit soon renounced the temptations of pleasure, for the graver follies of fame and dominion: the garment of Saladin was a coarse woollen; water was his only drink; and, while he emulated the temperance, he surpassed the chastity, of his Arabian prophet. Both in faith and practice he was a rigid Musulman; he ever deplored that the defence of religion had not allowed him to accomplish the pilgrimage of Mecca; but at the stated hours, five times each day, the sultan devoutly prayed with his brethren: the involuntary omission of fasting was scrupulously repaid; and his perusal of the Koran, on horseback between the approaching armies, may be quoted as a proof, however ostentatious, of piety and courage.[54] The superstitious doctrine of the sect of Shafei was the only study that he deigned to encourage: the poets were safe in his contempt; but all profane science was the object of his aversion; and a philosopher, who had vented some speculative novelties, was seized and strangled by the command of the royal saint. The justice of his divan was accessible to the meanest suppliant against himself and his ministers; and it was only for a kingdom that Saladin would deviate from the rule of equity. While the descendants of Seljuk and Zenghi held his stirrup and smoothed his garments, he was affable and patient with the meanest of his servants. So boundless was his liberality, that he distributed twelve thousand horses at the siege of Acre; and, at the time of his death, no more than forty-seven drams of silver and one piece of gold coin were found in the treasury; yet in a martial reign, the tributes were diminished, and the wealthy

took the guilt for themselves, and left the reward to their innocent collaterals (Excerpt. p. 10.).

53. See his life and character in Renaudot, p. 537–548.

54. His civil and religious virtues are celebrated in the first chapter of Bohadin (p. 4–30.), himself an eye-witness, and an honest bigot.

citizens enjoyed without fear or danger the fruits of their industry. Egypt, Syria, and Arabia, were adorned by the royal foundations of hospitals, colleges, and moschs; and Cairo was fortified with a wall and citadel; but his works were consecrated to public use,[55] nor did the sultan indulge himself in a garden or palace of private luxury. In a fanatic age, himself a fanatic, the genuine virtues of Saladin commanded the esteem of the Christians: the emperor of Germany gloried in his friendship:[56] the Greek emperor solicited his alliance;[57] and the conquest of Jerusalem diffused, and perhaps magnified, his fame both in the East and West.

His conquest of the kingdom. A.D. 1187, July 3.

During its short existence, the kingdom of Jerusalem[58] was supported by the discord of the Turks and Saracens; and both the Fatimite caliphs and the sultans of Damascus were tempted to sacrifice the cause of their religion to the meaner considerations of private and present advantage. But the powers of Egypt, Syria, and Arabia, were now united by an hero, whom nature and fortune had armed against the Christians. All without, now bore the most threatening aspect; and all was feeble and hollow in the internal state of Jerusalem. After the two first Baldwins, the brother and cousin of Godfrey of Bouillon, the sceptre devolved by female succession to Melisenda, daughter of the second Baldwin, and her husband Fulk, count of Anjou, the father, by a former marriage, of our English Plantagenets. Their two sons, Baldwin the third and Amaury, waged a strenuous, and not unsuccessful, war against the infidels; but the son of Amaury, Baldwin the fourth, was deprived, by the leprosy, a gift of the crusades, of the faculties both of mind and body. His sister Sybilla, the mother of Baldwin the fifth, was his natural heiress: after the suspicious death of her child, she crowned her second husband, Guy of Lusignan, a prince of a handsome person, but of such base renown, that his own brother Jeffrey was heard to exclaim, "Since they have made *him* a king, surely they would have made *me* a god!" The choice was generally blamed; and the most powerful vassal, Raymond count of Tripoli, who had been excluded from the succession and regency, entertained an implacable hatred against the king, and exposed his honour and conscience to the temptations of the sultan. Such were the guardians of the holy city; a leper, a child, a

55. In many works, particularly Joseph's well in the castle of Cairo, the sultan and the patriarch have been confounded by the ignorance of natives and travellers.

56. Anonym. Canisii, tom. iii. p. ii. p. 504.

57. Bohadin, p. 129, 130.

58. For the Latin kingdom of Jerusalem, see William of Tyre, from the ix[th] to the xxii[d] book. Jacob. à Vitriaco, Hist. Hierosolem. l. i. and Sanutus, Secreta Fidelium Crucis, l. iii. p. vi, vii, viii, ix.

woman, a coward, and a traitor: yet its fate was delayed twelve years by some supplies from Europe, by the valour of the military orders, and by the distant or domestic avocations of their great enemy. At length, on every side the sinking state was encircled and pressed by an hostile line; and the truce was violated by the Franks, whose existence it protected. A soldier of fortune, Reginald of Chatillon, had seized a fortress on the edge of the desert, from whence he pillaged the caravans, insulted Mahomet, and threatened the cities of Mecca and Medina. Saladin condescended to complain; rejoiced in the denial of justice; and at the head of fourscore thousand horse and foot, invaded the Holy Land. The choice of Tiberias for his first siege was suggested by the count of Tripoli, to whom it belonged; and the king of Jerusalem was persuaded to drain his garrisons, and to arm his people, for the relief of that important place.[59] By the advice of the perfidious Raymond, the Christians were betrayed into a camp destitute of water: he fled on the first onset with the curses of both nations:[60] Lusignan was overthrown with the loss of thirty thousand men; and the wood of the true cross, a dire misfortune! was left in the power of the infidels. The royal captive was conducted to the tent of Saladin; and as he fainted with thirst and terror, the generous victor presented him with a cup of sherbet cooled in snow, without suffering his companion, Reginald of Chatillon, to partake of this pledge of hospitality and pardon. "The person and dignity of a king," said the sultan, "are sacred; but this impious robber must instantly acknowledge the prophet, whom he has blasphemed, or meet the death which he has so often deserved." On the proud or conscientious refusal of the Christian warrior, Saladin struck him on the head with his scymetar, and Reginald was dispatched by the guards.[61] the trembling Lusignan was sent to Damascus to an honourable prison and speedy ransom; but the victory

59. Templarii ut apes bombabant et Hospitalarii ut venti stridebant, et barones se exitio offerebant, et Turcopuli (the Christian light troops) semet ipsi in ignem injiciebant (Ispahani de Expugnatione Kudsiticâ, p. 18. apud Schultens); a specimen of Arabian eloquence, somewhat different from the style of Xenophon!.

60. The Latins affirm, the Arabians insinuate, the treason of Raymond; but had he really embraced their religion, he would have been a saint and a hero in the eyes of the latter.

61. Renaud, Reginald, or Arnold de Chatillon, is celebrated by the Latins in his life and death; but the circumstances of the latter are more distinctly related by Bohadin and Abulfeda; and Joinville (Hist. de St. Louis, p. 70.) alludes to the practice of Saladin, of never putting to death a prisoner who had tasted his bread and salt. Some of the companions of Arnold had been slaughtered, and almost sacrificed, in a valley of Mecca, ubi sacrificia mactantur (Abulfeda, p. 32.).

was stained by the execution of two hundred and thirty knights of the hospital, the intrepid champions and martyrs of their faith. The kingdom was left without a head; and of the two grand masters of the military orders, the one was slain and the other was a prisoner. From all the cities, both of the sea-coast and the inland country, the garrisons had been drawn away for this fatal field: Tyre and Tripoli alone could escape the rapid inroad of Saladin; and three months after the battle of Tiberias he appeared in arms before the gates of Jerusalem.[62]

and city of Jerusalem, A.D. 1187, October 2.

He might expect, that the siege of a city, so venerable on earth and in heaven, so interesting to Europe and Asia, would rekindle the last sparks of enthusiasm; and that, of sixty thousand Christians, every man would be a soldier, and every soldier a candidate for martyrdom. But queen Sybilla trembled for herself and her captive husband; and the barons and knights, who had escaped from the sword and chains of the Turks, displayed the same factious and selfish spirit in the public ruin. The most numerous portion of the inhabitants was composed of the Greek and Oriental Christians, whom experience had taught to prefer the Mahometan before the Latin yoke;[63] and the holy sepulchre attracted a base and needy crowd, without arms or courage, who subsisted only on the charity of the pilgrims. Some feeble and hasty efforts were made for the defence of Jerusalem; but in the space of fourteen days, a victorious army drove back the sallies of the besieged, planted their engines, opened the wall to the breadth of fifteen cubits, applied their scaling-ladders, and erected on the breach twelve banners of the prophet and the sultan. It was in vain that a bare-foot procession of the queen, the women, and the monks, implored the Son of God to save his tomb and his inheritance from impious violation. Their sole hope was in the mercy of the conqueror, and to the first suppliant deputation that mercy was sternly denied. "He had sworn to avenge the patience and long-suffering of the Moslems; the hour of forgiveness was elapsed, and the moment was now arrived to expiate in blood, the innocent blood, which had been spilt by Godfrey and the first crusaders." But a desperate and successful struggle of the Franks admonished the sultan that his triumph was not yet secure; he listened with reverence to a solemn adjuration in the name of the common father of mankind; and a sentiment of human sympathy mollified the rigour of fanaticism and

62. Vertot, who well describes the loss of the kingdom and city (Hist. des Chevaliers de Malthe, tom. i. l. ii. p. 226–278.), inserts two original epistles of a knight templar.

63. Renaudot, Hist. Patriarch. Alex. p. 545.

conquest. He consented to accept the city, and to spare the inhabitants. The Greek and Oriental Christians were permitted to live under his dominion; but it was stipulated, that in forty days all the Franks and Latins should evacuate Jerusalem, and be safely conducted to the sea-ports of Syria and Egypt; that ten pieces of gold should be paid for each man, five for each woman, and one for every child; and that those who were unable to purchase their freedom should be detained in perpetual slavery. Of some writers it is a favourite and invidious theme to compare the humanity of Saladin with the massacre of the first crusade. The difference would be merely personal; but we should not forget that the Christians had offered to capitulate, and that the Mahometans of Jerusalem sustained the last extremities of an assault and storm. Justice is indeed due to the fidelity with which the Turkish conqueror fulfilled the conditions of the treaty; and he may be deservedly praised for the glance of pity which he cast on the misery of the vanquished. Instead of a rigorous exaction of his debt, he accepted a sum of thirty thousand byzants, for the ransom of seven thousand poor; two or three thousand more were dismissed by his gratuitous clemency; and the number of slaves was reduced to eleven or fourteen thousand persons. In his interview with the queen, his words, and even his tears, suggested the kindest consolations; his liberal alms were distributed among those who had been made orphans or widows by the fortune of war; and while the knights of the hospital were in arms against him, he allowed their more pious brethren to continue, during the term of a year, the care and service of the sick. In these acts of mercy the virtue of Saladin deserves our admiration and love: he was above the necessity of dissimulation, and his stern fanaticism would have prompted him to dissemble, rather than to affect, this profane compassion for the enemies of the Koran. After Jerusalem had been delivered from the presence of the strangers, the sultan made his triumphant entry, his banners waving in the wind and to the harmony of martial music. The great mosch of Omar, which had been converted into a church, was again consecrated to one God and his prophet Mahomet; the walls and pavement were purified with rose water; and a pulpit, the labour of Noureddin, was erected in the sanctuary. But when the golden cross that glittered on the dome was cast down, and dragged through the streets, the Christians of every sect uttered a lamentable groan, which was answered by the joyful shouts of the Moslems. In four ivory chests the patriarch had collected the crosses, the images, the vases, and the relics, of the holy place: they were seized by the conqueror, who was desirous of presenting the caliph with the trophies of Christian idolatry. He was persuaded however to entrust them to the patriarch and prince of Antioch; and the pious pledge was redeemed by Richard of England, at the expence of fifty-two thousand byzants of gold.[64]

The third crusade, by sea, A.D. 1188.

The nations might fear and hope the immediate and final expulsion of the Latins from Syria; which was yet delayed above a century after the death of Saladin.[65] In the career of victory, he was first checked by the resistance of Tyre; the troops and garrisons, which had capitulated, were imprudently conducted to the same port: their numbers were adequate to the defence of the place; and the arrival of Conrad of Montferrat inspired the disorderly crowd with confidence and union. His father, a venerable pilgrim, had been made prisoner in the battle of Tiberias; but that disaster was unknown in Italy and Greece, when the son was urged by ambition and piety to visit the inheritance of his royal nephew, the infant Baldwin. The view of the Turkish banners warned him from the hostile coast of Jaffa; and Conrad was unanimously hailed as the prince and champion of Tyre, which was already besieged by the conqueror of Jerusalem. The firmness of his zeal, and perhaps his knowledge of a generous foe, enabled him to brave the threats of the sultan, and to declare, that should his aged parent be exposed before the walls, he himself would discharge the first arrow, and glory in his descent from a Christian martyr.[66] The Egyptian fleet was allowed to enter the harbour of Tyre; but the chain was suddenly drawn, and five gallies were either sunk or taken: a thousand Turks were slain in a sally; and Saladin, after burning his engines, concluded a glorious campaign by a disgraceful retreat to Damascus. He was soon assailed by a more formidable tempest. The pathetic narratives, and even the pictures, that represented in lively colours the servitude and profanation of Jerusalem, awakened the torpid sensibility of Europe: the emperor, Frederic Barbarossa, and the kings of France and England, assumed the cross; and the tardy magnitude of their armaments was anticipated by the maritime

64. For the conquest of Jerusalem, Bohadin (p. 67–75.) and Abulfeda (p. 40–43.) are our Moslem witnesses. Of the Christian, Bernard Thesaurarius (c. 151–167.) is the most copious and authentic; see likewise Matthew Paris (p. 120–124.).

65. The sieges of Tyre and Acre are most copiously described by Bernard Thesaurarius (de Acquisitione Terræ Sanctæ, c. 167–179.), the author of the Historia Hierosolymitana (p. 1150–1172. in Bongarsius), Abulfeda (p. 43–50.), and Bohadin (p. 75–179.).

66. I have followed a moderate and probable representation of the fact: by Vertot, who adopts without reluctance a romantic tale, the old marquis is actually exposed to the darts of the besieged.

states of the Mediterranean and the Ocean. The skilful and provident Italians first embarked in the ships of Genoa, Pisa, and Venice. They were speedily followed by the most eager pilgrims of France, Normandy, and the Western Isles. The powerful succour of Flanders, Frise, and Denmark, filled near an hundred vessels; and the northern warriors were distinguished in the field by a lofty stature and a ponderous battle-axe.[67] Their encreasing multitudes could no longer be confined within the walls of Tyre, or remain obedient to the voice of Conrad. They pitied the misfortunes, and revered the dignity, of Lusignan, who was released from prison, perhaps, to divide the army of the Franks. He proposed the recovery of Ptolemais, or Acre, thirty miles to the south of Tyre; and the place was first invested by two thousand horse and thirty thousand foot under his nominal command. I shall not expatiate on the story of this memorable siege; which lasted near two years, and consumed in a narrow space, the forces of Europe and Asia. Never did the flame of enthusiasm burn with fiercer and more destructive rage; nor could the true believers, a common appellation, who consecrated their own martyrs, refuse some applause to the mistaken zeal and courage of their adversaries. At the sound of the holy trumpet, the Moslems of Egypt, Syria, Arabia, and the Oriental provinces, assembled under the servant of the prophet:[68] his camp was pitched and removed within a few miles of Acre; and he laboured, night and day, for the relief of his brethren and the annoyance of the Franks. Nine battles, not unworthy of the name, were fought in the neighbourhood, of mount Carmel, with such vicissitude of fortune, that in one attack, the sultan forced his way into the city; that in one sally, the Christians penetrated to the royal tent. By the means of divers and pigeons, a regular correspondence was maintained with the besieged: and, as often as the sea was left open, the exhausted garrison was withdrawn, and a fresh supply was poured into the place. The Latin camp was thinned by famine, the sword, and the climate; but the tents of the dead were replenished with new pilgrims, who exaggerated the strength and speed of their approaching countrymen. The vulgar was astonished by the report, that the pope himself, with an innumerable crusade, was advanced as far as

Siege of Acre, A.D. 1189, July–A.D. 1191, July.

67. Northmanni et Gothi, et cæteri populi insularum quæ inter occidentem et septemtrionem sitæ sunt, gentes bellicosæ, corporis proceri, mortis intrepidæ, bipennibus armatæ, navibus rotundis quæ Ysnachiæ dicuntur advectæ.

68. The historian of Jerusalem (p. 1108.) adds the nations of the East from the Tigris to India, and the swarthy tribes of Moors and Getulians, so that Asia and Africa fought against Europe.

Constantinople. The march of the emperor filled the East with more serious alarms; the obstacles which he encountered in Asia, and perhaps in Greece, were raised by the policy of Saladin; his joy on the death of Barbarossa was measured by his esteem; and the Christians were rather dismayed that encouraged at the sight of the duke of Swabia and his way-worn remnant of five thousand Germans. At length, in the spring of the second year, the royal fleets of France and England cast anchor in the bay of Acre, and the siege was more vigorously prosecuted by the youthful emulation of the two kings, Philip Augustus and Richard Plantagenet. After every resource had been tried, and every hope was exhausted, the defenders of Acre submitted to their fate; a capitulation was granted, but their lives and liberties were taxed at the hard conditions of a ransom of two hundred thousand pieces of gold, the deliverance of one hundred nobles and fifteen hundred inferior captives, and the restoration of the wood of the holy cross. Some doubts in the agreement, and some delay in the execution, rekindled the fury of the Franks, and three thousand Moslems, almost in the sultan's view, were beheaded by the command of the sanguinary Richard.[69] By the conquest of Acre, the Latin powers acquired a strong town and a convenient harbour; but the advantage was most dearly purchased. The minister and historian of Saladin computes, from the report of the enemy, that their numbers, at different periods, amounted to five or six hundred thousand; that more than one hundred thousand Christians were slain; that a far greater number was lost by disease or shipwreck; and that a small portion of this mighty host could return in safety to their native countries.[70]

Richard of England, in Palestine, A.D. 1191, 1192.

Philip Augustus, and Richard the first, are the only kings of France and England, who have fought under the same banners; but the holy service, in which they were enlisted, was incessantly disturbed by their national jealousy; and the two factions, which they protected in Palestine, were more averse to each other than

69. Bohadin, p. 180.; and this massacre is neither denied nor blamed by the Christian historians. Alacriter jussa complentes (the English soldiers), says Galfridus à Vinesauf (l. iv. c. 4. p. 346.), who fixes at 2700 the number of victims; who are multiplied to 5000 by Roger Hoveden (p. 697, 698.). The humanity or avarice of Philip Augustus was persuaded to ransom his prisoners (Jacob. à Vitriaco, l. i. c. 98. p. 1122.).

70. Bohadin, p. 14. He quotes the judgment of Balianus, and the prince of Sidon, and adds, ex illo mundo quasi hominum paucissimi redierunt. Among the Christians who died before St. John d'Acre, I find the English names of de Ferrers earl of Derby (Dugdale, Baronage, part i. p. 260.), Mowbray (idem. p. 124.), de Mandevil, de Fiennes, St. John, Scrope, Pigot, Talbot, &c.

to the common enemy. In the eyes of the Orientals, the French monarch was superior in dignity and power; and in the emperor's absence, the Latins revered him as their temporal chief.[71] His exploits were not adequate to his fame. Philip was brave, but the statesman predominated in his character; he was soon weary of sacrificing his health and interest on a barren coast; the surrender of Acre became the signal of his departure; nor could he justify this unpopular desertion, by leaving the duke of Burgundy, with five hundred knights and ten thousand foot, for the service of the Holy Land. The king of England, though inferior in dignity, surpassed his rival in wealth and military renown;[72] and if heroism be confined to brutal and ferocious valour, Richard Plantagenet will stand high among the heroes of the age. The memory of *Cœur de Lion*, of the lion-hearted prince, was long dear and glorious to his English subjects; and, at the distance of sixty years, it was celebrated in proverbial sayings by the grandsons of the Turks and Saracens, against whom he had fought: his tremendous name was employed by the Syrian mothers to silence their infants; and if an horse suddenly started from the way, his rider was wont to exclaim, "Dost thou think king Richard is in that bush?"[73] His cruelty to the Mahometans was the effect of temper and zeal; but I cannot believe that a soldier, so free and fearless in the use of his lance, would have descended to whet a dagger against his valiant brother Conrad of Montferrat, who was slain at Tyre by some secret assassins.[74] After the surrender of Acre, and the departure of Philip, the king of England led the crusaders to the recovery of the sea-coast; and the cities of Cæsarea and Jaffa were added to the fragments of the kingdom of Lusignan. A march of one hundred miles from Acre to Ascalon, was a great and perpetual battle of eleven days. In the disorder of his troops, Saladin remained on the field with seventeen guards, without lowering

71. Magnus hic apud eos, interque reges eorum tum virtute, tum majestate eminens ... summus rerum arbiter (Bohadin, p. 159.). He does not seem to have known the names either of Philip or Richard.

72. Rex Angliæ, præstrenuus ... rege Gallorum minor apud eos censebatur ratione regni atque dignitatis; sed tum divitiis florentior, tum bellicâ virtute multo erat celebrior (Bohadin, p. 161.). A stranger might admire those riches; the national historians will tell with what lawless and wasteful oppression they were collected.

73. Joinville, p. 17. Cuides-tu que ce soit le roi Richart?

74. Yet he was guilty in the opinion of the Moslems, who attest the confession of the assassins, that they were sent by the king of England (Bohadin, p. 225.); and his only defence is an absurd and palpable forgery (Hist. de l'Academie des Inscriptions, tom. xvi. p. 155–163.), a pretended letter from the prince of the assassins, the Sheich, or old man of the mountain, who justified Richard, by assuming to himself the guilt or merit of the murder.

his standard, or suspending the sound of his brazen kettle-drum: he again rallied and renewed the charge; and his preachers or heralds called aloud on the *unitarians*, manfully to stand up against the Christian idolaters. But the progress of these idolaters was irresistible: and it was only by demolishing the walls and buildings of Ascalon, that the sultan could prevent them from occupying an important fortress on the confines of Egypt. During a severe winter, the armies slept; but in the spring, the Franks advanced within a day's march of Jerusalem, under the leading standard of the English king; and his active spirit intercepted a convoy, or caravan, of seven thousand camels. Saladin[75] had fixed his station in the holy city; but the city was struck with consternation and discord: he fasted; he prayed; he preached; he offered to share the dangers of the siege; but his Mamalukes, who remembered the fate of their companions at Acre, pressed the sultan with loyal or seditious clamours, to reserve *his* person and *their* courage for the future defence of the religion and empire.[76] The Moslems were delivered by the sudden, or, as they deemed, the miraculous, retreat of the Christians;[77] and the laurels of Richard were blasted by the prudence, or envy, of his companions. The hero, ascending an hill, and veiling his face, exclaimed with an indignant voice, "Those who are unwilling to rescue, are unworthy to view, the sepulchre of Christ!" After his return to Acre, on the news that Jaffa was surprised by the sultan, he sailed with some merchant vessels, and leaped foremost on the beach; the castle was relieved by his presence; and sixty thousand Turks and Saracens fled before his arms. The discovery of his weakness provoked them to return in the morning; and they found him carelessly encamped before the gates with only seventeen knights and three hundred archers. Without counting their numbers, he sustained their charge; and we learn from the evidence of his enemies, that the king of England, grasping his lance, rode furiously along their front, from the right to the

75. See the distress and pious firmness of Saladin, as they are described by Bohadin (p. 7–9. 235–237.), who himself harangued the defenders of Jerusalem; their fears were not unknown to the enemy (Jacob. à Vitriaco, l. i. c. 100. p. 1123. Vinisauf, l. v. c. 50. p. 399.).

76. Yet unless the sultan, or an Ayoubite prince, remained in Jerusalem, nec Curdi, Turcis, nec Turci essent obtemperaturi Curdis (Bohadin, p. 236.). He draws aside a corner of the political curtain.

77. Bohadin (p. 237.) and even Jeffrey de Vinisauf (l. vi. c. 1–8. p. 403–409.) ascribe the retreat to Richard himself; and Jacobus à Vitriaco observes, that in his impatience to depart, in alterum virum mutatus est (p. 1123.). Yet Joinville, a French knight, accuses the envy of Hugh duke of Burgundy (p. 116.), without supposing, like Matthew Paris, that he was bribed by Saladin.

left wing, without meeting an adversary who dared to encounter his career.[78] Am I writing the history of Orlando or Amadis?

His treaty and departure, A.D. 1192, September.

During these hostilities, a languid and tedious negociation[79] between the Franks and Moslems, was started, and continued, and broken, and again resumed, and again broken. Some acts of royal courtesy, the gift of snow and fruit, the exchange of Norway hawks and Arabian horses, softened the asperity of religious war: from the vicissitude of success, the monarchs might learn to suspect that Heaven was neuter in the quarrel; nor, after the trial of each other, could either hope for a decisive victory.[80] The health both of Richard and Saladin appeared to be in a declining state; and they respectively suffered the evils of distant and domestic warfare: Plantagenet was impatient to punish a perfidious rival who had invaded Normandy in his absence; and the indefatigable sultan was subdued by the cries of the people, who was the victim, and of the soldiers, who were the instruments, of his martial zeal. The first demands of the king of England were the restitution of Jerusalem, Palestine, and the true cross; and he firmly declared, that himself and his brother pilgrims would end their lives in the pious labour, rather than return to Europe with ignominy and remorse. But the conscience of Saladin refused, without some weighty compensation, to restore the idols, or promote the idolatry, of the Christians: he asserted, with equal firmness, his religious and civil claim to the sovereignty of Palestine; descanted on the importance and sanctity of Jerusalem; and rejected all terms of the establishment, or partition, of the Latins. The marriage which Richard proposed, of his sister with the sultan's brother,

78. The expeditions to Ascalon, Jerusalem, and Jaffa, are related by Bohadin (p. 184–249.) and Abulfeda (p. 51, 52.). The author of the Itinerary, or the monk of St. Alban's, cannot exaggerate the Cadhi's account of the prowess of Richard (Vinisauf, l. vi. c. 14–24. p. 412–421. Hist. Major, p. 137–143.); and on the whole of this war, there is a marvellous agreement between the Christian and Mahometan writers, who mutually praise the virtues of their enemies.

79. See the progress of negociation and hostility in Bohadin (p. 207–260.), who was himself an actor in the treaty. Richard declared his intention of returning with new armies to the conquest of the Holy Land; and Saladin answered the menace with a civil compliment (Vinisauf, l. vi. c. 28. p. 423.).

80. The most copious and original account of this holy war, is Galfridi à Vinisauf Itinerarium Regis Anglorum Richardi et aliorum in Terram Hierosolymorum, in six books, published in the ii[d] volume of Gale's Scriptores Hist. Anglicanæ (p. 247–429.). Roger Hoveden and Matthew Paris afford likewise many valuable materials; and the former describes, with accuracy, the discipline and navigation of the English fleet.

was defeated by the difference of faith: the princess abhorred the embraces of a Turk; and Adel, or Saphadin, would not easily renounce a plurality of wives. A personal interview was declined by Saladin, who alleged their mutual ignorance of each other's language; and the negociation was managed with much art and delay by their interpreters and envoys. The final agreement was equally disapproved by the zealots of both parties, by the Roman pontiff and the caliph of Bagdad. It was stipulated that Jerusalem and the holy sepulchre should be open, without tribute or vexation, to the pilgrimage of the Latin Christians; that, after the demolition of Ascalon, they should inclusively possess the sea-coast from Jaffa to Tyre; that the count of Tripoli and the prince of Antioch should be comprised in the truce; and that, during three years and three months, all hostilities should cease. The principal chiefs of the two armies swore to the observance of the treaty; but the monarchs were satisfied with giving their word and their right-hand; and the royal majesty was excused from an oath, which always implies some suspicion of falsehood and dishonour. Richard embarked for Europe to seek a long captivity and a premature grave; and the space of a few months concluded the life and glories of Saladin. The Orientals describe his edifying death, which happened at Damascus; but they seem ignorant of the equal distribution of his alms among the three religions,[81] or of the display of a shroud, instead of a standard, to admonish the East of the instability of human greatness. The unity of empire was dissolved by his death; his sons were oppressed by the stronger arm of their uncle Saphadin; the hostile interests of the sultans of Egypt, Damascus, and Aleppo,[82] were again revived; and the Franks or Latins stood, and breathed, and hoped, in their fortresses along the Syrian coast.

Death of Saladin, A.D. 1193, March 4.

Innocent III. A.D. 1198–1216.

The noblest monument of a conqueror's fame, and of the terror which he inspired, is the Saladine tenth, a general tax, which was imposed on the laity, and even the clergy, of the Latin church for the service of the holy war. The practice was too lucrative to expire with the occasion; and this tribute became the foundation of all the tithes and tenths on ecclesiastical benefices, which have been granted by the Roman pontiffs to Catholic sovereigns, or reserved for

81. Even Vertot (tom. i. p. 251.) adopts the foolish notion of the indifference of Saladin, who professed the Koran with his last breath.

82. See the succession of the Ayoubites, in Abulpharagius (Dynast. p. 277, &c.), and the tables of M. de Guignes, l'Art de Verifier les Dates, and the Bibliotheque Orientale.

the immediate use of the apostolic see.[83] This pecuniary emolument must have tended to encrease the interest of the popes in the recovery of Palestine; after the death of Saladin they preached the crusade, by their epistles, their legates, and their missionaries; and the accomplishment of the pious work might have been expected from the zeal and talents of Innocent the third.[84] Under that young and ambitious priest, the successors of St. Peter attained the full meridian of their greatness; and in a reign of eighteen years, he exercised a despotic command over the emperors and kings, whom he raised and deposed; over the nations, whom an interdict of months or years deprived, for the offence of their rulers, of the exercise of Christian worship. In the council of the Lateran he acted as the ecclesiastical, almost as the temporal, sovereign of the East and West. It was at the feet of his legate that John of England surrendered his crown; and Innocent may boast of the two most signal triumphs over sense and humanity, the establishment of transubstantiation, and the origin of the inquisition. At his voice, two crusades, the fourth and the fifth, were undertaken; but, except a king of Hungary, the princes of the second order were at the head of the pilgrims; the forces were inadequate to the design; nor did the effects correspond with the hopes and wishes of the pope and the people. The fourth crusade was diverted from Syria to Constantinople; and the conquest of the Greek or Roman empire by the Latins will form the proper and important subject of the next chapter. In the fifth,[85] two hundred thousand Franks were landed at the eastern mouth of the Nile. They reasonably hoped that Palestine must be subdued in Egypt, the seat and storehouse of the sultan; and, after a siege of sixteen months, the Moslems deplored the loss of Damietta. But the Christian army was ruined by the pride and insolence of the legate Pelagius, who, in the pope's name, assumed the character of general: the sickly Franks were

The fourth crusade, A.D. 1203.

The fifth, A.D. 1218.

83. Thomassin (Discipline de l'Eglise, tom. iii. p. 311–374.) has copiously treated of the origin, abuses, and restrictions of these *tenths*. A theory was started, but not pursued, that they were rightfully due to the pope, a tenth of the Levites' tenth to the high priest (Selden on Tithes; see his Works, vol. iii. p. ii. p. 1083.).

84. See the Gesta Innocentii III. in Muratori, Script. Rer. Ital. (tom. iii. p. i. p. 486–568.).

85. See the vth crusade, and the siege of Damietta, in Jacobus à Vitriaco (l. iii. p. 1125–1149. in the Gesta Dei of Bongarsius), an eye-witness, Bernard Thesaurarius (in Script. Muratori, tom. vii. p. 825–846. c. 190–207.), a contemporary, and Sanutus (Secreta Fidel. Crucis, l. iii. p. xi. c. 4–9.), a diligent compiler; and of the Arabians, Abulpharagius (Dynast. p. 294.), and the Extracts at the end of Joinville (p. 533. 537. 540. 547, &c.).

encompassed by the waters of the Nile and the Oriental forces; and it was by the evacuation of Damietta that they obtained a safe retreat, some concessions for the pilgrims, and the tardy restitution of the doubtful relic of the true cross. The failure may in some measure be ascribed to the abuse and multiplication of the crusades, which were preached at the same time against the Pagans of Livonia, the Moors of Spain, the Albigeois of France, and the kings of Sicily, of the Imperial family.[86] In these meritorious services, the volunteers might acquire at home the same spiritual indulgence, and a larger measure of temporal rewards; and even the popes, in their zeal against a domestic enemy, were sometimes tempted to forget the distress of their Syrian brethren. From the last age of the crusades they derived the occasional command of any army and revenue; and some deep reasoners have suspected that the whole enterprise, from the first synod of Placentia, was contrived and executed by the policy of Rome. The suspicion is not founded, either in nature or in fact. The successors of St. Peter appear to have followed, rather than guided, the impulse of manners and prejudice; without much foresight of the seasons, or cultivation of the soil, they gathered the ripe and spontaneous fruits of the superstition of the times. They gathered these fruits without toil or personal danger: in the council of the Lateran, Innocent the third declared an ambiguous resolution of animating the crusaders by his example; but the pilot of the sacred vessel could not abandon the helm; nor was Palestine ever blessed with the presence of a Roman pontiff.[87]

The emperor Frederic II. in Palestine, A.D. 1228.

The persons, the families, and estates of the pilgrims, were under the immediate protection of the popes; and these spiritual patrons soon claimed the prerogative of directing their operations, and enforcing, by commands and censures, the accomplishment of their vow. Frederic the second,[88] the grandson of Barbarossa, was successively the pupil, the enemy, and the victim, of the

86. To those who took the cross against Mainfroy, the pope (A.D. 1255) granted plenissimam peccatorum remissionem. Fideles mirabantur quòd tantum eis promitteret pro sanguine Christianorum effundendo quantum pro cruore infidelium aliquando (Matthew Paris, p. 785.). A high flight for the reason of the xiii[th] century.

87. This simple idea is agreeable to the good sense of Mosheim (Institut. Hist. Eccles. p. 332.) and the fine philosophy of Hume (Hist. of England, vol. i. p. 330.).

88. The original materials for the crusade of Frederic II. may be drawn from Richard de St. Germano (in Muratori, Script. Rerum Ital. tom. vii. p. 1002–1013.) and Matthew Paris (p. 286. 291. 300. 302. 304.). The most rational moderns are, Fleury (Hist. Eccles. tom. xvi.), Vertot (Chevaliers

church. At the age of twenty-one years, and in obedience to his guardian Innocent the third, he assumed the cross; the same promise was repeated at his royal and imperial coronations; and his marriage with the heiress of Jerusalem for ever bound him to defend the kingdom of his son Conrad. But as Frederic advanced in age and authority, he repented of the rash engagements of his youth: his liberal sense and knowledge taught him to despise the phantoms of superstition and the crowns of Asia: he no longer entertained the same reverence for the successors of Innocent; and his ambition was occupied by the restoration of the Italian monarchy from Sicily to the Alps. But the success of this project would have reduced the popes to their primitive simplicity; and, after the delays and excuses of twelve years, they urged the emperor, with intreaties and threats, to fix the time and place of his departure for Palestine. In the harbours of Sicily and Apulia, he prepared a fleet of one hundred gallies, and of one hundred vessels, that were framed to transport and land two thousand five hundred knights, with their horses and attendants; his vassals of Naples and Germany formed a powerful army; and the number of English crusaders was magnified to sixty thousand by the report of fame. But the inevitable, or affected, slowness of these mighty preparations, consumed the strength and provisions of the more indigent pilgrims: the multitude was thinned by sickness and desertion, and the sultry summer of Calabria anticipated the mischiefs of a Syrian campaign. At length the emperor hoisted sail at Brundusium, with a fleet and army of forty thousand men; but he kept the sea no more than three days; and his hasty retreat, which was ascribed by his friends to a grievous indisposition, was accused by his enemies as a voluntary and obstinate disobedience. For suspending his vow, was Frederic excommunicated by Gregory the ninth; for presuming, the next year, to accomplish his vow, he was again excommunicated by the same pope.[89] While he served under the banner of the cross, a crusade was preached against him in Italy; and after his return he was compelled to ask pardon for the injuries which he had suffered. The clergy and military orders of Palestine were previously instructed to renounce his communion and dispute his commands; and in his own kingdom, the emperor was forced to consent that the orders of the camp should be issued in the name of God and of the Christian republic. Frederic entered Jerusalem in triumph; and with his own hands (for no

---

de Malthe, tom. i. l. iii.), Giannone (Istoria Civile di Napoli, tom. ii. l. xvi.), and Muratori (Annali d'Italia, tom. x.).

89. Poor Muratori knows what to think, but knows not what to say, "Chino qûi il capo," &c. p. 322.

priest would perform the office) he took the crown from the altar of the holy sepulchre. But the patriarch cast an interdict on the church which his presence had profaned; and the knights of the hospital and temple informed the sultan how easily he might be surprised and slain in his unguarded visit to the river Jordan. In such a state of fanaticism and faction, victory was hopeless and defence was difficult; but the conclusion of an advantageous peace may be imputed to the discord of the Mahometans and their personal esteem for the character of Frederic. The enemy of the church is accused of maintaining with the miscreants an intercourse of hospitality and friendship, unworthy of a Christian; of despising the barrenness of the land; and of indulging a profane thought, that if Jehovah had seen the kingdom of Naples, he never would have selected Palestine for the inheritance of his chosen people. Yet Frederic obtained from the sultan the restitution of Jerusalem, of Bethlem and Nazareth, of Tyre and Sidon: the Latins were allowed to inhabit and fortify the city; an equal code of civil and religious freedom was ratified for the sectaries of Jesus and those of Mahomet; and, while the former worshipped at the holy sepulchre, the latter might pray and preach in the mosch of the temple,[90] from whence the prophet undertook his nocturnal journey to heaven. The clergy deplored this scandalous toleration; and the weaker Moslems were gradually expelled; but every rational object of the crusades was accomplished without bloodshed; the churches were restored, the monasteries were replenished; and, in the space of fifteen years, the Latins of Jerusalem exceeded the number of six thousand. This peace and prosperity, for which they were ungrateful to their benefactor, was terminated by the irruption of the strange and savage hords of Carizmians.[91] Flying from the arms of the Moguls, those shepherds of the Caspian rolled headlong on Syria; and the union of the Franks with the sultans of Aleppo, Hems, and Damascus, was insufficient to stem the violence of the torrent. Whatever stood against them, was cut off by the sword, or dragged into captivity; the military orders were almost exterminated in a single battle; and in the pillage of the city, in the profanation of the holy sepulchre, the Latins confess and regret the modesty and discipline of the Turks and Saracens.

Invasion of the Carizmians, A.D. 1243.

90. The clergy artfully confounded the mosch or church of the temple with the holy sepulchre, and their wilful error has deceived both Vertot and Muratori.

91. The irruption of the Carizmians, or Corasmins, is related by Matthew Paris (p. 546, 547.), and by Joinville, Nangis, and the Arabians (p. 111, 112. 191, 192. 528. 530.).

St. Louis, and the sixth crusade, A.D. 1248–1254.

Of the seven crusades, the two last were undertaken by Louis the ninth, king of France; who lost his liberty in Egypt, and his life on the coast of Africa. Twenty-eight years after his death, he was canonized at Rome; and sixty-five miracles were readily found, and solemnly attested, to justify the claim of the royal saint.[92] The voice of history renders a more honourable testimony, that he united the virtues of a king, an hero, and a man; that his martial spirit was tempered by the love of private and public justice; and that Louis was the father of his people, the friend of his neighbours, and the terror of the infidels. Superstition alone, in all the extent of her baleful influence,[93] corrupted his understanding and his heart; his devotion stooped to admire and imitate the begging friars of Francis and Dominic; he pursued with blind and cruel zeal the enemies of the faith; and the best of kings twice descended from his throne to seek the adventures of a spiritual knight-errant. A monkish historian would have been content to applaud the most despicable part of his character; but the noble and gallant Joinville,[94] who shared the friendship and captivity of Louis, has traced with the pencil of nature the free portrait of his virtues as well as of his failings. From this intimate knowledge, we may learn to suspect the political views of depressing their great vassals, which are so often imputed to the royal authors of the crusades. Above all the princes of the middle ages, Louis the ninth successfully laboured to restore the prerogatives of the crown; but it was at home, and not in the East, that he acquired for himself and his posterity; his vow was the result of enthusiasm and sickness; and if he were the promoter, he was likewise the victim, of this holy madness. For the invasion of Egypt, France was exhausted of her troops and treasures; he covered the sea of Cyprus with eighteen hundred sails; the most modest enumeration amounts to fifty

92. Read, if you can, the life and miracles of St. Louis, by the confessor of queen Margaret (p. 291–523. Joinville, du Louvre).

93. He believed all that mother church taught (Joinville, p. 10.), but he cautioned Joinville against disputing with infidels. "L'omme lay (said he in his old language) quand il ot medire de la loy Crestienne, ne doit pas deffendre la loy Crestienne ne mais que de l'espée, dequoi il doit donner parmi le ventre dedens, tant comme elle y peut entrer" (p. 12.).

94. I have two editions of Joinville, the one (Paris, 1668) most valuable for the observations of Ducange; the other (Paris au Louvre, 1761) most precious for the pure and authentic text, a MS. of which has been recently discovered. The last editor proves, that the history of St. Louis was finished A.D. 1309, without explaining, or even admiring, the age of the author, which must have exceeded ninety years (Preface, p. xi. Observations de Ducange, p. 17.).

thousand men; and, if we might trust his own confession, as it is reported by Oriental vanity, he disembarked nine thousand five hundred horse, and one hundred and thirty thousand foot, who performed their pilgrimage under the shadow of his power.[95]

He takes Damietta, A.D. 1249.

In complete armour, the oriflamme waving before him, Louis leaped foremost on the beach; and the strong city of Damietta, which had cost his predecessors a siege of sixteen months, was abandoned on the first assault by the trembling Moslems. But Damietta was the first and the last of his conquests; and in the fifth and sixth crusades, the same causes, almost on the same ground, were productive of similar calamities.[96] After a ruinous delay, which introduced into the camp the seeds of an epidemical disease, the Franks advanced from the sea-coast towards the capital of Egypt, and strove to surmount the unseasonable inundation of the Nile, which opposed their progress. Under the eye of their intrepid monarch, the barons and knights of France displayed their invincible contempt of danger and discipline: his brother, the count of Artois, stormed with inconsiderate valour the town of Massoura; and the carrier pigeons announced to the inhabitants of Cairo, that all was lost. But a soldier, who afterwards usurped the sceptre, rallied the flying troops: the main body of the Christians was far behind their vanguard; and Artois was overpowered and slain. A shower of Greek fire was incessantly poured on the invaders; the Nile was commanded by the Egyptian gallies, the open country by the Arabs; all provisions were intercepted; each day aggravated the sickness and famine; and about the same time a retreat was found to be necessary and impracticable. The Oriental writers confess, that Louis might have escaped, if he would have deserted his subjects: he was made prisoner, with the greatest part of his nobles; all who could not redeem their lives by service or ransom, were inhumanly massacred; and the walls of Cairo were decorated with a circle of Christian heads.[97] The king of France was loaded with chains; but the generous victor, a great grandson of the brother of Saladin, sent a robe of honour to his royal captive; and his deliverance,

His captivity in Egypt,

95. Joinville, p. 32. Arabic Extracts, p. 549.

96. The last editors have enriched their Joinville with large and curious extracts from the Arabic historians, Macrizi, Abulfeda, &c. See likewise Abulpharagius (Dynast. p. 322–325.), who calls him by the corrupt name of *Redefrans*. Matthew Paris (p. 683, 684.) has described the rival folly of the French and English who fought and fell at Massoura.

97. Savary, in his agreeable Lettres sur l'Egypte, has given a description of Damietta (tom. i. lettre xxiii. p. 274–290.), and a narrative of the expedition of St. Louis (xxv. p. 306–350.).

with that of his soldiers, was obtained by the restitution of Damietta[98] and the payment of four hundred thousand pieces of gold. In a soft and luxurious climate, the degenerate children of the companions of Noureddin and Saladin were incapable of resisting the flower of European chivalry: they triumphed by the arms of their slaves or Mamalukes, the hardy natives of Tartary, who at a tender age had been purchased of the Syrian merchants, and were educated in the camp and palace of the sultan. But Egypt soon afforded a new example of the danger of prætorian bands; and the rage of these ferocious animals, who had been let loose on the strangers, was provoked to devour their benefactor. In the pride of conquest, Touran Shaw, the last of his race, was murdered by his Mamalukes; and the most daring of the assassins entered the chamber of the captive king, with drawn scymetars, and their hands imbrued in the blood of their sultan. The firmness of Louis commanded their respect;[99] their avarice prevailed over cruelty and zeal; the treaty was accomplished; and the king of France, with the relics of his army, was permitted to embark for Palestine. He wasted four years within the walls of Acre, unable to visit Jerusalem, and unwilling to return without glory to his native country.

A.D. 1250 April 5–May 6

The memory of his defeat excited Louis, after sixteen years of wisdom and repose, to undertake the seventh and last of the crusades. His finances were restored, his kingdom was enlarged; a new generation of warriors had arisen, and he embarked with fresh confidence at the head of six thousand horse and thirty thousand foot. The loss of Antioch had provoked the enterprise: a wild hope of baptising the king of Tunis, tempted him to steer for the African coast; and the report of an immense treasure reconciled his troops to the delay of their voyage to the Holy Land. Instead of a proselyte, he found a siege; the French panted and died on the burning sands; St. Louis expired in his tent; and no sooner had he closed his eyes, than his son and successor

His death before Tunis, in the

98. For the ransom of St. Louis, a million of byzants was asked and granted; but the sultan's generosity reduced that sum to 800,000 byzants, which are valued by Joinville at 400,000 French livres of his own time, and expressed by Matthew Paris by 100,000 marks of silver (Ducange, Dissertation xx. sur Joinville).

99. The idea of the emirs to chuse Louis for their sultan, is seriously attested by Joinville (p. 77, 78.), and does not appear to me so absurd as to M. de Voltaire (Hist. Generale, tom. ii. p. 386, 387.). The Mamalukes themselves were strangers, rebels, and equals; they had felt his valour, they hoped his conversion; and such a motion, which was not seconded, might be made, perhaps by a secret Christian, in their tumultuous assembly.

seventh crusade, A.D. 1270, August 25. gave the signal of the retreat.[100] "It is thus," says a lively writer, "that a Christian king died near the ruins of Carthage, waging war against the sectaries of Mahomet, in a land to which Dido had introduced the deities of Syria."[101]

The Mamalukes of Egypt, A.D. 1250–1517. A more unjust and absurd constitution cannot be devised, than that which condemns the natives of a country to perpetual servitude, under the arbitrary dominion of strangers and slaves. Yet such has been the state of Egypt above five hundred years. The most illustrious sultans of the Baharite and Borgite dynasties,[102] were themselves promoted from the Tartar and Circassian bands; and the four-and-twenty beys or military chiefs, have ever been succeeded, not by their sons, but by their servants. They produce the great charter of their liberties, the treaty of Selim the first with the republic;[103] and the Othman emperor still accepts from Egypt a slight acknowledgment of tribute and subjection. With some breathing intervals of peace and order, the two dynasties are marked as a period of rapine and bloodshed:[104] but their throne, however shaken, reposed on the two pillars of discipline and valour; their sway extended over Egypt, Nubia, Arabia, and Syria; their Mamalukes were multiplied from eight hundred to twenty-five thousand horse; and their numbers were encreased by a provincial militia of one hundred and seven thousand foot, and the occasional aid of sixty-six thousand Arabs.[105] Princes of such power and spirit could not long endure on their coast an hostile and independent

100. See the expedition in the Annals of St. Louis, by William de Nangis, p. 270–287. and the Arabic Extracts, p. 545. 555. of the Louvre edition of Joinville.

101. Voltaire, Hist. Generale, tom. ii. p. 391.

102. The chronology of the two dynasties of Mamalukes, the Baharites, Turks or Tartars of Kipzak, and the Borgites, Circassians, is given by Pocock (Prolegom. ad Abulpharag. p. 6–31.) and de Guignes (tom. i. p. 264–270.); their history from Abulfeda, Macrizi, &c. to the beginning of the xv[th] century, by the same M. de Guignes (tom. iv. p. 110–328.).

103. Savary, Lettres sur l'Egypte, tom. ii. lettre xv. p. 189–208. I much question the authenticity of this copy; yet it is true, that sultan Selim concluded a treaty with the Circassians or Mamalukes of Egypt, and left them in possession of arms, riches, and power. See a new Abregé de l'Histoire Ottomane, composed in Egypt, and translated by M. Digeon (tom. i. p. 55–58. Paris, 1781), a curious, authentic, and national history.

104. Si totum quo regnum occupârunt tempus respicias, presertim quod fini propius, reperies illud bellis, pugnis, injuriis, ac rapinis refertum (Al Jannabi, apud Pocock, p. 31.). The reign of Mohammed (A.D. 1311–1341) affords an happy exception (de Guignes, tom. iv. p. 208–210.).

105. They are now reduced to 8500: but the expence of each Mamaluke may be rated at 100 louis; and Egypt groans under the avarice and insolence of these strangers (Voyages de Volney, tom. i. p. 89–187.).

nation; and if the ruin of the Franks was postponed about forty years, they were indebted to the cares of an unsettled reign, to the invasion of the Mogols, and to the occasional aid of some warlike pilgrims. Among these, the English reader will observe the name of our first Edward, who assumed the cross in the lifetime of his father Henry. At the head of a thousand soldiers, the future conqueror of Wales and Scotland delivered Acre from a siege; marched as far as Nazareth with an army of nine thousand men; emulated the fame of his uncle Richard; extorted, by his valour, a ten years truce; and escaped, with a dangerous wound, from the dagger of a fanatic *assassin*.[106] Antioch,[107] whose situation had been less exposed to the calamities of the holy war, was finally occupied and ruined by Bondocdar, or Bibars, sultan of Egypt and Syria; the Latin principality was extinguished; and the first seat of the Christian name was dispeopled by the slaughter of seventeen, and the captivity of one hundred, thousand of her inhabitants. The maritime towns of Laodicea, Gabala, Tripoli, Berytus, Sidon, Tyre, and Jaffa, and the stronger castles of the Hospitalers and Templars, successively fell; and the whole existence of the Franks was confined to the city and colony of St. John of Acre, which is sometimes described by the more classic title of Ptolemais.

Loss of Antioch, A.D. 1268, June 12.

After the loss of Jerusalem, Acre,[108] which is distant about seventy miles, became the metropolis of the Latin Christians, and was adorned with strong and stately buildings, with aqueducts, an artificial port, and a double wall. The population was encreased by the incessant streams of pilgrims and fugitives: in the pauses of hostility, the trade of the East and West was attracted to this convenient station; and the market could offer the produce of every clime and the interpreters of every tongue. But in this conflux of nations, every vice was propagated and practised: of all the disciples of Jesus and Mahomet, the male and female inhabitants of Acre were esteemed the most corrupt; nor could the abuse of religion be corrected by the discipline of law. The city had many sovereigns, and no government. The kings of Jerusalem and Cyprus, of the house of

106. See Carte's History of England, vol. ii. p. 165–175. and his original authors, Thomas Wikes and Walter Hemingford (l. iii. c. 34, 35.), in Gale's Collection (tom. ii. p. 97. 589–592). They are both ignorant of the princess Eleanor's piety in sucking the poisoned wound, and saving her husband at the risk of her own life.

107. Sanutus, Secret. Fidelium Crucis, l. iii. p. xii. c. 9. and de Guignes, Hist. des Huns, tom. iv. p. 143. from the Arabic historians.

108. The state of Acre is represented in all the chronicles of the times, and most accurately in John Villani, l. vii. c. 144. in Muratori, Scriptores Rerum Italicarum, tom. xiii. p. 337, 338.

Lusignan, the princes of Antioch, the counts of Tripoli and Sidon, the great masters of the hospital, the temple, and the Teutonic order, the republics of Venice, Genoa, and Pisa, the pope's legate, the kings of France and England, assumed an independent command: seventeen tribunals exercised the power of life and death; every criminal was protected in the adjacent quarter; and the perpetual jealousy of the nations often burst forth in acts of violence and blood. Some adventurers, who disgraced the ensign of the cross, compensated their want of pay by the plunder of the Mahometan villages: nineteen Syrian merchants, who traded under the public faith, were despoiled and hanged by the Christians; and the denial of satisfaction justified the arms of the sultan Khalil. He marched against Acre, at the head of sixty thousand horse and one hundred and forty thousand foot: his train of artillery (if I may use the word) was numerous and weighty; the separate timbers of a single engine were transported in one hundred waggons; and the royal historian Abulfeda, who served with the troops of Hamah, was himself a spectator of the holy war. Whatever might be the vices of the Franks, their courage was rekindled by enthusiasm and despair; but they were torn by the discord of seventeen chiefs, and overwhelmed on all sides by the powers of the sultan. After a siege of thirty-three days, the double wall was forced by the Moslems; the principal tower yielded to their engines; the Mamalukes made a general assault; the city was stormed; and death or slavery was the lot of sixty thousand Christians. The convent, or rather fortress, of the Templars resisted three days longer; but the great master was pierced with an arrow; and, of five hundred knights, only ten were left alive, less happy than the victims of the sword, if they lived to suffer on a scaffold in the unjust and cruel proscription of the whole order. The king of Jerusalem, the patriarch, and the great master of the hospital, effected their retreat to the shore; but the sea was rough; the vessels were insufficient; and great numbers of the fugitives were drowned before they could reach the isle of Cyprus, which might comfort Lusignan for the loss of Palestine. By the command of the sultan, the churches and fortifications of the Latin cities were demolished: a motive of avarice or fear still opened the holy sepulchre to some devout and defenceless pilgrims; and a mournful and solitary silence prevailed along the coast which had so long resounded with the WORLD'S DEBATE.[109]

The loss of Acre and the Holy Land, A.D. 1291, May 18.

109. See the final expulsion of the Franks, in Sanutus, l. iii. p. xii. c. 11–22. Abulfeda, Macrizi, &c. in de Guignes, tom. iv. p. 162. 164. and Vertot, tom. i. l. iii. p. 407–428.

CHAPTER LX

Schism of the Greeks and Latins. – State of Constantinople. – Revolt of the Bulgarians. – Isaac Angelus dethroned by his Brother Alexius. – Origin of the Fourth Crusade. – Alliance of the French and Venetians with the Son of Isaac. – Their naval Expedition to Constantinople. – The two Sieges and final Conquest of the City by the Latins.

Schism of the Greeks.

The restoration of the Western empire by Charlemagne, was speedily followed by the separation of the Greek and Latin churches.[1] A religious and national animosity still divides the two largest communions of the Christian world; and the schism of Constantinople, by alienating her most useful allies and provoking her most dangerous enemies, has precipitated the decline and fall of the Roman empire in the East.

Their aversion to the Latins.

In the course of the present history, the aversion of the Greeks for the Latins has been often visible and conspicuous. It was originally derived from the disdain of servitude, inflamed, after the time of Constantine, by the pride of equality or dominion; and finally exasperated by the preference which their rebellious subjects had given to the alliance of the Franks. In every age, the Greeks were proud of their superiority in profane and religious knowledge: they had first received the light of Christianity; they had pronounced the decrees of the seven general councils: they alone possessed the language of scripture and philosophy; nor should the Barbarians, immersed in the darkness of the West,[2] presume to argue on the high and mysterious questions of theological science. Those Barbarians despised in their turn the restless and subtle levity of the Orientals, the authors of every heresy; and blessed

1. In the successive centuries, from the ixth to the xviiith, Mosheim traces the schism of the Greeks, with learning, clearness, and impartiality: the *filioque* (Institut. Hist. Eccles. p. 277.), Leo III. p. 303. Photius, p. 307, 308. Michael Cerularius, p. 370, 371, &c.

2. Ανδρες δυσσεβεις και αποτροπαιοι, ανδρες εκ σκοτους αναδυντες, της γαρ 'Εσπεριου μοιρας ὑπηρχον γεννηματα (Phot. Epist. p. 47. edit. Montacut.). The Oriental patriarch continues to apply the images of thunder, earthquake, hail, wild-boar, præcursors of Antichrist, &c. &c.

their own simplicity, which was content to hold the tradition of the apostolic church. Yet in the seventh century, the synods of Spain, and afterwards of France, improved or corrupted the Nicene creed, on the mysterious subject of the third person of the Trinity.[3] In the long controversies of the East, the nature and generation of the Christ had been scrupulously defined; and the well-known relation of father and son seemed to convey a faint image to the human mind. The idea of birth was less analogous to the Holy Spirit, who, instead of a divine gift or attribute, was considered by the Catholics, as a substance, a person, a god; he was not begotten, but in the orthodox style he *proceeded*. Did he proceed from the Father alone, perhaps *by* the Son? or from the Father and the Son? The first of these opinions was asserted by the Greeks, the second by the Latins; and the addition to the Nicene creed of the word *filioque*, kindled the flame of discord between the Oriental and the Gallic churches. In the origin of the dispute, the Roman pontiffs affected a character of neutrality and moderation:[4] they condemned the innovation, but they acquiesced in the sentiment, of their Transalpine brethren: they seemed desirous of casting a veil of silence and charity over the superfluous research; and in the correspondence of Charlemagne and Leo the third, the pope assumes the liberality of a statesman, and the prince descends to the passions and prejudices of a priest.[5] But the orthodoxy of Rome spontaneously obeyed the impulse of her temporal policy; and the *filioque*, which Leo wished to erase, was transcribed in the symbol and chaunted in the liturgy of the Vatican. The Nicene and Athanasian creeds are held as the Catholic faith, without which none can be saved; and both Papists and Protestants must now sustain and return the anathemas of the Greeks, who deny the procession of the Holy Ghost from the Son, as well as from the Father. Such articles of faith are not susceptible of treaty; but the

Procession of the Holy Ghost.

Variety of ecclesiastical discipline.

3. The mysterious subject of the procession of the Holy Ghost, is discussed in the historical, theological, and controversial sense, or nonsense, by the Jesuit Petavius (Dogmata Theologica, tom. ii. l. vii. p. 362–440.).

4. Before the shrine of St. Peter, he placed two shields of the weight of 94½ pounds of pure silver; on which he inscribed the text of both creeds (utroque symbolo), pro amore et *cautelâ* orthodoxæ fidei (Anastas. in Leon. III. in Muratori, tom. iii. pars i. p. 208.). His language most clearly proves, that neither the filioque, nor the Athanasian creed, were received at Rome about the year 830.

5. The Missi of Charlemagne pressed him to declare, that all who rejected the *filioque*, at least the doctrine, must be damned. All, replies the pope, are not capable of reaching the altiora mysteria; qui potuerit, et non voluerit, salvus esse non potest (Collect. Concil. tom. ix. p. 277–286.). The *potuerit* would leave a large loop-hole of salvation!

rules of discipline will vary in remote and independent churches; and the reason, even of divines, might allow, that the difference is inevitable and harmless. The craft or superstition of Rome has imposed on her priests and deacons the rigid obligation of celibacy; among the Greeks, it is confined to the bishops; the loss is compensated by dignity or annihilated by age; and the parochial clergy, the papas, enjoy the conjugal society of the wives whom they have married before their entrance into holy orders. A question concerning the *Azyms* was fiercely debated in the eleventh century, and the essence of the Eucharist was supposed in the East and West, to depend on the use of leavened or unleavened bread. Shall I mention in a serious history the furious reproaches that were urged against the Latins, who, for a long while remained on the defensive? They neglected to abstain, according to the apostolical decree, from things strangled, and from blood: they fasted, a Jewish observance! on the Saturday of each week: during the first week of Lent they permitted the use of milk and cheese;[6] their infirm monks were indulged in the taste of flesh; and animal grease was substituted for the want of vegetable oil: the holy chrism of unction in baptism, was reserved to the episcopal order: the bishops, as the bridegrooms of their churches, were decorated with rings; their priests shaved their faces, and baptized by a single immersion. Such were the crimes which provoked the zeal of the patriarchs of Constantinople; and which were justified with equal zeal by the doctors of the Latin church.[7]

Ambitious quarrels of Photius, patriarch of Constantinople, with the popes, A.D. 857–886.

Bigotry and national aversion are powerful magnifiers of every object of dispute; but the immediate cause of the schism of the Greeks may be traced in the emulation of the leading prelates, who maintained the supremacy of the old metropolis superior to all, and of the reigning capital, inferior to none, in the Christian world. About the middle of the ninth century, Photius,[8] an ambitious layman, the captain of the guards and principal secretary, was promoted by merit and favour to the more

6. In France, after some harsher laws, the ecclesiastical discipline is now relaxed: milk, cheese, and butter, are become a perpetual, and eggs an annual, indulgence in Lent (Vie privée des François, tom. ii. p. 27–38.).

7. The original monuments of the schism, of the charges of the Greeks against the Latins, are deposited in the Epistles of Photius (Epist. Encyclica, ii. p. 47–61.) and of Michael Cerularius (Canisii Antiq. Lectiones, tom. iii. p. i. p. 281–324. edit. Basnage, with the prolix answer of cardinal Humbert).

8. The xth volume of the Venice edition of the Councils, contains all the acts of the synods, and history of Photius: they are abridged, with a faint tinge of prejudice or prudence, by Dupin and Fleury.

desirable office of patriarch of Constantinople. In science, even ecclesiastical science, he surpassed the clergy of the age; and the purity of his morals has never been impeached: but his ordination was hasty, his rise was irregular; and Ignatius, his abdicated predecessor, was yet supported by the public compassion and the obstinacy of his adherents. They appealed to the tribunal of Nicholas the first, one of the proudest and most aspiring of the Roman pontiffs, who embraced the welcome opportunity of judging and condemning his rival of the East. Their quarrel was embittered by a conflict of jurisdiction over the king and nation of the Bulgarians; nor was their recent conversion to Christianity of much avail to either prelate, unless he could number the proselytes among the subjects of his power. With the aid of his court the Greek patriarch was victorious; but in the furious contest he deposed in his turn the successor of St. Peter, and involved the Latin church in the reproach of heresy and schism. Photius sacrificed the peace of the world to a short and precarious reign: he fell with his patron, the Cæsar Bardas; and Basil the Macedonian performed an act of justice in the restoration of Ignatius, whose age and dignity had not been sufficiently respected. From his monastery, or prison, Photius solicited the favour of the emperor by pathetic complaints and artful flattery; and the eyes of his rival were scarcely closed, when he was again restored to the throne of Constantinople. After the death of Basil, he experienced the vicissitudes of courts and the ingratitude of a royal pupil: the patriarch was again deposed, and in his last solitary hours he might regret the freedom of a secular and studious life. In each revolution, the breath, the nod, of the sovereign had been accepted by a submissive clergy; and a synod of three hundred bishops was always prepared to hail the triumph, or to stigmatize the fall, of the holy, or the execrable, Photius.[9] By a delusive promise of succour or reward, the popes were tempted to countenance these various proceedings; and the synods of Constantinople were ratified by their epistles or legates. But the court and the people, Ignatius and Photius, were equally adverse to their claims; their ministers were insulted or imprisoned; the procession of the Holy Ghost was forgotten; Bulgaria was for ever annexed to the Byzantine throne; and the schism was prolonged by their rigid censure of all the multiplied ordinations of an irregular patriarch. The darkness and corruption of the tenth century

9. The synod of Constantinople, held in the year 869, is the viii[th] of the general councils, the last assembly of the East which is recognised by the Roman church. She rejects the synods of Constantinople of the years 867 and 879, which were, however, equally numerous and noisy; but they were favourable to Photius.

suspended the intercourse, without reconciling the minds, of the two nations. But when the Norman sword restored the churches of Apulia to the jurisdiction of Rome, the departing flock was warned, by a petulant epistle of the Greek patriarch, to avoid and abhor the errors of the Latins. The rising majesty of Rome could no longer brook the insolence of a rebel; and Michael Cerularius was excommunicated in the heart of Constantinople by the pope's legates. Shaking the dust from their feet, they deposited on the altar of St. Sophia a direful anathema,[10] which enumerates the seven mortal heresies of the Greeks, and devotes the guilty teachers, and their unhappy sectaries, to the eternal society of the devil and his angels. According to the emergencies of the church and state, a friendly correspondence was sometimes resumed; the language of charity and concord was sometimes affected; but the Greeks have never recanted their errors; the popes have never repealed their sentence: and from this thunderbolt we may date the consummation of the schism. It was enlarged by each ambitious step of the Roman pontiffs: the emperors blushed and trembled at the ignominious fate of their royal brethren of Germany; and the people was scandalized by the temporal power and military life of the Latin clergy.[11]

The popes excommunicate the patriarch of Constantinople and the Greeks, A.D. 1054, July 16.

The aversion of the Greeks and Latins was nourished and manifested in the three first expeditions to the Holy Land. Alexius Comnenus contrived the absence at least of the formidable pilgrims: his successors, Manuel and Isaac Angelus, conspired with the Moslems for the ruin of the greatest princes of the Franks; and their crooked and malignant policy was seconded by the active and voluntary obedience of every order of their subjects. Of this hostile temper, a large portion may doubtless be ascribed to the difference of language, dress, and manners, which severs and alienates the nations of the globe. The pride, as well as the prudence, of the sovereign, was deeply wounded by the intrusion of foreign armies, that claimed a right of traversing his dominions and passing under the walls of his capital: his subjects were insulted and plundered by the rude strangers of the West; and the hatred of the pusillanimous Greeks was sharpened by secret envy of the bold and pious enterprises of the Franks. But these profane

Enmity of the Greeks and Latins, A.D. 1100–1200.

10. See this anathema in the Councils, tom. xi. p. 1457–1460.

11. Anna Comnena (Alexiad, l. i. p. 31–33.) represents the abhorrence, not only of the church, but of the palace, for Gregory VII. the popes, and the Latin communion. The style of Cinnamus and Nicetas is still more vehement. Yet how calm is the voice of history compared with that of polemics!

causes of national enmity were fortified and inflamed by the venom of religious zeal. Instead of a kind embrace, an hospitable reception from their Christian brethren of the East, every tongue was taught to repeat the names of schismatic and heretic, more odious to an orthodox ear than those of pagan and infidel: instead of being loved for the general conformity of faith and worship, they were abhorred for some rules of discipline, some questions of theology, in which themselves or their teachers might differ from the Oriental church. In the crusade of Louis the seventh, the Greek clergy washed and purified the altars which had been defiled by the sacrifice of a French priest. The companions of Frederic Barbarossa deplore the injuries which they endured, both in word and deed, from the peculiar rancour of the bishops and monks. Their prayers and sermons excited the people against the impious Barbarians; and the patriarch is accused of declaring, that the faithful might obtain the redemption of all their sins by the extirpation of the schismatics.[12] An enthusiast, named Dorotheus, alarmed the fears, and restored the confidence, of the emperor, by a prophetic assurance, that the German heretic, after assaulting the gate of Blachernes, would be made a signal example of the divine vengeance. The passage of these mighty armies were rare and perilous events; but the crusades introduced a frequent and familiar intercourse between the two nations, which enlarged their knowledge, without abating their prejudices. The wealth and luxury of Constantinople demanded the productions of every climate: these imports were balanced by the art and labour of her numerous inhabitants; her situation invites the commerce of the world; and, in every period of her existence, that commerce has been in the hands of foreigners. After the decline of Amalphi, the Venetians, Pisans, and Genoese, introduced their factories and settlements into the capital of the empire: their services were rewarded with honours and immunities; they acquired the possession of lands and houses; their families were multiplied by marriages with the natives; and, after the toleration of a

The Latins at Constantinople:

12. His anonymous historian (de Expedit. Asiat. Fred. I. in Canisii Lection. Antiq. tom. iii. pars ii. p. 511. edit. Basnage) mentions the sermons of the Greek patriarch, quomodo Græcis injunxerat in remissionem peccatorum peregrinos occidere et delere de terra. Tagino observes (in Scriptores Freher. tom. i. p. 409. edit. Struv.), Græci hæreticos nos appellant: clerici et monachi dictis et factis persequuntur. We may add the declaration of the emperor Baldwin fifteen years afterwards: Hæc est *(gens)* quæ Latinos omnes non hominum nomine, sed canum dignabatur; quorum sanguinem effundere penè inter merita reputabant (Gesta Innocent. III. c. 92. in Muratori, Script. Rerum Italicarum. tom. iii. pars i. p. 536.). There may be some exaggeration, but it was as effectual for the action and re-action of hatred.

Mahometan mosch, it was impossible to interdict the churches of the Roman rite.[13] The two wives of Manuel Comnenus[14] were of the race of the Franks; the first, a sister-in-law of the emperor Conrad; the second, a daughter of the prince of Antioch: he obtained for his son Alexius a daughter of Philip Augustus king of France; and he bestowed his own daughter on a marquis of Montferrat, who was educated and dignified in the palace of Constantinople. The Greek encountered the arms, and aspired to the empire, of the West; he esteemed the valour, and trusted the fidelity, of the Franks;[15] their military talents were unfitly recompensed by the lucrative offices of judges and treasurers; the policy of Manuel had solicited the alliance of the pope; and the popular voice accused him of a partial bias to the nation and religion of the Latins.[16] During his reign, and that of his successor Alexius, they were exposed at Constantinople to the reproach of foreigners, heretics, and favourites; and this triple guilt was severely expiated in the tumult, which announced the return and elevation of Andronicus.[17] The people rose in arms; from the Asiatic shore the tyrant dispatched his troops and gallies to assist the national revenge; and the hopeless resistance of the strangers served only to justify the rage, and sharpen the daggers, of the assassins. Neither age, nor sex, nor the ties of friendship or kindred, could save the victims of national hatred, and avarice, and religious zeal: the Latins were slaughtered in their houses and in the streets; their quarter was reduced to ashes; the clergy was burnt in their churches, and the sick in their hospitals; and some estimate may be formed of the slain from the clemency which sold above four thousand Christians in perpetual slavery to the Turks. The priests and monks were the loudest and most active in the destruction of the schismatics; and they chaunted a thanksgiving to

their massacre, A.D. 1183.

13. See Anna Comnena (Alexiad, l. vi. p. 161, 162.), and a remarkable passage of Nicetas (in Manual. l. v. c. 9.), who observes of the Venetians, *κατα σμηνη και φρατριας την Κωνσταντινου πολιν της οικειας ηλλαξαντο*, &c.

14. Ducange, Fam. Byzant. p. 186, 187.

15. Nicetas in Manuel. l. vii. c. 2. Regnante enim (Manuele) ... apud eum tantam Latinus populus repererat gratiam ut neglectis Græculis suis tanquam viris mollibus et effœminatis, ... solis Latinis grandia committeret negotia ... erga eos profusâ liberalitate abundabat ... ex omni orbe ad eum tanquam ad benefactorem nobiles et ignobiles concurrebant. Willerm. Tyr. xxii. c. 10.

16. The suspicions of the Greeks would have been confirmed, if they had seen the political epistles of Manuel to pope Alexander III. the enemy of his enemy Frederic I. in which the emperor declares his wish of uniting the Greeks and Latins as one flock under one shepherd, &c. (See Fleury, Hist. Eccles. tom. xv. p. 187. 213, 243.)

17. See the Greek and Latin narratives in Nicetas (in Alexio Comneno, c. 10.) and William of Tyre (l. xxii. c. 10, 11, 12, 13.); the first soft and concise, the second loud, copious, and tragical.

the Lord, when the head of a Roman cardinal, the pope's legate, was severed from his body, fastened to the tail of a dog, and dragged, with savage mockery, through the city. The more diligent of the strangers had retreated, on the first alarm, to their vessels, and escaped through the Hellespont from the scene of blood. In their flight, they burnt and ravaged two hundred miles of the sea-coast; inflicted a severe revenge on the guiltless subjects of the empire; marked the priests and monks as their peculiar enemies; and compensated, by the accumulation of plunder, the loss of their property and friends. On their return, they exposed to Italy and Europe the wealth and weakness, the perfidy and malice, of the Greeks, whose vices were painted as the genuine characters of heresy and schism. The scruples of the first crusaders had neglected the fairest opportunities of securing, by the possession of Constantinople, the way to the Holy Land: a domestic revolution invited, and almost compelled, the French and Venetians to atchieve the conquest of the Roman empire of the East.

Reign and character of Isaac Angelus, A.D. 1185–1195, Sept. 12.

In the series of the Byzantine princes, I have exhibited the hypocrisy and ambition, the tyranny and fall, of Andronicus, the last male of the Comnenian family who reigned at Constantinople. The revolution, which cast him headlong from the throne, saved and exalted Isaac Angelus,[18] who descended by the females from the same Imperial dynasty. The successor of a second Nero might have found it an easy task to deserve the esteem and affection of his subjects: they sometimes had reason to regret the administration of Andronicus. The sound and vigorous mind of the tyrant was capable of discerning the connection between his own and the public interest; and while he was feared by all who could inspire him with fear, the unsuspected people, and the remote provinces, might bless the inexorable justice of their master. But his successor was vain and jealous of the supreme power, which he wanted courage and abilities to exercise; his vices were pernicious, his virtues (if he possessed any virtues) were useless, to mankind; and the Greeks, who imputed their calamities to his negligence, denied him the merit of any transient or accidental benefits of the times. Isaac slept on the throne, and was awakened only by the sound of pleasure: his vacant hours were amused by comedians and buffoons, and even to these buffoons the emperor was an object of contempt; his feasts and buildings exceeded the examples of royal luxury;

18. The history of the reign of Isaac Angelus is composed, in three books, by the senator Nicetas (p. 228–290.); and his offices of logothete, or principal secretary, and judge of the veil or palace, could not bribe the impartiality of the historian. He wrote, it is true, after the fall and death of his benefactor.

the number of his eunuchs and domestics amounted to twenty thousand; and a daily sum of four thousand pounds of silver would swell to four millions sterling the annual expence of his household and table. His poverty was relieved by oppression; and the public discontent was inflamed by equal abuses in the collection, and the application, of the revenue. While the Greeks numbered the days of their servitude, a flattering prophet, whom he rewarded with the dignity of patriarch, assured him of a long and victorious reign of thirty-two years; during which he should extend his sway to mount Libanus, and his conquests beyond the Euphrates. But his only step towards the accomplishment of the prediction, was a splendid and scandalous embassy to Saladin,[19] to demand the restitution of the holy sepulchre, and to propose an offensive and defensive league with the enemy of the Christian name. In these unworthy hands, of Isaac and his brother, the remains of the Greek empire crumbled into dust. The island of Cyprus, whose name excites the ideas of elegance and pleasure, was usurped by his namesake, a Comnenian prince: and by a strange concatenation of events, the sword of our English Richard bestowed that kingdom on the house of Lusignan, a rich compensation for the loss of Jerusalem.

Revolt of the Bulgarians, A.D. 1186.

The honour of the monarchy, and the safety of the capital, were deeply wounded by the revolt of the Bulgarians and Walachians. Since the victory of the second Basil, they had supported, above an hundred and seventy years, the loose dominion of the Byzantine princes; but no effectual measures had been adopted to impose the yoke of laws and manners on these savage tribes. By the command of Isaac, their sole means of subsistence, their flocks and herds, were driven away, to contribute towards the pomp of the royal nuptials; and their fierce warriors were exasperated by the denial of equal rank and pay in the military service. Peter and Asan, two powerful chiefs, of the race of the ancient kings,[20] asserted their own rights and the national freedom: their dæmoniac impostors proclaimed to the crowd, that their glorious patron St. Demetrius had for ever deserted the cause of the Greeks; and the conflagration spread from the banks of the Danube to

19. See Bohadin, Vit. Saladin. p. 129–131. 226. vers. Schultens. The ambassador of Isaac was equally versed in the Greek, French, and Arabic languages; a rare instance in those times. His embassies were received with honour, dismissed without effect, and reported with scandal in the West.

20. Ducange, Familiæ Dalmaticæ, p. 318, 319, 320. The original correspondence of the Bulgarian king and the Roman pontiff, is inscribed in the Gesta Innocent. III. c. 66–82. p. 513–525.

the hills of Macedonia and Thrace. After some faint efforts, Isaac Angelus and his brother acquiesced in their independence; and the Imperial troops were soon discouraged by the bones of their fellow-soldiers, that were scattered along the passes of mount Hæmus. By the arms and policy of John or Joannices, the second kingdom of Bulgaria was firmly established. The subtle Barbarian sent an embassy to Innocent the third, to acknowledge himself a genuine son of Rome in descent and religion;[21] and humbly received from the pope, the licence of coining money, the royal title, and a Latin archbishop or patriarch. The Vatican exulted in the spiritual conquest of Bulgaria, the first object of the schism; and if the Greeks could have preserved the prerogatives of the church, they would gladly have resigned the rights of the monarchy.

Usurpation and character of Alexius Angelus, A.D. 1195–1203, April 8.

The Bulgarians were malicious enough to pray for the long life of Isaac Angelus, the surest pledge of their freedom and prosperity. Yet their chiefs could involve in the same indiscriminate contempt, the family and nation of the emperor. "In all the Greeks," said Asan to his troops, "the same climate, and character, and education, will be productive of the same fruits. Behold my lance," continued the warrior, "and the long streamers that float in the wind. They differ only in colour; they are formed of the same silk and fashioned by the same workman; nor has the stripe that is stained in purple, any superior price or value above its fellows."[22] Several of these candidates for the purple successively rose and fell under the empire of Isaac; a general who had repelled the fleets of Sicily, was driven to revolt and ruin by the ingratitude of the prince; and his luxurious repose was disturbed by secret conspiracies and popular insurrections. The emperor was saved by accident, or the merit of his servants: he was at length oppressed by an ambitious brother, who, for the hope of a precarious diadem, forgot the obligations of nature, of loyalty, and of friendship.[23] While Isaac in the Thracian vallies pursued the idle and solitary pleasures of the chace, his brother, Alexius Angelus,

21. The pope acknowledges his pedigree, a nobili urbis Romæ prosapiâ genitores tui originem traxerunt. This tradition, and the strong resemblance of the Latin and Walachian idioms, is explained by M. d'Anville (Etats de l'Europe, p. 258–262.). The Italian colonies of the Dacia of Trajan, were swept away by the tide of emigration from the Danube to the Volga, and brought back by another wave from the Volga to the Danube. Possible, but strange!

22. This parable is in the best savage style; but I wish the Walach had not introduced the classic name of Mysians, the experiment of the magnet or loadstone, and the passage of an old comic poet (Nicetas, in Alex. Comneno, l. i. p. 299, 300.).

23. The Latins aggravate the ingratitude of Alexius, by supposing that he had been released by his brother Isaac from Turkish

was invested with the purple, by the unanimous suffrage of the camp: the capital and the clergy subscribed to their choice; and the vanity of the new sovereign rejected the name of his fathers, for the lofty and royal appellation of the Comnenian race. On the despicable character of Isaac, I have exhausted the language of contempt; and can only add, that in a reign of eight years, the baser Alexius[24] was supported by the masculine vices of his wife Euphrosyne. The first intelligence of his fall was conveyed to the late emperor by the hostile aspect and pursuit of the guards, no longer his own: he fled before them above fifty miles as far as Stagyra in Macedonia; but the fugitive, without an object or a follower, was arrested, brought back to Constantinople, deprived of his eyes, and confined in a lonesome tower, on a scanty allowance of bread and water. At the moment of the revolution, his son Alexius, whom he educated in the hope of empire, was twelve years of age. He was spared by the usurper, and reduced to attend his triumph both in peace and war; but as the army was encamped on the sea-shore, an Italian vessel facilitated the escape of the royal youth; and, in the disguise of a common sailor, he eluded the search of his enemies, passed the Hellespont, and found a secure refuge in the isle of Sicily. After saluting the threshold of the apostles, and imploring the protection of pope Innocent the third, Alexius accepted the kind invitation of his sister Irene, the wife of Philip of Swabia, king of the Romans. But in his passage through Italy, he heard that the flower of Western chivalry was assembled at Venice for the deliverance of the Holy Land; and a ray of hope was kindled in his bosom, that their invincible swords might be employed in his father's restoration.

The fourth crusade, A.D. 1198.

About ten or twelve years after the loss of Jerusalem, the nobles of France were again summoned to the holy war by the voice of a third prophet, less extravagant, perhaps, than Peter the hermit, but far below St. Bernard in the merit of an orator and a statesman. An illiterate priest of the neighbourhood of Paris, Fulk of Neuilly,[25] forsook his parochial duty, to assume the more flattering character of a popular and itinerant missionary. The fame of his sanctity and miracles was spread over the land; he declaimed, with severity and

captivity. This pathetic tale had doubtless been repeated at Venice and Zara: but I do not readily discover its grounds in the Greek historians.

24. See the reign of Alexius Angelus, or Comnenus, in the three books of Nicetas, p. 291–352.

25. See Fleury, Hist. Eccles. tom. xvi. p. 26, &c. and Villehardouin, N° 1. with the observations of Ducange, which I always mean to quote with the original text.

vehemence, against the vices of the age; and his sermons, which he preached in the streets of Paris, converted the robbers, the usurers, the prostitutes, and even the doctors and scholars of the university. No sooner did Innocent the third ascend the chair of St. Peter, than he proclaimed in Italy, Germany, and France, the obligation of a new crusade.[26] The eloquent pontiff described the ruin of Jerusalem, the triumph of the Pagans, and the shame of Christendom: his liberality proposed the redemption of sins, a plenary indulgence to all who should serve in Palestine, either a year in person, or two years by a substitute;[27] and among his legates and orators who blew the sacred trumpet, Fulk of Neuilly was the loudest and most successful. The situation of the principal monarchs was averse to the pious summons. The emperor Frederic the second was a child; and his kingdom of Germany was disputed by the rival houses of Brunswick and Swabia, the memorable factions of the Guelphs and Ghibelines. Philip Augustus of France had performed, and could not be persuaded to renew, the perilous vow; but as he was not less ambitious of praise than of power, he chearfully instituted a perpetual fund for the defence of the Holy Land. Richard of England was satiated with the glory and misfortunes of his first adventure, and he presumed to deride the exhortations of Fulk of Neuilly, who was not abashed in the presence of kings. "You advise me," said Plantagenet, "to dismiss my three daughters, pride, avarice, and incontinence. I bequeath them to the most deserving; my pride to the knights-templars, my avarice to the monks of Cisteaux, and my incontinence to the prelates." But the preacher was heard and obeyed by the great vassals, the princes of the second order; and Theobald, or Thibaut, count of Champagne, was the foremost in the holy race. The valiant youth, at the age of twenty-two years, was encouraged by the domestic examples of his father, who marched in the second crusade, and of his elder brother, who had ended his days in Palestine with the title of king of Jerusalem: two thousand two hundred knights owed service and homage to his peerage:[28] the nobles of Champagne excelled in all the exercises of

Embraced by the barons of France.

26. The contemporary life of pope Innocent III. published by Baluze and Muratori (Scriptores Rerum Italicarum, tom. iii. pars i. p. 486–568.), is most valuable for the important and original documents which are inserted in the text. The bull of the crusade may be read, c. 84, 85.

27. Por-ce que cil pardon fut issi gran, si s'en esmeurent mult li cuers des genz, et mult s'en croisierent, porce que li pardons ere si gran. Villehardouin, N° 1. Our philosophers may refine on the causes of the crusades, but such were the genuine feelings of a French knight.

28. This number of fiefs (of which 1800 owed liege homage) was enrolled in the

war;[29] and by his marriage with the heiress of Navarre, Thibaut could draw a band of hardy Gascons from either side of the Pyrenæan mountains. His companion in arms was Louis, count of Blois and Chartres; like himself of regal lineage, for both the princes were nephews, at the same time, of the kings of France and England. In a crowd of prelates and barons, who imitated their zeal, I distinguish the birth and merit of Matthew of Montmorency; the famous Simon of Montfort, the scourge of the Albigeois; and a valiant noble, Jeffrey of Villehardouin,[30] marshal of Champagne,[31] who has condescended, in the rude idiom of his age and country,[32] to write or dictate[33] an original narrative of the councils and actions, in which he bore a memorable part. At the same time, Baldwin count of Flanders, who had married the sister of Thibaut, assumed the cross at Bruges, with his brother Henry and the principal knights and citizens of that rich and industrious province.[34] The vow which the chiefs had pronounced in churches, they ratified in tournaments: the operations of the war were debated in full and frequent assemblies; and it was resolved to seek the deliverance of Palestine in Egypt, a country, since Saladin's death, which was almost ruined by famine and civil war. But the fate of so many royal armies displayed the

church of St. Stephen at Troyes, and attested A.D. 1213, by the marshal and butler of Champagne (Ducange, Observ. p. 254.).

29. Campania ... militiæ privilegio singularius excellit ... in tyrociniis ... prolusione armorum, &c. Ducange, p. 249. from the old Chronicle of Jerusalem, A.D. 1177–1199.

30. The name of Ville-hardouin, was taken from a village and castle in the diocese of Troyes, near the river Aube, between Bar and Arceis. The family was ancient and noble; the elder branch of our historian existed after the year 1400; the younger, which acquired the principality of Achaia, merged in the house of Savoy (Ducange, p. 235–245.).

31. This office was held by his father and his descendants, but Ducange has not hunted it with his usual sagacity. I find that, in the year 1356, it was in the family of Conflans; but these provincial, have been long since eclipsed by the national, marshals of France.

32. This language, of which I shall produce some specimens, is explained by Vigenere and Ducange in a version and glossary. The president des Brosses (Mechanisme des Langues, tom. ii. p. 83.) gives it as the example of a language which has ceased to be French, and is understood only by grammarians.

33. His age, and his own expression, moi qui ceste oeuvre *dicta* (N° 62, &c.), may justify the suspicion (more probable than Mr. Wood's on Homer), that he could neither read nor write. Yet Champagne may boast of the two first historians, the noble authors of French prose, Villehardouin and Joinville.

34. The crusade and reigns of the counts of Flanders, Baldwin and his brother Henry, are the subject of a particular history by the Jesuit Doutremens (Constantinopolis Belgica; Turnaci, 1638, in 4to), which I have only seen with the eyes of Ducange.

toils and perils of a land expedition; and, if the Flemings dwelt along the ocean, the French barons were destitute of ships and ignorant of navigation. They embraced the wise resolution of chusing six deputies or representatives, of whom Villehardouin was one, with a discretionary trust to direct the motions, and to pledge the faith, of the whole confederacy. The maritime states of Italy were alone possessed of the means of transporting the holy warriors with their arms and horses; and the six deputies proceeded to Venice to solicit, on motives of piety or interest, the aid of that powerful republic.

State of the Venetians, A.D. 697–1200.

In the invasion of Italy by Attila, I have mentioned[35] the flight of the Venetians from the fallen cities of the continent, and their obscure shelter in the chain of islands that line the extremity of the Adriatic gulf. In the midst of the waters, free, indigent, laborious, and inaccessible, they gradually coalesced into a republic: the first foundations of Venice were laid in the island of Rialto; and the annual election of the twelve tribunes was superseded by the permanent office of a duke or doge. On the verge of the two empires the Venetians exult in the belief of primitive and perpetual independence.[36] Against the Latins, their antique freedom has been asserted by the sword, and may be justified by the pen. Charlemagne himself resigned all claims of sovereignty to the islands of the Adriatic gulf; his son Pepin was repulsed in the attacks of the *lagunas* or canals, too deep for the cavalry, and too shallow for the vessels; and in every age, under the German Cæsars, the lands of the republic have been clearly distinguished from the kingdom of Italy. But the inhabitants of Venice were considered by themselves, by strangers, and by their sovereigns, as an inalienable portion of the Greek empire;[37] in the ninth and tenth centuries, the proofs of their subjection are numerous and unquestionable; and the vain titles, the servile honours,

35. History, &c. vol. ii. p. 345–7.

36. The foundation and independence of Venice, and Pepin's invasion, are discussed by Pagi (Critica, tom. iii. A.D. 810, N° 4, &c.) and Beretti (Dissert. Chorograph. Italiæ medii Ævi, in Muratori, Script. tom. x. p. 153.). The two critics have a slight bias, the Frenchman adverse, the Italian favourable, to the republic.

37. When the son of Charlemagne asserted his right of sovereignty, he was answered by the loyal Venetians, ὀτι ἡμεις δουλοι θελομεν ειναι του Ρωμαιων βασιλεως (Constantin. Porphyrogenit. de Administrat. Imperii, pars ii. c. 28. p. 85.); and the report of the ix[th], establishes the fact of the xth century, which is confirmed by the embassy of Liutprand of Cremona. The annual tribute, which the emperor allows them to pay to the king of Italy, alleviates, by doubling, their servitude; but the hateful word δουλοι must be translated, as in the charter of 827 (Laugier, Hist. de Venise, tom. i. p. 67, &c.), by the softer appellation of *subditi*, or *fideles*.

of the Byzantine court, so ambitiously solicited by their dukes, would have degraded the magistrates of a free people. But the bands of this dependence, which was never absolute or rigid, were imperceptibly relaxed by the ambition of Venice and the weakness of Constantinople. Obedience was softened into respect, privilege ripened into prerogative, and the freedom of domestic government was fortified by the independence of foreign dominion. The maritime cities of Istria and Dalmatia bowed to the sovereigns of the Adriatic; and when they armed against the Normans in the cause of Alexius, the emperor applied, not to the duty of his subjects, but to the gratitude and generosity of his faithful allies. The sea was their patrimony:[38] the western parts of the Mediterranean, from Tuscany to Gibraltar, were indeed abandoned to their rivals of Pisa and Genoa; but the Venetians acquired an early and lucrative share of the commerce of Greece and Egypt. Their riches encreased with the encreasing demand of Europe: their manufactures of silk and glass, perhaps the institution of their bank, are of high antiquity; and they enjoyed the fruits of their industry in the magnificence of public and private life. To assert her flag, to avenge her injuries, to protect the freedom of navigation, the republic could launch and man a fleet of an hundred gallies; and the Greeks, the Saracens, and the Normans, were encountered by her naval arms. The Franks of Syria were assisted by the Venetians in the reduction of the sea-coast; but their zeal was neither blind nor disinterested; and in the conquest of Tyre, they shared the sovereignty of a city, the first seat of the commerce of the world. The policy of Venice was marked by the avarice of a trading, and the insolence of a maritime, power; yet her ambition was prudent; nor did she often forget that if armed gallies were the effect and safeguard, merchant vessels were the cause and supply, of her greatness. In her religion, she avoided the schism of the Greeks, without yielding a servile obedience to the Roman pontiff; and a free intercourse with the infidels of every clime appears to have allayed betimes the fever of superstition. Her primitive government was a loose mixture of democracy and monarchy: the doge was elected by the votes of the general assembly; as long as he was popular and successful, he reigned with the pomp and authority of a prince; but

38. See the xxv[th] and xxx[th] dissertations of the Antiquitates medii Ævi of Muratori. From Anderson's History of Commerce, I understand that the Venetians did not trade to England before the year 1323. The most flourishing state of their wealth and commerce in the beginning of the xv[th] century, is agreeably described by the Abbé Dubos (Hist. de la Ligue de Cambray, tom. ii. p. 443–480.).

in the frequent revolutions of the state, he was deposed, or banished, or slain, by the justice or injustice of the multitude. The twelfth century produced the first rudiments of the wise and jealous aristocracy, which has reduced the doge to a pageant and the people to a cypher.[39]

Alliance of the French and Venetians, A.D. 1201.

When the six ambassadors of the French pilgrims arrived at Venice, they were hospitably entertained in the palace of St. Mark, by the reigning duke: his name was Henry Dandolo;[40] and he shone in the last period of human life as one of the most illustrious characters of the times. Under the weight of years, and after the loss of his eyes,[41] Dandolo retained a sound understanding and a manly courage; the spirit of an hero, ambitious to signalize his reign by some memorable exploits, and the wisdom of a patriot, anxious to build his fame on the glory and advantage of his country. He praised the bold enthusiasm and liberal confidence of the barons and their deputies; in such a cause, and with such associates, he should aspire, were he a private man, to terminate his life; but he was the servant of the republic, and some delay was requisite to consult, on this arduous business, the judgment of his colleagues. The proposal of the French was first debated by the six *sages* who had been recently appointed to control the administration of the doge: it was next disclosed to the forty members of the council of state; and finally communicated to the legislative assembly of four hundred and fifty representatives, who were annually chosen in the six quarters of the city. In peace and war, the doge was still the chief of the republic; his legal authority was supported by the personal reputation of Dandolo: his

39. The Venetians have been slow in writing and publishing their history. Their most ancient monuments are, 1. The rude Chronicle (perhaps) of John Sagorninus (Venezia, 1765, in octavo), which represents the state and manners of Venice in the year 1008. 2. The larger history of the doge (1342–1354) Andrew Dandolo, published for the first time in the xii[th] tom. of Muratori, A.D. 1728. The History of Venice by the Abbé Laugier (Paris, 1728), is a work of some merit, which I have chiefly used for the constitutional part.

40. Henry Dandolo was eighty-four at his election (A.D. 1192), and ninety-seven at his death (A.D. 1205). See the Observations of Ducange sur Villehardouin, N° 204. But this *extraordinary* longevity is not observed by the original writers, nor does there exist another example of an hero near an hundred years of age. Theophrastus might afford an instance of a writer of ninety-nine; but instead of εννενηκοντα (Procem. ad Character.), I am much inclined to read ἑβδομηκοντα, with his last editor Fischer, and the first thoughts of Casaubon. It is scarcely possible that the powers of the mind and body should support themselves till such a period of life.

41. The modern Venetians (Laugier, tom. ii. p. 119.) accuse the emperor Manuel: but the calumny is refuted by Villehardouin and the older writers, who suppose that Dandolo lost his eyes by a wound (N° 34. and Ducange).

arguments of public interest were balanced and approved; and he was authorised to inform the ambassadors of the following conditions of the treaty.[42] It was proposed that the crusaders should assemble at Venice, on the feast of St. John of the ensuing year: that flat-bottomed vessels should be prepared for four thousand five hundred horses, and nine thousand squires, with a number of ships sufficient for the embarkation of four thousand five hundred knights, and twenty thousand foot: that during a term of nine months they should be supplied with provisions, and transported to whatsoever coast the service of God and Christendom should require; and that the republic should join the armament with a squadron of fifty gallies. It was required that the pilgrims should pay, before their departure, a sum of eighty-five thousand marks of silver; and that all conquests, by sea and land, should be equally divided between the confederates. The terms were hard; but the emergency was pressing, and the French barons were not less profuse of money than of blood. A general assembly was convened to ratify the treaty: the stately chapel and place of St. Mark were filled with ten thousand citizens; and the noble deputies were taught a new lesson of humbling themselves before the majesty of the people. "Illustrious Venetians," said the marshal of Champagne, "we are sent by the greatest and most powerful barons of France, to implore the aid of the masters of the sea for the deliverance of Jerusalem. They have enjoined us to fall prostrate at your feet; nor will we rise from the ground, till you have promised to avenge with us the injuries of Christ." The eloquence of their words and tears,[43] their martial aspect, and suppliant attitude, were applauded by an universal shout; as it were, says Jeffrey, by the sound of an earthquake. The venerable doge ascended the pulpit to urge their request by those motives of honour and virtue, which alone can be offered to a popular assembly: the treaty was transcribed on parchment; attested with oaths and seals, mutually accepted by the weeping and joyful representatives of France and Venice; and dispatched to Rome for the approbation of pope Innocent the third. Two thousand marks were borrowed of the merchants for the first expences of the armament. Of the six deputies, two repassed the Alps to

42. See the original treaty in the Chronicle of Andrew Dandolo, p. 323–326.

43. A reader of Villehardouin must observe the frequent tears of the marshal and his brother knights. Sachiez que la ot mainte lerme plorée de pitié (N° 17.); mult plorant (ibid.); mainte lerme plorée (N° 34.); si orent mult pitié et plorerent mult durement (N° 60.); i ot maint lerme plorée de pitié (N° 202.). They weep on every occasion of grief, joy, or devotion.

announce their success, while their four companions made a fruitless trial of the zeal and emulation of the republics of Genoa and Pisa.

Assembly and departure of the crusade from Venice, A.D. 1202, October 8.

The execution of the treaty was still opposed by unforeseen difficulties and delays. The marshal, on his return to Troyes, was embraced and approved by Thibaut count of Champagne, who had been unanimously chosen general of the confederates. But the health of that valiant youth already declined, and soon became hopeless; and he deplored the untimely fate, which condemned him to expire, not in a field of battle, but on a bed of sickness. To his brave and numerous vassals, the dying prince distributed his treasures: they swore in his presence to accomplish his vow and their own; but some there were, says the marshal, who accepted his gifts and forfeited their word. The more resolute champions of the cross held a parliament at Soissons for the election of a new general; but such was the incapacity, or jealousy, or reluctance, of the princes of France, that none could be found both able and willing to assume the conduct of the enterprise. They acquiesced in the choice of a stranger, of Boniface marquis of Montferrat, descended of a race of heroes, and himself of conspicuous fame in the wars and negociations of the times;[44] nor could the piety or ambition of the Italian chief decline this honourable invitation. After visiting the French court, where he was received as a friend and kinsman, the marquis, in the church of Soissons, was invested with the cross of a pilgrim and the staff of a general; and immediately repassed the Alps, to prepare for the distant expedition of the East. About the festival of the Pentecost he displayed his banner, and marched towards Venice at the head of the Italians: he was preceded or followed by the counts of Flanders and Blois, and the most respectable barons of France; and their numbers were swelled by the pilgrims of Germany,[45] whose object and motives were similar to their own. The Venetians had fulfilled, and even surpassed, their engagements: stables were constructed for the horses, and barracks for the troops; the magazines were abundantly replenished with forage and provisions; and the fleet of transports, ships, and gallies, was ready to hoist sail, as soon as the republic had received

44. By a victory (A.D. 1191) over the citizens of Asti, by a crusade to Palestine, and by an embassy from the pope to the German princes (Muratori, Annali d'Italia, tom. x. p. 163. 202.).

45. See the crusade of the Germans in the Historia C. P. of Gunther (Canisii Antiq. Lect. tom. iv. p. v–viii.), who celebrates the pilgrimage of his abbot Martin, one of the preaching rivals of Fulk of Neuilly. His monastery, of the Cistercian order, was situate in the diocese of Basil.

the price of the freight and armament. But that price far exceeded the wealth of the crusaders who were assembled at Venice. The Flemings, whose obedience to their count was voluntary and precarious, had embarked in their vessels for the long navigation of the ocean and Mediterranean; and many of the French and Italians had preferred a cheaper and more convenient passage from Marseilles and Apulia to the Holy Land. Each pilgrim might complain, that after he had furnished his own contribution he was made responsible for the deficiency of his absent brethren: the gold and silver plate of the chiefs, which they freely delivered to the treasury of St. Mark, was a generous but inadequate sacrifice; and after all their efforts, thirty-four thousand marks were still wanting to complete the stipulated sum. The obstacle was removed by the policy and patriotism of the doge, who proposed to the barons, that if they would join their arms in reducing some revolted cities of Dalmatia, he would expose his person in the holy war, and obtain from the republic a long indulgence, till some wealthy conquest should afford the means of satisfying the debt. After much scruple and hesitation they chose rather to accept the offer than to relinquish the enterprise; and the first hostilities of the fleet and army were directed against Zara,[46] a strong city of the Sclavonian coast, which had renounced its allegiance to Venice, and implored the protection of the king of Hungary.[47] The crusaders burst the chain or boom of the harbour; landed their horses, troops, and military engines; and compelled the inhabitants, after a defence of five days, to surrender at discretion; their lives were spared, but the revolt was punished by the pillage of their houses and the demolition of their walls. The season was far advanced; the French and Venetians resolved to pass the winter in a secure harbour and plentiful country; but their repose was disturbed by national and tumultuous quarrels of the soldiers and mariners. The conquest of Zara had scattered the seeds of discord and scandal: the arms of the allies had been stained in their outset with the blood, not of infidels, but of Christians: the king

Siege of Zara, Nov. 10.

46. Jadera, now Zara, was a Roman colony, which acknowledged Augustus for its parent. It is now only two miles round, and contains five or six thousand inhabitants; but the fortifications are strong, and it is joined to the main land by a bridge. See the travels of the two companions, Spon and Wheeler (Voyage de Dalmatie, de Grece, &c. tom. i. p. 64–70. Journey into Greece, p. 8–14.); the last of whom, by mistaking *Sestertia* for *Sestertii*, values an arch with statues and columns at twelve pounds. If, in his time, there were no trees near Zara, the cherry-trees were not yet planted which produce our incomparable *marasquin*.

47. Katona (Hist. Critica Reg. Hungariæ, Stirpis Arpad. tom. iv. p. 536–558.) collects all the facts and testimonies most adverse to the conquerors of Zara.

of Hungary and his new subjects were themselves enlisted under the banner of the cross; and the scruples of the devout, were magnified by the fear or lassitude of the reluctant, pilgrims. The pope had excommunicated the false crusaders who had pillaged and massacred their brethren,[48] and only the marquis Boniface and Simon of Montfort escaped these spiritual thunders; the one by his absence from the siege, the other by his final departure from the camp. Innocent might absolve the simple and submissive penitents of France; but he was provoked by the stubborn reason of the Venetians, who refused to confess their guilt, to accept their pardon, or to allow, in their temporal concerns, the interposition of a priest.

Alliance of the crusaders with the Greek prince, the young Alexius.

The assembly of such formidable powers by sea and land, had revived the hopes of young[49] Alexius; and, both at Venice and Zara, he solicited the arms of the crusaders, for his own restoration and his father's[50] deliverance. The royal youth was recommended by Philip king of Germany: his prayers and presence excited the compassion of the camp; and his cause was embraced and pleaded by the marquis of Montferrat and the doge of Venice. A double alliance, and the dignity of Cæsar, had connected with the Imperial family the two elder brothers of Boniface:[51] he expected to derive a kingdom from the important service; and the more generous ambition of Dandolo was eager to secure the inestimable benefits of trade and dominion that might accrue to his country.[52] Their influence procured a favourable audience for the ambassadors of Alexius; and if the magnitude of his offers excited some suspicion, the motives and rewards

48. See the whole transaction, and the sentiments of the pope, in the Epistles of Innocent III. Gesta, c. 86, 87, 88.

49. A modern reader is surprised to hear of the valet de Constantinople, as applied to young Alexius, on account of his youth, like the *infants* of Spain, and the *nobilissimus puer* of the Romans. The pages and *valets* of the knights were as noble as themselves (Villehardouin and Ducange, N° 36.).

50. The emperor Isaac is styled by Villehardouin, *Sursac* (N° 35, &c.), which may be derived from the French *Sire*, or the Greek *Κυρ* (κυριος) melted into his proper name; the farther corruptions of Tursac and Conserac will instruct us what licence may have been used in the old dynasties of Assyria and Egypt.

51. Reinier and Conrad; the former married Maria, daughter of the emperor Manuel Comnenus; the latter was the husband of Theodora Angela, sister of the emperors Isaac and Alexius. Conrad abandoned the Greek court and princess for the glory of defending Tyre against Saladin (Ducange, Fam. Byzant. p. 187. 203.).

52. Nicetas (in Alexio Comneno, l. iii. c. 9.) accuses the doge and Venetians as the first authors of the war against Constantinople, and considers only as a κυμα ὑπερ κυματι, the arrival and shameful offers of the royal exile.

which he displayed might justify the delay and diversion of those forces which had been consecrated to the deliverance of Jerusalem. He promised, in his own and his father's name, that as soon as they should be seated on the throne of Constantinople, they would terminate the long schism of the Greeks, and submit themselves and their people to the lawful supremacy of the Roman church. He engaged to recompense the labours and merits of the crusaders, by the immediate payment of two hundred thousand marks of silver; to accompany them in person to Egypt; or, if it should be judged more advantageous, to maintain, during a year, ten thousand men, and, during his life, five hundred knights, for the service of the Holy Land. These tempting conditions were accepted by the republic of Venice; and the eloquence of the doge and marquis persuaded the counts of Flanders, Blois, and St. Pol, with eight barons of France, to join in the glorious enterprise. A treaty of offensive and defensive alliance was confirmed by their oaths and seals; and each individual, according to his situation and character, was swayed by the hope of public or private advantage; by the honour of restoring an exiled monarch; or by the sincere and probable opinion, that their efforts in Palestine would be fruitless and unavailing, and that the acquisition of Constantinople must precede and prepare the recovery of Jerusalem. But they were the chiefs or equals of a valiant band of freemen and volunteers, who thought and acted for themselves: the soldiers and clergy were divided; and, if a large majority subscribed to the alliance, the numbers and arguments of the dissidents were strong and respectable.[53] The boldest hearts were appalled by the report of the naval power and impregnable strength of Constantinople; and their apprehensions were disguised to the world, and perhaps to themselves, by the more decent objections of religion and duty. They alleged the sanctity of a vow, which had drawn them from their families and homes to the rescue of the holy sepulchre; nor should the dark and crooked counsels of human policy divert them from a pursuit, the event of which was in the hands of the Almighty. Their first offence, the attack of Zara, had been severely punished by the reproach of their conscience and the censures of the pope; nor would they again imbrue their hands in the blood of their fellow-christians. The apostle of Rome had pronounced; nor would they usurp the right of avenging with the sword the schism of the Greeks and the doubtful

53. Villehardouin and Gunther represent the sentiments of the two parties. The abbot Martin left the army at Zara, proceeded to Palestine, was sent ambassador to Constantinople, and became a reluctant witness of the second siege.

usurpation of the Byzantine monarch. On these principles or pretences, many pilgrims, the most distinguished for their valour and piety, withdrew from the camp; and their retreat was less pernicious than the open or secret opposition of a discontented party, that laboured, on every occasion, to separate the army and disappoint the enterprise.

Voyage from Zara to Constantinople, A.D. 1203, April 7–June 24.

Notwithstanding this defection, the departure of the fleet and army was vigorously pressed by the Venetians; whose zeal for the service of the royal youth concealed a just resentment to his nation and family. They were mortified by the recent preference which had been given to Pisa the rival of their trade; they had a long arrear of debt and injury to liquidate with the Byzantine court; and Dandolo might not discourage the popular tale, that he had been deprived of his eyes by the emperor Manuel, who perfidiously violated the sanctity of an ambassador. A similar armament, for ages, had not rode the Adriatic: it was composed of one hundred and twenty flat-bottomed vessels or *palanders* for the horses; two hundred and forty transports filled with men and arms; seventy storeships laden with provisions; and fifty stout gallies, well prepared for the encounter of an enemy.[54] While the wind was favourable, the sky serene, and the water smooth, every eye was fixed with wonder and delight on the scene of military and naval pomp which overspread the sea. The shields of the knights and squires, at once an ornament and a defence, were arranged on either side of the ships; the banners of the nations and families were displayed from the stern; our modern artillery was supplied by three hundred engines for casting stones and darts: the fatigues of the way were cheered with the sound of music; and the spirits of the adventurers were raised by the mutual assurance, that forty thousand christian heroes were equal to the conquest of the world.[55] In the navigation[56] from Venice and Zara, the fleet was successfully steered by the skill and experience of the Venetian pilots: at Durazzo, the con-

54. The birth and dignity of Andrew Dandolo gave him the motive and the means of searching in the archives of Venice the memorable story of his ancestor. His brevity seems to accuse the copious and more recent narratives of Sanudo (in Muratori, Script. Rerum Italicarum, tom. xxii.), Blondus, Sabellicus, and Rhamnusius.

55. Villehardouin, N° 62. His feelings and expressions are original; he often weeps, but he rejoices in the glories and perils of war with a spirit unknown to a sedentary writer.

56. In this voyage, almost all the geographical names are corrupted by the Latins. The modern appellation of Chalcis, and all Eubœa, is derived from its *Euripus*, *Evripo*, *Negri-po*, *Negropont*, which dishonours our maps (d'Anville, Geographie Ancienne, tom. i. p. 263.).

federates first landed on the territories of the Greek empire: the isle of Corfu afforded a station and repose; they doubled without accident the perilous cape of Malea, the southern point of Peloponesus or the Morea; made a descent in the islands of Negropont and Andros; and cast anchor at Abydus on the Asiatic side of the Hellespont. These preludes of conquest were easy and bloodless; the Greeks of the provinces, without patriotism or courage, were crushed by an irresistible force; the presence of the lawful heir might justify their obedience; and it was rewarded by the modesty and discipline of the Latins. As they penetrated through the Hellespont, the magnitude of their navy was compressed in a narrow channel; and the face of the waters was darkened with innumerable sails. They again expanded in the bason of the Propontis, and traversed that placid sea, till they approached the European shore, at the abbey of St. Stephen, three leagues to the west of Constantinople. The prudent doge dissuaded them from dispersing themselves in a populous and hostile land; and, as their stock of provisions was reduced, it was resolved, in the season of harvest, to replenish their storeships in the fertile islands of the Propontis. With this resolution, they directed their course; but a strong gale, and their own impatience, drove them to the eastward; and so near did they run to the shore and the city, that some vollies of stones and darts were exchanged between the ships and the rampart. As they passed along, they gazed with admiration on the capital of the East, or, as it should seem, of the earth; rising from her seven hills, and towering over the continents of Europe and Asia. The swelling domes and lofty spires of five hundred palaces and churches, were gilded by the sun and reflected in the waters; the walls were crowded with soldiers and spectators, whose numbers they beheld, of whose temper they were ignorant; and each heart was chilled by the reflection, that, since the beginning of the world, such an enterprise had never been undertaken by such an handful of warriors. But the momentary apprehension was dispelled by hope and valour; and every man, says the marshal of Champagne, glanced his eye on the sword or lance which he must speedily use in the glorious conflict.[57] The Latins cast anchor before Chalcedon; the mariners only were left in the vessels; the soldiers, horses, and arms, were safely landed, and, in the luxury of an Imperial palace, the barons tasted the first fruits of their success. On the third day, the fleet and army moved towards Scutari, the Asiatic suburb of Constantinople; a detachment of five

57. Et sachiez que il ne ot si hardi cui le cuer ne fremist (c. 67.) ... Chascuns regardoit ses armes ... que par tems en aront mestier (c. 68.). Such is the honesty of courage.

hundred Greek horse was surprised and defeated by fourscore French knights; and in a halt of nine days, the camp was plentifully supplied with forage and provisions.

Fruitless negociation of the emperor.

In relating the invasion of a great empire, it may seem strange that I have not described the obstacles which should have checked the progress of the strangers. The Greeks, in truth, were an unwarlike people; but they were rich, industrious, and subject to the will of a single man: had that man been capable of fear, when his enemies were at a distance, or of courage, when they approached his person. The first rumour of his nephew's alliance with the French and Venetians was despised by the usurper Alexius; his flatterers persuaded him, that in this contempt he was bold and sincere; and each evening in the close of the banquet, he thrice discomfited the Barbarians of the West. These Barbarians had been justly terrified by the report of his naval power; and the sixteen hundred fishing-boats of Constantinople[58] could have manned a fleet, to sink them in the Adriatic, or stop their entrance in the mouth of the Hellespont. But all force may be annihilated by the negligence of the prince and the venality of his ministers. The great duke, or admiral, made a scandalous, almost a public, auction of the sails, the masts and the rigging: the royal forests were reserved for the more important purpose of the chace; and the trees, says Nicetas, were guarded by the eunuchs, like the groves of religious worship.[59] From his dream of pride, Alexius was awakened by the siege of Zara and the rapid advances of the Latins; as soon as he saw the danger was real, he thought it inevitable; and his vain presumption was lost in abject despondency and despair. He suffered these contemptible Barbarians to pitch their camp in the sight of the palace; and his apprehensions were thinly disguised by the pomp and menace of a suppliant embassy. The sovereign of the Romans was astonished (his ambassadors were instructed to say) at the hostile appearance of the strangers. If these pilgrims were sincere in their vow for the deliverance of Jerusalem, his voice must applaud, and his treasures should assist, their pious design; but should they dare to invade the sanctuary of empire, their numbers, were they ten times more considerable, should not protect them from his just resentment. The

58. Eandem urbem plus in solis navibus piscatorum abundare, quam illos in toto navigio. Habebat enim mille et sexcentas piscatorias naves ... Bellicas autem sive mercatorias habebant infinitæ multitudinis et portum tutissimum. Gunther, Hist. C. P. c. 8. p. 10.

59. *Καθαπερ ἱερων αλσεων, ειπειν δε και θεοφυτευτων παραδεισων εφειδοντο τουτωνι.* Nicetas in Alex. Comneno, l. iii. c. 9. p. 348.

answer of the doge and barons was simple and magnanimous. "In the cause of honour and justice," they said, "we despise the usurper of Greece, his threats, and his offers. *Our* friendship and *his* allegiance are due to the lawful heir, to the young prince who is seated among us, and to his father, the emperor Isaac, who has been deprived of his sceptre, his freedom, and his eyes, by the crime of an ungrateful brother. Let that brother confess his guilt, and implore forgiveness, and we ourselves will intercede, that he may be permitted to live in affluence and security. But let him not insult us by a second message: our reply will be made in arms, in the palace of Constantinople."

Passage of the Bosphorus, July 6.

On the tenth day of their encampment at Scutari, the crusaders prepared themselves, as soldiers and as catholics, for the passage of the Bosphorus. Perilous indeed was the adventure; the stream was broad and rapid; in a calm the current of the Euxine might drive down the liquid and unextinguishable fires of the Greeks; and the opposite shores of Europe were defended by seventy thousand horse and foot in formidable array. On this memorable day, which happened to be bright and pleasant, the Latins were distributed in six battles or divisions; the first, or vanguard, was led by the count of Flanders, one of the most powerful of the Christian princes in the skill and number of his cross-bows. The four successive battles of the French were commanded by his brother Henry, the counts of St. Pol and Blois, and Matthew of Montmorency, the last of whom was honoured by the voluntary service of the marshal and nobles of Champagne. The sixth division, the rear-guard and reserve of the army, was conducted by the marquis of Montferrat, at the head of the Germans and Lombards. The chargers, saddled, with their long caparisons dragging on the ground, were embarked in the flat *palanders*;[60] and the knights stood by the side of their horses, in complete armour, their helmets laced, and their lances in their hands. Their numerous train of *serjeants*[61] and archers occupied the transports; and each transport was towed by the strength and swiftness

60. From the version of Vignere I adopt the well-sounding word *palander*, which is still used, I believe, in the Mediterranean. But had I written in French, I should have preferred the original and expressive denomination of *vessiers* or *huissiers*, from the *huis*, or door, which was let down as a draw-bridge; but which, at sea, was closed into the side of the ship (see Ducange au Villehardouin, N° 14. and Joinville, p. 27, 28. edit. du Louvre).

61. To avoid the vague expressions of followers, &c. I use, after Villehardouin, the word *serjeants* for all horsemen who were not knights. There were serjeants at arms, and serjeants at law; and if we visit the parade and Westminster-hall, we may observe the strange result of the distinction (Ducange, Glossar. Latin. *Servientes*, &c. tom. vi. p. 226–231.).

of a galley. The six divisions traversed the Bosphorus, without encountering an enemy or an obstacle; to land the foremost was the wish, to conquer or die was the resolution, of every division and of every soldier. Jealous of the pre-eminence of danger, the knights in their heavy armour leaped into the sea, when it rose as high as their girdle; the serjeants and archers were animated by their valour; and the squires, letting down the draw-bridges of the palanders, led the horses to the shore. Before the squadrons could mount, and form, and couch their lances, the seventy thousand Greeks had vanished from their sight; the timid Alexius gave the example to his troops; and it was only by the plunder of his rich pavillions that the Latins were informed that they had fought against an emperor. In the first consternation of the flying enemy, they resolved by a double attack to open the entrance of the harbour. The tower of Galata,[62] in the suburb of Pera, was attacked and stormed by the French, while the Venetians assumed the more difficult task of forcing the boom or chain that was stretched from that tower to the Byzantine shore. After some fruitless attempts, their intrepid perseverance prevailed: twenty ships of war, the relics of the Grecian navy, were either sunk or taken: the enormous and massy links of iron were cut asunder by the shears, or broken by the weight, of the gallies;[63] and the Venetian fleet, safe and triumphant, rode at anchor in the port of Constantinople. By these daring atchievements, a remnant of twenty thousand Latins solicited the licence of besieging a capital which contained above four hundred thousand inhabitants,[64] able, though not willing, to bear arms in the defence of their country. Such an account would indeed suppose a population of near two millions; but whatever abatement may be required

62. It is needless to observe, that on the subject of Galata, the chain, &c. Ducange is accurate and full. Consult likewise the proper chapters of the C. P. Christiana of the same author. The inhabitants of Galata were so vain and ignorant, that they applied to themselves St. Paul's Epistle to the Galatians.

63. The vessel that broke the chain was named the Eagle, *Aquila* (Dandol. Chronicon. p. 322.), which Blondus (de Gestis Venet.) has changed into *Aquilo* the north-wind. Ducange, Observations, N° 83. maintains the latter reading; but he had not seen the respectable text of Dandolo, nor did he enough consider the topography of the harbour. The south-east would have been a more effectual wind.

64. Quatre cens mil homes ou plus (Villehardouin, N° 134.), must be understood of *men* of a military age. Le Beau (Hist. du Bas Empire, tom. xx. p. 417.) allows Constantinople a million of inhabitants, of whom 60,000 horse, and an infinite number of foot soldiers. In its present decay, the capital of the Ottoman empire may contain 400,000 souls (Bell's Travels, vol. ii. p. 401, 402.); but as the Turks keep no registers, and as circumstances are fallacious, it is impossible to ascertain (Niebuhr, Voyage en Arabie, tom. i. p. 18, 19.) the real populousness of their cities.

in the numbers of the Greeks, the *belief* of those numbers will equally exalt the fearless spirit of their assailants.

First siege and conquest of Constantinople by the Latins, July 7–18.

In the choice of the attack, the French and Venetians were divided by their habits of life and warfare. The latter affirmed with truth, that Constantinople was most accessible on the side of the sea and the harbour. The former might assert with honour, that they had long enough trusted their lives and fortunes to a frail bark and a precarious element, and loudly demanded a trial of knighthood, a firm ground, and a close onset, either on foot or horseback. After a prudent compromise, of employing the two nations by sea and land, in the service best suited to their character, the fleet covering the army, they both proceeded from the entrance to the extremity of the harbour: the stone bridge of the river was hastily repaired; and the six battles of the French formed their encampment against the front of the capital, the basis of the triangle which runs about four miles from the port to the Propontis.[65] On the edge of a broad ditch, at the foot of a lofty rampart, they had leisure to contemplate the difficulties of their enterprise. The gates to the right and left of their narrow camp poured forth frequent sallies of cavalry and light-infantry, which cut off their stragglers, swept the country of provisions, sounded the alarm five or six times in the course of each day, and compelled them to plant a pallisade, and sink an entrenchment, for their immediate safety. In the supplies and convoys the Venetians had been too sparing, or the Franks too voracious: the usual complaints of hunger and scarcity were heard, and perhaps felt: their stock of flour would be exhausted in three weeks; and their disgust of salt meat tempted them to taste the flesh of their horses. The trembling usurper was supported by Theodore Lascaris, his son-in-law, a valiant youth, who aspired to save and to rule his country; the Greeks, regardless of that country, were awakened to the defence of their religion; but their firmest hope was in the strength and spirit of the Varangian guards, of the Danes and English, as they are named in the writers of the times.[66] After ten days incessant labour, the ground was levelled, the ditch filled, the approaches of the besiegers were regularly made, and two hundred and fifty engines of assault exercised

65. On the most correct plans of Constantinople, I know not how to measure more than 4000 paces. Yet Villehardouin computes the space at three leagues (N° 86.). If his eye were not deceived, he must reckon by the old Gallic league of 1500 paces, which might still be used in Champagne.

66. The guards, the Varangi, are styled by Villehardouin (N° 89. 95, &c.), Englois et

their various powers to clear the rampart, to batter the walls, and to sap the foundations. On the first appearance of a breach, the scaling-ladders were applied: the numbers that defended the vantage ground repulsed and oppressed the adventurous Latins; but they admired the resolution of fifteen knights and serjeants, who had gained the ascent, and maintained their perilous station till they were precipitated or made prisoners by the Imperial guards. On the side of the harbour the naval attack was more successfully conducted by the Venetians; and that industrious people employed every resource that was known and practised before the invention of gunpowder. A double line, three bow-shots in front, was formed by the gallies and ships; and the swift motion of the former was supported by the weight and loftiness of the latter, whose decks, and poops, and turret, were the platforms of military engines, that discharged their shot over the heads of the first line. The soldiers, who leaped from the gallies on shore, immediately planted and ascended their scaling-ladders, while the large ships, advancing more slowly into the intervals, and lowering a draw-bridge, opened a way through the air from their masts to the rampart. In the midst of the conflict, the doge, a venerable and conspicuous form, stood aloft in complete armour on the prow of his galley. The great standard of St. Mark was displayed before him; his threats, promises, and exhortations, urged the diligence of the rowers; his vessel was the first that struck; and Dandolo was the first warrior on the shore. The nations admired the magnanimity of the blind old man, without reflecting that his age and infirmities diminished the price of life, and enhanced the value of immortal glory. On a sudden, by an invisible hand (for the standard-bearer was probably slain), the banner of the republic was fixed on the rampart: twenty-five towers were rapidly occupied; and, by the cruel expedient of fire, the Greeks were driven from the adjacent quarter. The doge had dispatched the intelligence of his success, when he was checked by the danger of his confederates. Nobly declaring that he would rather die with the pilgrims than gain a victory by their destruction, Dandolo relinquished his advantage, recalled his troops, and hastened to the scene of action. He found the six weary diminutive *battles* of the French encompassed by sixty squadrons of the Greek cavalry, the least of which was more numerous than the largest of their divisions. Shame and despair had provoked Alexius to the last effort of a general sally; but he was awed by the firm order and manly aspect of the Latins;

Danois avec leurs haches. Whatever had been their origin, a French pilgrim could not be mistaken in the nations of which they were at that time composed.

and, after skirmishing at a distance, withdrew his troops in the close of the evening. The silence or tumult of the night exasperated his fears; and the timid usurper, collecting a treasure of ten thousand pounds of gold, basely deserted his wife, his people, and his fortune; threw himself into a bark, stole through the Bosphorus, and landed in shameful safety in an obscure harbour of Thrace. As soon as they were apprised of his flight, the Greek nobles sought pardon and peace in the dungeon where the blind Isaac expected each hour the visit of the executioner. Again saved and exalted by the vicissitudes of fortune, the captive in his Imperial robes was replaced on the throne, and surrounded with prostrate slaves, whose real terror and affected joy he was incapable of discerning. At the dawn of day, hostilities were suspended; and the Latin chiefs were surprised by a message from the lawful and reigning emperor, who was impatient to embrace his son and to reward his generous deliverers.[67]

Restoration of the emperor Isaac Angelus, and his son Alexius, July 19.

But these generous deliverers were unwilling to release their hostage, till they had obtained from his father the payment, or at least the promise, of their recompense. They chose four ambassadors, Matthew of Montmorency, our historian the marshal of Champagne, and two Venetians, to congratulate the emperor. The gates were thrown open on their approach, the streets on both sides were lined with the battle-axes of the Danish and English guard: the presence-chamber glittered with gold and jewels, the false substitutes of virtue and power; by the side of the blind Isaac, his wife was seated, the sister of the king of Hungary; and by her appearance, the noble matrons of Greece were drawn from their domestic retirement, and mingled with the circle of senators and soldiers. The Latins, by the mouth of the marshal, spoke like men, conscious of their merits, but who respected the work of their own hands; and the emperor clearly understood, that his son's engagements with Venice and the pilgrims must be ratified without hesitation or delay. Withdrawing into a private chamber with the empress, a chamberlain, an interpreter, and the four ambassadors, the father of young Alexius enquired with some anxiety into the nature of his stipulations. The submission of the Eastern

67. For the first siege and conquest of Constantinople, we may read the original letter of the crusaders to Innocent III. Gesta, c. 91. p. 533, 534. Villehardouin, N° 75–99. Nicetas in Alexio Comnen. l. iii. c. 10. p. 349–352. Dandolo, in Chron. p. 322. Gunther, and his abbot Martin, were not yet returned from their obstinate pilgrimage to Jerusalem, or St. John d'Acre, where the greatest part of the company had died of the plague.

empire to the pope, the succour of the Holy Land, and a present contribution of two hundred thousand marks of silver – "These conditions are weighty," was his prudent reply; "they are hard to accept, and difficult to perform. But no conditions can exceed the measure of your services and deserts." After this satisfactory assurance, the barons mounted on horseback, and introduced the heir of Constantinople to the city and palace: his youth and marvellous adventures engaged every heart in his favour, and Alexius was solemnly crowned with his father in the dome of St. Sophia. In the first days of his reign, the people, already blessed with the restoration of plenty and peace, was delighted by the joyful catastrophe of the tragedy; and the discontent of the nobles, their regret, and their fears, were covered by the polished surface of pleasure and loyalty. The mixture of two discordant nations in the same capital, might have been pregnant with mischief and danger; and the suburb of Galata, or Pera, was assigned for the quarters of the French and Venetians. But the liberty of trade and familiar intercourse was allowed between the friendly nations; and each day the pilgrims were tempted by devotion or curiosity to visit the churches and palaces of Constantinople. Their rude minds, insensible perhaps of the finer arts, were astonished by the magnificent scenery: and the poverty of their native towns enhanced the populousness and riches of the first metropolis of Christendom.[68] Descending from his state, young Alexius was prompted by interest and gratitude to repeat his frequent and familiar visits to his Latin allies; and in the freedom of the table, the gay petulance of the French sometimes forgot the emperor of the East.[69] In their more serious conferences, it was agreed, that the re-union of the two churches must be the result of patience and time; but avarice was less tractable than zeal; and a large sum was instantly disbursed to appease the wants, and silence the importunity, of the crusaders.[70] Alexius was alarmed by the approaching hour of their departure: their absence might have relieved him from the engagement which he was yet incapable of performing; but his friends

68. Compare, in the rude energy of Villehardouin (N° 66. 100.), the inside and outside views of Constantinople, and their impression on the minds of the pilgrims: cette ville (says he) que de totes les autres ére souveraine. See the parallel passages of Fulcherius Carnotensis, Hist. Hierosol. l. i. c. 4. and Will. Tyr. ii. 3. xx. 26.

69. As they played at dice, the Latins took off his diadem, and clapped on his head a woollen or hairy cap, το μεγαλοπρεπες και παγκλἔιστον κατερρυπαινεν ονομα (Nicetas, p. 358.). If these merry companions were Venetians, it was the insolence of trade and a commonwealth.

70. Villehardouin, N° 101. Dandolo, p. 322. The doge affirms, that the Venetians were paid more slowly than the French;

would have left him, naked and alone, to the caprice and prejudice of a perfidious nation. He wished to bribe their stay, the delay of a year, by undertaking to defray their expence, and to satisfy, in their name, the freight of the Venetian vessels. The offer was agitated in the council of the barons; and, after a repetition of their debates and scruples, a majority of votes again acquiesced in the advice of the doge and the prayer of the young emperor. At the price of sixteen hundred pounds of gold, he prevailed on the marquis of Montferrat to lead him with an army round the provinces of Europe; to establish his authority, and pursue his uncle, while Constantinople was awed by the presence of Baldwin and his confederates of France and Flanders. The expedition was successful; the blind emperor exulted in the success of his arms, and listened to the predictions of his flatterers, that the same Providence which had raised him from the dungeon to the throne, would heal his gout, restore his sight, and watch over the long prosperity of his reign. Yet the mind of the suspicious old man was tormented by the rising glories of his son: nor could his pride conceal from his envy, that, while his own name was pronounced in faint and reluctant acclamations, the royal youth was the theme of spontaneous and universal praise.[71]

Quarrel of the Greeks and Latins.

By the recent invasion, the Greeks were awakened from a dream of nine centuries; from the vain presumption that the capital of the Roman empire was impregnable to foreign arms. The strangers of the West had violated the city, and bestowed the sceptre, of Constantine: their Imperial clients soon became as unpopular as themselves: the well-known vices of Isaac were rendered still more contemptible by his infirmities; and the young Alexius was hated as an apostate who had renounced the manners and religion of his country. His secret covenant with the Latins was divulged or suspected; the people, and especially the clergy, were devoutly attached to their faith and superstition; and every convent, and every shop, resounded with the danger of the church and the tyranny of the pope.[72] An empty treasury could ill supply the demands of regal luxury and foreign extortion: the

but he owns, that the histories of the two nations differed on that subject. Had he read Villehardouin? The Greeks complained, however, quòd totius Græciæ opes transtulisset (Gunther, Hist. C. P. c. 13.). See the lamentations and invectives of Nicetas (p. 355.).

71. The reign of Alexius Comnenus occupies three books in Nicetas, p. 291–352. The short restoration of Isaac and his son is dispatched in five chapters, p. 352–362.

72. When Nicetas reproaches Alexius for his impious league, he bestows the harshest names on the pope's new religion; *μειζον και ατοπωτατον ... παρεκτροπην πιστεως ... των του Παπα προνομιων καινισμον*

Greeks refused to avert, by a general tax, the impending evils of servitude and pillage; the oppression of the rich excited a more dangerous and personal resentment; and if the emperor melted the plate, and despoiled the images, of the sanctuary, he seemed to justify the complaints of heresy and sacrilege. During the absence of marquis Boniface and his Imperial pupil, Constantinople was visited with a calamity which might be justly imputed to the zeal and indiscretion of the Flemish pilgrims.[73] In one of their visits to the city, they were scandalized by the aspect of a mosch or synagogue, in which one God was worshipped, without a partner or a son. Their effectual mode of controversy was to attack the infidels with the sword, and their habitation with fire: but the infidels, and some Christian neighbours, presumed to defend their lives and properties; and the flames which bigotry had kindled consumed the most orthodox and innocent structures. During eight days and nights, the conflagration spread above a league in front, from the harbour to the Propontis, over the thickest and most populous regions of the city. It is not easy to count the stately churches and palaces that were reduced to a smoking ruin, to value the merchandise that perished in the trading streets, or to number the families that were involved in the common destruction. By this outrage, which the doge and the barons in vain affected to disclaim, the name of the Latins became still more unpopular; and the colony of that nation, above fifteen thousand persons, consulted their safety in a hasty retreat from the city to the protection of their standard in the suburb of Pera. The emperor returned in triumph; but the firmest and most dextrous policy would have been insufficient to steer him through the tempest, which overwhelmed the person and government of that unhappy youth. His own inclination, and his father's advice, attached him to his benefactors; but Alexius hesitated between gratitude and patriotism, between the fear of his subjects and of his allies.[74] By his feeble and fluctuating conduct he lost the esteem and confidence of both; and, while he invited the marquis of Montferrat to occupy the palace, he

... *μεταθεσιν τε και μεταποιησιν των παλαιων Ρωμαιοις εθων* (p. 348.). Such was the sincere language of every Greek to the last gasp of the empire.

73. Nicetas (p. 355.) is positive in the charge, and specifies the Flemings (*Φλαμιονες*), though he is wrong in supposing it an ancient name. Villehardouin (N° 107.) exculpates the barons, and is ignorant (perhaps affectedly ignorant) of the names of the guilty.

74. Compare the suspicions and complaints of Nicetas (p. 359–362.) with the blunt charges of Baldwin of Flanders (Gesta Innocent. III. c. 92. p. 534.), cum patriarcha et mole nobilium, nobis promissis perjurus et mendax.

suffered the nobles to conspire, and the people to arm, for the deliverance of their country. Regardless of his painful situation, the Latin chiefs repeated their demands, resented his delays, suspected his intentions, and exacted a decisive answer of peace or war. The haughty summons was delivered by three French knights and three Venetian deputies, who girded their swords, mounted their horses, pierced through the angry multitude, and entered with a fearless countenance the palace and presence of the Greek emperor. In a peremptory tone, they recapitulated their services and his engagements; and boldly declared, that unless their just claims were fully and immediately satisfied, they should no longer hold him either as a sovereign or a friend. After this defiance, the first that had ever wounded an Imperial ear, they departed without betraying any symptoms of fear; but their escape from a servile palace and a furious city astonished the ambassadors themselves; and their return to the camp was the signal of mutual hostility.

The war renewed, A.D. 1204.

Among the Greeks, all authority and wisdom were overborne by the impetuous multitude, who mistook their rage for valour, their numbers for strength, and their fanaticism for the support and inspiration of Heaven. In the eyes of both nations Alexius was false and contemptible: the base and spurious race of the Angeli was rejected with clamorous disdain; and the people of Constantinople encompassed the senate, to demand at their hands a more worthy emperor. To every senator, conspicuous by his birth or dignity, they successively presented the purple: by each senator the deadly garment was repulsed: the contest lasted three days; and we may learn from the historian Nicetas, one of the members of the assembly, that fear and weakness were the guardians of their loyalty. A phantom, who vanished in oblivion, was forcibly proclaimed by the crowd;[75] but the author of the tumult, and the leader of the war, was a prince of the house of Ducas; and his common appellation of Alexius must be discriminated by the epithet of Mourzoufle,[76] which in the vulgar idiom expressed the close junction of his black and shaggy eye-brows. At once a patriot and a courtier, the perfidious Mourzoufle, who was not destitute of cunning and courage, opposed the Latins both in speech and action, inflamed the passions and

75. His name was Nicholas Canabus; he deserved the praise of Nicetas and the vengeance of Mourzoufle (p. 362.).

76. Villehardouin (N° 116.) speaks of him as a favourite, without knowing that he was a prince of the blood, *Angelus* and *Ducas*. Ducange, who pries into every corner, believes him to be the son of Isaac Ducas Sebastocrator, and second cousin of young Alexius.

prejudices of the Greeks, and insinuated himself into the favour and confidence of Alexius, who trusted him with the office of great chamberlain, and tinged his buskins with the colours of royalty. At the dead of night he rushed into the bed-chamber with an affrighted aspect, exclaiming, that the palace was attacked by the people and betrayed by the guards. Starting from his couch, the unsuspecting prince threw himself into the arms of his enemy, who had contrived his escape by a private staircase. But that staircase terminated in a prison; Alexius was seized, stripped, and loaded with chains; and, after tasting some days the bitterness of death, he was poisoned, or strangled, or beaten with clubs, at the command, and in the presence, of the tyrant. The emperor Isaac Angelus soon followed his son to the grave, and Mourzoufle, perhaps, might spare the superfluous crime of hastening the extinction of impotence and blindness.

Alexius and his father deposed by Mourzoufle, February 8.

The death of the emperors, and the usurpation of Mourzoufle, had changed the nature of the quarrel. It was no longer the disagreement of allies who over-valued their services, or neglected their obligations: the French and Venetians forgot their complaints against Alexius, dropt a tear on the untimely fate of their companion, and swore revenge against the perfidious nation who had crowned his assassin. Yet the prudent doge was still inclined to negociate; he asked as a debt, a subsidy, or a fine, fifty thousand pounds of gold, about two millions sterling; nor would the conference have been abruptly broken, if the zeal, or policy, of Mourzoufle had not refused to sacrifice the Greek church to the safety of the state.[77] Amidst the invectives of his foreign and domestic enemies, we may discern, that he was not unworthy of the character which he had assumed, of the public champion: the second siege of Constantinople was far more laborious than the first; the treasury was replenished, and discipline was restored, by a severe inquisition into the abuses of the former reign; and Mourzoufle, an iron mace in his hand, visiting the posts, and affecting the port and aspect of a warrior, was an object of terror, to his soldiers, at least, and to his kinsmen. Before and after the death of Alexius, the Greeks made two vigorous and well-conducted attempts to burn the navy in the harbour; but the skill and courage of the Venetians repulsed the fire-ships; and the vagrant flames wasted themselves without injury in

Second siege, January–April.

77. This negociation, probable in itself, and attested by Nicetas (p. 365.), is omitted as scandalous by the delicacy of Dandolo and Villehardouin.

the sea.[78] In a nocturnal sally, the Greek emperor was vanquished by Henry, brother of the count of Flanders: the advantages of number and surprise aggravated the shame of his defeat; his buckler was found on the field of battle; and the Imperial standard,[79] a divine image of the Virgin, was presented, as a trophy and a relic, to the Cistercian monks, the disciples of St. Bernard. Near three months, without excepting the holy season of Lent, were consumed in skirmishes and preparations, before the Latins were ready or resolved for a general assault. The land-fortifications had been found impregnable; and the Venetian pilots represented, that, on the shore of the Propontis, the anchorage was unsafe, and the ships must be driven by the current far away to the streights of the Hellespont; a prospect not unpleasing to the reluctant pilgrims, who sought every opportunity of breaking the army. From the harbour, therefore, the assault was determined by the assailants, and expected by the besieged; and the emperor had placed his scarlet pavillions on a neighbouring height, to direct and animate the efforts of his troops. A fearless spectator, whose mind could entertain the ideas of pomp and pleasure, might have admired the long array of two embattled armies, which extended above half a league, the one on the ships and gallies, the other on the walls and towers raised above the ordinary level by several stages of wooden turrets. Their first fury was spent in the discharge of darts, stones, and fire, from the engines; but the water was deep; the French were bold; the Venetians were skilful; they approached the walls; and a desperate conflict of swords, spears, and battle-axes, was fought on the trembling bridges that grappled the floating, to the stable, batteries. In more than an hundred places, the assault was urged, and the defence was sustained; till the superiority of ground and numbers finally prevailed, and the Latin trumpets sounded a retreat. On the ensuing days, the attack was renewed with equal vigour and a similar event; and, in the night, the doge and the barons held a council, apprehensive only for the public danger: not a voice pronounced the words of escape or treaty; and each warrior, according to his temper, embraced the hope of victory or the assurance of a glorious death.[80] By the experience of the former siege,

78. Baldwin mentions both attempts to fire the fleet (Gest. c. 92. p. 534, 535.); Villehardouin (N° 113–115.) only describes the first. It is remarkable, that neither of these warriors observe any peculiar properties in the Greek fire.

79. Ducange (N° 119.) pours forth a torrent of learning on the *Gonfanon Imperial*. This banner of the Virgin is shewn at Venice as a trophy and relic: if it be genuine, the pious doge must have cheated the monks of Citeaux.

80. Villehardouin (N° 126.) confesses, that mult ere grant peril; and Guntherus (Hist.

the Greeks were instructed, but the Latins were animated; and the knowledge, that Constantinople *might* be taken, was of more avail than the local precautions which that knowledge had inspired for its defence. In the third assault, two ships were linked together to double their strength; a strong north wind drove them on the shore; the bishops of Troyes and Soissons led the van; and the auspicious names of the *pilgrim* and the *paradise* resounded along the line.[81] The episcopal banners were displayed on the walls; an hundred marks of silver had been promised to the first adventurers; and if their reward was intercepted by death, their names have been immortalised by fame. Four towers were scaled; three gates were burst open; and the French knights, who might tremble on the waves, felt themselves invincible on horseback on the solid ground. Shall I relate that the thousands who guarded the emperor's person fled on the approach and before the lance of a single warrior? Their ignominious flight is attested by their countryman Nicetas; an army of phantoms marched with the French hero, and he was magnified to a giant in the eyes of the Greeks.[82] While the fugitives deserted their posts and cast away their arms, the Latins entered the city under the banners of their leaders; the streets and gates opened for their passage; and either design or accident kindled a third conflagration, which consumed in a few hours the measure of three of the largest cities of France.[83] In the close of evening, the barons checked their troops and fortified their stations; they were awed by the extent and populousness of the capital, which might yet require the labour of a month, if the churches and palaces were conscious of their internal strength. But in the morning, a suppliant procession, with crosses and images, announced the submission of the Greeks, and deprecated the wrath of the conquerors: the usurper escaped through the golden gate; the palaces of Blachernæ and Boucoleon were occupied by the count of Flanders and the marquis of Montferrat;

C. P. c. 13.) affirms, that nulla spes victoriæ arridere poterat. Yet the knight despises those who thought of flight, and the monk praises his countrymen who were resolved on death.

81. Baldwin, and all the writers, honour the names of these two gallies, felici auspicio.

82. With an allusion to Homer, Nicetas calls him ἐννεα οργυιας, nine orgyæ, or eighteen yards high, a stature which would indeed have excused the terror of the Greek. On this occasion, the historian seems fonder of the marvellous, than of his country, or perhaps of truth. Baldwin exclaims in the words of the psalmist, persequitur unus ex nobis centum alienos.

83. Villehardouin (N° 130.) is again ignorant of the authors of *this* more legitimate fire, which is ascribed by Gunther to a quidam comes Teutonicus (c. 14.). They seem ashamed, the incendiaries!

and the empire which still bore the name of Constantine, and the title of Roman, was subverted by the arms of the Latin pilgrims.[84]

Pillage of Constantinople.

Constantinople had been taken by storm; and no restraints, except those of religion and humanity, were imposed on the conquerors by the laws of war. Boniface marquis of Montferrat still acted as their general; and the Greeks, who revered his name as that of their future sovereign, were heard to exclaim in a lamentable tone, "Holy marquis-king, have mercy upon us!" His prudence or compassion opened the gates of the city to the fugitives; and he exhorted the soldiers of the cross to spare the lives of their fellow-Christians. The streams of blood that flow down the pages of Nicetas, may be reduced to the slaughter of two thousand of his unresisting countrymen;[85] and the greater part was massacred, not by the strangers, but by the Latins, who had been driven from the city, and who exercised the revenge of a triumphant faction. Yet of these exiles, some were less mindful of injuries than of benefits; and Nicetas himself was indebted for his safety to the generosity of a Venetian merchant. Pope Innocent the third accuses the pilgrims of respecting, in their lust, neither age nor sex, nor religious profession; and bitterly laments that the deeds of darkness, fornication, adultery, and incest, were perpetrated in open day; and that noble matrons and holy nuns were polluted by the grooms and peasants of the Catholic camp.[86] It is indeed probable that the licence of victory prompted and covered a multitude of sins: but it is certain, that the capital of the East contained a stock of venal or willing beauty, sufficient to satiate the desires of twenty thousand pilgrims; and female prisoners were no longer subject to the right or abuse of domestic slavery. The marquis of Montferrat was the patron of discipline and decency; the count of Flanders was the mirrour

84. For the second siege and conquest of Constantinople, see Villehardouin (N° 113–132.), Baldwin's ii[d] Epistle to Innocent III. (Gesta, c. 92. p. 534–537.), with the whole reign of Mourzoufle, in Nicetas (p. 363–375.); and borrow some hints from Dandolo (Chron. Venet. p. 323–330.) and Gunther (Hist. C. P. c. 14–18.), who add the decorations of prophecy and vision. The former produces an oracle of the Erythræan sybil, of a great armament on the Adriatic, under a blind chief, against Byzantium, &c. Curious enough, were the prediction anterior to the fact.

85. Ceciderunt tamen eâ die civium quasi duo millia, &c. (Gunther, c. 18.) Arithmetic is an excellent touchstone to try the amplifications of passion and rhetoric.

86. Quidam (says Innocent III. Gesta, c. 94. p. 538.) nec religioni, nec ætati, nec sexui pepercerunt: sed fornicationes, adulteria, et incestus in occulis omnium exercentes, non solùm maritatas et viduas, sed et matronas et virgines Deoque dicatas, exposuerunt spurcitiis garcionum. Villehardouin takes no notice of these common incidents.

of chastity: they had forbidden, under pain of death, the rape of married women, or virgins, or nuns; and the proclamation was sometimes invoked by the vanquished[87] and respected by the victors. Their cruelty and lust were moderated by the authority of the chiefs, and feelings of the soldiers; for we are no longer describing an irruption of the northern savages; and however ferocious they might still appear, time, policy, and religion, had civilized the manners of the French, and still more of the Italians. But a free scope was allowed to their avarice, which was glutted, even in the holy week, by the pillage of Constantinople. The right of victory, unshackled by any promise or treaty, had confiscated the public and private wealth of the Greeks; and every hand, according to its size and strength, might lawfully execute the sentence and seize the forfeiture. A portable and universal standard of exchange was found in the coined and uncoined metals of gold and silver, which each captor at home or abroad might convert into the possessions most suitable to his temper and situation. Of the treasures, which trade and luxury had accumulated, the silks, velvets, furs, the gems, spices, and rich moveables, were the most precious, as they could not be procured for money in the ruder countries of Europe. *Division of the spoil.* An order of rapine was instituted; nor was the share of each individual abandoned to industry or chance. Under the tremendous penalties of perjury, excommunication and death, the Latins were bound to deliver their plunder into the common stock: three churches were selected for the deposit and distribution of the spoil: a single share was allotted to a foot soldier; two for a serjeant on horseback; four to a knight; and larger proportions according to the rank and merit of the barons and princes. For violating this sacred engagement, a knight belonging to the count of St. Paul was hanged with his shield and coat of arms round his neck: his example might render similar offenders more artful and discreet; but avarice was more powerful than fear; and it is generally believed, that the secret far exceeded the acknowledged plunder. Yet the magnitude of the prize surpassed the largest scale of experience or expectation.[88] After the whole had been equally divided between the French and Venetians, fifty thousand marks were deducted to satisfy the debts of the former and the demands of the latter. The

87. Nicetas saved, and afterwards married, a noble virgin (p. 380.), whom a soldier επι μαρτυσι πολλοις ονηδον επιβρωμωμενος, had almost violated in spite of the εντολαι, ενταλματα ευ γεγονοτων.

88. Of the general mass of wealth, Gunther observes, ut de pauperibus et advenis cives ditissimi redderentur (Hist. C. P. c. 18.); Villehardouin (N° 132.), that since the creation, ne fu tant gaaignié dans une ville; Baldwin (Gesta, c. 92.), ut tantum tota non videatur possidere Latinitas.

residue of the French amounted to four hundred thousand marks of silver,[89] about eight hundred thousand pounds sterling; nor can I better appreciate the value of that sum in the public and private transactions of the age, than by defining it as seven times the annual revenue of the kingdom of England.[90]

Misery of the Greeks.

In this great revolution we enjoy the singular felicity of comparing the narratives of Villehardouin and Nicetas, the opposite feelings of the marshal of Champagne and the Byzantine senator.[91] At the first view it should seem that the wealth of Constantinople was only transferred from one nation to another; and that the loss and sorrow of the Greeks is exactly balanced by the joy and advantage of the Latins. But in the miserable account of war, the gain is never equivalent to the loss, the pleasure to the pain: the smiles of the Latins were transient and fallacious; the Greeks for ever wept over the ruins of their country; and their real calamities were aggravated by sacrilege and mockery. What benefits accrued to the conquerors from the three fires which annihilated so vast a portion of the buildings and riches of the city? What a stock of such things, as could neither be used nor transported, was maliciously or wantonly destroyed? How much treasure was idly wasted in gaming, debauchery, and riot? And what precious objects were bartered for a vile price by the impatience or ignorance of the soldiers, whose reward was stolen by the base industry of the last of the Greeks? These alone, who had nothing to lose, might derive some profit from the revolution; but the misery of the upper ranks of society is strongly painted in the personal adventures of Nicetas himself. His stately palace had been reduced to ashes in the second conflagration; and the senator, with his family and friends, found an obscure shelter in another house which he possessed near the church of St. Sophia. It was the door of this mean habitation that his friend the Venetian merchant guarded in the disguise of a soldier,

89. Villehardouin, N° 133–135. Instead of 400,000, there is a various reading of 500,000. The Venetians had offered to take the whole booty, and to give 400 marks to each knight, 200 to each priest and horseman, and 100 to each foot-soldier: they would have been great losers (Le Beau, Hist. du Bas-Empire, tom. xx. p. 506. I know not from whence).

90. At the council of Lyons (A.D. 1245), the English ambassadors stated the revenue of the crown as below that of the foreign clergy, which amounted to 60,000 marks a year (Matthew Paris, p. 451. Hume's History of England, vol. ii. p. 170.).

91. The disorders of the sack of Constantinople, and his own adventures, are feelingly described by Nicetas, p. 367–369. and in the Status Urb. C. P. p. 375–384. His complaints even of sacrilege are justified by Innocent III. (Gesta, c. 92.); but Villehardouin does not betray a symptom of pity or remorse.

till Nicetas could save, by a precipitate flight, the relics of his fortune and the chastity of his daughter. In a cold wintry season, these fugitives, nursed in the lap of prosperity, departed on foot; his wife was with child; the desertion of their slaves compelled them to carry their baggage on their own shoulders; and their women, whom they placed in the centre, were exhorted to conceal their beauty with dirt, instead of adorning it with paint and jewels. Every step was exposed to insult and danger: the threats of the strangers were less painful than the taunts of the plebeians, with whom they were now levelled; nor did the exiles breathe in safety till their mournful pilgrimage was concluded at Selymbria, above forty miles from the capital. On the way they overtook the patriarch, without attendance and almost without apparel, riding on an ass, and reduced to a state of apostolical poverty, which, had it been voluntary, might perhaps have been meritorious. In the mean while, his desolate churches were profaned by the licentiousness and party zeal of the Latins. After stripping the gems and pearls, they converted the chalices into drinking-cups; their tables, on which they gamed and feasted, were covered with the pictures of Christ and the saints; and they trampled under foot the most venerable objects of the Christian worship. In the cathedral of St. Sophia, the ample veil of the sanctuary was rent asunder for the sake of the golden fringe; and the altar, a monument of art and riches, was broken in pieces and shared among the captors. Their mules and horses were laden with the wrought silver and gilt carvings, which they tore down from the doors and pulpit; and if the beasts stumbled under the burthen, they were stabbed by their impatient drivers, and the holy pavement streamed with their impure blood. A prostitute was seated on the throne of the patriarch; and that daughter of Belial, as she is styled, sung and danced in the church, to ridicule the hymns and processions of the Orientals. Nor were the repositories of the royal dead secure from violation: in the church of the apostles, the tombs of the emperors were rifled; and it is said, that after six centuries the corpse of Justinian was found without any signs of decay or putrefaction. In the streets, the French and Flemings clothed themselves and their horses in painted robes and flowing head-dresses of linen; and the coarse intemperance of their feasts[92] insulted the splendid sobriety of the East. To expose the arms of a people of scribes and scholars, they affected to display a pen, an ink-

Sacrilege and mockery.

92. If I rightly apprehend the Greek of Nicetas's receipts, their favourite dishes were boiled buttocks of beef, salt pork and pease, and soup made of garlic and sharp or sour herbs (p. 382).

horn, and a sheet of paper, without discerning that the instruments of science and valour were *alike* feeble and useless in the hands of the modern Greeks.

Destruction of the statues.

Their reputation and their language encouraged them, however, to despise the ignorance, and to overlook the progress, of the Latins.[93] In the love of the arts, the national difference was still more obvious and real; the Greeks preserved with reverence the works of their ancestors, which they could not imitate; and, in the destruction of the statues of Constantinople, we are provoked to join in the complaints and invectives of the Byzantine historian.[94] We have seen how the rising city was adorned by the vanity and despotism of the Imperial founder: in the ruins of paganism, some gods and heroes were saved from the axe of superstition; and the forum and hippodrome were dignified with the relics of a better age. Several of these are described by Nicetas,[95] in a florid and affected style; and, from his descriptions, I shall select some interesting particulars. 1. The victorious charioteers were cast in bronze, at their own, or the public, charge, and fitly placed in the hippodrome: they stood aloft in their chariots, wheeling round the goal; the spectators could admire their attitude, and judge of the resemblance; and of these figures, the most perfect might have been transported from the Olympic stadium. 2. The sphynx, river-horse, and crocodile, denote the climate and manufacture of Egypt, and the spoils of that ancient province. 3. The she-wolf suckling Romulus and Remus; a subject alike pleasing to the *old* and the *new* Romans; but which could rarely be treated before the decline of the Greek sculpture. 4. An eagle holding and tearing a serpent in his talons; a domestic monument of the Byzantines, which they ascribed, not to a human artist, but to the magic power of the philosopher

93. Nicetas uses very harsh expressions, *παρ' αγραμματοις Βαρβαροις, και τελεον αναλφαβητοις* (Fragment. apud Fabric. Bibliot. Græc. tom. vi. p. 414.). This reproach, it is true, applies most strongly to their ignorance of Greek and of Homer. In their own language, the Latins of the xii[th] and xiii[th] centuries were not destitute of literature. See Harris's Philological Inquiries, p. iii. c. 9, 10, 11.

94. Nicetas was of Chonæ in Phrygia (the old Colossæ of St. Paul): he raised himself to the honours of senator, judge of the veil, and great logothete; beheld the fall of the empire, retired to Nice, and composed an elaborate history from the death of Alexius Comnenus to the reign of Henry.

95. A manuscript of Nicetas in the Bodleian library, contains this curious fragment on the statues of Constantinople, which fraud, or shame, or rather carelessness, has dropt in the common editions. It is published by Fabricius (Bibliot. Græc. tom. vi. p. 405–416.), and immoderately praised by the late ingenious Mr. Harris of Salisbury (Philological Inquiries, p. iii. c. 5. p. 301–312.).

Apollonius, who, by this talisman, delivered the city from such venomous reptiles. 5. An ass and his driver; which were erected by Augustus in his colony of Nicopolis, to commemorate a verbal omen of the victory of Actium. 6. An equestrian statue; which passed, in the vulgar opinion, for Joshua, the Jewish conqueror, stretching out his hand to stop the course of the descending sun. A more classical tradition recognised the figures of Bellerophon and Pegasus; and the free attitude of the steed seemed to mark that he trod on air, rather than on the earth. 7. A square and lofty obelisk of brass; the sides were embossed with a variety of picturesque and rural scenes: birds singing; rustics labouring, or playing on their pipes; sheep bleating; lambs skipping; the sea, and a scene of fish and fishing; little naked cupids laughing, playing, and pelting each other with apples; and, on the summit, a female figure turning with the slightest breath, and thence denominated *the wind's attendant*. 8. The Phrygian shepherd presenting to Venus the prize of beauty, the apple of discord. 9. The incomparable statue of Helen; which is delineated by Nicetas in the words of admiration and love: her well-turned feet, snowy arms, rosy lips, bewitching smiles, swimming eyes, arched eye-brows, the harmony of her shape, the lightness of her drapery, and her flowing locks that waved in the wind: a beauty that might have moved her Barbarian destroyers to pity and remorse. 10. The manly or divine form of Hercules,[96] as he was restored to life by the master-hand of Lysippus; of such magnitude, that his thumb was equal to the waist, his leg to the stature, of a common man;[97] his chest ample, his shoulders broad, his limbs strong and muscular, his hair curled, his aspect commanding. Without his bow, or quiver, or club, his lion's skin carelessly thrown over him, he was seated on an osier basket, his right leg and arm stretched to the utmost, his left knee bent, and supporting his elbow, his head reclining on his left hand, his countenance indignant and pensive. 11. A colossal statue of Juno, which had once adorned her temple of Samos; the enormous head by four yoke of oxen was laboriously drawn to the palace. 12. Another colossus, of Pallas or Minerva, thirty feet in height, and representing with admirable spirit the attributes and character of the martial maid. Before

96. To illustrate the statue of Hercules, Mr. Harris quotes a Greek epigram, and engraves a beautiful gem, which does not however copy the attitude of the statue: in the latter, Hercules had not his club, and his right leg and arm were extended.

97. I transcribe these proportions, which appear to me inconsistent with each other; and may possibly shew, that the boasted taste of Nicetas was no more than affectation and vanity.

we accuse the Latins, it is just to remark, that this Pallas was destroyed after the first siege, by the fear and superstition of the Greeks themselves.[98] The other statues of brass which I have enumerated, were broken and melted by the unfeeling avarice of the crusaders: the cost and labour were consumed in a moment; the soul of genius evaporated in smoke; and the remnant of base metal was coined into money for the payment of the troops. Bronze is not the most durable of monuments: from the marble forms of Phidias and Praxiteles, the Latins might turn aside with stupid contempt;[99] but unless they were crushed by some accidental injury, those useless stones stood secure on their pedestals.[100] The most enlightened of the strangers, above the gross and sensual pursuits of their countrymen, more piously exercised the right of conquest in the search and seizure of the relics of the saints.[101] Immense was the supply of heads and bones, crosses and images, that were scattered by this revolution over the churches of Europe; and such was the encrease of pilgrimage and oblation, that no branch, perhaps, of more lucrative plunder was imported from the East.[102] Of the writings of antiquity, many that still existed in the twelfth century are now lost. But the pilgrims were not solicitous to save or transport the volumes of an unknown tongue: the perishable substance of paper or parchment can only be preserved by the multiplicity of copies; the literature of the Greeks had almost centered in the metropolis; and, without computing the extent of our loss, we may drop a tear over the libraries that have perished in the triple fire of Constantinople.[103]

98. Nicetas in Isaaco Angelo et Alexio, c. 3. p. 359. The Latin editor very properly observes, that the historian, in his bombast style, produces ex pulice elephantem.

99. In two passages of Nicetas (edit. Paris, p. 360. Fabric. p. 408.), the Latins are branded with the lively reproach of *όι του καλου ανεραστοι βαρβαροι*, and their avarice of brass is clearly expressed. Yet the Venetians had the merit of removing four bronze horses from Constantinople to the place of St. Mark (Sanuto, Vite del Dogi, in Muratori, Script. Rerum Italicarum, tom. xxii. p. 534.).

100. Winckelman, Hist. de l'Art, tom. iii. p. 269, 270.

101. See the pious robbery of the abbot Martin, who transferred a rich cargo to his monastery of Paris, diocese of Basil (Gunther, Hist. C. P. c. 19. 23, 24.). Yet in secreting this booty, the saint incurred an excommunication, and perhaps broke his oath.

102. Fleury, Hist. Eccles. tom. xvi. p. 139–145.

103. I shall conclude this chapter with the notice of a modern history, which illustrates the taking of Constantinople by the Latins; but which has fallen somewhat late into my hands. Paolo Ramusio, the son of the compiler of voyages, was directed by the senate of Venice to write the history of the conquest; and this order, which he received in his youth, he executed in a mature age, by an elegant Latin work, de Bello Constantinopolitano et Imper-

atoribus Comnenis per Gallos et Venetos restitutis (Venet. 1635, in folio). Ramusio, or Rhamnusius, transcribes and translates sequitur ad unguem, a MS. of Villehardouin, which he possessed; but he enriches his narrative with Greek and Latin materials, and we are indebted to him for a correct state of the fleet, the names of the fifty Venetian nobles who commanded the gallies of the republic, and the patriot opposition of Pantaleon Barbus to the choice of the doge for emperor.

CHAPTER LXI

Partition of the Empire by the French and Venetians. – Five Latin Emperors of the Houses of Flanders and Courtenay. – Their Wars against the Bulgarians and Greeks. – Weakness and Poverty of the Latin Empire. – Recovery of Constantinople by the Greeks. – General Consequences of the Crusades.

Election of the emperor Baldwin I. A.D. 1204, May 9–16.

After the death of the lawful princes, the French and Venetians, confident of justice and victory, agreed to divide and regulate their future possessions.[1] It was stipulated by treaty, that twelve electors, six of either nation, should be nominated; that a majority should chuse the emperor of the East; and that, if the votes were equal, the decision of chance should ascertain the successful candidate. To him, with all the titles and prerogatives of the Byzantine throne, they assigned the two palaces of Boucoleon and Blachernæ, with a fourth part of the Greek monarchy. It was defined that the three remaining portions should be equally shared between the republic of Venice and the barons of France; that each feudatory, with an honourable exception for the doge, should acknowledge and perform the duties of homage and military service to the supreme head of the empire: that the nation which gave an emperor, should resign to their brethren the choice of a patriarch; and that the pilgrims, whatever might be their impatience to visit the Holy Land, should devote another year to the conquest and defence of the Greek provinces. After the conquest of Constantinople by the Latins, the treaty was confirmed and executed; and the first and most important step was the creation of an emperor. The six electors of the French nation were all ecclesiastics, the abbot of Loces, the archbishop elect of Acre in Palestine, and the bishops of Troyes, Soissons, Halberstadt, and Bethlehem, the last of whom exercised in the camp the office of pope's legate: their profession and knowledge were respectable; and as

1. See the original treaty of partition, in the Venetian Chronicle of Andrew Dandolo, p. 326–330. and the subsequent election in Villehardouin, N° 136–140. with Ducange in his Observations, and the i[st] book of his Histoire de Constantinople sous l'Empire des François.

they could not be the objects, they were best qualified to be the authors, of the choice. The six Venetians were the principal servants of the state, and in this list the noble families of Querini and Contarini are still proud to discover their ancestors. The twelve assembled in the chapel of the palace; and after the solemn invocation of the Holy Ghost, they proceeded to deliberate and vote. A just impulse of respect and gratitude prompted them to crown the virtues of the doge; his wisdom had inspired their enterprise; and the most youthful knights might envy and applaud the exploits of blindness and age. But the patriot Dandolo was devoid of all personal ambition, and fully satisfied that he had been judged worthy to reign. His nomination was over-ruled by the Venetians themselves: his countrymen, and perhaps his friends,[2] represented, with the eloquence of truth, the mischiefs that might arise to national freedom and the common cause, from the union of two incompatible characters, of the first magistrate of a republic and the emperor of the East. The exclusion of the doge left room for the more equal merits of Boniface and Baldwin; and at their names all meaner candidates respectfully withdrew. The marquis of Montferrat was recommended by his mature age and fair reputation, by the choice of the adventurers and the wishes of the Greeks; nor can I believe that Venice, the mistress of the sea, could be seriously apprehensive of a petty lord at the foot of the Alps.[3] But the count of Flanders was the chief of a wealthy and warlike people; he was valiant, pious, and chaste; in the prime of life, since he was only thirty-two years of age; a descendant of Charlemagne, a cousin of the king of France, and a compeer of the prelates and barons who had yielded with reluctance to the command of a foreigner. Without the chapel, these barons, with the doge and marquis at their head, expected the decision of the twelve electors. It was announced by the bishop of Soissons, in the name of his colleagues: "Ye have sworn to obey the prince whom we should chuse; by our unanimous suffrage, Baldwin count of Flanders and Hainault is now your sovereign, and the emperor of the East." He was saluted with loud applause, and the proclamation was re-echoed through the city by

2. After mentioning the nomination of the doge by a French elector, his kinsman Andrew Dandolo approves his exclusion, quidam Venetorum fidelis et nobilis senex, usus oratione satis probabili, &c. which has been embroidered by modern writers from Blondus to Le Beau.

3. Nicetas (p. 384.), with the vain ignorance of a Greek, describes the marquis of Montferrat as a *maritime* power. *Λαμπαρδιαν δε οικεισθαι παραλιον.* Was he deceived by the Byzantine theme of Lombardy, which extended along the coast of Calabria?

the joy of the Latins and the trembling adulation of the Greeks. Boniface was the first to kiss the hand of his rival, and to raise him on the buckler; and Baldwin was transported to the cathedral, and solemnly invested with the purple buskins. At the end of three weeks he was crowned by the legate, in the vacancy of a patriarch; but the Venetian clergy soon filled the chapter of St. Sophia, seated Thomas Morosini on the ecclesiastical throne, and employed every art to perpetuate in their own nation the honours and benefices of the Greek church.[4] Without delay, the successor of Constantine instructed Palestine, France, and Rome, of this memorable revolution. To Palestine he sent, as a trophy, the gates of Constantinople, and the chain of the harbour;[5] and adopted, from the Assise of Jerusalem, the laws or customs best adapted to a French colony and conquest in the East. In his epistles, the natives of France are encouraged to swell that colony, and to secure that conquest, to people a magnificent city and a fertile land, which will reward the labours both of the priest and the soldier. He congratulates the Roman pontiff on the restoration of his authority in the East; invites him to extinguish the Greek schism by his presence in a general council; and implores his blessing and forgiveness for the disobedient pilgrims. Prudence and dignity are blended in the answer of Innocent.[6] In the subversion of the Byzantine empire, he arraigns the vices of man, and adores the providence of God: the conquerors will be absolved or condemned by their future conduct; the validity of their treaty depends on the judgment of St. Peter; but he inculcates their most sacred duty of establishing a just subordination of obedience and tribute, from the Greeks to the Latins, from the magistrate to the clergy, and from the clergy to the pope.

Division of the Greek empire.

In the division of the Greek provinces,[7] the share of the Venetians was more ample than that of the Latin emperor. No

4. They exacted an oath from Thomas Morosini to appoint no canons of St. Sophia, the lawful electors, except Venetians who had lived ten years at Venice, &c. But the foreign clergy was envious, the pope disapproved this national monopoly, and of the six Latin patriarchs of Constantinople, only the first and the last were Venetians.

5. Nicetas, p. 383.

6. The Epistles of Innocent III. are a rich fund for the ecclesiastical and civil institution of the Latin empire of Constantinople; and the most important of these epistles (of which the collection in 2 vols. in folio, is published by Stephen Baluze) are inserted in his Gesta, in Muratori, Script. Rerum Italicarum, tom. iii. p. i. c. 94–105.

7. In the treaty of partition, most of the names are corrupted by the scribes: they might be restored, and a good map suited to the last age of the Byzantine empire, would be an improvement of geography. But, alas! d'Anville is no more!

more than one fourth was appropriated to his domain; a clear moiety of the remainder was reserved for Venice; and the other moiety was distributed among the adventurers of France and Lombardy. The venerable Dandolo was proclaimed despot of Romania, and invested after the Greek fashion with the purple buskins. He ended at Constantinople his long and glorious life; and if the prerogative was personal, the title was used by his successors till the middle of the fourteenth century, with the singular though true addition of lords of one fourth and a half of the Roman empire.[8] The doge, a slave of state, was seldom permitted to depart from the helm of the republic; but his place was supplied by the *bail* or regent, who exercised a supreme jurisdiction over the colony of Venetians: they possessed three of the eight quarters of the city; and his independent tribunal was composed of six judges, four counsellors, two chamberlains, two fiscal advocates, and a constable. Their long experience of the Eastern trade enabled them to select their portion with discernment: they had rashly accepted the dominion and defence of Adrianople; but it was the more reasonable aim of their policy to form a chain of factories, and cities, and islands, along the maritime coast, from the neighbourhood of Ragusa to the Hellespont and the Bosphorus. The labour and cost of such extensive conquests exhausted their treasury: they abandoned their maxims of government, adopted a feudal system, and contented themselves with the homage of their nobles,[9] for the possessions which these private vassals undertook to reduce and maintain. And thus it was, that the family of Sanut acquired the dutchy of Naxos, which involved the greatest part of the Archipelago. For the price of ten thousand marks, the republic purchased of the marquis of Montferrat the fertile island of Crete or Candia with the ruins of an hundred cities;[10] but its improvement was stinted by the proud and narrow spirit of an aristocracy;[11] and the wisest senators would confess that the sea, not the

8. Their style was dominus quartæ partis et dimidiæ imperii Romani, till Giovanni Dolfino who was elected doge in the year 1356 (Sanuto, p. 530. 641.). For the government of Constantinople, see Ducange, Histoire de C. P. i. 37.

9. Ducange (Hist. de C. P. ii. 6.) has marked the conquests made by the state or nobles of Venice of the islands of Candia, Corfu, Cephalonia, Zante, Naxos, Paros, Melos, Andros, Mycone, Scyro, Cea, and Lemnos.

10. Boniface sold the isle of Candia, August 12, A.D. 1204. See the act in Sanuto, p. 533.: but I cannot understand how it could be his mother's portion, or how she could be the daughter of an emperor Alexius.

11. In the year 1212, the doge Peter Zani sent a colony to Candia, drawn from every

land, was the treasury of St. Mark. In the moiety of the adventurers, the marquis Boniface might claim the most liberal reward; and, besides the isle of Crete, his exclusion from the throne was compensated by the royal title and the provinces beyond the Hellespont. But he prudently exchanged that distant and difficult conquest for the kingdom of Thessalonica or Macedonia, twelve days journey from the capital, where he might be supported by the neighbouring powers of his brother-in-law the king of Hungary. His progress was hailed by the voluntary or reluctant acclamations of the natives; and Greece, the proper and ancient Greece, again received a Latin conqueror,[12] who trod with indifference that classic ground. He viewed with a careless eye the beauties of the valley of Tempe; traversed with a cautious step the streights of Thermopylæ; occupied the unknown cities of Thebes, Athens, and Argos; and assaulted the fortifications of Corinth and Napoli,[13] which resisted his arms. The lots of the Latin pilgrims were regulated by chance, or choice, or subsequent exchange; and they abused, with intemperate joy, their triumph over the lives and fortunes of a great people. After a minute survey of the provinces, they weighed in the scales of avarice the revenue of each district, the advantage of the situation, and the ample or scanty supplies for the maintenance of soldiers and horses. Their presumption claimed and divided the long-lost dependencies of the Roman sceptre: the Nile and Euphrates rolled through their imaginary realms; and happy was the warrior who drew for his prize the palace of the Turkish sultan of Iconium.[14] I shall not descend to the pedigree of families and the rent-roll of estates, but I wish to specify that the counts of Blois and St. Pol were invested with the dutchy of Nice and the lordship of

---

quarter of Venice. But in their savage manners and frequent rebellions, the Candiots may be compared to the Corsicans under the yoke of Genoa; and when I compare the accounts of Belon and Tournefort, I cannot discern much difference between the Venetian and the Turkish island.

12. Villehardouin (N° 159, 160. 173–177.) and Nicetas (p. 387–394.) describe the expedition into Greece of the marquis Boniface. The Choniate might derive his information from his brother Michael, archbishop of Athens, whom he paints as an orator, a statesman, and a saint. His encomium of Athens, and the description of Tempe, should be published from the Bodleian MS. of Nicetas (Fabric. Bibliot. Græc. tom. vi. p. 405.), and would have deserved Mr. Harris's enquiries.

13. Napoli di Romania, or Nauplia, the ancient sea-port of Argos, is still a place of strength and consideration, situate on a rocky peninsula, with a good harbour (Chandler's Travels into Greece, p. 227.).

14. I have softened the expression of Nicetas, who strives to expose the presumption of the Franks. See de Rebus post C. P. expugnatam, p. 375–384.

Demotica:[15] the principal fiefs were held by the service of constable, chamberlain, cup-bearer, butler, and chief cook; and our historian, Jeffrey of Villehardouin, obtained a fair establishment on the banks of the Hebrus, and united the double office of marshal of Champagne and Romania. At the head of his knights and archers, each baron mounted on horseback to secure the possession of his share, and their first efforts were generally successful. But the public force was weakened by their dispersion; and a thousand quarrels must arise under a law, and among men, whose sole umpire was the sword. Within three months after the conquest of Constantinople, the emperor and the king of Thessalonica drew their hostile followers into the field; they were reconciled by the authority of the doge, the advice of the marshal, and the firm freedom of their peers.[16]

Revolt of the Greeks, A.D. 1204, &c.

Two fugitives, who had reigned at Constantinople, still asserted the title of emperor; and the subjects of their fallen throne might be moved to pity by the misfortunes of the elder Alexius, or excited to revenge by the spirit of Mourzoufle. A domestic alliance, a common interest, a similar guilt, and the merit of extinguishing his enemies, a brother and a nephew, induced the more recent usurper to unite with the former the relics of his power. Mourzoufle was received with smiles and honours in the camp of his father Alexius; but the wicked can never love, and should rarely trust, their fellow-criminals: he was seized in the bath, deprived of his eyes, stripped of his troops and treasures, and turned out to wander an object of horror and contempt to those who with more propriety could hate, and with more justice could punish, the assassin of the emperor Isaac, and his son. As the tyrant, pursued by fear or remorse, was stealing over to Asia, he was seized by the Latins of Constantinople, and condemned, after an open trial, to an ignominious death. His judges debated the mode of his execution, the axe, the wheel, or the stake; and it was resolved that Mourzoufle[17] should ascend the Theodosian column, a pillar of white

15. A city surrounded by the river Hebrus, and six leagues to the south of Adrianople, received from its double wall the Greek name of Didymoteichos, insensibly corrupted into Demotica and Dimot. I have preferred the more convenient and modern appellation of Demotica. This place was the last Turkish residence of Charles XII.

16. Their quarrel is told by Villehardouin (N° 146–158.) with the spirit of freedom. The merit and reputation of the marshal are acknowledged by the Greek historian (p. 387.), μεγα παρα τοις Λατινων δυναμενου στρατευμασι: unlike some modern heroes, whose exploits are only visible in their own memoirs.

17. See the fate of Mourzoufle, in Nicetas (p. 393.), Villehardouin (N° 141–145. 163.), and Guntherus (c. 20, 21.). Neither the marshal nor the monk afford a grain of

marble of one hundred and forty-seven feet in height.[18] From the summit he was cast down headlong, and dashed in pieces on the pavement, in the presence of innumerable spectators, who filled the forum of Taurus, and admired the accomplishment of an old prediction, which was explained by this singular event.[19] The fate of Alexius is less tragical: he was sent by the marquis a captive to Italy, and a gift to the king of the Romans; but he had not much to applaud his fortune, if the sentence of imprisonment and exile were changed from a fortress in the Alps to a monastery in Asia. But his daughter, before the national calamity, had been given in marriage to a young hero who continued the succession, and restored the throne, of the Greek princes.[20] The valour of Theodore Lascaris was signalised in the two sieges of Constantinople. After the flight of Mourzoufle, when the Latins were already in the city, he offered himself as their emperor to the soldiers and people: and his ambition, which might be virtuous, was undoubtedly brave. Could he have infused a soul into the multitude, they might have crushed the strangers under their feet: their abject despair refused his aid, and Theodore retired to breathe the air of freedom in Anatolia, beyond the immediate view and pursuit of the conquerors. Under the title, at first of despot, and afterwards of emperor, he drew to his standard the bolder spirits, who were fortified against slavery by the contempt of life; and as every means was lawful for the public safety, implored without scruple the alliance of the Turkish sultan. Nice, where Theodore established his residence, Prusa and Philadelphia, Smyrna and Ephesus, opened their gates to their deliverer: he derived strength and reputation from his victories, and even from his defeats; and the successor of Constantine preserved a fragment of the empire from the banks of the Mæander to the suburbs of Nicomedia, and at length of

Theodore Lascaris, emperor of Nice. A.D. 1204–1222.

---

pity for a tyrant or rebel, whose punishment, however, was more unexampled than his crime.

18. The column of Arcadius, which represents in basso-relievo his victories, or those of his father Theodosius, is still extant at Constantinople. It is described and measured, Gyllius (Topograph. iv. 7.), Banduri (ad l. i. Antiquit. C. P. p. 507, &c.), and Tournefort (Voyage du Levant, tom. ii. lettre xii. p. 231.).

19. The nonsense of Gunther and the modern Greeks concerning this *columna fatidica*, is unworthy of notice: but it is singular enough, that fifty years before the Latin conquest, the poet Tzetzes (Chiliad, ix. 277.) relates the dream of a matron, who saw an army in the forum, and a man sitting on the column, clapping his hands, and uttering a loud exclamation.

20. The dynasties of Nice, Trebizond, and Epirus (of which Nicetas saw the origin without much pleasure or hope), are learnedly explored, and clearly represented, in the Familiæ Byzantinæ of Ducange.

The dukes and emperors of Trebizond.

Constantinople. Another portion, distant and obscure, was possessed by the lineal heir of the Comneni, a son of the virtuous Manuel, a grandson of the tyrant Andronicus. His name was Alexius; and the epithet of great was applied perhaps to his stature, rather than to his exploits. By the indulgence of the Angeli, he was appointed governor or duke of Trebizond:[21] his birth gave him ambition, the revolution independence; and without changing his title, he reigned in peace from Sinope to the Phasis, along the coast of the Black Sea. His nameless son and successor is described as the vassal of the sultan, whom he served with two hundred lances; that Comnenian prince was no more than duke of Trebizond, and the title of emperor was first assumed by the pride and envy of the grandson of Alexius. In the West,

The despots of Epirus.

a third fragment was saved from the common shipwreck by Michael, a bastard of the house of Angeli, who, before the revolution, had been known as an hostage, a soldier, and a rebel. His flight from the camp of the marquis Boniface secured his freedom; by his marriage with the governor's daughter, he commanded the important place of Durazzo, assumed the title of despot, and founded a strong and conspicuous principality in Epirus, Ætolia, and Thessaly, which have ever been peopled by a warlike race. The Greeks, who had offered their service to their new sovereigns, were excluded by the haughty Latins[22] from all civil and military honours, as a nation born to tremble and obey. Their resentment prompted them to shew that they might have been useful friends, since they could be dangerous enemies: their nerves were braced by adversity: whatever was learned or holy, whatever was noble or valiant, rolled away into the independent states of Trebizond, Epirus, and Nice; and a single patrician is marked by the ambiguous praise of attachment and loyalty to the Franks. The vulgar herd of the cities and the country, would have gladly submitted to a mild and regular servitude;

21. Except some facts in Pachymer and Nicephorus Gregoras, which will hereafter be used, the Byzantine writers disdain to speak of the empire of Trebizond, or principality of the *Lazi*; and among the Latins, it is conspicuous only in the romances of the xiv[th] or xv[th] centuries. Yet the indefatigable Ducange has dug out (Fam. Byz. p. 192.) two authentic passages in Vincent of Beauvais (l. xxxi. c. 144.), and the protonotary Ogerius (apud Wading, A.D. 1279, N° 4.).

22. The portrait of the French Latins, is drawn in Nicetas by the hand of prejudice and resentment: *ουδεν των αλλων εθνων εις Αρεος εργα παρασυμβεβλησθαι ηνειχοντο, αλλ' ουδε τις των χαριτων η των μουσων παρα τοις βαρβαροις τουτοις επεξενιζετο, και παρα τουτο οιμαι την φυσιν ησαν ανημεροι, και τον χολον ειχον του λογου προτρεχοντα.*

and the transient disorders of war would have been obliterated by some years of industry and peace. But peace was banished, and industry was crushed, in the disorders of the feudal system. The *Roman* emperors of Constantinople, if they were endowed with abilities, were armed with power for the protection of their subjects: their laws were wise, and their administration was simple. The Latin throne was filled by a titular prince, the chief, and often the servant, of his licentious confederates: the fiefs of the empire, from a kingdom to a castle, were held and ruled by the sword of the barons: and their discord, poverty, and ignorance, extended the ramifications of tyranny to the most sequestered villages. The Greeks were oppressed by the double weight of the priest, who was invested with temporal power, and of the soldier, who was inflamed by fanatic hatred; and the insuperable bar of religion and language for ever separated the stranger and the native. As long as the crusaders were united at Constantinople, the memory of their conquest, and the terror of their arms, imposed silence on the captive land: their dispersion betrayed the smallness of their numbers and the defects of their discipline; and some failures and mischances revealed the secret, that they were not invincible. As the fear of the Greeks abated, their hatred encreased. They murmured; they conspired; and before a year of slavery had elapsed, they implored, or accepted, the succour of a Barbarian, whose power they had felt, and whose gratitude they trusted.[23]

The Bulgarian war, A.D. 1205.

The Latin conquerors had been saluted with a solemn and early embassy from John, or Joannice, or Calo-John, the revolted chief of the Bulgarians and Walachians. He deemed himself their brother, as the votary of the Roman pontiff, from whom he had received the regal title and an holy banner; and in the subversion of the Greek monarchy, he might aspire to the name of their friend and accomplice. But Calo-John was astonished to find, that the count of Flanders had assumed the pomp and pride of the successors of Constantine; and his ambassadors were dismissed with an haughty message, that the rebel must deserve a pardon, by touching with his forehead the footstool of the Imperial throne. His resentment[24] would have exhaled in

23. I here begin to use, with freedom and confidence, the eight books of the Histoire de C. P. sous l'Empire des François, which Ducange has given as a supplement to Villehardouin; and which, in a barbarous style, deserves the praise of an original and classic work.

24. In Calo-John's answer to the pope, we may find his claims and complaints (Gesta Innocent. III. c. 108, 109.); he was cherished at Rome as the prodigal son.

acts of violence and blood; his cooler policy watched the rising discontent of the Greeks; affected a tender concern for their sufferings; and promised, that their first struggles for freedom should be supported by his person and kingdom. The conspiracy was propagated by national hatred, the firmest band of association and secrecy: the Greeks were impatient to sheath their daggers in the breasts of the victorious strangers; but the execution was prudently delayed, till Henry, the emperor's brother, had transported the flower of his troops beyond the Hellespont. Most of the towns and villages of Thrace were true to the moment and the signal: and the Latins, without arms or suspicion, were slaughtered by the vile and merciless revenge of their slaves. From Demotica, the first scene of the massacre, the surviving vassals of the count of St. Pol escaped to Adrianople; but the French and Venetians, who occupied that city, were slain or expelled by the furious multitude; the garrisons that could effect their retreat, fell back on each other towards the metropolis; and the fortresses, that separately stood against the rebels, were ignorant of each other's and of their sovereign's fate. The voice of fame and fear announced the revolt of the Greeks and the rapid approach of their Bulgarian ally; and Calo-John, not depending on the forces of his own kingdom, had drawn from the Scythian wilderness a body of fourteen thousand Comans, who drank, as it was said, the blood of their captives, and sacrificed the Christians on the altars of their gods.[25]

Alarmed by this sudden and growing danger, the emperor dispatched a swift messenger to recall count Henry and his troops; and had Baldwin expected the return of his gallant brother, with a supply of twenty thousand Armenians, he might have encountered the invader with equal numbers and a decisive superiority of arms and discipline. But the spirit
March. of chivalry could seldom discriminate caution from cowardice; and the emperor took the field with an hundred and forty knights, and their train of archers and serjeants. The marshal, who dissuaded and obeyed, led the vanguard in their march to Adrianople; the main body was commanded by the count of Blois; the aged doge of Venice followed with the rear; and their scanty numbers were encreased from all sides by the fugitive Latins. They undertook to besiege the rebels of Adrianople; and such was the pious tendency of the crusades, that they employed the

25. The Comans were a Tartar or Turkman hord, which encamped in the xii[th] and xiii[th] centuries on the verge of Moldavia. The greater part were pagans, but some were Mahometans, and the whole hord was converted to Christianity (A.D. 1370) by Lewis king of Hungary.

holy week in pillaging the country for their subsistence, and in framing engines for the destruction of their fellow-christians. But the Latins were soon interrupted and alarmed by the light cavalry of the Comans, who boldly skirmished to the edge of their imperfect lines: and a proclamation was issued by the marshal of Romania, that, on the trumpet's sound, the cavalry should mount and form; but that none, under pain of death, should abandon themselves to a desultory and dangerous pursuit. This wise injunction was first disobeyed by the count of Blois, who involved the emperor in his rashness and ruin. The Comans, of the Parthian or Tartar school, fled before their first charge; but after a career of two leagues, when the knights and their horses were almost breathless, they suddenly turned, rallied, and encompassed the heavy squadrons of the Franks. The count was slain on the field; the emperor was made prisoner; and if the one disdained to fly, if the other refused to yield, their personal bravery made a poor atonement for their ignorance, or neglect, of the duties of a general.[26]

Defeat and captivity of Baldwin, A.D. 1205, April 15.

Proud of his victory and his royal prize, the Bulgarian advanced to relieve Adrianople and atchieve the destruction of the Latins. They must inevitably have been destroyed, if the marshal of Romania had not displayed a cool courage and consummate skill; uncommon in all ages, but most uncommon in those times, when war was a passion, rather than a science. His grief and fears were poured into the firm and faithful bosom of the doge; but in the camp he diffused an assurance of safety, which could only be realized by the general belief. All day he maintained his perilous station between the city and the Barbarians: Villehardouin decamped in silence, at the dead of night; and his masterly retreat of three days would have deserved the praise of Xenophon and the ten thousand. In the rear, the marshal supported the weight of the pursuit; in the front, he moderated the impatience of the fugitives; and wherever the Comans approached, they were repelled by a line of impenetrable spears. On the third day, the weary troops beheld the sea, the solitary town of Rodosto,[27] and their friends, who had landed from

Retreat of the Latins.

26. Nicetas, from ignorance or malice, imputes the defeat to the cowardice of Dandolo (p. 383.); but Villehardouin shares his own glory with his venerable friend, qui viels home ére et gote ne veoit, mais mult ére sages et preus et vigueros (N° 193.).

27. The truth of geography, and the original text of Villehardouin (N° 194.), place Rodosto three days journey (trois jornées) from Adrianople; but Vigenere, in his version, has most absurdly substituted *trois heures*; and this error, which is not corrected by Ducange, has entrapped several moderns, whose names I shall spare.

the Asiatic shore. They embraced, they wept; but they united their arms and counsels; and, in his brother's absence, count Henry assumed the regency of the empire, at once in a state of childhood and caducity.[28] If the Comans withdrew from the summer heats, seven thousand Latins, in the hour of danger, deserted Constantinople, their brethren, and their vows. Some partial success was overbalanced by the loss of one hundred and twenty knights in the field of Rusium; and of the Imperial domain, no more was left, than the capital, with two or three adjacent fortresses on the shores of Europe and Asia. The king of Bulgaria was resistless and inexorable; and Calo-John respectfully eluded the demands of the pope, who conjured his new proselyte to restore peace and the emperor to the afflicted Latins. The deliverance of Baldwin was no longer, he said, in the power of man: that prince had died in prison; and the manner of his death is variously related by ignorance and credulity. The lovers of a tragic legend will be pleased to hear, that the royal captive was tempted by the amorous queen of the Bulgarians; that his chaste refusal exposed him to the falsehood of a woman and the jealousy of a savage; that his hands and feet were severed from his body; that his bleeding trunk was cast among the carcases of dogs and horses; and that he breathed three days, before he was devoured by the birds of prey.[29] About twenty years afterwards, in a wood of the Netherlands, an hermit announced himself as the true Baldwin, the emperor of Constantinople, and lawful sovereign of Flanders. He related the wonders of his escape, his adventures, and his penance, among a people prone to believe and to rebel; and, in the first transport, Flanders acknowledged her long-lost sovereign. A short examination before the French court detected the impostor, who was punished with an ignominious death; but the Flemings still adhered to the pleasing error; and the countess Jane is accused by the gravest historians of sacrificing to her ambition the life of an unfortunate father.[30]

Death of the emperor.

28. The reign and end of Baldwin are related by Villehardouin and Nicetas (p. 386–416.): and their omissions are supplied by Ducange in his Observations, and to the end of his first book.

29. After brushing away all doubtful and improbable circumstances, we may prove the death of Baldwin, 1. By the firm belief of the French barons (Villehardouin, N° 230.). 2. By the declaration of Calo-John himself, who excuses his not releasing the captive emperor, quia debitum carnis exsolverat cum carcere teneretur (Gesta Innocent. III. c. 109.).

30. See the story of this impostor from the French and Flemish writers in Ducange, Hist. de C. P. iii. 9. and the ridiculous fables that were believed by the monks of St. Alban's, in Matthew Paris, Hist. Major, p. 271, 272.

Reign and character of Henry, A.D. 1206, August 20–A.D. 1216, June 11.

In all civilized hostility, a treaty is established for the exchange or ransom of prisoners; and if their captivity be prolonged, their condition is known, and they are treated according to their rank with humanity or honour. But the savage Bulgarian was a stranger to the laws of war; his prisons were involved in darkness and silence; and above a year elapsed before the Latins could be assured of the death of Baldwin, before his brother, the regent Henry, would consent to assume the title of emperor. His moderation was applauded by the Greeks as an act of rare and inimitable virtue. Their light and perfidious ambition was eager to seize or anticipate the moment of a vacancy, while a law of succession, the guardian both of the prince and people, was gradually defined and confirmed in the hereditary monarchies of Europe. In the support of the Eastern empire, Henry was gradually left without an associate, as the heroes of the crusade retired from the world or from the war. The doge of Venice, the venerable Dandolo, in the fulness of years and glory, sunk into the grave. The marquis of Montferrat was slowly recalled from the Peloponnesian war to the revenge of Baldwin and the defence of Thessalonica. Some nice disputes of feudal homage and service, were reconciled in a personal interview between the emperor and the king: they were firmly united by mutual esteem and the common danger; and their alliance was sealed by the nuptial of Henry with the daughter of the Italian prince. He soon deplored the loss of his friend and father. At the persuasion of some faithful Greeks, Boniface made a bold and successful inroad among the hills of Rhodope: the Bulgarians fled on his approach; they assembled to harass his retreat. On the intelligence that his rear was attacked, without waiting for any defensive armour, he leaped on horseback, couched his lance, and drove the enemies before him; but in the rash pursuit he was pierced with a mortal wound; and the head of the king of Thessalonica was presented to Calo-John, who enjoyed the honours, without the merit, of victory. It is here, at this melancholy event, that the pen or the voice of Jeffrey of Villehardouin seems to drop or to expire;[31] and if he still exercised his military office of marshal of Romania, his subsequent exploits are buried in oblivion.[32] The character of Henry was not unequal

31. Villehardouin, N° 257. I quote, with regret, this lamentable conclusion, where we lose at once the original history, and the rich illustrations of Ducange. The last pages may derive some light from Henry's two Epistles to Innocent III. (Gesta, c. 106, 107.)

32. The marshal was alive in 1212, but he probably died soon afterwards, without returning to France (Ducange, Observations sur Villehardouin, p. 238.). His fief of Messinople, the gift of Boniface, was the

to his arduous situation: in the siege of Constantinople, and beyond the Hellespont, he had deserved the fame of a valiant knight and a skilful commander; and his courage was tempered with a degree of prudence and mildness unknown to his impetuous brother. In the double war against the Greeks of Asia and the Bulgarians of Europe, he was ever the foremost on shipboard or on horseback; and though he cautiously provided for the success of his arms, the drooping Latins were often roused by his example to save and to second their fearless emperor. But such efforts, and some supplies of men and money from France, were of less avail than the errors, the cruelty, and death, of their most formidable adversary. When the despair of the Greek subjects invited Calo-John as their deliverer, they hoped that he would protect their liberty and adopt their laws: they were soon taught to compare the degrees of national ferocity, and to execrate the savage conqueror, who no longer dissembled his intention of dispeopling Thrace, of demolishing the cities, and of transplanting the inhabitants beyond the Danube. Many towns and villages of Thrace were already evacuated: an heap of ruins marked the place of Philippopolis, and a similar calamity was expected at Demotica and Adrianople, by the first authors of the revolt. They raised a cry of grief and repentance to the throne of Henry; the emperor alone had the magnanimity to forgive and trust them. No more than four hundred knights, with their serjeants and archers, could be assembled under his banner; and with this slender force he sought and repulsed the Bulgarian, who, besides his infantry, was at the head of forty thousand horse. In this expedition, Henry felt the difference between an hostile and a friendly country; the remaining cities were preserved by his arms; and the savage, with shame and loss, was compelled to relinquish his prey. The siege of Thessalonica was the last of the evils which Calo-John inflicted or suffered: he was stabbed in the night in his tent; and the general, perhaps the assassin, who found him weltering in his blood, ascribed the blow with general applause to the lance of St. Demetrius.[33] After several victories, the prudence of Henry concluded an honourable peace with the successor of the tyrant, and with the Greek princes of Nice and Epirus. If he ceded some doubtful limits, an ample kingdom was reserved

---

ancient Maximianopolis, which flourished in the time of Ammianus Marcellinus, among the cities of Thrace (N° 141.).

33. The church of this patron of Thessalonica was served by the canons of the holy sepulchre, and contained a divine ointment which distilled daily and stupendous miracles (Ducange, Hist. de C. P. ii. 4.).

for himself and his feudatories; and his reign, which lasted only ten years, afforded a short interval of prosperity and peace. Far above the narrow policy of Baldwin and Boniface, he freely entrusted to the Greeks the most important offices of the state and army: and this liberality of sentiment and practice, was the more seasonable, as the princes of Nice and Epirus had already learned to seduce and employ the mercenary valour of the Latins. It was the aim of Henry to unite and reward his deserving subjects of every nation and language; but he appeared less solicitous to accomplish the impracticable union of the two churches. Pelagius, the pope's legate, who acted as the sovereign of Constantinople, had interdicted the worship of the Greeks, and sternly imposed the payment of tithes, the double procession of the Holy Ghost, and a blind obedience to the Roman pontiff. As the weaker party, they pleaded the duties of conscience, and implored the rights of toleration: "Our bodies," they said, "are Cæsar's, but our souls belong only to God." The persecution was checked by the firmness of the emperor;[34] and if we can believe that the same prince was poisoned by the Greeks themselves, we must entertain a contemptible idea of the sense and gratitude of mankind. His valour was a vulgar attribute, which he shared with ten thousand knights; but Henry possessed the superior courage to oppose, in a superstitious age, the pride and avarice of the clergy. In the cathedral of St. Sophia he presumed to place his throne on the right-hand of the patriarch; and this presumption excited the sharpest censure of pope Innocent the third. By a salutary edict, one of the first examples of the laws of mortmain, he prohibited the alienation of fiefs; many of the Latins, desirous of returning to Europe, resigned their estates to the church for a spiritual or temporal reward; these holy lands were immediately discharged from military service; and a colony of soldiers would have been gradually transformed into a college of priests.[35]

Peter of Courtenay, emperor of Constantinople, A.D. 1217, April 9.

The virtuous Henry died at Thessalonica, in the defence of that kingdom, and of an infant, the son of his friend Boniface. In the two first emperors of Constantinople the male line of the counts of Flanders was extinct. But their sister Yolande was the wife of a French prince, the mother of a

34. Acropolita (c. 17.) observes the persecution of the legate, and the toleration of Henry (ʻ*Ερη* as he calls him), *κλυδωνα κατεστορεσε*.

35. See the reign of HENRY, in Ducange (Hist. de C. P. l. i. c. 35–41. l. ii. c. 1–22.), who is much indebted to the Epistles of the Popes. Le Beau (Hist. du Bas-Empire, tom. xxi. p. 120–122.) has found, perhaps in Doutreman, some laws of Henry, which determined the service of fiefs, and the prerogatives of the emperor.

numerous progeny; and one of her daughters had married Andrew king of Hungary, a brave and pious champion of the cross. By seating him on the Byzantine throne, the barons of Romania would have acquired the forces of a neighbouring and warlike kingdom; but the prudent Andrew revered the laws of succession; and the princess Yolande, with her husband Peter of Courtenay, count of Auxerre, was invited by the Latins to assume the empire of the East. The royal birth of his father, the noble origin of his mother, recommended to the barons of France the first cousin of their king. His reputation was fair, his possessions were ample, and, in the bloody crusade against the Albigeois, the soldiers and the priests had been abundantly satisfied of his zeal and valour. Vanity might applaud the elevation of a French emperor of Constantinople; but prudence must pity, rather than envy, his treacherous and imaginary greatness. To assert and adorn his title, he was reduced to sell or mortgage the best of his patrimony. By these expedients, the liberality of his royal kinsman Philip Augustus, and the national spirit of chivalry, he was enabled to pass the Alps at the head of one hundred and forty knights, and five thousand five hundred serjeants and archers. After some hesitation, pope Honorius the third was persuaded to crown the successor of Constantine; but he performed the ceremony in a church without the walls, lest he should seem to imply or to bestow any right of sovereignty over the ancient capital of the empire. The Venetians had engaged to transport Peter and his forces beyond the Adriatic, and the empress, with her four children, to the Byzantine palace; but they required, as the price of their service, that he should recover Durazzo from the despot of Epirus. Michael Angelus, or Comnenus, the first of his dynasty, had bequeathed the succession of his power and ambition to Theodore, his legitimate brother, who already threatened and invaded the establishments of the Latins. After discharging his debt by a fruitless assault, the emperor raised the siege to prosecute a long and perilous journey over land from Durazzo to Thessalonica. He was soon lost in the mountains of Epirus: the passes were fortified; his provisions exhausted: he was delayed and deceived by a treacherous negociation; and, after Peter of Courtenay and the Roman legate had been arrested in a banquet, the French troops, without leaders or hopes, were eager to exchange their arms for the delusive promise of mercy and bread. The Vatican thundered; and the impious Theodore was threatened with the vengeance of earth and heaven; but the captive emperor and his soldiers were forgotten, and the reproaches of the pope are confined to the imprisonment of his legate. No sooner was he satisfied by the deliverance of the priest and a

His captivity and death, A.D. 1217–1219.

promise of spiritual obedience, than he pardoned and protected the despot of Epirus. His peremptory commands suspended the ardour of the Venetians and the king of Hungary; and it was only by a natural or untimely death[36] that Peter of Courtenay was released from his hopeless captivity.[37]

Robert emperor of Constantinople, A.D. 1221–1228.

The long ignorance of his fate, and the presence of the lawful sovereign, of Yolande, his wife or widow, delayed the proclamation of a new emperor. Before her death, and in the midst of her grief, she was delivered of a son, who was named Baldwin, the last and most unfortunate of the Latin princes of Constantinople. His birth endeared him to the barons of Romania; but his childhood would have prolonged the troubles of a minority, and his claims were superseded by the elder claims of his brethren. The first of these, Philip of Courtenay, who derived from his mother the inheritance of Namur, had the wisdom to prefer the substance of a marquisate to the shadow of an empire; and on his refusal, Robert, the second of the sons of Peter and Yoland, was called to the throne of Constantinople. Warned by his father's mischance, he pursued his slow and secure journey through Germany and along the Danube: a passage was opened by his sister's marriage with the king of Hungary; and the emperor Robert was crowned by the patriarch in the cathedral of St. Sophia. But his reign was an æra of calamity and disgrace; and the colony, as it was styled, of NEW FRANCE yielded on all sides to the Greeks of Nice and Epirus. After a victory, which he owed to his perfidy rather than his courage, Theodore Angelus entered the kingdom of Thessalonica, expelled the feeble Demetrius, the son of the marquis Boniface, erected his standard on the walls of Adrianople; and added, by his vanity, a third or a fourth name to the list of rival emperors. The relics of the Asiatic province were swept away by John Vataces, the son-in-law and successor of Theodore Lascaris, and who, in a triumphant reign of thirty-three years, displayed the virtues both of peace and war. Under his discipline the swords of the French mercenaries were the most effectual instrument of his conquests, and

36. Acropolita (c. 14.) affirms, that Peter of Courtenay died by the sword (*εργον μαχαιρας γενεσθαι*): but from his dark expressions, I should conclude a previous captivity, *ως παντας αρδην δεσμωτας ποιησαι συν πασι σκευεσι*. The Chronicle of Auxerre delays the emperor's death till the year 1219; and Auxerre is in the neighbourhood of Courtenay.

37. See the reign and death of Peter of Courtenay, in Ducange (Hist. de C. P. l. ii. c. 22–28.), who feebly strives to excuse the neglect of the emperor by Honorius III.

their desertion from the service of their country was at once a symptom and a cause of the rising ascendant of the Greeks. By the construction of a fleet, he obtained the command of the Hellespont, reduced the islands of Lesbos and Rhodes, attacked the Venetians of Candia, and intercepted the rare and parsimonious succours of the West. Once, and once only, the Latin emperor sent an army against Vataces; and in the defeat of that army, the veteran knights, the last of the original conquerors, were left on the field of battle. But the success of a foreign enemy was less painful to the pusillanimous Robert than the insolence of his Latin subjects, who confounded the weakness of the emperor and of the empire. His personal misfortunes will prove the anarchy of the government and the ferociousness of the times. The amorous youth had neglected his Greek bride, the daughter of Vataces, to introduce into the palace a beautiful maid, of a private, though noble, family of Artois; and her mother had been tempted by the lustre of the purple to forfeit her engagements with a gentleman of Burgundy. His love was converted into rage; he assembled his friends, forced the palace gates, threw the mother into the sea, and inhumanly cut off the nose and lips of the wife or concubine of the emperor. Instead of punishing the offender, the barons avowed and applauded the savage deed,[38] which, as a prince and as a man, it was impossible that Baldwin should forgive. He escaped from the guilty city to implore the justice or compassion of the pope: the emperor was coolly exhorted to return to his station; before he could obey, he sunk under the weight of grief, shame, and impotent resentment.[39]

Baldwin II. and John of Brienne, emperors of Constantinople, A.D. 1228–1237.

It was only in the age of chivalry, that valour could ascend from a private station to the thrones of Jerusalem and Constantinople. The titular kingdom of Jerusalem had devolved to Mary, the daughter of Isabella and Conrad of Montferrat, and the grand-daughter of Almeric or Amaury. She was given to John of Brienne, of a noble family in Champagne, by the public voice, and the judgment of Philip Augustus, who named him as the most worthy champion of the Holy Land.[40] In the fifth crusade, he

38. Marinus Sanutus (Secreta Fidelium Crucis, l. ii. p. iv. c. 18. p. 73.) is so much delighted with this bloody deed, that he has transcribed it in his margin as a bonum exemplum. Yet he acknowledges the damsel for the lawful wife of Robert.

39. See the reign of Robert, in Ducange (Hist. de C. P. l. iii. c. 1–12.).

40. Rex igitur Franciæ, deliberatione habitâ respondit nuntiis, se daturum hominem Syriæ partibus aptum; in armis probum *(preux)*, in bellis securum, in agendis providum, Johannem comitem Brennensem. Sanut. Secret. Fidelium, l. iii. p. xi. c. 4. p. 205. Matthew Paris, p. 159.

led an hundred thousand Latins to the conquest of Egypt; by him the siege of Damietta was atchieved; and the subsequent failure was justly ascribed to the pride and avarice of the legate. After the marriage of his daughter with Frederic the second,[41] he was provoked by the emperor's ingratitude to accept the command of the army of the church; and though advanced in life and despoiled of royalty, the sword and spirit of John of Brienne were still ready for the service of Christendom. In the seven years of his brother's reign, Baldwin of Courtenay had not emerged from a state of childhood, and the barons of Romania felt the strong necessity of placing the sceptre in the hands of a man and an hero. The veteran king of Jerusalem might have disdained the name and office of regent; they agreed to invest him for his life with the title and prerogatives of emperor, on the sole condition, that Baldwin should marry his second daughter, and succeed at a mature age to the throne of Constantinople. The expectation, both of the Greeks and Latins, was kindled by the renown, the choice, and the presence of John of Brienne: and they admired his martial aspect, his green and vigorous age of more than fourscore years, and his size and stature, which surpassed the common measure of mankind.[42] But avarice, and the love of ease, appear to have chilled the ardour of enterprise: his troops were disbanded, and two years rolled away without action or honour, till he was awakened by the dangerous alliance of Vataces emperor of Nice, and of Azan king of Bulgaria. They besieged Constantinople by sea and land, with an army of one hundred thousand men, and a fleet of three hundred ships of war; while the entire force of the Latin emperor was reduced to one hundred and sixty knights, and a small addition of serjeants and archers. I tremble to relate, that instead of defending the city, the hero made a sally at the head of his cavalry; and that of forty-eight squadrons of the enemy, no more than three escaped from the edge of his invincible sword. Fired by his example, the infantry and the citizens boarded the vessels that anchored close to the walls; and twenty-five were dragged in triumph into the harbour of Constantinople. At the summons of the emperor, the vassals and allies armed in her defence; broke through every obstacle that

41. Giannone (Istoria Civile, tom. ii. l. xvi. p. 380–385.) discusses the marriage of Frederic II. with the daughter of John of Brienne, and the double union of the crowns of Naples and Jerusalem.

42. Acropolita, c. 27. The historian was at that time a boy, and educated at Constantinople. In 1233, when he was eleven years old, his father broke the Latin chain, left a splendid fortune, and escaped to the Greek court of Nice, where his son was raised to the highest honours.

opposed their passage; and, in the succeeding year, obtained a second victory over the same enemies. By the rude poets of the age, John of Brienne is compared to Hector, Roland, and Judas Machabæus:[43] but their credit, and his glory, receives some abatement from the silence of the Greeks. The empire was soon deprived of the last of her champions; and the dying monarch was ambitious to enter paradise in the habit of a Franciscan friar.[44]

Baldwin II. A.D. 1237, March 23– A.D. 1261, July 25.

In the double victory of John of Brienne, I cannot discover the name or exploits of his pupil Baldwin; who had attained the age of military service, and who succeeded to the Imperial dignity on the decease of his adoptive father.[45] The royal youth was employed on a commission more suitable to his temper; he was sent to visit the Western courts, of the pope more especially, and of the king of France; to excite their pity by the view of his innocence and distress; and to obtain some supplies of men or money, for the relief of the sinking empire. He thrice repeated these mendicant visits, in which he seemed to prolong his stay and postpone his return; of the five-and-twenty years of his reign, a greater number were spent abroad than at home; and in no place did the emperor deem himself less free and secure, than in his native country, and his capital. On some public occasions, his vanity might be soothed by the title of Augustus, and by the honours of the purple; and at the general council of Lyons, when Frederic the second was excommunicated and deposed, his Oriental colleague was enthroned on the right-hand of the pope. But how often was the exile, the vagrant, the Imperial beggar, humbled with scorn, insulted with pity, and degraded in his own eyes and those of the nations? In his first visit to England, he was stopped at Dover, by a severe reprimand, that he should presume, without leave, to enter an independent kingdom. After some delay, Baldwin however was permitted to pursue his journey, was entertained with cold civility, and thankfully departed with a present of seven

43. Philip Mouskes, bishop of Tournay (A.D. 1274–1282), has composed a poem, or rather a string of verses, in bad old Flemish French, on the Latin emperors of Constantinople, which Ducange has published at the end of Villehardouin; see p. 224. for the prowess of John of Brienne.

N'Aie, Ector, Roll' ne Ogiers
Ne Judas Machabeus li fiers
Tant ne fit d'armes en estors
Com fist li Rois Jehans cel jors
Et il defors et il dedans
La paru sa force et ses sens
Et li hardiment qu'il avoit.

44. See the reign of John de Brienne, in Ducange, Hist. de C. P. l. iii. c. 13–26.

45. See the reign of Baldwin II. till his expulsion from Constantinople, in Ducange, Hist. de C. P. l. iv. c. 1–34. the end l. v. c. 1–33.

hundred marks.[46] From the avarice of Rome, he could only obtain the proclamation of a crusade and a treasure of indulgences; a coin, whose currency was depreciated by too frequent and indiscriminate abuse. His birth and misfortunes recommended him to the generosity of his cousin Louis the ninth; but the martial zeal of the saint was diverted from Constantinople to Egypt and Palestine; and the public and private poverty of Baldwin was alleviated, for a moment, by the alienation of the marquisate of Namur and the lordship of Courtenay, the last remains of his inheritance.[47] By such shameful or ruinous expedients, he once more returned to Romania, with an army of thirty thousand soldiers, whose numbers were doubled in the apprehension of the Greeks. His first dispatches to France and England announced his victories and his hopes: he had reduced the country round the capital to the distance of three days journey; and if he succeeded against an important, though nameless, city (most probably Chiorli), the frontier would be safe and the passage accessible. But these expectations (if Baldwin was sincere) quickly vanished like a dream; the troops and treasures of France melted away in his unskilful hands; and the throne of the Latin emperor was protected by a dishonourable alliance with the Turks and Comans. To secure the former, he consented to bestow his niece on the unbelieving sultan of Cogni; to please the latter, he complied with their Pagan rites; a dog was sacrificed between the two armies; and the contracting parties tasted each other's blood, as a pledge of their fidelity.[48] In the palace or prison of Constantinople, the successor of Augustus demolished the vacant houses for winter-fuel, and stripped the lead from the churches for the daily expence of his family. Some usurious loans were dealt with a scanty hand by the merchants of Italy; and Philip, his son and heir, was pawned at Venice as the security for a debt.[49] Thirst, hunger, and nakedness, are positive evils; but wealth is relative; and a prince, who would be rich in a private

46. Matthew Paris relates the two visits of Baldwin II. to the English court, p. 396. 637.: his return to Greece armatâ manû, p. 407.: his letters of his nomen formidabile, &c. p. 481. (a passage which had escaped Ducange): his expulsion, p. 850.

47. Louis IX. disapproved and stopped the alienation of Courtenay (Ducange, l. iv. c. 23.). It is now annexed to the royal demesne, but granted for a term (*engagé*) to the family of Boulainvilliers. Courtenay, in the election of Nemours in the Isle de France, is a town of 900 inhabitants with the remains of a castle (Melanges tirés d'une grand Bibliotheque, tom. xlv. p. 74–77.).

48. Joinville, p. 104. edit. du Louvre. A Coman prince, who died without baptism, was buried at the gates of Constantinople with a live retinue of slaves and horses.

49. Sanut. Secret. Fidel. Crucis, l. ii. p. iv. c. 18. p. 73.

station, may be exposed by the encrease of his wants to all the anxiety and bitterness of poverty.

The holy crown of thorns. But in this abject distress, the emperor and empire were still possessed of an ideal treasure, which drew its fantastic value from the superstition of the Christian world. The merit of the true cross was somewhat impaired by its frequent division; and a long captivity among the infidels might shed some suspicion on the fragments that were produced in the East and West. But another relic of the Passion was preserved in the Imperial chapel of Constantinople; and the crown of thorns which had been placed on the head of Christ was equally precious and authentic. It had formerly been the practice of the Egyptian debtors to deposit, as a security, the mummies of their parents; and both their honour and religion were bound for the redemption of the pledge. In the same manner, and in the absence of the emperor, the barons of Romania borrowed the sum of thirteen thousand one hundred and thirty-four pieces of gold,[50] on the credit of the holy crown: they failed in the performance of their contract; and a rich Venetian, Nicholas Querini, undertook to satisfy their impatient creditors, on condition that the relic should be lodged at Venice, to become his absolute property, if it were not redeemed within a short and definite term. The barons apprised their sovereign of the hard treaty and impending loss; and as the empire could not afford a ransom of seven thousand pounds sterling, Baldwin was anxious to snatch the prize from the Venetians, and to vest it with more honour and emolument in the hands of the most Christian king.[51] Yet the negociation was attended with some delicacy. In the purchase of relics, the saint would have started at the guilt of simony; but if the mode of expression were changed, he might lawfully repay the debt, accept the gift, and acknowledge the obligation. His ambassadors, two Dominicans, were dispatched to Venice, to redeem and receive the holy crown, which had escaped the dangers of the sea and the gallies of Vataces. On opening a wooden box, they recognised the seals of the doge and barons, which were applied on a shrine of silver: and within this shrine, the monument of the Passion was inclosed in a golden vase. The

50. Under the words, *Perparus, Perpera, Hyperperum*, Ducange is short and vague: Monetæ genus. From a corrupt passage of Guntherus (Hist. C. P. c. 8. p. 10.), I guess, that the Perpera was the nummus aureus, the fourth part of a mark of silver, or about ten shillings sterling in value. In lead, it would be too contemptible.

51. For the translation of the holy crown, &c. from Constantinople to Paris, see Ducange (Hist. de C. P. l. iv. c. 11–14. 24. 35.) and Fleury (Hist. Eccles. tom. xvii. p. 201–204.).

reluctant Venetians yielded to justice and power: the emperor Frederic granted a free and honourable passage; the court of France advanced as far as Troyes in Champagne, to meet with devotion this inestimable relic: it was borne in triumph through Paris by the king himself, barefoot, and in his shirt; and a free gift of ten thousand marks of silver reconciled Baldwin to his loss. The success of this transaction tempted the Latin emperor to offer with the same generosity the remaining furniture of his chapel;[52] a large and authentic portion of the true cross; the baby-linen of the Son of God; the lance, the spunge, and the chain, of his Passion; the rod of Moses, and part of the skull of St. John the baptist. For the reception of these spiritual treasures, twenty thousand marks were expended by St. Louis on a stately foundation, the holy chapel of Paris, on which the muse of Boileau has bestowed a comic immortality. The truth of such remote and ancient relics, which cannot be proved by any human testimony, must be admitted by those who believe in the miracles which they have performed. About the middle of the last age, an inveterate ulcer was touched and cured by an holy prickle of the holy crown:[53] the prodigy is attested by the most pious and enlightened Christians of France; nor will the fact be easily disproved, except by those who are armed with a general antidote against religious credulity.[54]

Progress of the Greeks, A.D. 1237–1261.

The Latins of Constantinople[55] were on all sides encompassed and pressed: their sole hope, the last delay of their ruin, was in the division of their Greek and Bulgarian enemies; and of this hope they were deprived by the superior arms and policy of Vataces emperor of Nice. From the Propontis to the rocky coast of

52. Melanges tirés d'une grande Bibliothéque, tom. xliii. p. 201–205. The Lutrin of Boileau exhibits the inside, the soul and manners of the *Sainte Chapelle*; and many facts relative to the institution are collected and explained by his commentators, Brossette and de St. Marc.

53. It was performed A.D. 1656, March 24, on the niece of Pascal; and that superior genius, with Arnauld, Nicole, &c. were on the spot to believe and attest a miracle which confounded the Jesuits, and saved Port Royal (Oeuvres de Racine, tom. vi. p. 176–187. in his eloquent History of Port Royal).

54. Voltaire (Siecle de Louis XIV. c. 37. Oeuvres, tom. ix. p. 178, 179.) strives to invalidate the fact: but Hume (Essays, vol. ii. p. 483, 484.), with more skill and success, seizes the battery, and turns the cannon against his enemies.

55. The gradual losses of the Latins may be traced in the third, fourth, and fifth books of the compilation of Ducange: but of the Greek conquests he has dropped many circumstances, which may be recovered from the larger history of George Acropolita, and the three first books of Nicephorus Gregoras, two writers of the Byzantine series, who have had the good fortune to meet with learned editors, Leo Allatius at Rome, and John Boivin in the Academy of Inscriptions of Paris.

Pamphylia, Asia was peaceful and prosperous under his reign: and the events of every campaign extended his influence in Europe. The strong cities of the hills of Macedonia and Thrace, were rescued from the Bulgarians; and their kingdom was circumscribed by its present and proper limits, along the southern banks of the Danube. The sole emperor of the Romans could no longer brook that a lord of Epirus, a Comnenian prince of the West, should presume to dispute or share the honours of the purple; and the humble Demetrius changed the colour of his buskins, and accepted with gratitude the appellation of despot. His own subjects were exasperated by his baseness and incapacity: they implored the protection of their supreme lord. After some resistance, the kingdom of Thessalonica was united to the empire of Nice; and Vataces reigned without a competitor from the Turkish borders to the Adriatic gulf. The princes of Europe revered his merit and power; and had he subscribed an orthodox creed, it should seem that the pope would have abandoned without reluctance the Latin throne of Constantinople. But the death of Vataces, the short and busy reign of Theodore his son, and the helpless infancy of his grandson John, suspended the restoration of the Greeks. In the next chapter, I shall explain their domestic revolutions; in this place, it will be sufficient to observe, that the young prince was oppressed

Michael Palæologus, the Greek emperor, A.D. 1259, December 1.

by the ambition of his guardian and colleague Michael Palæologus, who displayed the virtues and vices that belong to the founder of a new dynasty. The emperor Baldwin had flattered himself, that he might recover some provinces or cities by an impotent negociation. His ambassadors were dismissed from Nice with mockery and contempt. At every place which they named, Palæologus alleged some special reason, which rendered it dear and valuable in his eyes: in the one he was born; in another he had been first promoted to military command; and in a third he had enjoyed, and hoped long to enjoy, the pleasures of the chace. "And what then do you propose to give us?" said the astonished deputies. "Nothing," replied the Greek, "not a foot of land. If your master be desirous of peace, let him pay me as an annual tribute, the sum which he receives from the trade and customs of Constantinople. On these terms, I may allow him to reign. If he refuses, it is war. I am not ignorant of the art of war, and I trust the event to God and my sword."[56] An expedition against the despot of Epirus was the first prelude of his arms. If a victory was followed by a defeat; if the race of the Comneni or Angeli survived in those mountains

56. George Acropolita, c. 78. p. 89, 90. edit. Paris.

his efforts and his reign; the captivity of Villehardouin, prince of Achaia, deprived the Latins of the most active and powerful vassal of their expiring monarchy. The republics of Venice and Genoa disputed, in the first of their naval wars, the command of the sea and the commerce of the East. Pride and interest attached the Venetians to the defence of Constantinople: their rivals were tempted to promote the designs of her enemies, and the alliance of the Genoese with the schismatic conqueror provoked the indignation of the Latin church.[57]

Constantinople recovered by the Greeks, A.D. 1261, July 25.

Intent on his great object, the emperor Michael visited in person and strengthened the troops and fortifications of Thrace. The remains of the Latins were driven from their last possessions: he assaulted without success the suburb of Galata; and corresponded with a perfidious baron, who proved unwilling, or unable, to open the gates of the metropolis. The next spring, his favourite general, Alexius Strategopulus, whom he had decorated with the title of Cæsar, passed the Hellespont with eight hundred horse and some infantry,[58] on a secret expedition. His instructions enjoined him to approach, to listen, to watch, but not to risk any doubtful or dangerous enterprise against the city. The adjacent territory between the Propontis and the Black Sea, was cultivated by an hardy race of peasants and outlaws, exercised in arms, uncertain in their allegiance, but inclined by language, religion, and present advantage, to the party of the Greeks. They were styled the *volunteers*,[59] and by their free service, the army of Alexius, with the regulars of Thrace and the Coman auxiliaries,[60] was augmented to the number of five-and-twenty thousand men. By the ardour of the volunteers, and by his own ambition, the Cæsar was stimulated to disobey the precise orders of his master, in the just confidence that success would

57. The Greeks, ashamed of any foreign aid, disguise the alliance and succour of the Genoese; but the fact is proved by the testimony of J. Villani (Chron. l. vi. c. 71. in Muratori, Script. Rerum Italicarum, tom. xiii. p. 202, 203.) and William de Nangis (Annales de St. Louis, p. 248. in the Louvre Joinville), two impartial foreigners; and Urban IV. threatened to deprive Genoa of her archbishop.

58. Some precautions must be used in reconciling the discordant numbers; the 800 soldiers of Nicetas, the 25,000 of Spandugino (apud Ducange, l. v. c. 24.); the Greeks and Scythians of Acropolita, and the numerous army of Michael, in the Epistles of Pope Urban IV. (i. 129.).

59. Θεληματαριοι. They are described and named by Pachymer (l. ii. c. 14.).

60. It is needless to seek these Comans in the deserts of Tartary, or even of Moldavia. A part of the hord had submitted to John Vataces, and was probably settled as a nursery of soldiers on some waste lands of Thrace (Cantacuzen, l. i. c. 2.).

plead his pardon and reward. The weakness of Constantinople, and the distress and terror of the Latins, were familiar to the observation of the volunteers: and they represented the present moment as the most propitious to surprise and conquest. A rash youth, the new governor of the Venetian colony, had sailed away with thirty gallies and the best of the French knights, on a wild expedition to Daphnusia, a town on the Black Sea, at the distance of forty leagues; and the remaining Latins were without strength or suspicion. They were informed that Alexius had passed the Hellespont; but their apprehensions were lulled by the smallness of his original numbers; and their imprudence had not watched the subsequent encrease of his army. If he left his main body to second and support his operations, he might advance unperceived in the night with a chosen detachment. While some applied scaling-ladders to the lowest part of the walls, they were secure of an old Greek, who would introduce their companions through a subterraneous passage into his house; they could soon on the inside break an entrance through the golden gate, which had been long obstructed; and the conqueror would be in the heart of the city, before the Latins were conscious of their danger. After some debate, the Cæsar resigned himself to the faith of the volunteers; they were trusty, bold, and successful; and in describing the plan, I have already related the execution and success.[61] But no sooner had Alexius passed the threshold of the golden gate, than he trembled at his own rashness; he paused, he deliberated; till the desperate volunteers urged him forwards, by the assurance that in retreat lay the greatest and most inevitable danger. Whilst the Cæsar kept his regulars in firm array, the Comans dispersed themselves on all sides; an alarm was sounded, and the threats of fire and pillage compelled the citizens to a decisive resolution. The Greeks of Constantinople remembered their native sovereigns; the Genoese merchants their recent alliance and Venetian foes; every quarter was in arms; and the air resounded with a general acclamation of "Long life and victory to Michael and John, the august emperors of the Romans!" Their rival, Baldwin, was awakened by the sound; but the most pressing danger could not prompt him to draw his sword in the defence of a city which he deserted, perhaps, with more pleasure than regret: he fled from the palace to the sea-shore, where he descried the welcome sails of the fleet returning from the vain and fruitless attempt

61. The loss of Constantinople is briefly told by the Latins: the conquest is described with more satisfaction by the Greeks; by Acropolita (c. 85.), Pachymer (l. ii. c. 26, 27.), Nicephorus Gregoras (l. iv. c. 1, 2.). See Ducange, Hist. de C. P. l. v. c. 19–27.

on Daphnusia. Constantinople was irrecoverably lost; but the Latin emperor and the principal families embarked on board the Venetian gallies, and steered for the isle of Eubœa, and afterwards for Italy, where the royal fugitive was entertained by the pope and Sicilian king with a mixture of contempt and pity. From the loss of Constantinople to his death, he consumed thirteen years, soliciting the Catholic powers to join in his restoration; the lesson had been familiar to his youth; nor was his last exile more indigent or shameful than his three former pilgrimages to the courts of Europe. His son Philip was the heir of an ideal empire; and the pretensions of *his* daughter Catherine were transported by her marriage to Charles of Valois, the brother of Philip the Fair king of France. The house of Courtenay was represented in the female line by successive alliances, till the title of emperor of Constantinople, too bulky and sonorous for a private name, modestly expired in silence and oblivion.[62]

General consequences of the crusades.

After this narrative of the expeditions of the Latins to Palestine and Constantinople, I cannot dismiss the subject without revolving the general consequences on the countries that were the scene, and on the nations that were the actors, of these memorable crusades.[63] As soon as the arms of the Franks were withdrawn, the impression, though not the memory, was erazed in the Mahometan realms of Egypt and Syria. The faithful disciples of the prophet were never tempted by a prophane desire to study the laws or language of the idolators; nor did the simplicity of their primitive manners receive the slightest alteration from their intercourse in peace and war with the unknown strangers of the West. The Greeks, who thought themselves proud, but who were only vain, shewed a disposition somewhat less inflexible. In the efforts for the recovery of their empire, they emulated the valour, discipline, and tactics, of their antagonists. The modern literature of the West they might justly despise; but its free spirit would

62. See the three last books (l. v–viii.), and the genealogical tables of Ducange. In the year 1382, the titular emperor of Constantinople was James de Baux, duke of Andria in the kingdom of Naples, the son of Margaret, daughter of Catherine de Valois, daughter of Catherine, daughter of Philip, son of Baldwin II. (Ducange, l. viii. c. 37, 38.) It is uncertain whether he left any posterity.

63. Abulfeda, who saw the conclusion of the crusades, speaks of the kingdoms of the Franks, and those of the Negroes, as equally unknown (Prolegom. ad Geograph.). Had he not disdained the Latin language, how easily might the Syrian prince have found books and interpreters?

instruct them in the rights of man; and some institutions of public and private life were adopted from the French. The correspondence of Constantinople and Italy diffused the knowledge of the Latin tongue; and several of the fathers and classics were at length honoured with a Greek version.[64] But the national and religious prejudices of the Orientals were inflamed by persecution; and the reign of the Latins confirmed the separation of the two churches.

If we compare, at the æra of the crusades, the Latins of Europe with the Greeks and Arabians, their respective degrees of knowledge, industry, and art, our rude ancestors must be content with the third rank in the scale of nations. Their successive improvement and present superiority may be ascribed to a peculiar energy of character, to an active and imitative spirit, unknown to their more polished rivals, who at that time were in a stationary or retrograde state. With such a disposition, the Latins should have derived the most early and essential benefits from a series of events which opened to their eyes the prospect of the world, and introduced them to a long and frequent intercourse with the more cultivated regions of the East. The first and most obvious progress was in trade and manufactures, in the arts which are strongly prompted by the thirst of wealth, the calls of necessity, and the gratification of the sense or vanity. Among the crowd of unthinking fanatics, a captive or a pilgrim might sometimes observe the superior refinements of Cairo and Constantinople: the first importer of windmills[65] was the benefactor of nations; and if such blessings are enjoyed without any grateful remembrance, history has condescended to notice the more apparent luxuries of silk and sugar, which were transported into Italy from Greece and Egypt. But the intellectual wants of the Latins were more slowly felt and supplied; the ardour of studious curiosity was awakened in Europe by different causes and more recent events; and, in the age of the crusades, they viewed with careless indifference the literature of the Greeks and Arabians. Some rudiments of mathematical and medicinal knowledge might be imparted in practice and in figures; necessity might produce some interpreters for the grosser business of merchants and soldiers; but the commerce of the

64. A short and superficial account of these versions from Latin into Greek, is given by Huet (de Interpretatione et de claris Interpretibus, p. 131–135.). Maximus Planudes, a monk of Constantinople (A.D. 1327–1353), has translated Cæsar's Commentaries, the Somnium Scipionis, the Metamorphoses and Heroides of Ovid, &c. (Fabric. Bib. Græc. tom. x. p. 533.).

65. Windmills, first invented in the dry country of Asia Minor, were used in Normandy as early as the year 1105 (Vie privée des François, tom. i. p. 42, 43. Ducange, Gloss. Latin. tom. iv. p. 474.).

Orientals had not diffused the study and knowledge of their languages in the schools of Europe.[66] If a similar principle of religion repulsed the idiom of the Koran, it should have excited their patience and curiosity to understand the original text of the Gospel; and the same grammar would have unfolded the sense of Plato and the beauties of Homer. Yet in a reign of sixty years the Latins of Constantinople disdained the speech and learning of their subjects; and the manuscripts were the only treasures which the natives might enjoy without rapine or envy. Aristotle was indeed the oracle of the Western universities; but it was a barbarous Aristotle; and, instead of ascending to the fountain-head, his Latin votaries humbly accepted a corrupt and remote version from the Jews and Moors of Andalusia. The principle of the crusades was a savage fanaticism; and the most important effects were analogous to the cause. Each pilgrim was ambitious to return with his sacred spoils, the relics of Greece and Palestine;[67] and each relic was preceded and followed by a train of miracles and visions. The belief of the Catholics was corrupted by new legends, their practice by new superstitions; and the establishment of the inquisition, the mendicant orders of monks and friars, the last abuse of indulgences, and the final progress of idolatry, flowed from the baleful fountain of the holy war. The active spirit of the Latins preyed on the vitals of their reason and religion; and if the ninth and tenth centuries were the times of darkness, the thirteenth and fourteenth were the age of absurdity and fable.

In the profession of Christianity, in the cultivation of a fertile land, the northern conquerors of the Roman empire insensibly mingled with the provincials, and rekindled the embers of the arts of antiquity. Their settlements about the age of Charlemagne had acquired some degree of order and stability, when they were overwhelmed by new swarms of invaders, the Normans, Saracens,[68] and Hungarians, who replunged the western countries of Europe into their former state of anarchy and barbarism. About the eleventh century, the second tempest had subsided

66. See the complaints of Roger Bacon (Biographia Britannica, vol. i. p. 418. Kippis's edition). If Bacon himself, or Gerbert, understood *some* Greek, they were prodigies, and owed nothing to the commerce of the East.

67. Such was the opinion of the great Leibnitz (Oeuvres de Fontenelle, tom. v. p. 458.), a master of the history of the middle ages. I shall only instance the pedigree of the Carmelites, and the flight of the house of Loretto, which were both derived from Palestine.

68. If I rank the Saracens with the Barbarians, it is only relative to their wars, or rather inroads, in Italy and France, where their sole purpose was to plunder and destroy.

by the expulsion or conversion of the enemies of Christendom: the tide of civilization, which had so long ebbed, began to flow with a steady and accelerated course; and a fairer prospect was opened to the hopes and efforts of the rising generations. Great was the increase, and rapid the progress, during the two hundred years of the crusades; and some philosophers have applauded the propitious influence of these holy wars, which appear to me to have checked rather than forwarded the maturity of Europe.[69] The lives and labours of millions, which were buried in the East, would have been more profitably employed in the improvement of their native country: the accumulated stock of industry and wealth would have overflowed in navigation and trade; and the Latins would have been enriched and enlightened by a pure and friendly correspondence with the climates of the East. In one respect I can indeed perceive the accidental operation of the crusades, not so much in producing a benefit as in removing an evil. The larger portion of the inhabitants of Europe was chained to the soil, without freedom, or property, or knowledge; and the two orders of ecclesiastics and nobles, whose numbers were comparatively small, alone deserved the name of citizens and men. This oppressive system was supported by the arts of the clergy and the swords of the barons. The authority of the priests operated in the darker ages as a salutary antidote: they prevented the total extinction of letters, mitigated the fierceness of the times, sheltered the poor and defenceless, and preserved or revived the peace and order of civil society. But the independence, rapine, and discord, of the feudal lords were unmixed with any semblance of good; and every hope of industry and improvement was crushed by the iron weight of the martial aristocracy. Among the causes that undermined that Gothic edifice, a conspicuous place must be allowed to the crusades. The estates of the barons were dissipated, and their race was often extinguished, in these costly and perilous expeditions. Their poverty extorted from their pride those charters of freedom which unlocked the fetters of the slave, secured the farm of the peasant and the shop of the artificer, and gradually restored a substance and a soul to the most numerous and useful part of the community. The conflagration which destroyed the tall and barren trees of the forest gave air and scope to the vegetation of the smaller and nutritive plants of the soil.

---

69. On this interesting subject, the progress of society in Europe, a strong ray of philosophic light has broke from Scotland in our own times; and it is with private, as well as public regard, that I repeat the names of Hume, Robertson, and Adam Smith.

Digression on the Family of Courtenay.

The purple of three emperors, who have reigned at Constantinople, will authorise or excuse a digression on the origin and singular fortunes of the house of COURTENAY,[70] in the three principal branches, I. Of Edessa; II. Of France; and, III. Of England, of which the last only has survived the revolutions of eight hundred years.

Origin of the family of Courtenay, A.D. 1020.

I. Before the introduction of trade, which scatters riches, and of knowledge, which dispels prejudice, the prerogative of birth is most strongly felt and most humbly acknowledged. In every age, the laws and manners of the Germans have discriminated the ranks of society: the dukes and counts, who shared the empire of Charlemagne, converted their office to an inheritance; and to his children, each feudal lord bequeathed his honour and his sword. The proudest families are content to lose in the darkness of the middle ages, the tree of their pedigree, which, however deep and lofty, must ultimately rise from a plebeian root; and their historians must descend ten centuries below the Christian æra, before they can ascertain any lineal succession by the evidence of surnames, of arms, and of authentic records. With the first rays of light,[71] we discern the nobility and opulence of Atho, a French knight: his nobility, in the rank and title of a nameless father; his opulence, in the foundation of the castle of Courtenay in the district of Gatinois, about fifty-six miles to the south of Paris. From the reign of Robert, the son of Hugh Capet, the barons of Courtenay are conspicuous among the immediate vassals of the crown; and Joscelin, the grandson of Atho and a noble dame, is enrolled among the heroes of the first crusade.

I. The counts of Edessa, A.D. 1101–1152.

A domestic alliance (their mothers were sisters) attached him to the standard of Baldwin of Bruges, the second count of Edessa: a princely fief, which he was worthy to receive, and able to maintain, announces the number of his martial

70. I have applied, but not confined, myself to *A genealogical History of the noble and illustrious Family of Courtenay, by Ezra Cleaveland, Tutor to Sir William Courtenay, and Rector of Honiton; Exon.* 1735. *in folio.* The first part is extracted from William of Tyre, the second from Bouchet's French history; and the third from various memorials, public, provincial, and private, of the Courtenays of Devonshire. The rector of Honiton has more gratitude than industry, and more industry than criticism.

71. The primitive record of the family, is a passage of the continuator of Aimoin, a monk of Fleury, who wrote in the xii[th] century. See his Chronicle, in the Historians of France (tom. xi. p. 276.).

followers: and after the departure of his cousin, Joscelin himself was invested with the county of Edessa on both sides of the Euphrates. By the œconomy in peace, his territories were replenished with Latin and Syrian subjects; his magazines with corn, wine, and oil; his castles with gold and silver, with arms and horses. In a holy warfare of thirty years, he was alternately a conqueror and a captive; but he died like a soldier, in an horse-litter at the head of his troops; and his last glance beheld the flight of the Turkish invaders who had presumed on his age and infirmities. His son and successor, of the same name, was less deficient in valour than in vigilance; but he sometimes forgot that dominion is acquired and maintained by the same arts. He challenged the hostility of the Turks, without securing the friendship of the prince of Antioch; and, amidst the peaceful luxury of Turbessel, in Syria,[72] Joscelin neglected the defence of the Christian frontier beyond the Euphrates. In his absence, Zenghi, the first of the Atabeks, besieged and stormed his capital, Edessa, which was feebly defended by a timorous and disloyal crowd of Orientals: the Franks were oppressed in a bold attempt for its recovery, and Courtenay ended his days in the prison of Aleppo. He still left a fair and ample patrimony. But the victorious Turks oppressed on all sides the weakness of a widow and orphan; and, for the equivalent of an annual pension, they resigned to the Greek emperor the charge of defending, and the shame of losing, the last relics of the Latin conquest. The countess-dowager of Edessa retired to Jerusalem with her two children: the daughter, Agnes, became the wife and mother of a king; the son, Joscelin the third, accepted the office of senechal, the first of the kingdom, and held his new estates in Palestine by the service of fifty knights. His name appears with honour in all the transactions of peace and war; but he finally vanishes in the fall of Jerusalem; and the name of Courtenay, in this branch of Edessa, was lost by the marriage of his two daughters with a French and a German baron.[73]

II. The Courtenays of France.

II. While Joscelin reigned beyond the Euphrates, his elder brother Milo, the son of Joscelin, the son of Atho, continued, near the Seine, to possess the castle of their fathers, which was at length inherited by Rainaud, or Reginald, the youngest of his three

72. Turbessel, or as it is now styled Telbesher, is fixed by d'Anville four-and-twenty miles from the great passage over the Euphrates at Zeugma.

73. His possessions are distinguished in the Assises of Jerusalem (c. 326.) among the feudal tenures of the kingdom, which must therefore have been collected between the years 1153 and 1187. His pedigree may be found in the Lignages d'Outremer, c. 16.

sons. Examples of genius or virtue must be rare in the annals of the oldest families; and, in a remote age, their pride will embrace a deed of rapine and violence; such, however, as could not be perpetrated without some superiority of courage, or, at least, of power. A descendant of Reginald of Courtenay may blush for the public robber, who stripped and imprisoned several merchants, after they had satisfied the king's duties, at Sens and Orleans. He will glory in the offence, since the bold offender could not be compelled to obedience and restitution till the regent and the count of Champagne prepared to march against him at the head of an army.[74] Reginald bestowed his estates on his eldest daughter, and his daughter on the seventh son of king Louis the Fat; and their marriage was crowned with a numerous offspring. We might expect that a private should have merged in a royal name; and that the descendants of Peter of France and Elizabeth of Courtenay would have enjoyed the title and honours of princes of the blood. But this legitimate claim was long neglected and finally denied; and the causes of their disgrace will represent the story of this second branch. 1. Of all the families now extant, the most ancient, doubtless, and the most illustrious, is the house of France, which has occupied the same throne above eight hundred years, and descends, in a clear and lineal series of males, from the middle of the ninth century.[75] In the age of the crusades, it was already revered both in the East and West. But from Hugh Capet to the marriage of Peter, no more than five reigns or generations had elapsed; and so precarious was their title, that the eldest sons, as a necessary precaution, were previously crowned during the lifetime of their fathers.

Their alliance with the royal family, A.D. 1150.

74. The rapine and satisfaction of Reginald de Courtenay, are preposterously arranged in the Epistles of the abbot and regent Suger (cxiv. cxvi.), the best memorials of the age (Duchesne, Scriptores Hist. Franc. tom. iv. p. 530.).

75. In the beginning of the xith century, after naming the father and grandfather of Hugh Capet, the monk Glaber is obliged to add, cujus genus valde in-ante reperitur obscurum. Yet we are assured that the great grandfather of Hugh Capet was Robert the Strong, count of Anjou (A.D. 863–873), a noble Frank of Neustria, Neustricus ... generosæ stirpis, who was slain in the defence of his country against the Normans, dum patriæ fines tuebatur. Beyond Robert, all is conjecture or fable. It is a probable conjecture, that the third race descended from the second by Childebrand, the brother of Charles Martel. It is an absurd fable, that the second was allied to the first by the marriage of Ansbert, a Roman senator and the ancestor of St. Arnoul, with Blitilde, a daughter of Clotaire I. The Saxon origin of the house of France is an ancient but incredible opinion. See a judicious memoir of M. de Foncemagne (Memoires de l'Academie des Inscriptions, tom. xx. p. 548–579.). He had promised to declare his own opinion in a second memoir, which has never appeared.

The peers of France have long maintained their precedency before the younger branches of the royal line; nor had the princes of the blood, in the twelfth century, acquired that hereditary lustre which is now diffused over the most remote candidates for the succession. 2. The barons of Courtenay must have stood high in their own estimation, and in that of the world, since they could impose on the son of a king the obligation of adopting for himself and all his descendants the name and arms of their daughter and his wife. In the marriage of an heiress with her inferior or her equal, such exchange was often required and allowed: but as they continued to diverge from the regal stem, the sons of Louis the Fat were insensibly confounded with their maternal ancestors; and the new Courtenays might deserve to forfeit the honours of their birth, which a motive of interest had tempted them to renounce. 3. The shame was far more permanent than the reward, and a momentary blaze was followed by a long darkness. The eldest son of these nuptials, Peter of Courtenay, had married, as I have already mentioned, the sister of the counts of Flanders, the two first emperors of Constantinople: he rashly accepted the invitation of the barons of Romania; his two sons, Robert and Baldwin, successively held and lost the remains of the Latin empire in the East, and the grand-daughter of Baldwin the second again mingled her blood with the blood of France and of Valois. To support the expences of a troubled and transitory reign, their patrimonial estates were mortgaged or sold; and the last emperors of Constantinople depended on the annual charity of Rome and Naples.

While the elder brothers dissipated their wealth in romantic adventures, and the castle of Courtenay was profaned by a plebeian owner, the younger branches of that adopted name were propagated and multiplied. But their splendour was clouded by poverty and time; after the decease of Robert, great butler of France, they descended from princes to barons; the next generations were confounded with the simple gentry; the descendants of Hugh Capet could no longer be visible in the rural lords of Tanlay and of Champignelles. The more adventurous embraced without dishonour the profession of a soldier: the least active and opulent might sink, like their cousins of the branch of Dreux, into the condition of peasants. Their royal descent, in a dark period of four hundred years, became each day more obsolete and ambiguous: and their pedigree, instead of being enrolled in the annals of the kingdom, must be painfully searched by the minute diligence of heralds and genealogists. It was not till the end of the sixteenth century on the accession of a family, almost as remote as their own, that the princely spirit of the Courtenays again revived; and the question of the nobility, provoked them to assert the royalty, of their blood. They appealed to the justice and compassion of Henry the fourth; obtained a favourable opinion from twenty lawyers of Italy and Germany, and modestly compared themselves to the descendants of king David, whose prerogatives were not impaired by the lapse of ages or the trade of a carpenter.[76] But every ear was deaf, and every circumstance was adverse, to their lawful claims. The Bourbon kings were justified by the neglect of the Valois: the princes of the blood more recent and lofty, disdained the alliance of this humble kindred: the parliament, without denying their proofs, eluded a dangerous precedent by an arbitrary distinction, and established St. Louis as the first father of the royal line.[77] A repetition of complaints and protests was repeatedly disregarded: and the hopeless pursuit was terminated in the present century by the death of the last male of the family.[78] Their painful and anxious situation was alleviated by the pride of conscious virtue: they sternly rejected the temptations of fortune and favour; and a dying Courtenay would have sacrificed his son, if the youth could have renounced, for any temporal interest, the right and title of a legitimate prince of the blood of France.[79]

76. Of the various petitions, apologies, &c. published by the *princes* of Courtenay, I have seen the three following, all in octavo: 1. De Stirpe et Origine Domus de Courtenay: addita sunt Responsa celeberrimorum Europæ Jurisconsultorum: Paris, 1607. 2. Representation du Procedé tenû a l'instance faicte devant le Roi, par Messieurs de Courtenay, pour la conservation de l'Honneur et Dignité de leur Maison, branche de la royalle Maison de France: à Paris, 1613. 3. Representation du subject qui a porté Messieurs de Salles et de Fraville, de la Maison de Courtenays, à se retirer hors du Royaume, 1614. It was an homicide, for which the Courtenays expected to be pardoned, or tried, as princes of the blood.

77. The sense of the parliaments is thus expressed by Thuanus: Principis nomen nusquam in Galliâ tributum, nisi iis qui per mares e regibus nostris originem repetunt: qui nunc tantum a Ludovico nono beatæ memoriæ numerantur: nam *Cortinæi* et Drocenses, a Ludovico crasso genus ducentes, hodie inter eos minime recensentur. A distinction of expediency, rather than justice. The sanctity of Louis IX. could not invest him with any special prerogative, and all the descendants of Hugh Capet must be included in his original compact with the French nation.

78. The last male of the Courtenays was Charles Roger, who died in the year 1730, without leaving any sons. The last female was Helene de Courtenay, who married Louis de Beaufremont. Her title of Princesse du Sang Royal de France, was suppressed (February 7th, 1737) by an *arrêt* of the parliament of Paris.

79. The singular anecdote to which I allude, is related in the Recueil des Pieces interessantes et peu connues (Maestricht, 1786, in 4 vols. 12mo); and the unknown editor quotes his author, who had received it from Helene de Courtenay, marquise de Beaufremont.

III. The Courtenays of England. III. According to the old register of Ford Abbey, the Courtenays of Devonshire are descended from prince *Florus*, the second son of Peter, and the grandson of Louis the Fat.[80] This fable of the grateful or venal monks was too respectfully entertained by our antiquaries, Cambden[81] and Dugdale:[82] but it is so clearly repugnant to truth and time, that the rational pride of the family now refuses to accept this imaginary founder. Their most faithful historians believe, that after giving his daughter to the king's son, Reginald of Courtenay abandoned his possessions in France, and obtained from the English monarch a second wife and a new inheritance. It is certain, at least, that Henry the second distinguished in his camps and councils, *a* Reginald, of the name and arms, and, as it may be fairly presumed, of the genuine race, of the Courtenays of France. The right of wardship enabled a feudal lord to reward his vassal with the marriage and estate of a noble heiress; and Reginald of Courtenay acquired a fair establishment in Devonshire, where his posterity has been seated above six hundred years.[83] From a Norman baron, Baldwin de Brioniis, who had been invested by the Conqueror, Hawise, the wife of Reginald, derived the honour of Okehampton, which was held by the service of ninety-three knights; and a female might claim the manly offices of hereditary viscount or sheriff, and of captain of the royal castle of Exeter. Their son Robert married the sister of the earl of Devon; at the end of a century, on the failure of the family of Rivers,[84] his great-grandson, Hugh the second, succeeded to a title which was still considered as a territorial dignity; and twelve *The earls of Devonshire.* earls of Devonshire, of the name of Courtenay, have flourished in a period of two hundred and twenty years. They were ranked

80. Dugdale, Monasticon Anglicanum, vol. i. p. 786. Yet this fable must have been invented before the reign of Edward III. The profuse devotion of the three first generations to Ford abbey, was followed by oppression on one side and ingratitude on the other; and in the sixth generation, the monks ceased to register the births, actions, and deaths of their patrons.

81. In his Britannia, in the list of the earls of Devonshire. His expression, e regio sanguine ortos credunt, betrays however some doubt or suspicion.

82. In his Baronage, P. i. p. 634. he refers to his own Monasticon. Should he not have corrected the register of Ford abbey, and annihilated the phantom Florus, by the unquestionable evidence of the French historians?

83. Besides the third and most valuable book of Cleaveland's History, I have consulted Dugdale, the father of our genealogical science (Baronage, P. i. p. 634–643.).

84. This great family, de Ripuariis, de Redvers, de Rivers, ended, in Edward the First's time, in Isabella de Fortibus, a famous and potent dowager, who long survived her brother and husband (Dugdale, Baronage, P. i. p. 254–257.).

among the chief of the barons of the realm; nor was it till after a strenuous dispute, that they yielded to the fief of Arundel, the first place in the parliament of England: their alliances were contracted with the noblest families, the Veres, Despensers, St. Johns, Talbots, Bohuns, and even the Plantagenets themselves; and in a contest with John of Lancaster, a Courtenay, bishop of London, and afterwards archbishop of Canterbury, might be accused of profane confidence in the strength and number of his kindred. In peace, the earls of Devon resided in their numerous castles and manors of the west: their ample revenue was appropriated to devotion and hospitality; and the epitaph of Edward, surnamed, from his misfortune, the *blind*, from his virtues, the *good*, earl, inculcates with much ingenuity a moral sentence, which may however be abused by thoughtless generosity. After a grateful commemoration of the fifty-five years of union and happiness, which he enjoyed with Mabel his wife, the good earl thus speaks from the tomb:

What we gave, we have;
What we spent, we had;
What we left, we lost.[85]

But their *losses*, in this sense, were far superior to their gifts and expences; and their heirs, not less than the poor, were the objects of their paternal care. The sums which they paid for livery and seisin, attest the greatness of their possessions; and several estates have remained in their family since the thirteenth and fourteenth centuries. In war, the Courtenays of England fulfilled the duties, and deserved the honours, of chivalry. They were often entrusted to levy and command the militia of Devonshire and Cornwall; they often attended their supreme lord to the borders of Scotland; and in foreign service, for a stipulated price, they sometimes maintained fourscore men at arms and as many archers. By sea and land they fought under the standard of the Edwards and Henries: their names are conspicuous in battles, in tournaments, and in the original list of the order of the garter; three brothers shared the Spanish victory of the Black Prince; and in the lapse of six generations, the English Courtenays had learned to despise the nation and country from which they derived their origin. In the quarrel of the two roses, the earls of Devon adhered to the house of Lancaster, and three brothers successively died, either in the field or on the scaffold. Their honours and estates were restored by Henry

85. Cleaveland, p. 142. By some, it is assigned to a Rivers earl of Devon: but the English denotes the xv[th], rather than the xiii[th], century.

the seventh; a daughter of Edward the fourth was not disgraced by the nuptials of a Courtenay; their son, who was created marquis of Exeter, enjoyed the favour of his cousin Henry the eighth; and in the camp of Cloth of Gold, he broke a lance against the French monarch. But the favour of Henry was the prelude of disgrace; his disgrace was the signal of death; and of the victims of the jealous tyrant, the marquis of Exeter is one of the most noble and guiltless. His son Edward lived a prisoner in the Tower, and died an exile at Padua; and the secret love of queen Mary, whom he slighted, perhaps for the princess Elizabeth, has shed a romantic colour on the story of this beautiful youth. The relics of his patrimony were conveyed into strange families by the marriages of his four aunts; and his personal honours, as if they had been legally extinct, were revived by the patents of succeeding princes. But there still survived a lineal descendant of Hugh the first earl of Devon, a younger branch of the Courtenays, who have been seated at Powderham castle above four hundred years from the reign of Edward the third to the present hour. Their estates have been encreased by the grant and improvement of lands in Ireland, and they have been recently restored to the honours of the peerage. Yet the Courtenays still retain the plaintive motto, which asserts the innocence, and deplores the fall, of their ancient house.[86] While they sigh for past greatness, they are doubtless sensible of present blessings: in the long series of the Courtenay annals, the most splendid æra is likewise the most unfortunate; nor can an opulent peer of Britain be inclined to envy the emperors of Constantinople, who wandered over Europe to solicit alms for the support of their dignity and the defence of their capital.

86. *Ubi lapsus! Quid feci?* a motto which was probably adopted by the Powderham branch, after the loss of the earldom of Devonshire, &c. The primitive arms of the Courtenays were, *or, three torteaux, gules*, which seem to denote their affinity with Godfrey of Bouillon, and the ancient counts of Boulogne.

CHAPTER LXII

The Greek Emperors of Nice and Constantinople. – Elevation and Reign of Michael Palæologus. – His false Union with the Pope and the Latin Church. – Hostile Designs of Charles of Anjou. – Revolt of Sicily. – War of the Catalans in Asia and Greece. – Revolutions and present State of Athens.

Restoration of the Greek empire.

The loss of Constantinople restored a momentary vigour to the Greeks. From their palaces, the princes and nobles were driven into the field; and the fragments of the falling monarchy were grasped by the hands of the most vigorous or the most skilful candidates. In the long and barren pages of the Byzantine annals,[1] it would not be an easy task to equal the two characters of Theodore Lascaris and John Ducas Vataces,[2] who replanted and upheld the Roman standard at Nice in Bithynia. The difference of their virtues was happily suited to the diversity of their situation. In his first efforts, the fugitive Lascaris commanded only three cities and two thousand soldiers: his reign was the season of generous and active despair: in every military operation he staked his life and crown; and his enemies, of the Hellespont and the Mæander, were surprised by his celerity and subdued by his boldness. A victorious reign of eighteen years expanded the principality of Nice to the magnitude of an empire. The throne of his successor and son-in-law Vataces was founded on a more solid basis, a larger scope, and more plentiful resources; and it was the temper, as well as the interest, of Vataces to calculate the risk, to expect the moment, and to ensure the success, of his ambitious designs. In the decline of the Latins, I have briefly

Theodore Lascaris, A.D. 1204–1222.

John Ducas Vataces, A.D. 1222–1255, October 30.

1. For the reigns of the Nicene emperors, more especially of John Vataces and his son, their minister, George Acropolita, is the only genuine contemporary: but George Pachymer returned to Constantinople with the Greeks, at the age of nineteen (Hanckius, de Script. Byzant. c. 33, 34. p. 564–578. Fabric, Bibliot. Græ. tom. vi. p. 448–460). Yet the history of Nicephorus Gregoras, though of the xiv[th] century, is a valuable narrative from the taking of Constantinople by the Latins.

2. Nicephorus Gregoras (l. ii. c. 1.) distinguishes between the οξεια ὁρμη of Lascaris, and the ευσταθεια of Vataces. The two portraits are in a very good style.

exposed the progress of the Greeks; the prudent and gradual advances of a conqueror, who, in a reign of thirty-three years, rescued the provinces from national and foreign usurpers, till he pressed on all sides the Imperial city, a leafless and sapless trunk which must fall at the first stroke of the axe. But his interior and peaceful administration is still more deserving of notice and praise.[3] The calamities of the times had wasted the numbers and the substance of the Greeks: the motives and the means of agriculture were extirpated; and the most fertile lands were left without cultivation or inhabitants. A portion of this vacant property was occupied and improved by the command, and for the benefit, of the emperor: a powerful hand and a vigilant eye supplied and surpassed, by a skilful management, the minute diligence of a private farmer: the royal domain became the garden and granary of Asia; and without impoverishing the people, the sovereign acquired a fund of innocent and productive wealth. According to the nature of the soil, his lands were sown with corn or planted with vines: the pastures were filled with horses and oxen, with sheep and hogs; and when Vataces presented to the empress a crown of diamonds and pearls, he informed her with a smile that this precious ornament arose from the sale of the eggs of his innumerable poultry. The produce of his domain was applied to the maintenance of his palace and hospitals, the calls of dignity and benevolence: the lesson was still more useful than the revenue: the plough was restored to its ancient security and honour; and the nobles were taught to seek a sure and independent revenue from their estates, instead of adorning their splendid beggary by the oppression of the people, or (what is almost the same) by the favours of the court. The superfluous stock of corn and cattle was eagerly purchased by the Turks, with whom Vataces preserved a strict and sincere alliance; but he discouraged the importation of foreign manufactures, the costly silks of the East, and the curious labours of the Italian looms. "The demands of nature and necessity," was he accustomed to say, "are indispensable; but the influence of fashion may rise and sink at the breath of a monarch;" and both his precept and example recommended simplicity of manner and the use of domestic industry. The education of youth and the revival of learning were the most serious objects of his care; and, without deciding the precedency, he pronounced with truth, that a prince and a philosopher[4] are the two most eminent characters of

3. Pachymer, l. i. c. 23, 24. Nic. Greg. l. ii. c. 6. The reader of the Byzantines must observe how rarely we are indulged with such precious details.

4. *Μονοι γαρ ἁπαντων ανθρωπων ονομαστοτατοι βασιλευς και φιλοσοφος* (Greg.

human society. His first wife was Irene, the daughter of Theodore Lascaris, a woman more illustrious by her personal merit, the milder virtues of her sex, than by the blood of the Angeli and Comneni, that flowed in her veins, and transmitted the inheritance of the empire. After her death he was contracted to Anne or Constance, a natural daughter of the emperor Frederic the second; but as the bride had not attained the years of puberty, Vataces placed in his solitary bed an Italian damsel of her train; and his amorous weakness bestowed on the concubine the honours, though not the title, of lawful empress. His frailty was censured as a flagitious and damnable sin by the monks; and their rude invectives exercised and displayed the patience of the royal lover. A philosophic age may excuse a single vice, which was redeemed by a crowd of virtues; and in the review of his faults, and the more intemperate passions of Lascaris, the judgment of their contemporaries was softened by gratitude to the second founders of the empire.[5] The slaves of the Latins, without law or peace, applauded the happiness of their brethren who had resumed their national freedom; and Vataces employed the laudable policy of convincing the Greeks of every dominion that it was their interest to be enrolled in the number of his subjects.

Theodore Lascaris II. A.D. 1255, October 30– A.D. 1259, August.

A strong shade of degeneracy is visible between John Vataces and his son Theodore; between the founder who sustained the weight, and the heir who enjoyed the splendour, of the Imperial crown.[6] Yet the character of Theodore was not devoid of energy; he had been educated in the school of his father, in the exercise of war and hunting: Constantinople was yet spared; but in the three years of a short reign, he thrice led his armies into the heart of Bulgaria. His virtues were sullied by a choleric and suspicious temper: the first of these may be ascribed to the ignorance of controul; and the second might naturally arise from a dark and imperfect view of the corruption of mankind. On a march in Bulgaria, he consulted on a question of policy his principal ministers; and the Greek logothete, George Acropolita, presumed to offend him by the declaration of a free and honest opinion. The emperor half-unsheathed his scymetar; but his

Acropol. c. 32.). The emperor, in a familiar conversation, examined and encouraged the studies of his future logothete.

5. Compare Acropolita (c. 18. 52.), and the two first books of Nicephorus Gregoras.

6. A Persian saying, that Cyrus was the *father*, and Darius the *master*, of his subjects, was applied to Vataces and his son. But Pachymer (l. i. c. 23.) has mistaken the mild Darius for the cruel Cambyses, despot or tyrant of his people. By the institution of taxes, Darius had incurred the less odious, but more contemptible, name of Καπηλος, merchant or broker (Herodotus, iii. 89.).

more deliberate rage reserved Acropolita for a baser punishment. One of the first officers of the empire was ordered to dismount, stripped of his robes, and extended on the ground in the presence of the prince and army. In this posture he was chastised with so many and such heavy blows from the clubs of two guards or executioners, that when Theodore commanded them to cease, the great logothete was scarcely able to arise and crawl away to his tent. After a seclusion of some days, he was recalled by a peremptory mandate to his seat in council; and so dead were the Greeks to the sense of honour and shame, that it is from the narrative of the sufferer himself that we acquire the knowledge of his disgrace.[7] The cruelty of the emperor was exasperated by the pangs of sickness, the approach of a premature end, and the suspicion of poison and magic. The lives and fortunes, the eyes and limbs, of his kinsmen and nobles, were sacrificed to each sally of passion; and before he died, the son of Vataces might deserve from the people, or at least from the court, the appellation of tyrant. A matron of the family of the Palæologi had provoked his anger by refusing to bestow her beauteous daughter on the vile plebeian who was recommended by his caprice. Without regard to her birth or age, her body, as high as the neck, was enclosed in a sack with several cats, who were pricked with pins to irritate their fury against their unfortunate fellow-captive. In his last hours, the emperor testified a wish to forgive and be forgiven, a just anxiety for the fate of John his son and successor, who, at the age of eight years, was condemned to the dangers of a long minority. His last choice entrusted the office of guardian to the sanctity of the patriarch Arsenius, and to the courage of George Muzalon, the great domestic, who was equally distinguished by the royal favour and the public hatred. Since their connection with the Latins, the names and privileges of hereditary rank had insinuated themselves into the Greek monarchy; and the noble families[8] were provoked by the elevation of a worthless favourite, to whose influence they imputed the errors and calamities of the late reign. In the first council, after the emperor's death, Muzalon, from a lofty throne, pronounced a laboured apology of his conduct and intentions: his

Minority of John Lascaris, A.D. 1259, August.

7. Acropolita (c. 63.) seems to admire his own firmness in sustaining a beating, and not returning to council till he was called. He relates the exploits of Theodore, and his own services, from c. 53. to c. 74. of his history. See the third book of Nicephorus Gregoras.

8. Pachymer (l. i. c. 21.) names and discriminates fifteen or twenty Greek families, *και ὁσοι αλλοι, ὁις ἡ μεγαλογενης σειρα και χρυση συγκεκροτητο*. Does he mean, by this decoration, a figurative, or a real golden chain? Perhaps, both.

modesty was subdued by an unanimous assurance of esteem and fidelity; and his most inveterate enemies were the loudest to salute him as the guardian and saviour of the Romans. Eight days were sufficient to prepare the execution of the conspiracy. On the ninth, the obsequies of the deceased monarch were solemnised in the cathedral of Magnesia,[9] an Asiatic city, where he expired, on the banks of the Hermus and at the foot of mount Sipylus. The holy rites were interrupted by a sedition of the guards: Muzalon, his brothers, and his adherents, were massacred at the foot of the altar; and the absent patriarch was associated with a new colleague, with Michael Palæologus, the most illustrious, in birth and merit, of the Greek nobles.[10]

Family and character of Michael Palæologus.

Of those who are proud of their ancestors, the far greater part must be content with local or domestic renown; and few there are who dare trust the memorials of their family to the public annals of their country. As early as the middle of the eleventh century, the noble race of the Palæologi[11] stands high and conspicuous in the Byzantine history: it was the valiant George Palæologus who placed the father of the Comneni on the throne; and his kinsmen or descendants continue, in each generation, to lead the armies and councils of the state. The purple was not dishonoured by their alliance; and had the law of succession, and female succession, been strictly observed, the wife of Theodore Lascaris must have yielded to her elder sister, the mother of Michael Palæologus, who afterwards raised his family to the throne. In his person, the splendour of birth was dignified by the merit of the soldier and statesman: in his early youth he was promoted to the office of *constable* or commander of the French mercenaries; the private expence of a day never exceeded three pieces of gold; but his ambition was rapacious and profuse; and his gifts were doubled by the graces of his conversation and manners. The love of the soldiers and people excited the jealousy of the court; and Michael thrice escaped from the dangers in which he was involved by his own

9. The old geographers, with Cellarius and d'Anville, and our travellers, particularly Pocock and Chandler, will teach us to distinguish the two Magnesias of Asia Minor, of the Mæander and of Sipylus. The latter, our present object, is still flourishing for a Turkish city, and lies eight hours, or leagues, to the north-east of Smyrna (Tournefort, Voyage du Levant, tom. iii. lettre xxii. p. 365–370. Chandler's Travels into Asia Minor, p. 267.).

10. See Acropolita (c. 75, 76, &c.), who lived too near the times; Pachymer (l. i. c. 13–25.), Gregoras (l. iii. c. 3, 4, 5.).

11. The pedigree of Palæologus is explained by Ducange (Famil. Byzant. p. 230, &c.): the events of his private life are related by Pachymer (l. i. c. 7–12.) and Gregoras (l. ii. 8. l. iii. 2. 4. l. iv. 1.), with visible favour to the father of the reigning dynasty.

imprudence or that of his friends. I. Under the reign of Justice and Vataces, a dispute arose[12] between two officers, one of whom accused the other of maintaining the hereditary right of the Palæologi. The cause was decided, according to the new jurisprudence of the Latins, by single combat: the defendant was overthrown; but he persisted in declaring that himself alone was guilty; and that he had uttered these rash or treasonable speeches without the approbation or knowledge of his patron. Yet a cloud of suspicion hung over the innocence of the constable: he was still pursued by the whispers of malevolence; and a subtle courtier, the archbishop of Philadelphia, urged him to accept the judgment of God in the fiery proof of the ordeal.[13] Three days before the trial, the patient's arm was enclosed in a bag, and secured by the royal signet; and it was incumbent on him to bear a red-hot ball of iron three times from the altar to the rails of the sanctuary, without artifice and without injury. Palæologus eluded the dangerous experiment with sense and pleasantry. "I am a soldier," said he, "and will boldly enter the lists with my accusers: but a layman, a sinner like myself, is not endowed with the gift of miracles. *Your* piety, most holy prelate, may deserve the interposition of heaven, and from your hands I will receive the fiery globe, the pledge of my innocence." The archbishop started; the emperor smiled; and the absolution or pardon of Michael was approved by new rewards and new services. II. In the succeeding reign, as he held the government of Nice, he was secretly informed, that the mind of the absent prince was poisoned with jealousy; and that death, or blindness, would be his final reward. Instead of awaiting the return and sentence of Theodore, the constable, with some followers, escaped from the city and the empire; and though he was plundered by the Turkmans of the desert, he found an hospitable refuge in the court of the sultan. In the ambiguous state of an exile, Michael reconciled the duties of gratitude and loyalty: drawing his sword against the Tartars; admonishing the garrisons of the Roman limit; and promoting by his influence, the restoration of peace, in which his pardon and recall were honourably included. III. While he guarded the West against the despot of Epirus, Michael was again suspected and condemned

12. Acropolita (c. 50.) relates the circumstances of this curious adventure, which seem to have escaped the more recent writers.

13. Pachymer (l. i. c. 12.), who speaks with proper contempt of this barbarous trial, affirms, that he had seen in his youth many persons who had sustained, without injury, the fiery ordeal. As a Greek, he is credulous: but the ingenuity of the Greeks might furnish some remedies of art or fraud against their own superstition, or that of their tyrant.

in the palace; and such was his loyalty or weakness, that he submitted to be led in chains above six hundred miles from Durazzo to Nice. The civility of the messenger alleviated his disgrace; the emperor's sickness dispelled his danger; and the last breath of Theodore, which recommended his infant son, at once acknowledged the innocence and the power of Palæologus.

His elevation to the throne.

But his innocence had been too unworthily treated, and his power was too strongly felt, to curb an aspiring subject in the fair field that was opened to his ambition.[14] In the council after the death of Theodore, he was the first to pronounce, and the first to violate, the oath of allegiance to Muzalon; and so dextrous was his conduct, that he reaped the benefit, without incurring the guilt, or at least the reproach, of the subsequent massacre. In the choice of a regent, he balanced the interests and passions of the candidates; turned their envy and hatred from himself against each other, and forced every competitor to own, that after his own claims, those of Palæologus were best entitled to the preference. Under the title of great duke, he accepted or assumed, during a long minority, the active powers of government; the patriarch was a venerable name; and the factious nobles were seduced, or oppressed, by the ascendant of his genius. The fruits of the œconomy of Vataces were deposited in a strong castle on the banks of the Hermus, in the custody of the faithful Varangians; the constable retained his command or influence over the foreign troops; he employed the guards to possess the treasure, and the treasure to corrupt the guards; and whatsoever might be the abuse of the public money, his character was above the suspicion of private avarice. By himself, or by his emissaries, he strove to persuade every rank of subjects, that their own prosperity would rise in just proportion to the establishment of his authority. The weight of taxes was suspended, the perpetual theme of popular complaint; and he prohibited the trials by the ordeal and judicial combat. These Barbaric institutions were already abolished or undermined in France[15] and England;[16] and

14. Without comparing Pachymer to Thucydides or Tacitus, I will praise his narrative (l. i. c. 13–32. l. ii. c. 1–9.), which pursues the ascent of Palæologus with eloquence, perspicuity, and tolerable freedom. Acropolita is more cautious, and Gregoras more concise.

15. The judicial combat was abolished by St. Louis in his own territories; and his example and authority were at length prevalent in France (Esprit des Loix, l. xxviii. c. 29.).

16. In civil cases Henry II. gave an option to the defendant: Glanville prefers the proof by evidence, and that by judicial combat is reprobated in the Fleta. Yet the trial by battle has never been abrogated in the English law, and it was ordered by the judges as late as the beginning of the last century.

the appeal to the sword offended the sense of a civilized,[17] and the temper of an unwarlike, people. For the future maintenance of their wives and children, the veterans were grateful: the priest and the philosopher applauded his ardent zeal for the advancement of religion and learning; and his vague promise of rewarding merit, was applied by every candidate to his own hopes. Conscious of the influence of the clergy, Michael successfully laboured to secure the suffrage of that powerful order. Their expensive journey from Nice to Magnesia, afforded a decent and ample pretence: the leading prelates were tempted by the liberality of his nocturnal visits; and the incorruptible patriarch was flattered by the homage of his new colleague, who led his mule by the bridle into the town, and removed to a respectful distance the importunity of the crowd. Without renouncing his title by royal descent, Palæologus encouraged a free discussion into the advantages of elective monarchy; and his adherents asked, with the insolence of triumph, what patient would trust his health, or what merchant would abandon his vessel, to the *hereditary* skill of a physician or a pilot? The youth of the emperor, and the impending dangers of a minority, required the support of a mature and experienced guardian; of an associate, raised above the envy of his equals, and invested with the name and prerogatives of royalty. For the interest of the prince and people, without any selfish views for himself or his family, the great duke consented to guard and instruct the son of Theodore; but he sighed for the happy moment when he might restore to his firmer hands the administration of his patrimony, and enjoy the blessings of a private station. He was first invested with the title and prerogatives of *despot*, which bestowed the purple ornaments, and the second place in the Roman monarchy. It was afterwards agreed that John and Michael should be proclaimed as joint-emperors, and raised on the buckler, but that the pre-eminence should be reserved for the birth-right of the former. A mutual league of amity was pledged between the royal partners; and in case of a rupture, the subjects were bound, by their oath of allegiance, to

17. Yet an ingenious friend has urged to me in mitigation of this practice, 1. *That* in nations emerging from barbarism, it moderates the licence of private war and arbitrary revenge. 2. *That* it is less absurd than the trials by the ordeal, or boiling water, or the cross, which it has contributed to abolish. 3. *That* it served at least as a test of personal courage; a quality so seldom united with a base disposition, that the danger of the trial might be some check to a malicious prosecutor, and an useful barrier against injustice supported by power. The gallant and unfortunate earl of Surrey might probably have escaped his unmerited fate, had not his demand of the combat against his accuser been over-ruled.

declare themselves against the aggressor, an ambiguous name, the seed of discord and civil war. Palæologus was content; but on the day of the coronation, and in the cathedral of Nice, his zealous adherents most vehemently urged the just priority of his age and merit. The unseasonable dispute was eluded by postponing to a more convenient opportunity the coronation of John Lascaris; and he walked with a slight diadem in the train of his guardian, who alone received the Imperial crown from the hands of the patriarch. It was not without extreme reluctance that Arsenius abandoned the cause of his pupil; but the Varangians brandished their battle-axes; a sign of assent was extorted from the trembling youth; and some voices were heard, that the life of a child should no longer impede the settlement of the nation. A full harvest of honours and employments was distributed among his friends by the grateful Palæologus. In his own family he created a despot and two sebastocrators; Alexius Strategopulus was decorated with the title of Cæsar; and that veteran commander soon repaid the obligation, by restoring Constantinople to the Greek emperor.

Michael Palæologus emperor, A.D. 1260, January 1.

Recovery of Constantinople, A.D. 1261, July 25.

It was in the second year of his reign, while he resided in the palace and gardens of Nymphæum[18] near Smyrna, that the first messenger arrived at the dead of night; and the stupendous intelligence was imparted to Michael, after he had been gently waked by the tender precaution of his sister Eulogia. The man was unknown or obscure; he produced no letters from the victorious Cæsar; nor could it easily be credited after the defeat of Vataces and the recent failure of Palæologus himself, that the capital had been surprised by a detachment of eight hundred soldiers. As an hostage, the doubtful author was confined, with the assurance of death or an ample recompense; and the court was left some hours in the anxiety of hope and fear, till the messengers of Alexius arrived with the authentic intelligence, and displayed the trophies of the conquest, the sword and sceptre,[19] the buskins and bonnet,[20] of the usurper Baldwin, which he

18. The site of Nymphæum is not clearly defined in ancient or modern geography. But from the last hours of Vataces (Acropolita, c. 52.), it is evident the palace and gardens of his favourite residence were in the neighbourhood of Smyrna. Nymphæum might be loosely placed in Lydia (Gregoras, l. vi. 6.).

19. This sceptre, the emblem of justice and power, was a long staff, such as was used by the heroes in Homer. By the latter Greeks it was named *Dicanice*, and the Imperial sceptre was distinguished as usual by the red or purple colour.

20. Acropolita affirms (c. 87.), that this bonnet was after the French fashion; but

had dropped in his precipitate flight. A general assembly of the bishops, senators, and nobles, was immediately convened, and never perhaps was an event received with more heartfelt and universal joy. In a studied oration, the new sovereign of Constantinople congratulated his own and the public fortune. "There was a time," said he, "a far distant time, when the Roman empire extended to the Adriatic, the Tigris, and the confines of Æthiopia. After the loss of the provinces, our capital itself, in these last and calamitous days, has been wrested from our hands by the Barbarians of the West. From the lowest ebb, the tide of prosperity has again returned in our favour; but our prosperity was that of fugitives and exiles; and when we were asked, which was the country of the Romans, we indicated with a blush the climate of the globe and the quarter of the heavens. The divine Providence has now restored to our arms the city of Constantine, the sacred seat of religion and empire; and it will depend on our valour and conduct to render this important acquisition the pledge and omen of future victories." So eager was the impatience of the prince and people, that Michael made his triumphal entry into Constantinople only twenty days after the expulsion of the Latins. The golden gate was thrown open at his approach; the devout conqueror dismounted from his horse; and a miraculous image of Mary the Conductress was borne before him, that the divine Virgin in person might appear to conduct him to the temple of her son, the cathedral of St. Sophia. But after the first transport of devotion and pride, he sighed at the dreary prospect of solitude and ruin. The palace was defiled with smoke and dirt, and the gross intemperance of the Franks; whole streets had been consumed by fire, or were decayed by the injuries of time; the sacred and profane edifices were stripped of their ornaments; and, as if they were conscious of their approaching exile, the industry of the Latins had been confined to the work of pillage and destruction. Trade had expired under the pressure of anarchy and distress; and the numbers of inhabitants had decreased with the opulence of the city. It was the first care of the Greek monarch to reinstate the nobles in the palaces of their fathers; and the houses or the ground which they occupied were restored to the families that could exhibit a legal right of inheritance. But the far greater part was extinct or lost; the vacant property had devolved to the lord; he repeopled Constantinople by a

Return of the Greek emperor, A.D. 1261, August 14.

from the ruby at the point or summit, Ducange (Hist. de C. P. l. v. c. 28, 29.) believes that it was the high-crowned hat of the Greeks. Could Acropolita mistake the dress of his own court?

liberal invitation to the provinces; and the brave *volunteers* were seated in the capital which had been recovered by their arms. The French barons and the principal families had retired with their emperor; but the patient and humble crowd of Latins was attached to the country, and indifferent to the changes of masters. Instead of banishing the factories of the Pisans, Venetians, and Genoese, the prudent conqueror accepted their oaths of allegiance, encouraged their industry, confirmed their privileges, and allowed them to live under the jurisdiction of their proper magistrates. Of these nations, the Pisans and Venetians preserved their respective quarters in the city; but the services and power of the Genoese deserved at the same time the gratitude and the jealousy of the Greeks. Their independent colony was first planted at the sea-port town of Heraclea in Thrace. They were speedily recalled and settled in the exclusive possession of the suburb of Galata, an advantageous post, in which they revived the commerce, and insulted the majesty, of the Byzantine empire.[21]

Palæologus blinds and banishes the young emperor, A.D. 1261, Dec. 25.

The recovery of Constantinople was celebrated as the æra of a new empire: the conqueror, alone, and by the right of the sword, renewed his coronation in the church of St. Sophia; and the name and honours of John Lascaris, his pupil and lawful sovereign, were insensibly abolished. But his claims still lived in the minds of the people; and the royal youth must speedily attain the years of manhood and ambition. By fear or conscience, Palæologus was restrained from dipping his hands in innocent and royal blood; but the anxiety of an usurper and a parent urged him to secure his throne, by one of those imperfect crimes so familiar to the modern Greeks. The loss of sight incapacitated the young prince for the active business of the world: instead of the brutal violence of tearing out his eyes, the visual nerve was destroyed by the intense glare of a red-hot bason,[22] and John Lascaris was removed to a distant castle, where he spent many years in privacy and oblivion. Such cool and deliberate guilt may seem incompatible with remorse; but if Michael could trust the mercy

21. See Pachymer (l. ii. c. 28–33.), Acropolita (c. 88.), Nicephorus Gregoras (l. iv. 7.), and for the treatment of the subject Latins, Ducange (l. v. c. 30, 31.).

22. This milder invention for extinguishing the sight, was tried by the philosopher Democritus on himself, when he sought to withdraw his mind from the visible world: a foolish story! The word *abacinare*, in Latin and Italian, has furnished Ducange (Gloss. Latin.) with an opportunity to review the various modes of blinding: the more violent were scooping, burning with an iron, or hot vinegar, and binding the head with a strong cord till the eyes burst from their sockets. Ingenious tyrants!

of heaven, he was not inaccessible to the reproaches and vengeance of mankind, which he had provoked by cruelty and treason. His cruelty imposed on a servile court the duties of applause or silence; but the clergy had a right to speak in the name of their invisible master; and their holy legions were led by a prelate, whose character was above the temptations of hope or fear. After a short abdication of his dignity, Arsenius[23] had consented to ascend the ecclesiastical throne of Constantinople, and to preside in the restoration of the church. His pious simplicity was long deceived by the arts of Palæologus; and his patience and submission might soothe the usurper and protect the safety of the young prince. On the news of his inhuman treatment, the patriarch unsheathed the spiritual sword; and superstition, on this occasion, was enlisted in the cause of humanity and justice. In a synod of bishops, who were stimulated by the example of his zeal, the patriarch pronounced a sentence of excommunication; though his prudence still repeated the name of Michael in the public prayers. The eastern prelates had not adopted the dangerous maxims of ancient Rome; nor did they presume to enforce their censures, by deposing princes, or absolving nations from their oaths of allegiance. But the Christian, who had been separated from God and the church, became an object of horror; and, in a turbulent and fanatic capital, that horror might arm the hand of an assassin, or inflame a sedition of the people. Palæologus felt his danger, confessed his guilt, and deprecated his judge: the act was irretrievable; the prize was obtained; and the most rigorous penance, which he solicited, would have raised the sinner to the reputation of a saint. The unrelenting patriarch refused to announce any means of atonement or any hopes of mercy; and condescended only to pronounce, that, for so great a crime, great indeed must be the satisfaction. "Do you require," said Michael, "that I should abdicate the empire?" And at these words, he offered, or seemed to offer, the sword of state. Arsenius eagerly grasped this pledge of sovereignty; but when he perceived that the emperor was unwilling to purchase absolution at so dear a rate, he indignantly escaped to his cell, and left the royal sinner kneeling and weeping before the door.[24]

is excommunicated by the patriarch Arsenius, A.D. 1262–1268.

23. See the first retreat and restoration of Arsenius, in Pachymer (l. ii. c. 15. l. iii. c. 1, 2.), and Nicephorus Gregoras (l. iii. c. 1. l. iv. c. 1.). Posterity justly accused the *αφελεια* and *ραθυμια* of Arsenius, the virtues of an hermit, the vices of a minister (l. xii. c. 2.).

24. The crime and excommunication of Michael are fairly told by Pachymer (l. iii. c. 10. 14. 19, &c.) and Gregoras (l. iv. c. 4.). His confession and penance restored their freedom.

Schism of the Arsenites, A.D. 1266–1312.

The danger and scandal of this excommunication subsisted above three years, till the popular clamour was assuaged by time and repentance; till the brethren of Arsenius condemned his inflexible spirit, so repugnant to the unbounded forgiveness of the gospel. The emperor had artfully insinuated, that, if he were still rejected at home, he might seek, in the Roman pontiff, a more indulgent judge; but it was far more easy and effectual to find or to place that judge at the head of the Byzantine church. Arsenius was involved in a vague rumour of conspiracy and disaffection; some irregular steps in his ordination and government were liable to censure; a synod deposed him from the episcopal office; and he was transported under a guard of soldiers to a small island of the Propontis. Before his exile, he sullenly requested that a strict account might be taken of the treasures of the church; boasted that his sole riches, three pieces of gold, had been earned by transcribing the psalms; continued to assert the freedom of his mind; and denied, with his last breath, the pardon which was implored by the royal sinner.[25] After some delay, Gregory, bishop of Adrianople, was translated to the Byzantine throne; but his authority was found insufficient to support the absolution of the emperor; and Joseph, a reverend monk, was substituted to that important function. This edifying scene was represented in the presence of the senate and people; at the end of six years, the humble penitent was restored to the communion of the faithful; and humanity will rejoice, that a milder treatment of the captive Lascaris was stipulated as a proof of his remorse. But the spirit of Arsenius still survived in a powerful faction of the monks and clergy, who persevered above forty-eight years in an obstinate schism. Their scruples were treated with tenderness and respect by Michael and his son; and the reconciliation of the Arsenites was the serious labour of the church and state. In the confidence of fanaticism, they had proposed to try their cause by a miracle; and when the two papers, that contained their own and the adverse cause, were cast into a fiery brasier, they expected that the Catholic verity would be respected by the flames. Alas! the two papers were indiscriminately consumed, and this unforeseen accident produced the union of a day, and renewed the quarrel of an age.[26] The final treaty displayed the victory of the Arsenites: the clergy abstained during forty

25. Pachymer relates the exile of Arsenius (l. iv. c. 1–16.): he was one of the commissaries who visited him in the desert island. The last testament of the unforgiving patriarch is still extant (Dupin. Bibliotheque Ecclesiastique, tom. x. p. 95.).

26. Pachymer (l. vii. c. 22.) relates this miraculous trial like a philosopher, and

days from all ecclesiastical functions; a slight penance was imposed on the laity; the body of Arsenius was deposited in the sanctuary; and in the name of the departed saint, the prince and people were released from the sins of their fathers.[27]

Reign of Michael Palæologus, A.D. 1259, Dec. 1– A.D. 1282, Dec. 11. Reign of Andronicus the Elder, A.D. 1273, Nov. 8– A.D. 1332, February 13.

The establishment of his family was the motive, or at least the pretence, of the crime of Palæologus; and he was impatient to confirm the succession, by sharing with his eldest son the honours of the purple. Andronicus, afterwards surnamed the Elder, was proclaimed and crowned emperor of the Romans, in the fifteenth year of his age; and, from the first æra of a prolix and inglorious reign, he held that august title nine years as the colleague, and fifty as the successor, of his father. Michael himself, had he died in a private station, would have been thought more worthy of the empire: and the assaults of his temporal and spiritual enemies, left him few moments to labour for his own fame or the happiness of his subjects. He wrested from the Franks several of the noblest islands of the Archipelago, Lesbos, Chios, and Rhodes: his brother Constantine was sent to command in Malvasia and Sparta; and the eastern side of the Morea, from Argos and Napoli to Cape Tænarus, was repossessed by the Greeks. This effusion of Christian blood was loudly condemned by the patriarch; and the insolent priest presumed to interpose his fears and scruples between the arms of princes. But in the prosecution of these western conquests, the countries beyond the Hellespont were left naked to the Turks; and their depredations verified the prophecy of a dying senator, that the recovery of Constantinople would be the ruin of Asia. The victories of Michael were atchieved by his lieutenants; his sword rusted in the palace; and in the transactions of the emperor with the popes and the king of Naples, his political arts were stained with cruelty and fraud.[28]

---

treats with similar contempt a plot of the Arsenites, to hide a revelation in the coffin of some old saint (l. vii. c. 13.). He compensates this incredulity by an image that weeps, another that bleeds (l. vii. c. 30.), and the miraculous cures of a deaf and a mute patient (l. xi. c. 32.).

27. The story of the Arsenites is spread through the thirteen books of Pachymer. Their union and triumph are reserved for Nicephorus Gregoras (l. vii. 9.), who neither loves nor esteems these sectaries.

28. Of the xiii books of Pachymer, the first six (as the iv[th] and v[th] of Nicephorus Gregoras) contain the reign of Michael, at the time of whose death he was forty years of age. Instead of breaking, like his editor the Pere Poussin, his history into two parts, I follow Ducange and Cousin, who number the xiii books in one series.

His union with the Latin church, A.D. 1274–1277.

I. The Vatican was the most natural refuge of a Latin emperor, who had been driven from his throne; and pope Urban the fourth appeared to pity the misfortunes, and vindicate the cause, of the fugitive Baldwin. A crusade, with plenary indulgence, was preached by his command against the schismatic Greeks; he excommunicated their allies and adherents; solicited Louis the ninth in favour of his kinsman; and demanded a tenth of the ecclesiastic revenues of France and England for the service of the holy war.[29] The subtle Greek, who watched the rising tempest of the West, attempted to suspend or soothe the hostility of the pope, by suppliant embassies and respectful letters; but he insinuated that the establishment of peace must prepare the reconciliation and obedience of the Eastern church. The Roman court could not be deceived by so gross an artifice; and Michael was admonished, that the repentance of the son should precede the forgiveness of the father; and that *faith* (an ambiguous word) was the only basis of friendship and alliance. After a long and affected delay, the approach of danger, and the importunity of Gregory the tenth, compelled him to enter on a more serious negociation: he alleged the example of the great Vataces; and the Greek clergy, who understood the intentions of their prince, were not alarmed by the first steps of reconciliation and respect. But when he pressed the conclusion of the treaty, they strenuously declared, that the Latins, though not in name, were heretics in fact, and that they despised those strangers as the vilest and most despicable portion of the human race.[30] It was the task of the emperor to persuade, to corrupt, to intimidate, the most popular ecclesiastics, to gain the vote of each individual, and alternately to urge the arguments of Christian charity and the public welfare. The texts of the fathers and the arms of the Franks were balanced in the theological and political scale; and without approving the addition to the Nicene creed, the most moderate were taught to confess, that the two hostile propositions of proceeding from the Father BY the Son, and of proceeding from the Father AND the Son, might be reduced to a safe and Catholic sense.[31] The supremacy of

29. Ducange, Hist. de C. P. l. v. c. 33, &c. from the Epistles of Urban IV.

30. From their mercantile intercourse with the Venetians and Genoese, they branded the Latins as *καπηλοι* and *βαναυσοι* (Pachymer, l. v. c. 10.). "Some are heretics in name; others, like the Latins, in fact," said the learned Veccus (l. v. c. 12.), who soon afterwards became a convert (c. 15, 16.) and a patriarch (c. 24.).

31. In this class, we may place Pachymer himself, whose copious and candid narrative occupies the vth and vith books of his history. Yet the Greek is silent on the council of Lyons, and seems to believe that the popes always resided in Rome and Italy (l. v. c. 17. 21.).

the pope was a doctrine more easy to conceive, but more painful to acknowledge; yet Michael represented to his monks and prelates, that they might submit to name the Roman bishop as the first of the patriarchs; and that their distance and discretion would guard the liberties of the Eastern church from the mischievous consequences of the right of appeal. He protested that he would sacrifice his life and empire, rather than yield the smallest point of orthodox faith or national independence; and this declaration was sealed and ratified by a golden bull. The patriarch Joseph withdrew to a monastery, to resign or resume his throne, according to the event of the treaty: the letters of union and obedience were subscribed by the emperor, his son Andronicus, and thirty-five archbishops and metropolitans, with their respective synods; and the episcopal list was multiplied by many dioceses which were annihilated under the yoke of the infidels. An embassy was composed of some trusty ministers and prelates; they embarked for Italy, with rich ornaments and rare perfumes, for the altar of St. Peter; and their secret orders authorised and recommended a boundless compliance. They were received in the general council of Lyons, by pope Gregory the tenth, at the head of five hundred bishops.[32] He embraced with tears his long-lost and repentant children; accepted the oath of the ambassadors, who abjured the schism in the name of the two emperors; adorned the prelates with the ring and mitre; chaunted in Greek and Latin the Nicene creed with the addition of *filioque*; and rejoiced in the union of the East and West, which had been reserved for his reign. To consummate this pious work, the Byzantine deputies were speedily followed by the pope's nuncios; and their instruction discloses the policy of the Vatican, which could not be satisfied with the vain title of supremacy. After viewing the temper of the prince and people, they were enjoined to absolve the schismatic clergy, who should subscribe and swear their abjuration and obedience; to establish in all the churches the use of the perfect creed; to prepare the entrance of a cardinal legate, with the full powers and dignity of his office; and to instruct the emperor in the advantages which he might derive from the temporal protection of the Roman pontiff.[33]

32. See the acts of the council of Lyons in the year 1274. Fleury, Hist. Ecclesiastique, tom. xviii. p. 181–199. Dupin, Bibliot. Eccles. tom. x. p. 135.

33. This curious instruction, which has been drawn with more or less honesty by Wading and Leo Allatius from the archives of the Vatican, is given in an abstract or version by Fleury (tom. xviii. p. 252–258.).

His persecution of the Greeks, A.D. 1277–1282.

But they found a country without a friend, a nation in which the names of Rome and Union were pronounced with abhorrence. The patriarch Joseph was indeed removed; his place was filled by Veccus, an ecclesiastic of learning and moderation; and the emperor was still urged by the same motives, to persevere in the same professions. But in his private language, Palæologus affected to deplore the pride, and to blame the innovations, of the Latins; and while he debased his character by this double hypocrisy, he justified and punished the opposition of his subjects. By the joint suffrage of the new and the ancient Rome, a sentence of excommunication was pronounced against the obstinate schismatics: the censures of the church were executed by the sword of Michael; on the failure of persuasion, he tried the arguments of prison and exile, of whipping and mutilation; those touch-stones, says an historian, of cowards and the brave. Two Greeks still reigned in Ætolia, Epirus, and Thessaly, with the appellation of despots: they had yielded to the sovereign of Constantinople, but they rejected the chains of the Roman pontiff, and supported their refusal by successful arms. Under their protection, the fugitive monks and bishops assembled in hostile synods; and retorted the name of heretic with the galling addition of apostate: the prince of Trebizond was tempted to assume the forfeit title of emperor; and even the Latins of Negropont, Thebes, Athens, and the Morea, forgot the merits of the convert, to join, with open or clandestine aid, the enemies of Palæologus. His favourite generals, of his own blood and family, successively deserted, or betrayed, the sacrilegious trust. His sister Eulogia, a niece, and two female cousins, conspired against him; another niece, Mary queen of Bulgaria, negociated his ruin with the sultan of Egypt; and, in the public eye, their treason was consecrated as the most sublime virtue.[34] To the pope's nuncios, who urged the consummation of the work, Palæologus exposed a naked recital of all that he had done and suffered for their sake. They were assured that the guilty sectaries, of both sexes and every rank, had been deprived of their honours, their fortunes, and their liberty; a spreading list of confiscation and punishment, which involved many persons, the dearest to the emperor, or the best deserving of his favour. They were conducted to the prison, to behold four princes of the royal blood chained in the

34. This frank and authentic confession of Michael's distress, is exhibited in barbarous Latin by Ogerius, who signs himself Protonotarius Interpretum, and transcribed by Wading from the MSS. of the Vatican (A.D. 1278, Nº 3.). His Annals of the Franciscan order, the Fratres Minores, in xvii volumes in folio (Rome, 1741), I have now accidentally seen among the waste paper of a bookseller.

four corners, and shaking their fetters in an agony of grief and rage. Two of these captives were afterwards released; the one by submission, the other by death: but the obstinacy of their two companions was chastised by the loss of their eyes; and the Greeks, the least adverse to the union, deplore that cruel and inauspicious tragedy.[35] Persecutors must expect the hatred of those whom they oppress; but they commonly find some consolation in the testimony of their conscience, the applause of their party, and, perhaps, the success of their undertaking. But the hypocrisy of Michael, which was prompted only by political motives, must have forced him to hate himself, to despise his followers, and to esteem and envy the rebel champions by whom he was detested and despised. While his violence was abhorred at Constantinople, at Rome his slowness was arraigned and his sincerity suspected; till at length pope Martin the fourth excluded the Greek emperor from the pale of a church, into which he was striving to reduce a schismatic people. No sooner had the tyrant expired, than the union was dissolved, and abjured by unanimous consent; the churches were purified; the penitents were reconciled; and his son Andronicus, after weeping the sins and errors of his youth, most piously denied his father the burial of a prince and a Christian.[36]

The union dissolved, A.D. 1283.

Charles of Anjou subdues Naples and Sicily. A.D. 1266, February 26.

II. In the distress of the Latins, the walls and towers of Constantinople had fallen to decay: they were restored and fortified by the policy of Michael, who deposited a plenteous store of corn and salt provisions, to sustain the siege which he might hourly expect from the resentment of the Western powers. Of these, the sovereign of the two Sicilies was the most formidable neighbour; but as long as they were possessed by Mainfroy, the bastard of Frederic the second, his monarchy was the bulwark rather than the annoyance of the Eastern empire. The usurper, though a brave and active prince, was sufficiently employed in the defence of his throne: his proscription by successive popes had separated Mainfroy from the common cause of the Latins; and the forces that might have besieged Constantinople, were detained in a crusade against the domestic enemy of Rome. The prize of her avenger, the crown of the two Sicilies, was won and worn by the brother of St. Louis, by Charles count of Anjou

35. See the vi[th] book of Pachymer, particularly the chapters, 1. 11. 16. 18. 24–27. He is the more credible, as he speaks of this persecution with less anger than sorrow.

36. Pachymer, l. vii. c. 1–11. 17. The speech of Andronicus the elder (l. xii. c. 2.) is a curious record, which proves, that if the Greeks were the slaves of the emperor, the emperor was not less the slave of superstition and the clergy.

and Provence, who led the chivalry of France on this holy expedition.[37] The disaffection of his Christian subjects compelled Mainfroy to enlist a colony of Saracens whom his father had planted in Apulia: and this odious succour will explain the defiance of the Catholic hero, who rejected all terms of accommodation. "Bear this message," said Charles, "to the sultan of Nocera, that God and the sword are umpire between us; and that he shall either send me to paradise, or I will send him to the pit of hell." The armies met, and though I am ignorant of Mainfroy's doom in the other world, in this he lost his friends, his kingdom, and his life, in the bloody battle of Benevento. Naples and Sicily were immediately peopled with a warlike race of French nobles; and their aspiring leader embraced the future conquest of Africa, Greece, and Palestine. The most specious reasons might point his first arms against the Byzantine empire; and Palæologus, diffident of his own strength, repeatedly appealed from the ambition of Charles to the humanity of St. Louis, who still preserved a just ascendant over the mind of his ferocious brother. For a while the attention of that brother was confined at home by the invasion of Conradin, the last heir of the Imperial house of Swabia: but the hapless boy sunk in the unequal conflict; and his execution on a public scaffold taught the rivals of Charles to tremble for their heads as well as their dominions. A second respite was obtained by the last crusade of St. Louis to the African coast; and the double motive of interest and duty urged the king of Naples to assist, with his powers and his presence, the holy enterprise. The death of St. Louis released him from the importunity of a virtuous censor; the king of Tunis confessed himself the tributary and vassal of the crown of Sicily; and the boldest of the French knights were free to enlist under his banner against the Greek empire. A treaty and a marriage united his interest with the house of Courtenay; his daughter Beatrice was promised to Philip, son and heir of the emperor Baldwin; a pension of six hundred ounces of gold was allowed for his maintenance; and his generous father distributed among his allies the kingdoms and provinces of the East, reserving only Constantinople, and one day's journey round the

Threatens the Greek empire, A.D. 1270, &c.

37. The best accounts, the nearest the time, the most full and entertaining, of the conquest of Naples by Charles of Anjou, may be found in the Florentine Chronicles of Ricordano Malespina (c. 175–193.) and Giovanni Villani (l. vii. c. 1–10. 25–30.), which are published by Muratori in the viii[th] and xiii[th] volumes of the historians of Italy. In his Annals (tom. xi. p. 56–72.), he has abridged these great events, which are likewise described in the Istoria Civile of Giannone, tom. ii. l. xix. tom. iii. l. xx.

city, for the Imperial domain.[38] In this perilous moment, Palæologus was the most eager to subscribe the creed, and implore the protection, of the Roman pontiff, who assumed, with propriety and weight, the character of an angel of peace, the common father of the Christians. By his voice, the sword of Charles was chained in the scabbard; and the Greek ambassadors beheld him, in the pope's antichamber, biting his ivory sceptre in a transport of fury, and deeply resenting the refusal to enfranchise and consecrate his arms. He appears to have respected the disinterested mediation of Gregory the tenth; but Charles was insensibly disgusted by the pride and partiality of Nicholas the third; and his attachment to his kindred, the Ursini family, alienated the most strenuous champion from the service of the church. The hostile league against the Greeks, of Philip the Latin emperor, the king of the two Sicilies, and the republic of Venice, was ripened into execution; and the election of Martin the fourth, a French pope, gave a sanction to the cause. Of the allies, Philip supplied his name, Martin, a bull of excommunication, the Venetians, a squadron of forty gallies; and the formidable powers of Charles consisted of forty counts, ten thousand men at arms, a numerous body of infantry, and a fleet of more than three hundred ships and transports. A distant day was appointed for assembling this mighty force in the harbour of Brindisi: and a previous attempt was risked with a detachment of three hundred knights, who invaded Albania and besieged the fortress of Belgrade. Their defeat might amuse with a triumph the vanity of Constantinople; but the more sagacious Michael, despairing of his arms, depended on the effects of a conspiracy; on the secret workings of a rat, who gnawed the bow-string[39] of the Sicilian tyrant.

Palæologus instigates the revolt of Sicily, A.D. 1280.

Among the proscribed adherents of the house of Swabia, John of Procida forfeited a small island of that name in the bay of Naples. His birth was noble, but his education was learned; and in the poverty of exile, he was relieved by the practice of physic, which he had studied in the school of Salerno. Fortune had left him nothing to lose, except life; and to despise life is the first qualification of a rebel. Procida was endowed with the art of negociation, to enforce his reasons, and disguise his motives; and in his various

38. Ducange, Hist. de C. P. l. v. c. 49–56. l. vi. c. 1–13. See Pachymer, l. iv. c. 29. l. v. c. 7–10. 25. l. vi. c. 30. 32, 33. and Nicephorus Gregoras, l. iv. 5. l. v. 1. 6.

39. The reader of Herodotus will recollect how miraculously the Assyrian host of Sennacherib was disarmed and destroyed (l. ii. c. 141.).

transactions with nations and men, he could persuade each party that he laboured solely for *their* interest. The new kingdoms of Charles were afflicted by every species of fiscal and military oppression;[40] and the lives and fortunes of his Italian subjects were sacrificed to the greatness of their master and the licentiousness of his followers. The hatred of Naples was repressed by his presence; but the looser government of his vicegerents excited the contempt, as well as the aversion, of the Sicilians: the island was roused to a sense of freedom by the eloquence of Procida; and he displayed to every baron his private interest in the common cause. In the confidence of foreign aid, he successively visited the courts of the Greek emperor, and of Peter king of Arragon,[41] who possessed the maritime countries of Valencia and Catalonia. To the ambitious Peter a crown was presented, which he might justly claim by his marriage with the sister of Mainfroy, and by the dying voice of Conradin, who from the scaffold had cast a ring to his heir and avenger. Palæologus was easily persuaded to divert his enemy from a foreign war by a rebellion at home; and a Greek subsidy of twenty-five thousand ounces of gold was most profitably applied to arm a Catalan fleet, which sailed under an holy banner to the specious attack of the Saracens of Africa. In the disguise of a monk or beggar, the indefatigable missionary of revolt flew from Constantinople to Rome, and from Sicily to Saragossa: the treaty was sealed with the signet of pope Nicholas himself, the enemy of Charles; and his deed of gift transferred the fiefs of St. Peter from the house of Anjou to that of Arragon. So widely diffused and so freely circulated, the secret was preserved above two years with impenetrable discretion; and each of the conspirators imbibed the maxim of Peter, who declared that he would cut off his left-hand if it were conscious of the intentions of his right. The mine was prepared with deep and dangerous artifice; but it may be questioned, whether the instant explosion of Palermo were the effect of accident or design.

The Sicilian Vespers,

On the vigil of Easter, a procession of the disarmed citizens visited a church without the walls; and a noble damsel was

40. According to Sabas Malaspina (Hist. Sicula, l. iii. c. 16. in Muratori, tom. viii. p. 832.), a zealous Guelph, the subjects of Charles, who had reviled Mainfroy as a wolf, began to regret him as a lamb: and he justifies their discontent by the oppressions of the French government (l. vi. c. 2. 7.). See the Sicilian manifesto in Nicholas Specialis (l. i. c. 11. in Muratori, tom. x. p. 930.).

41. See the character and counsels of Peter king of Arragon, in Mariana (Hist. Hispan. l. xiv. c. 6. tom. ii. p. 133.). The reader forgives the Jesuit's defects, in favour, always of his style, and often of his sense.

A.D. 1282, March 30. rudely insulted by a French soldier.[42] The ravisher was instantly punished with death; and if the people was at first scattered by a military force, their numbers and fury prevailed: the conspirators seized the opportunity; the flame spread over the island; and eight thousand French were exterminated in a promiscuous massacre, which has obtained the name of the SICILIAN VESPERS.[43] From every city the banners of freedom and the church were displayed: the revolt was inspired by the presence or the soul of Procida; and Peter of Arragon, who sailed from the African coast to Palermo, was saluted as the king and saviour of the isle. By the rebellion of a people on whom he had so long trampled with impunity, Charles was astonished and confounded; and in the first agony of grief and devotion, he was heard to exclaim, "Oh God! if thou hast decreed to humble me, grant me at least a gentle and gradual descent from the pinnacle of greatness!" His fleet and army, which already filled the sea-ports of Italy, were hastily recalled from the service of the Grecian war; and the situation of Messina exposed that town to the first storm of his revenge. Feeble in themselves, and yet hopeless of foreign succour, the citizens would have repented, and submitted on the assurance of full pardon and their ancient privileges. But the pride of the monarch was already rekindled; and the most fervent intreaties of the legate could extort no more than a promise, that he would forgive the remainder, after a chosen list of eight hundred rebels had been yielded to his discretion. The despair of the Messinese renewed their courage: Peter of Arragon approached to their relief;[44] and his rival was driven back by the failure of provision and the terrors of the equinox to the Calabrian shore.

Defeat of Charles, October 2. At the same moment, the Catalan admiral, the famous Roger de Loria, swept the channel with an invincible squadron: the French fleet, more numerous in transports than in gallies, was either

42. After enumerating the sufferings of his country, Nicholas Specialis adds, in the true spirit of Italian jealousy, Quæ omnia et graviora quidem, ut arbitror, patienti animo Siculi tolerassent, nisi (quod primum cunctis dominantibus cavendum est), alienas fœminas invassissent (l. i. c. 2. p. 924.).

43. The French were long taught to remember this bloody lesson: "If I am provoked (said Henry the fourth), I will breakfast at Milan, and dine at Naples." "Your majesty (replied the Spanish ambassador) may perhaps arrive in Sicily for vespers."

44. This revolt, with the subsequent victory, are related by two national writers, Bartholemy à Neocastro (in Muratori, tom. xiii.) and Nicholas Specialis (in Muratori, tom. x.), the one a contemporary, the other of the next century. The patriot Specialis disclaims the name of rebellion, and all previous correspondence with Peter of Arragon (nullo communicato consilio), who *happened* to be with a fleet and army on the African coast (l. i. c. 4. 9.).

burnt or destroyed; and the same blow assured the independence of Sicily and the safety of the Greek empire. A few days before his death, the emperor Michael rejoiced in the fall of an enemy whom he hated and esteemed; and perhaps he might be content with the popular judgment, that had they not been matched with each other, Constantinople and Italy must speedily have obeyed the same master.[45] From this disastrous moment, the life of Charles was a series of misfortunes; his capital was insulted, his son was made prisoner, and he sunk into the grave without recovering the isle of Sicily, which, after a war of twenty years, was finally severed from the throne of Naples, and transferred, as an independent kingdom, to a younger branch of the house of Arragon.[46]

The service and war of the Catalans in the Greek empire, A.D. 1303–1307.

I shall not, I trust, be accused of superstition: but I must remark, that, even in this world, the natural order of events will sometimes afford the strong appearances of moral retribution. The first Palæologus had saved his empire by involving the kingdoms of the West in rebellion and blood; and from these seeds of discord, uprose a generation of iron men, who assaulted and endangered the empire of his son. In modern times, our debts and taxes are the secret poison, which still corrodes the bosom of peace; but in the weak and disorderly government of the middle ages, it was agitated by the present evil of the disbanded armies. Too idle to work, too proud to beg, the mercenaries were accustomed to a life of rapine: they could rob with more dignity and effect under a banner and a chief; and the sovereign, to whom their service was useless and their presence importunate, endeavoured to discharge the torrent on some neighbouring countries. After the peace of Sicily, many thousands of Genoese, *Catalans*,[47] &c. who had fought, by sea and land, under the standard of Anjou or Arragon, were blended into one nation by the resemblance of their manners and interest. They heard that the Greek provinces of Asia were invaded by the Turks: they resolved to share the harvest of pay and plunder; and Frederic king of Sicily most liberally

45. Nicephorus Gregoras (l. v. c. 6.) admires the wisdom of Providence in this equal balance of states and princes. For the honour of Palæologus, I had rather this balance had been observed by an Italian writer.

46. See the Chronicle of Villani, the xi[th] volume of the Annali d'Italia of Muratori, and the xx[th] and xxi[st] books of the Istoria Civile of Giannone.

47. In this motley multitude, the Catalans and Spaniards, the bravest of the soldiery, were styled, by themselves and the Greeks, *Amogavares*. Moncada derives their origin from the Goths, and Pachymer (l. xi. c. 22.) from the Arabs; and in spite of national and religious pride, I am afraid the latter is in the right.

contributed the means of their departure. In a warfare of twenty years, a ship, or a camp, was become their country; arms were their sole profession and property; valour was the only virtue which they knew; their women had imbibed the fearless temper of their lovers and husbands: it was reported, that, with a stroke of their broad-sword, the Catalans could cleave a horseman and an horse; and the report itself was a powerful weapon. Roger de Flor was the most popular of their chiefs: and his personal merit overshadowed the dignity of his prouder rivals of Arragon. The offspring of a marriage between a German gentleman of the court of Frederic the second and a damsel of Brindisi, Roger was successively a templar, an apostate, a pirate, and at length the richest and most powerful admiral of the Mediterranean. He sailed from Messina to Constantinople, with eighteen gallies, four great ships, and eight thousand adventurers; and his previous treaty was faithfully accomplished by Andronicus the elder, who accepted with joy and terror this formidable succour. A palace was allotted for his reception, and a niece of the emperor was given in marriage to the valiant stranger, who was immediately created great duke or admiral of Romania. After a decent repose, he transported his troops over the Propontis, and boldly led them against the Turks: in two bloody battles thirty thousand of the Moslems were slain: he raised the siege of Philadelphia, and deserved the name of the deliverer of Asia. But after a short season of prosperity, the cloud of slavery and ruin again burst on that unhappy province. The inhabitants escaped (says a Greek historian) from the smoke into the flames; and the hostility of the Turks was less pernicious than the friendship of the Catalans. The lives and fortunes which they had rescued, they considered as their own: the willing or reluctant maid was saved from the race of circumcision for the embraces of a Christian soldier: the exaction of fines and supplies was enforced by licentious rapine and arbitrary executions; and, on the resistance of Magnesia, the great duke besieged a city of the Roman empire.[48] These disorders he excused by the wrongs and passions of a victorious army; nor would his own authority or person have been safe, had he dared to punish his faithful followers, who were defrauded of the just and covenanted price of their services. The threats and complaints of Andronicus disclosed the nakedness of the empire. His golden bull had invited no more than five hundred horse and a thousand foot soldiers; yet the crowds of volunteers, who migrated to the East, had been enlisted and fed by his

48. Some idea may be formed of the population of these cities, from the 36,000 inhabitants of Tralles, which, in the preceding reign, was rebuilt by the emperor, and ruined by the Turks (Pachymer, l. vi. c. 20, 21.).

spontaneous bounty. While his bravest allies were content with three byzants, or pieces of gold, for their monthly pay, an ounce, or even two ounces, of gold were assigned to the Catalans, whose annual pension would thus amount to near an hundred pounds sterling: one of their chiefs had modestly rated at three hundred thousand crowns the value of his *future* merits; and above a million had been issued from the treasury for the maintenance of these costly mercenaries. A cruel tax had been imposed on the corn of the husbandman: one third was retrenched from the salaries of the public officers; and the standard of the coin was so shamefully debased, that of the four-and-twenty parts only five were of pure gold.[49] At the summons of the emperor, Roger evacuated a province which no longer supplied the materials of rapine; but he refused to disperse his troops; and while his style was respectful, his conduct was independent and hostile. He protested, that if the emperor should march against him, he would advance forty paces to kiss the ground before him, but in rising from this prostrate attitude Roger had a life and sword at the service of his friends. The great duke of Romania condescended to accept the title and ornaments of Cæsar; but he rejected the new proposal of the government of Asia with a subsidy of corn and money, on condition that he should reduce his troops to the harmless number of three thousand men. Assassination is the last resource of cowards. The Cæsar was tempted to visit the royal residence of Adrianople: in the apartment, and before the eyes, of the empress, he was stabbed by the Alani guards; and, though the deed was imputed to their private revenge, his countrymen, who dwelt at Constantinople in the security of peace, were involved in the same proscription by the prince or people. The loss of their leader intimidated the crowd of adventurers, who hoisted the sails of flight, and were soon scattered round the coasts of the Mediterranean. But a veteran band of fifteen hundred Catalans or French stood firm in the strong fortress of Gallipoli on the Hellespont, displayed the banners of Arragon, and offered to revenge and justify their chief by an equal combat of ten or an hundred warriors. Instead of accepting this bold defiance, the

49. I have collected these pecuniary circumstances from Pachymer (l. xi. c. 21. l. xii. c. 4, 5. 8. 14. 19.), who describes the progressive degradation of the gold coin. Even in the prosperous times of John Ducas Vataces, the byzants were composed in equal proportions of the pure and the baser metal. The poverty of Michael Palæologus compelled him to strike a new coin, with nine parts, or carats, of gold, and fifteen of copper alloy. After his death, the standard rose to ten carats, till in the public distress it was reduced to the moiety. The prince was relieved for a moment, while credit and commerce were for ever blasted. In France, the gold coin is of twenty-two carats (one-twelfth alloy), and the standard of England and Holland is still higher.

emperor Michael, the son and colleague of Andronicus, resolved to oppress them with the weight of multitudes: every nerve was strained to form an army of thirteen thousand horse and thirty thousand foot; and the Propontis was covered with the ships of the Greeks and Genoese. In two battles by sea and land, these mighty forces were encountered and overthrown by the despair and discipline of the Catalans; the young emperor fled to the palace; and an insufficient guard of light-horse was left for the protection of the open country. Victory renewed the hopes and numbers of the adventurers: every nation was blended under the name and standard of the *great company*; and three thousand Turkish proselytes deserted from the Imperial service to join this military association. In the possession of Gallipoli, the Catalans intercepted the trade of Constantinople and the Black Sea, while they spread their devastations on either side of the Hellespont over the confines of Europe and Asia. To prevent their approach, the greatest part of the Byzantine territory was laid waste by the Greeks themselves: the peasants and their cattle retired into the city; and myriads of sheep and oxen, for which neither place nor food could be procured, were unprofitably slaughtered on the same day. Four times the emperor Andronicus sued for peace, and four times he was inflexibly repulsed, till the want of provisions, and the discord of the chiefs, compelled the Catalans to evacuate the banks of the Hellespont and the neighbourhood of the capital. After their separation from the Turks, the remains of the great company pursued their march through Macedonia and Thessaly, to seek a new establishment in the heart of Greece.[50]

Revolutions of Athens, A.D. 1204–1456.

After some ages of oblivion, Greece was awakened to new misfortunes by the arms of the Latins. In the two hundred and fifty years between the first and the last conquest of Constantinople, that venerable land was disputed by a multitude of petty tyrants; without the comforts of freedom and genius, her ancient cities were again plunged in foreign and intestine war; and, if servitude

50. The Catalan war is most copiously related by Pachymer, in the xi[th], xii[th], and xiii[th] books, till he breaks off in the year 1308. Nicephorus Gregoras (l. vii. 3–6.) is more concise and complete. Ducange, who adopts these adventurers as French, has hunted their footsteps with his usual diligence (Hist. de C. P. l. vi. c. 22–46.). He quotes an Arragonese history, which I have read with pleasure, and which the Spaniards extol as a model of style and composition (Expedicion de los Catalanes y Arragoneses contra Turcos y Griegos; Barcelona, 1623, in quarto; Madrid, 1777, in octavo). Don Francisco de Moncada, Conde de Osona, may imitate Cæsar or Sallust; he may transcribe the Greek or Italian contemporaries: but he never quotes his authorities, and I cannot discern any national records of the exploits of his countrymen.

be preferable to anarchy, they might repose with joy under the Turkish yoke. I shall not pursue the obscure and various dynasties, that rose and fell on the continent or in the isles; but our silence on the fate of ATHENS,[51] would argue a strange ingratitude to the first and purest school of liberal science and amusement. In the partition of the empire, the principality of Athens and Thebes was assigned to Otho de la Roche, a noble warrior of Burgundy,[52] with the title of great duke,[53] which the Latins understood in their own sense, and the Greeks more foolishly derived from the age of Constantine.[54] Otho followed the standard of the marquis of Montferrat; the ample state which he acquired by a miracle of conduct or fortune,[55] was peaceably inherited by his son and two grandsons, till the family, though not the nation, was changed, by the marriage of an heiress, into the elder branch of the house of Brienne. The son of that marriage, Walter de Brienne, succeeded to the dutchy of Athens; and, with the aid of some Catalan mercenaries, whom he invested with fiefs, reduced above thirty castles of the vassal or neighbouring lords. But when he was informed of the approach and ambition of the great company, he collected a force of seven hundred knights, six thousand four hundred horse, and eight thousand foot, and boldly met them on the banks of the river Cephisus in Bœotia. The Catalans amounted to no more than three thousand five hundred horse, and four thousand foot: but the deficiency of numbers was compensated by stratagem and order. They formed round their camp an artificial inundation: the duke and his knights advanced without fear or precaution on the verdant meadow: their horses plunged into the bog; and he was cut

51. See the laborious histories of Ducange, whose accurate table of the French dynasties, recapitulates the thirty-five passages in which he mentions the dukes of Athens.

52. He is twice mentioned by Villehardouin with honour (N° 151. 235.); and under the first passage, Ducange observes all that can be known of his person and family.

53. From these Latin princes of the xiv[th] century, Boccace, Chaucer and Shakespeare, have borrowed their Theseus *duke* of Athens. An ignorant age transfers its own language and manners to the most distant times.

54. The same Constantine gave to Sicily a king, to Russia the *magnus dapifer* of the empire, to Thebes the *primicerius*: and these absurd fables are properly lashed by Ducange (ad Nicephor. Greg. l. vii. c. 5.). By the Latins, the Lord of Thebes was styled by corruption the Megas Kurios, or Grand Sire!

55. *Quodam miraculo*, says Alberic. He was probably received by Michael Choniates, the archbishop who had defended Athens against the tyrant Leo Sgurus (Nicetas in Baldwino). Michael was the brother of the historian Nicetas; and his encomium of Athens is still extant in MS. in the Bodleian library (Fabric. Bibliot. Græc. tom. vi. p. 405.).

in pieces, with the greatest part of the French cavalry. His family and nation were expelled; and his son Walter de Brienne, the titular duke of Athens, the tyrant of Florence, and the constable of France, lost his life in the field of Poitiers. Attica and Bœotia were the rewards of the victorious Catalans: they married the widows and daughters of the slain; and during fourteen years, the great company was the terror of the Grecian states. Their factions drove them to acknowledge the sovereignty of the house of Arragon; and during the remainder of the fourteenth century, Athens, as a government or an appanage, was successively bestowed by the kings of Sicily. After the French and Catalans, the third dynasty was that of the Accaioli, a family, plebeian at Florence, potent at Naples, and sovereign in Greece. Athens, which they embellished with new buildings, became the capital of a state, that extended over Thebes, Argos, Corinth, Delphi, and a part of Thessaly; and their reign was finally determined by Mahomet the second, who strangled the last duke, and educated his sons in the discipline and religion of the seraglio.

Present state of Athens. Athens,[56] though no more than the shadow of her former self, still contains about eight or ten thousand inhabitants: of these, three-fourths are Greeks in religion and language; and the Turks, who compose the remainder, have relaxed, in their intercourse with the citizens, somewhat of the pride and gravity of their national character. The olive-tree, the gift of Minerva, flourishes in Attica; nor has the honey of mount Hymettus lost any part of its exquisite flavour:[57] but the languid trade is monopolised by strangers; and the agriculture of a barren land is abandoned to the vagrant Walachians. The Athenians are still distinguished by the subtlety and acuteness of their understandings: but these qualities, unless ennobled by freedom and enlightened by study, will degenerate into a low and selfish cunning: and it is a proverbial saying of the country, "From the Jews of Thessalonica, the Turks of Negropont, and the Greeks of Athens, good Lord deliver us!" This artful people has eluded the tyranny of the Turkish bashaws, by an expedient which

56. The modern account of Athens, and the Athenians, is extracted from Spon (Voyage en Grece, tom. ii. p. 79–199.) and Wheeler (Travels into Greece, p. 337–414.), Stuart (Antiquities of Athens, passim) and Chandler (Travels into Greece, p. 23–172.). The first of these travellers visited Greece in the year 1676, the last 1765; and ninety years had not produced much difference in the tranquil scene.

57. The ancients, or at least the Athenians, believed that all the bees in the world had been propagated from mount Hymettus. They taught, that health might be preserved, and life prolonged, by the external use of oil, and the internal use of honey (Geoponica, l. xv. c. 7. p. 1089–1094. edit. Niclas).

alleviates their servitude and aggravates their shame. About the middle of the last century, the Athenians chose for their protector the Kislar Aga, or chief black eunuch of the seraglio. This Æthiopian slave, who possesses the sultan's ear, condescends to accept the tribute of thirty thousand crowns: his lieutenant, the Waywode, whom he annually confirms, may reserve for his own about five or six thousand more; and such is the policy of the citizens, that they seldom fail to remove and punish an oppressive governor. Their private differences are decided by the archbishop, one of the richest prelates of the Greek church, since he possesses a revenue of one thousand pounds sterling; and by a tribunal of the eight *geronti* or elders, chosen in the eight quarters of the city: the noble families cannot trace their pedigree above three hundred years; but their principal members are distinguished by a grave demeanour, a fur-cap, and the lofty appellation of *archon*. By some, who delight in the contrast, the modern language of Athens is represented as the most corrupt and barbarous of the seventy dialects of the vulgar Greek:[58] this picture is too darkly coloured; but it would not be easy, in the country of Plato and Demosthenes, to find a reader, or a copy, of their works. The Athenians walk with supine indifference among the glorious ruins of antiquity; and such is the debasement of their character, that they are incapable of admiring the genius of their predecessors.[59]

58. Ducange, Glossar. Græc. Præfat. p. 8. who quotes for his author Theodosius Zygomalas, a modern grammarian. Yet Spon (tom. ii. p. 194.) and Wheeler (p. 355.), no incompetent judges, entertain a more favourable opinion of the Attic dialect.

59. Yet we must not accuse them of corrupting the name of Athens, which they still call Athini. From the *εις την Αθηνην*, we have formed our own barbarism of *Setines*.

CHAPTER LXIII

Civil Wars, and Ruin of the Greek Empire. – Reigns of Andronicus, the Elder and Younger, and John Palæologus. – Regency, Revolt, Reign, and Abdication of John Cantacuzene. – Establishment of a Genoese Colony at Pera or Galata. – Their Wars with the Empire and City of Constantinople.

Superstition of Andronicus and the times, A.D. 1282–1320.

The long reign of Andronicus[1] the elder is chiefly memorable, by the disputes of the Greek church, the invasion of the Catalans, and the rise of the Ottoman power. He is celebrated as the most learned and virtuous prince of the age; but such virtue, and such learning, contributed neither to the perfection of the individual, nor to the happiness of society. A slave of the most abject superstition, he was surrounded on all sides by visible and invisible enemies; nor were the flames of hell less dreadful to his fancy, than those of a Catalan or Turkish war. Under the reign of the Palæologi, the choice of the patriarch was the most important business of the state; the heads of the Greek church were ambitious and fanatic monks; and their vices or virtues, their learning or ignorance, were equally mischievous or contemptible. By his intemperate discipline, the patriarch Athanasius[2] excited the hatred of the clergy and people: he was heard to declare, that the sinner should swallow the last dregs of the cup of penance; and the foolish tale was propagated, of his punishing a sacrilegious ass that had tasted the lettuce of a convent garden. Driven from the throne by the universal clamour, Athanasius composed before his retreat two papers of a very opposite cast. His public testament was in the tone of charity and resignation; the private codicil breathed the direst anathemas against the authors of his disgrace, whom he excluded for ever from the communion

1. Andronicus himself will justify our freedom in the invective (Nicephorus Gregoras, l. i. c. 1.), which he pronounced against historic falsehood. It is true, that his censure is more pointedly urged against calumny than against adulation.

2. For the anathema in the pigeon's nest, see Pachymer (l. ix. c. 24.), who relates the general history of Athanasius (l. viii. c. 13–16. 20–24. l. x. c. 27–29. 31–36. l. xi. c. 1–3. 5, 6. l. xiii. c. 8. 10. 23. 35.), and is followed by Nicephorus Gregoras (l. vi. 5. 7. l. vii. c. 1. 9.), who includes the second retreat of this second Chrysostom.

of the holy trinity, the angels, and the saints. This last paper he inclosed in an earthen pot, which was placed, by his order, on the top of one of the pillars in the dome of St. Sophia, in the distant hope of discovery and revenge. At the end of four years, some youths, climbing by a ladder in search of pigeons nests, detected the fatal secret; and, as Andronicus felt himself touched and bound by the excommunication, he trembled on the brink of the abyss which had been so treacherously dug under his feet. A synod of bishops was instantly convened to debate this important question: the rashness of these clandestine anathemas was generally condemned; but as the knot could be untied only by the same hand, as that hand was now deprived of the crosier, it appeared that this posthumous decree was irrevocable by any earthly power. Some faint testimonies of repentance and pardon were extorted from the author of the mischief; but the conscience of the emperor was still wounded, and he desired, with no less ardour than Athanasius himself, the restoration of a patriarch, by whom alone he could be healed. At the dead of night, a monk rudely knocked at the door of the royal bed-chamber, announcing a revelation of plague and famine, of inundations and earthquakes. Andronicus started from his bed, and spent the night in prayer, till he felt, or thought that he felt, a slight motion of the earth. The emperor on foot led the bishops and monks to the cell of Athanasius; and, after a proper resistance, the saint, from whom this message had been sent, consented to absolve the prince, and govern the church, of Constantinople. Untamed by disgrace, and hardened by solitude, the shepherd was again odious to the flock; and his enemies contrived a singular, and as it proved a successful, mode of revenge. In the night, they stole away the footstool or foot-cloth of his throne, which they secretly replaced with the decoration of a satirical picture. The emperor was painted with a bridle in his mouth, and Athanasius leading the tractable beast to the feet of Christ. The authors of the libel were detected and punished; but as their lives had been spared, the Christian priest in sullen indignation retired to his cell; and the eyes of Andronicus, which had been opened for a moment, were again closed by his successor.

If this transaction be one of the most curious and important of a reign of fifty years, I cannot at least accuse the brevity of my materials, since I reduce into some few pages the enormous folios of Pachymer,[3] Cantacuzene,[4]

3. Pachymer, in seven books, 377 folio pages, describes the first twenty-six years of Andronicus the Elder; and marks the date of his composition by the current news or lye of the day (A.D. 1308). Either death or disgust prevented him from resuming the pen.

4. After an interval of twelve years, from

and Nicephorus Gregoras,[5] who have composed the prolix and languid story of the times. The name and situation of the emperor John Cantacuzene might inspire the most lively curiosity. His memorials of forty years extend from the revolt of the younger Andronicus to his own abdication of the empire; and it is observed, that, like Moses and Cæsar, he was the principal actor in the scenes which he describes. But in this eloquent work, we should vainly seek the sincerity of an hero or a penitent. Retired in a cloyster from the vices and passions of the world, he presents not a confession, but an apology, of the life of an ambitious statesman. Instead of unfolding the true counsels and characters of men, he displays the smooth and specious surface of events, highly varnished with his own praises and those of his friends. Their motives are always pure; their ends always legitimate: they conspire and rebel without any views of interest; and the violence which they inflict or suffer is celebrated as the spontaneous effect of reason and virtue.

First disputes between the elder and younger Andronicus, A.D. 1320.

After the example of the first of the Palæologi, the elder Andronicus associated his son Michael to the honours of the purple; and from the age of eighteen to his premature death, that prince was acknowledged, above twenty-five years, as the second emperor of the Greeks.[6] At the head of an army, he excited neither the fears of the enemy nor the jealousy of the court: his modesty and patience were never tempted to compute the years of his father; nor was that father compelled to repent of his liberality either by the virtues or vices of his son. The son of Michael was named Andronicus from his grandfather, to whose early favour he was introduced by that nominal resemblance. The blossoms of wit and beauty increased the fondness of the elder Andronicus; and, with the common vanity of age, he expected to realize in the second, the hope which had been

---

the conclusion of Pachymer, Cantacuzenus takes up the pen; and his first book (c. 1–59. p. 9–150.) relates the civil war, and the eight last years of the elder Andronicus. The ingenious comparison with Moses and Cæsar, is fancied by his French translator, the president Cousin.

5. Nicephorus Gregoras more briefly includes the entire life and reign of Andronicus the Elder (l. vi. c. 1–l. x. c. 1. p.96–291.). This is the part of which Cantacuzene complains as a false and malicious representation of his conduct.

6. He was crowned May 21st, 1295, and died October 12th, 1320 (Ducange, Fam. Byz. p. 239.). His brother Theodore, by a second marriage, inherited the marquisate of Montferrat, apostatised to the religion and manners of the Latins (ὁτι και γνωμῃ και πιστει και σχηματι, και γενειων κουρα και πασιν εθεσιν Λατινος ην ακραιφνης. Nic. Greg. l. ix. c. 1.), and founded a dynasty of Italian princes, which was extinguished A.D. 1533 (Ducange, Fam. Byz. p. 249–253.).

disappointed in the first, generation. The boy was educated in the palace as an heir and a favourite; and, in the oaths and acclamations of the people, the *august triad* was formed by the names of the father, the son, and the grandson. But the younger Andronicus was speedily corrupted by his infant greatness, while he beheld with puerile impatience the double obstacle that hung, and might long hang, over his rising ambition. It was not to acquire fame, or to diffuse happiness, that he so eagerly aspired: wealth and impunity were in his eyes the most precious attributes of a monarch; and his first indiscreet demand was the sovereignty of some rich and fertile island, where he might lead a life of independence and pleasure. The emperor was offended by the loud and frequent intemperance which disturbed his capital: the sums which his parsimony denied were supplied by the Genoese usurers of Pera; and the oppressive debt, which consolidated the interest of a faction, could be discharged only by a revolution. A beautiful female, a matron in rank, a prostitute in manners, had instructed the younger Andronicus in the rudiments of love; but he had reason to suspect the nocturnal visits of a rival; and a stranger passing through the street was pierced by the arrows of his guards, who were placed in ambush at her door. That stranger was his brother, prince Manuel, who languished and died of his wound; and the emperor Michael, their common father, whose health was in a declining state, expired on the eighth day, lamenting the loss of both his children.[7] However guiltless in his intention, the younger Andronicus might impute a brother's and a father's death to the consequence of his own vices; and deep was the sigh of thinking and feeling men, when they perceived, instead of sorrow and repentance, his ill-dissembled joy on the removal of two odious competitors. By these melancholy events, and the increase of his disorders, the mind of the elder emperor was gradually alienated; and, after many fruitless reproofs, he transferred on another grandson[8] his hopes and affection. The change was announced by the new oath of allegiance to the reigning sovereign, and the *person* whom he should appoint for his successor; and the acknowledged heir, after a repetition of insults and complaints, was exposed to the indignity of a public trial. Before the sentence, which would probably have condemned him to a

7. We are indebted to Nicephorus Gregoras (l. viii. c. 1.) for the knowledge of this tragic adventure; while Cantacuzene more discreetly conceals the vices of Andronicus the Younger, of which he was the witness, and perhaps the associate (l. i. c. 1, &c.).

8. His destined heir was Michael Catharus, the bastard of Constantine his second son. In this project of excluding his grandson Andronicus, Nicephorus Gregoras (l. viii. c. 3.) agrees with Cantacuzene (l. i. c. 1, 2.).

dungeon or a cell, the emperor was informed that the palace courts were filled with the armed followers of his grandson; the judgment was softened to a treaty of reconciliation; and the triumphant escape of the prince encouraged the ardour of the younger faction.

Three civil wars between the two emperors, A.D. 1321, April 20– A.D. 1328, May 24.

Yet the capital, the clergy, and the senate, adhered to the person, or at least to the government, of the old emperor; and it was only in the provinces, by flight, and revolt, and foreign succour, that the malecontents could hope to vindicate their cause and subvert his throne. The soul of the enterprise was the great domestic John Cantacuzene: the sally from Constantinople is the first date of his actions and memorials; and if his own pen be most descriptive of his patriotism, an unfriendly historian has not refused to celebrate the zeal and ability which he displayed in the service of the young emperor. That prince escaped from the capital under the pretence of hunting; erected his standard at Adrianople; and, in a few days, assembled fifty thousand horse and foot, whom neither honour nor duty could have armed against the Barbarians. Such a force might have saved or commanded the empire; but their counsels were discordant, their motions were slow and doubtful, and their progress was checked by intrigue and negociation. The quarrel of the two Andronici was protracted, and suspended, and renewed, during a ruinous period of seven years. In the first treaty, the relics of the Greek empire were divided: Constantinople, Thessalonica, and the islands, were left to the elder, while the younger acquired the sovereignty of the greatest part of Thrace, from Philippi to the Byzantine limit. By the second treaty, he stipulated the payment of his troops, his immediate coronation, and an adequate share of the power and revenue of the state. The third civil war was terminated by the surprise of Constantinople, the final retreat of the old emperor, and the sole reign of his victorious grandson. The reasons of this delay may be found in the characters of the men and of the times. When the heir of the monarchy first pleaded his wrongs and his apprehensions, he was heard with pity and applause: and his adherents repeated on all sides the inconsistent promise, that he would increase the pay of the soldiers and alleviate the burthens of the people. The grievances of forty years were mingled in his revolt; and the rising generation was fatigued by the endless prospect of a reign, whose favourites and maxims were of other times. The youth of Andronicus had been without spirit, his age was without reverence: his taxes produced an annual revenue of five hundred thousand pounds; yet the richest of the sovereigns of Christendom was

Coronation of the younger Andronicus, A.D. 1325, February 2.

incapable of maintaining three thousand horse and twenty gallies, to resist the destructive progress of the Turks.[9] "How different," said the younger Andronicus, "is my situation from that of the son of Philip! Alexander might complain, that his father would leave him nothing to conquer: alas! my grandsire will leave me nothing to lose." But the Greeks were soon admonished, that the public disorders could not be healed by a civil war; and that their young favourite was not destined to be the saviour of a falling empire. On the first repulse, his party was broken by his own levity, their intestine discord, and the intrigues of the ancient court, which tempted each malcontent to desert or betray the cause of rebellion. Andronicus the younger was touched with remorse, or fatigued with business, or deceived by negociation: pleasure rather than power was his aim; and the licence of maintaining a thousand hounds, a thousand hawks, and a thousand huntsmen, was sufficient to sully his fame and disarm his ambition.

The elder Andronicus abdicates the government, A.D. 1328, May 24.

Let us now survey the catastrophe of this busy plot, and the final situation of the principal actors.[10] The age of Andronicus was consumed in civil discord; and, amidst the events of war and treaty, his power and reputation continually decayed, till the fatal night in which the gates of the city and palace were opened without resistance to his grandson. His principal commander scorned the repeated warnings of danger; and retiring to rest in the vain security of ignorance, abandoned the feeble monarch, with some priests and pages, to the terrors of a sleepless night. These terrors were quickly realized by the hostile shouts, which proclaimed the titles and victory of Andronicus the younger; and the aged emperor, falling prostrate before an image of the Virgin, dispatched a suppliant message to resign the sceptre, and to obtain his life at the hands of the conqueror. The answer of his grandson was decent and pious; at the prayer of his friends, the younger Andronicus assumed the sole administration; but the elder still enjoyed the name and pre-eminence of the first emperor, the use of the great palace, and a pension of twenty-four thousand pieces of gold, one half of which was assigned on the royal treasure, and the other on the fishery

9. See Nicephorus Gregoras, l. viii. c. 6. The younger Andronicus complained, that in four years and four months, a sum of 350,000 byzants of gold was due to him for the expences of his household (Cantacuzen. l. i. c. 48.). Yet he would have remitted the debt, if he might have been allowed to squeeze the farmers of the revenue.

10. I follow the chronology of Nicephorus Gregoras, who is remarkably exact. It is proved, that Cantacuzene has mistaken the dates of his own actions, or rather that his text has been corrupted by ignorant transcribers.

of Constantinople. But his impotence was soon exposed to contempt and oblivion; the vast silence of the palace was disturbed only by the cattle and poultry of the neighbourhood, which roved with impunity through the solitary courts; and a reduced allowance of ten thousand pieces of gold[11] was all that he could ask, and more than he could hope. His calamities were embittered by the gradual extinction of sight; his confinement was rendered each day more rigorous; and during the absence and sickness of his grandson, his inhuman keepers, by the threats of instant death, compelled him to exchange the purple for the monastic habit and profession. The monk *Antony* had renounced the pomp of the world: yet he had occasion for a coarse fur in the winter season, and as wine was forbidden by his confessor, and water by his physician, the sherbet of Egypt was his common drink. It was not without difficulty that the late emperor could procure three or four pieces to satisfy these simple wants; and if he bestowed the gold to relieve the more painful distress of a friend, the sacrifice is of some weight in the scale of humanity and religion. Four years after his abdication, Andronicus or Antony expired in a cell, in the seventy-fourth year of his age: and the last strain of adulation could only promise a more splendid crown of glory in heaven, than he had enjoyed upon earth.[12]

His death, A.D. 1332, February 13.

Reign of Andronicus the younger, A.D. 1328, May 24– A.D. 1341, June 15.

Nor was the reign of the younger, more glorious or fortunate than that of the elder, Andronicus.[13] He gathered the fruits of ambition; but the taste was transient and bitter: in the supreme station he lost the remains of his early popularity; and the defects of his character became still more conspicuous to the world. The public reproach urged him to march in person against the Turks; nor did his courage fail in the hour of trial; but a defeat and a wound were the only trophies of his expedition in Asia, which confirmed the establishment of the Ottoman monarchy. The abuses of the civil government attained their full maturity and perfection: his neglect of forms, and the confusion of national dresses, are deplored by the Greeks

11. I have endeavoured to reconcile the 24,000 pieces of Cantacuzene (l. ii. c. 1.) with the 10,000 of Nicephorus Gregoras (l. ix. c. 2.); the one of whom wished to soften, the other to magnify, the hardships of the old emperors.

12. See Nicephorus Gregoras (l. ix. 6, 7, 8. 10. 14. l. x. c. 1.). The historian had tasted of the prosperity, and shared the retreat, of his benefactor; and that friendship, which "waits or to the scaffold or the cell," should not lightly be accused as "a hireling, a prostitute to praise."

13. The sole reign of Andronicus the younger is described by Cantacuzene (l. ii. c. 1–40. p. 191–339.) and Nicephorus Gregoras (l. ix. c. 7–l. xi. c. 11. p. 262–361.).

as the fatal symptoms of the decay of the empire. Andronicus was old before his time: the intemperance of youth had accelerated the infirmities of age; and after being rescued from a dangerous malady by nature, or physic, or the Virgin, he was snatched away before he had accomplished his forty-fifth year. He was twice married; and as the progress of the Latins in arms and arts had softened the prejudices of the Byzantine court, his two wives were chosen in the princely houses of Germany and Italy. The first, Agnes at home, Irene in Greece, was daughter of the duke of Brunswick. Her father[14] was a petty lord[15] in the poor and savage regions of the north of Germany:[16] yet he derived some revenue from his silver-mines;[17] and his family is celebrated by the Greeks as the most ancient and noble of the Teutonic name.[18] After the death of this childless princess, Andronicus sought in marriage Jane, the sister of the count of

His two wives.

14. Agnes, or Irene, was the daughter of duke Henry the Wonderful, the chief of the house of Brunswick, and the fourth in descent from the famous Henry the Lion, duke of Saxony and Bavaria, and conqueror of the Slavi on the Baltic coast. Her brother Henry was surnamed the *Greek*, from his two journies into the East: but these journies were subsequent to his sister's marriage; and I am ignorant *how* Agnes was discovered in the heart of Germany, and recommended to the Byzantine court (Rimius, Memoirs of the House of Brunswick, p. 126–137.).

15. Henry the Wonderful was the founder of the branch of Grubenhagen, extinct in the year 1596 (Rimius, p. 287.). He resided in the castle of Wolfenbuttel, and possessed no more than a sixth part of the allodial estates of Brunswick and Luneburgh, which the Guelph family had saved from the confiscation of their great fiefs. The frequent partitions among brothers, had almost ruined the princely houses of Germany, till that just, but pernicious, law was slowly superseded by the right of primogeniture. The principality of Grubenhagen, one of the last remains of the Hercynian forest, is a woody, mountainous, and barren tract (Busching's Geography, vol. vi. p. 270–286. English translation.).

16. The royal author of the Memoirs of Brandenburgh will teach us, how justly, in a much later period, the north of Germany deserved the epithets of poor and barbarous (Essai sur les Mœurs, &c.). In the year 1306, in the woods of Luneburgh, some wild people of the Vened race were allowed to bury alive their infirm and useless parents (Rimius, p. 136.).

17. The assertion of Tacitus, that Germany was destitute of the precious metals, must be taken, even in his own time, with some limitation (Germania, c. 5. Annal. xi. 20.). According to Spener (Hist. Germaniæ Pragmatica, tom. i. p. 351.), *Argentifodinæ* in Hercyniis montibus, imperante Othone magno (A.D. 968) primum apertæ, largam etiam opes augendi dederunt copiam: but Rimius (p. 258, 259.) defers till the year 1016 the discovery of the silver mines of Grubenhagen, or the Upper Hartz, which were productive in the beginning of the xiv[th] century, and which still yield a considerable revenue to the house of Brunswick.

18. Cantacuzene has given a most honourable testimony, *ην δ' εκ Γερμανων ἀυτη θυγατηρ δουκος ντι μπρουζουικ* (the modern Greeks employ the *ντ* for the *δ*, and the *μπ* for the *β*, and the whole will read in the Italian idiom di Brunzuic),

Savoy;[19] and his suit was preferred to that of the French king.[20] The count respected in his sister the superior majesty of a Roman empress: her retinue was composed of knights and ladies; she was regenerated and crowned in St. Sophia, under the more orthodox appellation of Anne; and, at the nuptial feast, the Greeks and Italians vied with each other in the martial exercises of tilts and tournaments.

Reign of John Palæologus, A.D. 1341, June 15–A.D. 1391. Fortune of John Cantacuzenus.

The empress Anne of Savoy survived her husband: their son, John Palæologus, was left an orphan and an emperor, in the ninth year of his age; and his weakness was protected by the first and most deserving of the Greeks. The long and cordial friendship of his father for John Cantacuzene is alike honourable to the prince and the subject. It had been formed amidst the pleasures of their youth: their families were almost equally noble;[21] and the recent lustre of the purple was amply compensated by the energy of a private education. We have seen that the young emperor was saved by Cantacuzene from the power of his grandfather; and, after six years of civil war, the same favourite brought him back in triumph to the palace of Constantinople. Under the reign of Andronicus the younger, the great domestic ruled the emperor and the empire; and it was by his valour and conduct that the isle of Lesbos and the principality of Ætolia were restored to their ancient allegiance. His enemies confess, that, among the public robbers, Cantacuzene alone was moderate and abstemious; and the free and voluntary account which he produces of his own wealth[22] may sustain the presumption that it was devolved by inheritance, and not accumulated by rapine. He does not indeed specify the value of his money, plate, and jewels; yet, after a voluntary gift of two hundred vases of silver, after much had been secreted by his friends and plundered by his foes, his forfeit treasures were sufficient for the equipment of a fleet of seventy gallies. He does not measure the size and number of his estates;

του παρ' αυτοις επιφανεστατου, και λαμπροτητι παντας τους ὁμοφυλους ὑπερβαλλοντος του γενους. The praise is just in itself, and pleasing to an English ear.

19. Anne, or Jane, was one of the four daughters of Amedée the Great, by a second marriage, and half sister of his successor Edward count of Savoy (Anderson's Tables, p. 650.). See Cantacuzene (l. i. c. 40–42.).

20. That king, if the fact be true, must have been Charles the Fair, who in five years (1321–1326) was married to three wives (Anderson, p. 628.). Anne of Savoy arrived at Constantinople in February 1326.

21. The noble race of the Cantacuzeni (illustrious from the xi[th] century in the Byzantine annals) was drawn from the Paladins of France, the heroes of those romances which in the xiii[th] century were translated and read by the Greeks (Ducange, Fam. Byzant. p. 258.).

22. See Cantacuzene (l. iii. c. 24. 30. 36.).

but his granaries were heaped with an incredible store of wheat and barley; and the labour of a thousand yoke of oxen might cultivate, according to the practice of antiquity, about sixty-two thousand five hundred acres of arable land.[23] His pastures were stocked with two thousand five hundred brood mares, two hundred camels, three hundred mules, five hundred asses, five thousand horned cattle, fifty thousand hogs, and seventy thousand sheep:[24] a precious record of rural opulence, in the last period of the empire, and in a land, most probably in Thrace, so repeatedly wasted by foreign and domestic hostility. The favour of Cantacuzene was above his fortune. In the moments of familiarity, in the hour of sickness, the emperor was desirous to level the distance between them, and pressed his friend to accept the diadem and purple. The virtue of the great domestic, which is attested by his own pen, resisted the dangerous proposal; but the last testament of Andronicus the younger named him the guardian of his son, and the regent of the empire.

He is left regent of the empire.

His regency is attacked, A.D. 1341,

Had the regent found a suitable return of obedience and gratitude, perhaps he would have acted with pure and zealous fidelity in the service of his pupil.[25] A guard of five hundred soldiers watched over his person and the palace; the funeral of the late emperor was decently performed; the capital was silent and submissive; and five hundred letters, which Cantacuzene dispatched in the first month, informed the provinces of their loss and their duty. The prospect of a tranquil minority was blasted by the great duke or admiral Apocaucus; and to exaggerate *his* perfidy, the Imperial historian is pleased to magnify his own imprudence, in raising him to that office against the advice of his more sagacious sovereign. Bold and subtle, rapacious and profuse, the avarice and ambition of Apocaucus were by turns subservient to each other; and his talents were applied to the ruin of his country. His

by Apocaucus;

23. Saserna, in Gaul, and Columella, in Italy or Spain, allow two yoke of oxen, two drivers, and six labourers, for two hundred jugera (125 English acres) of arable land, and three more men must be added if there be much underwood (Columella de Re Rusticâ, l. ii. c. 13. p. 441. edit. Gesner).

24. In this enumeration (l. iii. c. 30.), the French translation of the president Cousin is blotted with three palpable and essential errors. 1. He omits the 1000 yoke of working oxen. 2. He interprets the πεντακοσιαι προς δισχιλιαις, by the number of fifteen hundred. 3. He confounds myriads with chiliads, and gives Cantacuzene no more than 5000 hogs. Put not your trust in translations!

25. See the regency and reign of John Cantacuzenus, and the whole progress of the civil war, in his own history (l. iii. c. 1–100. p. 348–700.), and in that of Nicephorus Gregoras (l. xii. c. 1 – l. xv. c. 9. p. 353–492.).

arrogance was heightened by the command of a naval force and an impregnable castle, and under the mask of oaths and flattery he secretly conspired against his benefactor. The female court of the empress was bribed and directed: he encouraged Anne of Savoy to assert, by the law of nature, the tutelage of her son; the love of power was disguised by the anxiety of maternal tenderness; and the founder of the Palæologi had instructed his posterity to dread the example of a perfidious guardian. The patriarch John of Apri, was a proud and feeble old man, encompassed by a numerous and hungry kindred. He produced an obsolete epistle of Andronicus, which bequeathed the prince and people to his pious care: the fate of his predecessor Arsenius prompted him to prevent, rather than punish, the crimes of an usurper; and Apocaucus smiled at the success of his own flattery, when he beheld the Byzantine priest assuming the state and temporal claims of the Roman pontiff.[26] Between three persons so different in their situation and character, a private league was concluded: a shadow of authority was restored to the senate; and the people was tempted by the name of freedom. By this powerful confederacy, the great domestic was assaulted at first with clandestine, at length with open, arms. His prerogatives were disputed; his opinions slighted; his friends persecuted; and his safety was threatened both in the camp and city. In his absence on the public service, he was accused of treason; proscribed as an enemy of the church and state; and delivered, with all his adherents, to the sword of justice, the vengeance of the people, and the power of the devil: his fortunes were confiscated; his aged mother was cast into prison; all his past services were buried in oblivion; and he was driven by injustice to perpetrate the crime of which he was accused.[27] From the review of his preceding conduct, Cantacuzene appears to have been guiltless of any treasonable designs; and the only suspicion of his innocence must arise from the vehemence of his protestations, and the sublime purity which he ascribes to his own virtue. While the empress and the patriarch still affected the appearances of harmony, he repeatedly solicited the permission of retiring

by the empress Anne of Savoy;

by the patriarch.

26. He assumed the royal privilege of red shoes or buskins; placed on his head a mitre of silk and gold; subscribed his epistles with hyacinth or green ink, and claimed for the new, whatever Constantine had given to the ancient, Rome (Cantacuzen. l. iii. c. 36. Nic. Gregoras, l. xiv. c. 3.).

27. Nic. Gregoras (l. xii. c. 5.) confesses the innocence and virtues of Cantacuzenus, the guilt and flagitious vices of Apocaucus; nor does he dissemble the motive of his personal and religious enmity to the former; *νυν δε δια κακιαν αλλων, αιτιος ὁ πραοτατος της των ὁλων εδοξεν ειναι φθορας.*

to a private, and even a monastic, life. After he had been declared a public enemy, it was his fervent wish to throw himself at the feet of the young emperor, and to receive without a murmur the stroke of the executioner: it was not without reluctance that he listened to the voice of reason, which inculcated the sacred duty of saving his family and friends, and proved that he could only save them by drawing the sword and assuming the Imperial title.

Cantacuzene assumes the purple, A.D. 1341, October 26.

In the strong city of Demotica, his peculiar domain, the emperor John Cantacuzenus was invested with the purple buskins: his right-leg was clothed by his noble kinsmen, the left by the Latin chiefs, on whom he conferred the order of knighthood. But even in this act of revolt, he was still studious of loyalty; and the titles of John Palæologus and Anne of Savoy were proclaimed before his own name and that of his wife Irene. Such vain ceremony is a thin disguise of rebellion, nor are there perhaps any *personal* wrongs that can authorise a subject to take arms against his sovereign: but the want of preparation and success may confirm the assurance of the usurper, that this decisive step was the effect of necessity rather than of choice. Constantinople adhered to the young emperor: the king of Bulgaria was invited to the relief of Adrianople: the principal cities of Thrace and Macedonia, after some hesitation, renounced their obedience to the great domestic; and the leaders of the troops and provinces were induced, by their private interest, to prefer the loose dominion of a woman and a priest. The army of Cantacuzene, in sixteen divisions, was stationed on the banks of the Melas to tempt or intimidate the capital: it was dispersed by treachery or fear; and the officers, more especially the mercenary Latins, accepted the bribes, and embraced the service, of the Byzantine court. After this loss, the rebel emperor (he fluctuated between the two characters) took the road of Thessalonica with a chosen remnant; but he failed in his enterprise on that important place; and he was closely pursued by the great duke, his enemy Apocaucus, at the head of a superior power by sea and land. Driven from the coast, in his march, or rather flight, into the mountains of Servia, Cantacuzene assembled his troops to scrutinize those who were worthy and willing to accompany his broken fortunes. A base majority bowed and retired; and his trusty band was diminished to two thousand, and at last to five hundred, volunteers. The *cral*,[28] or despot of the Servians, received him with generous

28. The princes of Servia (Ducange, Famil. Dalmaticæ, &c. c. 2, 3, 4. 9.) were styled Despots in Greek, and Cral, in their native idiom (Ducange, Gloss. Græc.

hospitality; but the ally was insensibly degraded to a suppliant, an hostage, a captive; and, in this miserable dependence, he waited at the door of the Barbarian, who could dispose of the life and liberty of a Roman emperor. The most tempting offers could not persuade the cral to violate his trust; but he soon inclined to the stronger side; and his friend was dismissed without injury to a new vicissitude of hopes and perils. Near six years the flame of discord burnt with various success and unabated rage: the cities were distracted by the faction of the nobles and the plebeians; the Cantacuzeni and Palæologi: and the Bulgarians, the Servians, and the Turks, were invoked on both sides as the instruments of private ambition and the common ruin. The regent deplored the calamities, of which he was the author and victim: and his own experience might dictate a just and lively remark on the different nature of foreign and civil war. "The former," said he, "is the external warmth of summer, always tolerable, and often beneficial; the latter is the deadly heat of a fever, which consumes without a remedy the vitals of the constitution."[29]

The civil war, A.D. 1341–1347.

Victory of Cantacuzene.

The introduction of barbarians and savages into the contests of civilized nations, is a measure pregnant with shame and mischief; which the interest of the moment may compel, but which is reprobated by the best principles of humanity and reason. It is the practice of both sides to accuse their enemies of the guilt of the first alliances; and those who fail in their negociations, are loudest in their censure of the example which they envy, and would gladly imitate. The Turks of Asia were less barbarous perhaps than the shepherds of Bulgaria and Servia; but their religion rendered them the implacable foes of Rome and Christianity. To acquire the friendship of their emirs, the two factions vied with each other in baseness and profusion: the dexterity of Cantacuzene obtained the preference: but the succour and victory were dearly purchased by the marriage of his daughter with an infidel, the captivity of many thousand Christians, and the passage of the Ottomans into Europe, the last and fatal stroke in the fall of the Roman empire. The inclining

p. 751.). That title, the equivalent of king, appears to be of Sclavonic origin, from whence it has been borrowed by the Hungarians, the modern Greeks, and even by the Turks (Leunclavius, Pandect. Turc. p. 422.), who reserve the name of Padishah for the emperor. To obtain the latter instead of the former, is the ambition of the French at Constantinople (Avertissement à l'Histoire de Timur Bec, p. 39.).

29. Nic. Gregoras, l. xii. c. 14. It is surprising, that Cantacuzene has not inserted this just and lively image in his own writings.

scale was decided in his favour by the death of Apocaucus, the just, though singular, retribution of his crimes. A crowd of nobles or plebeians, whom he feared or hated, had been seized by his orders in the capital and the provinces; and the old palace of Constantine was assigned for the place of their confinement. Some alterations in raising the walls, and narrowing the cells, had been ingeniously contrived to prevent their escape, and aggravate their misery; and the work was incessantly pressed by the daily visits of the tyrant. His guards watched at the gate, and as he stood in the inner-court to overlook the architects, without fear or suspicion, he was assaulted and laid breathless on the ground, by two resolute prisoners of the Palæologian race,[30] who were armed with sticks, and animated by despair. On the rumour of revenge and liberty, the captive multitude broke their fetters, fortified their prison, and exposed from the battlements the tyrant's head, presuming on the favour of the people and the clemency of the empress. Anne of Savoy might rejoice in the fall of an haughty and ambitious minister, but while she delayed to resolve or to act, the populace, more especially the mariners, were excited by the widow of the great duke to a sedition, an assault, and a massacre. The prisoners (of whom the far greater part were guiltless or inglorious of the deed) escaped to a neighbouring church: they were slaughtered at the foot of the altar; and in his death the monster was not less bloody and venomous than in his life. Yet his talents alone upheld the cause of the young emperor; and his surviving associates, suspicious of each other, abandoned the conduct of the war, and rejected the fairest terms of accommodation. In the beginning of the dispute, the empress felt and complained, that she was deceived by the enemies of Cantacuzene: the patriarch was employed to preach against the forgiveness of injuries; and her promise of immortal hatred was sealed by an oath, under the penalty of excommunication.[31] But Anne soon learned to hate without a teacher: she beheld the misfortunes of the empire with the indifference of a stranger: her jealousy was exasperated by the competition of a rival empress; and on the first symptoms of a more yielding temper, she threatened the patriarch to convene a synod, and degrade him from his office. Their incapacity and discord would have afforded the most decisive

30. The two avengers were both Palæologi, who might resent, with royal indignation, the shame of their chains. The tragedy of Apocaucus may deserve a peculiar reference to Cantacuzene (l. iii. c. 86.) and Nic. Gregoras (l. xiv. c. 10.).

31. Cantacuzene accuses the patriarch, and spares the empress, the mother of his sovereign (l. iii. 33, 34.), against whom Nic. Gregoras expresses a particular ani-

advantage; but the civil war was protracted by the weakness of both parties; and the moderation of Cantacuzene has not escaped the reproach of timidity and indolence. He successively recovered the provinces and cities; and the realm of his pupil was measured by the walls of Constantinople; but the metropolis alone counterbalanced the rest of the empire; nor could he attempt that important conquest till he had secured in his favour the public voice and a private correspondence. An Italian, of the name of Facciolati,[32] had succeeded to the office of great duke: the ships, the guards, and the golden gate, were subject to his command; but his humble ambition was bribed to become the instrument of treachery; and the revolution was accomplished without danger or bloodshed. Destitute of the powers of resistance, or the hope of relief, the inflexible Anne would have still defended the palace, and have smiled to behold the capital in flames, rather than in the possession of a rival. She yielded to the prayers of her friends and enemies; and the treaty was dictated by the conqueror, who professed a loyal and zealous attachment to the son of his benefactor. The marriage of his daughter with John Palæologus was at length consummated: the hereditary right of the pupil was acknowledged; but the sole administration during ten years was vested in the guardian. Two emperors and three empresses were seated on the Byzantine throne; and a general amnesty quieted the apprehensions, and confirmed the property, of the most guilty subjects. The festival of the coronation and nuptials was celebrated with the appearances of concord and magnificence, and both were equally fallacious. During the late troubles, the treasures of the state, and even the furniture of the palace, had been alienated or embezzled: the royal banquet was served in pewter or earthen-ware; and such was the proud poverty of the times, that the absence of gold and jewels was supplied by the paltry artifices of glass and gilt-leather.[33]

He re-enters Constantinople, A.D. 1347, January 8.

I hasten to conclude the personal history of John Cantacuzene.[34] He triumphed and reigned; but his reign and triumph were clouded by the discontent of his own and the

Reign of John Cantacuzene, A.D. 1347,

mosity (l. xiv. 10, 11. xv. 5.). It is true, that they do not speak exactly of the same time.

32. The traitor and treason are revealed by Nic. Gregoras (l. xv. c. 8.): but the name is more discreetly suppressed by his great accomplice (Cantacuzen, l. iii. c. 99.).

33. Nic. Greg. l. xv. 11. There were however some true pearls, but very thinly sprinkled. The rest of the stones had only παντοδαπην χροιαν προς το διαυγες.

34. From his return to Constantinople, Cantacuzene continues his history, and that of the empire, one year beyond the abdication of his son Matthew, A.D. 1357 (l. iv. c. 1–50. p. 705–911.). Nicephorus Gregoras

adverse faction. His followers might style the general amnesty, an act of pardon for his enemies, and of oblivion for his friends:[35] in his cause, their estates had been forfeited or plundered; and as they wandered naked and hungry through the streets, they cursed the selfish generosity of a leader; who, on the throne of the empire, might relinquish without merit his private inheritance. The adherents of the empress blushed to hold their lives and fortunes by the precarious favour of an usurper; and the thirst of revenge was concealed by a tender concern for the succession, and even the safety, of her son. They were justly alarmed by a petition of the friends of Cantacuzene, that they might be released from their oath of allegiance to the Palæologi; and entrusted with the defence of some cautionary towns; a measure supported with argument and eloquence; and which was rejected (says the Imperial historian) "by *my* sublime, and almost incredible, virtue." His repose was disturbed by the sound of plots and seditions; and he trembled, lest the lawful prince should be stolen away by some foreign or domestic enemy, who would inscribe his name and his wrongs in the banners of rebellion. As the son of Andronicus advanced in the years of manhood, he began to feel and to act for himself; and his rising ambition was rather stimulated than checked by the imitation of his father's vices. If we may trust his own professions, Cantacuzene laboured with honest industry to correct these sordid and sensual appetites, and to raise the mind of the young prince to a level with his fortune. In the Servian expedition, the two emperors shewed themselves in cordial harmony to the troops and provinces; and the younger colleague was initiated by the elder in the mysteries of war and government. After the conclusion of the peace, Palæologus was left at Thessalonica, a royal residence, and a frontier station, to secure by his absence the peace of Constantinople, and to withdraw his youth from the temptations of a luxurious capital. But the distance weakened the powers of control, and the son of Andronicus was surrounded with artful or unthinking companions, who taught him to hate his guardian, to deplore his exile, and to vindicate his rights. A private treaty with the cral or despot of Servia, was soon followed by an

January 8–A.D. 1355, January.

ends with the synod of Constantinople, in the year 1351 (l. xxii. c. 3. p. 660. the rest to the conclusion of the xxivth book, p. 717. is all controversy); and his fourteen last books are still MSS. in the king of France's library.

35. The emperor (Cantacuzen, l. iv. c. 1.) represents his own virtue, and Nic. Gregoras (l. xv. c. 11.) the complaints of his friends, who suffered by its effects. I have lent them the words of our poor cavaliers after the restoration.

open revolt; and Cantacuzene, on the throne of the elder Andronicus, defended the cause of age and prerogative, which in his youth he had so vigorously attacked. At his request, the empress mother undertook the voyage of Thessalonica, and the office of mediation: she returned without success; and unless Anne of Savoy was instructed by adversity, we may doubt the sincerity, or at least the fervour, of her zeal. While the regent grasped the sceptre with a firm and vigorous hand, she had been instructed to declare, that the ten years of his legal administration would soon elapse; and that after a full trial of the vanity of the world, the emperor Cantacuzene sighed for the repose of a cloyster, and was ambitious only of an heavenly crown. Had these sentiments been genuine, his voluntary abdication would have restored the peace of the empire, and his conscience would have been relieved by an act of justice. Palæologus alone was responsible for his future government; and whatever might be his vices, they were surely less formidable than the calamities of a civil war, in which the Barbarians and infidels were again invited to assist the Greeks in their mutual destruction. By the arms of the Turks, who now struck a deep and everlasting root in Europe, Cantacuzene prevailed in the third contest in which he had been involved; and the young emperor, driven from the sea and land, was compelled to take shelter among the Latins of the isle of Tenedos. His insolence and obstinacy provoked the victor to a step which must render the quarrel irreconcilable: and the association of his son Matthew, whom he invested with the purple, established the succession in the family of the Cantacuzeni. But Constantinople was still attached to the blood of her ancient princes: and this last injury accelerated the restoration of the rightful heir. A noble Genoese espoused the cause of Palæologus, obtained a promise of his sister, and atchieved the revolution with two gallies and two thousand five hundred auxiliaries. Under the pretence of distress, they were admitted into the lesser port; a gate was opened, and the Latin shout of, "long life and victory to the emperor, John Palæologus!" was answered by a general rising in his favour. A numerous and loyal party yet adhered to the standard of Cantacuzene: but he asserts in his history (does he hope for belief?) that his tender conscience rejected the assurance of conquest; that, in free obedience to the voice of religion and philosophy, he descended from the throne, and embraced with pleasure the monastic habit and profession.[36] So soon as

John Palæologus takes up arms against him, A.D. 1353.

36. The awkward apology of Cantacuzene (l. iv. c. 39–42.), who relates, with visible confusion, his own downfall, may be supplied by the less accurate, but more honest

he ceased to be a prince, his successor was not unwilling that he should be a saint: the remainder of his life was devoted to piety and learning; in the cells of Constantinople and mount Athos, the monk Joasaph was respected as the temporal and spiritual father of the emperor; and if he issued from his retreat, it was as the minister of peace, to subdue the obstinacy, and solicit the pardon, of his rebellious son.[37]

Abdication of Cantacuzene, A.D. 1355, January.

Yet in the cloyster, the mind of Cantacuzene was still exercised by theological war. He sharpened a controversial pen against the Jews and Mahometans;[38] and in every state, he defended with equal zeal the divine light of mount Thabor, a memorable question which consummates the religious follies of the Greeks. The fakirs of India,[39] and the monks of the Oriental church, were alike persuaded, that, in total abstraction of the faculties of the mind and body, the purer spirit may ascend to the enjoyment and vision of the Deity. The opinion and practice of the monasteries of mount Athos[40] will be best represented in the words of an abbot, who flourished in the eleventh century. "When thou art alone in thy cell," says the ascetic teacher, "shut thy door, and seat thyself in a corner; raise thy mind above all things vain and transitory; recline thy beard and chin on thy breast; turn thy eyes and thy thought towards the middle of thy belly, the region of the navel; and search the place of the heart, the seat of the soul. At first, all will be dark and comfortless; but if you persevere day and night, you will feel an ineffable joy; and no sooner has the soul discovered the place of the heart, than it is involved in a mystic and etherial light." This light, the production of a distempered

Dispute concerning the light of mount Thabor, A.D. 1341–1351.

---

narratives of Matthew Villani (l. iv. c. 46. in the Script. Rerum Ital. tom. xiv. p. 268.) and Ducas (c. 10, 11.).

37. Cantacuzene, in the year 1375, was honoured with a letter from the pope (Fleury, Hist. Eccles. tom. xx. p. 250.). His death is placed by respectable authority on the 20th of November 1411 (Ducange, Fam. Byzant. p. 260.). But if he were of the age of his companion Andronicus the Younger, he must have lived 116 years; a rare instance of longevity, which in so illustrious a person would have attracted universal notice.

38. His four discourses, or books, were printed at Basil 1543 (Fabric. Bibliot. Græc. tom. vi. p. 473.). He composed them to satisfy a proselyte who was assaulted with letters from his friends of Ispahan. Cantacuzene had read the Koran; but I understand from Maracci, that he adopts the vulgar prejudices and fables against Mahomet and his religion.

39. See the Voyages de Bernier, tom. i. p. 127.

40. Mosheim, Institut. Hist. Eccles. p. 522, 523. Fleury, Hist. Eccles. tom. xx. p. 22. 24. 107–114, &c. The former unfolds the causes with the judgment of a philosopher, the latter transcribes and translates with the prejudices of a Catholic priest.

fancy, the creature of an empty stomach and an empty brain, was adored by the Quietists as the pure and perfect essence of God himself; and as long as the folly was confined to mount Athos, the simple solitaries were not inquisitive how the divine essence could be a *material* substance, or how an *immaterial* substance could be perceived by the eyes of the body. But in the reign of the younger Andronicus, these monasteries were visited by Barlaam,[41] a Calabrian monk, who was equally skilled in philosophy and theology; who possessed the languages of the Greeks and Latins; and whose versatile genius could maintain their opposite creeds, according to the interest of the moment. The indiscretion of an ascetic revealed to the curious traveller the secrets of mental prayer; and Barlaam embraced the opportunity of ridiculing the Quietists, who placed the soul in the navel; of accusing the monks of mount Athos of heresy and blasphemy. His attack compelled the more learned to renounce or dissemble the simple devotion of their brethren; and Gregory Palamas introduced a scholastic distinction between the essence and operation of God. His inaccessible essence dwells in the midst of an uncreated and eternal light; and this beatific vision of the saints had been manifested to the disciples on mount Thabor, in the transfiguration of Christ. Yet this distinction could not escape the reproach of polytheism; the eternity of the light of Thabor was fiercely denied; and Barlaam still charged the Palamites with holding two eternal substances, a visible and an invisible God. From the rage of the monks of mount Athos, who threatened his life, the Calabrian retired to Constantinople, where his smooth and specious manners introduced him to the favour of the great domestic and the emperor. The court and the city were involved in this theological dispute, which flamed amidst the civil war; but the doctrine of Barlaam was disgraced by his flight and apostacy: the Palamites triumphed; and their adversary, the patriarch John of Apri, was deposed by the consent of the adverse factions of the state. In the character of emperor and theologian, Cantacuzene presided in the synod of the Greek church, which established, as an article of faith, the uncreated light of mount Thabor; and, after so many insults, the reason of mankind was slightly wounded by the addition of a single absurdity. Many rolls of paper or parchment have been blotted; and the impenitent sectaries, who refused

41. Basnage (in Canisii Antiq. Lectiones, tom. iv. p. 363–368.) has investigated the character and story of Barlaam. The duplicity of his opinions had inspired some doubts of the identity of his person. See likewise Fabricius (Bibliot. Græc. tom. x. p. 427–432.).

to subscribe the orthodox creed, were deprived of the honours of Christian burial; but in the next age the question was forgotten; nor can I learn that the axe or the faggot were employed for the extirpation of the Barlaamite heresy.[42]

Establishment of the Genoese at Pera or Galata, A.D. 1261–1347.

For the conclusion of this chapter, I have reserved the Genoese war, which shook the throne of Cantacuzene, and betrayed the debility of the Greek empire. The Genoese, who, after the recovery of Constantinople, were seated in the suburb of Pera or Galata, received that honourable fief from the bounty of the emperor. They were indulged in the use of their laws and magistrates; but they submitted to the duties of vassals and subjects: the forcible word of *liegemen*[43] was borrowed from the Latin jurisprudence; and their *podesta*, or chief, before he entered on his office, saluted the emperor with loyal acclamations and vows of fidelity. Genoa sealed a firm alliance with the Greeks; and, in case of a defensive war, a supply of fifty empty gallies, and a succour of fifty gallies completely armed and manned, was promised by the republic to the empire. In the revival of a naval force, it was the aim of Michael Palæologus to deliver himself from a foreign aid; and his vigorous government contained the Genoese of Galata within those limits which the insolence of wealth and freedom provoked them to exceed. A sailor threatened that they should soon be masters of Constantinople, and slew the Greek who resented this national affront; and an armed vessel, after refusing to salute the palace, was guilty of some acts of piracy in the Black Sea. Their countrymen threatened to support their cause; but the long and open village of Galata was instantly surrounded by the Imperial troops; till, in the moment of the assault, the prostrate Genoese implored the clemency of their sovereign. The defenceless situation which secured their obedience, exposed them to the attack of their Venetian rivals, who, in the reign of the elder Andronicus, presumed to violate the majesty of the throne. On the approach of their fleets, the Genoese, with their families and effects, retired into the city:

42. See Cantacuzene (l. ii. c. 39, 40. l. iv. c. 3. 23, 24, 25.), and Nic. Gregoras (l. xi. c. 10. l. xv. 3, 7, &c.), whose last books, from the xixth to the xxivth, are almost confined to a subject so interesting to the authors. Boivin (in Vit. Nic. Gregoræ), from the unpublished books, and Fabricius (Bibliot. Græc. tom. x. p. 462–473.), or rather Montfaucon, from the MSS. of the Coislin library, have added some facts and documents.

43. Pachymer (l. v. c. 10.) very properly explains λιζιους (*ligios*) by ιδιους. The use of these words in the Greek and Latin of the feudal times, may be amply understood from the Glossaries of Ducange (Græc. p. 811, 812. Latin. tom. iv. p. 109–111.).

their empty habitations were reduced to ashes; and the feeble prince, who had viewed the destruction of his suburb, expressed his resentment, not by arms, but by ambassadors. This misfortune, however, was advantageous to the Genoese, who obtained, and imperceptibly abused, the dangerous licence of surrounding Galata with a strong wall; of introducing into the ditch the waters of the sea; of erecting lofty turrets; and of mounting a train of military engines on the rampart. The narrow bounds in which they had been circumscribed, were insufficient for the growing colony; each day they acquired some addition of landed property; and the adjacent hills were covered with their villas and castles, which they joined and protected by new fortifications.[44] The navigation and trade of the Euxine was the patrimony of the Greek emperors, who commanded the narrow entrance, the gates, as it were, of that inland sea. In the reign of Michael Palæologus, their prerogative was acknowledged by the sultan of Egypt, who solicited and obtained the liberty of sending an annual ship for the purchase of slaves in Circassia and the Lesser Tartary; a liberty pregnant with mischief to the Christian cause; since these youths were transformed by education and discipline into the formidable Mamalukes.[45] From the colony of Pera, the Genoese engaged with superior advantage in the lucrative trade of the Black Sea; and their industry supplied the Greeks with fish and corn; two articles of food almost equally important to a superstitious people. The spontaneous bounty of nature appears to have bestowed the harvests of the Ukraine, the produce of a rude and savage husbandry; and the endless exportation of salt fish and caviar is annually renewed by the enormous sturgeons that are caught at the mouth of the Don or Tanais, in their last station of the rich mud and shallow water of the Mæotis.[46] The waters of the Oxus, the Caspian, the Volga, and the Don, opened a rare and laborious passage

Their trade and insolence.

44. The establishment and progress of the Genoese at Pera, or Galata, is described by Ducange (C. P. Christiana, l. i. p. 68, 69.) from the Byzantine historians, Pachymer (l. ii. c. 35. l. v. 10. 30. l. ix. 15. l. xii. 6. 9.), Nicephorus Gregoras (l. v. c. 4. l. vi. c. 11. l. ix. c. 5. l. xi. c. 1. l. xv. c. 1. 6.), and Cantacuzene (l. i. c. 12. l. ii. c. 29, &c.).

45. Both Pachymer (l. iii. c. 3, 4, 5.) and Nic. Gregoras (l. iv. c. 7.) understand and deplore the effects of this dangerous indulgence. Bibars, sultan of Egypt, himself a Tartar, but a devout Musulman, obtained from the children of Zingis the permission to build a stately mosque in the capital of Crimæa (de Guignes, Hist. des Huns, tom. iii. p. 343.).

46. Chardin (Voyages en Perse, tom. i. p. 48.) was assured at Caffa, that these fishes were sometimes twenty-four or twenty-six feet long, weighed eight or nine hundred pounds, and yielded three or four quintals of caviar. The corn of the Bosphorus had supplied the Athenians in the time of Demosthenes.

for the gems and spices of India; and, after three months march, the caravans of Carizme met the Italian vessels in the harbours of Crimæa.[47] These various branches of trade were monopolised by the diligence and power of the Genoese. Their rivals of Venice and Pisa were forcibly expelled; the natives were awed by the castles and cities, which arose on the foundations of their humble factories; and their principal establishment of Caffa[48] was besieged without effect by the Tartar powers. Destitute of a navy, the Greeks were oppressed by these haughty merchants, who fed, or famished, Constantinople, according to their interest. They proceeded to usurp the customs, the fishery, and even the toll, of the Bosphorus; and while they derived from these objects a revenue of two hundred thousand pieces of gold, a remnant of thirty thousand was reluctantly allowed to the emperor.[49] The colony of Pera or Galata acted, in peace and war, as an independent state; and, as it will happen in distant settlements, the Genoese podesta too often forgot that he was the servant of his own masters.

Their war with the emperor Cantacuzene, A.D. 1348.

These usurpations were encouraged by the weakness of the elder Andronicus, and by the civil wars that afflicted his age and the minority of his grandson. The talents of Cantacuzene were employed to the ruin, rather than the restoration, of the empire; and after his domestic victory, he was condemned to an ignominious trial, whether the Greeks or the Genoese should reign in Constantinople. The merchants of Pera were offended by his refusal of some contiguous lands, some commanding heights, which they proposed to cover with new fortifications; and in the absence of the emperor, who was detained at Demotica by sickness, they ventured to brave the debility of a female reign. A Byzantine vessel, which had presumed to fish at the mouth of the harbour, was sunk by these audacious strangers; the fishermen were murdered. Instead of suing for pardon, the Genoese demanded satisfaction; required in an haughty strain, that the Greeks should renounce the exercise of navigation; and encountered with regular arms the first sallies of the popular indignation. They instantly occupied the debateable land; and by the labour of a whole people, of either sex

47. De Guignes, Hist. des Huns, tom. iii. p. 343, 344. Viaggi di Ramusio, tom. i. fol. 400. But this land or water carriage could only be practicable when Tartary was united under a wise and powerful monarch.

48. Nic. Gregoras (l. xiii. c. 12.) is judicious and well-informed on the trade and colonies of the Black Sea. Chardin describes the present ruins of Caffa, where, in forty days, he saw above 400 sail employed in the corn and fish trade (Voyages en Perse, tom. i. p. 46–48.).

49. See Nic. Gregoras, l. xvii, c. 1.

and of every age, the wall was raised, and the ditch was sunk, with incredible speed. At the same time, they attacked and burnt two Byzantine gallies; while the three others, the remainder of the Imperial navy, escaped from their hands: the habitations without the gates, or along the shore, were pillaged and destroyed; and the care of the regent, of the empress Irene, was confined to the preservation of the city. The return of Cantacuzene dispelled the public consternation: the emperor inclined to peaceful counsels; but he yielded to the obstinacy of his enemies, who rejected all reasonable terms, and to the ardour of his subjects, who threatened, in the style of scripture, to break them in pieces like a potter's vessel. Yet they reluctantly paid the taxes, that he imposed for the construction of ships, and the expences of the war; and as the two nations were masters, the one of the land, the other of the sea, Constantinople and Pera were pressed by the evils of a mutual siege. The merchants of the colony, who had believed that a few days would terminate the war, already murmured at their losses; the succours from their mother-country were delayed by the factions of Genoa; and the most cautious embraced the opportunity of a Rhodian vessel to remove their families and effects from the scene of hostility. In the spring, the Byzantine fleet, seven gallies and a train of smaller vessels, issued from the mouth of the harbour, and steered in a single line along the shore of Pera; unskilfully presenting their sides to the beaks of the adverse squadron. The crews were composed of peasants and mechanics; nor was their ignorance compensated by the native courage of Barbarians: the wind was strong, the waves were rough; and no sooner did the Greeks perceive a distant and inactive enemy, than they leaped headlong into the sea, from a doubtful, to an inevitable, peril. The troops that marched to the attack of the lines of Pera were struck at the same moment with a similar panic; and the Genoese were astonished, and almost ashamed, at their double victory. Their triumphant vessels, crowned with flowers, and dragging after them the captive gallies, repeatedly passed and repassed before the palace: the only virtue of the emperor was patience; and the hope of revenge his sole consolation. Yet the distress of both parties interposed a temporary agreement; and the shame of the empire was disguised by a thin veil of dignity and power. Summoning the chiefs of the colony, Cantacuzene affected to despise the trivial object of the debate; and, after a mild reproof, most liberally granted the lands, which had been previously resigned to the seeming custody of his officers.[50]

Destruction of his fleet, A.D. 1349.

50. The events of this war are related by Cantacuzene (l. iv. c. 11.) with obscurity and confusion, and by Nic. Gregoras (l. xvii. c. 1–7.) in a clear and honest narrative.

Victory of the Genoese over the Venetians and Greeks, A.D. 1352, February 13.

But the emperor was soon solicited to violate the treaty, and to join his arms with the Venetians, the perpetual enemies of Genoa and her colonies. While he compared the reasons of peace and war, his moderation was provoked by a wanton insult of the inhabitants of Pera, who discharged from their rampart a large stone that fell in the midst of Constantinople. On his just complaint, they coldly blamed the imprudence of their engineer; but the next day the insult was repeated, and they exulted in a second proof that the royal city was not beyond the reach of their artillery. Cantacuzene instantly signed his treaty with the Venetians; but the weight of the Roman empire was scarcely felt in the balance of these opulent and powerful republics.[51] From the streights of Gibraltar to the mouth of the Tanais, their fleets encountered each other with various success; and a memorable battle was fought in the narrow sea, under the walls of Constantinople. It would not be an easy task to reconcile the accounts of the Greeks, the Venetians, and the Genoese;[52] and while I depend on the narrative of an impartial historian,[53] I shall borrow from each nation the facts that redound to their own disgrace, and the honour of their foes. The Venetians, with their allies the Catalans, had the advantage of number; and their fleet, with the poor addition of eight Byzantine gallies, amounted to seventy-five sail: the Genoese did not exceed sixty-four; but in those times their ships of war were distinguished by the superiority of their size and strength. The names and families of their naval commanders, Pisani and Doria, are illustrious in the annals of their country; but the personal merit of the former was eclipsed by the fame and abilities of his rival. They engaged in tempestuous weather; and the tumultuary conflict was continued from the dawn to the extinction of light. The enemies of the Genoese applaud their prowess: the friends of the Venetians are dissatisfied with their behaviour; but all parties agree in praising the skill and boldness of the Catalans, who, with many wounds, sustained

---

The priest was less responsible than the prince for the defeat of the fleet.

51. This second war is darkly told by Cantacuzene (l. iv. c. 18. p. 24, 25. 28–32.), who wishes to disguise what he dares not deny. I regret this part of Nic. Gregoras, which is still in MS. at Paris.

52. Muratori (Annali d'Italia, tom. xii. p. 144.) refers to the most ancient Chronicles of Venice (Caresinus, the continuator of Andrew Dandulus, tom. xii. p. 421, 422.) and Genoa (George Stella, Annales Genuenses, tom. xvii. p. 1091, 1092.); both which I have diligently consulted in his great Collection of the Historians of Italy.

53. See the Chronicle of Matteo Villani of Florence, l. ii. c. 59, 60. p. 145–147. c. 74, 75. p. 156, 157. in Muratori's Collection, tom. xiv.

the brunt of the action. On the separation of the fleets, the event might appear doubtful; but the thirteen Genoese gallies, that had been sunk or taken, were compensated by a double loss of the allies; of fourteen Venetians, ten Catalans, and two Greeks; and even the grief of the conquerors expressed the assurance and habit of more decisive victories. Pisani confessed his defeat, by retiring into a fortified harbour, from whence, under the pretext of the orders of the senate, he steered with a broken and flying squadron for the isle of Candia, and abandoned to his rivals the sovereignty of the sea. In a public epistle,[54] addressed to the doge and senate, Petrarch employs his eloquence to reconcile the maritime powers, the two luminaries of Italy. The orator celebrates the valour and victory of the Genoese, the first men in the exercise of naval war: he drops a tear on the misfortunes of their Venetian brethren; but he exhorts them to pursue with fire and sword the base and perfidious Greeks; to purge the metropolis of the East from the heresy with which it was infected. Deserted by their friends, the Greeks were incapable of resistance; and three months after the battle, the emperor Cantacuzene solicited and subscribed a treaty, which for ever banished the Venetians and Catalans, and granted to the Genoese a monopoly of trade, and almost a right of dominion. The Roman empire (I smile in transcribing the name) might soon have sunk into a province of Genoa, if the ambition of the republic had not been checked by the ruin of her freedom and naval power. A long contest of one hundred and thirty years was determined by the triumph of Venice; and the factions of the Genoese compelled them to seek for domestic peace under the protection of a foreign lord, the duke of Milan, or the French king. Yet the spirit of commerce survived that of conquest; and the colony of Pera still awed the capital and navigated the Euxine, till it was involved by the Turks in the final servitude of Constantinople itself.

Their treaty with the empire, May 6.

54. The Abbé de Sade (Memoires sur la Vie de Petrarque, tom. iii. p. 257–263.) translates this letter, which he had copied from a MS. in the king of France's library. Though a servant of the duke of Milan, Petrarch pours forth his astonishment and grief at the defeat and despair of the Genoese in the following year (p. 323–332.).

CHAPTER LXIV

Conquests of Zingis Khan and the Moguls from China to Poland. – Escape of Constantinople and the Greeks. – Origin of the Ottoman Turks in Bithynia. – Reigns and Victories of Othman, Orchan, Amurath the First, and Bajazet the First. – Foundation and Progress of the Turkish Monarchy in Asia and Europe. – Danger of Constantinople and the Greek Empire.

From the petty quarrels of a city and her suburbs, from the cowardice and discord of the falling Greeks, I shall now ascend to the victorious Turks; whose domestic slavery was ennobled by martial discipline, religious enthusiasm, and the energy of the national character. The rise and progress of the Ottomans, the present sovereigns of Constantinople, are connected with the most important scenes of modern history: but they are founded on a previous knowledge of the great eruption of the Moguls and Tartars; whose rapid conquests may be compared with the primitive convulsions of nature, which have agitated and altered the surface of the globe. I have long since asserted my claim to introduce the nations, the immediate or remote authors of the fall of the Roman empire; nor can I refuse myself to those events, which, from their uncommon magnitude, will interest a philosophic mind in the history of blood.[1]

Zingis Khan, first emperor of the Moguls and Tartars, A.D. 1206–1227.

From the spacious highlands between China, Siberia, and the Caspian Sea, the tide of emigration and war has repeatedly been poured. These ancient seats of the Huns and Turks were occupied in the twelfth century by many pastoral tribes, of the same descent and similar manners, which were united and led to conquest by the formidable Zingis. In his ascent to greatness, that Barbarian (whose private appellation was Temugin) had trampled on the necks of his equals. His birth was noble: but it was in the pride of

1. The reader is invited to review the chapters of the second and third volumes; the manners of pastoral nations, the conquests of Attila and the Huns, which were composed at a time when I entertained the wish, rather than the hope, of concluding my history.

victory, that the prince or people deduced his seventh ancestor from the immaculate conception of a virgin. His father had reigned over thirteen hords, which composed about thirty or forty thousand families: above two-thirds refused to pay tithes or obedience to his infant son; and at the age of thirteen, Temugin fought a battle against his rebellious subjects. The future conqueror of Asia was reduced to fly and to obey: but he rose superior to his fortune, and in his fortieth year he had established his fame and dominion over the circumjacent tribes. In a state of society, in which policy is rude and valour is universal, the ascendant of one man must be founded on his power and resolution to punish his enemies and recompense his friends. His first military league was ratified by the simple rites of sacrificing an horse and tasting of a running stream: Temugin pledged himself to divide with his followers the sweets and the bitters of life; and, when he had shared among them his horses and apparel, he was rich in their gratitude and his own hopes. After his first victory, he placed seventy chaldrons on the fire, and seventy of the most guilty rebels were cast headlong into the boiling water. The sphere of his attraction was continually enlarged by the ruin of the proud and the submission of the prudent; and the boldest chieftains might tremble, when they beheld, enchased in silver, the skull of the khan of the Keraites;[2] who, under the name of Prester John, had corresponded with the Roman pontiff and the princes of Europe. The ambition of Temugin condescended to employ the arts of superstition; and it was from a naked prophet, who could ascend to heaven on a white horse, that he accepted the title of Zingis,[3] the *most great*; and a divine right to the conquest and dominion of the earth. In a general *couroultai*, or diet, he was seated on a felt, which was long afterwards revered as a relic, and solemnly proclaimed great khan, or emperor, of the Moguls[4] and Tartars.[5] Of these kindred, though

2. The khans of the Keraites were most probably incapable of reading the pompous epistles composed in their name by the Nestorian missionaries, who endowed them with the fabulous wonders of an Indian kingdom. Perhaps these Tartars (the Presbyter or Priest John) had submitted to the rites of baptism and ordination (Asseman, Bibliot. Orient. tom. iii. P. ii. p. 487–503.).

3. Since the history and tragedy of Voltaire, *Gengis*, at least in French, seems to be the more fashionable spelling: but Abulghazi Khan must have known the true name of his ancestor. His etymology appears just: *Zin*, in the Mogul tongue, signifies *great*, and *gis* is the superlative termination (Hist. Genealogique des Tatars, part iii. p. 194, 195.). From the same idea of magnitude, the appellation of *Zingis* is bestowed on the ocean.

4. The name of Moguls has prevailed among the Orientals, and still adheres to the titular sovereign, the Great Mogul, of Hindostan.

5. The Tartars (more properly Tatars) were

rival, names, the former had given birth to the Imperial race; and the latter has been extended, by accident or error, over the spacious wilderness of the north.

His laws. The code of laws which Zingis dictated to his subjects, was adapted to the preservation of domestic peace, and the exercise of foreign hostility. The punishment of death was inflicted on the crimes of adultery, murder, perjury, and the capital thefts of an horse or ox; and the fiercest of men were mild and just in their intercourse with each other. The future election of the great khan was vested in the princes of his family and the heads of the tribes; and the regulations of the chace were essential to the pleasures and plenty of a Tartar camp. The victorious nation was held sacred from all servile labours, which were abandoned to slaves and strangers; and every labour was servile except the profession of arms. The service and discipline of the troops, who were armed with bows, scymetars, and iron maces, and divided by hundreds, thousands, and ten thousands, were the institutions of a veteran commander. Each officer and soldier was made responsible, under pain of death, for the safety and honour of his companions; and the spirit of conquest breathed in the law, that peace should never be granted unless to a vanquished and suppliant enemy. But it is the religion of Zingis that best deserves our wonder and applause. The Catholic inquisitors of Europe, who defended nonsense by cruelty, might have been confounded by the example of a Barbarian, who anticipated the lessons of philosophy,[6] and established by his laws a system of pure theism and perfect toleration. His first and only article of faith was the existence of one God, the author of all good; who fills by his presence the heavens and earth, which he has created by his power. The Tartars and Moguls were addicted to the idols of their peculiar tribes; and many of them had been converted by the foreign missionaries to the religions of Moses, of Mahomet, and of Christ. These various systems in freedom and concord, were taught and practised within the precincts of the same camp; and the Bonze, the Imam, the Rabbi, the Nestorian and the Latin priest, enjoyed the same

---

descended from Tatar Khan, the brother of Mogul Khan (see Abulghazi, part i and ii.), and once formed a hord of 70,000 families on the borders of Kitay (p. 103–112.). In the great invasion of Europe (A.D. 1238), they seem to have led the vanguard; and the similitude of the name of *Tartarei*, recommended that of Tartars to the Latins (Matt. Paris, p. 398, &c.).

6. A singular conformity may be found between the religious laws of Zingis Khan and of Mr. Locke (Constitutions of Carolina, in his works, vol. iv. p. 535. 4[to] edition, 1777).

honourable exemption from service and tribute: in the mosch of Bochara, the insolent victor might trample the Koran under his horses feet, but the calm legislator respected the prophets and pontiffs of the most hostile sects. The reason of Zingis was not informed by books; the khan could neither read nor write; and, except the tribe of the Igours, the greatest part of the Moguls and Tartars were as illiterate as their sovereign. The memory of their exploits was preserved by tradition: sixty-eight years after the death of Zingis, these traditions were collected and transcribed;[7] the brevity of their domestic annals may be supplied by the Chinese,[8] Persians,[9] Armenians,[10] Syrians,[11] Arabians,[12] Greeks,[13]

7. In the year 1294, by the command of Cazan, khan of Persia, the fourth in descent from Zingis. From these traditions, his vizir Fadlallah composed a Mogul history in the Persian language, which has been used by Petis de la Croix (Hist. de Genghizcan, p. 537–539.). The Histoire Genealogique des Tatars (à Leyde, 1726, in 12mo, 2 tomes) was translated by the Swedish prisoners in Siberia from the Mogul MS. of Abulgasi Bahadur Khan, a descendant of Zingis, who reigned over the Usbeks of Charasm, or Carizme (A. D. 1644–1663). He is of most value and credit for the names, pedigrees, and manners of his nation. Of his nine parts, the i^st^ descends from Adam to Mogul Khan; the ii^d^, from Mogul to Zingis; the iii^d^, is the life of Zingis; the iv^th^, v^th^, vi^th^, and vii^th^, the general history of his four sons, and their posterity; the viii^th^ and ix^th^, the particular history of the descendants of Sheibani Khan, who reigned in Maurenahar and Charasm.

8. Histoire de Gentchiscan, et de toute la Dinastie des Mongous ses Successeurs, Conquerans de la Chine; tirée de l'Histoire de la Chine, par le R. P. Gaubil, de la Societé de Jesus, Missionaire à Peking; à Paris, 1739, in 4to. This translation is stamped with the Chinese character of domestic accuracy and foreign ignorance.

9. See the Histoire du Grand Genghizcan, premier Empereur des Mogols et Tartares, par M. Petis de la Croix, à Paris, 1710, in 12mo: a work of ten years labour, chiefly drawn from the Persian writers, among whom Nisavi, the secretary of sultan Gelaleddin, has the merit and prejudices of a contemporary. A slight air of romance is the fault of the originals, or the compiler. See likewise the articles of *Genghizcan*, *Mohammed*, *Gelaleddin*, &c. in the Bibliotheque Orientale of d'Herbelot.

10. Haithonus, or Aithonus, an Armenian prince, and afterwards a monk of Premontré (Fabric. Bibliot. Lat. medii Ævi, tom. i. p. 34.), dictated in the French language, his book de *Tartaris*, his old fellow-soldiers. It was immediately translated into Latin, and is inserted in the Novus Orbis of Simon Grynæus (Basil, 1555, in folio).

11. Zingis Khan, and his first successors, occupy the conclusion of the ix^th^ Dynasty of Abulpharagius (vers. Pocock, Oxon. 1663, in 4to); and his x^th^ Dynasty is that of the Moguls of Persia. Assemannus (Bibliot. Orient. tom. ii.) has extracted some facts from his Syriac writings, and the lives of the Jacobite maphrians, or primates of the East.

12. Among the Arabians, in language and religion, we may distinguish Abulfeda, sultan of Hamah in Syria, who fought in person, under the Mamaluke standard, against the Moguls.

13. Nicephorus Gregoras (l. ii. c. 5, 6.) has felt the necessity of connecting the Scythian and Byzantine histories. He

Russians,[14] Poles,[15] Hungarians,[16] and Latins;[17] and each nation will deserve credit in the relation of their own disasters and defeats.[18]

His invasion of China, A.D. 1210–1214.

The arms of Zingis and his lieutenants successively reduced the hords of the desert, who pitched their tents between the wall of China and the Volga; and the Mogul emperor became the monarch of the pastoral world, the lord of many millions of shepherds and soldiers, who felt their united strength, and were impatient to rush on the mild and wealthy climates of the south. His ancestors had been the tributaries of the Chinese emperors; and Temugin himself had been disgraced by a title of honour and servitude. The court of Pekin was astonished by an embassy from its former vassal, who, in the tone of the king of nations, exacted the tribute and obedience which he had paid, and who affected to treat the *son of heaven* as the most contemptible of mankind. An haughty answer disguised their secret apprehensions; and their fears were soon justified by the march of innumerable squadrons, who pierced on all sides the feeble rampart of the great wall. Ninety

---

describes with truth and elegance the settlement and manners of the Moguls of Persia, but he is ignorant of their origin, and corrupts the names of Zingis and his sons.

14. M. Levesque (Histoire de Russie, tom. ii.) has described the conquest of Russia by the Tartars, from the patriarch Nicon, and the old chronicles.

15. For Poland, I am content with the Sarmatia Asiatica et Europea of Matthew à Michou, or de Michoviâ, a canon and physician of Cracow (A.D. 1506), inserted in the Novus Orbis of Grynæus. Fabric. Bibliot. Latin mediæ et infimæ Ætatis, tom. v. p. 56.

16. I should quote Thuroczius, the oldest general historian (pars ii. c. 74. p. 150.), in the i[st] volume of the Scriptores Rerum Hungaricarum, did not the same volume contain the original narrative of a contemporary, an eye-witness, and a sufferer (M. Rogerii, Hungari, Varadiensis Capituli Canonici, Carmen miserabile, seu Historia super Destructione Regni Hungariæ, Temporibus Belæ IV. Regis per Tartaros facta, p. 292–321.): the best picture that I have ever seen of all the circumstances of a Barbaric invasion.

17. Matthew Paris has represented, from authentic documents, the danger and distress of Europe (consult the word *Tartari* in his copious Index). From motives of zeal and curiosity, the court of the great Khan, in the xiii[th] century, was visited by two friars, John de Plano Carpini, and William Rubruquis, and by Marco Polo, a Venetian gentleman. The Latin relations of the two former are inserted in the i[st] volume of Hackluyt; the Italian original or version of the third (Fabric. Bibliot. Latin. medii Ævi, tom. ii. p. 198. tom. v. p. 25.) may be found in the ii[d] tome of Ramusio.

18. In his great History of the Huns, M. de Guignes has most amply treated of Zingis Khan and his successors. See tom. iii. l. xv–xix. and in the collateral articles of the Seljukians of Roum, tom. ii. l. xi. the Carizmians, l. xiv. and the Mamalukes, tom. iv. l. xxi.: consult likewise the tables of the i[st] volume. He is ever learned and accurate; yet I am only indebted to him for a general view, and some passages of Abulfeda, which are still latent in the Arabic text.

cities were stormed, or starved, by the Moguls; ten only escaped; and Zingis, from a knowledge of the filial piety of the Chinese, covered his vanguard with their captive parents; an unworthy, and by degrees a fruitless, abuse of the virtue of his enemies. His invasion was supported by the revolt of an hundred thousand Khitans, who guarded the frontier: yet he listened to a treaty; and a princess of China, three thousand horses, five hundred youths and as many virgins, and a tribute of gold and silk, were the price of his retreat. In his second expedition, he compelled the Chinese emperor to retire beyond the yellow river to a more southern residence. The siege of Pekin[19] was long and laborious: the inhabitants were reduced by famine to decimate and devour their fellow-citizens; when their ammunition was spent, they discharged ingots of gold and silver from their engines; but the Moguls introduced a mine to the centre of the capital; and the conflagration of the palace burnt above thirty days. China was desolated by Tartar war and domestic faction; and the five northern provinces were added to the empire of Zingis.

of Carizme, Transoxiana, and Persia, A.D. 1218–1224.

In the West, he touched the dominions of Mohammed sultan of Carizme, who reigned from the Persian Gulf to the borders of India and Turkestan; and who, in the proud imitation of Alexander the Great, forgot the servitude and ingratitude of his fathers to the house of Seljuk. It was the wish of Zingis to establish a friendly and commercial intercourse with the most powerful of the Moslem princes; nor could he be tempted by the secret solicitations of the caliph of Bagdad, who sacrificed to his personal wrongs the safety of the church and state. A rash and inhuman deed provoked and justified the Tartar arms in the invasion of the southern Asia. A caravan of three ambassadors and one hundred and fifty merchants, was arrested and murdered at Otrar, by the command of Mohammed; nor was it till after a demand and denial of justice, till he had prayed and fasted three nights on a mountain, that the Mogul emperor appealed to the judgment of God and his sword. Our European battles, says a philosophic writer,[20] are petty skirmishes, if compared to the numbers that have fought and fallen in the fields of Asia. Seven hundred thousand Moguls and Tartars are said

19. More properly *Yen-king*, an ancient city, whose ruins still appear some furlongs to the south-east of the modern *Pekin*, which was built by Cublai Khan (Gaubel, p. 146.). Pe-king and Nan-king are vague titles, the courts of the north and of the south. The identity and change of names perplex the most skilful readers of the Chinese geography (p. 177.).

20. M. de Voltaire, Essai sur l'Histoire Generale, tom. iii. c. 60. p. 8. His account of Zingis and the Moguls contains, as usual, much general sense and truth, with some particular errors.

to have marched under the standard of Zingis and his four sons. In the vast plains that extend to the north of the Sihon or Jaxartes, they were encountered by four hundred thousand soldiers of the sultan; and in the first battle, which was suspended by the night, one hundred and sixty thousand Carizmians were slain. Mohammed was astonished by the multitude and valour of his enemies: he withdrew from the scene of danger, and distributed his troops in the frontier towns, trusting that the Barbarians, invincible in the field, would be repulsed by the length and difficulty of so many regular sieges. But the prudence of Zingis had formed a body of Chinese engineers, skilled in the mechanic arts, informed perhaps of the secret of gunpowder, and capable, under his discipline, of attacking a foreign country with more vigour and success than they had defended their own. The Persian historians will relate the sieges and reduction of Otrar, Cogende, Bochara, Samarcand, Carizme, Herat, Merou, Nisabour, Balch, and Candahar; and the conquest of the rich and populous countries of Transoxiana, Carizme, and Chorasan. The destructive hostilities of Attila and the Huns have long since been elucidated by the example of Zingis and the Moguls; and in this more proper place I shall be content to observe, that, from the Caspian to the Indus, they ruined a tract of many hundred miles, which was adorned with the habitations and labours of mankind, and that five centuries have not been sufficient to repair the ravages of four years. The Mogul emperor encouraged or indulged the fury of his troops: the hope of future possession was lost in the ardour of rapine and slaughter; and the cause of the war exasperated their native fierceness by the pretence of justice and revenge. The downfal and death of the sultan Mohammed, who expired unpitied and alone, in a desert island of the Caspian Sea, is a poor atonement for the calamities of which he was the author. Could the Carizmian empire have been saved by a single hero, it would have been saved by his son Gelaleddin, whose active valour repeatedly checked the Moguls in the career of victory. Retreating, as he fought, to the banks of the Indus, he was oppressed by their innumerable host, till, in the last moment of despair, Gelaleddin spurred his horse into the waves, swam one of the broadest and most rapid rivers of Asia, and extorted the admiration and applause of Zingis himself. It was in this camp that the Mogul conqueror yielded with reluctance to the murmurs of his weary and wealthy troops, who sighed for the enjoyment of their native land. Incumbered with the spoils of Asia, he slowly measured back his footsteps, betrayed some pity for the misery of the vanquished, and declared his intention of rebuilding the cities which had been swept away by the tempest of his arms. After he had repassed the Oxus and Jaxartes, he was joined by two generals, whom he had detached with thirty thousand horse, to subdue the western provinces of Persia. They had trampled on the nations which opposed their passage, penetrated through the gates of Derbend, traversed the Volga and the Desert, and accomplished the circuit of the Caspian Sea, by an expedition which had never been attempted, and has never been repeated. The return of Zingis was signalized by the overthrow of the rebellious or independent kingdoms of Tartary; and he died in the fulness of years and glory, with his last breath exhorting and instructing his sons to atchieve the conquest of the Chinese empire.

His death A.D. 1227.

Conquests of the Moguls under the successors of Zingis, A.D. 1227–1295.

The haram of Zingis was composed of five hundred wives and concubines; and of his numerous progeny, four sons, illustrious by their birth and merit, exercised under their father the principal offices of peace and war. Toushi was his great huntsman, Zagatai[21] his judge, Octai his minister, and Tuli his general; and their names and actions are often conspicuous in the history of his conquests. Firmly united for their own and the public interest, the three brothers and their families were content with dependent sceptres; and Octai, by general consent, was proclaimed great khan, or emperor of the Moguls and Tartars. He was succeeded by his son Gayuk, after whose death the empire devolved to his cousins Mangou and Cublai, the sons of Tuli, and the grandsons of Zingis. In the sixty-eight years of his four first successors, the Mogul subdued almost all Asia, and a large portion of Europe. Without confining myself to the order of time, without expatiating on the detail of events, I shall present a general picture of the progress of their arms; I. In the East; II. In the South; III. In the West; and IV. In the North.

Of the northern empire of China, A.D. 1234.

I. Before the invasion of Zingis, China was divided into two empires or dynasties of the North and South;[22] and the difference of origin and interest was smoothed by a general

21. Zagatai gave his name to his dominions of Maurenahar, or Transoxiana; and the Moguls of Hindostan, who emigrated from that country, are styled Zagatais by the Persians. This certain etymology, and the similar example of Uzbek, Nogai, &c. may warn us not absolutely to reject the derivations of a national, from a personal, name.

22. In Marco Polo, and the Oriental geographers, the names of Cathay and Mangi distinguish the northern and southern empires, which, from A.D. 1234 to 1279, were those of the Great Khan, and of the Chinese. The search of Cathay, after China had been found, excited and misled our navigators of the sixteenth century, in their attempts to discover the north-east passage.

conformity of laws, language, and national manners. The Northern empire, which had been dismembered by Zingis, was finally subdued seven years after his death. After the loss of Pekin, the emperor had fixed his residence at Kaifong, a city many leagues in circumference, and which contained, according to the Chinese annals, fourteen hundred thousand families of inhabitants and fugitives. He escaped from thence with only seven horsemen, and made his last stand in a third capital, till at length the hopeless monarch, protesting his innocence and accusing his fortune, ascended a funeral pile, and gave orders, that, as soon as he had stabbed himself, the fire should be kindled by his attendants. The dynasty of the *Song*, the native and ancient sovereigns of the whole empire, survived about forty-five years the fall of the northern usurpers; and the perfect conquest was reserved for the arms of Cublai. During this interval, the Moguls were often diverted by foreign wars; and, if the Chinese seldom dared to meet their victors in the field, their passive courage presented an endless succession of cities to storm and of millions to slaughter. In the attack and defence of places, the engines of antiquity and the Greek fire were alternately employed: the use of gunpowder in cannon and bombs appears as a familiar practice;[23] and the sieges were conducted by the Mahometans and Franks, who had been liberally invited into the service of Cublai. After passing the great river, the troops and artillery were conveyed along a series of canals, till they invested the royal residence of Hamcheu, or Quinsay, in the country of silk, the most delicious climate of China. The emperor, a defenceless youth, surrendered his person and sceptre; and before he was sent in exile into Tartary he struck nine times the ground with his forehead, to adore in prayer or thanksgiving the mercy of the great khan. Yet the war (it was now styled a rebellion) was still maintained in the southern provinces from Hamcheu to Canton; and the obstinate remnant of independence and hostility was transported from the land to the sea. But when the fleet of the *Song* was surrounded and oppressed by a superior

Of the southern, A.D. 1279.

23. I depend on the knowledge and fidelity of the Pere Gaubil, who translates the Chinese text of the Annals of the Moguls or Yuen (p. 71. 93. 153.); but I am ignorant at what time these annals were composed and published. The two uncles of Marco Polo, who served as engineers at the siege of Siengyangfou (l. ii. c. 61. in Ramusio, tom. ii. See Gaubil, p. 155. 157.), must have felt and related the effects of this destructive powder, and their silence is a weighty, and almost decisive, objection. I entertain a suspicion, that the recent discovery was carried from Europe to China by the caravans of the xv[th] century, and falsely adopted as an old national discovery before the arrival of the Portuguese and Jesuits in the xvi[th]. Yet the Pere Gaubil affirms, that the use of gunpowder has been known to the Chinese above 1600 years.

armament, their last champion leaped into the waves with his infant emperor in his arms. "It is more glorious," he cried, "to die a prince, than to live a slave." An hundred thousand Chinese imitated his example; and the whole empire, from Tonkin to the great wall, submitted to the dominion of Cublai. His boundless ambition aspired to the conquest of Japan: his fleet was twice shipwrecked; and the lives of an hundred thousand Moguls and Chinese were sacrificed in the fruitless expedition. But the circumjacent kingdoms, Corea, Tonkin, Cochinchina, Pegu, Bengal, and Thibet, were reduced in different degrees of tribute and obedience by the effort or terror of his arms. He explored the Indian ocean with a fleet of a thousand ships: they sailed in sixty-eight days, most probably to the isle of Borneo, under the equinoctial line; and though they returned not without spoil or glory, the emperor was dissatisfied that the savage king had escaped from their hands.

Of Persia, and the empire of the caliphs, A.D. 1258.

II. The conquest of Hindostan by the Moguls, was reserved in a later period for the house of Timour; but that of Iran, or Persia, was atchieved by Holagou Khan, the grandson of Zingis, the brother and lieutenant of the two successive emperors, Mangou and Cublai. I shall not enumerate the crowd of sultans, emirs, and atabeks, whom he trampled into dust: but the extirpation of the *Assassins*, or Ismaelians[24] of Persia, may be considered as a service to mankind. Among the hills to the south of the Caspian, these odious sectaries had reigned with impunity above an hundred and sixty years; and their prince, or Imam, established his lieutenant to lead and govern the colony of mount Libanus, so famous and formidable in the history of the crusades.[25] With the fanaticism of the Koran, the Ismaelians had blended the Indian transmigration, and the visions of their own prophets: and it was their first duty to devote their souls and bodies in blind obedience to the vicar of God. The daggers of his missionaries were felt both in the East and West: the Christians and the Moslems enumerate, and perhaps multiply, the illustrious victims that were sacrificed to the zeal, avarice, or resentment of *the old man* (as he was corruptly styled) *of the mountain*. But these daggers, his only arms, were broken by the sword of Holagou, and not a vestige is left of the enemies of mankind, except

24. All that can be known of the Assassins of Persia and Syria, is poured from the copious, and even profuse, erudition of M. Falconet, in two *memoires* read before the Academy of Inscriptions (tom. xvii. p. 127–170.).

25. The Ismaelians of Syria, 40,000 Assassins, had acquired or founded ten castles in the hills above Tortosa. About the year 1280, they were extirpated by the Mamalukes.

the word *assassin*, which, in the most odious sense, has been adopted in the languages of Europe. The extinction of the Abbassides cannot be indifferent to the spectators of their greatness and decline. Since the fall of their Seljukian tyrants, the caliphs had recovered their lawful dominion of Bagdad and the Arabian Irak; but the city was distracted by theological factions, and the commander of the faithful was lost in a haram of seven hundred concubines. The invasion of the Moguls he encountered with feeble arms and haughty embassies. "On the divine decree," said the caliph Mostasem, "is founded the throne of the sons of Abbas: and their foes shall surely be destroyed in this world and in the next. Who is this Holagou that dares to arise against them? If he be desirous of peace, let him instantly depart from the sacred territory; and perhaps he may obtain from our clemency the pardon of his fault." This presumption was cherished by a perfidious vizir, who assured his master, that, even if the Barbarians had entered the city, the women and children, from the terraces, would be sufficient to overwhelm them with stones. But when Holagou touched the phantom, it instantly vanished into smoke. After a siege of two months, Bagdad was stormed and sacked by the Moguls: and their savage commander pronounced the death of the caliph Mostasem, the last of the temporal successors of Mahomet; whose noble kinsmen, of the race of Abbas, had reigned in Asia above five hundred years. Whatever might be the designs of the conqueror, the holy cities of Mecca and Medina[26] were protected by the Arabian desert; but the Moguls spread beyond the Tigris and Euphrates, pillaged Aleppo and Damascus, and threatened to join the Franks in the deliverance of Jerusalem. Egypt was lost, had she been defended only by her feeble offspring: but the Mamalukes had breathed in their infancy the keenness of a Scythian air: equal in valour, superior in discipline, they met the Moguls in many a well-fought field; and drove back the stream of hostility to the eastward of the Euphrates. But it overflowed with resistless violence the kingdoms of Armenia and Anatolia, of which the former was possessed by the Christians, and the latter by the Turks. The sultans of Iconium opposed some resistance to the Mogul arms, till Azzadin sought a refuge among the Greeks of Constantinople, and his feeble successors, the last of the Seljukian dynasty, were finally extirpated by the khans of Persia.

Of Anatolia, A.D. 1242–1272.

26. As a proof of the ignorance of the Chinese in foreign transactions, I must observe, that some of their historians extend the conquests of Zingis himself to Medina, the country of Mahomet (Gaubil, p. 42.).

Of Kipzak, Russia, Poland, Hungary, &c. A.D. 1235–1245.

III. No sooner had Octai subverted the northern empire of China, than he resolved to visit with his arms, the most remote countries of the West. Fifteen hundred thousand Moguls and Tartars were inscribed on the military roll; of these the great khan selected a third, which he entrusted to the command of his nephew Batou, the son of Tuli; who reigned over his father's conquests to the north of the Caspian Sea. After a festival of forty days, Batou set forwards on this great expedition; and such was the speed and ardour of his innumerable squadrons,that in less than six years they had measured a line of ninety degrees of longitude, a fourth part of the circumference of the globe. The great rivers of Asia and Europe, the Volga and Kama, the Don and Borysthenes, the Vistula and Danube, they either swam with their horses, or passed on the ice, or traversed in leathern boats, which followed the camp, and transported their waggons and artillery. By the first victories of Batou, the remains of national freedom were eradicated in the immense plains of Turkestan and Kipzak.[27] In his rapid progress, he overran the kingdoms, as they are now styled, of Astracan and Cazan; and the troops which he detached towards mount Caucasus, explored the most secret recesses of Georgia and Circassia. The civil discord of the great dukes, or princes, of Russia, betrayed their country to the Tartars. They spread from Livonia to the Black Sea, and both Moscow and Kiow, the modern and the ancient capitals, were reduced to ashes; a temporary ruin, less fatal than the deep, and perhaps indelible, mark, which a servitude of two hundred years has imprinted on the character of the Russians. The Tartars ravaged with equal fury the countries which they hoped to possess, and those which they were hastening to leave. From the permanent conquest of Russia, they made a deadly, though transient, inroad into the heart of Poland, and as far as the borders of Germany. The cities of Lublin and Cracow were obliterated: they approached the shores of the Baltic; and in the battle of Lignitz, they defeated the dukes of Silesia, the Polish palatines, and the great master of the Teutonic order, and filled nine sacks with the right-ears of the slain. From Lignitz, the extreme point of their western march, they turned aside to the invasion of Hungary; and the presence or spirit of Batou inspired the host of five hundred thousand men: the Carpathian hills could not be long impervious to their divided columns; and their

27. The *Dashté Kipzak*, or plain of Kipzak, extends on either side of the Volga, in a boundless space towards the Jaik and Borysthenes, and is supposed to contain the primitive name and nation of the Cosacks.

approach had been fondly disbelieved till it was irresistibly felt. The king, Bela the fourth, assembled the military force of his counts and bishops: but he had alienated the nation by adopting a vagrant hord of forty thousand families of Comans, and these savage guests were provoked to revolt by the suspicion of treachery and the murder of their prince. The whole country north of the Danube was lost in a day, and depopulated in a summer; and the ruins of cities and churches were overspread with the bones of the natives, who expiated the sins of their Turkish ancestors. An ecclesiastic, who fled from the sack of Waradin, describes the calamities which he had seen or suffered; and the sanguinary rage of sieges and battles is far less atrocious than the treatment of the fugitives, who had been allured from the woods under a promise of peace and pardon, and who were coolly slaughtered as soon as they had performed the labours of the harvest and vintage. In the winter, the Tartars passed the Danube on the ice, and advanced to Gran or Strigonium, a German colony, and the metropolis of the kingdom. Thirty engines were planted against the walls; the ditches were filled with sacks of earth and dead bodies; and after a promiscuous massacre, three hundred noble matrons were slain in the presence of the khan. Of all the cities and fortresses of Hungary, three alone survived the Tartar invasion, and the unfortunate Bela hid his head among the islands of the Adriatic.

The Latin world was darkened by this cloud of savage hostility: a Russian fugitive carried the alarm to Sweden; and the remote nations of the Baltic and the ocean trembled at the approach of the Tartars,[28] whom their fear and ignorance were inclined to separate from the human species. Since the invasion of the Arabs in the eighth century, Europe had never been exposed to a similar calamity; and if the disciples of Mahomet would have oppressed her religion and liberty, it might be apprehended that the shepherds of Scythia would extinguish her cities, her arts, and all the institutions of civil society. The Roman pontiff attempted to appease and convert these invincible Pagans by a mission of Franciscan and Dominican friars; but he was astonished by the reply of the khan, that the sons of God and of Zingis were invested with a divine power to

28. In the year 1238, the inhabitants of Gothia *(Sweden)* and Frise were prevented, by their fear of the Tartars, from sending, as usual, their ships to the herring-fishery on the coast of England; and as there was no exportation, forty or fifty of these fish were sold for a shilling (Matthew Paris, p. 396.). It is whimsical enough, that the orders of a Mogul khan, who reigned on the borders of China, should have lowered the price of herrings in the English market.

subdue or extirpate the nations; and that the pope would be involved in the universal destruction, unless he visited in person, and as a suppliant, the royal hord. The emperor Frederic the second embraced a more generous mode of defence; and his letters to the kings of France and England, and the princes of Germany, represented the common danger, and urged them to arm their vassals in this just and rational crusade.[29] The Tartars themselves were awed by the fame and valour of the Franks: the town of Newstadt in Austria was bravely defended against them by fifty knights and twenty cross-bows; and they raised the siege on the appearance of a German army. After wasting the adjacent kingdoms of Servia, Bosnia, and Bulgaria, Batou slowly retreated from the Danube to the Volga to enjoy the rewards of victory in the city and palace of Serai, which started at his command from the midst of the desert.

Of Siberia A.D. 1242, &c.

IV. Even the poor and frozen regions of the North attracted the arms of the Moguls: Sheibani Khan, the brother of the great Batou, led an hord of fifteen thousand families into the wilds of Siberia; and his descendants reigned at Tobolskoy above three centuries, till the Russian conquest. The spirit of enterprise which pursued the course of the Oby and Yenisei must have led to the discovery of the icy sea. After brushing away the monstrous fables, of men with dogs heads and cloven feet, we shall find, that, fifteen years after the death of Zingis, the Moguls were informed of the name and manners of the Samoyedes in the neighbourhood of the polar circle, who dwelt in subterraneous huts, and derived their furs and their food from the sole occupation of hunting.[30]

The successors of Zingis, A.D. 1227–1259.

While China, Syria, and Poland, were invaded at the same time by the Moguls and Tartars, the authors of the mighty mischief were content with the knowledge and declaration, that their word was the sword of death. Like the first caliphs, the first successors of Zingis seldom appeared in person at the head of

29. I shall copy his characteristic or flattering epithets of the different countries of Europe: Furens ac fervens ad arma Germania, strenuæ militiæ genetrix et alumna Francia, bellicosa et audax Hispania, virtuosa viris et classe munita fertilis Anglia, impetuosis bellatoribus referta Alemannia, navalis Dacia, indomita Italia, pacis ignara Burgundia, inquieta Apulia, cum maris Græci, Adriatici et Tyrrheni insulis pyraticis et invictis, Cretâ, Cypro, Siciliâ, cum Oceano conterminis insulis, et regionibus, cruenta Hybernia, cum agili Wallia, palustris Scotia, glacialis Norwegia suam electam militiam sub vexillo Crucis destinabunt, &c. (Matthew Paris, p. 498.).

30. See Carpin's relation in Hackluyt, vol. i. p. 30. The pedigree of the khans of Siberia is given by Abulghazi (part viii. p. 485–495.). Have the Russians found no Tartar chronicles at Tobolskoi?

their victorious armies. On the banks of the Onon and Selinga, the royal or *golden hord* exhibited the contrast of simplicity and greatness; of the roasted sheep and mare's milk which composed their banquets; and of a distribution in one day of five hundred waggons of gold and silver. The ambassadors and princes of Europe and Asia were compelled to undertake this distant and laborious pilgrimage; and the life and reign of the great dukes of Russia, the kings of Georgia and Armenia, the sultans of Iconium, and the emirs of Persia, were decided by the frown or smile of the great khan. The sons and grandsons of Zingis had been accustomed to the pastoral life; but the village of Caracorum[31] was gradually ennobled by their election and residence. A change of manners is implied in the removal of Octai and Mangou from a tent to an house; and their example was imitated by the princes of their family and the great officers of the empire. Instead of the boundless forest, the inclosure of a park afforded the more indolent pleasures of the chace; their new habitations were decorated with painting and sculpture; their superfluous treasures were cast in fountains, and basons, and statues of massy silver; and the artists of China and Paris vied with each other in the service of the great khan.[32] Caracorum contained two streets, the one of Chinese mechanics, the other of Mahometan traders; and the places of religious worship, one Nestorian church, two moschs, and twelve temples of various idols, may represent in some degree the number and division of inhabitants. Yet a French missionary declares, that the town of St. Denys, near Paris, was more considerable than the Tartar capital; and that the whole palace of Mangou was scarcely equal to a tenth part of that Benedictine abbey. The conquests of Russia and Syria might amuse the vanity of the great khans; but they were seated on the borders of China; the acquisition of that empire was the nearest and most interesting object; and they might learn from their pastoral œconomy, that it is for the advantage of the shepherd to protect and propagate his flock. I have already celebrated the wisdom and virtue of a Mandarin, who prevented the desolation of five populous and cultivated

adopt the manners of China, A.D. 1259–1368.

31. The Map of d'Anville, and the Chinese Itineraries (de Guignes, tom. i. part ii. p. 57.), seem to mark the position of Holin, or Caracorum, about six hundred miles to the north-west of Pekin. The distance between Selinginsky and Pekin is near 2000 Russian versts, between 1300 and 1400 English miles (Bell's Travels, vol. ii. p. 67.).

32. Rubruquis found at Caracoram his countryman *Guillaume Boucher orfevre de Paris*, who had executed for the khan a silver tree, supported by four lions, and ejecting four different liquors. Abulghazi (part iv. p. 366.) mentions the painters of Kitay or China.

provinces. In a spotless administration of thirty years, this friend of his country and of mankind continually laboured to mitigate, or suspend, the havock of war; to save the monuments, and to rekindle the flame, of science; to restrain the military commander by the restoration of civil magistrates; and to instill the love of peace and justice into the minds of the Moguls. He struggled with the barbarism of the first conquerors; but his salutary lessons produced a rich harvest in the second generation. The northern, and by degrees the southern, empire, acquiesced in the government of Cublai, the lieutenant, and afterwards the successor, of Mangou; and the nation was loyal to a prince who had been educated in the manners of China. He restored the forms of her venerable constitution; and the victors submitted to the laws, the fashions, and even the prejudices, of the vanquished people. This peaceful triumph, which has been more than once repeated, may be ascribed in a great measure to the numbers and servitude of the Chinese. The Mogul army was dissolved in a vast and populous country; and their emperors adopted with pleasure a political system, which gives to the prince the solid substance of despotism, and leaves to the subject the empty names of philosophy, freedom, and filial obedience. Under the reign of Cublai, letters and commerce, peace and justice, were restored; the great canal, of five hundred miles, was opened from Nankin to the capital; he fixed his residence at Pekin; and displayed in his court the magnificence of the greatest monarch of Asia. Yet this learned prince declined from the pure and simple religion of his great ancestor; he sacrificed to the idol Fo; and his blind attachment to the lamas of Thibet and the bonzes of China[33] provoked the censure of the disciples of Confucius. His successors polluted the palace with a crowd of eunuchs, physicians, and astrologers, while thirteen millions of their subjects were consumed in the provinces by famine. One hundred and forty years after the death of Zingis, his degenerate race, the dynasty of the Yuen, was expelled by a revolt of the native Chinese; and the Mogul emperors were lost in the oblivion of the desert. Before this revolution, they had forfeited their supremacy over the dependent branches of their house, the khans of Kipzak and Russia, the khans of Zagatai

Division of the Mogul empire, A.D. 1259–1300.

33. The attachment of the khans, and the hatred of the mandarins, to the bonzes and lamas (Duhalde, Hist. de la Chine, tom. i. p. 502, 503.) seems to represent them as the priests of the same god, of the Indian *Fo*, whose worship prevails among the sects of Hindostan, Siam, Thibet, China, and Japan. But this mysterious subject is still lost in a cloud, which the researches of our Asiatic Society may gradually dispel.

or Transoxiana, and the khans of Iran or Persia. By their distance and power these royal lieutenants had soon been released from the duties of obedience; and, after the death of Cublai, they scorned to accept a sceptre or a title from his unworthy successors. According to their respective situation they maintained the simplicity of the pastoral life, or assumed the luxury of the cities of Asia; but the princes and their hords were alike disposed for the reception of a foreign worship. After some hesitation between the Gospel and the Koran, they conformed to the religion of Mahomet; and while they adopted for their brethren the Arabs and Persians, they renounced all intercourse with the ancient Moguls, the idolaters of China.

Escape of Constantinople and the Greek empire from the Moguls, A.D. 1240–1304.

In this shipwreck of nations, some surprise may be excited by the escape of the Roman empire, whose relics, at the time of the Mogul invasion, were dismembered by the Greeks and Latins. Less potent than Alexander, they were pressed, like the Macedonian, both in Europe and Asia, by the shepherds of Scythia; and had the Tartars undertaken the siege, Constantinople must have yielded to the fate of Pekin, Samarcand, and Bagdad. The glorious and voluntary retreat of Batou from the Danube was insulted by the vain triumph of the Franks and Greeks;[34] and in a second expedition death surprised him in full march to attack the capital of the Cæsars. His brother Borga carried the Tartar arms into Bulgaria and Thrace; but he was diverted from the Byzantine war by a visit to Novogorod, in the fifty-seventh degree of latitude, where he numbered the inhabitants and regulated the tributes of Russia. The Mogul khan formed an alliance with the Mamalukes against his brethren of Persia: three hundred thousand horse penetrated through the gates of Derbend; and the Greeks might rejoice in the first example of domestic war. After the recovery of Constantinople, Michael Palæologus,[35] at a distance from his court and army, was surprised and surrounded in a Thracian castle by twenty thousand Tartars. But the object of their march was a private interest: they came to the deliverance of Azzadin, the Turkish sultan; and were content with his person and the treasure of the emperor. Their general Noga, whose name is perpetuated in the hords

34. Some repulse of the Moguls in Hungary (Matthew Paris, p. 545, 546.) might propagate and colour the report of the union and victory of the kings of the Franks on the confines of Bulgaria. Abulpharagius (Dynast. p. 310.), after forty years, beyond the Tigris, might be easily deceived.

35. See Pachymer, l. iii. c. 25. and l. ix. c. 26, 27.: and the false alarm at Nice, l. iii. c. 27. Nicephorus Gregoras, l. iv. c. 6.

of Astracan, raised a formidable rebellion against Mengo Timour, the third of the khans of Kipzak; obtained in marriage Maria the natural daughter of Palæologus; and guarded the dominions of his friend and father. The subsequent invasions of a Scythian cast were those of outlaws and fugitives; and some thousands of Alani and Comans, who had been driven from their native seats, were reclaimed from a vagrant life, and enlisted in the service of the empire. Such was the influence in Europe of the invasion of the Moguls. The first terror of their arms secured, rather than disturbed, the peace of the Roman Asia. The sultan of Iconium solicited a personal interview with John Vataces; and his artful policy encouraged the Turks to defend their barrier against the common enemy.[36] That barrier indeed was soon overthrown; and the servitude and ruin of the Seljukians exposed the nakedness of the Greeks. The formidable Holagou threatened to march to Constantinople at the head of four hundred thousand men; and the groundless panic of the citizens of Nice will present an image of the terror which he had inspired. The accident of a procession, and the sound of a doleful litany, "From the fury of the Tartars, good Lord deliver us," had scattered the hasty report of an assault and massacre. In the blind credulity of fear, the streets of Nice were crowded with thousands of both sexes, who knew not from what or to whom they fled; and some hours elapsed before the firmness of the military officers could relieve the city from this imaginary foe. But the ambition of Holagou and his successors was fortunately diverted by the conquest of Bagdad, and a long vicissitude of Syrian wars: their hostility to the Moslems inclined them to unite with the Greeks and Franks;[37] and their generosity or contempt had offered the kingdom of Anatolia as the reward of an Armenian vassal. The fragments of the Seljukian monarchy were disputed by the emirs who had occupied the cities or the mountains; but they all confessed the supremacy of the khans of Persia; and he often interposed his authority, and sometimes his arms, to check their depredations, and to preserve the peace and balance of his Turkish frontier. The death of Cazan,[38] one of the greatest and most accomplished

Decline of the Mogul khans of Persia, A.D. 1304, May 31.

36. G. Acropolita, p. 36, 37. Nic. Gregoras, l. ii. c. 6. l. iv. c. 5.

37. Abulpharagius, who wrote in the year 1284, declares, that the Moguls, since the fabulous defeat of Batou, had not attacked either the Franks or Greeks; and of this he is a competent witness. Hayton, likewise the Armeniac prince, celebrates their friendship for himself and his nation.

38. Pachymer gives a splendid character of Cazan Khan, the rival of Cyrus and Alexander (l. xii. c. 1.). In the conclusion of his history (l. xiii. c. 36.), he *hopes* much from the arrival of 30,000 Tochars or

princes of the house of Zingis, removed this salutary control; and the decline of the Moguls gave a free scope to the rise and progress of the OTTOMAN EMPIRE.[39]

Origin of the Ottomans, A.D. 1240, &c.

After the retreat of Zingis, the sultan Gelaleddin of Carizme had returned from India to the possession and defence of his Persian kingdoms. In the space of eleven years, that hero fought in person fourteen battles; and such was his activity, that he led his cavalry in seventeen days from Teflis to Kerman, a march of a thousand miles. Yet he was oppressed by the jealousy of the Moslem princes, and the innumerable armies of the Moguls; and after his last defeat, Gelaleddin perished ignobly in the mountains of Curdistan. His death dissolved a veteran and adventurous army, which included under the name of Carizmians or Corasmins many Turkman hords, that had attached themselves to the sultan's fortune. The bolder and more powerful chiefs invaded Syria, and violated the holy sepulchre of Jerusalem: the more humble engaged in the service of Aladin, sultan of Iconium; and among these were the obscure fathers of the Ottoman line. They had formerly pitched their tents near the southern banks of the Oxus, in the plains of Mahan and Nesa; and it is somewhat remarkable, that the same spot should have produced the first authors of the Parthian and Turkish empires. At the head, or in the rear, of a Carizmian army, Soliman Shah was drowned in the passage of the Euphrates: his son Orthogrul became the soldier and subject of Aladin, and established at Surgut, on the banks of the Sangar, a camp of four hundred families or tents, whom he governed fifty-two years both in peace and war. He was the father of Thaman, or Athman, whose Turkish name has been melted into the appellation of the caliph Othman; and if we describe that pastoral chief as a shepherd and a robber, we must separate from those characters all idea of ignominy and baseness. Othman possessed, and perhaps surpassed, the ordinary virtues of a soldier; and the circumstances of time and place were propitious to his independence and success. The Seljukian dynasty was no more; and the distance and decline of the Mogul khans soon enfranchised him from the control of a superior. He was situate on the verge of the Greek empire: the Koran

Reign of Othman, A.D. 1299–1326.

Tartars, who were ordered by the successor of Cazan to restrain the Turks of Bithynia, A.D. 1308.

39. The origin of the Ottoman dynasty is illustrated by the critical learning of M. M. de Guignes (Hist. des Huns, tom. iv. p. 329–337.) and d'Anville (Empire Turc, p. 14–22.), two inhabitants of Paris, from whom the Orientals may learn the history and geography of their own country.

sanctified his *gazi*, or holy war, against the infidels; and their political errors unlocked the passes of mount Olympus, and invited him to descend into the plains of Bithynia. Till the reign of Palæologus, these passes had been vigilantly guarded by the militia of the country, who were repaid by their own safety and an exemption from taxes. The emperor abolished their privilege and assumed their office; but the tribute was rigorously collected, the custody of the passes was neglected, and the hardy mountaineers degenerated into a trembling crowd of peasants without spirit or discipline. It was on the twenty-seventh of July, in the year twelve hundred and ninety-nine of the Christian æra, that Othman first invaded the territory of Nicomedia;[40] and the singular accuracy of the date seems to disclose some foresight of the rapid and destructive growth of the monster. The annals of the twenty-seven years of his reign would exhibit a repetition of the same inroads; and his hereditary troops were multiplied in each campaign by the accession of captives and volunteers. Instead of retreating to the hills, he maintained the most useful and defensible posts; fortified the towns and castles which he had first pillaged; and renounced the pastoral life for the baths and palaces of his infant capitals. But it was not till Othman was oppressed by age and infirmities, that he received the welcome news of the conquest of Prusa, which had been surrendered by famine or treachery to the arms of his son Orchan. The glory of Othman is chiefly founded on that of his descendants; but the Turks have transcribed or composed a royal testament of his last counsels of justice and moderation.[41]

40. See Pachymer, l. x. c. 25, 26. l. xiii. c. 33, 34. 36.; and concerning the guard of the mountains, l. i. c. 3–6.: Nicephorus Gregoras, l. vii. c. 1. and the 1st book of Laonicus Chalcocondyles, the Athenian.

41. I am ignorant whether the Turks have any writers older than Mahomet II. nor can I reach beyond a meagre chronicle (Annales Turcici ad Annum 1550), translated by John Gaudier, and published by Leunclavius (ad calcem Laonic. Chalcond. p. 311–350.), with copious pandects, or commentaries. The History of the Growth and Decay (A.D. 1300–1683) of the Othman Empire, was translated into English from the Latin MS. of Demetrius Cantemir, prince of Moldavia (London, 1734, in folio). The author is guilty of strange blunders in Oriental history; but he was conversant with the language, the annals, and institutions of the Turks. Cantemir partly draws his materials from the Synopsis of Saadi Effendi of Larissa, dedicated in the year 1696 to sultan Mustapha, and a valuable abridgment of the original historians. In one of the Ramblers, Dr. Johnson praises Knolles (a General History of the Turks to the present Year. London, 1603) as the first of historians, unhappy only in the choice of his subject. Yet I much doubt whether a partial and verbose compilation from Latin writers, thirteen hundred folio pages of speeches and battles, can either instruct or amuse an enlightened

Reign of Orchan, A.D. 1326–1360.

From the conquest of Prusa, we may date the true æra of the Ottoman empire. The lives and possessions of the Christian subjects were redeemed by a tribute or ransom of thirty thousand crowns of gold; and the city, by the labours of Orchan, assumed the aspect of a Mahometan capital; Prusa was decorated with a mosch, a college, and an hospital, of royal foundation; the Seljukian coin was changed for the name and impression of the new dynasty: and the most skilful professors, of human and divine knowledge, attracted the Persian and Arabian students from the ancient schools of Oriental learning. The office of vizir was instituted for Aladin, the brother of Orchan; and a different habit distinguished the citizens from the peasants, the Moslems from the infidels. All the troops of Othman had consisted of loose squadrons of Turkman cavalry; who served without pay and fought without discipline: but a regular body of infantry was first established and trained by the prudence of his son. A great number of volunteers was enrolled with a small stipend, but with the permission of living at home, unless they were summoned to the field: their rude manners, and seditious temper, disposed Orchan to educate his young captives as his soldiers and those of the prophet; but the Turkish peasants were still allowed to mount on horseback, and follow his standard, with the appellation and the hopes of *freebooters*. By these arts he formed an army of twenty-five thousand Moslems: a train of battering engines was framed for the use of sieges; and the first successful experiment was made on the cities of Nice and Nicomedia. Orchan granted a safe-conduct to all who were desirous of departing with their families and effects; but the widows of the slain were given in marriage to the conquerors; and the sacrilegious plunder, the books, the vases, and the images, were sold or ransomed at Constantinople. The emperor Andronicus the younger was vanquished and wounded by the son of Othman:[42] he subdued the whole province or kingdom of Bithynia, as far as the shores of the Bosphorus and Hellespont; and the Christians confessed the justice and clemency of a reign, which claimed the voluntary attachment of the Turks of Asia. Yet Orchan was content with the modest title of emir; and

His conquest of Bithynia, A.D. 1326–1339.

age, which requires from the historian some tincture of philosophy and criticism.

42. Cantacuzene, though he relates the battle and heroic flight of the younger Andronicus (l. ii. c. 6, 7, 8.), dissembles by his silence the loss of Prusa, Nice, and Nicomedia, which are fairly confessed by Nicephorus Gregoras (l. viii. 15. ix. 9. 13. xi. 6.). It appears that Nice was taken by Orchan in 1330, and Nicomedia in 1339, which are somewhat different from the Turkish dates.

Division of Anatolia among the Turkish emirs, A.D. 1300, &c.

in the list of his compeers, the princes of Roum or Anatolia,[43] his military forces were surpassed by the emirs of Ghermian and Caramania, each of whom could bring into the field an army of forty thousand men. Their dominions were situate in the heart of the Seljukian kingdom: but the holy warriors, though of inferior note, who formed new principalities on the Greek empire, are more conspicuous in the light of history. The maritime country from the Propontis to the Mæander and the isle of Rhodes, so long threatened and so often pillaged, was finally lost about the thirtieth year of Andronicus the elder.[44] Two Turkish chieftains, Sarukhan and Aidin, left their names to their conquests, and their conquests to their posterity. The captivity or ruin of the *seven* churches of Asia was consummated; and the barbarous lords of Ionia and Lydia still trample on the monuments of classic and Christian antiquity. In the loss of Ephesus, the Christians deplored the fall of the first angel, the extinction of the first candlestick, of the revelations:[45] the desolation is complete; and the temple of Diana, or the church of Mary, will equally elude the search of the curious traveller. The circus and three stately theatres of Laodicea are now peopled with wolves and foxes; Sardes is reduced to a miserable village; the God of Mahomet, without a rival or a son, is invoked in the moschs of Thyatira and Pergamus; and the populousness of Smyrna is supported by the foreign trade of the Franks and Armenians. Philadelphia alone has been saved by prophecy, or courage. At a distance from the sea, forgotten by the emperors, encompassed on all sides by the Turks, her valiant citizens defended their religion and freedom above fourscore years; and at length capitulated with the proudest of the Ottomans. Among the Greek colonies and churches of Asia, Philadelphia is still erect; a column in a scene of ruins; a pleasing example, that the paths of honour and safety may sometimes be the same. The servitude of Rhodes was delayed above two centuries by the establishment of the knights

Loss of the Asiatic provinces, A.D. 1312, &c.

The knights of Rhodes, A.D. 1310,

43. The partition of the Turkish emirs is extracted from two contemporaries, the Greek Nicephorus Gregoras (l. vii. 1.) and the Arabian Marakeschi (de Guignes, tom. ii. P. ii. p. 76, 77.). See likewise the first book of Laonicus Chacondyles.

44. Pachymer, l. xiii. c. 13.

45. See the Travels of Wheeler and Spon, of Pococke and Chandler, and more particularly Smith's Survey of the Seven Churches of Asia, p. 205–276. The more pious antiquaries labour to reconcile the promises and threats of the author of the Revelations with the *present* state of the seven cities. Perhaps it would be more prudent to confine his predictions to the characters and events of his own times.

of St. John of Jerusalem:[46] under the discipline of the order, that island emerged into fame and opulence; and the noble and warlike monks were renowned by land and sea; and the bulwark of Christendom provoked, and repelled, the arms of the Turks and Saracens.

August 15– A.D. 1523, January 1.

First passage of the Turks into Europe A.D. 1341–1347.

The Greeks, by their intestine divisions, were the authors of their final ruin. During the civil wars of the elder and younger Andronicus, the son of Othman atchieved, almost without resistance, the conquest of Bithynia; and the same disorders encouraged the Turkish emirs of Lydia and Ionia to build a fleet, and to pillage the adjacent islands and the sea-coast of Europe. In the defence of his life and honour, Cantacuzene was tempted to prevent, or imitate, his adversaries; by calling to his aid the public enemies of his religion and country. Amir, the son of Aidin, concealed under a Turkish garb the humanity and politeness of a Greek; he was united with the great domestic by mutual esteem and reciprocal services; and their friendship is compared, in the vain rhetoric of the times, to the perfect union of Orestes and Pylades.[47] On the report of the danger of his friend, who was persecuted by an ungrateful court, the prince of Ionia assembled at Smyrna a fleet of three hundred vessels, with an army of twenty-nine thousand men; sailed in the depth of winter, and cast anchor at the mouth of the Hebrus. From thence, with a chosen band of two thousand Turks, he marched along the banks of the river, and rescued the empress, who was besieged in Demotica by the wild Bulgarians. At that disastrous moment, the life or death of his beloved Cantacuzene was concealed by his flight into Servia: but the grateful Irene, impatient to behold her deliverer, invited him to enter the city, and accompanied her message with a present of rich apparel, and an hundred horses. By a peculiar strain of delicacy, the gentle Barbarian refused, in the absence of an unfortunate friend, to visit his wife, or to taste the luxuries of the palace; sustained in his tent the rigour of the winter; and rejected the hospitable gift, that he might share the hardships of two thousand companions, all as deserving

46. Consult the iv[th] book of the Histoire de l'Ordre de Malthe, par l'Abbé de Vertot. That pleasing writer betrays his ignorance, in supposing that Othman, a freebooter of the Bithynian hills, could besiege Rhodes by sea and land.

47. Nicephorus Gregoras has expatiated with pleasure on this amiable character (l. xii. 7. xiii. 4. 10. xiv. 1. 9. xvi. 6.). Cantacuzene speaks with honour and esteem of his ally (l. iii. c. 56, 57. 63, 64. 66, 67, 68. 86. 89. 95, 96.); but he seems ignorant of his own sentimental passion for the Turk, and indirectly denies the possibility of such unnatural friendship (l. iv. c. 40.).

as himself of that honour and distinction. Necessity and revenge might justify his prædatory excursions by sea and land: he left nine thousand five hundred men for the guard of his fleet; and persevered in the fruitless search of Cantacuzene, till his embarkation was hastened by a fictitious letter, the severity of the season, the clamours of his independent troops, and the weight of his spoil and captives. In the prosecution of the civil war, the prince of Ionia twice returned to Europe; joined his arms with those of the emperor; besieged Thessalonica, and threatened Constantinople. Calumny might affix some reproach on his imperfect aid, his hasty departure, and a bribe of ten thousand crowns, which he accepted from the Byzantine court; but his friend was satisfied; and the conduct of Amir is excused by the more sacred duty of defending against the Latins his hereditary dominions. The maritime power of the Turks had united the pope, the king of Cyprus, the republic of Venice, and the order of St. John, in a laudable crusade; their gallies invaded the coast of Ionia; and Amir was slain with an arrow, in the attempt to wrest from the Rhodian knights the citadel of Smyrna.[48] Before his death, he generously recommended another ally of his own nation; not more sincere or zealous than himself, but more able to afford a prompt and powerful succour, by his situation along the Propontis and in the front of Constantinople. By the prospect of a more advantageous treaty, the Turkish prince of Bithynia was detached from his engagements with Anne of Savoy; and the pride of Orchan dictated the most solemn protestations, that if he could obtain the daughter of Cantacuzene, he would invariably fulfil the duties of a subject and a son. Parental tenderness was silenced by the voice of ambition; the Greek clergy connived at the marriage of a Christian princess with a sectary of Mahomet; and the father of Theodora describes, with shameful satisfaction, the dishonour of the purple.[49] A body of Turkish cavalry attended the ambassadors, who disembarked from thirty vessels before his camp of Selybria. A stately pavillion was erected, in which the empress Irene passed the night with her daughters. In the morning, Theodora

Marriage of Orchan with a Greek princess, A.D. 1346.

48. After the conquest of Smyrna by the Latins, the defence of this fortress was imposed by pope Gregory XI. on the knights of Rhodes (see Vertot. l. v.).

49. See Cantacuzenus, l. iii. c. 95. Nicephorus Gregoras, who, for the light of mount Thabor, brands the emperor with the names of tyrant and Herod, excuses, rather than blames, this Turkish marriage, and alleges the passion and power of Orchan, *εγγυτατος, και τη δυναμει τους κατ' αυτον ηδη Περσικους* (Turkish) *ὑπεραιρων Σατραπας* (l. xv. 5.). He afterwards celebrates his kingdom and armies. See his reign in Cantemir, p. 24–30.

ascended a throne, which was surrounded with curtains of silk and gold: the troops were under arms; but the emperor alone was on horseback. At a signal the curtains were suddenly withdrawn, to disclose the bride, or the victim, encircled by kneeling eunuchs and hymenæal torches: the sound of flutes and trumpets proclaimed the joyful event; and her pretended happiness was the theme of the nuptial song, which was chaunted by such poets as the age could produce. Without the rites of the church, Theodora was delivered to her barbarous lord: but it had been stipulated, that she should preserve her religion in the haram of Bursa; and her father celebrates her charity and devotion in this ambiguous situation. After his peaceful establishment on the throne of Constantinople, the Greek emperor visited his Turkish ally, who with four sons, by various wives, expected him at Scutari, on the Asiatic shore. The two princes partook, with seeming cordiality, of the pleasures of the banquet and the chace; and Theodora was permitted to repass the Bosphorus, and to enjoy some days in the society of her mother. But the friendship of Orchan was subservient to his religion and interest; and in the Genoese war he joined without a blush the enemies of Cantacuzene.

Establishment of the Ottomans in Europe, A.D. 1353.

In the treaty with the empress Anne, the Ottoman prince had inserted a singular condition, that it should be lawful for him to sell his prisoners at Constantinople, or transport them into Asia. A naked crowd of Christians of both sexes and every age, of priests and monks, of matrons and virgins, was exposed in the public market; the whip was frequently used to quicken the charity of redemption; and the indigent Greeks deplored the fate of their brethren, who were led away to the worst evils of temporal and spiritual bondage.[50] Cantacuzene was reduced to subscribe the same terms; and their execution must have been still more pernicious to the empire: a body of ten thousand Turks had been detached to the assistance of the empress Anne; but the entire forces of Orchan were exerted in the service of his father. Yet these calamities were of a transient nature; as soon as the storm had passed away, the fugitives might return to their habitations; and at the conclusion of the civil and foreign wars, Europe was completely evacuated by the Moslems of Asia. It was in his last quarrel with his pupil that Cantacuzene inflicted the deep and deadly wound, which could never be healed by his successors, and which is poorly expiated by his theological dialogues against the prophet Mahomet. Ignorant of their

50. The most lively and concise picture of this captivity, may be found in the history of Ducas (c. 8.), who fairly describes what Cantacuzene confesses with a guilty blush!

own history, the modern Turks confound their first and their final passage of the Hellespont,[51] and describe the son of Orchan as a nocturnal robber, who, with eighty companions, explores by stratagem an hostile and unknown shore. Soliman, at the head of ten thousand horse, was transported in the vessels, and entertained as the friend, of the Greek emperor. In the civil wars of Romania, he performed some service and perpetrated more mischief; but the Chersonesus was insensibly filled with a Turkish colony; and the Byzantine court solicited in vain the restitution of the fortresses of Thrace. After some artful delays between the Ottoman prince and his son, their ransom was valued at sixty thousand crowns, and the first payment had been made, when an earthquake shook the walls and cities of the provinces; the dismantled places were occupied by the Turks; and Gallipoli, the key of the Hellespont, was rebuilt and repeopled by the policy of Soliman. The abdication of Cantacuzene dissolved the feeble bands of domestic alliance; and his last advice admonished his countrymen to decline a rash contest, and to compare their own weakness with the numbers and valour, the discipline and enthusiasm, of the Moslems. His prudent counsels were despised by the headstrong vanity of youth, and soon justified by the victories of the Ottomans. But as he practised in the field the exercise of the *jerid*, Soliman was killed by a fall from his horse; and the aged Orchan wept and expired on the tomb of his valiant son.

Death of Orchan and his son Soliman.

The reign and European conquests of Amurath I. A.D. 1360–1389, September.

But the Greeks had not time to rejoice in the death of their enemies; and the Turkish scymetar was wielded with the same spirit by Amurath the first, the son of Orchan and the brother of Soliman. By the pale and fainting light of the Byzantine annals,[52] we can discern, that he subdued without resistance the whole province of Romania or Thrace, from the Hellespont to mount Hæmus, and the verge of the capital; and that Adrianople was chosen for the royal seat of his government and religion in Europe. Constantinople, whose decline is almost coeval with her foundation, had often, in the lapse of a thousand years, been assaulted by the Barbarians

51. In this passage, and the first conquests in Europe, Cantemir (p. 27, &c.) gives a miserable idea of his Turkish guides: nor am I much better satisfied with Chalcondyles (l. i. p. 12, &c.). They forget to consult the most authentic record, the iv[th] book of Cantacuzene. I likewise regret the last books, which are still manuscript, of Nicephorus Gregoras.

52. After the conclusion of Cantacuzene and Gregoras, there follows a dark interval of an hundred years. George Phranza, Michael Ducas, and Laonicus Chalcondyles, all three wrote after the taking of Constantinople.

of the East and West; but never till this fatal hour had the Greeks been surrounded, both in Asia and Europe, by the arms of the same hostile monarchy. Yet the prudence or generosity of Amurath postponed for a while this easy conquest; and his pride was satisfied with the frequent and humble attendance of the emperor John Palæologus and his four sons, who followed at his summons the court and camp of the Ottoman prince. He marched against the Sclavonian nations between the Danube and the Adriatic, the Bulgarians, Servians, Bosnians, and Albanians; and these warlike tribes, who had so often insulted the majesty of the empire, were repeatedly broken by his destructive inroads. Their countries did not abound either in gold or silver; nor were their rustic hamlets and townships enriched by commerce or decorated by the arts of luxury. But the natives of the soil have been distinguished in every age by their hardiness of mind and body; and they were converted by a prudent institution into the firmest and most faithful supporters of the Ottoman greatness.[53] The vizir of Amurath reminded his sovereign that, according to the Mahometan law, he was entitled to a fifth part of the spoil and captives; and that the duty might easily be levied, if vigilant officers were stationed at Gallipoli, to watch the passage, and to select for his use the stoutest and most beautiful of the Christian youth. The advice was followed; the edict was proclaimed; many thousands of the European captives were educated in religion and arms; and the new militia was consecrated and named by a celebrated dervish. Standing in the front of their ranks, he stretched the sleeve of his gown over the head of the foremost soldier, and his blessing was delivered in these words: "Let them be called janizaries (*Yengi cheri*, or new soldiers); may their countenance be ever bright! their hand victorious! their sword keen! may their spear always hang over the heads of their enemies! and wheresoever they go, may they return with a *white face*!"[54] Such was the origin of these haughty troops, the terror of the nations, and sometimes of the sultans themselves. Their valour has declined, their discipline is relaxed, and their tumultuary array is incapable of contending with the order and weapons of modern tactics; but at the time of their institution, they possessed a decisive superiority in war; since a regular body of infantry, in constant exercise and pay, was not maintained by any of the princes of

The Janizaries.

53. See Cantemir, p. 37–41. with his own large and curious annotations.

54. *White* and *black* face are common and proverbial expressions of praise and reproach in the Turkish language. Hic *niger* est, hunc tu Romane caveto, was likewise a Latin sentence.

Christendom. The Janizaries fought with the zeal of proselytes against their *idolatrous* countrymen; and in the battle of Cossova, the league and independence of the Sclavonian tribes was finally crushed. As the conqueror walked over the field, he observed that the greatest part of the slain consisted of beardless youths; and listened to the flattering reply of his vizir, that age and wisdom would have taught them not to oppose his irresistible arms. But the sword of his Janizaries could not defend him from the dagger of despair; a Servian soldier started from the crowd of dead bodies, and Amurath was pierced in the belly with a mortal wound. The grandson of Othman was mild in his temper, modest in his apparel, and a lover of learning and virtue; but the Moslems were scandalised at his absence from public worship; and he was corrected by the firmness of the mufti, who dared to reject his testimony in a civil cause: a mixture of servitude and freedom not unfrequent in Oriental history.[55]

The reign of Bajazet I. Ilderim, A.D. 1389–1403, March 9.

The character of Bajazet, the son and successor of Amurath, is strongly expressed in his surname of *Ilderim*, or the lightning; and he might glory in an epithet, which was drawn from the fiery energy of his soul and the rapidity of his destructive march. In the fourteen years of his reign,[56] he incessantly moved, at the head of his armies, from Boursa to Adrianople, from the Danube to the Euphrates; and, though he strenuously laboured for the propagation of the law, he invaded, with impartial ambition, the Christian and Mahometan princes of Europe and Asia. From Angora to Amasia and Erzeroum, the northern regions of Anatolia were reduced to his obedience: he stripped of their hereditary possessions, his brother emirs of Ghermian and Caramania, of Aidin and Sarukhan; and after the conquest of Iconium, the ancient kingdom of the Seljukians again revived in the Ottoman dynasty. Nor were the conquests of Bajazet less rapid or important in Europe. No sooner had he imposed a regular form of servitude on the Servians and

His conquests, from the Euphrates to the Danube.

55. See the life and death of Morad, or Amurath I. in Cantemir (p. 33–45.), the i[st] book of Chalcondyles, and the Annales Turcici of Leunclavius. According to another story, the sultan was stabbed by a Croat in his tent: and this accident was alleged to Busbequius (Epist. i. p. 98.) as an excuse for the unworthy precaution of pinioning, as it were, between two attendants, an ambassador's arms, when he is introduced to the royal presence.

56. The reign of Bajazet I. or Ilderim Bayazid, is contained in Cantemir (p. 46.), the ii[d] book of Chalcondyles, and the Annales Turcici. The surname of Ilderim, or lightning, is an example, that the conquerors and poets of every age have *felt* the truth of a system which derives the sublime from the principle of terror.

Bulgarians, than he passed the Danube to seek new enemies and new subjects in the heart of Moldavia.[57] Whatever yet adhered to the Greek empire in Thrace, Macedonia, and Thessaly, acknowledged a Turkish master: an obsequious bishop led him through the gates of Thermopylæ into Greece; and we may observe, as a singular fact, that the widow of a Spanish chief, who possessed the ancient seat of the oracle of Delphi, deserved his favour by the sacrifice of a beauteous daughter. The Turkish communication between Europe and Asia had been dangerous and doubtful, till he stationed at Gallipoli a fleet of gallies, to command the Hellespont and intercept the Latin succours of Constantinople. While the monarch indulged his passions in a boundless range of injustice and cruelty, he imposed on his soldiers the most rigid laws of modesty and abstinence; and the harvest was peaceably reaped and sold within the precincts of his camp. Provoked by the loose and corrupt administration of justice, he collected in a house the judges and lawyers of his dominions, who expected that in a few moments the fire would be kindled to reduce them to ashes. His ministers trembled in silence: but an Æthiopian buffoon presumed to insinuate the true cause of the evil; and future venality was left without excuse, by annexing an adequate salary to the office of cadhi.[58] The humble title of emir was no longer suitable to the Ottoman greatness; and Bajazet condescended to accept a patent of sultan from the caliphs who served in Egypt under the yoke of the Mamalukes:[59] a last and frivolous homage that was yielded by force to opinion; by the Turkish conquerors to the house of Abbas and the successors of the Arabian prophet. The ambition of the sultan was inflamed by the obligation of deserving this august title; and he turned his arms against the kingdom of Hungary, the perpetual theatre of the Turkish victories and defeats. Sigismond, the Hungarian king, was the son and brother of the emperors of the West: his cause was that of Europe and the church: and, on the report of his danger, the bravest knights of France and Germany

57. Cantemir, who celebrates the victories of the great Stephen over the Turks (p. 47.), had composed the ancient and modern state of his principality of Moldavia, which has been long promised, and is still unpublished.

58. Leunclav. Annal. Turcici, p. 318, 319. The venality of the cadhis has long been an object of scandal and satire; and if we distrust the observations of our travellers, we may consult the feeling of the Turks themselves (d'Herbelot, Bibliot. Orientale, p. 216, 217. 229, 230.).

59. The fact, which is attested by the Arabic history of Ben Schounah, a contemporary Syrian (de Guignes, Hist. des Huns, tom. iv. p. 336.), destroys the testimony of Saad Effendi and Cantemir (p. 14, 15.), of the election of Othman to the dignity of sultan.

Battle of Nicopolis, A.D. 1396, Sept. 28.

were eager to march under his standard and that of the cross. In the battle of Nicopolis, Bajazet defeated a confederate army of an hundred thousand Christians, who had proudly boasted, that if the sky should fall they could uphold it on their lances. The far greater part were slain or driven into the Danube; and Sigismond, escaping to Constantinople by the river and the Black Sea, returned after a long circuit to his exhausted kingdom.[60] In the pride of victory, Bajazet threatened that he would besiege Buda; that he would subdue the adjacent countries of Germany and Italy; and that he would feed his horse with a bushel of oats on the altar of St. Peter at Rome. His progress was checked, not by the miraculous interposition of the apostle, not by a crusade of the Christian powers, but by a long and painful fit of the gout. The disorders of the moral, are sometimes corrected by those of the physical, world; and an acrimonious humour falling on a single fibre of one man, may prevent or suspend the misery of nations.

Crusade and captivity of the French princes, A.D. 1396–1398.

Such is the general idea of the Hungarian war; but the disastrous adventure of the French has procured us some memorials which illustrate the victory and character of Bajazet.[61] The duke of Burgundy, sovereign of Flanders, and uncle of Charles the sixth, yielded to the ardour of his son, John count of Nevers; and the fearless youth was accompanied by four princes, *his* cousins, and those of the French monarch. Their inexperience was guided by the sire de Coucy, one of the best and oldest captains of Christendom;[62] but the constable, admiral, and marshal, of France[63] commanded an army which did not exceed the number of a thousand knights and squires.

60. See the Decades Rerum Hungaricarum (Dec. iii. l. ii. p. 379.) of Bonfinius, an Italian, who, in the xv[th] century, was invited into Hungary to compose an eloquent history of that kingdom. Yet, if it be extant and accessible, I should give the preference to some homely chronicle of the time and country.

61. I should not complain of the labour of this work, if my materials were always derived from such books as the chronicle of honest Froissard (vol. iv. c. 67. 69. 72. 74. 79–83. 85. 87. 89.), who read little, enquired much, and believed all. The original Memoirs of the marechal de Boucicault (Partie i. c. 22–28.), add some facts, but they are dry and deficient, if compared with the pleasant garrulity of Froissard.

62. An accurate memoir on the life of Enquerrand VII. sire de Coucy, has been given by the baron de Zurlauben (Hist. de l'Academie des Inscriptions, tom. xxv.). His rank and possessions were equally considerable in France and England; and, in 1375, he led an army of adventurers into Switzerland, to recover a large patrimony which he claimed in right of his grandmother, the daughter of the emperor Albert I. of Austria (Sinner, Voyage dans la Suisse Occidentale, tom. i. p. 118–124.).

63. That military office, so respectable at present, was still more conspicuous when it

These splendid names were the source of presumption and the bane of discipline. So many might aspire to command, that none were willing to obey; their national spirit despised both their enemies and their allies; and in the persuasion that Bajazet *would* fly, or *must* fall, they began to compute how soon they should visit Constantinople and deliver the holy sepulchre. When their scouts announced the approach of the Turks, the gay and thoughtless youths were at table, already heated with wine; they instantly clasped their armour, mounted their horses, rode full speed to the vanguard, and resented as an affront the advice of Sigismond, which would have deprived them of the right and honour of the foremost attack. The battle of Nicopolis would not have been lost, if the French would have obeyed the prudence of the Hungarians: but it might have been gloriously won, had the Hungarians imitated the valour of the French. They dispersed the first line, consisting of the troops of Asia; forced a rampart of stakes, which had been planted against the cavalry; broke, after a bloody conflict, the Janizaries themselves; and were at length overwhelmed by the numerous squadrons that issued from the woods, and charged on all sides this handful of intrepid warriors. In the speed and secrecy of his march, in the order and evolutions of the battle, his enemies felt and admired the military talents of Bajazet. They accuse his cruelty in the use of victory. After reserving the count of Nevers, and four-and-twenty lords, whose birth and riches were attested by his Latin interpreters, the remainder of the French captives, who had survived the slaughter of the day, were led before his throne; and, as they refused to abjure their faith, were successively beheaded in his presence. The sultan was exasperated by the loss of his bravest Janizaries; and if it be true, that, on the eve of the engagement, the French had massacred their Turkish prisoners,[64] they might impute to themselves the consequences of a just retaliation. A knight, whose life had been spared, was permitted to return to Paris, that he might relate the deplorable tale, and solicit the ransom of the noble captives. In the mean while, the count of Nevers, with the princes and barons of France, were dragged along in the marches of the Turkish camp, exposed as a grateful trophy to the Moslems of Europe and Asia, and strictly confined at Boursa, as often as Bajazet resided in

---

was divided between two persons (Daniel, Hist. de la Milice Françoise, tom. ii. p. 5.). One of these, the marshal of the crusade, was the famous Boucicault, who afterwards defended Constantinople, governed Genoa, invaded the coast of Asia, and died in the field of Azincour.

64. For this odious fact, the Abbé de Vertot quotes the Hist. Anonyme de St. Denys, l. xvi. c. 10, 11. (Ordre de Malthe, tom. ii. p. 310.).

his capital. The sultan was pressed each day to expiate with their blood the blood of his martyrs; but he had pronounced, that they should live, and either for mercy or destruction his word was irrevocable. He was assured of their value and importance by the return of the messenger, and the gifts and intercessions of the kings of France and of Cyprus. Lusignan presented him with a gold salt-cellar of curious workmanship, and of the price of ten thousand ducats; and Charles the sixth dispatched by the way of Hungary a cast of Norwegian hawks, and six horse-loads of scarlet cloth, of fine linen of Rheims, and of Arras tapestry, representing the battles of the great Alexander. After much delay, the effect of distance rather than of art, Bajazet agreed to accept a ransom of two hundred thousand ducats for the count of Nevers and the surviving princes and barons: the marshal Boucicault, a famous warrior, was of the number of the fortunate; but the admiral of France had been slain in the battle; and the constable, with the sire de Coucy, died in the prison of Boursa. This heavy demand, which was doubled by incidental costs, fell chiefly on the duke of Burgundy, or rather on his Flemish subjects, who were bound by the feudal laws to contribute for the knighthood and captivity of the eldest son of their lord. For the faithful discharge of the debt, some merchants of Genoa gave security to the amount of five times the sum; a lesson to those warlike times, that commerce and credit are the links of the society of nations. It had been stipulated in the treaty, that the French captives should swear never to bear arms against the person of their conqueror; but the ungenerous restraint was abolished by Bajazet himself. "I despise," said he to the heir of Burgundy, "thy oaths and thy arms. Thou art young, and mayest be ambitious of effacing the disgrace or misfortune of thy first chivalry. Assemble thy powers, proclaim thy design, and be assured that Bajazet will rejoice to meet thee a second time in a field of battle." Before their departure, they were indulged in the freedom and hospitality of the court of Boursa. The French princes admired the magnificence of the Ottoman, whose hunting and hawking equipage was composed of seven thousand huntsmen and seven thousand falconers.[65] In their presence, and at his command, the belly of one of his chamberlains was cut open, on a complaint against him for drinking the goats-milk of

65. Sherefeddin Ali (Hist. de Timour Bec, l. v. c. 13.) allows Bajazet a round number of 12,000 officers and servants of the chace. A part of his spoils was afterwards displayed in a hunting-match of Timour: 1. hounds with sattin housings; 2. leopards with collars set with jewels; 3. Grecian greyhounds; and, 4. dogs from Europe, as strong as African lions (idem, l. vi. c. 15). Bajazet was particularly fond of flying his hawks at cranes (Chalcondyles, l. ii. p. 35.).

a poor woman. The strangers were astonished by this act of justice; but it was the justice of a sultan who disdains to balance the weight of evidence or to measure the degrees of guilt.

The emperor John Palæologus, A.D. 1355, January 8– A.D. 1391.

After his enfranchisement from an oppressive guardian, John Palæologus remained thirty-six years, the helpless, and as it should seem, the careless, spectator, of the public ruin.[66] Love, or rather lust, was his only vigorous passion; and in the embraces of the wives and virgins of the city, the Turkish slave forgot the dishonour of the emperor of the *Romans*. Andronicus, his eldest son, had formed, at Adrianople, an intimate and guilty friendship with Sauzes the son of Amurath; and the two youths conspired against the authority and lives of their parents. The presence of Amurath in Europe soon discovered and dissipated their rash counsels; and, after depriving Sauzes of his sight, the Ottoman threatened his vassal with the treatment of an accomplice and an enemy, unless he inflicted a similar punishment on his own son. Palæologus trembled and obeyed; and a cruel precaution involved in the same sentence the childhood and innocence of John the son of the criminal. But the operation was so mildly, or so unskilfully, performed, that the one retained the sight of an eye, and the other was afflicted only with the infirmity of squinting. Thus excluded from the succession, the two princes were confined in the tower of Anema; and the piety of Manuel, the second son of the reigning monarch, was rewarded with the gift of the Imperial crown. But at the end of two years, the turbulence of the Latins and the levity of the Greeks produced a revolution; and the two emperors were buried in the tower from whence the two prisoners were exalted to the throne. Another period of two years afforded Palæologus and Manuel the means of escape: it was contrived by the magic, or subtlety, of a monk, who was alternately named the angel or the devil: they fled to Scutari; their adherents armed in their cause; and the two Byzantine factions displayed the ambition and animosity, with which Cæsar and Pompey had disputed the empire of the world. The Roman world was now contracted to a corner of Thrace, between the Propontis and the Black Sea, about fifty miles in length and thirty in breadth; a space of ground not more extensive than the lesser principalities of Germany or Italy, if the remains of Constantinople had not still represented the wealth and populousness of a kingdom. To restore

Discord of the Greeks.

66. For the reigns of John Palæologus and his son Manuel, from 1354 to 1402, see Ducas, c. 9–15. Phranza, l. i. c. 16–21. and the i[st] and ii[d] books of Chalcondyles, whose proper subject is drowned in a sea of episode.

the public peace, it was found necessary to divide this fragment of the empire; and while Palæologus and Manuel were left in possession of the capital, almost all that lay without the walls was ceded to the blind princes, who fixed their residence at Rhodosto and Selybria. In the tranquil slumber of royalty, the passions of John Palæologus survived his reason and his strength; he deprived his favourite and heir of a blooming princess of Trebizond; and while the feeble emperor laboured to consummate his nuptials, Manuel, with an hundred of the noblest Greeks, was sent on a peremptory summons to the Ottoman *porte.* They served with honour in the wars of Bajazet; but a plan of fortifying Constantinople excited his jealousy: he threatened their lives; the new works were instantly demolished; and we shall bestow a praise, perhaps above the merit of Palæologus, if we impute this last humiliation as the cause of his death.

The emperor Manuel, A.D. 1391–1425, July 25.

The earliest intelligence of that event was communicated to Manuel, who escaped with speed and secrecy from the palace of Boursa to the Byzantine throne. Bajazet affected a proud indifference at the loss of this valuable pledge; and while he pursued his conquests in Europe and Asia, he left the emperor to struggle with his blind cousin John of Selybria, who, in eight years of civil war, asserted his right of primogeniture. At length the ambition of the victorious sultan pointed to the conquest of Constantinople; but he listened to the advice of his vizir, who represented, that such an enterprise might unite the powers of Christendom in a second and more formidable crusade. His epistle to the emperor was conceived in these words: "By the divine clemency, our invincible scymetar has reduced to our obedience almost all Asia, with many and large countries in Europe, excepting only the city of Constantinople; for beyond the walls thou hast nothing left. Resign that city; stipulate thy reward; or tremble, for thyself and thy unhappy people, at the consequences of a rash refusal." But his ambassadors were instructed to soften their tone, and to propose a treaty, which was subscribed with submission and gratitude. A truce of ten years was purchased by an annual tribute of thirty thousand crowns of gold: the Greeks deplored the public toleration of the law of Mahomet, and Bajazet enjoyed the glory of establishing a Turkish cadhi, and founding a royal mosch in the metropolis of the Eastern church.[67] Yet this truce was soon violated by the restless

Distress of Constantinople, A.D. 1395–1402.

67. Cantemir, p. 50–53. Of the Greeks, Ducas alone (c. 13. 15.) acknowledges the Turkish cadhi at Constantinople. Yet even Ducas dissembles the mosch.

sultan: in the cause of the prince of Selybria, the lawful emperor, an army of Ottomans, again threatened Constantinople, and the distress of Manuel implored the protection of the king of France. His plaintive embassy obtained much pity and some relief; and the conduct of the succour was entrusted to the marshal Boucicault,[68] whose religious chivalry was inflamed by the desire of revenging his captivity on the infidels. He sailed with four ships of war, from Aiguesmortes to the Hellespont; forced the passage, which was guarded by seventeen Turkish gallies; landed at Constantinople a supply of six hundred men at arms and sixteen hundred archers; and reviewed them in the adjacent plain, without condescending to number or array the multitude of Greeks. By his presence, the blockade was raised both by sea and land; the flying squadrons of Bajazet were driven to a more respectful distance; and several castles in Europe and Asia were stormed by the emperor and the marshal, who fought with equal valour by each other's side. But the Ottomans soon returned with an encrease of numbers; and the intrepid Boucicault, after a year's struggle, resolved to evacuate a country which could no longer afford either pay or provisions for his soldiers. The marshal offered to conduct Manuel to the French court, where he might solicit in person a supply of men and money; and advised in the mean while, that, to extinguish all domestic discord, he should leave his blind competitor on the throne. The proposal was embraced: the prince of Selybria was introduced to the capital; and such was the public misery, that the lot of the exile seemed more fortunate than that of the sovereign. Instead of applauding the success of his vassal, the Turkish sultan claimed the city as his own; and on the refusal of the emperor John, Constantinople was more closely pressed by the calamities of war and famine. Against such an enemy, prayers and resistance were alike unavailing; and the savage would have devoured his prey, if, in the fatal moment, he had not been overthrown by another savage stronger than himself. By the victory of Timour or Tamerlane, the fall of Constantinople was delayed about fifty years; and this important, though accidental, service may justly introduce the life and character of the Mogul conqueror.

68. Memoirs du bon Messire Jean le Maingre, dit *Boucicault*, Maréchal de France, partie i[re], c. 30–35.

CHAPTER LXV

Elevation of Timour or Tamerlane to the Throne of Samarcand. – His Conquests in Persia, Georgia, Tartary, Russia, India, Syria, and Anatolia. – His Turkish War. – Defeat and Captivity of Bajazet. – Death of Timour. – Civil War of the Sons of Bajazet. – Restoration of the Turkish Monarchy by Mahomet the First. – Siege of Constantinople by Amurath the Second.

Histories of TIMOUR, or Tamerlane.

The conquest and monarchy of the world was the first object of the ambition of TIMOUR. To live in the memory and esteem of future ages was the second wish of his magnanimous spirit. All the civil and military transactions of his reign were diligently recorded in the journals of his secretaries:[1] the authentic narrative was revised by the persons best informed of each particular transaction; and it is believed in the empire and family of Timour, that the monarch himself composed the *commentaries*[2] of his life, and the *institutions*[3] of his government.[4] But these cares were ineffectual for the preservation of his fame, and these

1. These journals were communicated to Sherefeddin, or Cherefeddin Ali, a native of Yezd, who composed in the Persian language a history of Timour Beg, which has been translated into French by M. Petis de la Croix (Paris, 1722, in 4 vols. 12mo), and has always been my faithful guide. His geography and chronology are wonderfully accurate; and he may be trusted for public facts, though he servilely praises the virtue and fortune of the hero. Timour's attention to procure intelligence from his own and foreign countries, may be seen in the Institutions, p. 215. 217. 349. 351.

2. These Commentaries are yet unknown in Europe: but Mr. White gives some hope, that they may be imported and translated by his friend Major Davy, who had read in the East this "minute and faithful narrative of an interesting and eventful period."

3. I am ignorant whether the original institution, in the Turkish or Mogul language, be still extant. The Persic version, with an English translation and most valuable index, was published (Oxford, 1783, in 4to) by the joint labours of Major Davy, and Mr. White the Arabic professor. This work has been since translated from the Persic into French (Paris, 1787) by M. Langlès, a learned Orientalist, who has added the life of Timour, and many curious notes.

4. Shaw Allum, the present Mogul, reads, values, but cannot imitate, the institutions of his great ancestor. The English translator replies on their internal evidence: but if any suspicions should arise of fraud and fiction, they will not be dispelled by Major Davy's letter. The Orientals have never cultivated the art of criticism; the patronage

precious memorials in the Mogul or Persian language were concealed from the world, or at least from the knowledge of Europe. The nations which he vanquished exercised a base and impotent revenge; and ignorance has long repeated the tale of calumny,[5] which had disfigured the birth and character, the person, and even the name, of *Tamerlane.*[6] Yet his real merit would be enhanced, rather than debased, by the elevation of a peasant to the throne of Asia; nor can his lameness be a theme of reproach, unless he had the weakness to blush at a natural, or perhaps an honourable, infirmity.

In the eyes of the Moguls, who held the indefeasible succession of the house of Zingis, he was doubtless a rebel subject; yet he sprang from the noble tribe of Berlass: his fifth ancestor, Carashar Nevian, had been the vizir of Zagatai, in his new realm of Transoxiana; and in the ascent of some generations, the branch of Timour is confounded, at least by the females,[7] with the Imperial stem.[8] He was born forty miles to the south of Samarcand, in the village of Sebzar, in the fruitful territory of Cash, of which his fathers were the hereditary chiefs, as well as of a toman of ten thousand horse.[9] His birth[10] was cast on one of those periods of

of a prince, less honourable perhaps, is not less lucrative than that of a bookseller: nor can it be deemed incredible, that a Persian, the *real* author, should renounce the credit, to raise the value and price, of the work.

5. The original of the tale is found in the following work, which is much esteemed for its florid elegance of style: *Ahmedis Arabsiadæ* (Ahmed Ebn Arabshah) *Vitæ et Rerum gestarum Timuri. Arabice et Latine. Edidit Samuel Henricus Manger. Franequeræ,* 1767, 2 *tom. in* 4to. This Syrian author is ever a malicious, and often an ignorant, enemy: the very titles of his chapters are injurious; as how the wicked, as how the impious, as how the viper, &c. The copious article of TIMUR, in Bibliothéque Orientale, is of a mixed nature, as d'Herbelot indifferently draws his materials (p. 877–888.) from Khondemir, Ebn Schounah, and the Lebtarikh.

6. *Demir,* or *Timour,* signifies, in the Turkish language, Iron; and *Beg* is the appellation of a lord or prince. By the change of a letter or accent, it is changed into *Lenc,* or lame; and a European corruption confounds the two words in the name of Tamerlane.

7. After relating some false and foolish tale of Timour *Lenc,* Arabshah is compelled to speak truth, and to own him for a kinsman of Zingis, per mulieres (as he peevishly adds) laqueos Satanæ (pars i. c. 1. p. 25.). The testimony of Abulghazi Khan (P. ii. c. 5. P. v. c. 4.) is clear, unquestionable, and decisive.

8. According to one of the pedigrees, the fourth ancestor of Zingis, and the ninth of Timour, were brothers; and they agreed, that the posterity of the elder should succeed to the dignity of khan, and that the descendants of the younger should fill the office of their minister and general. This tradition was at least convenient to justify the *first* steps of Timour's ambition (Institutions, p. 24, 25. from the MS. fragments of Timour's history).

9. See the preface of Sherefeddin, and Abulfeda's Geography (Chorasmiæ, &c. Descriptio, p. 60, 61.), in the iii[d] volume of Hudson's Minor Greek Geographers.

10. See his nativity in Dr. Hyde (Syntagma

anarchy which announce the fall of the Asiatic dynasties, and open a new field to adventurous ambition. The khans of Zagatai were extinct; the emirs aspired to independence; and their domestic feuds could only be suspended by the conquest and tyranny of the khans of Kashgar, who, with an army of Getes or Calmucks,[11] invaded the Transoxian kingdom.

His first adventures, A.D. 1361–1370.

From the twelfth year of his age, Timour had entered the field of action; in the twenty-fifth, he stood forth as the deliverer of his country; and the eyes and wishes of the people were turned towards an hero who suffered in their cause. The chiefs of the law and of the army had pledged their salvation to support him with their lives and fortunes; but in the hour of danger they were silent and afraid; and, after waiting seven days on the hills of Samarcand, he retreated to the desert with only sixty horsemen. The fugitives were overtaken by a thousand Getes, whom he repulsed with incredible slaughter, and his enemies were forced to exclaim, "Timour is a wonderful man: fortune and the divine favour are with him." But in this bloody action his own followers were reduced to ten, a number which was soon diminished by the desertion of three Carizmians. He wandered in the desert with his wife, seven companions, and four horses; and sixty-two days was he plunged in a loathsome dungeon, from whence he escaped by his own courage, and the remorse of the oppressor. After swimming the broad and rapid stream of the Jihoon, or Oxus, he led, during some months, the life of a vagrant and outlaw, on the borders of the adjacent states. But his fame shone brighter in adversity; he learned to distinguish the friends of his person, the associates of his fortune, and to apply the various characters of men for their advantage, and above all for his own. On his return to his native country, Timour was successively joined by the parties of his confederates, who anxiously sought him in the desert; nor can I refuse to describe, in his pathetic simplicity, one of their fortunate encounters. He presented himself as a guide to three chiefs, who were at

Dissertat. tom. ii. p. 466.), as it was cast by the astrologers of his grandson Ulugh Beg. He was born A.D. 1336, April 9, 11° 57 P. M. lat. 36. I know not whether they can prove the great conjunction of the planets from whence, like other conquerors and prophets, Timour derived the surname of Saheb Keran, or master of the conjunctions (Bibliot. Orient. p. 878.).

11. In the Institutions of Timour, these subjects of the khan of Kashgar are most improperly styled Ouzbegs, or Uzbeks, a name which belongs to another branch and country of Tartars (Abulghazi, P. v. c. 5. P. vii. c. 5.). Could I be sure that this word is in the Turkish original, I would boldly pronounce, that the Institutions were framed a century after the death of Timour, since the establishment of the Uzbeks in Transoxiana.

the head of seventy horse. "When their eyes fell upon me," says Timour, "they were overwhelmed with joy; and they alighted from their horses; and they came and kneeled; and they kissed my stirrup. I also came down from my horse, and took each of them in my arms. And I put my turban on the head of the first chief; and my girdle, rich in jewels and wrought with gold, I bound on the loins of the second; and the third, I clothed in my own coat. And they wept, and I wept also; and the hour of prayer was arrived, and we prayed. And we mounted our horses, and came to my dwelling; and I collected my people, and made a feast." His trusty bands were soon encreased by the bravest of the tribes; he led them against a superior foe; and after some vicissitudes of war, the Getes were finally driven from the kingdom of Transoxiana. He had done much for his own glory; but much remained to be done, much art to be exerted, and some blood to be spilt, before he could teach his equals to obey him as their master. The birth and power of emir Houssein compelled him to accept a vicious and unworthy colleague, whose sister was the best beloved of his wives. Their union was short and jealous; but the policy of Timour, in their frequent quarrels, exposed his rival to the reproach of injustice and perfidy: and, after a final defeat, Houssein was slain by some sagacious friends, who presumed, for the last time, to disobey the commands of their lord. At the age of thirty-four,[12] and in a general diet or *couroultai*, he was invested with *Imperial* command, but he affected to revere the house of Zingis; and while the emir Timour reigned over Zagatai and the East, a nominal khan served as a private officer in the armies of his servant. A fertile kingdom, five hundred miles in length and in breadth, might have satisfied the ambition of a subject; but Timour aspired to the dominion of the world; and before his death, the crown of Zagatai was one of the twenty-seven crowns which he had placed on his head. Without expatiating on the victories of thirty-five campaigns; without describing the lines of march, which he repeatedly traced over the continent of Asia; I shall briefly represent his conquests in, I. Persia, II. Tartary, and, III. India,[13] and

He ascends the throne of Zagatai, A.D. 1370, April.

12. The i[st] book of Sherefeddin is employed on the private life of the hero; and he himself, or his secretary (Institutions, p. 3–77.), enlarges with pleasure on the thirteen designs and enterprises which most truly constitute his *personal* merit. It even shines through the dark colouring of Arabshah, P. i. c. 1–12.

13. The conquests of Persia, Tartary, and India, are represented in the ii[d] and iii[d] books of Sherefeddin, and by Arabshah, c. 13–55. Consult the excellent Indexes to the Institutions.

from thence proceed to the more interesting narrative of his Ottoman war.

His conquests, A.D. 1370–1400. I. Of Persia, A.D. 1380–1393.

I. For every war, a motive of safety or revenge, of honour or zeal, of right or convenience, may be readily found in the jurisprudence of conquerors. No sooner had Timour re-united to the patrimony of Zagatai the dependent countries of Carizme and Candahar, than he turned his eyes towards the kingdoms of Iran or Persia. From the Oxus to the Tigris, that extensive country was left without a lawful sovereign since the death of Abousaid, the last of the descendants of the great Holacou. Peace and justice had been banished from the land above forty years; and the Mogul invader might seem to listen to the cries of an oppressed people. Their petty tyrants might have opposed him with confederate arms: they separately stood, and successively fell; and the difference of their fate was only marked by the promptitude of submission or the obstinacy of resistance. Ibrahim, prince of Shirwan or Albania, kissed the footstool of the Imperial throne. His peace-offerings of silks, horses, and jewels, were composed, according to the Tartar fashion, each article of nine pieces; but a critical spectator observed, that there were only eight slaves. "I myself am the ninth," replied Ibrahim, who was prepared for the remark; and his flattery was rewarded by the smile of Timour.[14] Shah Mansour, prince of Fars, or the proper Persia, was one of the least powerful, but most dangerous, of his enemies. In a battle under the walls of Shiraz, he broke, with three or four thousand soldiers, the *coul* or main-body of thirty thousand horse, where the emperor fought in person. No more than fourteen or fifteen guards remained near the standard of Timour: he stood firm as a rock, and received on his helmet two weighty strokes of a scymetar:[15] the Moguls rallied; the head of Mansour was thrown at his feet, and he declared his esteem of the valour of a foe, by extirpating all the males of so intrepid a race. From Shiraz, his troops advanced to the Persian gulf; and the richness and weakness of Ormuz[16] were displayed

14. The reverence of the Tartars for the mysterious number of nine, is declared by Abulghazi Khan, who, for that reason, divides his Genealogical History into nine parts.

15. According to Arabshah (P. i. c. 28. p. 183.), the coward Timour ran away to his tent, and hid himself from the pursuit of Shah Mansour under the women's garments. Perhaps Sherefeddin (l. iii. c. 25.) has magnified his courage.

16. The history of Ormuz is not unlike that of Tyre. The old city, on the continent, was destroyed by the Tartars, and renewed in a neighbouring island without fresh water or vegetation. The kings of Ormuz, rich in the Indian trade and the pearl fishery, possessed large territories both in Persia and Arabia; but they were at first the tributaries of the sultans of Kerman, and

in an annual tribute of six hundred thousand dinars of gold. Bagdad was no longer the city of peace, the seat of the caliphs; but the noblest conquest of Houlacou could not be overlooked by his ambitious successor. The whole course of the Tigris and Euphrates, from the mouth to the sources of those rivers, was reduced to his obedience: he entered Edessa; and the Turkmans of the black sheep were chastised for the sacrilegious pillage of a caravan of Mecca. In the mountains of Georgia, the native Christians still braved the law and the sword of Mahomet; by three expeditions he obtained the merit of the *gazie*, or holy war; and the prince of Teflis became his proselyte and friend.

II. Of Turkestan, A.D. 1370–1383.

II. A just retaliation might be urged for the invasion of Turkestan, or the eastern Tartary. The dignity of Timour could not endure the impunity of the Getes: he passed the Sihoon, subdued the kingdom of Cashgar, and marched seven times into the heart of their country. His most distant camp was two months journey, or four hundred and eighty leagues to the north-east of Samarcand; and his emirs, who traversed the river Irtish, engraved in the forests of Siberia a rude memorial of their exploits. The conquest of Kipzak, or the western Tartary,[17] was founded on the double motive of aiding the distressed, and chastising the ungrateful. Toctamish, a fugitive prince, was entertained and protected in his court: the ambassadors of Auruss Khan were dismissed with an haughty denial, and followed on the same day by the armies of Zagatai; and their success established Toctamish in the Mogul empire of the north. But after a reign of ten years, the new khan forgot the merits and the strength of his benefactor; the base usurper, as he deemed him, of the sacred rights of the house of Zingis. Through the gates of Derbend, he entered Persia at the head of ninety thousand horse: with the innumerable forces of Kipzak, Bulgaria, Circassia, and Russia, he passed the Sihoon, burnt the palaces of Timour, and compelled him, amidst the winter snows, to contend for Samarcand and his life. After a mild expostulation and a glorious victory, the emperor resolved on revenge: and by the east, and the west, of the Caspian, and the Volga, he

at last were delivered (A.D. 1505) by the Portuguese tyrants from the tyranny of their own vizirs (Marco Polo, l. i. c. 15, 16. fol. 7, 8. Abulfeda Geograph. tabul. xi. p. 261, 262. an original Chronicle of Ormuz, in Texeira, or Stevens' History of Persia, p. 376–416. and the Itineraries inserted in the i[st] volume of Ramusio, of Ludovico Barthema (1503), fol. 167. of Andrea Corsali (1517), fol. 202, 203, and of Odoardo Barbessa (in 1516), fol. 315–318.).

17. Arabshah had travelled into Kipzak, and acquired a singular knowledge of the geography, cities, and revolutions, of that northern region (P. i. c. 45–49.).

of Kipzak, Russia, &c. A.D. 1390–1396.

twice invaded Kipzak with such mighty powers, that thirteen miles were measured from his right to his left wing. In a march of five months, they rarely beheld the footsteps of man; and their daily subsistence was often trusted to the fortune of the chace. At length the armies encountered each other; but the treachery of the standard-bearer, who, in the heat of action, reversed the Imperial standard of Kipzak, determined the victory of the Zagatais; and Toctamish (I speak the language of the institutions) gave the tribe of Toushi to the wind of desolation.[18] He fled to the Christian duke of Lithuania; again returned to the banks of the Volga; and, after fifteen battles with a domestic rival, at last perished in the wilds of Siberia. The pursuit of a flying enemy carried Timour into the tributary provinces of Russia: a duke of the reigning family was made prisoner amidst the ruins of his capital; and Yeletz, by the pride and ignorance of the Orientals, might easily be confounded with the genuine metropolis of the nation. Moscow trembled at the approach of the Tartar, and the resistance would have been feeble, since the hopes of the Russians were placed in a miraculous image of the Virgin, to whose protection they ascribed the casual and voluntary retreat of the conqueror. Ambition and prudence recalled him to the South, the desolate country was exhausted, and the Mogul soldiers were enriched with an immense spoil of precious furs, of linen of Antioch,[19] and of ingots of gold and silver.[20] On the banks of the Don, or Tanais, he received an humble deputation from the consuls and merchants of Egypt,[21] Venice, Genoa, Catalonia, and Biscay, who occupied the commerce and city of Tana, or Azoph, at the mouth of the river. They offered their gifts, admired his magnificence, and trusted his royal word. But the peaceful visit of an emir, who explored the state of

18. Institutions of Timour, p. 123. 125. Mr. White, the editor, bestows some animadversion on the superficial account of Sherefeddin (l. iii. c. 12, 13, 14.), who was ignorant of the designs of Timour, and the true springs of action.

19. The furs of Russia are more credible than the ingots. But the linen of Antioch has never been famous; and Antioch was in ruins. I suspect that it was some manufacture of Europe, by which the Hanse merchants had imported by the way of Novogorod.

20. M. Levésque (Hist. de Russie, tom. ii. p. 247. Vie de Timour, p. 64–67. before the French version of the Institutes) has corrected the error of Sherefeddin, and marked the true limit of Timour's conquests. His arguments are superfluous, and a simple appeal to the Russian Annals is sufficient to prove that Moscow, which six years before had been taken by Toctamish, escaped the arms of a more formidable invader.

21. An Egyptian consul from Grand Cairo, is mentioned in Barbaro's voyage to Tana in 1436, after the city had been rebuilt (Ramusio, tom. ii. fol. 92.).

the magazines and harbour, was speedily followed by the destructive presence of the Tartars. The city was reduced to ashes; the Moslems were pillaged and dismissed; but all the Christians, who had not fled to their ships, were condemned either to death or slavery.[22] Revenge prompted him to burn the cities of Serai and Astrachan, the monuments of rising civilization; and his vanity proclaimed, that he had penetrated to the region of perpetual daylight, a strange phenomenon, which authorised his Mahometan doctors to dispense with the obligation of evening prayer.[23]

III. Of Hindostan, A.D. 1398, 1399.

III. When Timour first proposed to his princes and emirs the invasion of India or Hindostan,[24] he was answered by a murmur of discontent: "The rivers! and the mountains and deserts! and the soldiers clad in armour! and the elephants, destroyers of men!" But the displeasure of the emperor was more dreadful than all these terrors; and his superior reason was convinced, that an enterprise of such tremendous aspect was safe and easy in the execution. He was informed by his spies of the weakness and anarchy of Hindostan: the Soubahs of the provinces had erected the standard of rebellion; and the perpetual infancy of sultan Mahmood was despised even in the haram of Delhi. The Mogul army moved in three great divisions: and Timour observes with pleasure, that the ninety-two squadrons of a thousand horse most fortunately corresponded with the ninety-two names or epithets of the prophet Mahomet. Between the Jihoon and the Indus, they crossed one of the ridges of mountains, which are styled by the Arabian geographers The stony girdles of the earth. The highland robbers were subdued or extirpated; but great numbers of men and horses perished in the snow; the emperor himself was let down a precipice on a portable scaffold, the ropes were one hundred and fifty cubits in length; and, before he could

22. The sack of Azoph is described by Sherefeddin (l. iii. c. 55.); and much more particularly by the author of an Italian chronicle (Andreas de Redusiis de Quero, in Chron. Tarvisiano, in Muratori Script. Rerum Italicarum, tom. xix. p. 802–805.). He had conversed with the Mianis, two Venetian brothers, one of whom had been sent a deputy to the camp of Timour, and the other had lost at Azoph three sons and 12,000 ducats.

23. Sherefeddin only says (l. iii. c. 13.), that the rays of the setting, and those of the rising sun, were scarcely separated by any interval; a problem which may be solved in the latitude of Moscow (the 56th degree), with the aid of the Aurora Borealis, and a long summer twilight. But a *day* of forty days (Khondemir apud d'Herbelot, p. 880.) would rigorously confine us within the polar circle.

24. For the Indian war, see the Institutions (p. 129–139.), the fourth book of Sherefeddin, and the history of Ferishta (in Dow, vol. ii. p. 1–20.), which throws a general light on the affairs of Hindostan.

reach the bottom, this dangerous operation was five times repeated. Timour crossed the Indus at the ordinary passage of Attok; and successively traversed, in the footsteps of Alexander, the *Punjab*, or five rivers,[25] that fall into the master-stream. From Attok to Delhi, the high road measures no more than six hundred miles; but the two conquerors deviated to the south-east; and the motive of Timour was to join his grandson, who had atchieved by his command the conquest of Moultan. On the eastern bank of the Hyphasis, on the edge of the desert, the Macedonian hero halted and wept: the Mogul entered the desert, reduced the fortress of Batnir, and stood in arms before the gates of Delhi, a great and flourishing city, which had subsisted three centuries under the dominion of the Mahometan kings. The siege, more especially of the castle, might have been a work of time; but he tempted, by the appearance of weakness, the sultan Mahmoud and his vizir to descend into the plain, with ten thousand cuirassiers, forty thousand of his foot-guards, and one hundred and twenty elephants, whose tusks are said to have been armed with sharp and poisoned daggers. Against these monsters, or rather against the imagination of his troops, he condescended to use some extraordinary precautions of fire and a ditch, of iron spikes and a rampart of bucklers; but the event taught the Moguls to smile at their own fears; and, as soon as these unwieldy animals were routed, the inferior species (the men of India) disappeared from the field. Timour made his triumphal entry into the capital of Hindostan; and admired, with a view to imitate, the architecture of the stately mosch; but the order or licence of a general pillage and massacre polluted the festival of his victory. He resolved to purify his soldiers in the blood of the idolaters, or Gentoos, who still surpass, in the proportion of ten to one, the numbers of the Moslems. In this pious design, he advanced one hundred miles to the north-east of Delhi, passed the Ganges, fought several battles by land and water, and penetrated to the famous rock of Coupele, the statue of the cow, that *seems* to discharge the mighty river, whose source is far distant among the mountains of Thibet.[26] His return was along the skirts of the northern

25. The rivers of the Punjab, the five eastern branches of the Indus, have been laid down for the first time with truth and accuracy in Major Rennel's incomparable map of Hindostan. In his Critical Memoir, he illustrates with judgment and learning the marches of Alexander and Timour.

26. The two great rivers, the Ganges and Burrampooter, rise in Thibet, from the opposite ridges of the same hills, separate from each other to the distance of 1200 miles, and, after a winding course of 2000 miles, again meet in one point near the gulf of Bengal. Yet so capricious is Fame, that the Burrampooter is a late discovery, while his brother Ganges has been the

hills; nor could this rapid campaign of one year justify the strange foresight of his emirs, that their children in a warm climate would degenerate into a race of Hindoos.

His war against sultan Bajazet, A.D. 1400, September 1.

It was on the banks of the Ganges that Timour was informed, by his speedy messengers, of the disturbances which had arisen on the confines of Georgia and Anatolia, of the revolt of the Christians, and the ambitious designs of the sultan Bajazet. His vigour of mind and body was not impaired by sixty-three years, and innumerable fatigues; and, after enjoying some tranquil months in the palace of Samarcand, he proclaimed a new expedition of seven years into the western countries of Asia.[27] To the soldiers who had served in the Indian war, he granted the choice of remaining at home or following their prince; but the troops of all the provinces and kingdoms of Persia were commanded to assemble at Ispahan, and wait the arrival of the Imperial standard. It was first directed against the Christians of Georgia, who were strong only in their rocks, their castles, and the winter season; but these obstacles were overcome by the zeal and perseverance of Timour: the rebels submitted to the tribute or the Koran; and if both religions boasted of their martyrs, that name is more justly due to the Christian prisoners, who were offered the choice of abjuration or death. On his descent from the hills, the emperor gave audience to the first ambassadors of Bajazet, and opened the hostile correspondence of complaints and menaces; which fermented two years before the final explosion. Between two jealous and haughty neighbours, the motives of quarrel will seldom be wanting. The Mogul and Ottoman conquests now touched each other in the neighbourhood of Erzerum, and the Euphrates; nor had the doubtful limit been ascertained by time and treaty. Each of these ambitious monarchs might accuse his rival of violating his territory; of threatening his vassals; and protecting his rebels; and, by the name of rebels, each understood the fugitive princes, whose kingdoms he had usurped, and whole life or liberty he implacably pursued. The resemblance of character was still more dangerous than the opposition of interest; and in their victorious career, Timour was impatient of an equal, and Bajazet was ignorant of a superior. The first epistle[28] of the Mogul

theme of ancient and modern story. Coupele, the scene of Timour's last victory, must be situate near Loldong, 1100 miles from Calcutta; and, in 1774, a British camp! (Rennel's Memoir, p. 7. 59. 90, 91. 99.).

27. See the Institutions, p. 141. to the end of the i[st] book, and Sherefeddin (l. v. c. 1–16.), to the entrance of Timour into Syria.

28. We have three copies of these hostile epistles in the Institutions (p. 147.), in Sherefeddin (l. v. c. 14.), and in Arabshah (tom. ii. c. 19. p. 183–201.); which agree with

emperor must have provoked, instead of reconciling the Turkish sultan; whose family and nation he affected to despise.[29] "Dost thou not know, that the greatest part of Asia is subject to our arms and our laws? that our invincible forces extend from one sea to the other? that the potentates of the earth form a line before our gate? and that we have compelled fortune herself to watch over the prosperity of our empire? What is the foundation of thy insolence and folly? Thou hast fought some battles in the woods of Anatolia; contemptible trophies! Thou hast obtained some victories over the Christians of Europe; thy sword was blessed by the apostle of God; and thy obedience to the precept of the Koran, in waging war against the infidels, is the sole consideration that prevents us from destroying thy country, the frontier and bulwark of the Moslem world. Be wise in time; reflect; repent; and avert the thunder of our vengeance, which is yet suspended over thy head. Thou art no more than a pismire; why wilt thou seek to provoke the elephants? Alas, they will trample thee under their feet." In his replies, Bajazet poured forth the indignation of a soul which was deeply stung by such unusual contempt. After retorting the basest reproaches on the thief and rebel of the desert, the Ottoman recapitulates his boasted victories in Iran, Touran, and the Indies; and labours to prove, that Timour had never triumphed unless by his own perfidy and the vices of his foes. "Thy armies are innumerable: be they so; but what are the arrows of the flying Tartar against the scymetars and battle-axes of my firm and invincible Janizaries? I will guard the princes who have implored my protection: seek them in my tents. The cities of Arzingan and Erzeroum are mine; and unless the tribute be duly paid, I will demand the arrears under the walls of Tauris and Sultania." The ungovernable rage of the sultan at length betrayed him to an insult of a more domestic kind. "If I fly from thy arms," said he, "may *my* wives be thrice divorced from my bed: but if thou hast not courage to meet me in the field, mayest thou again receive *thy* wives after they have thrice endured the embraces of a stranger."[30] Any violation by word or deed of

---

each other in the spirit and substance rather than in the style. It is probable, that they have been translated, with various latitude, from the Turkish original into the Arabic and Persian tongues.

29. The Mogul emir distinguishes himself and his countrymen by the name of *Turks*, and stigmatises the race and nation of Bajazet with the less honourable epithet of *Turkmans*. Yet I do not understand how the Ottomans could be descended from a Turkman sailor; those inland shepherds were so remote from the sea, and all maritime affairs.

30. According to the Koran (c. 2. p. 27. and Sale's Discourses, p. 134.), a Musulman who had thrice divorced his wife (who had thrice repeated the words of a divorce), could not take her again, till after she had been married *to*, and repudiated *by*, another

the secrecy of the Haram is an unpardonable offence among the Turkish nations;[31] and the political quarrel of the two monarchs was embittered by private and personal resentment. Yet in his first expedition, Timour was satisfied with the siege and destruction of Siwas or Sebaste, a strong city on the borders of Anatolia; and he revenged the indiscretion of the Ottoman, on a garrison of four thousand Armenians, who were buried alive for the brave and faithful discharge of their duty. As a Musulman he seemed to respect the pious occupation of Bajazet, who was still engaged in the blockade of Constantinople: and after this salutary lesson, the Mogul conqueror checked his pursuit, and turned aside to the invasion of Syria and Egypt. In these transactions, the Ottoman prince, by the Orientals, and even by Timour, is styled the *Kaissar of Roum*, the Cæsar of the Romans: a title which, by a small anticipation, might be given to a monarch who possessed the provinces, and threatened the city, of the successors of Constantine.[32]

Timour invades Syria, A.D. 1400.

The military republic of the Mamalukes still reigned in Egypt and Syria: but the dynasty of the Turks was overthrown by that of the Circassians;[33] and their favourite Barkok, from a slave and a prisoner, was raised and restored to the throne. In the midst of rebellion and discord, he braved the menaces, corresponded with the enemies, and detained the ambassadors, of the Mogul, who patiently expected his decease, to revenge the crimes of the father on the feeble reign of his son Farage. The Syrian emirs[34] were assembled at Aleppo to repel the invasion: they confided in the fame and discipline of the Mamalukes, in the temper of

husband: an ignominious transaction, which it is needless to aggravate by supposing, that the first husband must see her enjoyed by a second before his face (Rycaut's State of the Ottoman Empire, l. ii. c. 21.).

31. The common delicacy of the Orientals, in never speaking of their women, is ascribed in a much higher degree by Arabshah to the Turkish nations; and it is remarkable enough, that Chalcondyles (l. ii. p. 55.) had some knowledge of the prejudice, and the insult.

32. For the style of the Moguls, see the Institutions (p. 131. 147.), and for the Persians, the Bibliotheque Orientale (p. 882.): but I do not find that the title of Cæsar has been applied by the Arabians, or assumed by the Ottomans themselves.

33. See the reigns of Barkok and Pharadge, in M. de Guignes (tom. iv. l. xxii.), who, from the Arabic texts of Aboulmahasen, Ebn Schounah, and Aintabi, has added some facts to our common stock of materials.

34. For these recent and domestic transactions, Arabshah, though a partial, is a credible, witness (tom. i. c. 64–68. tom. ii. c. 1–14.). Timour must have been odious to a Syrian; but the notoriety of facts would have obliged him, in some measure, to respect his enemy and himself. His bitters may correct the luscious sweets of Sherefeddin (l. v. c. 17–29.).

their swords and lances of the purest steel of Damascus, in the strength of their walled cities, and in the populousness of sixty thousand villages: and instead of sustaining a siege, they threw open their gates, and arrayed their forces in the plain. But these forces were not cemented by virtue and union; and some powerful emirs had been seduced to desert or betray their more loyal companions. Timour's front was covered with a line of Indian elephants, whose turrets were filled with archers and Greek fire: the rapid evolutions of his cavalry completed the dismay and disorder; the Syrian crowds fell back on each other; many thousands were stifled or slaughtered in the entrance of the great street; the Moguls entered with the fugitives; and, after a short defence, the citadel, the impregnable citadel of Aleppo, was surrendered by cowardice or treachery. Among the suppliants and captives, Timour distinguished the doctors of the law, whom he invited to the dangerous honour of a personal conference.[35] The Mogul prince was a zealous Musulman; but his Persian schools had taught him to revere the memory of Ali and Hosain; and he had imbibed a deep prejudice against the Syrians, as the enemies of the son of the daughter of the apostle of God. To these doctors he proposed a captious question, which the casuists of Bochara, Samarcand, and Herat, were incapable of resolving. "Who are the true martyrs, of those who are slain on my side, or on that of my enemies?" But he was silenced, or satisfied, by the dexterity of one of the cadhis of Aleppo, who replied, in the words of Mahomet himself, that the motive, not the ensign, constitutes the martyr; and that the Moslems of either party, who fight only for the glory of God, may deserve that sacred appellation. The true succession of the caliphs was a controversy of a still more delicate nature and the frankness of a doctor, too honest for his situation, provoked the emperor to exclaim, "Ye are as false as those of Damascus: Moawiyah was an usurper, Yezid a tyrant, and Ali alone is the lawful successor of the prophet." A prudent explanation restored his tranquillity; and he passed to a more familiar topic of conversation. "What is your age?" said he to the cadhi. "Fifty years." – "It would be the age of my eldest son: you see me here (continued Timour) a poor, lame, decrepit mortal. Yet by my arm has the Almighty been pleased to subdue the kingdoms of Iran, Touran, and the Indies. I am not a man of blood; and God is my witness, that in all my wars I have never been the

Sacks Aleppo, A.D. 1400, Nov. 11.

35. Those interesting conversations appear to have been copied by Arabshah (tom. i. c. 68. p. 625–645.) from the cadhi and historian Ebn Schounah, a principal actor. Yet how could he be alive seventy-five years afterwards (d'Herbelot, p. 792.)?

aggressor, and that my enemies have always been the authors of their own calamity." During this peaceful conversation, the streets of Aleppo streamed with blood, and re-echoed with the cries of mothers and children, with the shrieks of violated virgins. The rich plunder that was abandoned to his soldiers might stimulate their avarice; but their cruelty was enforced by the peremptory command of producing an adequate number of heads, which, according to his custom, were curiously piled in columns and pyramids: the Moguls celebrated the feast of victory, while the surviving Moslems passed the night in tears and in chains. I shall not dwell on the march of the destroyer from Aleppo to Damascus, where he was rudely encountered, and almost overthrown, by the armies of Egypt. A retrograde motion was imputed to his distress and despair: one of his nephews deserted to the enemy; and Syria rejoiced in the tale of his defeat, when the sultan was driven by the revolt of the Mamalukes to escape with precipitation and shame to his palace of Cairo. Abandoned by their prince, the inhabitants of Damascus still defended their walls; and Timour consented to raise the siege, if they would adorn his retreat with a gift or ransom; each article of nine pieces. But no sooner had he introduced himself into the city, under colour of a truce, than he perfidiously violated the treaty; imposed a contribution of ten millions of gold; and animated his troops to chastise the posterity of those Syrians who had executed, or approved, the murder of the grandson of Mahomet. A family which had given honourable burial to the head of Hosein, and a colony of artificers whom he sent to labour at Samarcand, were alone reserved in the general massacre; and, after a period of seven centuries, Damascus was reduced to ashes, because a Tartar was moved by religious zeal to avenge the blood of an Arab. The losses and fatigues of the campaign obliged Timour to renounce the conquest of Palestine and Egypt; but in his return to the Euphrates, he delivered Aleppo to the flames; and justified his pious motive by the pardon and reward of two thousand sectaries of Ali, who were desirous to visit the tomb of his son. I have expatiated on the personal anecdotes which mark the character of the Mogul hero; but I shall briefly mention,[36] that he erected on the ruins of Bagdad a pyramid of ninety thousand heads; again visited Georgia; encamped on the banks of Araxes; and proclaimed his resolution of marching against the Ottoman emperor. Conscious of the importance of the war, he collected

Damascus, A.D. 1401, January 23.

and Bagdad, A.D. 1401, July 23.

36. The marches and occupations of Timour between the Syrian and Ottoman wars, are represented by Sherefeddin (l. v. c. 29–43.) and Arabshah (tom. ii. c. 15–18.).

his forces from every province: eight hundred thousand men were enrolled on his military list;[37] but the splendid commands of five, and ten, thousand horse, may be rather expressive of the rank and pension of the chiefs, than of the genuine number of effective soldiers.[38] In the pillage of Syria, the Moguls had acquired immense riches: but the delivery of their pay and arrears for seven years, more firmly attached them to the Imperial standard.

Invades Anatolia, A.D. 1402.

During this diversion of the Mogul arms, Bajazet had two years to collect his forces for a more serious encounter. They consisted of four hundred thousand horse and foot,[39] whose merit and fidelity were of an unequal complexion. We may discriminate the Janizaries who have been gradually raised to an establishment of forty thousand men; a national cavalry, the Spahis of modern times; twenty thousand cuirassiers of Europe, clad in black and impenetrable armour; the troops of Anatolia, whose princes had taken refuge in the camp of Timour, and a colony of Tartars, whom he had driven from Kipzak, and to whom Bajazet had assigned a settlement in the plains of Adrianople. The fearless confidence of the sultan urged him to meet his antagonist; and, as if he had chosen that spot for revenge, he displayed his banners near the ruins of the unfortunate Suvas. In the mean while, Timour moved from the Araxes through the countries of Armenia and Anatolia: his boldness was secured by the wisest precautions; his speed was guided by order and discipline; and the woods, the mountains, and the rivers, were diligently explored by the flying squadrons, who marked his road and preceded his standard. Firm in his plan of fighting in the heart of the Ottoman kingdom, he avoided their camp; dextrously inclined to the left; occupied Cæsarea; traversed the salt desert and the river Halys; and

37. This number of 800,000 was extracted by Arabshah, or rather by Ebn Schounah, ex rationario Timuri, on the faith of a Carizmian officer (tom. i. c. 68. p. 617.); and it is remarkable enough, that a Greek historian (Phranza, l. i. c. 29.) adds no more than 20,000 men. Poggius reckons 1,000,000; another Latin contemporary (Chron. Tarvisianum, apud Muratori, tom. xix. p. 800.) 1,100,000; and the enormous sum of 1,600,000 is attested by a German soldier, who was present at the battle of Angora (Leunclav. ad Chalcondyl. l. iii. p. 82.). Timour, in his Institutions, has not deigned to calculate his troops, his subjects, or his revenues.

38. A wide latitude of non-effectives was allowed by the Great Mogul for his own pride and the benefit of his officers. Bernier's patron was Penge-Hazari, commander of 5000 horse; of which he maintained no more than 500 (Voyages, tom. i. p. 288, 289.).

39. Timour himself fixes at 400,000 men the Ottoman army (Institutions, p. 153.), which is reduced to 150,000 by Phranza (l. i. c. 29.), and swelled by the German soldier to 1,400,000. It is evident, that the Moguls were the more numerous.

invested Angora: while the sultan, immoveable and ignorant in his post, compared the Tartar swiftness to the crawling of a snail:[40] he returned on the wings of indignation to the relief of Angora; and as both generals were alike impatient for action, the plains round that city were the scene of a memorable battle, which has immortalised the glory of Timour and the shame of Bajazet. For this signal victory, the Mogul emperor was indebted to himself, to the genius of the moment, and the discipline of thirty years. He had improved the tactics, without violating the manners, of his nation,[41] whose force still consisted in the missile weapons, and rapid evolutions, of a numerous cavalry. From a single troop to a great army, the mode of attack was the same: a foremost line first advanced to the charge, and was supported in a just order by the squadrons of the great vanguard. The general's eye watched over the field, and at his command the front and rear of the right and left wings successively moved forwards in their several divisions, and in a direct or oblique line: the enemy was pressed by eighteen or twenty attacks; and each attack afforded a chance of victory. If they all proved fruitless or unsuccessful, the occasion was worthy of the emperor himself, who gave the signal of advancing to the standard and main body, which he led in person.[42] But in the battle of Angora, the main body itself was supported, on the flanks and in the rear, by the bravest squadrons of the reserve, commanded by the sons and grandsons of Timour. The conqueror of Hindostan ostentatiously shewed a line of elephants, the trophies, rather than the instruments, of victory: the use of the Greek fire was familiar to the Moguls and Ottomans: but had they borrowed from Europe the recent invention of gunpowder and cannon, the artificial thunder, in the hands of either nation, must have turned the fortune of the day.[43] In that day, Bajazet displayed the qualities of a soldier and a chief: but his genius

Battle of Angora, A.D. 1402, July 28.

40. It may not be useless to mark the distances between Angora and the neighbouring cities, by the journies of the caravans, each of twenty or twenty-five miles: to Smyrna xx. to Kiotahia x. to Boursa x. to Cæsarea viii. to Sinope x. to Nicomedia ix. to Constantinople xii. or xiii. (see Tournefort, Voyage au Levant, tom. ii. lettre xxi.).

41. See the Systems of Tactics in the Institutions, which the English editors have illustrated with elaborate plans (p. 373–407.).

42. The sultan himself (says Timour) must then put the foot of courage into the stirrup of patience. A Tartar metaphor, which is lost in the English, but preserved in the French, version of the Institutes (p. 156, 157.).

43. The Greek fire, on Timour's side, is attested by Sherefeddin (l. v. c. 47.); but Voltaire's strange suspicion, that some cannon, inscribed with strange characters, must have been sent by that monarch to Delhi, is refuted by the universal silence of contemporaries.

sunk under a stronger ascendant; and from various motives, the greatest part of his troops failed him in the decisive moment. His rigour and avarice had provoked a mutiny among the Turks; and even his son Soliman too hastily withdrew from the field. The forces of Anatolia, loyal in their revolt, were drawn away to the banners of their lawful princes. His Tartar allies had been tempted by the letters and emissaries of Timour;[44] who reproached their ignoble servitude under the slaves of their fathers; and offered to their hopes the dominion of their new, or the liberty of their ancient, country. In the right wing of Bajazet, the cuirassiers of Europe charged, with faithful hearts and irresistible arms; but these men of iron were soon broken by an artful flight and headlong pursuit: and the Janizaries, alone, without cavalry or missile weapons, were encompassed by the circle of the Mogul hunters. Their valour was at length oppressed by heat, thirst, and the weight of numbers; and the unfortunate sultan, afflicted with the gout in his hands and feet, was transported from the field on the fleetest of his horses. He was pursued and taken by the titular khan of Zagatai; and, after his capture, and the defeat of the Ottoman powers, the kingdom of Anatolia submitted to the conqueror, who planted his standard at Kiotahia, and dispersed on all sides the ministers of rapine and destruction. Mirza Mehemmed Sultan, the eldest and best beloved of his grandsons, was dispatched to Boursa with thirty thousand horse: and such was his youthful ardour, that he arrived with only four thousand at the gates of the capital, after performing in five days a march of two hundred and thirty miles. Yet fear is still more rapid in its course: and Soliman, the son of Bajazet, had already passed over to Europe with the royal treasure. The spoil, however, of the palace and city was immense: the inhabitants had escaped; but the buildings, for the most part of wood, were reduced to ashes. From Boursa, the grandson of Timour advanced to Nice, even yet a fair and flourishing city; and the Mogul squadrons were only stopped by the waves of the Propontis. The same success attended the other mirzas and emirs in their excursions: and Smyrna, defended by the zeal and courage of the Rhodian knights, alone deserved the presence of the emperor himself. After an obstinate defence, the place was taken by storm; all that breathed was put to the sword; and the heads of the

Defeat and captivity of Bajazet.

44. Timour has dissembled this secret and important negociation with the Tartars, which is indisputably proved by the joint evidence of the Arabian (tom. i. c. 47. p. 391.), Turkish (Annal. Leunclav. p. 321.), and Persian historians (Khondemir, apud d'Herbelot, p. 882.).

Christian heroes were launched from the engines, on board of two carracks, or great ships of Europe, that rode at anchor in the harbour. The Moslems of Asia rejoiced in their deliverance from a dangerous and domestic foe, and a parallel was drawn between the two rivals, by observing that Timour, in fourteen days, had reduced a fortress which had sustained seven years the siege, or at least the blockade, of Bajazet.[45]

The story of his iron cage

The *iron cage* in which Bajazet was imprisoned by Tamerlane, so long and so often repeated as a moral lesson, is now rejected as a fable by the modern writers, who smile at the vulgar credulity.[46] They appeal with confidence to the Persian history of Sherefeddin Ali, which has been given to our curiosity in a French version, and from which I shall collect and abridge a more specious narrative of this memorable transaction. No sooner was Timour informed that the captive Ottoman was at the door of his tent, than he graciously stept forwards to receive him, seated him by his side, and mingled with just reproaches a soothing pity for his rank and misfortune. "Alas!" said the emperor, "the decree of fate is now accomplished by your own fault: it is the web which you have woven, the thorns of the tree which yourself have planted. I wished to spare, and even to assist, the champion of the Moslems: you braved our threats; you despised our friendship; you forced us to enter your kingdom with our invincible armies. Behold the event. Had you vanquished, I am not ignorant of the fate which you reserved for myself and my troops. But I disdain to retaliate: your life and honour are secure; and I shall express my gratitude to God by my clemency to man." The royal captive shewed some signs of repentance, accepted the humiliation of a robe of honour, and embraced with tears his son Mousa, who, at his request, was sought and found among the captives of the field. The Ottoman princes were lodged in a splendid pavillion; and the respect of the guards could be surpassed only by their vigilance. On the arrival of the haram from Boursa, Timour restored the queen Despina and her daughter to their

disproved by the Persian historian of Timour;

45. For the war of Anatolia or Roum, I add some hints in the Institutions, to the copious narratives of Sherefeddin (l. v. c. 44–65.) and Arabshah (tom. ii. c. 20–35.). On this part only of Timour's history, it is lawful to quote the Turks (Cantemir, p. 53–55. Annal. Leunclav. p. 320–322.) and the Greeks (Phranza, l. i. c. 29. Ducas, c. 15–17. Chalcondyles, l. iii.).

46. The scepticism of Voltaire (Essai sur l'Histoire Generale, c. 88.) is ready on this, as on every occasion, to reject a popular tale, and to diminish the magnitude of vice and virtue; and on most occasions his incredulity is reasonable.

father and husband; but he piously required, that the Servian princess, who had hitherto been indulged in the profession of Christianity, should embrace without delay the religion of the prophet. In the feast of victory, to which Bajazet was invited, the Mogul emperor placed a crown on his head and a sceptre in his hand, with a solemn assurance of restoring him with an increase of glory to the throne of his ancestors. But the effect of this promise was disappointed by the sultan's untimely death: amidst the care of the most skilful physicians, he expired of an apoplexy at Akshehr, the Antioch of Pisidia, about nine months after his defeat. The victor dropped a tear over his grave; his body, with royal pomp, was conveyed to the mausoleum which he had erected at Boursa; and his son Mousa, after receiving a rich present of gold and jewels, of horses and arms, was invested by a patent in red ink with the kingdom of Anatolia.

Such is the portrait of a generous conqueror, which has been extracted from his own memorials, and dedicated to his son and grandson, nineteen years after his decease;[47] and, at a time when the truth was remembered by thousands, a manifest falsehood would have implied a satire on his real conduct. Weighty indeed is this evidence, adopted by all the Persian histories;[48] yet flattery, more especially in the East, is base and audacious; and the harsh and ignominious treatment of Bajazet is attested by a chain of witnesses, some of whom shall be produced in the order of their time and country. 1. The reader has not forgot the garrison of French, whom the marshal Boucicault left behind him for the defence of Constantinople. They were on the spot to receive the earliest and most faithful intelligence of the overthrow of their great adversary; and it is more than probable, that some of them accompanied the Greek embassy to the camp of Tamerlane. From their account, the *hardships* of the prison and death of Bajazet are affirmed by the marshal's servant and historian, within the distance of seven years.[49] 2. The name of

attested, 1. by the French;

2. by the Italians;

47. See the history of Sherefeddin (l. v. c. 49. 52, 53. 59, 60.). This work was finished at Shiraz, in the year 1424, and dedicated to sultan Ibrahim, the son of Sharokh, the son of Timour, who reigned in Farsistan in his father's lifetime.

48. After the perusal of Khondemir, Ebn Schounah, &c. the learned d'Herbelot (Bibliot. Orientale, p. 882.) may affirm, that this fable is not mentioned in the most authentic histories: but his denial of the visible testimony of Arabshah, leaves some room to suspect his accuracy.

49. Et fut lui-meme *(Bajazet)* pris, et mené en prison, en laquelle mourut de *dure mort*! Memoires de Boucicault, P. i. c. 37. These memoirs were composed while the marshal was still governor of Genoa, from whence he was expelled in the year 1409, by a popular insurrection (Muratori, Annali d'Italia, tom. xii. p. 473, 474.).

Poggius the Italian[50] is deservedly famous among the revivers of learning in the fifteenth century. His elegant dialogue on the vicissitudes of fortune[51] was composed in his fiftieth year, twenty-eight years after the Turkish victory of Tamerlane;[52] whom he celebrates as not inferior to the illustrious Barbarians of antiquity. Of his exploits and discipline Poggius was informed by several ocular witnesses; nor does he forget an example so apposite to his theme as the Ottoman monarch, whom the Scythian confined like a wild beast in an iron cage, and exhibited a spectacle to Asia. I might add the authority of two Italian chronicles, perhaps of an earlier date, which would prove at least that the same story, whether false or true, was imported into Europe with the first tidings of the revolution.[53] 3. At the time when Poggius flourished at Rome, Ahmed Ebn Arabshah composed at Damascus the florid and malevolent history of Timour, for which he had collected materials in his journies over Turkey and Tartary.[54] Without any possible correspondence between the Latin and the Arabian writer, they agree in the fact of the iron cage; and their agreement is a striking proof of their common veracity. Ahmed Arabshah likewise relates another outrage, which Bajazet endured, of a more domestic and tender nature. His indiscreet mention of women and divorces was deeply resented by the jealous Tartar: in the feast of victory, the wine was served by female cup-bearers, and the sultan beheld his own concubines and wives confounded among the slaves, and exposed without a veil to the eyes of intemperance. To escape a similar indignity, it is said, that his successors, except in a single instance, have abstained from legitimate nuptials; and the Ottoman practice and

3. by the Arabs;

50. The reader will find a satisfactory account of the life and writings of Poggius, in the Poggiana, an entertaining work of M. Lenfant, and in the Bibliotheca Latina mediæ et infimæ Ætatis of Fabricius (tom. v. p. 305–308.). Poggius was born in the year 1380, and died in 1459.

51. The dialogue de Varietate Fortunæ (of which a complete and elegant edition has been published at Paris in 1723, in 4to), was composed a short time before the death of pope Martin V. (p. 5.), and consequently about the end of the year 1430.

52. See a splendid and eloquent encomium of Tamerlane, p. 36–39. ipse enim novi (says Poggius) qui fuere in ejus castris . . . Regem vivum cepit, caveâque in modum feræ inclusum per omnem Asiam circumtulit egregium admirandumque spectaculum fortunæ.

53. The Chronicon Tarvisianum (in Muratori, Script. Rerum Italicarum, tom. xix. p. 800.), and the Annales Estenses (tom. xviii. p. 974.). The two authors, Andrea de Redusiis de Quero, and James de Delayto, were both contemporaries, and both chancellors, the one of Trevigi, the other of Ferrara. The evidence of the former is the most positive.

54. See Arabshah, tom. ii. c. 28. 34. He travelled in regiones Rumæas, A.H. 839 (A.D. 1435, July 27), tom. ii. c. 2. p. 13.

belief, at least in the sixteenth century, is attested by the observing Busbequius,[55] ambassador from the court of Vienna to the great Soliman.

4. by the Greeks; 4. Such is the separation of language, that the testimony of a Greek is not less independent than that of a Latin or an Arab. I suppress the names of Chalcondyles and Ducas, who flourished in a later period, and who speak in a less positive tone; but more attention is due to George Phranza,[56] protovestiare of the last emperors, and who was born a year before the battle of Angora. Twenty-two years after that event, he was sent ambassador to Amurath the second; and the historian might converse with some veteran Janizaries, who had been made prisoners with the sultan, and had themselves seen him in his iron cage. *5. by the Turks.* 5. The last evidence, in every sense, is that of the Turkish annals, which have been consulted or transcribed by Leunclavius, Pocock, and Cantemir.[57] They unanimously deplore the captivity of the iron cage; and some credit may be allowed to national historians, who cannot stigmatize the Tartar without uncovering the shame of their king and country.

Probable conclusion. From these opposite premises, a fair and moderate conclusion may be deduced. I am satisfied that Sherefeddin Ali has faithfully described the first ostentatious interview, in which the conqueror whose spirits were harmonised by success, affected the character of generosity. But his mind was insensibly alienated by the unseasonable arrogance of Bajazet; the complaints of his enemies, the Anatolian princes, were just and vehement; and Timour betrayed a design of leading his royal captive in triumph to Samarcand. An attempt to facilitate his escape, by digging a mine under the tent, provoked the Mogul emperor to impose a harsher restraint; and in his perpetual marches, an iron cage on a waggon might be invented, not as a wanton insult, but as a rigorous precaution. Timour had read in some fabulous history a similar treatment of one of his predecessors, a king of Persia; and Bajazet was condemned to represent the person, and expiate the guilt, of the Roman Cæsar.[58] But the strength

55. Busbequius in Legatione Turcicâ, epist. i. p. 52. Yet his respectable authority is somewhat shaken by the subsequent marriages of Amurath II. with a Servian, and of Mahomet II. with an Asiatic, princess (Cantemir, p. 83. 93.).

56. See the testimony of George Phranza (l. i. c. 29.), and his life in Hanckius de Script. Byzant. P. i. c. 40.). Chalcondyles and Ducas speak in general terms of Bajazet's *chains*.

57. Annales Leunclav. p. 321. Pocock, Prolegomen. ad Abulpharag. Dynast. Cantemir, p. 55.

58. A Sapor, king of Persia, had been made prisoner and inclosed in the figure of a cow's hide by Maximian or Galerius Cæsar. Such is the fable related by Eutychius (Annal. tom. i. p. 421. vers. Pocock). The recollection of the true history (Decline

Death of Bajazet, A.D. 1403, March 9.

of his mind and body fainted under the trial, and his premature death might, without injustice, be ascribed to the severity of Timour. He warred not with the dead; a tear and a sepulchre were all that he could bestow on a captive who was delivered from his power; and if Mousa, the son of Bajazet, was permitted to reign over the ruins of Boursa, the greatest part of the provinces of Anatolia had been restored by the conqueror to their lawful sovereign.

Term of the conquests of Timour, A.D. 1403.

From the Irtish and Volga to the Persian Gulf, and from the Ganges to Damascus and the Archipelago, Asia was in the hand of Timour; his armies were invincible, his ambition was boundless, and his zeal might aspire to conquer and convert the Christian kingdoms of the West, which already trembled at his name. He touched the utmost verge of the land; but an insuperable, though narrow, sea rolled between the two continents of Europe and Asia;[59] and the lord of so many *tomans*, or myriads, of horse, was not master of a single galley. The two passages of the Bosphorus and Hellespont, of Constantinople and Gallipoli, were possessed, the one by the Christians, the other by the Turks. On this great occasion, they forgot the difference of religion to act with union and firmness in the common cause: the double streights were guarded with ships and fortifications; and they separately withheld the transports, which Timour demanded of either nation, under the pretence of attacking their enemy. At the same time, they soothed his pride with tributary gifts and suppliant embassies, and prudently tempted him to retreat with the honours of victory. Soliman, the son of Bajazet, implored his clemency for his father and himself; accepted, by a red patent, the investiture of the kingdom of Romania, which he already held by the sword; and reiterated his ardent wish, of casting himself in person at the feet of the king of the world. The Greek emperor[60] (either John or Manuel) submitted to pay the same tribute which he had stipulated with the Turkish sultan, and ratified the treaty by an oath of

and Fall, &c. vol. i. p. 376–84.) will teach us to appreciate the knowledge of the Orientals of the ages which precede the Hegira.

59. Arabshah (tom. ii. c. 25.) describes, like a curious traveller, the streights of Gallipoli and Constantinople. To acquire a just idea of these events, I have compared the narratives and prejudices of the Moguls, Turks, Greeks, and Arabians. The Spanish ambassador mentions this hostile union of the Christians and Ottomans (Vie de Timour, p. 96.).

60. Since the name of Cæsar had been transferred to the sultans of Roum, the Greek princes of Constantinople (Sherefeddin, l. v. c. 54.) were confounded with the Christian *lords* of Gallipoli, Thessalonica, &c. under the title of *Tekkur*, which is derived by corruption from the genitive του κυριου (Cantemir, p. 51.).

allegiance, from which he could absolve his conscience so soon as the Mogul arms had retired from Anatolia. But the fears and fancy of nations ascribed to the ambitious Tamerlane a new design of vast and romantic compass; a design of subduing Egypt and Africa, marching from the Nile to the Atlantic Ocean, entering Europe by the Streights of Gibraltar, and, after imposing his yoke on the kingdoms of Christendom, of returning home by the deserts of Russia and Tartary. This remote, and perhaps imaginary, danger was averted by the submission of the sultan of Egypt: the honours of the prayer and the coin, attested at Cairo the supremacy of Timour; and a rare gift of a *giraffe*, or camelopard, and nine ostriches, represented at Samarcand the tribute of the African world. Our imagination is not less astonished by the portrait of a Mogul, who, in his camp before Smyrna, meditates and almost accomplishes the invasion of the Chinese empire.[61] Timour was urged to this enterprise by national honour and religious zeal. The torrents which he had shed of Musulman blood could be expiated only by an equal destruction of the infidels; and as he now stood at the gates of paradise, he might best secure his glorious entrance by demolishing the idols of China, founding moschs in every city, and establishing the profession of faith in one God, and his prophet Mahomet. The recent expulsion of the house of Zingis was an insult on the Mogul name; and the disorders of the empire afforded the fairest opportunity for revenge. The illustrious Hongvou, founder of the dynasty of *Ming*, died four years before the battle of Angora; and his grandson, a weak and unfortunate youth, was burnt in his palace, after a million of Chinese had perished in the civil war.[62] Before he evacuated Anatolia, Timour dispatched beyond the Sihoon a numerous army, or rather colony, of his old and new subjects, to open the road, to subdue the Pagan Calmucks and Mungals, and to found cities and magazines in the desert; and, by the diligence of his lieutenant, he soon received a perfect map and description of the unknown regions, from the source of the Irtish to the wall of China. During these preparations, the emperor atchieved the final conquest of Georgia; passed the winter on the banks of the Araxes; appeased the troubles of Persia; and slowly returned to his capital, after a campaign of four years and nine months.

61. See Sherefeddin, l. v. c. 4. who marks, in a just itinerary, the road to China, which Arabshah (tom. ii. c. 33.) paints in vague and rhetorical colours.

62. Synopsis Hist. Sinicæ, p. 74–76 (in the iv[th] part of the Relations de Thevenot), Duhalde, Hist. de la Chine (tom. i. p. 507, 508. folio edition); and for the chronology of the Chinese emperors, de Guignes, Hist. des Huns, tom. i. p. 71, 72.

His triumph at Samarcand, A.D. 1404, July– A.D. 1405, January 8.

On the throne of Samarcand,[63] he displayed in a short repose his magnificence and power; listened to the complaints of the people; distributed a just measure of rewards and punishments; employed his riches in the architecture of palaces and temples; and gave audience to the ambassadors of Egypt, Arabia, India, Tartary, Russia, and Spain, the last of whom presented a suit of tapestry which eclipsed the pencil of the Oriental artists. The marriage of six of the emperor's grandsons was esteemed an act of religion, as well as of paternal tenderness; and the pomp of the ancient caliphs was revived in their nuptials. They were celebrated in the gardens of Canighul, decorated with innumerable tents and pavilions, which displayed the luxury of a great city and the spoils of a victorious camp. Whole forests were cut down to supply fuel for the kitchens; the plain was spread with pyramids of meat, and vases of every liquor, to which thousands of guests were courteously invited: the orders of the state, and the nations of the earth, were marshalled at the royal banquet; nor were the ambassadors of Europe (says the haughty Persian) excluded from the feast; since even the *casses*, the smallest of fish, find their place in the ocean.[64] The public joy was testified by illuminations and masquerades; the trades of Samarcand passed in review; and every trade was emulous to execute some quaint device, some marvellous pageant, with the materials of their peculiar art. After the marriage-contracts had been ratified by the cadhis, the bridegrooms and their brides retired to the nuptial chambers; nine times, according to the Asiatic fashion, they were dressed and undressed; and at each change of apparel, pearls and rubies were showered on their heads, and contemptuously abandoned to their attendants. A general indulgence was proclaimed: every law was relaxed, every pleasure was allowed; the people was free, the sovereign was idle; and the historian of Timour may remark, that, after devoting fifty years to the attainment of empire, the only happy period of his life were the two months in which he ceased to exercise his power. But he was soon awakened to the cares of government and war. The standard was unfurled for the invasion of China: the emirs made their report of

63. For the return, triumph, and death of Timour, see Sherefeddin (l. vi. c. 1–30.) and Arabshah (tom. ii. c. 35–47.).

64. Sherefeddin (l. vi. c. 24.) mentions the ambassadors of one of the most potent sovereigns of Europe. We know that it was Henry III. king of Castile; and the curious relation of his two embassies is still extant (Mariana, Hist. Hispan. l. xix. c. 11. tom. ii. p. 329, 330. Avertissement à l'Hist. de Timur Bec, p. 28–33.). There appears likewise to have been some correspondence between the Mogul emperor, and the court of Charles VII. king of France (Histoire de France, par Velly et Villaret, tom. xii. p. 336.).

two hundred thousand, the select and veteran soldiers of Iran and Touran: their baggage and provisions were transported by five hundred great waggons, and an immense train of horses and camels; and the troops might prepare for a long absence, since more than six months were employed in the tranquil journey of a caravan from Samarcand to Pekin. Neither age, nor the severity of the winter, could retard the impatience of Timour; he mounted on horseback, passed the Sihoon on the ice, marched seventy-six parasangs, three hundred miles, from his capital, and pitched his last camp in the neighbourhood of Otrar, where he was expected by the angel of death. Fatigue, and the indiscreet use of iced water, accelerated the progress of his fever; and the conqueror of Asia expired in the seventieth year of his age, thirty-five years after he had ascended the throne of Zagatai. His designs were lost; his armies were disbanded; China was saved; and fourteen years after his decease, the most powerful of his children sent an embassy of friendship and commerce to the court of Pekin.[65]

His death on the road to China, A.D. 1405, April 1.

Character and merits of Timour.

The fame of Timour has pervaded the East and West; his posterity is still invested with the Imperial *title*; and the admiration of his subjects, who revered him almost as a deity, may be justified in some degree by the praise or confession of his bitterest enemies.[66] Although he was lame of an hand and foot, his form and stature were not unworthy of his rank; and his vigorous health, so essential to himself and to the world, was corroborated by temperance and exercise. In his familiar discourse he was grave and modest, and if he was ignorant of the Arabic language, he spoke with fluency and elegance the Persian and Turkish idioms. It was his delight to converse with the learned on topics of history and science; and the amusement of his leisure hours was the game of chess, which he improved or corrupted with new refinements.[67] In his religion, he was a zealous, though not perhaps an orthodox, Musulman;[68] but his sound understanding may tempt us to believe,

65. See the translation of the Persian account of their embassy, a curious and original piece (in the iv[th] part of the Relations de Thevenot). They presented the emperor of China with an old horse which Timour had formerly rode. It was in the year 1419, that they departed from the court of Herat, to which place they returned in 1422 from Pekin.

66. From Arabshah, tom. ii. c. 96. The bright or softer colours are borrowed from Sherefeddin, d'Herbelot, and the Institutions.

67. His new system was multiplied from 32 pieces and 64 squares, to 56 pieces and 110 or 130 squares. But, except in his court, the old game has been thought sufficiently elaborate. The Mogul emperor was rather pleased than hurt, with the victory of a subject: a chess-player will feel the value of this encomium!

68. See Sherefeddin, l. v. c. 15. 25. Arab-

that a superstitious reverence for omens and prophecies, for saints and astrologers, was only affected as an instrument of policy. In the government of a vast empire, he stood alone and absolute, without a rebel to oppose his power, a favourite to seduce his affections, or a minister to mislead his judgment. It was his firmest maxim, that whatever might be the consequence, the word of the prince should never be disputed or recalled; but his foes have maliciously observed, that the commands of anger and destruction were more strictly executed than those of beneficence and favour. His sons and grandsons, of whom Timour left six-and-thirty at his decease, were his first and most submissive subjects; and whenever they deviated from their duty, they were corrected, according to the laws of Zingis, with the bastonade, and afterwards restored to honour and command. Perhaps his heart was not devoid of the social virtues; perhaps he was not incapable of loving his friends and pardoning his enemies; but the rules of morality are founded on the public interest; and it may be sufficient to applaud the *wisdom* of a monarch, for the liberality by which he is not impoverished, and for the justice by which he is strengthened and enriched. To maintain the harmony of authority and obedience, to chastise the proud, to protect the weak, to reward the deserving, to banish vice and idleness from his dominions, to secure the traveller and merchant, to restrain the depredations of the soldier, to cherish the labours of the husbandman, to encourage industry and learning, and, by an equal and moderate assessment, to encrease the revenue, without encreasing the taxes, are indeed the duties of a prince; but, in the discharge of these duties, he finds an ample and immediate recompense. Timour might boast, that at his accession to the throne, Asia was the prey of anarchy and rapine, whilst under his prosperous monarchy a child, fearless and unhurt, might carry a purse of gold from the East to the West. Such was his confidence of merit, that from this reformation he derived an excuse for his victories, and a title to universal dominion. The four following observations will serve to appreciate his claim to the public gratitude; and perhaps we shall conclude, that the Mogul emperor was rather the scourge than the benefactor of mankind. 1. If some partial disorders, some local oppressions, were healed by the sword of Timour, the remedy was far more pernicious than the disease.

---

shah (tom. ii. c. 96. p. 801. 803.) reproves the impiety of Timour and the Moguls, who almost preferred to the Koran, the *Yacsa*, or Law of Zingis (cui Deus maledicat): nor will he believe that Sharokh had abolished the use and authority of that Pagan code.

By their rapine, cruelty, and discord, the petty tyrants of Persia might afflict their subjects; but whole nations were crushed under the footsteps of the reformer. The ground which had been occupied by flourishing cities, was often marked by his abominable trophies, by columns, or pyramids, of human heads. Astracan, Carizme, Delhi, Ispahan, Bagdad, Aleppo, Damascus, Boursa, Smyrna, and a thousand others, were sacked, or burnt, or utterly destroyed, in his presence, and by his troops; and perhaps his conscience would have been startled, if a priest or philosopher had dared to number the millions of victims whom he had sacrificed to the establishment of peace and order.[69] 2. His most destructive wars were rather inroads than conquests. He invaded Turkestan, Kipzak, Russia, Hindostan, Syria, Anatolia, Armenia, and Georgia, without a hope or a desire of preserving those distant provinces. From thence he departed, laden with spoil; but he left behind him neither troops to awe the contumacious, nor magistrates to protect the obedient, natives. When he had broken the fabric of their ancient government, he abandoned them to the evils which his invasion had aggravated or caused; nor were these evils compensated by any present or possible benefits. 3. The kingdoms of Transoxiana and Persia were the proper field which he laboured to cultivate and adorn, as the perpetual inheritance of his family. But his peaceful labours were often interrupted, and sometimes blasted, by the absence of the conqueror. While he triumphed on the Volga or the Ganges, his servants, and even his sons, forgot their master and their duty. The public and private injuries were poorly redressed by the tardy rigour of enquiry and punishment; and we must be content to praise the *Institutions* of Timour, as the specious idea of a perfect monarchy. 4. Whatsoever might be the blessings of his administration, they evaporated with his life. To reign, rather than to govern, was the ambition of his children and grandchildren;[70] the enemies of each other and of the people. A fragment of the empire was upheld with some glory by Sharokh his youngest son; but after *his* decease, the scene was again involved in

69. Besides the bloody passages of this narrative, I must refer to an anticipation in the third volume of the Decline and Fall, which, in a single note (vol. ii. p. 305. Note 25.), accumulates near 300,000 heads of the monuments of his cruelty. Except in Rowe's play on the fifth of November, I did not expect to hear of Timour's amiable moderation (White's preface, p. 7.). Yet I can excuse a generous enthusiasm in the reader, and still more in the editor, of the *Institutions*.

70. Consult the last chapters of Sherefeddin and Arabshah, and M. de Guignes (Hist. des Huns, tom. iv. l. xx.). Fraser's History of Nadir Shah, p. 1–62. The story of Timour's descendants is imperfectly told: and the second and third parts of Sherefeddin are unknown.

darkness and blood; and before the end of a century, Transoxiana and Persia were trampled by the Uzbeks from the north, and the Turkmans of the black and white sheep. The race of Timour would have been extinct, if an hero, his descendant in the fifth degree, had not fled before the Uzbek arms to the conquest of Hindostan. His successors (the great Moguls[71]) extended their sway from the mountains of Cashmir to Cape Comorin, and from Candahar to the gulf of Bengal. Since the reign of Aurungzebe, their empire has been dissolved; their treasures of Delhi have been rifled by a Persian robber; and the richest of their kingdoms is now possessed by a company of Christian merchants, of a remote island in the Northern ocean.

Civil wars of the sons of Bajazet, A.D. 1403–1421.

Far different was the fate of the Ottoman monarchy. The massy trunk was bent to the ground, but no sooner did the hurricane pass away, than it again rose with fresh vigour and more lively vegetation. When Timour, in every sense, had evacuated Anatolia, he left the cities without a palace, a treasure, or a king. The open country was overspread with hords of shepherds and robbers of Tartar or Turkman origin; the recent conquests of Bajazet were restored to the emirs, one of whom, in base revenge, demolished his sepulchre; and his five sons were eager, by civil discord, to consume the remnant of their patrimony. I shall enumerate their names in the order of their age and actions.[72] 1. It is doubtful, whether I relate the story of the true *Mustapha*, or of an impostor, who personated that lost prince. He fought by his father's side in the battle of Angora: but when the captive sultan was permitted to enquire for his children, Mousa alone could be found; and the Turkish historians, the slaves of the triumphant faction, are persuaded that his brother was confounded among the slain. If Mustapha escaped from that disastrous field, he was concealed twelve years from his friends and enemies; till he emerged in Thessaly, and was hailed by a numerous party, as the son and successor of Bajazet. His first defeat would have been his last, had not the true, or false, Mustapha been saved by the Greeks, and restored, after the decease of his brother Mahomet, to liberty and empire. A degenerate mind seemed to argue his spurious birth; and if, on the throne of Adrianople,

1. Mustapha;

71. Shah Allum, the present Mogul, is in the fourteenth degree from Timour by Miran Shah, his third son. See the ii[d] volume of Dow's History of Hindostan.

72. The civil wars, from the death of Bajazet to that of Mustapha, are related, according to the Turks, by Demetrius Cantemir (p. 58–82.). Of the Greeks, Chalcondyles (l. iv and v.), Phranza (l. i. c. 30–32.), and Ducas (c. 18–27.), the last is the most copious and best informed.

he was adored as the Ottoman sultan; his flight, his fetters, and an ignominious gibbet, delivered the impostor to popular contempt. A similar character and claim was asserted by several rival pretenders; thirty persons are said to have suffered under the name of Mustapha; and these frequent executions may perhaps insinuate, that the Turkish court was

2. Isa; not perfectly secure of the death of the lawful prince. 2. After his father's captivity, Isa[73] reigned for some time in the neighbourhood of Angora, Sinope, and the Black Sea; and his ambassadors were dismissed from the presence of Timour with fair promises and honourable gifts. But their master was soon deprived of his province and life, by a jealous brother, the sovereign of Amasia; and the final event suggested a pious allusion, that the law of Moses and Jesus, of *Isa* and *Mousa*, had been

3. Soliman, A.D. 1403–1410. abrogated by the greater *Mahomet*. 3. *Soliman* is not numbered in the list of the Turkish emperors: yet he checked the victorious progress of the Moguls; and after their departure, united for a while the thrones of Adrianople and Boursa. In war he was brave, active, and fortunate: his courage was softened by clemency; but it was likewise inflamed by presumption, and corrupted by intemperance and idleness. He relaxed the nerves of discipline, in a government where either the subject or the sovereign must continually tremble: his vices alienated the chiefs of the army and the law; and his daily drunkenness, so contemptible in a prince and a man, was doubly odious in a disciple of the prophet. In the slumber of intoxication, he was surprised by his brother Mousa; and as he fled from Adrianople towards the Byzantine capital, Soliman was overtaken and slain in a bath, after a reign of seven years and ten months.

4. Mousa, A.D. 1410. 4. The investiture of Mousa degraded him as the slave of the Moguls: his tributary kingdom of Anatolia was confined within a narrow limit, nor could his broken militia and empty treasury contend with the hardy and veteran bands of the sovereign of Romania. Mousa fled in disguise from the palace of Boursa; traversed the Propontis in an open boat; wandered over the Walachian and Servian hills; and after some vain attempts, ascended the throne of Adrianople, so recently stained with the blood of Soliman. In a reign of three years and an half, his troops were victorious against the Christians of Hungary and the Morea; but Mousa was ruined by his timorous disposition and unseasonable clemency. After resigning the sovereignty of Anatolia, he fell a victim to the perfidy of his ministers, and the superior ascendant of his brother Mahomet.

73. Arabshah, tom. ii. c. 26. whose testimony on this occasion is weighty and valuable. The existence of Isa (unknown to the Turks) is likewise confirmed by Sherefeddin (l. v. c. 57.).

5. The final victory of Mahomet was the just recompense of his prudence and moderation. Before his father's captivity, the royal youth had been entrusted with the government of Amasia, thirty days journey from Constantinople, and the Turkish frontier against the Christians of Trebizond and Georgia. The castle, in Asiatic warfare, was esteemed impregnable; and the city of Amasia,[74] which is equally divided by the river Iris, rises on either side in the form of an amphitheatre, and represents on a smaller scale the image of Bagdad. In his rapid career, Timour appears to have overlooked this obscure and contumacious angle of Anatolia; and Mahomet, without provoking the conqueror, maintained his silent independence, and chased from the province the last stragglers of the Tartar host. He relieved himself from the dangerous neighbourhood of Isa; but in the contests of their more powerful brethren, his firm neutrality was respected; till, after the triumph of Mousa, he stood forth the heir and avenger of the unfortunate Soliman. Mahomet obtained Anatolia by treaty and Romania by arms; and the soldier who presented him with the head of Mousa was rewarded as the benefactor of his king and country. The eight years of his sole and peaceful reign were usefully employed in banishing the vices of civil discord, and restoring on a firmer basis the fabric of the Ottoman monarchy. His last care was the choice of two vizirs, Bajazet and Ibrahim,[75] who might guide the youth of his son Amurath; and such was their union and prudence, that they concealed above forty days the emperor's death, till the arrival of his successor in the palace of Boursa. A new war was kindled in Europe by the prince, or impostor, Mustapha; the first vizir lost his army and his head; but the more fortunate Ibrahim, whose name and family are still revered, extinguished the last pretender to the throne of Bajazet, and closed the scene of domestic hostility.

5. Mahomet I. A.D. 1413–1421.

Reign of Amurath II. A.D. 1421–1451, February 9.

In these conflicts, the wisest Turks, and indeed the body of the nation, were strongly attached to the unity of the empire; and Romania and Anatolia, so often torn asunder by private ambition, were animated by a strong and invincible tendency of cohesion. Their efforts might have instructed the Christian powers;

Re-union of the Ottoman empire, A.D. 1421.

74. Arabshah, loc. citat. Abulfeda, Geograph. tab. xvii. p. 302. Busbequius, epist. i. p. 96, 97. in Itinere C. P. et Amasiano.

75. The virtues of Ibrahim are praised by a contemporary Greek (Ducas, c. 25.). His descendants are the sole nobles in Turkey: they content themselves with the administration of his pious foundations, are excused from public offices, and receive two annual visits from the sultan (Cantemir, p. 76.).

and had they occupied with a confederate fleet, the streights of Gallipoli, the Ottomans, at least in Europe, must have been speedily annihilated. But the schism of the West, and the factions and wars of France and England, diverted the Latins from this generous enterprise: they enjoyed the present respite, without a thought of futurity; and were often tempted by a momentary interest, to serve the common enemy of their religion. A colony of Genoese,[76] which had been planted at Phocæa[77] on the Ionian coast, was enriched by the lucrative monopoly of alum;[78] and their tranquillity, under the Turkish empire, was secured by the annual payment of tribute. In the last civil war of the Ottomans, the Genoese governor, Adorno, a bold and ambitious youth, embraced the party of Amurath; and undertook with seven stout gallies to transport him from Asia to Europe. The sultan and five hundred guards embarked on board the admiral's ship; which was manned by eight hundred of the bravest Franks. His life and liberty were in their hands; nor can we, without reluctance, applaud the fidelity of Adorno, who, in the midst of the passage, knelt before him, and gratefully accepted a discharge of his arrears of tribute. They landed in sight of Mustapha and Gallipoli; two thousand Italians, armed with lances and battle-axes, attended Amurath to the conquest of Adrianople; and this venal service was soon repaid by the ruin of the commerce and colony of Phocæa.

State of the Greek empire, A.D. 1402–1425.

If Timour had generously marched at the request, and to the relief, of the Greek emperor, he might be entitled to the praise and gratitude of the Christians.[79] But a Musulman, who carried into Georgia the sword of persecution, and respected

76. See Pachymer (l. v. 29.), Nicephorus Gregoras (l. ii. c. 1.), Sherefeddin (l. v. c. 57.), and Ducas (c. 25.). The last of these, a curious and careful observer, is entitled, from his birth and station, to particular credit in all that concerns Ionia and the islands. Among the nations that resorted to New Phocæa, he mentions the English (*Ιγγληνοι*); an early evidence of Mediterranean trade.

77. For the spirit of navigation, and freedom of ancient Phocæa, or rather of the Phocæans, consult the 1st book of Herodotus, and the Geographical Index of his last and learned French translator, M. Larcher (tom. vii. p. 299.).

78. Phocæa is not enumerated by Pliny (Hist. Nat. xxxv. 52.) among the places productive of alum; he reckons Egypt as the first, and for the second the isle of Melos, whose alum mines are described by Tournefort (tom. i. lettre iv.), a traveller and a naturalist. After the loss of Phocæa, the Genoese, in 1459, found that useful mineral in the isle of Ischia (Ismael. Bouillaud, ad Ducam, c. 25.).

79. The writer who has the most abused this fabulous generosity, is our ingenious Sir William Temple (his works, vol. iii. p. 349, 350. octavo edition), that lover of exotic virtue. After the conquest of Russia, &c. and the passage of the Danube, his Tartar hero relieves, visits, admires, and refuses the city of Constantine. His flatter-

the holy warfare of Bajazet, was not disposed to pity or succour the *idolaters* of Europe. The Tartar followed the impulse of ambition; and the deliverance of Constantinople was the accidental consequence. When Manuel abdicated the government, it was his prayer, rather than his hope, that the ruin of the church and state might be delayed beyond his unhappy days; and after his return from a western pilgrimage, he expected every hour the news of the sad catastrophe. On a sudden he was astonished and rejoiced by the intelligence of the retreat, the overthrow, and the captivity of the Ottoman. Manuel[80] immediately sailed from Modon in the Morea; ascended the throne of Constantinople; and dismissed his blind competitor to an easy exile in the isle of Lesbos. The ambassadors of the son of Bajazet were soon introduced to his presence; but their pride was fallen, their tone was modest; they were awed by the just apprehension, lest the Greeks should open to the Moguls the gates of Europe. Soliman saluted the emperor by the name of father; solicited at his hands the government or gift of Romania; and promised to deserve his favour by inviolable friendship, and the restitution of Thessalonica, with the most important places along the Strymon, the Propontis, and the Black Sea. The alliance of Soliman exposed the emperor to the enmity and revenge of Mousa: the Turks appeared in arms before the gates of Constantinople; but they were repulsed by sea and land; and unless the city was guarded by some foreign mercenaries, the Greeks must have wondered at their own triumph. But, instead of prolonging the division of the Ottoman powers, the policy or passion of Manuel was tempted to assist the most formidable of the sons of Bajazet. He concluded a treaty with Mahomet, whose progress was checked by the insuperable barrier of Gallipoli: the sultan and his troops were transported over the Bosphorus; he was hospitably entertained in the capital; and his successful sally was the first step to the conquest of Romania. The ruin was suspended by the prudence and moderation of the conqueror: he faithfully discharged his own obligations and those of Soliman, respected the laws of gratitude and peace; and left the emperor guardian of his two younger sons, in the vain hope of saving them from the jealous cruelty of their brother Amurath. But the execution of his last testament would have offended

ing pencil deviates in every line from the truth of history: yet his pleasing fictions are more excusable than the gross errors of Cantemir.

80. For the reigns of Manuel and John, of Mahomet I. and Amurath II. see the Othman history of Cantemir (p. 70–95.), and the three Greeks, Chalcondyles, Phranza, and Ducas, who is still superior to his rivals.

the national honour and religion: and the divan unanimously pronounced, that the royal youths should never be abandoned to the custody and education of a Christian dog. On this refusal, the Byzantine councils were divided: but the age and caution of Manuel yielded to the presumption of his son John; and they unsheathed a dangerous weapon of revenge, by dismissing the true or false Mustapha, who had long been detained as a captive and hostage, and for whose maintenance they received an annual pension of three hundred thousand aspers.[81] At the door of his prison, Mustapha subscribed to every proposal; and the keys of Gallipoli, or rather of Europe, were stipulated as the price of his deliverance. But no sooner was he seated on the throne of Romania, than he dismissed the Greek ambassadors with a smile of contempt, declaring, in a pious tone, that, at the day of judgment, he would rather answer for the violation of an oath, than for the surrender of a Musulman city into the hands of the infidels. The emperor was at once the enemy of the two rivals; from whom he had sustained, and to whom he had offered, an injury; and the victory of Amurath was followed, in the ensuing spring, by the siege of Constantinople.[82]

Siege of Constantinople by Amurath II. A.D. 1422, June 10–August 24.

The religious merit of subduing the city of the Cæsars, attracted from Asia a crowd of volunteers, who aspired to the crown of martyrdom: their military ardour was inflamed by the promise of rich spoils and beautiful females; and the sultan's ambition was consecrated by the presence and prediction of Seid Bechar,a descendant of the prophet,[83] who arrived in the camp, on a mule, with a venerable train of five hundred disciples. But he might blush, if a fanatic could blush, at the failure of his assurances. The strength of the walls resisted an army of two hundred thousand Turks: their assaults were repelled by the sallies of the Greeks and their foreign mercenaries; the old resources of defence were opposed to the

81. The Turkish asper (from the Greek *ασπρος*) is, or was, a piece of *white* or silver money, at present much debased, but which was formerly equivalent to the 54th part, at least, of a Venetian ducat or sequin; and the 300,000 aspers, a princely allowance or royal tribute, may be computed at 2500l. sterling (Leunclav. Pandect. Turc. p. 406–408.).

82. For the siege of Constantinople in 1422, see the particular and contemporary narrative of John Cananus, published by Leo Allatius, at the end of his edition of Acropolita (p. 188–199.).

83. Cantemir, p. 80. Cananus, who describes Seid Bechar without naming him, supposes that the friend of Mahomet assumed in his amours the privilege of a prophet, and that the fairest of the Greek nuns were promised to the saint and his disciples.

new engines of attack; and the enthusiasm of the dervish, who was snatched to heaven in visionary converse with Mahomet, was answered by the credulity of the Christians, who *beheld* the Virgin Mary, in a violet garment, walking on the rampart and animating their courage.[84] After a siege of two months, Amurath was recalled to Boursa by a domestic revolt, which had been kindled by Greek treachery, and was soon extinguished by the death of a guiltless brother. While he led his Janizaries to new conquests in Europe and Asia, the Byzantine empire was indulged in a servile and precarious respite of thirty years. Manuel sunk into the grave; and John Palæologus was permitted to reign, for an annual tribute of three hundred thousand aspers, and the dereliction of almost all that he held beyond the suburbs of Constantinople.

The emperor John Palæologus II. A.D. 1425, July 21– A.D. 1448, October 31.

Hereditary succession and merit of the Ottomans.

In the establishment and restoration of the Turkish empire, the first merit must doubtless be assigned to the personal qualities of the sultans; since, in human life, the most important scenes will depend on the character of a single actor. By some shades of wisdom and virtue, they may be discriminated from each other; but, except in a single instance, a period of nine reigns, and two hundred and sixty-five years, is occupied, from the elevation of Othman to the death of Soliman, by a rare series of warlike and active princes, who impressed their subjects with obedience and their enemies with terror. Instead of the slothful luxury of the seraglio, the heirs of royalty were educated in the council and the field: from early youth they were entrusted by their fathers with the command of provinces and armies; and this manly institution, which was often productive of civil war, must have essentially contributed to the discipline and vigour of the monarchy. The Ottomans cannot style themselves, like the Arabian caliphs, the descendants or successors of the apostle of God; and the kindred which they claim with the Tartar khans of the house of Zingis, appears to be founded in flattery rather than in truth.[85] Their origin is obscure; but their sacred and indefeasible right, which no time can erase and no violence can infringe, was soon and unalterably implanted in the minds of their subjects. A weak or vicious sultan may be deposed and strangled; but his inheritance devolves to an infant or an ideot: nor has the most

84. For this miraculous apparition, Cananus appeals to the Musulman saint; but who will bear testimony for Seid Bechar?

85. See Rycaut (l. i. c. 13.). The Turkish sultans assume the title of khan. Yet Abulghazi is ignorant of his Ottoman cousins.

daring rebel presumed to ascend the throne of his lawful sovereign.[86] While the transient dynasties of Asia have been continually subverted by a crafty vizir in the palace or a victorious general in the camp, the Ottoman succession has been confirmed by the practice of five centuries, and is now incorporated with the vital principle of the Turkish nation.

Education and discipline of the Turks.

To the spirit and constitution of that nation, a strong and singular influence may however be ascribed. The primitive subjects of Othman were the four hundred families of wandering Turkmans, who had followed his ancestors from the Oxus to the Sangar; and the plains of Anatolia are still covered with the white and black tents of their rustic brethren. But this original drop was dissolved in the mass of voluntary and vanquished subjects, who, under the name of Turks, are united by the common ties of religion, language, and manners. In the cities, from Erzeroum to Belgrade, that national appellation is common to all the Moslems, the first and most honourable inhabitants; but they have abandoned, at least in Romania, the villages, and the cultivation of the land, to the Christian peasants. In the vigorous age of the Ottoman government, the Turks were themselves excluded from all civil and military honours; and a servile class, an artificial people, was raised by the discipline of education to obey, to conquer, and to command.[87] From the time of Orchan and the first Amurath, the sultans were persuaded that a government of the sword must be renewed in each generation with new soldiers; and that such soldiers must be sought, not in effeminate Asia, but among the hardy and warlike natives of Europe. The provinces of Thrace, Macedonia, Albania, Bulgaria, and Servia, became the perpetual seminary of the Turkish army; and when the royal fifth of the captives was diminished by conquest, an inhuman tax, of the fifth child, or of every fifth year, was rigorously levied on the Christian families. At the age of twelve or fourteen years, the most robust youths were torn from their parents; their names were enrolled in a book; and from that moment they were clothed, taught, and maintained, for the

86. The third grand vizir of the name of Kiuperli, who was slain at the battle of Salankanen in 1691 (Cantemir, p. 382.), presumed to say, that all the successors of Soliman had been fools or tyrants, and that it was time to abolish the race (Marsigli Stato Militare, &c. p. 28.). This political heretic was a good whig, and justified against the French ambassador the revolution of England (Mignot, Hist. Ottomans, tom. iii. p. 434.). His presumption condemns the singular exception of continuing offices in the same family.

87. Chalcondyles (l. v.) and Ducas (c. 23.) exhibit the rude lineaments of the Ottoman policy, and the transmutation of Christian children into Turkish soldiers.

public service. According to the promise of their appearance, they were selected for the royal schools of Boursa, Pera, and Adrianople, entrusted to the care of the bashaws, or dispersed in the houses of the Anatolian peasantry. It was the first care of their masters to instruct them in the Turkish language: their bodies were exercised by every labour that could fortify their strength; they learned to wrestle, to leap, to run, to shoot with the bow, and afterwards with the musket; till they were drafted into the chambers and companies of the Janizaries, and severely trained in the military or monastic discipline of the order. The youths most conspicuous for birth, talents, and beauty, were admitted into the inferior class of *Agiamoglans*, or the more liberal rank of *Ichoglans*, of whom the former were attached to the palace, and the latter to the person of the prince. In four successive schools, under the rod of the white eunuchs, the arts of horsemanship and of darting the javelin were their daily exercise, while those of a more studious cast applied themselves to the study of the Koran, and the knowledge of the Arabic and Persian tongues. As they advanced in seniority and merit, they were gradually dismissed to military, civil, and even ecclesiastical employments: the longer their stay, the higher was their expectation; till, at a mature period, they were admitted into the number of the forty agas, who stood before the sultan, and were promoted by his choice to the government of provinces and the first honours of the empire.[88] Such a mode of institution was admirably adapted to the form and spirit of a despotic monarchy. The ministers and generals were, in the strictest sense, the slaves of the emperor, to whose bounty they were indebted for their instruction and support. When they left the seraglio, and suffered their beards to grow as the symbol of enfranchisement, they found themselves in an important office, without faction or friendship, without parents and without heirs, dependent on the hand which had raised them from the dust, and which, on the slightest displeasure, could break in pieces these statues of glass, as they are aptly termed by the Turkish proverb.[89] In the slow and painful steps of education, their characters and talents were unfolded to a discerning eye: the *man*, naked and alone, was reduced to the standard of his personal

88. This sketch of the Turkish education and discipline, is chiefly borrowed from Rycaut's State of the Ottoman Empire, the Stato Militare del' Imperio Ottomanno of Count Marsigli (in Haya, 1732, in folio), and a Description of the Seraglio, approved by Mr. Greaves himself, a curious traveller, and inserted in the second volume of his works.

89. From the series of cxv vizirs till the siege of Vienna (Marsigli, p. 13.), their place may be valued at three years and a half purchase.

merit; and, if the sovereign had wisdom to choose, he possessed a pure and boundless liberty of choice. The Ottoman candidates were trained by the virtues of abstinence to those of action; by the habits of submission to those of command. A similar spirit was diffused among the troops; and their silence and sobriety, their patience and modesty, have extorted the reluctant praise of their Christian enemies.[90] Nor can the victory appear doubtful, if we compare the discipline and exercise of the Janizaries with the pride of birth, the independence of chivalry, the ignorance of the new levies, the mutinous temper of the veterans, and the vices of intemperance and disorder, which so long contaminated the armies of Europe.

Invention and use of gunpowder.

The only hope of salvation for the Greek empire and the adjacent kingdoms, would have been some more powerful weapon, some discovery in the art of war, that should give them a decisive superiority over their Turkish foes. Such a weapon was in their hands; such a discovery had been made in the critical moment of their fate. The chymists of China or Europe had found, by casual or elaborate experiments, that a mixture of saltpetre, sulphur, and charcoal, produces, with a spark of fire, a tremendous explosion. It was soon observed, that if the expansive force were compressed in a strong tube, a ball of stone or iron might be expelled with irresistible and destructive velocity. The precise æra of the invention and application of gunpowder[91] is involved in doubtful traditions and equivocal language; yet we may clearly discern, that it was known before the middle of the fourteenth century; and that before the end of the same, the use of artillery in battles and sieges, by sea and land, was familiar to the states of Germany, Italy, Spain, France, and England.[92] The priority of nations is of small account; none could derive any exclusive benefit from their previous or superior knowledge; and in the common improvement they stood on the same level of relative

90. See the entertaining and judicious letters of Busbequius.

91. The i[st] and ii[d] volumes of Dr. Watson's Chemical Essays, contain two valuable discourses on the discovery and composition of gunpowder.

92. On this subject, modern testimonies cannot be trusted. The original passages are collected by Ducange (Gloss. Latin. tom. i. p. 675. *Bombarda*). But in the early doubtful twilight, the name, sound, fire, and effect, that seem to express *our* artillery, may be fairly interpreted of the old engines and the Greek fire. For the English cannon at Crecy, the authority of John Villani (Chron. l. xii. c. 65.), must be weighed against the silence of Froissard. Yet Muratori (Antiquit. Italiæ medii Ævi, tom. ii. Dissert. xxvi. p. 514, 515.) has produced a decisive passage from Petrarch (de Remediis utriusque Fortunæ Dialog.), who, before the year 1344, execrates this terrestrial thunder, *nuper* rara, *nunc* communis.

power and military science. Nor was it possible to circumscribe the secret within the pale of the church; it was disclosed to the Turks by the treachery of apostates and the selfish policy of rivals; and the sultans had sense to adopt, and wealth to reward, the talents of a Christian engineer. The Genoese, who transported Amurath into Europe, must be accused as his preceptors; and it was probably by their hands that his cannon was cast and directed at the siege of Constantinople.[93] The first attempt was indeed unsuccessful; but in the general warfare of the age, the advantage was on *their* side, who were most commonly the assailants; for a while the proportion of the attack and defence was suspended; and this thundering artillery was pointed against the walls and towers which had been erected only to resist the less potent engines of antiquity. By the Venetians, the use of gunpowder was communicated without reproach to the sultans of Egypt and Persia, their allies against the Ottoman power; the secret was soon propagated to the extremities of Asia; and the advantage of the European was confined to his easy victories over the savages of the new world. If we contrast the rapid progress of this mischievous discovery with the slow and laborious advances of reason, science, and the arts of peace, a philosopher, according to his temper, will laugh or weep at the folly of mankind.

93. The Turkish cannon, which Ducas (c. 30.) first introduces before Belgrade (A.D. 1436), is mentioned by Chalcondyles (l. v. p. 123.) in 1422, at the siege of Constantinople.

CHAPTER LXVI.

Applications of the Eastern Emperors to the Popes. – Visits to the West, of John the First, Manuel, and John the Second, Palæologus. – Union of the Greek and Latin Churches, promoted by the Council of Basil, and concluded at Ferrara and Florence. – State of Literature at Constantinople. – Its Revival in Italy by the Greek Fugitives. – Curiosity and Emulation of the Latins.

Embassy of the younger Andronicus to pope Benedict XII. A.D. 1339.

In the four last centuries of the Greek emperors, their friendly or hostile aspect towards the pope and the Latins, may be observed as the thermometer of their prosperity or distress; as the scale of the rise and fall of the Barbarian dynasties. When the Turks of the house of Seljuk pervaded Asia and threatened Constantinople, we have seen at the council of Placentia, the suppliant ambassadors of Alexius, imploring the protection of the common father of the Christians. No sooner had the arms of the French pilgrims removed the sultan from Nice to Iconium, than the Greek princes resumed, or avowed, their genuine hatred and contempt for the schismatics of the West, which precipitated the first downfal of their empire. The date of the Mogul invasion is marked in the soft and charitable language of John Vataces. After the recovery of Constantinople, the throne of the first Palæologus was encompassed by foreign and domestic enemies: as long as the sword of Charles was suspended over his head, he basely courted the favour of the Roman pontiff; and sacrificed to the present danger, his faith, his virtue, and the affection of his subjects. On the decease of Michael, the prince and people asserted the independence of their church and the purity of their creed: the elder Andronicus neither feared nor loved the Latins; in his last distress, pride was the safeguard of superstition, nor could he decently retract in his age the firm and orthodox declarations of his youth. His grandson, the younger Andronicus, was less a slave in his temper and situation; and the conquest of Bithynia by the Turks, admonished him to seek a temporal and spiritual alliance with the western princes. After a separation and silence of fifty years, a secret agent, the monk Barlaam, was dispatched to pope Benedict the twelfth; and his artful instructions appear to have

The arguments for a crusade and union.

been drawn by the master-hand of the great domestic.[1] "Most holy father," was he commissioned to say, "the emperor is not less desirous than yourself of an union between the two churches: but in this delicate transaction, he is obliged to respect his own dignity and the prejudices of his subjects. The ways of union are two-fold; force, and persuasion. Of force, the inefficacy has been already tried; since the Latins have subdued the empire, without subduing the minds, of the Greeks. The method of persuasion, though slow, is sure and permanent. A deputation of thirty or forty of our doctors would probably agree with those of the Vatican, in the love of truth and the unity of belief: but on their return, what would be the use, the recompense of such agreement? the scorn of their brethren, and the reproaches of a blind and obstinate nation. Yet that nation is accustomed to reverence the general councils, which have fixed the articles of our faith; and if they reprobate the decrees of Lyons, it is because the Eastern churches were neither heard nor represented in that arbitrary meeting. For this salutary end, it will be expedient, and even necessary, that a well-chosen legate should be sent into Greece, to convene the patriarchs of Constantinople, Alexandria, Antioch, and Jerusalem; and, with their aid, to prepare a free and universal synod. But at this moment," continued the subtle agent, "the empire is assaulted and endangered by the Turks, who have occupied four of the greatest cities of Anatolia. The Christian inhabitants have expressed a wish of returning to their allegiance and religion; but the forces and revenues of the emperor are insufficient for their deliverance: and the Roman legate must be accompanied, or preceded, by an army of Franks, to expel the infidels, and open a way to the holy sepulchre." If the suspicious Latins should require some pledge, some previous effect of the sincerity of the Greeks, the answers of Barlaam were perspicuous and rational. "1. A general synod can alone consummate the union of the churches; nor can such a synod be held till the three Oriental patriarchs, and a great number of bishops, are enfranchised from the Mahometan yoke. 2. The Greeks are alienated by a long series of oppression and injury: they must be reconciled by some act of brotherly love, some effectual succour, which may fortify the authority and argu-

1. This curious instruction was transcribed (I believe) from the Vatican archives, by Odoricus Raynaldus, in his continuation of the Annals of Baronius (Romæ, 1646–1677, in x volumes in folio). I have contented myself with the abbé Fleury (Hist. Ecclesiastique, tom. xx. p. 1–8.), whose abstracts I have always found to be clear, accurate, and impartial.

ments, of the emperor, and the friends of the union. 3. If some difference of faith or ceremonies should be found incurable, the Greeks however are the disciples of Christ; and the Turks are the common enemies of the Christian name. The Armenians, Cyprians, and Rhodians, are equally attacked; and it will become the piety of the French princes to draw their swords in the general defence of religion. 4. Should the subjects of Andronicus be treated as the worst of schismatics, of heretics, of pagans, a judicious policy may yet instruct the powers of the West to embrace an useful ally, to uphold a sinking empire, to guard the confines of Europe; and rather to join the Greeks against the Turks, than to expect the union of the Turkish arms with the troops and treasures of captive Greece." The reasons, the offers, and the demands, of Andronicus, were eluded with cold and stately indifference. The kings of France and Naples declined the dangers and glory of a crusade: the pope refused to call a new synod to determine old articles of faith: and his regard for the obsolete claims of the Latin emperor and clergy, engaged him to use an offensive superscription: "To the *moderator*[2] of the Greeks, and the persons who style themselves the patriarchs of the Eastern churches." For such an embassy, a time and character less propitious could not easily have been found. Benedict the twelfth[3] was a dull peasant, perplexed with scruples, and immersed in sloth and wine: his pride might enrich with a third crown the papal tiara, but he was alike unfit for the regal and the pastoral office.

Negociation of Cantacuzene with Clement VI. A.D. 1348.

After the decease of Andronicus, while the Greeks were distracted by intestine war, they could not presume to agitate a general union of the Christians. But as soon as Cantacuzene had subdued and pardoned his enemies, he was anxious to justify, or at least to extenuate, the introduction of the Turks into Europe, and the nuptials of his daughter with a Musulman prince. Two officers

2. The ambiguity of this title is happy or ingenious; and *moderator*, as synonymous to *rector, gubernator*, is a word of classical, and even Ciceronian, Latinity, which may be found, not in the Glossary of Ducange, but in the Thesaurus of Robert Stephens.

3. The first Epistle (sine titulo) of Petrarch, exposes the danger of the *bark*, and the incapacity of the *pilot*. Hæc inter, vino madidus, ævo gravis ac soporifero rore perfusus, jamjam nutitat, dormitat, jam somno præceps, atque (utinam solus) ruit ... Heu quanto felicius patrio terram sulcasset aratro, quam scalmum piscatorium ascendisset. This satire engages his biographer to weigh the virtues and vices of Benedict XII. which have been exaggerated by Guelphs and Ghibelines, by Papists and Protestants (see Memoires sur la Vie de Petrarque, tom. i. p. 259. ii. not. xv. p. 13–16.). He gave occasion to the saying, Bibamus papaliter.

of state, with a Latin interpreter, were sent in his name to the Roman court, which was transplanted to Avignon, on the banks of the Rhône, during a period of seventy years; they represented the hard necessity which had urged him to embrace the alliance of the miscreants, and pronounced by his command the specious and edifying sounds of union and crusade. Pope Clement the sixth,[4] the successor of Benedict, received them with hospitality and honour, acknowledged the innocence of their sovereign, excused his distress, applauded his magnanimity, and displayed a clear knowledge of the state and revolutions of the Greek empire, which he had imbibed from the honest accounts of a Savoyard lady, an attendant of the empress Anne.[5] If Clement was ill-endowed with the virtues of a priest, he possessed however the spirit and magnificence of a prince, whose liberal hand distributed benefices and kingdoms with equal facility. Under his reign, Avignon was the seat of pomp and pleasure: in his youth he had surpassed the licentiousness of a baron; and the palace, nay, the bed-chamber of the pope, was adorned, or polluted, by the visits of his female favourites. The wars of France and England were adverse to the holy enterprise; but his vanity was amused by the splendid idea; and the Greek ambassadors returned with two Latin bishops, the ministers of the pontiff. On their arrival at Constantinople, the emperor and the nuncios admired each other's piety and eloquence: and their frequent conferences were filled with mutual praises and promises, by which both parties were amused, and neither could be deceived. "I am delighted," said the devout Cantacuzene, "with the project of our holy war, which must redound to my personal glory, as well as to the public benefit of Christendom. My dominions will give a free passage to the armies of France: my troops, my gallies, my treasures, shall be consecrated to the common cause; and happy would be my fate, could I deserve and obtain the crown of martyrdom. Words are insufficient to express the ardour with which I sigh for the reunion of the scattered members of Christ. If my death could avail, I would gladly present my sword and my neck: if

4. See the original lives of Clement VI. in Muratori (Script. Rerum Italicarum, tom. iii. P. ii. p. 550–589.). Matteo Villani (Chron. l. iii. c. 43. in Muratori, tom. xiv. p. 186.), who styles him, molto cavallaresco, poco religioso; Fleury (Hist. Eccles. tom. xx. p. 126.), and the Vie de Petrarque (tom. ii. p. 42–45.). The abbé de Sade treats him with the most indulgence; but *he* is a gentleman as well as a priest.

5. Her name (most probably corrupted) was Zampea. She had accompanied, and alone remained with her mistress at Constantinople, where her prudence, erudition, and politeness, deserved the praises of the Greeks themselves (Cantacuzen. l. i. c. 42.).

the spiritual phœnix could arise from my ashes, I would erect the pile and kindle the flame with my own hands." Yet the Greek emperor presumed to observe, that the articles of faith which divided the two churches had been introduced by the pride and precipitation of the Latins: he disclaimed the servile and arbitrary steps of the first Palæologus; and firmly declared, that he would never submit his conscience unless to the decrees of a free and universal synod. "The situation of the times," continued he, "will not allow the pope and myself to meet either at Rome or Constantinople; but some maritime city may be chosen on the verge of the two empires, to unite the bishops, and to instruct the faithful, of the East and West." The nuncios seemed content with the proposition; and Cantacuzene affects to deplore the failure of his hopes, which were soon overthrown by the death of Clement and the different temper of his successor. His own life was prolonged, but it was prolonged in a cloister; and, except by his prayers, the humble monk was incapable of directing the counsels of his pupil or the state.[6]

Treaty of John Palæologus I. with Innocent VI. A.D. 1355.

Yet of all the Byzantine princes, that pupil, John Palæologus, was the best disposed to embrace, to believe, and to obey, the shepherd of the West. His mother, Anne of Savoy, was baptized in the bosom of the Latin church: her marriage with Andronicus imposed a change of name, of apparel, and of worship; but her heart was still faithful to her country and religion; she had formed the infancy of her son, and she governed the emperor, after his mind, or at least his stature, was enlarged to the size of man. In the first year of his deliverance and restoration, the Turks were still masters of the Hellespont; the son of Cantacuzene was in arms at Adrianople; and Palæologus could depend neither on himself nor on his people. By his mother's advice, and in the hope of foreign aid, he abjured the rights both of the church and state; and the act of slavery,[7] subscribed in purple ink, and sealed with the *golden* bull, was privately intrusted to an Italian agent. The first article of the treaty is an oath of fidelity and obedience to Innocent the sixth and his successors, the supreme pontiffs of the Roman and Catholic church. The emperor promises to entertain with due reverence their legates and nuncios; to assign a palace for their residence and a temple

6. See this whole negociation in Cantacuzene (l. iv. c. 9.), who, amidst the praises and virtues which he bestows on himself, reveals the uneasiness of a guilty conscience.

7. See this ignominious treaty in Fleury (Hist. Eccles. p. 151–154.), from Raynaldus, who drew it from the Vatican archives. It was not worth the trouble of a pious forgery.

for their worship; and to deliver his second son Manuel as the hostage of his faith. For these condescensions, he requires a prompt succour of fifteen gallies, with five hundred men at arms, and a thousand archers, to serve against his Christian and Musulman enemies. Palæologus engages to impose on his clergy and people the same spiritual yoke; but as the resistance of the Greeks might be justly foreseen, he adopts the two effectual methods of corruption and education. The legate was empowered to distribute the vacant benefices among the ecclesiastics who should subscribe the creed of the Vatican: three schools were instituted to instruct the youth of Constantinople in the language and doctrine of the Latins; and the name of Andronicus, the heir of the empire, was enrolled as the first student. Should he fail in the measures of persuasion or force, Palæologus declares himself unworthy to reign; transfers to the pope all regal and paternal authority; and invests Innocent with full power to regulate the family, the government, and the marriage, of his son and successor. But this treaty was neither executed nor published: the Roman gallies were as vain and imaginary as the submission of the Greeks; and it was only by the secrecy, that their sovereign escaped the dishonour, of this fruitless humiliation.

Visit of John Palæologus to Urban V. at Rome, A.D. 1369. October 13. &c.

The tempest of the Turkish arms soon burst on his head; and, after the loss of Adrianople and Romania, he was enclosed in his capital, the vassal of the haughty Amurath, with the miserable hope of being the last devoured by the savage. In this abject state, Palæologus embraced the resolution of embarking for Venice, and casting himself at the feet of the pope; he was the first of the Byzantine princes who had ever visited the unknown regions of the West, yet in them alone he could seek consolation or relief; and with less violation of his dignity he might appear in the sacred college than at the Ottoman *Porte*. After a long absence, the Roman pontiffs were returning from Avignon to the banks of the Tyber; Urban the fifth,[8] of a mild and virtuous character, encouraged or allowed the pilgrimage of the Greek prince; and, within the same year, enjoyed the glory of receiving in the Vatican the two Imperial shadows, who represented the majesty of Constantine and Charlemagne. In this suppliant visit, the emperor of Constantinople,

8. See the two first original lives of Urban V. (in Muratori, Script. Rerum Italicarum, tom. iii. P. ii. p. 623. 635.), and the Ecclesiastical Annals of Spondanus (tom. i. p. 573. A.D. 1369, N° 7.) and Raynaldus (Fleury, Hist. Eccles. tom. xx. p. 223, 224.). Yet, from some variations, I suspect the papal writers of slightly magnifying the genuflexions of Palæologus.

whose vanity was lost in his distress, gave more than could be expected of empty sounds and formal submissions. A previous trial was imposed; and in the presence of four cardinals, he acknowledged, as a true Catholic, the supremacy of the pope, and the double procession of the Holy Ghost. After this purification, he was introduced to a public audience in the church of St. Peter: Urban, in the midst of the cardinals, was seated on his throne; the Greek monarch, after three genuflexions, devoutly kissed the feet, the hands, and at length the mouth, of the holy father, who celebrated high mass in his presence, allowed him to lead the bridle of his mule, and treated him with a sumptuous banquet in the Vatican. The entertainment of Palæologus was friendly and honourable; yet some difference was observed between the emperors of the East and West;[9] nor could the former be entitled to the rare privilege of chaunting the gospel in the rank of a deacon.[10] In favour of his proselyte, Urban strove to rekindle the zeal of the French king, and the other powers of the West; but he found them cold in the general cause, and active only in their domestic quarrels. The last hope of the emperor was in an English mercenary, John Hawkwood,[11] or Acuto, who with a band of adventurers, the white brotherhood, had ravaged Italy from the Alps to Calabria; sold his services to the hostile states; and incurred a just excommunication by shooting his arrows against the papal residence. A special licence was granted to negociate with the outlaw, but the forces, or the spirit, of Hawkwood were unequal to the enterprise; and it was for the advantage perhaps of Palæologus to be disappointed of a succour, that must have been costly, that could not be effectual, and which might have been

9. Paullo minus quam si fuisset Imperator Romanorum. Yet his title of Imperator Græcorum was no longer disputed (Vit. Urban V. p. 623.).

10. It was confined to the successors of Charlemagne, and to them only on Christmas day. On all other festivals, these Imperial deacons were content to serve the pope, as he said mass, with the book and the *corporal*. Yet the abbé de Sade generously thinks, that the merits of Charles IV. might have entitled him, though not on the proper day (A.D. 1368, November 1.), to the whole privilege. He seems to affix a just value on the privilege and the man (Vie de Petrarque, tom. iii. p. 735.).

11. Through some Italian corruptions, the etymology of *Falcone in bosco* (Matteo Villani, l. xi. c. 79. in Muratori, tom. xv. p. 746.), suggests the English word *Hawkwood*, the true name of our adventurous countryman (Thomas Walsingham, Hist. Anglican. inter Scriptores Cambdeni, p. 184.). After two-and-twenty victories, and one defeat, he died, in 1394, General of the Florentines, and was buried with such honours as the republic has not paid to Dante or Petrarch (Muratori, Annali d'Italia, tom. xii. p. 212–371.).

dangerous.[12] The disconsolate Greek[13] prepared for his return, but even his return was impeded by a most ignominious obstacle. On his arrival at Venice, he had borrowed large sums at exorbitant usury; but his coffers were empty, his creditors were impatient, and his person was detained as the best security for the payment. His eldest son Andronicus, the regent of Constantinople, was repeatedly urged to exhaust every resource; and, even by stripping the churches, to extricate his father from captivity and disgrace. But the unnatural youth was insensible of the disgrace, and secretly pleased with the captivity of the emperor; the state was poor, the clergy was obstinate; nor could some religious scruple be wanting to excuse the guilt of his indifference and delay. Such undutiful neglect was severely reproved by the piety of his brother Manuel, who instantly sold or mortgaged all that he possessed, embarked for Venice, relieved his father, and pledged his own freedom to be responsible for the debt. On his return to Constantinople, the parent and king distinguished his two sons with suitable rewards; but the faith and manners of the slothful Palæologus had not been improved by his Roman pilgrimage; and his apostacy or conversion, devoid of any spiritual or temporal effects, was speedily forgotten by the Greeks and Latins.[14]

His return to Constantinople, A.D. 1370.

Thirty years after the return of Palæologus, his son and successor, Manuel, from a similar motive, but on a larger scale, again visited the countries of the West. In a preceding chapter I have related his treaty with Bajazet, the violation of that treaty, the siege or blockade of Constantinople, and the French succour under the command of the gallant Boucicault.[15] By his ambassadors, Manuel had solicited the Latin powers; but it was thought that the presence of a distressed monarch would draw tears and supplies from the hardest Barbarians;[16]

Visit of the emperor Manuel

12. This torrent of English (by birth or service) overflowed from France into Italy after the peace of Bretigny in 1360. Yet the exclamation of Muratori (Annali, tom. xii. p. 197) is rather true than civil. "Ci mancava ancor questo, che dopo essere calpestrata l'Italia da tanti masnadieri Tedeschi ed Ungheri, venissero fin dall' Inghilterra nuovi *cani* a finire di divorarla."

13. Chalcondyles, l. i. p. 25, 26. The Greek supposes his journey to the king of France, which is sufficiently refuted by the silence of the national historians. Nor am I much more inclined to believe, that Palæologus departed from Italy, valde bene consolatus et contentus (Vit. Urban V. p. 623.).

14. His return in 1370, and the coronation of Manuel, Sept. 25, 1373 (Ducange, Fam. Byzant. p. 241.), leaves some intermediate æra for the conspiracy and punishment of Andronicus.

15. Memoires de Boucicault, P. i. c. 35, 36.

16. His journey into the west of Europe, is slightly, and I believe reluctantly, noticed by Chalcondyles (l. ii. 44–50.) and Ducas (c. 14.).

and the marshal who advised the journey, prepared the reception, of the Byzantine prince. The land was occupied by the Turks; but the navigation of Venice was safe and open: Italy received him as the first, or, at least, as the second of the Christian princes; Manuel was pitied as the champion and confessor of the faith; and the dignity of his behaviour prevented that pity from sinking into contempt. From Venice he proceeded to Padua and Pavia; and even the duke of Milan, a secret ally of Bajazet, gave him safe and honourable conduct to the verge of his dominions.[17]

to the court of France, A.D. 1400, June 3;

On the confines of France,[18] the royal officers undertook the care of his person, journey, and expences; and two thousand of the richest citizens, in arms and on horseback, came forth to meet him as far as Charenton, in the neighbourhood of the capital. At the gates of Paris, he was saluted by the chancellor and the parliament; and Charles the sixth, attended by his princes and nobles, welcomed his brother with a cordial embrace. The successor of Constantine was clothed in a robe of white silk, and mounted on a milk-white steed; a circumstance, in the French ceremonial, of singular importance: the white colour is considered as the symbol of sovereignty; and, in a late visit, the German emperor, after an haughty demand and a peevish refusal, had been reduced to content himself with a black courser. Manuel was lodged in the Louvre; a succession of feasts and balls, the pleasures of the banquet and the chace, were ingeniously varied by the politeness of the French, to display their magnificence and amuse his grief: he was indulged in the liberty of his chapel; and the doctors of the Sorbonne were astonished, and possibly scandalised, by the language, the rites, and the vestments, of his Greek clergy. But the slightest glance on the state of the kingdom, must teach him to despair of any effectual assistance. The unfortunate Charles, though he enjoyed some lucid intervals, continually relapsed into furious or stupid insanity: the reins of government were alternately seized by his brother and uncle, the dukes of Orleans and Burgundy, whose factious competition prepared the miseries of civil war. The former was a gay youth, dissolved in luxury and love: the latter was the father of John count of Nevers, who had so

17. Muratori, Annali d'Italia, tom. xii. p. 406. John Galeazzo was the first and most powerful duke of Milan. His connection with Bajazet is attested by Froissard; and he contributed to save and deliver the French captives of Nicopolis.

18. For the reception of Manuel at Paris, see Spondanus (Annal. Eccles. tom. i. p. 676, 677. A.D. 1400, N° 5.), who quotes Juvenal des Ursins, and the monk of St. Denys; and Villaret (Hist. de France, tom. xii. p. 331–334.), who quotes nobody, according to the last fashion of the French writers.

lately been ransomed from Turkish captivity; and, if the fearless son was ardent to revenge his defeat, the more prudent Burgundy was content with the cost and peril of the first experiment. When Manuel had satiated the curiosity, and perhaps fatigued the patience, of the French, he resolved on a visit to the adjacent island. In his progress from Dover, he was entertained at Canterbury with due reverence by the prior and monks of St. Austin; and, on Blackheath, king Henry the fourth, with the English court, saluted the Greek hero (I copy our old historian), who, during many days, was lodged and treated in London as emperor of the East.[19] But the state of England was still more adverse to the design of the holy war. In the same year, the hereditary sovereign had been deposed and murdered; the reigning prince was a successful usurper, whose ambition was punished by jealousy and remorse: nor could Henry of Lancaster withdraw his person or forces from the defence of a throne incessantly shaken by conspiracy and rebellion. He pitied, he praised, he feasted, the emperor of Constantinople; but if the English monarch assumed the cross, it was only to appease his people, and perhaps his conscience, by the merit or semblance of this pious intention.[20] Satisfied, however, with gifts and honours, Manuel returned to Paris; and, after a residence of two years in the West, shaped his course through Germany and Italy, embarked at Venice, and patiently expected, in the Morea, the moment of his ruin or deliverance. Yet he had escaped the ignominious necessity of offering his religion to public or private sale. The Latin church was distracted by the great schism: the kings, the nations, the universities, of Europe, were divided in their obedience between the popes of Rome and Avignon; and the emperor, anxious to conciliate the friendship of both parties, abstained from any correspondence with the indigent and unpopular rivals. His journey coincided with the year of the jubilee; but he passed through Italy without desiring, or deserving, the plenary indulgence which abolished the guilt or penance of the sins of the faithful. The Roman pope was offended by this neglect; accused him of irreverence to an image of Christ; and exhorted

of England, A.D. 1400, December.

His return to Greece, A.D. 1402.

19. A short note of Manuel in England, is extracted by Dr. Hody from a MS. at Lambeth (de Græcis illustribus, p. 14.), C. P. Imperator, diu variisque et horrendis Paganorum insultibus coartatus, ut pro eisdem resistentiam triumphalem perquireret Anglorum Regem visitare decrevit, &c. Rex (says Walsingham, p. 364.) nobili apparatû ... suscepit (ut decuit) tantum Heroa, duxitque Londonias, et per multos dies exhibuit gloriose, pro expensis hospitii sui solvens, et eum respiciens tanto fastigio donativis. He repeats the same in his Upodigma Neustriæ, p. 556.

20. Shakespeare begins and ends the play of Henry IV. with that prince's vow of a crusade, and his belief that he should die in Jerusalem.

the princes of Italy to reject and abandon the obstinate schismatic.[21]

Greek knowledge and descriptions

During the period of the crusades, the Greeks beheld with astonishment and terror the perpetual stream of emigration that flowed, and continued to flow, from the unknown climates of the West. The visits of their last emperors removed the veil of separation, and they disclosed to their eyes the powerful nations of Europe, whom they no longer presumed to brand with the name of Barbarians. The observations of Manuel, and his more inquisitive followers, have been preserved by a Byzantine historian of the times:[22] his scattered ideas I shall collect and abridge; and it may be amusing enough, perhaps instructive, to contemplate the rude pictures of Germany, France, and England, whose ancient and modern state are so familiar to *our* minds.

of Germany;

I. GERMANY (says the Greek Chalcondyles) is of ample latitude from Vienna to the Ocean; and it stretches (a strange geography) from Prague in Bohemia to the river Tartessus, and the Pyrenæan mountains.[23] The soil, except in figs and olives, is sufficiently fruitful; the air is salubrious; the bodies of the natives are robust and healthy; and these cold regions are seldom visited with the calamities of pestilence, or earthquakes. After the Scythians or Tartars, the Germans are the most numerous of nations; they are brave and patient, and were they united under a single head, their force would be irresistible. By the gift of the pope, they have acquired the privilege of chusing the Roman emperor;[24] nor is any people more devoutly attached to the faith and obedience of

21. This fact is preserved in the Historia Politica, A.D. 1391–1478, published by Martin Crusius (Turco Græcia, p. 1–43.). The image of Christ, which the Greek emperor refused to worship, was probably a work of sculpture.

22. The Greek and Turkish history of Laonicus Chalcondyles ends with the winter of 1463, and the abrupt conclusion seems to mark, that he laid down his pen in the same year. We know that he was an Athenian, and that some contemporaries of the same name contributed to the revival of the Greek language in Italy. But in his numerous digressions, the modest historian has never introduced himself; and his editor Leunclavius, as well as Fabricius (Bibliot. Græc. tom. vi. p. 474.), seems ignorant of his life and character. For his descriptions of Germany, France, and England, see l. ii. p. 36, 37. 44–50.

23. I shall not animadvert on the geographical errors of Chalcondyles. In this instance, he perhaps followed, and mistook, Herodotus (l. ii. c. 33.), whose text may be explained (Herodote de Larcher, tom. ii. p. 219, 220.), or whose ignorance may be excused. Had these modern Greeks never read Strabo, or any of their lesser geographers?

24. A citizen of new Rome, while new Rome survived, would have scorned to dignify the German *Ρηξ* with the titles of *Βασιλευς*, or *Αὐτοκρατωρ Ρωμαιων*: but all pride was extinct in the bosom of Chalcondyles; and he describes the Byzantine prince, and his subject, by the proper, though humble names of *Ἑλληνες*, and *Βασιλευς Ἑλληνων*.

the Latin patriarch. The greatest part of the country is divided among the princes and prelates; but Strasburgh, Cologne, Hamburgh, and more than two hundred free cities, are governed by sage and equal laws, according to the will, and for the advantage, of the whole community. The use of duels, or single combats on foot, prevails among them in peace and war; their industry excels in all the mechanic arts, and the Germans may boast of the invention of gunpowder and cannon, which is now diffused over the greatest part of the world. II. The kingdom of FRANCE is spread above fifteen or twenty days journey from *of France;* Germany to Spain, and from the Alps to the British Ocean; containing many flourishing cities, and among these Paris, the seat of the king, which surpasses the rest in riches and luxury. Many princes and lords alternately wait in his palace, and acknowledge him as their sovereign; the most powerful are the dukes of Bretagne and Burgundy, of whom the latter possesses the wealthy province of Flanders, whose harbours are frequented by the ships and merchants of our own and the more remote seas. The French are an ancient and opulent people: and their language and manners, though somewhat different, are not dissimilar from those of the Italians. Vain of the Imperial dignity of Charlemagne, of their victories over the Saracens, and of the exploits of their heroes, Oliver and Rowland;[25] they esteem themselves the first of the western nations: but this foolish arrogance has been recently humbled by the unfortunate events of their wars against the English, the inhabitants of the British island. III. BRITAIN, in the ocean, and opposite to the shores *of England.* of Flanders, may be considered either as one, or as three islands; but the whole is united by a common interest, by the same manners, and by a similar government. The measure of its circumference is five thousand stadia: the land is overspread with towns and villages: though destitute of wine, and not abounding in fruit-trees, it is fertile in wheat and barley; in honey and wool; and much cloth is manufactured by the inhabitants. In populousness and power, in riches and luxury, London,[26] the metropolis of the isle, may claim a pre-eminence over all the cities of the West. It is situate on the Thames, a broad and rapid river, which at the distance

25. Most of the old romances were translated in the xiv[th] century into French prose, and soon became the favourite amusement of the knights and ladies in the court of Charles VI. If a Greek believed in the exploits of Rowland and Oliver, he may surely be excused, since the monks of St. Denys, the national historians, have inserted the fables of archbishop Turpin in their Chronicles of France.

26. *Λονδινη . . . δε τε πολις δυναμει τε προεχουσα των εν τη νυσῳ ταυτη πασων πολεων, ολβῳ τε και τῃ αλλη ευδαιμονιᾳ ουδεμιας των προς ἑσπεραν λειπομενη.* Even since the time of Fitzstephen (the xii[th] century), London appears to have main-

of thirty miles falls into the Gallic Sea; and the daily flow and ebb of the tide, affords a safe entrance and departure to the vessels of commerce. The king is the head of a powerful and turbulent aristocracy; his principal vassals hold their estates by a free and unalterable tenure; and the laws define the limits of his authority and their obedience. The kingdom has been often afflicted by foreign conquest and domestic sedition; but the natives are bold and hardy, renowned in arms and victorious in war. The form of their shields or targets is derived from the Italians, that of their swords from the Greeks; the use of the long bow is the peculiar and decisive advantage of the English. Their language bears no affinity to the idioms of the continent; in the habits of domestic life, they are not easily distinguished from their neighbours of France: but the most singular circumstance of their manners is their disregard of conjugal honour and of female chastity. In their mutual visits, as the first act of hospitality, the guest is welcomed in the embraces of their wives and daughters: among friends they are lent and borrowed without shame; nor are the islanders offended at this strange commerce, and its inevitable consequences.[27] Informed as we are of the customs of old England, and assured of the virtue of our mothers, we may smile at the credulity, or resent the injustice, of the Greek, who must have confounded a modest salute[28] with a criminal embrace. But his credulity and injustice may teach an important lesson; to distrust the accounts of foreign and remote nations, and to suspend our belief of every tale that deviates from the laws of nature and the character of man.[29]

Indifference of Manuel towards the Latins, A.D. 1402–1417.

After his return, and the victory of Timour, Manuel reigned many years in prosperity and peace. As long as the sons of Bajazet solicited his friendship and spared his dominions, he was satisfied with the national religion; and his leisure was employed in composing twenty theological

tained this pre-eminence of wealth and magnitude; and her gradual increase has, at least, kept pace with the general improvement of Europe.

27. If the double sense of the verb *Κυω* (osculor, and in utero gero) be equivocal, the context and pious horror of Chalcondyles can leave no doubt of his meaning and mistake (p. 49.).

28. Erasmus (Epist. Fausto Andrelino) has a pretty passage on the English fashion of kissing strangers on their arrival and departure, from whence, however, he draws no scandalous inferences.

29. Perhaps we may apply this remark to the community of wives among the old Britons, as it is supposed by Cæsar and Dion (Dion Cassius, l. lxii. tom. ii. p. 1007.), with Reimar's judicious annotation. The *Arreoy* of Otaheite, so certain at first, is become less visible and scandalous, in proportion as we have studied the manners of that gentle and amorous people.

dialogues for its defence. The appearance of the Byzantine ambassadors at the council of Constance[30] announces the restoration of the Turkish power, as well as of the Latin church; the conquest of the sultans, Mahomet and Amurath, reconciled the emperor to the Vatican; and the siege of Constantinople almost tempted him to acquiesce in the double procession of the Holy Ghost. When Martin the fifth ascended without a rival the chair of St. Peter, a friendly intercourse of letters and embassies was revived between the East and West. Ambition on one side, and distress on the other, dictated the same decent language of charity and peace: the artful Greek expressed a desire of marrying his six sons to Italian princesses; and the Roman, not less artful, dispatched the daughter of the marquis of Montferrat, with a company of noble virgins, to soften by their charms the obstinacy of the schismatics. Yet under this mask of zeal, a discerning eye will perceive that all was hollow and insincere in the court and church of Constantinople. According to the vicissitudes of danger and repose, the emperor advanced or retreated; alternately instructed and disavowed his ministers; and escaped from an importunate pressure by urging the duty of enquiry, the obligation of collecting the sense of his patriarchs and bishops, and the impossibility of convening them at a time when the Turkish arms were at the gates of his capital. From a review of the public transactions it will appear, that the Greeks insisted on three successive measures, a succour, a council, and a final re-union, while the Latins eluded the second, and only promised the first, as a consequential and voluntary reward of the third. But we have an opportunity of unfolding the most secret intentions of Manuel, and he explained them in a private conversation without artifice or disguise. In his declining age, the emperor had associated John Palæologus, the second of the name, and the eldest of his sons, on whom he devolved the greatest part of the authority and weight of government. One day, in the presence only of the historian Phranza,[31] his favourite chamberlain, he opened to his colleague and

His negociations, A.D. 1417–1425.

His private motives.

30. See Lenfant, Hist. du Concile de Constance, tom. ii. p. 576.; and for the ecclesiastical history of the times, the Annals of Spondanus, the Bibliotheque of Dupin, tom. xii. and xxi[st] and xxii[d] volumes of the History, or rather the Continuation, of Fleury.

31. From his early youth, George Phranza, or Phranzes, was employed in the service of the state and palace; and Hanckius (de Script. Byzant. P. i. c. 40.) has collected his life from his own writings. He was no more than four-and-twenty years of age at the death of Manuel, who recommended him in the strongest terms to his successor: Imprimis vero hunc Phranzen tibi commendo, qui ministravit mihi fideliter et diligenter (Phranzes, l. ii. c. 1.). Yet the emperor John was cold, and he preferred the service of the despots of Peloponnesus.

successor the true principle of his negociations with the pope.[32] "Our last resource," said Manuel, "against the Turks is their fear of our union with the Latins, of the warlike nations of the West, who may arm for our relief and for their destruction. As often as you are threatened by the miscreants, present this danger before their eyes. Propose a council; consult on the means; but ever delay and avoid the convocation of an assembly, which cannot tend either to our spiritual or temporal emolument. The Latins are proud; the Greeks are obstinate; neither party will recede or retract; and the attempt of a perfect union will confirm the schism, alienate the churches, and leave us, without hope or defence, at the mercy of the Barbarians." Impatient of this salutary lesson, the royal youth arose from his seat, and departed in silence; and the wise monarch (continues Phranza), casting his eyes on me, thus resumed his discourse: "My son deems himself a great and heroic prince; but, alas! our miserable age does not afford scope for heroism or greatness. His daring spirit might have suited the happier times of our ancestors; but the present state requires not an emperor, but a cautious steward of the last relics of our fortunes. Well do I remember the lofty expectations which he built on our alliance with Mustapha; and much do I fear, that his rash courage will urge the ruin of our house, and that even religion may precipitate our downfal." Yet the experience and authority of Manuel preserved the peace and eluded the council; till, in the seventy-eighth year of his age, and in the habit of a monk, he terminated his career, dividing his precious moveables among his children and the poor, his physicians and his favourite servants. Of his six sons,[33] Andronicus the second was invested with the principality of Thessalonica, and died of a leprosy soon after the sale of that city to the Venetians and its final conquest by the Turks. Some fortunate incidents had restored Peloponnesus, or the Morea, to the empire; and in his more prosperous days, Manuel had fortified the narrow isthmus of six miles[34] with a stone wall and one hundred and fifty-three towers. The wall was overthrown by the first

His death.

32. See Phranzes, l. ii. c. 13. While so many manuscripts of the Greek original are extant in the libraries of Rome, Milan, the Escurial, &c. it is a matter of shame and reproach, that we should be reduced to the Latin version, or abstract, of James Pontanus (ad calcem Theophylact Simocattæ; Ingolstadt, 1604), so deficient in accuracy and elegance (Fabric. Bibliot. Græc. tom. vi. p. 615–620.).

33. See Ducange, Fam. Byzant. p. 243–248.

34. The exact measure of the Hexamilion, from sea to sea, was 3,800 orgygiæ, or *toises*, of six Greek feet (Phranzes, l. i. c. 38.), which would produce a Greek mile, still smaller than that of 660 French *toises*, which is assigned by d'Anville as still in use in

blast of the Ottomans: the fertile peninsula might have been sufficient for the four younger brothers, Theodore and Constantine, Demetrius and Thomas; but they wasted in domestic contests the remains of their strength; and the least successful of the rivals were reduced to a life of dependence in the Byzantine palace.

Zeal of John Palæologus II. A.D. 1425–1437.

The eldest of the sons of Manuel, John Palæologus the second, was acknowledged, after his father's death, as the sole emperor of the Greeks. He immediately proceeded to repudiate his wife, and to contract a new marriage with the princess of Trebizond: beauty was in his eyes the first qualification of an empress; and the clergy had yielded to his firm assurance, that unless he might be indulged in a divorce, he would retire to a cloister, and leave the throne to his brother Constantine. The first, and in truth the only, victory of Palæologus was over a Jew,[35] whom, after a long and learned dispute, he converted to the Christian faith; and this momentous conquest is carefully recorded in the history of the times. But he soon resumed the design of uniting the East and West; and, regardless of his father's advice, listened, as it should seem with sincerity, to the proposal of meeting the pope in a general council beyond the Adriatic. This dangerous project was encouraged by Martin the fifth, and coldly entertained by his successor Eugenius, till, after a tedious negociation, the emperor received a summons from a Latin assembly of a new character, the independent prelates of Basil, who styled themselves the representatives and judges of the Catholic church.

Corruption of the Latin church.

The Roman pontiff had fought and conquered in the cause of ecclesiastical freedom; but the victorious clergy were soon exposed to the tyranny of their deliverer; and his sacred character was invulnerable to those arms which they found so keen and effectual against the civil magistrate. Their great charter, the right of election, was annihilated by appeals, evaded by trusts or commendams, disappointed by reversionary grants, and superseded by previous and arbitrary reservations.[36] A public auction was instituted in the court of Rome: the

---

Turkey. Five miles are commonly reckoned for the breadth of the Isthmus. See the Travels of Spon, Wheeler, and Chandler.

35. The first objection of the Jews, is on the death of Christ: if it were voluntary, Christ was a suicide; which the emperor parries with a mystery. They then dispute on the conception of the virgin, the sense of the prophecies, &c. (Phranzes, l. ii. c. 12. a whole chapter).

36. In the treatise delle Materie Beneficiarie of Fra-Paolo (in the iv[th] volume of the last and best edition of his works), the papal system is deeply studied and freely

cardinals and favourites were enriched with the spoils of nations; and every country might complain that the most important and valuable benefices were accumulated on the heads of aliens and absentees. During their residence at Avignon, the ambition of the popes subsided in the meaner passions of avarice[37] and luxury: they rigorously imposed on the clergy the tributes of first-fruits and tenths; but they freely tolerated the impunity of vice, disorder, and corruption. These manifold scandals were aggravated by the great schism of the West, which continued above fifty years. In the furious conflicts of Rome and Avignon, the vices of the rivals were mutually exposed; and their precarious situation degraded their authority, relaxed their discipline, and multiplied their wants and exactions. To heal the wounds, and restore the monarchy, of the church, the synods of Pisa and Constance[38] were successively convened; but these great assemblies, conscious of their strength, resolved to vindicate the privileges of the Christian aristocracy. From a personal sentence against two pontiffs, whom they rejected, and a third, their acknowledged sovereign, whom they deposed, the fathers of Constance proceeded to examine the nature and limits of the Roman supremacy; nor did they separate till they had established the authority, above the pope, of a general council. It was enacted, that, for the government and reformation of the church, such assemblies should be held at regular intervals; and that each synod, before its dissolution, should appoint the time and place of the subsequent meeting. By the influence of the court of Rome, the next convocation at Sienna was easily eluded; but the bold and vigorous proceedings of the council of Basil[39] had almost been fatal to the reigning pontiff, Eugenius the fourth. A just suspicion of his design prompted

Schism, A.D. 1377–1429.

Council of Pisa, A.D. 1409. of Constance, A.D. 1414–1418.

described. Should Rome and her religion be annihilated, this golden volume may still survive, a philosophical history, and a salutary warning.

37. Pope John XXII. (in 1334) left behind him, at Avignon, eighteen millions of gold florins, and the value of seven millions more in plate and jewels. See the Chronicle of John Villani (l. xi. c. 20. in Muratori's Collection, tom. xiii. p. 765.), whose brother received the account from the papal treasurers. A treasure of six or eight millions sterling in the xiv[th] century is enormous, and almost incredible.

38. A learned and liberal protestant, M. Lenfant, has given a fair history of the councils of Pisa, Constance, and Basil, in six volumes in quarto: but the last part is the most hasty and imperfect, except in the account of the troubles of Bohemia.

39. The original acts or minutes of the council of Basil, are preserved in the public library, in twelve volumes in folio. Basil was a free city, conveniently situate on the Rhine, and guarded by the arms of the neighbouring and confederate Swiss. In 1459, the university was founded by pope Pius II. (Æneas Sylvius), who had been

of Basil, A.D. 1431–1443.

the fathers to hasten the promulgation of their first decree, that the representatives of the church-militant on earth were invested with a divine and spiritual jurisdiction over all Christians, without excepting the pope; and that a general council could not be dissolved, prorogued, or transferred, unless by their free deliberation and consent. On the notice that Eugenius had fulminated a bull for that purpose, they ventured to summon, to admonish, to threaten, to censure, the contumacious successor of St. Peter. After many delays, to allow time for repentance, they finally declared, that, unless he submitted within the term of sixty days, he was suspended from the exercise of all temporal and ecclesiastical authority. And to mark their jurisdiction over the prince as well as the priest, they assumed the government of Avignon, annulled the alienation of the sacred patrimony, and protected Rome from the imposition of new taxes. Their boldness was justified, not only by the general opinion of the clergy, but by the support and power of the first monarchs of Christendom: the emperor Sigismond declared himself the servant and protector of the synod; Germany and France adhered to their cause; the duke of Milan was the enemy of Eugenius; and he was driven from the Vatican by an insurrection of the Roman people. Rejected at the same time by his temporal and spiritual subjects, submission was his only choice: by a most humiliating bull, the pope repealed his own acts, and ratified those of the council; incorporated his legates and cardinals with that venerable body; and *seemed* to resign himself to the decrees of the supreme legislature. Their fame pervaded the countries of the East; and it was in their presence that Sigismond received the ambassadors of the Turkish sultan,[40] who laid at his feet twelve large vases, filled with robes of silk and pieces of gold.

Their opposition to Eugenius IV.

Negociations with the Greeks, A.D. 1434–1437.

The fathers of Basil aspired to the glory of reducing the Greeks, as well as the Bohemians, within the pale of the church; and their deputies invited the emperor and patriarch of Constantinople to unite with an assembly which possessed the confidence of the Western nations. Palæologus was not averse to the proposal; and his ambassadors were introduced with due honours into the Catholic senate. But the choice of the place appeared to be an insuperable obstacle, since he refused to pass the Alps, or the sea of Sicily,

secretary to the council. But what is a council, or an university, to the presses of Froben and the studies of Erasmus?

40. This Turkish embassy, attested only by Crantzius, is related with some doubt by the annalist Spondanus, A.D. 1433, N° 25. tom. i. p. 824.

and positively required that the synod should be adjourned to some convenient city in Italy, or at least on the Danube. The other articles of this treaty were more readily stipulated: it was agreed to defray the travelling expences of the emperor, with a train of seven hundred persons,[41] to remit an immediate sum of eight thousand ducats[42] for the accommodation of the Greek clergy; and in his absence to grant a supply of ten thousand ducats, with three hundred archers and some gallies, for the protection of Constantinople. The city of Avignon advanced the funds for the preliminary expences; and the embarkation was prepared at Marseilles with some difficulty and delay.

John Palæologus embarks in the pope's gallies, A.D. 1437, Nov. 24.

In his distress, the friendship of Palæologus was disputed by the ecclesiastical powers of the West; but the dextrous activity of a monarch prevailed over the slow debates and inflexible temper of a republic. The decrees of Basil continually tended to circumscribe the despotism of the pope, and to erect a supreme and perpetual tribunal in the church. Eugenius was impatient of the yoke; and the union of the Greeks might afford a decent pretence for translating a rebellious synod from the Rhine to the Po. The independence of the fathers was lost if they passed the Alps: Savoy or Avignon, to which they acceded with reluctance, were described at Constantinople as situate far beyond the pillars of Hercules;[43] the emperor and his clergy were apprehensive of the dangers of a long navigation; they were offended by an haughty declaration, that after suppressing the *new* heresy of the Bohemians, the council would soon eradicate the *old* heresy of the Greeks.[44] On the side of Eugenius, all was smooth, and yielding, and respectful: and he invited the Byzantine

41. Syropulus, p. 19. In this list, the Greeks appear to have exceeded the real numbers of the clergy and laity which afterwards attended the emperor and patriarch, but which are not clearly specified by the great ecclesiarch. The 75,000 florins which they asked in this negociation of the pope (p. 9.), were more than they could hope or want.

42. I use indifferently the words, *ducat* and *florin*, which derive their names, the former from the *dukes* of Milan, the latter from the republic of *Florence*. These gold pieces, the first that were coined in Italy, perhaps in the Latin world, may be compared in weight and value to one-third of the English guinea.

43. At the end of the Latin version of Phranzes, we read a long Greek epistle or declamation of George of Trebizond, who advises the emperor to prefer Eugenius and Italy. He treats with contempt the schismatic assembly of Basil, the Barbarians of Gaul and Germany, who had conspired to transport the chair of St. Peter beyond the Alps: οἱ αθλιοι (says he) σε και την μετα σου συνοδον εξω των Ἡρακλειων στηλων και περα Γαδηρων εξαξουσι. Was Constantinople unprovided with a map?

44. Syropulus (p. 26–31.) attests his own

monarch to heal by his presence the schism of the Latin, as well as of the Eastern, church. Ferrara, near the coast of the Adriatic, was proposed for their amicable interview; and with some indulgence of forgery and theft, a surreptitious decree was procured, which transferred the synod, with its own consent, to that Italian city. Nine gallies were equipped for this service at Venice, and in the isle of Candia; their diligence anticipated the slower vessels of Basil: the Roman admiral was commissioned to burn, sink, and destroy;[45] and these priestly squadrons might have encountered each other in the same seas where Athens and Sparta had formerly contended for the pre-eminence of glory. Assaulted by the importunity of the factions, who were ready to fight for the possession of his person, Palæologus hesitated before he left his palace and country on a perilous experiment. His father's advice still dwelt on his memory: and reason must suggest, that since the Latins were divided among themselves, they could never unite in a foreign cause. Sigismond dissuaded the unseasonable adventure; his advice was impartial, since he adhered to the council; and it was enforced by the strange belief, that the German Cæsar would nominate a Greek his heir and successor in the empire of the West.[46] Even the Turkish sultan was a counsellor whom it might be unsafe to trust, but whom it was dangerous to offend. Amurath was unskilled in the disputes, but he was apprehensive of the union, of the Christians. From his own treasures, he offered to relieve the wants of the Byzantine court; yet he declared with seeming magnanimity, that Constantinople should be secure and inviolate, in the absence of her sovereign.[47] The resolution of Palæologus was decided by the most splendid gifts and the most specious promises: he wished to escape for a while from a scene of danger and distress; and after dismissing with an

---

indignation, and that of his countrymen: and the Basil deputies, who excused the rash declaration, could neither deny nor alter an act of the council.

45. Condolmieri, the pope's nephew and admiral, expressly declared, *ὁτι ὁρισμον εχει παρα του Παπα ἱνα πολεμηση ὁπου αν ευρη τα κατεργα της Συνοδου, και ει δυνηθη καταδυση και αφανιση*. The naval orders of the synod were less peremptory, and, till the hostile squadrons appeared, both parties tried to conceal their quarrel from the Greeks.

46. Syropulus mentions the hopes of Palæologus (p. 36.), and the last advice of Sigismond (p. 57.). At Corfu, the Greek emperor was informed of his friend's death; had he known it sooner, he would have returned home (p. 79.).

47. Phranzes himself, though from different motives, was of the advice of Amurath (l. ii. c. 13.). Utinam ne synodus ista unquam fuisset, si tantas offensiones et detrimenta paritura erat. This Turkish embassy is likewise mentioned by Syropulus (p. 58.); and Amurath kept his word. He might threaten (p. 125. 219.), but he never attacked the city.

ambiguous answer the messengers of the council, he declared his intention of embarking in the Roman gallies. The age of the patriarch Joseph was more susceptible of fear than of hope; he trembled at the perils of the sea, and expressed his apprehension, that his feeble voice, with thirty perhaps of his orthodox brethren, would be oppressed in a foreign land by the power and numbers of a Latin synod. He yielded to the royal mandate, to the flattering assurance, that he would be heard as the oracle of nations, and to the secret wish of learning from his brother of the West, to deliver the church from the yoke of kings.[48] The five *cross-bearers* or dignitaries of St. Sophia, were bound to attend his person; and one of these, the great ecclesiarch or preacher, Sylvester Syropulus,[49] has composed[50] a free and curious history of the *false* union.[51] Of the clergy that reluctantly obeyed the summons of the emperor and the patriarch, submission was the first duty, and patience the most useful virtue. In a chosen list of twenty bishops, we discover the metropolitan titles of Heraclea and Cyzicus, Nice and Nicomedia, Ephesus and Trebizond, and the personal merit of Mark and Bessarion, who, in the confidence of their learning and eloquence, were promoted to the episcopal rank. Some monks and philosophers were named to display the science and sanctity of the Greek church: and the service of the choir was performed by a select band of singers and musicians. The patriarchs of Alexandria, Antioch, and Jerusalem, appeared by their genuine or fictitious deputies;

48. The reader will smile at the simplicity with which he imparted these hopes to his favourites: *τοιαυτην πληροφοριαν σχησειν ηλπιζε και δια του Παπα εθαρρει ελευθερωσαι την εκκλησιαν απο της αποτεθεισης αυτου δουλειας παρα του βασιλεως* (p. 92.). Yet it would have been difficult for him to have practised the lessons of Gregory VII.

49. The Christian name of Sylvester is borrowed from the Latin calendar. In modern Greek, *πουλος*, as a diminutive, is added to the end of words: nor can any reasoning of Creyghton, the editor, excuse his changing into *Sguro*pulus (Sguros, fuscus) the Syropulus of his own manuscript, whose name is subscribed with his own hand in the acts of the council of Florence. Why might not the author be of Syrian extraction?

50. From the conclusion of the history, I should fix the date to the year 1444, four years after the synod, when the great ecclesiarch had abdicated his office (sectio xii. p. 330–350.). His passions were cooled by time and retirement, and, although Syropulus is often partial, he is never intemperate.

51. *Vera historia unionis non veræ inter Græcos et Latinos* (*Hagæ Comitis*, 1660, in folio), was first published with a loose and florid version, by Robert Creyghton, chaplain to Charles II. in his exile. The zeal of the editor has prefixed a polemic title, for the beginning of the original is wanting. Syropulus may be ranked with the best of the Byzantine writers for the merit of his narration, and even of his style: but he is excluded from the orthodox collections of the councils.

the primate of Russia represented a national church, and the Greeks might contend with the Latins in the extent of their spiritual empire. The precious vases of St. Sophia were exposed to the winds and waves, that the patriarch might officiate with becoming splendour; whatever gold the emperor could procure, was expended in the massy ornaments of his bed and chariot:[52] and while they affected to maintain the prosperity of their ancient fortune, they quarrelled for the division of fifteen thousand ducats, the first alms of the Roman pontiff. After the necessary preparations, John Palæologus, with a numerous train, accompanied by his brother Demetrius, and the most respectable persons of the church and state, embarked in eight vessels with sails and oars, which steered through the Turkish streights of Gallipoli to the Archipelago, the Morea, and the Adriatic Gulf.[53]

His triumphal entry at Venice, A.D. 1438, February 9;

After a tedious and troublesome navigation of seventy-seven days, this religious squadron cast anchor before Venice; and their reception proclaimed the joy and magnificence of that powerful republic. In the command of the world, the modest Augustus had never claimed such honours from his subjects as were paid to his feeble successor by an independent state. Seated on the poop, on a lofty throne, he received the visit, or, in the Greek style, the *adoration*, of the doge and senators.[54] They sailed in the Bucentaur, which was accompanied by twelve stately gallies: the sea was overspread with innumerable gondolas of pomp and pleasure; the air resounded with music and acclamations; the mariners, and even the vessels, were dressed in silk and gold; and in all the emblems and pageants, the Roman eagles were blended with the lions of St. Mark. The triumphal procession, ascending the great canal, passed under the bridge of the Rialto; and the eastern strangers gazed with admiration

52. Syropulus (p. 63.) simply expresses his intention: ἰν' ὁυτω πομπαων εν Ιταλοις μεγας βασιλευς παρ' εκεινων νομιζοιτο; and the Latin of Creyghton may afford a specimen of his florid paraphrase. Ut pompâ circumductus noster Imperator Italiæ populis aliquis deauratus Jupiter crederetur, aut Crœsus ex opulenta Lydia.

53. Although I cannot stop to quote Syropulus for every fact, I will observe, that the navigation of the Greeks from Constantinople to Venice and Ferrara is contained in the iv[th] section (p. 67–100.), and that the historian has the uncommon talent of placing each scene before the reader's eye.

54. At the time of the synod, Phranzes was in Peloponnesus; but he received from the despot Demetrius, a faithful account of the honourable reception of the emperor and patriarch both at Venice and Ferrara (Dux ... sedentem Imperatorem *adorat*), which are more slightly mentioned by the Latins (l. ii. c. 14, 15, 16.).

on the palaces, the churches, and the populousness of a city that seems to float on the bosom of the waves.[55] They sighed to behold the spoils and trophies with which it had been decorated after the sack of Constantinople. After an hospitable entertainment of fifteen days, Palæologus pursued his journey by land and water from Venice to Ferrara: and on this occasion, the pride of the Vatican was tempered by policy to indulge the ancient dignity of the emperor of the East.

into Ferrara, February 28. He made his entry on a *black* horse; but a milk-white steed, whose trappings were embroidered with golden eagles, was led before him; and the canopy was borne over his head by the princes of Este, the sons or kinsmen of Nicholas, marquis of the city, and a sovereign more powerful than himself.[56] Palæologus did not alight till he reached the bottom of the stair-case: the pope advanced to the door of the apartment; refused his proffered genuflexion; and, after a paternal embrace, conducted the emperor to a seat on his left-hand. Nor would the patriarch descend from his galley, till a ceremony, almost equal, had been stipulated between the bishops of Rome and Constantinople. The latter was saluted by his brother with a kiss of union and charity: nor would any of the Greek ecclesiastics submit to kiss the feet of the Western primate. On the opening of the synod, the place of honour in the centre was claimed by the temporal and ecclesiastical chiefs; and it was only by alleging that his predecessors had not assisted in person at Nice or Chalcedon, that Eugenius could evade the ancient precedents of Constantine and Marcian. After much debate, it was agreed that the right and left sides of the church should be occupied by the two nations: that the solitary chair of St. Peter should be raised the first of the Latin line; and that the throne of the Greek emperor, at the head of his clergy, should be equal and opposite to the second place, the vacant seat of the emperor of the West.[57]

55. The astonishment of a Greek prince and a French ambassador (Memoires de Philippe de Comines, l. vii. c. 18.) at the sight of Venice, abundantly prove, that in the xvth century it was the first and most splendid of the Christian cities. For the spoils of Constantinople at Venice, see Syropulus (p. 87.).

56. Nicholas III. of Este, reigned forty-eight years (A.D. 1393–1441), and was lord of Ferrara, Modena, Reggio, Parma, Rovigo, and Commachio. See his life in Muratori (Antichità Estense, tom. ii. p. 159–201.).

57. The Latin vulgar was provoked to laughter at the strange dresses of the Greeks, and especially the length of their garments, their sleeves, and their beards; nor was the emperor distinguished, except by the purple colour, and his diadem or tiara with a jewel on the top (Hody de Græcis Illustribus, p. 31.). Yet another spectator confesses, that the Greek fashion was piu grave e piu degna than the Italian

Council of the Greeks and Latins at Ferrara and Florence, A.D. 1438, October 8– A.D. 1439, July 6.

But as soon as festivity and form had given place to a more serious treaty, the Greeks were dissatisfied with their journey, with themselves, and with the pope. The artful pencil of his emissaries had painted him in a prosperous state; at the head of the princes and prelates of Europe, obedient, at his voice, to believe and to arm. The thin appearance of the universal synod of Ferrara betrayed his weakness; and the Latins opened the first session with only five archbishops, eighteen bishops, and ten abbots, the greatest part of whom were the subjects or countrymen of the Italian pontiff. Except the duke of Burgundy, none of the potentates of the West condescended to appear in person, or by their ambassadors; nor was it possible to suppress the judicial acts of Basil against the dignity and person of Eugenius, which were finally concluded by a new election. Under these circumstances, a truce or delay was asked and granted, till Palæologus could expect from the consent of the Latins some temporal reward for an unpopular union; and, after the first session, the public proceedings were adjourned above six months. The emperor, with a chosen band of his favourites and *Janizaries*, fixed his summer residence at a pleasant spacious monastery, six miles from Ferrara; forgot, in the pleasures of the chace, the distress of the church and state; and persisted in destroying the game, without listening to the just complaints of the marquis or the husbandman.[58] In the mean while, his unfortunate Greeks were exposed to all the miseries of exile and poverty; for the support of each stranger, a monthly allowance was assigned of three or four gold florins; and although the entire sum did not amount to seven hundred florins, a long arrear was repeatedly incurred by the indigence or policy of the Roman court.[59] They sighed

(Vespasiano, in Vit. Eugen. IV. in Muratori, tom. xxv. p. 261.).

58. For the emperor's hunting, see Syropulus (p. 143, 144. 191.). The pope had sent him eleven miserable hacks: but he bought a strong and swift horse that came from Russia. The name of *Janizaries* may surprise: but the name, rather than the institution, had passed from the Ottoman, to the Byzantine, court; and is often used in the last age of the empire.

59. The Greeks obtained, with much difficulty, that instead of provisions, money should be distributed, four florins *per* month to the persons of honourable rank, and three florins to their servants, with an addition of thirty more to the emperor, twenty-five to the patriarch, and twenty to the prince or despot Demetrius. The payment of the first month amounted to 691 florins, a sum which will not allow us to reckon above 200 Greeks of every condition (Syropulus, p. 104, 105.). On the 20th October 1438, there was an arrear of four months; in April 1439, of three; and of five and a half in July, at the time of the union (p. 172. 225. 271.).

for a speedy deliverance, but their escape was prevented by a triple chain: a passport from their superiors was required at the gates of Ferrara; the government of Venice had engaged to arrest and send back the fugitives; and inevitable punishment awaited them at Constantinople; excommunication, fines, and a sentence, which did not respect the sacerdotal dignity, that they should be stripped naked and publicly whipped.[60] It was only by the alternative of hunger or dispute that the Greeks could be persuaded to open the first conference; and they yielded with extreme reluctance to attend from Ferrara to Florence the rear of a flying synod. This new translation was urged by inevitable necessity: the city was visited by the plague; the fidelity of the marquis might be suspected; the mercenary troops of the duke of Milan were at the gates; and as they occupied Romagna, it was not without difficulty and danger that the pope, the emperor, and the bishops, explored their way through the unfrequented paths of the Apennine.[61]

Yet all these obstacles were surmounted by time and policy. The violence of the fathers of Basil rather promoted than injured the cause of Eugenius: the nations of Europe abhorred the schism, and disowned the election, of Felix the fifth, who was successively a duke of Savoy, an hermit, and a pope; and the great princes were gradually reclaimed by his competitor to a favourable neutrality and a firm attachment. The legates, with some respectable members, deserted to the Roman army, which insensibly rose in numbers and reputation: the council of Basil was reduced to thirty-nine bishops, and three hundred of the inferior clergy;[62] while the Latins of Florence could produce the subscriptions of the pope himself, eight cardinals, two patriarchs, eight archbishops, fifty-two bishops, and forty-five abbots, or chiefs of religious orders. After the labour of nine months, and the debates of twenty-five sessions, they attained the advantage and glory of the re-union of the Greeks. Four principal questions had been agitated between the two churches: 1. The

60. Syropulus (p. 141, 142. 204. 221.) deplores the imprisonment of the Greeks, and the tyranny of the emperor and patriarch.

61. The wars of Italy are most clearly represented in the xiiith volume of the Annals of Muratori. The schismatic Greek, Syropulus (p. 145.), appears to have exaggerated the fear and disorder of the pope in his retreat from Ferrara to Florence, which is proved by the acts to have been somewhat more decent and deliberate.

62. Syropulus is pleased to reckon seven hundred prelates in the council of Basil. The error is manifest, and perhaps voluntary. That extravagant number could not be supplied by *all* the ecclesiastics of every degree who were present at the council, nor by *all* the absent bishops of the West, who, expressly or tacitly, might adhere to its decrees.

use of unleavened bread in the communion of Christ's body. 2. The nature of purgatory. 3. The supremacy of the pope. And, 4. The single or double procession of the Holy Ghost. The cause of either nation was managed by ten theological champions: the Latins were supported by the inexhaustible eloquence of cardinal Julian; and Mark of Ephesus and Bessarion of Nice were the bold and able leaders of the Greek forces. We may bestow some praise on the progress of human reason, by observing, that the first of these questions was *now* treated as an immaterial rite, which might innocently vary with the fashion of the age and country. With regard to the second, both parties were agreed in the belief of an intermediate state of purgation for the venial sins of the faithful; and whether their souls were purified by elemental fire, was a doubtful point, which in a few years might be conveniently settled on the spot by the disputants. The claims of supremacy appeared of a more weighty and substantial kind; yet by the Orientals the Roman bishop had ever been respected as the first of the five patriarchs; nor did they scruple to admit, that his jurisdiction should be exercised agreeable to the holy canons; a vague allowance, which might be defined or eluded by occasional convenience. The procession of the Holy Ghost from the Father alone, or from the Father and the Son, was an article of faith which had sunk much deeper into the minds of men; and in the sessions of Ferrara and Florence, the Latin addition of *filioque* was subdivided into two questions, whether it were legal, and whether it were orthodox. Perhaps it may not be necessary to boast on this subject of my own impartial indifference; but I must think that the Greeks were strongly supported by the prohibition of the council of Chalcedon, against adding any article whatsoever to the creed of Nice, or rather of Constantinople.[63] In earthly affairs, it is not easy to conceive how an assembly of legislators can bind their successors invested with powers equal to their own. But the dictates of inspiration must be true and unchangeable; nor should a private bishop, or a provincial synod, have presumed to innovate against the judgment of the Catholic church. On the substance of the doctrine, the controversy was equal and endless: reason is confounded by the procession of a deity; the gospel, which lay on the altar, was silent; the various texts of the fathers might be corrupted by fraud or entangled by sophistry; and the Greeks

63. The Greeks, who disliked the union, were unwilling to sally from this strong fortress (p. 178. 193. 195. 202. of Syropulus). The shame of the Latins was aggravated by their producing an old MS. of the second council of Nice, with *filioque* in the Nicene creed: a palpable forgery! (p. 173.)

were ignorant of the characters and writings of the Latin saints.[64] Of this at least we may be sure, that neither side could be convinced by the arguments of their opponents. Prejudice may be enlightened by reason, and a superficial glance may be rectified by a clear and more perfect view of an object adapted to our faculties. But the bishops and monks had been taught from their infancy to repeat a form of mysterious words; their national and personal honour depended on the repetition of the same sounds; and their narrow minds were hardened and inflamed by the acrimony of a public dispute.

Negociations with the Greeks. While they were lost in a cloud of dust and darkness, the pope and emperor were desirous of a seeming union, which could alone accomplish the purposes of their interview; and the obstinacy of public dispute was softened by the arts of private and personal negociation. The patriarch Joseph had sunk under the weight of age and infirmities; his dying voice breathed the counsels of charity and concord, and his vacant benefice might tempt the hopes of the ambitious clergy. The ready and active obedience of the archbishops of Russia and Nice, of Isidore and Bessarion, was prompted and recompensed by their speedy promotion to the dignity of cardinals. Bessarion, in the first debates, had stood forth the most strenuous and eloquent champion of the Greek church; and if the apostate, the bastard, was reprobated by his country,[65] he appears in ecclesiastical story a rare example of a patriot who was recommended to court-favour by loud opposition and well-timed compliance. With the aid of his two spiritual coadjutors, the emperor applied his arguments to the general situation and personal characters of the bishops, and each was successively moved by authority and example. Their revenues were in the hands of the Turks, their persons in those of the Latins: an episcopal treasure, three robes and forty ducats, was soon exhausted:[66] the hopes of their return still depended on the ships of Venice and the alms of Rome; and such was their indigence, that their

64. *‘Ως εγω* (said an eminent Greek) *οταν εις ναον εισελθω Λατινων ου προσκυνω τινα των εκεισε ἁγιων, επει ουδε γνωριζω τινα* (Syropulus, p. 109.). See the perplexity of the Greeks (p. 217, 218. 252, 253. 273.).

65. See the polite altercation of Mark and Bessarion in Syropulus (p. 257.), who never dissembles the vices of his own party, and fairly praises the virtues of the Latins.

66. For the poverty of the Greek bishops, see a remarkable passage of Ducas (c. 31.). One had possessed, for his whole property, three old gowns, &c. By teaching one-and-twenty years in his monastery, Bessarion himself had collected forty gold florins; but of these, the archbishop had expended twenty-eight in his voyage from Peloponnesus, and the remainder at Constantinople (Syropulus, p. 127.).

arrears, the payment of a debt, would be accepted as a favour, and might operate as a bribe.[67] The danger and relief of Constantinople might excuse some prudent and pious dissimulation; and it was insinuated, that the obstinate heretics who should resist the consent of the East and West, would be abandoned in a hostile land to the revenge or justice of the Roman pontiff.[68] In the first private assembly of the Greeks, the formulary of union was approved by twenty-four, and rejected by twelve, members: but the five *cross-bearers* of St. Sophia, who aspired to represent the patriarch, were disqualified by ancient discipline; and their right of voting was transferred to an obsequious train of monks, grammarians, and profane laymen. The will of the monarch produced a false and servile unanimity, and no more than two patriots had courage to speak their own sentiments and those of their country. Demetrius, the emperor's brother, retired to Venice, that he might not be witness of the union; and Mark of Ephesus, mistaking perhaps his pride for his conscience, disclaimed all communion with the Latin heretics, and avowed himself the champion and confessor of the orthodox creed.[69] In the treaty between the two nations, several forms of consent were proposed, such as might satisfy the Latins, without dishonouring the Greeks: and they weighed the scruples of words and syllables, till the theological balance trembled with a slight preponderance in favour of the Vatican. It was agreed (I must intreat the attention of the reader), that the Holy Ghost proceeds from the Father *and* the Son, as from one principle and one substance; that he proceeds *by* the Son, being of the same nature and substance, and that he proceeds from the Father *and* the Son, by one *spiration* and production. It is less difficult to understand the articles of the preliminary treaty; that the pope should defray all the expences of the Greeks in their return home; that he should annually maintain two gallies and three hundred soldiers for the defence of Constantinople; that all the ships which transported pilgrims to Jerusalem, should be obliged to touch at that port; that as often as they were required, the pope should

67. Syropulus denies that the Greeks received any money before they had subscribed the act of union (p. 283.): yet he relates some suspicious circumstances; and their bribery and corruption are positively affirmed by the historian Ducas.

68. The Greeks most piteously express their own fears of exile and perpetual slavery (Syropul. p. 196.): and they were strongly moved by the emperor's threats (p. 260.).

69. I had forgot another popular and orthodox protester; a favourite hound, who usually lay quiet on the foot-cloth of the emperor's throne; but who barked most furiously while the act of union was reading, without being silenced by the soothing or the lashes of the royal attendants (Syropul. p. 265, 266.).

furnish ten gallies for a year, or twenty for six months; and that he should powerfully solicit the princes of Europe, if the emperor had occasion for land-forces.

Eugenius deposed at Basil, A.D. 1438, June 25.

The same year, and almost the same day, were marked by the deposition of Eugenius at Basil; and, at Florence, by his re-union of the Greeks and Latins. In the former synod (which he styled indeed an assembly of dæmons), the pope was branded with the guilt of simony, perjury, tyranny, heresy, and schism;[70] and declared to be incorrigible in his vices, unworthy of any title, and incapable of holding any ecclesiastical office. In the latter, he was revered as the true and holy vicar of Christ, who, after a separation of six hundred years, had reconciled the Catholics of the East and West, in one fold, and under one shepherd. The act of union was subscribed by the pope, the emperor, and the principal member of both churches; even by those who, like Syropulus,[71] had been deprived of the right of voting. Two copies might have sufficed for the East and West; but Eugenius was not satisfied, unless four authentic and similar transcripts were signed and attested as the monuments of his victory.[72] On a memorable day, the sixth of July, the successors of St. Peter and Constantine ascended their thrones; the two nations assembled in the cathedral of Florence; their representatives, cardinal Julian and Bessarion archbishop of Nice, appeared in the pulpit, and, after reading in their respective tongues the act of union, they mutually embraced in the name and the presence of their applauding brethren. The pope and his ministers then officiated according to the Roman liturgy; the creed was chaunted with the addition of *filioque*; the acquiescence of the Greeks was poorly excused by their ignorance of the

Re-union of the Greeks at Florence, A.D. 1438, July 6.

70. From the original Lives of the Popes, in Muratori's Collection (tom. iii. P. ii. tom. xxv.), the manners of Eugenius IV. appear to have been decent, and even exemplary. His situation, exposed to the world and to his enemies, was a restraint, and is a pledge.

71. Syropulus, rather than subscribe, would have assisted, as the least evil, at the ceremony of the union. He was compelled to do both; and the great ecclesiarch poorly excuses his submission to the emperor (p. 290–292.).

72. None of these original acts of union can at present be produced. Of the ten MSS. that are preserved (five at Rome, and the remainder at Florence, Bologna, Venice, Paris, and London), nine have been examined by an accurate critic (M. de Brequigny), who condemns them for the variety and imperfections of the Greek signatures. Yet several of these may be esteemed as authentic copies, which were subscribed at Florence before (26th of August 1439) the final separation of the pope and emperor (Memoires de l'Academie des Inscriptions, tom. xliii. p. 287–311.).

harmonious, but inarticulate, sounds;[73] and the more scrupulous Latins refused any public celebration of the Byzantine rite. Yet the emperor and his clergy were not totally unmindful of national honour. The treaty was ratified by their consent: it was tacitly agreed that no innovation should be attempted in their creed or ceremonies; they spared, and secretly respected, the generous firmness of Mark of Ephesus; and on the decease of the patriarch, they refused to elect his successor, except in the cathedral of St. Sophia. In the distribution of public and private rewards, the liberal pontiff exceeded their hopes and his promises: the Greeks, with less pomp and pride, returned by the same road of Ferrara and Venice; and their reception at Constantinople was such as will be described in the following chapter.[74] The success of the first trial encouraged Eugenius to repeat the same edifying scenes; and the deputies of the Armenians, the Maronites, the Jacobites of Syria and Egypt, the Nestorians and the Æthiopians, were successively introduced, to kiss the feet of the Roman pontiff, and to announce the obedience and the orthodoxy of the East. These Oriental embassies, unknown in the countries which they presumed to represent,[75] diffused over the West the fame of Eugenius: and a clamour was artfully propagated against the remnant of a schism in Switzerland and Savoy, which alone impeded the harmony of the Christian world. The vigour of opposition was succeeded by the lassitude of despair: the council of Basil was silently dissolved; and Fœlix, renouncing the tiara, again withdrew to the devout or delicious hermitage of Ripaille.[76] A general peace was secured by mutual acts of oblivion and indemnity: all ideas of reformation subsided; the popes continued to exercise and abuse their ecclesiastical despotism; nor has Rome been since disturbed by the mischiefs of a contested election.[77]

Their return to Constantinople, A.D. 1440, February 1.

Final peace of the church, A.D. 1449.

73. Ἡμιν δε ὡς ασημοι εδοκουν φωναι (Syropul. p. 297.).

74. In their return, the Greeks conversed at Bologna with the ambassadors of England; and after some questions and answers, these impartial strangers laughed at the pretended union of Florence (Syropul. p. 307.).

75. So nugatory, or rather so fabulous, are these reunions of the Nestorians, Jacobites, &c. that I have turned over, without success, the Bibliotheca Orientalis of Assemannus, a faithful slave of the Vatican.

76. Ripaille is situate near Thonon in Savoy, on the southern side of the lake of Geneva. It is now a Carthusian abbey; and Mr. Addison (Travels into Italy, vol. ii. p. 147, 148. of Baskerville's edition of his works) has celebrated the place and the founder. Æneas Sylvius, and the fathers of Basil, applaud the austere life of the ducal hermit; but the French and Italian proverbs most unluckily attest the popular opinion of his luxury.

77. In this account of the councils of Basil, Ferrara, and Florence, I have consulted the

State of the Greek language at Constantinople, A.D. 1300–1453.

The journies of three emperors were unavailing for their temporal, or perhaps their spiritual, salvation; but they were productive of a beneficial consequence; the revival of the Greek learning in Italy, from whence it was propagated to the last nations of the West and North. In their lowest servitude and depression, the subjects of the Byzantine throne were still possessed of a golden key that could unlock the treasures of antiquity; of a musical and prolific language, that gives a soul to the objects of sense, and a body to the abstractions of philosophy. Since the barriers of the monarchy, and even of the capital, had been trampled under foot, the various Barbarians had doubtless corrupted the form and substance of the national dialect; and ample glossaries have been composed, to interpret a multitude of words, of Arabic, Turkish, Sclavonian, Latin, or French origin.[78] But a purer idiom was spoken in the court and taught in the college; and the flourishing state of the language is described, and perhaps embellished, by a learned Italian,[79] who, by a long residence and noble marriage,[80] was naturalized at Constantinople about thirty years before the Turkish conquest. "The vulgar speech," says Philelphus,[81] "has been

original acts, which fill the xvii[th] and xviii[th] tomes of the edition of Venice, and are closed by the perspicuous, though partial, history of Augustin Patricius, an Italian of the xv[th] century. They are digested and abridged by Dupin (Bibliotheque Eccles. tom. xii.), and the continuator of Fleury (tom. xxii.); and the respect of the Gallican church for the adverse parties confines their members to an awkward moderation.

78. In the first attempt, Meursius collected 3600 Græco-barbarous words, to which, in a second edition, he subjoined 1800 more; yet what plenteous gleanings did he leave to Portius, Ducange, Fabrotti, the Bollandists, &c. (Fabric. Bibliot. Græc. tom. x. p. 101, &c.) *Some* Persic words may be found in Xenophon, and some Latin ones in Plutarch; and such is the inevitable effect of war and commerce: but the form and substance of the language were not affected by this slight alloy.

79. The life of Francis Philelphus, a sophist, proud, restless, and rapacious, has been diligently composed by Lancelot (Memoires de l'Academie des Inscriptions, tom. x. p. 691–751.) and Tiraboschi (Istoria della Letteratura Italiana, tom. vii. p. 282–294.), for the most part from his own letters. His elaborate writings, and those of his contemporaries, are forgotten: but their familiar epistles still describe the men and the times.

80. He married, and had perhaps debauched, the daughter of John, and the grand-daughter of Manuel Chrysoloras. She was young, beautiful, and wealthy; and her noble family was allied to the Dorias of Genoa and the emperors of Constantinople.

81. Græci quibus lingua depravata non sit ... ita loquuntur vulgo hâc etiam tempestate ut Aristophanes comicus, aut Euripides tragicus, ut oratores omnes ut historiographi ut philosophi ... litterati autem homines et doctius et emendatius ... Nam viri aulici veterem sermonis dignitatem atque elegantiam retinebant in primisque ipsæ nobiles mulieres; quibus cum nullum esset omnino cum viris peregrinis

depraved by the people, and infected by the multitude of strangers and merchants, who every day flock to the city and mingle with the inhabitants. It is from the disciples of such a school that the Latin language received the versions of Aristotle and Plato; so obscure in sense, and in spirit so poor. But the Greeks who have escaped the contagion, are those whom *we* follow; and they alone are worthy of our imitation. In familiar discourse, they still speak the tongue of Aristophanes and Euripides, of the historians and philosophers of Athens; and the style of their writings is still more elaborate and correct. The persons who, by their birth and offices, are attached to the Byzantine court, are those who maintain, with the least alloy, the ancient standard of elegance and purity; and the native graces of language most conspicuously shine among the noble matrons, who are excluded from all intercourse with foreigners. With foreigners do I say? They live retired and sequestered from the eyes of their fellow-citizens. Seldom are they seen in the streets; and when they leave their houses, it is in the dusk of evening, on visits to the churches and their nearest kindred. On these occasions, they are on horseback, covered with a veil, and encompassed by their parents, their husbands, or their servants."[82]

Among the Greeks, a numerous and opulent clergy was dedicated to the service of religion: their monks and bishops have ever been distinguished by the gravity and austerity of their manners; nor were they diverted, like the Latin priests, by the pursuits and pleasures of a secular, and even military, life. After a large deduction for the time and talents that were lost in the devotion, the laziness, and the discord, of the church and cloyster, the more inquisitive and ambitious minds would explore the sacred and profane erudition of their native language. The ecclesiastics presided over the education of youth; the schools of philosophy and eloquence were perpetuated till the fall of the empire; and it may be affirmed, that more books and more knowledge were included within the walls of Constantinople than could be dispersed over the extensive countries of the West.[83] But an important distinction has been already noticed: the Greeks were stationary or retrograde, while the Latins were advancing with a rapid and progressive motion.

Comparison of the Greeks and Latins.

---

commercium, merus ille ac purus Græcorum sermo servabatur intactus (Philelph. Epist. ad ann. 1451, apud Hodium, p. 188, 189.). He observes in another passage, uxor illa mea Theodora locutione erat admodum moderatâ et suavi et maxime Atticâ.

82. Philelphus, absurdly enough, derives this Greek or Oriental jealousy from the manners of ancient Rome.

83. See the state of learning in the xiii[th] and xiv[th] centuries, in the learned and judicious Mosheim (Institut. Hist. Eccles. p. 434–440. 490–494.).

The nations were excited by the spirit of independence and emulation; and even the little world of the Italian states contained more people and industry than the decreasing circle of the Byzantine empire. In Europe, the lower ranks of society were relieved from the yoke of feudal servitude; and freedom is the first step to curiosity and knowledge. The use, however rude and corrupt, of the Latin tongue had been preserved by superstition; the universities, from Bologna to Oxford,[84] were peopled with thousands of scholars; and their misguided ardour might be directed to more liberal and manly studies. In the resurrection of science, Italy was the first that cast away her shroud; and the eloquent Petrarch, by his lessons and his example, may justly be applauded as the first harbinger of day. A purer style of composition, a more generous and rational strain of sentiment, flowed from the study and imitation of the writers of ancient Rome; and the disciples of Cicero and Virgil approached, with reverence and love, the sanctuary of their Grecian masters. In the sack of Constantinople, the French, and even the Venetians, had despised and destroyed the works of Lysippus and Homer: the monuments of art may be annihilated by a single blow; but the immortal mind is renewed and multiplied by the copies of the pen; and such copies it was the ambition of Petrarch and his friends to possess and understand. The arms of the Turks undoubtedly pressed the flight of the muses; yet we may tremble at the thought, that Greece might have been overwhelmed, with her schools and libraries, before Europe had emerged from the deluge of barbarism; that the seeds of science might have been scattered by the winds, before the Italian soil was prepared for their cultivation.

Revival of the Greek learning in Italy.

The most learned Italians of the fifteenth century have confessed and applauded the restoration of Greek literature, after a long oblivion of many hundred years.[85] Yet in that country, and beyond the Alps, some names are quoted; some profound scholars, who in the darker ages were honourably distinguished by their

84. At the end of the xvth century, there existed in Europe about fifty universities, and of these the foundation of ten or twelve is prior to the year 1300. They were crowded in proportion to their scarcity. Bologna contained 10,000 students, chiefly of the civil law. In the year 1357 the number at Oxford had decreased from 30,000 to 6000 scholars (Henry's History of Great Britain, vol. iv. p. 478.). Yet even this decrease is much superior to the present list of the members of the university.

85. Of those writers who professedly treat of the restoration of the Greek learning in Italy, the two principal are Hodius, Dr. Humphrey Hody (de Græcis Illustribus, Linguæ Græcæ Literarumque humaniorum Instauratoribus; Londini, 1742, in large octavo), and Tiraboschi (Istoria della Letteratura Italiana, tom. v. p. 364–377.

knowledge of the Greek tongue; and national vanity has been loud in the praise of such rare examples of erudition. Without scrutinizing the merit of individuals, truth must observe that their science is without a cause, and without an effect; that it was easy for them to satisfy themselves and their more ignorant contemporaries; and that the idiom, which they had so marvellously acquired, was transcribed in few manuscripts, and was not taught in any university of the West. In a corner of Italy, it faintly existed as the popular, or at least as the ecclesiastical, dialect.[86] The first impression of the Doric and Ionic colonies has never been completely erazed: the Calabrian churches were long attached to the throne of Constantinople; and the monks of St. Basil pursued their studies in mount Athos and the schools of the East. Calabria was the native country of Barlaam, who has already appeared as a sectary and an ambassador; and Barlaam was the first who revived, beyond the Alps, the memory, or at least the writings, of Homer.[87] He is described, by Petrarch and Boccace,[88] as a man of a diminutive stature, though truly great in the measure of learning and genius; of a piercing discernment, though of a slow and painful elocution. For many ages (as they affirm) Greece had not produced his equal in the knowledge of history, grammar, and philosophy; and his merit was celebrated in the attestations of the princes and doctors of Constantinople. One of these attestations is still extant; and the emperor Cantacuzene, the protector of his adversaries, is forced to allow that Euclid, Aristotle, and Plato, were familiar to that profound and subtle logician.[89] In the court of Avignon, he formed an intimate connection with Petrarch,[90] the first of the Latin scholars; and the desire of mutual instruction was the principle of their literary commerce. The Tuscan applied himself with eager curiosity and assiduous

Lessons of Barlaam, A.D. 1339.

---

tom. vii. p. 112–143.). The Oxford professor is a laborious scholar, but the librarian of Modena enjoys the superiority of a modern and national historian.

86. In Calabria quæ olim magna Græcia dicebatur, coloniis Græcis repleta, remansit quædam linguæ veteris cognitio (Hodius, p. 2.). If it were eradicated by the Romans, it was revived and perpetuated by the monks of St. Basil, who possessed seven convents at Rossano alone (Giannone, Istoria di Napoli, tom. i. p. 520.).

87. Ii Barbari (says Petrarch, the French and Germans) vix, non dicam libros sed nomen Homeri audiverunt. Perhaps, in that respect, the xiii[th] century was less happy than the age of Charlemagne.

88. See the character of Barlaam, in Boccace de Genealog. Deorum, l. xv. c. 6.

89. Cantacuzen. l. ii. c. 36.

90. For the connection of Petrarch and Barlaam, and the two interviews at Avignon in 1339, and at Naples in 1342, see the excellent Memoires sur la Vie de Petrarque, tom. i. p. 406–410. tom. ii. p. 75–77.

Studies of Petrarch, A.D. 1339–1374.

diligence to the study of the Greek language; and in a laborious struggle with the dryness and difficulty of the first rudiments, he began to reach the sense, and to feel the spirit, of poets and philosophers, whose minds were congenial to his own. But he was soon deprived of the society and lessons of this useful assistant: Barlaam relinquished his fruitless embassy; and, on his return to Greece, he rashly provoked the swarms of fanatic monks, by attempting to substitute the light of reason to that of their navel. After a separation of three years, the two friends again met in the court of Naples; but the generous pupil renounced the fairest occasion of improvement; and by his recommendation Barlaam was finally settled in a small bishopric of his native Calabria.[91] The manifold avocations of Petrarch, love and friendship, his various correspondence and frequent journies, the Roman laurel, and his elaborate compositions in prose and verse, in Latin and Italian, diverted him from a foreign idiom; and as he advanced in life, the attainment of the Greek language was the object of his wishes, rather than of his hopes. When he was about fifty years of age, a Byzantine ambassador, his friend, and a master of both tongues, presented him with a copy of Homer; and the answer of Petrarch is at once expressive of his eloquence, gratitude, and regret. After celebrating the generosity of the donor, and the value of a gift more precious in his estimation than gold or rubies, he thus proceeds: "Your present of the genuine and original text of the divine poet, the fountain of all invention, is worthy of yourself and of me: you have fulfilled your promise, and satisfied my desires. Yet your liberality is still imperfect: with Homer you should have given me yourself; a guide, who could lead me into the fields of light, and disclose to my wondering eyes the specious miracles of the Iliad and Odyssey. But, alas! Homer is dumb, or I am deaf; nor is it in my power to enjoy the beauty which I possess. I have seated him by the side of Plato, the prince of poets near the prince of philosophers; and I glory in the sight of my illustrious guests. Of their immortal writings, whatever had been translated into the Latin idiom, I had already acquired; but, if there be no profit, there is some pleasure, in beholding these venerable Greeks in their proper and national habit. I am delighted with the aspect of Homer;

91. The bishopric to which Barlaam retired, was the old Locri, in the middle ages S[cta] Cyriaca, and by corruption Hieracium, Gerace (Dissert. Chorographica Italiæ medii Ævi, p. 312.). The dives opum of the Norman times soon lapsed into poverty, since even the church was poor: yet the town still contains 3000 inhabitants (Swinburne, p. 340.).

and as often as I embrace the silent volume, I exclaim with a sigh, illustrious bard! with what pleasure should I listen to thy song, if my sense of hearing were not obstructed and lost by the death of one friend, and in the much-lamented absence of another. Nor do I yet despair; and the example of Cato suggests some comfort and hope, since it was in the last period of age that he attained the knowledge of the Greek letters."[92]

Of Boccace, A.D. 1360. &c.

The prize which eluded the efforts of Petrarch, was obtained by the fortune and industry of his friend Boccace,[93] the father of the Tuscan prose. That popular writer, who derives his reputation from the Decameron, an hundred novels of pleasantry and love, may aspire to the more serious praise of restoring in Italy the study of the Greek language. In the year one thousand three hundred and sixty, a disciple of Barlaam, whose name was Leo, or Leontius Pilatus, was detained in his way to Avignon by the advice and hospitality of Boccace, who lodged the stranger in his house, prevailed on the republic of Florence to allow him an annual stipend, and devoted his leisure to the first Greek professor, who taught that language in the Western countries of Europe. The appearance of Leo might disgust the most eager disciple; he was clothed in the mantle of a philosopher, or a mendicant; his countenance was hideous; his face was overshadowed with black hair; his beard long and uncombed; his deportment rustic; his temper gloomy and inconstant; nor could he grace his discourse with the ornaments, or even the perspicuity, of Latin elocution. But his mind was stored with a treasure of Greek learning: history and fable, philosophy and grammar, were alike at his command; and he read the poems of Homer in the schools of Florence. It was from his explanation that Boccace composed and transcribed a literal prose version of the Iliad and Odyssey, which satisfied

Leo Pilatus, first Greek professor at Florence, and in the West, A.D. 1360–1363.

92. I will transcribe a passage from this epistle of Petrarch (Famil. ix. 2.): Donasti Homerum non in alienum sermonem violento alveo derivatum, sed ex ipsis Græci eloquii scatebris, et qualis divino illi profluxit ingenio ... Sine tuâ voce Homerus tuus apud me mutus, immo vero ego apud illum surdus sum. Gaudeo tamen vel adspectû solo, ac sæpe illum amplexus atque suspirans dico, O magne vir, &c.

93. For the life and writings of Boccace, who was born in 1313, and died in 1375, Fabricius (Bibliot. Latin. medii Ævi, tom. i. p. 248, &c.) and Tiraboschi (tom. v. p. 83. 439–451.) may be consulted. The editions, versions, imitations of his novels, are innumerable. Yet he was ashamed to communicate that trifling, and perhaps scandalous, work to Petrarch his respectable friend, in whose letters and memoirs he conspicuously appears.

the thirst of his friend Petrarch, and which perhaps, in the succeeding century, was clandestinely used by Laurentius Valla, the Latin interpreter. It was from his narratives that the same Boccace collected the materials for his treatise on the genealogy of the heathen gods, a work, in that age, of stupendous erudition, and which he ostentatiously sprinkled with Greek characters and passages, to excite the wonder and applause of his more ignorant readers.[94] The first steps of learning are slow and laborious; no more than ten votaries of Homer could be enumerated in all Italy; and neither Rome, nor Venice, nor Naples, could add a single name to this studious catalogue. But their numbers would have multiplied, their progress would have been accelerated, if the inconstant Leo, at the end of three years, had not relinquished an honourable and beneficial station. In his passage, Petrarch entertained him at Padua a short time; he enjoyed the scholar, but was justly offended with the gloomy and unsocial temper of the man. Discontented with the world and with himself, Leo depreciated his present enjoyments, while absent persons and objects were dear to his imagination. In Italy he was a Thessalian, in Greece a native of Calabria; in the company of the Latins he disdained their language, religion, and manners; no sooner was he landed at Constantinople, than he again sighed for the wealth of Venice and the elegance of Florence. His Italian friends were deaf to his importunity; he depended on their curiosity and indulgence, and embarked on a second voyage; but on his entrance into the Adriatic, the ship was assailed by a tempest, and the unfortunate teacher, who like Ulysses had fastened himself to the mast, was struck dead by a flash of lightning. The humane Petrarch dropt a tear on his disaster; but he was most anxious to learn whether some copy of Euripides or Sophocles might not be saved from the hands of the mariners.[95]

Foundation of the Greek language in Italy

But the faint rudiments of Greek learning, which Petrarch had encouraged and Boccace had planted, soon withered and expired. The succeeding generation was content for a while

94. Boccace indulges an honest vanity: Ostentationis causâ Græca carmina adscripsi ... jure utor meo; meum est hoc decus mea gloria scilicet inter Etruscos Græcis uti carminibus. Nonne ego fui qui Leontium Pilatum, &c. (de Genealogia Deorum, l. xv. c. 7. a work which, though now forgotten, has run through thirteen or fourteen editions.)

95. Leontius, or Leo Pilatus, is sufficiently made known by Hody (p. 2–11.), and the Abbé de Sade (Vie de Petrarque, tom. iii. p. 625–634. 670–673.), who has very happily caught the lively and dramatic manner of his original.

by Manuel Chrysoloras, A.D. 1390–1415.

with the improvement of Latin eloquence: nor was it before the end of the fourteenth century, that a new and perpetual flame was rekindled in Italy.[96] Previous to his own journey, the emperor Manuel dispatched his envoys and orators to implore the compassion of the Western princes. Of these envoys, the most conspicuous, or the most learned, was Manuel Chrysoloras,[97] of noble birth, and whose Roman ancestors are supposed to have migrated with the great Constantine. After visiting the courts of France and England, where he obtained some contributions and more promises, the envoy was invited to assume the office of a professor; and Florence had again the honour of this second invitation. By his knowledge, not only of the Greek, but of the Latin, tongue, Chrysoloras deserved the stipend, and surpassed the expectation, of the republic: his school was frequented by a crowd of disciples of every rank and age; and one of these, in a general history, has described his motives and his success. "At that time," says Leonard Aretin,[98] "I was a student of the civil law; but my soul was inflamed with the love of letters; and I bestowed some application on the sciences of logic and rhetoric. On the arrival of Manuel, I hesitated whether I should desert my legal studies, or relinquish this golden opportunity; and thus, in the ardour of youth, I communed with my own mind – Wilt thou be wanting to thyself and thy fortune? Wilt thou refuse to be introduced to a familiar converse with Homer, Plato, and Demosthenes? with those poets, philosophers, and orators, of whom such wonders are related, and who are celebrated by every age as the great masters of human science? Of professors and scholars in civil law, a sufficient supply will always be found in our universities; but a teacher,

96. Dr. Hody (p. 54.) is angry with Leonard Aretin, Guarinus, Paulus Jovius, &c. for affirming, that the Greek letters were restored in Italy *post septingentos annos*; as if, says he, they had flourished till the end of the vii[th] century. These writers most probably reckoned from the last period of the exarchate; and the presence of the Greek magistrates and troops at Ravenna and Rome, must have preserved, in some degree, the use of their native tongue.

97. See the article of Emanuel, or Manuel Chrysoloras, in Hody (p. 12–54.) and Tiraboschi (tom. vii. p. 113–118.). The precise date of his arrival floats between the years 1390 and 1400, and is only confined by the reign of Boniface IX.

98. The name of *Aretinus* has been assumed by five or six natives of *Arezzo* in Tuscany, of whom the most famous and the most worthless lived in the xvi[th] century. Leonardus Brunus Aretinus, the disciple of Chrysoloras, was a linguist, an orator, and an historian, the secretary of four successive popes, and the chancellor of the republic of Florence, where he died A.D. 1444, at the age of seventy-five (Fabric. Bibliot. medii Ævi, tom. i. p. 190, &c. Tiraboschi, tom. vii. p. 33–38.).

and such a teacher, of the Greek language, if he once be suffered to escape, may never afterwards be retrieved. Convinced by these reasons, I gave myself to Chrysoloras; and so strong was my passion, that the lessons which I had imbibed in the day were the constant subject of my nightly dreams."[99] At the same time and place, the Latin classics were explained by John of Ravenna, the domestic pupil of Petrarch:[100] the Italians, who illustrated their age and country, were formed in this double school; and Florence became the fruitful seminary of Greek and Roman erudition.[101] The presence of the emperor recalled Chrysoloras from the college to the court; but he afterwards taught at Pavia and Rome with equal industry and applause. The remainder of his life, about fifteen years, was divided between Italy and Constantinople, between embassies and lessons. In the noble office of enlightening a foreign nation, the grammarian was not unmindful of a more sacred duty to his prince and country; and Emanuel Chrysoloras died at Constance on a public mission from the emperor to the council.

The Greeks in Italy, A.D. 1400–1500.

After his example, the restoration of the Greek letters in Italy was prosecuted by a series of emigrants, who were destitute of fortune, and endowed with learning, or at least with language. From the terror or oppression of the Turkish arms, the natives of Thessalonica and Constantinople escaped to a land of freedom, curiosity, and wealth. The synod introduced into Florence the lights of the Greek church and the oracles of the Platonic philosophy: and the fugitives who adhered to the union, had the double merit of renouncing their country, not only for the Christian, but for the Catholic, cause. A patriot, who sacrifices his party and conscience to the allurements of favour, may be possessed however of the private and social virtues: he no longer hears the reproachful epithets of slave and apostate; and the consideration which he acquires among his new associates, will restore in his own eyes

99. See the passage in Aretin. Commentario Rerum suo Tempore in Italia gestarum, apud Hodium, p. 28–30.

100. In this domestic discipline, Petrarch, who loved the youth, often complains of the eager curiosity, restless temper, and proud feelings, which announce the genius and glory of a riper age (Memoires sur Petrarque, tom. iii. p. 700–709.).

101. Hinc Græcæ Latinæque scholæ exortæ sunt, Guarino Philelpho, Leonardo Aretino, Caroloque, ac plerisque aliis tanquam ex equo Trojano prodeuntibus, quorum emulatione multa ingenia deinceps at laudem excitata sunt (Platina in Bonifacio IX.). Another Italian writer adds the names of Paulus Petrus Vergerius, Omnibonus Vincentius, Poggius, Franciscus Barbarus, &c. But I question whether a rigid chronology would allow Chrysoloras *all* these eminent scholars (Hodius, p. 25–27, &c.).

Cardinal Bessarion, &c.

the dignity of his character. The prudent conformity of Bessarion was rewarded with the Roman purple: he fixed his residence in Italy; and the Greek cardinal, the titular patriarch of Constantinople, was respected as the chief and protector of his nation:[102] his abilities were exercised in the legations of Bologna, Venice, Germany, and France; and his election to the chair of St. Peter floated for a moment on the uncertain breath of a conclave.[103] His ecclesiastical honours diffused a splendour and pre-eminence over his literary merit and service: his palace was a school; as often as the cardinal visited the Vatican, he was attended by a learned train of both nations;[104] of men applauded by themselves and the public; and whose writings, now overspread with dust, were popular and useful in their own times. I shall not attempt to enumerate the restorers of Grecian literature in the fifteenth century: and it may be sufficient to mention with gratitude the names of Theodore Gaza, of George of Trebizond, of John Argyropulus, and Demetrius Chalcocondyles, who taught their native language in the schools of Florence and Rome. Their labours were not inferior to those of Bessarion, whose purple they revered, and whose fortune was the secret object of their envy. But the lives of these grammarians was humble and obscure: they had declined the lucrative paths of the church; their dress and manners secluded them from the commerce of the world; and since they were confined to the merit, they might be content with the rewards, of learning. From this character, Janus Lascaris[105] will deserve an exception. His eloquence, politeness, and Imperial descent, recommended him to the French monarchs; and in the same cities he

Their faults and merits.

102. See in Hody the article of Bessarion (p. 136–177.): Theodore Gaza, George of Trebizond, and the rest of the Greeks whom I have named or omitted, are inserted in their proper chapters of his learned work. See likewise Tiraboschi, in the 1st and 2d parts of the vith tome.

103. The cardinals knocked at his door, but his conclavist refused to interrupt the studies of Bessarion; "Nicholas," said he, "thy respect has cost thee an hat, and me the tiara."

104. Such as George of Trebizond, Theodore Gaza, Argyropulus Andronicus of Thessalonica, Philelphus, Poggius, Blondus, Nicholas Perrot, Valla, Campanus, Platina, &c. Viri (says Hody, with the pious zeal of a scholar) nullo ævo perituri (p. 156.).

105. He was born before the taking of Constantinople, but his honourable life was stretched far into the xvith century (A.D. 1535). Leo X. and Francis I. were his noblest patrons, under whose auspices he founded the Greek colleges of Rome and Paris (Hody, p. 247–275.). He left posterity in France; but the counts de Vintimille, and their numerous branches, derive the name of Lascaris, from a doubtful marriage in the xiiith century with the daughter of a Greek emperor (Ducange, Fam. Byzant. p. 224–230.).

was alternately employed to teach and to negociate. Duty and interest prompted them to cultivate the study of the Latin language; and the most successful attained the faculty of writing and speaking with fluency and elegance in a foreign idiom. But they ever retained the inveterate vanity of their country: their praise, or at least their esteem, was reserved for the national writers, to whom they owed their fame and subsistence; and they sometimes betrayed their contempt in licentious criticism or satire on Virgil's poetry and the oratory of Tully.[106] The superiority of these masters arose from the familiar use of a living language; and their first disciples were incapable of discerning how far they had degenerated from the knowledge, and even the practice, of their ancestors. A vicious pronunciation,[107] which they introduced, was banished from the schools by the reason of the succeeding age. Of the power of the Greek accents they were ignorant: and those musical notes, which, from an Attic tongue, and to an Attic ear, must have been the secret soul of harmony, were to their eyes, as to our own, no more than mute and unmeaning marks; in prose superfluous, and troublesome in verse. The art of grammar they truly possessed: the valuable fragments of Apollonius and Herodian were transfused into their lessons; and their treatises of syntax and etymology, though devoid of philosophic spirit, are still useful to the Greek student. In the shipwreck of the Byzantine libraries, each fugitive seized a fragment of treasure, a copy of some author, who, without his industry, might have perished: the transcripts were multiplied by an assiduous, and sometimes an elegant, pen; and the text was corrected and explained by their own

106. Two of his epigrams against Virgil, and three against Tully, are preserved and refuted by Franciscus Floridus, who can find no better names than Græculus ineptus et impudens (Hody, p. 274.). In our own times, an English critic has accused the Æneid of containing, multa languida, nugatoria, spiritû et majestate carminis heroici defecta; many such verses as he, the said Jeremiah Markland, would have been ashamed of owning (præfat. ad Statii Sylvas, p. 21, 22.).

107. Emanuel Chrysoloras, and his colleagues, are accused of ignorance, envy, or avarice (Sylloge, &c. tom. ii. p. 235.). The modern Greek pronounce the β as a V consonant, and confound three vowels (η ι υ), and several diphthongs. Such was the vulgar pronunciation which the stern Gardiner maintained by penal statutes in the university of Cambridge: but the monosyllable βη represented to an Attic ear the bleating of sheep; and a bell-wether is better evidence than a bishop or a chancellor. The treatises of those scholars, particularly Erasmus, who asserted a more classical pronunciation, are collected in the Sylloge of Havercamp (2 vols. in octavo, Lugd. Bat. 1736, 1740): but it is difficult to paint sounds by words; and in their reference to modern use, they can be understood only by their respective countrymen. We may observe, that our peculiar pronunciation of the θ, *th*, is approved by Erasmus (tom. ii. p. 130.).

comments, or those of the elder scholiasts. The sense, though not the spirit, of the Greek classics, was interpreted to the Latin world: the beauties of style evaporate in a version; but the judgment of Theodore Gaza selected the more solid works of Aristotle and Theophrastus, and their natural histories of animals and plants opened a rich fund of genuine and experimental science.

The Platonic philosophy.

Yet the fleeting shadows of metaphysics were pursued with more curiosity and ardour. After a long oblivion, Plato was revived in Italy by a venerable Greek,[108] who taught in the house of Cosmo of Medicis. While the synod of Florence was involved in theological debate, some beneficial consequences might flow from the study of his elegant philosophy; his style is the purest standard of the Attic dialect; and his sublime thoughts are sometimes adapted to familiar conversation, and sometimes adorned with the richest colours of poetry and eloquence. The dialogues of Plato are a dramatic picture of the life and death of a sage; and, as often as he descends from the clouds, his moral system inculcates the love of truth, of our country, and of mankind. The precept and example of Socrates recommended a modest doubt and liberal enquiry: and if the Platonists, with blind devotion, adored the visions and errors of their divine master, their enthusiasm might correct the dry, dogmatic method of the Peripatetic school. So equal, yet so opposite, are the merits of Plato and Aristotle, that they may be balanced in endless controversy; but some spark of freedom may be produced by the collision of adverse servitude. The modern Greeks were divided between the two sects: with more fury than skill they fought under the banner of their leaders; and the field of battle was removed in their flight from Constantinople to Rome. But this philosophical debate soon degenerated into an angry and personal quarrel of grammarians: and Bessarion, though an advocate for Plato, protected the national honour, by interposing the advice and authority of a mediator. In the gardens of the Medici, the academical doctrine was enjoyed by the polite and learned: but their philosophic society was quickly dissolved; and if the writings of the Attic sage were perused in the closet, the more powerful Stagyrite continued to reign, the oracle of the church and school.[109]

108. George Gemistus Pletho, a various and voluminous writer, the master of Bessarion, and all the Platonists of the times. He visited Italy in his old age, and soon returned to end his days in Peloponnesus. See the curious Diatribe of Leo Allatius de Georgiis, in Fabricius (Bibliot. Græc. tom. x. p. 739–756.).

109. The state of the Platonic philosophy in Italy, is illustrated by Boivin (Mem. de

Emulation and progress of the Latins.

I have fairly represented the literary merits of the Greeks; yet it must be confessed, that they were seconded and surpassed by the ardour of the Latins. Italy was divided into many independent states; and at that time, it was the ambition of princes and republics to vie with each other in the encouragement and reward of literature. The fame of Nicholas the fifth[110] has not been adequate to his merits. From a plebeian origin, he raised himself by his virtue and learning: the character of the man prevailed over the interest of the pope; and he sharpened those weapons which were soon pointed against the Roman church.[111] He had been the friend of the most eminent scholars of the age: he became their patron; and such was the humility of his manners, that the change was scarcely discernible either to them or to himself. If he pressed the acceptance of a liberal gift, it was not as the measure of desert, but as the proof of benevolence; and when modest merit declined his bounty, "accept it," would he say with a consciousness of his own worth; "you will not always have a Nicholas among ye." The influence of the holy see pervaded Christendom; and he exerted that influence in the search, not of benefices, but of books. From the ruins of the Byzantine libraries, from the darkest monasteries of Germany and Britain, he collected the dusty manuscripts of the writers of antiquity; and wherever the original could not be removed, a faithful copy was transcribed and transmitted for his use. The Vatican, the old repository for bulls and legends, for superstition and forgery, was daily replenished with more precious furniture; and such was the industry of Nicholas, that in a reign of eight years, he formed a library of five thousand volumes. To his munificence, the Latin world was indebted for the versions of Xenophon, Diodorus, Polybius, Thucydides, Herodotus, and Appian; of Strabo's geography, of the Iliad, of the most valuable works of Plato and Aristotle, of Ptolemy and Theophrastus, and of the fathers of the Greek church. The example of the Roman pontiff was preceded or imitated by a Florentine merchant, who governed the

Nicholas V. A.D. 1447–1455.

---

l'Acad. des Inscriptions, tom. ii. p. 715–729.) and Tiraboschi (tom. vi. P. i. p. 259–288.).

110. See the life of Nicholas V. by two contemporary authors, Janottus Manettus (tom. iii. P. ii. p. 905–962.) and Vespasian of Florence (tom. xxv. p. 267–290.), in the collection of Muratori; and consult Tiraboschi (tom. vi. P. i. 46–52. 109.) and Hody in the articles of Theodore Gaza, George of Trebizond, &c.

111. Lord Bolingbroke observes, with truth and spirit, that the popes in this instance were worse politicians than the muftis, and that the charm which has bound mankind for so many ages, was broken by the magicians themselves (Letters on the Study of History, l. vi. p. 165, 166. octavo edition, 1779).

Cosmo and Lorenzo of Medicis, A.D. 1428–1492.

republic without arms and without a title. Cosmo of Medicis[112] was the father of a line of princes, whose name and age are almost synonymous with the restoration of learning: his credit was ennobled into fame; his riches were dedicated to the service of mankind; he corresponded at once with Cairo and London: and a cargo of Indian spices and Greek books was often imported in the same vessel. The genius and education of his grandson Lorenzo rendered him, not only a patron, but a judge and candidate, in the literary race. In his palace, distress was entitled to relief, and merit to reward: his leisure hours were delightfully spent in the Platonic academy: he encouraged the emulation of Demetrius Chalcocondyles and Angelo Politian; and his active missionary Janus Lascaris returned from the East with a treasure of two hundred manuscripts, fourscore of which were as yet unknown in the libraries of Europe.[113] The rest of Italy was animated by a similar spirit, and the progress of the nation repaid the liberality of her princes. The Latins held the exclusive property of their own literature: and these disciples of Greece were soon capable of transmitting and improving the lessons which they had imbibed. After a short succession of foreign teachers, the tide of emigration subsided; but the language of Constantinople was spread beyond the Alps; and the natives of France, Germany, and England,[114] imparted to their country the sacred fire which they had kindled in the schools of Florence and Rome.[115] In the

112. See the literary history of Cosmo and Lorenzo of Medicis, in Tiraboschi (tom. vi. P. i. l. i. c. 2.), who bestows a due measure of praise on Alphonso of Arragon, king of Naples, the dukes of Milan, Ferrara, Urbino, &c. The republic of Venice has deserved the least from the gratitude of scholars.

113. Tiraboschi (tom. vi. P. i. p. 104.), from the preface of Janus Lasçaris to the Greek Anthology, printed at Florence 1494. Latebant (says Aldus in his preface to the Greek Orators, apud Hodium, p. 249.) in Atho Thraciæ monte. Eas Lascaris ... in Italiam reportavit. Miserat enim ipsum Laurentius ille Medices in Græciam ad inquirendos simul, et quantovis emendos pretio bonos libros. It is remarkable enough, that the research was facilitated by sultan Bajazet II.

114. The Greek language was introduced into the university of Oxford in the last years of the xv[th] century, by Grocyn, Linacer, and Latimer, who had all studied at Florence under Demetrius Chalcocondyles. See Dr. Knight's curious Life of Erasmus. Although a stout academical patriot, he is forced to acknowledge, that Erasmus learned Greek at Oxford, and taught it at Cambridge.

115. The jealous Italians were desirous of keeping a monopoly of Greek learning. When Aldus was about to publish the Greek scholiasts on Sophocles and Euripides, Cave (said they), cave hoc facias, ne *Barbari* istis adjuti domi maneant, et pauciores in Italiam ventitent (Dr. Knight, in his Life of Erasmus, p. 365. from Beatus Rhenanus).

productions of the mind, as in those of the soil, the gifts of nature are excelled by industry and skill: the Greek authors, forgotten on the banks of the Ilissus, have been illustrated on those of the Elbe and the Thames: and Bessarion or Gaza might have envied the superior science of the Barbarians; the accuracy of Budæus, the taste of Erasmus, the copiousness of Stephens, the erudition of Scaliger, the discernment of Reiske, or of Bentley. On the side of the Latins, the discovery of printing was a casual advantage: but this useful art has been applied by Aldus, and his innumerable successors, to perpetuate and multiply the works of antiquity.[116] A single manuscript imported from Greece is revived in ten thousand copies; and each copy is fairer than the original. In this form, Homer and Plato would peruse with more satisfaction their own writings: and their scholiasts must resign the prize to the labours of our western editors.

Use and abuse of ancient learning.

Before the revival of classic literature, the Barbarians in Europe were immersed in ignorance; and their vulgar tongues were marked with the rudeness and poverty of their manners. The students of the more perfect idioms of Rome and Greece, were introduced to a new world of light and science; to the society of the free and polished nations of antiquity; and to a familiar converse with those immortal men who spoke the sublime language of eloquence and reason. Such an intercourse must tend to refine the taste, and to elevate the genius, of the moderns: and yet, from the first experiment, it might appear that the study of the ancients had given fetters, rather than wings, to the human mind. However laudable, the spirit of imitation is of a servile cast; and the first disciples of the Greeks and Romans were a colony of strangers in the midst of their age and country. The minute and laborious diligence which explored the antiquities of remote times, might have improved or adorned the present state of society: the critic and metaphysician were the slaves of Aristotle; the poets, historians, and orators, were proud to repeat the thoughts and words of the Augustan

116. The press of Aldus Manutius, a Roman, was established at Venice about the year 1494: he printed above sixty considerable works of Greek literature, almost all for the first time; several containing different treatises and authors, and of several authors two, three, or four editions (Fabric. Bibliot. Græc. tom. xiii. p. 605, &c.). Yet his glory must not tempt us to forget, that the first Greek book, the Grammar of Constantine Lascaris, was printed at Milan in 1476; and that the Florence Homer of 1488 displays all the luxury of the typographical art. See the Annales Typographici of Mattaire, and the Bibliographie Instructive of de Bure, a knowing bookseller of Paris.

age; the works of nature were observed with the eyes of Pliny and Theophrastus; and some Pagan votaries professed a secret devotion to the gods of Homer and Plato.[117] The Italians were oppressed by the strength and number of their ancient auxiliaries: the century after the deaths of Petrarch and Boccace was filled with a crowd of Latin imitators, who decently repose on our shelves; but in that æra of learning, it will not be easy to discern a real discovery of science, a work of invention or eloquence, in the popular language of the country.[118] But as soon as it had been deeply saturated with the celestial dew, the soil was quickened into vegetation and life; the modern idioms were refined: the classics of Athens and Rome inspired a pure taste and a generous emulation; and in Italy, as afterwards in France and England, the pleasing reign of poetry and fiction was succeeded by the light of speculative and experimental philosophy. Genius may anticipate the season of maturity; but in the education of a people, as in that of an individual, memory must be exercised, before the powers of reason and fancy can be expanded; nor may the artist hope to equal or surpass, till he has learned to imitate, the works of his predecessors.

117. I will select three singular examples of this classic enthusiasm. 1. At the synod of Florence, Gemistus Pletho said, in familiar conversation to George of Trebizond, that in a short time mankind would unanimously renounce the Gospel and the Koran for a religion similar to that of the Gentiles (Leo Allatius, apud Fabricium, tom. x. p. 751.). 2. Paul II. persecuted the Roman academy, which had been founded by Pomponius Lætus; and the principal members were accused of heresy, impiety, and *paganism* (Tiraboschi, tom. vi. P. i. p. 81, 82.). 3. In the next century, some scholars and poets in France celebrated the success of Jodelle's tragedy of Cleopatra, by a festival of Bacchus, and as it is said, by the sacrifice of a goat (Bayle, Dictionaire, JODELLE. Fontenelle, tom. iii. p. 56–61.). Yet the spirit of bigotry might often discern a serious impiety in the sportive play of fancy and learning.

118. The survivor Boccace died in the year 1375; and we cannot place before 1480, the composition of the Morgante Maggiore of Pulci, and the Orlando Inamorato of Boyardo (Tiraboschi, tom. vi. P. ii. p. 174–177.).

CHAPTER LXVII

Schism of the Greeks and Latins. – Reign and Character of Amurath the Second. – Crusade of Ladislaus King of Hungary. – His Defeat and Death. – John Huniades. – Scanderbeg. – Constantine Palæologus last Emperor of the East.

Comparison of Rome and Constantinople. The respective merits of Rome and Constantinople are compared and celebrated by an eloquent Greek the father of the Italian schools.[1] The view of the ancient capital, the seat of his ancestors, surpassed the most sanguine expectations of Emanuel Chrysoloras; and he no longer blamed the exclamation of an old sophist, that Rome was the habitation, not of men, but of gods. Those gods, and those men, had long since vanished; but, to the eye of liberal enthusiasm, the majesty of ruin restored the image of her ancient prosperity. The monuments of the consuls and Cæsars, of the martyrs and apostles, engaged on all sides the curiosity of the philosopher and the Christian; and he confessed, that in every age the arms and the religion of Rome were destined to reign over the earth. While Chrysoloras admired the venerable beauties of the mother, he was not forgetful of his native, country, her fairest daughter, her Imperial colony; and the Byzantine patriot expatiates with zeal and truth, on the eternal advantages of nature, and the more transitory glories of art and dominion, which adorned, or had adorned, the city of Constantine. Yet the perfection of the copy still redounds (as he modestly observes) to the honour of the original, and parents are delighted to be renewed, and even excelled, by the superior merit of their children. "Constantinople," says the orator, "is situate on a commanding point, between Europe and Asia, between the Archipelago

1. The epistle of Manuel Chrysoloras to the emperor John Palæologus, will not offend the eye or ear of a classical student (ad calcem Codini de Antiquitatibus C. P. p. 107–126.). The superscription suggests a chronological remark, that John Palæologus II. was associated in the empire before the year 1414, the date of Chrysoloras's death. A still earlier date, at least 1408, is deduced from the age of his youngest sons, Demetrius and Thomas, who were both *Porphyrogeniti* (Ducange, Fam. Byzant. p. 244. 247.).

and the Euxine. By her interposition, the two seas, and the two continents, are united for the common benefit of nations; and the gates of commerce may be shut or opened at her command. The harbour, encompassed on all sides by the sea and the continent, is the most secure and capacious in the world. The walls and gates of Constantinople may be compared with those of Babylon: the towers are many; each tower is a solid and lofty structure; and the second wall, the outer fortification, would be sufficient for the defence and dignity of an ordinary capital. A broad and rapid stream may be introduced into the ditches; and the artificial island may be encompassed, like Athens,[2] by land or water." Two strong and natural causes are alleged for the perfection of the model of new Rome. The royal founder reigned over the most illustrious nations of the globe; and in the accomplishment of his designs, the power of the Romans was combined with the art and science of the Greeks. Other cities have been reared to maturity by accident and time; their beauties are mingled with disorder and deformity; and the inhabitants, unwilling to remove from their natal spot, are incapable of correcting the errors of their ancestors, and the original vices of situation or climate. But the free idea of Constantinople was formed and executed by a single mind; and the primitive model was improved by the obedient zeal of the subjects and successors of the first monarch. The adjacent isles were stored with an inexhaustible supply of marble; but the various materials were transported from the most remote shores of Europe and Asia; and the public and private buildings, the palaces, churches, aqueducts, cisterns, porticoes, columns, baths, and hippodromes, were adapted to the greatness of the capital of the East. The superfluity of wealth was spread along the shores of Europe and Asia; and the Byzantine territory, as far as the Euxine, the Hellespont, and the long wall, might be considered as a populous suburb and a perpetual garden. In this flattering picture, the past and the present, the times of prosperity and decay, are artfully confounded; but a sigh and a confession escape from the orator, that his wretched country was the shadow and sepulchre of its former self. The works of ancient sculpture had been defaced by Christian zeal or Barbaric violence; the fairest structures were demolished; and the marbles of Paros or Numidia were burnt for lime, or applied to the meanest uses. Of many

2. Somebody observed, that the city of Athens might be circumnavigated (*τις ειπεν την πολιν των Αθηναιων δυνασθαι και παραπλειν και περιπλειν*). But what may be true in a rhetorical sense of Constantinople, cannot be applied to the situation of Athens, five miles from the sea, and not intersected or surrounded by any navigable streams.

a statue, the place was marked by an empty pedestal; of many a column, the size was determined by a broken capital; the tombs of the emperors were scattered on the ground; the stroke of time was accelerated by storms and earthquakes; and the vacant space was adorned, by vulgar tradition, with fabulous monuments of gold and silver. From these wonders, which lived only in memory or belief, he distinguishes however the porphyry pillar, the column and colossus of Justinian,[3] and the church, more especially the dome, of St. Sophia; the best conclusion, since it could not be described according to its merits, and after it no other object could deserve to be mentioned. But he forgets, that a century before, the trembling fabrics of the colossus and the church had been saved and supported by the timely care of Andronicus the elder. Thirty years after the emperor had fortified St. Sophia with two new buttresses or pyramids, the eastern hemisphere suddenly gave way; and the images, the altars, and the sanctuary, were crushed by the falling ruin. The mischief indeed was speedily repaired; the rubbish was cleared by the incessant labour of every rank and age; and the poor remains of riches and industry were consecrated by the Greeks to the most stately and venerable temple of the East.[4]

The Greek schism after the council of Florence, A.D. 1440–1448.

The last hope of the falling city and empire was placed in the harmony of the mother and daughter, in the maternal tenderness of Rome, and the filial obedience of Constantinople. In the synod of Florence, the Greeks and Latins had embraced, and subscribed, and promised; but these signs of friendship were perfidious or fruitless;[5] and the baseless fabric of the union vanished like a dream.[6] The emperor and his prelates returned home in

3. Nicephorus Gregoras has described the colossus of Justinian (l. vii. 12.): but his measures are false and inconsistent. The editor Boivin consulted his friend Girardon; and the sculptor gave him the true proportions of an equestrian statue. That of Justinian was still visible to Peter Gyllius, not on the column, but in the outward court of the seraglio; and he was at Constantinople when it was melted down, and cast into a brass cannon (de Topograph. C. P. l. ii. c. 17.).

4. See the decay and repairs of St. Sophia, in Nicephorus Gregoras (l. vii. 12. l. xv. 2.). The building was propped by Andronicus in 1317, the eastern hemisphere fell in 1345. The Greeks, in their pompous rhetoric, exalt the beauty and holiness of the church, an earthly heaven, the abode of angels, and of God himself, &c.

5. The genuine and original narrative of Syropulus (p. 312–351.) opens the schism from the first *office* of the Greeks at Venice, to the general opposition at Constantinople of the clergy and people.

6. On the schism of Constantinople, see Phranza (l. ii. c. 17.), Laonicus Chalcondyles (l. vi. p. 155, 156.), and Ducas (c. 31.); the last of whom writes with truth and freedom. Among the moderns we may distinguish the continuator of Fleury (tom. xxii. p. 338, &c. 401. 420, &c.), and Spon-

the Venetian gallies; but as they touched at the Morea and the isles of Corfu and Lesbos, the subjects of the Latins complained that the pretended union would be an instrument of oppression. No sooner did they land on the Byzantine shore than they were saluted, or rather assailed, with a general murmur of zeal and discontent. During their absence, above two years, the capital had been deprived of its civil and ecclesiastical rulers: fanaticism fermented in anarchy; the most furious monks reigned over the conscience of women and bigots; and the hatred of the Latin name was the first principle of nature and religion. Before his departure for Italy, the emperor had flattered the city with the assurance of a prompt relief and a powerful succour; and the clergy, confident in their orthodoxy and science, had promised themselves and their flocks an easy victory over the blind shepherds of the West. The double disappointment exasperated the Greeks; the conscience of the subscribing prelates was awakened; the hour of temptation was past; and they had more to dread from the public resentment, than they could hope from the favour of the emperor or the pope. Instead of justifying their conduct, they deplored their weakness, professed their contrition, and cast themselves on the mercy of God and of their brethren. To the reproachful question, what had been the event or the use of their Italian synod? they answered with sighs and tears, "Alas! we have made a new faith; we have exchanged piety for impiety; we have betrayed the immaculate sacrifice; and we are become *Azymites*." (The Azymites were those who celebrated the communion with unleavened bread; and I must retract or qualify the praise which I have bestowed on the growing philosophy of the times.) "Alas! we have been seduced by distress, by fraud, and by the hopes and fears of a transitory life. The hand that has signed the union should be cut off; and the tongue that has pronounced the Latin creed deserves to be torn from the root." The best proof of their repentance was an encrease of zeal for the most trivial rites and the most incomprehensible doctrines; and an absolute separation from all, without excepting their prince, who preserved some regard for honour and consistency. After the decease of the patriarch Joseph, the archbishops of Heraclea and Trebizond had courage to refuse the vacant office; and cardinal Bessarion preferred the warm and comfortable shelter of the Vatican. The choice of the emperor and his clergy was confined to Metrophanes of Cyzicus: he was consecrated in St. Sophia, but the temple was vacant. The cross-

danus (A.D. 1440–50.). The sense of the latter is drowned in prejudice and passion, as soon as Rome and religion are concerned.

bearers abdicated their service; the infection spread from the city to the villages; and Metrophanes discharged, without effect, some ecclesiastical thunders against a nation of schismatics. The eyes of the Greeks were directed to Mark of Ephesus, the champion of his country; and the sufferings of the holy confessor were repaid with a tribute of admiration and applause. His example and writings propagated the flame of religious discord; age and infirmity soon removed him from the world; but the gospel of Mark was not a law of forgiveness; and he requested with his dying breath, that none of the adherents of Rome might attend his obsequies or pray for his soul.

Zeal of the Orientals and Russians.

The schism was not confined to the narrow limits of the Byzantine empire. Secure under the Mamaluke sceptre, the three patriarchs of Alexandria, Antioch, and Jerusalem, assembled a numerous synod; disowned their representatives at Ferrara and Florence; condemned the creed and council of the Latins; and threatened the emperor of Constantinople with the censures of the Eastern church. Of the sectaries of the Greek communion, the Russians were the most powerful, ignorant, and superstitious. Their primate, the cardinal Isidore, hastened from Florence to Moscow,[7] to reduce the independent nation under the Roman yoke. But the Russian bishops had been educated at mount Athos; and the prince and people embraced the theology of their priests. They were scandalised by the title, the pomp, the Latin cross of the legate, the friend of those impious men who shaved their beards, and performed the divine office with gloves on their hands and rings on their fingers: Isidore was condemned by a synod; his person was imprisoned in a monastery; and it was with extreme difficulty, that the cardinal could escape from the hands of a fierce and fanatic people.[8] The Russians refused a passage to the missionaries of Rome who aspired to convert the Pagans beyond the Tanais;[9] and their refusal

7. Isidore was metropolitan of Kiow, but the Greeks subject to Poland have removed that see from the ruins of Kiow to Lemberg, or Leopold (Herbestein, in Ramusio, tom. ii. p. 127.). On the other hand, the Russians transferred their spiritual obedience to the archbishop, who became, in 1588, the patriarch, of Moscow (Levesque, Hist. de Russie, tom. iii. p. 188. 190. from a Greek MS. at Turin, Iter et labores Archiepiscopi Arsenii).

8. The curious narrative of Levesque (Hist. de Russie, tom. ii. p. 242–247.) is extracted from the patriarchal archives. The scenes of Ferrara and Florence are described by ignorance and passion; but the Russians are credible in the account of their own prejudices.

9. The Shamanism, the ancient religion of the Samanæans and Gymnosophists, has been driven by the more popular Bramins from India into the northern deserts; the naked philosophers were compelled to wrap themselves in fur; but they insensibly

was justified by the maxim, that the guilt of idolatry is less damnable than that of schism. The errors of the Bohemians were excused by their abhorrence for the pope; and a deputation of the Greek clergy solicited the friendship of those sanguinary enthusiasts.[10] While Eugenius triumphed in the union and orthodoxy of the Greeks, his party was contracted to the walls, or rather to the palace, of Constantinople. The zeal of Palæologus had been excited by interest; it was soon cooled by opposition: an attempt to violate the national belief might endanger his life and crown; nor could the pious rebels be destitute of foreign and domestic aid. The sword of his brother Demetrius, who in Italy had maintained a prudent and popular silence, was half unsheathed in the cause of religion; and Amurath, the Turkish sultan, was displeased and alarmed by the seeming friendship of the Greeks and Latins.

Reign and character of Amurath II. A.D. 1421–1451, February 9.

"Sultan Murad or Amurath, lived forty-nine, and reigned thirty years, six months and eight days. He was a just and valiant prince, of a great soul, patient of labours, learned, merciful, religious, charitable; a lover and encourager of the studious, and of all who excelled in any art or science; a good emperor, and a great general. No man obtained more or greater victories than Amurath: Belgrade alone withstood his attacks. Under his reign, the soldier was ever victorious, the citizen rich and secure. If he subdued any country, his first care was to build moschs and caravanseras, hospitals, and colleges. Every year he gave a thousand pieces of gold to the sons of the prophet; and sent two thousand five hundred to the religious persons of Mecca, Medina, and Jerusalem."[11] This portrait is transcribed from the historian of the Othman empire: but the applause of a servile and superstitious people has been lavished on the worst of tyrants; and the virtues of a sultan are often the vices most useful to himself, or most agreeable to his subjects. A nation ignorant of the equal benefits of liberty

---

sunk into wizards and physicians. The Mordvans and Tcheremisses in the European Russia adhere to this religion, which is formed on the earthly model of one king or God, his ministers or angels, and the rebellious spirits who oppose his government. As these tribes of the Volga have no images, they might more justly retort on the Latin missionaries the name of idolaters (Levesque, Hist. des Peuples soumis à la Domination des Russes, tom. i. p. 194–237. 423–460.).

10. Spondanus, Annal. Eccles. tom. ii. A.D. 1451, N° 13. The Epistle of the Greeks, with a Latin version, is extant in the college library at Prague.

11. See Cantemir, History of the Othman Empire, p. 94. Murad, or Morad, may be more correct: but I have preferred the popular name, to that obscure diligence which is rarely successful in translating an Oriental, into the Roman, alphabet.

and law, must be awed by the flashes of arbitrary power: the cruelty of a despot will assume the character of justice; his profusion, of liberality; his obstinacy, of firmness. If the most reasonable excuse be rejected, few acts of obedience will be found impossible; and guilt must tremble, where innocence cannot always be secure. The tranquillity of the people, and the discipline of the troops, were best maintained by perpetual action in the field; war was the trade of the Janizaries: and those who survived the peril, and divided the spoil, applauded the generous ambition of their sovereign. To propagate the true religion, was the duty of a faithful Musulman: the unbelievers were *his* enemies, and those of the prophet; and, in the hands of the Turks, the scymetar was the only instrument of conversion. Under these circumstances, however, the justice and moderation of Amurath are attested by his conduct, and acknowledged by the Christians themselves; who consider a prosperous reign and a peaceful death as the reward of his singular merits. In the vigour of his age and military power, he seldom engaged in war till he was justified by a previous and adequate provocation: the victorious sultan was disarmed by submission; and in the observance of treaties, his word was inviolate and sacred.[12] The Hungarians were commonly the aggressors; he was provoked by the revolt of Scanderbeg; and the perfidious Caramanian was twice vanquished, and twice pardoned, by the Ottoman monarch. Before he invaded the Morea, Thebes had been surprised by the despot: in the conquest of Thessalonica, the grandson of Bajazet might dispute the recent purchase of the Venetians; and after the first siege of Constantinople, the sultan was never tempted, by the distress, the absence, or the injuries of Palæologus, to extinguish the dying light of the Byzantine empire.

His double abdication, A.D. 1442–1444.

But the most striking feature in the life and character of Amurath, is the double abdication of the Turkish throne; and, were not his motives debased by an alloy of superstition, we must praise the royal philosopher,[13] who at the age of forty could discern the vanity of human greatness. Resigning the sceptre to his son, he retired to the pleasant residence of Magnesia; but he retired to the society of saints and hermits. It was not till the fourth century of the

12. See Chalcondyles (l. vii. p. 186. 198.), Ducas (c. 33.), and Marinus Barletius (in Vit. Scanderbeg, p. 145, 146.). In his good faith towards the garrison of Sfetigrade, he was a lesson and example to his son Mahomet.

13. Voltaire (Essai sur l'Histoire Generale, c. 89. p. 283, 284.) admires *le Philosophe Turc*; would he have bestowed the same praise on a Christian prince for retiring to a monastery? In his way, Voltaire was a bigot, an intolerant bigot.

Hegira, that the religion of Mahomet had been corrupted by an institution so adverse to his genius; but in the age of the crusades, the various orders of Dervishes were multiplied by the example of the Christian, and even the Latin, monks.[14] The lord of nations submitted to fast, and pray, and turn round in endless rotation with the fanatics, who mistook the giddiness of the head for the illumination of the spirit.[15] But he was soon awakened from this dream of enthusiasm, by the Hungarian invasion; and his obedient son was the foremost to urge the public danger and the wishes of the people. Under the banner of their veteran leader, the Janizaries fought and conquered; but he withdrew from the field of Varna, again to pray, to fast, and to turn round with his Magnesian brethren. These pious occupations were again interrupted by the danger of the state. A victorious army disdained the inexperience of their youthful ruler: the city of Adrianople was abandoned to rapine and slaughter; and the unanimous divan implored his presence to appease the tumult, and prevent the rebellion, of the Janizaries. At the well-known voice of their master, they trembled and obeyed; and the reluctant sultan was compelled to support his splendid servitude, till, at the end of four years, he was relieved by the angel of death. Age or disease, misfortune or caprice, have tempted several princes to descend from the throne; and they have had leisure to repent of their irretrievable step. But Amurath alone, in the full liberty of choice, after the trial of empire and solitude, has *repeated* his preference of a private life.

Eugenius forms a league against the Turks, A.D. 1443.

After the departure of his Greek brethren, Eugenius had not been unmindful of their temporal interest; and his tender regard for the Byzantine empire was animated by a just apprehension of the Turks, who approached, and might soon invade, the borders of Italy. But the spirit of the crusades had expired; and the coldness of the Franks was not less unreasonable than their headlong passion. In the eleventh century, a fanatic monk could precipitate Europe on Asia for the recovery of the holy sepulchre; but in the fifteenth, the most pressing motives of religion and policy were

14. See the articles *Dervische, Fakir, Nasser, Rohbaniat*, in d'Herbelot's Bibliotheque Orientale. Yet the subject is superficially treated from the Persian and Arabian writers. It is among the Turks that these orders have principally flourished.

15. Rycaut (in the present State of the Ottoman Empire, p. 242–268.) affords much information, which he drew from his personal conversation with the heads of the dervishes, most of whom ascribed their origin to the time of Orchan. He does not mention the *Zichidæ* of Chalcondyles (l. vii. p. 286.), among whom Amurath retired: the *Seids* of that author are the descendants of Mahomet.

insufficient to unite the Latins in the defence of Christendom. Germany was an inexhaustible store-house of men and arms:[16] but that complex and languid body required the impulse of a vigorous hand; and Frederic the third was alike impotent in his personal character and his Imperial dignity. A long war had impaired the strength, without satiating the animosity of France and England:[17] but Philip, duke of Burgundy, was a vain and magnificent prince; and he enjoyed, without danger or expence, the adventurous piety of his subjects, who sailed, in a gallant fleet, from the coast of Flanders to the Hellespont. The maritime republics of Venice and Genoa were less remote from the scene of action; and their hostile fleets were associated under the standard of St. Peter. The kingdoms of Hungary and Poland, which covered as it were the interior pale of the Latin church, were the most nearly concerned to oppose the progress of the Turks. Arms were the patrimony of the Scythians and Sarmatians, and these nations might appear equal to the contest, could they point, against the common foe, those swords that were so wantonly drawn in bloody and domestic quarrels. But the same spirit was adverse to concord and obedience: a poor country and a limited monarch are incapable of maintaining a standing force; and the loose bodies of Polish and Hungarian horse were not armed with the sentiments and weapons which, on some occasions, have given irresistible weight to the French chivalry. Yet, on this side, the designs of the Roman pontiff, and the eloquence of cardinal Julian, his legate, were promoted by the circumstances of the times;[18] by the union of the two crowns on the head of Ladislaus,[19] a

16. In the year 1431, Germany raised 40,000 horse, men at arms, against the Hussites of Bohemia (Lenfant, Hist. du Concile de Basle, tom. i. p. 318.). At the siege of Nuys on the Rhine in 1474, the princes, prelates, and cities, sent their respective quotas: and the bishop of Munster (qui n'est pas des plus grands) furnished 1400 horse, 6000 foot, all in green, with 1200 waggons. The united armies of the king of England and the duke of Burgundy scarcely equalled one-third of this German host (Memoires de Philippe de Comines, l. iv. c. 2.). At present, six or seven hundred thousand men are maintained in constant pay and admirable discipline, by the powers of Germany.

17. It was not till the year 1444, that France and England could agree on a truce of some months (See Rymer's Fœdera, and the chronicles of both nations).

18. In the Hungarian crusade, Spondanus (Annal. Eccles. A.D. 1443, 1444.) has been my leading guide. He has diligently read, and critically compared, the Greek and Turkish materials, the historians of Hungary, Poland, and the West. His narrative is perspicuous; and where he can be free from a religious bias, the judgment of Spondanus is not contemptible.

19. I have curtailed the harsh letter (Wladislaus) which most writers affix to his name, either in compliance with the Polish pronunciation, or to distinguish him from his rival the infant Ladislaus of Austria. Their competition for the crown of Hungary is described by Callimachus (l. i, ii. p. 447–486.), Bonfinius (Decad. iii. l. iv.), Spondanus, and Lenfant.

young and ambitious soldier; by the valour of an hero, whose name, the name of John Huniades, was already popular among the Christians, and formidable to the Turks. An endless treasure of pardons and indulgences was scattered by the legate; many private warriors of France and Germany enlisted under the holy banner; and the crusade derived some strength, or at least some reputation, from the new allies, both of Europe and Asia. A fugitive despot of Servia exaggerated the distress and ardour of the Christians beyond the Danube, who would unanimously rise to vindicate their religion and liberty. The Greek emperor,[20] with a spirit unknown to his fathers, engaged to guard the Bosphorus, and to sally from Constantinople at the head of his national and mercenary troops. The sultan of Caramania[21] announced the retreat of Amurath, and a powerful diversion in the heart of Anatolia; and if the fleets of the West could occupy at the same moment the streights of the Hellespont, the Ottoman monarchy would be dissevered and destroyed. Heaven and earth must rejoice in the perdition of the miscreants; and the legate, with prudent ambiguity, instilled the opinion of the invisible, perhaps the visible, aid, of the Son of God, and his divine Mother.

Ladislaus, king of Poland and Hungary, marches against them.

Of the Polish and Hungarian diets, a religious war was the unanimous cry; and Ladislaus, after passing the Danube, led an army of his confederate subjects as far as Sophia, the capital of the Bulgarian kingdom. In this expedition they obtained two signal victories, which were justly ascribed to the valour and conduct of Huniades. In the first, with a vanguard of ten thousand men, he surprised the Turkish camp; in the second, he vanquished and made prisoner the most renowned of their generals, who possessed the double advantage of ground and numbers. The approach of winter, and the natural and artificial obstacles of mount Hæmus, arrested the progress of the hero, who measured a narrow interval of six days march from the foot of the mountains to the hostile towers of Adrianople, and the friendly capital of the Greek empire. The retreat was undisturbed; and the entrance into Buda was at once a military and religious triumph. An ecclesiastical procession was followed by the king and his warriors on

20. The Greek historians, Phranza, Chalcondyles, and Ducas, do not ascribe to their prince a very active part in this crusade, which he seems to have promoted by his wishes, and injured by his fears.

21. Cantemir (p. 88.) acribes to his policy the original plan, and transcribes his animating epistle to the king of Hungary. But the Mahometan powers are seldom informed of the state of Christendom; and the situation and correspondence of the knights of Rhodes must connect them with the sultan of Caramania.

foot: he nicely balanced the merits and rewards of the two nations; and the pride of conquest was blended with the humble temper of Christianity. Thirteen bashaws, nine standards, and four thousand captives, were unquestionable trophies; and as all were willing to believe, and none were present to contradict, the crusaders multiplied, with unblushing confidence, the myriads of Turks whom they had left on the field of battle.[22] The most solid proof, and the most salutary consequence, of victory, was a deputation from the divan to solicit peace, to restore Servia, to ransom the prisoners, and to evacuate the Hungarian frontier. By this treaty, the rational objects of the war were obtained: the king, the despot, and Huniades himself, in the diet of Segedin, were satisfied with public and private emolument; a truce of ten years was concluded; and the followers of Jesus and Mahomet, who swore on the Gospel and the Koran, attested the word of God as the guardian of truth and the avenger of perfidy. In the place of the Gospel, the Turkish ministers had proposed to substitute the Eucharist, the real presence of the Catholic deity; but the Christians refused to profane their holy mysteries; and a superstitious conscience is less forcibly bound by the spiritual energy, than by the outward and visible symbols, of an oath.[23]

The Turkish peace.

Violation of the peace, A.D. 1444.

During the whole transaction, the cardinal legate had observed a sullen silence, unwilling to approve, and unable to oppose, the consent of the king and people. But the diet was not dissolved before Julian was fortified by the welcome intelligence, that Anatolia was invaded by the Caramanian, and Thrace by the Greek emperor; that the fleets of Genoa, Venice, and Burgundy, were masters of the Hellespont; and that the allies, informed of the victory, and ignorant of the treaty, of Ladislaus, impatiently waited for the return of his victorious army. "And is it thus," exclaimed the cardinal,[24] "that you

22. In their letters to the emperor Frederic III. the Hungarians slay 30,000 Turks in one battle; but the modest Julian reduces the slaughter to 6000, or even 2000 infidels (Æneas Sylvius in Europ. c. 5. and epist. 44. 81. apud Spondanum).

23. See the origin of the Turkish war, and the first expedition of Ladislaus, in the vth and vith books of the iii^{d} Decad of Bonfinius, who, in his division and style, copies Livy with tolerable success. Callimachus (l. ii. p. 487–496) is still more pure and authentic.

24. I do not pretend to warrant the literal accuracy of Julian's speech, which is variously worded by Callimachus (l. iii. p. 505–507.), Bonfinius (Dec. iii. l. vi. p. 457, 458.), and other historians, who might indulge their own eloquence, while they represent one of the orators of the age. But they all agree in the advice and arguments for perjury, which in the field of controversy are fiercely attacked by the Protestants, and feebly defended by the Catholics. The latter are discouraged by the misfortune of Warna.

will desert their expectations and your own fortune? It is to them, to your God, and your fellow-Christians, that you have pledged your faith; and that prior obligation annihilates a rash and sacrilegious oath to the enemies of Christ. His vicar on earth is the Roman pontiff; without whose sanction you can neither promise nor perform. In his name I absolve your perjury and sanctify your arms: follow my footsteps in the paths of glory and salvation; and if still ye have scruples, devolve on my head the punishment and the sin." This mischievous casuistry was seconded by his respectable character, and the levity of popular assemblies: war was resolved, on the same spot where peace had so lately been sworn; and, in the execution of the treaty, the Turks were assaulted by the Christians; to whom, with some reason, they might apply the epithet of infidels. The falsehood of Ladislaus to his word and oath, was palliated by the religion of the times: the most perfect, or at least the most popular, excuse would have been the success of his arms and the deliverance of the Eastern church. But the same treaty which should have bound his conscience, had diminished his strength. On the proclamation of the peace, the French and German volunteers departed with indignant murmurs: the Poles were exhausted by distant warfare, and perhaps disgusted with foreign command; and their palatines accepted the first licence, and hastily retired to their provinces and castles. Even Hungary was divided by faction, or restrained by a laudable scruple; and the relics of the crusade that marched in the second expedition, were reduced to an inadequate force of twenty thousand men. A Walachian chief, who joined the royal standard with his vassals, presumed to remark that their numbers did not exceed the hunting retinue that sometimes attended the sultan; and the gift of two horses of matchless speed, might admonish Ladislaus of his secret foresight of the event. But the despot of Servia, after the restoration of his country and children, was tempted by the promise of new realms; and the inexperience of the king, the enthusiasm of the legate, and the martial presumption of Huniades himself, were persuaded that every obstacle must yield to the invincible virtue of the sword and the cross. After the passage of the Danube, two roads might lead to Constantinople and the Hellespont; the one direct, abrupt, and difficult, through the mountains of Hæmus; the other more tedious and secure, over a level country, and along the shores of the Euxine; in which their flanks, according to the Scythian discipline, might always be covered by a moveable fortification of waggons. The latter was judiciously preferred: the Catholics marched through the plains of Bulgaria, burning, with wanton cruelty, the churches and villages of the Christian natives;

and their last station was at Warna, near the sea-shore; on which the defeat and death of Ladislaus have bestowed a memorable name.[25]

Battle of Warna, A.D. 1444, Nov. 10.

It was on this fatal spot, that, instead of finding a confederate fleet to second their operations, they were alarmed by the approach of Amurath himself, who had issued from his Magnesian solitude, and transported the forces of Asia to the defence of Europe. According to some writers, the Greek emperor had been awed, or seduced, to grant the passage of the Bosphorus; and an indelible stain of corruption is fixed on the Genoese, or the pope's nephew, the Catholic admiral, whose mercenary connivance betrayed the guard of the Hellespont. From Adrianople, the sultan advanced by hasty marches, at the head of sixty thousand men; and when the cardinal, and Huniades, had taken a nearer survey of the numbers and order of the Turks, these ardent warriors proposed the tardy and impracticable measure of a retreat. The king alone was resolved to conquer or die; and his resolution had almost been crowned with a glorious and salutary victory. The princes were opposite to each other in the centre; and the Beglerbegs, or generals of Anatolia and Romania, commanded on the right and left against the adverse divisions of the despot and Huniades. The Turkish wings were broken on the first onset: but the advantage was fatal; and the rash victors, in the heat of the pursuit, were carried away far from the annoyance of the enemy or the support of their friends. When Amurath beheld the flight of his squadrons, he despaired of his fortune and that of the empire: a veteran Janizary seized his horse's bridle; and he had magnanimity to pardon and reward the soldier who dared to perceive the terror, and arrest the flight, of his sovereign. A copy of the treaty, the monument of Christian perfidy, had been displayed in the front of battle; and it is said, that the sultan in his distress, lifting his eyes and his hands to heaven, implored the protection of the God of truth; and called on the prophet Jesus himself to avenge the impious mockery of his name and religion.[26] With inferior numbers and disordered ranks, the king of Hungary rushed

25. Warna, under the Grecian name of Odessus, was a colony of the Milesians, which they denominated from the hero Ulysses (Cellarius, tom. i. p. 374. d'Anville, tom. i. p. 312.). According to Arrian's Periplus of the Euxine (p. 24, 25. in the 1st volume of Hudson's Geographers), it was situate 1740 stadia, or furlongs, from the mouth of the Danube, 2140 from Byzantium, and 360 to the north of a ridge or promontory of mount Hæmus, which advances into the sea.

26. Some Christian writers affirm, that he drew from his bosom the host or wafer on which the treaty had *not* been sworn. The Moslems suppose, with more simplicity, an appeal to God and his prophet Jesus, which is likewise insinuated by Callimachus (l. iii. p. 516. Spondan. A.D. 1444, N° 8.).

forwards in the confidence of victory, till his career was stopped by the impenetrable phalanx of the Janizaries. If we may credit the Ottoman annals, his horse was pierced by the javelin of Amurath;[27] he fell among the spears of the infantry; and a Turkish soldier proclaimed with a loud voice, "Hungarians, behold the head of your king!" The death of Ladislaus was the signal of their defeat. On his return from an intemperate pursuit, Huniades deplored his error and the public loss: he strove to rescue the royal body, till he was overwhelmed by the tumultuous crowd of the victors and vanquished; and the last efforts of his courage and conduct were exerted to save the remnant of his Walachian cavalry. Ten thousand Christians were slain in the disastrous battle of Warna: the loss of the Turks, more considerable in numbers, bore a smaller proportion to their total strength; yet the philosophic sultan was not ashamed to confess, that his ruin must be the consequence of a second and similar victory. At his command a column was erected on the spot where Ladislaus had fallen; but the modest inscription, instead of accusing the rashness, recorded the valour, and bewailed the misfortune, of the Hungarian youth.[28]

Death of Ladislaus.

Before I lose sight of the field of Warna, I am tempted to pause on the character and story of two principal actors, the cardinal Julian and John Huniades. Julian[29] Cæsarini was born of a noble family of Rome: his studies had embraced both the Latin and Greek learning, both the sciences of divinity and law; and his versatile genius was equally adapted to the schools, the camp, and the court. No sooner had he been invested with the Roman purple, than he was sent into

The cardinal Julian.

27. A critic will always distrust these *spolia opima* of a victorious general, so difficult for valour to obtain, so easy for flattery to invent (Cantemir, p. 90, 91.). Callimachus (l. iii. p. 517.) more simply and probably affirms, supervenientibus Janizaris, telorum multitudine, non tam confossus est, quam obrutus.

28. Besides some valuable hints from Æneas Sylvius, which are diligently collected by Spondanus, our best authorities are three historians of the xv[th] century, Philippus Callimachus (de Rebus a Vladislao Polonorum atque Hungarorum Rege gestis, libri iii. in Bel. Script. Rerum Hungaricarum, tom. i. p. 433–518.), Bonfinius (decad iii. l. v. p. 460–467.), and Chalcocondyles (l. vii. p. 165–179.). The two first were Italians, but they passed their lives in Poland and Hungary (Fabric. Bibliot. Latin. med. et infimæ Ætatis, tom. i. p. 324. Vossius de Hist. Latin. l. iii. c. 8. 11. Bayle, Dictionnaire, BONFINIUS). A small tract of Fælix Petancius, chancellor of Segnia (ad calcem Cuspinian. de Cæsaribus, p. 716–722.), represents the theatre of the war in the xv[th] century.

29. M. Lenfant has described the origin (Hist. du Concile de Basle, tom. i. p. 247, &c.), and Bohemian campaign (p. 315, &c.), of cardinal Julian. His services at Basil and Ferrara, and his unfortunate end, are occasionally related by Spondanus, and the continuator of Fleury.

Germany to arm the empire against the rebels and heretics of Bohemia. The spirit of persecution is unworthy of a Christian; the military profession ill becomes a priest; but the former is excused by the times; and the latter was ennobled by the courage of Julian, who stood dauntless and alone in the disgraceful flight of the German host. As the pope's legate, he opened the council of Basil; but the president soon appeared the most strenuous champion of ecclesiastical freedom; and an opposition of seven years was conducted by his ability and zeal. After promoting the strongest measures against the authority and person of Eugenius, some secret motive of interest or conscience engaged him to desert on a sudden the popular party. The cardinal withdrew himself from Basil to Ferrara; and, in the debates of the Greeks and Latins, the two nations admired the dexterity of his arguments and the depth of his theological erudition.[30] In his Hungarian embassy we have already seen the mischievous effects of his sophistry and eloquence, of which Julian himself was the first victim. The cardinal, who performed the duties of a priest and a soldier, was lost in the defeat of Warna. The circumstances of his death are variously related; but it is believed, that a weighty incumbrance of gold impeded his flight, and tempted the cruel avarice of some Christian fugitives.

John Corvinus Huniades.

From an humble, or at least a doubtful origin, the merit of John Huniades promoted him to the command of the Hungarian armies. His father was a Walachian, his mother a Greek; her unknown race might possibly ascend to the emperors of Constantinople; and the claims of the Walachians, with the surname of Corvinus, from the place of his nativity, might suggest a thin pretence for mingling his blood with the patricians of ancient Rome.[31] In his youth he served in the wars of Italy; and was retained, with twelve horsemen, by the bishop of Zagrab: the valour of the *white knight*[32] was soon conspicuous; he encreased his fortunes by a noble and wealthy marriage; and in the defence of the Hungarian borders, he won in the same year three battles against the Turks. By his influence, Ladislaus of Poland obtained the

30. Syropulus honourably praises the talents of an enemy (p. 117.): *τοιαυτα τινα ειπεν ὁ Ιουλιανος, πεπλατυσμενως αγαν και λογικως, και μετ' επιστημης και δεινοτητος ῾Ρητορικης.*

31. See Bonfinius, decad iii. l. iv. p. 423. Could the Italian historian pronounce, or the king of Hungary hear, without a blush, the absurd flattery, which confounded the name of a Walachian village with the casual, though glorious, epithet of a single branch of the Valerian family at Rome?

32. Philip de Comines (Memoires, l. vi. c. 13.), from the tradition of the times, mentions him with high encomiums, but under the whimsical name of the Chevalier Blanc de Valaigne (Valachia). The Greek Chalcocondyles, and the Turkish Annals of Leunclavius, presume to accuse his fidelity or valour.

crown of Hungary; and the important service was rewarded by the title and office of Waivod of Transylvania. The first of Julian's crusades added two Turkish laurels on his brow; and in the public distress the fatal errors of Warna were forgotten. During the absence and minority of Ladislaus of Austria, the titular king, Huniades was elected supreme captain and governor of Hungary; and if envy at first was silenced by terror, a reign of twelve years supposes the arts of policy as well as of war. Yet the idea of a consummate general is not delineated in his campaigns; the white knight fought with the hand rather than the head, as the chief of desultory Barbarians, who attack without fear and fly without shame; and his military life is composed of a romantic alternative of victories and escapes. By the Turks, who employed his name to frighten their perverse children, he was corruptly denominated *Jancus Lain*, or the Wicked: their hatred is the proof of their esteem; the kingdom which he guarded was inaccessible to their arms; and they felt him most daring and formidable, when they fondly believed the captain and his country irrecoverably lost. Instead of confining himself to a defensive war, four years after the defeat of Warna he again penetrated into the heart of Bulgaria; and in the plain of Cossova sustained, till the third day, the shock of the Ottoman army, four times more numerous than his own. As he fled alone through the woods of Walachia, the hero was surprised by two robbers; but while they disputed a gold chain that hung at his neck, he recovered his sword, slew the one, terrified the other, and, after new perils of captivity or death, consoled by his presence an afflicted kingdom. But the last and most glorious action of his life was the defence of Belgrade against the powers of Mahomet the second in person. After a siege of forty days, the Turks, who had already entered the town, were compelled to retreat; and the joyful nations celebrated Huniades and Belgrade as the bulwarks of Christendom.[33] About a month after this great deliverance, the champion expired; and his most splendid epitaph is the regret of the Ottoman prince, who sighed that he could no longer hope for revenge against the single antagonist who had triumphed over his arms. On the first vacancy of the throne, Matthias Corvinus, a youth of eighteen years of age, was elected and crowned by the grateful Hungarians. His reign was prosperous and long: Matthias aspired to the glory of a conqueror and a saint; but his

His defence of Belgrade, and death, A.D. 1456, July 22, Sept. 4.

33. See Bonfinius (decad iii. l. viii. p. 492.) and Spondanus (A.D. 1456, N° 1–7.). Huniades shared the glory of the defence of Belgrade with Capistran, a Franciscan friar; and in their respective narratives, neither the saint nor the hero condescend to take notice of his rival's merit.

purest merit is the encouragement of learning; and the Latin orators and historians, who were invited from Italy by the son, have shed the lustre of their eloquence on the father's character.[34]

Birth and education of Scanderbeg, prince of Albania, A.D. 1404–1413, &c.

In the list of heroes, John Huniades and Scanderbeg are commonly associated:[35] and they are both entitled to our notice, since their occupation of the Ottoman arms delayed the ruin of the Greek empire. John Castriot, the father of Scanderbeg,[36] was the hereditary prince of a small district of Epirus or Albania, between the mountains and the Adriatic sea. Unable to contend with the sultan's power, Castriot submitted to the hard conditions of peace and tribute: he delivered his four sons as the pledges of his fidelity; and the Christian youths, after receiving the mark of circumcision, were instructed in the Mahometan religion, and trained in the arms and arts of Turkish policy.[37] The three elder brothers were confounded in the crowd of slaves; and the poison to which their deaths are ascribed, cannot be verified or disproved by any positive evidence. Yet the suspicion is in a great measure removed by the kind and paternal treatment of George Castriot, the fourth brother, who from his tender youth, displayed the strength and spirit of a soldier. The successive overthrow of a Tartar and two Persians, who carried a proud defiance to the Turkish court, recommended him to the favour of Amurath, and his Turkish appellation of Scanderbeg (*Iskender Beg*), or the lord Alexander, is an indelible memorial of his glory and servitude. His father's principality was reduced into a province: but the loss was compensated by the rank and title of

34. See Bonfinius, decad iii. l. viii.–decad iv. l. viii. The observations of Spondanus on the life and character of Matthias Corvinus, are curious and critical (A.D. 1464, N° 1. 1475, N° 6. 1476, N° 14–16. 1490, N° 4, 5.). Italian fame was the object of his vanity. His actions are celebrated in the Epitome Rerum Hungaricarum (p. 322–412.) of Peter Ranzanus, a Sicilian. His wise and facetious sayings are registered by Galestus Martius of Narni (528–568.): and we have a particular narrative of his wedding and coronation. These three tracts are all contained in the 1st vol. of Bel's Scriptores Rerum Hungaricarum.

35. They are ranked by Sir William Temple, in his pleasing Essay on Heroic Virtue (works, vol. iii. p. 385.), among the seven chiefs who have deserved, without wearing, a royal crown; Belisarius, Narses, Gonsalvo of Cordova, William first prince of Orange, Alexander duke of Parma, John Huniades, and George Castriot, or Scanderbeg.

36. I could wish for some simple, authentic memoirs of a friend of Scanderbeg, which would introduce me to the man, the time, and the place. In the old and national history of Marinus Barletius, a priest of Scodra (de Vitâ, Moribus, et Rebus gestis Georgii Castrioti, &c. libri xiii. pp. 367. Argentorat. 1537, in fol.), his gawdy and cumbersome robes are stuck with many false jewels. See likewise Chalcocondyles, l. vii. p. 185. l. viii. p. 229.

37. His circumcision, education, &c. are marked by Marinus with brevity and reluctance (l. i. p. 6, 7.).

Sanjiak, a command of five thousand horse, and the prospect of the first dignities of the empire. He served with honour in the wars of Europe and Asia; and we may smile at the art or credulity of the historian, who supposes, that in every encounter he spared the Christians, while he fell with a thundering arm on his Musulman foes. The glory of Huniades is without reproach; he fought in the defence of his religion and country; but the enemies who applaud the patriot, have branded his rival with the name of traitor and apostate. In the eyes of the Christians, the rebellion of Scanderbeg is justified by his father's wrongs, the ambiguous death of his three brothers, his own degradation, and the slavery of his country; and they adore the generous, though tardy, zeal, with which he asserted the faith and independence of his ancestors. But he had imbibed from his ninth year the doctrines of the Koran; he was ignorant of the Gospel; the religion of a soldier is determined by authority and habit; nor is it easy to conceive what new illumination at the age of forty[38] could be poured into his soul. His motives would be less exposed to the suspicion of interest or revenge, had he broken his chain from the moment that he was sensible of its weight: but a long oblivion had surely impaired his original right; and every year of obedience and reward had cemented the mutual bond of the sultan and his subject. If Scanderbeg had long harboured the belief of Christianity and the intention of revolt, a worthy mind must condemn the base dissimulation, that could serve only to betray, that could promise only to be foresworn, that could actively join in the temporal and spiritual perdition of so many thousands of his unhappy brethren. Shall we praise a secret correspondence with Huniades, while he commanded the vanguard of the Turkish army? shall we excuse the desertion of his standard, a treacherous desertion which abandoned the victory to the enemies of his benefactor? In the confusion of a defeat, the eye of Scanderbeg was fixed on the Reis Effendi or principal secretary: with the dagger at his breast, he extorted a firman or patent for the government of Albania; and the murder of the guiltless scribe and his train, prevented the consequences of an immediate discovery. With some bold companions, to whom he had revealed his design, he escaped in the night, by rapid

His revolt from the Turks, A.D. 1443, Nov. 28.

38. Since Scanderbeg died A.D. 1466, in the lxiii[d] year of his age (Marinus, l. xiii. p. 370.), he was born in 1403; since he was torn from his parents by the Turks, when he was *novennis* (Marinus, l. i. p. 1. 6.), that event must have happened in 1412, nine years before the accession of Amurath II. who must have inherited, not acquired, the Albanian slave. Spondanus has remarked this inconsistency, A.D. 1431, N° 31. 1443, N° 14.

marches, from the field of battle to his paternal mountains. The gates of Croya were opened to the royal mandate; and no sooner did he command the fortress, than George Castriot dropt the mask of dissimulation; abjured the prophet and the sultan, and proclaimed himself the avenger of his family and country. The names of religion and liberty provoked a general revolt: the Albanians, a martial race, were unanimous to live and die with their hereditary prince; and the Ottoman garrisons were indulged in the choice of martyrdom or baptism. In the assembly of the states of Epirus, Scanderbeg was elected general of the Turkish war; and each of the allies engaged to furnish his respective proportion of men and money. From these contributions, from his patrimonial estate, and from the valuable salt-pits of Selina, he drew an annual revenue of two hundred thousand ducats;[39] and the entire sum, exempt from the demands of luxury, was strictly appropriated to the public use. His manners were popular; but his discipline was severe; and every superfluous vice was banished from his camp: his example strengthened his command; and under his conduct, the Albanians were invincible in their own opinion and that of their enemies. The bravest adventurers of France and Germany were allured by his fame and retained in his service: his standing militia consisted of eight thousand horse and seven thousand foot; the horses were small, the men were active: but he viewed with a discerning eye the difficulties and resources of the mountains; and, at the blaze of the beacons, the whole nation was distributed in the strongest posts. With such unequal arms, Scanderbeg resisted twenty-three years the powers of the Ottoman empire; and two conquerors, Amurath the second, and his greater son, were repeatedly baffled by a rebel, whom they pursued with seeming contempt and implacable resentment. At the head of sixty thousand horse and forty thousand Janizaries, Amurath entered Albania; he might ravage the open country, occupy the defenceless towns, convert the churches into moschs, circumcise the Christian youths, and punish with death his adult and obstinate captives: but the conquests of the sultan were confined to the petty fortress of Sfetigrade; and the garrison, invincible to his arms, was oppressed by a paltry artifice and a superstitious scruple.[40] Amurath retired with shame and loss from the walls of Croya, the castle and residence of the Castriots; the march, the siege, the retreat,

His valour,

39. His revenue and forces are luckily given by Marinus (l. ii. p. 44.).

40. There were two Dibras, the upper and lower, the Bulgarian and Albanian: the former, 70 miles from Croya (l. i. p. 17.), was contiguous to the fortress of Sfetigrade, whose inhabitants refused to drink from a well into which a dead dog had traiterously been cast (l. v. p. 139, 140.). We want a good map of Epirus.

were harassed by a vexatious, and almost invisible, adversary;[41] and the disappointment might tend to embitter, perhaps to shorten, the last days of the sultan.[42] In the fulness of conquest, Mahomet the second still felt at his bosom this domestic thorn: his lieutenants were permitted to negociate a truce; and the Albanian prince may justly be praised as a firm and able champion of his national independence. The enthusiasm of chivalry and religion has ranked him with the names of Alexander and Pyrrhus; nor would they blush to acknowledge their intrepid countrymen: but his narrow dominion, and slender powers, must leave him at an humble distance below the heroes of antiquity, who triumphed over the East and the Roman legions. His splendid atchievements, the bashas whom he encountered, the armies that he discomfited, and the three thousand Turks who were slain by his single hand, must be weighed in the scales of suspicious criticism. Against an illiterate enemy, and in the dark solitude of Epirus, his partial biographers may safely indulge the latitude of romance: but their fictions are exposed by the light of Italian history; and they afford a strong presumption against their own truth, by a fabulous tale of his exploits, when he passed the Adriatic with eight hundred horse to the succour of the king of Naples.[43] Without disparagement to his fame, they might have owned that he was finally oppressed by the Ottoman powers: in his extreme danger, he applied to pope Pius the second for a refuge in the ecclesiastical state; and his resources were almost exhausted, since Scanderbeg died a fugitive at Lissus on the Venetian territory.[44] His sepulchre was soon violated by the Turkish conquerors; but the Janizaries, who wore his bones enchased in a bracelet, declared by this superstitious

and death, A.D. 1467, January 17.

41. Compare the Turkish narrative of Cantemir (p. 92.), with the pompous and prolix declamation in the iv[th], v[th], and vi[th] books of the Albanian priest, who has been copied by the tribe of strangers and moderns.

42. In honour of his hero, Barletius (l. vi. p. 188–192.) kills the sultan, by disease indeed, under the walls of Croya. But this audacious fiction is disproved by the Greeks and Turks, who agree in the time and manner of Amurath's death at Adrianople.

43. See the marvels of his Calabrian expedition in the ix[th] and x[th] books of Marinus Barletius, which may be rectified by the testimony or silence of Muratori (Annali d'Italia, tom. xiii. p. 291.), and his original authors (Joh. Simonetta de Rebus Francisci Sfortiæ, in Muratori, Script. Rerum Ital. tom. xxi. p. 728. et alios). The Albanian cavalry, under the name of *Stradiots*, soon became famous in the wars of Italy (Memoires de Comines, l. viii. c. 5.).

44. Spondanus, from the best evidence and the most rational criticism, has reduced the giant Scanderbeg to the human size (A.D. 1461, N° 20. 1463, N° 9. 1465, N° 12, 13. 1467, N° 1.). His own letter to the pope, and the testimony of Phranza (l. iii. c. 28.), a refugee in the neighbouring isle of Corfu, demonstrate his last distress, which is awk-

amulet their involuntary reverence for his valour. The instant ruin of his country may redound to the hero's glory; yet, had he balanced the consequences of submission and resistance, a patriot perhaps would have declined the unequal contest which must depend on the life and genius of one man. Scanderbeg might indeed be supported by the rational, though fallacious, hope, that the pope, the king of Naples, and the Venetian republic, would join in the defence of a free and Christian people, who guarded the sea-coast of the Adriatic, and the narrow passage from Greece to Italy. His infant son was saved from the national shipwreck; the Castriots[45] were invested with a Neapolitan dukedom, and their blood continues to flow in the noblest families of the realm. A colony of Albanian fugitives obtained a settlement in Calabria, and they preserve at this day the language and manners of their ancestors.[46]

Constantine, the last of the Roman or Greek emperors, A.D. 1448, Nov. 1–A.D. 1453, May 29.

In the long career of the decline and fall of the Roman empire, I have reached at length the last reign of the princes of Constantinople, who so feebly sustained the name and majesty of the Cæsars. On the decease of John Palæologus, who survived about four years the Hungarian crusade,[47] the royal family, by the death of Andronicus and the monastic profession of Isidore, was reduced to three princes, Constantine, Demetrius, and Thomas, the surviving sons of the emperor Manuel. Of these the first and the last were far distant in the Morea; but Demetrius, who possessed the domain of Selybria, was in the suburbs, at the head of a party: his ambition was not chilled by the public distress; and his conspiracy with the Turks and the schismatics had already disturbed the peace of his country. The funeral of the late emperor was accelerated with singular and even suspicious haste; the claim of Demetrius to the vacant throne was justified by a trite and flimsy sophism, that he was born in the purple, the eldest son of his father's reign. But the empress-mother, the senate and soldiers, the clergy and people, were unanimous in the cause of the lawful successor; and the despot Thomas, who, ignorant of the change, accidentally returned to the capital, asserted with becoming zeal the

---

wardly concealed by Marinus Barletius (l. x.).

45. See the family of the Castriots, in Ducange (Fam. Dalmaticæ, &c. xviii. p. 348–350.).

46. This colony of Albanese is mentioned by Mr. Swinburne (Travels into the Two Sicilies, vol. i. p. 350–354.).

47. The chronology of Phranza is clear and authentic; but instead of four years and seven months, Spondanus (A.D. 1445. N° 7.) assigns seven or eight years to the reign of the last Constantine, which he deduces from a spurious epistle of Eugenius IV. to the king of Æthiopia.

interest of his absent brother. An ambassador, the historian Phranza, was immediately dispatched to the court of Adrianople. Amurath received him with honour and dismissed him with gifts; but the gracious approbation of the Turkish sultan announced his supremacy, and the approaching downfal of the Eastern empire. By the hands of two illustrious deputies, the Imperial crown was placed at Sparta on the head of Constantine. In the spring he sailed from the Morea, escaped the encounter of a Turkish squadron, enjoyed the acclamations of his subjects, celebrated the festival of a new reign, and exhausted by his donatives the treasure, or rather the indigence, of the state. The emperor immediately resigned to his brothers the possession of the Morea; and the brittle friendship of the two princes, Demetrius and Thomas, was confirmed in their mother's presence by the frail security of oaths and embraces. His next occupation was the choice of a consort. A daughter of the doge of Venice had been proposed; but the Byzantine nobles objected the distance between an hereditary monarch and an elective magistrate; and in their subsequent distress, the chief of that powerful republic was not unmindful of the affront. Constantine afterwards hesitated between the royal families of Trebizond and Georgia; and the embassy of Phranza represents in his public and private life the last days of the Byzantine empire.[48]

Embassies of Phranza, A.D. 1450–1452.

The *protovestiare*, or great chamberlain, Phranza sailed from Constantinople as the minister of a bridegroom; and the relics of wealth and luxury were applied to his pompous appearance. His numerous retinue consisted of nobles and guards, of physicians and monks; he was attended by a band of music; and the term of his costly embassy was protracted above two years. On his arrival in Georgia or Iberia, the natives from the towns and villages flocked around the strangers; and such was their simplicity, that they were delighted with the effects, without understanding the cause, of musical harmony. Among the crowd was an old man, above an hundred years of age, who had formerly been carried away a captive by the Barbarians,[49] and who amused his hearers with a tale of the wonders of India,[50] from whence

48. Phranza (l. iii. c. 1–6.) deserves credit and esteem.

49. Suppose him to have been captured in 1394, in Timour's first war in Georgia (Sherefeddin, l. iii. c. 50.); he might follow his Tartar master into Hindostan in 1398, and from thence sail to the spice islands.

50. The happy and pious Indians lived an hundred and fifty years, and enjoyed the most perfect productions of the vegetable and mineral kingdoms. The animals were on a large scale; dragons seventy cubits,

he had returned to Portugal by an unknown sea.[51] From this hospitable land, Phranza proceeded to the court of Trebizond, where he was informed by the Greek prince of the recent decease of Amurath. Instead of rejoicing in the deliverance, the experienced statesman expressed his apprehension, that an ambitious youth would not long adhere to the sage and pacific system of his father. After the sultan's decease, his Christian wife Maria,[52] the daughter of the Servian despot, had been honourably restored to her parents: on the fame of her beauty and merit, she was recommended by the ambassador as the most worthy object of the royal choice; and Phranza recapitulates and refutes the specious objections that might be raised against the proposal. The majesty of the purple would ennoble an unequal alliance; the bar of affinity might be removed by liberal alms and the dispensation of the church; the disgrace of Turkish nuptials had been repeatedly overlooked; and, though the fair Maria was near fifty years of age, she might yet hope to give an heir to the empire. Constantine listened to the advice, which was transmitted in the first ship that sailed from Trebizond; but the factions of the court opposed his marriage; and it was finally prevented by the pious vow of the sultana, who ended her days in the monastic profession. Reduced to the first alternative, the choice of Phranza was decided in favour of a Georgian princess; and the vanity of her father was dazzled by the glorious alliance. Instead of demanding, according to the primitive and national custom, a price for his daughter,[53] he offered a portion of fifty-six thousand, with an annual pension of five thousand, ducats; and the services of the ambassador were repaid by an assurance, that, as his son had been adopted in baptism by the emperor, the establishment of his daughter should be the peculiar care of the empress of Constantinople. On the return of Phranza, the treaty was ratified by the Greek monarch, who with his

---

ants (the *formica Indica*) nine inches long, sheep like elephants, elephants like sheep. Quidlibet audendi, &c.

51. He sailed in a country vessel from the spice island to one of the ports of the exterior India, invenitque navem grandem *Ibericam*, quâ in *Portugalliam* est delatus. This passage, composed in 1477 (Phranza, l. iii. c. 30.), twenty years before the discovery of the Cape of Good Hope, is spurious or wonderful. But this new geography is sullied by the old and incompatible error which places the source of the Nile in India.

52. Cantemir (p. 83.), who styles her the daughter of Lazarus Ogli, and the Helen of the Servians, places her marriage with Amurath in the year 1424. It will not easily be believed, that in six-and-twenty years cohabitation, the sultan corpus ejus non tetigit. After the taking of Constantinople, she fled to Mahomet II. (Phranza, l. iii. c. 22.).

53. The classical reader will recollect the offers of Agamemnon (Iliad I. v. 144.), and the general practice of antiquity.

own hand impressed three vermillion crosses on the golden bull, and assured the Georgian envoy, that in the spring his gallies should conduct the bride to her Imperial palace. But Constantine embraced his faithful servant, not with the cold approbation of a sovereign, but with the warm confidence of a friend, who, after a long absence, is impatient to pour his secrets into the bosom of his friend. "Since the death of my mother and of Cantacuzene, who alone advised me without interest or passion,[54] I am surrounded," said the emperor, "by men whom I can neither love, nor trust, nor esteem. You are not a stranger to Lucas Notaras, the great admiral; obstinately attached to his own sentiments, he declares, both in private and public, that his sentiments are the absolute measure of my thoughts and actions. The rest of the courtiers are swayed by their personal or factious views; and how can I consult the monks on questions of policy and marriage? I have yet much employment for your diligence and fidelity. In the spring you shall engage one of my brothers to solicit the succour of the Western powers; from the Morea you shall sail to Cyprus on a particular commission; and from thence proceed to Georgia to receive and conduct the future empress." "Your commands," replied Phranza, "are irresistible; but deign, great sir," he added, with a serious smile, "to consider, that if I am thus perpetually absent from my family, my wife may be tempted either to seek another husband, or to throw herself into a monastery." After laughing at his apprehensions, the emperor more gravely consoled him by the pleasing assurance, that *this* should be his last service abroad, and that he destined for his son, a wealthy and noble heiress; for himself, the important office of great logothete, or principal minister of state. The marriage was immediately stipulated; but the office, however incompatible with his own, had been usurped by the ambition of the admiral. Some delay was requisite to negociate a consent and an equivalent; and the nomination of Phranza was half declared, and half suppressed, lest it might be displeasing to an insolent and powerful favourite. The winter was spent in the preparations of his embassy; and Phranza had resolved, that the youth his son should embrace this opportunity of foreign travel, and be left, on the appearance of danger, with his maternal kindred of the Morea. Such were the private and public designs, which were interrupted by a Turkish war, and finally buried in the ruins of the empire.

State of the Byzantine court.

54. Cantacuzene (I am ignorant of his relation to the emperor of that name) was great domestic, a firm asserter of the Greek creed, and a brother of the queen of Servia, whom he visited with the character of ambassador (Syropulus, p. 37, 38. 45.).

CHAPTER LXVIII

Reign and Character of Mahomet the Second. – Siege, Assault, and final Conquest, of Constantinople by the Turks. – Death of Constantine Palæologus. – Servitude of the Greeks. – Extinction of the Roman Empire in the East. – Consternation of Europe. – Conquests and Death of Mahomet the Second.

Character of Mahomet II. The siege of Constantinople by the Turks attracts our first attention to the person and character of the great destroyer. Mahomet the second[1] was the son of the second Amurath; and though his mother has been decorated with the titles of Christian and princess, she is more probably confounded with the numerous concubines who peopled from every climate the haram of the sultan. His first education and sentiments were those of a devout Musulman; and as often as he conversed with an infidel, he purified his hands and face by the legal rites of ablution. Age and empire appear to have relaxed this narrow bigotry: his aspiring genius disdained to acknowledge a power above his own; and in his looser hours he presumed (it is said) to brand the prophet of Mecca as a robber and impostor. Yet the sultan persevered in a decent reverence for the doctrine and discipline of the Koran:[2] his private indiscretion must have been sacred from the vulgar ear; and we should suspect the credulity of strangers and sectaries, so prone to believe that a mind which is hardened against truth, must be armed with superior contempt for absurdity and error. Under the tuition of the most skilful masters, Mahomet advanced with an early and rapid progress in the paths of knowledge; and besides his native tongue, it is affirmed that he spoke or

1. For the character of Mahomet II. it is dangerous to trust either the Turks or the Christians. The most moderate picture appears to be drawn by Phranza (l. i. c. 33.), whose resentment had cooled in age and solitude; see likewise Spondanus (A.D. 1451, N° 11.) and the continuator of Fleury (tom. xxii. p. 552.), the *Elogia* of Paulus Jovius (l. iii. p. 164–166.), and the Dictionaire de Bayle (tom. iii. p. 272–279.).

2. Cantemir (p. 115), and the moschs which he founded, attest his public regard for religion. Mahomet freely disputed with the patriarch Gennadius on the two religions (Spond. A.D. 1453, N° 22.).

understood five languages,[3] the Arabic, the Persian, the Chaldæan or Hebrew, the Latin, and the Greek. The Persian might indeed contribute to his amusement, and the Arabic to his edification; and such studies are familiar to the Oriental youth. In the intercourse of the Greeks and Turks, a conqueror might wish to converse with the people over whom he was ambitious to reign: his own praises in Latin poetry[4] or prose[5] might find a passage to the royal ear; but what use or merit could recommend to the statesman or the scholar the uncouth dialect of his Hebrew slaves? The history and geography of the world were familiar to his memory: the lives of the heroes of the East, perhaps of the West,[6] excited his emulation: his skill in astrology is excused by the folly of the times, and supposes some rudiments of mathematical science; and a profane taste for the arts is betrayed in his liberal invitation and reward of the painters of Italy.[7] But the influence of religion and learning were employed without effect on his savage and licentious nature. I will not transcribe, nor do I firmly believe, the stories of his fourteen pages, whose bellies were ripped open in search of a stolen melon; or of the beauteous slave, whose head he severed from her body, to convince the Janizaries that their master was not the votary of love. His sobriety is attested by the silence of the Turkish annals, which accuse three, and three only, of the Ottoman line of the vice of drunkenness.[8] But it cannot

3. Quinque linguas præter suam noverat; Græcam, Latinam, Chaldaicam, Persicam. The Latin translator of Phranza has dropt the Arabic, which the Koran must recommend to every Musulman.

4. Philelphus, by a Latin ode, requested and obtained the liberty of his wife's mother and sisters from the conqueror of Constantinople. It was delivered into the sultan's hands by the envoys of the duke of Milan. Philelphus himself was suspected of a design of retiring to Constantinople; yet the orator often sounded the trumpet of holy war (see his Life by M. Lancelot, in the Memoires de l'Academie des Inscriptions, tom. x. p. 718. 724, &c.).

5. Robert Valturio published at Verona, in 1483, his xii books de Re Militari, in which he first mentions the use of bombs. By his patron Sigismond Malatesta, prince of Rimini, it had been addressed with a Latin epistle to Mahomet II.

6. According to Phranza, he assiduously studied the lives and actions of Alexander, Augustus, Constantine, and Theodosius. I have read somewhere, that Plutarch's Lives were translated by his orders into the Turkish language. If the sultan himself understood Greek, it must have been for the benefit of his subjects. Yet these lives are a school of freedom as well as of valour.

7. The famous Gentile Bellino, whom he had invited from Venice, was dismissed with a chain and collar of gold, and a purse of 3000 ducats. With Voltaire, I laugh at the foolish story of a slave purposely beheaded, to instruct the painter in the action of the muscles.

8. These Imperial drunkards were Soliman I. Selim II. and Amurath IV. (Cantemir, p. 61.). The sophis of Persia can produce a more regular succession; and in the last age, our European travellers were the witnesses and companions of their revels.

be denied that his passions were at once furious and inexorable; that in the palace, as in the field, a torrent of blood was spilt on the slightest provocation; and that the noblest of the captive youth were often dishonoured by his unnatural lust. In the Albanian war, he studied the lessons, and soon surpassed the example, of his father; and the conquest of two empires, twelve kingdoms, and two hundred cities, a vain and flattering account, is ascribed to his invincible sword. He was doubtless a soldier, and possibly a general; Constantinople has sealed his glory; but if we compare the means, the obstacles, and the atchievements, Mahomet the second must blush to sustain a parallel with Alexander or Timour. Under his command, the Ottoman forces were always more numerous than their enemies; yet their progress was bounded by the Euphrates and the Adriatic; and his arms were checked by Huniades and Scanderbeg, by the Rhodian knights and by the Persian king.

His reign, A.D. 1451, February 9–A.D. 1481, July 2.

In the reign of Amurath, he twice tasted of royalty, and twice descended from the throne: his tender age was incapable of opposing his father's restoration, but never could he forgive the vizirs who had recommended that salutary measure. His nuptials were celebrated with the daughter of a Turkman emir; and, after a festival of two months, he departed from Adrianople with his bride, to reside in the government of Magnesia. Before the end of six weeks, he was recalled by a sudden message from the divan, which announced the decease of Amurath, and the mutinous spirit of the Janizaries. His speed and vigour commanded their obedience: he passed the Hellespont with a chosen guard; and at the distance of a mile from Adrianople, the vizirs and emirs, the imams and cadhis, the soldiers and the people, fell prostrate before the new sultan. They affected to weep, they affected to rejoice; he ascended the throne at the age of twenty-one years, and removed the cause of sedition by the death, the inevitable death, of his infant brothers.[9] The ambassadors of Europe and Asia soon appeared to congratulate his accession and solicit his friendship; and to all he spoke the language of moderation and peace. The confidence of the Greek emperor was revived by the solemn oaths and fair assurances, with which he sealed the ratification of the treaty: and a rich domain on the banks of the Strymon was assigned for the annual payment of three

9. Calapin, one of these royal infants, was saved from his cruel brother, and baptised at Rome under the name of Callistus Othomannus. The emperor Frederic III. presented him with an estate in Austria, where he ended his life; and Cuspinian, who in his youth conversed with the aged prince at Vienna, applauds his piety and wisdom (de Cæsaribus, p. 672, 673).

hundred thousand aspers, the pension of an Ottoman prince, who was detained at his request in the Byzantine court. Yet the neighbours of Mahomet might tremble at the severity with which a youthful monarch reformed the pomp of his father's household: the expences of luxury were applied to those of ambition, and an useless train of seven thousand falconers was either dismissed from his service or enlisted in his troops. In the first summer of his reign, he visited with an army the Asiatic provinces; but after humbling the pride, Mahomet accepted the submission, of the Caramanian, that he might not be diverted by the smallest obstacle from the execution of his great design.[10]

Hostile intentions of Mahomet, A.D. 1451.

The Mahometan, and more especially the Turkish casuists, have pronounced that no promise can bind the faithful against the interest and duty of their religion; and that the sultan may abrogate his own treaties and those of his predecessors. The justice and magnanimity of Amurath had scorned this immoral privilege; but his son, though the proudest of men, could stoop from ambition to the basest arts of dissimulation and deceit. Peace was on his lips, while war was in his heart: he incessantly sighed for the possession of Constantinople; and the Greeks, by their own indiscretion, afforded the first pretence of the fatal rupture.[11] Instead of labouring to be forgotten, their ambassadors pursued his camp, to demand the payment, and even the encrease, of their annual stipend: the divan was importuned by their complaints, and the vizir, a secret friend of the Christians, was constrained to deliver the sense of his brethren. "Ye foolish and miserable Romans,"

10. See the accession of Mahomet II. in Ducas (c. 33.), Phranza (l. i. c. 33. l. iii. c. 2.), Chalcocondyles (l. vii. p. 199), and Cantemir (p. 96.).

11. Before I enter on the siege of Constantinople I shall observe, that except the short hints of Cantemir and Leunclavius, I have not been able to obtain any Turkish account of this conquest: such an account as we possess of the siege of Rhodes by Soliman II. (Memoires de l'Academie des Inscriptions, tom. xxvi. p. 723–769.). I must therefore depend on the Greeks, whose prejudices, in some degree, are subdued by their distress. Our standard texts are those of Ducas (c. 34–42.), Phranza (l. iii. c. 7–20.), Chalcocondyles (l. viii. p. 201–214.), and Leonardus Chiensis (Historia C.P. a Turco expugnatæ. Norimberghæ, 1544, in 4to, 20 leaves). The last of these narratives is the earliest in date, since it was composed in the isle of Chios, the 16th of August 1453, only seventy-nine days after the loss of the city, and in the first confusion of ideas and passions. Some hints may be added from an epistle of cardinal Isidore (in Farragine Rerum Turcicarum, ad calcem Chalcocondyl. Clauseri, Basil, 1556) to pope Nicholas V. and a tract of Theodosius Zygomala, which he addressed in the year 1581 to Martin Crusius (Turco-Græcia, l. i. p. 74–98. Basil, 1584). The various facts and materials are briefly, though critically, reviewed by Spondanus (A.D. 1453, N° 1–27.). The hearsay relations of Monstrelet and the distant Latins, I shall take leave to disregard.

said Calil, "we know your devices, and ye are ignorant of your own danger! the scrupulous Amurath is no more; his throne is occupied by a young conqueror, whom no laws can bind and no obstacles can resist: and if you escape from his hands, give praise to the divine clemency, which yet delays the chastisement of your sins. Why do ye seek to affright us by vain and indirect menaces? Release the fugitive Orchan, crown him sultan of Romania; call the Hungarians from beyond the Danube; arm against us the nations of the West: and be assured, that you will only provoke and precipitate your ruin." But, if the fears of the ambassadors were alarmed by the stern language of the vizir, they were soothed by the courteous audience and friendly speeches of the Ottoman prince; and Mahomet assured them that on his return to Adrianople he would redress the grievances, and consult the true interest, of the Greeks. No sooner had he repassed the Hellespont than he issued a mandate to suppress their pension, and to expel their officers from the banks of the Strymon: in this measure he betrayed an hostile mind; and the second order announced, and in some degree commenced, the siege of Constantinople. In the narrow pass of the Bosphorus, an Asiatic fortress had formerly been raised by his grandfather: in the opposite situation, on the European side, he resolved to erect a more formidable castle; and a thousand masons were commanded to assemble in the spring on a spot named Asomaton, about five miles from the Greek metropolis.[12] Persuasion is the resource of the feeble; and the feeble can seldom persuade: the ambassadors of the emperor attempted, without success, to divert Mahomet from the execution of his design. They represented, that his grandfather had solicited the permission of Manuel to build a castle on his own territories; but that this double fortification, which would command the streight, could only tend to violate the alliance of the nations; to intercept the Latins who traded in the Black Sea, and perhaps to annihilate the subsistence of the city. "I form no enterprise," replied the perfidious sultan, "against the city; but the empire of Constantinople is measured by her walls. Have you forgot the distress to which my father was reduced, when you formed a league with the Hungarians; when they invaded our country by land, and the Hellespont was occupied by the French gallies? Amurath was compelled to force the passage of the

12. The situation of the fortress, and the topography of the Bosphorus, are best learned from Peter Gyllius (de Bosphoro Thracio, l. ii. c. 13), Leunclavius (Pandect. p. 445.), and Tournefort (Voyage dans le Levant, tom. ii. lettre xv. p. 413, 444.); but I must regret the map or plan which Tournefort sent to the French minister of the marine. The reader may turn back to vol. ii. ch. 17. of this History.

Bosphorus; and your strength was not equal to your malevolence. I was then a child at Adrianople; the Moslems trembled; and for a while the *Gabours*[13] insulted our disgrace. But when my father had triumphed in the field of Warna, he vowed to erect a fort on the western shore, and that vow it is my duty to accomplish. Have ye the right, have ye the power, to control my actions on my own ground? For that ground *is* my own: as far as the shores of the Bosphorus, Asia is inhabited by the Turks, and Europe is deserted by the Romans. Return, and inform your king that the present Ottoman is far different from his predecessors; that *his* resolutions surpass *their* wishes; and that *he* performs more than *they* could resolve. Return in safety – but the next who delivers a similar message may expect to be flayed alive." After this declaration, Constantine, the first of the Greeks in spirit as in rank,[14] had determined to unsheathe the sword, and to resist the approach and establishment of the Turks on the Bosphorus. He was disarmed by the advice of his civil and ecclesiastical ministers, who recommended a system less generous, and even less prudent, than his own, to approve their patience and long-suffering, to brand the Ottoman with the name and guilt of an aggressor, and to depend on chance and time for their own safety and the destruction of a fort which could not long be maintained in the neighbourhood of a great and populous city. Amidst hope and fear, the fears of the wise and the hopes of the credulous, the winter rolled away; the proper business of each man, and each hour, was postponed; and the Greeks shut their eyes against the impending danger, till the arrival of the spring and the sultan decided the assurance of their ruin.

He builds a fortress on the Bosphorus, A.D. 1452, March.

Of a master who never forgives, the orders are seldom disobeyed. On the twenty-sixth of March, the appointed spot of Asomaton was covered with an active swarm of Turkish artificers; and the materials by sea and land, were diligently transported from Europe and Asia.[15] The lime had been burnt in Cataphrygia; the timber was cut down in the woods of Heraclea and

13. The opprobrious name which the Turks bestow on the Infidels, is expressed *Καβουρ* by Ducas, and *Giaour* by Leunclavius and the moderns. The former term is derived by Ducange (Gloss. Græc. tom. i. p. 530) from *Καβουρον* in vulgar Greek, a tortoise, as denoting a retrograde motion from the faith. But, alas! *Gabour* is no more than *Gheber*, which was transferred from the Persian to the Turkish language, from the worshippers of fire to those of the crucifix (d'Herbelot, Bibliot. Orient. p. 375.).

14. Phranza does justice to his master's sense and courage. Calliditatem hominis non ignorans Imperator prior arma movere constituit, and stigmatises the folly of the cum sacri tum profani proceres, which he had heard, amentes spe vanâ pasci. Ducas was not a privy-counsellor.

15. Instead of this clear and consistent

Nicomedia; and the stones were dug from the Anatolian quarries. Each of the thousand masons was assisted by two workmen; and a measure of two cubits was marked for their daily task. The fortress[16] was built in a triangular form; each angle was flanked by a strong and massy tower; one on the declivity of the hill, two along the sea-shore: a thickness of twenty-two feet was assigned for the walls, thirty for the towers; and the whole building was covered with a solid platform of lead. Mahomet himself pressed and directed the work with indefatigable ardour: his three vizirs claimed the honour of finishing their respective towers; the zeal of the cadhis emulated that of the Janizaries; the meanest labour was ennobled by the service of God and the sultan; and the diligence of the multitude was quickened by the eye of a despot, whose smile was the hope of fortune, and whose frown was the messenger of death. The Greek emperor beheld with terror the irresistible progress of the work; and vainly strove, by flattery and gifts, to assuage an implacable foe, who sought, and secretly fomented, the slightest occasion of a quarrel. Such occasions must soon and inevitably be found. The ruins of stately churches, and even the marble columns which had been consecrated to St. Michael the archangel, were employed without scruple by the profane and rapacious Moslems; and some Christians, who presumed to oppose the removal, received from their hands the crown of martyrdom. Constantine had solicited a Turkish guard to protect the fields and harvests of his subjects: the guard was fixed; but their first order was to allow free pasture to the mules and horses of the camp, and to defend their brethren if they should be molested by the natives. The retinue of an Ottoman chief had left their horses to pass the night among the ripe corn: the damage was felt; the insult was resented; and several of both nations were slain in a tumultuous conflict. Mahomet listened with joy to the complaint; and a detachment was commanded to exterminate the guilty village: the guilty had fled; but forty innocent and unsuspecting reapers were massacred by the soldiers. Till this provocation, Constantinople had been open to the visits of commerce and curiosity: on the first alarm, the gates were shut; but the emperor, still anxious for peace, released on the third day his Turkish

The Turkish war, June;

account, the Turkish Annals (Cantemir, p. 97.) revived the foolish tale of the ox's hide, and Dido's stratagem in the foundation of Carthage. These annals (unless we are swayed by an antichristian prejudice) are far less valuable than the Greek historians.

16. In the dimensions of this fortress, the old castle of Europe, Phranza does not exactly agree with Chalcocondyles, whose description has been verified on the spot by his editor Leunclavius.

captives;[17] and expressed, in a last message, the firm resignation of a Christian and a soldier. "Since neither oaths, nor treaty, nor submission, can secure peace, pursue," said he to Mahomet, "your impious warfare. My trust is in God alone: if it should please him to mollify your heart, I shall rejoice in the happy change; if he delivers the city into your hands, I submit without a murmur to his holy will. But until the Judge of the earth shall pronounce between us, it is my duty to live and die in the defence of my people." The sultan's answer was hostile and decisive: his fortifications were completed; and before his departure for Adrianople, he stationed a vigilant Aga and four hundred Janizaries, to levy a tribute of the ships of every nation that should pass within the reach of their cannon. A Venetian vessel, refusing obedience to the new lords of the Bosphorus, was sunk with a single bullet. The master and thirty sailors escaped in the boat; but they were dragged in chains to the *porte:* the chief was impaled; his companions were beheaded; and the historian Ducas[18] beheld, at Demotica, their bodies exposed to the wild beasts. The siege of Constantinople was deferred till the ensuing spring; but an Ottoman army marched into the Morea to divert the force of the brothers of Constantine. At this æra of calamity, one of these princes, the despot Thomas, was blessed or afflicted with the birth of a son; "the last heir," says the plaintive Phranza, "of the last spark of the Roman empire".[19]

September 1;

A.D. 1453, January 17.

Preparations for the siege of Constantinople, A.D. 1452, September–A.D. 1453, April.

The Greeks and the Turks passed an anxious and sleepless winter: the former were kept awake by their fears, the latter by their hopes; both by the preparations of defence and attack; and the two emperors, who had the most to lose or to gain, were the most deeply affected by the national sentiment. In Mahomet, that sentiment was inflamed by the ardour of his youth and temper: he amused his leisure with building at Adrianople[20] the lofty palace of Jehan Numa (the watch-tower of the world); but his serious thoughts were irrevocably bent on

17. Among these were some pages of Mahomet so conscious of his inexorable rigour, that they begged to lose their heads in the city unless they could return before sun-set.

18. Ducas, c. 35. Phranza (l. iii. c. 3.), who had sailed in his vessel, commemorates the Venetian pilot as a martyr.

19. Auctum est Palæologorum genus, et Imperii successor, parvæque Romanorum scintillæ hæres natus, Andreas, &c. (Phranza, l. iii. c. 7.) The strong expression was inspired by his feelings.

20. Cantemir, p. 97, 98. The sultan was either doubtful of his conquest, or ignorant of the superior merits of Constantinople. A city or a kingdom may sometimes be ruined by the Imperial fortune of their sovereign.

the conquest of the city of Cæsar. At the dead of night, about the second watch, he started from his bed, and commanded the instant attendance of his prime vizir. The message, the hour, the prince, and his own situation, alarmed the guilty conscience of Calil Basha; who had possessed the confidence, and advised the restoration, of Amurath. On the accession of the son, the vizir was confirmed in his office and the appearances of favour; but the veteran statesman was not insensible that he trod on a thin and slippery ice, which might break under his footsteps, and plunge him in the abyss. His friendship for the Christians, which might be innocent under the late reign, had stigmatised him with the name of Gabour Ortachi, or foster-brother of the infidels;[21] and his avarice entertained a venal and treasonable correspondence, which was detected and punished after the conclusion of the war. On receiving the royal mandate, he embraced, perhaps for the last time, his wife and children; filled a cup with pieces of gold, hastened to the palace, adored the sultan, and offered, according to the Oriental custom, the slight tribute of his duty and gratitude.[22] "It is not my wish," said Mahomet, "to resume my gifts, but rather to heap and multiply them on thy head. In my turn I ask a present far more valuable and important; – Constantinople." As soon as the vizir had recovered from his surprise, "the same God," said he, "who has already given thee so large a portion of the Roman empire, will not deny the remnant, and the capital. His providence, and thy power, assure thy success; and myself, with the rest of thy faithful slaves, will sacrifice our lives and fortunes." "Lala,"[23] (or preceptor), continued the sultan, "do you see this pillow? all the night, in my agitation, I have pulled it on one side and the other; I have risen from my bed, again have I lain down; yet sleep has not visited these weary eyes. Beware of the gold and silver of the Romans: in arms we are superior; and with the aid of God, and the prayers of the prophet, we shall speedily become masters

21. Συντροφος, by the president Cousin, is translated *pere* nourricier, most correctly indeed from the Latin version; but in his haste, he has overlooked the note by which Ismael Boillaud (ad Ducam, c. 35) acknowledges and rectifies his own error.

22. The Oriental custom of never appearing without gifts before a sovereign or a superior, is of high antiquity, and seems analogous with the idea of sacrifice, still more ancient and universal. See the examples of such Persian gifts, Ælian, Hist. Var. l. i. c. 31, 32, 33.

23. The *Lala* of the Turks (Cantemir, p. 34.), and the *Tata* of the Greeks (Ducas, c. 35.), are derived from the natural language of children; and it may be observed, that all such primitive words which denote their parents, are the simple repetition of one syllable, composed of a labial or dental consonant and an open vowel (des Brosses, Mechanisme des Langues, tom. i. p. 231–247.).

of Constantinople." To sound the disposition of his soldiers, he often wandered through the streets alone and in disguise: and it was fatal to discover the sultan, when he wished to escape from the vulgar eye. His hours were spent in delineating the plan of the hostile city: in debating with his generals and engineers, on what spot he should erect his batteries; on which side he should assault the walls; where he should spring his mines; to what place he should apply his scaling-ladders: and the exercises of the day repeated and proved the lucubrations of the night.

The great cannon of Mahomet.

Among the implements of destruction, he studied with peculiar care the recent and tremendous discovery of the Latins; and his artillery surpassed whatever had yet appeared in the world. A founder of cannon, a Dane or Hungarian, who had been almost starved in the Greek service, deserted to the Moslems, and was liberally entertained by the Turkish sultan. Mahomet was satisfied with the answer to his first question, which he eagerly pressed on the artist. "Am I able to cast a cannon capable of throwing a ball or stone of sufficient size to batter the walls of Constantinople? I am not ignorant of their strength, but were they more solid than those of Babylon, I could oppose an engine of superior power: the position and management of that engine must be left to your engineers." On this assurance, a foundery was established at Adrianople: the metal was prepared; and at the end of three months, Urban produced a piece of brass ordnance of stupendous, and almost incredible, magnitude; a measure of twelve palms is assigned to the bore; and the stone bullet weighed above six hundred pounds.[24] A vacant place before the new palace was chosen for the first experiment; but, to prevent the sudden and mischievous effects of astonishment and fear, a proclamation was issued, that the cannon would be discharged the ensuing day. The explosion was felt or heard in a circuit of an hundred furlongs: the ball, by the force of gunpowder, was driven above a mile; and on the spot where it fell, it buried itself a fathom deep in the ground. For the conveyance of this destructive engine, a frame or carriage of thirty waggons was linked together and drawn along by a team of sixty oxen: two hundred men on both sides were stationed to poise and support the rolling weight; two hundred and fifty workmen marched before to smooth the way and repair the bridges; and near two months were

24. The Attic talent weighed about sixty minæ, or averdupois pounds (see Hooper on Ancient Weights, Measures, &c.): but among the modern Greeks, that classic appellation was extended to a weight of one hundred, or one hundred and twenty-five pounds (Ducange, ταλαντον). Leonardus Chiensis measured the ball or stone of the *second* cannon: Lapidem, qui palmis undecim ex meis ambibat in gyro.

employed in a laborious journey of one hundred and fifty miles. A lively philosopher[25] derides on this occasion the credulity of the Greeks, and observes, with much reason, that we should always distrust the exaggerations of a vanquished people. He calculates, that a ball, even of two hundred pounds, would require a charge of one hundred and fifty pounds of powder; and that the stroke would be feeble and impotent, since not a fifteenth part of the mass could be inflamed at the same moment. A stranger as I am to the art of destruction, I can discern that the modern improvements of artillery prefer the number of pieces to the weight of metal; the quickness of the fire to the sound, or even the consequence, of a single explosion. Yet I dare not reject the positive and unanimous evidence of contemporary writers; nor can it seem improbable, that the first artists, in their rude and ambitious efforts, should have transgressed the standard of moderation. A Turkish cannon, more enormous than that of Mahomet, still guards the entrance of the Dardanelles; and if the use be inconvenient, it has been found on a late trial that the effect was far from contemptible. A stone bullet of *eleven* hundred pounds weight was once discharged with three hundred and thirty pounds of powder; at the distance of six hundred yards it shivered into three rocky fragments, traversed the streight, and, leaving the waters in a foam, again rose and bounded against the opposite hill.[26]

Mahomet II. forms the siege of Constantinople, A.D. 1453, April 6.

While Mahomet threatened the capital of the East, the Greek emperor implored with fervent prayers the assistance of earth and heaven. But the invisible powers were deaf to his supplications; and Christendom beheld with indifference the fall of Constantinople, while she derived at least some promise of supply from the jealous and temporal policy of the sultan of Egypt. Some states were too weak, and others too remote; by some the danger was considered as imaginary, by others as inevitable: the Western princes were involved in their endless and domestic quarrels; and the Roman pontiff was exasperated by the falsehood or obstinacy of the Greeks. Instead of employing in their favour the arms and treasures of Italy, Nicholas the fifth had foretold their approaching ruin; and his honour was engaged in the accomplishment of his prophecy. Perhaps he

25. See Voltaire (Hist. Generale, c. xci. p. 294, 295.). He was ambitious of universal monarchy; and the poet frequently aspires to the name and style of an astronomer, a chymist, &c.

26. The Baron de Tott (tom. iii. p. 85–89.), who fortified the Dardanelles against the Russians, describes in a lively, and even comic, strain his own prowess, and the consternation of the Turks. But that adventurous traveller does not possess the art of gaining our confidence.

was softened by the last extremity of their distress; but his compassion was tardy; his efforts were faint and unavailing; and Constantinople had fallen, before the squadrons of Genoa and Venice could sail from their harbours.[27] Even the princes of the Morea and of the Greek islands affected a cold neutrality: the Genoese colony of Galata negociated a private treaty; and the sultan indulged them in the delusive hope, that by his clemency they might survive the ruin of the empire. A plebeian crowd, and some Byzantine nobles, basely withdrew from the danger of their country; and the avarice of the rich denied the emperor, and reserved for the Turks, the secret treasures which might have raised in their defence whole armies of mercenaries.[28] The indigent and solitary prince prepared however to sustain his formidable adversary; but if his courage were equal to the peril, his strength was inadequate to the contest. In the beginning of the spring, the Turkish vanguard swept the towns and villages as far as the gates of Constantinople: submission was spared and protected; whatever presumed to resist was exterminated with fire and sword. The Greek places on the Black Sea, Mesembria, Acheloum, and Bizon, surrendered on the first summons; Selybria alone deserved the honours of a siege or blockade; and the bold inhabitants, while they were invested by land, launched their boats, pillaged the opposite coast of Cyzicus, and sold their captives in the public market. But on the approach of Mahomet himself all was silent and prostrate: he first halted at the distance of five miles; and from thence advancing in battle array, planted before the gate of St. Romanus the Imperial standard; and, on the sixth day of April, formed the memorable siege of Constantinople.

Forces of the Turks;

The troops of Asia and Europe extended on the right and left from the Propontis to the harbour: the Janizaries in the front were stationed before the sultan's tent; the Ottoman line was covered by a deep intrenchment; and a subordinate army inclosed the suburb of Galata, and watched the doubtful faith of the Genoese. The inquisitive

27. Non audivit, indignum ducens, says the honest Antoninus; but as the Roman court was afterwards grieved and ashamed, we find the more courtly expression of Platina, in animo fuisse pontifici juvare Græcos, and the positive assertion of Æneas Sylvius, structam classem, &c. (Spond. A.D. 1453, N° 3.).

28. Antonin. in Proem. – Epist. Cardinal. Isidor. apud Spondanum; and Dr. Johnson, in the tragedy of Irene, has happily seized this characteristic circumstance:

The groaning Greeks dig up the golden caverns,
The accumulated wealth of hoarding ages;
That wealth which, granted to their weeping prince,
Had rang'd embattled nations at their gates.

Philelphus, who resided in Greece about thirty years before the siege, is confident, that all the Turkish forces, of any name or value, could not exceed the number of sixty thousand horse and twenty thousand foot; and he upbraids the pusillanimity of the nations, who had tamely yielded to an handful of Barbarians. Such indeed might be the regular establishment of the *Capiculi,*[29] the troops of the Porte, who marched with the prince, and were paid from his royal treasury. But the bashaws, in their respective governments, maintained or levied a provincial militia; many lands were held by a military tenure; many volunteers were attracted by the hope of spoil; and the sound of the holy trumpet invited a swarm of hungry and fearless fanatics, who might contribute at least to multiply the terrors, and in a first attack to blunt the swords, of the Christians. The whole mass of the Turkish powers is magnified by Ducas, Chalcocondyles, and Leonard of Chios, to the amount of three or four hundred thousand men; but Phranza was a less remote and more accurate judge; and his precise definition of two hundred and fifty-eight thousand does not exceed the measure of experience and probability.[30] The navy of the besiegers was less formidable: the Propontis was overspread with three hundred and twenty sail; but of these no more than eighteen could be rated as gallies of war; and the far greater part must be degraded to the condition of storeships and transports, which poured into the camp

of the Greeks.

fresh supplies of men, ammunition, and provisions. In her last decay, Constantinople was still peopled with more than an hundred thousand inhabitants; but these numbers are found in the accounts, not of war, but of captivity; and they mostly consisted of mechanics, of priests, of women, and of men devoid of that spirit which even women have sometimes exerted for the common safety. I can suppose, I could almost excuse, the reluctance of subjects to serve on a distant frontier, at the will of a tyrant; but the man who dares not expose his life in the defence of his children and his property has lost in society the first and most active energies of nature. By the emperor's command, a particular enquiry had been made through the streets and houses, how many of the

29. The palatine troops are styled *Capiculi*, the provincials, *Seratculi:* and most of the names and institutions of the Turkish militia existed before the *Canon Nameh* of Soliman II. from which, and his own experience, count Marsigli has composed his military state of the Ottoman empire.

30. The observation of Philelphus is approved by Cuspinian in the year 1508 (de Cæsaribus, in Epilog. de Militiâ Turcicâ, p. 697.). Marsigli proves, that the effective armies of the Turks are much less numerous than they appear. In the army that besieged Constantinople, Leonardus Chiensis reckons no more than 15,000 Janizaries.

citizens, or even of the monks, were able and willing to bear arms for their country. The lists were entrusted to Phranza;[31] and, after a diligent addition, he informed his master, with grief and surprise, that the national defence was reduced to four thousand nine hundred and seventy *Romans*. Between Constantine and his faithful minister, this comfortless secret was preserved; and a sufficient proportion of shields, cross-bows, and muskets, was distributed from the arsenal to the city bands. They derived some accession from a body of two thousand strangers, under the command of John Justiniani, a noble Genoese; a liberal donative was advanced to these auxiliaries; and a princely recompense, the isle of Lemnos, was promised to the valour and victory of their chief. A strong chain was drawn across the mouth of the harbour: it was supported by some Greek and Italian vessels of war and merchandise; and the ships of every Christian nation, that successively arrived from Candia and the Black Sea, were detained for the public service. Against the powers of the Ottoman empire, a city of the extent of thirteen, perhaps of sixteen, miles was defended by a scanty garrison of seven or eight thousand soldiers. Europe and Asia were open to the besiegers; but the strength and provisions of the Greeks must sustain a daily decrease; nor could they indulge the expectation of any foreign succour or supply.

False union of the two churches, A.D. 1452, Dec. 12.

The primitive Romans would have drawn their swords in the resolution of death or conquest. The primitive Christians might have embraced each other, and awaited in patience and charity the stroke of martyrdom. But the Greeks of Constantinople were animated only by the spirit of religion, and that spirit was productive only of animosity and discord. Before his death, the emperor John Palæologus had renounced the unpopular measure of an union with the Latins; nor was the idea revived, till the distress of his brother Constantine imposed a last trial of flattery and dissimulation.[32] With the demand of temporal aid, his ambassadors were instructed to mingle the assurance of spiritual obedience: his neglect of the church was excused by the urgent cares of the state; and his orthodox wishes solicited the presence of a Roman legate. The Vatican had been too often

31. Ego, eidem (Imp.) tabellas extribui non absque dolore et mœstitia, mansitque apud nos duos aliis occultus numerus (Phranza, l. iii. c. 8.). With some indulgence for national prejudices, we cannot desire a more authentic witness, not only of public facts, but of private counsels.

32. In Spondanus, the narrative of the union is not only partial, but imperfect. The bishop of Pamiers died in 1642, and the history of Ducas, which represents these scenes (c. 36, 37.) with such truth and spirit, was not printed till the year 1649.

deluded; yet the signs of repentance could not decently be overlooked; a legate was more easily granted than an army; and about six months before the final destruction, the cardinal Isidore of Russia appeared in that character with a retinue of priests and soldiers. The emperor saluted him as a friend and father; respectfully listened to his public and private sermons; and with the most obsequious of the clergy and laymen subscribed the act of union, as it had been ratified in the council of Florence. On the twelfth of December, the two nations, in the church of St. Sophia, joined in the communion of sacrifice and prayer; and the names of the two pontiffs were solemnly commemorated; the names of Nicholas the fifth, the vicar of Christ, and of the patriarch Gregory who had been driven into exile by a rebellious people.

Obstinacy and fanaticism of the Greeks.

But the dress and language of the Latin priest who officiated at the altar, were an object of scandal; and it was observed with horror, that he consecrated a cake or wafer of *unleavened* bread, and poured cold water into the cup of the sacrament. A national historian acknowledges with a blush, that none of his countrymen, not the emperor himself, were sincere in this occasional conformity.[33] Their hasty and unconditional submission was palliated by a promise of future revisal; but the best, or the worst, of their excuses was the confession of their own perjury. When they were pressed by the reproaches of their honest brethren, "Have patience," they whispered, "have patience till God shall have delivered the city from the great dragon who seeks to devour us. You shall then perceive whether we are truly reconciled with the Azymites." But patience is not the attribute of zeal; nor can the arts of a court be adapted to the freedom and violence of popular enthusiasm. From the dome of St. Sophia, the inhabitants of either sex, and of every degree, rushed in crowds to the cell of the monk Gennadius,[34] to consult the oracle of the church. The holy man was invisible; entranced, as it should seem, in deep meditation, or divine rapture: but he had exposed on the door of his cell, a speaking tablet; and they successively withdrew

33. Phranza, one of the conforming Greeks, acknowledges that the measure was adopted only propter spem auxilii; he affirms with pleasure, that those who refused to perform their devotions in St. Sophia, extra culpam et in pace essent (l. iii. c. 20.).

34. His primitive and secular name was George Scholarius, which he changed for that of Gennadius, either when he became a monk or a patriarch. His defence, at Florence, of the same union which he so furiously attacked at Constantinople, has tempted Leo Allatius (Diatrib. de Georgiis, in Fabric. Bibliot. Græc. tom. x. p. 760–786.) to divide him into two men; but Renaudot (p. 343–384.) has restored the identity of his person and the duplicity of his character.

after reading these tremendous words: "O miserable Romans, why will ye abandon the truth; and why, instead of confiding in God, will ye put your trust in the Italians? In losing your faith, you will lose your city. Have mercy on me, O Lord! I protest in thy presence, that I am innocent of the crime. O miserable Romans, consider, pause, and repent. At the same moment that you renounce the religion of your fathers, by embracing impiety, you submit to a foreign servitude." According to the advice of Gennadius, the religious virgins, as pure as angels and as proud as dæmons, rejected the act of union, and abjured all communion with the present and future associates of the Latins; and their example was applauded and imitated by the greatest part of the clergy and people. From the monastery, the devout Greeks dispersed themselves in the taverns; drank confusion to the slaves of the pope; emptied their glasses in honour of the image of the holy Virgin; and besought her to defend against Mahomet, the city which she had formerly saved from Chosroes and the Chagan. In the double intoxication of zeal and wine, they valiantly exclaimed, "What occasion have we for succour, or union, or Latins? far from us be the worship of the Azymites!" During the winter that preceded the Turkish conquest, the nation was distracted by this epidemical frenzy; and the season of Lent, the approach of Easter, instead of breathing charity and love, served only to fortify the obstinacy and influence of the zealots. The confessors scrutinised and alarmed the conscience of their votaries, and a rigorous penance was imposed on those, who had received the communion from a priest, who had given an express or tacit consent to the union. His service at the altar propagated the infection to the mute and simple spectators of the ceremony: they forfeited, by the impure spectacle, the virtue of the sacerdotal character; nor was it lawful, even in danger of sudden death, to invoke the assistance of their prayers or absolution. No sooner had the church of St. Sophia been polluted by the Latin sacrifice, than it was deserted as a Jewish synagogue, or an heathen temple, by the clergy and people: and a vast and gloomy silence prevailed in that venerable dome, which had so often smoked with a cloud of incense, blazed with innumerable lights, and resounded with the voice of prayer and thanksgiving. The Latins were the most odious of heretics and infidels; and the first minister of the empire, the great duke, was heard to declare, that he had rather behold in Constantinople the turban of Mahomet, than the pope's tiara or a cardinal's hat.[35] A sentiment so unworthy of Christians and patriots, was

35. *Φακιολιον, καλυπτρα*, may be fairly translated a cardinal's hat. The difference of the Greek and Latin habits embittered the schism.

familiar and fatal to the Greeks: the emperor was deprived of the affection and support of his subjects; and their native cowardice was sanctified by resignation to the divine decree, or the visionary hope of a miraculous deliverance.

Siege of Constantinople by Mahomet II. A.D. 1453, April 6– May 29.

Of the triangle which composes the figure of Constantinople, the two sides along the sea were made inaccessible to an enemy; the Propontis by nature, and the harbour by art. Between the two waters, the basis of the triangle, the land side was protected by a double wall, and a deep ditch of the depth of one hundred feet. Against this line of fortification, which Phranza, an eye-witness, prolongs to the measure of six miles,[36] the Ottomans directed their principal attack; and the emperor, after distributing the service and command of the most perilous stations, undertook the defence of the external wall. In the first days of the siege, the Greek soldiers descended into the ditch, or sallied into the field; but they soon discovered, that, in the proportion of their numbers, one Christian was of more value than twenty Turks: and, after these bold preludes, they were prudently content to maintain the rampart with their missile weapons. Nor should this prudence be accused of pusillanimity. The nation was indeed pusillanimous and base; but the last Constantine deserves the name of an hero: his noble band of volunteers was inspired with Roman virtue; and the foreign auxiliaries supported the honour of the Western chivalry. Their incessant vollies of lances and arrows were accompanied with the smoke, the sound, and the fire, of their musketry and cannon. Their small arms discharged at the same time either five, or even ten, balls of lead, of the size of a walnut; and, according to the closeness of the ranks and the force of the powder, several breastplates and bodies were transpierced by the same shot. But the Turkish approaches were soon sunk in trenches, or covered with ruins. Each day added to the science of the Christians; but their inadequate stock of gunpowder was wasted in the operations of each day. Their ordnance was not powerful, either in size or number; and if they possessed some heavy cannon, they feared to plant them on the walls, lest the aged structure should be shaken and overthrown by the explosion.[37] The same

36. We are obliged to reduce the Greek miles to the smallest measure which is preserved in the wersts of Russia, of 547 French *toises*, and of $104\frac{2}{5}$ to a degree. The six miles of Phranza do not exceed four English miles (d'Anville, Mesures Itineraires, p. 61. 123, &c.).

37. At indies doctiores nostri facti paravere contra hostes machinamenta, quæ tamen avare dabantur. Pulvis erat nitri modica exigua; tela modica; bombardæ, si aderant incommoditate loci primum hostes offendere maceriebus alveisque tectos non poterant. Nam siquæ magnæ erant, ne murus

destructive secret had been revealed to the Moslems; by whom it was employed with the superior energy of zeal, riches, and despotism. The great cannon of Mahomet has been separately noticed; an important and visible object in the history of the times: but that enormous engine was flanked by two fellows almost of equal magnitude:[38] the long order of the Turkish artillery was pointed against the walls; fourteen batteries thundered at once on the most accessible places; and of one of these it is ambiguously expressed, that it was mounted with one hundred and thirty guns, or that it discharged one hundred and thirty bullets. Yet, in the power and activity of the sultan, we may discern the infancy of the new science. Under a master who counted the moments, the great cannon could be loaded and fired no more than seven times in one day.[39] The heated metal unfortunately burst; several workmen were destroyed; and the skill of an artist was admired who bethought himself of preventing the danger and the accident, by pouring oil, after each explosion, into the mouth of the cannon.

Attack and defence.

The first random shots were productive of more sound than effect; and it was by the advice of a Christian, that the engineers were taught to level their aim against the two opposite sides of the salient angles of a bastion. However imperfect, the weight and repetition of the fire made some impression on the walls; and the Turks, pushing their approaches to the edge of the ditch, attempted to fill the enormous chasm, and to build a road to the assault.[40] Innumerable fascines, and hogsheads, and trunks of trees, were heaped on each other; and such was the impetuosity of the throng, that the foremost and the weakest were pushed headlong down the precipice, and instantly buried under the accumulated mass. To fill the ditch, was the toil of the besiegers; to clear away the rubbish, was the safety of the besieged; and, after a long and bloody conflict, the web that had been woven in the day was still

---

concuteretur noster, quiescebant. This passage of Leonardus Chiensis is curious and important.

38. According to Chalcocondyles and Phranza, the great cannon burst; an accident which, according to Ducas, was prevented by the artist's skill. It is evident that they do not speak of the same gun.

39. Near an hundred years after the siege of Constantinople, the French and English fleets in the Channel were proud of firing 300 shot in an engagement of two hours (Memoires de Martin du Bellay, l. x. in the Collection Generale, tom. xxi. p. 239.).

40. I have selected some curious facts, without striving to emulate the bloody and obstinate eloquence of the abbé de Vertot, in his prolix descriptions of the sieges of Rhodes, Malta, &c. But that agreeable historian had a turn for romance, and as he wrote to please the order, he has adopted the same spirit of enthusiasm and chivalry.

unravelled in the night. The next resource of Mahomet was the practice of mines; but the soil was rocky; in every attempt he was stopped and undermined by the Christian engineers; nor had the art been yet invented of replenishing those subterraneous passages with gunpowder, and blowing whole towers and cities into the air.[41] A circumstance that distinguishes the siege of Constantinople, is the re-union of the ancient and modern artillery. The cannon were intermingled with the mechanical engines for casting stones and darts; the bullet and the battering-ram were directed against the same walls; nor had the discovery of gunpowder superseded the use of the liquid and unextinguishable fire. A wooden turret of the largest size was advanced on rollers: this portable magazine of ammunition and fascines was protected by a threefold covering of bulls hides; incessant vollies were securely discharged from the loop-holes; in the front, three doors were contrived for the alternate sally and retreat of the soldiers and workmen. They ascended by a stair-case to the upper platform; and, as high as the level of that platform, a scaling-ladder could be raised by pullies to form a bridge and grapple with the adverse rampart. By these various arts of annoyance, some as new as they were pernicious to the Greeks, the tower of St. Romanus was at length overturned: after a severe struggle, the Turks were repulsed from the breach and interrupted by darkness; but they trusted, that with the return of light they should renew the attack with fresh vigour and decisive success. Of this pause of action, this interval of hope, each moment was improved by the activity of the emperor and Justiniani, who passed the night on the spot, and urged the labours which involved the safety of the church and city. At the dawn of day, the impatient sultan perceived, with astonishment and grief, that his wooden turret had been reduced to ashes: the ditch was cleared and restored; and the tower of St. Romanus was again strong and entire. He deplored the failure of his design; and uttered a profane exclamation, that the word of the thirty-seven thousand prophets should not have compelled him to believe that such a work, in so short a time, could have been accomplished by the infidels.

Succour and victory of four ships.

The generosity of the Christian princes was cold and tardy; but in the first apprehension of a siege, Constantine had negociated, in the isles of the Archipelago, the Morea, and Sicily,

41. The first theory of mines with gunpowder appears in 1480, in a MS. of George of Sienna (Tiraboschi, tom. vi. P. i. p. 324.). They were first practised at Sarzanella, in 1487; but the honour and improvement in 1503 is ascribed to Peter of Navarre, who used them with success in the wars of Italy (Hist. de la Ligue de Cambray, tom. ii. p. 93–97.).

the most indispensable supplies. As early as the beginning of April, five[42] great ships, equipped for merchandise and war, would have sailed from the harbour of Chios, had not the wind blown obstinately from the north.[43] One of these ships bore the Imperial flag; the remaining four belonged to the Genoese; and they were laden with wheat and barley, with wine, oil, and vegetables, and, above all, with soldiers and mariners, for the service of the capital. After a tedious delay, a gentle breeze, and, on the second day, a strong gale from the south, carried them through the Hellespont and the Propontis: but the city was already invested by sea and land; and the Turkish fleet, at the entrance of the Bosphorus, was stretched from shore to shore, in the form of a crescent, to intercept, or at least to repel, these bold auxiliaries. The reader who has present to his mind the geographical picture of Constantinople, will conceive and admire the greatness of the spectacle. The five Christian ships continued to advance with joyful shouts, and a full press, both of sails and oars, against an hostile fleet of three hundred vessels; and the rampart, the camp, the coasts of Europe and Asia, were lined with innumerable spectators, who anxiously awaited the event of this momentous succour. At the first view that event could not appear doubtful; the superiority of the Moslems was beyond all measure or account; and, in a calm, their numbers and valour must inevitably have prevailed. But their hasty and imperfect navy had been created, not by the genius of the people, but by the will of the sultan: in the height of their prosperity, the Turks have acknowledged, that if God had given them the earth, he had left the sea to the infidels;[44] and a series of defeats, a rapid progress of decay, has established the truth of their modest confession. Except eighteen gallies of some force, the rest of their fleet consisted of open boats, rudely constructed and awkwardly managed, crowded with troops, and destitute of cannon; and, since courage arises in a great measure from the consciousness of strength, the bravest of the Janizaries might tremble on a

42. It is singular that the Greeks should not agree in the number of these illustrious vessels; the *five* of Ducas, the *four* of Phranza and Leonardus, and the *two* of Chalcocondyles, must be extended to the smaller, or confined to the larger, size. Voltaire, in giving one of these ships to Frederic III. confounds the emperors of the East and West.

43. In bold defiance, or rather in gross ignorance, of language and geography, the president Cousin detains them at Chios with a south, and wafts them to Constantinople with a north, wind.

44. The perpetual decay and weakness of the Turkish navy, may be observed in Rycaut (State of the Ottoman Empire, p. 372–378.), Thevenot (Voyages, P. i. p. 229–242.), and Tott (Memoires, tom iii.); the last of whom is always solicitous to amuse and amaze his reader.

new element. In the Christian squadron, five stout and lofty ships were guided by skilful pilots, and manned with the veterans of Italy and Greece, long practised in the arts and perils of the sea. Their weight was directed to sink or scatter the weak obstacles that impeded their passage: their artillery swept the waters: their liquid fire was poured on the heads of the adversaries, who, with the design of boarding, presumed to approach them; and the winds and waves are always on the side of the ablest navigators. In this conflict, the Imperial vessel, which had been almost overpowered, was rescued by the Genoese; but the Turks, in a distant and a closer attack, were twice repulsed with considerable loss. Mahomet himself sat on horseback on the beach, to encourage their valour by his voice and presence, by the promise of reward, and by fear, more potent than the fear of the enemy. The passions of his soul, and even the gestures of his body,[45] seemed to imitate the actions of the combatants; and, as if he had been the lord of nature, he spurred his horse with a fearless and impotent effort into the sea. His loud reproaches, and the clamours of the camp, urged the Ottomans to a third attack, more fatal and bloody than the two former; and I must repeat, though I cannot credit, the evidence of Phranza, who affirms, from their own mouth, that they lost above twelve thousand men in the slaughter of the day. They fled in disorder to the shores of Europe and Asia, while the Christian squadron, triumphant and unhurt, steered along the Bosphorus, and securely anchored within the chain of the harbour. In the confidence of victory, they boasted that the whole Turkish power must have yielded to their arms; but the admiral, or captain bashaw, found some consolation for a painful wound in his eye, by representing that accident as the cause of his defeat. Baltha Ogli was a renegade of the race of the Bulgarian princes: his military character was tainted with the unpopular vice of avarice; and under the despotism of the prince or people, misfortune is a sufficient evidence of guilt. His rank and services were annihilated by the displeasure of Mahomet. In the royal presence, the captain bashaw was extended on the ground by four slaves, and received one hundred strokes with a golden rod:[46] his death had been pronounced; and he adored the clemency of the sultan, who was satisfied with the milder punishment of confiscation and exile. The introduction of this supply revived the hopes of the

45. I must confess, that I have before my eyes the living picture which Thucydides (l. vii. c. 71.) has drawn of the passions and gestures of the Athenians in a naval engagement in the great harbour of Syracuse.

46. According to the exaggeration or corrupt text of Ducas (c. 38.), this golden bar was of the enormous and incredible weight of 500 libræ, or pounds. Bouillaud's

Greeks, and accused the supineness of their western allies. Amidst the deserts of Anatolia and the rocks of Palestine, the millions of the crusades had buried themselves in a voluntary and inevitable grave; but the situation of the Imperial city was strong against her enemies, and accessible to her friends; and a rational and moderate armament of the maritime states might have saved the relics of the Roman name, and maintained a Christian fortress in the heart of the Ottoman empire. Yet this was the sole and feeble attempt for the deliverance of Constantinople: the more distant powers were insensible of its danger; and the ambassador of Hungary, or at least of Huniades, resided in the Turkish camp, to remove the fears, and to direct the operations, of the sultan.[47]

Mahomet transports his navy over land.

It was difficult for the Greeks to penetrate the secret of the divan; yet the Greeks are persuaded, that a resistance, so obstinate and surprising, had fatigued the perseverance of Mahomet. He began to meditate a retreat, and the siege would have been speedily raised if the ambition and jealousy of the second vizir had not opposed the perfidious advice of Calil Bashaw, who still maintained a secret correspondence with the Byzantine court. The reduction of the city appeared to be hopeless, unless a double attack could be made from the harbour as well as from the land; but the harbour was inaccessible: an impenetrable chain was now defended by eight large ships, more than twenty of a smaller size, with several gallies and sloops; and, instead of forcing this barrier, the Turks might apprehend a naval sally, and a second encounter in the open sea. In this perplexity, the genius of Mahomet conceived and executed a plan of a bold and marvellous cast, of transporting by land his lighter vessels and military stores from the Bosphorus into the higher part of the harbour. The distance is about ten miles; the ground is uneven, and was overspread with thickets; and, as the road must be opened behind the suburb of Galata, their free passage or total destruction must depend on the option of the Genoese. But these selfish merchants were ambitious of the favour of being the last devoured; and the deficiency of art was supplied by the strength of obedient myriads. A level way was covered with a broad platform of strong and solid planks; and to render them more slippery and smooth, they were anointed with

reading of 500 drachms, or five pounds, is sufficient to exercise the arm of Mahomet, and bruise the back of his admiral.

47. Ducas, who confesses himself ill informed of the affairs of Hungary, assigns a motive of superstition, a fatal belief that Constantinople would be the term of the Turkish conquests. See Phranza (l. iii. c. 20.) and Spondanus.

the fat of sheep and oxen. Fourscore light gallies and brigantines of fifty and thirty oars, were disembarked on the Bosphorus shore; arranged successively on rollers; and drawn forwards by the power of men and pullies. Two guides or pilots were stationed at the helm, and the prow, of each vessel; the sails were unfurled to the winds; and the labour was cheered by song and acclamation. In the course of a single night, this Turkish fleet painfully climbed the hill, steered over the plain, and was launched from the declivity into the shallow waters of the harbour, far above the molestation of the deeper vessels of the Greeks. The real importance of this operation was magnified by the consternation and confidence which it inspired: but the notorious, unquestionable, fact was displayed before the eyes, and is recorded by the pens, of the two nations.[48] A similar stratagem had been repeatedly practised by the ancients;[49] the Ottoman gallies (I must again repeat) should be considered as large boats; and, if we compare the magnitude and the distance, the obstacles and the means, the boasted miracle[50] has perhaps been equalled by the industry of our own times.[51] As soon as Mahomet had occupied the upper harbour with a fleet and army; he constructed, in the narrowest part, a bridge, or rather mole, of fifty cubits in breadth and one hundred in length: it was formed of casks and hogsheads; joined with rafters, linked with iron, and covered with a solid floor. On this floating battery, he planted one of his largest cannon, while the fourscore gallies, with troops and scaling-ladders, approached the most accessible side, which had formerly been stormed by the Latin conquerors. The indolence of the Christians has been accused for not destroying these unfinished works; but their fire, by a superior fire was controlled and silenced; nor were they wanting in a nocturnal attempt to burn the vessels as well as the bridge of the sultan. His vigilance prevented their approach; their foremost galliots were sunk or taken; forty youths, the bravest of Italy and Greece, were inhumanly

48. The unanimous testimony of the four Greeks is confirmed by Cantemir (p. 96.) from the Turkish annals: but I could wish to contract the distance of *ten* miles, and to prolong the term of *one* night.

49. Phranza relates two examples of a similar transportation over the six miles of the Isthmus of Corinth; the one fabulous, of Augustus after the battle of Actium; the other true, of Nicetas, a Greek general in the xth century. To these he might have added a bold enterprise of Hannibal, to introduce his vessels into the harbour of Tarentum (Polybius, l. viii. p. 749 edit. Gronov.).

50. A Greek of Candia, who had served the Venetians in a similar undertaking (Spond. A.D. 1438, N° 37.), might possibly be the adviser and agent of Mahomet.

51. I particularly allude to our own embarkations on the lakes of Canada in the years 1776 and 1777, so great in the labour, so fruitless in the event.

massacred at his command; nor could the emperor's grief be assuaged by the just though cruel retaliation, of exposing from the walls the heads of two hundred and sixty Musulman captives. After a siege of forty days, the fate of Constantinople could no longer be averted. The diminutive garrison was exhausted by a double attack: the fortifications, which had stood for ages against hostile violence, were dismantled on all sides by the Ottoman cannon: many breaches were opened; and near the gate of St. Romanus, four towers had been levelled with the ground. For the payment of his feeble and mutinous troops, Constantine was compelled to despoil the churches with the promise of a fourfold restitution; and his sacrilege offered a new reproach to the enemies of the union. A spirit of discord impaired the remnant of the Christian strength: the Genoese and Venetian auxiliaries asserted the pre-eminence of their respective service; and Justiniani and the great duke, whose ambition was not extinguished by the common danger, accused each other of treachery and cowardice.

Distress of the city.

During the siege of Constantinople, the words of peace and capitulation had been sometimes pronounced; and several embassies had passed between the camp and the city.[52] The Greek emperor was humbled by adversity; and would have yielded to any terms compatible with religion and royalty. The Turkish sultan was desirous of sparing the blood of his soldiers; still more desirous of securing for his own use the Byzantine treasures; and he accomplished a sacred duty in presenting to the *Gabours*, the choice of circumcision, of tribute, or of death. The avarice of Mahomet might have been satisfied with an annual sum of one hundred thousand ducats: but his ambition grasped the capital of the East: to the prince he offered a rich equivalent, to the people a free toleration, or a safe departure: but after some fruitless treaty, he declared his resolution of finding either a throne, or a grave, under the walls of Constantinople. A sense of honour, and the fear of universal reproach, forbade Palæologus to resign the city into the hands of the Ottomans; and he determined to abide the last extremities of war. Several days were employed by the sultan in the preparations of the assault; and a respite was granted by his favourite science of astrology, which had fixed on the twenty-ninth of May, as the fortunate and fatal hour. On the evening of the twenty-seventh, he issued his final orders; assembled in his presence the military chiefs; and dispersed

Preparations of the Turks for the general assault, May 26.

52. Chalcocondyles and Ducas differ in the time and circumstances of the negociation; and as it was neither glorious nor salutary, the faithful Phranza spares his prince even the thought of a surrender.

his heralds through the camp to proclaim the duty, and the motives, of the perilous enterprise. Fear is the first principle of a despotic government; and his menaces were expressed in the Oriental style, that the fugitives and deserters, had they the wings of a bird,[53] should not escape from his inexorable justice. The greatest part of his bashaws and Janizaries were the offspring of Christian parents; but the glories of the Turkish name were perpetuated by successive adoption; and in the gradual change of individuals, the spirit of a legion, a regiment, or an *oda*, is kept alive by imitation and discipline. In this holy warfare, the Moslems were exhorted to purify their minds with prayer, their bodies with seven ablutions; and to abstain from food till the close of the ensuing day. A crowd of dervishes visited the tents to instil the desire of martyrdom, and the assurance of spending an immortal youth amidst the rivers and gardens of paradise, and in the embraces of the black-eyed virgins. Yet Mahomet principally trusted to the efficacy of temporal and visible rewards. A double pay was promised to the victorious troops; "The city and the buildings," said Mahomet, "are mine: but I resign to your valour the captives and the spoil, the treasures of gold and beauty: be rich and be happy. Many are the provinces of my empire: the intrepid soldier who first ascends the walls of Constantinople, shall be rewarded with the government of the fairest and most wealthy; and my gratitude shall accumulate his honours and fortunes above the measure of his own hopes." Such various and potent motives diffused among the Turks a general ardour, regardless of life and impatient for action: the camp re-echoed with the Moslem shouts of, "God is God, there is but one God,

53. These wings (Chalcocondyles, l. viii. p. 208.) are no more than an Oriental figure: but in the tragedy of Irene, Mahomet's passion soars above sense and reason:

> Should the fierce North, upon his frozen wings,
> Bear him aloft above the wondering clouds,
> And seat him in the Pleiads golden chariot –
> Thence should my fury drag him down to tortures.

Besides the extravagance of the rant, I must observe, 1. That the operation of the winds must be confined to the *lower* region of the air. 2. That the name, etymology, and fable of the Pleiads are purely Greek (Scholiast ad Homer. Σ 686. Eudocia in Ioniâ, p. 339. Apollodor. l. iii. c. 10. Heine, p. 229. Not. 682.), and had no affinity with the astronomy of the East (Hyde ad Ulugbeg, Tabul. in Syntagma Dissert. tom. i. p. 40. 42. Goguet, Origine des Arts, &c. tom. vi. p. 73–78. Gebelin, Hist. du Calendrier, p. 73.), which Mahomet had studied. 3. The golden chariot does not exist either in science or fiction; but I much fear that Dr. Johnson has confounded the Pleiads with the great bear or waggon, the zodiac with a northern constellation:

> Αρκτον θ' ἣν και ἁμαξαν επικλησιν καλεουσι.

and Mahomet is the apostle of God;"[54] and the sea and land, from Galata to the seven towers, were illuminated by the blaze of their nocturnal fires.

Last farewel of the emperor and the Greeks.

Far different was the state of the Christians; who, with loud and impotent complaints, deplored the guilt, or the punishment, of their sins. The celestial image of the Virgin had been exposed in solemn procession; but their divine patroness was deaf to their entreaties; they accused the obstinacy of the emperor for refusing a timely surrender; anticipated the horrors of their fate; and sighed for the repose and security of Turkish servitude. The noblest of the Greeks, and the bravest of the allies, were summoned to the palace, to prepare them, on the evening of the twenty-eighth, for the duties and dangers of the general assault. The last speech of Palæologus was the funeral oration of the Roman empire:[55] he promised, he conjured, and he vainly attempted to infuse the hope which was extinguished in his own mind. In this world all was comfortless and gloomy; and neither the gospel nor the church have proposed any conspicuous recompense to the heroes who fall in the service of their country. But the example of their prince, and the confinement of a siege, had armed these warriors with the courage of despair; and the pathetic scene is described by the feelings of the historian Phranza, who was himself present at this mournful assembly. They wept, they embraced; regardless of their families and fortunes, they devoted their lives; and each commander, departing to his station, maintained all night a vigilant and anxious watch on the rampart. The emperor, and some faithful companions, entered the dome of St. Sophia, which in a few hours was to be converted into a mosch; and devoutly received, with tears and prayers, the sacrament of the holy communion. He reposed some moments in the palace, which resounded with cries and lamentations; solicited the pardon of all whom he might have injured;[56] and mounted on horseback to visit the guards, and explore the motions of the enemy. The distress and

54. Phranza quarrels with these Moslem acclamations, not for the name of God, but for that of the prophet: the pious zeal of Voltaire is excessive, and even ridiculous.

55. I am afraid that this discourse was composed by Phranza himself: and it smells so grossly of the sermon and the convent, that I almost doubt whether it was pronounced by Constantine. Leonardus assigns him another speech, in which he addresses himself more respectfully to the Latin auxiliaries.

56. This abasement, which devotion has sometimes extorted from dying princes, is an improvement of the gospel doctrine of the forgiveness of injuries: it is more easy to forgive 490 times, than once to ask pardon of an inferior.

fall of the last Constantine are more glorious than the long prosperity of the Byzantine Cæsars.

The general assault, May 29.

In the confusion of darkness an assailant may sometimes succeed; but in this great and general attack, the military judgment and astrological knowledge of Mahomet advised him to expect the morning, the memorable twenty-ninth of May, in the fourteen hundred and fifty-third year of the Christian æra. The preceding night had been strenuously employed: the troops, the cannon, and the fascines, were advanced to the edge of the ditch, which in many parts presented a smooth and level passage to the breach; and his fourscore gallies almost touched with the prows and their scaling-ladders, the less defensible walls of the harbour. Under pain of death, silence was enjoined: but the physical laws of motion and sound are not obedient to discipline or fear; each individual might suppress his voice and measure his footsteps; but the march and labour of thousands must inevitably produce a strange confusion of dissonant clamours, which reached the ears of the watchmen of the towers. At day-break, without the customary signal of the morning gun, the Turks assaulted the city by sea and land; and the similitude of a twined or twisted thread had been applied to the closeness and continuity of their line of attack.[57] The foremost ranks consisted, of the refuse of the host, a voluntary crowd who fought without order or command; of the feebleness of age or childhood, of peasants and vagrants, and of all who had joined the camp in the blind hope of plunder and martyrdom. The common impulse drove them onwards to the wall: the most audacious to climb were instantly precipitated; and not a dart, not a bullet, of the Christians, was idly wasted on the accumulated throng. But their strength and ammunition were exhausted in this laborious defence: the ditch was filled with the bodies of the slain; they supported the footsteps of their companions; and of this devoted vanguard, the death was more serviceable than the life. Under their respective bashaws and sanjaks, the troops of Anatolia and Romania were successively led to the charge: their progress was various and doubtful; but, after a conflict of two hours, the Greeks still maintained, and improved, their advantage; and the voice of the emperor was heard, encouraging his soldiers to atchieve, by a last effort, the deliverance of their country. In that fatal moment, the Janizaries arose, fresh, vigorous, and invincible. The sultan himself on horseback, with an iron mace in his hand, was the spectator and judge of their

57. Besides the 10,000 guards, and the sailors and the marines, Ducas numbers in this general assault 250,000 Turks both horse and foot.

valour: he was surrounded by ten thousand of his domestic troops, whom he reserved for the decisive occasions; and the tide of battle was directed and impelled by his voice and eye. His numerous ministers of justice were posted behind the line, to urge, to restrain, and to punish; and if danger was in the front, shame and inevitable death were in the rear, of the fugitives. The cries of fear and of pain were drowned in the martial music of drums, trumpets, and attaballs; and experience has proved, that the mechanical operation of sounds, by quickening the circulation of the blood and spirits, will act on the human machine more forcibly than the eloquence of reason and honour. From the lines, the gallies, and the bridge, the Ottoman artillery thundered on all sides; and the camp and city, the Greeks and the Turks, were involved in a cloud of smoke, which could only be dispelled by the final deliverance or destruction of the Roman empire. The single combats of the heroes of history or fable, amuse our fancy and engage our affections: the skilful evolutions of war may inform the mind, and improve a necessary, though pernicious, science. But in the uniform and odious pictures of a general assault, all is blood, and horror, and confusion; nor shall I strive, at the distance of three centuries and a thousand miles, to delineate a scene, of which there could be no spectators, and of which the actors themselves were incapable of forming any just or adequate idea.

The immediate loss of Constantinople may be ascribed to the bullet, or arrow, which pierced the gauntlet of John Justiniani. The sight of his blood, and the exquisite pain, appalled the courage of the chief, whose arms and counsels were the firmest rampart of the city. As he withdrew from his station in quest of a surgeon, his flight was perceived and stopped by the indefatigable emperor. "Your wound," exclaimed Palæologus, "is slight; the danger is pressing; your presence is necessary; and whither will you retire?" "I will retire," said the trembling Genoese, "by the same road which God has opened to the Turks;" and at these words he hastily passed through one of the breaches of the inner wall. By this pusillanimous act, he stained the honours of a military life; and the few days which he survived in Galata, or the isle of Chios, were embittered by his own and the public reproach.[58] His example was imitated by the greatest part of

58. In the severe censure of the flight of Justiniani, Phranza expresses his own feelings, and those of the public. For some private reasons, he is treated with more lenity and respect by Ducas; but the words of Leonardus Chiensis express his strong and recent indignation, gloriæ salutis suique oblitus. In the whole series of their Eastern policy, his countrymen, the Genoese, were always suspected, and often guilty.

the Latin auxiliaries, and the defence began to slacken when the attack was pressed with redoubled vigour. The number of the Ottomans was fifty, perhaps an hundred, times superior to that of the Christians: the double walls were reduced by the cannon to an heap of ruins: in a circuit of several miles, some places must be found more easy of access, or more feebly guarded; and if the besiegers could penetrate in a single point, the whole city was irrecoverably lost. The first who deserved the sultan's reward was Hassan the Janizary, of gigantic stature and strength. With his scymetar in one hand and his buckler in the other, he ascended the outward fortification: of the thirty Janizaries, who were emulous of his valour, eighteen perished in the bold adventure. Hassan and his twelve companions had reached the summit; the giant was precipitated from the rampart; he rose on one knee, and was again oppressed by a shower of darts and stones. But his success had proved that the atchievement was possible: the walls and towers were instantly covered with a swarm of Turks; and the Greeks, now driven from the vantage ground, were overwhelmed by encreasing multitudes. Amidst these multitudes, the emperor,[59] who accomplished all the duties of a general and a soldier, was long seen, and finally lost. The nobles, who fought round his person, sustained till their last breath the honourable names of Palæologus and Cantacuzene: his mournful exclamation was heard, "Cannot there be found a Christian to cut off my head?"[60] and his last fear was that of falling alive into the hands of the infidels.[61] The prudent despair of Constantine cast away the purple: amidst the tumult he fell by an unknown hand, and his body was buried under a mountain of the slain. After his death, resistance and order were no more: the Greeks fled towards the city; and many were pressed and stifled in the narrow pass of the gate of St. Romanus. The

Death of the emperor Constantine Palæologus.

59. Ducas kills him with two blows of Turkish soldiers; Chalcocondyles wounds him in the shoulder, and then tramples him in the gate. The grief of Phranza carrying him among the enemy, escapes from the precise image of his death; but we may, without flattery, apply these noble lines of Dryden:

As to Sebastian, let them search the field;
And where they find a mountain of the slain;
Send one to climb, and looking down beneath,
There they will find him at his manly length,
With his face up to heaven, in that red monument
Which his good sword had digged.

60. Spondanus (A.D. 1453, N° 10.), who has hopes of his salvation, wishes to absolve this demand from the guilt of suicide.

61. Leonardus Chiensis very properly observes, that the Turks, had they known the emperor, would have laboured to save and secure a captive so acceptable to the sultan.

victorious Turks rushed through the breaches of the inner wall; and as they advanced into the streets, they were soon joined by their brethren, who had forced the gate Phenar on the side of the harbour.[62] In the first heat of the pursuit, about two thousand Christians were put to the sword; but avarice soon prevailed over cruelty; and the victors acknowledged, that they should immediately have given quarter if the valour of the emperor and his chosen bands had not prepared them for a similar opposition in every part of the capital. It was thus, after a siege of fifty-three days, that Constantinople, which had defied the power of Chosroes, the Chagan, and the caliphs, was irretrievably subdued by the arms of Mahomet the second. Her empire only had been subverted by the Latins: her religion was trampled in the dust by the Moslem conquerors.[63]

Loss of the city and empire.

The Turks enter and pillage Constantinople.

The tidings of misfortune fly with a rapid wing; yet such was the extent of Constantinople, that the more distant quarters might prolong some moments the happy ignorance of their ruin.[64] But in the general consternation, in the feelings of selfish or social anxiety, in the tumult and thunder of the assault, a *sleepless* night and morning must have elapsed; nor can I believe that many Grecian ladies were awakened by the Janizaries from a sound and tranquil slumber. On the assurance of the public calamity, the houses and convents were instantly deserted, and the trembling inhabitants flocked together in the streets, like an herd of timid animals; as if accumulated weakness could be productive of strength, or in the vain hope, that amid the crowd, each individual might be safe and invisible. From every part of the capital, they flowed into the church of St. Sophia: in the space of an hour, the sanctuary, the choir, the nave, the upper and lower galleries, were filled with the multitudes of fathers and husbands, of women and children, of priests, monks, and religious virgins: the doors were barred on the inside, and they sought protection from the sacred dome, which they had so lately abhorred as a profane and polluted edifice. Their confidence was

62. Cantemir, p. 96. The Christian ships in the mouth of the harbour, had flanked and retarded this naval attack.

63. Chalcocondyles most absurdly supposes, that Constantinople was sacked by the Asiatics in revenge for the ancient calamities of Troy; and the grammarians of the xv[th] century are happy to melt down the uncouth appellation of Turks, into the more classical name of *Teucri*.

64. When Cyrus surprised Babylon during the celebration of a festival, so vast was the city, and so careless were the inhabitants, that much time elapsed before the distant quarters knew that they were captives. Herodotus (l. i. c. 191.), and Usher (Annal. p. 78.), who has quoted from the prophet Jeremiah a passage of similar import.

founded on the prophecy of an enthusiast or impostor; that one day the Turks would enter Constantinople, and pursue the Romans as far as the column of Constantine in the square before St. Sophia: but that this would be the term of their calamities: that an angel would descend from heaven, with a sword in his hand, and would deliver the empire, with that celestial weapon, to a poor man seated at the foot of the column. "Take this sword," would he say, "and avenge the people of the Lord." At these animating words, the Turks would instantly fly, and the victorious Romans would drive them from the West, and from all Anatolia, as far as the frontiers of Persia. It is on this occasion, that Ducas, with some fancy and much truth, upbraids the discord and obstinacy of the Greeks. "Had that angel appeared," exclaims the historian, "had he offered to exterminate your foes if you would consent to the union of the church, even then, in that fatal moment, you would have rejected your safety or have deceived your God."[65]

Captivity of the Greeks. While they expected the descent of the tardy angel, the doors were broken with axes; and as the Turks encountered no resistance, their bloodless hands were employed in selecting and securing the multitude of their prisoners. Youth, beauty, and the appearance of wealth, attracted their choice; and the right of property was decided among themselves by a prior seizure, by personal strength, and by the authority of command. In the space of an hour, the male captives were bound with cords, the females with their veils and girdles. The senators were linked with their slaves; the prelates, with the porters, of the church; and young men of a plebeian class, with noble maids, whose faces had been invisible to the sun and their nearest kindred. In this common captivity, the ranks of society were confounded; the ties of nature were cut asunder; and the inexorable soldier was careless of the father's groans, the tears of the mother, and the lamentations of the children. The loudest in their wailings were the nuns, who were torn from the altar with naked bosoms, outstretched hands, and dishevelled hair: and we should piously believe that few could be tempted to prefer the vigils of the haram to those of the monastery. Of these unfortunate Greeks, of these domestic animals, whole strings were rudely driven through the streets; and as the

65. This lively description is extracted from Ducas (c. 39.), who two years afterwards was sent ambassador from the prince of Lesbos to the sultan (c. 44.). Till Lesbos was subdued in 1463 (Phranza, l. iii. c. 27.), that island must have been full of the fugitives of Constantinople, who delighted to repeat, perhaps to adorn, the tale of their misery.

conquerors were eager to return for more prey, their trembling pace was quickened with menaces and blows. At the same hour, a similar rapine was exercised in all the churches and monasteries, in all the palaces and habitations of the capital; nor could any place, however sacred or sequestered, protect the persons or the property of the Greeks. Above sixty thousand of this devoted people were transported from the city to the camp and fleet; exchanged or sold according to the caprice or interest of their masters, and dispersed in remote servitude through the provinces of the Ottoman empire. Among these we may notice some remarkable characters. The historian Phranza, first chamberlain and principal secretary, was involved with his family in the common lot. After suffering four months the hardships of slavery, he recovered his freedom; in the ensuing winter he ventured to Adrianople, and ransomed his wife from the *mir bashi* or master of the horse; but his two children, in the flower of youth and beauty, had been seized for the use of Mahomet himself. The daughter of Phranza died in the seraglio, perhaps a virgin: his son, in the fifteenth year of his age, preferred death to infamy, and was stabbed by the hand of the royal lover.[66] A deed thus inhuman, cannot surely be expiated by the taste and liberality with which he released a Grecian matron, and her two daughters, on receiving a Latin ode from Philelphus, who had chosen a wife in that noble family.[67] The pride or cruelty of Mahomet would have been most sensibly gratified by the capture of a Roman legate; but the dexterity of cardinal Isidore eluded the search, and he escaped from Galata in a plebeian habit.[68] The chain and entrance of the outward harbour was still occupied by the Italian ships of merchandise and war. They had signalised their valour in the siege; they embraced the moment of retreat, while the Turkish mariners were dissipated in the pillage of the city. When they hoisted sail, the beach was covered with a suppliant and lamentable crowd: but the means of

66. See Phranza, l. iii. c. 20, 21. His expressions are positive: Ameras suâ manû jugulavit ... volebat enim eo turpiter et nefarie abuti. Me miserum et infelicem. Yet he could only learn from report, the bloody or impure scenes that were acted in the dark recesses of the seraglio.

67. See Tiraboschi (tom. vi. P. i. p. 290.) and Lancelot (Mem. de l'Academie des Inscriptions, tom. x. p. 718.). I should be curious to learn how he could praise the public enemy, whom he so often reviles as the most corrupt and inhuman of tyrants.

68. The Commentaries of Pius II. suppose, that he craftily placed his cardinal's hat on the head of a corpse which was cut off and exposed in triumph, while the legate himself was bought and delivered, as a captive of no value. The great Belgic Chronicle adorns his escape with new adventures, which he suppressed (says Spondanus, A.D. 1453, N° 15.) in his own letters, lest he should lose the merit and reward of suffering for Christ.

transportation were scanty: the Venetians and Genoese selected their countrymen; and, notwithstanding the fairest promises of the sultan, the inhabitants of Galata evacuated their houses, and embarked with their most precious effects.

Amount of the spoil. In the fall and the sack of great cities, an historian is condemned to repeat the tale of uniform calamity: the same effects must be produced by the same passions; and when those passions may be indulged without control, small, alas! is the difference between civilized and savage man. Amidst the vague exclamations of bigotry and hatred, the Turks are not accused of a wanton or immoderate effusion of Christian blood: but according to their maxims (the maxims of antiquity), the lives of the vanquished were forfeited; and the legitimate reward of the conqueror was derived from the service, the sale, or the ransom, of his captives of both sexes.[69] The wealth of Constantinople had been granted by the sultan to his victorious troops: and the rapine of an hour is more productive than the industry of years. But as no regular division was attempted of the spoil, the respective shares were not determined by merit; and the rewards of valour were stolen away by the followers of the camp, who had declined the toil and danger of the battle. The narrative of their depredations could not afford either amusement or instruction: the total amount, in the last poverty of the empire, has been valued at four millions of ducats;[70] and of this sum, a small part was the property of the Venetians, the Genoese, the Florentines, and the merchants of Ancona. Of these foreigners, the stock was improved in quick and perpetual circulation: but the riches of the Greeks were displayed in the idle ostentation of palaces and wardrobes, or deeply buried in treasures of ingots and old coin, lest it should be demanded at their hands for the defence of their country. The profanation and plunder of the monasteries and churches, excited the most tragic complaints. The dome of St. Sophia itself, the earthly heaven, the second firmament, the vehicle of the cherubim, the throne of the glory of God,[71] was despoiled of the oblations of ages; and the gold and silver, the pearls and jewels, the vases and sacerdotal ornaments, were most wickedly converted to the service of

69. Busbequius expatiates with pleasure and applause on the rights of war, and the use of slavery, among the ancients and the Turks (de Legat. Turcicâ, epist. iii. p. 161.).

70. This sum is specified in a marginal note of Leunclavius (Chalcocondyles, l. viii. p. 211), but in the distribution to Venice, Genoa, Florence, and Ancona, of 50, 20, 20, and 15,000 ducats, I suspect that a figure has been dropt. Even with the restitution, the foreign property would scarcely exceed one-fourth.

71. See the enthusiastic praises and lamentations of Phranza (l. iii. c. 17.).

mankind. After the divine images had been stripped of all that could be valuable to a profane eye, the canvass, or the wood, was torn, or broken, or burnt, or trod under foot, or applied, in the stables or the kitchen, to the vilest uses. The example of sacrilege was imitated however from the Latin conquerors of Constantinople; and the treatment which Christ, the Virgin, and the saints, had sustained from the guilty Catholic, might be inflicted by the zealous Musulman on the monuments of idolatry. Perhaps, instead of joining the public clamour, a philosopher will observe, that in the decline of the arts, the workmanship could not be more valuable than the work, and that a fresh supply of visions and miracles would speedily be renewed by the craft of the priest and the credulity of the people. He will more seriously deplore the loss of the Byzantine libraries, which were destroyed or scattered in the general confusion: one hundred and twenty thousand manuscripts are said to have disappeared;[72] ten volumes might be purchased for a single ducat; and the same ignominious price, too high perhaps for a shelf of theology, included the whole works of Aristotle and Homer, the noblest productions of the science and literature of ancient Greece. We may reflect with pleasure, that an inestimable portion of our classic treasures was safely deposited in Italy; and that the mechanics of a German town had invented an art which derides the havock of time and barbarism.

Mahomet II. visits the city, St. Sophia, the palace, &c.

From the first hour[73] of the memorable twenty-ninth of May, disorder and rapine prevailed in Constantinople, till the eighth hour of the same day; when the sultan himself passed in triumph through the gate of St. Romanus. He was attended by his vizirs, bashaws, and guards, each of whom (says a Byzantine historian) was robust as Hercules, dextrous as Apollo, and equal in battle to any ten of the race of ordinary mortals. The conqueror[74] gazed with satisfaction and wonder on the strange though splendid appearance of the domes and palaces, so dissimilar from the style of Oriental architecture. In the hippodrome, or *atmeidan*, his eye was attracted by the twisted column of the three serpents; and, as a trial of his strength, he shattered with his iron mace or battle-axe the

72. See Ducas (c. 43.), and an epistle, July 15th, 1453, from Laurus Quirinus to pope Nicholas V. (Hody de Græcis, p. 192. from a MS. in the Cotton library).

73. The Julian Calendar, which reckons the days and hours from midnight, was used at Constantinople. But Ducas seems to understand the natural hours from sunrise.

74. See the Turkish Annals, p. 329. and the Pandects of Leunclavius, p. 448.

under jaw of one of these monsters,[75] which in the eyes of the Turks were the idols or talismans of the city. At the principal door of St. Sophia, he alighted from his horse, and entered the dome: and such was his jealous regard for that monument of his glory, that on observing a zealous Musulman in the act of breaking the marble pavement, he admonished him with his scymetar, that, if the spoil and captives were granted to the soldiers, the public and private buildings had been reserved for the prince. By his command, the metropolis of the Eastern church was transformed into a mosch: the rich and portable instruments of superstition had been removed; the crosses were thrown down; and the walls, which were covered with images and mosaics, were washed and purified, and restored to a state of naked simplicity. On the same day, or on the ensuing Friday, the *muezin* or crier ascended the most lofty turret, and proclaimed the *ezan*, or public invitation in the name of God and his prophet; the imam preached; and Mahomet the second performed the *namaz* of prayer and thanksgiving on the great altar, where the Christian mysteries had so lately been celebrated before the last of the Cæsars.[76] From St. Sophia he proceeded to the august, but desolate, mansion of an hundred successors of the great Constantine; but which in a few hours had been stripped of the pomp of royalty. A melancholy reflection on the vicissitudes of human greatness, forced itself on his mind; and he repeated an elegant distich of Persian poetry: "The spider has wove his web in the Imperial palace; and the owl hath sung her watch-song on the towers of Afrasiab."[77]

His behaviour to the Greeks. Yet his mind was not satisfied, nor did the victory seem complete, till he was informed of the fate of Constantine; whether he had escaped, or been made prisoner, or had fallen in the battle. Two Janizaries claimed the honour and reward of his death: the body, under an heap of slain, was discovered by the golden eagles embroidered on his shoes: the Greeks acknowledged with tears the head of their late emperor; and, after exposing the bloody trophy,[78] Mahomet

75. I have had occasion (vol. i. p. 597.) to mention this curious relic of Græcian antiquity.

76. We are obliged to Cantemir (p. 102.) for the Turkish account of the conversion of St. Sophia, so bitterly deplored by Phranza and Ducas. It is amusing enough to observe, in what opposite lights the same object appears to a Musulman and a Christian eye.

77. This distich, which Cantemir gives in the original, derives new beauties from the application. It was thus that Scipio repeated, in the sack of Carthage, the famous prophecy of Homer. The same generous feeling carried the mind of the conqueror to the past or the future.

78. I cannot believe with Ducas (see Spondanus, A.D. 1453, N° 13.), that Mahomet

bestowed on his rival the honours of a decent funeral. After his decease, Lucas Notaras, great duke,[79] and first minister of the empire, was the most important prisoner. When he offered his person and his treasures at the foot of the throne, "And why," said the indignant sultan, "did you not employ these treasures in the defence of your prince and country?" "They were yours," answered the slave, "God had reserved them for your hands." "If he reserved them for me," replied the despot, "how have you presumed to with-hold them so long by a fruitless and fatal resistance?" The great duke alleged the obstinacy of the strangers, and some secret encouragement from the Turkish vizir; and from this perilous interview, he was at length dismissed with the assurance of pardon and protection. Mahomet condescended to visit his wife, a venerable princess oppressed with sickness and grief; and his consolation for her misfortunes was in the most tender strain of humanity and filial reverence. A similar clemency was extended to the principal officers of state, of whom several were ransomed at his expence; and during some days he declared himself the friend and father of the vanquished people. But the scene was soon changed; and before his departure, the hippodrome streamed with the blood of his noblest captives. His perfidious cruelty is execrated by the Christians: they adorn with the colours of heroic martyrdom the execution of the great duke and his two sons; and his death is ascribed to the generous refusal of delivering his children to the tyrant's lust. Yet a Byzantine historian has dropt an unguarded word of conspiracy, deliverance, and Italian succour: such treason may be glorious; but the rebel who bravely ventures, has justly forfeited, his life; nor should we blame a conqueror for destroying the enemies whom he can no longer trust. On the eighteenth of June, the victorious sultan returned to Adrianople; and smiled at the base and hollow embassies of the Christian princes, who viewed their approaching ruin in the fall of the Eastern empire.

He repeoples and adorns Constantinople.

Constantinople had been left naked and desolate, without a prince or a people. But she could not be despoiled of the incomparable situation which marks her for the metropolis of a great empire; and the genius of the place will ever triumph over the accidents of time and fortune. Boursa and Adrianople, the ancient seats

---

sent round Persia, Arabia, &c. the head of the Greek emperor: he would surely content himself with a trophy less inhuman.

79. Phranza was the personal enemy of the Greek duke; nor could time, or death, or his own retreat to a monastery, extort a feeling of sympathy or forgiveness. Ducas is inclined to praise and pity the martyr; Chalcocondyles is neuter, but we are indebted to him for the hint of the Greek conspiracy.

of the Ottomans, sunk into provincial towns; and Mahomet the second established his own residence, and that of his successors, on the same commanding spot which had been chosen by Constantine.[80] The fortifications of Galata, which might afford a shelter to the Latins, were prudently destroyed; but the damage of the Turkish cannon was soon repaired; and before the month of August, great quantities of lime had been burnt for the restoration of the walls of the capital. As the entire property of the soil and buildings, whether public or private, or profane or sacred, was now transferred to the conqueror, he first separated a space of eight furlongs from the point of the triangle for the establishment of his seraglio or palace. It is here, in the bosom of luxury, that the *grand signor* (as he has been emphatically named by the Italians) appears to reign over Europe and Asia; but his person on the shores of the Bosphorus may not always be secure from the insults of an hostile navy. In the new character of a mosch, the cathedral of St. Sophia was endowed with an ample revenue, crowned with lofty minarets, and surrounded with groves and fountains, for the devotion and refreshment of the Moslems. The same model was imitated in the *jami* or royal moschs; and the first of these was built, by Mahomet himself, on the ruins of the church of the holy apostles and the tombs of the Greek emperors. On the third day after the conquest, the grave of Abu Ayub or Job, who had fallen in the first siege of the Arabs, was revealed in a vision; and it is before the sepulchre of the martyr, that the new sultans are girded with the sword of empire.[81] Constantinople no longer appertains to the Roman historian; nor shall I enumerate the civil and religious edifices that were profaned or erected by its Turkish masters: the population was speedily renewed; and before the end of September, five thousand families of Anatolia and Romania had obeyed the royal mandate, which enjoined them, under pain of death, to occupy their new habitations in the capital. The throne of Mahomet was guarded by the numbers and fidelity of his Moslem subjects: but his rational policy aspired to collect the remnant of the

80. For the restitution of Constantinople and the Turkish foundations, see Cantemir (p. 102–109.), Ducas (c. 42.), with Thevenot, Tournefort, and the rest of our modern travellers. From a gigantic picture of the greatness, population, &c. of Constantinople and the Ottoman empire (Abregé de l'Histoire Ottomane, tom. i. p. 16–21.), we may learn, that in the year 1586, the Moslems were less numerous in the capital than the Christians, or even the Jews.

81. The *Turbé*, or sepulchral monument of Abou Ayub, is described and engraved in the Tableau General de l'Empire Ottoman (Paris, 1787, in large folio), a work of less use, perhaps, than magnificence (tom. i. p. 305, 306.).

Greeks; and they returned in crowds, as soon as they were assured of their lives, their liberties, and the free exercise of their religion. In the election and investiture of a patriarch, the ceremonial of the Byzantine court was revived and imitated. With a mixture of satisfaction and horror, they beheld the sultan on his throne; who delivered into the hands of Gennadius the crosier or pastoral staff, the symbol of his ecclesiastical office; who conducted the patriarch to the gate of the seraglio, presented him with an horse richly caparisoned, and directed the vizirs and bashaws to lead him to the palace which had been allotted for his residence.[82] The churches of Constantinople were shared between the two religions: their limits were marked; and, till it was infringed by Selim the grandson of Mahomet, the Greeks[83] enjoyed above sixty years the benefit of this equal partition. Encouraged by the ministers of the divan, who wished to elude the fanaticism of the sultan, the Christian advocates presumed to allege that this division had been an act, not of generosity, but of justice; not a concession, but a compact; and that if one half of the city had been taken by storm, the other moiety had surrendered on the faith of a sacred capitulation. The original grant had indeed been consumed by fire: but the loss was supplied by the testimony of three aged Janizaries who remembered the transaction; and their venal oaths are of more weight in the opinion of Cantemir, than the positive and unanimous consent of the history of the times.[84]

Extinction of the Imperial families

The remaining fragments of the Greek kingdom in Europe and Asia I shall abandon to the Turkish arms; but

82. Phranza (l. iii. c. 19.) relates the ceremony, which has possibly been adorned in the Greek reports to each other, and to the Latins. The fact is confirmed by Emanuel Malaxus, who wrote, in vulgar Greek, the History of the Patriarchs after the taking of Constantinople, inserted in the Turco-Græcia of Crusius (l. v. p. 106–184.). But the most patient reader will not believe that Mahomet adopted the Catholic form, "Sancta Trinitas quæ mihi donavit imperium te in patriarcham novæ Romæ deligit."

83. From the Turco-Græcia of Crusius, &c. Spondanus (A.D. 1453, N° 21. 1458, N° 16.) describes the slavery and domestic quarrels of the Greek church. The patriarch who succeeded Gennadius, threw himself in despair into a well.

84. Cantemir (p. 101–105.) insists on the unanimous consent of the Turkish historians, ancient as well as modern, and argues, that they would not have violated the truth to diminish their national glory, since it is esteemed more honourable to take a city by force than by composition. But, 1. I doubt this consent, since he quotes no particular historian, and the Turkish Annals of Leunclavius affirm, without exception, that Mahomet took Constantinople *per vim* (p. 329.). 2. The same argument may be turned in favour of the Greeks of the times, who would not have forgotten this honourable and salutary treaty. Voltaire, as usual, prefers the Turks to the Christians.

of Comnenus and Palæologus. the final extinction of the two last dynasties[85] which have reigned in Constantinople, should terminate the decline and fall of the Roman empire in the East. The despots of the Morea, Demetrius and Thomas,[86] the two surviving brothers of the name of PALÆOLOGUS, were astonished by the death of the emperor Constantine, and the ruin of the monarchy. Hopeless of defence, they prepared with the noble Greeks who adhered to their fortune, to seek a refuge in Italy, beyond the reach of the Ottoman thunder. Their first apprehensions were dispelled by the victorious sultan, who contented himself with a tribute of twelve thousand ducats; and while his ambition explored the continent and the islands in search of prey, he indulged the Morea in a respite of seven years. But this respite was a period of grief, discord, and misery. The *hexamilion*, the rampart of the Isthmus, so often raised and so often subverted, could not long be defended by three hundred Italian archers: the keys of Corinth were seized by the Turks: they returned from their summer excursions with a train of captives and spoil; and the complaints of the injured Greeks were heard with indifference and disdain. The Albanians, a vagrant tribe of shepherds and robbers, filled the peninsula with rapine and murder: the two despots implored the dangerous and humiliating aid of a neighbouring bashaw; and when he had quelled the revolt, his lessons inculcated the rule of their future conduct. Neither the ties of blood, nor the oaths which they repeatedly pledged in the communion and before the altar, nor the stronger pressure of necessity, could reconcile or suspend their domestic quarrels. They ravaged each other's patrimony with fire and sword: the alms and succours of the West were consumed in civil hostility; and their power was only exerted in savage and arbitrary executions. The distress and revenge of the weaker rival invoked their supreme lord; and, in the season of maturity and revenge, Mahomet declared himself the friend of Demetrius, and

Loss of the Morea, A.D. 1460; marched into the Morea with an irresistible force. When he had taken possession of Sparta, "You are too weak," said the sultan, "to control this turbulent province: I will take your daughter to my bed; and you shall pass the remainder of your life in security and

85. For the genealogy and fall of the Comneni of Trebizond, see Ducange (Fam. Byzant. p. 195.); for the last Palæologi, the same accurate antiquarian (p. 244. 247, 248.). The Palæologi of Montferrat were not extinct till the next century; but they had forgotten their Greek origin and kindred.

86. In the worthless story of the disputes and misfortunes of the two brothers, Phranza (l. iii. c. 21–30.) is too partial on the side of Thomas; Ducas (c. 44, 45.) is too brief, and Chalcocondyles (l. viii, ix, x.) too diffuse and digressive.

honour." Demetrius sighed and obeyed; surrendered his daughter and his castles; followed to Adrianople his sovereign and son; and received for his own maintenance, and that of his followers, a city in Thrace, and the adjacent isles of Imbros, Lemnos, and Samothrace. He was joined the next year by a companion of misfortune, the last of the COMNENIAN race, who, after the taking of Constantinople by the Latins, had founded a new empire on the coast of the Black Sea.[87] In the progress of his Anatolian conquests, Mahomet invested with a fleet and army the capital of David, who presumed to style himself emperor of Trebizond;[88] and the negociation was comprised in a short and peremptory question, "Will you secure your life and treasures by resigning your kingdom? or had you rather forfeit your kingdom, your treasures, and your life?" The feeble Comnenus was subdued by his own fears, and the example of a Musulman neighbour, the prince of Sinope,[89] who, on a similar summons, had yielded a fortified city with four hundred cannon and ten or twelve thousand soldiers. The capitulation of Trebizond was faithfully performed; and the emperor, with his family, was transported to a castle in Romania: but on a slight suspicion of corresponding with the Persian king, David, and the whole Comnenian race, were sacrificed to the jealousy or avarice of the conqueror. Nor could the name of father long protect the unfortunate Demetrius from exile and confiscation; his abject submission moved the pity and contempt of the sultan; his followers were transplanted to Constantinople; and his poverty was alleviated by a pension of fifty thousand aspers, till a monastic habit and a tardy death released Palæologus from an earthly master. It is not easy to pronounce whether the servitude of Demetrius, or the exile of his brother Thomas,[90]

of Trebizond, A.D. 1461.

87. See the loss or conquest of Trebizond in Chalcocondyles (l. ix. p. 263–266.), Ducas (c. 45.), Phranza (l. iii. c. 27.), and Cantemir (p. 107.).

88. Though Tournefort (tom. iii. lettre xvii. p. 179.) speaks of Trebizond as mal peuplée, Peyssonel, the latest and most accurate observer, can find 100,000 inhabitants (Commerce de la Mer Noire, tom. ii. p. 72. and for the province, p. 53–90.). Its prosperity and trade are perpetually disturbed by the factious quarrels of two *odas* of Janizaries, in one of which 30,000 Lazi are commonly enrolled (Memoires de Tott, tom. iii. p. 16, 17.).

89. Ismael Beg, prince of Sinope or Sinople, was possessed (chiefly from his copper mines) of a revenue of 200,000 ducats (Chalcocond. l. ix. p. 258, 259.). Peyssonel (Commerce de la Mer Noire, tom. ii. p. 100.) ascribes to the modern city 60,000 inhabitants. This account seems enormous: yet it is by trading with a people that we become acquainted with their wealth and numbers.

90. Spondanus (from Gobelin Comment. Pii II. l. v.) relates the arrival and reception of the despot Thomas at Rome (A.D. 1461, N° 3.).

be the most inglorious. On the conquest of the Morea, the despot escaped to Corfu, and from thence to Italy, with some naked adherents: his name, his sufferings, and the head of the apostle St. Andrew, entitled him to the hospitality of the Vatican; and his misery was prolonged by a pension of six thousand ducats from the pope and cardinals. His two sons, Andrew and Manuel, were educated in Italy; but the eldest, contemptible to his enemies and burthensome to his friends, was degraded by the baseness of his life and marriage. A title was his sole inheritance; and that inheritance he successively sold to the kings of France and Arragon.[91] During his transient prosperity, Charles the eighth was ambitious of joining the empire of the East with the kingdom of Naples: in a public festival, he assumed the appellation and the purple of *Augustus*: the Greeks rejoiced, and the Ottoman already trembled, at the approach of the French chivalry.[92] Manuel Palæologus, the second son, was tempted to revisit his native country: his return might be grateful, and could not be dangerous, to the Porte: he was maintained at Constantinople in safety and ease; and an honourable train of Christians and Moslems attended him to the grave. If there be some animals of so generous a nature that they refuse to propagate in a domestic state, the last of the Imperial race must be ascribed to an inferior kind: he accepted from the sultan's liberality two beautiful females; and his surviving son was lost in the habit and religion of a Turkish slave.

Grief and terror of Europe, A.D. 1453.

The importance of Constantinople was felt and magnified in its loss: the pontificate of Nicholas the fifth, however peaceful and prosperous, was dishonoured by the fall of the Eastern empire; and the grief and terror of the Latins revived, or seemed to revive, the old enthusiasm of the crusades. In one of the most distant countries of the West, Philip duke of Burgundy entertained, at Lisle in Flanders, an assembly of his nobles; and the pompous pageants of the

91. By an act dated A.D. 1494, Sept. 6. and lately transmitted from the archives of the Capitol to the royal library of Paris, the despot Andrew Palæologus, reserving the Morea, and stipulating some private advantages, conveys to Charles VIII. king of France the empires of Constantinople and Trebizond (Spondanus, A.D. 1495, N° 2.). M. de Foncemagne (Mem. de l'Academie des Inscriptions, tom. xvii. p. 539–578.) has bestowed a dissertation on this national title, of which he had obtained a copy from Rome.

92. See Philippe de Comines (l. vii. c. 14.), who reckons with pleasure the number of Greeks who were prepared to rise, 60 miles of an easy navigation, eighteen days journey from Valona to Constantinople, &c. On this occasion the Turkish empire was saved by the policy of Venice.

feast were skilfully adapted to their fancy and feelings.[93] In the midst of the banquet, a gigantic Saracen entered the hall, leading a fictitious elephant, with a castle on his back: a matron in a mourning robe, the symbol of religion, was seen to issue from the castle; she deplored her oppression, and accused the slowness of her champions: the principal herald of the golden fleece advanced, bearing on his fist a live pheasant, which, according to the rites of chivalry, he presented to the duke. At this extraordinary summons, Philip, a wise and aged prince, engaged his person and powers in the holy war against the Turks; his example was imitated by the barons and knights of the assembly; they swore to God, the Virgin, the ladies, and the *pheasant*; and their particular vows were not less extravagant than the general sanction of their oath. But the performance was made to depend on some future and foreign contingency; and, during twelve years, till the last hour of his life, the duke of Burgundy might be scrupulously, and perhaps sincerely, on the eve of his departure. Had every breast glowed with the same ardour; had the union of the Christians corresponded with their bravery; had every country, from Sweden[94] to Naples, supplied a just proportion of cavalry and infantry, of men and money, it is indeed probable that Constantinople would have been delivered, and that the Turks might have been chased beyond the Hellespont or the Euphrates. But the secretary of the emperor, who composed every epistle, and attended every meeting, Æneas Sylvius,[95] a statesman and orator, describes from his own experience the repugnant state and spirit of Christendom. "It is a body," says he, "without an head; a republic without laws or magistrates. The pope and the emperor may shine as lofty titles, as splendid images; but *they* are unable to command, and none are willing to obey: every state has a separate prince, and every prince has a separate interest. What eloquence could unite so many discordant and hostile powers under the same standard? Could they be assembled in arms, who would dare to assume the office of general? What order could be maintained? – what military discipline? Who would undertake to feed such an enormous multitude?

93. See the original feast in Olivier de la Marche (Memoires, P. i. c. 29, 30.), with the abstract and observations of M. de S[te] Palaye (Memoires sur la Chevalerie, tom. i. P. iii. p. 182–185.). The peacock and the pheasant were distinguished as royal birds.

94. It was found by an actual enumeration, that Sweden, Gothland, and Finland, contained 1,800,000 fighting men, and consequently were far more populous than at present.

95. In the year 1454 Spondanus has given, from Æneas Sylvius, a view of the state of Europe, enriched with his own observations. That valuable annalist, and the Italian Muratori, will continue the series of events from the year 1453 to 1481, the end of Mahomet's life, and of this chapter.

Who would understand their various languages, or direct their stranger and incompatible manners? What mortal could reconcile the English with the French, Genoa with Arragon, the Germans with the natives of Hungary and Bohemia? If a small number enlisted in the holy war, they must be overthrown by the infidels; if many, by their own weight and confusion." Yet the same Æneas, when he was raised to the papal throne, under the name of Pius the second, devoted his life to the prosecution of the Turkish war. In the council of Mantua he excited some sparks of a false or feeble enthusiasm; but when the pontiff appeared at Ancona to embark in person with the troops, engagements vanished in excuses; a precise day was adjourned to an indefinite term; and his effective army consisted of some German pilgrims, whom he was obliged to disband with indulgences and alms. Regardless of futurity, his successors and the powers of Italy were involved in the schemes of present and domestic ambition; and the distance or proximity of each object determined, in their eyes, its apparent magnitude. A more enlarged view of their interest would have taught them to maintain a defensive and naval war against the common enemy; and the support of Scanderbeg and his brave Albanians, might have prevented the subsequent invasion of the kingdom of Naples. The siege and sack of Otranto by the Turks, diffused a general consternation; and pope Sixtus was preparing to fly beyond the Alps, when the storm was instantly dispelled by the death of Mahomet the second, in the fifty-first year of his age.[96] His lofty genius aspired to the conquest of Italy: he was possessed of a strong city and a capacious harbour; and the same reign might have been decorated with the trophies of the NEW and the ANCIENT ROME.[97]

Death of Mahomet II. A.D. 1481, May 3, or July 2.

96. Besides the two annalists, the reader may consult Giannone (Istoria Civile, tom. iii. p. 449–455.) for the Turkish invasion of the kingdom of Naples. For the reign and conquests of Mahomet II. I have occasionally used the Memorie Istoriche de Monarchi Ottomanni di Giovanni Sagredo (Venezia, 1677, in 4[to]). In peace and war, the Turks have ever engaged the attention of the republic of Venice. All her dispatches and archives were open to a procurator of St. Mark, and Sagredo is not contemptible either in sense or style. Yet he too bitterly hates the infidels; he is ignorant of their language and manners; and his narrative, which allows only seventy pages to Mahomet II. (p. 69–140.), becomes more copious and authentic as he approaches the years 1640 and 1644, the term of the historic labours of John Sagredo.

97. As I am now taking an everlasting farewell of the Greek empire, I shall briefly mention the great collection of Byzantine writers, whose names and testimonies have been successively repeated in this work. The Greek presses of Aldus and the Italians, were confined to the classics of a better age; and the first rude editions of Procopius,

Agathias, Cedrenus, Zonaras, &c. were published by the learned diligence of the Germans. The whole Byzantine series (xxxvi volumes in folio) has gradually issued (A.D. 1648, &c.) from the royal press of the Louvre, with some collateral aid from Rome and Leipsic; but the Venetian edition (A.D. 1729), though cheaper and more copious, is not less inferior in correctness than in magnificence to that of Paris. The merits of the French editors are various; but the value of Anna Comnena, Cinnamus, Villehardouin, &c. is enhanced by the historical notes of Charles du Fresne du Cange. His supplemental works, the Greek Glossary, the Constantinopolis Christiana, the Familiæ Byzantinæ, diffuse a steady light over the darkness of the Lower Empire.

CHAPTER LXIX

State of Rome from the Twelfth Century. – Temporal Dominion of the Popes. – Seditions of the City. – Political Heresy of Arnold of Brescia. – Restoration of the Republic. – The Senators. – Pride of the Romans. – Their Wars. – They are deprived of the Election and Presence of the Popes, who retire to Avignon. – The Jubilee. – Noble Families of Rome. – Feud of the Colonna and Ursini.

State and revolutions of Rome, A.D. 1100–1500.

In the first ages of the decline and fall of the Roman empire, our eye is invariably fixed on the royal city, which had given laws to the fairest portion of the globe. We contemplate her fortunes, at first with admiration, at length with pity, always with attention; and when that attention is diverted from the Capitol to the provinces, they are considered as so many branches which have been successively severed from the Imperial trunk. The foundation of a second Rome, on the shores of the Bosphorus, has compelled the historian to follow the successors of Constantine; and our curiosity has been tempted to visit the most remote countries of Europe and Asia, to explore the causes and the authors of the long decay of the Byzantine monarchy. By the conquests of Justinian, we have been recalled to the banks of the Tyber, to the deliverance of the ancient metropolis; but that deliverance was a change, or perhaps an aggravation, of servitude. Rome had been already stripped of her trophies, her gods, and her Cæsars: nor was the Gothic dominion more inglorious and oppressive than the tyranny of the Greeks. In the eighth century of the Christian æra, a religious quarrel, the worship of images, provoked the Romans to assert their independence: their bishop became the temporal, as well as the spiritual, father of a free people; and of the Western empire, which was restored by Charlemagne, the title and image still decorate the singular constitution of modern Germany. The name of Rome must yet command our involuntary respect: the climate (whatsoever may be its influence) was no longer the same:[1] the purity of blood had been contaminated through a

1. The abbé Dubos, who, with less genius than his successor Montesquieu, has asserted and magnified the influence of climate, objects to himself the degeneracy of the Romans and Batavians. To the first of these examples he replies, 1. That the

thousand channels; but the venerable aspect of her ruins, and the memory of past greatness, rekindled a spark of the national character. The darkness of the middle ages exhibits some scenes not unworthy of our notice. Nor shall I dismiss the present work till I have reviewed the state and revolutions of the ROMAN CITY, which acquiesced under the absolute dominion of the popes about the same time that Constantinople was enslaved by the Turkish arms.

The French and German emperors of Rome, A.D. 800–1100.

In the beginning of the twelfth century,[2] the æra of the first crusade, Rome was revered by the Latins, as the metropolis of the world, as the throne of the pope and the emperor, who, from the eternal city, derived their title, their honours, and the right or exercise of temporal dominion. After so long an interruption, it may not be useless to repeat that the successors of Charlemagne and the Othos were chosen beyond the Rhine in a national diet; but that these princes were content with the humble names of kings of Germany and Italy, till they had passed the Alps and the Apennine, to seek their Imperial crown on the banks of the Tyber.[3] At some distance from the city, their approach was saluted by a long procession of the clergy and people with palms and crosses; and the terrific emblems of wolves and lions, of dragons and eagles, that floated in the military banners, represented the departed legions and cohorts of the republic. The royal oath to maintain the liberties of Rome was thrice reiterated, at the bridge, the gate, and on the stairs of the Vatican; and the distribution of a customary donative feebly imitated the magnificence of the first Cæsars. In the church of St. Peter, the coronation was performed by his successor: the voice of God was confounded with that of the people; and the public consent was declared in the acclamations of, "Long life and victory to our lord the pope! Long life and victory to our lord the emperor! Long life and victory to the Roman and Teutonic armies!"[4] The

change is less real than apparent, and that the modern Romans prudently conceal in themselves the virtues of their ancestors. 2. That the air, the soil, and the climate of Rome have suffered a great and visible alteration (Reflexions sur la Poesie et sur la Peinture, part. ii. sect. 16.).

2. The reader has been so long absent from Rome, that I would advise him to recollect or review the xlix[th] chapter, in the vth volume of this History.

3. The coronation of the German emperors at Rome, more especially in the xi[th] century, is best represented from the original monuments by Muratori (Antiquitat. Italiæ medii Ævi, tom. i. dissertat. ii. p. 99, &c.), and Cenni (Monument. Domin. Pontif. tom. ii. diss. vi. p. 261.), the latter of whom I only know from the copious extract of Schmidt (Hist. des Allemands, tom. iii. p. 255–266.)

4. Exercitui Romano et Teutonico! The latter was both seen and felt; but the former was no more than magni nominis umbra.

names of Cæsar and Augustus, the laws of Constantine and Justinian, the example of Charlemagne and Otho, established the supreme dominion of the emperors; their title and image was engraved on the papal coins;[5] and their jurisdiction was marked by the sword of justice, which they delivered to the præfect of the city. But every Roman prejudice was awakened by the name, the language, and the manners, of a Barbarian lord. The Cæsars of Saxony or Franconia were the chiefs of a feudal aristocracy; nor could they exercise the discipline of civil and military power, which alone secures the obedience of a distant people, impatient of servitude, though perhaps incapable of freedom. Once, and once only, in his life, each emperor, with an army of Teutonic vassals, descended from the Alps. I have described the peaceful order of his entry and coronation; but that order was commonly disturbed by the clamour and sedition of the Romans, who encountered their sovereign as a foreign invader: his departure was always speedy, and often shameful; and, in the absence of a long reign, his authority was insulted and his name was forgotten. The progress of independence in Germany and Italy undermined the foundations of the Imperial sovereignty, and the triumph of the popes was the deliverance of Rome.

Authority of the popes in Rome,

Of her two sovereigns, the emperor had precariously reigned by the right of conquest; but the authority of the pope was founded on the soft, though more solid, basis of opinion and habit. The removal of a foreign influence restored and endeared the shepherd to his flock. Instead of the arbitrary or venal nomination of a German court, the vicar of Christ was freely chosen by the college of cardinals, most of whom were either natives or inhabitants of the city.

from affection;

The applause of the magistrates and people confirmed his election; and the ecclesiastical power that was obeyed in Sweden and Britain, had been ultimately derived from the suffrage of the Romans. The same suffrage gave a prince, as well as a pontiff, to the capital. It was universally believed, that Constantine had invested the popes with the temporal dominion of Rome; and the boldest civilians, the most profane sceptics, were satisfied with disputing the right of the emperor and the validity of his gift. The truth of the fact, the authenticity of his donation, was deeply rooted in the ignorance and tradition of four centuries: and

5. Muratori has given the series of the papal coins (Antiquitat. tom. ii. diss. xxvii. p. 548–554.). He finds only two more early than the year 800: fifty are still extant from Leo III. to Leo IX. with addition of the reigning emperor; none remain of Gregory VII. or Urban II.; but in those of Paschal II. he seems to have renounced this badge of dependence.

the fabulous origin was lost in the real and permanent effects. The name of *Dominus* or Lord was inscribed on the coin of the bishops: their *right;* title was acknowledged by acclamations and oaths of allegiance, and with the free, or reluctant, consent of the German Cæsars, they had long exercised a supreme or subordinate jurisdiction over the city and patrimony of St. Peter. The reign of the popes, which gratified the prejudices, was not incompatible with the liberties, of Rome; and a more critical enquiry would have revealed a still nobler source of their power; the gratitude of a nation, whom they had rescued from the heresy and oppression of the Greek tyrant. In an age of superstition, it should seem that the union of the royal and sacerdotal characters would mutually fortify each other; and that the keys of paradise would be the surest pledge of earthly obedience. The sanctity of the office might indeed be degraded by the personal vices of the man. But the scandals of the tenth century were obliterated by the austere and more dangerous virtues *virtue;* of Gregory the seventh and his successors; and in the ambitious contests which they maintained for the rights of the church, their sufferings or their success must equally tend to encrease the popular veneration. They sometimes wandered in poverty and exile, the victims of persecution; and the apostolic zeal with which they offered themselves to martyrdom, must engage the favour and sympathy of every Catholic breast. And sometimes, thundering from the Vatican, they created, judged, and deposed the kings of the world: nor could the proudest Roman be disgraced by submitting to a priest, whose feet were kissed, and whose stirrup was held, by the successors of Charlemagne.[6] Even the temporal interest of the city should have protected in peace and honour the residence of the popes; from whence a vain and lazy people derived the greatest part of their subsistence and riches. The fixed revenue of *benefits.* the popes was probably impaired: many of the old patrimonial estates, both in Italy and the provinces, had been invaded by sacrilegious hands; nor could the loss be compensated by the claim, rather than the possession, of the more ample gifts of Pepin and his descendants. But the Vatican and Capitol were nourished by the incessant and encreasing swarms of pilgrims and suppliants: the pale of Christianity was enlarged, and the pope and cardinals were overwhelmed by the judgment of

6. See Ducange, Gloss. mediæ et infimæ Latinitat. tom. vi. p. 364, 365. STAFFA. This homage was paid by kings to archbishops, and by vassals to their lords (Schmidt, tom. iii. p. 262.); and it was the nicest policy of Rome, to confound the marks of filial and of feudal subjection.

ecclesiastical and secular causes. A new jurisprudence had established in the Latin church the right and practice of appeals;[7] and, from the north and west, the bishops and abbots were invited or summoned to solicit, to complain, to accuse, or to justify, before the threshold of the apostles. A rare prodigy is once recorded, that two horses, belonging to the archbishops of Mentz and Cologne, repassed the Alps, yet laden with gold and silver:[8] but it was soon understood, that the success, both of the pilgrims and clients, depended much less on the justice of their cause than on the value of their offering. The wealth and piety of these strangers were ostentatiously displayed; and their expences, sacred or profane, circulated in various channels for the emolument of the Romans.

Inconstancy of superstition. Such powerful motives should have firmly attached the voluntary and pious obedience of the Roman people to their spiritual and temporal father. But the operation of prejudice and interest is often disturbed by the sallies of ungovernable passion. The Indian who fells the tree, that he may gather the fruit,[9] and the Arab who plunders the caravans of commerce, are actuated by the same impulse of savage nature, which overlooks the future in the present, and relinquishes for momentary rapine the long and secure possession of the most important blessings. And it was thus, that the shrine of St. Peter was profaned by the thoughtless Romans; who pillaged the offerings, and wounded the pilgrims, without computing the number and value of similar visits, which they prevented by their inhospitable sacrilege. Even the influence of superstition is fluctuating and precarious: and the slave, whose reason is subdued, will often be delivered by his avarice or pride. A credulous devotion for the fables and oracles of the priesthood, most powerfully acts on the mind of a Barbarian: yet such a mind is the least capable of preferring imagination to sense, of sacrificing to a distant motive, to an

7. The appeals from all the churches to the Roman pontiff, are deplored by the zeal of St. Bernard (de Consideratione, l. iii. tom. ii. p. 431–442. edit. Mabillon, Venet. 1750) and the judgment of Fleury (Discours sur l'Hist. Ecclesiastique, iv. & vii.). But the saint, who believed in the false decretals, condemns only the abuse of these appeals; the more enlightened historian investigates the origin, and rejects the principles, of this new jurisprudence.

8. Germanici . . . summarii non levatis sarcinis onusti nihilominus repatriant inviti. Nova res! quando hactenus aurum Roma refudit? Et nunc Romanorum consilio id usurpatum non credimus (Bernard de Consideratione, l. iii. c. 3. p. 437.). The first words of the passage are obscure, and probably corrupt.

9. Quand les sauvages de la Louisiane veulent avoir du fruit, ils coupent l'arbre au pied et cueillent le fruit. Voila le gouvernement despotique (Esprit des Loix, l.v. c. 13.); and passion and ignorance are always despotic.

invisible, perhaps an ideal, object, the appetites and interests of the present world. In the vigour of health and youth, his practice will perpetually contradict his belief; till the pressure of age, or sickness, or calamity, awakens his terrors, and compels him to satisfy the double debt of piety and remorse. I have already observed, that the modern times of religious indifference, are the most favourable to the peace and security of the clergy. Under the reign of superstition, they had much to hope from the ignorance, and much to fear from the violence, of mankind. The wealth, whose constant encrease must have rendered them the sole proprietors of the earth, was alternately bestowed by the repentant father and plundered by the rapacious son: their persons were adored or violated; and the same idol, by the hands of the same votaries, was placed on the altar or trampled in the dust. In the feudal system of Europe, arms were the title of distinction and the measure of allegiance; and amidst their tumult, the still voice of law and reason was seldom heard or obeyed. The turbulent Romans disdained the yoke, and insulted the impotence, of their bishop;[10] nor would his education or character allow him to exercise, with decency or effect, the power of the sword. The motives of his election and the frailties of his life were exposed to their familiar observation; and proximity must diminish the reverence, which his name and his decrees impressed on a barbarous world. This difference has not escaped the notice of our philosophic historian: "Though the name and authority of the court of Rome were so terrible in the remote countries of Europe, which were sunk in profound ignorance, and were entirely unacquainted with its character and conduct, the pope was so little revered at home, that his inveterate enemies surrounded the gates of Rome itself, and even controlled his government in that city; and the ambassadors, who, from a distant extremity of Europe, carried to him the humble, or rather abject, submissions of the greatest potentate of the age, found the utmost difficulty to make their way to him, and to throw themselves at his feet."[11]

Seditions of Rome against the popes.

10. In a free conversation with his countryman Adrian IV. John of Salisbury accuses the avarice of the pope and clergy: Provinciarum deripiunt spolia, ac si thesauros Crœsi studeant reparare. Sed recte cum eis agit Altissimus, quoniam et ipsi aliis et sæpe vilissimis hominibus dati sunt in direptionem (de Nugis Curialium, l. vi. c. 24. p. 387.). In the next page, he blames the rashness and infidelity of the Romans, whom their bishops vainly strove to conciliate by gifts, instead of virtues. It is pity that this miscellaneous writer has not given us less morality and erudition, and more pictures of himself and the times.

11. Hume's History of England, vol. i. p. 419. The same writer has given us, from Fitz-Stephen, a singular act of cruelty per-

Successors of Gregory VII. A.D. 1086–1305.

Since the primitive times, the wealth of the popes was exposed to envy, their power to opposition, and their persons to violence. But the long hostility of the mitre and the crown encreased the numbers, and inflamed the passions, of their enemies. The deadly factions of the Guelphs and Ghibelines, so fatal to Italy, could never be embraced with truth or constancy by the Romans, the subjects and adversaries both of the bishop and emperor; but their support was solicited by both parties; and they alternately displayed in their banners the keys of St. Peter and the German eagle. Gregory the seventh, who may be adored or detested as the founder of the papal monarchy, was driven from Rome, and died in exile at Salerno. Six-and-thirty of his successors,[12] till their retreat to Avignon, maintained an unequal contest with the Romans: their age and dignity were often violated; and the churches, in the solemn rites of religion, were polluted with sedition and murder. A repetition[13] of such capricious brutality, without connection or design, would be tedious and disgusting; and I shall content myself with some events of the twelfth century, which represent the state of the popes and the city. On Holy Thursday, while

Paschal II. A.D. 1099–1118.

Paschal officiated before the altar, he was interrupted by the clamours of the multitude, who imperiously demanded the confirmation of a favourite magistrate. His silence exasperated their fury: his pious refusal to mingle the affairs of earth and heaven was encountered with menaces and oaths, that he should be the cause and the witness of the public ruin. During the festival of Easter, while the bishop and the clergy, barefoot and in procession, visited the tombs of the martyrs, they were twice assaulted, at the bridge of St. Angelo, and before the Capitol, with vollies of stones and darts. The houses of his

---

petrated on the clergy by Geoffrey, the father of Henry II. "When he was master of Normandy, the chapter of Seez presumed, without his consent, to proceed to the election of a bishop: upon which he ordered all of them, with the bishop elect, to be castrated, and made all their testicles be brought him in a platter." Of the pain and danger they might justly complain; yet, since they had vowed chastity, he deprived them of a superfluous treasure.

12. From Leo IX. and Gregory VII. an authentic and contemporary series of the lives of the popes by the cardinal of Arragon, Pandulphus Pisanus, Bernard Guido, &c. is inserted in the Italian Historians of Muratori (tom. iii. P. i. p. 277–685.), and has been always before my eyes.

13. The dates of years in the margin, may throughout this chapter be understood as tacit references to the Annals of Muratori, my ordinary and excellent guide. He uses, and indeed quotes, with the freedom of a master, his great Collection of the Italian Historians, in xxviii. volumes; and as that treasure is in my library, I have thought it an amusement, if not a duty, to consult the originals.

adherents were levelled with the ground: Paschal escaped with difficulty and danger: he levied an army in the patrimony of St. Peter; and his last days were embittered by suffering and inflicting the calamities of civil war. The scenes that followed the election of his successor Gelasius the second were still more scandalous to the church and city. Cencio Frangipani,[14] a potent and factious baron, burst into the assembly furious and in arms: the cardinals were stripped, beaten, and trampled under foot; and he seized, without pity or respect, the vicar of Christ by the throat. Gelasius was dragged by his hair along the ground, buffeted with blows, wounded with spurs, and bound with an iron chain in the house of his brutal tyrant. An insurrection of the people delivered their bishop: the rival families opposed the violence of the Frangipani; and Cencio, who sued for pardon, repented of the failure, rather than of the guilt, of his enterprise. Not many days had elapsed, when the pope was again assaulted at the altar. While his friends and enemies were engaged in a bloody contest he escaped in his sacerdotal garments. In this unworthy flight, which excited the compassion of the Roman matrons, his attendants were scattered or unhorsed; and, in the fields behind the church of St. Peter, his successor was found alone and half-dead with fear and fatigue. Shaking the dust from his feet, the *apostle* withdrew from a city in which his dignity was insulted and his person was endangered; and the vanity of sacerdotal ambition is revealed in the involuntary confession, that one emperor was more tolerable than twenty.[15] These examples might suffice; but I cannot forget the sufferings of two pontiffs of the same age, the second and third of the name of Lucius. The former, as he ascended in battle-array to assault the Capitol, was struck on the temple by a stone, and expired in a few days. The latter was severely wounded in the persons of his servants. In a civil commotion, several of his priests had been made prisoners; and the inhuman Romans, reserving one as a guide for his brethren, put out their eyes, crowned them with ludicrous mitres,

Gelasius II. A.D. 1118, 1119.

Lucius II. A.D. 1144, 1145. Lucius III. A.D. 1181–1185.

14. I cannot refrain from transcribing the high-coloured words of Pandulphus Pisanus (p. 384.): Hoc audiens inimicus pacis atque turbator jam fatus Centius Frajapane, more draconis immanissimi sibilans, et ab imis pectoribus trahens longa suspiria, accinctus retro gladio sine more cucurrit, valvas ac fores confregit. Ecclesiam furibundus introiit, inde custode remoto papam per gulam accepit, distraxit, pugnis calcibusque percussit, et tanquam brutum animal intra limen ecclesiæ acriter calcaribus cruentavit; et latro tantum dominum per capillos et brachia, Jesû bono interim dormiente, detraxit ad domum, usque deduxit, inibi catenavit et inclusit.

15. Ego coram Deo et ecclesiâ dico, si unquam possibile esset, mallem unum imperatorem quam tot dominos (Vit. Gelas. II. p. 398.).

mounted them on asses with their faces to the tail, and extorted an oath, that, in this wretched condition, they should offer themselves as a lesson to the head of the church. Hope or fear, lassitude or remorse, the characters of the men, and the circumstances of the times, might sometimes obtain an interval of peace and obedience; and the pope was restored with joyful acclamations to the Lateran or Vatican, from whence he had been driven with threats and violence. But the root of mischief was deep and perennial; and a momentary calm was preceded and followed by such tempests as had almost sunk the bark of St. Peter. Rome continually presented the aspect of war and discord: the churches and palaces were fortified and assaulted by the factions and families; and, after giving peace to Europe, Calistus the second alone had resolution and power to prohibit the use of private arms in the metropolis. Among the nations who revered the apostolic throne, the tumults of Rome provoked a general indignation; and, in a letter to his disciple Eugenius the third, St. Bernard, with the sharpness of his wit and zeal, has stigmatised the vices of the rebellious people.[16] "Who is ignorant," says the monk of Clairvaux, "of the vanity and arrogance of the Romans? a nation nursed in sedition, cruel, untractable, and scorning to obey, unless they are too feeble to resist. When they promise to serve, they aspire to reign; if they swear allegiance, they watch the opportunity of revolt; yet they vent their discontent in loud clamours if your doors, or your counsels, are shut against them. Dextrous in mischief, they have never learnt the science of doing good. Odious to earth and heaven, impious to God, seditious among themselves, jealous of their neighbours, inhuman to strangers, they love no one, by no one are they beloved; and while they wish to inspire fear, they live in base and continual apprehension. They will not submit; they know not how to govern; faithless to their superiors, intolerable to their equals, ungrateful to their benefactors, and alike impudent in their demands and their refusals. Lofty in promise, poor in execution: adulation and calumny, perfidy and treason, are the familiar arts of their policy." Surely this dark portrait is not coloured by the pencil of Christian charity;[17] yet the features, however

Calistus II. A.D. 1119–1124.

Innocent II. A.D. 1130–1143.

Character of the Romans by St. Bernard.

16. Quid tam notum seculis quam protervia et cervicositas Romanorum? Gens insueta paci, tumultui assueta, gens immitis et intractabilis usque adhuc, subdi nescia, nisi cum non valet resistere (de Considerat. l. iv. c. 2. p. 441.). The saint takes breath, and then begins again: Hi, invisi terræ et cœlo, utrique injecere manus, &c. (p. 443.).

17. As a Roman citizen, Petrarch takes leave to observe, that Bernard, though a

harsh and ugly, express a lively resemblance of the Romans of the twelfth century.[18]

Political heresy of Arnold of Brescia, A.D. 1140.

The Jews had rejected the Christ when he appeared among them in a plebeian character; and the Romans might plead their ignorance of his vicar when he assumed the pomp and pride of a temporal sovereign. In the busy age of the crusades, some sparks of curiosity and reason were rekindled in the Western world: the heresy of Bulgaria, the Paulician sect, was successfully transplanted into the soil of Italy and France; the Gnostic visions were mingled with the simplicity of the gospel; and the enemies of the clergy reconciled their passions with their conscience, the desire of freedom with the profession of piety.[19] The trumpet of Roman liberty was first sounded by Arnold of Brescia,[20] whose promotion in the church was confined to the lowest rank, and who wore the monastic habit rather as a garb of poverty than as an uniform of obedience. His adversaries could not deny the wit and eloquence which they severely felt: they confess with reluctance the specious purity of his morals; and his errors were recommended to the public by a mixture of important and beneficial truths. In his theological studies, he had been the disciple of the famous and unfortunate Abelard,[21] who was likewise involved in the suspicion of heresy: but the lover of Eloisa was of a soft and flexible nature; and his ecclesiastic judges were edified and disarmed by the humility of his repentance. From this master, Arnold most probably imbibed some metaphysical definitions of the

---

saint, was a man; that he might be provoked by resentment, and possibly repent of his hasty passion, &c. (Memoires sur la Vie de Petrarque, tom. i. p. 330.)

18. Baronius, in his index to the xii[th] volume of his Annals, has found a fair and easy excuse. He makes two heads, of Romani *Catholici*, and *Schismatici*: to the former he applies all the good, to the latter all the evil, that is told of the city.

19. The heresies of the xii[th] century may be found in Mosheim (Institut. Hist. Eccles. p. 419–427.), who entertains a favourable opinion of Arnold of Brescia. In the vth volume, I have described the sect of the Paulicians, and followed their migration from Armenia to Thrace and Bulgaria, Italy and France.

20. The original pictures of Arnold of Brescia, are drawn by Otho bishop of Frisingen (Chron. l. vii. c. 31. de Gestis Frederici I. l. i. c. 27. l. ii. c. 21.), and in the iii[d] book of the Ligurinus, a poem of Gunther, who flourished A.D. 1200, in the monastery of Paris near Basil (Fabric. Bibliot. Latin. med. et infimæ Ætatis, tom. iii. p. 174, 175.). The long passage that relates to Arnold, is produced by Guilliman (de Rebus Helveticis, l. iii. c. 5. p. 108.).

21. The wicked wit of Bayle was amused in composing, with much levity and learning, the articles of ABÉLARD, FOULQUES, HELOISE, in his Dictionnaire Critique. The dispute of Abelard and St. Bernard, of scholastic and positive divinity, is well understood by Mosheim (Institut. Hist. Eccles. p. 412–415.).

Trinity, repugnant to the taste of the times: his ideas of baptism and the eucharist are loosely censured; but a *political* heresy was the source of his fame and misfortunes. He presumed to quote the declaration of Christ, that his kingdom is not of this world: he boldly maintained, that the sword and the sceptre were entrusted to the civil magistrate; that temporal honours and possessions were lawfully vested in secular persons; that the abbots, the bishops, and the pope himself, must renounce either their state or their salvation; and that after the loss of their revenues, the voluntary tithes and oblations of the faithful would suffice, not indeed for luxury and avarice, but for a frugal life in the exercise of spiritual labours. During a short time, the preacher was revered as a patriot; and the discontent, or revolt, of Brescia against her bishop, was the first fruits of his dangerous lessons. But the favour of the people is less permanent than the resentment of the priest; and after the heresy of Arnold had been condemned by Innocent the second,[22] in the general council of the Lateran, the magistrates themselves were urged by prejudice and fear to execute the sentence of the church. Italy could no longer afford a refuge; and the disciple of Abelard escaped beyond the Alps, till he found a safe and hospitable shelter in Zurich, now the first of the Swiss cantons. From a Roman station,[23] a royal villa, a chapter of noble virgins, Zurich had gradually encreased to a free and flourishing city; where the appeals of the Milanese were sometimes tried by the Imperial commissaries.[24] In an age less ripe for reformation, the præcursor of Zuinglius was heard with applause: a brave and simple people imbibed and long retained the colour of his opinions; and his art, or merit, seduced the bishop of Constance,

22.

—— Damnatus ab illo
Præsule, qui numeros vetitum
contingere nostros
Nomen ab *innocuâ* ducit laudabile vitâ.

We may applaud the dexterity and correctness of Ligurinus, who turns the unpoetical name of Innocent II. into a compliment.

23. A Roman inscription of Statio Turicensis has been found at Zurich (d'Anville, Notice de l'ancienne Gaule, p. 642–644.): but it is without sufficient warrant, that the city and canton have usurped, and even monopolised, the names of Tigurum and Pagus Tigurinus.

24. Guilliman (de Rebus Helveticis, l. iii. c. 5. p. 106.) recapitulates the donation (A.D. 833) of the emperor Lewis the Pious to his daughter the abbess Hildegardis. Curtim nostram Turegum in ducatû Alamanniæ in pago Durgaugensi, with villages, woods, meadows, waters, slaves, churches, &c. a noble gift. Charles the Bald gave the jus monetæ, the city was walled under Otho I. and the line of the bishop of Frisingen,

Nobile Turegum multarum copiâ
rerum,

is repeated with pleasure by the antiquaries of Zurich.

and even the pope's legate, who forgot, for his sake, the interest of their master and their order. Their tardy zeal was quickened by the fierce exhortations of St. Bernard;[25] and the enemy of the church was driven by persecution to the desperate measure of erecting his standard in Rome itself, in the face of the successor of St. Peter.

He exhorts the Romans to restore the republic, A.D. 1144–1154.

Yet the courage of Arnold was not devoid of discretion; he was protected, and had perhaps been invited, by the nobles and people; and in the service of freedom, his eloquence thundered over the seven hills. Blending in the same discourse the texts of Livy and St. Paul, uniting the motives of gospel, and of classic, enthusiasm, he admonished the Romans, how strangely their patience and the vices of the clergy had degenerated from the primitive times of the church and the city. He exhorted them to assert the inalienable rights of men and Christians; to restore the laws and magistrates of the republic; to respect the *name* of the emperor; but to confine their shepherd to the spiritual government of his flock.[26] Nor could his spiritual government escape the censure and control of the reformer; and the inferior clergy were taught by his lessons to resist the cardinals, who had usurped a despotic command over the twenty-eight regions or parishes of Rome.[27] The revolution was not accomplished without rapine and violence, the effusion of blood and the demolition of houses: the victorious faction was enriched with the spoils of the clergy and the adverse nobles. Arnold of Brescia enjoyed, or deplored, the effects of his mission: his reign continued above ten years, while two popes, Innocent the second and Anastasius the fourth, either trembled in the Vatican, or wandered as exiles in the adjacent cities. They were succeeded by a more vigorous and fortunate pontiff, Adrian the fourth,[28]

25. Bernard, epistol. cxcv, cxcvi. tom. i. p. 187–190. Amidst his invectives he drops a precious acknowledgment, qui, utinam quam sanæ esset doctrinæ quam districtæ est vitæ. He owns that Arnold would be a valuable acquisition for the church.

26. He advised the Romans,

> Consiliis armisque sua moderamina summa
> Arbitrio tractare suo: nil juris in hâc re
> Pontifici summo, modicum concedere regi
> Suadebat populo. Sic læsâ stultus utrâque
> Majestate, reum geminæ se fecerat aulæ.

Nor is the poetry of Gunther different from the prose of Otho.

27. See Baronius (A.D. 1148, N° 38, 39.) from the Vatican MSS. He loudly condemns Arnold (A.D. 1141, N° 3.) as the father of the political heretics, whose influence then hurt him in France.

28. The English reader may consult the Biographia Britannica, ADRIAN IV. but our own writers have added nothing to the fame or merits of their countryman.

the only Englishman who has ascended the throne of St. Peter; and whose merit emerged from the mean condition of a monk, and almost a beggar, in the monastery of St. Albans. On the first provocation, of a cardinal killed or wounded in the streets, he cast an interdict on the guilty people; and from Christmas to Easter, Rome was deprived of the real or imaginary comforts of religious worship. The Romans had despised their temporal prince; they submitted with grief and terror to the censures of their spiritual father; their guilt was expiated by penance, and the banishment of the seditious preacher was the price of their absolution. But the revenge of Adrian was yet unsatisfied, and the approaching coronation of Frederic Barbarossa was fatal to the bold reformer, who had offended, though not in an equal degree, the heads of the church and state. In their interview at Viterbo, the pope represented to the emperor the furious ungovernable spirit of the Romans: the insults, the injuries, the fears, to which his person and his clergy were continually exposed; and the pernicious tendency of the heresy of Arnold, which must subvert the principles of civil, as well as ecclesiastical, subordination. Frederic was convinced by these arguments, or tempted by the desire of the Imperial crown; in the balance of ambition, the innocence or life of an individual is of small account; and their common enemy was sacrificed to a moment of political concord. After his retreat from Rome, Arnold had been protected by the viscounts of Campania, from whom he was extorted by the power of Cæsar: the præfect of the city pronounced his sentence; the martyr of freedom was burnt alive in the presence of a careless and ungrateful people; and his ashes were cast into the Tyber, lest the heretics should collect and worship the relics of their master.[29] The clergy triumphed in his death: with his ashes, his sect was dispersed; his memory still lived in the minds of the Romans. From his school they had probably derived a new article of faith, that the metropolis of the Catholic church is exempt from the penalties of excommunication and interdict. Their bishops might argue, that the supreme jurisdiction, which they exercised over kings and nations, more specially embraced the city and diocese of the prince of the apostles. But they preached to the winds, and the same principle that weakened the effect, must temper the abuse, of the thunders of the Vatican.

His execution, A.D. 1155.

29. Besides the historian and poet already quoted, the last adventures of Arnold are related by the Biographer of Adrian IV. (Muratori, Script. Rerum Ital. tom. iii. P. i. p. 441, 442.)

Restoration of the senate, A.D. 1144.

The love of ancient freedom has encouraged a belief, that as early as the tenth century, in their first struggles against the Saxon Othos, the commonwealth was vindicated and restored by the senate and people of Rome; that two consuls were annually elected among the nobles, and ten or twelve plebeian magistrates revived the name and office of the tribunes of the commons.[30] But this venerable structure disappears before the light of criticism. In the darkness of the middle ages, the appellations of senators, of consuls, of the sons of consuls, may sometimes be discovered.[31] They were bestowed by the emperors, or assumed by the most powerful citizens, to denote their rank, their honours,[32] and perhaps the claim of a pure and patrician descent: but they float on the surface, without a series or a substance, the titles of men, not the orders of government;[33] and it is only from the year of Christ one thousand one hundred and forty-four, that the establishment of the senate is dated, as a glorious æra, in the acts of the city. A new constitution was hastily framed by private ambition or popular enthusiasm; nor could Rome, in the twelfth century, produce an antiquary to explain, or a legislator to restore, the harmony and proportions of the ancient model. The assembly of a free, of an armed, people, will

30. Ducange (Gloss. Latinitatis mediæ et infimi Ætatis, DECARCHONES, tom. ii. p. 726.) gives me a quotation from Blondus (decad ii. l. ii.): Duo consules ex nobilitate quotannis fiebant, qui ad vetustum consulum exemplar summæ rerum præessent. And in Sigonius (de Regno Italiæ, l. vi. opp. tom. ii. p. 400.) I read of the consuls and tribunes of the xth century. Both Blondus, and even Sigonius, too freely copied the classic method of supplying from reason or fancy the deficiency of records.

31. In the panegyric of Berengarius (Muratori, Script. Rer. Ital. tom. ii. P. i. p. 408.), a Roman is mentioned as consulis natus in the beginning of the xth century. Muratori (dissert. v.) discovers in the years 952 and 956, Gratianus in Dei nomine consul et dux, Georgius consul et dux; and in 1015, Romanus, brother of Gregory VIII. proudly, but vaguely, styles himself consul et dux et omnium Romanorum senator.

32. As late as the xth century, the Greek emperors conferred on the dukes of Venice, Naples, Amalphi, &c. the title of ὕπατος, or consuls (see Chron. Sagornini, passim); and the successors of Charlemagne would not abdicate any of their prerogative. But in general, the names of *consul* and *senator*, which may be found among the French and Germans, signify no more than count and lord (*Signeur*, Ducange, Glossar.). The monkish writers are often ambitious of fine classic words.

33. The most constitutional form, is a diploma of Otho III. (A.D. 998), Consulibus senatûs populique Romani; but the act is probably spurious. At the coronation of Henry I. A.D. 1014, the historian Dithmar (apud Muratori, dissert. xxiii.) describes him, a senatoribus duodecim vallatum, quorum sex rasi barbâ, alii prolixâ, mystice incedebant cum baculis. The senate is mentioned in the panegyric of Berengarius (p. 406.).

ever speak in loud and weighty acclamations. But the regular distribution of the thirty-five tribes, the nice balance of the wealth and numbers of the centuries, the debates of the adverse orators, and the slow operation of votes and ballots, could not easily be adapted by a blind multitude, ignorant of the arts, and insensible of the benefits, of legal government. It was proposed by Arnold to revive and discriminate the equestrian order; but what could be the motive or measure of such distinction?[34] The pecuniary qualification of the knights must have been reduced to the poverty of the times: those times no longer required their civil functions of judges and farmers of the revenue; and their primitive duty, their military service on horseback, was more nobly supplied by feudal tenures and the spirit of chivalry. The jurisprudence of the republic was useless and unknown: the nations and families of Italy who lived under the Roman and Barbaric laws were insensibly mingled in a common mass; and some faint tradition, some imperfect fragments, preserved the memory of the Code and Pandects of Justinian. With their liberty the Romans might doubtless have restored the appellation and office of consuls; had they not disdained a title so promiscuously adopted in the Italian cities, that it has finally settled on the humble station of the agents of commerce in a foreign land. But the rights of the tribunes, the formidable word that arrested the public counsels, suppose or must produce a legitimate democracy. The old patricians were the subjects, the modern barons the tyrants, of the state; nor would the enemies of peace and order, who insulted the vicar of Christ, have long respected the unarmed sanctity of a plebeian magistrate.[35]

The Capitol. In the revolution of the twelfth century, which gave a new existence and æra to Rome, we may observe the real and important events that marked or confirmed her political independence. I. The

34. In ancient Rome, the equestrian order was not ranked with the senate and people as a third branch of the republic till the consulship of Cicero, who assumes the merit of the establishment (Plin. Hist. Natur. xxxiii. 3. Beaufort, Republique Romaine, tom. i. p. 144–155.).

35. The republican plan of Arnold of Brescia is thus stated by Gunther:

> Quin etiam titulos urbis renovare vetustos;
> Nomine plebeio secernere nomen equestre,
> Jura tribunorum, sanctum reparare senatum,
> Et senio fessas mutasque reponere leges.
> Lapsa ruinosis, et adhuc pendentia muris
> Reddere primævo Capitolia prisca nitori.

But of these reformations, some were no more than ideas, others no more than words.

Capitoline hill, one of her seven eminences,[36] is about four hundred yards in length, and two hundred in breadth. A flight of an hundred steps led to the summit of the Tarpeian rock; and far steeper was the ascent before the declivities had been smoothed and the precipices filled by the ruins of fallen edifices. From the earliest ages, the Capitol had been used as a temple in peace, a fortress in war: after the loss of the city, it maintained a siege against the victorious Gauls; and the sanctuary of empire was occupied, assaulted, and burnt, in the civil wars of Vitellius and Vespasian.[37] The temples of Jupiter and his kindred deities had crumbled into dust; their place was supplied by monasteries and houses; and the solid walls, the long and shelving porticoes, were decayed or ruined by the lapse of time. It was the first act of the Romans, an act of freedom, to restore the strength, though not the beauty, of the Capitol; to fortify the seat of their arms and counsels; and as often as they ascended the hill, the coldest minds must have glowed with the remembrance of their ancestors. II. The first Cæsars had been invested with the exclusive coinage of the gold and silver; to the senate they abandoned the *The coin.* baser metal of bronze or copper:[38] the emblems and legends were inscribed on a more ample field by the genius of flattery; and the prince was relieved from the care of celebrating his own virtues. The successors of Diocletian despised even the flattery of the senate: their royal officers at Rome, and in the provinces, assumed the sole direction of the mint; and the same prerogative was inherited by the Gothic kings of Italy, and the long series of the Greek, the French, and the German dynasties. After an abdication of eight hundred years, the Roman senate asserted this honourable and lucrative privilege; which was tacitly renounced by the popes, from Paschal the second to the establishment of their residence beyond the Alps. Some of these republican coins of the twelfth and thirteenth centuries, are shewn in the cabinets of the curious. On one of these, a gold medal, Christ is depictured holding in his left hand a book with this inscription: "THE VOW OF THE ROMAN SENATE AND PEOPLE: ROME THE CAPITAL OF THE WORLD;" on the reverse, St.

36. After many disputes among the antiquaries of Rome, it seems determined, that the summit of the Capitoline hill next the river is strictly the Mons Tarpeius, the Arx; and that on the other summit, the church and convent of Araceli, the barefoot friars of St. Francis, occupy the temple of Jupiter (Nardini, Roma Antica, l. v. c. 11–16.).

37. Tacit. Hist. iii. 69, 70.

38. This partition of the noble and baser metals between the emperor and senate, must however be adopted, not as a positive fact, but as the probable opinion of the best antiquaries (see the Science des Medailles of the Pere Joubert, tom. ii. p. 208–211. in the improved and scarce edition of the Baron de la Bastie).

Peter delivering a banner to a kneeling senator in his cap and gown, with the name and arms of his family impressed on a shield.[39] III. With the empire, the præfect of the city had declined to a municipal officer; yet he still exercised in the last appeal the civil and criminal jurisdiction; and a drawn sword, which he received from the successors of Otho, was the mode of his investiture and the emblem of his functions.[40] The dignity was confined to the noble families of Rome: the choice of the people was ratified by the pope; but a triple oath of fidelity must have often embarrassed the præfect in the conflict of adverse duties.[41] A servant, in whom they possessed but a third share, was dismissed by the independent Romans: in his place they elected a patrician; but this title, which Charlemagne had not disdained, was too lofty for a citizen or a subject; and, after the first fervour of rebellion, they consented without reluctance to the restoration of the præfect. About fifty years after this event, Innocent the third, the most ambitious, or at least the most fortunate, of the pontiffs, delivered the Romans and himself from this badge of foreign dominion: he invested the præfect with a banner instead of a sword, and absolved him from all dependence of oaths or service to the German emperors.[42] In his place an ecclesiastic, a present or future cardinal, was named by the pope to the civil government of Rome; but his jurisdiction has been reduced to a narrow compass; and in the days of freedom, the right or exercise was derived from the senate and people. IV. After the revival of the

The præfect of the city.

A.D. 1198–1216.

39. In his xxvii[th] dissertation on the Antiquities of Italy (tom. ii. p. 559–569.), Muratori exhibits a series of the senatorian coins, which bore the obscure names of *Affortiati, Infortiati, Provisini, Paparini.* During this period all the popes, without excepting Boniface VIII. abstained from the right of coining, which was resumed by his successor Benedict XI. and regularly exercised in the court of Avignon.

40. A German historian, Gerard of Reichерspeg (in Baluz. Miscell. tom. v. p. 64. apud Schmidt, Hist. des Allemands, tom. iii. p. 265.), thus describes the constitution of Rome in the xi[th] century: Grandiora urbis et orbis negotia spectant ad Romanum pontificem itemque ad Romanum imperatorem; sive illius vicarium urbis præfectum, qui de suâ dignitate respicit utrumque, videlicet dominum papam cui facit hominum, et dominum imperatorum a quo accipit suæ potestatis insigne, scilicet gladium exertum.

41. The words of a contemporary writer (Pandulph. Pisan. in Vit. Paschal. II. p. 357, 358.) describe the election and oath of the præfect in 1118, inconsultis patribus ... loca præfectoria ... Laudes præfectoriæ ... comitiorum applausum ... juraturum populo in ambonem sublevant ... confirmari eum in urbe præfectum petunt.

42. Urbis præfectum ad ligiam fidelitatem recepit, et per mantum quod illi donavit de præfecturâ eum publice investivit, qui usque ad id tempus juramento fidelitatis imperatori fuit obligatus et ab eo præfecturæ tenuit honorem (Gesta Innocent. III. in Muratori, tom. iii. P. i. p. 487.).

Number and choice of the senate.

senate,[43] the conscript fathers (if I may use the expression) were invested with the legislative and executive power; but their views seldom reached beyond the present day; and that day was most frequently disturbed by violence and tumult. In its utmost plenitude, the order or assembly consisted of fifty-six senators,[44] the most eminent of whom were distinguished by the title of counsellors; they were nominated, perhaps annually, by the people; and a previous choice of their electors, ten persons in each region or parish, might afford a basis for a free and permanent constitution. The popes, who in this tempest submitted rather to bend than to break, confirmed by treaty the establishment and privileges of the senate, and expected from time, peace, and religion, the restoration of their government. The motives of public and private interest might sometimes draw from the Romans an occasional and temporary sacrifice of their claims; and they renewed their oath of allegiance to the successor of St. Peter and Constantine, the lawful head of the church and the republic.[45]

The office of senator.

The union and vigour of a public council was dissolved in a lawless city; and the Romans soon adopted a more strong and simple mode of administration. They condensed the name and authority of the senate in a single magistrate, or two colleagues; and as they were changed at the end of a year, or of six months, the greatness of the trust was compensated by the shortness of the term. But in this transient reign, the senators of Rome indulged their avarice and ambition: their justice was perverted by the interest of their family and faction; and as they punished only their enemies, they were obeyed only by their adherents. Anarchy, no longer tempered by the pastoral care of their bishop, admonished the Romans that they were incapable of governing themselves; and they sought abroad those blessings which they were hopeless of finding

43. See Otho Frising. Chron. vii. 31. de Gest. Frederic. I. l. i. c. 27.

44. Our countryman, Roger Hoveden, speaks of the single senators, of the *Capuzzi* family, &c. quorum temporibus melius regebatur Roma quam nunc (A.D. 1194) est temporibus lvi. senatorum (Ducange, Gloss. tom. vi. p. 191. SENATORES).

45. Muratori (dissert. xlii. tom. iii. p. 785–788.) has published an original treaty: Concordia inter D. nostrum papam Clementem III. et senatores populi Romani super regalibus et aliis dignitatibus urbis, &c. anno 44° senatûs. The senate speaks, and speaks with authority: Reddimus ad præsens ... habebimus ... dabitis presbyteria ... jurabimus pacem et fidelitatem, &c. A chartula de Tenimentis Tusculani, dated in the 47th year of the same æra, and confirmed decreto amplissimi ordinis senatûs, acclamatione P. R. publice Capitolio consistentis. It is there we find the difference of senatores consiliarii and simple senators (Muratori, dissert. xlii. tom. iii. p. 787–789.).

at home. In the same age, and from the same motives, most of the Italian republics were prompted to embrace a measure, which, however strange it may seem, was adapted to their situation, and productive of the most salutary effects.[46] They chose, in some foreign but friendly city, an impartial magistrate of noble birth and unblemished character, a soldier and a statesman, recommended by the voice of fame and his country, to whom they delegated for a time the supreme administration of peace and war. The compact between the governor and the governed was sealed with oaths and subscriptions; and the duration of his power, the measure of his stipend, the nature of their mutual obligations, were defined with scrupulous precision. They swore to obey him as their lawful superior: he pledged his faith to unite the indifference of a stranger with the zeal of a patriot. At his choice, four or six knights and civilians, his assessors in arms and justice, attended the *Podesta*,[47] who maintained at his own expence a decent retinue of servants and horses: his wife, his son, his brother, who might bias the affections of the judge, were left behind; during the exercise of his office he was not permitted to purchase land, to contract an alliance, or even to accept an invitation in the house of a citizen; nor could he honourably depart till he had satisfied the complaints that might be urged against his government.

Brancaleone, A.D. 1252–1258.

It was thus, about the middle of the thirteenth century, that the Romans called from Bologna the senator Brancaleone,[48] whose fame and merit have been rescued from oblivion by the pen of an English historian. A just anxiety for his reputation, a clear foresight of the difficulties of the task, had engaged him to refuse the honour of their choice: the statutes of Rome were suspended, and his office prolonged to the term of three years. By the guilty and licentious he was accused as cruel; by the clergy he was suspected as partial; but the friends of peace and order applauded the firm and upright magistrate by

46. Muratori (dissert. xlv. tom. iv. p. 64–92.) has fully explained this mode of government; and the *Oculus Pastoralis*, which he has given at the end, is a treatise or sermon on the duties of these foreign magistrates.

47. In the Latin writers, at least of the silver age, the title of *Potestas* was transferred from the office to the magistrate:

Hujus qui trahitur prætextam sumere mavis.
An Fidenarum Gabiorumque esse *Potestas*.

(Juvenal. Satir. x. 99.)

48. See the life and death of Brancaleone, in the Historia Major of Matthew Paris, p. 741. 757. 792. 797. 799. 810. 823. 833. 836. 840. The multitude of pilgrims and suitors connected Rome and St. Alban's; and the resentment of the English clergy prompted them to rejoice whenever the popes were humbled and oppressed.

whom those blessings were restored. No criminals were so powerful as to brave, so obscure as to elude, the justice of the senator. By his sentence two nobles of the Annibaldi family were executed on a gibbet; and he inexorably demolished, in the city and neighbourhood, one hundred and forty towers, the strong shelters of rapine and mischief. The bishop, as a simple bishop, was compelled to reside in his diocese; and the standard of Brancaleone was displayed in the field with terror and effect. His services were repaid by the ingratitude of a people unworthy of the happiness which they enjoyed. By the public robbers, whom he had provoked for their sake, the Romans were excited to depose and imprison their benefactor; nor would his life have been spared, if Bologna had not possessed a pledge for his safety. Before his departure, the prudent senator had required the exchange of thirty hostages of the noblest families of Rome: on the news of his danger, and at the prayer of his wife, they were more strictly guarded; and Bologna, in the cause of honour, sustained the thunders of a papal interdict. This generous resistance allowed the Romans to compare the present with the past; and Brancaleone was conducted from the prison to the Capitol amidst the acclamations of a repentant people. The remainder of his government was firm and fortunate; and as soon as envy was appeased by death, his head, enclosed in a precious vase, was deposited on a lofty column of marble.[49]

Charles of Anjou, A.D. 1265–1278.

The impotence of reason and virtue recommended in Italy a more effectual choice: instead of a private citizen, to whom they yielded a voluntary and precarious obedience, the Romans elected for their senator some prince of independent power, who could defend them from their enemies and themselves. Charles of Anjou and Provence, the most ambitious and warlike monarch of the age, accepted at the same time the kingdom of Naples from the pope, and the office of senator from the Roman people.[50] As he passed through the city, in his road to victory, he received their oath of allegiance, lodged

49. Matthew Paris thus ends his account: Caput vero ipsius Brancaleonis in vase pretioso super marmoream columnam collocatum, in signum sui valoris et probitatis, quasi reliquias, superstitiose nimis et pompose sustulerunt. Fuerat enim superborum potentum et malefactorum urbis malleus et exstirpator, et populi protector et defensor, veritatis et justitiæ imitator et amator (p. 840.). A biographer of Innocent IV. (Muratori, Script. tom. iii. P. i. p. 591, 592.) draws a less favourable portrait of this Ghibelline senator.

50. The election of Charles of Anjou to the office of perpetual senator of Rome, is mentioned by the historians in the viii[th] volume of the Collection of Muratori, by Nicholas de Jamsilla (p. 592.), the monk of Padua (p. 724.), Sabas Malaspina (l. ii. c. 9. p. 808.), and Ricordano Malespini (c. 177. p. 999.).

in the Lateran palace, and smoothed in a short visit the harsh features of his despotic character. Yet even Charles was exposed to the inconstancy of the people, who saluted with the same acclamations the passage of his rival, the unfortunate Conradin; and a powerful avenger, who reigned in the Capitol, alarmed the fears and jealousy of the popes. The absolute term of his life was superseded by a renewal every third year; and the enmity of Nicholas the third obliged the Sicilian king to abdicate the government of Rome. In his bull, a perpetual law, the imperious pontiff asserts the truth, validity, and use, of the donation of Constantine, not less essential to the peace of the city than to the independence of the church; establishes the annual election of the senator; and formally disqualifies all emperors, kings, princes, and persons of an eminent and conspicuous rank.[51] This prohibitory clause was repealed in his own behalf by Martin the fourth, who humbly solicited the suffrage of the Romans. In the presence, and by the authority, of the people, two electors conferred, not on the pope, but on the noble and faithful Martin, the dignity of senator, and the supreme administration of the republic,[52] to hold during his natural life, and to exercise at pleasure by himself or his deputies. About fifty years afterwards, the same title was granted to the emperor Lewis of Bavaria; and the liberty of Rome was acknowledged by her two sovereigns, who accepted a municipal office in the government of their own metropolis.

Pope Martin IV. A.D. 1281.

The emperor Lewis of Bavaria, A.D. 1328.

Addresses of Rome to the emperors.

In the first moments of rebellion, when Arnold of Brescia had inflamed their minds against the church, the Romans artfully laboured to conciliate the favour of the empire, and to recommend their merit and services in the cause of Cæsar. The style of their ambassadors to Conrad the third and Frederic the first, is a mixture of flattery and pride, the tradition and the ignorance of their own history.[53] After some complaint of his silence and neglect,

Conrad III. A.D. 1144.

51. The high-sounding bull of Nicholas III. which founds his temporal sovereignty on the donation of Constantine, is still extant; and as it has been inserted by Boniface VIII. in the *Sexte* of the Decretals, it must be received by the Catholics, or at least by the Papists, as a sacred and perpetual law.

52. I am indebted to Fleury (Hist. Eccles. tom. xviii. p. 306.) for an extract of this Roman act, which he has taken from the Ecclesiastical Annals of Odericus Raynaldus, A.D. 1281, N° 14, 15.

53. These letters and speeches are preserved by Otho bishop of Frisingen (Fabric. Bibliot. Lat. med. et infim. tom. v. p. 186, 187.), perhaps the noblest of historians: he was son of Leopold marquis of Austria, his mother, Agnes, was daughter of the emperor Henry IV. and he was half-brother and uncle to Conrad III. and Frederic I. He has left, in seven books, a Chron-

they exhort the former of these princes to pass the Alps, and assume from their hands the Imperial crown. "We beseech your majesty, not to disdain the humility of your sons and vassals, not to listen to the accusations of our common enemies; who calumniate the senate as hostile to your throne, who sow the seeds of discord, that they may reap the harvest of destruction. The pope and the *Sicilian* are united in an impious league to oppose *our* liberty and *your* coronation. With the blessing of God, our zeal and courage has hitherto defeated their attempts. Of their powerful and factious adherents, more especially the Frangipani, we have taken by assault the houses and turrets: some of these are occupied by our troops, and some are levelled with the ground. The Milvian bridge, which they had broken, is restored and fortified for your safe passage; and your army may enter the city without being annoyed from the castle of St. Angelo. All that we have done, and all that we design, is for your honour and service, in the loyal hope, that you will speedily appear in person, to vindicate those rights which have been invaded by the clergy, to revive the dignity of the empire, and to surpass the fame and glory of your predecessors. May you fix your residence in Rome, the capital of the world; give laws to Italy, and the Teutonic kingdom; and imitate the example of Constantine and Justinian,[54] who by the vigour of the senate and people obtained the sceptre of the earth."[55] But these splendid and fallacious wishes were not cherished by Conrad the Franconian, whose eyes were fixed on the Holy Land, and who died without visiting Rome soon after his return from the Holy Land.

Frederic I. A.D. 1155.

His nephew and successor Frederic Barbarossa, was more ambitious of the Imperial crown; nor had any of the successors of Otho acquired such absolute sway over the kingdom of Italy. Surrounded by his ecclesiastical and secular princes, he gave audience in his camp at Sutri to the ambassadors of Rome, who thus addressed him in a free and florid oration: "Incline your ear to the queen of cities; approach with a peaceful and friendly mind the precincts of Rome, which has cast away the yoke of the clergy, and is impatient to crown her legitimate emperor. Under your auspicious influence, may the primitive times be restored. Assert the prerogatives of the eternal city, and reduce under her

---

icle of the Times; in two, the Gesta Frederici I. the last of which is inserted in the vi[th] volume of Muratori's historians.

54. We desire (said the ignorant Romans) to restore the empire in eum statum, quo fuit tempore Constantini et Justiniani, qui totum orbem vigore senatûs et populi Romani suis tenuere manibus.

55. Otho Frising. de Gestis Frederici I. l. i. c. 28. p. 662–664.

monarchy, the insolence of the world. You are not ignorant, that, in former ages, by the wisdom of the senate, by the valour and discipline of the equestrian order, she extended her victorious arms to the East and West, beyond the Alps, and the islands of the ocean. By our sins, in the absence of our princes, the noble institution of the senate has sunk in oblivion: and with our prudence, our strength has likewise decreased. We have revived the senate, and the equestrian order; the counsels of the one, the arms of the other, will be devoted to your person and the service of the empire. Do you not hear the language of the Roman matron? You were a guest, I have adopted you as a citizen; a Transalpine stranger, I have elected you for my sovereign;[56] and given you myself, and all that is mine. Your first and most sacred duty, is to swear and subscribe, that you will shed your blood for the republic; that you will maintain in peace and justice, the laws of the city and the charters of your predecessors; and that you will reward with five thousand pounds of silver the faithful senators who shall proclaim your titles in the Capitol. With the name, assume the character, of Augustus." The flowers of Latin rhetoric were not yet exhausted; but Frederic, impatient of their vanity, interrupted the orators in the high tone of royalty and conquest. "Famous indeed have been the fortitude and wisdom of the ancient Romans: but your speech is not seasoned with wisdom, and I could wish that fortitude were conspicuous in your actions. Like all sublunary things, Rome has felt the vicissitudes of time and fortune. Your noblest families were translated to the East, to the royal city of Constantine; and the remains of your strength and freedom have long since been exhausted by the Greeks and Franks. Are you desirous of beholding the ancient glory of Rome, the gravity of the senate, the spirit of the knights, the discipline of the camp, the valour of the legions? you will find them in the German republic. It is not empire, naked and alone, the ornaments and virtues of empire have likewise migrated beyond the Alps to a more deserving people:[57] they will be employed in your defence, but they claim your obedience. You pretend that myself or my predecessors have been invited by the Romans: you mistake the word, they were not invited; they were implored. From its foreign and domestic tyrants, the city was rescued by Charlemagne and Otho, whose ashes repose in our country: and their dominion was

56. Hospes eras, civem feci. Advena fuisti ex Transalpinis partibus; principem constitui.

57. Non cessit nobis nudum imperium, virtute sua amictum venit, ornamenta sua secum traxit. Penes nos sunt consules tui, &c. Cicero or Livy would not have rejected these images, the eloquence of a Barbarian born and educated in the Hercynian forest.

the price of your deliverance. Under that dominion your ancestors lived and died. I claim by the right of inheritance and possession, and who shall dare to extort you from my hands? Is the hand of the Franks[58] and Germans enfeebled by age? Am I vanquished? Am I a captive? Am I not encompassed with the banners of a potent and invincible army? You impose conditions on your master; you require oaths: if the conditions are just, an oath is superfluous; if unjust, it is criminal. Can you doubt my equity? It is extended to the meanest of my subjects. Will not my sword be unsheathed in the defence of the Capitol? By that sword the northern kingdom of Denmark has been restored to the Roman empire. You prescribe the measure and the objects of my bounty, which flows in a copious but a voluntary stream. All will be given to patient merit; all will be denied to rude importunity."[59] Neither the emperor nor the senate could maintain these lofty pretensions of dominion and liberty. United with the pope, and suspicious of the Romans, Frederic continued his march to the Vatican: his coronation was disturbed by a sally from the Capitol; and if the numbers and valour of the Germans prevailed in the bloody conflict, he could not safely encamp in the presence of a city of which he styled himself the sovereign. About twelve years afterwards, he besieged Rome, to seat an antipope in the chair of St. Peter; and twelve Pisan gallies were introduced into the Tyber: but the senate and people were saved by the arts of negociation and the progress of disease; nor did Frederic or his successors reiterate the hostile attempt. Their laborious reigns were exercised by the popes, the crusades, and the independence of Lombardy and Germany; they courted the alliance of the Romans; and Frederic the second offered in the Capitol the great standard, the *Caroccio* of Milan.[60] After the extinction of the house of Swabia, they

58. Otho of Frisingen, who surely understood the language of the court and diet of Germany, speaks of the Franks in the xii[th] century as the reigning nation (Proceres Franci, equites Franci, manus Francorum): he adds, however, the epithet of *Teutonici*.

59. Otho Frising. de Gestis Frederici I. l. ii. c. 22. p. 720–723. These original and authentic acts I have translated and abridged with freedom, yet with fidelity.

60. From the Chronicles of Ricobaldo and Francis Pipin, Muratori (dissert. xxvi. tom. ii. p. 492.) has transcribed this curious fact with the doggrel verses that accompanied the gift.

Ave decus orbis ave! victus tibi destinor, ave!
Currus ab Augusto Frederico Cæsare justo.
Væ Mediolanum! jam sentis spernere vanum
Imperii vires, proprias tibi tollere vires.
Ergo triumphorum urbs potes memor esse priorum
Quos tibi mittebant reges qui bella gerebant.

Ne si dee tacere (I now use the Italian Dissertations, tom. i. p. 444.) che nell'anno

were banished beyond the Alps; and their last coronations betrayed the impotence and poverty of the Teutonic Cæsars.[61]

Wars of the Romans against the neighbouring cities.

Under the reign of Adrian, when the empire extended from the Euphrates to the ocean, from mount Atlas to the Grampian hills, a fanciful historian[62] amused the Romans with the picture of their infant wars. "There was a time," says Florus, "when Tibur and Præneste, our summer retreats, were the objects of hostile vows in the Capitol, when we dreaded the shades of the Arician groves, when we could triumph without a blush over the nameless villages of the Sabines and Latins, and even Corioli could afford a title not unworthy of a victorious general." The pride of his contemporaries was gratified by the contrast of the past and the present: they would have been humbled by the prospect of futurity; by the prediction, that after a thousand years, Rome, despoiled of empire and contracted to her primæval limits, would renew the same hostilities, on the same ground which was then decorated with her villas and gardens. The adjacent territory on either side of the Tyber was always claimed, and sometimes possessed, as the patrimony of St. Peter, but the barons assumed a lawless independence, and the cities too faithfully copied the revolt and discord of the metropolis. In the twelfth and thirteenth centuries, the Romans incessantly laboured to reduce or destroy the contumacious vassals of the church and senate; and if their headstrong and selfish ambition was moderated by the pope, he often encouraged their zeal by the alliance of his spiritual arms. Their warfare was that of the first consuls and dictators, who were taken from the plow. They assembled in arms at the foot of the Capitol; sallied from the gates, plundered or burnt the harvests of their neighbours, engaged in tumultuary conflict, and returned home after an expedition of fifteen or twenty days. Their sieges were tedious and unskilful: in the use of victory, they indulged the meaner passions of

---

1727, una copia desso Caroccio in marmo dianzi ignoto si scopri nel Campidoglio, presso alle carcere di quel luogo, dove Sisto V. l'avea falto rinchiudere. Stava esso posto sopra quatro colonne di marmo fino colla sequente inscrizione, &c. to the same purpose as the old inscription.

61. The decline of the Imperial arms and authority in Italy, is related with impartial learning in the Annals of Muratori (tom. x, xi, xii.); and the reader may compare his narrative with the Histoire des Allemands (tom. iii, iv.), by Schmidt, who has deserved the esteem of his countrymen.

62. Tibur nunc suburbanum, et æstivæ Præneste deliciæ, nuncupatis in Capitolio votis petebantur. The whole passage of Florus (l. i. c. 11.) may be read with pleasure, and has deserved the praise of a man of genius (Œuvres de Montesquieu, tom. iii. p. 634, 635. quarto edition).

jealousy and revenge; and instead of adopting the valour, they trampled on the misfortunes, of their adversaries. The captives, in their shirts, with a rope round their necks, solicited their pardon: the fortifications and even the buildings of the rival cities were demolished, and the inhabitants were scattered in the adjacent villages. It was thus that the seats of the cardinal bishops, Porto, Ostia, Albanum, Tusculum, Præneste, and Tibur or Tivoli, were successively overthrown by the ferocious hostility of the Romans.[63] Of these,[64] Porto and Ostia, the two keys of the Tyber, are still vacant and desolate: the marshy and unwholesome banks are peopled with herds of buffalos, and the river is lost to every purpose of navigation and trade. The hills which afford a shady retirement from the autumnal heats, have again smiled with the blessings of peace: Frescati has arisen near the ruins of Tusculum: Tibur or Tivoli has resumed the honours of a city,[65] and the meaner towns of Albano and Palestrina are decorated with the villas of the cardinals and princes of Rome. In the work of destruction, the ambition of the Romans was often checked and repulsed by the neighbouring cities and their allies: in the first siege of Tibur, they were driven from their camp; and the battles of Tusculum[66] and Viterbo[67] might be compared in their relative state to the memorable fields of Thrasymene and Cannæ. In the first of these petty wars, thirty thousand Romans were overthrown by a thousand German horse, whom Frederic Barbarossa had detached to the relief of Tusculum; and if we number the slain at three, the prisoners at two, thousand, we shall embrace the most authentic and moderate account.

Battle of Tusculum, A.D. 1167.

63. Ne a feritate Romanorum, sicut fuerant Hostienses, Portuenses, Tusculanenses, Albanenses, Labicenses, et nuper Tiburtini destruerentur (Matthew Paris, p. 757.). These events are marked in the Annals and Index (the xviii[th] volume) of Muratori.

64. For the state or ruin of these suburban cities, the banks of the Tyber, &c. see the lively picture of the P. Labat (Voyage en Espagne et en Italie), who had long resided in the neighbourhood of Rome; and the more accurate description of which P. Eschinard (Roma, 1750, in octavo) has added to the topographical map of Cingolani.

65. Labat (tom. iii. p. 233.) mentions a recent decree of the Roman government, which has severely mortified the pride and poverty of Tivoli: in civitate Tiburtinâ non vivitur civiliter.

66. I depart from my usual method, of quoting only by the date the Annals of Muratori, in consideration of the critical balance in which he has weighed nine contemporary writers who mention the battle of Tusculum (tom. x. p. 42–44.).

67. Matthew Paris, p. 345. This bishop of Winchester was Peter de Rupibus, who occupied the see thirty-two years (A.D. 1206–1238), and is described, by the English historian, as a soldier and a statesman (p. 178. 399.).

Battle of Viterbo, A.D. 1234. Sixty-eight years afterward they marched against Viterbo in the ecclesiastical state with the whole force of the city; by a rare coalition, the Teutonic eagle was blended, in the adverse banners, with the keys of St. Peter; and the pope's auxiliaries were commanded by a count of Tholouse and a bishop of Winchester. The Romans were discomfited with shame and slaughter; but the English prelate must have indulged the vanity of a pilgrim, if he multiplied their numbers to one hundred, and their loss in the field to thirty, thousand men. Had the policy of the senate and the discipline of the legions been restored with the Capitol, the divided condition of Italy would have offered the fairest opportunity of a second conquest. But in arms, the modern Romans were not *above*, and in arts, they were far *below*, the common level of the neighbouring republics. Nor was their warlike spirit of any long continuance; after some irregular sallies, they subsided in the national apathy, in the neglect of military institutions, and in the disgraceful and dangerous use of foreign mercenaries.

The election of the popes. Ambition is a weed of quick and early vegetation in the vineyard of Christ. Under the first Christian princes, the chair of St. Peter was disputed by the votes, the venality, the violence, of a popular election: the sanctuaries of Rome were polluted with blood; and, from the third to the twelfth century, the church was distracted by the mischief of frequent schisms. As long as the final appeal was determined by the civil magistrate, these mischiefs were transient and local: the merits were tried by equity or favour; nor could the unsuccessful competitor long disturb the triumph of his rival. But after emperors had been divested of their prerogatives, after a maxim had been established, that the vicar of Christ is amenable to no earthly tribunal, each vacancy of the holy see might involve Christendom in controversy and war. The claims of the cardinals and inferior clergy, of the nobles and people, were vague and litigious: the freedom of choice was over-ruled by the tumults of a city that no longer owned or obeyed a superior. On the decease of a pope, two factions proceeded in different churches to a double election: the number and weight of votes, the priority of time, the merit of the candidates, might balance each other: the most respectable of the clergy were divided; and the distant princes, who bowed before the spiritual throne, could not distinguish the spurious, from the legitimate, idol. The emperors were often the authors of the schism, from the political motive of opposing a friendly to an hostile pontiff; and each of the competitors was reduced to suffer the insults of his enemies, who were not awed by conscience; and to purchase the support of his adherents, who were

Right of the cardinals established by Alexander III. A.D. 1179.

instigated by avarice or ambition. A peaceful and perpetual succession was ascertained by Alexander the third,[68] who finally abolished the tumultuary votes of the clergy and people, and defined the right of election in the sole college of cardinals.[69] The three orders of bishops, priests, and deacons, were assimilated to each other by this important privilege: the parochial clergy of Rome obtained the first rank in the hierarchy; they were indifferently chosen among the nations of Christendom; and the possession of the richest benefices, of the most important bishoprics, was not incompatible with their title and office. The senators of the Catholic church, the coadjutors and legates of the supreme pontiff, were robed in purple, the symbol of martyrdom or royalty; they claimed a proud equality with kings; and their dignity was enhanced by the smallness of their number, which, till the reign of Leo the tenth, seldom exceeded twenty, or twenty-five, persons. By this wise regulation, all doubt and scandal were removed, and the root of schism was so effectually destroyed, that in a period of six hundred years a double choice has only once divided the unity of the sacred college. But as the concurrence of two thirds of the votes had been made necessary, the election was often delayed by the private interest and passions of the cardinals; and while they prolonged their independent reign, the Christian world was left destitute of an head. A vacancy of almost three years had preceded the elevation of Gregory the tenth, who resolved to prevent the future abuse; and his bull, after some opposition, has been consecrated in the code of the canon law.[70] Nine days are allowed for the obsequies of the deceased pope, and the arrival of the absent cardinals; on the tenth, they are imprisoned, each with one domestic, in a common apartment or *conclave*, without any separation of walls or curtains; a small window is reserved for the introduction of necessaries; but the door is locked on both sides, and guarded by the

Institution of the conclave by Gregory X. A.D. 1274.

68. See Mosheim, Institut. Hist. Ecclesiast. p. 401. 403. Alexander himself had nearly been the victim of a contested election; and the doubtful merits of Innocent had only preponderated by the weight of genius and learning which St. Bernard cast into the scale (see his life and writings).

69. The origin, titles, importance, dress, precedency, &c. of the Roman cardinals, are very ably discussed by Thomassin (Discipline de l'Eglise, tom. i. p. 1262–1287.); but their purple is now much faded. The sacred college was raised to the definite number of seventy-two, to represent, under his vicar, the disciples of Christ.

70. See the bull of Gregory X. (approbante sacro concilio), in the *Sexte* of the Canon Law (l. i. tit. 6. c. 3.), a supplement to the Decretals, which Boniface VIII. promulgated at Rome in 1298, and addressed to all the universities of Europe.

magistrates of the city, to seclude them from all correspondence with the world. If the election be not consummated in three days, the luxury of their table is contracted to a single dish at dinner and supper; and after the eighth day, they are reduced to a scanty allowance of bread, water, and wine. During the vacancy of the holy see, the cardinals are prohibited from touching the revenues, or assuming, unless in some rare emergency, the government, of the church: all agreements and promises among the electors are formally annulled; and their integrity is fortified by their solemn oath and the prayers of the Catholics. Some articles of inconvenient or superfluous rigour have been gradually relaxed, but the principle of confinement is vigorous and entire: they are still urged, by the personal motives of health and freedom, to accelerate the moment of their deliverance; and the improvement of ballot or secret votes has wrapt the struggles of the conclave[71] in the silky veil of charity and politeness.[72] By these institutions, the Romans were excluded from the election of their prince and bishop; and in the fever of wild and precarious liberty, they seemed insensible of the loss of this inestimable privilege. The *A.D. 1328.* emperor Lewis of Bavaria revived the example of the great Otho. After some negociation with the magistrates, the Roman people was assembled[73] in the square before St. Peter's; the pope of Avignon, John the twenty-second, was deposed; the choice of his successor was ratified by their consent and applause. They freely voted for a new law, that their bishop should never be absent more than three months in the year, and two days journey from the city; and that if he neglected to return on the

71. The genius of cardinal de Retz had a right to paint a conclave (of 1655), in which he was a spectator and an actor (Memoires, tom. iv. p. 15–57.): but I am at a loss to appreciate the knowledge or authority of an anonymous Italian, whose history (Conclavi de' Pontifici Romani, in 4to, 1667) has been continued since the reign of Alexander VII. The accidental form of the work furnishes a lesson, though not an antidote, to ambition. From a labyrinth of intrigues, we emerge to the adoration of the successful candidate: but the next page opens with his funeral.

72. The expressions of cardinal de Retz are positive and picturesque: On y veçut toujours ensemble avec le même respect, et la même civilité que l'on observe dans le cabinet des rois, avec la même politesse qu'on avoit dans la cour de Henri III. avec la même familiarité que l'on voit dans les colleges; avec la même modestie, qui se remarque dans les noviciats; et avec la même charité, du moins en apparence, qui pourroit être entre des freres parfaitement unis.

73. Rechiesti per bando (says John Villani) sanatori di Roma, e 52 del popolo, et capitani de' 25. e consoli *(consoli?)*, et 13 buone huomini, uno per rione. Our knowledge is too imperfect to pronounce, how much of this constitution was temporary, and how much ordinary and permanent. Yet it is faintly illustrated by the ancient statutes of Rome.

third summons, the public servant should be degraded and dismissed.[74] But Lewis forgot his own debility and the prejudices of the times: beyond the precincts of a German camp, his useless phantom was rejected; the Romans despised their own workmanship; the antipope implored the mercy of his lawful sovereign;[75] and the exclusive right of the cardinals was more firmly established by this unseasonable attack.

Absence of the popes from Rome.

Had the election been always held in the Vatican, the rights of the senate and people would not have been violated with impunity. But the Romans forgot, and were forgotten, in the absence of the successors of Gregory the seventh, who did not keep as a divine precept their ordinary residence in the city and diocese. The care of that diocese was less important than the government of the universal church; nor could the popes delight in a city in which their authority was always opposed and their person was often endangered. From the persecution of the emperors, and the wars of Italy, they escaped beyond the Alps into the hospitable bosom of France; from the tumults of Rome they prudently withdrew to live and die in the more tranquil stations of Anagni, Perugia, Viterbo, and the adjacent cities. When the flock was offended or impoverished by the absence of the shepherd, they were recalled by a stern admonition, that St. Peter had fixed his chair, not in an obscure village, but in the capital of the world; by a ferocious menace that the Romans would march in arms to destroy the place and people that should dare to afford them a retreat. They returned with timorous obedience; and were saluted with the account of an heavy debt, of all the losses which their desertion had occasioned, the hire of lodgings, the sale of provisions, and the various expences of servants and strangers who attended the court.[76] After a short interval of peace, and perhaps of

74. Villani (l. x. c. 68–71. in Muratori, Script. tom. xiii. p. 641–645.) relates this law, and the whole transaction, with much less abhorrence than the prudent Muratori. Any one conversant with the darker ages must have observed how much the sense (I mean the nonsense) of superstition is fluctuating and inconsistent.

75. In the 1st volume of the Popes of Avignon, see the second original Life of John XXII. p. 142–145. the confession of the antipope, p. 145–152. and the laborious notes of Baluze, p. 714, 715.

76. Romani autem non valentes nec volentes ultra suam celare cupiditatem gravissimam contra papam movere cœperunt questionem, exigentes ab eo urgentissime omnia quæ subierant per ejus absentiam damna et jacturas, videlicet in hospitiis locandis, in mercimoniis, in usuris, in redditibus, in provisionibus, et in aliis modis innumerabilibus. Quôd cum audisset papa, præcordialiter ingemuit et se comperiens *muscipulatum*, &c. Matt. Paris, p. 757. For the ordinary history of the popes, their life and death, their residence and absence, it is enough to refer to the ecclesiastical annalists, Spondanus and Fleury.

authority, they were again banished by new tumults, and again summoned by the imperious or respectful invitation of the senate. In these occasional retreats, the exiles and fugitives of the Vatican were seldom long, or far, distant from the metropolis; but in the beginning of the fourteenth century the apostolic throne was transported, as it might seem for ever, from the Tyber to the Rhône; and the cause of the transmigration may be deduced from the furious contest between Boniface the eighth and the king of France.[77] The spiritual arms of excommunication and interdict were repulsed by the union of the three estates, and the privileges of the Gallican church; but the pope was not against the carnal weapons which Philip the Fair had courage to employ. As the pope resided at Anagni, without the suspicion of danger, his palace and person were assaulted by three hundred horse, who had been secretly levied by William of Nogaret, a French minister, and Sciarra Colonna, of a noble but hostile family of Rome. The cardinals fled; the inhabitants of Anagni were seduced from their allegiance and gratitude; but the dauntless Boniface, unarmed and alone, seated himself in his chair, and awaited, like the conscript fathers of old, the swords of the Gauls. Nogaret, a foreign adversary, was content to execute the orders of his master: by the domestic enmity of Colonna, he was insulted with words and blows; and during a confinement of three days his life was threatened by the hardships which they inflicted on the obstinacy which they provoked. Their strange delay gave time and courage to the adherents of the church, who rescued him from sacrilegious violence; but his imperious soul was wounded in a vital part; and Boniface expired at Rome in a frenzy of rage and revenge. His memory is stained with the glaring vices of avarice and pride; nor has the courage of a martyr promoted this ecclesiastical champion to the honours of a saint; a magnanimous sinner (say the chronicles of the times), who entered like a fox, reigned like a lion, and died like a dog. He was succeeded by Benedict the eleventh, the mildest of mankind. Yet he excommunicated the impious emissaries of Philip, and devoted the city and people of Anagni by a tremendous curse, whose effects are still visible to the eyes of superstition.[78]

Boniface VIII. A.D. 1294–1303.

77. Besides the general historians of the church of Italy and of France, we possess a valuable treatise composed by a learned friend of Thuanus, which his last and best editors have published in the appendix (Histoire particuliere du grand Differend entre Boniface VIII. et Philippe le Bel, par Pierre du Puis, tom. vii. P. xi. p. 61–82.).

78. It is difficult to know whether Labat (tom. iv. p. 53–57.) be in jest or in earnest, when he supposes that Anagni still feels the weight of this curse, and that the corn-

Translation of the holy see to Avignon, A.D. 1309.

After his decease, the tedious and equal suspense of the conclave was fixed by the dexterity of the French faction. A specious offer was made and accepted, that, in the term of forty days, they would elect one of the three candidates who should be named by their opponents. The archbishop of Bourdeaux, a furious enemy of his king and country, was the first on the list; but his ambition was known; and his conscience obeyed the calls of fortune and the commands of a benefactor, who had been informed by a swift messenger that the choice of a pope was now in his hands. The terms were regulated in a private interview; and with such speed and secresy was the business transacted, that the unanimous conclave applauded the elevation of Clement the fifth.[79] The cardinals of both parties were soon astonished by a summons to attend him beyond the Alps; from whence, as they soon discovered, they must never hope to return. He was engaged, by promise and affection, to prefer the residence of France; and, after dragging his court through Poitou and Gascogny, and devouring, by his expence, the cities and convents on the road, he finally reposed at Avignon,[80] which flourished above seventy years[81] the seat of the Roman pontiff and the metropolis of Christendom. By land, by sea, by the Rhone, the position of Avignon was on all sides accessible: the southern provinces of France do not yield to Italy itself; new palaces arose for the accommodation of the pope and cardinals; and the arts of luxury were soon attracted by the treasures of the church. They were already possessed of the

---

fields, or vineyards, or olive-trees, are annually blasted by nature, the obsequious handmaid of the popes.

79. See in the Chronicle of Giovanni Villani (l. viii. c. 63, 64. 80. in Muratori, tom. xiii.) the imprisonment of Boniface VIII. and the election of Clement V. the last of which, like most anecdotes, is embarrassed with some difficulties.

80. The original lives of the eight popes of Avignon, Clement V. John XXII. Benedict XII. Clement VI. Innocent VI. Urban V. Gregory XI. and Clement VII. are published by Stephen Baluze (Vitæ Paparum Avenionensium; Paris, 1693, 2 vols. in 4to) with copious and elaborate notes, and a second volume of acts and documents. With the true zeal of an editor and a patriot, he devoutly justifies or excuses the characters of his countrymen.

81. The exile of Avignon is compared by the Italians with Babylon, and the Babylonish captivity. Such furious metaphors, more suitable to the ardour of Petrarch than to the judgment of Muratori, are gravely refuted in Baluze's preface. The abbé de Sade is distracted between the love of Petrarch and of his country. Yet he modestly pleads, that many of the local inconveniences of Avignon are now removed; and many of the vices against which the poet declaims, had been imported with the Roman court by the strangers of Italy (tom. i. p. 23–28.).

adjacent territory, the Venaissin county,[82] a populous and fertile spot; and the sovereignty of Avignon was afterwards purchased from the youth and distress of Jane, the first queen of Naples and countess of Provence, for the inadequate price of fourscore thousand florins.[83] Under the shadow of the French monarchy, amidst an obedient people, the popes enjoyed an honourable and tranquil state, to which they long had been strangers: but Italy deplored their absence; and Rome, in solitude and poverty, might repent of the ungovernable freedom which had driven from the Vatican the successor of St. Peter. Her repentance was tardy and fruitless: after the death of the old members, the sacred college was filled with French cardinals,[84] who beheld Rome and Italy with abhorrence and contempt, and perpetuated a series of national, and even provincial, popes, attached by the most indissoluble ties to their native country.

Institution of the jubilee, or holy year, A.D. 1300.

The progress of industry had produced and enriched the Italian republics: the æra of their liberty is the most flourishing period of population and agriculture, of manufactures and commerce; and their mechanic labours were gradually refined into the arts of elegance and genius. But the position of Rome was less favourable, the territory less fruitful; the character of the inhabitants was debased by indolence and elated by pride; and they fondly conceived that the tribute of subjects must for ever nourish the metropolis of the church and empire. This prejudice was encouraged in some degree by the resort of pilgrims to the shrines of the apostles; and the last legacy of the popes, the institution of the HOLY

82. The comtat Venaissin was ceded to the popes in 1273 by Philip III. king of France, after he had inherited the dominions of the count of Tholouse. Forty years before, the heresy of count Raymond had given them a pretence of seizure, and they derived some obscure claim from the xi[th] century to some lands citra Rhodanum (Valesii Notitia Galliarum, p. 459. 610. Longuerue, Description de la France, tom. i. p. 376–381.).

83. If a possession of four centuries were not itself a title, such objections might annul the bargain; but the purchase-money must be refunded, for indeed it was paid. Civitatem Avenionem emit ... per ejusmodi venditionem pecuniâ redundantes, &c. (ii[da] Vita Clement. VI. in Baluz. tom. i. p. 272. Muratori, Script. tom. iii. P. ii. p. 565.) The only temptation for Jane and her second husband was ready money, and without it they could not have returned to the throne of Naples.

84. Clement V. immediately promoted ten cardinals, nine French and one English (Vita iv[ta], p. 63. et Baluz. p. 625, &c.). In 1331, the pope refused two candidates recommended by the king of France, quod xx. Cardinales, de quibus xvii. de regno Franciæ originem traxisse noscuntur in memorato collegio existant (Thomassin, Discipline de l'Eglise, tom. i. p. 1281.).

YEAR,[85] was not less beneficial to the people than to the clergy. Since the loss of Palestine, the gift of plenary indulgences, which had been applied to the crusades, remained without an object; and the most valuable treasure of the church was sequestered above eight years from public circulation. A new channel was opened by the diligence of Boniface the eighth, who reconciled the vices of ambition and avarice; and the pope had sufficient learning to recollect and revive the secular games, which were celebrated in Rome at the conclusion of every century. To sound without danger the depth of popular credulity, a sermon was seasonably pronounced, a report was artfully scattered, some aged witnesses were produced; and on the first of January of the year thirteen hundred, the church of St. Peter was crowded with the faithful, who demanded the *customary* indulgence of the holy time. The pontiff, who watched and irritated their devout impatience, was soon persuaded by ancient testimony of the justice of their claim; and he proclaimed a plenary absolution to all Catholics who, in the course of that year, and at every similar period, should respectfully visit the apostolic churches of St. Peter and St. Paul. The welcome sound was propagated through Christendom; and at first from the nearest provinces of Italy, and at length from the remote kingdoms of Hungary and Britain, the highways were thronged with a swarm of pilgrims who sought to expiate their sins in a journey, however costly or laborious, which was exempt from the perils of military service. All exceptions of rank or sex, of age or infirmity, were forgotten in the common transport; and in the streets and churches many persons were trampled to death by the eagerness of devotion. The calculation of their numbers could not be easy nor accurate; and they have probably been magnified by a dextrous clergy, well apprised of the contagion of example: yet we are assured by a judicious historian, who assisted at the ceremony, that Rome was never replenished with less than two hundred thousand strangers; and another spectator has fixed at two millions the total concourse of the year. A trifling oblation from each individual would accumulate a royal treasure; and two priests stood night and day, with rakes in their hands, to collect, without counting, the heaps of gold and silver that were poured on the altar of St. Paul.[86] It was

85. Our primitive account is from cardinal James Caietan (Maxima Bibliot. Patrum, tom. xxv.); and I am at a loss to determine whether the nephew of Boniface VIII. be a fool or a knave: the uncle is a much clearer character.

86. See John Villani (l. viii. c. 36.) in the xii[th], and the Chronicon Astense, in the xi[th] volume (p. 191, 192.) of Muratori's Collection. Papa innumerabilem pecuniam ab eisdem accepit, nam duo clerici, cum rastris, &c.

fortunately a season of peace and plenty; and if forage was scarce, if inns and lodgings were extravagantly dear, an inexhaustible supply of bread and wine, of meat and fish, was provided by the policy of Boniface and the venal hospitality of the Romans. From a city without trade or industry, all casual riches will speedily evaporate: but the avarice and envy of the next generation solicited Clement the sixth[87] to anticipate the distant period of the century. The gracious pontiff complied with their wishes; afforded Rome this poor consolation for his loss; and justified the change by the name and practice of the Mosaic Jubilee.[88] His summons was obeyed; and the number, zeal, and liberality, of the pilgrims did not yield to the primitive festival. But they encountered the triple scourge of war, pestilence, and famine: many wives and virgins were violated in the castles of Italy; and many strangers were pillaged or murdered by the savage Romans, no longer moderated by the presence of their bishop.[89] To the impatience of the popes we may ascribe the successive reduction to fifty, thirty-three, and twenty-five, years; although the second of these terms is commensurate with the life of Christ. The profusion of indulgences, the revolt of the Protestants, and the decline of superstition, have much diminished the value of the jubilee: yet even the nineteenth and last festival was a year of pleasure and profit to the Romans; and a philosophic smile will not disturb the triumph of the priest or the happiness of the people.[90]

The second jubilee, A.D. 1350.

The nobles or barons of Rome.

In the beginning of the eleventh century, Italy was exposed to the feudal tyranny alike oppressive to the sovereign and the people. The rights of human nature were vindicated by her numerous republics, who soon extended their liberty and dominion from the city to the adjacent country. The sword of the nobles was broken; their slaves were enfranchised; their castles were demolished; they assumed the

87. The two bulls of Boniface VIII. and Clement VI. are inserted in the Corpus Juris Canonici (Extravagant. Commun. l. v. tit. ix. c. 1, 2.).

88. The sabbatic years and jubilees of the Mosaic law (Car. Sigon. de Republicâ Hebræorum, Opp. tom. iv. l. iii. c. 14, 15. p. 151, 152.), the suspension of all care and labour, the periodical release of lands, debts, servitude, &c. may seem a noble idea, but the execution would be impracticable in a *profane* republic; and I should be glad to learn that this ruinous festival was observed by the Jewish people.

89. See the Chronicle of Matteo Villani (l. i. c. 56.) in the xiv[th] volume of Muratori, and the Memoires sur la Vie de Petrarque, tom. iii. p. 75–89.

90. The subject is exhausted by M. Chais, a French minister at the Hague, in his Lettres Historiques et Dogmatiques, sur les Jubiles et les Indulgences; la Haye, 1751, 3 vols. in 12[mo]; an elaborate and pleasing work, had not the author preferred the character of a polemic to that of a philosopher.

habits of society and obedience; their ambition was confined to municipal honours, and in the proudest aristocracy of Venice or Genoa, each patrician was subject to the laws.[91] But the feeble and disorderly government of Rome was unequal to the task of curbing her rebellious sons, who scorned the authority of the magistrate within and without the walls. It was no longer a civil contention between the nobles and plebeians for the government of the state: the barons asserted in arms their personal independence; their palaces and castles were fortified against a siege; and their private quarrels were maintained by the numbers of their vassals and retainers. In origin and affection, they were aliens to their country:[92] and a genuine Roman, could such have been produced, might have renounced these haughty strangers, who disdained the appellation of citizens, and proudly styled themselves the princes, of Rome.[93] After a dark series of revolutions, all records of pedigree were lost; the distinction of surnames was abolished; the blood of the nations was mingled in a thousand channels; and the Goths and Lombards, the Greeks and Franks, the Germans and Normans, had obtained the fairest possessions by royal bounty, or the prerogative of valour. These examples might be readily presumed: but the elevation of an Hebrew race to the rank of senators and consuls, is an event without a parallel in the long captivity of these miserable exiles.[94] In the time of Leo the ninth, a wealthy and learned Jew was converted to christianity; and honoured at his baptism with the name of his godfather, the reigning pope. The zeal and courage of Peter the son of Leo were signalised in the cause of Gregory the seventh, who entrusted his faithful adherent with the government of Adrian's mole, the tower of Crescentius, or, as it is now called, the castle of St. Angelo. Both the father and the son were the parents of

Family of Leo the Jew.

91. Muratori (Dissert. xlvii.) alleges the Annals of Florence, Padua, Genoa, &c. the analogy of the rest, the evidence of Otho of Frisingen (de Gest. Fred. I. l. ii. c. 13.), and the submission of the marquis of Este.

92. As early as the year 824, the emperor Lothaire I. found it expedient to interrogate the Roman people, to learn from each individual, by what national law he chose to be governed (Muratori, Dissert xxii.).

93. Petrarch attacks these foreigners, the tyrants of Rome, in a declamation or epistle, full of bold truths and absurd pedantry, in which he applies the maxims, and even prejudices, of the old republic to the state of the xiv[th] century (Memoires, tom. iii. p. 157–169.).

94. The origin and adventures of this Jewish family are noticed by Pagi (Critica, tom. iv. p. 435. A.D. 1124, N° 3, 4.), who draws his information from the Chronographus Maurigniacensis, and Arnulphus Sagiensis de Schismate (in Muratori, Script. Ital. tom. iii. P. i. p. 423–432.). The fact must in some degree be true; yet I could wish that it had been coolly related, before it was turned into a reproach against the antipope.

a numerous progeny; their riches, the fruits of usury, were shared with the noblest families of the city; and so extensive was their alliance, that the grandson of the proselyte was exalted by the weight of his kindred to the throne of St. Peter. A majority of the clergy and people supported his cause; he reigned several years in the Vatican, and it is only the eloquence of St. Bernard, and the final triumph of Innocent the second, that has branded Anacletus with the epithet of antipope. After his defeat and death, the posterity of Leo is no longer conspicuous; and none will be found of the modern nobles ambitious of descending from a Jewish stock. It is not my design to enumerate the Roman families, which have failed at different periods, or those which are continued in different degrees of splendour to the present time.[95] The old consular line of the *Frangipani* discover their name in the generous act of *breaking* or dividing bread in a time of famine; and such benevolence is more truly glorious than to have enclosed, with their allies the *Corsi*, a spacious quarter of the city in the chains of their fortifications: the *Savelli*, as it should seem a Sabine race, have maintained their original dignity; the obsolete surname of the *Capizucchi* is inscribed on the coins of the first senators; the *Conti* preserve the honour, without the estate, of the counts of Signia; and the *Annibaldi* must have been very ignorant, or very modest, if they had not descended from the Carthaginian hero.[96]

The Colonna, But among, perhaps above, the peers and princes of the city,

95. Muratori has given two dissertations (xli and xlii.) to the names, surnames, and families of Italy. Some nobles, who glory in their domestic fables, may be offended with his firm and temperate criticism; yet surely some ounces of pure gold are of more value than many pounds of base metal.

96. The cardinal of St. George, in his poetical, or rather metrical, history of the election and coronation of Boniface VIII. (Muratori, Script. Ital. tom. iii. P. i. p. 641, &c.), describes the state and families of Rome at the coronation of Boniface VIII. (A.D. 1295):

Interea titulis redimiti sanguine et armis
Illustresque viri Romanâ a stirpe trahentes
Nomen in emeritos tantæ virtutis honores
Intulerant sese medios festumque colebant
Aurata fulgentes toga sociante catervâ.
Ex ipsis devota domus præstantis ab *Ursâ*
Ecclesiæ, vultumque gerens demissius altum
Festa *Columna* jocis, necnon *Sabellia* mitis;
Stephanides senior, *Comites, Anibalica* proles,
Præfectusque urbis magnum sine viribus nomen.

(l. ii. c. 5. 100. p. 647, 648.).

The ancient statutes of Rome (l. iii. c. 59. p. 174, 175.) distinguish eleven families of barons, who are obliged to swear in concilio communi, before the senator, that they would not harbour or protect any malefactors, outlaws, &c. – a feeble security!

I distinguish the rival houses of COLONNA and URSINI, whose private story is an essential part of the annals of modern Rome. I. The name and arms of Colonna[97] have been the theme of much doubtful etymology; nor have the orators and antiquarians overlooked either Trajan's pillar, or the columns of Hercules, or the pillar of Christ's flagellation, or the luminous column that guided the Israelites in the desert. Their first historical appearance in the year eleven hundred and four, attests the power and antiquity, while it explains the simple meaning, of the name. By the usurpation of Cavæ, the Colonna provoked the arms of Paschal the second; but they lawfully held in the Campagna of Rome, the hereditary fiefs of Zagarola and *Colonna*; and the latter of these towns was probably adorned with some lofty pillar, the relic of a villa or temple.[98] They likewise possessed one moiety of the neighbouring city of Tusculum; a strong presumption of their descent from the counts of Tusculum, who in the tenth century were the tyrants of the apostolic see. According to their own and the public opinion, the primitive and remote source was derived from the banks of the Rhine;[99] and the sovereigns of Germany were not ashamed of a real or fabulous affinity with a noble race, which in the revolutions of seven hundred years has been often illustrated by merit, and always by fortune.[100] About the end of the thirteenth century, the most powerful branch was composed of an uncle and six brothers, all conspicuous in arms, or in the honours of the church. Of these, Peter was elected senator of Rome, introduced to the Capitol in a triumphant car, and hailed in some vain acclamations with

97. It is pity that the Colonna themselves have not favoured the world with a complete and critical history of their illustrious house. I adhere to Muratori (Dissert. xlii. tom. iii. p. 647, 648.).

98. Pandulph. Pisan. in Vit. Paschal. II. in Muratori, Script. Ital. tom. iii. P. i. p. 335. The family has still great possessions in the Campagna of Rome; but they have alienated to the Rospigliosi this original fief of *Colonna* (Eschinard, p. 258, 259.).

99.

> Te longinqua dedit tellus et pascua
> Rheni,

says Petrarch; and, in 1417, a duke of Guelders and Juliers acknowledges (Lenfant, Hist. du Concile de Constance, tom. ii. p. 539.) his descent from the ancestors of Martin V. (Otho Colonna): but the royal author of the Memoirs of Brandenburg observes, that the sceptre in his arms has been confounded with the column. To maintain the Roman origin of the Colonna, it was ingeniously supposed (Diario di Monaldeschi, in the Script. Ital. tom. xii. p. 533.), that a cousin of the emperor Nero escaped from the city, and founded Mentz in Germany.

100. I cannot overlook the Roman triumph or ovation of Marco Antonio Colonna, who had commanded the pope's gallies at the naval victory of Lepanto (Thuan. Hist. l. 7. tom. iii. p. 55, 56. Muret. Oratio x. Opp. tom. i. p. 180–190.).

the title of Cæsar; while John and Stephen were declared marquis of Ancona and count of Romagna, by Nicholas the fourth, a patron so partial to their family, that he has been delineated in satirical portraits, imprisoned as it were in a hollow pillar.[101] After his decease, their haughty behaviour provoked the displeasure of the most implacable of mankind. The two cardinals, the uncle and the nephew, denied the election of Boniface the eighth; and the Colonna were oppressed for a moment by his temporal and spiritual arms.[102] He proclaimed a crusade against his personal enemies; their estates were confiscated; their fortresses on either side of the Tyber were besieged by the troops of St. Peter and those of the rival nobles; and after the ruin of Palestrina or Præneste, their principal seat, the ground was marked with a ploughshare, the emblem of perpetual desolation. Degraded, banished, proscribed, the six brothers, in disguise and danger, wandered over Europe without renouncing the hope of deliverance and revenge. In this double hope, the French court was their surest asylum: they prompted and directed the enterprise of Philip; and I should praise their magnanimity, had they respected the misfortune and courage of the captive tyrant. His civil acts were annulled by the Roman people, who restored the honours and possessions of the Colonna; and some estimate may be formed of their wealth by their losses, of their losses by the damages of one hundred thousand gold florins which were granted them against the accomplices and heirs of the deceased pope. All the spiritual censures and disqualifications were abolished[103] by his prudent successors; and the fortune of the house was more firmly established by this transient hurricane. The boldness of Sciarra Colonna was signalised in the captivity of Boniface; and long afterwards in the coronation of Lewis of Bavaria; and by the gratitude of the emperor, the pillar in their arms was encircled with a royal crown. But the first of the family in fame and merit was the elder Stephen, whom Petrarch loved

101. Muratori, Annali d'Italia, tom. x. p. 216. 220.

102. Petrarch's attachment to the Colonna, has authorised the abbé de Sade to expatiate on the state of the family in the fourteenth century, the persecution of Boniface VIII. the character of Stephen and his sons, their quarrels with the Ursini, &c. (Memoires sur Petrarque, tom. i. p. 98–110. 146–148. 174–176. 222–230. 275–280.) His criticism often rectifies the hearsay stories of Villani, and the errors of the less diligent moderns. I understand the branch of Stephen to be now extinct.

103. Alexander III. had declared the Colonna who adhered to the emperor Frederic I. incapable of holding any ecclesiastical benefice (Villani, l. v. c. 1.); and the last stains of annual excommunication, were purified by Sixtus V. (Vita di Sisto V. tom. iii. p. 416.). Treason, sacrilege, and proscription, are often the best titles of ancient nobility.

and esteemed as an hero superior to his own times, and not unworthy of ancient Rome. Persecution and exile displayed to the nations his abilities in peace and war; in his distress, he was an object, not of pity, but of reverence; the aspect of danger provoked him to avow his name and country: and when he was asked, "where is now your fortress?" he laid his hand on his heart, and answered, "here." He supported with the same virtue the return of prosperity; and, till the ruin of his declining age, the ancestors, the character, and the children of Stephen Colonna, exalted his dignity in the Roman republic, and at the court of Avignon. II. The Ursini migrated from Spoleto;[104] the sons of Ursus, as they are *and Ursini.* styled in the twelfth century, from some eminent person who is only known as the father of their race. But they were soon distinguished among the nobles of Rome, by the number and bravery of their kinsmen, the strength of their towers, the honours of the senate and sacred college, and the elevation of two popes, Celestin the third and Nicholas the third, of their name and lineage.[105] Their riches may be accused as an early abuse of nepotism: the estates of St. Peter were alienated in their favour by the liberal Celestin;[106] and Nicholas was ambitious for their sake to solicit the alliance of monarchs; to found new kingdoms in Lombardy and Tuscany; and to invest them with the perpetual office of senators of Rome. All that has been observed of the greatness of the Colonna, will likewise redound to the glory of the Ursini, their constant and equal antagonists in the long hereditary feud, which distracted above *Their hereditary feuds.* two hundred and fifty years the ecclesiastical state. The jealousy of pre-eminence and power was the true ground of their quarrel;

104.

—— Vallis te proxima misit
Appenninigenæ quâ prata virentia sylvæ
Spoletana metunt armenta greges protervi.

Monaldeschi (tom. xii. Script. Ital. p. 533.) gives the Ursini a French origin, which may be remotely true.

105. In the metrical life of Celestin V. by the cardinal of St. George (Muratori, tom. iii. P. i. p. 613, &c.), we find a luminous, and not inelegant passage (l. i. c. 3. p. 203, &c.):

—— genuit quem nobilis Ursæ (*Ursi?*)
Progenies, Romana domus, veterataque magnis
Fascibus in clero, pompasque experta senatûs,
Bellorumque manû grandi stipata parentum
Cardineos apices necnon fastigia dudum
Papatûs *iterata* tenens.

Muratori (Dissert. xlii. tom. iii.) observes, that the first Ursini pontificate of Celestin III. was unknown: he is inclined to read *Ursi* progenies.

106. Filii Ursi, quondam Cœlestini papæ nepotes, de bonis ecclesiæ Romanæ ditati (Vit. Innocent. III. in Muratori, Script. tom. iii. P. i.). The partial prodigality of Nicholas III. is more conspicuous in Villani and Muratori. Yet the Ursini would disdain the nephews of a *modern* pope.

but as a specious badge of distinction, the Colonna embraced the name of Ghibelines and the party of the empire; the Ursini espoused the title of Guelphs and the cause of the church. The eagle and the keys were displayed in their adverse banners; and the two factions of Italy most furiously raged when the origin and nature of the dispute were long since forgotten.[107] After the retreat of the popes to Avignon, they disputed in arms the vacant republic: and the mischiefs of discord were perpetuated by the wretched compromise of electing each year two rival senators. By their private hostilities, the city and country were desolated, and the fluctuating balance inclined with their alternate success. But none of either family had fallen by the sword, till the most renowned champion of the Ursini was surprised and slain by the younger Stephen Colonna.[108] His triumph is stained with the reproach of violating the truce; their defeat was basely avenged by the assassination, before the church door, of an innocent boy and his two servants. Yet the victorious Colonna, with an annual colleague, was declared senator of Rome during the term of five years. And the muse of Petrarch inspired a wish, a hope, a prediction, that the generous youth, the son of his venerable hero, would restore Rome and Italy to their pristine glory; that his justice would extirpate the wolves and lions, the serpents and *bears*, who laboured to subvert the eternal basis of the marble COLUMN.[109]

107. In his li[st] Dissertation on the Italian Antiquities, Muratori explains the factions of the Guelphs and Ghibelines.

108. Petrarch (tom. i. p. 222–230.) has celebrated this victory according to the Colonna; but two contemporaries, a Florentine (Giovanni Villani, l. x. c. 220.), and a Roman (Ludovico Monaldeschi, p. 533, 534.), are less favourable to their arms.

109. The abbé de Sade (tom. i. Notes, p. 61–66.) has applied the vi[th] Canzone of Petrarch, *Spirto Gentil*, &c. to Stephen Colonna the younger:

Orsi, lupi, leoni, aquile e serpi
Ad una gran marmorea *colonna*
Fanno noja sovente e à se damno.

CHAPTER LXX

Character and Coronation of Petrarch. – Restoration of the Freedom and Government of Rome by the Tribune Rienzi. – His Virtues and Vices, his Expulsion and Death. – Return of the Popes from Avignon. – Great Schism of the West. – Re-union of the Latin Church. – Last Struggles of Roman Liberty. – Statutes of Rome. – Final Settlement of the Ecclesiastical State.

Petrarch, A.D. 1304, June 19– A.D. 1374, July 19.

In the apprehension of modern times, Petrarch[1] is the Italian songster of Laura and love. In the harmony of his Tuscan rhymes, Italy applauds, or rather adores, the father of her lyric poetry: and his verse, or at least his name, is repeated by the enthusiasm, or affectation, of amorous sensibility. Whatever may be the private taste of a stranger, his slight and superficial knowledge should humbly acquiesce in the judgement of a learned nation: yet I may hope or presume, that the Italians do not compare the tedious uniformity of sonnets and elegies, with the sublime compositions of their epic muse, the original wildness of Dante, the regular beauties of Tasso, and the boundless variety of the incomparable Ariosto. The merits of the lover, I am still less qualified to appreciate: nor am I deeply interested in a metaphysical passion for a nymph so shadowy, that her existence has been questioned;[2] for a matron so prolific,[3] that she was delivered of eleven legitimate children,[4]

1. The Memoires sur la Vie de François Petrarque (Amsterdam, 1764, 1767. 3 vols. in 4to), form a copious, original, and entertaining work, a labour of love, composed from the accurate study of Petrarch and his contemporaries; but the hero is too often lost in the general history of the age, and the author too often languishes in the affectation of politeness and gallantry. In the preface to his first volume, he enumerates and weighs twenty Italian biographers, who have professedly treated of the same subject.

2. The allegorical interpretation prevailed in the xv[th] century; but the wise commentators were not agreed whether they should understand by Laura, religion, or virtue, or the blessed Virgin, or ——. See the prefaces to the i[st] and ii[d] volume.

3. Laure de Noves, born about the year 1307, was married in January 1325 to Hugues de Sade, a noble citizen of Avignon, whose jealousy was not the effect of love, since he married a second wife within seven months of her death, which happened the 6th of April 1348, precisely one-and-twenty years after Petrarch had seen and loved her.

4. Corpus crebris partubus exhaustum; from one of these is issued, in the tenth

while her amorous swain sighed and sung at the fountain of Vaucluse.[5] But in the eyes of Petrarch, and those of his graver contemporaries, his love was a sin, and Italian verse a frivolous amusement. His Latin works of philosophy, poetry, and eloquence, established his serious reputation, which was soon diffused from Avignon over France and Italy: his friends and disciples were multiplied in every city; and if the ponderous volume of his writings[6] be now abandoned to a long repose, our gratitude must applaud the man, who by precept and example revived the spirit and study of the Augustan age. From his earliest youth, Petrarch aspired to the poetic crown. The academical honours of the three faculties had introduced a royal degree of master or doctor in the art of poetry;[7] and the title of poet-laureat, which custom, rather than vanity, perpetuates in the English court,[8] was first invented by the Cæsars of Germany. In the musical games of antiquity, a prize was bestowed on the victor:[9] the belief that Virgil and Horace had been crowned in the Capitol, inflamed the emulation of a Latin bard;[10] and the

---

degree, the abbé de Sade, the fond and grateful biographer of Petrarch; and this domestic motive most probably suggested the idea of his work, and urged him to enquire into every circumstance that could affect the history and character of his grandmother (see particularly tom. i. p. 122–133. notes, p. 7–58. tom. ii. p. 455–495. not. p. 76–82.).

5. Vaucluse, so familiar to our English travellers, is described from the writings of Petrarch, and the local knowledge of his biographer (Memoires, tom. i. p. 340–359.). It was, in truth, the retreat of an hermit; and the moderns are much mistaken, if they place Laura and an happy lover in the grotto.

6. Of 1250 pages, in a close print, at Basil in the xvi[th] century, but without the date of the year. The abbé de Sade calls aloud for a new edition of Petrarch's Latin works; but I much doubt whether it would redound to the profit of the bookseller, or the amusement of the public.

7. Consult Selden's Titles of Honour, in his works (vol. iii. p. 457–466.). An hundred years before Petrarch, St. Francis received the visit of a poet, qui ab imperatore fuerat coronatus et exinde rex versuum dictus.

8. From Augustus to Louis, the muse has too often been false and venal: but I much doubt whether any age or court can produce a similar establishment of a stipendiary poet, who in every reign, and at all events, is bound to furnish twice a year a measure of praise and verse, such as may be sung in the chapel, and, I believe, in the presence, of the sovereign. I speak the more freely, as the best time for abolishing this ridiculous custom, is while the prince is a man of virtue, and the poet a man of genius.

9. Isocrates (in Panegyrico, tom. i. p. 116, 117. edit. Battie, Cantab. 1729) claims for his native Athens the glory of first instituting and recommending the *αγωνας και τα αθλα μεγιστα μη μονον ταχους και ρωμης, αλλα και λογων και γνωμης*. The example of the Panathenæa was imitated at Delphi; but the Olympic games were ignorant of a musical crown, till it was extorted by the vain tyranny of Nero (Sueton. in Nerone, c. 23.; Philostrat. apud Casaubon ad locum; Dion Cassius, or Xiphilin, l. lxiii. p. 1032. 1041. Potter's Greek Antiquities, vol. i. p. 445. 450.).

10. The Capitoline games (certamen

laurel[11] was endeared to the lover by a verbal resemblance with the name of his mistress. The value of either object was enhanced by the difficulties of the pursuit; and if the virtue or prudence of Laura was inexorable,[12] he enjoyed, and might boast of enjoying, the nymph of poetry. His vanity was not of the most delicate kind, since he applauds the success of his own *labours*; his name was popular; his friends were active; the open or secret opposition of envy and prejudice, was surmounted by the dexterity of patient merit. In the thirty-sixth year of his age, he was solicited to accept the object of his wishes: and on the same day, in the solitude of Vaucluse, he received a similar and solemn invitation from the senate of Rome and the university of Paris. The learning of a theological school, and the ignorance of a lawless city, were alike unqualified to bestow the ideal though immortal wreath which genius may obtain from the free applause of the public and of posterity: but the candidate dismissed this troublesome reflection, and, after some moments of complacency and suspense, preferred the summons of the metropolis of the world.

His poetic coronation at Rome, A.D. 1341, April 8.

The ceremony of his coronation[13] was performed in the Capitol, by his friend and patron the supreme magistrate of the republic. Twelve patrician youths were arrayed in scarlet; six representatives of the most illustrious families, in green robes, with garlands of flowers, accompanied the procession; in the midst of the princes and nobles, the senator, count of Anguillara, a kinsman of the Colonna, assumed his throne; and at the voice of an herald Petrarch arose. After discoursing on a text of Virgil, and thrice repeating his vows for the prosperity of Rome, he knelt before the throne

---

quinquennale, *musicum*, equestre, gymnicum), were instituted by Domitian (Sueton. c. 4.) in the year of Christ 86 (Censorin. de Die Natali, c. 18. p. 100. edit. Havercamp), and were not abolished in the iv[th] century (Ausonius de Professoribus Burdegal. V.). If the crown were given to superior merit, the exclusion of Statius (Capitolia nostræ inficiata lyræ, Silv. l. iii. v. 31.) may do honour to the games of the Capitol; but the Latin poets who lived before Domitian were crowned only in the public opinion.

11. Petrarch and the senators of Rome were ignorant that the laurel was not the Capitoline, but the Delphic, crown (Plin. Hist. Natur. xv. 39. Hist. Critique de la Republique des Lettres, tom. i. p. 150–220.). The victors in the Capitol were crowned with a garland of oak leaves (Martial, l. iv. epigram 54.).

12. The pious grandson of Laura has laboured, and not without success, to vindicate her immaculate chastity against the censures of the grave and the sneers of the profane (tom. ii. notes, p. 76–82.).

13. The whole process of Petrarch's coronation is accurately described by the abbé de Sade (tom. i. p. 425–435. tom. ii. p. 1–6. notes, p. 1–13.) from his own writings, and the Roman Diary of Ludovico Monaldeschi, without mixing in this authentic narrative the more recent fables of Sannuccio Delbene.

and received from the senator a laurel crown, with a more precious declaration, "This is the reward of merit." The people shouted, "Long life to the Capitol and the poet!" A sonnet in praise of Rome was accepted as the effusion of genius and gratitude; and after the whole procession had visited the Vatican, the profane wreath was suspended before the shrine of St. Peter. In the act or diploma[14] which was presented to Petrarch, the title and prerogatives of poet laureat are revived in the Capitol, after the lapse of thirteen hundred years; and he receives the perpetual privilege of wearing, at his choice, a crown of laurel, ivy, or myrtle, of assuming the poetic habit, and of teaching, disputing, interpreting, and composing, in all places whatsoever, and on all subjects of literature. The grant was ratified by the authority of the senate and people; and the character of citizen was the recompense of his affection for the Roman name. They did him honour, but they did him justice. In the familiar society of Cicero and Livy, he had imbibed the ideas of an ancient patriot; and his ardent fancy kindled every idea to a sentiment, and every sentiment to a passion. The aspect of the seven hills and their majestic ruins, confirmed these lively impressions; and he loved a country by whose liberal spirit he had been crowned and adopted. The poverty and debasement of Rome excited the indignation and pity of her grateful son: he dissembled the faults of his fellow-citizens; applauded with partial fondness the last of their heroes and matrons; and in the remembrance of the past, in the hope of the future, was pleased to forget the miseries of the present time. Rome was still the lawful mistress of the world: the pope and the emperor, her bishop and general, had abdicated their station by an inglorious retreat to the Rhône and the Danube; but if she could resume her virtue, the republic might again vindicate her liberty and dominion. Amidst the indulgence of enthusiasm and eloquence,[15] Petrarch, Italy, and Europe, were astonished by a revolution which realized for a moment his most splendid visions. The rise and fall of the tribune Rienzi will occupy the following pages:[16] the subject is interesting, the

14. The original act is printed among the Pieces Justificatives in the Memoires sur Petrarque, tom. iii. p. 50–53.

15. To find the proofs of his enthusiasm for Rome, I need only request that the reader would open, by chance, either Petrarch, or his French biographer. The latter has described the poet's first visit to Rome (tom. i. p. 323–335.). But in the place of much idle rhetoric and morality, Petrarch might have amused the present and future age with an original account of the city and his coronation.

16. It has been treated by the pen of a Jesuit, the P. du Cerçeau, whose posthumous work (Conjuration de Nicolas Gabrini, dit de Rienzi Tyran de Rome, en 1347) was published at Paris 1748, in 12mo. I am indebted to him for some facts and documents in John Hocsemius, canon of Liege, a contem-

materials are rich, and the glance of a patriot-bard[17] will sometimes vivify the copious, but simple, narrative of the Florentine,[18] and more especially of the Roman,[19] historian.

Birth, character, and patriotic designs of Rienzi.

In a quarter of the city which was inhabited only by mechanics and Jews, the marriage of an innkeeper and a washerwoman produced the future deliverer of Rome.[20] From such parents Nicholas Rienzi Gabrini could inherit neither dignity nor fortune; and the gift of a liberal education, which they painfully bestowed, was the cause of his glory and untimely end. The study of history and eloquence, the writings of Cicero, Seneca, Livy, Cæsar, and Valerius Maximus, elevated above his equals and contemporaries the genius of the young plebeian: he perused with indefatigable diligence the manuscripts and marbles of antiquity; loved to dispense his knowledge in familiar language; and was often provoked to exclaim, "Where are now these Romans? their virtue, their justice, their power? why was I not born in those happy times?"[21] When the republic addressed to the

---

porary historian (Fabricius, Bibliot. Latin. med. Ævi, tom. iii. p. 273. tom. iv. p. 85.).

17. The abbé de Sade, who so freely expatiates on the history of the xivth century, might treat, as his proper subject, a revolution in which the heart of Petrarch was so deeply engaged (Memoires, tom. ii. p. 50, 51. 320–417. notes, p. 70–76. tom. iii. p. 221–243. 366–375.). Not an idea or a fact in the writings of Petrarch has probably escaped him.

18. Giovanni Villani, l. xii. c. 89. 104. in Muratori, Rerum Italicarum Scriptores, tom. xiii. p. 969, 970. 981–983.

19. In his iii^{d} volume of Italian Antiquities (p. 249–548.), Muratori has inserted the Fragmenta Historiæ Romanæ ab Anno 1327 usque ad Annum 1354, in the original dialect of Rome or Naples in the xivth century, and a Latin version for the benefit of strangers. It contains the most particular and authentic life of Cola (Nicholas) di Rienzi; which had been printed at Bracciano 1627, in 4to, under the name of Tomaso Fortifiocca, who is only mentioned in this work as having been punished by the tribune for forgery. Human nature is scarcely capable of such sublime or stupid impartiality: but whosoever is the author of these Fragments, he wrote on the spot and at the time, and paints, without design or art, the manners of Rome and the character of the tribune.

20. The first and splendid period of Rienzi, his tribunitian government, is contained in the xviiith chapter of the Fragments (p. 399–479.), which, in the new division, forms the ii^{d} book of the history in xxxviii smaller chapters or sections.

21. The reader may be pleased with a specimen of the original idiom: Fò da soa juventutine nutricato di latte de eloquentia, bono gramatico, megliore rettuorico, autorista bravo. Deh como et quanto era veloce leitore! moito usava Tito Livio, Seneca, et Tullio, et Balerio Massimo, moito li dilettava le magnificentie di Julio Cesare raccontare. Tutta la die se speculava negl' intagli di marmo lequali iaccio intorno Roma. Non era altri che esso, che sapesse lejere li antichi patassii. Tutte scritture antiche vulgarizzava; quesse fiure di marmo justamente interpretava. Oh come spesso diceva, "Dove suono quelli buoni Romani? dove ene loro somma justitia? poleramme trovare in tempo che quessi fiuriano!"

throne of Avignon an embassy of the three orders, the spirit and eloquence of Rienzi recommended him to a place among the thirteen deputies of the commons. The orator had the honour of haranguing pope Clement the sixth, and the satisfaction of conversing with Petrarch, a congenial mind: but his aspiring hopes were chilled by disgrace and poverty; and the patriot was reduced to a single garment and the charity of the hospital. From this misery he was relieved by the sense of merit or the smile of favour; and the employment of apostolic notary afforded him a daily stipend of five gold florins, a more honourable and extensive connection, and the right of contrasting, both in words and actions, his own integrity with the vices of the state. The eloquence of Rienzi was prompt and persuasive: the multitude is always prone to envy and censure: he was stimulated by the loss of a brother and the impunity of the assassins; nor was it possible to excuse or exaggerate the public calamities. The blessings of peace and justice, for which civil society has been instituted, were banished from Rome: the jealous citizens, who might have endured every personal or pecuniary injury, were most deeply wounded in the dishonour of their wives and daughters:[22] they were equally oppressed by the arrogance of the nobles and the corruption of the magistrates; and the abuse of arms or of laws was the only circumstance that distinguished the lions, from the dogs and serpents, of the Capitol. These allegorical emblems were variously repeated in the pictures which Rienzi exhibited in the streets and churches; and while the spectators gazed with curious wonder, the bold and ready orator unfolded the meaning, applied the satire, inflamed their passions, and announced a distant hope of comfort and deliverance. The privileges of Rome, her eternal sovereignty over her princes and provinces, was the theme of his public and private discourse; and a monument of servitude became in his hands a title and incentive of liberty. The decree of the senate, which granted the most ample prerogatives to the emperor Vespasian, had been inscribed on a copper-plate still extant in the choir of the church of St. John Lateran.[23] A numerous assembly of nobles and plebeians was invited to this political lecture, and a convenient theatre was erected for their reception. The notary appeared, in a magnificent and mysterious habit, explained the inscription by a version and com-

22. Petrarch compares the jealousy of the Romans, with the easy temper of the husbands of Avignon (Memoires, tom. i. p. 330.).

23. The fragments of the *Lex Regia* may be found in the Inscriptions of Gruter, tom. i. p. 242. and at the end of the Tacitus of Ernesti, with some learned notes of the editor, tom. ii.

mentary,[24] and descanted with eloquence and zeal on the ancient glories of the senate and people, from whom all legal authority was derived. The supine ignorance of the nobles was incapable of discerning the serious tendency of such representations: they might sometimes chastise with words and blows the plebeian reformer; but he was often suffered in the Colonna palace to amuse the company with his threats and predictions; and the modern Brutus[25] was concealed under the mask of folly and the character of a buffoon. While they indulged their contempt, the restoration of the *good estate,* his favourite expression, was entertained among the people as a desirable, a possible, and at length as an approaching, event; and while all had the disposition to applaud, some had the courage to assist, their promised deliverer.

He assumes the government of Rome, A.D. 1347, May 20;

A prophecy, or rather a summons, affixed on the church door of St. George, was the first public evidence of his designs; a nocturnal assembly of an hundred citizens on mount Aventine, the first step to their execution. After an oath of secrecy and aid, he represented to the conspirators the importance and facility of their enterprise; that the nobles, without union or resources, were strong only in the fear of their imaginary strength; that all power, as well as right, was in the hands of the people; that the revenues of the apostolical chamber might relieve the public distress; and that the pope himself would approve their victory over the common enemies of government and freedom. After securing a faithful band to protect his first declaration, he proclaimed through the city, by sound of trumpet, that on the evening of the following day all persons should assemble without arms, before the church of St. Angelo, to provide for the re-establishment of the good estate. The whole night was employed in the celebration of thirty masses of the Holy Ghost; and in the morning, Rienzi, bareheaded, but in complete armour, issued from the church, encompassed by the hundred conspirators. The pope's vicar, the simple bishop of Orvieto, who had been persuaded to sustain a part in this singular ceremony, marched on his right-hand; and three great standards

24. I cannot overlook a stupendous and laughable blunder of Rienzi. The Lex Regia empowers Vespasian to enlarge the Pomœrium, a word familiar to every antiquary. It was not so to the tribune; he confounds it with pomarium an orchard, translates lo Jardino de Roma cioene Italia, and is copied by the less excusable ignorance of the Latin translator (p. 406.) and the French historian (p. 33.). Even the learning of Muratori has slumbered over the passage.

25. Priori *(Bruto)* tamen similior, juvenis uterque, longe ingenio quam cujus simulationem induerat, ut sub hoc obtentû liberator ille P. R. aperiretur tempore suo ... Ille regibus, hic tyrannis contemptus (Opp. p. 536.).

were borne aloft as the emblems of their design. In the first, the banner of *liberty*, Rome was seated on two lions, with a palm in one hand and a globe in the other: St. Paul, with a drawn sword, was delineated in the banner of *justice*; and in the third, St. Peter held the keys of *concord* and *peace*. Rienzi was encouraged by the presence and applause of an innumerable crowd, who understood little, and hoped much; and the procession slowly rolled forwards from the castle of St. Angelo to the Capitol. His triumph was disturbed by some secret emotions which he laboured to suppress: he ascended without opposition, and with seeming confidence, the citadel of the republic; harangued the people from the balcony; and received the most flattering confirmation of his acts and laws. The nobles, as if destitute of arms and counsels, beheld in silent consternation this strange revolution; and the moment had been prudently chosen, when the most formidable, Stephen Colonna, was absent from the city. On the first rumour, he returned to his palace, affected to despise this plebeian tumult, and declared to the messenger of Rienzi, that at his leisure he would cast the madman from the windows of the Capitol. The great bell instantly rang an alarm, and so rapid was the tide, so urgent was the danger, that Colonna escaped with precipitation to the suburb of St. Laurence: from thence, after a moment's refreshment, he continued the same speedy career till he reached in safety his castle of Palestrina; lamenting his own imprudence, which had not trampled the spark of this mighty conflagration. A general and peremptory order was issued from the Capitol to all the nobles, that they should peaceably retire to their estates: they obeyed; and their departure secured the tranquillity of the free and obedient citizens of Rome.

with the title and office of tribune.

But such voluntary obedience evaporates with the first transports of zeal; and Rienzi felt the importance of justifying his usurpation by a regular form and a legal title. At his own choice, the Roman people would have displayed their attachment and authority, by lavishing on his head the names of senator or consul, of king or emperor: he preferred the ancient and modest appellation of tribune; the protection of the commons was the essence of that sacred office; and they were ignorant, that it had never been invested with any share in the legislative or executive powers of the republic. In this character, and with the consent of the Romans, the tribune enacted the most salutary laws for the restoration and maintenance of the good estate. By the first he fulfils the wish of honesty and inexperience, that no civil suit should be protracted beyond the term of fifteen days. The danger of frequent perjury might justify the pronouncing against a false accuser the same

Laws of the good estate.

penalty which his evidence would have inflicted: the disorders of the times might compel the legislator to punish every homicide with death, and every injury with equal retaliation. But the execution of justice was hopeless till he had previously abolished the tyranny of the nobles. It was formally provided, that none, except the supreme magistrate, should possess or command the gates, bridges, or towers, of the state: that no private garrisons should be introduced into the towns or castles of the Roman territory; that none should bear arms or presume to fortify their houses in the city or country; that the barons should be responsible for the safety of the highways and the free passage of provisions; and that the protection of malefactors and robbers should be expiated by a fine of a thousand marks of silver. But these regulations would have been impotent and nugatory; had not the licentious nobles been awed by the sword of the civil power. A sudden alarm from the bell of the Capitol, could still summon to the standard above twenty thousand volunteers: the support of the tribune and the laws required a more regular and permanent force. In each harbour of the coast, a vessel was stationed for the assurance of commerce; a standing militia of three hundred and sixty horse and thirteen hundred foot was levied, cloathed, and paid in the thirteen quarters of the city: and the spirit of a commonwealth may be traced in the grateful allowance of one hundred florins, or pounds, to the heirs of every soldier who lost his life in the service of his country. For the maintenance of the public defence, for the establishment of granaries, for the relief of widows, orphans, and indigent convents, Rienzi applied, without fear of sacrilege, the revenues of the apostolic chamber: the three branches of hearth-money, the salt-duty, and the customs, were each of the annual produce of one hundred thousand florins;[26] and scandalous were the abuses, if in four or five months the amount of the salt-duty could be trebled by his judicious œconomy. After thus restoring the forces and finances of the republic, the tribune recalled the nobles from their solitary independence; required their personal appearance in the Capitol; and imposed an oath, of allegiance to the new government, and of submission to the laws of the good estate. Apprehensive for their safety, but still more apprehensive of the danger of a refusal, the princes and barons returned to their houses at Rome in the garb of simple and

26. In one MS. I read (l. ii. c. 4. p. 409.) perfumante quatro *solli*, in another quatro *florini*, an important variety, since the florin was worth ten Roman *solidi* (Muratori, dissert. xxviii.). The former reading would give us a population of 25,000, the latter of 250,000 families; and I much fear, that the former is more consistent with the decay of Rome and her territory.

peaceful citizens: the Colonna and Ursini, the Savelli and Frangipani, were confounded before the tribunal of a plebeian, of the vile buffoon whom they had so often derided, and their disgrace was aggravated by the indignation which they vainly struggled to disguise. The same oath was successively pronounced by the several orders of society, the clergy and gentlemen, the judges and notaries, the merchants and artisans, and the gradual descent was marked by the increase of sincerity and zeal. They swore to live and die with the republic and the church, whose interest was artfully united by the nominal association of the bishop of Orvieto, the pope's vicar, to the office of tribune. It was the boast of Rienzi, that he had delivered the throne and patrimony of St. Peter from a rebellious aristocracy; and Clement the sixth, who rejoiced in its fall, affected to believe the professions, to applaud the merits, and to confirm the title, of his trusty servant. The speech, perhaps the mind, of the tribune, was inspired with a lively regard for the purity of the faith; he insinuated his claim to a supernatural mission from the Holy Ghost: enforced by an heavy forfeiture the annual duty of confession and communion; and strictly guarded the spiritual as well as temporal welfare of his faithful people.[27]

Freedom and prosperity of the Roman republic.

Never perhaps has the energy and effect of a single mind been more remarkably felt than in the sudden, though transient, reformation of Rome by the tribune Rienzi. A den of robbers was converted to the discipline of a camp or convent: patient to hear, swift to redress, inexorable to punish, his tribunal was always accessible to the poor and stranger; nor could birth, or dignity, or the immunities of the church, protect the offender or his accomplices. The privileged houses, the private sanctuaries in Rome, on which no officer of justice would presume to trespass, were abolished; and he applied the timber and iron of their barricades in the fortifications of the Capitol. The venerable father of the Colonna was exposed in his own palace to the double shame of being desirous, and of being unable, to protect a criminal. A mule, with a jar of oil, had been stolen near Capranica; and the lord, of the Ursini family, was condemned to restore the damage, and to discharge a fine of four hundred florins for his negligence in guarding the highways. Nor were the persons of the barons more inviolate than their lands or houses: and either from accident or design, the same impartial rigour was exercised against the heads of the adverse factions.

27. Hocsemius, p. 398. apud du Cerçeau, Hist. de Rienzi, p. 194. The fifteen tribunitian laws may be found in the Roman historian (whom for brevity I shall name) Fortifiocca, l. ii. c. 4.

Peter Agapet Colonna, who had himself been senator of Rome, was arrested in the street for injury or debt; and justice was appeased by the tardy execution of Martin Ursini, who, among his various acts of violence and rapine, had pillaged a shipwrecked vessel at the mouth of the Tyber.[28] His name, the purple of two cardinals, his uncles, a recent marriage, and a mortal disease, were disregarded by the inflexible tribune, who had chosen his victim. The public officers dragged him from his palace and nuptial bed: his trial was short and satisfactory: the bell of the Capitol convened the people: stripped of his mantle, on his knees, with his hands bound behind his back, he heard the sentence of death; and after a brief confession, Ursini was led away to the gallows. After such an example, none who were conscious of guilt could hope for impunity, and the flight of the wicked, the licentious, and the idle, soon purified the city and territory of Rome. In this time (says the historian) the woods began to rejoice that they were no longer infested with robbers; the oxen began to plow; the pilgrims visited the sanctuaries; the roads and inns were replenished with travellers; trade, plenty, and good faith were restored in the markets; and a purse of gold might be exposed without danger in the midst of the highway. As soon as the life and property of the subject are secure, the labours and rewards of industry spontaneously revive: Rome was still the metropolis of the Christian world; and the fame and fortunes of the tribune were diffused in every country by the strangers who had enjoyed the blessings of his government.

The tribune is respected in Italy, &c.

The deliverance of his country inspired Rienzi with a vast, and perhaps visionary, idea of uniting Italy in a great fœderative republic, of which Rome should be the ancient and lawful head, and the free cities and princes the members and associates. His pen was not less eloquent than his tongue; and his numerous epistles were delivered to swift and trusty messengers. On foot, with a white wand in their hand, they traversed the forests and mountains; enjoyed, in the most hostile states, the sacred security of ambassadors; and reported, in the style of flattery or truth, that the highways along their passage were lined with

28. Fortifiocca, l. ii. c. 11. From the account of this shipwreck, we learn some circumstances of the trade and navigation of the age. 1. The ship was built and freighted at Naples for the ports of Marseilles and Avignon. 2. The sailors were of Naples and the isle of Œnaria, less skilful than those of Sicily and Genoa. 3. The navigation from Marseilles was a coasting voyage to the mouth of the Tyber, where they took shelter in a storm, but, instead of finding the current, unfortunately ran on a shoal: the vessel was stranded, the mariners escaped. 4. The cargo, which was pillaged, consisted of the revenue of Provence for the royal treasury, many bags of pepper and cinnamon, and bales of French cloth, to the value of 20,000 florins: a rich prize.

kneeling multitudes, who implored Heaven for the success of their undertaking. Could passion have listened to reason; could private interest have yielded to the public welfare; the supreme tribunal and confederate union of the Italian republic might have healed their intestine discord, and closed the Alps against the Barbarians of the North. But the propitious season had elapsed; and if Venice, Florence, Sienna, Perugia, and many inferior cities, offered their lives and fortunes to the good estate, the tyrants of Lombardy and Tuscany must despise, or hate, the plebeian author of a free constitution. From them, however, and from every part of Italy, the tribune received the most friendly and respectful answers: they were followed by the ambassadors of the princes and republics; and in this foreign conflux, on all the occasions of pleasure or business, the low-born notary could assume the familiar or majestic courtesy of a sovereign.[29] The most glorious circumstance of his reign was an appeal to his justice from Lewis king of Hungary, who complained, that his brother, and her husband, had been perfidiously strangled by Jane queen of Naples:[30] her guilt or innocence was pleaded in a solemn trial at Rome; but after hearing the advocates,[31] the tribune adjourned this weighty and invidious cause, which was soon determined by the sword of the Hungarian. Beyond the Alps, more especially at Avignon, the revolution was the theme of curiosity, wonder, and applause. Petrarch had been the private friend, perhaps the secret counsellor, of Rienzi: his writings breathe the most ardent spirit of patriotism and joy; and all respect for the pope, all gratitude for the Colonna, was lost in the superior duties of a Roman citizen. The poet-laureat of the Capitol maintains the act, applauds the hero, and mingles with some apprehension and advice the most lofty hopes of the permanent and rising greatness of the republic.[32]

and celebrated by Petrarch.

29. It was thus that Oliver Cromwell's old acquaintance, who remembered his vulgar and ungracious entrance into the House of Commons, were astonished at the ease and majesty of the protector on his throne (see Harris's Life of Cromwell, p. 27–34. from Clarendon, Warwick, Whitelocke, Waller, &c.). The consciousness of merit and power, will sometimes elevate the manners to the station.

30. See the causes, circumstances, and effects of the death of Andrew, in Giannone (tom. iii. l. xxiii, p. 220–229.), and the Life of Petrarch (Memoires, tom. ii. p. 143–148. 245–250. 375–379. notes, p. 21–37.). The Abbé de Sade *wishes* to extenuate her guilt.

31. The advocate who pleaded against Jane, could add nothing to the logical force and brevity of his master's epistle. Johanna! inordinata vita præcedens, retentio potestatis in regno, neglecta vindicta, vir alter susceptus, et excusatio subsequens, necis viri tui te probant fuisse participem et consortem. Jane of Naples, and Mary of Scotland, have a singular conformity.

32. See the Epistola Hortatoria de Capessenda Republica, from Petrarch to Nicholas Rienzi (Opp. p. 535–540.), and the vth

His vices and follies.

While Petrarch indulged these prophetic visions, the Roman hero was fast declining from the meridian of fame and power; and the people, who had gazed with astonishment on the ascending meteor, began to mark the irregularity of its course, and the vicissitudes of light and obscurity. More eloquent than judicious, more enterprising than resolute, the faculties of Rienzi were not balanced by cool and commanding reason: he magnified in a tenfold proportion the objects of hope and fear; and prudence, which could not have erected, did not presume to fortify, his throne. In the blaze of prosperity, his virtues were insensibly tinctured with the adjacent vices; justice with cruelty, liberality with profusion, and the desire of fame with puerile and ostentatious vanity. He might have learned, that the ancient tribunes, so strong and sacred in the public opinion, were not distinguished in style, habit, or appearance, from an ordinary plebeian;[33] and that as often as they visited the city on foot, a single *viator*, or beadle, attended the exercise of their office. The Gracchi would have frowned or smiled, could they have read the sonorous titles and epithets of their successor, "NICHOLAS, SEVERE AND MERCIFUL; DELIVERER OF ROME; DEFENDER OF ITALY;[34] FRIEND OF MANKIND, AND OF LIBERTY, PEACE, AND JUSTICE; TRIBUNE AUGUST:" his theatrical pageants had prepared the revolution; but Rienzi abused, in luxury and pride, the political maxim of speaking to the eyes, as well as the understanding, of the multitude. From nature he had received the gift of an handsome person,[35] till it was swelled and disfigured by intemperance; and his propensity to laughter was corrected in the magistrate by the affectation of gravity and sternness. He was cloathed, at least on public occasions, in a party-coloured robe of velvet

---

eclogue or pastoral, a perpetual and obscure allegory.

33. In his Roman Questions, Petrarch (Opuscul. tom. i. p. 505, 506. edit. Græc. Hen. Steph.) states, on the most constitutional principles, the simple greatness of the tribunes, who were not properly magistrates, but a check on magistracy. It was their duty and interest *ὁμοιουσθαι σχηματι, και στολῃ και διαιτῃ τοις επιτυγχανουσι των πολιτων ... καταπατεισθαι δει* (a saying of C. Curio) *και μη σεμνον ειναι τῃ δημαρχον οψει ... οσῳ δε μαλλον εκταπεινουται τω σωματι, τοσουτῳ μαλλον αυξεται τῃ δυναμει*, &c. Rienzi, and Petrarch himself, were incapable perhaps of reading a Greek philosopher; but they might have imbibed the same modest doctrines from their favourite Latins, Livy and Valerius Maximus.

34. I could not express in English the forcible, though barbarous title of *Zelator* Italiæ, which Rienzi assumed.

35. Era bell' homo (l. ii. c. 1. p. 399.). It is remarkable, that the riso sarcastico of the Bracciano edition is wanting in the Roman MS. from which Muratori has given the text. In his second reign, when he is painted almost as a monster, Rienzi travea una ventresca tonna trionfale, a modo de uno Abbate Asiano, or Asinino (l. iii. c. 18. p. 523.).

or sattin, lined with fur, and embroidered with gold: the rod of justice, which he carried in his hand, was a sceptre of polished steel, crowned with a globe and cross of gold, and enclosing a small fragment of the true and holy wood. In his civil and religious processions through the city, he rode on a white steed, the symbol of royalty: the great banner of the republic, a sun with a circle of stars, a dove with an olive branch, was displayed over his head; a shower of gold and silver was scattered among the populace; fifty guards with halberds encompassed his person; a troop of horse preceded his march; and their tymbals and trumpets were of massy silver.

The pomp of his knighthood, A.D. 1347, August 1.

The ambition of the honours of chivalry[36] betrayed the meanness of his birth, and degraded the importance of his office; and the equestrian tribune was not less odious to the nobles, whom he adopted, than to the plebeians, whom he deserted. All that yet remained of treasure, or luxury, or art, was exhausted on that solemn day. Rienzi led the procession from the Capitol to the Lateran; the tediousness of the way was relieved with decorations and games; the ecclesiastical, civil, and military orders marched under their various banners; the Roman ladies attended his wife; and the ambassadors of Italy might loudly applaud, or secretly deride, the novelty of the pomp. In the evening, when they had reached the church and palace of Constantine, he thanked and dismissed the numerous assembly, with an invitation to the festival of the ensuing day. From the hands of a venerable knight he received the order of the Holy Ghost; the purification of the bath was a previous ceremony; but in no step of his life did Rienzi excite such scandal and censure as by the prophane use of the porphyry vase, in which Constantine (a foolish legend) had been healed of his leprosy by pope Sylvester.[37] With equal presumption the tribune watched or reposed within the consecrated precincts of the baptistery; and the failure of his state-bed was interpreted as an omen of his approaching downfal. At the

36. Strange as it may seem, this festival was not without a precedent. In the year 1327, two barons, a Colonna, and an Ursini, the usual balance, were created knights by the Roman people: their bath was of rose-water, their beds were decked with royal magnificence, and they were served at St. Maria of Araceli in the Capitol, by the twenty-eight *buoni huomini*. They afterwards received from Robert king of Naples the sword of chivalry (Hist. Rom. l. i. c. 2. p. 259.).

37. All parties believed in the leprosy and bath of Constantine (Petrarch, Epist. Famil. vi. 2.), and Rienzi justified his own conduct by observing to the court of Avignon, that a vase which had been used by a Pagan, could not be profaned by a pious Christian. Yet this crime is specified in the bill of excommunication (Hocsemius, apud du Cerçeau, p. 189, 190.).

hour of worship he shewed himself to the returning crowds in a majestic attitude, with a robe of purple, his sword, and gilt spurs; but the holy rites were soon interrupted by his levity and insolence. Rising from his throne, and advancing towards the congregation, he proclaimed in a loud voice: "We summon to our tribunal pope Clement; and command him to reside in his diocese of Rome: we also summon the sacred college of cardinals.[38] We again summon the two pretenders, Charles of Bohemia and Lewis of Bavaria, who style themselves emperors: we likewise summon all the electors of Germany, to inform us on what pretence they have usurped the inalienable right of the Roman people, the ancient and lawful sovereigns of the empire."[39] Unsheathing his maiden-sword, he thrice brandished it to the three parts of the world, and thrice repeated the extravagant declaration, "And this too is mine!" The pope's vicar, the bishop of Orvieto, attempted to check this career of folly; but his feeble protest was silenced by martial music; and instead of withdrawing from the assembly, he consented to dine with his brother tribune, at a table which had hitherto been reserved for the supreme pontiff. A banquet, such as the Cæsars had given, was prepared for the Romans. The apartments, porticoes, and courts, of the Lateran were spread with innumerable tables for either sex, and every condition; a stream of wine flowed from the nostrils of Constantine's brazen horse; no complaint, except of the scarcity of water, could be heard; and the licentiousness of the multitude was curbed by discipline and fear. A subsequent *and coronation.* day was appointed for the coronation of Rienzi;[40] seven crowns of different leaves or metals were successively placed on his head by the most eminent of the Roman clergy; they represented the seven gifts of the Holy Ghost; and he still professed to imitate the example of the ancient tribunes. These extraordinary spectacles might deceive or flatter the people; and their own vanity was gratified in the vanity of their leader. But in his private life he soon deviated from the strict rule of frugality and abstinence; and the plebeians, who were awed by the splendour of the nobles, were provoked by the luxury of their equal. His

38. This *verbal* summons of pope Clement VI. which rests on the authority of the Roman historian and a Vatican MS. is disputed by the biographer of Petrarch (tom. ii. not. p. 70–76.) with arguments rather of decency than of weight. The court of Avignon might not chuse to agitate this delicate question.

39. The summons of the two rival emperors, a monument of freedom and folly, is extant in Hocsemius (Cerçeau, p. 163–166.).

40. It is singular, that the Roman historian should have overlooked this sevenfold coronation, which is sufficiently proved by internal evidence, and the testimony of Hocsemius, and even of Rienzi (Cerçeau, p. 167–170. 229.).

wife, his son, his uncle (a barber in name and profession), exposed the contrast of vulgar manners and princely expence; and without acquiring the majesty, Rienzi degenerated into the vices, of a king.

Fear and hatred of the nobles of Rome.

A simple citizen describes with pity, or perhaps with pleasure, the humiliation of the barons of Rome. "Bare-headed, their hands crossed on their breast, they stood with downcast looks in the presence of the tribune; and they trembled, good God, how they trembled!"[41] As long as the yoke of Rienzi was that of justice and their country, their conscience forced them to esteem the man, whom pride and interest provoked them to hate: his extravagant conduct soon fortified their hatred by contempt; and they conceived the hope of subverting a power which was no longer so deeply rooted in the public confidence. The old animosity of the Colonna and Ursini was suspended for a moment by their common disgrace: they associated their wishes, and perhaps their designs; an assassin was seized and tortured; he accused the nobles; and as soon as Rienzi deserved the fate, he adopted the suspicions and maxims, of a tyrant. On the same day, under various pretences, he invited to the Capitol his principal enemies, among whom were five members of the Ursini and three of the Colonna name. But instead of a council or a banquet, they found themselves prisoners under the sword of despotism or justice; and the consciousness of innocence or guilt might inspire them with equal apprehensions of danger. At the sound of the great bell the people assembled; they were arraigned for a conspiracy against the tribune's life; and though some might sympathise in their distress, not a hand, nor a voice, was raised to rescue the first of the nobility from their impending doom. Their apparent boldness was prompted by despair; they passed in separate chambers a sleepless and painful night; and the venerable hero, Stephen Colonna, striking against the door of his prison, repeatedly urged his guards to deliver him by a speedy death from such ignominious servitude. In the morning they understood their sentence from the visit of a confessor and the tolling of the bell. The great hall of the Capitol had been decorated for the bloody scene with red and white hangings; the countenance of the tribune was dark and severe; the swords of the executioners were unsheathed; and the barons were interrupted in their dying speeches by the sound of trumpets. But in this decisive moment, Rienzi was not less anxious or

41. Puoi se faceva stare denante a se, mentre sedeva, li baroni tutti in piedi ritti co le vraccia piecate, e co li capucci tratti. Deh como stavano paurosi! (Hist. Rom. l. ii. c. 20. p. 439.). He saw them, and we see them.

apprehensive than his captives: he dreaded the splendour of their names, their surviving kinsmen, the inconstancy of the people, the reproaches of the world; and, after rashly offering a mortal injury, he vainly presumed that, if he could forgive, he might himself be forgiven. His elaborate oration was that of a Christian and a suppliant; and, as the humble minister of the commons, he entreated his masters to pardon these noble criminals, for whose repentance and future service he pledged his faith and authority. "If you are spared," said the tribune, "by the mercy of the Romans, will you not promise to support the good estate with your lives and fortunes?" Astonished by this marvellous clemency, the barons bowed their heads; and, while they devoutly repeated the oath of allegiance, might whisper a secret, and more sincere, assurance of revenge. A priest, in the name of the people, pronounced their absolution: they received the communion with the tribune, assisted at the banquet, followed the procession; and, after every spiritual and temporal sign of reconciliation, were dismissed in safety to their respective homes, with the new honours and titles of generals, consuls, and patricians.[42]

They oppose Rienzi in arms.

During some weeks they were checked by the memory of their danger, rather than of their deliverance, till the most powerful of the Ursini, escaping with the Colonna from the city, erected at Marino the standard of rebellion. The fortifications of the castle were hastily restored; the vassals attended their lord; the outlaws armed against the magistrate; the flocks and herds, the harvests and vineyards, from Marino to the gates of Rome, were swept away or destroyed; and the people arraigned Rienzi as the author of the calamities which his government had taught them to forget. In the camp, Rienzi appeared to less advantage than in the rostrum: and he neglected the progress of the rebel barons till their numbers were strong and their castles impregnable. From the pages of Livy he had not imbibed the art, or even the courage, of a general: an army of twenty thousand Romans returned without honour or effect from the attack of Marino: and his vengeance was amused by painting his enemies, their heads downwards, and drowning two dogs (at least they should have been bears) as the representatives of the Ursini. The belief of his incapacity encouraged their operations: they were invited by their secret adherents; and the barons attempted with four thousand foot and sixteen hundred horse, to enter Rome by force or

42. The original letter, in which Rienzi justifies his treatment of the Colonna (Hocsemius, apud du Cerçeau, p. 222–229.), displays, in genuine colours, the mixture of the knave and the madman.

surprise. The city was prepared for their reception: the alarm-bell rung all night; the gates were strictly guarded, or insolently open; and after some hesitation they sounded a retreat. The two first divisions had passed along the walls, but the prospect of a free entrance tempted the headstrong valour of the nobles in the rear; and after a successful skirmish, they were overthrown and massacred without quarter by the crowds of the Roman people. Stephen Colonna the younger, the noble spirit to whom Petrarch ascribed the restoration of Italy, was preceded or accompanied in death by his son John, a gallant youth, by his brother Peter, who might regret the ease and honours of the church, by a nephew of legitimate birth, and by two bastards of the Colonna race; and the number of seven, the seven crowns, as Rienzi styled them, of the Holy Ghost, was completed by the agony of the deplorable parent, of the veteran chief, who had survived the hope and fortune of his house. The vision and prophecies of St. Martin and pope Boniface had been used by the tribune to animate his troops:[43] he displayed, at least in the pursuit, the spirit of an hero; but he forgot the maxims of the ancient Romans, who abhorred the triumphs of civil war. The conqueror ascended the Capitol; deposited his crown and sceptre on the altar; and boasted with some truth, that he had cut off an ear which neither pope nor emperor had been able to amputate.[44] His base and implacable revenge denied the honours of burial; and the bodies of the Colonna, which he threatened to expose with those of the vilest malefactors, were secretly interred by the holy virgins of their name and family.[45] The people sympathised in their grief, repented of their own

Defeat and death of the Colonna, Nov. 20.

43. Rienzi, in the above-mentioned letter, ascribes to St. Martin the tribune, Boniface VIII. the enemy of Colonna, himself, and the Roman people, the glory of the day, which Villani likewise (l. xii. c. 104.) describes as a regular battle. The disorderly skirmish, the flight of the Romans, and the cowardice of Rienzi, are painted in the simple and minute narrative of Fortifiocca, or the anonymous Citizen (l. ii. c. 34–37.).

44. In describing the fall of the Colonna, I speak only of the family of Stephen the elder, who is often confounded by the P. du Cerçeau, with his son. That family was extinguished, but the house has been perpetuated in the collateral branches, of which I have not a very accurate knowledge. Circumspice (says Petrarch) familiæ tuæ statum, Columniensium *domos*: solito pauciores habeat columnas. Quid ad rem? modo fundamentum stabile, solidumque permaneat.

45. The convent of St. Silvester was founded, endowed, and protected by the Colonna cardinals, for the daughters of the family who embraced a monastic life, and who, in the year 1318, were twelve in number. The others were allowed to marry with their kinsmen in the fourth degree, and the dispensation was justified by the small number and close alliances of the noble families of Rome (Memoires sur Petrarque, tom. i. p. 110. tom. ii. p. 401.).

fury, and detested the indecent joy of Rienzi, who visited the spot where these illustrious victims had fallen. It was on that fatal spot, that he conferred on his son the honour of knighthood: and the ceremony was accomplished by a slight blow from each of the horsemen of the guard, and by a ridiculous and inhuman ablution from a pool of water, which was yet polluted with patrician blood.[46]

Fall and flight of the tribune Rienzi, A.D. 1347, Dec. 15.

A short delay would have saved the Colonna, the delay of a single month, which elapsed between the triumph and the exile of Rienzi. In the pride of victory, he forfeited what yet remained of his civil virtues, without acquiring the fame of military prowess. A free and vigorous opposition was formed in the city; and when the tribune proposed in the public council[47] to impose a new tax, and to regulate the government of Perugia, thirty-nine members voted against his measures; repelled the injurious charge of treachery and corruption; and urged him to prove, by their forcible exclusion, that, if the populace adhered to his cause, it was already disclaimed by the most respectable citizens. The pope and the sacred college had never been dazzled by his specious professions; they were justly offended by the insolence of his conduct; a cardinal legate was sent to Italy, and after some fruitless treaty, and two personal interviews, he fulminated a bull of excommunication, in which the tribune is degraded from his office, and branded with the guilt of rebellion, sacrilege, and heresy.[48] The surviving barons of Rome were now humbled to a sense of allegiance; their interest and revenge engaged them in the service of the church; but as the fate of the Colonna was before their eyes, they abandoned to a private adventurer the peril and glory of the revolution. John Pepin, count of Minorbino[49] in the kingdom of Naples, had been

46. Petrarch wrote a stiff and pedantic letter of consolation (Fam. l. vii. epist. 13. p. 682, 683.). The friend was lost in the patriot. Nulla toto orbe principum familia carior; carior tamen respublica, carior Roma, carior Italia.

Je rends graces aux Dieux de n'etre pas Romain.

47. This council and opposition is obscurely mentioned by Pollistore, a contemporary writer, who has preserved some curious and original facts (Rer. Italicarum, tom. xxv. c. 31. p. 798–804.).

48. The briefs and bulls of Clement VI. against Rienzi, are translated by the P. du Cerçeau (p. 196. 232.) from the Ecclesiastical Annals of Odericus Raynaldus (A.D. 1347, N° 15. 17. 21, &c.), who found them in the archives of the Vatican.

49. Matteo Villani describes the origin, character, and death of this count of Minorbino, a man de natura inconstante e senza fede, whose grandfather, a crafty notary, was enriched and ennobled by the spoils of the Saracens of Nocera (l. vii. c. 102, 103.). See his imprisonment, and the efforts of Petrarch, tom. ii. p. 149–151.

condemned for his crimes, or his riches, to perpetual imprisonment: and Petrarch, by soliciting his release, indirectly contributed to the ruin of his friend. At the head of one hundred and fifty soldiers, the count of Minorbino introduced himself into Rome; barricaded the quarter of the Colonna; and found the enterprise as easy as it had seemed impossible. From the first alarm, the bell of the Capitol incessantly tolled; but, instead of repairing to the well-known sound, the people was silent and inactive; and the pusillanimous Rienzi, deploring their ingratitude with sighs and tears, abdicated the government and palace of the republic.

Revolutions of Rome, A.D. 1347–1354.

Without drawing his sword, count Pepin restored the aristocracy and the church; three senators were chosen, and the legate assuming the first rank, accepted his two colleagues from the rival families of Colonna and Ursini. The acts of the tribune were abolished, his head was proscribed; yet such was the terror of his name, that the barons hesitated three days before they would trust themselves in the city, and Rienzi was left above a month in the castle of St. Angelo, from whence he peaceably withdrew, after labouring, without effect, to revive the affection and courage of the Romans. The vision of freedom and empire had vanished: their fallen spirit would have acquiesced in servitude, had it been smoothed by tranquillity and order: and it was scarcely observed, that the new senators derived their authority from the Apostolic See, that four cardinals were appointed to reform with dictatorial power the state of the republic. Rome was again agitated by the bloody feuds of the barons, who detested each other, and despised the commons: their hostile fortresses, both in town and country, again rose and were again demolished; and the peaceful citizens, a flock of sheep, were devoured, says the Florentine historian, by these rapacious wolves. But when their pride and avarice had exhausted the patience of the Romans, a confraternity of the Virgin Mary protected or avenged the republic: the bell of the Capitol was again tolled, the nobles in arms trembled in the presence of an unarmed multitude; and of the two senators, Colonna escaped from the window of the palace, and Ursini was stoned at the foot of the altar. The dangerous office of tribune was successively occupied by two plebeians, Cerroni and Baroncelli. The mildness of Cerroni was unequal to the times; and after a faint struggle, he retired with a fair reputation and a decent fortune to the comforts of rural life. Devoid of eloquence or genius, Baroncelli was distinguished by a resolute spirit: he spoke the language of a patriot, and trode in the footsteps of tyrants; his suspicion was a sentence of death, and his own death was the reward of his cruelties. Amidst the public misfortunes, the faults of Rienzi were forgotten; and the Romans sighed for the peace and prosperity of the good estate.[50]

Adventures of Rienzi.

After an exile of seven years, the first deliverer was again restored to his country. In the disguise of a monk or a pilgrim, he escaped from the castle of St. Angelo, implored the friendship of the king of Hungary at Naples, tempted the ambition of every bold adventurer, mingled at Rome with the pilgrims of the jubilee, lay concealed among the hermits of the Apennine, and wandered through the cities of Italy, Germany, and Bohemia. His person was invisible, his name was yet formidable; and the anxiety of the court of Avignon supposes, and even magnifies, his personal merit. The emperor Charles the fourth gave audience to a stranger, who frankly revealed himself as the tribune of the republic; and astonished an assembly of ambassadors and princes, by the eloquence of a patriot and the visions of a prophet, the downfal of tyranny and the kingdom of the Holy Ghost.[51] Whatever had been his hopes, Rienzi found himself a captive; but he supported a character of independence and dignity, and obeyed, as his own choice, the irresistible summons of the supreme pontiff. The zeal of Petrarch, which had been cooled by the unworthy conduct, was rekindled by the sufferings and the presence, of his friend; and he boldly complains of the times, in which the saviour of Rome was delivered by her emperor into the hands of her bishop. Rienzi was transported slowly, but in safe custody, from Prague to Avignon: his entrance into the city was that of a malefactor; in his prison he was chained by the leg; and four cardinals were named to enquire into the crimes of heresy and rebellion. But his trial and condemnation would have involved some questions, which it was more prudent to leave under the veil of mystery: the temporal supremacy of the popes; the duty of residence; the civil and ecclesiastical privileges of the clergy and people of Rome. The reigning pontiff well deserved the appellation of *Clement*: the strange vicissitudes and magnanimous spirit of the captive excited his pity and esteem; and

A prisoner at Avignon, A.D. 1351.

50. The troubles of Rome, from the departure to the return of Rienzi, are related by Matteo Villani (l. ii. c. 47. l. iii. c. 33. 57. 78.) and Thomas Fortifiocca (l. iii. c. 1–4.). I have slightly passed over these secondary characters, who imitated the original tribune.

51. These visions, of which the friends and enemies of Rienzi seem alike ignorant, are surely magnified by the zeal of Pollistore, a Dominican inquisitor (Rer. Ital. tom. xxv. c. 36. p. 819.). Had the tribune taught, that Christ was succeeded by the Holy Ghost, that the tyranny of the pope would be abolished, he might have been convicted of heresy and treason, without offending the Roman people.

Petrarch believes that he respected in the hero the name and sacred character of a poet.[52] Rienzi was indulged with an easy confinement and the use of books; and in the assiduous study of Livy and the bible, he sought the cause and the consolation of his misfortunes.

Rienzi, senator of Rome, A.D. 1354.

The succeeding pontificate of Innocent the sixth opened a new prospect of his deliverance and restoration; and the court of Avignon was persuaded, that the successful rebel could alone appease and reform the anarchy of the metropolis. After a solemn profession of fidelity, the Roman tribune was sent into Italy, with the title of senator; but the death of Baroncelli appeared to supersede the use of his mission; and the legate, cardinal Albornoz,[53] a consummate statesman, allowed him with reluctance, and without aid, to undertake the perilous experiment. His first reception was equal to his wishes: the day of his entrance was a public festival; and his eloquence and authority revived the laws of the good estate. But this momentary sunshine was soon clouded by his own vices and those of the people: in the Capitol he might often regret the prison of Avignon; and after a second administration of four months, Rienzi was massacred in a tumult which had been fomented by the Roman barons. In the society of the Germans and Bohemians, he is said to have contracted the habits of intemperance and cruelty: adversity had chilled his enthusiasm, without fortifying his reason or virtue; and that youthful hope, that lively assurance, which is the pledge of success, was now succeeded by the cold impotence of distrust and despair. The tribune had reigned with absolute dominion, by the choice, and in the hearts, of the Romans: the senator was the servile minister of a foreign court; and while he was suspected by the people, he was abandoned by the prince. The legate Albornoz, who seemed desirous of his ruin, inflexibly refused all supplies of men and money; a faithful subject could no longer presume to touch the revenues of the apostolical chamber; and the first idea of a tax was the signal of clamour and sedition. Even his justice was tainted with the guilt or reproach of selfish cruelty: the most virtuous citizen of Rome was sacrificed to his

52. The astonishment, the envy almost, of Petrarch is a proof, if not of the truth of this incredible fact, at least of his own veracity. The abbé de Sade (Memoires, tom. iii. p. 242.) quotes the vi[th] epistle of the xiii[th] book of Petrarch, but it is of the royal MS. which he consulted, and not of the ordinary Basil edition (p. 920.).

53. Ægidius, or Giles Albornoz, a noble Spaniard, archbishop of Toledo, and cardinal legate in Italy (A.D. 1353–1367), restored, by his arms and counsels, the temporal dominion of the popes. His life has been separately written by Sepulveda; but Dryden could not reasonably suppose, that his name, or that of Wolsey, had reached the ears of the Mufti in Don Sebastian.

jealousy; and in the execution of a public robber, from whose purse he had been assisted, the magistrate too much forgot, or too much remembered, the obligations of the debtor.[54] A civil war exhausted his treasures, and the patience of the city: the Colonna maintained their hostile station at Palestrina; and his mercenaries soon despised a leader whose ignorance and fear were envious of all subordinate merit. In the death as in the life of Rienzi, the hero and the coward were strangely mingled. When the Capitol was invested by a furious multitude, when he was basely deserted by his civil and military servants, the intrepid senator, waving the banner of liberty, presented himself on the balcony, addressed his eloquence to the various passions of the Romans, and laboured to persuade them, that in the same cause himself and the republic must either stand or fall. His oration was interrupted by a volley of imprecations and stones; and after an arrow had transpierced his hand, he sunk into abject despair, and fled weeping to the inner chambers, from whence he was let down by a sheet before the windows of the prison. Destitute of aid or hope, he was besieged till the evening: the doors of the Capitol were destroyed with axes and fire; and while the senator attempted to escape in a plebeian habit, he was discovered and dragged to the platform of the palace, the fatal scene of his judgments and executions. A whole hour, without voice or motion, he stood amidst the multitude half naked and half dead; their rage was hushed into curiosity and wonder; the last feelings of reverence and compassion yet struggled in his favour; and they might have prevailed, if a bold assassin had not plunged a dagger in his breast. He fell senseless with the first stroke; the impotent revenge of his enemies inflicted a thousand wounds; and the senator's body was abandoned to the dogs, to the Jews, and to the flames. Posterity will compare the virtues and failings of this extraordinary man; but in a long period of anarchy and servitude, the name of Rienzi has often been celebrated as the deliverer of his country, and the last of the Roman patriots.[55]

His death, A.D. 1354, September 8.

The first and most generous wish of Petrarch was the restoration of a free republic; but after the exile and death of

Petrarch invites and upbraids

54. From Matteo Villani, and Fortifiocca, the P. du Cerçeau (p. 344–394.) has extracted the life and death of the chevalier Montreal, the life of a robber and the death of an hero. At the head of a free company, the first that desolated Italy, he became rich and formidable: he had money in all the banks, 60,000 ducats in Padua alone.

55. The exile, second government, and death of Rienzi, are minutely related by the anonymous Roman, who appears neither his friend nor his enemy (l. iii. c. 12–25.). Petrarch, who loved the *tribune*, was indifferent to the fate of the *senator*.

the emperor Charles IV. A.D. 1355, January–May.

his plebeian hero, he turned his eyes from the tribune, to the king, of the Romans. The Capitol was yet stained with the blood of Rienzi, when Charles the fourth descended from the Alps to obtain the Italian and Imperial crowns. In his passage through Milan he received the visit, and repaid the flattery, of the poet-laureat; accepted a medal of Augustus; and promised, without a smile, to imitate the founder of the Roman monarchy. A false application of the names and maxims of antiquity was the source of the hopes and disappointments of Petrarch; yet he could not overlook the difference of times and characters; the immeasurable distance between the first Cæsars and a Bohemian prince, who by the favour of the clergy had been elected the titular head of the German aristocracy. Instead of restoring to Rome her glory and her provinces, he had bound himself, by a secret treaty with the pope, to evacuate the city on the day of his coronation; and his shameful retreat was pursued by the reproaches of the patriot bard.[56]

He solicits the popes of Avignon to fix their residence at Rome.

After the loss of liberty and empire, his third and more humble wish, was to reconcile the shepherd with his flock; to recal the Roman bishop to his ancient and peculiar diocese. In the fervour of youth, with the authority of age, Petrarch addressed his exhortations to five successive popes, and his eloquence was always inspired by the enthusiasm of sentiment and the freedom of language.[57] The son of a citizen of Florence invariably preferred the country of his birth to that of his education: and Italy, in his eyes, was the queen and garden of the world. Amidst her domestic factions, she was doubtless superior to France both in art and science, in wealth and politeness; but the difference could scarcely support the epithet of barbarous, which he promiscuously bestows on the countries beyond the Alps. Avignon, the mystic Babylon, the sink of vice and corruption, was the object of his hatred and contempt; but he forgets that her scandalous vices were not the growth of the soil, and that in every residence they

56. The hopes and the disappointment of Petrarch, are agreeably described in his own words by the French biographer (Memoires, tom. iii. p. 375–413.); but the deep, though secret, wound, was the coronation of Zanubi the poet laureat by Charles IV.

57. See in his accurate and amusing biographer, the application of Petrarch and Rome to Benedict XII. in the year 1334 (Memoires, tom. i. p. 261–265.), to Clement VI. in 1342 (tom. ii. p. 45–47.), and to Urban V. in 1366 (tom. iii. p. 677–691.): his praise (p. 711–715.) and excuse (p. 771.) of the last of these pontiffs. His angry controversy on the respective merits of France and Italy may be found (Opp. p. 1068–1085.).

would adhere to the power and luxury of the papal court. He confesses, that the successor of St. Peter is the bishop of the universal church; yet it was not on the banks of the Rhône, but of the Tyber, that the apostle had fixed his everlasting throne: and while every city in the Christian world was blessed with a bishop, the metropolis alone was desolate and forlorn. Since the removal of the Holy See, the sacred buildings of the Lateran and the Vatican, their altars and their saints, were left in a state of poverty and decay; and Rome was often painted under the image of a disconsolate matron, as if the wandering husband could be reclaimed by the homely portrait of the age and infirmities of his weeping spouse.[58] But the cloud which hung over the seven hills, would be dispelled by the presence of their lawful sovereign: eternal fame, the prosperity of Rome, and the peace of Italy, would be the recompence of the pope who should dare to embrace this generous resolution. Of the five whom Petrarch exhorted, the three first, John the twenty-second, Benedict the twelfth, and Clement the sixth, were importuned or amused by the boldness of the orator; but the memorable change which had been attempted by Urban the fifth, was finally accomplished by Gregory the eleventh. The execution of their design was opposed by weighty and almost insuperable obstacles. A king of France who has deserved the epithet of wise, was unwilling to release them from a local dependence: the cardinals, for the most part his subjects, were attached to the language, manners, and climate, of Avignon; to their stately palaces; above all, to the wines of Burgundy. In their eyes, Italy was foreign or hostile; and they reluctantly embarked at Marseilles, as if they had been sold or banished into the land of the Saracens. Urban the fifth resided three years in the Vatican with safety and honour: his sanctity was protected by a guard of two thousand horse; and the king of Cyprus, the queen of Naples, and the emperors of the East and West devoutly saluted their common father in the chair of St. Peter. But the joy of Petrarch and the Italians was soon turned into grief and indignation.

Return of Urban V. A.D. 1367, October 16– A.D. 1370, April 17.

58.
Squalida sed quoniam facies, neglecta cultû
Cæsaries; multisque malis lassata senectus
Eripuit solitam effigiem: vetus accipe nomen;
Roma vocor.

(Carm. l. 2. p. 77.)

He spins this allegory beyond all measure or patience. The Epistles to Urban V. in prose, are more simple and persuasive (Senilium, l. vii. p. 811–827. l. ix. epist. i. p. 844–854.).

Some reasons of public or private moment, his own impatience or the prayers of the cardinals, recalled Urban to France; and the approaching election was saved from the tyrannic patriotism of the Romans. The powers of heaven were interested in their cause: Bridget of Sweden, a saint and pilgrim, disapproved the return, and foretold the death, of Urban the fifth; the migration of Gregory the eleventh was encouraged by St. Catherine of Sienna, the spouse of Christ and ambassadress of the Florentines; and the popes themselves, the great masters of human credulity, appear to have listened to these visionary females.[59] Yet those celestial admonitions were supported by some arguments of temporal policy. The residence of Avignon had been invaded by hostile violence: at the head of thirty thousand robbers, an hero had extorted ransom and absolution from the vicar of Christ and the sacred college; and the maxim of the French warriors, to spare the people and plunder the church, was a new heresy of the most dangerous import.[60] While the pope was driven from Avignon, he was strenuously invited to Rome. The senate and people acknowledged him as their lawful sovereign, and laid at his feet the keys of the gates, the bridges, and the fortresses; of the quarter at least beyond the Tyber.[61] But this loyal offer was accompanied by a declaration, that they could no longer suffer the scandal and calamity of his absence; and that his obstinacy would finally provoke them to revive and assert the primitive right of election. The abbot of mount Cassin had been consulted, whether he would accept the triple crown[62] from the clergy and

Final return of Gregory XI. A.D. 1377, January 17.

59. I have not leisure to expatiate on the legends of St. Bridget or St. Catherine, the last of which might furnish some amusing stories. Their effect on the mind of Gregory XI. is attested by the last solemn words of the dying pope, who admonished the assistants, ut caverent ab hominibus, sive viris, sive mulieribus, sub specie religionis loquentibus visiones sui capitis, quia per tales ipse seductus, &c. (Baluz. Not. ad Vit. Pap. Avenionensium, tom. i. p. 1223.).

60. This predatory expedition is related by Froissard (Chronique, tom. i. p. 230.), and in the life of du Guesclin (Collection Generale des Memoires Historiques, tom. iv. c. 16. p. 107–113.). As early as the year 1361, the court of Avignon had been molested by similar freebooters, who afterwards passed the Alps (Memoires sur Petrarque, tom. iii. p. 563–569.).

61. Fleury alleges, from the Annals of Odericus Raynaldus, the original treaty which was signed the 21st of December 1376, between Gregory XI. and the Romans (Hist. Eccles. tom. xx. p. 275.).

62. The first crown or regnum (Ducange, Gloss. Latin. tom. v. p. 702.) on the episcopal mitre of the popes, is ascribed to the gift of Constantine, or Clovis. The second was added by Boniface VIII. as the emblem not only of a spiritual, but of a temporal, kingdom. The three states of the church are represented by the triple crown

people: "I am a citizen of Rome,"[63] replied that venerable ecclesiastic, "and my first law is the voice of my country."[64]

His death, A.D. 1378, March 27.

If superstition will interpret an untimely death;[65] if the merit of counsels be judged from the event; the heavens may seem to frown on a measure of such apparent reason and propriety. Gregory the eleventh did not survive above fourteen months his return to the Vatican; and his decease was followed by the great schism of the West, which distracted the Latin church above forty years. The sacred college was then composed of twenty-two cardinals: six of these had remained at Avignon; eleven Frenchmen, one Spaniard, and four Italians, entered the conclave in the usual form. Their choice was not yet limited to the purple; and their unanimous votes acquiesced in the archbishop of Bari, a subject of Naples, conspicuous for his zeal and learning, who ascended the throne of St. Peter under the name of Urban the sixth. The epistle of the sacred college affirms his free and regular election; which had been inspired, as usual, by the Holy Ghost: he was adored, invested, and crowned, with the customary rights; his temporal authority was obeyed at Rome and Avignon, and his ecclesiastical supremacy was acknowledged in the Latin world. During several weeks, the cardinals attended their new master with the fairest professions of attachment and loyalty; till the summer-heats permitted a decent escape from the city. But as soon as they were united at Anagni and Fundi, in a place of security, they cast aside the mask, accused their own falsehood and hypocrisy, excommunicated the apostate and antichrist of Rome, and proceeded to a new election of Robert of

Election of Urban VI. April 9.

---

which was introduced by John XXII. or Benedict XII. (Memoires sur Petrarque, tom. i. p. 258, 259.).

63. Baluze (Not. ad Pap. Avenion. tom. i. p. 1194, 1195.) produces the original evidence which attests the threats of the Roman ambassadors, and the resignation of the abbot of mount Cassin, qui, ultro se offerens, respondit se civem Romanum esse, et illud velle quod ipsi vellent.

64. The return of the popes from Avignon to Rome, and their reception by the people, are related in the original Lives of Urban V. and Gregory XI. in Baluze (Vit. Paparum Avenionensium, tom. i. p. 363–486.) and Muratori (Script. Rer. Italicarum, tom. iii. P. i. p. 610–712.). In the disputes of the schism, every circumstance was severely, though partially, scrutinised; more especially in the great inquest, which decided the obedience of Castile, and to which Baluze, in his notes, so often and so largely appeals, from a MS. volume in the Harley library (p. 1281, &c.).

65. Can the death of a good man be esteemed a punishment by those who believe in the immortality of the soul? They betray the instability of their faith. Yet as a mere philosopher, I cannot agree with the Greeks, ὁν οι θεοι φιλουσιν αποθνησκει νεος (Brunck. Poetæ Gnomici, p. 231.). See in Herodotus (l. i. c. 31.) the moral and pleasing tale of the Argive youths.

Election of Clement VII. Sept. 21.

Geneva, Clement the seventh, whom they announced to the nations as the true and rightful vicar of Christ. Their first choice, an involuntary and illegal act, was annulled by the fear of death and the menaces of the Romans; and their complaint is justified by the strong evidence of probability and fact. The twelve French cardinals, above two-thirds of the votes, were masters of the election; and whatever might be their provincial jealousies, it cannot fairly be presumed that they would have sacrificed their right and interest to a foreign candidate, who would never restore them to their native country. In the various, and often inconsistent, narratives,[66] the shades of popular violence are more darkly or faintly coloured: but the licentiousness of the seditious Romans was inflamed by a sense of their privileges, and the danger of a second emigration. The conclave was intimidated by the shouts, and encompassed by the arms, of thirty thousand rebels; the bells of the Capitol and St. Peter's rang an alarm; "Death, or an Italian pope!" was the universal cry; the same threat was repeated by the twelve bannerets or chiefs of the quarters, in the form of charitable advice; some preparations were made for burning the obstinate cardinals; and had they chosen a Transalpine subject, it is probable that they would never have departed alive from the Vatican. The same constraint imposed the necessity of dissembling in the eyes of Rome and of the world: the pride and cruelty of Urban presented a more inevitable danger; and they soon discovered the features of the tyrant, who could walk in his garden and recite his breviary, while he heard from an adjacent chamber six cardinals groaning on the rack. His inflexible zeal, which loudly censured their luxury and vice, would have attached them to the stations and duties of their parishes at Rome; and had he not fatally delayed a new promotion, the French cardinals would have been reduced to an helpless minority in the sacred college. For these reasons, and in the hope of repassing the Alps, they rashly violated the peace and unity of the church; and the merits of their double choice are yet agitated in the Catholic schools.[67]

66. In the first book of the Histoire du Concile de Pise, M. Lenfant has abridged and compared the original narratives of the adherents of Urban and Clement, of the Italians and Germans, the French and Spaniards. The latter appear to be the most active and loquacious, and every fact and word in the original Lives of Gregory XI. and Clement VII. are supported in the notes of their editor Baluze.

67. The ordinal numbers of the popes seem to decide the question against Clement VII. and Benedict XIII. who are boldly stigmatised as anti-popes by the Italians, while the French are content with authorities and reasons to plead the cause of doubt and toleration (Baluz. in Prefat.). It is singular, or rather it is not singular, that saints, visions, and miracles, should be common to both parties.

The vanity, rather than the interest, of the nation determined the court and clergy of France.[68] The states of Savoy, Sicily, Cyprus, Arragon, Castille, Navarre, and Scotland, were inclined by their example and authority to the obedience, of Clement the seventh, and, after his decease, of Benedict the thirteenth. Rome and the principal states of Italy, Germany, Portugal, England,[69] the Low Countries, and the kingdoms of the North, adhered to the prior election of Urban the sixth, who was succeeded by Boniface the ninth, Innocent the seventh, and Gregory the twelfth.

Great schism of the West, A.D. 1378–1418.

From the banks of the Tyber and the Rhône, the hostile pontiffs encountered each other with the pen and the sword: the civil and ecclesiastical order of society was disturbed; and the Romans had their full share of the mischiefs of which they may be arraigned as the primary authors.[70] They had vainly flattered themselves with the hope of restoring the seat of the ecclesiastical monarchy, and of relieving their poverty with the tributes and offerings of the nations; but the separation of France and Spain diverted the stream of lucrative devotion; nor could the loss be compensated by the two jubilees which were crowded into the space of ten years. By the avocations of the schism, by foreign arms, and popular tumults, Urban the sixth and his three successors were often compelled to interrupt their residence in the Vatican. The Colonna and Ursini still exercised their deadly feuds: the bannerets of Rome asserted and abused the privileges of a republic: the vicars of Christ, who had levied a military force, chastised their rebellion with the gibbet, the sword, and the dagger; and, in a friendly conference, eleven deputies of the people were perfidiously murdered and cast into the street. Since the invasion of Robert the Norman, the Romans had pursued their domestic quarrels without the dangerous interposition of a stranger. But in the disorders of the schism, an aspiring neighbour, Ladislaus king of Naples, alternately supported and betrayed the pope and the people: by the former, he was declared *gonfalonier*, or general, of the church, while the latter submitted to his

Calamities of Rome.

68. Baluze strenuously labours (Not. p. 1271–1280.) to justify the pure and pious motives of Charles V. king of France; he refused to hear the arguments of Urban; but were not the Urbanists equally deaf to the reasons of Clement, &c.?

69. An epistle, or declamation, in the name of Edward III. (Baluz. Vit. Pap. Avenion. tom. i. p. 553.) displays the zeal of the English nation against the Clementines. Nor was their zeal confined to words: the bishop of Norwich led a crusade of 60,000 bigots beyond sea (Hume's History, vol. iii. p. 57, 58.).

70. Besides the general historians, the Diaries of Delphinus Gentilis, Peter Antonius, and Stephen Infessura, in the great Collection of Muratori, represent the state and misfortunes of Rome.

choice the nomination of their magistrates. Besieging Rome by land and water, he thrice entered the gates as a Barbarian conqueror; profaned the altars, violated the virgins, pillaged the merchants, performed his devotions at St. Peter's, and left a garrison in the castle of St. Angelo. His arms were sometimes unfortunate, and to a delay of three days he was indebted for his life and crown; but Ladislaus triumphed in his turn, and it was only his premature death that could save the metropolis and the ecclesiastical state from the ambitious conqueror, who had assumed the title, or at least the powers, of king of Rome.[71]

Negociations for peace and union, A.D. 1392–1407.

I have not undertaken the ecclesiastical history of the schism; but Rome, the object of these last chapters, is deeply interested in the disputed succession of her sovereigns. The first counsels for the peace and union of Christendom arose from the university of Paris, from the faculty of the Sorbonne, whose doctors were esteemed, at least in the Gallican church, as the most consummate masters of theological science.[72] Prudently waving all invidious enquiry into the origin and merits of the dispute, they proposed, as an healing measure, that the two pretenders of Rome and Avignon should abdicate at the same time, after qualifying the cardinals of the adverse factions to join in a legitimate election; and that the nations should *substract*[73] their obedience, if either of the competitors preferred his own interest to that of the public. At each vacancy, these physicians of the church deprecated the mischiefs of an hasty choice; but the policy of the conclave and the ambition of its members were deaf to reason and entreaties; and whatsoever promises were made, the pope could never be bound by the oaths of the cardinal. During fifteen years, the pacific designs of the university were eluded by the arts of the rival pontiffs, the scruples or passions of their adherents, and the vicissitudes of French factions, that ruled the insanity of Charles the sixth. At length a vigorous resolution was

71. It is supposed by Giannone (tom. iii. p. 292.) that he styled himself Rex Romæ, a title unknown to the world since the expulsion of Tarquin. But a nearer inspection has justified the reading of Rex Ramæ, of Rama, an obscure kingdom annexed to the crown of Hungary.

72. The leading and decisive part which France assumed in the schism, is stated by Peter du Puis in a separate history, extracted from authentic records, and inserted in the vii[th] volume of the last and best edition of his friend Thuanus (P. xi. p. 110–184.).

73. Of this measure, John Gerson, a stout doctor, was the author or the champion. The proceedings of the university of Paris and the Gallican church were often prompted by his advice, and are copiously displayed in his theological writings, of which Le Clerc (Bibliotheque Choisie, tom. x. p. 1–78.) has given a valuable extract. John Gerson acted an important part in the councils of Pisa and Constance.

embraced; and a solemn embassy, of the titular patriarch of Alexandria, two archbishops, five bishops, five abbots, three knights, and twenty doctors, was sent to the courts of Avignon and Rome, to require, in the name of the church and king, the abdication of the two pretenders, of Peter de Luna, who styled himself Benedict the thirteenth, and of Angelo Corrario, who assumed the name of Gregory the twelfth. For the ancient honour of Rome, and the success of their commission, the ambassadors solicited a conference with the magistrates of the city, whom they gratified by a positive declaration, that the most Christian king did not entertain a wish of transporting the holy see from the Vatican, which he considered as the genuine and proper seat of the successor of St. Peter. In the name of the senate and people, an eloquent Roman asserted their desire to co-operate in the union of the church, deplored the temporal and spiritual calamities of the long schism, and requested the protection of France against the arms of the king of Naples. The answers of Benedict and Gregory were alike edifying and alike deceitful; and, in evading the demand of their abdication, the two rivals were animated by a common spirit. They agreed on the necessity of a previous interview, but the time, the place, and the manner, could never be ascertained by mutual consent. "If the one advances," says a servant of Gregory, "the other retreats; the one appears an animal fearful of the land, the other a creature apprehensive of the water. And thus for a short remnant of life and power, will these aged priests endanger the peace and salvation of the Christian world."[74]

Council of Pisa, A.D. 1409.

The Christian world was at length provoked by their obstinacy and fraud: they were deserted by their cardinals, who embraced each other as friends and colleagues; and their revolt was supported by a numerous assembly of prelates and ambassadors. With equal justice, the council of Pisa deposed the popes of Rome and Avignon; the conclave was unanimous in the choice of Alexander the fifth, and his vacant seat was soon filled by a similar election of John the twenty-third, the most profligate of mankind. But instead of extinguishing the schism, the rashness of the French and Italians had given a third pretender to the chair of St. Peter. Such new claims of the synod and conclave were disputed: three kings, of Germany, Hungary, and Naples, adhered to the cause of Gregory the twelfth; and Benedict the thirteenth, himself a

74. Leonardus Brunus Aretinus, one of the revivers of classic learning in Italy, who, after serving many years as secretary in the Roman court, retired to the honourable office of chancellor of the republic of Florence (Fabric. Bibliot. medii Ævi, tom. i. p. 290.). Lenfant has given the version of this curious epistle (Concile de Pise, tom. i. p. 192–195.).

Spaniard, was acknowledged by the devotion and patriotism of that powerful nation. The rash proceedings of Pisa were corrected by the council of Constance; the emperor Sigismond acted a conspicuous part as the advocate or protector of the Catholic church; and the number and weight of civil and ecclesiastical members might seem to constitute the states general of Europe. Of the three popes, John the twenty-third was the first victim: he fled and was brought back a prisoner: the most scandalous charges were suppressed; the vicar of Christ was only accused of piracy, murder, rape, sodomy, and incest; and after subscribing his own condemnation, he expiated in prison the imprudence of trusting his person to a free city beyond the Alps. Gregory the twelfth, whose obedience was reduced to the narrow precincts of Rimini, descended with more honour from the throne, and his ambassador convened the session, in which he renounced the title and authority of lawful pope. To vanquish the obstinacy of Benedict the thirteenth or his adherents, the emperor in person undertook a journey from Constance to Perpignan. The kings of Castille, Arragon, Navarre, and Scotland, obtained an equal and honourable treaty: with the concurrence of the Spaniards, Benedict was deposed by the council; but the harmless old man was left in a solitary castle to excommunicate twice each day the rebel kingdoms which had deserted his cause. After thus eradicating the remains of the schism, the synod of Constance proceeded with slow and cautious steps, to elect the sovereign of Rome and the head of the church. On this momentous occasion, the college of twenty-three cardinals was fortified with thirty deputies; six of whom were chosen in each of the five great nations of Christendom, the Italian, the German, the French, the Spanish, and the *English*:[75] the

Council of Constance, A.D. 1414–1418.

75. I cannot overlook this great national cause, which was vigorously maintained by the English ambassadors against those of France. The latter contended, that Christendom was essentially distributed into the four great nations and votes, of Italy, Germany, France, and Spain; and that the lesser kingdoms (such as England, Denmark, Portugal, &c.) were comprehended under one or other of these great divisions. The English asserted, that the British islands, of which they were the head, should be considered as a fifth and co-ordinate nation, with an equal vote; and every argument of truth or fable was introduced to exalt the dignity of their country. Including England, Scotland, Wales, the four kingdoms of Ireland, and the Orknies, the British islands are decorated with eight royal crowns, and discriminated by four or five languages, English, Welsh, Cornish, Scotch, Irish, &c. The greater island from north to south measures 800 miles, or 40 days journey; and England alone contains 32 counties, and 52,000 parish churches, (a bold account!) besides cathedrals, colleges, priories, and hospitals. They celebrate the mission of St. Joseph of Arimathea, the birth of Constantine, and the legantine powers of the two primates, without forgetting the testimony of Bartholemy de

interference of strangers was softened by their generous preference of an Italian and a Roman; and the hereditary, as well as personal, merit of Otho Colonna recommended him to the conclave. Rome accepted with joy and obedience the noblest of her sons, the ecclesiastical state was defended by his powerful family, and the elevation of Martin the fifth is the æra of the restoration and establishment of the popes in the Vatican.[76]

Election of Martin V.

Martin V. A.D. 1417. Eugenius IV. A.D. 1431. Nicholas V. A.D. 1447.

The royal prerogative of coining money, which had been exercised near three hundred years by the senate, was *first* resumed by Martin the fifth,[77] and his image and superscription introduce the series of the papal medals. Of his two immediate successors, Eugenius the fourth was the *last* pope expelled by the tumults of the Roman people,[78] and Nicholas the fifth, the *last* who was importuned by the presence of a Roman emperor.[79] I. The conflict of Eugenius, with the fathers of Basil, and the weight or apprehension of a new excise, emboldened and provoked the Romans to usurp the temporal government of the city. They rose in arms, elected seven governors of the republic, and a constable of the Capitol; imprisoned the Pope's nephew; besieged his person in the palace; and shot vollies of arrows into his bark

Last revolt of Rome, A.D. 1434, May 29– October 26.

Glanville (A.D. 1360), who reckons only four Christian kingdoms, 1. of Rome, 2. of Constantinople, 3. of Ireland, which had been transferred to the English monarchs, and, 4. of Spain. Our countrymen prevailed in the council, but the victories of Henry V. added much weight to their arguments. The adverse pleadings were found at Constance by Sir Robert Wingfield, ambassador from Henry VIII. to the emperor Maximilian I. and by him printed in 1517 at Louvain. From a Leipsic MS. they are more correctly published in the Collection of Von der Hardt, tom. v.; but I have only seen Lenfant's abstract of these acts (Concile de Constance, tom. ii. p. 447. 453, &c.).

76. The histories of the three successive councils, Pisa, Constance, and Basil, have been written with a tolerable degree of candour, industry, and elegance, by a Protestant minister, M. Lenfant, who retired from France to Berlin. They form six volumes in quarto; and as Basil is the worst, so Constance is the best, part of the collection.

77. See the xxvii[th] Dissertation of the Antiquities of Muratori, and the i[st] Instruction of the Science des Medailles of the Pere Joubert and the Baron de la Bastie. The Medallic History of Martin V. and his successors, has been composed by two monks, Moulinet a Frenchman, and Bonanni an Italian: but I understand, that the first part of the series is restored from more recent coins.

78. Besides the Lives of Eugenius IV. (Rerum Italic. tom. iii. P. i. p. 869. and tom. xxv. p. 256.), the Diaries of Paul Petroni and Stephen Infessura are the best original evidence for the revolt of the Romans against Eugenius IV. The former, who lived at the time and on the spot, speaks the language of a citizen, equally afraid of priestly and popular tyranny.

79. The coronation of Frederic III. is described by Lenfant (Concile de Basle, tom. ii. p. 276–288.); from Æneas Sylvius, a spectator and actor in that splendid scene.

as he escaped down the Tyber in the habit of a monk. But he still possessed in the castle of St. Angelo a faithful garrison and a train of artillery: their batteries incessantly thundered on the city, and a bullet more dextrously pointed broke down the barricade of the bridge, and scattered with a single shot the heroes of the republic. Their constancy was exhausted by a rebellion of five months. Under the tyranny of the Ghibeline nobles, the wisest patriots regretted the dominion of the church; and their repentance was unanimous and effectual. The troops of St. Peter again occupied the Capitol; the magistrates departed to their homes; the most guilty were executed or exiled; and the legate, at the head of two thousand foot and four thousand horse, was saluted as the father of the city. The synods of Ferrara and Florence, the fear or resentment of Eugenius, prolonged his absence: he was received by a submissive people; but the pontiff understood from the acclamations of his triumphal entry, that to secure their loyalty and his own repose, he must grant without delay the abolition of the odious excise. II. Rome was restored, adorned, and enlightened, by the peaceful reign of Nicholas the fifth. In the midst of these laudable occupations, the pope was alarmed by the approach of Frederic the third of Austria; though his fears could not be justified by the character or the power of the Imperial candidate. After drawing his military force to the metropolis, and imposing the best security of oaths[80] and treaties, Nicholas received with a smiling countenance the faithful advocate and vassal of the church. So tame were the times, so feeble was the Austrian, that the pomp of his coronation was accomplished with order and harmony: but the superfluous honour was so disgraceful to an independent nation, that his successors have excused themselves from the toilsome pilgrimage to the Vatican; and rest their Imperial title on the choice of the electors of Germany.

Last coronation of a German emperor, Frederic III. A.D. 1452, March 18.

The statutes and government of Rome.

A citizen has remarked, with pride and pleasure, that the king of the Romans, after passing with a slight salute the cardinals and prelates who met him at the gate, distinguished the dress and person of the senator of Rome; and in this last farewel, the pageants of the empire and the republic were clasped in a friendly embrace.[81]

80. The oath of fidelity imposed on the emperor by the pope, is recorded and sanctified in the Clementines (l. ii. tit. ix.); and Æneas Sylvius, who objects to this new demand, could not foresee, that in a few years he should ascend the throne, and imbibe the maxims, of Boniface VIII.

81. Lo senatore di Roma, vestito di brocarto con quella beretta, e con quelle maniche, et ornamenti di pelle, co' quali va alle feste di Testaccio e Nagone, might escape the eye of Æneas Sylvius, but he is

According to the laws of Rome,[82] her first magistrate was required to be a doctor of laws, an alien, of a place at least forty miles from the city; with whose inhabitants he must not be connected in the third canonical degree of blood or alliance. The election was annual: a severe scrutiny was instituted into the conduct of the departing senator; nor could he be recalled to the same office till after the expiration of two years. A liberal salary of three thousand florins was assigned for his expence and reward; and his public appearance represented the majesty of the republic. His robes were of gold brocade or crimson velvet, or in the summer season of a lighter silk; he bore in his hand an ivory sceptre; the sound of trumpets announced his approach; and his solemn steps were preceded at least by four lictors or attendants, whose red wands were enveloped with bands or streamers of the golden colour or livery of the city. His oath in the Capitol proclaims his right and duty, to observe and assert the laws, to control the proud, to protect the poor, and to exercise justice and mercy within the extent of his jurisdiction. In these useful functions he was assisted by three learned strangers; the two *collaterals*, and the judge of criminal appeals: their frequent trials of robberies, rapes, and murders, are attested by the laws; and the weakness of these laws connives at the licentiousness of private feuds and armed associations for mutual defence. But the senator was confined to the administration of justice: the Capitol, the treasury, and the government of the city and its territory were entrusted to the three *conservators*, who were changed four times in each year: the militia of the thirteen regions assembled under the banners of their respective chiefs, or *caporioni*; and the first of these was distinguished by the name and dignity of the *prior*. The popular legislature consisted of the secret and the common councils of the Romans. The former was composed of the magistrates and their immediate predecessors, with some fiscal and legal officers, and three classes of thirteen, twenty-six, and forty, counsellors; amounting in the whole to about one hundred and twenty persons. In the common council all male citizens had a right to vote; and the value of their privilege was enhanced by the care with which any foreigners were prevented from usurping the title and character of Romans. The tumult of a democracy was checked by wise and jealous

---

viewed with admiration and complacency by the Roman citizen (Diario di Stephano Infessura, p. 1133.).

82. See in the statutes of Rome, the *senator and three judges* (l. i. c. 3–14.), the *conservators* (l. i. c. 15, 16, 17. l. iii. c. 4.), the *caporioni* (l. i. c. 18. l. iii. c. 8.), the *secret council* (l. iii. c. 2.), the *common council* (l. iii. c. 3.). The title of *feuds, defiances, acts of violence,* &c. is spread through many a chapter (c. 14–40.) of the second book.

precautions: except the magistrates, none could propose a question; none were permitted to speak, except from an open pulpit or tribunal; all disorderly acclamations were suppressed; the sense of the majority was decided by a secret ballot; and their decrees were promulgated in the venerable name of the Roman senate and people. It would not be easy to assign a period in which this theory of government has been reduced to accurate and constant practice, since the establishment of order has been gradually connected with the decay of liberty. But in the year one thousand five hundred and eighty, the ancient statutes were collected, methodised in three books, and adapted to present use, under the pontificate, and with the approbation, of Gregory the thirteenth:[83] this civil and criminal code is the modern law of the city; and, if the popular assemblies have been abolished, a foreign senator, with the three conservators, still resides in the palace of the Capitol.[84] The policy of the Cæsars has been repeated by the popes; and the bishop of Rome affected to maintain the form of a republic, while he reigned with the absolute powers of a temporal, as well as spiritual, monarch.

Conspiracy of Porcaro, A.D. 1453, January 9.

It is an obvious truth, that the times must be suited to extraordinary characters, and that the genius of Cromwell or Retz might now expire in obscurity. The political enthusiasm of Rienzi had exalted him to a throne; the same enthusiasm, in the next century, conducted his imitator to the gallows. The birth of Stephen Porcaro was noble, his reputation spotless; his tongue was armed with eloquence, his mind was enlightened with learning; and he aspired, beyond the aim of vulgar ambition, to free his country and immortalise his name. The dominion of priests is most odious to a liberal spirit: every scruple was removed by the recent knowledge of the fable and forgery of Constantine's donation; Petrarch was now the oracle of the Italians; and as often as Porcaro revolved the ode which describes the patriot and hero of Rome, he applied to himself the visions of the prophetic bard. His first trial of the popular feelings was at the funeral of Eugenius the fourth: in an elaborate speech he called the Romans to liberty and arms;

83. *Statuta almæ Urbis Romæ Auctoritate S. D. N. Gregorii* XIII. *Pont. Max. a Senatû Populoque Rom. reformata et edita. Romæ*, 1580, *in folio.* The obsolete, repugnant statutes of antiquity, were confounded in five books, and Lucas Pætus, a lawyer and antiquarian, was appointed to act as the modern Tribonian. Yet I regret the old code, with the rugged crust of freedom and barbarism.

84. In my time (1765), and in M. Grosley's (Observations sur l'Italie, tom. ii. p. 361.), the senator of Rome was M. Bielke, a noble Swede, and a proselyte to the Catholic faith. The pope's right to appoint the senator and the conservator is implied, rather than affirmed, in the Statutes.

and they listened with apparent pleasure, till Porcaro was interrupted and answered by a grave advocate, who pleaded for the church and state. By every law the seditious orator was guilty of treason; but the benevolence of the new pontiff, who viewed his character with pity and esteem, attempted by an honourable office to convert the patriot into a friend. The inflexible Roman returned from Anagni with an encrease of reputation and zeal; and, on the first opportunity, the games of the place Navona, he tried to inflame the casual dispute of some boys and mechanics into a general rising of the people. Yet the humane Nicholas was still averse to accept the forfeit of his life; and the traitor was removed from the scene of temptation to Bologna, with a liberal allowance for his support, and the easy obligation of presenting himself each day before the governor of the city. But Porcaro had learned from the younger Brutus, that with tyrants no faith or gratitude should be observed: the exile declaimed against the arbitrary sentence; a party and a conspiracy was gradually formed; his nephew, a daring youth, assembled a band of volunteers; and on the appointed evening a feast was prepared at his house for the friends of the republic. Their leader, who had escaped from Bologna, appeared among them in a robe of purple and gold: his voice, his countenance, his gestures, bespoke the man who had devoted his life or death to the glorious cause. In a studied oration, he expatiated on the motives and the means of their enterprise: the name and liberties of Rome; the sloth and pride of their ecclesiastical tyrants; the active or passive consent of their fellow-citizens; three hundred soldiers, and four hundred exiles, long exercised in arms or in wrongs; the licence of revenge to edge their swords, and a million of ducats to reward their victory. It would be easy (he said), on the next day, the festival of the Epiphany, to seize the pope and the cardinals before the doors, or at the altar, of St. Peter's; to lead them in chains under the walls of St. Angelo; to extort by the threat of their instant death a surrender of the castle; to ascend the vacant Capitol; to ring the alarm-bell; and to restore in a popular assembly the ancient republic of Rome. While he triumphed, he was already betrayed. The senator, with a strong guard, invested the house: the nephew of Porcaro cut his way through the crowd; but the unfortunate Stephen was drawn from a chest, lamenting that his enemies had anticipated by three hours the execution of his design. After such manifest and repeated guilt, even the mercy of Nicholas was silent. Porcaro, and nine of his accomplices, were hanged without the benefit of the sacraments; and amidst the fears and invectives of the papal court, the Romans pitied, and almost applauded, these martyrs of their country.[85] But their applause was mute, their pity ineffectual, their liberty for ever extinct; and, if they have since risen in a vacancy of the throne or a scarcity of bread, such accidental tumults may be found in the bosom of the most abject servitude.

Last disorders of the nobles of Rome.

But the independence of the nobles, which was fomented by discord, survived the freedom of the commons, which must be founded in union. A privilege of rapine and oppression was long maintained by the barons of Rome; their houses were a fortress and a sanctuary: and the ferocious train of banditti and criminals whom they protected from the law, repaid the hospitality with the service of their swords and daggers. The private interest of the pontiffs, or their nephews, sometimes involved them in these domestic feuds. Under the reign of Sixtus the fourth, Rome was distracted by the battles and sieges of the rival houses: after the conflagration of his palace, the protonotary Colonna was tortured and beheaded; and Savelli, his captive friend, was murdered on the spot, for refusing to join in the acclamations of the victorious Ursini.[86] But the popes no longer trembled in the Vatican: they had strength to command, if they had resolution to claim, the obedience of their subjects; and the strangers, who observed these partial disorders, admired the easy taxes and wise administration of the ecclesiastical state.[87]

The popes acquire the absolute dominion of Rome, A.D. 1500, &c.

The spiritual thunders of the Vatican depend on the force of opinion: and, if that opinion be supplanted by reason or passion, the sound may idly waste itself in the air; and the helpless priest is exposed to the brutal violence of a noble or a plebeian adversary. But after their return from Avignon, the

85. Besides the curious though concise narrative of Machiavel (Istoria Fiorentina, l. vi. Opere, tom. i. p. 210, 211. edit. Londra, 1747, in 4[to]), the Porcarian conspiracy is related in the Diary of Stephen Infessura (Rer. Ital. tom. iii. P. ii. p. 1134, 1135.), and a separate tract by Leo Baptista Alberti (Rer. Ital. tom. xxv. p. 609–614.). It is amusing to compare the style and sentiments of the courtier and citizen. Facinus profecto quo ... neque periculo horribilius, neque audaciâ detestabilius, neque crudelitate tetrius, a quoquam perditissimo uspiam excogitatum sit ... Perdette la vita quell' huomo da bene, e amatore dello bene et libertà di Roma.

86. The disorders of Rome, which were much inflamed by the partiality of Sixtus IV. are exposed in the Diaries of two spectators, Stephen Infessura, and an anonymous citizen. See the troubles of the years 1484, and the death of the protonotary Colonna, in tom. iii. P. ii. p. 1083. 1158.

87. Est toute la terre de l'eglise troublée pour cette partialité (des Colonnes et des Ursins), come nous dirions Luce et Grammont, ou en Hollande Houc et Caballan; et quand ce ne seroit ce differend la terre de l'eglise seroit la plus heureuse habitation pour les sujets, qui soit dans tout le monde (car ils ne payent ni tailles ni gueres autres choses), et seroient toujours bien conduits (car toujours les papes sont sages et bien conseillés); mais très souvent en advient de grands et cruels meurtres et pilleries.

keys of St. Peter were guarded by the sword of St. Paul. Rome was commanded by an impregnable citadel: the use of cannon is a powerful engine against popular seditions: a regular force of cavalry and infantry was enlisted under the banners of the pope: his ample revenues supplied the resources of war; and, from the extent of his domain, he could bring down on a rebellious city an army of hostile neighbours and loyal subjects.[88] Since the union of the dutchies of Ferrara and Urbino, the ecclesiastical state extends from the Mediterranean to the Adriatic, and from the confines of Naples to the banks of the Po; and as early as the sixteenth century, the greater part of that spacious and fruitful country acknowledged the lawful claims and temporal sovereignty of the Roman pontiffs. Their claims were readily deduced from the genuine, or fabulous, donations of the darker ages: the successive steps of their final settlement would engage us too far in the transactions of Italy, and even of Europe; the crimes of Alexander the sixth, the martial operations of Julius the second, and the liberal policy of Leo the tenth, a theme which has been adorned by the pens of the noblest historians of the times.[89] In the first period of their conquests, till the expedition of Charles the eighth, the popes might successfully wrestle with the adjacent princes and states, whose military force was equal, or inferior, to their own. But as soon as the monarchs of France, Germany, and Spain, contended with gigantic arms for the dominion of Italy, they supplied with art the deficiency of strength; and concealed, in a labyrinth of wars and treaties, their aspiring views, and the immortal hope of chacing the Barbarians beyond the Alps. The nice balance of the Vatican was often subverted by the soldiers of the North and West, who were united under the standard of Charles the fifth: the feeble and fluctuating policy of Clement the seventh exposed his person and dominions to the conqueror; and Rome was abandoned seven months to a lawless army, more cruel and rapacious than the Goths and Vandals.[90] After this severe lesson, the popes contracted their

88. By the œconomy of Sixtus V. the revenue of the ecclesiastical state was raised to two millions and a half of Roman crowns (Vita, tom. ii. p. 291–296.); and so regular was the military establishment, that in one month Clement VIII. could invade the duchy of Ferrara with three thousand horse and twenty thousand foot (tom. iii. p. 64.). Since that time (A.D. 1597.), the papal arms are happily rusted; but the revenue must have gained some nominal encrease.

89. More especially by Guicciardini and Machiavel; in the general history of the former, in the Florentine history, the Prince, and the political discourses of the latter. These, with their worthy successors, Fra-Paolo and Davila, were justly esteemed the first historians of modern languages, till, in the present age, Scotland arose, to dispute the prize with Italy herself.

90. In the history of the Gothic siege, I have compared the Barbarians with the

ambition, which was almost satisfied, resumed the character of a common parent, and abstained from all offensive hostilities, except in an hasty quarrel, when the vicar of Christ and the Turkish sultan were armed at the same time against the kingdom of Naples.[91] The French and Germans at length withdrew from the field of battle: Milan, Naples, Sicily, Sardinia, and the sea-coast of Tuscany, were firmly possessed by the Spaniards; and it became their interest to maintain the peace and dependence of Italy, which continued almost without disturbance from the middle of the sixteenth to the opening of the eighteenth century. The Vatican was swayed and protected by the religious policy of the Catholic king: his prejudice and interest disposed him in every dispute to support the prince against the people; and instead of the encouragement, the aid, and the asylum, which they obtained from the adjacent states, the friends of liberty, or the enemies of law, were enclosed on all sides within the iron circle of despotism. The long habits of obedience and education subdued the turbulent spirit of the nobles and commons of Rome. The barons forgot the arms and factions of their ancestors, and insensibly became the servants of luxury and government. Instead of maintaining a crowd of tenants and followers, the produce of their estates was consumed in the private expences, which multiply the pleasures, and diminish the power, of the lord.[92] The Colonna and Ursini vied with each other in the decoration of their palaces and chapels; and their antique splendour was rivalled or surpassed by the sudden opulence of the papal families. In Rome the voice of freedom and discord is no longer heard; and, instead of the foaming torrent, a smooth and stagnant lake reflects the image of idleness and servitude.

The ecclesiastical government. A Christian, a philosopher,[93] and a patriot, will be equally scandalized by the temporal kingdom of the clergy; and the

---

subjects of Charles V. (vol. ii. p. 207–9.); an anticipation, which, like that of the Tartar conquests, I indulged with the less scruple, as I could scarcely hope to reach the conclusion of my work.

91. The ambitious and feeble hostilities of the Caraffa pope, Paul IV. may be seen in Thuanus (l. xvi–xviii.) and Giannone (tom. iv. p. 149–163.). Those Catholic bigots, Philip II. and the duke of Alva, presumed to separate the Roman prince from the vicar of Christ: yet the holy character, which would have sanctified his victory, was decently applied to protect his defeat.

92. This gradual change of manners and expence, is admirably explained by Dr. Adam Smith (Wealth of Nations, vol. i. p. 495–504.), who proves, perhaps too severely, that the most salutary effects have flowed from the meanest and most selfish causes.

93. Mr. Hume (Hist. of England, vol. i. p. 389.) too hastily concludes, that if the civil and ecclesiastical powers be united in the same person, it is of little moment whether he be styled prince or prelate, since the temporal character will always predominate.

local majesty of Rome, the remembrance of her consuls and triumphs, may seem to embitter the sense, and aggravate the shame, of her slavery. If we calmly weigh the merits and defects of the ecclesiastical government, it may be praised in its present state as a mild, decent, and tranquil system, exempt from the dangers of a minority, the sallies of youth, the expences of luxury, and the calamities of war. But these advantages are overbalanced by a frequent, perhaps a septennial, election of a sovereign, who is seldom a native of the country: the reign of a *young* statesman of threescore, in the decline of his life and abilities, without hope to accomplish, and without children to inherit, the labours of his transitory reign. The successful candidate is drawn from the church, and even the convent; from the mode of education and life the most adverse to reason, humanity, and freedom. In the trammels of servile faith, he has learned to believe because it is absurd, to revere all that is contemptible, and to despise whatever might deserve the esteem of a rational being; to punish error as a crime, to reward mortification and celibacy, as the first of virtues; to place the saints of the kalendar[94] above the heroes of Rome and the sages of Athens; and to consider the missal, or the crucifix, as more useful instruments than the plough or the loom. In the office of nuncio, or the rank of cardinal, he may acquire some knowledge of the world, but the primitive stain will adhere to his mind and manners; from study and experience he may suspect the mystery of his profession; but the sacerdotal artist will imbibe some portion of the bigotry which he inculcates. The genius of Sixtus the fifth[95] burst from the gloom of a Franciscan cloister. In a reign of five years, he exterminated the outlaws and banditti, abolished the *profane* sanctuaries of Rome,[96] formed a naval and military force, restored and emulated the monuments of

Sixtus V. A.D. 1585–1590.

94. A protestant may disdain the unworthy preference of St. Francis or St. Dominic, but he will not rashly condemn the zeal or judgment of Sixtus V. who placed the statues of the apostles, St. Peter and St. Paul, on the vacant columns of Trajan and Antonine.

95. A wandering Italian, Gregorio Leti, has given the Vita di Sisto-Quinto (Amstel. 1721, 3 vols. in 12mo), a copious and amusing work, but which does not command our absolute confidence. Yet the character of the man, and the principal facts, are supported by the Annals of Spondanus and Muratori (A.D. 1585–1590), and the contemporary history of the great Thuanus (l. lxxxii. c. 1, 2. l. lxxxiv. c. 10. l. c. c. 8.).

96. These privileged places, the *quartieri* or *franchises*, were adopted from the Roman nobles by the foreign ministers. Julius II. had once abolished the abominandum et detestandum franchitiarum hujusmodi nomen; and after Sixtus V. they again revived. I cannot discern either the justice or magnanimity of Louis XIV. who in 1687 sent his ambassador, the marquis de Lavardin, to Rome, with an armed force of a thousand officers, guards, and domestics, to maintain this iniquitous claim,

antiquity, and after a liberal use and large encrease of the revenue, left five millions of crowns in the castle of St. Angelo. But his justice was sullied with cruelty, his activity was prompted by the ambition of conquest; after his decease, the abuses revived; the treasure was dissipated; he entailed on posterity thirty-five new taxes and the venality of offices; and, after his death, his statue was demolished by an ungrateful, or an injured, people.[97] The wild and original character of Sixtus the fifth stands alone in the series of the pontiffs: the maxims and effects of their temporal government may be collected from the positive and comparative view of the arts and philosophy, the agriculture and trade, the wealth and population, of the ecclesiastical state. For myself, it is my wish to depart in charity with all mankind; nor am I willing, in these last moments, to offend even the pope and clergy of Rome.[98]

---

and insult pope Innocent XI. in the heart of his capital (Vita di Sisto V. tom. iii. p. 260–278. Muratori, Annali d'Italia, tom. xv. p. 494–496. and Voltaire, Siecle de Louis XIV. tom. ii. c. 14. p. 58, 59.).

97. This outrage produced a decree, which was inscribed on marble, and placed in the Capitol. It is expressed in a style of manly simplicity and freedom: Si quis, sive privatus, sive magistratum gerens de collocandâ *vivo* pontifici statuâ mentionem facere ausit, legitimo S. P. Q. R. decreto in perpetuum infamis et publicorum munerum expers esto. MDXC. mense Augusto (Vita di Sisto V. tom. iii. p. 469.). I believe that this decree is still observed, and I know that every monarch who deserves a statue, should himself impose the prohibition.

98. The histories of the church, Italy, and Christendom, have contributed to the chapter which I now conclude. In the original Lives of the Popes, we often discover the city and republic of Rome; and the events of the xiv[th] and xv[th] centuries are preserved in the rude and domestic chronicles which I have carefully inspected, and shall recapitulate in the order of time.

1. Monaldeschi (Ludovici Boncomitis) Fragmenta Annalium Roman. A.D. 1328, in the Scriptores Rerum Italicarum of Muratori, tom. xii. p. 525. N.B. The credit of this fragment is somewhat hurt by a singular interpolation, in which the author relates *his own death* at the age of 115 years.

2. Fragmenta Historiæ Romanæ (vulgo Thomas Fortifioccæ), in Romano Dialecto vulgari (A.D. 1327–1354, in Muratori, Antiquitat. medii Ævi Italiæ, tom. iii. p. 247–548.): the authentic ground-work of the history of Rienzi.

3. Delphini (Gentilis) Diarium Romanum (A.D. 1370–1410), in the Rerum Italicarum, tom. iii. P. ii. p. 846.

4. Antonii (Petri) *Diarium* Rom. (A.D. 1404–1417.), tom. xxiv. p. 969.

5. Petroni (Pauli) Miscellanea Historica Romana (A.D. 1433–1446), tom. xxiv. p. 1101.

6. Volaterrani (Jacob.) Diarium Rom. (A.D. 1472–1484), tom. xxiii. p. 81.

7. Anonymi Diarium Urbis Romæ (A.D. 1481–1492), tom. iii. P. ii. p. 1069.

8. Infessuræ (Stephani) Diarium Romanum (A.D. 1294, or 1378–1494.), tom. iii. P. ii. p. 1109.

9. Historia Arcana Alexandri VI. sive Excerpta ex Diario Joh. Burcardi (A.D. 1492–1503), edita a Godefr. Gulielm. Leibnizio, Hanover, 1697, in 4to. The large and valuable Journal of Burcard might be completed from the MSS. in different libraries

of Italy and France (M. de Foncemagne, in the Memoires de l'Acad. des Inscript. tom. xvii. p. 597–606.).

Except the last, all these fragments and diaries are inserted in the Collections of Muratori, my guide and master in the history of Italy. His country, and the public, are indebted to him for the following works on that subject: 1. *Rerum Italicarum Scriptores* (A.D. 500–1500), *quorum potissima pars nunc primum in lucem prodit*, &c. xxviii vols. in folio, Milan, 1723–1738. 1751. A volume of chronological and alphabetical tables is still wanting as a key to this great work, which is yet in a disorderly and defective state: 2. *Antiquitates Italiæ medii Ævi*, vi vols. in folio, Milan, 1738–1743, in lxxv curious dissertations on the manners, government, religion, &c. of the Italians of the darker ages, with a large supplement of charters, chronicles, &c. 3. *Dissertioni sopra le Antiquita Italiane*, iii vols. in 4to, Milano, 1751, a free version by the author, which may be quoted with the same confidence as the Latin text of the Antiquities. 4. *Annali d'Italia*, xviii vols. in octavo, Milan, 1753–1756, a dry, though accurate and useful, abridgement of the history of Italy from the birth of Christ to the middle of the xviiith century. 5. *Dell' Antichita Estense ed Italiane*, ii vols. in folio, Modena, 1717. 1740. In the history of this illustrious race, the parent of our Brunswick kings, the critic is not seduced by the loyalty or gratitude of the subject. In all his works, Muratori approves himself a diligent and laborious writer, who aspires above the prejudices of a Catholic priest. He was born in the year 1672, and died in the year 1750, after passing near sixty years in the libraries of Milan and Modena (Vita del Proposto Ludovico Antonio Muratori, by his nephew and successor Gian. Francesco Soli Muratori, Venezia, 1756, in 4to).

CHAPTER LXXI

Prospect of the Ruins of Rome in the Fifteenth Century. – Four Causes of Decay and Destruction. – Example of the Coliseum. – Renovation of the City. – Conclusion of the whole Work.

View and discourse of Poggius from the Capitoline hill, A.D. 1430.

In the last days of pope Eugenius the fourth, two of his servants, the learned Poggius[1] and a friend, ascended the Capitoline hill; reposed themselves among the ruins of columns and temples; and viewed from that commanding spot the wide and various prospect of desolation.[2] The place and the object gave ample scope for moralising on the vicissitudes of fortune, which spares neither man nor the proudest of his works, which buries empires and cities in a common grave; and it was agreed, that in proportion to her former greatness, the fall of Rome was the more awful and deplorable. "Her primæval state, such as she might appear in a remote age, when Evander entertained the stranger of Troy,[3] has been delineated by the fancy of Virgil. This Tarpeian rock was then a savage and solitary thicket: in the time of the poet, it was crowned with the golden roofs of a temple; the temple is overthrown, the gold has been pillaged, the wheel of fortune has accomplished her revolution, and the sacred ground is again disfigured with thorns and brambles. The hill of the Capitol, on which we sit, was formerly the head of the Roman empire, the citadel of the earth, the terror of kings; illustrated by the footsteps of so many triumphs, enriched with the spoils and tributes of so many nations. This spectacle of the world, how is it fallen! how changed! how defaced! the path of victory

1. I have already (not. 50, 51. on chap. 65.) mentioned the age, character, and writings of Poggius; and particularly noticed the date of this elegant moral lecture on the varieties of fortune.

2. Consedimus in ipsis Tarpeiæ arcis ruinis, pone ingens portæ cujusdam, ut puto, templi, marmoreum limen, plurimasque passim confractas columnas, unde magnâ ex parte prospectus urbis patet (p. 5.).

3. Æneid viii. 97–369. This ancient picture, so artfully introduced, and so exquisitely finished, must have been highly interesting to an inhabitant of Rome; and our early studies allow us to sympathise in the feelings of a Roman.

is obliterated by vines, and the benches of the senators are concealed by a dunghill. Cast your eyes on the Palatine hill, and seek among the shapeless and enormous fragments, the marble theatre, the obelisks, the colossal statues, the porticoes of Nero's palace: survey the other hills of the city, the vacant space is interrupted only by ruins and gardens. The forum of the Roman people, where they assembled to enact their laws and elect their magistrates, is now enclosed for the cultivation of pot-herbs, or thrown open for the reception of swine and buffaloes. The public and private edifices, that were founded for eternity, lie prostrate, naked, and broken, like the limbs of a mighty giant; and the ruin is the more visible, from the stupendous relics that have survived the injuries of time and fortune."[4]

His description of the ruins.

These relics are minutely described by Poggius, one of the first who raised his eyes from the monuments of legendary, to those of classic, superstition.[5] 1. Besides a bridge, an arch, a sepulchre, and the pyramid of Cestius, he could discern, of the age of the republic, a double row of vaults in the salt-office of the Capitol, which were inscribed with the name and munificence of Catulus. 2. Eleven temples were visible in some degree, from the perfect form of the Pantheon, to the three arches and a marble column of the temple of peace, which Vespasian erected after the civil wars and the Jewish triumph. 3. Of the number, which he rashly defines, of seven *thermæ* or public baths, none were sufficiently entire to represent the use and distribution of the several parts; but those of Diocletian and Antoninus Caracalla still retained the titles of the founders, and astonished the curious spectator, who, in observing their solidity and extent, the variety of marbles, the size and multitude of the columns, compared the labour and expence with the use and importance. Of the baths of Constantine, of Alexander, of Domitian, or rather of Titus, some vestige might yet be found. 4. The triumphal arches of Titus, Severus, and Constantine, were entire, both the structure and the inscriptions; a falling fragment was honoured with the name of Trajan; and two arches, then extant, in the Flaminian way, have been ascribed to the baser memory of Faustina and Gallienus. 5. After the wonder of the Coliseum, Poggius might have overlooked a

4. Capitolium adeo ... immutatum ut vineæ in senatorum subsellia successerint, stercorum ac purgamentorum receptaculum factum. Respice ad Palatinum montem ... vasta rudera ... cæteros colles perlustra omnia vacua ædificiis, ruinis vineisque oppleta conspicies (Poggius de Varietat. Fortunæ, p. 21.).

5. See Poggius, p. 8–22.

small amphitheatre of brick, most probably for the use of the prætorian camp: the theatres of Marcellus and Pompey were occupied in a great measure by public and private buildings; and in the Circus, Agonalis and Maximus, little more than the situation and the form could be investigated. 6. The columns of Trajan and Antonine were still erect; but the Egyptian obelisks were broken or buried. A people of gods and heroes, the workmanship of art, was reduced to one equestrian figure of gilt brass, and to five marble statues, of which the most conspicuous were the two horses of Phidias and Praxiteles. 7. The two mausoleums or sepulchres of Augustus and Hadrian could not totally be lost; but the former was only visible as a mound of earth; and the latter, the castle of St. Angelo, had acquired the name and appearance of a modern fortress. With the addition of some separate and nameless columns, such were the remains of the ancient city: for the marks of a more recent structure might be detected in the walls, which formed a circumference of ten miles, included three hundred and seventy-nine turrets, and opened into the country by thirteen gates.

Gradual decay of Rome.

This melancholy picture was drawn above nine hundred years after the fall of the Western empire, and even of the Gothic kingdom of Italy. A long period of distress and anarchy, in which empire, and arts, and riches, had migrated from the banks of the Tyber, was incapable of restoring or adorning the city; and, as all that is human must retrograde if it do not advance, every successive age must have hastened the ruin of the works of antiquity. To measure the progress of decay, and to ascertain at each æra the state of each edifice, would be an endless and a useless labour, and I shall content myself with two observations which will introduce a short enquiry into the general causes and effects. 1. Two hundred years before the eloquent complaint of Poggius, an anonymous writer composed a description of Rome.[6] His ignorance may repeat the same objects under strange and fabulous names. Yet this barbarous topographer had eyes and ears, he could observe the visible remains, he could listen to the tradition of the people, and he distinctly

6. Liber de Mirabilibus Romæ, ex Registro Nicolai Cardinalis de Arragoniâ, in Bibliothecâ St. Isidori Armario IV. N° 69. This treatise, with some short but pertinent notes, has been published by Montfaucon (Diarium Italicum, p. 283–301.), who thus delivers his own critical opinion: Scriptor xiii^{mi} circiter sæculi, ut ibidem notatur; antiquariæ rei imperitus, et, ut ab illo ævo, nugis et anilibus fabellis refertus: sed, quia monumenta quæ iis temporibus Romæ supererant pro modulo recenset, non parum inde lucis mutuabitur qui Romanis antiquitatibus indagandis operam navabit (p. 283.).

enumerates seven theatres, eleven baths, twelve arches, and eighteen palaces, of which many had disappeared before the time of Poggius. It is apparent, that many stately monuments of antiquity survived till a late period,[7] and that the principles of destruction acted with vigorous and encreasing energy in the thirteenth and fourteenth centuries. 2. The same reflection must be applied to the three last ages; and we should vainly seek the Septizonium of Severus,[8] which is celebrated by Petrarch and the antiquarians of the sixteenth century. While the Roman edifices were still entire, the first blows, however weighty and impetuous, were resisted by the solidity of the mass and the harmony of parts; but the slightest touch would precipitate the fragments of arches and columns, that already nodded to their fall.

Four causes of destruction:

After a diligent enquiry, I can discern four principal causes of the ruin of Rome, which continued to operate in a period of more than a thousand years. I. The injuries of time and nature. II. The hostile attacks of the Barbarians and Christians. III. The use and abuse of the materials. And, IV. The domestic quarrels of the Romans.

I. The injuries of nature;

I. The art of man is able to construct monuments far more permanent than the narrow span of his own existence: yet these monuments, like himself, are perishable and frail; and in the boundless annals of time, his life and his labours must equally be measured as a fleeting moment. Of a simple and solid edifice, it is not easy however to circumscribe the duration. As the wonders of ancient days, the pyramids[9] attracted the curiosity of the ancients: an hundred generations, the leaves of autumn,[10] have dropt into the grave; and after the fall of the Pharaohs and Ptolemies, the Cæsars and caliphs, the same pyramids stand erect and unshaken above the floods of the Nile. A complex figure of various and minute parts is more accessible to injury and decay; and the silent lapse

7. The Pere Mabillon (Analecta, tom. iv. p. 502.) has published an anonymous pilgrim of the ix[th] century, who, in his visit round the churches and holy places of Rome, touches on several buildings, especially porticoes, which had disappeared before the xiii[th] century.

8. On the Septizonium, see the Memoires sur Petrarque (tom. i. p. 325.), Donatus (p. 338.), and Nardini (p. 117. 414.).

9. The age of the pyramids is remote and unknown, since Diodorus Siculus (tom. i. l. i. c. 44. p. 72.) is unable to decide whether they were constructed 1000, or 3400, years before the clxxx[th] Olympiad. Sir John Marsham's contracted scale of the Egyptian dynasties would fix them about 2000 years before Christ (Canon. Chronicus, p. 47.).

10. See the speech of Glaucus in the Iliad (*Z*. 146.). This natural but melancholy image is familiar to Homer.

hurricanes and earthquakes; of time is often accelerated by hurricanes and earthquakes, by fires and inundations. The air and earth have doubtless been shaken; and the lofty turrets of Rome have tottered from their foundations: but the seven hills do not appear to be placed on the great cavities of the globe; nor has the city, in any age, been exposed to the convulsions of nature, which, in the climate of Antioch, Lisbon, or Lima, have crumbled in a few moments the works of ages into dust.

fires; Fire is the most powerful agent of life and death: the rapid mischief may be kindled and propagated by the industry or negligence of mankind; and every period of the Roman annals is marked by the repetition of similar calamities. A memorable conflagration, the guilt or misfortune of Nero's reign, continued, though with unequal fury, either six, or nine days.[11] Innumerable buildings, crowded in close and crooked streets, supplied perpetual fewel for the flames; and when they ceased, four only of the fourteen regions were left entire; three were totally destroyed, and seven were deformed by the relics of smoking and lacerated edifices.[12] In the full meridian of empire, the metropolis arose with fresh beauty from her ashes; yet the memory of the old deplored their irreparable losses, the arts of Greece, the trophies of victory, the monuments of primitive or fabulous antiquity. In the days of distress and anarchy, every wound is mortal, every fall irretrievable; nor can the damage be restored either by the public care of government or the activity of private interest. Yet two causes may be alleged, which render the calamity of fire more destructive to a flourishing than a decayed city. 1. The more combustible materials of brick, timber, and metals, are first melted or consumed; but the flames may play without injury or effect on the naked walls, and massy arches, that have been despoiled of their ornaments. 2. It is among the common and plebeian habitations, that a mischievous spark is most easily blown

11. The learning and criticism of M. des Vignoles (Histoire Critique de la Republique des Lettres, tom. viii. p. 74–118. ix. p. 172–187.) dates the fire of Rome from A.D. 64, July 19, and the subsequent persecution of the Christians from November 15, of the same year.

12. Quippe in regiones quatuordecim Roma dividitur, quarum quatuor integræ manebant, tres solo tenus dejectæ: septem reliquis pauca tectorum vestigia supererant, lacera et semiusta. Among the old relics that were irreparably lost, Tacitus enumerates the temple of the moon of Servius Tullius; the fane and altar consecrated by Evander præsenti Herculi; the temple of Jupiter Stator, a vow of Romulus; the palace of Numa; the temple of Vesta cum Penatibus populi Romani. He then deplores the opes tot victoriis quæsitæ et Græcarum artium decora ... multa quæ seniores meminerant, quæ reparari nequibant (Annal. xv. 40, 41.).

to a conflagration; but as soon as they are devoured, the greater edifices which have resisted or escaped, are left as so many islands in a state of solitude and safety. From her situation, Rome is exposed to the danger of frequent inundations. Without excepting the Tyber, the rivers *inundations.* that descend from either side of the Apennine have a short and irregular course: a shallow stream in the summer heats; an impetuous torrent, when it is swelled in the spring or winter, by the fall of rain, and the melting of the snows. When the current is repelled from the sea by adverse winds, when the ordinary bed is inadequate to the weight of waters, they rise above the banks, and overspread, without limits or control, the plains and cities of the adjacent country. Soon after the triumph of the first Punic war, the Tyber was encreased by unusual rains; and the inundation, surpassing all former measure of time and place, destroyed all the buildings that were situate below the hills of Rome. According to the variety of ground, the same mischief was produced by different means; and the edifices were either swept away by the sudden impulse, or dissolved and undermined by the long continuance, of the flood.[13] Under the reign of Augustus, the same calamity was renewed: the lawless river overturned the palaces and temples on its banks;[14] and, after the labours of the emperor in cleansing and widening the bed that was incumbered with ruins,[15] the vigilance of his successors was exercised by similar dangers and designs. The project of diverting into new channels the Tyber itself, or some of the dependent streams, was long opposed by superstition and local

13. A.U.C. 507, repentina subversio ipsius Romæ prævenit triumphum Romanorum ... diversæ ignium aquarumque clades pene absumsere urbem. Nam Tiberis insolitis auctus imbribus et ultra opinionem, vel diurnitate vel magnitudine redundans, *omnia* Romæ ædificia in plano posita delevit. Diversæ qualitates locorum ad unam convenere perniciem: quoniam et quæ segnior inundatio tenuit madefacta dissolvit, et quæ cursus torrentis invenit impulsa dejecit (Orosius, Hist. l. iv. c. 11. p. 244. edit. Havercamp). Yet we may observe, that it is the plan and study of the Christian apologist, to magnify the calamities of the pagan world.

14.

Vidimus flavum Tiberim, retortis
Littore Etrusco violenter undis
Ire dejectum monumenta Regis
Templaque Vestæ.
(Horat. Carm. I. 2.)

If the palace of Numa, and temple of Vesta, were thrown down in Horace's time, what was consumed of those buildings by Nero's fire could hardly deserve the epithets of vetustissima or incorrupta.

15. Ad coercendas inundationes alveum Tiberis laxavit, ac repurgavit, completum olim ruderibus, et ædificiorum prolapsionibus coarctatum (Suetonius in Augusto, c. 30.).

interests;[16] nor did the use compensate the toil and cost of the tardy and imperfect execution. The servitude of rivers is the noblest and most important victory which man has obtained over the licentiousness of nature;[17] and if such were the ravages of the Tyber under a firm and active government, what could oppose, or who can enumerate, the injuries of the city after the fall of the Western empire? A remedy was at length produced by the evil itself: the accumulation of rubbish and the earth, that has been washed down from the hills, is supposed to have elevated the plain of Rome, fourteen or fifteen feet, perhaps, above the ancient level;[18] and the modern city is less accessible to the attacks of the river.[19]

II. The hostile attacks of the Barbarians and Christians.

II. The crowd of writers of every nation, who impute the destruction of the Roman monuments to the Goths and the Christians, have neglected to enquire how far they were animated by an hostile principle, and how far they possessed the means and the leisure to satiate their enmity. In the preceding volumes of this History, I have described the triumph of barbarism and religion; and I can only resume, in a few words, their real or imaginary connection with the ruin of ancient Rome. Our fancy may create, or adopt, a pleasing romance, that the Goths and Vandals sallied from Scandinavia, ardent to avenge the flight of Odin,[20] to break the chains, and to chastise the oppressors, of mankind; that they wished to burn the records of classic literature, and to found their national architecture on the broken members of the Tuscan and Corinthian orders. But in simple truth, the northern conquerors were

16. Tacitus (Annal. i. 79.) reports the petitions of the different towns of Italy to the senate against the measure; and we may applaud the progress of reason. On a similar occasion, local interests would undoubtedly be consulted: but an English house of commons would reject with contempt the arguments of superstition, "that nature had assigned to the rivers their proper course, &c."

17. See the Epoques de la Nature of the eloquent and philosophic Buffon. His picture of Guyana in South America, is that of a new and savage land, in which the waters are abandoned to themselves, without being regulated by human industry (p. 212. 561. quarto edition).

18. In his Travels in Italy, Mr. Addison (his works, vol. ii. p. 98. Baskerville's edition) has observed this curious and unquestionable fact.

19. Yet in modern times, the Tyber has sometimes damaged the city; and in the years 1530, 1557, 1598, the Annals of Muratori record three mischievous and memorable inundations (tom. xiv. p. 268. 429. tom. xv. p. 99, &c.).

20. I take this opportunity of declaring, that in the course of twelve years I have forgotten, or renounced, the flight of Odin from Azoph to Sweden, which I never very seriously believed (vol. i. p. 257.). The Goths are apparently Germans: but all beyond Cæsar and Tacitus, is darkness or fable, in the antiquities of Germany.

neither sufficiently savage, nor sufficiently refined, to entertain such aspiring ideas of destruction and revenge. The shepherds of Scythia and Germany had been educated in the armies of the empire, whose discipline they acquired, and whose weakness they invaded: with the familiar use of the Latin tongue, they had learned to reverence the name and titles of Rome; and, though incapable of emulating, they were more inclined to admire, than to abolish, the arts and studies of a brighter period. In the transient possession of a rich and unresisting capital, the soldiers of Alaric and Genseric were stimulated by the passions of a victorious army; amidst the wanton indulgence of lust or cruelty, portable wealth was the object of their search; nor could they derive either pride or pleasure from the unprofitable reflection, that they had battered to the ground the works of the consuls and Cæsars. Their moments were indeed precious; the Goths evacuated Rome on the sixth,[21] the Vandals on the fifteenth, day;[22] and, though it be far more difficult to build than to destroy, their hasty assault would have made a slight impression on the solid piles of antiquity. We may remember, that both Alaric and Genseric affected to spare the buildings of the city; that they subsisted in strength and beauty under the auspicious government of Theodoric;[23] and that the momentary resentment of Totila[24] was disarmed by his own temper and the advice of his friends and enemies. From these innocent Barbarians, the reproach may be transferred to the Catholics of Rome. The statues, altars, and houses, of the dæmons were an abomination in their eyes; and in the absolute command of the city, they might labour with zeal and perseverance to eraze the idolatry of their ancestors. The demolition of the temples in the East[25] affords to *them* an example of conduct, and to *us* an argument of belief; and it is probable, that a portion of guilt or merit may be imputed with justice to the Roman proselytes. Yet their abhorrence was confined to the monuments of heathen superstition; and the civil structures that were dedicated to the business or pleasure of society might be preserved without injury or scandal. The change of religion was accomplished, not by a popular tumult, but by the decrees of the emperors, of the senate, and of time. Of the Christian hierarchy, the bishops of Rome were commonly the most

21. History of the Decline, &c. vol. ii. p. 209.
22. ——vol. ii. p. 360.
23. ——vol. ii. p. 548–50.
24. ——vol. ii. p. 749. 754.
25. History of the Decline, &c. vol. ii. c. xxviii. p. 79–81.

prudent and least fanatic: nor can any positive charge be opposed to the meritorious act of saving and converting the majestic structure of the Pantheon.[26]

III. The use and abuse of the materials.

III. The value of any object that supplies the wants or pleasures of mankind, is compounded of its substance and its form, of the materials and the manufacture. Its price must depend on the number of persons by whom it may be acquired and used; on the extent of the market; and consequently on the ease or difficulty of remote exportation, according to the nature of the commodity, its local situation, and the temporary circumstances of the world. The Barbarian conquerors of Rome usurped in a moment the toil and treasure of successive ages; but, except the luxuries of immediate consumption, they must view without desire all that could not be removed from the city in the Gothic waggons or the fleet of the Vandals.[27] Gold and silver were the first objects of their avarice; as in every country, and in the smallest compass, they represent the most ample command of the industry and possessions of mankind. A vase or a statue of those precious metals might tempt the vanity of some Barbarian chief; but the grosser multitude, regardless of the form, was tenacious only of the substance; and the melted ingots might be readily divided and stamped into the current coin of the empire. The less active or less fortunate robbers were reduced to the baser plunder of brass, lead, iron, and copper: whatever had escaped the Goths and Vandals was pillaged by the Greek tyrants; and the emperor Constans, in his rapacious visit, stripped the bronze tiles from the roof of the Pantheon.[28] The edifices of Rome might be considered as a vast and

26. Eodem tempore petiit a Phocate principe templum, quod appellatur *Pantheon*, in quo fecit ecclesiam Sanctæ Mariæ semper Virginis, et omnium martyrum; in quâ ecclesiæ princeps multa bona obtulit (Anastasius vel potius Liber Pontificalis in Bonifacio IV. in Muratori, Script. Rerum Italicarum, tom. iii. P. i. p. 135.). According to the anonymous writer in Montfaucon, the Pantheon had been vowed by Agrippa to Cybele and Neptune, and was dedicated by Boniface IV. on the calends of November to the Virgin, quæ est mater omnium sanctorum (p. 297, 298.).

27. Flaminius Vacca (apud Montfaucon, p. 155, 156. His Memoir is likewise printed, pp. 21. at the end of the Roma Antica of Nardini), and several Romans, doctrinâ graves, were persuaded that the Goths buried their treasures at Rome, and bequeathed the secret marks filiis nepotibusque. He relates some anecdotes to prove, that in his own time, these places were visited and rifled by the Transalpine pilgrims, the heirs of the Gothic conquerors.

28. Omnia quæ erant in ære ad ornatum civitatis deposuit: sed et ecclesiam B. Mariæ ad martyres quæ de tegulis æreis cooperta discooperuit (Anast. in Vitalian. p. 141.). The base and sacrilegious Greek had not even the poor pretence of plundering an heathen temple; the Pantheon was already a Catholic church.

various mine; the first labour of extracting the materials was already performed; the metals were purified and cast; the marbles were hewn and polished; and after foreign and domestic rapine had been satiated, the remains of the city, could a purchaser have been found, were still venal. The monuments of antiquity had been left naked of their precious ornaments, but the Romans would demolish with their own hands the arches and walls, if the hope of profit could surpass the cost of the labour and exportation. If Charlemagne had fixed in Italy the seat of the Western empire, his genius would have aspired to restore, rather than to violate, the works of the Cæsars: but policy confined the French monarch to the forests of Germany; his taste could be gratified only by destruction; and the new palace of Aix la Chapelle was decorated with the marbles of Ravenna[29] and Rome.[30] Five hundred years after Charlemagne, a king of Sicily, Robert, the wisest and most liberal sovereign of the age, was supplied with the same materials by the easy navigation of the Tyber and the sea; and Petrarch sighs an indignant complaint, that the ancient capital of the world should adorn from her own bowels the slothful luxury of Naples.[31] But these examples of plunder or purchase were rare in the darker

29. For the spoils of Ravenna (musiva atque marmora) see the original grant of pope Adrian I. to Charlemagne (Codex Carolin. epist. lxvii. in Muratori, Script. Ital. tom. iii. P. ii. p. 223.).

30. I shall quote the authentic testimony of the Saxon poet (A.D. 887–899), de Rebus gestis Caroli magni, l. v. 437–440. in the Historians of France (tom. v. p. 180.):

> Ad quæ marmoreas præstabat ROMA columnas,
> Quasdam præcipuas pulchra Ravenna dedit
> De tam longinquâ poterit regione vetustas.
> Illius ornatum Francia ferre tibi.

And I shall add, from the Chronicle of Sigebert (Historians of France, tom. v. p. 378.), extruxit etiam Aquisgrani basilicam plurimæ pulchritudinis, ad cujus structuram a ROMA et Ravenna columnas et marmora devehi fecit.

31. I cannot refuse to transcribe a long passage of Petrarch (Opp. p. 536, 537. in Epistolâ hortatoria ad Nicolaum Laurentium); it is so strong and full to the point: Nec pudor aut pietas continuit quominus impii spoliata Dei templa, occupatas arces, opes publicas regiones urbis, atque honores magistratûum inter se divisos; *(habeant?)* quam unâ in re, turbulenti ac seditiosi homines et totius reliquæ vitæ consiliis et rationibus discordes, inhumani fœderis stupendâ societate convenerant, in pontes et mœnia atque immeritos lapides desævirent. Denique post vi vel senio collapsa palatia, quæ quondam ingentes tenuerunt viri, post diruptos arcus triumphales (unde majores horum forsitan corruerunt), de ipsius vetustatis ac propriæ impietatis fragminibus vilem questûm turpi mercimonio captare non puduit. Itaque nunc, heu dolor! heu scelus indignum! de vestris marmoreis columnis, de liminibus templorum (ad quæ nuper ex orbe toto concursus devotissimus fiebat), de imaginibus sepulchrorum sub quibus patrum vestrorum venerabilis civis *(cinis?)* erat, ut reliquas sileam, desidiosa Neapolis ador-

ages; and the Romans, alone and unenvied, might have applied to their private or public use the remaining structures of antiquity, if in their present form and situation they had not been useless in a great measure to the city and its inhabitants. The walls still described the old circumference, but the city had descended from the seven hills into the Campus Martius; and some of the noblest monuments which had braved the injuries of time were left in a desert, far remote from the habitations of mankind. The palaces of the senators were no longer adapted to the manners or fortunes of their indigent successors: the use of baths[32] and porticoes was forgotten: in the sixth century, the games of the theatre, amphitheatre, and circus, had been interrupted: some temples were devoted to the prevailing worship; but the Christian churches preferred the holy figure of the cross; and fashion, or reason, had distributed after a peculiar model the cells and offices of the cloyster. Under the ecclesiastical reign, the number of these pious foundations was enormously multiplied; and the city was crowded with forty monasteries of men, twenty of women, and sixty chapters and colleges of canons and priests,[33] who aggravated, instead of relieving, the depopulation of the tenth century. But if the forms of ancient architecture were disregarded by a people insensible of their use and beauty, the plentiful materials were applied to every call of necessity or superstition; till the fairest columns of the Ionic and Corinthian orders, the richest marbles of Paros and Numidia, were degraded, perhaps to the support of a convent or a stable. The daily havock which is perpetrated by the Turks in the cities of Greece and Asia, may afford a melancholy example; and in the gradual destruction of the monuments of Rome, Sixtus the fifth may alone be excused for employing the stones of the Septizonium in the glorious edifice of St. Peter's.[34] A fragment, a ruin, howsoever mangled or profaned, may be viewed with pleasure and regret; but the greater part of the marble was deprived of substance, as well as of place and proportion; it was burnt to lime for the purpose of cement. Since the arrival of Poggius, the temple of Concord,[35] and many capital structures, had

natur. Sic paullatim ruinæ ipsæ deficiunt. Yet king Robert was the friend of Petrarch.

32. Yet Charlemagne washed and swam at Aix la Chapelle with an hundred of his courtiers (Eginhart, c. 22. p. 108, 109.), and Muratori describes as late as the year 814, the public baths which were built at Spoleto in Italy (Annali, tom. vi. p. 416.).

33. See the Annals of Italy, A.D. 988. For this and the preceding fact, Muratori himself is indebted to the Benedictine history of Pére Mabillon.

34. Vita di Sisto Quinto, da Gregorio Leti, tom. iii. p. 50.

35. Porticus ædis Concordiæ, quam cum primum ad urbem accessi vidi fere inte-

vanished from his eyes; and an epigram of the same age expresses a just and pious fear, that the continuance of this practice would finally annihilate all the monuments of antiquity.[36] The smallness of their numbers was the sole check on the demands and depredations of the Romans. The imagination of Petrarch might create the presence of a mighty people;[37] and I hesitate to believe, that, even in the fourteenth century, they could be reduced to a contemptible list of thirty-three thousand inhabitants. From that period to the reign of Leo the tenth, if they multiplied to the amount of eighty-five thousand,[38] the encrease of citizens was in some degree pernicious to the ancient city.

IV. The domestic quarrels of the Romans.

IV. I have reserved for the last, the most potent and forcible cause of destruction, the domestic hostilities of the Romans themselves. Under the dominion of the Greek and French emperors, the peace of the city was disturbed by accidental, though frequent, seditions: it is from the decline of the latter, from the beginning of the tenth century, that we may date the licentiousness of private war, which violated with impunity the laws of the Code and the Gospel; without respecting the majesty of the absent sovereign, or the presence and person of the vicar of Christ. In a dark period of five hundred years, Rome was perpetually afflicted by the sanguinary quarrels of the nobles and the people, the Guelphs and Ghibelines, the Colonna and Ursini; and if much has escaped the knowledge, and much is unworthy of the notice, of history, I have exposed in the two preceding chapters, the causes and effects of the public disorders. At

---

gram opere marmoreo admodum specioso: Romani postmodum ad calcem ædem totam et porticûs partem disjectis columnis sunt demoliti (p. 12.). The temple of Concord was therefore *not* destroyed by a sedition in the xiii[th] century, as I have read in a MS. treatise del' Governo civile di Rome, lent me formerly at Rome, and ascribed (I believe falsely) to the celebrated Gravina. Poggius likewise affirms, that the sepulchre of Cæcilia Metella was burnt for lime (p. 19, 20.).

36. Composed by Æneas Sylvius, afterwards pope Pius II. and published by Mabillon from a MS. of the queen of Sweden (Musæum Italicum, tom. i. p. 97.).

Oblectat me, Roma, tuas spectare ruinas;
Ex cujus lapsû gloria prisca patet.
Sed tuus hic populus muris defossa vetustis
Calcis in obsequium marmora dura coquit
Impia tercentum si sic gens egerit annos
Nullum hinc indicium nobilitatis erit.

37. Vagabamur pariter in illâ urbe tam magnâ; quæ, cum propter spatium vacua videretur, populum habet immensum (Opp. p. 605. Epist. Familiares, ii. 14.).

38. These states of the population of Rome at different periods, are derived from an ingenious treatise of the physician Lancisi, de Romani Cœli Qualitatibus (p. 122.).

such a time, when every quarrel was decided by the sword; and none could trust their lives or properties to the impotence of law; the powerful citizens were armed for safety or offence, against the domestic enemies, whom they feared or hated. Except Venice alone, the same dangers and designs were common to all the free republics of Italy; and the nobles usurped the prerogative of fortifying their houses, and erecting strong towers[39] that were capable of resisting a sudden attack. The cities were filled with these hostile edifices; and the example of Lucca, which contained three hundred towers; her law, which confined their height to the measure of fourscore feet, may be extended with suitable latitude to the more opulent and populous states. The first step of the senator Brancaleone in the establishment of peace and justice, was to demolish (as we have already seen) one hundred and forty of the towers of Rome; and, in the last days of anarchy and discord, as late as the reign of Martin the fifth, forty-four still stood in one of the thirteen or fourteen regions of the city. To this mischievous purpose, the remains of antiquity were most readily adapted: the temples and arches afforded a broad and solid basis for the new structures of brick and stone; and we can name the modern turrets that were raised on the triumphal monuments of Julius Cæsar, Titus, and the Antonines.[40] With some slight alterations, a theatre, an amphitheatre, a mausoleum, was transformed into a strong and spacious citadel. I need not repeat, that the mole of Adrian has assumed the title and form of the castle of St. Angelo;[41] the Septizonium of Severus was capable of standing against a royal army;[42] the sepulchre of Metella has sunk under its outworks;[43] the theatres of Pompey and Marcellus

39. All the facts that relate to the towers at Rome, and in other free cities of Italy, may be found in the laborious and entertaining compilation of Muratori, Antiquitates Italiæ medii Ævi, dissertat. xxvi. (tom. ii. p. 493–496. of the Latin, tom. i. p. 446. of the Italian work).

40. As for instance, Templum Jani nunc dicitur, turris Centii Frangapanis; et sane Jano impositæ turris lateritiæ conspicua hodieque vestigia supersunt (Montfaucon Diarium Italicum, p. 186.). The anonymous writer (p. 285.) enumerates, arcus Titi, turris Cartularia; Arcus Julii Cæsaris et Senatorum, turres de Bratis; arcus Antonini, turris de Cosectis, &c.

41. Hadriani molem ... magna ex parte Romanorum injuria ... disturbavit: quod certe funditus evertissent, si eorum manibus pervia, absumptis grandibus saxis, reliqua moles exstitisset (Poggius de Varietate Fortunæ, p. 12.).

42. Against the emperor Henry IV. (Muratori, Annali d'Italia, tom. ix. p. 147.).

43. I must copy an important passage of Montfaucon: Turris ingens rotunda ... Cæciliæ Metellæ ... sepulchrum erat, cujus muri tam solidi, ut spatium perquam minimum intus vacuum supersit: et *Torre di Bove* dicitur, a boum capitibus muro inscriptis. Huic sequiori ævo, tempore intestinorum bellorum, ceu urbecula adjuncta fuit, cujus mœnia et turres etiamnum visuntur; ita ut sepulchrum

were occupied by the Savelli and Ursini families;[44] and the rough fortress has been gradually softened to the splendour and elegance of an Italian palace. Even the churches were encompassed with arms and bulwarks, and the military engines on the roof of St. Peter's were the terror of the Vatican and the scandal of the Christian world. Whatever is fortified will be attacked; and whatever is attacked may be destroyed. Could the Romans have wrested from the popes the castle of St. Angelo, they had resolved by a public decree to annihilate that monument of servitude. Every building of defence was exposed to a siege; and in every siege the arts and engines of destruction were laboriously employed. After the death of Nicholas the fourth, Rome, without a sovereign or a senate, was abandoned six months to the fury of civil war. "The houses," says a cardinal and poet of the times,[45] "were crushed by the weight and velocity of enormous stones;[46] the walls were perforated by the strokes of the battering-ram; the towers were involved in fire and smoke; and the assailants were stimulated by rapine and revenge." The work was consummated by the tyranny of the laws; and the factions of Italy alternately exercised a blind and thoughtless vengeance on their adversaries, whose houses and castles they razed to the ground.[47] In comparing the *days* of foreign, with the *ages* of domestic, hostility, we must pronounce, that the latter have been far more ruinous to the city, and our opinion is confirmed by

---

Metellæ quasi arx oppiduli fuerit. Ferventibus in urbe partibus, cum Ursini atque Columnenses mutuis cladibus perniciem inferrent civitati, in utriusve partis ditionem cederet magni momenti erat (p. 142.).

44. See the testimonies of Donatus, Nardini, and Montfaucon. In the Savelli palace, the remains of the theatre of Marcellus are still great and conspicuous.

45. James cardinal of St. George, ad velum aureum, in his metrical Life of Pope Celestin V. (Muratori, Script. Ital. tom. i. P. iii. p. 621. l. i. c. 1. ver. 132, &c.)

Hoc dixisse sat est, Romam caruisse
Senatû
Mensibus exactis heu sex; belloque
vocatum (*vocatos*)
In scelus, in socios fraternaque vulnera
patres:
Tormentis jecisse viros immania saxa;
Perfodisse domus trabibus, fecisse ruinas
Ignibus; incensas turres, obscurataque
fumo
Lumina vicino, quo sit spoliata supellex.

46. Muratori (Dissertazione sopra le Antiquitá Italiane, tom. i. p. 427–431.) finds, that stone bullets of two or three hundred pounds weight were not uncommon; and they are sometimes computed at xii or xviii *cantari* of Genoa, each *cantaro* weighing 150 pounds.

47. The vi^th law of the Visconti prohibits this common and mischievous practice; and strictly enjoins, that the houses of banished citizens should be preserved pro communi utilitate (Gualvaneus de la Flamma, in Muratori, Script. Rerum Italicarum, tom. xii. p. 1041.).

the evidence of Petrarch. "Behold," says the laureat, "the relics of Rome, the image of her pristine greatness! neither time nor the Barbarian can boast the merit of this stupendous destruction: it was perpetrated by her own citizens, by the most illustrious of her sons; and your ancestors (he writes to a noble Annibaldi) have done with the battering-ram, what the Punic hero could not accomplish with the sword."[48] The influence of the two last principles of decay must in some degree be multiplied by each other; since the houses and towers, which were subverted by civil war, required a new and perpetual supply from the monuments of antiquity.

The Coliseum or amphitheatre of Titus.

These general observations may be separately applied to the amphitheatre of Titus, which has obtained the name of the COLISEUM,[49] either from its magnitude or from Nero's colossal statue: an edifice, had it been left to time and nature, which might perhaps have claimed an eternal duration. The curious antiquaries, who have computed the numbers and seats, are disposed to believe that above the upper row of stone steps, the amphitheatre was encircled and elevated with several stages of wooden galleries, which were repeatedly consumed by fire, and restored by the emperors. Whatever was precious, or portable, or profane, the statues of gods and heroes, and the costly ornaments of sculpture, which were cast in brass, or overspread with leaves of silver and gold, became the first prey of conquest or fanaticism, of the avarice of the Barbarians or the Christians. In the massy stones of the Coliseum, many holes are discerned; and the two most probable conjectures represent the various accidents of its decay. These stones were connected by solid links of

48. Petrarch thus addresses his friend who, with shame and tears, had shewn him the mœnia, laceræ specimen miserabile Romæ, and declared his own intention of restoring them (Carmina Latina, l. ii. epist. Paulo Annibalensi, xii. p. 97, 98.):

Nec te parva manet servatis fama ruinis
Quanta quod integræ fuit olim gloria Romæ
Reliquiæ testantur adhuc; quas longior ætas
Frangere non valuit; non vis aut ira cruenti
Hostis, ab egregiis franguntur civibus heu! heu!
—— Quod *ille* nequivit (*Hannibal*)
Perficit hic aries. ——

49. The fourth part of the Verona Illustrata of the Marquis Maffei, professedly treats of amphitheatres, particularly those of Rome and Verona, of their dimensions, wooden galleries, &c. It is from magnitude that he derives the name of *Colosseum*, or *Coliseum*: since the same appellation was applied to the amphitheatre of Capua, without the aid of a colossal statue; since that of Nero was erected in the court *(in atrio)* of his palace, and not in the Coliseum (P. iv. p. 15–19. l. i. c. 4.).

brass or iron, nor had the eye of rapine overlooked the value of the baser metals:[50] the vacant space was converted into a fair or market; the artisans of the Coliseum are mentioned in an ancient survey; and the chasms were perforated or enlarged to receive the poles that supported the shops or tents of the mechanic trades.[51] Reduced to its naked majesty, the Flavian amphitheatre was contemplated with awe and admiration by the pilgrims of the North; and their rude enthusiasm broke forth in a sublime proverbial expression, which is recorded in the eighth century, in the fragments of the venerable Bede: "As long as the Coliseum stands, Rome shall stand; when the Coliseum falls, Rome will fall; when Rome falls, the world will fall."[52] In the modern system of war, a situation commanded by three hills would not be chosen for a fortress; but the strength of the walls and arches could resist the engines of assault; a numerous garrison might be lodged in the enclosure; and while one faction occupied the Vatican and the Capitol, the other was intrenched in the Lateran and the Coliseum.[53]

Games of Rome.

The abolition at Rome of the ancient games must be understood with some latitude; and the carnival sports, of the Testacean mount and the Circus Agonalis,[54] were regulated by the law[55] or custom of the city. The senator presided with dignity and

50. Joseph Maria Suarés, a learned bishop, and the author of an history of Præneste, has composed a separate dissertation on the seven or eight probable causes of these holes, which has been since reprinted in the Roman Thesaurus of Sallengre. Montfaucon (Diarium, p. 233.) pronounces the rapine of the Barbarians to be the unam germanamque causam foraminum.

51. Donatus, Roma Vetus et Nova, p. 285.

52. Quamdiu stabit Colyseus, stabit et Roma; quando cadet Colyseus, cadet Roma; quando cadet Roma, cadet et mundus (Beda in Excerptis seu Collectaneis apud Ducange Glossar. med. et infimæ Latinitatis, tom. ii. p. 407. edit. Basil). This saying must be ascribed to the Anglo-Saxon pilgrims who visited Rome before the year 735, the æra of Bede's death; for I do not believe that our venerable monk ever passed the sea.

53. I cannot recover in Muratori's original Lives of the Popes (Script. Rerum Italicarum, tom. iii. P. i.) the passage that attests this hostile partition, which must be applied to the end of the xi[th] or the beginning of the xii[th] century.

54. Although the structure of the Circus Agonalis be destroyed, it still retains its form and name (Agona, Nagona, Navona): and the interior space affords a sufficient level for the purpose of racing. But the Monte Testaceo, that strange pile of broken pottery, seems only adapted for the annual practice of hurling from top to bottom some waggon-loads of live hogs for the diversion of the populace (Statuta Urbis Romæ, p. 186.).

55. See the Statuta Urbis Romæ, l. iii. c. 87, 88, 89. p. 185, 186. I have already given an idea of this municipal code. The races of Nagona and Monte Testaceo are likewise mentioned in the Diary of Peter Antonius from 1404 to 1417 (Muratori, Script. Rerum Italicarum, tom. xxiv. p. 1124.).

pomp to adjudge and distribute the prizes, the gold ring, or the *pallium*,[56] as it was styled, of cloth or silk. A tribute on the Jews supplied the annual expence;[57] and the races, on foot, on horseback, or in chariots, were ennobled by a tilt and tournament of seventy-two of the Roman youth. In the year one thousand three hundred and thirty-two, a bull-feast, after the fashion of the Moors and Spaniards, was celebrated in the Coliseum itself; and the living manners are painted in a diary of the times.[58] A convenient order of benches was restored; and a general proclamation, as far as Rimini and Ravenna, invited the nobles to exercise their skill and courage in this perilous adventure. The Roman ladies were marshalled in three squadrons, and seated in three balconies, which on this day, the third of September, were lined with scarlet cloth. The fair Jacova di Rovere led the matrons from beyond the Tyber, a pure and native race, who still represent the features and character of antiquity. The remainder of the city was divided as usual between the Colonna and Ursini: the two factions were proud of the number and beauty of their female bands: the charms of Savella Ursini are mentioned with praise; and the Colonna regretted the absence of the youngest of their house, who had sprained her ancle in the garden of Nero's tower. The lots of the champions were drawn by an old and respectable citizen; and they descended into the *arena*, or pit, to encounter the wild-bulls, on foot as it should seem, with a single spear. Amidst the crowd, our annalist has selected the names, colours, and devices, of twenty of the most conspicuous knights. Several of the names are the most illustrious of Rome, and the ecclesiastical state; Malatesta, Polenta, della Valle, Cafarello, Savelli, Capoccio, Conti, Annibaldi, Altieri, Corsi; the colours were adapted to their taste and situation; the devices are expressive of hope or despair, and breathe the spirit of gallantry and arms. "I am alone, like the youngest of the

A bull-feast in the Coliseum, A.D. 1332, September 3.

56. The *Pallium*, which Menage so foolishly derives from *Palmarium*, is an easy extension of the idea and the words, from the robe or cloak, to the materials, and from thence to their application as a prize (Muratori, dissert. xxxiii.).

57. For these expences, the Jews of Rome paid each year 1130 florins, of which the odd thirty represented the pieces of silver for which Judas had betrayed his master to their ancestors. There was a foot-race of Jewish, as well as of Christian youths (Statuta Urbis, ibidem).

58. This extraordinary bull-feast in the Coliseum, is described from tradition, rather than memory, by Ludovico Buonconte Monaldesco, in the most ancient fragments of Roman annals (Muratori, Script. Rerum Italicarum, tom. xii. p. 535, 536.): and however fanciful they may seem, they are deeply marked with the colours of truth and nature.

Horatii," the confidence of an intrepid stranger: "I live disconsolate," a weeping widower: "I burn under the ashes," a discreet lover: "I adore Lavinia, or Lucretia," the ambiguous declaration of a modern passion: "My faith is as pure," the motto of a white livery: "Who is stronger than myself?" of a lion's hide: "If I am drowned in blood, what a pleasant death," the wish of ferocious courage. The pride or prudence of the Ursini restrained them from the field, which was occupied by three of their hereditary rivals, whose inscriptions denoted the lofty greatness of the Colonna name: "Though sad, I am strong:" "Strong as I am great:" "If I fall," addressing himself to the spectators, "you fall with me:" – intimating (says the contemporary writer) that while the other families were the subjects of the Vatican, they alone were the supporters of the Capitol. The combats of the amphitheatre were dangerous and bloody. Every champion successively encountered a wild bull; and the victory may be ascribed to the quadrupedes, since no more than eleven were left on the field, with the loss of nine wounded and eighteen killed on the side of their adversaries. Some of the noblest families might mourn, but the pomp of the funerals, in the churches of St. John Lateran and St. Maria Maggiore, afforded a second holiday to the people. Doubtless it was not in such conflicts that the blood of the Romans should have been shed; yet in blaming their rashness, we are compelled to applaud their gallantry; and the noble volunteers, who display their magnificence, and risk their lives, under the balconies of the fair, excite a more generous sympathy than the thousands of captives and malefactors who were reluctantly dragged to the scene of slaughter.[59].

Injuries,

This use of the amphitheatre was a rare, perhaps a singular, festival: the demand for the materials was a daily and continual want, which the citizens could gratify without restraint or remorse. In the fourteenth century, a scandalous act of concord secured to both factions the privilege of extracting stones from the free and common quarry of the Coliseum;[60] and Poggius laments that the greater part of these stones had been burnt to lime by the folly of the Romans.[61] To check this abuse,

59. Muratori has given a separate dissertation (the xxix[th]) to the games of the Italians in the middle ages.

60. In a concise but instructive memoir, the abbé Barthelemy (Memoires de l'Academie des Inscriptions, tom. xxviii. p. 585.) has mentioned this agreement of the factions of the xiv[th] century, de Tiburtino faciendo in the Coliseum, from an original act in the archives of Rome.

61. Coliseum ... ob stultitiam Romanorum *majori ex parte* ad calcem deletum, says the indignant Poggius (p. 17.): but his expression, too strong for the present age, must be very tenderly applied to the xv[th] century.

and to prevent the nocturnal crimes that might be perpetrated in the vast and gloomy recess, Eugenius the fourth surrounded it with a wall; and, by a charter long extant, granted both the ground and edifice to the monks of an adjacent convent.[62] After his death, the wall was overthrown in a tumult of the people; and had they themselves respected the noblest monument of their fathers, they might have justified the resolve that it should never be degraded to private property. The inside was damaged; but in the middle of the sixteenth century, an æra of taste and learning, the exterior circumference of one thousand six hundred and twelve feet was still entire and inviolate; a triple elevation of fourscore arches, which rose to the height of one hundred and eight feet. Of the present ruin, the nephews of Paul the third are the guilty agents; and every traveller who views the Farnese palace may curse the sacrilege and luxury of these upstart princes.[63] A similar reproach is applied to the Barberini; and the repetition of injury might be dreaded from every reign, till the Coliseum was placed under the safeguard of religion, by the most liberal of the pontiffs, Benedict the fourteenth, who consecrated a spot which persecution and fable had stained with the blood of so many Christian martyrs.[64]

and consecration of the Coliseum.

Ignorance and barbarism of the Romans.

When Petrarch first gratified his eyes with a view of those monuments, whose scattered fragments so far surpass the most eloquent descriptions, he was astonished at the supine indifference[65] of the Romans themselves;[66] he was humbled rather than

62. Of the Olivetan monks, Montfaucon (p. 142.) affirms this fact from the memorials of Flaminius Vacca (N° 72.). They still hoped, on some future occasion, to revive and vindicate their grant.

63. After measuring the priscus amphitheatri gyrus, Montfaucon (p. 142.) only adds, that it was entire under Paul III.; tacendo clamat. Muratori (Annali d'Italia, tom. xiv. p. 371.) more freely reports the guilt of the Farnese pope, and the indignation of the Roman people. Against the nephews of Urban VIII. I have no other evidence than the vulgar saying, "Quod non fecerunt Barbari, fecere Barbarini," which was perhaps suggested by the resemblance of the words.

64. As an antiquarian and a priest, Montfaucon thus deprecates the ruin of the Coliseum: Quôd si non suopte merito atque pulchritudine dignum fuisset quod improbas arceret manus, indigna res utique in locum tot martyrum cruore sacrum tantopere sævitum esse.

65. Yet the Statutes of Rome (l. iii. c. 81. p. 182.) impose a fine of 500 *aurei* on whosoever shall demolish any ancient edifice, ne ruinis civitas deformetur, et ut antiqua ædificia decorem urbis perpetuo representent.

66. In his first visit to Rome (A.D. 1337. See Memoires sur Petrarque, tom. i. p. 322, &c.), Petrarch is struck mute miraculo rerum tantarum, et stuporis mole obrutus ... Præsentia vero, mirum dictû, nihil imminuit: vere major fuit Roma majoresque sunt reliquiæ quam rebar. Jam non orbem ab hâc urbe domitum, sed tam sero domitum, miror (Opp. p. 605. Familiares, ii. 14. Joanni Columnæ).

elated by the discovery, that, except his friend Rienzi and one of the Colonna, a stranger of the Rhône was more conversant with these antiquities than the nobles and natives of the metropolis.[67] The ignorance and credulity of the Romans are elaborately displayed in the old survey of the city which was composed about the beginning of the thirteenth century; and, without dwelling on the manifold errors of name and place, the legend of the Capitol[68] may provoke a smile of contempt and indignation. "The Capitol," says the anonymous writer, "is so named as being the head of the world; where the consuls and senators formerly resided for the government of the city and the globe. The strong and lofty walls were covered with glass and gold, and crowned with a roof of the richest and most curious carving. Below the citadel stood a palace, of gold for the greatest part, decorated with precious stones, and whose value might be esteemed at one third of the world itself. The statues of all the provinces were arranged in order, each with a small bell suspended from its neck; and such was the contrivance of art or magic,[69] that if the province rebelled against Rome, the statue turned round to that quarter of the heavens, the bell rang, the prophet of the Capitol reported the prodigy, and the senate was admonished of the impending danger." A second example of less importance, though of equal absurdity, may be drawn from the two marble horses, led by two naked youths, which have since been transported from the baths of Constantine to the Quirinal hill. The groundless application of the names of Phidias and Praxiteles may perhaps be excused; but these Grecian sculptors should not have been removed above four hundred years from the age of Pericles to that of Tiberius: they should not have been transformed into two philosophers

67. He excepts and praises the *rare* knowledge of John Colonna. Qui enim hodie magis ignari rerum Romanarum, quam Romani cives? Invitus dico nusquam minus Roma cognoscitur quam Romæ.

68. After the description of the Capitol, he adds, statuæ erant quot sunt mundi provinciæ; et habebat quælibet tintinnabulum ad collum. Et erant ita per magicam artem dispositæ, ut quando aliqua regio Romano Imperio rebellis erat, statim imago illius provinciæ vertebat se contra illam; unde tintinnabulum resonabat quod pendebat ad collum; tuncque vates Capitolii qui erant custodes senatui, &c. He mentions an example of the Saxons and Suevi, who, after they rebelled: tintinnabulum sonuit; sacerdos qui erat in speculo in hebdomadâ senatoribus nuntiavit: Agrippa marched back and reduced the — Persians (Anonym. in Montfaucon, p. 297, 298.).

69. The same writer affirms, that Virgil captus a Romanis invisibiliter exiit, ivitque Neapolim. A Roman magician, in the xi[th] century, is introduced by William of Malmsbury (de Gestis Regum Anglorum, l. ii. p. 86.); and in the time of Flaminius Vacca (N° 81. 103.) it was the vulgar belief that the strangers (the *Goths*) invoked the dæmons for the discovery of hidden treasures.

or magicians, whose nakedness was the symbol of truth and knowledge, who revealed to the emperor his most secret actions; and, after refusing all pecuniary recompense, solicited the honour of leaving this eternal monument of themselves.[70] Thus awake to the power of magic, the Romans were insensible to the beauties of art: no more than five statues were visible to the eyes of Poggius; and of the multitudes which chance or design had buried under the ruins, the resurrection was fortunately delayed till a safer and more enlightened age.[71] The Nile, which now adorns the Vatican, had been explored by some labourers in digging a vineyard near the temple, or convent, of the Minerva; but the impatient proprietor, who was tormented by some visits of curiosity, restored the unprofitable marble to its former grave.[72] The discovery of a statue of Pompey, ten feet in length, was the occasion of a law-suit. It had been found under a partition-wall: the equitable judge had pronounced, that the head should be separated from the body to satisfy the claims of the contiguous owners; and the sentence would have been executed, if the intercession of a cardinal, and the liberality of a pope, had not rescued the Roman hero from the hands of his barbarous countrymen.[73]

Restoration and ornaments of the city, A.D. 1420, &c.

But the clouds of barbarism were gradually dispelled; and the peaceful authority of Martin the fifth and his successors, restored the ornaments of the city as well as the order of the ecclesiastical state. The improvements of Rome, since the fifteenth century, have not been the spontaneous produce of freedom and industry. The first and most natural root of a great city, is the labour and populousness of the adjacent country, which supplies the materials of subsistence, of manufactures, and of foreign trade. But the greater part of the Campagna of Rome is reduced to a dreary and desolate

70. Anonym. p. 289. Montfaucon (p. 191.) justly observes, that if Alexander be represented, these statues cannot be the work of Phidias (Olympiad lxxxiii.) or Praxiteles (Olympiad civ.), who lived before that conqueror (Plin. Hist. Natur. xxxiv. 19.).

71. William of Malmsbury (l. ii. p. 86, 87.) relates a marvellous discovery (A.D. 1046) of Pallus, the son of Evander, who had been slain by Turnus; the perpetual light in his sepulchre, a Latin epitaph, the corpse, yet entire, of a young giant, the enormous wound in his breast (pectus perforat ingens), &c. If this fable rests on the slightest foundation, we may pity the bodies, as well as the statues, that were exposed to the air in a barbarous age.

72. Prope porticum Minervæ, statua est recubantis, cujus caput integrâ effigie, tantæ magnitudinis, ut signa omnia excedat. Quidam ad plantandos arbores scrobes faciens detexit. Ad hoc visendum cum plures in dies magis concurrerent, strepitum adeuntium fastidiumque pertæsus, horti patronus congestâ humo texit (Poggius de Varietate Fortunæ, p. 12.).

73. See the Memorials of Flaminius Vacca, N° 57. p. 11, 12. at the end of the Roma Antica of Nardini (1704, in 4to).

wilderness: the overgrown estates of the princes and the clergy are cultivated by the lazy hands of indigent and hopeless vassals; and the scanty harvests are confined or exported for the benefit of a monopoly. A second and more artificial cause of the growth of a metropolis, is the residence of a monarch, the expence of a luxurious court, and the tributes of dependent provinces. Those provinces and tributes had been lost in the fall of the empire: and if some streams of the silver of Peru and the gold of Brasil have been attracted by the Vatican; the revenues of the cardinals, the fees of office, the oblations of pilgrims and clients, and the remnant of ecclesiastical taxes, afford a poor and precarious supply, which maintains however the idleness of the court and city. The population of Rome, far below the measure of the great capitals of Europe, does not exceed one hundred and seventy thousand inhabitants;[74] and within the spacious inclosure of the walls, the largest portion of the seven hills is overspread with vineyards and ruins. The beauty and splendour of the modern city may be ascribed to the abuses of the government, to the influence of superstition. Each reign (the exceptions are rare) has been marked by the rapid elevation of a new family, enriched by the childless pontiff at the expence of the church and country. The palaces of these fortunate nephews are the most costly monuments of elegance and servitude; the perfect arts of architecture, painting, and sculpture, have been prostituted in their service, and their galleries and gardens are decorated with the most precious works of antiquity, which taste or vanity has prompted them to collect. The ecclesiastical revenues were more decently employed by the popes themselves in the pomp of the Catholic worship; but it is superfluous to enumerate their pious foundations of altars, chapels, and churches, since these lesser stars are eclipsed by the sun of the Vatican, by the dome of St. Peter, the most glorious structure that ever has been applied to the use of religion. The fame of Julius the second, Leo the tenth, and Sixtus the fifth, is accompanied by the superior merit of Bramante and Fontana, of Raphael and Michael-Angelo: and the same munificence which had been displayed in palaces and temples, was directed with equal zeal to revive and emulate the labours of antiquity. Prostrate obelisks were raised from the ground, and erected in the most conspicuous places; of the eleven aqueducts of

74. In the year 1709, the inhabitants of Rome (without including eight or ten thousand Jews) amounted to 138,568 souls (Labat, Voyages en Espagne et en Italie, tom. iii. p. 217, 218.). In 1740 they had increased to 146,080; and in 1765, I left them, without the Jews, 161,899. I am ignorant whether they have since continued in a progressive state.

the Cæsars and consuls, three were restored; the artificial rivers were conducted over a long series of old, or of new, arches, to discharge into marble basins a flood of salubrious and refreshing waters: and the spectator, impatient to ascend the steps of St. Peter's, is detained by a column of Egyptian granite, which rises between two lofty and perpetual fountains, to the height of one hundred and twenty feet. The map, the description, the monuments of ancient Rome, have been elucidated by the diligence of the antiquarian and the student:[75] and the footsteps of heroes, the relics, not of superstition, but of empire, are devoutly visited by a new race of pilgrims from the remote, and once savage, countries of the North.

Final conclusion. Of these pilgrims, and of every reader, the attention will be excited by an history of the decline and fall of the Roman empire; the greatest, perhaps, and most awful scene, in the history of mankind. The various causes and progressive effects are connected with many of the events most interesting in human annals: the artful policy of the Cæsars, who long maintained the name and image of a free republic; the disorders of military despotism; the rise, establishment, and sects of Christianity; the foundation of Constantinople; the division of the monarchy; the invasion and settlements of the Barbarians of Germany and Scythia; the institutions of the civil law; the character and religion of Mahomet; the temporal sovereignty of the popes; the restoration and decay of the Western empire of Charlemagne; the crusades of the Latins in the East; the conquests of the Saracens and Turks; the ruin of the Greek empire; the state and revolutions of Rome in the middle age. The

75. The Pere Montfaucon distributes his own observations into twenty days, he should have styled them weeks, or months, of his visits to the different parts of the city (Diarium Italicum, c. 8–20. p. 104–301.). That learned Benedictine reviews the topographers of ancient Rome; the first efforts of Blondus, Fulvius, Martianus, and Faunus, the superior labours of Pyrrhus Ligorius, had his learning been equal to his labours; the writings of Onuphrius Panvinius, qui omnes obscuravit, and the recent but imperfect books of Donatus and Nardini. Yet Montfaucon still sighs for a more complete plan and description of the old city, which must be attained by the three following methods: 1. The measurement of the space and intervals of the ruins. 2. The study of inscriptions, and the places where they were found. 3. The investigation of all the acts, charters, diaries of the middle ages, which name any spot or building of Rome. The laborious work, such as Montfaucon desired, must be promoted by princely or public munificence: but the great modern plan of Nolli (A.D. 1748) would furnish a solid and accurate basis for the ancient topography of Rome.

historian may applaud the importance and variety of his subject; but, while he is conscious of his own imperfections, he must often accuse the deficiency of his materials. It was among the ruins of the Capitol, that I first conceived the idea of a work which has amused and exercised near twenty years of my life, and which, however inadequate to my own wishes, I finally deliver to the curiosity and candour of the Public.

LAUSANNE,
June 27, 1787.

APPENDIX I

Deviations from Copy Text

The copy texts for volumes 5 and 6 are the first editions of 1788 (*1788*). These have been corrected as specified below. The form of the entries is the same as in appendix 2 to volume 1.

Ch. XLVIII

74; Turkish camp,] Turkish campaign,
74; and the fifteenth] and, in the fifteenth

Ch. XLIX

87; he skull] the skull
90; nich] niche
101, n. 37; defensensione] defensione
116, n. 71; Farsense] Farfense
116, n. 72; 580.] 580.).
116, n. 75; offered] offered by
117, n. 76; chose] chose que
117, n. 76; lengono] tengono
137; Vatican an] Vatican and
142, n. 142; bones] flesh
143; counts] abbots

Ch. L

151; koran] Koran
157, n. 20; Sural] Surat
160, n. 30; ridicuously] ridiculously
160, n. 30; Holtinger,] Hottinger,
161; meanner] meaner
161, n. 32; de] (de
161, n. 32; tom,] tom.
166; a honoured] an honoured

167; line nor] linen or
170, n. 58; de] et
177, n. 75; Holtinger,] Hottinger,
177, n. 76; c. 4.] (c. 4.
184, n. 99; Holtinger,] Hottinger,
193; 662.] 622.
211; bid] bade *G. MS*
216, n. 162; pœnis] penis

Ch. LI

240, n. 19; 16th] (16th
248; Bocara,] Bochara,
249, n. 46; Paw] Pauw
255; koran] Koran
271; war degraded] was degraded
279, n. 103; l'Egypt] l'Egypte
279, n. 106; Nieubuhr] Niebuhr
288, n. 129; Mason's,] Mason's
296; others] other's
307, n. 179; tables,] table,
311, n. 187; Conimbra] Coimbra

Ch. LII

324, n. 2; Constantinah] Constantin.
327; Walid sat] Waled sat
329, n. 12; eat,] ate,
341, n. 37; Dioclesian] Diocletian
342; 1755.] 755.
342, n. 37; caussam] causam
343, n. 43; it] it is
344, n. 43; Christain] Christian
357; Sicily[83]] Sicily[82]
363, n. 91; circumstance] circumstances
365, n. 96; Theophilus] Theophilus,
366; paricide,] parricide,
366, n. 100; Mostanser,] Montasser,

Ch. LIII

379, n. 3; Deslisle,] Delisle
386; free -Laconians.[16]] free-Laconians.[16]
394; steward, of the public] steward of the public,
395; *Panhypersebastor;*] *Panhypersebastos;*
395; amy.] army.

399, n. 53; Codin,] Codin.
400, n. 58; Famiilæ Byzantine] Familiæ Byzantinæ
401, n. 62; *Ουγονως*).] *Ουγονως*.
408, n. 78; Tactic,] Tactic.
419, n. 109; Greca] Græca

Ch. LIV

429, n. 15; martydom] martyrdom

Ch. LV

441; Borythenes,] Borysthenes,
455, n. 45, 458, n. 50, 460, n. 55, 461, n. 59, 461, n. 62; Leveque] Levesque
444; Christian,] Christian?
444; "it] "It
444; peace.] peace?
448, n. 26; Leveque] Levesque
454, n. 42 Geisla] Geisa
457, n. 48; (Glossar] (Glossar.
458, n. 50; remain] remains
468, endignantly] indignantly
469, n. 80; Elzeivir:] Elzevir:

Ch. LVI

471, n. 1; Mark,] Marc,
479; assimilitated] assimilated
479, n. 19 quoscunque] quoscumque
490, n. 47; Lettetura] Letteratura
515, n. 118; Nihilhominus] Nihilominus
520, n. 136; Siculi in ter] Siculi inter

Ch. LVII

525; Dehli,] Delhi,
525, n. 6, n. 7; Hindoostan] Hindostan
527, n. 9; Dehli,] Delhi,
536, n. 30; Deslile,] Delisle,
536, n. 32; exhanged] exchanged
551, n. 68; Nieubuhr] Niebuhr
552, n. 71; Kartona] Katona

Ch. LVIII

573; Tyrensis] Tyriensis
580, n. 58; &c.] &c.).
590, n. 80; 1192] 1092 *G. MS*
590, n. 82; Herman] Hernan *G. MS*
602; a idle] an idle
603; described] descried *G. MS*
608, n. 119; xxi.] xxi.)
613, n. 142; peuble] peuple

Ch. LIX

618, n. 13; Cinnanum,] Cinnamum,
652; condems] condemns *G. MS*

Ch. LX

679; Grece] Greece
681; former affirmed] latter affirmed
681; latter might] former might
691, n. 86; nec, ætati] nec ætati,
691, n. 86; maritatas] maritatas
698, n. 103; Rhamnusus] Rhamnusius *G. MS*

Ch. LXI

703, n. 12; Villehardoin] Villehardouin
712, n. 32; Maximianoplis,] Maximianopolis
719, n. 47; 77.] 77.).
726; wind-mills[65]] windmills[65]
727, n. 66; Greeks,] Greek, *G. MS*
729; ranks f] ranks of
735; dispise] despise

Ch. LXII

758; has] hast
761, n. 49; ten cartas,] ten carats,

Ch. LXIII

781, n. 35; virtues,] virtue,
781, n. 35; it's] its

785, n. 42; Montfauçon,] Montfaucon
790; epistle,] epistle, [54]

Ch. LXIV

794; koran] Koran
794, n. 7; Petit] Petis
802; hastened] hastening *G. MS*
803; Bata] Bela *G. MS*
814; pavillon] pavillion
820, n. 61; 28.);]28.),
821, n. 63; afterwards afterwards] afterwards *G. MS*

Ch. LXV

826, n. 1; native,] native of Yezd, *G. MS*
826, n. 3; Turki] Turkish
835, n. 26; 99.] 99.).
841, n. 43; Dehli,] Delhi,
847; province] provinces
847; sovereigns.] sovereign.
850; for intranquil] in the tranquil *G. MS*
850; hast] has *G. MS*
861; leap] leap,

Ch. LXVI

867, n. 4; reliogoso;] religioso;
871, n. 12; Inghliterra] Inghilterra
873, n. 19; 556.).] 556.
869; transferred] transfers
879; she design] the design
885; fortune;] fortune,
900; manner;] manners;
901, n. 96; affiming] affirming
906; iterature] literature
908, n. 116; Manutus,] Manutius,

Ch. LXVII

913, n. 6; 1440–30.).] 1440–50.).
921; fortune.] fortune?
929, n. 43; (Annali,] (Annali

Ch. LXVIII

939; [36]] [13]
939; yet he power,] ye the power,
946, n. 30; numerou] numerous
958, n. 42; larger] the larger
963, n. 63; Chaloccondyles] Chalcocondyles
963, n. 64; captives (Herodotus,] captives. Herodotus (

Ch. LXIX

982, n. 8; nihillominus] nihilominus
986; know how] know not how
987, n. 21; ABE'LARD] ABÉLARD
992, n. 34; eslablishment] establishment
994, n. 40; hominium,] hominum,
996; statesmen,] statesman,
996, n. 46; *Occulus*] *Oculus*
1001; besiged] besieged
1003, n. 63; Albananses,] Albanenses,
1005, n. 70; concilio,] concilio),
1010, n. 84; iv^{2},] iv^{ta},
1017, n. 105; iii. p. .)] iii.)
1017, n. 105; Celestine III.] Celestin III.
1018, n. 109; savente] sovente

Ch. LXX

1019; taste] judgement *G. MS*
1020, n. 10; quinquenale,] quinquennale,
1023, n. 21; suoco] suono
1036, n. 44; solidumq;] solidumque
1040, n. 53; cars] ears
1045, n. 64; Harlay] Harley
1051, n. 77; Metallic] Medallic
1056, n. 87; autres autres] autres
1060, n. 98; Romana] Romano

Ch. LXXI

1068, n. 19; memorablein undations] memorable inundations
1070, n. 27; Monfaucon] Montfaucon
1071, n. 31; desæeirent.] desævirent.
1081; art magic,] art or magic,

APPENDIX 2
Gibbon's Marginalia

Two sets of *The Decline and Fall* in the British Library contain extensive marginalia in Gibbon's hand. Those in C.60.m.1 were made probably in 1790/1; those in C.135.h.3 are harder to date. (Patricia Craddock speculated on the date and purpose of the marginalia in C.60.m.1 in 'Gibbon's Revision of the *Decline and Fall*', *Studies in Bibliography*, 21 [1968], 191–204; and she reprinted a selection of the marginalia in that set in *The English Essays of Edward Gibbon* [Oxford, 1972], 338–52.) All marginalia in both sets are printed below. The volume, page, note (where appropriate) and line numbers, if unbracketed, refer to the present edition; those in square brackets refer to the original volumes. ^ is the symbol used by Gibbon to indicate an insertion point.

C.60.m.1

In this set there are marginalia in all volumes, except volume 3, though the nature of the marginalia differs markedly from volume to volume. The early pages of volume 1 are heavily marked with substantial comments, and there are no corrections of accidentals. Thereafter, the marginalia are less the result of major rethinking than of a desire to tidy the text of misprints and inaccuracies. [. . .] indicates a lacuna caused by the trimming of the page; see the headnote to *C.135.h.3* below for an explanation of how these lacunae were caused.

i, 31, 14 [1, 1, 15]
empire;] ^empire;

In margin:
^times

In margin and at foot:
+ Should I not have given the history of that fortunate period which was interposed between two Iron ages? Should I not have deduced the decline of the Empire from the civil Wars, that ensued after the fall of Nero or even from the tyranny which succeeded the reign of Augustus? Alas! I should: but of what avail is this tardy knowledge? Where error is irretrievable, repentance is useless.

i, 31, 15–17 [1, 2, 1–3]
to . . . earth.] ^^ ~~to . . .~~ ^^ ~~a . . . earth.~~

In margin:
^^"to prosecute the decline and fall of the Empire of Rome: of whose language, Religion and laws the impression will be long preserved in our own, and the neighbouring countries of Europe." N.B. Mr. Hume told me that in correcting his history, he always laboured to reduce superlatives, and soften positives. Have Asia and Africa, from Japan to Morocco, any feeling or memory of the Roman Empire?

i, 31, 22–3 [1, 2, 9]
a . . . triumphs;] a . . . triumphs;

In margin:
Excursion I, on the succession of Roman triumphs

i, 32, 20 [1, 3, 12]
boundaries;] boundaries+;

In margin:
+.Incertum metû an per invidiam (Tacit. Annal. I. ii) Why must rational advice be imputed to a base or foolish motives? To what cause, error, malevolence or flattery shall I ascribe this unworthy alternative? Was the historian dazzled by Trajan's conquests?

i, 35, 12 [1, 6, 23]
soul [15].] soul [15]. +

In margin:
+.Julian assigns this Theological cause of whose power he himself might be conscious ~~himself~~ (Caesares p 327.) Yet I am not assured that the Religion of Zamolxis subsisted in the time of Trajan, or that his Dacians were the same people with the Getæ of Herodotus. The transmigration of the Soul has been believed by many ~~other~~ nations, warlike as the Celts, or pusillanimous like the Hindoos. When speculative opinion is ~~kindlet~~ kindled into practical enthusiasm, its operation will be determined by the prævious character of the man or the nation.

i, 35, 28 [1, 7, 16]
benefactors,] benefactors, +

In margin:
+The first place in the temple of fame is due and is assigned to the successful heroes who had struggled with adversity; who, after signalizing their valour in the deliverance of their country have displayed their wisdom and virtue in foundation or government of a flourishing state Such men as Moses, Cyrus Alfred, Gustavus Vasa Henry iv of France &c.

i, 35, 29–32 [1, 7, 18–22]
characters . . . he] ^^ ~~characters . . . he~~

At foot:
^minds. Late generations, and far distant climates may impute their calamities to the immortal author of the Iliad. The spirit of Alexander was inflamed by the praises of Achilles: and succeeding Heroes have been ambitious to tread in the footsteps of Alexander. Like him the Emperor Trajan aspired to the conquest of the East; but ~~he lamen~~ the Roman lamented with a sigh &c

i, 39, 6 [1, 11, 24]
South:] South+:

At foot:
+ The distinction of North and South is real and intelligible; and our pursuit is terminated on either side by the poles of the Earth. But the difference of East and West is arbitrary, and shifts round the globe. As the men of the North not of the West the legions of Gaul and Germany were superior to the south-eastern natives of Asia and Egypt. It is the triumph of cold over heat; which may however and has been surmounted by moral causes.

i, 41, 27 [1, 15, 12]
centurions.] centurions. +

In margin and at foot:
+ The composition of the Roman officers was very faulty. 1. It was late before a Tribune was fixed to each cohort. Six tribunes were chosen for the entire legion, which two of them commanded by turns (Polyb. L vi p 526 Edit Schweighæuser) for the space of two months. 2. Our long subordination from the Colonel to the Corporal was unknown. I cannot discern any intermediate ranks between the Tribune and the Centurion the Centurion, and the Manipularis or private legionary. 3 As the Tribunes were often without experience, the Centurions were often without education, mere soldiers of fortune who had risen from the ranks (eo immitior, quia toleraverat. Tacit. Annal i.20). A body equal to eight or nine of our battalions might be commanded by half a dozen young gentlemen and fifty or sixty old serjeants Like the legion, our great ships of war may seem ill-provided with officers: but in both cases the deficiency is corrected by strong principles of discipline and vigour.

i, 43, n. 53, 1–2 [1, 17, n. 53, 1–2]
As . . . Agricola.] ~~As . . . Agricola.~~^

In margin and at foot:
53^Quôd mihi pareret legio Romana Tribuno. (Horat Serm. L i.vi, 45); a worthy commander, of three and twenty from the schools of Athens! Augustus was indulgent to noble birth, liberis Senatorum . . . militiam auspicantibus non tribunatum modo legionum, sed et præfecturas alarum dedit (Sueton. C 38)

i, 54, n. 86, 7–8 [1, 32, n. 86, 7–8]
a . . . sea,] a . . . sea,

In margin and at foot:
More correctly, according to Mr Bouguer, 2500 Toises (Buffon Supplement Tom. V p 304). The height of Mont Blanc is now fixed at 2426 Toises. (Saussure Voyage dans les

Alpes Tom i p 495): but the lowest ground from whence it can be seen is itself greatly elevated above the level of the sea. He who sails by the isle of Teneriff, contemplates the entire Pike, from the foot to the summit.

i, 863 [2, 353]

In margin:
το τεχνιον πασα γαια τρεφει was the boast and comfort of Nero the musician (Sueton. C 40). But the applause of venal or trembling crowds was dispelled by the first manifesto of the Rebels, which pronounced him a most execrable performer; ~~and~~ (C 41) and could he have survived his descent from the throne, it is more than probable, that he would have been soon hissed from the stage. The present King of N is satisfied that, in case of a revolution, he could subsist by the trade of a fisherman or a pastry-cook. Perhaps he would be disappointed. The amusement of a hour must not contend with the labour of a life. Frederic alone, of the monarchs of the age, was capable, like Julian, of making his own fortune

ii, 527 [4, iv]
should . . . still] ~~should . . . still~~
crown.] crown. +

In margin:
[. . .] ve been silent, as long [. . .] he

At foot:
+ In the years 1776 when I published the first Volume, in 1781 when I published the second and third, Lord North was first Lord of the treasury. I was his friend and follower, a Member of parliament and a Lord of trade: but I disdained to sink the Scholar in the politician.

ii, 540, n. 22, 1 [4, 13, n. 22, 3]
προτιω] *προτιῳ*

In margin:
/

ii, 545, n. 46, 5 [4, 20, n. 46, 5]
dromonibas,] dromonib~~a~~s,

In margin:
/u

ii, 547, n. 55, 8 [4, 22, n. 55, 8]
Cotlian] Cot~~l~~ian

In margin:
/t

ii, 581, 26 [4, 67, 4]
finance;] finance$^{\vee}_{\wedge}$;

In margin:
$^{\vee}_{\wedge}$s

ii, 595, n. 88, 6 [4, 85, n. 88, 6]
Cain,] $^{\vee}_{\wedge}$Cain,

In margin:
$^{\vee}_{\wedge}$of

ii, 605 [4, 98], shoulder note
Fortification] Fortification$^{\vee}_{\wedge}$

In margin:
$^{\vee}_{\wedge}$s

ii, 609, 13 [4, 103, 3]
piety [122].] piety [~~122~~].

In margin:
/del.

ii, 103, 16 [4, 103, 6]
retainers.] retainers.$^{\vee}_{\wedge}$

In margin:
$^{\vee}_{\wedge}$122

ii, 617, 2 [4, 112, 22]
and his] and $^{\vee}_{\wedge}$his

In margin:
$^{\vee}_{\wedge}$that

ii, 629, 31 [4, 129, 23]
patrons.] patron~~s~~.

In margin:
/del s

ii, 955, 7 [4, 553, 28]
partia] partia$^{\vee}_{\wedge}$

In margin:
$^{\vee}_{\wedge}$l

ii, 966, n. 63, 1 [4, 568, n. 63, 1]
περι βοητος] *περι‿βοητος*

In margin:
/

ii, 966, n. 63, 15 [4, 569, n. 63, 14]
Ειρηρη] *Ειρηρη*

In margin:
/ν

iii, 211, 8 [5, 247, 13]
bid] ~~bid~~‸

In margin:
‸bade

iii, 304, 13 [5, 367, 13]
that . . . sea.] ‸~~that . . . sea.~~

In margin:
‸and small isle on the western side of the bay of Gibraltar

iii, 590, n. 80, 2 [6, 41, n. 80, 5]
1192] 1~~1~~92

In margin:
/o

iii, 590, n. 82, 3 [6, 42, n. 82, 3]
Herman] Her~~m~~an

In margin:
/n

iii, 603, 3 [6, 57, 27]
described] descri~~b~~ed

In margin:
/del. b

iii, 632, 22 [6, 93, 15]
despoised] despoi~~s~~ed

In margin:
/l

iii, 652, 6 [6, 117, 15]
condems] condem‸s

In margin:
‸n

iii, 698, n. 103, 3 [6, 173, n. 103, 13]
Rhamnusus,] Rhamnus‸us,

In margin:
‸i

iii, 727, n. 66, 4 [6, 208, n. 66, 4]
Greeks,] Greek~~s~~,

In margin:
/del. s

iii, 727, 15 [6, 209, 5]
Palestine [67];] Palestine ~~[67]~~;

iii, 727, 16 [6, 209, 6]
visions.] visions.‸

In margin:
‸A cross, or a crown of thorns might be easily transported; since the house of the Virgin Mary was carried through the air two thousand miles, from Nazareth to Loretto[67], a perpetual monument[67^2] of priestly fraud, and popular credulity.[67^3]

iii, 727, 23 [6, 209, 14]
fable.] fable.[67^4]

iii, 727, n. 67, 1 [6, 209, n. 67, 1]
67] ~~67~~

In margin:
67 [4]

iii, 727, n. 67, 4–7 [6, 209, n. 67, 3–6]
I . . . Palestine.] ~~I . . . Palestine~~.

iii, 735, 33 [6, 219, 16]
dispise] d~~i~~spise
In margin:
/e

iii, 794, 6 [6, 291, 27–8]
the . . . Tartars] ^~~the . . . Tartars~~

In margin:
^the præceptors of the North, his native subjects

iii, 794, 9 [6, 292, 3]
their domestic annals] ~~their domestic annals~~

In margin:
^the Mogul annals

iii, 794, 10 [6, 292, 3]
Chinese[8],] ^Chinese[8],

In margin:
^Japanese[7^2]

iii, 795, 2 [6, 293, 2]
defeats[18].] defeats~~[18]~~.^

In margin:
^The zeal[17^2] and curiosity [17^3] of Europe soon explored the Empire of the Great Khan; and the monuments of Tartar history have been illustrated by the learning of modern times.[18]

iii, 802, 26 [6, 302, 12]
hastened] hasten~~ed~~

In margin:
/ing

iii, 803, 21 [6, 303, 15]
Bata] ~~Bata~~^

In margin:
^Bela

iii, 821, n. 63, 5 [6, 324, n. 63, 7]
afterwards] ~~afterwards~~

In margin:
/del

iii, 826, n. 1, 2 [6, 331, n. 1, 2]
a native,] a native^,

In margin:
^of Yezd

iii, 850, 5 [6, 360, 21]
for intranquil] ~~for in~~tranquil

In margin:
^in the

iii, 850, 17 [6, 361, 3]
hast] ~~hast~~^

In margin:
^has

iii, 1019, 7 [6, 567, 7]
taste] ^~~taste~~

In margin:
^judgement

C.135.h.3

In this set there are marginalia in only volume 1. When Gibbon annotated this copy, the leaves were still uncut, and he wrote close to the edge and foot of the page. When the leaves were subsequently trimmed by a binder, leaves bearing marginal comments were left untrimmed, and were folded back so as not to obtrude beyond the side and edge of the volume. However, three leaves bearing marginal comments on the verso were accidentally trimmed, and some of the annotation was therefore lost. In these cases [...] indicates a lacuna caused by the trimming of the page.

i, 53, 26 [1, 31, 14]
inundations.] inundations.^

In margin:
^ 85.[2] Egypt occupies a large space on the Maps; but the soil which is susceptible of cultivation must be reduced to a long narrow valley and to a triangular island (the Delta) divided and perhaps created by the Nile. The cultivated parts of Egypt cannot exceed 2100 square leagues, and are equal only to one twelfth of the Kingdom of France which contains at least 25.000. see d'Anville Description de l'Egypte p 30.

i, 55, 25 [1, 33, 27]
Western] ^ ~~Western~~]

In margin:
^ Atlantic

i, 55, 25 [I, 33, 27]
Euphrates;] Euphrates,^

In margin:
^and the Tigris; 88[2]

In margin and at foot:
88.[2] According to the Geography of Ptolemy that interval affords seventy degrees of Longitude which must be computed in ['~~at~~ *below* 'in'] that Paralel at four thousand two hundred Roman miles. But it has been justly observed that the progress of knowledge tends to enlarge the Cœlestial, and to contract the Terrestrial space. The extent of the Mediterranean was reduced from 1160 to 860 Leagues by the accurate Delisle (Oeuvres de Fontenelle Tom vi p 301 dans son Eloge) Yet the maps of Delisle still remain erroneously large. His Italy contains 13200 square leagues instead of 10650, which form the true size of that Country as it is measured by the masterly hand of d'Anville (Analyse de sa Carte d'Italie p 286) Lewis XIV had reason to say that he lost more land by his Geographers than he gained by his Generals.

i, 70, 2 [I, 52, 4]
persons:] persons^61[2].

i, 70, 4 [I, 52, 6]
government.] government.62[2]

In margin and at foot:
[...] have good authority to [...] at 7.500.000 persons were [...] to the Capitation tax in [...] ithout including the great [...] pulous City of Alexandria [...] de Bell. Jud. L ii C 16 p. 190 [...] Edit Havercamp). From [...] <u>ata</u> afforded by Pliny (Hist. [...] L iii C 4). I should be inclined [...] ed that Spain contained [...] even millions of free Inhabi

There follows a space of approximately one inch presumably separating the text of 61[2] *from 62*[2].

[...] a however may claim ~~an~~ [...] superior degree of population [...] redit can be given to the po: [...] stimony of a Missionary and [...] e. Father Ko asserts that in [...] a legal <u>denombrement</u> was [...] which produced the enormous [...] 198.214.555 persons in the [...] extent of the Chinese Empire. [...] thstanding the notoriety of this [...] should chuse to suspend my [...] till the proofs and circumstances [...] airly stated to the public (see Memoires

^Yet the extreme populousness of China cannot admit of any rational doubt.

i, 75, 35 [I, 59, 26]
three hundred and sixty cities,] ^~~three hundred and sixty~~ cities,

In margin:
^four hundred

i, 76, n. 77 [I, 59, n. 77]
35.] 35.^

The list . . . distinguished.] *scored through vertically.*

In margin, and scored through diagonally:

˅˄Of these, twenty six were Colonies, twenty two had obtained the ~~freedom of the~~ Roman City and fifty more the inferior privileges of Latium.

At foot:

˅˄Of these, twenty six were Colonies; twenty two consisted of Roman Citizens: fifty had obtained the inferior privileges of the Latins; six were distinguished by the title of Free; four were honoured with the name of Allies, and the remainder was composed of two hundred and ninety one Tributary Cities. Besides these, in the province of Tarraconensis alone there were two hundred and ninety four towns or Cities, included within the territory and jurisdiction of some of the former.

i, 95, 18 [1, 85, 18]

The obscure . . . Aricia.] ˅˄~~The obscure name of [Octavianus, he derived from a mean family, in the little town of Aricia.~~]

In margin:

˅˄The descendants of the Patricians and Consuls of ancient Rome might disdain the yoke of an ignoble Master who derived from the little town of Velitræ[24.2] the obscure name of the Octavian family.[24.3]

At foot:

24.[2] One of the Cities of the Volsci in the Country of Latium, distinguished by a bold and obstinate resistance to the arms of Rome from whence it was distant only twenty two miles. see Cluver. ~~Tom. ii p 1~~ Italia Antiq. Tom ii p 1015. The contemptuous Epithet of <u>Aricinus</u>, was used by Marc Antony to stigmatize the maternal descent of his Rival from the town of Aricia; which ~~is~~ on this occasion is placed in a conspicuous light by the eloquence of Cicero. Phillipic. iii. 6.

24.[3] We may observe as an unfavourable symptom, that Virgil never alludes to the Octavian name. The ancestors of Augustus were exalted by flattery into Heroes and Patricians; and degraded by calumny into the vilest Mechanics. The prudent Monarch who despised these opposite exagerations, always declared, that he descended from an old and wealthy family of Equestrian rank, and that his father was the first, who obtained a seat in the Senate. See the accurate Suetonius in the first Chapters of the life of Augustus.

i, 96 [1, 87]

n. 27 *enclosed in a box and crossed out.*

In margin and at foot:

27. The merit or at least the fame of the Ides of March has cast a veil over the faults of the <u>Patriot Assassin</u>. After the battle of Pharsalia, when Cicero was in ~~exile~~ retirement, Marcellus in exile, and Cato in arms, the nephew of Cato submitted tamely to the Conqueror, and ungenerously revealed whatever he knew or suspected of the designs of Pompey. While the standard of Liberty was still flying in Africa, Brutus accepted as the Lieutenant of Caesar the important command of the Cisalpine Gaul, and wantonly exposed his virtue to the alternative of betraying either his trust or his Country. The return of the Conqueror to the insolent triumph which displayed the bleeding Image of

Cato was graced by the attendance of his obsequious Nephew. By ~~cons~~ soliciting the honours and offices which were bestowed by the arbitrary will of a single Man, Brutus consented to the establishment of Tyranny; and he even courted the opportunity of binding himself by a solemn oath to the person and government of Cæsar about three months before he plunged a dagger into his breast. In a much earlier period of his life, the avarice and cruelty of the Usurer Brutus towards his unhappy Debtors of the Isle of Cyprus cannot easily be reconciled with the applauded Character of a friend of justice and of mankind.

i, 184, 14 [I, 200, 20]
state.] state.[109][2]

In margin:
[. . .] e conduct of Augustus was [. . .] egulated by the most disinte- [. . .] inciples. He never accepted the [. . .] of strangers; and he never suf [. . .] friends to deprive their chil: [. . .] any part of their patrimony [. . .] in August. C 66). Yet Augus: [. . .] to declare in his own Will, [. . .] the last twenty years of his [. . .] had received from Testamentary [. . .] aterdecies Millies; fourteen Millions. [. . .] ces, (Id. ib. C 101.); or in English Money £11.786.457. [. . .] wenty years his personal tax would amount to [. . .] ix hundred thousand pounds Sterling.

i, 215, 14–24 [I, 240, I–12]
I. During . . . prophet.] *enclosed in a box and crossed out,* ‸ *inserted before* 'I.'.
n. 7 and n. 8 *enclosed in a box and crossed out.*

i, 216, 10 [I, 241, 3]
ferences with the Deity. Every] [~~ferences with the Deity.~~] ‸Every

n. 9 *crossed out.*

i, 217, 2 [I, 242, 5]
articles] ‸articles
In margin:
‸p
n. 11 and n. 12 *crossed out.*

i, 217 [I, 242–3]
The theology . . . Nature[13].] *enclosed in a box and crossed out.*

i, 217 [I, 243]
n. 13 *enclosed in a box and crossed out.*

i, 240, n. 42 [I, 272, n. 42]
May . . . empire.] *crossed out,* ‸ *after* empire.
In the year . . . xlv.] *enclosed in a box and crossed out.*

In margin:

^As early as ~~Yet in~~ the year 854, when ~~the~~ Arischarius, the first Christian Missionary visited Sweden, the King was reduced to the condition of a Magistrate, vested only with the legal right of summoning the Assemblies, and of executing the decrees, of a popular Legislature: see a very curious detail in the authentic life of Ariscarius written by his successor Archbishop Rembert N°. 47. 48 ap Fleury Hist Eccles. Tom X p 484. 485 In the year 1072, Adam of Bremen (ap. Grotium. Hist Goth. p 102) adds ~~a~~ a remarkable testimony to the freedom of the Swedish Constitution.

i, 321 [1, 376]

n. 78 *crossed out.*

In margin and at foot:

[...] withstanding the traditions [...] and the new World a pure [...] nent Society of Amazons [...] mpatible with the prin: [...] human Nature. Particu: [...] ples of female heroism [...] sted in every age, especi: [...] ong the warlike nations [...] ea and Sarmatia. In the [...] bles of Poland (1764) the [...] sister of Prince Radzivil, fought on horseback by ~~the~~ his side; and managed their sabres [...] much courage and dexterity as the bravest of his Heydamacks. In the heat of a bloody action [...] the Russians, his sister, a young and beautiful woman, distinguished the grace and [...] of an obscure Officer, conceived an instant passion, and married him a few days afterwards

i, 344, n. 53 [1, 405, n. 53]

language;] language;^

246.] 246.^

In margin:

^and the fact must rest on his own authority.

At foot:

^Shall I abuse the privilege of a Note If I dwell for a moment on this interesting subject? The nocturnal ~~warfare~~ victory [*above word crossed out*] of young Hercules ~~with~~ ^~~the fifty~~ [*in margin:* ^ over Fifty Virgins, the] daughters of Thestius has justly been reckoned the most marvellous of his labours, (Diodor. Sicul L 18 p 274. Edit Wesseling. Pausanias L ix p 763. Arnobius L iv p 145).

——Vagæ post crimina Noctis
Thespius obstupuit toties Socer——

Stat Silv. L iii Ep. i V 42.

But the merit of the <u>toties</u> is strangely reduced by some rational Mythologists, who extend the Nuptials of Hercules to seven (Herodotus ap. Athenæum. Deipnosoph. L xiii p 556) or even to fifty, nights (Apollodor ~~Bibliot~~ Hist Poet. ~~L iv~~ L ii C 4. p 96). Mahomet was no more than a Prophet Yet he was able to prove, within the compass of ~~an~~ a single [*above word crossed out*] hour that he deserved the affection of his Eleven wives. See Observations de Bélon. L iii C x. p 179. and Maracci. Alcoran. Tom i Prodrom. iv p 55.

APPENDIX 3

A Vindication (1779)

In draft 'E' of his *Memoirs*, Gibbon described how he came to compose the *Vindication*. Amidst the storm of protest against the two final chapters of volume 1 dealing with Christianity, 'I adhered to the wise resolution of trusting myself and my writings to the candour of the Public, till Mr. Davies of Oxford presumed to attack, not the faith, but the good faith, of the historian. My *Vindication*, expressive of less anger than contempt, amused for a moment the busy and idle metropolis; and the most rational part of the Laity, and even of the Clergy, appears to have been satisfied of my innocence and accuracy' (*A*, 316–17). Although the *Vindication* was keenly appreciated when first published (a second edition was required within a few weeks of the publication of the first), and has delighted connoisseurs of polemical writing ever since, it is arguably the work of Gibbon's which stands in sorest need of contextualization.

The *Vindication* is published here alongside *The Decline and Fall* in defiance of Gibbon's wishes. In his *Memoirs* he tells us that he had insisted on the *Vindication*'s being published in octavo, 'for I would not print it in quarto, lest it should be bound and preserved with the History itself' (*A*, 316, n. 34).

The text reprinted here is that of the second edition, which was revised and enlarged. The following corrections have been made to the copy text (*I* indicates a reading to be found in the first edition):

1116; Tacitus,] Tacitus.
1126; *Hiberis*] *Hibernis I*
1148; note[(7)]?] note?''[75]
1177; aknowledged] acknowledged *I*
1177; Licinus] Licinius

Footnotes have been renumbered in a single sequence throughout the text, and repeated references have been simplified to 'Ibid.' or 'Id.' in accordance with the pagination of this edition. Shoulder headings have been set as centred headings, and page references to *The Decline and Fall* have been amended in accordance with the pagination of this edition.

A VINDICATION

OF

SOME PASSAGES

IN THE

Fifteenth and Sixteenth Chapters

OF THE

History of the Decline and Fall of the Roman Empire.

BY THE AUTHOR.

LONDON:

PRINTED FOR W. STRAHAN; AND T. CADELL, IN THE STRAND.

MDCCLXXIX.

A VINDICATION,

&c. &c.

Perhaps it may be necessary to inform the Public, that not long since an Examination of the Fifteenth and Sixteenth Chapters of the History of the Decline and Fall of the Roman Empire was published by Mr. Davis. He styles himself a Bachelor of Arts, and a Member of Baliol College in the University of Oxford. His title-page is a declaration of war, and in the prosecution of his religious crusade, he assumes a privilege of disregarding the ordinary laws which are respected in the most hostile transactions between civilized men or civilized nations. Some of the harshest epithets in the English language are repeatedly applied to the historian, a part of whose work Mr. Davis has chosen for the object of his criticism. To this author Mr. Davis imputes the crime of betraying the confidence and seducing the faith of those readers, who may heedlessly stray in the flowery paths of his diction, without perceiving the poisonous snake that lurks concealed in the grass. *Latet anguis in herbâ.* The Examiner has assumed the province of reminding them of "the unfair proceedings of such an insidious friend, who offers the deadly draught in a golden cup, that they may be less sensible of the danger.[1] In order to which, Mr. Davis has selected several of the more notorious instances of his misrepresentations and errors; reducing them to their respective heads, and subjoining a long list of almost incredible inaccuracies: and such striking proofs of servile plagiarism, as the world will be surprised to meet with in an author who puts in so bold a claim to originality and extensive reading?"[2] Mr. Davis prosecutes this attack through an octavo volume of not less than two hundred and eighty-four pages with the same implacable spirit; perpetually charges his adversary with perverting the ancients, and transcribing the moderns; and, inconsistently enough, imputes to him the opposite crimes of art and carelessness, of gross ignorance and of wilful falsehood. The Examiner closes his work[3] with

1. Davis, Preface, p. ii.
2. Ibid. Preface, p. iii.
3. Id. p. 282, 283.

a severe reproof of those feeble critics who have allowed any share of knowledge to an odious antagonist. He presumes to pity and to condemn the first historian of the present age, for the generous approbation which he had bestowed on a writer who is content that Mr. Davis should be his enemy, whilst he has a right to name Dr. Robertson for his friend.

When I delivered to the world the First Volume of an important History, in which I had been obliged to connect the progress of Christianity with the civil state and revolutions of the Roman Empire, I could not be ignorant that the result of my inquiries might offend the interest of some and the opinions of others. If the whole work was favourably received by the Public, I had the more reason to expect that this obnoxious part would provoke the zeal of those who consider themselves as the Watchmen of the Holy City. These expectations were not disappointed; and a fruitful crop of Answers, Apologies, Remarks, Examinations &c. sprung up with all convenient speed. As soon as I saw the advertisement, I generally sent for them; for I have never affected, indeed I have never understood, the stoical apathy, the proud contempt of criticism, which some authors have publicly professed. Fame is the motive, it is the reward, of our labours; nor can I easily comprehend how it is possible that we should remain cold and indifferent with regard to the attempts which are made to deprive us of the most valuable object of our possessions, or at least of our hopes. Besides this strong and natural impulse of curiosity, I was prompted by the more laudable desire of applying to my own, and the public, benefit, the well-grounded censures of a learned adversary; and of correcting those faults which the indulgence of vanity and friendship had suffered to escape without observation. I read with attention several criticisms which were published against the Two last Chapters of my History, and unless I much deceive myself, I weighed them in my own mind without prejudice and without resentment. After I was clearly satisfied that their principal objections were founded on misrepresentation or mistake, I declined with sincere and disinterested reluctance the odious task of controversy, and almost formed a tacit resolution of committing my intentions, my writings, and my adversaries to the judgment of the Public, of whose favourable disposition I had received the most flattering proofs.

The reasons which justified my silence were obvious and forcible: the respectable nature of the subject itself, which ought not to be rashly violated by the rude hand of controversy; the inevitable tendency of dispute, which soon degenerates into minute and personal altercation; the indifference of the Public for the discussion of such questions as neither relate to the business nor the amusement of the present age. I calculated the possible loss of temper and the certain loss of time, and considered, that while I was laboriously engaged in a humiliating task, which could add nothing to my own reputation, or to the entertainment of my readers, I must interrupt the prosecution of a work which claimed my whole attention, and which the Public, or at least my friends, seemed to require with some impatience at my hands. The judicious lines of Dr. Young sometimes offered themselves to my memory, and I felt the truth of his observation, That every author lives or dies by his own pen, and that the unerring sentence of Time assigns its proper rank to every composition and to every criticism, which it preserves from oblivion.

I should have consulted my own ease, and perhaps I should have acted in stricter conformity to the rules of prudence, if I had still persevered in patient silence. But Mr. Davis may, if he pleases, assume the merit of extorting from me the notice which I had refused to more honourable foes. I had declined the consideration of their *literary Objections*; but he has compelled me to give an answer to his *criminal Accusations*. Had he confined himself to the ordinary, and indeed obsolete charges of impious principles, and mischievous intentions, I should have acknowledged with readiness and pleasure that the religion of Mr. Davis appeared to be very different from mine. Had he contented himself with the use of that style which decency and politeness have banished from the more liberal part of mankind, I should have smiled, perhaps with some contempt, but without the least mixture of anger or resentment. Every animal employs the note, or cry, or howl, which is peculiar to its species; every man expresses himself in the dialect the most congenial to his temper and inclination, the most familiar to the company in which he has lived, and to the authors with whom he is conversant; and while I was disposed to allow that Mr. Davis had made some proficiency in Ecclesiastical Studies, I should have considered the difference of our language and manners as an unsurmountable bar of separation between us. Mr. Davis has overleaped that bar, and forces me to contend with him on the very dirty ground which he has chosen for the scene of our combat. He has judged, I know not with how much propriety, that the support of a cause, which would disclaim such unworthy assistance, depended on the ruin of my moral and literary character. The different misrepresentations, of which he has drawn out the ignominious catalogue, would materially affect my credit as an historian, my reputation as a scholar, and even my honour and veracity as a gentleman. If I am indeed incapable of understanding what I read, I can no longer claim a place among those writers who merit the esteem and confidence of the Public. If I am capable of wilfully perverting what I understand, I no longer deserve to live in the society of those men, who consider a strict and inviolable adherence to truth, as the foundation of every thing that is virtuous or honourable in human nature. At the same time, I am not insensible that his mode of attack has given a transient pleasure to my enemies, and a transient uneasiness to my friends. The size of his volume, the boldness of his assertions, the acrimony of his style, are contrived with tolerable skill to confound the ignorance and candour of his readers. There are few who will examine the truth or justice of his accusations; and of those persons who have been directed by their education to the study of ecclesiastical antiquity, many will believe, or will affect to believe, that the success of their champion has been equal to his zeal, and that the *serpent* pierced with an hundred wounds lies expiring at his feet. Mr. Davis's book *will* cease to be read (perhaps the grammarians may already reproach me for the use of an improper tense); but the oblivion towards which it seems to be hastening, will afford the more ample scope for the artful practices of those, who may not scruple to affirm, or rather to insinuate, that Mr. Gibbon was publickly convicted of falsehood and misrepresentation; that the evidence produced against him was unanswerable; and that his silence was the effect and the proof of conscious guilt. Under the hands of a malicious surgeon, the sting of a wasp may continue to fester and inflame, long after the vexatious little insect has left its venom and its life in the wound.

The defence of my own honour is undoubtedly the first and prevailing motive which urges me to repel with vigour an unjust and unprovoked attack; and to undertake a tedious vindication, which, after the perpetual repetition of the vainest and most disgusting of the pronouns, will only prove that *I* am innocent; and that Mr. Davis, in his charge, has very frequently subscribed his own condemnation. And yet I may presume to affirm, that the Public have some interest in this controversy. They have some interest to know, whether the writer whom they have honoured with their favour is deserving of their confidence, whether they must content themselves with reading the History of the Decline and Fall of the Roman Empire as a *tale amusing enough*, or whether they may venture to receive it as a fair and authentic history. The general persuasion of mankind, that where *much* has been positively asserted, *something* must be true, may contribute to encourage a secret suspicion, which would naturally diffuse itself over the whole body of the work. Some of those friends who may now tax me with imprudence for taking this public notice of Mr. Davis's book, have perhaps already condemned me for silently acquiescing under the weight of such serious, such direct, and such circumstantial imputations.

Mr. Davis, who in the last page of his[4] Work appears to have recollected that modesty is an amiable and useful qualification, affirms, that his plan required only that he should consult the authors to whom he was directed by my references; and that the judgment of riper years was not so necessary to enable him to execute with success the pious labour to which he had devoted his pen. Perhaps, before we separate, a moment to which I most fervently aspire, Mr. Davis may find that a mature judgment is indispensably requisite for the successful execution of *any* work of literature, and more especially of criticism. Perhaps he will discover, that a young student, who hastily consults an unknown author, on a subject with which he is unacquainted, cannot always be guided by the most accurate reference to the knowledge of the sense, as well as to the sight of the passage which has been quoted by his adversary. Abundant proofs of these maxims will hereafter be suggested. For the present, I shall only remark, that it is my intention to pursue in my defence the order, or rather the course, which Mr. Davis has marked out in his Examination; and that I have numbered the several articles of my impeachment according to the most natural division of the subject. And now let me proceed on this hostile march over a dreary and barren desert, where thirst, hunger, and intolerable weariness, are much more to be dreaded, than the arrows of the enemy.

I.
Quotations in general.

"The remarkable mode of quotation which Mr. Gibbon adopts must immediately strike every one who turns to his notes. He sometimes only mentions the author, perhaps the book; and often leaves the reader the toil of finding out, or rather guessing at the passage. The policy, however, is not without its design and use. By endeavouring to deprive us of the means of comparing him with the authorities he cites, he flattered himself, no doubt, that he might safely have recourse to *misrepresentation*."[5] Such is the style of Mr. Davis; who in another place[6] mentions this mode of quotation "as a good artifice to escape detection;" and applauds, with

4. Davis, p. 284.
5. Id. Preface, p. ii.
6. Id. p. 230.

an agreeable irony, his own labours in turning over a *few* pages of the Theodosian Code.

I shall not descend to animadvert on the rude and illiberal strain of this passage, and I will frankly own that my indignation is lost in astonishment. The Fifteenth and Sixteenth Chapters of my History are illustrated by three hundred and eighty-three Notes; and the nakedness of a few Notes, which are not accompanied by any quotation, is amply compensated by a much greater number, which contain two, three, or perhaps four distinct references; so that upon the whole my stock of quotations which support and justify my facts cannot amount to less than eight hundred or a thousand. As I had often felt the inconvenience of the loose and general method of quoting which is so falsely imputed to me, I have carefully distinguished the *books*, the *chapters*, the *sections*, the *pages* of the authors to whom I referred, with a degree of accuracy and attention, which might claim some gratitude, as it has seldom been so regularly practised by any historical writers. And here I must confess some obligation to Mr. Davis, who, by staking my credit and his own on a circumstance so obvious and palpable, has given me this early opportunity of submitting the merits of our cause, or at least of our characters, to the judgment of the Public. Hereafter, when I am summoned to defend myself against the imputation of misquoting the text, or misrepresenting the sense of a Greek or Latin author, it will not be in my power to communicate the knowledge of the languages, or the possession of the books, to those readers who may be destitute either of one or of the other, and the part which *they* are obliged to take between assertions equally strong and peremptory, may sometimes be attended with doubt and hesitation. But, in the present instance, every reader who will give himself the trouble of consulting the First Volume of my History, is a competent judge of the question. I exhort, I solicit him to run his eye down the columns of Notes, and to count *how many* of the quotations are minute and particular, *how few* are vague and general. When he has satisfied himself by this easy computation, there *is* a word which may naturally suggest itself; an epithet, which I should be sorry either to deserve or use; the boldness of Mr. Davis's assertion, and the confidence of my appeal will tempt, nay, perhaps, will force him to apply that epithet either to one or to the other of the adverse parties.

I have confessed that a critical eye may discover *some* loose and general references; but as they bear a very *inconsiderable* proportion to the whole mass, they cannot support, or even excuse, a false and ungenerous accusation, which must reflect dishonour either on the object or on the author of it. If the examples in which I have occasionally deviated from my ordinary practice were specified and examined, I am persuaded that they might always be fairly attributed to one of the following reasons. 1 In some *rare* instances, which I have never attempted to conceal, I have been obliged to adopt quotations which were expressed with less accuracy than I could have wished. 2. I may have accidentally recollected the sense of a passage which I had formerly read, without being able to find the place, or even to transcribe from memory the precise words. 3. The whole tract (as in a remarkable instance of the second Apology of Justin Martyr) was so short, that a more particular description was not required. 4. The form of the composition supplied the want of a local reference; the preceding mention of the *year* fixed the passage of the annalist; and the reader was guided to the proper spot in the commentaries of Grotius, Valesius, or Godefroy, by the more accurate citation of their original author. 5. The idea which I was desirous of communicating to the reader, was sometimes the general result of the author or treatise that I had quoted; nor was it possible to confine, within the narrow limits of a particular reference, the sense or spirit which was mingled with the whole mass. These motives are either laudable, or at least innocent. In two of these exceptions, my ordinary mode of citation was superfluous; in the other three, it was impracticable.

In quoting a comparison which Tertullian had used to express the rapid increase of the Marcionites, I expressly declared that I was obliged to quote it from memory.[7] If I have been guilty of comparing them to *bees* instead of *wasps*, I can however most sincerely disclaim the sagacious suspicion of Mr. Davis,[8] who imagines that I was tempted to amend the simile of Tertullian from an improper partiality for those odious Heretics.

A rescript of Diocletian, which declared *the* old law (not *an* old law[9]), had been alleged by me on the respectable authority of Fra-Paolo. The Examiner, who thinks that he has turned over the pages of the Theodosian Code, informs[10] his reader that it may be found, I. vi. tit. xxiv. 8.; he will be surprised to learn that this rescript could not be *found* in a code where it does not exist, but that it may distinctly be read in the same number, the same title, and the same book of the CODE OF JUSTINIAN. He who is severe should at least be just: yet I should probably have disdained this

7. Gibbon's History, p. 458. I shall usually refer to the third edition, unless there are any various readings.

8. Davis, p. 144.

9. Gibbon, p. 492.

10. Davis, p. 230.

minute animadversion, unless it had served to display the general ignorance of the critic in the History of the Roman Jurisprudence. If Mr. Davis had not been an absolute stranger, the most treacherous guide could not have persuaded him that a rescript of Diocletian was to be found in the Theodosian Code, which was designed only to preserve the laws of Constantine and his successors. Compendiosam (says Theodosius himself) Divalium Constitutionum scientiam, ex D. Constantini temporibus roboramus. (Novell. ad calcem Cod. Theod. l. i. tit. i. leg. 1.)

II.
Errors of the press.

Few objects are below the notice of Mr. Davis, and his criticism is never so formidable as when it is directed against the guilty corrector of the press, who on some occasions has shewn himself negligent of my fame and of his own. Some errors have arisen from the omission of letters; from the confusion of cyphers, which perhaps were not very distinctly marked in the original manuscript. The *two* of the Roman, and the *eleven* of the Arabic, numerals have been unfortunately mistaken for each other; the similar forms of a 2 and a 3, a 5 and a 6, a 3 and an 8, have improperly been transposed; Antolycus for Autolycus, Idolatria for Ido*lo*latria, Holsterius for Holste*n*ius, had escaped my own observation, as well as the diligence of the person who was employed to revise the sheets of my History. These important errors, from the indulgence of a deluded Public, have been multiplied in the numerous impressions of three different editions; and for the present I can only lament my own defects, whilst I deprecate the wrath of Mr. Davis, who seems ready to infer that I cannot either read or write. I sincerely admire his patient industry, which I despair of being able to imitate; but if a future edition should ever be required, I could wish to obtain, on any reasonable terms, the services of so useful a corrector.

III.
Difference of editions.

Mr. Davis had been directed by my references to several passages of Optatus Milevitanus,[11] and of the Bibliotheque Ecclesiastique of M.

11. Davis, p. 73.

Dupin.[12] He eagerly consults those places, is unsuccessful, and is happy. Sometimes the place which I have quoted does not offer any of the circumstances which I had alleged, sometimes only a few; and sometimes the same passages exhibit a sense totally adverse and repugnant to mine. These shameful misrepresentations incline Mr. Davis to suspect that I have never consulted the original (not even of a common French book!), and he asserts his right to censure my presumption. These important charges form two distinct articles in the list of *Misrepresentations*; but Mr. Davis has amused himself with adding to the slips of the pen or of the press, some complaints of his ill success, when he attempted to verify my quotations from Cyprian and from Shaw's Travels.[13]

The success of Mr. Davis would indeed have been somewhat extraordinary, unless he had consulted the same *editions*, as well as the same places. I shall content myself with mentioning the editions which I have used, and with assuring him, that if he renews his search, he will not, or rather that he will, be disappointed.

Mr. Gibbon's Editions.	Mr. Davis's Editions.
Optatus Milevitanus, by Dupin, fol. Paris, 1700.	Fol. Antwerp, 1702.
Dupin, Bibliotheque Ecclesiastique, 4to. Paris, 1690.	8vo. Paris, 1687.
Cypriani Opera, Edit. Fell, fol. Amsterdam, 1700.	Most probably Oxon. 1682.
Shaw's Travels, 4to. London, 1757.	The folio Edition.

IV.
Jewish history, Tacitus.

The nature of my subject had led me to mention, not the real origin of the Jews, but their first *appearance* to the eyes of other nations; and I cannot avoid transcribing the short passage in which I had introduced them. "The Jews, who under the Assyrian and Persian monarchies had languished for many ages the most despised portion of their slaves, emerged from their obscurity under the successors of Alexander. And as they multiplied to a surprising degree in the East, and afterwards in the West, they soon excited the curiosity and wonder of other nations."[14]

12. Davis, p. 132–136.
13. Id. p. 151. 155.
14. Gibbon, p. 44.

This simple abridgment seems in its turn to have excited the wonder of Mr. Davis, whose surprise almost renders him eloquent. "What a strange assemblage," says he, "is here? It is like Milton's Chaos, without bound, without dimension, where time and place are lost. In short, what does this display afford us, but a deal of boyish colouring to the prejudice of much good history?"[15] If I rightly understand Mr. Davis's language, he censures, as a piece of confused declamation, the passage which he has produced from my History; and if I collect the angry criticisms which he has scattered over twenty pages of controversy,[16] I think I can discover that there is hardly a period, or even a word, in this unfortunate passage, which has obtained the approbation of the Examiner.

As nothing can escape his vigilance, he censures me for including the twelve tribes of Israel under the common appellation of JEWS,[17] and for extending the name of ASSYRIANS to the subjects of the Kings of Babylon;[18] and again censures me, because some facts which are affirmed or insinuated in my text, do not agree with the strict and proper limits which he has assigned to those national denominations. The name of *Jews* has indeed been established by the scepter of the tribe of *Judah*, and, in the times which precede the captivity, it is used in the more general sense with some sort of impropriety; but surely I am not peculiarly charged with a fault which has been consecrated by the consent of twenty centuries, the practice of the best writers, ancient as well as modern (See Josephus and Prideaux, even in the titles of their respective works), and by the usage of modern languages, of the Latin, the Greek, and, if I may credit Reland, of the Hebrew itself (See Palestin. l. i. c. 6.). With regard to the other word, that of Assyrians, most assuredly I will not lose myself in the labyrinth of the Asiatic monarchies before the age of Cyrus; nor indeed is any more required for my justification, than to prove that Babylon was considered as the capital and royal seat of Assyria. If Mr. Davis were a man of learning, I might be morose enough to censure his ignorance of ancient geography, and to overwhelm him under a load of quotations, which might be collected and transcribed with very little trouble: But as I *must* suppose that he has received a classical education, I might have expected him to have read the first book of Herodotus, where that historian describes, in the clearest and most elegant terms, the situation and greatness of Babylon: *Της δε Ασσυριης τα μεν κου και αλλα πολισματα μεγαλα πολλα, το δε ονομαστοτατον και ισχυροτατον*

15. Davis, p. 5.
16. Id. p. 2–22.
17. Id. p. 3.
18. Id. p. 2.

και ενθα σφι, Νινου αναστατου γενομενης, τα βασιληια κατεστηκεε, την Βαβυλων. (Clio, c. 178.) I may be surprised that he should be so little conversant with the Cyropœdia of Xenophon, in the whole course of which the King of Babylon, the adversary of the Medes and Persians, is repeatedly mentioned by the style and title of THE ASSYRIAN, *'Οδε Ασσυριος, ὁ Βαβυλωνα τε εχων και την αλλην Ασσυριαν*. (l. ii. p. 102, 103, Edit. Hutchinson.) But there remains something more: and Mr. Davis must apply the same reproaches of *inaccuracy, if not ignorance*, to the Prophet Isaiah, who, in the name of Jehovah, announcing the downfal of Babylon and the deliverance of Israel, declares with an oath; "And as I have purposed the thing shall stand: to crush the ASSYRIAN in my land, and to trample him on my mountains. Then shall his yoke depart from off them; and his burthen shall be removed from off their shoulders." (Isaiah, xiv. 24, 25. Lowth's new translation. See likewise the Bishop's note, p. 98.) Our old translation expresses, with less elegance, the same meaning; but I mention with pleasure the labours of a respectable Prelate, who in this, as well as in a former work, has very happily united the most critical judgment, with the taste and spirit of poetry.

The jealousy which Mr. Davis affects for the honour of the Jewish people, will not suffer him to allow that they were *slaves* to the conquerors of the East; and while he acknowledges that they were tributary and dependent, he seems desirous of introducing, or even inventing, some milder expression of the state of vassalage and *subservience*;[19] from whence Tacitus assumed the words of *despectissima pars servientium*. Has Mr. Davis never heard of the distinction of civil and political slavery? Is he ignorant that even the natural and victorious subjects of an Asiatic despot have been deservedly marked with the opprobrious epithet of slaves by every writer acquainted with the name and advantage of freedom? Does he not know that, under such a government, the yoke is imposed with double weight on the necks of the vanquished, as the rigour of tyranny is aggravated by the abuse of conquest. From the first invasion of Judæa by the arms of the Assyrians, to the subversion of the Persian monarchy by Alexander, there elapsed a period of above four hundred years, which included about twelve ages or generations of the human race. As long as the Jews asserted their independence, they repeatedly suffered every calamity which the rage and insolence of a victorious enemy could inflict; the throne of David was overturned, the temple and city were reduced to ashes, and the whole land, a circumstance perhaps unparalleled in

19. Davis, p. 6.

history, remained three-score and ten years without inhabitants, and without cultivation. (2 Chronicles, xxxvi. 21.) According to an institution which has long prevailed in Asia, and particularly in the Turkish government, the most beautiful and ingenious youths were carefully educated in the palace, where superior merit sometimes introduced these fortunate *slaves* to the favour of the conqueror, and to the honours of the state. (See the book and example of Daniel.) The rest of the unhappy Jews experienced the hardships of captivity and exile in distant lands, and while individuals were oppressed, the nation seemed to be dissolved or annihilated. The gracious edict of Cyrus was offered to all those who worshipped the God of Israel in the temple of Jerusalem; but it was accepted by no more than forty-two thousand persons of either sex and of every age, and of these about thirty thousand derived their origin from the Tribes of Judah, of Benjamin, and of Levi. (See Ezra, i. Nehemiah, vii. and Prideaux's Connections, vol. i. p. 107. fol. Edit. London, 1718.) The inconsiderable band of exiles, who returned to inhabit the land of their fathers, cannot be computed as the hundred and fiftieth part of the mighty people that had been numbered by the impious rashness of David. After a survey, which did not comprehend the Tribes of Levi and Benjamin, the monarch was assured that he reigned over *one million five hundred and seventy thousand men* that drew sword (1 Chronicles, xxi. 1–6), and the country of Judæa must have contained near seven millions of free inhabitants. The progress of restoration is always less rapid than that of destruction; Jerusalem, which had been ruined in a few months, was rebuilt by the slow and interrupted labours of a whole century; and the Jews, who gradually multiplied in their native seats, enjoyed a servile and precarious existence, which depended on the capricious will of their master. The books of Ezra and Nehemiah do not afford a very pleasing view of their situation under the Persian Empire; and the book of Esther exhibits a most extraordinary instance of the degree of estimation in which they were held at the Court of Susa. A Minister addressed his King in the following words, which may be considered as a Commentary on the *despectissima pars servientium* of the Roman historian: "And Haman said to King Ahasuerus, There is a certain people scattered abroad, and dispersed among the people in all the provinces of thy kingdom; and their laws are diverse from all people, neither keep they the King's laws; therefore it is not for the King's profit to suffer them. If it please the King, let it be written that they may be destroyed; and I will pay ten thousand talents of silver to the hands of those that have the charge of the business, to bring it to the King's treasuries. And the king took his ring from his hand, and gave it to Haman, the son of Hammedatha the Agagite, the Jews' enemy. And the king said unto Haman, The silver is given unto thee; the people also, to do with them as it seemeth good to thee." (Esther, iii. 8–11.) This trifling favour was asked by the Minister, and granted by the Monarch, with an easy indifference, which expressed their contempt for the lives and fortunes of the Jews; the business passed without difficulty through the forms of office; and had Esther been less lovely, or less beloved, a single day would have consummated the universal slaughter of a submissive people, to whom no legal defence was allowed, and from whom no resistance seems to have been dreaded. I am a stranger to Mr. Davis's political principles; but I should think that the epithet of *slaves*, and of despised slaves, may, without injustice, be applied to a captive nation, over whose head the sword of tyranny was suspended by so slender a thread.

The policy of the Macedonians was very different from that of the Persians; and yet Mr. Davis, who reluctantly confesses that the Jews were oppressed by the former, does not understand how long they were favoured and protected by the latter.[20] In the shock of those revolutions which divided the empire of Alexander, Judæa, like the other provinces, experienced the transient ravages of an advancing or retreating enemy, who led away a multitude of captives. But, in the age of Josephus, the Jews still enjoyed the privileges granted by the Kings of Asia and Egypt, who had fixed numerous colonies of that nation in the new cities of Alexandria, Antioch, &c. and placed them in the same honourable condition (ισοπολιτας, ισοτιμους) as the Greeks and Macedonians themselves. (Joseph. Antiquitat. l. xii. c. 1. 3. p. 585. 596. Vol. i. edit. Havercamp.) Had they been treated with less indulgence, their settlement in those celebrated cities, the seats of commerce and learning, was enough to introduce them to the knowledge of the world, and to justify my *absurd* proposition, that they emerged from obscurity under the successors of Alexander.

The Jews remained and flourished under the mild dominion of the Macedonian Princes, till they were compelled to assert their civil and religious rights against Antiochus Epiphanes, who had adopted new maxims of tyranny; and the age of the Maccabees is perhaps the most glorious period of the Hebrew annals. Mr. Davis, who on this occasion is bewildered by the subtlety of Tacitus, does not comprehend why the historian should ascribe the independence of the Jews to three *negative*

20. Davis, p. 4.

causes, "Macedonibus invalidis, Parthis nondum adultis, et Romani procul aberant." To the understanding of the critic, Tacitus might as well have observed, that the Jews were not destroyed by a plague, a famine, or an earthquake; and Mr. Davis cannot see, for his own part, any reason why they might not have elected Kings of their own two or three hundred years before.[21] Such indeed was not the reason of Tacitus: he probably considered that every nation, depressed by the weight of a foreign power, naturally rises towards the surface, as soon as the pressure is removed; and he might think that, in a short and rapid history of the independence of the Jews, it was sufficient for him to shew that the obstacles did not exist, which, in an earlier or in a later period, would have checked their efforts. The curious reader, who has leisure to study the Jewish and Syrian history, will discover, that the throne of the Asmonæan Princes was confirmed by the two great victories of the Parthians over Demetrius Nicator, and Antiochus Sidetes (See Joseph. Antiquitat. Jud. l. xiii. c. 5, 6. 8, 9. Justin, xxxvi. 1. xxxviii. 10. with Usher and Prideaux, before Christ 141 and 130); and the expression of Tacitus, the more closely it is examined, will be the more rationally admired.

My Quotations[22] are the object of Mr. Davis's criticism,[23] as well as the Text of this short, but obnoxious passage. He corrects the error of my memory, which had suggested *servitutis* instead of *servientium*; and so natural is the alliance between truth and moderation, that on this occasion he forgets his character, and candidly acquits me of any malicious design to misrepresent the words of Tacitus. The other references, which are contained in the first and second Notes of my Fifteenth Chapter, are connected with each other, and can only be mistaken after they have been forcibly separated. The silence of Herodotus is a fair evidence of the obscurity of the Jews, who had escaped the eyes of so curious a traveller. The Jews are first mentioned by Justin, when he relates the siege of Jerusalem by Antiochus Sidetes; and the conquest of Judæa, by the arms of Pompey, engaged Diodorus and Dion to introduce that singular nation to the acquaintance of their readers. These epochs, which are within seventy years of each other, mark the age in which the Jewish people, emerging from their obscurity, began to act a part in the society of nations, and to excite the curiosity of the Greek and Roman historians. For that purpose only, I had appealed to the authority of Diodorus Siculus, of Justin, or rather of Trogus Pompeius, and of Dion Cassius. If

21. Davis, p. 8.
22. Gibbon, p. 447. Note 1, 2.
23. Davis, p. 10. 11. 20.

I had designed to investigate the Jewish Antiquities, reason, as well as faith, must have directed my inquiries to the Sacred Books, which, even as human productions, would deserve to be studied as one of the most curious and original monuments of the East.

I stand accused, though not indeed by Mr. Davis, for profanely depreciating the *promised* Land, as well as the *chosen* People. The Gentleman without a name has placed this charge in the front of his battle,[24] and if my memory does not deceive me, it is one of the few remarks in Mr. Apthorpe's book, which have any immediate relation to my History. They seem to consider in the light of a reproach, and of an unjust reproach, the idea which I had given of Palestine, as of a territory scarcely superior to Wales in extent and fertility;[25] and they strangely convert a geographical observation into a theological error. When I recollect that the imputation of a similar error was employed by the implacable Calvin, to precipitate and to justify the execution of Servetus, I must applaud the felicity of this country, and of this age, which has disarmed, if it could not mollify, the fierceness of ecclesiastical criticism (see Dictionaire Critique de Chaffeupié, tom. iv. p. 223).

As I had compared the narrow extent of Phœnicia and Palestine with the important blessings which those celebrated countries had diffused over the rest of the earth, their minute size became an object not of censure but of praise.

Ingentes animos angusto in pectore versant.

The precise measure of Palestine was taken from Templeman's Survey of the Globe: he allows to Wales 7011 square English miles, to the Morea, or Peloponnesus, 7220, to the Seven United Provinces 7546, and to Judæa or Palestine 7600. The difference is not very considerable, and if any of these countries has been magnified beyond its real size, Asia is more liable than Europe to have been affected by the inaccuracy of Mr. Templeman's maps. To the authority of this modern survey, I shall only add the ancient and weighty testimony of Jerom, who passed in Palestine above thirty years of his life. From Dan to Bershebah, the two fixed and proverbial boundaries of the Holy Land, he reckons no more than one hundred and sixty miles (Hieronym. ad Dardanum, tom. iii. p. 66), and the breadth of Palestine cannot by any expedient be stretched to one half of its length (see Reland, Palestin. l. ii. c. 5. p. 421).

The degrees and limits of fertility cannot be ascertained with the

24. Remarks, p. 1.

25. Gibbon, p. 53.

strict simplicity of geographical measures. Whenever we speak of the productions of the earth, in different climates, our ideas must be relative, our expressions vague and doubtful; nor can we always distinguish between the gifts of Nature and the rewards of Industry. The Emperor Frederick II., the enemy and the victim of the Clergy, is accused of saying, after his return from his Crusade, that the God of the Jews would have despised his promised land, if he had once seen the fruitful realms of Sicily and Naples (See Giannone Istoria Civile del Regno di Napoli, tom. ii. p. 245). This raillery, which malice has perhaps falsely imputed to Frederick, is inconsistent with truth and piety; yet it must be confessed, that the soil of Palestine does not contain that inexhaustible, and as it were spontaneous, principle of fecundity, which, under the most unfavourable circumstance, has covered with rich harvests the banks of the Nile, the fields of Sicily, or the plains of Poland. The Jordan is the only navigable river of Palestine: a considerable part of the narrow space is occupied, or rather lost, in the *Dead Sea,* whose horrid aspect inspires every sensation of disgust, and countenances every tale of horror. The districts which border on Arabia partake of the sandy quality of the adjacent desert. The face of the country, except the sea-coast and the valley of the Jordan, is covered with mountains, which appear for the most part as naked and barren rocks; and in the neighbourhood of Jerusalem there is a real scarcity of the two elements of earth and water (See Maundrel's Travels, p. 65, and Reland Palestin. tom. i. p. 238–395). These disadvantages, which now operate in their fullest extent, were formerly corrected by the labours of a numerous people, and the active protection of a wise government. The hills were clothed with rich beds of artificial mould, the rain was collected in vast cisterns, a supply of fresh water was conveyed by pipes and aqueducts to the dry lands, the breed of cattle was encouraged in those parts which were not adapted for tillage, and almost every spot was compelled to yield some production for the use of the inhabitants. (See the same testimonies and observations of Maundrel and Reland.)

——Pater ipse colendi
Haud facilem esse viam voluit, primusque per artem
Movit agros; curi acuens mortalia corda
Nec torpere gravi passus SUA REGNA veterno.

Such are the useful victories which have been atchieved by MAN on the lofty mountains of Switzerland, along the rocky coast of Genoa, and upon the barren hills of Palestine; and since Wales has flourished under the influence of English freedom, that rugged country has surely acquired some share of the same industrious merit and the same artificial fertility. Those Critics who interpret the comparison of Palestine and Wales as a tacit libel on the former, are themselves guilty of an unjust satire against the latter, of those countries. Such is the injustice of Mr. Apthorpe and of the anonymous *Gentleman*: but if Mr. Davis (as we may suspect from his name) is himself of Cambrian origin, his patriotism on this occasion has protected me from his zeal.

V.

I shall begin this article by the confession of an error which candour might perhaps excuse, but which my Adversary magnifies by a pathetic interrogation. "When he tells us, that he has carefully examined all the original materials, are we to believe him? or is it his design to try how far the credulity and easy disposition of the age will suffer him to proceed unsuspected and undiscovered?"[26] *Quousque tandem abuteris Catilina patientiâ nostrâ?*

In speaking of the danger of idolatry, I had quoted the pictoresque expression of Tertullian, "Recogita sylvam et quantæ latitant spinæ," and finding it marked c. 10 in my Notes, I hastily, though naturally, added *de Idololatria*, instead of *de Corona Militis*, and referred to one Treatise of Tertullian instead of another.[27] And now let me ask in my turn, whether Mr. Davis had any real knowledge of the passage which I had misplaced, or whether he made an ungenerous use of his advantage, to insinuate that I had invented or perverted the words of Tertullian? Ignorance is less criminal than malice, and I shall be satisfied if he will plead guilty to the milder charge.

The same observation may be extended to a passage of Le Clerc, which asserts, in the clearest terms, the ignorance of the more ancient Jews with regard to a future state. Le Clerc lay open before me, but while my eye moved from the book to the paper, I transcribed the reference c. 1. sect. 8. instead of sect. 1. c. 8. from the natural, but erroneous persuasion, that *Chapter* expressed the larger, and *Section* the smaller division:[28] and this difference, of such trifling moment and so easily rectified, holds a dis-

26. Davis, p. 25.
27. Gibbon, p. 460. Note 40.
28. Id. p. 465, Note 58.

tinguished place in the list of Misrepresentations which adorn Mr. Davis's Table of Contents.[29] But to return to Tertullian.

The *infernal* picture, which I had produced[30] from that vehement writer, which excited the horror of every humane reader, and which even Mr. Davis will not explicitly defend, has furnished him with a few critical cavils.[31] Happy should I think myself, if the materials of my History could be always exposed to the Examination of the Public; and I shall be content with appealing to the impartial Reader, whether my Version of this Passage is not as fair and as faithful, as the more literal translation which Mr. Davis has exhibited in an opposite column. I shall only justify two expressions which have provoked his indignation. 1. I had observed that the zealous African pursues the infernal description in a long variety of affected and unfeeling witticisms; the instances of Gods, of Kings, of Magistrates, of Philosophers, of Poets, of Tragedians, were introduced into my Translation. Those which I had omitted relate to the Dancers, the Charioteers, and the Wrestlers; and it is almost impossible to express those conceits which are connected with the language and manners of the Romans. But the reader will be *sufficiently* shocked, when he is informed that Tertullian alludes to the improvement which the agility of the Dancers, the *red* livery of the Charioteers, and the attitudes of the Wrestlers, would derive from the effects of fire. "Tunc histriones cognoscendi solutiores multo per ignem; tunc spectandus Auriga in flammea rota totus ruber. Tunc Xystici contemplandi, non in Gymnasiis, sed in igne jaculati." 2. I cannot refuse to answer Mr. Davis's very particular question, Why I appeal to Tertullian for the condemnation of the wisest and most virtuous of the Pagans? *Because* I am inclined to bestow that epithet on Trajan and the Antonines, Homer and Euripides, Plato and Aristotle, who are all manifestly included within the fiery description which I had produced.

I am accused of misquoting Tertullian ad Scapulam,[32] as an evidence that Martyrdoms were lately introduced into Africa.[33] Besides Tertullian, I had quoted from Ruinart (Acta Sincera, p. 84.) the Acts of the Scyllitan Martyrs; and a very moderate knowledge of Ecclesiastical History would have informed Mr. Davis, that the two authorities thus connected establish the proposition asserted in my Text. Tertullian, in the above-mentioned Chapter, speaks of one of the Proconsuls of Africa, Vigellius Saturninus, "qui *primus hic* gladium in nos egit;" the Acta Sincera rep-

29. Davis, p. 19.
30. Gibbon, p. 471.
31. Davis, p. 29–33.
32. Id. p. 35, 36.
33. Gibbon, p. 504–5, Note 172.

resent the same Magistrate as the Judge of the Scyllitan Martyrs; and Ruinart, with the consent of the best Critics, ascribes their sufferings to the persecution of Severus. Was it my fault if Mr. Davis was incapable of supplying the intermediate ideas?

Is it likewise necessary that I should justify the frequent use which I have made of Tertullian? His copious writings display a lively and interesting picture of the primitive Church, and the scantiness of original materials scarcely left me the liberty of choice. Yet as I was sensible, that the Montanism of Tertullian is the convenient screen which our orthodox Divines have placed before his errors, I have, with peculiar caution, confined myself to those works which were composed in the more early and sounder part of his life.

As a collateral justification of my frequent appeals to this African Presbyter, I had introduced, in the third edition of my History, two passages of Jerom and Prudentius, which prove that Tertullian was the master of Cyprian, and that Cyprian was the master of the Latin Church.[34] Mr. Davis assures me, however, that I should have done better not to have "added this note,[35] as I have only accumulated my inaccuracies." One inaccuracy he had indeed detected, an error of the press, Hieronym. de Viris illustribus, c. 53 for 63; but this advantage is dearly purchased by Mr. Davis. *Επιδος τον διδασκαλον*, which he produces as the original words of Cyprian, has a braver and more learned sound, than *Da magistrum*; but the quoting in Greek, a sentence which was pronounced, and is recorded, in Latin, seems to bear the mark of the most ridiculous pedantry; unless Mr. Davis, consulting for the first time the Works of Jerom, mistook the Version of Sophronius, which is printed in the opposite column, for the Text of his original Author. My reference to Prudentius, Hymn. xiii. 100. cannot so easily be justified, as I presumptuously believed that my critics would continue to read till they came to a full stop. I shall now place before them, not the first verse only, but the entire period, which they will find full, express, and satisfactory. The Poet says of St. Cyprian, whom he places in Heaven,

> Nec minus involitat terris, nec ab hoc recedit orbe:
> Disserit, eloquitur, tractat, docet, instruit, prophetat;
> Nec *Libyæ populos* tantum regit, exit usque in ortum
> Solis, et usque obitum; *Gallos* fovet, imbuit *Britannos*,
> Presidet *Hesperiæ*, Christum serit ultimis *Hibernis*.

34. Gibbon, p. 471. N. 72.
35. Davis, p. 145.

VI.
Sulpicius Severus and Fra-Paolo.

On the subject of the imminent dangers which the Apocalypse has so narrowly escaped,[36] Mr. Davis accuses me of misrepresenting the sentiments of Sulpicius Severus and Fra-Paolo,[37] with this difference, however, that I was incapable of reading or understanding the text of the Latin author; but that I wilfully perverted the sense of the Italian historian. These imputations I shall easily wipe away, by shewing that, in the first instance, I am probably in the right, and that, in the second, he is certainly in the wrong.

1. The concise and elegant Sulpicius, who has been justly styled the Christian Sallust, after mentioning the exile and Revelations of St. John in the Isle of Patmos, observes (and surely the observation is in the language of complaint), "Librum sacræ Apocalypsis, qui quidem *a plerisque* aut stulte aut impie non recipitur, conscriptum edidit." I am found guilty of supposing *plerique* to signify *the greater number*; whereas Mr. Davis, with Stephen's Dictionary in his hand, is able to prove that *plerique* has not *always* that extensive meaning, and that a classic of good authority has used the word in a much more limited and qualified sense. Let the Examiner therefore try to apply his exception to this particular case. For my part, *I* stand under the protection of the general usage of the Latin language, and with a strong presumption in favour of the justice of my cause, or at least of the innocence and fairness of my intentions; since I have translated a familiar word, according to its acknowledged and ordinary acceptation.

But, "if I had looked into the passage, and found that Sulpicius Severus there expressly tells us, that the Apocalypse was the work of St. John, I could not have committed so unfortunate a *blunder*, as to cite this Father as saying, That the greater number of Christians denied its Canonical authority."[38] Unfortunate indeed would have been my blunder, had I asserted that the same Christians who denied its Canonical authority, admitted it to be the work of an Apostle. Such indeed was the opinion of Severus himself, and his opinion has obtained the sanction of the Church; but the Christians whom he taxes with folly or impiety for rejecting this sacred book, must have supported their error by attributing the Apocalypse to some uninspired writer; to John the Presbyter, or to Cerinthus the Heretic.

36. Gibbon, p. 468, 469. N. 67.
37. Davis, p. 40–44.
38. Id. p. 270.

If the rules of grammar and of logic authorise, or at least allow me to translate *plerique* by the *greater number*, the Ecclesiastical History of the fourth century illustrates and justifies this obvious interpretation. From a fair comparison of the populousness and learning of the Greek and Latin Churches, may I not conclude that the former contained the *greater number* of Christians qualified to pass sentence on a mysterious prophecy composed in the Greek language? May I not affirm, on the authority of St. Jerom, that the Apocalypse was generally rejected by the Greek Churches? "Quod si eam (the Epistle to the Hebrews) Latinorum consuetudo non recipit inter Scripturas Canonicas; nec Græcorum Ecclesiæ Apocalypsim Johannis eadem libertate suscipiunt. Et tamen nos utramque suscipimus, nequaquam hujus temporis consuetudinem, sed veterum auctoritatem sequentes." Epistol. ad Dardanum, tom. iii. p. 68.

It is not my design to enter any farther into the controverted history of that famous book; but I am called upon[39] to defend my Remark that the Apocalypse was tacitly excluded from the sacred canon by the council of Laodicea (Canon LX.) To defend my Remark, I need only state the fact in a simple, but more particular manner. The assembled Bishops of Asia, after enumerating all the books of the Old and New Testament which should be read in churches, omit the Apocalypse, and the Apocalypse alone; at a time when it was rejected or questioned by many pious and learned Christians, who might deduce a very plausible argument from the silence of the Synod.

2. When the Council of Trent resolved to pronounce sentence on the Canon of Scripture, the opinion which prevailed, after some debate, was to declare the Latin Vulgate authentic and *almost* infallible; and this sentence, which was guarded by formidable Anathemas, secured all the books of the Old and New Testament which composed that ancient version, "che si dichiarassero tutti in tutte le parte come si trovano nella Biblia Latina, esser di Divina è ugual autorita." (Istoria del Concilio Tridentino, l. ii. p. 147. Helmstadt (*Vicenza*) 1761.) When the merit of that version was discussed, the majority of the Theologians urged, with confidence and success, that it was absolutely necessary to receive the Vulgate as authentic and inspired, unless they wished to abandon the victory to the Lutherans, and the honours of the Church to the Grammarians. "In contrario della maggior parte dè Teologi era detto ... che questi nuovi Grammatici confonderanno ogni cosa, e sarà fargli giudici e arbitri della fede; e in luogo dè Teologi e Canonisti, converrà tener il

39. By Mr. Davis, p. 41. and by Dr. Chelsum, Remarks, p. 57.

primo conto nell' assumere a Vescovati e Cardinalati dè pedanti." (Istoria del Concilio Tridentino, l. ii. p. 149.) The sagacious Historian, who had studied the Council, and the judicious Le Courayer, who had studied his Author (Histoire du Concile de Trente, tom. i. p. 245. Londres 1736) consider this *ridiculous* reason as the most powerful argument which influenced the debates of the Council: But Mr. Davis, jealous of the honour of a Synod which placed tradition on a level with the Bible, affirms that Fra-Paolo has given another more substantial reason on which these Popish Bishops built their determination, That after dividing the books under their consideration into three classes; of those which had been always held for divine; of those whose authenticity had formerly been doubted, but which by use and custom had acquired canonical authority; and of those which had never been properly certified; the Apocalypse was judiciously placed by the Fathers of the Council in the second of these classes.

The Italian passage, which, for that purpose, Mr. Davis has alleged at the bottom of his page, is indeed taken from the text of Fra-Paolo: but the reader who will give himself the trouble, or rather the pleasure, of perusing that incomparable historian, will discover that Mr. Davis has *only* mistaken a motion of the opposition, for a measure of the administration. He will find, that this critical division, which is so erroneously ascribed to the public reason of the Council, was no more than the ineffectual proposal of a temperate minority, which was soon over-ruled by a majority of artful Statesmen, bigotted Monks, and dependent Bishops.

"We have here an evident proof that Mr. Gibbon is equally expert in misrepresenting a modern as an ancient writer, or that he wilfully conceals the most material reason, with a design, no doubt, to instil into his Reader a notion, that the authenticity of the Apocalypse is built on the slightest foundation."[40]

VII.
Clemens.

I had cautiously observed (for I was apprised of the obscurity of the subject) that the Epistle of Clemens does not lead us to discover any traces of Episcopacy either at Corinth or Rome.[41] In this observation I

40. Davis, p. 44.
41. Gibbon, p. 481. N. 110.

particularly alluded to the republican form of salutation, "The Church of God inhabiting Rome, to the Church of God inhabiting Corinth;" without the least mention of a Bishop or President in either of those ecclesiastical assemblies.

Yet the piercing eye of Mr. Davis[42] can discover not only traces, but evident proofs, of Episcopacy, in this Epistle of Clemens; and he actually quotes two passages, in which he distinguishes by capital letters the word BISHOPS, whose institution Clemens refers to the Apostles themselves. But can Mr. Davis hope to gain credit by such egregious trifling? While we are searching for the origin of Bishops, not merely as an ecclesiastical title, but as the peculiar name of an order distinct from that of Presbyters, he idly produces a passage, which, by declaring that the Apostles established in every place *Bishops* and *Deacons,* evidently confounds the *Presbyters* with one or other of those two ranks. I have neither inclination nor interest to engage in a controversy which I had considered only in an historical light; but I have already said enough to shew, that there are more traces of a disingenuous mind in Mr. Davis, than of an Episcopal Order in the Epistle of Clemens.

VIII.
Eusebius.

Perhaps, on some future occasion, I may examine the historical character of Eusebius; perhaps I may enquire, how far it appears from his words and actions, that the learned Bishop of Cæsarea was averse to the use of fraud, when it was employed in the service of Religion. At present, I am only concerned to defend my own truth and honour, from the reproach of misrepresenting the sense of the Ecclesiastical Historian. Some of the charges of Mr. Davis on this head are so strong, so pointed, so vehemently urged, that he seems to have staked, on the event of the trial, the merits of our respective characters. If his assertions are true, I deserve the contempt of learned, and the abhorrence of good, men. If they are false, ******

1. I had remarked, without any malicious intention, that one of the seventeen Christians who suffered at Alexandria was likewise *accused* of robbery.[43] Mr. Davis[44] seems enraged because I did not add that he was

42. Davis, p. 44, 45.

43. Gibbon, p. 472, N. 75.

44. Davis, p. 61, 62, 63. This ridiculous charge is repeated by another *Sycophant* (in the Greek sense of the word), and forms one of the *valuable* communications, which

falsely accused, takes some unnecessary pains to convince me that the Greek word *εσυκοφαντηθη* signifies *falso accusatus*, and "can hardly think that any one who had looked into the original, would dare thus absolutely to contradict the plain testimony of the author he *pretends* to follow." A simple narrative of this fact, in the relation of which Mr. Davis has *really* suppressed several material circumstances, will afford the clearest justification.

Eusebius has preserved an original letter from Dionysius Bishop of Alexandria to Fabius Bishop of Antioch, in which the former relates the circumstances of the persecution which had lately afflicted the capital of Egypt. He allows a rank among the martyrs to one Nemesion, an Egyptian, who was falsely or maliciously accused as a companion of robbers. Before the Centurion he justified himself from this calumny, which did not relate to him; but being charged as a Christian, he was brought in chains before the Governor. That unjust magistrate, after inflicting on Nemesion *a double measure of stripes and tortures*, gave orders that he should be *burnt with the robbers*. (Dionys. apud Euseb. l. vi. c. 41.).

It is evident that Dionysius represents the religious sufferer as innocent of the criminal accusation which had been falsely brought against him. It is no less evident, that whatever might be the opinion of the Centurion, the supreme magistrate considered Nemesion as guilty, and that he affected to shew, by the measure of his tortures, and by the companions of his execution, that he punished him, not only as a Christian, but as a robber. The evidence against Nemesion, and that which might be produced in his favour, are equally lost; and the question (which fortunately is of little moment) of his guilt or innocence rests solely on the opposite judgments of his ecclesiastical and civil superiors. I could easily perceive that both the Bishop and the Governor were actuated by different passions and prejudices towards the unhappy sufferer; but it was impossible for me to decide which of the two was the most likely to indulge his prejudices and passions at the expence of truth. In this doubtful situation, I conceived that I had acted with the most unexceptionable caution, when I contented myself with observing that Nemesion was *accused*; a circumstance of a public and authentic nature, in which both parties were agreed.

Mr. Davis will no longer ask, "what possible evasion then can Mr. Gibbon have recourse to, to convince the world that I have *falsely* accused *him* of a gross misrepresentation of Eusebius?"

2. Mr. Davis[45] charges me with falsifying (*falsifying* is a very serious

---

the learning of a Randolph suggested to the candour of a Chelsum. See Remarks, p. 209.

45. Davis, p. 64, 65.

word) the testimony of Eusebius; because it suited my purpose to magnify the humanity and even kindness of Maxentius towards the afflicted Christians.[46] To support this charge, he produces some part of a chapter of Eusebius, the English in his text, the Greek in his notes, and makes the Ecclesiastical Historian express himself in the following terms: "Although Maxentius at first favoured the Christians with a view of popularity, yet afterwards, being addicted to magic, and every other impiety, HE exerted himself in persecuting the Christians, in a more severe and destructive manner than his predecessors had done before him."

If it were in my power to place the volume and chapter of Eusebius (Hist. Eccles. l. viii. c. 14.) before the eyes of every reader, I should be satisfied and silent. I should not be under the necessity of protesting, that in the passage quoted, or rather abridged, by my adversary, the second member of the period, which alone contradicts my account of Maxentius, has not the most distant reference to that odious tyrant. After distinguishing the mild conduct which *he* affected towards the Christians, Eusebius proceeds to animadvert with becoming severity on the general vices of his reign; the rapes, the murders, the oppression, the promiscuous massacres, which I had faithfully related in their proper place, and which the Christians, not in their religious, but in their civil capacity, must occasionally have shared with the rest of his unhappy subjects. The Ecclesiastical Historian then makes a transition to *another tyrant*, the cruel Maximin, who carried away from his friend and ally Maxentius the prize of superior wickedness; for HE was addicted to magic arts, and was a cruel persecutor of the Christians. The evidence of words and facts, the plain meaning of Eusebius, the concurring testimony of Cæcilius or Lactantius, and the superfluous authority of Versions and Commentators, establish beyond the reach of doubt or cavil, that Maximin, and not Maxentius, is stigmatized as a persecutor, and that Mr. Davis alone has deserved the reproach of *falsifying* the testimony of Eusebius.

Let him examine the chapter on which he founds his accusation. If in that moment his feelings are not of the most painful and humiliating kind, he must indeed be an object of pity!

3. *A gross blunder* is imputed to me by this polite antagonist,[47] for quoting under the name of Jerom, the Chronicle which I ought to have described as the work and property of Eusebius,[48] and Mr. Davis kindly points out the occasion of my blunder, That it was the consequence of

46. Gibbon, p. 504, N. 168.

47. Davis, p. 66.

48. Gibbon, p. 489, N. 125.

my looking no farther than Dodwell for this remark, and of not rightly understanding his reference. Perhaps the Historian of the Roman Empire may be credited, when he affirms that he frequently consulted a Latin Chronicle of the affairs of that Empire; and he may the sooner be credited, if he shews that he knows something more of this Chronicle besides the name and the title-page.

Mr. Davis, who talks so familiarly of the Chronicle of Eusebius, will be surprised to hear that the Greek original no longer exists. Some chronological fragments, which had successively passed through the hands of Africanus and Eusebius, are still extant, though in a very corrupt and mutilated state, in the compilations of Syncellus and Cedrenus. They have been collected, and disposed by the labour and ingenuity of Joseph Scaliger; but that proud Critic, always ready to applaud his own success, did not flatter himself, that he had restored the hundredth part of the genuine Chronicle of Eusebius. "Ex eo (*Syncello*) omnia Eusebiana excerpsimus quæ quidem deprehendere potuimus; quæ, quanquam ne centesima quidem pars eorum esse videtur quæ ab Eusebio relicta sunt, aliquod tamen justum volumen explere possunt." (Jos. Scaliger Animadversiones in Græca Eusebii in Thesauro Temporum, p. 401. Amstelod. 1658.) While the Chronicle of Eusebius was perfect and entire, the second book was translated into Latin by Jerom, with the freedom, or rather licence, which that voluminous Author, as well as his friend or enemy Rufinus, always assumed. "Plurima in vertendo mutat, infulcit, præterit," says Scaliger himself, in the Prolegomena, p. 22. In the persecution of Aurelian, which has so much offended Mr. Davis, we are able to distinguish the work of Eusebius from that of Jerom, by comparing the expressions of the Ecclesiastical History with those of the Chronicle. The former affirms, that, towards the end of his reign, Aurelian was moved by some councils to excite a persecution against the Christians; that his design occasioned a great and general rumour; but that when the letters were prepared, and as it were signed, Divine Justice dismissed him from the world. *Ηδη τισι βουλαις ως αν διωγμον καθ' ἡμων εγειρειεν ανεκινειτο. πολυς τε ην ὁ παρα πασι περι τουτου λογος. μελλοντα δε ηδη και σχεδον ειπειν τοις καθ' ἡμων γραμμασιν υποσημειουμενον, θεια μετεισιν δικη*. Euseb. Hist. Eccles. l. vii. c. 30. Whereas the Chronicle relates, that Aurelian was killed after he had excited or moved a persecution against the Christians, "cum adversum nos persecutionem movisset."

From this manifest difference I assume a right to assert; first, that the expression of the Chronicle of *Jerom*, which is always proper, became in this instance necessary; and secondly, that the language of the Fathers is so ambiguous and incorrect, that we are at a loss how to determine how far Aurelian had carried his intention before he was assassinated. I have neither perverted the *fact*, nor have I been guilty of *a gross blunder.*

IX.
Justin Martyr.

"The persons accused of Christianity had a convenient time allowed them to settle their domestic concerns, and to prepare their answer."[49] This observation had been suggested, partly by a general expression of Cyprian (de Lapsis, p. 88. Edit. Fell. Amstelod. 1700), and more especially by the second Apology of Justin Martyr, who gives a particular and curious example of this legal delay.

The expressions of Cyprian, "dies negantibus præstitutus, &c.", which Mr. Davis most prudently suppresses, are illustrated by Mosheim in the following words: "Primum qui delati erant aut suspecti, illis certum dierum spatium judex definiebat, quo decurrente, secum deliberare poterant, utrum profiteri Christum an negare mallent; *explorandæ fidei præfiniebantur dies*, per hoc tempus liberi manebant in domibus suis; nec impediebat aliquis quod ex consequentibus apparet, ne fugâ sibi consulerent. Satis hoc erat humanum." (De Rebus Christianis ante Constantinum, p. 480.) The practice of Egypt was sometimes more expeditious and severe; but this humane indulgence was still allowed in Africa during the persecution of Decius.

But my appeal to Justin Martyr is encountered by Mr. Davis with the following declaration:[50] "The reader will observe, that Mr. Gibbon does not make any reference to any section or division of this part of Justin's work; with what view we may shrewdly suspect, when I tell him, that after an accurate perusal of the whole second Apology, I can boldly affirm, that the following instance is the only one that bears the most distant similitude to what Mr. Gibbon relates as above on the authority of Justin. What I find in Justin is as follows: "A woman being converted to Christianity, is afraid to associate with her husband, because he is an abandoned reprobate, lest she should partake of his sins. Her husband, not being able to accuse *her*, vents his rage in this manner on one Ptolemæus, a teacher of Christianity, and who had converted her, *&c.*"

49. Gibbon, p. 548.
50. Davis, p. 71, 72.

Mr. Davis then proceeds to relate the severities inflicted on Ptolemæus, who made a frank and instant profession of his faith: and he sternly exclaims, that if I take every opportunity of passing encomiums on the humanity of Roman magistrates, it is incumbent on me to produce better evidence than this.

His demand may be easily satisfied, and I need only for that purpose transcribe and translate the words of Justin, which *immediately* precede the Greek quotation alleged at the bottom of my adversary's page. I am possessed of two editions of Justin Martyr, that of Cambridge, 1768, in 8vo, by Dr. Ashton, who only published the two Apologies; and that of all his works, published in fol. Paris, 1742, by the Benedictines of the Congregation of St. Maar: the following curious passage may be found, p. 164, of the former, and p. 89 of the latter Edition. *κατηγοριαν πεποιηται, λεγων αυτην χριστιανην ειναι, και ἡ μεν βιβλιδιον σοι τω αυτοκρατορι αναδεδωκε, προτερον συνχωρηθηναι αυτη διοικησασθαι τα εαυτης αξιουσα. επειτα απολογησασθαι περι του κατηγορματος, μετα την των πραγματων αυτης διοικησιν. και συνεχωρησας τουτο.* "He brought an accusation against her, saying, that she was a Christian. But she presented a petition to the Emperor, praying that she might first be allowed to settle her domestic concerns; and promising, that after she had settled them, she would then put in her answer to the accusation. This you granted."

I disdain to add a single reflection; nor shall I qualify the conduct of my adversary with any of those harsh epithets, which might be interpreted as the expressions of resentment, though I should be constrained to use them as the only words in the English language, which could accurately represent my cool and unprejudiced sentiments.

X.
Lactantius.

In stating the toleration of Christianity during the greatest part of the reign of Diocletian, I had observed,[51] that the principal officers of the palace, whose names and functions were particularly specified, enjoyed, with their wives and children, the free exercise of the Christian religion. Mr. Davis twice affirms,[52] in the most deliberate manner, that this pretended fact, which is asserted on the sole authority, is contradicted by

51. Gibbon, p. 559. N. 133, 134.
52. Davis, p. 75, 76.

the positive evidence, of Lactantius. In both these *affirmations* Mr. Davis is inexcusably mistaken.

1. When the storms of persecution arose, the Priests, who were offended by the sign of the Cross, obtained an order from the Emperor, that the profane, the Christians, who accompanied him to the Temple, should be compelled to offer sacrifice; and this incident is mentioned by the Rhetorician, to whom I shall not at present refuse the name of Lactantius. The act of idolatry, which, at the expiration of eighteen years, was required of the officers of Diocletian, is a manifest proof that their religious freedom had hitherto been inviolate, except in the single instance of waiting on their master to the Temple; a service less criminal than the profane compliance for which the Minister of the King of Syria solicited the permission of the Prophet of Israel.

2. The reference which I made to Lactantius expressly pointed out this exception to their freedom. But the proof of the toleration was built on a different testimony, which my disingenuous adversary has concealed; an ancient and curious instruction, composed by Bishop Theonas, for the use of Lucian, and the other Christian eunuchs of the palace of Diocletian. This authentic piece was published in the Spicilegium of Dom Luc d'Acheri; as I had not the opportunity of consulting the original, I was contented with quoting it on the faith of Tillemont, and the reference to it immediately precedes (ch. xvi. note 133.) the citation of Lactantius (note 134).

Mr. Davis may now answer his own question, "What apology can be made for thus asserting, on the sole authority of Lactantius, facts which Lactantius so expressly denies?"

XI.
Dion Cassius.

"I have already given a curious instance of our Author's asserting, on the authority of Dion Cassius, a fact not mentioned by that Historian. I shall now produce a very singular proof of his endeavouring to conceal from us a passage really contained in him."[53] Nothing but the angry vehemence with which these charges are urged, could engage me to take the least notice of them. In themselves they are doubly contemptible; they are trifling, and they are false.

1. Mr. Davis[54] had imputed to me as a crime, that I had mentioned,

53. Davis, p. 83.

54. Id. p. 11.

on the sole testimony of Dion (l. lxviii. p. 1145.), the spirit of rebellion which inflamed the Jews, from the reign of Nero to that of Antoninus Pius,[55] whilst the passage of that Historian is confined to an insurrection in Cyprus and Cyrene, which broke out within that period. The Reader who will cast his eye on the Note (ch. xvi. note 1.), which is supported by that quotation from Dion, will discover that it related only to *this* particular fact. The general position, which is indeed too notorious to require any proof, I had carefully justified in the course of the same paragraph; partly by another reference to Dion Cassius, partly by an allusion to the well-known History of Josephus, and partly by *several* quotations from the learned and judicious Basnage, who has explained, in the most satisfactory manner, the principles and conduct of the rebellious Jews.

2. The passage of Dion, which I am accused of endeavouring to conceal, might perhaps have remained invisible, even to the piercing eye of Mr. Davis, if *I* had not carefully reported it in its proper place:[56] and it was in my power to report it, without being guilty of any *inconsiderate contradiction*. I had observed, that, in the large history of Dion Cassius, Xiphilin had not been able to discover the name of *Christians*: yet I afterwards quote a passage in which Marcia, the favourite Concubine of Commodus, is celebrated as the Patroness of the *Christians*. Mr. Davis has transcribed my quotation, but *he* has concealed the important words which I now distinguish by Italics (ch. xvi. note 106. Dion Cassius, *or rather his abbreviator Xiphilin*, l. lxxii. p. 1206.) The reference is fairly made and cautiously qualified: I am already secure from the imputations of fraud or inconsistency; and the opinion which attributes the last-mentioned passage to the Abbreviator, rather than to the original Historian, may be supported by the most unexceptionable authorities. I shall protect myself by those of Reimar (in his Edition of Dion Cassius, tom. ii. p. 1207. note 34.), and of Dr. Lardner; and shall only transcribe the words of the latter, in his Collection of Jewish and Heathen Testimonies, vol. iii. p. 57.

"This paragraph I rather think to be Xiphilin's than Dion's. The style at least is Xiphilin's. In the other passages before quoted, Dion speaks of *Impiety*, or *Atheism*, or *Judaism*; but never useth the word *Christians*. Another thing that may make us doubt whether this observation be entirely Dion's, is the phrase, "it is related (ιστορειται)." For at the beginning of the reign of Commodus, he says, "These things, and what follows, I write not from the report of others, but from my own knowledge and observation." However, the sense may be Dion's; but I

55. Gibbon, p. 515–16.

56. Id. p. 551. N. 107.

wish we had also his style without any adulteration." For my own part, I must, in my private opinion, ascribe even the sense of this passage to Xiphilin. The *Monk* might eagerly collect and insert an anecdote which related to the domestic history of the church; but the religion of a courtezan must have appeared an object of very little moment in the eyes of a *Roman Consul*, who, at least in every other part of his history, disdained or neglected to mention the name of the Christians.

"What shall we say now? Do we not discover the name of Christians in the History of Dion? With what *assurance* then can Mr. Gibbon, after asserting a fact manifestly *untrue*, lay claim to the merits of diligence and accuracy, the indispensable duty of an Historian. Or can he expect us to credit his assertion, that he has carefully examined all the original materials?"[57]

Mr. Gibbon may still maintain the character of an Historian; but it is difficult to conceive how Mr. Davis will support his pretensions, if he aspires to that of a Gentleman.

I almost hesitate whether I should take any notice of another ridiculous charge which Mr. Davis includes in the article of Dion Cassius. My adversary owns, that I have occasionally produced the several passages of the Augustan History which relate to the Christians; but he fiercely contends that they amount to more than *six lines*.[58] I really have not measured them: nor did I mean that loose expression as a precise and definite number. If, on a nicer survey, those short hints, when they are brought together, should be found to exceed six of the long lines of my folio edition, I am content that my critical Antagonist should substitute eight, or ten, or twelve, lines: nor shall I think either my learning or my veracity much interested in this important alteration.

XII.
Pliny, &c.

After a short description of the unworthy conduct of those Apostates who, in a time of persecution, deserted the Faith of Christ, I produced the evidence of a Pagan Proconsul,[59] and of two Christian Bishops, Pliny, Dionysius of Alexandria, and Cyprian. And here the unforgiving Critic remarks, "That Pliny has not particularized that difference of conduct (in the different Apostates) which Mr. Gibbon here describes: yet his

57. Davis, p. 83.
58. Gibbon, p. 525. N. 24.
59. Id. p. 549. N. 102.

name stands at the head of those Authors whom he has cited on the occasion. It is allowed indeed that this distinction is made by the other Authors; but as Pliny, the first referred to by Mr. Gibbon, gives him no cause or reason to use *them*," (I cannot help Mr. Davis's bad English) "it is certainly very reprehensible in our Author, thus to confound their testimony, and to make a needless and improper reference."[60]

A criticism of this sort can only tend to expose Mr. Davis's total ignorance of historical composition. The Writer who aspires to the name of Historian, is obliged to consult a variety of original testimonies, each of which, taken separately, is perhaps imperfect and partial. By a judicious re-union and arrangement of these dispersed materials, he endeavours to form a consistent and interesting narrative. Nothing ought to be inserted which is not proved by some of the witnesses; but their evidence must be so intimately blended together, that as it is unreasonable to expect that each of them should vouch for the whole, so it would be impossible to define the boundaries of their respective property. Neither Pliny, nor Dionysius, nor Cyprian, mention *all* the circumstances and *distinctions* of the conduct of the Christian Apostates; but if any of them was withdrawn, the account which I have given would, in some instance, be defective.

Thus much I thought necessary to say, as several of the subsequent *misrepresentations* of Orosius, of Bayle, of Fabricius, of Gregory of Tours, &c.,[61] which provoked the fury of Mr. Davis, are derived only from the ignorance of this common historical principle.

Another class of Misrepresentations, which my Adversary urges with the same degree of vehemence (See in particular those of Justin, Diodorus Siculus, and even Tacitus), requires the support of another principle, which has not yet been introduced into the art of criticism; *that* when a modern historian appeals to the authority of the ancients for the truth of any particular fact; he makes himself answerable, I know not to what extent, for all the circumjacent errors or inconsistencies of the authors whom he has quoted.

XIII.
Ignatius.

I am accused of throwing out a false accusation against this Father,[62]

60. Davis, p. 87, 88.
61. Id. p. 88. 90. 137.
62. Id. p. 100, 101.

because I had observed[63] that Ignatius, defending against the Gnostics the resurrection of Christ, employs a vague and doubtful tradition, instead of quoting the certain testimony of the Evangelists: and this observation was justified by a remarkable passage of Ignatius, in his Epistle to the Smyrnæans, which I cited according to the volume and the page of the best edition of the Apostolical Fathers, published at Amsterdam, 1724, in two volumes in folio. The Criticism of Mr. Davis is announced by one of those solemn declarations which leave not any refuge, if they are convicted of falsehood. "I cannot find any passage that bears the least affinity to what Mr. Gibbon observes, in the whole Epistle, which I have read over more than once."

I had already marked the *situation*; nor is it in my power to prove the *existence*, of this passage, by any other means than by producing the words of the original. *Εγω γαρ και μετα την αναστασιν εν σαρκι αυτον οιδα και πιστευω οντα, και οτε προς τους περι Πετρον ηλθεν, εφη αυτοις, λαβετε, ψυλαφησατε με, και ιδετε οτι ουκ' ειμι δαιμονιον ασωματον. και ευθυς αυτου ἥψαντο, και επιστευσαν.* "I have known, and I believe, that after his resurrection likewise he existed in the flesh: And when he came to Peter, and to the rest, he said unto them, Take, handle me, and see that I am not an incorporal dæmon or spirit. And they touched him, and believed." The faith of the Apostles confuted the impious error of the Gnostics, which attributed only the *appearances* of a human body to the Son of God: and it was the great object of Ignatius, in the last moments of his life, to secure the Christians of Asia from the snares of those dangerous Heretics. According to the tradition of the modern Greeks, Ignatius was the child whom Jesus received into his arms (See Tillemont Mem. Eccles. tom. ii. part ii. p. 43.); yet as he could scarcely be old enough to remember the resurrection of the Son of God, he must have derived his knowledge *either* from our present Evangelists, *or* from some Apocryphal Gospel, *or* from some unwritten tradition.

1. The Gospels of St. Luke and St. John would undoubtedly have supplied Ignatius with the most invincible proofs of the reality of the body of Christ, when he appeared to the Apostles after his resurrection; but neither of those Gospels contain the characteristic words of *ουκ δαιμονιον ασωματον*, and the important circumstance that either Peter, or *those* who were with Peter, touched the body of Christ and believed. Had the saint designed to quote the Evangelist on a very nice subject of controversy, he would not surely have exposed himself, by an inaccurate,

63. Gibbon, p. 458. Note 35.

or rather by a false, reference, to the just reproaches of the Gnostics. On this occasion, therefore, Ignatius did not employ, as he might have done, against the Heretics, the certain testimony of the Evangelists.

2. Jerom, who cites this remarkable passage from the Epistle of Ignatius to the Smyrnæans (See Catalog. Script. Eccles. in Ignatio, tom. i. p. 273. edit. Erasm. Basil, 1537), is of opinion that it was taken from the *Gospel* which he himself had lately translated: and *this*, from the comparison of two other passages in the same Work (in Jacob. et in Matthæo, p. 264), appears to have been the Hebrew Gospel, which was used by the Nazarenes of Beræa, as the genuine composition of St. Matthew. Yet Jerom mentions another Copy of this Hebrew Gospel (so different from the Greek Text), which was extant in the library formed at Cæsarea, by the care of Pamphilus: while the learned Eusebius, the friend of Pamphilus and the Bishop of Cæsarea, very frankly declares (Hist. Eccles. l. iii. c. 36.), that *he* is ignorant from whence Ignatius borrowed those words, which are the subject of the present Inquiry.

3. The doubt which remains, is only whether he took them from an Apocryphal Book, or from *unwritten tradition*: and I thought myself safe from every species of Critics, when I embraced the rational sentiment of Casaubon and Pearson. I shall produce the words of the Bishop. "Præterea iterum observandum est, quod de hac re scripsit Isaacus Casaubonus, *Quinetiam fortasse verius, non ex Evangelio Hebraico, Ignatium illa verba descripsisse, verum traditionem allegasse non scriptam, quæ postea in literas fuerit relata, et Hebraico Evangelio, quod Matthæo tribuebant, inserta.* Et hoc quidem mihi multo verisimilius videtur." (Pearson. Vindiciæ Ignatianæ, part ii. c. ix. p. 396. in tom. ii. Patr. Apostol.)

I may now submit to the judgment of the Public, whether I have looked into the Epistle which I cite with such a parade of learning, and *how profitably* Mr. Davis has read it over more than once.

XIV.
Mosheim.

The learning and judgment of Mosheim had been of frequent use in the course of my Historical Inquiry, and I had not been wanting in proper expressions of gratitude. My vexatious Adversary is always ready to start from his ambuscade, and to harass my march by a mode of attack, which cannot easily be reconciled with the laws of honourable war. The greatest part of the Misrepresentations of Mosheim, which Mr. Davis has imputed to me,[64] are of such a nature, that I must indeed be humble, if I could persuade myself to bestow a moment of serious attention on them. *Whether* Mosheim could prove that an absolute community of goods was not established among the first Christians of Jerusalem; *whether* he suspected the purity of the Epistles of Ignatius; *whether* he censured Dr. Middleton with temper or indignation (in this cause I must challenge Mr. Davis as an incompetent judge); *whether* he corroborates the *whole* of my description of the prophetic office; *whether* he speaks with approbation of the humanity of Pliny, and *whether* he attributed the same sense to the *malefica* of Suetonius, and the *exitiabilis* of Tacitus? These questions, even as Mr. Davis has stated them, lie open to the judgment of every reader, and the superfluous observations which I could make, would be an abuse of their time and of my own. As little shall I think of consuming their patience, by examining whether Le Clerc and Mosheim *labour* in the interpretation of some texts of the Fathers, and particularly of a passage of Irenæus, which seem to favour the pretensions of the Roman Bishop. The material part of the passage of Irenæus consists of about *four lines*; and in order to shew that the interpretations of Le Clerc and Mosheim are not *laboured*, Mr. Davis abridges them as much as possible in the space of *twelve pages*. I known not whether the perusal of my History will justify the suspicion of Mr. Davis, that I am secretly inclined to the interest of the Pope: but I cannot discover how the Protestant cause can be affected, if Irenæus in the second, or Palavicini in the seventeenth century, were tempted, by any private views, to countenance in their writings the system of ecclesiastical dominion, which has been pursued in every age by the aspiring Bishops of the Imperial city. Their conduct was adapted to the revolutions of the Christian Republic, but the same spirit animated the haughty breasts of Victor the First, and of Paul the Fifth.

There still remain one or two of these imputed Misrepresentations, which appear, and indeed only appear, to merit a little more attention. In stating the opinion of Mosheim with regard to the progress of the Gospel, Mr. Davis boldly declares, "that I have *altered the truth* of Mosheim's history, that I might have an opportunity of contradicting the belief and wishes of the Fathers."[65] In other words, I have been guilty of uttering a malicious falsehood.

I had endeavoured to mitigate the sanguine expression of the Fathers of the second century, who had too hastily diffused the light of Christianity over every part of the globe, by observing, as an undoubted fact,

64. Davis, p. 95–97. 104–107. 114–132.
65. Id. p. 127.

"that the Barbarians of Scythia and Germany, who subverted the Roman Monarchy, were involved in the errors of Paganism; and that even the conquest of Iberia, of Armenia, or of Æthiopia, was not attempted with any degree of success, till the scepter was in the hands of an orthodox Emperor."[66] I had referred the curious reader to the fourth century of Mosheim's General History of the Church: Now Mr. Davis has discovered, and can prove, from that excellent work, "that Christianity, not long after its first rise, had been introduced into the less as well as greater Armenia; that part of the Goths, who inhabited Thracia, Mæsia, and Dacia, had received the Christian religion long before this century; and that Theophilus, their Bishop, was present at the Council of Nice."[67]

On this occasion, the reference was made to a popular work of Mosheim, for the satisfaction of the reader, that he might obtain the general view of the progress of Christianity in the fourth century, which I had gradually acquired by studying with some care the Ecclesiastic Antiquities of the Nations beyond the limits of the Roman Empire. If I had reasonably supposed that the result of our common inquiries must be the same, should I have deserved a very harsh censure for my unsuspecting confidence? Or if I had declined the invidious task of separating a few immaterial errors, from a just and judicious representation, might not my respect for the name and merit of Mosheim, have claimed some indulgence? But I disdain those excuses, which only a candid adversary would allow. I can meet Mr. Davis on the hard ground of controversy, and retort on his own head the charge of concealing a part of the truth. He himself has dared to suppress the words of my text, which immediately followed his quotation. "Before that time the various accidents of war and commerce might indeed diffuse an imperfect knowledge of the Gospel among the tribes of Caledonia, and among the borderers of the Rhine, the Danube, and the Euphrates;" and Mr. Davis has likewise suppressed one of the justificatory Notes on this passage, which expressly points out the time and circumstances of the first Gothic conversions. These exceptions, which I had cautiously inserted, and Mr. Davis has cautiously concealed, are superfluous for the provinces of Thrace, Mæsia, and the Lesser Armenia, which were contained within the precincts of the Roman Empire. They allow an ample scope for the more early conversion of some independent districts of Dacia and the Greater Armenia, which bordered on the Danube and Euphrates; and the entire

66. Gibbon, p. 506, 507.
67. Davis, p. 126, 127.

sense of this passage, which Mr. Davis first mutilates and then attacks, is perfectly consistent with the original text of the learned Mosheim.

And yet I will fairly confess, that, after a nicer inquiry into the epoch of the Armenian Church, I am not satisfied with the accuracy of my own expression. The assurance that the first Christian King, and the first Archbishop, Tiridates, and St. Gregory the Illuminator, were still alive several years after the death of Constantine, inclined me to believe, that the conversion of Armenia was posterior to the auspicious Revolution, which had given the scepter of Rome to the hands of an orthodox Emperor. But I had not enough considered the two following circumstances. 1. I might have recollected the dates assigned by Moses of Chorene, who, on this occasion, may be regarded as a competent witness. Tiridates ascended the throne of Armenia in the third year of Diocletian (Hist. Armeniæ, l. ii. c. 79. p. 207.), and St. Gregory, who was invested with the Episcopal character in the seventeenth year of Tiridates, governed almost thirty years the Church of Armenia, and disappeared from the world in the forty-sixth year of the reign of the same Prince. (Hist. Armeniæ, l. ii. c. 88. p. 224, 225.) The consecration of St. Gregory must therefore be placed A.D. 303, and the conversion of the King and kingdom was soon atchieved by that successful missionary. 2. The unjust and inglorious war which Maximin undertook against the Armenians, the ancient faithful allies of the Republic, was evidently derived from a motive of superstitious zeal. The historian Eusebius (Hist. Eccles. l. ix. c. 8. p. 448. edit. Cantab.) considers the pious Armenians as a nation of Christians, who bravely defended themselves from the hostile oppression of an idolatrous tyrant. Instead of maintaining "that the conversion of Armenia was not attempted with any degree of success till the scepter was in the hands of an orthodox Emperor," I ought to have observed, that the seeds of the faith were deeply sown during the season of the last and greatest persecution, that many Roman exiles might assist the labours of Gregory, and that the renowned Tiridates, the hero of the East, may dispute with Constantine the honour of being the first Sovereign who embraced the Christian religion.

In a future edition, I shall rectify an expression which, in strictness, can only be applied to the kingdoms of Iberia and Æthiopia. Had the error been exposed by Mr. Davis himself, I should not have been ashamed to correct it; but *I am* ashamed at being reduced to contend with an adversary who is unable to discover, or to improve, his own advantages.

But, instead of prosecuting any inquiry from whence the public might have gained instruction, and himself credit, Mr. Davis chuses to perplex his readers with some angry cavils about the progress of the Gospel in the second century. What does he mean to establish or to refute? Have I denied, that before the end of that period Christianity was very widely diffused both in the East and in the West? Has not Justin Martyr affirmed, without exception or limitation, that it was already preached to *every* nation on the face of the earth? Is that proposition true at present? Could it be true in the time of Justin? Does not Mosheim acknowledge the exaggeration? "Demus, nec enim quæ in oculos incurrunt infitiari audemus, esse in his verbis exaggerationis nonnihil. Certum enim est diu post Justini ætatem, multas orbis terrarum gentes cognitione Christi caruisse." (Mosheim de Rebus Christianis, p. 203.) Does he not expose (p. 205.), with becoming scorn and indignation, the falsehood and vanity of the hyperboles of Tertullian? "bonum hominem æstu imaginationis elatum non satis adtendisse ad ea quæ litteris consignabat."

The high esteem which Mr. Davis expresses for the writings of Mosheim, would alone convince me how little he has read them, since he must have been perpetually offended and disgusted by a train of thinking, the most repugnant to his own. His jealousy, however, for the honour of Mosheim, provokes him to arraign the boldness of Mr. Gibbon who presumes *falsely* to charge such an eminent man with *unjustifiable assertions.*[68] I might observe, that my style, which on this occasion was more modest and moderate, has acquired, perhaps undesignedly, an illiberal cast from the rough hand of Mr. Davis. But as my veracity is impeached, I may be less solicitous about my politeness; and though I have repeatedly declined the fairest opportunities of correcting the errors of my predecessors, yet, as long as I have truth on my side, I am not easily daunted by the names of the most eminent men.

The assertion of Mosheim, which did not seem to be justified[69] by the authority of Lactantius, was, that the wife and daughter of Diocletian, Prisca and *Valeria*, had been privately *baptized*. Mr. Davis is sure that the words of Mosheim, "Christianis sacris clam initiata," need not be confined to the rite of baptism; and he is equally sure, that the reference to Mosheim does not lead us to discover even the name of Valeria. In both these assurances he is grossly mistaken; but it is the misfortune of controversy, that an error may be committed in three or four words, which cannot be rectified in less than thirty or forty lines.

1. The true and the sole meaning of the Christian initiation, one of the familiar and favourite allusions of the Fathers of the fourth century,

68. Davis, p. 131.

69. Gibbon, p. 558, Note 132.

is clearly explained by the exact and laborious Bingham. "The baptized were also styled *ὅι μεμυημενοι*, which the Latins call *initiati*, the initiated, that is admitted to the use of the *sacred* offices, and knowledge of the *sacred* mysteries of the Christian Religion. Hence came that form of speaking so frequently used by St. Chrysostom, and other ancient writers, when they touched upon any doctrines or mysteries which the Catechumens understood not, *ισασιν ὁι μεμυημενοι*, the initiated know what is spoken. St. Ambrose writes a book to these *initiati*; Isidore of Pelusium and Hesychius call them *μυσται* and *μυσταγωγητοι*. Whence the Catechumens have the contrary names, *Αμυστοι, Αμυητοι, Αμυσταγωγητοι*, the uninitiated or unbaptized." (Antiquities of the Christian Church, l. i. c. 4. N° 2. vol. i. p. 11. fol. edit.) Had I presumed to suppose that Mosheim was capable of employing a technical expression in a loose and equivocal sense, I should indeed have violated the respect which I have always entertained for his learning and abilities.

2. But Mr. Davis cannot discover in the text of Mosheim the name of Valeria. In that case Mosheim would have suffered another slight inaccuracy to drop from his pen, as the passage of Lactantius, "sacrificio pollui coëgit," on which he founds his assertion, includes the names both of Prisca and Valeria. But I am not reduced to the necessity of accusing another in my own defence. Mosheim has properly and expressly declared that Valeria imitated the pious example of her mother Prisca, "Gener Diocletiani uxorem habebat *Valeriam* matris exemplum pietate erga Deum imitantem et a cultu fictorum Numinum alienam." (Mosheim, p. 913.) Mr. Davis has a bad habit of greedily snapping at the first words of a reference, without giving himself the trouble of going to the end of the page or paragraph.

These trifling and peevish cavils would, perhaps, have been confounded with some criticisms of the same stamp, on which I had bestowed a slight, though sufficient notice, in the beginning of this article of Mosheim; had not my attention been awakened by a peroration worthy of Tertullian himself, if Tertullian had been devoid of eloquence as well as of moderation – "Much less does the Christian Mosheim give our *infidel Historian* any pretext for inserting that *illiberal malignant insinuation*, "That Christianity has, in every age, acknowledged its important obligations to FEMALE devotion;" the remark is truly *contemptible*."[70]

It is not my design to fill whole pages with a tedious enumeration of the many illustrious examples of female Saints, who, in every age, and almost in every country, have promoted the interest of Christianity. Such

70. Davis, p. 132.

instances will readily offer themselves to those who have the slightest knowledge of Ecclesiastical History; nor is it necessary that I should remind them how much the charms, the influence, the devotion of Clotilda, and of her great-grand-daughter Bertha, contributed to the conversion of France and England. Religion may accept, without a blush, the services of the purest and most gentle portion of the human species: but there are some advocates who would disgrace Christianity, if Christianity could be disgraced, by the manner in which they defend her cause.

XV.
Tillemont.

As I could not readily procure the works of Gregory of Nyssa, I borrowed[71] from the accurate and indefatigable Tillemont, a passage in the Life of Gregory Thaumaturgus, or the Wonder-worker, which affirmed that when the Saint took possession of his Episcopal See, he found only SEVENTEEN *Christians* in the city of Neo-Cæsarea, and the adjacent country, "Les environs, la Campagne, le pays d'alentour." (Mem. Eccles. Tom. iv. p. 677. 691. Edit. Brusselles, 1706). These expressions of Tillemont, to whom I explicitly acknowledged my obligation, appeared synonymous to the word *Diocese*, the whole territory intrusted to the pastoral care of the Wonder-worker, and I added the epithet of *extensive*; because I was apprised that Neo-Cæsarea was the capital of the Polemoniac Pontus, and that the whole kingdom of Pontus, which stretched above five hundred miles along the coast of the Euxine, was divided between sixteen or seventeen Bishops. (See the Geographia Ecclesiastica of Charles de St. Paul, and Lucas Holstenius, p. 249, 250, 251.) Thus far I may not be thought to have deserved any censure; but the omission of the subsequent part of the same passage, which imports that at his death the Wonder-worker left no more than *seventeen Pagans*, may seem to wear a partial and suspicious aspect.

Let me therefore first observe, as some evidence of an impartial disposition, that I *easily* admitted, as the cool observation of the philosophic Lucian, the angry and interested complaint of the false prophet Alexander, that Pontus was filled with Christians. This complaint was made under the reigns of Marcus or of Commodus, with whom the impostor so admirably exposed by Lucian was contemporary: and I had

71. Gibbon, p. 501. N. 156.

contented myself with remarking that the numbers of Christians must have been very unequally distributed in the several parts of Pontus, since the diocese of Neo-Cæsarea contained, above sixty years afterwards, only seventeen Christians. Such was the inconsiderable flock which Gregory began to feed about the year two hundred and forty, and the real or fabulous conversions ascribed to that Wonder-working Bishop during a reign of thirty years, are totally foreign to the state of Christianity in the preceding century. This obvious reflection may serve to answer the objection of Mr. Davis,[72] and of another adversary,[73] who on this occasion is more liberal than Mr. Davis of those harsh epithets so familiar to the tribe of Polemics.

XVI.
Pagi.

"Mr. Gibbon says,[74] "Pliny was sent into Bithynia (according to Pagi) in the year 110."

"Now that accurate Chronologer places it in the year 102. See the fact *recorded* in his Critica-Historico-Chronologica in Annales C. Baronii, A.D. 102. p. 99. fæc. ii. § 3."

"I appeal to my reader, Whether this anachronism does not plainly prove that our Historian never looked into Pagi's Chronology, though he has not hesitated to make a pompous reference to him in his note?"[75]

I cannot help observing, that either Mr. Davis's Dictionary is extremely confined, or that in his Philosophy all sins are of equal magnitude. Every error of fact or language, every instance where he does not know to reconcile the original and the reference, he expresses by the gentle word of *misrepresentation*. An inaccurate appeal to the sentiment of Pagi, on a subject where I must have been perfectly disinterested, might have been styled a lapse of memory, instead of being censured as the effect of vanity and ignorance. Pagi is neither a difficult nor an uncommon writer, nor could I hope to derive much additional fame from a *pompous* quotation of his writings, which I had never seen.

The words employed by Mr. Davis, of *fact*, of *record*, of *anachronism*, are unskilfully chosen, and so unhappily applied, as to betray a very shameful

72. Davis, p. 136, 137.

73. Dr. Randolph, in Chelsum's Remarks, p. 159, 160.

74. Gibbon, p. 501. N. 157.

75. Davis, p. 140.

ignorance, either of the English language, or of the nature of this Chronological Question. The date of Pliny's government of Bithynia is not a fact recorded by any ancient writer, but an opinion which modern critics have variously formed, from the consideration of presumptive and collateral evidence. Cardinal Baronius placed the consulship of Pliny one year too late, and, as he was persuaded that the old practice of the republic still subsisted, he naturally supposed that Pliny obtained his province immediately after the expiration of his consulship. He therefore sends him into Bithynia in the year which, according to his erroneous computation, coincided with the year one hundred and four (Baron. Annal. Eccles. A.D. 103. N° 1. 104. N° 1), or, according to the true chronology, with the year one hundred and two, of the Christian Æra. This mistake of Baronius, Pagi, with the assistance of his friend Cardinal Noris, undertakes to correct. From an accurate parallel of the Annals of Trajan and the Epistles of Pliny, he deduces his proofs that Pliny remained at Rome several years after his Consulship; by his own ingenious, though sometimes fanciful theory, of the imperial Quinquennalia, &c. Pagi at last discovers that Pliny made his entrance into Bithynia in the year one hundred and ten. "Plinius igitur anno Christi CENTESIMO DECIMO Bithyniam intravit." Pagi, tom. i. p. 100.

I will be more indulgent to my adversary than he has been to me: I will admit, that he has *looked into Pagi*; but I must add, that he has only looked into that accurate Chronologer. To rectify the errors, which, in the course of a laborious and original work, had escaped the diligence of the Cardinal, was the arduous task which Pagi proposed to execute: and for the sake of perspicuity, he distributes his criticisms according to the particular dates, whether just or faulty, of the Chronology of Baronius himself. Under the year 102, Mr. Davis confusedly saw a long argument about Pliny and Bithynia, and without condescending to read the Author whom he *pompously* quotes, this hasty Critic imputes to him the opinion which he had so laboriously destroyed.

My readers, if any readers have accompanied me thus far, must be satisfied, and indeed satiated, with the repeated proofs which I have made of the weight and temper of my adversary's weapons. They have, in every assault, fallen dead and lifeless to the ground: they have more than once recoiled, and dangerously wounded the unskilful hand that had presumed to use them. I have now examined all the *misrepresentations* and *inaccuracies*, which even for a moment could perplex the ignorant, or deceive the credulous: the *few* imputations which I have neglected, are still more palpably false, or still more evidently trifling, and even the friends of Mr. Davis will scarcely continue to ascribe my contempt to my fear.

Plagiarisms.

The first part of his Critical Volume might admit, though it did not deserve, a particular reply. But the easy, though tedious compilation, which fills the remainder,[76] and which Mr. Davis has produced as the evidence of my shameful *plagiarisms*, may be set in its true light by three or four short and general reflexions.

I. Mr. Davis has disposed, in two columns, the passages which he thinks proper to select from my Two last Chapters, and the corresponding passages from Middleton, Barbeyrac, Beausobre, Dodwell, &c., to the most important of which he had been regularly guided by my own quotations. According to the opinion which he has conceived of literary property, to *agree* is to *follow*, and to *follow* is to *steal*. He celebrates his own sagacity with loud and reiterated applause, and declares with infinite facetiousness, that if he restored to every author the passages which Mr. Gibbon has purloined, *he* would appear as naked as the proud and gaudy Daw in the Fable, when each bird had plucked away its own plumes. Instead of being angry with Mr. Davis for the parallel which he has extended to so great a length, I am under some obligation to his industry for the copious proofs which he has furnished the reader, that my representation of some of the most important facts of Ecclesiastical Antiquity, is supported by the authority or opinion of the most ingenious and learned of the modern writers. The Public may not, perhaps, be very eager to assist Mr. Davis in his favourite amusement of *depluming* me. They may think, that if the materials which compose my Two last Chapters are curious and valuable, it is of little moment to whom they properly belong. If my readers are satisfied with the form, the colours, the new arrangement which I have given to the labours of my predecessors, they may perhaps consider me not as a contemptible Thief, but as an honest and industrious Manufacturer, who has fairly procured the raw materials, and worked them up with a laudable degree of skill and success.

II. About two hundred years ago, the Court of Rome discovered that the system which had been erected by ignorance must be defended and

76. Davis, p. 168–274.

countenanced by the aid, or at least by the abuse, of science. The grosser legends of the middle ages were abandoned to contempt, but the supremacy and infallibility of two hundred Popes, the virtues of many thousand Saints, and the miracles which they either performed or related, have been laboriously consecrated in the Ecclesiastical Annals of Cardinal Baronius. A Theological Barometer might be formed, of which the Cardinal and our countryman Dr. Middleton should constitute the opposite and remote extremities, as the former sunk to the lowest degree of credulity, which was compatible with learning, and the latter rose to the highest pitch of scepticism, in any wise consistent with Religion. The intermediate gradations would be filled by a line of ecclesiastical critics, whose rank has been fixed by the circumstances of their temper and studies, as well as by the spirit of the church or society to which they were attached. It would be amusing enough to calculate the weight of prejudice in the air of Rome, of Oxford, of Paris, and of Holland; and sometimes to observe the irregular tendency of Papists towards freedom, sometimes to remark the unnatural gravitation of Protestants towards slavery. But it is useful to borrow the assistance of so many learned and ingenious men, who have viewed the first ages of the church in every light, and from every situation. If we skilfully combine the passions and prejudices, the hostile motives and intentions, of the several theologians, we may frequently extract knowledge from credulity, moderation from zeal, and impartial truth from the most disingenuous controversy. It is the right, it is the duty of a critical historian to collect, to weigh, to select the opinions of his predecessors; and the more diligence he has exerted in the search, the more rationally he may hope to add some improvement to the stock of knowledge, the use of which has been common to all.

III. Besides the ideas which may be suggested by the study of the most learned and ingenious of the moderns, the historian may be indebted to them for the occasional communication of some passages of the ancients, which might otherwise have escaped his knowledge or his memory. In the consideration of any extensive subject, none will pretend to have read all that has been written, or to recollect all that they have read: nor is there any disgrace in recurring to the writers who have professionally treated any questions, which, in the course of a long narrative, we are called upon to mention in a slight and incidental manner. If I touch upon the obscure and fanciful theology of the Gnostics, I can accept without a blush the assistance of the candid Beausobre; and when, amidst the fury of contending parties, I trace the progress of ecclesiastical dominion, I am not ashamed to confess myself the grateful disciple of the impartial

Mosheim. In the next Volume of my History, the Reader and the Critic must prepare themselves to see me make a still more liberal use of the labours of those indefatigable workmen who have dug deep into the mine of antiquity. The Fathers of the fourth and fifth centuries are far more voluminous than their predecessors; the writings of Jerom, of Augustin, of Chrysostom, *&c.* cover the walls of our libraries. The smallest part is of the historical kind: yet the treatises which seem the least to invite the curiosity of the reader, frequently conceal very useful hints, or very valuable facts. The polemic, who involves himself and his antagonists in a cloud of argumentation, sometimes relates the origin and progress of the heresy which he confutes; and the preacher who declaims against the luxury, describes the manners, of the age; and seasonably introduces the mention of some public calamity, that he may ascribe it to the justice of offended Heaven. It would surely be unreasonable to expect that the historian should peruse enormous volumes, with the uncertain hope of extracting a few interesting lines, or that he should sacrifice whole days to the momentary amusement of his Reader. Fortunately for us both, the diligence of ecclesiastical critics has facilitated our inquiries: the compilations of Tillemont might alone be considered as an immense repertory of truth and fable, of almost all that the Fathers have preserved, or invented, or believed; and if we equally avail ourselves of the labours of contending sectaries, we shall often discover, that the same passages which the prudence of one of the disputants would have suppressed or disguised, are placed in the most conspicuous light by the active and interested zeal of his adversary. On these occasions, what is the duty of a faithful historian, who derives from some modern writer the knowledge of some ancient testimony, which he is desirous of introducing into his own narrative? It is his duty, and it has been my invariable practice, to consult the original; to study with attention the words, the design, the spirit, the context, the situation of the passage to which I had been referred; and before I appropriated it to my own use, to justify my own declaration, "that I had carefully examined all the original materials that could illustrate the subject which I had undertaken to treat." If this important obligation has sometimes been imperfectly fulfilled, I have only omitted what it would have been impracticable for me to perform. The greatest city in the world is still destitute of that useful institution, a public library; and the writer who has undertaken to treat any large historical subject, is reduced to the necessity of purchasing, for his private use, a numerous and valuable collection of the books which must form the basis of his work. The diligence of his booksellers will not always prove successful; and the candour of his readers will not *always* expect, that, for the sake of verifying an accidental quotation of ten lines, he should load himself with an useless and expensive series of ten volumes. In a very few instances, where I had not the opportunity of consulting the originals, I have adopted their testimony on the faith of modern guides, of whose fidelity I was satisfied; but on these occasions,[77] instead of decking myself with the borrowed plumes of Tillemont or Lardner, I have been most scrupulously exact in marking the extent of my reading, and the source of my information. This distinction, which a sense of truth and modesty had engaged me to express, is ungenerously abused by Mr. Davis, who seems happy to inform his readers, that "in ONE instance (Chap. xvi. 164. or, in the first edition, 163.) I have, by an unaccountable oversight, unfortunately for myself, forgot to drop the modern, and that I modestly disclaim all knowledge of Athanasius, but what I had picked up from Tillemont."[78] Without animadverting on the decency of these expressions, which are now grown familiar to me, I shall content myself with observing, that as I had frequently quoted Eusebius, or Cyprian, or Tertullian, *because* I had read them; so, in this instance, I only made my reference to Tillemont, *because* I had not read, and did not possess, the works of Athanasius. The progress of my undertaking has since directed me to peruse the Historical Apologies of the Archbishop of Alexandria, whose life is a very interesting part of the age in which he lived; and if Mr. Davis should have the curiosity to look into my Second Volume, he will find that I make a free and frequent appeal to the writings of Athanasius. Whatever may be the opinion or practice of my adversary, this I apprehend to be the dealing of a fair and honourable man.

IV. The historical monuments of the three first centuries of ecclesiastical antiquity are neither very numerous, nor very prolix. From the end of the Acts of the Apostles, to the time when the first Apology of Justin Martyr was presented, there intervened a dark and doubtful period of fourscore years; and, even if the Epistles of Ignatius should be approved by the critic, they could not be very serviceable to the historian. From the middle of the second, to the beginning of the fourth, century, we gain knowledge of the state and progress of Christianity from the successive Apologies which were occasionally composed by Justin, Athenagoras, Tertullian, Origen, *&c.*; from the Epistles of Cyprian; from a few *sincere*

77. Gibbon, p. 501, N. 156; p. 502, N. 161; p. 503, N. 164; p. 506, N. 178.

78. Davis, p. 273.

acts of the Martyrs; from some moral or controversial tracts, which indirectly explain the events and manners of the times; from the rare and accidental notice which profane writers have taken of the Christian sect; from the declamatory Narrative which celebrates the deaths of the persecutors; and from the Ecclesiastical History of Eusebius, who has preserved some valuable fragments of more early writers. Since the revival of letters, these original materials have been the common fund of critics and historians: nor has it ever been imagined, that the absolute and exclusive property of a passage in Eusebius or Tertullian was acquired by the first who had an opportunity of quoting it. The learned work of Mosheim, *de Rebus Christianis ante Constantinum*, was printed in the year 1753; and if I were possessed of the patience and disingenuity of Mr. Davis, I would engage to find all the ancient testimonies that he has alleged, in the writings of Dodwell or Tillemont, which were published before the end of the last century. But if I were animated by any malevolent intentions against Dodwell or Tillemont, I could as easily, and as unfairly, fix on *them* the guilt of Plagiarism, by producing the same passages transcribed or translated at full length in the Annals of Cardinal Baronius. Let not criticism be any longer disgraced by the practice of such unworthy arts. Instead of admitting suspicions as false as they are ungenerous, candour will acknowledge, that Mosheim or Dodwell, Tillemont or Baronius, enjoyed the same right, and often were under the same obligation, of quoting the passages which they had read, and which were indispensably requisite to confirm the truth and substance of their similar narratives. Mr. Davis is so far from allowing me the benefit of this common indulgence, or rather of this common right, that he stigmatizes with the name of *Plagiarism* a close and literal agreement with Dodwell in the account of some parts of the persecution of Diocletian, where a few chapters of Eusebius and Lactantius, perhaps of Lactantius alone, are the sole materials from whence our knowledge could be derived, and where, if I had not transcribed, I must have invented. He is even bold enough (*bold* is not the *proper* word) to conceive some hopes of persuading his readers, that an Historian who has employed several years of his life, and several hundred pages, on the Decline and Fall of the Roman Empire, had never read Orosius, or the Augustan History; and that he was forced to borrow, at second-hand, his quotations from the Theodosian Code. I cannot profess myself very desirous of Mr. Davis's acquaintance; but if he will take the trouble of calling at my house any afternoon when I am *not* at home, my servant shall shew him my library, which he will find tolerably well furnished with the useful authors, ancient as well as modern, ecclesiastical as well as profane, who have *directly* supplied me with the materials of my History.

The peculiar reasons, and they are not of the most flattering kind, which urged me to repel the furious and feeble attack of Mr. Davis, have been already mentioned. But since I am drawn thus reluctantly into the lists of controversy, I shall not retire till I have saluted, either with stern defiance or gentle courtesy, the theological champions who have signalized their ardour to break a lance against the shield of a *Pagan* adversary. The Fifteenth and Sixteenth Chapters have been honoured with the notice of several writers, whose names and characters seemed to promise more maturity of judgment and learning than could reasonably be expected from the unfinished studies of a Batchelor of Arts. The Reverend Mr. Apthorpe, Dr. Watson, the Regius Professor of Divinity in the University of Cambridge, Dr. Chelsum of Christ Church, and his associate Dr. Randolph, President of Corpus Christi College, and the Lady Margaret's Professor of Divinity in the University of Oxford, have given me a fair right, which, however, I shall not abuse, of freely declaring my opinion on the subject of their respective criticisms.

Mr. Apthorpe.

If I am not mistaken, Mr. Apthorpe was the first who announced to the Public his intention of examining the interesting subject which I had treated in the Two last Chapters of my History. The multitude of collateral and accessary ideas which presented themselves to the Author, insensibly swelled the bulk of his papers to the size of a large volume in octavo; the publication was delayed many months beyond the time of the first advertisement; and when Mr. Apthorpe's Letters appeared, I was surprised to find, that I had *scarcely* any interest or concern in their contents. They are filled with general observations on the Study of History, with a large and useful catalogue of Historians, and with a variety of reflections, moral and religious, all preparatory to the direct and formal consideration of my Two last Chapters, which Mr. Apthorpe seems to reserve for the subject of a Second Volume. I sincerely respect the learning, the piety, and the candour of this Gentleman, and must consider it as a mark of his esteem, that he has thought proper to begin his approaches at so great a distance from the fortifications which he designed to attack.

Dr. Watson.

When Dr. Watson gave to the Public his Apology for Christianity, in a Series of Letters, he addressed them to the Author of the Decline and Fall of the Roman Empire, with a just confidence that he had considered this important object in a manner not unworthy of his antagonist or of himself. Dr. Watson's mode of thinking bears a liberal and philosophic cast; his thoughts are expressed with spirit, and that spirit is always tempered by politeness and moderation. Such is the man whom I should be happy to call my friend, and whom I should not blush to call my antagonist. But the same motives which might tempt me to accept, or even to solicit, a private and amicable conference, dissuaded me from entering into a public controversy with a Writer of so respectable a character; and I embraced the earliest opportunity of expressing to Dr. Watson himself, how sincerely I agreed with him in thinking, "That as the world is now possessed of the opinion of us both upon the subject in question, it may be perhaps as proper for us both to leave it in this state."[79] The nature of the ingenious Professor's Apology contributed to strengthen the insuperable reluctance to engage in hostile altercation which was common to us both, by convincing me, that such an altercation was unnecessary as well as unpleasant. He very justly and politely declares, that a considerable part, near seventy pages, of his small volume are not directed to me,[80] but to a set of men whom he places in an odious and contemptible light. He leaves to other hands the defence of the leading Ecclesiastics, even of the primitive church; and without being *very* anxious, either to soften their vices and indiscretion, or to aggravate the cruelty of the Heathen Persecutors, he passes over in silence the greatest part of my Sixteenth Chapter. It is not so much the purpose of the Apologist to examine the facts which have been advanced by the Historian, as to remove the impressions which may have been formed by many of his Readers; and the remarks of Dr. Watson consist more properly of general argumentation than of particular criticism. He fairly owns, that I have expressly allowed the full and irresistible weight of the *first* great cause of the success of Christianity,[81] and he is too candid to deny that the five *secondary* causes, which I had attempted to explain, operated with *some* degree of active energy towards the accomplishment of that great event. The only question which remains between us, relates

79. Watson's Apology for Christianity, p. 200.

80. Id. p. 202–268.

81. Id. p. 5.

to the *degree* of the weight and effect of those secondary causes; and as I am persuaded that our philosophy is not of the dogmatic kind, we should soon acknowledge that this precise degree cannot be ascertained by reasoning, nor perhaps be expressed by words. In the course of this inquiry, some incidental difficulties have arisen, which I had stated with impartiality, and which Dr. Watson resolves with ingenuity and temper. If in some instances he seems to have misapprehended my sentiments, I may hesitate whether I should impute the fault to my own want of clearness or to his want of attention, but I can never entertain a suspicion that Dr. Watson would descend to employ the disingenuous arts of vulgar controversy.

There is, however, one passage, and one passage only, which must not pass without some explanation; and I shall the more eagerly embrace this occasion to illustrate what I had said, as the misconstruction of my true meaning seems to have made an involuntary, but unfavourable, impression on the liberal mind of Dr. Watson. As I endeavour *not* to palliate the severity, but to discover the motives, of the Roman Magistrates, I had remarked, "it was in vain that the oppressed Believer asserted the unalienable rights of conscience and private judgment. Though his situation might excite the pity, his arguments could never reach the understanding, either of the philosophic or of the believing part of the Pagan world."[82] The humanity of Dr. Watson takes fire on the supposed provocation, and he asks with unusual quickness, "How, Sir, are the arguments for liberty of conscience so exceedingly inconclusive, that you think them incapable of reaching the understanding even of philosophers?"[83] He continues to observe, that a captious adversary would embrace with avidity the opportunity this passage *affords*, of blotting my character with the odious stain of being a Persecutor; a stain which no learning can wipe out, which no genius or ability can render amiable; and though he himself does not entertain such an opinion of my principles, his ingenuity tries in vain to provide me with means of escape.

I must lament that I have not been successful in the explanation of a very simple notion of the spirit both of philosophy and of polytheism, which I have repeatedly inculcated. The arguments which assert the rights of conscience are not inconclusive in themselves, but the understanding of the Greeks and Romans was fortified against their evidence by an invincible prejudice. When we listen to the voice of Bayle, of Locke, and of genuine reason, in favour of religious toleration, we shall easily perceive

82. Gibbon, p. 518.
83. Watson, p. 185.

that our most forcible appeal is made to our mutual feelings. If the Jew were allowed to argue with the Inquisitor, he would request that for a moment they might exchange their different situations, and might safely ask his Catholic Tyrant, whether the fear of death would compel *him* to enter the synagogue, to receive the mark of circumcision, and to partake of the paschal lamb. As soon as the case of persecution was brought home to the breast of the Inquisitor, he must have found some difficulty in suppressing the dictates of natural equity, which would insinuate to his conscience, that he could have no right to inflict those punishments which, under similar circumstances, he would esteem it as his duty to encounter. But this argument could not reach the understanding of a Polytheist, or of an ancient Philosopher. The former was ready, whenever he was summoned, or indeed without being summoned, to fall prostrate before the altars of any Gods who were adored in any part of the world, and to admit a vague persuasion of the *truth* and divinity of the most different modes of religion. The Philosopher, who considered them, at least in their literal sense, as equally *false* and absurd, was not ashamed to disguise his sentiments, and to frame his actions according to the laws of his country, which imposed the same obligation on the philosophers and the people. When Pliny declared, that whatever was the opinion of the Christians, their obstinacy deserved punishment, the absurd cruelty of Pliny was excused in his own eye, by the consciousness that, in the situation of the Christians, he would not have refused the religious compliance which he exacted. I shall not repeat, that the Pagan worship was a matter, not of *opinion*, but of *custom*; that the toleration of the Romans was confined to nations or families who followed the practice of their ancestors; and that in the first ages of Christianity their persecution of the individuals who departed from the established religion was neither moderated by pure reason, nor inflamed by exclusive zeal. But I only desire to appeal, from the hasty apprehension to the more deliberate judgment, of Dr. Watson himself. Should there still remain any difference of opinion between us, I shall be satisfied, if he will consider me as a sincere, though perhaps unsuccessful, lover of truth, and as a firm friend to civil and ecclesiastical freedom.

Dr. Chelsum and Dr. Randolph.

Far be it from me, or from any faithful Historian, to impute to respectable societies the faults of some individual members. Our two Universities most undoubtedly contain the same mixture, and most probably the same proportions, of zeal and moderation, of reason and superstition. Yet there is much less difference between the smoothness of the Ionic, and the roughness of the Doric dialect, than may be found between the polished style of Dr. Watson, and the coarse language of Mr. Davis, Dr. Chelsum, or Dr. Randolph. The second of these Critics, Dr. Chelsum of Christ Church, is unwilling that the world should forget that *he* was the first who sounded to arms, that *he* was the first who furnished the antidote to the poison, and who, as early as the month of October of the year 1776, published his *Strictures* on the Two last Chapters of Mr. Gibbon's History. The success of a pamphlet, which he modestly styles imperfect and ill-digested, encouraged him to resume the controversy. In the beginning of the present year, his Remarks made their second appearance, with some alteration of form, and a large increase of bulk; and the author who seems to fight under the protection of two episcopal banners, has prefixed, in the front of his volume, his name and titles, which in the former edition he had less honourably suppressed. His confidence is fortified by the alliance and communications of a *distinguished* Writer, Dr. Randolph, &c. who, on a proper occasion, would, no doubt, be ready to bear as honourable testimony to the merit and reputation of Dr. Chelsum. The two friends are indeed so happily united by art and nature, that if the author of the Remarks had not pointed out the valuable communications of the Margaret Professor, it would have been impossible to separate their respective property. Writers who possess any freedom of mind, may be known from each other by the peculiar character of their style and sentiments; but the champions who are inlisted in the service of Authority, commonly wear the uniform of the regiment. Oppressed with the same yoke, covered with the same trappings, they heavily move along, perhaps not with an equal pace, in the same beaten track of prejudice and preferment. Yet I should expose my own injustice, were I absolutely to confound with Mr. Davis the two Doctors in Divinity, who are joined in one volume. The three Critics appear to be animated by the same implacable resentment against the Historian of the Roman Empire; they are alike disposed to support the same opinions by the same arts; and if in the language of the two latter, the disregard of politeness is somewhat less gross and indecent, the difference is not of such a magnitude as to excite in my breast any lively sensations of gratitude. It was the misfortune of Mr. Davis that he undertook to *write* before he had *read*. He set out with the stock of authorities which he found in my quotations, and boldly ventured to play his reputation against mine. Perhaps he may now repent of a loss which is not easily recovered; but if I had not surmounted my almost insuperable reluctance to a public dispute, many a reader might still be dazzled by the vehemence of his assertions, and might still believe that Mr. Davis had detected several wilful and important misrepresentations in my Two last Chapters. But the confederate Doctors appear to be scholars of a higher form and longer experience; they enjoy a certain rank in their academical world; and as their zeal is enlightened by some rays of knowledge, so their desire to ruin the credit of their adversary is occasionally checked by the apprehension of injuring their own. These restraints, to which Mr. Davis was a stranger, have confined them to a very narrow and humble path of historical criticism; and if I were to correct, according to their wishes, all the particular facts against which they have advanced any objections, these corrections, admitted in their fullest extent, would hardly furnish materials for a decent list of *errata.*

The *dogmatical* part of their work, which in every sense of the word deserves that appellation, is ill adapted to engage my attention. I had declined the consideration of theological arguments, when they were managed by a candid and liberal adversary; and it would be inconsistent enough, if I should have refused to draw my sword in honourable combat against the keen and well-tempered weapon of Dr. Watson, for the sole purpose of encountering the rustic cudgel of two staunch and sturdy Polemics.

I shall not enter any farther into the character and conduct of Cyprian, as I am sensible that, if the opinion of Le Clerc, Mosheim, and myself, is reprobated by Dr. Chelsum and his ally, the difference must subsist, till we shall entertain the same notions of moral virtue and Ecclesiastical power.[84] If Dr. Randolph will allow that the primitive Clergy received, managed, and distributed the tythes, and other charitable donations of the faithful, the dispute between *us*, will be a dispute of words.[85] I shall not amuse myself with proving that the learned Origen must have derived from the *inspired* authority of the Church his knowledge, not indeed of the *authenticity*, but of the *inspiration* of the *four* Evangelists, *two* of whom are not in the rank of the Apostles.[86] I shall submit to the judgment of the Public, whether the Athanasian Creed is not read and received in the Church of England, and whether the wisest and most virtuous of the

84. Gibbon, p. 464, 465. Chelsum, p. 132–139.

85. Gibbon, p. 491. Randolph in Chelsum, p. 122.

86. Gibbon, p. 458. Note 33. Chelsum, p. 39.

Pagans[87] believed the Catholic faith, which is declared in the Athanasian Creed to be absolutely necessary for salvation. As little shall I think myself interested in the elaborate disquisitions with which the Author of the Remarks has filled a great number of pages, concerning the famous testimony of Josephus, the passages of Irenæus and Theophilus, which relate to the gift of miracles, and the origin of circumcision in Palestine or in Egypt.[88] If I have rejected, and rejected with some contempt, the *interpolation* which pious fraud has very aukwardly inserted in the text of Josephus, I may deem myself secure behind the shield of learned and pious critics (See in particular Le Clerc, in his Ars Critica, part iii. sect. i. c. 15. and Lardner's Testimonies, Vol. i. p. 150, &c.), who have condemned this passage: and I think it very natural that Dr. Chelsum should embrace the contrary opinion, which is not destitute of able advocates. The passages of Irenæus and Theophilus were thoroughly sifted in the controversy about the duration of Miracles; and as the Works of Dr. Middleton may be found in every library, so it is not impossible that a diligent search may still discover some remains of the writings of his adversaries. In mentioning the confession of the Syrians of Palestine, that they had received from Egypt the rite of circumcision, I had simply alleged the testimony of Herodotus, without expressly adopting the sentiment of Marsham. But I had always imagined, that in these doubtful and indifferent questions, which have been solemnly argued before the tribunal of the Public, every scholar was at liberty to chuse his side, without assigning his reasons; nor can I yet persuade myself, that either Dr. Chelsum, or myself, are likely to enforce, by any new arguments, the opinions which we have respectively followed. The only novelty for which I can perceive myself indebted to Dr. Chelsum, is the very extraordinary Scepticism which he insinuates concerning the time of Herodotus, who, according to the chronology of some, flourished during the time of the Jewish captivity.[89] Can it be necessary to inform a Divine, that the captivity which lasted seventy years, according to the prophecy of Jeremiah, was terminated in the year 536 before Christ, by the edict which Cyrus published in the first year of his reign (Jeremiah, xxv. 11, 12. xxix. 10. Ezra, i. 1. &c. Usher and Prideaux, under the years 606 and 536.)? Can it be necessary to inform a man of letters, that Herodotus was fifty-three years old at the commencement of the Peloponnesian war

87. Gibbon, p. 470, Note 70. Chelsum, p. 66.

88. Chelsum's Remarks, p. 13–19. 67–91. 180–185.

89. Id. p. 15.

(Aulus Gellius, Noct. Attic. xv. 23. from the commentaries of Pamphila), and consequently that he was born in the year before Christ 484, fifty-two years after the end of the Jewish captivity? As this well attested fact is not exposed to the slightest doubt or difficulty, I am somewhat curious to learn the names of those unknown authors, whose chronology Dr. Chelsum has allowed as the specious foundation of a probable hypothesis. The Author of the Remarks does not seem indeed to have cultivated, with much care or success, the province of literary history; as a very moderate acquaintance with that useful branch of knowledge would have saved him from a positive mistake, much less excusable than the doubt which he entertains about the time of Herodotus. He styles Suidas "a *Heathen* writer, who lived about the end of the *tenth* century."[90] I admit the period which he assigns to Suidas; and which is well ascertained by Dr. Bentley (See his Reply to Boyle, p. 22, 23.). We are led to fix this epoch, by the chronology which this *Heathen* writer has deduced from Adam, to the death of the emperor John Zimisces, A.D. 975: and a crowd of passages might be produced, as the unanswerable evidence of his Christianity. But the most unanswerable of all is the very date, which is not disputed between us. The philosophers who flourished under Justinian (See Agathias, l. ii. p. 65, 66.), appear to have been the last of the Heathen writers: and the ancient religion of the Greeks was annihilated almost four hundred years before the birth of Suidas.

After this animadversion, which is not intended either to insult the failings of my Adversary, or to provide a convenient excuse for my own errors, I shall proceed to select *two* important parts of Dr. Chelsum's Remarks, from which the candid reader may form some opinion of the whole. They relate to the military service of the first Christians, and to the historical character of Eusebius; and I shall review them with the less reluctance, as it may not be impossible to pick up something curious and useful even in the barren waste of controversy.

I.
Military Service of the first Christians.

In representing the errors of the primitive Christians, which flowed from an excess of virtue, I had observed, *that* they exposed themselves to the reproaches of the Pagans, by their obstinate refusal to take an active part

90. Chelsum, p. 73.

in the civil administration, or military defence of the empire; *that* the objections of Celsus appear to have been mutilated by his adversary Origen, and *that* the Apologists, to whom the public dangers were urged, returned obscure and ambiguous answers, as they were unwilling to disclose the true ground of their security, their opinion of the approaching end of the world.[91] In another place I had related, from the Acts of Ruinart, the action and punishment of the Centurion Marcellus, who was put to death for renouncing the service in a public and seditious manner.[92]

On this occasion Dr. Chelsum is extremely alert. He denies my facts, controverts my opinions, and, with a politeness worthy of Mr. Davis himself, insinuates that I borrowed the story of Marcellus, not from Ruinart, but from Voltaire. My learned Adversary thinks it highly improbable that Origen should dare to *mutilate* the objections of Celsus, "whose work was, in all probability, extant at the time he made this reply. In such case, had he even been inclined to treat his adversary unfairly, he must yet surely have been with-held from the attempt, through the fear of detection."[93] The experience both of ancient and modern controversy, had indeed convinced me that this reasoning, just and natural as it may seem, is totally inconclusive, and that the generality of disputants, especially in religious contests, are of a much more daring and intrepid spirit. For the truth of this remark, I shall content myself with producing a recent and very singular example, in which Dr. Chelsum himself is personally interested. He charges[94] me with passing over in "silence the important and unsuspected testimony of a Heathen historian (Dion Cassius) to the persecution of Domitian; and he affirms, that I have produced that testimony so far only as it relates to Clemens and Domitilla; yet in the very same passage follows immediately, that on a like accusation MANY OTHERS were also condemned. Some of them were put to death, others suffered the confiscation of their goods."[95] Although I should not be ashamed to undertake the apology of Nero or Domitian, if I thought them innocent of any particular crime with which zeal or malice had unjustly branded their memory; yet I should indeed blush, if, in favour of tyranny, or even in favour of virtue, I had suppressed the truth and evidence of historical facts. But the Reader will feel some surprise, when he has convinced himself that, in the three editions of my First Volume,

91. Gibbon, p. 481, 482.
92. Id. p. 562.
93. Chelsum, p. 118, 119.
94. Id. p. 188.
95. Gibbon, p. 534.

after relating the death of Clemens, and the exile of Domitilla, I continue to allege the ENTIRE TESTIMONY of Dion, in the following words: "and sentences either of death, or of confiscation, were pronounced against a GREAT NUMBER OF PERSONS who were involved in the SAME accusation. The guilt imputed to their charge, was that of Atheism and Jewish manners; a singular association of ideas which cannot with any propriety be applied except to the Christians, as they were obscurely and imperfectly viewed by the magistrates and writers of that period." Dr. Chelsum has not been deterred, by the fear of detection, from this scandalous mutilation of the popular work of a living adversary. But Celsus had been dead above fifty years before Origen published his Apology; and the copies of an ancient work, instead of being instantaneously multiplied by the operation of the press, were separately and slowly transcribed by the labour of the hand.

If any modern Divine should still maintain that the fidelity of Origen was secured by motives more honourable than the fear of detection, he may learn from Jerom the difference of the *gymnastic* and *dogmatic* styles. Truth is the object of the one, Victory of the other; and the same arts which would disgrace the sincerity of the teacher, serve only to display the skill of the disputant. After justifying his own practice by that of the orators and philosophers, Jerom defends himself by the more respectable authority of Christian Apologists. "How many thousand lines, says he, have been composed against *Celsus* and Porphyry, by *Origen*, Methodius, Eusebius, Apollinaris? Consider with what arguments, with what slippery problems, they elude the inventions of the Devil; and how in their controversy with the Gentiles, they are sometimes obliged to speak, not what they really think, but what is most advantageous for the cause they defend." "Origenes, &c. multis versuum millibus scribunt adversus Celsum et Porphyrium. Considerate quibus argumentis et quam lubricis problematibus diaboli spiritu contexta subvertunt: et quia interdum coguntur loqui, non quod sentiunt, sed quod necesse est dicunt adversus ea quæ dicunt Gentiles." (Pro Libris advers. Jovin an. Apolog. Tom. ii. p. 135.)

Yet Dr. Chelsum may still ask, and he has a right to ask, why in this particular instance I suspect the pious Origen of mutilating the objections of his adversary. From a very obvious, and, in my opinion, a very decisive, circumstance. Celsus was a Greek philosopher, the friend of Lucian; and I thought that, although he might support error by sophistry, he would not write nonsense in his own language. I renounce my suspicion, if the most attentive reader is able to understand the design and purport of a passage which is given as a formal quotation from Celsus, and which begins with the following words: *Ου μην ουδε εκεινο ανεκτον σου λεγοντος, ως*, &c. (Origen contr. Celsum, l. viii. p. 425. edit. Spencer, Cantab. 1677.) I have carefully inspected the original, I have availed myself of the learning of Spencer, and even Bouhereau (for I shall always disclaim the absurd and affected pedantry of using without scruple a Latin version, but of despising the aid of a French translation), and the ill success of my efforts has countenanced the suspicion to which I still adhere, with a just mixture of doubt and hesitation. Origen very boldly denies, that any of the Christians have affirmed what is imputed to them by Celsus, in this unintelligible quotation; and it may easily be credited, that none had maintained what none can comprehend. Dr. Chelsum has produced the words of Origen; but on this occasion there is a strange ambiguity in the language of the modern Divine,[96] as if he wished to insinuate what he dared not affirm; and every reader must conclude, from his state of the question, that Origen expressly denied the truth of the *accusation* of Celsus, who had *accused* the Christians of declining to assist their fellow-subjects in the military defence of the empire, assailed on every side by the arms of the Barbarians.

Will Dr. Chelsum justify to the world, can he justify to his own feelings, the abuse which he has made even of the privileges of the Gymnastic style? Careless and hasty indeed must have been his perusal of Origen, if he did not perceive that the ancient Apologist, who makes a stand on some incidental question, admits the accusation of his adversary, that the Christians *refused* to bear arms even at the command of their Sovereign. "*και ου συστρατευομεθα μην αυτῳ, καν επειγῃ.*" (Origen, l. viii. p. 427.) He endeavours to palliate this undutiful refusal, by representing that the Christians had their peculiar camps, in which they incessantly combated for the safety of the emperor and the empire, by lifting up their right hands – in prayer. The Apologist seems to hope that his country will be satisfied with this spiritual aid, and dexterously confounding the colleges of Roman priests with the multitudes which swelled the Catholic Church, he claims for his brethren, in all the provinces, the exemption from military service, which was enjoyed by the sacerdotal order. But as this excuse might not readily be allowed, Origen looks forwards with a lively faith to that auspicious Revolution, which Celsus had rejected as impossible, when all the nations of the habitable earth, renouncing their passions and their arms, should embrace the pure doctrines of the Gospel, and lead a life of peace and innocence under the immediate protection

96. Chelsum, p. 118.

of Heaven. The faith of Origen seems to be principally founded on the predictions of the Prophet Zephaniah (See iii. 9, 10.); and he prudently observes, that the Prophets often speak secret things (εν απορρητω λεγουσι, p. 426.), which may be understood by those who can understand them; and that if this stupendous change cannot be effected while we retain our bodies, it may be accomplished as soon as we shall be released from them. Such is the reasoning of Origen: though I have not followed the order, I have faithfully preserved the substance, of it; which fully justifies the truth and propriety of my observations.

The execution of Marcellus, the Centurion, is naturally connected with the Apology of Origen, as the former declared by his actions, what the latter affirmed in his writings, that the conscience of a devout Christian would not allow him to bear arms, even at the command of his Sovereign. I had represented this religious scruple as *one* of the motives which provoked Marcellus; on the day of a public festival, to throw away the ensigns of his office; and I presumed to observe, that such an act of desertion would have been punished in any government according to martial or even civil law. Dr. Chelsum[97] very *bluntly* accuses me of misrepresenting the story, and of suppressing those circumstances which would have defended the Centurion from the unjust imputation thrown by me upon his conduct. The dispute between the Advocate for Marcellus and myself, lies in a very narrow compass; as the whole evidence is comprised in a short, simple, and, I believe, authentic narrative.

1. In another place I observed, and even pressed the observation, "that the innumerable Deities and rites of Polytheism were closely interwoven with every circumstance of business or pleasure, of public or of private life;" and I had particularly specified how much the Roman discipline was connected with the national superstition. A solemn oath of fidelity was repeated every year in the name of the Gods and of the genius of the Emperor, public and daily sacrifices were performed at the head of the camp, the legionary was continually tempted, or rather compelled, to join in the idolatrous worship of his fellow-soldiers, and had not any scruples been entertained of the lawfulness of war, it is not easy to understand how any serious Christian could inlist under a banner which has been justly termed the *rival of the Cross*. "Vexilla æmula Christi." (Tertullian de Corona Militis, c. xi.) With regard to the soldiers, who before their conversion were already engaged in the military life, fear, habit, ignorance, necessity might bend them to some acts of occasional

97. Chelsum, p. 114–117.

conformity; and as long as they abstained from absolute and intentional idolatry, their behaviour was excused by the indulgent, and censured by the more rigid casuists. (See the whole Treatise *De Corona Militis*.) We are ignorant of the adventures and character of the Centurion Marcellus, how long he had conciliated the profession of arms and of the Gospel, whether he was only a Catechumen, or whether he was initiated by the Sacrament of Baptism. We are likewise at a loss to ascertain the particular act of idolatry which so suddenly and so forcibly provoked his pious indignation. As he declared his faith in the midst of a public entertainment given on the birth-day of Galerius, he must have been startled by some of the sacred and convivial rites (Convivia ista profana reputans) of prayers, or vows, or libations, or, perhaps, by the offensive circumstance of eating the meats which had been offered to the idols. But the scruples of Marcellus were not confined to these accidental impurities; they evidently reached the essential duties of his profession; and when before the tribunal of the magistrates, he avowed his faith at the hazard of his life, the Centurion declared, as his cool and determined persuasion, that it does not become a Christian man, who is the soldier of the Lord Christ, to bear arms for any object of earthly concern. "Non enim decebat Christianum hominem molestiis secularibus militare, qui Christo Domino militat." A formal declaration, which clearly disengages from each other the different questions of war and idolatry. With regard to both these questions, as they were understood by the primitive Christians, I wish to refer the Reader to the sentiments and authorities of Mr. Moyle, a bold and ingenious critic, who read the Fathers as their judge, and not as their slave, and who has refuted, with the most patient candour, all that learned prejudice could suggest in favour of the silly story of the Thundering Legion. (See Moyle's Works, Vol. ii. p. 84–88. 111–116. 163–212. 298–302. 327–341.) And here let me add, that the passage of Origen, who in the name of his brethren disclaims the duty of military service, is understood by Mr. Moyle in its true and obvious signification.

2. I know not where Dr. Chelsum has imbibed the principles of logic or morality which teach him to approve the conduct of Marcellus, who threw down his rod, his belt, and his arms, at the head of the legion, and publicly renounced the military service, *at the very time* when he found himself obliged to offer sacrifice. Yet surely this is a very false notion of the condition and duties of a Roman Centurion. Marcellus was bound, by a solemn oath, to serve with fidelity till he should be regularly discharged; and according to the sentiments which Dr. Chelsum ascribes to him, he was not released from this oath by any mistaken opinion of

the unlawfulness of war. I would propose it as a case of conscience to any philosopher, or even to any casuist in Europe, Whether a particular order, which cannot be reconciled with virtue or piety, dissolves the ties of a general and lawful obligation? And whether, if they had been consulted by the Christian Centurion, they would not have directed him to increase his diligence in the execution of his military functions, to refuse to yield to any act of idolatry, and patiently to expect the consequences of such a refusal? But, instead of obeying the mild and moderate dictates of religion, instead of distinguishing between the duties of the soldier and of the Christian, Marcellus, with imprudent zeal, rushed forwards to seize the crown of martyrdom. He might have privately confessed himself guilty to the tribune or præfect under whom he served: he chose on the day of a public festival to disturb the order of the camp. He insulted without necessity the religion of his Sovereign and of his country, by the epithets of contempt which he bestowed on the Roman Gods. "Deos vestros ligneos et lapideos, adorare contemno, quæ sunt idola surda et muta." Nay more: at the head of the legion, and in the face of the standards, the Centurion Marcellus openly renounced his allegiance to the Emperors. "Ex hoc militare IMPERATORIBUS VESTRIS desisto." From this moment I no longer serve YOUR EMPERORS, are the important words of Marcellus, which his advocate has not thought proper to translate. I again make my appeal to any lawyer, to any military man, Whether, under such circumstances, the pronoun *your* has not a seditious and even treasonable import? And whether the officer who should make this declaration, and at the same time throw away his sword at the head of the regiment, would not be condemned for mutiny and desertion by any court-martial in Europe? I am the rather disposed to judge favourably of the conduct of the Roman government, as I cannot discover any desire to take advantage of the indiscretion of Marcellus. The Commander of the Legion seemed to lament that it was not in his power to dissemble this rash action. After a delay of more than three months, the Centurion was examined before the Vice-præfect, his superior Judge, who offered him the fairest opportunities of explaining or qualifying his seditious expressions, and at last condemned him to lose his head; not simply because he was a Christian, but because he had violated his military oath, thrown away his belt, and publicly blasphemed the Gods and the Emperors. Perhaps the impartial reader will confirm the sentence of the Vice-Præfect Agricolanus, "Ita se habent facta Marcelli, ut hæc *disciplinâ* debeant vindicari."

Notwithstanding the plainest evidence, Dr. Chelsum will not believe that either Origen in Theory, or Marcellus in Practice, could seriously object to the use of arms; "because it is well known, that far from declining the business of war altogether, whole legions of Christians served in the Imperial armies."[98] I have not yet discovered, in the Author or Authors of the Remarks, many traces of a clear and enlightened understanding, yet I cannot suppose them so destitute of every reasoning principle, as to imagine that they here allude to the conduct of the Christians who embraced the profession of arms after their religion had obtained a public establishment. Whole legions of Christians served under the banners of Constantine and Justinian, as whole regiments of Christians are now inlisted in the service of France or England. The representation which I had given, was confined to the principles and practice of the Church of which Origen and Marcellus were members, before the sense of public and private interest had reduced the lofty standard of Evangelical perfection to the ordinary level of human nature. In those primitive times, where are the Christian legions that served in the Imperial armies? Our Ecclesiastical Pompeys may stamp with their foot, but no armed men will arise out of the earth, except the ghosts of the Thundering and the Thebæan legions, the former renowned for a Miracle, and the latter for a Martyrdom. Either the two Protestant Doctors must acquiesce under some imputations which are better understood than expressed, or they must prepare, in the full light and freedom of the eighteenth century, to undertake the defence of two obsolete legends, the least absurd of which staggered the well-disciplined credulity of a Franciscan Friar. (See Pagi Critic. ad Annal. Baronii, A.D. 174. tom. i. p. 168.) Very different was the spirit and taste of the learned and ingenuous Dr. Jortin, who after treating the silly story of the Thundering Legion with the contempt it deserved, continues in the following words: "Moyle wishes no greater penance to the believers of the Thundering Legion, than that they may also believe the Martyrdom of the Thebæan Legion. (Moyle's Works, vol. ii. p. 103): to which good wish, I say with Le Clerc (Bibliotheque A. et M. tom. xxvii. p. 193) AMEN.

Qui Bavium non odit, amet tua carmina, Mævi."

(Jortin's Remarks on Ecclesiastical History, vol. i. p. 367. 2d edition. London, 1767.)

Yet I shall not attempt to conceal a formidable army of Christians and even of Martyrs, which is ready to inlist under the banners of the

98. Chelsum, p. 113.

confederate Doctors, if they will accept their service. As a specimen of the extravagant legends of the middle age, I had produced the instance of ten thousand Christian soldiers supposed to have been crucified on Mount Ararat, by the order either of Trajan or Hadrian.[99] For the mention and for the confutation of this story, I had appealed to a Papist and a Protestant, to the learned Tillemont (Mem. Ecclesiast. tom. ii. part ii. p. 438), and to the diligent Geddes (Miscellanies, vol. ii. p. 203), and when Tillemont was not afraid to say that there are few histories which appear more fabulous, I was not ashamed of dismissing the *Fable* with silent contempt. We may trace the degrees of fiction as well as those of credibility, and the impartial Critic will not place on the same level the baptism of Philip and the donation of Constantine. But in considering the crucifixion of the ten thousand Christian soldiers, we are not reduced to the necessity of weighing any internal probabilities, or of disproving any external testimonies. This legend, the absurdity of which must strike every *rational* mind, stands naked and unsupported by the authority of any writer who lived within a thousand years of the age of Trajan, and has not been able to obtain the poor sanction of the uncorrupted Martyrologies which were framed in the most credulous period of Ecclesiastical History. The two Protestant Doctors will probably reject the unsubstantial present which has been offered them: yet there is one of my adversaries, the *anonymous Gentleman*, who boldly declares himself the votary of the ten thousand Martyrs, and challenges me "to discredit a FACT which hitherto by many has been looked upon as well established."[100] It is pity that a prudent confessor did not whisper in his ear, that, although the martyrdom of these military Saints, like that of the eleven thousand Virgins, may contribute to the edification of the faithful, these wonderful tales should not be rashly exposed to the jealous and inquisitive eye of those profane Critics, whose examination always precedes, and sometimes checks, their Religious Assent.

II.
Character and credit of Eusebius.

A grave and pathetic complaint is introduced by Dr. Chelsum, into his preface,[101] that Mr. Gibbon, who has often referred to the Fathers of the

99. Gibbon, p. 541. Note 74.
100. Remarks, p. 65, 66, 67.
101. P. ii, iii.

Church, seems to have entertained a general distrust of those respectable witnesses. The Critic is scandalized at the epithets of scanty and *suspicious*, which are applied to the materials of Ecclesiastical History; and if he cannot impeach the truth of the former, he censures in the most angry terms the injustice of the latter. He assumes, with peculiar zeal, the defence of Eusebius, the venerable parent of Ecclesiastical History, and labours to rescue his character from the *gross misrepresentation* on which Mr. Gibbon has openly insisted.[102] He observes, as if he sagaciously foresaw the objection, "That it will not be sufficient here to allege a few instances of apparent credulity in some of the Fathers, in order to fix a general charge of *suspicion* on all." But it *may* be sufficient to allege a clear and fundamental principle of historical as well as legal Criticism, that whenever we are destitute of the means of comparing the testimonies of the opposite parties, the evidence of *any* witness, however illustrious by his rank and titles, is justly to be *suspected* in his own cause. It is unfortunate enough, that I should be engaged with adversaries, whom their habits of study and conversation appear to have left in total ignorance of the principles which universally regulate the opinions and practice of mankind.

As the ancient world was not distracted by the fierce conflicts of hostile sects, the free and eloquent writers of Greece and Rome had few opportunities of indulging their passions, or of exercising their impartiality in the relation of religious events. Since the origin of Theological Factions, some Historians, Ammianus Marcellinus, Fra-Paolo, Thuanus, Hume, and perhaps a few others, have deserved the singular praise of holding the balance with a steady and equal hand. Independent and unconnected, they contemplated with the same indifference, the opinions and interests of the contending parties; or, if they were seriously attached to a particular system, they were armed with a firm and moderate temper, which enabled them to suppress their affections, and to sacrifice their resentments. In this small, but *venerable* Synod of Historians, Eusebius cannot claim a seat. I had acknowledged, and I still think, that his character was less tinctured with credulity than that of most of his contemporaries; but as his enemies must admit, that he was sincere and earnest in the profession of Christianity, so the warmest of his admirers, or at least of his readers, must discern, and will probably applaud, the religious zeal which disgraces or adorns every page of his Ecclesiastical History. This laborious and useful work was published at a time, between

102. Chelsum and Randolph, p. 220–238.

the defeat of Licinius and the Council of Nice, when the resentment of the Christians was still warm, and when the Pagans were astonished and dismayed by the recent victory and conversion of the great Constantine. The materials, I shall dare to repeat the invidious epithets of scanty and suspicious, were extracted from the accounts which the Christians themselves had given of their *own* sufferings, and of the cruelty of their enemies. The Pagans had so long and so contemptuously neglected the rising greatness of the Church, that the Bishop of Cæsarea had little either to hope or to fear from the writers of the opposite party; almost all of that *little* which did exist, has been accidentally lost, or purposely destroyed; and the candid enquirer may vainly wish to compare with the History of Eusebius, some Heathen narrative of the persecutions of Decius and Diocletian. Under these circumstances, it is the duty of an impartial judge to be counsel for the prisoner, who is incapable of making any defence for himself; and it is the first office of a counsel to examine with distrust and *suspicion*, the interested evidence of the accuser. Reason justifies the suspicion, and it is confirmed by the constant experience of modern History, in almost every instance where we have an opportunity of comparing the mutual complaints and apologies of the religious factions, who have disturbed each other's happiness in this world, for the sake of securing it in the next.

As we are deprived of the means of contrasting the adverse relations of the Christians and Pagans; it is the more incumbent on us to improve the opportunities of trying the narratives of Eusebius, by the original, and sometimes occasional, testimonies of the more ancient writers of his own party. Dr. Chelsum[103] has observed, that the celebrated passage of Origen, which has so much thinned the ranks of the army of Martyrs, must be confined to the persecutions that had already happened. I cannot dispute this sagacious remark, but I shall venture to add, that this passage more immediately relates to the religious tempests which had been excited in the time and country of Origen; and still more particularly to the city of Alexandria, and to the persecution of Severus, in which young Origen successfully exhorted his father, to sacrifice his life and fortune for the cause of Christ. From such unquestionable evidence, I am authorised to conclude, that the number of holy victims who sealed their faith with their blood, was not, on this occasion, very considerable: but I cannot reconcile this fair conclusion with the positive declaration of Eusebius (l. vi. c. 2. p. 258), that at Alexandria, in the persecution of

103. Gibbon, p. 540. Chelsum, p. 204–207.

Severus, an innumerable, at least an indefinite multitude (*μυριοι*) of Christians were honoured with the Crown of Martyrdom. The advocates for Eusebius may exert their critical skill in proving that *μυριοι* and *ολιγοι* *many* and *few*, are synonymous and convertible terms, but they will hardly succeed in diminishing so palpable a contradiction, or in removing the suspicion which deeply fixes itself on the historical character of the Bishop of Cæsarea. This unfortunate experiment taught me to read, with becoming caution, the loose and declamatory style which *seems* to magnify the multitude of Martyrs and Confessors, and to aggravate the nature of their sufferings. From the same motives I selected, with careful observation, the more certain account of the number of persons who actually suffered death in the province of Palestine, during the whole eight years of the last and most rigorous persecution.

Besides the reasonable grounds of suspicion, which suggest themselves to every liberal mind, against the credibility of the Ecclesiastical Historians, and of Eusebius, their venerable leader, I had taken notice of two very remarkable passages of the Bishop of Cæsarea. He frankly, or at least indirectly, declares, that in treating of the last persecution, "he has related whatever might redound to the glory, and suppressed all that could tend to the disgrace, of Religion."[104] Dr. Chelsum, who, on this occasion, most lamentably exclaims that we should hear Eusebius, before we utterly condemn him, has provided, with the assistance of his worthy colleague, an elaborate defence for their common patron; and as if he were secretly conscious of the weakness of the cause, he has contrived the resource of intrenching himself in a very muddy soil, behind three several fortifications, which do not exactly support each other. The advocate for the sincerity of Eusebius maintains: 1st, That he never made such a declaration: 2dly, That he had a right to make it: and, 3dly, That he did not observe it. These separate and almost inconsistent apologies, I shall separately consider.

1. Dr. Chelsum is at a loss how to reconcile, – I beg pardon for weakening the force of his dogmatic style; he declares that, "It is plainly impossible to reconcile the express words of the charge exhibited, with any part of either of the passages appealed to in support of it."[105] If he means, as I think he must, that the *express words* of my text cannot be found in that of Eusebius, I congratulate the importance of the discovery. But was it possible? Could it be my design to quote the words of Eusebius, when I reduced into one sentence the spirit and substance of two diffuse and distinct passages? If I have given the true sense and meaning of the

104. Gibbon, p. 577.

105. Chelsum, p. 232.

Ecclesiastical Historian, I have discharged the duties of a fair Interpreter; nor shall I refuse to rest the proof of my fidelity on the translation of those two passages of Eusebius, which Dr. Chelsum produces in his favour.[106] "But it is not our part to describe the sad calamities which at last befel them (the *Christians*), since it does not agree with our plan to relate their dissentions and wickedness before the persecution; on which account we have determined to relate nothing more concerning them than may serve to justify the Divine Judgment. We therefore have not been induced to make mention either of those who were tempted in the persecution, or of those who made utter shipwreck of their salvation, and who were sunk of their own accord in the depths of the storm; but shall only add those things to our General History, which may in the first place be profitable to ourselves, and afterwards to posterity." In the other passage, Eusebius, after mentioning the dissentions of the Confessors among themselves, again declares that it is his intention to pass over all these things. "Whatsoever things, (continues the Historian, in the words of the Apostle, who was recommending the practice of virtue) whatsoever things are honest, whatsoever things are of good report, if there be any virtue, and if there be any praise; these things Eusebius thinks most suitable to a History of Martyrs;" of *wonderful* Martyrs, is the splendid epithet which Dr. Chelsum had not thought proper to translate. I should betray a very mean opinion of the judgment and candour of my readers, if I added a single reflection on the clear and obvious tendency of the two passages of the Ecclesiastical Historian. I shall only observe, that the Bishop of Cæsarea seems to have claimed a privilege of a still more dangerous and extensive nature. In one of the most learned and elaborate works that antiquity has left us, the Thirty-second Chapter of the Twelfth Book of his Evangelical Preparation bears for its title this scandalous Proposition, "How it may be lawful and fitting to use falsehood as a medicine, and for the benefit of those who want to be deceived." *Οτι δεησει ποτε τῳ ψευδει αντι φαρμακου χρησθαι επι ωφελεια των δεομενων του τοιουτου τροπου*. (P. 356, Edit. Græc. Rob. Stephani, Paris 1544.) In this chapter he alleges a passage of Plato, which approves the occasional practice of pious and salutary frauds; nor is Eusebius ashamed to justify the sentiments of the Athenian philosopher by the example of the sacred writers of the Old Testament.

2. I had contented myself with observing, that Eusebius had violated one of the fundamental laws of history, *Ne quid veri dicere non audeat*; nor

106. P. 228. 231.

could I imagine, if the *fact* was allowed, that any question could possibly arise upon the matter of *right*. I was indeed mistaken; and I now begin to understand why I have given so little satisfaction to Dr. Chelsum, and to other critics of the same complexion, as our ideas of the duties and the privileges of an historian appear to be so widely different. It is alleged, that "every writer has a right to chuse his subject, for the particular benefit of his reader; that he has explained his own plan consistently; that he considers himself, according to it, not as a complete historian of the times, but rather as a *didactic* writer, whose main object is to make his work, like the Scriptures themselves, PROFITABLE FOR DOCTRINE; that, as he treats only of the affairs of the Church, the plan is at least excusable, perhaps peculiarly proper; and that he has conformed himself to the principal duty of an historian, while, according to his immediate design, he has not particularly related any of the transactions which could tend to the disgrace of religion."[107] The historian must indeed be generous, who will conceal, by his own disgrace, that of his country, or of his religion. Whatever subject he has chosen, whatever persons he introduces, he owes to himself, to the present age, and to posterity, a just and perfect delineation of all that may be praised, of all that may be excused, and of all that must be censured. If he fails in the discharge of his important office, he partially violates the sacred obligations of truth, and disappoints his readers of the instruction which they might have derived from a fair parallel of the vices and virtues of the most illustrious characters. Herodotus might range without controul in the spacious walks of the Greek and Barbaric domain, and Thucydides might confine his steps to the narrow path of the Peloponnesian war; but those historians would never have deserved the esteem of posterity, if they had designedly suppressed or transiently mentioned those facts which could tend to the disgrace of Greece or of Athens. These unalterable dictates of conscience and reason have been *seldom* questioned, though they have been seldom observed; and we must sincerely join in the honest complaint of Melchior Canus, "that the lives of the philosophers have been composed by Laertius, and those of the Cæsars by Suetonius, with a much stricter and more severe regard for historic truth, than can be found in the lives of saints and martyrs, as they are described by Catholic writers." (See Loci Communes, l. xi. p. 650, apud Clericum, Epistol. Critic. v. p. 136.) And yet the partial representation of truth is of far more pernicious consequence in ecclesiastical, than in civil, history. If Laertius had con-

107. Chelsum, p. 229, 230, 231.

cealed the defects of Plato, or if Suetonius had disguised the vices of Augustus, we should have been deprived of the knowledge of some curious, and perhaps instructive, facts, and our idea of those celebrated men might have been more favourable than they deserved; but I cannot discover any practical inconveniencies which could have been the result of our ignorance. But if Eusebius had fairly and circumstantially related the scandalous dissentions of the Confessors; if he had shewn that their virtues were tinctured with pride and obstinacy, and that their lively faith was not exempt from some mixture of enthusiasm; he would have armed his readers against the excessive veneration for those holy men, which imperceptibly degenerated into religious worship. The success of these *didactic* histories, by concealing or palliating every circumstance of human infirmity, was one of the most efficacious means of consecrating the memory, the bones, and the writings of the saints of the prevailing party; and a great part of the errors and corruptions of the Church of Rome may fairly be ascribed to this criminal dissimulation of the ecclesiastical historians. As a Protestant Divine, Dr. Chelsum must abhor these corruptions; but as a Christian, he should be careful lest his apology for the prudent choice of Eusebius should fix an indirect censure on the unreserved sincerity of the four Evangelists. Instead of confining their narrative to those things which are virtuous and of good report, instead of following the plan which is here recommended as *peculiarly proper* for the affairs of the Church, the inspired writers have thought it their duty to relate the most minute circumstances of the fall of St. Peter, without considering whether the behaviour of an Apostle, who thrice denied his Divine Master, might redound to the honour, or to the disgrace, of Christianity. If Dr. Chelsum should be frightened by this unexpected consequence, if he should be desirous of saving his faith from *utter shipwreck*, by throwing over-board the useless lumber of memory and reflection, I am not enough his enemy to impede the success of his honest endeavours.

The didactic method of writing history was still more profitably exercised by Eusebius in another work, which he has intitled,. The Life of Constantine, his gracious patron and benefactor. Priests and poets have enjoyed in every age a privilege of flattery; but if the actions of Constantine are compared with the perfect idea of a royal saint, which, under his name, has been delineated by the zeal and gratitude of Eusebius, the most indulgent reader will confess, that when I styled him a *courtly Bishop,*[108] I could only be restrained by my respect for the episcopal

108. Gibbon, p. 580.

character from the use of a much harsher epithet. The other appellation of a *passionate declaimer*, which seems to have sounded still more offensive in the tender ears of Dr. Chelsum,[109] was not applied by me to Eusebius, but to Lactantius, or rather to the author of the historical declamation, *De mortibus persecutorum*; and indeed it is much more properly adapted to the Rhetorician, than to the Bishop. Each of those authors was alike studious of the glory of Constantine; but each of them directed the torrent of his invectives against the tyrant, whether Maxentius or Licinius, whose recent defeat was the actual theme of popular and Christian applause. This simple observation may serve to extinguish a very trifling objection of my critic, That Eusebius has not represented the tyrant Maxentius under the character of a Persecutor.

Without scrutinizing the considerations of interest which might support the integrity of Baronius and Tillemont, I may fairly observe, that both those learned Catholics have acknowledged and condemned the dissimulation of Eusebius, which is partly denied, and partly justified, by my adversary. The honourable reflection of Baronius well deserves to be transcribed. "Hæc (the passages already quoted) de suo in conscribendâ persecutionis historia Eusebius; parum explens numeros sui muneris; dum perinde ac si panegyrim scriberet non historiam, triumphos dumtaxat martyrum atque victorias, non autem lapsus jacturamque fidelium posteris scripturæ monumentis curaret." (Baron. Annal. Ecclesiast. A.D. 302, N° 11. See likewise Tillemont, Mem. Eccles. tom. v. p. 62. 156; tom. vii. p. 130.) In a former instance, Dr. Chelsum appeared to be more credulous than a Monk: on the present occasion, he has shewn himself less sincere than a Cardinal, and more obstinate than a Jansenist.

3. Yet the advocate for Eusebius has still another expedient in reserve. Perhaps he made the unfortunate declaration of his partial design, perhaps he had a right to make it; but at least his accuser must admit, that he has saved his honour by not keeping his word; since I myself have taken notice of THE CORRUPTION OF MANNERS AND PRINCIPLES among the Christians, SO FORCIBLY LAMENTED by Eusebius.[110] He has indeed indulged himself in a strain of *loose* and *indefinite* censure, which may generally be just, and which cannot be personally offensive, which is alike incapable of wounding or of correcting, as it seems to have no fixed object or certain aim. Juvenal might have read his satire against women in a circle of Roman ladies, and each of them might have listened with pleasure to the amusing description of the various vices and follies, from

109. Chelsum, p. 234.
110. Id. p. 226, 227.

which she herself was so perfectly free. The moralist, the preacher, the ecclesiastical historian, enjoy a still more ample latitude of invective; and as long as they abstain from any particular censure, they may securely expose, and even exaggerate, the sins of the multitude. The precepts of Christianity seem to inculcate a style of mortification, of abasement, of self-contempt; and the hypocrite who aspires to the reputation of a saint, often finds it convenient to affect the language of a penitent. I should doubt whether Dr. Chelsum is much acquainted with the comedies of Moliere. If he has ever read that inimitable master of human life, he may recollect whether Tartuffe was very much inclined to confess his real guilt, when he exclaimed,

> Oui, mon Frere, je suis un mechant, un coupable;
> Un malheureux pécheur, tout plein d'iniquité;
> Le plus grand scelerat qui ait jamais été.
> Chaque instant de ma vie est chargé de souillures,
> Elle n'est qu'un amas de crimes et d'ordures.
>
> . . . .
>
> Oui, mon cher fils, parlex, traitez moi de perfide,
> D'infame, de perdu, de voleur, d'homicide;
> Accablez moi de noms encore plus detestés:
> Je n'y contredis point, je les ai merités,
> Et j'en veux à genoux souffrir l'ignominie,
> Comme une honte due aux crimes de ma vie.

It is not my intention to compare the character of Tartuffe with that of Eusebius; the former pointed his invectives against himself, the latter directed them against the times in which he had lived: but as the prudent Bishop of Cæsarea did not specify any place or person for the object of his censure, he cannot justly be accused, even by his friends, of violating the *profitable* plan of his *didactic* history.

The extreme caution of Eusebius, who declines any mention of those who were tempted and who fell during the persecution, has countenanced a suspicion that he himself was one of those unhappy victims, and that his tenderness for the wounded fame of his brethren arose from a just apprehension of his own disgrace. In one of my notes,[III] I had observed, that he was charged with the guilt of some criminal compliances, in his own presence, and in the Council of Tyre. I am therefore accountable for the reality only, and not for the truth, of the accusation:

III. Gibbon, p. 577, N. 178.

but as the two Doctors, who on this occasion unite their forces, are angry and clamorous in asserting the innocence of the Ecclesiastical Historian,[112] I shall advance one step farther, and shall maintain, that the charge against Eusebius, though not legally proved, is supported by a reasonable share of presumptive evidence.

I have often wondered why our orthodox Divines should be so earnest and zealous in the defence of Eusebius; whose moral character cannot be preserved, unless by the sacrifice of a more illustrious, and, as I really believe, of a more innocent victim. Either the Bishop of Cæsarea, on a very important occasion, violated the laws of Christian charity and civil justice, or we must fix a charge of calumny, almost of forgery, on the head of the great Athanasius, the standard-bearer of the Homoousian cause, and the firmest pillar of the Catholic faith. In the Council of Tyre, he was accused of murdering, or at least of mutilating, a Bishop, whom he produced at Tyre alive and unhurt (Athanas. tom. i. p. 783. 786.); and of sacrilegiously breaking a consecrated chalice, in a village where neither church, nor altar, nor chalice, could possibly have existed. (Athanas. tom. i. p. 731, 732. 802.) Notwithstanding the clearest proofs of his innocence, Athanasius was oppressed by the Arian faction; and Eusebius of Cæsarea, the venerable father of ecclesiastical history, conducted this iniquitous prosecution from a motive of personal enmity. (Athanas. tom. i. p. 728. 795. 797.) Four years afterwards, a national council of the Bishops of Egypt, forty-nine of whom had been present at the Synod of Tyre, addressed an epistle or manifesto in favour of Athanasius to all the Bishops of the Christian world. In this epistle they assert, that some of the Confessors, who accompanied them to Tyre, had accused Eusebius of Cæsarea of an act relative to idolatrous sacrifice. *ουκ Ευσεβιος ὁ εν Καισερειᾳ της Παλαιστινης επι θυσιᾳ κατηγορειτο ὑπο των συν ἡμιν ὁμολογητων.* (Athanas. tom. i. p. 728.) Besides this short and authentic memorial, which escaped the knowledge or the candour of our confederate Doctors, a consonant but more circumstantial narrative of the accusation of Eusebius may be found in the writings of Epiphanius (Hæres. lxviii. p. 723, 724.), the learned Bishop of Salamis, who was born about the time of the Synod of Tyre. He relates that, in one of the sessions of the Council, Potamon, Bishop of Heraclea in Egypt, addressed Eusebius in the following words: "How now, Eusebius, can this be borne, that you should be seated as a judge, while the innocent Athanasius is left standing as a criminal? Tell me, continued Potamon, were we not in

112. Chelsum and Randolph, p. 236, 237, 238.

prison together during the persecution? For my own part, I lost an eye for the sake of the truth; but I cannot discern that *you* have lost any one of your members. You bear not any marks of your sufferings for Jesus Christ; but here you are, full of life, and with all the parts of your body sound and entire. How could you contrive to escape from prison, unless you stained your conscience, either by actual guilt or by a criminal promise to our persecutors." Eusebius immediately broke up the meeting, and discovered by his anger, that he was confounded or provoked by the reproaches of the Confessor Potamon.

I should despise myself, if I were capable of magnifying, for a present occasion, the authority of the witness whom I have produced. Potamon was most assuredly actuated by a strong prejudice against the personal enemy of his Primate; and if the transaction to which he alluded had been of a private and doubtful kind, I would not take any ungenerous advantage of the respect which my Reverend Adversaries must entertain for the character of a Confessor. But I cannot distrust the veracity of Potamon, when he confined himself to the assertion of a fact, which lay within the compass of his personal knowledge: and collateral testimony (See Photius, p. 296, 297.) attests, that Eusebius was long enough in prison to assist his friend, the Martyr Pamphilus, in composing the first five books of his Apology for Origen. If we admit that Eusebius was imprisoned, he must have been discharged, and his discharge must have been either honourable, or criminal, or innocent. If his patience vanquished the cruelty of the Tyrant's Ministers, a short relation of his own confession and sufferings would have formed an useful and edifying Chapter in his Didactic History of the Persecution of Palestine; and the Reader would have been satisfied of the veracity of an Historian who valued truth above his life. If it had been in his power to justify, or even to excuse, the manner of his discharge from prison, it was his interest, it was his duty, to prevent the doubts and suspicions which must arise from his silence under these delicate circumstances. Notwithstanding these urgent reasons, Eusebius has observed a profound, and perhaps a prudent, silence: though he frequently celebrates the merit and martyrdom of his friend Pamphilus (p. 371. 394. 419. 427. Edit. Cantab.), he never insinuates that he was his companion in prison; and while he copiously describes the eight years persecution in Palestine, he never represents himself in any other light than that of a spectator. Such a conduct in a Writer, who relates with a visible satisfaction the honourable events of his own life, if it be not absolutely considered as an evidence of conscious guilt, must excite, and may justify, the suspicions of the most candid Critic.

Yet the firmness of Dr. Randolph is not shaken by these rational suspicions; and he condescends, in a magisterial tone, to inform me, "That it is highly improbable, from the general well-known decision of the Church in such cases, that had his apostacy been known, he would have risen to those high honours which he attained, or been admitted at all indeed to any other than lay-communion." This weighty objection did not surprise me, as I had already seen the substance of it in the Prolegomena of Valesius; but I safely disregarded a difficulty which had not appeared of any moment to the national council of Egypt; and I still think that an hundred Bishops, with Athanasius at their head, were as competent judges of the discipline of the fourth Century, as even the Lady Margaret's Professor of Divinity in the University of Oxford. As a work of supererogation, I have consulted, however, the Antiquities of Bingham (see l. iv. c. 3. f. 6, 7. vol. i. p. 144, &c. fol. edit.), and found, as I expected, that much real learning had made him cautious and modest. After a careful examination of the facts and authorities already known to me, and of those with which I was supplied by the diligent Antiquarian, I am persuaded that the theory and the practice of discipline were not invariably the same, that particular examples cannot always be reconciled with general rules, and that the stern laws of justice often yielded to motives of policy and convenience. The temper of Jerom towards those whom he considered as Heretics, was fierce and unforgiving; yet the Dialogue of Jerom against the Luciferians, which I have read with infinite pleasure (tom. ii. p. 135–147. Edit. Basil. 1536.), is the seasonable and dextrous performance of a Statesman, who felt the expediency of soothing and reconciling a numerous party of offenders. The most rigid discipline, with regard to the Ecclesiastics who had fallen in time of persecution, is expressed in the 10th Canon of the Council of Nice; the most remarkable indulgence was shewn by the Fathers of the same Council to the *lapsed*, the degraded, the schismatic Bishop of Lycopolis. Of the penitent sinners, some might escape the shame of a public conviction or confession, and others might be exempted from the rigour of clerical punishment. If Eusebius incurred the guilt of a sacrilegious promise (for we are free to accept the milder alternative of Potamon), the proofs of this criminal transaction might be suppressed by the influence of money or favour; a seasonable journey into Egypt might allow time for the popular rumours to subside. The crime of Eusebius might be protected by the impunity of many Episcopal Apostates (see Philostorg. l. ii. c. 15. p. 21. Edit. Gothofred.); and the Governors of the Church very reasonably desired to retain in their service the most learned Christian of the Age.

Before I return these sheets to the press, I must not forget an anonymous pamphlet, which, under the title of *A Few Remarks*, &c. was published against my History in the course of the last summer. The unknown writer has thought proper to distinguish himself by the emphatic, yet vague, appellation of A GENTLEMAN: but I must lament that he has not considered, with becoming attention, the duties of that respectable character. I am ignorant of the motives which can urge a man of a liberal mind, and liberal manners, to attack without provocation, and without tenderness, any work which may have contributed to the information, or even to the amusement, of the Public. But I am well convinced, that the author of such a work, who boldly gives his name and his labours to the world, imposes on his adversaries the fair and honourable obligation of encountering him in open day-light, and of supporting the weight of their assertions by the credit of their names. The effusions of wit, or the productions of reason, may be accepted from a secret and unknown hand. The critic who attempts to injure the reputation of another, by strong imputations which may possibly be false, should renounce the ungenerous hope of concealing behind a mask the vexation of disappointment, and the guilty blush of detection.

After this remark, which I cannot make without some degree of concern, I shall frankly declare, that it is not my wish or my intention to prosecute with this *Gentleman* a literary altercation. There lies between us a broad and unfathomable gulph; and the heavy mist of prejudice and superstition, which has in a great measure been dispelled by the free inquiries of the present age, still continues to involve the mind of my Adversary. He fondly embraces those phantoms (for instance, an imaginary Pilate[113]), which can scarcely find a shelter in the gloom of an Italian convent; and the resentment which he points against me, might frequently be extended to the most enlightened of the PROTESTANT, or, in his opinion, of the HERETICAL critics. His observations are divided into a number of unconnected paragraphs, each of which contains some quotation from my History, and the angry, yet commonly trifling, expression of his disapprobation and displeasure. Those sentiments I cannot hope to remove; and as the religious opinions of this *Gentleman* are principally founded on the infallibility of the Church,[114] they are not calculated to make a very deep impression on the mind of an English reader. The view of *facts* will be materially affected by the contagious influence of *doctrines*. The man who refuses to judge of the conduct of Lewis XIV. and

113. Remarks, p. 100.

114. Id. p. 15.

Charles V. towards their Protestant subjects[115] declares himself incapable of distinguishing the limits of persecution and toleration. The devout Papist, who has implored on his knees the intercession of St. Cyprian, will seldom presume to examine the actions of the Saint by the rules of historical evidence and of moral propriety. Instead of the homely likeness which I had exhibited of the Bishop of Carthage, my Adversary has substituted a life of Cyprian,[116] full of what the French call *onction*, and the English, *canting* (See Jortin's Remarks, Vol. ii. p. 239.): to which I can only reply, that those who are dissatisfied with the principles of Mosheim and Le Clerc, *must* view with eyes very different from mine, the Ecclesiastical History of the third century.

It would be an *endless* discussion (*endless* in every sense of the word), were I to examine the cavils which start up and expire in every page of this criticism, on the inexhaustible topic of opinions, characters, and intentions. Most of the instances which are here produced, are of so brittle a substance that they fall in pieces as soon as they are touched: and I searched for some time before I was able to discover an example of some moment where the *Gentleman* had fairly staked his veracity against some positive fact asserted in the Two last Chapters of my History. At last I perceived that he has absolutely denied[117] that any thing can be gathered from the Epistles of St. Cyprian, or from his treatise *De Unitate Ecclesiæ*, to which I had referred, to justify my account of the spiritual pride and licentious manners of some of the Confessors.[118] As the *numbers* of the Epistles are not the same in the edition of Pamelius and in that of Fell, the Critic may be excused for mistaking my quotations, if he will acknowledge that he was ignorant of ecclesiastical history, and that he never heard of the troubles excited by the spiritual pride of the Confessors, who usurped the privilege of giving letters of communion to penitent sinners. But my reference to the treatise *De Unitate Ecclesiæ* was clear and direct; the treatise itself contains only ten pages, and the following words might be distinctly read by any person who understood the Latin language. "Nec quisquam miretur, dilectissimi fratres, etiam de confessoribus quosdam ad ista procedere, inde quoque aliquos tam nefanda tam gravia peccare. Neque enim confessio immunem facit ab insidiis diaboli; aut contra tentationes, et pericula, et incursus atque impetus seculares adhuc in seculo positum perpetuâ securitate defendit: ceterum nunquam in confessoribus, *fraudes*, et *stupra*, et *adulteria* post-

115. Remarks, p. 111.
116. Id. p. 72–88.
117. Id. p. 90, 91.
118. Gibbon, p. 546, Note 91.

modum videremus, quæ nunc in quibusdam videntes ingemiscimus et dolemus." This formal declaration of Cyprian, which is followed by several long periods of admonition and censure, is alone sufficient to expose the scandalous vices of some of the Confessors, and the disingenuous behaviour of my concealed adversary.

After this example, which I have fairly chosen as one of the most specious and important of his objections, the candid Reader would excuse me, if from this moment I declined *the Gentleman*'s acquaintance. But as two topics have occurred, which are intimately connected with the subject of the preceding sheets, I have inserted each of them in its proper place, as the conclusion of the fourth article of my answers to Mr. Davis, and of the first article of my reply to the confederate Doctors, Chelsum and Randolph.

It is not without some mixture of mortification and regret, that I now look back on the number of hours which I have consumed, and the number of pages which I have filled, in vindicating my literary and moral character from the charge of wilful *Misrepresentations*, gross *Errors*, and servile *Plagiarisms*. I cannot derive any triumph or consolation from the occasional advantages which I may have gained over three adversaries, whom it is impossible for me to consider as objects either of terror or of esteem. The spirit of resentment, and every other lively sensation, have long since been extinguished; and the pen would long since have dropped from my weary hand, had I not been supported in the execution of this ungrateful task, by the consciousness, or at least by the opinion, that I was discharging a debt of honour to the Public and to myself. I am impatient to dismiss, and to dismiss FOR EVER, this odious controversy, with the success of which I cannot surely be elated; and I have only to request, that, as soon as my Readers are convinced of my innocence, they would forget my Vindication.

Bentinck-Street,
February 3, 1779.

FINIS.

N.B. If any slips of the pen, or errors of the press, should still remain in this *second* Edition, I must make my appeal, not to the candour of my Adversaries, but to the indulgence of the Public.

BIBLIOGRAPHICAL INDEX

On 17 November 1790, Gibbon wrote to his publisher, Thomas Cadell, to propose 'a seventh, or supplemental' volume to *The Decline and Fall*, part of which was to be a 'critical review of all the authors whom I have used and quoted' (*L*, iii, 209). This notion had been with him since the mid-1770s, when in the 'Advertisement' to the first edition of volume I (1776) he had written:

> Should I ever complete the extensive design which has been sketched out in the Preface, I might perhaps conclude it with a critical account of the authors consulted during the progress of the whole work; and however such an attempt might incur the censure of ostentation, I am persuaded, that it would be susceptible of entertainment as well as information.

Although Gibbon collected some materials for this projected seventh volume (*EE*, 338–52), it was never published. However, Gibbon was surely right that a bibliographical supplement to *The Decline and Fall* would be 'entertaining, as well as useful'.

This index takes its cue from Gibbon's envisaged but abandoned project. It is for the most part an index to authors, although some particularly important publications, and publications with multiple authors (such as the *Mémoires de l'Académie des Inscriptions*) are listed separately. Roman numerals refer to chapters; arabic numerals to foot-notes.

This is not an index to proper names in the notes; rather an index to citations. But this is a shade of distinction which is often minute, and on many occasions I can feel, where I cannot explain, the motives of my choice. Where Gibbon's reference is accompanied with a critical judgement, I have quoted it before the number of the footnote where it is to be found.

Gibbon sometimes added footnotes after the main text had been composed. In n. 136 to chapter XLVII, for example, he referred to Volney's

Voyage en Syrie, a work first published in 1787, although in the *Memoirs* Gibbon tells us that this chapter was completed shortly after he arrived in Lausanne in the summer of 1784 (*A*, 331–2). Some of the more lengthy of the notes, particularly in the later volumes, may thus have been added in an interim stage between the composition of the narrative and the anticipated composition of the proposed supplement. They certainly read, at times, as if they were so written. The result is that, although Gibbon never completed his supplement, we can glimpse what it might have been like. For the first time, the reader of *The Decline and Fall* can now easily ascertain to which previous writers Gibbon referred; the frequency, extent and location of those references; and occasionally Gibbon's often pungent opinions of the writer. Moreover, the extent and depth of Gibbon's reading in Renaissance and post-Renaissance scholarship now come into sharp focus. The number of works referred to which were published during the composition of *The Decline and Fall* is particularly remarkable, and provides evidence for the view that Gibbon's intellectual appetite was not sated by the process of composition.

Bibliographical details are provided for the works of most post-classical writers cited in *The Decline and Fall*. Where a particular edition is specified, it is an edition noted by Gibbon in *The Decline and Fall* itself, an edition in his library, as recorded in G. Keynes, *The Library of Edward Gibbon* (London, 1940), or a particularly common edition. Where Gibbon's library contained more than one edition of a work, the place and date of all such editions are given.

Although, as the *Vindication* shows, Gibbon prided himself on what he took to be his meticulousness of reference, the compiler of this index has been obliged to struggle with the elusive, the cryptic, the ambiguous and the inconsistent. Undoubtedly there are errors. I can only hope that they do not reveal too shameful an ignorance, and that readers will be kind enough to inform me of slips and blunders.

A

Abauzit, Firmin [1679–1767; theologian; author of a *Discours historique sur l'Apocalipse*, and of the article 'Apocalipse' in the *Encyclopédie*; Gibbon owned his *Œuvres diverses* (London, 1770) and *Miscellanies on Historical, Theological, and Critical Subjects* (London, 1774)]: XV.154.

Abdel Balcides [historian of Abyssinia]: LI.97.

Ablavius: X.5; XXVI.72.

Abraham, Rabbi: VIII.28.

Abu al-Fida [1273–1331; referred to by Gibbon as Abulfeda; Ayoubite prince of Hamah; geographer and historian; Gibbon owned his *Annales Moslemici Latinos ex Arabicis fecit J. J. Reiske*

(Leipzig, 1774), *Annales Muslemici, Opera J. J. Reiskii*, 3 vols. (Copenhagen, 1789–91), *Chorasmide et Mawaralnahræ* (London, 1650), *De Vita et Rebus Gestis Mohammedis. Latine vertit J. Gagnier* (Oxford, 1723), *Descriptio Ægypti. Latine vertit J. D. Michaelis* (Göttingen, 1776), *Opus Geographicum. Latinum fecit J. Reiske* (Hamburg, 1770, 1771) and *Tabula Syriæ Arabicé edidit, Latiné vertit J. B. Kochler* (Leipzig, 1766)]: I.2; XXIV.52; XXVI.46; XXVII.112; XLII.97; XLVI.68; XLVII.54, 56, 57; XLIX.16; 'the most copious and correct account of the peninsula' L.2, 3, 15, 16, 17, 18, 46, 48, 51, 64, 65, 66, 68, 69, 70, 73, 95, 98, 'the silence of Abulfeda is worthy of a prince and a philosopher' 99, 'an enlightened prince' 111, 113, 115, 118, 119, 120, 121, 122, 125, 128, 130, 134, 135, 136, 138, 140, 142, 143, 144, 146, 147, 148, 149, 150, 153, 158, 161, 162, 165, 166, 168, 169, 'a moderate Sonnite' 175, 184; LI.1, 2, 3, 4, 5, 6, 7, 8, 9, 'the best of our Chronicles' 13, 21, 24, 34, 35, 36, 38, 41, 49, 52, 60, 61, 'the description of Syria, his native country, is the most interesting and authentic portion' 67, 72, 74, 78, 88, 91, 96, 117, 137, 139, 144, 156, 165, 170, 190; 'Abulfeda, whose testimony I esteem the most convenient and creditable' LII.1, 2, 12, 13, 15, 37, 38, 45, 46, 48, 61, 76, 78, 85, 96, 99, 100, 101, 103, 105, 108, 115, 116, 118; LIII.88; LVII.3, 6, 7, 10, 14, 30, 38, 52, 73; LVIII.90, 102; LIX.7, 38, 45, 48, 49, 52, 61, 64, 65, 78, 102, 109; LXI.63; LXIV.12, 18; LXV.9, 16, 74.

Abudacnus, Joseph [author of *Historia Jacobitarum* (Oxford, 1675)]: XLVII.149; LVII.66.

Abulfeda, *see* Abu al-Fida.

Abulghazi Bahadur Khan [1603–63; Khan of Khowaresm, author of the *Genealogical History of the Tatars*]: IX.14; X.28, 95; XXVI.7, 13, 16, 26, 29, 46, 50, 55; XXXIV.7, 42; XXXV.67; 'Gen. Obs.'.6; XL.138; XLII.25, 26, 33; XLVII.117; LI.34; LV.24; LVII.11, 17; LXIV.3, 5, 'the Histoire Genealogique des Tatars . . . was translated by the Swedish prisoners in Siberia from the Mogul MS. of Abulgasi Bahadur Khan, a descendant of Zingis, who reigned over the Usbeks of Charasm, or Carizme . . . He is of most value and credit for the names, pedigrees, and manners of his nation' 7, 30, 32; LXV.7, 11, 14, 85.

Abulmahasen [or Aboulmahasen; historian of Egypt]: LVII.21, 38; LVIII.99, 110; LIX.36; LXV.33.

Abulpharagius, Gregory [or Bar Hebraeus; 1226–86; Jacobite primate of the East; author of *De Rebus Gestis Richardi, Angliæ Regis, in Palæstina: Excerpta ex Chronico Syriaco* (Oxford, 1780), *Historia Compendiosa Dynastiarum, edita ab E. Pocockio* (Oxford, 1663), and *Specimen Historiæ Arabum, sive de Origine et Moribus Arabum, Opera E. Pocockii* (Oxford, 1650)]: VIII.5; XXXIV.7; XLII.45; XLVI.22, 59, 64; XLVII.19, 57, 101, 110, 132, 137; XLIX.16; L.8, 66, 97, 100, 134, 138, 144, 148, 166, 170; LI.3, 4, 5, 6, 7, 8, 9, 13, 'thoughtless chronology' 19, 31, 38, 60, 92, 116, 156, 170; LII.5, 13, 15, 35, 38, 'a number of literary anecdotes of philosophers, physicians, &c. who have flourished under each caliph, form the principal merit of the Dynasties of Abulpharagius' 53, 54, 57, 60, 63, 70, 78, 94, 96, 100, 101, 103, 110, 118; LIII.87, 88, 99; LVII.12, 22, 33, 38, 73; LVIII.93, 99, 110; LIX.38, 40, 42, 82, 85, 96, 102; LXIV.11, 34, 37.

Académie des Inscriptions, Mémoires de l', 43 vols. (Paris, 1736–86): I.18, 20, 38, 63, 74; II.50, 51, 70, 83; III.19, 22; 'it is seldom that the antiquarian and the philosopher are so happily blended' IX.86; X.69, 76, 166, 176; XI.23, 50; XIII.59; XIV.76, 88; XV.94; XVI.136, 149; XVII.15, 16, 30, 37, 92, 132; XIX.92; XX.45, 82, 117; XXI.170, 172; XXII.7; XXIII.105; XXIV.15, 54, 65; XXV.46, 155; XXVI.5, 25, 30, 52, 60; XXVII.1; XXVIII.41, 52; XXXI.27, 64, 86, 88, 115, 123; XXXII.1; XXXV.16, 26, 27;

Académie des Inscriptions, Mémoires de l'— *contd* XXXVIII.7, 13, 29, 51, 58, 62, 110, 118; XXXIX.63; XL.68, 97, 129, 140; XLI.32, 77; XLII.29, 45, 71; XLIII.25, 78; XLIV.17, 35, 56, 84; XLVI.22, 28, 65, 85, 90, 118; XLIX.112; LI.36, 99, 138; LVII.58; LIX.74; LXI.75; LXIV.24, 62; LXVI.72, 79, 109; LXVIII.4, 11, 67, 91; LXXI.60.

Acheri, Jean Luc d' [or Achery; 1609–85; author of *Veterum aliquot Scriptorum . . . Spicilegium*, 13 vols. (Paris, 1655–77), *Spicilegium* (Paris, 1723) and *Asceticorum, vulgò Spiritualium, Opusculum* (Paris, 1671)]: XVI.133; LVIII.48.

Acholius: XI.18.

Acropolita, George [1217–82; Byzantine statesman and historian]: LXI.36, 42, 55, 56, 58, 61; LXII.1, 4, 5, 7, 10, 12, 14, 18, 20, 21; LXIV.36; LXV.82.

Acta Proconsularia: XVI.86, 87.

Acta Sanctorum [possibly the collection in two volumes by S. E. Assemanus (Rome, 1748), or that by Charles Marie de Veil (London, 1684), or that by Giacomo Laderchi (Rome, 1723)]: 'an undertaking, which, through the medium of fable and superstition, communicates much historical and philosophical instruction' XXXIII.46.

Acts of the Apostles: XV.130; XVI.26; XLVIII.35.

Adam of Bremen [or Adam Bremensis; fl. eleventh century]: X.7, 9; LV.32, 52, 53, 80.

Adam, Robert [1728–92; architect and designer; Gibbon owned his *Ruins of the Palace of the Emperor Diocletian, at Spalatro* (London, 1764)]: XIII.117, 'Messieurs Adam and Clerisseau . . . visited Spalatro in the month of July 1757. The magnificent work which their journey produced, was published in London seven years afterwards' 121.

Addison, Joseph [1672–1719; essayist, poet, dramatist and politician; Gibbon owned his *Works*, 4 vols. (Birmingham, 1761), *De la religion chrétienne*, 3 vols. (Geneva, 1771), *The Freeholder* (London, 1761) and *The Spectator*, 8 vols. (London, n.d.)]: XXXI.4, 5; 'among the herd of bigots who are forcibly driven from this convenient, but untenable, post, I am ashamed, with the Grabes, Caves, Tillemonts, &c. to discover Mr. Addison, an English gentleman . . .; but his superficial tract on the Christian religion owes its credit to his name, his style, and the interested applause of our clergy' XLIX.9; LIII.18; LXVI.76; LXXI.18.

Administration des terres chez les Romains: XLIV.138.

Adrastus, of Cyzicus [mathematician]: XLIII.78.

Ælianus, Claudius [170–235]: II.74; XL.116; XLI.44; XLV.46; XLVI.81; LI.107; LXVIII.22.

Æschines, Socraticus [390–314 BC; Greek orator; Gibbon owned three copies of his *Dialogi Tres* (Amsterdam, 1711, Amsterdam, 1740, and Leipzig, 1766)]: XLIV.194.

Afer, John Leo [author of *De Medicis et Philosophis Arabibus*]: LVI.57.

Africanus, Leo [or Giovanni Leone; more accurately, Hasan b. Muhammad Wazzân, al-Fâsî; *c.*1485–*c.*1554; author of the work known in Europe as *Joannis Leonis Africani de Totius Africæ Descriptione*, tr. Joannes Florianus (Antwerp, 1556)]: XXV.125; XLI.45; 'a Moor, a scholar, and a traveller, who composed or translated his African geography in a state of captivity at Rome, where he had assumed the name and religion of pope Leo X' LI.140, 148, 149, 152, 154, 158, 161, 163, 213; LII.54; LVI.105.

Africanus, Sextus Julius [*c.*180–*c.*250; Christian historian; author of *Chronographia*]: XV.62.

Agatharcides [or Agatharchides; geographer of Arabia; author of *De Mari Rubro*]: L.2, 7, 32, 45.

Agathias [*c.*536–582; Byzantine poet and historian; author of *De Imperio et Rebus Gestis Iustiniarii Imperatoris*]: VIII.2, 23, 34; X.86; XII.72; XVII.134; XVIII.54; XXXII.64; XXXIV.31; XXXV.18;

xxxviii.45, 61; xl.13, 14, 15, 91, 101, 103, 155; xli.102, 103; xlii.5, 6, 19, 42, 47, 49, 53, 54, 64, 83, 85, 86, 88, 90; xliii.46, 47, 49, 50, 52, 54, 61, 62, 64, 83, 86, 88; xlvi.7; liii.94; lxviii.97.

Agiles, Raimondus d' [historian of the Crusades]: lviii.19, 41, 51, 79, 100.

Agnellus [or Andreas; abbot of St Maria ad Blachernas; author of the *Liber Pontificalis, sive, Vitæ Pontificum Ravennatum*]: xlv.16; xlix.37, 39, 60, 62, 67.

Agobard [779–840; st; abp of Lyons; French historian]: xxxviii.82, 83, 84.

Ahmed Ben Joseph [or Ahmad b. Yûsuf, al-Tarfashî, author of a work on precious stones]: l.121, 148.

Ahmed Ebn Arabshah [or Ahmed Arabsiades; author of a history of Tamerlane, translated into Latin and edited by Samuel Hendrik Manger, and published as *Vitæ et Rerum Gestarum Timuri* (Franequeræ, 1767)]: xix.55; xxxiv.25; 'ever a malicious, and often an ignorant, enemy: the very titles of his chapters are injurious' lxv.5, 7, 'the dark colouring of Arabshah' 12, 13, 15, 17, 28, 'for these recent and domestic transactions, Arabshah, though a partial, is a credible, witness' 34, 35, 36, 37, 45, 48, 54, 59, 61, 63, 66, 68, 70, 'Arabshah . . . whose testimony on these occasions is weighty and valuable' 73, 74.

Aimoin [960–1010; monk of Fleury; chronicler]: xxxviii.26, 31, 56; xli.101, 111; xliii.48; lxi.71.

Aintabi [Arabic writer]: lxv.33.

Albert of Stade: lix.14.

Alberti, Leandro [1479–1553?; author of the *Descrittione di tutta l'Italia* (Venice, 1577)]: xxx.40; xxxix.107; lvi.18.

Alberti, Leo Baptista [1404–72; historian of the Porcarian conspiracy]: lxx.85.

Alciat [or Andreas Alciatus; 1492–1550]: xliii.69; xliv.79.

Aldus, *see* Manutius, Aldus.

Alemannus, Nicolaus [commentator on Procopius]: xl.4, 14, 17, 'the learned notes of Alemannus' 20, 21, 22, 23, 28, 29, 36, 37, 39, 43, 45, 47, 49, 85, 94, 108, 154; xli.5, 7, 52, 95, 112, 114; xlii.63; xliii.21, 26, 67, 72, 95; xliv.94, 198; xlvii.80, 82, 83, 87.

Alembert, Jean le Rond d' [1717–83; *philosophe*; Gibbon owned his *Sur la destruction des Jésuites en France* (Paris?, 1765)]: xliii.76.

Alexander, Natalis [or Noël Alexandre; 1639–1724; author of *Historia Ecclesiastica*]: xlix.18, 30, 55, 70, 77, 83, 84, 94.

Alexandrian Chronicle, see Paschal Chronicle.

Allatius, Leo [or Leone Allacci; 1586–1669; Italian editor of Byzantine texts]: liii.109, 113; lxi.55; lxii.33; lxv.82; lxvi.108, 117; lxviii.34.

Alvarez, Francisco [d.1540?; Portuguese traveller]: xlii.99.

Ambrose [*c.*339–397; st; bp of Milan]: xx.33, 108; xxi.56; xxiii.80; xxvii.4, 14, 15, 17, 19, 21, 57, 62, 63, 64, 69, 73, 77, 80, 83, 91, 92, 96, 98, 103, 107, 120, 121; xxviii.1, 11, 12, 17; xliv.50, 166.

Amelius: xxi.18, 20.

Amelot de la Houssaie, Abraham Nicolas [1634–1706; historian; author of the *Histoire du gouvernement de Venise*, 3 vols. (Amsterdam, 1714)]: xxxv.58; xlv.18, 24.

Ameti [cartographer]: xxxi.89.

Ammianus Marcellinus [*c.*330–395; soldier and historian; Gibbon owned three copies of his *Rerum Gestarum Libri* (Augsburg, 1533, Leyden, 1693, and Leipzig, 1773)]: ii.43; vii.10, 51, 52; viii.2, 18, 27, 57, 58; ix.78, 82; x.32, 141, 175; xii.92; xiii.55, 62, 68, 72, 79; xiv.10, 11, 25, 55; xv.165; xvii.61, 87, 123, 126, 129, 131, 138, 139, 140, 141, 159, 161, 167, 179; xviii.5, 11, 17, 31, 32, 37, 45, 59, 60, 61, 67, 94, 100; xix.1, 8, 10, 16, 17, 18, 20, 21, 23, 24, 26, 30, 31, 32, 35, 36, 38, 39, 40, 41, 42, 45, 47, 49, 50, 51, 52, 53, 54, 57, 58, 59, 60, 62, 63, 64, 65, 67, 68, 70, 71, 72, 73, 'inflated eloquence' 74, 77, 78, 80, 82, 83, 85, 86, 88, 89, 90; xx.94; xxi.3,

Ammianus Marcellinus—*contd*
13, 91, 98, 125, 128, 140, 152, 161, 168; XXII.1, 2, 'the memory of Ammianus must have been inaccurate, and his language incorrect' 4, 'affected language' 5, 6, 10, 13, 15, 16, 19, 20, 21, 22, 23, 25, 26, 27, 28, 33, 34, 35, 36, 38, 39, 40, 41, 42, 43, 44, 50, 53, 61, 62, 65, 66, 67, 69, 71, 74, 77, 83; XXIII.4, 33, 34, 35, 36, 44, 46, 70, 78, 83, 89, 105, 113, 119, 122, 128; XXIV.6, 10, 16, 20, 21, 22, 23, 31, 32, 39, 40, 41, 42, 43, 44, 45, 46, 50, 51, 52, 53, 57, 61, 62, 63, 64, 68, 69, 72, 73, 75, 77, 78, 85, 87, 90, 91, 93, 95, 'an intelligent spectator' 99, 100, 102, 103, 108, 110, 111, 119, 'Ammianus and Eutropius may be admitted as fair and credible. witnesses of the public language and opinions' 122, 124, 125, 128, 133, 140; XXV.12, 13, 16, 'unmindful of his usual candour and good sense' 17, 20, 21, 24, 25, 26, 27, 28, 32, 33, 34, 35, 37, 39, 40, 41, 42, 52, 53, 55, 58, 59, 63, 64, 65, 85, 86, 88, 89, 90, 91, 92, 93, 94, 95, 96, 97, 98, 100, 106, 118, 120, 121, 'the chronology of Ammianus is loose and obscure' 122, 123, 124, 133, 136, 139, 143, 144, 145, 147, 149, 150, 'becoming asperity' 151, 153, 'Ammianus is so eloquent, that he writes nonsense' 154, 156, 157; 'such is the bad taste of Ammianus . . . that it is not easy to distinguish his facts from his metaphors' XXVI.1, 55, 57, 'the text of Ammianus seems to be imperfect, or corrupt' 60, 62, 'the chronology of Ammianus is obscure and imperfect' 63, 'he [Ammianus] often takes a false measure of . . . importance; and his superflouous prolixity is disagreeably balanced by his unseasonable brevity' 65, 67, 'a patriot historian' 69, 70, 71, 74, 75, 78, 80, 'those turgid metaphors, those false ornaments, that perpetually disfigure the style of Ammianus' 81, 'the historian might have viewed these plains [at the mouth of the Danube], either as a soldier, or as a traveller. But his modesty has suppressed the adventures of his own life subsequent to the Persian wars of Constantius and Julian. We are ignorant of the time when he quitted the service, and retired to Rome, where he appears to have composed his History of his Own Times' 82, 83, 84, 85, 'the full and impartial narrative of Ammianus' 87, 88, 89, 90, 'we might censure the vices of his style, the disorder and perplexity of his narrative: but we must now take leave of this impartial historian; and reproach is silenced by our regret for such an irreparable loss' 91, 92, 93, 94, 97, 98, 103, 110, 'the first thirteen books, a superficial epitome of two hundred and fifty years, are now lost: the last eighteen, which contain no more than twenty-five years, still preserve the copious and authentic history of his own times' 113, 'the last subject of Rome who composed a profane history in the Latin language' 114; XXVII.6; XXVIII.40; XXIX.43; XXXI.20, 31, 34, 35, 38, 60, 61, 65, 154; XXXIV.8; XXXVI.112; XXXVII.14; XXXIX.3, 24; XL.67; XLIII.62; XLV.10; L.29, 159; LI.48, 101, 121; LXI.32.

Ammonius [fl. 440 AD; poet]: XXXII.40.

Anastasius, bibliothecarius [*c.*810–*c.*878; Gibbon owned his *Historia de Vitis Romanorum Pontificum* (Paris, 1649)]: XXXIX.78, 82, 88; XL.33; XLI.91, 94, 109, 116; XLIII.7, 13; XLV.16; XLVII.94; XLIX.31, 'the style is barbarous, the narrative partial, the details are trifling – yet it must be read as a curious and authentic record of the times' 32, 38, 50, 64, 91, 93, 130; LII.32, 86, 'our authentic and contemporary guide' 90; LIII.96; LV.3; LX.4; LXXI.26, 28.

Anderson, Adam [1692?–1765; historian of commerce; Gibbon owned his *An Historical and Chronological Deduction of the Origin of Commerce*, 2 vols. (London, 1764)]: LIII.27; 'the trade of the Baltic, and the Hanseatic league, are carefully treated in Anderson's Historical

Deduction of Commerce; at least in *our* languages, I am not acquainted with any book so satisfactory' LV.52; LX.38.

Anderson, James [1680?–1739; preacher and miscellaneous writer; Gibbon owned his *Royal Genealogies* (London, 1736)]: LXIII.19, 20.

Anianinus, Benedict [monastic reformer, compiler of the *Codex Regularum*]: XXXVII.36, 37, 41, 42, 43, 49, 50.

Annales Bertiniani [early medieval annals of the abbey of St Bertin]: XLIX.93.

Annibalensi, Paulo [editor of Petrarch]: LXXI.48.

Anonymi Ravennatis qui circa Sæculum VII Vixit De Geographia Libri Quinque (Paris, 1688) [the 'Geographer of Ravenna']: X.68; XLI.36.

Anonym. Vales., *see Valesian Fragment.*

Anquetil, Louis Pierre d' [1723–1806; historian; author of *L'Esprit de la Ligue, ou histoire politique des troubles de France pendant les XVI*[e] *& XVII*[e] *siècles*, 3 vols. (Paris, 1767), and *L'Intrigue du Cabinet sous Henri IV. et Louis XIII., terminée par la Fronde*, 4 vols. (Maestricht, 1782)]: VIII.8, 10; XLII.49, 53.

Anquetil, M. Perron d' [or Abraham Hyacinthe Anquetil-Duperron; 1731–1805; traveller and orientalist]: XLVI.90.

Anthemius, of Tralles [mathematician]: XL.97.

Antioch, John, *see* John Scholasticus.

Antiochus [monk of St Saba]: 'whose one hundred and twenty-nine homilies are still extant, if what no one reads may be said to be extant' XLVI.60.

Antoninus [1389–1459; st; abp of Florence]: XLV.62.

Antonius, Peter: LXX.70, 98; LXXI.55.

Anville, Jean Baptiste Bourguignon d' [1697–1782; geographer; Gibbon owned his *Analyse de la carte, intitulée, les côtes de la Grèce, et l'Archipel* (Paris, 1757), *Analyse géographique de l'Italie* (Paris, 1744), *Antiquité géographique de l'Inde, et de plusieurs autres contrées de la haute Asie* (Paris, 1755), *Atlas ancien et moderne* (n.p., n.d.), *Dissertation sur l'étendue de l'ancienne Jérusalem et de son temple* (Paris, 1747), *Éclaircissemens géographiques sur l'ancienne Gaule* (Paris, 1741), *Éclaircissemens géographiques sur la carte de l'Inde* (Paris, 1753), *L'Empire de Russie, son origine, et ses acroissemens* (Paris, 1772), *L'Empire turc consideré dans son établissement et dans ses accroissements successifs* (Paris, 1772), *États formés en Europe après la chute de l'empire romain en Occident* (Paris, 1771), *Géographie ancienne abrégée* (Paris, 1768 and 1769), *Mémoire sur la Chine* (Paris, 1776), *Mémoire sur la mer Caspienne* (Paris, 1777), *Mémoires sur l'Égypte ancienne et moderne* (Paris, 1766), *Notice de l'ancienne Gaule tirée des monumens romains* (Paris, 1760), *Traité des mesures itinéraires* (Paris, 1769), and *Twelve Maps of Antient Geography* (London, 1757)]: I.18, 70, 72; II.85, 97; VIII.35, 38; 'his incomparable map of Europe' X.23, 29; XI.23; XII.108; XIII.79, 120; XIV.53, 87, 88; 'even that ingenious geographer is too fond of supposing new, and perhaps imaginary *measures*, for the purpose of rendering ancient writers as accurate as himself' XVII.15, 30, 33, 34, 36, 37, 47, 184, 185; 'the skill and accuracy which always distinguishes that excellent writer' XVIII.36, 71, 96; XIX.61, 86, 92; XX.117; 'for my own justification, I am obliged to mention the *only* error [the mislocation of the passes of Succi] which I have discovered in the maps or writings of that admirable geographer' XXII.33; XXIII.60, 77, 98; XXIV.34, 54, 65, 81, 105, 118; XXV.75, 90, 102, 120, 134; XXVI.4, 52, 59, 76, 86, 112; XXVII.112, 117; XXIX.2, 52; XXXI.88, 174; XXXII.14, 84; XXXIV.24; XXXV.11, 41; XXXVII.12; XXXVIII.137; XL.1, 71, 112, 114, 126, 131, 134, 137, 139; XLI.19, 28, 68, 71, 73, 77; XLII.33, 60, 62; XLIII.25, 34; XLVI.28, 65, 82, 'admirable skill and learning' 85, 90, 91; XLVII.56, 73, 122, 151; 'concise, but correct and original' XLIX.105; L.2, 17, 24, 51, 58, 174; 'equally at home in every age and

Anville, Jean Baptiste Bourguignon d'—*contd* every climate of the world' LI.16, 23, 74, 83, 106, 'the master hand of the first of geographers' 111, 127, 134, 136, 166, 175, 182, 185, 193; LII.28, 37, 41, 76, 94, 98, 117; 'the prince of geographers [Delisle], till the appearance of the greater d'Anville' LIII.3, 13; LIV.11; LV.6, 43, 70; LVI.66; LVII.6; LVIII.60, 87, 104, 107, 111; LX.21, 56; 'a good map suited to the last age of the Byzantine empire, would be an improvement of geography. But, alas! d'Anville is no more!' LXI.7, 72; LXII.9; LXIV.31, 'from whom the Orientals may learn the history and geography of their own country' 39; LXVI.34; LXVII.25; LXVIII.36; LXIX.23.

Apocalypse, *see* Revelation.

Apollodorus of Athens [fl. 140 BC; Gibbon owned the *Bibliothecæ Libri Tres*, 4 vols. (Göttingen, 1782, 1783), erroneously attributed to Apollodorus]: L.164; LXVIII.53.

Appianus, of Alexandria [fl. second century AD; historian]: I.12, 28, 71; II.24; III.8; V.70; VI.91; VIII.31; X.99, 114; XIII.27; XV.200; 'Gen. Obs.'.4; XL.13; XLII.77, 78; XLIV.184; LI.133, 172.

Appulus, William [or the Apulian, or of Apulia; poet]: LIV.28; 'they [William Appulus and Galfridus Malaterra] wrote on the spot, . . . and with the spirit of freemen' LVI.15, 19, 24, 25, 29, 30, 'the national, is counterbalanced by the clerical, prejudice' 33, 34, 37, 41, 45, 49, 51, 59, 60, 'bold and positive' 62, 63, 69, 71, 74, 76, 79, 85, 86, 88, 90, 91, 92, 94.

Apuleius, Lucius: II.38, 39, 60; XV.150, 172; XLIV.112.

Aquensis, Albertus [historian of the Crusades]: LVIII.2, 19, 35, 41, 94, 103; LIX.8.

Arabian Nights: XXXII.77; 'a faithful and amusing picture of the Oriental world' LI.199.

Arbuthnot, John [1667–1735; mathematician and physician; member of the Scriblerus Club; Gibbon owned his *Tables of Coins, Weights and Measures* (London, 1727)]: II.108; XIX.87; XXIV.15; XXXI.33, 56; XLIV.27; LI.133; LIII.72.

Aretinus, Leonardus Brunus [or Leonardo Bruni; *c.*1370–1444]: XL.14; LXVI.98, 99.

Argelatus, Philip [or Filippo Argellati; 1685–1755; editor of early Italian historians]: XLV.15; XLIX.27.

Ariosto, Lodovico [1474–1533; poet]: 'this incomparable poem' XLIX.74; LVIII.54.

Aristenus, Alexis [deacon of St Sophia]: XX.28.

Aristides [early Christian apologist]: II.35, 83, 109; XV.151.

Aristo of Pella: XV.20.

Aristophanes [*c.*450–*c.*388 BC; comic playwright]: XXIII.20; XLIV.51; LIII.110.

Aristotle [384–322 BC; philosopher]: XXI.58; XXII.48, 70; XLV.44, 46; XLVI.66; LI.115.

Aristus: XLIV.18.

Arnobius [the elder; fl. fourth century AD; Christian apologist]: XVI.141; L49.

Arnold of Lübeck: LVI.140; LIX.14.

Arrianus, Flavius [fl. second century A D.; biographer of Alexander the Great; follower of Epictetus]: I.48, 54, 58, 59, 82; VIII.35; X.105, 107, 109; XLII.15, 65; XLIV.18; XLVI.40; L.9, 24, 39; LXVII.25.

Art de verifier les dates des faits historiques . . . depuis la naissance de Notre-Seigneur, ed. Maur François Dantine et al. (Paris, 1750): XVI.131; XVII.170; XL.161; XLVII.140; L.66; LI.86; LVI.127; LIX.82.

Artemidorus of Daldia [fl. second century AD; author of *De Somniorum Interpretatione*]: L.2.

Artigny, Antoine Gachet d' [1704–78; author of the *Nouveaux memoires d'histoire, de critique, et de littérature*, 7 vols. (Paris, 1749–56)]: LIV.35.

Arvieux, Chevalier Laurent d' [1635–1702; author of *Mémoires*, 6 vols. (Paris, 1735), and *Voyage dans la Palestine* (Amsterdam, 1718)]: L.10, 12, 34, 40, 64; LVII.66.

Ascelin: XXVI.7.

Asclepiades of Bithynia: XLIV.18.

Assemanus, Joseph Simon [Gibbon owned his *Bibliotheca Orientalis Clementino-Vaticana*, 3 vols. (Rome, 1719–28)]: XV.182; XXXII.80, 87; XXXIII.44, 45; XXXVII.21, 70; XL.74, 79, 135, 155; XLII.39, 45, 48; XLVI.59, 108; XLVII.19, 'a learned and modest slave' 40, 52, 55, 57, 72, 86, 96, 101, 109, 110, 111, 'I am deeply indebted to . . . Assemannus. . . . As a native and as a scholar, he possessed the Syriac literature; and, though a dependent of Rome, he wishes to be moderate and candid' 112, 113, 114, 'his learned researches are digested in the most lucid order' 115, 116, 117, 118, 120, 124, 125, 127, 128, 129, 130, 131, 132, 135, 138, 141, 149, 153, 156; XLIX.8, 10; L.30, 'some valuable remarks' 44, 58, 148; LI.92, 214, 216; LII.57; LVII.62; LXIV.2, 11; 'a faithful slave of the Vatican' LXVI.75.

Asterius of Amasia: XVII.122; XXXII.12.

Aterianus, Julius: XI.47.

Athanasius [*c*.293–373; st]: XVI.164; XVIII.50, 52, 90; XX.39, 55, 81; 'his expressions have an uncommon energy; and as he was writing to Monks, there could not be any occasion for him to *affect* a rational language' XXI.32, 36, 63, 70, 81, 83, 86, 92, 94, 96, 99, 100, 101, 103, 104, 105, 107, 108, 109, 116, 118, 119, 120, 121, 122, 128, 132, 133, 134, 135, 136, 143, 144, 145, 149, 151; XXIII.129; XXIV.39, 134; XXV.4, 8; XXXVII.7, 8, 20; XLVII.3.

Athenæus: II.22, 54; XXXI.120; XL.150 L.164.

Athenagoras [fl. second century A D; Christian philosopher and apologist]: XV.38, 75, 95; XVI.19; XXI.50.

Aubigné, Théodore Agrippa d' [1552–1630; author of *Histoire universelle*, 3 vols. (1616–20), and *Mémoires écrits par lui-même*, 2 vols. (Amsterdam, 1731)]: XXVIII.86.

Augustan History: I.24, 25, 26, 27, 29, 40; II.50, 67, 104, 110; III.41, 43, 44, 45, 47, 48, 49; IV.1, 2, 3, 5, 7, 15, 16, 17, 23, 24, 28, 29, 32, 35, 38, 43, 44, 47, 49, 54, 56; V.6, 10, 13, 14, 17, 18, 19, 21, 23, 24, 28, 29, 30, 34, 36, 37, 45, 47, 48, 51, 57, 59, 62, 63, 65; VI.1, 4, 5, 11, 14, 15, 16, 24, 27, 31, 41, 44, 47, 54, 56, 57, 59, 60, 61, 63, 66, 67, 68, 69, 71, 72, 73, 74, 78, 79, 80, 111, 115; VII.2, 3, 4, 5, 9, 11, 14, 15, 16, 17, 18, 20, 22, 23, 25, 26, 27, 30, 31, 36, 37, 38, 39, 42, 43, 45, 47, 49, 51, 55; VIII.42, 43, 50; IX.82; X.22, 35, 40, 42, 49, 63, 64, 88, 94, 123, 125, 128, 135, 137, 140, 147, 152, 157, 150, 163, 164, 165, 167, 169, 172, 174, 178, 180, 181; XI.2, 5, 7, 10, 11, 12, 13, 15, 16, 17, 18, 19, 21, 22, 25, 30, 32, 35, 39, 42, 45, 47, 48, 49, 50, 53, 54, 56, 59, 60, 63, 66, 70, 72, 73, 74, 75, 76, 77, 82, 83, 84, 85, 86, 87, 88, 90, 91, 95, 96; XII.1, 2, 4, 8, 10, 11, 13, 14, 15, 16, 17, 20, 21, 22, 23, 25, 26, 27, 28, 30, 32, 33, 34, 35, 39, 40, 47, 48, 49, 51, 53, 54, 55, 57, 59, 61, 65, 66, 68, 69, 71, 74, 76, 79, 81, 82, 83, 86, 89, 101, 102, 103, 105, 107, 109; XIII.5, 113; XV.138, 163; XVI.4, 24, 108, 111, 114, 116, 126; XVII.97, 148; XIX.6; XXIII.104, 109; XXXI.47, 57; XL.64, 65, 120; XLIV.196.

Augustine [or Augustin; 354–430; st]: I.23; II.37, 38; XV.26, 37, 91; XVI.181; XVII.68, 183; XVIII.51; XXI.6, 20, 52; XXIV.78, 127; XXV.48; XXVI.105; XXVII.66, 69, 91, 'the grave energy of Augustin' 96, 98, 101, 120, 121; XXVIII.56, 57, 60, 65, 77, 'Augustin composed the two-and-twenty books de Civitate Dei in the space of thirteen years . . . His learning is too often borrowed, and his arguments are too often his own; but the whole work claims the merit of a magnificent design, vigorously, and not unskilfully executed' 79, 80, 84; XXX.77, 92; XXXI.100, 101, 103, 104, 109, 125; XXXIII.10, 'St. Augustin altered his opinion with regard to the proper treatment of heretics. His pathetic declaration of pity and indulgence for the Manichæans, has been inserted by Mr. Locke . . . among the choice specimens

Augustine—*contd*
of his common-place book. Another philosopher, the celebrated Bayle . . ., has refuted, with superfluous diligence and ingenuity, the arguments, by which the bishop of Hippo justified, in his old age, the persecution of the Donatists' 20, 29; XXXVII.30; XLIII.78; XLIV.166, 177; XLVII.12; XLIX.3.

Augustus, Antoninus [or Augustinus; legal scholar;]: XLIV.76, 92.

Aulus Gellius [fl. second century AD]: II.33, 69; VI.64; XV.41; XXIV.62; XLI.75; XLIII.92; XLIV.20, 51, 52, 63, 107, 117, 120, 124, 148, 159, 170, 173, 178; LI.121; LIII.112.

Aurelius, Marcus [emperor]: III.44; IV.4; VI.8; XV.191; XVI.95.

Aurelius Victor, Sextus [*c.*320–389; historian; author of *De Cæsaribus*, abbreviated as *Aurelii Victoris Historiæ Abbreviatæ*]: I.17; III.39, 41; IV.39, 56; V.35, 58; VI.14, 15; VII.3, 21, 49, 52; IX.82; X.33, 45, 47, 77, 80, 'his complaints breathe an uncommon spirit of freedom' 90; X.2, 50, 54, 58, 62, 65, 66, 66, 85, 123, 138, 147, 181; XI.2, 8, 13, 34, 45, 48, 50, 51, 83, 89, 90, 92, 94, 96; XII.1, 18, 19, 20, 58, 59, 74, 76, 79, 82, 93, 106, 109; XIII.1, 4, 5, 8, 9, 10, 20, 24, 30, 31, 41, 53, 64, 69, 70, 75, 90, 93, 94, 102, 105, 108, 112, 114; XIV.5, 15, 22, 32, 36, 43, 44, 46, 66, 74, 75, 78, 80, 92, 109, 111; XVII.95, 97, 141; XVIII.2, 3, 16, 23, 34, 35, 47, 52, 68, 69, 70, 78, 79, 87, 88, 90, 91, 98; XIX.9, 13, 15, 35, 48; XX.23, 30; XXII.2; XXIII.56; XXIV.77, 103; XXV.21, 54, 95, 154; XXVI.87, 94, 105; XXVII.6, 7, 79, 83; XLIV.196.

Ausonius, Decimus Magnus [*c.*310–395; poet]: X.78; XIII.38, 90; XVII.81, 82, 85, 89; XX.94; XXV.93; XXVII.1, 2, 77, 78; XXXI.120, 123, 155, 167; XXXIII.38; XXXVI.22; XXXIX.68; XL.25; LXX.10.

Austin [or Augustine; st; d. 604]: LIV.6.

Avitus [st; abp of Vienne]: XXXVII.87; XXXVIII.38, 39.

B

Baillet, Adrien [1649–1706; author of *Jugemens des savans sur les principaux ouvrages des auteurs*, 8 vols. (Paris, 1722–30)]: XXXII.3.

Bailly, Jean Sylvain [1763–93; author of *Histoire de l'astronomie ancienne* (Paris, 1781), *Histoire de l'astronomie indienne et orientale* (Paris, 1787), *Histoire de l'astronomie moderne*, 3 vols. (Paris, 1785), *Lettre sur l'Atlantide de Platon et sur l'ancienne histoire de l'Asie* (London and Paris, 1779) and *Lettres sur l'origine des sciences et sur celle des peuples de l'Asie* (London and Paris, 1777)]: 'This ingenious writer is a worthy disciple of the great Buffon: nor is it easy for the coldest reason to withstand the magic of their philosophy' XXXIX.42.

Baldric [or Baldricus; abp of Dol; poet and historian of the Crusades]: LVIII.15, 19, 41, 61, 79, 85, 94.

Balduinus, Franciscus [or François Bauduin]: XLIV.82.

Baldus: XXXII.19.

Baldwin of Flanders [author of *Gesta Innocent III.*]: LX.74, 78, 81, 82, 84, 86, 88, 91; LXI.24, 29, 31.

Balsamon, Theodoros [*c.*1105–*c.*1195; jurist and patriarch of Antioch]: XX.28.

Baluze, Étienne [1613–1718; publisher]: LX.26; LXI.6; LXIX.75, 'copious and elaborate notes . . . With the true zeal of an editor and a patriot, he devoutly justifies or excuses the characters of his countrymen' 80, 81, 83, 84; LXX.59, 63, 64, 66, 67, 68, 69.

Banduri, Anselme [1671–1743; editor of *Imperium Orientale, sive, Antiquitates Constantinopolitanæ*]: X.60; XVII.42, 48; XX.11; XL.27, 103; XLIII.67; LII.11; LIII.3, 12; LV.66, 76; LXI.18.

Banier, Antoine [1673–1741; author of *La Mythologie et les fables expliquées par l'histoire*, 3 vols. (Paris, 1715), 8 vols. (Paris, 1764)]: LVI.73.

Baratier, Jean Philippe [1721–40; translated

Benjamin of Tudela as *Voyages . . . en Europe, en Asie, et en Afrique*, 2 vols. (Amsterdam, 1734)]: LIII.14, 'the Hebrew text has been translated into French by that marvellous child Baratier, who has added a volume of crude learning' 28, 36; LVIII.36.

Barbarus, Hermolaus [or Ermolao Barbaro; 1453–93; classical scholar; editor of Pomponius Mela and Pliny]: LVI.66.

Barbessa, Odoardo: LXV.16.

Barbeyrac, Jean [1674–1744; author of *Histoire des anciens traités* (Amsterdam, 1739); Gibbon owned his *Traité de la morale des pères de l'église* (Amsterdam, 1728)]: 'very judicious' XV.87, 93, 100; XXVII.92; XXXVIII.96; XLI.107; XLII.90; XLIV.40, 166.

Barclay, Robert [1648–90; author of *An Apology for the True Christian Divinity, as the Same is held forth by the People called Quakers* (London, 1736)]: XV.100.

Bardesanes [*c.*154–*c.*222; Gnostic]: XV.182.

Bargæus, Petrus Angelius [author of *Commentarius de Obelisco* (Rome, 1586)]: XIX.46; XXXI.106.

Barletius, Marinus [priest of Scodra; author of *De Vitâ, Moribus, et Rebus Gestis Georgii Castrioti* [i.e. Scanderbeg] *Libri XIII* (Argentorat., 1537)]: LXVII.12, 'in the old and national history of Marinus Barletius . . . his [Scanderbeg's] gawdy and cumbersome robes are stuck with many false jewels' 36, 37, 38, 39, 40, 42, 43, 44.

Barnabas, Epistle of: XV.61.

Barnes, Joshua [1654–1712; editor of Euripides]: XXXI.152.

Baronius, Cæsar [1538–1607; cardinal; Gibbon owned his *Annales Ecclesiastici*, 12 vols. (Cologne, 1622–7)]: XI.82; XX.6, 9, 34, 35, 43, 53, 64, 69, 75, 106, 108, 115; XXI.2, 70, 77, 88, 123, 131, 142; XXIII.5, 65, 140; XXIV.129; XXV.65, 77, 82; XXVI.104; XXVII.22, 74; XXVIII.27, 33, 72, 77; XXIX.37, 38, 47, 56; XXX.33, 104, 111; XXXI.19, 20, 23, 37, 85, 101, 102, 125; XXXII.58, 60, 'Baronius is copious and florid; but he is accused of placing the lies of different ages on the same level of authenticity' 76; XXXIII.23, 45; XXXIV.52; XXXV.66; XXXVI.77, 82, 109, 132, 136, 141; XXXVII.134, 139; XXXVIII.28; XXXIX.62, 76, 81, 82, 91, 100, 108; XL.6, 9, 17, 40, 44; XLI.2, 22, 25, 62, 91, 98, 99; XLII.98; XLIII.7, 69; XLV.3, 14, 15, 33, 57, 58, 63, 'a copious but partial history' 64, 73; XLVI.29, 48, 60, 61, 62, 63, 76, 111; XLVII.27, 28, 31, 41, 42, 62, 'cardinal Baronius is firm and hard as the rock of St. Peter' 74, 78, 84, 92, 102, 104, 107, 108, 126, 147; XLIX.18, 27, 33, 75, 76, 77, 84, 116, 124, 127, 128; LI.86, 169, 171; LII.25, 34, 80, 90, 113; LV.5, 27, 38; LVI.1, 4, 10, 15, 18, 35, 44, 62, 82; LVII.69, 72, 74; LVIII.6, 26, 84; LXVI.1; LXIX.18, 27.

Barrington, hon. Daines [1727–1800; author of *Miscellanies* (London, 1781); Gibbon owned his *Observations on the More Ancient Statutes* (London, 1759), and may have bought his copy of P. de Marca's *Hispanica*]: XLVII.123.

Barthelemy, Jean-Jacques [1716–95]: XXXIX.63; LXXI.60.

Barthema, Ludovico [or Varthema; *c.*1465–1517; traveller]: LXV.16.

Barthius [commentator on Eutropius]: 'Barthius, who adored his author [Eutropius] with all the blind superstition of a commentator' XXXII.3.

Bartolus de Saxoferrato [1313–57; jurist]: XXXII.19; 'the great Bartolus' XLIV.89.

Basil [*c.*329–379; st; abp of Cæsarea]: XXV.71, 72; XXVI.64; XXVII.97; XLIV.166.

Basnage, Henri, sieur de Beauval [1656–1710; author of the *Histoire des Juifs*, 15 vols. (The Hague, 1716)]: VIII.29; XV.3, 11, 14, 162; XVI.3, 5, 6, 31, 46; 'the curious diligence of this writer pursues the Jewish exiles to the extremities of the globe' XX.78; XXI.12, 14, 17, 18, 29; XXIII.55, 58, 79; XXVIII.80, 84; XXXVII.138, 140; XXXIX.86; XLII.98; XLVII.3, 'learned and impartial' 88; L.60.

Basnage, Jacques, sieur de Beauval [1653–1723; author of the *Histoire des églises reformées*; editor of Canisius]: XLVII. 'most learned and rational' 19, 'a work of controversy' 35, 40, 71, 'too firmly resolved to depreciate the authority and character of the popes' 94, 96, 107; XLIX.3, 'he [Basnage] was a protestant, but of a manly spirit; and on this head [worship of images] the protestants are so notoriously in the right, that they can venture to be impartial' 6, 18, 'the cautious Basnage' 29, 77; LIX.10; LX.7, 12; LXIII.41.

Battie, William [1704–76; editor of Isocrates]: LIV.36; LXX.9.

Bayer, Gottlieb Siegfried [author of *Historia Osrhoena et Edessena, ex Nummis Illustrata* (St Petersburg, 1734) and *Historia Regni Græcorum Bactriani* (St Petersburg, 1738)]: VIII.44, 45, 46; XL.141; 'the learned Bayer' LV.22, 'I have perused, with pleasure and profit, a dissertation de Origine Russorum . . ., by Theophilus Sigefrid Bayer, a learned German, who spent his life and labours in the service of Russia' 43, 44, 46, 47, 49, 51, 53, 59.

Bayle, Pierre [1647–1706; Gibbon owned his *Œuvres diverses*, 4 vols. (The Hague, 1727–31), *Analyse raisonnée de Bayle, ou abregé de ses ouvrages*, 8 vols. (London, 1755–70), *Critique générale de l'histoire du calvinisme de Mr. Maimbourg* ('Villefranche', 1683), *Dictionnaire historique et critique*, 4 vols. (Amsterdam, 1740), *Nouvelles de la république des lettres*, 8 vols. (Amsterdam, 1685–87), *Nouvelles lettres*, 2 vols. (The Hague, 1739), and *Pensées diverses, à l'occasion de comète qui parut au mois de Décembre 1680*, 2 vols. (Rotterdam, 1683)]: VII.28; IX.15; XII.9; XV.34, 54, 97; XVI.37; XX.20; 'profound and interesting' XXI.34, 65; 'the sceptic of Rotterdam exhibits, according to his custom, a strange medley of loose knowledge, and lively wit' XXV.45, 'acute logic' 46; XXVII.92; XXVIII.2, 48; XXIX.33; XXXIII.20; XXXVII.5; XL.14, 150; XLIII.80; XLIV.200; XLV.62; XLVI.48; 'in the article of NESTORIUS, Bayle has scattered some loose philosophy on the worship of the Virgin Mary' XLVII.36; XLIX.72, 132; 'in the article of Mahomet, Bayle has shewn how indifferently wit and philosophy supply the absence of genuine information' L.110, 148, 151; 'more merit for lively reflection than original research' LII.25, 72; LIV.39; LVI.83; LXVI.117; LXVII.28; LXVIII.1; 'wicked wit' LXIX.21.

Beaufort, Louis de [*c.*1720–95; Gibbon owned his *La République romaine*, 2 vols. (The Hague, 1766) and *Dissertation sur l'incertitude des cinq premiers siècles de l'histoire romaine* (The Hague, 1750)]: I.52; II.23; III.19; XXVIII.3; XXXI.9, 115; XLIV.28, 40, 201; 'who will not be accused of too much credulity for the early ages of Rome' XLIX.43; LXIX.34.

Beaumanoir, Philippe de Remi, sire de [poet and author of *Coutumes de Beauvoisis* (Bourges, 1690)]: LVIII.132.

Beauplan, G. le Vasseur, sieur de [author of *Description d'Ukraine* (Rouen, 1660)]: LV.54, 'his descriptions are lively, his plans accurate' 58.

Beausobre, Isaac de [1659–1738; author of the *Histoire critique de Manichée et du manichëisme*, 2 vols. (Amsterdam, 1734–39)]: XV.26; XV.30, 32, 52, 91, 182; 'M. de Beausobre . . . has exposed with great spirit, the disingenuous arts of Augustin and Pope Leo I.' XVI.21, 48; XX.127; XXI.2, 21, 26, 27, 30, 35, 48, 54; XXII.22; XXVIII.75, 'M. de Beausobre . . . a Protestant, but a philosopher, has represented, with candour and learning, the introduction of *Christian idolatry* in the fourth and fifth centuries' 88; 'a treasure of ancient philosophy and theology. The learned historian spins with incomparable art the systematic thread of opinion, and transforms himself by turns into the person of a saint, a sage, or an heretic. Yet his refinement is sometimes excessive: he betrays an amiable partiality in favour of the weaker side, and, while he guards against calumny, he does not allow sufficient scope for superstition and fanaticism' XLVII.1, 'most learned and rational' 19; XLIX.7, 'equal reason and wit' 11, 13; 'the candid Beausobre' L.76, 88, 89, 90; LIV.6, 9.

Beauvais, Vincent de [1190–1264; st]: LVI.111.

Bede [673–735; Gibbon owned his *Historiæ Ecclesiasticæ Gentis Anglorum Libri Quinque* (Cambridge, 1722)]: XXXI.177, 178; XXXVII.81, 136; XXXVIII.122, 126, 130, 131, 138, 145, 148, 151, 152, 156; XL.161; XLV.8; XLVII.108; LXXI.52.

Beidawi, Al [commentator on the Koran]: L.74, 99, 103, 109.

Bel, Matyas [historian and editor of *Scriptores Rerum Hungaricarum*]: XXXIV.2; LXVII.28, 34.

Bell of Antermony, John [1691–1780; Gibbon owned his *Travels from St. Petersburg in Russia, to diverse parts of Asia* (Glasgow, 1763)]: X.28; 'that honest and intelligent traveller' XXVI.7, 32, 50; XLII.31, 89; XLVI.6; LII.47; LV.25; LX.64; LXIV.31.

Bellarmino, Roberto Francesco R. [1542–1621; st; cardinal]: XLIX.27, 'honest Bellarmin' 28.

Bellay, Guillaume du, seigneur de Langey [1491–1543; author of the *Epitome de l'antiquité des Gaules et de France* (Paris, 1556)]: XXX.93.

Bellay, Martin du, seigneur de Langey [fl. 1559; author of *Les Memoires de mess. Martin du Bellay* (Paris, 1569)]: LXVIII.39.

Belon, Pierre [1518–64; Gibbon owned his *Les Obseruations de plusieurs singularitez et choses memorables, trouuées en . . . pays estranges* (Paris, 1555) and *La Nature & diuersité des poissons* (Paris, 1555)]: XVII.14, 23; L.162; LII.79; LIII.13.

Benelathir: LIX.38.

Benjamin of Tudela [fl. twelfth century]: LII.41; LIII.14, 'the errors and fictions of the Jewish rabbi, are not a sufficient ground to deny the reality of his travels' 28, 36; LVIII.36.

Benschounah [or Ben Schounah, or Ebn Schounah; historian and epitomizer of Abu al-Fida]: LVII.38; LVIII.102; LIX.38; LXIV.59; LXV.5, 33, 35, 37, 48.

Bentivoglio, Guido [1579–1644; cardinal; Gibbon owned his *Opere* (Paris, 1645) and *Relationi, date in luce de E. Puteano* (Cologne, 1630)]: 'curious, well-informed, but somewhat partial' XX.25.

Bentley, Richard [1662–1742; classical scholar; master of Trinity College, Cambridge; Gibbon owned his *A Dissertation upon the Epistles of Phalaris* (London, 1699) and two copies of *Remarks Upon a Late Discourse of Free-Thinking* (London, 1713, and Cambridge, 1743)]: XXIV.26; 'This intricate subject of the Sicilian and Roman money, is ably discussed by Dr. Bentley . . ., whose powers in this controversy [the Epistles of Phalaris] were called forth by honour and resentment' XLIV.14, 'the critical sagacity of Bentley' 17, 55, 63; LII.67.

Berengarius [*c.*999–1088; archdeacon of Angers; author of panegyric]: LXIX.31, 33.

Bérenger, Jean Pierre [1740–1807; editor of Büsching]: XLVII.154; L.2.

Beretta, Giovanni Gasparo [referred to by Gibbon as Berretti, or Beretti; Gibbon owned his *De Italiâ Medii Ævi Dissertatio Chorographica* (Milan, 1727)]: XXXV.56; XLV.19, 'excellent' 37; XLIX.42, 63, 105; LII.89; LV.4; LX.36; LXVI.91.

Bergeron, Pierre [fl. 1637; Gibbon owned his *Voyages faits principalement en Asie*, 2 vols. (The Hague, 1735)]: LVII.52.

Bergier, Nicolas [1557–1623; Gibbon owned his *Histoire des grands chemins de l'empire romain*, 2 vols. (Brussels, 1736)]: I.88; II.87, 88, 91; XXIV.29; XXXI.88; XLI.73.

Berkelius, Abraham [editor of Stephanus Byzantinus]: XXX.60.

Bermudez, John: 'John Bermudez, whose relation, printed at Lisbon, 1569, was

Bermudez, John—*contd* translated into English by Purchas . . ., and from thence into French by La Croze . . . The piece is curious; but the author may be suspected of deceiving Abyssinia, Rome, and Portugal. His title to the rank of patriarch is dark and doubtful' XLVII.158.

Bernard of Clairvaux [1090–1153; st]: XV.81, LVIII.37; LIX.28, 29, 30, 31, 32, 33, 34, 35; LXIX.7, 8, 25, 68.

Bernard, Edward [1638–96; Gibbon owned his *De Mensuris et Ponderibus Antiquis* (Oxford, 1688)]: LI.133.

Bernier, François [fl. 1610; Gibbon owned his *Voyages*, 2 vols. (Amsterdam, 1723–4)]: VIII.41; XXXIV.44; LXIII.39; LXV.38.

Bernoulli, Johann [1667–1748]: XLIII.80.

Bertholdus: LVIII.6.

Beveridge, William [1637–1708; abp of St Asaph; author of *Pandectæ*]: XX.28, 114, 129; XXI.110; XXVII.97; XXXVII.56.

Bèze, Théodore de [or Beza; 1519–1605; Protestant nobleman and scholar]: XV.195; XXXVII.120.

Bianchini: XLIX.32, 155.

Bibliothèque Bunavianæ: XLIX.117.

Bibliothèque germanique, ou histoire littéraire de l'Allemagne et des pays du nord, 76 vols. (Amsterdam, 1720–60): XLIX.11.

Bibliothèque italique ou histoire littéraire de l'Italie, 18 vols. (Geneva, 1728–34): XLIX.155; LVI.97.

Bibliothèque raisonnée de la diplomatique: XLIV.47, 84.

Bibliothèque raisonnée des ouvrages des savans de l'Europe, 52 vols. (Paris, 1728–35): IX.1, 42; X.9; XVI.144; XXXIV.2; XXXVIII.44.

Biet, Antoine [b. *c.*1620]: 'much learning and good sense' XIX.66; XXXVIII.14, 17.

Bingham, Joseph [1668–1723; author of *Christian Antiquities*; Gibbon owned his *Works*, 2 vols. (London, 1726)]: XX.5, 'a Protestant reader will depend with more confidence on the learned Bingham' 63, 67, 84, 86, 'moderate' 88, 'by each of these learned but partial critics [Bingham and Thomassin], one half of the truth is produced, and the other is concealed' 93, 95, 122; XXII.22; XXVII.49; XXXI.187; XXXVII.1, 32; XLIV.121.

Biographia Britannica, 6 vols. (London, 1747–66): XXXIX.99; LII.24; LXI.66; LXIX.28.

Blackstone, Sir William [1723–80; jurist and legal historian; Gibbon owned two copies of his *Commentaries on the Laws of England*, 4 vols. (Oxford, 1773, and London, 1774), his *Law Tracts*, 2 vols. (Oxford, 1762), and *Tracts Chiefly Relating to the Antiquities and Laws of England* (Oxford, 1771)]: XXV.44; XLIV.145, 146; LIV.41.

Blair, Hugh [1718–1800; author of *Dissertation on Ossian*; Gibbon owned his *Lectures on Rhetoric and Belles Lettres*, 2 vols. (London, 1783), and two copies of his *Sermons* (Edinburgh, 1777, and, 3 vols., London, 1779–92)]: XXV.114.

Blanc, François le [d. 1698; author of *Traité historique des monnoyes de France*, (Amsterdam, 1692)]: XXXVIII.60; 'an elaborate, though partial, dissertation' XLIX.61, 71, 136.

Blancus, Horatius: XLV.15.

Blastares, Matthæus [fl. fourteenth century; monk and legal historian]: LIII.98.

Blondel, David [1591–1655; Gibbon owned his *De la primauté en l'église* (Geneva, 1641), *Apologia pro Sententia Hieronymi de Episcopis et Presbyteris* (Amsterdam, 1646) and *Des sybilles celebrées cant par l'antiquité que par les saincts pères* (Charenton, 1649)]: XV.109; XVIII.11; XX.60; XLIX.132.

Blondus, Flavius [or Flavio Biondo; 1392–1463; Italian historian]: LX.54, 63; LXI.2; 'both Blondus, and even Sigonius, too freely copied the classic method of supplying from reason or fancy the deficiency of records' LXIX.30; LXXI.75.

Boccaccio, Giovanni [1313–75; Gibbon owned two copies of the *Decameron*: *Decamerone*, 2 vols. (Amsterdam, 1761), and *Il Decamerone* (Florence, 1761)]: XXX.62; XLV.51; 'an ignorant age transfers its own language and manners to the most distant times' LXII.53; LXVI.88, 93, 94.

Bochari, Al: L.121, 168.

Boetius, Anicius Manlius Severinus [or Boethius; *c*.470–524; author of *De Consolatione Philosophiæ*]: XXI.53; XXXIX.84, 87, 89, 92, 93, 94, 97, 101.

Bohadin [biographer of Saladin]: LVIII.108; LIX.14, 20, 25, 42, 45, 48, 'an eye-witness, and an honest bigot' 54, 57, 61, 64, 65, 69, 70, 71, 72, 74, 75, 'he draws aside a corner of the political curtain' 76, 77, 78, 79; LX.19.

Boileau-Despréaux, Nicolas [1636–1711; French poet and critic; Gibbon owned three copies of his *Œuvres*, 5 vols. (Paris, 1747), 2 vols. (Paris, 1750) and 5 vols. (Amsterdam, 1772), and his *Poésies*, 2 vols. (Paris, 1781)]: XIX.86; XX.42; 'the sage Boileau' XLIV.74; 'the beautiful lines of Boileau's Lutrin' LII.26; LXI.52.

Boillaud, Ismael [or Bouillaud; editor of Ducas]: LXV.78; LXVIII.21, 46.

Boivin de Villeneuve, Jean [1663–1726; editor at the Academy of Inscriptions, Paris; biographer and editor of Nicephorus Gregoras]: LXI.55; LXIII.42; LXVI.109; LXVII.3.

Bolingbroke, *see* St John, Henry, viscount Bolingbroke.

Bologninus, Ludovicus: XLIV.89, 92.

Bonamy, Pierre Nicolas [1694–1770]: X.176; XIX.92; XXII.7; 'formal and elaborate' XXV.155; XXXVIII.118.

Bonanni [monk; compiler of a medallic history of Martin V]: LXX.77.

Bondari [Arabian historian of the Seljukides]: LVII.23.

Bonfinius, Antonius [*c*.1427–1502; author of *Decades Rerum Hungaricarum*]: 'an Italian, who, in the xv[th] century, was invited into Hungary to compose an eloquent history of that kingdom' LXIV.60; LXVII.19, 'Bonfinius, who, in his division and style, copies Livy with tolerable success' 23, 24, 28, 31, 33, 34.

Bongars, Jacques [or Bongarsius]: LVIII.19, 88; LIX.65, 85.

Boniface [st]: XXXVII.81.

Bossuet, Jacques-Bénigne [1627–1704; bp of Meaux; French divine; Gibbon owned two copies of his *Discours sur l'histoire universelle* (Paris, 1732, and, 2 vols., Lyons, 1782), two copies of its English translation as *An Universal History*, 4 vols. (London, 1736) and 21 vols. (London, 1747), his *Exposition de la doctrine de l'église catholique sur les matières de controverse* (Paris, 1680), his *Histoire des variations des églises protestantes*, 4 vols. (Paris, 1718–30) and two copies of his *Recueil des oraisons funèbres* (Paris, 1754, and Paris, 1761)]: II.3; XV.70; XX.20; 'the sublime Bossuet' XXVII.8; XXXI.117.

Bouchaud, Matthieu Antoine [1719–1804; Gibbon owned his *De l'impôt du vingtième sur la succession et de l'impôt sur les marchandises chez les Romains* (Paris, 1772)]: 'a very prolix commentary' VI.100; XX.130; XLIV.35.

Bouchet, Jean [1476–1550; French historian]: LXI.70.

Boucicault, Jean le Maingre, *dit* [1365–1421; marshal of France; Crusader; author of *Memoirs*]: 'the original Memoirs of the marechal de Boucicault . . .; add some facts, but they are dry and deficient' LXIV.61, 68; 'these memoirs were composed while the marshal was still governor of Genoa, from whence he was expelled in the year 1409, by a popular insurrection' LXV.49; LXVI.15.

Bougainville, Louis Antoine de [1729–1811; Gibbon owned his *A Voyage round the World* (London, 1772)]: XLII.71.

Boulainvilliers, Henri de [1658–1722; Gibbon owned his *Mémoires historiques sur l'état de la France*, 3 vols. ('London', 1727–8) and *La Vie de Mahomed* ('London', 1730)]: XXXVIII.12, 'the free spirit of the Count de Boulainvilliers' 64, 'The count de Boulainvilliers . . . shews a strong understanding, through a cloud of ignorance, and prejudice' 87, 103; XLVI.68, 'wicked intentions' 69;

Boulainvilliers, Henri de—*contd* L.71, 'the adverse wish of finding an impostor or an hero, has too often corrupted the learning of the doctor [Prideaux] and the ingenuity of the count' 111, 112; LVIII.11.

Bouquet, Martin [1685–1754; chief editor of the compilation, which Gibbon owned, entitled *Recueil des historiens des Gaules et de la France*, 13 vols. (Geneva, 1781)]: XIX.81; XXXI.139, 140; XXXV.8, 15, 16, 18, 20, 26, 33, 34, 38; XXXVII.35, 137, 139; 'By the labour of Dom. Bouquet, and the other Benedictines, all the original testimonies, as far as A.D. 1060, are disposed in chronological order, and illustrated with learned notes. Such a national work, which will be continued to the year 1500, might provoke our emulation' XXXVIII.1, 10, 21, 63, 68, 'I dislike the style; I detest the superstition' 125, 158; XLI.101, 103, 111; XLII.34; XLIII.48; XLVI.33; LI.184; LII.25, 27; LIII.66; LVII.70; LXI.71; LXXI.30.

Boyardo, Matteo Maria, conte di Scandiano [or Boiardo; 1441–94; author of *Orlando Inamorato*]: LXVI.118.

Boyle, Charles [1676–1731; earl of Orrery; Gibbon owned his *Dr. Bentley's Dissertations on the Epistles of Phalaris and the Fables of Æsop, Examin'd* (London, 1745)]: LII.67.

Boze, Claude Gros de: II.83; XI.50; XVI.136, 149; XLII.29.

Brenckman, Hendrik [or Brencmannus; Gibbon owned his *Historia Pandectarum* (Utrecht, 1722)]: 'the diligent Brenckman' XLIV.75, 87, 88, 89, 91, 'Henry Brenckman, a Dutchman, undertook a pilgrimage to Florence, where he employed several years in the study of a single manuscript. His Historian Pandectarum Florentinorum . . ., though a monument of industry, is a small portion of his original design' 92; XLV.35; 'an excellent dissertation' LVI.5, 'indefatigable' 48.

Brequigny, Louis Georges Oudart Feudrix de [*c.*1716–95]: X.76, 166; 'an accurate critic' LXVI.72.

Brisson, Barnabé [or Brissonius; 1531–91; Gibbon owned his *De Regio Persarum Principatu* (Strasburg, 1710), referred to by Gibbon as *De Regno Persico*]: XVII.160; XIX.53; XXIV.88, 104; XLII.43, 86; XLVI.11.

Brodeau, Jean [or Brodæus; 1500–63; editor of the *Anthologia Græca*]: XLVII.25, 63; LIII.10, 32.

Brosses, Charles de [1709–77; historian and editor of Sallust; Gibbon owned his *Traité de la formation mécanique des langues*, 4 vols. (Paris, 1765), and *Histoire des navigations aux terres Australes*, 2 vols. (Paris, 1756)]: XVII.154; XVIII.64; XLII.65; LII.23; LIV.10; LX.32; LXVIII.23.

Brossette, Claude [1671–1746; editor of Boileau]: LXI.52.

Brotier, Gabriel [1723–89; Jesuit; editor of Pliny and Tacitus]: XXXI.45, 73; 'learned Jesuit' XL.61.

Brouwer, Hendrik [or Brouer; Gibbon owned his *De Jure Connubiorum apud Batavo Recepto* (Delft, 1714)]: XVIII.51.

Browne, Edward [1644–1708; Gibbon owned his *A Brief Account of some Travels in Divers Parts of Europe* (London, 1685)]: XVIII.80, 82.

Brucker, Johann Jacob [Gibbon owned his *Historia Critica Philosophiæ*, 6 vols. (Leipzig, 1767)]: XXI.12, 13, 15, 18, 30; 'the learned Brucker . . . has employed much labour to illustrate their [Plotinus's, Porphyry's and Iamblichus's] obscure lives, and incomprehensible doctrines' XXIII.16, 47; XXXIX.91, 99; XL.149, 152, 153.

Brunck, R. F. P. [Gibbon owned his *Analecta Veterum Poetarum Græcorum*, 3 vols. (Strasburg, 1772–6)]: LIII.10, 32; LXX.65.

Bruyn, Cornelis de [or de Bruin; Gibbon owned his *Voyage au Levant* (Paris, 1714) and *Voyages par la Moscovie, en Perse, et aux Indes Orientales*, 2 vols. (Amsterdam, 1718)]: XXIII.62; XL.138; LI.31.

Bryan, Augustine [or Brian; d. 1726; eighteenth-century editor of Plutarch]: XVII.28; XXX.13.

Buat-Nançay, Louis Gabriel, comte de [1732–87; author of the *Histoire des anciens peuples de l'Europe*]: XVII.72; 'very accurate' XVIII.40; XXV.94, 'more industry than success' 141, 145; XXVI.61, 119; 'an elaborate work, which I had not the advantage of perusing till the year 1777' XXX.86, 'whose laborious accuracy may sometimes fatigue a superficial reader' 101; XXXIII.6; XXXIV.4, 12, 43, 'the scepticism of the count de Buat . . . cannot be reconciled with any principles of reason or criticism' XXXV.35, 45, 'laborious and minute diligence' 71; XXXVI.46, 120, 125; 'the patient reader may plunge into the dark and minute researches of M. de Buat' XXXIX.37, 'The Count de Buat was French minister at the court of Bavaria: a liberal curiosity prompted his enquiries into the antiquities of the country, and the curiosity was the *germ* of twelve respectable volumes' 44, 'I will neither hear nor reconcile the long and contradictory arguments of the Abbé Dubos and the Count de Buat, about the wars of Burgundy' 50; XL.7; XLI.53, 56; XLII.10, 13; XLIII.6, 44; 'any fragment of Bavarian antiquity excites the indefatigable diligence of the count de Buat' XLV.50; XLVI.23, 32.

Buchanan, George [1506–82; Gibbon owned his *Opera*, 2 vols. (Edinburgh, 1715)]: I.11; 'the earliest, or at least the most celebrated, of the reformers, who has justified the theory of resistance' XX.21; XXXVII.24.

Buckley, Samuel [editor of de Thou]: LI.155.

Bufalini, Leonardo [or Buffalino; cartographer of Rome]: XLI.89.

Buffon, Georges Louis Le Clerc, comte de [1707–88; Gibbon owned his *Histoire naturelle, générale et particulière*, 35 vols. (Paris, 1749–88), and *Collection complette des œuvres*, 45 vols. (Paris, 1769–85)]: I.86; IV.32, 34; IX.4; X.183; XI.74; XXIV.61; XXV.128; XXVI.57; XXXI.45; XXXIII.16; XXXIV.6; XXXIX.41, 42; 'the immortal Buffon' XL.99; XLI.35, 104; XLII.73, 92; XLIII.82; XLV.44, 47, 66; XLVII.152; L.11; LV.28; 'eloquent and philosophic' LXXI.17.

Bull, George [1634–1710; bp of St David's; Gibbon owned his *Defensio Fidei Nicenæ* (Oxford, 1685) and his *Opera Omnia* (London, 1703)]: XX.57; XXI.17, 19, 23, 25, 39, 40, 50, 57, 59, 60, 69.

Buondelmonte [traveller to Constantinople]: XVII.48.

Burchardus, Joannes [or Burcard; bp of Cività Castellana and Orte; Gibbon owned his *Historia Arcana, sive de Vita Alexandri VI Papæ, seu Excerpta ex Diario J. Burchardi edita a G. G. Leibnizio* (Hanover, 1697)]: 'large and valuable' LXX.98.

Bure, Guillaume François de [1731–82; Gibbon owned his *Bibliographie instructive*, 7 vols. (Paris, 1763–8)]: 'a knowing bookseller of Paris' LXVI.116.

Burette, Pierre Jean [1665–1747; historian of the art of pantomime]: XXXI.64.

Burigny, Jean Lévesque de [1692–1785; Gibbon owned his *Vie d'Érasme*, 2 vols. (Paris, 1757) and his *Vie de Grotius*, 2 vols. (Paris, 1752)]: II.50, 51.

Burmannus, Petrus [1668–1741; Gibbon owned his *Anthologia Veterum Latinorum Epigrammatum et Poematum*, 2 vols. (Amsterdam, 1759, 1773), *Poetæ Latini Minores*, 2 vols. (Leyden, 1731), and *Vectigalia Populi Romani* (Leyden, 1734)]: VI.111.

Burnet, Gilbert [1643–1715; bp of Salisbury; historian; Gibbon owned his *History of His Own Time*, 4 vols. (London, 1753), *The History of the Reformation of the Church of England*, 3 vols. (London, 1679–1753), and *Travels* (London, 1737)]: XV.170; LIV.33, 37, 38.

Burnet, Thomas [1635?–1715; Gibbon owned his *The Sacred Theory of the Earth*, 2 vols. (London, 1759), and *De Statu*

Burnet, Thomas—*contd*
Mortuorum et Resurgentium Liber (London, 1727)]: 'Dr. Burnet . . . has discussed the first chapters of Genesis with too much wit and freedom' XV.28, 61, 'every reader of taste will be entertained with the third part of Burnet's Sacred Theory. He blends philosophy, scripture, and tradition, into one magnificent system; in the description of which, he displays a strength of fancy not inferior to that of Milton himself' 69; XXVIII.81.

Busbequius, Augerius Gislenius: XVII.24; XVIII.80; XL.126; XLII.89; LIII.45; LXIV.55; LXV.55, 74, 90; LXVIII.69.

Büsching, Anton Friedrich [1724–93; geographer; Gibbon owned his *A New System of Geography*, 6 vols. (London, 1762), *Géographie, ornée d'un précis de l'histoire de chaque état par M. Bérenger*, 12 vols. (Lausanne, 1776–82), and *Caractère de Frédéric II., roi de Prusse*, 2 vols. (Berne, 1788)]: XVIII.82; XXVII.53; XLVII.154; L.2; LXIII.15.

Butler, Alban [1711–73; author of *Lives of the Saints*, 4 vols. (London, 1756–9)]: 'a work of merit; the sense and learning belong to the author – his prejudices are those of his profession' XLV.67; XLVI.19, 63.

Bynkershoek, C. von [or Binkershoek; 1673–1743; jurist; Gibbon owned his *Opera Omnia* (Geneva, 1761)]: XXV.60; XLIV.5, 8, 12, 81, 114, 139, 178, 206.

C

Cadomensis, Radulphus [biographer of Tancred]: LVIII.19, 41, 79, 88, 91, 92, 94, 100.

Cæcilius, *see* Lactantius.

Cæsar, Gaius Julius [100–44 BC]: II.5, 29; III.12; IX.5, 19, 26, 27, 36, 47, 48, 51, 69, 77; X.84, 87; XIII.18; XV.53; XXV.104, 109; XXVI.99; 'the simplicity of truth [in Cæsar] is far greater than the amplifications of Lucan' XXX.78; XXXVIII.18, 85, 100; 'the simple and masterly narrative of Cæsar himself' LVI.72; LXXI.20.

Caietan, James [cardinal; nephew of Boniface VIII]: LXIX.85.

Caius [or Gaius; fl. 130–80 AD; Roman jurist; author of *Institutes*]: XLIV.137, 149, 157, 158.

Callimachus, Philippus [pseud. for Filippo Buonaccorsi; 1437–96; Italian historian of Hungary; author of *De Rebus a Vladislao Polonorum atque Hungarorum Rege Gestis, Libri III*]: LXVII.19, 'still more pure and authentic [than Bonfinius]' 23, 24, 26, 27, 28.

Callistus, Nicephorus: XVII.21; XXXIV.50; XLI.74.

Calmet, Augustin [1672–1757; Gibbon owned his *Dissertations qui peuvent servir de prolégomènes de l'écriture sainte*, 3 vols. (Paris, 1720) and *Histoire ecclésiastique et civile de la Lorraine* (Nancy, 1728)]: XV.194; XVI.105; XXI.16; L.24.

Calphurnius: XI.81, 93; XII.70, 84, 87, 92, 95, 97, 98.

Camden, William [or Cambden; 1551–1623; Gibbon owned his *Britannia* (London, 1607), tr. E. Gibson, 2 vols. (London, 1753) and *Anglica, Hibernica, Normannica, Cambrica a Veteribus Scripta* (Frankfort, 1603)]: I.8; XII.46; 'the British Strabo' XXV.109, 116; XXVII.11, 55; 'the great Cambden himself' XXXI.173; XXXVII.22; XXXVIII.134, 143, 160; LVI.17, 37; LVIII.47; LXI.81; LXVI.11.

Camus [editor of Aristotle]: XLV.46.

Camusat, Denis François [1695–1732; Gibbon owned his *Histoire critique des journaux*, 2 vols. (Amsterdam, 1734)]: LIII.108.

Cananus, Joannes [author of an account of the siege of Constantinople in 1422]: LXV.82, 83, 84.

Candidus, Joannes: XXVI.114; XXXVI.112, 124; XXXIX.9.

Canisius, Henricus [editor of *Antiquæ Lectionis tomus I (–VI)* (Ingolstadt, 1601–4)]: XLVII.71, 94; LIX.10, 19, 23, 24, 25, 56; LX.7, 12, 45; LXIII.41.

Cannegieter, Hermannus [author of *Observationum Juris Romani Libri Quatuor* (Lugd. Bat., 1772)]: XLIV.19.

Cantacuzen, John [or Cantacuzenus, or Cantacuzene; fourteenth-century Byzantine statesman, regent, and eventually emperor; composed a history of his own times, and works of polemical theology]: LXI.60; LXIII.4, 5, 7, 8, 9, 'his text has been corrupted by ignorant transcribers' 10, 11, 12, 13, 18, 19, 22, 24, 25, 26, 29, 30, 31, 32, 34, 'the emperor . . . represents his own virtues' 35, 36, 'his four discourses, or books, were printed at Basil 1543 . . . He composed them to satisfy a proselyte who was assaulted with letters from his friends of Ispahan. Cantacuzene had read the Koran; but I understand from Maracci, that he adopts the vulgar prejudices and fables against Mahomet and his religion' 38, 42, 44, 'obscurity and confusion' 50, 'Cantacuzene . . ., who wishes to disguise what he dares not deny' 51; LXIV.42, 47, 49, 50, 51, 52; LXVI.5, 6, 89.

Cantelorius, Felix: XVII.109.

Cantemir, Demetrius [1673–1723; prince of Moldavia; author of the *History of the Othman Empire*]: XVII.70; L.23, 186; LII.4; 'the author is guilty of strange blunders in Oriental history; but he was conversant with the language, the annals, and institutions of the Turks' LXIV.41, 49, 'a miserable idea of his Turkish guides' 51, 'large and curious annotations' 53, 55, 56, 57, 59, 67; LXV.45, 55, 57, 60, 72, 75, 'gross errors' 79, 80, 83, 86; LXVII.11, 21, 27, 41, 52; LXVIII.2, 8, 10, 11, 15, 20, 23, 48, 62, 76, 77, 80, 84, 87.

Capaccio, Giulio Cesare [Gibbon owned his *Neapolitanæ historiæ tomus primus* (Naples, 1607)]: XLI.67.

Capecelatro, Francesco: 'in the Bibliotheque Italique . . . I find an useful abstract of Capecelatro, a modern Neapolitan, who has composed, in two volumes, the history of his country from Roger I. to Frederic II. inclusive' LVI.97.

Capellus, James: XLIV.79.

Capitolinus, Julius: IV.49, 52, 'if we credit Capitolinus (which is rather difficult)' 54; XII.27, 89; XLIV.43.

Caracciolus, Antonius [editor of *Antiqui Chronologi Quatuor, Herempertus Langobardus* (Naples, 1626)]: LVI.9.

Cardonne, Denis Dominique [1720–83; Gibbon owned his *Histoire de l'Afrique et de l'Espagne sous les Arabes*, 3 vols. (Paris, 1765), and *Mélanges de littérature orientale*, 2 vols. (Paris, 1770)]: XXXI.142; LI.138, 153, 170, 'inexcusably ignorant or careless' 171, 184, 188, 191, 194, 207; LII.25, 39, 49, 50, 88, 104; LVI.103.

Caresinus [Venetian chronicler]: LXIII.52.

Carisius [editor of Hugo Falcundus]: LIII.21.

Carmen de Providentiâ Divinâ: XXX.91.

Carpini, Joannes de Plano [or Carpin; c.1180–1252; abp of Antivari; historian of the Mongols]: XXVI.7.

Carte, Thomas [1686–1754; Gibbon owned his *A General History of England*, 4 vols. (London, 1747–55), *A Collection of Original Letters and Papers concerning the Affairs of England found among the Duke of Ormonde's Papers*, 2 vols. (London, 1739), and *A History of the Life of James, Duke of Ormond*, 3 vols. (London, 1735–6)]: XIV.8; XXVII.10; XXX.94; 'the laborious Mr. Carte' XXXVIII.127, 147, 150, 155; LIX.106.

Casaubon, Isaac [1559–1614; classical scholar]: IV.16, 26; V.29; VII.26; XI.79; XII.12, 14, 22, 81; XV.6; XVI.4; XVII.1, 97; XXIII.104; XXIV.106, 136; XXXI.120; XLIII.65, 70, 71; XLIV.15, 180; LIII.3, 61; LX.40; LXX.9.

Casiri, Miguel [1710–91; librarian of the Escurial; Gibbon owned his *Bibliotheca Arabica-Hispana Escurialensis*, 2 vols. (Madrid, 1760, 1770)]: L.38, 39, 41; LI.43, 166, 'the librarian of the Escurial has not satisfied my hopes: yet he appears to have searched with diligence

Casiri, Miguel—*contd* his broken materials' 170, 176, 186, 189, 190, 192, 193, 'I am happy enough to possess a splendid and interesting work, which has only been distributed in presents by the court of Madrid . . . The execution of this work does honour to the Spanish press; the MSS. to the number of MDCCCLI, are judiciously classed by the editor, and his copious extracts throw *some* light on the Mahometan literature and history of Spain' 195, 210, 212; LII.23, 39, 54, 55, 57, 60, 64, 68; LVI.57.

Cassari [author of *Annal. Genuenses*]: LVI.138.

Cassianus, Joannes [or Cassian; 360–435; st; author of *Institutes*, and *Collations* or *Conferences*]: XXXVII.3, 33, 34, 40, 44, 45, 47, 48, 50, 52, 60, 61, 64, 65; XLVII.12, 13.

Cassiodorus [or, erroneously, Cassiodorius; *c.*480–575; statesman and historian of Theodoric the Great and the Ostrogoths]: X.4; XVII.150; XXV.100; XXVI.72; XXX.45; XXXI.17; XXXIII.8, 13; XXXIV.6; XXXV.7, 33, 43, 44, 57; XXXVI.123; XXXVII.52; XXXVIII.24, 49, 56; XXXIX.1, 16, 'loyal and credulous' 22, 32, 33, 36, 39, 45, 'liberal and classic style' 46, 49, 50, 54, 56, 57, 'ostentatious, though agreeable learning' 60, 'his descriptions are not unworthy of the reader's perusal' 63, 64, 65, 72, 74, 79, 82, 84, 91, 92, 95, 'In the fanciful eloquence of Cassiodorius, the variety of sea and river-fish are an evidence of extensive dominion' 102, 105, 106, 109; XL.42, 59, 156; XLI.49, 52, 53, 54, 71; XLII.11; XLIII.43; LIII.41.

Castor [mathematician]: XLIII.78.

Catalani, Giuseppe [author of *Critical Prefaces Annali d'Italia*]: XLIX.59.

Cato, Marcus Porcius, the elder [234–149 BC]: XLIV.148, 167.

Catrou, François [1659–1737; commentator on Virgil]: XXXI.40.

Catullus, Valerius [84–54 BC]: XV.44; XLIV.180.

Cave, William [1637–1713; Gibbon owned his *Primitive Christianity*, 2 vols. (London, 1673) and his *Scriptorum Ecclesiasticorum Historia Literaria* (Geneva, 1720)]: XV.147; XXXVII.124; XXXVIII.94.

Cedrenus [eleventh-century Byzantine historian]: VI.62; XIV.50; XVII.43, 66; XVIII.35; XXI.90; XXVI.2; XXVII.91; XXXII.74; XXXVI.64, 69; XL.11, 78; XLIII.68; XLIV.198; XLV.4, 23, 28, 30; XLVI.22, 42, 47, 49, 53, 54; XLVII.135; XLIX.10, 15, 18, 24, 26; L.145; LI.10, 114; LII.2, 15, 17, 74, 78, 80, 96, 118; LIII.29, 65, 83, 95, 103, 105, 106; LIV.16, 17, 'without their [Genesius's and Constantine Porphyrogenitus's] passions or their knowledge' 19, 'how elegant is the Greek tongue, even in the mouth of Cedrenus!' 20, 21; LV.6, 13, 34, 55, 56, 57, 61, 63, 'they [Cedrenus and Zonaras] grow more weighty and credible as they draw near to their own times' 64, 72; LVI.22, 23, 30; LVII.15, 19, 25, 26; LXVIII.97.

Cellarius, Christopherus [1638–1707; Gibbon owned his *Historia Nova, hoc est XVI. et XVII. Sæculorum* (Halle, 1696) and his *Notitia Orbis Antiqui*, 2 vols. (Cambridge and Amsterdam, 1703–6)]: X.179; XIII.1; XIV.10, 66; XVI.82; XVII.61; XVIII.36; XX.117; XXI.150; XXIV.66; XXV.41, 120; XXVI.76; XXIX.52; XXX.18; XXXII.24; XXXIII.26; XXXVII.121; XXXIX.2; XL.129; XLII.21, 81; LI.74; LIII.13; LVIII.87; LIX.7; LXII.9; LXVII.25.

Celsius, Olof [1670–1756; bp of Lund; writer on Gothic antiquities]: IX.16.

Celsus: XV.184, 187, 192; XVI.8, 13.

Cenni, Gaetano [editor of *Monumenta Dominationis Pontificæ*, 2 vols. (Rome, 1760–1)]: LXIX.3.

Censorinus [Gibbon owned his *Liber de Die Natali* (Leyden, 1767)]: VII.32, 57; X.38; XXV.24; XXXV.75; XLIV.8; LXX.10.

'Centuriators of Magdeburg': XX.53; XLIX.29.

Cerceau [Jesuit; author of the *Conjuration*

de Nicolas Gabrini, dit de Rienzi Tyran de Rome, en 1347 (Paris, 1748)]: LXX.16, 27, 37, 39, 40, 42, 44, 48, 54.

Cerularius, Michael: LX.1, 7.

Cervantes Saavedra, Miguel de [1547–1616; Gibbon owned his *El Ingenioso Hidalgo Don Quixote de la Mancha*, 4 vols. (Madrid, 1782), *The Life and Exploits of Don Quixote, translated by C. Jarvis*, 2 vols. (London, 1742) and *The History and Adventures of Don Quixote, translated by T. Smollett*, 2 vols. (London, 1755) and 4 vols. (London, 1770)]: LI.176, 'La Mancha, which the pen of Cervantes has transformed into classic ground to the readers of every nation' 177; LVIII.27.

Chais, Charles [1701–85; French minister at the Hague; Gibbon owned his *Lettres historiques et dogmatiques sur les jubilés et les indulgences*, 3 vols. (The Hague, 1751)]: VII.56; XXVIII.70; LVIII.22; 'an elaborate and pleasing work, had not the author preferred the character of a polemic to that of a philosopher' LXIX.90.

Chalcocondyles, Laonicus [*c.*1423–1490?; historian of Byzantium]: L.151; LIII.102; LV.7; LXIV.40, 41, 43, 51, 52, 55, 56, 65, 'Chalcocondyles, whose proper subject is drowned in a sea of episode' 66; LXV.31, 37, 45, 56, 72, 80, 87, 93; LXVI.13, 16, 'in his numerous digressions, the modest historian has never introduced himself' 22, 23, 'all pride was extinct in the bosom of Chalcocondyles' 24, 27; LXVII.6, 12, 15, 20, 28, 32, 36; LXVIII.10, 11, 16, 38, 42, 52, 53, 59, 63, 70, 79, 'too diffuse and digressive' 86, 87, 89.

Chandler, Richard [1738–1810; Gibbon owned his *Travels in Asia Minor* (Oxford, 1775) and *Travels in Greece* (Oxford, 1776)]: II.81; XXX.9, 18, 19; LXI.13; LXII.9, 56; LXIV.45; LXVI.34.

Chappe d'Auteroche, Jean Baptiste [1722–69; Gibbon owned his *Voyage en Siberie fait en 1761* (Amsterdam, 1769, 1770)]: XLII.24.

Chardin, Jean [1643–1713; Gibbon owned his *Voyages en Perse*, 4 vols. (Amsterdam, 1735)]: III.52, 54; VIII.36, 58; X.119; XIX.53; 'the most judicious of modern travellers' XXIV.88; XL.115; XLII.43, 44, 'his observations are judicious; and his own adventures in the country are still more instructive than his observations' 67, 68, 74, 'an absurdity unworthy of that judicious traveller' 75, 81; XLVI.10, 84, 86, 87; XLVII.143; L.18, 53, 79, 80, 97, 99, 'the jeweller Chardin had the eyes of a philosopher' 101, 141, 'Sir John Chardin has too faithfully copied the fables and errors of the modern Persians' 166, 'their master, Chardin' 171, 172, 173, 'a traveller whom I have often praised' 180, 185; LI.31, 50, 'not indeed the most learned, but the most judicious and inquisitive, of our modern travellers' 206; LII.63; LVII.29, 44; LXIII.46, 48.

Chardon, Charles Mathias [1695–1771; author of *Histoire des sacremens* (Paris, 1745)]: XX.5, 67, 68, 87, 'very clear and concise' 88, 114; XXVII.97, 108; XXVII.34, 129; XLIV.121.

Charlevoix, Pierre François Xavier de [1684–1761; Gibbon owned his *Histoire de l'isle Espagnole ou de S. Domingue*, 2 vols. (Paris, 1730–1), and *Journal of a Voyage to North America*, 2 vols. (London, 1761)]: IX.7.

Chaucer, Geoffrey [*c.*1340–1400; Gibbon owned his *Works*, ed. J. Urry (London, 1721), *The Canterbury Tales Modernis'd by Several Hands*, 3 vols. (London, 1741), and *The Canterbury Tales, with an Essay and Notes by T. Tyrwhitt*, 5 vols. (London, 1775–8)]: 'an ignorant age transfers its own language and manners to the most distant times' LXII.53.

Chauffepié, Jacques Georges de [1702–86; Gibbon owned his *Nouveau dictionnaire historique et critique*, 4 vols. (Amsterdam, 1750–6)]: XX.20, 42, 53; LIV.35.

Cherefeddin Ali [or Sherefeddin; more accurately, Sharāf al-Din; Gibbon owned his *Histoire de Timur Bec, traduite*

Cherefeddin Ali—*contd*
par Pétis de la Croix, 4 vols. (Paris, 1722), and *The History of Timur-Bec*, 2 vols. (London, 1723)]: II.84, XIX.55, 61; XXXIV.14, 'servile panegyrist' 25; XLVI.89; LI.72, 85, 199; LXIII.28; LXIV.65; 'my faithful guide. His geography and chronology are wonderfully accurate; and he may be trusted for public facts, though he servilely praises the virtue and fortune of the hero' LXV.1, 9, 12, 13, 15, 23, 24, 27, 28, 34, 36, 43, 45, 47, 59, 60, 61, 63, 64, 66, 68, 70, 73, 76; LXVII.49.

Chi'en-Lung [emperor of China; Gibbon owned his *Éloge de la ville de Moukden. Poëme composé Par Kien-long, empereur de la Chine, traduit par le P. Amiot* (Paris, 1770)]: XXVI.12, 31, 40.

Chiensis, Leonardus [fifteenth-century author of *Historia C.P. a Turco Expugnatæ* (Norimberghæ, 1544)]: LXVIII.11, 24, 30, 'curious and important' 37, 42, 55, 58, 61.

Chillingworth, William [1602–44; theologian; Gibbon owned his *Works* (London, 1674) and *Religion of Protestants a Safe Way to Salvation* (London, 1674)]: LIV.38.

Chishull, Edmund [1671–1733; Gibbon owned his *Antiquitates Asiaticæ* (London, 1728) and *Travels in Turkey* (London, 1747)]: 'a curious traveller' XXVI.66; 'Chishull . . . proceeded from Gallipoli, through Hadrianople, to the Danube, in about fifteen days. He was in the train of an English ambassador, whose baggage consisted of seventy-one waggons. That learned traveller has the merit of tracing a curious and unfrequented route' XXXII.38.

Chislet [editor of Vigilius of Thapsus]: XXXVII.113.

Choniates, Michael [*c.*1140–*c.*1220; abp; brother of the historian Nicetas Acominatus]: LXII.55.

Choniates, Nicetas, *see* Nicetas Acominatus.

Christodorus: 'a Theban poet in genius as well as in birth' XVII.51.

Chron. Paschal., *see Paschal Chronicle*

Chron. Saxonicum: XXXVIII.126, 139, 142.

Chron. Venet.: XLV.18.

2 Chronicles: XXIII.74.

Chronicon Astense: LXIX.86.

Chronicon Farfense: XLIX.71.

Chroniques de St Denys: XXXVIII.31.

Chrysolaurus, Manuel: LXVI.97, 98, 101.

Chrysostom, Dio [*c.*40–*c.*112 AD; orator]: XVIII.24; XXIII.25.

Chrysostom, St John [*c.*347–407]: XV.159, 161, 170; XX.68; XXIII.81, 112; XXIV.11; 'the Christian orator attempts to comfort a widow by the examples of illustrious misfortunes . . . Such vague consolations have never wiped away a single tear' XXV.18; XXVI.115; XXVII.43, 89, 90; XXVIII.70; XXXII.1, 6, 10, 29, 30, 35, 41, 42, 46, 54; XXXIV.34; XXXVII.25, 'one of the most eloquent and successful advocates for the monastic life' 27; XLIV.166; XLVII.28; LIV.5.

Ciampini, Giovanni Giustino: XLIX.32.

Cicero, Marcus Tullius [106–43 BC]: I.36, 62; II.6, 10, 48; III.8, 11, 24, 60; IV.20; V.7; VI.83, 108; VII.27; VIII.25; X.114; XV.5, 51, 53, 75, 192; XVI.10; XVII.73, 164, 176; XX.29, 47, 59; XXI.11, 33; 'Cicero . . . has beautifully expressed the common sense of mankind' XXIII.64; XXVI.3; XXVIII.3, 5, 26; XXX.59; XXXI.41, 51; XXXII.53, 54; 'the story of Damocles, which Cicero . . . had so inimitably told' XXXVI.3, 143; XL.146; XLI.58; XLIV.13, 19, 21, 26, 29, 49, 52, 53, 54, 55, 57, 60, 142, 175, 177, 181, 203; XLV.21; XLVI.80; XLVII.6, 12; L.155; LII.117; LXIX.57.

Cingolani, Giovanni Battista [surveyor, and cartographer of Rome]: XXXI.89; XLI.87; LXIX.64.

Cinnamus: LII.18; LVI.102, 109, 110, 'a diffuse narrative' 112, 113, 114, 117, 120, 121, 122, 123, 125; LIX.9, 13, 15, 'infected with national prejudice and pride' 16, 18, 19; LX.10; LXVIII.97.

Clarke, Samuel [1675–1729; latitudinarian divine; author of *The Scripture-Doctrine of the Trinity* (1712) and commentator on Homer]: XXI.36, 49; LI.162; LIV.38.

Clarke, William [1696–1771; editor of *Leges Wallicæ Ecclesiasticæ et Civiles*]: XXXVIII.126.

Claudianus, Claudius [*c.*370–*c.*404; poet]: IX.78; XVII.59, 83, 84, 85, 86, 88, 'lively and fanciful' 90, 121, 150, 193; XXV.119; XXVI.71, 125, 127, 128, 136; XXVII.79, 83, 109, 114, 116, 'Claudian's wit is intolerable' 118, 120, 121, 123; XXIX.1, 7, 8, 11, 12, 16, 17, 19, 21, 22, 23, 24, 25, 27, 28, 29, 30, 'the *dissection* of Rufinus, which Claudian performs with the savage coolness of an anatomist . . ., is likewise specified by Zosimus and Jerom' 31, 33, 35, 36, 37, 38, 39, 40, 41, 42, 43, 44, 45, 46, 48, 49, 53, 54, 58, 59, 62; XXX.1, 2, 5, 8, 9, 10, 16, 18, 22, 24 25, 26, 27, 30, 31, 32, 34, 35, 36, 38, 41, 42, 46, 47, 48, 49, 52, 53, 60, 70, 83, 87, 89, 90, 94, 100, 114, 115, 116, 117, 118, 119, 'the rigid critics reproach the exotic weeds, or flowers, which spring too luxuriantly in his Latian soil' 120; XXXI.5, 6, 13, 18, 21, 22, 25, 35; 'they [the two books which Claudian composed against Eutropius] are indeed a very elegant and spirited satire; and would be more valuable in an historical light, if the invective were less vague, and more temperate' XXXII.3, 4, 'Claudian . . ., with that mixture of indignation and humour, which always pleases in a satiric poet, describes the insolent folly of the eunuch, the disgrace of the empire, and the joy of the Goths' 5, 6, 7, 8, 9, 11, 12, 15, 21, 22, 23, 25, 26, 27, 29, 30; XXXIV.16; XXXV.76; XXXVI.7, 63; LIII.1.

Cleaveland, Ezra [rector of Honiton; Gibbon owned his *A Genealogical History of the Noble and Illustrious Family of Courtenay* (Exeter, 1735)]: 'the rector of Honiton has more gratitude than industry, and more industry than criticism' LXI.70, 83, 85.

Clemens of Alexandria: XV.31, 71, 89, 90, 107; XVI.21; L.49.

Clérisseau, Charles Louis [1721–1820; architect and painter]: 'Messieurs Adam and Clerisseau . . . visited Spalatro in the month of July 1757. The magnificent work which their journey produced, was published in London seven years afterwards' XIII.121.

Clitarchus: XLIV.18.

Cluverius, Philippus [or Cluvier; 1580–1622; Gibbon owned his *Germaniæ Antiquæ Libri Tres* (Leyden, 1616) and *Italia Antiqua*, 2 vols. (Leyden, 1624)]: VII.34; IX.6, 9, 18, 22, 50, 62, 76, 78; X.25, 69, 73, 82; XI.1; XII.36, 41; XXII.29; XXV.101; XXVII.117; XXX.44, 60, 74; XXXI.4, 5, 89, 112, 128; XXXVI.35; XXXIX.72, 109; XLI.13, 60, 66, 70, 71; XLII.8; XLIII.8, 35, 42, 43; XLV.32.

Cochlœus, Joannes [1479–1552; Gibbon owned his *Vita Theoderici Regis Ostrogothorum et Italiæ* (Stockholm, 1699)]: XXXIX.1, 58, 70.

Codex Carolinus: XLIX.51, 52, 53, 59, 62, 65, 66, 67, 68; LXXI.29.

Codex Gregorian.: XLIV.186.

Codex Justiniani: XVII.59, 60, 100, 101, 107, 108, 111, 114, 115, 118, 151, 166, 176, 183; XX.8; XXII.84; XXV.60; XXVII.3, 5; XXXVII.102, 125; XL.28, 60, 122; XLIV.186, 190, 197.

Codex Theodosiani: II.88; IV.30; XIII.96, 103; XIV.72, 76, 77, 93, 95, 96, 97, 105, 113; XVI.143; XVII.26, 41, 56, 59, 62, 65, 71, 72, 74, 75, 79, 80, 98, 99, 109, 117, 118, 123, 127, 128, 130, 135, 136, 137, 138, 142, 151, 153, 155, 157, 161, 166, 167, 171, 172, 173, 174, 176, 177, 178, 183, 188, 190, 192; XVIII.12, 18, 58; XX.7, 8, 9, 30, 33, 37, 74, 96, 100, 102, 109, 110, 113; XXI.4, 169, 170, 173; XXII.67, 77, 84; XXIII.55, 91; XXIV.101; XXV.2, 48, 51, 61, 62, 65, 74, 77; XXVI.76, 77, 117; XXVII.22, 48, 76, 95, 99; XXVIII.25, 28, 53, 54, 55, 67; XXIX.6, 8, 34, 55; XXX.29, 56, 72, 110, 116; XXXI.3, 27, 31, 53, 55, 95, 111, 143, 148; XXXII.4, 18, 31, 65, 67; XXXIII.7, 19, 34; XXXIV.40, 52; XXXVI.36, 39, 40, 41, 43,

Codex Theodosiani—contd 44, 83; xl.60, 120; xlii.87; xliv.46, 70, 111, 130, 186, 196, 197; xlvii.24, 31.

Codinus, George [curopalata and author of *De Officiis Ecclesiæ et Aulæ C. P.*]: XVII.31, 39, 42, 'in a single page of Codinus we may detect twelve unpardonable mistakes' 53, 'full of fictions and inconsistencies' 55, 58, 'the authority of Codinus is of little weight' 64; XVIII.17, 21; XL.103; LIII.41, 45, 'his elaborate though trifling work' 48, 53, 55, 68; LV.48, 66; LXVII.1.

Columella, Lucius Junius M. [fl. first century AD; author of *De Re Rustica*]: II.40; XXXI.30; XLII.14; LXIII.23.

Commelinus, Hieronymus [editor of Eunapius]: XXI.108; XXIII.11; XXX.7.

Commines, Philippe de [1445–1509; historian; Gibbon owned his *Mémoires* (Leyden, 1648, and, 4 vols., London and Paris, 1747)]: XXVI.71; XXXIV.30; LXVI.55; LXVII.16, 32, 43; LXVIII.92.

Comnena, Anna [author of the *Alexiad*]: XLIX.81; LII.20; 'Anna Comnena, who, except in filial piety, may be compared with Mademoiselle de Montpensier' LIII.39, 40, 44; LIII.111; LIV.23, 24, 25; LV.70; LVI.37, 38, 59, 61, 62, 64, 68, 74, 75, 78, 80, 81, 84, 88, 91, 93; LVII.46, 49, 51, 55; LVIII.2, 40, 46, 50, 62, 63, 'brief and ignorant' 64, 70, 71, 76, 79, 86, 94, 'so prone to exaggeration, that she magnifies the exploits of the Latins' 98, 99; LIX.1, 3, 5, 8, 11; LX.10, 13; LXVIII.97.

Complutensian Bible: XXXVII.116, 119, 120.

Concil. [or *Acts of the Councils*; the Venice edition]: XX.27; XLVII.36, 39, 41, 42, 43, 46, 47, 49, 50, 51, 53, 60, 61, 62, 63, 64, 66, 67, 74, 75, 79, 94, 97, 98, 99, 103, 104, 106, 107, 108, 109, 113, 126, 134; XLIX.18, 32, 33, 'a faithful version, with some critical notes, would provoke, in different readers, a sigh or a smile' 78, 82, 84, 87, 89; LVIII.3, 7, 14, 28, 75; LX.5, 8, 10.

Conringius, Hermannus [author of *De Finibus Imperii Germanici* (Frankfort, 1680)]: XLIX.118.

Constantine the Great [c.280–337; emperor]: XIII.118, 119; XVI.156; XX.13, 59; XLIV.175.

Constantine Porphyrogenitus [905–59; emperor]: 'I am aware that he was a Greek of the tenth century and that his accounts of ancient history are frequently confused and fabulous. But on this occasion [war with the Chersonites, AD 332] his narrative is, for the most part, consistent and probable' XVIII.44, 45; XXXIX.9; LI.89, 94; LII.11, 21, 80, 84, 95; LIII.1, 10, 12, 15, 17, 20, 36, 37, 40, 54, 56, 58, 62, 74, 76, 77, 78, 81, 109; LIV.19; LV.10, 11, 16, 20, 40, 48, 49, 54, 55, 71, 75; LVI.3, 11, 23; LVII.4, 30, 60; LX.37.

Corippus, Flavius Crescerius [fl. sixth century AD; poet]: XVII.158; XL.83, 91; XLV.2, 3, 5, 6, 15, 24, 25; XLVI.17; LIII.41.

Corneille, Pierre [1606–84; French playwright; Gibbon owned his *Chefs-d'œuvre* (Oxford, 1746) and two copies of his *Théâtre*, ed. Voltaire, 12 vols. (Amsterdam, 1764) and 10 vols. (n.p., 1776)]: XVI.94; XXXIV.15; XXXV.68; XLVI.46, 110.

Cornelius Nepos [c.100–c.25 BC]: II.56; XIII.2.

Corpus Juris Canonici Academicum, ed. Christoph Heinrich Freiesleben (Prague, 1728): LXIX.87.

Corsali, Andrea: LXV.16.

Corsini, Edoardo [Gibbon owned his *Fasti Attici*, 4 vols. (Florence, 1744–56), *De Præfectis Urbis* (Pisa, 1766) and *Dissertationes IV. Agonisticæ* (Leipzig, 1752)]: XL.150; XLIV.172.

Cosmas Indicopleustes [sixth-century traveller, and author of the *Christian Topography*]: XXXVII.70; XL.72, 73, 74, 'this work . . ., which displays the prejudices of a monk, with the knowledge of a merchant' 77, 133, 134; XLII.95; 'it was the design of the author to confute the impious heresy of those who maintain that the earth is a globe, and not a flat oblong table, as it is represented in the Scriptures . . . But the nonsense of the monk is mingled with the practical knowledge of the traveller' XLVII.116.

Cotelier, Jean Baptiste [or Cotelerius; 1629–86; Gibbon owned his *SS. Patrum qui Temporibus Apostolicis Floruerunt Opera* (Amsterdam, 1724)]: XV.132; XXI.28; XL.85; L.86.

Cousin, Louis [1627–1707; historian, and editor of and commentator on Greek literature; Gibbon owned his *Histoire de l'empire d'Occident*, 2 vols. (Paris, 1684), and *Histoire de Constantinople*, 8 vols. (Paris, 1684)]: XXIV.132; XXXVIII.128; 'may not be implicitly trusted' XLI.1, 'Did he never think?' 10; XLIII.39, 95; LVI.73, 84; LXII.28; LXIII.4, 'the French translation of the president Cousin is blotted with three palpable and essential errors . . . Put not your trust in translations!' 24; LXVIII.21, 'in bold defiance, or rather in gross ignorance, of language and geography, the president Cousin detains them at Chios with a south, and wafts them to Constantinople with a north, wind' 43.

Cowley, Abraham [1618–67; poet; Gibbon owned his *Works* (London, 1700) and *Select Works*, 2 vols. (London, 1772)]: XXX.30, 'in this passage, Cowley is perhaps superior to his original [Claudian]; and the English poet, who was a good botanist, has concealed the *oaks*, under a more general expression' 31.

Coxe, William [1747–1828; Gibbon owned his *Travels into Poland, Russia, Sweden, and Denmark*, 2 vols. (London, 1784), *Account of the Russian Discoveries between Europe and America* (London, 1780) and *Lettres sur l'état politique, civil et naturel de la Suisse*, 2 vols. (Paris, 1782)]: LV.45, 77, 81.

Crantzius [or Cranz, D.; Gibbon owned his *The History of Greenland*, 2 vols. (London, 1767)]: LXVI.40.

Creyghton, Robert [1593–1672; chaplain to Charles II; bp of Bath and Wells; editor and translator of Sylvester Syropulus]: 'loose and florid' LXVI.51, 52.

Crinitus: XLIII.69.

Crusias, Martin [or Martinus Crusius; author of *Turco Græcia Libri Octo* (Basle, 1584)]: LXVI.21; LXVIII.82, 83.

Ctesias [b. *c.*416 BC]: XLVI.101.

Cudworth, Ralph [1617–88; Gibbon owned his *The True Intellectual System of the Universe* (London, 1743)]: XXI.12, 18, 51, 59.

Cujacius, Jacobus [jurist]: XLIV.3, 48.

Cumberland, Richard [1631–1718; bp of Peterborough], *see* Sanchoniathon..

Cuper, Gijsbert [or Cuperus; editor of Lactantius; author of *De Elephantis*; Gibbon owned his *Apotheosis, vel Consecratio Homeri* (Amsterdam, 1683)]: XII.87, 99; XIV.84; XX.35; XXXIX.67.

Curtius, Quintus: VII.46; VIII.49; XVII.164; XXIV.60, 138; XXXII.23; LIX.26.

Cuspinianus, Joannes [author of *De Cæsaribus*]: LXVII.28; LXVIII.9, 30.

Cyprian [st; bp of Carthage]: XV.97, 115, 117, 118, 124, 125, 126, 132, 135, 139, 140, 146, 149, 190; XVI.69, 76, 77, 79, 83, 90, 91, 99, 102, 103, 112, 118, 122; XLIV.166.

Cyril of Alexandria [*c.*375–444; st; opponent of Nestorianism]: XXI.88; XXIII.14, 19, 21, 31, 73; XLVII.20, 34.

D

Da Giovenazzo, Matteo Spinello [Italian historian]: LVI.139.

Dacier, André [1651–1722; editor of Horace and Varro]: X.161; XIII.2, 89; XIX.3; XXV.47; XL.63; XLIV.27; XLVI.103; LI.162.

Daillé, Jean [1594–1670; Gibbon owned his *De Imaginibus* (Leyden, 1642) and *De Usu Patrum ad ea Definienda Religionis Capita quæ sunt hodie Controversa* (Geneva, 1656)]: XV.64; XXI.39.

Dalin: IX.1, 42; X.9.

Dalmatinus, Juvencus Cælius Calanus [biographer of Attila the Hun]: XXXIV.1.

Dalrymple, Sir David [1726–92; Gibbon owned his *Annals of Scotland*, 2 vols. (Edinburgh, 1776–9)]: XXV.115.

Damascius the Syrian: XXVIII.45; XXXVI.89; XL.147, 153.

Damian, Peter [or Damianus; st; cardinal; bp of Ostia; biographer of St Dominic Loricatus]: LVIII.26.

Dampier, William [1651–1715; traveller and author of various collections of voyages]: 'Gen. Obs.'.10; XL.70.

Dandolo, Andrea [or Dandulus; doge of Venice; historian of Venice]: LV.212; LVI.91, 109, 111; LX.39, 42, 54, 63, 67, 70, 77, 84; LXI.1, 2; LXIII.52.

Daniel [Old Testament prophet]: XV.63; 'Gen. Obs.'.5.

Daniel [d. 745; first bp of Winchester]: XXXVII.81, 82.

Daniel, Gabriel [1649–1728; Gibbon owned his *Histoire de la milice françoise*, 2 vols. (Amsterdam, 1724), and *Histoire de France*, 7 vols. (Amsterdam, 1720–5)]: XIX.66; XXXV.19; 'whose ideas were superficial and modern' XXXVI.61; XLIII.51; LXIV.63.

Daubuz, Charles [or Daubus; fl. 1625–30]: XVI.36.

Davila, Henri Catherin [1577–1631; historian]: IX.37; LXX.89.

Davis [editor of Maximus of Tyre]: L.155.

Davy, Major William [editor (with Joseph White) of Tamerlane's *Institutes* (Oxford, 1783)]: LXV.2, 3, 4.

Dawkins [*see* Wood, Robert]: XI.69; 'every preceding account is eclipsed by the magnificent description and drawings of M.M. Dawkins and Wood, who have transported into England the ruins of Palmyra and Baalbeck' LI.71.

De Hoveden, Roger [d. 1201; historian]: LVI.92, 137, 140; LIX.69, 80; LXIX.44.

De Quero, Andreas de Redusiis [Italian chronicler; chancellor of Trevigi]: LXV.22, 53.

Delayto, James de [Italian chronicler; chancellor of Ferrara]: LXV.53.

Delbene, Sannuccio [Italian historian]: LXX.13.

Delisle, William [cartographer]: XLII.60; LII.11; 'the prince of geographers, till the appearance of the greater d'Anville' LIII.3; LVI.23; LVII.30.

Della Valle, Pietro [1586–1652; traveller; Gibbon owned his *Viaggi, Divisi in tre Parti*, 4 vols. (Rome, 1650–63)]: XIX.59; XXIV.49, 'a gentleman and a scholar, but intolerably vain and prolix' 65; XLII.84; LI.23, 'that vain and curious traveller' 27, 135, 206; LII.41.

Demetrius of Scepsis: XVII.19.

Demosthenes [d. 413 BC]: XLII.3, 29; XLIV.19; 'the simple and sublime logic of Demosthenes' L.33; LV.75.

Denisart, Jean Baptiste [1713–65; Gibbon owned his *Collection de décisions nouvelles et de notions relatives à la jurisprudence*, 3 vols. (Paris, 1771)]: XXV.44; XXXVII.35; XLIV.154.

Des Vignoles, Alphonse [1649–1744; *érudit*; author of *Histoire critique de la république des lettres*]: LXX.11; LXXI.11.

Description of the World, see Expositio totius Mundi.

Deuteronomy: XV.12; XIX.1; XLIV.143; L.124.

Dexippus, Publius Herennius [*c.*210–270?]: X.88, 123; XI.16, 21, 25, 27, 28, 31, 33.

Dicæarchus [fl. *c.*320 BC]: II.71; XL.144.

Dictionnaire diplomatique [or *Dictionnaire raisonnée de la diplomatique*]: IX.16; XVII.170; XL.161; LIII.43.

Dictionnaire de Trevoux [or *Dictionnaire universel françois et latin*]: XXXVIII.47.

Digeon, J. M. [1730–1812; translator of the *Abrégé de l'histoire ottomane* (Paris, 1781); Gibbon owned his *Nouveaux contes turcs et arabes*, 2 vols. (Paris, 1781)]: 'a curious, authentic, and national history' LIX.103; LXVIII.80.

Dinarchus [*c.*360–292? BC; orator]: XLI.10.

Diodorus Siculus[fl. first century BC]: II.47; VI.92; IX.3, 69, 71; X.169, 171, 173; XV.2; XVII.164; XX.42, 94; XXVI.4, 76; XXVIII.39; XXXII.2; 'Gen. Obs.'.10; XLII.69; XLIV.16, 20, 200; XLVI.11, 101; L.2, 26, 32, 35, 45, 55, 164; LI.107; LXXI.9.

Diogenes Laertius [fl. third century AD]: II.8; VI.7; XVI.140; XL.145, 146, 150.

Diogilo, Odo de: LIX.13.

Dion Cassius [c.150–235; historian]: I.1, 2, 4, 14, 17, 21, 24, 25, 29, 56, 65, 84; II.15, 25, 31, 44, 110; III.3, 'prolix and bombast' 4, 6, 8, 12, 19, 25, 28, 36, 38, 39, 48, 50; IV.5, 8, 13, 15, 17, 22, 23, 25, 28, 32, 34, 38, 41, 42, 44, 49, 50, 51, 52, 55, 56; V.1, 3, 6, 10, 12, 14, 15, 24, 32, 33, 36, 38, 39, 49, 50, 51, 54, 55, 56, 57, 59, 67, 68, 69, 71; VI.2, 3, 6, 8, 12, 14, 15, 16, 17, 21, 23, 25, 26, 28, 34, 35, 36, 37, 38, 39, 42, 44, 45, 46, 47, 49, 50, 51, 55, 58, 59, 61, 62, 67, 75, 76, 80, 102, 114; VIII.5, 37, 42, 43, 45; IX.81, 85; X.85; XII.87; XIII.54; XV.2, 20, 200; XVI.1, 2, 24, 28, 30, 46, 53, 54, 56, 107, 117; XVII.96, 103, 115, 146, 147, 148; XIX.5; XXXI.29, 40, 88; XL.62, 95, 112, 148; XLI.71; XLII.79; XLIV.34, 'the universal censure which freedom and criticism have pronounced against that slavish historian' 38, 155; L.24; LI.172, 183; LXVI.29; LXX.9.

Dion of Naples [mathematician]: XLIII.78.

Dionysius [geographer]: XL.134; XLII.69; L.2; 'this poetical geographer lived in the age of Augustus, and his description of the world is illustrated by the Greek commentary of Eustathius, who paid the same compliment to Homer and Dionysius' LI.68, 70; LII.79.

Dionysius [c.200–265; st; bp of Alexandria]: X.182; XVI.102.

Dionysius of Corinth: XV.142, 146.

Dionysius of Halicarnassus [fl. 20 BC]: I.22, 30, 44; II.14, 41; V.7; VI.81; XII.3; XXVIII.3; XXXI.50; XXXVI.81; XL.143; 'Dionysius Halicarnassensis . . ., who sometimes betrays the character of a rhetorician and a Greek' XLIV.6, 8, 'How concise and animated is the Roman [Livy] – how prolix and lifeless the Greek? Yet he has admirably judged the masters, and defined the rules, of historical composition' 11, 15, 27, 103, 115, 124; L.2.

Diophantus of Alexandria [fl. 250 AD]: LII.60.

Ditmar [or Dithmar; 975–1018; bp of Merseburg; German historian]: XLIX.138; LV.47; LXIX.33.

Dodechin: LVIII.6.

Dodwell, Henry [1641–1711; Gibbon owned his *De Veteribus Græcorum Romanorumque Cyclis* (Oxford, 1701–2) and *Prælectiones Academicæ in Schola Historices Camdeniana* (Oxford, 1692)]: III.38; XV.77, 97, 122; XVI.43, 90, 125, 165; XVII.149; XL.144; XLIV.34, 'Dodwell . . ., who wanders from the subject in confused reading and feeble paradox' 36, 43; L.45; LIII.15.

Donatus [or Donati, A.; Jesuit; author of the *Roma Antiqua et Nova*; properly, *Roma vetus et recens*, of which Gibbon owned two copies (Rome, 1639, and Rome, 1738)]: II.72; V.5; XVI.34; XIX.46; XXV.82; XXVIII.34; XXXI.107; XXXVI.7, 81; XLI.80; XLIII.23; LVI.87; LXXI.8, 44, 51, 75.

Doutremens [Jesuit; author of the *Constantinopolis Belgica* (Turnaci, 1638)]: LX.34; LXI.35.

Dow, Alexander [d. 1779; translator of Ferishta's *The History of Hindostan*, 3 vols. (London, 1770–2); *see also* Ferishta]: 'he styles himself the translator of the Persian Ferishta; but in his florid text, it is not easy to distinguish the version and the original' LVII.1, 5, 6, 7, 9, 10, 'I have copied this passage as a specimen of the Persian manner; but I suspect, that by some odd fatality, the style of Ferishta has been improved by that of Ossian' 13, 14; LXV.24, 71.

Drakenborch, Arnold [editor of Silius Italicus]: XXIII.13; XXXI.9.

Dryden, John [1631–1700; poet; Gibbon owned his *Miscellaneous Works*, 4 vols. (London, 1760) and his *Plays*, 6 vols. (London, 1762)]: XXX.62; LXVIII.59; LXX.53.

Du Halde, Jean Baptiste [1674–1743; Jesuit; author of the *Description de la Chine*]: XXVI.7.

Du Perron, Jacques Davy [1556–1618; abp of Sens; cardinal]: XLIX.28, 76.

Du Puis, Pierre [friend of de Thou; author of the *Histoire particulière du grand differend entre Boniface VIII. et Philippe le Bel*]: LXIX.77; LXX.72.

Du Soul, Moïse [fl. 1720; translator]: XL.148.

Du Tillet, Jean [bp of Meaux; editor of *Leges. Burgundicæ*]: XXXVIII.82.

Du Voisin, Jean Baptiste: XX.38, 'an Apology, which deserves the praise of learning and moderation' 53.

Dubos, Jean-Baptiste [1670–1742; Gibbon owned two copies of his *Réflexions critiques sur la poésie et sur la peinture* (Paris, 1755, and 3 vols., Paris, 1770), *Histoire critique de l'établissement de la monarchie française dans les Gaules*, 2 vols. (Paris, 1742), and *Histoire de la Ligue faite à Cambray*, 2 vols. (Paris, 1709)]: 'attempts, with very little success, to prove that the assemblies of Gaul were continued under the emperors' II.29; IX.2, 35; XVII.125, 187; 'the best commentary [on Sidonius Apollinaris on the Saxon pirates]' XXV.105; XXX.89, 97; XXXI.172, 176, 190, 191; 'the second book of the Histoire Critique de l'Etablissement de la Monarchie Françoise . . ., throws great light on the state of Gaul, when it was invaded by Attila; but the ingenious author, the Abbé Dubos, too often bewilders himself in system and conjecture' XXXV.3, 8, 9, 20, 24, 44, 66, 76; XXXVI.18, 31, 52, 61, 91, 113; XXXVIII.9, 12, 14, 20, 42, 48, 55, 59, 63, 'the learned ingenuity of the Abbé Dubos' 64, 113; 'I will neither hear nor reconcile the long and contradictory arguments of the Abbé Dubos and the Count de Buat, about the wars of Burgundy' XXXIX.50, 66; XLI.38; XLV.70; LXVIII.41; 'the Abbé Dubos, who, with less genius than his successor Montesquieu, has asserted and magnified the influence of climate, objects to himself the degeneracy of the Romans and Batavians' LXIX.1.

Ducange, Charles du Fresne, seigneur [1610–88; Gibbon owned his *Glossarium ad Scriptores Mediæ et Infimæ Græcitatis*, 2 vols. (Leyden, 1688), and *Glossarium ad Scriptores Mediæ et Infimæ Latinitatis*, 6 vols. (Basle, 1762)]: XVII.2, 13, 27, 31, 32, 35, 44, 46, 49, 51, 68, 69; XVIII.7, 8, 13, 18; XX.11, 33; XXI.173; XXII.45, 73; XXV.1, 27, 34, 38; XXVII.32; XXIX.20; XXXI.75, 133; XXXII.70; XXXIII.32; XXXV.28; XXXVI.76, 111, 126; XXXVIII.47, 97; XL.50, 51, 'the great Byzantine antiquarian' 103, 108, 159; XLI.20, 76; XLIII.20, 21, 73; XLV.1, 5, 24; XLVI.50, 52, 99; XLVII.38, 64; XLIX.11, 45, 58, 59, 88, 134, 144, 145; LI.51, 58; 'our sure and indefatigable guide in the middle ages and Byzantine history, Charles du Fresne du Cange, has treated in several places of the Greek fire, and his collections leave few gleanings behind' LII.16, 22; LIII.1, 12, 20, 'Ducange, the Tillemont of the middle ages. Never has laborious Germany produced two antiquarians more laborious and accurate, than these two natives of lively France' 31, 35, 38, 40, 42, 44, 45, 53, 58, 97, 103, 111, 112, 113; LIV.24, 26, 29; LV.10, 13, 48, 69; LVI.7, 31, 37, 'just and moderate' 40, 50, 54, 68, 75, 80, 81, 110; LVII.4, 32, 35, 55, 57; LVIII.2, 16, 17, 18, 32, 58, 59, 63, 66, 67, 71, 72, 81, 86, 124, 130; LIX.2, 4, 13, 18, 21, 50, 94, 98; LX.14, 20, 25, 28, 29, 30, 31, 32, 34, 40, 41, 49, 51, 60, 61, 'accurate and full' 62, 63, 'Ducange, who pries into every corner' 76, 'Ducange . . . pours forth a torrent of learning on the *Gonfanon Imperial*' 79; LXI.1, 8, 9, 20, 'the indefatigable Ducange' 21, 23, 27, 28, 30, 31, 32, 33, 35, 37, 39, 43, 44, 45, 46, 47, 'short and vague' 50, 51, 55, 58, 61, 62, 65; LXII.11, 20, 21, 22, 28, 29, 38, 'his usual diligence' 50, 51, 52, 54, 58; LXIII.6, 21, 28, 37, 43, 44; LXV.92; LXVI.2, 14, 33, 78, 105; LXVII.1, 45; LXVIII.13, 24, 'accurate antiquarian' 85, 'his supplemental works . . . diffuse a steady light over the darkness of the Lower Empire' 97; LXIX.6, 30, 32, 44; LXX.62; LXXI.52.

Ducas, Michael [Byzantine historian]: XVII.8; LXIII.36; LXIV.50, 66, 67; LXV.45, 56, 'the most copious and best informed' 72, 75, 'a curious and careful observer, . . . entitled, from his birth and station, to particular credit in all that concerns Ionia and the islands' 76, 'still superior to his rivals' 80, 87, 93; LXVI.16, 66; 'writes with truth and freedom' LXVII.6, 12, 20; LXVIII.10, 11, 13, 14, 18, 21, 23, 'such truth and spirit' 32, 38, 42, 46, 47, 52, 58, 59, 65, 72, 73, 76, 78, 79, 80, 'too brief' 86, 87.

Duchesne, André [1584–1640; editor of *Historiæ Francorum Scriptores*, 5 vols. (Paris, 1636–49)]: XIII.23; LVIII.19, 88; LIX.9, 22; LXI.74.

Duck, Sir Arthur [1580–1648; lawyer; Gibbon owned his *De Usu et Authoritate Juris Civilis Romanorum* (London, 1689)]: XLIV.2.

Dufresnoy, Nicolas Lenglet [1674–1755; editor of Lactantius; author of *Méthode pour étudier l'histoire*, 2 vols. (Paris, 1713)]: XX.1.

Dugdale, Sir William [1605–86; author of *Monasticon Anglicanum*; Gibbon owned his *The Baronage of England*, 3 vols. (London, 1675–6)]: LVIII.77; LIX.70; LXI.80, 82, 'the father of our genealogical science' 83, 84.

Duhalde, Jean Baptiste [1674–1743; Gibbon owned his *Description de l'empire de la Chine et de la Tartarie Chinoise*, 4 vols. (Paris, 1735), and its English translation, *The General History of China*, 4 vols. (London, 1736)]: XXVI.12, 28, 33, 35, 39; XL.75; LXIV.33; LXV.62.

Duker, Carolus Andreas [Gibbon owned his *Opuscula Varia de Latinitate Iurisconsultorum Veterum* (Leyden, 1711)]: XLIII.90; XLIV.8, 79.

Dupin, Louis-Ellies [1657–1719; Gibbon owned his *Nouvelle bibliothèque des auteurs ecclésiastiques*, 19 vols. (Paris, Mons, Amsterdam, 1690–1715)]: II.42; XV.66, 98, 120, 148; XVI.159; XVIII.9; XXI.6, 157; XXI.31, 69; XXV.71; 'the good sense of the latter [Dupin] is always restrained by prudential considerations' XXXII.42; XXIII.28, 35, 66, 123; XXXIII.17; XXXV.61; XXXVIII.39; XXXIX.23; XLI.26; XLV.64, 72; XLVII.19, 20, 94, 107; XLIX.5, 77; LIV.2; 'a faint tinge of prejudice or prudence' LX.8; LXII.25, 32; LXVI.30; LXVI.77.

Dupuys, Pierre: 'a scholar and a mathematician' XL.97.

Duquesseau [legal scholar]: XLIV.150.

Dutens, Louis [1730–1812; Gibbon owned his *Œuvres* (London, 1777), *Des pierres précieuses et des pierres fines* (London, 1777), *An Inquiry into the Origin of the Discoveries Attributed to the Moderns* (London, 1769) and *Itinéraire des routes les plus fréquentées, ou journal d'un voyage aux villes principales de l'Europe en 1768–1771* (London, 1777)]: LII.23.

E

Ebed-Jesu [Nestorian]: XLVII.52, 110.

Ebn Alwardi: LI.219.

Ebn Khateb: 'an historian, geographer, physician, poet, etc.' LI.190.

Ecchellensis, Abraham: XLVII.149.

Ecclesiastes: XLI.33.

Ecclesiastical History of Alexandria: XX.100.

Edrissi, Sherif al [geographer; author of *Geographia Nubiensis*]: XLVII.154; L.2; LI.52, 185; LVI.57, 104.

Eggehardus [Russian chronicler]: LV.51.

Eginhardus [or Eginard, or Eginhart; 770–840; historian; Gibbon owned his *De Vita et Gestis Caroli Magni* (Bonn, 1711)]: XLV.12, 37; 'Eginhard understood the world, the court, and the Latin language' XLIX.57, 91, 92, 93, 97, 99, 102, 106, 113, 120; LII.26, 27; LVII.60; LXXI.32.

Eisenschmidius, Joannes Casparus [or Eisenschmidt; Gibbon owned his *De Ponderibus et Mensuris Veterum Romanorum* (Strasburg, 1737)]: XLIV.27.

Elmacinus, Georgius [historian of the Saracens; author of *Historia Saracenica . . . operâ et studio Thomæ Erpinii* (Lugd. Batavorum, 1625)]: XXXI.142; XLVI.59, 64, 100; XLVII.150; XLIX.16; L.66, 134, 137, 138, 148, 166; LI.4, 5, 6, 7, 8, 9, 'often deficient in style and sense' 13, 17, 24, 38, 42, 60, 61, 86, 112, 117, 126, 133, 'cloudy' 144, 156, 170, 179; LII.2, 8, 13, 15, 38, 44, 78, 96, 100, 101, 103, 110, 114, 118; LIII.65; LVII.2, 22, 24, 33, 38, 39, 67, 73; LVIII.110.

Emlyn, Thomas [1663–1741; Socinian]: XXI.38; XXXVII.116.

Encyclopédie: 'the editors . . . have reason to be proud of *this* article [CONCILE]. Those who consult their immense compilation, seldom depart so well satisfied' XX.130; XLIII.76.

Encyclopédie méthodique [Gibbon owned vols. 1–9 (Paris, 1782–3)]: XLIV.162.

Ennodius, Magnus Felix [473/4–521; st; bp of Pavia; writer of epigrams]: XXXVI.55, 103, 104, 'his narrative, verbose and turgid as it must appear, illustrates some curious passages in the fall of the Western empire' 105, 115, 116, 119, 135; XXXIX.3, 4, 10, 17, 18, 19, 'loyal and credulous' 22, 23, 27, 33, 45, 49, 69, 73, 77, 79, 81, 83, 84, 92; XLII.11.

Enoch: L.81.

Epictetus [fl. 500 BC]: XV.191; XVI.95.

Epiphanius [*c.*315–403; st]: XV.22, 23, 33, 36, 154; XVI.21; XXI.43, 62; XXIII.119, 122; XLVII.4; XLIX.3.

Erasmus, Desiderius [*c.*1466–1536; humanist; Gibbon owned his *Opera*, 10 vols. (Leyden, 1703–6), *Adagiorum Chiliades* (Geneva, 1606), *The Apophthegms of the Ancients*, 2 vols. (London, 1753), *Colloquia* (Leyden, 1729), *Epistolarum Opus* (Basle, 1558), *Epistolarum D. Erasmi Libri XXXI* (London, 1642) and his *Epistolæ Selectiores* (Basle, 1719)]: XV.60; 'admirable sense and freedom' XXI.64; XXIII.66; XXXI.42; 'The moderate Erasmus . . .. His vivacity and good sense were his own; his errors, in the uncultivated state of ecclesiastical antiquity, were almost inevitable' XXXII.41, 'the good taste of the former [Erasmus] is sometimes vitiated by an excessive love of antiquity' 42; XXXVII.34, 119, 120; XLVII.5; XLVII5, 'the father of rational theology' 38; LXVI.28, 39, 107.

Eratosthenes 276–194 BC; astronomer]: L.2.

Erchempert [or Herempert; ninth-century Italian historian; *see also* Caracciolus, Antonius]: LVI.4, 9, 10.

Ernesti, Johann August [editor of classical texts, including Ammianus Marcellinus and Tacitus; Gibbon owned his *Clavis Ciceroniana* (Halle, 1757)]: XIX.63; XXX.117; XLIV.53, 148, 193; LXX.23.

Erpenius, Thomas [orientalist; translator of the *Historia Saracenica*]: LII.44; LVII.24.

Erricus [author of *Monach. in Vit. St Germani*]: XXXI.175.

Eschinardi, Francesco [Gibbon owned his *Descrizione di Roma et dell'Agro Romano* (Rome, 1750)]: XXXI.90; XLI.87, 89; LXIX.64, 98.

Eschines [author of *De Falsa Legatione*]: XLI.107; LI.30.

Esprit des croisades: LVIII.19, 29, 34, 42, 48, 88, 'sense and erudition' 106.

Estius, Gulielmus: 'Estius, who so accurately defined the limits of Omnipotence, was a Dutchman by birth, and by trade a scholastic divine' XXI.69.

Eugippius [or Eugipius; abbot of Lucullano; biographer of St Severinus]: XXXVI.121, 132, 137.

Eulogius of Alexandria: XLVII.68, 'more conspicuous for subtlety than eloquence' 146.

Eumenius [fl. 300 AD; orator]: II.97; XI.52, 53; XIII.19, 26, 39, 44, 111, 123; XIV.16, 17, 18, 33, 35, 40; XVII.173, 185, 186; XX.12.

Eunapius [*c.*345–*c.*420; Gibbon owned his *De Vitis Philosophorum et Sophistarum* (Antwerp, 1568)]: XVII.110, 123; XIX.51, 83; XXI.108; XXII.10; XXIII.11, 'a partial and fanatical history' 16, 22, 'unsuspecting simplicity' 23, 46, 48, 92; XXIV.25, 28, 30, 42, 52; XXV.146, 148;

xxvi.65, 68, 98, 102, 116, 135; xxviii.47, 68; xxix.11; xxx.7, 15; xxxii.13.

Eunomius c.335–c.394; Arian]: xxi.68.

Euripides [c.484–406 BC]: x.97; xv.42; xxxi.152.

Eusebius [fl. fourth century; historian]: iv.14; viii.42; x.61, 175, 176, 181, 182; xi.13, 45, 50, 85; xii.29, 64; xiii.36, 40, 45, 53, 85; xiv.1, 14, 18, 37, 39, 45, 46, 48, 56, 65, 69, 70, 92, 97, 102, 110, 112; xv.17, 19, 20, 21, 22, 23, 31, 34, 62, 96, 126, 142, 146, 155, 162, 169, 171, 181, 182, 185, 187; xvi.20, 21, 36, 50, 53, 60, 62, 71, 75, 78, 81, 98, 102, 110, 112, 115, 117, 119, 120, 122, 123, 124, 125, 128, 130, 135, 144, 152, 154, 155, 156, 161, 162, 163, 165, 167, 168, 173, 174, 175, 176, 177, 178, 179, 180, 'artful management . . . all who, like Eusebius, had been conversant with the Egyptians, delighted in an obscure and intricate style' 182; xvii.2, 48, 103, 105, 141; xviii.1, 5, 6, 10, 19, 29, 33, 34, 45, 46, 47, 48, 53, 56; xx.3, 5, 6, 7, 10, 14, 15, 22, 23, 24, 26, 28, 31, 34, 36, 48, 52, 56, 58, 64, 66, 69, 70, 74, 76, 77, 103, 104, 110, 128; xxi.1, 15, 62, 77, 78, 80, 84, 104, 106, 164, 165, 166, 167; xxiii.60, 62, 112; xxv.151; xxviii.69; xxxvii.2; xlii.79; xlix.7, 8; l.49, 75; li.79.

Eusebius Scholasticus [poet and soldier]: xxxii.40.

Eustathius [of Antioch; st]: xl.95, 134; xlii.69; xliii.24; li.68, 70; liii.109.

Eustathius [d. c.1194; abp of Thessalonica; commentator on Homer]: lvi.125.

Eutropius [historian]: i.17, 20; iii.37; iv.56; v.35; vii.36, 52; viii.42; x.2, 61, 62, 80, 100, 138, 181; xi.2, 13, 22, 45, 50, 65, 83, 89, 92, 96, 18, 59, 64, 71, 74, 76, 82, 105, 106, 108, 109; xiii.1, 10, 22, 24, 25, 30, 31, 36, 44, 64, 68, 73, 81, 87, 102, 106, 112; xiv.2, 3, 9, 41, 92, 103, 112; xvii.69; xviii.2, 3, 10, 16, 18, 26, 27, 34, 45, 49, 52, 60, 61, 68, 73, 87; xix.15, 35; 'a respectable witness' xxii.11; xxiii.110; xxiv.111, 'Ammianus and Eutropius may be admitted as fair and credible witnesses of the public language and opinions' 122; xxv.16; xxvi.128; xxvii.114; xxxiv.16; xlii.79.

Eutychius [patriarch of Alexandria, historian]: viii.2, 33, 54; xv.164; xx. 127; xxxiii.43; xlii.38, 42, 45; xlvi.15, 22, 56, 58, 59, 60, 83, 'an insufficient author' 91, 108, 111; xlvii.55, 57, 105, 109, 129, 133, 144; l.76; li.4, 5, 6, 7, 8, 9, 61, 100, 112, 113, 117, 126, 132, 142, 215, 217; lii.38, 78; liii.88; lxv.58.

Evagrius [346–99; mystic]: xviii.19; xxxii.34, 77, 79; xxxiv.18, 52; xxxvi.4, 11, 30; xxxvii.7, 67, 70, 71; xxxix.14; xl.11, 15, 17, 46, 48, 78, 81, 87, 103, 118, 136; xli.74; xliii.38, 88, 91, 94; xlv.23, 26, 28, 30, 31; xlvi.7, 20, 22; xlvii.41, 45, 47, 51, 52, 55, 'the hard and stupid fanatic' 58, 61, 62, 66, 72, 79, 80, 93, 94, 100, 128; xlix.10.

Evodius [bp of Uzalis]: xxviii.80.

Excerpta Legationum, *see* Priscus of Panium.

Excerpt. Valesian.: xxv.11.

Exodus: xv.12; xxi.174; xliv.20.

Expositio totius Mundi (Lugd. Bat., 1700): xxxi.54; xxxiii.38, 39; l.31.

F

Fabretti, Raffaello [Gibbon owned his *De Aquis et Aquæductibus Veteris Romæ*]: ii.73; xli.87.

Fabricius, Johann Albert [1668–1736; Gibbon owned his *Bibliotheca Græca*, 14 vols. (Hamburg, 1705–28), *Bibliotheca Latina*, 2 vols. (Leipzig, 1773–4), *Bibliotheca Latina Mediæ et Infimæ Ætatis*, 6 vols. (Padua, 1754), *Codex Apocryphus Novi Testamenti*, 3 vols. (Hamburg, 1719), *Codex Pseudepigraphus Veteris Testamenti*, 2 vols. (Hamburg, 1722–3), and *Imp. Cæs. Augusti Temporum Notatio, Genus, et Scriptorum Fragmenta* (Hamburg, 1727)]: ii.74; vii.49; xiii.124; xvi.37; xvii.121; xviii.14; xix.91; xx.45, 58; xxi.68, 169; xxii.10; xxiii.30; xxiv.18, 28, 40, 135; xxvi.2,

Fabricius, Johann Albert—*contd* 95; XXX.118; XXXI.67; XXXII.75; XXXIV.41; XXXVII.124; 'Gen. Obs.'.1; XXXIX.57, 89; XL.12, 95, 152; XLI.3; XLII.15, 54; XLIV.73, 'the indefatigable Fabricius' 76; XLVI.40; XLVII.25, 113, 116, 143, 147, 148, 160, 161; XLIX.69, 139; L.45, 81, 86; LI.68, 70, 115; LII.51, 54, 56, 60; LIII.4, 5, 6, 71, 73, 98, 106, 107, 'the Bibliotheca Greca of Fabricius; a laborious work, yet susceptible of a better method and many improvements' 109; LVI.57; LVIII.10; LX.93, 95, 99; LXI.12, 64; LXII.1, 55; LXIII.38, 41, 42; LXIV.10, 15, 17; LXV.50; LXVI.22, 32, 78, 93, 98, 108, 116, 117; LXVII.28; LXVIII.34; LXX.16, 74.

Fabrotus, Charles Annibal [1580–1659; editor of the *Basilics* (Paris, 1647)]: LIII.5; LXVI.78.

Facundus the African [bp of Hermiane]: XLVII.80, 94.

Fadlallah [vizir to Zingis Khan; Mogul historian]: LXIV.7.

Falconet, Claude [1740–72]: 'all that can be known of the Assassins of Persia and Syria, is poured from the copious, and even profuse, erudition of M. Falconet' LXIV.24.

Falcundus, Hugo [twelfth-century historian of Sicily; author of *Historia Sicula*]: LIII.21, 24; LVI.108, 122, 'Falcundus has been styled the Tacitus of Sicily; and, after a just, but immense, abatement, from the I[st] to the XIIth century, from a senator to a monk, I would not strip him of his title: his narrative is rapid and perspicuous, his style bold and elegant, his observation keen; he had studied mankind, and feels like a man. I can only regret the narrow and barren field on which his labours have been cast' 126, 127, 128, 129, 130, 131, 132, 133, 134, 135, 136.

Faunus [topographer of Rome]: LXXI.75.

Faustus [*c.*400–*c.*490; st]: XV.26.

Feithius, Everhardus [or Feith; commentator on Homer; Gibbon owned his *Antiquitatum Homericarum Libri IV.* (Strasburg, 1743)]: XXVIII.26.

Fell, John [1625–86; bp of Oxford; editor of Arrian, Cyprian and Lactantius]: XV.115; XVI.83, 90.

Ferdusi [or Ferdoussi; *c.*935–*c.*1020; poet]; 'the Homer of Persia' XXVI.20; XLII.49.

Ferishta [or Firishtah; *c.*1570–*c.*1620; Persian historian; Gibbon owned his *The History of Hindostan*, tr. Alexander Dow, 3 vols. (London, 1770–2)]: LVII.1, 5, 7, 13; LXV.24.

Ferraras, Jean de [translator of Mariana into French as *Histoire de l'Espagne*]: XVI.43; 'Ferreras, an industrious compiler, reviews his [Mariana's] facts, and rectifies his chronology' XXXVII.126, 130, 132; 'very accurate and useful' XXXVIII.124.

Festus, S. Pompeius: XII.76, 78; XIII.64, 68; XVII.139; XXI.173; XLIV.27; LI.162.

Fielding, Henry [1707–54; dramatist and novelist; Gibbon owned his *Works*, 8 vols. (London, 1771)]: 'I am almost tempted to quote the romance of a great master . . ., which may be considered as the history of human nature' XXXII.13.

Firmicius Maternus, Julius: XIV.10.

Fischer, Johann Eberhard [Gibbon owned his *Quæstiones Petropolitanæ* (Göttingen and Gotha, 1770)]: LV.22, 25.

Fischer, Johann Friedrich [editor of Theophrastus]: LX.40.

Fléchier, Valentin Esprit [1632–1710; bp of Nîmes; Gibbon owned his *Histoire de Théodose le Grand* (Paris, 1679 and 1680) and *Recueil des oraisons funèbres* (Paris, 1761)]: 'Flechier, afterwards Bishop of Nismes, was a celebrated preacher; and his history [of Theodosius the Great] is adorned, or tainted, with pulpit-eloquence; but he takes his learning from Baronius, and his principles from St. Ambrose and St. Augustine' XXVI.104.

Fleury, Claude [1640–1723; Gibbon owned his *Discours sur l'histoire ecclésiastique* (Paris, 1764 and 1771), *Histoire ecclésiastique*, 21 vols. (Brussels, 1713–26), *Institution au droit ecclésiastique*, 2 vols. (Paris, 1767), and *Les mœurs des*

Israélites et des Chrétiens (Paris, 1712)]: XVIII.1, 51; XX.41, 'the subject of ecclesiastical jurisdiction has been involved in a mist of passion. Two of the fairest books which have fallen into my hands are the Institutes of Canon Law, by the Abbé de Fleury, and the Civil History of Naples, by Giannone. Their moderation was the effect of situation as well as of temper. Fleury was a French ecclesiastic, who respected the authority of the parliaments; Giannone was an Italian lawyer, who dreaded the power of the church' 111; XXVIII.83; XXIX.14; XXXVII.63, 86; XXXVIII.115; XL.6; 'the good sense of Fleury' XLV.64, 69, 73; XLVI.61; LI.187, 211, 218; LII.34; 'the detail [of the persecution of the Albigeois] may be found in the ecclesiastical historians, ancient and modern, Catholics and Protestants; and among these Fleury is the most impartial and moderate' LIV.30; LV.17; 'an accurate and rational view of the causes and effects of the crusades' LVIII.21, 26; LIX.88; 'a faint tinge of prejudice or prudence' LX.8, 16, 25, 102; LXI.51; LXII.32, 33; LXIII.37, '[Fleury] transcribes and translates with the prejudices of a Catholic priest' 40; 'Fleury . . ., whose abstracts I have always found to be clear, accurate, and impartial' LXVI.1, 4, 7, 8, 30, 77; LXVII.6, 29; LXVIII.1; LXIX.7, 52, 76; LXX.61.

Floridus, Franciscus: LXVI.106.

Florus, Lucius Annæus [fl. first century AD]: I.76; II.47; XX.47; XXXIV.28; XXXV.64; XXXVI.48; XLI.107; XLIV.185; LXIX.62.

Fœlix of Thibara, or Tibiur: XVI.158.

Foggini, Pietro Francesco [editor of Corippus, and of George of Pisidia; Gibbon owned his *Corporis Historiæ Byzantinæ Nova Appendix* (Rome, 1777)]: XLV.5; XLVI.53, 78, 81, 95.

Folard, Jean Charles, Chevalier de [1669–1752]: 'the subject of the ancient machines is treated with great knowledge and ingenuity by the Chevalier Folard' I.59; V.54; XI.1; XIV.53; 'the Chevalier Folard, the once famous editor of Polybius, who fashioned to his own habits and opinions all the military operations of antiquity' XLIII.51.

Foncemagne, Étienne Lauréault de [1694–1779; historian of the Franks]: XXXV.26, 27; 'a correct and elegant dissertation' XXXVIII.62; LXI.75; LXVIII.91.

Fontanini, Giusto [abp of Ancyra]: XLV.34.

Fontenelle, Bernard le Bouyer de [1657–1757; Gibbon owned his *Œuvres*, 10 vols. (Paris, 1758) and 11 vols. (Paris, 1766)]: XII.70; XVII.70; XXX.37; 'an ingenious, though feeble, comedy' XL.89; XLIII.80, 81; XLIV.74; XLIX.155; LII.56; LXI.67; LXVI.117.

Forster, R. [or Foster; author of 'Dissertation' in Spelman's tr. of Xenophon]: XIII.66; XXIV.41, 84; XLII.77.

Fortifiocca, Tomaso [fourteenth-century biographer of Rienzi]: 'the most particular and authentic life of Cola (Nicholas) di Rienzi . . . under the name of Tomaso Fortifiocca, who is only mentioned in this work as having been punished by the tribune for forgery. Human nature is scarcely capable of such sublime or stupid impartiality: but whosoever is the author of these Fragments, he wrote on the spot and at the time, and paints, without design or art, the manners of Rome and the character of the tribune' LXX.19, 20, 21, 27, 28, 43, 50, 54, 55, 'the authentic ground-work of the history of Rienzi' 98.

Fortis, Alberto [author of *Viaggio in Dalmazia*]: I.80; XIII.116, 117, 122.

Fortunatus, Venantius Honorius C. [*c.*540–*c.*600; bp of Poitiers; poet]: IX.16; XXXVIII.56, 108; XLI.30.

Fourmont, Claude Louis [1703–80; Persian scholar; author of *Description historique et géographique des ruines d'Héliopolis et de Memphis* (Paris, 1755)]: XLII.45; XLVI.22.

Fraser, James [Gibbon owned his *History of Nadir Shah* (London, 1742)]: LXV.70.

Freculphus [bp of Lisieux]: XXVIII.80.

Fredegarius, scholasticus [fl. seventh century AD; historian of France]: XXXV.21, 33; XXXVIII.15, 26, 31, 56; XLVI.33; LII.29.

Freher, Marquard [Roman antiquarian and scholar]: XLIX.104.

Freind, John [1675–1728; physician and politician]: XLIII.89.

Frenshemius, Johann [or Freinshemius, or Frensheim; classical scholar]: IX.41; XXX.50; XLIV.147; LI.119.

Fréret, Nicolas [1688–1749; Gibbon owned his *Défense de la chronologie, fondée sur les monumens de l'histoire ancienne, contre le système de M. Newton* (Paris, 1758) and *Examen critique des apologistes de la religion chrétienne* (London, 1767)]: I.20, 74; VIII.31; X.69; XX.45; 'judicious observations' XXV.129; XXVI.5; XXVIII.52; XL.129; XLIII.78; 'how laboriously does the curious spirit of Europe explore the darkest and most distant antiquities' LI.18, 36.

Frigeridus, Renautus Profuturus: XXX.88; XXXI.150; XXXIII.9; XXXV.6.

Frisingen, Otho [or of Frisingen; bp of Frisingen; historian; author of *De Gestis Frederici I*]: LIII.22; LVI.109, 113, 114; LVIII.38; LIX.9, 31; LXIX.20, 26, 43, 53, 55, 56, 'Cicero or Livy would not have rejected these images, the eloquence of a Barbarian born and educated in the Hercynian forest' 57, 58, 59, 91.

Froissart, Jean [*c.* 1337–1404; historian; Gibbon owned his *Le Premier (–Quart) Volume de l'histoire et cronique*, 4 vols. in 1 (Lyons, 1559–61)]: XIII.17; LVIII.63; 'I should not complain of the labour of this work, if my materials were always derived from such books as the chronicle of honest Froissard . . ., who read little, enquired much, and believed all . . . the pleasant garrulity of Froissard' LXIV.61; LXV.92; LXVI.17; LXX.60.

Frontinus, Sextus Julius [*c.*35–*c.*103; Gibbon owned his *De Aquæductibus Urbis Romæ* (Padua, 1722) and *Libri Quatuor Strategematicon, curante F. Oudendorpio* (Leyden, 1779)]: I.62; XLI.87.

Fulcherius Carnotensis [or of Chartres; *c.*1059–*c.*1127; historian of the Crusades]: LVIII.15, 19, 41, 74, 88, 94, 100; LX.68.

Fulgentius [st; bp of Ruspæ]: XXXVII.96, 112, 117.

Fulvius, Andreas [topographer and antiquarian of Rome]: LXXI.75.

Fuselin [editor of Simler]: X.74; XXVI.71.

G

Gagnier, John [1670–1740; editor of *Ismael Abulfeda de Vita et Rebus Gestis Mohammedis* (Oxford, 1723); Gibbon owned his *La Vie de Mahomet*, 2 vols. (Amsterdam, 1748)]: XLVI.4, 68; L.13, 20, 40, 43, 48, 52, 59, 64, 65, 68, 69, 70, 71, 72, 73, 95, 98, 99, 'the best and most authentic of our guides' 111, 113, 119, 120, 'the honest Gagnier' 121, 122, 125, 128, 130, 134, 135, 137, 138, 140, 142, 143, 144, 145, 146, 147, 148, 149, 150, 151, 153, 'impartial pen' 157, 158, 162, 165, 168; LI.26, 97, 108, 139, 200; LII.51.

Gaillard, Gabriel Henri [1726–1806; Gibbon owned his *Histoire de Charlemagne*, 4 vols. (Paris, 1782), *Histoire de François I*[er], 7 vols. (Paris, 1766–9), and *Histoire de la rivauté de la France et de l'Angleterre*, 11 vols. (Paris, 1771–7)]: XLIX.92, 94, 'the author is a man of sense and humanity; and his work is laboured with industry and elegance' 95, 96, 98, 99, 102, 103, 104, 107, 112, 113, 115, 116, 121, 122.

Galand, Antoine [1646–1715; compiler, with Denis Dominique Cardonne, of *Contes et fables indiennes*, 3 vols. (Paris, 1778)]: XLII.55; L.2.

Galanus, Clemens [author of the *Armenian History*, 3 vols. (Rome, 1650–51)]: 'the work of a Jesuit must have sterling merit when it is praised by La Croze' XLVII.139.

Gale, Thomas [1635?–1702; British antiquary; author of *Antoninus's Itinerary in Britain*; editor of Gildas and Nennius;

Gibbon owned his *Historiæ Poeticæ Scriptores Antiqui Græci et Latini* (Paris, 1675), *Opuscula Mythologica Physica et Ethica* (Amsterdam, 1688) and *Rerum Anglicarum Scriptorum Veterum*, 3 vols. (Oxford, 1684–91)]: II.85; XXXI.29; XXXVIII.126, 132, 138; LIX.80, 106.

Galenus, Claudius: XV.191; XL.95; XLIII.43.

Galiani, Ferdinando [or Galliani; 1728–87; Gibbon owned his *Dialogues sur le commerce des blés* (London, 1770)]: 'that laughing philosopher' LII.27.

Gallienus [*c*.218–68; emperor]: X.153.

Garretius, Joh.[editor of the *Variarum Libri XII*]: XXXIX.25.

Gaubil, Antoine [1689–1759; Jesuit; editor and translator of the *Histoire de la dynastie des Mongous* (Paris, 1739)]: XXVI.40; XXXIV.22, 23; XXXV.48; LV.23; 'this translation is stamped with the Chinese character of domestic accuracy and foreign ignorance' LXIV.8, 19, 23, 26.

Gaudier, John [translator of *Annales Turcici ad Annum 1550*]: LXIV.41.

Gazæus, Æneas: XXXVII.124.

Gébelin, Antoine Court de [1728–84; author of the *Histoire du calendrier* and *Monde primitif analysé et comparé avec le monde moderne*, 9 vols. (Paris, 1773–82)]: LXVIII.53.

Geddes, Michael [1650?–1713; Gibbon owned his *The Church-history of Æthiopia* (London, 1696), *The Council of Trent no Free Assembly* (London, 1714), *The History of the Church of Malabar* (London, 1694), *Miscellaneous Tracts*, 3 vols. (London, 1730) and *Several Tracts against Popery* (London, 1715)]: XV.25, 176; XVI.74; XXI.115; XXVIII.66; XXXVII.21; XLVII.124, 161.

Gedoyn, Nicolas: XXIII.105.

Gelasius [d. 496; st; pope]: XLVII.74.

Gelasius, Cyzicenus [bp of Cæsarea]: XX.51.

Gemeticensis, William [or of Jumieges; author of *De Ducibus Normannis*]: LVI.17, 37; LVIII.47.

Genesis: XXXI.86; XL.55; XLIV.143; L.21, 24.

Genesius de Sepulveda, Joseph [fl. tenth century; Gibbon owned his *Opera*, 4 vols. (Madrid, 1780), and *De Rebus Constantinopolitanis* (Venice, 1733)]: LII.80, 96; LIV.19.

Gentilis, Delphinus: LXX.70, 98.

Geographia Nubiensis, Recens ex Arabico in Latinum versa a Gabriele Sionita et Joanne Hesronita (Paris, 1619) [*see also* Edrissi, Sherif al]: XIX.58; L.2, 16, 132; LI.20, 23, 25, 34, 52, 102, 166, 174; LII.41.

Geoponica. Geoponicorum sive de Re Rustica Libri XX. C. Basso Collectore, 2 vols. (Leipzig, 1781): LXII.57.

George of Malatia: VIII.44.

George of Pisidia [fl. seventh century; poet]: XLVI.51, 53, 74, 75, 78, 79, 81, 82, 93, 95, 'the smoke of George of Pisidia' 97, 107, 110, 112.

George of Sienna [military historian]: LXVIII.41.

Gerard of Reicherspeg [German historian]: LXIX.40.

Gerbillon, Jean François [1654–1707; Jesuit]: 'Gerbillon . . . who accurately surveyed the Chinese Tartary' XXVI.7, 12.

Gesner, Johann Matthias [editor of Columella and Varro]: XXXI.30; XLII.14; XLIV.138; LXIII.23.

Gesta Anglorum post Bedam: LV.38.

Gesta Impiorum per Francos, sive Gesta Francorum per Impios, or *Anonymi Gesta Francorum*, or *Gesta Dei per Francos* [*see also* Fredegarius and William of Tyre]: XXXI.169; XXXV.22; XXXVIII.33, 46, 47, 52, 55, 56; LVIII.9, 19, 41, 84, 95.

Giannone, Pietro [1676–1748; Gibbon owned his *Istoria Civile del Regno di Napoli*, 4 vols. (The Hague, 1753), and *Opere Posthume in Difesa della sua Storia Civile del Regno di Napoli* (Lausanne, 1760)]: 'the subject of ecclesiastical jurisdiction has been involved in a mist of passion. Two of the fairest books which have fallen into my hands are the Institutes of Canon Law, by the Abbé de Fleury, and the Civil History of Naples, by Giannone. Their moderation was

Giannone, Pietro—*cont* the effect of situation as well as of temper. Fleury was a French ecclesiastic, who respected the authority of the parliaments; Giannone was an Italian lawyer, who dreaded the power of the church' XX.111, 129; 'Giannone . . . has treated the interesting subject [Valentinian's establishment of professorships] with the zeal and curiosity of a man of letters, who studies his domestic history' XXV.61; XXXIX.53, 'patriotic diligence' 55, 56; XLI.67; XLIV.135; XLV.37, 51, 52; 'a disciple of the Gallican school' XLIX.30, 86, 94, 110, 148; LII.66; LIII.5, 47; LVI.1, 15, 25, 'the origin and nature of the papal investitures are ably discussed by Giannone . . . as a lawyer and antiquarian. Yet he vainly strives to reconcile the duties of patriot and catholic, adopts an empty distinction of "Ecclesia Romana non dedit sed accepit," and shrinks from an honest but dangerous confession of the truth' 36, 39, 43, 46, 47, 56, 58, 96, 97, 101, 139; LIX.88; LXI.41; LXII.37, 46; LXVI.86; LXVIII.96; LXX.30, 71, 91.

Gibson, Edmund [1669–1748; bp of London; editor of the *Chronicon Saxonicum* (Oxford, 1692)]: XXXVIII.126.

Gildas [d. 570?; st]: XXXVIII.126, 132, 136.

Gilles, Pierre [or Gyllius; 1490–1555; Gibbon owned his *De Bosporo Thracio* (Lyons, 1561)]: XVII.3, 5, 11, 35, 48, 51, 57; XL.103, 108; XLIII.73; XLVI.44; LVIII.66; LXI.18; LXVII.3; LXVIII.12.

Giornale de Letterati d'Italia, 40 vols. (Venice, 1710–40): XL.14.

Giphanius, Obertus [editor of Homer and Lucretius]: XLI.5.

Giraldus Cambrensis: XXXVIII.159, 160.

Giustiniani, Giambattista: XIII.116.

Glaber, Rudolphus [*c.*985–*c.*1047; monk and French historian]: LVII.69, 70, 71.

Glycas, Michael [fl. twelfth century; historian]: XLIX.15; LIII.103; LVII.38.

Gmelin, Johann Georg [traveller in Siberia]: XXVI.32; XXXIX.41.

Goar, Jacobus [1601–53; editor of Theophanes, commentator on George Codinus, curopalata]: LII.1; LIII.48.

Godefroy, Jacques [or Gothofredus; 1587–1652; historian and jurist; editor of the *Theodosian Code*, of Libanius, and of Philostorgius]: II.88; III.19; IV.30; XIII.96; XIV.76, 93; 'the commentary of Godefroy on the whole title well deserves to be consulted' XVII.41, 62, 71, 98, 102, 123, 127, 128, 137, 153, 155, 161, 173, 178; XVIII.11, 12, 15, 18, 58; XX.9, 16, 33, 53, 74, 80, 'illustrated with tolerable candour by the learned Godefroy, whose mind was balanced by the opposite prejudices of a civilian and a protestant' 96, 100, 110; XXI.44, 'more attached to his principles than to his author [Philostorgius]' 67, 71, 81, 90, 99, 147, 167, 169, 173; XXII.44, 67, 77, 84; XXIII.55, 91, 118, 121; XXV.2, 3, 20, 23, 36, 48, 51, 61, 62, 66, 74, 77; XXVI.76, 105, 117; XXVII.6, 22, 48, 76, 95, 106, 122; XXVIII.24, 53; XXIX.3, 8, 30; XXX.56, 63, 72, 115; XXXI.3, 31, 53, 74, 91, 150; XXXII.18, 20, 28, 61, 65; XXXIII.3, 9; XXXVI.40; XL.120, 121; XLII.87; XLIV.41, 70, '[Godefroy] pours a flood of ancient and modern learning over these penal laws' 111, 130, 196; XLVII.31.

Godfrey of Bouillon [*c.*1060–1100; Crusader;]: LVIII.132, 133, 136, 141, 143; LXI.73.

Godfrey of Viterbo: XLIX.139; LIX.13, 14.

Goguet, Antoine Yves [1716–58; Gibbon owned his (together with A. C. Fugère) *De l'origine des loix, des arts et des sciences, et de leur progrès chez les anciens peuples*, 6 vols. (Paris, 1758)]: XIX.1; XXXI.141; 'learned and rational' 'Gen. Obs.'.11; 'The president Goguet . . . will amuse and satisfy the reader. I doubt whether his book, especially in England, is as well known as it deserves to be' XL.59, 133; XLVI.101; LI.132; LXVIII.53.

Goldast, Melchior [scholar of German history; editor of Eginhardus]: XLV.12.

Goltz, Hubert [or Goltzius; Dutch classical scholar and antiquarian]: XIII.21.

Grabe, Johann Ernst: XXI.25, 59.

Grævius, Joannes Georgius [author of *Thesaurus Antiquitatum Romanorum*, 12 vols. (Lugd. Bat., 1694–9)]: XIX.46; XLIV.34; XLV.21.

Grainville, Charles Joseph de Lespine de: XX.38.

Grammaticus, Leo [Byzantine historian]: LV.34, 61, 63.

Gratian [359–83; emperor]: XVII.82.

Gravina, Giovanni Vincenzo [Gibbon owned his *Opera, seu Originum Juris Civilis Libri Tres* (Leipzig, 1737), *Esprit des lois romaines*, 3 vols. (Amsterdam, 1766), and *Raison ou idée de la poésie*, 2 vols. (Paris, 1755)]: XLIV.7, 22, 40, 41, 52, 53, 'the classic Latinity of the Roman Gravina' 54, 58, 61, 71, 163, 173, 193, 201; XLIX.154; LXXI.35.

Gray, Thomas [1716–71; poet; Gibbon owned his *Poems. To which are Prefixed Memoirs of his Life and Writings, by W. Mason* (York, 1775)]: XXXI.127; 'from a college at Cambridge, the poetic eye of Gray had *seen* the same objects [the Nile] with a keener glance' LI.129.

Greaves, John [1602–52; Gibbon owned his *Miscellaneous Works*, 2 vols. (London, 1737)]: VII.37; X.130; XVII.180; XXVIII.52; 'the learned Greaves' XXXVI.42; XXXVII.9; XL.103; L.2, 41, 118; 'a curious traveller' LXV.88.

Gregory I [c.540–604;]: XXXVII.125, 134; XXXIX.108; XLV.14, 36, 60, 'the writings of Gregory himself attest his innocence of any classic taste or literature' 61, 63, 64, 65, 68; XLVI.48.

Gregory II [669–731]: XLIX.10, 21, 33.

Gregory VII: LVIII.3.

Gregory Bar-Hebræus, *see* Abulpharagius, Gregory.

Gregory of Nazianzen [c.330–c.389; st]: XIII.100; XIX.11, 29; XX.33; XXI.96, 111, 139, 162; XXII.11, 30, 41, 42, 44, 60, 83; XXIII.2, 3, 5, 7, 8, 11, 24, 28, 33, 36, 40, 48, 51, 53, 54, 68, 76, 82, 85, 88, 90, 94, 96, 97, 100, 102, 103, 118, 119, 129, 134, 135, 137, 139, 140, 141; XXIV.20, 57, 72, 77, 78, 99, 111, 130, 137; XXV.4, 9, 67, 73, 84; XXVII.25, 26, 29, 30, 34, 35, 38, 41, 44, 45; XL.45; L.163.

Gregory of Nyssa [c.335–c.394; brother of St Basil]: XV.91; XXIX.9; XLIV.166.

Gregory Thaumaturgus [st; third-century bishop of Neo-Cæsarea]: X.110, 132; XVI.78; LIV.13.

Gregory of Tours [538/9–594/5]: X.67; XV.173; XVIII.16; XXVII.105; XXX.88; XXXIII.9, 43; XXXV.6, 16, 18, 22, 33, 35, 46, 47; XXXVI.15, 25, 29, 30, 34, 61, 94, 96, 113, 120; XXXVII.89, 128, 130; XXXVIII.8, 11, 12, 15, 19, 20, 22, 24, 26, 30, 31, 32, 36, 37, 38, 40, 41, 42, 45, 46, 53, 56, 57, 61, 68, 78, 92, 95, 96, 98, 99, 102, 104, 105, 106, 107, 110, 'His style is equally devoid of elegance and simplicity. In a conspicuous station he still remained a stranger to his own age and country; and in a prolix work . . . he has omitted almost every thing that posterity desires to learn. I have tediously acquired, by a painful perusal, the right of pronouncing this unfavourable sentence' 111, 113, 114, 116, 117, 121, 122, 136, 164; XLI.101, 104; XLII.34; XLIII.48, 88; XLV.7, 8, 33, 59.

Grelot, Guillaume Joseph [traveller; Gibbon owned his *Relation d'un voyage de Constantinople* (Paris, 1680)]: XL.103.

Gretser, Jacob [Jesuit; author of *Syntagma de Imaginibus non Manû factis*]: 'equal learning and bigotry . . . the ass, or rather the fox, of Ingoldstadt' XLIX.11, 13; 'Gretser, a learned Jesuit' LIII.48; LVI.88.

Gronovius, Jacobus [Gibbon owned his *De Sestertiis* (Leyden, 1671)]: I.35; III.19; VI.38; XVI.32; XIX.63; XXIV.44, 136; XXV.112; XXVIII.1; 'Gen. Obs.'.1; XLIV.147; XLIX.47; 'the most virulent of critics' LI.150; LII.28; LXVIII.49.

Gronovius, Joannes Fredericus: XLIV.40, 163.

Grosier, Jean Baptiste Gabriel Alexandre [1743–1823; editor of the *Histoire générale de la Chine*, or the *Tong-Kien-Kang-Mou*]: XXVI.25, 34, 38, 40, 41, 44, 52.

Grosley, Pierre Jean [1718–85; Gibbon owned his *Observations sur l'Italie*, 4 vols. (London, 1774)]: XIV.53; LXX.84.

Grotius, Hugo [1583–1645; Dutch jurist and historian; Gibbon owned his *Opera Omnia Theologica*, 3 vols. (Amsterdam, 1679), *Annales et Historiæ de Rebus Belgicis* (Amsterdam, 1657), and Amsterdam, 1658), *De Jure Belli ac Pacis* (Amsterdam, 1689), *Le Droit de la guerre et de la paix* (Basle, 1746), *De Veritate Religionis Christianæ* (The Hague, 1729), *Epistolæ* (Amsterdam, 1687), *Excerpta Tragœdiis et Comœdiis Græcis* (Paris, 1626), *Historia Gothorum, Vandalorum et Langobardorum* (Amsterdam, 1655) and *Poemata* (Leyden, 1617)]: IX.45; 'the excellent edition published by Grotius, of the Gothic writers' X.4, 7, 9; XIV.38; XV.16, 60, 130; XVI.185, 186; XVIII.43, 45; 'Grotius was a republican and an exile, but the mildness of his temper inclined him to support the established powers' XX.18; XXV.142; XXVI.72; XXX.4, 77; XXXI.99, 155; 'He has laboriously, but vainly, attempted to form a reasonable system of jurisprudence, from the various and discordant modes of royal succession, which have been introduced by fraud, or force, by time, or accident' XXXIII.4; XXXV.38; XXXVII.135; 'the character of Grotius inclines me to believe, that he has not substituted the *Rhine* for the *Rhone* . . . without the authority of some MS.' XXXVIII.5; 96; XXXIX.1, 43, 104; XL.156; 'the first scholar of a learned age' XLI.1, 'the learned and free-spirited Grotius' 33, 46, 64, 76, 'Grotius himself is lost in an idle distinction between the jus naturæ and the jus gentium' 107; XLII.8; XLIII.31; L.148, 154; LI.73; LII.32; LIV.38, 40; LV.28, 53; LVI.12.

Gruter, Jan [Gibbon owned his *Inscriptiones Antiquæ Totius Orbis Romani*, 4 vols. (Amsterdam, 1707)]: II.49; III.14; XI.37; XIV.20; XVI.43, 166, 167, 169; XVII.148; XX.43; XXV.86; XXXI.11; XLIV.10; LXX.23.

Grynæus, Simon [Gibbon owned his *Novus Orbis Regionum ac Insularum Veteribus Incognitarum* (Basil, 1555)]: LXIV.10, 15.

Guazzesi, Lorenzo [or Guazzezi; Gibbon owned his *Dell'Antico Dominio del Vescovo di Arezzo in Cortona* (Pisa, 1760)]: XLIII.35.

Gude, Gottlieb Friedrich: LIII.71.

Guenée, Antoine [1717–1803]: XXXII.79.

Guibert [or Guibertus; abbot of Nogent; historian of the Crusades]: LVII.53, 57; LVIII.2, 8, 9, 15, 19, 28, 30, 31, 'Guibert . . . paints in lively colours this general emotion [of the Crusaders]. He was one of the few contemporaries who had genius enough to feel the astonishing scenes that were passing before their eyes' 33, 41, 45, 'ever the lively and interesting Guibert' 49, 75, 78, 79, 94, 97; LIX.50, 68.

Guicciardini, Francesco [1483–1540; Gibbon owned his *La Historia d'Italia*, 2 vols. (Geneva, 1636), and *Della Istoria d'Italia*, 4 vols. (Florence, 1775–6)]: 'the great, but unfinished, history of Guicciardini' XXXI.116; 'a servant of the popes' XLIX.73; LXX.89.

Guicciardini, Lodovico [Gibbon owned his *Il Sacco di Roma* (Cologne, 1758) and *Belgicæ sive Inferioris Germaniæ Descriptio* (Amsterdam, 1635)]: XXXI.104, 116.

Guido, Bernardus [biographer of Urban VII]: LVIII.4; LXIX.12.

Guignes, Joseph de [1721–1800; Gibbon owned his *Histoire Générale des Huns, des Turcs, des Mongols, et des autres Peuples Tartares Occidentaux*, 4 vols. in 5 (Paris, 1756–58)]: II.2; XIII.59; XXV.97; 'a skilful and laborious interpreter of the Chinese language; who has thus laid open new and important scenes in the history of mankind' XXVI.10, 14, 25, 27, 30, 33, 37, 41, 42, 43, 45, 53, 55; XXX.64; XXXIV.5, 13, 14, 23; 'extraordinary knowledge of the Chinese language and writers' XXXV.71; XXXVIII.58; XL.68; XLII.25, 30, 31, 32, 35; XLVI.98; L.22; LI.14, 36, 42, 133, 170, 179, 184; LII.33, 85, 88, 'M. de

Guignes, who sometimes leaps, and sometimes stumbles, in the gulph between Chinese and Mahometan story' 97, 103, 'to escape the reproach of error, I must criticise the inaccuracies of M. de Guignes . . . concerning the Edrisites' 105, 107; LV.23; LVI.103; LVII.1, 'his division of nations often disturbs the series of time and place' 2, 12, 18, 21, 'that learned author' 23, 'the accuracy of de Guignes' 25, 29, 31, 38, 39, 'without these two learned Frenchmen [d'Herbelot and de Guignes], I should be blind indeed in the Eastern world' 41, 47, 51, 'very learned' 58, 73, 75; LVIII.80, 89, 99, 101, 102, 110, 122, 123; LIX.6, 36, 37, 38, 45, 46, 82, 102, 104, 107, 109; LXIII.45, 47; 'in his great History of the Huns, M. de Guignes has most amply treated of Zingis Khan and his successors . . . He is ever learned and accurate; yet I am only indebted to him for a general view' LXIV.18, 31, 'from whom the Orientals may learn the history and geography of their own country' 39, 43, 59; LXV.33, 62, 70.

Guillimannus, Franciscus [or Guilliman; Swiss historian; author of *De Rebus Helveticis*]: XXXVIII.23, 24; LXIX.20, 24.

Guischardt, Carl Gottlieb [or Guichardt, or Guischard, or 'Quintus Icilius'; military historian; Gibbon owned his *Mémoires critiques et historiques sur plusieurs points d'antiquités militaires*, 4 vols. (Berlin, 1774), and *Mémoires Militaires sur les Grecs et les Romains*, 2 vols. (Lyons, 1760)]: 'M. Guichard . . . has treated the subject [of troop dispositions] like a scholar and an officer' I.47, 61 'see those evolutions [of the legion] admirably well explained by M. Guichard' 64; XXIV.83, 'his Analysis of the two Campaigns in Spain and Africa, is the noblest monument that has ever been raised to the fame of Cæsar' 117; XXV.104; XLI.17; 'a good edition of all the Scriptores Tactici would be a task not unworthy of a scholar . . . But this scholar should be likewise a soldier; and, alas! Quintus Icilius is no more' LIII.9; 'it is pity that Quintus Icilius (M. Guischard) did not live to analyse these operations [those between Cæsar and Pompey], as he has done the campaigns of Africa and Spain' LVI.72.

Gundling: XLIX.117.

Gunther [or Guntherus; thirteenth-century monk in the monastery of Paris near Basil; poet of the *Ligurinus*; historian of the Crusades]: XLIX.146; LX.45, 53, 58, 67, 70, 80, 83, 84, 85, 88, 101; LXI.17, 19, 50; LXIX.20, 22, 26, 35.

Gussanvillus, Petrus: XLV.72.

Gutherius, Jacobus [author of the *De Officiis Domus Augustae*]: XVII.144.

H

Hadrian [76–138; emperor]: XLIV.175, 188.

Haiton the Armenian [or Hayton, or Haithonus, or Aithonus; Armenian prince and latterly monk of Premontré; historian of the Tartars]: LVII.52; LXIV.10, 37.

Hakluyt, Richard [1552–1616; Gibbon owned his *The Principal Nauigations, Voyages, Traffiques and Discoueries of the English Nation*, 3 vols. (London, 1599–1600)]: XL.69; LXIV.17, 30.

Halley, Edmond [1656–1742; astronomer]: XI.69; XLIII.76.

Hamartolus, George: LIII.112; LV.61, 63.

Hanke, Martin [or Hankius, or Hanckius; Gibbon owned his *De Byzantinarum Rerum Scriptoribus Græcis* (Leipzig, 1677)]: XLVI.57; LI.10; LIII.8, 107; LXII.1; LXV.56; LXVI.31.

Hanselman: XII.44.

Hanway, Jonas [Gibbon owned his *An Historical Account of the British Trade over the Caspian Sea: with a Journal of Travels, to which are added the Revolutions of Persia*, 4 vols. in 3 (London, 1753)]: XL.69.

Hardouin, Jean [1646–1729; Jesuit; Pyrrhonist; editor of Pliny and Themistius]: XV.122; XVII.55; XXV.10; 'learned Jesuit' XL.61; LVI.66.

Harmer, Thomas [1714–88; Gibbon owned his *Observations on Divers Passages of Scripture*, 4 vols. (London, 1776–87)]: XIX.59.

Harris, James [1709–80; Gibbon owned his *Hermes, or a Philosophical Inquiry Concerning Universal Grammar* (London, 1771), *Philological Enquiries* (London, 1781), *Philosophical Arrangements* (London, 1775) and *Three Treatises* (London, 1772)]: LI.98; 'the learned and amiable Mr. Harris of Salisbury' LII.48, 'the most elegant commentary on the Categories or Predicaments of Aristotle, may be found in the Philosophical Arrangements of Mr. James Harris . . ., who laboured to revive the studies of Grecian literature and philosophy' 59; 'Philosophical Arrangements, opus senile' LIII.109; LX.93, 'a manuscript of Nicetas in the Bodleian library . . . is . . . immoderately praised by the late ingenious Mr. Harris of Salisbury' 95, 96; LXI.12.

Harris, John [1666–1719; Gibbon owned his *Navigantium atque Itinerantium Bibliotheca, or, a Complete Collection of Voyages and Travels*, 2 vols. (London, 1764)]: XVIII.80; XXVI.32; LV.25.

Harris, William [1720–70; Gibbon owned his *An Historical and Critical Account of the Life of Charles I.* (London, 1772), *An Historical and Critical Account of the Life of Charles the Second*, 2 vols. (London, 1766), *An Historical and Critical Account of the Life of James the First* (London, 1772) and *An Historical and Critical Account of the Life of Oliver Cromwell* (London, 1772)]: LXX.29.

Harte, Walter [1709–74; Gibbon owned his *History of the Life of Gustavus Adolphus*, 2 vols. (London, 1759) and his *Essays on Husbandry* (Bath, 1764, and, 2 vols., London, 1770)]: II.100; X.8; XXVI.100; XXXI.102.

Hauteville, John de [or Hanville; monk and poet]: XXII.7.

Havercamp, Sigebertus [editor of Eutropius, Censorinus, Orosius and Josephus]: XVIII.3, 26, 68; XXIII.74; XXV.122; XXVI.87; XXVIII.46, 48; XXXV.75; XLII.79; XLIV.18, 37, 133; LI.53; LXVI.107; LXX.10; LXXI.13.

Hayley, William [1745–1820; Gibbon owned his *Plays*, 2 vols. (London, 1779–80), *Poems*, 2 vols. (London, 1782–4), *Poems and Plays*, 3 vols. (London, 1774) and 6 vols. (London, 1785), and *Two Dialogues containing a Comparative View of the Lives, Characters and Writings of Philip, the late Earl of Chesterfield, and Dr. Samuel Johnson* (London, 1787)]: XLIII.29.

Hegesippus [fl. second century AD]: XV.31; XVI.50.

Heinecke, Johann Christian G. [or Heineccius; 1681–1741; Gibbon owned his *Antiquitatum Romanarum Jurisprudentiam Illustrantium Syntagma*, 2 vols. (Utrecht, 1745), *Elementa Juris Civilis Secundum Ordinem Institutorum* (Leyden, 1751), *Elementa Juris Civilis Secundum Ordinem Pandectarum*, 2 vols. (Utrecht, 1772), and *Historia Juris Civilis Romani ac Germanici* (Leyden, 1740)]: VI.32, 106; XVII.100, 107, 114, 120, 165; XXIV.97; XXV.51; XXIX.26; XXXI.70, 110; 'the discreet Heineccius' XXXII.19; XXXVIII.63, 'he considers, and tries to excuse, the defects of that barbarous jurisprudence [German law]' 65, 66, 72, 76, 77, 93, 95, 97; XLIII.21, 22, 86; XLIV.2, 3, 'At the head of these guides [to Roman law], I shall respectfully place the learned and perspicuous Heineccius' 4, 5, 8, 12, 19, 22, 30, 34, 'the master-hand of Heineccius' 35, 41, 49, 51, 52, 53, 58, 61, 71, 98, 101, 105, 128, 135, 137, 163, 193, 201; XLV.1; LIII.5, 98.

Hélyot, Pierre [1660–1716; Gibbon owned his *Histoire des ordres monastiques, religieux et militaires*, 8 vols. (Paris, 1714–19)]: XXXVII.1, 5, 18.

Hemingford, Walter de [fl. 1300; English chronicler]: LIX.106.

Henoticon, *see* Zeno, emperor of the East

Henry of Huntingdon [1084?–1155; English historian]: XXXVIII.134.

Henry, Robert [1718–90; historian; Gibbon owned his *The History of Great Britain*, 5 vols. (London, 1771)]: 'useful and laborious' XXXVIII.148; LXVI.84.

Herbelot de Molainville, Barthélemy d' [Gibbon owned his *Bibliothèque orientale* (Paris, 1697)]: VIII.4, 26, 55; X.150; XII.72; XIII.61; XVII.70; XVIII.54, 55; XIX.55, 58; XX.79; XXIV.50; XXVI.13, 20, 46; XXXIII.48; XXXIV.24; XL.135, 138, 142; XLII.23, 38, 45, 52, 62, 91, 100; XLV.5; XLVI.4, 8, 10, 21, 22, 67, 87, 108; L.2, 12, 18, 19, 20, 22, 34, 36, 40, 43, 47, 57, 60, 65, 77, 83, 84, 85, 91, 95, 97, 103, 110, 111, 117, 118, 131, 134, 142, 166, 173, 176, 181, 183, 184, 185; LI.4, 5, 6, 7, 8, 9, 11, 12, 'for the character of the respectable author, consult his friend Thevenot . . . His work is an agreeable miscellany, which must gratify every taste; but I never can digest the alphabetical order, and I find him more satisfactory in the Persian than the Arabic history' 15, 22, 23, 25, 28, 29, 31, 33, 38, 39, 42, 52, 79, 84, 105, 133, 156, 159, 166, 198, 202, 203, 205, 208, 217, 219; LII.2, 13, 36, 38, 41, 45, 48, 57, 69, 73, 'that learned collector has shewn much taste in stripping the Oriental chronicles of their instructive and amusing anecdotes' 75, 96, 98, 100, 101, 103, 'the most interesting facts had already been drained by the diligence of M. d'Herbelot' 106; LIII.45; LVI.57; LVII.1, 3, 4, 8, 12, 14, 17, 18, 22, 'the wealth of d'Herbelot' 25, 26, 28, 33, 38, 39, 'without these two learned Frenchmen [d'Herbelot and de Guignes], I should be blind indeed in the Eastern world' 41, 42, 43, 47, 67; LVIII.101; LIX.37, 38, 42, 'very incorrect' 45, 82; LXIV.9, 58; LXV.5, 10, 23, 32, 35, 44, 48, 66; LXVII.14; LXVIII.13.

Herberstein, Siegmund [Russian historian]: LV.77.

Hericourt du Vatier, Louis d' [Gibbon owned his *Les loix ecclesiastiques de France* (Paris, 1771)]: XVIII.51.

Hermant, Godefroi [Gibbon owned his *La vie de saint Ambroise* (Paris, 1678) and *La vie de saint Jean Chrysostome*, 2 vols. (Lyons, 1683)]: XXVII.90.

Herodian [d. 238?]: IV.10, 11, 15, 17, 19, 23, 25, 27, 28, 35, 44, 45, 52, 56; V.10, 22, 24, 25, 27, 30, 33, 36, 38, 40, 43, 47, 49, 51, 54, 55, 57, 63, 66, 69; VI.11, 12, 17, 18, 19, 20, 22, 23, 26, 35, 39, 40, 41, 44, 47, 49, 51, 53, 55, 58, 61, 67, 68, 80; VII.3, 6, 9, 12, 14, 20, 24, 25, 26, 30, 31, 32, 34, 35, 36, 40, 41, 44; VIII.5, 43, 48, 51, 53, 56, 58; IX.3, 23.

Herodotus [*c.*484–*c.*430 BC]: I.15; 'there is not any writer who describes in so lively a manner as Herodotus, the true genius of Polytheism' II.3, 21; VIII.12, 47, 58; XIII.82; XV.1; XVII.9, 15, 17, 48; XIX.53; XXII.81; XXIV.52, 56, 61, 79, 96; XXVI.3, 19, 58; XXVIII.52; XXX.6; XXXII.14; XXXIV.10; XXXVIII.16; 'the tone half sceptical, half superstitious, of Herodotus' XL.132; XLI.31; 'It will be a pleasure, not a task, to read Herodotus . . . The conversation of Xerxes and Demaratus at Thermopylæ, is one of the most interesting and moral scenes in history' XLII.1, 46, 51, 69, 73, 76, 85; XLIV.10, 18, 192; XLV.21; XLVI.11, 96; XLVII.160; L.53, 106; LI.107, 162; LIII.49; LIV.10; LVII.28; LXII.6, 39; LXV.77; LXVI.23; LXVIII.64; LXX.65.

Heroldus: XXXVIII.63, 71.

Hesychius of Miletus: XLIV.74; XLVII.25.

Heylin, Peter [or Heylyn; 1600–62; author of *Life of Archbishop Laud, History of St George*]: XX.123; XXIII.126.

Heyne, Christian Gottlob [classical scholar]: XLI.75, 84; 'the excellent editor of Virgil' XLIII.46; 'usual good taste' XLIV.171, 'the best of his [Virgil's] editors' 208; L.164; LXVIII.53.

Hierocles [fl. *c.*430]: X.29; XXVII.31; XL.54.

Hilary [or Hilarius; *c.*315–*c.*367; st; bp of Poitiers]: XXI.65, 66, 70, 71, 72, 110, 124, 128.

Hill, Sir John [1716–75; translator of Theophrastus]: XL.133.

Hincmar of Rheims [*c.*806–882; historian

Hincmar of Rheims—*contd*
of France, and biographer of Remigius]: XXXI.190, 191; XXXV.22; XXXVIII.28, 29.

Hirtius, Aulus [*c.*90–43 BC]: XIII.43; XLI.17.

Histoire des camisards: 'accurate and impartial. It requires some attention to discover the religion of the author' XXI.159.

Histoire de la conquête de la Chine, par les Tartares Mantcheoux, see Jouve, Joseph.

Histoire générale des voyages, see Prévost d'Exiles, Antoine François de.

Histoire générale de la Chine, see Grosier, Jean Baptiste G. A.

Histoire de la Ligue Faite à Cambray, see Dubos, Jean-Baptiste.

Histoire politique et philosophique des . . . deux Indes, see Raynal, Guillaume Thomas F.

Historia Miscella: XLII.34, 35, 82; XLIII.37; XLIX.31.

Historiens de France [or *Recueil des historiens des Gaules et de la France*], *see* Bouquet, Martin.

History of Nader Shah, see Jones, Sir William.

Hoadley, Benjamin [1676–1761; bp of Bangor, Hereford, Salisbury and Winchester; latitudinarian; Gibbon owned his *An Account of the State of the Roman Catholick Religion* (London, 1715)]: LIV.38.

Hocsemius, John [fourteenth-century canon of Liège; historian]: LXX.16, 27, 37, 39, 40, 42.

Hody, Humphrey [1659–1707; Gibbon owned his *De Græcis Illustribus Linguæ Græcæ Literarumque Humaniorum Instauratoribus* (London, 1742)]: XL.11; LXVI.19, 57, 'a laborious scholar' 85, 86, 95, 96, 97, 99, 102, 'the pious zeal of a scholar' 104, 105, 106, 110, 113; LXVIII.72.

Hoeschelius, David, of Augsburgh [printer of the *editio princeps* of Procopius]: XL.14; XLI.59; XLVII.116.

Holstenius, Lucas [1596–1661; Gibbon owned his *Annotationes in Geographiam Sacram Caroli à S. Paulo; Italiam Antiquam Cluverii, et Thesaurum Geographicum Ortelli* (Rome, 1666)]: XVI.172; XX.86; XXXVII.13, 32, 36; XLIII.35; XLV.32; XLIX.32, 86.

Homer: II.4, 94; XV.54; XVII.18, 19, 20; XIX.37; XXI.174; XXIII.87; XXIV.96; XXV.130; XXVI.17; XXVIII.26; XXX.11, 12, 14; XXXI.42; 'Gen. Obs.'.14; 'read and feel the xxiiid book of the Iliad, a living picture of manners, passions, and the whole form and spirit of the chariot race' XL.41, 57; 'How concise – how just – how beautiful is the whole picture! I see the attitudes of the archer – I hear the twanging of the bow' XLI.9, 12, 107; XLIII.24; XLIV.64, 192; XLV.46; 'in every light superior to his age and country' XLVI.35; XLVII.148; LI.68, 162; LII.36, 70, 79; LV.35, 'by such a picture [of the cookery of Achilles], a modern epic poet would disgrace his work and disgust his reader; but the Greek verses are harmonious, a dead language can seldom appear low or familiar; and at the distance of two thousand seven hundred years, we are amused with the primitive manners of antiquity' 68, 78, 79, 89; LX.33, 82, 93; LXII.19; LXVII.53; LXVIII.53, 77; LXXI.9.

Hooker, Richard [1554?–1600; Gibbon owned his *Works* (London, 1723)]: XV.108.

Hooper, George [1640–1727; bp of Bath and Wells; Gibbon owned his *An Inquiry into the State of the Ancient Measures* (London, 1721)]: VI.89; XXIV.56; XLI.10; LII.8; LXVIII.24.

Horace [65–8 BC]: II.41; III.23; VI.107; VII.58; X.161; 'the little river or rather torrent of Metaurus near Fano, has been immortalized, by finding such an historian as Livy, and such a poet as Horace' XI.36; XIII.2, 89; XV.55; XIX.3; XXV.47; XXXI.62; XXXVI.3; XL.25, 63; XLI.14, 66, 71; XLIII.14; XLIV.53, 63, 177, 180; XLV.55; L.27; LVI.67, 95; LXXI.14.

Horsley, John [1685–1732; antiquary; Gibbon owned his *Britannia Romana* (London, 1732)]: I.8, 10.

Hotman, François [or Hottoman; 1524–90; French jurist; author of the *Anti-Tribonianus* and *Franco-Gallia*]: XLIV.3, 78.

Hottinger, Johann Heinrich [1620–67; Gibbon owned his *Historia Orientalis* (Zurich, 1651, and Heidelberg, 1658) and *Promtuarium sive Bibliotheca Orientalis* (Heidelberg, 1658)]: L.30, 57, 60, 63, 68, 75, 99, 148, 'gross bigotry' 149; LI.197, 201.

Howard, John [1726–90; author of the *State of Prisons in England and Wales* (Warrington, 1780)]: XXXVII.46.

Howell, William [1638–83; author of *An Institution of General History, from the Beginning of the World to the Monarchy of Constantine the Great* (London, 1661)]: XVII.102, 'that learned historian, who is not sufficiently known' 130, 189; XX.75.

Hudson, John [1662–1719; classical scholar; Gibbon owned his *Geographiæ Veteris Scriptores Græci Minores*, 4 vols. (Oxford, 1698–1712)]: XVII.3; XXIII.108; XXIV.12, 86; XXVI.46; XXVIII.3, 40; XXXI.50, 54, 155; XXXIII.38; XL.67, 134, 143, 144; XLII.65; L.2, 14, 15, 24, 30, 31, 32, 45; LI.34, 41; LIII.15; LXV.9; LXVII.25.

Huet, Pierre Daniel [1630–1721; bp of Avranches; Gibbon owned his *Commentarius de Rebus ad eum Pertinentibus* (Amsterdam, 1718), *De Interpretatione* (Paris, 1661), *Histoire du Commerce et de la Navigation des Anciens* (Lyons, 1763), *Huetiana, ou Pensées Diverses de M. Huet* (Amsterdam, 1723) and *Tractatus de Situ Paradisi Terrestris* (Amsterdam, 1698)]: XXXI.155; XL.14; LXI.64.

Hughes, John [1677–1720; dramatist; author of the *Siege of Damascus*]: 'one of our most popular tragedies, and which possesses the rare merit of blending nature and history, the manners of the times and the feelings of the heart. The foolish delicacy of the players compelled him to soften the guilt of the hero and the despair of the heroine . . . A frigid catastrophe!' LI.62.

Humbertus [*c.*1000–1051; bp of Silva Candida; cardinal]: LX.7.

Hume, David [1711–76; philosopher; Gibbon owned his *Dialogues Concerning Natural Religion* (London, 1779) and, *Essays and Treatises on Several Subjects*, 4 vols. (London, 1760), 2 vols. (London, 1768, and London, 1777) and 8 vols. (London, 1770, and, London, 1778)]: II.3; V.30; VI.18; VIII.24; IX.2, 40, 87; XV.114; XVI.153; XVII.169; XXI.173; XXII.17; XXIII.12; XXIV.91; XXVIII.85; XXXI.25, 'admirable good sense and scepticism' 66; XXXVIII.128; XLIV.140, 174; LIII.115; LVI.8; LVIII.112; 'the fine philosophy of Hume' LIX.87; LX.90; LXI.54, 69; LXIX.11; LXX.69, 93.

Hunter, John [1728–93; writer on medical subjects]: XLIII.90.

Hurd, Richard [1720–1808; bp of Worcester; editor of Cowley; Gibbon owned his *An Introduction to the Study of the Prophecies Concerning the Christian Church, and, in particular, Concerning the Church of Papal Rome* (London, 1772) and *Moral and Political Dialogues* (London, 1759, and, 3 vols., London, 1771)]: XV.67; XXX.30.

Hutchinson, Thomas [1698–1769; editor of Xenophon]: IX.3; X.108; XXIV.37, 41; XXXII.23; XLI.44; XLII.77; XLVI.79.

Hyde, Thomas [1636–1703; Gibbon owned his *Syntagma Dissertationum* (Oxford, 1767) and *Veterum Persarum et Parthorum et Medorum Religionis Historia* (Oxford, 1760)]: VIII.7, 9, 10, 16, 17, 26, 30; XXXI.46; XLII.36, 38, 56, 85; L.57, 'the original ideas of the Magi are darkly and doubtfully explored by their apologist Dr. Hyde' 110; 'how laboriously does the curious spirit of Europe explore the darkest and most distant antiquities' LI.18, 198; LII.62, 102; LVII.45; LXV.10; LXVIII.53.

I

Ibelin, Jean d' [count of Jaffa and Ascalon; restorer of the *Assises de Jerusalem*]:

Ibelin, Jean d'—*cont*
LVIII.135, 136, 137, 138, 141, 143; LXI.73.

Ibn Chaukel: LI.72.

Ibn Said: LIX.7.

'Icilius, Quintus', *see* Guischardt, Carl Gottlieb.

Idatius [historian; bp of Iria Flavia]: XI.45; XVIII.11, 53; XIX.13, 50; XXVI.94, 105, 112, 119, 123; XXVIII.27; XXXI.135, 147, 150, 156, 157, 166; XXXIII.12, 14, 15, 37; XXXV.4, 15, 33, 35, 44, 59, 78; XXXVI.4, 11, 23, 27, 30, 47, 53, 54, 73.

Ignatius [abp of Nicæa]: XV.35, 113; XVI.70, 93; XXXVII.62.

Infessura, Stefano: LXX.70, 78, 81, 85, 86, 98.

Ingulphus [secretary to William the Conqueror; abbot of Croyland; author of a chronicle of Croyland Abbey]: LVII.72.

Innocent III [1160/61–1216]: LIX.20; LX.48, 86, 91; 'the epistles of Innocent III. are a rich fund for the ecclesiastical and civil institution of the Latin empire of Constantinople' LXI.6.

Institutes, *see* Justinian.

Irenæus [*c.*120–*c.*200; st]: XV.33, 63, 74, 77, 111, 124, 132, 177; XVI.21; XLVII.11, 45; XLIX.3.

Isæus [Greek orator]: XLIV.144, 151.

Isæus, Josephus [editor of Lactantius]: XX.2.

Isaiah: XV.63.

Isidore of Charax [or Characensis; writer on Persian geography]: XL.67.

Isidore Pacensis [bp of Beja; chronicler of the Arabs in Spain]: LII.25.

Isidore of Pelusium [st]: XLVII.21, 'Isidore is a saint, but he never became a bishop; and I half suspect that the pride of Diogenes trampled on the pride of Plato' 32, 36.

Isidore of Seville [*c.*560–636; st; bp of Seville, cardinal]: XVIII.43, 45; XXX.77; XXXI.80, 99, 155, 166; XXXIII.14, 37; XXXV.33, 44, 59; XXXVI.16; XXXVII.96, 139; XXXVIII.21, 56, 122; XXXIX.104; XLI.46, 48; LXVIII.11, 28.

Isocrates: LIV.36; LXX.9.

Italicus, Silius [25?–101 AD]: XXIII.13; XXXI.5; XLI.66.

Itinerary of Antoninus: XXVI.79; XXVII.30.

Ives, Isbrand: XXVI.32.

J

Jablonski, Paul Ernst [Gibbon owned his *Institutiones Historiæ Christianæ*, 3 vols. (Frankfort-on-Oder, 1766–7)]: 'most learned and rational' XLVII.19, 40, 'The learned but cautious Jablonski did not always speak the whole truth' 59, 138.

Jallaloddin: L.103.

James of Sarug: XXXIII.45.

Jamsilla, Nicholas de: LVI.139; LXIX.50.

Jeffrey of Monmouth [or Geoffrey; 1100?–1154]: XIV.8; XXXVIII.129, 146.

Jenisch, Graf Bernard von [Oriental scholar]: LI.203.

Jennabi, Al [or Jannabi; Arabian historian]: L.48, 98, 'credulous' 99, 'a credulous doctor' 111, 119, 121, 122, 128, 143, 145, 150, 152, 162, 168, 108; LIX.104.

Jeremiah: LXVIII.64.

Jerome [*c.*347–419/20; st]: I.24; X.88; XI.45, 65, 82; XII.76, 105, 106; XIII.10, 36; XIV.112; XV.22, 72, 93, 109, 185; XVI.65, 115, 125; XVII.42; XVIII.9, 16, 23, 35, 45, 49, 59, 60, 76; XIX.15; XX.29, 52; XXI.33, 47, 75, 76, 149; XXII.21; XXIII.35, 61, 63, 67, 92, 131; XXV.16, 64, 72, 76, 78, 79, 80, 81, 87, 100, 'whose veracity I find no reason to question' 117, 124, 128, 151, 153, 154; XXVI.2, 'fair, though concise' 69, 85, 87, 94, 101; XXVII.8, 34, 35, 36, 52, 96; XXVIII.20, 23, 35, 71, 72, 73, 82; XXIX.11, 18, 31; XXX.3, 8, 28, 29, 85, 91; XXXI.11, 28, 48, 76, 101, 104, 113, 114, 153, 186; XXXII.12, 55, 62; XXXIII.28; XXXIV.16; XXXVII.7, 10, 11, 13, 16, 17, 21, 'Jerom's devout ladies form a very considerable portion of his works: the particular treatise, which he styles the Epitaph of Paula . . ., is an elaborate and extravagant panegyric. The exordium is ridiculously turgid . . .' 28, 29, 34, 44, 54, 65; 'Gen. Obs.'.5; XLIV.125, 129, 166; XLVII.10; L.24; LIV.5.

Jobert, Louis [or Joubert; 1676–1756; Gibbon owned his *La Science des medailles*, 2 vols. (Paris, 1739)]: XXXIII.32; LXIX.38; LXX.77.

Johan. Antiochen., *see* John Scholasticus.

St John: XXI.20, 21; XLVII.7, 14.

1 John: XXXVII.115; XLVII.10.

John of Biclar [historian of the Visigoths]: XXXVIII.122.

John Damascenus [*c.*675–749]: XLIX.10, 13, 19, 22, 23, 25.

John the Deacon: XLV.64, 65, 68, 71; XLIX.91.

John Philoponus: LI.115.

John of Salisbury [1115/20–1180; Gibbon owned his *Policraticus, sive de Nugis Curialium et Vestigiis Philosophorum* (Leyden, 1639)]: XXXVIII.95; XLV.62; 'it is a pity that this miscellaneous writer has not given us less morality and erudition, and more pictures of himself and the times' LXIX.10.

John Scholasticus [or John Antioch; *c.*503–577; patriarch of Constantinople]: XIII.50; XXV.11.

John of Tinemouth [fl. 1366]: XXXVIII.150.

Johnson, Samuel [1709–84; poet, essayist, critic and lexicographer; Gibbon owned his *A Dictionary of the English Language*, 2 vols. (London, 1755), *The Idler*, 2 vols. (London, 1761, and London, 1783), *A Journey to the Western Islands of Scotland* (London, 1775), *Letters to and from the late Samuel Johnson*, 2 vols. (London, 1788), *Political Tracts* (London, 1776), *The Prince of Abissinia* (London, 1759), *The Rambler*, 4 vols. (London, 1752, and London, 1784), *Taxation no Tyranny* (London, 1775) and *The Works of the English Poets*, 68 vols. (London, 1779–81)]: 'Dr. Johnson affirms, that *few* English words are of British extraction. Mr. Whitaker, who understands the British language, has discovered more that *three thousand*, and actually produces a long and various catalogue' XXXVIII.144; LII.50; 'a critic of high renown' LVII.40; 'the workings of a bigotted though vigorous mind, greedy of every pretence to hate and persecute those who dissent from his creed' LVIII.20; 'in one of the Ramblers, Dr. Johnson praises Knolles . . . as the first of historians, unhappy only in the choice of his subject. Yet I much doubt whether a partial and verbose compilation from Latin writers, thirteen hundred folio pages of speeches and battles, can either instruct or amuse an enlightened age, which requires from the historian some tincture of philosophy and criticism' LXIV.41; LXVIII.28, 'above sense and reason' 53.

Joinville, Jean, sire de [1224–1319]: LII.22; LIII.35, 40; LIX.50, 61, 73, 77, 85, 91, 92, 93, 94, 95, 96, 98, 99, 100; 'Champagne may boast of the two first historians, the noble authors of French prose, Villehardouin and Joinville' LX.33, 60; LXI.48, 57.

Jones, Sir William [1746–94; orientalist; Gibbon owned his *An Essay on the Law of Bailments* (London, 1781), *Poems, consisting chiefly of Translations from the Asiatic Languages* (Oxford, 1772) and *Poeseos Asiaticæ Commentatiorum Libri Sex* (London, 1774); translator of the *History of Nader Shah*]: XXVI.20; XLII.49, 53; 'a scholar, a lawyer, and a man of genius' XLIV.144, 151, 168; XLVI.89; L.41, 171, 176; 'I have perused, with much pleasure, Sir William Jones's Latin Commentary on Asiatic poetry . . ., which was composed in the youth of that wonderful linguist. At present, in the maturity of his taste and judgment, he would perhaps abate of the fervent, and even partial, praise which he has bestowed on the Orientals' LII.71; 'an excellent discourse' LVII.42.

Jordan, Johann Christoph von [Gibbon owned his *De Originibus Sclavicis*, 2 vols. (Vindobonæ, 1745)]: 'his collections and researches are useful to elucidate the antiquities of Bohemia and the adjacent countries: but his plan is narrow, his style barbarous, his criticism shallow, and the Aulic counsellor is not free from the

Jordan, Johann Christoph von—*contd* prejudices of a Bohemian' LV.8, 9, 10.

Jornandes [properly, Jordanes; fl. mid sixth century AD; author of *De Rebus Geticis*]: IX.3; X.4, 5, 6, 18, 21, 26, 29, 36, 45, 47, 54, 56, 126, 127, 128; XI.24; XIII.69; XIV.101; XVIII.43, 45; XXV.140, 142, 149; XXVI.55, 56, 57, 'the rancour of a Goth' 58, 62, 65, 69, 72, 94, 118, 119, 121, 122, 129, 130; XXX.1, 4, 23, 27, 45, 60; XXXI.80, 99, 125, 129, 131, 136, 159, 160, 166; XXXIII.13; XXXIV.1, 6, 9, 12, 13, 15, 18, 26; XXXV.5, 15, 30, 33, 37, 38, 44, 46, 48, 49, 50, 65, 67, 69, 70; XXXVI.11, 16, 23, 27, 47, 88, 91, 94, 96, 102, 112, 120, 127; XXXVII.77; XXXVIII.6, 56; XXXIX.1, 2, 5, 12, 16, 36, 40, 45, 50, 105, 106; XL.7, 156; XLI.52, 64, 101, 110; XLII.10, 11, 16; XLIII.6, 26, 27, 40.

Jortin, John [1698–1770; Gibbon owned his *The Life of Erasmus*, 2 vols. (London, 1758–60), *Remarks on Ecclesiastical History*, 2 vols. (London, 1767), and *Tracts*, 2 vols. (London, 1790)]: XIV.38; XV.59; XVI.108; 'his usual freedom' XXI.45, 'Jortin . . . who examines the Arian controversy with learning, candour, and ingenuity' 58, 77, 86, 65; XXV.7, 69, 76; 'a correct and liberal scholar' XXVII.25; 'Jortin . . . censures, with becoming asperity, the style and sentiments of this intolerant law' XXVIII.55; XXX.29; XXXII.71; XXXVII.39; XL.11, 23.

Josephus ['false']: XVI.7.

Josephus, Flavius[37–*c.*100; historian]: I.39, 61, 62; II.63, 75, 79, 84; III.28; XV.4, 7, 8, 27, 59, 129, 200; XVI.1, 31, 36, 40, 42; XXI.11, 14; XXIII.74; XXVIII.48; XLII.79; XLIV.18, 133; XLVII.7; LI.53, 81; LVIII.106.

Journal de Henri IV, see L' Estoile, Pierre de.

Jouve, Joseph [1701–58; author of *Histoire de la conquête de la Chine, par les Tartares Mantcheoux*]: XXVI.36.

Jovius, Paulus: LXVIII.1.

Julian the Apostate [331–63; emperor]: I.4, 15, 17, 19; III.24, 26, 40, 44; IV.5, 46; VI.80; XI.6, 15, 86; XII.34, 60, 66; XIII.12, 15, 63; XIV.18, 42, 91, 100; XV.83, 143; 184; XVI.140; XVII.61, 63, 64, 69, 92; XVIII.4, 6, 10, 11, 25, 32, 33, 45, 51, 52, 57, 58, 60, 62, 63, 66, 70, 74, 77, 79, 83, 85, 86, 88, 89, 90, 92, 93, 94, 96, 98, 99; XIX.8, 15, 18, 24, 26, 27, 33, 34, 37, 38, 64, 67, 69, 70, 71, 76, 81, 82, 83, 84, 85, 87, 90, 92, 93, 94; XX.12; XXI.156; XXII.10, 12, 16, 18, 23, 24, 26, 36, 'the epistle to the Athenians . . . is one of the best manifestoes to be found in any language' 37, 42, 'much eloquence, and some affectation' 46, 47, 48, 49, 52, 57, 58, 59, 66, 70, 73, 75, 79, 'Julian's Latin style . . . is forcible and elaborate, but less pure than his Greek' 84; 'the variety and copiousness of the Greek tongue seems inadequate to the fervour of his devotion' XXIII.1, 4, 6, 10, 14, 15, 17, 18, 19, 20, 21, 26, 27, 34, 36, 37, 38, 39, 41, 42, 43, 45, 50, 52, 54, 73, 75, 86, 87, 88, 90, 111, 113, 114, 117, 120, 127, 128, 133, 134; XXIV.1, 2, 5, 9, 11, 13, 15, 16, 19, 23, 29, 30, 32, 33, 43, 152; LI.54.

Jungendorum Marium Fluviorumque Molimina, see Oberlin, Jérémie Jacques.

Justin [Marcus Junianus Justinus; fl. third century AD; historian of the East]: XIII.55; XV.2; XXVI.6, 47.

Justin Martyr [*c.*100–165]: XV.24, 38, 64, 65, 71, 75, 91, 93, 95, 131, 141, 177, 186, 193; XVI.12, 19, 21, 99; XX.29, 42; XXI.25; XLVII.2.

Justinian [483–565; emperor]: XVII.119, 156; XX.97, 105, 129; XXXVII.35; XL.29, 36, 56, 88, 113, 124, 157, 159; XLI.24, 27; XLIII.55, 57; XLIV.41, 64, 71, 75, 80, 106, 130, 149, 153, 157, 158, 175, 198; LIII.97.

Justinian Code, see Codex Justiniani.

Juvenal [Decimus Junius Juvenalis; 55–127 AD; satirist]: II.3, 9, 10, 43, 110; IV.36; V.64; VI.70; X.2; XV.53, 55; XIX.4; XXI.173; XXIV.60; XXXI.44, 52, 61, 69, 70, 88; XXXII.25; XXXIX.102; XLII.2; XLIII.45; XLIV.67, 125, 175, 180; LXIX.47.

K

Kämpfer, Engelbert [Gibbon owned his *Amœnitatum Exoticarum Politico-Physico-Medicarum Fasciculi V* (Lemgo, 1712) and *The History of Japan*, 2 vols. (London, 1728)]: 'the learned Kæmpfer, as a botanist, an antiquary, and a traveller, has exhausted . . . the whole subject of palm-trees' XXIV.55.

Kühn, Joachim [or Kahn; 1647–97; classical scholar]: XVIII.37; XXX.9.

Katona, István [1732–1811; Gibbon owned his *Historia Critica Primorum Hungariæ Ducum* (Pest, 1778) and *Historia Critica Regum Hungariæ Stirpis Arpadianæ*, 4 vols. (Pest, 1779–81)]: 'Katona . . . by his learning, judgment, and perspicuity, deserves the name of a critical historian' LV.18, 19, 20, 29, 30, 32, 34, 36, 39, 40, 41, 'his usual industry' 42, 62, 79, 82; LVII.71; LVIII.39, 59; LX.47.

Keating, Geoffrey [1570?–1644?; author of *The General History of Ireland* (Dublin, 1723)]: IX.13.

Khondemir [Persian historian; son of Mircond, and abbreviator of his father's work]: XLVI.15, 22; LXV.5, 23, 44, 48.

Kienlong, *see* Chi'en-Lung.

1 Kings: XXIII.74.

Kippis, Andrew [1725–95; Nonconformist divine and biographer; editor of *Biographia Britannica*]: LXI.66.

Knight, Samuel [1675–1746; Gibbon owned his *The Life of Dr. John Colet* (London, 1754) and *The Life of Erasmus* (Cambridge, 1726)]: 'curious' LXVI.114, 115.

Knolles, Richard [1550?–1610; author of *A General History of the Turks to the Present Year* (London, 1603)]: 'in one of the Ramblers, Dr. Johnson praises Knolles . . . as the first of historians, unhappy only in the choice of his subject. Yet I much doubt whether a partial and verbose compilation from Latin writers, thirteen hundred folio pages of speeches and battles, can either instruct or amuse an enlightened age, which requires from the historian some tincture of philosophy and criticism' LXIV.41.

Kochler, Adamus [commentator on Abulfeda]: LI.67.

Koran: XLVI.69; L.37, 38, 62, 65, 70, 72, 74, 76, 77, 78, 84, 85, 87, 88, 89, 91, 92, 96, 98, 99, 102, 103, 104, 107, 109, 110, 111, 114, 115, 123, 127, 131, 133, 147, 149, 158; LI.50, 56, 220; LXV.30; LXVIII.3.

Kuster, Ludolph [editor of Suidas and of Mill's *Prolegomena*]: XXXVII.75; XXXIX.8; XL.17; XLIV.72.

L

L'Estoile, Pierre de [editor of the *Journal de Henri IV*]: XXXI.76.

La Bastie, Joseph Bimard, baron de [1703–42; editor of Jobert's *Science des medailles*]: XX.82; XXI.170, 172; XXXIII.32; LXIX.38; LXX.77.

La Bléterie, Jean Philippe René de [1696–1772; Jansenist abbé; Gibbon owned his *Vie de l'empereur Julien* (Paris, 1746) and his *Histoire de l'empereur Jovien*, 2 vols. (n.p., 1748)]: III.19; IX.80; XII.43; XIII.99; XVI.37, 117; XVII.61, 'the Abbé de la Bleterie . . . who delights to pursue the vestiges of the old [Roman] constitution, and who sometimes finds them in his copious fancy' 92; XIX.27, 69, 81; XXI.137; XXII.12, 37, 'an elegant translation' 46, 'candour and ingenuity' 50, 58, 60, 73, 75, 79, 84; XXIII.23, 27, 31, 75, 115, 140; XXIV.1, 11, 20, 30, 40, 95, 'an elaborate history of his [Jovian's] short reign; a work remarkably distinguished by elegance of style, critical disquisition, and religious prejudice' 103, 113, 'a severe casuist . . . I have never found much delight or instruction in such political metaphysics' 123, 128, 129, 134; XXV.5, 10; XLI.32.

La Croze, Mathurin Veyssière de [1661–1739; orientalist; author of the *Christianisme des Indes*]: XL.77; 'most learned and rational' XLVII.19, 20, 33, 34, 35,

La Croze, Mathurin Veyssière de—*contd* 'the universal scholar' 40, 55, 59, 101, 111, 116, 118, 122, 'a learned and agreeable work' 124, 125, 127, 130, 131, 'the work of a Jesuit must have sterling merit when it is praised by La Croze' 139, 158, 160, 161.

La Flamma, Gualvaneus de [medieval Italian chronicler]: LXXI.47.

La Fontaine, Jean de [1621–95; poet and fabulist; Gibbon owned his *Œuvres diverses*, 4 vols. (Amsterdam, 1744), *Contes et nouvelles*, 2 vols. (London, 1755) and (The Hague, 1778), *Fables*, 2 vols. (Paris, 1757) and *Fables choisies*, 2 vols. (Geneva, 1777)]: XXXV.53; LVI.140.

La Marche, Olivier de [*c.*1425–1502; author of *Memoires*]: LXVIII.93.

La Mothe le Vayer, François de [1588–1672; Gibbon owned his *Œuvres*, 14 vols. (Dresden, 1756–9)]: XIII.51; XXI.29; XXXVII.4; XL.12, 23; XLI.97.

La Roque, Jean de [1661–1745; traveller; author of *Voyage de Syrie* (Amsterdam, 1723) and *Voyage de l'Arabie Heureuse* (Amsterdam, 1716)]: XLVII.135, 136, 138; L.2, 40.

La Thaumassière, Gaspard Thaumas de [fl. 1702–12]: LVIII.132.

Labat, Jean Baptiste [1663–1738; traveller; Gibbon owned his *Nouvelle relation de l'Afrique Occidentale*, 5 vols. (Paris, 1728), *Voyage aux isles françoises de l'Amerique* (The Hague, 1724), *Voyage du Chevalier Des Marchais en Guinée*, 4 vols. (Amsterdam, 1731), and *Voyages en Espagne et en Italie*, 8 vols. (Amsterdam, 1731)]: XXXVII.5, 31; XLI.78, 88; 'his usual pleasantry' LI.173; 'very lively' LVIII.27; LXIX.64, 65, 78; LXXI.74.

Labbé, Charles [1648–1723; Gibbon owned his *Cyrilli Philoxeni, Aliorumque Veterum Glossaria Latino-Græca et Græco-Latina a Labbæo Collecta* (Paris, 1679)]: XLIX.5, 18.

Labbe, Philippe [or Labb; 1607–67; editor of the *Notitia Dignitatum Imperii Romani*]: XXII.31.

Lactantius, Lucius Cælius Firmianus [*c.*240–*c.*320; probable author of the work *De Mortibus Persecutorum* ascribed in MS. to Cæcilius]: XI.22; XIII.3, 8, 9, 10, 35, 53, 62, 63, 85, 86, 91, 92, 93, 94, 103, 104, 107; XIV.4, 5, 6, 7, 13, 14, 17, 18, 21, 22, 26, 28, 30, 32, 34, 35, 37, 39, 63, 69, 70, 73, 79, 80, 81, 82, 83, 84, 85; XV.38, 62, 64, 68, 88, 193; XVI.64, 121, 125, 132, 134, 137, 142, 147, 148, 150, 151, 152, 154, 155, 156, 161, 165, 173, 174, 176, 184; XX.1, 2, 14, 15, 17, 22, 35, 'it is certain, that this historical declamation [*De Mortibus Persecutorum*] was composed and published, while Licinius, sovereign of the East, still preserved the friendship of Constantine, and of the Christians. Every reader of taste must perceive, that the style is of a very different and inferior character to that of Lactantius; and such indeed is the judgement of Le Clerc and Lardner . . . Three arguments from the title of the book, and from the names of Donatus and Cæcilius, are produced by the advocates for Lactantius . . . Each of these proofs is singly weak and defective; but their concurrence has great weight. I have often fluctuated, and shall *tamely* follow the Colbert MS. in calling the author (whoever he was) Cæcilius' 40, 41, 101; XXI.35; XXVII.96; XXX.57; 'an elegant and specious work [*Institutes of Christianity*]' XLIV.97, 142, 166; 'the last, as well as the most eloquent, of the Latin apologists' XLIX.2.

Lamberti, Arcangelo [author of *Relation de la Mingrelie*]: 'all the knowledge and prejudices of a missionary' XLII.67, 75, 83.

Lambertus [1025–*c.*1088; chronicler]: LVII.72.

Lameti [cartographer of Rome]: XLI.87.

Lami, Giovanni [1719–70; classical scholar and ecclesiastical historian; editor of Meursius; Gibbon owned his *De Eruditione Apostolorum*, 2 vols. (Florence, 1766)]: XLIV.47; 'the learned John Lami' LIII.4.

Lampridius, Ælius: VI.47; XIX.6; XLIV.196; XLIX.3.

Lancelot, Claude [1615–95; grammarian; biographer of Francis Philelphus; Gibbon owned his *Le Jardin de racines grecques mises en vers français* (Paris, 1741) and *Nouvelle méthode pour apprendre facilement la langue grecque* [The Grammar of Port Royal] (Paris, 1754)]: LXVI.79; LXVIII.4, 67.

Lancisi, Giovanni Maria [1654–1720; physician; Gibbon owned his *Dissertatio de Nativis deque Adventitiis Romani Cœli Qualitatibus* (Rome, 1711)]: 'an ingenious treatise' LXXI.38.

Lange, Pierre de [traveller]: XLII.89.

Langlès, Louis Matthieu [1763–1824; French orientalist; translator of Tamerlane's *Institutes* (Paris, 1787)]: 'learned' LXV.3, 20, 42.

Larcher, Pierre Henri [1726–1812; Hellenist; commentator on and translator of, Herodotus]: XLII.85; XLIV.10; 'learned' LXV.77; LXVI.23.

Lardner, Nathaniel [1684–1768; Nonconformist divine; biblical and patristic scholar; Gibbon owned his *A Large Collection of Ancient Jewish and Heathen Testimonies to the Truth of the Christian Religion*, 4 vols. (London, 1764–7), and *The Credibility of the Gospel History*, 17 vols. (London, 1741–62)]: XV.153, 'the learned Dr. Lardner' 161, 191, 195; XVI.32, 41, 57, 138; XVIII.9; XX.1, 40; XXI.2, 167; XXIII.30, 84; XXIV.28; 'Lardner . . . has copiously and fairly examined this dark transaction [the persecution of Antioch] of the reign of Valens' XXV.49; 'pure learning, good sense, and moderation' XXVII.51, 56; XXVIII.13, 29, 45, 57; XXXI.90; XLIX.3, 'the candid Lardner' 9.

Lascaris, Janus [1445–1534; humanist and Byzantinist]: LXVI.113.

Laugier, Marc Antoine [1713–69; author of the *Histoire de Venise* (Paris, 1728)]: LX.37, 'a work of some merit, which I have chiefly used for the constitutional part' 39, 41.

Launoy, Jean de [1603–78; ecclesiastical historian and theologian]: XLIX.30, 55, 57.

Le Beau, Jean Baptiste [1602–1670; antiquarian and writer on the Roman legion]: 'that learned academician, in a series of memoirs, has collected all the passages of the ancients that relate to the Roman legion' I.38.

Le Beau, Charles [1701–78; author of *Histoire du Bas-empire*, 10 vols. (Paris, 1757–66)]: XLIX.77; LIII.34; LX.64, 89; LXI.2, 35.

Le Bœuf, Jean [1687–1760; abbé and antiquarian; Gibbon owned his *Dissertation sur l'état des anciens habitans du Soissonois* (Paris, 1735)]: 'an antiquarian, whose name was happily expressive of his talents' XIX.66; XXXV.18; XXXVIII.52, 54.

Le Clerc, Jean [1657–1736; Arminian scholar; Gibbon owned his *Ars Critica*, 2 vols. (Amsterdam, 1697, and Amsterdam, 1730), *Bibliothèque ancienne et moderne*, 29 vols. (The Hague, 1726–30), *Bibliothèque choisie*, 28 vols. (Amsterdam, 1718), *Bibliothèque universelle et historique*, 26 vols. (Amsterdam, 1700–13), *Harmonia Evangelica* (Amsterdam, 1699), *Historia Ecclesiastica Duorum Primorum a Christo Nato Sæculorum* (Amsterdam, 1716) and *Parrhasiana, ou pensées diverses*, 2 vols. (Amsterdam, 1699–1701)]: XV.19, 22, 23, 'dull, but exact' 32, 58, 113, 118, 124, 195; XVI.31, 32, 36, 76; XVII.4; XX.40; XXI.11, 12, 17, 18, 22, 25, 38, 39, 51, 53, 55, 80; XXIII.74, 101; XXVII.27, 41, 44; XXVIII.56; XXXIII.31; XXXIV.2; XXXIX.89; XLIV.143; 'the Arminian Le Clerc . . . was free both in his temper and situation; his sense is clear, but his thoughts are narrow; he reduces the reason or folly of ages to the standard of his private judgment, and his impartiality is sometimes quickened, and sometimes tainted, by his opposition to the fathers' XLVII.1, 'most learned and rational' 19; L.24; 'a

Le Clerc, Jean—*contd* modern (John Le Clerc), who sometimes assumed the same name, was equal to old Philoponus in diligence, and far superior in good sense and real knowledge' LI.115; LIII.110; LIV.38; LVI.83; 'honest and rational' LVIII.119; LXX.73.

Le Comte, Louis Daniel [1655–1729; editor of *Mémoires sur la Chine*, 2 vols. (Paris, 1696)]: XV.144; XXVI.31, 51; 'Gen. Obs.'.6; XL.61.

Le Fevre, Tanneguy [1615–72; editor of the works of Horace as *Opera* (Saumur, 1671)]: XIII.89; XVI.36.

Le Grand, Joachim [1653–1733]: XV.25.

Le Maire, Jacques Joseph [cartographer]: XLIII.35.

Leges. Burgundicæ, see Du Tillet, Jean.

Leges Wallicæ Ecclesiasticæ et Civiles, see Clarke, William.

Legrand d'Aussy, Pierre Jean B. [1737–1800; historian; author of *Vie privée des François*, 3 vols. (Paris, 1782)]: XLVI.25; LX.6; LXI.65.

Leibnitz, Gottfried Wilhelm von, [1646–1716; philosopher, mathematician and political adviser; Gibbon owned his *Esprit de Leibnitz*, 2 vols. (Lyons, 1772), *Essais de Théodicée*, 2 vols. (Lausanne, 1709, and Lausanne, 1760), and *Origines Guelficæ*, 5 vols. (Hanover, 1750–80)]: X.68; 'accurate chronology' XLIX.129, 140; LIV.39; 'critical industry' LVI.60; 'the great Leibnitz . . ., a master of the history of the middle ages' LXI.67; LXX.98.

Leich, Johann Heinrich [eighteenth-century Byzantinist; Gibbon owned his edition (with J. J. Reiske) of Constantine Porphyrogenitus, *De Ceremoniis*, 2 vols. (Leipzig, 1751–4)]: 'a splendid MS. of Constantine . . . was published in a splendid edition by Leich and Reiske . . ., with such lavish praise as editors never fail to bestow on the worthy or worthless object of their toil' LIII.2, 56.

Lenfant, Jacques [1661–1728; church historian; Gibbon owned his *Préservatif contre la réunion avec le siège de Rome*, 4 vols. (Amsterdam, 1723), *Histoire du concile de Constance*, 2 vols. (Amsterdam, 1714, and Amsterdam, 1727), and *Histoire du concile de Pise*, 2 vols. (Amsterdam, 1724, and Utrecht, 1731); he also composed a *Histoire du concile de Basle*]: XLIX.132, 153; LXV.50; LXVI.30, 'a learned and liberal protestant' 38; LXVII.16, 19, 29; LXIX.99; LXX.66, 74, 75, 'the histories of the three successive councils, Pisa, Constance, and Basil, have been written with a tolerable degree of candour, industry, and elegance, by a Protestant minister, M. Lenfant, who retired from France to Berlin. They form six volumes in quarto; and as Basil is the worst, so Constance is the best, part of the collection' 76, 79.

Leo III: LX.1.

Leo Africanus, *see* Africanus, Leo.

Leo the Deacon [or Leo Diaconus]: LII.116, 117, 118; LV.69, 72; LVI.20.

Leo [or the Philosopher; emperor; author of works of military strategy]: LIII.67, 71, 73, 77, 78, 79, 80, 82, 'the XVIIIth chapter of the tactics of the different nations, is the most historical and useful of the whole Collection of Leo. The manners and arms of the Saracens . . ., the Roman emperor was too frequently called upon to study' 84, 85, 90, 93; LV.27, 29; LVI.8.

Leontius [bp of Neapolis; biographer of St John the Almsgiver (or the Eleemosynary)]: XLVI.61; XLVII.147.

Leontius [first Greek professor at Florence], *see* Pilatus, Leo.

Lequien de la Neufville, Jacques [1647–1728; historian; editor of John Damascenus]: XLIX.10, 22.

Les Mois [French poet]: XXXVI.139.

Lestocq, Jean Louis [or Johann Ludwig; 1712–79; lawyer]: XX.40.

Leti, Gregorio [1630–1701; author of *Conclavi de' Pontfici Romani* (Rome, 1667); Gibbon owned his *Vita di Sisto-Quinto*,

3 vols. (Amsterdam, 1721), and *Il Sindicato di Alexandro VII. Con il suo Viaggio nell'altro Mondo* (1668)]: LXIX.71; 'a copious and amusing work, but which does not command our absolute confidence' LXX.95, 96, 97; LXXI.34.

Leunclavius, Joannes [Gibbon owned his *Historiæ Musulmanæ Turcorum Libri XVIII* (Frankfort, 1591)]: XVII.8; LIII.5; LXIII.28, 41; LXIV.55, 56, 58; LXV.37, 44, 45, 57, 81; LXVI.22; LXVII.32; LXVIII.11, 12, 13, 16, 70, 74, 84.

Lévesque, Pierre Charles [1736–1812; historian and translator; Gibbon owned his *Histoire de Russie et des peuples soumis à la domination russe*, 8 vols. (Yverdon, 1783)]: XXXIX.41; LIII.65; LV.26, 45, 50, 55, 59, 62, 65, 67, 'M. Levesque has extracted, from old chronicles and modern researches, the most satisfactory account of the religion of the *Slavi*, and the conversion of Russia' 74, 81; LXIV.14; LXV.20; LXVII.7, 'curious narrative' 8, 9.

Libanius [314–93; sophist and rhetorician]: II.41, 89; XIII.91; XIV.18; XVI.13, 162; XVIII.33, 60, 62, 97; XIX.8, 12, 29, 33, 64, 71, 73, 77, 78, 79, 80, 81, 83, 84, 86, 91; XXI.3, 167, 168, 169; XXII.10, 16, 17, 21, 23, 30, 35, 43, 44, 49, 50, 53, 55, 57, 62, 63, 69, 72, 77, 82, 83; XXIII.11, 26, 27, 29, 32, 33, 34, 36, 43, 46, 48, 50, 53, 87, 95, 97, 100, 104, 113; XXIV.10, 16, 17, 18, 19, 20, 23, 24, 25, 26, 'the vain, prolix, but curious narrative of his own life' 28, 43, 51, 57, 58, 64, 67, 68, 72, 74, 76, 77, 78, 87, 90, 94, 99, 108, 111, 112, 119, 120, 121, 130, 133, 134, 139; XXV.9, 43, 113; XXVI.2, 95, 133; XXVII.84, 85, 86, 90; XXVIII.24, 27, 28, 29, 32, 42, 53, 58, 59, 61, 63.

Liberatus: XXXIX.10; XLI.91; XLVII.41, 47, 51, 61, 62, 66, 72, 79, 94, 97, 128, 141, 145.

Lignages d'outremer: LXI.73.

Ligorio, Pirro [or Ligorius; 1510–83; architect and painter; topographer of Rome]: LXXI.75.

Limborch, Philippus van [Gibbon owned his *De Veritate Religionis Christianæ* (Gouda, 1687) and *Historia Inquisitionis* (Amsterdam, 1692)]: XV.15; XXI.24; 'they [the Acts of the Inquisition of Tholouse] deserved a more learned and critical editor' LIV.31, 38.

Lindenbrog, Friedrich [or Lindenbrogius; editor of Ammianus Marcellinus]: XVII.139; XIX.45; XXII.13; XXXIV.8; XXXVIII.63, 71, 99, 148.

Lipsius, Justus [or Joest Lips; 1547–1606; Gibbon owned his *Opera*, 4 vols. (Antwerp, 1637)]: I.45, 61, 65, 68; II.37; III.15; IV.36, 55; V.1; VI.22, 96; IX.79, 42; XII.9; XIV.10; XVI.32, 37; XVII.106, 148, 191; XVIII.51; XX.29; XXV.98; XXVIII.4; XXX.55; XXXI.66, 69; XXXVII.4; XL.62; XLI.81, 86; XLIII.17; XLIV.7, 31, 114, 189, 205.

Liutprand [*c*.920–*c*.972; Lombard diplomat and historian; bp of Cremona]: XVII.53; XXXV.50; XLIX.44, 45, 125, 127, 128, 133, 137; LII.111, 114; LIII.11, 19, 33, 35, 38, 'the two embassies of Liutprand to Constantinople, all that he saw or suffered in the Greek capital, are pleasantly described by himself' 50, 51, 'it must not be forgot, that the bishop of Cremona was a lover of scandal' 63, 69, 70, 86, 88, 91, 92, 101; lv.14, 16, 'his colours are glaring' 31, 34, 36, 37, 38, 44, 63; LVI.6, 14, 20; LX.37.

Livy [Titus Livius; 59 BC–AD 17; historian]: I.21, 51; II.17; III.7, 8; IV.53; V.7, 9; VI.82; VII.57; IX.34, 41; X.2, 52; 'the little river or rather torrent of Metaurus near Fano, has been immortalized, by finding such an historian as Livy, and such a poet as Horace' XI.36; XII.3, 58; XIII.88; XV.168, 176, 200; XVII.25, 93, 133; XX.47; XXII.81; XXIII.13; XXVI.93, 130; XXVIII.3; XXX.6, 42, 50, 73; XXXI.7, 9, 10, 14, 15, 32, 50; XXXVI.87, 128; XLIII.15, 36; XLIV.6, 11, 15, 23, 24, 107, 120, 171, 174, 176, 181, 191; XLVI.103; XLIX.48; LI.119; LVIII.60; LXIX.57; LXX.33.

Lobo, Jeronymo [Gibbon owned his *Voyage*

Lobo, Jeronymo—*contd*
historique d'Abissinie (Paris, 1728)]: XV.25; XLII.93.

Locke, John [1632–1704; philosopher and political theorist; Gibbon owned his *Works*, 3 vols. (London, 1759) and 4 vols. (London, 1777)]: XXI.66; XXXIII.20; LIV.39; LXIV.6.

Logothet., Symeon: LV.61, 63.

Longinus [fl. first century AD]: 'here too we may say of Longinus, "his own example strengthens all his laws." Instead of proposing his sentiments with a manly boldness, he insinuates them with the most guarded caution, puts them into the mouth of a friend; and as far as we can collect from a corrupted text, makes a shew of refuting them himself' II.111; XX.42; LIII.112.

Longuerue, Louis Dufour de [1652–1733; historian and *érudit*; Gibbon owned his *Description historique et géographique de la France ancienne et moderne*, 2 vols. (Paris, 1722), and *Longueruana*, 2 vols. (Berlin, 1754)]: XVI.36, 169; XVIII.71, 96; XIX.92; XXIII.125; XXX.4; XXXII.1; XXXV.23; XXXVIII.40, 103, 137; XLIX.108; LI.170; LVI.106; LVIII.1, 44, 50; LXIX.82.

Longus [fl. second to third centuries AD; poet]: XLI.18.

Lowth, Robert [1710–87; bp of London; Gibbon owned his *De Sacra Poesi Hebræorum Prælectiones* (Oxford, 1775), *A Letter to the Author of 'The Divine Legation of Moses Demonstrated'* (London, 1766), *The Life of William of Wykeham* (London, 1758) and *A Short Introduction to English Grammar* (London, 1784)]: 'in the examination of the fourth eclogue, the respectable bishop of London has displayed learning, taste, ingenuity, and a temperate enthusiasm, which exalts his fancy without degrading his judgment' XX.62; L.94, 115, 'a respectable prelate' 116.

Lowthorp: XI.69.

Lucan [Marcus Annæus Lucanus; 39–65; epic poet]: II.40; III.24; V.41; VI.84; IX.63, 69; XIV.27; XV.199; XXIV.117; XXV.47; XXVIII.50; 'the simplicity of truth [in Cæsar] is far greater than the amplifications of Lucan' XXX.78; XLI.8, 71; XLVI.16.

Lucar, Cyril [1572–1638; patriarch of Constantinople]: XLVII.148.

Lucas Tudensis [Galician deacon of the thirteenth century]: LI.169.

Lucian [*c.*120–*c.*180; satirist]: I.29; II.110; X.101; XV.86, 143, 156, 192; XVI.95, 137; XXIII.20; XXIV.31; XXVIII.77; XXXI.64; XL.89, 95, 148.

Lucifer of Cagliari [d. *c.*370; bp of Cagliari; opponent of Arianism]: XXI.94; XXIII.130.

Lucretius [Titus Lucretius Carus; fl. first century BC; poet]: XLIII.90.

Ludewig, Johann Peter von [Gibbon owned his *Vita Justiniani M. atque Theodoræ Augustorum nec non Triboniani Jurisprudentiæ Justinianæ Proscenium* (Halle, 1731)]: XL.1, 3, 9, 27, 34; XLI.27; 'the pious Ludewig' XLII.17; XLIII.72; XLIV.1, 71, 'Ludewig . . . works hard, very hard, to white-wash – the black-a-moor' 72, 76, 77, 82, 94, 98; XLV.1.

Ludolf, Hiob [or Ludolphus; Gibbon owned his *Historia Æthiopica* (Frankfort, 1681)]: XV.25; XLII.92, 93, 96, 99; XLVII.111, 117, 151, 155, 'the mind of Ludolphus was a perfect blank' 156, 157, 158, 159, 160, 161.

St Luke: XVI.32; XLIV.131.

Lycophron [fl. third century BC]: XLIV.18.

Lysias [*c.*445–*c.*380 BC; Greek orator]: XLIV.179.

Lyttelton, George [1709–73; Gibbon owned his *History of the Life of King Henry the Second*, 4 vols. (London, 1767–71)]: XVI.89; XXV.115.

M

Mabillon, Jean [1632–1707; Gibbon owned the *Ouvrages posthumes de J. Mabillon et de Thierry Ruinart*, 3 vols. (Paris, 1724), and *Traité des études monastiques*, 2 vols. (Paris, 1692)]: XVI.73; XXXVII.26, 'an admirable discourse of the learned Mabillon . . .; who, on this occasion, seems to be inspired by the genius of humanity. For such an effort, I can forgive his defence of the holy tear of Vendome' 37, 51, 52, 88; XLV.69; XLIX.71; LVI.32; LVIII.129; LIX.28; LXIX.7; LXXI.7, 33.

Mably, Gabriel Bonnot de [1709–85; Gibbon owned his *Observations sur l'histoire de France*, 2 vols. (Geneva, 1765) and 6 vols. (Kehl, 1783), and *De la manière d'écrire l'histoire* (Paris, c. 1782)]: 'dry cold reason' IX.54; 'the good sense and diligence of the Abbé de Mably' XXXVIII.64, 71, 74, 87, 'His accurate distinction of *times* gives him a merit to which even Montesquieu is a stranger' 90, 97, 112, 120; XLIX.95; LVIII.11.

2 Maccabees: XXI.160.

Machiavelli, Niccolò [1469–1527; Florentine political theorist and historian; Gibbon owned his *Opere*, 6 vols. (Florence, 1782–3), and *Tutte le Opere*, 2 vols. (London, 1747)]: IX.37, 39; XXX.74; LIII.25; 'curious though concise' LXX.85, 89.

Macpherson, James [1736–96; Gibbon owned his *Introduction to the History of Great Britain and Ireland* (London, 1773), *The History of Great Britain*, 2 vols. (London, 1775), *The History and Management of the East India Company*, vol. 1 (London, 1779), and *Original Papers Containing the Secret History of Great Britain, from the Restoration to the Accession of the House of Hannover*, 2 vols. (London, 1775)]: XXV.110.

Macpherson, John [1710–65; Gibbon owned his *Critical Dissertations on the Origin, Antiquities, Language, Government, Manners and Religion of the Ancient Caledonians* (London, 1768)]: VI.14; XV.179; 'Dr. Macpherson was a minister in the Isle of Sky: and it is a circumstance honourable for the present age, that a work, replete with erudition and criticism, should have been composed in the most remote of the Hebrides' XXV.110, 114.

Macrizi [Arabic historian]: LIX.96, 102, 109.

Macrobius [fl. *c.*400]: II.18; XV.49; XXV.24; XXVIII.16, 38, 49; XXXI.48, 49; 'Gen. Obs.'.13; XLIV.19.

Maffei, Francesco Scipione, marchesi [Gibbon owned his *Osservazioni Letterarie che possono servir di Continuazione al Giornal de' Letterati d'Italia*, 6 vols. (Verona, 1737–40), *Istoria Diplomatica* (Mantua, 1727), *Verona Illustrata*, 2 vols. (Verona, 1731–2), and *Della Scienza Chiamata Cavalleresca* (Trento, 1717)]: I.75; 'the clearest and most comprehensive view of the state of Italy under the Cæsars' II.27, 65; III.19; IV.14; XII.91, 92, 93, 'he treats the very difficult subject [of the Coliseum] with all possible clearness, and like an architect, as well as an antiquarian' 94, 95; XIV.57, 62; XXIII.132; XXV.6; XXX.48, 182; XXXIV.1; 'the marquis Scipio Maffei has shewn himself equally capable of enlarged views and minute disquisitions' XXXV.54, 'Maffei . . . has translated and explained this curious letter, in the spirit of a learned antiquarian and a faithful subject, who considered Venice as the only legitimate offspring of the Roman republic' 57, 'taste and learning' 63; XXXVI.126; XXXIX.25, 'Maffei . . . exaggerates the injustice of the Goths, whom he hated as an Italian noble' 26, 56, 70, 71; XLI.108; XLIII.55; XLIV.10; 'Maffei .. and Muratori . . . have asserted the native claims of the Italian idiom: the former with enthusiasm, the latter with discretion; both with learning, ingenuity, and truth' XLV.38; LXXI.49.

Magini, Giovanni Antonio [1555–1617; astronomer, mathematician, geographer and cartographer; Gibbon owned his *Italia* (Bologna, 1620)]: XLIII.35.

Mahudel, Nicolas: XVII.16.

Mailla, Joseph Anne M. de Moyriac de [1679–1748; missionary, sinologist, geographer and translator of the *Histoire*

Mailla, Joseph Anne M. de Moyriac de—*contd* *générale de la Chine*, 12 vols. (Paris, 1777–85)]: XXVI.25, 34.

Maillet, Benoît de [1659–1738; diplomat and man of letters; Gibbon owned his *Description de l'Égypte* (Paris, 1735)]: LI.103, 129, 131, 'Maillet . . . seems to argue with candour and judgement. I am much better satisfied with the observations than with the reading of the French consul. He was ignorant of Greek and Latin literature, and his fancy is too much delighted with the fictions of the Arabs' 137.

Maimbourg, Louis [1610–86; Jesuit; author of *Histoire des iconoclastes*; Gibbon owned the *V. L. a Seckendorf Commentarius Historicus et Apologeticus de Lutheranismo, in quo L. Maimburgii Historia Lutheranismi Exhibetur* (Leipzig, 1694)]: XLIX.18, 38, 84; LVIII.65.

Mairan, Jean-Jacques Dortous de [1678–1771; physician; Gibbon owned his *Éloges des académiciens de l'Académie Royale des Sciences, morts en 1741, 1742, et 1743* (Paris, 1747) and *Lettres au R. P. Parrenin, contenant diverses questions sur la Chine* (Paris, 1770)]: XLIII.79.

Maittaire, Michael [or Mattaire; 1668–1747; Gibbon owned his *Annales Typographici*, 6 vols. (The Hague, 1719–41), *Græcæ Linguæ Dialecti* (The Hague, 1738), *Historia Typographorum Aliquot Parisiensium Vitas et Libros Complectens*, 2 vols. (London, 1717), *Marmorum Arundellianorum, Seldenianorum, aliorumque Academiæ Oxoniensi Donatorum, secunda editio* (London, 1732), *Miscellanea Græcorum Aliquot Scriptorum Carmina cum Versione Latina* (London, 1722) and *Stephanorum Historia, Vitas Ipsorum ac Libros Complectens*, 2 vols. (London, 1709)]: XXXVII.119; XL.14; XLIV.83; LXVI.116.

Malalas, Joannes [or Malala, or Malela; *c.*491–*c.*578; Byzantine chronicler; Gibbon owned his *Historia Chronica* (Oxford, 1691)]: V.22; X.143, 148; XII.67, 98; XIII.32, 44; XV.160; 'a writer whose merit and authority are confined within the limits of his native city' XXIII.107; XXIV.20, 43; XXXII.74, 'in the domestic history of Antioch, John Malala becomes a writer of good authority' 79, 81; XL.11, 35, 38, 46, 48, 49, 52, 86, 90, 100, 107, 123, 154; XLII.42, 82, 94; XLIII.68, 74, 83; 'John Malala . . . who deserves more credit as he draws towards his end' XLVII.84, 90; LI.87.

Malaspina, Saba [thirteenth-century Italian chronicler; author of *Historia Sicula*]: 'a zealous Guelph' LXII.40; LXIX.50.

Malaterra, Galfridus [or Jeffrey; chronicler]: 'they [William Appulus and Galfridus Malaterra] wrote on the spot, . . . and with the spirit of freemen' LVI.15, 22, 25, 26, 'the national, is counterbalanced by the clerical, prejudice' 33, 37, 45, 52, 53, 55, 56, 58, 59, 62, 63, 69, 77, 'authentic, circumstantial, and fair' 86, 92, 93; LVII.32.

Malaxus, Emanuel [author of a *History of the Patriarchs*]: LXVIII.82.

Malchus [historian]: XXVI.114; XXXVI.86, 112, 116, 124; XXXIX.5, 9, 11, 12, 14, 15.

Malespina, Ricordano [Florentine chronicler]: LXII.37; LXIX.50.

Mallet, Paul Henri [1730–1807; historian; Gibbon owned his *Carte du pays de Vaud* (n.p., n.d.), *Des intérêts et des devoirs d'un republicain, par un citoyen de Raguse* (Yverdon, 1770), *Histoire de Danemark*, 6 vols. (Lyons, 1766), and *Introduction à l'histoire de Dannemarc*, 2 vols. (Copenhagen, 1755–6)]: IX.70; X.10, 11.

Maltret, Claude [or Maltretus; 1621–74; Hellenist; Jesuit; editor of Procopius]: XL.14; XLI.61; XLIII.39.

Mamachi, Tommaso Maria [1713–92; Dominican: author of *Antiquitates Christianæ*]: XX.6, 'his great but imperfect work' 76.

Mamertinus, Claudius [fl. *c.*360 AD]: XIII.29, 34; XVII.81, 92, 122; XIX.8, 89, 90; XXII.3, 32, 44, 50, 53, 'lively and forcible' 56, 61, 'an eloquent slave' 74, 78.

Manasses, Constantine [d. 1187; chronicler]: XLIX.15, 18; LIII.95, 103, 113; LVII.36, 38.

Manettus, Janottus [biographer of Nicholas V]: LXVI.110.

Manger, Samuel Hendrik [orientalist; translator and editor of Ahmed Ebn Arabshah]: LXV.5.

Manutius, Aldus [or Aldo Manuzio; 1547–97; editor and printer of classical texts]: XXIII.54; LXVI.113, 116; LXVIII.97.

Manutius, Paulus [or Paolo Manuzio; 1512–74; editor of classical texts]: XXXI.51.

Maracci [author of the *Version and Confutation of the Koran*]: XXXIII.2, 47; XLII.50; L.65, 68, 72, 79, 87, 88, 90, 91, 92, 93, 96, 97, 98, 99, 'a partial accuser' 101, 102, 105, 107, 109, 'virulent, but learned' 110, 111, 114, 123, 127, 131, 'gross bigotry' 149, 158, 162; LXIII.38.

Marakeschi [Arabian historian]: LXIV.43.

Marca, Pierre de [1594–1662; historian and theologian; abp of Paris; Gibbon owned his *Hispanica* (Paris, 1688)]: XVIII.71; XLIX.105.

Marcellinus [count; chronicler]: XXVI.105, 119; XXVII.24; XXVIII.43; XXIX.16, 30; XXX.80; XXXI.106, 118, 135, 146, 150; XXXII.10, 70, 77, 81; XXXIII.37; XXXIV.18, 20, 35, 51; XXXV.4, 30, 68; XXXVI.4, 11, 59, 112; XXXVII.125; XXXVIII.57; XXXIX.9, 12, 13, 16, 'Marcellinus spits the venom of a Greek subject' 22, 45; XL.11, 44, 52, 53, 123, 136; XLI.62, 95, 101, 117; XLII.11, 57; XLIII.6, 16, 30, 40, 88; XLVII.30, 78.

Marcian [jurist]: XLIV.110.

Marcian of Heraclea [geographer]: L.14.

Marei [historian of Egypt]: LVII.67.

Mariana, Juan de [1536–1624; Jesuit; Gibbon owned his *Historiæ de Rebus Hispanicis*, 4 vols. (The Hague, 1733)]: IX.39; XV.176; XXXI.158; XXXVI.92; 'Mariana almost forgets that he is a Jesuit, to assume the style and spirit of a Roman classic' XXXVII.126; XLI.46, 48; 'that historian has infused into his noble work . . . the style and spirit of a Roman classic; and after the XIIth century, his knowledge and judgment may be safely trusted. But the Jesuit is not exempt from the prejudices of his order; he adopts and adorns, like his rival Buchanan, the most absurd of the national legends; he is too careless of criticism and chronology, and supplies, from a lively fancy, the chasms of historical evidence' LI.167, 169, 171, 210; LII.65; 'the reader forgives the Jesuit's defects, in favour, always of his style, and often of his sense' LXII.41; LXV.64.

Marianus, scotus [1028–*c.*1082; chronicler]: XLIX.130; LVII.72.

Marinus [Gibbon owned his *Procli Philosophi Platonici Vita* (Hamburg, 1700)]: XL.151, 152.

Marius Aviticensis [chronicler]: xxxix.61; XLI.101.

St Mark: XLIV.131.

Markland, Jeremiah [1693–1776; classical scholar; editor of Statius; Gibbon owned his *Remarks on the Epistles of Cicero to Brutus, and of Brutus to Cicero* (London, 1745)]: XLI.66; LXVI.106.

Marmol-Caravajal, Luis del [Gibbon owned his *L'Afrique*, tr. N. Perrot, 3 vols. (Paris, 1667)]: XVI.82; XXV.120, 125; XXXIII.26; XLI.19, 23, 45; XLIII.4; 'in . . . captivity among the Moors, the Spaniard Marmol, a soldier of Charles V. compiled his Description of Africa, translated by d'Ablancourt into French (Paris, 1667, 3 vols.. in 4to). Marmol had read and seen, but he is destitute of the curious and extensive observation which abounds in the original work of Leo the African' LI.140, 147, 148, 149, 152, 154, 161.

Marmontel, Jean-François [1723–99; Gibbon owned his *Bélisaire* (Paris, 1767), *Contes moraux*, 3 vols. (Paris, 1765, and Paris, 1775), *Les Incas*, 2 vols. (Paris, 1777) and *Poétique françoise*, 2 vols. (Paris, 1763)]: XLI.34.

Marsham, Sir John [1602–85; Gibbon owned his *Canon Chronicus* (London, 1672, and Frankfort, 1696): XXI.11; XXII.81; XXIII.55; XLIII.85; XLIV.172; XLVII.160; L.35, 49, 'the learned Sir John Marsham' 50, 53, 56, 82, 'our learned countryman' 106; LI.160; LXXI.9.

Marsigli, Luigi Fernando, count [Gibbon owned his *Stato Militare dell'Imperio Ottomano* (The Hague, 1732)]: XL.112, 114; L.23; LIV.27; LVIII.60; LXV.86, 88, 89; LXVIII.29, 30.

Martène, Edmond [or Martenne; 1654–1739; author of *De Antiquis Ecclesiæ Ritibus Libri Quatuor*]: XX.67; LVIII.88.

Martial [38/41–c.103]: II.40; XII.95; XVI.45, 47; XXX.61; XXXI.44; XLIV.125; LXX.11.

Martianus, Prosper [topographer of Rome]: LXXI.75.

Martius of Narni, Galestus [biographer of Matthias Corvinus]: LXVII.34.

Martyn, John [or Martin; 1699–1768; botanist; commentator on Virgil; Gibbon owned his *Dissertations and Critical Remarks upon the Æneids of Virgil* (London, 1770)]: XLI.75; XLIII.17.

Mascov, Johann Jacob [or Mascow, or Mascou; Gibbon owned his *History of the Ancient Germans*, 2 vols. (London, 1738)]: X.22, 110; XXV.90, 149; XXX.54, 67, 86; XXXI.132, 136, 168, 169, 171; XXXIV.1, 26, 43; XXXV.25, 47; XXXVIII.24, 37, 38, 'very accurate and useful' 124; XXXIX.32, 60, 82; XL.43; XLI.39, 109; 'The patient reader may draw some light from Mascou' XLII.10, 15; XLIII.6, 30, 44; XLIV.7, 'the ineffectual cavils of Mascou' 58.

Mascov, Gottfried [author of *De Sectis Jurisconsultorum* (Lipsiæ, 1728); confused by Gibbon with Johann Jacob Mascov]: 'a learned treatise on a narrow and barren ground' XLIV.62, 63, 65, 66, 69.

Mason, William [1724–97; poet; friend and editor of Gray; Gibbon owned his *The English Garden* (York, 1783), *An Heroic Epistle to Sir W. Chambers* (London, 1773) and *Poems* (York, 1774)]: XXXI.127; LI.129.

Massieu, Guillaume [1665–1722; historian of the oaths of the ancients]: XXXI.86.

Maternus, Julius Firmicus [author of *De Errore Profan. Relig.*]: XXV.112; XXVIII.1.

St Matthew: XV.60; XLIV.131; XLVII.4.

Maundrell, Henry [1665–1701; Gibbon owned his *A Journey from Aleppo to Jerusalem* (Oxford, 1721)]: XLIII.84; XLVII.89; LI.52, 63, 71; LVII.65; LVIII.104, 107.

Maurice [c.539–602; emperor; author of *Strategems*]: XLII.15, 20; XLVI.40.

Maxima Bibliotheca Patrum [probably the *Maxima Bibliotheca Veterum Patrum*, ed. Philippe Despont and Marguerin de La Bigne, 28 vols. (Lugd. Bat., 1677–1707); also published in a two-volume abridgement by Philipp Puetner (Aug. Vind., 1719)]: XXXVII.81, 90, 96.

Maximus [st; bp of Turin]: XX.29.

Maximus of Tyre [or Tyrius]: XLVII.6; L.49, 155.

Mead, Richard [1673–1754; Gibbon owned his *A Short Discourse Concerning Pestilential Contagion* (London, 1722), *A Mechanical Account of Poisons* (London, 1745) and *Oratio Anniversaria Harveiana Habita 1723. Adjecta est Dissertatio de Nummis quibusdam a Smyrnæis in Medicorum Honorem Percussis* (London, 1724)]: 'I have read with pleasure Mead's short but elegant treatise concerning Pestilential Disorders' XLIII.87, 92, 93.

Meerman, Gerard [jurist; author of the *Novus Thesaurus Juris Civ. et Can.*]: LIII.5.

Mela, Pomponius [fl. 43 AD]: I.7; IX.1; XIII.46; XV.56; XVIII.71; XXV.127; XL.131; XLI.41; XLIII.63, 84; LI.150.

Mélanges tirés d'une grande bibliothèque, ed. M. A. R. de Voyer d'Argenson, marquis de Paulmy, and A. G. Coutant d'Orville, 61 vols. (Paris, 1779): LVIII.13, 52; LIX.29; LXI.47, 52.

Melot, Anicet [1697–1759; author of *Catalogus Codicum Manuscriptorum Bibliothecæ Regiæ*]: XXXI.115.

Memnon of Heraclea: II.31; XLIV.18.

Mémoires sur la Chine, see Le Comte, Louis Daniel.

Mémoires de la Societé de Bern: IX.36.

Ménage, Gilles [1613–92; Gibbon owned the *Ménagiana*, 4 vols. (Amsterdam, 1713)]: VI.7; XL.23, 150.

Menander [*c.*342–*c.*292 BC; comic playwright]: XIX.2; LIII.110.

Menander [fl. sixth century AD; historian]: XL.67, 76; XLII.24, 30, 32, 34, 35, 'the Extracts of Menander . . ., in which we often regret the want of order and connection' 37, 52, 90; XLIII.56; XLV.6, 7, 11, 33; XLVI.2, 7, 23, 27; L.29.

Messance [or Messange; fl. 1765–85; Gibbon owned his *Recherches sur la population des généralités d'Auvergne, de Lyon, de Rouen* (Paris, 1766)]: II.55; XVII.184; 'that accurate writer' XXXI.9, 72; LI.132.

Metrical History of the First Crusade: 'of small value or account' LVIII.19.

Meursius, Joannes [1579–1639; Greek scholar; editor of Constantine Porphyrogenitus; Gibbon owned his *Opera Omnia*, 12 vols. (Florence, 1741–63), *Ceramicus Geminus* (Utrecht, 1663), *Creta, Cyprus, Rhodus* (Amsterdam, 1765), *Græcia Ludibunda, siue de Ludis Græcorum Liber* (Leyden, 1625), *Miscellanea Laconica* (Amsterdam, 1661) and *Regnum Atticum* (Amsterdam, 1633)]: II.22; XIV.106; XVIII.45; XL.144; XLIV.172; XLVII.25; LI.94; LII.20, 79, 112, 115; LIII.3, 4, 71, 73; LXVI.78.

Méziriac, Claude Gaspar Bachet, sieur de [1581–1638; poet and classical scholar]: XXVIII.4; LII.60.

Michaelis, Johann David [orientalist and theologian; editor of Abulfeda's *Descriptio Ægypti* (Göttingen, 1776)]: XXVII.112; XLVII.54, 56; L.94, 115, 116, 137; 'the learned and orthodox Michaelis' LII.37.

Michou, Matthew à [or de Michoviâ; canon and physician of Cracow; author of *Sarmatia Asiatica et Europea*]: LXIV.15.

Middleton, Conyers [1683–1750; polemicist and divine; Gibbon owned his *Miscellaneous Works*, 4 vols. (London, 1752), *The History of the Life of M. T. Cicero*, 3 vols. (London, 1741), and *The Origin of Printing* [with Supplement by Bowyer and Nichols] (London, 1776–81)]: II.57; XV.73, 74, 79; XVI.90; XXVIII.90; XXXIV.37; 'Dr. Middleton . . . liberally censures the conduct and writings of Chrysostom, one of the most eloquent and successful advocates for the monastic life' XXXVII.27, 62; XLVII.14; LIV.5.

Mignot, Vincent [*c.*1730–*c.*1790; author of *Histoire de l'empire ottoman . . . jusqu'à . . . 1740*, 4 vols. (Paris, 1771)]: LXV.86.

Mill, John [1645–1707; author of *Prolegomena to the New Testament*]: XV.153; XXXVII.75, 'in 1689, the papist Simon strove to be free; in 1707, the protestant Mill wished to be a slave; in 1751, the Arminian Wetstein used the liberty of his times, and of his sect' 115; XLVII.5, 35, 111.

Miller, Philip [or Millar; 1691–1771; Gibbon owned his *The Gardener's Dictionary* (London, 1761)]: XLII.14; LI.25.

Milton, John [1608–74; Gibbon owned his *Poetical Works*, 2 vols. (London, 1753) and 3 vols. (London, 1761), and his *Works, Historical, Political and Miscellaneous*, 2 vols. (London, 1753)]: XV.9, 69; XXII.30; XLIII.81; XLIV.93; 'our great poet' l.6; LII.46.

Minutius Fælix: II.19; XV.95, 184; XVI.8, 9, 'elegant and circumstantial' 19; XX.29.

Mircond [or Mirchond, or Mirkhond; more correctly, Mir Khwand; 1433–98; Persian historian; see also Khondemir and Teixeira, Pedro]: XLVI.22; L.111; LI.202, 'Mirchond . . ., a native of Herat, composed in the Persian language a general history of the East, from the creation to the year of the Hegira 875 . . . In the year 904 (A.D. 1498) the historian obtained the command of a princely library, and his applauded work, in seven or twelve parts, was abbreviated in three volumes by his son Khondemir' 203, 204; LII.106.

Missy, César de [1703–75; Gibbon owned his *Paraboles ou fables, mises en vers* (London, 1769)]: XXXVII.116; XLVII.17.

Modestinus, Herennius: XLIV.175.

Monachus Albericus: LVI.77.

Monachus, Robertus: LVIII.9, 15, 17, 19, 41, 61, 91, 94.

Monaldeschi, Ludovico Buonconte [or Monaldesco; Italian historian]: LXIX.99, 104, 108; LXX.13, 'N.B. The credit of this fragment is somewhat hurt by a singular interpolation, in which the author relates *his own death* at the age of 115 years' 98; 'the most ancient fragments of Roman annals . . . and however fanciful they may seem, they are deeply marked with the colours of truth and nature' LXXI.58.

Moncada, Francisco de [Gibbon owned his *Expedicion de los Catalanes y Arragoneses contra Turcos y Griegos* (Barcelona, 1623, and Madrid, 1777)]: LXII.47, 'an Arragonese history, which I have read with pleasure, and which the Spaniards extol as a model of style and composition . . .. Don Francisco de Moncada, Conde de Osona, may imitate Cæsar or Italian contemporaries: but he never quotes his authorities, and I cannot discern any national records of the exploits of his countrymen' 50.

Mongault, Nicolas Hubert de [1674–1746; editor of Cicero's letters to Atticus]: III.22.

Monstrelet, Enguerrand de [*c.*1390–1453; chronicler]: LXVIII.11.

Montagu, Richard [or Montacul, or Montacut; 1577–1641; bp of Norwich; translator of Eusebius; editor of Photius and Gregory of Nazianzen]: XLVII.142; LV.73; LX.2.

Montaigne, Michel Eyquem de [1538–92; essayist and philosopher; Gibbon owned his *Essais*, 3 vols. (London, 1724) and 10 vols. (London, 1754), and the *Journal du voyage de M. de Montaigne en Italie* (Rome and Paris, 1774)]: X.133; XII.85; XLIV.82.

Montesquieu, Charles de Sécondat, baron de la Brède et de [1689–1755; *philosophe* and historian; Gibbon owned his *Œuvres*, 3 vols. (Amsterdam and Leipzig, 1758, and London, 1772), *Œuvres posthumes* (Lausanne, 1784), *Considérations sur les causes de la grandeur des Romains, et de leur décadence* (Paris, 1755) and *Lettres* (London, 1767)]: V.52; 'spirited and even . . . sublime' VII.33, 54; IX.38, 'brilliant imagination' 54; X.37; 'lively fancy' XI.11; XIV.1; XVII.54, 168; XX.110; XXII.68; XXIV.97; XXV.45; 'Montesquieu, who has used, and abused, the relations of travellers' XXVI.11, 15, 47, 56, 'the president Montesquieu seems ignorant, that the Goths, after the defeat of Valens, *never* abandoned the Roman territory . . . The error is inexcusable; since it disguises the principal and immediate cause of the fall of the Western Empire of Rome' 136; XXVII.100; XXVIII.17; XXIX.10; XXX.73; XXXI.137, 176; 'a bold and easy pencil' XXXIV.38; XXXVI.90; XXXVIII.50, 'the comprehensive genius of the president de Montesquieu' 64, 71, 74, 78, 'the philosopher is sometimes lost in the legal antiquarian' 80, 84, 86, 87, 90, 112, 119, 125; XXXIX.24; XL.19, 111; XLII.70; 'on this occasion he throws aside the gown and cap of a President à Mortier' XLIV.95, 156, 163, 164, 'that eloquent philosopher conciliates the rights of liberty and of nature, which should never be placed in opposition to each other' 199, 206; XLV.54; XLIX.95, 101; 'in the forty years since its publication [that of the *Esprit des Loix*], no work has been more read and criticised; and the spirit of enquiry which it has excited, is not the least of our obligations to the author' LVIII.139; LXII.15; LXIX.1, 9, 'a man of genius' 62.

Montfaucon, Bernard de [1655–1741; *érudit*; Gibbon owned his *L'Antiquité expliquée et représentée*, 10 vols. (Paris, 1719–24), *Diarium Italicum* (Paris, 1702) and *Les Monuments de la monarchie fran-*

çoise, 5 vols. (Paris, 1729–33)]: II.73, 86; XIV.74; XV.47; XVII.83; XX.2; XXIII.81, 112; XXV.18; XXVI.115; XXVII.88, 90; XXVIII.8, 49; XXXII.1, 6, 29, 'Father Montfaucon . . . has perused those works [the works of Chrysostom] with the curious diligence of an editor, discovered several new homilies, and again reviewed and composed the life of Chrysostom' 41, 51; XXXV.17; XL.72, 77; XLI.22, 109; XLIV.84; XLVII.116; LXIII.42; LXXI.6, 26, 27, 40, 43, 44, 50, 62, 63, 64, 68, 69, 70, 'that learned Benedictine' 75.

Monument. Antiq.: XVI.127.

Monuments de la monarchie françoise: XXXV.17.

More, Sir Thomas [1478–1535; Gibbon owned his *De Optimo Reipublicæ Statu, deque Nova Insula Utopia Libri II* (Glasgow, 1750)]: XV.128.

Moses: VIII.19; LI.115.

Moses of Chorene (or Chorenensis): VIII.2, 6, 27, 52; X.134; XIII.52, 55, 56, 57, 58, 60, 62, 67, 76, 82; XV.178; XVI.162; XVIII.58; XXIV.38, 74; XXV.133, 136, 139; 'Deficient as he is in every qualification of a good historian, his local information, his passions, and his prejudices, are strongly expressive of a native and contemporary' XXXII.82, 84, 85, 86, 87; XLII.50.

Mosheim, Johann Lorenz von [1694–1755; ecclesiastical historian; Gibbon owned his *De Rebus Christianorum ante Constantinum Magnum Commentarii* (Helmstadt, 1753), *Dissertationum ad Historiam Ecclesiasticam Pertinentium Volumen Primum et Alterum*, 2 vols. (Altona and Lübeck, 1767), *An Ecclesiastical History*, 2 vols. (London, 1765) and 6 vols. (London, 1782), and *Institutionum Historiæ Ecclesiasticæ Libri Quatuor* (Helmstadt, 1764)]: 'this masterly performance' XV.18, 21, 29, 'ingenious and candid' 32, 34, 66, 80, 99, 'learned and candid' 105, 106, 113, 116, 119, 120, 124, 127, 130, 133, 'learned and copious' 145; 173, 174, 177, 178; XVI.16, 18, 27, 32, 35, 57, 97, 101, 104, 110, 116, 123, 129, 152, 163; XX.5, 'ingenious, subtle, prolix' 16; XXI.22, 23, 30, 41, 54, 102; XXXVII.79; 'less profound than Petavius, less independent than Le Clerc, less ingenious than Beausobre, the historian Mosheim is full, rational, correct, and moderate' XLVII.1, 15, 'most learned and rational' 19, 40, 85; XLIX.62, 77, 88, 126, 132; L.88, 148; LII.58; 'the errors and virtues of the Paulicians are weighed, with his usual judgment and candour, by the learned Mosheim' LIV.1, 9, 25, 28, 30, 'the opinions and proceedings of the reformers are exposed in the second part of the general history of Mosheim: but the balance, which he has held with so clear an eye, and so steady an hand, begins to incline in favour of his Lutheran brethren' 32; 'Mosheim's excellent History of the Church' LV.78, 82; LVII.29, 63, 64, 66; 'the good sense of Mosheim' LIX.87; 'Mosheim traces the schism of the Greeks, with learning, clearness, and impartiality' LX.1; '[Mosheim] unfolds the causes with the judgement of a philosopher' LXIII.40; 'the learned and judicious Mosheim' LXVI.83; LXIX.19, 21, 68.

Moulinet [monk; compiler of a medallic history of Martin V]: LXX.77.

Mouskes, Philip [*c.*1215–1283; bp of Tournay; amateur poet]: LXI.43.

Moyle, Walter [1672–1721; Gibbon owned his *Works*, 3 vols. (London, 1726–7)]: VIII.7, 31; XV.170; 'admirable criticism' XVI.106, 107, 113; XX.19; 'an English Whig, as well as . . . a Roman antiquary' XXVIII.3, 12; XLIV.34.

Muratori, Giovanni Francesco Soli [nephew and biographer of L. A. Muratori; Gibbon owned his *Vita del Proposto Ludovico Antonio Muratori* (Venice, 1756)]: LXX.98.

Muratori, Lodovico Antonio [1672–1750; antiquarian; Gibbon owned his *Annali d'Italia*, 18 vols. (Milan, 1753–6), *Antiquitates Italicæ Medii Aevi*, 6 vols. (Milan,

Muratori, Lodovico Antonio—*contd* 1738–42), *Delle Antichità Estensi ed Italiane*, 2 vols. (Modena, 1717–40), *Dissertazioni sopra le Antichità Italiane*, 3 vols. (Milan, 1751), and *Novus Thesaurus Veterum Inscriptionum*, 4 vols. (Milan, 1739–42)]: VII.32, 34, 55; XVI.73; XXIV.40; XXVI.89; XXX.37, 38, 72; XXXI.116; XXXIII.5; XXXV.51; XXXVI.4, 109, 133, 140; XXXVIII.79, 97; XXXIX.21, 'the plebeian Muratori crouches under their [the Goths'] oppression' 26, 53, 55, 88, 93, 105, 107; XLI.22, 52, 62, 63, 64, 69, 98, 108, 109, 110; XLII.10; XLIII.6, 13, 33; XLV.10, 12, 13, 15, 'correct and critical' 20, 'of all chronological guides, Muratori is the safest' 22, 33, 'Muratori, as the servant of the house of Este, is not free from partiality and prejudice' 34, 'Maffei .. and Muratori . . . have asserted the native claims of the Italian idiom: the former with enthusiasm, the latter with discretion; both with learning, ingenuity, and truth' 38, 45, 48, 49, 52, 53, 57, 64, 71; XLVI.23, 70; XLVII.98; XLIX.31, 32, 33, 39, 41, 46, 49, 51, 53, 54, 58, 63, 65, 70, 71, 85, 91, 93, 94, 110, 116, 119, 124, 126, 127, 128, 'accurate chronology' 129, 135, 139, 140, 141, 143, 145, 147; LII.66, 82, 85; LIII.11, 21, 22, 25, 26, 62, 64, 69, 93, 95, 96; LIV.28; LV.12, 27, 31, 33, 37, 44; 'Muratori's great collection of the *Scriptores Rerum Italicarum*' LVI.1, 9, 10, 15, 21, 31, 32, 43, 47, 50, 'critical industry' 60, 64, 69, 77, 82, 86, 91, 92, 97, 99, 101, 108, 109, 110, 115, 116, 118, 119, 121, 122, 124, 126, 128, 137, 138, 139, 140; LVIII.4, 17, 19, 22, 38, 53, 54, 81, 86, 120; LIX.13, 84, 85, 88, 'poor Muratori knows what to think, but knows not what to say' 89, 90, 108; LX.4, 12, 26, 36, 38, 39, 44, 54, 99; LXI.6, 57; LXII.37, 40, 44, 46; LXIII.36, 52, 53; LXV.22, 37, 53, 92; LXVI.4, 8, 9, 11, 12, 13, 17, 37, 56, 57, 61, 70, 110; LXVII.43; LXVIII.95; LXIX.3, 5, 12, 'my ordinary and excellent guide. He uses, and indeed quotes, with the freedom of a master, his great Collection of the Italian Historians, in xxviii. volumes; and as that treasure is in my library, I have thought it an amusement, if not a duty, to consult the originals' 13, 29, 31, 33, 39, 42, 45, 46, 49, 50, 53, 60, 'impartial learning' 61, 63, 66, 74, 79, 83, 86, 89, 91, 92, 94, 95, 96, 97, 98, 99, 101, 105, 106, 107; LXX.18, 19, 24, 26, 35, 51, 64, 70, 77, 78, 85, 95, 96, 'my guide and master in the history of Italy . . . In all his works, Muratori approves himself a diligent and laborious writer, who aspires above the prejudices of a Catholic priest' 98; LXXI.19, 26, 29, 32, 33, 'laborious and entertaining compilation' 39, 42, 45, 46, 47, 53, 55, 56, 59, 63.

Muret, Jean Louis [1715–96; economist]: IX.36.

Murtadã [Gibbon owned his *L'Égypte*, tr. P. Vattier (Paris, 1666)]: LI.80, 'he expatiates on the subject with the zeal and minuteness of a citizen and a bigot, and his local traditions have a strong air of truth and accuracy' 104, 112, 117, 125, 'the antiquities of Egypt are wild and legendary: but the writer deserves credit and esteem for his account of the conquest and geography of his native country' 128, 130.

Musson, Pierre [fl. 1620–35; Gibbon owned his *Ordres monastiques*, 5 vols. (Berlin, 1751)]: XXXVII.5, 50.

Mylius, Johann Heinrich [commentator on Theophilus]: XLIV.42.

N

Nangis, William de [chronicler; author of the *Annales de St Louis*]: LIX.100; LXI.57.

Nardini, Famiano [Gibbon owned his *Roma Antica* (Rome, 1704)]: II.72; IV.23; V.5; VI.18, 81; XI.43; XVI.34; XXXI.24, 71, 105, 107; XXXVI.81, 'it would require a tedious dissertation to mark the circumstances, in which I am declined to depart from the topography of that learned Roman' 108; XXXIX.64,

66; 'the accurate eye of Nardini' XLI.79, 84, 85, 89; XLIII.23; XLV.68; LXIX.36; LXXI.8, 27, 44, 73, 75.

Nauze, Louis Jouard de [1696–1773; *érudit*]: XVII.16.

Nazarius, Joannes Paulus: IX.78; XIV.49, 69, 71, 76, 94, 98; XX.46.

Necker, Jacques [1732–1804; financier and politician; Gibbon owned his *Œuvres*, 4 vols. (Lausanne, 1786), *De l'administration des finances de la France*, 3 vols. (1784), *De l'importance des opinions religieuses* (Liège, 1788), *Du pouvoir exécutif dans les grands états*, 2 vols. (Paris, 1792), *Éloge de J.-B. Colbert* (Paris, 1773), *Sur la législation et le commerce des grains* (Paris, 1776) and *Sur le compte rendu au roi en 1781. Nouveaux éclaircissements* (Lyons, 1783)]: XLIII.93; XLIX.108; LVIII.47.

Nemesianus, Marcus Aurelius Olympianus [fl. 280 AD]: XII.77, 80, 100, 101.

Nennius [fl. 796; abbot of Bangor; early British historian]: XXXVIII.128, 129, 138, 140.

Neocastrato, Bartholemy à [historian]: LXII.44.

Nestor [early Russian historian]: LIII.65; 'Nestor, the first and best of these ancient annalists [of Russia], was a monk of Kiow, who died in the beginning of the XIIth century; but his Chronicle was obscure, till it was published at Petersburgh, 1767' LV.45, 55, 62, 65.

Nestorius [d. *c.*451; patriarch of Constantinople]: XLVII.58.

Newton, Sir Isaac [1642–1727; Gibbon owned his *The Chronology of Ancient Kingdoms Amended* (London, 1728) and *Opticks* (London, 1704)]: VII.59; XLIII.76; XLVII.17.

Nicephorus [d. 829; Byzantine historian; author of *Breviarium Historicum* (Paris, 1648); patriarch of Constantinople]: XXI.90, 155; XXXII.74; XLVI.54, 57, 71, 73, 76, 83, 110, 111; XLVII.28; XLIX.18; LI.10, 109, 114, 157, 159; LII.2, 6, 14, 15; LV.3.

Nicephorus Bryennius Cæsar [1062–1137; Byzantine statesman; husband of Anna Comnena]: LVII.15, 25, 32, 35, 36, 37, 38, 51; LVIII.64.

Nicephorus Gregoras [*c.*1265–*c.*1335; Byzantine historian]: LV.6; LXI.21, 55, 61; 'a valuable narrative from the taking of Constantinople by the Latins' LXII.1, 2, 3, 5, 7, 10, 11, 14, 18, 21, 23, 24, 27, 28, 38, 45, 50, 54; LXIII.1, 2, 5, 6, 7, 8, 9, 'remarkably exact' 10, 11, 12, 13, 25, 26, 27, 29, 30, 31, 32, 33, 34, 35, 42, 44, 45, 'judicious and well-informed on the trade and colonies of the Black Sea' 48, 49, 'a clear and honest narrative' 50, 51; 'Nicephorus Gregoras . . . has felt the necessity of connecting the Scythian and Byzantine histories. He describes with truth and elegance the settlement and manners of the Moguls of Persia, but he is ignorant of their origin, and corrupts the names of Zingis and his sons' LXIV.13, 35, 36, 40, 42, 43, 47, 49, 51, 52; LXV.76; LXVII.3, 4.

Nicetas Acominatus [or Nicetas Choniates; *c.*1150–1213; Byzantine senator and historian]: XLVII.142; XLIX.17; LIII.23, 42; LV.66; LVI.109, 111, 112, 121, 123, 'Nicetas . . . who now becomes a respectable contemporary. As he survived the emperor and the empire, he is above flattery: but the fall of Constantinople exasperated his prejudices against the Latins' 125; LIX.9, 10, 16, 17; LX.10, 13, 15, 'soft and concise' 17, 'his offices of logothete, or principal secretary, and judge of the veil or palace, could not bribe the impartiality of the historian. He wrote, it is true, after the fall and death of his benefactor [Isaac Angelus]' 18, 22, 24, 52, 59, 67, 69, 70, 71, 72, 73, 74, 75, 77, 82, 84, 87, 91, 92, 93, 'Nicetas was of Chonæ in Phrygia (the old Colossæ of St. Paul): he raised himself to the honours of senator, judge of the veil, and great logothete; beheld the fall of the empire, retired to Nice, and composed an elaborate history from the death of Alexius

Nicetas Acominatus—*contd*
Comnenus to the reign of Henry' 94, 95, 'the boasted taste of Nicetas was no more than affectation and vanity' 97, 98, 99; 'the vain ignorance of a Greek' LXI.3, 5, 12, 14, 17, 20, the portrait of the French Latins, is drawn in Nicetas by the hand of prejudice and resentment' 22, 26, 28, 58; LXII.55.

Nicolson, William [or Nicholson; 1655–1727; bp of Derry; Gibbon owned his *The English, Scotch, and Irish Historical Libraries* (London, 1736)]: XXXVIII.150.

Niclas, Johann Nicolaus [eighteenth-century Byzantinist; editor of the *Geoponics* (Lipsiæ, 1781)]: LIII.6; LXII.57.

Nicon [or Nikita Minin; sixth patriarch of Russia; historian]: LV.62.

Niebuhr, Carsten [1733–1815; Gibbon owned his *Voyage en Arabie*, 2 vols. (Amsterdam, 1776–80), and *Description de l'Arabie* (Copenhagen, 1773)]: XVII.12; XVIII.64, 66; 'a learned and accurate Dane' XIX.55; XXIV.41, 52, 85; XLVI.102, 138; L.2, 'the last and most judicious of our Syrian travellers' 10, 12, 15, 23, 25, 34, 37, 39, 137, 141, 171, 175, 180, 186; LI.1, 23, 102, 106, 111, 220; LII.41; 'industrious' LVII.68; LX.64.

Nigellus, Ermoldus: XXXVIII.81, 84.

Nivernois, Louis Jules Barbon-Mancini-Mazarini, duc de [1716–98; writer and statesman]: XXXVIII.13.

Nolli, Giovanni Battista [cartographer of modern Rome]: XXXI.105; XLI.77, 82, 85, 89, 92; LXXI.75.

Nonnius, Ludovicus [author of *Hispania Illustrata*]: XXXI.155; 'a work of correct and concise knowledge' LI.175, 178, 183.

Noodt, Gerard: III.19; XXV.60; XLIV.40, 'learned and rational' 101, 114, 141, 160, 163, 166, 169, 201.

Noris, Enrico [1631–1704; archaeologist; historian, theologian and polemicist; cardinal; Gibbon owned his *Cenotaphia Pisana Caii et Lucii Cæsarum* (Venice, 1681) and *Annus et Epochæ Syro-macedonum in Vetustis Urbium Syriæ Nummis Expositæ* (Florence, 1691)]: XI.80; 'learned' XII.29; XVI.31; XXIII.98, 107; XXVII.87; XXXI.36; XXXIX.90.

Nouvelles de la république des lettres: X.155.

Novairi [or Thomas Obicinus; orientalist]: L.111; LI.138, 147, 153, 170, 179, 184, 190; LII.25; LVI.103; LVII.38, 73.

Numatianus, Rutilius: XXX.113; XXXI.112, 145, 183; XXXVI.7.

Numbers: XV.10.

O

Oberlin, Jérémie Jacques [1735–1806; author of *Jungendorum Marium Fluviorumque Molimina* (Strasburg, 1770)]: 'a learned thesis' LI.127.

Obsequens, Julius: XV.200.

Ockley, Simon [1678–1720; orientalist; Gibbon owned his *The Conquest of Syria, Persia, and Ægypt, by the Saracens* (i.e. *The History of the Saracens*), 2 vols. (London, 1708, 1718)]: XXVI.97; L.40, 69, 79, 149, 166, 167, 168, 170, 173, 'I have abridged the interesting narrative of Ockley . . . . It is long and minute; but the pathetic, almost always, consists in the detail of little circumstances' 179; LI.11, 12, 16, 19, 28, 40, 'learned and spirited . . . I am sorry to think that the labours of Ockley were consummated in a jail' 44, 45, 51, 59, 65, 66, 75, 76, 80, 84, 86, 88, 91, 92, 99, 100, 125, 142, 154, 156, 164; LII.2, 'these domestic revolutions are related in a clear and natural style, in the second volume of Ockley's History of the Saracens, ... Besides our printed authors, he draws his materials from the Arabic MSS. of Oxford, which he would have more deeply searched, had he been confined to the Bodleian library instead of the city jail; a fate how unworthy of the man and of his country!' 7.

Odo [*c*.879–942; abbot of Cluny; biographer of Gregory of Tours]: XXXVIII.110.

Ogearius [or Ogerius; protonotary]: LXI.21; LXII.34.

Olahus, Nicolas [abp of Gran; biographer of Attila the Hun]: XXXIV.1.

Olearius, Adam [Gibbon owned his *Voyages, faits en Moscovie, Tartarie, et Perse* (Leyden, 1718)]: XXVI.2; XL.138, 148; XLI.18, 44; XLII.89; XLVI.12, 89; XLVII.143; L.185; LI.206; LV.50.

Olivet, Pierre Joseph Thoulier d', [1682–1768; historian; classical and literary scholar]: XVI.10; XLIV.177.

Olympiodorus: XXVI.114; XXX.68, 81, 95, 106; XXXI.26, 27, 58, 67, 74, 80, 84, 91, 93, 138, 144, 150, 152, 154, 161, 164, 166: XXXIII.1, 3, 10; XLI.50; LI.30.

Opsopæus, Vincentius: XLI.61.

Optatianus Porfyrius, Publius: XIV.99.

Optatus of Milevis [or Optatus Milevitanus]: XVI.159, 160, 170; XXI.6, 7, 9, 157, 158; XXIII.35, 123, 136; XXXIII.17; XXXVII.122; XLI.26.

Oricellarius, Bernardus [or Rucellai; author of *Descriptio Urbis Romæ* (MS)]: 'a MS. description of ancient Rome . . . of which I obtained a copy from the library of the Canon Ricardi at Florence' II.72.

Origen [*c.*185–*c.*254]: XV.35, 101, 103, 132, 166, 183, 184, 187, 192, 195; XVI.8, 13, 36, 72, 119; 'his moderate opinions were too repugnant to the zeal of the church, and he was found guilty of the heresy of reason' XLVII.95.

Oróbio de Castro, Baltasar: XV.15; XXI.24.

Orosius, Paulus [fl. 414–17]: I.67; III.1; X.88, 100, 123, 181; XIII.36, 44, 64, 68; XIV.1, 9; XVI.28, 118, 125; XVIII.16; XXI.164, 173; XXIII.92, 139; XXV.16, 70, 76, 99, 100, 106, 122, 124, 138; XXVI.87, 94, 105; XXVII.12, 'how many interesting facts might Orosius have inserted in the vacant space which is devoted to pious nonsense!' 77, 104, 120, 121; 'though a bigot and a controversial writer, Orosius seems to blush' XXVIII.46, 57; XXIX.16, 18, 45, 47, 49, 50, 51, 53, 57; XXX.26, 43, 45, 77, 79, 81, 'The bloody actor is less detestable than the cool unfeeling historian' 82, 85, 88, 95, 'abominably partial' 102, 106, 109; XXXI.80, 83, 96, 98, 99, 107, 108, 118, 130, 131, 135, 146, 150, 156, 158, 159, 165, 166, 168; XXXVII.80, 85; LI.121; LXXI.13.

Orville, Jacques Philippe d' [Gibbon owned his *Sicula* (Amsterdam, 1764)]: XLI.58; LVI.98.

'Ossian' [Gibbon owned *The Works of Ossian, translated from the Galic Language by J. Macpherson* (London, 1765)]: I.12; VI.13, 14; XV.179.

Ostiensis, Leo: LVI.24.

Otrokosci [or Ferencz Foris, author of *Origines Hungaricæ* (Franqueræ, 1693)]: 'a learned Hungarian' XXXIV.43.

Otter, Jean [1707–48; orientalist; Gibbon owned his *Voyage en Turquie et en Perse*, 2 vols. (Paris, 1748)]: XIX.55; XXIV.52; XLVI.79; LI.20, 23, 29, 72, 99, 138, 147, 153, 157; LII.19, 41; LIV.18; LVIII.87, 90.

Otto, Everard [author of *De Stoica Jurisconsultorum Philosophia*]: XLIV.58.

Ovid [Publius Ovidius Naso; 43 BC–AD 17]: I.22; II.15; III.58; IV.18; VI.79; IX.3, 57; XV.49, 199; XVIII.39, 40, 41; XXV.50; XXVI.9; XXX.2; XXXI.77, 156; XXXVI.80; XXXVII.97; XL.58, 61; XLI.70; XLIV.195; LIII.18; LV.15.

P

Pacatus Drepanius, Latinus: XXV.119, 138; XXVI.105, 108, 109, 111, 129; XXVII.11, 15, 54, 59, 72, 77, 78, 79, 80, 81.

Pachomius [*c.*290–346; st]: XXXVII.43, 47, 59.

Pachymer, George [1242–*c.*1310; Byzantine historian]: XLII.55; LIII.44; LXI.21, 59, 61; LXII.1, 3, 6, 8, 10, 11, 'as a Greek, he is credulous' 13, 'without comparing Pachymer to Thucydides or Tacitus, I will praise his narrative . . ., which pursues the ascent of Palæologus with eloquence, perspicuity, and tolerable freedom' 14, 21, 23, 24, 25, 26, 27, 28, 30, 'copious and candid narrative' 31, 35, 36, 38, 47, 48, 49, 50; LXIII.2, 3, 4, 43, 44, 45; LXIV.35, 38, 40, 44; LXV.76.

Pæanius: VII.36; XIII.36; XVIII.3.

Pætus, Lucas [fifteenth-century lawyer and antiquarian; compiler of the *Statuta*

Pætus, Lucas—*contd* *Urbis Romæ*]: LXX.83; LXXI.54, 55, 57, 65.

Pagi, Antoine [1624–95; chronologist; Gibbon owned his *Critica Historico-Chronologica in Universos Annales Ecclesiasticos Baronii*, 4 vols. (Antwerp, 1727), and *Dissertatio Hypatica, seu de Consulibus Cæsareis* (Lyons, 1682)]: XII.71; XIII.85, 109; XV.157; XVI.31; XX.41; XXV.37; XXVII.99; XXVIII.43; XXIX.8; XXX.72; XXXIII.14; XXXVI.107, 133; XXXVIII.28, 57; XXXIX.88; XL.13, 76, 94, 155, 159; XLI.74; XLII.42, 52, 57; XLIII.6, 88; XLV.3, 15, 33, 64; XLVI.4, 17, 68, 82; XLVII.31, 41, 62, 64, 72, 77, 78, 107, 108, 128, 135, 140; 'the perplexity of poor friar Pagi' XLIX.6, 12, 16, 18, 30, 33, 36, 49, 55, 58, 65, 68, 77, 84, 94, 123, 127, 'accurate chronology' 129, 132; LI.86, 114, 157, 167, 170, 171, 181, 184, 185, 209, 212; LII.1, 14, 25, 33, 84, 90, 93, 112, 118; LIII.62, 64, 65; LV.27, 31, 72, 77; LVI.1, 15, 20, 101, 106; LVII.60, 69, 74; LVIII.128; LX.36; LXIX.94.

Pagi, François [1654–1721; historian; Gibbon owned his *Breviarium Historico-Chronologico-Criticum Illustriora Pontificum Romanorum Gesta, Conciliorum Generalium Acta Complectens*, 3 vols. (Antwerp, 1717–18)]: XXXIX.81, 82, 88, 93; XLIII.7.

Palladius [*c.*363–431; bp of Helenopolis]: XXI.142; XXVII.113; XXXII.43, 45, 50; XXXVII.33, 54, 65.

Pancirolli, Guido [or Pancirolus; 1523–99; jurist]: XVII.72, 'his explanations are obscure, and he does not sufficiently distinguish the painted emblems from the effective ensigns of office' 76, 78, 102, 110, 111, 132, 158; XL.120.

Pandects: V.71; XVII.77, 100, 108, 114, 116, 148, 162, 166, 167.

Panegyrici Veteres, Illustravit J. de la Baume (Paris, 1676): XII.50; XIII.7, 8, 9, 11, 20, 27, 33, 34, 37, 42, 61, 110, 111; XIV.14, 31, 32, 33, 34, 35, 41, 45, 47, 48, 50, 51, 52, 58, 59, 60, 63, 65, 67, 68, 71, 73, 75, 76, 94, 98; XVII.81, 92, 122, 173, 185, 186; XIX.89; XX.12, 16, 44, 46; XXII.3, 32, 50, 53, 74; XXV.119, 138; XXVI.104, 129; XXVII.11, 16, 54, 59, 77, 78.

Panvinius, Onuphrius [Gibbon owned his *De Ludis Circensibus. De Triumphis* (Padua, 1642)]: VII.26; XL.43; LXXI.75.

Papinianus, Æmilianus: XLIV.103.

Paris, Matthew [d.1259; Gibbon owned his *Historia Major* (London, 1684)]: LIV.26; LVIII.63, 130; LIX.9, 12, 64, 77, 78, 80, 86, 88, 91, 96, 98; LX.90; LXI.30, 40, 46; LXIV.5, 17, 28, 29, 34; LXIX.48, 49, 63, 67, 76.

Pascal, Blaise [1623–62; mathematician, physicist and moralist; Gibbon owned his *Pensées* (Paris, 1761) and *Les Provinciales* (Cologne, 1698, Paris, 1754, and, 4 vols., Leyden, 1761)]: 'that superior genius' LXI.53.

Paschal Chronicle [or *Alexandrian Chronicle*]: XII.6, 24, 104; XIII.49; XVII.44, 51, 67; XVIII.8, 11, 31, 49, 53, 63; XXI.90; XXIV.126; XXV.29, 58; XXXI.162; XXXII.39, 52, 74, 79, 81; XXXIV.18, 50; 'the Alexandrian or Paschal Chronicle, which introduces this haughty message, during the lifetime of Theodosius, may have anticipated the date; but the dull annalist was incapable of inventing the original and genuine style of Attila' XXXV.2; XXXVI.107; XXXVIII.57; XL.52; XLVI.42, 47, 54, 71, 'the Paschal Chronicle, which was composed, perhaps at Alexandria, under the reign of Heraclius' 72, 'a minute and authentic narrative of the siege and deliverance of Constantinople' 97, 104, 106, 109.

Pasquier, Étienne [1529–1615; Gibbon owned his *Les Recherches de la France* (Paris, 1633) and *Œuvres*, 2 vols. (Amsterdam, 1723)]: LVI.50.

Patricius, Augustus [fifteenth-century Italian church historian]: 'perspicuous, though partial' LXVI.77.

Paucton, Alexis Jean Pierre [*c.*1732–1798; mathematician; Gibbon owned his *Métrologie ou traité des mesures, poids, et* *monnoies* (Paris, 1780)]: 'useful and laborious' XLIV.116; 'laborious' LII.61.

St Paul: XV.60; XV.107; XLVII.17; LIX.7; LX.62.

Paul the Deacon [or Paulus Diaconus, or Paul Warnefrid; *c*.720–*c*.799; author of *De Gestis Langobardorum*]: IX.37; XXXIII.49; XXXV.50, 54; XXXVI.137; XXXVII.135; XXXVIII.122; XXXIX.55; XLI.76, 100; XLII.8, 9, 10; XLIII.30, 31, 38, 50, 56, 88; XLV.7, 'his pictures of national manners, though rudely sketched, are more lively and faithful than those of Bede, or Gregory of Tours' 8, 10, 11, 12, 13, 15, 16, 17, 19, 20, 22, 'some curious and authentic facts' 28, 29, 33, 39, 40, 42, 43, 44, 49, 50, 52, 57, 64, 66; XLVI.23, 29, 70; XLIX.31, 49, 61; LI.146; LII.32; LIII.96, 100; LV.4; LVI.12.

Paulinus, Fabius: XLIII.91.

Paulinus of Nola [353–431; st; deacon; biographer of St Ambrose]: XXIII.66; XXVII.61, 69, 70, 91, 92, 98, 121; XXVIII.60; XXX.33, 76; XXXI.21.

Paulinus of Périgord: XXXV.9.

Paulus, Julius [or Paul; jurist]: XLIV.114, 146, 175, 186, 188, 189, 206.

Pausanias [fl. 143–176; Greek traveller and geographer]: I.27; II.28, 70; XVII.48; XVIII.38; XXX.9; XL.62, 144; XLI.107; L.164; LIII.16.

Pauw, Cornelius de [Gibbon owned his *Recherches philosophiques sur les Américains*, 3 vols. (Berlin, 1777), two copies of *Recherches philosophiques sur les Égyptiens et les Chinois*, 2 vols. (Berlin, 1773, and London, 1774), and *Recherches philosophiques sur les Grecs*, 2 vols. (Berlin, 1788)]: IX.17, 29; XII.44; XV.25, 144; XVIII.39; XLVII.148, 160; LI.46, 'some peevish cavils' 134, 135; LII.69.

Pearson, John [1613–86; bp of Chester; author of the *Vindiciæ Epistolarum s. Ignatii* (Cambridge, 1672)]: XV.109, 122, 164; XVI.93.

Pedianus, Asconius: XLIV.203.

Pellegrino, Camillo [1527–1603; Gibbon owned his *Discorsi della Campania Felice* (Naples, 1651) and *Apparato alle Antichità di Capua* (Naples, 1651)]: XXXI.40; XLIII.42; XLV.37; XLIX.34; LV.4; 'Camillo Pellegrino, a learned Capuan of the last century, has illustrated the history of the dutchy of Beneventum, in his two books' LVI.2, 6, 9, 10.

Pelloutier, Simon [1694–1757; historian; Gibbon owned his *Histoire des Celtes*, 8 vols. (Paris, 1769–71)]: II.12; IX.2, 16, 69.

Pennant, Thomas [1726–98; traveller and naturalist; Gibbon owned his *Synopsis of Quadrupeds* (Chester, 1771), *Arctic Zoology*, 2 vols. (London, 1784–7), *British Zoology*, 4 vols. (London, 1768–70), *A History of Quadrupeds*, 2 vols. (London, 1781), *The Journey to Snowdon* (London, 1781), *Some Account of London* (London, 1791), *A Tour in Scotland*, 3 vols. (London, 1776), and *A Tour in Wales* (London, 1778)]: XXXI.45; XXXVIII.157; XXXIX.41; XL.110; XLV.44.

Pergæus, Apollonius [Greek mathematician]: LII.56.

Perieget., *see* Dionysius Periegetes.

Peringskiöld, Johann Fredrik [Swedish commentator on Cochlæus]: XXXIX.1, 70.

Persius [34–62 AD; satirist]: XV.55.

Persona, Christopher [early Latin translator of Procopius]: XL.14.

Petancius, Fælix [fifteenth-century chancellor of Segnia; historian]: LXVII.28.

Petau, Denis [or Petavius; 1583–1652; *érudit*; Jesuit; translator and editor of Julian the Apostate, Synesius, Cicero and St Nicephorus, patriarch of Constantinople]: XII.73; XIII.99; XX.39, 116; XXI.19, 30, 36, 37, 39, 59, 62, 74; XXII.47; XXIII.54; XXX.8, 20; XXXVII.114; XLVI.94; 'a work [the *Dogmata Theologica*] of incredible labour and compass; . . . The Jesuit's learning is copious and correct; his latinity is pure, his method clear, his argument profound and well connected: but he is the slave of the fathers, the scourge of

Petau, Denis—*contd* heretics, and the enemy of truth and candour, as often as *they* are inimical to the Catholic cause' XLVII.1, 3, 19, 34, 37, 39, 65, 72, 76, 102; LI.54; LII.1; LX.3.

Peter the Deacon [or Petrus Diaconus]: LVI.69.

Peter the Jacobite [historian]: XLVII.149.

Peter Patricius [or Peter the Patrician]: X.19, 139, 146, 149; XIII.74, 76, 79, 84; XIV.91; XVIII.75; XIX.50,

Pétis de la Croix, François (the elder) [1622–95; orientalist; Gibbon owned his *Histoire du grand Genghizcan* (Paris, 1710; tr. London, 1722), to which he commonly referred as the *Vie de Gengiscan*]: XXVI.12, 14, 46; XXXIV.7, 23, 45; XL.138; XLII.33; XLVII.117; LI.12, 41, 203; LVI.57; LVII.50; LXIV.7, 'a work of ten years labour, chiefly drawn from the Persian writers, among whom Nisavi, the secretary of sultan Gelaleddin, has the merit and prejudices of a contemporary. A slight air of romance is the fault of the originals, or the compiler' 9.

Pétis de la Croix, François (the younger) [1653–1713; translator of Cherefeddin Ali's history of Tamerlane, published as the *Histoire de Timur Bec* (Paris, 1722)]: LXV.1, 64.

Petrarca, Francesco [1304–74; scholar, poet and humanist]: XXXVI.43; XLIX.150; LXV.92; LXVI.3, 87, 92, 93, 99; LXIX.17, 81, 'bold truths and absurd pedantry' 93, 99, 102, 108, 109; LXX.15, 17, 22, 37, 46, 52, 58; LXXI.31, 37, 48, 66, 67.

Petrone, Paolo di Lello: '[Petroni], who lived at the time and on the spot, speaks the language of a citizen, equally afraid of priestly and popular tyranny' LXX.78, 98.

Petronius, Jerom: LIII.112.

Petronius Arbiter, Gaius [d. AD 66]: VI.107; XLV.55.

Peyssonnel, Claude Charles de [1700–57; Gibbon owned his *Observations historiques et géographiques sur les peuples barbares qui ont habité les bords du Danube et du Pont-Euxin* (Paris, 1765) and *Examen du livre intitulé Considérations sur la guerre actuelle des Turcs, par M. Volney* (Amsterdam, 1788)]: X.96; XVIII.44; XL.126; XLII.28, 'his erudition is less valuable than his experience' 67, 81; 'the latest and most accurate observer' LXVIII.88, 89.

Pezron, Paul Yves [1639–1706; Gibbon owned his *Défense de l'Antiquité des Tems* (Paris, 1704) and *L'Antiquité des Tems, rétablie et défendue contre les Juifs et les nouveaux chronologistes* (Paris, 1687)]: XL.160.

Pfeffel von Kriegelstein, Christian Friedrich [Gibbon owned his *Nouvel abrégé chronologique de l'histoire et du droit public d'Allemagne* (Paris, 1766, and, 2 vols., Paris, 1776)]: XLIX.116, 134, 'the author of the best constitutional history that I know of any country . . . . His learning and judgment have discerned the most interesting facts; his simple brevity comprises them in a narrow space; his chronological order distributes them under the proper dates; and an elaborate index collects them under their respective heads' 149.

Phædrus [*c.*15 BC–*c.*AD 50; poet; author of *Fabulæ*]: XXXV.53; XXXVI.129.

Philelphus, Francis: 'a sophist, proud, restless, and rapacious . . . His elaborate writings, and those of his contemporaries, are forgotten: but their familiar epistles still describe the men and the times' LXVI.79, 81, 82; LXVIII.4, 30.

Philip of Side: 'a prolix and contemptible writer' XXIII.31.

Philo: XV.6; XV.8, 129, 162; XXI.15, 17.

Philopatris: XII.75; XVI.11.

Philosophical Transactions [of the Royal Society]: XI.69.

Philostorgius [*c.*368–*c.*433; Byzantine historian; Gibbon owned the *Ecclesiasticæ Historiæ Libri XII* (Geneva, 1643)]: XVII.29, 58, 64; XVIII.16, 23, 50; XIX.13, 21, 25; XX.80, 92; 'the credibility of Philostorgius is lessened, in the eyes of the orthodox, by his Arianism; and in those of rational critics, by his passion, his prejudice, and his ignorance' XXI.44, 67, 68, 71, 81, 84, 90, 93, 99, 114, 119, 130, 147, 148; XXII.44; XXIII.118, 'cautious malice' 121; XXV.2, 3, 20, 23, 25, 36, 66; XXVI.105; XXVII.6, 'The Eunomian historian has been carefully strained through an orthodox sieve' 40, 103, 109, 122; XXIX.3, 30; XXX.106; XXXI.74, 91, 92, 95, 97, 106, 125, 144, 150; XXXII.28, 32, 61, 72; XXXIII.3, 9; XXXIV.16; XXXVII.74, 76; XL.121; XLVII.18; XLIX.7.

Philostratus: II.68, 69, 70, 79, 110; XVI.55; XL.148; XLI.65; LXX.9.

Phlegon of Tralles: XV.196.

Photius [c.820–891?; patriarch of Constantinople and historian]: XIV.50; XVII.122; XXI.153; XXVII.122; XXXII.49; XXXII.75; 'wretchedly concise' XXXIV.27; XXXVI.112; XXXIX.9; XL.15, 77, 143; XLI.115; XLII.94; XLIV.18; 'the life of Maurice was composed about the year 628 . . . by Theophylact Simocatta, ex-præfect, a native of Egypt. Photius, who gives an ample extract of the work . . ., gently reproves the affectation and allegory of the style. His preface is a dialogue between Philosophy and History; they seat themselves under a plane-tree, and the latter touches her lyre' XLVI.55; XLVII.9, 11, 68, 116, 142, 146; LI.10; LII.77; LIII.107, 108; LIV.1; LV.60, 73; LX.1, 2, 7, 8, 9.

Phranza, George [or Phranzes; chamberlain to the emperor Manuel; Byzantine historian]: LXIV.52, 66; LXV.37, 39, 45, 56, 72, 80; LXVI.31, 32, 34, 35, 43, 47, 54; LXVII.6, 20, 44, 47, 'deserves credit and esteem' 48, 51, 52; 'the most moderate picture [of Mahomet II] appears to be drawn by Phranza . . ., whose resentment had cooled in age and solitude' LXVIII.1, 3, 6, 10, 11, 14, 16, 18, 19, 'with some indulgence for national prejudices, we cannot desire a more authentic witness, not only of public facts, but of private counsels' 31, 33, 36, 38, 42, 47, 49, 52, 54, 55, 58, 59, 65, 66, 71, 76, 79, 82, 'too partial' 86, 87.

Pighius, Stephanus Vinandus [Gibbon owned his *Annales Romanorum*, 3 vols. (Antwerp, 1615)]: XXXI.14; XLIV.34.

Pignoria, Lorenzo [Gibbon owned his *De Servis Commentarius* (Padua, 1656)]: II.58.

Pilatus, Leo [or Leontius; first Greek professor at Florence]: LXVI.95.

Pindar [c.518–c.438 BC]: XV.54; XXX.17; XLI.14.

Pipin, Francis [Italian chronicler]: LXIX.60.

Pisanus, Pandulphus [biographer of Urban II]: LVIII.4; LXIX.12, 14, 15, 16, 41, 42, 98.

Piso: XII.90.

Pithou, Pierre [or Pithæus; 1539–96; French jurist]: XLIV.122.

Planudes, Maximus [fourteenth-century Constantinopolitan monk and translator of classical Latin works into Greek]: LII.60; LXI.64.

Platina [or Bartholomæus Sacchi]: LXVI.101; LXVIII.27.

Plato [428/7–348/7 BC]: VIII.21; XV.128; XVI.10; XXI.11, 18, 33; L.155; 'the artful dialogues of Plato' LIII.111.

Plautus [c.254–184 BC]: XVII.139; LI.162.

Pletho, George Gemistus [c.1355–c.1450]: 'a various and voluminous writer, the master of Bessarion, and all the Platonists of the times' LXVI.108.

Pliny the Elder [23–79; author of the *Natural History*]: I.2, 52, 77; II.32, 37, 54, 61, 72, 76, 77, 92, 95, 98, 99, 101, 103, 107, 109; III.33; VI.83, 94, 98; VIII.22, 32, 39; IX.1; X.11, 17, 38, 38, 71, 122, 129, 170; XI.40, 41, 68; XII.90, 96; XV.197, 198; XVII.175; XVIII.41; XIX.44, 59, 65; XXI.173; XXIV.6, 15, 80; XXV.41, 129, 130; XXVI.67; XXVII.31; XXVIII.50; XXX.19, 60; XXXI.32, 37, 45, 79, 126; XXXVI.7, 129, 142; XXXVII.6, 121, 130; XXXIX.64; XL.61, 63, 72, 110, 116, 128, 131; XLI.44, 77; XLII.2, 14, 66, 68, 72; XLIII.35, 59, 79; XLIV.13, 18, 27, 75, 118, 138, 184, 207; XLV.10, 46; XLVI.6; L.2, 6, 16, 17, 20, 27, 30, 53; LI.95, 103, 150, 151; LII.18, 19; LIII.16;

Pliny the Elder—*contd*
LVI.66, 77; LXV.78; LXIX.34; LXX.11; LXXI.70.

Pliny the Younger [61–113; author of the *Epistles*]: I.13, 16, 40; II.26, 66, 90; III.15, 16, 36; VI.105, 107, 109, 111, 113; VII.15; XIII.98; XV.84, 158, 188, 191; XVI.14, 17, 23, 54, 56, 57, 58, 59, 82, 102; XVII.73, 148; XXI.38; XXV.99; XXVIII.5, 9, 'in the form and disposition of his ten books of epistles, he [Symmachus] imitated the younger Pliny; whose rich and florid style he was supposed, by his friends, to equal or excel' 16; XXXI.39, 63; XXXVI.13; XLI.55; XLIII.71; XLIV.45.

Plotinus [205–70]: X.154; XIII.124; XXI.18.

Plutarch [46–*c*.119]: I.67, 71; II.31, 46; III.8; V.9; VI.83, 86; IX.10, 34, 61; X.39, 114; XII.3; XIII.65; XV.191, 200; XVI.45; XVII.28, 133; XVIII.64; XX.42, 85; XXI.65; XXIV.37, 89; XXVI.9; XXVIII.39; XXX.11, 13; XXXI.8, 51; XXXIV.46; XXXVI.85, 130, 131; XXXVIII.100; 'Gen. Obs.'.1, 13; XL.143; XLI.16; XLII.78; XLIV.18, 65, 115, 123, 124, 151, 152, 167, 176, 181, 183; XLVI.5; LII.70; LXVI.78; 'these lives are a school of freedom as well as of valour' LXVIII.6; LXX.33.

Pocock, Edward [1604–91; orientalist; editor of *Annales Eutychii*, 2 vols. (Oxford, 1656), and of Abulpharagius (Oxford, 1663)]: VIII.54; XV.109, 164; XX.127; XXIV.50; XXXIII.43; XXXIV.7; XLII.38, 40, 59, 100; XLVI.4, 56; XLVII.101, 133; L.2, 'a classic and original work on the Arabian antiquities' 8, 10, 13, 16, 18, 20, 28, 30, 31, 33, 36, 39, 41, 43, 'profound erudition' 44, 46, 47, 52, 54, 57, 59, 60, 61, 65, 66 67, 70, 79, 93, 97, 99, 100, 115, 154; 'a pompous edition of an indifferent author, translated by Pocock to gratify the presbyterian prejudices of his friend Selden' LI.3, 13, 'the English scholar understood more Arabic than the Mufti of Aleppo' 16, 52, 60, 97, 100, 116, 210; LII.5, 38, 53; LIII.99; LVII.73; LIX.38, 42, 102; LXIV.11; LIX.104; LXV.57, 58.

Pocock, Richard [1704–65; bp of Meath; Gibbon owned his *A Description of the East*, 2 vols. (London, 1743, 1745)]: V.60; X.116; 'his plan of the seven hills is clear and accurate. That traveller is seldom so satisfactory' XVII.22, 45, 48; XLIII.84; XLVII.56; 'a work of superior learning and dignity; but the author too often confounds what he had seen and what he had read' LI.67, 'the pompous folio of Doctor Pocock' 71, 85, 103, 106, 111; LVIII. 90; LXII.9; LXIV.45.

Poggius [Poggio Bracciolini, G. F.; 1380–1459; Italian humanist; Gibbon owned his *Historiæ de Varietate Fortunæ Libri Quatuor* (Paris, 1723)]: LXV.37, 'a complete and elegant edition' 50, 52; LXXI.1, 2, 4, 5, 35, 41, 61, 72.

Politianus, Angelus [or Poliziano; 1454–94; poet and humanist; Gibbon owned his *Epistolæ* (Hanover, 1622) and *Conjurationis Pactianæ Anni MCCCCLXXVIII. Commentarium* (Naples, 1769)]: XLIV.76, 87, 92.

Pollio, Trebellius: X.157; XI.2, 12, 15, 16, 49, 50, 54, 73, 83; XL.120.

Pollistore [fourteenth-century Italian historian; Dominican inquisitor]: 'a contemporary writer, who has preserved some curious and original facts' LXX.47, 51.

Pollux, Julius [Gibbon owned his *Onomasticon*, 2 vols. (Amsterdam, 1706)]: XL.150; XLIV.51.

Polo, Marco [Gibbon owned his *De Regionibus Orientalibus Libri III* (Berlin, 1671)]: LXV.16.

Polonus, Martinus: XLIX.130.

Polyænus [Gibbon owned his *Strategematon libri octo* (Leyden, 1690)]: XX.42; XLI.44.

Polybius [*c*.200–*c*.118 BC; statesman and historian]: I.41, 44, 49, 61; II.9; III.11; VI.90; XVII.1, 23; XXIV.106; XXVI.93; XXX.17; XXXII.37; XXXVI.48; 'Gen. Obs.'.1, 2, 3, 4; XLIII.41, 84; XLIV.15, 147, 'how much is the cool, rational evidence of Polybius . . . superior to vague, indiscriminate applause' 159,

204; XLVI.11; XLIX.47; LII.28; LIII.3, 61; LXVIII.49.

Pomponius [Roman lawyer of the Antonine age]: XLIV.5, 8, 12, 32, 53, 61, 85.

Pontanus, Jacobus [or Giovanni Pontano; 1426–1503; Italian humanist]: XLIII.69; 'so deficient in accuracy and elegance' LXVI.32.

Ponticus, Heraclides: XLIV.18.

Pontius [deacon of Carthage; biographer of St Cyprian]: XVI.82, 84, 85, 86, 87, 88.

Pope, Alexander [1688–1744; poet, editor and translator; Gibbon owned his *Works, with the Notes of Mr. Warburton*, 9 vols. (London, 1751), *Poetical Works*, 3 vols. (Glasgow, 1785), and *Works*, 9 vols. (London, 1770)]: II.4; XL.30; LVII.40.

Population de la France, see Messance.

Porphyrius [or Porphyry; *c.*234–*c.*305]: VII.49; X.154; XIII.124; XXI.18; XXIII.32; L.51, 56; LIV.5.

Portius, Simon [Gibbon owned his *Lexicon Latinum, Græco-Barbarum, et Literale* (Paris, 1635)]: LVI.81; LXVI.78.

Possidius [st; bp of Calama; biographer of St Augustine]: XXXIII.15, 25, 36.

Posthumian: XXXVII.33.

Potter, John [1674?–1747; abp of Canterbury; Gibbon owned his *Archæologia Græca*, 2 vols. (London, 1764)]: XLIV.172; LXX.9.

Poussin [editor of George Pachymer]: XLII.55; LXII.28.

Praxagoras: XIV.12, 50.

Praxeas: XXI.41, 54.

Pray, George [Gibbon owned his *Dissertationes Historico-Criticæ in Annales Veteres Hunnorum, Avarum et Hungarorum* (Vienna, 1775)]: 'Pray . . . embraces a large and often conjectural space' LV.18, 'this rude annalist' 19, 21, 22, 25, 34, 40.

Prémare, Joseph Henri [1666–1736; missionary and sinologist; author of *Lettres édifiantes*]: XLIV.200; XLVII.154.

Prévost d'Exiles, Antoine François de [1697–1763; editor of *Histoire générale des voyages*]: XX.79; XXV.131; XXVI.26, 32; XXXIV.7, 44; XXXIX.43; XL.70, 110; XLV.44.

Prideaux, Humphrey [1648–1724; orientalist; Gibbon owned his *The Old and New Testament Connected in the History of the Jews* (London, 1718, and London, 1749), and *The True Nature of Imposture Fully Displayed in the Life of Mahomet* (London, 1718)]: VIII.7, 12; XV.4, 132; XL.104; L.20, 65, 72, 96, 98, 104, 'the adverse wish of finding an impostor or an hero, has too often corrupted the learning of the doctór and the ingenuity of the count [Boulainvilliers]' 111, 112, 121, 'gross bigotry' 149, 158; LI.12, 198; LVI.57.

Priestley, Joseph [1733–1804; theologian and scientist; Gibbon owned his *Disquisitions Relating to Matter and Spirit*, 2 vols. (Birmingham, 1782), *A Free Discussion of the Doctrines of Materialism and Philosophical Necessity, in a Correspondence between Dr. Price and Dr. Priestley* (London, 1778), *An History of the Corruptions of Christianity*, 2 vols. (Birmingham, 1782), *Letters to a Philosophical Unbeliever. Part II, Containing a State of the Evidence of Revealed Religion, with Animadversions on the Two Last Chapters of the First Volume of Mr. Gibbon's History* (Birmingham, 1787) and *The Rudiments of English Grammar* (London, 1768)]: 'the miraculous conception is one of the last articles which Dr. Priestley has curtailed from his scanty creed' XLVII.4; 'I shall recommend to public animadversion two passages in Dr. Priestley, which betray the ultimate tendency of his opinions. At the first of these . . ., the priest; at the second . . ., the magistrate, may tremble!' LIV.42.

Prior, Matthew [1664–1721; poet and diplomat; Gibbon owned his *Poems on Several Occasions* (London, 1718)]: XLI.33; 'verbose but eloquent' LII.50.

Priscus of Panium: X.19, 53; XIII.74, 76; XVIII.75; XIX.50, 83; XXV.146; XXVI.72;

Priscus of Panium—*contd* XXXII.78; XXXIV.1, 4, 5, 9, 11, 13, 17, 18, 26, 29, 31, 32, 35, 36, 38, 39, 'Priscus was a native of Panium in Thrace, and deserved, by his eloquence, an honourable place among the sophists of the age. His Byzantine history, which related to his own times, was comprised in seven books. . . . Notwithstanding the charitable judgment of the critics, I suspect that Priscus was a Pagan' 41, 42, 43, 47, 49; XXXV.1, 7, 18, 26, 29, 65, 69; XXXVI.47, 49, 60, 62, 106, 126;. XL.67, 76; XLII.24, 34, 90; XLIII.41; XLV.6, 11, 33; XLVI.7, 23, 27; L.29.

Proclus: XXIII.25.

Procopius of Cæsarea [historian]: II.88; X.17, 148; XIII.48, 49, 78; XIV.10; XVII.12, 91; XXIV.104; XXV.133; XXVI.48, 56; XXIX.61; XXX.60, 65; XXXI.94, 98, 101, 106, 149, 177, 186; XXXII.63, 64, 82, 84; XXXIII.3, 11, 15, 16, 33, 34, 41; XXXIV.19, 36, 52; XXXV.49, 'a fabulous writer for the events which precede his own memory' 74; XXXVI.4, 11, 32, 50, 52, 54, 59, 62, 66, 84, 86, 87, 90, 106, 117, 119; XXXVII.90, 100, 102, 125; XXXVIII.5, 35, 36, 42, 45, 47, 56, 59, 136, 161, 163; XXXIX.3, 16, 'an impartial sceptic' 22, 24, 26, 27, 28, 30, 37, 40, 43, 50, 52, 54, 56, 64, 68, 79, 86, 101, 103, 104, 106; XL.4, 5, 8, 9, 13, 'the literary fate of Procopius has been somewhat unlucky. 1. His books de Bello Gothico were stolen by Leonard Aretin, and published . . . in his own name . . . 2. His works were mutilated by the first Latin translators, Christopher Persona . . . and Raphael de Volaterra . . ., who did not even consult the MS. of the Vatican library, of which they were præfects . . . 3. The Greek text was not printed till 1607, by Hoeschelius of Augsburgh . . . 4. The Paris edition was imperfectly executed by Calude Maltret, a Jesuit of Tholouse (in 1663), far distant from the Louvre press and the Vatican MS. from which, however, he obtained some supplements. His promised commentaries, &c. have never appeared. The Agathias of Leyden (1594) has been wisely reprinted by the Paris editor, with the Latin version of Bonaventura Vulcanius, a learned interpreter' 14, 'a Christian, as well as a courtly style' 16, 17, 18, 20, 22, 23, 24, 26, 31, 32, 35, 38, 45, 46, 47, 'the doubtful credit of Procopius' 48, 49, 52, 53, 65, 66, 67, 73, 76, 80, 82, 84, 92, 93, 94, 101, 102, 103, 106, 109, 110, 112, 118, 124, 125, 126, 127, 130, 132, 133, 135, 136, 137, 139, 142, 158; 'happy would be my lot, could I always tread in the footsteps of such a guide' XLI.1, 5, 6, 7, 8, 10, 14, 15, 20, 23, 28, 30, 35, 37, 39, 40, 42, 43, 45, 47, 49, 51, 52, 54, 56, 57, 59, 60, 61, 62, 63, 74, 80, 81, 82, 84, 85, 86, 87, 91, 93, 95, 96, 97, 100, 101, 105, 111, 'Of these strange Anecdotes, a part may be true, because probable – and a part true, because improbable. Procopius must have *known* the former, and the latter he could scarcely *invent*' 112, 113, 114, 115, 117; XLII.3, 4, 6, 10, 12, 15, 16, 18, 19, 20, 22, 28, 39, 41, 42, 43, 51, 57, 58, 60, 61, 62, 63, 64, 80, 83, 85, 89, 90, 94, 100; 'I neither have nor desire another guide than Procopius, whose eye contemplated the image, and whose ear collected the reports, of the memorable events of his own times' XLIII.1, 2, 3, 5, 6, 7, 9, 10, 11, 12, 17, 19, 20, 21, 22, 23, 24, 26, 28, 29, 30, 32, 36, 40, 42, 'We must now relinquish a statesman and soldier, to attend the footsteps of a poet and rhetorician [Agathias]' 47, 58, 60, 61, 62, 63, 66, 71, 72, 73, 74, 83, 89, 94, 95; XLIV.72, 74, 96, 198; XLVII.80, 81, 82, 83, 87, 90, 91, 93, 'he seems to promise an ecclesiastical history. It would have been curious and impartial' 97, 145; XLIX.10; L.9, 24, 29, 38, 52, 174; LII.18, 23; LXVIII.97.

Propertius, Sextus Aurelius [*c*.55–*c*.16 BC]: XXXI.5; XLIV.30.

Prosper-Tyro [or of Aquitaine; c.390–463; st; historian of France]: XI.82; XXVI.105; XXVIII.33, 43; XXX.45, 80, 84; XXXI.144, 150, 166, 169; XXXIII.12, 35, 37; XXXIV.18, 20, 33; XXXV.8, 9, 15, 30, 33, 59; XXXVI.11.

Protospata, Lupus [chronicler]: LVI.30, 69, 76.

Proverbs: XLI.33.

Prudentius Clemens, Aurelius: XV.72, 134; XX.32, 33; XXI.173; 'the consciousness of a generous sentiment seems to have raised the Christian poet above his usual mediocrity' XXII.85; XXVIII.8, 15, 17, 18, 19, 21, 22, 62; XXX.47, 49, 57; XXXI.19.

Psellus, Michael [1018–c.1078; Byzantine scholar]: LIII.109, 110.

Ptolemy [fl. 127–45 AD]: I.85; IX.18; X.11, 15; XIII.77; XXIV.6; XXV.101; XXVII.31; XLI.15; L.2, 30; LVIII.73.

Pulci, Luigi [1432–84; poet; author of the *Morgante Maggiore*]: LXVI.118.

Purchas, Samuel [1575?–1626; Gibbon owned his *Hakluytus Posthumus, or Purchas his Pilgrimes*, 5 vols. (London, 1625–6)]: XLII.93; XLVII.158.

Purpurius: XXI.7.

Q

Quadratus, Asinius: X.86.

Quadrigarius, Claudius [annalist]: XLIV.107.

Quesnel, Pierre [1699–1774; Gibbon owned his *Histoire de Don Inigo de Guipuscoa*, 2 vols. (The Hague, 1738)]: XXXVII.114.

Quintilianus, Marcus Fabius [c.35–c.96 AD]: II.40; VII.46; XXXI.63; XL.25; 'that judicious critic' LI.123.

Quirini, Angelo Maria [Gibbon owned the *Commentarii de Rebus Pertinentibus ad Ang: Mar: S. R. E. Cardinalem Quirinum pars prima*, 5 vols. (Brescia, 1749–61), *De Monastica Italiæ Historia Conscribenda Dissertatio* (Rome, 1717), *Liber Singularis de Optimorum Scriptorum Editionibus quæ Romæ Primum Prodierunt* (Lindau, 1761) and *Epistolæ* (Venice, 1756)]: XLIX.71.

Quirinus, Lauro: LXVIII.72.

R

Racine, Jean [1639–99; playwright; Gibbon owned his *Œuvres*, 7 vols. (Paris and London, 1768), and the *Lettres de Racine et mémoires sur sa vie* (Lausanne, 1747)]: XVIII.25; XXX.12; XLIV.133; 'the judicious Racine' LIII.60; LXI.53.

Rader, Matthæus [or Raderus; Jesuit; editor of Petrus Siculus, *Historia de Vana Manichæorum Hæresi* (Ingolstadt, 1604)]: LIV.1.

Ramusio, Giovanni Battista [1485–1557; humanist and geographer; Gibbon owned his *Navigationi et Viaggi*, 3 vols. (Venice, 1550–6)]: XXV.125; XXXIII.26; XLI.45; XLII.93, 99; LI.140; LVI.105; LVII.52; LXIII.47; LXIV.17, 23; LXV.16, 21; LXVII.7.

Ramusio, Paolo [or Rhamnusus, or Rhamnusius; historian of the conquest of Constantinople by the Latins]: LX.54, 'I shall conclude this chapter with the notice of a modern history, which illustrates the taking of Constantinople by the Latins; but which has fallen somewhat late into my hands. Paolo Ramusio, the son of the compiler of voyages, was directed by the senate of Venice to write the history of the conquest; and this order, which he received in his youth, he executed in a mature age, by an elegant Latin work, de Bello Constantinopolitano et Imperatoribus Comnenis per Gallos et Venetos restitutis (Venet. 1635, in folio). Ramusio, or Rhamnusus, transcribes and translates sequitur ad unguem, a MS. of Villehardouin, which he possessed; but he enriches his narrative with Greek and Latin materials, and we are indebted to him for a correct state of the fleet, the names of the fifty Venetian nobles who commanded the gallies of the republic,

Ramusio, Paolo—*contd* and the patriot opposition of Pantaleon Barbus to the choice of the doge for emperor' 103.

Ranzanus, Petrus [bp of Lucera; Sicilian historian of Hungary; author of *Epitome Rerum Hungaricarum*]: LV.42; LXVII.34.

Rapin-Thoyras, Paul de [1661–1725; historian; Gibbon owned his *Histoire de l'Angleterre*, 13 vols. (The Hague, 1724–36)]: XXXVIII.128.

'Ravenna, Geographer of', *see Anonymi Ravennatis*. . .

Raynal, Guillaume Thomas F. [1713–96; Gibbon owned his *Histoire philosophique et politique des . . . deux Indes*, 7 vols. (The Hague, 1774) and 4 vols. (Geneva, 1780)]: XX.74; XXI.163; XXV.132; XXXI.79; XL.70; LI.23, 25.

Raynaldus, Odoricus [or Odericus; continuator of Baronius's *Annals*, 10 vols. (Rome, 1646–77)]: LXVI.1, 7, 8; LXIX.52; LXX.48, 61.

Réaumur, René Antoine Ferchault de [1683–1757; Gibbon owned his *L'Art de faire éclorre et d'élever des oiseaux domestiques*, 2 vols. (Paris, 1749), and *Mémoires pour servire à l'histoire des insectes*, 6 vols. (Paris, 1734–42) and 12 vols. (Amsterdam, 1737–48)]: LII.52.

Recherches sur l'administration des terres chez les Romains: XXXVI.138.

Recueil de pièces intèressantes et peu connues, 4 vols. (Maestricht, 1786): LXI.79.

Reimarus, Hermann Samuel [or Reimar, or Reymar; 1694–1768; editor of Dion Cassius]: I.1; III.25; VI.76; XVI.46; XXXI.88; XL.62, 112, 148; XLII.79; XLIV.38, 155; LXVI.29.

Reiske, Johann Jacob [1716–74; editor of Abulfeda's *Annales Moslemici*; author of *Prodidagmata* (Lipsiæ, 1766); Gibbon owned his *Oratorum Græcorum, quorum Princeps est Demosthenes, quæ Supersunt Monumenta Ingenii*, 12 vols. (Leipzig, 1770)]: XLI.10; XLII.3, 29; XLIV.19, 179, 194; L.49, 'pride and acrimony' 130, 161, 169; LI.12, 13, 21, 30, 'petulant' 44, 60, 67, 138, 165; LII.2, 61, 108, 116; 'a splendid MS. of Constantine . . . was published in a splendid edition by Leich and Reiske . . ., with such lavish praise as editors never fail to bestow on the worthy or worthless object of their toil' LIII.2, 35, 40, 52, 56; LV.16, 48; LVII.3, 14, 67; LVIII.90; LIX.7.

Reitz, Johann Frederik [editor of Lucian]: XXIV.31; XXXI.64; XL.148; XLIV.33, 42.

Reland, Adrian [author of *De Religione Mohammedicâ* (Utrecht, 1717); Gibbon owned his *De Spoliis Templi Hierosolymitani in Arcu Titiano* (Utrecht, 1716), *Dissertationum Miscellanearum Pars Prima (–Tertia)*, 3 vols. (Utrecht, 1706–8) and *Palæstina ex Monumentis Veteribus Illustrata*, 2 vols. (Utrecht, 1714)]: XXIII.57, 59, 138; 'learned and accurate' XXXVI.8; XXXVII.6; 'much superfluous learning' L.4, 47, 53, 70, 79, 80, 'his excellent treatise de Religione Mohammedicâ . . . Reland, a judicious student, had travelled over the East in his closet at Utrecht' 101, 'candid' 108, 110, 'the learned Reland' 126, 127, 141, 151, 154, 173; LI.48, 49, 50, 64, 69, 'this learned professor was equal to the task of describing the Holy Land, since he was alike conversant with Greek and Latin, with Hebrew and Arabian literature' 74, 79, 118, 196, 201, 217; LVIII.107, 108.

Remigius [*c*.437–*c*.533; st]: XXXVIII.27, 28.

Remond [author of *Observations sur les voyages de Coxe dans la Suisse*]: XL.128.

Renaudot, Eusèbe [1646–1720; Gibbon owned his *Historia Patriarcharum Alexandrinorum Jacobitarum* (Paris, 1713), *Anciennes relations des Indes et de la Chine* (Paris, 1718) and *Ancient Accounts of India and China, by two Mahommedan Travellers* (London, 1733)]: XV.164; XX.79; XL.70; XLII.54; XLIV.200; XLVII.23, 73, 109, 125, 129, 141, 144, 'Renaudot's motley work, neither a translation nor an original' 149, 150, 151, 154, 155, 156; L.148; LI.110, 112, 'I may distinguish with honour the rational scepticism of Renaudot' 116,

122, 135, 208, 213, 215; LII.51, 54, 57, 81; LVII.67; LVIII.102, 116; LIX.41, 45, 53, 63; LXVIII.34.

Rennell, James [or Rennel; 1742–1830; historian and cartographer of India; Gibbon owned his *Memoir of a Map of Hindoostan* (London, 1783, and London, 1788)]: 'If he extends the sphere of his enquiries with the same critical knowledge and sagacity, he will succeed, and may surpass the first of modern geographers [d'Anville]' XL.71; 'his excellent Memoir on his map of Hindostan' LVII.6, 7; 'the rivers of the Punjab, the five eastern branches of the Indus, have been laid down for the first time with truth and accuracy in Major Rennel's incomparable map of Hindostan' LXV.25, 26.

Resnel, Pierre de [fl. 1677]: XXXVIII.51.

Retz, Jean François Paul de Gondi, cardinal de [1613–79; statesman; Gibbon owned his *Mémoires*, 4 vols. (Amsterdam, 1731, and Geneva, 1777)]: XXVII.64; 'genius' LXIX.71, 72.

Revelation [or Apocalypse]: XV.63, 67, 110; LXIV.45.

Rhegino: LV.29.

Richard of Cirencester [author of *De Sitû Britanniæ*]: I.11; II.32; XIII.25; XXXI.181.

Ricobaldo [Italian chronicler]: LXIX.60.

Riedesel, Johann Hermann, Freiherr von [Gibbon owned his *Travels through Sicily*, tr. J. R. Forster (London, 1773)]: XLIII.18; LVI.98.

Rimius, Henry [author of *Memoirs of the House of Brunswick* (London, 1750)]: LXIII.14, 15, 16, 17.

Robertson, William [1721–93; historian; Gibbon owned his *The History of America*, 3 vols. (London, 1788), *The History of Scotland during the Reigns of Queen Mary and of King James VI* (London, 1759), *The History of Scotland*, 2 vols. (London, 1787), and *The History of the Reign of the Emperor Charles V*, 3 vols. (London, 1769) and 4 vols. (London, 1787)]: IX.40, 66; 'learned and judicious' XXV.126; 'an admirable narrative' XXXI.116; XLIX.95, 'that masterly sketch which traces even the modern changes of the Germanic body' 149; LVIII.82, 141; LXI.69.

Rocca, Angelo [Roman antiquary]: XLV.65.

Roderic of Toledo, *see* Ximines, Roderic.

Rogerius, M. [thirteenth-century Hungarian historian; author of *Carmen Miserabile, seu Historia super Destructione Regni Hungariæ . . . per Tartaros Facta*]: 'the original narrative of a contemporary, an eye-witness, and a sufferer . . .: the best picture that I have ever seen of all the circumstances of a Barbaric invasion' LXIV.16.

Rollin, Charles [1661–1741; *érudit*; Gibbon owned his *De la manière d'enseigner et d'étudier les belles-lettres*, 4 vols. (Paris, 1726–8)]: XLI.77.

Romuald of Salerno [chronicler]: LVI.92, 122.

Rorico [historian of France]: XXXVIII.56.

Rossi, Bastiano de' [topographer of Rome]: XLI.77.

Rosweydus, Heribertus [or Rosweide; Jesuit; publisher of the *History of the Fathers of the Desert*; Gibbon owned his *Vitæ Patrum* (Antwerp, 1615)]: XXI.100; XXVII.113; XXIX.9; XXXVII.7, 9, 38, 47, 73.

Rousseau, Jean-Jacques [1728–78; *philosophe*; Gibbon owned his *Œuvres diverses*, 3 vols. (Amsterdam, 1734), *Œuvres*, 9 vols. (Amsterdam, 1769), *Collection complète des œuvres*, 17 vols. (Geneva, 1782–9), *Supplément aux œuvres* (Amsterdam, 1767), *Les confessions*, 2 vols. (The Hague, 1782), *Du contrat social* (Amsterdam, 1762), *Lettre à M. de Beaumont* (Amsterdam, 1764), *Lettres écrites de la montagne* (Amsterdam, 1764) and *Recueil de lettres, et autres pièces* (London, 1766)]: XXVI.9; 'much good taste' XLVI.96; XLVII.16.

Rowe, Nicholas [1674–1718; playwright]: XXXVIII.163; LXV.69.

Rowlands, Henry [1655–1723; author of *Mona Antiqua Restaurata* (Dublin, 1723)]: XXVII.10.

Rubruguis [or Rubruquis, or Willem van Ruysbroek; traveller]: XXVI.7; XXXIV.44; LXIV.32,

Rudbeck, Olaus: 'the authority of Rudbeck is much to be suspected' IX.8, 15.

Ruddiman, Thomas [editor of George Buchanan]: XX.21; XXXVII.24.

Rufinus Tyrannius [*c.*345–410]: XIV.45; XX.76, 112, 125; XXI.134, 138; XXIV.116; XXVII.113; XXVIII.35, 40, 48; XXXVII.14, 15, 29, 33, 58, 63, 65, 70.

Rufus, Sextus: X.147; XI.22, 65; XII.76; XIV.36.

Ruinart, Thierry [1657–1709; editor of Gregory of Tours; Gibbon owned his *Acta Primorum Martyrum* (Amsterdam, 1713) and *Historia Persecutionis Vandalicæ* (Paris, 1694)]: XV.172, 173; XVI.65, 145, 146, 158, 171, 179; XX.98; XXIII.116; XXVIII.78; XXXIII.11, 15, 25, 36, 42; XXXV.4; 'copious and learned' XXXVII.90, 92, 95, 96, 123, 125; XXXVIII.107, 109; XLI.2.

Ruotgerus, Coloniensis [biographer of St Bruno]: XLIX.117.

Rycaut, Sir Paul [1628–1700; Gibbon owned his *The History of the Present State of the Ottoman Empire* (London, 1675)]: XL.114; XLIV.200; LII.4; LIII.44; LXV.30, 85, 88; LXVII.15; LXVIII.44.

Rymer, Thomas [1641–1713; author of *Fœdera*]: LVIII.68; LXVII.17.

S

Saadi Essendi of Larissa: 'a valuable abridgement of the original historians' LXIV.41, 59.

Sabellicus, Marcus Antonius Coccius [historian of Venice]: LX.54.

Sabellius [heretic]: XXI.41, 42.

Sabinus: XXI.70.

Sabinus, Floridus [or Franciscus Floridus]: XLIV.79.

Sadder, The: VIII.11, 14, 20.

Sade, Jacques François P. A. de [1705–78; ecclesiastic and man of letters; Gibbon owned his *Mémoires pour la vie de François Pétrarque*, 3 vols. (Amsterdam, 1764–7)]: XLIX.151; LXIII.54; LXVI.3, 'a gentleman as well as a priest' 4, 10, 'excellent' 90, 95, 99; LXIX.17, 81, 89, 93, 'his criticism often rectifies the hearsay stories of Villani, and the errors of the less diligent moderns' 102, 109; 'a copious, original, and entertaining work, a labour of love, composed from the accurate study of Petrarch and his contemporaries; but the hero is too often lost in the general history of the age, and the author too often languishes in the affectation of politeness and gallantry' LXX.1, 2, 4, 5, 6, 12, 13, 14, 15, 'not an idea or a fact in the writings of Petrarch has probably escaped him' 17, 22, 30, 38, 45, 52, 56, 'accurate and amusing' 57, 60, 62; LXXI.8, 66.

Saferna: LXIII.23.

Sagorninus, John [alleged author of anonymous eleventh-century chronicle of Venice]: XLIX.49; LV.12; LX.39; LXIX.32.

Sagredo, Giovanni [Gibbon owned his *Memorie Istoriche de' Monarchi Ottomanni* (Venice, 1677)]: 'Sagredo is not contemptible in either sense or style. Yet he too bitterly hates the infidels; he is ignorant of their language and manners; and his narrative, which allows only seventy pages to Mahomet II. . . ., becomes more copious and authentic as he approaches the years 1640 and 1644, the term of the historic labours of John Sagredo' LXVIII.96.

Sainte-Croix, Guillaume de Clermont-Lodève, baron de [1746–1809; Gibbon owned his *Examen critique des anciens historiens d'Alexandre-le-Grand* (Paris, 1775), and *Mémoires por servir à l'histoire de la religion secrète des anciens peuples: ou recherches sur les mystères de paganisme* (Paris, 1784)]: XXVI.21; XLIV.17; LI.34.

St Germano, Richard de [chronicler]: LVI.128, 139; LIX.88.

St John, Henry, viscount Bolingbroke [1678–1751; English politician and man of letters; Gibbon owned his *Works, published by D. Mallet*, 11 vols. (London,

1754–83), *Letters on the Spirit of Patriotism* (London, 1750) and *Memoirs* (London, 1752)]: LXVI.111.

Saint-Marc, Charles Hugues Lefebvre de [1698–1769; Gibbon owned his *Abrégé chronologique de l'histoire générale d'Italie*, 6 vols. (Paris, 1761–70)]: XLIX.58, 65, 94, 127, 144; LIII.62, 64; 'a work which, under a superficial title, contains much genuine learning and industry' LVI.1, 7, 13, 15, 32, 35, 43, 'St. Marc . . . labours the case with the diligence of a Sicilian lawyer' 58, 82, 83; LXI.52.

Saint-Palaye, Jean Baptiste de la Curne de [1697–1781; historian; author of *Mémoires sur l'ancienne chevalerie*]: XLV.48; LVIII.58; LXVIII.93.

Saint-Paul, Charles Vialart de [bp of Avranches; author of *Geographia Sacra* (Amsterdam, 1704)]: XVI.172; XX.86, 117; XXXI.90; LII.92.

Saint-Pierre, Charles Irénée Castel de [1658–1743; author of *Annales politiques* ('London' [Paris], 1757)]: XLIV.99.

Sale, George [1697–1736; orientalist; Persian scholar; editor of the Koran]: XLII.50, 100; 'our honest and learned translator' XLVI.69; L.20, 37, 38, 42, 'clearly and concisely interpreted' 44, 47, 54, 57, 60, 'half a Musulman' 65, 70, 72, 74, 80, 87, 88, 91, 92, 98, 102, 103, 104, 107, 109, 110, 111, 114, 124, 127, 'learned and rational' 147, 149, 160, 182; LXV.30.

Sallengre, Albert Henri de [1694–1723; Gibbon owned his *Novus Thesaurus Antiquitatum Romanarum*, 3 vols. (The Hague, 1716–19)]: LXXI.50.

Sallust [Gaius Sallustius Crispus; *c.*86–*c.*35 BC]: I.30; XV.53; XVII.94; XVIII.64; XXIV.60; 'The historian Sallust, who usefully practised the vices which he has so eloquently censured' XXXI.105; 'Gen. Obs.'.3; XLI.40; XLII.65; XLIII.10; XLVII.30; XLIX.48; LII.23; LIV.10.

Salmasius, Claudius [or Claude de Saumaise; 1588–1653; *érudit*]: IV.26; VI.115; VII. 16; XI.19; XII.14, 22, 81, 99; XVI.126; XXII.51; 'the profound, diffuse, and obscure researches of the great Salmasius' XL.64, 65, 72, 148; XLIII.45; L.148; LI.70, 150, 'Salmasius appears to exhaust the subject [of citrus trees], but he too often involves himself in the web of his disorderly erudition' 151, 160.

Salvianus of Marseilles [Gibbon owned his *De Gubernatione Dei* (Paris, 1608)]: XXX.91; XXXI.167; XXXIII.12, 38, 40; XXXV.12, 15, 25, 'His immoderate freedom serves to prove the weakness, as well as the corruption, of the Roman government' 77, 78; XXXVII.78, 84.

Sanadon, Noël Étienne [1676–1733; editor and translator of Horace]: X.161; XXV.47.

Sanchoniathon [historian; Gibbon owned his *Phœnician History, Translated from the First Book of Eusebius De Præparatione Evangelica*, by R. Cumberland (London, 1720)]: L.50.

Sandoval, Alonso de [historian]: LI.187.

Sandys, George [1578–1644; Gibbon owned his *Travels* (London, 1673)]: 'that judicious traveller' XVII.14; XXIII.62; LVII.65.

Sanfelicius, Antonius [or San Felice; Gibbon owned his *Campania* (Naples, 1726)]: XXXI.40.

Sanuto, Marino [or Sanudo; 1466–1535; author of *Vite del Dogi*]: LX.54, 99; LXI.8, 10.

Sanutus, Marinus [called Torsello; author of *Secreta Fidelium Crucis*]: LVIII.118, 123, 124, 125, 127, 135; LIX.27, 58, 85, 107, 109; LXI.38, 40, 49.

Saribariensis, Joan.: LVIII.72.

Sarpi, Paolo [1552–1623; historian; Gibbon owned his *Opere*, 6 vols. (Helmstatt, 1761–65) and *Istoria del Concilio Tridentino*, 2 vols. (London, 1757, and London, 1736)]: XV.67, 104, 132, 134, 137; XVI.186; XVIII.51; 'an excellent discourse' XX.113; XXI.55; XLVII.121; L.87; 'the papal system is deeply studied and freely described. Should Rome and her religion be annihilated, this golden volume may

Sarpi, Paolo—*contd*
still survive, a philosophical history, and a salutary warning' LXVI.36; LXX.89.

Savaron, Jean [*c.*1550–1622; editor of Sidonius Apollinaris]: XXXVI.13, 46, 62; XXXVIII.103.

Savary, Claude Étienne [1750–88; traveller and orientalist; Gibbon owned two copies of his *Lettres sur l'Égypte* (Paris, 1785, and Paris, 1786)]: L.111; LI.111, 137; LIX.44, 'agreeable' 97, 103.

Savile, Sir Henry [1549–1622; warden of Merton; provost of Eton; classical scholar; editor of St John Chrysostom; translator of Tacitus; Gibbon owned his *Rerum Anglicarum Scriptores post Bedam Præcipui* (Frankfort, 1601)]: IX.74; XV.159.

Saxe, Christoph [author of *Onomasticon*]: XXXIX.23, 135.

Saxo Grammaticus [fl. twelfth century; Danish historian]: X.7; LV.48.

Scaliger, Joseph Justus [1540–1609; classical scholar; Gibbon owned his *Opus de Emendatione Temporum* (Geneva, 1629) and the *Scaligerana* (Cologne, 1695)]: X.176; XII.64, 99; XIII.16, 40; XVII.2; XVIII.14; XXIII.92; XXV.72, 151; XXVI.105, 123; XXVII.121; XXXI.145; XXXVII.125; XL.8; XLII.79; XLIII.45; XLIV.12; XLIX.11; L.81.

Schardius, Simon [author of *De Potestate Imperiali Ecclesiasticâ*]: XLIX.72.

Scheffer, Johannes Gerhard [classical scholar; editor of Arrianus]: XLII.15; XLVI.40.

Schelestrate: XLIX.32.

Schickard, Wilhelm [or Schikard; Gibbon owned his *Tarich, hoc est, Series Regum Persiæ* (Tübingen, 1628)]: XVIII.54; XLII.45; XLVI.22.

Schmidt, Michael Ignaz [Gibbon owned his *Histoire des Allemands*, 6 vols. (Liège, Rheims, 1784–6)]: XLIX.100, 103, 109, 116, 134, 138, 142, 146; LVIII.23; LXIX.3, 40, 'Schmidt, who has deserved the esteem of his countrymen' 61.

Schminke, Johann Hermann [commentator on, and editor of, Eginhardus]: XLIX.97; LII.26.

Schœpflin, Johann Daniel [or Schæpflin; Gibbon owned his *Commentationes Historicæ et Criticæ* (Basle, 1741)]: XII.43; XLIX.112.

Schultens, Albert [orientalist]: 'a work from which I have obtained much *Oriental* knowledge' XXIV.36; XLVI.79, 90; L.94; LI.52, 136; LVIII.90; LIX.7, 45, 46, 'we are indebted to the professor Schultens . . . for the richest and most authentic materials' 48, 51, 59; LX.19.

Schultingius, Antonius [or Schulting; jurist; author of *Jurisprudentia Ante-Justinianea*]: XLIV.48, 50, 78, 98, 105, 122, 152, 175, 186.

Schweighæuser, Johann [editor of Appianus]: 'the last and best edition' XLII.77; XLIV.184.

Schweitzer, Johann Caspar [or Suicer.; author of *Thesaurus Ecclesiasticus* (Amsterdam, 1682)]: XXXVII.4, 66; XLIV.77.

Scotus, Marianus, *see* Marianus, scotus.

Scylitzes, Joannes [fl. eleventh century; curopalata; continuator of Cedrenus]: LII.80; LVII.25, 27, 35, 36, 38, 51.

Seckendorf, Veit Ludwig von [author of the *Commentarius Historicus et Apologeticus de Lutheranismo*]: XXXI.117.

Secundinus the Manichæan: XXXI.23.

Secundus [historian]: XLV.33.

Selden, John [1584–1654; jurist; Gibbon owned his *Opera Omnia*, 3 vols. (London, 1726), and *The Historie of Tithes* (London, 1618)]: XV.9; XLIV.86, 119, 121, 129, 131; 'The learned Selden has given the history of transubstantiation in a comprehensive and pithy sentence. "This opinion is only rhetoric turned into logic."' XLIX.1, 56, 101, 144; 'the learning and credulity of Selden' L.82, 160; LI.13; 'our learned Selden' LIII.49; LVI.17; LVIII.55, 58; LIX.83; LXX.7.

Sellius, Homerus [commentator on Menander]: LIII.110.

Sematsien [Chinese chronologist and historian]: XXVI.23.

Seneca [Lucius Annæus Seneca; *c.*4 BC–AD 65]: II.13, 30, 40, 53; XV.43, 191, 197; XXI.73; 'Seneca . . . shews the feelings of a man' XXX.59; XXXI.25, 29, 37, 43, 52, 59; XXXVI.128; XXXVII.97; XXXIX.94; XLI.3; XLIII.75; XLIV.109, 125, 167, 175; 'the narrow stoicism of Seneca . . ., whose wisdom, on this occasion [Livy's praise of the Alexandrian library], deviates into nonsense' LI.119.

Sephadius: L.33.

Sepulveda, Juan Gines de [biographer of Giles Albornoz, abp of Toledo and cardinal legate in Italy]: LXX.53.

Servius Honoratus, Maurus [commentator on Virgil]: XV.45; XXI.173; XXXI.170; XLIII.46; XLIV.122.

Severini, Joannes [Gibbon owned his *Pannonia Veterum Monumentis Illustrata* (Leipzig, 1770)]: I.79; XIV.36; XXXIX.2.

Severus [tenth-century bp of Hermapolis Magna, or Ashmunein]: 'who can never be trusted, unless our assent is extorted by the internal evidence of facts' XLVII.23; LI.110, 112.

Severus, Sulpicius [*c.*363–*c.*420; author of the *Historia Sacra, Dialogues* and a life of St Martin]: XV.17, 21, 67, 171, 172; XVI.92, 112; XVIII.84; XX.84, 89; XXI.76, 85, 87, 95, 97, 127, 132, 149; XXVII.12, 16, 51, 52, 58, 59, 'facts adapted to the grossest barbarism, in a style not unworthy of the Augustan age' 60, 72; XXVIII.30, 76; XXXI.188; XXXVII.19, 20, 33, 38, 52, 65, 73.

Sextus Rufus: I.20; XVIII.45, 56, 60, 61; XXIII.110; XXIV.71, 72, 77, 109, 113, 127.

Shakespeare, William [1564–1616; Gibbon owned his *Plays, to which are added notes by Sam. Johnson*, 8 vols. (London, 1765), *Works. With notes by L. Theobald*, 8 vols. (London, 1773) and *The Plays of William Shakespeare. To which are added notes by S. Johnson and G. Steevens. (Supplement [by E. Malone].)*, 12 vols. (London, 1778–80)]: 'his mother-tongue, the language of nature' XXVII.29; 'our English poet' XLIII.54; 'a breed of barren metal, exclaims Shakespeare [about usury] – and the stage is the echo of the public voice' XLIV.167; 'the natural feelings of enthusiasm' LVIII.20; 'an ignorant age transfers its own language and manners to the most distant times' LXII.53; LXVI.20.

Shaw Abbas [or Abbas I, shah of Persia, author of *Binarum Litterarum Copia* (Brussels, 1611)]: L.53.

Shaw, Thomas [1694–1751; Gibbon owned his *Travels, or Observations Relating to Several Parts of Barbary and the Levant* (London, 1757)]: I.86; V.60; VII.13; XI.72; XVI.82; XIX.59; 'our blind travellers seldom possess any previous knowledge of the countries which they visit. Shaw and Tournefort deserve an honourable exception' XXIV.49; XXXIII.26; XXXVI.52, 87; XLI.15, 17, 19, 29, 35, 'Shaw . . . is the best commentator on the poet [Virgil] and the geographer [Pomponius Mela]' 41, 45; XLIII.4; L.2, 5, 17, 129; LI.103, 106, 143, 147, 148, 154, 161, 163; LVI.105.

Sicard, Claude [1677–1726; Jesuit missionary]: XXXVII.10, 11, 69; XLVII.139, 149; XLIX.17; LI.106.

Sicard of Cremona [Italian chronicler]: LVI.124.

Siculus, Petrus [author of the *Historia de Vana Manichæorum Hæresi*, ed. Matthæus Rader (Ingolstadt, 1604)]: LIV.1, 3, 4, 7, 8, 14, 15, 16, 17, 22.

Sidonius, C. Sollius Modestus Apollinaris [*c.*430–*c.*479; poet; bp of Clermont]: XII.76; XVII.57, 181; XVIII.17, 28; XX.90; XXV.104, 'the best original account of the Saxon pirates may be found in Sidonius Apollinaris' 105, 107; XXX.60, 61, 96; XXXI.153, 163, 184, 190; XXXV.4, 9, 10, 13, 14, 15, 19, 23, 24, 31, 32, 36, 39, 59, 60, 73, 76; XXXVI.1, 2, 3, 5, 11, 12, 13, 14, 21, 24, 26, 28, 31, 33, 36, 38, 45, 46, 49, 51, 56, 57, 60, 62, 63, 71, 72, 73, 74, 75, 'If Jerom was scourged by the angels for only reading Virgil; the bishop of Clermont,

Sidonius, C. Sollius Modestus Apollinaris—*cont* for such a vile imitation, deserved an additional whipping from the muses' 79, 'an imperfect but original picture of Gaul' 93, 94, 95, 96, 'The prose of Sidonius, however vitiated by a false and affected taste, is much superior to his insipid verses' 97, 101, 114, 134; XXXVII.87, 89; XXXVIII.4, 6, 16, 27, 101, 103; XLV.48.

Sigebert of Gembloux [*c*.1030–1112; chronicler]: XLIX.130; LV.38; LXXI.30.

Sigonius, Charles [historian; Gibbon owned his *Historiarum de Regno Italiæ Libri Quindecim* (Frankfort, 1575) and *Opera*, 6 vols. (Milan, 1732–7)]: XXX.38; XXXV.51; XXXVI.109; XXXIX.20; XL.150; XLI.62, 63; XLIII.6; XLIV.28, 173, 201; 'eloquent narrative' XLV.20, 75; XLIX.27, 48, 65, 93, 94, 135, 137, 139, 140; LVI.1, 15, 82; 'both Blondus, and even Sigonius, too freely copied the classic method of supplying from reason or fancy the deficiency of records' LXIX.30, 88.

Sike, Henricus [commentator on the Apocrypha]: L.86.

Silentiarius, Paulus [poet]: XL.39, 101, 103, 'dark and poetic language' 105.

Simler, Josias [author of *De Republica Helvetiorum* (Zurich, 1734)]: X.74; XIV.53; XXVI.71.

Simocatta, Theophylactus [historian; author of the *History of the Emperor Maurice*]: XL.76; XLII.30, 32; XLV.9, 27, 28, 'prolix and florid history' 30, 33; XLVI.7, 9, 11, 13, 14, 15, 20, 22, 23, 24, 25, 26, 27, 30, 31, 'If he were a writer of taste or genius, we might suspect him of an elegant irony: but Theophylact is surely harmless' 34, 36, 37, 38, 'his want of judgment renders him diffuse in trifles and concise in the most interesting facts' 39, 41, 42, 43, 44, 45, 47, 51, 'the life of Maurice was composed about the year 628 . . . by Theophylact Simocatta, ex-præfect, a native of Egypt. Photius, who gives an ample extract of the work . . ., gently reproves the affectation and allegory of the style. His preface is a dialogue between Philosophy and History; they seat themselves under a plane-tree, and the latter touches her lyre' 55, 77; XLIX.12; LXVI.32.

Simon, Richard [1638–1712; Gibbon owned his *Bibliothèque critique: ou recueil de diverses pièces critiques, publiées par Mr. de Sainjore*, 4 vols. (Basle, 1709–10), *Histoire critique des principaux commentateurs du nouveau Testament* (Rotterdam, 1693), *Histoire critique des versions du nouveau Testament* (Rotterdam, 1689), *Histoire critique du vieux Testament* (Amsterdam, 1685) and *Réponse au livre [by J. le Clerc] intitulé Sentimens de quelques théologiens de Hollande sur l'histoire critique du vieux Testament* (Amsterdam, '1621')]: XXXVII.75, 'in 1689, the papist Simon strove to be free; in 1707, the protestant Mill wished to be a slave; in 1751, the Arminian Wetstein used the liberty of his times, and of his sect' 115; XLVII.5, 111; L.62; LIV.4.

Simoneta, Giovanni [author of *De Rebus Francisci Sfortiæ*]: LXVII.43.

Simplicius [fl. *c*.530; author of *De Cœlo*]: L.56.

Sinner, Jean Rodolphe [Gibbon owned his *Voyage historique et littéraire dans la Suisse Occidentale*, 2 vols. (Neuchâtel, 1781)]: XXXIX.97; LXIV.62.

Sionita, Gabriel [translator of Edrisi's *Geographia Nubiensis*]: L.148; LI.52.

Sirmond, Jacques [or Sirmondus; 1559–1651; *érudit*; editor of Sidonius Apollinaris and Ennodius; Gibbon owned his *Opera Varia*, 5 vols. (Paris, 1696)]: XVII.57, 181; XX.125; XXV.81, 105; XXX.96; XXXI.111, 153, 163, 184, 190; XXXV.59; XXXVI.13, 46, 55, 57, 62, 95, 97, 100, 103, 104, 115, 116, 119, 134, 135; XXXVII.89; XXXVIII.103; XXXIX.3, 10, 23, 77; XLII.11; XLVII.94; XLIX.79; LII.113.

Smith, Adam [1723–90; political economist and moral philosopher; Gibbon owned his *An Inquiry into the Nature and Causes of the Wealth of Nations*, 2 vols. (London, 1776), and *The Theory of Moral Sentiments* (London, 1767, and London, 1790)]: 'the work of a sage and a friend' XXIV.15; XL.87, 'a judicious philosopher' 148; LXI.69; 'Smith . . . who proves, perhaps too severely, that the most salutary effects have flowed from the meanest and most selfish causes' LXX.92.

Smith, John [1659–1715; editor of Bede]: XXXVII.81, 136; XXXVIII.126.

Smith, Thomas [1638–1710; author of the *Remarks upon the Manners, Religion and Government of the Turks. Together with a Survey of the Seven Churches of Asia, as they now lye in their Ruines: and A Brief Description of Constantinople* (London, 1678)]: LXIV.45.

Socrates [*c*.380–*c*.450; historian]: XV.25; XVI.13, 143; XVII.48, 58, 63, 137; XVIII.45, 76, 78, 98; XIX.12; XXI.5, 42, 45, 70, 80, 82, 84, 86, 93, 96, 104, 119, 151, 153, 154, 155, 164; XXII.53, 82; XXIII.7, 32, 94, 96, 134; XXIV.10, 'inaccurate' 75, 76, 102; XXV.3, 9, 23, 68, 70, 76, 154, 155; XXVI.88, 94, 105; XXVII.14, 20, 24, 37, 43, 84, 98, 104, 115, 122; XXVIII.35; XXIX.30; XXX.102, 109, 120; XXXII.21, 29, 33, 39, 40, 41, 44, 50, 51, 52, 57, 65, 72, 74, 75, 79, 81; XXXIII.3; XXXIV.3, 40; XXXVII.74, 80; XLVII.18, 22, 23, 27, 29, 30, 41, 47, 51.

Socrates [*c*.470–399 BC; Greek philosopher]: XV.43; XLVII.16; L.155.

Solinus, Caius Julius [Gibbon owned his *Polyhistor* (Leipzig, 1777) and *Cl. Salmasii Plinianæ Exercitationes in C. Julii Solini Polyhistora. Item C. J. Solini Polyhistor Emendatus*, 2 vols. (Utrecht, 1688–9)]: XL.72; L.53; LI.160.

Soyouthi [chronicler of the caliphs]: LVII.38.

Sozomen [*c*.400–*c*.450]: VIII.29; XIV.92, 112, 25; XVII.21, 48, 55, 58, 63, 68; XVIII.45, 76, 98; XIX.64; XX.37, 76, 110; XXI.5, 45, 84, 86, 93, 94, 96, 98, 103, 104, 119, 133, 141, 149, 151, 153, 154, 155, 164; XXIII.7, 35, 88, 93, 94, 99, 104, 118, 134, 137, 138; XXIV.40, 43, 102, 132; XXV.2, 16, 22, 23, 65, 68; XXVI.2, 56, 64, 94, 105; XXVII.14, 20, 23, 24, 32, 37, 43, 46, 50, 65, 91, 98, 102, 109, 114, 121; XXVIII.31, 52; XXIX.9, 30; XXX.102, 105, 106; XXXI.74, 78, 91, 92, 95, 97, 102, 150, 151, 156; XXXII.16, 21, 33, 39, 41, 44, 51, 66, 68, 72; XXXIII.3; XXXVII.4, 40, 68, 74; XLVII.18.

Spandugino, Theodoro: LXI.58.

Spanheim, Ezechiel [1629–1710; *érudit*; editor of Julian the Apostate; Gibbon owned his *Dissertationes de Præstantia et Usu Numismatum Antiquorum*, 2 vols. (London, Amsterdam, 1717), *In Callimachi Hymnos Observationes* (Utrecht, 1697) and *Orbis Romanus* (London, 1703)]: I.4, 15; II.33, 34, 52; III.40; IV.5, 31; V.60; VI.40; VII.10; X.155; XI.86; XIII.9, 13, 15, 97, 101; XIV.91, 100; XV.83, 122, 127, 184; XVI.18, 46, 140; XVII.63, 64, 107; XVIII.6, 10, 31, 33, 45, 60, 62, 63, 74, 96; XIX.90; XX.12; XXI.156; XXIII.19, 20, 54; 'coarse, languid, and correct' XXIV.1, 'Spanheim . . . has most learnedly discussed the etymology, origin, resemblance, and disagreement of the Greek *satyrs*' 2; XLIV.28; LI.54.

Spanheim, Frederick (the younger) [1632–1701; theologian; author of *Historia Imaginum Restituta*; Gibbon owned his *Opera*, 3 vols. (Leyden, 1701–3)]: XVI.120; XLIX.15, 18, 'truth and ingenuity' 19, 20, 24, 29, 40, 77, 82; 'after refuting the absurd charge against the emperor [Leo the Isaurian], Spanheim . . ., like a true advocate, proceeds to doubt or deny the reality of the fire, and almost of the library [of the royal college of Constantinople]', 94, 132 LIII.103.

Spartianus, Ælius: 'undigested collections' V.17, 23, 55.

Specialis, Nicholas [Italian historian]: LXII.40, 'the true spirit of Italian jealousy' 42, 44.

Spelman, Edward [translator of Xenophon]: XIII.66, XXIV.41, 48; XLII.77.

Spence, Joseph [1699–1768; Gibbon owned his *Polymetis* (London, 1755) and *An Essay on Mr. Pope's Odyssey* (London, 1747)]: XL.42.

Spener, Jacob Carl [Gibbon owned his *Historia Germaniæ Universalis et Pragmatica*, 2 vols. (Leipzig and Halle, 1716–17)]: LXIII.17.

Spon, Jacob [1647–85; Gibbon owned his *Histoire de Genève*, 4 vols. (Geneva, 1730), and *Voyage d'Italie, de Dalmatie, de Grèce et du Levant*, 3 vols. (Amsterdam, 1678–9)]: V.60; LX.46; LXII.56, 58; LXIV.45; LXVI.34.

Sponde, Henri de [or Spondanus; 1568–1643; bp of Pamiers; church historian; author of *Ecclesiastical Annals*]: LXVI.8, 18, 30, 40; 'the sense of the latter [Spondanus] is drowned in prejudice and passion, as soon as Rome and religion are concerned' LXVII.6, 10, 'in the Hungarian crusade, Spondanus . . . has been my leading guide. He has diligently read, and critically compared, the Greek and Turkish materials, the historians of Hungary, Poland, and the West. His narrative is perspicuous; and where he can be free from a religious bias, the judgment of Spondanus is not contemptible' 18, 19, 22, 26, 28, 29, 33, 'curious and critical' 34, 38, 44, 47; LXVIII.1, 2, 11, 27, 28, 32, 47, 50, 60, 68, 78, 83, 90, 91, 'that valuable annalist' 95; LXIX.76; LXX.95.

Statius, Publius Papinianus: XXV.119; 'an elegant epistle' XLI.66; L.164; LXX.10.

Stella, George [historian of Genoa; author of *Annales Genuenses*]: LXIII.52.

Stephanus Byzantinus [or Stephen of Byzantium; author of *Gentilia per Epitomen, antehac de Urbibus Inscripta* (Leyden, 1694)]: X.11, 31; XVII.61; XXX.60; L.30.

Stephanus, Henricus [or Henri Étienne; 1528–98; classical scholar; editor of the *Anthologia Græca*, and of Plutarch]: XXXIX.68; XL.143; XLI.16, 81, 105; XLIV.18; L.155; LI.162; LXX.33.

Stephanus, Robertus [or Robert Estienne; 1503–59; classical scholar and author of *Thesaurus Linguæ Latinæ*]: XXXVII.2, 116, 120; XL.42; LXVI.2.

Sterne, Laurence [1713–68; Gibbon owned his *A Sentimental Journey through France and Italy* (London, 1768) and *Works*, 10 vols. (London, 1783)]: 'poor Sterne' LVI.14.

Stevens, John [d. 1726; author of *The History of Persia* (London, 1715)]: XLII.38, 45; XLVI.22; LXV.16.

Stobæus, Joannes: XXIII.25; LIII.109.

Strabo [*c*.64 BC–AD 23]: I.2, 70, 85; II.38, 78, 82, 96, 103; VI.87, 93, 95; VIII.40; IX.71, 83; X.11, 98, 103, 115, 121, 129, 131, 177; XII.41; XIII.46, 83; XVII.11, 19, 20, 23, 40, 154; XVIII.41; XXI.13; XXII.80; XXIII.104; XXIV.52, 79, 81, 130; XXX.19, 60; XXXI.40, 89; XXXII.23; XXXVI.85; XXXVII.14; XXXIX.64; XL.129; XLI.15, 58; XLII.7, 66, 68, 75, 79; XLIII.14, 45; XLV.10, 43; XLVI.10; L.2, 19, 27, 32; 'an accurate and attentive spectator' LI.101; LII.19; LIII.15, 16; LIV.12; LVI.18; LIX.7; LXVI.23.

Strada, Famianus [Gibbon owned his *De Bello Belgico*, 2 vols. (Leyden, 1643–8), and *Prolusiones Academicæ* (Oxford, 1745)]: XXX.120.

Strahlenberg, Philip Johann Tabbert von [Gibbon owned his *An Historico-geographical description of the North and Eastern Parts of Europe and Asia; but more particularly of Russia, Siberia, and Great Tartary* (London, 1738)]: XLII.24, 36.

Stritter, John Gotthelf [author of *Memoriæ Populorum, ad Danubium, Pontum Euxinum, Paludem Mæotidem, Caucasum, Mare Caspium, et inde magis ad Septentriones Incolentium*, 6 vols. (Petropoli, 1771–9)]: 'all the passages of the Byzantine history which relate to the Barbarians, are compiled, methodised, and transcribed in a Latin version, by the laborious John Gotthelf Stritter . . . But the fashion has not enhanced the price of these raw materials' LV.I, 13, 56; LVII.28, 31.

Struve, Burcard Gotthelf [Gibbon owned his *Bibliotheca Historica*, vols. 1 and 2 (Leipzig, 1782–5), *Corpus Historiæ Germanicæ*, 2 vols. (Jena, 1730), and *Introductio in Notitiam Rei Litterariæ* (Frankfort and Leipzig, 1729)]: XLIX.98, 106, 117, 149, 152; LVIII.5; LIX.9, 10, 14; LX.12.

Stuart, James [1713–88; with Nicholas Revett, author of *The Antiquities of Athens* (1762)]: LXII.56.

Studites, Theodore: XLIX.79.

Stukeley, William [1687–1765; antiquarian; Gibbon owned his *The Medallic History of M. A. Valerius Carausius, Emperor in Britain*, 2 vols. (London, 1757–9)]: II.85; XIII.25, 28, 30.

Stylites, Josue: XL.136.

Suarès, Joseph Maria [bp; Gibbon owned his *Prænestes Antiquæ Libri Duo* (Rome, 1655)]: LXXI.50.

Suetonius Tranquillus, Gaius [*c.*69–*c.*122 AD]: I.3; II.11, 45, 64; III.2, 3, 4, 17, 19, 28, 29, 32, 33, 35, 50, 57; IV.48; V.2, 3, 6, 20; XI.79; XIII.89; XV.6, 41; XVI.25, 28, 30, 35, 45, 47, 52, 55; XVII.97, 138, 147, 148, 149; XIX.4, 5; XXII.51, 52; XXIV.136; XXVIII.9; XXXI.40, 44, 56, 88; XXXIV.11; XLII.79; XLIII.65, 70, 71; XLIV.25, 30, 45, 68, 152, 181, 187; XLIX.92; LIII.59, 60; LXX.9, 10; LXXI.15.

Suicer, *see* Schweitzer, Johann Caspar.

Suidas [Gibbon owned his *Lexicon*, 3 vols. (Cambridge, 1705)]: XIII.50; XVIII.16; XXI.108; XXV.29; XXVII.28; XXVIII.45; XXIX.4, 11, 25; XXXII.10, 13, 69, 72; XXXV.52; XXXVI.58; XXXIX.8, 9; XL.17, 78, 152; XLIII.62; XLIV.72, 73, 74; XLVI.113; XLVII.25; LI.107; LIII.109, 110.

Sulpicius Alexander [*c.*106–43 BC]: XXVII.105.

Sulpicius, Servius [jurist]: XLIV.54.

Swinburne, Henry [1743–1803; Gibbon owned his *Travels in the Two Sicilies*, 2 vols. (London, 1783–5), and *Travels through Spain*, 3 vols. (London, 1779)]: LI.83, 177, 185; LII.49; LVI.90, 98; LXVI.91; LXVII.46.

Sylvius, Æneas [1405–64; Pius II]: LXVI.39, 76; LXVII.22, 28; LXVIII.27, 95; LXX.79, 80, 81; LXXI.36.

Symmachus, Quintus Aurelius [d. 524]: XVII.73, 150; XXI.171; XXV.107; 'in the form and disposition of his ten books of epistles, he imitated the younger Pliny; whose rich and florid style he was supposed, by his friends, to equal or excel' XXVIII.16, 17; XXIX.40; XLIII.43.

Syncellus, Georgius [author of *Chronographia*]: X.118, 120, 123, 124; XI.56; XII.76; L.81.

Synesius of Cyrene [bp of Ptolemais; Gibbon owned his *Opera quæ Extant Omnia* (Paris, 1612)]: XII.73; XIII.99; XX.116, 117, 118, 119, 120, 121; 'the philosophic bishop of Cyrene was near enough to judge; and he was sufficiently removed from the temptation of fear, or flattery' XXVI.131; XXX.8, 20, 21; XXXVII.8; XLVII.25.

Synodicon adversus Tragædiam Irenæi: XLVII.47, 49, 50, 51, 52.

Syropulus, Sylvester [Greek schismatic and ecclesiarch; author of *Vera Historia Unionis non Veræ inter Græcos et Latinos* (The Hague, 1660)]: LXVI.41, 44, 46, 47, 49, 'although Syropulus is often partial, he is never intemperate' 50, 'Syropulus may be ranked with the best of the Byzantine writers for the merit of his narration, and even of his style: but he is excluded from the orthodox collections of the councils' 51, 52, 'the historian has the uncommon talent of placing each scene before the reader's eye' 53, 55, 58, 59, 60, 61, 62, 63, 64, 'Syropulus . . ., who never dissembles the vices of his own party, and fairly praises the virtues of the Latins' 65, 66, 67, 68, 69, 71, 73, 74; 'genuine and original narrative' LXVII.5, 30, 54.

Syrus, Publius: XL.63.

T

Tableau général de l'empire ottoman (Paris, 1787): 'a work of less use, perhaps, than magnificence' LXVIII.81.

Tacitus, Gaius Cornelius [*c.*56–*c.*120; historian]: I.3, 4, 5, 6, 8, 9, 34, 55, 57, 65, 66; II.15, 20, 36, 38, 59, 80, 101, 106; III.4, 15, 18, 19, 28, 29, 30, 34, 46, 50, 55, 57, 59; IV.55; V.1, 3, 4, 8; VI.28, 30, 33, 38, 65, 77, 85, 95, 97, 101, 110; VIII.39; IX.1, 9, 12, 16, 20, 21, 24, 25, 27, 28, 30, 31, 32, 33, 41, 43, 44, 45, 49, 51, 52, 53, 55, 56, 58, 'somewhat too florid' 59, 60, 61, 62, 64, 65, 67, 68, 71, 72, 74, 75, 79, 80, 81, 83; X.13, 14, 20, 24, 27, 43, 46, 72, 81, 100, 103, 129, 131, 162; XI.44; XII.9, 37, 38, 42, 43; XIII.83; XIV.61; XV.1, 2, 8, 13, 27, 43, 167, 191; XVI.28, 30, 32, 33, 35, 37, 38, 39, 51; XVII.10, 23, 73, 95, 96, 103, 105, 106, 124, 145, 146, 148, 163; XVIII.42, 51; XIX.43; XXI.173; XXII.14, 38, 82; XXV.48, 50, 98, 103, 109, 119, 142; XXVIII.37; XXX.69, 74; XXXI.11, 12, 16, 30; XXXIV.31; XXXV.17; 'the revolution of ages may bring round the same calamities; but ages may revolve, without producing a Tacitus to describe them' XXXVI.110, 138; XXXVII.98; XXXVIII.2, 3; XXXIX.39, 43; XL.62; XLI.65; XLII.7; XLIII.10, 71; XLIV.23, 'This deep disquisition fills only two pages; but they are the pages of Tacitus' 24, 31, 63, 68, 113, 164, 189, 205; XLV.12; XLVI.1, 18; XLVII.136; L.178; LI.73, 99, 172; LIII.57; LV.28; LVIII.56, 69, 'the masterly description of Tacitus' 105, 106, 108; LXII.14; LXIII.17; LXIX.37; LXX.23; LXXI.12, 16, 20.

Tagino [historian of the third crusade]: LIX.10, 25; LX.12.

Tasso, Torquato [1544–95; poet; Gibbon owned his *Aminta* (Venice, 1736), *Il Goffredo, ovvero Gerusalemme Liberata*, (Padua, 1763, and, 2 vols., Venice, 1760–1) and *Jerusalem Delivered, done into English by E. Fairfax* (London, 1749)]: XLIII.29; XLIV.93; LVIII.54, 80, 109.

Tatius, Achilles: XLI.18.

Taurellus, Franciscus [sixteenth-century editor of the *Pandects*]: XLIV.92.

Tavernier, Jean-Baptiste [or Taberna; 1605–89; Gibbon owned his *Six voyages en Turquie, en Perse et aux Indes*, 2 vols. (Paris, 1692), and *Recueil de plusieurs relations et traitez* (Paris, 1692)]: II.105; VIII.35, 49; XIX.55; XXIV.49, 52, 79, 81; XLII.74; 'perfectly conversant with the roads of Asia' XLVI.84, 91; 'that rambling jeweller, who had read nothing, but had seen so much and so well' XLVII.143; LI.23, 85, 206; LII.41; LVII.9, 48; LIX.46.

Tayler [editor of Olympiodorus]: LI.30.

Taylor, John [1704–66; civilian lawyer; Gibbon owned his *Elements of the Civil Law* (Cambridge, 1755)]: XVIII.51; 'a work of amusing, though various, reading; but which cannot be praised for philosophical precision' XLIV.132, 'a learned, rambling, spirited writer' 150, 179.

Tegrimi, Nicholas [biographer of Castruccio Casticani]: LIII.25.

Teixeira, Pedro [translator of Mircond as *History of Persia*]: XL.135; XLII.38, 45; XLVI.22; LXV.16.

Tellez, Balthazar [Jesuit; editor of *General History* (Coimbra, 1660)]: XLII.93; XLVII.161.

Temple, Sir William [1628–99; statesman and man of letters; Gibbon owned his *Works*, 2 vols. (London, 1721) and 4 vols. (London, 1770)]: IX.38; 'lively exotic fancies' LI.124; LII.23, 'the strange errors and fancies of Sir William Temple' 40; 'the excellent chapter of Sir William Temple on the religion of the United Provinces' LIV.40; 'our ingenious Sir William Temple . . ., that lover of exotic virtue . . . His flattering pencil deviates in every line from the truth of history: yet his pleasing fictions are more excusable than the gross errors of Cantemir' LXV.79; 'his pleasing Essay on Heroic Virtue' LXVII.35.

Templeman, Thomas [Gibbon owned his *A New Survey of the Globe* (London, 1729)]: 'I distrust both the doctor's learning and his maps' I.89.

Terence [*c.*186–*c.*159 BC]: XIX.2; XLIII.65.

Terrasson, Antoine [1705–82; author of the *Histoire de la jurisprudence romaine* (Paris, 1750)]: 'a work of more promise than performance' XLIV.9, 22, 44, 71.

Tertullianus, Quintus Septimius [c.155–c.220]: II.16, 109; IV.9; XV.23, 36, 39, 40, 42, 46, 48, 50, 72, 75, 76, 85, 90, 95, 101, 102, 111, 114, 116, 121, 124, 127, 131, 136, 141, 172, 174, 177, 179, 189, 196; XVI.19, 22, 23, 31, 59, 61, 64, 66, 69, 96, 100, 108, 109; XX.19, 29, 39; XXI.19, 30, 34, 41, 54, 173; XXVII.96; XXXI.86; XLIV.37, 113.

Teutoburgicus, Peter: LV.53.

Thalelæus [Byzantine jurist]: LIII.98.

Thegan [chorepiscope of Trèves; biographer of Lewis the Pious, i.e. Louis I, emperor of Germany]: XLIX.116.

Themistius: XVII.55, 64, 65; XVIII.79; XIX.50; XXII.2, 46; XXIII.25; XXV.10, 33, 42, 'a whole oration of Themistius . . . full of adulation, pedantry, and common-place morality . . . the virtues and genius of Themistius, who was not unworthy of the age in which he lived' 63, 70, 'servile eloquence' 149; XXVI.105, 110, 119, 123, 128, 'an elaborate and rational apology, which is not, however, exempt from the puerilities of Greek rhetoric' 132.

Theodore of Mopsuestia: 'if he composed 10,000 volumes, as many errors would be a charitable allowance' XLVII.96.

Theodoret [c.393–c.458; bp of Cyrrhus]: XVIII.65; XX.10, 76, 83, 112; XXI.79, 80, 84, 93, 96, 119, 122, 128, 149, 164; XXIII.76, 96, 134, 140; XXIV.30, 102, 116; XXV.7, 8, 22, 68; XXVI.105, 110; XXVII.23, 39, 91, 'the copious narrative of Theodoret . . . must be used with precaution' 98, 119, 121; XXVIII.27, 31, 35, 60; XXX.58; XXXII.33, 35, 41, 57, 73, 80; ; XXXIV.3, 27; XXXVII.67, 70, 74, 83; XLVII.18, 113; LIV.2.

Theodorus the Reader [fl. sixth century]: XXXIV.50; XL.11; XLVII.69, 79, 114.

Theodosian Code, see Codex Theodosiani.

Theodulphus [ninth-century bp of Orléans]: XLIX.91.

Theophanes [c.752–c.818; st; the Confessor; monk, theologian and chronicler; author of *Chronographia*, ed. J. Goar (Paris, 1648)]: XVII.21; XVIII.35; XX.37; XXVII.91; XXXIII.3; XXXIV.18; XXXIV.52; XXXVI.11, 64, 68, 84, 88, 90, 107, 112, 122; XXXIX.3, 6, 10, 16, 51, 88; XL.38, 39, 46, 50, 52, 53, 76, 123, 136; XLI.116; XLII.11, 34, 35, 82, 'full of strange blunders' 100; XLIII.3, 37, 53, 56, 64, 66, 68, 74, 83, 86, 88; XLIV.198; XLV.4, 23, 26, 28, 30; XLVI.7, 42, 47, 53, 54, 'a courtier who became a monk' 57, 58, 62, 67, 83, 88, 91, 97, 104, 105, 106, 110; XLVII.78, 86, 87, 90, 106, 135; XLIX.18, 21, 24, 26, 38, 85, 93, 121; 'the most ancient of the Greeks, and the father of many a lie' L.63, 145, 146, 149; LI.10, 32, 'brief and obscure' 77, 82, 86, 92, 93, 94, 109, 114, 141, 'his chronology is loose and inaccurate' 145, 146, 157, 217; LII.1, 2, 5, 'just and pointed' 6, 9, 14, 15, 17, 38, 74, 78, 80, 82, 93, 96; LIII.29, 34, 75, 95; LIV.17, 21; LV.3, 61.

Theophilus [or Theophylus; Christian Maronite of Mount Libanus]: XV.78; XX.79; XLIV.33, 42, 64, 'loose prolixity' 137, 149, 157, 158, 186; LII.70.

Theophrastus: XL.133, 150; XLIV.18; LX.40.

Theopompus of Chios: XLIV.18.

Thesaurarius, Bernardus [historian of the Crusades]: LVIII.19, 41, 45, 94, 120; LIX.14, 64, 65, 85.

Thévenot, Jean de [1633–67; traveller; Gibbon owned his *Voyages tant en Europe qu'en Asie et en Afrique*, 5 vols. (Paris, 1689), and *Travels into the Levant* (London, 1687)]: XVII.12, 14, 34, 48; XXIV.81, 86, 118; XL.69; L.18; LI.15, 23, 52, 111, 135, 206; LII.4, 41; LVII.65; LXVIII.44, 80.

Thévenot, Melchisedec [1620–92; traveller; author of *Relations de divers voyages curieux*, 2 vols. (Paris, 1696)]: XL.77; XLII.67, 93; XLVII.116; LI.37; LXV.62, 65.

Thevrocz, János [or Thuroczius, or Thuroczy; Hungarian historian]: XXXIV.1; LXIV.16.

Thiers, Jean Baptiste [1636–1703; theologian; Gibbon owned his *Dissertation sur la Sainte Larme de Vendôme* (Paris, 1699), *Dissertations ecclésiastiques sur les principaux autels des églises, les jubés, la clôture du chœur* (Paris, 1688), *Traité de l'exposition du st. sacrement de l'autel* (Paris, 1683), *Traité de la clôture des religieuses* (Paris, 1681), *Traité des superstitions que regardent tous les sacrements*, 3 vols. (Paris, 1703–4), and *Traité des superstitions selon l'écriture sainte, des décrets des conciles et les sentiments des SS. pères et des théologiens* (Paris, 1687)]: XX.63.

Thomas [commentator on Themistius]: 'eloquent' XXV.63.

Thomassin, Louis [1637–1718; bp of Sisteron; Gibbon owned his *Ancienne et nouvelle discipline de l'église touchant les bénéfices et les bénéficiers*, 3 vols. (Paris, 1725)]: XX.87, 88, 92, 'by each of these learned but partial critics [Bingham and Thomassin], one half of the truth is produced, and the other is concealed' 93, 95, 107, 108, 122; XXI.146; XXXVII.1, 26, 30, 32, 51, 53, 56, 66; XXXVIII.94; XLV.18; XLVII.29, 119; XLIX.86, 126; LI.47; LIII.89; LV.6; LIX.83; LXIX.69, 84.

Thou, Jacques Auguste de [or Thuanus; 1553–1617; historian; Gibbon owned his *Doctorum Virorum Elogia Thuanea* (London, 1671), *Historiarum Sui Temporis Libri CXXXVIII*, 7 vols. (London, 1733), and *Histoire Universelle*, 16 vols. (London, 1734)]: XLI.19; LI.155; LVI.105; LXI.77; LXIX.100; LXX.72, 91, 'the great Thuanus' 95.

Thucydides [fl. fifth century BC]: XIV.106; XXVI.18; XLIII.90, 91; XLIV.18, 182; LXII.14; 'the living picture which Thucydides . . . has drawn' LXVIII.45.

Tibullus [c.55–c.19 BC]: XV.199.

Tillemont, Louis Sébastien le Nain de [1637–98; ecclesiastical historian; Gibbon owned his *Histoire des empereurs*, 5 vols. (Brussels, 1707) and 6 vols. (Paris, 1720–38), and *Mémoires pour servir à l'histoire ecclésiastique des six premiers siècles*, 10 vols. (Brussels, 1706)]: IV.6, 27; V.37, 42, 51; 'Tillemont is miserably embarrassed with a passage of Dion' VI.3, 10, 80; VII.31, 32, 55; VIII.51; X.19, 44, 63, 66, 70, 93, 150, 159, 166; XI.46, 50, 61; XII.73; XIII.6, 11, 14, 79, 100, 109; XIV.9, 23, 29, 69; XV.24, 50, 'the learned M. de Tillemont never dismisses a virtuous emperor without pronouncing his damnation' 70, 156, 171, 173, 180, 186; XVI.21, 27, 42, 48, 53, 74, 76, 78, 88, 113, 133, 154, 157, 164, 166, 178, 181; XVII.56, 64, 67, 84, 121; XVIII.8, 9, 13, 14, 53, 56, 60, 63, 84, 95; XIX.11, 13, 28, 51; XX.1, 5, 16, 41, 49, 50, 55, 71, 73, 84, 112, 118, 126, 127, 128; XXI.2, 6, 8, 10, 46, 55, 62, 63, 70, 77, 88, 94, 'The diligence of Tillemont . . . has collected every fact, and examined every difficulty' 96, 100, 109, 110, 112, 115, 117, 123, 126, 129, 139, 142, 143, 144, 148, 149, 157, 162; XXII.45, 60, 66; XXIII.9, 48, 56, 61, 65, 'Tillemont . . . who treats his [St Cyril's] memory with tenderness and respect, has thrown his virtues into the text, and his faults into the notes, in decent obscurity, at the end of the volume' 69, 90, 101, 112, 123, 130, 132, 134, 137, 140, 141; XXIV.14, 28, 30, 46, 'the *military* criticisms of the saint [Gregory of Nazianzen] are devoutly copied by Tillemont, his faithful slave' 57, 116, 131; XXV.4, 6, 29, 31, 37, 52, 53, 66, 'immense compilations' 68, 71, 74, 'the devout eyes of Tillemont' 80, 86, 112, 121, 'the patient and sure-footed mule of the Alps may be trusted in the most slippery paths' 122, 135, 151, 157; XXVI.63, 64, 85, 90, 96, 106, 108, 115, 135; XXVII.4, 20, 23, 27, 28, 31, 33, 39, 42, 43, 44, 46, 'Tillemont . . . has raked together all the dirt of the fathers: an useful scavenger!' 51, 56, 61, 67, 71, 75, 78, 88, 90, 'the honest efforts of Tillemont' 99, 113; XXVIII.43, 44, 47, 77, 79; XXIX.2, 6, 7, 8, 9, 13, 14, 46, 47; XXX.3, 20, 27, 43, 71, 72, 94, 104,

107; XXXI.19, 28, 78, 113, 122, 133, 'peevish' 136, 145, 154, 172; XXXII.12, 31, 35, 41, 'the learned Tillemont . . .; who compiles the lives of the saints with incredible patience, and religious accuracy' 41, 43, 47, 49, 51, 56, 59, 64, 65, 68, 72, 80; XXXIII.10, 17, 21, 22, 23, 24, 'the diligence of that learned Jansenist was excited, on this occasion [composition of the life of St Augustine], by factious and devout zeal for the founder of his sect' 27; XXXIV.3, 15, 21, 26, 48; XXXV.72; XXXVI.17, 29, 'always scandalized by the virtues of Infidels' 58, 65, 84, 86, 104, 121, 132; XXXVII.8, 12, 18, 30, 68, 70, 84, 106, 114; XXXIX.9; XL.44, 132; XLI.22; XLVI.19; XLVII.18, 21, 24, 28, 39, 41, 42, 44, 47, 51, 62, 74, 76, 'here I must take leave for ever of that incomparable guide – whose bigotry is overbalanced by the merits of erudition, diligence, veracity, and scrupulous minuteness' 79; 'Ducange, the Tillemont of the middle ages. Never has laborious Germany produced two antiquarians more laborious and accurate, than these two natives of lively France' LIII.31.

Tillotson, John [1630–94; abp of Canterbury; latitudinarian; Gibbon owned his *Works*, 10 vols. (Dublin, 1739)]: LIV.38.

Timosthenes [Greek historian]: XLII.72.

Timotheus of Gaza [playwright]: XL.78.

Tiraboschi, Girolamo [1731–94; historian of Italian literature; Gibbon owned his *Storia della Letteratura Italiana*, 10 vols. (Modena, 1786–90), and *Histoire de la littérature d'Italie*, 5 vols. (Berne, 1784)]: XXXIX.25, 57, 71, 89, 98; LVI.47; LXVI.79, 'the librarian of Modena enjoys the superiority of a modern and national historian' 85, 93, 97, 98, 102, 109, 110, 112, 113, 117, 118; LXVIII.41, 67.

Tobit: XLVI.10.

Tolet., Roderic., *see* Ximines, Roderic.

Tollius: 'his own character, literary as well as moral, is not free from reproach' XX.42; XLI.38.

Torrentius, Lævinus [bp of Antwerp; poet; editor of Suetonius and Horace]: XXXI.56; XL.25, 63.

Tott, François, baron de [1733–93; Gibbon owned his *Mémoires sur les Turcs et les Tartares* (Amsterdam, 1784)]: XL.126; LI.127; 'the state and defence of the Dardanelles is exposed in the memoirs of the Baron de Tott . . ., who was sent to fortify them against the Russians. From a principal actor, I should have expected more accurate details; but he seems to write for the amusement, rather than the instruction, of his reader' LII.3; LVII.53; 'the Baron de Tott . . ., who fortified the Dardanelles against the Russians, describes in a lively, and even comic, strain his own prowess, and the consternation of the Turks. But that adventurous traveller does not possess the art of gaining our confidence' LXVIII.26, 'always solicitous to amuse and amaze his reader' 44, 88.

Tournefort, Joseph Pitton de [1656–1708; traveller; Gibbon owned his *Relation d'un voyage du Levant*, 3 vols. (Lyon, 1717)]: I.78; VI.95; X.104, 109; XIV.108; XVII.3, 5, 12, 'the extravagant computation of Tournefort . . . is a strange departure from his usual character' 34, 40, 47; 'our blind travellers seldom possess any previous knowledge of the countries which they visit. Shaw and Tournefort deserve an honourable exception' XXIV.49; XL.128; XLVI.84; XLVII.143; L.101; LII.77, 79; LIV.11; LXI.18; LXII.9; LXV.40, 78; LXVIII.12, 80, 88.

Tribonian [d. 545; jurist]: XLIV.5.

Tritheim, Johann [or Tritheimius]: XXVII.13.

Tudebodus, Petrus [historian of the Crusades]: LVIII.19.

Tzetzes, Joannes [fl. twelfth century; monk, historian and poet]: XL.95, 97; XLIII.69; LIII.109, 113; LXI.19.

U

Ullug Beig [or Ulugh Beg; 1394–1449; grandson of Tamerlane; Gibbon owned his *Epochæ Celebriores* (London, 1650)]: L.118.

Ulpian [Domitius Ulpianus; d. AD 228; Roman jurist]: XVII.108, 113, 148, 162, 166; XLIV.32, 57, 103, 105, 122, 137, 139, 152, 188.

Universal History, 7 vols. (London, 1736–44): XV.12; 'the authors of that unequal work have compiled the Sassanian dynasty with erudition and diligence: but it is a preposterous arrangement to divide the Roman and Oriental accounts into two distinct histories' XXV.137; 'these learned bigots' XLVI.3; L.21, 47, 'the writers of the Modern Universal History . . . have compiled . . . the life of Mahomet and the annals of the caliphs. They enjoyed the advantage of reading, and sometimes correcting, the Arabic texts; yet, notwithstanding their high-sounding boasts, I cannot find, after the conclusion of my work, that they have afforded me much (if any) additional information. The dull mass is not quickened by a spark of philosophy or taste: and the compilers indulge the criticism of acrimonious bigotry against . . . all who have treated Mahomet with favour, or even justice' 187; 'the self-sufficient compilers of the Modern Universal History' LI.125; LII.8.

Urban IV [*c.*1200–1264]: LXI.58.

Ursinus, Fulvius . [sixteenth-century Byzantinist; editor of *De Legationibus* (Antwerp, 1582)]: LIII.7.

Usher, James [or Ussher; 1581–1656; abp of Armagh; historian and chronologist; Gibbon owned his *Britannicarum Ecclesiarum Antiquitates* (London, 1687) and *Annales Veteris et Novi Testamenti* (Geneva, 1722)]: XXVII.13; XXX.94; XXXI.189; 'all that learning can extract from the rubbish of the dark ages is copiously stated by archbishop Usher' XXXVII.23, 24; LI.90, 119; LVIII.73; LXVIII.64.

V

Vacca, Flaminio [*c.*1538–*c.*1592; sculptor and antiquarian]: XIV.74; LXXI.27, 62, 69, 73.

Valerius Maximus: II.15, 31, 45; III.7; XV.56; XVII.95; XX.47; XXXI.25; XLIV.124, 126, 127, 180, 185; LXX.33.

Valesian Fragment [or Anonym. Vales.]: XIV.86, 107, 110, 112; XVII.55, 61; XVIII.31, 34, 45; XXXVI.112, 118, 121, 127; XXXIX.3, 10, 16, 22, 'The author's name is unknown, and his style is barbarous; but in his various facts he exhibits the knowledge, without the passions of a contemporary' 24, 31, 36, 59, 61, 65, 74, 75, 78, 79, 87, 88, 97, 98, 101, 105, 107.

Valesius, Hadrian [or Adrien de Valois, seigneur de la Mare; 1607–92; historian; Gibbon owned his *Notitia Galliarum Ordine Litterarum Digesta* (Paris, 1675)]: XIX.92; XXV.27; XXXI.174, 175; XXXVIII.109, 137; XLIX.105, 140; LII.27; LVIII.1, 11, 43; LXIX.82.

Valesius, Henry [or Henri de Valois, seigneur d'Orcé; 1603–76; *érudit*; translator of Eusebius; editor of Ammianus Marcellinus, Evagrius and *De Virtutibus et Vitiis* (Paris, 1634)]: VII.10; X.79; XI.28; XIII.79; XIV.25, 32, 90, 92, 111; XV.169; XVI.49, 162, 182; XVII.58, 61, 87, 126, 139, 161; XVIII.31; XIX.20, 51, 65, 81, 92; XX.5, 84; XXI.3, 91, 112, 140, 142, 155; XXII.6, 66, 67, 69; XXIV.23; XXV.7, 13, 24, 27, 34, 40, 59, 86, 'a long and good note on the master of the offices' 88; XXVI.74, 80, 92, 97; XXXI.31, 38; XXXIV.8, 50; XXXV.11, 21, 23, 41, 42; XXXVI.112; XXXIX.80; XLVII.26, 77; LIII.7.

Valla, Laurentius [1407–57; humanist, philosopher and critic; Gibbon owned his *Elegantiarum Linguæ Latinæ Libri Sex* (Lyons, 1556)]: 'a fastidious grammarian of the XVth century' XLIV.79.

Vallemont, Pierre le Lorrain de [1649–1721; scholar and historian]: X.155.

Valmont de Bomare, Jacques-Christoph [1731–1807; Gibbon owned his *Dictionnaire raisonné universel d'histoire naturelle*, 9 vols. (Paris, 1775) and 8 vols. (Lyons, 1791)]: XLII.14; XLIII.82; XLV.44; LI.25.

Valsecchi: VI.62.

Valturio, Robert [author of *De Re Militari Libri XII* (Verona, 1483)]: LXVIII.5.

Vandale [or Jacobus van Dalen]: 'it would be easier for me to copy, than it has been to verify, the quotations of that learned Dutchman' III.21; XIII.100; XXIII.106.

Varro, Marcus Terrentius [116–27 BC]: I.36; VII.57, 58; XXXI.45; XXXV.75, 76; XL.1; XLIII.78; XLIV.138; XLVI.103.

Vega, Garcilasso de la [1539–1616; Spanish historian]: XLIV.200.

Vegetius Renatus, Flavius: I.32, 37, 42, 43, 44, 50, 58, 59, 60, 61, 63, 68; XIII.95; XVII.135; XXVI.80; XXVII.125.

Velleius Paterculus, Gaius [*c.*19 BC–AD 30]: I.3; II.24, 38; III.32; V.26, 31; VI.79, 88, 92; VII.33; VIII.1; IX.83; XII.41; XLII.7; XLIII.45; LI.90, 160; LII.28; LVI.52.

Velly, Paul François [*c.*1709–1759; historian; Gibbon owned his (with others including Claude Villaret) *Histoire de France*, 30 vols. (Paris, 1761–86)]: XLIX.116; LXV.64; 'who quotes nobody, according to the last fashion of the French writers' LXVI.18.

Velserus, Marcus [author of *Rerum Boicarum Libri Quinque*; editor of Apollonius of Tyre]: XLI.5.

Venantius Fortunatus: IX.16.

Verbiest, Ferdinand [1623–88; astronomer]: XXVI.12.

Vertot d'Auberf, René Aubert de [1655–1735; historian; Gibbon owned his *Histoire des chevaliers hospitaliers de S. Jean de Jérusalem*, 4 vols. (Paris, 1726) and 5 vols. (Amsterdam, 1780), *Histoire critique de l'établissement des Bretons dans les Gaules*, 2 vols. (Paris, 1720), *Histoire des révolutions arrivées dans le gouvernement de la république romaine*, 2 vols. (Paris, 1722), *Histoire des révolutions de Suède*, 2 vols. (Amsterdam, 1722, and Paris, 1772), and *Révolutions de Portugal* (Paris, 1758, and The Hague, 1769)]: 'this fable . . . whose slight foundations the Abbé Vertot . . . has undermined, with profound respect, and consummate dexterity' XXXVIII.29, 137, 160; LVI.105; 'a fair, and sometimes flattering, picture of the order' LVIII.131; LIX.45, 62, 'Vertot, who adopts without reluctance a romantic tale' 66, 81, 88, 90, 109; 'that pleasing writer' LXIV.46, 48, 64; 'I have selected some curious facts, without striving to emulate the bloody and obstinate eloquence of the abbé Vertot, in his prolix descriptions of the sieges of Rhodes, Malta, &c. But that agreeable historian had a turn for romance, and as he wrote to please the order, he has adopted the same spirit of enthusiasm and chivalry' LXVIII.40.

Vespasiano of Florence [biographer of Eugenius IV and Nicholas V]: LXVI.57, 110.

Victor, *see* Aurelius Victor, Sextus.

Victor, Publius [author of a description of Rome]: XLIV.126.

Victor Tunnunensis [bp of Tunnunum; chronicler]: XXXVI.28; XXXVII.96; XL.8, 11, 39; XLI.49; XLIII.88; XLVII.71, 78, 92, 94, 97, 145.

Victor Vitensis [bp of Vita; author of *Historia Persecutionis Vandalicæ*]: XX.98; XXXIII.15, 25, 28, 35, 41; XXXV.4; XXXVI.10, 62; XXXVII.88, 90, 91, 92, 93, 94, 95, 99, 101, 102, 103, 104, 105, 106, 108, 109, 110, 111, 117, 123.

Vie privée des François, *see* Legrand d'Aussy, Pierre Jean B.

Vigenère, Blaise de [1523–96; Byzantinist; translator of Laonicus Chalcocondyles]: LX.32.

Vigilius [bp of Thapsus]: XXXVII.113, 117.

Villani, John [or Giovanni; Florentine; d. 1348; chronicler of Florence]: LIX.108; LXI.57; LXII.37, 46; LXV.92; LXVI.37; LXIX.73, 74, 86, 108; LXX.18, 43.

Villani, Matteo [or Matthew; historian of his own times]: LVI.139; LXIII.36, 53; LXVI.4, 11; LXIX.89, 102, 103, 106; LXX.49, 50, 54.

Villehardouin, Geoffroy de [fl. 1223; marshal of Champagne; historian]: XVII.13; LIII.45; LIV.26; LVIII.114; LX.25, 27, 'Champagne may boast of the two first historians, the noble authors of French prose, Villehardouin and Joinville' 33, 40, 41, 43, 49, 50, 53, 'his feelings and expressions are original; he often weeps, but he rejoices in the glories and perils of war with a spirit unknown to a sedentary writer' 55, 'such is the honesty of courage' 57, 60, 61, 64, 65, 66, 67, 'rude energy' 68, 70, 73, 76, 77, 78, 80, 83, 84, 86, 88, 89, 91; LXI.1, 12, 'the spirit of freedom' 16, 17, 23, 26, 27, 28, 29, 31, 32, 43; LXII.52; LXVIII.97.

Villioson, Jean Baptiste G. d'Ansse de [1750–1805; Hellenist; author of *Anecdota Græca*, 2 vols. (Venice, 1781)]: LII.10.

Vincent of Beauvais: LXI.21.

Vincentius Lirinensis [or St Vincent of Lerino]: XXI.8.

Vinesauf, Galfridus à [or Jeffrey de Vinisauf]: LIX.69, 75, 77, 78, 79, 'the most copious and original account of this holy war [the third Crusade]' 80.

Virgil [Publius Virgilius Maro; 70–19 BC]: I.46; II.41; VII.34; IX.3; XII.70; XIV.26; XV.45, 54, 199; XX.60, 61; XXI.173; XXIV.3; XXV.50; XXVI.67; XXVII.78; XXVIII.53; XXIX.1; XXX.48; XXXI.5, 40, 101, 170; XXXV.63; XL.62; XLI.14, 41, 66, 75, 84; XLIII.17, 46; XLIV.74, 134, 171, 208; XLVI.86; LIII.59; LVI.67, 79, 89; LXXI.3, 69.

Visdelou, Claude de [1656–1737; missionary; orientalist; Gibbon owned his (together with Antoine Galand) *Bibliothèque orientale* (The Hague, 1779)]: XLII.27, 30; 'a medley of tales, proverbs, and Chinese antiquities' LI.15.

Vitalis, Ordericus: LVI.70.

Vitriaco, Jacob a [or Jacques de Vitra, or James de Vitry; historian of Jerusalem; author of *Historia Hierosolimita*]: XLVII.119, 137; LI.212; LII.18; LVII.20, 28; LVIII.118, 124; LIX.43, 58, 69, 75, 77, 85.

Vitruvius Pollio, Marcus: X.129; XXXI.68.

Vives, Ludovicus [or Juan Luis Vives]: XLIV.34.

Viviani, Vincenzo [geometrician]: 'the mathematical divination of Viviani' LII.56.

Volaterranus, Raphael Maffeius [early Latin translator of Homer, Procopius and St Basil]: XL.14; XLIII.69; LXX.98.

Volney, Constantin François de Chassebœuf, comte de [1757–1820; *philosophe*, historian and orientalist; Gibbon owned his *Voyage en Syrie et en Égypte*, 2 vols. (Paris, 1787), and *Considérations sur la guerre actuelle des Turcs* (London, 1788)]: XLVII.136, 'the judicious Volney' 138; 'the last and most judicious of our Syrian travellers' L.10; LI.111, 'I wish the latter [Volney] could travel over the globe' 137; 'recent and instructive' LVII.68; LIX.105.

Voltaire, François Marie Arouet de [1694–1778; *philosophe*; man of letters; Gibbon owned his *History of the War of 1741* (London, 1756), *Mémoires écrits par lui-même* (Amsterdam, 1785), *Le Siècle de Louis XIV* (London, 1752) and the *Collection complette des œuvres*, 30 vols. (Geneva, 1768–77) and 57 vols. (Lausanne, 1780–1)]: I.69, 'M. de Voltaire . . . unsupported by either fact or probability, has generously bestowed the Canary Islands on the Roman empire' 87; II.62; X.8; XVIII.20; XIX.23; XX.41; XXI.86; XXVI.6; 'compare the tenth book of the Henriade, and the Journal de Henri IV. . . . and observe that a plain narrative of facts is much more pathetic, than the most laboured descriptions of epic poetry' XXXI.76; 'Gen. Obs.'.9; XLVII.118; XLIX.95, 'Voltaire, whose pictures are sometimes just, and always pleasing' 116; L.40, 139, 156; 'Voltaire . . . casts a keen and lively glance over the surface of history' LI.55,

168; 'the mistakes of Voltaire proceeded from the want of knowledge or reflection' LII.40, 'the splendid and interesting tragedy of *Tancrede* would adapt itself much better to this epoch [the ninth century], than to the date (A.D. 1005) which Voltaire has chosen. But I must gently reproach the poet, for infusing into the Greek subjects the spirit of modern knights and ancient republicans' 83, 87; 'Voltaire might wonder at this alliance [the marriage between Henri I and a Russian princess]; but he should not have owned his ignorance of the country, religion, &c. of Jeroslaus – a name so conspicuous in the Russian annals' LIII.66; LVI.12; 'the prejudice of a philosopher is less excusable than that of a Jesuit [Maimbourg]' LVIII.65, 'lively scepticism' 106, 113; LIX.99, 101; LXI.54; LXIII.16; LXIV.3, 'as usual, much general sense and truth, with some particular errors' 20; LXV.43, 'the scepticism of Voltaire . . . is ready on this, as on every occasion, to reject a popular tale, and to diminish the magnitude of vice and virtue; and on most occasions his incredulity is reasonable' 46; 'Voltaire . . . admires *le Philosophe Turc* [Amurath II]; would he have bestowed the same praise on a Christian prince for retiring to a monastery? In his way, Voltaire was a bigot, an intolerant bigot' LXVII.13; LXVIII.7, 25, 42, 'the pious zeal of Voltaire is excessive, and even ridiculous' 54, 'Voltaire, as usual, prefers the Turks to the Christians' 84; LXX.96.

Vopiscus, Flavius: XI.25, 30, 35, 39, 45, 50, 53, 63, 66, 70, 74, 76, 77, 82, 83, 85, 87, 91, 92, 95, 96; XII.1, 2, 4, 8, 10, 14, 15, 17, 22, 23, 26, 30, 32, 33, 39, 40, 47, 51, 53, 54, 61, 65, 66, 79, 82, 83, 86, 101, 102, 107; XIII.113; XXXI.47, 57; XL.65.

Vossius, Gerardus Joannes [1577–1649; Gibbon owned his *Etymologicon Linguæ Latinæ* (Leyden, 1664), *De Historicis Græcis* (Leyden, 1651), *De Historicis Latinis* (Leyden, 1651), *De Studiorum Ratione Opuscula* (Utrecht, 1651), *De Septuaginta Interpretibus* (The Hague, 1661–3) and *Opera*, 6 vols. (Amsterdam, 1701)]: XXI.173; XXII.48; XXVI.114; XXVIII.36; XXXI.47; XXXVII.114, 133; XL. 12, 14; XLIX.72; LIII.110; LXVII.28.

Vossius, Isaacius [Gibbon owned his *Variarum Observationum Liber* (London, 1685)]: XI.42; XXV.72, 127; XXVI.39; XXXI.66, 68; XLIII.84; LI.150.

Vulcanius, Bonaventura [classical scholar]: 'a learned interpreter' XL.14.

W

Wadding, Luke [or Wading; 1588–1657; historian of the Franciscans; author of *Annales Minorum*, 4 vols. (Lugd. Bat., 1625–37)]: LXII.33, 'his Annals of the Franciscan order . . . I have now accidentally seen among the waste paper of a bookseller' 34.

Wakidi, Al: 'Al Wakidi has the double merit of antiquity and copiousness. His tales and traditions afford an artless picture of the men and the times. Yet his narrative is too often defective, trifling, and improbable' LI.44, 45, 51, 59, 60, 84, 86, 92, 100.

Wallace, Robert [1697–1771; Gibbon owned his *A Dissertation on the Numbers of Mankind* (Edinburgh, 1753)]: IX.87; XLIV.140; LVI.98.

Walpole, Horace [1717–97; man of letters; Gibbon owned his *Anecdotes of Painting in England*, 5 vols. (Strawberry Hill, 1762–71), *The Castle of Otranto* (London, 1782) and *Historic Doubts of the Life and Reign of King Richard the Third* (London, 1768)]: LV.37.

Walsingham, Thomas [d. 1422?; early English historian]: LXVI.11, 19.

Walton, Brian [1600?–1661; bp of Chester; biblical scholar; author of *The Considerator Considered: or, A Brief View of Certain Considerations upon the Biblia Polyglotta, the Prolegomena and Appendix therof* (London, 1659)]: XLVII.111; L.62.

Warburton, William [1698–1779; bp of Gloucester; Gibbon owned his *The Divine Legation of Moses Demonstrated*, 5 vols. (London, 1765), *The Alliance between Church and State* (London, 1736), *The Doctrine of Grace*, 2 vols. (London, 1763), *Julian* (London, 1751) and *Tracts* (London, 1789)]: XV.57; XVI.32; XIX.43; 'learned' XXIII.25, 'the secret intentions of Julian are revealed by the late bishop of Gloucester, the learned and dogmatic Warburton; who, with the authority of a theologian, prescribes the motives and conduct of the Supreme Being. The discourse entitled *Julian* . . . is strongly marked with all the peculiarities which are imputed to the Warburtonian school' 71, 72, 79, 83, 85; 'learned and rational' XXIV.98; XXVIII.89, 90; XL.30, 55.

Warnefrid, Paul, *see* Paul the Deacon.

Warton, Thomas [1728–90; historian of English poetry; Gibbon owned his *History of English Poetry*, 3 vols. (London, 1774–81), *Life of Sir Thomas Pope* (London, 1772) and *Observations on the Fairy Queen of Spenser*, 2 vols. (London, 1762)]: XXII.7; 'the taste of a poet, and the minute diligence of an antiquarian' XXXVIII.141; XLII.55.

Watson, Richard [1737–1816; bp of Llandaff; Gibbon owned his *An Apology for Christianity in a Series of Letters Addressed to Edward Gibbon* (London, 1776), *Chemical Essays*, 3 vols. (London, 1781–2), and *Sermons on Public Occasions, and Tracts on Religious Subjects* (Cambridge, 1788)]: XLIII.82; 'on the different sorts of oils and bitumens, see Dr. Watson's (the present bishop of Llandaff's) Chemical Essays, . . . a classic book, the best adapted to infuse the taste and knowledge of chemistry' LII.19, 69; LXV.91.

Watteville, Alexandre Louis de [Gibbon owned his *Histoire de la confédération helvétique* (Berne, 1757)]: XXXVIII.22.

Wechel, André [*c.*1510–1581; classical scholar]: XXX.11; 'Gen. Obs.'.1; XLVII.63.

Wells, Edward [1667–1727; editor of Xenophon]: L.3.

Wesselingius, Petrus [or Wesseling; editor of Diodorus Siculus; Gibbon owned his *Vetera Romanorum Itineraria* (Amsterdam, 1735)]: II.85; VII.13; IX.3; X.29, 31, 112, 171; XIII.115; XX.94, 117; XXI.150; 'learned and judicious' XXIII.63, 68, 98, 104; XXIV.29; XXV.15; XXVI.4, 76, 79; XXVII.30, 31; XXVIII.39; XXX.39; XXXI.6; XXXII.2; XXXVII.121; 'Gen. Obs.'.10; XL.54; XLII.46, 60, 69; XLIII.34, 62, 63; XLV.32; XLVI.79, 101; L.2, 26; LI.63, 107; LII.115; LVI.65; LVII.28.

West, Gilbert [1703–56; translator of Pindar; author of *Dissertation on the Olympic Games*]: XXX.17; XL.41; XLIX.47; LVIII.57.

Wetstein, Johann Jacob: XXI.113; XXXVII.75, 'in 1689, the papist Simon strove to be free; in 1707, the protestant Mill wished to be a slave; in 1751, the Arminian Wetstein used the liberty of his times, and of his sect' 115, 116, 118; XLVII.5, 111; LI.122; LIV.4.

Wheeler, Sir George [Gibbon owned his *A Journey into Greece* (London, 1682) and *Voyage de Dalmatie, de Grèce, et du Levant* (The Hague, 1723)]: V.60; XXX.9, 19; LX.46; LXII.56, 58; LXIV.45; LXVI.34.

Whiston, William [1667–1752; Gibbon owned two copies of his *Memoirs* (London, 1773, and London, 1787)]: XLII.50; 'honest, pious, visionary Whiston' XLIII.77; 'the fanatic Whiston' LIV.34.

Whitaker, John [1735–1808; historian; Gibbon owned his *History of Manchester*, 2 vols. (London, 1771–5), *Mary Queen of Scots Vindicated*, 3 vols. (London, 1787–8), and *Genuine History of the Britons Asserted* (London, 1772)]: I.73; II.32; VI.14; 'learned' IX.19; 'the lively spirit of the learned and ingenious antiquarian has tempted him to forget the nature of a question, which he so *vehemently* debates, and so *absolutely* decides' XXV.111; XXX.94; XXXI.185; 'the ingenious Mr. Whitaker' XXXVIII.127, 130, 133, 'I am surprised that Mr. Whitaker . . . should so faithfully transcribe the gross ignorance of Carte, whose venial errors he has so rigorously chastised' 136, 140, 'Dr. Johnson affirms, that *few* English words are of British extraction. Mr. Whitaker, who understands the British language, has discovered more than *three thousand*, and actually produces a long and various catalogue' 144.

White, Joseph [1745–1814; orientalist; Bampton lecturer; Gibbon owned his *Sermons Preached before the University of Oxford* (London, 1785); editor (with Major Davy) of Tamerlane's *Institutes* (Oxford, 1783)]: 'his arguments are far from satisfactory' L.70; 'I sincerely doubt whether the Oxford mosch would have produced a volume of controversy so elegant and ingenious as the sermons lately preached by Mr. White, the Arabic professor, at Mr. Bampton's lecture. His observations on the character and religion of Mahomet, are always adapted to his argument, and generally founded in truth and reason. He sustains the part of a lively and eloquent advocate; and sometimes rises to the merit of an historian and philosopher' LII.30; LXV.2, 'the Persic version, with an English translation and most valuable index, was published . . . by the joint labours of Major Davy, and Mr. White the Arabic professor' 3, 8, 11, 12, 'excellent Indexes' 13, 18, 24, 27, 28, 32, 37, 39, 41, 42, 45, 66, 'I did not expect to hear of Timour's amiable moderation . . . Yet I can excuse a generous enthusiasm in the reader, and still more in the editor, of the *Institutions*' 69.

Wibert [seventeenth-century biographer of St Leo IX]: LVI.29, 'deeply tinged with the passions and prejudices of the age' 32.

Wikes, Thomas [fl. 1258–93; English historian]: LIX.106.

Wilkins, David [1685–1745; author of *Leges Anglo-Saxonicæ Ecclesiasticæ et Civiles* (London, 1721)]: XXXVII.137; XXXVIII.126, 154.

William of Malmesbury [d. 1143?]: XVII.27; XXXVIII.135, 151; XLVII.123; 'William of Malmsbury . . ., who appreciates, like a philosophic historian, the vices and virtues of the Saxons and Normans. England was assuredly a gainer by the conquest' LVI.28, 40, 70, 92, 94; LVII.64; LVIII.77, 78; LXXI.69, 71.

William of Poitiers: XXXVIII.158.

William of Tyre [abp of Tyre; historian of the Crusades]: XLVII.137; LVII.11, 16, 20, 'the most authentic and deplorable account of these Turkish conquests [in the Middle East]' 56, 'our best fund for the history of Jerusalem from Heraclius to the crusades, is contained in two large and original passages of William Archbishop of Tyre . . ., the principal author of the Gesta Dei per Francos' 58, 'the latinity of William of Tyre is by no means contemptible' 59, 61, 74, 76; LVIII.2, 15, 19, 41, 45, 'the only historian of the crusades who has any knowledge of antiquity' 87, 91, 94, 97, 103, 115, 117, 118, 120, 121, 128; LIX.9, 12, 39, 40, 41, 45, 58; LX.15, 'loud, copious, and tragical' 17, 68; LXI.70.

Winckelman, Johann Joachim [1717–68; historian of art; Gibbon owned his *Histoire de l'art chez les anciens*, 2 vols. (Amsterdam, 1766), *Histoire de l'art de l'antiquité*, 3 vols. (Leipzig, 1781), and *Lettre sur les découvertes d'Herculanum* (Dresden, 1764)]: XXXIX.66; XLI.83; XLIII.70; LX.100.

Witichind [monk of Corbey; Saxon historian]: LV.36.

Wolf, Johann Christoph [or Wolfius; 1683–1739; translator and editor of the letters of Libanius]: XXIII.100, 101; XXIV.25.

Wood, Robert [1717?–1771; Gibbon owned his *The Ruins of Balbec* (London, 1757) and *An Essay on the Original*

Wood, Robert—*contd*
Genius and Writings of Homer (London, 1775)]: XI.69; 'I have, with pleasure, selected this remark from an author who in general seems to have disappointed the expectation of the public as a critic, and still more as traveller' XVII.18; XLI.12; 'every preceding account is eclipsed by the magnificent description and drawings of M.M. Dawkins and Wood, who have transported into England the ruins of Palmyra and Baalbeck' LI.71; LX.33.

Wotton, William [1666–1727; Gibbon owned his *The History of Rome from the Death of Antoninus Pius to the Death of Severus Alexander* (London, 1701) and *Reflections upon Ancient and Modern Learning* (London, 1694, and London, 1697)]: IV.12, 27; VI.37, 45, 52, 80; IX.84; 'solid sense' LI.124; 'his reputation has been unworthily depreciated by the wits in the controversy of Boyle and Bentley' LII.67, 69.

Wowerus [or Joannes à Wower of Antwerp; classical scholar]: XV.184.

X

Xenophon [431–*c*.350 BC; historian]: VIII.47, 58; IX.3; X.108; XIII.65, 66, 71, 80; XVII.160; XIX.7; XXII.47; XXIV.37, 41, 'this pleasing work [the *Anabasis*] is original and authentic. Yet Xenophon's memory, perhaps many years after the expedition, has sometimes betrayed him' 47, 107, 114, 'the *Cyropædia* is vague and languid: the *Anabasis* circumstantial and animated. Such is the eternal difference between fiction and truth' 115; XXXII.23; 'After a long and tedious conversation with the Byzantine declaimers, how refreshing is the truth, the simplicity, the elegance of an Attic writer!' XL.117, 124, 129; XLI.12, 44; XLII.77, 85; XLVI.79, 80, 92; L.3, 155; LIII.9; LIX.47; LXVI.78.

Ximines, Roderic [abp of Toledo; author of the *Historia Arabum*]: XXXI.142; LI.179; LII.25, 29, 31, 38, 39.

Xiphilin, Joannes (the younger): I.24; VI.46, 62; XVI.24, 107; XL.148; XLII.79; LXX.9.

Z

Zabari, Al: 'the great Al Zabari' L.137.

Zaccagni, Lorenzo Alessandro [or Zacagni; editor of the *Collectanea Monumentorum Veterum Ecclesiæ Græcæ, ac Latinæ, quæ hactenus in Vaticana Bibliotheca Dilituerunt* (Rome, 1698)]: XLV.34.

Zacharias [bp of Mitylene; ecclesiastical historian]: XLVII.55.

Zendavesta: VIII.15, 26.

Zeno [d. 491; emperor of the East; author of *Henoticon*]: XLVII.70, 72.

Zonaras [twelfth-century Byzantine historian]: VI.62; 'little dependence is to be had on the authority of a modern Greek, so grossly ignorant of the history of the third century, that he creates several imaginary emperors, and confounds those who really existed' VII.29; X.1, 3, 31, 41, 47, 51, 59, 91, 123, 133, 139, 144, 181; XI.2, 9, 10, 11, 13, 14, 56; XII.2, 6, 17, 18, 20, 52, 76; XIV.50, 112; XVII.21, 66; XVIII.7, 8, 67, 68, 72, 76, 85, 86, 88, 92, 98; XIX.19, 25, 50; XX.28; XXII.22, 'Zonaras . . . who, on this occasion, appears to have possessed and used some valuable materials' 23, 53, 54; XXIV.78; XXV.16, 29; XXVII.91; XXXII.74; XXXVI.64, 90; XL.4, 11, 52, 53, 76, 81, 86, 95, 96; XLIII.68; XLIV.198; XLV.4, 23, 28, 30; XLVI.22, 42, 47, 54; XLVII.61; XLIX.15, 18, 26; L.145, 149; LI.10, 93; LII.2, 15, 78, 112, 118; LIII.29, 30, 65, 83, 95, 103, 104, 105, 106, 111; LIV.17, 23; LV.13, 56, 61, 63, 'they [Cedrenus and Zonaras] grow more weighty and credible as they draw near to their own times' 64, 72; LVI.22; LVII.4, 15, 19, 25, 32, 36, 38; LXVIII.97.

Zoroaster: VIII.15, 19.

Zosimus [count; historian]: VII.12, 26, 52, 58; X.1, 3, 36, 44, 47, 55, 57, 62, 75, 89, 102, 106, 111, 113, 117, 123, 127, 136,

Zosimus—*contd*
139, 142, 145, 181; xi.2, 13, 16, 20, 25, 45, 56, 60, 62, 64, 67, 72, 74, 89, 92, 96; xii.2, 17, 18, 20, 31, 32, 35, 47, 48, 50, 51, 56; xiii.33; xiv.9, 13, 14, 22, 28, 32, 35, 39, 42, 43, 46, 49, 51, 56, 69, 70, 71, 75, 76, 78, 79, 'the descriptions of Zosimus are rhetorical rather than military' 89, 90, 92, 99, 103, 104, 107, 108, 109, 111, 112; XVII.21, 44, 48, 55, 63, 65, 98, 99, 126, 128, 189; XVIII.1, 2, 4, 7, 15, 16, 22, 23, 28, 30, 45, 52, 53, 63, 70, 72, 77, 81, 85, 88, 91, 93, 94, 97, 98; XIX.13, 18, 32, 35, 64, 72, 75, 76, 77, 82, 83, 85, 84, 87; XX.4, 26, 56, 65, 69, 73; XXI.172; XXII.10, 13, 20, 23, 32, 35, 37, 76; XXIV.10, 43, 45, 46, 51, 57, 69, 72, 73, 'artful or ignorant' 75, 78, 87, 90, 108, 111, 119, 121, 125, 127, 128; XXV.12, 16, 20, 22, 31, 41, 42, 52, 64, 65, 89, 91, 95, 149, 150, 154, 155, 157; XXVI.2, 56, 64, 65, 68, 'according to the ecclesiastical critics . . . the praise of Zosimus is disgrace . . . His prejudice and ignorance undoubtedly render him a very questionable judge of merit' 90, 94, 'Zosimus . . . whom we are now reduced to cherish' 98, 'curious and copious' 103, 105, 110, 112, 114, 118, 119, 120, 122, 124, 125, 'Zosimus . . . too frequently betrays his poverty of judgment, by disgracing the most serious narratives with trifling and incredible circumstances' 126, 129, 'the partial invectives of Zosimus' 131, 'a long and ridiculous story' 134, 135; XXVII.7, 9, 11, 12, 14, 18, 75, 77, 82, 85, 91, 101, 104, 109, 110, 111, 115, 121, 123, 124; XXVIII.6, 18, 19, 27, 'Zosimus, who styles himself Count and Ex-advocate of the Treasury, reviles, with partial and indecent bigotry, the Christian princes, and even the father of his sovereign. His work must have been privately circulated, since it escaped the invectives of the ecclesiastical historians prior to Evagrius' 64; XXIX.5, 6, 7, 11, 12, 13, 15, 16, 25, 30, 31, 32, 35, 39, 45, 51, 53, 'the narrative of Zosimus, which, in its crude simplicity, is almost incredible' 57, 60; XXX.1, 5, 8, 16, 26, 66, 'In good policy, we must use the service of Zosimus, without esteeming or trusting him' 71, 80, 88, 95, 97, 99, 102, 103, 104, 105, 106, 107, 108, 112, 113; XXXI.1, 2, 3, 74, 77, 80, 81, 82, 83, 84, 85, 86, 87, 91, 92, 93, 95, 'Credulous and partial as he is, we must take our leave of that historian with some regret' 97, 134, 135, 150, 173, 180; XXXII.10, 12, 13, 14, 17, 21, 24, 30, 32, 33, 34, 37, 39, 50, 51, 52, 59; XXXVII.55; XL.78.

Zurlauben, baron de [biographer of Enquerrand VII, sire de Coucy]: LXIV.62.

Zwingli, Ulrich [or Zuinglius; 1484–1531; Swiss reformer]: XV.70.

Zygomalas, Theodosius [or Zygomala; grammarian]: LXII.58; LXVIII.11.

GENERAL INDEX

In the preface to the final instalment of 1788, Gibbon drew the attention of his reader to the 'General Index to the Six Volumes, which has been drawn up by a person frequently employed in works of this nature'. This index has received no attention from Gibbon scholars: it has never been reprinted in subsequent editions of *The Decline and Fall*, and there have been no attempts to discover the identity of its compiler. Yet the original index is full of fascinating information about how *The Decline and Fall* was received by its first readership. The topics which this professional indexer thought would interest his contemporaries (and also what he left out) are rich in implication. Three conclusions emerge. First, the anti-clericalism of *The Decline and Fall* is far more naked in the index than in the history itself: read and relish the entries for '*Acacius*', '*Ambrose*', '*Apollinaris*, patriarch of Alexandria', '*Damasus*, bishop of Rome', '*Ennodius*', '*Fornication*', '*John* of Cappadocia', '*Marcellus*, bishop of Rome', '*Marcia*', '*Marozia*', '*Mary*, Virgin', '*Moses*', '*Noah*', '*Sigismond*, king of the Burgundians' and '*Valens*, the Arian bishop of Mursa'. Second, the index directs the reader towards the proliferation of minute and particular information contained in *The Decline and Fall*: see, for instance, the entries for '*Pheasant*' and '*Veratius*'. Third, the index reveals a great interest in commerce and in what we might call general social history: consider, for example, the thoroughness with which the Roman trade in silk has been indexed, by examining the entries for '*Caravans*', '*Ceos*', '*China*', '*Elagabalus*', '*Italy*', '*Justinian*', '*Persia*', '*Pinna* marina', '*Rome*', '*Sicily*' and '*Virgil*', as well as '*Silk*'. Nor was our indexer without a sense of the possibilities for wit afforded by his craft: read the entry for '*Sylvania*', turn to the text, and appreciate his alertness to how the act of chasing a reference might provide the timing for a joke.

The index is reprinted here exactly as it first appeared, except that slips have been silently corrected, and the division of large entries into separate sections according to volume now follows the three-volume organization of the present edition, rather than the original six-volume division. Where the subject extends over more than one page (e.g. '*Courtenay*, history of the family of'), the index refers the reader to only the first page.

N. B. The Roman Numerals refer to the Volume and the Figures to the Page.

A

Aban, the Saracen, heroism of his widow, iii.256.

Abbassides, elevation of the house of, to the office of caliph of the Saracens, iii.339.

Abdallah, the Saracen, his excursion to plunder the fair of Abyla, iii.261. His African expedition, 290.

Abdalmalek, caliph of the Saracens, refuses tribute to the emperor of Constantinople, and establishes a national mint, iii.326.

Abdalrahman, the Saracen, establishes his throne at Cordova in Spain, iii.342. Splendour of his court, 345. His estimate of his happiness, 346.

Abdelazir, the Saracen, his treaty with Theodemir the Gothic prince of Spain, iii.310. His death, 312.

Abderame, his expedition to France, and victories there, iii.335. His death, 338.

Abdol Motalleb, the grandfather of the prophet Mahomet, his history, iii.172.

Abgarus, inquiry into the authenticity of his correspondence with Jesus Christ, iii.89.

Abgarus, the last king of Edessa, sent in chains to Rome, i.225.

Ablavius, the confidential præfect under Constantine the Great, a conspiracy formed against him on that emperor's death, i.661. Is put to death, 663.

Abu Ayub, his history, and the veneration paid to his memory by the Mahometans, iii.325. 970.

Abu Caab commands the Andalusian Moors who subdued the island of Crete, iii.357.

Abu Sophian, prince of Mecca, conspires the death of Mahomet, iii.193. Battles of Beder and Ohud, 199. Besieges Medina without success, 200. Surrenders Mecca to Mahomet, and receives him as a prophet, 204.

Abu Taher, the Carmathian, pillages Mecca, iii.368.

Abubeker, the friend of Mahomet, is one of his first converts, iii.190. Flies from Mecca with him, 193. Succeeds Mahomet as caliph of the Saracens, 219. His character, 235.

Abulfeda, his account of the splendour of the caliph Moctader, iii.344.

Abulpharagius, primate of the Eastern Jacobites, some account of, ii.989. His encomium on wisdom and learning, iii.347.

Abundantius, general of the East, and patron of the eunuch Eutropius, is disgraced and exiled by him, ii.242.

Abyla, the fair of, plundered by the Saracens, iii.262.

Abyssinia, the inhabitants of, described, ii.727. Their alliance with the emperor Justinian, 729. Ecclesiastical history of, 997.

Acacius, bishop of Amida, an uncommon instance of episcopal benevolence, ii.269.

Achaia, its extent, i.52.

Acre, the memorable siege of, by the crusaders, iii.639. Final loss of, 654.

Actions, institutes of Justinian respecting, ii.826.

Actium, a review of Roman affairs after the battle of, i.85.

Adauctus, the only martyr of distinction

during the persecution under Diocletian, i.571.

Adolphus, the brother of Alaric, brings him a reinforcement of troops, ii.192. Is made count of the domestics to the new emperor Attalus, 197. Succeeds his brother as king of the Goths, and concludes a peace with Honorius, 212.

Adoption, the two kinds of, under the Greek empire, iii.584 *note*.

Adoration of the Roman emperor, custom of, and derivation of the term, iii.397.

Adorno, the Genoese governor of Phocæa, conveys Amurath II. from Asia to Europe, iii.856.

Adrian I. pope, his alliance with Charlemagne against the Lombards, iii.109. His reception of Charlemagne at Rome, 112. Asserts the fictitious donation of Constantine the Great, 115.

Adultery, distinctions of, and how punished by Augustus, ii.837. By the Christian emperors, 838.

Ægidius, his character, and revolt in Gaul, ii.380. His son Syagrius, 455.

Ælia Capitolina founded on mount Sion by Hadrian, i.454.

Ælius Paetus, his *Tripartite*, the oldest work of Roman jurisprudence, ii.792.

Æmilianus, governor of Pannonia and Mæsia, routs the barbarous invaders of the empire, and is declared emperor by his troops, i.266.

Æneas of Gaza, his attestation of the miraculous gift of speech to the Catholic confessors of Tipasa, whose tongues had been cut out, ii.444.

Æneas Sylvius, his account of the impracticability of an European crusade against the Turks, iii.975. His epigram on the destruction of ancient buildings in Rome, 1073 *note*.

Æra of the world, remarkable epochas in, pointed out, ii.167 *note*.

——, Gelalæan, of the Turks, when settled, iii.543.

Aerial tribute, in the Eastern empire, what, ii.588.

Ætius, surnamed the Atheist, his character and adventures, i.786. 794. 808 *note*.

Ætius, the Roman general under Valentinian III. his character, ii.277. His treacherous scheme to ruin count Boniface, 278. Is forced to retire into Pannonia, 287. His invitation of the Huns into the empire, 295. Seizes the administration of the Western empire, 324. His character as given by Renatus a contemporary historian, 325. Employs the Huns and Alani in the defence of Gaul, 325. Concludes a peace with Theodoric, 329. Raises the siege of Orleans, 336. Battle of Châlons, 338. His prudence on the invasion of Italy by Attila, 347. Is murdered by Valentinian, 352.

Africa, its situation and revolutions i.53. Great revenue raised from, by the Romans, 180. Progress of Christianity there, 504. Is distracted with religious discord in the time of Constantine the Great, 768. Character and revolt of the Circumcellions, 821. Oppressions of, under the government of count Romanus, 1002. General state of Africa, 1006.

——, Revolt of count Boniface there, ii.278. Arrival of Genseric king of the Vandals, 280. Persecution of the Donatists, 281. Devastation of, by the Vandals, 284. Carthage surprised by Genseric, 288. Persecution of the Catholics, 435. Expedition of Belisarius to, 625. Is recovered by the Romans, 636. The government of, settled by Justinian, 637. Revolt of the troops there, under Stoza, 732. Devastation of the war, 735.

——, Invasion of, by the Saracens, iii.290. Conquest of, by Akbah, 294. Decline and extinction of Christianity there, 318. Revolt and independence of the Saracens there, 370.

Aglabites, the Saracen dynasty of, iii.370.

Aglae, a Roman lady, patronises St. Boniface, i.572.

Agricola, review of his conduct in Britain, i.34.

Agriculture, great improvement of, in the western countries of the Roman empire, i.78. State of, in the Eastern empire, under Justinian, ii.578.

Aiznadin, battle of, between the Saracens and the Greeks, iii.253.

Ajax, the sepulchre of, how distinguished, i.591.

Akbah, the Saracen, his exploits in Africa, iii.294.

Alani, occupation of these people invading Asia, i.333. Conquest of, by the Huns, 1042. Join the Goths who had emigrated into Thrace, 1058. See *Goths*, and *Vandals*.

Alaric, the Goth, learns the art of war under Theodosius the Great, ii.65. Becomes the leader of the Gothic revolt, and ravages Greece, 122. Escapes from Stilicho, 126. Is appointed master general of the Eastern Illyricum, 128. His invasion of Italy, 129. Is defeated by Stilicho at Pollentia, 134. Is driven out of Italy, 137. Is, by treaty with Honorius, declared master-general of the Roman armies throughout the præfecture of Illyricum, 155. His pleas and motives for marching to Rome, 166. Encamps under the walls of that city, 168. Accepts a ransom, and raises the siege, 191. His negociations with the emperor Honorius, 192. His second siege of Rome, 196. Places Attalus on the Imperial throne, 197. Degrades him, 199. Seizes the city of Rome, 200. His sack of Rome compared with that by the emperor Charles V. 207. Retires from Rome, and ravages Italy, 209. His death and burial, 211.

Alaric II. king of the Goths, his overthrow by Clovis king of the Franks, ii.465.

Alberic, the son of Marozia, his revolt, and government of Rome, iii.140.

Albigeois of France, persecution of, iii.435.

Alboin, king of the Lombards, his history, ii.848. His alliance with the Avars against the Gepidæ, 849. Reduces the Gepidæ, 850. He undertakes the conquest of Italy, 851. Overruns what is now called Lombardy, 853. Assumes the regal title there, 854. Takes Pavia, and makes it his capital city, 855. Is murdered at the instigation of his queen Rosamond, 855.

Alchemy, the books of, in Egypt, destroyed by Diocletian, i.372.

Aleppo, siege and capture of, by Saracens, iii.270. Is recovered by the Greeks, 346. Is taken and sacked by Tamerlane, 838.

Alexander III. pope, establishes the papal election in the college of cardinals, iii.1005.

Alexander, archbishop of Alexandria, excommunicates Arius for his heresy, i.779.

Alexander Severus, is declared Cæsar by the emperor Elagabalus, i.169. Is raised to the throne, 170. Examination into his pretended victory over Artaxerxes, 226. Shewed a regard for the Christian religion, 553.

Alexandria, a general massacre there, by order of the emperor Caracalla, i.158. The city described, 292. Is ruined by ridiculous intestine commotions, 293. By famine and pestilence, 294. Is besieged and taken by Diocletian, 370. The Christian theology reduced to a systematical form in the school of, 503. Number of martyrs who suffered there in the persecution by Decius, 541. The theological system of Plato taught in the school of, and received by the Jews there, 772. Questions concerning the nature of the trinity, agitated in the philosophical and Christian schools of, 775. 779. History of the archbishop St. Athanasius, 796. Outrages attending his expulsion and the establishment of his successor, George of Cappadocia, 811. The city distracted by pious factions, 815. Disgraceful life and tragical death of George of Cappadocia, 901. Restoration of Athanasius, 904. Athanasius banished by Julian, 905. Suffers greatly by an earthquake, 1023.

——, History of the temple of Serapis there, ii.81. This temple, and the famous library, destroyed by bishop Theophilus, 82.

——, Is taken by Amrou the Saracen, iii.282. The famous library destroyed, 284.

Alexius Angelus, his usurpation of the Greek empire, and character, iii.664. Flies before the crusaders, 680.

Alexius I. *Comnenus*, emperor of Constantinople, iii.69. New titles of dignity invented by him, 394. Battle of Durazzo, 500. Solicits the aid of the emperor Henry III. 503. Solicits the aid of the Christian princes against the Turks, 559. His suspicious policy on the arrival of the crusaders, 582. Exacts homage from them, 584. Profits by the success of the crusaders, 615.

Alexius II. *Comnenus*, emperor of Constantinople, iii.74.

Alexius Strategopulus, the Greek general, retakes Constantinople from the Latins, iii.723.

Alexius, the son of Isaac Angelus, his escape from his uncle, who had deposed his father, iii.665. His treaty with the crusaders for his restoration, 674. Restoration of his father, 683. His death, 688.

Alfred sends an embassy to the shrine of St. Thomas in India, ii.985.

Algebra, by whom invented, iii.350.

Ali, joins Mahomet in his prophetical mission, iii.191. His heroism, 201. 203. His character, 218. Is chosen caliph of the Saracens, 220. Devotion paid at his tomb, 224. His posterity, 225.

Aligern, defends Cumæ, for his brother Teias, king of the Goths, ii.757. Is reduced, 759.

Allectus murders Carausius, and usurps his station, i.367.

Allemanni, the origin and warlike spirit of, i.272. Are driven out of Italy by the senate and people, 272. Invade the empire under Aurelian, 306. Are totally routed, 308. Gaul delivered from their depradations by Constantius Chlorus, 369. Invade and establish themselves in Gaul, 711. Are defeated at Strasburgh by Julian, 715. Are reduced by Julian in his expeditions beyond the Rhine, 720. Invade Gaul under the emperor Valentinian, 989. Are reduced by Jovinus, 990. And chastised by Valentinian, 991.

——, Are subdued by Clovis king of the Franks, ii.456.

Alp Arslan, sultan of the Turks, his reign, iii.534.

Alypius, governor of Britain, is commissioned by the emperor Julian to rebuild the temple of Jerusalem, i.889.

Amala, king of the Goths, his high credit among them, i.258.

Amalasontha, queen of Italy, her history and character, ii.648. Her death, 650.

Amalphi, description of the city, and its commerce, iii.491.

Amazons, improbability of any society of, i.321 *note*.

Ambition, reflections on the violence, and various operations of that passion, iii.83.

Ambrose, St. composed a treatise on the trinity, for the use of the emperor Gratian, ii.20 *note*. His birth, and promotion to the archbishopric of Milan, 40. Opposes the Arian worship of the empress Justina, 41. Refuses obedience to the Imperial power, 44. Controls the emperor Theodosius, 58. Imposes penance on Theodosius for his cruel treatment of Thessalonica, 59. Employed his influence over Gratian and Theodosius, to inspire them with maxims of persecution, 71. Opposes Symmachus, the advocate for the old Pagan religion, 75. Comforts the citizens of Florence with a dream, when besieged by Radagaisus, 145.

Amida, siege of, by Sapor, king of Persia, i.706. Receives the fugitive inhabitants of Nisibis, 956.

——, Is besieged and taken by Cabades king of Persia, ii.607.

Amir, prince of Ionia, his character, and passage into Europe, iii.813.

Ammianus, the historian, his religious character of the emperor Constantius, i.794. His remark on the enmity of Christians toward each other, 823. His account of the fiery obstructions to restoring the temple of Jerusalem, 890. His account of the hostile contest of Damasus and Ursinus for the bishopric of Rome, 986. Testimony in favour of his historical merit, 1073. His character of the nobles of Rome, ii.175.

Ammonius, the mathematician, his measurement of the circuit of Rome, ii.186.

Ammonius, the monk of Alexandria, his martyrdom, ii.946.

Amorium, siege and destruction of, by the caliph Motassem, iii.363.

Amphilochus, bishop of Iconium, gains the favour of the emperor Theodosius by an orthodox *bon mot*, ii.27.

Amphitheatre at Rome, a description of, i.353. iii.1076.

Amrou, his birth and character, iii.276. His invasion and conquest of Egypt, 277. His administration there, 286. His description of the country, 288.

Amurath I. sultan of the Turks, his reign, iii.816.

Amurath II. sultan, his reign and character, iii.915.

Anachorets, in monkish history, described, ii.426.

Anacletus, pope, his Jewish extraction, iii.1014.

Anastasius I. marries the empress Ariadne, ii.528. His war with Theodoric, the Ostrogoth king of Italy, 538. His œconomy celebrated, 585. His long wall from the Propontis to the Euxine, 602. Is humbled by the Catholic clergy, 966.

Anastasius II. emperor of Constantinople, iii.36. His preparations of defence against the Saracens, 327.

Anastasius, St. his brief history and martyrdom, ii.910 *note*.

Anatho, the city of, on the banks of the Euphrates, described, i.923.

Andalusia, derivation of the name of that province, iii.301 *note*.

Andronicus, president of Lybia, excommunicated by Synesius bishop of Ptolemais, i.762.

Andronicus Comnenus, his character, and first adventures, iii.74. Seizes the empire of Constantinople, 79. His unhappy fate, 83.

Andronicus the Elder, emperor of Constantinople, his superstition, iii.766. His war with his grandson, and abdication, 770.

Andronicus the Younger, emperor of Constantinople, his licentious character, iii.769. His civil war against his grandfather, 770. His reign, 772. Is vanquished and wounded by sultan Orchan, 811. His private application to pope Benedict XII of Rome, 864.

Angora, battle of, between Tamerlane and Bajazet, iii.841.

Anianus, bishop of Orleans, his pious anxiety for the relief of that city when besieged by Attila the Hun, ii.335.

Anician family at Rome, brief history of, ii.170.

Anne Comnena, character of her history of her father, Alexius I. emperor of Constantinople, iii.69. Her conspiracy against her brother John, 71.

Anthemius, emperor of the West, his descent, and investiture by Leo the Great, ii.385. His election confirmed at Rome, 385. Is killed in the sack of Rome by Ricimer, 398.

Anthemius, præfect of the East, character of his administration, in the minority of the emperor Theodosius the younger, ii.262.

Anthemius, the architect, instances of his great knowledge in mechanics, ii.593. Forms the design of the church of St. Sophia at Constantinople, 595.

Anthony, St. father of the Egyptian monks, his history, ii.413.

Anthropomorphites, among the early Christians, personifiers of the Deity, ii.938.

Antioch, taken and destroyed by Sapor king

of Persia, i.284. Flourishing state of the Christian church there, in the reign of Theodosius, 501. History of the body of St. Babylas, bishop of, 898. The cathedral of, shut up, and its wealth confiscated, by the emperor Julian, 899. Licentious manners of the citizens, 912. Popular discontents during the residence of Julian there, 913.

——, Sedition there, against the emperor Theodosius, ii.53. The city pardoned, 55. Is taken, and ruined, by Chosroes king of Persia, 711. Great destruction there by an earthquake, 771. Is again seized by Chosroes II. 908.

——, Is reduced by the Saracens, and ransomed, iii.271. Is recovered by the Greeks, 376. Besieged and taken by the first crusaders, 593.

Antonina, the wife of Belisarius, her character, ii.623. Examines and convicts pope Silverius of treachery, 667. Her activity during the siege of Rome, 669. Her secret history, 680. Founds a convent for her retreat, 767.

Antoninus, a Roman refugee at the court of Sapor king of Persia, stimulates him to an invasion of the Roman provinces, i.704.

Antoninus Pius, his character, and that of Hadrian, compared, i.37. Is adopted by Hadrian, 100.

Antoninus Marcus, his defensive wars, i.38. Is adopted by Pius at the instance of Hadrian, 101. His character, 108. His war against the united Germans, 250. Suspicious story of his edict in favour of the Christians, 550.

Aper, Arrius, prætorian præfect, and father-in-law to the emperor Numerian, is killed by Diocletian as the presumptive murderer of that prince, i.357.

Apharban, the Persian, his embassy from Narses king of Persia, to the emperor Galerius, i.379.

Apocalypse, why now admitted into the canon of the Scriptures, i.468 *note*.

Apocaucus, admiral of Constantinople, his confederacy against John Cantacuzene, iii.775. His death, 779.

Apollinaris, bishop of Laodicea, his hypothesis of the divine incarnation of Jesus Christ, ii.939.

Apollinaris, patriarch of Alexandria, butchers his flock in defence of the Catholic doctrine of the incarnation, ii.994.

Apollonius of Tyana, his doubtful character, i.315 *note*.

Apotheosis of the Roman emperors, how this custom was introduced, i.94.

Apsimar dethrones Leontius emperor of Constantinople, and usurps his place, iii.33.

Apulia, is conquered by the Normans, iii.480. Is confirmed to them by papal grant, 485.

Aquileia, besieged by the emperor Maximin, i.202. Is taken and destroyed by Attila king of the Huns, ii.343.

Aquitain, is settled by the Goths, under their king Wallia, ii.228. Is conquered by Clovis king of the Franks, 468.

Arabia, its situation, soil, and climate, iii.151. Its division into the *Sandy*, the *Stony*, and the *Happy*, 153. The pastoral Arabs, 154. Their horses and camels, 155. Cities of, 155. Manners and customs of the Arabs, 156. Their language, 164. Their benevolence, 165. History and description of the Caaba of Mecca, 167. Religions, 170. Life and doctrine of Mahomet, 172. Conquest of, by Mahomet, 205. Character of the caliphs, 235. Rapid conquests of, 237. Limits of their conquests, 323. Three caliphs established, 343. Introduction of learning among the Arabians, 347. Their progress in the sciences, 349. Their literary deficiencies, 352. Decline and fall of the caliphs, 369.

Arbetio, a veteran under Constantine the Great, leaves his retirement to oppose the usurper Procopius, i.973.

Arbogastes, the Frank, his military promotion under Theodosius in Gaul, and conspiracy against Valentinian the Younger, ii.62. Is defeated and killed by Theodosius, 67.

Arcadius, son of the emperor Theodosius, succeeds to the empire of the East, ii.98. His magnificence, 237. Extent of his dominions, 238. Administration of his favourite eunuch Eutropius, 239. His cruel law against treason, 244. Signs the condemnation of Eutropius, 247. His interview with the revolters Tribigild and Gainas, 250. His death, and supposed testament, 261.

Architecture, Roman, the general magnificence of, indicated by the existing ruins, i.70.

Ardaburius, his expedition to Italy, to reduce the usurper John, ii.274.

Argonauts, the object of their expedition to Colchos, ii.716.

Ariadne, daughter of the emperor Leo, and wife of Zeno, her character, and marriage afterward with Anastasius, ii.528.

Arii, a tribe of the Lygians, their terrific mode of waging war, i.339.

Arinthæus, is appointed general of the horse by the emperor Julian of his Persian expedition, ii.922. Distinguishes himself against the usurper Procopius, 972.

Ariovistus seizes two-thirds of the lands of the Sequani in Gaul, for himself and his German followers, ii.478.

Aristobulus, principal minister of the house of Carus, is received into confidence by the emperor Diocletian, i.359.

Aristotle, his logic better adapted to the detection of error, than for the discovery of truth, iii.350.

Arius, is excommunicated for heretical notions concerning the Trinity, i.779. Strength of his party, 780. His opinions examined in the council of Nice, 782. Account of Arian sects, 785. Council of Rimini, 788. His banishment and recall, 791. His suspicious death, 791.

——, The Arians persecute the Catholics in Africa, ii.435.

Armenia, is seized by Sapor king of Persia, i.282. Tiridates restored, 373. He is again expelled by the Persians, 376. Is resigned to Tiridates by treaty between the Romans and Persians, 382. Is rendered tributary to Persia, on the death of Tiridates, 666. Character of Arsaces Tiranus king of, and his conduct toward the emperor Julian, 920. Is reduced by Sapor to a Persian province, 1009.

——, Its distractions and division between the Persians and the Romans, ii.270. History of Christianity there, 991.

Armies of the Eastern empire, state of, under the emperor Maurice, ii.898.

Armorica, the provinces of, form a free government independent of the Romans, ii.231. Submits to Clovis the king of the Franks, 460. Settlement of Britons in, 499.

Armour, defensive, is laid aside by the Romans, and adopted by the Barbarians, ii.70.

Arnold of Brescia, his heresy, and history, iii.987.

Arragon, derivation of the name of that province, i.48 *note*.

Arrian, his visit to, and description of, Colchos, ii.719.

Arsaces Tiranus, king of Armenia, his character, and disaffection to the emperor Julian, i.920. Withdraws his troops treacherously from the Roman service, 935. His disastrous end, 1008.

Arsenius, patriarch of Constantinople, excommunicates the emperor Michael Palæologus, iii.748. Faction of the Arsenites, 749.

Artaban, king of Parthia, is defeated and slain by Artaxerxes king of Persia, i.215.

Artaban, his conspiracy against the emperor Justinian, ii.747. Is intrusted with the conduct of the armament sent to Italy, 750.

Artasires, king of Armenia, is deposed by the Persians at the instigation of his own subjects, ii.271.

Artavasdes, his revolt against the Greek emperor Constantine V. at Constantinople, iii.96.

Artaxerxes, restores the Persian monarchy, i.215. Prohibits every worship but that of Zoroaster, 220. His war with the

Romans, 225. His character and maxims, 228.

Artemius, duke of Egypt under Constantius, is condemned to death under Julian, for cruelty and corruption, i.857.

Arthur, king of the Britons, his history obscured by monkish fictions, ii.499.

Arvandus, prætorian præfect of Gaul, his trial and condemnation by the Roman senate, ii.393.

Ascalon, battle of, between Godfrey king of Jerusalem, and the sultan of Egypt, iii.606.

Ascetics, in ecclesiastical history, account of, ii.411.

Asclepiodatus, reduces and kills the British usurper Allectus, i.367.

Asia, summary view of the revolutions in that quarter of the world, i.213.

Asia Minor described, i.52. Amount of its tribute to Rome, 179. Is conquered by the Turks, iii.545.

Asiarch, the nature of this office among the ancient Pagans, i.497.

Aspar is commissioned by Theodosius the Younger to conduct Valentinian III. to Italy, ii.274. Places his steward Leo on the throne of the Eastern empire, 384. He and his sons murdered by Leo, 527.

Assassins, the principality of, destroyed by the Moguls, iii.800.

Assemblies of the people abolished under the Roman emperors, i.92. The nature of, among the ancient Germans, 240.

Assyria, the province of, described, i.925. Is invaded by the emperor Julian, 926. His retreat, 940.

Astarte, her image brought from Carthage to Rome, as a spouse for Elagabalus, i.167.

Astolphus, king of the Lombards, takes the city of Ravenna, and attacks Rome, iii.107. Is repelled by Pepin king of France, 107.

Astrology, why cultivated by the Arabian astronomers, iii.351.

Athalaric, the son of Amalasontha queen of Italy, his education and character, ii.649.

Athanaric, the Gothic chief, his war against the emperor Valens, i.1016. His allegiance with Theodosius, his death and funeral, 1077.

Athanasius, St. confesses his understanding bewildered by meditating on the divinity of the Logos, i.775. General view of his opinions, 783. Is banished, 791. His character and adventures, 796. 904. 960. 982. Was not the author of the famous creed under his name, ii.441.

Athanasius, patriarch of Constantinople, his contests with the Greek emperor Andronicus the Elder, iii.766.

Athenais, daughter of the philosopher Leontius. See *Eudocia*.

Athens, the libraries in that city, why said to have been spared by the Goths, i.282. Naval strength of the republic of, during its prosperity, 441 *note*.

——, is laid under contribution by Alaric the Goth, ii.123. Review of the philosophical history of, 610. The schools of, silenced by the emperor Justinian, 615.

——, Revolutions of, after the crusades, and its present state, iii.762.

Athos, mount, beatific visions of the monks of, iii.783.

Atlantic Ocean, derivation of its name, i.54.

Attacotti, a Caledonian tribe of cannibals, account of, i.1000.

Attalus, præfect of Rome, is chosen emperor by the senate, under the influence of Alaric, ii.197. Is publicly degraded, 200. His future fortune, 222.

Attalus, a noble youth of Auvergne, his adventures, ii.485.

Attila, the Hun, ii.296. Description of his person and character, 296. His conquests, 298. His treatment of his captives, 304. Imposes terms of peace on Theodosius the Younger, 308. Oppresses Theodosius by his ambassadors, 310. Description of his royal residence, 314. His reception of the ambassadors of Theodosius, 316. His behaviour on discovering the scheme of Theodosius to get him assassinated, 319. His haughty messages to the

Attila—contd
emperors of the East and West 323. His invasion of Gaul, 334. His oration to his troops on the approach of Ætius and Theodoric, 339. Battle of Châlons, 340. His invasion of Italy, 343. His retreat purchased by Valentinian, 347. His death, 350.

Atys and *Cybele*, the fable of, allegorised by the pen of Julian, i.869.

Augurs, Roman, their number and peculiar office, ii.72.

Augustin, his account of the miracles wrought by the body of St. Stephen, ii.93. Celebrates the piety of the Goths in the sacking of Rome, 202. Approves the persecution of the Donatists of Africa, 282. His death, character, and writings, 285. History of his relics, 635 *note*.

Augustulus, son of the patrician Orestes, is chosen emperor of the West, ii.402. Is deposed by Odoacer, 402. His banishment to the Lucullan villa in Campania, 405.

Augustus and *Cæsar*, those titles explained and discriminated, i.95.

Augustus, emperor, his moderate exercise of power, i.31. Is imitated by his successors, 32. His naval regulations, 46. His division of Gaul, 48. His situation after the battle of Actium, 85. He reforms the senate, 86. Procures a senatorial grant of the Imperial dignity, 87. Division of the provinces between him and the senate, 89. Is allowed his military command and guards in the city of Rome, 89. Obtains the consular and tribunitian offices for life, 90. His character and policy, 96. Adopts Tiberius, 98. Formed an accurate register of the revenues and expenses of the empire, 179. Taxes instituted by him, 181. His naval establishments at Ravenna, ii.139.

Aurelian, emperor, his birth and services, i.303. His expedition against Palmyra, 315. His triumph, 320. His cruelty, and death, 324.

Aurengzebe, account of his immense camp, i.223 *note*.

Aureolus is invested with the purple on the Upper Danube, i.295.

Ausonius, the tutor of the emperor Gratian, his promotions, ii.20 *note*.

Autharis, king of the Lombards in Italy, his wars with the Franks, ii.863. His adventurous gallantry, 869.

Autun, the city of, stormed and plundered by the legions in Gaul, i.312.

Auvergne, province and city of, in Gaul, revolutions of, ii.343.

Auxiliaries, Barbarian, fatal consequences of their admission into the Roman armies, i.623.

Avars, are discomfited by the Turks, ii.697. Their embassy to the emperor Justinian, 698. Their conquests in Poland and Germany, 699. Their embassy to Justin II. 846. They join the Lombards against the Gepidæ, 849. Pride, policy, and power, of their chagan Baian, 893. Their conquests, 895. Invest Constantinople, 922.

Averroes, his religious infidelity, how far justifiable, iii.353 *note*.

Aversa, a town near Naples, built as a settlement for the Normans, iii.479.

Avienus, his character and embassy from Valentinian III. to Attila king of the Huns, ii.348.

Avignon, the holy see how transferred from Rome to that city, iii.1009. Return of pope Urban V. to Rome, 1043.

Avitus, his embassy from Ætius to Theodoric king of the Visigoths, ii.336. Assumes the empire, 362. His deposition and death, 368.

Axuch, a Turkish slave, his generous friendship to the princess Anne Comnena, iii.71. And to Manuel Comnenus, 72.

Azimuntium, the citizens of, defend their privileges against Peter, brother of the Eastern emperor Maurice, ii.897.

Azimus, remarkable spirit shewn by the citizens of, against Attila and his Huns, ii.309.

B

Baalbec, description of the ruins of, iii.263.

Babylas, St. bishop of Antioch, his posthumous history, i.898.

Bagaudæ, in Gaul, revolt of, its occasion and suppression by Maximian, i.363.

Bagdad becomes the royal residence of the Abbassides, iii.343. Derivation of the name, 343 *note*. The fallen state of the caliphs of, 372. The city of, stormed and sacked by the Moguls, 801.

Bahram, the Persian general, his character and exploits, ii.885. Is provoked to rebellion, 887. Dethrones Chosroes, 889. His usurpation and death, 891.

Baian, chagan of the Avars, his pride, policy, and power, ii.893. His perfidious seizure of Sirmium and Singidunum, 895. His conquests, 896. His treacherous attempt to seize the emperor Heraclius, 914. Invests Constantinople in conjunction with the Persians, 921. Retires, 923.

Bajazet I. sultan of the Turks, his reign, iii.818. His correspondence with Tamerlane, 836. Is defeated and captured by Tamerlane, 842. Inquiry into the story of the iron cage, 843. His sons, 853.

Balbinus elected joint emperor with Maximus, by the senate, on the deaths of the two Gordians, i.198.

Baldwin, count of Flanders, engages in the fourth crusade, iii.667. Is chosen emperor of Constantinople, 700. Is taken prisoner by Calo-John, king of the Bulgarians, 709. His death, 710.

Baldwin II. emperor of Constantinople, iii.716. His distresses and expedients, 718. His expulsion from that city, 725.

Baldwin, brother of Godfrey of Bouillon, accompanies him on the first crusade, iii.575. Founds the principality of Edessa, 593.

Baltic Sea, progressive subsidence of the water of, i.231 *note*. How the Romans acquired a knowledge of the naval powers of, 994 *note*.

Baptism, theory and practice of, among the primitive Christians, i.746.

Barbary, the name of that country whence derived, iii.299 *note*. The Moors of, converted to the Mahometan faith, 301.

Barbatio, general of infantry in Gaul under Julian, his misconduct, i.715.

Barchochebas, his rebellion against the emperor Hadrian, i.516.

Bardas, Cæsar, one of the restorers of learning, iii.417.

Bards, British, their peculiar office and duties, ii.504.

Bards, Celtic, their power of exciting a martial enthusiasm in the people, i.246.

Bari is taken from the Saracens by the joint efforts of the Latin and Greek empires, iii.472.

Barlaam, a Calabrian monk, his dispute with the Greek theologians about the light of mount Thabor, iii.784. His embassy to Rome, from Andronicus the Younger, 864. His literary character, 897.

Basil I. the Macedonian, emperor of Constantinople, iii.49. Reduces the Paulicians, 432.

Basil II. emperor of Constantinople, iii.60. His great wealth, 390. His inhuman treatment of the Bulgarians, 445.

Basil, archbishop of Cæsarea, no evidence of his having been persecuted by the emperor Valens, ii.509. Insults his friend Gregory Nazianzen, under the appearance of promotion, ii.29. The father of the monks of Pontus, 415.

Basiliscus, brother of the empress Verina, is entrusted with the command of the armament sent against the Vandals in Africa, ii.389. His fleet destroyed by Genseric, 390. His promotion to the empire, and death, 527.

Bassianus, high priest of the sun, his parentage, i.163. Is proclaimed emperor at Emesa, 163. See *Elagabalus*.

Bassianus, brother-in-law to Constantine, revolts against him, i.434.

Bassora, its foundation and situation, iii.241.

Baths, public, of Rome, described, ii.184.

Batnæ, reception of the emperor Julian there, i.918.

Beasts, wild, the variety of, introduced in the circus, for the public games at Rome, i.352.

Beausobre, M. de, character of his *Histoire Critique du Manicheisme*, ii.993 *note.*

Beder, battle of, between Mahomet and the Koreish of Mecca, iii.199.

Bedoweens of Arabia, their mode of life, iii.154.

Bees, remarks on the structure of their combs and cells, iii.347 *note.*

Belisarius, his birth and military promotion, ii.621. Is appointed by Justinian to conduct the African war, 623. Embarkation of his troops, 625. Lands in Africa, 627. Defeats Gelimer, 629. Is received into Carthage, 631. Second defeat of Gelimer, 633. Reduction of Africa, 636. Surrender of Gelimer, 639. His triumphant return to Constantinople, 640. Is declared sole consul, 641. He menaces the Ostrogoths of Italy, 646. He seizes Sicily, 650. Invades Italy, 654. Takes Naples, 656. He enters Rome, 658. He is besieged in Rome by the Goths, 658. The siege raised, 670. Causes Constantine, one of his generals, to be killed, 672. Siege of Ravenna, 675. Takes Ravenna by stratagem, 677. Returns to Constantinople, 678. His character and behaviour, 679. Scandalous life of his wife Antonina, 680. His disgrace and submission, 684. Is sent into the East to oppose Chosroes king of Persia, 712. His politic reception of the Persian ambassadors, 713. His second campaign in Italy, 789. His ineffectual attempt to raise the siege of Rome, 742. Dissuades Totila from destroying Rome, 744. Recovers the city, 745. His final recall from Italy, 746. Rescues Constantinople from the Bulgarians, 765. His disgrace and death, 766.

Benefice, in feudal language, explained, ii.480.

Benevento, battle of, between Charles of Anjou, and Mainfroy the Sicilian usurper, iii.755.

Beneventum, anecdotes relating to the siege of, iii.475.

Benjamin of Tudela, his account of the riches of Constantinople, iii.390.

Beræa, or Aleppo, reception of the emperor Julian there, i.917.

Bernard, St. his character and influence in promoting the second crusade, iii.624. His character of the Romans, 986.

Bernier, his account of the camp of Aurengzebe, i.223 *note.*

Berytus, account of the law school established there, i.591. Is destroyed by an earthquake, ii.771.

Bessarion, cardinal, his character, iii.903.

Bessas, governor of Rome for Justinian, his rapacity during the siege of that city by Totila the Goth, ii.741. Occasions the loss of Rome, 743.

Bezabde, is taken and garrisoned by Sapor king of Persia, i.708. Is ineffectually besieged by Constantius, 710.

Bindoes, a Sassanian prince, deposes Hormouz king of Persia, ii.887.

Birthright, the least invidious of all human distinctions, i.188.

Bishops, among the primitive Christians, the office of, explained, i.484. Progress of episcopal authority, 487. Assumed dignity of episcopal government, 496. Number of, at the time of Constantine the Great, 752. Mode of their election, 753. Their power of ordination, 754. The ecclesiastical revenue of each diocese how divided, 758. Their civil jurisdiction, 759. Their spiritual censures, 760. Their legislative assemblies, 764.

Bishops, rural, their rank and duties, i.752.

Bissextile, superstitious regard to this year by the Romans, i.966.

Bithynia, the cities of, plundered by the Goths, i.277.

Blemmyes, their revolt against the emperor Diocletian, i.370.

Boccace, his literary character, iii.899.

Boethius, the learned senator of Rome, his

history, ii.550. His imprisonment and death, 553.

Bohemond, the son of Robert Guiscard, his character and military exploits, iii.502. 577. His route to Constantinople on the crusade, 582. His flattering reception by the emperor Alexius Comnenus, 585. Takes Antioch, and obtains the principality of it, 595. His subsequent transactions, and death, 616.

Boniface, St. his history, i.573.

Boniface, count, the Roman general under Valentinian III. his character, ii.277. Is betrayed into a revolt by Ætius, 278. His repentance, 283. Is besieged in Hippo Regius by Genseric king of the Vandals. 284. Returns to Italy, and is killed by Ætius, 286.

Boniface VIII. pope, his violent contest with Philip the Fair king of France, and his character, iii.1008. Institutes the jubilee, 1010.

Boniface, marquis of Montferrat, is chosen general of the fourth crusade to the Holy Land, iii.672. Is made king of Macedonia, 703. Is killed by the Bulgarians, 711.

Bosphorus, revolutions of that kingdom, i.274. Is seized by the Goths, 274. The strait of, described, 587.

Bosra, siege of, by the Saracens, iii.250.

Botheric, the Imperial general in Thessalonica, murdered in a sedition, ii.56.

Boucicault, marshal, defends Constantinople against Bajazet, iii.825.

Boulogne, the port of, recovered from Carausius, by Constantius Chlorus, i.366.

Bowides, the Persian dynasty of, iii.372.

Brancaleone, senator of Rome, his character, iii.996.

Bretagne, the province of, in France, settled by Britons, ii.498.

Britain, reflections on the conquest of, by the Romans, i.33. Description of, 49. Colonies planted in, 64 *note*. A colony of Vandals settled there by Probus, 342. Revolt of Carausius, 364. How first peopled, 996. Invasions of, by the Scots and Picts, 999. Is restored to peace by Theodosius, 1001.

——, Revolt of Maximus there, ii.23. Revolt of the troops there against Honorius, 151. Is abandoned by the Romans, 231. State of, until the arrival of the Saxons, 232. Descent of the Saxons on, 494. Establishment of the Saxon heptarchy, 495. Wars in, 496. Saxon devastation of the country, 501. Manners of the independent Britons, 504. Description of, by Procopius, 505. Conversion of the Britons by a mission from pope Gregory the Great, 877. The doctrine of the incarnation received there, 977.

Brutus the Trojan, his colonization of Britain now given up by intelligent historians, i.997 *note*.

Buffon, M. his extraordinary burning mirrors, ii.593 *note*.

Bulgarians, their character, ii.690. Their inroads on the Eastern empire, 692. Invasion of, under Zabergan, 764. Repulsed by Belisarius, 765.

——, The kingdom of, destroyed by Basil II. the Greek emperor, iii.61. 445. Revolt of, from the Greek empire, and submission to the pope of Rome, 663. War with the Greeks under Calo-John, 707.

Bull-feast, in the Coliseum at Rome, described, iii.1078.

Burgundians, their settlement on the Elbe, and maxims of government, i.992. Their settlement in Gaul, ii.229. Limits of the kingdom of, under Gundobald, 461. Are subdued by the Franks, 464.

Burnet, character of his *Sacred Theory of the Earth*, i. 470 *note*.

Burrampooter, source of that river, iii.834 *note*.

Busir, in Egypt, four several places known under this name, iii.341 *note*.

Buzurg, the philosophical preceptor of Hormouz king of Persia, his high reputation, ii.883 *note*.

Byzantine historians, list and character of, iii.976 *note*.

Byzantium, siege of, by the emperor Severus, i.142. Is taken by Maximin, 430. Siege of, by Constantine the Great, 443. Its situation described, 586. By whom founded, 586. *note*. See *Constantinople.*

C

Caaba, or temple of Mecca, described, iii.167. The idols in, destroyed by Mahomet, 205.

Cabades, king of Persia, besieges and takes Amida, ii.607. Seizes the straits of Caucasus, 609. Vicissitudes of his reign, 702.

Cadesia, battle of, between the Saracens and the Persians, iii.239.

Cadijah, her marriage with Mahomet, iii.173. Is converted by him to his new religion, 190. Her death, 193. Mahomet's veneration for her memory, 217.

Cæcilian, the peace of the church in Africa disturbed by him and his party, i.768.

Cæcilius, the authority of his account of the famous vision of Constantine the Great, inquired into, i.738.

Cælestian, senator of Carthage, his distress on the taking of that city by Genseric, ii.290.

Cæsar and *Augustus*, those titles explained and discriminated, i.95.

Cæsar, Julius, his inducement to the conquest of Britain, i.33. Degrades the senatorial dignity, 86 *note*. Assumes a place among the tutelar deities of Rome, in his lifetime, 94. His address in appeasing a military sedition, 176 *note*. His prudent application of the coronary gold presented to him, 641.

Cæsarea, capital of Cappadocia, taken by Sapor king of Persia, i.329. Is reduced by the Saracens, iii.273.

Cæsars, of the emperor Julian, the philosophical fable of that work delineated, i.909.

Cahina, queen of the Moors of Africa, her policy to drive the Arabs out of the country, iii.300.

Cairoan, the city of, founded in the kingdom of Tunis, iii.296.

Caled, deserts from the idolatrous Arabs to the party of Mahomet, iii.204. His gallant conduct at the battle of Muta, 208. His victories under the caliph Abubeker, 239. Attends the Saracen army on the Syrian expedition, 250. His valour at the siege of Damascus, 252. Distinguishes himself at the battle of Aiznadin, 254. His cruel treatment of the refugees from Damascus, 260. Joins in plundering the fair of Abyla, 261. Commands the Saracens at the battle of Yermuk, 266. His death, 274.

Caledonia, and its ancient inhabitants, described, i.997.

Caledonian war, under the emperor Severus, an account of, i.151.

Caliphs of the Saracens, character of, iii.235. Their rapid conquests, 237. Extent and power of, 321. Triple division of the office, 343. They patronise learning, 347. Decline and fall of their empire, 369. 801.

Callinicum, the punishment of a religious sedition in that city, opposed by St. Ambrose, ii.58.

Callinicus of Heliopolis, assists in defending Constantinople against the Saracens, by his chymical inflammable compositions, iii.330.

Calmucks, black, recent emigration of, from the confines of Russia to those of China, i.1041.

Calo-John, the Bulgarian chief, his war with Baldwin, the Latin emperor of the Greeks, iii.707. Defeats, and takes him prisoner, 709. His savage character and death, 712.

Calocerus, a camel-driver, excites an insurrection in the island of Cyprus, i.655.

Calphurnius, the machinery of his eclogue on the accession of the emperor Carus, i.347.

Calvin, the reformer, his doctrine of the Eucharist, iii.437. Examination of his conduct to Servetus, 438.

Camel, of Arabia, described, iii.155.

Camisards of Languedoc, their enthusiasm compared with that of the Circumcellions of Numidia, i.822.

Campania, the province of, desolated by the ill policy of the Roman emperors, i.635. Description of the Lucullan villa in, ii.406.

Canada, the present climate and circumstances of, compared with those of ancient Germany, i.232.

Cannon, enormous one of the sultan Mahomet II. described, iii.943. Bursts, 951.

Canoes, Russian, a description of, iii.460.

Cantacuzene, John, character of his Greek History, iii.768. His good fortune under the younger Andronicus, 774. Is driven to assume the purple, 777. His lively distinction between foreign and civil war, 778. His entry into Constantinople, and reign, 780. Abdicates, and turns monk, 783. His war with the Genoese factory at Pera, 787. Marries his daughter to a Turk, 814. His negociation with pope Clement VI. 866.

Cantemir's History of the Ottoman Empire, a character of, iii.810 *note*.

Capelianus, governor of Mauritania, defeats the younger Gordian, and takes Carthage, i.198.

Capitation-tax, under the Roman emperors, an account of, i.636.

Capito, Ateius, the civilian, his character, ii.795.

Capitol of Rome, burning and restoration of, i.531.

Cappadocia, famous for its fine breed of horses, i.629.

Capraria, isle of, character of the monks there, ii.166.

Captives, how treated by the Barbarians, ii.304. 482.

Caracalla, son of the emperor Severus, his fixed antipathy to his brother Geta, i.150. Succeeds to the empire jointly with him, 153. Tendency of his edict to extend the privileges of Roman citizens to all the free inhabitants of his empire, 178. His view in this transaction, 184. Doubles the tax on legacies and inheritances, 185.

Caracorum, the Tartar settlement of, described, iii.805.

Carausius, his revolt in Britain, i.364. Is acknowledged by Diocletian and his colleagues, 366.

Caravans, Sogdian, their route to and from China, for silk, to supply the Roman empire, ii.581.

Carbeas, the Paulician, his revolt from the Greek emperor to the Saracens, iii.430.

Cardinals, the election of a pope vested in them, iii.1005. Institution of the conclave, 1005.

Carduene, situation and history of that territory, i.382.

Carinus, the son of Carus, succeeds his father in the empire, jointly with his brother Numerian, i.349.

Carizmians, their invasion of Syria, iii.648.

Carlovingian race of kings, commencement of, in France, iii.109.

Carmath, the Arabian reformer, his character, iii.367. His military exploits, 368.

Carmelites, from whom they derive their pedigree, ii.412 *note*.

Carpathian mountains, their situation, i.231.

Carthage, the bishopric of, bought for Majorinus, i.556 *note*. Religious discord generated there by the factions of Cæcilian and Donatus, 768.

——, The temple of Venus there, converted into a Christian church, ii.80. Is surprised by Genseric of the Vandals, 288. The gates of, opened to Belisarius, 631. Natural alterations produced by time in the situation of this city, 632 *note*. The walls of, repaired by Belisarius, 633. Insurrection of the Roman troops there, 732.

——, Is reduced and pillaged by Hassan the Saracen, iii.298. Subsequent history of, 299.

Carthagena, an extraordinary rich silver mine worked there for the Romans, i.180.

Carus, emperor, his election and character, i.346.

Caspian and Iberian gates of mount Caucasus, distinguished, ii.609.

Cassians, the party of, among the Roman civilians, explained, ii.796.

Cassiodorus, his Gothic history, i.255. His account of the infant state of the republic of Venice, ii.346. His long and prosperous life, 541.

Castriot, George. See *Scanderbeg*.

Catalans, their service and war in the Greek empire, iii.759.

Catholic church, the doctrines of, how discriminated from the opinions of the Platonic School, i.776. The authority of, extended to the minds of mankind, 778. Faith of the Western or Latin church, 787. Is distracted by factions in the cause of Athanasius, 797. The doxology, how introduced, and how perverted, 815. The revenue of, transferred to the heathen priests, by Julian, 890.

——, Edict of Theodosius for the establishment of the Catholic faith, ii.26. The progressive steps of idolatry in, 90. Persecution of the Catholics in Africa, 435. Pious frauds of the Catholic clergy, 441. How bewildered by the doctrine of the incarnation, 941. Union of the Greek and Latin churches, 977.

——, Schism of the Greek church, iii.655.

Celestine, pope espouses the party of Cyril against Nestorius, and pronounces the degradation of the latter from his episcopal dignity, ii.949.

Celtic language, driven to the mountains by the Latin, i.65, and *note*.

Censor, the office of, revived under the emperor Decius, i.262. But without effect, 263.

Ceos, the manufacture of silk, first introduced to Europe from that island, ii.579.

Cerca, the principal queen of Attila king of the Huns, her reception of Maximin the Roman ambassador, ii.315.

Cerinthus, his opinion of the twofold nature of Jesus Christ, ii.938.

Ceylon, ancient names given to that island, and the imperfect knowledge of, by the Romans, i.910 *note*.

Chalcedon, the injudicious situation of this city stigmatised by proverbial contempt, i.588. A tribunal erected there by the emperor Julian, to try and punish the evil ministers of his predecessor Constantius, 855.

——, A stately church built there by Rufinus, the infamous minister of the emperor Theodosius, ii.101. Is taken by Chosroes II. king of Persia, 910.

Chalcondyles, the Greek historian, his remarks on the several nations of Europe, iii.874.

Châlons, battle of, between the Romans and Attila the king of the Huns, ii.340.

Chamavians reduced and generously treated by Julian, i.718.

Chancellor, the original and modern application of this word compared, i.351.

Characters, national, the distinctions of, how formed, i.1025.

Chariots of the Romans described, ii.176 *note*.

Charlemagne conquers the kingdom of Lombardy, iii.109. His reception at Rome, 112. Eludes fulfilling the promises of Pepin and himself to the Roman pontiff, 114. His coronation at Rome by the pope Leo III. 123. His reign and character, 124. Extent of his empire, 127. His neighbours and enemies, 130. His successors, 132. His negociations and treaty with the Eastern empire, 134. State of his family and dominions in the tenth century, 411.

Charles the Fat emperor of the Romans, iii.133.

Charles of Anjou subdues Naples and Sicily, iii.754. The *Sicilian Vespers*, 757. His character as a senator of Rome, 997.

Charles IV. emperor of Germany, his weakness and poverty, ii.147. His public ostentation, 148. Contrast between him and Augustus, 149.

Charles V. emperor, parallel between him and Diocletian, i.466. And between the sack of Rome by him, and that by

Alaric the Goth, ii.207.

Chastity, its high esteem among the ancient Germans, i.243. And the primitive Christians, 480.

Chemistry, the art of, from whom derived, iii.352.

Chersonesus, Thracian, how fortified by the emperor Justinian, ii.602.

Chersonites assist Constantine the Great against the Goths, i.658. Are cruelly persecuted by the Greek emperor Justinian II., iii.34.

Chess, object of the game of, and by whom invented, ii.708.

Childeric, king of France, deposed under papal sanction, iii.110.

Children, the exposing of, a prevailing vice of antiquity, ii.811. Natural, according to the Roman laws, what, 818.

China, how distinguished in ancient history, i.375 *note*. Great numbers of children annually exposed there, 494 *note*. Its situation, 1034. The high chronology claimed by the historians of, 1034. The great wall of, when erected, 1036. Was twice conquered by the northern tribes, 1038.

——, The Romans supplied with silk by the caravans from, ii.581.

——, Is conquered by the Moguls, iii.798. 806. Expulsion of the Moguls, 806.

Chivalry, origin of the order of, iii.577.

Chnodomar, prince of the Alemanni, taken prisoner by Julian at the battle of Strasburg, i.717.

Chosroes, king of Armenia, assassinated by the emissaries of Sapor king of Persia, i.282.

Chosroes, son of Tiridates, king of Armenia, his character, i.666.

Chosroes I. king of Persia, protects the last surviving philosophers of Athens, in his treaty with the emperor Justinian, ii.615. Review of his history, 703. Sells a peace to Justinian, 708. His invasion of Syria, 710. His negociations with Justinian, 725. His prosperity, 726. Battle of Melitene, 882. His death, 883.

Chosroes II. king of Persia, is raised to the throne on the deposition of his father Hormouz, ii.888. Is reduced to implore the assistance of the emperor Maurice, 889. His restoration and policy, 893. Conquers Syria, 908. Palestine, 908. Egypt and Asia Minor, 909. His reign and magnificence, 910. Rejects the Mahometan religion, 912. Imposes an ignominious peace on the emperor Heraclius, 914. His flight, deposition, and death, 926.

Chozars, the hord of, sent by the Turks to the assistance of the emperor Heraclius, ii.923.

Christ, the festival of his birth, why fixed by the Romans at the winter solstice, i.841 *note*.

Christianity, enquiry into the progress and establishment of, i.446. Religion and character of the Jews, 447. The Jewish religion the basis of Christianity, 451. Is offered to all mankind, 451. The sects into which the Christians divided, 453. The theology of, reduced to a systematical form in the school of Alexandria, 503. Injudicious conduct of its early advocates, 511. Its persecutions, 514. First erection of churches, 553. The system of, found in Plato's doctrine of the *Logos*, 775.

——, Salutary effects resulting from the conversion of the barbarous nations, ii.432.

——, Its progress in the north of Europe, iii.468.

Christians, primitive, the various sects into which they branched out, i.453. Ascribed the Pagan idolatry to the agency of dæmons, 459. Believed the end of the world to be near at hand, 466. The miraculous powers ascribed to the primitive church, 471. Their faith stronger than in modern times, 475. Their superior virtue and austerity, 475. Repentance a virtue in high esteem among them, 476. Their notions of marriage and chastity, 479. They disclaim war and government, 481. Were active however in the internal

Christians—contd
government of their own society, 482. Bishops, 484. Synods, 486. Metropolitans and primates, 488. Bishop of Rome, 489. Their probable proportion to the Pagan subjects of the empire before the conversion of Constantine the Great, 507. Enquiry into their persecutions, 514. Why more odious to the governing powers than the Jews, 517. Their religious meetings suspected, 520. Are persecuted by Nero, as the incendiaries of Rome, 527. Instructions of the emperor Trajan to Pliny the Younger for the regulation of his conduct toward them, 535. Remained exposed to popular resentment on public festivities, 536. Legal mode of proceeding against them, 537. The ardour with which they courted martyrdom, 546. When allowed to erect places for public worship, 553. Their persecution under Diocletian and his associates, 564. An edict of toleration for them published by Galerius just before his death, 574. Some considerations necessary to be attended to in reading the sufferings of the martyrs, 577. Edict of Milan published by Constantine the Great, 729. Political recommendations of the Christian morality to Constantine, 730. Theory and practice of passive obedience, 731. Their loyalty and zeal, 734. The sacrament of baptism, how administered in early times, 746. Extraordinary propagation of Christianity after it obtained the Imperial sanction, 748. Becomes the established religion of the Roman empire, 750. Spiritual and temporal powers distinguished, 750. Review of the episcopal order in the church, 752. The ecclesiastical revenue of each diocese, how divided, 758. Their legislative assemblies, 764. Edict of Constantine the Great against heretics, 766. Mysterious doctrine of the Trinity, 775. The doctrines of the Catholic church, how discriminated from the opinions of the Platonic school, 776. General character of the Christian sects, 823. Christian schools prohibited by the emperor Julian, 892. They are removed from all offices of trust, 894. Are obliged to reinstate the Pagan temples, 895. Their imprudent and irregular zeal against idolatry, 906.

——, distinction of, into *vulgar* and *ascetic*, ii.411. Conversion of the barbarous nations, 429.

Chrysaphius the Eunuch, engages Edecon, to assassinate his king Attila, ii.319. Is put to death by the empress Pulcheria, 321. Assisted at the second council of Ephesus, 957.

Chrysocheir, general of the revolted Paulicians, over-runs and pillages Asia Minor, iii.431. His death, 431.

Chrysoloras, Manuel, the Greek envoy, his character, iii.900. His admiration of Rome and Constantinople, 910.

Chrysopolis, battle of, between Constantine the Great and Licinus, i.532.

Chrysostom, St. his account of the pompous luxury of the emperor Arcadius, ii.237. Protects his fugitive patron the eunuch Eutropius, 248. History of his promotion to the archiepiscopal see of Constantinople, 252. His character and administration, 253. His persecution, 256. His death, 259. His relics removed to Constantinople, 259. His encomium on the monastic life, 416 *note*.

Churches, Christian, the first erection of, i.553. Demolition of, under Diocletian, 568. Splendour of, under Constantine the Great, 757. Seven, of Asia, the fate of, iii.812.

Cibalis, battle of, between Constantine the Great and Licinius, i.435.

Cicero, his view of the philosophical opinions as to the immortality of the soul, i.463. His encomium on the study of the law, ii.783. System of his *republic*, 793.

Cimmerian darkness, the expression of, whence derived, ii.177 *note*.

Circumcellions of Africa, Donatist schismatics, history of their revolt, i.821.

Their religious suicides, 823. Persecution of, by the emperor Honorius, ii.281.

Circumcision of both sexes, a physical custom in Æthiopia, unconnected with religion, ii.1001.

Circus, Roman, the four factions in, described ii.570. Constantinople, and the Eastern empire, distracted by these factions, 571.

Cities in the Roman empire enumerated, i.75.

——, Commercial, of Italy, rise, and government of, iii.143.

Citizens of Rome, motive of Caracalla for extending the privileges of, to all the free inhabitants of the empire, i.178. 185. Political tendency of this grant, 186.

City, the birth of a new one, how celebrated by the Romans, i.593 *note*.

Civilians of Rome, origin of the profession, and the three periods in the history of, ii.791.

Civilis, the Batavian, his successful revolt against the Romans, i.248.

Claudian the poet, and panegyrist of Stilicho, his works supply the deficiencies of history, ii.106. Celebrates the murder of Rufinus, 110. His death and character, 162. His character of the eunuch Eutropius, 241.

Claudius, emperor, chosen by the Prætorian guards, without the concurrence of the senate, i.97.

Claudius, emperor, successor to Gallienus, his character and elevation to the throne, i.297.

Cleander, minister of the emperor Commodus, his history, i.114.

Clemens, Flavius, and his wife Domitilla, why distinguished as Christian martyrs, i.534.

Clement III. pope, and the emperor Henry III. mutually confirm each other's sovereign characters, iii.504.

Clement V. pope, transfers the holy see from Rome to Avignon, iii.1009.

Clergy, when first distinguished from the laity, i.490 750. The ranks and numbers of, how multiplied, 756. Their property, 756. Their offences only cognisable by their own order, 760. Valentinian's edict to restrain the avarice of, 985.

Clodion, the first of the Merovingian race of kings of the Franks in Gaul, his reign, ii.330.

Clodius Albinus, governor of Britain, his steady fidelity during the revolutions at Rome, i.132. Declares himself against Julianus, 133.

Clotilda, niece of the king of Burgundy, is married to Clovis king of the Franks, and converts her Pagan husband, ii.458. Exhorts her husband to the Gothic war, 465.

Clovis, king of the Franks, his descent, and reign, ii.453.

Cluverius, his account of the objects of adoration among the ancient Germans, i.245 *note*.

Cochineal, importance of the discovery of, in the art of dying, ii.578 *note*.

Code of Justinian, how formed, ii.799. New edition of, 805.

Codicils, how far admitted by the Roman law respecting testaments, ii.825.

Cœnobites, in monkish history, described, ii.426.

Coinage, how regulated by the Roman emperors, iii.993.

Colchos, the modern Mingrelia, described, ii.714. Manners of the natives, 716. Revolt of, from the Romans to the Persians, and repentance, 720. Colchian war, in consequence, 723.

Coliseum, of the emperor Titus, observations on, iii.1076. Exhibition of a bull feast in, 1078.

Collyridian heretics, an account of, iii.177.

Colonies, Roman, how planted, i.63.

Colonna, history of the Roman family of, iii.1014.

Colossus of Rhodes, some account of, iii.275.

Columns of Hercules, their situation, i.54.

Comana, the rich temple of, suppressed, and the revenues confiscated, by the emperors of the East, i.629.

Combat, judicial, origin of, in the Salic laws, ii.477. The laws of, according to the Assize of Jerusalem, iii.612. Apology for the practice of, 743 *note*.

Comets, account of those which appeared in the reign of Justinian, ii.770.

Commentiolus, his disgraceful warfare against the Avars, ii.897.

Commodus, emperor, his education, character, and reign, i.109.

Comneni, origin of the family of, on the throne of Constantinople, iii.64. Its extinction, 972.

Conception, immaculate, of the Virgin Mary, the doctrine of, from whence derived, iii.180.

Concubine, according to the Roman civil law, explained, ii.817.

Conflagration, general, ideas of the primitive Christians, concerning, i.469.

Conquest, the vanity of, not so justifiable as the desire of spoil, i.1000. Is rather achieved by art, than personal valour, ii.297.

Conrad III. emperor, engages in the second crusade, iii.617. His disastrous expedition, 622.

Conrad of Montferrat, defends Tyre against Saladin, iii.638. Is assassinated, 641.

Constance, treaty of, iii.144.

Constans, the third son of Constantine the Great, is sent to govern the western provinces of the empire, i.654. Division of the empire among him and his brothers, on the death of their father, 663. Is invaded by his brother Constantine, 670. Is killed, on the usurpation of Magnentius, 673. Espoused the cause of Athanasius against his brother Constantius, 802.

Constans II. emperor of Constantinople, iii.29.

Constantia, princess, grand-daughter of Constantine the Great, is carried by her mother to the camp of the usurper Procopius, i.971. Narrowly escapes falling into the hands of the Quadi, 1018. Marries the emperor Gratian, 1021.

Constantina, daughter of Constantine the Great, and widow of Hannibalianus, places the diadem on the head of the general Vetranio, i.673. Is married to Gallus, 687. Her character, 687. Dies, 690.

Constantina, widow of the Eastern emperor Maurice, the cruel fate of, and her daughters, ii.904.

Constantine the Great, the several opinions as to the place of his birth, i.403. His history, 404. He is saluted emperor by the British legions on the death of his father, 405. Marries Fausta, the daughter of Maximian, 410. Puts Maximian to death, 415. General review of his administration in Gaul, 417. Undertakes to deliver Rome from the tyranny of Maxentius, 420. Defeats Maxentius, and enters Rome, 426. His alliance with Licinius, 430. Defeats Licinius, 435. Peace concluded with Licinius, 436. His laws, 437. Chastises the Goths, 439. Second civil war with Licinius, 440. Motives which induced him to make Byzantium the capital of his empire, 586. Declares his determination to spring from divine command, 592. Despoils other cities of their ornaments to decorate his new capital, 596. Ceremony of dedicating his new city, 601. Form of civil and military administration established there, 602. Separates the civil from the military administration, 618. Corrupted military discipline, 619. His character, 643. Account of his family, 646. His jealousy of his son Crispus, 648. Mysterious deaths of Crispus and Licinius, 650. His repentance and acts of atonement inquired into, 651. His sons and nephews, 653. Sends them to superintend the several provinces of the empire, 654. Assists the Sarmatians, and provokes the Goths, 657. Reduces the Goths to peace, 658. His death, 660.

Attempt to ascertain the date of his conversion to Christianity, 726. His Pagan superstition, 727. Protects the Christians in Gaul, 728. Publishes the edict of Milan, 729. Motives which recommended the Christians to his favour, 730. Exhorts his subjects to embrace the Christian profession, 733. His famous standard the *Labarum* described, 737. His celebrated vision previous to his battle with Maxentius, 738. Story of the miraculous cross in the air, 740. His conversion accounted for, from natural and probable causes, 742. His theological discourses, 744. His devotion and privileges, 745. The delay of his baptism accounted for, 746. Is commemorated as a saint by the Greeks, 747. His edict against heretics, 766. Favours the cause of Cæcilian against Donatus, 769. His sensible letter to the bishop of Alexandria, 789. How prevailed on to ratify the Nicene creed, 790. His levity in religion, 792. Granted a toleration to his Pagan subjects, 825. His reform of Pagan abuses, 826. Was associated with the Heathen Deities after his death, by a decree of the senate, 827. His discovery of the holy sepulchre, 886.

——, Publication of his fictitious donation to the bishops of Rome, iii.115. Fabulous interdiction of marriage with strangers, ascribed to him, 400.

Constantine II. the son of Constantine the Great, is sent to preside over Gaul, i.654. Division of the empire among him and his brothers, on the death of their father, 663. Invades his brother Constans, and is killed, 671.

Constantine III. emperor of Constantinople, iii.28.

Constantine IV. Pogonatus, emperor of Constantinople, iii.30.

Constantine V. Copronymus, emperor of Constantinople, iii.37. Fates of his five sons, 39. Revolt of Artavasdes, and troubles on account of image worship, 96. Abolishes the monkish order, 96.

Constantine VI. emperor of Constantinople, iii.40.

Constantine VII. Porphyrogenitus, emperor of Constantinople, iii.54. His cautions against discovering the secret of the Greek fire, 332. Account of his works, 379. Their imperfections pointed out, 380. His account of the ceremonies of the Byzantine court, 399. Justifies the marriage of his son with the princess Bertha of France, 400.

Constantine VIII. emperor of Constantinople, iii.55.

Constantine IX. emperor of Constantinople, iii.58.

Constantine X. Monomachus, emperor of Constantinople, iii.63.

Constantine XI. Ducas, emperor of Constantinople, iii.65.

Constantine Palæologus, the last of the Greek emperors, his reign, iii.930.

Constantine Sylvanus, founder of the Paulicians, his death, iii.428.

Constantine, a private soldier in Britain, elected emperor, for the sake of his name, ii.152. He reduces Gaul and Spain, 153. 219. His reduction and death, 220.

Constantine, general under Belisarius in Italy, his death, ii.672.

Constantinople, its situation described, with the motives which induced Constantine the Great to make this city the capital of his empire, i.586. Its local advantages, 591. Its extent, 593. Progress of the work, 595. Principal edifices, 596. How furnished with inhabitants, 598. Privileges granted to it, 600. Its dedication, 601. Review of the new form of civil and military administration established here, 602. Is allocated to Constantine the Younger, in the division of the empire, on the emperor's death, 663. Violent contests there between the rival bishops, Paul and Macedonius, 817. Bloody engagement between the Athanasians and Arians on the removal of the body of Constantine, 819. Triumphant entry of

Constantinople—contd
the emperor Julian, 849. The senate of, allowed the same powers and honours as that at Rome, 860. Arrival of Valens, as emperor of the East, 969. Revolt of Procopius, 970.

——, Continued the principal seat of the Arian heresy, during the reigns of Constantius and Valens, ii.28. Is purged from Arianism by the emperor Theodosius, 31. Council of, 33. Is enriched by the bodies of saints and martyrs, 91. Insurrection against Gainas and his Arian Goths, 250. Persecution of the archbishop, St. Chrysostom, 256. Popular tumults on his account, 257. Earthquake there, 303. The city and eastern empire distracted by the factions of the circus, 571. Foundation of the church of St. Sophia, 594. Other churches erected there by Justinian, 598. Triumph of Belisarius over the Vandals, 640. The walls of, injured by an earthquake, 764. State of the armies, under the emperor Maurice, 898. The armies and city revolt against him, 900. Deliverance of the city from the Persians and Avars, 921. Religious war about the Trisagion, 965.

——, Prospectus of remaining history of the Eastern empire, iii.23. Summary review of the five dynasties of the Greek empire, 83. Tumults in the city to oppose the destruction of images, 95. Abolition of the monkish order by Constantine, 96. First siege of, by the Saracens, 323. Second siege by the Saracens, 327. Review of the provinces by the Greek empire, in the tenth century, 383. Riches of the city of Constantinople, 390. The imperial palace of, 391. Officers of state, 395. Military character of the Greeks, 407. The name and character of Romans, supported to the last, 416. Decline, and revival of literature, 417. The city menaced by the Turks, 452. Account of the Varangians, 456. Naval expeditions of the Russians against the city, 460. Origin of the separation of the Greek and Latin churches, 655. Massacre of the Latins, 661. Invasion of the Greek empire, and conquest of Constantinople by the crusaders, 678. The city taken, and Isaac Angelus restored, 683. Part of the city burned by the Latins, 686. Second siege of the city by the Latins, 688. Is pillaged, 691. Account of the statues destroyed, 695. Partition of the Greek empire by the French and Venetians, 699. The Greeks rise against their Latin conquerors, 708. The city retaken by the Greeks, 723. The suburb of Galata, assigned to the Genoese, 785. Hostilities between the Genoese and the emperor, 787. How the city escaped the Moguls, 807. Is besieged by the sultan Amurath II., 858. Is compared with Rome, 910. Is besieged by Mahomet II. sultan of the Turks, 944. Is stormed and taken, 963. Becomes the capital of the Turkish empire, 969.

Constantius Chlorus, governor of Dalmatia, was intended to be adopted by the emperor Carus, in the room of his vicious son Carinus, i.351. Is associated as Cæsar by Diocletian in his administration, 361. Assumes the title of Augustus, on the abdication of Diocletian, 400. His death, 405. Granted a toleration to the Christians, 571.

Constantius, the second son of Constantine the Great, his education, i.653. Is sent to govern the Eastern provinces of the empire, 654. Seizes Constantinople on the death of his father, 662. Conspires the deaths of his kinsmen, 662. Division of the empire among him and his brothers, 663. Restores Chosroes king of Armenia, 666. Battle of Singara with Sapor king of Persia, 667. Rejects the offers of Magnentius and Vetranio, on the plea of a vision, 674. His oration to the Illyrian troops at the interview with Vetranio, 676. Defeats Magnentius at the battle of Mursa, 678. His councils governed by eunuchs, 684. Education of his cousins Gallus and Julian, 686.

Disgrace and death of Gallus, 690. Sends for Julian to court, 695. Invests him with the title of Cæsar, 696. Visits Rome, 698. Presents an obelisk to that city, 700. The Quadian and Sarmatian wars, 700. His Persian negociations, 703. Mismanagement of affairs in the East, 709. Favours the Arians, 792. His religious character by Ammianus the historian, 793. His restless endeavours to establish an uniformity of Christian doctrine, 795. Athanasius driven into exile by the council of Antioch, 801. Is intimidated by his brother Constans, and invites Athanasius back again, 803. His severe treatment of those bishops who refused to concur in deposing Athanasius, 807. His scrupulous orthodoxy, 808. His cautious conduct in expelling Athanasius from Alexandria, 809. His strenuous efforts to seize his person, 812. Athanasius writes invectives to expose his character, 814. Is constrained to restore Liberius bishop of Rome, 817. Supports Macedonius, bishop of Constantinople, and countenances his persecutions of the Catholics and Novations, 819. His conduct toward his Pagan subjects, 826. Envies the fame of Julian, 831. Recalls the legions from Gaul, 831. Negociations between him and Julian, 840. His preparations to oppose Julian, 847. His death and character, 848.

Constantius, general, relieves the British emperor Constantine when besieged in Arles, ii.220. His character and victories, 220. His marriage with Placidia, and death, 273.

Constantius, secretary to Attila king of the Huns, his matrimonial negociation at the court of Constantinople, ii.311.

Consul, the office of explained, i.90. Alterations this office underwent under the emperors, and when Constantinople became the seat of empire, 605. The office of, suppressed by the emperor Justinian, ii.616. Is now sunk to a commercial agent, iii.992.

Contracts, the Roman laws respecting, ii.827.

Copts of Egypt, brief history of, ii.993.

Corinth, reviving as a Roman colony, celebrates the Isthmian games, under the emperor Julian, i.860. The isthmus of, fortified by the emperor Justinian, ii.601.

Cornwal, reduction of, by the Saxons, ii.499.

Coronary gold, nature of those offerings to the Roman emperors, i.640.

Corvinus, Matthias, king of Hungary, his character, iii.925.

Cosmas Indicopleustes, account of his Christian topography, ii.585 *note*. 982 *note*.

Cosmo of Medicis, his character, iii.907.

Councils and synods of
- Antioch, i.801.
- Arles, i.805.
- Basil, iii.881.
- Carthage, ii.437. 637.
- Chalcedon, ii.256. 958.
- Clermont, iii.560.
- Constance, iii.877. 880. 1050.
- Constantinople, ii.33. 973. 976. iii.94. 658.
- Ephesus, ii.949. 957.
- Ferrara, iii.887.
- Florence, iii.888.
- Frankfort, iii.120.
- Lyons, ii.462. iii.718. 752.
- Milan, i.805.
- Nice, i.782. iii.188.
- Pisa, iii.880. 1049.
- Placentia, iii.559.
- Rimini, i.788.
- Sardica, i.802.
- Toledo, ii.447. 449. 492.
- Tyre, i.799.

Count, great difference between the ancient and modern application of this title, i.619. By whom first invented, 619. Of the sacred largesses, under Constantine the Great, his office, 628. Of the domestics in the Eastern empire, his office, 629.

Courtenay, history of the family of, iii.729.

Crescentius, consul of Rome, his vicissitudes, and disgraceful death, iii.141.

Crete, the isle of, subdued by the Saracens, iii.356. Is recovered by Nicephorus Phocas, 374. Is purchased by the Venetians, 702.

Crimes, how distinguished by the penal laws of the Romans, ii.836.

Crispus, son of Constantine the Great, is declared Cæsar, i.437. Distinguishes his valour against the Franks and Alemanni, 439. Forces the passage of the Hellespont, and defeats the fleet of Licinius, 443. His character, 647. His mysterious death, 649.

Crispus, the Patrician, marries the daughter of Phocas, and contributes to depose him, ii.905. Is obliged to turn monk, 906.

Croatia, account of the kingdom of, iii.442.

Cross, the different sentiments entertained of this instrument of punishment, by the Pagan and Christian Romans, i.736. The famous standard of, in the army of Constantine the Great described, 737. His visions of, 738. 740. The holy sepulchre and cross of Christ discovered, 887. The cross of Christ undiminished by distribution to pilgrims, 887.

Crown of thorns, its transfer from Constantinople to Paris, iii.720.

Crowns, mural and obsidional, the distinction between, i.930 *note*.

Crusade, the first resolved on at the council of Clermont, iii.562. Enquiry into the justice of the holy war, 563. Examination into the private motives of the crusaders, 567. Departure of the crusaders, 570. Account of the chiefs, 574. Their march to Constantinople, 580. Review of their numbers, 587. They take Nice, 590. Battle of Dorylæum, 591. They take Antioch, 593. Their distresses, 596. Are relieved by the discovery of the holy lance, 598. Siege and conquest of Jerusalem, 603. Godfrey of Bouillon chosen king of Jerusalem, 606. The second crusade, 617. The crusaders ill treated by the Greek emperors, 620. The third crusade, 638. Siege of Acre, 639. Fourth and fifth crusades, 645. Sixth crusade, 649. Seventh crusade, 651. Recapitulation of the fourth crusade, 672. General consequences of the crusades, 725.

Ctesiphon, the city of, plundered by the Romans, i.224. Its situation described, 931. Julian declines the siege of that city, 936. Is sacked by the Saracens, iii.242.

Cublai, emperor of China, his character, iii.806.

Curopalata, his office under the Greek emperors, iii.395.

Customs, duties of, imposed by Augustus, i.181.

Cycle of indictions, the origin of, traced, and how now employed, i.633 *note*.

Cyprian, bishop of Carthage, his history and martyrdom, i.541.

Cyprus, the kingdom of, bestowed on the house of Lusignan, by Richard I. of England, iii.663.

Cyrene, the Greek colonies there finally exterminated by Chosroes II. king of Persia, ii.909.

Cyriades, an obscure fugitive, is set up by Sapor the Persian monarch, as emperor of Rome, i.284.

Cyril, bishop of Jerusalem, his pompous relation of the miraculous appearance of a celestial cross, i.793. His ambiguous character, 888.

Cyril, patriarch of Alexandria, his life and character, ii.942. Condemns the heresy of Nestorius, 949. Procures the decision of the council of Ephesus against Nestorius, 949. His court intrigues, 953.

Cyzicus, how it escaped destruction from the Goths, i.278. Is at length ruined by them, 279. The island and city of, seized by the usurper Procopius, 971.

D

Dacia, conquest of, by the emperor Trajan, i.35. Its situation, 51. Is over-run by the Goths, 260. Is resigned to them by Aurelian, 305.

Dæmons, supposed to be the authors and objects of Pagan idolatry, by the primitive Christians, i.459.

Dagisteus, general of the emperor Justinian, besieges Petra, ii.722. Commands the Huns in Italy under Narses, 752.

Daimbert, archbishop of Pisa, installed patriarch of Jerusalem, iii.607.

Dalmatia described, i.51. Produce of a silver mine there, 180 *note*.

Dalmatius, nephew of Constantine the Great, is created Cæsar, i.653. Is sent to govern the Gothic frontier, 654. Is cruelly destroyed by Constantius, 662.

Damascus, siege of, by the Saracens, iii.252. The city reduced both by storm and by treaty, 257. Remarks on Hughes's tragedy of this siege, 259 *note*. Taken and destroyed by Tamerlane, 839.

Damasus, bishop of Rome, edict of Valentinian addressed to him, to restrain the crafty avarice of the Roman clergy, i.985. His bloody contest with Ursinus for the episcopal dignity, 987.

Dames, the Arab, his gallant enterprise against the castle of Aleppo, iii.270.

Damietta, is taken by Louis IX. of France, iii.650.

Damophilus, archbishop of Constantinople, resigns his see, rather than subscribe the Nicene creed, ii.31.

Dandalo, Henry, doge of Venice, his character, iii.670. Is made despot of Romania, 702.

Daniel, first bishop of Winchester, his instructions to St. Boniface, for the conversion of infidels, ii.431.

Danielis, a Grecian matron, her presents to the emperor Basil, iii.388. Her visit to him at Constantinople, 393. Her testament, 394.

Danube, course of the river, and the provinces of, described, i.50.

Daphne, the sacred grove and temple of, at Antioch, described, i.896. Is converted to Christian purposes by Gallus, and restored to the Pagans by Julian, 898. The temple burned, 899.

Dara, the fortification of Justinian, described, ii.608. The demolition of, by the Persians, prevented by peace, 708. Is taken by Chosroes king of Persia, 882.

Darius, his scheme for connecting the continents of Europe and Asia, i.588.

Darkness, præternatural, at the time of the passion, is unnoticed by the heathen philosophers and historians, i.512.

Dastagard, the Persian royal seat of, plundered by the emperor Heraclius, ii.926.

Datianus, governor of Spain, yields ready obedience to the Imperial edicts against the Christians, i.570.

Datius, bishop of Milan, instigates the revolt of the Ligurians to Justinian, ii.669. Escapes to Constantinople on the taking of Milan by the Burgundians, 673.

Debtors, insolvent, cruel punishment of, by the law of the twelve tables, ii.833.

Decemvirs, review of the laws of their twelve tables, ii.781. These laws superseded by the perpetual edict, 786. Severity of, 831.

Decius, his exaltation to the empire, i.254. Was a persecutor of the Christians, 555.

Decurions, in the Roman empire, are severely treated by the Imperial laws, i.634.

Deification of the Roman emperors, how this species of idolatry was introduced, i.94.

Delators, are encouraged by the emperor Commodus, to gratify his hatred of the senate, i.112. Are suppressed by Pertinax, 123.

Delphi, the sacred ornaments of the temple of, removed to Constantinople by Constantine the Great, i.597 *note*.

Democracy, a form of government unfavourable to freedom in a large state. i.61.

Demosthenes, governor of Cæsarea, his gallant defence against, and heroic escape from, Sapor king of Persia, i.284.

Deogratias, bishop of Carthage, humanely succours the captives brought from Rome by Genseric king of the Vandals, ii.362.

Derar the Saracen, his character, iii.254.

Desiderius, the last king of the Lombards, conquered by Charlemagne, iii.109.

Despot, nature of that title in the Greek empire, iii.395.

Despotism originates in superstition, i.240 *note.*

Diadem assumed by Diocletian, what, i.388.

Diamonds, the art of cutting them, unknown to the ancients, i.182 *note.*

Didius Julianus, purchases the imperial dignity at a public auction, i.130.

Dioceses of the Roman empire, their number and government, i.613.

Diocletian, the manner of his military election to the empire, i.356. his birth and character, 358. Takes Maximian for his colleague, 360. Associates as Cæsars, Galerius and Constantius Clorus, 361. His triumph in conjunction with Maximian, 383. Fixes his court at the city of Nicomedia, 385. Abdicates the empire, 391. Parallel between him and the emperor Charles V. 391. Passes his life in retirement at Salona, 393. His impartial behaviour towards the Christians, 558. Causes that produced the persecution of the Christians under his reign, 559.

Dion Cassius the historian, screened from the fury of the soldiers, by the emperor Alexander Severus, i.175.

Dioscorus, patriarch of Alexandria, his outrageous behaviour at the second council of Ephesus, ii.957. Is deposed by the council of Chalcedon, 959.

Disabul, great khan of the Turks, his reception of the ambassadors of Justinian, ii.700.

Divorce, the liberty and abuse of, by the Roman laws, ii.813. Limitations of, 815.

Docetes, their peculiar tenets, i.774, ii.936. Derivation of their name, i.775 *note.*

Dominic, St. Loricatus, his fortitude in flagellation, iii.566.

Dominus, when this epithet was applied to the Roman emperors, i.387.

Domitian, emperor, his treatment of his kinsmen Flavius Sabinus, and Flavius Clemens, i.533.

Domitian, the Oriental prefect, is sent by the emperor Constantius, to reform the state of the East, then oppressed by Gallus, i.689. Is put to death there, 690.

Donatus, his contest with Cæcilian for the see of Carthage, i.768. History of the schism of the Donatists, 769, 821. Persecution of the Donatists by the emperor Honorius, ii.281.

Dorylæum, battle of between sultan Soliman and the first crusaders, iii.591.

Doxology, how introduced in the church-service, and how perverted, i.815.

Dramatic representations at Rome, a character of, ii.185.

Dreams, the popular opinion of the preternatural origin of, favourable to that of Constantine, previous to his battle with Maxentius, i.738.

Dromedary, extraordinary speed of this animal, i.318 *note.*

Dromones of the Greek empire, described, iii.405.

Druids, their power in Gaul suppressed by the emperors Tiberius and Claudius, i.60.

Druses of mount Libanus, a character of, iii.551 *note.*

Duke, derivation of that title, and great change in the modern, from the ancient application of it, i.619.

Durazzo, siege of, by Robert Guiscard, iii.497. Battle of, between him and the Greek emperor Alexius, 500.

E

Earthquake, an extraordinary one over the great part of the Roman empire, i.1023. Account of those that happened in the reign of Justinian, ii.772.

East India, the Roman commercial intercourse with that region, i.81. Commodities of, taxed by Alexander Severus, 182.

Ebionites, account of that sect, i.454. A confutation of their errors, supposed by the primitive fathers, to be a particular object in the writings of St. John the

Evangelist, i.773.
——, Their ideas of the person of Jesus Christ, ii.933.
Ecclesiastes, the book of, why not likely to be the production of king Solomon, ii.641 *note*.
Ecclesiastical and civil powers, distinguished, by the fathers of the Christian church, i.750.
Ecdicius, son of the emperor Avitus, his gallant conduct in Gaul, ii.393.
Ecthesis of the emperor Heraclius, ii.975.
Edda of Iceland, the system of mythology in, i.256.
Edecon, is sent from Attila king of the Huns, as his ambassador to the emperor Theodosius the Younger, ii.312. Engages in a proposal to assassinate Attila, 319. His son Odoacer, the first Barbarian king of Italy, 403.
Edessa, the purest dialect of the Syriac language spoken there, i.224 *note*. The property of the Christians there, confiscated by the emperor Julian, for the disorderly conduct of the Arians, 903. Revolt of the Roman troops there, ii.899. The city and principality of, seized by Baldwin the Crusader, iii.593. Is retaken by Zhengi, 627. The counts of, 729.
Edict of Milan, published by Constantine the Great, i.729.
Edicts of the prætors of Rome, under the republic, their nature and tendency, ii.785.
Edom, why that name was applied to the Roman empire by the Jews, i.517 *note*.
Edrisites, the Saracen dynasty of, iii.370.
Edward I. of England, his crusade to the Holy Land, iii.653.
Egypt, general description of, i.53. The superstitions of, with difficulty tolerated at Rome, 60. Amount of its revenues, 179. Public works executed there by Probus, 345. Conduct of Diocletian there, 370. Progress of Christianity there, 503. Edict of the emperor Valens, to restrain the number of recluse monks there, 984.
——, The worship of Serapis how introduced there, ii.81. This temple, and the Alexandrian library destroyed by bishop Theophilus, 82. Origin of monkish institutions in, 413. Great supplies of wheat furnished by, for the city of Constantinople, in the time of Justinian, 578. Ecclesiastical history of, 993.
——, Reduced by the Saracens, iii.277. Capture of Alexandria, 282. Administration of, 286. Description of, by Amrou, 288. The Egyptians take Jerusalem from the Turks, 601. Egypt conquered by the Turks, 628. Government of the Mamalukes there, 652.
Elagabalus, is declared emperor by the troops at Emesa, i.163. Was the first Roman who wore garments of pure silk, ii.580.
Elephants, enquiry into the numbers of, brought into the field by the ancient princes of the East, i.226 *note*. With what view introduced in the circus at Rome in the first Punic war, 353.
Eleusinian mysteries, why tolerated by the emperor Valentinian, i.981.
Elizabeth, queen of England, the political use she made of the national pulpits, i.763 *note*.
Emigration of the ancient northern nations, the nature and motives of, examined, i.239.
Emperors of Rome, a review of their constitutions, ii.787. Their legislative power, 788. Their rescripts, 789.
——, of Germany, their limited powers, iii.145. Of Constantinople, their pomp and luxury, 391. Officers of the palace, state, and army, 395. Adoration of the emperor, mode of, 397. Their public appearance, 398. Their despotic power, 403. Their navy, 404. They retain the name of Romans to the last, 416.
Empire, Roman, division of, into the *East* and *West* empires by Valentinian, i.968. Extinction of the Western empire, ii.404.
Encampment, Roman, described, i.44.

Ennodius, the servile flatterer of Theodoric the Ostrogoth king of Italy, is made bishop of Pavia, ii.534 *note*.

Epagathus, leader of the mutinous prætorians, who murdered their præfect Ulpian, punished by the emperor Alexander Severus, i.175.

Ephesus, the famous temple of Diana at, destroyed by the Goths, i.281. Council of, ii.949. Episcopal riots there, 951.

Epicurus, his legacy to his philosophical disciples at Athens, ii.613.

Epirus, despots of, on the dismemberment of the Greek empire, iii.706.

Equitius, master general of the Illyrian frontier, is defeated by the Sarmatians, i.1019.

Erasmus, his merit as a reformer, iii.438.

Essenians, their distinguishing tenets and practices, i.502.

Eucharist a knotty subject to the first reformers, iii.437.

Eudes, duke of Aquitain, repels the first Saracen invasion of France, iii.334. Implores the aid of Charles Martel, 336. Recovers his dukedom, 338.

Eudocia, her birth, character, and marriage, with the emperor Theodosius the Younger, ii.266. Her disgrace and death, 268.

Eudoxia, her marriage with the emperor Arcadius, ii.104. Stimulates him to give up his favourite Eutropius, 248. Persecutes St. Chrysostom, 256. Her death and character, 260.

Eudoxia, the daughter of Theodosius the Younger, is betrothed to the young emperor Valentinian III. of the West, ii.276. Her character, 354. Is married to the emperor Maximus, 359. Invites Genseric king of the Vandals to Italy, 360.

Eudoxus, bishop of Constantinople, baptises the emperor Valens, i.982.

Eugenius, the Rhetorician is made emperor of the West by Arbogastes the Frank, ii.63. Is defeated and killed by Theodosius, 67.

Eugenius, IV. pope, his contest with the council of Basil, iii.881. Procures a reunion of the Latin and Greek churches, 892. Forms a league against the Turks, 917. Revolt of the Roman citizens against him, 1051.

Eumenius the Orator, some account of, i.398 *note*.

Eunapius the Sophist, his character of monks, and of the objects of their worship, ii.90.

Eunomians, punishment of, by the edict of the emperor Theodosius against heretics, ii.37.

Eunuchs, enumerated in the list of Eastern commodities imported and taxed in the time of Alexander Severus, i.182. They infest the palace of the third Gordian, 205. Their ascendancy in the court of Constantius, 684. Why they favoured the Arians, 792 *note*. Procure the banishment of Liberius bishop of Rome, 816.

——, A conspiracy of, disappoint the schemes of Rufinus, and marry the emperor Arcadius to Eudoxia, ii.104. They distract the court of the emperor Honorius, 194. And govern that of Arcadius, 239. Scheme of Chrysaphius to assassinate Attila king of the Huns, 319.

——, The bishop of Seez and his whole chapter castrated, iii.984 *note*.

Euric, king of the Visigoths in Gaul, his conquests in Spain, ii.392. Is vested with all the Roman conquests beyond the Alps by Odoacer king of Italy, 452.

Europe, evidences that the climate of, was much colder in ancient than in modern times, i.231. This alteration accounted for, 232.

——, Final division of, between the Western and Eastern empires, ii.98. Is ravaged by Attila king of the Huns, 302. Is now, one great republic, 511.

Eusebia, empress, wife of Constantius, her steady friendship to Julian, i.693. 694. Is accused of arts to deprive Julian of children, 697.

Eusebius, his character of the followers of

Artemon, i.509. His own character, 577. His story of the miraculous appearance of the cross in the sky to Constantine the Great, 741.

Eutropius the Eunuch, great chamberlain to the emperor Arcadius, concerts his marriage with Eudoxia, in opposition to the views of Rufinus, ii.104. Succeeds Rufinus in the emperor's confidence, 111. His character and administration, 239. Provides for his own security, in a new law against treason, 244. Takes sanctuary with St. Chrysostom, 248. His death, 249.

Eutyches, his opinion on the subject of the incarnation supported by the second council at Ephesus, ii.957. And adhered to by the Armenians, 992.

Euxine Sea, description of the vessels used in navigating, i.275.

Exaltation of the cross, origin of the annual festival of, ii.930.

Exarch, under the Greek empire, the office and rank of, iii.111. Of Ravenna, the government of Italy settled in, and administered by, ii.762. 864.

Excise duties imposed by Augustus, i.182.

Excommunication from Christian communion, the origin of, i.494, 761.

Exile, voluntary, under accusation and conscious guilt, its advantage among the Romans, ii.841.

F

Faith and its operations defined, i.475.

Falcandus, Hugo, character of his *Historia Sicula*, iii.518 *note.* His lamentation on the transfer of the sovereignty of the island to the emperor Henry VI. 519.

Fathers of the Christian church, cause of their austere morality, i.477.

Fausta, empress, wife of Constantine the Great, causes of her being put to death, i.652.

Faustina, wife of Marcus Antonius, her character, i.108.

Faustina, the widow of the emperor Constantius, countenances the revolt of Procopius against the emperor Valens, i.971.

Festivals, Pagan, great offence taken at, by the primitive Christians, i.462.

Feudal government, the rudiments of, to be found among the Scythians, i.1032.

Figures, numeral, occasion of their first public and familiar use, iii.327.

Finances of the Roman empire, when the seat of it was removed to Constantinople, reviewed, i.632.

Fingal, his questionable history, whether to be connected with the invasion of Caledonia by the emperor Severus, i.151.

Fire, Greek, the Saracen fleet destroyed by, in the harbour of Constantinople, iii.329. Is long preserved as a secret, 332. Its effects not to be compared with gunpowder, 407.

Firmus, an Egyptian merchant, his revolt against the emperor Aurelian, i.319.

Firmus the Moor, history of his revolt against the emperor Valentinian, i.1004.

Flagellation, its efficacy in penance, and how proportioned, iii.566.

Flamens, Roman, their number, and peculiar office, ii.72.

Flaminian way, its course described, ii.753 *note.*

Flavian, archbishop of Constantinople, is killed at the second council of Ephesus, ii.958.

Fleece, golden, probable origin of the fable of, ii.716.

Florence, the foundation of that city, ii.145 *note.* Is besieged by Radagaisus, and relieved by Stilicho, 145.

Florentius, prætorian præfect of Gaul under Constantius, his character, i.722. 833. Is condemned by the tribunal of Chalcedon, but suffered to escape by Julian, 856.

Florianus, brother of the emperor Tacitus, his eager usurpation of the Imperial dignity, i.334.

Fœlix is consecrated bishop of Rome, to supersede Liberius who was exiled, i.816. He is violently expelled, and his adherents slaughtered, 817.

Fœlix, an African bishop, his martyrdom, i.567.

Fornication, a doubtful plea for divorce, by gospel authority, ii.816 *note*.

France, modern, computation of the number of its inhabitants, and the average of their taxation, i.638.

——, The name of, whence derived, ii.483. Derivation of the French language, 489 *note*.

——, Childeric deposed, and Pepin appointed king, by papal sanction, iii.110. Reign and character of Charlemagne, 124. Invasion of, by the Saracens, 333.

Frangipani, Censio, his profane violation of the persons of pope Gelasius II. and his college of cardinals, iii.985. Derivation of his family name, 1014.

Franks, their origin and confederacy, i.269. They invade Gaul, and ravage Spain, 270. They pass over into Africa, 271. Bold and successful return of a colony of, from the sea of Pontus, by sea, 342. They over-run and establish themselves at Toxandria in Germany, 711.

——, Their fidelity to the Roman government, ii.148. Origin of the Merovingian race of their kings, 329. How converted to Christianity, 431. Reign of their king Clovis, 453. Final establishment of the French monarchy in Gaul, 470. Their laws, 472. Give the name of *France* to their conquest in Gaul, 483. They degenerate into a state of anarchy, 489. They invade Italy, 673. 759.

——, Their military character, iii.411.

Fravitta the Goth, his character, and deadly quarrel with his countryman Priulf, i.1083. His operations against Gainas, ii.251.

Frederic I. emperor of Germany, his tyranny in Italy, iii.143. Engages in the third crusade, 617. His disastrous expedition, 622. 638. Sacrifices Arnold of Brescia to the pope, 990. His reply to the Roman ambassadors, 1000.

Frederic II. is driven out of Italy, iii.144. His disputes with the pope, and reluctant crusade, 638. Exhorts the European princes to unite in opposing the Tartars, 804.

Frederic III. the last emperor crowned at Rome, iii.1052.

Freedmen, among the Romans, their rank in society, ii.807.

Freemen of Laconia, account of, iii.386.

Fritigern, the Gothic chief, extricates himself from the hands of Lupicinus, governor of Thrace, i.1052. Defeats him, 1053. Battle of Salices, 1056. His strength recruited by the accession of new tribes, 1058. Negociates with Valens, 1062. Battle of Hadrianople, 1063. The union of the Gothic tribes broken by his death, 1076.

Frumentius was the first Christian missionary in Abyssinia, i.749.

Fulk of Neuilly, his ardour in preaching the fourth crusade, iii.665.

G

Gabinius, king of the Quadi, is treacherously murdered by Marcellinus governor of Valeria, i.1018.

Gaillard, M. character of his *Histoire de Charlemagne*, iii.124 *note*.

Gainas the Goth is commissioned by Stilicho to execute his revenge on Rufinus, præfect of the East, ii.110. His conduct in the war against the revolter Tribigild, 247. Joins him, 249. His flight and death, 252.

Gala, probable derivation of the term, iii.398 *note*.

Galata, the suburb of, at Constantinople, assigned to the Genoese, iii.785.

Galerius is associated in the administration, as Cæsar, by the emperor Diocletian, i.361. Is defeated by the Persians, 376. Surprises and overthrows Narses, 378. Assumes the title of Augustus, on the abdication of Diocletian, 400. His jealousy of Constantine, 404. Deems it prudent to acknowledge him Cæsar, 406. His unsuccessful invasion of Italy,

411. Invests Licinius with the purple on the death of Severus, 413. His death, 415. From what causes he entertained an aversion to the Christians, 561. Obtains the countenance of Diocletian for persecuting them, 562. Publishes an edict of toleration just before his death, 574.

Galilæans, twofold application of that name in the infancy of Christianity, i.531. Why the emperor Julian applied this name to the Christians, 891.

Gallienus, son of the emperor Valerian, is associated by him in the Imperial throne, i.268. Prohibits the senators from exercising military employments, 273. Character of his administration after the captivity of his father, 286. Names Claudius for his successor, 296. Favoured the Christians, 555.

Gallies of the Greek empire, described, iii.405.

Gallus elected emperor, on the minority of Hostilianus, the son of Decius, i.265.

Gallus, nephew of Constantine the Great, his education, i.686. Is invested with the title of Cæsar, 687. His cruelty and imprudence, 687. His disgrace and death, 690. Embraced the doctrine, but neglected the precepts of Christianity, 866. Converts the grove of Daphne at Antioch to a Christian burial place, 895.

Games, public, of the Romans, described, i.211. 351. ii.185. Account of the factions of the circus, 570.

Ganges, source of that river, iii.834 *note.*

Gaudentius, the notary, is condemned to death under the emperor Julian, i.857.

Gaul, the province of, described, i.48. The power of the druids suppressed there by Tiberius and Claudius, 60. Cities in, 59. Amount of the tribute paid by that province to Rome, 180. Is defended against the Franks by Posthumus, 270. Succession of usurpers there, 311. Invasion of, by the Lygians, 339. Revolt of the Bagaudæ suppressed by Maximian, 363. Progress of Christianity there, 505. Proportion of the capitation tax levied there by the Roman emperors, 636. Is invaded by the Germans, 710. The government of, assigned to Julian, 711. His civil administration, 721. Is invaded by the Alemanni, under the emperor Valentinian, 989. And under Gratian, 1059.

——, Destruction of idols and temples there, by Martin bishop of Tours, ii.79. Is over-run by the barbarous troops of Radagaisus, after his defeat by Stilicho, 149. Is settled by the Goths, Burgundians, and Franks, 229. Assembly of the seven provinces in, 235. Reign of Theodoric king of the Visigoths in, 327. Origin of the Merovingian race of kings of the Franks in, 329. Invasion of, by Attila king of the Huns, 334. Battle of Châlons, 340. Revolutions of, on the death of the emperor Majorian, 392. Conversion of, to Christianity, by the Franks, 444. Representation of the advantages it enjoyed under Roman government, 451. Conquests and prosperity of Euric king of the Visigoths, 452. Character and reign of Clovis, 453. The Alemanni conquered, 456. Submission of the Armoricans, and the Roman troops, 460. Final establishment of the French monarchy in Gaul, 470. History of the Salic laws, 472. The lands of, how claimed and divided by the Barbarian conquerors of, 478. Domain and benefices of the Merovingian princes, 480. Usurpations of the *Seniors*, 481. Privileges of the Romans in, 487.

Gedrosia, revolutions of the sea coast of, i.222 *note.*

Gelalæan æra of the Turks, when settled, iii.543.

Gelasius, pope, his zeal against the celebration of the feast of Lupercalia, ii.388. Deplores the miserable decay of Italy, 409.

Gelasius II. pope, his rough treatment by Censio Frangipani, iii.985.

Gelimer deposes Hilderic the Vandal king of Africa, and usurps the government, ii.619. Is defeated by Belisarius, 629.

Gelimer—contd
His final defeat, 633. His distressful flight, 638. Surrenders himself to Belisarius, 639. Graces his triumph, 641. His peaceful retirement, 642.

General of the Roman army, his extensive power, i.87.

Generosity, Arabian, striking instances of, iii.165.

Gennadius, the monk, his denunciation against a Greek union with the Latin church, iii.948.

Gennerid, the Roman general, under the emperor Honorius, his character, ii.194.

Genoese, their mercantile establishment in the suburb of Pera at Constantinople, iii.785. Their war with the emperor Cantacuzenus, 787.

Genseric, king of the Vandals in Spain, his character, ii.279. Goes over to Africa on the invitation of count Boniface, 280. His successes there by the assistance of the Donatists, 282. Devastation of Africa by his troops, 284. Besieges Boniface in Hippo Regius, 284. His treacherous surprisal of Carthage, 288. Strengthens himself by an alliance with Attila king of the Huns, 301. His brutal treatment of his son's wife, daughter of Theodoric, 329. Raises a naval force, and invades Italy, 357. His sack of Rome, 360. Destroys the fleet of Majorian, 378. His naval depredations on Italy, 381. His claims on the Eastern empire, 382. Destroys the Roman fleet under Basilicus, 390. Was an Arian, and persecuted his Catholic subjects, 435.

Gentleman, etymology of the term, iii.578 *note*.

Geoponics of the emperor of Constantine Porphyrogenitus, account of, iii.380.

George of Cappadocia supersedes Athanasius in the see of Alexandria, i.810. His scandalous history, and tragical death, 902. Becomes the tutelar saint of England, 903.

Gepidæ, their incroachments on the Eastern empire checked by the Lombards, ii.688. Are reduced by them, 850.

Germanus, nephew of the emperor Justinian, his character and promotion to the command of the army sent to Italy, ii.750. His death, 751.

Germany, the rude institutions of that country the original principles of European laws and manners, i.230. Its ancient extent, 230. How peopled, 233. The natives unacquainted with letters in the time of Tacitus, 234. Had no cities, 235. Manners of the ancient Germans, 237. Population, 238. State of liberty among them, 239. Authority of their magistrates, 241. Conjugal faith and chastity, 243. Their religion, 245. Arms and discipline, 247. Their feuds, 249. General idea of the German tribes, 251. Probus carries the Roman arms into Germany, 339. A frontier wall built by Probus, from the Rhine to the Danube, 340. Invasions of Gaul by the Germans, 710. 989.

——, State of, under the emperor Charlemagne, iii.129. The Imperial crown established in the name and nation of Germany, by the first Otho, 133. Division of, among independent princes, 145. Formation of the Germanic constitution, 146. State assumed by the emperor, 148.

Gerontius, count, sets up Maximus as emperor in Spain, and loses his life in the attempt, ii.219.

Geta and Caracalla, sons of the emperor Severus, their fixed antipathy to each other, i.150.

Ghebers of Persia, history of, iii.316.

Gibraltar, derivation of the name of, iii.305.

Gildo the Moor, his revolt in Africa, ii.113. His defeat and death, 118.

Gladiators, desperate enterprise and fate of a party of, reserved for the triumph of Probus, i.344. The combats of, abolished by the emperor Honorius, ii.138.

Glycerius is first emperor of Rome, and then bishop of Salona, ii.399. Murders Julius Nepos, and is made archbishop of Milan, 401.

Gnostics, character and account of the sect of, i.456. Principal sects into which they divided, 457. Their peculiar tenets, 774. ii.936.

Godfrey of Bouillon, his character, and engagement in the first crusade, iii.574. His route to Constantinople, 580. 583. Is elected king of Jerusalem, 606. Compiles the Assize of Jerusalem, 610. Form of his administration, 611.

Gog and Magog, the famous rampart of, described, ii.610.

Goisvintha, wife of Leovigild, king of Spain, her pious cruelty to the princess Ingundis, ii.445.

Gold of affliction, the tax so denominated in the Eastern empire abolished by the emperor Anastasius, ii.585.

Golden horn, why the Bosphorus obtained this appellation in remote antiquity, i.588.

Gordianus, proconsul of Africa, his character and elevation to the empire of Rome, i.194. His son associated with him in the imperial dignity, 195.

Gordian, the third and youngest, declared Cæsar, i.200. Is declared emperor by the army, on the murder of Maximus and Balbinus, 207.

Goths of Scandinavia, their origin, i.255. Their religion, 256. The Goths and Vandals supposed to be originally one great people, 258. Their emigration to Prussia and the Ukraine, 258. They invade the Roman provinces, 260. They receive tribute from the Romans, 265. They subdue the Bosphorus, 274. Plunder the cities of Bithynia, 277. They ravage Greece, 279. Conclude a treaty with the emperor Aurelian, 304. They ravage Illyricum, and are chastised by Constantine the Great, 439. Their war with the Sarmatians, 657. Are again routed by Constantine, 658. Gothic war under the emperors Valentinian and Valens, 1014. Are defeated by the Huns, 1044. They implore the protection of the emperor Valens, 1046. They are received into the empire, 1048. They are oppressed by the Roman governors of Thrace, 1050. Are provoked to hostilities, and defeat Lupicinus, 1053. They ravage Thrace, 1053. Battle of Salices, 1056. They are strengthened by fresh swarms of their countrymen, 1057. Battle of Hadrianople, 1063. Scour the country from Hadrianople to Constantinople, 1066. Massacre of the Gothic youth in Asia, 1069. Their formidable union broken by the death of Fritigern, 1076. Death and funeral of Athanaric, 1077. Invasion and defeat of the Ostrogoths, 1078. Are settled in Thrace by Theodosius, 1080. Their hostile sentiments, 1082.

——, Revolt of the Goths under Honorius, ii.121. They ravage Greece, under the command of Alaric, 122. They invade Italy, 129. The sack of Rome by, 200. Death of Alaric, 211. Victories of Wallia in Spain, 227. They are settled in Aquitain, 228. See *Gaul*, and *Theodoric*. Conquest of the Visigoths in Gaul and Spain, 392. How the Goths were converted to the Christian religion, 429. 445. Reign of Theodoric king of the Ostrogoths, 525. The Goths in Italy, extinguished, 762.

Government, civil, the origin of, i.240.

Governors of provinces, under the emperors, their great power and influence, i.617.

Gratian was the first emperor who refused the pontifical robe, i.827 *note*. Marries the princess Constantia, and succeeds to the empire, 1021. Defeats the Alemanni in Gaul, 1059. Invests Theodosius with the empire of the East, 1070.

——, His character and conduct, ii.19. His flight from Maximus and death, 23. Overthrew the ecclesiastical establishment of Paganism, 73.

Greece, is ravaged by the Goths, i.279. Is overrun by Alaric the Goth, ii.122. Is reduced by the Turks, iii.971.

Greek church, origin of the schism of, iii.655. 892. 912.

Greek empire. See *Constantinople.*

Greek learning, revival of, in Italy, iii.896.

Greeks, why averse to the Roman language and manners, i.65. The Greek becomes a scientific language among the Romans, 66. Character of the Greek language of Constantinople, iii.894. When first taught in Italy, 900.

Gregory the Great, pope, his pious presents to Recared king of Spain, ii.447. Exhorts Theodelinda queen of the Lombards to propagate the Nicene faith, 448. His enmity to the venerable buildings and learning of Rome, 873. His birth and early profession, 874. His elevation to the pontificate, 876. Sends a mission to convert the Britons, 877. Sanctifies the usurpation of the emperor Phocas, 903.

Gregory II. pope, his epistles to Leo III. emperor of Constantinople, iii.99. Revolts against the Greek emperor, 101.

Gregory VII. pope, his ambitious schemes, iii.139. His contest with the emperor Henry III, 504. His retreat to Salerno, 505. 984.

Gregory, præfect of Africa, history of him and his daughter, iii.291.

Gregory Nazianzen, his lamentation on the disgraceful discord among Christians, i.824. Loads the memory of the emperor Julian with invective, 865. Censures Constantius for having spared his life, 874 *note.*

——, is presented to the wretched see of Sasima by his friend archbishop Basil, ii.29. His mission to Constantinople, 30. Is placed on the archiepiscopal throne by Theodosius, 32. His resignation and character, 35.

Grumbates, king of the Chionites, attends Sapor king of Persia, in his invasion of Mesopotamia, i.705. Loses his son at the siege of Amida, 706. Returns home in grief, 708.

Guardianship, how vested and exercised, according to the Roman civil laws, ii.818.

Gubazes, king of Colchos, his alliance with Chosroes king of Persia, ii.721. Returns to his former connexion with the emperor Justinian, 722. Is treacherously killed, 725.

Guelphs and Ghibelines, the parties of, in Italy, iii.144. 1081.

Guilt, the degrees of, in the penal laws of the Romans, ii.836.

Guiscard, Robert, his birth and character, iii.485. Acquires the dukedom of Apulia, 488. His Italian conquests, 489. Besieges Durazzo, 496. Defeats the Greek emperor Alexius there, 500. Engages in the cause of pope Gregory VII. 505. His second expedition to Greece, and death, 506.

Gundobald, king of the Burgundians, is reduced by Clovis king of the Franks, ii.462. His mode of justifying the judicial combat, 477.

Gunpowder, the invention and use of, iii.862.

Guy of Lusignan, king of Jerusalem, his character, iii.364. Is defeated and taken prisoner by Saladin, 635.

Gyarus, a small island in the Ægean sea, an instance of its poverty, i.180.

H

Hadrian, emperor, relinquishes the eastern conquests of Trajan, i.36. Their characters compared, 37. His character contrasted with that of Antoninus Pius, 37. His several adoptions of successors, 100. Founds the city of Ælia Capitolina on mount Sion, 454.

——, Reforms the laws of Rome in the perpetual edict, ii.786.

Hadrianople, battle of, between Constantine the Great, and Licinius, i.442. Is ineffectually besieged by Fritigern the Goth, 1054. Battle of, between the emperor Valens and the Goths, 1063.

Hakem, caliph of the Saracens, assumes a divine character to supplant the Mahometan faith, iii.551.

Hamadanites, the Saracen dynasty of, in Mesopotamia, iii.371.

Hannibal, review of the state of Rome when he besieged that city, ii.168.

Hannibalianus, nephew of Constantine the Great, is dignified with the title of king, i.653. Provinces assigned to him for a kingdom, 654. Is cruelly destroyed by Constantius, 662.

Happiness, instance how little it depends on power and magnificence, iii.345.

Harmozan, the Persian satrap, his interview with the caliph Omar, iii.245.

Harpies, in ancient mythologic history, Le Clerc's conjecture concerning, i.587 *note*.

Harun al Rashid, caliph, his friendly correspondence with the emperor Charlemagne, iii.131. His wars with the Greek empire, 353.

Hassan, the Saracen, conquers Carthage, iii.298.

Hawking, the art and sport of, introduced into Italy, by the Lombards, ii.868.

Hegira, the æra of, how fixed, iii.194.

Helena, the mother of Constantine, her parentage ascertained, i.403. Was converted to Christianity by her son, 727 *note*.

Helena, sister of the emperor Constantius, married to Julian, i.695. Is reported to be deprived of children by the arts of the empress Eusebia, 697. Her death, 840.

Heliopolis taken by the Saracens, iii.264.

Hell, according to Mahomet, described, iii.187.

Hellespont, described i.589.

Helvetia, amount of its population in the time of Cæsar, i.239 *note*.

Hengist, his arrival in Britain, with succours for Vortigern, against the Caledonians, ii.494. His establishment in Kent, 495. 497.

Henoticon of the emperor Zeno, character of, ii.963.

Henry succeeds his brother Baldwin as emperor of Constantinople, iii.711. His character and administration, 711.

Henry III. emperor, his contest with pope Gregory VII. iii.504. Takes Rome, and sets up pope Clement III. 504.

Henry VI. emperor, conquers and pillages the island of Sicily, iii.520.

Henry the Fowler, emperor of Germany, defeats the Turkish invaders, iii.452.

Heptarchy, Saxon, establishment of, in Britain, ii.495. Review of the state of, 501.

Heracleonas, emperor of Constantinople, iii.28.

Heraclian, count of Africa, retains that province in obedience to Honorius, ii.199. His cruel usage of the refugees from the sack of Rome by Alaric, 207. His revolt and death, 217.

Heraclius, deposes the Eastern usurper Phocas, and is chosen emperor, ii.905. Conquests of Chosroes II. king of Persia, 908. His distressful situation, 912. Accepts an ignominious peace from Chosroes, 914. His first expedition against the Persians, 916. His second Persian expedition, 918. Strengthens himself by an alliance with the Turks, 923. His third Persian expedition, 924. His treaty of peace with Persia, 929. His triumph and pilgrimage to Jerusalem, 930. His theological inquiries, 974.

——, marries his niece Martina, iii.27. Leaves his two sons joint successors to the empire, 27. Invasion of his provinces by the Saracens, 253. Flies from Syria, 271.

Heraclius the præfect, his expedition against the Vandals in Africa, ii.389.

Heraclius the eunuch, instigates the emperor Valentinian III. to the murder of the patrician Ætius, ii.352. His death, 354.

Herbelot, character of his *Bibliotheque Orientale* iii.238 *note*.

Hercynian forest, the extent of, unknown in the time of Cæsar, i.232 *note*.

Heresy in religion, the origin of, traced, i.457. Edict of Constantine the Great, against, 766.

Hermanric king of the Ostrogoths, his conquests, i.1013. His death, 1045.

Hermenegild prince of Bœtica, his marriage with Ingundis princess of Austrasia, and conversion to the Nicene faith, ii.445. Revolt and death, 446.

Hermits of the East, their mortified course of life, ii.426. Miracles performed by them and their relics, 428.

Hermodorus, the Ephesian, assists the Romans in compiling their twelve tables of laws, ii.781.

Hermogenes, master general of the cavalry, is killed in the attempt to banish Paul, bishop of Constantinople, i.818.

Hero and Leander, the story of, by whom controverted and defended, i.590 *note*.

Herodian, his life of Alexander Severus, why preferable to that in the Augustan history, i.178 *note*.

Herodes Atticus, his extraordinary fortune and munificence, i.72.

Herodotus, his character of the Persian worship, i.217.

Heruli, of Germany and Poland, their character, ii.537.

Hilarion, the monk of Palestine, account of, ii.415.

Hilary, bishop of Poitiers, his remarkable observations on the diversity of Christian doctrines, i.785. His exposition of the term Homoiousion, 787.

Hilary, pope, censures the emperor Anthemius for his tolerating principles, ii.386.

Hilderic the Vandal king of Africa, his indulgence to his Catholic subjects displeases both the Arians and Athanasians, ii.619. Is deposed by Gelimer, 619. Is put to death, 630.

Hindoos of the East, not the disciples of Zoroaster, iii.316 *note*.

Hindostan, conquest of, by Tamerlane, iii.833.

Hippo Regius, siege of, by Genseric king of the Vandals, ii.284.

History, the principal subjects of, i.252.

Holy war, the justice of it enquired into, iii.563.

Homicide, how commuted by the Salic laws, ii.474.

Homoousion, origin, and use of that term at the council of Nice, i.782. And Homoiousion, the distinction between, 787.

Honain, war of, iii.206.

Honoratus, archbishop of Milan, is, with his clergy, driven from his see, by the Lombards, ii.854.

Honoria, princess, sister of the emperor Valentinian III. her history, ii.332.

Honorius, son of Theodosius the Great, is declared emperor of the West, by his dying father, ii.68. Marries Maria, daughter of Stilicho, 119. His character, 120. Flies from Milan on the invasion of Italy by Alaric, 133. His triumphant entry into Rome, 137. Abolishes the combats of gladiators, 138. Fixes his residence at Ravenna, 139. Orders the death of Stilicho, 160. His impolitic measures, and cruelty unite his barbarian soldiers against him under Alaric, 166. His councils distracted by the eunuchs, 194. His abject overtures to Attalus and Alaric, 198. His last acts, and death, 218. His triumph for the reduction of Spain by Wallia the Goth, 228. Is suspected of incest with his sister Placidia, 274. His persecution of the Donatists in Africa, 281.

Honour, the new ranks of, introduced in the city of Constantinople, i.604. iii.394.

Hormisdas, a fugitive Persian prince, in the court of the emperor Constantius, his remarks on the city of Rome, i.699. *note*. His history, and station under Julian, 922.

Hormouz, the son of Chosroes, king of Persia, his accession, ii.883. His character, 884. Is deposed, and at length killed, 887.

Horses, of Arabia, their peculiar qualities, iii.155.

Hosein, the son of Ali, his tragical death, iii.226.

Hospitallers, knights of St. John of Jerusalem, popularity and character of the order of, iii.609.

Hostilianus, the minor son of the emperor Decius, elected emperor under the guardianship of Gallus, i.265.

Hugh, king of Burgundy, his marriage with Marozia, and expulsion from Rome by Alberic, iii.140.

Hugh, count of Vermandois, engages in the first crusade, iii.575. Is shipwrecked and made captive by the Greek emperor Alexius Comnenus, 582. His return, 598.

Human nature, its propensities, i.478.

Hume, Mr. his natural history of religion, the best commentary on the polytheism of the ancients, i.57 *note.* His difficulty as to the extent of the Imperial palace at Rome, resolved, 153 *note.* Charges the most refined and philosophic sects with intolerancy, 220 *note.*

Hungary, establishment of the Huns in, ii.294. State of, under the emperor Charlemagne, iii.130. Terror excited by their first approach to Europe, 445. Their character, 448.

Huniades, John, his exploits gainst the Turks, iii.919. His defence of Belgrade, and death, 925.

Hunneric, the son of Genseric, king of the Vandals, persecutes his Catholic subjects, ii.436. His cruelty to the Catholics of Tipasa, 443.

Huns, their original seat, and their conquests, i.1035. Their decline, 1038. Their emigrations, 1040. Their victories over the Goths, 1044. 1045.

——, They drive other barbarous tribes before them, upon the Roman provinces, ii.142. Their establishment in Hungary, 294. Character of their king Attila, 296. Their invasion of Persia, 300. The empire of, extinguished by the death of Attila, 351.

Hunting of wild beasts, when a virtue, and when a vice, i.117. Is the school of war, 1030.

Hypatia, the female philosopher, murdered in the church at Alexandria, ii.946.

Hypatius, sedition of, at Constantinople, ii.576.

I & J

Jacobites of the East, history of the sect of, ii.987.

James, St. his legendary exploits in Spain, i.506.

Janizaries, first institution of those troops, iii.817.

Iberian and Caspian gates of mount Caucasus, distinguished, ii.609. The Iberian gates occupied by Cabades king of Persia, 609.

Idatius, his account of the misfortunes of Spain by an irruption of the barbarous nations, ii.225.

Idolatry ascribed to the agency of dæmons, by the primitive Christians, i.459. Derivation of the term, and its successive applications, 828 *note.*

Jerom, his extravagant representation of the devastation of Pannonia by the Goths, i.1068. His influence over the widow Paula, ii.417.

Jerusalem, its situation, destruction, and profanation, i.885. Pilgrimages to, and curious relics preserved there, 886. Abortive attempt of the emperor Julian to rebuild the temple, 888.

——, A magnificent church erected there to the Virgin Mary by Justinian, ii.598. The vessels of the temple brought from Africa to Constantinople by Belisarius, 641. Is conquered by Chosroes II. king of Persia, 908. Insurrection of the monks there, 962.

——, The city conquered by the Saracens, iii.267. Great resort of pilgrims to, 548. Conquest of, by the Turks, 553. Is taken from the Turks by the Egyptians, 601. Is taken by the crusaders, 605. Is erected into a kingdom under Godfrey of Bouillon, 606. Succession of its Christian princes, 634. Is pillaged by the Carizmians, 648.

Jerusalem, New, described according to the ideas of the primitive Christians, i.468.

Jesuits, Portuguese, persecute the Eastern Christians, ii.986. Their labours in, and expulsion from Abyssinia, 1000.

Jews, an obscure, unsocial, obstinate race of men, i.447. Review of their history, 448. Their religion the basis of Christianity, 451. The promises of divine favour extended by Christianity to all mankind, 451. The immortality of the soul not inculcated in the law of Moses, 466. Why there are no Hebrew gospels extant, 499. Provoked the persecutions of the Roman emperors, 515. Those of a more liberal spirit adopted the theological system of Plato, 772. Their condition under the emperors Constantine and Constantius, 884. Abortive attempt of Julian to rebuild the temple of Jerusalem, 888.

——, Miraculous conversion of a number of, at Minorca, ii.95 *note*. Persecution of, in Spain, 448. Are persecuted by the Catholics in Italy, 548. And by Cyril at Alexandria, 944. How plagued by the emperor Justinian, 970.

——, Those in Arabia subdued by Mahomet, iii.201. Assist the Saracens in the reduction of Spain, 307. Massacres of, by the first crusaders, 571.

Jezdegerd, king of Persia, is said to be left guardian to Theodosius the Younger, by the emperor Arcadius, ii.261. His war with Theodosius, 268.

Igilium, the small island of, serves as a place of refuge for Romans who flew from the sack of Rome by Alaric, ii.206.

Ignatius, bishop of Antioch, the Christian fortitude displayed in his epistles, i.546.

Ikshidites, the Saracen dynasty of, iii.371.

Illustrious, the title of, how limited in the times of Roman simplicity, and how extended when Constantinople became the seat of empire, i.604.

Illyricum described, i.50.

Images, introduction of, into the Christian church, iii.86. The worship of, derived from Paganism, 87. Are condemned by the council of Constantinople, 94. The adoration of, justified by pope Gregory II. 99. And sanctified by the second council of Nice, 118.

Imperator, in the Roman history, explained, i.87 *note*. The Imperial prerogatives, 91. The court, 93. The sense of this appellation altered by long use, 387.

Incarnation, theological history of the doctrine of, ii.932.

Incest, natural, and arbitrary, distinguished, ii.817.

India, account of the Christians of St. Thomas in, ii.985. Persecution of, by the Portuguese, 985.

Indictions, the memorable æra of, whence dated, i.425 *note*. The name and use of, in the middle ages, whence derived, 633.

Indulgences in the Romish church, the nature of, explained, iii.566.

Ingundis, princess of Austrasia, is married to Hermenegild prince of Boetica, and cruelly treated by his mother Goisvintha, ii.445.

Inheritance, paternal, subject to parental discretion among the Romans, i.183. The Roman law of, ii.821. Testamentary dispositions of property, 823. The Voconian law, how evaded, 826.

Injuries, review of the Roman laws for the redress of, ii.830.

Innocent III. pope, enjoyed the plenitude of papal power, iii.644.

Inquisition, the first erection of that tribunal, iii.645.

Institutes of Justinian, an analysis of, ii.805.

Interest of money, how regulated by the Roman laws, ii.829.

Joan, pope, the story of fictitious, iii.138.

John, principal secretary to the emperor Honorius, usurps the empire after his death, ii.274.

John the almsgiver, archbishop of Alexandria, relieves the Jewish refugees when Jerusalem was taken by the Persians, ii.909. His extraordinary liberality of the church treasure, 994.

John, bishop of Antioch, arrives at Ephesus after the meeting of the council, and, with his bishops, decides against Cyril, ii.951. Coalition between him and Cyril, 953.

John of Apri, patriarch of Constantinople,

his pride, and confederacy against John Cantacuzene, iii.776.

John of Brienne, emperor of Constantinople, iii.716.

John of Cappadocia, prætorian præfect of the East, under the emperor Justinian, his character, ii.590. Is disgraced by the empress Theodora, and becomes a bishop, 591. Opposes the African war, 620. His fraud in supplying the army with bread, 626.

John Comnenus, emperor of Constantinople, iii.70.

John Damascenus, St. his history, iii.96 *note*.

John of Lycopolis, the hermit, his character and oracular promise to the emperor Theodosius the Great, ii.64.

John, the Monophysite bishop of Asia, is employed by the emperor Justinian to root out Pagans and heretics, ii.969.

John XII. pope, his flagitious character, iii.138.

John XXIII. pope, his profligate character, iii.1049.

John, St. the evangelist, reveals the true sense of Plato's doctrine of the *Logos*, i.773.

John the Sanguinary, seizes the Gothic treasures in Picenum, and obliges Vitiges to raise the siege of Rome, ii.969.

John Zimisces, murders the Greek emperor Nicephorus, and succeeds him, iii.58. His Eastern victories, 375. Defeats Swatoslaus, czar of Russia, 464.

Iona, one of the Hebride islands, its ancient monastic eminence, ii.416.

Jonas, renegado of Damascus, story of, iii.259.

Jordan, character of his work, *De Originibus Sclavicis*, iii.442 *note*.

Joseph the Carizmian, governor of Berzem, kills the sultan Alp Arslan, iii.540.

Josephus, the mention of Jesus Christ in his history, a forgery, i.529 *note*. His opinion, that Plato derived knowledge from the Jews, controverted, 771 *note*.

Jovian is elected emperor by the troops of Julian, on their retreat from Assyria, i.947. His treaty with Sapor king of Persia, 949. His death, 963.

Jovians and Herculians, new bodies of guards instituted to supersede the Prætorian bands, i.386.

Jovinian of Verona, his punishment by a Roman synod, for heresy, ii.130.

Jovinus reduces the Alemanni, who had invaded Gaul, i.990.

——, Account of his revolt against the emperor Honorius in Germany, ii.221.

Jovius, prætorian præfect under the emperor Honorius, succeeds Olympius as his confidential minister, ii.194. His negociations with Alaric obstructed, 195. Deserts Honorius, and goes over to Alaric, and the new emperor Attalus, 198.

Irene, her marriage with the Greek emperor Leo, iii.40. Her ambition, and barbarity to her son Constantine, 41. Restores images to public devotion, 118.

Ireland was first colonised from Scotland, i.998. Derivation of the name of its tutelar saint, Patrick, ii.405 *note*.

Isaac I. *Comnenus*, emperor of Constantinople, iii.64.

Isaac II. *Angelus*, emperor of Constantinople, iii.83. His character and reign, 662. Is deposed by his brother Alexius, 664. Is restored by the crusaders, 683. His death, 688.

Isaac, archbishop of Armenia, his apology for the vices of king Artasires, ii.271.

Isauria, the rebellion there against the emperor Gallienus, i.293.

Isaurians, reduction of, by the Eastern emperors, ii.602.

Isidore, cardinal, his ill treatment in Russia, iii.194. Receives an act of union from the Greek clergy at Constantinople, 948.

Isocrates, his price for the tuition of his pupils, ii.612.

Italy, the dominion of, under Odoacer, succeeds the extinction of the Western empire, ii.403. Its miserable state at this æra, 409. Conversion of the Lombards of, to the Nicene faith, 448. Is reduced by Theodoric the Ostrogoth, 533. His

Italy—contd
administration, 534. Government of, according to the Roman law, by Theodoric, 540. Its flourishing state at this time, 544. How supplied with silk from China, 580. History of Amalasontha, queen of Italy, 648. Invasion of, by Belisarius, 654. Siege of Rome by the Goths, 658. Invasion of Italy by the Franks, 673. Revolt of the Goths, 735. Expedition of the eunuch Narses, 751. Invasion of, by the Franks and Alemanni, 759. Government of, under the exarchs of Ravenna, 762. Conquests of Alboin king of the Lombards in, 853. Distress of, 862. How divided between the Lombards, and the exarchs of Ravenna, 864.

——, Growth of the papal power in, iii.97. Revolt of, against the Greek emperors, 102. The exarchate of Ravenna granted to the pope, 113. Extent of the dominion of Charlemagne there, 129. The power of the German Cæsars destroyed by the rise of the commercial cities there, 143. Factions of the Guelphs and Ghibelins, 144. Conflict of the Saracens, Latins, and Greeks in, 471. Revival of Greek learning in, 896. Authors consulted for the history of, 1060 *note.*

Jubilee, popish, a revival of the secular games, i.211 *note.* iii.1010. The return of, accelerated, 1012.

Jude, St. examination of his grandsons before the tribunal of the procurator of Judæa, i.532.

Judgments of God, in the Salic laws, how determined, ii.476.

Judgments, popular, of the Romans, displayed, ii.839.

Julia Domna, wife of the emperor Severus, her character, i.150. Her death, 163.

Julian, the nephew of Constantine the Great, his education, i.686. His dangerous situation on the death of his brother Gallus, 692. Is sent to Athens, where he cultivates philosophy, 693. Is recalled by Constantius, 695. Is invested with the title of Cæsar, 696. Is appointed to the government of Gaul, 711. His first campaign, 713. Battle of Strasburgh, 715. Reduces the Franks at Toxandria, 718. His three expeditions beyond the Rhine, 719. Restores the cities of Gaul, 720. His civil administration, 721. His account of the theological calamities of the empire under Constantius, 820. Constantius grows jealous of him, 831. The Gaulish legions are ordered into the East, 831. Is saluted emperor by the troops, 835. His embassy and epistle to Constantius, 837. His fourth and fifth expeditions beyond the Rhine, 839. Declares war against Constantius, and abjures the Christian religion, 841. His march from the Rhine into Illyricum, 843. Enters Sirmium, 845. Publishes apologies for his conduct, 846. His triumphant entry into Constantinople on the death of Constantius, 849. His private life and civil government, 850. His reformations in the Imperial palace, 853. Becomes a sloven to avoid foppery, 854. Erects a tribunal for the trial of the evil ministers of Constantius, 855. Dismisses the spies and informers employed by his predecessor, 857. His love of freedom and the republic, 858. His kindnesses to the Grecian cities, 860. His abilities as an orator, 861. And as a judge, 862. His character, 863. His apostacy accounted for, 865. Adopts the Pagan mythology, 867. His theological system, 870. His initiation into the Eleusinian mysteries, and his fanaticism, 871. His hypocritical duplicity, 873. Writes a vindication of his apostacy, 875. His edict for a general toleration, 876. His Pagan superstitious zeal, 877. His circular letters for the reformation of the Pagan religion, 879. His industry in gaining proselytes, 882. His address to the Jews, 884. History of his attempt to rebuild the temple at Jerusalem, 888. Transfers the revenues of the Christian church, to the heathen priests, 892. Prohibits Christian schools, 892.

Obliges the Christians to reinstate the Pagan temples, 895. Restores the sacred grove and temple of Daphne, 898. Punishes the Christians of Antioch for burning that temple, 899. His treatment of the cities of Edessa and Alexandria, 903. Banishes Athanasius, 905. The philosophical fable of his *Cæsars*, delineated, 909. Meditates the conquest of Persia, 910. Popular discontents during his residence at Antioch, 913. Occasion of writing his *Misopogon*, 915. His march to the Euphrates, 917. He enters the Persian territories, 921. Invades Assyria, 926. His personal conduct in this enterprise, 929. His address to his discontented troops, 930. His successful passage over the Tigris, 933. Burns his fleet, 937. His retreat and distress, 940. His death, 943. His funeral, 957.

Julian, count, offers to betray Spain into the hands of the Arabs, iii.302. His advice to the victorious Turks, 306.

Julian, the papal legate, exhorts Ladislaus king of Hungary and Poland to breach of faith with the Turks, iii.920. His death and character, 923.

Julius, master-general of the troops in the Eastern empire, concerts a general massacre of the Gothic youth in Asia, i.1069.

Jurisprudence, Roman, a review of, ii.778. Was polished by Grecian philosophy, 793. Abuses of, 842.

Justin the Elder, his military promotion, ii.558. His elevation to the empire, and character, 558. His death, 561.

Justin II. emperor, succeeds his uncle Justinian, ii.846. His firm behaviour to the ambassadors of the Avars, 847. His abdication, and investiture of Tiberius, as his successor, 858.

Justin Martyr, his decision in the case of the Ebionites, i.455. His extravagant account of the progress of Christianity, 506. Occasion of his own conversion, 508.

Justina, the popular story of her marriage with the emperor Valentinian examined, i.1021. Her infant son Valentinian II. invested with the imperial ensigns, on the death of his father, 1022. Her contest with Ambrose archbishop of Milan, ii.41. Flies from the invasion of Maximus, with her son, 46.

Justinian, emperor of the East, his birth and promotion, ii.557. His orthodoxy, 560. Is invested with the diadem by his uncle Justin, 561. Marries Theodora, 566. Patronizes the blue faction of the circus, 572. State of agriculture and manufacture in his provinces, 577. Introduces the culture of the silk worm, and manufacture of silk, into Greece, 583. State of his revenue, 585. His avarice and profusion, 586. Taxes and monopolies, 588. His ministers, 590. His public buildings, 592. Founds the church of St. Sophia at Constantinople, 594. His other public works, 598. His European fortifications, 599. His Asiatic fortifications, 604. He suppresses the schools of Athens, 610. And the consular dignity, 616. Purchases a peace from the Persians, 618. 708. Undertakes to restore Hilderic king of Carthage, 620. Reduction of Africa, 636. His instructions for the government of, 637. His acquisitions in Spain, 646. His deceitful negociations in Italy, 650. Weakness of his empire, 686. Receives an embassy from the Avars, 698. And from the Turks, 699. Persian war, 712. His negociations with Chosroes, 725. His alliance with the Abyssinians, 729. Neglects the Italian war under Belisarius, 739. Settles the government of Italy under the exarch of Ravenna, 762. Disgrace and death of Belisarius, 766. His death and character, 768. Comets and calamities in his reign, 770. His Code, Pandects, and Institutes, 778. His theological character and government, 967. His persecuting spirit, 969. His orthodoxy, 971. Died a heretic, 974.

Justinian II. emperor of Constantinople, iii.32.

Justinian, the son of Germanus, his conspiracy with the empress Sophia, and successes against the Persians, ii.860.

Juvenal, his remarks on the crowded state of the inhabitants of Rome, ii.187.

K

Khan, import of this title in the northern parts of Asia, i.1031. ii.142.

Kindred, degrees of, according to the Roman civil law, ii.822.

King, the title of, conferred by Constantine the Great on his nephew Hannibalianus, i.653.

Knighthood, how originally conferred, and its obligations, iii.578.

Koran of Mahomet, account and character of, iii.181.

Koreish, the tribe of, acquire the custody of the Caaba at Mecca, iii.168. Pedigree of Mahomet, 172. They oppose his pretensions to a prophetical character, 192. Flight of Mahomet, 193. Battle of Beder, 199. Battle of Ohud, 200. Mecca surrendered to Mahomet, 204.

L

Labarum, or standard of the cross, in the army of Constantine the Great, described, i.736.

Labeo, the civilian, his diligence in business and composition, ii.792. His professional character, 795.

Lactantius, difficulties in ascertaining the date of his *Divine Institutions*, i.725 *note*. His flattering prediction of the influence of Christianity among mankind, 731. Inculcates the divine right of Constantine to the empire, 732.

Ladislaus, king of Hungary and Poland, leads an army against the Turks, iii.919. His breach of faith with them, 920.

Ladislaus, king of Naples, harasses Rome during the schism of the papacy, iii.1048.

Lætus, prætorian præfect, conspires the death of Commodus, and confers the empire on Pertinax, i.120.

Laity, when first distinguished from the clergy, i.490.

Lampadius, a Roman senator, boldly condemns the treaty with Alaric the Goth, ii.157.

Lance, holy, narrative of the miraculous discovery of, iii.598.

Land, how assessed by the Roman emperors, i.634. How divided by the Barbarians, ii.478. Allodial, and Salic, distinguished, 481. Of Italy, how partitioned by Theodoric the Ostrogoth, 536.

Laodicea, its ancient splendor, i.76.

Lascaris, Theodore, establishes an empire at Nice, iii.705. His character, 737.

Lascaris, Theodore II. his character, iii.739.

Lascaris, Janus, the Greek grammarian, his character, iii.903.

Latin church, occasion of its separation from the Greek church, iii.655. Corruption and schism of, 880. Reunion of, with the Greek church, 892. The subsequent Greek schism, 912.

Latium, the right of, explained, i.64.

Laura, in monkish history, explained, ii.426.

Law, review of the profession of, under the emperors, i.616.

Laws of Rome, a review of, ii.778. Those of the kings, 779. Of the twelve tables, 781. Of the people, 784. Decrees of the senate, and edicts of the prætors, 785. Constitutions of the emperors, 787. Their rescripts, 789. The forms of, 789. Succession of civil lawyers, 791. Reformation of, by Justinian, 797. Abolition and revival of the penal laws, 833.

Lazi, the tribe of, in Colchos, account of, ii.720.

Le Clerc, character of his ecclesiastical history, ii.933 *note*.

Legacies and inheritances taxed by Augustus, i.183. How regulated by the Roman law, ii.825.

Legion, in the Roman army under the emperors, described, i.41. General distribution of the legions, 45. The size of, reduced by Constantine the Great, 621.

Leo of Thrace is made emperor of the East, by his master Aspar, ii.384. Was the first Christian potentate who was crowned by a priest, 384. Confers the empire of the West on Anthemius, 385. His armament against the Vandals in Africa, 388. Murders Aspar and his sons, 527.

Leo III. emperor of Constantinople, iii.36. His edicts against images in churches, 93. Revolt of Italy, 102.

Leo IV. emperor of Constantinople, iii.38.

Leo V. emperor of Constantinople, iii.43.

Leo VI. the philosopher, emperor of Constantinople, iii.53. Extinguishes the power of the senate, 403.

Leo, bishop of Rome, his character and embassy from Valentinian III. to Attila king of the Huns, ii.348. Intercedes with Genseric king of the Vandals for clemency to the city of Rome, 360. Calls the council of Chalcedon, ii.959.

Leo III. pope, his miraculous recovery from the assaults of assassins, iii.123. Crowns Charlemagne emperor of the Romans, 123.

Leo IV. pope, his reign, iii.360. Founds the Leonine city, 362.

Leo IX. pope, his expedition against the Normans of Apulia, iii.484. His treaty with them, 485.

Leo, archbishop of Thessalonica, one of the restorers of Greek learning, iii.417.

Leo, general of the East, under the emperor Arcadius, his character, ii.247.

Leo Pilatus, first Greek professor at Florence, and in the West, his character, iii.899.

Leo, the Jew proselyte, history of his family, iii.1013.

Leonas, the quæstor, his embassy from Constantius to Julian, i.841.

Leonine city at Rome founded, iii.362.

Leontius is taken from prison, and chosen emperor of Constantinople, on the deposition of Justinian II. iii.32.

Leovigild, Gothic king of Spain, his character, ii.445. Revolt and death of his son Hermenegild, 445.

Letters, a knowledge of, the test of civilization in a people, i.234.

Lewis the Pious, emperor of the Romans, iii.132.

Lewis II. emperor of the Romans, iii.133. His epistle to the Greek emperor Basil I., 472.

Libanius, his account of the private life of the emperor Julian, i.851. And of his divine visions, 873. Applauds the dissimulation of Julian, 874. His character, 916. His eulogium on the emperor Valens, 1065.

Liberius, bishop of Rome, is banished by the emperor Constantius, for refusing to concur in deposing Athanasius, i.807. 816.

Liberty, public, the only sure guardians of, against an aspiring prince, i.85.

Licinius, is invested with the purple by the emperor Galerius, i.413. His alliance with Constantine the Great, 430. Defeats Maximin, 430. His cruelty, 431. Is defeated by Constantine at Cibalis, 435. And at Mardia, 435. Peace concluded with Constantine, 437. Second civil war with Constantine, 440. His humiliation, and death, 444. Fate of his son, 650. Concurred with Constantine in publishing the edict of Milan, 729. Violated this engagement by oppressing the Christians, 733. Cæcilius's account of his vision, 739.

Lieutenant, Imperial, his office and rank, i.77.

Lightning, superstition of the Romans with reference to persons and places struck with, i.350.

Limigantes, Sarmatian slaves, expel their masters, and usurp possession of their country, i.659. Extinction of, by Constantius, 701.

Literature, revival of, in Italy, iii.896. Ancient, use and abuse of, 908.

Lithuania, its late conversion to Christianity, iii.469.

Litorius, count, is defeated and taken captive, in Gaul by Theodoric, ii.328.

Liutprand, king of the Lombards, attacks the city of Rome, iii.106.

Liutprand, bishop of Cremona, ambassador to Constantinople, ceremony of his audience with the emperor, iii.397.

Logos, Plato's doctrine of, i.771. Is expounded by St. John the Evangelist, 773. Athanasius confesses himself unable to comprehend it, 775. Controversies on the eternity of, 779.

Logothete, great, his office under the Greek emperors, iii.395.

Lombards, derivation of their name, and review of their history, ii.688. Are employed by the emperor Justinian to check the Gepidæ, 690. Actions of their king Alboin, 848. They reduce the Gepidæ, 850. They over-run that part of Italy now called Lombardy, 853. Extent of their kingdom, 866. Language and manners of the Lombards, 866. Government and laws, 870.

Lombardy, ancient, described, i.49. Conquest of, by Charlemagne, iii.109.

Longinus, his representation of the degeneracy of his age, i.84. Is put to death by Aurelian, 319.

Longinus, is sent to supersede Narses, as exarch of Ravenna, ii.852. Receives Rosamond the fugitive queen of the Lombards, 856.

Lothaire I. emperor of the Romans, iii.132.

Louis VII. of France is rescued from the treachery of the Greeks by Roger king of Sicily, iii.513. Undertakes the second crusade, 617. His disastrous expedition, 622.

Louis IX. of France, his crusades to the Holy Land, iii.649. His death, 651. Procured a valuable stock of relics from Constantinople, 721.

Lucian, the severity of his satire against the Heathen mythology, accounted for, i.58.

Lucian, count of the East, under the emperor Arcadius, his cruel treatment by the præfect Rufinus, ii.103.

Lucian, presbyter of Jerusalem, his miraculous discovery of the body of St. Stephen, the first Christian martyr, ii.92.

Lucilian, governor of Illyricum, is surprised, and kindly treated by Julian, i.854. His death, 962.

Lucilla, sister of the emperor Commodus, her attempt to get him assassinated, i.111.

Lucius II. and III. popes, their disastrous reigns, iii.985.

Lucrine lake described, with its late destruction, ii.177 *note*.

Lucullan villa in Campania, its description and history, ii.405.

Lupercalia, the feast of, described, and continued under the Christian emperors, ii.387.

Lupicinus, the Roman governor of Thrace, oppresses the Gothic emigrants there, i.1050. Rashly provokes them to hostilities, 1052. Is defeated by them, 1053.

Lustral contribution in the Roman empire, explained, i.640.

Luther, Martin, his character as a reformer, iii.436.

Luxury the only means of correcting the unequal distribution of property, i.80.

Lygians, a formidable German nation, account of, i.339.

Lyons, battle of, between the competitors Severus and Albinus, i.141.

M

Macedonius, the Arian bishop of Constantinople, his contests with his competitor Paul, i.817. Fatal consequences on his removing the body of the emperor Constantine to the church of St. Acacius, 819. His cruel persecutions of the Catholics and Novatians, 819. His exile, ii.966.

Macrianus, prætorian præfect under the emperor Valerian, his character, i.283.

Macrinus, his succession to the empire predicted by an African, i.159. Accelerates the completion of the prophecy, 159. Purchases a peace with Parthia, 222.

Madayn, the capital of Persia, sacked by the

Saracens, iii.242.
Mæonius of Palmyra assassinates his uncle Odenathus, i.314.
Mæsia, its situation, i.51.
Magi, the worship of, in Persia, reformed by Artaxerxes, i.215. Abridgment of the Persian theology, 216. Simplicity of their worship, 217. Ceremonies and moral precepts, 218. Their power, 219.
Magic, severe prosecution of persons for the crime of, at Rome and Antioch, i.974.
Magnentius assumes the empire in Gaul, i.672. Death of Constans, 673. Sends an embassy to Constantius, 674. Makes war against Constantius, 677. Is defeated at the battle of Mursa, 678. Kills himself, 683.
Mahmud, the Gaznevide, his twelve expeditions into Hindostan, iii.523. His character, 526.
Mahomet, the prophet, his embassy to Chosroes II. king of Persia, ii.912.
——, His genealogy, birth, and education, iii.172. His person and character, 179. Assumes his prophetical mission, 176. Inculcated the unity of God, 178. His reverential mention of Jesus Christ, 179. His Koran, 181. His miracles, 182. His precepts, 184. His Hell, and Paradise, 187. The best authorities for his history, 190 *note*. Converts his own family, 190. Preaches publicly at Mecca, 191. Escapes from the Koreishites there, 193. Is received as prince of Medina, 194. His regal dignity, and sacerdotal office, 195. Declares war against infidels, 196. Battle of Beder, 199. Battle of Ohud, 200. Subdues the Jews of Arabia, 201. Submission of Mecca to him, 203. He conquers Arabia, 205. His sickness and death, 210. His character, 212. His private life, 214. His wives, 215. His children, 217. His posterity, 228. Remarks on the great spread and permanency of his religion, 230.
Mahomet, the son of Bajazet, his reign, iii.855.
Mahomet II. sultan of the Turks, his character, iii.934. His reign, 936. Indications of his hostile intentions against the Greeks, 937. He besieges Constantinople, 944. Takes the city by storm, 963. His entry into the city, 967. Makes it his capital, 969. His death, 976.
Mahometism, by what means propagated, iii.315. Toleration of Christianity under, 320.
Majorian, his history, character, and elevation to the Western empire, ii.370. His epistle to the senate, 371. His salutary laws, 372. His preparations to invade Africa, 375. His fleet destroyed by Genseric, 378. His death, 379.
Malaterra, his character of the Normans, iii.481.
Malek Shah, sultan of the Turks, his prosperous reign, iii.541. Reforms the Eastern calendar, 543. His death, 543.
Mallius Theodorus, the great civil honours to which he attained, i.616 *note*.
Mamæa, mother of the young emperor Alexander Severus, acts as regent of the empire, i.170. Is put to death with him, 191. Her conference with Origen, 553.
Mamalukes, their origin and character, iii.651. Their establishment in Egypt, 652.
Mamgo, an Armenian noble, his history, i.375.
Man, the only animal that can accommodate himself to all climates, i.233 *note*.
Mancipium, in the Roman law, explained, ii.820.
Manichæans are devoted to death, by the edict of Theodosius against heretics, ii.36.
Manuel Comnenus, emperor of Constantinople, iii.72. He repulses the Normans, 513. But fails in his scheme of subduing the Western empire, 516. His ill treatment of the crusaders, 620.
Maogamalcha, a city of Assyria, reduced and destroyed by the emperor Julian, i.927.
Marble, the four species of, most esteemed by the Romans, i.194 *note*.
Marcellinus, count of the sacred largesses under the emperor Constans in Gaul,

Marcellinus—contd
assists the usurpation of Magnentius, i.672. His embassy to Constantius, 674. Was killed in the battle of Mursa, 683.

Marcellinus, his revolt in Dalmatia, and character, ii.380. Joins the emperor Anthemius, and expels the Vandals from Sardinia, 388. His death, 391.

Marcellinus, son of the præfect Maximin, his treacherous murder of Gabinius king of the Quadi, i.1018.

Marcellus the centurion martyred for desertion, i.562.

Marcellus, bishop of Rome, exiled to restore peace to the city, i.572.

Marcellus, bishop of Apamea in Syria, loses his life in destroying the Pagan temples, ii.80.

Marcia, the concubine of the emperor Commodus, a patroness of the Christians, i.551.

Marcian, senator of Constantinople, marries the empress Pulcheria, and is acknowledged emperor, ii.321. His temperate refusal of the demands of Attila the Hun, 323.

Marcianopolis, the city of, taken by the Goths, i.261.

Marcomanni are subdued and punished by Marcus Antoninus, i.251. Alliance made with, by the emperor Gallienus, 273.

Marcus, elected bishop of the Nazarenes, i.454.

Mardia, battle of, between Constantine the Great and Licinius, i.435.

Margus, battle of, between Diocletian and Carinus, i.357.

Margus, bishop of, betrays his episcopal city into the hands of the Huns, ii.302.

Maria, daughter of Eudæmon of Carthage, her remarkable adventures, ii.290.

Mariana, his account of the misfortunes of Spain, by an irruption of the barbarous nations, ii.225.

Marinus, a subaltern officer, chosen emperor by the legions of Mæsia, i.253.

Marius the armourer, a candidate for the purple among the competitors against Gallienus, his character, i.289.

Mark, bishop of Arethusa, is cruelly treated by the emperor Julian, i.895.

Maronga, engagement there between the emperor Julian, and Sapor king of Persia, i.941.

Maronites of the East, character and history of, ii.989.

Marozia, a Roman prostitute, the mother, grandmother, and great-grandmother, of three popes, iii.138.

Marriage, regulations of, by the Roman laws, ii.812. Of Roman citizens with strangers, proscribed by their jurisprudence, iii.400.

Martel, Charles, duke of the Franks, his character, iii.336. His politic conduct on the Saracen invasion of France, 337. Defeats the Saracens, 338. Why he was consigned over to hell flames by the clergy, 339.

Martin, bishop of Tours, destroys the idols and Pagan temples in Gaul, ii.79. His monkish institutions there, 415.

Martina marries her uncle, the emperor Heraclius, iii.27. Endeavours to share the Imperial dignity with her sons, 27. Her fate, 29.

Martinianus receives the title of Cæsar, from the emperor Licinius, i.444.

Martyrs, primitive, an inquiry into the true history of, i.514. The several inducements to martyrdom, 546. Three methods of escaping it, 548. Marks by which learned Catholics distinguish the relics of the martyrs, 540 *note*. The worship of, and their relics, introduced, ii.90.

Mary, Virgin, her immaculate conception, borrowed from the Koran, iii.180.

Mascazel, the persecuted brother of Gildo the Moor, takes refuge in the Imperial court of Honorius, ii.115. Is intrusted with troops to reduce Gildo, 115. Defeats him, 117. His suspicious death, 118.

Master of the offices, under Constantine the Great, his functions, i.625.

Maternus, his revolt and conspiracy against

the emperor Commodus, i.113.
Matthew, St. his gospel originally composed in Hebrew, i.499 *note.* ii.934 *note.*
Maurice, his birth, character, and promotion to the Eastern empire, ii.861. Restores Chosroes II. king of Persia, 890. His war against the Avars, 896. State of his armies, 898. His abdication and death, 901.
Mauritania, ancient, its situation and extent, i.54. Character of the native Moors of, ii.281.
Maxentius, the son of Maximian, declared emperor at Rome, i.408. His tyranny in Italy and Africa, 418. The military force he had to oppose Constantine, 420. His defeat and death, 427. His politic humanity to the Christians, 571.
Maximian, associate in the empire with Diocletian, his character, i.360. Triumphs with Diocletian, 383. Holds his court at Milan, 384. Abdicates the empire along with Diocletian, 393. He resumes the purple, 409. Reduces Severus, and puts him to death, 409. His second resignation, and unfortunate end, 415. His aversion to the Christians accounted for, 561.
Maximilianus, the African, a Christian martyr, i.562.
Maximin, his birth, fortune and elevation to the empire of Rome, i.188. Why deemed a persecutor of the Christians, 554.
Maximin is declared Cæsar, on the abdication of Diocletian, i.402. Obtains the rank of Augustus, from Galerius, 413. His defeat and death, 431. Renewed the persecution of the Christians after the toleration granted by Galerius, 575.
Maximin, the cruel minister of the emperor Valentinian, promoted to the præfecture of Gaul, i.978.
Maximin, his embassy from Theodosius the Younger, to Attila king of the Huns, ii.312.
Maximus and Balbinus elected joint emperors by the senate, on the deaths of the two Gordians, i.198.
Maximus, his character and revolt in Britain, ii.22. His treaty with the emperor Theodosius, 24. Persecutes the Priscillianists, 38. His invasion of Italy, 45. His defeat and death, 49.
Maximus, the Pagan preceptor of the emperor Julian, initiates him into the Eleusinian mysteries, i.872. Is honourably invited to Constantinople by his Imperial pupil, 881. Is corrupted by his residence at court, 882.
Maximus, Petronius, his wife ravished by Valentinian III. emperor of the West, ii.354. His character, and elevation to the empire, 358.
Mebodes, the Persian general, ungratefully treated by Chosroes, ii.704.
Mecca, its situation, and description, iii.157. The Caaba, or temple of, 167. Its deliverance from Abrahah, 173. The doctrine of Mahomet opposed there, 192. His escape, 193. The city of, surrendered to Mahomet, 204. Is pillaged by Abu Taher, 368.
Medina, reception of Mahomet there, on his flight from Mecca, iii.194.
Megalesia, the festival of, at Rome, described, i.113 *note.*
Meletians, an Egyptian sect, persecuted by Athanasius, i.795.
Melitene, battle of, between the Eastern emperor Tiberius, and Chosroes king of Persia, ii.882.
Melo, citizen of Bari, invites the Normans into Italy, iii.478.
Memphis, its situation, and reduction by the Saracens, iii.278.
Merovingian kings of the Franks in Gaul, origin of, ii.329. Their domain and benefices, 480.
Mervan, caliph of the Saracens, and the last of the house of Ommiyah, his defeat and death, iii.341.
Mesopotamia, invasion of by the emperor Julian, i.922. Described by Xenophon, 923.
Messala, Valerius, the first præfect of Rome, his high character, i.611 *note.*

Messiah, under what character he was expected by the Jews, i.451. His birthday, how fixed by the Romans, 841 *note.*
Metals and money, their operation in improving the human mind, i.236.
Metellus Numidicus, the censor, his invective against women, i.171 *note.*
Metius Falconius, his artful speech to the emperor Tacitus in the senate on his election, i.331.
Metrophanes of Cyzicus, is made patriarch of Constantinople, iii.913.
Metz, cruel treatment of, by Attila king of the Huns, ii.335.
Michael I. Rhangabe, emperor of Constantinople, iii.913.
Michael II. the Stammerer, emperor of Constantinople, iii.44.
Michael III. emperor of Constantinople, iii.47. Is defeated by the Paulicians, 431.
Michael IV. the Paphlagonian, emperor of Constantinople, iii.62.
Michael V. Calaphates, emperor of Constantinople, iii.62.
Michael VI. Stratioticus, emperor of Constantinople, iii.63.
Michael VII. Parapinaces, emperor of Constantinople, iii.66.
Milan, how the Imperial court of the Western empire came to be transferred from Rome to that city, i.384. Famous edict of Constantine the Great in favour of the Christians, published there, 729.
——, St. Ambrose elected archbishop of that city, ii.40. Tumults occasioned by his refusing a church for the Arian worship of the empress Justina and her son, 42. Revolt of, to Justinian, 669. Is taken and destroyed by the Burgundians, 674.
——, Is again destroyed by Frederic I. iii.144.
Military force, its strength and efficacy dependent on a due proportion to the number of the people, i.127.
Military officers of the Roman empire at the time of Constantine the Great, a review of, i.617.
Millennium, the doctrine of, explained, i.467.
Mingrelia. See *Colchos.*
Minority, two distinctions of, in the Roman law, ii.108 *note.*
Miracles, those of Christ and his apostles, escaped the notice of the heathen philosophers and historians, i.512. Account of those wrought by the body of St. Stephen, ii.92.
Miraculous powers of the primitive church, an enquiry into, i.471.
Misitheus, chief minister and father-in-law of the third Gordian, his character, i.208.
Misopogon of the emperor Julian, on what occasion written, i.915.
Missorium, or great golden dish of Adolphus king of the Visigoths, history of, ii.215.
Moawiyah, assumes the title of caliph, and makes war against Ali, iii.223. His character and reign, 224. Lays siege to Constantinople, 323.
Modar, prince of the Amali, seduced by the emperor Theodosius, turns his arms against his own countrymen, i.1077.
Moguls, primitive, their method of treating their conquered enemies, ii.304. Reign and conquests of Zingis, iii.791. Conquests of his successors, 798. See *Tamerlane.*
Moguntiacum, the city of, surprised by the Alemanni, i.991.
Mokawkas the Egyptian, his treaty with the Saracen Amrou, iii.280.
Monarchy defined, i.85. Hereditary, ridiculous in theory, but salutary in fact, 187. The peculiar objects of cruelty and of avarice under, 632.
Monastic institutions, the seeds of, sown by the primitive Christians, i.481. Origin, progress, and consequences of, ii.411.
Money, the standard and computation of, under Constantine the Great, and his successors, i.636 *note.*
Monks have embellished the sufferings of the primitive martyrs by fictions, i.538.
——, Character of, by Eunapius, ii.90. By Rutilius, 116. Origin and history of, 411. Their industry in making pros-

elytes, 416. Their obedience, 418. Their dress and habitations, 420. Their diet, 420. Their manual labour, 422. Their riches, 423. Their solitude, 424. Their devotion and visions, 424. Their division into the classes of *Cœnobites* and *Anachorets*, 426.

——, Suppression of, at Constantinople, by Constantine V. iii.96.

Monophysites of the East, history of the sect of, ii.987.

Monothelite controversy, account of, ii.974.

Montesquieu, his description of the military government of the Roman empire, i.210. His opinion that the degrees of freedom in a state are measured by taxation, controverted, 632.

Montius, quæstor of the palace, is sent by the emperor Constantius, with Domitian, to correct the administration of Gallus in the East, i.689. Is put to death there, 690.

Moors of Barbary, their miserable poverty, ii.638. Their invasion of the Roman province punished by Solomon the Eunuch, 645.

Morea is reduced by the Turks, iii.972.

Morosini, Thomas, elected patriarch of Constantinople by the Venetians, iii.701.

Moseilama, an Arabian chief, endeavours to rival Mahomet in his prophetical character, iii.234.

Moses, the doctrine of the immortality of the soul not inculcated in his law, i.465. His sanguinary laws compared with those of Mahomet, iii.197.

Mosheim, character of his work *De rebus Christianis ante Constantinum*, ii.933 *note.*

Moslemah the Saracen, besieges Constantinople, iii.328.

Motassem, the last caliph of the Saracens, his wars with the Greek emperor Theophilus, iii.362. Is killed by the Moguls, 801.

Mourzoufle, usurps the Greek empire, and destroys Isaac Angelus, and his son Alexius, iii.687. Is driven from Constantinople by the Latins, 690. His death, 704.

Mousa, the son of Bajazet, invested with the kingdom of Anatolia, by Tamerlane, iii.844. His reign, 854.

Mozarabes, in the history of Spain, explained, iii.319.

Municipal cities, their advantages, i.64.

Muratori, his literary character, iii.1060 *note.*

Mursa, battle of, between the emperor Constantius, and the usurper Magnentius, i.678.

Musa the Saracen, his conquest of Spain, iii.308. His disgrace, 311. His death, 312.

Mustapha, the supposed son of Bajazet, his story, iii.853.

Muta, battle of, between the forces of the emperor Heraclius and those of Mahomet, iii.208.

Mygdonius, river, the course of, stopped by Sapor king of Persia, at the siege of Nisibis, i.669.

N

Narbonne is besieged by Theodoric, and relieved by count Litorius, ii.327.

Nacoragan, the Persian general, his defeat by the Romans, and cruel fate, ii.724.

Naissus, battle of, between the emperor Claudius and the Goths, i.301.

Naples is besieged and taken by Belisarius, ii.655. Extent of the dutchy of, under the exarchs of Ravenna, 865.

Narses, his embassy from Sapor king of Persia to the emperor Constantius, i.703.

Narses, king of Persia, prevails over the pretensions of his brother Hormuz, and expels Tiridates king of Armenia, i.376. Overthrows Galerius, 376. Is surprised and routed by Galerius, 378. Articles of peace between him and the Romans, 381.

Narses, the Persian general of the emperor Maurice, restores Chosroes II. king of Persia, ii.890. His revolt against Phocas, and cruel death, 907.

Narses, the eunuch, his military promotion, and dissension with Belisarius, ii.672. His character and expedition to Italy, 751. Battle of Tagina, 754. Takes Rome, 755. Reduces and kills Teias, the last king of the Goths, 757. Defeats the Franks and Alemanni, 760. Governs Italy in the capacity of exarch, 762. His disgrace, and death, 852.

Naulobatus, a chief of the Heruli, enters into the Roman service, and is made consul, i.280.

Navy of the Roman empire described, i.46

Nazarene church at Jerusalem, account of, i.453.

Nazarius the Pagan orator, his account of miraculous appearances in the sky in favour of Constantine the Great, i.740.

Nebridius, prætorian præfect in Gaul, is maimed and superseded, by his indiscrete opposition to the troops of Julian, i.843.

Nectarius is chosen archbishop of Constantinople, ii.36.

Negroes of Africa, evidences of their intellectual inferiority to the rest of mankind, i.1008.

Nennius, his account of the arrival of the Saxons in Britain, different from that of Gildas, Bede, and Witikind, ii.494 *note*.

Nepos, Julius, is made emperor of the West by Leo the Great, ii.399.

Nepotian, account of his revolt in Italy, i.680.

Nero, persecutes the Christians as the incendiaries of Rome, i.527.

Nerva, emperor, his character, and prudent adoption of Trajan, i.99.

Nestorius, archbishop of Constantinople, his character, ii.946. His heresy concerning the incarnation, 947. His dispute with Cyril of Alexandria, 948. Is condemned, and degraded from his episcopal dignity, by the council of Ephesus, 951. Is exiled, 954. His death, 956. His opinions still retained in Persia, 980. Missions of his disciples in the East Indies, 982.

Nevers, John, count of, disastrous fate of him and his party at the battle of Nicopolis, iii.820.

Nice becomes the capital residence of sultan Soliman, iii.547. Siege of, by the first crusaders, 589.

Nicephorus I. emperor of Constantinople, iii.42. His wars with the Saracens, 354. His death, 443.

Nicephorus II. *Phocas*, emperor of Constantinople, iii.57. His military enterprizes, 374.

Nicephorus III. *Botaniates*, emperor of Constantinople, iii.67. Was raised to the throne by sultan Soliman, 546.

Nicetas, senator of Constantinople, his flight, on the capture of the city by the Latins, iii.693. His brief history, 695 *note*. His account of the statues destroyed at Constantinople, 695.

Nicholas, patriarch of Constantinople, opposes the fourth marriage of the emperor Leo the philosopher, iii.54.

Nicholas V. pope, his character, iii.906. How interested in the fall of Constantinople, 944.

Nicomedia, the court of Diocletian held there, and the city embellished by him, i.385. The church of, demolished by Diocletian, 563. His palace fired, 566.

Nicopolis, battle of, between sultan Bajazet, and Sigismond king of Hungary, iii.820.

Nika, the sedition of, at Constantinople, ii.573.

Nineveh, battle of, between the emperor Heraclius, and the Persians, ii.925.

Nisibis, the city of, described, and its obstinate defence against the Persians, i.669. Is yielded to Sapor by treaty, 950.

Nizam, the Persian vizir, his illustrious character, and unhappy fate, iii.543.

Noah, his ark very convenient for resolving the difficulties of Mosaic antiquarians, i.233.

Nobilissimus, a title invented by Constantine the Great, to distinguish his nephew Hannibalianus, i.653.

Noricum described, i.50.

Normans, their settlement in the province of Normandy in France, iii.477. Their introduction to Italy, 478. They serve in Sicily, 479. They conquer Apulia, 480. Their character, 481. Their treaty with the pope, 485.

Noureddin, sultan, his exalted character, iii.627.

Novatians, are exempted by Constantine the Great, in a particular edict from the general penalties of heresy, i.767. Are cruelly persecuted by Macedonius bishop of Constantinople, 820.

Novels of Justinian, how formed, and their character, ii.805.

Nubia, conversion of, to Christianity, ii.997.

Numerian, the son of Carus, succeeds his father in the empire, in conjunction with his brother Carinus, i.349.

Numidia, its extent at different æras of the Roman history, i.54.

O

Oasis, in the deserts of Lybia, described, ii.243 *note*. Three places under this name pointed out, 955 *note*.

Obedience, passive, theory and practice of the Christian doctrine of, i.731.

Obelisks, Egyptian, the purpose of their erection, i.699.

Oblations to the church, origin of, i.490.

Obligations, human, the sources of, ii.826. Laws of the Romans respecting, 827.

Odenathus, the Palmyrene, his successful opposition to Sapor king of Persia, i.285. Is associated in the empire by Gallienus, 290. Character and fate of his queen Zenobia, 312.

Odin, the long reign of his family in Sweden, i.240 *note*. His history, 256.

Odoacer, the first barbarian king of Italy, ii.403. His character and reign, 407. Resigns all the Roman conquests beyond the Alps, to Euric king of the Visigoths, 452. Is reduced and killed by Theodoric the Ostrogoth, 532.

Ohud, battle of, between Mahomet and Abu Sophian prince of Mecca, iii.200.

Olga, princess of Russia, her baptism, iii.467.

Olive, its introduction into the western world, i.79.

Olybrius is raised to the Western empire by count Ricimer, ii.397.

Olympic games compared with the tournaments of the Goths, iii.579.

Olympiodorus, his account of the magnificence of the city of Rome, ii.172. His account of the marriage of Adolphus king of the Visigoths, with the princess Placidia, 215.

Olympius, favourite of the emperor Honorius, alarms him with unfavourable suspicions of the designs of Stilicho, ii.158. Causes Stilicho to be put to death, 160. His disgrace, and ignominious death, 194.

Omar, caliph of the Saracens, iii.219. His character, 236. His journey to Jerusalem, 268.

Ommiyah, elevation of the house of, to the office of caliph of the Saracens, iii.224. Why not the objects of public favour, 339. Destruction of, 341.

Oracles, Heathen, are silenced by Constantine the Great, i.825.

Orchan, emir of the Ottomans, his reign, iii.811. Marries the daughter of the Greek emperor Cantacuzene, 814.

Ordination of the clergy in the early ages of the church, an account of, i.754.

Orestes is sent ambassador from Attila king of the Huns, to the emperor Theodosius the Younger, ii.312. His history and promotion under the Western emperors, 401. His son Augustulus, the last emperor of the West, 402.

Orestes, prætor of Egypt, is insulted by a monkish mob in Alexandria, ii.945.

Origen declares the number of primitive martyrs to be very inconsiderable, i.540. His conference with the empress Mammæa, 553. His memory persecuted by the emperor Justinian and his clergy, ii.972.

Orleans besieged by Attila king of the Huns, and relieved by Ætius and Theodoric, ii.335.

Osius, bishop of Cordova, his great influence with Constantine the Great, i.743. Prevails on Constantine to ratify the Nicene creed, 790. Is with difficulty prevailed on to concur in deposing Athanasius, 807.

Osrhoene, the small kingdom of, reduced by the Romans, i.224.

Ossian, his poems, whether to be connected with the invasion of Caledonia by the emperor Severus, i.152. Is said to have disputed with a Christian missionary, 507 *note*.

Ostia, the port of, described, ii.196.

Othman, caliph of the Saracens, iii.220.

Othman, the father of the Ottomans, his reign, iii.809.

Otho I. king of Germany, restores and appropriates the Western empire, iii.133. Claims by treaty the nomination of the pope of Rome, 137. Defeats the Turks, 453.

Otho II. deposes pope John XII. and chastises his party at Rome, iii.141.

Otho, bishop of Frisingen, his character as an historian, iii.998 *note*.

Ottomans, origin and history of, iii.809. They obtain an establishment in Europe, 815.

Ovid is banished to the banks of the Danube, i.656.

Oxyrinchus, in Egypt, monkish piety of that city, ii.414.

P

Pacatus, his encomium on the emperor Theodosius the Great, ii.52.

Pæderasty, how punished by the Scatinian law, ii.837. By Justinian, 838.

Pagan, derivation and revolutions of the term, i.827 *note*.

Paganism, the ruin of, suspended by the divisions among the Christians, i.827. Theological system of the emperor Julian, 870.

——, General review of the ecclesiastical establishment and jurisdiction of, before it was subverted by Christianity, ii.72. Is renounced by the Roman senate, 76. The Pagan sacrifices prohibited, 77. The temples demolished, 78. The ruin of, deplored by the sophists, 90. Pagan ceremonies revived in Christian churches, 96.

Palæologus, Constantine, Greek emperor, his reign, iii.930. Is killed in the storm of Constantinople by the Turks, 962.

Palæologus, John, emperor of Constantinople, iii.774. Marries the daughter of John Cantacuzene, 780. Takes up arms against Cantacuzene, and is reduced to flight, 782. His restoration, 782. Discord between him and his sons, 823. His treaty with pope Innocent VI. 868. His visit to pope Urban V. at Rome, 869.

Palæologus, John II. Greek emperor, his zeal, iii.879. His voyage to Italy, 882.

Palæologus, Manuel, associated with his father John, in the Greek empire, iii.823. Tribute exacted from him by sultan Bajazet, 824. His treaties with Soliman and Mahomet, the sons of Bajazet VI. 857. His visit to the courts of Europe, 871. Private motives of his European negociations explained, 877. His death, 878.

Palæologus, Michael, emperor of Nice, his brief replies to the negociations of Baldwin II. emperor of Constantinople, iii.722. His family and character, 741. His elevation to the throne, 743. His return to Constantinople, 746. Blinds and banishes his young associate John Lascaris, 747. He is excommunicated by the patriarch Arsenius, 748. Associates his son Andronicus in the empire, 750. His union with the Latin church, 751. Instigates the revolt of Sicily, 756.

Palatines and Borderers, origin and nature of these distinctions in the Roman troops, i.620.

Palermo, taken by Belisarius by stratagem, ii.651.

Palestine, a character of, i.52.

Palladium of Rome, described, ii.72 *note*.

Palladius, the notary, sent by Valentinian to

Africa to inquire into the government of count Romanus, connives with him in oppressing the province, i.1003.

Palmyra, description of, and its destruction by the emperor Aurelian, i.316.

Panætius, was the first teacher of the Stoic philosophy at Rome, ii.794 *note*.

Pandects of Justinian, how formed, ii.799.

Panhypersebastos, import of that title in the Greek empire, iii.395.

Pannonia described, i.50.

Pantheon at Rome, by whom erected, i.71 *note*. Is converted into a Christian church, ii.81.

Pantomimes, Roman, described, ii.186.

Paper, where and when the manufacture of, was first found out, iii.248.

Papinian, the celebrated lawyer, created prætorian præfect, by the emperor Severus, i.147. His death, 156.

Papirius, Caius, reasons for concluding that he could not be the author of the *Jus Papirianum*, ii.780 *note*.

Papists, proportion their number bore to that of the Protestants in England, at the beginning of the last century, i.734 *note*.

Para, king of Armenia, his history, i.1011. Is treacherously killed by the Romans, 1012.

Parabolani of Alexandria, account of, ii.944 *note*.

Paradise, Mahomet's, described, iii.187.

Paris, description of that city, under the government of Julian, i.723. Situation of his palace, 835 *note*.

Parthia, subdued by Artaxerxes king of Persia, i.221. Its constitution of government similar to the feudal system of Europe, 221. Recapitulation of the war with Rome, 222.

Paschal II. pope, his troublesome pontificate, iii.984.

Pastoral manners, much better adapted to the fierceness of war, than to peaceful innocence, i.1025.

Paternal authority, extent of, by the Roman laws, ii.808. Successive limitations of, 809.

Patras, extraordinary deliverance of, from the Sclavonians and Saracens, iii.386.

Patricians, the order of, under the Roman republic, and under the emperors, compared, i.607. Under the Greek empire, their rank explained, iii.111.

Patrick, the tutelar saint of Ireland, derivation of his name, ii.405 *note*.

Paul of Samosata, bishop of Antioch, his character and history, i.556.

Paul, archbishop of Constantinople, his fatal contest with his competitor Macedonius, i.818.

Paula, a Roman widow, her illustrious descent, ii.169. Was owner of the city of Nicopolis, 173. Her monastic zeal, 417.

Paulicians, origin and character of, iii.424. Are persecuted by the Greek emperors, 428. They revolt, 430. They are reduced, and transplanted to Thrace, 432. Their present state, 434.

Paulina, wife of the tyrant Maximin, softens his ferocity by gentle counsels, i.192 *note*.

Paulinus, master of the offices to Theodosius the Younger, his crime, and execution, ii.268.

Paulinus, bishop of Nola, his history, ii.209.

Paulinus, patriarch of Aquileia, flies from the Lombards with his treasure, into the island of Grado, ii.854.

Pavia, massacre of the friends of Stilicho there, by the instigations of Olympius, ii.158. Is taken by Alboin king of the Lombards, who fixes his residence there, ii.854.

Pegasians, the party of, among the Roman civilians, explained, ii.796.

Pekin, the city of, taken by Zingis the Mogul emperor, iii.796.

Pelagian controversy agitated by the Latin clergy, ii.150. And in Britain, 234.

Pella, the church of the Nazarenes settled there on the destruction of Jerusalem, i.453.

Peloponnesus, state of, under the Greek empire, iii.384. Manufactures, 387.

Penal laws of Rome, the abolition, and revival of, ii.833.

Pendragon, his office and power in Britain, ii.234.

Penitentials, of the Greek and Latin churches, history of, iii.565.

Pepin, king of France, assists the pope of Rome against the Lombards, iii.107. Receives the title of king by papal sanction, 110. Grants the exarchate to the pope, 113.

Pepin, John, count of Minorbino, reduces the tribune Rienzi, and restores aristocracy and church government at Rome, iii.1037.

Pepper, its high estimation and price at Rome, ii.191 *note*.

Perennis, minister of the emperor Commodus, his great exaltation and downfall, i.112.

Perisabor, a city of Assyria, reduced and burned by the emperor Julian, i.927.

Perozes, king of Persia, his fatal expedition against the Nephthalites, ii.606.

Persecutions, ten, of the primitive Christians, a review of, i.550.

Perseus, amount of the treasures taken from that prince, i.179.

Persia, the monarchy of, restored by Artaxerxes, i.214. The religion of the magi reformed, 215. Abridgment of the Persian theology, 216. Simplicity of their worship, 217. Ceremonies and moral precepts, 218. Every other mode of worship prohibited but that of Zoroaster, 220. Extent and population of the country, 222. Its military power, 228. Account of the audience given by the emperor Carus to the ambassadors of Varanes, 348. The throne of, disputed by the brothers Narses and Hormuz, 376. Galerius defeated by the Persians, 376. Narses overthrown in his turn by Galerius, 378. Articles of peace agreed on between the Persians and the Romans, 381. War between Sapor king of, and the emperor Constantius, 667. Battle of Singara, 667. Sapor invades Mesopotamia, 705. The Persian territories invaded by the emperor Julian, 921. Passage of the Tigris, 933. Julian harassed in his retreat, 940. Treaty of peace between Sapor and the emperor Jovian, 949. Reduction of Armenia, and death of Sapor, 1008.

——, The silk trade, how carried on from China through Persia, for the supply of the Roman empire, ii.580. Death of Perozes, in an expedition against the white Huns, 606. Review of the reigns of Cabades, and his son Chosroes, 702. Anarchy of, after the death of Chosroes II. 928. Ecclesiastical history of, 980.

——, Invasion of, by the caliph Abubeker, iii.239. Battle of Cadesia, 239. Sack of Ctesiphon, 242. Conquest of, by the Saracens, 244. The magian religion supplanted by Mahometism, 317. The power of the Arabs crushed by the dynasty of the Bowides, 372. Persia subdued by the Turks, 529. Conquest of, by the Moguls, 800. By Tamerlane, 830.

Pertinax, his character, and exaltation to the Imperial throne, i.120. His funeral and apotheosis, 138.

Pescennius Niger, governor of Syria, assumes the Imperial dignity on the death of Pertinax, i.133.

Petavius, character of his *Dogmata Theologica*, ii.932 *note*.

Peter, brother of the Eastern emperor Maurice, his injurious treatment of the citizens of Azimuntium, and flight from thence, ii.897.

Peter I. czar of Russia, his conduct toward his son, contrasted with that of Constantine the Great, i.650.

Peter of Arragon, assumes the kingdom of Sicily, iii.758.

Peter Bartholemy, his miraculous discovery of the Holy Lance, iii.598. His strange death, 600.

Peter of Courtenay, emperor of Constantinople, iii.713.

Peter the hermit, his character and scheme to recover the Holy Land from the infidels, iii.557. Leads the first crusaders, 570. Failure of his zeal, 598.

Petra, the city of, taken by the Persians, ii.721. Is besieged by the Romans, 722. Is demolished, 723.

Petrarch, his studies and literary character, iii.898. And history, 1019. His account of the ruin of the ancient buildings of Rome, 1076.

Pfeffel, character of his history of Germany, iii.147 *note*.

Phalanx, Grecian, compared with the Roman legion, i.42.

Pharamond, the actions, and foundation of the French monarchy by him, of doubtful authority, ii.229.

Pharas commands the Heruli, in the African war, under Belisarius, ii.623. Pursues Gelimer, 638. His letter to Gelimer, 639.

Pharisees, account of that sect among the Jews, i.466.

Phasis, river, its course described, ii.715.

Pheasant, derivation of the name of that bird, ii.716.

Philelphus, Francis, his character of the Greek language of Constantinople, iii.894.

Philip I. of France, his limited dignity and power, iii.561.

Philip Augustus of France engages in the third crusade, iii.640.

Philip, prætorian præfect under the third Gordian, raised to the empire on his death, i.209. Was a favourer of the Christians, 554.

Philip, prætorian præfect of Constantinople, conveys the bishop Paul into banishment clandestinely, i.818.

Philippicus, emperor of Constantinople, iii.35.

Philippopolis taken and sacked by the Goths, i.261.

Philo, a character of his works, i.772.

Philosophy, Grecian, review of the various sects of, i.58.

Phineus, the situation of his palace, i.587.

Phocæa is settled by the Genoese, who trade in allum, iii.856.

Phocas, a centurion, is chosen emperor by the disaffected troops of the Eastern empire, ii.900. Murders the emperor Maurice, and his children, 902. His character, 903. His fall, and death, 905.

Phœnicia described, i.53.

Photius, the son of Antonina, distinguishes himself at the siege of Naples, ii.681. Is exiled, 682. Betrays his mother's vices to Belisarius, 682. Turns monk, 683.

Phranza, George, the Greek historian, some account of, iii.877 *note*. His embassies, 931. His fate on the taking of Constantinople by the Turks, 965.

Picardy, derivation of the name of that province, iii.557 *note*.

Pilate, Pontius, his testimony in favour of Jesus Christ, much improved by the primitive fathers, i.550.

Pilpay's fables, history and character of, ii.707.

Pinna marina, a kind of silk manufactured from the threads spun by this fish, by the Romans, ii.580.

Pipa, a princess of the Marcomanni, espoused by the emperor Gallienus, i.273.

Piso, Calphurnius, one of the competitors against Gallienus, his illustrious family and character, i.289.

Pityus, the city of, destroyed by the Goths, i.276.

Placidia, daughter of Theodosius the Great, her history, and marriage with Adolphus king of the Goths, ii.213. Is injuriously treated by the usurper Singeric, after the death of her husband, 226. Her marriage with Constantius, and retreat to Constantinople, 273. Her administration in the West, as guardian of her son the emperor Valentinian III. 276. History of her daughter Honoria, 332. Her death and burial, 352 *note*.

Plague, origin and nature of this disease, ii.774. Great extent, and long duration of that in the reign of Justinian, 776.

Plato, his theological system, i.771. Is received by the Alexandrian Jews, 772. And expounded by St. John the Evangelist, 773. The theological system of the emperor Julian, 870.

Platonic philosophy introduced into Italy, iii.905.

Platonists, new, an account of, i.398. Unite with the heathen priests to oppose the Christians, 561.

Plautianus, prætorian præfect under the emperor Severus, his history, i.146.

Plebeians of Rome, state and character of, ii.181.

Pliny the Younger, examination of his conduct toward the Christians, i.534.

Poet laureat, a ridiculous appointment, iii.1020 *note*.

Poggius, his reflections on the ruin of ancient Rome, iii.1062.

Poitiers, battle of, between Clovis king of the Franks, and Alaric the Goth, ii.467.

Pollentia, battle of, between Stilicho the Roman general, and Alaric the Goth, ii.134.

Polytheism of the Romans, its origin, and effects, i.56. How accounted for by the primitive Christians, 459. Scepticism of the people at the time of the publication of Christianity, 498. The Christians, why more odious to the Pagans than the Jews, 517. The ruin of, suspended by the divisions among Christians, 827. Theological system of the emperor Julian, 870.

——, Review of the Pagan ecclesiastical establishment, ii.72. Revival of, by the Christian monks, 94.

Pompeianus, præfect of Rome, proposes to drive Alaric from the walls by spells, ii.190.

Pompeianus, Ruricius, general under Maxentius, defeated and killed by Constantine the Great, i.424.

Pompey, his discretional exercise of power during his command in the East, i.88. Increase of the tributes of Asia by his conquests, 179.

Pontifex Maximus, in Pagan Rome, by whom that office was exercised, i.750.

Pontiffs, Pagan, their jurisdiction, ii.72.

Popes of Rome, the growth of their power, iii.97. Revolt of, from the Greek emperors, 101. Origin of their temporal dominion, 113. Publication of the Decretals, and of the fictitious donation of Constantine the Great, 115. Authority of the German emperors in their election, 136. Violent distractions in their election, 137. Foundation of their authority at Rome, 980. Their mode of election settled, 1004. Schism in the papacy, 1045. They acquire the absolute dominion of Rome, 1056. The ecclesiastical government, 1058.

Population of Rome, a computation of, ii.186.

Porcaro, Stephen, his conspiracy at Rome, iii.1054.

Posthumus, the Roman general under the emperor Gallienus, defends Gaul against the incursions of the Franks, i.273. Is killed by his mutinous troops, 311.

Power, absolute, the exercise of, how checked, iii.404.

Præfect of the sacred bed-chamber, under Constantine the Great, his office, i.625.

Præfects of Rome and Constantinople, under the emperors, the nature of their offices, i.611. The office revived at Rome, iii.994.

Prætextatus, præfect of Rome under Valentinian, his character, i.988.

Prætorian bands, in the Roman army, an account of, i.127. They sell the empire of Rome by public auction, 129. Are disgraced by the emperor Severus, 138. A new establishment of them, 146. Authority of the prætorian præfect, 146. Are reduced, their privileges abolished, and their place supplied, by the Jovians and Herculians, 386. Their desperate courage under Maxentius, 426. Are totally suppressed by Constantine the Great, 428.

Prætorian præfect, revolutions of this office under the emperors, i.609. Their functions when it became a civil office, 610.

Prætors of Rome, the nature and tendency of their edicts explained, ii.785.

Preaching, a form of devotion unknown in the temples of Paganism, i.762. Use, and abuse of, 763.

Predestination, influence of the doctrine of, on the Saracens and Turks, iii.198.

Presbyters, among the primitive Christians, the office explained, i.484.

Prester, John, origin of the romantic stories concerning, ii.983.

Priestley, Dr. the ultimate tendency of his opinions, pointed out, iii.439 *note*.

Priests, no distinct order of men among the ancient Pagans, i.497. 751.

Primogeniture, the prerogative of, unknown to the Roman law, ii.822.

Prince of the waters, in Persia, his office, ii.705 *note*.

Priscillian, bishop of Avila in Spain, is, with his followers, put to death for heresy, ii.38.

Priscus the historian, his conversation with a captive Greek, in the camp of Attila, ii.307. His character, 311 *note*.

Priscus, the Greek general, his successes against the Avars, ii.898.

Proba, widow of the præfect Petronius, her flight from the sack of Rome by Alaric, ii.207.

Probus assumes the Imperial dignity in opposition to Florianus, i.334. His character and history, 335.

Probus, prætorian præfect of Illyricum, preserves Sirmium from the Quadi, i.1019.

Probus, Sicorius, his embassy from the emperor Diocletian to Narses, king of Persia, i.380.

Procida, John of, instigates the revolt of Sicily from John of Anjou, iii.758.

Proclus, story of his extraordinary brazen mirror, ii.592.

Proclus, the platonic philosopher of Athens, his superstition, ii.614.

Proconsuls of Asia, Achaia, and Africa, their office, i.613.

Procopia, wife of the Greek emperor Michael I. her martial inclinations, iii.42.

Procopius, his history, and revolt against Valens, emperor of the East, i.969. Is reduced, and put to death, 973.

——, His account of the testament of the emperor Arcadius, ii.261. His account of Britain, 505. Character of his histories, 561. Accepts the office of secretary under Belisarius, 622. His defence of the Roman archers, 624. His account of the desolation of the African province by war, 735.

Proculians, origin of the sect of, in the Roman civil law, ii.795.

Proculus, his extraordinary character, and his rebellion against Probus in Gaul, i.344.

Prodigies in ancient history, a philosophical resolution of, i.740.

Promises, under what circumstances the Roman law enforced the fulfilment of, ii.827.

Promotus, master-general of the infantry under Theodosius, is ruined by the enmity of Rufinus, ii.100.

Property, personal, the origin of, ii.819. How ascertained by the Roman laws, 820. Testamentary dispositions of, how introduced, 823.

Prophets, their office among the primitive Christians, i.484.

Propontis described, i.589.

Proterius, patriarch of Alexandria, his martial episcopacy, and violent death, ii.963.

Protestants, their resistance of oppression, not consistent with the practice of the primitive Christians, i.732. Proportion of their number, to that of the Catholics, in France, at the beginning of the last century, 734 *note*. Estimate of their reformation of Popery, iii.436.

Protosebastos, import of that title in the Greek empire, iii.395.

Proverbs, the book of, why not likely to be the production of king Solomon, ii.641 *note*.

Provinces of the Roman empire described, i.47. Distinction between Latin and Greek provinces, 65. Account of the tributes received from, 179. Their number and government after the seat of empire was removed to Constantinople, 614.

Prusa, conquest of, by the Ottomans, iii.810.

Prussia, emigration of the Goths to, i.257.

Pulcheria, sister of the emperor Theodosius the Younger, her character and administration, ii.262. Her lessons to her brother, 264. Her contests with the empress Eudocia, 267. Is proclaimed empress of the East, on the death of Theodosius, 321. Her death and canonization, 383.

Purple, the royal colour of, among the ancients, far surpassed by the modern discovery of cochineal, ii.578 *note*.

Pygmies of Africa, ancient fabulous account of, i.1007.

Q

Quadi, the inroads of, punished by the emperor Constantius, i.700. Revenge the treacherous murder of their king Gabinius, 1018.

Quæstor, historical review of this office, i.626.

Question, criminal, how exercised under the Roman emperors, i.631.

Quintilian brothers, Maximus and Condianus, their history, i.112.

Quintilius, brother of the emperor Claudius, his ineffectual effort to succeed him, i.303.

Quintus Curtius, an attempt to decide the age in which he wrote, i.207 *note*.

Quirites, the effect of that word when opposed to *soldiers*, i.176 *note*.

R

Radagaisus, king of the Goths, his formidable invasion of Italy, ii.143. His savage character, 145. Is reduced by Stilicho, and put to death, 145.

Radiger, king of the Varni, compelled to fulfil his matrimonial obligations by a British heroine, ii.506.

Ramadan, the month of, how observed by the Turks, iii.186.

Rando, a chieftain of the Alemanni, his unprovoked attack on Moguntiacum, i.991.

Ravenna, the ancient city of, described, ii.139. The emperor Honorius fixes his residence there, 139.

——, Invasion of, by a Greek fleet, iii.102. Is taken by the Lombards, and recovered by the Venetians, 106. Final conquest of, by the Lombards, 107. The exarchate of, bestowed by Pepin on the pope, 113.

Raymond of Tholouse, the crusader, his character, iii.576. His route to Constantinople, 581. His bold behaviour there, 585.

Raymond, count of Tripoli, betrays Jerusalem into the hands of Saladin, iii.635.

Raynal, Abbé, mistaken in asserting that Constantine the Great suppressed Pagan worship, i.824.

Rebels, who the most inveterate of, iii.430.

Recared, the first Catholic king of Spain, converts his Gothic subjects, iii.550.

Reformation from popery, the amount of, estimated, iii.436. A secret reformation still working in the reformed churches, 438.

Rein-deer, this animal driven northward by the improvement of climate from cultivation, i.231.

Relics, the worship of, introduced by the monks, ii.90. A valuable cargo of, imported from Constantinople by Louis IX. of France, iii.721.

Remigius, bishop of Rheims, converts Clovis king of the Franks, ii.458.

Repentance, its high esteem, and extensive operation, among the primitive Christians, i.476.

Resurrection, general, the Mahometan doctrine of, iii.187.

Retiarius, the mode of his combat with the secutor, in the Roman amphitheatre, i.119.

Revenues of the primitive church, how distributed, i.493. 758. Of the Roman empire, when removed to Constantinople, a review of, 632.

Rhæteum, city of, its situation, i.591.

Rhætia described, i.50.

Rhazates, the Persian general, defeated and killed by the emperor Heraclius, ii.925.

Rhetoric, the study of, congenial to a popular state, ii.612.

Rhine, the banks of, fortified by the emperor Valentinian, i.992.

Rhodes, account of the colossus of, iii.275. The knights of, 812.

Richard I. of England, engages in the third crusade, iii.640. Bestows the island of Cyprus on the house of Lusignan, 663. His reply to the exhortations of Fulk of Neuilly, 666.

Richard, monk of Cirencester, his literary character, ii.232 *note*.

Ricimer, count, his history, ii.369. Permits Majorian to assume the Imperial dignity in the Western empire, 371. Enjoys supreme power under cover of the name of the emperor Libius Severus, 379, Marries the daughter of the emperor Anthemius, 385. Sacks Rome, and kills Athemius, 398. His death, 399.

Rienzi, Nicholas di, his birth, character, and history, iii.1023.

Roads, Roman, the construction and great extent of, i.77.

Robert, count of Flanders, his character and engagement in the first crusade, iii.575.

Roderic, the Gothic king of Spain, his defeat and death by Tarik the Arab, iii.305.

Rodugune, probable origin of her character, in Rowe's *Royal Convert*, ii.506.

Roger, count of Sicily, his exploits, and conquest of that island, iii.492.

Roger, son of the former, the first king of Sicily, iii.508. His military atchievements in Africa and Greece, 510.

Roger de Flor, engages as an auxiliary in the service of the Greek emperor Andronicus, iii.760. His assassination, 761.

Romanus I. Lecapenus, emperor of Constantinople, iii.55.

Romanus II. emperor of Constantinople, iii.57.

Romanus III. Argyrus, emperor of Constantinople, iii.61.

Romanus IV. Diogenes, emperor of Constantinople, iii.66. Is defeated and taken prisoner by the Turkish sultan Alp Arslan, 537. His treatment, deliverance, and death, 538.

Romanus, count, governor of Africa, his corrupt administration, i.1002.

Romanus, governor of Bosra, betrays it to the Saracens, iii.251.

Rome, the three periods of its decline pointed out, i. *Preface*. Its prosperous circumstances in the second century, 31. The principal conquests of, atchieved under the republic, 31. Conquests under the emperors, 33. Military establishment of the emperors, 38. Naval force of the empire, 46. View of the provinces of the empire, 47. Its general extent, 55. The union and internal prosperity of the empire, in the age of the Antonines, accounted for, 56. Treatment of the provinces, 62. Benefits included in the freedom of the city, 64. Distinction between the Latin and Greek provinces, 65. Prevalence of the Greek, as a scientific language, 66. Numbers and condition of the Roman slaves, 67. Populousness of the empire, 69. Unity and power of the government, 70. Monuments of Roman architecture, 70. The Roman magnificence chiefly displayed in public buildings, 73. Principal cities in the empire, 75. Public roads, 77. Great improvements of agriculture in the western countries of the empire, 78. Arts of luxury, 80. Commerce with the East, 81. Contemporary representation of the prosperity of the empire, 82. Decline of courage and genius, 83. A review of public affairs after the battle of Actium, 85. The Imperial power and dignity confirmed to Augustus by the senate, 87. The various characters and powers vested in the emperor, 90. General idea of the Imperial system, 93. Abortive attempt of the senate to resume its rights after the murder of Caligula, 97. The emperors associate their intended

Rome—contd
successors to power, 98. The most happy period in the Roman history pointed out, 103. Their peculiar misery under their tyrants, 104. The empire publicly sold by auction by the prætorian guards, 129. Civil wars of the Romans, how generally decided, 141. When the army first received regular pay, 178. How the citizens were relieved from taxation, 179. General estimate of the Roman revenue from the provinces, 181. Miseries flowing from the succession to the empire being elective, 188. A summary review of the Roman history, 211. Recapitulation of the war with Parthia, 222. Invasion of the provinces by the Goths, 260. The office of censor revived by the emperor Decius, 262. Peace purchased of the Goths, 265. The emperor Valerian taken prisoner by Sapor king of Persia, 283. The popular conceit of the thirty tyrants of Rome investigated, 288. Famine and pestilence throughout the empire, 294. The city fortified against the inroads of the Alemanni, 310. Remarks on the alleged sedition of the officers of the mint under Aurelian, 323. Observations on the peaceful interregnum after the death of Aurelian, 328. Colonies of barbarians introduced into the provinces by Probus, 341. Exhibition of the public games by Carinus, 351. Treaty of peace between the Persians and the Romans, 381. The last triumph celebrated at Rome, 383. How the imperial courts came to be transferred to Milan and Nicomedia, 384. The prætorian bands superseded by the Jovian and Herculean guards, 386. The power of the senate annihilated, 387. Four divisions of the empire under four conjunct princes, 389. Their expensive establishments call for more burdensome taxes, 390. Diocletian and Maximian abdicate the empire, 391. Six emperors existing at one time, 413. The senate and people apply to Constantine to deliver them from the tyranny of Maxentius, 419. Constantine enters the city victorious, 427. Laws of Constantine, 437. Constantine remains sole emperor, 445. History of the progress and establishment of Christianity, 446. Pretensions of the bishop of Rome, whence deduced, 489. State of the church at Rome at the time of the persecution of Nero, 503. Narrative of the fire of Rome, in the reign of Nero, 526. The Christians persecuted as the incendiaries, 527. The memorable edicts of Diocletian and his associates against the Christians, 564. Account of the building and establishment of the rival city of Constantinople, 586. New forms of administration established there, 602. Division of the empire among the sons of Constantine, 663. Establishment of Christianity as the national religion, 750. Tumults excited by the rival bishops, Liberius and Fælix, 816. Paganism restored by Julian, 876. And Christianity by Jovian, 959. The empire divided into the *East* and *West*, by the emperor Valentinian, 968. Civil institutions of Valentinian, 978. The crafty avarice of the clergy restrained by Valentinian, 985. Bloody contest of Damasus and Ursinus for the bishopric of Rome, 987. Great earthquake, 1023.

——, The emperor Theodosius visits the city, ii.50. Inquiry into the cause of the corruption of morals in his reign, 69. Review of the Pagan establishment, 72. The Pagan religion renounced by the senate, 76. Sacrifices prohibited, 78. The Pagan religion prohibited, 86. Triumph of Honorius and Stilicho, over Alaric the Goth, 137. Alaric encamps under the walls of the city, 168. Retrospect of the state of the city when besieged by Hannibal, 168. Wealth of the nobles, and magnificence of the city, 172. Character of the nobles of, by Ammianus Marcellinus, 175. State and character of the common people, 181. Public distributions of bread, &c. 183. Public baths, 184. Games and spectacles, 185. Attempts to ascertain the population of the city, 186. The citizens suffer by famine, 189. Plague, 189. The retreat of Alaric purchased by a ransom, 191. Is again besieged by Alaric, 196. The senate unites with him in electing Attalus emperor, 197. The city seized by Alaric, and plundered, 200. Comparison between this event, and the sack of Rome by the emperor Charles V. 207. Alaric quits Rome, and ravages Italy, 209. Laws passed for the relief of Rome, and Italy, 216. Triumph of Honorius for the reduction of Spain by Wallia, 228. Is preserved from the hands of Attila by a ransom, 349. Indications of the ruin of the empire, at the death of Valentinian III. 355. Sack of the city by Genseric, king of the Vandals, 360. The public buildings of, protected from depredation by the laws of Majorian, 374. Is sacked again by the patrician Ricimer, 398. Augustulus, the last emperor of the West, 402. The decay of the Roman spirit remarked, 407. History of monastic institutions in, 414. General observations on the history of the Roman empire, 508. Italy conquered by Theodoric the Ostrogoth, 532. Prosperity of the city under his government, 542. Account of the four factions in the circus, 570. First introduction of silk among the Romans, 580. The office of consul suppressed by Justinian, 616. The city receives Belisarius, 658. Siege of, by the Goths, 658. Distressful siege of, by Totila the Goth, 740. Is taken, 743. Is recovered by Belisarius, 745. Is again taken by Totila, 748. Is taken by the eunuch Narses, 755. Extinction of the senate, 756. The city degraded to the second rank under the exarchs of Ravenna, 763. A review of the Roman laws, 778. Extent of the dutchy of, under the exarchs of Ravenna, 865. Miserable state of the city, 872. Pontificate of Gregory the Great, 876.

——, The government of the city new modelled under the popes, after their revolt from the Greek emperors, iii.104. Is attacked by the Lombards, and delivered by king Pepin, 105. The office and rank of exarchs and patricians explained, 111. Reception of Charlemagne by pope Adrian I. 112. Is menaced by the Saracens, 359. Prosperous pontificate of Leo IV. 360. Is besieged and taken by the emperor Henry III. 504. Great part of the city burnt by Robert Guiscard, in the cause of pope Gregory VII. 505. The history of, resumed, after the capture of Constantinople by the Turks, 978. French and German emperors of, 979. Authority of the popes, 980. Restoration of the republican form of government, 991. Office of senator, 995. Wars against the neighbouring cities, 1002. Institution of the Jubilee, 1010. Revolution in the city, by the tribune Rienzi, 1023. Calamities flowing from the schism of the papacy, 1046. Statutes and government of the city, 1052. Porcaro's conspiracy, 1054. The ecclesiastical government of, 1058. Reflections of Poggius on the ruin of the city, 1062. Four principal causes of its ruin specified, 1065. The Coliseum of Titus, 1076. Restoration and ornaments of the city, 1082.

Romilda, the betrayer of Friuli to the Avars, her cruel treatment by them, ii.912.

Rosamond, daughter of Cunimund king of the Gepidæ, her marriage with Alboin king of the Lombards, ii.849. Conspires his murder, 855. Her flight and death, 856.

Roum, the Seljukian kingdom of, formed, iii.546.

Rudbeck, Olaus, summary abridgment of the argument in his *Atlantica*, i.234.

Rufinus, the confidential minister of the emperor Theodosius the Great, stimulates his cruelty against Thessalonica, ii.56. His character and administration, 99. His death, 110.

Rugilas the Hun, his settlement in Hungary, ii.295.

Runic characters, the antiquity of, traced, i.234.

Russia, origin of the monarchy of, iii.455. Geography and trade of, 457. Naval expeditions of the Russians against Constantinople, 460. Reign of the czar Swatoslaus, 463. The Russians converted to Christianity, 466. Is conquered by the Moguls, 802.

Rustan, a Persian nobleman, a saying of his, expressive of the danger of living under despots, i.105.

Rutilius, his character of the monks of Capraria, ii.166.

S

Sabellius the heresiarch, his opinions afterward adopted by his antagonists, i.778. His doctrine of the Trinity, 781. The Sabellians unite with the Tritheists at the council of Nice to overpower the Arians, 783.

Sabians, their astronomical mythology, iii.170.

Sabinian obtains the command of the Eastern provinces from Constantius, i.709.

Sabinian, general of the East, is defeated by Theodoric the Ostrogoth king of Italy, ii.538.

Sabinians, origin of the sect of, in the Roman civil law, ii.795.

Sadducees, account of that sect among the Jews, i.466.

Saladin, his birth, promotion, and character, iii.631. Conquers the kingdom of Jerusalem, 634. His ineffectual siege of Tyre, 638. Siege of Acre, 639. His negociations with Richard I. of England, 643. His death, 644.

Salerno, account of the medical school of, iii.490.

Salic laws, history of, ii.472.

Sallust, the præfect, and friend of the emperor Julian, declines the offer of the diadem on his death, i.946. Declines it again, on the death of Jovian, 964. Is retained in his employment by the emperor Valentinian, 968.

Sallust, the historian, by what funds he raised his palace on the Quirinal hill, ii.205 *note*.

Salona, the retreat of the emperor Diocletian, described, i.395.

Salvian, his account of the distress and rebellion of the Bagaudæ, ii.356 *note*.

Samanides, the Saracen dynasty of, iii.371.

Samaritans, persecution and extinction of, by the emperor Justinian, ii.970.

Samuel the prophet, his ashes conveyed to Constantinople, ii.91.

Sapor, king of Persia, procures the assassination of Chosroes king of Armenia, and seizes the country, i.282. Defeats the emperor Valerian, and takes him prisoner, 283. Sets up Cyriades as successor to Valerian in the Roman empire, 284. Over-runs Syria, Cilicia, and Cappadocia, 284. His death, 318.

Sapor, the son of Hormouz, is crowned king of Persia before his birth, i.664. His character and early heroism, 664. Harasses the eastern provinces of the Roman empire, 667. Battle of Singara, against the emperor Constantius, 667. His son brutally killed by Constantius, 668. His several attempts on Nisibis, 669. Concludes a truce with Constantius, 670. His haughty propositions to Constantius, 703. Invades Mesopotamia, 705. Reduces Amida, 706. Returns home, 709. His peaceful overtures to the emperor Julian, 911. His consternation at the successes of Julian, 936. Harasses the retreat of the Romans, 940. His treaty with the emperor Jovian, 949. His reduction of Armenia, and death, 1008.

Saracen, various definitions of that appellation, iii.160 *note*.

Saracens, succession of the caliphs of, iii.219. Their rapid conquests, 237. Conquest of Persia, 244. Siege of Damascus, 252. Battle of Yermuck, and conquest of Syria, 264. Of Egypt, 276. Invasions of Africa, 290. Their military character, 409.

Sarbar, the Persian general, joins the Avars in besieging Constantinople, ii.922. Revolts to the emperor Heraclius, 924.

Sardinia, expulsion of the Vandals from, by Marcellinus, ii.389. Is conquered by Zano, the brother of Gelimer king of the Vandals, 633. Is surrendered to Belisarius, 636.

Sarmatians, memorable defeat of, by the emperor Carus, i.347. Their manners described, 655. Brief history of, 656. They apply to Constantine the Great for assistance against the Goths, 657. Are expelled their country by the Limigantes, 659. Are restored by Constantius, 703.

Sarus the Goth, plunders the camp of Stilicho, and drives him into the hands of the emperor at Ravenna, ii.159. Insults Alaric, and occasions the sacking of Rome, 200. Is killed by Adolphus king of the Visigoths, 223.

Saturninus, one of the competitors for empire against Gallienus, his observation on his investiture, i.290.

Saturninus, lieutenant under the emperor Probus, in the East, is driven into rebellion by his troops, i.343.

Savage manners, a brief view of, i.237. Are more uniform than those of civilised nations, 1025.

Saxons, ancient, an account of, i.994. Their piratical confederations, 995. Their invasions of Gaul checked by the Romans, 996.

——, How converted to Christianity, ii.431. Descent of the Saxons on Britain, 494. Their brutal desolation of the country, 501.

Scanderbeg, prince of Albania, his history, iii.926.

Scatinian law of the Romans, account of, ii.837.

Scaurus, the patrician family of, how reduced under the emperors, i.608 *note*.

Schism in religion, the origin of, traced, i.549.

Science reducible to four classes, iii.349.

Sclavonians, their national character, ii.690. Their barbarous inroads on the Eastern empire, 692. Of Dalmatia, account of, iii.442.

Scots and Picts, the nations of, how distinguished, i.996. Invasions of Britain by, 999.

Scythians, this name vaguely applied to mixed tribes of barbarians, i.281. Their pastoral manners, 1025. Extent and boundaries of Scythia, 1033.

——, Revolutions of, ii.141. Their mode of war, 303.

Sebastian, master-general of the infantry under the emperor Valens, his successful expedition agains the Goths, i.1061. Is killed in the battle of Hadrianople, 1065.

Sebastian, the brother of the usurper Jovinus, is associated with him in his assumed Imperial dignities, ii.222.

Sebastocrator, import of that title in the Greek empire, iii.394.

Seez, in Normandy, the bishop, and chapter of, all castrated, iii.983 *note.*

Segestan, the princes of, support their independency obstinately against Artaxerxes, i.221 *note.*

Segued, emperor of Abyssinia, is with his whole court, converted by the Jesuits, ii.1000.

Selden, his sententious character of transubstantiation, iii.86 *note.*

Seleucia, the great city of, ruined by the Romans, i.223.

Seleucus Nicator, number of cities founded by him, i.221 *note.*

Seljuk, Turkish dynasty of the house of, iii.530. Division of their empire, 544.

Senate of Rome, is reformed by Augustus, i.86. Its legislative and judicial powers, 92. Abortive attempt of, to resume its rights after the murder of Caligula, 97. Its legal jurisdiction over the emperors, 122. Is subjected to military despotism, by Severus, 147. Women excluded from this assembly by a solemn law, 171. The form of a secret meeting, 196. Measures taken to support the authority of the two Gordians, 197. The senate elect

Senate of Rome—contd
Maximus and Balbinus emperors on the deaths of the Gordians, 198. They drive the Alemanni out of Italy, 272. The senators forbid to exercise military employments by Gallienus, 273. Elect Tacitus, the father of the senate, emperor, 329. Prerogatives gained to the senate, by this election, 331. Their power and authority annihilated by Diocletian, 386. Amount of the coronary gold, or customary free gift of, to the emperors, 641. The claim of Julian to the empire admitted, 847.

——, Petitions of, to the emperors, for the restoration of the altar of victory, ii.74. The Pagan religion renounced, 76. Debates of, on the proposals of Alaric the Goth, 156. Genealogy of the senators, 169. Passes a decree for putting to death Serena the widow of Stilicho, 189. Under the influence of Alaric, elects Attalus emperor, 197. Trial of Arvandus, prætorian præfect of Gaul, 393. Surrenders the sovereign power of Italy to the emperor of the East, 404. Extinction of that illustrious assembly, 756.

——, Restoration of, in the twelfth century, iii.991. The assembly resolved into single magistrates, 995. 1052.

Serapion, his lamentation for the loss of a personified deity, ii.938.

Serapis, history of his worship, and of his temple at Alexandria, ii.82. The temple destroyed, 84.

Serena, niece of the emperor Theodosius, married to his general Stilicho, ii.107. Is cruelly strangled by order of the Roman senate, 189.

Serjeant, legal and military import of that term, iii.679 *note*.

Severinus, St. encourages Odoacer to assume the dominion of Italy, ii.403. His body, how disposed of, 407 *note*.

Severus is declared Cæsar on the abdication of Diocletian and Maximian, i.402. His defeat and death, 409.

Severus is appointed general of the cavalry in Gaul under Julian, i.714.

Severus, Septimius, general of the Pannonian legions, assumes the purple on the death of Pertinax, i.135. His conduct toward the Christians, 552.

Shepherds and warriors, their respective modes of life compared, i.1025.

Shiites, a sect of Mahometans, their distinction from the Sonnites, iii.220.

Siberia, extreme coldness of the climate, and miserable state of the natives of, i.1035. Is seized and occupied by the Tartars, iii.804.

Sicily, reflections on the distractions in that island, i.292.

——, Is conquered by the Saracens, iii.357. Introduction of the silk manufacture there, 389. Exploits of the Normans there, 479. Is conquered by count Roger, 492. Roger, son of the former, made king of, 508. Reign of William the Bad, 518. Reign of William the Good, 518. Conquest of, by the emperor Henry VI. 520. Is subdued by Charles of Anjou, 754. The *Sicilian Vespers*, 758.

Sidonius Apollinaris the poet, his humorous treatment of the capitation tax, i.637. His character of Theodoric king of the Visigoths in Gaul, ii.364. His panegyric on the emperor Avitus, 368. His panegyric on the emperor Anthemius, 386.

Sigismond, king of the Burgundians, murders his son, and is canonised, ii.464. Is overwhelmed by an army of Franks, 464.

Silentiarius, Paul, his account of the various species of stone and marble, employed in the church of St. Sophia at Constantinople, ii.597 *note*.

Silk, first manufactured in China, and then in the small Grecian island of Ceos, ii.579. A peculiar kind of silk procured from the pinna marina, 580. The silk worm, how introduced to Greece, 583. Progress of the manufacture of, in the tenth century, iii.389.

Simeon, persecutor of the Paulicians,

becomes a proselyte to their opinions, iii.429.

Simeon, king of Bulgaria, his exploits, iii.444.

Simony, an early instance of, i.556 *note.*

Simplicius, one of the last surviving Pagan philosophers of Athens, his writings, and character, ii.615.

Singara, battle of, between the emperor Constantius, and Sapor king of Persia, i.667. The city of, reduced by Sapor, 708. Is yielded to him by Jovian, 950.

Singeric, brother of Sarus, is made king of the Goths, ii.226.

Singidunum is perfidiously taken by Baian chagan of the Avars, ii.895.

Sirmium is perfidiously taken by Baian chagan of the Avars, ii.895.

Siroes deposes and murders his father Chosroes II. king of Persia, ii.928. His treaty of peace with the emperor Heraclius, 929.

Sisebut, a Gothic king of Spain, persecutes the Jews there, ii.449.

Sixtus V. pope, character of his administration, iii.1059.

Slave, strange perversion of the original sense of that appellation, iii.442.

Slavery, personal, imposed on captives by the barbarous nations, ii.482.

Slaves, among the Romans, who, and their condition described, i.67.

Sleepers, seven, narrative of the legendary tale of, ii.291.

Smyrna, capture of, by Tamerlane, iii.842.

Society, philosophical reflections on the revolutions of, ii.515.

Soffarides, the Saracen dynasty of, iii.370.

Soldiers, Roman, their obligations and discipline, i.39. When they first received regular pay, 178.

Soliman, sultan, conquers Asia Minor, iii.546. Fixes his residence at Nice, 547. Nice taken by the first crusaders, 590. Battle of Dorylæum, 591.

Soliman, the son of Bajazet, his character, iii.854. His alliance with the Greek emperor Manuel Palæologus, 857.

Solomon, king of the Jews, not the author of the book which bears the name of his *Wisdom*, i.772. Reasons for supposing he did not write either the book of *Ecclesiastes* or the *Proverbs*, ii.641 *note.*

Solomon the eunuch relieves the Roman province in Africa, from the depredations of the Moors, ii.644. Revolt of his troops at Carthage, 732. Is defeated and killed by Antalus the Moor, 735.

Solyman, caliph of the Saracens, undertakes the siege of Constantinople, iii.327. His enormous appetite and death, 329.

Sonnites, in the Mahometan religion, their tenets, iii.221.

Sopator, a Syrian philosopher, beheaded by Constantine the Great, on a charge of binding the wind by magic, i.800 *note.*

Sophia, the widow of Justin II. her conspiracy against the emperor Tiberius, ii.860.

Sophia, St. foundation of the church of, at Constantinople, ii.594. Its description, 595. Is converted into a mosch, iii.968.

Sophian, the Arab, commands the first siege of Constantinople, iii.323.

Sophronia, a Roman matron, kills herself to escape the violence of Maxentius, i.418 *note.*

Sortes Sanctorum, a mode of Christian divination, adopted from the Pagans, ii.467 *note.*

Soul, uncertain opinions of the ancient philosophers as to the immortality of, i.463. This doctrine more generally received among the barbarous nations, and for what reason, 465. Was not taught by Moses, 465. Four different prevailing doctrines as to the origin of, ii.935.

Sozopetra destroyed by the Greek emperor Theophilus, iii.362.

Spain, the province of, described, i.47. Great revenues raised from this province by the Romans, 180. Is ravaged by the Franks, 270.

——, Review of the history of, ii.224. Is invaded by the barbarous nations, 225. The invaders conquered by Wallia king

Spain—*contd*
of the Goths, 227. Successes of the Vandals there, 279. Expedition of Theodoric king of the Visigoths into, 366. The Christian religion received there, 444. Revolt and martyrdom of Hermenegild, 445. Persecution of the Jews in, 448. Legislative assemblies of, 491. Acquisitions of Justinian there, 646.

——, State of, under the emperor Charlemagne, iii.128. First introduction of the Arabs into the country, 301. Defeat and death of Roderic the Gothic king of, 305. Conquest of, by Musa, 308. Its prosperity under the Saracens, 313. The Christian faith there, supplanted by that of Mahomet, 319. The throne of Cordova filled by Abdalrahman, 342.

Stadium, Olympic, the races of, compared with those in the Roman circus, ii.570.

Stauracius, emperor of Constantinople, iii.42.

Stephen, a freedman of Domitilla, assassinates the emperor Domitian, i.534.

Stephen, count of Chartres, his character and engagement in the first crusade, iii.575. Deserts his standard, 598.

Stephen, St. the first Christian martyr, miraculous discovery of his body, and the miracles worked by it, ii.93.

Stephen the Savage, sent by the Greek emperor Justinian II. to exterminate the Chersonites, iii.34.

Stephen III. pope, solicits the aid of Pepin king of France, against the Lombards, under the character of St. Peter, iii.108. Crowns king Pepin, 110.

Stilicho, the great general of the Western empire under the emperor Honorius, his character, ii.106. Puts to death Rufinus the tyrannical præfect of the East, 109. His expedition against Alaric in Greece, 125. His diligent endeavours to check his progress in Italy, 131. Defeats Alaric at Pollentia, 134. Drives him out of Italy, 137. His triumph at Rome, 137. His preparations to oppose the invasion of Radagaisus, 144. Reduces and puts him to death, 147. Supports the claims of Alaric in the Roman senate, 155. Is put to death at Ravenna, 159. His memory persecuted, 160.

Stoza heads the revolted troops of the emperor Justinian in Africa, ii.732.

Strasburgh, battle of, between Julian and the Alemanni, i.715.

Successianus defends the Roman frontier against the Goths, i.276.

Suevi, the origin and renown of, i.271.

Suicide applauded and pitied by the Romans, ii.841.

Sulpicius, Servius, was the highest improver of the Roman jurisprudence, ii.792.

Sultan, origin and import of this title of Eastern sovereignty, iii.524.

Sumnat, description of the pagoda of, in Guzarat, and its destruction by Sultan Mahmud, iii.525.

Sun, the worship of, introduced at Rome by the emperor Elagabalus, i.166. Was the peculiar object of the devotion of Constantine the Great, before his conversion, 728. And of Julian, after his apostacy, 877.

Susa, the city of, taken by Constantine the Great, i.422.

Swatoslaus, czar of Russia, his reign, iii.463.

Swiss cantons, the confederacy of, how far similar to that of the ancient Franks, i.270.

Sword of Mars, the sacred weapon of the Huns, history of, ii.297.

Syagrius, king of the Franks and Burgundians, his character, ii.455.

Sylla the dictator, his legislative character, ii.835.

Syllanus the consul, his speech to the senate, recommending the election of the two Gordians to their approbation, i.196.

Sylvania, sister of the præfect Rufinus, her uncommon sanctity, ii.111 *note*.

Sylvanus, general in Gaul under Constantius, is ruined by treachery, i.697.

Sylverius, pope, is degraded and sent into exile by Belisarius for an attempt to betray the city of Rome to the Goths, ii.667. His death, 737 *note.*

Symmachus, his account of the Pagan conformity of the emperor Constantius, during his visit to Rome, i.827. Pleads in behalf of the ancient Pagan religion of Rome, to the emperor Valentinian, ii.74.

Synesius, bishop of Ptolemais, excommunicates the president Andronicus, i.761. His extraordinary character, 761. *note.* His advice to the Eastern emperor Arcadius, ii.127.

Synods, provincial, in the primitive churches, institution of, i.486. Nature of those assemblies, 764. See *Councils.*

Syria, its revolutions and extent, i.52. Is reduced by Chosroes II. king of Persia, ii.908. General description of, iii.262. Is conquered by the Saracens, 264. Invasion of, by Tamerlane, 837.

Syriac language, where spoken in the greatest purity, i.224 *note.*

Syrianus, duke of Egypt, surprises the city of Alexandria, and expels Athanasius the primate of Egypt, i.810.

T

Tabari, the Arabian historian, account of his work, iii.238 *note.*

Tabenne, the island of, in upper Thebais, is settled with monks, by Pachomius, ii.414.

Table of emerald, in the Gothic treasury in Sapin, account of, ii.216.

Tacitus, emperor, his election and character, i.329.

Tacitus the historian, his character of the principles of the portico, i.102 *note.* The intention of his episodes, 213. His character as a historian, 230. His account of the ancient Germans, 234. His history how preserved and transmitted down to us, 330 *note.* His account of the persecution of the Christians as the incendiaries of Rome, 527.

Tactics of Leo and Constantine, character of, iii.381. Military character of the Greeks, 407.

Tagina, battle of, between the eunuch Narses, and Totila king of the Goths in Italy, ii.754.

Taherites, the Saracen dynasty of, iii.370.

Tamerlane, his birth, reign, and conquests, iii.827. His letter to Bajazet, 836, His conference with the doctors of the law, at Aleppo, 838. Defeats and takes Bajazet prisoner, 842. How kept out of Europe, 847. His triumph at Samarcand, 849. Dies on a march to China, 850. His character, 850.

Tancred, the crusader, his character, iii.577. His bold behaviour at Constantinople, 586.

Tarasius, secretary to the empress Irene, made patriarch of Constantinople, iii.117. Presides at, and frames the decrees of, the second council of Nice, 118.

Tarik, the Arab, his descent on Spain, iii.304. Defeats and kills Roderic the Gothic king of, 306. His disgrace, 309, 312.

Tarragona, the city of, almost destroyed by the Franks, i.270.

Tartars. See *Scythians.*

Tartary, Eastern conquest of, by Tamerlane, iii.831.

Tatian, and his son Proculus, destroyed by the base arts of Rufinus, the confidential minister of the emperor Theodosius, ii.100.

Taurus, the consul, is banished by the tribunal of Chalcedon, i.856.

Taxes, how the Roman citizens were exonerated from the burden of, i.179. Account of those instituted by Augustus, 181. How raised under Constantine the Great, and his successors, 633.

Tayef, siege of, by Mahomet, iii.206.

Teias, the last king of the Goths, defeated and killed by the eunuch Narses, ii.757.

Telemachus, an Asiatic monk, loses his life at Rome, in an attempt to prevent the combat of the gladiators, ii.139.

Temple of Jerusalem, burned, i.531. History of the emperor Julian's attempt to restore it, 888.

Temugin. See *Zingis*.

Tephrice, is occupied and fortified by the Paulicians, iii.430.

Tertullian, his pious exultation in the expected damnation of all the Pagan world, i.471. Suggests desertion to Christian soldiers, 482. His suspicious account of two edicts of Tiberius and Marcus Antoninus, in favour of the Christians, 550.

Testaments, the Roman laws for regulating, ii.823. Codicils, 825.

Tetricus assumes the empire in Gaul, at the instigation of Victoria, i.311. Betrays his legions into the hand of Aurelian, 312. Is led in triumph by Aurelian, 321.

Thabor, mount, dispute concerning the light of, iii.784.

Thanet, the island of, granted by Vortigern, as a settlement for his Saxon auxiliaries, ii.495.

Theatrical entertainments of the Romans described, ii.185.

Thebæan legion, the martyrdom of, apocryphal, i.561.

Theft, the Roman laws relating to, ii.830, 834, 836.

Themes, or military governments of the Greek empire, account of, iii.383.

Themistius, the orator, his encomium on religious toleration, i.961.

Theodatus, his birth and elevation to the throne of Italy, ii.650. His disgraceful treaties with the emperor Justinian, and revolt against them, 652. His deposition and death, 657.

Theodebert, king of the Franks in Austrasia, joins the Goths in the siege and destruction of Milan, ii.673. Invades Italy, 673. His death, 675.

Theodemir, a Gothic prince of Spain, copy of his treaty of submission to the Saracens, iii.310.

Theodora, empress, her birth, and early history, ii.563. Her marriage with Justinian, 565. Her tyranny, 567. Her virtues, 568. Her death, 569. Her fortitude during the Nika sedition, 576. Account of her palace and gardens of Heræum, 599. Her pious concern for the conversion of Nubia, 997.

Theodora, wife of the Greek emperor Theophilus, her history, iii.47. Restored the worship of images, 119. Provokes the Paulicians to rebellion, 430.

Theodora, daughter of the Greek emperor Constantine IX. her history, iii.61.

Theodora, widow of Baldwin III. king of Jerusalem, her adventures as the concubine of Andronicus Comnenus, iii.78.

Theodore Angelus, despot of Epirus, seizes Peter of Courtenay, emperor of Constantinople, prisoner, iii.714. Possesses himself of Thessalonica, 715.

Theodoric, acquires the Gothic sceptre by the murder of his brother Torismond, ii.364. His character by Sidonius, 364. His expedition into Spain, 366.

Theodoric, the son of Alaric, his prosperous reign over the Visigoths in Gaul, ii.327. Unhappy fates of his daughters, 329. Is prevailed on by Ætius to join his forces against Attila, 337. Is killed at the battle of Châlons, 340.

Theodoric the Ostrogoth, his birth and education, ii.525. Is forced by his troops into a revolt against the emperor Zeno, 528. He undertakes the conquest of Italy, 530. Reduces and kills Odoacer, 533. Is acknowledged king of Italy, 534. Review of his administration, 534. His visit to Rome, and care of the public buildings, 542. His religion, 546. His remorse, and death, 555.

Theodosiopolis, the city of, in Armenia, built, ii.271.

Theodosius the Great, his distinction between a Roman prince and a Parthian monarch, i.642 *note*. The province of Mæsia preserved by his valour, 1019. Is associated by Gratian as emperor of the East, 1071. His birth and character, 1071. His prudent and successful conduct of the Gothic war, 1075.

Defeats an invasion of the Ostrogoths, 1078.

——, His treaty with Maximus, ii.25. His baptism, and edict to establish orthodox faith, 26. Purges the city of Constantinople from Arianism, 31. Enforces the Nicene doctrine throughout the East, 32. Convenes a council at Constantinople, 33. His edicts against heresy, 36. Receives the fugitive family of Valentinian, and marries his sister Galla, 48. Defeats Maximus, and visits Rome, 49. His character, 50. His lenity to the city of Antioch, 47. His cruel treatment of Thessalonica, 56. Submits to the penance imposed by St. Ambrose, for his severity to Thessalonica, 58. Restores Valentinian, 61. Consults John of Lycopolis the hermit on the intended war against Eugenius, 64. Defeats Eugenius, 65. His death, 68. Procured a senatorial renunciation of the Pagan religion, 76. Abolishes Pagan rites, 78. Prohibits the Pagan religion, 85.

Theodosius the Younger, his birth, ii.260. Is said to be left by his father Arcadius, to the care of Jezdegerd king of Persia, 261. His education and character, 264. His marriage with Eudocia, 266. His war with Persia, 268. His pious joy on the death of John, the usurper of the West, 275. His treaty with the Huns, 295. His armies defeated by Attila, 301. Is reduced to accept a peace dictated by Attila, 308. Is oppressed by the embassies of Attila, 310. Embassy of Maximin to Attila, 312. Is privy to a scheme for the assassination of Attila, 319. Attila's embassy to him on that occasion, 320. His death, 321. His perplexity at the religious feuds between Cyril and Nestorius, 952. Banishes Nestorius, 955.

Theodosius III. emperor of Constantinople, iii.36.

Theodosius, the father of the emperor, his successful expedition to Britain, i.1001. Suppresses the revolt of Firmus the Moor, in Africa, 1004. Is beheaded at Carthage, 1006.

Theodosius, patriarch of Alexandria, his competition with Gaian, how decided, ii.993. His negociations at the court of Byzantium, 995.

Theodosius, the deacon, grandson of the emperor Heraclius, murdered by his brother Constans II. iii.30.

Theodosius, the lover of Antonina, detected by Belisarius, ii.681. Turns monk to escape her, 682. His death, 683.

Theodosius, president of the council of Hierapolis under Constantius, his ridiculous flattery to that emperor, i.847.

Theophano, wife of the Greek emperor Romanus II. poisons both him and his father, iii.57. Her connexion with Nicephorus Phocas, 58. His murder, and her exile, 59.

Theophilus, emperor of Constantinople, iii.45. His Amorian war with the caliph Motassem, 362.

Theophilus, archbishop of Alexandria, destroys the temple of Serapis, and the Alexandrian library, ii.83. Assists the persecution of St. Chrysostom, 256. His invective against him, 259 *note*.

Theophilus, his pious embassy from the emperor Constantius to the East Indies, i.750.

Theophobus, the Persian, his unfortunate history, iii.46.

Therapeutæ, or Essenians, some account of, i.502.

Thermopylæ, the straits of, fortified by the emperor Justinian, ii.601.

Thessalonica, sedition and massacre there, ii.56. Cruel treatment of the citizens, 57. Penance of Theodosius for this severity, 58.

Theudelinda, princess of Bavaria, married to Autharis king of the Lombards, ii.869.

Thibaut, count of Champagne, engages in the fourth crusade, iii.666.

Thomas the Cappadocian, his revolt against the Greek emperor Michael II. and cruel punishment, iii.45.

Thomas of Damascus, his exploits against the Saracens when besieging that city, iii.256.

Thomas, St. account of the Christians of, in India, ii.985. Persecution of, by the Portuguese, 986.

Thrace, is colonised by the Bastarnæ, in the reign of Probus, i.342. The fugitive Goths permitted to settle there by the emperor Valens, 1048. Is ravaged by them, 1053. The Goths settled there by Theodosius, 1080.

Thrasimund, king of the Vandals, his character, ii.436.

Three Chapters, the famous dispute concerning, ii.972.

Thundering Legion, the story concerning, of suspicious veracity, i.551.

Tiberius, is adopted by Augustus, i.98. Reduces the Pannonians, 134. Reduces Cappadocia, 182 *note*. Suspicious story of his edict in favour of the Christians, 550.

Tiberius is invested by Justin II. as his successor in the empire of the East, ii.858. His character and death, 860.

Timasius, master-general of the army under the emperor Theodosius, is disgraced and exiled under Arcadius, ii.242.

Timothy the Cat conspires the murder of Proterius archbishop of Alexandria, and succeeds him, ii.963.

Tipasa, miraculous gift of speech bestowed on the Catholics, whose tongues had been cut out there, ii.443.

Tiridates, king of Armenia, his character and history, i.373. Is restored to his kingdom by Diocletian, 374. Is expelled by the Persians, 376. Is restored again by treaty between the Romans and Persians, 352. His conversion to Christianity and death, 666.

Titus admitted to share the Imperial dignity with his father Vespasian, i.98.

Togrul Beg, sultan of the Turks, his reign and character, iii.530. He rescues the caliph of Bagdad from his enemies, 532.

Toledo taken by the Arabs under Tarik, iii.306.

Toleration, universal, its happy effects in the Roman empire, i.56. What sects the most intolerant, 220 *note*.

Tollius, objections to his account of the vision of Antigonus, i.739 *note*.

Torismond, son the Theodoric king of the Visigoths, attends his father against Attila king of the Huns, ii.337. Battle of Châlons, 340. Is acknowledged king on the death of his father in the field, 342. Is killed by his brother Theodoric, 364.

Torture, how admitted in the criminal law of the Romans under the emperors, i.631.

Totila is elected king of Italy by the Goths, ii.736. His justice and moderation, 737. Besieges and takes the city of Rome, 743. Is induced to spare Rome from destruction, at the instance of Belisarius, 744. Takes Rome again, 748. Plunders Sicily, 749. Battle of Tagina, 754. His death, 755.

Toulunides, the Saracen dynasty of, iii.371.

Tournaments, preferable exhibitions to the Olympic games, iii.579.

Tours, battle of, between Charles Martel and the Saracens, iii.337.

Toxandria, in Germany, is overrun and occupied by the Franks, i.711.

Traditors, in the primitive church, who, i.568.

Trajan, emperor, his conquest of Dacia, i.35. His conquests in the East, 35. Contrast between the characters of him and Hadrian, 37. His pillar described, 74. Why adopted by the emperor Nerva, 99. His instructions to Pliny the Younger for his conduct toward the Christians, 535. Description of his famous bridge over the Danube, ii.600 *note*.

Transubstantiation, the doctrine of, when established, iii.645.

Trebizond, the city of, taken and plundered by the Goths, i.276. The dukes of, become independent on the Greek empire, iii.706. Is yielded to the Turks, 973.

Tribigild the Ostrogoth, his rebellion in Phrygia against the emperor Arcadius, iii.292.

Tribonian, his genius and character, ii.797. Is employed by Justinian to reform the code of Roman laws, 799.

Tribune, the office of, explained, i.90.

Trinity, the mysterious doctrine of, i.775. Is violently agitated in the schools of Alexandria, 779. Three systems of, 780. Decisions of the council of Nice concerning, 782. Different forms of the doxology, 815. Frauds used to support the doctrine of, ii.442.

Tripoli, the confederacy of, cruelly oppressed under the government of count Romanus, i.1002.

Trisagion, religious war concerning, ii.965.

Troops, Roman, their discipline, i.39. when they first received pay, 179. Cause of the difficulty in levying them, 622. See *Jovians*, *Palatines*, and *Prætorian bands*.

Troy, the situation of that city, and of the Grecian camp of besiegers, described, i.591.

Turin, battle of, between Constantine the Great and the lieutenants of Maxentius, i.422.

Turisund, king of the Gepidæ, his honourable reception of Alboin the Lombard, who had slain his son in battle, ii.848.

Turks, their origin, ii.694. Their primitive institutions, 696. Their conquests, 696. Their alliance with the emperor Justinian, 700. Send auxiliaries to Heraclius, 923.

——, They grow powerful and licentious under the Saracens, iii.365. Terror excited by their menacing Europe, 445. Their military character, 449. They extend themselves over Asia, 523. Reign of Mahmud the Gaznevide, 523. Their manners and emigration, 527. They subdue Persia, 529. Dynasty of the Seljukians, 530. They invade the provinces of the Greek empire, 533. Reformation of the Eastern calendar, 543. They conquer Asia Minor, 545. Their capital city, Nice, taken by the crusaders, 589. The seat of government removed to Iconium, 617. Valour and conquests of Zenghi, 627. Character of sultan Noureddin, 627. Conquest of Egypt, 628. Origin and history of the Ottomans, 809. Their first passage into Europe, 813. Their education and discipline, 860. Embassy from, to the emperor Sigismund, 881. Take the city of Constantinople, 963.

Turpin, the romance of, by whom, and when written, iii.560 *note*.

Twelve Tables, review of the laws of, ii.781. Their severity, 831. How the criminal code of, sunk into disuse, 833.

Tyrants of Rome, the popular conceit of the thirty is investigated, i.288.

Tyre is besieged by Saladin, iii.638.

Tythes assigned to the clergy as well by Zoroaster as by Moses, i.219. Were first granted to the church by Charlemagne, iii.216.

U & V

Vadomair, prince of the Alemanni, is sent prisoner to Sapin by the emperor Julian, i.839. His son murdered by the Romans, 991.

Valens, general of the Illyrian frontier, receives the title of Cæsar from Licinius, i.435. Loses his new title and his life, 436.

Valens, the brother of the emperor Valentinian, is associated with him in the empire, i.967. Obtains from his brother the Eastern portion of the empire, 968. His timidity on the revolt of Procopius, 972. His character, 976. Is baptised by Eudoxus, and patronises the Arians, 982. Is vindicated from the charge of persecution, 983. His edict against the Egyptian monks, 985. His war with the Goths, 1015. Receives the suppliant Goths into the Roman territories, 1046. His war with them, 1055. Is defeated and killed at the battle of Hadrianople, 1064. His eulogium by Libanius, 1065.

Valens, the Arian bishop of Mursa, his crafty pretension to divine revelation, i.793.

Valentia, a new province in Britain, settled by Theodosius, i.1002.

Valentinian I. his election to the empire, and character, i.965. Associates his brother Valens with him, 967. Divides the empire into the *East* and *West*, and retains the latter, 968. His cruelty, 976. His civil institutions, 978. His edicts to restrain the avarice of the clergy, 985. Chastises the Alemanni, and fortifies the Rhine, 992. His expedition to Illyricum, and death, 1019. Is vindicated from the charge of polygamy, 1021.

Valentinian II. is invested with the Imperial ornaments in his mother's arms, on the death of his father, i.1022. Is refused, by St. Ambrose, the privilege of a church for him and his mother Justina, on account of their Arian principles, ii.42. His flight from the invasion of Maximus, 46. Is restored by the emperor Theodosius, 61. His character, 61. His death, 63.

Valentinian III. is established emperor of the West, by his cousin Theodosius the Younger, ii.275. Is committed to the guardianship of his mother Placidia, 277. Flies, on the invasion of Italy by Attila, 347. Sends an embassy to Attila to purchase his retreat, 348. Murders the patrician Ætius, 353. Ravishes the wife of Petronius Maximus, 354. His death, and character, 354.

Valentinians, their confused ideas of the divinity of Jesus Christ, ii.939 *note*.

Valeria, empress, widow of Galerius, the unfortunate fates of her and her mother, i.431.

Valerian, is elected censor under the emperor Decius, i.263. His elevation to the empire, and his character, 268. Is defeated and taken prisoner by Sapor king of Persia, 283. His treatment, 286. His inconsistent behaviour toward the Christians, 555.

Vandals. See *Goths*.

——, Their successes in Spain, ii.279. Their expedition into Africa under Genseric, 279. They raise a naval force and invade Italy, 357. Sack of Rome, 360. Their naval depredations on the coasts of the Mediterranean, 381. Their conversion to the Christian religion, 430. Persecution of the Catholics, 435. Expedition of Belisarius against Gelimer, 625. Conquest of, 636. Their name and distinction lost in Africa, 642. Remains of their nation still found in Germany, 643.

Varanes. See *Bahram*.

Varangians of the north, origin and history of, iii.456.

Varronian, the infant son of the emperor Jovian, his history, i.964.

Vataces, John, his long and prosperous reign at Nice, iii.715. 721. His character, 737.

Vegetius, his remarks on the degeneracy of the Roman discipline at the time of Theodosius the Great, ii.70.

Veii, the siege of that city, the æra of the Roman army first receiving regular pay, i.178.

Venice, foundation of that republic, ii.345. Its infant state under the exarchs of Ravenna, 865.

——, Its growth and prosperity at the time of the fourth crusade, iii.668. Alliance with France, 670. Divides the Greek empire with the French, 699.

Veratius, his mode of obeying the law of the twelve tables respecting personal insults, ii.830.

Verina, empress, the widow of Leo, deposes Zeno, ii.527. Her turbulent life, 528.

Verona, siege of, by Constantine the Great, i.423. Battle of, between Stilicho the Roman general, and Alaric the Goth, ii.137.

Verres, why his punishment was inadequate to his offences, ii.835.

Vespasian, his prudence in sharing the Imperial dignity with his son Titus, i.98.

Vestals, Roman, their number, and peculiar office, ii.72.

Vetranio, the Roman general in Illyricum, assumes the purple, and enters into an alliance with the Gaulish usurper Magnentius, i.673. Is reduced to abdicate his new dignity, 676.

Victoria, exercises the government over the legions and province of Gaul, i.311.

Victory, her statue and altar, in the senate house at Rome, described, ii.73. The senate petitions the Christian emperors to have it restored, 74.

Vigilantius, the presbyter, is abused by Jerom for opposing monkish superstition, ii.91 *note*.

Vigilius, interpreter to the embassy from Theodosius the younger to Attila, is privy to a scheme for the assassination of Attila, ii.312. Is detected by Attila, 319.

Vigilius, purchases the papal chair of Belisarius and his wife, ii.667. Instigates the emperor Justinian to resume the conquest of Italy, 750.

Vine, its progress, from the time of Homer, i.79.

Virgil, his fourth eclogue interpreted into a prophecy of the coming of the Messiah, i.744. Is the most ancient writer who mentions the manufacture of silk, ii.579.

Vitalian, the Gothic chief, is treacherously murdered at Constantinople, ii.559.

Vitalianus, prætorian præfect under the emperor Maximin, put to death by order of the senate, i.197.

Vitellius, emperor, his character, i.104.

Vitiges, general of the Barbarians under Theodatus king of Italy, is by his troops declared king of Italy, ii.657. He besieges Belisarius in Rome, 658. Is forced to raise the siege, 670. He is besieged by Belisarius in Ravenna, 671. Is taken prisoner in Ravenna, 677. Conforms to the Athanasian faith, and is honourably settled in Asia, 678. His embassy to Chosroes king of Persia, 709.

Vitruvius, the architect, his remarks on the buildings of Rome, ii.187.

Vizir, derivation of that appellation, iii.191 *note*.

Ukraine, description of that country, i.260.

Uldin, king of the Huns, reduces and kills Gainas the Goth, ii.252. Is driven back by the vigilance of the Imperial ministers, 262.

Ulphilas, the apostle of the Goths, his pious labours, ii.429. Propagated Arianism, 434.

Ulpian, the lawyer, placed at the head of the council of state, under the emperor Alexander Severus, i.171. Is murdered by the Prætorian guards, 175.

Voconian law abolished the right of female inheritance, ii.823. How evaded, 826.

Voltaire, prefers the labarum of Constantine to the angel of Licinius, i.739 *note*. His reflections on the expenses of a siege, ii.514 *note*.

Vortigern, king of South Britain, his invitation of the Saxons for assistance against his enemies, ii.494.

Vouti, emperor of China, his exploits against the Huns, i.1038.

Upsal, anciently famous for its Gothic temple, i.256.

Urban II. pope, patronises Peter the Hermit in his project for recovering the Holy Land, iii.558. Exhorts the people to a crusade, at the council of Clermont, 562.

Urban V. pope, removes the papal court from Avignon to Rome, iii.1043.

Urban VI. pope, his disputed election, iii.1045.

Ursacius, master of the offices under the emperor Valentinian, occasions a revolt of the Alemanni by his parsimony, i.989.

Ursicinus, a Roman general, his treacherous conduct to Sylvanus in Gaul, i.698. Is superseded in his command over the Eastern provinces, 709. Is sent back again to conduct the war with Persia under Sabinian, 709. Is again disgraced, 710.

Ursini, history of the Roman family of, iii.1017.

Ursulus, treasurer of the empire under Constantius, unjustly put to death by the tribunal of Chalcedon, i.856.

Usury. See *Interest of money*.

W

Walachians, the present, descendants from the Roman settlers in ancient Dacia, i.306 *note*.

Wales is settled by British refugees from Saxon tyranny, ii.498. 501. The bards of, 504.

Wallia is chosen king of the Goths, ii.227. He reduces the barbarous invaders of Spain, 227. Is settled in Aquitain, 228.

War and robbery, their difference, iii.162. Evolutions and military exercise of the Greeks, 407. Military character of the Saracens, 409. Of the Franks and Latins, 411.

Warburton, bishop of Gloucester, his literary character, i.888 *note*. His labours to establish the miraculous interruption to Julian's building the temple of Jerusalem, 890 *notes*.

Warna, battle of, between the sultan Amurath II. and Ladislaus king of Hungary and Poland, iii.922.

Werdan, the Greek general, defeated by the Saracens at Aiznadin, iii.254.

Wheat, the average price of, under the successors of Constantine the Great, i.913 *note*.

Whitaker, Mr. remarks on his account of the Irish descent of the Scottish nation, i.999 *note*.

White, Mr. Arabic professor at Oxford, character of his sermons at Bampton's lecture, iii.336 *note*.

Wilfrid, the apostle of Sussex, his benevolent establishment at Selsey, ii.503.

William I. the Bad, king of Sicily, iii.518.

William II. the Good, king of Sicily, iii.518.

Windmills, the use of, from whence derived, iii.726.

Wine, the use of, expressly prohibited by Mahomet, iii.186.

Wisdom of Solomon, when, and by whom that book was written, i.772.

Wolodomir, great prince of Russia, marries Anne, daughter of the emperor Romanus, iii.402. His conversion to Christianity, 467.

Women, in hereditary monarchies, allowed to exercise sovereignty, though incapable of subordinate state offices, i.170. How treated by the Roman civil laws, ii.811. The Voconian law, how evaded, 826. Are not excluded from Paradise by Mahomet, iii.189.

X

Xenophon, his description of the desert of Mesopotamia, i.923.

Xerxes, the situation of his bridge of boats for passing over to Europe, pointed out, i.590.

Y

Yermuk, battle of, between the Greeks and the Saracens, iii.264.

Yezdegerd, king of Persia, his reign the æra of the fall of the Sassanian dynasty, and of the religion of Zoroaster, iii.240.

Yezid, caliph of the Saracens, iii.225.

Z

Zabergan invades the Eastern empire with an army of Bulgarians, ii.764. Is repulsed by Belisarius, 765.

Zachary, pope, pronounces the deposition of Childeric king of France, and the appointment of Pepin to succeed him, iii.110.

Zano, brother of Gelimer the Vandal usurper, conquers Sardinia, ii.633. Is recalled to assist his brother, 633. Is killed, 634.

Zara, a city on the Sclavonian coast, reduced by the crusaders for the republic of Venice, iii.673.

Zenghi, sultan, his valour and conquests, iii.627.

Zeno, emperor of the East, receives a surrender of the Imperial government of the Western empire, from the senate of Rome, ii.404. The vicissitudes of his life and reign, 527. His Henoticon, 963.

Zenobia, queen of Palmyra, her character and history, i.312.

Zingis, first emperor of the Moguls and Tartars, parallel between him and Attila, king of the Huns, ii.297. His proposal for improving his conquests in China, 304. His birth and early military exploits, iii.791. His laws, 793. His invasion of China, 795. Carisme, Transoxiana, and Persia, 796. His death, 798.

Zizais, a noble Sarmatian, is made king of that nation by the emperor Constantius, i.703.

Zobeir, the Saracen, his bravery in the invasion of Africa, iii.292.

Zoe, first the concubine, becomes the fourth wife of the emperor Leo the philosopher, iii.54.

Zoe, wife of Romanus III. and Michael IV. emperors, iii.62.

Zoroaster, the Persian prophet, his high antiquity, i.215 *note*. Abridgement of his theology, 216. Provides for the encouragement of agriculture, 218. Assigns tythes to the priests, 219.

Zosimus, his representation of the oppression of the lustral contribution, i.640.

Zuinglius the reformer, his conceptions of the Eucharist, iii.436.

Zurich, brief history of that city, iii.988.

THE END.